The American Directory of

Writer's Guidelines

A Compilation of Information for Freelancers from More Than 1,500 Magazine Editors and Book Publishers

4th Edition

Compiled by
Brigitte M. Phillips,
Susan D. Klassen
and Doris Hall

Quill
Driver
Books
Q

Sanger, California

Published by
Quill Driver Books/Word Dancer Press, Inc.
1831 Industrial Way #101
Sanger, CA 93657
(559) 876-2170
FAX (559) 876-2180
QuillDriverBooks.com

Printed in The United States of America

Quill Driver Books/Word Dancer Press books may be purchased at special prices for educational, fund-raising, business or promotional use. Please contact:

Special Markets
Quill Driver Books\Word Dancer Press, Inc.
1831 Industrial Way #101
Sanger, CA 93657
SpecialMarkets@QuillDriverBooks.com
1-800-497-4909

To order an additional copy of this book
please call 1-800-497-4909 or visit
QuillDriverBooks.com

Quill Driver Books/Word Dancer Press, Inc. project cadre:
Doris Hall, Susan Klassen, David Marion,
Stephen Blake Mettee, Brigitte Phillips

ISBN 1884956-40-8

QUILL DRIVER BOOKS and colophon are trademarks of Quill Driver Books/Word Dancer Press, Inc.

Library of Congress Cataloging-in-Publication Data

The American directory of writer's guidelines : a compilation of information for freelancers from more than 1,500 magazine editors and book publishers, 4th edition / edited and compiled by Brigitte M. Phillips, Susan D. Klassen and Doris Hall
    p. cm.
 ISBN 1-884956-40-8
 1. Authorship—Handbooks, manuals, etc. 2. Journalism—Authorship—Handbooks, manuals, etc. I. Phillips, Brigitte M., 1979- II. Klassen, Susan D., 1957- III Hall, Doris, 1932-

PN147.A479 2004
808'.02—dc22
                                    2004011497

USE THIS BOOK TO:

- ## FIND A PUBLISHER

  Search *The American Directory of Writer's Guidelines'* "Topic Index" to find a publisher interested in the subject you wish to write about, then turn to that publisher's guidelines for more information, including the name and address of the editor to whom you should send query letters, manuscripts, book proposals or other submissions. Periodical publisher guidelines are listed alphabetically beginning on page 1. Guidelines for book publishers begin on page 559.

- ## POLISH YOUR SUBMISSION

  When you already know which periodical you would like to target or which book publisher you wish to approach, look up the appropriate guidelines and use the information provided to fine-tune your submission.

- ## BRAINSTORM IDEAS

  A primary value of *The American Directory of Writer's Guidelines* is its ability to be browsed. Use the guidelines and the "Topic Index" to brainstorm ideas for everything from nonfiction articles to short stories, from brief fillers to full-length books.

- ## EXPLOIT YOUR EXPERTISE

  Many regularly published writers use the same material for more than one article or project. If you are an expert in a certain area or have collected an abundance of material on a subject about which you would like to write, use the "Topic Index" to locate a number of publishers interested in your subject and then contact each individually slanting your approach to fit the individual publisher's wants and needs.

- ## LOOK LIKE A PRO

  Anything less than a businesslike manuscript format will brand you as a beginner. See page xxi for an example of proper manuscript format.

- ## TRACK YOUR SUBMISSIONS

  A "Submission Tracking Sheet" appears on page xxiii. Photocopy this form to record the progress of each of your submissions.

WHAT ARE WRITER'S GUIDELINES?

For years, editors at magazines have prepared writer's guidelines to advise and direct freelance writers who wish to write for their magazines. Today, editors at many book publishers also prepare writer's guidelines for writers with book-length projects in mind.

Yet, while supporting writers is important to editors (who are most often writers themselves), they don't provide writer's guidelines for purely altruistic reasons. They do it with the hope that the pool of material submitted to them will increase both in quality and in adherence to the needs of the press.

In theory, the editor's ability to pick and choose from this enriched reservoir will enhance the publisher's success—and the editor's job security.

Whether this works as anticipated is a still a topic of discussion among editors—most material that arrives on an editor's desk still does not fit the editor's needs. What is certain is that savvy writers save time and limit the number of rejection slips they receive by perusing a publisher's guidelines before querying or submitting material.

The best writer's guidelines convey a plethora of information. The basics, such as whether material should be fiction or nonfiction, which subject matters or topics are to be dealt with, and the approximate word count required, are almost universally spelled out. Yet, many guidelines go well beyond the basics, instructing the writer in such matters as tone, voice, use of first person or third person point of view, use of humor, and the appropriateness of political, sexual, or violent content.

Guidelines often provide information about photographs and other illustrations to be used, deadlines for seasonal material, which rights are acquired, which columns or features are open to freelancers and which are staff written, and which style guide (*The Associated Press Stylebook and Libel Manual* and *The Chicago Manual of Style* are two common examples) the publisher wishes the author to follow. Some guidelines even list the rates the publisher will pay.

HOW THIS BOOK IS ORGANIZED

This book is broken into two main sections, "Periodicals' Guidelines," which lists guidelines for magazines and other periodicals in alphabetical order, and "Book Publishers' Guidelines," which does the same for book publishing houses. Contact information—with names of the editors to whom submissions should be addressed—follows each of the guidelines. Since editors change jobs and publishers change addresses, it is wise to invest in a phone call to verify this information before submitting.

The "Topic Index" beginning on page 755 lists publishers by areas of interest. This is the place to start when you know what subject you want to write about.

CONTENTS

PERIODICALS' GUIDELINES

Book Publishers' Guidelines

QUERY LETTERS

The job of a query letter is to convince an editor to ask to see a full book proposal or to assign an article to you.

The first rule of a query letter is to address it to the proper editor—by name. Never use "Dear Editor" or "To Whom It May Concern." Triple-check the correct spelling of the editor's name.

The second rule is to be brief. What's brief? Conventional wisdom dictates never exceeding one page in length, but Donna Elizabeth Boetig, author of *Feminine Wiles: Creative Techniques for Writing Women's Feature Stories that Sell,* says this advice is "a scam propagated by published writers who want to keep new ones from nipping at their assignments." She advises, "...don't shortchange yourself. If you've got something to say—and you better if you're writing to [an editor]—then relax and allow yourself space to make your point." Boetig says for her, "...one and a half to two pages seems comfortable."

A query letter should begin with an opening that will "hook" the editor. This might be a colorful anecdote, an intriguing question, or some other arresting device. Whatever you use, the first paragraph or two must pique the editor's interest, or he may not read on.

WRITING "ON SPEC"

If you are a new writer, an editor interested in the article you are suggesting may ask to see it "on spec." On spec is short for "on speculation," meaning the author writes the article speculating that the editor will purchase it. While, at this point, the editor *has* shown an interest in the article, all he has agreed to do is to consider it when it comes in. This is a common practice and may be necessary for the new author trying to break in.

After you have caught his attention, explain why you have chosen to contact this particular editor. How do the interests of his magazine or book publishing house coincide with what you are proposing?

Your query must present a specific idea. Don't ask if the editor would like an article on snowboarding; ask if he would like one on septuagenarians who snowboard in their underwear.

Describe the main points your article or book will cover and how the reader will benefit from having read it. Suggest a catchy title for the work. Explain how your article or book will be fresh and different than other articles or books on the same subject.

Explain why you are the one to write the article or book. How will you get your material? Will you research the subject, conduct polls, interview experts?

Estimate the approximate word count for the project, fitting this number to what you have learned from this publisher's writer's guidelines.

Throughout the query, show your passion for the subject.

WHEN NOT TO QUERY

Most publishers of short stories don't wish to receive a query letter. They prefer that the complete short story be submitted. In fact, many suggest foregoing a cover letter as well, the point being that the short story must stand on its own—without any tangential information that is included in the cover letter—when published.

If you have already written a nonfiction article—and tailored it to a specific periodical—you might wish to send the whole article with a short cover letter explaining what the article is about and why you chose to send it to this particular periodical.

When you are suggesting a nonfiction book project to a publisher, Stephen Blake Mettee, author of *The Fast-Track Course on Writing a Nonfiction Book Proposal,* advises skipping the query letter stage and instead submitting a full proposal. He contends a query letter asking if an editor wishes to see a full book proposal is simply giving the editor an additional chance to say no. Where the full proposal might secure a contract with the editor, a query letter never will. If you choose to skip the query stage, a brief cover letter explaining why you chose to contact this particular editor would be appropriate.

QUERY LETTER FORMAT

Query letters are business letters and as such take the form of business letters. Single space queries. Use a businesslike font such as Times New Roman. Use your letterhead or center your name and contact information at the top of the sheet.

SELF-ADDRESSED, STAMPED ENVELOPES (SASEs)

It is customary for an author to enclose a self-addressed, stamped envelope with unsolicited queries, book proposals, or other submissions. This isn't absolutely necessary; if the editor is interested in what you are suggesting, he will undoubtedly contact you, but, if he isn't, most will simply trash or recycle your material without responding.

This may sound harsh and unbusiness like, but an editor who receives hundreds or even thousands of submissions each year, as most do, simply doesn't have the time to address and affix the correct postage to that many envelopes.

While a business-sized (#10) envelope will suffice, it is a good idea to enclose a self-addressed, stamped envelope large enough to return everything you sent—many editors jot notes on the material and these notes may provide information you can use to tweak your submission when sending it out to another editor.

SELLING YOUR BOOK TO A PUBLISHER

NONFICTION BOOKS

Most nonfiction books, even those by first-time authors, are sold to a publisher before the book has been completely written. This is done via a ten- to fifty-page book proposal.

Most successful book proposals have the following five components:

- A synopsis of the book, including a suggested title, the subject matter and how it will be approached, the main points the book will cover, the book's potential readership, other similar books and how yours will be different or better, the anticipated word count, and why you are the person to write this book.
- A table of contents
- A chapter-by-chapter outline
- Two or three sample chapters
- Additional supporting material. This may be copies of charts or photographs to be included in the book, current newspaper clippings that deal with the subject matter, photocopies or a list of your previously published works, and any other material that will help the editor get an overall view of the project.

For more on writing nonfiction book proposals, including a successful proposal and sample book contracts, see *The Fast-Track Course on How to Write a Nonfiction Book Proposal* by Stephen Blake Mettee.

NOVELS

First-time novelists usually acquire the attention of an agent or an editor by submitting a complete synopsis of the book and the first two or three chapters. The synopsis should provide an overview of the main characters and the intricacies of the plot and subplots. Unlike with nonfiction book publishers, most publishers of novels will want to see the complete novel before offering a contract to a first-time author.

"TWAINISMS"

Few writers had so much to say or said it as well as humorist Mark Twain. Here's a couple of comments he had for writers.

"The difference between the right word and the almost-right word is the difference between the lightning and the lightning bug."

"Truth is stranger than fiction, because fiction is obliged to stick to possibilities. Truth isn't."

THE AUTHOR'S BUNDLE OF RIGHTS

According to United States copyright law, the writer's work is considered copyrighted from the moment it is written. This automatically gives the author ownership of a bundle of rights to his or her work.

This bundle of rights may be divided and sold in any number of pieces and with any limitations the author can conceive of and get a publisher to agree to. The writer assigns the right to use the work to a publisher according to the contract between the writer and the publisher.

While it isn't necessary, many people in the industry suggest that writers list on the manuscript just what rights are being offered. For example, type "First North American Serial Rights" on the upper right hand corner of a short story or article, just above the word count. Always check your contract (or letter of acceptance from the editor) to see what rights the publisher expects to receive.

Below is a brief summary of some of the components of the bundle of rights. For specific questions, it is always best to consult an attorney who specializes in communications, copyright, or publication law.

All rights—This is just what it suggests. When a writer sells "all rights" to a work to a publisher, the writer no longer has any say in future publication of the piece. If he wants to use it again, say to include it in an anthology, he would need to get permission from the publisher to whom he sold the rights. It's always a good idea to avoid selling "all rights," unless the amount offered is excellent or the writer decides that the sale—for prestige or another reason—is worth abdicating all rights to the piece.

Electronic rights—This is a term used to define a bundle of rights related to computer technology. It may include the right to reproduce the material on CD-ROMs, in online databases, in multimedia or interactive media, on web sites, or with publishing-on-demand systems. Just like all other rights, an author may wish to assign certain electronic rights and retain others.

First North American rights—A specific form of first serial rights. This is an agreement to let a periodical publish the material before any other periodical within North America publishes it. This is probably the most common type of rights purchased when short stories and articles are acquired by a periodical published in the United States.

First serial rights—The right to be the first periodical to publish the material. May be limited geographically.

Foreign language rights—The right to reproduce the material in one or more foreign languages. This also may involve geographic limitations, such as Spanish language rights for Mexico, but not Spain.

Foreign rights—These include the right to publish the material outside of the originating country. These may be broken down by country or by some other geographical division, such as European rights, and may involve foreign language rights.

One-time rights—This is generally used when a writer sells an article to more than one noncompeting newspaper or magazine. This means the periodical buys non-exclusive rights to use the piece once.

Second serial rights—Also called reprint rights. This gives a periodical the right to print a piece that has already appeared somewhere else. Like one-time rights, these are usually nonexclusive.

Simultaneous rights—The right to publish the material at the same time as another publisher. An example would be when a writer sells the same article to more than one of the many regional periodicals published.

Subsidiary rights—This is a term that refers to any secondary rights including, but not limited to:

- Audio rights
- Book club rights
- Condensation rights
- TV rights
- Film rights
- Mass-market paperback rights
- Merchandising rights
- Trade paperback rights
- Translation rights

Subsidiary rights usually come into play with books. Often an author will assign these rights to a book publisher with the agreement that the author will share in the profits when the publisher exploits these rights or licenses others to exploit them.

DEALING WITH REJECTION

There are many reasons a publishing company turns down a project that have nothing to do with the quality of the work or its publishability. When you get a form rejection letter, don't get discouraged. It may be that the editor used a form letter because he didn't want to tell you how awful your work was, but chances are, something else came into play.

There are at least four other reasons editors are reluctant to give you a concrete reason for declining your work:

- It takes time out of an already too-busy day.
- Giving a reason suggests that the door is still open and appears to the author as an opportunity to begin a dialogue with the editor, when, if he wanted to discuss your fixing or changing something and resubmitting the work, he would have said so.
- Explaining how elements particular to his company's publishing program came into play to nix your project might be sharing confidential corporate information with an outsider.
- Editors know they aren't the final authority on what will please the reading public and they don't want to discourage you.

Persistence is frequently the key to getting published. Mark Victor Hansen and Jack Canfield had their fabulously successful *Chicken Soup for the Soul* rejected by publishers 140 times before Health Communications picked it up.

Rejection is part of most writers' lives. Remember, you aren't defeated until you quit submitting.

12 Ancient Storytelling Elements You Can Use to Attract and Hold Your Readers

By Stephen Blake Mettee

Have you ever noticed that certain elements in novels and movies seem to repeat themselves? For instance, in most stories the hero is reluctant to take the particular action that it is necessary for him to take for the story to begin. In private-eye novels, the detective initially balks at accepting the case, protesting that he doesn't do divorce work or that the police are more equipped to locate missing persons.

Then, after expressing this initial reluctance, the hero decides to do—or is forced to do—that which he resisted and, having accepted (or having been forced to accept) this "call to action," takes the first step on a journey from which there is no turning back. In J. R. R. Tolkien's *The Lord of the Rings,* Frodo leaves the Shire and cannot return until he has destroyed the "one" ring.

During his journey, Frodo is assisted by the wizard Gandolf who dispenses sage advice. This hero-meets-mentor stage is also a reoccurring element in stories.

These elements, which surface to one degree or another in almost all stories, are old as storytelling itself. It was mythologist Joseph Campbell who first identified twelve universal road marks in what has become known as the "hero's journey." Campbell found these stages to exist in everything from ancient Sumerian myths to the work of film maker George Lucas.

That these elements exist is important information for the novelist—or the memoir writer— because, on some primal level, readers are strongly drawn to stories that possess all or most of these stages. If, as you write, you keep these stages in mind or even use them as an outline for your story, you are more likely to tap into this unconscious hunger.

While the order of the twelve stages as listed below is common, the sequence often varies from story to story.

- Ordinary world—The reader is allowed to see the hero in his everyday world.
- Call to adventure—The incident that beckons the hero to start his journey.
- Refusal of the call—The hero's reluctance to leave the ordinary world.
- Meeting the mentor—The mentor can be anyone from a hooker with a heart of gold to an alien. As with Frodo, the mentor may appear numerous times and there is often more than one mentor.
- Crossing the first threshold—The action the hero takes from which there is no turning back.
- Tests, Allies, Enemies—The meat of the story where most of the action plays out.

- Approach to the inmost cave—At this stage the hero prepares to cross another threshold, one after which he must confront the most frightening or most critical part of his journey.
- Supreme ordeal—This is the hero's greatest challenge. Here his character, intelligence, or strength are put to the maximum test. The hero often appears to die—metaphorically or otherwise—at this stage.
- The seizing of the sword—This is the point at which the hero accomplishes his task. His triumph may not last, or it may have unexpected consequences.
- The road back—Most heros attempt to return to the ordinary world and experience further adventures or difficulties on the way back.
- Resurrection—The hero has been changed by his experiences. In one sense his old self has died and his new self born. To the reader, this transformation or growth is often the most satisfying part of the story.
- Return with the Elixir—After the hunt, the hero returns with his kill and shares it with those who stayed in the village. Often the hero, since he has changed, no longer fits in the ordinary world and must ride off into the sunset unable to stay and enjoy the fruits of his journey.

The hero's journey is something that lives within us all. Even with the process of our writing we travel a hero's journey. The more we can tap into these elements within us, the more we will capture our reader's hearts, minds and souls.

ADVICE FROM WRITERS
WHO WRITE HOW-TO-WRITE BOOKS

"As you write your first draft, let it flow through you—bubbling from the wellspring of your soul, coursing through your cerebral cortex, pouring down your arms and out your fingertips, flooding your computer's Pentium memory with brilliance."
—Jim Denney, author of *Quit Your Day Job: How to Sleep Late, Do What You Enjoy, and Make a Ton of Money as a Writer!*

"To dramatize a scene, you need to introduce a sense of immediacy—convey the impression that the scene is unfolding before the reader's eyes in the present moment, the way a scene is enacted on the stage or screen."
—Fred D. White, Ph.D. author of *LifeWriting: Drawing from Personal Experience to Create Features You Can Publish*

"You should choose an agent as carefully as you'd choose a cardiac specialist because either one can break your heart."
—Marc McCutcheon, author of *Damn! Why Didn't I Write That?: How Ordinary People are Raking in $100,000...or More Writing Nonfiction Books & How You Can Too!*

STANDARD MANUSCRIPT FORMAT

There is no single correct page format for a manuscript, but following common format conventions, as shown here, is a good way to say to an editor: "I am a professional." Always use letter-sized, white paper. Always be sure the print is dark and legible. Paper clip sheets together or use a manuscript box; never staple. Be sure to check individual guidelines for special requirements.

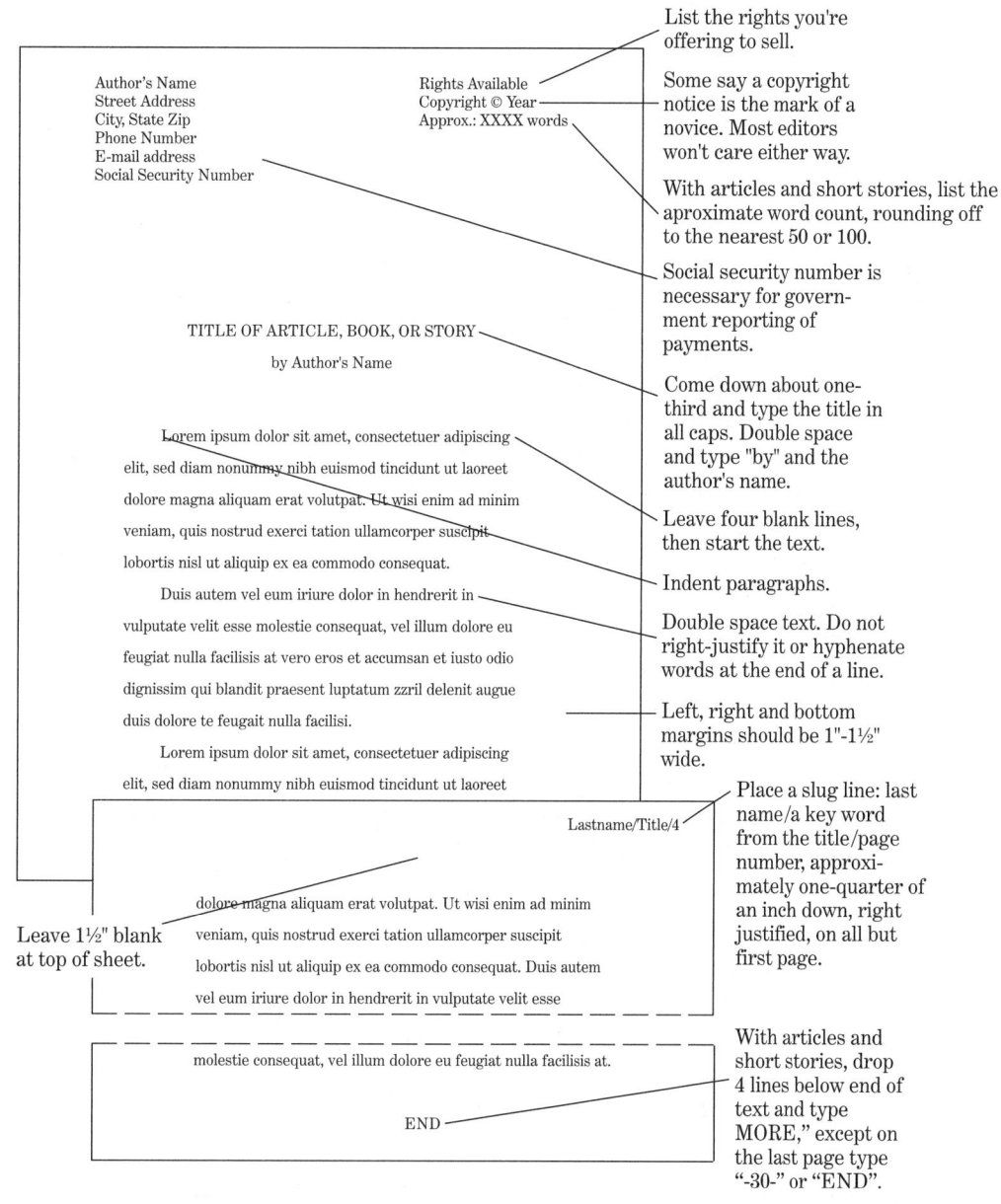

List the rights you're offering to sell.

Some say a copyright notice is the mark of a novice. Most editors won't care either way.

With articles and short stories, list the aproximate word count, rounding off to the nearest 50 or 100.

Social security number is necessary for government reporting of payments.

Come down about one-third and type the title in all caps. Double space and type "by" and the author's name.

Leave four blank lines, then start the text.

Indent paragraphs.

Double space text. Do not right-justify it or hyphenate words at the end of a line.

Left, right and bottom margins should be 1"-1½" wide.

Place a slug line: last name/a key word from the title/page number, approximately one-quarter of an inch down, right justified, on all but first page.

With articles and short stories, drop 4 lines below end of text and type MORE," except on the last page type "-30-" or "END".

Leave 1½" blank at top of sheet.

WRITERS ON WRITER'S BLOCK

Wherever writers gather, the conversation is, sooner or later, bound to turn to writer's block. Here are some thoughts on it by some of the best in the business.

"Generally, when I hit writer's block, I stop. I can break away and work on other books. Or, I will pace around in circles downstairs in my house and talk to my dog about it."
—Amelia Atwater-Rhodes, author of *In the Forests of the Night*

"I think writer's block is simply the dread that you are going to write something horrible. But as a writer, I believe that if you sit down at the keys long enough, sooner or later something will come out."
—Roy Blount, Jr. author of *Crackers* and *One Fell Soup*

"You don't know what it is to stay a whole day with your head in your hands trying to squeeze your unfortunate brain so as to find a word."
—Gustave Flaubert, author of *Madame Bovary*

"Writer's block is only a failing of the ego."
—Norman Mailer, author of *The Naked and the Dead*

"This may seem oversimple, but if you think you have writer's block or are taking too long to write, the problem is probably that you are spending too much time writing (or trying to) and not enough time thinking."
—Steven D. Stark, author of *Writing to Win*

"I was trained as a newspaper reporter, so there's no such thing as writer's block. You get fired for having writer's block."
—Nora Ephron, author of *When Harry Met Sally*

"If I don't know my character well enough, then I'll have writer's block. That's a clear sign I haven't delved deep enough into the personalities of my characters."
—Lee Wardlaw, author of *Punia and the King of Sharks*

"If I'm stuck, I write something else, do laundry, or take a nap."
—Karen Cushman, author of *Catherine Called Birdy*

"I've never had the luxury of having writer's block. When I do, I think about my mortgage."
—Larry Dane Brimner author of *The Littlest Wolf*

"Trust the process. Acknowledge your doubts and then write anyway."
—Mary Pearson author of *Scribbler of Dreams*

SUBMISSION TRACKING SHEET

Photocopy this page and use for each item submitted

Title: _____

Notes:

① Publisher: _____ Editor: _____ Phone: _____

Address: _____ Date submitted: _____ Multiple Submission? No Yes

Date to follow up: _____ Date followed up: _____ Follow-up note: _____

Date accepted: _____ Pub date: _____ Payment due date: _____ Payment amount: _____ Clips received: _____ Rejection date: _____

② Publisher: _____ Editor: _____ Phone: _____

Address: _____ Date submitted: _____ Multiple Submission? No Yes

Date to follow up: _____ Date followed up: _____ Follow-up note: _____

Date accepted: _____ Pub date: _____ Payment due date: _____ Payment amount: _____ Clips received: _____ Rejection date: _____

③ Publisher: _____ Editor: _____ Phone: _____

Address: _____ Date submitted: _____ Multiple Submission? No Yes

Date to follow up: _____ Date followed up: _____ Follow-up note: _____

Date accepted: _____ Pub date: _____ Payment due date: _____ Payment amount: _____ Clips received: _____ Rejection date: _____

④ Publisher: _____ Editor: _____ Phone: _____

Address: _____ Date submitted: _____ Multiple Submission? No Yes

Date to follow up: _____ Date followed up: _____ Follow-up note: _____

Date accepted: _____ Pub date: _____ Payment due date: _____ Payment amount: _____ Clips received: _____ Rejection date: _____

⑤ Publisher: _____ Editor: _____ Phone: _____

Address: _____ Date submitted: _____ Multiple Submission? No Yes

Date to follow up: _____ Date followed up: _____ Follow-up note: _____

Date accepted: _____ Pub date: _____ Payment due date: _____ Payment amount: _____ Clips received: _____ Rejection date: _____

Periodicals' Guidelines

Periodicals

12th Planet Literary Journal

You have entered the realm of *12th Planet*, one of the premiere internet literary magazines. In existence since, February of 1999 (a dinosaur in on-line time!) we are proud to have showcased some of the best authors on the web.

Submission Guidelines

We welcome your work! Please submit your poetry and/or essays according to the following guidelines!

WHAT WE ACCEPT

You may submit up to 3 poems at one time. We tend to shy away from rhyming poetry and gravitate towards poems that are rich in imagery.

You may also submit one essay at one time. We are looking for essays with a satirical bent. Think "A Modest Proposal".

Please do not submit additional work until we have responded to your initial submission. Any additional work submitted before we have a chance to respond to your initial submission will not be reviewed and will be deleted or destroyed.

We do NOT publish chapbooks or collections of poetry. Please do not query us asking how we can publish your manuscript!

HOW TO SUBMIT YOUR WORK

All e-mail submissions must be submitted in the body of an the e-mail. NO ATTACHMENTS ARE ACCEPTED!!!! To forewarn you, we delete any submission that is in attachment form. E-mail your submissions to twelfthplanet@worldnet.att.net. Please list "submission" in the subject line, and enclose all work in ONE e-mail.

All snail mail submissions must be accompanied by a self-addressed stamped envelope (SASE) or an e-mail address to which we can respond. We are usually slower at responding to snail mail submissions, since we function mainly electronically. However, we understand not everyone feels comfortable using email, and may not have easy access to the Internet. That being said, please address submissions to:

NOTE! U.S. Postal prices are increasing, effective June 30. If you send a submission via the mail from this point on, please be certain the SASE has enough postage.

PAYMENT & COPYRIGHT

We pay $10 per accepted piece, payable upon publication.

We claim one-time electronic publishing rights. After publication all rights revert back to the author. If your piece is published in another forum at a later date, you must list *12th Planet* at the original publisher. We also retain the right to re-publish your work in print, should we decide to do a "Best of" collection in the future. At that time we would notify you of our intent to publish your work in this forum, which will include further monetary compensation.

We will do our best to reply to your submission within 2 months. However, the volume of submissions we receive does not always allow for this. If you haven't heard from us by then, please drop us a line to make certain we received your original submission!

Finally, please make certain that the email address you use to make your submission will be valid for the next 2-3 months. We get email returned to us on a regular basis because the address is not longer in use, or the mailbox is full. If you do not hear from us, make certain it isn't for this reason!

Categories: Poetry—Short Stories

CONTACT: Rachel Baron, Editor
Material: All
4111 Circle Court, Ste. 1
Williamsville NY 14221
E-mail: twelfthplanet@worldnet.att.net
Website: www.12thplanetmagazine.com

4-Wheel Drive & Sport Utility

Circulation: 50,440
Frequency: monthly
Published by the PRIMEDIA Enthusiast Group.

Features in-depth articles about Jeeps, Broncos, Explorers, Blazers and domestic and imported four-wheel drive trucks and sport utility vehicles. Editorial also includes technical how-to information and reviews of aftermarket products and accessories.

For more information, visit the magazine's Web site at: www.4wdandsportutility.com.

Editorial submissions are welcomed, but the editor recommends that contributors query first. All contributions must be accompanied by a self-addressed, stamped envelope. Solicitations for editorial coverage, including car feature articles, should be submitted via US mail. Please include a photograph of the vehicle/project, a quick reference sheet and a few paragraphs detailing the editorial significance of your work. Due to busy travel and work schedules, the editor is not able to field calls related to potential editorial coverage. We assume no responsibility for loss or damage of any unsolicited materials.

Due to the volume of letters received we cannot directly answer any tech inquiry letter. Published letters may be edited for style, length or content. Be sure to include your full name and mailing address in all correspondence.

Categories: Nonfiction—Automobiles—Sports/Recreation—Technical

CONTACT: Editor
Material: All
PRIMEDIA Anaheim (McMullen Argus)
2400 E. Katella Ave, Ste 1100
Anaheim CA 92806
Phone: 714-939-2400
Fax: 714-939-6390
E-mail: 4wd@mc mcmullenargus.com
Website: www.mcmullenargus.com

5.0 Mustang & Super Fords

Formal guidelines not available. Please read a number of issues to ascertain the publication's style and needs.

Send queries to address below.

Categories: Nonfiction—Automobiles—Hobbies—Technical

CONTACT: Steve Turner, Editor-in-Chief
Material: All
3816 Industry Blvd.
Lakeland FL 33811
Phone: 863-644-0449
Website: www.50mustangandsuperfords.com

5678 Country
5678 Swing

Champion Media Group publishes two magazines *5678 Swing* and *5678 Swing*. Each is published six times per year focused on dance in its perspective genre. *5678* is a niche publication that has approximately 10,000 readers per month. *5678 Country* features articles pertaining to Country Western couples, line, and team dancing in its many forms.

5678 Swing features articles pertaining to West coast Swing, Lindy Hop, Salsa, Shag, Hustle and other forms of Swing Type social dance.

Areas of Interest:

We are interested in articles of many different natures.

• *Celebrity Interviews:* Today's stars of the dance world
• *Dance Technique:* How to do the steps, connection, lead and follow and more

- *Event Reviews:* How did it go?
- *Social Dancing:* Where to go, what to do, who does what where.
- *Personal Profiles*: Teachers, Studios, Dance Clubs.... what's up?
- *Dance Humor:* Something true or fictitious.... just funny.
- *Just Dance:* Doesn't fit into a category above, so what, if it's dance we might just want it.

Submission Format:

All articles accepted by email or attached file only. We accept Microsoft Word or a text file.

We pay upon printing of the article and purchase all rights. We pay anywhere from $35 to $100 for features. Material is subject to editing for length, style and format. We encourage photos and prefer to receive them by email as well in 300 dpi jpeg format at regular size. If that is not possible they can be sent hard copy. Photos are paid depending on quantity of use and size.

Categories: Fiction—Nonfiction—Arts—Dance—Entertainment—Music

CONTACT: Barry Durand, Publisher
Material: All
PO Box 8886
Gaithersburg MD 20898
E-mail: durand5678@aol.com
Website: www.5678magazine.com

96 Inc.

About *96 Inc*: *96 Inc* Artists' Collaborative has received national attention over the past twelve years for its innovative ways of supporting new and established artists. Its goal is that of integrating the arts into the community and to bring together the professional and the beginner, the artist and the artisan. Using writing and literature as a base, *96 Inc* has created and presented new works in usual and unusual spaces. Since February 1995, 96 has been the resident company at the Lansdowne Street Playhouse, where it presented the New Works on Tuesdays series and afternoon workshops for high school students. Founded on inclusiveness, *96 Inc* places a strong belief in the potential of young people and in the potential and accomplishments of young artists of all ages.

96 Inc magazine has a national distribution in bookstores and is currently being used in several high schools and colleges in other parts of the country—Colorado, Kentucky, Minnesota, Ohio, South Carolina, Vermont, and West Virginia. In addition, the Lithuanian Translators Society translates the magazine and uses it in literature and language classes at the University of Vilnius.

Submissions: *96 Inc* considers submissions in short fiction and poetry.

When to Submit: *96 Inc* accepts submissions on an ongoing basis. The magazine is published annually.

Payment: Writers whose submissions are accepted for publication receive four free copies of the magazine.

Categories: Fiction—Arts—Poetry—Short Stories

CONTACT: Vera Gold or Nancy Mehegan, Editors
Material: All
PO Box 15559
Boston MA 02215
Phone: 617-267-0543
Fax: 617-262-3568
E-mail: mail@96inc.com
Website: www.96inc.com

AAA Going Places

Please refer to *Going Places*

AAA Midwest Traveler

Please refer to *Midwest Traveler*

AAA Southern Traveler

Please refer to *Southern Traveler.*

AARP, The Magazine

Please refer to *Modern Maturity.*

ABA Journal

Thank you for your inquiry about submitting an article. The *ABA Journal*, the official magazine of the American Bar Association, is published 12 times a year and distributed to more than 376,000 readers. We also publish the *ABA Journal* eReport, a weekly e-mail publication that is sent to more than 200,000 members who have submitted their e-mail addresses.

The *ABA Journal* does not publish unsolicited manuscripts. Our articles are written by in-house legal writers or by freelance journalists we hire for specific assignments.

The Journal will consider queries. We prefer to hire freelancers who have a law degree and experience as a reporter for a legal or consumer publication. If you are interested in freelancing for the Journal, we urge you to include your resumé and published clips when you contact us with story ideas.

We are interested in queries about legal news or practice-oriented topics.

Please send queries to Sarah Randag by e-mail at releases@abanet.org or by fax to (312) 988-6025.

WRITERS' GUIDELINES

The *ABA Journal*'s content is designed to appeal to the association's diverse membership, with some emphasis on general practitioners in smaller law firms.

In writing an article for possible publication in the Journal, please be familiar with the following guidelines:

1. Type of article. The focus of the Journal is on current events in the law and on ideas that will help lawyers to practice better and more efficiently. Articles should emphasize practical, rather than theoretical or esoteric material.

2. Readership. As you write, keep your audience in mind. The typical reader of the Journal is a lawyer whose age is 43, and who is in private practice in a small law firm. Most are general practitioners.

3. Writing Style. The Journal is a magazine that covers topical issues involving lawyers. STORIES WRITTEN IN THE STYLE OF LAW REVIEWS, ACADEMIC JOURNALS OR LEGAL BRIEFS WILL NOT BE ACCEPTED. Articles should be written in an informal, journalistic style. Short quotations from people and specific examples will improve an article.

4. Length. Feature articles should be NO MORE THAN 3,500 WORDS. News stories or departments are 650 words.

5. Title. Developing a working title for an article may help you keep it in focus. The working title may be accepted as is or altered by the Journal staff as it deems appropriate.

6. Editing. All articles are subject to editing by the Journal. All articles are edited to conform to the Journal editorial style, which generally follows the AP Stylebook. The Journal inserts subheads, captions and readouts as needed.

7. Copyright. By having an article published in the Journal, authors thereby grant all property rights in the article to the American Bar Association and consent to an unqualified right by the ABA to copyright the work. This grant includes the right of the ABA to republish the article in other media, including electronic databases. This applies unless other arrangements are made in writing.

8. Citations. Citations to cases and other materials should be incorporated into the text; FOOTNOTES ARE NOT PERMITTED.

9. Structure. It is suggested that articles open with an interesting catchy lead, followed by a "nut paragraph" that tersely states the gist of the article.

10. Biographical data. At the end of an article, give your name, whether you are a lawyer, your place of employment, and whether you serve on an ABA committee or other entity. This data may be shortened.

11. Manuscripts. Manuscripts should be typewritten in a standard font (not all italics or all capitals) and double spaced. A cover letter should accompany the manuscript, indicating your name, address and telephone number. You also can submit your article via e-mail to releases@abanet.org.

12. Graphics. The Journal obtains appropriate artwork or photographs, if any, to illustrate articles.

Categories: Nonfiction—Law

CONTACT: Debra Cassens, Managing Editor
Material: All
American Bar Association
750 N. Lake Shore Drive
Chicago IL 60611
Phone: 312-988-6009
Fax: 312-988-6025
Website: abanet.org/journal

Abilities
Canada's Lifestyle Magazine for People with Disabilities

ABILITIES is Canada's foremost cross-disability lifestyle magazine. It is widely read by people with disabilities, their families and professionals engaged in disability issues.

The mission of the magazine is to provide:

INFORMATION: to the readership about stories, events and services.

INSPIRATION: to the readership to participate in organizations and events that are or could/should be made accessible to them.

OPPORTUNITY: to the readership through exposure, four times a year, to a wealth of Canadian resources that facilitate self-empowerment of people with disabilities.

ABILITIES is distributed nationally and internationally. The publication is available in print, on audio cassette and on computer disk. Back issues are also available on the Internet. In addition to its subscriber base, ABILITIES is circulated to every organization across Canada committed to the advancement and well-being of people with disabilities, as well as thousands of professionals, corporations and government agencies.

The editorial scope of the magazine includes travel, health, sport, recreation, employment, education, transportation, housing, social policy, sexuality, movie/book reviews and personality profiles. Other topics such as specific events or conferences are also considered.

The style of the magazine is "conversational" in that it is important for each article to be appreciated by as many of the readers as possible.

Articles are considered on the following basis:

Organizations and businesses are welcome to purchase space in the ABILITIES Forum section, as long as the editorial provided is of relevance to our readership and falls within the guidelines of the publication's philosophy. A one-page space in the magazine accommodates approximately 900 words - or fewer if a photograph or illustration is to be incorporated. "Advertorial" that is strictly product or com-

pany specific will be tagged as advertising. Information considered of generic interest may be treated simply as editorial.

Voluntary contributors wishing to shed light on a particular area of interest or provide personal perspective on any given matter are encouraged to submit a brief abstract of their idea for consideration, accompanied by a writing sample. The magazine cannot be responsible for unsolicited material. A self-addressed stamped envelope should be included. Finished articles, in general terms, should be between 500 and 2000 words.

Professional writers are welcome to submit abstracts or proposals for consideration, accompanied by writing samples, or unsolicited completed manuscripts. ABILITIES, as a not-for-profit organization, is generally able to award only honoraria as remuneration for professional work. Honoraria range from $50 to $350, depending on the length of the article and whether it was assigned by ABILITIES as needed information or brought to the publication as a matter of interest. Again, a self-addressed, stamped envelope should be included with any submission. Finished articles, unless otherwise specified, should range from 500 to 2000 words. We prefer not to receive simultaneous submissions.

Written contributions may also target specific regular departments in ABILITIES, such as coping methods in "FYI," and humour in "The Lighter Side."

Please note that all queries and manuscripts submitted by e-mail for consideration must include the writer's full regular mailing address and phone number.

ABILITIES purchases first-time rights only for all material used. This includes the right to publish all material printed in ABILITIES in our alternate formats as well as in electronic format on the Internet. A "kill fee" of 50% is available to writers where a financial agreement has been established.

If possible, all material should be provided both electronically (computer disk or e-mail), and as hard copy. The hard copy can be mailed, but faxing or e-mail is essential if it is close to a deadline. The disk should be in an IBM-compatible format. Any available photographs that illustrate an article should also be collected and included.

All material is subject to the editorial prerogative of the publication as to word count, logical flow, grammatical accuracy and choice of terms as they relate to people with disabilities.

Categories: Nonfiction—Disabilities—Lifestyle

CONTACT: Lisa Bendall, Managing Editor
Material: All
Canadian Abilities Foundation
340 College St., Ste. 650
Toronto, Ontario M5T 3A9
Phone: 416-923-1885
Fax: 416-923-9829
E-mail: lisa@abilities.ca
Website: www.abilities.ca

Absolute Write

Absolute Write is seeking original and reprint articles. We publish articles and interviews related to the craft and/or marketing of writing only— please do not submit fiction! We recommend that writers read articles published on this site to get an idea of our style and the types of articles that we publish. We are not geared to beginners; our target audience is intermediate and advanced-level writers. Very occasionally, we publish articles about the "basics," but in general, we're looking for articles that will be helpful to writers who have already had work published, taken writing courses, etc.

Article Submissions

Absolute Write is seeking "how-to" type articles about any branch of writing— screenwriting, freelance writing, technical writing, greeting cards, novels, nonfiction, playwriting, comic writing, and so on.

If you have never been published, please don't submit an article about how to get published. If you've never sold a screenplay, please don't submit an article about how to sell a screenplay. (You'd think this would be obvious, right?)

We are ALSO looking for the following things:

Interviews with working writers or those connected to the publishing or film industries— we particularly need interviews with agents, editors, and producers.

News stories or trends related to writing.

Perspectives from working writers. Can cover any aspect of a writer's life— business, craft, or "life" (balancing work and family, overcoming writer's block, increasing creativity, etc.).

Departments

• Debate Desk: be controversial. Tackle a subject like writing on spec, writing for free, plagiarism, etc. Don't be afraid to be opinionated!

• First Person: first-person essays about writing.

• Just for Fun: humor columns and funny poetry about writing.

Articles should be approximately 800-2000 words in length. Feel free to query first if you're considering writing an original article for us. For reprints, just send the complete manuscript with original publication name and date in the BODY of the e-mail message (please, no attachments, except for photos. We delete them unread, as we've gotten far too many viruses— even from writers who didn't know they had them).

We particularly like informational and humorous articles... the best are the ones that manage to combine those two qualities. You are welcome to write from a first-person perspective and editorialize, as long as your subject matter is relevant to other writers.

Articles must be the work of the original author. We accept simultaneous submissions. *Absolute Write* retains non-exclusive electronic publishing rights with the right to archive the material indefinitely on the website— thought the writer can ask me to pull it down at any time, and I'm happy to comply. All other rights remain with the author.

Bios

It'll save time if you include the bio that you'd like us to include along with the article. Of course, you can always send it after we accept an article, but if you have it ready, please send it along when you submit. (Just paste it below the article.)

All submissions should be sent to managing editor Amy Brozio-Andrews at amy@absolutewrite.com.

Payment

Did you skip right to this section? (Yeah, can't blame you.) I don't want to let you down, but we probably won't make you rich. There are two payment options:

• We pay $5 per article, interview, essay, or column— originals or reprints. We do not pay for book reviews (but, of course, you keep any book we send you). We also do not pay for syndicated columns (those that are published widely on the 'net). That said, it's very unlikely for us to accept a column that's been widely published on the 'net. Payments can be made by PayPal or check.

• Or you can have a free 1-year subscription to the Absolute Markets Premium Edition (a $15 value— see www.absolutemarkets.com).

We are happy to run your bio (with any links you like), your photo, ordering info if you've got books published. We have more than 72,000 subscribers and hope it brings you great publicity!

Product and Book Submissions

If you would like to submit your product or book for review by *Absolute Write* staff, or for use as a prize in our writing contests, please e-mail amy@absolutewrite.com to let us know. I'm sorry, but we do NOT review self-published/vanity-published/subsidy-published books anymore.

Categories: Nonfiction—Book Reviews—Interview—Writing

CONTACT: Amy Brozio-Andrews, Managing Editor
Material: All
E-mail: amy@absolutewrite.com
Website: www.absolutewrite.com

Accounting Today

Accounting Today is mostly staff-written, though we do occasionally run articles, commentaries and opinion pieces from outside, generally ranging from 600-1,200 words. They must be of specific interest to our readership of practicing accountants. There's no need to query first, though you may if you like; all submissions should be made via e-mail or snail mail — no phone calls or faxes.

Categories: Money & Finances—Accounting/CPAs

CONTACT: Bill Carlino, Editor-in-Chief
Material: All other
CONTACT: John Covaleski, Senior Editor
Material: Technology
395 Hudson St., 5th Floor
New York NY 10014
Phone: 212-337-8433

ACM
Another Chicago Magazine

We happily read submissions between February 1 and August 31; submissions received any other time are returned unread.

• Please send a SASE for reply.

• Double-space all fiction and keep stories under 25 pages (though once or twice we've published stories a little longer).

• Send one story only, unless you write shorts, and then you may send up to three (if indeed they are very short).

• It's very unlikely we would accept a "strictly genre" piece (e.g., Fantasy, Mystery, Scifi, etc.)

• No inspirational or religious stuff.

• Keep poetry to 4 pages unless you're convinced your long poem is irresistible.

• We welcome creative non-fictions personal essay, memoir, pastiche-that are factual and urgent, that had to be written. We publish short-short essays as well as longer pieces.

• Simultaneous submissions are okay, but we expect to be notified immediately when work has been accepted elsewhere and is therefore withdrawn from ACM consideration.

Replies/Acceptance/Payments: Like most literary magazines, we're a nonprofit, struggling operation which can't afford to pay much- a barely token honorarium when funding permits; but you do get a contributor's copy and a year's subscription. We try to send notice within 10 weeks, though it too often takes longer. We get about 75 manuscripts a week, which is a lot for your volunteer editors to handle.

If we accept the work, we understand you grant us first serial rights; all subsequent rights are yours, though we expect any future publication to carry acknowledgment that the work first appeared in ACM.

Photo guidelines—We're especially interested in presenting strong documentary photography and possibly some fine art photography. For more information, contact photo editor Karen Kring kkring@anotherchicagomag.com. You may include a URL for reviewing images on the web. No attachments please. Submitting scans or prints for production purposes-this work will be returned promptly.

Support literary publishing—To ensure the survival of literary journals—and a place to publish your writing—consider subscribing to at least one literary journal (if you don't already). If not ours, another.

Thanks—Tom Moss

Categories: Fiction—Poetry—Short Stories

CONTACT: Editors
Material: All
3709 N Kenmore
Chicago IL 60613
E-mail: editors@anotherchicagomag.com
Website: www.anotherchicagomag.com

Acoustic Guitar

QUERIES

If you are working on an assignment for Acoustic Guitar, you can skip this section. If you want an assignment, send a written query to the editors describing your proposed submission and your interest in the subject. If you have a manuscript, send it with a self-addressed stamped envelope. If you have previously published work that will give us a sense of your writing, send a copy with the understanding that it will not be returned. We will respond to your query within 60 days.

ASSIGNMENTS

If we assign you an article, we will send you two copies of a letter confirming the details of the assignment (deadline, length, content, etc.) and your acceptance of the terms of these Guidelines; please sign one copy and return it to us in the envelope provided. Even if we do not receive your signed copy, your submission of an assigned article constitutes agreement to the terms of the letter and the Guidelines.

CONTENT

The readers of Acoustic Guitar are musicians and/or instrument makers, so you may safely suppose that all have some basic knowledge of musicianship, music reading, etc. Remember, however, that many guitarists are self-taught or play only by ear, and that their musical interests and ability levels vary widely. Try to keep your article accessible and interesting to a reader who might be unfamiliar with the genre or style you are discussing, without getting bogged down in explaining every musical detail. Similarly, articles about guitars and gear should be catered to players, but they need to speak to readers with greatly varying degrees of knowledge and expertise.

INTERVIEWS/PROFILES

We publish stories on individual players because their musical contributions are enduring and important. Your job is to bring those contributions to light in an entertaining and illuminating way, not to hype them as personalities or stars. Treat artists with respect, but don't suspend your critical faculties or shy away from difficult questions. The musician-to-musician communication in the magazine should be as open and honest as possible.

• A sidebar list of recommended, currently available recordings is often useful for readers. Supply listings with full title, record company (with mail, phone, and Web address if it's a small label), catalog number, and year. If videos, publications, or Web sites relating to the artist's work are available, include details on those as well.

• Artist profiles written for the magazine's feature section, Song Craft, Jump Street, or Off the Record should include a "What They Play" sidebar on the artist's choice of guitar(s) and related equipment: strings, picks, and other accessories, plus stage amplification and recording setups. Include addresses for any small, hard-to-find companies. The best "What They Play" sidebars are more than straight listings, including quotes from the artists on why they use a particular piece of gear.

REVIEWS

We expect all writers who are evaluating products or the work of an artist to be free from conflicts of interest. If you have any questions about what might constitute a conflict of interest, speak to your editor.

FORMAT

Please submit your article electronically as well as on hard copy. If you're working on a PC, send us files in Microsoft Word for Windows (versions up to 97), RTF, or text-only format. If you use a Macintosh, send Word, WordPerfect, RTF, or text-only files. Stories should be emailed (preferably as attached Word files) to the editor who assigned the piece or editors.ag@stringletter.com.

FACTS

Make sure all name spellings, album titles, song titles, dates, company and product names, and other facts are correct when you're writing, and double-check them before you submit an article. We do as much fact-checking of material as we can, but our resources are limited, so don't count on us to catch errors. It can be useful to check facts with your original sources, but do not submit your full manuscript to an artist or company you're writing about. Doing so frequently leads to disagreements over the content and will compromise the integrity of your article.

MUSIC

If your contribution includes previously published music, we need either the original or a clear photocopy of the published example (original preferred), including full identification of the publisher and name of work. If the music has not been published, please provide a fair copy and any relevant information about the composer, copyright, etc. In the case of a transcription from a recording, we will need the same type of information. Whenever possible, please provide computer-notated scores on a disk in Encore or Finale (up to version 2002) format or as a standard MIDI file. Include a printout of the piece with the disk. Music files can be emailed to music editor Andrew DuBrock: andrew@stringletter.com. Details about our notation style can be found in the Music Style Guide, which is available from our music editor.

PHOTOS

If you are providing black-and-white prints, please be sure they are on glossy paper; sized as large as possible, up to 8" x 10"; clearly identified; properly credited to the photographer and/or owner of copyright; safely packed (not paperclipped!); and unmarred by writing on front or back. We can also use color transparencies or good-quality color prints. You may e-mail JPEG or TIFF photo files (300 dpi or better and as large as possible) to agart@stringletter.com.

DEADLINES

For magazine articles, we need your draft manuscript approximately 120 days before the cover date (the magazine actually comes out a month before the cover date). Your exact deadline will be included in your assignment letter.

PROOFS

After initial editing, we will send proofs for your approval.

PAYMENT

For all articles except Hit List reviews and Great Acoustics articles, you will be paid 25 cents per word, upon publication. We pay a flat rate of $75 for Great Acoustics and $25 per published Hit List review. For instructional articles, you will be paid $75 per published page of music that you contribute. Consult the editors about rates for photographs. On the rare occasion when we find an assigned article to be unpublishable, we will pay you 50 percent of the fee for that article at its assigned length, up to $200. (For example, the normal fee for a 1,000-word article would be $250, so the "kill fee" for that article would be $125.) We do not pay kill fees for unpublished Hit List reviews. See below for information on payments for article reprints. You will receive two complimentary copies of the issue in which your contribution appears. As a contributor, you may purchase any of our products (magazine subscriptions or back issues) at a 50 percent discount.

EXPENSES

We do not reimburse you for routine expenses such as phone calls, postage, or local travel. If you anticipate unusual expenses, please discuss these in advance with your editor.

COPYRIGHT

By submitting a manuscript, you are representing to us that you are its original author and that it has not been published previously. You must notify us in advance if your article contains any copyrighted material (whether text, artwork, or music), or if any of it has appeared, or is slated to appear, in another publication. The entire content of each issue of Acoustic Guitar is copyrighted as "work for hire," meaning that we, not you, hold the copyright. This copyright covers all uses of the material, including electronic or digital reproduction and our Web site. If you are providing us with a work that is already under copyright, such as an excerpt from a book, please furnish complete copyright information. If you are authorized to give permission to reprint it, please do so in writing. If someone else must grant us permission, furnish us with their name, address, and phone number. If you wish us to reassign the copyright to you, please consult your editor.

REPRINT RIGHTS

String Letter Publishing has an active book publishing program in which we frequently reprint material written for the magazine; we also reprint material written for our books in the magazine. If we reprint your article, you will be notified in advance and paid 12.5 cents per word for the reprinted text. (The rate for reprinted music will depend on whether you provide a recording for a lesson book/CD). The same principle applies when other publishers request permission to reprint articles. In the case of a publisher with limited resources and circulation-a local guitar club newsletter or a fan Web site, for example-we generally assign permission without a fee. But in the case of a publication that can pay for rights, we will negotiate the fee and share the reprint proceeds with you on a 50/50 basis.

—Scott Nygaard, Editor

Categories: Nonfiction—Biography—Music

CONTACT: Derk Richardson, Associate Editor
Material: All
255 West End
San Rafael, CA 94901
Phone: 415-485-6946 ext. 611
Fax: 415-485 0831
Website: www.acousticguitar.com

Adirondack Life

Editorial Guidelines

Adirondack Life is the only publication that addresses the unique natural and social aspects of New York State's Adirondack Park, and that gives those concerns local and national exposure. The magazine offers an important window into understanding this region.

In addition to the regular bimonthly issues of *Adirondack Life* — describing the history, culture, recreation, wildlife and personalities of the area—are two special issues: the Annual Guide to the Adirondacks and the Collectors Issue. The Guide's emphasis is on outdoorsy how-to and where-to articles that meet the needs of new visitors and offer in-depth information about an array of recreational offerings. The theme of the Collectors Issue changes each year—the premiere Collectors Issue was "At Home in the Adirondacks" and in 1999 that issue celebrated the magazine's thirtieth anniversary.

Writers should become familiar with the magazine and can do so by requesting a sample copy. Please send an address label and a check for $3.00 to cover postage. Along with a writer's query we like to see a few published stories. For new writers, the best way to break into the magazine is through departments, which, save for Adirondack Made (see below), run from 1,200 to 2,400 words. Features run from approximately 2,500 to 5,000 words.

Payment is $0.25 per published word approximately sixty days after acceptance. Currently we are not interested in poetry, editorial cartoons or short essays of less than 1,000 words.

All work submitted must be the original property of the writer and should not have appeared in another publication. *Adirondack Life* buys first North American serial print rights.

Facts in all articles must be verified or substantiated in the text. Please double space manuscripts. Include an SASE with all correspondence.

Departments

Special Places: Focused articles about unique locations that underline the special character of the Adirondacks. Recent examples include a visit to Up Yonda Farm, in Bolton Landing, and a history of the Crater Club, on Lake Champlain. Watercraft: Pieces on boats, boatbuilders and boat-related events. A recent example profiled sailboat builder Jack Manley, of Northville.

Barkeater: Short essays, from personal to political. Recent examples: an essay on winter camping on Azure Mountain's summit and a proposal for a trail around the Hudson River Gorge.

Wilderness: Descriptions of specific wild places and observations about legal or environmental issues affecting wilderness areas. In 1998 we described the search, semantical and actual, for "pristine" ponds.

Working: Stories of uncommon occupations in the Adirondack Park as well as characteristic employment. Recent Working departments include a story on a theatrical-lighting company in North Creek and a reflection on summer jobs in Lake George.

Home: Stories of Adirondack crafts or skills and techniques of interest to homeowners. A recent example describes family tree farms.

Yesteryears: Vignettes from regional history. Recent examples include an account of the former keeper of the Arab Mountain fire tower and a profile of "The Bishop of North Lake."

Adirondack Made: Short (500-600 words) describing a unique Adirondack business, past or present, and the people behind it. Recent examples profiled the Sunfeather Natural Soap Company, in Parishville, and the Crown Point Bread Company.

Other departments include Kitchen (distinctly Adirondack recipes), Profile (local individuals and families), Historic Preservation (important structures), North Country (catch-all), Sporting Scene (outdoor recreation and competitions), Environment and Wildlife.

The *Annual Guide* generally includes departments on hiking, biking, paddling, climbing, fishing, family activities, touring, access, learning and so forth.

*We accept queries, BUT NOT UNSOLICITED MANU-SCRIPTS, via e-mail.

Categories: Nonfiction—Architecture—Conservation—Culture—Ecology—Environment—Fishing—Gardening—History—Lifestyle—Outdoors—Photography—Recreation—Regional—Sports/Recreation—Travel

CONTACT: Galen Crane or Mary Thill, Editors
Material: All
PO Box 410
Jay NY 12941-0410
Phone: 518-946-2191
Website: www.adirondacklife.com

Affaire de Coeur

1. AFFAIRE DE COEUR no longer accept short stories, except through our contest. For the contest we will accept short stories of two thousand words maximum. *Short stories must be stories of romance with the following guidelines:*

a. There are no limitations with regard to setting. Time of setting may be historical, contemporary or futuristic.

b. Plots may be general romance or may include suspense, mystery or intrigue.

c. There are no age restrictions on the couple. Romances can range from young adult romances to twilight romances. There are no restrictions on previous relationship.

d. There are no racial or ethnic restrictions on the couple. We welcome diversity as long as the portrayal of the race or ethnic groups are realistic and non-stereotypical.

e. Because of the short length of the story, we discourage a love scene unless it is vital to the story.

f. The story should end on a positive note. That does not necessarily mean that the couple ends up together and lives happily ever after. It may mean that the heroine realizes she is better off without the hero or vice versa.

g. In order to avoid the feel of a true confession we encourage the author to write the story in the third person. However, if he/she does write it in the first person and it works, it may be accepted.

2. AFFAIRE will not accept previously printed short stories. We require a contract to the effect that the work submitted is original.

3. AFFAIRE pays up to $35.00 per published short story depending on the length. Payment is made at the end of the quarter in which the story appears.

4. AFFAIRE reserves the right to edit all short stories. While it is not our intent to change the context or complexion of a story, we will alter it for the purposes of length and correct spelling or grammar.

5. Short stories printed in AFFAIRE become the property of AFFAIRE DE COEUR magazine and may not be reprinted without the expressed written permission of AFFAIRE DE COEUR.

Categories: Fiction—African-American—Reference—Romance—Women's Fiction

CONTACT: Submissions Editor
Material: All
3976 Oak Hill Rd.
Oakland CA 94605
Phone: 510-569-5675
Fax: 510-632-8868
E-mail: Sseven@aol.com
Website: www.affairedecoeur.com

Affilia
Journal of Women and Social Work

The Editorial Board of *Affilia: Journal of Women and Social Work* invites the submission of manuscripts, poetry, articles, reports, essays, and literary pieces that relate to its mission: to the discussion and development of feminist values, theories, and knowledge as they relate to social work and social welfare, research, education, and practice. All forms of writing and analysis will be considered and a range of feminist perspectives will be encouraged. The intent of *Affilia* is to bring insight and knowledge to the task of eliminating discrimination and oppression, especially with respect to gender, race, ethnicity, class, age, disability, and sexual and affectional preference. The editors seek manuscripts from people both in and outside the field of social work that offer a critical analysis of the condition of women in this and other societies, apply these ideas to social welfare purposes, and work toward the empowerment of women in an equitable society.

Manuscripts should be submitted in quadruplicate, typewritten and double spaced in 12-point font. Maximum length of a manuscript for an article is 20 pages (25 pages for manuscripts reporting on qualitative research), including text, tables, references, and all else. Authors are requested to submit manuscripts in the reference style specified in the *Publication Manual of the American Psychological Association* (5th ed.). Authors should supply a separate cover sheet with name of the author(s) and other identifying information. An abstract of fewer than 100 words should accompany the manuscript. It is assumed that manuscripts are submitted for exclusive consideration of *Affilia* and have not been simultaneously submitted elsewhere.

Authors are required to submit written permission to reprint, from the original publisher, any quoted material of 300 words or more from a single source (journal article or book); any quoted material from a newspaper (especially the *New York Times*), a poem, or a song (even a phrase); and any table or figure reproduced from another work.

After editing, a corrected copy of the manuscript saved on a disk as an ASCII text file must be returned with the final hard copy (see letter of acceptance). Authors are requested to submit manuscripts in the reference style specified in the Publication Manual of the American Psychological Association (5th ed.). Text references use the author's surname and the year of publication; superior figures are not used. The References section at the end of each article contains the full citation, alphabetized by author, with initials for the author's first name, followed by the year of publication in parentheses. Titles of articles, chapters, and books are to be typed lowercase except for the initial letter, and no quotation marks are used with titles of articles or chapters. Titles of journals and publishing companies, however, follow the

usual style of capitalizing the appropriate letters. This style affords no place for notes or comments in the References section or footnotes in the text. Such notes should be incorporated into the text if they are pertinent. Simple asides will not be included.

Submission of a manuscript implies commitment to publish in this journal. Authors submitting manuscripts to the journal should not simultaneously submit them to another journal, nor should manuscripts have been published elsewhere in substantially similar content. Authors in doubt about what constitutes prior publication should consult the editor.

Categories: Nonfiction—Feminism—Social Work

CONTACT: Miriam Dinerman, Editor-in-Chief, *Affilia*
Material: All
School of Social Work
Yeshiva University
2495 Amsterdam Ave.
New York, NY 10033.
Phone: 212-960-5289
E-mail: editor-in-chief@affiliajournal.org
Website: www.affiliajournal.org

African American Family

Please refer to *Metro Parent Magazine*.

The African American Pulpit!

Unsolicited materials are gladly received. Please follow these specifications for publication: Only sermons and articles by African American preachers will be published. Any sermon submitted for consideration should be prefaced with a brief synopsis of its context and point of origin.

Submission of material to Judson Press or to the editors assumes the right of Judson Press to publish the material in an issue of *The African American Pulpit*. Prior to actual publication, the writers will sign a formal publishing agreement granting permission to Judson Press to publish the piece. All manuscripts submitted for publication to *The African American Pulpit* are subject to editorial revision (grammar, punctuation, conformity with house style, and length). Only original work will be considered. Any previously published material chosen for use will be obtained by the editorial team.

The following are some specifics to remember:

• Written manuscripts should be submitted printed on 8 1/2" x 11" paper, typed double-spaced, and on computer diskette (a non-MAC format). Sermons should not exceed 2,500 words. Articles should not exceed 1,500 words.•

• When a Scripture verse is quoted or paraphrased, make sure to specify chapter, verses, and version used.•

• Sources of direct quotations must be cited with full publishing author, title, place of publication, publisher, year of publication, and page number(s) of quoted material. For periodicals, include author, title of article, name of periodical, date, volume and number if applicable, and page number(s).•

• For quotations longer than one sentence, contributors must supply a photocopy of the original. If this is not available, the editors will, in most instances, paraphrase or delete the quotation rather than risk reprinting it incorrectly.•

• Permission from the copyright holder is needed for any quote of significant length and for any music or poetry that is not in public domain.•

• Please be sure to include a photograph (black and white preferred) of yourself with your submission. If your submission is published, we will include your photograph alongside your piece.

Categories: Nonfiction—African-American—Book Reviews—Christian Interests—Inspirational—Men's Issues—Multicultural—Music—Poetry—Public Speaking—Religion—Spiritual—Sermans—Women's Issues—Homiletics

CONTACT: Editorial Department—Judson Press
Material: All
Judson Press, 588 North Gulph Road
King of Prussia PA 19406
Phone: 610-768-2128

African American Review

African American Review publishes essays on African American literature, theater, film, art, and culture generally; interviews; poetry; fiction; bibliographies; and book reviews.

Those submitting article manuscripts should prepare them in accordance with the most recent edition of The MLA Style Manual, which encourages the use of intratextual documentation wherever possible and mandates the inclusion of a list of works cited (with full pagination) at the manuscript's end. Send three copies of submissions (2,500-5,000 words are preferred), along with a self-addressed envelope and sufficient postage to permit your manuscript's return, to the Editor, *African American Review*, Shannon Hall 119, Saint Louis University, 220 N. Grand Blvd., St. Louis, Missouri 63103.

Poets should submit two copies of no more than six poems at a time, along with a self-addressed, stamped envelope (sufficient postage to permit your work's return), to the Editor at the above address.

Fiction writers should also submit two copies of a story, along with a self-addressed, stamped envelope (sufficient postage to permit your work's return), to the Editor at the above address. (Stories between 2,500-5,000 words are preferred.)

Inquiries regarding book review assignments should be addressed to, Dr. Yoshinobu Hakutani, Book Review Editor—AAR, Kent State University, Dept. of English, Kent, OH 44242, yhakutan@kent.edu.

Individuals whose works are accepted for publication must provide *African American Review* with a brief biographical sketch. Moreover, because the magazine is set from computer disk, accepted work should, whenever possible, be provided on floppy diskette.

The editors do not assume responsibility for loss of or damage to submitted materials. Materials published in AfricanAmerican Review do not necessarily represent the views of the journal's editors, staff, or financial supporters, and these parties therefore disavow any legal responsibility for the materials.

Categories: African-American—Literature

CONTACT: Dr. Joe Weixlmann, Editor
Material: All
Shannon Hall 119, Saint Louis University, 220 N. Grand
St. Louis MO 63103
Phone: 314-977-3703

African-American Career World

Please refer to Equal Opportunity Publications, Inc.

Agni

AGNI publishes poetry, short fiction, and essays. Writers whose work has appeared in the magazine include Derek Walcott, Seamus Heaney, Joyce Carol Oates, Jhumpa Lahiri, Louise Gluck, Ha Jin, Olga Broumas, Tom Sleigh, Jill McCorkle, Ilan Stavans, Thomas Sayers Ellis, Gail Mazur, Noam Chomsky, and Rosanna Warren. AGNI also focuses on featuring emerging writers. The magazine appears twice yearly, in Spring and Fall.

For AGNI's next open reading period, please call us. We adhere strictly to postmark dates, and manuscripts received outside that period will be returned unread, provided that sufficient return postage is included. The editors suggest submissions of no more than one story or essay or five poems. Poetry, fiction, and non-fiction should be submitted SEPARATELY (i.e., with separate SASE's) and addressed to the Fiction, Poetry, or

Non-fiction Editor. Translations and essays are welcomed. Please enclose a self-addressed, stamped envelope (SASE) for our response or we will be unable to reply. Envelopes which are too small or have insufficient postage for a manuscript's return will only get our response, and the manuscript will be recycled.

Note that we CANNOT CURRENTLY ACCEPT EMAIL SUBMISSIONS (although this may change in the coming year as our website is developed—please check there periodically, and before you submit, for changes in our submission policies). Simultaneous submissions are acceptable with notice of such, but please notify us immediately if the work we are considering has been accepted elsewhere. AGNI's reporting time is approximately 2-4 months. While we endeavor to deal with each submission quickly and fairly, we cannot, due to the overwhelming number of submissions we receive, accept responsibility for unsolicited manuscripts. Do not send us your only copy.

We strongly suggest that potential contributors unfamiliar with AGNI read a recent issue (preferably more) before submitting to ensure that your work is appropriate for the journal. Sample copies are available for $10. Subscriptions are $17 for 1 year, or $31 for 2 years and a free back issue. (Add $3/year for Canadian addresses, $6/year for other international orders). Make checks payable to AGNI, and please specify the issue you would like to start with and your preferences for back issues, if any.

PS. Please note our new web address, where guidelines are also posted.

Categories: Fiction—Poetry—Short Stories

CONTACT: Submissions Editor or Managing Editor
Material: All
Creative Writing Dept, Boston University
236 Bay State Rd.
Boston MA 02215
Website: www.bu.edu/AGNI

Alabama Living

Alabama Living

A Publication of the Alabama Rural Electric Association of Cooperatives

Ceased publication.

Alaska Business Monthly

Alaska Business Monthly is written, edited and published by Alaskans for Alaskans and other U.S. and international audiences interested in the business affairs of the 49th state. Its goal is to provide thorough and objective analysis of the issues and trends affecting Alaska's businesses, and to feature stories on the individuals, organizations and companies that shape the Alaska economy. *Alaska Business Monthly* emphasizes the importance of all enterprise, and stresses a statewide approach to business coverage.

We seek informative, entertaining articles on everything from entrepreneurs to heavy industry. We cover all Alaska industry to include mining, tourism, timber, transportation, oil & gas, fisheries, finance, insurance, real estate, communications, medical services, technology and construction. We also cover Native and environmental issues, and occasionally feature Seattle and other communities in the Pacific Northwest.

As our magazine is on most in-state airlines and in many major hotels, our reach extends beyond the businessperson to include tourists and the general public. Though circulation is at minimum 10,000 issues per month, we have a total statewide readership of approximately 100,000 individuals per month.

SUBMISSION CRITERIA

Approximately 80 percent of the features appearing in *Alaska Business Monthly* are written by free-lancers. All queries should be directed to the editor via mail, e-mail (editor@akbizmag.com), mail, fax or phone. We also welcome queries from individuals who would like to write columns in their fields of expertise. Anyone interested in writing for *Alaska Business Monthly* should submit three clips or sample articles.

Articles are assigned at least two months in advance. Each year we publish an editorial calendar that lists about half of each issue's topics. A copy of the editorial calendar will be provided upon request.

We purchase all rights of articles and reserve the right to make reprints of articles or to republish them in special ABM editions (such as an anniversary edition). We generally do not provide additional payment for such uses.

If we use the article in one of our specialty publications, we will provide additional payment. When we receive reprint requests from other publications, we direct such solicitations to the writer.

We prefer submissions on disk or transmitted via e-mail. When submitting by disk, please note formatting information on the disk (Word 2.0, for example) and provide a hard copy. When submitting by e-mail, send the article as an attachment, and also place a copy of the text in the e-mail itself.

PAYMENT

In a survey done in 1996, we discovered that *Alaska Business Monthly* pays the second-highest free-lance rates of any statewide business magazine in the western states. *Payment for articles is set at the time of assignment and will generally conform to the following standards:*

Business Spotlight	1-2 sources	500 words	$100
Short Feature	1-2 sources	500-750 words	$125
Short Feature	3+ sources	500-850 words	$150
Regular Feature	1-2 sources	750-1,000 words	$150
Regular Feature	Multi-source	1,000-1,500 words	$175
Full-length Feature	Multi-source	1,500-1,800 words	$200
Full-length Feature	Multi-source	1,800-2,000 words	$250
Full-length Feature	Multi-source	2,000+ words	$300
Sidebar to Feature			$15-$50

We will reimburse writers for long-distance charges, provided total charges for any article do not exceed $20. Charges in excess of $20 must be approved in advance. We generally do not reimburse for other expenses (gas, travel, meals). Writers must invoice for payment.

PHOTOGRAPHY GUIDELINES

We accept black-and-white prints or negatives, color slides, color prints and color negatives. We prefer color slides. The name and address of the photographer should be on the back of every print or on the margin of every slide.

Our preferred color slide film is Fujichrome, ASA 100 or slower. For black-and-white photography, please try to use 400 ASA film or slower. We can scan prints, 35 mm slides and 35 mm negatives in-house.

Photo payment is determined by the published size of the photograph, unless otherwise agreed upon at the time of assignment. Generally, the following rates for payment will apply for one-time use of an assigned photograph. (When we are asked for reprints of articles or sections of our magazine, we generally do not provide additional payment to the photographer). Payment for stock photography is less.

Cover:	up to $400
Stock:	up to $100
Full-page:	up to $200 color
	up to $175 B/W
Stock:	up to $50
Three-quarters-page:	up to $150 color
	up to $125 B/W
Stock:	up to $40
Half-page:	up to $125 color
	up to $100 B/W
Stock:	up to $35
Quarter-page:	up to $75 color
	up to $50 B/W
Stock:	up to $25

ABM will only pay full-price for photography that is professionally done. Payment for slides and photographs of lesser quality will be substantially less. There is no payment for photos provided by businesses or non-profits. In special cases ABM will reimburse the photographer for film and processing. Arrangements should be made with the editor at the time of assignment. Photographers must invoice for payment. (Call or e-mail editor for amount to invoice.)

CONTACT: Debbie Cutler, Editor
Material: All
PO Box 241288
Anchorage AK 99524-1288
Phone: 907-276-4373

Alberta Views

Writers/Illustrators/Photographers

AlbertaViews is a bimonthly magazine dedicated to providing well-written and well-researched commentary on the culture, politics and economy of Alberta. Each issue contains three feature articles of between 3000–5000 words on matters of social concern to Albertans. *AlbertaViews* is a regional magazine; therefore we are only interested in articles with a strong Albertan focus.

Please do not send unsolicited manuscripts.

AlbertaViews will consider synopses for feature ideas, reviews and garden articles, as well as reprints from various Alberta media of up to 1000 words for our readings section entitled Eye on Alberta. We also accept queries from photographers for submissions to View, our regular photographic feature on the inside front cover, or from artists who wish to showcase their work in Eye on Alberta. We do not accept unsolicited fiction or poetry. No materials will be returned without a self-addressed, stamped envelope (S.A.S.E.).

WE DO NOT ACCEPT PHONE QUERIES. But email is an excellent way to query us.

Queries:

Please read *AlbertaViews* before querying in order to fully understand the mandate of the magazine. With at least two months lead time for every issue, *AlbertaViews* covers issues as opposed to news, so please be aware of time-sensitive material or ideas. Back issues of the magazine are available for $5, which includes first class postage.

In any query, please include:

1) A written proposal of 300–500 words outlining your intended contribution to *AlbertaViews*, why you feel qualified to write about your chosen subject and what sources you intend to use.

2) A resume outlining your experience and education, complete with references and their phone numbers.

3) Recent examples of your published work (tear sheets).

4) A self-addressed stamped envelope (S.A.S.E.) if you require your submission material returned.

To submit a piece that has been previously published–such as an editorial or news item relevant to a current issue–please e-mail us the text and send a clear photocopy of the published piece. Provide the name of the publication and the date the piece appeared. We do not pay for reprints, art or anything else published in the Eye on Alberta section of the magazine, but we are interested in receiving speeches, memos, e-mails, web site excerpts and letters that might be of interest to the public.

For queries, expect a reply in six to eight weeks.

Format

For matters of style such as spelling, please refer to the Canadian Oxford Dictionary and the Globe and Mail style guide. Send all material in a double-spaced, paragraphed format with one space after periods.

Provide us with both a hard copy of the text (preferably mailed) and a computer version on disk or via e-mail. When e-mailing text, please attach the file if it is a Microsoft Word document, and include plain text in the body of the e-mail if you are not using Word. We require disks to be IBM or PC formatted (Microsoft Word if possible. If not, please send plain text).

Accompanying artwork or photos are welcome, but please provide them as 5x7 or 4x5 transparencies, 35 mm slides, or on disk, saved as Adobe Photoshop scans of a minimum 300 dpi using the CMYK color system and saved as a .tiff file.

For clarity of communication, we expect all writers to sign an agreement. We buy First North American Serial Rights, and the right to use an excerpt of the article on our web site. *AlbertaViews* pays about $.30 to $.50 per word depending on the writer's experience and qualifications. We pay about $50.00 for reviews. Photos vary. We pay upon publication. The writer must also provide a brief autobiographical sketch to be included with the article, a title for the article and suggested pull quotes. For emailing, please send only 3 to 5 files (no larger than 100kb each). Thank you.

Thank you for your interest in *AlbertaViews*. If you have any further questions, please feel free to e-mail us.

If you would like *AlbertaViews* to see your work, please send samples to: Scott Dutton, Art Director (see address below).

Categories: Nonfiction—Arts—Culture—Economics—Politics—Regional

CONTACT: Jackie Flanagan, Publisher and Executive Editor
Material: Queries
(QUERIES) 320 23rd Ave SW Ste 208
Calgary AB P2SOJ2
Phone: 403-243-5334
Fax: 403-243-8599
E-mail: (QUERIES) contactus@albertaviews.ab.ca
CONTACT: Scott Dutton, Art Director
Material: Photos and Illustrations
602 - 815 1st Street SW
Calgary AB T2P 1N3
E-mail: (PHOTOS, ILLUSTRATION)
creative@albertaviews.ab.ca
Website: www.albertaviews.ab.ca

Alfred Hitchcock Mystery Magazine

Finding new authors is a great pleasure for all of us here, and we look forward to reading the fiction you send us. Since we do read all submissions, there is no need to query first; please send the entire story. You don't need an agent.

Because this is a mystery magazine, the stories we buy must fall into that genre in some sense or another. We are interested in nearly every kind of mystery, however: stories of detection of the classic kind, police procedurals, private eye tales, suspense, courtroom dramas, stories of espionage, and so on. We ask only that the story be about a crime (or the threat or fear of one). We sometimes accept ghost stories or supernatural tales, but those also should involve a crime.

You might find it useful to read one or more issues of *AHMM*; that should give you an idea of the kind of fiction we buy. For a sample copy, send a check made out to *AHMM* for $5.00 to 475 Park Ave. South, 11th floor, New York, NY 10016.

Style. We prefer that stories not be longer than 10,000 words; most of the stories in the magazine are considerably shorter than that. They should, of course, be well-written. We are looking for stories that have not been previously published elsewhere, and among them for those that are fresh, well-told, and absorbing. They should be entirely fiction: please do not send us stories based on actual crimes, for instance, or other real-life events.

Manuscript preparation. Manuscripts should be typed on plain white paper (not erasable paper) and double-spaced (not space-and-a-half), with your name and address at the top of the first page. The title of the story as well as the byline you want to use should be on the first page of the story also. (We prefer that there not be a separate title page.) If you use a word processor, please do not justify the right-hand margin. Every page of the story should be numbered, preferably in the upper right-hand corner. If you number the pages by hand, be sure before you start that no page has been omitted. Do not use the italic, large-size, or boldface characters some computers are capable of generating. Underline words to indicate italics.

Indent for each paragraph. Do not leave 1-line spaces between paragraphs. The number of lines per page should be uniform, or mostly so.

Stories should be mailed to us flat, with the pages bound together by a paper clip only —— not stapled or enclosed in a binder. A cover letter isn't necessary. If you want the manuscript returned in the event we cannot use it, you must include a self-addressed stamped envelope; contributors outside the U.S.A. should send International Reply Coupons in lieu of stamps. If you have sent us a photocopy and do not want it back, please advise us of that and enclose a smaller SASE for our response. Please keep a copy of any material submitted, since we cannot be responsible for lost or misdelivered mail.

Revisions. Revised versions of a story should be submitted only on our request, as a rule. At the very least, tell us in a cover letter that the story has been submitted before but has been revised, and explain how.

NOTE: Stories submitted to *AHMM* are not also considered by or for *Ellery Queen's Mystery Magazine*, though we share the same address. Submissions to *EQMM* must be made separately. We do not accept simultaneous submissions.

Categories: Fiction—Crime—Mystery—Short Stories

CONTACT: Submissions Editor
Material: All
AHMM
475 Park Ave. South, 11th Floor
New York NY 10016
Phone: 212-686-7188
Website: www.themysteryplace.com

A-E

Alive Now

Our Mission
Alive Now is a devotional magazine that supports the spiritual lives of small groups as well as individuals. The magazine invites readers to enter an ever-deepening relationship with God, helps them reflect on contemporary issues from a faith perspective, and supports them in acting on these issues.

General Guidelines
Each issue of this bimonthly, 64-page magazine focuses on a contemporary topic that impacts the faith life. Divided into sections that move readers through exploration and reflection on the theme, the magazine may be used weekly by individuals or members of small groups. The sections contain scripture, prayers, meditations, stories, poetry, reflection aids, photographs, and art. Seasonal material, both theological and liturgical, is appropriate.

Readership
Alive Now is ecumenical, including both lay persons and church professionals. Our readers are primarily adults — from young adults to older adults — and include persons of many cultures and ethnic backgrounds.

Style and Format
Your submissions should invite readers to seek God in the midst of daily life by exploring how contemporary issues impact their faith lives. We do not pretend to have the final answer to life's dilemmas. But we hope that the magazine will provide a glimpse of the life of faith to which we all are called.

Submit for a theme. We make selections based on a list of upcoming themes. Manuscripts which do not fit a theme will be returned. To receive a current themes list by mail, please send your request to us with a self-addressed, stamped envelope. (See *Alive Now* address below.) *Alive Now* also posts upcoming themes online. We place manuscripts on long-term hold for specific issues. Authors are free to request that their manuscripts be returned to them at any time during the long-term hold.

Meditations and stories should be 250 to 500 words. Send your best work. Use language that is inclusive. Material that contains sexist language and imagery is difficult to use.

Manuscript Preparation
Contributions should be typed, double-spaced, on 8 1/2" x 11" paper and should be accompanied by a self-addressed, stamped envelope for return. If you are submitting material for more than one theme, send an SASE for each theme represented. On each page you submit, include your name, address, and the theme for which the piece is being sent.

Notification and Payment
Payment will be made at the time of acceptance for publication. We will notify contributors of manuscript status when we make final decisions for a theme, three months before the issue date. Unusable material will be returned if an SASE was sent with the manuscript. We purchase newspaper, periodical, and electronic rights so that we can respond to requests for reprints from local church publications and other periodicals as well as promote the magazine on the World Wide Web. We may purchase one-time use. The usual fee is $35 and up.

Categories: Arts—Inspirational—Photography—Poetry—Religion—Spiritual

CONTACT: Melissa Tidwell
Material: All
1908 Grand Ave.
PO Box 340004
Nashville TN 37203-0004
Phone: 615-340-7216
E-mail: AliveNow@upperroom.org
Website: www.alivenow.org

Alive!
A Magazine for Christian Senior Adults

Alive! A Magazine for Christian Senior Adults is currently published quarterly. Editor is J. David Lang; Office Editor is A. June Lang. Please send all communication to the address below.

FORMAT: 2 colors, 24 pages 8 1/2 x 11. Manuscripts should be typed double-spaced on good quality paper (no erasable bond). Letter quality computer print-outs acceptable (no matrix, please). No FAX please. Length may vary from 600 to 1200 words.

MARKET: Christian senior adults approximately 55 years of age or older. Timely articles about Christian seniors in vital and productive life styles, travel, or ministries. The character of the magazine is upbeat and activity oriented rather than nostalgic. We can use fiction, jokes, articles about needs and interests of seniors, appropriate cartoons, and biographical sketches of active Christian senior adults.

RIGHTS: Prefer first rights, but will consider second rights and simultaneous submissions.

SUBMISSIONS: Prefer complete manuscripts rather than queries. Material cannot be returned unless SASE is enclosed. Request for samples should include $1.06 for mailing and handling.

RATES: 4-6 cents per word. Payment on publication.

PHOTOS: A limited number of free-lance black and white photos will be accepted. Photos with articles are welcomed, and will be paid for at our rates according to the quality.

Categories: Fiction—Nonfiction—Christian Interests—Health—Relationships—Senior Citizen—Short Stories—Spiritual—Travel—Humor

CONTACT: A. June Lang, Office Editor
Material: All
PO Box 46464
Cincinnati OH 45246
Phone: 1-800-35ALIVE or 513-825-3681
Website: www.missionsalive.org/csf

All About Kids

About Us
All About Kids, now in its 17th year of production, is a local, national award-winning magazine that serves as the premier parenting resource in the Greater Cincinnati and Northern Kentucky area.

All About Kids is a valuable guide for parents, educators and child care providers. Each monthly issue features timely articles on a variety of parenting topics, as well as a comprehensive calendar of family events.

Pick up a free copy at any Greater Cincinnati or Northern Kentucky Kroger Store or one of our more than 600 distribution points throughout the area including The Museum Center, The Art Museum, Cincinnati Public Libraries and a multitude of local public, private and parochial schools.

If you have any questions, comments or suggestions please contact us at:

All About Kids is nearly 100% freelance written and depends on talented freelance writers to fill the magazine with timely and informative editorial content each month.

Although we utilize an annual editorial calendar, there are some topics you simply can't plan for; thus, assignments become critical and maintaining a wide variety of talented writers is crucial.

We accept queries via e-mail, phone, fax and mail. Please note that we do adhere to AP style and require documentation of all sources.

Each issue also includes regular columns such as Expert Advice, Middle Years, Rave Reviews, Women's and Family Health, News You Can Use and our award-winning Calendar of Family Events.

For more information, or to submit an article, please e-mail our the Editor.

Categories: Nonfiction—Children—Parenting—Relationships—Teen—Women's Issues

CONTACT: Shelly Bucksot, Editor
Material: All
Midwest Parenting Publications
1077 Celestial St. Ste. #101
Cincinnati OH 45202-1629
Phone: 513-684-0501
Fax: 513-684-0507
E-mail: editor@aak.com
Website: www.aak.com

All For You

ALL for YOU's Philosophy
ALL for YOU is in business to help people discover feeling good everyday, so we print only positive stories about life experiences. ALL for YOU does not dwell on negative aspects of any related subject matter. Please do not be critical of competing products or services. If you do mention a product or service, please give us a contact name for possible advertising.

ALL for YOU's Editorial Requirements
ALL for YOU is interested in where to go and how to do it stories on fitness, nutrition, self-health/alternative health options in the Chicagoland suburbs, primarily western and northwest. Material should provide information readers can use in this immediate vicinity and in areas they can travel to on weekends or a short vacation.

The accent in ALL for YOU is on:
- Fitness
- Nutrition
- Health
- Spirituality
- Healing Arts

Related subjects are healthy eating/cooking, well-being, massage, meditation, acupuncture, hypnosis, intuitive healing, bicycling, yoga, pilates, golf, education related to any of these areas, intuitive/awareness information, chiropractic.

Remember, you are writing for publication one or two months in advance, and your subject matter should reflect that time lapse if necessary. We never want to lose sight of our primary goal which is to provide useful information for the reader.

Any material accepted is subject to such revision as is necessary to meet the requirements of this publication. Manuscripts and photos not used will be returned if a stamped, self-addressed envelope is provided, but we assume no responsibility for lost materials.

Please include a title of the article on each page. Also include an overline or subtitle (example: Pilates: The Miracle I Found). Include a byline and page number on each page and please include your social security number. If you submit a timely item, please indicate the month for suggested use.

ALL for YOU's Acceptance Policy
Please read before calling.

If you make an editorial submission to ALL for YOU and it is not returned in 30 days, you can assume we do plan to use it. However, we do keep some material for as long as 12 to 18 months before using it.

ALL for YOU Web Site Permission Form
The ALL for YOU web site may feature a sampling of articles found in the magazine. These articles are chosen at random from the current issue. If your article appears in ALL for YOU and you do not wish to see it on the web page, please let us know. The use of an article on the web site involves no additional compensation from ALL for YOU.

ALL for YOU Deadline Schedule:
35 Days Preceding Publication. Example: April 25th for the June issue.

Stories
- Should be accompanied by jpg, tif or gif files, black and white or color photos

- Should be between 600 and 1,200 words with shorter stories preferred. The story's focus should be on where to and how to. Stories should impart information in an entertaining fashion, and not in a text book or preachy tone.
- Can be submitted in the following forms:
—via e-mail. We have had best results with email.
—on a 3½" diskette if you use a Macintosh or IBM computer. We use Microsoft Word for word processing.

Photos
- ALL for YOU can accept color or black and white or color slides. A good photo is usually one that catches the action of the story.
- Please send no more than 3 to 4 photos per story.
- You must place your return address on the back of the photo if you want it returned. Caption sheet, with the title of the story it accompanies should be taped to the back of the photo. There is no better way to insure that your photo will not be used with another writer's story.

Important Checklist before Sending in Material
- Your name is on all pages and photos.
- You have included your social security number.
- You have indicated what month the material is for.
- You have written a headline and subheadline.
- You have written a caption for each photo.

Please Remember: If we do not plan on using your material, it will be returned to you within 10 days of receipt.

Categories: Food/Drink—Health—Spiritual

CONTACT: Submissions Editor
Material: All
161 Hawkins Circle
Wheaton IL 60187
E-mail: ALL4YOUWRITERS@aol.com

America@Work

About Us
America@work (monthly magazine). Union leaders and front-line activists creating change for working families find their ideas, info and ammo in America@work, the monthly magazine of the AFL-CIO. The AFL-CIO was formed in 1955 by the merger of the American Federation of Labor and the Congress of Industrial Organizations.

What is the AFL-CIO?
The American Federation of Labor-Congress of Industrial Organizations (AFL-CIO) is the voluntary federation of America's unions, representing more than 13 million working women and men nationwide.

Guidelines
Formal guidelines not available. Please read a number of issues to ascertain the publication's style and needs.

Send queries to address below.

Categories: Nonfiction, Careers

CONTACT: Submissions Editor
Material: All
AFL-CIO, 815 16th Street, N.W.
Washington DC 20006
Phone: 202-637-5000
Fax: 202-637-5058
Website: www.aflcio.org

America West

Published by Skyword Marketing Inc., *America West* magazine is the monthly publication aboard *America West* Airlines. Each month, more than 1.6 million passengers fly on *America West* to destinations across the continental United States, several Canadian cities, Mexico and Costa Rica. The airline's operational hubs are Phoenix and Las Vegas.

Feature

• One Good Read: The magazine's centerpiece story might be a thoughtful news feature, an essay, a piece of fiction (short story or excerpt from a longer work) or a photo essay. Subjects that evoke a strong sense of place within the airline's route system are particularly welcome. The length ranges from 1,500- 3,000 words; sidebars often are staff-generated.

Departments

• Flights of Fancy: A regular compendium of fribble and froth to amuse and inform. Discrete components of short narratives and lists in a graphically sharp design. Demands excellent research, reporting and snappy writing with an attitude. Staff written. Each issue includes several of the following, plus other material as warranted:

• Dept. of Commerce: A look at new and notable business trends in *America West* destination cities. Approximately 450 words; assigned to a regular contributor.

• Dateline: Las Vegas—a monthly slice of commercial, cultural or recreational life in and around • Las Vegas. 300-400 words; assigned to a regular contributor.

• Language Arts—words, phrases, vocabulary. Etymology rendered entertainment.

• Briefs—goofy news stories, trivia and cool stuff we can't fit anywhere else.

• Creature Feature—descriptions of bizarre animals, traits, animal behavior and research.

• Extreme Science—reports of wacky research studies we wonder ever got funded.

• Who, What, When, Where, Why?—brief descriptions of quirks in history keyed to destination cities.

The length of this section ranges from 1,200-2,000; currently staff written and not open to freelancers.

• Opposites Attract: Two writers assume opposing positions on a topic of wide interest. Balanced, civil expressions by people with no agenda other than to communicate well a passionate belief; politicians, stuffy academics need not apply. The length is 500-800 words each; open to freelancers and contributors among our readers.

• City Lights: a digest of interesting, entertaining and serviceable information about our cover destination. The length is 500 words; assigned to a regular contributor.

• Transitions: how people solved problems, confronted demons and prejudices, or overcame odds in business, personal relationships, adventure/survival, competition, etc. The length is 1,000- 1,500 words; open to freelancers.

• Location, Location, Location: Real estate writ engagingly conceptual and pegged to destination cities. The length is 1,000- 1,500 words; open to freelancers.

• Hometown: Writers wax eloquent/amusing/ passionate/quirky about an aspect of their city of origin or residence. No sweeping "everything you always wanted to know about" destination stories. Must be personal and opinionated. No wimps allowed. The length is 1,000-1,500 words; open to freelancers.

• Who's On First?: A humorous, sports-information Q&A with questions submitted by our readers. The length is 1,000- 1,500 words; assigned to a regular contributor.

Terms and Rights

The magazine buys first North American print rights and pays on acceptance. Rates range from 60 cents to $1 per word, depending on the degree of difficulty and research. If, after one rewrite as directed by the editor, the work is not suitable for publication, the kill fee is 25%. Reasonable expenses are reimbursed if cleared with the editor in advance and invoiced with reciepts and a Social Security number.

Terms and Assignments

Please query the editors by snail mail at the address below. Expect four to eight weeks for a reply. A business-sized SASE guarantees a faster response. Sample copies are available for $3: Please include an self-addressed, 9-inch by 12-inch envelope with sample-copy requests. Stories are assigned four to six months in advance of publi-

cation. Assignments must be submitted via e-mail or on disk in Microsoft Word. Meeting deadlines is critical. Writers should also be prepared to submit a list of source material for fact-checking.

Categories: Fiction—Nonfiction—Adventure—Animals—Careers—Comedy—Conservation—Cooking—Culture— Entertainment—Family—Food/Drink—General Interest— Inspirational—Language—Literature—Money and Finances—Multicultural—Native Americans—Photography—Recreation—Rural America—Science— Short Stories—Society—Travel—Western—Writing

CONTACT: Ellen Alperstein, Editor in Chief
Material: All
CONTACT: David Proffit, Associate Editor
Skyword Publishing
4636 E. Elwood St., Ste. 5
Phoenix, AZ 85040-1963
Phone: 602-997-7200
Website: www.skyword.com

American Artist
Watercolor

What we are looking for:

The readers of *American Artist* and *Watercolor* magazines are professional or advanced amateur artists who want to learn from other artists. Our articles therefore profile an accomplished artist in any fine-art medium (no photography) and his or her techniques, featuring large full-color reproductions of the artwork and a step-by-step demonstration whenever possible. The artists are primarily realists, interested in traditional techniques and subjects.

American Artist always features a "Watercolor Page" and a "Pastel Page." These articles are often written by the artist (or ghost-written in the artist's voice) and focus on one technical aspect, rather than providing an overview of the artist's work. In addition, the "Business & Professional Practices" articles cover the business side of being an artist, such as gallery representation, pricing artwork, framing, and obtaining grants and fellowships.

The stories in *Watercolor* are similar in content to those in *American Artist*, except that they must be on watermedia (acrylic on paper, casein, gouache, and watercolor). *Watercolor* often features a "Lives in Art" story that focuses on one artist's career path.

In both magazines we also publish stories with an art historical bent. These stories are always oriented toward what a practicing artist today can learn from a master of a certain medium or technique.

Finally, some of our stories focus on recent exhibitions. In these pieces, we aim to provide insight into an assembled group of pictures in terms of their subject matter. In this way, we hope to provide readers with a greater understanding of how contemporary artists are incorporating more meaningful content into their work.

What to submit:

For editorial consideration, please send a letter outlining your proposal, along with your résumé. (A Web site address is not acceptable.) Be as specific, and concise, as possible in your proposal.

Please send a stamped return envelope with your submission.

What we pay:

Upon the article's publication, we generally pay $500 for articles of about 1,500 to 2,000 words.

Final notes:

We acquire the copyright for the article, but not the artwork.

We receive a large volume of material every day. It can take six to eight weeks for us to respond to your query. Please be patient. We seriously consider every proposal we receive.

We work about four and a half months in advance of the publication date.

Categories: Arts—Biography—Trade: Art Exhibition

CONTACT: M. Stephen Doherty, Editor-in-Chief
American Artist and Watercolor
770 Broadway
New York, NY 10003
Phone: 646-654-5506
Website: www.myamericanartist.com

American Business Review

The American Business Review welcomes both empirical and theoretical articles that can be applied or be pertinent to current business issues and practices or contribute to academic research in finance and business.

Authors' articles should not exceed 25 double-spaced typewritten pages, and footnotes should appear on a separate page and follow A.P.A. style. The author should send three copies of his manuscript plus a short biography. Include also an abstract of not more than 75 words summarizing the paper.

All articles are anonymously reviewed by the editorial board entirely in terms of scholarly content.

Previously published articles cannot be accepted.

Categories: Nonfiction—Business—Money & Finances

CONTACT: Editor
Material: All
University of New Haven, 300 Orange Ave.
West Haven CT 06516
Phone: 203-932-7118
Fax: 203-931-6084
E-mail: mharvey@newhaven.org

American Bungalow

Inquiry Letter: Please send a brief pitch letter with a summary of the article you propose and several photographs of the subject matter if possible. We will return any materials with a SASE. Expect a response within six weeks and include an e-mail address if at all possible.

Clips: If you are a published writer, please include one to three samples of your previous work. If you write for competitive magazines, or if the material you are pitching has been published previously, please let us know the names of those publications.

Topics: American Bungalow covers a wide range of topics: the Arts and Crafts movement, collecting, bungalow neighborhoods, new construction, gardens, art, period lodges and home renovation, among others. Surprise us; we love to publish little-known gems.

Tone: We're looking for writers whose personalities come through in their work, and first-person storytelling is fine. Factual information should be leavened with quotes when possible, and please avoid footnotes and other academic approaches.

Length: Typically, American Bungalow articles run between 800 and 1,200 words. Sidebars containing resource information, brief historical overviews, etc. are also fine to include. Short (100–400 word) pieces may be published in our b&w newsletter within the magazine without compensation.

Format: If your idea is accepted for further development, you may submit final text in a hard copy, an MS Word-based floppy or an electronic document.

Artwork: Strong graphic elements are very important to the look of American Bungalow. Your proposal has a much better chance of being accepted if you are able to provide quality photographs, drawings or period illustrations to accompany your piece.

Some specifics: We can work with transparencies, slides or prints of photographs. Scanned images need to be saved at 300 dpi; please do not e-mail photos to us without prior arrangement. Please include the name of the photographer so we can give them proper credit. Period photos are welcome as well. Elevations, floor plans and the like should be a reasonable size—they need to fit on our scanners. We are happy to return all of your materials, but will need to work with them for approximately three months.

Show Us What You've Done: American Bungalow publishes architect and homeowner renovations, and new construction articles that have slightly different guidelines than our features. We're looking for firsthand experiences—the challenges or special characteristics of your project and how you solved them—that will resonate for other readers. Humor, how the experience impacted your family, what made you decide to build a bungalow—all are welcome. These articles are also the one category where we can accept amateur snapshots—but we still need sharp, well-exposed photos to illustrate the piece. Flash-on-camera interiors are often unusable, so if you're shooting indoors, please use a tripod and available light. Professional-quality photography is most welcome as well, and elevations, floor plans and resource lists are strongly encouraged.

Compensation: American Bungalow will send you several copies of the issue in which your article appears, along with your returned art materials. Articles are often written in exchange for a nationally published clip, a comp book from the Bungalow Bookstore, or a subscription to the magazine. If you have a business that deals with Arts and Crafts products or services, we may be able to trade out ad space for the feature; each case is unique, so please let us know on what basis your proposal is predicated. We do offer modest compensation for some features, in the $175–$250 range.

Back Issues: If you are not a regular reader, the best way to get a sense of our style is to review several back issues of American Bungalow. The current issue is posted on our website, www.ambungalow.com, and past issues are available through the site or by calling 800 350-3363.

We look forward to receiving your proposals; thanks for your inquiry.

Categories: Nonfiction—Architecture—Collectibles—History—Sheltor

CONTACT: Michelle Gringeri-Brown, Editor
Material: All
PO Box 756
Sierra Madre, CA 91025-0756
Phone: 800-350-3363
E-mail: editor@ambungalow.com
Website: www.ambungalow.com

American Careers

American Careers is published once a year for high school students and once a year for middle/junior high school students. Each issue contains up-to-date career information, how-to articles, self-assessments and other stories designed to promote career development and career education.

Assignment Procedures

1. Individuals in business, government and education provide some stories at no charge. Career Communications, Inc., makes work-for-hire assignments or buys all rights for other stories in *American Careers*.

2. Often stories are assigned based on ideas proposed by writers. Before making assignments, we need a résumé and writing samples on file.

3. We assign stories by phone, letter or e-mail detailing the story idea and focus, possible contacts, deadline, etc. We may ask you to in-

clude photographs or request photographs or other art from interviewees to illustrate your article.

4. A signed contract must be on file before any payment is made.

5. We accept late copy only if you consult with us first. Writers who do not meet deadlines may not receive future assignments.

Payment

1. Payment rate varies with assignment.

2. Payment is made within 30 days of receipt of assigned work.

3. Reasonable expenses, approved in advance and documented, will be reimbursed within 30 days.

Copy/Photo Requirements

1. You may e-mail your manuscript using Macintosh-compatible Microsoft Word or QuarkXPress programs. We also request a hard copy of your manuscript, which you may submit by fax or mail. Use 1" margins, double-space your copy and place a page number on each page.

2. Include a one-sentence author biography at the end of your story.

3. Submit a list of all resources and the names, addresses, phone numbers and e-mail addresses of interviewees with each article.

4. When possible, we would appreciate photographs complementing your article, particularly photos of specific people addressed in your story. Submit permission slips or release forms from all people photographed and all photographers.

Style

1. Reading Level/Story Length. Articles should be written at a seventh-grade reading level, or they will be returned for rewrite. Articles in *American Careers* usually run from 300-750 words. Some topics may require additional space for impact and clarity. These topics are discussed on an individual basis. Sometimes we run half-page or single-page items on topics such as recent career news or people who have been successful climbing the career ladder.

2. Focus. Stories should exhibit a balanced national focus, unless the assignment covers only one region or school.

3. Style. Use the Associated Press Stylebook as a guide for style. Style matters particular to *American Careers* will be handled in editing. Career Communications, Inc., reserves the right to edit and revise all materials for publication.

Categories: Nonfiction—Careers—Education

CONTACT: Submissions Editor
Material: All
6701 W. 64th St.
Overland Park KS 66202
Phone: 800-669-7795
Fax: 913-362-4864
E-mail: ccinfo@carcom.com

American City & County

General Information

American City & County is received by more than 70,000 elected and appointed local government officials and public and private engineers. Included in the circulation list are administrators, supervisors and department heads of municipal, county, township, state and special district governments.

The interests of these readers span all areas of local government concern, including, but not limited to: street and highway construction and maintenance, water supply, wastewater collection and treatment, solid waste collection and disposal, resource recovery, street lighting, public transit, parks and recreation, traffic engineering, public housing, urban renewal, financing, community development, office automation and computer application, management techniques, and security and public safety.

Our goal is to provide a voice for local government by addressing the issues and concerns of public officials, offering ideas and solutions to problems and publishing information of interest to managers at all levels of local government. This goal is accomplished through the publi-

cation of in-depth discussions of major topics and supporting features, shorter news and feature items and various departments devoted to federal legislation, news of people in the industry, new products, product literature and manufacturers' news.

Before submitting any editorial material, you should take a few moments to read a copy of the magazine. This should give you information about what we cover and at whom our editorial material is aimed. Be aware of several things, including:

• We use only third-person articles. We do not tell the reader what to do; we offer the facts and assume the reader will make his or her own informed decision;

• We cover city and county government and state highway departments. We do not cover state legislatures or the federal government, except as they affect local government;

• If you are submitting a case history or application story, be aware that a company or product may be mentioned once in the article unless a byline is included, in which case the author's bio will list the company. We do not run articles about products no matter how clever or useful. To be considered, the article must be about the product's usefulness to a particular city or county. In other words, tell us how the product or service helped the local government solve a unique problem. Only in rare instances will we use quotes from company spokespeople; quotes must generally be from city or county officials.

What We Use
FEATURES AND SPECIAL REPORTS

Each month, three to five major topics are given in-depth coverage of 1,500 to 2,200 words. These stories are written in news magazine format and are generally authored by magazine staff members or paid freelancers. Occasionally, however, experts on particular subjects are retained to write features. Sources and ideas for these articles must be approved by the editor in order to assure placement and proper writing style. Features should generally discuss all pertinent aspects of a subject and use quotes from local government officials and industry leaders. Dissertations or thesis-like articles are not used for features, nor is promotional copy.

ISSUES AND TRENDS

This section includes three articles per month on rotating topics that include public safety (including EMS services and 911 systems,) water supply, wastewater, grounds maintenance (including landscaping and pest control,) information technology (including GIS, imaging, surveying and computer services,) fleet maintenance (including trucks and automated fleet systems,) streets and highways and solid waste collection and disposal. These 300- to 500-word articles should reflect information on timely developments and trends within the specific topics. Graphics are encouraged.

DOTTED LINE

Briefs on services offered or contracts awarded are used in this department. A local government or government agency must be involved. We do not use material about mergers, acquisitions or contracts between private companies.

ROLL CALL

This department reports on promotions, job changes, new appointments and honors received by local government officials or those companies that serve the municipal and county market. Releases should include the name of the individual community or company name, location and the person's responsibilities. Black and white photographs will be considered.

PROJECT PROFILES

Case histories between 500 and 800 words appear in this section. When available, color or black-and-white photographs or artwork should accompany the case history. They should be written from the local government perspective and should not be promotional in nature. Case histories should discuss how a particular local government solved a unique problem and should be non-technical in nature.

ACROSS AMERICA

Short news articles of general interest to local governments are included in this section. Technical or dated material will not be used.

Articles should not be promotional but may mention company names germane to the subject matter. Articles about community projects should be written in a third person, news feature format with quotes from local officials. Items that include black-and-white prints or color slides are preferred. Articles should not exceed 600 words.

FINANCIAL MANAGEMENT

This column is bylined by experts in local government financing, both from the public and private sectors. These 500- to 600-word articles discuss local government financial options and techniques in generic terms. Published articles will include a byline and brief biography; no other reference to a company or specific service is allowed. Ideas for submission should be cleared with the editor first. Deadline is six weeks prior to publication.

GOVERNMENT TECHNOLOGY

This column is bylined by public officials or companies serving local governments. It deals with information technology trends in local government operations. This 500- to 700-word column is not limited to administrative operations; discussions of the automation of public works functions are equally important. The contributor receives a byline and short biography for this generic article. Ideas should be cleared with the editor. Deadline is six weeks prior to publication.

BUYER'S INDEX

Items should include a brief, clearly written summary of important features of the product, video or literature and the significance to the local government field. We file the hundreds of product releases we receive each week, so we would prefer that you not call to request information on the status of a particular one. We clean out these files every six months, so, if your product release has not appeared within that time, it most likely will not appear. You are welcome to re-submit releases. Black and white photos are encouraged. Length: 50 - 100 words.

Submitting Articles

American City & County accepts articles on CDs and via e-mail. We will also accept a clean, double-spaced manuscript for scanning. The magazine's word processing software is Microsoft Word, and its desktop publishing software is Adobe InDesign. Other software can be translated. Editorial is prepared two months in advance of the publication date. Signed copyright forms are required and will be sent out before publication. Advance phone calls and query letters are welcome but not necessary, except regarding feature stories.

You should be aware of certain considerations, including:

• We do accept unsolicited articles, which we keep on file for a year. We use these articles when the topic appears on the editorial calendar. It is generally a good idea to call to make sure your article has been received, although it is unlikely that you will receive the promise of a certain publication date;

• Rather than calling with an article query, it is generally better to write a short paragraph describing a potential story idea and to follow up a week or so later with a phone call;

• We will never guarantee either publication or placement of a story. We deal with too many variables — space considerations, length of other articles, etc. If we specifically ask you to write an article for us, we will do everything possible to see that it is published;

• Our copyright forms are not open to negotiation. They basically serve to protect us against the possibility of your article appearing in our magazine and those of our competitors. We don't want that, and neither do they. If your article has been accepted for publication elsewhere, please inform us of that fact, so we do not count on it;

• Your article has a better chance of being published if it is accompanied by artwork (photographs, charts or graphics.) Color slides are preferred, but we will accept black and white and color photographs, as well as digital images. Please call if you have questions about digital formats;

• We stick closely to our editorial calendar, so if the topic of your article is not listed on the calendar, it is highly unlikely we will make an exception and publish it;

• We edit all submitted material for style. We will try to work with you on edits if we get the material early enough; however, we cannot guarantee that you will see the finished article before it is published.

Categories: Nonfiction—Government

CONTACT: Bill Wolpin, Editorial Director
770-618-0112, (bwolpin@primediabusiness.com)
Material: Feature Articles
CONTACT: Lindsay Isaacs, Managing Editor
770-618-0199, (lisaacs@primediabusiness.com)
Material: Government Technology and Project Profiles.
CONTACT: Ellen Howle, Associate Editor
770-618-0120, (ehowle@primediabusiness.com)
Material: Financial Management and Issue & Trends
CONTACT: Wendy Angel, Assistant Editor
770-618-0202, (wangel@primediabusiness.com)
Material: All product releases and submissions for Across America
6151 Powers Ferry Rd. NW, Ste. 200
Atlanta, GA 30339-2941
Fax: 770- 618-0349
Website: www.americancityandcounty.com

The American Dissident

Read the FOCUS section of *The American Dissident* to better understand what this literary journal is about and what it seeks to publish. Send no more than three or four well-written, unpublished poems and/or one unpublished essay (250-950 words max), preferably relating or stemming from a PERSONAL EXPERIENCE with corruption, any kind, and, even better yet, that RISKED something on the part of the poet/writer, be it ostracism from fellow poets or even one's job because it was published or read in public. Include an SASE. Send books for review consideration. Pays one copy. Acquires first North American serial rights. Submit a short biography not including credits or letters of recommendation, but rather deprogramming and personal dissident information. What pushed you to shed the various skins of indoctrination? When did you stand apart from your friends or colleagues to "speak the rude truth" a la Emerson? Why are you submitting poems to a journal called The American Dissident? Subscriptions are $18 per year (two issues). Purchase one copy of the most recent issue for $8. *The American Dissident* is professionally printed, flatbound and 48-56 tight pages virtually crammed, though neatly, with poems, essays, book reviews, literary letters, tough rude truth quotations, and sociopolitical cartoons and drawings. All correspondence should be sent to and checks made out to G. Tod Slone, Ed., The American Dissident, 1837 Main St., Concord, MA 01742 -3811. E-mail submissions accepted only from subscribers.

Categories: Nonfiction—Literature—Poetry

CONTACT: G. Tod Slone, Editor
Material: All
ContraOstrich Press
1837 Main St.
Concord MA 01742-3811

American Fitness

American Fitness welcomes unsolicited and queried manuscripts for publication on the subjects of health, fitness, aerobic exercise, sports nutrition, sports medicine, innovations and trends in aerobic sports, fitness marketing, tips on teaching exercise and humorous accounts of fitness motivation, physiology and women's health and fitness issues (pregnancy, family, pre- and post-natal, menopause and eating disorders). Profiles and biographical accounts of fitness leaders are also used. Query with published clips or send complete manuscript. Length: 800-1,200 words. Pays $140-180. No first person accounts.

American Fitness also accepts material for its columns and departments: "Adventure" (treks, trails and global challenges), "Strength" (the latest breakthroughs in weight training), "Clubscene" (profiles and highlights of the fitness club industry), "Food" (low-fat/non-fat, high-flavor dishes), "Homescene" (home workout alternatives) and "Clip 'n' Post" (concise exercise research to post in health clubs, offices or refrigerators). Query with published clips or send complete manuscript. Length: 800-1,000 words. Pays $100-140.

Review: All manuscripts are reviewed, refereed and edited according to the editors' discretion. Solicited manuscripts receive referee notification within three to four months. Only accurate, scientifically valid and well-documented material is accepted for educational articles. Manuscripts that deal with lighter, non academic material are not processed through the editorial review board.

Preparation: Manuscripts should be typed, double-spaced, with 1.25-inch margins. Due to our scanning capabilities, dot matrix submissions are now unacceptable. Manuscripts must be submitted on pure white paper with no last-minute, penciled notations. All italic type must be indicated with an underline. Electronic submissions on Macintosh compatible disks in Microsoft Word are welcome. SASE must be enclosed. Every attempt will be made to return artwork, line drawings, photographs and slides. However, neither the editors nor AFAA are responsible for lost or damaged submissions.

Exclusivity: It is understood that accepted manuscripts are not being considered for publication in any other magazine or journal.

Categories: Nonfiction—Adventure—Alternate Life-style—Children—Consumer—Food/Drink—Health—History—Inspirational—Interview—Physical Fitness—Senior Citizen—Sports/Recreation—Travel—Nutrition—Nostalgia—Personal Experience—Pregnancy—Medicine—Home—Eating Disorders—Humor

CONTACT: Meg Jordan, Editor-at-large
Material: All
15250 Ventura Blvd.
Sherman Oaks CA 91403
Phone: 818-905-0040
Fax: 818-990-5468

American Forests

American Forests—the magazine of trees and forests for those interested in all facets of forestry—is the nation's oldest conservation magazine, having begun regular publication in 1894. It emphasizes the trends, issues, policies, management, and enjoyment of America's forest resources, including trees in and around communities. The best way to get an idea of the kind of articles and photographs we commission and buy is to study the magazine. A sample copy will be sent to those who send a self-addressed, magazine-size envelope with $1.70 in postage.

ARTICLES FORMAT: We're looking for factual articles that are well written, well illustrated, and will inform, entertain, and perhaps inspire. Most of our articles are now assigned, but we welcome informative news stories on controversial or current topics, as long as they are well documented and present the issue fairly. We do not, at this time, accept fiction or poetry. Articles should be neither too elementary nor too technical. About 80 percent of our readers have had college training, and about 30 percent have either a Master's or a Ph.D. degree.

Written queries are required, and we work four to 12 months in advance of an issue.

Most of our published manuscripts come to us on disc. Because the magazine is produced on Macintosh computers, we prefer Microsoft Word, but we can accept WordPerfect saved as ASCII text (DOS). Your disc must be accompanied by a paper manuscript. We can also accept articles via e-mail [or mailed] to the address below.

Although we are always willing to consider a submission, the acceptance of an article for review in no way constitutes a contract for publication. All submissions and queries are reviewed by the editors, and the author is informed of our decision within eight weeks.

PAY RATES: Payment for full-length articles—with photo or other illustrative support—ranges from $250 to $800, and is authorized upon acceptance.

PHOTOGRAPHS
FORMAT: Many of the photos used in American Forests are sent by the authors to illustrate their articles. These photographs should be related to the article and must be clear and sharp. A caption sheet, keyed to numbers on the photos, should describe each shot and name any people shown.

In black-and-white photos, we prefer 8"x10" glossies. In color, we need original—not duplicate—transparencies; 35mm is the most common, although 4"x5" or 5"x7" transparencies are good choices for cover shots. Fuji Velvia and Kodachrome 64 are two of the best color films for our purposes. We accept good quality digital images, that are at least 300 dpi.

PAY RATE: Payment for cover photos is $300. For photos submitted with articles, payment is included in a check to the author. Inside shots not submitted with an article are paid for at a rate that depends on size, quality and placement in the magazine.

SUBMITTING ARTICLES AND/OR PHOTOGRAPHS
All material will be returned, provided a self-addressed, stamped envelope of suitable size accompanies your submission. Send submissions to the address below.

ADDITIONAL INFORMATION FOR PHOTOGRAPHERS
American Forests has long been noted for its coffee table—quality covers and inside photographs, and we intend to improve upon that reputation. We strive for the photos in our magazine to be more than simply a record of a place or event, but rather a creative interpretation that's pleasing to the eye and evokes an understanding of what is happening in the scene and/or a longing to be in that particular place, usually outdoors. Some detailed guidelines on outdoor photography follow for the semi-pros and nonprofessionals among our contributors.

FILM TYPE: For optimum reproduction, film should be a smooth-grained type such as Fuji Velvia or Kodachrome 64. Because of the relatively slow ASA speed of such films, there are times when a higher-speed film is needed—low-light conditions, for example. Under those conditions, the first option would be to use a longer exposure time with a camera mounted on a tripod. If the subject is stationary, shoot at 1/60th or 1/30th of a second. If that's not possible, the other alternative is to shoot high-speed Ektachrome with an ASA of 400. It's better to have a grainy photo than none at all.

BEST TIME OF DAY: The ideal time to photograph is when the sun is low on the horizon—from sunrise until about 10:30 and from 3:30 until sunset. A low sun lights a person's face or any vertical object, so that you can distinguish detail. When the sun is directly overhead, all the features are in dark shadows. Also, the light of a low sun is warmer, because it is passing through more atmosphere on its slanted approach.

Obviously, there are situations when the time of day cannot be prearranged and photographs must be taken when the opportunity arises.

POSING YOUR SUBJECTS: When working with people in your photos, it's best to have them doing their "thing," whatever that may be, rather than looking at the camera. If they are scientists, for example, they should appear to be studying some object that relates to the article. Posed shots usually are undesirable; when taking a portrait, strive for a more relaxed shot.

CAMERA EQUIPMENT: Because we are trying to portray a three-dimensional subject in two-dimensional form without the help of other senses, you should portray nature not exactly the way it appears, but a bit larger than life. To accomplish this, most photographers use lenses other than the "normal" 50mm lens that comes on most cameras. The lenses used most by professional photographers are wide-angle—either 35mm or 28mm—or short telephotos of 75mm or 135mm. These lenses produce a slightly exaggerated view of nature and appear fresh to the reader, who with the unaided eye has never seen nature quite that way.

It's impossible to provide detailed advice about camera selection here, but it pays to use the best you can buy or borrow. Even the newer point-and-shoot cam-eras, if they have a quality lens, can produce reproduction-quality photographs.

Packages to be handled by Federal Express, UPS, or other fast-delivery services should be sent to our street address below.

Categories: Nonfiction—Conservation—Ecology—Environment—General Interest—Outdoors—Public Policy/Politics—Recreation—Reference

CONTACT: Michelle Robbins, Editor
Material: All
734 15th St NW, 8th Floor
Washington DC 20005
Phone: 202-737-1944, x203
Fax: 202-737-2457
E-mail: mrobbins@amfor.org
Website: www.americanforests.org

The American Gardener

The American Gardener is the official publication of the American Horticultural Society (AHS), a national, nonprofit, membership organization for gardeners founded in 1922. By advancing the art and science of horticulture through its publications and programs, AHS is dedicated to educating and inspiring people of all ages to become successful and environmentally responsible gardeners.

The bimonthly *American Gardener* goes out to the more than 30,000 members of the American Horticultural Society. Another 2,500 issues are sold on newsstands nationwide.

EDITORIAL CONTENT

The magazine is primarily free-lance written, and its content differs considerably from that of other gardening publications. Our readers are mainly experienced amateur gardeners; about 20 percent are horticultural professionals. Articles are intended to bring this knowledgeable group new information, ranging from the latest scientific findings that affect plants, to the history of gardening and gardens in America. We introduce readers to unusual plants, personalities, and issues that will enrich what we assume is already a passionate commitment to gardening.

Among the topics of particular interest to us are profiles of individual plant groups; innovative approaches to garden design; profiles of prominent horticulturists whose work has a national impact; plant research and plant hunting; plant conservation, biodiversity, and heirloom gardening; events or personalities in horticultural history; people-plant relationships (horticultural therapy, ethnobotany, and community gardening); environmentally appropriate gardening (choosing plants suited to one's region, using native plants, conserving water, etc.); and plant lore and literature. We are also seeking articles that describe and show how to construct simple garden features such as ponds or paths, or illustrate gardening techniques such as grafting, pollarding, or propagation.

We stress environmentally-responsible gardening: minimal use of synthetic pesticides and water, not collecting plants from the wild, and avoiding plants with the potential to escape and damage natural ecosystems. Proposals for articles on specific plants or plant families, public or private gardens, or garden design should stress a unique approach to the topic.

QUERIES

We prefer that authors query us before developing a manuscript. Queries must be accompanied by a self-addressed stamped envelope. Please note: We do not accept phone, fax, or e-mail queries, or simultaneous submissions.

Queries should include a description of the proposed topic and an explanation of why it is of interest to a national audience of knowledgeable gardeners, as well as an outline of the major points to be covered in the manuscript.

When querying for the first time, authors should submit relevant writing samples, and explain why they believe they are qualified to write on the subject they are proposing. We look for writers with a knowledge of plants, but also an ability to write in a strong journalistic style, complete with lively quotes from interviews or written sources. While ideas for articles are evaluated separately from photographs or artwork, it is helpful to the evaluation process for submissions to include information on possible sources for photographs or illustrations.

Acceptance of an idea outlined in a query does not constitute acceptance of an article. All contributors to *The American Gardener* are sent a formal contract outlining the rights being purchased, payment terms, and deadlines.

Feature articles run 1,500 to 2,500 words, depending on subject and assignment.

DEPARTMENTS

The American Gardener has a number of departments for which we accept free-lance submissions.

• Natural Connections. Explains a natural phenomenon or symbiotic relationship-plant and pollinator relationships, plant and fungus relationships, plant and soil relationships, parasites, etc.-that may be observed in nature or in the garden. Runs 750- 1,000 words.

• Conservationist's Notebook. Articles about individuals or organizations attempting to save endangered species or protect natural areas, or about control of pests that threaten ornamental plants or natural ecosystems. Runs 750 -1,000 words.

POLICIES

We make every effort to report back to the author within 90 days of receiving a query. Accepted articles are scheduled and published at the discretion of the editorial staff.

We do not knowingly consider manuscripts simultaneously submitted to other publishers, and we retain the right to return at any time manuscripts that appear or have been published as a whole or in part in another publication, regardless of whether the manuscripts have already been accepted or scheduled.

The staff of *The American Gardener* retains the right to edit manuscripts as it deems necessary, for clarity, style, length, and accuracy. We do not as a matter of policy provide authors with revised manuscripts prior to publication. However, this can sometimes be negotiated at the time that an article is accepted.

Although all work submitted to *The American Gardener* is handled with great care, the Society cannot accept responsibility for any materials that are lost or damaged.

PAYMENT

Payment for feature articles ranges from $300 to $500 upon publication, depending on the article's length and complexity, and the author's horticultural background and publishing experience. Reimbursement for travel and other expenses can sometimes be negotiated.

Payment for departments is $150 to $200. Payment for photographs used with department articles is $50 each.

We pay a 25-percent kill fee in those instances where an author has completed revisions of the text requested by our editorial staff, and the article is still for any reason considered unacceptable.

All contributors receive three complimentary copies of the issue in which their work is published. Additional copies are available to contributors at a reduced rate of $1 each; shipping fees will be charged for contributor orders of 10 copies or more. Extra copies must be ordered prior to publication in order to ensure availability and avoid additional handling fees.

RIGHTS

Information on specific rights purchased is included in a contract sent to all contributors. All articles in *The American Gardener* are also published in the members-only section of the American Horticultural Society's Web site (www.ahs.org).

Mechanical Requirements On ACCEPTANCE

• Submit material typewritten and double spaced. Include a self-addressed, stamped return envelope.

• Accompany the article with a brief biography plus your name, address, social security number, and telephone number.

• After a manuscript has been accepted, it is a great help to us to receive manuscripts on computer disks or via e-mail. Please send articles in Rich Text Format (.rtf) or in Microsoft Word. In preparing a computer document, please do not include formatting such as automatic indents, centering, italics, etc.

• Feature articles should be limited, whenever possible, to eight to 10 double-spaced, typewritten pages, excluding bibliography or sidebars.

• Avoid using footnotes. Incorporate citations or attributions in the body of the text. To assist us in editing, authors should include a bibliography of reference books or previously published articles used for background, and addresses, telephone numbers, and e-mail addresses of individuals interviewed.

• For articles relating to particular plants or types of plants, we appreciate a list of retail mail-order sources-including the names, addresses, phone numbers, and web site-and whether the nurseries charge for their plant lists or catalogs.

• Authors who are submitting photographs or illustrations to accompany an article should request a copy of our Photographer's Guidelines before doing so. Authors writing in detail about plants should request a copy of our "Rules for Botanical Nomenclature."

SAMPLE COPIES

Sample copies of the magazine are available for $5; specific back issues are available for $8. Send checks payable to AHS with your request for sample issues or back issues to the address below; back issues can also be ordered by credit card from the AHS Web site (www.ahs.org). Photographer's guidelines are available by e-mail to editor@ahs.org or by sending an SASE with the request to the address below.

Categories: Ecology—Environment—Gardening

CONTACT: David J. Ellis, Editor
Material: All
7931 E. Boulevard Dr.
Alexandria VA 22308
Phone: 703-768-5700

American Girl

Thanks for your interest in writing for American Girl.

American Girl is a bimonthly, four-color magazine for girls ages 8 and up. Our mission is to celebrate girls. American Girl readers are girls in the formative years, girls who dream big dreams. We hope to encourage that dreaming and to reinforce each reader's self-confidence, curiosity, and self-esteem as she prepares to navigate adolescence in the years ahead. Our lead time is approximately six months.

Fiction

We're looking for contemporary fiction up to 2,300 words. The protagonist should be a girl between 8 and 12 who captures the hopes, thoughts, and emotions unique to that precarious age between childhood and teenager. We look for top quality writing and thoughtfully developed characters and plots. Stories should engage readers quickly and have a satisfying conclusion. We are always looking for humor and seasonal stories. We don't publish science fiction, romance, or horror stories.

Nonfiction

We're looking for individual girls, or groups of girls who are doing something other girls would love to read and learn about. Find a topic about which girls are passionate. Past pieces have featured synchronized swimmers, rhythmic gymnasts, ballerinas, and girl bands. Some of our most successful pieces are sports-related, but that doesn't mean we won't consider other contemporary topics or profiles. Look for new twists on familiar topics. Please send queries rather than finished manuscripts.

Girls Express

This section offers the most opportunities for freelance writers. We're looking for short profiles of girls who are into sports, the arts,

interesting hobbies, cultural activities, and other areas. We are also looking for true stories about girls who have had unusual experiences. The girl must be the "star" and the story must be from her point of view. Be sure the include the age of the girls you're pitching to us. Let us know if you have any photo leads. We also welcome how-to stories, such as how to send away for free things, hot ideas for a cold day, or how to write the President and get a response. Stories should be no more than 150 words. In addition, we're looking for easy crafts and recipes that can be explained in a few simple steps, ideas for contests, and current products and trends for girls to review.

Craft and Cooking

We welcome original craft and cooking ideas that are new and exciting to our readers. Projects should require limited parental involvement and supplies should be inexpensive and readily available. Keep in mind the skill level of our readers. Safety is a priority. Query with a short explanation of the project and an example, photograph, or sketch.

Giggle Gang

We're looking for visual puzzles, mazes, math puzzles, word games, simple crosswords, cartoons, and other ideas. Seasonal ideas are especially welcome.

Sample issues

American Girl costs $3.95 per issue and is available in many children's bookstores. To get a sample copy, send a check for $3.95 made out to American Girl, plus a self-addressed stamped 9x12 envelope with $1.94 in postage on it.

Please Note

American Girl cannot reply or return a manuscript unless you enclose a self-addressed stamped envelope. Please allow at least 12 weeks for a reply.

Categories: Fiction—Nonfiction—Children—Cooking—Crafts/Hobbies—Entertainment—Games—Juvenile—Teen

CONTACT: Magazine Editorial Assistant
Material: All queries and requests for sample magazines
PO Box 620986
8400 Fairway Place
Middleton WI 53562
Phone: 608-836-4848
Website: americangirl.com

American History

Please refer to Primedia History Group

American Hunter

American Hunter, an official journal of the National Rifle Association, is one of the most popular hunting magazines in the nation. Approximately 1.3 million NRA members receive it each month. For most issues, American Hunter buys out 50 percent or more of its editorial material and photos. The following information is intended to reduce confusion during the query, submission, and publication process and to inform contributors of our editorial needs and policies.

Feature Articles-American Hunter feature stories typically run 1,800 to 2,000 words. However, the editors are more concerned with content than length. If an article is short (1,000 to 1,500 words) but good, we'll buy it. Subject matter for feature articles falls into five general categories that run in each issue: deer, big game, upland birds, waterfowl, and varmints/small game. Features may be written in a number of styles, including expository how-to, where-to, and general-interest pieces; humor; personal narratives; and technical articles on firearms, ammunition, optics, wildlife management, or hunting. American Hunter does not buy poetry or articles on firearms legislation. Story angles should be narrow, but coverage must have depth. How-to articles are popular with readers and might range from methods for hunting to techniques on making gear used on successful hunts. Where-to articles should contain contacts and information needed to arrange a similar hunt. All submissions are judged on three criteria: story angle (it should be fresh, interesting, and informative); quality of writing (clear and lively-capable of holding the readers' attention throughout); and quality and quantity of accompanying photos (sharpness, reproduction quality, and connection to the text are most important).

Departments-We solicit material for three monthly departments: "Public Hunting Ground," "Hunting Skills," and "Hardware." "PHG" covers how to and where to hunt different game on public lands throughout the nation. "Skills" covers techniques and "tricks of the trade" used in the field; marksmanship, first aid, field-dressing, and calling techniques are just some worthy topics. "Hardware" is our technical department covering new firearms, ammunition, and optics used for hunting. Contributors should study back issues for appropriate subject matter and style for this column. Copy length should be 800 to 1,200 words.

Photographs-Photo requirements are demanding. We use color transparencies and prints throughout the magazine to illustrate features and departments. The editors prefer article packages containing a good selection of 35mm color transparencies. We will accept color prints, however, overall criteria for selection includes content and technique. Captions should be detailed and should explain how the photo relates to the text. Photos should be given an identifying code to correspond to the caption sheet, and the name of the photographer should appear on every print or slide. Color slides should be protected in plastic sleeves (either individually or within sheets that hold 20 or more). If a submitted photograph has been published previously, photographers are required to advise the editor of the title and date of publication. *American Hunter rates for photographs submitted and purchased separately and not as part of a photo package supporting a manuscript are:*

- Cover: $450-$600
- Centerspread, full bleed: $300-$400
- Two-page spread, partial coverage: $250-$300
- Full page: $200-$250
- Fractional page: $75-$150

Query Letters-Although unsolicited manuscripts are welcomed, detailed query letters outlining a proposed topic and approach are appreciated and will save both writers and editor and given direction on how we'd like the topic covered. American Hunter accepts all manuscript and photographs for consideration on a speculative basis only. On those rare occasions when an advance assignment is made, it will be done in writing only if signed by the Editor or the Executive Editor of American Hunter.

Payment-We pay for articles on acceptance and for freelance photos on publication. We purchase first North American serial rights plus the subsequent reprint rights for NRA Publications. *American Hunter* currently pays up to $800 for full-length feature articles with complete photo packages. Payment may be reduced if we have to supplement your photo package or if your manuscript requires extensive clean-up or rewrite. Payment for departments and other short articles ranges from $300 to $450. Upon publication, all photographs and other material is returned to the contributor. *American Hunter* does not pay kill fees.

Specifications-All manuscripts must be typed double-spaced. No photocopied or hand-written submissions will be accepted and simultaneous submissions will not receive consideration. Please avoid script typefaces. Manuscripts should be submitted in both hard-copy form and on 3 s considerable time. If we like your story idea you will be contacted by mail, phone, or e-mail ½-inch, IBM-compatible diskettes in Microsoft Word or WordPerfect word-processing programs. We work specifically with Word, and would rather see the article come in on this program, but others are accepted so long as we can open a file and read it. Disks will be returned after publication or upon decline or purchase.

Replies-*American Hunter* receives more than a thousand queries and manuscripts a year, and although the editors try to respond within a month it may take longer for an author to receive a reply. The editors are not responsible for unsolicited manuscripts or photos.

Categories: Nonfiction—Animals—Computers—Fishing—General Interest—Internet—Law—Outdoors—Politics—Recreation—Sports/Recreation—Hunting——Humor—Firearms—Personal Experience—How-to: Camping

CONTACT: Scott Olmstead, Editor in Chief
Material: All
11250 Waples Mill Rd.
Fairfax VA 22030-9400
Phone: 703-267-1335
Fax: 703-267-3971

American Indian Art Magazine

American Indian Art Magazine is a quarterly art journal that presents the art of the American Indian through articles and illustrations appealing to both lay people and professionals. We prefer articles that utilize the magazine's illustrated format—in other words, articles that tie the illustrations to the text. Our readers are collectors, dealers, scholars, students and other interested individuals. Some of our readers are knowledgeable about the field and some know very little; American Indian Art Magazine seeks articles which offer something to both groups.

Manuscript Review

Any article, whether solicited or volunteered, is subject to review by members of the magazine's Editorial Advisory Board and/or other authorities in the field. These readers may suggest revisions to be made by authors or may recommend additional material and illustrations. Manuscripts will be returned to the author for any substantive changes. An article must be approved by members of the Editorial Advisory Board before it is published in the magazine. Articles reflecting original research and expressing new hypotheses are preferred over summaries and reviews of previously discussed material. Acceptance of an article for publication does not guarantee its appearance in the next issue of the magazine.

In addition to research articles, the magazine publishes museum collection and exhibition features that are designed to give readers a sense of the overall strengths and weaknesses of the collection, in addition to answering questions about collection history, quality or problems of documentation and the like.

Style

Manuscripts published in the magazine generally run between twelve and eighteen pages in typescript form, exclusive of bibliography, captions and footnotes. We prefer to receive manuscripts on computer disc (Macintosh Microsoft Word) with a hard copy.

We would like an article to be as detailed and specific as possible; try to limit the article to a particular subject, small geographical area, particular object(s) or selected design style. For example, if the subject is Plains Indian shields, try to limit the article to one group or one type of shield or design. In an article discussing changes in style with time, try to explain how to date the changes, and what other contemporaneous styles were. Authors should discuss aesthetics as well as the anthropological context of a subject, if possible.

An article usually requires between eight and fifteen photographs, with a choice from both black and white and color. It is often a good idea to shoot all the subjects in both ways so that the article can be adapted to the technical limitations of the printing process. Please send photographs in individual sleeves with figure numbers clearly marked.

In obtaining photographs, make certain the photographer and processor know that the photographs will be used for reproduction in a magazine. Black-and-white photographs should be glossy 8"x10" prints. Color photographs should be transparencies and 35mm slides are acceptable. Use plain backdrops.

As a matter of policy, we prefer to illustrate material from public collections, avoiding items in private collections unless comparable material is not available elsewhere.

Other Illustrations

Occasionally an article will require a diagrammatic drawing to illustrate a particular manufacturing method. If the author provides a clear sketch or a standard reference source, the magazine will prepare a reproducible line drawing.

Permission

American Indian Art Magazine needs permission in writing to use illustrations which belong to other publications, historical societies, institutions, and private individuals. Sometimes it is necessary to obtain permission separately from the owner of the object in the picture, as well as from the owner of the photograph and/or photographer. With contemporary objects it is also necessary to obtain permission from the artist. Obtaining such permission is the responsibility of the author.

The magazine can supply copies of the printed article to the person or institution allowing use of the photograph; this is frequently a condition for receiving permission. Make certain any special phrases— e.g., "used by permission of"—stipulated by the permission-giver are included in the photograph caption.

Photograph Usage and Fees

American Indian Art Magazine buys onetime publication rights to photographs and returns the originals after the magazine has been printed. Fee schedules and reimbursable expenses are arranged for single photographs and for multiple photograph assignments; the magazine and the author jointly decide on these arrangements.

Conclusion

The Editor and staff of American Indian Art Magazine make every effort to help authors in preparing manuscripts, obtaining illustrations and permission, and generally assisting in article preparation. Authors are encouraged to make preliminary contact with the magazine before committing many long hours to work on the article: proposals and draft outlines will be reviewed if an author requests.

Style

Note: In preparing accepted manuscripts for publication, the editorial staff of the magazine attempts to conform to standard spelling and usage procedures. Reference works consulted include Webster's Ninth Collegiate Dictionary (Merriam-Webster Inc., Springfield, Massachusetts, 1985); A Manual of Style (University of Chicago Press, 1969, twelfth edition, revised); and Ethnographic Bibliography of North America by George Peter Murdock and Timothy J. O'Leary (Human Relations Area Files Press, New Haven, 1975, fourth edition).

Categories: Nonfiction—Arts—Native American

CONTACT: Roanne Goldfein, Editor
Material: All
7314 E. Osborn Dr.
Scottsdale AZ
Phone: 480-994-5445
Fax: 480-945-9533

American Indian Quarterly

The complexity and excitement of the burgeoning field of Native American studies are captured in *American Indian Quarterly* (AIQ), a peer reviewed interdisciplinary journal of the histories, anthropologies, literatures, religions, and arts of Native America. Wide-ranging in its coverage of issues and topics, AIQ is devoted to charting and inciting debate about the latest developments in method and theory. It publishes original articles, shorter contributions, review articles, and book reviews.

Subscription Information

Quarterly/ISSN 0095-182X
Individuals $25.00
Institutions $50.00
Single issue $14.00

For foreign subscriptions please add $20.00. Payment must accompany order. Make checks payable to University of Nebraska Press and mail to:

University of Nebraska Press
233 N 8th St
Lincoln, NE 68588-0255
or call: 1-800-755-1105 U.S. Orders and customer service.
1-800-526-2617 U.S. Fax orders and customer service.
1-402-472-3584 Foreign orders and customer service.
1-402-472-6214 Main fax line.
Telephone and fax orders must be prepaid.

Submission Information

AIQ accepts submissions that make original contributions to scholarship within the broad interdisciplinary framework of American Indian Studies and that meet the following requirements:

- 35 pages or less
- submit 4 copies
- prepare according to Chicago Manual of Style, 14th edition
- include a one-sentence personal bio
- typed double-spaced (including quotations and endnotes)
- 8 1/2 x 11" paper
- 1" margins
- 12 pt. type
- paragraphs not blocked
- footnotes and author date systems are not acceptable

Authors whose manuscripts are accepted for publication will be required to submit their article on a 3.5-inch Macintosh-formatted disk. Submissions to AIQ will not be returned to authors and all submissions, except for book reviews, will be subjected to peer review. All reviewers will remain anonymous unless specifically requesting otherwise. The decisions of the editor with respect to the acceptance of manuscripts are final.

All material published in AIQ is copyrighted by the University of Nebraska Press. Photocopies for course or research use that are supplied to the end user at no cost may be made without explicit permission or fee. Photocopies that are provided to end users for a photocopying fee may not be made without payment of permissions fees to the University of Nebraska Press.

Categories: Nonfiction—Culture—Health—History—Native American

CONTACT: Devon A. Mihesuah, Editor
Material: All
Department of Applied Indigenous Studies
Northern Arizona University
PO Box 15020
Flagstaff AZ 86011-5020
Phone: 928-523-5159
Website: jan.ucc.nau.edu/~mihesuah/aiq/

The American Legion Magazine

The American Legion Magazine — The 22nd largest magazine in the U.S.— is an award-winning leader among national general-interest publications.

It is published monthly by The American Legion for its 2.6 million-plus members, and is also widely read by members of the Washington establishment and other policy makers.

Working through 15,000 community-level posts, the honorably discharged wartime veterans of The American Legion dedicate themselves to God, country and traditional American values. They believe in a strong defense; adequate and compassionate care for veterans and their families; community service; and the wholesome development of our nation's youth.

We publish articles that reflect these values. We inform our readers and their families of significant trends and issues affecting our nation, the world and the way we live.

Our major features focus on national security, foreign affairs, business trends, social issues, health, education, ethics, military history and the arts. We also publish selected general feature articles, articles of special interest to veterans, and question-and-answer interviews with prominent national and world figures.

Format and Style: Ideally, issues should be covered in human terms, but expository articles should also include current facts, vivid examples and expert opinions needed to (a) tell the story, and (b) make the writer's case. Use a compelling lead and an engaging writing style.

Sources: We will not accept just a warmed-over compilation of quotes and background material taken from other publications (with or without attribution). Our authors must be willing to undertake first-hand research.

Query Required: We make all assignments based on a one or two-page query letter. It should show the general thrust of the article, outline its basic structure and content, and demonstrate the writer's firm understanding of the proposed topic. The best query clearly states the article's angle or point, explains why readers will want to read about this subject, and begins with an enticing proposed title for the article. Writers should include sample clips and list relevant experience or background.

Documentation: Completed articles must include appropriate documentation of facts and citations verifying all quotations and statements from sources. This is especially important when quoting people whose professional reputations could be damaged through improper quoting. All material published in *The American Legion Magazine* must first survive a legal reading by the Legion's in-house counsel.

Rights: We purchase First North American serial rights, unless otherwise negotiated, and those rights include the option to re-publish or use in other American Legion publications, including publication on the magazine's web site. This does not limit the contributor's option to re-sell the materials to other organizations.

Payment, Length, Queries: Payment is individually negotiated depending on complexity of subject matter and current needs. Kill fees and reimbursement of expenses are available to writers working on assignment. The minimum we normally pay for an accepted article is 50 cents per published word.

Manuscript length varies from 500 words to about 2,500; most features are in the 1,000 to 2,000-word range.

We report on queries within six to eight weeks. We will consider unsolicited manuscripts.

Queries, manuscripts and art must be accompanied by a self-addressed, stamped envelope (SASE) if the writer desires that they be returned. We cannot assume any financial liability for the loss of any submissions.

Sample Magazines: The best way to get a feel for our type of article is to read several issues of the magazine. For a sample copy, send $3.50 to NATIONAL HEADQUARTERS, PO BOX 1055, INDIANAPOLIS, IN 46206-1055.

Categories: Nonfiction—Arts—Business—Children—Education—Family—Health—Military—Politics—Religion—Society—Morality

CONTACT: John B. Raughter, Editor
Material: All
PO Box 1055
Indianapolis IN 46206-1055
Phone: 317-630-1200
Fax: 317-630-1280
E-mail: magazine@legion.org
Website: www.legion.org

> *Remember: Editors change jobs and publishers change addresses. It is wise to invest in a phone call for the current information before submitting.*

American Letters & Commentary

American Letters & Commentary is a literary annual particularly interested in innovative and challenging writing. Past contributors include Charles Bernstein, Gillian Conoley, Lydia Davis, Stephen Dixon, Stephen Dixon, Elaine Equi, Barbara Guest, Ann Lauterbach, Donald Revell, Stephanie Strickland, Cole Swensen, Susan Wheeler, C.D. Wright, and John Yau. Writers unfamiliar with these names are encouraged to read a copy of the magazine before submitting material. For a sample send $6.00 to the address below, requesting a sample back issue.

All submissions must include a self-addressed stamped envelope (SASE) for response. We cannot be responsible for returning items without an SASE. A brief cover letter is always welcome, but please do not send resumes, reviews of your work, or lengthy lists of previous publications. Submit to the address below.

Only previously unpublished work is considered. Simultaneous submissions are accepted providing we are notified at once should the work be accepted elsewhere.

Poetry

Send 3 to 5 poems, 10 pages maximum. We prefer that poetry submissions be sent in a standard #10 envelope.

Fiction

Stories of 12 pages or less have the best chance. Most of our stories are shorter than that. Please query before sending more than 20 pages of fiction.

Non-fiction (essays, reviews)

We are interested in personal literary essay and in critical essays on writers that are slanted for the general reader (i.e., not academic prose). Please see past issues for examples. Reviews are usually assigned. If you are interested in reviewing books, please query first. We regret the size of our staff makes these restrictions necessary. We also regret that the publication of just one issue each year means that we must turn down many worthy pieces that come our way.

Payment is in copies. All rights are returned to the author upon publication.

Thank you for your interest in our magazine.

Categories: Fiction—Nonfiction—Poetry—Short Stories

CONTACT: Submissions Editor
Material: All
850 Park Avenue, Suite 5B
New York NY 10021
Website: www.amletters.org

American Libraries

American Libraries is ALA's [American Library Association] four-color monthly magazine and the primary perquisite of membership in the Association. Each issue features articles on professional concerns and developments, along with news of the Association, library-related legislation, and libraries around the country and the world. Expression of diverse viewpoints and critical interpretation of professional issues make the magazine the premier forum for the exchange of ideas crucial to the fulfillment of ALA Goal 2000. Annual subscriptions are available to institutions at $60, $70 foreign.

STYLE: Informal, but informative. Factual article must be inviting and readable, with all statements backed by responsible research and interviews. The Chicago Manual of Style may be used in styling articles for publication, but extensive footnoting is discouraged.

FORMAT: Letter- or near-letter quality. One copy suffices.

SUBMISSIONS BY E-MAIL: In addition to considering manuscripts submitted by surface mail, American Libraries considers manuscripts sent by e-mail. When e-mailing a submission, please include your surface-mail address to expedite our sending a contributor's contract if your submission is accepted for publication.

WORD PROCESSING REQUIREMENTS: Manuscripts should be submitted via email or on a 3½" diskette (high density, 1.44 megabytes in size) and accompanied by a paper printout of the text. While American Libraries is capable of handling a wide range of word processing programs in both the PC and Mac formats, we prefer that manuscripts be in Word 6.x for Windows. When submitting a manuscript, indicate the word processing program used.

LENGTH: 600-2,000 words.

PAYMENT: Honoraria of $100 to $250 are offered for most articles, paid upon receipt of an acceptable manuscript.

EXCLUSIVE SUBMISSION: It is assumed that no other publisher is or will be simultaneously considering a manuscript submitted to American Libraries until that manuscript is returned or written permission is provided by the *American Libraries* editors.

RIGHTS: According to the contract provided to authors, exclusive North American rights are retained until three months after publication, unless another arrangement is made in writing. American Libraries retains rights to have the published material reproduced, distributed, and sold in microform or electronic text.

REPRINT POLICY: No reprints can be provided, but permission is usually granted for authors to reproduce their contributions as published in American Libraries. Others wishing to republish the text of an article are referred to the author for permission and fee information. A reasonable number of copies are sent to each author. Special arrangements may be necessary to reproduce illustrations.

ACKNOWLEDGEMENT: Unsolicited manuscripts are acknowledged when received.

REPORTS: The editors try to report on manuscripts within 4-8 weeks. Written reminders from the author after this period are welcome, and usually result in a prompt reply.

PUBLICATION DATE: On acceptance, an estimated date of publication may be provided to the author. Usually manuscripts can be published no sooner than two months after receipt.

EDITING: On accepted manuscripts, the editors reserve the right to make editorial revisions, deletions, or additions which, in their opinion, support the author's intent. When changes are substantial, every effort is made to work with the author.

GALLEYS: Galleys are not provided to the author.

PHOTOGRAPHS: Color prints, taken in natural light, are preferred for use with manuscripts or as picture stories. Transparencies and black-and-white prints are also considered for possible use. High-resolution digital photos (300 dpi, approximate size of 3 x 5 inches) can be sent to americanlibrariesproduction@ala.org. Payment is negotiated.

CARTOONS: Cartoons of the highest professional quality that relate to library interests and avoid librarian stereotypes will be considered. Average payment $50.

ILLUSTRATIONS: Illustrations are commissioned for certain articles and features.

Categories: Education—Trade—Libraries

CONTACT: Submissions Editor
Material: All
50 E. Huron
Chicago IL 60611
Phone: 312-280-4216
Fax: 312-440-0901
E-mail: americanlibraries@ala.org
Website: www.ala.org

American Medical News

American Medical News is the nation's most widely circulated newspaper focusing on socioeconomic issues in medicine. Published weekly by the American Medical Association, AMN covers the full spectrum of non-clinical news affecting physicians' practices. Our primary readers are about 320,000 physicians, most of whom receive the publication free as part of their AMA membership. Readers also include administrators of health-care organizations, government health-care policymakers and others with a professional interest in physicians and the U.S. health-care system.

AMN contracts with a relatively small group of freelance writers for news and feature articles that focus on policy development, legislation, regulation, economic trends, and physician-impact coverage in the categories that follow. We also seek articles about innovative efforts by individuals or groups to improve health-system functioning or physician practice in these areas.

Population health & related trends

• Health promotion and disease prevention: tobacco, alcohol and drug use; family and community violence; maternal and child health, including immunization; clinical preventive services

• Infectious diseases: AIDS; tuberculosis

• Treatment issues: health of targeted groups, including minorities, women, children, adolescents elderly and disabled; access to care for homeless, medically indigent and rural residents; organ transplantation

• Health protection: environmental and occupational health; accident prevention; food and drug safety• Impact of health care market trends and policy developments on patients and population health

• How doctors are helping to implement public health goals

• Physician health, well-being and job satisfaction

• Physician-patient relationships

• Consumerism and patients' rights

Topic Editor: Wayne Hearn

Professional issues

• Medical education and training, including undergraduate, graduate and continuing medical education, specialty training, certification, credentialing and physician supply issues

• Medical-legal matters, including professional liability, antitrust, fraud, abuse and related questions

• Quality assurance, including licensure, discipline, professional regulation, peer review, outcomes measurement and practice standards

• Professional and clinical ethics

• Technology, medical informatics, the pharmaceutical industry and related biomedical research

• The institution of organized medicine

Health system structure and finance

• Developments in public policy and the private marketplace that affect the structure of the health care industry and determine the conditions, quality and financial rewards of the practice of medicine

• Physician services financing issues, including Medicare, Medicaid, other government payers, Blue Cross and Blue Shield, commercial insurers and managed care; physician pay

• Physician relations with health care delivery systems, including HMOs, PPOs, group practices, hospitals and integrated hospital/physician networks

• Workforce issues: supply of physicians, the mix between specialists and generalists, relations between physicians and other health professions

• Federal and state health system reform efforts

Business

• Practice management, including general small-business issues (i.e. taxes, employment policies, salary and benefits), small-business issues unique to medical practices (i.e. CPT coding, relations with other physicians and third-party payers), contracting with insurers, strategic planning, raising capital, integrating new technology in practice settings, forming partnerships and managing groups

Please submit written queries of about one typewritten page, containing a detailed account of what you intend to cover and beginning with a lead you consider suitable for a finished article. Alternatively, you may submit the story to us on speculation.

Categories: Health—Medicine

CONTACT: Kathryn Trombatore, Editor
Material: All

515 N. State St.
Chicago IL 60610
Phone: 312-464-4429
Fax: 312-464-4445

The American Poetry Review

The American Poetry Review is unique in American publishing. With its eclectic editing, its newsprint- tabloid format, and its circulation of 17,000, APR reaches a worldwide audience six times a year with the poetry and prose of living modern masters, of new poets and critics just arriving on the scene, and of a diverse range of cultures and ethnic groups. Over the past 30 years, the magazine has helped to make poetry a more public art form without compromising the art of poetry.

Writers' Guidelines

The American Poetry Review publishes original poetry, literary criticism, interviews, essays and social commentary. Please use the following guidelines when submitting manuscripts for consideration.

Manuscripts should snail mailed. Do not send manuscripts by fax or E-mail.

Each manuscript must be accompanied by a self-addressed envelope, stamped with sufficient postage for its return. (International submissions should be accompanied by Universal Postal Union International Response Coupons.) No reply will be made to unaccepted manuscripts that are not accompanied by sufficient return postage.

Keep a copy of your manuscript and an accurate record of the date you mailed it.

Do not send previously published material or material that is currently under consideration by another magazine or periodical. Please do not send work that is under consideration by APR to another magazine or periodical.

Our reporting time is approximately ten weeks. We will inform you of acceptance or return your manuscript. Please do not inquire about the status of your manuscript during the ten-week reporting period.

All work submitted to APR is considered for publication in *The American Poetry Review* only.

Copyright: APR holds first serial rights for material that we publish. The copyright automatically reverts to the author upon publication. We do not require that material be copyrighted prior to submission.

Contests: APR does not conduct a poetry contest. All work submitted to APR is considered for publication in *The American Poetry Review* only.

Prizes: The Jerome J. Shestack Poetry Prizes of $1000 are awarded annually to each of two poets whose work has appeared in APR during the preceding calendar year.

Thank you and best wishes. The Editors

Categories: Literature—Poetry—Writing

CONTACT: The Editors
Material: All
117 South 17th Street Ste 910
Philadelphia PA 19103
Phone: 215-496-0439
Website: www.aprweb.org

American Profile

American Profile's audience lives in communities with an average population of 7,000. Our articles are useful, informative, human, and concise; full of detail and color, writing and reporting at its best. Our readers are intelligent and discriminating, our standards are high. This is not a market for beginners; send only your most professional work. No fiction, nostalgia, or poetry. Coverage of people and places must be enlightening and instructional, and have a broad regional or national relevance. We also cover health, food, gardening, home projects, nature, and finances. Articles should be topical, but have a long shelf life. Length varies from 450 to 1,200 words. Payment within 45 days of acceptance. Fees are competitive but vary widely. Byline and one-sentence bio given. Mostly freelance written. No reprints. Buys exclusive first-time print rights and all electronic rights to unpublished pieces for six months, non-exclusive rights thereafter.

Queries: Send a one-paragraph query with clips and SASE. No phone, fax, or e-mail submissions.

Categories: African-American—Asian-American—Children—Consumer—Disabilities—Education—Family—Gardening—Health—Hispanic—Inspirational—Money & Finances—Multicultural—Native American—Outdoors—Parenting—Religion—Rural America—Spiritual—Sports/Recreation

CONTACT: Peter V. Fossel, Executive Editor
Material: All
Publishing Group of America
341 Cool Springs Blvd., Suite 400
Franklin TN 37067
Phone: 615-468-6000
Fax: 800-720-6323

American Rifleman

WRITER'S AND PHOTOGRAPHER'S GUIDELINES

The publisher of *American Rifleman* regularly purchases material submitted by freelancers. While we buy only a small portion of the material submitted, we do pay upon acceptance. Articles are received on speculation only, and we do not pay kill fees. Assignments are made only on written approval of the editor or the executive editor of *American Rifleman*. The editorial staff is not responsible for unsolicited manuscripts and/or photographs.

WHAT WE ARE LOOKING FOR: We want fresh material on all aspects of firearms and shooting. These can include gunsmithing, handloading, gun collecting, law enforcement training, competitive shooting, blackpowder, handguns, rifles or shotguns. Personality and firearms industry-related feature articles are also considered.

WHAT WE DON'T NEED: While we can use equipment-related articles that involve hunting, we do not run straight hunting pieces. Consider sending those to American Hunter at the same address. Nor can we use verse, fiction, essays or articles on gun legislation. We occasionally purchase pieces on the gun control issue, but the circumstances must be compelling or the material a new scholarly contribution to the literature.

NRA DOES NOT BUY GUN TESTS: Tests of new firearms and related equipment are conducted exclusively by the NRA Technical Staff and Contributing Editors.

ILLUSTRATIONS: Pictures sell articles. We need good quality color images. We want technically excellent photographs that are well-focused and properly exposed. We can supplement photo packages but give first consideration to articles that have good photo support. A completed NRA Publications Division Model Release Form is required for each identifiable individual appearing in a photograph. (They will be supplied upon request.) While we can handle other formats, we strongly prefer 35 mm slides or medium-or large-format transparencies. We may be able to get more out of them than your local processor. You may submit images electronically as high-resolution (300 d.p.i.) RGB, TIF, or .JPG files. The file size needs to be large enough for magazine format publication (example, 4"x 6" photo'8mgs; full page '25mgs.) We return illustrative material approximately three months after publication.

ARTICLE PREPARATION: Articles should be typed double-spaced, with only one space between sentences, with 22" margins and may range in length from 1,600 to 2,200 words. Manuscripts may be submitted on 32" disks or via e-mail (addressed to Publications@NRAHQ.org) on an IBM compatible operating system. Articles may be submitted in WordPerfect versions 4.2, 5.0, 5.1 or 6.0 or in other convertible word processing format (Microsoft Word) or in ASCII format along with a legible printout. Disks will be returned after publication or upon decline of purchase. Submissions must be accompanied by a postage-paid, self-addressed return envelope.

REPLIES: We generally purchase or reject manuscripts within 3 months of receipt. Occasionally, this process may take a little longer.

WRITING FOR US: Aspiring writers should study carefully the content of past issues of the magazine to get an understanding of the type of material we publish. Inexperienced writers might consider first submitting a AFavorite Firearms@ article for publication. While American Rifleman does not currently pay for these pieces, they generally represent good, concise writing and provide an opportunity for new writers to Atest the water.@

COPYRIGHT: The Copyright Law Revision of January, 1978 provides that, unless otherwise stipulated, a publisher purchases first publication rights only. The purpose of this notice is to include in addition to first publication rights the NRA's right to reprint any manuscript or illustrative material purchased by the NRA in future publications of the NRA. The right to offer this material to publishers other than the NRA remains with the author.

Categories: Nonfiction—Firearms—Shooting
CONTACT: Mark A. Keefe IV, Executive Editor
Material: All
11250 Waples Mill Rd.
Fairfax VA 22030-9400
Phone: 703-267-1300
Fax: 703-267-3971
Website: www.nra.org

American Salesman

The *American Salesman* is a monthly magazine for sales professionals. Its primary objective is to provide informative articles which develop the attitudes, skills, personal and professional qualities of the sales representative, enabling them to use more of their potential to increase their productivity and achieve goals.

CONTENT: *The American Salesman* contains seven feature articles each month. Most of the articles are contributed by people with practical experience in sales. No advertising is used in this publication. Articles involving successful and innovative sales trends or case histories are considered.

NEEDS: We are interested in articles addressing the following: improving sales productivity, reviewing sales fundamentals, motivating sales staff, determining customer needs, customer service, knowing and analyzing competition, making sales presentations, handling objections, closing sales, following up, telephone selling, managing sales territory, planning, goal setting, time management and new innovative sales concepts.

SUBMISSION OF ARTICLES: We work in advance. Therefore, articles may be retained up to six months before tentative scheduling. Finished articles should contain from 900 to 1,200 words. A sample is mailed to the copy originator.

Manuscripts should be high-quality typed (suitable for scanning—do not submit articles on a low quality dot matrix printer). The Associated Press Stylebook is followed for editing. The author should indicate address, current byline containing background employment, company affiliation and educational degrees listing alma mater. Submissions must include a stamped, self-addressed return envelope.

Your experience and your ideas are valuable. We are always happy to receive inquiries from potential writers.

Categories: Business—Careers—Economics—Money & Finances—Sales

CONTACT: Teresa Levinson, Editor
Material: All

National Research Bureau, 320 Valley St.
Burlington IA 52601-5513
Phone: 319-752-5415

The American Scholar
Phi Beta Kappa

Articles

The Scholar is a quarterly journal published by Phi Beta Kappa for general circulation. Our intent is to have articles by scholars and experts but written in non-technical language for an intelligent audience. The material that appears in the magazine covers a wide range of subject matter in the arts, sciences, current affairs, history, and literature. We prefer articles between 3,500 and 4,000 words, and we pay up to $500. To be accepted for publication, a manuscript must receive the affirmative votes of the editor and at least two members of the editorial board.

Poetry

Poems for submission to *The Scholar* should be typewritten, on one side of the paper, and each sheet of paper should bear the name and address of the author and the name of the poem. We have no special requirements of length, form, or content for original poetry. A look at several recent issues of the Scholar should give a good idea of the kind of poetry we publish and the way poems look on our pages. We suggest, too, that, from the author's point of view, it is probably most effective if not more than three or four poems are submitted at any one time. We pay $50.00 for each accepted poem.

We do not have arrangements for sending sample copies of the Scholar to prospective contributors. It would be possible, of course, for you to purchase the latest issue for $8.00. If you do not care to purchase a copy, your library would probably have copies you could see.

Categories: Nonfiction—Arts—General Interest—History—Literature—Poetry

CONTACT: Submissions Editor
Material: All
Phi Beta Kappa Society
1606 New Hampshire Ave., N.W.
Washington DC 20009
Phone: 202-265-3808
Website: www.pbk.org

American Snowmobiler
The North American Enthusiast Magazine

Formal guidelines not available. Please read a number of issues to ascertain the publication's style and needs.

Send queries to address below.

Categories: Nonfiction—Outdoors—Sports/Recreation

CONTACT: Editor
Material: All
Kalmbach Publishing Co.
21027 Crossroads Circle
Waukesha, WI 53187-1612
Phone: 262-796-8776

AmericanStyle

AmericanStyle is a magazine for people who love art. Our mandate is to nurture collectors with information that will increase their knowledge of and passion for contemporary craft and the artists who create it.

AUDIENCE:

AmericanStyle's primary audience is contemporary craft collectors and enthusiasts. Readers are primarily college educated, age 35-

plus, high-income earners with the financial means to collect art and craft, and to travel to national art and craft events in pursuit of their passions.

CONTENTS:

Every issue of *AmericanStyle* contains a wealth of information about American crafts in all mediums, including a collector profile, a city/regional arts tour, interviews with artists, museum curators and gallery directors, visits to regional arts enclaves, and state-by-state listings of museum and gallery craft exhibitions, retail craft fairs and annual craft events. About 75 percent of the articles in *AmericanStyle* are written by freelancers; the balance is staff-produced.

AmericanStyle is interested in purchasing well-researched articles on themes in contemporary craft art; profiles of American craft collectors; arts tours of American cities or regions of the country; major craft fairs and events; established craft artists and their work; trends in studio art; and regional art enclaves, craft workshops and educational institutions.

It is essential that stories be written for readers who already have considerable expertise and background knowledge of studio art and contemporary crafts; straight general interest articles will be discouraged.

STORY CONSIDERATIONS:

Regular features in *AmericanStyle* include collector profiles, arts tours, Collector's Corner articles, themes in craft art and artist profiles. Keep in mind the following as you work to complete manuscripts in these specific areas:

COLLECTOR PROFILE:

Article should be written in a clear, lively, conversational style, and answer the following questions of the subject being interviewed: how did you first become interested in collecting? how has your collection grown and/or changed over the years? how do you feel about these works from an investment standpoint? what advice would you give to a new collector? did you have a mentor when you first started collecting? how do you make your selections? where do you find new talent? is your family involved in your collecting endeavors?

Profiles generally run 1000-1200 words, with possible accompanying sidebars on topics such as a brief history of a particular craft medium; information on technique or a brief profile of a specific artist in the collection.

ARTS TOUR:

City and regional arts tours in *AmericanStyle* focus specifically on art, artists, galleries, museums and arts-oriented open studios, tours and events in a given city or region. They are NOT generic travel stories and should not be written as such.

Stories generally run about 900 words for the main feature, and are accompanied by possible sidebars of varying lengths that highlight gallery group events, gallery crawls, interesting arts centers, sculpture gardens or art coops, plus a mandatory "If You Go" box with details about contacting travel bureaus and arts organizations for more information.

The main story must include quotes from a variety of gallery owners, artists or museum directors about the city or region's growing arts scene.

For this assignment, the writer is also expected to ask galleries contacted to supply 35mm slides, transparencies, or high-resolution electronic images of their establishments and/or artists' works for the feature. All slides will be returned by *AmericanStyle* to the galleries after publication.

The arts tour also includes a list of galleries and art museums in the city or region being featured. A primary list of galleries in the region will be supplied to the writer at the time the assignment is made; the writer, in turn, is expected to compile the galleries and museums sidebar for the arts tour, with specifics on address, phone number and a brief description of what a reader can expect of the establishment and its artists.

ARTS WALK:

Arts Walk is a regular department of the magazine that virtually walks readers through an arts enclave, small arts town or gallery district. Stories generally run 600-800 words, with addresses and phone numbers for each gallery highlighted included in parentheses in the running text. General guidelines for writing Arts Walk columns follow the same considerations as for Arts Tours (see above).

ARTIST PORTFOLIO:

A regular department of the magazine, the Portfolio column focuses on emerging artists and their work, and provides readers with details about their background and education, ongoing editions of their work, gallery affiliations and, where applicable, museum representation.

Portfolio columns run approximately 600 words and should be written in a lively conversational style. Hints: focus on the human side of craft artists, uncovering for the reader interesting tidbits about where artists get their inspiration, what their work space is like, how they came to work in their chosen medium, who their mentors were/are, and what path their work is now taking.

For Portfolio submissions, the writer is also expected to ask the artist to supply 4 to 8 35mm slides, transparencies, or high-resolution electronic images of their recent work PLUS a color slide, transparency, or electronic image of themselves, preferably a candid (rather than formal) portrait at work in their studio.

SUBMISSION REQUIREMENTS:

Most manuscripts are transmitted electronically by e-mail to hoped@rosengrp.com, followed by hard-copy manuscripts (to verify materials and proof against) sent by regular mail.

QUERIES:

Freelancers interested in contributing to *AmericanStyle* should submit a clear, specific, concise outline of the topic they wish to write about. They should explain why they think it would be of interest to *AmericanStyle* readers and also provide reasons why they have the background or experience to sucessfully carry out the assignment. Subject, sources, projected length of the article, types of interviews and angle should all be clearly explained in written form. Submissions by e-mail are acceptable and generally assure a quicker response.

First-time writers submit articles on speculation; after an article has been accepted, the editor will negotiate a fee with the writer for the material to be used. Payment is made for published stories at the time of publication.

When an article is assigned to a writer, article length is set by the editor at the time the assignment is made. The average length of feature articles in *AmericanStyle* is about 1000-1200 words; lengths of secondary features, columns and departments at the front and back of the magazine range from 500 to 800 words.

AmericanStyle buys First North American serial rights to all its articles. Contributors are free to resell their articles after publication, but not before.

AmericanStyle's lead time is 6 to 12 months.

Categories: Arts—Collectibles—Crafts/Hobbies—Interview

CONTACT: Hope Daniels, Editor
Material: All
3000 Chestnut Ave., #304
Baltimore, MD 21211
Phone: Non phone queries
E-mail: hoped@rosengrp.com
Website: www.americanstyle.com

American Theatre

When submitting material, please allow for *American Theatre's* two month lead time for each issue.

Writers Guidelines

American Theatre typically publishes two or three features and four to six back-of-the-book articles covering trends and events in all types of theatre, as well as economic and legislative developments affecting the arts. The main focus, however, is on professional, nonprofit theatre. We usually are not interested in academic or community theatre, nor in "how-to" articles. While significant productions are highlighted in our "Critic's Notebook" section, *American Theatre* does not publish reviews.

Writers wishing to submit articles to *American Theatre* should send a query letter to editor Jim O'Quinn outlining a particular proposal; unsolicited material is rarely accepted. Please include a brief resume and sample clips, along with a self-addressed, stamped envelope—average response time is two months. Lead time for finished pieces is at least two months. While fees are negotiated per manuscript, *American Theatre* pays on average $350 for full-length (2500-3500 words) features, less for shorter pieces, upon publication. All manuscripts are subject to editing.

Categories: Arts—Drama

CONTACT: Jim O'Quinn, Editor
Material: All
American Theatre
520 8th Ave., 24th Floor
New York, NY 10018
Website: www.tcg.org

American Turf Monthly

Specific approaches or insights relating to Thoroughbred handicapping, researched angles, methods or trends, non-fiction stories of general racing interest, interviews with racing personalities.

Double-spaced manuscripts, three to five typewritten pages. For handicapping angles and systems, accompanying past performance lines, results charts and workout of results preferred

Unsolicited manuscripts and photographs O.K. Queries welcome. Fee: Approx. $75 per published page.

Categories: Nonfiction—Book Reviews—Games—Sports/Recreation—Gambling—Equine—Sports Betting

CONTACT: James Corbett, Editor-in-Chief
Material: All
All Star Sports, Inc.
299 East Shore Rd., Ste. 204
Great Neck, NY 11023
Phone: 516-773-4075

American Visions

What kind of magazine is *American Visions*?

American Visions is the official magazine of the African-American Museums Association. It was launched in 1986 as the official publication of the Martin Luther King, Jr. national holiday. The magazine focuses on the "culturally active" African-American adult with editorial on culture, art, history, theater, music, dance, film, travel and technology from a unique cultural perspective. Its mission-in line with that of the American Visions Society is to promote an appreciation of black culture. Each issue also contains a cultural calendar of major local and regional events throughout the country.

Who reads *American Visions*?

Some 125,000 members of the *American Visions* Society and the general public read *American Visions*. Each issue is passed along to an average of 5 additional readers, for a total readership of more than 625,000.

What kind of articles does *American Visions* look for?

American Visions is interested in stories that present the elegant,

sophisticated side of African-American culture in a pop-scholarly fashion. Topics covered include the arts, history, literature, cuisine, genealogy and travel-all filtered through the prism of the African-American experience. We frequently include a historical perspective on a topic, but we are not a scholarly publication. The magazine is reportorial, current and objective rather than academic or polemical. Departments include: Arts Scene, Books, Calendar, Computers & Technology, Cuisine, Film, Genealogy, Music Notes and Travel. Special Supplements, covering specific geographic areas and topics, are featured throughout the year as well.

When submitting material to *American Visions*...

Propose your ideas by letter or e-mail. Be specific: What will you write about the subject? Why will readers of *American Visions* find your story interesting?

Once we agree on a subject and an approach, we will work out length and scheduling details. Authors must provide good four-color or black-and-white illustrations where appropriate and must obtain permission from photographers and illustrators for the use of copyrighted materials. Editorial and word processing specifications are available upon request.

Writer's and Word Processing Guidelines

American Visions is the only magazine of its kind, in that it presents the elegant, sophisticated side of the African-American culture in a pop-scholarly fashion. Its scope includes the arts, history, literature, cuisine, genealogy and travel-all filtered through the prism of the African-American experience. Though we frequently include a historical perspective on a topic, we are not a scholarly publication.

Article Submissions

Manuscripts submitted for consideration should adhere to the following:

• Feature Articles: 10 pages.

• Department Articles: 4 to 6 pages.

• Length is ultimately determined by subject matter and illustration possibilities.

Submission Essentials:

• Manuscripts should be submitted on 3½" high-density or double-density diskette with a hard copy whenever possible. Microsoft Word 2.0 is the preferred format, but other word processing formats are acceptable. They are listed below.

• A brief (one or two sentence) biographical sketch of the author(s) should follow the body of the manuscript.

• Graphics are almost always essential. All graphic materials (photographs, maps, slides, illustrations, etc.) should be submitted with the manuscript.

Format

• The following word processing formats (in preferential order) are also accepted: ASCII, WordPerfect 5.0, 5.1, WordStar 3.3, 3.4, 4.0, 5.0 and Word for Macintosh 4.0, 5.0. (When using WordStar, turn off the Vari-Tab feature.)

Please Do:

• Use your word processor as a text entry vehicle only.

• Mark titles of books, reports, etc., by underlining or italicizing.

• Press the space bar only once after a period or colon.

Please Don't:

• Use tabs.

• Right-justify text.

• Use boldface or different fonts.

If you have not written for *American Visions* before, we suggest that you familiarize yourself with the magazine before querying us. Also take note of the following:

1.) Make query suggestions in writing of no more than one page, or submit a manuscript on speculation.

2.) Send three (3) samples of your writing.

3.) Send material(s) that you do not wish to have returned.

4.) Allow two to three (2-3) months for review.

Departments

Arts Scene: A potpourri of articles on current events in the realms of theater, film, television, dance, music, visual arts, literature and more.

Books/Recent & Relevant: Reviews of recent releases and their social relevance, as well as profiles of writers and suggested reading lists. Capsule book reviews.

Calendar: A vibrant section listing major cultural events of particular interest to the black community.

Computers & Technology: A section aimed at informing the African-American community of innovations, resources and advantages of computer use and available technology-with news on software, the information superhighway and the like.

Cuisine: A column devoted to defining an African-American cuisine, sometimes discussing specific foods, sometimes offering profiles of black chefs and restaurateurs, nearly always including a recipe or two.

Film: Articles on the film industry, ranging from profiles of actors, producers, directors and technicians to reviews of theatrical releases.

Genealogy: Essays that encourage readers to explore their ancestry by recommending ideas and strategies, and by relating the adventures of others.

Music Notes/Earworthy: Interviews with musicians, as well as essays on the genres and literature of black music. Capsule reviews of newly released recordings.

Travel: A historical and pleasure guide to areas of particular interest to African Americans.

Categories: Culture—Ethnic

CONTACT: Joanne Harris, Editor
Material: All
1101 Pennsylvania Ave NW Ste 820
Washington DC 20004
Phone: 202-347-3820
Fax: 202-347-1822
E-mail: edi@americanvisions.com

American Woodworker

The magazine has been repositioned and no longer purchases freelance articles. Thank you for your interest.

America's Civil War

Please refer to *Primedia History Group*

Analog Science Fiction and Fact

Story Content
Analog will consider material submitted by any writer, and consider it solely on the basis of merit. We are definitely eager to find and develop new, capable writers.

We have no hard-and-fast editorial guidelines, because science fiction is such a broad field that I don't want to inhibit a new writer's thinking by imposing Thou Shalt

Nots. Besides, a really good story can make an editor swallow his preconceived taboos.

Basically, we publish science fiction stories. That is, stories in which some aspect of future science or technology is so integral to the plot that, if that aspect were removed, the story would collapse. Try to picture Mary Shelley's Frankenstein without the science and you'll see what I mean. No story!

The science can be physical, sociological, psychological. The technology can be anything from electronic engineering to biogenetic engineering. But the stories must be strong and realistic, with believable people (who needn't be human) doing believable things—no matter how fantastic the background might be.

Fact
Articles for *Analog* should be about 4,000 words in length and should deal with subjects of not only current but future interest, i.e., with topics at the present frontiers of research whose likely future developments have implications of wide interest. Illustrations should be provided by the author in camera-ready form.

In writing for *Analog* readers, it is essential to keep in mind that they are, in general, very intelligent and technically knowledgeable, but represent a very wide diversity of backgrounds. Thus, specialized jargon and mathematical detail should be kept to a necessary minimum. Also, our readers are reading this magazine largely for entertainment, and a suitable style for our articles is considerably more informal than that in many professional journals. Manuscript Format Manuscripts must be computer-printed or typed, double-spaced, on white paper, one side of the sheet only. Please avoid unusual or very small typefaces. Indent paragraphs but do not leave extra space between them. Please do not put manuscripts in binders or folders. We do not accept e-mail or fax submissions.

Author's name and address should be on the first page of the manuscript. No material submitted can be returned or acknowledged unless accompanied by sufficient postage, stamped and addressed envelope (not a postcard), or stamped International Reply Coupons. No simultaneous submissions please.

Payment
Analog pays 6-8 cents per word for short stories up to 7,500 words, $450-600 for stories between 7,500 and 10,000 words, and 5-6 cents per word for longer material. We prefer lengths between 2,000 and 7,000 words for shorts, 10,000-20,000 words for novelettes, and 40,000-80,000 for serials. Fact articles are paid for at the rate of 6 cents per word. Other Information Please query first on serials only. A complete manuscript is strongly preferred for all shorter lengths.

Payment is on acceptance.
Categories: Fiction—Science—Science Fiction

CONTACT: Stanley Schmidt, Editor
Material: All
475 Park Ave. South, 11th Floor
New York NY 10016
Phone: 212-698-1313
E-mail: analog@dellmagazines.com
Website: analogsf.com

And Baby

About Us
When publisher Michelle Darné and her partner Kathleen Weiss made the commitment to become parents, they shared the excitement, fear and questioning that all parents-to-be experience. Yet as a lesbian couple, they had questions and concerns that others did not share.

They began to look for information appropriate to their needs. In the initial research, they were frustrated to find limited resources appropriate to the unique situations faced by gay parents. They networked profusely for feedback and advice on what options they had as gay parents, where to go and how to get started. They spent hours surfing the web for gay-friendly insemination doctors and donor facilities, went to every local bookstore in search of pregnancy and parenting guides and consulted several financial and legal advisors.

Most of the fragmented information they collected came from mainstream materials that did not address the unique obstacles faced by Gay/Lesbian/Bisexual/Transgender (GLBT) parents-to-be. The GLBT materials, on the other hand, did not include the broad scope or light-hearted content they liked seeing in mainstream publications. As a 20-year veteran of the advertising and publishing industries, Michelle realized the potential for a magazine that combined both sensibilities in a way that would appeal to a broad audience and be a valuable resource for others in the community looking for answers and inspiration. Twelve months later she launched *And Baby* Magazine.

Since our inception in July 2001, we have been embraced by experts, professionals, contributors, vendors and advertisers. And as our visibility increases, the positive response from the community, both here and abroad, has been overwhelming.

Submission guidelines:

All of *And Baby's* stories are written by assignment, work-for-hire projects.

Our editorial manifest is brainstormed at a staff meeting prior to each issue. Prior to each manifest meeting, an email is sent out to writers calling for ideas for stories, which they then write if the idea is selected.

If you would like to be included in the email call for story ideas, please email a few of your clips (or sample stories), copied into the email (not as an attachment) and a list of publications you have written for before to info@andbabymag.com.

If you're a good fit for *And Baby*, your name will be added to our list.

Categories: Gay Lesbian—Parenting

CONTACT: Editor
Material: All
E-mail: info@andbabymag.com
Website: www.andbabymag.com

Ancestry Magazine

Ancestry Magazine is a bimonthly publication of Myfamily.com, Inc. The magazine is primarily aimed at genealogists and hobbyists who are interested in getting the most out of their research. The focus on Column and Department articles is to instruct, inform, provide historical information, and help genealogists advance their work. Feature articles are given a more liberal approach. While still expected to be appealing and beneficial to genealogists, these articles should also generate interest and appeal among lay people. Topics should focus on human interest, historical, biographical, or personal aspects of genealogy, generally following a theme determined by *Ancestry*'s editorial staff.

Each issue of *Ancestry* also features a case study. The case study focuses on getting past a brick wall and the many unique discoveries a researcher makes that will benefit other family historians. The editors are interested in the unique story of your family as well as the steps you took to solve the problem, the research methods you used, and the sources you consulted. Illustrations and photographs are a plus. Entries should be between 1,800 and 2,000 words.

The final page of each issue of *Ancestry* is dedicated to a Bare Bones essay, limited to between 600 and 800 words. The essay is nostalgic, humorous, or sentimental in nature, and contributes largely to the human nature of family history.

Ancestry seeks articles that rise above the standard levels of writing, are informative, and appeal to its genealogy-focused audience. As a consequence of these expectations, the editor reserves the right to make alterations to an article to maintain consistency of tone, style, and clarity. Editors will make every effort to respect the author's voice and artistic freedom, within reasonable bounds. Writers should keep careful notes and provide sources and documentation for all facts. Articles should conform to The Chicago Manual of Style. Interested individuals are encouraged to submit articles appropriate to the focus and format of the publication. Family histories, genealogies, pedigree charts, and queries are not solicited.

Electronic text files must be submitted along with a double-spaced hard copy. Please label disks with the name of the article and program used. WordPerfect and Microsoft Word files are preferred; e-mail and faxed submissions are also acceptable. Authors should include a very brief biography with their submission. Quality illustrations or photographs that enhance the article are appreciated, but authors are not expected to generate headlines and titles or gather art.

The editor considers all submissions and usually responds within six weeks. Upon acceptance of an article, *Ancestry* sends the author a standard contract of agreement. An honorarium will be paid to the author upon publication.

Ancestry Magazine purchases the copyright as work for hire.
Categories: Nonfiction—Family—Geneology

CONTACT: Jennifer Utley, Managing Editor
Material: All
360 E. 4800 North
Provo UT 84602
Phone: 801-705-7301
Fax: 801-705-7120
E-mail: editoram@ancestry.com
Website: www.ancestry.com

Angels on Earth

Angels on Earth publishes true stories about God's messengers at work in today's world. We are interested in stories of heavenly angels and stories involving humans who have played angelic roles in daily life. The best stories are those where the narrator has been positively affected in some distinct way. Look for unusual situations; we have a surplus of stories about illness and car accidents. We are also especially on the lookout for recent stories. A typical *Angels on Earth* story is first-person narrative written in dramatic style, with a spiritual point that the reader can "take away" and apply to his or her own life. It may be your own or someone else's story. Please observe the following in writing your Angels on Earth story: ·The emphasis should be on one person, and is usually told from the vantage point of the individual most deeply affected by the angelic experience. But don't try to tell an entire life story; focus on one specific life event. Bring only as many people as needed to tell the story so the reader's interest stays with the dominant character. ·Decide what your spiritual point will be. We like to see a positive and specific change in the narrator as a result of the angelic experience. Don't forget: We want our readers to take away a message or insight they can use in their own lives. Everything in the story should be tied in with this specific and inspiring theme. ·Don't leave unanswered questions. Give all the relevant facts so the reader can clearly understand what took place. Let the reader feel as if he were there, seeing the characters, hearing them talk, feeling what they felt. Use dialogue, set scenes, build tension—dramatize the story. Show how the narrator becomes a new, or different person. ·The best rule of all: STUDY THE MAGAZINE! Payments: ·For full-length manuscripts (1500 words): $100 - $400, and is made when the story is approved and scheduled for publication. ·For quotes, anecdotes to use as fillers, and material for our short features (50 - 250 words): ·"Messages": brief, mysterious happenings, or letters describing how a specific Angels on Earth article helped you. Payment is usually $25. ·"Earning Their Wings": unusual stories of good deeds worth imitating. Payment is usually $50. ·"Only Human?": short narratives in which the angelic character may or may not have been a human being. The narrator is pleasantly unsure and so is the reader. Payment is usually $100. Please do not send essays, sermons or fiction. We rarely use poetry and do not evaluate book-length material. We receive thousands of unsolicited manuscripts each month, so allow three months for a reply. At this time we cannot accept electronic submissions.

Categories: Nonfiction—Inspirational—Psychology—Religion—Self Help—Society—Personal Experience

CONTACT: The Editor
Material: All
16 East 34th St.
New York NY 10016
Phone: 212-251-8100
Fax: 212-684-0679
E-mail: submissions@angelsmag.com
Website: www.angelsonearth.com

Remember: Editors change jobs and publishers change addresses. It is wise to invest in a phone call for the current information before submitting.

Animal People

ANIMAL PEOPLE welcomes freelance submissions of articles, informed guest opinion columns, original art, and photography, subject to the following terms and conditions:

• Material submitted for our consideration must not be simultaneously submitted to any other animal-related publication of national distribution. We must be informed if an item is simultaneously submitted to or has previously been published by some other type of publication, e.g. a local humane society newsletter or a general circulation magazine or newspaper.

• All submissions of writing will be either accepted or rejected within two weeks of receipt. Our usual turn-around time is less than one day.

• We buy either first North American serial rights or one-time reprint rights, depending on whether or not the material has been previously published, including the right of publication in both our newsprint and electronic editions. All other rights remain with the author.

• Because we are a nonprofit publication, we prefer to receive freelance materials as donations. However, recognizing that many contributors need to earn their livings by their work, we do pay the following honorariums: $25 per assigned book review, $15 per photograph or drawing, 10¢ a word for profiles and features. Payment is upon acceptance. We do not pay for guest opinion columns.

• Assignments will be made (or confirmed) in writing only, and only to contributors whose work we have previously published. Please do not query by telephone.

• We do not assign spot news coverage to freelancers.

• Profile submissions are particularly welcome, especially if accompanied by photographs. Although we may occasionally be receptive to a profile of a well-known subject, or a subject who has engineered a uniquely effective protest, our preference is to salute seldom recognized individuals of unique and outstanding positive accomplishment, in any capacity that benefits animals or illustrates the intrinsic value of other species. We are also particularly interested in those individuals who combine active concern for animals with active concern for fellow human beings.

• Profiles of organizations should be accompanied by a copy of the organization's most recent IRS Form 990 (unless we already have it on file.)

• We require independent verification of the animal care conditions at facilities whose reputations and administrations are unknown to us.

• We prefer to consider photography and art submissions on a portfolio basis. Query first, with examples of your work. If we think we might be able to use your material with reasonable frequency, we will invite you to send us prints of photos that might be appropriate, as you take them, identified with your name on the back of each. We will file them according to subject (aardvark to zebra mussel), and use them and pay you for them as our need to illustrate news items requires.

• We do not publish fiction or poetry.

• We are not interested in atrocity stories, essays on why animals have rights, or material that promotes or defends animal abuse, including hunting, fishing, trapping, and slaughter. ANIMAL PEOPLE is the leading independent newspaper providing original investigative coverage of animal protection worldwide, founded in 1992. Our readership of 30,000-plus includes the decision-makers at more than 8,300 animal protection organizations. We have no alignment or affiliation with any other entity.

• We prefer to receive manuscript submissions by e-mail and/or in hard copy format.

Categories: Animals—Animal Protection

CONTACT: Submissions Editor
Material: All
PO Box 960
Clinton WA 98236-0960
Phone: 360-579-2505

Fax: 360-579-2575
E-mail: anmlpepl@whidbey.com
Website: www.animalpeoplenews.org

The Animals' Agenda
Helping People Help Animals

The *Animals' Agenda* is a bimonthly magazine that seeks to inspire action for animals by informing people about animal rights and cruelty-free living. Agenda is committed to serving —and fostering cooperation among—all animal advocates from the grassroots to the national levels. The magazine is published by The Animal Rights Network Inc., an IRS 501(c)(3) federal tax-exempt, not-for-profit organization founded in 1979.

Submissions

The *Animals' Agenda* does not accept unsolicited manuscripts.

Article proposals or outlines, as well as letters to the editor, should be sent to The *Animals' Agenda* mailing address (see below). Once an article has been commissioned, we prefer it to be submitted via e-mail or on a 3.5" computer disk saved in standard ASCII format (with hard copy attached). Typed copy may also be faxed (letters to the editor may be neatly handwritten). Articles are due two months preceding the month of publication, and may be edited for space or clarity. Agenda reprints articles infrequently. Please indicate if an article is being submitted to other publications in addition to Agenda. We generally welcome other periodicals' reprinting articles from Agenda if those articles are credited properly. Agenda generally does not offer payment for articles.

Contents

• Letters to the editor allow readers to comment on articles or letters that have appeared in previous issues of Agenda, to voice opinions about matters of concern to animal advocates, and to offer advice on solving animal-abuse problems. Maximum length: 300 words.

• "Bulletin Board" is a collection of concise and late-breaking news briefs relating to animals and their well-being. These items may be obtained from magazines, newspapers, newsletters, or computer forums. Contributors should identify the sources of the "Bulletin Board" items they submit. Maximum length: 100 words.

• "Making a Difference" highlights victories and successes on behalf of animals, and is similar in style and format to "Bulletin Board."

• "Happy Endings" briefly recounts the true story of an animal(s) who was rescued from abusive, exploitative, or dangerous conditions, and who now lives a comfortable and secure life. Must include a photo of the animal(s). Maximum length: 400 words.

• "News" is a compilation of brief reports that describe animal abuse or exploitation practices, organizational campaigns for animals, recent pertinent developments, etc. A report should include information on how readers can help and a contact organization (if applicable), and may be accompanied by a photo. Maximum length: text, 400 words; photo with caption, 100 words.

• "Unsung Heroes" profiles individuals who work diligently, without major recognition, to protect the well-being and/or rights of animals—whether through direct hands-on assistance or other ongoing advocacy efforts. The individual should reflect a "regular" activist, not movement leaders or other professional advocates. Must include a photo of the activist. Maximum length: 500 words.

• "Investigations" are based on investigative reporting. They present considerable detail about a major source of animal exploitation or about a campaign to reduce or eliminate that exploitation. Must include photographs and material for "Your Agenda," outlining action readers can take to help. Maximum length: 1,200 words.

• "Analysis" serves a variety of functions: discussing strategies to reduce or to end animal exploitation, reviewing in detail a book or movie about animals or animal liberation, presenting a historical analysis of some facet of animal abuse, discussing the status of animals in society, etc. Must include photographs and material for "Your Agenda." Maximum length: 1,200 words.

• The cover feature presents in-depth and extensively detailed coverage of a major news story or development concerning the treatment or status of animals. Must include photographs, at least one sidebar, and material for "Your Agenda." Maximum length: 2,500 words.

• "Resources" presents brief reviews describing recently produced materials including books, computer software, CDs, campaign matter, videos, etc. that are intended to serve as educational or activist tools. Maximum length: 100 words.

• Reviews, while generally devoted to books about animal liberation or abuse, also may discuss the latest movies or CDs that treat these subjects. Must include the dust jacket or cover of the work reviewed. Maximum length: 800 words.

• "Commentary," provides a forum for guest columnists to offer a perspective on important issues and developments affecting the animal rights movement. Must include a photo of the author. Maximum length: 700 words.

• "Toward Kinship," an essay in which an author is free to consider any aspect of animal rights, should approach its subject in a personal, expansive, even offbeat manner. Whenever appropriate, submit a photograph or other image to illustrate the text. Maximum length: 1,200 words.

• "Activities" lists forthcoming conferences, demonstrations, protests, seminars, and other events of interest to animal advocates. Must include the name of a person and/or organization to contact about the listed event, as well as the address and phone number of that individual or organization. Maximum length: 50 words.

Categories: Animals—Animal Rights

CONTACT: Kirsten Rosenberg, Managing Editor
Material: All
PO Box 25881
Baltimore MD 21224
Phone: 410-675-4566
Fax: 410-675-0066
E-mail: office@animalsagenda.org
Website: www.animalsagenda.org

Animals Magazine

Overview:
Animals is a full-color, quarterly magazine written and edited to deliver timely, reliable, and provocative coverage of wildlife issues, pet-care topics, and animal-protection concerns. It also publishes natural-history pieces that educate readers about animals' needs and behaviors.

The magazine circulates to a national audience (around 50,000), consisting mostly of members of the Massachusetts Society for the Prevention of Cruelty to Animals and the American Humane Education Society, its publishers.

What We Publish From Freelance Sources:
About 90 percent of our editorial coverage is from freelance sources.

Feature Stories: Well-researched articles (1,200 to 2,000 words) on national and international wildlife, domestic animals, wildlife/conservation issues, controversies involving animals and/or their use, animal-protection issues, pet health, and pet care. Articles must engage readers who are interested in knowing more about a variety of creatures as well as those who consider themselves animal protectionists.

Reviews: Newly released books and videos on animals, animal-related issues, and the environment. These reviews run from 300 to 500 words and are for our Books column.

Profiles: Short pieces on individuals at work to save both domestic and wild animals, to make conditions better for animals, or on others whose interactions with animals makes them of interest to a wide-ranging audience. These reviews run about 800 words and are published in our ProFiles column.

What We Pay:
Because payment depends on the length of the article and the amount of research necessary to complete it, payment varies.

How to Query:
Please query by letter and allow four to six weeks for a response. Query letters should include:

• a pointed summary describing the article's focus, purpose, approximate length, and finish date;

• a list of sources that you plan to contact or have already contacted. When dealing with controversies, sources should be from both sides of the issue;

• writing samples, preferably of comparable pieces;

• information on when and where you may have published, or plan to publish, a similar story, if applicable.

Additional Information:
For a sample copy of *Animals Magazine*, please send a check in the amount of $3.95, payable to Animals Magazine, to the address below.

For a copy of *Animals Magazine's* photography guidelines, please send a stamped, self-addressed envelope to the address below.

Thank you for your interest in *Animals Magazine*.

Categories: Animals

CONTACT: Paula Abend, Editor
Material: Wildlife and Pet/Domestic queries
350 S. Huntington Ave.
Boston MA 02130
Phone: 617-522-7400
Fax: 617-522-4885

Annals of Improbable Research (AIR)

The Journal of Record for Inflated Research and Personalities

The Annals of Improbable Research (AIR) publishes original articles, data, effluvia and news of improbable research. The material is intended to be humorous and/or educational, and sometimes is. We look forward to receiving your manuscripts, photographs, x-rays, drawings, etc. Please do not send biological samples. Photos should be black & white if possible. Reports of research results, modest or otherwise, are preferred to speculative proposals.

Keep it short, please. Articles are typically 500-2,000 words in length. (Items intended for mini-AIR* should be much, much, much shorter.) Please send two neatly printed copies. Alternatively, you may submit via e-mail, in ASCII format.

Please don't spend a lot of efforting in elaborate text formatting. If the article is accepted for publication we will take care of that.

Sincerely and improbably,
Marc Abrahams, Editor

Categories: Humor— Internet—Interview—Science

CONTACT: Submissions Editor
Material: All
PO Box 380853
Cambridge MA 02238
Phone: 617-491-4437
E-mail: AIR@improbable.com
Website: www.improbable.com

Antioch Review

SUGGESTIONS FOR
PROSPECTIVE CONTRIBUTORS

The best answer we can give on inquiries relating to what kind of material the ANTIOCH REVIEW uses is, "read the magazine." Look through a few representative issues for an idea of subjects, treatment, lengths of articles, and stories we have used; it will be far more rewarding than any theories we might try to formulate.Unfortunately, we cannot honor requests for free sample copies. The REVIEW is expensive to produce and operates on a precarious financial margin. If copies are not available at your local newsstand or library, we will be happy to send you a back issue for $6.00, which includes postage and handling.

ARTICLES

Our audience is made up of educated citizens, often professional people, who are interested in matters beyond their fields of special activity. With few exceptions, our subjects cover most of the range of social science and humanities. Our approach tries to steer a middle course between scholars speaking exclusively to other scholars in their field, and workaday journalists appealing to a broad popular audience; both these approaches have their own journals and audiences. We try for the interpretive essay on a topic of current importance, drawing on scholarly materials for its substance and appealing to the intellectual and social concerns of our readers. We are also interested in reviving the moribund art of literary journalism. We DO NOT read essays from June 1 to September 1.

FICTION

We seldom publish more than three short stories in each issue. Although the new writer as well as the previously published author is welcome, it is the story that counts, a story worthy of the serious attention of the intelligent reader, a story that is compelling, written with distinction. Only rarely do we publish translations of well known or new foreign writers; a chapter of a novel is welcome only if it can be read complete in itself as a short story. We DO NOT read fiction from June 1 to September 1.

POETRY

Like fiction, we get far more poetry than we can possibly accept, and the competition is keen. Here, where form and content are so inseparable and reaction is so personal, it is difficult to state requirements or limitations. Studying recent issues of the REVIEW should be helpful. No "light" or inspirational verse. Any poetry received without a self addressed stamped envelope will be discarded if rejected and no notice will be sent. No need to enclose a post card for the purpose of acknowledging receipt of a submission. Do not mix poetry and prose in the same envelope. Please submit three to six poems at one time. We DO NOT read poetry from May 1 to September 1.

REVIEWS

We do not publish unsolicited book reviews and very seldom do we publish essays on literary problems or the canons of significant contemporary writers. The editors and their associates regularly prepare a section of short book evaluations, selectively treating recent publications.

STYLE, LENGTHS, PAYMENT, ETC.

Our literary standards are as high as we can enforce them; we do not have the staff to engage in major editorial rewriting, except on rare occasions when the content justifies the effort.

Actually, we have no rigid expectations of length, preferring the content and treatment to determine size. Rarely, however, do we use articles or stories over 5,000 words—and 8,000 at the outside limit.

In order to be returned to you, all manuscripts must be accompanied by a self-addressed stamped envelope. We cannot be responsible for the return of manuscripts for which the postage has not been provided. If you want the ms. discarded, say so and enclose a postcard or stamped envelope which we can use if we do not accept your submission.

Manuscripts should be typed, double-spaced on one side of white, 8.5 x 11 paper. Please spare the editors the task of reading carbons or dirty Xerox copies or pages with excessive inter-linear corrections and revisions. We also prefer manuscripts to be mailed flat, fastened by paper clip only, and one at a time (does not apply for poetry). Do not mix prose and poetry in the same envelope, please.

We try to report on manuscripts within five weeks, but because material that interests us is occasionally read by several members of our staff, the process can sometimes take up to six or eight weeks. We acknowledge receipt of a manuscript only if it is accompanied by a return postcard for that purpose.

Payment is upon printed publication at the rate of $10.00 per printed page (about 425 words) plus 2 copies of the issue. Authors may buy additional copies at an authors' discount of 40% off the cover price.

All material sent to the ANTIOCH REVIEW is read and considered, although we cannot comment on each rejection. However, we do not read simultaneous submissions.

Categories: Fiction—Nonfiction—Literature—Poetry

CONTACT: Robert Fogarty, Editor
Material: Fiction, Nonfiction
CONTACT: Judith Hall, Poetry Editor
Material: Poetry
PO Box 148
Yellow Springs OH 45387
Phone: 937-769-1365
Website: www.antioch.edu/review/home.html

Antique Trader Weekly

Editorial Submissions

Unsolicited manuscripts are welcome, but must include a self-addressed, stamped envelope (SASE) with sufficient return postage. Query letters are appreciated with samples of the author's previously published writing. Writers are encouraged to send in completed articles for consideration.

Queries are accepted via e-mail at korbecks@krause.com.

Content

Antique Trader is published weekly and includes feature stories, news items and regular columns. Articles are of general interest to collectors, dealers and others actively involved in the antiques and collectibles hobby.

What are we looking for?

• *Profiles.* These 500 to 800-word profiles could feature interesting stories about "super" collectors, enterprising dealers, fledgling businesses or other personalities in the hobby. They should be creatively written in story form, rather than question and answer format.

• *Feature stories.* Subject matter should focus on the collectibility of specific antiques or manufacturers' lines. Features should not be too narrow, but rather hit the highlights of a particular type of antique. Smaller features may focus on more specific topics (tin wind-up toys, Wallace Nutting furniture, Red Wing pottery, milk glass, etc.)

• *Event coverage. Antique Trader* regularly covers news of events such as antique shows and auctions. These features should include highlights of the events (special guests, prices realized, major announcements), quotes from promoters, dealers and attendees and high-quality photos with identification.

Most stories bear an author's byline, and all stories are subject to editing and rewriting for accuracy, clarity, conciseness and space considerations.

Current values of antique and other pricing information should be incorporated into features or placed in an accompanying sidebar. Our readers want to know not only the historical information about toys, but also what is available and how much it's worth. Please note the source of the pricing (online auction, auction prices realized, dealer list, etc.).

• *Word count.* To accommodate our new, more user-friendly design, word count should be limited to 500 to 800 words. Sidebar and pricing text is not included in that count.

• *Illustrations.* Appropriate photos (line art, illustrations, etc.) must accompany each column. This can include color or black/white slides, prints or transparencies or digital images. Digital images (TIFF or JPG) must be at least 200 dpi (72 dpi JPGs are NOT acceptable for print) and sent via e-mail, disk or CD. Images downloaded from Web sites are discouraged since screen resolution does not frequently translate well to print.

Photos should be identified on a separate sheet or on a Post-It note on the back of the photo. Do NOT use ink on the backs of photos.

It is the columnist's responsibility to secure photos for his/her column; photos from outside sources are acceptable with proper permissions. Photos should not be indiscriminately downloaded from Web sites without the owners' and/or author's permission. Photos must not be taken from other books or publications without permission from the respective publishers.

• *Quotes.* In an effort to make our editorial content more interactive and community driven, quotes from at least two outside sources must be incorporated into each column or feature. Depending on content, these quotes could be from dealers, collectors, show promoters, clubs or other related sources. Sources should be tapped to comment on what's hot, what's not, a particular controversy, a new product, an old standard or anything applicable to your column that month.

• *Sidebars.* At least one sidebar must be included with each column or feature. Sample sidebars could include (but are not limited to):

• Resources (clubs, books, web sites, etc.)

• *Hot News.* (a late-breaking addition, an especially interesting trend or controversy, a show report, historical timeline, etc.)

• *Pricing.* All features must include secondary market pricing or retail pricing (depending on what is appropriate). Pricing sidebars can include values from various sources including Krause Publications price guides, secondary market dealers, retail price lists, other outside "expert" resources or prices realized (from auctions or completed online auctions). In any case, proper citation must be given.

Prices should be worked into a sidebar, but you are also free to incorporate pricing into the body of the column or feature. Top 10 lists are encouraged as well (top-selling Rookwood, best bets of the month, etc.).

Rights and Payment

Krause Publications purchases exclusive rights to manuscripts for *Antique Trader* Publications. Krause Publications retains the right to republish the material (online or in other Krause publications).

Previously published articles can be submitted for consideration; please specify previous publisher/date with query.

Editorial contracts are mailed out after the article has been accepted, but the editor retains the right to withhold publication due to space, time or other considerations. At such time, a lesser kill fee may be offered.

Payment for articles accepted is based on a per-story basis (story plus illustrative material) at the editor's discretion. Payment is upon publication, unless other arrangements have been agreed upon. Contact Editor Sharon Korbeck for specific, current rates.

Manuscript Format

Hard copy submitted must be typewritten and double-spaced on white paper with the author's name, address and phone number at the top. Please leave at least one-inch margins on all sides of the page. Do not submit copy typed in ALL CAPS.

Computer submissions should be on a DS/HD disk in ASCII (text) or Microsoft Word format with accompanying hard copy.

Electronic submissions are accepted only for solicited or assigned stories. No unsolicited manuscripts via e-mail, please. Send e-mail submissions to korbecks@krause.com.

Style

We follow the basic journalistic style guidelines in *The Associated Press Stylebook.* Consult Strunk & White's *The Elements of Style* for additional considerations. Please proofread stories carefully before submitting them.

Publication

Authors will not be notified prior to publication and will be sent two copies of the issue containing their story.

Please note: Publication time may be anywhere from two months to 24 months following acceptance.

Contact

Interested free-lance writers should query via mail or via e-mail. For a sample copy of *Antique Trader* or other Krause publications, call (800) 258-0929.

For more information about our company's books and magazines, visit our Web sites www.krause.com or www.collect.com.

Categories: Nonfiction—Antiques—Collectibles—Hobbies

CONTACT: Sharon Korbeck, Editor
Material: Queries
700 E. State St.
Iola WI 54990-0001
Phone: 715-445-4612, ext. 468v
Fax: 715-445-4087
E-mail: korbecks@krause.com
Website: www.krause.com

Antiques & Collecting Magazine

We accept freelance material for publication in *Antiques & Collecting Magazine* and would be pleased to have you submit an article on speculation at your convenience.

We are looking for manuscripts about a particular antique, collectible, artist, or company that produced the collectibles. Although some collectibles made after the 1980s are considered, we prefer to focus on antiques and collectibles made before 1980. We hope both the novice and seasoned collector will appreciate the article.

Length should be approximately 1300-1600 words. We prefer that you send a hard copy in the mail (please include computer disc), or send the article as an attachment via email.

• Include the current value of the items. Our readers need to know!

• If possible, include the names of clubs or organizations whose members specialize in that particular collectible. The more information the better.

• Please provide a list of books on the topic if you can.

We require six to ten well-lit, high quality photographs to illustrate the article. Polaroid, color copies and computer-generated images do not reproduce as well as "real" photographs or slides. If you would like to send digital images (jpgs, tiffs), scan them in at 300 DPI or more, or 170 LPI for the best reproduction. Please do not crop objects, and include a shot of maker's marks if possible. We love variety!

We purchase first-rights only and our pay scale ranges from $100-$250, depending on the quality of the article and photos submitted. Material is subject to editing for length, style and format. We offer alternative advertising compensation, and will be happy to provide you with details if you are interested.

Payment is made upon publication of the article. We also provide you with four complimentary copies of the issue in which your article appears. Please submit your material to the Editorial Department at the above address. You may also send the article via email.

Thanks for your interest!

Categories: Nonfiction—Arts—Crafts/Hobbies—Hobbies

CONTACT: Therese Nolan, Editor
Material: All

Lighner Publishing Corp.
1006 S. Michigan Ave.
Chicago IL 60605
Phone: 312-939-4767
Fax: 312-939-0053
E-mail: acmeditor@interaccess.com

Anvil Magazine

For the past 21 years, ANVIL Magazine has been The Voice of the Farrier and Blacksmith. This international monthly is distributed throughout the United States and in over 20 foreign countries and enjoys a readership of over 10,000 per issue.

Our staff is always interested in your submission. We read and consider every contribution forwarded, as we sincerely believe that the responsibility of a good editor is to listen to many voices and to encourage writers to grow. We appreciate the efforts of our contributors, and when editing is necessary, we attempt to offer comment that promotes clarity. We reserve the right to edit in the interests of available space and clarity.

Contribution Categories

• Feature/Pictorial Events, personal profiles, question-and-answer interviews, local color, points of interest (e.g., museums, schools)

• Blacksmithing

• How-To-Do-It articles—illustrated step-by-step smithing processes. Metallurgy, history, craft hints, tools and techniques

• Farriery

• How-To-Do-It articles—illustrated step-by-step shoeing processes. Craft hints and techniques, shoeing experience with horses.

• Veterinary/Technical: Research, studies, documented reports by professional individuals.

• Equine Training Information

• Reports, studies and personal experiences related to handling, training and locomotion of the horse.

• Humor: As it pertains to the farrier and blacksmith.

• Safety/Health/Psychology: Personal aspects of the industry: individual experiences, shop safety tips, exercise and nutrition information, psychology of working with horses.

• Book Reviews on books of interest to the industry.

• Business articles for the farrier and equine industry.

• Guest Editorial: Personal opinion or consideration of an existing condition within the industry. Individual's name must be included with submission.

• Horse Owner Information: Equine hoof, nutrition and handling, pertaining to farriery, written to inform the horse owner.

Submission Format and Requirements

Text: Formats listed in order of preference.

1. Commitment of material to a 5¼" or 3½" floppy disk with one (1) hard copy representation (printout, typewritten text, photocopy) of each submission. Computer files must be IBM compatible and utilize either WordPerfect, Word or ASCII text files. Hard copies are required, should there be complications involved in disk submission retrieval.

2. Computer printout or photocopy of typewritten material.

3. Handwritten articles.

All submissions must be legible and must include the name, address and phone number of author. If previously published material, full credit information of prior publication and written release to reprint are required. In the case of technical, historical or controversial submissions, the reference sources, bibliography or verification may be requested. Illustrations in the form of original art work and photographs enhance the literature. Contributors are encouraged to illustrate articles whenever possible.

Photography: Formats listed in order of preference.

1. High-contrast, high-clarity black-and-white 5"x7" photographs, labeled on backs for article reference.

2. Black-and-white proof sheets with negatives.

3. High-contrast color photographs.

4. Color slides.

All photo submissions must be clearly identified and must include photographer's name, address and phone number. Each individual photo should be clearly marked, preferably with paper label on the back with reference to the article. Names of subjects, dates and places or reference numbers to written sheet of captions are required. If previously published material, include full credit information of prior publication and written release to reprint.

Cartoons, Graphics, Illustrations: Must be original and the work of the artist of submission. Submissions must be clearly marked with name, address and phone number of the artist. In the case of illustration to text referrals, illustrations must be clearly marked in sequence. Black-and-white material is preferred. Computer files (TIFF or other formats) of art work are welcomed.

Submission Dates

Material targeted for a particular issue must be in our editorial offices two months prior to the first day of the month of issue. In case of important events, special arrangements can be made to accommodate time-sensitive material.

Publishing Policy

ANVIL Magazine publishes first-run material and reprints of previously published articles. We reserve the right to reject material and to professionally edit any first-run works submitted.

ANVIL Magazine reserves the right to offer articles for reprints, which are available at cost.

In addition, ANVIL Magazine reserves the right to place articles on the ANVIL Magazine World Wide Web Page. These articles will carry the copyright of the author, e.g., "© John Smith." The ANVIL Magazine Web Page is an information resource.

Material Appearance Policy

First-run material under contract to ANVIL Magazine may not appear in another publication prior to its appearance in ANVIL Magazine.

No material will be accepted for publication prior to review. No material will be considered in part, but must be forwarded in its entirety for editorial review.

Tear sheets of article/graphic appearance and a complimentary copy of the issue in which it appears are forwarded directly to author within 30 days of publication.

Disclaimer

ANVIL Magazine and its staff do not manufacture, test, warrant, guarantee or endorse any of the tools, materials, instructions or products contained in any articles published. ANVIL Magazine disclaims any responsibility or liability for damages or injuries as a result of the use or application of any information published in ANVIL Magazine.

Payment for Contributions

Payment for submissions is made directly to the author within 30 days of material acceptance. Rate of payment is determined on each individual submission and is based upon, but not limited to, article length, quality, complexity, timeliness and number of photos or graphics. ANVIL Magazine payments range from $25.00 to $250.00.

Categories: Book Reviews—Blacksmithing—Ferriery—Veterinary

CONTACT: Bob Edwards, Publisher/Editor
Material: All
PO Box 1810
Georgetown CA 95634
Phone: 530-333-2142
Fax: 530-333-2906

E-mail: anvil@anvilmag.com
Website: www.anvilmag.com

Appleseeds

General Information

APPLESEEDS is a 36-page, multidisciplinary, nonfiction social studies magazine for children ages 8 and up (primarily in grades 3 & 4). Writers are encouraged to study recent back issues for content and style. (Sample issues are available at $4.95 plus $2.00 shipping and handling. Send 7 1/2 " x 10 1/2 " self-addressed envelope.) We are looking for articles that are lively, age-appropriate, and exhibit an original approach to the theme. Scientific and historical accuracy is extremely important. Authors are urged to use primary sources and up-to-date resources for their research. And remember, your article must stimulate the curiosity of a child. APPLESEEDS purchases all rights to material.

Procedure

Writers may propose an article for any issue. The article idea must be closely related to the theme of the issue. Please include a completed query.

• Each query must be written separately; however, you may mail / email them together.

• Feel free to include copies of published writing samples with your query if you have not yet written for APPLESEEDS.

• After the deadline for query proposals has passed, the editors will review the suggestions and assign articles. This may take several months - don't despair! We may suggest modifications to your original proposal or assign an entirely new idea.

Please do not begin work until you've received a detailed assignment sheet from us!

Guidelines

Feature articles:
1-4 pages, (Most issues contain about 6-8 feature articles.)
Includes: nonfiction, interviews, and how-to
Departments:
• Fun Stuff (games or activities relating to the theme, 2 pages)
• Reading Corner (literature piece, 2-4 pages)
• By the Numbers (math activities relating to the theme, 1 page)
• Where in the World (map activities, 2 pages)
• Your Turn (theme-related opportunities for children to take action, 1 page)
• Experts in Action (short profile of professional in field related to theme, 1 page)
• The Artist's Eye (fine or folk art relating to theme, 1 page)
• From the Source (age-appropriate primary source material, 1-2 pages)
Assume 150 words per page; payment approximately $50 per page

Photo Guidelines

To be considered for publication, photographs must relate to a specific theme. Writers are encouraged to submit available photos with their query or article. We buy one-time use.

Our suggested fee range for professional quality photographs follows:

1/4 page	to	full page
b/w $15	to	$100
color $25	to	$100

• Please note that fees for non-professional quality photographs are negotiated.

• Cover fees are set on an individual basis for one-time use, plus promotional use. All cover images are color.

• Prices set by museums, societies, stock photography houses, etc., are paid or negotiated. Photographs that are promotional in nature (e.g., from tourist agencies, organizations, special events, etc.) are usually submitted at no charge.

• If you have photographs pertaining to any upcoming theme, please contact the editor by mail or fax, or send them with your query. You may also send images on speculation.

Write a brief description of your idea, including a list of sources you plan to use, your intended word length, and any unique angle or hook you think will make your piece irresistible to its intended audience (8 - 10-year-olds and their teachers and parents).

• E-mail queries are preferred. To avoid problems in downloading attachments, always include your query in the body of the email. You may also include attachments if you wish.

• If you mail your queries by regular mail, include one SASE (only one is required, no matter how many queries you submit).

• Queries may be submitted at any time before the deadline, but queries sent well in advance of deadline MAY NOT BE ANSWERED FOR SEVERAL MONTHS.

• Assignments are made approximately one month before manuscripts are due.

E-mail queries to: swbuc@aol.com
Or mail them to: Susan Buckley, Editor
APPLESEEDS Magazine
140 E 83rd St.
New York, NY 10028
Mail sample requests to:
Editorial Department
Cobblestone Publishing
Attn: Sample Requests
30 Grove Street, Suite C
Peterborough, NH 03458
Categories: Nonfiction—Children—History—Juvenile—Science—Society

CONTACT: Susan Buckley, Co-Editor
Material: All
Cobblestone Publishing
140 E 83rd St.
New York NY 10028
E-mail: swbuc@aol.com
Website: www.cobblestonepub.com

The Appraisers Standard

• Articles should be approximately 700 words in length. Longer articles may be broken in two or more parts if necessary in order to cover the topic as required.

• Black and white photos should accompany the article and assist the reader with appraising the articles being covered.

• Current auction/market prices should be included whenever applicable.

• Topics for articles should be appropriate for appraisers of personal as well as real estate property.

• Articles should be geared to provide information which will help the appraisers with ascertaining value, detecting forgeries or reproductions, or simply providing advice on appraising the articles.

• A short biography of the author should be sent to be added to story to supply reader with credentials of author.

• Payment of $50 is made when story is published.
Categories: Nonfiction—Antiques—Arts—Collectibles—Appraising

CONTACT: Linda Tucker, Editor
Material: All
5 Gill Terrace
Ludlow VT 05149-1003
Phone: 802-228-7444

AQR
Alaska Quarterly Review

Alaska Quarterly Review, a journal devoted to contemporary literary art, and published by the University of Alaska Anchorage, invites submissions in the following areas:

FICTION: Short stories and novel excerpts in traditional and experimental styles (generally not exceeding 50 pages).

POETRY: Poems in traditional and experimental styles but no light verse (up to 20 pages).

PROSE: Literary nonfiction in traditional and experimental styles (generally not exceeding 50 pages).

DRAMA: Short plays in traditional and experimental styles (generally not exceeding 50 pages).

No cover letter is necessary. Your submission will be judged on its own merits. If you do send a letter, please include your publication credits. You may submit a legible photocopy. Unless a SASE is enclosed with your submission, you will not hear from us unless we are interested in publishing your manuscript. We try to reply within 4 to 12 weeks. Unsolicited manuscripts are welcome between August 15 and May 15.

Rates for individuals: $10.00 (1 yr.); $20.00 (2 yrs.); $30.00 (3 yrs.)

Rates for institutions: $10.00 (1 yr.); $20.00 (2 yrs.); $30.00 (3 yrs.)

Note: Add $4.00 per year for subscriptions outside of the USA.

Sample copies: $6.00 (Outside the USA add $2.00)

Prices for back issues and special issues available upon request.

Please make checks payable to: *Alaska Quarterly Review.*

Categories: Fiction—Nonfiction—Poetry

CONTACT: Editor
Material: All
University of Alaska Anchorage, 3211 Providence Dr.
Anchorage AK 99508
Phone: 907-786-6916
Fax: 907-786-6916
Website: aqr.uaa.alaska.edu

Archaeology

Archaeology magazine is one of two publications of the Archaeological Institute of America. While our sister publication, the *American Journal of Archaeology*, is widely read in the academic world, Archaeology shares this world of discovery with a general audience. Our circulation is 225,000.

Our readers are well-read, well-traveled professionals interested in global history, discovery, culture and adventure. They are acutely aware of the fact that archaeology often corrects and rewrites history, and provides a voice to peoples whom often have had no presence in the historical record.

Authors include not only professional journalists but professional archaeologists as well. If you are a scientist interested in writing about your research for *Archaeology*, see below for tips and suggestions on writing for a general audience.

What we publish:

Our feature—length articles cover all corners of the globe, from frozen settlements in Alaska to ancient temples on South Asian islands. Archaeology isn't just about digging, and we're always looking for a new angle on a subject. Recent articles (which generally range from 1,000 to 3,500 words) have covered such diverse topics as how to make a mummy, the terror of Moche ritual sacrifice, cultural heritage in Afghanistan under the Taliban, objects featured in the odd paintings of Hieronymous Bosch that have been found in excavations of his hometown, how increased tourism has boosted archaeological investigation in Old Havana, and royal nomad burials in Kazakhstan;

as well as photo essays on Angkor Wat, the artifacts of the steel industry, and Australian rock art; and profiles of people who have made great contributions to archaeology, from volcanologists to tree-ring specialists to Mayanists to novelists. Archaeology encompasses the full breadth of human history—there's a lot out there; don't be afraid to think outside the box.

Along with new archaeological discoveries, our news department publishes short (250 to 500 word) articles on criminal, environmental, and political developments that impact global heritage. Significant or exclusive archaeological news is featured in our 1,000-1,500-word *Special Report section*. Recent Special Reports have included an unlikely Israeli-Palestinian archaeological program that sprung up during the current Intifada, as well as prospects for archaeology and the preservation of cultural heritage in Pakistan during military actions in neighboring Afghanistan.

Our reviews department looks for short (250 to 500 word) articles on museums, books, television shows, movies, and websites of interest to our readers. While the material reviewed may not be purely archaeological in nature, it should have a strong archaeological element to it. Reviews should not simply summarize the material, but provide an critical evaluation.

Letter From... is often a personal rumination on a particular topic or site. Recent "Letters" have included a look at how metal detectorists and archaeologists in Britain have learned to cooperate, the ongoing dispute over construction work at Jerusalem's ancient Temple Mount, and a humble stone monument that keeps causing a lot of political friction between Japan and Korea. "Letters" are usually about 2,500-3,000 words in length.

Conversations is a one-page interview in Q&A format with someone who has made a considerable impact on the field of archaeology. The interview may explain the researcher's general approach to his or her subject, or concentrate on a specific, and often controversial, discovery or theory.

Field Note: features a compelling and intriguing photograph of someone (layperson or professional) involved in an archaeological activity, together with a 300-word first-person narrative of what the subject in the photograph is doing and thinking.

We do not accept fiction, poetry, or previously published articles.

Queries: Preliminary queries should be no more than one or two pages (500 words max.) in length and may be sent to the Editor-in-Chief, *Archaeology*, 36-36 33rd Street, Long Island City, NY 11106 or via email to editorial@archaeology.org. If you would like a reply to your query mailed to you, please enclose a self-addressed stamped envelope. We do not accept telephone queries. Check our online index (link) to make sure that we have not already published a similar article.

Your query should tell us the following: who you are, why you are qualified to cover the subject, how you will cover the subject, and why our readers would be interested in the subject. Clips and credentials are helpful.

While illustrations are not the responsibility of the author, it helps to give us a sense of how the article could be illustrated; if possible, email an example of 2 or 3 images that might accompany the article. Please do not email unusually large images or too many images at a time; we will request additional images if needed. Please do not mail us unsolicited diskettes, photographs, or transparencies as they will not be returned. If you do not have access to images, referrals to professional photographers with relevant material are appreciated.

Unsolicited queries should receive a reply within six to eight weeks. Commissioned articles found unsuitable for publication will receive a kill fee of one-quarter of the agreed payment price.

Please be familiar with our magazine and what we publish before you write up a query. For a sample copy of *Archaeology*, send a self-addressed stamped 9"x12" envelope to Guidelines, *Archaeology*, 36-36 33rd Street, Long Island City, NY 11106. Back issues can be ordered on our website.

Manuscripts: Accepted manuscripts should be sent electronically in a universal format, with no embedded images. The author's name, social security number and contact information must be included. Authors should be prepared to provide a list of publications and people consulted, along with contact information for each source. In addition, we request a list of five to seven general-interest books and/or websites, with a brief description of each, that may be of interest to readers who would like to learn more about the subject you've written about.

Style: Dates use A.D. and B.C., measures must be in miles and feet. When in doubt, refer to *The Chicago Manual of Style*.

Rights and payment: Payments range from $100 for a short news article to $1500 for a feature. We purchase non-exclusive worldwide publication rights for texts and photographs. News and review articles are included in full on the magazine's website; feature articles are abstracted. Material published in *Archaeology* may be reproduced on our web site as purchasable html or pdf format files, and via third-party data bases such as EBSCO, in books of collected articles from Archaeology, and in translated form.

Things to keep in mind when writing for a general audience: This is not an academic publication. It's critically important to remember that less than one-half of one percent of our readers are professional archaeologists. Your proposed article must clearly spell out why the other 99.5% of our readers—bank tellers, doctors, librarians, corporate raiders—would be interested in your story. Some research—say, the variance in arsenic levels of metal objects produced in the Near East from the beginning to end of the Assyrian period—is a hard sell for a popular publication. On the other hand, such unlikely topics as Sumerian beer and a fish bone conference have made for entertaining and accessible articles that give our readers what they're looking for—a fresh and interesting perspective on human history.

Put yourself in the piece: Many scientists are consistently surprised by the fact that the general public is not just interested in what they do, but who they are. This is especially true for archaeologists: chances are you've traveled to a lot more interesting places, met a lot more interesting people, and had many more interesting adventures than most people. Nobody becomes an archaeologist to get rich, they do it for the experience; let the guy who grew up wanting to be an archaeologist but ended up a lawyer live vicariously through you!

Enable your readers to see through your eyes, but don't lose them in technical details. If you're writing about a fabulous discovery you made in the depths of the rain forest, bring the complete experience to your readers: what does the jungle look like, smell like? What sort of animals are about? What's camp like? If you only have a limited number of sentences to evoke a site for a lay reader, you're better off describing the looming mountains or sun-baked bricks rather than the fact that the 4.5x10-foot structure is 3.3 feet south of the 15-foot-square platform, which is 10 feet from the two cooking pits, each averaging 24 inches in diameter. Explain or avoid technical or local terms.

Engage the locals: If you're ready to tell us about the remarkable discoveries you've made in your ten years of work at site X, solicit thoughts and opinions from the people who live around site X. Does it give them a new perspective on where they live? Has it taught them something about themselves? How has having an archaeological expedition around for a decade affected their lives? What role will they have in managing the site you've excavated? Are they glad to see your noisy Land Rovers go?

Talk to us: *Archaeology* understands the importance of sharing your research with the public, and we've been helping archaeologists do just that for over fifty years. If you'd like to explore the possibility of publishing your work in the world's largest-circulation archaeology magazine, please contact us at editorial@archaeology.org and we'll put you in touch with the editor who can best assist you.

Categories: Nonfiction—Environment—Politics—Science—Archaeology

CONTACT: Editor-in-Chief
Material: All

36-36 33rd St.
Long Island City NY 11106
Phone: 718-472-3050
Fax: 718-472-3051
E-mail: edit@archaeology.org
Website: www.archaeology.org

Architectural Digest

Thank you for contacting *Architectural Digest* regarding how to submit to the magazine. Due to the volume of submissions we adhere to a strict policy.

Below is the best way to submit a project or person for publication consideration:

Our submission procedure requires that the designer, architect, resident (or representative) send 35mm transparencies, slides or prints to the attention of Ms. Paige Rense, Editor-in-Chief, 6300 Wilshire Boulevard, Los Angeles, CA 90048. *We do not accept anything via e-mail, disk, fax or cd-rom.*

For a private home, these images should cover the main rooms of the residence, (living room, dining room and master bedroom in particular) as well as a few exterior shots. We are not necessarily interested in bathrooms or kitchens unless they are extremely interesting or spectacular as they are rarely featured. Children's rooms and nurseries are not normally featured either.

Please include information on antiques, art works, and special design elements as well. Please also make sure information is typed and legible. Please also include a short bio on the owners of the property as well as the architect and or interior designer. With any and all submissions, we would like to know if the residence has been published previously.

To submit for an artist, photographs of different works as well as a bio will be sufficient. Please also send a list of your clients, designer and architects, who shop with you or have used your work. Send this information to Nina Farrell at the above address. I am sorry to say that we do not feature commercial spaces, except for hotels, gardens and museums.

After the editors have carefully reviewed the images, the submitter will be notified of our decision. If selected for publication, we will assign a photographer and a writer to do the story. If not, all materials will be returned. We do not visit or 'scout' homes in person. Normally it takes at least seven months from the submission date for the article to be published.

This letter is not a solicitation for materials and *Architectural Digest* is not responsible for unsolicited photos and other submitted materials.

Thank you for your interest in *Architectural Digest* and please let me know if I may be of further assistance.

Categories: Nonfiction—Architecture

CONTACT: Ms. Paige Rense, Editor-in-Chief
Material: Architectural Reviews
CONTACT: Nina Farrell
Material: Artist Reviews
6300 Wilshire Blvd.
Los Angeles CA 90048
Website: www.condenet.com/mags/archdigest

Area Development

Area Development is an economic development publication. It has consistently maintained a quality of editorial unmatched by any other magazine in this field. Writers for *Area Development* should have an understanding of its advertising market and readership to avoid submission of unsuitable material.

Area Development's advertising market consists of countries, states, provinces, counties, cities, utilities, railroads, industrial and business parks, industrial real estate firms, port authorities, foreign-trade zones, enterprise zones, and location specialists/ consultants. These advertisers are in *Area Development* because they want to attract industry to their areas. However, editorial in *Area Development* is not directed towards its advertisers.

Editorial in *Area Development* is directed to corporate decision-makers responsible for selecting sites and planning facilities for their companies. The magazine's more than 40,000 readers are primarily chief executives of industrial corporations. Feature articles must be useful to them in making decisions involving expansion or relocation. A basic guideline for editorial is stated in the magazine's masthead: "sites and facility planning." *This broad statement covers various factors including the following:*

- Labor availability and costs
- Availability of raw materials
- Infrastructure (highways, rail service, airports, ocean ports, inland ports and waterways)
- Proximity to (and association with) colleges and universities
- Utilities (electricity and gas availability and costs)
- Financing and incentives
- Training of employees
- Taxes
- Quality-of-life factors (schools, housing, cultural opportunities, recreational facilities)
- Availability of land and facilities for future expansion
- Community acceptance and relations
- Government requirements and controls
- Telecommunications requirements and services
- Access to markets
- Security (crime prevention, fire protection)
- Support services for constructing and maintaining plants and equipment
- Pollution controls and environmental regulations
- Legislation affecting economic development
- Working with architects, construction companies, and construction management firms
- Technical equipment (such as robotics and CAD/CAM) when it is a factor in site selection and facility planning.
- Start-up and operating costs

When writing feature articles for *Area Development*, it is necessary to avoid blatant promotional or "puff" material. It is also necessary to avoid negative comments about any areas or comparisons of areas. With a few exceptions, *Area Development* does not publish case studies or information specifically about any area.

If there are any questions about the suitability of feature material for *Area Development*, please call the editor.

Categories: Business—Site and Facility Planning

CONTACT: Geraldine Gambale, Editor
Material: All
400 Post Ave.
Westbury NY 11590
Phone: 516-338-0900
Fax: 516-338-0100
E-mail: readev@areadevelopment.com
Website: www.areadevelopment.com

Arizona Foothills Magazine

Formal guidelines not available. Please read a number of issues to ascertain the publication's style and needs.

Send queries to address below.

Categories: General Interest—Lifestyle—Regional

CONTACT: Melissa Castleman, Features Editor
Material: Features
CONTACT: Elizabeth Exline, Departments Editor
Material: Departments
8132 N. 87th Place
Scottsdale AZ 85258

Phone: 480-460-5203
Fax: 480-443-1517
E-mail: publishersassistant@azfoothillsmag.com
Website: www.azfoothillsmag.com

Arizona Highways

Arizona Highways is a monthly magazine that encourages travel to and within Arizona. It does this by featuring stories on places to go and things to do, on the state's unique scenic environment, on its flora and fauna, on its people and on the history and culture of the Old West. We use experience-based travel stories, rather than guidebook or list stories, and we particularly like adventure-travel stories and stories on Indian arts, crafts and customs.

CIRCULATION: The magazine sells about 350,000 copies monthly, mostly to subscribers outside Arizona (about 25 percent are in Arizona). The magazine circulates in every state and in about two-thirds of the countries of the world.

AUDIENCE: Our typical reader is a 50-something person with the time, the inclination and the means to travel. Our subscribers are equally divided between men and women, are outdoor-oriented and have a strong interest in the Old West and in the arts, crafts and culture of Native Americans.

QUERIES: Nearly all the features and departments are free-lance written and photographed. And nearly all assignments result from written queries. We prefer query letters that are brief and to the point, by e-mail. The letter should detail the story, the angle or angles you will pursue; what makes this story important and useful for *Arizona Highways*; and why you are the person to write it. We do not accept queries for fiction, humor stories or Along the Way columns. For these, we must see the manuscript before making a decision to purchase. If you include a SASE, we normally respond to queries within a month. Replies to manuscript submissions may take longer. No phone queries, please.

BREAKING IN: The easiest way to break into the magazine for writers new to us is to (1) propose short items for the Off-ramp section, (2) contribute short humor anecdotes for the Humor page, or (3) submit 650-word pieces for the Along the Way column.

DEPARTMENTS: The maximum word length and fees paid for departments are: Along the Way (650 words, $450), Back Road Adventure (1,000 words, $900), Hike of the Month (500 words, $275), Humor (200 words, $50), Off-ramp (200 words, $50), Destination (1,000 words, $750). Check the magazine for content of these departments.

FEATURES: Feature stories should be between 1,200 and 1,800 words (two-page stories should be 650 to 800 words), depending on the subject. Travel stories, cover stories and lead stories pay $1 a word. Other features pay 55 cents a word.

TRAVEL STORIES: Our travel stories are of three types: travel-destination (involves experience at a specific location/tourist attraction), travel adventure (involves hiking, climbing, boating or some other physical activity) and travel history (involves a backdrop or running theme of a historical event/person). We have a style for travel stories that is distinctly Arizona Highways. As this style starts with outstanding photographs that not only depict an area but interpret it as well, our travel stories need not dwell on descriptions of what can be seen.

Concentrate instead on the experience of being there, whether the destination is a hiking trail, a ghost town, a trout stream, a forest or an urban area. What thoughts and feelings did the experience evoke? What was happening? What were the mood and comportment of the people? What were the sounds and smells? What was the feel of the area? Did bugs get into the sleeping bag? Were the crows curious about intruders? Could you see to the bottom of the lake, and if so, what was there? We want to know why you went there, what you experienced and what impressions you came away with.

These experiences and impressions should be focused into a story with a beginning, middle and end, and it should be as evocative and interesting as you can make it. We do not want a rambling series of thoughts or vignettes, diary entries or a travelogue (a piece that begins in the morning, goes hour-by-hour through the day and ends in the evening). We want a story that opens by introducing us to a story line or theme, then develops the tale and finally concludes. We want an ending, a logical conclusion to the story we are telling. Just stopping the story won't do.

Because the piece will not be a general guide to an area, we need a short sidebar detailing the service information. (Some departments also require this sidebar.)

The sidebar, called "When You Go," should explain how to get to the destination, where to stay, restrictions, special requirements and what to see and do in the area. It also should include places to call for further information. (You will receive a separate format sheet with contractual paperwork.)

APPROACH: Our style is informal yet polished, with a readable, literary quality. The story should use the techniques of the fiction writer to create a narrative the reader will be unable to put down. We do not want choppy, shallow/Sunday-supplement treatments. First-person or third-person narrative is okay; present tense, fine. Use strong verbs in the active voice and avoid overuse of the verb "to be" in all its forms, especially "it was" and "there are."

CONTRACT AND PAYMENT: We buy first print rights, and we expect original work. Payment is 35 cents to $1 a word, on acceptance. For travel stories as well as cover stories and lead stories (determined by the editor), we pay $1 a word.

SUBMISSIONS: We require written queries, preferably on page; no unsolicited manuscripts (except for consideration for Fiction or Along the Way). Send all queries to Arizona Highways, Query Editor, 2039 W. Lewis Ave., Phoenix, AZ 85009. Send short humorous anecdotes to Humor Department, editor@arizonahighways.com. Queries may be sent via e-mail to: queryeditor@arizonahighways.com. Effective March 2002.

Categories: Adventure—Culture—Environment—History—Regional—Travel—Western

CONTACT: Query Editor
<queryeditor@arizonahighways.com >
Material: Queries
CONTACT: Humor Dept. <editor@arizonahighways.com>
Material: Short humorous anecdotes
CONTACT: Photography Editor
Material: Photographs
2039 W. Lewis Ave.
Phoenix AZ 85009-9988
Website: www.arizhwys.com

Arkansas Review
A Journal of Delta Studies

Arkansas Review: A Journal of Delta Studies focuses on the seven-state Mississippi River Delta. Interdisciplinary in scope, we welcome contributions from all the humanities and social sciences, including anthropology, art history, folklore studies, history, literature, musicology, political science, and sociology. Articles should be aimed at a general academic audience and follow the format specified in the Chicago Manual of Style, 14th edition. Submit articles in hard copy and on disk to the General Editor.

Photographs and other visual materials to accompany articles are encouraged. Do not submit originals until after the article has been accepted. When submitted, photographs should be black-and-white prints no larger that 8"x10" in either glossy or matte finish.

Arkansas Review also publishes creative material, especially fiction, poetry, essays, and visual art that evoke or respond to the Delta cultural and natural experience.

All material sent to the *Arkansas Review* will be refereed by the relevant editor and at least one other reviewer—in the case of articles, a specialist in the field of the article. We will attempt to respond to submissions within four months.

Contributors may also want to submit proposals for special issues of the *Review*, ones dealing with specific Delta topics. Such proposals should be sent to the General Editor.

Contributors will receive five copies of the issue of the *Arkansas Review* in which their work appears.

Categories: Fiction—Nonfiction—African-American—Arts—Culture—History—Literature—Multicultural—Music—Poetry—Regional—Short Stories

CONTACT: Tom Williams, General Editor and Creative Materials Editor
Material: All written submissions
CONTACT: Kim Vickrey, Art Editor
Material: Visual Art
PO Box 1890
State University AR 72467-1890
Phone: 870-972-3043
Fax: 870-972-2795
E-mail: delta@astate.edu
Website: www.clt.astate.edu/arkreview

Army Magazine

Length

Features are usually 1,000 to 1,500 words long. Shorter articles such as sidebars to features or photo essays are from 250 to 500 words.

Include a brief explanation of why your submission (if it is a feature article) is timely, innovative or important.

Book reviews, guest columns (such as "Sounding Off") and articles for "Front & Center" are preferably 500 to 1,000 words long. (We do not accept unsolicited book reviews. If you are interested in book reviewing, write us regarding your areas of interest and expertise. Send writing samples also.)

Format

Please send your article on a floppy disk, indicating the type of software used, and also send a triple- or double-spaced hard copy.

Photographs and Other Artwork

We are interested in seeing photographs or artwork that may enhance your article. We can use black and white or color prints as well as color slides. Please include caption and credit information with each photograph.

Headlines

We take your suggestions for headlines seriously. Please send headline suggestions with your article.

Author Biographies

Biographical information should be submitted with the text of the article. Include as much information as possible, preferably a vita.

Submissions

Please do not send us articles that have been submitted or published elsewhere. We do not accept simultaneous submissions.

Categories: Military

CONTACT: Editor in Chief, Army Magazine
Material: All
2425 Wilson Blvd.
Arlington VA 22210

Art&Antiques

Art & Antiques

Proposal Tips

Art & Antiques is the authoritative source for elegant, sophisticated coverage of the treasures collectors love, the places to discover them and the unique ways collectors use them to enrich their environments. From fine art to folk art, from Louis XIV to Louis Tiffany, *Art & Antiques'* award-winning articles and lush photography meld the past to the present to reflect the passion of collecting.

Submission Guidelines: Unless noted above, query first with visuals of the subject. No article will be considered without scouting shots (pre-printed material is accepted, but slides or transparencies are better. All material will be returned.) Editorial lead-time: 6 months. Payment upon acceptance.

Unless otherwise noted, send proposals to Patti Verbanas, Managing Editor, *Art & Antiques* Magazine, 2100 Powers Ferry Rd., Ste. 300, Atlanta, GA 30339.

No phone calls, please.

Ideas pitched for any of these departments are also considered for feature treatment.

Art & Antiques Update

Definition: A mix of trend coverage and timely news of the issues and personalities that move the world of art and antiques. Word length: 100-350.

Visuals not necessary for pitch, but must be attainable if assigned. We are seeking these pitches on an on-going basis.

Send proposals for this section directly to Rebecca Grilliot at rgrilliot@billian.com or to Rebecca via regular mail.

Buying Buzz

Definition: A monthly, 300-word column that focuses on emerging collecting trends. Writers interview top dealers and auctioneers. While this column does report post-sale results from a few key events, its goal is to provide collectors with practical information rather than to merely report the latest market news. If a writer attends a fair and learns from several sources that a certain type of furniture is likely to skyrocket in value, those interviews and related sales figures could form the basis for an excellent Buying Buzz column. A general post-mortem on the fair itself would be of less interest. Writers are responsible for providing a few high-quality images of artworks/antiques, along with the appropriate caption and credit information. Send proposals for this section directly to Rebecca Grilliot at rgrilliot@billian.com or to Joel via regular mail. Fee: $300.

Review

Definition: A criticisms on a variety of worldwide art exhibitions throughout the year. If it is a European show, it must have a destination in the United States. Visuals preferred, but not necessary. Word length: 600-800.

Value Judgments

Definition: Experts in various fields highlight popular to undiscovered areas of collecting and discuss crucial aspects of connoisseurship. Provides readers with an in-depth look at specific categories of high-end art and antiques collecting. Pitches should include recent auction results and why now is an important time to report on this collectible. This is a popular department; competition is stiff. Visuals required. Word length: 600-900.

Emerging Artists

Definition: This department highlights an artist on the cusp of discovery. What "unknowns" should readers be watching? Send the artist's c.v. and 7-15 slides or cards to show work. Entrants are juried by an international team of art scholars, and response time can reach 10-12 months. Word length: 600-800.

Features

Definition: Features are expanded, more in-depth articles that fit into any of the other categories noted here. We publish one "interior design with art and antiques" focus feature a month. Visuals required for all feature pitches. Word length: 1,000-2,000.

A&A Insider

Definition: A "How-To" column for beginning an expert collectors on how to collect and collecting issues. Examples include: "How To Collect Contemporary Art," "Best Lighting Techniques," "How to Find an Art Advisor," etc. Word length: 800–900. Fee: $750.

Discoveries

Definition: Art & Antiques takes to the road to seek out collections in lesser-known museums and homes that are open to the public. It is similar to the Traveling Collector, but without shopping as the focus. In your proposal note why now (issue month) is the time to visit? Visuals required. Word length: 800-900.

Studio Session

Definition: A peek into the studio of an artist who currently is hot or is a revered veteran that allows the reader to watch the artist in action. In your proposal, note a timely angle to the story and if we should look at the pitch for a particular month). This is a very competitive department. Visuals required. Word length: 800-900.

Then & Now

Definition: Highlights the best reproductions being created today and the craftspeople behind the work. In your proposal, tell us the artists who would be discussed as the "Thens" and the contemporary artists/manufacturers who are the "Nows." Visuals required. Word length: 800-900.

World View

Definition: A report on major art and antiques news worldwide. Visuals preferred, but not necessary. Do let us know where we would be able to obtain images and how easy that will be. Word length: 600-800.

Traveling Collector

Definition: Guides readers to the hottest art and antiques destinations.

Featured are the best in local art and antiques, and unique places and events of interest to readers in their many travels. Destinations are selected one time a year (during Editorial Calendar meeting in May); suggestions are welcomed. Visuals necessary. In the past, the winning destinations have been those where the writer sends us a contact list of the galleries and antiques shops that can be profiled. Word length: 800-1,800.

Essay

Definition: A forum for the writer's opinion, expressed within the magazine's guidelines. It is a first-person piece that tackles a topic in a non-academic way. Can send completed manuscript. Visuals preferred, but not necessary. Word length: 600-800.

Categories: Nonfiction—Antiques—Arts

CONTACT: Patti Verbanas, Managing Editor
Material: All
TransWorld Publishing, Inc.
2100 Powers Ferry Rd. Ste. 300
Altanta GA 30339
Website: www.artantiquesmag.com

ART PAPERS

Art Papers

GENERAL GUIDELINES

We prefer proposals to completed articles. For features, the proposal should be 125—250 words; for columns and reviews, 50 words is plenty. Tell us what and who you want to discuss, and what you plan to say. If you haven't written for ART PAPERS before, please include two brief writing samples (1,000—2,000 words), together with a short bio (40 words) describing your background and interests. We evaluate proposals based on quality, appropriateness and available space, and strive to notify writers of a decision within two months. Proposals may be submitted either by email to editor@artpapers.org or by post to Art Papers, PO Box 5748, Atlanta GA 31107. We do not return support materials. We will not consider queries not accompanied by writing samples.

If we accept your proposal, we will negotiate a mutually acceptable length, deadline and fee. We reserve the right to terminate our acceptance of your proposal without compensation if we discover you have misrepresented yourself, or if the final form of the article diverges markedly from the agreed-upon topic, format or deadline.

TYPES OF ARTICLES

Features range from 2,400 to 2,700 words, and express fully developed viewpoints about a particular work, artist or trend.

The staff of ART PAPERS, Inc. appreciates the value of historical investigation and academic work. However, ART PAPERS does not print densely theoretical arguments or detailed archival research. Nonetheless, we expect our writers to develop and support their theses rigorously, and to have a sophisticated understanding of any philosophies, histories or theoretical concepts they invoke.

Columns in ART PAPERS cover a wide range of topics ("Surviving," "Readings," "IN," "Studio Visit," etc.). These columns differ from those of most other magazines in that none of them appear regularly and they do not "belong" to any one writer. Rather, our columns offer opportunities for writers to address topics of current interest in brief, exploratory essays. These pieces generally are around 1,000 words, with one or two pictures.

Reviews cover solo and group shows of regional, national or international significance. We are especially interested in regionally significant artists who have not yet reached a national or international audience. Reviews are 600 words when covering the work of a single artist and 800 words when discussing the work of more than one artist (in both cases, plus or minus ten words). Faculty and student exhibitions do not constitute acceptable group shows.

CONFLICT OF INTEREST

a) The editors will not consider submissions in which a writer: writes about his/her work, the work of someone with whom the writer has a personal relationship, the work of someone with whom the writer has a financial relationship, any gallery that represents his/her work, any relative, any gallery institutionally related to the organization employing the writer or a colleague in the institution employing the writer.

b) The editors will not consider submissions by a writer who has been hired to write a catalogue essay for the same artist or gallery within the past year. The exception, to be determined by the editors, shall be a curator who has shown an artist's work and whose expertise on the artist would be considered an advantage in writing the article.

c) The editors will not consider submissions by a writer whom the gallery or artist has paid or commissioned to write the article in question. Suggestions from galleries are permitted but the editors make the final decision.

d) The editors will not consider a submission by a writer who collects the work of the artist in question.

e) Writers may not write reviews or articles for ART PAPERS on exhibitions that they already have covered for other publications.

f) The editors shall decide whether to cover exhibitions curated by, featuring or including the work of any writer for ART PAPERS.

Categories: Arts

CONTACT: Charles Reeve, Editor-in-Chief
Material: All
PO Box 5748
Atlanta GA 31107
Phone: 404-588-1837 ext 14

Fax: 404-588-1836
E-mail: editor@artpapers.org
Website: www.artpapers.org

Art Times

WRITER'S GUIDELINES FOR FIRST SERIAL RIGHTS
FICTION: Short Stories up to 1,500 words. All subjects but no excessive sex, violence or racist themes. Our prime requisite is high literary quality and professional presentation. Pay $25 upon publication, six extra copies of issue in which work appears and one year's complimentary subscription beginning with that issue. We do not publish reprints.

POETRY: Up to 20 lines. All topics; all forms. Same requisite high quality as above. Pay is six extra copies of issue in which work appears and one year's complimentary subscription beginning with that issue. We do not publish reprints. We do not encourage simultaneous submissions of poetry.

(Note: We are usually on about a 36-month lead for fiction; 24-month lead for poetry.)

Readers of ART TIMES are generally over 40, literate and arts conscious. Our distribution is heaviest in New York State (along the "Hudson River Corridor" from Albany into Manhattan). We are sold by subscription; copies may be obtained free at selected art galleries. Subscription copies are mailed across the US and abroad. In addition to short fiction and poetry, feature essays on the arts make up the bulk of our editorial. (Note: Articles and Essays are not solicited).

Sample copy: $1.75 plus 9"x12" SASE with 3 first class stamps.

Categories: Arts—Crafts/Hobbies—Culture—Dance—Drama—Entertainment—Film/Video—Literature—Multicultural—Music—Poetry—Short Stories—Theatre

CONTACT: Submissions Editor
Material: All
PO Box 730
Mt. Marion NY 12456-0730
Phone: 845-246-6944
Fax: 845-246-6944
E-mail: info@arttimesjournal.com

Artemis Magazine
Science and Fiction for a Space-Faring Age

About the Magazine: *Artemis Magazine* publishes science for an educated audience interested in space development, flight, and travel and the best in near-term, near-Earth, hard science fiction. Formed as an adjunct to the Artemis Project (a commercial venture to build a lunar colony), *Artemis Magazine* and its parent company, LRC Publications, are independent entities.

Science: Articles should generally be limited to 5,000 words. We're looking for articles related to the devvelopment of lunar and near-Earth industries, including the role of the Moon in further development of space travel. Remember that the readers, in general, want to know how to get to, build, and live in a lunar colony. Target your work toward a general audience of educated, but not necessarily technically sophisticated, people. Include charts, tables, or photos if necessary, and explain them in the text.

Illustrations should be separate from the text, with captions on a separate page.

Fiction: We're looking for near-term, near-Earth, hard science fiction. As a supporter of the Artemis Project, we're looking especially for stories that aim at lunar and space development, but a good story is a good story. We want well-plotted, character-oriented stories. Technical accuracy is an absolute requirement, but don't bog down the story with unnecessary technical detail; remember that in good "science fiction", both terms ought to receive equal emphasis.

We'll consider any length up to 15,000 words. Shorter is better.

Mechanics: This is standard: on the first page, put your name, address(es), and phone number in the upper left corner; put the word count in the upper right corner.

Print your manuscript double-spaced on 8.5" x 11" paper (or the local equivalent) in a legible font with 1-inch margins all around. Do not put it in a binder or staple the pages together. You don't need a separate title page. On every page after the first, in the upper right-hand corner, put your name, the page number, and enough of the title that we can reassemble your manuscript after we drop it on the floor and get it mixed up with a bunch of other papers.

Don't use your word processor's ability to do fancy fonts, italics, or typesetting. Simply underline text to be italicized.

Include an "about the author" paragraph with your manuscript.

Include a self-addressed envelope with your manuscript with sufficient postage to get it back to you. If you don't want your manuscript back, mark it DISPOSABLE and include a business-size self-addressed, stamped envelope for our reply (it's very difficult to fold a check into a postcard). From outside the US, include International Reply Coupons. We will not respond to any submissions without return postage. And no, we do NOT accept electronic submissions.

Art: We need artists to illustrate articles and stories. Send disposable photocopies of examples of your work along with notes about prior publication and the type of art you prefer to do.

Cartoons and stock submissions are welcome.

Payment: We pay be on acceptance, 3 to 5 cents a word, for science and fiction.

About the Artemis Project: The Artemis Project is a commercial venture to establish a permanent lunar colony and to exploit the Moon's resources for profit. Our strategy for this project is to use its entertainment value as much as possible to pay for its initial development. The Project is sponsored by The Lunar Resources Company. For more information on the Project, check out the web site at http://www.asi.org.

A final note: These guidelines describe what we want. If you can write something that fits this bill, we want you. However, we're also open-minded enough to be interested in a story that contradicts everything written here, and yet won't let us reject it. You want us to read your manuscript: save us both some time, and read the magazine first.

Categories: Fiction—Nonfiction—Adventure—Agriculture—Architecture—Arts—Aviation—Business—Careers—Cartoons—Children—Comedy—Computers—Conservation—Consumer—Cooking—Crafts/Hobbies—Ecology—Economics—Education—Electronics—Engineering—Entertainment—Environment—Fashion—Food/Drink—Games—General Interest—Government—Health—History—Hobbies—Interview—Law—Lifestyle—Literature—Military—Money & Finances—Outdoors—Photography—Physical Fitness—Politics—Psychology—Recreation—Recreation Vehicles—Reference—Regional—Satire—Science—Science Fiction—Short Stories—Society—Software—Sports/Recreation—Technical—Trade—Travel—Aerospace

CONTACT: The Editor
Material: All
Ian Randal Strock, Editor
Material:1380 E. 17th St., Suite 201
Brooklyn NY 11230-6011
Phone: 718-375-3862

ARTFUL DODGE

Artful Dodge
The College of Wooster

Even from the beginning, *Artful Dodge* has strived to expand the wide but not infinite boundaries of American literature. We have developed an ongoing interest in translation, especially from Eastern Europe and Third World, and have published well-received special sections on poetry from the Polish underground and the Middle East. One of our more recent issues, *Artful Dodge* 31/32, featured a section of poetry written and translated from the Native American Ahtna by John Smelcer accompanied by an eye-opening essay entitled "Poems from a Vanishing Language."

Rather than looking at these other literatures as rare exotica, we recognize that American literature right now is particularly open to writing form other languages, to fresh air from mythologies beyond our huge but not infinite cultural and metaphorical borders. We are always on the look out for excellent translations of contemporary literature.

However, *Artful Dodge*'s doors are open to much more than just translations or works rooted in foreign culture. What it boils down to is this: *Artful Dodge* has always been attracted to writing with a sense of place and looks for work that combines the aesthetic and the human in fresh, unexpected ways. However, don't ask us what that statement means—all we can say is that the work we print shows awareness of the cultural landscape out of which it comes, the words and deeds of people, the language of the bus stop and bar. It involves an illumination of the particular and the concrete, and the transforming of this here-at-hand to the level of the permanent, the mythic. This can be accomplished in ways as diverse as William Carlos Williams' wheelbarrows, Elizabeth Bishop's maps, Langston Hughes' rivers, or William S. Burroughs' disrobed lunches. But some sort of interplay between focus and transcendence must be at work.

So, read *Artful Dodge* to get an idea of what we print. If you can't afford a copy, then ask your local library to order a subscription—it might as well be *Artful Dodge* (or some other literary journal) sitting on those shelves instead of Fortune and Cosmo and Gourmet. And, after you've taken a look at the world around you, at the words surrounding you, take a deep breath and send us your work.

Some basic guidelines for submitting work to *Artful Dodge* are as follows: SASE, typed manuscripts; no simultaneous submissions or previously published material; allow one week to six months for response. Please send no more than 30 pages of prose or six poems, though long poems are encouraged. We pay in copies, plus $5 a page. Translations should be submitted with original texts. We also prefer that you indicate you have copyright clearance and/or author permission.

Categories: Fiction—Poetry

CONTACT: Daniel Bourne, Editor
Material: All
Dept. of English, The College of Wooster
Wooster OH 44691
Phone: 330-263-2577
Website: www.wooster.edu/artfuldodge

Arthritis Today

About *Arthritis Today*

Arthritis Today is an award-winning, national consumer health magazine published by the Arthritis Foundation. It is written for the 43 million Americans who have arthritis or an arthritis-related condition as well as for the millions of other people whose lives are touched by these conditions. The magazine is a comprehensive and authorita-

tive source of information about arthritis research, treatment, self-care and emotional coping.

Our magazine has a diverse audience because there are more than 100 arthritis-related conditions, including osteoarthritis, rheumatoid arthritis, fibromyalgia and lupus. These conditions can affect anyone of any age, from children and young adults to middle-aged and older people. Our magazine speaks to all of these groups.

The editorial content of *Arthritis Today* is designed to empower people with arthritis to live healthier lives overall, emphasizing up-beat, informative articles that provide practical advice and inspiration. Feature articles of approximately 1,000 to 4,000 words focus on treatment options, research advances, ways of coping with physical and emotional challenges, empowerment, and exercise. Our "Research Spotlight" section reports on research advances in the understanding and treatment of arthritis, based on studies from respected medical journals and scientific meetings. The magazine also includes shorter items that address the whole person, such as brief items of 150 to 300 words on general health and medical topics, travel, nutrition, hobbies, leisure and relationships. We also include personal, inspirational essays of 500 to 1,200 words written by people who have arthritis-related conditions. Each issue is extensively reviewed by our medical editor, by the Arthritis Foundation's medical director and by individual experts on our medical advisory board.

What we're looking for in a freelance writer

We prefer to work with professional writers who have experience writing for other consumer magazines, but will consider pieces – specifically first-person accounts of life with arthritis or a related condition – from people who have not been previously published.

What we need from you

A resume and nonreturnable clips of articles you've written that have been published in other consumer magazines plus a query for article(s) you are interested in writing.

Queries should include the following information:

• a general synopsis of the idea and the specific angle to be addressed in the article;

• research or other material you plan to cite to support the article;

• experts, such as researchers, health professionals or real people, whom you plan to interview and quote in the article.

When you can expect to hear from us

After reviewing your query, the editors will respond within six to eight weeks. At that time, we may ask for more details or request the manuscript on speculation.

A caveat

We prefer not to receive unsolicited manuscripts or telephone queries.

Tell Us Your Personal Story

Hardly a day goes by that we at Arthritis Today don't hear from readers who want a chance to share a personal story about how they've encountered – and bested – arthritis.

Categories: Nonfiction—Consumer—Health

CONTACT: Assistant Editor
Material: All
1330 West Peachtree St.
Atlanta GA 30309
Phone: 404-872-7100
Fax: 404-872-9559
E-mail: writers@arthritis.org. (queries)
E-mail: my.story@arthritis.org. (poem or personal essay)
Website: www.arthritis.org/resources/arthritistoday

The Artist's Magazine

Article Submission Guidelines

The Artist's Magazine is a monthly publication for working artists. Unlike coffee-table magazines for art collectors, *The Artist's Magazine* is a nuts-and bolts, instructional resource for the working artist in search of artistic and professional success. We show readers how other artists have dealt with various issues-painting techniques, media and materials, design and composition, specific subjects, special effects, marketing and other business topics.

Opportunities for professional artists and writers to work with *The Artist's Magazine* lie basically with feature articles. Freelance writers must have the ability to write from the artist's viewpoint using the language of art.

Where to Start

Artists and writers should query in advance rather than send unsolicited manuscripts. Queries should include:

• A cover letter giving us a clear picture of the slant and purpose of the proposed article (including a possible title and subtitle).

• The artist's résumé, credits and approximately 8-12 slides or larger transparencies of his or her work. (Note: All slides should be in protective plastic slide sleeves.)

• The writer's résumé, credits and photocopies of no more than two clips (if different than the artist).

• A self-addressed stamped envelope (SASE) large enough and with sufficient postage for returning the slides.

Note: We cannot accept digital images on disk or sent by e-mail, or a referral to an artist's Web site, in lieu of slides or transparencies. Our publication decisions are based heavily on the quality of the artwork submitted, and we've found that slides and transparencies capture the color, depth and texture of a painting in a way that digital images cannot. The only exception to this requirement would be in the case of digitally-created art, but we very rarely feature computer-generated art in *The Artist's Magazine*.

Let your query demonstrate that you know where you want to go and how to get there. If we like your idea, we'll do one of two things: 1) ask for a comprehensive, detailed outline or 2) assign the piece to you. We will attempt to respond to your query within three months.

All About Features

Our most consistent need is for instructional articles written in the artist's voice, rather than in newspaper-style reporting or Q&A interview styles. All features should emphasize the how-to: how an artist works with a medium, solves problems and conducts business. You're talking to artists, not the general public, so techniques and methods must be specifically explained and demonstrated. Writers should try to avoid clichés and concentrate on basic, practical, step-by-step instruction with a friendly, conversational tone. The goal is for the reader to be able to pick up a brush (or whatever) and duplicate the described process or technique after reading the article.

Feature themes will generally fall into the following categories:

• Genres of art, including basic, new or unusual techniques of still life, landscape, portraiture or wildlife painting. Example: 10 ways to arrange a still life.

• Specific objects, such as flowers, animals, trees—objects commonly found in paintings and drawings. Example: the visual structure in painting a sky.

• Basic application techniques and how they're used with different media. Examples: color mixing in watercolors, drybrushing with acrylics.

• Special effects, covering new or time-tested techniques in any one medium. Example: using stencils with water-based media.

• Introduction to unusual media, including the necessary tools, materials and basic techniques of mastering a medium. Examples: alkyds, encaustics, casein.

• Techniques of the masters—how a great artist created his or her works. Example: paint like the Impressionists.

• New markets for art sales, including the scope and potential of market categories, and how an artist can break in. Examples: religious market, romance book cover market.

• Business articles on any subject that the beginning artist needs to master to become a professional. Examples: recordkeeping, pricing, selling, portfolio building, etc.

One tip: The Artist's Magazine typically deals with realistic and semi-realistic painting; we rarely feature abstract art. Therefore, we suggest that you peruse recent copies of the magazine and compare them to the work of the artist you have in mind before you send in your submission.

Feature articles typically range from 1,200 to 2,200 words. Pay is $300 for most features. Articles are usually used within one year of acceptance.

Manuscripts should be submitted as typed, double-spaced hard copy and on a 3-1/2" disk if possible, and should include captions, author bio and artist bio. The artwork package should contain at least 8-12 slides or larger transparencies of the artist's work for use in illustrating the article. It should also include at least one set of progressives—a series of slides that show how a painting is developed from concept to finish; include at least four distinct steps per set. The slides/transparencies should be professionally shot, either by yourself or by a photographer; poorly shot artwork will not be reproducible. All slides should be correctly labeled with artist's name, address, medium, dimensions, title and indication of top and front. (For more information on correctly shooting slides of artwork, please see our Photography Guidelines.) A complete set of writer's guidelines will be provided upon acceptance of query. Slides and transparencies will be returned after publication of the article.

Inside Our Columns

Artists interested in submitting for a particular column should clearly indicate which one, both in the query letter and on the envelope. We recommend that potential contributors familiarize themselves with the structure and style of several recent columns before submitting. Queries should include a brief outline of the topic and how it would be approached, illustrations and/or slides as appropriate, and an artist's résumé including any expertise or credentials especially relevant to the topic. Payment varies by column and length.

• Drawing Board covers basic drawing skills. Recent examples include improving your sketching techniques, using grids to improve composition, drawing realistic trees and grass, and rendering textural hair and fur.

• Color Corner focuses on how to use color effectively in your paintings. Some recent examples include tips for using white, possibilities for fleshtones, and how to make use of sedimentary colors.

• Landscape Basics deals with issues fundamental to landscape painting. Recent examples include autumn scenes, painting wind and rain, and painting mountains.

• Brushing Up is concerned with defining and illustrating art terms. Recent examples include pointillism, contour drawings and underpainting.

• The Business column deals with the business-related issues of artmaking. Recent examples include hanging art for shows, writing news releases, entering the greeting card market, and writing the artist's résumé.

For More Information

Query letters with art should be sent to: Editor, *The Artist's Magazine*, 4700 E. Galbraith Rd., Cincinnati OH 45236. Sample copies can be ordered by sending $6.50 per copy to: Back Issue Manager, *The Artist's Magazine*, PO Box 2031, Harlan IA 51593.

Categories: Nonfiction—Arts—Business—Painting

CONTACT: The Editor
Material: Queries
4700 E. Galbraith Rd.
Cincinnati OH 45236
Phone: 513-531-2690 ext. 1467
Fax: 513-531-2902
E-mail: TAMedit@fwpubs.com

The Asian Pacific American Journal

The Asian Pacific American Journal is now accepting submission. THERE IS NO SPECIFIC THEME — so send those essays, short stories, poems, plays and art pieces that have been ripening in the deepest caverns of your heart and mind.

Send four typed copies with your name, address, email and phone number on each piece (all pages must be numbered and double-spaced, only one story/essay per submission). Include cover letter with a list of submitted pieces, brief author bio and SASE for reply. Please send print-outs of manuscripts, no disks please. We do not take general submissions by email. Please send art in transparency or slide form. Due to the volume of submissions, manuscripts cannot be returned.

Categories: Nonfiction—Arts—Asian-American—Drama—Poetry—Short Stories

CONTACT: Editors
Material: All
16 West 32nd Street, Ste 10A
New York NY 10001
Phone: 212-228-7718
Fax: 212-228-7718
E-mail: apaj@aaww.org

Asimov's Science Fiction

PAYMENT & RIGHTS *Asimov's Science Fiction* magazine is an established market for science fiction stories. We pay on acceptance, and beginners get 6.0 cents a word to 7,500 words, 5.0 cents a word for stories longer than 12,500 words, and $450 for stories between those lengths. We seldom buy stories longer than 15,000 words, and we don't serialize novels. We pay $1 a line for poetry, which should not exceed 40 lines. We buy First English Language serial rights plus certain non-exclusive rights explained in our contract. We do not publish reprints, and we do not accept "simultaneous submissions," (stories sent at the same time to a publication other than Asimov's). Asimov's will consider material submitted by any writer, previously published or not. We've bought some of our best stories from people who have never sold a story before.

STORY CONTENT In general, we're looking for "character oriented" stories, those in which the characters, rather than the science, provide the main focus for the reader's interest. Serious, thoughtful, yet accessible fiction will constitute the majority of our purchases, but there's always room for the humorous as well. Borderline fantasy is fine, but no Sword & Sorcery, please. Neither are we interested in explicit sex or violence. A good overview would be to consider that all fiction is written to examine or illuminate some aspect of human existence, but that in science fiction the backdrop you work against is the size of the Universe.

MANUSCRIPT FORMAT Manuscripts submitted to Asimov's must be neatly typed, double-spaced on one side of the sheet only, on bond paper (no erasable paper, please). Any ms. longer than 5 pages should be mailed to us flat. Dot matrix printouts are acceptable only if they are easily readable. Please do NOT send us submissions on disk. When using a word processor, please do not justify the right margin. If sending a printout, separate the sheets first. The ms. should include the title, your name and address, and the number of words in your story.

Enclose a cover letter if you like. All manuscripts must be accompanied by a self-addressed stamped envelope (if ms. is over 5 pages, use a 9" x 12" envelope) carrying enough postage to return the ms. If you wish to save on postage, you may submit a clear copy of your story along with a standard (#10) envelope, also self-addressed and stamped. Mark your ms. "DISPOSABLE," and you will receive our reply only. We do not suggest that you have us dispose of your original typescript. If you live overseas or in Canada, use International Reply Coupons for postage, along with a self-addressed envelope.

OUR REPLY Finally, we regret that it's become necessary for us to use form letters for rejecting manuscripts, but time limitations are such that we have no choice. Unfortunately, we are unable to provide specific criticism of each story. Our response time runs about five weeks. If you have not heard from us within three months from the day you mailed your ms., you can assume it was lost in the mail, and are welcome to resubmit it to us. We do NOT keep a record of submissions, but if you would like to know if we received your story or poem, include a self-addressed stamped postcard, which we will return to you on the day it arrives in the office. Thanks for your interest in Asimov's and good luck!

Categories: Fiction—Fantasy—Science Fiction

CONTACT: Sheila Williams, Editor
Material: All
475 Park Ave. South, 11th Floor
New York NY 10016
Phone: 212-686-7188
E-mail: asimovs@asimovs.com
Website: www.asimovs.com

Aspen Magazine

Aspen Magazine is published six times a year with a mission of providing a voice for the life of the town. We strive to capture the flavor of all that is Aspen—the latest news, local personalities, businesses, controversies, the best dining, skiing, gallery openings, live music, outdoor adventure, festivals, and events. Stories are geared towards a well-traveled, well-educated, savvy audience with a special interest in the area, either as resident or as tourist.

Guidelines
• Issues appear in January (Midwinter), March (Spring), May (Summer), July (Midsummer), August (Fall), and November (Holiday). Lineups are created no later than two-and-a-half months before the publication date and writing deadlines fall no later than a month-and-a-half before

publication. For example, a story for the Midsummer issue (on sale by mid-July) would be assigned no later than early May and due in early June.

• Queries are accepted ONLY in writing. We look for an "only in Aspen" angle: whether it be a local triumph or tragedy or a special event, it must be timely and newsworthy.

• We do not accept unsolicited articles.

• Aspen Magazine buys first North American serial rights to any work assigned and must be notified if articles of similar content will appear in any other publications.

Departments
• Aspen Insider. Short takes on the latest news, personalities, or businesses. Departments include Around Town, Sports, Arts & Performance, Shopping, Home & Lifestyle, Design, and Health. About 50 to 150 words.

• Middle-of-the-Book. Voice-oriented, mid-length stories for departments including Art, Trends, Business, Film, Health. About 500 to 1,000 words.

• Features. In depth coverage of any number of cutting-edge Aspen-related topics. About 1000 to 3500 words.

• Scene. Short, newsy, and up-to-date information on the latest in events, art, dining, and nightlife in Aspen and the Roaring Fork valley. Written in a sophisticated tone, usually about 150 to 300 words per piece.

Categories: Nonfiction—Adventure—Arts—Automobiles—Business—Computers—Conservation—Culture—Entertainment—Health—Lifestyle—Outdoors—Recreation—Regional—Rural America—Sports/Recreation—Travel

CONTACT: Dana Butler, Managing Editor
Material: All
720 E. Durant Ave Ste E8
Aspen CO 81611
Phone: 970-920-4040
Fax: 970-920-4044
E-mail: edit@aspenmagazine.com

ASU Travel Guide
The Guide for Airline Employee Discounts

The *ASU Travel Guide* is published quarterly: January (winter issue); April (spring issue); July (summer issue); and October (fall issue). The publication comprises two sections. The first section contains four travel articles and other pertinent editorial matter. The second section, which is the bulk of the publication, is a directory of discounts available only to airline employees, their families, parents of airline employees and retired airline employees. Articles must be aimed at this well-traveled audience.

Style: Clean and simple; use active verbs. You may use whatever narrative you deem best. Focus on what is unique about a destination: do not write descriptions that could apply to any tourist destination.

Photographs: We do not buy photos. They are mostly obtained from tourist and convention bureaus.

Payment: $200 upon acceptance-including one rewrite if needed—for 1,800-word articles.

Tips:
• Reader surveys indicate that most of our subscribers are interested in how to visit a destination inexpensively, so please include some cost-cutting hints.

• If you have information indirectly related to the article, such as a side trip, it is best presented as a sidebar.

• Send us a sample of your published travel writing and a list of destinations about which you can write. A list of recent articles is shown below. Be aware that we publish travel destination articles only (i.e., do not submit pieces on luggage or currency tips).

• Be patient. The next year's editorial calendar is made each April, so an idea may not be acted upon immediately. We answer all mail as long as a self-addressed, stamped envelope is enclosed. To receive a sample copy of the publication, please submit a 6"x9" envelope (minimum) with $1.41 postage affixed.

Categories: Travel—Airline

CONTACT: Christopher Gil, Managing Editor
Material: All
1525 Francisco Blvd. E
San Rafael CA 94901
Phone: 415-459-0300
Fax: 415-459-0494
E-mail: christopher_gil@asutravelguide.com
Website: www.asutravelguide.com

Atlanta Baby

Please refer to *Atlanta Parent*.

Atlanta Homes and Lifestyles

GENERAL GUIDELINES

Atlanta Homes & Lifestyles is published twelve times a year. Much of the content is written by freelance writers working on assignment for the magazine. Writers are paid between $100 and $500 per article, depending on the assignment.

We always welcome inquiries from qualified freelance writers. Interested parties should submit a resume and photocopies of three published articles to Lisa Frederick, Managing Editor, *Atlanta Homes & Lifestyles*, 1100 Johnson Ferry Road, Suite 595, Atlanta, GA 30342. We regret we cannot return writing samples or unsolicited photos.

We will review story proposals, but such queries should be limited to lifestyle topics, personality profiles or home and garden feature candidates in the Atlanta area. Food, wine and garden stories are written by regular columnists and are not generally assigned to outside freelancers.

Thank you for your interest in *Atlanta Homes & Lifestyles*. We look forward to hearing from you.

ADDITIONAL GUIDELINES

Features—home or garden

Length is 500-800 words (approximately 2-4 pages, double-spaced). All articles should include three suggested heads and two to three decks (subheads). Please include cutlines (captions) and resources (study our format for both; Resources is located in the back of the magazine). *When writing the article, keep the following guidelines in mind:*

• Homeowners are first introduced in the story as, for example, John and Jane Doe (not Mr. and Mrs. Doe, except where appropriate, such as former President and Mrs. Carter). In subsequent mentions, they are referred to as John and Jane. Professionals associated with the home, such as builders, interior designers and landscape architects, are mentioned by last name on second reference. (In departments, such as Short Takes or Snapshots, all second references are with last names.)

• Limit discussion of rooms or gardens to areas seen in photography (if photos are available at the time), unless it's particularly relevant or self-explanatory even without a photo.

• Avoid stating the obvious, such as the colors of things (unless particularly relevant) or furniture arrangement. Captions, also, should state some new information: what type of furnishings, from where, why bought, etc.

• Avoid including overused phrases, such as "I wanted to create an environment that reflects me" or "I created this garden because flowers bring such joy." Focus instead on unusual angles or approaches in design. Some features might be slanted towards the homeowner and his or her interests and talents; a remodeling story, on the other hand, may deal primarily with the chronological progress of the project.

• Avoid lapses into first-person reporting.•

• No gushing over the homeowner or home.

• Remember that houses are not homes until someone is living in them. A "new home" is realtor-speak. Condominiums and apartments can also be homes, of course.

• Don't include specific streets where gardens or homes are located; we don't print that. Add geographical interest, though, by being more specific than "north Atlanta," such as "a quiet cul-de-sac near Roswell's historic square."

Features—Food & Entertaining

In general, F & E articles should have no more than 500 words intro before recipes. Sidebars elaborating on something mentioned in the article are encouraged. As always, include three suggested heads and decks, plus cutlines with the article. Recipe guidelines:

• Must include name of dish and source of recipe, if known.

• List yield at end of recipe.

• Teaspoon, tablespoon, pounds, etc. are always spelled out.

• Ingredients listed in the order they're used.

• List generic rather than brand names, when possible (mayonnaise vs. Hellman's).

• Try to keep directions as succinct as possible without confusing the reader.

Department — A la Carte (restaurants)

Themed to a specific topic (best chicken salad, al fresco dining, for example), this 300-500 word article usually includes one intro paragraph and paragraphs on four or five restaurants.

Include phone number and general location (Virginia-Highland area, historic Marietta, for example) for each restaurant. Mention several special dishes, but no more than six for each restaurant. No overly negative comments. Text should be personal without being written in first person.

Department—Short Takes

Short Takes articles can range in size from one paragraph to 500 words; brevity is always appreciated! Topics may include Finds (new, unique stores; new products or services); People (focus on an entrepreneur or personality in one of our subject matters); or Causes (charities with some tie-in to our subjects). Stories should focus on a benefit to the reader, and what's unusual about the subject. Include a phone number and Web site (if applicable).

Department—Big Fix or Quick Fix

Most articles should have a before-after component and be written with a Problem-Solution-Cost intro (see past issues for examples). Articles should also include a Spec Sheet, a listing of professionals and products involved in the project. Any projects under $5,000 are considered a Quick Fix. Average length is 300-500 words.

Department—Great Escapes (travel)

All hotels, inns, etc. mentioned must include prices/packages, and phone numbers. Average length is 500 words. Travel features should go beyond brochures and press kit copy, focusing on unique finds and interesting anecdotes about the area. We like off-the-beaten-path suggestions.

Department—House Hunting (real estate)

Subjects can be broad, such as "Who's Buying What Where," unusual subdivision amenities or female builders; can be a real estate-related web-site; can be a blurb, sidebar or one-page article, depending on subject. Includes a one-page "Homing in On" article about a specific area, i.e., Vinings, Marietta, Decatur. Write articles to be of the most benefit to readers. All must have a metro Atlanta-area slant. Whenever possible, include house prices, square footage, etc.

Remember: a house on the market isn't a "home" yet, no matter what the real estate agents call it.

Whenever possible, obtain supplied photography.

Department—Second Home

An article about an Atlantan's vacation home, approximately 400-500 words. Articles should have an emphasis on the area, the home itself and the activities the Atlantans enjoy there. (Avoid overused phrases such as "We designed this second home for relaxing.")

Department-Cheap Chic

This short (200-300 words) article focuses on a clever idea that doesn't cost a lot. It can be written from a how-to standpoint or one person's story of how he or she executed the idea. Often we have two examples of a related idea, such as two inexpensive headboards or two uses of outdoor furniture in an indoors setting. Writing tone is light.

ADDITIONAL GUIDELINES

Please obtain very specific resources from designers, architects and homeowners when applicable (any home piece). This is a service to our readers. Resources can include builders, designers, architects, cabinetry, wallpaper (pattern name and manufacturer), paint (manufacturer, color name or number), furniture, accessories, window treatments, flooring, landscaping, artwork, etc. Please provide phone numbers as well.

Include photography (preferably slides or transparencies) with your article if you are able to. If more photography is needed or you are unable to obtain photography, please include suggestions for photography. Also provide a contact name and phone number for the subject to be photographed. Please suggest specific shots, as you wrote the article and are most familiar with the subject matter.

Include the names, addresses and phone numbers of anyone contacted, quoted or mentioned in the article so that we can send them a complimentary copy of the magazine.

List several suggestions for a story head (headline should be catchy) and deck (should be an explanatory sentence).

Please include an invoice for your services with your article. Delays can occur if your paperwork is not submitted.

If you have photos for the article, please write cutlines (captions). This helps us tremendously.

Provide both a hard copy of your article and a disk (on Microsoft Word 6.0 or a compatible software). If you are using a PC save as rich text or Microsoft Word. You may also e-mail to lfrederick@ atlantahomesmag,com.

Strange things happen to text in our computers, so please follow these formatting guidelines. Don't use tabs or indent paragraphs in your text. And, though it goes against everything you were taught, please try to leave only one space after a period. Also, no fancy organizing, styling (like bold or italics) or centering of text is necessary (we try to let the art director have some fun). Simply double space, justify left and return to start a new paragraph.

We refer to homeowners in a feature by their first names (after first mention of first and last names) and designers, architect, etc., by their last names (unless homeowner is anonymous and designer or architect is the primary interviewee). In department articles refer to people by their last names after first mention (unless it is a couple with the same last name).

Spell out all numbers from one to nine. Over nine use the numeral, unless it is the first word of a sentence. In feature articles always spell out state names. (ex. The beach house in Mobile, Alabama, is tacky. In departments use state abbreviations (AP style).

When in doubt, refer to the *AP Style Book* and *Webster's Unabridged Dictionary.*

Categories: Nonfiction—Antiques—Architecture—Arts—Book Reviews—Cooking—Food/Drink—Gardening—Lifestyle—Real Estate—Regional—Society—Travel

CONTACT: Lisa G. Frederick, Managing Editor
Material: All
Weisner Publishing LLC, 1100 Johnson Ferry Rd., Suite 595
Atlanta GA 30342
Phone: 404-965-4471
Fax: 404-252-6673
E-mail: lfrederick@atlantahomesmag.com
Website: www.atlantahomesmag.com

Atlanta Parent
Atlanta Baby

Atlanta Parent Magazine is a monthly magazine aimed at parents with children from birth to 18 years old.

Atlanta Baby is aimed at parents from the time of pregnancy through when baby is 2 years old. *Atlanta Baby* is published 2 times a year.

For both publications:

• Send submissions to: adusek@atlantaparent.com (in word attachments); 2346 Perimeter Park Drive, Suite 101, Atlanta, Georgia 30341; 770-454-7699 (fax). E-mailed submissions are preferred.

• Authors should include name, address, phone number and e-mail address at the top of the first page, along with the word count. On the following pages, please include your name - top pages frequently get detached from the rest of the manuscript.

• For publication in our magazines, please use only one space after a period at the end of a sentence - not two. All articles should be typed and double-spaced. Lengths typically run from 800 to 1,200 words. Indent paragraphs with a tab.

• Articles should address the parent, not the child.

• All of our articles are very down-to-earth - we do not print philosophical or theoretical articles. Most are third person - we do VERY

little first person, except for humor pieces. We do not publish short stories, poetry or fiction.

• *Atlanta Parent* Magazine and *Atlanta Baby* are both service journalism publications. When writing about a problem, give parents the symptoms or signs of the problem and then the solution or where they can turn to for help. We encourage you to include the addresses, phone numbers and web addresses for local and national resources and support groups so our readers can obtain reliable information.

• We will not accept articles with quotes from experts located in only one region of the country. For *Atlanta Parent* Magazine and *Atlanta Baby*, the article should include either quotes from local experts or experts from around the country.

• Our readers also want to read articles that are activity-based. Keep the instructions short and to the point. Using the directions, do the activity yourself or ask another person to follow the instructions to make sure they are accurate.

• Articles will not be returned.

• All articles are submitted on speculation unless specifically assigned in advance.

• If we like your article but have no immediate plans to use it, our normal procedure is to keep your article on file for possible future publication.

• Photos and illustrations may be submitted with the story. Nominal payment may be offered, if used.

• Payment is upon publication.

Categories: Nonfiction—Children—Family—Lifestyle—Parenting

CONTACT: Peggy Middendorf, Editor
Material: All
2346 Perimeter Park Dr, Ste 101
Atlanta GA 30341
Phone: 770-454-7599
Fax: 770-454-7699
E-mail: adusek@atlantaparent.com (in word attachments)
Website: www.atlantaparent.com

The Atlantic Monthly

The *Atlantic Monthly* is always interested in poetry, fiction, and articles of the highest quality. A general familiarity with what we have published in the past is your best guide to what we're looking for. Simply send your manuscript—typewritten, double-spaced, and accompanied by a stamped self-addressed envelope.

Categories: Fiction—General Interest—Poetry

CONTACT: Submissions Editor
Material: All
77 North Washington St.
Boston MA 02114
Website: www.atlantic.com

Attaché
The Inflight Magazine of US Airways

Attaché, the inflight magazine of US Airways, is published by Pace Communications, Inc., for the passengers who fly US Airways. The magazine's 400,000 monthly copies reach 2.3 million readers. Articles for the magazine are written by in-house staff, freelance writers, and contributing editors. An average of 70 percent of the editorial is written out-of-house.

Attaché's mission is to bring the best of the world to the business traveler. The heart of the magazine is superlatives—the best of any category.

What We're Looking For

We look for cleverly written, entertaining articles with a unique angle, particularly pieces that focus on "the best of" something.

We request that writers send clips of previously published work along with their queries.

Attaché is a heavily departmentalized magazine with a preferred format for most departments and some features. Please study sample copies, which are available for $7.50 each from Lynn Gianiny at our address. Checks must be made payable to Pace Communications. Writers can also get a sense of the magazine by visiting our Web site at www.attachemag.com

Please make yourself aware of US Airways' destinations. The most common error made by prospective writers is to propose stories on locations to which we do not fly.

Queries should be concise. Writers must include a stamped, self-addressed envelope with all correspondence to ensure a reply/return of their materials. We try to report on queries within six weeks. *Attaché* assumes no responsibility for safekeeping or return of unsolicited art, photographs, manuscripts, or other material. Do not send originals of any kind.

Article delivery@very via an on-line service or through an Internet account is preferable but should first be arranged through the assigning editor.

Payment for articles is upon acceptance and the return of a signed contract. Amount of pay depends on length of article and varies somewhat according to experience. Due to our international circulation, we buy First Global Serial Rights for most articles.

Features

Each monthly issue has three main feature articles ranging in length from 1500-2000 words. Features are highly visual, focusing on anything from the painter Maxfield Parrish to championship rose-growing competitions. We consider ourselves curious about the world and are interested in finding stories that are either slightly off-beat (crossword puzzle tournaments) or which cover a little-known aspect of the world (a man who makes books in the style used during the 17th century).

Departments

Most of the departments are handled by regular columnists, but submissions will be reviewed.

Paragons features short lists of the best in a particular field or category, as well as 350-word pieces describing the best of something—for example, the best home tool, the best ice cream in Paris, and the best reading library. Each piece should lend itself to highly visual art.

Passions includes several topics such as "Vices", "Food" "Golf," "Sporting," and "Things That Go."

Informed Sources are departments of expertise and first-person accounts. They include "How It Works," "Home Front," "Improvement" and "Genius at Work."

Photography

Attaché works solely with professional photographers and stock houses. We discourage writers from sending their own photos or stock lists. Please do not send unsolicited selections of photography. We assume no responsibility for the safety or return of material that we do not expressly request to receive. Only assigned writers who are also published photographers should submit color transparencies with their articles.

Categories: General Interest

CONTACT: Submissions Editor
Material: All
CONTACT: Attaché Art Dept.
Material: Photography, Illustrations & Art
Pace Communications, Inc.
1301 Carolina St.
Greensboro NC 27401
Phone: 910-378-6065
Fax: 910-275-2864
Website: www.attachemag.com

Audio Amateur Corporation

Before You Write

It's always a good idea to query us before submitting an article. If you have an idea, draw up a brief outline of what you plan to do. If the idea is something we can use, we will give you the go-ahead. If, however, someone is working on a similar project or we do not foresee a need for such an article, we will let you know so that you won't waste time preparing a full-fledged manuscript.

Tone

Many technical writers use a highly impersonal style of writing, relying heavily on the passive voice and avoiding all personal pronouns. We want you to write as though you were talking to your best friend. Use "I" rather than the editorial "we" and don't be afraid to address the reader as "you" instead of the objective "one." Avoid constructions such as "It was found that..." and instead tell us who found what and how: "I found that this design worked better because..."

Organization

Writing in a personal style does not mean dashing off your article in longhand or not taking the time to correct typing errors. We strongly suggest you generate your manuscript on computer disk and include a neat printout. Make sure you keep a copy of the article in case we misplace ours or you have any questions about our editing. Every manuscript page, including labels, parts lists and artwork, should carry your name and the article title.

In addition to a working title for your submission, include a description (20-30 words) summarizing your article and stating its benefit to the reader.

For example: This article discusses feedback effects and shows you how you can reduce distortion while improving the stability of your audio system.

Also include a short (30-40 words) biographical sketch with your article. It should contain your related work experience and relevant educational background and interests.

Be concise, but explain all technical terms. The first time an abbreviation or acronym appears, spell out the full term for which it stands. Do not assume that the reader will know what you are talking about. Our readers are at different levels of technical expertise, and we don't want to lose any of them with obscure writing.

Your lead paragraph should state the problem at hand and how you solved it. Then you can go on to explain any background material and design concepts. If your article involves construction, tell the reader how you designed (briefly) and built the equipment. Include a clear description of how the unit works, and be prepared to submit your prototype for verification and testing. (Transport and insurance will be at our expense.)

Sometimes you can convey material better in a table or diagram. Tables should be self-explanatory and should supplement, not duplicate, the text. Submit each table and its title on a separate sheet of paper, but remember to reference at the appropriate spot in the text. Parts lists and specifications should also be printed on separate sheets. Make sure you double-check them against text references and figures.

Pages should be numbered consecutively. Number your diagrams and photos in the order in which you refer to them in the text. Supply captions for all photographs and artwork. Include caption information on a separate sheet, and make sure each piece of art is labeled with the appropriate number, your name, and the article title.

Artwork

Make all drawings large and clear, giving all component designators (R1, R2, etc.) and parts values on the drawing. They need not be inked art, as we will redraw them for publication. If you can do acceptable reproduction drawings, we will pay an extra fee for their use. Please include pinouts for all ICs and solid-state devices on your schematics. Specify top or bottom view. Diagrams are usually set up with the input on the left and the signal or control moving to the output on the right, where possible. Use connector dots where crossing lines are connected, and "run arounds" for those crossing lines which are not connected.

Use the traditional ground sign for power ground, and the other one for chassis ground. Schematics parts designators should include a part number as well as the value, capacitor and diode max voltages, and polarity signs. Do not include tolerances on the schematic. Much of our schematic capture is now done with OrCAD SDT, a fine software package which is easy to use, flexible, and customizable. If you have access to a drafting package, be sure to tell us what you used.

Please make a separate parts list to accompany schematics. In your parts list(s), be sure to include all wattages of resistors, type and voltage ratings of capacitors, and current ratings of transformers, chokes and diodes. List PIV (peak inverse voltage) ratings of rectifiers-even if you list a "1N" number as well. If tolerances are important, state them. If you use special or surplus parts, give the reader a readily available replacement and name the supplier and their address.

Schematic Conventions (others and our own)

1. Number parts with designators (R1, C1) on all construction schematics from input to output, top to bottom. This gives readers a handle for asking about any particular component in a design.

2. Put part details beyond designator, value, and rating in your parts list. Keep special notes to a minimum by putting such information in the caption, or in the parts list.

3. Arrange your drawing of a schematic from input on the left side to output on the right side of the sheet.

4. Capacitor values. We prefer to use the standard nano- prefix for fractional farads as follows:

micro (m)	nano (n)	pico (p)
0.001	1	1,000
0.01	10	10,000
0.1	100	100,000

Thus, 100n (nanofarads) = 0.1m

Use 1n (nanofarads), NOT 1,000pF or 0.001mF

Use 100pF, NOT 0.0001m

(Note: micro = millionth, nano = billionth, and pico = trillionth. Thanks a lot, Michael Faraday.)

5. We believe it is safer to use the quantity unit to replace the decimal in many fractional values of capacitance and resistance to avoid confusion or to avoid the risk of the decimal disappearing on the fifth copy of the schematic.

5R4 vs. 5.4W   (R is used in values below 10)

6K8 vs. 6.8K

6p8 vs. 6.8p This technique works best for small values of capacitance.

6. Please do not use lowercase "m" as an abbreviation for the micro- prefix. The "m" is reserved to represent the prefix "milli-" as in -amperes, -henries, -seconds, -volts, and so on. If you cannot access the Greek letter "m" (Alt+109 on the keypad from the Symbol font in most word processors), use the Roman lowercase letter "u."

If you use perforated or etched boards for construction, please include component layout diagrams. (As with other drawings, put designators on your layout diagrams, and values on your part list.) If you use an etched board, submit a black and white film of the foil pattern, negative or positive, same size or 2 .

Photos should be clear, black and white, or color, at least 3 5, but if you prefer to submit negatives and con tact prints, we will be glad to consider these, even in 35mm form.

Please consider Seattle FilmWorks, PO Box 34056, Seattle WA 98124 who will send you two rolls of free film on request. They offer to put your photos on a 3.5" disk and supply the software, PC or MAC, for viewing. These files can be submitted to us with articles on a 3.5" disk. Cost is $4. for 22 photos on disk. These may also be downloaded from their website: http://www.filmworks.com. This is the very best way we know of to get your photos into your article.

The most important consideration in photographing equipment is light. The best results I've ever achieved in black and white resulted when I took photos against a neutral background, outside, on an overcast day, placing the equipment on it and shooting three frames: bracketing the exposure, one stop above, one at, and one below the computed exposure value. Halogen-type lights are becoming much more common and cheaper. These pointed at a light colored, reflecting surface, rather than directly at the object, give excellent results. Do not locate them close to flammable materials, however.

We welcome your photos for covers and will pay $50 each for those accepted-on acceptance.

We have a reprint of an article on how to photograph your work, which is an excellent source of information. If you'd like to receive it, just send us a SASE with enough postage to cover 2 oz. (outside the US, two postal coupons).

Do not write on your photographs. Use pencil to write on adhesive labels, then affix them to the photo. Don't use felt tip pens on photos. We pay from $5 to $7 per picture, depending on its quality.

References

If you quote others or refer to material published elsewhere, give full reference information, preferably within the text. Alternatively, you may number each reference and list them all at the end of the article. References should include the author's name, full title of the publication, place and date of publication, volume number (if applicable), and page number. Oblique references to so-and-so's design are not acceptable. Readers want to know where they can find additional information about that de sign, and authors should be given full credit for their work. If you use a long quote or copyright material, you must secure the owner's permission. Fees for such usage are subject to negotiation. Audio Amateur Corporation, assumes no responsibility for this type of material unless fees are agreed to in writing.

Final Considerations

We will acknowledge your submission upon receipt, then either accept or reject it (or ask for an extension) within six weeks. Include a self-addressed envelope and loose stamps for your manuscript in case we can't use it.

We hope that you will consider submitting articles to one or all of our publications, and that you will be as attentive to detail as we try to be. After all, we both want the same thing: to let other hobbyists in on the latest in audio design.

Communications

If you need to communicate with us quickly, our FAX ma chine is open 24 hours a day at (603) 924-9467. Please do not FAX manuscripts-only correspondence and corrections will be accepted via FAX. Our 924-9464 line is switched to an answering machine at 4:15 pm every day, M-F, and is operative on weekends around the clock. You can also E-mail submissions at editorial@ audioxpress.com.

About Letters

We have always made it a policy to safeguard the privacy of all authors. We do not give your address or telephone number to readers. Audiophiles like to talk and would love it if you were willing to redesign their systems or recommend the best choice of equipment. (If you mention in your MS that readers may contact you, we will, of course, publish your address.)

When we receive a letter from a reader about your article, it may or may not be for publication. If we indicate it is not, you are entirely free to decide whether you wish to take the time to answer. If the question is frivolous or asking for too much of your time, you need not answer. It will help if you return the author's letter in the envelope we have provided with a polite refusal.

If the letter is marked for publication, we will have kept a copy of the reader's letter. Please send your reply to the author directly in the envelope he supplies, and a copy of your reply to us. We'll provide an envelope for returning the copy to us.

It helps a lot if we can have the text on a disk. When providing us with a stamped envelope, please include loose stamps (i.e., not glued to the envelope). This is especially important for overseas mail.

We do not ask you to answer letters which we aren't going to use. But it does happen that some letters inevitably get left behind and are finally killed. We regret that, but can't think of any way to avoid it.

It would be difficult to overestimate the value of published correspondence. I try to keep it centered on the subject and to edit personal acrimony. If you think the reader or another author is being excessively personal, please indicate your opinion and I'll be certain to cut or temper the respondent's terminology if I agree with you.

Computers

We receive manuscripts (and letter replies if possible) on 3½² 1.4M and 720K types in any of the IBM formats. We are also able to translate directly from Macintosh disks. We can now also manage almost any IBM word processor which you may be using. We can translate 32 word processor formats to and from each other. We have recently abandoned our practice of returning author disks, since the cost of return postage approaches today's cost for disks.

Please do not apply any fancy formatting to your text in an effort to duplicate our style. Text should be flush left (no indented left margins), with one space between paragraphs, no proportional spacing, and only a single spacebar between sentences. Also, please indicate clearly not only which word processor you are using but also which version. If you are submitting computer-generated figures, do not embed them into the text file-create a separate file for figures only.

We now have Microsoft Word 97 for direct use of your disks. Those of you who use computers are probably aware of how much help spreadsheet packages can provide in your writing and designing. If you haven't discovered them yet, these programs are well worth the effort of learning. Our new favorite is MS Excel 97. The graphical capabilities of this program, along with its total compatibility with Lotus 1-2-3, is outstanding. These are fine tools and can enhance any technical writer's capabilities significantly. We highly recommend MS Excel for data presentation in graphical form, although Quattro Pro and Lotus perform graphical charts as well. Excel is also fine for drawings.

Categories: Audio

CONTACT: Marianne M. Norris, Editor
Material: All
PO Box 876
305 Union Street
Peterborough NH 03458-0576
Phone: 603-924-9464
Fax: 603-924-9467
E-mail: editorial@audioXpress.com

Audio Video Interiors

Rarely accepts unsolicited submissions.
Categories: Nonfiction—Technical—Technology—Audio-Video

CONTACT: Mary Ann Giorgio, Editor
Material: All
774 S. Placentia Ave
Placentia CA
92870
Phone: 714-939-2628
E-mail: magiorgio@mcmullenargus.com
Website: www.audiovideointeriors.com

Audubon

Audubon articles deal with the natural and human environment. They cover the remote as well as the familiar. What they all have in common, however, is that they have a story to tell, one that will not only interest *Audubon* readers, but that will interest everyone with a concern for the affairs of humans and nature.

We want good solid journalism. We want stories of people and places, good news and bad; humans and nature in conflict, humans and nature working together, humans attempting to comprehend, restore and renew the natural world.

We are looking for new voices and fresh ideas. Read the magazine, both features and departments before sending queries. Every story suggestion should be submitted in a brief query letter, accompanied by a stamped, self-addressed envelope; no telephone or FAX que-

ries please. Be sure the query not only outlines the subject matter, but also indicates the approach you would take and how you would handle the material. Please estimate how many words you would need to cover the subject. Also, include some samples of your writing.

Among the types of stories we seek: profiles of individuals whose life and work illuminate some issues relating to natural history, the environment, conservation, etc.; balanced reporting on environmental issues and events here in North America; analyses of events, policies, and issues from fresh points of view. We do not publish fiction or poetry. We're not seeking first person meditations on "nature," or accounts of wild animal rescue or taming.

Queries should be accompanied by a stamped, self-addressed envelope of sufficient size. If you are submitting photographs with a queries, be sure your submission includes the stiffeners, sufficient postage, and instructions we need to return the photos the way you want them returned.

Author identification should be included; name, address, telephone number, fax number. Computer printouts and photocopies are acceptable though we will not consider simultaneous submissions. *Audubon* is vigorously fact-checked. Once an article is accepted, the author must be prepared to submit source materials that back up the text and enable us to verify all facts.

We pay for articles on acceptance, and our rates vary according to length, the amount of work and thought required.

Categories: Nonfiction—Book Reviews—Conservation—Ecology—Environment—History—Interview—Outdoors—Nature—Essay—Humor —Opinion

CONTACT: The Editor
Material: All
700 Broadway
New York NY 10003-9501
Website: magazine.audubon.org

Austin Monthly
"Austin's City Magazine"

Heading:
At the top of each story please include, in this complete format:
• Full Name
• Contact Info (E-mail &/or Phone No.)
• Section article goes in (e.g. Talk, Character, Features)
• Month & Year article will be in: Nov. 2003
• Word Count
• Suggested Title(s) of the Article:
• Suggested Deck (An auxiliary headline that adds info. to the title):
• Image Status: (Here, TK, on CD, etc.)
(Note: You can usually check your word count in Microsoft Word under Tools on the Menu bar.)

Please do not include notes to the staff, invoices, etc. within the same document as your story. Please put this information in the e-mail itself or a separate attachment.

Submission:
Please submit your stories in a Microsoft Word or Quark document, if possible, and note if you use a computer other than a Macintosh (We receive stories on Macs.). Please submit your stories via e-mail to srichardson@austin.rr.com and editor@austinmonthly.com. Please do not send images to these addresses! (See Photography and Artwork section.)

Photography and Artwork:
If you need our office to supply imagery for your piece, please let us know as soon as possible.

To aid in caption writing, please submit the following, complete information along with each image:
Full names (correct spellings) of everyone in the picture

As many details as you can: who it is, what it's of, where it was taken, when it was taken and why the event was held or why it was important.

Any images used in the magazine need to be a minimum of 300 dpi, preferably in TIF format (JPEG as a second option). Images must be able to be enlarged to a minimum of 5x7 and maintain a 300 dpi. Slides are also acceptable, but transparencies should be used as a last resort.

Please send all images to designer@austin.rr.com. Images are due by the 10th of the month (same time as the stories); however, if the image cannot be submitted by the deadline, please let Shannon Richardson (editor) or Lyn Brady (publisher) know. (Images for features are due on the 10th three months in advance, unless the photos cannot be taken until a later date.) We understand that photographers usually have to read the story before they can shoot pictures and extensions will be given when necessary.

Text:

Articles should be single-spaced with an extra space in between paragraphs. Please do not make indentions.

Please fact check all of your work: This means verifying all facts with a credible source, especially the spellings of all proper names. Please contact a credible source directly (in person, by phone or e-mail) and avoid using the phone book or Internet as references—they might not always be accurate.

Carefully edit the entire story for errors in spelling, grammar and punctuation before submission.

Please write like you know your topic intimately. If you're writing about someone, meet him or her in person. If you're writing about a place, visit it.

Style:

We follow AP Style (*The Associated Press Stylebook and Briefing on Media Law*, Norm Goldstein, ed., 2002) and refer to *The Elements of Style* (William Strunk Jr. and E.B. White, 2000) and a standard English dictionary, in addition to the following *Austin Monthly* modifications/additions:

• Attribution: Please use present tense ("says", not "said") and keep it in subject-verb order ("Bob says", not "says Bob"). We do not use courtesy titles (Miss, Ms., Mrs., Mr.), and we generally use last names for reference unless the piece is especially personal or informal ("Smith ran," not "Bob ran").

• Composition Titles: Italicize the names of movies, books, newspapers, magazines, plays, songs, TV shows, etc. Don't use quotes.

• Fonts: To bold a word, please insert double brackets around the bolded word: [[bold]]. To italicize a word, please insert single fancy brackets around the italicized word: {*italicize*}. This way, when your document is transferred to our designers who work in Quark (our layout program), we won't lose any of your bolded or italicized words.

• Foreign Words: Italicize non-English words, and provide a translation if the word is not commonly known.

• Percentages: Use the numeral and the word "percent" spelled out (14 percent; 6.5 percent)

• Phone Numbers: Use hyphens only (263-9133; 214-561-0341). The local area code 512 is not needed.

• The University of Texas at Austin: Use this as the official name on first reference. On second reference, The University is acceptable when referring to the University of Texas at Austin. Use the university on second reference for another institution of higher learning. UT is used only as a modifier, not a noun.

• Street names: Every street mentioned should have a St., Blvd., Ave., Road, Circle, etc. with it. Follow AP Style to determine what's abbreviated and what's not.

• Time of Day: We use Central Daylight (CDT) time or Central Standard Time (CST). We use a.m. and p.m. (not am, AM, pm, or PM) with numerals. Use midnight or noon, not 12 a.m. or 12 p.m.

• Web addresses: Please use this format for a Web site: www.austinmonthly.com

Grammar and Punctuation Reminders:

• Commas: In a series of three or more terms with a single conjunction, use a comma after each term except the last (apples, oranges and bananas; not apples, oranges, and bananas). Place a comma before a conjunction introducing an independent clause. Do not join independent clauses with a comma.

• Dashes (———), rather than hyphens (-), should be used within a sentence to designate abrupt change or a series within a phrase. Hyphens are often used in order to avoid ambiguity or with compound modifiers. There should be no spaces on either side of a dash or hyphen.

Be aware of:

• Dangling modifiers—The writer knows what is intended but doesn't say it, forcing the reader to rearrange a sentence to grasp its meaning (Short and readable, I finished it in about 45 minutes.) Avoid these!

• Misuse of relative pronouns—Who is nominative, like the personal pronouns he, she and they. Whom is objective, like him, her and them.

• Possessives—Singular common nouns ending in s take 's unless the next word begins with s: the hostess' invitation; the hostess' seat.

• Singular proper nouns ending in s take only an apostrophe: Socrates' life.

• Cliches—Try to avoid and instead come up with fresh, original language

• Clutter—Avoid unnecessary words; be concise.

• Passive Voice—Active voice (the subject performs the action) is preferred over passive voice (the subject is acted upon).

QUERY PROCEDURE

Editorial mission

Austin Monthly is not content to sit back and watch the city; we are active participants, chronicling and contributing to the vitality of the community. We strive to create a magazine that is lively and relevant—a utilitarian "owner's manual," written with an insider's edge, geared to help life-long residents and newcomers alike get the most out of living in this city. We will challenge the status quo, criticize when warranted, heap praise when deserved and season everything with a passion for this place we call home.

Austin Monthly stories are by, for and about this city. The magazine examines our city's people, politics, services, development, economy, culture, shopping, faults, quirks—everything that makes the city unique—through useful service pieces, personality profiles and investigative stories.

The editorial style of *Austin Monthly* is bright, lively and utilitarian wherever possible. We like to feature at least one sidebar per story (features and departments)—they don't have to be long, just relevant to the piece. We must lead readers into each story, making it relevant to their lives, answering the "so what/what's in it for me" and trying to anticipate readers' questions. Pieces should provide insight into the subject that goes beyond the obvious, beyond what the dailies and weeklies are saying, and provide insider information the reader cannot find elsewhere. Stories should be well researched and facts triple-checked (including phone numbers, addresses, titles, etc.).

Target reader

Austin Monthly is targeted to an urban, affluent Austin metro resident. Primary age range: 30s-60s. 60% female, 40% male. They live in Austin, the surrounding city neighborhoods and suburbs. They are into cooking, dining out, the restaurant scene, their homes, fitness/outdoor activities, their children, style, shopping, culture, art, music and events—but they also want to read in greater depth about politics, personalities and other important issues that shape the city and come with rapid growth (crime, traffic, city government, public transportation, etc.).

Editorial format and departments

On average we run three to four feature stories per issue, each one usually opening with a two-page spread. We have several regular departments in the magazines as well as several rotating departments. Please study the magazine before you query us to know what types of stories we like to run. You'll be way ahead of the game if you query us with a story idea for a specific department or genre in the magazine.

Query Procedure

WE DO NOT ACCEPT QUERIES OVER THE PHONE.

Queries should be submitted in writing via e-mail, fax or mail and consist of three parts:

1. What is the story? A brief synopsis written in the style of your proposed piece.

2. How will you tell it? Detail what sources you will use and how you will research the story.

3. Why? Answer the "so what?" Why is this story important now? Why should you be the one to tell it? Why is this story right for *Austin Monthly*?

PLEASE ALSO SEND THREE OF YOUR BEST MAGAZINE-STYLE WRITING CLIPS.

How will I know if you've accepted my query?

Sometimes it takes us months to get around to reading queries. We will do our best to respond to your query in the timeliest manner possible. We prefer that you follow up with us via email. NO PHONE CALLS PLEASE.

Sometimes your pitch isn't exactly what we're looking for, but we like your tone, your approach and the way you think. If that happens, we'll usually keep your pitch and clips on file and contact you if a story comes up that we think you might be interested in.

If you want the opportunity to sell your story to another publication after we've had a chance to review it, please indicate a time frame (e.g. "If I don't hear from you within 30 days, I'll assume you're not interested and will begin to pitch the story to other publications.") We won't take it personally.

If you are to get an assignment from us, style and content, as well as deadline and payment, are negotiated when the assignment is made.

Questions?

For questions concerning editorial matters, contact Jeff Brady, managing editor, at editor@austinmonthly.com.

We cannot be responsible for unsolicited manuscripts, slides, photographs or other **material.**

Categories: Non-Fiction—Art—Business—Cooking—Children—Culture—Economy—Family—Food/Drink—General Interest—Government—Lifestyle—Music—Politics—Regional

CONTACT: Submissions Editor
Material: All
11612 Bee Caves Rd., Bldg. II, Ste. 125
Austin, TX 78738
Phone: 512-263-9133
Fax: 512-263-1370
E-mail: editor@austinmonthly.com
Website: www.austinmonthly.com

Authorship

Purpose: Authorship magazine is the "in-house" publication for the National Writers Assn. It is read by the thousands of members on a bi-monthly basis. Currently the magazine is a 32 page publication with slick 2 color cover.

Scope: Articles submitted for consideration to *Authorship* should have a writing slant. Material should deal with writing "how-to's" or current market trends. We are overstocked on inspirational "How I became a successful writer…" type material and will not be interested in any of these articles. Articles slanted toward aspects of fiction–creating characters, setting scenes, etc. are of interest and will be our primary interest. Humor is a plus–writing is serious enough without a totally serious article.

We do not accept fiction. Poetry is published in our January/February issue, if it has a writing theme.

Submissions: All submissions should be in standard manuscript format, approximately 750 words, accompanied by an SASE if the material is to be returned. *Authorship* used AP style with the exception of state abbreviations. If the author is not aware of proper manu-

script format, they should request NWA RR#35 prior to submitting. Manuscripts accepted for publication will be requested on disk 3½ IBM compatible in WordPerfect 5.1 or Microsoft Word format in text files with line breaks. NO tabs, fancy fonts, bullets, charts, or tables. If charts or tables are necessary submit them like art work. Disks will be given preferred treatment as this prevents typos in final copy. Sharp clear photos of article authors will be requested if material is accepted.

Payment: We are currently paying $10 honorarium per article or a $10 reduction on membership dues.

Reporting Time: Currently we are reporting in approximately 8 weeks, however this varies at different times of the year and with the amount of material received.

Themes: The issues will have the following themes: Jan/Feb-Poetry, March/April-Creative Nonfiction, May/June-Conference, July/Aug-Children's Writing, Sept/Oct-The Business of Writing, Nov/Dec-Fiction and Screenplays.

Categories: Nonfiction—Associations—Book Reviews—Literature—Writing

CONTACT: Kathi Gustafson, Editor
Material: All
CONTACT: Sandy Whelchel, Managing Editor
Material: All
National Writers Association
3140 S. Peoria #295
Aurora CO 80014
Phone: 303-841-0246
Fax: 303-751-8593

Auto Sound & Security

Circulation: 44,754
Frequency: monthly
Published by the PRIMEDIA Enthusiast Group.

Showcases the excitement, quality and technology of sound systems designed for specific use in vehicles, whether simply for the listener's enjoyment or as the hottest equipment competing in sound-off events. Features include coverage of industry events, vehicle protection, and sound-system protection tips.

For more information, visit the magazine's Website.

Editorial submissions are welcomed, but the editor recommends that contributors query first. All contributions must be accompanied by a self-addressed, stamped envelope. Solicitations for editorial coverage, including car feature articles, should be submitted via US mail. Please include a photograph of the vehicle/project, a quick reference sheet and a few paragraphs detailing the editorial significance of your work. Due to busy travel and work schedules, the editor is not able to field calls related to potential editorial coverage. We assume no responsibility for loss or damage of any unsolicited materials.

Categories: Nonfiction—Automobiles

CONTACT: Editorial Feedback, Submissions
Material: All
McMullen Argus Publishing Inc.
2400 E. Katella Ave., 11th Floor
Anaheim CA 92806
Phone: 714-939-2400
Fax: 714-978-6390
Website: www.autosoundsecurityweb.com

Automated Builder

Automated Builder publishes articles on all seven segments of the automated building industry: Production (Big Volume Site) Builders; Panelized/Precut (including Log and Dome) Home Manufacturers; Residential Modular Manufacturers; Commercial (Special Unit)

Modular; HUD-Code Home Manufacturers; Component Manufacturers and Dealers and Builders for the above companies.

Deadlines

Editorial deadlines are the 21st day of the second preceding month. Advertising deadlines are on the first day of the preceding month. Call for extensions.

Profile Features

Articles range in length from 500 to 1,000 words with a preferred length of 750 words. Color photographs (slides, prints or electronic format) are required. A query about subject matter is suggested before submitting work.

General News

Automated Builder publishes departmental items in these categories: newslines (general industry news); company news, coming events, letters to the editor, new software, new literature and new products.

Electronic Specifications

Material sent for publication should be submitted on floppy (3.5) diskette, CD, ZIP disk or JAZ disk, formatted for IBM PC. Fonts and images used in the material submitted should accompany the material on the disk.

Text should be formatted in text (.txt) or MSWord. If files are compressed, please include the unzipping utility on the disk.

Image files should be saved in .tif or .eps format at 300 dpi. Line art should be scanned at 800 dpi or above and saved in .tif format.

Automated Builder used Pagemaker 6.5 and Photoshop 5.0 for IBM and processes 1200 dpi negative film. Copy should also be submitted in hard copy form.

Categories: Nonfiction—Business—Trade: Building & Construction

CONTACT: Don O. Carlsen, Editor, Publisher
Material: All
CMN Associates, Inc.
1445 Donlon St., Ste 16
Ventura Ca 93303
Phone: 805-642-9735
Fax: 805-642-8820
E-mail: info@automatedbuilder.com
Website: www.automatedbuilder.com

Automobile Quarterly
The Connoisseur's Magazine of Motoring Today, Yesterday, and Tomorrow

Automobile Quarterly is a quality hardbound, advertising-free, 112-page journal of automotive history with excellent photography. Established in 1962, circ. approx. 10,000. It is 85% freelance written.

Submission and Style

Contact for queries and submissions: Tracy Powell, managing editor. No phone calls please. Query by e-mail, fax or snail mail.

AQ accepts queries regarding historical stories about automakers, individual automobile models, and historical figures, past competition, automotive art and collectibles, as well as automotive technology. Queries need to address available sources of information and illustrative materials. Queries will be responded to within 2 weeks, manuscripts within 2 months. Although AQ reviews unsolicited manuscripts, queries are preferred. Unsolicited manuscripts will be returned only if accompanied by a self-addressed, stamped envelope. Submissions should arrive on disc (3 1/2-in. floppy, zip or CD) and hard copy (8 1/2 x 11, double-spaced). Although we prefer Word for Mac, we can convert most PC-based word-processing programs. AQ expects its stories to be based on original and primary research sources and to be accurate and well written. Previously published sources must be used sparingly and be carefully documented. The magazine does not accept repackaged stories that have already been published in English.

Sections frequently freelanced include:
- Brass Era (1904-1917)
- Grand Classic (1918-1929)
- Racing History
- Great Cars of the 30s
- Great Cars of the 40s
- Great Cars of the 50s
- Of Inventors & Innovations
- Of Collectors and Collections
- Art Gallery
- Short-Lived Marque
- Cars of the World
- Biography

AQ's audience consists of enthusiasts from all eras, a group of knowledgeable car aficionados that pay a premium subscription for lively, insightful stories accompanied by top-notch photography. For a sample of what AQ is looking for, visit www.autoquarterly.com and read Featured Articles, or request an issue for $20 (normal price: $25.99). Style bibles include the latest *AP Stylebook* and *Webster's Ninth Collegiate Dictionary*. Bylines are given; authors receive one comp issue.

Photos

AQ reviews 4x5, 35mm and 120 transparencies, historical prints, and high-resolution digital photography (300 dpi minimum).

Compensation

AQ pays on acceptance within 30 days of assigned deadline, unless otherwise contracted. Feature stories range from 1,500 to 4,500 words. Payment is negotiated (depending primarily on word length, the writer's expertise, writing ability and professionalism) but generally ranges between $500 and $2,000 per story. AQ often relies on authors to assist in locating and supplying historical photos. Writer/photographers are sometimes used to provide a complete package of words and color or black-and-white images. Fees will be negotiated. AQ offers a 33% kill fee. Manuscripts are published an average 1 year after acceptance with byline. Editorial lead time: 9 months. Currently, AQ purchases first international rights for articles (including excerpting for book compilation and Web site use) and all rights for photographs.

Contributors receive two (2) complimentary copies; additional copies are available at $15 per copy.

Categories: Nonfiction—Automobiles—Consumer—History

CONTACT: Tracy Powell, Managing Editor
Material: Queries and submissions
137 E. Market St.
New Albany IN 47150
Phone: 866-838-2886
Fax: 812-948-2816
E-mail: editor@autoquarterly.com
Website: www.autoquarterly.com

Aviation History

Please refer to PRIMEDIA History Group.

Aviation Maintenance

About Us

Monthly—12 issues.

Aviation Maintenance is the number-one source for information on the worldwide aviation aftermarket. Maintenance managers in all segments of the industry—corporate flight departments, regional and major airlines, general aviation, repair stations and the military turn to *Aviation Maintenance* for the latest new business trends, regulatory developments, technical advancements, and new products and services. Subscriptions to *Aviation Maintenance* are complimentary to aviation maintenance industry professionals.

Guidelines

No formal guidelines, but writers must be intimately familiar with the Aviation Industry, especially the maintenance side of the industry.

Categories: Nonfiction—Aviation—Trade: Aircraft Maintenance Issues

CONTACT: Matt Thurber, Editor
Material: All
Access Intelligence, LLC
1201 Seven Locks Rd, Ste 300
Potomac MD 20854
Phone: 301-354-2000
Website: www.aviationmx.com

Babybug

For a sample issue of BABYBUG, please send $5.00 to: BABYBUG Sample Copy • P.O. Box 300 • Peru, IL 61354. **NOTE:** Sample copy requests from foreign countries must be accompanied by International Postal Reply Coupons (IRCs) valued at US $5.00. Please do NOT send a check or money order.

BABYBUG, a listening and looking magazine for infants and toddlers ages six months to two years, is published by Cricket Magazine Group. BABYBUG features simple stories and poems, words and concepts, illustrated in full color by the best children's artists from around the world. BABYBUG measures 6-1/4" x 7", contains 24 pages, and is printed in large (26-point) type on high-quality cardboard stock with rounded corners and no staples. We hope that the following information will be useful to prospective contributors.

Published: Monthly, except for combined May/June and July/August issues.

Price: $35.97 for 1-year subscription (ten issues)

Manuscripts: Stories very simple and concrete; 4 to 6 short sentences maximum.

Poems: rhythmic, rhyming; 8 lines maximum.

Nonfiction: very basic words and concepts; 10 words maximum.

Activities: parent/child interaction; 8 line maximum. Rates vary $25 minimum.

Payment upon publication.

Art by assignment only: Artists should submit review samples of artwork to be kept in our illustrator files. We prefer to see tear sheets or photoprints/photocopies of art.

• If you wish to send an original art portfolio for review, package it carefully, insure the package, and be sure to include return packing materials and postage.

• Author-illustrators may submit a complete manuscript with art samples. The manuscript will be evaluated for quality of concept and text before the art is considered.

• Rate: $500/spread ($250/page).

• Payment within 45 days of acceptance. We purchase all rights; physical art remains the property of the illustrator and may be used for artist's self promotion.

Comments:

• BABYBUG would like to reach as many children's authors and artists as possible for original contributions, but our standards are very high, and we will accept only top-quality material. Before attempting to write for BABYBUG, be sure to familiarize yourself with this age child.

• PLEASE DO NOT QUERY FIRST. We will consider any manuscripts or art samples sent on speculation and accompanied by a self-addressed, stamped envelope. Submissions without a SASE will be discarded.

• Please allow 8 to 10 weeks response time for manuscripts, 12 weeks for art samples.

• We do not distribute theme lists for upcoming issues.

BABYBUG normally purchases the following rights. For stories and poems previously unpublished, BABYBUG purchases all rights.

Payment is made upon publication. For stories and poems previously published, BABYBUG purchases second North American publication rights. Fees vary, but are generally less than fees for first publication rights. Payment is made upon publication. Same applies to accompanying art.

For recurring features, BABYBUG purchases the material outright. The work becomes the property of BABYBUG and is copyrighted in the name of Carus Publishing Company. A flat fee per feature is usually negotiated. Payment is made upon publication.

For commissioned artwork, BABYBUG purchases all rights plus promotional rights. (promotions, advertising, or in any other form not offered for sale to the general public without payment of an additional fee) subject to the terms outlined below:

(a) Physical art remains the property of the illustrator.

(b) Payment is made within 45 days of acceptance.

(c) Illustrator may use artwork for self promotion.

Categories: Fiction—Nonfiction—Children—Literature—Poetry—Short Stories

CONTACT: Submissions Editor
Material: Manuscripts
CONTACT: Suzanne Beck, Art Director
Material: Art Samples
Cricket Magazine Group
PO Box 300
Peru IL 61354
Website: www.cricketmag.com or www.cobblestonepub.com

BabyLife

Please refe to *ParentLife.*

BabyTalk

BabyTalk reaches 1.8 million readers, primarily women, who are expecting a child or are the parents of a child under the age of 18 months. Every area we cover–pregnancy, the basics of baby care, infant health, growth and development, juvenile equipment and toys, work and day care, marriage and relationships–is approached from a how-to service perspective. The message "here's what you need to know and why" is delivered with smart, crisp style. The tone is confident and reassuring (and, when appropriate, humorous and playful)–advice you can trust, backed up by experts, from someone who's been there.

BabyTalk is largely freelance written, although we use regular contributors for many of the departments. Fees average a dollar a word, depending on the degree of difficulty and the writer's previous experience. Features generally run between 1,000 and 2,000 words. Departments range from 100 to 1,000 words.

Queries should be addressed to the editor of the department in question (Your Body Editor, Table for 2 Editor, Healthy Baby Editor) or, for essays or features, to the Articles Editor. Relevant clips and samples of your work are appreciated, although they can not be returned.

Put all queries in writing (no phone calls, please) and enclose a stamped, self-addressed business-size envelope for a reply. We cannot return any unsolicited manuscripts or material. Please allow at least six to eight weeks for a response. *BabyTalk* will not consider simultaneous submissions. We do not publish poetry.

The best guide for writers is *BabyTalk* itself. Please familiarize yourself with the magazine before submitting a query and take the time to focus your story idea; scattershot queries are a waste of time and postage. Thank you for your interest in *BabyTalk.*

Categories: Fiction—Nonfiction—Arts—Book Reviews—Cartoons—Conservation—Ecology—Environment—Recreation—Short Stories—Writing

CONTACT: Caitlin Stine, Editorial Assistant
Material: All
The Parenting Group, Inc.
530 5th Ave, 4th Floor
New York NY 10036
Phone: 212-522-8989
E-mail: letters@babytalk.com
Website: www.babytalk.com

Back Home in Kentucky

BACK HOME IN KENTUCKY is a beautiful, four-color, state-wide publication-the "coffee table magazine of choice" in Kentucky homes. We are now 10 issues per year with Jan/Feb and Nov/Dec being combined issues.BACK HOME IN KENTUCKY offers a glimpse of the state Kentuckians love—whether it's a drive down a country lane or a day spent in one of the state's cosmopolitan cities. Each time they browse through the publication, they'll find history, scenic beauty, the wildlife and natural history, as well as the "character" of the Commonwealth's people. Articles are designed to amuse, educate, and illustrate the Commonwealth, connecting the Highlands with the Purchase, the Pennyroyal with the Bluegrass.

GENERAL FEATURES

• *Fairs & Festivals*—This is an abbreviated listing of events taking place across the state over the two-month period of a particular issue. Color photos and slides are welcomed, as is listing information. Deadline: two months prior to issue date.

• *Pursuits*—This department features interviews with Kentuckians involved with interesting hobbies and avocations, as well as professional craftsmen and artisans. Past features have included a look at men and women involved in woodworking, quilting, metalworking, basketmaking, photography, and crop dusting. Publication quality color images required (slides or prints). Submissions encouraged.

• *In the Kitchen*—This department focuses on interesting dishes for entertaining and family fare, tying each issue's feature to seasonal or other themes. Recipes are contributed from readers and reprinted from cookbooks offered by various civic organizations. (Individual recipes accepted, as are civic group's cookbooks, from which we may reprint recipes in exchange for purchase information about the cookbook.)

• *Wildlife/Natural History*—These regular departments focus on flora and fauna native to the state of Kentucky as well as other aspects of the Commonwealth's natural history. From the mystery of a heronry to the stunning beauty of Pine Mountain, readers will find an interesting slice of Kentucky here.

• *County Lines*—A regular feature, the county salute covers a county's history, offers a present picture of the county and its communities, recreational opportunities, etc. We are actively seeking writers for county salutes in a variety of areas. Writers must provide photography to accompany the salute article (may be chamber or tourism furnished). Query first.

HISTORY

• *Memories*—This department features nostalgic writings offering the flavor of a slower, more friendly time submitted by our readers. Must be Kentucky-related. Black & white photos may accompany the submission. Images sent with submission enhance the chance of publication.

• *Chronicle*—A glimpse at the history of the state, this department explores some aspect of the Commonwealth's past in some depth. Themes have included: Kentucky women, Sports in Kentucky, Kentucky Inventors, Kentucky & World War II, Kentucky Medicine, etc. Queries encouraged.

• *Profiles*—This department captures the personality and characteristics of interesting Kentuckians who are no longer living. We feature well-known and lesser-known Kentucky men and women who have figured in the state's past. Queries and submissions encouraged.

• Departments for which submissions are most encouraged.

WRITER'S GUIDELINES

BACK HOME IN KENTUCKY is a regional hearth-and-home magazine reflecting a dynamic and contemporary Kentucky, yet one that is rich in history, hospitality, and natural beauty. BACK HOME fosters interest and pride in Kentucky, entertaining and educating the reader. The magazine covers the state's more obvious stories and sparks the interest with the lesser-known. Each issue focuses on one or more themes, which are outlined in the editorial calendar. We emphasizes the scenic beauty of the Commonwealth, as well as her wild creatures, natural history, and colorful characters.

We welcome queries and manuscripts on speculation that fall in these general areas: Kentucky history, Kentucky profiles, Kentucky nostalgia, county features, Kentucky crafts and craftspeople, and county features. Most articles must be accompanied by attractive, well-focused photographs. We have regular writers contributing features on wildlife, natural history, and cooking.

We particularly encourage submissions in these areas:

• *County Lines Assignments:* These are chosen about a year in advance, although the calendar is flexible. These features should be 2,000 to 3,000 words in length and feature interesting aspects of the county—history, famous natives, interesting historical sites, tourist spots, geographical information, and anything else of interest. Color photos are required, although these may be obtained from local tourism commissions, chambers of commerce, state parks, etc. (slides or prints).

• *Memories:* Submissions should be 500 to 900 words in length, written in first person. Stories should be of an anecdotal, "I remember when" style. Old family photos or photos pertaining to the story are greatly welcomed. Must be Kentucky related.

• *Pursuits:* These features can be from 1,000 to 2,500 words in length and should feature a Kentuckian with an interesting hobby or avocation. Publication-quality color images required (slides or prints).

• *Chronicle:* Perhaps our most popular feature, the Chronicle department in each issue covers a broad-based topic such as the history of medicine or aviation in Kentucky, Kentucky inventors, Kentucky women, etc. Feature length is 2,500 to 4,000 words. Submission of related historic images is encouraged.

• *Profiles:* Features about little-known or well-known deceased figures in the Commonwealth's history, with a focus on what makes them so interesting. Length is 1,000 to 3,000 words and a historic image of the person must be available.

• *Special Assignments:* There is always room for quality writing on a variety of Kentucky-related topics. Feel free to query the editor about any story ideas you think are feasible.

• *Payment:* Payment for all materials is upon publication, unless otherwise negotiated. Payment is for first-time North American rights, unless otherwise negotiated. Writers receive a byline and three copies of the magazine containing their work. Material is placed in the magazine as content merits and space allows. The editor determines the suitability of material for inclusion in BACK HOME, as well as in which issue material appears. Payment for articles varies and is negotiable with the editor. Generally, pay ranges from $15-100, depending on department.

• *Photographs:* Photos accompanying articles are paid for as part of the manuscript purchase. Photo essay submissions are welcome. BACK HOME welcomes submissions of color transparencies for cover consideration and color feature photos. We use about 25 photos/issue, less than 10% on assignment. Do not submit any photo without identifying it, and photos will be returned only if a stamped, self-addressed envelope is enclosed with the materials. Transparencies (35mm and larger format) and prints are accepted. Payment for these is individually negotiated. No payment is made for photos submitted for the Fairs & Festivals section, as it is assumed their publication benefits the event. For complete photo guidelines, contact the editor.

• *Deadlines:* BACK HOME editorial content is planned several months in advance. If an author wishes his/her work to appear in a particular month, he/she should work closely with the editor. Material should be in the editor's hands no later than ten weeks prior to the month of issue (that is, we need May/June material by February 15, and so forth).

• *Don't Forget:* All submissions should include the writer's/photographer's phone number for the editor's convenience if questions arise. A word count is required. We accept diskettes of articles in a variety of software—call to see if yours is compatible. Single issue copies available for $3.

Categories: Nonfiction—Animals—Antiques—Architecture—Arts—Biography—Civil War—Collectibles—Cooking—Crafts/Hobbies—History—Rural America—Travel—Regional (Kentucky-related only)

CONTACT: Nanci Gregg, Managing Editor
Material: All
CONTACT: Jerlene Rose, Editor
Material: All
PO Box 710
Clay City, KY 40312-0710
Phone: 606-663-1011
Fax: 606-663-1808
E-mail: info@backhomeinky.com

BackHome
Your Hands-On Guide to Sustainable Living

Suggestions for *BackHome* Contributors

BackHome is a down-to-earth, how-to magazine whose primary purpose is to help people gain more control over their own lives by doing more for themselves. We are looking for interesting, lively, preferably first-person articles based upon actual experience in the fields of gardening, home construction and repair, workshop projects, cooking, crafts, outdoor recreation, family activities and vacations, livestock, home business, home-based and other education, and community/neighborhood action.

In general, we'll consider any article that will help our readers improve the quality of life—for themselves, their families, their community, and their environment. We seldom publish essays or basically philosophical contemplations.

You can query or make submissions by e-mail (BackHome@ioa.com). We try to answer queries within a reasonable time. You are welcome to send complete articles, but in most cases sending a query in advance gives us a chance to help you develop the slant and focus we want for our readers. It also may save you the trouble of writing an article only to discover that we have a similar one in our files or have assigned the subject to someone else.

At present our base rate of pay is $35 a printed page, payable upon publication. We pay extra for good clear photographs: color prints are preferable but transparencies are OK. We return all photos sent to us. We prefer to buy first North American serial rights, in which case you're free to sell the article elsewhere after we run it, but we may hold your accepted submission for a considerable time before finding a spot for it. (We sometimes use second-rights material if its previous appearance was not in a major publication.) If after accepting an article we find we can't use it, we pay a kill fee of $25.

When submitting an article, please include your full name, address, and phone number. If you submit hard copy it is helpful if you can provide your manuscript on computer disk or transmit it by modem, but don't do so unless we request this—just let us know the possibilities. A stamped self-addressed envelope, or your e-mail address, will speed up our answers to your queries, and an envelope with correct postage is essential if you want your manuscript and photos returned. If you haven't seen *BackHome*, we strongly suggest you read at least an issue or two to get a better feel for the magazine before you try to write for us. If you can't find *BackHome* locally, you can order a sample from us for $5.00 or a one-year subscription for $21.97 (six issues).

Thank you very much for your interest in *BackHome*.
Lorna K. Loveless, Editor
To order the Current Issue as a Sample Copy for $5.00 Post paid, Call 1-800-992-2546. On the Web, backhomemagazine.com.

Categories: Ecology—Environment—Gardening—Rural America—Sustainable Living—Self-Sufficiency

CONTACT: Lorna K. Loveless, Editor
Material: All
Wordsworth Communications, Inc., PO Box 70
Hendersonville NC 28793
Phone: 828-696-3838
Website: wwwbackhomemagazine.com

Backpacker

BACKPACKER is a proud sponsor of Leave No Trace (check out our book, Leave No Trace, available from The Mountaineers Press). All articles and photos that appear in the magazine must adhere to Leave No Trace's ecologically friendly practices. Likewise, we do not promote motorized use in the wilderness or backcountry.

Our readers are knowledgeable and experienced backpackers, therefore we accept only authentic, well-researched, well-crafted stories (see the section on "Accuracy," below). We're not interested in slavish imitations of stories we've already done. As always, you should carefully study several issues of the magazine before submitting a query. The best articles have style, depth, emotional impact, and take-away value for the reader.

Good *BACKPACKER* articles contain the following attributes:

• Foot-based travel: BACKPACKER primarily covers hiking. When warranted, we cover canoeing, kayaking, snowshoeing, cross-country skiing, and other human-powered modes of travel.

• Wilderness or backcountry: The true backpacking experience means getting away from the trailhead and into the wilds. Whether a dayhike or a weeklong trip, out-of-the-way, unusual destinations are what we're looking for.

• North American destinations: We only occasionally cover foreign locales. Our defined market is North American destinations.

• Advice for improving the backcountry experience: Our readers want to know how to, when to, where to, and with what. Every *BACKPACKER* article incorporates one or more of these things. We write not merely to inspire our readers to do something, but to help them identify and research new places to go, techniques and skills to use, or the gear to take.

While a large portion of *BACKPACKER* is written by staff and regular contributors, we encourage freelance authors to submit query letters for features and departments. Approximately 50 percent of our features and more than half of our departments are written by freelancers. Please note that it's rare for a writer new to *BACKPACKER* to break into the magazine with a feature assignment. Direct your efforts toward establishing a working relationship with us via department assignments first.

FEATURES

BACKPACKER features usually fall into one of several distinct categories: destinations, personality, technique, or gear. Gear features are generally staff written. In order to make the grade, a potential feature needs an unusual hook, a compelling story, a passionate sense of place, or unique individuals finding unique ways to improve or enjoy the wilderness.

• Destinations: *BACKPACKER* uses pieces that go beyond a mere description of a trail or place. Our destination stories are almost always first person and based upon the author's recent trip experience. Readers should come away with a strong sense of that particular outdoor experience, a firm grasp of the location's character, and the inspiration to duplicate the trip. Journal-style articles are generally unacceptable. Typical word count is 1,250 to 1,750 words, plus a full Expedition sidebar (contact, permit, season, hazards, map, guidebook, and other useful information; look at past *BACKPACKER* issues for examples and style).

• Personality: Backpacking doesn't have star athletes like you find in bicycling or some other outdoor sports, but plenty of unique personalities exist to write about. Colorful, controversial, historically significant, amusing, unusual, or unique people are what we're looking for, especially those who have a direct impact on how or where others hike.

• Technique: Skill-based articles in *BACKPACKER* feature high levels of take-away value. A good technique piece also has information relevant to all skill levels (e.g., beginner, intermediate, and advanced hikers). Often our technique pieces take non-narrative forms.

• Gear: Our Field Tests and comparative gear reviews are always written by writers we've worked with before. If you're interested in writing such articles, start by querying our equipment editor about the Outfitting department (see "Departments," below).

DEPARTMENTS

Freelancers most often break into *BACKPACKER*'s pages in the departments. These shorter assignments (100 to 1,200 words) have specific topics and focus.

• Signpost: the news, issues, views, trends, and people that influence the backpacking world.

• Skills: the how-to, techniques, and tips department that covers all essential hiking and camping skills plus the following categories:

Food—centers on all aspects of trail nutrition, cooking, and food preparation. Tested recipes are a must.

Fitness/First Aid—covers the physical and psychological aspects of fitness, health, first aid, and occasionally nutrition as it relates to backpacking.

Wild Things—covers animals, plants, geology, any nature-oriented topic, provided it is presented in a way that provides substantive information a reader can actively apply on a backcountry trip.

• Outfitting: This department is filled with short reviews of gear that has been field-tested. Note: Outfitting, unlike the other departments, is done by assignment only. Instead of submitting a query regarding a specific piece of equipment, query the equipment editor with your qualifications for testing and reviewing gear. All gear reviewed in Outfitting is acquired by *BACKPACKER* editors only and shipped by us to assigned reviewers. All reviewed gear must be returned to us at the end of the test so that we may photograph it and return it to the manufacturer. This is not a way to fill your gear closet.

• Getaways: This is where we print short, fact-filled destination pieces on trails that can be hiked in a weekend or week. Destinations must be backcountry and offer overnight camping.

Most *BACKPACKER* departments take a single topic within the scope of that section and cover it thoroughly. Again, the more take-away value for the reader, the more appropriate it is for *BACK-PACKER*.

ACCURACY

BACKPACKER prides itself on providing outdoor enthusiasts with reliable information. It's important that our contributors check all facts and figures. A full set of guidelines for fact checking will be provided to you with your first contracted assignment for us. In general, however, we require:

Confirmation of all facts and figures used within an article from a primary source.

For medical, nutrition, and technical advice, direct quotes from accepted professionals or experts.

Full contact information for every source used in creating an article.

An extra copy for our files of any map, catalog, brochure, or other primary source you may have acquired from a land agency or manufacturer.

QUERIES

We prefer queries to completed manuscripts. Send samples of your published work with your first query. Include a SASE envelope if your samples must be returned. We are not responsible for unsolicited artwork, photographs, and manuscripts, so please don't send originals or anything that you can't afford to lose. Allow 6 to 8 weeks for replies.

ASSIGNMENTS AND PAYMENT

All *BACKPACKER* assignments are made in writing, and require a signed contract with you, the freelance author, in order to be valid. The contract will specify payment amount, payment terms, and rights purchased. In general, we pay on acceptance and buy all rights. We pay $.60 to $1.00 per word, depending upon the complexity and demands of the article, as well as the proven experience of the writer.

PHOTOGRAPHY

BACKPACKER uses stock photography and assigns photographers for magazine-sponsored trips. We use high-quality color transparencies in any format. We prefer photographs that meet the following requirements:

The activity shown does not violate local agency guidelines or Leave No Trace principles (e.g., unless specifically allowed in that location, no tents within 200 feet of water).

No visible roads and no frontcountry shots, unless specifically required by the article. *BACKPACKER* is about the backcountry experience and hiking in wildlands; photos taken at scenic outlooks on a road are not what the backpacking experience is about.

Packs and equipment shown in photos should reflect backpacking, not dayhiking or car camping. We're not likely to run a photo of someone wearing a fanny pack on a trail, nor are we likely to use a photo showing someone cooking on a two-burner stove set up on a campground table.

Because we use unbleached, recycled paper stock for the magazine, transparencies shot on film that saturates colors work best for us (e.g., Fuji Velvia, Fuji Provia, Kodak Ektachrome 100VS, etc.). This is especially true for gear photos.

Other things that we look for in photos, especially in gear shots for use in technique stories or • • • Outfitting: Hikers should not be shown wearing sneakers or jeans. At least one person should be in every shot to give a sense of scale to the equipment.

No dogs in the photo (unless we've requested it).

Packs should fit the hiker properly, and features like bottle holders should be utilized.

Tents should be fully staked out and the fly should be tight.

Smaller products, such as purifiers, stoves, and headlamps, should be shot in use.

A variety of images to choose from (two or three dozen), both vertical and horizontal, as well as varying viewpoints and framing.

• Stock Requirements: While we use a large amount of stock photography to illustrate articles, we usually have very specific requirements (e.g., "overnight hiker on McConnell Lake Trail, Desolation Wilderness, preferably with Horseshoe Lake in background"). For each issue, our photo editor sends out via e-mail a list of photos we need for upcoming articles. If you believe you have stock photos that may meet our needs, contact Liz Reap (lreap@*BACKPACKER*.com) indicating your interest in receiving our monthly call list. We require a stock list and a leave-behind example of your work. Portfolios are welcome, however please contact us first to let us know it's coming. If your work meets our photographic standards, you will be added to our database.

• Assignments: *BACKPACKER* is one of the few magazines that still hires photographers on a contract basis and sends them out on assignment. These assignments are grueling, as they often involve lots of mileage over rough terrain. Not only that, but you have to get your pictures while moving through the terrain, carrying your own photo and backpacking gear. Because we're a small publication, our budgets and time restraints are quite restrictive in this area, thus we tend to work only with photographers that we know to be capable of always bringing back results, no matter what the conditions. Interested photographers should contact photo editor Liz Reap and be prepared to present a portfolio of photographs taken in the backcountry.

Our pay rates for photography varies depending on how the photograph is used, and at what size:

• Cover photos: $550 to 800

Photo use inside magazine: $100 to 400 (depends upon size and placement)

Assignment day rate: $450 to 500

STATISTICS

Publishing frequency: 9 issues annually, one of which is the Gear Guide (March)

Circulation: 300,000 (2004)

Lead time: 6 months

Categories: Outdoor—Sports/Recreation—Travel

CONTACT: Peter Flax, Features Editor
Material: Features
E-mail: pflax@BACKPACKER.com
CONTACT: Dave Howard, Senior Associate Editor
E-mail: dhoward@BACKPACKER.com
Material: Getaways, Signpost
CONTACT: Michelle Hamilton, Assistant Editor
Material: Getaways, Skills
E-mail: mhamilton@BACKPACKER.com
CONTACT: Dennis Lewon, Equipment Editor,
Material: Outfitting
E-mail: dlewon@BACKPACKER.com
33 E. Minor St.
Emmaus, PA 18098.
Website: www.BACKPACKER.com

Backroads
Motorcycle Tour Magazine

Introduction

The concept of *Backroads* is simple. It is a publication created with the idea of giving our readers places of interest to ride to and getting the most enjoyment out of their motorcycles. Although *Backroads* is geared towards the motorcycling population, it is not by any means limited to just motorcycle riders. Non-motorcyclists enjoy great destinations too. As time has gone by, *Backroads* has developed more and more into a cutting edge touring publication. We like to see submissions that give the reader the distinct impression of being part of the ride they're reading. Words describing the feelings and emotions brought on by partaking in this great and exciting lifestyle are encouraged.

Aim and Query Before Shooting and Writing

Backroads does not send out rejection letters, just emails and notes to let you know we are interested. Being a touring publication, we are always interested in your travels, especially when they lead our readers to exciting new destinations, but sometimes we have a backlog of articles that cover the same area, idea or situation. To save you and us a lot of time, it is best to email us a note on your intentions regarding your article before submission.

We love pictures. The more the merrier. Particularly shots of motorcycles on the move, great scenery and creative photography. *Backroads* is about riding, and although we will use party pictures when appropriate, we discourage photography showing only indoor "end of the ride" shots.

Backroads Dos and Don't

What *Backroads* does not want is any "us vs. them" submissions. We are decidedly non-political and secular. *Backroads* is about getting out and riding, not getting down on any one particular group, nor do we feel this paper should be a pulpit for a writer's beliefs...be they religious, political or personal.

Please do not take any returns or criticism to heart. If we rejected an article perhaps another regional or national publication could use it. Don't give up or stop sending in submissions, you're already doing more than most folks...keep writing!

Backroads does not want submissions that push any one particular dealership or shop. Of course, if a shop is part of an event or charitable cause, mentioning the shop is the right thing to do. But a mention is not a 100 word description of everything the shop or dealer does. Articles are not ads, nor do we feature any one dealer or shop as an article by itself.

When writing a piece for *Backroads* try not to go overboard mentioning everybody's name. This paper is not here to make points for people personally. Stick to the story.

How to Submit

All submissions must be accompanied by images (negatives or slides), with an SASE of adequate size to return all material sent as well as a copy of the issue in which they were published, and a hard copy printout of the article, including your name, address and phone number. If none is enclosed, the materials will not be returned.

Text submissions are accepted via US mail on CD. Color images must be no smaller than 250 dpi, with B&W acceptable at 170 dpi. *Backroads* accepts both negatives, with accompanying prints for verification, and slides.

Please do not submit faded photocopies or badly developed film, as we will not use them. Photos should be properly exposed, neither light and washed out looking nor so dark that detail is hard to make out. Be aware of the five Ws of journalism, pertaining both to photography and writing: who, what, when, where and why. *Backroads* does not use photos that do not accompany an article, and vice versa.

What *Backroads* Is Looking For

Backroads has several monthly columns which are open to freelance writers. They include:

The Great All American Diner Run. An eatery destination story accompanied by directions, affectionately called a "Rip & Ride Route Sheet." These should be about 500 to 750 words, with a few good photos, at least one showing the eatery (with motorcycle in shot). Focus on ride area, eatery and what makes it a great motorcyclist's destination are suggestions for inclusioin. Payment on publication: $50

Big City Getaway. A day trip, either including a specific destination or just an enjoyable day's ride, about 500 to 750 words, with a few good photos along the route and of the destination, and route sheet. Payment on publication: $50

Mysterious America. Dr. Seymour O'Life founded this column. Since he is frequently gallivanting around the world, he needs help filling the spot. These stories should feature some mysterious, amazing, bizarre or just head-scratching destination. Story should be about 500 to 750 words, with photos, of course, of destination, although route sheet is not mandatory. Payment on publication: $50

We're Outta Here. *Backroads'* multi-day destination column, aimed towards couples looking for a quick weekend getaway, or perhaps a club ride, if the destination warrants larger groups. This should feature overnight accommodations, such as a hotel, B&B or such, route sheet, and photos of area and destination. Length from 500 to 750 words. Payment on publication: $50

Thoughts from the Road. This column gives the writer an opportunity to reflect on motorcycling, whether it be a specific instance that meant something in their life, a person that influenced them, or just something that ticked them off. As mentioned before, no pontificating, please, but rather thoughtful reflection. Length should be 400 to 600 words. Payment on publication: $50

Full Length Travel Features. This type of story offers a good opportunity for prospective contributors. They MUST feature spectacular photography, color preferable, and may be used as a cover story, if of acceptable quality. (Please query before submitting.) Payment on publication varies from .05¢ to .10¢ a word.

Travel Feature Dos and Don't

Don't write a blow-by-blow diary filled with minute, personal details. Structure your story with an opening that makes the reader want to read more. Include hotels or campgrounds in the area, key attractions and how to get to them, interesting places to eat, and special regional events, if applicable. Make sure that all information is current. A route sheet, with a loop of the area, would be a good feature. Photo suggestions include scenic shots with and without rider(s) and action shots. A mini tripod is always a good accessory to include in your tankbag on such trips.

Other avenues open to freelance are product review and Club Spotlights. Payment on publication varies–please query before submission.

Payment and Rights

Payment for all articles is upon publication, and varies from $50 and upward. *Backroads* buys one-time publication rights. We will accept articles that have been previously printed with a gap of at least six months from submission to *Backroads*. Please do not send us an article that has been simultaneously submitted to another publication! We reserve the right to edit any material we accept.

We hope these guidelines will be of help to you and we look forward to reading your submissions. If you have any questions regarding these guidelines, please drop us a line.

Categories: Adventure—Trade—Motorcycles Travel

CONTACT: Brian Rathjen, Publisher
Material: All
PO Box 317
Branchville NJ 07826
Phone: 973-948-4176
Fax: 973-948-0823
E-mail: editor@backroadsusa.com

Backwoodsman Magazine

Subjects: Muzzleloading guns, muzzleloading hunting, 19th century woodslore, early cartridge guns, primitive survival, craft items from yesteryear, American history, grass roots gardening, leather crafting projects, homesteading, log cabin construction, mountain men, Indians, Indian bow & arrow construction, building primitive weapons, etc.

We are not particularly interested in fictional stories, or material that has the tone of a novel. Any material of this type submitted to *Backwoodsman Magazine* will be sent back. It is important that any material submitted also have illustration or photo, many times this is the determining factor whether an article is published. Pen and ink drawings, or b/w and color pictures will reproduce. No pencil drawings. Length of material is left up to the author, but lengthy material that covers a subject in depth is always favored over a short piece. We do not count words at Backwoodsman, only the depth by which a subject is covered.

Pay: *Backwoodsman Magazine* is not a paying magazine. In the near future it's possible that we can become a paying magazine, but at this time we can't afford to pay. We are willing to trade a 1/24 page display ad (value $55) for each article submitted and accepted. Several of our regular writers who have something to sell have chosen this route. In the event you don't have anything to sell in the buckskinning field we are willing to trade a subscription for an article accepted. We want writers who care about a special publication, not writers who care more for the money they might earn. If you can gain satisfaction from submitting subject material of importance to our BWM family of readers, then you are our type of people.

Misc.: We do not deal in world affairs, personal vendettas, or bad mouthing products. Our whole basis is yesteryear. This is not to say that you can't speak your mind. We also do not publish racially motivated material of any type. We don't need a law suit.

If you desire correspondence with us, please send a SASE.

Categories: Crafts/Hobbies—History—Hobbies—Native American—Western—Buckskinning: Fur Trade—Historical (how-to)—Primitive Archery

CONTACT: Submissions Editor
Material: All
PO Box 627
Westcliffe CO 81252
Phone: 719-783-9028
Fax: 719-783-9028
E-mail: bwmmag@rif.net
Website: www.backwoodsmanmag.com

Balanced Living Magazine

We always encourage article submissions and welcome those who believe in our endeavor to make our world a healthier, happier place.

The following are editorial guidelines for preparing article submissions for *Balanced Living Magazine*.

1. Articles—length should be 700–1,000 words.
2. Mainstream Demographic—Assume a mainstream demographic of our readership. Assume that readers have little to no background knowledge of given subjects. Make sure articles begin with point A and follow through to point Z.
3. Clear Writing—Articles should be easy reads. While an article's subject matter may be complex, the writing style and presentation of information and/or ideas should be clear and deliberate. Utilize paragraphs that convey clear points and move successively from one point to the next. If an article is a difficult read due to writing style, a re-write will be requested of the author or the article will not be considered.
4. Mainstream Content—Content should not be too far from mainstream ideologies. Picture an "open-minded, mainstream reader" and present information they would be interested in and/or accept. We understand that this criterion is highly subjective because everyone has their own idea of what is mainstream; but aim to keep articles and ideas within an open-minded view of normalcy.
5. Formal Writing—Articles should embrace a standard of excellence. While certain magazine departments may accept a slightly casual style of writing, the overall aim should be to present information utilizing very professional literary and grammatical standards. A reader's willingness to accept a new idea hinges on the idea's presentation.
6. Keep it Balanced—Articles should not be overtly one-sided when arguing a sensitive point such as religion or politics. There may be an exception to this standard if we are preparing a Point/Counterpoint feature.
7. Accredited Writing—As much as possible, the author should have a demonstrated knowledge of subject matter.
8. Unbiased and Objective—Articles should be unbiased and objective, unless the article is specifically an opinion piece.
9. Supported Writing—Articles and points should be supported by facts and/or evidence wherever possible. Unsubstantiated statements or statements loaded with senseless propaganda and generalizations should be examined carefully or not submitted.

Categories: Nonfiction—Book Reviews—Environment—Health—Lifestyle—New Age—Physical Fitness—Psychology—Spiritual

CONTACT: Editor-in-Chief
Material: All
Balanced Living Magazine, LLC
13314 Detroit Ave.
Lakewood, OH 44017
Phone: 216-226-6094
Fax: 216-226-6095
E-mail: articles@balancedlivingmag.com
Website: www.balancedlivingmag.com

Balloon Life

Articles should be 1,000 to 1,500 words. Shorter articles in the 300 to 500 word range will be considered. Longer articles may be submitted, but are generally reserved for more technical or historical subjects. In addition, the writer may wish to present additional information as a separate item for use as a sidebar to the article.

Types of articles considered for publication:

• *Balloon events/rallies:* May be written on events that have recently taken place. Post-event articles should be submitted as soon as possible after the completion of the event. Types of information to include would be: the event's name, its history, its organizers, participating balloonists, other attractions in the area (famous restaurants, river raft trips, shopping, etc.), value of the event to the community, etc. Short articles (±300 words) will be accepted for our Logbook section, which deals with an event that has recently taken place.

• *Safety seminars:* Because this is an educational event, the article should be written as an educational piece that can be used by the readers to further their knowledge. If not written by the presenter whose information is being used, you must secure his/her permission.

• *Balloon clubs/organizations:* Tell us the history of the organization, what they do, meetings, events, projects, activities, etc. How the club helps to promote the sport of ballooning and handles public relations.

• *General interest stories:* Can be interviews or biographies of people that have made a contribution to the sport of hot air ballooning, or other general interest items.

• *Crew Quarters:* A regular column devoted to some aspect of crewing. May be educational, tell as story of a crew experience, or share some other aspect of the sport. 900 words preferred.

The above contributions should include pictures (color and black & white) with captions (pictures should be able to tell the story), charts, maps, or additional information that would be helpful in conveying the story to the readers.

All material submitted will be on a speculation basis only. The writer will be notified in writing within two weeks of receipt of the material whether it is being considered for publication. BALLOON LIFE will only consider articles for publication which have not previously been published. BALLOON LIFE will pay $50 for the first time North American rights of articles selected for publication and $20 for short article (our Logbook Section) balloon events that have recently taken place. Payment schedule for pictures is $15 inside and $50 for the cover.

Freelance pictures that are submitted will be considered for publication but generally only if they are of an unusual nature or used for the cover photo. See photo guidelines below for more information.

Those individuals who are interested in writing on a specific, technical topic may contact the editor to discuss subject areas, deadlines, and needs of the magazine. For these topics BALLOON LIFE will pay $100-200 for article(s) used on a specific subject, and provide assistance in researching the subject.

Photo Guidelines

BALLOON LIFE is a 4-color monthly magazine dedicated to the sport of hot air ballooning. Only photographs of the highest quality are considered. Photos should be of sharp exposure, good contrast and with excellent color saturation. The use of photos in the magazine is editorially driven; all photos, including the cover, must relate directly to inside editorial.

Submissions should be 35mm color transparencies. Color or black & white prints may also be acceptable. All photographs should be originals. (Duplicate transparencies will be considered but should be so identified.) Copyright must rest with photographer or written permission must be secured from third-party owners. Captions and model releases are preferred. Unless specific written assignment is made, all photos are accepted on a speculation basis only. Photographs will not be returned unless accompanied by a self-addressed, stamped envelope. The photographer generally will be notified within two weeks to confirm receipt of submissions. Simultaneous submissions and previously published work is okay.

• *Stock Needs:* BALLOON LIFE rarely buys stock photography. As mentioned above, the magazine is editorially driven. Occasionally we are interested in "stock subjects" such as winter flying, mountain flying, commercial balloons, special shape balloons, etc. Photographers should query first for information on these anticipated needs. Please include an indication of the contents of your files.

• *Event Coverage:* BALLOON LIFE targets a variety of balloon events for coverage each year and freelance photographs are often used with these articles. Photo coverage should include not only balloons, but other shots which help the reader to capture the true spirit of the event. For example, celebrities, scenics (with and without balloons) faces in the crowd, related events (arts & crafts fairs, chili cook-offs, polo games), etc. Photographers are welcome to query the magazine for interest if they will be attending an upcoming balloon event.

• *Assignments:* Occasionally assignments are made to shoot either specific events, flights, or subjects. In these cases, BALLOON LIFE will provide the photographer with specific direction, contacts and other assistance. Assignment rates are negotiable.

• *Rates:* BALLOON LIFE buys first North American serial rights. Payment schedule is $50 for the cover and $15 for inside color or B&W. Photos are returned and payment is made upon publication.

Categories: Nonfiction—Aviation—Outdoors—Sports/Recreation

CONTACT: Submissions Editor
Material: All
2336 47th Ave. SW
Seattle WA 98116-2331
Phone: 206-935-3649
Fax: 206-935-3326
E-mail: TOM@balloonlife.come
Website: www.balloonlife.com

Baltimore Magazine

As a regional magazine serving the Baltimore metropolitan area, we're almost obsessive in our focus on local people, events, trends, and ideas.

We sometimes write about national issues, but only those of immediate interest to our readers in Baltimore and surrounding counties. About 50 percent of our magazine is written by staff members.

We seek feature stories that are rich with character and drama or that provide new insight into local events. These stories range from 1,500 to 2,500 words. To propose one, send a query letter and clips.

Unless you already have a great set of feature clips and a powerful idea, though, the best way to break into Baltimore is through the shorter articles in the front of the magazine, in sections such as "B-Side" and "Baltimore Inc." To propose one, send a query letter and clips.

We generally develop story ideas ourselves and sometimes assign them to freelancers. To be considered for such assignments, send clips and a letter about your specialties.

Throughout the magazine we need originality, so don't propose anything that you've seen in *The Sun*, the *Baltimore Business Journal*, or other local media, unless you offer a fresh perspective or important new information. Because of our two-month lead time, we can't do much with breaking news.

You're most likely to impress us with writing that demonstrates how well you handle character, dramatic narrative, and factual analysis. We also admire inspired reporting and a clear, surprising style.

Your query should fit on one page. If you want a response, you must include a stamped, self-addressed envelope with your submission. Send correspondence to one of the editors listed.

Thank you for your interest.

Categories: Nonfiction—General Interest—Regional: Baltimore, Maryland

CONTACT: Submissions Editor
Material: All
Inner Harbor East
1000 Lancaster Street, Ste 400
Baltimore MD 21202
Phone: 410-752-4200
Fax: 410-625-0280

E-mail: iken@baltimoremag.com
Website: www.baltimoremagazine.com

The Baltimore Review

Submit 1 - 5 poems or 1 story of creative non-fiction. Traditional and experimental forms welcome. No themes. Length for essays and short stories: short-short to 6,000 words max. No previously published work. Simultaneous submissions are accepted, but notify us immediately if your work is accepted elsewhere.

Response time is 1 - 4 months and submissions are read year-round. Payment is in copies; readings are held for our local writers.

The Baltimore Review is distributed through:

Ingram Periodicals, Inc.—P.O. Box 7000–1240 Heil Quaker Blvd.— — Vergne, TN 37086-7000—(615) 793-5522

Categories: Poetry—Short Stories

CONTACT: Submissions Editor
Material: All
PO Box 36418
Towson MD 21286
Phone: 410-752-4200
Fax: 410-377-4325
E-mail: susanmd@global.com
Website: www.baltimorereview.org

The Baseball Research Journal

Please refer to the Society of American Baseball Research.

Bass West
A Magazine for Western Bass Anglers

Our goal is to make BASS WEST the most authoritative reference guide in the West. As western water problems continue to grow and fisheries budgets suffer more cutbacks, bass will become even more important to the western fishing scene. With your expertise, we can make BASS WEST a major resource for bass anglers in the West. BASS WEST magazine focuses on western techniques for the deep, clear water and tough fishing conditions found in the West. Each issue has three main sections:

1. Columns by western bass pros such as Mike Folkestad, Don Iovino, Jay Yelas, and Dub LaShot.

2. In-depth features of 2,000 to 3,000 words on western techniques, strategies, issues, etc. Additional standard-length articles of 750 to 1,800 words about projects, tips or other items of interest to western bass anglers.

3. Serious reports on the West's best bass destinations. Up to 4,500 words.

EDITORIAL REQUIREMENTS
• Content geared to both the serious western bass angler and occasional western tournament angler
• Lots of quotes from other authorities on the subject-guides, manufacturers, and biologists
• Specific lures and equipment and identification of manufacturers
• Articles based on current scientific research—western-based biological data
• New facts, not rehashed or outdated opinions
SPECIFICATIONS
• FEATURE ARTICLES: In-depth. hands-on western bass information including seasonal and regional variations-Southwest, Northwest and Intermountain may vary. Educational content is important, as are practical solutions to tough fishing problems. Subjects: techniques, biology, technology, seasonal conditions, etc. Include any slides, photos, charts, maps or illustrations you may have. We also like to clarify subjects with sidebar explanations, illustrations and charts or graphs.

• STANDARD ARTICLES: Unique projects, tidbits, short technical pieces, innovative projects, etc. If helpful, use quotes from experts. Include slides, diagrams, etc.

• DESTINATIONS ARTICLES: We want to know the nuts and bolts-why, where, how. Include information on seasonal variations, good detailed maps and interviews with experts-guides, biologists, and major tournament anglers. List lodges, guides and camping areas with phone numbers.

• PHOTOS AND ILLUSTRATIONS: We require 35mm color slides. We strongly encourage fishing action shots and photos showing tackle, techniques, rigging, lures, locations (especially western scenic locations) and some big fish photos. Please send photo captions with names, places and pertinent information.

• HUMOR/REAL LIFE ADVENTURES: Creative entertainment.

• PHOTOS: Cover shot must include angler; bass, western scenery, and action in one shot.

RATES

Rates are based upon how well the article is written and how closely the author follows the writers' guidelines. Payment for articles and photographs payable 30 to 45 days after publication.

• Feature articles: 2,000 to 3,000 words—$200 to $500.
• Standard articles: 750 to 1,800 words—$75 to $300.
• Destinations articles: 2,000 to 4,500 words—$200 to $500.
• Humor/real life adventure: 750 to 1,000 words—$75 to $250.
• Photos: Independent inside use—$25 to $75. Cover shot-angler, bass, western scenery, and action—Up to $400.

Categories: Fishing

CONTACT: Mark Mendez, Publisher
Material: All
1145 2nd St A-286
Brentwood CA 94513
Phone: 800-591-7111
Fax: 925-240-9450
E-mail: info@basswest.com
Phone: 800-240-9450
Website: www.basswest.com

Bay Area Parent

Please refer to United Parenting Publications.

Bay Area Parent's B.A.B.Y.

Formerly *Bay Area Baby*. Please refer to United Parenting Publications.

Bead & Button

Bead&Button is a bimonthly magazine devoted to techniques, projects and designs, and materials relating to beads, buttons, and accessories. Our readership includes both professional and amateur bead and button makers, hobbyists, and enthusiasts who find satisfaction in making beautiful things. Our authors are skilled artisans (not necessarily skilled writers) who are willing to share what they know, as well as professional writers with technical knowledge in the field.

Our format it 8.5 x 11, four-color throughout, and more than 50% graphic. Most articles are uninterrupted by advertising. Regular departments include: Letters, News & Reviews, Your Work, Origins, Tips & Techniques, Pattern Gallery, Anything Goes, and several projects.

We are looking for beadworking and button hobby articles about techniques, projects and patterns, materials, and people and design concentrated in the areas of jewelry, accessories, and clothing embellishment. We also examine fashion and style and present home furnishings.

Point of View

Our emphasis is on learning to design jewelry and accessories and developing the skills necessary for producing professional looking results. Most articles are or include projects and patterns, both for their own sake and also as a way to encourage experimentation in design. Thus we prefer projects that offer alternatives: in fashion—youthful, mature, and sophisticated styles; in design—suggestions for variation in size, materials, style or technique.

We report on what's available and new in tools, supplies, and materials. We review books, videos, schools or workshops, galleries, and organizations. We report on artists working with beads and buttons from the viewpoint of the enthusiast who is as curious about the artist's life as about her/his methods of work. And we explore trends in accessory fashion and contemporary beads and buttons.

Simultaneous Submissions

We don't accept simultaneous submissions. Please do not send your piece, proposal, or manuscript to us if you are sending it another magazine. If we seem slow in responding to your submission, please call or write to give us the opportunity to accept or release your submission within two weeks.

Article Proposals

If you want to write an article for *Bead&Button*, begin by sending us a proposal. Summarize your project, your knowledge of it, and the focus of your article in two or three paragraphs. Include an outline or a descriptive list of the topics and points you plan to cover. Please include photos and any supporting swatches, samples. And drawings you have or ideas about what you think should be illustrated. At this stage none of the art you submit needs to be publishable. We'll review your proposal and do our best to respond within eight weeks. Whenever sending us your goods, be sure to insure them

Manuscripts

When we ask you to proceed to a finished manuscript, we'll negotiate a deadline for the first draft of the text and supporting materials. For reference, please include all photos and drawings that you think the article requires (or sample of the work at the appropriate step for each photo), captioned and keyed to the text. The more good-quality visual information you can provide, especially photos of work in process that gives step-be-step information about how to make the item or shows what the tricky parts of the process are, the better the magazine article we can produce together.

We are most comfortable working with original color slides or transparencies—preferably 35mm—but sharply focused prints and negatives are fine. We usually arrange to reshoot step-by-step photos and finished work, but be sure to include photo and model credits and the photographer's and model's permission for us to use the photos. We will almost always redraw drawings; those you submit should be labeled so that all the information is clear.

If appropriate, include sources of supply with current addresses and phone numbers and an annotated Further reading list. We need your social security number for payment purposes, so please include it with your manuscript submission.

We'll evaluate your article and get back to you as soon as possible—our goal is within six weeks. We may accept the article immediately and tentatively schedule it for a particular issue (usually six months to a year hence); we may accept it but not yet schedule it (in this case the wait for publication might be up to two years); we may ask you to revise or rewrite before deciding, or we may reject the article. Because each issue of the magazine is a careful blend of techniques, projects, and information, our editorial scheduling must remain flexible. Acceptance of your article is not a promise to publish it but a good-faith acknowledgment of our intention to do so.

When your article has been scheduled for publication, an editor will be assigned to work with you throughout its production. This editor is likely to ask for revisions or clarification. She/he may ask for additional photography or for the loan of your item(s) so that we can rephotograph them. An illustrator will also be assigned to develop the final art for your article. In most cases, you will see an edited version of the manuscript before publication so that you can review it for accuracy and answer an outstanding questions.

Payment

Once we accept your article and have all the necessary materials, we'll send you copyright-agreement forms to sign. We pay for the article upon receipt of the signed contract. We'll also send you complimentary copies of the issue in which your article appears, and you'll have the right to buy up to 50 additional copies at half price while the issue is current. You must notify us before we go to press, however, if you want to buy more than 20 copies of the issue.

We'll reimburse you for out-of-pocket photo expenses that we request (film and processing only). All requests for reimbursement must be cleared with us in advance. We can only reimburse for expenses that are verified with dated receipts.

Contributing to Departments

To contribute to Tips & Techniques (hints, advice, sources for hard-to-find materials, techniques), you don't need to send a proposal. Just send the complete tip together with any necessary rough sketches or photos. For Patterns send a color diagram of your design. We'll pay $20 for each tip and $40 for each pattern upon receipt of your signed contract.

News & Reviews may be opinion or reportage (usually less than 400 words and one or two photos) on current or upcoming books, videos, or new products. A sample of the product must accompany the request for review samples will not be returned. Not all items submitted for review will appear in the magazine.

Anything Goes relates hilarious or amusing experiences with beads, buttons, or accessories or is a short article out of our normal format. Origins explains little-known facts, history, or superstitions about beads, buttons, or body or garment adornments. Your Work (unpaid) presents photos of readers' best work along with a short paragraph about it. Please address your proposals to the appropriate department.

We'd be delighted to discuss your article ideas with you or answer your questions.

Categories: Crafts/Hobbies

CONTACT: Editorial Submissions
Material: All
PO Box 1612
Waukesha, WI 53187-1612
Phone: 262-796-8776
E-mail: web@beadandbutton.com
Website: www.beadandbutton.com

Beadwork

Beadwork is a bi-monthly magazine devoted to every kind of bead stitching and bead making. Always providing clear-cut instruction for beaders of all skill levels, we also inspire readers to find their own creative voice. Articles focus on the latest innovations in the craft, including seed bead stitching, wireworking, lampwork, polymer clay, bead knitting, bead crochet, and beaded embroidery.

Beadwork welcomes fresh ideas to share with our readers, and we appreciate new approaches to standard topics. Our articles fall into two catagories:

Project instructions provide the basics for beginners, but challenge the advanced beadworker with new beadworking ideas. All are beautifully illustrated and provide clear step-by-step instructions.

Feature articles broaden our readers' perspective of their craft. This includes interviews of beadworking pros, exhibit and book reviews, historical surveys, and helpful tips.

Written proposals to *Beadwork* should display in-depth knowledge of the subject matter based on experience and research. Though the material is often technical, the tone of articles should be informal and accessible. If you are not already familiar with the content, style, and tone of the magazine, we suggest you read our previous issues.

Submissions

Send a detailed proposal or a completed manuscript along with supporting slides, sketches, and a brief biography. We do not accept articles that have been published, and discourage simultaneous submissions. If any portion of your submission has been published previously, please let us know when and by whom.

Manuscripts range from two to ten typed pages (from 500 to 2,500 words). Please submit your article on a 3 1/2" X 5" disk and include a hard copy of the article. Please save your files in Word for Windows 98, if possible. If not, our preference is Word 2.0, MS DOS-based Word, DOS-based WordPerfect, text only (*.txt), or a flat ASCII file. Although we can have MacIntosh disks read by our production department and emailed to us as flat ASCII files, we prefer DOS formats. Double-space your manuscript on 8 1/2 x 11 white bond paper with at least 1-inch margins. Place your name, address, and telephone number in the upper right-hand corner of each page. Photocopies and computer printouts should be legible. If you submit your article via fax or email, please follow your electronic submission with a hard copy and disk in the mail.

We will need to have your finished pieces at Interweave Press for at least eight to ten weeks for photography, illustration, and technical editing. If you need them returned by a specific date, please let us know.

Drawings and diagrams should be done in black ink on white paper ready for redrawing by a staff artist. All slides, artwork, and other materials will be returned.

Keep a copy of everything. Enclose a self-addressed envelope with sufficient return postage for return of your materials. Receipt of your submission will be promptly acknowledged, but please be patient while we decide whether to use it.

Deadlines and Payment

Submissions are accepted at any time and are scheduled as space permits. Projects are due about 4 1/2 months before publication date (ie. 8/16/00 project due date for Jan/Feb 2001 issue). About 1 month before the publication date, we will send a contract for you to sign which states that we are purchasing first North American serial rights for publication in *Beadwork* and subsequent nonexclusive rights for use in other Interweave Press publications and promotions. As author, you retain the publication rights for the original materials.

We reserve the right to edit your material as necessary to fit the style, format, or other requirements of *Beadwork*. A copy of the edited manuscript will be submitted to you for approval before publication.

Payment for *project instructions* is $50 per page. Payment for *feature articles* is 12.5 cents per published word. Payment is made upon publication unless other arrangements are made.

Categories: Nonfiction—Arts—Crafts/Hobbies—Hobbies

CONTACT: Submissions Editor
Material: Written and visual submissions
Interweave Press, Inc.
201 East Fourth St.
Loveland CO 80537
Phone: 970-669-7672 x 625
Fax: 970-669-6117
E-mail: beadwork@interweave.com
Website: www.interweave.com/bead

Remember: Editors change jobs and publishers change addresses. It is wise to invest in a phone call for the current information before submitting.

The Bear Deluxe Magazine

Thank you for your interest in *The Bear Deluxe* Magazine. Published quarterly, the magazine celebrates the big tent theory of literary arts, including investigative reporting, fiction, essay, poetry, news, creative opinion, reviews and interviews in each issue. Unsolicited submissions and query letters are encouraged. *The Bear Deluxe* has included nationally published authors as well as emerging and unpublished writers. As with any publication, writers are encouraged to review a sample copy for a clearer understanding of the magazine's editorial approach.

Established in 1993, *The Bear Deluxe* was recognized by *Utne Reader* as one of the country's best new titles and has received acclaim from media sources around the country. *The Bear Deluxe* is published by Orlo, a nonprofit organization exploring environmental issues through the creative arts. In 1998, *The Bear Deluxe* changed its name from *The Bear Essential.*

Nineteen thousand copies of each issue are distributed free of charge across the Western United States and beyond. Stories, however, are not limited to a regional focus.

While informative, the magazine has the additional goal of engaging new audiences. Cross-town appeal is achieved by including the full spectrum of literary forms and divergent styles, including satire and parody, while complementing the writing with original artwork and graphic design. Finally, the magazine draws connections to other related social concerns such as the media, social justice and human rights.

Nonfiction in General

Unsolicited nonfiction manuscripts are considered, but it is less common that they find a home in *The Bear Deluxe*. More often, nonfiction writers approach editors with a story idea or are asked to write on ideas generated by the magazine. Specific ideas should be presented in a query letter format and accompanied by writing samples and suggestions for artwork. Given its limited travel budget, the magazine is working to develop relationships with free-lance workers who can take assignments and offer story ideas from their home areas.

Features

Two to five independent features are included in each issue. Features are typically more timely, have an overarching perspective or appeal and require strong elements of reporting. Word range: 750-4000 words.

Departments

Portrait of an Artist: Profile of artist or arts group with unique environmental focus. 750-1500 words. Reviews: New titles, lost classics, films, videos, products, theater, fast food and pop corn. Almost anything goes. 100-1000 words. Sound Bites: Short, sometimes quirky news pieces. 100-500 words. New Dept.: Front of the Book: Unique mix of news shorts, lists, found writing, cartoons, opinion, others. 100-750 words.

Fiction/Essay/Poetry/Other

The Bear Deluxe maintains an open submission policy for fiction, essay, poetry and other forms. The Creative Review Group considers submissions on an ongoing basis. The magazine is moving away from using the term "environmental writing." Quality writing which furthers the magazine's goal of engaging new and divergent readers will garner the most attention. News essays, on occasion, are assigned out if they have a strong element of reporting.

The magazine welcomes submissions and appreciates writers who see it as appropriate for their work. Generally, authors are informed on their submissions 3-6 months after they are received. Manuscripts are returned only if accompanied by appropriate SASE. Fiction: 1-3 fiction pieces published per issue. 750-4000 words. Essays: Zero to two essays per issue. 750-3000 words. Poetry: 5-10 poems published per issue. Please submit only 3-5 poems.

Theme Section

One issue each year will focus on a specific theme. Theme stories tend to be developed in close consultation with the editorial staff. Contact the magazine for upcoming themes.

Copyright & Compensation

The Bear Deluxe pays for first time publishing rights only. After publication, all rights revert to the authors. *The Bear Deluxe* compensates its writers with five cents per published word ($10 per poem), contributor copies and a one-year subscription. The magazine may cover incidental costs (including phone and postage) upon prior agreement.

Deadlines

The magazine has moved away from strict deadlines and is considering submissions and story ideas on an ongoing basis. Writers are encouraged to join our e-mail list-serve for occasional updates on our publishing schedule.

E-mail Submissions

E-mail submissions are accepted but not roundly encouraged. Please send stories as e-mail text, not as attached documents. The magazine can only respond to those e-mail submissions chosen for publication.

Submission Formats

Submit double-spaced text on clean hard copy. Do not send discs. Writers are encouraged to suggest headlines, subheads and pull-quotes, though final decisions in these areas are made by the editorial staff. Include a 20-word biographical statement. Send submissions to appropriate editor: i.e. "poetry editor," "fiction editor," or "nonfiction editor." Do not send material to the street address.

Contact the editorial staff with further questions.

Categories: Fiction—Arts—Book Reviews—Interview—Literature—Poetry

CONTACT: Tom Webb, Editor
Material: Nonfiction
CONTACT: Poetry Editor
Material: Poetry
CONTACT: Fiction Editor
Material: Fiction
c/o Orlo
PO Box 10342
Portland OR 97296
Phone: 503-242-1047
Fax: 503-243-264
E-mail: bear@orlo.org
Website: www.orlo.org

The Beauty Spot
News You Can Use

Description: Quarterly publication of topics of interest to employees of Fortune 500 companies. Employees receive this publication at work.

(From permission form: "Very infrequently do we use freelance material. We do use material from press releases.")

No formal guidelines available

Categories: Nonfiction—Arts—Automobiles—Book Reviews—Business—Careers—Cartoons—Computers—Consumer—Cooking—Culture—Diet/Nutrition—Drama—Directories—Entertainment—Fashion—Feminism—Food/Drink—General Interest—Health—Internet—Interview—Lifestyle—Literature—Men's Issues—Money and Finances—Poetry—Public Speaking—Real Estate—Relationships—Society—Theater—Travel—Women's Issues

CONTACT: C.G. Bradford, Editor in Chief
Material: All
24 Fifth Ave., 6th Floor
New York, NY 10011
Phone: 212-614-9683

Remember: Editors change jobs and publishers change addresses. It is wise to invest in a phone call for the current information before submitting.

Beef Times

Please refer to *Farm Times*.

Bellevue Literary Review

Bellevue Hospital, the oldest public hospital in the United States, has been witness to nearly 270 years of human drama. In this tradition we have created the *Bellevue Literary Review*, a forum for illuminating humanity and human experience. *BLR* is published by the Department of Medicine at New York University. We invite submissions of previously unpublished works of fiction, nonfiction, and poetry that touch upon relationships to the human body, illness, health and healing. We encourage creative interpretation of these themes.

Submission Guidelines:

1. Prose should be limited to 5000 words. Please submit only one manuscript at a time. Manuscripts should be double-spaced with full author information (including address, phone number, email address) on the first page. Please specify word count, and indicate fiction or nonfiction.

2. Submit up to 3 poems at one time. Please do not submit poetry along with prose.

3. We read submissions year-round, but all of our reviewers and editors are volunteers. We strive to provide several readers for each manuscript in order to give it maximum exposure, but this takes time. We respectfully ask for your patience and forbearance. If you have not heard from us within six months, feel free to inquire about your manuscript.

4. *BLR* acquires first-time North American rights. After publication, all rights revert to the author and may be reprinted as long as appropriate acknowledgement to *BLR* is made.

5. Someday soon we hope to pay lavish stipends, but for now we will thank you with two copies of the issue in which your work appears, an additional 1-year subscription to the *BLR*, as well as a gift subscription for a lucky friend. You will also be eligible for an author discount when you purchase extra copies.

6. We now accept online submissions. To submit your manuscript electronically, please visit our website: www.BLReview.org

7. We continue to accept paper manuscripts. Please include SASE with sufficient postage for reply.

Categories: Fiction—Nonfiction—Poetry

CONTACT: Editor
Material: All
NYU School of Medicine
Dept. of Medicine, 550 First Ave., OBV-A612
New York, NY 10016
E-mail: info@BLReview.org
Website: www.BLReview.org

Bellingham Review

Simultaneous submissions are considered, as long as the *Bellingham Review* is notified immediately if the work is accepted elsewhere. All submissions must be previously unpublished in North America.

General Submission Guidelines

The *Bellingham Review* is a nonprofit literary arts magazine affiliated with Western Washington University. The magazine is bi-annual, published spring and fall. Sample copies are available for $7.00 each.

Our general submission period is from December 1st through March 15th; although, contest submission dates may vary. Manuscripts arriving between February 2nd and September 30th will be returned unread. The editors welcome submissions of poems, stories, and essays. There are no limitations on form or subject matter. Prose must be under 9,000 words. The editors prefer poetry submissions of 3-5 poems. Please indicate the approximate word count on prose pieces. We do not currently accept electronic mail submissions.

All submissions should be accompanied by a self-addressed stamped envelope (SASE). Submissions from other countries should be accompanied by a sufficient number of international postal reply coupons.

Reporting time normally varies from one to six months. We pay upon publication as funds permit.

Categories: Fiction—Nonfiction—Experimental Fiction—Poetry

CONTACT: Fiction Editor
Material: Fiction
CONTACT: Nonfiction Editor
Material: Nonfiction
CONTACT: Poetry Editor
Material: Poetry
MS—9053
Western Washington University
Bellingham WA 98225
Phone: 360-650-3242
Website: www.ac.wwu.edu/~bhreview

Bellowing Ark

We began publishing *Bellowing Ark* in 1984 because no market existed for the kind of literature that we wanted to read and wanted to see published; we set out to create such a market, and, by example, encourage others to do the same. We believe that there is more to art than the desire to shock and the glib and facile expression of nihilism and despair. We are also convinced that artists, particularly literary, have a responsibility to their audience and are required to present the world as meaningful, for, if the world has no meaning, how can life? The material we publish is the best expression of that responsibility that we can command.

We feel *Bellowing Ark* stands solidly in the Romantic tradition which passes from Blake and Wordsworth through the American Transcendentalists to Whitman, Frost, Roethke and Nelson Bentley then on to current writers Natalie Reciputi, Marshall Pipkin, L.L. Ollivier, Muriel Karr, Teresa Noelle Roberts and others. While we are in the Romantic tradition, we also take pride in being one of the most eclectic magazines ever published. There are essentially no restrictions on genre, length, or style.

We have published plays, serialized novels, short stories, poems, long-poems, epic poems (Nelson Bentley's Tracking the Transcendental Moose ran to 20,000 lines, published in 14 books, serialized sequentially), essays, memoirs, drawings, photographs, all forms of self expression, in fact, that we consider to meet our single, and sufficient criterion: everything that we publish demonstrates, to our satisfaction, that life is both meaningful and worth living. We are biased toward the narrative, both in poetry and fiction; that is, stories should have a plot, characterization, a beginning, a middle, and an end.

We have not, in our years of publication, ever published a fiction, nor anything pointlessly minimalist or surrealist—it seems to us that practitioners of those elegantly academic artforms have deliberately cut themselves off from an audience. We are interested in audience, since we believe art must be shared to be art.

We do ask that material submitted to *Bellowing Ark* be carefully presented. Please double-space prose, single space poetry, one poem

per page. If you use a dot-matrix printer please make sure the print is dark enough to be legible: we read hundreds of submissions every month and eyestrain is always a danger. And, always submit a stamped, self-addressed envelope with every submission. Note: we do not consider simultaneous submissions.

Payment is in copies of the issue containing the artist's work, that is, on publication. Sample copies, and it never hurts to read a magazine to see if your work fits, are $3.00, postpaid from the address below.

Thank you for your interest in *Bellowing Ark*; we do hope to hear from you again.

Robert R. Ward, Editor
Categories: Fiction—Literature—Poetry

CONTACT: Submissions Editor
Material: All
PO Box 55564
Seattle WA 98155
Phone: 206-440-0791

Beloit Poetry Journal

Beloit Poetry Journal is a quarterly in continuous publication since 1950. We have been the first or early publisher of such poets as Galway Kinnell, Anne Sexton, Sharon Olds, Maxine Kumin, W.S. Merwin, James Dickey, Philip Larkin, Charles Bukowski, Adrienne Rich, Philip Levine, and more recently Sherman Alexie, Victor Lodato, and Mary Leader.

We seek only unpublished poems or translations of poems (which we publish en face) not already available in English. The reviews are by our editors. The magazine is copyrighted, with rights reverting to the poet on publication. Payment is in copies.

We receive as many as twenty envelopes of poetry a day and return most within days of their arrival. The rest we circulate among the editors and continue to winnow. At quarterly meetings of the editorial board we read the surviving poems aloud and put together an issue of what we consider the best work. The Chad Walsh Poetry Award ($3000 in 2003) goes to the author of the poem or group of poems that the editors judge to be the strongest published during the previous year.

We prefer no particular forms or lengths or subjects. We are always watching for new poets, fresh insights, quickened language. Our occasional chapbooks are special collections of categories of poems we want to bring to our readers' attention, for example, Poets Under Twenty-Five.

How to Submit Poems-to the BPJ or Most Literary Magazines

1. Be familiar with any publication before you submit. Half of the poems we get are from poets who have obviously never seen an issue. A year's subscription to the BPJ is $18. A sample copy is only $5. Hundreds of libraries subscribe.

2. Type no more than one poem on a page, single-spaced. Put your name and address on every sheet.

3. Limit your submission to what will go for one first-class stamp-about four pages-unless it's a long poem or a poem sequence.

4. Always enclose an SASE (self-addressed stamped envelope). From overseas send an International Reply Coupon for each half-ounce (from Canada, U.S. or Canadian coins are acceptable), or include your email address and we'll respond by email. Tell us if you don't want your manuscript returned.

5. Keep copies of your work in case the originals disappear.

6. No cover note is necessary, unless you have something to say to us-but many other editors do like them. We use no contributors' notes. Our emphasis is on the poem.

7. Keep a record of when and where you mail every poem. Never send a poem to two places at once, unless they explicitly invite simultaneous submissions. We do not. If you have no reply after four months, send a query, including a new SASE. If after a month you still hear nothing, send a card announcing that you are withdrawing the poems.

8. Don't expect any comment on your work. Editors read as a labor of love, in spare moments, and if they fall behind they may have to read several hundred poems in a day.

9. Don't be discouraged by rejections. Just keep writing and mailing-and reading what is being published.

10. We do not accept electronic submissions.

For further information, consult our website: www.bpj.org.

Categories: Book Reviews—General Interest—Literature—Poetry

CONTACT: John Rosenwald and Lee Sharkey, Editors
Material: All
PO Box 151
Farmington, ME 04938
Phone: (207)778-0020
E-mail (for information only): sharkey@maine.edu
Website: www.bpj.org

Bend of the River Magazine

We are always looking for interesting articles about past events that have happened in Northwestern Ohio. Query or send 1500 word typewritten double-spaced hard copy with SASE.

It is our pleasure to include pictures of a nostalgic nature along with articles. We lean heavily on local history, but feature a nostalgic slant. We want positive, up-beat articles on "famous people" and or events that have their birth in the State of Ohio.

We buy one-time rights, pay accordingly one month after publication. And encourage first time writers and/or never published enthusiasts.

Thanks for your interest. We enjoy "delighting" our audience with wonderful, homespun stories of the early Black Swamp, life in Pioneer America, World War II and Great Depression subjects, along with the Prohibition Era.

Categories: Nonfiction—History—Regional

CONTACT: Submissions Editor
Material: All
PO Box 859
Maumee OH 43537
Phone: 419-893-0022

Benefit & Compensation Digest
(Formerly Employee Benefit Digest and Employee Benefit Journal)

The International Foundation Publications Department is looking for authors to write articles on the newest and most relevant employee benefits and compensation topics. We are looking for U.S. and Canadian articles in the areas of health care, pensions, retirement, and general benefits and compensation topics. If you would like to write an article for our publications, please see the following guidelines and suggested topics.

GENERAL INFORMATION

The guidelines are intended to make the writing process easier and more enjoyable for you. Please do not hesitate to call the Foundation editorial staff at any time. We re looking forward to working with you.

Our publications include articles on subjects directly or indirectly related to the employee benefits, compensation and related fields. Articles covering new or developing topics are particularly appropriate. We welcome queries or outlines of proposed articles. The editors will respond promptly.

We assume all material submitted is the original work of the listed authors and has not been accepted for publication elsewhere. In the event of any potential conflict, it is the author s responsibility to notify the editor prior to publication. We will ask you to sign a copyright transfer agreement.

ARTICLE LENGTH AND CONTENT

The recommended length for a printed article is 2,000-3,200 words.

In addition, we are accepting longer, in-depth articles of more than 3,200 words. We will post these longer articles on our Web site in a special online showcase called Web Exclusive. The full text of new articles, plus a permanent online archive of past articles, will be available to all on the Foundation Web site at www.ifebp.org, starting in Spetember. Follow the article submission guidelines included in this article.

You will be notified whether your article has been accepted within approximately two weeks.

Articles should be educational in nature. Pieces promoting a specific product or company will not be accepted.

WRITING THE ARTICLE

Organize your article carefully. Avoid overly specialized jargon.

HOW TO SUBMIT

Send your article via e-mail to sheilan@ifebp.org. or judys@ifebp.org.

CONTENT

Send us your complete manuscript in its final version, including any tables, graphs/charts, etc. at the same time.

REFERENCES

It is the author s responsibility to obtain any necessary permission for the use of lengthy quotations or other material (charts, surveys, etc.) originally prepared by others.

HEADINGS

Provide headings and subheadings that are succinct and that include words useful for information retrieval.

GRAPHS AND TABLES

If you use tables or graphs/charts, construct them so they are completely understandable on their own.

Tables and figures should be referenced correctly in the text.

If you are using:

Simple text tables: Tabular material can simply be part of your text document.

Pie charts/bar charts: Please DO NOT EMBED them into your Word documents. You may reference the placement, i.e., **Place table 3 here** but please do not embed any kind of image in Word. Please send charts and graphs as a separate file.

Best option: Separate high-resolution tif, eps or jpg files (600 dpi for line art or 300 ppi for grayscale or color), e.g., created in Illustrator or Photoshop.

Next best: Original Excel or PowerPoint documents. Do not make any conversions or embed them in Word; please send the original .xl or .ppt files.

Almost never usable: Charts taken from the Web, anything at 72 dpi or 96 dpi, Word charts.

LEGAL CASE CITATIONS

Check legal citations for accuracy. They will be included in the text as they are submitted.

COPYRIGHTED MATERIAL AND ACKNOWLEDGMENTS

If you use copyrighted materials from another publication, secure permission for reprint. Submit this with your manuscript, and inform the editor if a cost is associated with reprint approval.

AUTHOR NOTE

Write a brief biographical note, including present position title, responsibilities and address. Include a photo of the author at a resolution of 300 dpi or 600 dpi, whether scanned from hard copy or shot with a digital camera.

AUTHOR COPIES AND REPRINTS

Authors will receive ten copies of the issue containing their material. Reprints are available for a nominal charge.

Categories: Nonfiction—Employee Benefits

CONTACT: Sheila Nero, Editor, Publications Department
(sheilan@ifebp.org)
Material: All
CONTACT: Judith A. Sankey, CEBS, Editor, Publications
Department, (judys@ifebp.org);
Material: All
International Foundation of Employee Benefit Plans
18700 W. Bluemound Rd.
PO Box 69
Brookfield, WI 53008-0069
Phone: 262-786-6710 (ext. 8242 for Sheila; ext. 8244 for Judith)
Website: www.ifebp.org

Best of Times
Grandparents Magazine

Please refer to Metro Parent/Metro Baby.

Better Homes and Gardens

Only about ten percent of our editorial material comes from freelance writers, artists, and photographers; the rest is produced by staff.

We read all freelance articles submitted, but much prefer to see a letter of query than a finished manuscript. The query should be directed to the department where the story line is the strongest. See appropriate editor and department below.

A freelancer's best chance lies in the areas of travel, health, parenting and education. We do not deal with political subjects or with areas not connected with the home, community, and family. We use no poetry, beauty, or fiction. The best way to find out what we do use, and to get some idea of our style, is to study several of our most recent issues.

We buy all rights and pay on acceptance. Rates are based on our estimate of the length, quality, and importance of the published article.

Categories: Nonfiction—Automobiles—Computers—Cooking—Environment—Family—Gardening—Health—Home—Money & Finances—Parenting—Physical Fitness—Software—Travel—Decorating—Remodeling

CONTACT: Sarah Egge
Material: Home Design
CONTACT: Nancy Hopkins
Material: Food and Nutrition
CONTACT: Becky Mollenkamp
Material: Travel
CONTACT: Mark Kane
Material: Garden
CONTACT: Lamont Olson
Material: Money Management, Automotive
CONTACT: Lora O'neil
Material: Environment
CONTACT: Steve Mumford
Material: Environment
CONTACT: Martha Miller
Material: Health/Fitness, Cartoons
CONTACT: Richard Sowienski
Material: Education and Parenting, BH&G Kids
CONTACT: Stephen George
Material: Health/Fitness and Cartoons
CONTACT: Stephen George
Material: Education and Parenting, BH&G

1716 Locust St.
Des Moines IA 50309-3023
Phone: 515-284-3000
Website: www.bhg.com

Bible Advocate
Now What?

Identity

The Bible Advocate is one of the oldest religious magazines in America, founded in 1863. Now What? (formerly Bible Advocate Online) has been on the Internet since late 1996 (www.cog7.org/BA/NowWhat/). Both are published by the Bible Advocate Press, the publication agency of the General Conference of the Church of God (Seventh Day). Now What? is monthly; the print version is published ten times a year.

Readership

Readers of the print version have a wide range of denominational and religious backgrounds. About half of them are not members of the Church of God (Seventh Day).

Editorial focus

The Bible Advocate is geared to help Christians understand and obey God's Word, with articles on Bible doctrine, current social and religious issues, Christian living, Bible topics, textual or biblical book studies, prophecy, and personal experience. We also print fillers (sidebars), opinion pieces, and poetry (traditional, free, and blank verse).

Now What? addresses more of the "felt needs" of people (grief, depression, sickness, etc.). Each issue centers around a personal experience, with articles related to the topic. Material for this e-zine is more inclusive of non-Christians. Personal experience stories show a person's struggle that either led him to faith in Christ or deepened his walk with God. No opinion pieces or poetry.

Payment

We pay an honorarium, on publication, of $25 per printed magazine page, up to $55, for print and electronic rights. Online articles run $25-$55, depending on published length. For poetry and fillers, we pay $20. However, for opinion pieces, we only pay in copies of the magazine.

Rights

We buy first, electronic, and one-time rights. We also accept reprints and simultaneous submissions.

Format

Articles should be double-spaced on white paper, one side only, with a one-inch margin on each side. They can also be copied into the e-mail message box. No attachments, please.

Writers should include their name, address, telephone number, and Social Security number in the upper left-hand corner of the first page. The word count and indication of rights offered should appear in the upper right-hand corner of the first page.

Submissions

Please include an SASE or SASC with all hard copy submissions. Unsolicited manuscripts will not be returned unless accompanied by an SASE or SASC. Computer submissions on disk are welcomed if the material is compatible with our program. *The Bible Advocate* is produced in Word 2001 on Macintosh computers. Word programs that are 1998 and newer are compatible with ours.

Writers may also submit via e-mail at bibleadvocate@cog7.org. No fax or handwritten submissions, please.

Documentation

When stating important facts likely to be questioned, please list your sources so we can verify if necessary. When preparing a manuscript, writers should reference all Scripture quotations and enclose them in parentheses. Specify the main translation used, and note specifically where any other translation is used.

Length
• Feature articles 1000-1500 words
• Opinion pieces 600-650 words

• Fillers 100-400 words
• Poetry 5-20 lines
Online:
• Feature articles, 1,000-1500 words personal experience
Contact
Address manuscripts to the person listed below. Or send via e-mail to bibleadvocate@cog7.org. Allow 4-8 weeks for a response.
Tips
Articles must be in keeping with the doctrinal understanding of the Church of God (Seventh Day). Therefore, the writer should become familiar with what the Church generally accepts as truth as set forth in its doctrinal beliefs.

We reserve the right to edit manuscripts to fit our space requirements, doctrinal stands, and Church terminology. Significant changes are referred to writers for approval.

Categories: Nonfiction—Christian Interests—Culture—Family—Inspirational—Lifestyle—Marriage—Parenting—Relationships—Religion—Society—Spiritual

CONTACT: Sherri Langton, Associate Editor, Bible Advocate
Material: All
PO Box 33677
Denver, CO 80233
E-mail: bibleadvocate@cog7.org

Bibliophilos
A Journal of History, Literature, and the Liberal Arts

Audience: Literate persons, academically and scholastically-oriented. Topics range throughout the liberal arts, including fiction and non-fiction, literature and criticism, history, art, music, theology, philosophy, natural history, educational theory, contemporary issues and politics, sociology, economics. A refereed journal, with articles published in English, French, German, Romanian. Circulates throughout the United States, Canada, Mexico, United Kingdom, France, elsewhere. *Bibliophilos* was nominated for the Writer's Digest listing as one of the best 100 small press magazines in the country for the year 2000.

Bi-monthly magazine format: averages 72 pages per issue. Price $5.00 per issue, $18.00 per year, $35.00 for two years. Library rate available. Query first, unsolicited manuscripts not considered. MSS must be accompanied by large (#10) SASE (sufficient postage please–if it costs $1.03 to send the material to us, then it can't be returned with an SASE bearing only $.37.) Along with query or manuscript send check or money order for $5.00 handling fee, which also pays for sample issue along with our answer, and specifications. Initial answer in two weeks, final decision normally within thirty days. Payment varies, often including complimentary subscription, and money in some instances. Photocopied or simultaneous submissions ok, but we expect notification immediately if your material is accepted elsewhere. Acquires First North American Serial rights.

Non-fiction: Should be scholarly, with clarity of writing and well-defined and documented thesis. Footnotes are to be Turabian/Chicago Manual of Style only, and may be typed ordinally on the final page of the MS for convenience, but not in the text. Remember that paraphrased material must also be footnoted. The word "quote," moreover, is a verb, and not a noun. Lively and variegated prose is preferable to turgid thesis language. Literate and informative essays in literature, comparative studies, and critical review essays rather than the superficial standard "book review," are welcome. Length: 1500-3000 words for feature articles, 750-1250 words for reviews.

Fiction: Short stories, fantasy, satire, "genre pieces," mainstream, horror, humorous, historical, ethnic, regional and local color, suspense. Length 1500-3000 words, typed, double-spaced. We use 25-30 per year. Avoid obscenities and scatological language; curse words and vulgarisms should be minimized and serve a specific function. We do not use gay or lesbian themes, nor will we use historically anachronistic terminology for the sake of political correctness.

Poetry: we publish an annual poetry issue, containing the winners of an annual poetry contest. Send for a sample issue.

Photographs: we use a limited number, B & W submitted with MSS, glossies only; supply captions. Original art work and cartoons also welcome.

Reviews of books, art or photographic exhibitions, films: We assign almost all book reviews specifically, so do not submit unsolicited book reviews, please. We publish an annual book review number, but reviews are in every issue as well, averaging about 30+ per year. 750-1250 words. Consult the guidelines for book reviewers published in *Bibliophilos* Book Reviews '99, Vol. II, No. 3, pp. 188-191.

Notes & Notices section: for appropriate notices, plaudits, upcoming features announcements, and extravagant praise from readers. See sample issue. The majority of this is devoted to information about the contributors in that number, so if your material is accepted, we need 25-30 words about yourself. Best to send a brief biographical sketch with your original material.

Submissions are to be typed, double-spaced, on 8½" by 11" paper, with approximately 250 words per page, paper-clipped, not stapled, with pages numbered. Please do not clutter your query letters or MSS with e-mail addresses, fax numbers, and other electronic detritus, and please do not suggest that we use them to get in touch with you, because we will not. Please do not suggest that we telephone you, or that you will call us; we operate through the postal service only, such as it is.

MSS should be free as possible of jargon, cant, or short-cut language. The word is not "rehab," but rehabilitation, it is political science and not "poli sci," it is not "ad" but advertisement, not TV but television. Kindly remember that "quote" is a VERB, not a noun, and "access" is a NOUN, not a verb. If your material contains the word "hopefully" used as an expletive or adverbially, don't bother sending it at all. Grammar and punctuation and typographical errors should be fixed before sending your material. We want to invest our time considering its merit and literary value, not correcting apostrophes and possessives.

Kindly consult our listings in *The Writer's Market, the Poet's Market, the Novel & Short Story Writer's Market, The Writer magazine, the Small Press Review*, and the like to inform yourself of our tone and philosophy, and for further elaboration of some of the above items.

Recap for those publishing for the first time, or publishing with *Bibliophilos* for the first time:
1. *Query first*, before you send anything.
2. Along with your query (and again with any submitted material) send a large, self-addressed stamped envelope, with sufficient postage, and $5.00 for a sample issue, specifications, and answer.
3. *Nota Bene*. Once you have had your material accepted for publication, and an agreement has been concluded between you and the editor/staff, then embrace the words of Anthony Trollope that "some time must elapse before your story actually appears in print." Do not send us continual inquiries about "when will my stuff be published?" and thus force us to engage in needless extra correspondence, the normal volume of which is practically overwhelming as it is. The more you pester an editor, the farther down in the pile your story goes. We have a large backlog, we receive 20 submissions per week, at least, and answer each one personally, and with six issues annually it takes time to use up so much material. If you think your piece will appear two weeks after acceptance, you had better send it elsewhere.
4. *Equally important*: once your story has been accepted and/or published, this does not mean that you immediately send us another, or empty out your file cabinet and assume that you now have an automatic forum for everything you write. Query for each individual submission and expect each one to be judged on its own merits. But above all wait until submission #1 has been published before you start flooding us with Nos. 2, 3, and 4.

Categories: Fiction—Nonfiction—Adventure—Animals—Antiques—Architecture—Arts—Biography—Book Reviews—Cartoons—Civil War—Collectibles—College—Conservation—Culture—Drama—Economics—Education—Environment—Film/Video—Folklore—Food/Drink—General Interest—Government—History—Interview—Language—Law—Lifestyle—Military—Music—Poetry—Politics—Psychology—Regional—Satire—Short Stories—Theatre—Trade: Publishing—Travel—Western—Writing

CONTACT: Gerald J. Bobango, Editor
Material: All
The Bibliophile Publishing Co
200 Security Building
Fairmont WV 26554
Phone: 304-366-8107

Bike

Thank you for your interest in writing for *Bike* magazine. *Bike* delivers the excitement and passion of the sport better than the other mountain bike magazines do. We are vivid, unbiased, irreverent, probing, fun, humorous, funky, quirky, smart, good. And we're always on the lookout for new talent.

Bike has a section devoted to news and odds and ends. It has product reviews. It has travel stories that are *true* stories. It has unparalleled photography. It has regional columns. It has personality profiles, long and short ones. It has debates.

What *Bike* needs from you, then, are lots of story ideas. They can be about anything so long as there's a connection, however remote, to mountain biking. For instance, a Peace Corps worker describes what it was like peddling from village to village in Senegal. A whole essay devoted solely to the feeling of mud. Why bike messengers give us all a bad name. Odd things you've overheard. Whatever. Have fun, bust out, be a spin doctor, cut your teeth, tell us about things you'd tell a friend, write stories you've always wanted to write. Do anything. The only rule is that there are no rules.

We're vigorous editors, but we aren't saboteurs. You'll get great layouts with spectacular photography; in other words, your stuff will look good in *Bike*. As for buyouts, our basic rate is 50 cents per word. It's not a lot, but if you wanted riches you'd be an investment banker instead of some overgrown child splashing through creeks and whooping to an empty forest.

We'd love to hear what you've got to say, but we prefer that you say it in a certain way—as in a double-spaced, 12-point-font, typed hard copy. Feel free to include additional writing samples, photography (prints or slides) or anything else you think we should know about—within reason, of course. If we like what we see, we'll let you know. If we don't like what we see, we'll let you know too. So either way, we'll get back to you as soon as we're able. Oh, and kick us a SASE so we can return your materials. Thanks.

Categories: Nonfiction—Adventure—Recreation—Sports—Recreation

CONTACT: Sarah Smith
Material: All
33046 Calle Aviador
San Juan Capistrano, CA 92675
Phone: 949-661-5127
Fax: 949-496-7849
E-mail: sarah.smith@primedia.com
Website: www.bikemag.com

Birds & Blooms

There are plenty of opportunities to contribute to every issue of *Birds & Blooms*. Just jot down your personal backyard experiences and send us your photographs to help fill this magazine, which is basically ""written by our readers"". **If you'd like to share a story or photos, here are some guidelines:**

1. Be sure to print your name, address and daytime telephone number (and E-mail address, if you have one) on the first page of each item or manuscript. We receive a lot of mail, so please keep your stories under 800 words.

2. Print your name, city and state or province on the back of each photo lightly with pencil or indelible marker. Address labels work extremely well on the backs of photographs.

3. We do not publish fiction. Instead, we want you to tell us your real-life stories and share some of the tried-and-true tips and ideas that make your backyard a birds or blooms haven.

We can only print a limited amount of the mail we receive. Published stories are edited, and in many cases, only an excerpt of the original letter or manuscript is used.

4. Please enclose a self-addressed stamped envelope (SASE) if you want your materials returned or are requesting a response. Because of our small staff size and large mail volume, we simply cannot respond to most inquiries and letters.

Don't worry, submissions without SASEs are equally considered. We'll let you know if your story is published.

5. If you choose to enclose a SASE with your submission, please be patient. Submissions that do not fit in the magazine may be considered for our *Birds & Blooms* Web site (www.birdsandblooms.com) or for other projects.

6. Mail your submissions to *Birds & Blooms*, 5925 Country Lane, Greendale WI 53129.

7. Send E-mail submissions to editors@birdsandblooms.com. Be sure to include your full mailing address, daytime telephone number and E-mail address.

8. Feel free to E-mail electronic photographs. However, it's important that these photos are saved as ""jpeg"" files and measure at least 3 x 5 inches at 300 dpi (that's dots per inch).

We look forward to ""visiting"" with you through future issues.

Categories: Fiction—Animals—Family—Gardening—Hobbies—Lifestyle—Nature—Outdoors

CONTACT: Jeff Nowak, Managing Editor
Material: Manuscripts and manuscript/photo combination
CONTACT: Trudi Bellin, Photo Coordinator
Material: Photos Only
5400 S. 60th St
Greendale WI 53129
Phone: 414-423-0100
E-mail: editor@birdsandblooms.com
Website: www.birdsandblooms.com

BPR

Birmingham Poetry Review

Subscription Information
Birmingham Poetry Review is published semiannually in the fall and spring. Subscriptions are $4.00 per year. Sample copies are $2.00. Tax-deductible contributions of $10.00 or more are welcomed and entitle patrons to a two-year subscription.

Submission Information
Unsolicited manuscripts of no more than five poems are welcomed but must be accompanied by a stamped, self-addressed envelope for consideration. Deadlines are November 1 and May 1. At the present

time, we do not accept electronic submissions. Reprints are permitted with appropriate acknowledgement. All rights revert upon publication.

From Poet's Market:

Birmingham Poetry Review uses poetry that is, according to editor Robert Collins and associate editor Randy Blythe, of "any style, form, length, or subject. We are biased toward exploring the cutting edge of contemporary poetry. Style is secondary to the energy, the fire, the poem possesses. We don't want poetry with clichéé-bound, worn-out language."

The magazine is composed of 50 pages, 6" x 9" offset print, with a black and white cover, usually a photograph. The press run is 600 for fall and 500 for spring. Currently, we have over 300 subscriptions.

Guidelines for submission are available for a SASE. Pay is two copies and a one-year subscription. Authors should submit 3-5 poems, without cover letters "We are impressed by good poetry, not by publication credits." Be absolutely certain that you enclose sufficient postage on your SASE if you expect us to return your work. Simultaneous submissions are not accepted. Reprints are accepted in a very few cases — translations being the most common. We report on submissions within 1-3 months, and we occasionally comment on rejections. Our editors suggest that beginning writers "Read as much good contemporary poetry, national and international, as you can get your hands on. Then be persistent in finding your own voice."

Categories: Poetry

CONTACT: Robert Collins, Editor
Material: Any
CONTACT: Randy Blythe, Editor
Material: Any
English Department
University of Alabama - Birmingham
HB 205
1530 3RD AVE S
Birmingham AL 35294-1260
Phone: 202-934-4250
Fax: 205-975-8125
Website: www.uab.edu/english/bpr

The Birthkit

Please refer to *Midwifery Today*.

BLACK BELT.
COMMUNICATIONS INC.

Black Belt

Thank you for your interest in writing for *Black Belt*, the oldest martial arts publications in the United States. The magazine's subjects include martial arts styles and techniques, training methods, historical pieces, health and fitness articles, and interviews with prominent martial artists.

Before mailing a completed manuscript to *Black Belt*, we advise you to send a query letter. It will save your time and ours. Describe your proposed article, including a sample lead or story outline. If the subject attracts our interest and has not been covered too recently, we may request to see the article on a speculation basis. Please enclose a self-addressed stamped envelope if you want your materials returned.

Articles must address an area of specific interest or concern for the serious martial artist. The vast majority of our stories are educational; they either teach technical and strategic skills, or enlighten the reader about historical and philosophical matters. The writing should capture the reader's interest with a strong lead, then hold it with information that is exact, concrete and focused around a strong central theme. All quotes and anecdotes should pertain to that theme.

Black Belt seldom uses first-person accounts, because most are of interest only to the author and his or her friends. In addition, while many instructors are dedicated and high-ranking, the magazine rarely requests personality profiles. (If you do choose to write about an individual, your article should prove that your subject is unique or particularly significant in the martial arts community.) Remember: if you have a chance to meet or train with a great martial artist and want to write an article afterward, discuss what that person knows rather than how his or her life has unfolded.

All statements and quotes must be accurate and verifiable. Use authoritative sources and cross-check your information. Be certain of all spellings—especially names and foreign words—and define foreign terms in parentheses after first usage only.

Manuscripts should be 1,000 to 3,000 words long, typed and double-spaced. If you use a computer, feel free to send a floppy disk with a Microsoft Word or plain text (ASCII) file. Please include full-color lead and step-by-step photos—with the negatives, if possible—taken in front of a plain, contrasting background. Be careful not to chop off the subjects' feet or hands when you frame the image, and verify that your camera is focused on the subjects and not on the background. Feature articles receive $150 to $300, which is paid upon publication. Simultaneous or previously published submissions must be identified as such.

Categories: Martial Arts

CONTACT: Robert Young, Executive Editor
Material: All
Black Belt Communications, Inc.
24900 Anza Dr., Unit E
Valencia CA 91355
Phone: 661-257-4066
Fax: 661-257-3028

The Black Table

The Black Table welcomes a staggering array of submissions, from the serious to the satirical to the servicey and back again. Few topics are off limits, provided they are well written with a sharp point of view and cover something that hasn't completely saturated the media yet.

Before submitting, readers are encouraged to take some time to peruse the archive to get a feel for the tone, topics and treatment we give our stories. We're big fans of sidebars and artwork, so feel free to suggest stories that are driven by visuals, especially in service pieces. Q&A style interviews are always welcome and an easy way to break in, especially if the source or the line of questioning is especially sharp.

When it comes to length, *The Black Table* feels it's what you do with the words that counts most, so we refuse to adhere to a strict word count. Some of our stories have clocked in at 400 words and others have pushed 30,000. It all depends on the topic and what you have to say. Interviews can run long, whereas criticism should be kept short. Only professors like reading term papers. Typically, the best submissions are around 1,000 words.

The Black Table has few rules about what we will not run, but they're rather hard and fast. Excuse the boldness here, but *The Black Table* does not run personal reflections, or the kinds of first-person memoirs that show up on diary sites. We no longer run Life as a Loser, and we're not looking to publish personal essays, late-night musings or disposable tales of drunken mayhem. There are plenty of places for your personal essays to live outside of *The Black Table*. Generally speaking, we're aiming for original journalism here, hard-hitting stories that involve real people out there in the world, and a measure of reporting—not just one person's view on their own life.

It may be helpful to think of *The Black Table* as a home for the random magazine ideas you never have time to pitch or felt qualified enough to write. We're the excuse for you to write those. We're the place those can go.

Most come from like-minded strangers with good ideas, people with a passion for writing and a need to have that writing seen. We don't play favorites here, we just want good content on a daily basis. Don't be shy about dropping us a line.

All submissions are voted on by the editor-in-chief and the three managing editors and you're gonna need three votes in order for something to run. Our tastes kinda run the gamut, but we'll be very nice about it if we have to reject something. If you're accepted, you will be added to the masthead promptly.

Oh, yes. And *The Black Table* doesn't pay for stories, mostly because *The Black Table* has no money. Fire off your ideas to: theblacktable@hotmail.com.

See you on the playground.

Categories: Culture—Current Affairs—Humor—Interviews—Satire

CONTACT: Eric Gillin, Editor-in-Chief
Material: All
E-mail: theblacktable@hotmail.com
Website: www.blacktable.com

Black Warrior Review

The *Black Warrior Review* publishes contemporary fiction, poetry, reviews, essays, interviews, art, and photography. General guidelines are below (along with specific guidelines for each genre).

FICTION No page length requirements. We'd like to see more short-short fiction, but are open to longer work. Please send only one story or novel excerpt per envelope (short-shorts excluded). We generally consider excerpts only from novels already completed and contracted for publication.

POETRY Limit poetry submissions to seven poems. (For information about entering our chapbook competition, see announcement.)

ESSAYS We consider creative personal essays, lyric essays, and such. We do not typically publish academic articles.

ART Each issue of *Black Warrior Review* features cover art and a 6-12 page internal (black and white) feature on an artist. Usually we prefer to use artwork by Alabama or Southern artists.

SIMULTANEOUS SUBMISSIONS are fine, if noted (understanding that you must notify us immediately if the work is accepted somewhere else).

GENERAL GUIDELINES *Black Warrior Review* does NOT accept unsolicited email submissions. E-mail queries, however, are welcomed.

We read submissions year-round, though our response time is slower in the summer.

The average response time for submissions is between 2 and 4 months. If you have not received a response after 4 months (excepting the summer), send a query and SASE through the mail, or email us at <bwr@ua.edu>, and we'll check on the status of your submission.

Unsolicited manuscripts will not be returned unless accompanied by a self-addressed, stamped envelope (SASE) and proper postage.

We can't respond to submissions that come without an SASE.

Please do not mix genres in the same envelope.

We encourage you to read *Black Warrior Review* before submitting. Sample issues are available for $8; one-year subscriptions for $14.

Address all submissions and other correspondence to the attention of the appropriate editor.

RIGHTS Manuscripts accepted for publication become the property of the *Black Warrior Review* unless otherwise indicated. All rights reserved. All rights revert to the author upon publication.

PAYMENT *Black Warrior Review* pays a one-year subscription, and up to $150 for stories or $75 for poems.

AWARDS The annual *Black Warrior Review* Literary Awards, determined by independent judges, give $500 each to a fiction writer and to a poet whose work has been published in the previous fall and spring issues. These awards, announced each fall, are made possible through a gift from the Society of Fine Arts, the University of Alabama.

CIRCULATION *Black Warrior Review* is published bianually with a circulation of 2,000.

Categories: Fiction—Nonfiction—Poetry

CONTACT: Editor (Indicate Department)
Material: Queries and submissions
PO Box 862936
Tuscaloosa AL 35486-0027
Phone: 205-348-4578
E-mail: bwr@ua.edu (for queries only)
Website: www.webdelsol.com/bwr

Blackfire

Overview

Blackfire features the erotic images, experiences and fantasies of black men in the life. Without compromising the sensual spell, it also includes provocative articles, useful information, delicious interviews and fresh poetry. *Blackfire* is designed for the sophisticated reader as well as those who want to take matters into their own hands.

Submissions

Blackfire seeks stories, articles, photography, models, illustration and a very limited amount of poetry all related to black men unclothed or in erotic situations.

STORIES AND ARTICLES

The best way to determine our needs is to read and study several recent issues. Here is a partial list of our needs:

• Full-length erotic fiction of 2,000-4,000 words detailing the exploits of black men in the life.

• Nostalgia and humor pieces are welcome if they are black, ITL and erotic. We also publish historical articles and first-person accounts that meet these criteria.

• Where-to articles that include details on where black men in the life congregate. These can range from the latest local bar to out-of-the-way resorts. Thoroughness and accuracy are the keys to acceptance of these articles.

• Shorts. We use articles of 400 to 700 words with one to two photos for one-pagers. Subjects include fresh, sharply focused erotic ideas.

• We do not solicit product reviews, games or puzzles. Subjects considered inappropriate include stories that refer to minors, illegal drugs, bestiality, water sports and scat.

WRITING STYLE

Blackfire seeks erotic material of the highest quality, but it need not be written by professional writers. The most important thing is that the work be erotic and that it feature black men in the life or ITL themes. We are not interested in stories that demean black men or place them in stereotypical situations.

Erotic fiction can range from descriptions of idealized men having idealized sex ("his 13-inch dick spurted a cupful of love juice"), to depictions of typical men in plausible encounters ("homeboy didn't have no meat, but I didn't care; I wanted that booty"), to unconsummated hints at sex ("ballet is the politically correct way for men to stare at other men's dicks in public"). We are partial to the latter two categories.

We want to publish concise, well-organized articles, so material must be tightly written. We reserve the right to edit submissions and to change titles as necessary.

Study the magazine to see what we do and how we do it. Some fiction is very romantic; other is highly sexual. Most articles in *Blackfire* cater to black men between these two extremes.

SPECIFICS

Include your name and address on the title page as well as your pseudonym, if you intend to use one. If the work you submit to us is being submitting to others as well, please let us know.

RIGHTS

Blackfire secures first North American rights and the right to anthologize accepted work. You retain all other rights to your work. If the material you're submitting has appeared elsewhere, tell us when you submit it. Payment for articles averages about 10 cents per word. This payment is based on quality of the material, research required to complete the piece, length of the copy and how badly we want the story. Writers whose work is included in an anthology receive an additional payment.

ACCEPTANCE

Individuals whose works are accepted for publication must provide *Blackfire* with a brief biographical sketch. Accepted works should, whenever possible, be provided on diskette in either PC or Macintosh format. You should provide the original or a reproduction-quality duplicate of accepted artwork.

PEP TALK

Because you're reading these guidelines, you're one step closer to having us accept your work than are many others. We want to hear from you by way of a tantalizing query, a top-notch completed manuscript, or an article we can't resist featuring on the cover. Every year we work with a few unpublished writers, and in our pages you can also find the bylines and credits of established professionals. It doesn't matter if you're a pro or a novice. If the material meets our needs and standards, we use it.

PHOTOGRAPHY AND ILLUSTRATION

If you are a photographer or an artist, submit your work.

MODELS

If you have a nice face, a great body or are heavy in the meat department and want to appear in *Blackfire*, let us know. In fact, if you don't have a nice face, you've got an average body and God sent your dick elsewhere, and you want to appear in *Blackfire*, contact us anyway.

DEADLINES

We accept submissions year-round. Submit seasonal material six months in advance. For instance, a piece about Kwanzaa in December must be received in June, and an April piece about Easter must be in our hands in October.

DELIVERY

Submissions may be mailed to Editor, *Blackfire*, PO Box 83912, Los Angeles, CA 90083-0912. Please include a self-addressed, stamped envelope with adequate postage if you want your work returned. Submissions may be faxed to the Editor at 310-410-9250. Submissions may be emailed to: newsroom@blk.com. We usually respond within a month.

LEGALESE

The Editors do not assume responsibility for loss of or damage to submitted materials. Publication of the name, photograph or likeness of any person or organization in articles or advertising in *Blackfire* is not to be construed as any indication of the sexual orientation of such persons or organizations. The opinions of *Blackfire* are expressed only in editorials. Other opinions are those of the writers and do not necessarily represent the opinions of *Blackfire*.

Categories: Fiction—African-American—Erotica—Fantasy—Gay/Lesbian—Men's Fiction—Men's Issues—Poetry—Sexuality

CONTACT: Alan Bell, Editor
Material: All
PO Box 83912
Los Angeles CA 90083-0912
Phone: 310-410-0808
Fax: 310-410-9250
E-mail: newsroom@blk.com
Website: www.kuumba.net

The Blessed Bee

Please refer to *SageWoman Magazine*.

Bloomsbury Review

The Bloomsbury Review is a magazine about books that has been publishing since 1980 and is distributed throughout the U.S. and Canada. TBR accepts submissions of book reviews, essays, poetry, interviews, and other book-related articles.

Editorial Policy: *The Bloomsbury Review* does not announce reviews prior to publication. We do send copies of the issue to the publisher if and when a review appears. With that in mind, we ask that writers not contact the publisher or the author of a book when they have submitted a review to TBR.

TIPS ON WRITING A BOOK REVIEW

As in any good writing, there should be a strong introduction and conclusion, and smooth transitions between paragraphs. The writing should be intelligent without being too pedantic, critical without being condescending, and lively and colorful without being frivolous.

A good book review should tell the reader what the book is about, why the reader may or may not be interested in it, whether or not the author is successful in his/her intent, and whether or not the book should be read.

Never review a book on a subject you are not familiar with. It is not necessary to be an expert on the subject, but good working knowledge of the author or subject matter is imperative.

Be objective. Never review the work of a personal or ideological friend or enemy.

Never review a book you haven't read at least once and understood.

Review the author's ideas, not your own. Do not compete with the subject, but instead respond or react to it.

A review should be more than just a summary of the book's contents. It should be an involved and informed response to the style, theme, and content.

If you have any questions regarding the writing of a book review or any other feature, please do not hesitate to contact one of our editors. It is our obligation to provide our readers with informative, entertaining statements about books and the ideas presented in them.

For Style: Follow *The Chicago Manual of Style*. It is our policy to use nonsexist language. TBR's editors will make minor editorial alterations, if necessary, to conform to the house style. If substantial editing of your review is required, you will be notified and a copy of your edited review can be sent to you for your approval or final changes prior to publication.

Length: Upon assignment of a review or feature, an editor will assign an approximate length (usually from 100 to 1,000 words, as some subjects or books may warrant more or less space). If you find that a book you have been assigned does not warrant the time and effort it would take to review it, please contact your editor. This does not mean, however, that we will not publish negative criticism provided it is properly substantiated.

Quoted Material: It is extremely important to include a photocopy of all materials quoted in a review.

If the quotes are directly from the text of the book you are reviewing, please either photocopy those pages and indicate the passage quoted with brackets or, if you are returning the book to TBR along with the review, indicate on your manuscript (in the left margin) the page from which the quote is taken.

If you are quoting from a book other than the one you are reviewing, indicate the title of the book, the author, and the year of publication as well as a photocopy of the page with the quoted passage in brackets.

If you are quoting from a journal or magazine, please indicate the title of the periodical, the title of the article, the author of that piece, and the volume and issue date, as well as a photocopy of the quote.

Reviewer Information: Please include a bio/byline of up to 30 words at the end of each submission.

Headline: Writers are welcome to suggest a headline for their reviews, interviews, or essays, although such will be subject to editorial discretion and space limitations.

FORMAT FOR SUBMISSIONS

We use a PC. Our preferred format for submissions is in DOS text file stored on a 3¼" diskette (with one hard copy) formatted in Word Perfect version 5 or 5.1 or ASCII. We will also accept your review at our e-mail address (BloomsB@aol.com — only in ASCII or Word Perfect 6.0) or as hard or faxed copy. Please also send to our office one photocopy (keep your original), byped and double-spaced.

Please include your name, mailing address, and phone number on page 1, and your name only at the top of each following page; allow eight weeks for reply.

FORMAT FOR BOOK REVIEWS

At the top of the first page, include the following information:
1. Title of book
2. Subtitle (if any)
3. Author/Editor/Translator/Illustrator/Photographer
4. Publisher/price/binding/ISBN (please include price and ISBN for both cloth and paper editions, when available, as well as the address for small presses)
5. The year the book was published

Payment: Reviewers may opt for gift subscriptions in lieu of cash payment. The scale is as follows: book reviews (of 600 or more words) = $10 to $15 (1-year subscription); poetry = $5 to $10 per poem (1-year subscription); essays, features, and interviews = $20 to $50 (2- to 4-year subscription). Payment is made upon publication. Submissions of less than 600 words in length are welcome but not paid.

The book business is an exciting field, and we welcome your thoughts, comments, and submissions.

Categories: Fiction—Nonfiction—Book Reviews—Interview—Literature—Writing

CONTACT: Tom Auer, Publisher
Material: All
Marily Auer, Associate Publisher
1553 Platte St., Ste 206
Denver CO 80202-1667
Phone: 303-455-3123
Fax: 303-455-7039

Blue Ridge Country Magazine

Blue Ridge Country is a bi-monthly, full-color magazine embracing the feel and spirit of the Blue Ridge region–the traditions and recipes, the outdoor recreation and travel opportunities, the country stores and bed-and-breakfast inns, the things to visit and learn about. In short, it is everything that will allow and encourage the reader to "take a trip home for the weekend" even if he or she has never lived in the region.

Our territory extends from Western Maryland south through Virginia's Shenandoah Valley down into northern Georgia and including all territory within about a half day's drive of the parkway. It includes the mountain regions of Virginia, North Carolina, West Virginia, Tennessee, Maryland, Georgia, South Carolina, and Kentucky.

Main Pieces (750-2,000 words)

Places: Everything there is to find out and tell about a great Blue Ridge town, city, or locale. The history, the current economic status, the quaint spots and characters, the best places to eat. A profile so complete our readers can make hard decisions on going to spend a weekend or even moving there.

History & Legends: From people and events to unexplained occurrences or phenomena, the magazine prints fascinating tales of past and present.

The Blue Ridge Parkway and the Appalachian Trail: There's a wealth of wildlife, beauty, history and future plans involving the parkway and the trail and the new areas immediately surrounding each. We bring our readers a new piece of America's favorite scenes highway and favorite footpath in each issue.

General Articles: Anything that is well-researched, well-written and brings us some of the flavor of the region will get strong consideration. We'll be looking for at-home kinds of things–recipes and craft articles, natural history and wildlife, and especially pieces that embrace the whole of the region. Plus humor, first-person adventure or discovery and the "bests" of the region.

Departments: Very much like the main pieces, but in shorter versions; places to see, things to do, recipes to try, great people doing great things, new books, etc.–anything and everything that contributes to the sense of the place.

Rights: We buy exclusive first North American serial rights until the off-sale date of the issue in which material is published, as well as exclusive rights to the work for promotional reprint and use.

Pay: We pay from $25 (for department shorts) up to about $250 for major pieces. Payment is upon publication. Manuscripts not supplied on disk are paid 20% under the above rates.

Sample copies of the magazine are available. Send $3.00 and a magazine-size SASE.

Photography: We use primarily color slides, and pay $25 to $50 for exclusive first North American serial rights until the off-sale date of the issue in which the material is published, as well as rights to the work for promotional and reprint use.

Send queries, ideas, and stories with an SASE.

Categories: Nonfiction—Animals—Book Reviews—Civil War—Cooking—Environment—Family—Fishing—Folklore—Gardening—General Interest—History—Lifestyle—Multicultural—Outdoors—Photography—Recreation—Regional—Rural America—Senior Citizen—Travel—Appalachia Festivals

CONTACT: Kurt Rheinheimer, Chief Editor
Material: Features, Travel, History, Outdoors
CONTACT: Cara Ellen Modisett, Associate Editor
Material: Inns, Books, Environmental News, Festivals
CONTACT: William Alexander, Art Director
Material: Photos
PO Box 21535
Roanoke VA 24018
Phone: 540-989-6138
Fax: 540-989-7603
Website: www.blueridgecountry.com

Boat U.S. Magazine

Does not accept freelance submission.

Boating Life
An Authority on Recreational Boating

Boating Life is published 8 issues per year. BL does not have any formal writers' guidelines, but *we publishes articles on the following:*
- Adventure
- Boating in crafts up to 36 feet
- Boating Lifestyle
- Buyer's Guide
- Community
- Electronics
- Engines
- Fishing
- Gear
- Product Reviews
- Site Services

• Tips, Techniques, & Travel
• Water sports
Categories: Nonfiction—Adventure—Fishing—Lifestyle—Outdoors—Sports/Recreation—Travel

CONTACT: Robert Stephens, Executive Editor
Material: All
World Publications, LLC
460 N. Orlando Ave., Ste 200
Winter Park, Florida 32789
Phone: 407-628-4802
Website: www.boatinglifemag.com

Body & Soul

Thank you for your interest in contributing to BODY & SOUL magazine.

BODY & SOUL is a national bimonthly magazine. Our editorial objective is to serve as an inspirational guide for all those who want to live healthier, more balanced lives. We cover a wide range of subjects: integrative medicine, nutrition, self-help psychology, spirituality, the mind/body connection, work and money issues, and organic living. We provide the information readers need to take an active role in improving their lives and preserving the planet. We are looking for quality writing and thorough reporting to inform and entertain our audience. We are also interested in new, cutting-edge thinking.

We publish up to six features per issue (1,500 to 3,500 words); up to eight columns that run under headings such as Holistic Health, Food/Nutrition, Spirit, Home, Community, Travel and Life Lessons (600 to 1,300 words); book and music/media sections that include a variety of reviews (200 to 750 words); and an Insight section that includes short news items (50-250 words). Please note that we do not publish fiction, poetry, or previously published articles.

Our payment rates for published material are comparable to those of other small national magazines and range from $50 for a short news piece to $1,500 or more for a feature story. Fees are determined on an individual basis by assignment and vary depending on the nature of the story and the experience of the writer. Fees include the purchase of electronic rights.

Although we consider unsolicited manuscripts, it is best to send a query letter before preparing a lengthy article. When sending queries, please include clips of recent work and a résumé. Due to the volume of mail we receive, only manuscripts accompanied by an SASE with sufficient postage will be returned. We cannot consider submissions sent via e-mail. Please do not send originals, as the magazine cannot be held responsible for loss or damage of unsolicited material. We will attempt to respond to all submissions within 12 weeks of receipt. No phone calls please.

Categories: Nonfiction—Alternate Life-style—Arts—Book Reviews—Diet/Nutrition—Environment—Health—Inspirational—Lifestyle—Music—New Age—Physical Fitness—Self-Help—Spiritual

CONTACT: Liz Phillips, Executive Editor
Material: Spirituality, Work, Environment
CONTACT: Tania Hannan, Managing Editor
Material: Fitness, Health
CONTACT: Frances Lefkowitz, Senior Editor
Material: Food, Nutrition, Creativity
New Age Publishing, Editorial Department
42 Pleasant St.
Watertown MA 02472
Phone: 617-926-0200
Fax: 617-926-5021
E-mail: editor@bodyandsoulmag.com
Website: www.bodyandsoulmag.com

> *Remember: Editors change jobs and publishers change addresses. It is wise to invest in a phone call for the current information before submitting.*

Book/Mark Small Press Quarterly Review

Book/Mark Small Press Quarterly Review (1994-present) is dedicated to publishing reviews of books and magazines by small presses and non-corporate publishing entities. We are distributed by the Suffolk Cooperative Library System and can be found in the New York Public Library, in colleges, bookstores and arts councils on Long Island. We have subscribers and contributors across the country and abroad. *Book/Mark* is a member of CLMP, and is listed in, among other references, the *International Directory of Small Presses & Magazines* and *The American Humanities Index.*

We welcome inquiries regarding reviews, books (especially by local writers, artists, and faculty), and internship possibilities for students seeking experience in publishing/public relations. Our content is eclectic, including reviews of books on a variety of topics/genres (literary, political, popular culture, the arts, children's books, history, science, critical essay). *Book/Mark* seeks to promote and publicize the efforts of small press book publishers (including independents, university presses, cooperative, alternative and arts presses). We have sponsored literary forums such as a Women's History Month panel and discussion at Borders Books, and created/hosted the Long Island Small Press Book Fair.

Reviews generally run from 600 - 900 words (sometimes a bit longer, especially when using excerpts/author quotes).

Book/Mark is available by subscription: $12.00 yr/$15.00 Institutions; $3.50 a copy pp. Back issues available for $2.00 pp. Advertising rates available. We print gratis notices for arts/non-profits (readings/conferences/credible contests) and exchange ads where appropriate. We thank you for your interest and support!

Categories: Nonfiction—Book Reviews—Literature

CONTACT: Mindy Kronenberg, Editor-In-Chief
Material: All
PO Box 516
Miller Place NY 11764
Phone: 631-331-4118
E-mail: cyberpoet@msn.com

Books & Culture

Books and Culture magazine is a Christianity Today Publication.

Books and Culture magazine does not have any writers guidelines, however, we do accept unsolicited submissions.

See our website for an overview of our publication.

Categories: Christian Interests—Culture—Literature—Religion—Spiritual

CONTACT: John Wilson, Editor
Material: All
465 Gundersen Drive
Carol Stream IL 60188
Phone: 630-260-8428
E-mail: bceditor@booksandculture.com
Website: www.booksandculture.com

Boston Magazine

No formal guidelines available.

Categories: Book Reviews—Business—Culture—Economics—Education—Entertainment—Fashion—Food/Drink—General Interest—Health—Lifestyle—Politics—Real Estate

CONTACT: Jon Marcus, Editor
Material: All

CONTACT: Kim Atkinson, Executive Editor
Material: Lifestyle
CONTACT: Don Armstrong, Features Editor
Material: Features
Metro Corp
300 Massachusetts Ave.
Boston, MA 02115
Phone: 615-262-9700
Fax: 617-267-1774
E-mail: editor@bostonmagazine.com
Website: www.bostonmagazine.com

Boston Review

Boston Review is a bimonthly magazine of cultural and political analysis, reviews, fiction, and poetry. The editors are committed to a society and culture that foster human diversity and a democracy in which we seek common grounds of principle amidst our many differences. In the hope of advancing these ideals, the *Review* acts as a forum that seeks to enrich the language of public debate.

The best way to get a sense of the kind of material the *Review* is looking for is to read the magazine (sample copies are available for $5.00). Recent issues have featured articles by Stephen Lerner on rebuilding American unions, Sven Birkerts on the decline of reading, and Atilio Boron on prospects for Latin American democracy. Also poetry by Robert Pinsky, Charles Simic, and Jorie Graham, fiction by Tom Paine, Patricia Traxler, and Elizabeth Graver, and criticism by Richard Howard, Raphael Campo, and Marjorie Perloff.

FICTION: From Jodi Daynard, fiction editor: "I'm looking for stories that are emotionally and intellectually substantive and also interesting on the level of language. Things that are shocking, dark, lewd, comic, or even insane are fine so long as the fiction is controlled and purposeful in a masterly way. Subtlety, delicacy and lyricism are attractive too." Work should be polished—clearly revised, grammatical, proofread. Length should be no less than 1,200 and no more than 5,000 words.

NONFICTION: Please query with clips before devoting time to an article or essay. Also realize that the editors plan issues well in advance, and the *Review*'s bimonthly publication schedule often cannot accommodate topical or especially timebound material.

REVIEWS: We do not accept unsolicited book reviews: if you would like to be considered for *Review* assignments, please send your resume along with several published clips.

GENERAL: *Boston Review* acquires first serial rights on accepted pieces; copyright reverts to the author after publication. We do not consider previously published material. Simultaneous submissions are fine as long as we are notified of the fact; however, we do not accept electronic submissions. Payment varies. Response time is generally 6-8 weeks. A self-addressed stamped envelope must accompany all submissions.

Thank you for your interest in *Boston Review*.

Categories: Fiction—Nonfiction—Culture—Economics—Education—Literature—Multicultural—Poetry—Politics—Short Stories—Society—Writing

CONTACT: Jodi Daynard, Fiction Editor
Material: Short Stories
CONTACT: Mary Jo Bang, Timothy Donnelly, Poetry Editors
Material: Poetry
CONTACT: Ian Lague, Managing Editor
Material: Nonfiction Submissions
E53-407; MIT
30 Wadsworth St.
Cambridge MA 02139
Phone: 617-253-3642
Fax: 617-252-1549
E-mail: bostonreview@mit.edu

Bowling Magazine

No longer published.

BOYS' LIFE®

Boys' Life

Boys' Life is a general interest, four-color monthly, circulation 1.3 million, published by the Boy Scouts of America [BSA] since 1911. We buy first-time rights for original, unpublished material.

NONFICTION. Major articles run 500 to 1,500 words; payment is $400 to $1,500. Subject matter is broad. We cover everything from professional sports to American history to how to pack a canoe. A look at a current list of the BSA's more than 100 merit badge pamphlets gives an idea of the wide range of subjects possible. Even better, look at a year's worth of recent issues. We are found in libraries and BSA council offices.

Columns run 300 to 750 words; payment is $150 to $400. Column headings are science, nature, earth, health, sports, space and aviation, cars, computers, entertainment pets, history, music and others. Each issue uses seven columns, on average. We also have back-of-the-book how-to features that bring $250 to $300.

FICTION. Fiction runs 1,000 to 1,500 words. Payment is $750 and up. All stories feature a boy or boys. We use humor, mystery, science fiction and adventure. We use one short story per issue.

Articles for *Boys' Life* must interest and entertain boys ages 8 to 18. Write for a boy you know who is 12. Our readers demand crisp, punchy writing in relatively short, straightforward sentences. The editors demand well-reported articles that demonstrate high standards of journalism. We follow *The New York Times Manual of Style and Usage.*

We receive approximately 100 queries and unsolicited manuscripts and 75 fiction manuscripts per week. Unsolicited nonfiction manuscripts are returned unread.

Please query by mail, not by phone.

Thank you for your interest in *Boys' Life*.

Categories: Fiction—Nonfiction—Adventure—Animals—Automobiles—Aviation—Careers—Cartoons—Children—Computers—Conservation—Crafts/Hobbies—Ecology—Education—Electronics—Entertainment—Environment—Fishing—Games—General Interest—Health—History—Hobbies—Juvenile—Outdoors—Science—Science Fiction—Short Stories—Sports/Recreation—Humor—Technology

CONTACT: Rich Haddaway, Associate Editor
Material: Fiction Manuscripts
CONTACT: Mike Goldman, Articles Editor
Material: Nonfiction Queries (NO mss.)
1325 W. Walnut Hill Ln., PO Box 152079
Irving TX 75015-2079
Phone: 972-580-2355
Website: www.boyslife.org

Boys' Quest

A Word At The Outset:

Every BOYS' QUEST contributor must remember we publish only six issues a year, which means our editorial needs are extremely limited. It is obvious that we must reject far more contributions that we accept, no matter how outstanding they may seem to you or to us.

With that said, we would point out that BOYS' QUEST is a magazine created for boys from 6 to 13 years, with youngsters 8, 9, and 10 the specific target age. Our point of view is that every young boy deserves the right to be a young boy for a number of years before he becomes a young adult. As a result, BOYS' QUEST looks for articles, fiction, nonfiction, and poetry that deal with timeless topics, such as pets, nature, hobbies, science, games, sports, careers, simple cooking, and anything else likely to interest a young boy.Each issue revolves around a theme. A list of future themes can be view at our website.

Writers, we are looking for lively writing, most of it from a young boy's point of view - with the boy or boys directly involved in an activity that is both wholesome and unusual. We need nonfiction with photos and fiction stories - around 500 words - puzzles, poems, cooking, carpentry projects, jokes, and riddles. Nonfiction pieces that are accompanied by black and white photos are far more likely to be accepted than those that need illustrations.

The ideal length of a BOYS' QUEST piece - nonfiction or fiction - is 500 words. We will entertain simultaneous submissions as long as that fact is noted on the manuscript. Computer printouts are welcome if they are (as all submissions should be) double-spaced. BOYS' QUEST prefers to receive complete manuscripts with cover letters, although we do not rule out query letters. We do not answer submissions sent in by fax or e-mail. All submissions must be accompanied by a self-addressed, stamped envelope, with sufficient postage.

We will pay a minimum of five cents a word for both fiction and nonfiction, with additional payment given if the piece is accompanied by appropriate photos or art. We will pay a minimum of $10 per poem or puzzle, with variable rates offered for games, carpentry projects, etc.

BOYS' QUEST buys first American serial rights and pays upon publication. It welcomes the contributions of both published and unpublished writers. Sample copies are available for $4.00 within the US and $5.00 outside the US. All payment must be in US funds. A complimentary copy will be sent to each writer who has contributed to a given issue.

Photographers, we use a number of black and white photos inside the magazine, most in support of articles used. Payment is $5-10 per photo and $5 for color slides.

Artists, most art will be by assignment, in support of features used. The magazine is anxious to find artists capable of illustrating stories and features and welcomes copies of sample work, which will remain on file. Our work inside is pen and ink. We pay $35 for a full page and $25 for a partial page.

BOYS' QUEST is the companion to HOPSCOTCH magazine, and like HOPSCOTCH, the issues each revolve around a theme. We often choose new themes as the result of a submission on a topic we haven't covered. We work far into the future. If you don't receive a quick response on your submission, it means we are holding it and giving it serious consideration. We strive to treat all of our contributors and their work with respect and fairness.

Categories: Fiction—Nonfiction—Adventure—Animals—Cartoons—Children—Games—Hobbies—Nature—Outdoors—Sports/Recreation

CONTACT: Marilyn Edwards, Editor
Material: All
PO Box 227
Bluffton OH 45817-0227
Phone: 419-358-4610
Website: www.boysquest.com

BrandPackaging

We're always looking for good freelance articles, but they have to reflect business savvy and support our magazine's niche in the packaging industry. Freelancers should thoroughly understand our editorial platform before proposing articles. We focus on the marketing impact of packaging for marketing professionals at consumer packaged goods companies. We identify consumer and packaging industry trends at their earliest stages and publish articles that help marketers capitalize on these trends by more effectively using packaging as a marketing tool. Our readers include brand managers/marketers, product managers, category managers, senior vice president-marketing, package designers, and anyone else who is involved in package creation. They're very pressed for time, highly educated, cynical and dislike being sold to in print. They want ideas on how to innovate. Our job is to digest things down to the top-line information they want, written in the language of marketers. We do not publish "news," or "cover" industry events. Rather, we address topics such as color, shape, labels, special-effects materials, the psychology of packaging and the consumer's mindset when looking at packaging. We work from the premise that 70 percent of consumer buying decisions are made at the store shelf, and more than half of all brands carry no advertising support, so packaging must act as the "silent salesman."

Submission format: We prefer that articles be submitted electronically or provided on a CD. All "hard-packaging" articles that include information from packaging suppliers must include the name, phone number and e-mail address of the initial contact person at the supplier for our readers. Articles must be accompanied by well-lit, clear color photos or digital images of packaging referenced in the article. Photos should be either 4x6 or 5x7 in size, glossy finish. Digital images should be 300 dpi, jpeg or pdf format, 4 inches wide. We pay up to $1,200 for features, depending on length and complexity. We pay on acceptance and purchase all rights. Material is subject to editing for length, style and format. Tip: Our readers love bulleted and numbered lists, as well as sidebars. All articles should answer these three questions: What does it do? How does it do it? How can marketers use it in packaging to achieve their business objectives? Freelancers should look through the magazine archives at www.packaginginfo.com, and click on "Visit *BrandPackaging*" to familiarize themselves with our writing approach.

Categories: We are a "horizontal" magazine. We could use examples from a number of product categories in dissecting a trend in a single article. We also take an occasional look at product categories vertically. Our categories include food, beverage, housewares, hardware, automotive aftermarket, toys, health and beauty aids, and OTC drugs.

Categories: Packaging—Marketing

CONTACT: Bob Swientek, Editor-in-Chief
Material: All
CONTACT: Jim George, Senior Editor
Material: All
Independent Publishing Co.
210 S. Fifth St., Ste. 204
St. Charles IL 60174
Phone: 630-377-0100

Braveheart

BRAVE HEARTS is a quarterly magazine from Ogden Publications. The magazine is written by and for ordinary people who have an inspirational message to share.

BRAVE HEARTS seeks short manuscripts (up to 900 words), photographs, prayers, and related material on special inspirational subjects for each issue. A nominal payment of $5 to $12 is made upon publication. An additional payment of $2 is made for each item used on our Web site.

BRAVE HEARTS purchases all publishing rights to the items used. No simultaneous submissions are accepted. No e-mail submissions accepted.

Material should be submitted at least six months in advance of publication. Notification of acceptance or rejection will be made within approximately six months of receipt.

No queries: Send complete mss. to the address below.

Categories: Nonfiction—General Interest—Inspirational—Lifestyle—Religion—Romance—Spiritual

CONTACT: Ann Crahan, Editor-in-Chief
Material: All
1503 SW 42nd St
Topeka KS 66609
Phone: 785-274-4300
Fax: 785-274-4305
Website: www.braveheartsmagazine.com

Bridal Guide

Bridal Guide is interested in articles about relationships, marriage, sexuality, fitness, psychology, finance, and travel. Please do not send queries concerning fashion, beauty, or home design stories, since we produce these pages in house. We do accept wedding-planning ideas, but these should cover broad subjects, such as planning a long-distance or theme wedding, or emotional subjects, such as dealing with divorced parents. Shorter, how-to pieces (such as finding a band or choosing a cake) are written in-house. We also do not accept fiction or poetry.

We are looking for service-oriented, well researched pieces that are journalistically written and have a length of 1,000 to 2,000 words. Payment, made on acceptance, is 50 cents per word. Writers we work with consult at least 3 expert sources, such as physicians, book authors, and business people in the appropriate field. Our tone is conversational yet authoritative. Features are also generally filled with real-life anecdotes. We also do features that are completely real-person based–such as finding roundtables of bridesmaids discussing their experiences, or grooms-to-be talking about their feelings about getting married.

In queries, we are looking for a well thought-out idea, the specific angle or focus the writer intends to take, and the sources he or she intends to use. Queries should be brief and snappy–and titles should be supplied to give the editor an even better idea of the direction the writer is going in.

Feature ideas and ideas for the Confident Bride column should be sent to Cybele Eidenschenk, executive editor. Travel feature ideas should be directed to Laurie Bain Wilson, travel editor. Submit queries only, along with clips of work published in a national consumer magazine, and a self-addressed, stamped envelope. You will get a reply within one to three months, but we cannot return any materials such as manuscripts, clips, or photos, so do not send any originals.

Categories: Fiction—Nonfiction—Health—Marriage—Money & Finances—Poetry—Psychology—Relationships—Sexuality—Travel

CONTACT: Cybele Eidenschenk, Executive Editor
Material: Relationships, planning & financial issues
CONTACT: Laurie Bain Wilson, Travel Editor
Material: Honeymoon Travel
R.F.P., LLC.
3 East 54th St., 15th Floor
New York NY 10022
Phone: 212-838-7733

Bride's Magazine

Bride's magazine is written for the first— and second—time bride, the groom, their families, and their friends. The editorial goal is to help the couple plan their wedding and adjust to married life. *Bride's* does not publish fiction or poetry. Submit all travel queries directly to the Travel Department. Payment starts at $.50 per word.

Choosing a Topic:

1) Personal essays on wedding planning aspects of weddings or marriage. 800 words. Written by brides, grooms, attendants, family members, friends, in the first person. The writer's unique experience qualifies them to tell this story.

2) Articles on specific relationship and lifestyle issues. 700 words. Select a specialized topic in the areas of relationships, religion, in-laws, second marriage, finances, careers, sex. Written by freelancers who interview and quote experts and real couples.

3) In-depth explorations of relationship and lifestyle issues. 2,000 words. Well researched articles on sex, wedding and marriage trends. Should include statistics, quotes from experts and real couples, a resolution of the issues raised by each couple. Preparing an Article: First, familiarize yourself with the magazine by reading several of the most recent issues (also check the masthead; if you are writing to a specific editor, make sure she is still here). Next, send a detailed outline or query explaining how you would research and organize the piece, along with a self-addressed, stamped legal-size envelope and clippings of your previously published work. You should receive a response within eight-12 weeks. Please do not call to check on your query's status; each submission will be read and carefully considered.

Enrich your article with couple anecdotes and quotes from experts. Attribute all statistics to organizations or agencies. Include experts' full names, academic degrees and affiliations, cities and states; couples' first names, ages, occupations, cities and states. Do not cite secondary sources; use other magazine articles and books as background reading only (you may interview the authors of these sources).

Categories: Nonfiction—Family—Gardening—Marriage—Parenting—Relationships—Beauty—Home

CONTACT: Features Department
Material: All except Travel
CONTACT: Travel Department
Material: Travel
4 Times Square
New York NY 10036
Phone: 212-286-2860
Website: www.brides.com

Bridge

About

Bridge is a triannual publication, a hybrid of a journal and a magazine, as well as an event space at 119 North Peoria in Chicago.

The simple belief that provided the motivation to launch *Bridge* as a publication in November 2000 was that separate fields of inquiry can and should be thought of as having shared horizons. Every existing world view, whether scientific, philosophic, aesthetic, religious, political, or literary must acknowledge its limits or risk being defined as obsolete, unachievable, and incoherent. The goal of *Bridge* has been to make the relationships between these isolated fields of inquiry clear, exposing the basic humanity from which every idea originates.

This *idéée-force* led to the development of a publication where innovative and discerning artistic expression in the fields of literature, poetry, visual art, music, and more could be stated without inhibition, alongside intellectual work exploring a similarly unrestricted scope of thoughts, images and conceptions.

Our event space, launched in June 2002, is an extension of this purpose, a place where, through art events, symposia, author events, artists' talks, colloquia and more, an independent physical space can exist in which to put aside the incommensurability of these disparate fields of inquiry and participate in an examination of the particulars as well as the contexts of intelligibility that surround them.

General Editorial Guidelines

Submissions sent to *Bridge* should be addressed to the relevant department (Culture and Critique, Fiction, Literary Criticism, Poetry, Visual Arts, or Music), for which specific guidelines are available below. We consider unsolicited submissions.

For email submissions to all departments, please paste the first 300 words of your submission in the body of your email, and attach a Word document to that email, unless otherwise noted. Submissions shorter than 300 words need not be accompanied by a Word file. E-mail submissions are acceptable as an attachment in Microsoft Word format only. All email submissions must include the author's name, address, telephone number and date submitted. This will help us to prioritize. All email submissions should be sent to submissions@bridgemagazine.org. Please allow up to six months for a response, unless otherwise noted. After six months, please inquire as to the status of your submission with the appropriate editor or by email with Michael Workman, *Bridge* Publisher and Editor-in-Chief. If after completing these steps you receive no response, please feel free to submit elsewhere.

Editing of articles will consist primarily of lengthening or shortening, at the editor's discretion, to suit available space restrictions. Additionally, changes may be made to suit proper grammar. Editorial standards for nonfiction submissions are usually consistent with the most recent version of MLA style or *The Chicago Manual of Style: The Essential Guide for Writers, Editors, and Publishers* (14th Edition).

There is no payment for publication, unless otherwise noted. If we accept work for the print version, we will not necessarily accept that work for website publication.

Submission Guidelines for Bridge Readings Dept.

General Guidelines: Bridge is currently seeking submissions of ephemera, office memos, found notes, zine excerpts, website excerpts and the offbeat for its Readings department. Average length of submissions is 400 words unless otherwise stipulated by the editor. Material that otherwise fits into the Culture and Critique, Fiction, Literary Criticism, Poetry, Music, and Visual Arts Departments submitted for the Readings department should be sent directly to the editor of that department.

Submissions may be emailed directly to Michael Workman, Publisher and Editor-In-Chief, or mailed to us at *Bridge*, ATTN: Readings Department, 119 North Peoria, #3D, Chicago, IL 60607. E-mail submissions must include "Readings Section" in the subject line.

Submission Guidelines for Culture & Critique Dept.

General Guidelines: Essays should be submitted electronically as a Word attachment. Generally, they should be 500-2500 words long (although we will consider longer pieces) and double-spaced in a 12-point font. Endnotes are acceptable. The preferred citation method is the most recent version of MLA style; please triple-check quotations before submission. Essays may be emailed directly to Mark Tschaepe, Culture and Critique Editor-At-Large, or mailed to us at *Bridge*, ATTN: Culture & Critique Dept., 119 North Peoria, #3D, Chicago, IL 60607.

Culture and Critique department queries (preferred) and submissions should also include the following:

1) Two (2) writing samples
2) Curriculum Vitae
3) Letter of Intent

Culture and Critique Portfolio:

The Culture and Critique department at *Bridge* does not normally accept unsolicited essays for its portfolios—which are typically devoted to a single subject—but if you would like to submit an essay for possible inclusion in a future portfolio, contact Culture and Critique Editor-At-Large Mark Tschaepe to find out what the focus of our upcoming issue is.

Other: Bridge is also willing to publish high-quality cultural and critical writing outside its portfolio format. We seek analysis and exploration of contemporary theory and writing that actively participates in a critical exchange relevant to an identifiable public forum, from the institutional to the obscure. *Bridge* is not interested in peer review, writing that merely evidences a position or issue while offering unconditional support, political-scientific exegesis, or in mere discursive conceptual exercise, regardless how well-researched. Any discussion of ideas, concepts, methods and accessory citation of texts should only be used to support your own unique, cohesive argument.

Primarily, we are interested in philosophical writing that articulates qualitative distinctions and offers informed commentary on the practices of and tensions current in the social and cultural forces of the modern West. Strong writing for the Culture and Critique department will present thoroughly-examined investigations of particular subjects while providing contexts of intelligibility that successfully strive after verisimilitude. A readable prose that avoids utilizing literary devices is preferred, with styles that fall in the margin between academic journal writing and more popular intellectual writing (eg., *The New Yorker, Harper's, Atlantic Monthly*); unsolicited travel narratives or personal essays are not acceptable. No dissertation excerpts or class papers, please.

Feel free to submit unsolicited essays to the email address above, following the general guidelines. Allow up to six months for a response. Simultaneous submissions are fine so long as you contact *Bridge* immediately should your essay be accepted elsewhere.

Submission Guidelines for Fiction Dept.

General Guidelines: We are seeking provocative, well crafted short fiction by newer and established writers.

In broad terms, we eschew stories bound by expectations and allegiance to pre-defined 'schools', in favor of dynamic, risky material that forces the writer to take a stand on his or her intentions, rather than flooding the work with their authorial presence. Some developing veins of fictive expression which we admire include: the cunning consumerist dreams of George Saunders and Alex Shakar, the astringent moral landscapes of Denis Johnson and Thom Jones, the lapidary compressions of Stephen Milhauser and William Gaddis, the reactionary genre implosions of Robert Coover and James Ellroy, the psychopathic melodramas of Charles Willeford and Stephen Wright, the formalized rage of Mary Caponegro and Thomas Bernhard, the gonzo Gothic of Barry Hannah and Harry Crews, the broader disordered histories pursued by Don DeLillo. We welcome those writers cruising beneath radar who will cause us to re-calibrate these already stiffening priorities.

Younger writers, and those of culturally diverse or under-represented backgrounds, are particularly encouraged to submit. However, all interested writers are urged to read a recent issue of *Bridge* to consider the work we've already included, and likewise urged to read those writers who cut the paths we walk upon: John Barth, Flann O'Brien, Cynthia Ozick, Grace Paley, Donald Bartheleme, Flannery O'Connor, Thomas Pynchon, Joan Didion, Chester Himes, and many others.

The fine print: please send only previously unpublished, legible (non-dot matrix) manuscripts of approximately 2 - 20 pages, along with a business SASE for response (or an appropriately sized and stamped envelope for manuscript return). Simultaneous submissions are fine so long as you contact *Bridge* immediately should your work be accepted elsewhere. Fiction may be emailed directly to Mike Newirth, Fiction Editor

NOTE: Do Not send email attachments to this email address, please paste your submission in the body of the email or submit attachments to the main submission email address, submissions-@*Bridge*magazine.org), or mailed to us at *Bridge*, ATTN: Fiction Dept., 119 North Peoria, #3D, Chicago, IL 60607.

Submission Guidelines for Poetry Dept.

General Guidelines: We read with interest every poem submitted to *Bridge* and are, quite frankly, looking to be as much informed and inspired by our poets as the other way around. Our emphasis is on the new—or the newly discovered—and we entertain, if sometimes briefly, all arguments in sympathy with this idea.

Poetry submissions sent via email should be addressed to Greg Purcell, Poetry Editor, or send a typewritten group of two to six unpublished poems to *Bridge*, ATTN: Greg Purcell, Poetry Dept., 119 North Peoria, #3D, Chicago, IL 60607. Please include a self-addressed stamped envelope with your submission. Contributors living outside the United States should include international reply coupons. We will not consider simultaneous submissions or poems that have been previously published.

Several pieces of original poetry will appear per issue. We generally hold a standard of printing no more than ten (10) one-page poems per issue, but everything depends on the merit of the work we receive.

Submission Guidelines for Literary Criticism Dept.

General Guidelines: Essays should be submitted electronically as a Word attachment. Generally, they should be 5-10 pages long (although we will consider longer pieces) and double-spaced in a 12-point font. Footnotes are okay. The preferred citation method is the most recent version of MLA style; please triple-check quotations before submission. Essays may be emailed directly to David Andrews, Lit Crit Associate Editor, at or mailed to us at *Bridge*, ATTN: Literary Criticism Dept., 119 North Peoria, #3D, Chicago, IL 60607.

Critical Portfolios: The literary criticism department at *Bridge* does not normally accept unsolicited essays for its critical portfolios—which are typically devoted to a single literary figure—but if you would like to submit an essay for possible inclusion in a future portfolio, contact Lit Crit Associate Editor David Andrews to find out who the focus of our upcoming issue is.

Other: Bridge is also willing to publish high-quality critical essays outside its portfolio format. Feel free to submit unsolicited essays to the email address above, following the general guidelines. Typically, we are looking for analytical, text-based criticism rather than biography, anecdotal essays, or "art appreciation." And feel free, as well, to mix your media—*Bridge* always encourages this approach to the arts. Allow six to eight weeks for a response. Simultaneous submissions are fine so long as you contact *Bridge* immediately should your essay be accepted elsewhere.

Submission Guidelines for Music Dept.

General Guidelines: Bridge welcomes unsolicited articles on music-related topics for consideration and possible publication. We are looking for lucid and engaging writing on contemporary music as it relates to culture, art and society. Sample areas of interest include, but are not limited to: popular music, jazz, folk, blues, contemporary classical, oral histories, electronic music, experimental sound, independent or underground rock, politics and music, conceptual art, and music technology, as well as music-related fiction or artwork. Record reviews and band profiles are discouraged. Historical and musicological writing are welcome, but must be of interest to a general audience (not overly-technical or academic). Humor and wit are especially encouraged.

The above guidelines are flexible, and all works will be judged on their individual merits. Please proofread and fact-check before submitting. Submissions will not be returned without SASE. Essays may be emailed directly to Justin McKinley Niimi, Music Editor, at or mailed to us at *Bridge*, ATTN: Music Dept., 119 North Peoria, #3D, Chicago, IL 60607.

Submission Guidelines for Visual Art Dept.

General Guidelines, Writing: Bridge is interested in writing on contemporary art, though we're particularly interested in writing not limited to contemporary art. That is, we prefer writing that looks at work relevant to something old with a fresh eye. Strong writing will focus less on critique and more on theory, attempt to form ideologies based on trends in contemporary art and sum what's happening now as well as what's around the bend.

Essays should be submitted electronically as a Word attachment. Generally, they should be 500-2500 words long (although we will consider longer pieces) and double-spaced in a 12-point font. Endnotes are acceptable. The preferred citation method is the most recent version of MLA style; please triple-check quotations before submission. Essays may be emailed directly to Marie Walz, Art Editor, or Howard Fonda, Associate Art Editor, or mailed to us at *Bridge*, ATTN: Visual Art Dept., 119 North Peoria, #3D, Chicago, IL 60607. *Visual Art department queries (preferred) and submissions should also include the following:*

1) Two (2) writing samples
2) Curriculum Vitae
3) Letter of Intent

Images: If images are required, writers are responsible for making sure that *Bridge* receives an image to be published with the essay by the deadline. You may send the image yourself, or ask the artist, museum or gallery to send it. If mailed, an SASE must be included for return of materials. Images should be color where possible. Digital images should be Macintosh-formatted tif files, minimum 300 DPI. *Images must be labeled with the following information:*

• Artist's name
• Title of work, date, dimensions, media
• Credit line (photographer's name, gallery's name, etc.)

General Guidelines, Visual Art:

Slides or jpegs (via email) are acceptable. Include resume and artists statement. ALL materials must include a self-addressed, stamped envelope for return of materials. Inquiries may be emailed directly to Marie Walz, Art Editor, or Howard Fonda, Associate Art Editor, or mailed to us at *Bridge*, ATTN: Visual Art Dept., 119 North Peoria, #3D, Chicago, IL 60607.

Project Pages: Bridge does not normally accept unsolicited work for its project pages but if you would like to submit images for possible inclusion in a future project, contact Marie Walz, Art Editor, or Howard Fonda, Associate Art Editor or mailed to us at *Bridge*, ATTN: Visual Art Dept., 119 North Peoria, #3D, Chicago, IL 60607.

Sketchbook Pages: Bridge does not normally accept unsolicited work for its Sketchbook Pages, which appear only periodically in *Bridge*. Inquiries should be made to Marie Walz or Howard Fonda at the email addresses above or mailed to us at *Bridge*, ATTN: Visual Art Dept., Sketchbook Pages, 119 North Peoria, #3D, Chicago, IL 60607.

Comix Panels: Bridge does not normally accept unsolicited comix panels, which appear only periodically in *Bridge*. Inquiries should be made to Marie Walz or Howard Fonda at the email addresses above, to Michael Workman, or mailed to us at *Bridge*, ATTN: Visual Art Dept., Comix, 119 North Peoria, #3D, Chicago, IL 60607.

Illustrations: We are looking for spot illustrations and story-specific illustrations. Slides or jpegs (via email) are acceptable. Include resume and artists statement. ALL materials must include a self-addressed, stamped envelope for return of materials. Inquiries should be emailed to Howard Fonda or Marie Walz, or mailed to us at *Bridge*, ATTN: Visual Art Dept., Illustrations, 119 North Peoria, #3D, Chicago, IL 60607.

Online Book & Art Reviews: Bridge is currently accepting book reviews and reviews of art exhibitions to appear online ONLY. Art and book reviews will NOT be considered for publication in the print version of *Bridge*.

Online Book Reviews

Bridge does not publish unsolicited reviews. Writers wishing to be considered for book review assignments should send samples of previous reviews, a cover letter listing any areas of special interest (i.e., in covering contemporary experimental fiction, literature in translation, philosophy, etc.), and a brief resume.

Reviews are assigned by the editors. Ideas for reviews may also be pitched by writers. Reviews should be of contemporary authors publishing in the field of fiction, poetry, or an academic specialty (e.g. philosophy, psychology, literary or art criticism, etc.). For established authors or authors reviewed by *Bridge* in the past, reviews should be of new work. We generally do not review chapbooks, "pulp" fiction, online publishing, journal writing and reprints, etc.

Length:
- Short reviews: 500 words
- Long reviews: 750 words
- Unless otherwise stipulated by the editor.

Writing the review: Title information should appear in the upper left-hand corner of the first page of the review.

Information must include:
- Author's name/title of book
- Publisher name
- Publisher city/Year of publication
- ISBN #
- Hardcover or softcover/Page count/price

A review should include:
- Explanation of content - What is the subject matter?
- Contextualization - It is helpful to establish a context for the author's work in relation to his or her peers, in relation to the history in which they are participating (past and present), and in relation to his or her previous work.
- Interpretation - What does it mean?
- Judgment - Is it good or bad. Why? The writer's opinion of the work is the backbone of a review.

Fact-checking: Please take extra care with factual data (dates, spelling of names, and other information). We are not able to check every fact, and rely on the accuracy and integrity of our writers. If you mention a name or place, identify it, e.g. author Mary Caponegro.

Quotations: In general, reviews should not contain quotations. Avoid quoting the author or press release in reviews and do not extensively quote writers who have written reviews of the same title.

Byline: Include a writer's byline for yourself at the end of the review, such as "Sally Smith is a writer based in New York."

Editing: Reviews by writers who have not written for *Bridge* before are accepted "on spec."

All major editorial changes will be shown to the writer prior to publication. Unsatisfactory reviews will be returned for emendation.

Ethics and integrity: If you suspect an assignment may pose a potential conflict of interest, please check the situation with your editor. *Conflicts include, but are not limited to the following:*
- If you work for a commercial publisher, you may not review titles released by other publishers in your area.
- Do not review titles by people with whom you have personal relationships; i.e. relatives, close friends, significant others.
- Do not review titles with which you have any involvement (i.e. as an editor).
- Review content must be kept confidential until publication.

Bridge does not publish reviews of titles that are or will be reviewed by the writer in other publications.

Submitting: All review assignments must be cleared with your editor prior to submission. *Bridge* does not accept unsolicited reviews.

If possible, submit a press release from the publisher with your review. Sending the review via email is preferred. Send as an attached document in Microsoft Word format, or in the text of an e-mail message to: submissions@*Bridge*magazine.org and write "Book Review" in the subject line. Reviews may also be submitted on a 3.5" Macintosh floppy disk accompanied by a double-spaced hard copy.

Cover Images: Writers are responsible for making sure that *Bridge* receives a cover image of the title being reviewed. You may send the image yourself, or ask the publisher to send it. If mailed, an SASE

must be included for return of materials. Images should be color where possible. Digital images should be Macintosh-formatted jpg files. Images should be formatted for 3 x 5 inches for reviews.

Online Art Reviews

Bridge does not publish unsolicited reviews. Writers wishing to be considered for art review assignments should send samples of previous reviews, a cover letter listing any areas of special interest (i.e., in covering photography, performance art, film, etc.), and a brief resume.

Reviews are assigned by the editors. Ideas for reviews may also be pitched by writers. Reviews should be of contemporary artists showing at museums, galleries, or alternative spaces. The work should participate in current national and international dialogues on contemporary art in some way. For established artists or artists reviewed by *Bridge* in the past, reviews should be of new work. We generally do not review faculty shows, student shows, annual competitions and invitationals, etc.

Length:
- Short reviews:500 words
- Long reviews: 750 words
- Unless otherwise stipulated by the editor.

Writing the review: Exhibition information should appear in the upper left-hand corner of the first page of the review.

Information must include:
- Artist's name/title of show
- Gallery, museum, or other venue
- Gallery's street address, including city, state, and zip code
- Area code and phone number
- Dates of exhibition

A review should include:
- Physical description - Describe in detail what the work looks like: scale, materials, color, shape. The reader should be able to visualize the art from your brief descriptions of it. It is not necessary to mention every piece, likewise in a group show it is not necessary to mention every artist. Only write about those that substantiate the points you are making.
- Explanation of content - What is the subject matter?
- Contextualization - It is helpful to establish a context for the artist's work in relation to his or her peers, in relation to art history (past and present), and in relation to his or her previous work.
- Interpretation - What does it mean?
- Judgment - Is it good or bad. Why? The writer's opinion of the work is the backbone of a review.

Style: Write as clearly as possible. Reviews can become confusing when the writer relies too heavily on poetic license (ie, stretching the meaning of words), academic or theory-based language, or personal narrative and other prose or poetic structures.

As a rule, always use past tense. Exceptions are made if the show will still be on view when the review is published, or if you are discussing a piece that will still be in existence after the show closes (the work is not site-specific).

Fact-checking: Please take extra care with factual data (dates, spelling of names, and other information). We are not able to check every fact, and rely on the accuracy and integrity of our writers. If you mention a name or place, identify it, e.g. performance artist Meg Duguid.

Quotations: In general, reviews should not contain quotations. Avoid quoting the artist, press release, or catalogue in reviews and do not extensively quote writers in book reviews.

Byline: Include a writer's byline for yourself at the end of the review, such as "Sally Smith is a writer based in New York."

Editing: Reviews by writers who have not written for *Bridge* before are accepted "on spec."

All major editorial changes will be shown to the writer prior to publication. Unsatisfactory reviews will be returned for emendation.

Ethics and integrity: If you suspect an assignment may pose a potential conflict of interest, please check the situation with your editor. *Conflicts include, but are not limited to the following:*

• If you work for a commercial gallery, you may not review other commercial galleries in your area; likewise for alternative spaces, museums, schools, etc.

• Do not review exhibitions of work by people with whom you have personal relationships; i.e. relatives, close friends, significant others.

• Do not review exhibitions with which you have any involvement (i.e. as a catalogue essayist, guest lecturer, curator, or consultant).

• Review content must be kept confidential until publication.

• *Bridge* does not publish reviews of exhibitions that are or will be reviewed by the writer in other publications.

Submitting: All review assignments must be cleared with your editor prior to submission. *Bridge* does not accept unsolicited reviews.

If possible, submit a press release or announcement card from the exhibition with your review.

Sending the review via email is preferred. Send as an attached document in Microsoft Word format, or in the text of an e-mail message to: submissions@*Bridge*magazine.org and write "Art Review" in the subject line. Reviews may also be submitted on a 3.5" Macintosh floppy disk accompanied by a double-spaced hard copy.

Images: Writers are responsible for making sure that *Bridge* receives an image to be published with the review by the deadline. You may send the image yourself, or ask the museum or gallery to send it. If mailed, an SASE must be included for return of materials. Images should be color where possible. Digital images should be Macintosh-formatted jpg files. Images should be formatted for 3 x 5 inches for reviews.

Images must be labeled with the following information:
• Artist's name
• Title of show if it is a group show
• Title of work, date, dimensions, media
• Credit line (photographer's name, gallery's name, etc.)
Categories: Fiction—Arts—Culture—Literature—Music—Poetry

CONTACT: Michael Workman, Publisher and Editor-In-Chief
Material: Submission for Bridge Readings Dept
E-mail: mworkman@bridgemagazine.org
CONTACT: Mike Newirth, Fiction Editor
Material: Fiction
E-mail: submissions@bridgemagazine.org
CONTACT: Mark Tschaepe, Culture & Critique Editor
Material: Culture & Critique
CONTACT: Greg Purcell, Poetry Dept
Material: Poetry
CONTACT: David Andrews, Lit Crit Associate Editor
Material: Literary Criticism
CONTACT: Marie Walz, Art Editor
Material: Visual Art <mwalt@bridgemagazine.org> or
119 North Peoria, #3D
Chicago IL 60607
Phone: 312-421-2227
Fax: 312-421-2228
E-mail: submissions@bridgemagazines.com
Website: www.bridgemagazine.org

British Car Magazine

BRITISH CAR MAGAZINE is the only American magazine devoted exclusively to British automobiles. Our intention is to assist the active enthusiast in buying, using, maintaining, and enjoying his or her *British Car.*

In each issue, readers find a spectrum of articles on all facets of the cars and their hobby.

Classic profiles, providing historical information about a marque and model and a close-up of a specific car that typifies the marque being profiled are very popular, and we publish two to three in each issue.

Technical articles are intended to help readers understand basic technical principles, carry out general maintenance, and undertake restoration projects.

Historical articles provide readers with nostalgia and information on the cars and their development.

Articles about individual enthusiasts and their activities, such as long-distance tours, restoration projects, and unique personal histories also make entertaining reading, providing vicarious enjoyment.

Overall, the magazine is "the next best thing to driving your car."

FEATURES/PROFILES

Classic marque features including factual information and driving impressions are the core of the magazine, but should only be attempted by those with a good knowledge of the vehicles in question. All articles pertaining to a particular model or marque should be extremely well researched, compiled, and composed in such a way as to not sound like something that's been said many times before. A detailed article based around photographs of an excellent example of the model and marque and full of supporting facts and figures, current resources and historical background makes a desirable feature.

Articles can run from 1,500-4,000 words, depending on depth and scope, and should include a comprehensive set of pictures, preferable shot as slides, including front, back, sides, interior, engine compartment, trunk, and detail close-ups, plus attractive posed or driving shots.

TECHNICAL/HOW-TO ARTICLES

These articles must be well-researched. The author should have past hands-on experience and be considered an expert in the subject chosen. A query with a complete outline and introduction is acceptable for discussion prior to a completed manuscript. Step-by-step photos are, in most cases, required to illustrate the manuscript.

RESTORATION ARTICLES

British Car is always on the lookout for articles documenting complete restorations. These articles should provide a combination of specific tips on restoration of a particular model and marque, and general advice on how other readers can restore their own cars. Clear pictures documenting each step in the restoration, as well as attractive pictures of the final result are a critical element of these articles. Articles may be complete in one issue, or spread over two to three issues if they are very detailed.

ENTHUSIAST ACTIVITIES

Long tours, scenic drives, vintage races, and other organized or individual activities where the cars are put to active use are also desirable. These articles normally emphasize photography and use only a minimum of explanatory text to explain the event or activity.

"DESPATCHES"

Articles about specific field meets or events must be newsworthy, accurate, timely and well-written, accompanied preferably with one or two photos. Length should be one-half to one page, typed double-spaced. Contributors receive a small gift in return for their submission

YOUR CARS

This regular department features readers' personal cars owned by them now or in the past. Submissions should include clear photos of the car and from one to four pages typed manuscript, including history, technical information, anecdotes, funny stories, or other related information about the car Please include a SASE if you want photos returned. Upon publication a one-year subscription or renewal to *British Car* will be entered. No additional payments are made for "Your Car" articles.

SUBMISSION OF MANUSCRIPTS

Manuscripts should be submitted on computer disc, in either PC or MAC format, stored in MS Word or ASCII text and accompanied by typed hardcopy. Please do not fax manuscripts.

SUBMISSION OF PHOTOS

Well-focused, composed, and uncluttered photos are the best choice. For black and white reproduction, color prints with good contrast but without dark shadows are preferred, at least 4"x6" in size. For features, color transparencies (slides) are best. Slides should be submitted in plastic sheet slide protectors. All photos should be accompanied by captions detailing the pictures, including names of individuals pictured and identification of cars. Do not write on the backs of photos. Instead, please provide a typed manuscript sheet of captions, keyed to photo numbers.

PAYMENT

Standard payments are $75 to $100 per equivalent published page, including both text and photos, unless previous written agreement has been made, and is paid upon publication. For reprinted, previously published work, or work that requires extensive editing, the rate is $50 per equivalent page. *British Car* buys exclusive first North American publication rights as well as non-exclusive worldwide rights for manuscripts published, and any accompanying photos and artwork, including the non-exclusive right to reprint or republish the material in other electronic formats, unless other arrangements are made. The editorial staff reserves the right to edit for clarity and space without review or approval of the author.

ARRANGEMENTS AND CONSIDERATION

Before preparing material for submission, potential contributors are strongly encouraged to review several recent issues of the magazine to acquaint themselves with the approach, coverage, and format of editorial material.

Contributors wishing to have material considered for publication in *British Car* are encouraged to submit finished articles and/or photos for consideration. The staff will make every effort to acknowledge receipt of material that is not immediately returned, but can not make commitments as to publication potential.

Individuals who have had material published in other periodicals may submit proposals for specific articles if accompanied by samples of previously published work. Because of time constraints, the editorial staff can not respond by telephone or in writing to concepts or proposals for articles by individuals who do not have previous publication credits.

Categories: Automobiles

CONTACT: Gary Anderson, Editor and Publisher
Material: All
343 Second St., Ste. H
Los Altos CA 94022-3639
Phone: 650-941-3974
E-mail: editor@britishcar.com
Website: www.britishcar.com

British Heritage

Please refer to Primedia History Group

Budget Living

While, as a new magazine, we have yet to prepare formal guidelines, we are open to freelancers. Please take a look at a recent issue or our website to get an idea of how to target submissions.

Categories: Nonfiction—Antique—Consumer—Crafts/Hobbies—Fashion—Food/Drink—Money & Finances—Recreation—Travel

CONTACT: Caroline Whitbeck, Editorial Assist.
Material: All
317 Madison Ave Ste 2003
New York NY 10017
Phone: 212-657-6060
Website: www.budgetliving.com

Buffalo Spree

As Buffalo's only city magazine, *Buffalo Spree* tries to provide a wide range of engaging and compelling feature articles uniquely relevant to Buffalo and Western New York. We also offer regular coverage of home and garden design, arts and entertainment, food and dining, health and fitness, and travel and leisure. We prefer submissions in query format, rather than as unsolicited manuscripts. We encourage potential writers to keep Spree's mission as a city/regional publication in mind.

Spree accepts queries for possible feature or department articles. Send a letter with your story idea, along with samples of other published writing, and a resume to:

Categories: Fiction—Nonfiction—Arts—Entertainment—Health—Poetry—Regional—Short Stories

CONTACT: Elizabeth Licata, Editor
Material: Fiction and Nonfiction
CONTACT: Janet Goldenberg, Poetry Editor
Material: Poetry
5678 Main St.
Williamsville NY 14221
Phone: 716-839-3405
Fax: 716-839-4384
E-mail: elicata@buffalospree.com
E-mail: info@buffalospree.com
Website: www.buffalospree.com

The Bugle
Journal of Elk and the Hunt

The Bugle editorial staff is seeking manuscripts depicting the world of elk and the hunt. We accept fiction, non-fiction and scientific articles geared to the layman. Query letters are encouraged, but we also accept unsolicited manuscripts.

By reading Bugle prior to submitting (it's available on newsstands), you will gain a better sense of the kinds of stories we might publish. Thoughtful hunting stories and elk-related human interest stories are always high on our need list, as are essays on issues affecting hunting and conservation. Stories we use generally range from 1,500-4,500 words (1,000 to 3,000 words for departments like Women in the Outdoors or Situation Ethics), but we have no set length requirements.

We prefer hunting stories in which the hunter's satisfaction lies at least as much in appreciation for elk and other wildlife and for wild country and the total outdoors experience as in shooting a large bull. Sometimes it is the sheer difficulty or novelty of a hunt which attracts our interest. We do not publish how-to articles, or stories which indicate serious concern over who has taken the better trophy.

We will evaluate your story based on content, writing quality and our needs for the coming year. This process may take several months. If we decide not to publish it, the story will be returned in your self-addressed, stamped envelope with a letter to that effect.

The Rocky Mountain Elk Foundation is a nonprofit conservation organization committed to putting membership dollars into wildlife habitat, management and research. Donated manuscripts enable the Elk Foundation to devote more funds to habitat, and are tax deductible. We encourage and appreciate donated manuscripts, but gladly purchase them if that is the writer's preference. Our basic rate is 20 cents per word, paid on acceptance. Should your story appear in Bugle, you will receive three complimentary copies.

Please feel free to inquire into the status of your manuscript at any time.

Categories: Fiction—Nonfiction—Adventure—Animals—Conservation—Ecology—Environment—History—Humor—Outdoors—

Photography—Recreation—Science—Short Stories—Sports/Recreation—Hunting—Humor (elk-related)

CONTACT: Don Burgess, Hunting Editor
Material: Elk/Hunting
CONTACT: David Stalling, Conservation Editor
Material: Elk/Conservation/Natural History
CONTACT: Jan Brocci, Managing Editor
Material: Elk/Women Hunting
CONTACT: Lee Cromrich
Material: Elk/Poetry
PO Box 8249
Missoula MT 59807-8249
Phone: 406-523-4570
Fax: 406-543-7710
E-mail: dburgess@rmef.org
Website: www.rmef.org/bugle/bugle.html?main=/bugle/features.html

Business 2.0

Business 2.0 is the essential tool for navigating today's relentlessly changing marketplace, particularly as it's driven by the Internet and other technologies. It discovers and reports on the smartest, most innovative business practices and the people behind them. It delivers surprising, useful insights, and explains how to put them to work.

In the magazine we deliver great journalism that provides business people with useful, actionable insights to help them navigate and benefit from change.

On the website we offer daily editorial features and columns, in addition to resources that give readers an opportunity to research issues and network with people who have similar interests.

SUBMIT A PITCH

Our Website, www.business2.com/whatworks is a place for readers to share stories about successes and failures in the world of business and technology. We decided to create this feature online because we realized that our readers are eager to learn not just from the pages of *Business 2.0*, but also from each other. Our hope is that many of our hundreds of thousands of readers will provide their own personal "case studies" and that What Works will become the Web's greatest repository of grassroots information about what works (and what doesn't!) in business and technology. Please visit the website, if you'd like to share a story.

Note: If you are a software or hardware vendor, or a services provider, you'll do better if you get your customers to contact us directly with their stories, rather than you telling us what you've done for them.

Independent freelance writers and artists may send pitches, clips, and resumes to freelancers@business2.com with the words "freelance writer" or "freelance artist" in the subject line. (DO NOT, UNDER ANY CIRCUMSTANCES, SEND PR-RELATED MATERIALS TO THIS ADDRESS!) We use a few freelance writers, and the most successful freelance proposals come from established writers who have familiarized themselves with the magazine and our recent articles, and who can provide us with clear, smart, fresh-angled pitches on department topics. We're particularly interested in hearing about businesses that are using the Web or new technologies to achieve some measurable success.

We apologize that we can't respond directly to every e-mail, but we will contact you if we're interested in your work.

Categories: Business—Money & Finances—Technology

CONTACT: Submissions Editor
Material: Pitches, clips and resumes
One California St., 29th Floor
San Francisco CA 94111
Phone: 415-293-4800
Fax: 415-293-5900

E-mail: freelancers@business2.com (preferred submissions method)
Website: www.business2.com

Business Fleet

Business Fleet goes to 100,000 companies operating small fleets of from 10 to 50 vehicles. We run articles on such subjects as driver management, maximizing trade-in values, maintenance, telematics, fuel management, safety and accident prevention, dealer relationships, purchasing, and lifecycle costing.

We know that our target audience is very busy — they are often the owners of the company — so we make the magazine graphics-intensive and attractive to the eye. With the writing, we strive for readability and an informal tone, even while presenting material that is information-rich and sometimes slightly technical.

We pay $100 per page (500 words); in special circumstances (such as difficult assignments or short deadlines), we pay up to $150 per page. Our deadlines typically fall about three weeks after you receive an assignment. These assignments typically involve, in the case of *Business Fleet*, calling three or four vendors, such as fleet management or telematics companies, and three or four fleet managers and/or small company owners who use the products.

A good example of a recent *Business Fleet* article for which we used a freelancer is "Evaluating Diesel vs. Gasoline for Medium-Duty Trucks." This article (with background sources/leads provided by us) looked at the pros and cons of both fuels, including price, fuel efficiency, vehicle longevity, and other factors. It contained quotes from small-fleet managers in the field (we can help with these contacts) on why they chose one over the other.

We tend to go back again and again to authors who do a good job for us and demonstrate a willingness to get a "feel" for the magazines and for our target audiences, so there is an excellent possibility of an ongoing, mutually beneficial relationship.

The best way to get a feel for the "voice" of *Business Fleet* is to read a few back issues. These are available, free of charge, to serious and interested freelancers.

Categories: Nonfiction—Automobiles—Trade—Business Vehicles

CONTACT: Submissions Editor
Material: All
Bobit Publishing
21061 S. Western Ave.
Torrance CA 90501-1711
Phone: 310-533-2592
Fax: 310-533-2503
E-mail: Steve.Elliott@bobit.com
Website: www.businessfleet.com

Business Start-Ups Magazine

See *BizStartUp.com*.

Business Week

Does not accept unsolicited submission.

> *Remember: Editors change jobs and publishers change addresses. It is wise to invest in a phone call for the current information before submitting.*

ByLine

ByLine

Always include a self-addressed, stamped envelope with submissions. Manuscripts without SASE will not be read or returned. No e-mail submissions, please, but e-mail queries are okay.

We purchase first North American rights only; no reprints. Submissions must follow standard manuscript format. List your full name, address and telephone number in the upper left corner of the first page and an accurate word count (line count for poetry) in the upper right corner. Send a #10-sized SASE or larger.

Please do not confuse manuscript submissions with contest entries; these are two different processes. Send contest entries separately, following the rules on the contest page (see our website).

Manuscript Submission

Please do not e-mail complete manuscripts. Queries by e-mail are welcome, to MPreston@ByLineMag.com.

Fiction- *General short fiction, mainstream, literary or genre;* 2,000 to 4,000 words. Good writing is the main criterion. No explicit sex or violence. Payment is $100 on acceptance.

Features - *Instructive or motivational articles* that could be of genuine help to writers, especially how-to-write or how-to-sell to specific market areas. Length should be 1,500 to 1,800 words; query or submit full manuscript. We also solicit interviews with editors of freelancer-friendly publications for our Inside Information feature. Query with editor's name and sample of his publication; we'll provide specific guidelines. Payment is $75 on acceptance for all features.

End Piece - *A strong, thoughtful, first-person essay* of 700 words, related to writing. May be humorous, motivational or philosophical. Read several back issues as examples. Payment is $35 on acceptance.

Departments - *Read the magazine for examples.* First $ale carries 250-300 word accounts of a writer's first sale. Payment is $20 on acceptance. Writing-related humor of 50-600 words needed for Only When I Laugh. Pays $15 to $25 on acceptance. Great American Bookstores! features outstanding independent bookstores in 500-600 words. Stores should be unique in some way and also promote writers. No chains, children's only, or used bookstores. Pay is $30, or $40 with one good photo.

Poetry - *Our poetry also deals with the subject of writing.* We lean toward free verse but will accept skillful rhyme if it is not predictable. We seek good quality, serious or humorous poetry about the creative experience. Poems about writer's block, "the muse", and inspiration that comes in the middle of the night have been overdone. Payment for poems is $10.

How to subscribe

Mention our Web page when you subscribe and get a $5 coupon for contest entries by return mail. Send your check for $24 for one year (11 issues) or $42 for two years, along with your complete name and address (zip + four, please) to the address below.

For Canada: $28 per year in U.S. funds.

Overseas: $40 per year in U.S. funds.

To order ByLine with your credit card, see our website.

Sample copies are available from the same address for $5, postpaid.

Categories: Fiction—Literature—Poetry—Short Stories—Writing

CONTACT: Sandra Soli, Poetry Editor
Material: Poetry
CONTACT: Carolyn Wall, Fiction Editor
Material: Short stories
CONTACT: Marcia Preston, Editor
Material: All other manuscripts or queries
PO Box 5240
Edmond OK 73083-5240
Phone: 405-348-5591

E-mail: MPreston@ByLineMag.com (Queries only)
Website: www.bylinemag.com

Cadet Quest

Formerly Crusader: A Magazine for Cadets and Their Friends

About the Magazine

Cadet Quest is a Christian-oriented magazine for boys ages 9-14. It is published by the Calvinist Cadet Corps—a ministry of over 650 boys' clubs throughout churches in the United Sates and Canada. The goal of the Cadet Corps is "helping boys to grow more Christlike in all areas of life." *Cadet Quest* is one way we reach boys.

Cadet Quest is looking for fiction stories about sports, camping, athletes, or nature; craft and hobby projects; cartoon; puzzles; and illustrations.

Fiction (1000-1300 words)

Fast-moving, entertaining stories that appeal to a boy's sense of adventure or to his sense of humor are welcomed. Stories must present Christian life realistically and help boys relate Christian values to their own lives. Stories must have action without long dialogues. Favorite topics for boys include sports and athletes, humor, adventure, mystery, friends, etc. They must also fit the theme of that issue of *Cadet Quest*. Stories with preachiness and/or cliches are not of interest to us.

Nonfiction Articles (up to 1500 words)

Articles about Christian athletes, coaching tips, and developing Christian character through sports are appreciated. Photos of these sports or athletes are also welcomed. Be original in presenting these topics to boys.

Articles about camping, nature, and survival should be practical— the "how-to" approach is best. God in nature articles, if done without being preachy, are appreciated.

Nonfiction articles do not have to fit the issue's theme (though it helps, of course), but do need to fit within the *Cadet Quest* goals.

Project/Hobby Articles

Articles with clear and accurate instructions for projects boys can do with easily accessible materials are especially appreciated. Our artists can illustrate these articles, but photos are also appreciated.

Cartoons and Puzzles

Wholesome and boy-oriented, of course. Unique and/or theme puzzles or games appreciated—simple logic, crosswords, and hidden pictures are favorites.

Illustrations

Illustrations are done on a contracted basis to fit stories and articles. Send sample work for consideration. Photos should be at least 5x7, but snapshots are acceptable if sharp and clear. Action shots are preferred.

About *Cadet Quest* Readers

Generally speaking, *Cadet Quest* boys are active, inquisitive, and imaginative. They imitate their heroes and they love adventure. They are sociable and form groups easily. Many of them make decisions for Jesus Christ that will affect them the rest of their lives. Because our goal is to help boys see how God is working in and around them, every article and story for every issue is chosen for a specific purpose or reason. It must be wholesome, Christian, and age-appropriate.

Although *Cadet Quest* is the "official" publication of the Cadet Corps, it is designed to appeal to every pre-adolescent boy.

Method of Selection

Manuscripts submitted to *Cadet Quest* are read as they are received—we try to read them within four to eight weeks. If your manuscript doesn't fit our needs, it is returned in your SASE within one week of our decision, or recycled at your request or if you haven't included an SASE.

Themes for the new editorial season are chosen in January. By the end of April, all fiction selections are made for that editorial season. Fiction manuscripts are normally not purchased between May and December. After selecting material, we notify authors whose material will be published and return anything not selected. The new season's theme list is made available following their selection in January. (Include an SASE for your copy, or visit our website.)

Editing

The *Cadet Quest* staff reserves the right to edit any accepted manuscript or cartoon. Editing is done with a conscious effort to retain the author's style and intent.

Basis for Rejection of Material

1. Inappropriate. Does not show boys how God is working in their lives or world.

2. Not age/gender appropriate for 9-14 year old boys.

3. Simplistic, unrealistic, too predictable or preachy, or theological perspective too different from our own.

4. Does not fit themes.

5. Too similar to material already published/submitted.

6. Editorial needs already filled.

7. Very limited need for poetry.

8. Poor writing. Poor opening, transitions, grammar. Lacks excitement or adventure that appeals to readers.

Rights

We purchase all rights, first rights, and second rights. We have no qualms about purchasing rights to articles/stories that have been printed elsewhere, providing the audiences do not overlap.

Payment

Payment is made upon final acceptance of the material, varying according to the rights purchased and amount of editing needed. Current rates:

Manuscripts: 5¢ per word and up (first rights with no major editing)
Cartoons: $5 and up for single gags; $15 and up for full-page panels
Puzzles: Rates vary
Photos: $5 for each photo used with an article

Submissions

Please do not send queries before submitting a manuscript.

Mail: Send complete manuscript, typed, double-spaced, one-sided copy on white opaque paper. Include your name, desired byline, and address on the first page. Also indicate what publishing rights are offered and approximate number of words. On succeeding pages, include page number and your name.

Submit cartoons as camera-ready art.

Puzzle submissions must include answers.

Please include an SASE with correct postage if you would like your materials returned. Any material without an SASE will be recycled.

Online: Submit stories or articles (text) online at submissions@calvinistcadets.org. Submissions must be included in the body of the e-mail, not as an attachment. We will not open any material sent as attachments.

Tips for Acceptance

Write to our audience and to the issue's theme. Keep stories or articles exciting and entertaining. Include humor. The best time to send your submissions to Cadet Quest is between January and April. Remember our purpose of showing God's work in boys' lives!

Themes/Guidelines/Sample

For editorial theme list and/or author guidelines, send a #10 envelope with sufficient postage. For a free sample copy, simply write and ask, including a 9x12 SASE ($1.01 US postage, $1.14 Cdn postage). Requests sent without the required SASE will be recycled. Send your request to: Managing Editor, *Cadet Quest*, PO Box 7259, Grand Rapids, MI 49510-7259.

CONTACT: G. Richard Broeme, Editor
Material: All
PO Box 7259
Grand Rapids, MI 49510-7259
Phone: 616-241-5616
Fax: 616-241-5558
E-mail: submissions@calvinistcadets.org
Website: www.calvinistcadets.org

California Journal

Thank you for your interest in *California Journal.*

The *Journal* is a non-partisan monthly magazine that reports on California government and politics. Article submissions should be news-oriented and should focus on issues or personalities of statewide interest. The *Journal* puts a premium on lively, well-written articles that feature strong and original reporting. The editors usually assign stories on topics that are receiving widespread press coverage to *Journal* staff members, so these should be avoided unless some new, unreported angle is involved. Payment for stories is negotiated on an individual basis and ranges from $150 to $1,000, depending on the complexity of the story and the qualifications of the writer. Lengths vary according to subject. The *Journal* buys all rights to stories.

It is best to query a proposed article with the editor by phone, letter, or e-mail, and writers should establish their credentials on a given subject at the time an inquiry is made. Final submissions should be submitted on IBM-PC compatible disks or sent via fax or modem. Normally, the *Journal* does not pay a kill fee or expenses; however, these are negotiable. Payment for stories is normally made within two weeks after publication.

Categories: Government—Politics—Reference—Public Policy

CONTACT: A. G. Block, Editor
Material: Any
2101 K St.
Sacramento CA 95816
Phone: 916-552-7001
Fax: 916-444-2339
E-mail: AG_Block@sbcglobal.net

California Lawyer

California Lawyer is a monthly magazine about legal affairs, with related looks at business and politics. It is distributed to more than 140,000 California lawyers, plus 10,000 subscribers nationwide. We are interested in concise, well-researched articles on news and trends in the legal profession, legal aspects of current events, and general interest articles of benefit or interest to attorneys.

In an average month, we assign two feature articles. In addition, we publish columns on technology and strategies of sole practitioners.

In our California, Esq. section, we publish about six news stories on current case law, state and national politics, and shifts in the legal marketplace. In our Technicalities section, we assign case studies, reviews, and news articles on how software, hardware, and the Internet affect the practice of law.

Our editors will review unsolicited manuscripts, but we always prefer that contributors send query letters describing proposed articles. Letters should include a brief outline of the story and the intended approach. Please enclose copies of previously published work.

Payment for feature articles of 2,000-4,000 words ranges from $750 to $2,000, depending on the nature of the assignment and the writer's experience. Payment for columns of 1,000-1,500 words is $500. Payment for news articles and shorter technology pieces ranges from $50 to $350.

Articles should be double-spaced, with wide margins and numbered pages. Unsolicited manuscripts should be accompanied by a stamped, self-addressed envelope if you would like us to return your article. Please address correspondence to Tema Goodwin, Managing Editor.

Categories: Nonfiction—General Interest—Government—Politics—Society

CONTACT: Tema Goodwin, Managing Editor
Material: All
Daily Journal Corporation
44 Montgomery St., Ste. 250
San Francisco CA 94104
Fax: 415-296-2482

California Wild
California Academy of Sciences

CALIFORNIA WILD "Natural Sciences for Thinking Animals" (formerly Pacific Discovery) is a quarterly magazine published by the California Academy of Sciences, the research facility, natural history museum, and aquarium in San Francisco's Golden Gate Park. Circulation is approximately 30,000.

California Wild's readers are well-educated, and most are residents of California. They are concerned about environmental issues and are committed to informing themselves and others about the natural world. Our readers' interests range widely, from ecology to geology, from endangered species to anthropology, from field identification of plants and birds to an armchair understanding of complex scientific issues.

Articles should avoid a textbook style. It is not enough for a topic to be interesting scientifically, articles must also tell a story and illuminate for our readers the greater significance and timeliness of a topic. New information, new theories, new research should be featured prominently. Where there is controversy it is fine to take a stance, but opposing arguments should be aired. We prefer to emphasize possible solutions to conservation and environmental issues, rather than list problems. We're primarily looking for stories within our geographic region, which includes California and adjacent seas and regions, but almost every issue contains something farther afield.

Departments: Skywatcher: An account of recent research in a field of astronomy: 2,000-3,000 words. Wild Lives: A description of unusual behavior in a particular species or genus: 1,000 words plus excellent photos. Trail Less Traveled: A 1,000-word description of the fauna and flora seen along a little known, but not too strenuous, hike.

We purchase first North American serial rights and we also request electronic rights, as a version of *California Wild* is available through the Internet. Payment is 25 cents per word, two weeks prior to publication. Articles range in length from 1,000 to 3,000 words. Most authors are asked to submit on speculation; few assignments are given.

Authors of articles typically are well-informed professional writers or authoritative scientists with experience writing for popular audiences. Authors should interview and quote specialists and other authorities. There can be a primary source but use more than one source. Some first-hand experience with the subject is also appreciated.

Query letters: A proposal should take the form of the proposed story's opening paragraphs, followed by a description or outline of the remaining text. Faxed queries are fine, but we don't encourage e-mail queries.

Style of articles should be friendly, anecdotal, and thorough. We prefer to avoid technical language and to define specialized terms only when the words themselves and the concepts they embody are appropriate to the story. Regardless of the complexity of the subject matter, authors should try to write simply, using short sentences and paragraphs of not more than four or five sentences. Colloquial usages are fine as long as they're not carried to extremes. Stories should include fleshed out personalities, these may be scientists, environmentalists, or historical figures.

Manuscripts should be neat, with margins of not less than one and one-quarter inches all around. The author, abbreviated title, and page number should be typed in the upper right corner of every page. The first page must include the author's name, address, telephone number, social security number, and a close estimate of the number of words in the article. Once a manuscript is accepted, we will request a computer disk, if one is available. The story should be saved in ASCII or "text only."

Style Tips: Include scientific names in parentheses after common names of species. Spell out numbers from one to twelve and use numerals for measurements. Refer to *The Chicago Manual of Style*.

Source Documentation must be available for every manuscript. Authors should be prepared to provide a list including complete information about publications consulted and interviews conducted, including the name, title, address and telephone number of each source.

Photography: Photographs should be submitted in the form of original color transparencies or reproduction—quality dupes. Color slides must be mounted in flexible, page-size sleeves and must also be protected with individual slide protectors. Each transparency must be clearly marked on the cardboard mount itself with: the photographer's name and address, a sequencing number, and information describing the content of the photograph. Enclose a stamped, self-addressed envelope, return mailing instructions, and sufficient postage to cover safe return, including insurance if you wish. Our current photo needs are published in the Guilfoyle Report (Call 212-929-0959 for information).

Most articles are illustrated. If an author has no direct access to photographs (the author's own or others), referrals to photographers with professional-quality material are appreciated. We rarely use photographs without an accompanying text. But the right photos might inspire us to find one. We also use photographs which "tell a story" of a sequential event.

We purchase one-time publication rights to images. Payment ranges from $75 to $175 inside, and $200 for a cover. We may also use images as part of pages in promotional material. In the unlikely event that an original transparency is lost or damaged, the Academy's liability is limited to fair market value, and we are not bound by any arbitrary valuations.

Captions, typed on separate pages, must be numbered to correlate with numbers on the photographs. Captions should be written as complete sentences, providing both primary and secondary information about the subject of the photograph. If the photographs include people, their names must be noted with correct spelling. Plants and animals should be carefully identified.

For a sample copy, send a self-addressed, stamped envelope with postage-$1.75.

Categories: Animals—Book Reviews—Conservation—Ecology—Environment—Science

CONTACT: Keith Howell, Editor
Material: California Natural History/Traditional Cultures
Golden Gate Park
San Francisco CA 94118-4599
Phone: 415-750-7116
Fax: 415-221-4853

The Caller

Please refer to *Turkey Call*.

Calliope Magazine

General Information

CALLIOPE covers world history (East / West) and we are looking for lively, original approaches to the subject. Keep in mind that our magazine is aimed at youths from ages 8 to 14. Writers are encouraged to study recent back issues for content and style. (Sample issues are available at $4.95. Send 7 ½ " x 10 ½ " self-addressed $2.00 stamped envelope.) All material must relate to the theme of a specific upcoming issue in order to be considered. CALLIOPE purchases all rights to material.

Procedure

In order for your idea to be considered, a query must accompany each individual idea (however, you can mail them all together) and must include the following:

• A brief cover letter stating the subject and word length of the proposed article,

• A detailed one-page outline explaining the information to be presented in the article,

• An extensive bibliography of materials the author intends to use in preparing the article,

• A self-addressed stamped envelope.

Authors are urged to use primary resources and up-to-date scholarly resources in their bibliography. Writers new to CALLIOPE should send a writing sample with the query. If you would like to know if your query has been received, please also include a stamped postcard that requests acknowledgment of receipt. In all correspondence, please include your complete address as well as a telephone number where you can be reached.

A writer may send as many queries for one issue as he or she wishes, but each query must have a separate cover letter, outline, bibliography, and self-addressed stamped envelope. All queries must be typed.

Articles must be submitted on disk using a word processing program (preferably Microsoft Word - MAC). Text should be saved as ASCII text (in MS Word as "text only"). Disks should be either MAC - (preferred) or DOS - compatible 3½ ".

GUIDELINES

Feature Articles:

700-800 words

Includes: in-depth nonfiction, plays, and biographies

Supplemental Nonfiction:

300-600 words

Includes: subjects directly and indirectly related to the theme. Editors like little-known information but encourage writers not to overlook the obvious.

Fiction:

Up to 800 words

Includes: authentic historical and biographical fiction, adventure, retold legends, relating to the theme. The above three pay 20 to 25 cents per printed word.

Activities:

Up to 700 words.

Includes: crafts, recipes, woodworking, or any other interesting projects that can be done either by children alone or with adult supervision. Sketches and description of how activity relates to theme should accompany queries.

Poetry:

Up to 100 lines. Clear, objective imagery. Serious and light verse considered. Must relate to theme.

Puzzles and Games:

(please, no word finds). Crossword and other word puzzles using the vocabulary of the issue's theme. Mazes and picture puzzles that relate to the theme.

The above three pay on an individual basis.

Photo Guidelines

To be considered for publication, photographs must relate to a specific theme. Writers are encouraged to submit available photos with their query or article. We buy one-time use.

See our website for suggested fee range for professional quality photographs.

• Please note that fees for non-professional quality photographs are negotiated.

Cover fees are set on an individual basis for one-time use, plus promotional use. All cover images are color.

Prices set by museums, societies, stock photography houses, etc., are paid or negotiated.

Photographs that are promotional in nature (e.g., from tourist agencies, organizations,

special events, etc.) are usually submitted at no charge.

If you have photographs pertaining to any upcoming theme, please contact the editor by mail or fax, or send them with your query. You may also send images on speculation.

NOTE

Queries may be submitted at any time, but queries sent well in advance of deadline MAY NOT BE ANSWERED FOR SEVERAL MONTHS. Go-aheads requesting material proposed in queries are usually sent five months prior to publication date. Unused queries will be returned approximately three to four months prior to publication date. Hard copy queries ONLY, no email.

Categories: Children—History—Juvenile—Young Adult—World History

CONTACT: Rosalie Baker, Editor
Material: All Queries
Cobblestone Publishing
30 Grove Street, Suite C
Peterborough NH 03458
Phone: 603-924-7209
Fax: 603-924-7380
Website: www.cobblestonepub.com

Calyx Journal
A Journal of Art and Literature by Women

Thank you for your interest in CALYX. CALYX Journal accepts submissions of poetry, short fiction, visual art, essays, reviews, and interviews. *The writer's/artist's guidelines are as follows:*

Prose (includes essays) should not exceed 5,000 words.

Poetry submissions are limited to 6 poems.

Reviews should not exceed 1,000 words. If you are interested in reviewing books, please send a resume, published samples of writing, and an SASE. After reviewing these, you will be contacted about the book review list.

Interviews should be limited to 2,500 words.

Visual Art should be submitted on 35mm slides or 8"x10" or 5"x7" black and white glossy photographs (limit 6 slides or photos). All art media are considered. Please label all slides and photos with your name, titles, media, dimensions, and date. Also mark the top of the work. Do not write on photos! Attach all necessary information on a label. Include a brief biographical statement and a separate 50-word statement about your artwork. CALYX is always open for art submissions.

Black and white reproductions are used inside the Journal, so consider how well your work will look in black and white. Color is only used on the covers.

Submit art separately from prose and poetry.

All submissions should include author's name on each page and be accompanied by a brief (50-word or less) biographical statement, a self-addressed, stamped envelope (SASE), and a phone number. Even if you indicate that it is unnecessary to return submission(s), enclose an SASE for your notification. Prose and poetry should be submitted separately with separate SASEs for each submission category.

CALYX assumes no responsibility for submissions received without adequate return postage, packaging, or proper identification labels. Every effort is made to respond to submissions in a timely manner, but CALYX receives a large number of submissions when open, and it may take up to six to nine months to read and review everything received. Simultaneous submissions are accepted.

PLEASE NOTE: CALYX Journal is only open for submissions for prose and poetry once annually, October 1-December 31.

Sample copies of CALYX are available for $9.50 plus $2.00 postage and handling.

Thank you for your interest in CALYX.

We look forward to reviewing your work.

Categories: Fiction—Nonfiction—African-American—Asian-American—Feminism—Gay/Lesbian—General Interest—Hispanic—Literature—Multicultural—Native American—Poetry—Short Stories—Textbooks—Women's Fiction—Women's Issues

CONTACT: Micki Reaman, Managing Editor
Material: Any
CONTACT: Beverly McFarland, Senior Editor
Material: Any
PO Box B
Corvallis OR 97330
Phone: 541-753-9384
Fax: 541-753-0515
E-mail: calyx@proaxis.com

Camping Today

We appreciate your interest. *Camping Today* is a 32 page, ten times per year magazine which serves the 20,000 member families of the Family Campers & RVers (founded as NCHA, National Campers & Hikers Association). The July/August and January/February issues are combined. Because organization news is a priority we can only buy one or two articles a month. We print on a two month lead time.

75% of our readers are over age 55 and most are owners of recreational vehicles such as travel trailers, fifth wheels, and motorhomes. They enjoy reading nonfiction articles around 1,500 words on interesting places to visit by RV, how-to-do-it features related to camping, and topics of general interest to campers.

Payment is in the range of $35 to $125 depending on the type of article and photographs. Please send the photos with the article. We buy one time rights and will consider previously published articles (at minimum rates). We can't use poems or essays on "our first or worst campout."

Allow 60 days for a response.

Categories: Recreation Vehicles—RV/Camping

CONTACT: DeWayne Johnston, Editor
Material: RV Travel
126 Hermitage Rd.
Butler PA 16001
Phone: 724-283-7401

Campus Life

Meet *Campus Life*

Campus Life's contemporary and relevant editorial deals with the real life issues of high school and college students, including sex, spiritual concerns, friendships, school and music.

Campus Life is published bimonthly by Christianity Today International, 465 Gundersen Drive, Carol Stream, Illinois 60188. Please send all e-mail to clmag@campuslife.net

WRITER's GUIDELINES
Who Writes for *Campus Life*?

Writers who understand and empathize with a Christian world view is a good start, but that's not enough. Freelancers must be pros who understand our unique style and editorial philosophy. Don't query until you've studied at least one issue of *Campus Life* (Sample copy available for $3.00).

What Type of Article Works Best?

First-person stories that capture experiences from the lives of teenagers are our readers' favorite. These can be dramatic narratives or stories that highlight a "life lesson" learned through common everyday adolescent experiences. A first-person story must be highly descriptive and incorporate fictional technique. While avoiding simplistic religious answers, the story should demonstrate that Christian values or beliefs brought about a change in the young person's life. Since this is our editorial bread and butter, experienced freelancers should consider writing "as told to" first-person stories based on an experience from an interviewee's life Guidelines for writing first-person stories are available upon request.

What Else Does *Campus Life* Print?

Humor, fiction, and information for teens considering a Christian college. All such writings must be tied to the teenager's life experience. We also offer several regular departments that are largely staff written. Specific writer's guidelines for fiction, first person and humor pieces are available upon request.

What Doesn't Work?

Essays and how-to articles are not wanted. There are a few exceptions, yet even exceptions must be highly anecdotal and demonstrate a clear understanding of our style and editorial philosophy. Manuscripts are rejected if they: become moralistic or preachy; offer simplistic solutions; take an adult tone; use religious clichés and overuse/misuse religious language; lack respect and empathy for teenagers.

Guide for Writing First-Person Stories

The first-person or "as told to" first-person story is the best way for a new writer to break into our freelance pool. It is also the best way for a seasoned writer to remain there. It's no overstatement to say that the personal narrative is our editorial "mainstay." Follow these guidelines and your manuscript will receive serious consideration.

Study first-person stories. Guideposts© and *Reader's Digest*© are excellent resources. Most of all, study the first-person stories that appear in *Campus Life* before submitting anything. (Sample copy available for $3.00.).

Interview thoroughly. For "as told to" stories, be sure to tape a thorough interview with your subject. During the interview, probe for details that will add life and color to your story.

Show, don't tell. Appeal to the five senses through strong descriptive writing. Use fictional technique: Pay attention to plot (problem focus), character and scene development, setting, dialogue, and credible resolution.

Focus on the best scenes. Don't try to "tell it all." Pick scenes that are germane and develop those to the fullest. If possible, try to keep your story within a short interval of time.

Don't force your message. Weave your "life lessons" into the fabric of the story.

Think readers. Your story needs to have "universal appeal" to all of our teenage readers, both male and female.

Don't force religious values. A Christian world view should be represented, yet creatively and in a manner that won't alienate or puzzle the non-churched teenager. If the story becomes preachy, brings characters "out of character" to deliver a message or uses religious clichés, it won't work for us.

Mechanics. *Campus Life* does not accept unsolicited manuscripts. Query first. Requested manuscripts should be typed/keyboarded and double-spaced. Simultaneous submissions must be indicated on the first page. Length should be between 1,200 and 2,500 words. Based on difficulty and length, we pay 15 cents to 20 cents per word. Expect a response in three to six weeks.

Guide for Writing Fiction

It's not uncommon for a writer to query us with: "I know a teenager who had a problem and I have written a fictional piece based on that problem. …" Our usual response: "So why not tell the story in a true, first-person narrative?" That is the most helpful advice we can offer. At tops we print three short stories a year, and those are usually written by experienced, seasoned professionals. With that caution, consider these guidelines.

Know Campus Life. Do not query without a thorough understanding of this magazine. (Sample copy available for $3; when requesting a copy be sure to ask for fiction samples.).

Style and technique. Pay attention to strong descriptive scenes, credible dialogue, and realistic action, conflict and resolution.

Setting/perspective/tone. Story must take place in the world of today's high-school or college student and must be told from a teenager's perspective. Tone must not be condescending and/or adult. The overall "feel" must show a respect and empathy for the teenager's life and experiences.

Language. Strive for simplicity. Keep adjectives and adverbs to a minimum. Go instead with active, appropriate verbs. Remember: Lions roar, parents yell; rain trickles, people cry; cars travel, eyes look; etc. Exchange clichés for fresh expressions. Use metaphorical language sparingly and without mixing. Faddish, teen colloquialisms are not acceptable.

Predictability. We quickly reject stories that are simplistic, dependent on coincidences or end too neatly. A good fictional piece reflects life's shades of gray and complexities.

Point and message. In keeping with our editorial philosophy, each story we publish must contain a "lesson life" that represents a Christian world view. Yet this life lesson must be natural—not forced. "Religious message writing" is out. Give the reader credit for a good measure of intelligent, analytical thinking. Offer a credible resolution, yet strive for subtlety.

Mechanics. Campus Life does not accept unsolicited manuscripts. Query first. Requested manuscripts should be typed/keyboarded and double-spaced. Simultaneous submissions must be indicated on the first page. Length should be no longer than 2,000 words. Based on difficulty and length, we pay 15 cents to 20 cents per word. Expect a response in three to six weeks.

Categories: Campus Life—Education—Juvenile—Lifestyle—Music—Relationships—Sexuality—Spiritual—Young Adult

CONTACT: Marilyn Roe, Editorial Administrator
Material: All
Campus Life
465 Gundersen Drive
Carol Stream IL 60188
Phone: 630-260-6200
Fax: 630-260-0114
E-mail: clmag@campuslife.net
Website: www.christianitytoday.com

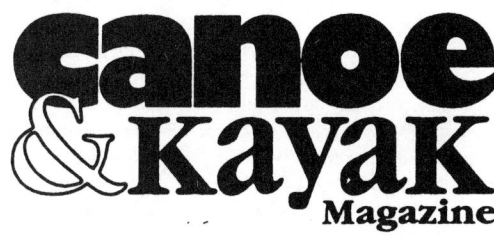

Canoe & Kayak Magazine

Editorial Submissions

Thank you for your interest in *Canoe & Kayak*! If you haven't already done so, we suggest that you review a recent issue of our magazine so that you can see what kinds of stories and photos we are using. You'll find *Canoe & Kayak* Magazine at many bookstores, large newsstands, and paddlesports retail shops. If you have trouble finding a copy, we'll send you a sample if you send us a self-addressed, 9-by-12-inch envelope with seven first-class stamps. Subscriptions are $17.95 per year.

Our readers include flatwater and whitewater canoeists and kayakers of all skill levels. We provide comprehensive information on destinations, technique, and equipment. Beyond that, we cover a variety of subjects of interest to our readers, including canoe and kayak camping, safety, the environment, and the history of boats and sport. We publish a limited number of personality pieces on people of national importance.

Most issues contain at least three feature articles of 2,000 to 2,500 words each. These features cover the range of subjects appropriate for our audience and are distinguished from departments by more in-depth coverage in the story and more liberal use of accompanying photographs. Regular departments, of 500 to 1,200 words, cover specific subjects such as techniques, new equipment, and boat reviews. Traditions and Take Out are devoted to reflective, personal essays on paddling.

The Put-In section uses short (700 words or less), newsy pieces that cover conservation, interesting people, and events. Keep in mind that you are writing for a national audience.

Our Destinations articles emphasize canoeing and kayaking trips that take no more than a few days to complete. Submissions should be a maximum of 1,500 words in length and include a map of the area showing the put-in, take-out, towns, tributaries, and features mentioned in the article; copies of materials we may need to check facts (name spelling, phone numbers, prices, etc.); a selection of quality color slides with captions; a sidebar giving driving directions to the put-in from the nearest town; trip length; seasonal information; permit requirements for paddling and camping; whitewater classification and hazards; recommended guidebooks (author, title, publishing information); and phone numbers of local sources.

Submissions

You can either query or submit material on speculation. If querying, give a brief outline of the proposed article. You can submit queries either by post or e-mail (editor@canoekayak.com). Allow at least six weeks for a response. To ensure return of your material, provide a self-addressed, stamped envelope of proper size. Please note: we will treat submissions with care, but we are not responsible for unsolicited manuscripts or photographs.

We prefer submissions in both hard copy and on disk. Please note whether your files are in Mac or IBM format on your disk, and please DO NOT double-space electronic copy or set tabs. We can accept most popular word-processing formats, but to be safe, please save a copy of the file in text format as well. Hard copies should be double-spaced.

We follow the *AP Stylebook* and *The Chicago Manual of Style.*

Preference will be given to writers who can supply color photographs with articles (see photo guidelines below).

Payment and Rights

Our base rate is 15¢ per published word. Rate for assigned articles may vary. Payment is made on publication. We purchase first international rights, which includes first anthology rights and electronic rights.

Photo Submissions

Canoe & Kayak is always looking for strong images appropriate for the magazine in 35mm, 2 1/4 x 2 1/4, or 4x5 slide formats. We prefer duplicates for selection purposes, provided that they are of good quality. We require a model release when the subject of the photo is easily identifiable.

We prefer unpublished images and do not use images that show a lack of common sense, lack of knowledge about paddlesports, or disregard for safety or the environment. People are usually wearing life preservers in photos we select. We do not use images of people in sailboats, rowing craft, or powerboats.

Payment

Canoe & Kayak Magazine pays on publication and purchases one-time or international serial rights. Rates are based on the published size and use (color or b/w) of the image:

Color
- $500 for a cover
- $350 for a full spread
- $300 for a three-quarter spread
- $250 for a full page
- $150 for a half page
- $75 for a quarter page or smaller
- $25 for second use of image in same publication

Black and White
- $200 for a full page
- $125 for a half page

• $75 for a quarter page or smaller
• $25 for second use of image in same publication

Place your name, address, and phone number on each image. *Canoe & Kayak* Magazine will handle each submission with due care, but we assume no liability for unsolicited original or duplicate slides, prints, or transparencies. Include a self-addressed envelope with proper postage for the return of your material. We normally reply to unsolicited material within six weeks.

Categories: Nonfiction—Adventure—Boating—Consumer—Family—Outdoors—Recreation—Sports/Recreation—Travel

CONTACT: Editor
Material: Editorial submissions
CONTACT: Art Director
Material: Photo submissions
PO Box 3146
10526 NE 68th St.
Kirkland WA 98033
Phone: 206-827-6363
Website: canoekayak.about.com

Capper's

ABOUT US

CAPPER'S has been taken to heart by families for more than 120 years, striving to enlighten and entertain while concentrating on traditional American values. CAPPER'S emphasizes life's positive perspectives and offers the opportunity to earnestly share joys and tears within the caring community of readers. CAPPER'S is a rural American tradition, growing from its Kansas roots to spread across the country. CAPPER'S takes a positive approach to the art of living, and subscribers in all 50 states love it and believe in it, often passing their copies among family and friends. Reader interest is the key to CAPPER'S continued popularity. The Heart of the Home is CAPPER'S most popular section. It is composed of reader-submitted letters, sharing humorous, heartwarming, poignant and nostalgic experiences of life. It also includes patterns and down-home recipes, including a special Kate Marchbanks feature recipe in every issue.

CAPPER'S columns include the well-loved Reader to Reader, in which subscribers help each other find old friends, family, and songs, and plan for reunions. Garden Clippings presents gardeners, old and new, with timely advice and suggestions for new plantings. Medical advice from Dr. Paul G. Donohue and a financial column by Bruce Williams are reader favorites. Reader questions are answered in Social Security Connections.

News stories, feature articles, photos, editorials and news briefs keep CAPPER'S readers in touch with the world.

CAPPER'S offers a wide selection of poetry in each issue, and serialized fiction remains a reader favorite.

SUBMISSION GUIDELINES

CAPPER's is a nationally distributed biweekly tabloid publication with a national paid circulation of approximately 240,000. It emphasizes home and family to readers who live mainly in the rural Midwest.

CAPPER's publishes manuscripts an average of two to 12 months after acceptance. It purchases first North American serial rights, with the exception of Heart of the Home letters, in which all rights are retained. Seasonal or holiday material should be submitted at least four months in advance. Notification of acceptance or rejection is made within two to three months, six months for serialized novels. No simultaneous submissions. Query for novel-length manuscripts only; submit all others complete.

If you wish to be notified of the status of your manuscript, please send a self-addressed, stamped envelope. If you wish to have your manuscript returned, send SASE with adequate postage. No manuscripts will be returned without adequate postage.

Features

CAPPER's uses historical, inspirational, nostalgic, family-oriented, travel and human-interest stories; unusual accomplishments, collections, occupations, hobbies, etc. Approximately 75 manuscripts are purchased annually (not including Heart of the Home). Use journalistic style. Payment is made upon publication at the rate of approximately $2.50 per printed inch. Length: 900 words maximum. Good quality accompanying photos considered.

CAPPER's uses 1-2 cartoons per issue Payment of $10-15 is made upon acceptance. Submit in batches of no more than 15.

Poetry

Free verse and light verse, traditional, nature and inspirational poems are purchased. Those selected are easy to read, with down-to-earth themes. Five or six poems are used in each issue. Limit submissions to batches of 5-6, length 4-16 lines. Payment of $10-$15 is made upon acceptance; tear sheet sent upon publication.

Jokes

CAPPER's buys 5-10 jokes per issue. Jokes published earn a $2 gift certificate. Limit submissions to batches of 5-6. Sorry, no jokes returned.

SERIALIZED NOVELS

Fiction: Query first, with brief description of plot and characters. Manuscripts accepted omit profanity, violence, sex and alcohol use. Four to six manuscripts are purchased annually. Payment of $100-$400 is made upon acceptance. Manuscripts of 12,000 to 25,000 words preferred; 7,500 words minimum, 50,000 maximum.

Manuscripts should be double-spaced with numbered pages and accurate word count. Use readable fonts; no italics or scripts.

PHOTOS

Color: Submit 35 mm color slides, transparencies or sharp color prints in batches of no more than 40. Include caption material. Payment of $40 for front page, $20-40 inside, made upon publication.

Black and white: Good quality photos accompanying manuscripts are considered. Payment is $5-15, depending on size and quality.

Heart of the Home

"Kate Marchbanks" uses letters sharing humorous, heartwarming, poignant and nostalgic experiences of life. These are mostly reader-written. Submissions may be held up to one year, especially if they are seasonal. Payment of $2 per printed inch is made upon publication. Length: 300 words maximum. Payment for recipes is $5 each. Hints used earn a $2 gift certificate.

"Space Place" is for original drawings, poems, jokes, stories, etc., by children 12 and under. Contributors receive T-shirts. (Include birth date, home address and shirt size with submission.)

CAPPER's retains all rights for Heart of the Home material.

We do not accept electronic submissions.

Items used on our Web site receive an additional $5.

Categories: Agriculture—Culture—Family—Gardening—General Interest—Inspirational—Lifestyle—Mystery—Outdoors—Poetry—Recreation—Regional—Romance—Rural America—Senior Citizen—Travel—Western

CONTACT: Ann Crahan, Editor-in-Chief
Material: All
c/o Ogden Publications, Inc.
1503 SW 42nd St
Topeka KS 66609
Phone: 785-274-4300
Fax: 785-274-4305
Website: www.cappers.com

Car and Driver

We do not accept unsolicited manuscripts, but story ideas in writing are accepted.

Categories: Nonfiction—Automobiles—History—Recreation—Sports/Recreation—Satire—Humor—Nostalgia

CONTACT: Csaba Csere, Editor-in-Chief
Material: All
2002 Hogback Rd.
Ann Arbor MI 48105-9736
Phone: 734-971-3600
Fax: 734-971-9188
E-mail: editors@caranddriver.com
Website: www.caranddriver.com

The Magazine For Those Who PLAY TO WIN!

Card Player

OUR MISSION STATEMENT
Our mission is to bring you a well-written, interesting, accurate, and informative magazine that will tweak your poker interest, knowledge, and comportment to make poker more enjoyable for you.

STANDARD TERMS AND CONDITIONS
These Standards Terms and Conditions (the "Standard Terms"), made and entered into as of the date of the Magazine Articles Submission Letter (the "Submission Letter"), are expressly incorporated into and made a part of the Submission Letter. The Standard Terms together with the Submission Letter govern the relationship between SM and Writer with respect to Writer submitting the Articles to SM for the purpose of being published in the Publication. (Capitalized terms not otherwise defined shall have the meanings set forth in Section 1 below.) By countersigning the Submission Letter, Writer is expressly agreeing to comply with and be bound by all the terms and conditions set forth in these Standard Terms and in the Submission Letter.

1. Definitions. As used herein, the following defined terms shall have the following meanings:

a. "Agreement" means, collectively, the Standard Terms and the Submission Letter.

b. "Articles" means, collectively, those magazine articles that Writer is submitting to SM for the purpose of being published in the Publication.

c. "SM" means Shulman Media, LLC, a Nevada limited liability company.

d. "Publication" means SM's biweekly publication entitled *"Card Player."*

e. "Writer" means the party who wrote the Articles and who is submitting the Articles to SM for the purpose of being published in the Publication.

2. Grant of Rights. For the consideration set forth in the Submission Letter, and subject to Section 3 below, Writer hereby irrevocably grants, conveys, and assigns exclusively to SM, forever and throughout the universe: (i) all right, title, and interest in and to the Articles, and any and all parts thereof, free and clear of any and all claims, liens, and encumbrances, including interactive media rights, Internet rights and book rights, and the right to utilize, reproduce, and exploit any of the foregoing rights; (ii) the right to utilize, reproduce, exploit, advertise, and promote Writer's name, likeness, photograph, and biography in connection with the Publication, SM's Web site located at www.cardplayer.com, and any advertising and public-

ity relating thereto; and (iii) the right to edit the Articles in any manner SM deems appropriate.

3. Rights Reserved to Writer. Notwithstanding the foregoing, Writer reserves the nonexclusive right to use and reuse the Articles in any form, manner, and media that Writer determines, so long as Writer does not use or reuse the Articles in connection with or for the benefit of any magazine that competes with the Publication. SM will have the sole discretion to determine whether a magazine competes with the Publication, and SM will periodically provide Writer with a list of those magazines that are determined to be in competition with the Publication. Presently, only Poker Pages and Poker Digest are prohibited publications. Except as set forth in the foregoing sentences, Writer reserves no other rights of any kind or nature whatsoever in or to the Articles, all such rights being granted to SM pursuant hereto.

4. Writer's Representations and Warranties. Writer hereby represents and warrants to SM that: (i) Writer has full and complete right, title, and interest in and to the Articles, has not sold, granted, conveyed, or assigned any of Writer's right, title, or interest in or to the Articles to any person or entity and has the full power, capacity, and authority to grant to SM the rights granted herein; (ii) no liens, encumbrances, claims, proceedings, and/or litigation presently exist or are pending with respect to the Articles; and (iii) the Articles are wholly original with Writer and shall not infringe upon or violate any statutory copyright, common law rights, proprietary rights or any other rights whatsoever of any person or entity.

5. Writer's Indemnification. Writer indemnifies, defends, protects, and holds harmless SM, and each of its members, managers, employees, licensees, agents, representatives, successors, and assigns, as well as any third parties claiming rights through SM, from and against any and all claims, liabilities, damages, losses, and costs of any kind resulting in connection with or otherwise resulting from the breach by Writer of any of the foregoing warranties.

6. Writer's Release. Writer releases, discharges, and acquits SM and each of its members, managers, employees, licensees, agents, representatives, successors, and assigns, from any and all claims, liabilities, damages, losses, and costs of any kind that Writer may now or hereafter have against SM, whether for defamation, invasion of right of privacy or publicity, or otherwise, arising out of or in connection with the exercise of any rights granted hereunder.

7. Entire Agreement. This Agreement constitutes the entire agreement among the parties and supersedes and cancels any prior agreements, representations, warranties, or communications, whether oral or written, among the parties to this Agreement relating to the transactions contemplated by this Agreement or the subject matter herein.

8. Miscellaneous. This Agreement will be governed by and construed in accordance with the laws of the state of Nevada (without regard to conflicts of law principles), and the parties hereby consent to the jurisdiction of Nevada State and Federal courts located within Clark County, over all matters relating hereto. In the event of any litigation between or among the parties arising out of this Agreement, the successful or prevailing party will be entitled to recover its reasonable attorneys' fees and other costs in connection therewith. This Agreement may not be amended, modified or supplemented except pursuant to an instrument in writing signed by each of the parties. This Agreement may not be assigned by any party without the other Party's prior written consent, and any attempted unauthorized assignment will be null and void.

Categories: Nonfiction—Games—Poker Gaming

CONTACT: Submissions Editor
Material: All
3140 S. Polaris, Ste. 8
Las Vegas NV 89102
Phone: 702-871-1720
Fax: 702-871-2674
E-mail: cardplay@wizard.com
Website: www.cardplayer.com

Careers & the Disabled

Please refer to Equal Opportunity Publications, Inc.

Caribbean Travel & Life

Caribbean Travel & Life is now in its 16th year of providing stories and photos about the fascinating region of the world that is the Caribbean. Potential writers for the magazine should understand, first and foremost, that our audience is made up of upscale, sophisticated and experienced Caribbean travelers: our research indicates that they visit the islands repeatedly. Therefore, our readers look to CT&L to guide them to the new and interesting places to visit, to explore the many facets of Caribbean culture and to highlight the fascinating people of the islands.

The editors of CT&L are always open to ideas from writers. Our only requirements are that the writing be superb, the subject be something unique and interesting, and the writer must know his/her subject. To understand what kind of stories we buy, read the magazine. We do NOT run generalized travelogues, guidebook-like island profiles, or stories about well-known, over-publicized or commonly visited places. Our readers demand behind-the-scenes stories, off-the-beaten-path destinations, ahead-of-the-curve knowledge about the Caribbean.

Most of the major features in CT&L are assigned to staff or to writers with whose work we are familiar. New writers will have better success starting off in one of our departments. Always keep in mind that the availability of good photographs to illustrate a story is essential.

TO SUBMIT

To submit a query, send a brief letter to Bob Friel, Editor, Caribbean Travel & Life, 460 N. Orlando Ave., Suite 200, Winter Park, FL 32790; FAX to 407-628-7061; or e-mail to editor@worldpub.net. Please do not call and do not send a complete manuscript unless requested by an editor.

Categories: Nonfiction—Culture—Entertainment—Regional—Travel

CONTACT: Bob Friel, Editor
Material: All
World Publications
460 N. Orlando Ave. Ste 200
Winter Park FL 32790
Phone: 407-628-4802
Fax: 407-628-7061
E-mail: editor@worldpub.net
Website: www.carribeantravelmag.com

Carolina Quarterly
The University of North Carolina

History

Since 1948 *The Carolina Quarterly* has served as a forum for the best work by writers with established reputations and by writers at the very beginnings of their careers. Among the many fine writers whose work has appeared in *The Carolina Quarterly* are Conrad Aiken, Wendell Berry, Anthony Burgess, Raymond Carver, Don DeLillo, Annie Dillard, Louise Erdrich, Lawrence Ferlinghetti, Paul Green, Michael S. Harper, Archibald MacLeish, Joyce Carol Oates, Reynolds Price, Kenneth Rexroth, and Thomas Wolfe. Among contributors to recent issues are Doris Batts, Mark Doty, Stephen Dunn, Clyde Edgerton, George Garrett, Barry Hannah, William Harmon, X. J. Kennedy, James Laughlin, Denise Levertov, Robert Morgan, and Gregory Orr.

Guidelines for Writers

The editorial board of *The Carolina Quarterly* welcomes submissions of fiction, poetry, reviews, nonfiction, and graphic art. Prose and poetry in all styles and on all subjects are of interest. The board also considers translations of work originally written in languages other than English. Black-and-white graphic art is used to illustrate prose in each issue and to decorate each cover.

Despite its name, *The Carolina Quarterly* goes to press three times a year, so manuscripts and artwork may be kept under serious consideration for four months or more. The editorial board considers unpublished work only and does not consider simultaneous submissions. All correspondence may be sent to the editorial board at the address below. Writers and artists should send only clear copies of their work.

Contributors of writing and art receive two copies of the issue in which their work appears and a 50% discount on additional copies. *The Carolina Quarterly* acquires first-publication rights to each work accepted for publication; subsequent to publication, rights revert to the author. Writers without major publication credits are eligible for the yearly Charles B. Wood Award for Distinguished Writing, a $500 prize for the best poem or story by an unestablished writer published in each volume.

Sample Copies and Subscriptions

Writers and artists may find it helpful to look at a sample copy of *The Carolina Quarterly*. A sample copy of a recent issue costs $5 (including shipping and handling). Yearly subscriptions to *The Carolina Quarterly* are just $12 to individuals. International subscriptions to individuals are $15.

Categories: Fiction—Nonfiction—African-American—Book Reviews—Gay/Lesbian—Interview—Literature—Men's Fiction—Men's Issues—Poetry—Short Stories—Women's Fiction—Women's Issues—Writing—Reviews

CONTACT: Fiction Editor
Material: Fiction
CONTACT: Poetry Editor
Material: Poetry
Editorial Board
CB 3520 Greenlaw Hall
University of North Carolina
Chapel Hill NC 27599-3520
Phone: 919-962-0244
Fax: 919-962-3520
Website: www.unc.edu/depts/cqonline

Cascades East Magazine
Central Oregon's Quarterly

Two types of articles offer limited opportunities for freelancers:
• First-Person Accounts of Outdoor Activities
• First-person accounts, with black & white or color photos, of outdoor activities in Central Oregon (Deschutes, Jefferson & Crook counties) are of particular need. Activities can include fishing, hunting, camping, hiking, backpacking, spelunking, etc. These would be strong narratives although treatment can be dramatic, factual or humorous. No "travel folder" tours. Queries are considered, however finished articles of 1,000 to 2,000 words are preferred.

Historical Features

Each issue includes a "Little Known Tales from Oregon History" feature. Query letters are preferred along with a statement of the availability of black & white photos. Length from 1,000 to 2,000 words.

Payment for the Above

5 to 15 cents a word with additional payment for photos. Payment is made upon publication.

Color Photos

Vertical, color transparencies of superior quality are needed, on a limited basis, for the magazine cover.

Editing

Any material accepted is subject to such revision necessary in our sole discretion to meet the requirements of *Cascades East*.

Categories: Adventure—Fishing—History—Outdoors—Physical Fitness—Recreation—Sports/Recreation

A-E

CONTACT: Geoff Hill, Editor
Material: All
PO Box 5784
Bend OR 97708
Phone: 541-382-0127
Fax: 541-382-7057
E-mail: Sunpub@sun-pub.com

Cat Fancy

Writing for Cat Fancy: Thank you for your interest in *Cat Fancy*, a consumer magazine directed to the general cat-owning population and dedicated to improving the lives of cats worldwide. We have listed below some of the publication requirements of our magazine.

Before you get started, we suggest that you read past issues of the magazine to acquaint yourself with the type of material we use. Past issues are available at many public libraries, or you may order a sample issue by sending $5.50 to the address on the back.

Unsolicited Manuscripts: *Cat Fancy* does not read or accept unsolicited manuscripts; however, the editors are happy to consider article queries. Unsolicited manuscripts sent with a self-addressed, stamped envelope are returned unread. Those without an SASE are discarded. Please query if you have an article idea in mind.

Feature Articles: While 90 percent of the feature articles that appear in *Cat Fancy* are assigned to writers we work with regularly, we do occasionally accept a feature or feature sidebar from a new contributor.

Each month, we try to provide our readers a mix of informative articles dealing with feline health, nutrition, grooming, behavior and training, as well as a fun feature or two on cat-related events, hobbies, etc. Breed profiles, run nearly every month, are usually assigned to a breeder or cat show judge. Occasionally, we run exceptional pieces of fiction or photo essays. We rarely use stories in which the cat speaks as if it were human.

While we assign most medical and behavior pieces to certified experts in the particular field, we will consider well-researched pieces by freelancers it experts are consulted. While there is no substitute for good writing, experts add credibility.

Department Articles: With few exceptions, our departments are written by regular columnists or by the editors. We occasionally accept articles of less than 1,000 words for our Cat Newsline column. Such articles should cover news items of national interest to cat lovers. Possible subjects include new legislation affecting cat owners, medical breakthroughs and trends in cat care.

We also use short stories, how-to pieces, word puzzles, quizzes and craft projects in our Kids for Cats column, a section aimed at our readers between 10 and 16 years old. Good-quality photographs are essential to craft projects.

The Feline Friends department is a column written by readers about their special cats. We accept Feline Friends submissions for consideration only once or twice a year. Check the end of the Feline Friends column in a current issue of the magazine for an announcement of when we will be accepting manuscripts again and for submission specifications. If no announcement appears, we are not currently accepting submissions.

Poetry: Poetry is the one exception to our query-first policy. The editors are happy to consider short, cat-related poems, which are used primarily as filler in the back of the magazine. We put no limit on the number of poems you may submit, but be sure to include a self-addressed, stamped envelope large enough for their return.

In general, we're looking for straightforward poems that capture the essence of the cat or of what owning a cat means to our readers. We rarely go for esoteric poems with deep hidden meanings. To get a feel for our readers, read back issues of the magazine.

The Query: *Following are a few points to consider when querying:* When possible, limit your query to one typewritten page.

We will be judging your writing ability on your query letter—put as much effort into your letter as you plan to put into your manuscript.

Research, research, research. Before sending a query, know the subject and be sure your letter reflects this knowledge. If you wish to write on a medical or behavioral subject in which you are not a certified expert, plan to interview an expert or two for your story. Include that information in your query.

Read back issues to find out whether we've recently covered your planned topic and to familiarize yourself with our style and readership.

If available, include one or two previously published writing samples.

Excellent-quality color photographs are essential to considering stories on regional events or cat-related attractions.

Please be patient. We'll make every effort to respond to your query within eight weeks. Occasionally, however, this simply isn't possible.

We do not consider fax, telephone or e-mail queries.

Submission Specifications: We only assign articles to writers with whom we work regularly; all others will be asked to submit work on speculation. After assignment or a go-ahead to send an article on speculation, your manuscript should be typewritten and double-spaced. Send both a hard copy and an electronic file in ASCII or text-only format on a 3.5 inch disk.

We prefer that articles be accompanied by appropriate art in the form of professional-quality transparencies or professional illustrations. We rarely use black-and-white photos. For more information, send for our photo guidelines, photo needs list and/or artist's guidelines.

With every submission, include a self-addressed, stamped envelope large enough to accommodate return of your materials.

Payment: *Cat Fancy* pays on publication. Article fees are based on the quality of the article and the experience of the author. We pay more for manuscripts accompanied by good-quality photographs.

You can expect payment to arrive in the latter part of the cover month in which the article appears (for example, if your piece appears in the November issue, your check should arrive in the latter part of November). We buy first North American Serial Rights on an exclusive basis; the nonexclusive right to use the article and/or artwork in electronic media; and the nonexclusive right to use the article and/or artwork as well as your name, image and biographical data in advertising and promotion.

Responsibility: We cannot assume responsibility for materials you submit, but we assure you that we will take all reasonable care in handling your work.

Miscellaneous: Inquiries should be in writing. While it may seem quicker to call, interruptions throughout the day will lead to a longer turnaround time for manuscripts and queries in the long run.

Additional guidelines are available for artists and photographers. Send an SASE with your request.

You must include a self-addressed, stamped envelope with every query or submission. We cannot respond to or acknowledge any correspondence or submission that does not include an SASE.

If you've been assigned an article and must send it via an express delivery service to meet your deadline, call our offices to get the street address. Please do not fax materials unless requested to do so by the editors.

Categories: Fiction—Nonfiction—Animals—Children—Crafts/Hobbies—Games—Health—History—Hobbies—Poetry—Short Stories—Pets—How To—Humor—Personal Experience—News

CONTACT: Steve Triolo, Assist. Editor
Material: All
PO Box 6050
Mission Viejo CA 92690
Phone: 949-855-8822
Fax: 949-855-3045
Website: www.catfancy.com

Catholic Digest

What material *Catholic Digest* uses:

Non-fiction articles: 1,000-3,500 words on almost any topic. Our readers have a wide range of interests—religion, family, science, health, human relationships, nostalgia, good works and more.• *Catholic Digest* article rates: $100 for reprints, $200-400 for originals. For re-use in electronic form, we pay half of all traceable revenue derived from use to owner/author. Online-only articles receive $100, plus half of any traceable revenue from electronic use. A copy of the issue is included with payment if published in *Catholic Digest*. Finders' fees: $15 per article published.• Send submissions to: Articles Editor, *Catholic Digest* Publications, P. O. Box 6001, Mystic, CT 06355, or by email to lwilson@bayardpubs.com. If submitting by mail, enclose a self-addressed, stamped envelope (SASE).

Monthly features include:

Open Door: Statements of true incidents through which people are brought into the Catholic faith, or recover the Catholic faith they had lost. (200-500 words)

People Are Like That: Original accounts of true incidents that illustrate the instinctive goodness of human nature. (200-500 words)

Perfect Assist: Original accounts of gracious or tactful remarks or actions. (200-500 words)**Fillers:** jokes, short anecdotes, quizzes. (one-liners to 500 words)

Catholic Digest filler rates:

To authors, we pay $2 per published line (full-page width) upon publication. For this payment, your filler may be published in any *Catholic Digest* publication, including *Catholic Digest*, Catholic Digest Reader Large Print, and HELLO HEAVEN, our online Web site (http://www.CatholicDigest.org). A copy of the issue is included with payment if published in *Catholic Digest*. Finders' fees are $5 or $10, depending on length.

Tips on selling a manuscript to *Catholic Digest*:

Before you submit a manuscript, study a copy of *Catholic Digest* for article tone and style, or check HELLO HEAVENO (http://www.CatholicDigest.org).We favor the anecdotal approach. Stories submitted must be strongly focused on a definite topic. This topic is to be illustrated for the reader by way of a well-developed series of true-life, interconnected vignettes. Most articles we use are reprinted—they have appeared in another periodical or newspaper. But we also consider original submissions. Don't query. Send the article itself. We don't consider fiction, poetry, or submissions simultaneously sent to other publications. Include your name, address, and telephone number on each submitted page. If you are submitting an article for reprint consideration, you must include the name, address, and editor of the original publication source, the copyright line from the original source, and the page number and date of the original publication.

If you are submitting an original manuscript by mail, please send a double-spaced, typewritten photocopy and, if possible, an ASCI text file saved on a 3.5-inch diskette; e-mail submissions should be included in the text of your message rather than as an attached file.

Categories: Nonfiction—Family—Health—Humor—Relationships—Religion—Science—Spiritual—Catholic Church

CONTACT: Articles Editor
Material: Non-Fiction
CONTACT: Filler Editor
Material: Filler: Jokes, short anecdotes and quizzes.
Catholic Digest Publications
P. O. Box 6001
Mystic CT 06355
Phone: 800-321-0411
E-mail: lwilson@bayardpubs.com

Catholic Near East

Please refer to *CNEW World*.

CC Motorcycle News Magazine

CC Motorcycle News Magazine *is always happy to review freelance articles, stories, and poetry, but will only accept unsolicited material that meets the following guidelines:*

1. Articles and stories must have a word count of no less than 750 words and no more than 2500 words. Poetry can be of varying lengths (within reason).

2. Articles, stories, and poetry can be about any subject, fiction or non-fiction, as long as the subject pertains to motorcycles or the world of motorcycling. Examples would include fiction or non-fiction stories about traveling cross-country on a motorcycle, biker lifestyle or perspective, motorcycling/biker humor, etc. Poetry can have a serious focus but light or humorous verse is generally preferred. Submissions need not be concerned about the date of the subject — motorcycling is rich in history, and stories about older bikes or past experiences are always welcome. Still, reading the publication thoroughly is the best way to understand what we seek from our writers.

3. Submissions MUST be sent in electronic form, on computer disk, text-only format or .rtf (Interchange Format) for IBM or Mac (Word 5.1 files may be sent as "Normal") or via e-mail with files attached. A printed copy is also welcome but is not necessary. If photos accompany an article or story, a written explanation for each photo MUST also be given. DO NOT write on the back of the photo (use Post-It™ notes or peel and stick labels). Identify the event, the motorcycles (if they are the subjects), and all people whose faces can be seen.

4. We will gladly return all submissions for which a SASE is provided.

We purchase all rights then license them back to you for $1.00 — this is because we need to own all rights for our copyright but also want to allow you to sell your work to other markets. Payment is $150 maximum for stories with photos from regular contributors; $10 minimum to $100 for all others depending on quality and need for editing. Tearsheets or contributor copies will be provided with payment. Payment is made at or within 30 days of publication.

Copies of current or past issues are available for $3.00 or you can read past articles on our website: www.motorcyclenews.cc.

Categories: Fiction—Nonfiction—Automobiles—Humor—Lifestyle—Short Stories—Travel

CONTACT: Mark Kalan
Material: All
Motomag Corp.
PO Box 808
Nyack NY 10960
Phone: 845-353-MOTO (6686)
Fax: 845-353-5240
E-mail: CCMNeditor@yahoo.com
E-mail: mark@motorcylenews.cc
Website: www.motorcylenews.cc

Central PA Magazine

EDITORIAL FOCUS

The central heartland of Pennsylvania ranges from rural expanses and small-town charm to vibrant cities with surprisingly diverse populations and cultural offerings. It's home to the state capital and Amish country, firehouse barbecues and world-class arts centers, ubiquitous outdoor recreation and a bustling economy. To sample the life of the region each month, *Central PA* magazine expresses a downhome knowledge of its territory with a sophisticated eye and literate writing. Our writers tell the stories of the region's people, history, places and events in intelligent prose and experiential narratives. Our storytelling component is tempered by analytical pieces on issues and initiatives that affect the region or informational articles about lifestyle trends that enable our readers to make better use of all the region has to offer.

MONTHLY FEATURES

Central Shorts and Central Stories comprise our opener section, with glances (175-750 words) into useful, suprising or quirky aspects of life in the region — the joys and trials of working as a costumed Hershey candy character, a look into the state treasury's mysterious underground vault, a visit to a ferret-rescue shelter or a local computer security firm with international scope. It's spiced with occasional quotes from the region's newspapers, mini-reviews of local books or CDs, or interesting local websites we've noticed.

In our departments, Opinion addresses an overlooked or unique angle on some aspect of state, local or national politics or public affairs. Our Essay department showcases the musings of some of the best writers in the region, on virtually any topic — humorous, serious, reflective or analytical, but always a good read. Our interview feature, Cameo, presents a monthly encounter with an interesting *Central PA* resident, from an opera singer to a rock vocalist, from the matron of a soft-pretzel empire to a female boxer.

Thirty Days is our events calender, highlighting noteworthy goings-on in 18 counties, plus a sprinkling of happenings in nearby urban areas.

Food is essential to identity in the region that invented shoofly pie, where (mostly locally produced) potato chips and pretzels take up a whole aisle in the grocery store, and where new dining establishments seem to be opening almost daily. Anchoring our Food section is The Phantom Diner, in which our anonymous restaurant critic sits down at one the region's tables each month and reports on the experience in detail. We also elicit a recipe and some thoughts on cooking from a *Central PA* chef each month, review cookbooks, provide entertaining tips and give a nod to local markets and drinking establishments.

A local duo of world-class puzzle creators whose credits include Atlantic Monthly and the Boston Globe supplies our crossword on *Central PA* themes.

ANNUAL FEATURES

In January, *Central PA* releases its much-awaited annual Dining Guide, with more than 1,000 restaurants throughout the region, picked by our readers as places where they like to eat. Winners are chosen in dozens of categories, including best overall restaurant in the region.

Our July issue is our annual Insider's Guide, giving natives and visitors alike a portrait of our 18-county region's offerings in the arts, educational and historic sites, tourist attractions and festivals, nightlife, day-trips, sports and outdoor recreation.

We finish off the year with a bow to the Best of *Central PA*, a lighthearted look by a panel of writers and editors at things throughout the region that stand out in their admittedly arbitrary categories.

WRITERS' GUIDELINES

Central PA magazine, a publication of WITF, Inc., is a general-interest regional magazine serving more than 43,000 families in 18 counties of Central Pennsylvania.

SUBJECT MATTER & POLICIES:

Central PA magazine publishes feature articles about interesting people, places, cultural and social issues, and activities that relate to life in Central Pennsylvania. The editorial content also includes essays, Q&As and short articles reviewing or discussing books, theater, music, news, food, dining, sports and outdoors. Features should be of broad interest, have a strong regional connection and be based on more than one source. The editors seek writing that is lively and literate. Writers must submit source information for fact-checking and be willing to work closely with editors before, during and after the submission process. Article lengths in the magazine range from 175-word vignettes to 3,000-word feature articles, although queries for the shorter pieces are much more likely to meet our editorial needs.

SUBMISSIONS:

Written queries are required for all articles and should be sent via mail, fax or e-mail to the attention of—Steve Kennedy, Senior Editor.

Telephone queries will not be accepted. Submissions will be considered on speculation only from writers with whom *Central PA* magazine has not previously worked. Articles are assigned by contract to established writers.

Revised 9/5/01

Categories: Nonfiction—Arts—Cooking—Culture—Education—Entertainment—Environment—Family—Food/Drink—Gardening—Health—History—Interview—Lifestyle—Multicultural—Outdoors—Regional

CONTACT: Steve Kennedy, Senior Editor
Material: All
CONTACT: Tracy Erb, Managing Editor
Material: All
WITF, Inc.
1982 Locust Lane
Harrisburg PA 17109
Phone: 717-221-2800 or 800-366-9483
Fax: 717-221-2630
E-mail: centralpa@centralpa.org
Website: www.centralpa.org

Ceramics Monthly

The following information is intended to serve as a guide for the submission of materials for publication in *Ceramics Monthly* magazine. If you have additional questions, please contact the editorial department: telephone (614) 794-5890; e-mail editorial@ceramicsmonthly.org.

About *Ceramics Monthly*

Recognized as "the world's most widely read ceramic arts magazine," *Ceramics Monthly* engages a wide variety of readers. Artists/potters, educators, students, gallery and museum personnel, and collectors alike enjoy full-color articles on studio artists/potters and exhibition coverage, as well as news, commentary and process-oriented articles.

Who Writes for *Ceramics Monthly*?

Our authors come from many walks of life. Although most are directly associated with ceramics, we also receive manuscripts from engineers, chemists, art critics, historians, collectors, publicists and others who have a topic of interest to CM subscribers.

What Kinds of Articles Are Needed?

Because of our readers' diverse interests, many kinds of articles are accepted, but the following categories are typical of what CM publishes most:

Profiles

This is perhaps the most popular article format in *Ceramics Monthly*. We prefer first-person accounts covering the full range of the potter's or sculptor's experience, including aesthetic concerns, business practices, technical data, etc. See "A Lot to Think About" by Craig Martell (May 2002) or "Intentional Serendipity" by Scott Ruescher (November 2001) as examples.

• Informational Articles: CM publishes a range of articles relating to the making and selling of ceramic art and craft. These include such topics as recipes for glazes and clay bodies, forming methods, innovative processes, studio layout and production flow, business practices, ceramics history, and ceramics in higher education. Technical articles on the leading edge of the field are also welcome.

• News and Exhibition Articles: Submissions concerning exhibitions, workshops, symposia and other ceramics-related events should include the location, date, names of the presenters/exhibitors (with their complete mailing addresses) and a description of the work(s) shown. Additional information (such as artists' statements, clay and glaze recipes, or details about forming or decorating techniques) may be of interest to a larger audience, thus increasing chances for publication.

For exhibition reviews, we prefer texts that include critical analysis of the work (what makes it good, bad, innovative, controversial, etc.), as well as pertinent background information of value to potters, ceramics sculptors, students and educators, and collectors. Publishable images of each work discussed must accompany the text.

• Commentary: Well-reasoned, substantiated thoughts on any ceramic craft- and art-related issues are particularly sought for the Comment column. (Responses to previous Comments are not eligible, but may be submitted to the Letters column.)

Manuscript Preparation

The average manuscript ranges from 1000 to 3000 words. Thus, it should be approximately 4 to 12 pages, typed double-spaced with ample margins. Please place your name, mailing address, telephone/fax number and e-mail address (if available) on the title page. Consecutively number each page, including the first. Unillustrated texts or submissions with digital graphics may be e-mailed to editorial@ceramicsmonthly.org, but please mail a printed copy as well. Texts submitted on disk (as a text-only file) should also be accompanied by a printed copy. We will need only one copy of your manuscript, but you may wish to keep a copy for your own reference.

Copyright

We ask for exclusive worldwide rights for the text (both print and electronic versions, including but not limited to publishing on demand, database online services, reprints or books), and nonexclusive rights for use of the photographic materials in print or electronic media.

Payment

We do not pay for news items or exhibition announcements. All other articles receive our standard fee following publication. Current rates are 10¢ per printed word and $25 per image. An article published in the Comment column receives the flat rate of $75.

Images

The quality of images is extremely important in determining manuscript acceptance. Slides and transparencies submitted for publication should be in focus, properly exposed and with a full range of contrast. No part of the work should be completely hidden by shadow. In most cases, the photographer should use a neutral background (typically gray, black, white or earthtones; avoid primary colors). Images of a work-in-progress should all have the same axis (either vertical or horizontal). It is best to submit as many images as possible (including bracketed exposure variations, if available).

• Slides/transparencies: We prefer professional-quality, large-format (2 1/4-inch-square or 4x5-inch) transparencies shot with any low ASA (ISO) film, but we can also work with original (not duplicate) 35mm color slides on a high-resolution film, such as Kodachrome 25 or Ektachrome 64T. Of course, slides or transparencies taken using other film types will also be considered, provided film grain or contrast does not detract from image quality.

• Photographs: Glossy prints in color or black-and-white are also used on occasion, primarily for candid action shots; however, color photocopies and laser prints are not suitable for publication.

• Digital images: We are very excited about this developing technology; however, consumer-level digital cameras do not produce acceptable images for high-quality print reproduction. Until the standards of film are matched, *Ceramics Monthly* will continue to work primarily from slides/transparencies.

The shortfall in resolution alone makes most digital images unacceptable. While the camera manufacturers may boast that their products can deliver high-resolution images, this is because they interpolate (invent) more information than is actually recorded.

The vast majority of consumer-level digital cameras have limited aperture settings and make exposure adjustments with an intense flash. Depth of field, range of contrast and color accuracy suffer as a result. As one professional photographer recently noted: "Until digital attains the dynamic range of the best large-format films, we need to stick with film."

Graphics

We also accept drawings for visual explanation of hard-to-photograph tools, equipment and processes, and charts for technical data.

Captions

Caption information should include the title of the work (when applicable), dimensions, specific ceramic medium (e.g., earthenware, stoneware, porcelain, etc.), brief description of forming and glazing techniques, firing temperature or cone, year made, and price (specify retail or wholesale). Number the slide mount or transparency sleeve and list captions with corresponding numbers on a separate sheet of paper.

Credits

Please provide the photographer's name so that credit may be duly noted. Whenever images by more than one photographer are used to illustrate an article, each photo should be identified with the appropriate photographer's name. It is the author's responsibility to secure permission to use photographic materials. CM does not credit collectors or collections.

Sending a Complete Submission

Enclose a cover letter, text, images and any other support materials in one package. Include a self-addressed, padded envelope with sufficient postage if you would like your materials to be returned. Protect the photographic materials with cardboard on both sides, and mark the package "Contains Photographs-Do Not Bend." Mail the package first class to: The Editor, *Ceramics Monthly*, P.O. Box 6136, Westerville, OH 43086-6136. Timely, unillustrated manuscripts may also be faxed to (614) 891-8960.

Evaluation and Acceptance

When your submission arrives, it will receive immediate attention. A member of the editorial staff will acknowledge receipt and perhaps ask for additional information or images. Once the submission is complete, the editors will consider it for publication.

Acceptance decisions are made at monthly review meetings, after which publication contracts are mailed to the authors. We ask that you give *Ceramics Monthly* exclusive worldwide rights to the text, and nonexclusive rights for any other use of the photographic materials in any other form, such as electronic media, reprints or books. This nonexclusive agreement allows for the continued use of the photographic material in any way the artist chooses after the article has The average time from acceptance to publication is between two months and one year, depending on article length and subject. The author and artist(s) are notified approximately one month prior to publication.

Editing and Proofs

Texts are edited first for style, grammar and punctuation, as well as technical accuracy, then to meet layout requirements. Because changes may take place up to the time the presses roll, we are unable to provide final proofs; however, galley proofs are available on request.

Layout

Article design takes place after initial editing. CM does not accept layouts from authors or subjects.

Copies

Following publication, two complimentary copies of the magazine containing your feature article will be mailed to you; additional copies are available for purchase on a first-come, first-served basis. Authors/subjects of Upfront items receive two page prints.

Categories: Arts—Ceramics—Crafts/Hobbies

CONTACT: Editor
Material: All
PO Box 6136
Westerville, OH 43086-6136
Phone: 614-895-4213
Fax: 614-891-8960
E-mail: editorial@ceramicsmonthly.org
Website: www.ceramicsmonthly.org

Change
The Magazine of Higher Learning

SCOPE

Change is a magazine dealing with contemporary issues in higher learning. It is intended to stimulate and inform reflective practitioners in colleges, universities, corporations, government, and elsewhere.

Using a magazine format, rather than that of an academic journal, *Change* spotlights trends, provides new insights and ideas, and analyzes the implications of educational programs, policies, and practices.

Over the past few years it has included articles on trend-setting institutions and individuals, innovative teaching methods, technology, liberal learning, the curriculum, the financing and management of higher education, for-profit and entrepreneurial higher education, faculty, the changing needs and nature of students, the undergraduate experience, administrative practice and governance, public policy, accountability, and the social role of higher education. The topics of the coming year's issues can be found on the Heldref Website, at http://www.heldref.org/. We encourage you to submit articles—whether brief expressions of a point of view (750 to 1,500 words) or more extended articles of from 2,500 to 5,000 words—on one of those topics or on others of current importance to higher education.

AUDIENCE

Change, which is published six times a year, is intended for individuals responsible for higher learning in college, university, and other settings, including faculty, administrators, trustees, state and federal officials, and students, as well as corporation, union, and foundation officers.

MANUSCRIPTS

Owned by Heldref Publications, a division of the nonprofit Helen Dwight Reid Education Foundation in Washington, *Change* is one of the 43 journals and magazines published by Heldref. The magazine staff at Heldref includes a full-time managing editor, Nanette Wiese, and an associate editor, Lea Pasternak. It is to Heldref that you direct all manuscripts, letters to the editor, and queries about guidelines for writers, as well as questions about advertising and subscriptions. (See below for relevant contact information.)

All manuscripts must be submitted in hard copy, on 8 1/2" x 11" paper, 12-point font, double-spaced, with one-inch margins, and page numbers, in triplicate. If the article is accepted, we will request an electronic copy of the article.

Because *Change* is a magazine rather than a journal, footnotes should not be included. References can be worked into the text or given parenthetically when necessary. A short list of "Related Readings" or "Resources" can be provided with the article where appropriate, and URLs can be provided for Web sites containing more extensive documentation.

A separate title page should provide short biographical information (up to four or five lines) and contact information, including the complete address, telephone, and fax number, and e-mail of the author(s). The first-named author of a multi-authored article will receive the notification of acceptance, rejection, or need for revision.

REVIEW PROCESS

When we receive your manuscript, we will send you a postcard verifying that your article has entered the review process. All manuscripts are read first by Barbara Cambridge to determine their suitability for *Change*. If the fit is not good, you will hear within six weeks. Those that are promising she sends to two consulting editors, who evaluate them for accuracy, argument, style, and interest to the readership. Barbara reads returned reviews to assign those that are positive to another executive editor. This process takes from three to four months to complete. (Should the manuscript be held for longer than usual, you will be notified at the end of four months and offered the option of withdrawing the manuscript from consideration.)

If the article is accepted, you will be contacted to discuss editing procedures and the production schedule for the issue of the magazine in which your article will appear. Each author receives six complimentary copies of the issue in which the article is included. Authors may also order additional copies or reprints (minimum order of 100) at their expense.

Manuscripts should be submitted exclusively to this publication.

CONTRIBUTING TO *Change*

By agreement with Heldref, AAHE is responsible for all editorial judgments about the magazine: its themes, articles, and editorial voice.

AAHE exercises that judgment through a team of four executive editors—Barbara Cambridge, Cheryl Fields, Peter Ewell, and Margaret Miller.

Even the best manuscripts compete for limited space: We publish just six times a year and given that many of the articles are solicited, we can use but 20 or so of the hundreds of manuscripts submitted. What accounts for acceptance or rejection? Topics that have been exhausted (the culture wars) or that are too broad (the history of universities in 2,000 words or less) or too specific for our broad audience (preventing dormitory theft) will not be published, nor will those written in the style of a journal—heavy on jargon and footnotes, light on analysis and point of view.

This last criterion is important. *Change* is a magazine, and the magazine article is a genre unto itself. A good article compels attention to an important matter. It shows a mind at work, one that reaches judgment and takes a stance. It is credible: it knows its subject and the context. And it is concrete: It names people, places, dates, and events. For a good idea of the kind of writing that works for *Change*, we encourage you to read a few past issues.

Change doesn't start with an ideological predisposition; we court good ideas from all sides. But tracts, broadsides, and grand plans seldom impress reviewers (or readers), who prefer real, usable ideas that someone has actually tried out and evaluated.

Beyond writing for *Change*, we encourage you to write to the magazine. Feedback is not plentiful in the magazine business, and any reader comment gets full attention. Your reactions to what we publish help your editors make *Change* better and more valuable for all of us.

—Barbara Cambridge, Cheryl Fields, Peter Ewell, and Margaret Miller

Categories: Nonfiction—College—Education

CONTACT: Managing Editor
Material: All
Heldref Publications
1319 Eighteenth Street, NW
Washington DC 20036-1802
Phone: 202-296-6267, Ext 222
Fax: 202-296-5149
E-mail: ch@heldref.org
Website: www.aahe.org/change

Charleston Magazine

Charleston Magazine has been a Low-country institution for more than 30 years, distilling the essence of Charleston and her outlying districts into a lively, informative, entertaining, and sophisticated resource. We welcome submissions and story proposals. These guidelines are intended to help writers match their story ideas to our editorial mission.

All articles must have a direct and obvious connection to Charleston. Ideally, each focuses on someone or something special to Charleston and contributes to a better understanding of this community's unique identity.

Typical issues of *Charleston* include articles on outstanding houses and gardens; notable residents; significant Charleston businesses and institutions; social and political issues facing Low country residents; local history, artists, and architecture; wildlife, natural history, and environmental research; antiques, wine, and food; and natural and cultural points of interest within the county. Stories with a visual nature are preferred. Articles range in length from 500-word profiles to 2,000-word features. We also publish illuminating personal narratives and reminiscences, think-pieces on Charleston subjects and occasional short fiction.

The pages of each bimonthly issue of *Charleston Magazine* deliver editorial and artistic excellence in a glossy, four-color format.

Editorial Content:
Profiles of the region's most provocative and influential personalities. Thorough reporting on issues and concerns facing Low country

residents today. Beautifully photographed, in-depth features revealing the subtle charms of our Low country lifestyle: uniquely beautiful homes and gardens, the natural beauty of the Low country and its environmental issues, our rich histories and traditions, and the lively arts community and cultural institutions.

Departments:

Channel Markers: Charleston's newsy snippets including The Insider and Mystery History.

Style File: Local style and fashion layouts for him, her, and home.

Local Seen: Outstanding, colorful Low country characters.

Southern View: Humorous first-person essays on life in the Low country.

In Good Taste/Chef at Home: Revolving departments featuring regional chefs, culinary trends, and recipes.

Fête Set: The Charleston social scene benefits good causes.

CityScape: A comprehensive guide to arts and events in Charleston: performing arts, visual arts and architecture, literary and cultural events, weddings, dining guides, sports and nature, family and youth activities, and special charitable events.

More! photo essays, history, and local weddings.

Categories: Nonfiction—Architecture—Arts—General Interest—Lifestyle—Regional

CONTACT: Darcy Shankland, Editor
Material: All
782 Johnnie Dodds Blvd., Suite C
Mt. Pleasant SC 29464
Phone: 843-971-9811
Fax: 843-971-0121
E-mail: dshankland@charlestonmag.com
Website: charlestonmag.com

The Chattahoochee Review
Georgia Perimeter College

The Chattahoochee Review pays $20.00 per Chattahoochee page for fiction, $15.00 per Chattahoochee page for essays, $100 per omnibook review, $50.00 per review of a single book, $100.00 per interview, and $50.00 per poem.

The aim of The *Chattahoochee Review* is to encourage unacknowledged writers and to provide printing space for published authors, striking a balance between the two. We are open to poetry and prose, both fiction and nonfiction. The *Chattahoochee Review* is copyrighted in its entirety. However, we are happy to grant reprint rights upon written request; we require only that the Review receive printed acknowledgement as first publisher.

All manuscripts should be typed. Prose should be double-spaced, and poetry should be single-spaced within stanzas, and double-spaced between stanzas. One poem to a page, please. Send originals or clear photocopies. The author's name, address, telephone numbers (including fax number, and e-mail address if available) should appear on the first page of each poem or prose piece. Send no more than one short story or nonfiction piece and no more than five (5) poems per submission. Your cover letter should provide sufficient information for us to compile a two- to three-sentence biography for our "Notes on Contributors" page, should the work be accepted. Do not send any work that is being simultaneously submitted to other publishers. Submit only work that has not been previously published.

Reviews: We usually review the categories that we publish: collections of poems or short stories. If you are submitting an omnibook review, please submit more of an essay than just a review-a piece that reflects the writer's other books and other relevant information. Please give the review a title inclusive of the book's title and provide the following bibliographic information: title of piece, author, title of book, publisher, date, number of pages, price.

Interviews: We are interested in a wide range of subjects, but favor interviews with notable Southern authors. If you wish to interview a writer for The *Chattahoochee Review,* please contact the editor.

Essays: We prefer literary essays that focus on aesthetics, essays that are intelligent, insightful, and artful. We also welcome essays that address literary trends and activities. Submissions of personal essays should reveal human truths in evocative styles: essays in the traditions of Thoreau, Monette, and Rodriguez-masters of the personal essay. The human experience is powerful, especially if shared with beautiful language, honest reflection, and clear prose.

Subscriptions: $16.00 per year, $30.00 for two years, $6.00 per copy.

Categories: Fiction—Nonfiction—Book Reviews—Literature—Poetry—Writing

CONTACT: Lawrence Hetrick, Editor
Material: Any
CONTACT: Jo Ann Yeager Adkins, Managing Editor
Material: Any
2101 Womack Rd.
Dunwoody GA 30338
Phone: 770-551-3019

Chef
The Food Magazine for Professionals

Chef magazine, "The Food Magazine for Professionals," focuses almost exclusively on food preparation and presentation for the modern chef and cook.

That's why we scheduled more than 100 food-related focuses in 2000. To that end, a writer for *Chef* should have a thorough knowledge of the food service industry and, more specifically, the needs of chefs and cooks in both commercial and noncommercial kitchens. Occasionally, we are happy to work with established writers with strong food backgrounds who may be less familiar with the food service industry, but are eager to learn.

Manuscripts for *Chef* magazine:

• speak to the professional, not the cooking enthusiast.

• tend to be short, usually no longer than 1,500 words; 1,200 words (including sidebar) is an average length. Our audience has little time to read, so we have to package features economically.

• usually feature a number of chefs in both commercial and noncommercial operations executing a particular application(s) or preparing a certain type or style of dish in a variety of markets nationwide.

• are light on basic information or instruction (such as history of an ingredient or how to prepare something simple or commonplace) and heavy on application, particularly novel or unique preparations and presentations. Our audience is almost solely professional, and mostly comprised of individuals who work in establishments grossing $1 million or more in F&B sales. We reach a negligible number of students.

Chef magazine does NOT accept:

• first-person editorials.

• travel features, except in very few cases, and then only when they have a strong cooking-application focus. (No "I dined on this here and on that there...")

• everything-you-wanted-to-know manuscripts on raw ingredients (garlic, pecans, watermelon, et al.).

• profiles of people or institutions, except when the angle is unusual and entertaining, and then only when that angle includes a strong cooking-application focus.

• manuscripts from representatives of entities selling a product or service.

• manuscripts on industry issues, except when real or potential impact on working chefs is considerable, and then only when they haven't been covered greatly in like publications or when the angle is unique.

• manuscripts on non-food-preparation topics such as management issues, computer software or the Internet, personal financial management, lifestyle issues and the like.

A few tips:

• Request our editorial calendar. We are committed to most of the focuses we plan for the year. We are interested, however, in topics not on the calendar, but you'll want to determine whether they've already been covered this year or soon will be.

• Read a sample issue or two to review our focus and style.

• Query with an idea in writing first, with published clips. Please include a daytime telephone number where you can be reached. Include in your letter why the topic you propose is of interest to our readers. Also, please make us aware of availability of color photography and the costs, if any, of such.

Payment starts at $300 for first-time North American serial rights, on acceptance, based on the writer's experience, expertise and relationship to our magazine. *Chef* will reimburse telephone and postage expenses. Other expenses must be approved prior to beginning assignment.

"Profiles" Articles Guidelines

Chef magazine "Profiles" are intended to be informational and educational articles that illustrate the breadth and variety of expertise in the culinary community. These articles identify the chefs who are influencing the industry, the new trends, and new upbeat ideas. These articles should inspire the reader through a clear description of the fresh and useful ideas of the chef being profiled. Profile articles "let the chef do the talking." Finished articles are approximately 750 words.

The "Profile" focuses attention on the chef's career by describing:

• Background;
• How the chef came to the industry;
• Mentors;
• Why the chef remains in the industry;
• Exciting accolades of the chef;
• What the chef is doing now;
• Areas of special interest;
• How he/she approaches challenges; and
• What he/she sees for the future.

The "Profile" article describes the chef's dishes by discussing:

• Some of the chef's techniques;
• Important steps in his/her procedures;
• The ingredients; and
• Advice and tips.

Artwork:

Artwork should reflect the personality of the chef. Authors are expected to provide suitable artwork.

A few Don'ts:

Do not include quotes or opinions that are negative or those that can have a deleterious effect on the industry, a supplier, or a market segment. Do not include quotes that reflect a political perspective or personal opinions of products or equipment. That's advertising.

Categories: Food—Design/Decor

CONTACT: Robert Benes, Senior Editor
Material: All
Melanie Wolkoff, Managing Editor
Material: All
20 W. Kinizig, Ste. 1200
Chicago, IL 60610
Phone: 312-849-2220
Fax: 312-849-2174
E-mail: ChefMag@aol.com
Website: www.chefmagazine.com

Chess Life
School Mates

WRITERS' & PHOTOGRAPHERS' GUIDELINES

Chess Life is the official publication of the United States Chess Federation. Each monthly issue covers news of many major chess events, both here and abroad, with special emphasis on the triumphs and exploits of American players. It also includes regular columns of instruction, general features on chess in other fields (computer science, psychology, art, war, etc.), historical articles, personality profiles, interviews, cartoons, quizzes, and humor.

Of special interest to free-lance writers is the feature section, which can include articles on relatively unknown chess personalities and "chess in everyday life," along with the usual chess news and tournament reports.

There is only one all-encompassing injunction: The game of chess must be central to every item. *Chess Life* readers include everyone from the professional grandmaster to the discerning amateur and hobbyist. Therefore, articles like "My first Chess Tournament" or quizzes containing the names of world champions have all been tried too many times before. We give little or no attention to other games or variants of chess. We no longer publish fiction.

School Mates is the national chess magazine for children. It includes instructional articles, chess news, tournament reports, quizzes, puzzles, humor, tips, cartoons, and pictures. Material is aimed at 8-12 year old beginning to intermediate chess players.

MANUSCRIPTS

Rates: Payment for *Chess Life* is generally $100 per page; a page is generally defined at 800 to 1,000 words. For the computer-minded, the general guide is approximately 5,000 bytes per page.) Writers with IM or GM titles should inquire about special rates. Payment is upon publication. This policy can be changed only under special circumstances.

Payment for *School Mates* is generally $50 per page (80-1000 words). Unsolicited promotional material is not paid.

TABLE FOR MANUSCRIPTS SUBMITTED TO *Chess Life*

The following shows a word count table for rates and dollar amounts based on such:

Size	Word Count	CL Rate
Full Page	900 to 1,100 words	$100 a pg.
2/3 Page	600 to 899 words	$6
1/2 Page	400 to 599 words	$50
1/3 Page	300 to 399 words	$35
1/4 page	200 to 299 words	$25
1/8 page or below	Below 200 words	$15

Writers with IM or GM titles should inquire about special rates. Payment is upon publication. This policy can be changed only under special circumstances.

TABLE FOR MANUSCRIPTS SUBMITTED TO *School Mates*

The following shows a word count table for rates and dollar amounts based on such:

Size	Word Count	SM Rate
Full Page	600 to 899 words	$50 a pg.
2/3 Page	450 to 599 words	$30
1/2 Page	300 to 449 words	$25
1/3 Page or below	Below 300 words	$10 or negotiable with editor

Writers with IM or GM titles should inquire about special rates. Payment is upon publication. This policy can be changed only under special circumstances.

Rights: All rights are reserved unless otherwise negotiated at the time the article is accepted.

Form: Submissions should be made on diskette (3½" or Zip and IBM compatible) or e-mailed. Word Perfect and Microsoft Word are acceptable word processing programs. If you don't have access to either, .txt or ASCII format is fine. Hard copy (printout) should be sent with the diskette.

The writer should include full name, address, telephone number, and e-mail address on the first page. Subsequent pages should include a short title and page number. Chess notation should be in simple algebraic (1. e4 e5 2.f4 exf4, etc.). Descriptive is, however, acceptable.

Getting in Touch: Unsolicited manuscripts, on speculation, are welcomed, but queries with clippings of the writer's previous work are preferred. No queries are necessary for fiction. Unsolicited manuscripts and query contents are not returned.

PHOTOGRAPHS

Inside: Chess Life: Black-and-white, one-time use: $25; color, one-time use: $35. *School Mates*: $25 for first time rights; $15 for each subsequent use. Additional photograph rights will be negotiated by the photographer and the editor.

Covers: Chess Life - up to $300. *School Mates* - up to $150 in special cases. All rights may be negotiated.

Format: Black-and-white: 5x7 or 8x10 glossies. Color: Slides are preferred, but 5x7 or 8x10 glossies are acceptable. FULL NAME MUST BE INCLUDED ON THE BACK OF EACH PHOTO. If this remains undone, we take no responsibility for either payment or for giving photo credit. Address and telephone number of the photographer must also accompany submissions. Captions and, when necessary, model releases must accompany each picture.

Getting in Touch: Unsolicited work, on speculation, is welcomed, but queries with contract sheets, samples, or clippings are preferred. Unsolicited photographs and query contents are not returned.

OTHER MATERIALS

Unsolicited cartoons, poems, puzzles and fillers submitted on speculation are welcomed. Payment is generally $25 upon acceptance for initial work. Subsequent work paid on publication. Rights purchased are the same as those for manuscripts. Cartoonists may submit sketches with captions and samples of published work. Unsolicited materials are not returned.

Contact Editor Peter Kurzdorfer for further information on *Chess Life* and *School Mates* (845) 562-8350 ext. 152 magazines@uschess.org

Categories: Children—Games—Sports/Recreation—Young Adult

CONTACT: Peter Kurzdorfer, Editor
Material: Chess
CONTACT: Jean Bernice, Editorial Asst.
Material: Chess
CONTACT: Jami Anson, Sr. Art Director
Material: Art, Photos
United States Chess Federation, 3054 US Route 9W
New Windsor NY 12553-7698
Phone: 845-562-8350, ext. 152
E-mail: 845-236-4852
Website: magazines@uschess.org

Chicago Magazine

A major magazine that covers a wide metropolitan area with a limited number of articles each month has to be highly selective about what it prints. Naturally, articles written with our readers in mind will interest us most. Our typical readers live along the lakefront or in other affluent communities, mainly in the suburbs. They have had more than four years of college and hold unusually high-paying jobs, often professional or managerial. Many are parents. They are well read and are interested in the arts and social issues. They go out several times a week to the city's theatres, music halls, and restaurants. They travel widely.

Procedures. Usually we assign or buy articles only after they have been discussed in editorial conferences, so put your queries in writing and send us samples of your best published work. In your query, tell us why you think your idea would interest our particular readers and why you are especially well qualified to write it.

Should we assign the story, you will be contacted by an articles editor, who will negotiate deadline and payment and outline the main features of the article we expect to receive. We will then send you a contract to sign and return.

Payment is on acceptance. What we pay depends on the length of your manuscript, the extent and nature of your research, and the importance we attach to the subject. You will be reimbursed for all reasonable expenses. *Although we have paid both more and less, the following ranges will give you an idea of our rates:*

• Feature articles (including sidebars) $350-$1,500
• Supplemental sidebars $150- $250
• Short articles (columns) $275- $600
• Standards. These are not hard-and-fast rules, and they don't apply to every article. If you have questions, discuss them with your articles editor.

1. A well-organized story usually answers a single question-often a very simple one. You may not know what it is at first, but after a little research you and your articles editor should be able to formulate one, and the answer ought to be the core of your story.

2. Your research should help you support a point of view. Your story is less likely to be successful if you merely present all sides of an issue and hope that the reader will discern the truth, or if you force a point of view that is not substantiated by your research, or if you tailor your research to validate a preconception.

3. A good magazine story is a good story. It doesn't just describe a state of affairs. It tells how and why the situation came about, who was instrumental in making it happen, what it means to the reader, and what the future holds. Often, novelistic devices can be effective: description, narrative, anecdote, dialogue, sensory detail. But if the situation in the story is not intrinsically interesting or does not have consequences that affect our readers, it might not be appropriate for us.

4. A good story usually focuses on individuals. Although institutions take action, it is ultimately individuals who make them act and whose lives are affected. A writer can make almost any story more vivid, and even more truthful, by concentrating on the people involved-their personalities, backgrounds, and motives-on what they stood to gain and lose, and on how they fared.

5. Good stories are rewritten stories. Our readers' time is limited; your manuscript should be a distilled version of your original draft. Remember: We don't pay by the word.

6. Above all, a good magazine story is believable and fair. Any person or institution whose character or actions have been impugned by the author or by anyone quoted in the article has a right to rebut those charges within the article. If that person or institution declines comment, say so in your story. Chicago magazine's libel insurance does not cover free-lance writers.

Chicago Magazine does not publish fiction, poetry or cartoons.

Categories: Fiction—Nonfiction—Literature—Poetry—Regional—Short Stories—Writing

CONTACT: Senior Editor
Material: All
CONTACT: Andrew Rathmann, Editor
Material: Nonfiction
5801 S. Kenwood Ave.
Chicago IL 60637
Phone: 773-702-0887
Fax: 773-702-0887
Website: www.chicagomagazine.com

Chicago Review

Thank you for your interest in *Chicago Review*. Since 1946, *Chicago Review* has published innovative fiction, poetry, and essays, including work by John Ashbery, Leslie Silko, Joyce Carol Oates, William Burroughs, Susan Sontag, Thom Gunn, Robert Pinsky, Nikki Giovanni, Charles Simic, and many others.

The editors welcome submissions of unpublished poetry, fiction, and nonfiction (i.e., reviews, interviews, essays, and the like). We strongly recommend that unsolicited authors familiarize themselves with recent issues of *Chicago Review* before submitting. Submissions that demonstrate familiarity with the journal tend to make it towards the top of the pile more quickly than those that appear to be part of a carpet-bombing campaign.

We have established the following guidelines for submission:

• All submissions should include a self-addressed, stamped envelope with sufficient postage or International Reply Coupons for return of manuscript.

• Simultaneous submissions are strongly discouraged. If work is accepted elsewhere, please notify our office at once.

• There are no strict length requirements. The poetry editors prefer 3-7 pages of poetry. Fiction and nonfiction submissions average about 20 pages.

• Citations follow the most recent edition of *The Chicago Manual of Style.*

• Contributors receive three copies of the issue in which their work appears, plus a one-year subscription.

• Due to the increasing volume of unsolicited submissions, the average response time is three to six months; it is especially slow during the summer.

• Unsolicited electronic submissions are gleefully deleted unread.

• Address submissions to the appropriate genre staff: Poetry, Fiction, or Nonfiction.

We do not accept submissions by e-mail or fax.

Potential contributors are encouraged to read a copy of *Chicago Review.* Many bookstores and libraries carry the magazine. Sample issues are available for $6; see our subscription page for more information.

Categories: Fiction—Poetry—Short Stories

CONTACT: Fiction Editor
Material: Fiction
CONTACT: Non-Fiction Editor
Material: Non-Fiction
CONTACT: Poetry Editor
Material: Poetry
5801 South Kenwood Ave.
Chicago IL 60637

The Chief of Police Magazine

Please refer to *Police Times Magazine.*

Child Life

Please refer to Children's Better Health Institute.

Child Magazine

Child Magazine is published 10 times a year, with combined issues in June/July and December/January.

Child provides parents of children from birth to age 12 with the newest thinking, information, and advice they need to raise their families in a constantly changing, time-pressed world.

Freelance writers are invited to submit query letters only, on the following topics:

• Children's health
• Parenting and marital relationship issues
• Child behavior and development
• Personal essays pertaining to family life

Child purchases first-time rights for articles and pays upon acceptance. Fees vary depending on length and positioning of articles.

Writers must include clips of previously published work and a SASE with their queries. Please allow 8 weeks for a reply. No electronic submissions will be accepted.

Categories: Nonfiction—Children—Consumer—Parenting

CONTACT: Submissons Editor
Material: All
Child Editorial Dept.
375 Lexington Ave., 9th Floor
New York NY 10017
Phone: 212-499-2000
Fax: 212-499-2038
E-mail: childmag@aol.com

Children's Better Health Institute

We at the Children's Better Health Institute have a constant need for high quality stories, articles, and activities with health related stories, articles, and activities with health-related themes. "Health" is a broad topic that includes exercise, sports, safety, nutrition, hygiene, and drug education.

Health information can be presented in a variety of formats, including fiction, nonfiction, poems, recipes, and puzzles. Fiction stories with a health message need not have health as the primary subject, but they should include it in some way in the course of events. Characters in fiction should adhere to good health practices, unless failure to do so is necessary to a story's plot.

Remember that characters in realistic stories should be up-to-date. Many of our readers have working mothers and/or come from single-parent homes. We need more stories that reflect these changing times but at the same time communicate good, wholesome values.

We are especially interested in material concerning sports and fitness, including profiles of famous amateur and professional athletes; "average" athletes (especially children) who have overcome obstacles to excel in their areas; and new or unusual sports, particularly those in which children can participate.

Nonfiction articles dealing with health subjects should be fresh and creative. Avoid an encyclopedic or "preachy" approach. We try to present our health material in a positive manner, incorporation humor and a light approach wherever possibly without minimizing the seriousness of the message.

We also welcome recipes that children can make on their own with minimal adult supervision. Ingredients should be healthful, so avoid using fats, sugars, salt, chocolate, and red meat. In all material submitted, please avoid reference to eating sugary foods, such as candy, cakes, cookies, and soft drinks.

Although our emphasis is on health, we certainly use material with more general themes. We would especially like to see more holiday stories, articles, and activities. Please send seasonal material at least eight months in advance.

Reading our writers guidelines is not enough. Careful study of current issues will acquaint writers with each title's "personality," various departments, and regular features, nearly all of which are open to freelancers. Sample copies are $1.75 each (U.S. currency) from the Children's Better Health Institute, P.O. Box 567, Indianapolis, IN 46206.

Periodicals We Publish

Turtle, Humpty Dumpty, Children's Playmate, Jack and Jill, Child Life, Children's Digest and *U.S. Kids.*

Manuscript Format

Manuscripts must be typewritten and double or triple-spaced. The author's name, address, telephone number, Social Security number, date of submission, and the approximate word count of the material should appear on the first page of the manuscript. Title pages are not necessary. Keep a copy of your work. We will handle your manuscript with care, but we cannot assume responsibility for its return. Please submit to a specific magazine, not just to CBHI or the Children's Better Health Institute. This aids us in tracking your manuscript.

Please send the entire manuscript. All work is on speculation only; queries are not accepted, nor are stories assigned. The editors cannot criticize, offer suggestions, or enter into correspondence with an author concerning manuscripts that are not accepted, nor can they suggest other markets for material that is not published. Material cannot be returned unless it is accompanied by a self-addressed stamped envelope and sufficient return postage.

Photos and Illustrations

We do not purchase single photographs. We do purchase short photo features (up to 6 or 8 Picture) or photos that accompany articles to help illustrate editorial material. (Please include captions and model releases.) Suggestions for illustrations are not necessary but are permissible. Please do not send drawings or artwork. We prefer to work with professional illustrators of our own choosing.

Review Time

About three months are required to review manuscripts properly. Please wait three months before sending status inquiries. If a manuscript is returned, it should not be resubmitted to a different you publication at this address. Each manuscript is carefully considered for possible use in all magazines, not only the one to which it was originally addressed.

Rates and Payment Policies

Turtle: up to 22¢ a word, Fiction/nonfiction — up to 350 words

Humpty Dumpty: up to 22¢ a word, Fiction/nonfiction — up to 350 words

Children's Playmate: up to 17¢ a word, Fiction/nonfiction — 300 to 700 words

Jack and Jill: up to 17¢ a word, Fiction/nonfiction — 500 to 800 words

Child Life: not accepting manuscripts at this time

Children's Digest: up to 12¢ a word, Fiction — 500 to 1500 words/nonfiction 500 to 1000 words

Poetry: $25.00 minimum

Photos: $15.00 minimum

Puzzles and games: no fixed rate

Rights

We purchase all rights to manuscripts. We buy one-time rights to photos. Simultaneous submissions are discouraged. One-time book rights may be returned when the author had found an interested publisher and can provide us with an approximate date of publication.

Children's Contributions

Except for items that are used in children's columns, the editors do not encourage submissions from children. Even highly talented young people are not usually experienced enough to compete on a professional level with adult authors. There is no payment for children's contributions.

ARTISTS GUIDELINES
Art Requirements

Artists interested in being considered for assignments may mail samples of their artwork accompanied by a stamped, self-addressed return envelope.

When an artist accepts an assignment, type proofs of the material are sent to him, together with layout sheets showing the page size of the magazine. Deadline dates for receipt of sketches and finished are included.

The artist should read the proofs carefully, then cut them close to the edge of the type matter and place the trimmed strips on the layout sheets. This will show how much space is available for illustration so artists can plan accordingly. Large illustrations for dramatic impact, and/or a scattering of small spots are preferred. Illustrations may bleed off the page, but any important art, such as lettering or parts of a person's body, must be kept within 1/4" from bleed lines, to avoid being cut when the magazine is trimmed. Avoid having a full page of copy without an illustration.

After the layout is planned and the type has been pasted down on the layout sheet, the artist should make actual-size sketches, the material is returned to the artist along with any comments and changes.

Sketches and finished artwork should be actual size. Sketches must be returned to us with the finished art for layout purposes. Color separations of the art are made on a color scanner; art must be prepared on a flexible surface to wrap around the scanner drum. The artist supplies color overlays for two-color work.

We welcome cover ideas with health, exercise, nutrition, and safety themes. Rough sketches should be submitted in color, the actual size of the magazine, with space allowed for the logo. The artist's name and return address should be noted on the back. These sketches are returned when the editors have reviewed them.

Payment for completed artwork is customarily mailed within a three-week period prior to the publication date. Each contributor is sent two copies of the printed issue containing his/her work. The art director should be contacted if additional copies are needed. All artwork is considered work for hire. We buy all rights and retain work after publication.

Art Payments

Rates for art payments for the following magazines — *Turtle, Humpty Dumpty, Children's Playmate, Jack and Jill, Child Life, Children's Digest* and *U.S. Kids* are as follows:

Cover Art $275.00

Inside Art	Full Page	1/2 Page	Spot
B/W	$90.00	$60.00	$35.00
2/C	$120.00	$90.00	$60.00
4/C	$155.00	$100.00	$70.00
Pre-separated 4/C	$190.00	$115.00	$80.00

Dimensions

Full page = 1/2 to 1 full page of art

1/2 page = 1/4 to 1/2 page of art

Spot = 1/4 page or less of art

Maximum payment per page will be full-page price — numerous small spots will not pay more.

All artwork is considered work for hire.

Kill fees rarely occur. If they should, they will be handled on a case-by-case basis.

The artist is responsible for any costs incurred in mailing sketches and finished artwork — please do not bill federal express or other mailing costs to us. Children's Better Health Institute is a non-profit organization; we do not pay state taxes on artwork.

An invoice should be submitted with your finished artwork. It should contain the following information: Your name, address, social security or federal tax reporting number, the date, the magazine for which the assignment has been made, the issue date, the title of the story and the total payment. The total is to be determined according to the above schedule and confirmed wit the art director at the time your sketches are submitted. We will hold your check until we have received your invoice.

Categories: Nonfiction—Health—Physical Fitness

CONTACT: Editor (Magazine Name)
Material: All
100 Waterway Blvd., Box 567
Indianapolis IN 46202
Phone: 317-634-1100
Fax: 317-684-8094
Website: www.cbhi.org

Children's Digest
Children's Playmate

Please refer to Children's Better Health Institute.

Chiron Review

Chiron Review presents the widest possible range of contemporary creative writing — fiction and non-fiction, traditional and off-beat — in an attractive, professional tabloid format, including artwork and photographs of featured writers.

All submissions are invited. No taboos. Send up to five poems, and/or one short story (up to 3000 words), typed or printed legibly. Photocopies are okay. We do NOT consider simultaneous submissions, previously published material or e-mail submissions. Must include SASE for reply. We recommend writers see a sample copy ($5) before submitting. Report in 2-6 weeks. Pays 1 copy. CR is copyrighted; writers retain all rights to their work.

About a quarter of each issue is devoted to news, views and reviews of interest to writers and the literary community. We are always on the lookout for intelligent non-fiction, as well as talented reviewers who wish to write in-depth, analytical reviews of literary books and magazines.

Past contributors include Charles Bukowski, William Stafford, Marge Piercy, Gavin Dillard, Edward Field, Antler, Robert Peters, Joan Jobe Smith, Fred Voss, Janice Eidus, Felice Picano, Lyn Lifshin, Will Inman, Richard Kostelanetz, Lorri Jackson, Ruth Moon Kempher, Charles Webb and a host of others, well-known and new.

A one-year subscription is $15 (four issues). A sample copy is $5.

Categories: Arts—Gay/Lesbian—Literature—Poetry

CONTACT: Michael Hathaway, Editor
Material: All
522 E. South Ave.
St. John KS 67576-2212
Phone: 620-786-4955
Website: geocities.com/SoHo/Nook/1748

Christian Camp & Conference Journal

PURPOSE: *Christian Camp & Conference Journal* is the bimonthly flagship publication of CCI/USA (Christian Camping International/USA) and seeks to inform, inspire, and motivate all who serve in Christian camps and conferences.

FOCUS: Inspirational, in-depth features related to what God is doing in and through Christian camp and conference ministries. Plus, practical "how-to" pieces in the following critical aspects of Christian camping ministries: Outdoor Setting; Purpose and Objectives; Administration and Organization; Camper/Guest Needs; Personnel Development; Programming; Health and Safety; Food Service; Site, Facilities, and Maintenance; Business and Operations; Marketing and Public Relations; and Fund Raising.

FORMAT: In-depth features in the Journal show (rather than tell) what God is doing in and through Christian camp and conference ministries. Overall, the Journal displays mostly third-person articles, and some profiles and question-and-answer interviews.

APPROACH: The Journal is published bimonthly on 8-1/4 by 10-5/8 inch matte stock with full color throughout. Article length for features is 1,200 - 1,500 words, "how-to" pieces is 1,000 - 1,200 words, and sidebars is 250-500 words. Please query first. Response to queries, photos/slides, and manuscripts are sent within one month. The Journal retains first rights.

PAYMENT: The Journal offers 16 cents per published word for articles contributed by individuals outside CCI/USA. Payment is sent upon publication. The Journal offers from $25 to $250 for photographs, depending on quality, position, and size used.

PHOTOS: Profiles on individuals should be accompanied by at least two clear pictures of the subject-one posed, one action. Sharp color shots are acceptable. Mood/action shots covering the gamut of emotion and activity in camp and conference ministries will be considered.

MISCELLANEOUS: Current circulation is nearly 8,000; the Journal is distributed primarily to individuals involved in all aspects of Christian camp and conference ministries. Byline and photo credits are given. Submit seasonal material queries six months in advance.

TIPS: Profiles/interviews and arresting photos/slides are the best bet for newcomers and freelancers. It is crucial to study a sample copy first and then query. Send $4.00 for a recent copy (this will also cover shipping and handling).

Categories: Associations—Christian Interests

CONTACT: Natalee Roth, Editor
Material: All
Christian Camping International U.S.A
PO Box 62189
Colorado Springs CO 80962-2189
E-mail: nroth@cciusa.org
Website: www.cciusa.org

The Christian Century

The editors assume that our readers are deeply engaged in thinking about the Christian faith and in trying to live it out. Many are church leaders, either in congregations or church-related agencies.

The Christian Century aims to be a magazine for Christians who are thoughtful about theology, church life, and contemporary culture, but who are not likely to be scholars of any academic discipline. We are not likely, therefore, to publish a treatise on, say, Augustine's doctrine of the Trinity. We might well be interested, however, in a fresh investigation of how that doctrine has been ignored—or perhaps made freshly relevant to contemporary life. Similarly, we probably won't publish an article on apocalyptic sects of the 19th century—but we might well be interested in an article on apocalyptic movements of our time and their relation to earlier groups.

When we read a submission, we tend to ask: Why this? Why now? What does this contribute to the ongoing discussion of the topic and people's everyday encounters? We also ask: What will cause someone to pick up this article? Is it lively? Is it provocative? Does it grab the reader with the importance of the subject? Does it generate some drama? Does it cover a neglected aspect of a familiar topic, or approach a classic topic in a new and engaging way?

If you are writing about a local event or program or about a conference, we encourage you to shape your account around the most crucial and broadly significant issues. No need to provide a step-by-step, or speaker-by-speaker, account.

Feature articles run about 3,000 words. Articles for the "comments and reports" section run about 1,500 words. We don't use footnotes or endnotes. We usually pay an honorarium of about $150 for feature articles.

We urge you to examine a copy of the magazine before submitting a manuscript. If you want your manuscript returned, please enclose a self-addressed stamped envelope.

Categories: Religion

CONTACT: Manuscripts, The Christian Century
Material: All
104 S. Michigan, Ste. 700
Chicago, IL 60603
Phone: 312-263-7510
E-mail: main@christiancentury.org
Website: www.christiancentury.org

Christian Health

Will no longer be published as of January 2003.

Christian History

A Christianity Today Publication.

Does not accept unsolicited submissions.

HOME & SCHOOL
CHRISTIAN

Christian Home & School

Christian Home & School is published by Christian Schools International for parents who send their children to Christian schools. The magazine aims to promote Christian education and to address a wide range of parenting topics. The magazine is published six times during the school year and has a circulation of 67,000 (75% U.S.; 25% Canada).

Some suggested topics can be found here, but don't limit yourself to these ideas. We are interested in articles that deal with timely issues that affect Christian parents. We are also interested in articles about Christian schooling and the relationship of parents to Christian schools. Each year we also include seasonal articles dealing with such topics as the beginning of the school year, Christmas, graduation, summer activities, and vacations. Send seasonal articles 4-5 months before the event. (We don't publish poetry or fillers.)

Articles should reflect a mature, biblical perspective. Use an informal, easy-to-read style rather than a philosophical, academic tone. Try to incorporate vivid imagery and concrete, practical examples from real life. You may wish to suggest a sidebar that contains further information or resources related to your subject.

A query is not necessary. Manuscripts can range from 1,000 to 2,000 words and should be typed (double spaced). Include your name and address at the top of the first page; also include a sentence or two about yourself for us to use as a contributor's note.

We pay $175-$250 upon publication, depending on the length of the edited article. We prefer to buy first rights only. We also look for brief parenting tips of 100 to 250 words for our Parentstuff pages and pay $25 to $40 for these.

If you would like a sample copy of the magazine, please send a 9" x12" self-addressed envelope with four first-class stamps affixed.

Categories: Nonfiction—Education—Family—Marriage

CONTACT: Roger W. Schmurr, Senior Editor
Material: All
3350 E. Paris Ave. SE
Grand Rapids MI 49512
Phone: 616-957-1070 ext. 239
Fax: 616-957-5022
E-mail: RogerS@CSIonline.org

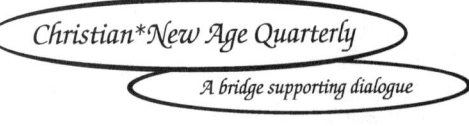

Christian*New Age Quarterly
A bridge supporting dialogue

Christian Living

Does not accept unsolicited submissions.

Christian*New Age Quarterly

Thank you for your interest in writing for *Christian*New Age Quarterly*. We welcome your creativity and insights, focused upon some facet of the *Christian-New Age* relationship.

C*NAQ is a forum for clear, respectful dialog between Christians and New Agers. Here we entertain, but do not assume, an underlying compatibility of the two. While we allow for the possibility of irreconcilable ideological differences, we have yet to see a single reason which precludes honest, mutually supportive communication. Moreover, we have discovered many reasons why such genuine communication is warranted, even crucial.

Our readership is comprised of Christians and New Agers, as well as those exploring other avenues of spiritual expression. While extraordinarily diverse, our readers also tend to be keenly observant, intelligent and in touch with spirituality. Consequently, we do not accept material marked by either a patronizing style, which assumes the reader needs to be taught some self-evident spiritual insight, or self-circular reasoning, which confuses subjective truth with observable fact.

As you select words for your insight or observation, aim for vital, flowing, yet precise language. C*NAQ especially looks for a certain caliber of vantage that surprises us with a slant we've yet to consider. Take a look at a topic, then wrestle with it, contemplatively and vigorously. Capture and submit it in simple style and fine polish.

If yours is a controversial theme, we would be pleased to consider it—as long as you have thought it through with research and sensitivity. Here, you needn't be wary of words considered taboo in other journals; "church," "Savior," "feminism" and "Goddess" are all functional terms in C*NAQ. But pieces that put forth an exclusivistic stance would best be submitted to one of the more singularly Christian or New Age periodicals which abound.

Besides staff-composed columns and "The Letters Library," we publish 2-3 articles per issue. Recommended word length is 400-1,500 words. The more peripheral the content is to our main focus, the shorter it needs to be. Articles with content especially pertinent may aim for the upper end of the range. Still, if you have composed an outstanding piece that exceeds length recommendations, we might consider it. We do try to be flexible when it comes to truly noteworthy pieces.

We do not accept poetry, photos, trendy pieces, channeled wisdom or fiction. We do, however, welcome original line drawings and cartoons. If you are in doubt regarding the propriety of an intended subject, feel free to query prior to investing your energies in its composition.

As to blind submissions, we at C*NAQ find it presumptuous when authors submit work with no knowledge of our periodical's focus. If one is drawn to Christian-New Age dialog to the extent that one would write on the subject, it would seem reasonable to expect interest in at least examining C*NAQ. Doing so provides the opportunity not only to explore our stylistic preferences, but also to learn from the views of other writers who are published here. Though our acceptances are not prejudiced by whether or not a writer reads C*NAQ, those who have familiarized themselves with our work are far more likely to create the kind of piece we seek to publish. If you are not currently a subscriber, you may obtain a sample by sending your check or money order, payable to *Christian*New Age Quarterly*, in the amount of $3.50.

C*NAQ rarely accepts material offered on a basis other than "first rights." Please indicate "first rights" on your manuscript or detail, in your cover letter, why first rights are not available. Never do we consider simultaneous submissions; don't send them here. We require a note of assurance, accompanying your submission, that we are the sole periodical considering the piece. After your work has been published in C*NAQ, you are free to submit it elsewhere.

We reserve the right to edit. Although C*NAQ honors the personal style of our authors, editing may be necessary for clarity or length. If you are opposed to revising your manuscript yourself or allowing us to do so, clearly state this in your cover letter. Our preliminary evaluation of submissions often is based on their "editability." Rest assured that we would not print a piece requiring substantial editing without first obtaining the author's approval on necessary changes.

The request of a revision does not ensure eventual acceptance. It does means we are seriously interested. But acceptance depends upon our approval of your final copy.

For accepted articles, you'll receive, as payment, a one-year complimentary subscription or an extension to your current subscription. For each drawing or cartoon, you'll receive one copy of the issue in which your work appears.

Our decisions are commitments. If we accept a piece for publication, you may rest assured that it will be published. Although we try to publish accepted material as soon as possible, we work carefully to achieve a balance of content in each issue. Therefore, we may wait upon an appropriate issue to include accepted articles.

Please enclose an SASE with sufficient postage in all correspondence. We are not responsible for returning manuscripts, advising you of our decision, or answering inquiries which arrive without SASEs. Please help us to be responsive to you!

C*NAQ's Editor, Catherine Groves—as well as our readers—will look forward to the opportunity to explore your thoughts.

Categories: Nonfiction—Christian Interests—New Age—Religion—Spiritual—Interfaith

CONTACT: Catherine Groves, Editor
Material: All
PO Box 276
Clifton NJ 07015-0276

Christian Parenting Today

Our Mission Statement:
To encourage and equip parents to nurture the spiritual and moral development of their children as they walk alongside them in a family journey of faith.

Our Philosophy:
We are a mission-driven magazine, defined by our goal of helping families grow spiritually. This mission will inform our choices when it comes to feature articles. If an idea doesn"t fit our focus, it won"t appear in the magazine. We are not a full-service parenting magazine.

We are a source of real, practical, trustworthy information. We ask writers to go to experts in spiritual development when applicable. Our goal is to take their theories and turn them into useful tools parents can use at home. We ask writers to look to primary sources whenever possible and avoid simply quoting other written material.

We are looking for articles that are fresh, friendly, informative, and useful. We look for biblically sound advice and practical application. Articles should feel lively and exciting, never dry or dull.

Our Articles:
We will only consider articles on the following subjects:
• Family Spirituality: Ideas for families to grow together
• Moral Development/Values: How we live as Christians
• Spiritual Disciplines: Specific how-to and why-to information on prayer, worship, fellowship, service, etc.
• The Big Picture: Reflective, philosophical pieces that encourage intentional spiritual development opportunities
• Pop Culture/Culture: How to help children deal with the influences outside the family (media issues would fall under this category)
• The Child in Community: How to help the child impact her world for Christ (friendships, school, and extra-curriculars would fall under this category)

• Discipline/Character Development: The nuts and bolts of discipline rooted in the belief that discipline is the tool we use to help shape our child"s character and develop his will to follow God"s own will, just as God uses loving discipline to develop our will to match his.

We do not accept unsolicited manuscripts. Please send a one-page query letter via regular mail or e-mail. Please include your address, social security number, a summary of the article, estimated word count, a list of sources, your qualifications, and a self-addressed, stamped envelope. We respond to most queries within 6-8 weeks. If, after reviewing your query, our editors feel that your article has potential, your manuscript will be requested on speculation. This does not guarantee purchase of the manuscript. Seasonal ideas should be queried six months to a year in advance. We do not accept fiction or poetry. We do not accept simultaneous submissions. Please note that Christian Parenting Today buys first rights only to material, with the right to include the article in our online version of the magazine.

Categories: Nonfiction—Children—Christian Interests—Family—Inspirational—Parenting—Religion—Spiritual

CONTACT: Editor
Material: All
Christianity Today Publications
465 Gundersen Drive
Carol Stream IL 60188
Phone: 719-531-7776
Fax: 719-535-0172
E-mail: cpt@christianparenting.net
Website: www.christianitytoday.com

Christian Reader
Stories of Faith, Hope and God's Love

Please refer to Today's Christian.

Christian Single

Thanks for your interest in writing for *Christian Single*. We are always looking for qualified Christian writers who deliver professional Christian journalism. These guidelines will give you a glimpse into who we are, what we look for in writers, our editorial voice, and how we work with writers.

WHO WE ARE
Our Vision
All articles submitted should be consistent with the vision for our publisher, LifeWay Christian Resources, as well as our magazine.

Christian Single vision: *Christian Single* is the magazine for successful single living, providing practical answers to the real-life needs of today's single adults, challenging them to intensify their faith and impact their community.

LifeWay vision: As God works through us…we will help people and churches know Jesus Christ and seek His kingdom by providing biblical solutions that spiritually transform individuals and cultures.

Our Audience
Our primary readership is comprised of men and women (approximately 40% male; 60% female) between the ages of 25 and 35. We also have secondary readership in the 20-25 and 35-45 age ranges. Approximately 70% have never been married, with 26% divorced or separated, and 4% widowed. Approximately 30% have completed at least some college, with 30% completing bachelor's degrees and 20% graduate degrees. The majority attend church more than once a week (65%) and half are involved in a singles group.

First Contact
Christian Single doesn't accept unsolicited queries or manuscripts. In your initial contact with our editors, we ask that you please provide the following:

1. Resume

Outline your qualifications as a writer, including but not limited to researching, interviewing, and writing skills or particular areas of expertise. What we tend to look for is (1) formal writing training (such as degrees in journalism, communications, English, etc.); (2) experience in feature writing (such as with newspapers, magazines, or books); and (3) recent publishing credits.

2. Clips

Send recently published pieces, including your original drafts as available. This is your opportunity to give us a look at your best work, and with the original drafts, it's our chance to see what it took to get it there.

3. Areas of interest

Share topics or areas of interest/expertise you'd be interested in covering for the magazine. We find that it's better for both the writers and editors if writers cover areas in which they already have an interest or investment.

4. A brief description of your testimony/journey with Christ.

It's important to us that our writers share the same worldview as our readers.

Journalists will be evaluated on the above and their ability to convey the tone and general worldview of the CS audience (see audience demographics above). What we hope to develop at CS are "surrogate staff writers"–a stable of strong writers who are able to deliver consistently in terms of reaching our audience and matching our editorial voice.

Categories: Nonfiction—Christian Interests—Lifestyle—Religion—Singles—Spiritual

CONTACT: Christian Single Writer
Material: All
127 Ninth Ave.
North TN 37234-0140
Phone: 615-251-2000

Christian Social Action

Christian Social Action

What is *Christian Social Action* magazine?

Christian Social Action is the official magazine of the General Board of Church and Society of The United Methodist Church. The bimonthly magazine seeks to explore contemporary social issues in the light of Christian faith, especially from the perspective of The United Methodist Church Social Principles and resolutions adopted by General Conference.

Who reads CSA?

The magazine as of May 2001 is sent to every United Methodist Church in the United States, to hundreds of Annual Conference leaders, Bishops and to about 3000 paid subscribers including many Christian social justice activists.

What are we looking for?

Articles published in CSA should be of interest to United Methodist pastors and laypersons who seek to connect justice with mercy. Articles should approach theologically what it means to challenge the powers and principalities of this world in pursuit of a more just creation for all of God's world. Teaching tools and practical applications of justice ministry are also important. The strongest articles provide a direct link to United Methodist policy and to a Christian understanding of the issue.. Writing should be clearl, persuasive and cover the topic in non-technical language or political jargon. We aim to educate, inspire, call, advocate, and witness to the needs of social justice and advocacy for all of God's children.

We are looking for the following kinds of articles:

Those that cover a contemporary social issue facing people in the church. These articles should educate and challenge the reader to action, using United Methodist Church social policies and resolutions as a guide.

First person stories from persons with a special vantage point or expertise on a contemporary social issue.

"How-to" articles that will explain and guide a local church to social action. Provide step by step, "it worked for us" language.

Interviews with leaders in social justice, witness and advocacy movements.

These articles should provide inspiration for the journey to our readers.

Photographs or artwork (color and b/w) or should be sent with any submission.

Please send a brief (one paragraph) summary of your suggested article topic and approach to the editor. Unsolicited manuscripts will be considered but cannot be acknowledged or returned unless selected for use in the magazine All manuscripts should be sent on floppy disk or via email and must be double spaced, about 1,500 to 1,700. E-mail ghakola@umc-gbcs.org, or via fax to 202-488-1617, or mail disk to Editor, *Christian Social Action*, 100 Maryland Ave NE, Washington, DC 20002.

What do we pay?

CSA pays up to $125 for first-rights materials. We pay less for reprints and other pieces. We also will pay on a per job basis for original artwork or color cover photos.

Categories: Nonfiction—Christian Interests—Religion—Society—Spiritual—Public Policy—Social Issues

CONTACT: Gretchen Hakola, Assistant Editor
Material: Article queries
100 Maryland Ave. NE
Washington DC 20002
Phone: 202-488-5600
Fax: 202-488-1617
E-mail: ghakola@umc-gbcs.org
Website: www.umc-gbcs.org/gbcs005.htm

CHRISTIANITY TODAY

Christianity Today

WHAT WE LOOK FOR IN CHRISTIANITY TODAY ARTICLES:

A. Good Thinking

1. Creative ideas; new angles on old themes.
2. Theses that fit the purpose and stance of CHRISTIANITY TODAY.
3. Fresh insights, wisdom, judgment, analysis, interpretation.
4. Of interest to and useful for CHRISTIANITY TODAY readers.

B. Evidence of Hard Work

1. No superficial generalities.
2. Strong supporting evidence for the article's thesis.
3. Careful diagnosis and solutions.
4. Related to the real world.
   a. Not limited to academic research.
   b. Addressing problems and needs Christians face.
5. Interaction with Christian values and principles.

C. A Strong Logical Case

1. Point-by-point, with transitions.
2. Show the reader where you are going and why.
3. Makes clear what you are trying to prove.

D. Compelling Opening and Conclusion

1. Introductory paragraphs that hold attention.

2. Thesis/transition sentence that clearly states the thesis.

3. An ending that summarizes and provokes thought.

E. Careful Craftsmanship.

1. High regard for language and style, words, punctuation, grammar, etc.

2. Colorful, vivid, moving language.

3. Simplicity, clarity, readability.

4. Generous, and appropriate, use of quotes, anecdotes, stories.

5. No technical jargon or professional academic language.

6. Adherence to our word limits, usually 1,500 to 3,000 words. The Speaking Out columns use 800-word articles. Book reviews are usually commissioned. Letters of inquiry are requested before these are sent out.

7. An electronic copy, as a text file or a Microsoft Word file, preferred. For hard copy we prefer a clean legible manuscript, double-spaced, typed. We prefer exclusive original submissions. If you have sent your manuscript to another magazine, please advise. We prefer these to be on 8-1/2 x 11 inch sheets.

8. Please include a self-addressed, stamped envelope with your submission.

CHRISTIANITY TODAY expects query letters before manuscripts are sent.

1. Material should not be submitted without first becoming thoroughly familiar with the magazine's content over a period of time.

2. Outline your article proposal. State your subject, theme, unique angle, proposition and your main points.

3. Outline your research, experience, qualifications.

4. Tell us something about yourself. Why are you qualified to write this particular article?

5. CT if NOT in the market for fiction or poetry.

PAYMENT SCHEDULE:

Articles are purchased at 20 cents per published word and higher. Reimbursement is usually sent upon publication.

Categories: Nonfiction—Christian Interests—Religion—Spiritual

CONTACT: Mark Galli, Managing Editor
Material: All (No poetry or fiction)
Christianity Today International
465 Gundersen Dr.
Carol Stream IL 60188
Phone: 630-260-6200
Fax: 630-260-8428
E-mail: cteditor@christianitytoday.com
Website: www.christianitytoday.com

Christian Women Today

Article Categories

• We publish non-fiction only; we do not publish poetry.

• Spiritual Content: Our prayer, life stories, spiritual growth and training tools channels are the heartbeat of the site. Suggested maximum word count: 800.

• Life Stories: We publish first-person life stories of Christian women that reflect how they have discovered the Holy Spirit's power for living. We value international representation in life stories. Word count: 500-800 words.

• Training Tools: This channel features practical, how-to articles that equip women for the ministries of prayer, evangelism and discipleship. We also have a special section for leaders in ministry. Word count: 500-800 words.

• Lifestyle Content: We seek authoritative, relevant articles on beauty, health, the workplace, personal finances, and parenting and relationships. Generally, lifestyle pieces are 200-500 words.

Writing for the Internet

To offer ease of online reading for our audience, we like to use sub-headings or bulleted lists that break up longer articles. For more information on writing for the Internet, see How Users Read on the Web.

Submissions

We ask that you complete a preliminary application form before submitting your article. (You will not have to fill out this form in the future if you decide to submit more articles.) Once your preliminary application is received, we will e-mail you information on how to submit articles.

The preliminary application form is available at http://www.christianwomentoday.com/volunteer/writingappl.html

Categories: Nonfiction—Beauty—Career—Christian Interest—Evangelism—Family—Health—Marriage—Ministry—Money and Finances—Parenting—Relationships—Spiritual

CONTACT: Editor
Material: All
Campus Crusade for Christ
Christian Women Today
Box 300 Stn A
Vancouver, BC V6C 2X3
Phone: 604-514-2000
Fax: 604-514-2124
E-mail: editor@christianwomantoday.com (preferred)
Website: www.christianwomentoday.com

Chronicle of the Old West

Chronicle of the Old West is a monthly 1800's newspaper for Old West enthusiasts. These are people for whom the Old West is a time and place of the heart.

WRITING STYLE: We are looking for articles that educate, entertain and excite people about the Old West. The articles should be historically accurate. – We do not do fiction. We are looking for the real flavor and atmosphere of the Old West, not technical or dry scholarly accounts. *Articles should be written as if the author is a reporter for* Chronicle of the Old West *writing about a current event. We want to give the reader the feeling the event just took place, and the reader is at the time and location of the subject of the article.* The author should not make reference to himself within the article. (A sample article is at the end of the writer's guidelines.)

Subjects can be about the adventure or daily life of outlaws and lawmen, ranchers and farmers, trappers and settlers, Native Americans and cavalry.

If the article is about a well-known person or event, it should include new or not commonly known information.

The format is newsprint tabloid size in sepia tone ink, giving the flavor of a vintage Old West newspaper.

We accept original or reprint articles. Please indicate if the material has previously been published and where. We purchase the rights not only to print the material in *Chronicle of the Old West*, but also the rights to reprint in our web site and an anthology.

Original sources are best (newspaper accounts, memoirs, documents), rather than compilations from previous publications. Do not include your sources within the article itself, but do include them as an addendum for our review.

So that our readers will get a better feeling of the timing of the article, it will appear in the issue of the month in which the article's final outcome took place.

TIMELINE & GEOGRAPHIC COVERAGE: The age of the Old West was from 1800 to1900. We give a special emphasis to what is known as the "Wild West" from 1860 to 1900. The Old West covers the Mississippi River to the Pacific Ocean, and the Canadian border to the Rio Grande River.

QUERY LETTER: Provide a one-page summary of the story with sources and short bio explaining your expertise and credits. If you would like your submission returned, please include a self-addressed stamped envelope.

SUBMISSIONS: Manuscripts should be typed, single space, on one side of standard white 8 ½ x 11 paper in Times or Arial fonts. Use bond paper and one inch margins on all sides. Name, address, telephone number and approximate word count should be at the top of the first page. Sources and additional reading should be included at the end of the manuscript. You can also submit manuscripts on an IBM compatible computer disk or via e-mail atOldPress@RavenHeart.com

In addition to byline and payment, we will provide authors with two copies of *Chronicle of the Old West* in which the article appears. When we buy a manuscript, we reserve the right to edit, rewrite and shorten it. Please allow up to two month's response time for queries and manuscripts.

PHOTOS/ART: Photos, maps and art are encouraged and may sway a decision. Material can be black and white, color slides or archival material. Private photos are especially valued. Submit photocopies with query.

ARTICLE LENGTH: Feature articles can vary in length from short 500 word clips to 1,500 word essays. Articles can be one-time, a series of related articles or a continuing saga. We also have special departments. *They include:*

- "The Chuck Wagon." Recipes of the Old West. It is necessary to include information on the history of the recipe.
- "The Old West on Celluloid." How current and past western movies portray the Old West.
- "The Old West Today." Descriptions of places and events where people can experience the Old West through participation and observation. This needs to be submitted four months prior to the event.

PAYMENT: Payment is made within 30 days following publication. *Chronicle of the Old West* pays five to eight cents per word with the exception of the column "The Chuck Wagon." The payment for "The Chuck Wagon" is $10.00 per recipe.

Categories: Nonfiction—History—Western

CONTACT: Dakota Livesay, Publisher
Material: All
PO Box 2859
Show Low AZ 85901
E-mail: info@chronicleoftheoldwest.com
Website: www.chronicleoftheoldwest.com

Chronicles
A Magazine of American Culture

CHRONICLES is a monthly magazine of ideas devoted to discussions of first principles in all branches of humane learning. It is not an academic journal. Our special concern is with the intersection of arts and letters with social and political issues. While our editorial policy can be described as traditionalist or conservative, our pages are open to a broad spectrum of opinions.

The ideal contributor to CHRONICLES is a writer or scholar who can express his ideas clearly enough to reach the general reader. We try to avoid both ideological polemics and academic jargon in favor of liveliness and clarity.

"VIEWS": Two or three essays are commissioned for each CHRONICLES issue and are usually devoted to some aspect of the issue's theme. These pieces run anywhere from 1,500-3,000 words long.

"OPINIONS": These are our longer review essays of about 1,500 words on a theme derived from a current book or number of books. The subject of the essay is not just the books themselves but a topic suggested by the books. The main part of the essay should be devoted to developing the writer's own ideas.

"REVIEWS": These are our shorter reviews in 500-1,200 words, reviewers are asked to identify the primary themes of a book and put them into perspective. In the case of fiction, please resist the temptation to summarize the plot.

"VITAL SIGNS": This is our cultural section, in which we run movie, theater, and art reviews. This is also the place for reportage on subjects such as legal cases, academic issues, and the like.

"CORRESPONDENCE": Our "Letters From..." fall into this section, which has the loosest criteria. In the past we have run reportage, personal essays, and more philosophical pieces.

When reviewing books, please be sure to include all book review information: title, author (or editor), publisher, city, state, price, and page number.

To assist us in fact-checking, please include at the end of the article sources of any quotations used within the text.

We will need you to provide us with a short bio, one or two sentences long.

CHRONICLES does not accept unsolicited fiction.

Categories: Nonfiction—Christian Interests—Culture—Education—Environment—Government—Literature—Poetry—Politics—Regional

CONTACT: Scott P. Richert, Exec. Editor
Material: All
928 N. Main St.
Rockford IL 61103
Phone: 815-964-5054
Fax: 815-964-9403
E-mail: submissions@chroniclesmagazine.org
Website: www.chroniclesmagazine.org

Chronogram

Chronogram is a regional magazine of arts, lifestyle, politics, environmental issues, holistic health and culture published monthly. *Chronogram* is an outlet for reportage and point of view that are not often found in the mainstream media. We like to think of ourselves as "progressive" in the broadest sense: We believe that an enlightened, democratic society is attainable as long as citizens-our readers a small group among them-are informed with reliable information. Our writers write the critiques, praises, philosophizings and personal anecdotes that provide the detail to the larger picture, the colors to the outline (often coloring outside the lines).

The editor's ears are always open for new voices and all story ideas are invited for pitching. *Chronogram* welcomes all voices and viewpoints as long as they are expressed well. We discriminate solely based on the quality of the writing, nothing else. The length of articles we usually run are from 1000-3500 words.

While for the most part *Chronogram* covers local events and profiles local people, our political and environmental coverage is nationally and internationally focused. *Chronogram* is also committed to publishing insightful first person essays, short stories and poetry.

Chronogram pays on a sliding scale based on a contract between the editor and the writer. We do not offer kill fees or any other compensation for stories we choose not to publish; we cannot afford that luxury. *Chronogram* reserves the right not to publish any story submitted to us if it does not meet our editorial standards, even if the editor has initially given a writer the 'go-ahead' for a story idea. If a story is purchased, *Chronogram* reserves first-time North American print and Web rights, which revert to the writer after a period of three months.

Now that you know what we want, get to it. For longer article ideas, please contact the editor, via e-mail bmahoney@chronogram.com, or regular post, before submitting the piece. Submissions should be double-spaced, with only one carriage return between paragraphs (no spaces between the paragraphs) and no paragraph indents. All accepted editorial submissions (not poetry) must be submitted electronically or on disk. Send it all, and if you want it returned, include an SASE.

Brian K. Mahoney, Editorial Director

***Chronogram* Artists' Guidelines**

Since *Chronogram* is a magazine of the arts, we strive to feature the best available art for our monthly Cover and Parting Shot features. Both are full page venues for local/semi-local artists to display their work. Along with both are (approximate) 100-word bios about the artist and gallery where and when to find the original work. Please send samples via e-mail or snail mail to the address above.

As well as the Cover and Parting Shot opportunities, there are many other ways artists can be seen in *Chronogram*. We are always looking for new talent to grace our pages. Assignment photographers, illustrators and cartoonists are needed every month! *Chronogram* pays $40-$80 per assignement. Please send samples via e-mail or snail mail to the address above.

COVER SUBMISSIONS:

Paintings/mixed media/photographs: original work*, large-format transparencies (sorry, no 35mm slides accepted for the cover)

PARTING SHOT SUBMISSIONS:

• Photographs/mixed media: original work* (no larger than 8.5x14), 35mm slide, large-format transparency, 300 dpi 8x10 BW scan (tiff/jpg/psd)

• Original work can be submitted, though is not recommended. We can direct large-format painters on how to get a 4x5 transparency shot for easier submission. Photographers, please submit original prints no larger than 8.5x14 inches.

Please note: Chronogram does not pay for Cover or Parting Shot art. All mailed artwork must come with a SASE in order to be returned. All measurement requirements listed above are in inches.

Categories: Nonfiction—Arts—Cartoons—Culture—Ecology—Interview—Music—Poetry—Regional

CONTACT: Brian K. Mahoney, Editorial Director
Material: All, except poetry
CONTACT: Franci Levine Grater, Poetry Director
Material: Poetry
Luminary Publishing, PO Box 459
New Paltz NY 12561
Phone: 845-255-4711
Website: www.chronogram.com

 THE CHRYSALIS READER

Chrysalis Reader
Journal of the Swedenborg Foundation

What Is the Chrysalis Reader? *Chrysalis*, originally a journal issued three times a year, has evolved into a book format that explores contemporary questions on spirituality. Each *Chrysalis Reader* seeks to give fresh and diverse perspectives on a theme through writing and art from many traditions. The *Chrysalis Reader* is published by the Swedenborg Foundation and includes spiritual insights of Emanuel Swedenborg (1688–1772)—scientist, inventor, and mystic—who used his rational and scientific orientation to explore the world of spirit.

Writer's Guidelines Essays, fiction, and poetry should focus on or expand one of the *Chrysalis Reader's* upcoming themes. In editing, our primary goal is maintaining the integrity of the author's style and point of view. Editing is designed to clarify and to keep the writing in the *Chrysalis Reader* vigorous and interesting.

The *Chrysalis Reader* does not accept material that has been published previously. We do accept simultaneous submissions.

The *Chrysalis Reader* style follows *The Chicago Manual of Style*. Manuscripts should be typed, double-spaced, and no longer than 3,000 words. The final copy of an accepted manuscript should be submitted in hard copy (snail mail) and electronically either on disc or as an attached file via e-mail. Manuscripts will not be returned to authors. Please keep a copy of your manuscript for your records and include a self-addressed, stamped envelope for our response and other correspondence.

The interval between submission of the accepted manuscript and the final draft may involve communication between author, reviewers, and editors. Our schedule is designed to allow flexibility and a liberal amount of time for such communication. If you have missed the date for a rough draft but feel you have a solid idea for a piece, send us an outline. We look forward to your contribution. Previously issued titles are $7 each. Issued titles are $10 each.

THE CHRYSALIS READER AUDIENCE The *Chrysalis Reader* audience includes people from many faiths and spiritual traditions, as well as seekers. Many of our readers work in psychology, education, religion, the arts, or one of the helping professions.

Categories: Fiction—Nonfiction—Arts—Literature—Poetry—Spiritual—Philosophy

CONTACT: Richard Butterworth, Editorial Associate
Material: All
Route 1, Box 4510
Dillwyn VA 23936
Phone: 434-983-3021
Fax: 434-983-1074
E-mail: chrysalis@hovac.com
Website: www.swedenborg.com

Cicada

Submissions Guidelines

For a sample issue of CICADA, please send $8.50 to CICADA Sample Copy • P.O. Box 300 • Peru, IL 61354 *NOTE: Sample copy requests from foreign countries must be accompanied by International Postal Reply Coupons (IRCs) valued at US $8.50. Please do NOT send a check or money order.* CICADA is a literary magazine for teenagers and young adults and is published by Cricket Magazine Group. CICADA, for ages 14 and up, publishes original short stories, poems, and first-person essays written for teens and young adults. In some cases, CICADA purchases rights for excerpts from books yet to be published. Each issue also includes several reprints of high-quality selections. CICADA measures 5-1/2" x 8-1/2", contains 128 pages, has a full-color cover, and is perfect bound. Black-and-white illustrations of the highest quality appear throughout the magazine. We hope the following information will be useful to prospective contributors. -Editor-in-Chief, Marianne Carus

Published: Bimonthly, 6 times a year.

Price: $35.97 for 1-year subscription (6 issues).

Comments:

CICADA would like to reach as many authors and illustrators as possible for original contributions, but our standards are very high, and we will accept only top-quality material. PLEASE DO NOT QUERY FIRST. CICADA will consider any manuscripts or art samples sent on speculation and accompanied by a self-addressed, stamped envelope. For art, send tear sheets or photoprints/photocopies. PLEASE DO NOT send original artwork. Be sure that each sample is marked with your name, address, and phone number. Allow 12 weeks for a reply.

CICADA normally purchases the following rights for works appearing in the magazine. For stories and poems previously unpublished, rights vary. Payment is made upon publication.

For stories and poems previously published, CICADA purchases second North American publication rights. Fees vary, but are generally less than fees for first publication rights. Payment is made upon publication. Same applies to accompanying art.

For recurring features, CICADA purchases the material outright. The work becomes the property of CICADA, and it is copyrighted in the name of Carus Publishing Company. A flat fee per feature is usually negotiated. Payment is made upon publication.

For commissioned artwork, rights vary, but in all cases the terms outlined below apply:

a. Physical art remains the property of the illustrator.

b. Payment is made within 45 days of acceptance.

c. Illustrators may use artwork for self promotion.

Manuscripts:

Fiction, realistic, contemporary, historical fiction, adventure, humor, fantasy, science fiction (Main protagonist should be age 14 or older; stories should have a genuine teen sensibility and be aimed at readers in high school or college). Nonfiction first-person experiences that are relevant and interesting to teenagers Poetry serious or humorous; rhymed or free verse. Other book reviews providing in-depth, thoughtful commentary. Length Fiction/articles up to 5,000 words .

Novellas up to 15,000 words (We run one novella per issue) .

Poems up to 25 lines.

Book review 300 to 700 words. An exact word count should be noted on each manuscript submitted. For poetry, indicate number of lines instead. Word count includes every word, but does not include the title of the manuscript or the author's name.

Rates:

Fiction and articles up to 25¢ per word.

Poems up to $3.00 per line.

Payment upon publication.

Categories Fiction—Nonfiction—Book Reviews—Juvenile—Poetry—Teen—Young Adult

CONTACT: Submissions Editor
Material: Manuscripts
CONTACT: Ron McCutchan, Senior Art Director
Material: Art
CONTACT: Diane Sikora, Rights and Permissions Coordinator
Material: Inquiries regarding permissions
PO Box 300
Peru IL 61354
Phone: 815-224-5803, ext. 656
Fax: 815-224-6615
Website: www.cricketmag.com

Cimarron Review

Please read carefully these guidelines before submitting.

We accept submissions year-round in poetry, fiction, non-fiction, and art. All work must be accompanied by a SASE. Cover letter encouraged.

Please send 3–6 poems, one piece of fiction or non-fiction (2–3 o.k. if work is under 1500 words), and prints for cover art and portfolios. Address all work to the appropriate editor (fiction, poetry, non-fiction, art) and mail to:

Cimarron Review
205 Morrill Hall, English Dept.
Oklahoma State University
Stillwater, OK 74078

We do not accept the following:

• Previously published work (includes work published online).

• E-mail submissions from authors living in the United States.

We will accept E-mail submissions from writers living outside the US, but please query first, and follow our guidelines listed here.

Simultaneous submissions are welcomed, but please notify us immediately through postal or E-mail should your work be accepted elsewhere.

We do not publish theme issues. We are interested in any strong writing of a literary variety, but are especially partial to poetry with an

awareness of narrative and fiction in the modern realist tradition. We have no set page lengths for any genre, but we seldom publish short-shorts or pieces over 25 pages. There are, however, exceptions to every rule. Our guiding aesthetic is the quality of the work itself.

We strongly encourage those interested in submitting to first read a copy of the magazine in order to better understand our likes and/or dislikes.

Categories: Fiction—Nonfiction—Culture—Literature—Native American—Poetry—Short Stories—Writing

CONTACT: Fiction Editor
Material: Fiction
CONTACT: Poetry Editor
Material: Poetry
CONTACT: Non-Fiction Editor
Material: Non-Fiction
CONTACT: Art Editor
Material: Art
205 Morrill Hall, English Dept.
Oklahoma State University
Stillwater OK 74078-4069
Phone:405-744-9476
Fax: 405-744-6326
E-mail: cimarronreview@yahoo.com (no submissions)
Website: www.cimarronreview.okstate.edu

Cincinnati Woman Magazine

Cincinnati Woman is a magazine relating to woman's issues in the Cincinnati area.

Please send a sample of your writing along with your story idea. E-mail submissions are okay.

Payment

$80 for feature stories of about 1,000 words.

$50 for other department articles.

Categories: Nonfiction—Arts—Book Reviews—Consumer—Cooking—Crafts/Hobbies—Culture—Diet/Nutrition—Dance—Drama—Entertainment—Family—Fashion—Film/Video—General Interest—Jewish Interest—Law—Lifestyle—Literature—Marriage—Money & Finances—Parenting—Physical Fitness—Real Estate—Relationships—Spiritual—Theatre—Women's Fiction—Women's Issues

CONTACT: Alicia Wiebe, Publisher
Material: All
Niche Publishing & Media, LLC
PO Box 8170
West Chester OH 45069-8170
Phone: 513-851-8916
Fax: 513-851-8916
E-mail: cincinnatiwoman@cinci.rr.com

CINEASTE
AMERICA'S LEADING MAGAZINE ON THE ART AND POLITICS OF THE CINEMA

Cineaste

Published quarterly, and appearing regularly since 1967, *Cineaste* is today internationally recognized as one of America's foremost film magazines. An independent publication, with no financial ties to the film industry or academic institutions, *Cineaste* features contributions from many of America's most articulate and outspoken writers, critics, and scholars. Focusing on both the art and politics of the cinema, and always stressing a popular, readable style displayed in an attractive, lavishly illustrated format, *Cineaste* offers colorful and thought-provoking coverage of the entire world of cinema, *including:*

• Probing and informative interviews with directors, screenwriters, performers and other creative and technical film production personnel.

• Feature articles on topical issues and contemporary film trends

• In-depth reviews of the latest Hollywood movies, independent productions and foreign films

• Regular coverage of films from developing nations in the Third world

• Critical symposiums and debates on such controversial films as *JFK, Do the Right Thing, Thelma & Louise, Boyz N the Hood,* and *Malcolm X*

• Special supplements on such subjects as Central and Eastern European Cinema, The Arab Image in American Cinema, The Restoration of Spartacus, and Sound and Music in the Movies

• A continuing series on "Race in Contemporary American Cinema"

• Regular columns such as "Book Reviews," "Homevideo," "A Second Look," "Festivals," and "Short Takes"

Guidelines for Writers

Cineaste offers a social, political and esthetic perspective on the cinema. We are not affiliated with any organization or institution. We are interested in all areas of the cinema, including Hollywood films (old and new), American independents, quality European films, and the cinema of the Third World. Familiarity with our editorial policies is a must for authors. The most frequent reason we reject material is that the potential contributor has sent material which, because of length or style or orientation, is clearly out of place in our pages.

STYLE: Our target audience is the intelligent general public, a public that is fairly sophisticated about both art and politics. No matter how complex the ideas or arguments advanced, we demand readability. We think it is the job of the writer to clarify his or her thoughts and not for the reader to decipher clumsy formulations. We dislike academic jargon, obtuse Marxist terminology, film buff trivia, trendy 'buzz' phrases, and show biz references. We do not want our writers to speak of how they have 'read' or 'decoded' a film, but to view, analyze and interpret same. The author's processes and quirks should be secondary to the interests of the reader. Warning the reader of problems with specific films is more important to us than artificially 'puffing' a film because its producers or politics are agreeable.

FEATURE ARTICLES: Articles should discuss the subject (a film, film genre, a career, a theory, a movement, etc.) in depth. The author should detail the particular sociopolitical and artistic content. When appropriate, provide documentation or quotes on the producer's intentions rather than your speculations. Be aware of the political implications of the work and its social perspectives, whatever the actual plot or genre. Whenever possible, sources should be incorporated into the text rather than footnoted. Preferred length for feature articles is 3,000-4,000 words. Send a letter of inquiry on a feature idea or provide an outline. Do not call the office to speak to an editor about article ideas. We want to see your proposal in writing.

One article format we encourage is an omnibus review of several current films, preferably those not reviewed in a previous issue. Such an article would focus on films that perhaps share a certain political perspective, subject matter, or generic concerns (e.g., films on suburban life, or urban violence, or revisionist Westerns). Like individual Film Reviews, these articles should incorporate a very brief synopsis of plots for those who haven't seen the films. The main focus, however, should be on the social issues manifested in each film and how it may reflect something about the current political/social/esthetic climate.

INTERVIEWS: Interviews may be with directors, performers, writers, composers, producers, distributors, technicians, or anyone else involved in the creative or business side of filmmaking. We expect the interview to be hard hitting in that challenging (not necessarily hostile) questions are posed and difficult or controversial points pursued. Our experience is that most interviewees respect a well-prepared interviewer who takes their work seriously enough to ask demanding questions. 'Puff' pieces are boring. We are interested in 1) In-depth career interviews with major personalities; 2) Medium-length interviews usually on a current production or issue; and 3) Very short interviews of a few questions which can be used as a sidebar interview with a review.

An interview is more than a transcript of questions and answers. Transcripts must be edited, condensed, and, if necessary, rearranged to bring major themes into focus. The interviewee should see this material for approval before submission to us. It is helpful, but not necessary, to provide a brief, straightforward introduction and a suggested title. Photos are also appreciated. We wish to emphasize that the focus of the interview is the interviewee, not the interviewer. A typical sign of a poor interview is the inordinate length of the questions which are as long, or even longer, than the answers.

FILM REVIEWS: We prefer reviews that focus on one current film. The review should tell what is of merit and what is not in the film under discussion. It should incorporate a very brief synopsis or description of the plot for those who haven't seen the film. Your review should not be a long plot outline with appended evaluations. We are concerned with esthetics as well as content, with how cinematic techniques affect a film's impact. Preferred length is about 1,500 words for feature reviews

BOOK REVIEWS: Book reviews should deal with newly published books, although recent books as much as two years old may be covered depending on the work's importance. Reviewers may focus on one title or cover several related ones. We encourage review-essays in which the discussion serves as a vehicle for a broader treatment of ideas or issues; but, to be fair to authors, their works deserve to be treated seriously rather than merely as launching pads for general essays. Preferred length for feature reviews is 1,000-2,000 words; capsule reviews are 300-400 words. Provide complete publication information (e.g., publisher, year of publication, number of pages, illus., etc.), following the format used in the "Book Reviews" section. In general, writers should query the Book Review Editor before submitting book reviews.

COLUMNS: "Homevideo" articles (1,000-1,500 words) should deal with topics of general interest or a related group of films; individual title reviews should be 300-500 words. "A Second Look" articles (1,000-1,500 words) should offer a new interpretation of a film classic or a reevaluation of an unjustly neglected release of more recent vintage. "Lost and Found" articles (1,000-1,500 words) should discuss a film that may or may not be released or otherwise seen in the U.S. but which is important enough to be brought to the attention of our readers. "Festivals" columns (1,000-1,500 words) should focus on film festivals of particular political importance, providing as much broader social and artistic context as possible for the specific films discussed since many of the latter may not be released or otherwise screened in the U.S.

SUBMISSIONS: We assume that all manuscripts are not reworked versions of previously published or simultaneously submitted material. Manuscripts will be responded to in from 2-4 weeks. Unsolicited material will be given serious consideration, but it is best to query first in case the film, book, or topic has already been assigned. No term papers, please! Do not call the office about submissions unless more than a month has elapsed since making your submission. Long distance phone calls will be returned collect.

REVISIONS: If we feel the material needs further work, we will either 1) Return the material to you with suggestions for changes, or 2) Make changes and submit the revised manuscript for your approval before publication. A Writer's Agreement Form will be sent for all manuscripts accepted for publication.

PAYMENT: We currently pay a minimum of $20 for film reviews and other short pieces, $12 for book or video reviews (the author also gets to retain the book or video reviewed), and a minimum of $25-$30 for feature material, on publication. Contributors also receive three copies of the issue for short pieces and six copies for feature material. We hope to raise these rates, knowing that good writing merits adequate compensation. Kill fees (50% of the above rates) may be paid for material originally solicited by the editors. Royalties from subsequent publication in foreign journals or anthologies will be split 50/50 with the author. Our percentage will be waived when the book is a collection of the author's work or is edited by the author.

All material submitted will be carefully read. Although we have published some of the best known writers on film, we have also been the first place of publication for many writers. All the editors are themselves writers and are aware of the curt treatment writers so often receive from indifferent editors. The least you can expect from us is a thoughtful reading of your work, even though we may not be able to write you with detailed comments.

Categories: Film/Video

CONTACT: Submissions Editor
Material: All
304 Hudson St., 6th Floor
New York NY 10013-1015
Phone: 212-366-5720
Fax: 212-366-5724
E-mail: CINEASTE@cineaste.com
Website: www.cineaste.com

Circle K

Thank you for your interest in CIRCLE K magazine. CIRCLE K is a sixteen-page collegiate publication distributed five times during each academic year (October, November/December, January/February, March, and April) to the 11,000 members of Circle K International, as well as additional subscribers.

Circle K International is the world's largest collegiate service organization, and its members are above-average college students, primarily residing in the United States and Canada, who are committed to community service and leadership development.

Articles published in CIRCLE K are of two types: serious and light nonfiction. Most articles purchased for publication in CIRCLE K address broad areas of interest to all college students but specifically to service-minded individuals, such as current trends (social, collegiate, etc.), leadership and career development, self-help, and community involvement. No fiction, short humor, or travel pieces are accepted. Also, we do not publish historical or philosophical pieces, nor do we accept profiles.

CIRCLE K articles average between 1,500 and 2,000 words (six to eight pages, typed double-spaced); payment is "on acceptance" and ranges from $150 to $400, depending on depth of treatment, appeal to our special audience, and other factors. Query letters are preferred to finished manuscripts.

Proposed articles are tested against two major criteria: They should (1) cover a broad subject rather than an individual person, place, or event; and (2) be applicable to the lives and concerns of today's college students.

Some of our recently published articles include "Student Legal Woes," "Mum's the Word" (political correctness), "The Black and White of How to Get a Job," "Cultural Diversity 101," "Television's College Cult," "Crossing the Student/Mentor Line," "When Children and Collegians Click," "The Graduate School Climb," "Last Call for Alcohol," and "Students of Divorce."

In all articles, treatment must be objective and in-depth, and each major point should be substantiated by illustrative examples and quotes from expert sources. Authors are required to base their stories on interviews and research rather than on personal insights and experiences, and serious articles should avoid intrusions of writers' views. Single-source articles and essays are quickly rejected.

Writing style should be smooth, personable, and to the point, with strong narration, anecdotes, and use of descriptive detail where appropriate. An article's lead must be strong, capturing the readers' attention and setting the tone of the piece. It should be followed by a clear thesis statement of the article's central point. The reader should know quickly what he or she is going to read about and why.

Treatment of light subjects must be as authoritative as serious subjects, but humorous examples and comparisons, as well as a lighter writing style, also are valued when appropriate.

Writers should be aware that CIRCLE K is not exclusively a US publication but has readers in Canada and the Caribbean as well. Avoid terms such as "our nation" and "our president," and strive for some quotes and examples from non-US sources, if practical.

Photographs (color and/or black-and-white) are not essential but are when they are of high quality and add substantially to the impact of article. Photos and artwork are purchased as part of the manuscript with consideration given to the extra time and expense of the author.

Mail or fax query letters.

Categories: Campus Life—College—Education—Young Adult

CONTACT: Amy Wiser, Executive Editor
Material: All
3636 Woodview Trace
Indianapolis IN 46268-3196
Phone: 317-875-8755
Fax: 317-879-0204
E-mail: ck.magazine@kiwanis.org

Circle Track

Circulation: 130,212
Frequency: monthly

Readers turn to *Circle Track* as the voice of authority and technical guide to oval track racing. The title focuses on the latest in racing technology and competition strategies. It also provides readers with in-depth articles on performance modifications.

Guidelines: *Circle Track* has no formal guidelines.

Visit *Circle Track* on-line at www.circletrack.com

Categories: Nonfiction—Automobiles—Sports/Recreation—Technology

CONTACT: Ron Lemaster Jr., Editor-in-Chief
Material: All
3816 Industry Blvd.
Lakeland FL 33811
Website: www.circletrack.com

The Circle

We love reading submissions. By submitting, you agree that if we chose to publish your work, we have permission to publish it in our print issue and put it on our website.

We pay in copies of the print edition (even if your work only appears on the website) so include your address with any submission.

Poetry
3-5 poems
No file attachments - put in body of email
any length/style
Note, however, that we have published only one rhyming poem since 1997.

Include your name, address, phone number & email address with submission. Submissions can be emailed to circlemag@aol.com or snail mailed.

Artwork/photographs
Please do not send originals until artwork is accepted! Attach as .jpg file or mail color photocopies. we are currently seeking art/photographs for cover and inside the print edition, as well as on the website. if the piece is for sale, please let us know that as well!

Submissions can be emailed to circlemag@aol.com or snail mailed.

Short stories

Word count is flexible but longer pieces have little chance of making the print issue most any style/topic - we shy away from anything religious or predictable can be attached as a TEXT FILE (not .doc) or in the body of email submissions can be emailed to circlemag@aol.com or snail mailed.

Features

Check with us first!

Columns

We are currently seeking new columnists on a weekly/monthly/quarterly basis. most of these columns will appear on the website with infrequent appearance in print edition. we are open to ideas and will work with writers to get their voice heard! email us for more information or with ideas. Note: pays in copies of print edition

Reviews

CD, website, movie, book, zine, etc. - email editor and ask! helpful suggestions

1. The word "you" is not spelled "u," nor is "your" or "you're" spelled "ur."

2. If English is not your native language, make sure we don't know it from your writing.

Categories: Fiction—Nonfiction—Arts—Comedy—Culture—Interview—Literature—Music—Paranormal—Photography—Poetry—Science—Science Fiction—Short Stories—Writing—Humor—Philosophy

CONTACT: Penny Talbert, Editor
Material: Short stories, Artwork, Photos, Poetry
173 Grandview Road
Wernersville PA 19565
Phone: 610-678-6550
Fax: 610-678-6550
E-mail: circlemag@aol.com
Website: www.circlemagazine.com

Civil War Times

Please refer to Primedia History Group

Clamor
New Perspectives on Politics, Culture, Media and Life

Clamor magazine is built from everyday folks like you. Please take some time to contact us if you have any ideas that you would like to see in clamor. *Below are the guidelines for contributing to clamor:*

REQUIREMENTS

When approaching us with a proposal, we simply need to know the topic, expected length, whether or not you will provide graphics to accompany your piece, and what deadline you can commit to.

Final drafts should be submitted via email or disk, and should include title, how you want to be credited (how you want your name listed), and a few lines of biographical inormation or the contributors page. You also need to tell us if want your address or e-mail to accompany your bio. This needs to be submitted with each article.

You always have the option of using your payment towards advertisement, a subscription, or a donation. Please let us know how you would like your payment (and what name to make payments to), when you submit your final draft.

PLEASE REMEMBER:

Do not feel obliged to send a big, feature length piece each time you contribute. We will happily take short columns, reviews, single panel/stand alone artwork and photography, etc.

WRITING REVIEWS FOR CLAMOR:

If you think you might be interested in writing reviews of books, zines, movies or CDs for *Clamor*, see our website for a list of available items.

Categories: Book Reviews—Film/Video—Mass Communications—Music

CONTACT: Submissions Editor
Materials: All
PO Box 1225
Bowling Green OH 43402
E-mail: info@clamormagazine.org
Website: www.clamormagazine.org

Classic Toy Trains

Formal guidelines not available. Please read a number of issues to ascertain the publication's style and needs.

Send queries to address below.

Categories: Antiques—Collectibles—Crafts/Hobbies—Hobbies—Juvenile

CONTACT: Kelly Shaw, Editorial Assistant
Material: All
Kalmbach Publishing Co.
21027 Crossroads Circle
Waukesha WI 53186
Phone: 262-796-8776

Click Magazine

Mission: The goal of CLICK is to allow young children access to the world of ideas and knowledge in an age-appropriate yet challenging way. It is often assumed that many areas of human endeavor and knowledge are uninteresting and beyond the understanding of young children. However, CLICK assumes otherwise and attempts to provide children with a clear and inviting introduction to many of the same phenomena and questions about the world that intrigue their adult counterparts. CLICK also attempts to introduce children to the processes of investigation and observation and encourages children to be active participants in the search for knowledge and understanding of their world.

Criteria for an Acceptable Article or Story: Each issue of CLICK is built around a central theme; CLICK themes introduce children to ideas and concepts within the natural, physical, or social sciences; the arts; technology; math; and history. CLICK presents nonfiction concepts to young children through a variety of formats, stories, articles, poems, photo essays, and activities. CLICK seeks **articles** that explain the how and why of something in a friendly, engaging, perhaps humorous way. CLICK prefers a more informal, conversational style to a formal, textbook style. The best articles tackle one idea or concept in depth rather than several ideas superficially. CLICK also seeks **stories** that contain and explain nonfiction concepts within them. Since it is part of CLICK's mission to encourage children to question, observe, and explore, successful stories often show children engaged in finding out about their universe—with the help of supportive, but not all-knowing, adults.

Queries: CLICK editors do not accept unsolicited manuscripts or queries. All articles published in CLICK are commissioned from professional authors. Authors interested in being considered for commissioned work should send a resume, writing samples, and detailed story ideas. Please allow 12 weeks for a reply.

Categories: Nonfiction—Arts—Children—Education—History—Juvenile—Nature—Science—Technology

CONTACT: Submissions Editor
Material: Queries
CONTACT: Art Director
Material: Art Samples
Carus Publishing Company

332 S. Michigan Ave., Ste 1100
Chicago IL 60604
Website: www.cricketmag.com

Climbing

Writers, Photographers, Illustrators and Artists
(digital media included)

Climbing magazine, which celebrates its 30th anniversary in 2000, covers the sport in all its forms. The magazine's editorial spectrum includes rock *Climbing* — from sport climbing to big walls — and mountaineering, with its steep ice routes, alpine classics, and expeditions to the world's great ranges. International in scope, but with a strong North American emphasis in its coverage, *Climbing* is published every six weeks.

If you are considering writing for *Climbing*, carefully read several recent issues to get an idea of our style and focus. Please query us prior to submitting any article, preferably enclosing a detailed outline of your proposal. E-mail queries are preferred. Also, mention the availability of photographs or illustrations to accompany the proposed article. *Send your query to:* climbing@climbing.com (formatted for Macintosh).

All written materials submitted should be typewritten and on disk if possible. Include a self-addressed, stamped envelope for their return.

Payment
Payment for photographs used is made on publication according to the following scale:
- Cover: $700
- Table of Contents: paid at rates listed below for size actually used, or $50/photo for second use in same issue.
- Two-page spread: $400
- Full page: $300
- 2/3 page: $200
- ½ page: $150
- 1/4 page & smaller: $75

Mailing Instructions
All editorial materials should be packaged carefully and shipped via certified or insured mail. All materials must include return postage.

Features
We publish both creative and documentary-type features. We strive to include personal accounts of climbing adventures, profiles of interesting climbers, and surveys of different areas in each issue. We look for lively, authoritative writing that captures the spirit of our varied sport. Think about the articles you've read that stimulated you to action, made your palms sweat, or gave you something new to dream about. That's the feeling we're looking for.

Features are from 2000 to 5000 words in length; payment, made on publication, is $.35 per word for final copy.

High-quality photography is another cornerstone of *Climbing*'s editorial product. A regular feature is the Climbing Gallery, a photo section that showcases our sport's finest images, from action shots to mountain scenery. Gallery pays $300 per photo.

Departments
- Off the Wall, Hot Flashes, and Inside Game: Off The Wall is a mostly lighthearted section that highlights the unusual and the humorous. Hot Flashes concentrates on state-of-the-art ascents, from rock to alpine.

Off the Wall and Hot Flashes are written by *Climbing* editors, although we do occasionally accept short news stories and pay $.25 per word. Otherwise, we welcome tips and information, and pay regular rates for photos used in both columns.

- Inside Game: We are on the lookout for correspondents; anyone interested should be involved in the local scene and willing to do the research required to provide accurate information. Competitions covers the rapidly growing field of local, national, and international climbing competitions; please call or write beforehand if you want to

cover an event. Photos are used liberally and are paid for at our regular rates.

- Roadworthy: These destination mini-features range from 500 to 1500 words, and are information-oriented. The story should both give a feel for the area and enough information for the reader to plan a trip. Stories pay $400, with regular rates for photos.

- High and Wild: These information-oriented stories are primers to both well-known and obscure mountain destinations. Include all pertinent information necessary for travel. Stories are 1000 to 2000 words. Pay is $500.

- Training: Subjects for this column can vary from nutrition to weight lifting. Concentrate on practical information for climbers of all levels, including theory and step-by-step workouts. Stories should be 1000 to 1500 words. Pay is $500.

- Medicine: Articles range from the prevention and treatment of tendinitis to what to take in an expedition medical kit. Length ranges from 1000 to 1500 words. Pay is $500.

- Equipment: This department reviews technical climbing gear, from rock shoes to bivy tents, and explains its use. Evaluations should be hard-hitting and research driven. Length varies from 1000 to 2000 words. Pay is $.35/word for final text.

- Just Out: Similar to our regular equipment reviews, but covers one piece of equipment only. Equipment reviewed should be new and innovative. Text reveals how a specific product worked in the field, based on the author's experiences. Length is 500 to 600 words. Pay is $150.

- Tech Tip: Concise how-to description of useful techniques for all types of climbing. Text is 250 to 500 words. Pay is $150.

- Players: Short (750-word) profiles of climbers. Players features those who are interesting as much or more for their personalities or lifestyle as their pure climbing accomplishments. Pay is $400.

- Reviews: This department covers new books, both fiction and non-fiction, as well as guidebooks, films, CD-ROMs, and videos. Length should be 200 to 300 words. Pay is $150.

- Perspective: The most varied department in the magazine, this is a personal opinion or experience column. Virtually any subject related to climbing is appropriate. Length should be 1000 to 1500 words. Pay is $300.

Photography
Climbing is renowned for its photography. While many of the images we use are solicited from regular contributors, we are always on the lookout for high-quality work.

Images must be sharp and properly exposed. If you are shooting for an article, variety is also important; a selection of both horizontal and vertical compositions, shot from different angles and with different lenses, will help us in layout. Please don't send multiple images that are virtually the same — edit your selection to "the best of the best." We accept negatives or prints, but typically use original 35mm transparencies. We also accept medium- and large-format transparencies. Please do not send duplicates. Submit your slides in plastic file sheets and make sure that your name and address are clearly printed on each slide mount. Include complete captions, including climbs' and climbers' names, for every photo submitted. Unsolicited submissions must be accompanied by return postage.

Contributor Guidelines for Illustrators and Artists
What happens to your art when we receive it?

Your illustrations will be scanned or downloaded to one of our Macintosh computers here in *Climbing*'s production department. Traditional art is scanned on an Agfa Studioscan IIsi 30bit color scanner. This is a high-quality flatbed scanner that is capable of scanning images at up to 2400dpi (with interpolation). In other words, if there are any marks on the art other than the art work it will digitize this information. We will only alter digitized information if it needs to be cleaned or if a file is not in the right format. Files that are already digitized will appear as you deliver them. The digitized files are imported into QuarkXPress and scaled to the layout.

Guidelines for traditional media illustrators.

All art should be as clean as possible. Your art will be digitized and everything you can see will be seen by the scanner. Keep art clean, please. Using high-quality art paper will minimize the chance that your original art will be altered by tonal adjustments after scanning.

Pen and ink drawings should have solid blacks and pure whites unless you desire a grayscale image. Again, working on high-quality paper will produce the best results.

Any text in your work should not be hand drawn unless you are asked to do so by an editor. We suggest using an overlay of tracing paper and making notes on the overlay to indicate where you would like text to be placed.

Color work should be cleared by the editor you are working with and a proof will ensure that your work looks the way you intend it to.

If you are sending original art you want returned, please include return address information. Protective covers are recommended for original art.

Guidelines for digital artwork.

We can translate most digital files, but if you are using an obscure or old program please contact us before sending files. If you are sending an illustration done in any vector-based drawing program, such as Adobe Illustrator or Macromedia Freehand, save in an EPS file format or as an Illustrator file.

Our primary graphic and photographic applications are:
• Adobe Illustrator (currently version 8.x-10.x)
• Adobe Photoshop (currently version 5.x-7.x)
• Fractal Design Painter (currently version 6.x-7.x)
• Macromedia Freehand (version 8.x-9.x)

If you are going to be adding your own text to a file please design using Helvetica unless we specify another font. If you are unsure of text use in the illustration you are submitting, print a copy/proof and attach a tracing-paper overlay to indicate text placement. Whenever possible convert text to outlines in programs such as Adobe Illustrator or Macromedia Freehand.

Important: Always include fonts for your work!

NOTE: The mandatory use of Helvetica font does not apply to advertisers or illustrations used in advertisements.

All digital files are imported into QuarkXPress. Please send all files as EPS. Send files at 100% size, or slightly oversized if you are unsure of our final layout size. If you want size information contact John McMullen <webmaster@climbing.com> or Mike Freeman <freeman@climbing.com> . Please notify us if you have any questions about the final size of your work.

The following are recommended settings for Adobe Photoshop 3.x-4.0 digital files:

Black and White EPS files can be bit mapped at 600dpi, 50% threshold (or your preference). *Save as EPS settings:*
• Macintosh (1 bit/pixel)
• Binary
• Halftone screens OFF
• Transfer function OFF
Grayscale EPS settings:
• Macintosh (8 bits/pixel)
• Binary
• Halftone screens OFF
• Transfer function OFF

Full- and spot-color files should be at least 288dpi (300dpi if you have enough room on your disk), converted to CMYK and saved as EPS files. *Settings should be:*
• Macintosh (8 bits/pixel)
• DCS, OFF
• Binary
• Halftone screens OFF
• Transfer function OFF

Disk drives we have available to read your data are:
• SyQuest 200c drive, reads 44MB, 88MB and 200MB SyQuest disks.
• SyQuest 540 drive, reads 540, 270 and 105 SyQuest disks.

• SyQuest 270 drive, reads 105 and 270 SyQuest disks.
• 600MB Sony Optical drive, reads double sided optical disks.
• 100MB Zip Drive.
• 1gig Jaz Drive.
• 2gig Jaz Drive, reads 1gig and 2gig disks.
• 1.4MB Super Floppy and 800k Floppy drives.
• CDROM and DVD readers.

If you are sending disks you will want returned, please include return address information.

Climbing is printed using a 155-line screen. You can set the resolution of your digital files using this information if disk space is tight. Scale them up just a bit to give us some working room.

If you need assistance with this please call, (970) 963-9449, or send e-mail to John McMullen <webmaster@climbing.com>

Thank you, and we look forward to seeing your work.

Categories: Nonfiction—Outdoors—Recreation—Sports,—Travel

CONTACT: Submissions Editor
Material: All
0326 Hwy 133, Ste 190
Carbondale CO 81623
Phone: 970-963-9449
Fax: 970-963-9442
E-mail: climbing@climbing.com
Website: www.climbing.com

Cloth Paper Scissors™

So, you want to write for us?

If you have a technique, project, or body of work to share, *Cloth Paper Scissors*™ Magazine would like to know about it. We want to show other artists—from beginners to the advanced—the latest, edgiest, most unusual collage and mixed media techniques and applications.

Who?

We are looking for writers who are artists themselves, with intimate knowledge of the subjects they wish to write about. We want sparkling, grammatically correct — even humorous — prose, of course, but what's most important is that you are an expert in your subject. Please note that regular features, including Artist Profiles, Product Reviews, Book Reviews, and Reader Challenges are all written by our in-house staff.

What?

Cloth Paper Scissors™ is most interested in publishing previously unpublished articles that cover unique collage and mixed media techniques geared to beginner, intermediate, or advanced artists. Feature articles may explore motifs and methods that will inspire and inform collage and mixed-media artists. Shorter "Spotlight" pieces focus on photos of projects with a brief explanation of how the work was done. *We are actively seeking queries on the following topics for publication:*
• Collage and mixed media artists to feature in our Artist Profiles (Please note: All profiles are written by CPS staff members.)
  • Collage techniques
  • Altered books
  • Art dolls
  • Assemblage
  • Image and text transfer techniques
  • Beaded embellishments
  • Working with found objects
  • Paper folding techniques
  • Transformative art
  • Embossing on fabric or paper
  • Unique painting and dyeing methods
  • Unusual stamping techniques

- Book arts
- Working with vintage materials
- Punching and cutting techniques
- Burning and distressing techniques
- Inspiration and the creative process

Bottom Line

So, what do we pay? The pay for feature articles in *Cloth Paper Scissors*™ (other than staff-written pieces) varies depending on the length of the piece and the depth of the subject matter, but generally we pay $150 and up for shorter pieces and $300 and up for longer ones. We pay within 45 days after publication.

Guidelines for Submissions

Query first, please. We prefer that you send us a query by mail only (no e-mails, please), that succinctly describes your story idea or your artwork and process, explaining how you would handle the story and summarizing your writing experience. Please include slides or prints of artwork or samples (these are just to give us an idea and do not need to be professionally shot.

Note: Our editors will consider complete articles submitted on spec, but queries will get first priority.

Consider our tone. We know, we know, we're just getting started, so you don't have much to go by. But here are some hints: *Cloth Paper Scissors*™ is fun, creative, quirky, spiritual, surprising, inspiring and sassy. We're upbeat. How-to articles should combine the excitement of discovery with accuracy and easy-to-follow instructions. Personal stories should show how you worked through a problem with your art and go on to show others how to use similar techniques or solve similar creative issues.

Give length some thought. Ultimately, we will decide how long the piece is, but please tell us what you have in mind. Though our story length varies greatly, main feature articles range from 800 to 2,500 words while shorter pieces run 400 to 1,000 words.

Include all your information. Please include your address, phone number, e-mail address, and a brief biographical paragraph that includes your title, affiliation, any other relevant experience, if applicable, as well as how you'd like your byline to appear. If you want us to return your query materials, please include a SASE (self-addressed, stamped envelope). Please do not send original artwork at this point in the process.

Copyright Issues

No submissions which may violate copyright laws will be accepted. If your artwork could be perceived by Quilting Arts, LLC as a potential copyright violation, please provide written consent by the party which may have standing with regard to the copyright issue. Thank you for cooperation.

Categories: Crafts/Hobbies

CONTACT: Patricia Bolton, Editor
Material: All
PO Box 685
Stow, MA 01775
Phone: 978-897-7750
E-mail: CPSEditor@quiltingartsllc.com
Website: www.quiltingarts.com

Club Connection

Club Connection, Girls Edition

Club Connection is an fun, full-color quarterly magazine for Missionettes ages 6 to 12. *Club Connection* includes articles dealing with girls' common interests such as school, friends, God, family, music, and fun activities like crafts, games, puzzles, snack recipes, etc. Also included are devotionals; fun facts and news; book, video, and music reviews; missions facts and trivia; a write-in question-and-answer column; and other great features. The salvation message is presented in each issue.

Club Connection, Leader Edition

Club Connection, Leader Edition, is targeted to leaders of Missionettes clubs. Leader's Connection provides leadership ideas and resources, discipleship materials, write-in questions and answers, fund-raising and graduation ideas, information on important current issues, and missions lesson plans that correspond with the missions features in the Girls Edition.

Topics for *Club Connection*, Girls Edition

- Fictional short stories
- Girls' personal experiences
- Adventures—Nature, camping, fine arts, professional, industrial
- Sports
- Unique craft and snack ideas
- Pets/animals
- Unique puzzles and games (Please do not send Word Search or Crossword puzzles)

Topics for *Club Connection*, Leader Edition

- Club meeting ideas
- Sponsors' personal experiences
- Social, Awards Presentation, Adventure (field trip) and project ideas
- Assisting girls with special needs
- Missionettes Celebrations
- Missionettes and outreach ministries
- Discipline in the clubroom
- Leadership development
- Spiritual growth
- Discipleship
- Program questions

SUBMITTING MANUSCRIPTS FOR *Club Connection*

Formatting

Copy should be typed double-spaced. Check grammar, spelling, and punctuation before submitting your manuscript. Make theologically correct statements, and confirm all illustrations, Scripture references, and facts (history, nature, etc.). Give the version of the Bible you are using when quoting Scripture.

Manuscripts 350 words or less will be considered a one-page article. Manuscripts 700 words or less will be two-page spreads.

Indicate if the manuscript is gratis, if the article has been submitted to another publisher, and if the article has previously been printed.

Please avoid any use of names of actual businesses and people. Also, indicate if your article is fact or fiction.

Print your name, address, and social security number on your manuscript, as well as the approximate number of words and a short bio. Include photos relevant to the manuscript (see "Photo Guidelines" below). Enclose a self-addressed stamped envelope if you would like your manuscript returned.

Photo Guidelines

Do not staple or paper clip photos to anything. Do not write directly on the back of photos. Instead attach a label or tape a piece of paper to the back of the photo with your name, address, and phone number and a fun caption describing the action or event. List the names and ages of girls who appear in the picture.

Photos which do not include name and address information cannot be returned.

Photos must be production quality-not blurry or over- or under-exposed.

Manuscript Evaluations

Each manuscript is read and evaluated, then either returned or held in a planning file for further evaluation and possible use. Because *Club Connection* is a quarterly publication, this process may take several months. If your material is published, you will be notified. Writers will receive payment upon publication, as well as two complimentary copies of the issue in which their article appears when the issue is printed. The editors of *Club Connection* reserve the right to edit your manuscript for clarity and space.

Enjoy writing!

Categories: Nonfiction—Children—Christian Interests—Inspirational—Girls

CONTACT: Kelly Kirksey, Associate Editor
Material: All
Assembly of God Publications
1445 N. Boonville Ave.
Springfield MO 65802-1894
Phone: 417-862-2781
E-mail: clubconnection@ag.org
Website: www.clubconnection@ag.org

Clubhouse

Clubhouse readers are 8- to 12-year-old boys and girls who desire to know more about God and the Bible. Their parents (who typically pay for the membership) want wholesome, educational material with Scriptural or moral insight. The kids want excitement, adventure, action, humor or mystery. Your job as a writer is to please both the parent and child with each article.

Fiction needs:
• humor with a point (500-1500 words)
• historical fiction featuring great Christians or Christians who lived during great times (1200-1500 words)
• contemporary, exotic settings (1200-1500 words)
• holiday material (Christmas, Thanksgiving, Easter, President's Day)
• parables (500-1000 words)
• fantasy, avoiding graphic descriptions of evil creatures and sorcery (1200-15– words)
• mystery stories (1200-1500 words)
• choose-your-own adventure stories (1500-1800 words)
• westerns (1200-1500 words)
• biblical: enhancing Bible stories without changing content or message (900 words)

Fiction flops:
• contemporary, middle-class family settings (existing authors meet this need)
• poems (rarely printed)
• stories dealing with boy-girl relationships

Nonfiction needs:
• fun-filled fact essays (12 to 18 off-the-wall facts on a certain subject or theme)
• interviews with noteworthy Christians or Christians who experienced noteworthy events
• scripts for Bible comics (10-12 panels)
• activity theme pages with 4 to 7 fun things for kids to do (800 words)

• top-10 how-to lists: 10 ways to get good grades, save money, etc.
• top-10 humor lists: 10 reasons to avoid family photograph sessions, 10 things not to do in a car while vacationing, 10 foods that do not mix well, etc.
• short, humorous essays with a point
• short news articles adapted to bring out a biblical lesson in a humorous way

Nonfiction flops:
• bible stories without a unique format or overt visual appeal
• information-only science or educational articles
• biographies told encyclopedia or textbook-style

Payment:
• 15 to 25 cents a word for nonfiction
• $200 on up for feature-length fiction stories
• $150 on up for Bible stories

Mail your article with a SASE.

You will receive a response within eight weeks. We accept printed manuscripts only; no query letters. Seasonal material should be sent at least 6 months in advance.

Categories: Fiction—Nonfiction—African-American—Asian-American—Children—Christian Interests—Cooking—Crafts/Hobbies—Family—Games—Hispanic—Home—Juvenile—Multicultural—Religion—Spiritual

CONTACT: Suzanne Hadley, Associate Editor
Material: All
Focus on the Family
8605 Explorer Dr.
Colorado Springs CO 80920
Phone: 719-531-3400

Clubmex

We look for positive, upbeat stories that pertain to a specific travel destination, a small village or big city in Mexico, that tells our readers where to go, what to see, where to stay and shop, and possible interesting things to do. The essential purpose of the Newsletter is to encourage our readers to drive into Mexico. Thus articles involving travel by air, train or ship will be less favored than those involving travel by auto, RV, or any road use vehicle.

For our feature articles, our large international readership base is interested in retirement area, fishing, camping, swimming, lodging (i.e., hotels, resorts, motels, RV parks, etc.), exploring, wind surfing, and/or snorkeling, boating, restaurants, shopping, whale watching, local colorful events—fiestas, and interesting people.

We pay $65.00 for the cover story and $50.00 for other articles, if and when used. Length can vary from 300 to 1000+ words. Photos or slides are strongly encouraged but not mandatory. We pay $5.00 for each photo or slide published.

We reserve the right to edit, delay printing and/or not print any and all stories due to editorial constraints and as space requirement dictate.

I sincerely hope that you send us some articles, photos and slides! I know that we would certainly appreciate your contribution. We will be looking forward to hearing from you soon.

Categories: Nonfiction—Hispanic—Travel

CONTACT: Chuck Stein, Vice President
Material: All
3450 Bonita Rd., Suite 103
Chula Vista CA 91910-5200
Phone: 619-422-3022
Fax: 619-422-2671
E-mail: igib@igib.com
Website: www.igib.com

CNEWA World

CNEWA World was formerly known as *Catholic Near East.*

CNEWA World magazine strives to educate its readers about the culture, faith, history, issues and people who form the Eastern Christian churches.

Established in 1974 by Catholic Near East Welfare Association, this bimonthly publication also attempts to inform its readers of the presence and work of the Association and its sister agency, the Pontifical Mission, in those nations that many Eastern Christians call home.

The goal of CNEWA World is to inform, but its contents should not be academic. People, details of contemporary life, history and "local color" should be woven together. Eastern Christians—Catholic and Orthodox—are frequently depicted as relics of the past. Our goal is to portray these communities as living bodies of men, women and children living and coping in a confused and often troubled world.

CNEWA World is also a tool of ecumenical and interreligious dialogue. Eastern forms of Christianity, Catholic and Orthodox, should be highlighted. However, the Jewish, Hindu and Muslim communities should not be ignored.

The most successful articles are written by those in the field. Stringers in each PM city and in other CNEWA countries offer the most objective, accurate and sensitive portraits of their subjects. Articles should not exceed 1,500 words. This stipulation allows for the lavish use of color photographs.

Photographers, if they are not writers as well, should work with the respective author (the editor should coordinate these efforts). Photographs must illustrate what is described in the article—people, places, festival, etc. General or thematic illustrations are exceptions.

Categories: Nonfiction—Christian Interests—Culture—History—Religion—Spiritual

CONTACT: Michael La Civita, Executive Editor
Material: All
1011 First Ave.,15th Floor
New York NY 10022-4195
Phone: 212-826-1480
Fax: 212-826-8979
E-mail: cnewa@snewa.org
Website: www.CNEWA.org

Coal People Magazine

THEME:

Coal industry business profiles; focus on people in different facets of the coal mining industry; and industry news and related features.

Please note: story ideas related to coal mining will be reviewed, however special assignments must be approved by the editors of COAL PEOPLE MAGAZINE.*

OTHER:

Payment upon publication only

All submissions must be typed or sent via email.

Computer CD acceptance (PC or Mac) in Word format

Please allow 3 months after date of submission.

Short Stories: $35.00 (1,500 words or under)

Regular Features: $60.00 (under 5,000 words)

Features: $75.00 (5,000 words or more)

Puzzles/Fillers: $15.00

Pictures: Cost, plus 15%

*Special assignment payments will be determined.

Categories: Fiction—Coal Mining

CONTACT: Submissions Editor
Material: All
PO Box 6247
Charleston WV 25362

Phone: 304-342-4129
Fax: 304-343-3124
E-mail: cpm@newwave.net or alskinner@ntelos.net
Website: www.coalpeople.com

Coast to Coast

Coast to Coast

As the membership publication for *Coast to Coast* Resorts, *Coast to Coast* is mailed to 200,000 readers eight times a year. *Coast to Coast* Resorts unites nearly 1,000 private camping and resort clubs across North America. A portion of the magazine is devoted to news about the *Coast to Coast* network: its programs, products and services, and, of course, its members. The remainder of the magazine focuses on travel, recreation and good times. *Coast to Coast* strives to be a fun, unpretentious but well-written and informative publication that offers a balanced mix of articles on things to do, places to visit, people to meet and ways to ensure a safe and happy trip.

Destination features in *Coast to Coast* should focus on a city or region of North America and should strive to convey the spirit of the place. The most readable place pieces go beyond typical tourist stops to interview locals and synthesize anecdotes and first-person observations in a way that is useful, entertaining and enlightening. Keep in mind that *Coast to Coast*'s readers already have more than 1,000 camping resorts at which to stay, so reporting on accommodations is almost always beside the point.

Activity or recreation features should introduce readers to or rekindle their interest in a sport, hobby or other diversion. As with the general public, most of our audience can be assumed to possess a basic knowledge of, say, golf or bicycling, but few have experienced rock climbing or skydiving. Nor would they care to, for the most part.

Many of our readers own recreational vehicles, so we feature the RV lifestyle in at least one article per issue. This is where lively, concise writing is especially in demand. If the writing is dry, the article will be, at best, unappealing; at worst, deadly. What's essential in these features is that readers identify with the situations they're reading about, that they pick up new information and at the same time are engaged and entertained.

The editors of *Coast to Coast* encourage queries and manuscripts. If you possess the requisite professional ability and have a lively writing style, please summarize your story idea, supplement it with a few opening paragraphs and forward it to our editorial offices with a selection of your best published clips or other writing samples. The editors are also pleased to review completed manuscripts.

Coast to Coast publishes first North American serial rights; articles must not appear in other publications for 90 days after they are first published in *Coast to Coast*. In accepting an assignment from *Coast to Coast*, writers agree to submit stories on or before the stated deadline and agree to rewrite them, if required, in a timely fashion. Assigned stories should be submitted electronically, either on disk or via e-mail, with an accompanying hard copy. Payment is made upon acceptance.

Categories: Recreation Vehicles—Travel

CONTACT: Valerie Law, Editorial Director
Material: All
2575 Vista Del Mar Dr.
Ventura CA 93001
Phone: 805-667-4100

Coastal Living

Welcome to the award-winning world of *Coastal Living* magazine. Many kudos have come our way since the first issue date, May-June 1997, but Folio: may have said it best. When this watchtower of the magazine industry presented its Editorial Excellence Award for Best Regional Magazine, *Coastal Living* was cited as "Beautifully designed, well written and nicely conceived and balanced. The breezy style, pace and rhythm of this issue make you want to shake the beach sand from its pages."

WHO WE ARE

Coastal Living is a lifestyle magazine that occupies a unique and well-defined niche. As stated on every cover, we are "The Magazine for People Who Love the Coast." Our editorial lineup takes readers to homes, destinations, activities, and people along the Atlantic, Pacific, and Gulf shores of North America. We include Hawaii and Alaska as well as coastal Canada and Mexico. We also visit the multinational Caribbean islands from time to time, and we recently expanded coverage to the waterside ways of life along the U.S. Great Lakes. Our rule of thumb: With the exception of features on the Great Lakes, or "North Coast," *Coastal Living* stories spotlight topics within sight, sound, taste, touch, or smell of salt water.

OUR VOICE

A tone of casual sophistication unfolds between the covers of *Coastal Living*. Regardless of the subject—decorating, entertaining, gardening, travel, nature, or zany beach characters—insider knowledge and ease prevail in the language of our stories. Our syntax welcomes humor but avoids cuteness.

Well-balanced and poised, *Coastal Living* is an accessory on the coffee table, a workhorse in the kitchen, and a friend in the hammock.

VITAL STATS

- *Frequency:* 6 times per year
- *Circulation:* 500,000 paid subscribers nationwide
- *Readership:* 1.5 million (average of 3 readers per issue)
- *Distribution:* 81% subscription; 19% newsstand
- *Editorial-to-Advertising Ratio:* +/-60 to +/-40
- *Publisher:* Southern Progress Corporation (SPC), a division of AOL Time Warner
- *SPC Editorial Offices:* 2100 Lakeshore Dr., Birmingham, AL 35209
- *Web site:* coastalliving.com
- *Word Counts:* 500-1,000

PLANNING SCHEDULE

Coastal Living stories are planned one year in advance during an annual series of editorial meetings from about November 1 through February 1. For example, the slate for 2003 was finalized as of February 2002. Flexibility allows some adjustment as the year progresses, but editors generally stick to the plan. That allows time for research, photography, writing, and production. This lead time is particularly crucial if a story has a seasonal angle, such as fall color or holiday decorating.

PRODUCTION SCHEDULE

Depending on the type of article, the deadline for text to be researched, written, and submitted to the assigning editor is four to six months prior to publication date.

OUR READERS

Subscription renewals and growing newsstand sales tell us that *Coastal Living* succeeds in transporting people to their dreams. Letters, E-mails, and focus groups reveal countless ways readers use our information to make those dreams come true. Surveys show the average time spent perusing a typical issue is 90 minutesan impressive statistic in this fast-paced age. Reader characteristics include:

- *Gender:* 65% women; 35% men
- *Median age:* 44.7
- *Median household income:* $84,824
- *Own a vacation home:* 28%
- *College educated:* 72%
- *Geographic location (percentages rounded):* South and Southeast47%; Northeast21%; West17%; Midwest15%.

- *Travel frequency:* 4.5 vacation trips per year; $4,000 + average annual vacation expenditure; 54% maintain a valid passport.

EDITORIAL DEPARTMENTS

Four overall subject areas (homes, travel, lifestyle, and food and entertaining) define the content of each issue. Divided into features and regular columns, stories depicting each of these areas are included in all three sections of the magazine: front of book, well (the middle section, with no advertising), and back of book.

The magazine also has special sections—such as ones focusing on summer entertaining and building a coastal home—typically written and produced by staff editors.

Behind every story, in all departments, is the desire to serve our readers—to give them ideas, techniques, or inspiration applicable to their own lives. Woven into our stories is an awareness of nature, the environment, and the importance of coastal conservation. Often those topics form the backbone of a story.

Homes

With a mission to promote comfort, livability, and style, the Homes section makes up more than 50% of editorial. Story focus may be on decorating, building and renovating, architecture, products, community development, or gardens and landscaping. Our tone of casual sophistication is unmistakable here: Informal scenes sport just-right touches of grace and taste; otherwise luxurious locations project a "come in and make yourself at home" personality. Homes stories are staff- and freelance-written.

Travel

Coastal Living issues a passport to fun in our destination, outdoor activity, nature experience, and lodging and dining stories. We strive for angles that reveal the essential character of a place in fresh and lively ways no other magazine would capture. The sight, sound, taste, touch, and smell of surf and sand are ever-present in text and photography. A travel/community hybrid is "So You Want to Live In . . . " This popular column, appearing in every issue, includes many of the earmarks of a travel story because it evokes a sense of place. But it takes the reader beyond what might otherwise be a great weekend getaway spot to the practicalities of year-round life with the resident cast and culture of a specific seaside town or village. Travel stories are staff- and freelance-written.

Lifestyle

Stories in this category may feature a family or other cluster of people with a common tie, or they may profile an individual person. They also may be hybrids—partly home/partly lifestyle. The latter depicts homeowners, architects, designers, or landscapers pertinent to the homes, gardens, or communities within the story. Lifestyle columns include:

"The Good Life," which showcases a person or family with a will to live on the coast and a way to do it.

"Coastal Character," which portrays one person who may be a quirky local or a semicelebrity but, either way, is intrinsically connected to the coastal environment.

"Collectibles" highlights rare, valuable, or otherwise treasured items and accessories with a marine connection or motif and is often presented in situ and/or with the owner's path in assembling the collection.

Lifestyle stories are staff- and freelance-written.

Food & Entertaining

In a word, "convivial" describes our approach to putting food and wine on the table or on the picnic cloth. We profile a lively gathering in each issue's well section feature. Other columns include:

"Seafood Primer," a popular what's it and how-to in each issue. The column features a type of (or method of cooking) fish or shellfish.

"Host Notes," which a modern-day Emily Post would find handy at the beach.

NOTE: Recipes in all food features and columns are professionally tested in the *Coastal Living* kitchens to ensure accuracy and quality. Food & entertaining stories are primarily staff-written. Currents—Encompassing the above subject areas, this section opens every issue of *Coastal Living* and is home to a variety of short items (25-200 words). Travel news, cool home products, beach fashion, and seaside events are among the topics that populate its pages. "Currents" is primarily staff-written.

FROM QUERY TO CONTRACT

No manuscripts, please! *Coastal Living* does not accept prepared text, but we are happy to consider a well-developed idea expressed in a query letter.

Winning Queries:

Indicate that the writer has read our magazine well enough to grasp our style and subject matter.

Do not propose a topic recently addressed in a published *Coastal Living* story.

Present a fresh and surprising angle on a widely acknowledged topic; or present a new story idea that is uniquely suited to *Coastal Living*.

Convince our editors that the writer is highly qualified to write on the topic according to his/her experience and familiarity with the subject.

Express the idea in language that captures and holds our attention.

Express the idea concisely.

Include scouting shots or photocopies of photographs whenever possible. This is mandatory for any query related to home and garden stories.

Maintain 100% perfect spelling and grammar.

Are accompanied by clips of published work by the writer unless samples are already on file with *Coastal Living*. (In the latter case, the cover letter should remind us that we have clips and offer to send more if necessary.)

NOTE: Query letters may be sent via e-mail, with clips sent by regular mail in a separate package, with a copy of the query enclosed.

Assignments

Assigning editors will contact the writer if *Coastal Living* decides to pursue an idea. The specific angle, fees, expenses, and deadlines are discussed. That editor prepares and sends a story-focus sheet to the writer to confirm the story approach.

NOTE: Per the planning process followed by *Coastal Living* editors (see Planning Schedule), queried ideas typically will be considered on an annual basis for a future editorial lineup. (For example, all 2003 stories are planned by early 2002.)

The *Coastal Living* office manager issues a story contract, which should be signed and promptly returned by the writer. Accompanying the contract are expense guidelines and a list of items for the writer's submitted story package to include. (The story Focus Sheet also may be included or may be sent separately—see above.)

FEES

Coastal Living typically pays $1 per word, plus reasonable expenses (such as transportation, lodging, and dining for travel stories) agreed upon in advance. Compliance of our expense guidelines is mandatory.

Payment is issued within 24 weeks of story acceptance. NOTE: Following story acceptance, the assigning editor may still request text revisions by the writer.

Kill fees are 25% of the assigned fee, as noted in the contract.

Finder's fees are paid when and where pertinent. The range varies according to the story.

PAYMENT

To ensure prompt payment, writers must:

Meet the deadline specified in the contract.

Send a complete story package to the assigning editor as specified in the directions that accompany the contract. That includes 1) story text; 2) all fact-checking material; 3) names and complete and legible addresses of all story sources or participants who should receive complimentary copies of the issue featuring the story.

Put themselves in the shoes of our fact checkers and think about what they need to do their job. Writers must not fail to include complete fact-checking material in the story package. This is mandatory

for payment. Such material includes but is not limited to: 1) names and contact points for all story sources and anyone quoted; 2) brochures and/or business cards showing up-to-date data pertinent to lodging and other referenced facilities; 3) restaurant menus if applicable; 4) photocopies of pages from historical documents, Web sites, or other information sources used.

Submit an invoice along with the complete story package. The contract does not serve as an invoice.

Categories: Nonfiction—Entertainment—Gardening—Home—Humor—Lifestyle—Regional

CONTACT: Jeff Book, Senior Editor
Material: Homes & gardens
Phone: 205-445-7083
E-mail: jeff_book@timeinc.com
CONTACT: Susan Haynes, Senior Editor
Material: West Coast travel
Phone: 205-445-8580
E-mail: susan_haynes@timeinc.com
CONTACT: Steve Millburg, Travel Editor
Material: All non-West Coast travel
Phone: 205-445-6294
E-mail: steve_millburg@timeinc.com
CONTACT: Jennifer Chappell, Lifestyle Editor
Material: Lifestyle
E-mail: jennifer_chappell@timeinc.com
Phone: 205-445-6264
CONTACT: Julia Rutland, Foods & Entertaining Editor
Material: Food & Entertaining
Phone: 205-445-6053
E-mail: julia_rutland@timeinc.com
2100 Lakeshore Dr.
Birmingham AL 35209
Phone: 205-445-6007
Fax: 205-445-8655
Website: www.coastalliving.com

Cobblestone Magazine
Discover American History

General Information

COBBLESTONE is interested in articles of historical accuracy and lively, original approaches to the subject at hand. Do not forget that our magazine is aimed at youths from ages 8 to 14. Writers are encouraged to study recent back issues for content and style. (Sample issues are available at $4.95. Send 7 ½ " x 10 ½ " self-addressed envelope with $2.00 worth of postage.) All material must relate to the theme of a specific upcoming issue in order to be considered. COBBLESTONE purchases all rights to material.

Procedure

In order for your idea to be considered, a query must accompany each individual idea (however, you can mail them all together) and must include the following:

• A brief cover letter stating the subject and word length of the proposed article,

• A detailed one-page outline explaining the information to be presented in the article,

• An extensive bibliography of materials the author intends to use in preparing the article,

• A self-addressed stamped envelope.

Authors are urged to use primary resources and up-to-date scholarly resources in their bibliography. Writers new to COBBLESTONE should send a writing sample with the query. If you would like to know if your query has been received, please also include a stamped postcard that requests acknowledgment of receipt. In all correspondence, please include your complete address as well as a telephone number where you can be reached.

A writer may send as many queries for one issue as he or she wishes, but each query must have a separate cover letter, outline, bibliography, and self-addressed stamped envelope. All queries must be typed.

Articles must be submitted on disk using a word processing program (preferably Microsoft Word - MAC). Text should be saved as ASCII text (in MS Word as "text only"). Disks should be either MAC - (preferred) or DOS - compatible 3 ½ ".

GUIDELINES

Feature Articles:

700-800 words

Includes: in-depth nonfiction, plays, first-person accounts, and biographies

Supplemental Nonfiction:

300-600 words

Includes: subjects directly and indirectly related to the theme. Editors like little-known information but encourage writers not to overlook the obvious.

Fiction:

up to 800 words

Includes: authentic historical and biographical fiction, adventure, retold legends, relating to the theme.

The above three pay 20 to 25 cents per printed word.

Activities:

Up to 700 words.

Includes: crafts, recipes, woodworking, or any other interesting projects that can be done either by children alone or with adult supervision. Sketches and description of how activity relates to theme should accompany queries.

Poetry:

up to 100 lines. Clear, objective imagery. Serious and light verse considered. Must relate to theme.

Puzzles and Games:

(please, no word finds). Crossword and other word puzzles using the vocabulary of the issue's theme. Mazes and picture puzzles that relate to the theme.

The above three pay on an individual basis.

Photo Guidelines

To be considered for publication, photographs must relate to a specific theme. Writers are encouraged to submit available photos with their query or article. We buy one-time use.

See our website for suggested fee range for professional quality photographs.

Please note that fees for non-professional quality photographs are negotiated.

Cover fees are set on an individual basis for one-time use, plus promotional use. All

cover images are color.

Prices set by museums, societies, stock photography houses, etc., are paid or negotiated.

Photographs that are promotional in nature (e.g., from tourist agencies, organizations,

special events, etc.) are usually submitted at no charge.

If you have photographs pertaining to any upcoming theme, please contact the editor by mail or fax, or send them with your query. You may also send images on speculation.

Note

Queries may be submitted at any time, but queries sent well in advance of deadline MAY NOT BE ANSWERED FOR SEVERAL MONTHS. Go-aheads requesting material

proposed in queries are usually sent five months prior to publication date. Unused queries will be returned approximately three to four months prior to publication date.

Categories: Fiction—Adventure—Biography—Games—History—Poetry

CONTACT: Meg Chorlian, Editor
Material: All

Cobblestone Publishing
30 Grove Street, Ste C
Peterborough NH 03458
Phone: 603-924-7209
Fax: 603-924-7380
Website: www.cobblestonepub.com

Collector Editions

PAYMENT: To be negotiated on an individual basis, meeting the agreement of both the writer and publisher. Payment will follow 60 days after publication. A complimentary copy of this issue will be mailed to the writer.

ARTICLE TOPICS: Free-lance articles introducing new artists in the collectibles and giftware industry; comprehensive documentaries of core companies. Contact the editor for assignments.

COPY: Electronic files are preferred. Submissions may be by e-mail, cd, floppy or zip discs.

ILLUSTRATIONS: 8–10 full color images for layout options. Electronic/digital images are preferred, hi res 300 dpi and approx. 4" x 5" or larger in size. MacIntosh platform; tifs, eps, jpeg, or hi res pdf files. High-quality color prints or transparencies will also be accepted. Materials are retained on file, unless return is requested by the author.

Categories: Collectibles

CONTACT: Joan Pursley, Editor
Material: All
Pioneer Communications, Inc.
PO Box 306
Grundy Center IA 50638
Phone: 800-352-8039
Fax: 319-824-3414
E-mail: lkruger@thepioneergroup.com
Website: www.collectors-news.com

Collectors News

SUBJECT MATTER: Free-lance article topics sought – 1. Articles about individuals & their collections, emphasizing personal insights. 2. Informational articles on antiques and collectibles: Farm-Country-Rural memorabilia, Care and/or Display of specific types of antiques and collectibles, Furniture, Glass, China, Music and related topics, Art, Transportation, Bottles, Timepieces, Jewelry, Lamps, Nostalgia, Political items, Western items, Textiles, and any 20th-century collectibles and timely subjects.

CONTENT: • Tips on how to collect, where to locate items, and brief histories with information that will enhance the collecting process are encouraged in copy whenever appropriate. • It is preferred that current values of your subject matter are included, either within copy or as a sidebar. Be sure to credit sources for the prices. • Sidebars containing Reproduction Alerts and/or topical Resources (books, clubs, etc.) also are recommended.

PHOTOS: Illustrations are required. Color electronic images at 300 resolution are best. Quality color or black-and-white prints are also satisfactory. Sharply focused pictures of individual items with an uncluttered background work best. When appropriate, images including collectors and/or a grouping of collectibles add interest to an article. A selection of 4 to 8 images is suggested.

FRONT PAGE PHOTOS: Articles are eligible for full-color front page consideration when accompanied by color electronic images, prints, or transparencies.

LENGTH: Shorter articles of 900 words or less are preferred; longer articles sometimes must await space availability or may be published in a serial.

COPY: Manuscripts are preferred in electronic files, but are accepted as typed double-spaced copy by mail. Specifics are available upon request.

PAYMENT: Basic payment is $1.10 per column inch, including space for published photos. Articles providing a color image selected for front page use receives an additional $25. Payment is routinely sent upon publication.

Basis of Purchase of Editorial Material by Collectors News:

All news articles and related editorial materials purchased by Collectors News are purchased on the basis of exclusive, First Serial Rights, for use in the magazine Collectors News and possible use on the Internet, unless otherwise stipulated by the author and agreed to by Collectors News at the time of submission and/or acceptance.

Categories: Nonfiction—Antiques—Collectibles—Hobbies

CONTACT: Linda Kruger, Managing Editor
Material: All
Pioneer Communications, Inc.
PO Box 306
Grundy Center IA 50638
Phone: 800-352-8039
Fax: 319-824-3414
E-mail: lkruger@thepioneergroup.com
Website: www.collectors-news.com

CollegeBound Teen

Misson:

CollegeBound Teen is designed to provide high school students with an inside look at all aspects of college life. College students (and those young at heart!) from around the country are welcome to serve as Correspondents to provide our teen readership with real-life accounts and cutting-edge, expert advice on the college admissions process and beyond.

Frequency:

CollegeBound Teen is published six times a year in New York, New Jersey, and Connecticut; in the fall, winter, and spring in California, Illinois, Florida, Texas, and New England; and nationally each September and February.

Style/Tone:

The tone of most articles in *CollegeBound Teen* is light-hearted and informative. Imagine you're relaying advice to a younger sibling or friend. You want to give them "the inside scoop" and offer helpful pointers for making a successful transition from high school to college. Teenage lingo and pop-culture references are totally acceptable (and encouraged!); however, a responsible journalistic blend of down-to-earth authority is important as well.

The Make-up:

CollegeBound Teen is comprised of departments, columns, and full feature articles. Our payment rates depend upon length of story, topic, and research involved.

Features:

Feature articles are usually 800-1,500 words. We look for well-researched articles packed with real-life student experiences and expert voices. Share with readers stories and survival tips on everything from dealing with dorm life, choosing the right college, and joining a fraternity or sorority, to college dating, cool campus happenings, scholarship scoring strategies, and other scholastic issues. Be original, real, and creative! Pays $70-$100.

Columns/Departments:

Straight Up Strategies (Think fun service pieces: Campus survival skills, admissions advice, professor tips, etc.—150-400 words); Cash Crunch (Money-related tips, scholarship advice, news—150-400 words); Savvy Scope (Lifestyle issues, student profiles, etc.—150-300 words); Athletics (standout student-athlete profiles—150-400 words); Celeb 101 (entertainment tidbits with a scholastic scope—200-600 words). Department payments range from $40-$75.

Rights/Payments:

We usually buy first rights to a piece; we also purchase electronic rights if we are interested in featuring the article at the online version of *CollegeBound Teen Magazine* (CollegeBoundTeen.com) or one of The CollegeBound Network affiliate sites (CollegeBound.net). We will not accept second rights to an article that has appeared in a similar publication. Payments are generated 60 days upon publication, with two complimentary issues.

All accepted articles must be accompanied by a source sheet (interview transcripts and research documentation may be requested).

How to Query Us:

Familiarize yourself first. Get to know our style and the kinds of articles we love. (You may receive a sample issue by sending a 9"x12" SASE [$3.85]).

We recommend you query us (via mail or e-mail) with a well-structured article proposal. *Hint:* Follow this format:

• Begin with the lead you expect to put in the article. Make it catchy—grab our attention!

• Write a summary of your intended areas of coverage, including sidebar ideas.

• Give specifics about experts you plan to interview, the types of student anecdotes you'll iclude, which resources you plan to utilize, and what conclusion the story might reach.

Writing Clips/Sample:

Send two or three clips or samples of your writing from your college newspaper, journalism class, etc. Photocopies are a good idea, as we do not return clips. All queries should be accompanied by a SASE. Our response time to all correspondence is approximately eight weeks.

Categories: Nonfiction—Campus Life—College—Education—Lifestyle—Self-Help—Teen—Young Adult

CONTACT: Gina LaGuardia, Editor-in-Chief
Material: All
CONTACT: Dawn Kessler, Senior Editor
Material: All
1200 South Ave., Ste. 202
Staten Island NY 10314
Phone: 718-761-4800
Fax: 718-761-3300
E-mail: editorial@collegebound.net
Website: www.collegebound.net

Colorado Homes & Lifestyles Magazine

1. Format: If possible, submit material by e-mail to mdakotah@coloradohomesmag.com. Please call to let us know it is on the way. Either send in the body of the letter, or attach as text only.

We use Microsoft Word 6.0 on an IBM computer system, so you can send a double-sided, double- or high density IBM disk formatted in Microsoft Word. Please save the information as a text-only file—even if you are using a Mac disk.

If you're mailing a disk, please include a hard copy of your article. Laser-printed, double-spaced copy in basic fonts (such as Courier, Times, or Helvetica) to allow us to scan the article into our system if your electronic transmission fails.

2. Style: *Colorado Homes & Lifestyles Magazine* uses the *Associated Press Stylebook* for style and punctuation. Other style guidelines:

• Do not use courtesy titles (such as Dr., Mr., Mrs.) unless the person is an actual medical doctor or if there is no other way to avoid confusion.

• Book titles, exhibition names and series are in italics. Place quotation marks around artwork titles.

• Italicize foreign words that are not shown in the dictionary in plain type.

• Write in present tense.

3. Headlines: Give your article three headline choices and three deck (article introduction or subtitle) choices. Headlines are usually 3-8 words. Decks can range from a phrase to two full sentences. Please look at past issues of the magazine for examples.

4. Source List: A list of sources used in the article should accompany your submission to be published on our Resources page. These should include the homeowner, the architect, the designer, artists, manufacturers, retailers, distributors, etc. Give the contact name, title and name of company, phone/fax number, mailing address, and e-mail address (if applicable).

5. References: If applicable to your article, include a publishable list of sources to which readers can refer to find out more about your topic. Sources include, books, people, organizations, and websites. Often this is used as sidebar material. This information should not be included in your total word count.

6. Sidebars: A story that falls under the heading of department may require a sidebar that includes such information as a reference-book listing, ingredients, facts, figures, etc.

7. Departments:

• **Travel:** Provide 35 mm slides or transparencies (that you've taken yourself or from other sources).

• **Artist's Workshop:** Ask artist to provide 35mm slides or transparencies of their work, and one of the artist as well—preferably showing him/her working.

• **Gardening:** Provide 35mm slides or transparencies of plants, flowers, etc. relevant to the story.

8. Photographers: Provide information on each photo (for editors to use in captioning), and full name/name of studio of photographer for proper photo credit.

9. Invoices: Submit an invoice for the contracted amount, plus expenses (previously agreed upon by editor and/or art director), along with your article or photography. Please include your name, address, phone/fax, and social security number on all invoices. Checks may be delayed if invoices are not included.

10. Length and Payment: Department articles usually run 1,000-1,200 words; payment is generally $150-$175. Features run 1,200-1,300 words; payment is generally $200-$250. Expenses must be approved before story is submitted.

11. Writer biography: Include a short (no more than two sentences) biography.

Categories: Nonfiction—Architecture—Cooking—Culture—Gardening—General Interest —Home—Lifestyle

CONTACT: Editor
Material: All
7009 S. Potomac St., Ste. 200
Centennial, CO 80112
Phone: 303-397-7600
Fax: 303-397-7619
E-mail: mdakotah@coloradohomesmag.com
Website: www.coloradohomesmag.com

ColoradoBiz Magazine

ColoradoBiz was formerly known as *Colorado Business Magazine*. With its January 1999 re-launch, *ColoradoBiz* took on a new tone, name, direction and look. We strive for fresh, vivid coverage of the people and issues affecting the entire state's business scene. Our readers are Colorado's business owners and top management, earning high-end and six-figure salaries. We seek and use writers who present accurate, professional work that's strong, humorous, touching, insightful, analytical, active, sound, witty, acerbic, droll, detailed, business-oriented — or any combination of those.

Queries

ColoradoBiz welcomes written, e-mail and phone queries with solid, original ideas and angles. In fact, it's required before we'll assign you a story.

We want analysis, forecasts, profiles, and pieces on trends, businesses, people and activities. As a full-color monthly, our editorial deadlines are about 10 to 12 weeks out from the first of the issue's month.

We seek features ranging between 650 and 1,200 words, and we always look for corresponding sidebar and chart material. Pay is a flat fee based on the story's complexity, length and time frame. Pay can range from $50 for a department item to $400 for a feature, including any sidebars. Our departments use stories in the 50- to 250-word range and cover people, companies, trends, unusual products, facts and more. *ColoradoBiz* also pays such expenses as phone and 25 cents a mile in certain cases.

We do not accept general business articles (they specifically must target Colorado's business scene), general how-to columns, book reviews, commentaries, collect calls, syndicated work, articles written by PR people about their clients, humor columns and poetry. Read back issues to gauge what we do want.

Photos

We usually shoot our own, although it can't hurt to ask sources to send us what they've got. If you shoot well, or know someone who does, we continuously seek contributions to our Last Look page in the back. This page tries to capture, in one shot, the unusual, offbeat, reminiscent, humorous or ironic in Colorado's business sectors.

What to Include

Although *ColoradoBiz* is a consumer magazine, our content is business-oriented. We want strong business angles, as well as clarity and accuracy.

Our features must start with a good lead and a clear (two- or three-line) nut graf summing up the story.

We like numbers. The more strong, solid, attributed numbers you include to support your story and facts, the better.

Active writing fits more into your word count and lessens your chances of heavy editing.

Do not use jargon

Do use several sources. Because this is a statewide magazine, include sources away from the Front Range.

Clearly attribute each quote. Include names, complete titles, company names, cities and for companies outside of Colorado, states.

Is it a public company? Include its stock exchange information: Wallace Computer Services (NYSE:WCS).

Where pertinent, include affiliates: Moore & Co. and Coldwell Banker Van Schaack, part of Parsippany, N.J.-based NRT Inc., a residential real estate brokerage and consolidator.

Verify data with the original source, especially with surveys and numbers. Do not use information published in other media, without verifying it for yourself. Get survey names, etc.

Check and double-check names and titles. Fact-check your work. We might, too.

Separately, give us your sources and phone numbers for photos and fact-checking.

We need your full name, address, phone, fax, e-mail, and Social Security number on the story to pay you. Include a brief biography of your experience.

Policies

New Wiesner Publishing policy requires a signed, dated, complete writer's contract for each article, before invoices will be paid. Do not alter the contracts. Please call Mike Taylor at 303-662-5223 with questions or comments.

Absolutely do not fax or send stories or portions of stories to anyone, including sources. We will read back direct quotes to sources after editing, if they want to know. If there are any questions about sources or anyone seeing a story, refer them to us.

Deadlines

Meet them. Call in advance if you can't. Have a good reason ready.

Format

Send the stories either on disk or via e-mail, in text or Word for Windows. Put MAC files on a PC disk in text. Include a hard copy.

Send attached e-mail files in text or paste the copy into your e-mail message.

Do not embellish the copy with indents of any kind, formatting of any kind, bold or italic type, or other aesthetic touches that we just have to take the time to remove.

Expenses

We pay long-distance phone bills for interviews (see writer contract). We also pay mileage (25 cents/mile) in some cases, which must be approved by the editor. *ColoradoBiz* is not responsible for expenses incurred without prior approval of the editor.

Photography and Illustration Guidelines

With its January 1999 relaunch, *ColoradoBiz* took on a new tone, name, direction and look. We are a full-color monthly business magazine that strives for fresh, vivid coverage of the people and issues affecting the entire state's business scene. Our readers are Colorado's business owners and top management, earning high-end and six-figure salaries.

We seek and use photographers and illustrators who want to have fun with their art, and who turn that into accurate, professional work with excellent composition, proper lighting, creative content and technical expertise. It should tell a story in itself and further the content of the article it illustrates. Our preference is for art with strong visual and emotional impact that captures the essence of the article.

Queries

ColoradoBiz welcomes written, e-mail and phone queries from artists and photographers. We use photos and renderings to illustrate articles on Colorado-specific business people, places, events, issues and concepts.

Last Look

Our Last Look page is dedicated to good photos and illustrations that make a fast and direct point. This page tries to capture, in one shot, the unusual, offbeat, reminiscent, humorous, ironic or other tones and looks of Colorado's business sectors.

Other photos and illustrations are by assignment for features or our departments. They may include studio shots, on-location shots and photojournalism. Read several issues of *ColoradoBiz* to gauge our style, tone and direction.

As a full-color monthly, our art deadlines are about three to four weeks out from the press date (typically the 3rd week of the month). Deadlines are assigned by the art director.

Format, Pay and Other Details

We use original color transparencies and slides, which we scan in-house. We also accept digital art and photos. Digital work should be scanned to 8 x 10, 300 dpi, CMYK in TIF format in MAC. We pay full- and half-day rates based on the assignment's complexity, length and size (no higher than $400 per day and no lower than $100 per half day). Pay is set by *ColoradoBiz* prior to the assignment, based on the assignment's logistics. The art director will state the pay at the time of the assignment. This rate is non-negotiable.

We also pay 25 cents a mile and reasonable film and processing expenses. Roughly, full-day rates apply to assignments of four ordered shots or more; half-day rates to three or fewer shots. Reasonable film and processing expenses are based on shooting 10 photos for every one ordered (five ordered, 50 shots).

All expenses must be approved by the art director prior to the shoot. *ColoradoBiz* is not responsible for expenses incurred without the art director's prior approval.

Illustrations should be distinctive, professional renderings in any media — preferably 8 x 10 or smaller, depending on its intended use. Digital renderings should follow the specifications for digital photos.

Rates for illustrations range from $45 to $350, depending on complexity and size, and include reasonable revisions or alterations at the art director's discretion.

Do not e-mail digital art.

ColoradoBiz pays on publication. Space may dictate how many photos ultimately will be used and when they will be used.

What to Include

Although *ColoradoBiz* is a consumer magazine, our content is business-oriented. We want art that renders a story in itself with a strong business focus.

ColoradoBiz is striving to move away from cliches and stereotypes in portraying business, whether in photos or illustrations. We do not want traditional posed shots, power shots, staid businessman shots, Venetian blinds, computers in the backgrounds and other dull office props - unless creatively used. We do want fresh, vivid work using activity, conceptualization, humor where appropriate, dignity where appropriate - in short, the photo (or art) should tell an interesting story.

Without fail, on photo shoots, get subjects' correct name spellings, complete titles, complete company names and locations, and their positions in the photos. Accuracy is critical for the cutlines.

Aside from good composition, proper lighting and creative content, art should be clear technically and in content. Focus photos. Some shots may be blown up several hundred percent.

Color should be well-saturated, not washed out, with good value contrast. As a general rule, use a variety of color. The paper we use may affect the colors. Check with the art director when in any doubt.

Art should have contrast in color, shape and sizes, and show attention to detail.

Read the stories (we will send the one you're illustrating for) to help determine art content. If you do not clearly understand or have difficulty with the assignment, contact the art director immediately. Reshoots are options only in special circumstances.

Do not show stories to sources. They are for your use only.

Photographers are responsible for arranging photo shoots with the subjects, which may include coordinating with art director and story author.

Wiesner Publishing requires a photographers' or illustrators' contract for each article illustrated (four articles or assignments, four contracts). These must be complete, signed, dated and returned in order to be paid. Do not alter the contract. Please call the managing editor with questions.

Provide exact wording for photo credits.

New artists also must fill out and return a W-9 before being paid.

Finally, we must have your full name, company name, address, phone, fax, e-mail and Social Security number with the photo in order to pay you. Expenses must have receipts. Please send contracts and invoices to Anne Kerven, managing editor, at the above address.

Upon submission, we must also have the photo credit wording and a brief two- or three-line bio of yourself for our contributors' list.

We will return art work to you after the issue is printed.

Deadlines

Meet them. Our production department generates a minimum of nine titles and extensive special projects. Our scanning schedule is tight. We schedule according to when your art is expected.

Categories: Nonfiction—Business

CONTACT: Robert Schwab, Editor, (303) 662-5283
Material: Manuscripts
CONTACT: Jurgen Mantzke, Art Director, (303) 662-5251
Material: Illustrations/Photography
7090 E. Potomac St.
Englewood CO 80112
Phone: 303-397-7600
Fax: 303-397-7619
E-mail: rschwab@cobizmag.com (Robert Schwab)
E-mail: jmantzke@wiesnerpublishing.com (Jurgen Mantzke)
Website: www.cobizmag.com

Colored Stone

Queries and Submissions: Because of the specialized nature of the colored stone trade, *Colored Stone* prefers to receive queries on story ideas before the manuscript itself is submitted.

Correspondents: The bulk of the articles published in each issue are generated from leads gathered by *Colored Stone* staff and assigned to one of a standard list of writers. If you do not have a specific story proposal, but would like to be considered for a story assignment, send your resume, and writing samples to the Editor at the below address. We also have "foreign correspondent" positions available for freelance writers in gem-producing or gem-trading centers outside the United States.

Readership: People in the wholesale end of the jewelry business, principally manufacturing jewelers and jewelry designers, gemstone dealers, and retail jewelers.

Subjects: New sources for colored gemstones, mining and processing, manufacturing, retail sales, consumer buying trends, marketing and promotion, gem cutting and jewelry design, and technological developments pertaining to the colored gemstone trade.

Style: Mostly feature style with an edge; some hard news.

NOTE: Because we are a trade magazine, our articles assume familiarity with the gem business, as well as a certain pre-knowledge about different types of colored gemstones, their sources, and how they are marketed and sold. If you are not familiar with the trade, we will provide background information for any articles we assign, and can also recommend some general reference books.

Length: Features: 1400-2000 words; Short Stories: 900-1200 words.

Artwork: Transparencies, slides, and prints. All photographs should be labeled and include captions. We prefer slides to prints and color to black and white. We cannot scan photos from pre-printed material such as postcards, brochures, or magazine pages.

Digital files submitted via e-mail are also acceptable. All pictures must be a minimum of 266 dpi at the size the picture will run in the magazine. We cannot take pictures directly from Web sites.

Manuscripts: E-mail submissions preferred, especially from writers outside the United States. Story text should be pasted into the body of the e-mail message rather than sent as an attached file.

Conditions: Writers must be able to substantiate any and all material as accurate. All articles are subject to editing. All material shall be submitted solely and exclusively for publication in *Colored Stone*, unless approved by the Editor in advance. Writers must sign a copyright agreement form before publication.

Fees: Payment is generally on a per-article rather than a per-word basis; fees are negotiated through the Editor. Fees generally run at 25-30 cents per word, depending on the complexity of the article, the experience of the writer, and the cost of living in the writer's home base. We pay a $15 finder's fee per photo submitted by the author and published. Phone/fax expenses are reimbursed upon submission of the phone bill; other expenses may be reimbursed with the pre-approval of the Editor.

Categories: Nonfiction—Trade—Gemstones

CONTACT: Morgan Beard, Editor-in-Chief
Material: All
60 Chestnut Ave., Suite 201
Devon PA 19333-1312
Phone: 610-964-6300
Fax: 610-293-0977
E-mail: Morgan_Beard@primediamags.com
Website: www.colored-stone.com

Commercial Investment Real Estate Magazine

Commercial Investment Real Estate magazine is the member publication of the CCIM Institute. *CIRE* provides practical, how-to information, market analyses and trends, and business strategies for commercial real estate professionals.

Selecting a Topic

CIRE readers are interested in how-to, trend, and forecast articles on a variety of topics, including development, brokerage, leasing, financing, property management, technology, and investment. Submit a detailed outline on a topic at least one month in advance of the manuscript. To discuss the topic with the editor, call (312) 321-4460.

Preparing the Manuscript

Submit articles as a Microsoft Word attachment to an e-mail. Article length should range between 1,800 and 3,000 words.

Supply a brief professional biography, including present title, designations, place of employment, published articles, and expertise in the subject about which you are writing.

Graphics

Include charts, graphs, original color or high-resolution digital photos, and illustrations when possible to emphasize and clarify points in your article.

Style

Aim for clear, concise, and lively writing, even if your topic is technical. *CIRE* follows AP style. When appropriate, include case studies.

Editors will remove any promotional material from articles before publication.

The Review Process

All articles are reviewed by the editorial review board, composed of commercial investment real estate professionals. The board determines whether an article is appropriate for publication in *CIRE*. If your manuscript is approved "with revisions," it may be returned with recommendations for more information or clarification. After receiving the revised article, the editor will discuss possible publication with you.

Copyright

CIRE is seeking original, unpublished material, and it owns the copyright for all of its contents. If your manuscript has been published elsewhere, please provide us with full information about the publication in which it appeared. Please inform us if your manuscript is currently under consideration or scheduled for publication elsewhere.

The Benefits of Writing

Share your knowledge and receive national recognition in your field by joining the ranks of well-respected CIRE authors. You will receive 10 complimentary copies of the issue in which your article appears. Online, your article will be linked to your e-mail address (if provided).

In addition, article reprints are available at a reasonable cost and make excellent handouts to current and potential clients.

Categories: Nonfiction—Associations—Business—Money & Finances—Real Estate

CONTACT: Jennifer Norbut, Editor (312-321-4531)
Material: Feature article ideas and outlines, regional info., CCIM Deal Makers submissions, and marketing information
CONTACT: Sara Drummond, Staff Editor (312-321-4469)
Material: Industry news
CONTACT: Sara Exley, Editorial Coordinator (312-321-4502)
Material: Product Information
430 N. Michigan Ave., Ste. 800
Chicago IL 60611-4092
Phone: 312-321-4460
Fax: 312-321-4530
E-mail: jnorbut@cciminstitute.com (Jennifer Norbut)

E-mail: sdrummond@cciminstitute.com (Sara Drummond)
Website: www.magazine@ccim.com

COMMONWEAL
Commonweal

COMMONWEAL is a biweekly journal of opinion edited by Catholic lay people. Founded in 1924, the magazine welcomes original manuscripts dealing with topical issues of the day on culture, religion, politics, and the arts. We look for articles that are timely, accurate, and well-written. *Articles fall into three categories:*

1. "Upfronts," running between 750-1,000 words, are brief, "newsy" reportorials, giving facts, information, and some interpretation behind the "headlines of the day."

2. Longer articles, running between 2,000-3,000 words, are more reflective and detailed, bringing new information or a different point of view to a subject, raising questions, and/or proposing solutions to the dilemmas facing the world, nation, church, or individual.

3. "Last Word" column, a 750-word reflection, usually of a personal nature, on some aspect of the human condition: spiritual, individual, political, or social.

Please send a query with outline and resume. We do not consider simultaneous submissions.

Articles should be written for a general but well-educated audience. While religious articles are always topical, we are less interested in devotional and churchy pieces than in articles which examine the links between "worldly" concerns and religious beliefs.

Notes and footnotes are discouraged. Please allow 3-4 weeks for an editorial decision.

Those with MS-DOS or Macintosh systems are encouraged to send the article on a diskette, along with hard copy. The diskette will be returned. Manuscripts can also be emailed (see below). Please send as a MS Word attachment. Payment for articles is generally made on publication.

Poetry: We publish about 20 high quality poems a year.

Categories: Nonfiction—Culture—Literature—Politics—Regional—Public Policy

CONTACT: Patrick Jordan, Managing Editor
Material: All
475 Riverside Dr., Ste. 405
New York NY 10115
Phone: 212-662-4200
E-mail: editors@commonwealmagazine.org
Website: www.commonwealmagazine.org

COMPLETE WOMAN
Complete Woman

Thank you for your interest in submitting material to *Complete Woman*. We welcome all manuscripts and cartoons or illustrations that address the concerns of today's woman. Topics may vary over a range, including positive approaches to home, family, career, health, relationships, and self-improvement. Subject matter is limited only by your imagination and understanding of what it means to be a complete woman in today's society.

Manuscripts should be between 1,000 and 2,200 words in length, including any sidebar or supplementary material. Because all materials are received on speculation only, we suggest you query us with clips before sending your articles.

Complete Woman is published bimonthly. We pay upon publication (during the month of the cover, and after publication).

We look forward to seeing your work.

Sincerely,

Bonnie L. Krueger, Editor-in-Chief

Categories: Confession—Diet/Nutrition—Entertainment—Fantasy—Fashion—General Interest—Interview—Lifestyle—Marriage—Physical Fitness—Relationships—Self Help—Sexuality—Singles—Teen—Women's Issues

CONTACT: Bonnie L. Krueger, Editor-in-Chief
Material: All
CONTACT: Lora M. Wintz, Executive Editor
Material: All
875 N. Michigan Ave., Ste. 3434
Chicago IL 60611-1901
Phone: 312-266-8680

The Compulsive Reader

The Compulsive Reader reviews literary fiction, cookbooks, and books for writers. If your book fits this category, please send a brief (1-2 paragraph) synopsis to maggieball@compulsivereader.com, and if we feel that the book fits the site, we will contact you directly to let you know where to send a review copy. Our reviews are quite detailed, honest, and specific, and will cover such things as stylistics, theme, characterisation, narrative voice, and plot development.

WHAT ARE WE LOOKING FOR IN REVIEW SUBMISSIONS?

We are looking for detailed, and informative reviews of literary fiction, cookbooks, or books for writers, as well as articles on any literary topic, including literary criticism. Reviewers retain all copyrights to their work and are free to publish their review or article in other venues as long as it doesn't conflict with our rights while your review remains on our site. Although we are unable to offer monetary compensation for reviews and articles at this time, we provide all contributors with a byline located directly under the title, up to six lines of Author Bio information at the end of the article, and links. Regular contributors are also featured in the "Who are We" section of our site and are offered books for review. Submit reviews in the body of the text (rather than as an attachment) to: maggieball@compulsivereader.com

Categories: Nonfiction—Book Reviews—Writing

CONTACT: Maggie Ball, Editor
Material: All
E-mail: maggieball@compulsivereader.com
Website: www.compulsivereader.com/html

Computer Bits

The best way for you to proceed from this point is to send us a list of topics that interest you. We accept submissions via U.S. Mail, but, really, we'd rather get them as e-mail. Proposals can be sent to our editor at editor@computerbits.com.

Here are a few considerations to keep in mind when you develop your topics list:

Write what you know. Our articles tend to be based more on an author's experience than his or her research. That doesn't mean that you won't want to do any research; it just means that you could probably outline your article off the top of your head, even if you'd have to do some checking to fill in all the details.

The vast majority of our feature articles fall into one of four categories:

• How-to—giving your readers information necessary to accomplish some computing task;

• Introductory—giving your readers an introduction to a new technology or resource;

• Round-up—giving your readers a survey of the hardware or software available in a given category;

• Whimsical—giving your readers a humorous or light-hearted look at the life and culture of computer users.

We tend to shy away from product reviews. That doesn't mean we won't consider printing a review, but you'll have to make a near airtight case for your idea before we'll consider it. The problem is that we have no testing lab, and no way of providing any editorial support for your conclusions. The major exception to this rule is for reviews of locally-produced hardware and software, which we're far more likely to accept.

The more specific and fully developed your topics are, the better. That said, it's more convenient for us and for you if you send in a proposal than a completed article. It gives us a chance to dialog about the direction you take before you take the plunge and begin writing.

For an idea of topics we've addressed recently, please visit our archives and survey the articles we've published in the past 10–12 months.

Before you ask:

Yes, we are a paying market. Payment for first NA rights plus e-rights runs $75 to $100 for articles in the range of 1,000 to 2,000 words; we pay within 30 days of publication. Feature articles are generally closer to 2,000 words.

The amount we offer for an article is not tied to its length, but rather to our perception of its value to us. It's entirely possible for a 1,000-word article to fetch $100, and for a 2000-word article to fetch $75.

Computer Bits magazine actively encourages our readers to contact our authors with questions or comments. Please copy editor@computerbits.com with these exchanges for possible publication in the printed mailbag column.

We really do prefer to get a proposal rather than a finished article. We hope to hear from you soon.

Categories: Nonfiction—Computers—Culture—Technology

CONTACT: Submissions Editor
Material: All
PO Box 329
Forest Grove OR 97116-0329
Phone: 503-359-9107
E-mail: editor@computerbits.com
Website: www.computerbits.com

Computer Shopper

Does not accept unsolicited submissions.

ComputorEdge
San Diego's Computer Magazine

ComputorEdge is the nation's largest regional computer weekly magazine, with editions in Southern California and Colorado.

A Profile of CE Writers

Freelance writers contribute to most sections of the magazine. CE writers use a style that is easily understood by novice and intermediate computer users, as well as well-educated readers and experts. Our writers are clear and conversational. They share their technical expertise in a relaxed, personable manner without unnecessary techno-jargon. This is a rare combination of talents.

Rights and Compensation

We buy First North American Serial Rights, as well as subsequent electronic publishing rights in order to maintain an archive on our Web site. Feature articles should be 1,000 to 1,200 words in length. The columns Mac Madness and I Don't Do Windows (alternative operating systems such as Linux, BeOS, Lindows, etc.) are open to freelance writers. They should consist of 800 to 900 words.

Payment is rendered 30 days after publication. The amount is based on the number of magazines in which an article is published, as follows: Feature articles: $100 for publication in one magazine; $150 for two. Columns pay $75 for one magazine; $110 for two.

How to Submit Your Ideas

Become familiar with the magazine-each issue has a specific theme. You'll find the current issue and archived copies of both magazines at www.computoredge.com. Access the Editorial Calendar at www.computoredge.com/sandiego/2003.htm or request one from editor@computoredge.com.

If you have a feature story or column idea for an upcoming issue, submit an e-mail query to submissions@computoredge.com. Do not include any attachments. We do not open attachments from unknown senders; your entire query will be deleted immediately. This is important: Put the Issue Number for which you wish to write in the Subject line of your e-mail message. Keep in mind that we assign stories three to five months ahead of the publication date. You should also provide:

• A brief but detailed description of the article you would like to write.

• A summary of your writing credits, credentials, or brief bio if you have never written for *ComputorEdge* before.

If your article is accepted, an editor will contact you. Be sure to provide your current e-mail address. If you do not hear from us within a reasonable amount of time, your submission has probably been rejected. If you wish, you may send a "reminder" e-mail to check on the status of your submission. Please do not send unsolicited manuscripts.

After Acceptance

When finalized, e-mail your accepted article or column to assigned@computoredge.com. It needs to be received by the Writer's Deadline, which is indicated on the Editorial Calendar. This is important:

In the Subject line of your e-mail, put "Issue Number" and the number of the issue for which your article is slated.

We prefer to receive the article in Microsoft Word format or as part of the body of the e-mail.

It is important that assigned articles be directed to assigned@computoredge.com. It is important that submissions be directed to submissions@computoredge.com. It is important that no other e-mail be directed to these mailboxes. Questions and comments should be addressed to editor@computoredge.com.

Acceptance of a piece does not guarantee its immediate publication. On occasion, a scheduled article may have to be moved to another issue.

Revised 1/15/04

Categories: Nonfiction—Computers—Technical—Technology

CONTACT: Submissions Editor
Material: All
3655 Ruffin Rd Ste 100
San Diego CA 92123
Phone: 858-573-0315
E-mail: editor@computoredge.com
Website: www.computoredge.com

Confrontation
A Literary Journal

Formal guidelines not available. Please read a number of issues to ascertain the publication's style and needs.

Send queries to address below.

Categories: Fiction—Nonfiction—Book Reviews—Drama—Experimental Fiction—Literature—Short Stories—Theatre—Writing

CONTACT: Jonna Semeiks, Associate Editor
Material: Fiction

CONTACT: Michael Hartnett, Assistant Editor
Material: Poetry
English Dept, C.W. Post of Long Island University
Brookville NY 11548
Phone: 516-299-2720

Conscience
The Newsjournal of Catholic Opinion

Conscience is a quarterly newsjournal of Catholic opinion, with a circulation of approximately 10,000, including members of Congress, librarians, members of the clergy, and members of the press.

Focusing on ideas and values, *Conscience* presents an ethical discussion of reproductive rights and choices, the role of women in society and the church, conscience and dissent in the church, church-state issues, and social conditions and policies affecting women's choices in childbearing and child-rearing.

The editor seeks manuscripts that will be of interest to concerned individuals of all denominations, as well as to leaders in the fields of theology, ethics, and women's studies. Articles should be written for an educated audience that is diverse professionally, culturally, and geographically.

Simultaneous submissions are acceptable, but writers should notify the editor at once when a manuscript is accepted elsewhere. Likewise, we ask writers to notify other publications considering the manuscript of any agreement to publish the article in *Conscience*. Some previously published articles are accepted; all such submissions must include the original publisher's name and address.

Manuscripts accepted for publication are subject to editing for clarity and conformity with *Conscience* style. Authors will generally receive an edited draft of the manuscript for evaluation before it is typeset and will be asked to answer any editorial queries and return the manuscript by a specified date. In the case of multiple authorship, one author should be designated as correspondent.

Submission
Manuscripts should be submitted in Microsoft Word version 6.0/95 or higher, and may be submitted on disk or via e-mail.

Length
Articles should be approximately 2,000 to 3,500 words; *Conscience* may run longer articles by agreement with the editor. Book reviews should be 800 to 1,500 words, and letters to the editor should be 100 to 350 words.

Title Page
In addition to the title of the manuscript, the title page should include the author's name, academic or professional title and degree, current affiliation, complete address, phone number, fax number, and e-mail address. For articles with multiple authorship, please provide complete information for each author.

Formatting
Submitted manuscripts should be double-spaced and use common system fonts such as Times New Roman, Courier, or Arial. Formatting, such as bolding, italics, underlining, tabs, indents, etc., should be kept to the minimum amount necessary to organize the text.

References
References should be numbered sequentially in the text, with full information for each citation. CFFC follows *The Chicago Manual of Style*, 14th Edition and the *Associated Press Stylebook*.

Illustrative Material
If permission to reproduce any illustration, photograph, or excerpt is needed, it is the responsibility of the author to secure such permission. Written notice of the permission should be included with the submission, or if the manuscript has been submitted via e-mail, sent via U.S. mail with the title page of the article to be published in *Conscience*.

When graphs, illustrations, line drawings, or other figures accompany the manuscript, they should be supplied as camera-ready art whenever possible. High-quality photographs that are relevant to the manuscript may be submitted. Accompanying tables should be put at the end of the manuscript, with a note in the text to show where they should appear in the published version.

Copyright
Conscience reserves first international rights to all original material accepted for publication unless otherwise specified. Thereafter, authors retain copyright of their work. Simultaneous submissions are accepted, but upon notice of intent to publish in *Conscience*, authors are expected to withdraw all simultaneous submissions.

Compensation
CFFC offers *Conscience* contributors five to ten copies of the issue in which their article appears; additional copies are available upon request. Some articles are paid on publication; payment for these is arranged on a case-by-case basis.

Categories: Nonfiction—Politics—Religion—Spiritual—Women's Issues—Catholics for a Free Choice

CONTACT: Submissions
1436 U Street, NW, Ste 301
Washington DC 20009-3997
Phone: 202-986-6093
Fax: 202-332-7995
E-mail: conscience@catholicsforchoice.org

Contract Management

The Magazine and Its Audience
Contract Management (CM) magazine is the NCMA flagship publication for people and businesses working in the buying and selling communities of both the public and private sectors.

CM is a full-color, monthly magazine written and edited specifically for contract management professionals. Each issue provides comprehensive reporting on issues and trends relevant to contract management of all shapes and sizes ¾ covering the public and private sectors.

Readers are usually members of National Contract Management Association (NCMA), typically with more than 15 years of contract management experience.

Before You Write
CM seeks original and useful articles dealing with contract management problems, insights, applications, and opinions. As a contract management professional, your personal experiences in the field can become valuable to readers. Apply your practical insights, solutions, and encountered problems to their situations. Focus on the lessons learned, rather than chronology of events. *Before you begin to write an article for CM, you should ask yourself these questions:*

- Is this topic practical to the reader?
- Do I have specific examples of lessons learned?
- How can other professionals adapt what I have done?
- What kinds of pitfalls might they run into?
- What are the costs involved?

Avoiding the Pitfalls
Articles often are not accepted in Contract Management magazine because the article topic:

- Is not related to contract management,
- Is poorly organized,
- Lacks valuable insight,
- Offers too few examples, or is overly promotional and self-serving.

In order to avoid these pitfalls, we recommend that you send an inquiry including a brief summary (150 words) of the proposed article to the editor-in-chief before you write the article.

If you cannot capture your idea in 150 words, you may be trying to tackle too broad of a topic. Your topic should be focused sufficiently in 12 to 30 pages, double-spaced, plus a double-spaced sidebar.

Your topic may not be best suited for a feature article, but rather a special interest corner article. Corner articles (four to 11 pages, double-spaced) can be written about the following topics: alternative disputes resolution, commercial contracting, construction contract management, environmental contracting, information technology, e-commerce, e-business, education, grants management, health care contracting, international acquisition, program management, small business, state and local government contracting, and professional development.

Writing Your Article

Here are our suggestions for an easy-to-read, successful CM article.

• Create a clever working title using active verbs. Try to keep it brief, between three and six words.

• Provide a byline. Include the author(s') full name(s), suffixes, degrees, etc.

• Provide a two- to three-line biography. Include the author's name, title, affiliation/employer, employer's city and state, and NCMA chapter membership information.

• Use subheadings in the article to help the reader focus on the direction of the story at least every two pages.

• Pay attention to tone. Avoid lecturing. Convey your ideas by showing the reader what to do, rather than telling them what to do. Explain your ideas clearly by avoiding excessive jargon, and define jargon you must use.

• Be comprehensive. Use details¾such as dates, statistics, references, and quantities¾to clarify and support your points. Sometimes pertinent information that is self-contained can be used as a sidebar. Steps of a process or a list of resources can be boxed off as a nice design element and easy-to-read sidebar.

• Explain the relevance to others. Make your points using examples from your experience, and then tell readers how they can apply your experience to their situations.

• Avoid the passive voice. Active language is straightforward and simple.

• Edit your article at least twice. Delete unnecessary words and phrases. Turn passive sentences into active ones. Move paragraphs to achieve continuity and use transition sentences to help paragraph-to-paragraph flow. Make sure paragraphs flow logically.

• Check the accuracy of your article. Using your original source material, verify every date, name, fact, and figure. Accuracy is your responsibility, not that of CM magazine editors.

• Test market your article. Ask a few colleagues to review your article. They may help point out ways to clarify your message.

Submitting Your Article

Members write most of the articles published in *Contract Management* (CM), although one does not have to be an NCMA member to be published in the magazine. Articles should concern some aspect of the contract management profession, whether at the level of a beginner or that of an advanced practitioner.

When submitting an article, accompany it with a cover letter that includes your daytime telephone number and preferred mailing address. If making a query, contact the Communications Team–see information below.

The Communications Team publishes an editorial calendar each year as a guide for potential writers on particular topics. Writers should not feel limited by the "topic of the month." CM is interested in receiving articles on all topics of interest to those engaged in the contract management profession. Particularly of interest are articles of a "how-to" nature with practical, problem-solving instruction that can be used on the job.

Note: The magazine has a three-month lead-time for any given issue.

Disk/Article submission guidelines

• Send the manuscript on a 3.5" disk formatted in Word or a compatible program; or e-mail your manuscript to miedema@ncmahq.org.

• Accompany the disk with hard copy, double-spaced on 8.5 x 11" sheets, on one side of each page only.

• Include a two to three sentence "abstract" describing what the article is about and how it will benefit the reader.

• Keep manuscripts in the range of 12 to 30 pages in length (double-spaced) for features, four to 12 pages in length for corners.

• Do not use all upper-case type for headings or text.

• Indent the beginning of each paragraph.

• Use illustrative charts, graphs, figures, and tables when appropriate.

• Use endnotes rather than footnotes.

• Include a brief biography of the author(s) at the end. This should include job title, employer name and location, and NCMA affiliation-chapter name, CPCM/CACM, Fellow, whether a member of a Special Topic Committee, etc.

Evaluation and Acceptance

The editor-in-chief will send an acknowledgment letter, but cannot guarantee when or if an article will be published. Articles are evaluated based on readability, soundness of content, timeliness, and interest to our readers. We also consider whether you support you ideas with concrete examples.

Articles that essentially only promote a particular company, product, and service are not considered publishable.

We may accept your article outright or accept it contingent on your revision. If an article is accepted, an editor will contact the author to advise him/her of the issue of publication. All accepted articles are subject to editing for style, clarity, language, and length.

Rejection of articles is confirmed through written correspondence.

Copyright Transfer

Once the article has been accepted and edited, you will be asked to sign a copyright release form that gives National Contract Management Association (NCMA) copyright to the article. The copyright only gives NCMA right to the copyedited version of your article in print and electronic format. You retain the rights to your original. If you have questions or concerns about copyright transfer, please call Amy Miedema, editor-in-chief, at 703-734-5412.

Categories: Nonfiction—Business—Government

CONTACT: Amy Miedema, Editor-in-Chief
Material: All
CONTACT: Kathryn Mullan, Assistant Editor
Material: All
National Contract Management Association
1912 Woodford Road
Vienna VA 22182
Phone: 703-448-9231 or 800-344-8096
Fax: 703-448-0939
E-mail: cm@ncmahq.org
E-mail: Miedema@ncmahq.org
Website: www.ncmahq.org

Conversely

IMPORTANT NOTICE: Conversely has switched to an online submissions system. E-mail or regular mail submissions are no longer be accepted. To submit online, please visit: www30.securedweb.net/conversely/wwwfp/Masth/onlin.shtml.

Conversely is looking for contributors

We welcome unsolicited submissions for each of our different 'categories'. Below are some general guidelines, followed by specific guidelines for each category. You will then find directions on next steps for submission, and a discussion of what we offer contributors.

What we're about:

At Conversely,

We believe that a romantic relationship is a crazy thing that grows out of words and actions, accidents and illusions. And lurking beneath this thing is an intricate web of motivations (frequently neglected, always confusing), a mysterious recess where feelings originate. We think there is, in probing these hidden places, a compelling, rewarding, perhaps even perverse pleasure.

We also believe that you can't take relationships, like many things in life, too seriously. We like the idea of smart, edgy commentary, but we like it even more if it's fun, if it's combined with humor and creativity. We think delving from new angles and hazarding multiple, preferably contrary opinions, is one great way to get things in the right perspective - though of course we have no idea what the right perspective is.

Our goal is a publication dedicated to exploring relationships - every aspect, every stage - through different forms of writing: essays, memoirs, fiction, etc. Our writing appeals to both women and men. It is entertaining, but not superficial. Intelligent, but not academic or presumptuous. Provocative, but not overbearing. Witty: definitely; sappy: absolutely not. In addition, we avoid being boring and formulaic. We do not recycle content. And we don't feature explicit sex.

What we're looking for:
General guidelines

We seek writers, new or established, who can produce articles and essays on all aspects of male-female relationships. Our readers are both female and male, primarily in their twenties and thirties. Thus, we focus on topics that relate to the types of relationships, and relationship issues, facing this group.

Specific guidelines

Writers should consider submitting to any of the following sections.

ANTIDOTE - Essays: opinion, observation, satire, and more

Antidote embraces essays ranging from personal opinion to social observation, intimate critique, satirical commentary, and factual reports. The goal is to explore the motivations and underlying emotions that are reflected in our behaviors.

Topics can be anything that has to do with relationships. Small topics are as valid as large ones, for example: the importance of remembering a phone number vs. the implications of marriage. For guidance on the kinds of themes we'd like to see, and the one's we'd prefer not to, please read our guidelines online at http://www.conversely.com/write.shtml.

While we don't expect essays to be arrow-straight and perfectly structured, this is our most "traditional" form: essays must make a point or have a thesis, and reach a conclusion.

Word count: 750 to 2,000

• For information on our Antidote essay contest, please visit: <http://www.conversely.com/Masth/conte.shtml>.

PERSONALS - Memoirs

Memoirs and personal stories about your own experience in or out of relationships. Writing that examines any or several aspects of relationships; preferably instances, or events, that haven't become clichéd. We prefer writing that is not overly dramatic or sentimental.

We look for honest, well structured pieces that carry the reader's attention throughout the narrative. In general, we expect stories in the first person.

Word count: 750 to 2,500

STORIES - Fiction

We're looking for stories that deal with romantic relationships: at any stage, from any angle. However, this is not to be confused with "romance genre" writing, which is not for us.

We prefer tales that focus on the inside as much as the outside, that reveal something unexpected and true about the characters and their motivations.

We focus on literary stories; gothic, sci-fi, fantasy and erotica are not for us. Memoirs are fine, but see "Personals" above. Both traditional and experimental forms are considered.

Word count: 750 to 3,000

UNHINGED - Oddities - creative non-fiction

If you have something that's not an essay, or a story, or a memoir, then it might be right for us. Unhinged serves as a catchall for writing that doesn't fit neatly into our other categories, such as non-fiction written in experimental, creative formats. It should have to do with relationships, or with the emotions and actions that are often associated with them. In some way it should reflect the writer's views or observations, that is, it should have a reason for being told, even if it's not told in the traditional forms.

Word count: 750 to 3,000

PLEASE NOTE: At this time, we do not need writers for our advice column. Also, we don't consider POETRY.

What next?

If you are interested, we want to hear from you!

Conversely accepts submissions only through our online submissions system at: www30.securedweb.net/conversely/wwwfp/Masth/onlin.shtml.

By following the above link you will reach our online submissions page, where you will be able to input all your personal information and upload or paste your manuscript. For further instructions and frequently asked questions, go to: https://www30.securedweb.net/conversely/wwwfp/Masth/onhlp.shtml <http://www.conversely.com/Masth/onhlp.shtml>.

We consider only new, never-before-published material (we do not accept previously published submissions). Generally, 'previously published' means it has been printed in a publication with circulation over 1,000, or it has appeared in an online magazine or similar site (with the exception of self-published, personal websites). If you have a question as to whether your submission qualifies as 'new', send us an e-mail query to query@conversely.com. We do accept simultaneous submissions, we only request that you inform us of this by checking the appropriate box during the online submission process.

PLEASE NOTE: There is no need to query before submitting. However, if you are wondering whether an idea would work for us, or if you have any other questions we haven't answered here, please contact us at the e-mail address above. We can not respond to queries, or send guidelines, over regular mail.

Acceptance of a submission may sometimes be contingent on editorial changes suggested by us. No changes will be made to submissions without the writer's consent. Writers will be able to review their posting before it goes live.

We respond within TWELVE weeks on submissions, less on queries. Our editorial lead times tend to be short, but they also vary widely.

Please check our online at http://www.conversely.com/Masth/submi.shtml often

for potential changes to our guidelines.

What do we offer?

Conversely pays $50 - $200 for accepted submissions. For very short pieces (under 1000 words), our rates may be lower.

Conversely provides bylines and we require that writers present a short bio with a photograph on the site.

Conversely buys the following rights:

• Exclusive electronic rights for NINETY days, and non-exclusive thereafter (this means we can keep the piece in our archives for as long as we think appropriate). Our electronic rights allow us to share the article with Partner Websites (http://www.conversely.com/Masth/partn.shtml), as long as that content is presented in Conversely format, with our logo, full credit to the author, and links back to the original publication page and the author's Conversely bio page;

• One-time print anthology rights.

After our exclusive electronic rights expire, the rights revert to the author, who is free to republish elsewhere. However, we do request that Conversely be credited as the place of original publication, with either a link to our homepage or our printed web address (www.conversely.com).

We pay within THIRTY days of initial posting (i.e., publication) on the site. We request that writers sign the contract (http://www.conversely.com/Masth/contr.shtml) at the time when we accept an article for publication.

Conversely reserves the right to make changes to these guidelines at any time. Any important changes will be noted on our guidelines page: <http://www.conversely.com/Masth/submi.shtml>.

(As of February 2004)

Categories: Fiction—Nonfiction—Relationships—Short Stories

CONTACT: Alejandro Gutierrez, Editor
Material: All

3053 Fillmore St., #121
San Francisco CA 94123-4009
E-mail: editor@conversely.com
Website: www.conversely.com

Cooking Light

Cooking Light, The Magazine of Food and Fitness, is the recipe for healthy living. Nearly 85% of our 5.2 million readers are women, most between the ages of 30 and 60. Our readers are affluent, sophisticated, well-educated, professional, and interested in living holistically healthy life styles. They come first to the magazine for our recipes, but the lively writing as well as health and fitness coverage help keep them coming back issue after is sue. *Here's what the editors of Cooking Light look for when assigning articles:*

• *Knowledge of the Magazines:* You can now find *Cooking Light* — the nation's largest epicurean magazine — at just about any supermarket or newsstand.

Lead Time: For food articles, it's anywhere from six months to a year, due largely to seasonality and the extensive work our Test Kitchens must do on every recipe. For healthy life styles articles, it's anywhere from three to eight months.

• *Story Ideas:* Those lead times acquire that our stories be seasonal, long-range, or forward-looking. A trend of today can be old news in a six months, so please keep that in mind when developing queries. We're looking for fresh, innovative stories that yield worthwhile information for our readers — a cooking tip, a trend, a suggestion of how they can use a particular recipe, nutritional information that may not be common knowledge, reassurance about their lifestyle or health concerns, etc.

• *Food Queries: Cooking Light* strives to offer new ideas and information than help readers make informed meal-planning, food-purchasing, and food-preparation decisions for a healthier way of eating — with more starch, dietary fiber, and water, but less fat, sodium, sugar, and alcohol. Our principles involve replacing the old, adapting the traditional, and creating the new. We expect our writers to adhere to the ethical standards set by the national Association of Food Journalists to keep our stories free of any commercial bias.

• *Submitting Queries:* All story ideas must be submitted in writing. Please enclose a paragraph or two about each idea, your resume, and some sample clips. Because of the volume of mail we receive, we guarantee a response only if you include a self-addressed, stamped envelope with your query. We'll get back to you, even if by form letter, within about a month.

Our street address (for overnight services) is 2100 Lakeshore Drive, Birmingham, AL 35209.

Categories: Nonfiction—Cooking—Diet/Nutrition—Food/Drink—Health—Physical Fitness—Travel

CONTACT: Jill Melton, Senior Food Editor
Material: Food
CONTACT: Phillip Rhodes, Associate Editor
Material: Fitness/Healthy Living
PO Box 1748
Birmingham AL 35201
Phone: 205-445-6000
Website: cookinglight.com

Cooks Illustrated

Does not accept unsolicited submissions.

Remember: Editors change jobs and publishers change addresses. It is wise to invest in a phone call for the current information before submitting.

The Cooperator
The Co-op and Condo Monthly

Requirements

Structure: Whereas newspaper articles are structured in a top-down format, *The Cooperator* articles are structures like those in magazines–composed as an entire piece. Every article must flow from beginning to end. Both a lead and a conclusion are necessary.

Title: Every title has a "header" and a "kicker"…Don't Get Soaked! *Waterproofing Your Masonry Facade,* Saving For a Rainy Day. *The Five-Year Budget Planning-Process*

Byline: Use capital B; no colon: By John Smith

Subheads: Sections of the article should be preceded with a subhead, organizing the information and breaking it up a bit. Arrange the article so that the story evolves from one section to the next.

Include @ 3 or 4 per article. Begin the body of the article with the first subhead following the introduction (around the second or third paragraph).

Subhead titles should generalize the information to follow, but be specific: "A Past of Many Disciplines" instead of just "the Past."

Author Blurb: (at end of article) indent blurb, and begin with Mr. Or Ms.: "Mr. Smith is a freelance writer based in Manhattan"; "Ms. Smith is executive director of the Bla Bla Foundation, a non-profit organization in Brooklyn that promotes safe bla bla practices."

Acronymns: First spell out the title and then put the acronym in parentheses. The acronym can then be used freely throughout the article: the Real Estate Board of New York (REBNY)…

Commas: Don't use a comma in a string of simple words: a dog, a cat and a bird.

Use comma in a string of phrases: The project succeeded because of a well-planned marketing program, long-term financing by several institutions, and much dedication from the developer's New York employees.

Colon: Capitalize the word following a colon only if it is a proper noun or the beginning of a new sentence.

Remember this: It is better to be…

There are two kinds: normal and strange.

Dash: Never use a dash to replace the words to or between and and: "10 a.m. to 11 a.m." instead of "10 a.m.-11 a.m." "Between eight and ten things" instead of "8-10"

Dates: Days of the week are not abbreviated: Monday instead of Mon.

Geography: Write out the names of cities, states and countries unless they are in a long list of cities and states or states and countries: New York, New York; or Philadelphia, PA, Knoxville, TN, and Quebec, Can.

Hyphens: Use hyphens when two or more words are used together as an adjective: five-year plan; 70-unit building.

Measurements: Use symbols when describing dimensions of furniture or space: The painting is 48" by 18".

Money:; Use decimal only if cents are indicated: $10 and $10.50.

Numbers: Spell out one through ten; use numerals above ten (11, 12…)–maintain this style within quotes.

BUT, spell out numerals when they begin a sentence.

Below one, use fractions: 3/4, 1/8…

For larger numbers, spell out: 16 million instead of 16,000,000.

Percent: Write out the word: two percent; 16 percent.

Quotes: All periods, commas, etc. fall inside quotes (even simple quotes): She says, "I love The Cooperator."

The meter dials had "turned over."

Quotes within quotes are single: According to Knight, "The coalition was created as a 'grassroots organization.'"

Quoting Sources: While it's not necessary to put every other sentence in quotes, back up much of what you say with "words" from a professional.

If a quote is not directly attributed to a person, make sure it's obvious who you're paraphrasing.

All quotes are present tense: So and so of blank says, "…"

Titles are lower case: Robert Grant, director of property management at Diversified Property Management in Brooklyn…

Give a brief description of the firm (what it is and where) unless it is obvious (like Diversified above): Jane Jones, president of Kaye Waterproofing, an exterior restoration firm in Manhattan.

Don't include words like "Inc." or "Co." unless it's a necessary part of a firm's title: "Insignia Financial Group" instead of "Insignia Financial Group, Inc."; "Samuel Klein & Co." is OK.

Text: Indent paragraphs ½"; double-space lines.

Use only one space between sentences.

Time: A.M. and P.M. are upper-case, "small caps" with periods and put a space between the number and the a or p.

Use colons only if minutes are indicated: "10 a.m. and 10:15 p.m."

Miscellaneous

"co-op" is hyphenated; "cooperative" isn't.

Generally use "co-op" for "cooperative" and "condo" for "condominium."

Use lower case for:
• the "b" in "board members"
• the "b" in "bylaws" (bylaws is not hyphenated)
• the "m" and "a" in "managing agent" (or the "a" in attorney, etc.)

Only use an ampersand (&) when it is part of a company's formal name.

Use the terms "managing agent" and "management company."

Simplify! It is better to break a sentence into two or three (or seven…) than to continue with a number of semi-colons, commas and dashes. If a sentence seems a bit confusing, that's because it is. The Cooperator's tone is one of straight-forward simplicity. Present things in "layman's" terms as clearly as possible.

Categories: Fiction—Business—Real Estate

CONTACT: Delora A. Estock, Editor
Material: All
Yale Robbins, LLC
31 E. 28th Street, 12th Floor
New York NY 10016
Phone: 212-683-5700
Website: www.cooperator.com

Cornerstone

These are the writers' guidelines for *Cornerstone* magazine. We appreciate your interest and hope you will find these guidelines helpful.

As of August 22, 2001, *Cornerstone* magazine will no longer be accepting unsolicited article manuscripts of any kind. Our publication dates (twice a year) preclude the likelihood that we would use any unsolicited materials, including general articles, book reviews, or fiction manuscripts.

Poetry:

One specific exception to this is poetry; we will still accept poetry submissions. We are interested in a variety of poetic styles (e.g., avant-garde, free and light verse, haiku), but if it has a "churchy," singsong rhythm or form, it is not for *Cornerstone*. We print 2 or 3 poems per issue at $10.00 per 1 to 15 line poem, $25.00 per 16+ line poem. We are looking for good use of imagery, words that elicit a sensory response, a poem that has memorable quality. The most important thing you can do: read the magazine. More poetry is rejected for not being familiar with *Cornerstone* than for any other reason. By reading back issues, you can familiarize yourself with our outlook on poetry.

Submissions:

Please send only email submissions (if email is unavailable to you, we accept hard copies—no SASEs please).

Send the submission in the body of the email message as ASCII or HTML text, or send as an attachment created in MS-Word, RTF (rich text format), or Word Perfect. If you send a file attachment, please tell us in the message body which word processor, version number, and operating system were used to produce it.

We do not mind simultaneous or previously published submissions.

Please DO NOT expect rejection slips. Due to the large volume of material we receive, we will only be able to respond to works we wish to publish. However, please rest assured that all material sent to *Cornerstone* is read and considered.

We look forward to hearing from you.

Sincerely,

Jon Trott, Editor in Chief

Categories: Christian Interests—Poetry

CONTACT: Book Review Editor
Material: Short Fiction, Articles
CONTACT: Tammy Perlmutter, Poetry Editor
Material: Poetry
Cornerstone Communications
939 W. Wilson
Chicago IL 60640
Phone: 773-561-2450
Fax: 773-989-2076
E-mail: poetry@cornerstonemag.com
Website: www.cornerstonemag.com

Corrections Compendium

Submission Guidelines

Corrections Compendium is a peer-reviewed research-oriented publication of the American Correctional Association (ACA). Its international readership includes individuals involved in every sector of the corrections and criminal justice fields.

Our readers are committed to the advancement of the corrections field. They cut across the spectrum of corrections, from individuals employed in correctional institutions, community corrections, and probation and parole, to those in juvenile services and academia.

AUTHOR GUIDELINES

What kind of articles do we want? We're very open-minded - as long as the article idea is interesting and relates to corrections. We are interested primarily in articles that are research-based and scholarly.

We don't like puff pieces or promotional articles. We want information that can help our readers better understand their profession and the critical issues they face day to day. For this reason, *our policy is that any article written by a consultant or an employee of a private firm must be co-authored by a corrections professional*. In other words, at least one author must be a practitioner employed by a public agency or nonprofit organization, or currently working in an adult/juvenile institutional or academic setting.

If you have not written for us before, send a written query telling us who you are and what kind of article you wish to submit. We'll let you know if your idea has possibilities. If you have an article that already is written and conforms to these guidelines, send the completed manuscript. All submitted manuscripts are reviewed by at least two members of the *Corrections Compendium* Editorial Advisory Board. Final publication decisions are based on the recommendations of these reviewers. We'll respond as soon as possible, usually within eight to 10 weeks.

What Makes a Good *CC* Article?

Most articles are organized in a simple format. First is the introduction. This captures the readers' attention and lets them know what the article will be about. It orients them to time and place and tells them why the subject is important enough for them to take the time to read about it.

The middle section of the article develops the topic. This is the meat of the article and should explain, simply and clearly, the important points you'd like to make about your research-oriented topic. When writing this section, try to put yourself in your readers' shoes. Make sure you're being detailed enough and giving enough examples to illustrate your point so they clearly understand the situation you are describing.

The final section is the conclusion. This should restate the main point of the article and should include any evaluations or recommendations you may have.

Finally, every good article has three main qualities: an interesting subject, thorough research and reporting, and an organized writing style. Your article doesn't have to be perfect - our editors will help you enhance it if it is accepted - but it's up to you to give the article focus.

Suggestions on Style

You can do a number of things to make your article come alive for readers. First, you should be familiar with the journal and the type of material we publish. Reading *Corrections Compendium* is the best way to figure out how to make your article fit our readers' needs.

Second, write clearly. In *The Elements of Style*, William Strunk makes these suggestions:

- use the active rather than passive voice;
- be specific, concrete and definite;
- don't overstate; and
- avoid fancy words and jargon.

Submission Specifics

Corrections Compendium is a peer-review publication. This means that unsolicited manuscripts are sent to editorial advisory board members with expertise in the article's subject area for evaluation. For this reason, you should provide us with two copies of the manuscript. Other submission guidelines include:

- Manuscripts must be typed and double-spaced. If possible, send us the article in WordPerfect 8.0 (or an earlier version of WordPerfect). (Note: We *can* convert other word processing programs, as long as they are IBM-compatible i.e., Microsoft Word). Manuscripts will not be returned.
- Ideally, articles should be 3,000 to 6,000 words.
- Include your name, title, agency name, address, office or home telephone number, and fax number.
- We must be notified in writing at the time of submission if you are submitting the article to any other publications. *Corrections Compendium* is a copyrighted journal.
- Do not use footnotes. Endnotes are fine.
- Any references discussed or referenced in the text must be cited in a reference list at the end of the article.
- Include a resume or biographical information with your article.
- Submit charts, graphs or diagrams at the end of the manuscript to illustrate the topic.

If Your Article Is Accepted

Articles published in *Corrections Compendium* will be edited to conform to Associated Press (AP) style. You will be given a chance to review the edited version of your article before publication. The Association reserves the right to write article headlines.

A Note on References

Please follow the guidelines below when submitting references:

- **Reference for a magazine article with one author:**

Doe, John. 1997. Rhetoric in contemporary culture. *Professional Writing Quarterly*.

Lanham, Md.: ACA Press. (November).

Doe, John. 1997. Rhetoric in contemporary culture. *Professional Writing Quarterly*, 40(3):151-155.

[40(3):151-155 refers to Volume 40, issue number 3, pages 151 through 155]

- **Starting a reference for an article/book with two or more authors:**

Doe, John and Jane Doe.

Doe, John, Jane Doe and James Doe.

- **Reference for a book:**

Doe, John. 1997. *Analyzing modern poetry*. Attica, N.Y.: Exciting Press.

- **Reference for a pamphlet/gov. document:**

Federal Bureau of Prisons. 1988. *A report to the attorney general on disturbances at the federal detention center*. Washington, D.C.: U.S. Government Printing Office. (February).

- **Reference for an article in a book with an editor(s):**

Doe, Jane. 1997. Perspectives on best practices in corrections. In *Exciting ideas in corrections*, ed. James Doe, 545-549. Washington, D.C.: Georgetown University Press.

Doe, Jane. 1997. Perspectives on best practices in corrections. In *Exciting ideas in corrections*, eds. James Doe and Jeffrey Doe, 545-549. Washington, D.C.: Georgetown University Press.

- **Reference for a speech/paper:**

Doe, Jeffrey. 1997. How to travel across country. Paper presented at the National Travel Symposium, 3-5 April in Pittsburgh, Pa.

*Note: If you are unable to attribute material within your text (i.e., According to researcher Michael Rutter of the University of Maryland, ...), and you need to use endnotes:

Please use one of the following methods of citation -

Positive interaction is critical to the development of healthy social relationships (Rutter, 1995).

Positive interaction is critical to the development of healthy social relationships.

Then, on a separate page at the end of the article:

1 Rutter, M. 1995. *Maternal deprivation reassessed*, second edition. New York: Penguin Books.

CONTACT: Managing Editor, *Corrections Compendium*
Material: All
American Correctional Association
4380 Forbes Blvd.
Lanham, MD 20706
Phone: 301-918-1890
Fax: 301-918-1886
E-mail: susanc@aca.org

Corrections Today

Submission Guidelines

Corrections Today is the professional membership publication of the American Correctional Association (ACA). Its international readership includes individuals involved in every sector of the corrections and criminal justice fields. The magazine, begun in 1939, currently has a circulation of 21,000, with a pass-along readership estimated as high as 65,000.

Our readers are committed to the advancement of the corrections field, and most play active roles in operating and administrating correctional facilities and systems. They cut across the spectrum of corrections, from individuals employed in correctional institutions, community corrections, and probation and parole to those in juvenile services and academia.

The magazine serves as a forum for presenting and discussing important issues related to corrections, including the presentation of minority or conflicting points of view. Its primary purpose is to offer practical information to promote the development of the field and those working in the field.

AUTHOR GUIDELINES

What kind of articles do we want? We're very open-minded - as long as the article idea is interesting and relates to corrections. We're interested in a variety of articles, including service ("how to") pieces, articles outlining new programs and case studies, and articles on how agencies or systems handle controversial issues. We also accept opinion pieces for our "Speak Out" column and personal accounts of on-the-job experiences for "A View From the Line."

We don't like puff pieces or promotional articles. There should be news, information or an opinion behind the story. Articles should be written in journalistic style using third person rather than first person (avoid using "I, we, me, us," etc.). We want information that can help our readers better understand their profession and the critical issues they face day to day. For this reason, our policy is that any article written by a consultant or an employee of a private firm must be co-authored by a corrections professional or academician. In other words, at least one author must be a practitioner employed by a public agency or non-profit organization, or currently working in an adult/juvenile institutional or academic setting.

If you have not written for us before, send a written query telling us who you are and what kind of article you wish to submit. We'll let you know if your idea has possibilities. If you have an article that already is written and conforms to these guidelines, send the completed manuscript. We'll respond as soon as possible, usually within eight to 10 weeks.

What Makes a Good *CT* Article?

Most magazine articles are organized in a simple format. First is the introduction. This captures the readers' attention and lets them know what the article will be about. It orients them to time and place and tells them why the subject is important enough for them to take the time to read about it. An anecdote or sample situation often is useful in the introduction - it can be a great way to pique readers' interest.

The middle section of the article develops the topic. This is the meat of the article and should explain, simply and clearly, the important points you'd like to make about your topic. When writing this section, try to put yourself in your readers' shoes. Make sure you're being detailed enough and giving enough examples to illustrate your point so they clearly understand the program, strategy or situation you are describing.

The final section is the conclusion. This should restate the main point of the article and should include any evaluations or recommendations you may have.

Finally, every good magazine article has three main qualities: an interesting subject, thorough research and reporting, and an organized writing style. Your article doesn't have to be perfect - our editors will help you enhance it if it is accepted - but it's up to you to give the article focus.

Suggestions on Style

You can do a number of things to make your article come alive for readers. First, you should be familiar with the magazine and the type of material we publish. Reading *Corrections Today* is the best way to figure out how to make your article fit our readers' needs.

Second, write clearly. In *The Elements of Style*, William Strunk makes these suggestions:
- use the active rather than passive voice;
- be specific, concrete and definite;
- don't overstate; and
- avoid fancy words and jargon.

Submission Specifics

Corrections Today is a peer-review publication. This means that unsolicited manuscripts are sent to ACA members with expertise in the article's subject area for evaluation. For this reason, you should provide us with two copies of the manuscript. Other submission guidelines include:

• Manuscripts must be typed and double-spaced. If possible, send us the disk with the article saved in WordPerfect 8.0 (or an earlier version of WordPerfect) or Microsoft Word. You also can e-mail manuscripts to with a WordPerfect or Microsoft attachment. Manuscripts will not be returned.

• Ideally, articles should be 8 to 10 double-spaced, typed pages (2,000 to 2,500 words).

• Include your name, title, agency name, mailing address, e-mail address, office or home telephone number, and fax number.

• We must be notified in writing at the time of submission if you are submitting the article to any other publications. *Corrections Today* is a copyrighted magazine.

• Any references discussed in the text must be cited at the end of the article.

• Please do not format the article, as it will need to be reformatted to fit the style of the magazine.

• Include a resume or biographical information with your article.

• Submit photos or slides, as well as charts, graphs or diagrams with the manuscript to illustrate the topic. These should be placed at the end of the document.

If Your Article Is Accepted

Articles published in *Corrections Today* will be edited to conform to AP style, as well as *Corrections Today* style. You will be given a chance to review the edited version of your article before publication. The Association reserves the right to write article headlines and photo captions and to illustrate articles with art or file photos when more suitable photos are not provided by you.

PHOTOGRAPHY GUIDELINES

Photos are the first thing readers see when they look at a page. Photos draw attention to the page, leading the eye to the text. Often, important copy goes unread because a photograph is not striking enough to stop the browsing reader.

Techniques

Two qualities of good photographs are technical excellence and composition of interesting subject matter. Detail is achieved through proper picture-taking, sharp focus, correct exposure and a steady hand. Photographs also must have satisfactory contrast: An ideal print for reproduction should have a full range of tones - from very white, through many intermediate grays, to deep black.

Make sure to carefully frame your pictures. Define what you want in both the foreground and background; this is called "composing" the picture. You should be certain that the subject appears level and then center on the subject. Move in as close as possible to eliminate nonessential details in the foreground, background and sides. If your camera takes pictures that are larger in one dimension than the other, don't forget to turn the camera to see if you can frame the subject better.

Types of Photos

The best photo is the one that appears unposed. Action photos make excellent shots. Action does not necessarily refer to physical movement, but rather to the subjects' keeping busy - their being occupied with something that holds their attention. This prevents a picture from appearing static.

Take photos showing people, focusing on one or two. Crowd scenes (unless you're showing prison crowding) make it difficult to see what you're trying to illustrate. A dramatic closeup photo may do a better job of making a statement.

If your article mentions a particular service, program or case study, photograph those involved - the employees, participants, family, etc. Familiar scenes can be photographed from an unusual perspective. For example, a typical counseling setting might dramatize the situation between a client and a correctional officer, capturing their facial expressions and body language.

Captions and Credits

Identify the subjects in the photos through a caption. Tell us what's going on and who's in the photo. Supply the name of the photographer or the person/agency who supplied the photo to you. But please do not write directly on the backs of photos because ink tends to bleed through and ruin the photo. It's best if you mount the photo on a piece of paper and write the necessary caption/credit information on it.

Photo Releases

When photographing inmates, whether juveniles or adults, a release must be signed by the individual or individuals giving permission for the photo to be taken for publication. We require a release for any person photographed - even if the photo shows a back or side view. A copy of an existing release already on file for a photo you are submitting also is permissible. Securing a release takes a little extra work, but in the long run, it protects you and *Corrections Today* from any liability.

A Note on References

Corrections Today encourages authors to include references with their articles to allow our readers to do follow-up reading on the subjects. Because *Corrections Today* is a magazine and not a scholarly journal per se, we favor the use of references in lieu of citations directly within the text. Please follow the guidelines below when submitting references:

• **Reference for a magazine article with one author:**

Doe, John. 1997. Rhetoric in contemporary culture. *Professional Writing Quarterly*, 40(3):151-155.

[40(3):151-155 refers to volume 40, issue number 3, pages 151 through 155] Lanham, Md.: ACA Press. (November).

- **Starting a reference for an article/book with two or more authors:**

Doe, John and Jane Doe.

Doe, John, Jane Doe and James Doe.

- **Reference for a book:**

Doe, John. 1997. *Analyzing modern poetry*. Attica, N.Y.: Exciting Press.

- **Reference for a pamphlet/government document:**

Federal Bureau of Prisons. 1988. *A report to the attorney general on disturbances at the federal detention center*. Washington, D.C.: U.S. Government Printing Office. (February).

- **Reference for an article in a book with an editor(s):**

Doe, Jane. 1997. Perspectives on best practices in corrections. In *Exciting ideas in corrections*, ed. James Doe, 545-549. Washington, D.C.: Georgetown University Press.

Doe, Jane. 1997. Perspectives on best practices in corrections. In *Exciting ideas in corrections*, eds. James Doe and Jeffrey Doe, 545-549. Washington, D.C.: Georgetown University Press.

- **Reference for a speech/paper:**

Doe, Jeffrey. 1997. How to travel across the country. Paper presented at the National Travel Symposium, 3-5 April in Pittsburgh, Pa.

If you are unable to attribute material within your text (i.e., According to researcher Michael Rutter of the University of Maryland, ...), and you need to use endnotes:

DO NOT use the following method of citation:

Positive interaction is critical to the development of healthy social relationships (Rutter, 1995).

DO use the following method of citation:

Positive interaction is critical to the development of healthy social relationships.

On a separate page at the end of the article:

[1] Rutter, M. 1995. *Maternal deprivation reassessed*, second edition. New York: Penguin Books.

CONTACT: Susan Clayton, Managing Editor
Material: All
American Correctional Association
4380 Forbes Blvd.
Lanham, MD 20706
Phone: 800-222-5646, ext. 1890, 301-918-1890
Fax: 301-918-1886
E-mail: susanc@aca.org

Corvette Fever

Writers and Photographers Guidelines

Thank you for your inquiry. *Corvette Fever* is devoted to Corvettes of all eras, although our readers have little interest in highly or unusually modified cars. All featured vehicles must have Corvette engines or they will be rejected outright. The major focus of the magazine is technical maintenance, restoration and hop-up articles, features about exceptional Corvettes and racing coverage.

Features

Photography for feature cars should be submitted in color using 35mm slides or medium format photography. Our graphic arts department likes 100 ASA slide film. For tech articles and certain historical features, 400 ASA black and white film would be preferable. When submitting B&W, please submit the negatives with contact sheets. Color prints are not acceptable for feature car photography. For small, secondary photos inside a story, color prints are acceptable, but not preferable. Features in *Corvette Fever* normally focus on restored older Corvettes and '84-and-up in exceptional condition with an interesting hook. Race cars are also featured on an occasional basis, but we focus more on actual racing events. If you are not sure if a car is suitable for publication, please check it with us.

Stories from readers on their own Corvettes are welcome for consideration in our "Editor's Spotlight" section each month, and for our annual "Corvettes USA" July issue. These use reader-generated photography and information, and are never assigned to professional journalist/photographers.

When photographing feature cars, be aware of background clutter and reflections; we need clean, simple backgrounds. We think *Corvette Fever* is a dynamic, stimulating magazine, so don't be afraid to experiment with dramatic or unusual camera angles. However, keep in mind the four basic shots we request for every feature car: an engine shot, interior shot, front three-quarter view and rear three-quarter view. Beyond that, feel free to let those creative juices flow!

Study recent issues for examples. Shoot interiors with the doors open; convertibles can be shot top up or down, although down is usually the better choice.

One commonly overlooked approach to feature car photography is action. If possible, have your subject drive by so you can pan to blur the background, wheels, and tires. We really enjoy action photography, so the extra effort often pays off. However, keep in mind the photos will be enlarged considerably and must be very sharp. Thus, get close to the subject and keep the car large in the frame. Use the fastest shutter speed possible that will not freeze the background or tires. The idea is to have a razor-sharp shot of the car with the background blurred. If you have the people, cars, and time, shooting car-to-car is the best way of getting these shots.

For text, the average two-page color feature story runs about 500 words, more for detailed historical features or interviews. When writing about feature cars, focus on the history and unusual characteristics of that particular car, with perhaps some general history of that model thrown in. Information like this can frequently best be presented in chart or graph form. When writing features, always remember our readers have heard the old historical stories too many times already. Strive to put the humanity behind the subject car into the story. Above all, make your feature text more-than a simple listing of what original parts remain on the car and what options were originally installed, or which aftermarket parts have been installed. With late model Corvettes, if feasible, document performance by quarter-mile time, lap times, top speed, lateral acceleration or whatever. We want to know how hard it runs besides how good it looks, when that is appropriate.

Technical

Our readers expect the very best, up-to-date, detailed, accurate tech advice on restoring, maintaining or improving performance on their Corvettes. Make sure B&W photography is sharp, not too dark or light, and crop as necessary ON THE CONTACT SHEET. Photos are sent to scan and cannot include crop marks for the process.

Categories: Nonfiction—Automobiles—Technical

CONTACT: Ronnie Hartman, Editor-in-Chief
Material: All
3816 Industrial Blvd.
Lakeland FL 33811
Phone: 863-644-0449
Website: www.corvettefever.com

Cosmopolitan

Cosmopolitan magazine aims at young career women. All nonfiction should tell readers how they can 1) improve their lives, 2) better enjoy their lives, and 3) live better lives. Within this sphere, articles can be of the widest range: career, man-woman relationships, health, emotions, celebrity profiles, how-to's ,etc. Crisp, incisive, entertaining writing is a must, with a heavy emphasis on reader involvement. Full length articles should be 2500-2700 words, features 1000-1800 words. New writers should accompany their pitches with a selection of previously published writing clips, if available.

Payment is open to negotiation.

Categories: Fiction—Nonfiction—Book Reviews—Careers—Diet/Nutrition—Entertainment—Fashion—Health—Lifestyle—Money & Finances—Physical Fitness—Relationships—Romance—Sexuality—Travel—Women's Issues—Self-Help—Beauty—Personal Development—Home —Essay—Interior Decorating—Celebrities—How-to—Humor—Personal Experience

CONTACT: Michele Promaulayko, Executive Editor
Material: All non-fiction
CONTACT: John Searles, Senior Books Editor
Material: Fiction
224 W. 57th St.
New York NY 10019
Phone: 212-649-2000
Fax: 212-956-3268
Website: www.hearstcorp.com

Country Living

Thank you for writing *Country Living* and for requesting our writer's guidelines.

While we do not commission work based on query letters, we are happy to review completed manuscripts.

Manuscripts should be triple-spaced, allowing wide margins on both sides, as well as at the top and bottom of the page. Please use white bond paper only.

Our fees vary depending on the nature of the work and on the inclusion of supplemental photos and/or art work.

All manuscripts should be sent to our Features Editor, Lynne Constantin, at the address below.

Sincerely,
The Editors

Categories: Nonfiction—Antiques—Collectibles—Conservation—Cooking—Crafts/Hobbies—Entertainment—Family—Food/Drink—Gardening—Hobbies—Marriage—Real Estate—Travel—Home—Interior Decorating—Nature

CONTACT: Lynne Constantin, Features Editor
Material: All
224 W. 57th St., 7th Floor
New York NY 10019
Phone: 212-649-3509

Country Magazine
Country Extra Magazine

Country is for people who "live in or long for the Country"—and our editorial matter reflects the rural life-style with relaxed, conversational writing and top-quality rural and scenic photography. We showcase the pleasures and benefits of Country life, the beauty of rural America and folks with interesting tales to tell. In fact, much of each issue is based on what we receive from our readers, who send us thousands of pieces of mail every month.

Country is full-color throughout, printed on high-quality glossy paper, with an extra-heavy varnished cover. Published six times per year, it contains no paid advertising and is available primarily by subscription. The magazine was launched in 1987 and has a very loyal following.

Country EXTRA includes the same type of photo and editorial material as *Country*. CX is published "in between" the bimonthly issues of *Country*, thereby offering these enthusiastic subscribers monthly frequency through six extra issues.

Each editorial and photo submission is reviewed thoroughly. The ideal time for free-lance submissions is 4 months before the issue date. Unless a specific assignment is made, all freelance material will be considered on a speculative basis.

Photography: We welcome submissions. See separate Reiman Publications Photo Guidelines for payment schedule.

Feature Articles: We are always looking for a variety of rural-oriented features. Past stories have covered such diverse topics as the reason most barns are red, an essay on windmills and a first-person account of riding on a cattle drive. At the end of many features, we ask readers to respond with their own stories and photos.

Payment, upon publication, varies according to length, quality of photos, and amount of editing required to make it fit the format and style of *Country* and CX.

In most cases, payment is $100-$200 per story.

"God's Country", the regular 10-page photo feature in *Country*, is paid at a flat rate of $1,000 for photos and text.

Aside from the above guidelines, editors will negotiate a package rate for other multi-page features that use extensive amounts of photography.

"Country People Section": "Country People" features brief articles about rural "characters" with unusual hobbies, interests and enterprises. Photo-illustrated pieces should be 500-1,000 words, with a conversational tone; at least half should be direct quotes. Payment, upon publication, ranges from $75-$150, depending on length and quality.

We prefer transparencies for all color work (including photos submitted along with feature articles). Color prints are acceptable if they are of high quality. Be sure every image is identified for proper return.

Potential contributors are encouraged to obtains samples of *Country* and CX to learn about our needs. With high production costs and our no-advertising policy—we're supported solely by subscriptions—we regret that we can't give away samples.

Issues are $2 plus a 9- x 12-inch envelope with $1.93 in postage. Freelancers may subscribe at a special rate of $10.98 per year (regularly $17.98). Contributors receive a complimentary copy of the issue in which their work appears. Always include return postage with submissions.

Please direct manuscripts and manuscript/photo combinations to Jerry Wiebel, editor. Photo submissions should be sent to Trudi Bellin, photo coordinator. The address for both is:

Categories: Nonfiction—Adventure—Agriculture—Animals—Cooking—Food/Drink—Lifestyle—Multicultural—Nature—Outdoors—Recreation—Rural America—Travel

CONTACT: Submissions Editor
Material: Manuscripts
CONTACT: Trudi Bellin, photo coordinator
Material: Photo submissions
5400 S. 60th St.
Greendale WI 53129
Phone: 414-423-0100
E-mail: editors@country-magazine.com
Website: www.country-magazine.com

Country Woman

Country Woman is a 68-page, full-color, bimonthly magazine for women who live in or long for the country. It is a positive, upbeat, entertaining publication that reflects the many interests and roles of its readers through short, photo-illustrated personality profiles of rural women...antiques and gardening articles...nostalgic photos and reader remembrances.

Free-lance material to be considered for publication should have a rural theme and be of specific interest to women who live on a farm or ranch, or women who live in a small town or country home and/or simply have an interest in country-oriented topics.

Many of the stories, columns, anecdotes and photos in CW come directly from its readers. But we count on free-lancers such as you for the balance of each issue. Here are some of our regular features that free-lancers help us with:

Features/Profile Stories...In each issue, we feature about half a dozen profile pieces, stories about ordinary country women doing in-

A-E

teresting and extraordinary things. Stories must be told in a light, entertaining, conversational style with plenty of direct quotes from the featured country woman. This is her story; let her tell it. Stories should have a strong, readily identifiable "angle", and must be focused throughout. Stories must be country related, and the "why" behind what the woman is doing must be clearly explained. Many of our profile pieces focus on cottage industries or small businesses women have started themselves. Recent issues have included profile pieces on: a farm woman who has become a wool spinner and whose husband has begun to make spinning wheels as a result of her craft...a country woman who makes rag rugs out of scraps of old cloth...a grade school teacher who takes the chicks she raises on her farm into her grade school classroom and uses them as "teaching aids". These profile pieces are not limited to farm women; however, features on women who live on a country place or in a small town are also acceptable. We are not interested in recent "transplants" to the country or in upscale "yuppie country" operations.

Bright and beautiful color photos must accompany all profile pieces. We prefer to work with 35 mm or 2-1/4 Kodachrome transparencies, but we have had remarkable luck with bright, clear color prints. CW is looking for top-quality color, focus and lighting in all photos. Profile pieces are most often rejected because of poor quality photos! Take good action, not posed, shots of your featured country woman in her natural environment-at work on the ranch, cutting out Christmas cookies, stitching a quilt or doing whatever it is that you are focusing on in your story. While your subject should be colorfully dressed, she should not be wearing much makeup-we prefer the "natural", wholesome look. Manuscript length should be about 1,000 words, accompanied by a good variety of photos-give us lots to choose from, please! Payment for photo-feature package, on acceptance: $100-$225. Generally, payment is in the $150 range, except for regular contributors, who are paid at the higher end of the scale.

Cover shots...We are always in the market for strong cover photos! Cover shots must be strong verticals, with bright and vibrant colors...focus must be razor-sharp-no soft-focus shots will be accepted. No hot spots either! Use fill-in lighting where necessary to avoid hulking shadows. We have found that Kodachrome film generally provides the best color saturation, although other brands in the hands of skilled photographers have also met our high standards. We can work from either 35 mm or 2-1/4 transparencies, but prefer the larger-format photos. Photos must focus on a close-up shot of a country woman in her natural surroundings. Subject should be attractive, but in a natural, wholesome way. She should not look "made up" or modelish or too dressed up. She must be a true country woman, preferably with a "traditional" family life. Prefer subjects in their 30's to mid-40's, although attractive older women are acceptable as well. It is our cover lady's "job" to invite the reader into the magazine. Subject should look as if she's just stopped whatever she was doing for a moment to glance up and smile warmly out at the reader. Try for as spontaneous a look as possible. While the magazine's logo does not overprint the cover photo, several small lines of type do-so try to plan a small solid area somewhere in the background to accommodate. When possible, covers should portray a strong seasonal look as well. Occasionally, we make cover assignments. More often, we find an acceptable shot from a standard feature/profile submission (see above). We always need at least one additional pose for the inside cover story. Cover prices are somewhat negotiable, but generally range around $300, depending on quality. Inside shot: $50-$75, depending on quality and size at which it's used.

Service Features...these must relate specifically to the lives of country women. Some "how-to" articles we've bought recently include: how to start your own at-home business...how to market your crafts...how to sell your work to publishers...how to preserve old family photos...a listing of mail-order sources for holiday baking. Maximum length: 500-600 words. Color photos where appropriate. Rate: $50-$75.

Country Crafts, Sewing, Needlework...emphasizing quick, easy and inexpensive country crafts. Prefer items that are utilitarian as well as pretty. Include a list of all materials needed, detailed patterns, in-structions and illustrations. Actual item must be enclosed so we can check it against instructions. Rate: $35-$75, depending on quality and degree of difficulty.

Also welcome features on contemporary sewing methods, ideas for "remakes," quilting tips, practical wardrobe planning, etc. Good color photos where appropriate. Rate: $35-$75.

Decorating...We're always looking for features on home improvements along with before and after photos, short tips on decorating and exciting features on how to accomplish that "country look". Again, good quality color transparencies are a must. Rate: $50-$125.

Nostalgia...We're looking for well-written nostalgic pieces that fall into three categories: "I Remember When..." is a country woman's recollection of a past event that the vast majority of readers can identify with; "I'll Never Forget..." is a more personal recollection describing an event unique to the writer; general nostalgia captured in fiction and poetry. Length: 750-1,000 words. Rate: $50-$75.

Inspirational...Material should reflect the positive way in which the country enhances your own life. Length: about 750 words. Rate: $50-$75.

Poetry...Must have a rural theme and be positive and upbeat. Always looking for good, seasonal poetry. We accept only traditional styles-poems must have rhythm and rhyme! Poems should be 4 to 25 lines in length, with some exceptions. Rate: $10-$25.

Fiction...Well-written short fiction is a continuing need. The subjects should center on life in the country, its problems and joys, as experienced by women, and contain a positive, upbeat message. The main character must be a country woman. Length: 1,000 words. Rate: $90-$125.

Unless a specific assignment is made, all free-lance material will be considered on a speculative basis. CW is published 6 times per year. The ideal deadline for free-lance material is 6 months before the date of the issue. Manuscripts should be typed and double-spaced. Please enclose a self-addressed stamped return envelope with all manuscript and photo submissions. For craft submissions, send return postage in the form of a check or money order. Submissions without adequate return postage will not be returned. CW is not responsible for lost material. *Country Woman* reserves the right to rewrite any and all material it buys to comply with our very particular in-house style. If you are not willing to have your material rewritten, do not submit it!

A decision on free-lance material is generally made within 2-3 months after receipt of the article. Payment is upon acceptance. If querying first (and do query on all feature/profile pieces), please enclose a self-addressed stamped envelope.

If you are notified that your manuscript is being held for future publication and later on you have an inquiry about its status, please enclose a self-addressed return envelope. Be sure to remind us of the subject matter of the article in your letter-don't just give the title. This will help us locate it in our files. Of course, articles we hold are not available for resale until we've notified you of publication. We sometimes hold articles several years or longer before publishing.

Contributors are strongly urged to study the magazine carefully before querying or submitting. CW is generally not available on the newsstand. Free-lancers may subscribe at a special rate of $10.98 per year (regularly $17.98). To obtain a sample copy, send $2.00.

Categories: Consumer—Cooking—Crafts/Hobbies—Family—Lifestyle—Rural America

CONTACT: Kathleen Anderson, Managing Editor
Material: All
5400 S. 60th St.
Greendale WI 53129
E-mail: editors@countrywomanmagazine.com
Website: www.countrywomanmagazine.com

Country Extra

Please refer to *Country Magazine*.

Crab Creek Review

POETRY

We publish an eclectic mix of energetic poems and remain more interested in powerful imagery than obscure literary allusion. Wit? Yes. Punch? Sure. Toast dry? No thank you. Translations are welcome. Send up to 5 poems.

SHORT FICTION

We accept stories up to 6000 words, with an admitted predilection for dynamic prose of distinct voice and strong images. Offer us a compelling view of the world in which we live and let us revel in your telling of it.

ART

High contrast black and white photography, pen or brushwork, any subject, preferably drawn to 9"h x6"w format size.

Remember to send your submissions with an SASE; without one we will not consider the work.

We accept submissions continuously, but ask that they be neither previously published nor under simultaneous consideration elsewhere. We aim for a response time between 2 and 4 months.

Our current payment is in the form of two copies of the issue for which your work has been accepted.

We buy first rights as well as the right to use your name and the accepted work (whole or in part) on our web site. Beyond this use, and following publication, rights revert to the author. We ask that Crab Creek Review be acknowledged in any subsequent publication of the work.

We are proud of our magazine and hope you will want to pursue a copy of your own. Hell, we want you to subscribe!

Thank you for your interest in Crab Creek Review. We look forward to reading your work.

Categories: Nonfiction—Arts—Poetry—Short Stories

CONTACT: Submissions Editor
Material: All
PO Box 840
Vashon WA 98070

The Cream City Review
University of Wisconsin, Milwaukee

The Cream City Review, founded in 1975, is a non-profit literary magazine operated entirely by students and published semi-annually in association with the creative writing concentration of the English Department of the University of Wisconsin—Milwaukee.

Our review takes its name from the "City of Cream-colored Bricks" or "Cream City," as Milwaukee was once known. The first "cream" brick was made in 1835. Pale yellow, the bricks proved more durable and aesthetically pleasing than the traditional red bricks produced by East Coast kilns. Popular throughout the 1800s, cream city bricks were used for ornamental architecture in the United States and Europe.

Our magazine is perfect bound in the standard magazine format of 5½"x8½" inches, with a four-color cover, averaging 250 pages. It is distributed to major university and public libraries and independent bookstores throughout the United States. We are indexed by *The American Humanities Index, the Index of American Periodical Verse*, and the *Annual Index to Poetry in Periodicals*, and are members of CLMP and COSMEP.

Submissions

Of course the best way to figure out what we really want is to read the magazine. Check out the samples and the preview of issue 19.2 or just go ahead and subscribe.

Submission Guidelines

First of all, we are sorry to say that we cannot accept electronic submissions at this time. We just don't yet have a reliable way of distributing an electronic manuscript among our various editors. So until further notice, you must rely on the US Postal Service.

Author's name and address should appear on the first page of the manuscript or on each individual piece of art work. Address submissions to the editors of the appropriate genre followed by our full address. Simultaneous submissions are acceptable as long as TCCR is notified at the time of submissions and in the event that work is accepted elsewhere. Submissions which do not include an SASE will not be read or returned.

We seek to publish all forms of writing, from traditional to experimental. We strive to produce issues which are challenging, diverse, and of lasting quality. We are not interested in sexist, homophobic, racist, or formulaic writings.

Please include a few lines about your publication history and other information you think of interest. TCCR seeks to publish not only a broad range of writing but a broad range of writers with diverse backgrounds as well. Both beginning and well established writers are welcome.

Reporting time is at least eight weeks. We do not read from April 1-Sept. 1. Contributors are given a one-year subscription to TCCR beginning with the issue in which their work appears. Copyright automatically reverts to the author upon publication, although TCCR retains the right to republish in future issues of the magazine.

GENRES

Fiction: Preferably under thirty pages, although we occasionally consider longer material. Please submit no more than one story at a time.

Poetry: No length restrictions. Please submit no more than five poems at a time.

Nonfiction: We are interested in reviews (one to ten pages), interviews, and personal essays.

Art: We are interested in camera-ready black-and-white artwork and photography. Please submit prints or slides. We use approximately twelve pieces of art per issue. As with text, we can accept submissions only through the mail.

Categories: Fiction—Nonfiction—Arts—Literature—Poetry—Short Stories—Writing

CONTACT: Erica Wiest
Material: Any
CONTACT: Beth Bretl or Jennifer Sworshack-Kinter, Poetry Editor
Material: Poetry
CONTACT: Steve Nelson or Zeke Jarvis, Fiction Editor
Material: Fiction
CONTACT: Oody Petty
Material: Nonfiction Editors
UW-Milwaukee English Dept., PO Box 413
Milwaukee WI 53201
Website: www.uwm.edu/Dept/English/ccr

Creative Crafter

GENERAL INFORMATION

Creative Crafter is published bimonthly (six times per year)-Jan./Feb., Mar./Apr., May/June, July/Aug., Sept./Oct. and Nov./Dec.

What do we mean by weekend crafts? Weekend crafts are projects that can be finished in a weekend - 48 hours or less. *Creative Crafter* will provide our readers with projects to decorate their home in upscale style or to proudly give as gifts. Projects will include clear and precise instructions and many will feature step-by-step photos of the project in progress. Projects will be grouped in coordinated room settings to give readers an idea of how the projects will look in their homes. Edible crafts and floral crafts will be featured in each issue. Popular decorating styles will be featured throughout the year.

Creative Crafter is always looking for:

Original, attractive designs and patterns for craft projects which readers of all skill levels can follow easily. Crafts we feature include, but are not limited to: needlework of all kinds, wood crafts, fabric crafts, mosaics, home decorating items, seasonal decorations, rubber stamping, polymer-clay projects, faux finishes, decorative painting, furniture refinishing, beading, metalwork, candle making, wire and glass projects, etc.

Your ideas for issue themes, project types to feature, etc.

New products and printed materials to review.

SUBMISSIONS

Project submissions or manuscripts

If we have not worked together before, we strongly recommend you first send an overview of your design concept, including a color sketch, project notes and a SASE. Include in the project notes the pertinent information about your craft, such as materials used, as well as any details that you feel will help "sell" your project.

While we will consider submission of completed projects, we reserve the right to request revisions to allow for photography in a coordinated setting with other projects.

Please make sure everything you submit is labeled with your name, complete address and daytime phone.

Accepted projects or manuscripts:

Once a concept is approved, you will need to provide complete written instructions for the project. Please observe the following guidelines.

Please type your instructions double-spaced on white paper, leaving generous margins all around. Label the first page with your name, complete address, daytime phone number and the title of your project; label all pages with your name and the title of the project. Number the pages if there are more than one.

Include a complete materials list for your project, listing each item on a separate line. The materials list should precede the instructions.

Give the size of your completed project when appropriate (child's small, adult medium, etc.). Needlework projects should include stitch count and measurement of the design area.

Give complete instructions on how the item is to be used. If it is a garment, give complete instructions as to how it is to be worn. If there are special instructions for care of the finished garment, be sure to include them. Label the top and bottom. It may be apparent to you, but it can be very confusing for us.

Give sources (including addresses and product numbers) for any products used in your project which are not readily available at any general craft or fabric store. Refer to specific brand names whenever possible; if the same kind of product is offered by different manufacturers under different names, include two or three of these options to give our readers a choice. When referring to specific brand names of materials, please be accurate.

List instruction steps numerically.

Label all diagrams, photos, etc.

If your project includes a color key, list it separately at the end of your manuscript, and provide a separate copy to paper-clip to the chart itself. Transfer symbols, color names and numbers carefully. Be sure to indicate which brand and type of fiber you are using.

If your project uses pattern pieces, please submit full-size pieces.

Proofread all aspects of your submission for accuracy. Are instructions clear? Is the materials list complete? Are all pattern pieces and diagrams labeled properly? Remember: Your instructions should be clearly understood by a beginner. We will return projects with instructions that are not written clearly enough for our needs, and will pay less if your instructions need considerable editorial help.

If at all possible, e-mail instructions directly to the editor or associate editor and include a hard copy in the box with the completed sample.

Mailing address: send submissions or proposals to Vicki Blizzard, *Creative Crafter*, 306 East Parr Road., Berne, IN 46711. E-mail submissions may be sent to Vicki at the above e-mail address.

CONTRACTS & PAYMENT

Once your project and instructions are approved, we will send an agreement with our payment offer and a pre-addressed envelope. You should complete it with your signature, phone number and Social Security number. Return the original to us in the pre-addressed envelope - the photocopy we send is for your records. (You always have the right to reject or negotiate a contractual offer.)

Payment is normally made upon acceptance.

We will keep your project until publication, so we may need to hold it for several months. Your project will be returned to you unless other arrangements are made. All manuscripts, diagrams, etc., remain our property. Since we purchase all rights to designs, you should not sell that design-or one very similar to it-to another publication. If you have questions as to what constitutes an original design, please give us a call.

We appreciate your interest in our magazines! These guidelines are meant to be just that - guidelines. If you have questions, special circumstances, etc., feel free to contact Vicki or Kelly. We will make every effort to work with you!

Categories: Nonfiction—Crafts/Hobbies—Hobbies

CONTACT: Vicki Blizzard, Editor
Material: All
306 East Parr Rd.
Berne IN 46711
Phone: 206-589-4000
Fax: 206-589-8093
E-mail: Vickie_Blizzard@whitebirches.com
Website: www.whitebirches.com

Creative Knitting

Creative Knitting is a full-color, 100-page bimonthly magazine.
Submissions

1. Project submissions or manuscripts:

• Send (1) proposal sketch with swatches; (2) your completed project; or (3) photo. Be sure to label everything with your name and address. Keep a copy of all materials.

• Project review: Knitting reviews are held six times a year for the magazine. Check the editorial calendar for dates. These projects are seasonal. Design topics and suggestions are sent to knitters in our database. They can also be requested.

• If we accept your design (s), we will contact you within two weeks after the swatch review date. Other designs will be returned within four weeks after the swatch review date.

2. Accepted projects or manuscripts:

• Be sure to label every page and tag every project with your name (as you would like it published) and e-mail and mailing address. Also list the publication in which the project will appear.

• Send the completed model and paper copy of instructions and drawings to Bobbie Matela (see address below).

• At the same time that you send the project and instructions, send us an electronic copy on disk (either MAC or PC files are acceptable) as well if you do not have email. If you have email, send a copy of magazine instructions to Joy Slayton at joyknits@joyknits.com.

• Put the pattern name in the subject line.

• In the message state Creative Knitting and the issue it will be in.

• If the instructions are sent as an attachment, state in the message what format it's in (MacWord, Wordperfect, Microsoft Word, etc.)

3. Writing guidelines:

• Type and double-space all instructions in step-by-step form, following a current magazine.

• Pay special attention to pattern stitch instructions, i.e. use k2, p2, not the upper case equivalent of K2, P2. Notice there is no space between the k or p and the stitch number.

• Do not use all caps for any part of the instructions.

• Do not use lowercase L's in place of numeral 1's.

• Complete and label graphs, diagrams and color keys. Do not use blue graph paper or a pencil because they do not photocopy well. Be sure lines are dark enough to photocopy, using ink if possible. Include charts of stitch patterns whenever possible.

• Use the abbreviations given in Creative Knitting magazine. Explain any non-standard abbreviations in your instructions.

• Write a descriptive sentence describing your project.

• State skill level, using the guidelines given in Creative Knitting magazine.

Give sizes (a minimum of three sizes, preferably four or five) and finished measurements.

• Give the model size in the instructions and on the tag on the project.

Include in the materials list the types of materials, quantities used (for all sizes) and ordering information if unavailable at most craft stores. Include any extras such as cable needles, stitch holders, markers, buttons.

• State needle size(s), including length of circular needles.

Give yardage and weight per skein/ball, fiber content, manufacturer and/or distributor (for imported yarns), color number and name (if given) and specify weight (baby/fingering, sport, DK, worsted, bulky).

• Send a yarn band for each color and kind of yarn if at all possible.

Give gauge (including approximate gauge before felting for a felted project). Measure stitches and rows/rnds over 4 inches/10cm and specify pattern (St st, stitch pattern, color pattern, etc.) and needle size used.

• Include source references for pattern stitches when available (such as Barbara Walker's books).

• Provide stitch counts at the end of all increase and decrease rows.

When increasing, specify type of increase: Knit in front & back of stitch, Make 1 (M1), etc. When decreasing, specify ssk, k2tog, etc.

• Write out any reverse shaping for all experience levels.

• Explain any technique a knitter of that experience level may not know.

4. Mailing address: Send submissions and completed projects to Bobbie Matela, Creative Knitting, 2420 Grand Avenue, Suite H, Vista, CA 92081.

5. Return of published projects: Projects accepted for publication will be returned to the designer (unless otherwise arranged) after the publication is printed. All manuscripts, diagrams, etc., remain the property of the publisher.

6. For all other questions, contact Bobbie Matela. If you have a question about the status of a design, contact Mary Ann Frits. If you have a question about pattern writing, contact Kathy Wesley.

Contracts and payment

When we receive the completed project, instructions and all related materials, we will send you a contract and a business-reply envelope. Sign the contract and return it in the postage-paid envelope. Keep the photocopy of the contract for your records and return the original to us.

Payment will be made within 45 days of the time we receive your signed contract. Amount will be determined by accuracy, creativity, workmanship, skill level, overall quality and instruction format. Average fees range from $50 to $550. Because all rights to designs are purchased, unless otherwise arranged, designers should not sell the purchased design or one very similar to it to another publisher.

We look forward to working with you in the coming months!

Categories: Nonfiction—Crafts—Hobbies

CONTACT: Bobbie Matela,, Editor
Material: All
2420 Grand Ave., Ste. H
Vista, CA 92081
Phone: 760-597-4801 ext. 129
E-mail: Bobbie_Matela@ASNpub.com
Website: www.knittingdigest.com

Creative Nonfiction

"Now that you have established this journal called *Creative Nonfiction*," people ask, "what does it mean?"

It's surprising how many writers (and readers) don't understand, exactly, the elements of the form in which they are writing. Some are attracted by the word "creative" and think that because their prose is unusual or distinctive and because the stories they are telling are true, they are writing "*Creative Nonfiction*."

Others, usually people with a journalistic background, are put off by the word "creative," maintaining that if it is creative, it certainly can't be accurate, believable, or ethical, which are the essence and anchor of nonfiction prose.

But there is no conflict between being a good "reporter" and a good writer, creative in technique and approach. The essays published in each issue of *Creative Nonfiction* are models of the truest forms of *Creative Nonfiction*, in that they simultaneously "showcase" or "frame" fact in creative context.

"Truth"—which should not be confused with the factual or informational aspects of the genre—is another important element of the "classic" *Creative Nonfiction* form-and often a more personal one. A writer's concept of the truth may not be universally accepted and may even conflict with the facts as others understand or remember them. Good *Creative Nonfiction* does not deny personal opinion: to the contrary, it welcomes the subjective voice.

Take, for example, Hilary Masters' essay, "Son of Spoon River," in our summer, 1996 "Five Fathers" issue. Masters discusses the ways in which the media and the publishing industry tend to brand or categorize people for their own comfort and pleasure, despite the personal and professional damage such "public" judgments may cause. Masters is the son of Edgar Lee Masters, of Spoon River Anthology fame; he and his father were the victims about whom he writes. The writer's message is often called the "theme" or "main point of focus."

As it was in Masters' piece, it is often the writer's personal depiction of the message that makes the work unique. Presenting the theme with a personal take makes the writer's work creative. But there are other ways in which writers can go about making their nonfiction creative.

Fiction techniques often capture a subject and add a distinctive feel that conventional journalism may not. Action-oriented scenes contain dialogue and evocative description with great specificity and detail. Fiction techniques include the use of dialogue, characterization, description, and point of view. But using the devices of fiction does not give the *Creative Nonfiction* writer a license to fabricate. John McPhee once noted that *Creative Nonfiction* is "an attempt to recognize that a piece of writing can be creative while using factual materials,that creative work can respect fact."

Writers must always respect fact-as distinguished from universal truth-in their work. Writers for *Creative Nonfiction* must present their personal interpretation of the truth without becoming overly experimental or egocentric. Though we encourage the subjective voice and encourage a unique approach, writers are still bound to the fundamental duty of journalism: to inform or teach the reader.

An essay from our third issue, "Emerging Women Writers," serves as a good example of a highly subjective voice that adheres to the principle of accuracy. The author, Lauren Slater, a practicing psychologist, used her skills as a fiction writer to give her readers insight into her struggles as a professional counselor and her own recovery from a debilitating mental illness. The reader feels close to Slater as she describes how she was assigned to counsel a patient in a hospital in which she herself had once been a patient. Every aspect of her essay was true, though she used scene and dialogue to embellish the facts into a larger and more universal truth.

There are no length requirements, although we are always searching for writers who can communicate a strong idea with drama and humor in a few pages. Payment is $10 per published page. We report in two months. Query for author profiles only.

Points to Remember When Submitting to *Creative Nonfiction*:
• Strong reportage.
• Well-written prose, attentive to language, rich with detail and distinctive voice.
• An informational quality or "teaching element" offering the reader something to learn-for example, an idea, concept, collection of facts-strengthened with insight, reflection, interpretation.
• A compelling, focused, sustained narrative that's well-structured, makes sense, and conveys a meaning.
• Manuscripts will not be accepted via fax.

Categories: Nonfiction—General Interest—Literature—Writing

CONTACT: Submissions Editor
Material: all
5501 Walnut St., Ste. 202
Pittsburgh PA 15232
Phone: 412-688-0304
Fax: 412-683-9173
E-mail: info@creativenonfiction.org

Creative With Words!

CWW will accept well-written manuscripts that focus on.
• Writing/Painting (why do I write/paint; why did I start, where do I plan to go with it)
• Photography (What can I photograph, how can I embellish my photographs, what will I do with my photographs?)
• Slogans/Idioms (take any slogan/idiom, research what it means, indicate for what purposes you would use it, whom have you convinced to use it as well)
• Quality of light, of water, of air, of fire
• Flashback (start your writing with "I remember..." or "I will never forget..."
• Wishes ("If I had, I would")
• I feel positive about.../I feel negative about...(write about it, how it influences your life; the life of others)
• Color (select a color, observe your environment for an entire day, jot down every time you see the color; then write a story about that particular color) When writing on the above topics, make sure you follow CWW's guideline before submitting your manuscripts. Manuscripts can be fiction or nonfiction.
• For further information, send CWW a FAX (831-655-8627) or an E-mail (cwwpub@usa.net),addressed to Brigitta Geltrich, Editor & Publisher; or visit CWW at its website: members.tripod.com
Creative With Words Standard Subscription Rates remain the same, please check CWW's guidelines.

CWW Guidelines

1. Focus: a) folkloristic matter; b) poetry, prose, language/ computer art by children (state age of child and verify authentic- city of writing); and by all ages; special interest groups, senior citizens (state age), disabled (state why), shut-ins (state why).

2. Language: English; translations by a native English speaker from another language. All manuscripts will be edited by CWW.

3. Manuscripts: Typed or legibly written: prose double-spaced, 1 poem per page, 1" margin (all sides); give name, home address, age (if child, up to 19) top left on every page; number pages.

Use standard font, size 12. Do not fax manuscripts. You may E-mail manuscripts. Send no more than 3 poems/prose by one author to any CWW theme.

4. Length: Poetry: up to 20 lines, up to 46 characters across any line. Prose: 800 words maximum. Shorter poems/prose have a better chance, if of quality. Our staff readers do count the words. Longer poems, if of quality, are converted to prose, or they are returned. Longer prose are returned with request to rewrite.

5. Format: Title poems (except haikus); do not indent each line differently, nor put a single word on a separate line. Title prose. If not titled, CWW will provide title.

6. Style: Poetry: any; folkloristic tales: any; folkloristic research: use MLA Handbook for Writers of Research Papers, Theses, and Dissertations. Prose: Quality writing. Use no brand names, names of companies, movies, television shows, etc. CWW is not their endorser.

7. Content: CWW publishes according to set themes. Violence of any nature, over-preoccupation with death, racial slurs or preferences, pornographic material, or current sensationalism will not be accepted.

8. Cover Letter: Include cover letter or CWW submittal form, stating name of project submitted to.

9. Multiple Submissions: Are not accepted.

10. Previously-Published Manuscripts: Are not accepted. If of folkloristic nature, permission of reprint must be enclosed.

11. SASE (self-addressed-stamped envelope with sufficient postage + 2 oz. for CWW material): Must accompany all manuscripts & correspondence. Rule: Manuscripts and correspondence submitted without SASE are destroyed at end of month submitted. A self- addressed envelope without postage is not a SASE. You may use E-mail, make sure to give return E-mail, for CWW to respond.

12. Query: Is preferred. CWW does not publish self- contained books. CWW publishes anthologies according to set themes. See theme list for the each year.

13. Copyright: CWW Publications. After publication, rights revert back to author for submission elsewhere. CWW requests a credit line be given to CWW for having published the item first. Content and graphics submitted must be copyright-free or a copyright-clearance statement must be included.

14. Evaluation: By CWW staff or guest readers; folkloristic items are read by guest scholars of folklore. CWW editors take the readers' and scholars' suggestions into consideration when further evaluating manuscripts. All manuscripts must reflect the standards of CWW. CWW offers suggestions how to improve rejected stories/ poems.

15. Reading Time: One month after deadline of theme. First notice might come one year after submitting to a specific theme. It is the writer's responsibility to notify CWW of any changes in the status of the manuscript or in change of writer's address.

16. Payment: Writers/poets published by CWW receive 20% discount on copies purchased of issue containing the writing; orders of 10 to 19 copies, writers receive a 30% discount; on orders of 20 or more copies, writers/schools/libraries receive 40% off. Note: A poet/writer does not have to order a copy to get published; however, a poet/writer should not use the services of CWW to claim "acceptance" only. There are neither tear sheets nor free copies. Accepted material is not returned. Byline: name of writer/ poet, age (if child/senior), city and state. "Best of the Month" writer receives 1 free copy (general anthologies) or US$10 plus 1 free copy (the Eclectics only). Final decision of CWW as to winners is not negotiable. Online contest winner receives a 3-month subscription to CWW, runner-ups receive a prize.

17. Contract: No contract. A statement of publishing intent is forwarded with acceptance notification and guidelines, at which time a writer/poet may withdraw manuscript within a given time.

18. Publications per Annum: 4-6 anthologies, written by all ages; 4 anthologies written by children (must be written by children, up to 19 years of age, not by well-meaning adults); 4 the Eclectics by adults (20 and over) only.

19. Market/Readership: Family, schools, libraries, universities- ties, editors,physicians, political and religious leaders, shut- ins. CWW publications are evaluated at trade fairs and trade conferences and are presented at book fairs; some are used in reading classes.

20. Editors/Advisors: Editor-in-Chief/Publisher: Brigitta Geltrich; Visiting Editor: Bert Hower; Advisor: D.G. Spencer Ludgate; Web-site advisors: D. G. Spencer Ludgate and K. Peter Geldreich; Nature Artist: Elaine Koppany; Humor/Folklore Artist J. F. Plotkin; Wood Sculpture;Artist: Henning Kristensen.

21. Editorial Office: P.O. Box 223226, Carmel, CA, USA 93922; FAX 831-655-8627 (this is not a telephone).

22. Cost of Issues: Single: US$11-13 ($11 for 50-60pp; $12 for 61-80pp; $13 for 81+ pp.). *Special:* US$15-20; Back Issues: US$6. Subscription: 12 issues for US$60; 6 issues for US$36; 3 issues for US$21 (state whether to include the four children only issues or the four adults only issues). Credit-card orders are not accepted at this time. Libraries and schools receive a 10% discount. Back-order status is set by CWW. Most issues do not make it to back- order status.

23. Reading Fees: Are reasonable and available. Write to CWW for information and fee, include SASE.

24. Check: Make check payable to: Brigitta Ludgate. Thank you! (Sorry, we must charge a $20 fine on returned checks.)

See our website to download the CWW Manuscript Submittal Form Thank you for submitting your manuscript to *Creative With Words* Publications (CWW). Manuscripts will be placed in appropriate theme file and processed after deadline of theme. You will be notified one way or the other within two to four weeks after deadline.

Categories: Fiction—Adventure—Animals—Children—Comedy—Culture—Education—Family—Gardening—History—Juvenile—Outdoors—Poetry—Relationships—Senior Citizen—Short Stories—Teen—Travel—Writing—Young Adult—Folklore—Humor—Nature

CONTACT: Brigitta Geltrich, Editor/Publisher
Material: All
PO Box 223226
Carmel CA 93922
Phone: 408-655-8627
Fax: 831-655-8627
E-mail: CWWPUB@USA.NET
Website: member.tripod.com/creativewithwords

Cricket

For a sample issue of CRICKET, please send $5.00 to: CRICKET Sample Copy • P.O. Box 300 • Peru, IL 61354. NOTE: Sample copy requests from foreign countries must be accompanied by International Postal Reply Coupons (IRCs) valued at US $5.00. Please do NOT send a check or money order. In September 1973, Open Court Publishing Company started publication of CRICKET, a literary magazine for young people. CRICKET is now published by Carus Publishing Company. CRICKET, for readers ages 9 to 14, publishes original stories, poems, and articles written by the world's best authors for children and young adults. In some cases, CRICKET purchases rights for excerpts from books yet to be published. Each issue also includes several reprints of high-quality selections. CRICKET measures 8" x 10", contains 64 pages, has a full-color cover, and is staple bound. Full-color and black-and-white illustrations of the highest quality appear throughout the magazine. We hope the following information will be useful to prospective contributors. —Editor-in-Chief, Marianne Carus

*Published:*12 months a year

Price: $35.97 for 1-year subscription (12 issues)

Comments: CRICKET would like to reach as many illustrators and authors as possible for original contributions, but our standards are very high, and we will accept only top-quality material. PLEASE DO NOT QUERY FIRST. CRICKET will consider any manuscripts or art samples sent on speculation and accompanied by a self-addressed, stamped envelope. For art, send tear sheets or photo prints/photocopies. PLEASE DO NOT send original artwork. Be sure that each sample is marked with your name, address, and phone number. Allow 12 weeks for a reply. Themes CRICKET does not publish an advance list of themes. Submissions on all appropriate topics will be considered at any time during the year. CRICKET normally purchases the following rights for works appearing in the magazine. For stories and poems previously unpublished, rights vary.

Payment is made upon publication.

For stories and poems previously published, CRICKET purchases second North American publication rights. Fees vary, but are generally less than fees for first publication rights. Payment is made upon publication. Same applies to accompanying art.

For recurring features, CRICKET purchases the material outright. The work becomes the property of CRICKET, and it is copyrighted in the name of Carus Publishing Company. A flat fee per feature is usually negotiated. Payment is made upon publication.

For commissioned artwork, rights vary. However, in all cases, the terms outlined below apply:

a. Physical art remains the property of the illustrator.

b. Payment is made within 45 days of acceptance.

c. Illustrator may use artwork for self promotion.

Art Submissions: CRICKET commissions all art separately from the text. Any review samples of artwork will be considered. Samples of both color and black-and-white work (where applicable) are appreciated. It is especially helpful to see pieces showing young people, animals, action scenes, and several scenes from a narrative (i.e., story) showing a character in different situations and emotional states. CRICKET accepts work in a number of different styles and media, including pencil, pen and ink, watercolor, acrylic, oil, pastels, scratch board, and woodcut. While we need humorous illustration, we cannot use work that is overly caricatured or "cartoony." We are always looking for strong realism. Many assignments will require artist's research into a particular scientific field, world culture, or historical period.

TYPES OF WORK IN CRICKET.

Fiction: realistic, contemporary, historical, humor, mysteries, fantasy, science fiction, folk tales, fairy tales, legends, myths.

Nonfiction: biography, history, science, technology, natural history, social science, archeology, architecture, geography, foreign culture, travel, adventure, sports (A bibliography is required for all nonfiction articles. Be prepared to send other backup materials and photo references—where applicable—upon request).

Poetry: serious, humorous, nonsense rhymes.

Other: crossword puzzles, logic puzzles, math puzzles, crafts, recipes, science experiments, games and activities from other countries, plays, music, art.

LENGTH

Stories: 200 to 2,000 words (2 to 8 pages).

Articles: 200 to 1,500 words (2 to 6 pages).

Poems: not longer than 50 lines (1 page, 2 pages maximum) An exact word count should be noted on each manuscript submitted. For poetry, indicate number of lines instead. Word count includes every word, but does not include the title of the manuscript or the author's name.

RATES

Stories and articles up to 25¢ per word

Poems up to $3.00 per line.

Payment upon publication.

Categories: Fiction—Nonfiction—Children—Literature—Poetry—Short Stories

CONTACT: Submissions Editor
Material: Manuscript Submissions
CONTACT: Ron McCutchan, Senior Art Director
Material: Art Samples
CONTACT: Mary Ann Hocking, Rights and Permissions Manager
Material: Rights and Permissions
PO Box 300
Peru IL 61354
Phone: 815-224-5803, ext. 656

Fax: 815-224-6615
Website: www.cricketmag.com

Crochet World

General Information
House of White Birches publishes *Crochet World* magazine, a full-color, 48-page bimonthly.

Submissions/Designer Guidelines
Project submissions or manuscripts:

Send (1) proposal sketch with swatches; (2) your completed project; or (3) photo. Be sure to label everything with your name and address. Keep a copy of all materials.

Project review: Reviews are held approximately every eight weeks. Check the editorial calendar for dates. Many of these projects are seasonal. Editorial calendars can be requested.

If we accept your design(s), we will contact you within two weeks after the review date. Other designs will be returned within four weeks after the review date.

E-mail projects or manuscripts:

If we have accepted your project after seeing the swatch or photo, e-mail the pattern instructions to Susan Hankins at shankins@conknet.com. Send the completed model and paper copy of the instructions and drawings to Susan Hankins.

Put the pattern name in the subject line.

In the message, state the project will appear in *Crochet World*.

If the instructions are sent as an attachment, state in the message what format they're in (MacWord, Microsoft Word, etc.)

Be sure to label every page and tag every project with your name (as you would like it published) and address.

Mailing address: Send submissions and completed projects to Susan Hankins, *Crochet World*, 6 Pearl Street, P.O. Box 776, Henniker, NH 03242-0776. Correct return postage is required.

Writing Guidelines:
Type and double-space all instructions in step-by-step form in 12 point font size, following a current publication.

Pay special attention to pattern stitch instructions

Do not use all caps for any part of the instructions.

Do not use lowercase L's in place of numeral 1's.

Complete and label graphs, diagrams and color keys. Do not use blue graph paper or a pencil because they do not photocopy well. Be sure lines are dark enough to photocopy, using ink if possible.

Use the abbreviations given in *Crochet World* magazine. Explain any non-standard abbreviations in your instructions.

Write a descriptive sentence describing your project.

State skill level: Beginner, intermediate or advanced.

Give sizes (a minimum of three sizes, preferably four or five) and finished measurements.

Give the model size in the instructions and on the tag of the project.

Include in the materials list the types of materials, quantities used and ordering information if unavailable at most craft stores. Include any extras such as stitch holders, markers, buttons, sequins, ribbon, fiberfill, etc.

State hook size(s).

Give yardage and weight per skein or ball, fiber content, manufacturer and/or distributor (for imported yarns), color number and name (if given) and specify weight (baby/fingering yarn, sport, DK, worsted, bulky, etc.)

Send a yarn or thread band (label) for each color and kind of yarn if at all possible.

Give gauge. Measure stitches and rows/rnds over 1 or 2 inches (example: 4 sc = 1 inch; 5 sc rows = 1 inch).

Provide stitch counts at the end of all increase and decrease rows.

Explain any technique a crocheter of that experience level may not know.

Small poems (less than 3 typeset column inches) pay $20; on rare occasions we publish non-pattern manuscripts that must relate to crochet in some way. They must be less than one typeset page.

Payment is $50-$100.

Proofread your instructions several times to eliminate possible errors. Suggestions: Have a crocheting friend read over your patterns to help spot errors or hard-to-follow sections.

House of White Birches will be responsible for all photography.

Contracts and payment
After our review and decision of acceptance, we will send you a contract and a business-reply envelope. Sign the contract and return it in the postage-paid envelope. Keep the photocopy of the contract for your records and return the original to us.

Payment will be made within 45 days of the time we receive your contract. Amount will be determined by accuracy, creativity, workmanship, skill level, overall quality and instruction format. Average fees range from $50 to $400. Because HWB purchases all rights to designs unless otherwise arranged, designers should not sell the purchased design or one very similar to it to another publisher.

If you have any questions, contact Susan Hankins.

jkn 02/02

Categories: Nonfiction—Crafts/Hobbies—Hobbies—Needlework

CONTACT: Susan Hankins, Editor
Material: All
6 Pearl Street
PO Box 776
Henniker NH 03242-0776
Phone: 206-589-4000
Fax: 206-589-8093
E-mail: shankins@conknet.com or
shankins@whitebirches.com
Website: www.crochet-world.com

CRONE CHRONICLES®
A Journal of Conscious Aging

Crone Chronicles
A Journal of Conscious Aging

General Information
Our readers are women (and some wonderful men) from their early 30's to 100, the majority of them from 40 to 80. Some come from New Age backgrounds, others are much more traditional. What we all have in common is a commitment to conscious aging, which includes transforming the derogatory meaning of the word "Crone". If you feel this kind of commitment yourself, then we welcome your contributions to the *Crone Chronicles*. Most of each issue is created from readers' contributions, so your willingness to share is vital to this journal!

Crone Chronicles is geared mainly towards women. However, we do not wish to limit our readers to women, nor to assume that men are excluded from the wisdom of Crone. Indeed, on an archetypal level, we assume that as each woman includes male and female elders within her, so does each man. With that understanding, both men and women are welcome to submit to this journal for possible publication.

The following guidelines may help you gear your submission to the context of *Crone Chronicles*.

Subject Matter
All submissions - whether written or artistic - should focus in some way on issues relating to the aging process itself or to perceptions of any subject which are altered or filtered through the process of "growing older". What we are looking for is the expression of "one's own unique Crone point of view". In other words, we wish to publish the wisdom you have gained from your experience, and strongly prefer submissions which are either written entirely from a personal point of view, or at least include personal experience as an example of what is being talked about. Thus, most of what we publish is non-fiction. Fic-

tion and myth will be considered, but only as they are particularly relevant to Crone.

Written Submissions

All written submissions should be the original work of the author. As a web-based magazine, we strongly prefer that all submissions be made by email. Items submitted in other ways may be delayed or ignored. Articles should be no more than 1000 words in length. Please include your name, address and phone number. Please be clear about the name under which you wish us to publish your material if we decide to use it.

We do edit for clarity, grammar, and sometimes for length. If you do not want your article edited in any way, please type "Do not edit" at the top of the manuscript clearly and in large letters. We will respect your wishes; however you should be aware that we are far less likely to publish manuscripts so marked.

Please include the article in the body of the email and NOT as an attached file. Apart from your name and contact information, please also tell us something about yourself when you email us. Accompanying artwork and photos are welcome. See guidelines below.

Writers: here is your chance to tell your stories! Personal essays, reviews, journal entries, dreams, jokes, cartoons, asides - all are welcome. *Crone Chronicles* is here to help document and report on the Crone archetype as she resurrects Herself from within the ashes of the patriarchal culture.

Graphic Art

All graphic art submissions should be the original work of the artist.

For the web issue, please submit your artwork in RGB JPEG format. If your artwork is line art, please also simultaneously submit a copy in GIF (89a) format with a transparent background. Graphic artwork can be in any size or dimensions in pixels. However, please ensure that the file you send is no larger than 100k. Should we decide to publish your artwork, we reserve the right to crop the image or alter its size. The resolution should be 72 dpi. If this is unacceptable to you, please state clearly at the time of submission.

Photography

All photographic submissions should be the original work of the photographer. If persons other than the photographer are shown, a signed release from said person(s) must be included in order for us to publish the photo. We are especially interested in photos of old women whose beauty of character shows in their faces and bodies; also in subject matter which is reminds us in some way of Crone. (For example, old trees, plants in their winter appearance, crossroads, gateways, etc.)

For the web issue, please submit your photos in RGB JPEG format Your photos can be in any size or dimensions in pixels, but the resolution should be screen resolution of 72 dpi. However, please ensure that the file you send is no larger than 100k. Should we decide to publish your artwork, we reserve the right to crop the image or alter its size. If this is unacceptable to you, please state clearly at the time of submission.

How to Submit

We prefer material that has not been published or seen previously - please inform us of multiple submissions or previous publication. For web issue submissions, please read the guidelines under the relevant sections above. You may submit material by email to the Editor.

Compensation and Rights

Unfortunately, *Crone Chronicles* does not offer cash compensation for unsolicited artwork, photography or written work.

If your material is published on the site, you will receive notification via email.

Copyright for all work reverts to authors and artists upon publication. However, we may also wish to reprint it in future *Crone Chronicles* collections. Please let us know if that is not possible.

If there are any questions which these guidelines do not cover, please feel free to call or email for more information, or simply to try out your ideas on us!. Please leave a message if we are not here to receive your call.

Thanks for your interest in *Crone Chronicles*. We look forward to hearing from you soon.

Blessings,

Ann Kreilkamp

Categories: Nonfiction—Biography—Culture—Feminism—Health—Inspirational—Interview—Lifestyle—Paranormal—Poetry—Psychology—Relationships—Religion—Senior Citizen—Sexuality—Spiritual—Women's Issues—New Age—Philosophy

CONTACT: Ann Kreilkamp, Editor
Material: All
PO Box 81
Kelly WY 83011
Phone: 307-733-5409
Fax: 307-733-8639
E-mail: submissions@cronechronicles.com
For FEDEX/UPS—c/o Jackson Holistic Center
70 Gros Ventre St.
Jackson WY 83001
Website: www.cronechronicles.com

Cross & Quill

The Christian Writers Newsletter

Cross & Quill
The Christian Writers Newsletter

Cross & Quill serves an audience of writers, speakers, editors, conference directors, group leaders, researchers, and agents involved in the Christian publishing industry. Please keep that in mind when submitting. Need more nuts and bolts (this is how to write it) articles. Rarely use personal experiences except for Writing Rainbows!

Our purpose is to inform, instruct, encourage, and equip Christians in publishing to produce writing of the highest biblical and professional standards.

OUR NEEDS ARE AS FOLLOWS:

Meet the Pro: Assigned. Front page features one of our professional members.

This Side of the Desk: Written in-house.

Writing Rainbows!: 500 to 600 word devotional thought including Scripture and prayer that comes from your writing experience. Give Bible translation.

Writers Helping Writers: 200 to 800 words. More instructional and how-to articles, fewer personal experiences. Need more articles directed to the veteran, rather than the beginning writer. (Feature Article)

Tots, Teens, & In Betweens: 200 to 800 word how-to and informational articles on writing for the juvenile marketplace. (Feature Article)

Editors Soapbox: Assigned. Dave Fessenden, Contributing Editor.

Editors Round Table: 200 to 800 word interviews with editors on current needs of the publication or publishing house. Ask questions that help writers understand the joys, frustrations, and challenges of editorial work. Find out what the editor has often wanted to tell writers to make the editor's and the writer's jobs easier, more productive, and more profitable. Professional quality photo of editor improves chances of acceptance. (Feature Article)

Computer Wise: Assigned. Kay Hall, Contributing Editor.

Business Wise: 200 to 800 how-to and informa tional articles on the business side of writing such as tax information, recordkeeping, and other related topics.

Legal Ease: 200 to 800 words on various legalities in the writing profession: contracts, copyright, etc. (Feature Article)

Connecting Points: 200 to 800 word how-to's on leading and attending writers groups. Especially want articles on how to critique various kinds of writing such as nonfiction, fiction, poetry, and others. Also group program ideas.

The Conference Circuit: Organizing and operating writers workshops and conferences â " successes and learning experiences. Also profiles of Christian writers conferences. State availability of photos.

Poetry: 1 to 8 line poems on helpful and inspirational topics, limit 3 per envelope.

Fillers: 25 to 100 word helpful hints, newsbreaks, tips, cartoons. Book and other writing product reviews, 100 to 300 words.

Submissions: Prefers complete manuscript submitted by regular mail. No simultaneous submissions.

Rights: Buys first or reprint rights. If manuscript is a reprint, state when and where the piece has been used.

Payment: Honorarium on publication for features as indicated above. For all others, payment in 3 contributors copies.

Sample copy of *Cross & Quill* available for $2 and 9x12 SASE w/ 2 first class stamps.

E-mail Submissions to This Address Only: CQArticles@cwfi-online.org.

Postal submissions not accompanied by SASE will not be returned.

Categories: Nonfiction—Arts—Associations—Careers—Christian Interests—Education—Internet—Language—Literature—Poetry—Religion—Writing

CONTACT: Sandy Brooks, Editor/Publisher
Material: All
c/o Christian Writers Fellowship International
1624 Jefferson Davis Rd.
Clinton SC 29325-6401
Phone: 864-697-6035
E-mail: CQArticles@cwfi-online.org (submissions)
E-mail: sandybrooks@cwfi-online.org
Website: www.cwfi-online.org

Cruising World

Although *Cruising World*'s editorial inventory is already planned and almost filled for 2002, we continue to welcome author inquiries and unsolicited manuscripts. All manuscripts should be typed double-spaced and accompanied by an electronic version, as well as by appropriate artwork such as transparencies or color prints. Color prints do not generally reproduce well, but if submitted should be accompanied by negatives. Good sketches are also acceptable. Manuscripts submitted for Feature consideration (center of the magazine) should be written in the first person and not exceed approximately 2,500 words. Manuscripts submitted for consideration as Non-features (technical articles and general interest, front and back of the magazine) should not exceed 2,000 words. "Log style" articles are generally unacceptable.

Due to the volume of manuscripts we receive, we regret we cannot offer critiques of unacceptable material. Payment varies depending on the type of article, ranging from $50 to $200 for short, newsworthy items and $300 to $800 for technical and feature articles. We buy all World Periodical Rights and pay within 90 days of acceptance.

Write your name and address on every page of your manuscript and on each photograph, slide or sketch. We cannot be responsible for anything that does not bear the sender's name. Also number and identify each slide and print on a brief caption sheet. If your manuscript involves a cruise, please include a photocopy of a map or chart with the places you visited clearly marked on it. Please enclose an author bio note with sailing history and identify the people and type of boat in the story.

Manuscripts submitted to *Cruising World* must not be sent to other magazines for consideration during the same time period. Such simultaneous submissions could cause an infringement of copyright laws. If, however, your manuscript has previously been published in part or in whole, let us know. Our rates vary with each individual submission.

Within about six weeks after we receive your manuscript, after the editors have had a chance to review your contribution, we will either accept it for publication or return it to you. Dates of publication remain tentative. Generally, it takes one year for a piece to reach publication.

Please be sure that you use a consistent permanent (not transient) address in all correspondence with *Cruising World*. Also, please note your telephone number and e-mail address on your cover letter, and enclose a self-addressed, stamped envelope large enough to contain your submission and any accompanying artwork.

Categories: Nonfiction—Boating—Lifestyle—Outdoors—Recreation—Sports/Recreation

CONTACT: Manuscripts Editor
Material: All
5 John Clarke Rd.
PO Box 3400
Newport RI 02840-0992
Phone: 401-845-5141
Website: www.cruisingworld.com

Crusader
A Magazine for Cadets and Their Friends

Please refer to *Cadet Quest* in the periodical section.

Custom Rodder

Circulation: 45,000
Frequency: Bi-monthly
Published by the PRIMEDIA Enthusiast Group.

Devoted to the modification and upgrading of American-made automobiles from the late forties to the present. Editors who appreciate and work on these cars themselves share their enthusiasm via on-the-spot participation and color coverage of events, immersing the leader in the beauty and nostalgia of these one-of-a-kind vehicles. Editorial includes how-to tech articles, tips, advice, and expertise. For more information, visit the magazine's Web site at: www.customrodderweb.com.

Editorial Submissions

Contributions Welcomed, but editors recommend that contributors query first. Contribution must be accompanied by return postage and we assume no responsibility for loss or damage thereto.

Manuscripts must be typewritten and submitted on white paper, with a disc copy enclosed enclosed (Microsoft Word format preferred). All photographs must be accompanied by captions.

Electronic images, Polaroid photographs and color copies are not acceptable for print publication. Photo model releases are required for all persons in photos.

Categories: Nonfiction—Automobiles—Hobbies

CONTACT: Editor
Material: All
Corporate Headquarters
McMullen Argus Publishing Inc.
2400 E. Katella Avenue, 11th Floor
Anaheim CA 92806
Phone: 714-939-2400
Fax: 714-978-6390
E-mail: robt@mcmullenargus.com
Website: www.customrodderweb.com

CutBank
University of Montana

Guidelines for Artists and Writers

CutBank is interested in art, poetry and fiction of high quality and serious intent. We regularly print work by both well-known and previously unpublished artists. All manuscripts are considered for the Richard Hugo Memorial Poetry Award and the A.B. Guthrie, Jr. Short Fiction Award.

We accept submissions from August 15 until March 15. The deadline for the spring issue is November 15, and for the fall issue it's March 15.

Include an SASE for response or return of submitted material.

Manuscripts must be typed or letter quality printout, double-spaced, and paginated. Your name should appear on each page. We encourage the use of paper clips over staples.

Fiction writers should submit only one story at a time, no longer than 40 pages. Poets may submit up to 5 poems.

Artists and photographers may submit up to 5 works at one time. Send slides or reproductions only; do not send original art.

If a piece has been submitted simultaneously to another publication, please let us know.

Please address all submissions to the appropriate editor—poetry, fiction, or art.

Categories: Fiction—Nonfiction—Poetry—Short Stories

CONTACT: Anne Holub, Poetry Editor
Material: Poetry
CONTAC: Siobhan Scarry, Fiction Editor
Material: Fiction/Nonfiction
Department of English
The University of Montana-Missoula
Missoula MT 59812
Phone: 406-243-6156
Fax: 406-243-4076
E-mail: cutbank@selway.umt.edu
Website: www.umt.edu/cutbank

Cutting Tool Engineering

Editorial Mission Statement:

CUTTING TOOL ENGINEERING is published for managers and engineers in the machining industry. The magazine provides timely and practical information on the procurement, use, and maintenance of cutting and grinding equipment, tools, and related accessories. CTE readers work in a wide variety of market segments, but the heaviest concentration is in the automotive and aerospace industries. The magazine has been published since 1955 and has a BPA-audited circulation of 35,000.

Submissions: We urge you to submit article documents electronically. In order of preference, documents may be sent in Word or Rich Text Format (RTF). E-mail communication is strongly encouraged, but disk or CD submission is acceptable. Artwork that illustrates the article is primarily your responsibility unless prior permission is granted in advance. The availability of artwork is a serious consideration for timely publication. Please review our artwork guidelines.

Style: We ask, if possible, that you follow the Associated Press writing style and use Webster's Ninth edition dictionary to resolve spelling and non-technical conflicts concerning word definition. Please write in the present tense. We encourage the use of common industry trade terms, but please spell out all acronyms on the first reference.

Any company mentioned in an article must include a city and state reference. Any person mentioned in the article must also include their job title, employer, city and state.

All articles must contain your byline. Please include a brief biography, including your current title and your employer's name and location.

Content: We will work with all authors to establish a working title. The author and editor work together to develop deadlines for an outline, first rough draft, final rough draft and the submission of artwork.

A narrow focus is essential. Providing relevant technical detail and a complete explanation of a subject are hallmarks of CTE articles. We ask that you maintain this tradition. If you can picture yourself telling a competent machine apprentice about why it works-and the cookbook recipe needed to correctly apply it on the shop floor-then you should find yourself at the right level of detail.

CTE readers are technically astute and very careful readers that want direct, unbiased information. Therefore, we do not accept so-called "advertorials," including case history/application stories. Submissions must be generic in nature and not specific to a single vendor's product or process unless that product or process is truly revolutionary and receives prior approval from CTE before an outline is submitted.

Length: Articles can range from 1,000 to 2,500 words, depending on the subject. However, our experience has shown that feature articles submitted below 2,000 words do not explain the subject in sufficient detail. On the other hand, articles that approach 3,000 words indicate a subject that is too broad for a magazine article.

Artwork: Photos, charts, graphs, and other visuals are necessary for any article that is being considered for publication. There is a distinct acceptance advantage for authors that can provide-or identify sources-of artwork for their articles. The most desirable photo shows a process in action, and an action photo is essential for a cover story. Unfortunately, great application photos are not commonplace in the industry. And most digital cameras that take great photos for Web pages and other types of screen viewing are useless for publication work. Technical requirements for submitting electronic files for publication in CUTTING TOOL ENGINEERING:

Photographic images: We accept black-and-white and 4-color photographic images, saved in either .TIFF or .EPS format.

To achieve the best print quality, images should have a resolution of approximately 266 dpi. Color images should be saved in CMYK (not RGB) format. Black-and-white images should be saved in grayscale mode. Mac files are preferable, but we can read correctly formatted images created on an IBM platform.

Art files (ads, illustrations, etc.): We accept black-and-white and color art files, MACINTOSH FORMAT ONLY, in the following applications: Quark Xpress, Adobe Illustrator, Adobe PageMaker, Adobe Photoshop, and Macromedia Freehand. All fonts and supporting graphics files used in creating the art must be included. Contact the production department for guidelines when preparing your files.

- *Quark/PageMaker:*
  Save files as native Quark or PageMaker files — do not save as EPS or postscript files.
  Include all linked images.
  Include all fonts used in document, (both screen and printer fonts).
  If your file is to print black-and-white, all graphic elements must be black-and-white.
  If your file is to print 4-color, graphic elements must be black-and-white or 4-color process (CMYK).
  If your file is to print with pms colors and includes color graphics, please contact production department to verify ad color.
  Provide a laser proof and/or a color proof.
- *Adobe Illustrator*
  Save files as Illustrator 6.0 or Illustrator EPS for Macintosh.
  Set preview to "Color Macintosh"
  Convert all text to outlines—or—include all fonts on disk (both screen and printer fonts).
  Provide a laser proof and/or a color proof.
- *Macromedia Freehand*
  Save files as Freehand Document or export as Macintosh EPS.
  Convert all text to paths - or — include all fonts on disk (both screen and printer fonts).
  Provide a laser proof and/or a color proof.

- *We accept electronic files on the following media only:*
  3.5" floppy (Mac or PC)
  Zip 100 disk (Mac or PC)
  Syquest 44MB, 88MB, 135 MB EZ-drive cartridges (Mac only)
  CD-Rom (Mac or PC)

We currently do not accept files over the Internet.

Questions?

Contact Claudia Gray, Art Director @ 847-714-0178.

Authors must plan for artwork very early. The author should submit possible sources of artwork with the outline. You may initially get very positive responses for artwork. But responses can and do get rescinded because of trade secret concerns or customer objectives. Progressive companies understand that continuous improvement is the key to protecting market position. Those companies will likely have an enlightened view regarding artwork-but don't count on it.

For more information contact Don Nelson, editorial director and publisher @ 847-714-0173 or dnelson@jwr.com.

Categories: Nonfiction—Engineering—Technical—Trade: Metal Working

CONTACT: Don Nelson, Editorial Director and Publisher
Material: All
John Wm.. Roberts & Associates, Inc.
400 Skokie Blvd., #395
Northbrook IL 60062-7903
Phone: 847-714-0175
E-mail: dnelson@jwr.com

Dakota Outdoors
Premier Outdoor Magazine of the Dakotas

Dakota Outdoors is a regional, monthly (12 issues per year) outdoor publication for and about the Dakotas. *Dakota Outdoors* contains feature articles about fishing, hunting and other outdoor pursuits. *Dakota Outdoors* focuses on how- and where-to articles, written by local sportsmen, that provide a local perspective on outdoor life in the Dakotas that you cannot get elsewhere. We also cover legislative, governmental and regulatory concerns, as well as product information, hints and tips, personalities, and humor relative to our *Dakota Outdoors*. Articles from writers outside our region are welcome, so long as they cover topics of concern to Dakotans.

Articles submitted should be applicable to the outdoor life in the Dakotas.

Topics: Topics should center on fishing and hunting experiences and advice. Other topics, such as boating, camping, hiking, environmental concerns and general nature, will be considered as well.

Rights: Exclusive rights to an article are not mandatory, but we would like to have exclusive rights in our area. Please inform us if the article has been, or will be, published elsewhere.

Deadlines: Timely articles are important. Typically, copy deadline is the 10th of the month prior to the month of publication.

Photos: Photos will also be considered for publication. Either color or black and white prints or negatives (not slides unless requested) are acceptable. If prints, a 5"x7" size is preferable, but larger or smaller sizes are acceptable. If submitted with an article, the photo should be pertinent to the article. All photos should be identified with the photographer's name and address as well as the name and address of the subject(s). The location where the photo was taken should be included as well. Photos will be returned with SASE.

Format: Articles should be submitted in typewritten form, double spaced. A headline and byline should be included on the submission. Articles will be accepted on computer disk in one of two forms. Either a 5.25" disk in an IBM compatible format with ASCII text or a 3.5" disk in an Apple Macintosh format will be acceptable. Computer disks will be returned after use. Please inquire for other formats. If submitting on disk, please let us know what format the file is in. Submissions will also be accepted on CompuServe at the address shown below.

Rates: Rates are negotiable and depend upon the quality of the article and the amount of work necessary to put it into final form. Rates typically run from $5 to $50 per article. If a specific rate is requested, the price should be negotiated prior to publication.

Kids Korner: *Dakota Outdoors* publishes a kids outdoors column each month. We look for articles addressing kids from 12 to 16 years of age, from 50 to 500 words in length. Payment will generally range for $5 to $15.

Shorts & Fillers: *Dakota Outdoors* accepts shorts and fillers and uses them on an as needed basis. There is generally no payment for these items. If you submit a short of filler item and require payment, please notify us in advance.

Payment: Payment will be made for articles and photos after the issue is published, unless other arrangements are made.

Categories: Fishing—Hunting

CONTACT: Rachel Engbrecht, Managing Editor
Material: All
PO Box 669
Pierre SD 57501-0669
Phone: 605-224-7301
Fax: 605-224-9210
E-mail: 73613.3456@compuserve.com

Dance Spirit

SUBJECT MATTER

DS is about all idioms of dance as well as choreography, fitness, nutrition, education and competitions. All articles are assigned; send pitches rather than unsolicited finished copy. Our approach is educational/instructional. Use quotes from the company or individual artist as a way of teaching the lesson to be learned.

The most successful queries demonstrate a familiarity with our regular columns and departments. When pitching, please send your resume, indicating all dance experience, as each issue focuses on a theme you may or may not be qualified to write about.

Readership: Most of our readers are in their mid-teens to mid-20s. They are pre-professional dancers with aspirations of careers on Broadway, in professional companies and in music videos. They want to know how to get there.

Language: upbeat and peppy, but intelligent

SUBMISSIONS

All submissions must be in electronic format. E-mail is preferred. Please include a title and a deck with all submissions. All manuscripts should follow Associated Press style.

Artwork: Art must be submitted with each story unless otherwise arranged. Do not pitch a story without first knowing that there is quality artwork to accompany it. Send as much art as you can so we have options. Performance photos are preferred. Label the back of each piece of artwork with a return address if you need it returned. Do not use a pen that will bleed ink onto another picture.

Caption and credit all artwork: Captions should include names of performers, name of choreographer, title of piece, name of company and photographer or photo credit. EX: Sally Smith and Jane Brown of Ballet Company in Susan Camp's [ital: Energetic Flight]. Credit: John Jump

We accept high-contrast photos, slides and e-mail submissions. Please make sure that the images submitted via e-mail are high-resolution, CMYK or greyscale and that they are 300 dpi (minimum). Images saved for Web pages are generally not acceptable as they are low-resolution.

When sending images taken by a digital camera, please capture them at the highest resolution setting the camera is capable of taking.

Manuscript: Do not use serial commas before "and". EX: ballet, jazz and modern. Use computer-generated em-dashes whenever possible; otherwise, use two hyphens, no spaces. We do not use en-dashes.

DO NOT FORMAT YOUR DOCUMENTS. All italics and bold-faced words should be in brackets, indicating the correct formatting. EX: [BF: Don't Forget:] George Delancey's piece [Ital: On The Fence] will be performed April 3.

Do not leave more than one space after periods.

Columns are 600 words; features are between 800 and 1200 words.

CONTRACT

Pay is received after your work is published. We own all rights to your work, including the right to post it on our website. Missed deadlines will not get you another assignment. We pay a 25 percent kill fee.

Categories: Nonfiction—Arts—Dance—Entertainment

CONTACT: Editor: Laura Teusink
Material: Broadway/Celebrities/Special Events & Awards/Hip Hop Dance/Dancewear/Dance Competitions & Conventions
CONTACT: Managing Editor: Sara Jarrett
Material: Features/Nutrition/Modern or Lyrical Dance/Dance Team
CONTACT: Senior Editor: Jessica Cassity
Material: Fitness/Dance News/Jazz/Tap/Ballet/Dance Books, Products and Shoes
Lifestyle Media, LLC
110 William St., 23rd Floor
New York NY 10038
Phone: 646-459-4800
Fax: 646-459-4890
E-mail: editor@dancespirit.com
Website: www.dancespirit.com

Dance Teacher
The Practical Magazine of Dance

Dance Teacher is the only magazine exclusively for and about dance education, founded in 1979. Its mission is to provide practical information that readers can put to immediate use, written in a clear, simple, conversational style, and to provide a forum for communication among dance educators.

Readership

Dance Teacher has a national circulation with additional subscribers in more than 35 countries. The readers are teachers, dancers, choreographers, and serious students in independent studios, dance departments and in the schools associated with major dance companies. They participate in all forms of dance—ballet, jazz, modern, tap, character, folk and ethnic, ballroom/dance sport, aerobic and fitness dance, dance drill, sacred dance and creative movement. Artistic directors, administrators of schools, dance historians, critics and writers also read *Dance Teacher*.

Topics

Articles focus on subjects specific to the teaching of dance; the business of running a studio; nutrition, injuries and health; publicity; performance production; issues in the profession of dance education; people in dance education; and other subjects of interest to dance educators.

Each issue includes a "Spotlight " on a successful teacher. This is a teacher or other dancer involved in dance education who has made an impact, and should include how-to information so readers can emulate, rather than merely admire, the success enjoyed by the subject. Each issue also highlights a studio/college dance department.

Special Sections

Dance Teacher has special sections in several issues throughout the year. Queries on articles appropriate to any of these sections are welcome, and should be submitted at least four months ahead of the first of the month of the issue.

January issue—Summer Study includes information on summer workshops for teachers and students and articles on summer dance activities.

July/August issue—Music & More is devoted to music and sound in the studio and for performance. It includes a "Buyers Guide" of dance records, audio tapes, and CDs. Feature articles are invited on the application of music to dance.

November issue—Costume & Production Preview is a separately bound supplement published in time to distribute at Costume Preview trade shows, which *Dance Teacher* sponsors in November and December. Articles on show production are needed.

December issue—Dance Education & Career Guide includes a directory of colleges and professional training programs. Articles to aid teachers in advising students on furthering their education toward a career in dance are welcome.

Length

Feature articles run 1,000 to 2,000 words and columns run between 500-1,000 words. All articles must have artwork accompanying them. Short pieces that focus on one problem and its solution may also be submitted as first person accounts of teaching/performing/choreographing issues.

Style

Articles are written in a conversational style, using the second-person pronoun. Take into consideration the body of knowledge readers of *Dance Teacher* already have about dance. Include dollar amounts, titles, dates, names—as many specifics as possible. Use direct quotes when possible. Include anecdotes, illustrations and examples.

Editing

All articles submitted are subject to editing for style and length. Stories will also be checked for accuracy. *Dance Teacher* generally follows the style rules of the Chicago Manual of Style, 13th edition.

Submissions

A query letter is preferred, but a completed article may be submitted for consideration. Online submissions or submissions on Mac disk or text-only on IBM compatible disk—along with a printed copy—are preferred; disks must be clearly labeled with program (Word or WordPerfect) and complete file names.

Otherwise, stories must be typed, double-spaced, with the author's name, address, telephone (and fax if appropriate) on the front page. Simultaneous submissions must be clearly indicated. Submissions will not be returned unless accompanied by a self-addressed, stamped envelope. Pre-publication drafts will be sent to the author and primary sources, so please provide names and addresses of persons quoted at length. An "author's bio" runs with each article. Please include a paragraph about yourself and your dance and writing credentials.

DT purchases all rights. Stories are given full author credit unless you request otherwise.

Photos/Illustrations

Dance Teacher uses photographs and artwork in conjunction with articles and pays one fee for text and artwork. All art must be royalty-free or cleared for publication by the artist or holder of copyright.

First generation slides, transparencies, or prints are acceptable. Color is preferred but we do accept black & white. In general, the closer-up and fewer people in a photograph, the better. Action photos are preferred. All photos or illustrations should be submitted with photographer's name and suggested caption clearly printed on an attached label.

Writers' Fees

Dance Teacher pays between $200-300 for feature articles and $100 for columns. We pay within 30 days of publication and after having received the appropriate invoice.

Thank you for your interest in *Dance Teacher*.

Categories: Arts—Dance—Drama

CONTACT: Caitlin Sims, Editor
Material: Queries and manuscripts
Lifestyle Ventures, LLC
250 West 57th Street, Ste 420
New York NY 10107
Phone: 212-265-8890

A-E

Fax: 212-265-8908
E-mail: csims@lifestyleventures.com
E-mail:Website:

DECA Dimensions

*DECA is...*the international association of marketing education students—ambitious, talented students eager to explore their career interests in marketing, merchandising, and entrepreneurship.

A nonprofit educational association, DECA has 180,000 members in all 50 states, Guam, Puerto Rico, Germany and Canada. The majority of members are of high school age, 15-19, while those in the post-secondary division, Delta Epsilon Chi, are 18 and older.

For more than 50 years, DECA has provided a program of leadership and professional development designed to merge with the marketing education curriculum. DECA is not extracurricular, but is a part of classroom instruction.

Working hand-in-hand with the education and business communities, DECA utilizes on-the-job experience, chapter projects and an outstanding program of competency based competitive events in specific occupational areas including sales, advertising, finance, retailing, wholesaling, fashion merchandising, restaurant management, tourism and hospitality among others.

Formerly known as the Distributive Education Clubs of America, DECA is governed by a board of directors and guided by councils of educators, as well as two advisory boards—the National Advisory Board (NAB) consists of representatives from more than 60 of America's major businesses and corporations; the Congressional Advisory Board (CAB) is made up of select members of the United States Congress.

DECA helps its members develop a "career success kit" to carry with them from school to work.

Dimensions is... the journal magazine for DECA's membership. Published four times a year during the school year, i.e., September/October, November/December, January/February and March/April, Dimensions reaches 160,000 young people and the adults who support their goals. It is a glossy publication, 8¼"x10¾", printed in four-color. Its audience is primarily high school students ages 15-19.

Because it is an education journal with a unique audience, Dimensions is a publication of substance but with the appeal of a commercial magazine for young adults. Its approach is direct and conversational—not academic.

Advertising and freelance articles are accepted. Topics covered include general business—corporate and small business; management and marketing—domestic and international; leadership development; entrepreneurship; fashion merchandising and trends; sales; business technology; personal and business finance; advertising and visual display; security; tourism and hospitality industries; food service—quick and full-serve; the retail food industry; career opportunities; employment and academic tips and helps; job skills; school-to-work incentives; current issues of interest to the association or audience, including school and peer issues.

Dimensions feature articles are approximately 1,000 words; columns approximately 500 words. A short bio statement should accompany bylined articles. Submissions on Mac disk along with hard copy are preferred. Small honorariums may be paid upon use.

Preparing to Write

Writing a column, a feature piece or a book is an experience that can be satisfying for you and rewarding for your reader. Producing a well-written, accurate work clearly conveys your knowledge and expertise to the audience. Each author has his own style and editors try

diligently to maintain that flavor in the finished piece. However, once your writing has been submitted to the publisher, it is assumed that editorial changes can and will be made as needed without consultation. Most often this will be done to accommodate available publication space.

To minimize editorial changes to your work, you will want to observe the following points:

• Keep in mind the audience you are trying to reach. The readers may be young, but they are knowledgeable in their areas and accustomed to a professional presentation. They will expect valuable, timely information that they can learn from or practice.

• Don't talk down to your reader, but at the same time don't use wordy or jargon-filled language. Whatever style you adopt, casual or formal, stay consistent throughout.

• Avoid language or content that could be interpreted as humiliating or slighting to any minority group or specific segment.

• The use of specific examples or stories to explain concepts is always a good idea.

• Laws governing what may or may not be used from another source are very complex and often difficult to interpret. You, as the author, are legally responsible for obtaining permissions, whether for text or illustration. Permission must be obtained not only for the directly quoted material but also for significant material that has been paraphrased or condensed. It is best to get permissions in writing and submit copies of them for our files along with your article. Sources must be acknowledged in the text or in a credit line.

Categories: Associations—Business—Careers—Education—Teen—Young Adult

CONTACT: Cindy Sweeney, Editor
Material: All
1908 Association Dr.
Reston VA 20191
Phone: 703-860-5000
Fax: 703-860-4013
E-mail: deca_dimensions@deca.org
Website: www.deca.org

Decorative Artist's Workbook

About Us

Decorative Artist's Workbook's mission is to inspire, instruct, inform and entertain decorative painters across the country and around the world. Our aim is to teach beginning, intermediate and advanced decorative painters the processes and techniques of painting firsthand from other artists via step-by-step instructions and illustrations. To encourage a reader's success, we: 1) provide patterns for every feature project, 2) teach the fundamentals of decorative painting, 3) present techniques in a variety of media, and 4) have experienced master painters answer their questions.

Writer's & Artist's Guidelines

Decorative Artist's Workbook (DAW) is a bimonthly publication for decorative painters of all skill levels. The magazine covers a wide range of decorative painting subjects, including folk art (such as rosemaling), stroke work, stenciling, fabric painting and faux finishing methods, just to name a few. Paintings are done in acrylics, oils, alkyds and watercolors on such surfaces as tin, wood, canvas, fabric and glass. Whatever the medium or surface, we're seeking the new, the unique and the traditional presented in a fresh way.

FEATURES

Our most consistent need is for instructional articles. We use between six and 10 features per issue, and all features should emphasize the how-to: the step-by-step process used to complete a project or master a technique. These features range from 1,000 to 2,000 words in length, but we certainly welcome short features on quick projects that can be explained in one or two pages.

Articles that introduce a traditional folk art style, for instance, or new technique, are usually combined with a finished project. This type of article explains how a style or technique originated, the history of the technique (if applicable), the materials used, and how it can be completed.

Pay for all features ranges from $200 to $300. and is, of course, dependent upon the complexity of the artwork, the writing, the article's length and the total package submitted by the writer. To submit a feature idea, see "How to Query" below.

COLUMNS

Opportunities with DAW lie primarily with feature articles. Most of the columns are written by our staff, contributing editors or editorial board members. We will, however, accept queries for "Stenciling," "By Design" (which covers the principles of design), "Home Decor" (decorative painting for the home), "Creative Painting" (new ideas, techniques and trends in decorative painting), and "Artist of the Issue" (profiles of up-and-coming artists).

Submissions for columns should follow the same format as for features. Pay varies depending on the length and content. To submit a column idea, see "How to Query" below.

OTHER NEEDS

"Ask the Masters" is a column that offers expert answers to your painting questions from the country's top decorative painters. To participate, send your questions to "Ask the Masters," *Decorative Artist's Workbook*. (See address below.)

In "Brush Talk," we share our reader mail – projects, creative ideas, painting solutions and opinions – that were inspired by the pages of *Decorative Artist's Workbook*. To participate, send your letters to "Brush Talk" at the address below.

ORIGINALITY AND RIGHTS

All material submitted must be original and unpublished. If accepted, DAW purchases First North American Serial Rights for one-time use in the magazine and all rights for use of the article (text and illustration/art) in any F&W promotional material/product or reprint.

You always retain copyright of your work and are free to use it in any way you wish after it appears in the magazine. We ask, however, that you do not publish this same material for at least six months from the time it appears in our publication.

HOW TO QUERY

Please query in advance rather than send unsolicited manuscripts and artwork. You may query with more than one idea at a time. Your query should include:

• A self-addressed, stamped envelope for the return of your material.

• A brief outline of the proposed article, telling us the skill level, medium and surface used, and anything else about the project that makes it special or unique.

• A color photo or slide of the project/s.

• A short biographical sketch. Include your accomplishments, address and a daytime phone number.

MANUSCRIPT SUBMISSION

Once your article query has been given the go-ahead, here's what you'll need to send next:

1. The Manuscript: This should be typed and double-spaced on white 8-1/2 x 11-inch paper. (If you have a computer, you may submit the article on a 3-1/2 inch disk along with the printed copy. Check with an editor for details.) Place your full name, address and phone number on the first page. *Your manuscript should include the following:*

• Title

• Introduction

• Describe an important point about your project or subject. What made you develop the idea or design for it? You might note an unusual technique, surface or medium, how it can be used, or why it's one of your favorites.

• Preparation: Explain any necessary pre-painting steps such as sanding, sealing, etc.

• Painting Instructions: Writing in a conversational style, go step-by-step through the painting process, explaining each point clearly and concisely, as if a beginning painter were looking over your shoulder.

Make sure you include every detail (such as the brush size and pigment being used). Spell out the full names of paint colors, and please don't shorten terms (e.g., P.G. for Paynes Gray).

• Finishing: Give complete instructions on how to finish the painted project (varnishing, sanding, heat setting, etc.).

• Closing: Close your article with a brief statement that ties everything together. Also, if you can, add an estimate of the approximate time needed to complete the project.

• Materials: Please provide a complete list of the materials used to complete the project. We ask that you include the following with the assumption that any product mentioned carries your endorsement for quality:

• Palette: paint brand, medium and colors (be sure these are spelled correctly).

• Brushes: brand name, type and size.

• Surface: size (if applicable), supplier's name, address, phone number and the price of the surface (including shipping charges).

• Miscellaneous: Note every other item used, from pencils to glue and sprays.

• About the Artist: This sidebar runs with every feature. Tell us about yourself, including the following information:

How long have you been painting and how did you get "hooked?"

Have you won any awards?

Have you published any painting books or pattern packets?

If you teach, give the what, when and how.

Any anecdotes about painting.

Your philosophy regarding decorative art.

Your advice for beginners.

Include a photo of yourself.

2. Visual Aides: Visual aids are an important part of instruction and are essential for project articles, so remember to submit quality painted work-sheets of key painting steps for each element of the design (such as petal leaves, and flower center). These work-sheets should show the painting progression, corresponding as much as possible with the written instructions.

For example, if the first step is base coating, the first illustration would show only that. If the second step is adding the shading, the second illustration would show that, and so on. (Please note: If adding written instructions on the illustrations, do not do so directly on the art. Instead, place them on a tracing paper overlay, and we'll compile the information into captions.)

Also include on the worksheets paint swatches for the paint mixtures used for the project.

Step-by-step worksheets should be painted on canvas, canvasette or sturdy paper, and should be neat and easy to see with plenty of contrast between the painted step and the background color. Also, keep plenty of blank space around each step as we may have to cut out illustrations for art purposes.

3. Sidebars: If a certain technique is important in the project, such as dry brushing or cross blending, make a suggestion for a special "sidebar" explaining that technique. Tips and hints to ensure success also make good sidebars.

4. Alternate Instructions: Whenever possible, we like to provide instructions for painting a project in an alternate medium. So, if you've painted your project in oils, for instance, and are able to translate those instructions or suggest tips for acrylic painters, please include them in your package.

5. The Pattern: Include a "drawn-to-scale" line drying of the pattern (neatly drawn with a technical pen) for inclusion in the pull-out pattern section of the magazine.

6. The Project: Please send the completed project, ready to be photographed. (If the project is on canvas or watercolor paper, please frame it.)

All artwork, photos and drawings will be returned after publication.

Categories: Arts—Crafts—Painting

CONTACT: Anne Hevener
Material:4700 E. Galbraith Rd.
Cincinnati OH 45236
Phone: 513-531-2690 ext. 1461
Fax: 513-531-2902
E-mail: dawedit@fwpubs.com
Website: www.decorativeartist.com

Defenders

General Information

DEFENDERS magazine is published quarterly for the membership of Defenders of Wildlife, a national nonprofit organization devoted to wildlife conservation. DEFENDERS has a circulation of about 260,000. Content reflects the organization's focus on endangered species, public lands, habitat and bio-diversity conservation, the international wildlife trade and similar subjects. Most issues contain four full-length features as well as departments and an organizational "newsletter." Most content deals with North American wildlife, although we print international articles from time to time. Please study an issue of the magazine and send a query before submitting any material.

Manuscripts

Query first. Include a self-addressed stamped reply envelope (SASE). Include a brief description of your background and qualifications along with some published writing samples. Most articles are assigned after a query.

We do not accept fiction or poetry. Essays are accepted rarely.

Length and Format

Usual length: 1,500 to 3,500 words.

Proposals and manuscripts submitted simultaneously to other publications are not acceptable, nor is previously published work.

The content is directed to a general audience, but scientific accuracy is essential. We do not want encyclopedia extracts or other second-hand natural history descriptions. We emphasize current threats to wild species and habitat, worthwhile action to save wildlife and informed discussions of government programs and policies. We seek to maintain a high literary, reportorial and graphic standard.

Categories: Nonfiction—Animals—Conservation—Ecology—Environment—Nature—Politics

CONTACT: Submissions Editor
Material: All
1101 Fourteenth Street, NW, Ste 1400
Washington DC 20005
Phone: 202-682-9400
Fax: 202-682-1331
E-mail: JDEANE@defenders.org
Website: www.defenders.org

Dermascope

As a trade publisher to the aesthetics, body therapy and spa industries, our subscribers have come to depend on DERMASCOPE as their source of clear educational information.

All articles submitted for consideration must meet the following criteria:

Style: Written from an aesthetic educators point-of-view, articles must be educational, comprehensive and positive. Whenever practical, alternative options and techniques should be mentioned. Overall, articles must remain generic in nature. Therefore, manuscripts cannot promote particular products, procedures or people. Instead, press releases, new products, industry profiles, news items, etc., will be considered for inclusion within courtesy sections: Essentials, or Pulse depending on space availability and other editorial criteria.

Furthermore, articles must not be slanted against a particular segment of the trade. Support your hypothesis based on documented facts about your subject; theory must be able to stand on its own merits, without referring negatively to other industry services, procedures or products. Please include research and other reference materials that support your claim.

Topics/Length: How-to, body therapy, diet, nutrition, spa, equipment, medical procedures, make-up and business articles should be approximately 1,500-2,000 words. Feature stories are usually between 1,800-2,500 words. Stories that are more than 2,500 may be printed in part and run in concurrent issues of the magazine.

Acceptance Policy: No simultaneous submissions, please. Reprints are rarely accepted.

All articles should be submitted in electronic form, whenever possible (MS Word), as well as a hard copy. (The hard copy will only serve as a backup, in case we are unable to read the electronic version.) The hard copy should be typed with 1" margins, double-spaced on single side of paper.

Artwork: Articles should include quality photographs or recommendations for photos, graphics, charts or other illustrations that would enhance the article. Electronic images (jpg or tiff) are preferred, but transparencies, slides, or glossy prints (no smaller than 3.5x5) may be acceptable.

Photo credits, model releases, and identification of subjects or techniques shown in photos are required. Side bars are a plus. Photos will not be returned, therefore we ask that you do NOT send Original artwork.

Authors are requested to supply their biographies, limited to a maximum of 80 words. A professional color headshot is also needed to accompany the bio. Photos will not be returned, therefore we ask that you do NOT send Original artwork.

DERMASCOPE acquires all rights and a signed release form is required. We publish manuscripts on an average of four to six months after acceptance and reserve the right to final edit all materials, kill an article or reschedule its publication date.

Categories: Nonfiction—Health—Aesthetics

CONTACT: Editorial Department
Material: All
2611 N. Belt Line Rd., Ste. 101
Sunnyvale TX 75182
Phone: 972-226-2309
Fax: 972-226-2339
E-mail: saundra@dermascope.com
Website: www.dermascope.com

Desktop Engineering

Desktop Engineering is for design and mechanical engineers who use and specify the purchase of computer hardware and software for the design for manufacture/process industries. DE covers all computer platforms, operating systems, applications software, and peripherals. DE clarifies technologies, explains operational theories and practices, and offers hands-on reports of how hardware and software affects engineers.

DE's readers are well educated and technically knowledgeable. They are interested in comprehensive technical and scientific information on new and existing technologies and products so that they can make informed business and technological decisions. They are not computer geeks, but they are computer savvy. They are engineers.

Write an Outline

Before you write an article for DE, please submit a complete outline. E-mail inquiries are acceptable. Please supply your daytime phone number.

An outline includes a working title, a paragraph or two summarizing the article's major points, a paragraph outlining the major graphical elements that will accompany your article, and a short biography detailing your qualifications to write on the subject matter.

If your idea is accepted, an editor will work with you on all other details, such as deadline and length.

Unacceptable and unsolicited manuscripts will be returned if accompanied by a self-addressed envelope with sufficient first-class postage.

What to Write

DE offers various types of articles, including focus topics, resource guides, features, application stories, and product reviews.

Focus topics, feature articles, and cover stories are in-depth discussions of leading-edge computer technologies. These articles range in size from 1,200 to 1,600 words.

Application stories and product reviews range in size from 900 to 1,200 words. Here, you test drive products and provide readers with a hands-on report.

Things to Remember

No matter what type of article you write, support and enhance your article visually. Visual information can include screen shots, photos, schematics, tables, charts, checklists, time lines, reading lists, and program code. The exact mix will depend on your particular article.

Your article also must be original, noncommercial, unpublished elsewhere, and not under consideration by another publication. All articles are subject to editing and significant rewrites. DE is not responsible for lost manuscripts, disks, or artwork.

Ethics Matter

DE will arrange to have products shipped to you. Never request a product from a company or accept one if offered. Please disclose any and all professional ties, grudges, or investments relating to companies or products you cover.

Submission Guidelines

Articles should be submitted via e-mail as Word attachments preferably saved in RTF or Text only format. Attach illustrations as well. Captions can be a separate attachment or be written at the end of the text of the article.

Print out all text and illustrations at the highest quality possible. Number illustrations sequentially and reference them in the text. Provide captions for all illustrations. Captions should not repeat the main text. Identify all printouts with your name and article title.

Reference sidebars, book lists, program code, and other textual elements in text by item title. Such elements should appear sequentially after the main text.

Submit graphics on disk, as color glossies or as slides (in that order of preference). Electronic files should be TIFF, JPG, or EPS (resolution must be 300+ dpi). Only use a common utility such as StuffIt or PKZip to compress graphics files. Please call about any images that must be sent on a CD-ROM, ZIP disk, or on another medium.

Acceptance & Payment

DE pays for articles upon publication. In most cases, all article rights revert to DE.

Categories: Nonfiction—Computers—Engineering—Trade—Design Engineering

CONTACT: Dennis Barker, Editor-in-Chief
Material: All
CONTACT: Jennifer Runyon, Managing Editor
Material: All
Helmers Publishing
174 Concord St., PO Box 874
Peterborough NH 03458
Phone: 603-924-9631
Fax: 603-924-4004
E-mail: DE-Editors@helmers.com

Remember: Editors change jobs and publishers change addresses. It is wise to invest in a phone call for the current information before submitting.

Development Director's Letter
Practical Advise for the Nonprofit Manager

We seek practical tips for nonprofit managers, particularly tips designed for fundraisers and executive directors. Typical areas of interest include: campaigns, direct mail, technology, proposal writing, public relations, Washington Watch and book reviews.

Articles are generally 500-800 words in length. We prefer articles based on interviews and which include a significant number of quotes.

Categories: Fundraising—Nonprofit Organizations

CONTACT: Lynn O'Connell, Editor
Material: All
4848 Virginia St.
Alexandria, VA 22312
Phone: 703-867-4942
Website: www.cdpublications.com/pubs/
developmentdirector.php

Devo'Zine

The daily meditations in *Devo'Zine* are written by real people — like you! These meditations are 250 words in length or less and are grouped according to weekly themes. Be sure to mention which theme you are writing for, and send your meditation to us by e-mail, Fax, US Mail, or submit it online.

WHAT IS THE PURPOSE?

Our purpose is to help youth develop a lifelong practice of prayer and spiritual reflection. *Devo'Zine* is designed to help readers grow in their faith and explore the relevancy of the Christian faith for the issues they face. Undergirded by scripture, *Devo'Zine* will aid youth in their prayer life, introduce them to spiritual disciplines, help them shape their concept of God, and encourage them in the life of discipleship.

WHAT IS Devo'Zine?

A bimonthly, 64-page magazine for youth

Written by youth and adults who care about them

Each issue focuses on nine themes.

Each theme includes weekday readings and weekend features, enough for two months.

Meditations may be read in chronological or random order.

Themes may be expressed through scripture, prose, poetry, prayers, stories, songs, art, or photographs.

Readers and writers include persons of many different denominations and cultures.

WHO WILL ENJOY IT?

Youth ages 12-18 who seek personal devotional readings

Youth groups who seek devotional reflections

Adults who seek to understand youth spirituality

HOW DO I WRITE FOR THE PUBLICATION?

Daily meditations should be 150-250 words long.

Poetry and prayers should be short to moderate in length — 10 to 20 lines.

Think about the purpose of the meditation — what do you want it to evoke in the reader?

Style notes: Simply written (preferably in youth language), realistic and relevant to life experiences of youth, does not need to be overtly religious but should help to open youth to the life of faith that we all seek, inclusive of multicultural experiences

Language guidelines: Try to use language that is non-sexist and inclusive of everyone (examples are words such as humankind, persons, or everyone instead of mankind or men in the familiar generic sense). We encourage the use of a wide range of biblical images for God.

May include scripture verse or suggested text (state version of Bible used)

May include a reflective element: brief prayers, quotes, reflection or journaling questions, action ideas, or other items. Prayers should use honest, straightforward, conversational language.

WHAT ARE SOME TIPS FOR DEVOTIONAL WRITING?

Devotional writing should invite people to come closer to God.

Devotional writing should tell about real experiences of real people who are struggling to apply their faith to daily life.

Devotional writing should express only one main idea. It should leave one memorable image with the reader.

Devotional writing should lead persons into further conversation with God after they finish reading the meditation.

Your journal can be a great source of devotional writing because your journal records your real thoughts about your experiences.

HOW DO I PREPARE MY MEDITATION?

Typed or handwritten, doubled-spaced on 8 1/2" x 11" paper/or on email

If the meditation is mailed in, it needs to be accompanied by a self-addressed, stamped envelope for return. We cannot acknowledge or return meditations submitted without an SASE, so please keep a copy of what you submit.

HOW WILL I KNOW IF MY MEDITATION IS ACCEPTED?

If we choose to use your meditation, we will notify you before publication. Otherwise, you will not hear from us unless you send an SASE.

We pay $25 for weekday meditations. Payment will be made at the time of acceptance.

HOW CAN I FIND OUT ABOUT UPCOMING THEMES?

Check out our upcoming themes — or send us an SASE to receive themes for upcoming issues.

WHAT OTHER INFORMATION DO I NEED TO INCLUDE?

Name

Age/Birthdate (if you are younger than 25)

Mailing Address

Phone /FAX

E-mail

You may have noticed that Devo'Zine's format includes brief devotional meditations to be read on the weekdays and a longer, more in-depth article for Saturday/Sunday reading. We invite you to consider writing one of these longer articles. The *Devo'Zine* staff assigns these articles; so if you'd like to write one, please contact us about what you'd like to write. We may have already assigned this particular article, so we don't want you to write an article for us that we can't publish. Contact us with your idea by mail or email. (See the last section of this document for addresses.) Give us as much notice as you can.

WHAT IS THE PURPOSE?

Our purpose is to help youth develop a lifetime pattern of prayer and spiritual reflection. *Devo'Zine* is designed to help readers grow in their faith and explore the relevancy of the Christian faith for the issues they face. Undergirded by scripture, it will aid youth in their prayer life, introduce them to spiritual disciplines, help them shape their concept of God, and encourage them in the life of discipleship.

WHAT IS Devo'Zine?

A bimonthly, 64-page magazine for youth

Written by youth and adults who care about them

Each issue focuses on nine themes

Each theme includes weekday readings and weekend features

Meditations may be read in chronological or random order

Themes may be expressed through scripture, prose, poetry, prayers, stories, songs, art, or photographs

Readers and writers include persons of many different denominations and cultures

WHO WILL ENJOY IT?

Youth ages 12-18 who seek personal devotional readings

Youth groups who seek devotional reflections

HOW SHOULD I WRITE?

Weekend feature articles should be 350-500 words long and should be related to the theme for the week — with a "twist."

Think about ideas for graphics and suggest them to the editor.

As you write, think about what you can do to give the feature a reflective element — the Next Day Stretch for the Sunday reading. You may want to use a question or questions, a suggestion for action, tips for ongoing practice of spiritual disciplines, a directed or open-ended prayer, or a suggestion for journaling or starting a journal.

Format. Try not to have long blocks of copy. Make your article invitational and reader-friendly. Use subtitles to break up copy; use sidebars; or use bulleted lists.

Language guidelines. We seek to use language that is non-sexist and inclusive of everyone (examples: humankind, persons, everyone, instead of mankind, men in the familiar generic sense). We encourage the use of a wide range of biblical images of God.

Payment is $100. Please include your legal name, name as you wish it to appear on article, address and email address, and a short bio (youth-friendly, please!).

MAIL, FAX, OR E-MAIL MANUSCRIPTS TO THE ADDRESS BELOW.

Categories: Arts—Christian Interests—Inspirational—Photography—Poetry—Religion—Spiritual

CONTACT: Sandy Miller, Managing Editor
Material: All
1908 Grand Avenue • PO Box 340004
Nashville TN 37203-0004
Phone: 615-340-7247/7270
Fax: 615-340-1783
E-mail: devozine@upperroom.org
Website: www.upperroom.org/devozine

Diabetes Self-Management

Diabetes Self-Management is written for the growing number of people with diabetes who want to know more about controlling and managing their diabetes. Our readers need up-to-date and authoritative information on nutrition, pharmacology, exercise, medical advances, self-help, and a host of other how-to subjects. We address the day-to-day and long-term concerns of our readers in a positive and upbeat manner and enable them to make informed choices about managing their diabetes.

The rule of thumb for any article we publish is that it must be clear, concise, interesting, useful, and instructive, and must have immediate application to the day-to-day life of our readers. For that reason, we do not publish personal experiences, personality profiles, exposés, or research breakthroughs.

Our audience ranges from the newly diagnosed diabetic—who has little knowledge of diabetes—to people who have been intimately involved in their own treatment for many years and often know more about diabetes than well-informed health writers. We do not assume knowledge of our audience, but we do assume intelligence and are careful not to write down to our readers.

Most articles range between 1,500 and 2,500 words. We do not accept previously published material. While we buy all rights, we are extremely generous regarding permission to republish. Articles are published with bylines and payment is made on publication. Payment rates vary depending on the quality of the material and the skill and effort required of the writer. Kill fees are 20%.

Tips

Use plain English; avoid medical jargon, but where appropriate for understanding, explain technical terms in simple, easily understood language. Writing style should be simple, upbeat, and leavened with tasteful humor where possible. Information should be accurate, up-to-date, and from reliable sources. References from lay publications are not acceptable.

Tables, charts, drawings, and sidebars are particularly useful when they are concise, illustrative, and help explain the text. Photographs are generally not accepted. Authors are required to include with their article a list of suggested reading to be published as a sidebar to the article.

Query with a one-page rationale and outline, and include writing samples. Reports will be made within six weeks. If your query is accepted, expect heavy editorial supervision.

Categories: Diet/Nutrition—Health

CONTACT: James Hazlett, Editor
Material: Any
CONTACT: Ingrid Strauch, Managing Editor
Material: Any
150 W. 22nd St.
New York NY 10011
Phone: 212-989-0200
Fax: 212-989-4786

Dialogue

Blindskills, Inc. welcomes the submission of freelance material from visually impaired authors for possible publication. The best way to get an idea of the kind of material we publish is to request a sample copy of DIALOGUE and review it. Sample copies are avaiable at no charge in large print, four-track cassette, braille or computer diskette. If the sample is requested by a fully sighted author, we will charge $7 to cover the cost of postage. Samples sent to blind and visually impaired individuals are shipped via the free matter for the blind designation.

Current Needs: Interviews of interest or assistance to newly blind and other visually impaired persons, examples of career and leisure experiences, fiction, humor, and coping methods.

Material that is religious, controversial, political, or contains explicit sex is not acceptable.

Payments: Since DIALOGUE is entirely dependent upon public contributions for its support, payment is necessarily low. We think we offer an unusual opportunity for beginning writers. We send an explanatory letter along with each returned manuscript. Those whose articles are published in DIALOGUE will receive a complimentary large print copy. Payment for fiction or non-fiction articles will be made at the rate of $15 to $35. All payments for articles used in a given issue will be made after all formats of DIALOGUE are shipped to our readers.

Rules:
1) No simultaneous submissions to other publications are allowed while being considered by Blindskills, Inc.

2) We reserve the right to do minor editing.

3) Manuscripts must be the original and unpublished work of the writer.

4) Authors who are legally blind are given priority. Exceptions are sometimes made when topics are judged to be of reader interest.

Rights:
We purchase all First North American rights. For reprint permission, contact Blindskills, Inc. in writing.

Deadlines: For publication in the Spring issue, material must be received by January 1; for the Summer issue by April 1; for the Fall issue by July 1; and for the Winter issue by October 1.

Specific Guidelines: Nonfiction: Though the freelance portion of any issue is generally representative of the kind of material we are buying, freelance pieces on subjects now being staff-written are always welcome. Currently, we are especially interested in first-person accounts of career or education experiences, travel experiences, articles about participation in sports, information on new products useful to people who are visually impaired, features on homemaking, and descriptions of feelings and methods experienced by those losing vision or who are blind.

Fiction: We are interested in well-written stories of many types: mystery, suspense, humor, adventure and romance. We prefer contemporary problem stories in which the protagonist solves his or her own problem. We are looking for strongly-plotted stories with definite beginnings, climaxes and endings. Characters may be blind, sighted, or

visually in-between. Because we want to encourage any writer who shows promise, we may return a story for revision when necessary. Fiction pieces should not exceed 1200 words.

Poetry: We are not accepting poetry until further notice.

Manuscripts: While we accept unsolicited manuscripts, we strongly prefer queries first. Both queries and manuscripts may be e-mailed, but the text of either the query or manuscript must be placed in the body of the message— absolutely no attachments, please. You may e-mail queries and/or manuscripts to blindskl@teleport.com.

Please accompany manuscripts with a cover letter that includes your mailing address, e-mail address, and telephone number. You may also submit material on a 3.5 inch disk. When doing so, include a hard copy of your letter and manuscript. Provide a self-addressed, stamped envelope if you would like your disk returned. Material submitted solely in typed form is acceptable. All submissions should be double-spaced on standard 8-1/2- by 11- inch paper, leaving at least a one-inch margin on all sides. On the first page be sure to type your name, complete address, phone number, and date of submission in the top left-hand corner. Center the title of the article. On all subsequent pages, be sure to include your name and the title of your submission in the top left corner and the page number in the top right corner.

Blindskills, Inc. cannot be responsible for manuscripts lost in the mail. Writers are therefore advised to retain a copy of each submission.

Length: Due to space limitations necessitated by quarterly publication, shorter lengths are preferred both for fiction and non-fiction. Stories and articles of more than 1200 words are rarely used. We do occasionally run long non- fiction articles if the importance of the topic or nature of the material warrants.

Receipt/Return: We acknowledge receipt of material by postcard. Only submissions accompanied by a self-addressed stamped envelope bearing sufficient postage will be returned upon rejection.

Time Needed For Reply: At least one month.

Categories: Nonfiction—Careers—Computers—Consumer—Disabilities—Family—Hobbies—Recreation—Senior Citizen—Sports/Recreation

CONTACT: Carol M. McCarl, Executive Director
Material: All
Blindskills, Inc.
PO Box 5181
Salem OR 97304-0181
Phone: 800-860-4224
Fax: 503-581-0178
E-mail: blindskl@teleport.com
Website: www.blindskills.com

The Diamond Registry Bulletin

Formal guidelines not available. Please read a number of issues to ascertain the publication's style and needs.

Send queries to address below.

Categories: Nonfiction—Fashion—Marriage—Trade—Diamonds and Jewelry

CONTACT: Submissions Editor
Materials: All
580 Fifth Ave.
New York NY 10036
Phone: 212-575-0445
Fax: 212-575-0722
E-mail: diamond@58@aol.com
Website: www.diamondregistry.com

Remember: Editors change jobs and publishers change addresses. It is wise to invest in a phone call for the current information before submitting.

Digger Magazine
Farwest Magazine

Publications

Digger Magazine—published monthly except August when it is replaced by *Farwest Magazine* for our annual Farwest Show trade show - is a trade publication produced by the Oregon Association of Nurseries. that serves the Northwest's nursery and greenhouse industry. Our circulation averages 5,000 monthly, 12,000 in August. Two-thirds of our readers are in the Northwest, and we have a growing national readership as well.

Purpose

The purposes of these publications include serving as:
• An association membership communication piece;
• A marketing vehicle for companies, the association and the Oregon nursery industry;
• Informing readers about industry news and providing information to make them better growers, retailers, suppliers, landscapers, etc.

Magazine Sections

The magazines are divided into these sections:
• Feature articles. About three to four features of varying lengths are used each month. Articles are staff- or freelance-written. Most of our freelance needs are for feature-length articles.
• Continuing departments: Northwest News, Events, Calendar, Around the State, New Members, New Products, National News and Bookshelf.
• Continuing columns by our executive director and president.
• *Farwest Magazine* only: Farwest Show information, including exhibitors listings, seminars information, Portland and Oregon attractions, in addition to extra feature articles to fill the triple-size issue.

Editorial Focus

Because we are an association title, our editorial - features and news items - mostly centers on our members (primarily those in the Northwest), their companies, products or information that can benefit them in keeping with our purpose. *Topics may include:* • New plants and cultivars.
• Industry trends. What do business and consumer markets demand now and in the future.
• Regulatory and legislative aspects. What regulations are upcoming, how regulations or legislation affect Oregon or Northwest nurserymen.
• Resource management. What demands are placed on resources (water, media, by-products, etc.) and how they are changing.
• Pests, disease and their management (specific pests, pesticide use, safety and IPM).
• Research. How we can apply horticultural research to practical use.
• Business skills. How the industry can improve its marketing, management, etc.

Editorial Calendar. Contact the editor for a list of topics for general or thematic issues. Our planned calendar is subject to change, however, as topics and space warrant.

Freelance Submissions

Contact the editor in advance of all submissions, for story ideas or for an assignment before you proceed. As a general rule, we do not buy unsolicited articles (manuscripts and related visuals). We are not responsible for unsolicited articles and related visuals. By visuals we generally mean photos, illustrations, graphs, charts, etc.

Acceptance. Articles accepted for publication are determined by the editor. We are under no obligation to publish an article and related visuals, either unsolicited or purchased. Usually, an agreement form will be provided by the editor to signal a commitment with an author for an article, news item or visual. We expect the author to fully honor the agreement. Conditions as stipulated are subject to change upon mutual agreement.

Upon acceptance of the topic and/or agreement form, the author shall provide Social Security number, address and telephone and fax numbers for our recordkeeping.

Credit. Author will be credited with by-line credit for feature articles, source credit for shorter pieces. Supplied visuals will be credited as to their source.

Deadlines. All articles and related visuals must be submitted at least by the first of the month in advance of the targeted issue. For features, we prefer submissions six weeks in advance of the scheduled run.

Length. Features generally run 800-2,000 words.

Articles format. We require articles to be submitted in the following formats (listed in order of preference):
• Microsoft Word or text file attached to e-mail sent to editor. Also include story in e-mail body text as a backup. Fax hard copy of article to editor, also as a backup.
• On CD a word-processing application (Microsoft Word desired) or ASCII text, and Macintosh (desired), Windows or DOS operating systems.

Visuals format. Visual elements include charts, tables and graphs, illustrations and photography. They should be submitted camera-ready—a useable electronic format is preferred—or in high-quality printout form.

Faxed visuals are meant to be an example only; an original must be delivered.

Computerized. Contact editor or graphic design coordinator for software compatibility of computer applications well in advance of submission deadline.
• Photography can be submitted as digital, prints, slides or negatives. Digital images should be high-resolution and can be emailed or sent on a CD. Prints should be 3"x5", 5"x7" or 8"x10" color gloss with no borders.

Permission. It is the responsibility of the author to secure any releases or other permission to use photographic images, logos, illustrations or other visual elements. Items will be returned to the author after publication upon request.

Visuals must include identification or description of subjects and products for cutlines. Visuals should be mailed to the editor's attention in protective packaging.

Payment

Rate of pay ranges from $125 for shorter articles to $400 for special feature-length articles and related visuals to qualified freelancers. Compensation depends on the quality of the article (length, number of sources, complexity of subject, etc.) as is solely the judgment of the editor.

Payment generally will be made two-four weeks upon receipt and acceptance of the article and all related visuals.

Certain expenses, such as film, film processing, and toll telephone calls, will be paid if agreed upon by editor and freelancer beforehand.

Right

Upon acceptance, the Oregon Association of Nurseries will assume first North American rights to the article and related visuals. The article shall not be published in other relevant industry publications (local, regional or international) before or concurrent with publication in *Digger* or *Farwest Magazine*, or the author forfeits compensation, unless prior agreement is reached. The author retains all copyrights. Editing. We reserve the right to edit all manuscripts and visuals for space, style, grammar or content at the discretion of the editor.

Manuscripts will be returned to author for major revisions.

Galleys

Proofs of articles will be provided upon request.

Thank you, OAN Publications Department

Categories: Nonfiction—Agriculture—Trade—Nursery—Greenhouse—Horticulture

CONTACT: Cam Sivesind, Editor
Material: All
Oregon Association of Nurseries

29750 S.W. Town Center Loop W.
Wilsonville OR 97070
Phone: 503-682-5089 or 800-342-6401
Fax: 503-682-5727
E-mail: csivesind@oan.org

DISCIPLESHIP JOURNAL

Discipleship Journal

OUR PURPOSE

Discipleship Journal strives to help believers develop a deeper relationship with Jesus Christ, and to provide practical help in understanding the Scriptures and applying them to daily life and ministry.

CONTENT

Most of the articles we publish fall into one of three categories:

• Teaching on a Scripture passage, such as a study of an Old Testament character or a short section of an episode, explaining the meaning and showing how to apply it to daily life

• Teaching on a topic, such as what Scripture says about forgiveness or materialism

• How-to, such as tips on deepening your devotional life or witnessing in the workplace

We *do not* publish testimonies, devotionals, purely theological material, book reviews, poetry, fiction, news articles, or articles about Christian organizations. We occasionally use profiles of lay people who exemplify a quality treated in a theme section.

TOPICS

About half of each issue is devoted to a theme section, which explores in-depth a subject such as busyness, evangelism, or leadership. However, we encourage first-time writers to write nontheme articles, which can touch on any aspect of living as a disciple of Christ. Recent issues have dealt with subjects such as rekindling passion for God, our focus in prayer, developing a gentle spirit, key dynamics for personal discipling, dealing with stress, and principles for reaching unbelieving friends.

We'd like to see more articles that (1) encourage involvement in world missions, (2) help readers in personal evangelism, follow-up, and Christian leadership, (3) show how to develop a deeper relationship with Jesus, or (4) show how to grow in an area of Christian character.

OUR READERS

Be sure to consider our audience as you choose a topic and approach:

• Slightly more than half are women.
• Median age is 44.
• Nearly all have regular personal devotions.
• More than half meet individually with younger Christians to help them grow.
• About half lead a small group Bible study.
• Most are professionals with at least some college education.
• Many consider busyness the greatest obstacle to their spiritual growth.

TIPS FOR SUCCESSFUL ARTICLES

• *Derive your main principles from a thorough study of Scripture.* You will probably want to include some personal experience and quotes from others, but these should not form the basis of your article. You need not always quote a verse or reference, but you should be able to support your assertions from the Bible.

• *Illustrate each principle.* Use analogies, examples, and illustrations to aid the reader.

• *Show how to put each principle into practice.* Show the reader what applying this principle would "look like" in everyday life.

• *Be vulnerable.* Show the reader that you have wrestled with the subject matter in your own life. Write from the perspective of a fellow pilgrim, not someone who has "arrived."

HOW TO SUBMIT A QUERY

Due to an increasing volume of submissions, we can no longer accept unsolicited manuscripts. Instead, send a query letter. Query letters should include (1) the working title (2) a clear statement of purpose, (3) a tentative outline, (4) some indication of the style and approach you plan to use, (5) the prospective length (generally 1000 to 3000 words), and (6) a short description of your qualifications to write the article.

• Before you submit a query, study several recent issues of *Discipleship Journal.* Look at the types of articles we publish, common writing styles, and the way our writers approach their topics. For samples, visit our archives at www.discipleshipjournal.com, or mail a request (see below).

• Please include a self-addressed, stamped envelope (SASE) with all query letters. If possible, include one or two samples of your published work. Queries may also be submitted by e-mail, using the same format. We do not accept phone queries or simultaneous queries.

• Queries may be mailed or e-mailed to Sue Kline, Editor, at the address below.

• Response time is usually within four to six weeks. Feel free to drop us a note if you haven't heard from us after two months; some manuscripts do get lost in the mail. If you receive a positive response to your query, you will be invited to send your article on speculation.

If Your Query Is Accepted

• All articles should be typed, double-spaced, on one side of the paper only. On the first page, type your name, address, phone number, and e-mail address in the upper left corner. At top right, indicate an approximate word count and rights offered (first or reprint). Please use page numbers.

• We prefer Bible quotes from the New International Version. If quoting from a version other than the NIV, indicate which version is being quoted with each reference.

• Requested manuscripts may be mailed or e-mailed to the address below. E-mailed articles may be attached (Word files are preferred) or pasted into the body of the message.

• Again, response time is four to six weeks. Articles will not be returned unless requested (include a SASE with appropriate postage.)

Payment

Payment is made upon acceptance. The current rate is 25 cents per word for first rights.

Reprints

Reprints from noncompeting publications are acceptable but must be queried in the same form as other articles. In your query letter, indicate the publication in which the article originally appeared and the date of publication. Reprints are paid at 5 cents per word.

Samples

To obtain a sample copy of *Discipleship Journal*, send a manila envelope with $2.64 in postage to the address below.

Departments

Separate guidelines are available for departments in *Discipleship Journal* (On the Home Front, Getting into God's Word, One to One, and DJ Plus). To request these guidelines, send an SASE to the address below.

Categories: Nonfiction—Christian Interests—Inspirational—Spiritual

CONTACT: Sue Kline, Editor
Material: All
PO Box 35004
Colorado Springs CO 80919
E-mail: dj.writers@naupress.com

Remember: Editors change jobs and publishers change addresses. It is wise to invest in a phone call for the current information before submitting.

Discover

Discover

If you are interested in writing for *Discover*, we encourage you to submit a focused article proposal. While we do not issue formal guidelines to prospective writers, we suggest that you look carefully at the style and content of articles in *Discover* and shape your story proposal accordingly. Include samples of your previously published work and a brief biography. We do not accept proposals for our R&D (news) section. Feature proposals should be sent to the attention of Submissions Editor, *Discover*, 114 Fifth Ave., 15th floor, New York, NY 10011. Due to the large volume of mail we receive, please allow six to eight weeks for a response.

Please note that we do not accept e-mail proposals.

Categories: Nonfiction—Health—Science—Medicine

CONTACT: Submissions Editor
Material: Feature Proposals
114 Fifth Ave., 15th floor
New York NY 10011
Website: www.discover.com

Diver

DIVER Magazine (ISSN 0706-5132) is published nine times a year by Seagraphic Publications Ltd. It is Canada's Premier *Diving Magazine. Subject matter includes the following:*

- Travel Adventures
- Canadian Diving
- U/W Photography
- Equipment Reviews
- Dive Boat Reviews
- Wreck Diving
- Marine Life
- Diving Medicine

EDITORIAL GUIDELINES

In order to have a manuscript considered for publication it must be submitted as follows:

Subject Preferences: Well written and illustrated Canadian and North American regional dive destination articles. Travel features should be brief and accompanied by a sleeve or more of outstanding original slides and/or prints and a map. Most travel articles are committed up to a year in advance and there is limited scope for new material.

Submission: Copy should be double spaced and typed, preferably on disc-PC or Mac in MS Word, with a hard copy. Copy should be concise and clear; other materials enclosed should be marked for easy identification and reference. Only complete articles as described with illustrations will be considered. Package only one completed article per submission.

Length: Between 500 and 1000 words. Shorter pieces are welcome.

Illustrations: Original slides, 5"x7" colour prints, glossy 5"x7" black and white prints, maps, drawings. Each item should be labelled with name, address and description. Captions and credits on separate sheet must be numbered to match. Photos by other than writer of article must be clearly indicated on each picture. (Payment made only to author or submitter.)

Return Envelope: Please enclose a self-addressed stamped envelope if you wish your manuscript returned. International Reply Coupons accepted. DIVER Magazine assumes no responsibility for loss or damage of unsolicited manuscripts or photographs.

Scheduling: Unsolicited travel articles will be viewed only from July through August for possible use in the following year (nine issues). Material sent prior to that period is subject to being unopened until then or returned. Photos only may be submitted after ascertaining what features are planned for the upcoming year. Photos will be considered only if approved manuscripts are not adequately supported by illustrations.

Acknowledgment: We will acknowledge receipt of articles or return immediately if not suitable. Acknowledgement does not mean acceptance. We may hold material for up to 90 days before deciding (except travel articles see "Scheduling" above).

Payment: Payment to author for text and photos will be made by cheque six to eight weeks after the date of publication. Rights purchased are First North American. Any story may be archived on our website unless its exemption is requested in writing. Rates are $2.50 per column inch text, $15 minimum for B&W and $20 minimum for color. Cover shots $200.

Categories: Nonfiction—Recreation—Regional—Sports/Recreation

CONTACT: Virginia Nuytten
Material: All
Seagraphic Publications Ltd
241 E 1st St
North Vancouver BC V7L 1B4 Canada
Phone: 604 980-6262
Fax: 604-980-6236
E-mail: divermag@axion.net
Website: www.divermag.com

Diversity
Career Opportunities & Insights

About Us

This publication was formerly called *EEO Bimonthly: Opportunity for Diversity.*

Guidelines

We would like to see samples of your work before we can assign or accept articles for

publication. When submitting ideas for our consideration, they must be sent both on disk and in hard copy.

Sincerely,

Valerie Anderson, Senior Editor

Categories: Nonfiction—African-American—Careers—Hispanic—Internet—Money & Finances

CONTACT: Valerie Anderson, Senior Editor
Material: All
Career Recruitment Media
1800 Sherman Ave.
Evanston IL 60201
Phone: 847-448-1000
Fax: 847-475-8839
E-mail: Valerie.Anderson@careermedia.com
Website: www.careermedia.com

Dog Gone Newsletter

EDITORIAL GUIDELINES

Dog Gone Newsletter is a 16-page printed, bimonthly publication about fun places to go and cool stuff to do with your dog. The editorial focus is split between travel pieces and activity articles, as well as regular columns. Dog-friendly vacation spots, resorts, hotels, campgrounds, beaches, hiking trails, dining and shopping establishments, weekend getaways, and festivals or events are profiled. Also highlighted are fun activities, such as: flyball, jogging, walking or skiing with your dog, lure coursing and obedience trials. In short, it's a travel and activity newsletter for dog owners - Travel & Leisure for our four-legged pals.

Dog Gone Newsletter readers range in age from young singles to families to retired folks. All are dog owners and their pooches range from the most highly prized pedigree to those of questionable ancestry. *Dog Gone Newsletter* readers are typically active folks who like to travel and never leave home without the dog. Many are outdoor types who enjoy hiking, camping, roller-blading, skiing, and other activities. Some subscribers are physically impaired and thus enjoy those activities that are conducive to their limitations. Some readers prefer luxury accommodations, while others are looking for moderate or budget lodgings. Some simply like to camp or stay in their RV.

What We're Looking For: *Dog Gone Newsletter* is looking for lively, entertaining, intelligently, and creatively written articles on travel and dog-friendly activities. A sampling of travel features includes resort destinations, B&Bs, camping, and air-travel tips - all written from a dog angle.

Activities features can be dog sports or people activities to enjoy with your best pal.

For travel pieces, resorts and inns which are especially dog-friendly (perhaps even offering a "Pampered Pooch Package") warrant a profile. Other accommodations that welcome dogs can be incorporated into a theme article (i.e. fall foliage destinations, ski resorts, or suite hotels).

For destination articles (such as "Boston With Terrier" or "Viszlas in Vegas"), it is important to find fun activities in the area for owners to take their dogs, such as nearby parks, hiking trails, pet-friendly tourist attractions, yearly festivals that allow dogs, gardens or zoos that permit pets, and transportation services that accommodate dogs. Our readers aren't bringing their dogs on vacation just to leave them in a hotel room! Destination features should include lodging recommendations that allow any size of dog. Contact phone numbers and addresses should be included, along with rates, number of dogs permitted in rooms, pet fees or deposits, and any pet restrictions.

Combination travel/activity articles include themes such as "dogs-allowed" beaches, hiking trails, skiing trails, etc.

Transportation articles could include international travel documentation requirements, railroads that permit pets, rating the airlines on their treatment of pet passengers, sailboat or houseboat travel with your dog, and the like.

Activity features will introduce readers to new hobbies to enjoy with their pooches. Dog-related sports, such as agility, field trials, skijoring, obedience trials, and pet therapy are possibilities, as are including your dog in your spare-time activities, such as backpacking, rock-hounding, cross-country skiing or bird-watching.

Short submissions are accepted for
Dog Gone Newsletter's **regular departments:**
• "Beyond Fetch (offering creative suggestions for games to play with your pooch)
• "Roving Rv'er (profiling pet-friendly campground resorts)
• "Road Trip" (featuring dog-allowed national, state, regional, or local parks, forests and recreations areas)
• "Dining With Dogs" (restaurants for dogs or that allow dogs. Photos are required for most submissions.
Style: Upbeat, humorous and/or easy-to-read articles are the main criteria for *Dog Gone Newsletter's* style. AP style is loosely adhered to; however, we prefer articles to sound colloquial. Therefore, a sentence does not necessarily have to be "complete" in a conversational style article. Because there are so many freelance writers who are not familiar with the publication, and thus the style, (and submit articles that are outside of the focus or style), freelancers are encouraged to subscribe to the newsletter ($25/6 issues), or to send $5 for a current

issue, to become better acquainted with the nature and focus of *Dog Gone Newsletter.*

Addresses and phone numbers of destinations and accommodations can be included in the text or can appear as a sidebar or blurb at the end of an article. All information should be fact-checked personally; chamber of commerce and other published info is often outdated. For activity articles, it is important to include contacts for further information, as we will only be able to introduce readers to the activity.

Articles can be anywhere from 300 to 750 words. An approximate word count will be agreed upon at acceptance so we can plan the rest of the newsletter accordingly. Articles may be submitted via e-mail or by snail mail (see addresses below). Articles with photos should be sent via USPS or other ground transportation. A SASE (9x12) is required for photos to be returned and a current newsletter sent to you.

Artwork: Articles MUST include photos. Location photos of guests with dogs are preferred.

Line art may be interspersed with photography, but it cannot be the sole graphic for a destination feature.

Color or B&W prints are accepted (no slides). Activity articles may be accompanied by a photograph of a dog and its owner participating in the featured activity.

Pay rate: This depends on the article. Generally speaking, however, an article of at least 300 words pays $35; 600 words pays $70; and 700-750 words pays $80-85. No article will pay more than $85 and there is no extra fee for photos or other graphics. A one-year subscription to *Dog Gone Newsletter* can be payment or partial payment for the article.

Queries: If you have an article you feel would fit into *Dog Gone Newsletter's* focus and format, submit a query or the actual article (including word count) in writing to: Robyn Peters, Owner and Publisher, *Dog Gone Newsletter*, PO Box 1846, Estes Park, CO 80517; or via e-mail to: roblipete@earthlink.net. Response time is generally 2-4 weeks. You may be requested to submit your entire article for consideration. All submissions are subject to editing if necessary.

(Articles may not have been published prior to acceptance and cannot be published elsewhere for a year after they appear in *Dog Gone Newsletter.*)

Categories: Nonfiction—Animals—Outdoors—Recreation—Senior Citizen—Sports/Recreation—Travel

CONTACT: Robyn Peters, Owner and Publisher
Material: Queries or articles
PO Box 1846
Estes Park, CO 80517
Phone: 303-449-2527
E-mail: roblipete@earthlink.net
Website: www.doggonefun.com

Doll World
The Magazine for Doll Lovers

General Information
Doll World is an 84-page, full-color, bimonthly magazine with readers from all age sectors. They are interested in informative, well-written articles about collectible dolls of all kinds, doll history, preservation, restoration, dollmakers, plus discerning articles about the world of dolls. Nostalgia and humor are welcome touches. We occasionally include full-size paper dolls.

SUBMISSIONS
1. Manuscript Submissions
• To submit your ideas: At the review date you may send an outline and summary of what you wish to cover in your story, as well as a list and color photocopies of the graphic images you will include. If accepted; send the complete manuscript at the manuscript deadline date listed.
• Complete manuscripts should include subtitles throughout, as well as a small paragraph at the beginning of the story as an introduc-

tion. Keep your photo captions short but lively, as some readers believe captions "tell the whole story!"

• You must include a SASE to receive a reply and have images or photos returned. Please allow one month for a response. Only written submissions will be considered. No phone or fax queries.

• Type your manuscript double-spaced on 8 1/2 x 11-inch white paper. Use one-inch margins. Be sure to number all pages. Our corporate style follows the Associate Press Style.

• Label everything! Be sure your name and contact information is on your written materials and photos or items to be photographed.

• Manuscripts should be written independently from the photos. Do not include any portion in the main text of the manuscript that would have to be cut if the photos were not printed. Captions should be at least two sentences in length and written on a separate page.

• Occasionally we use full-size paper dolls. This feature is a one-to two page spread. Color copies may be sent for query purposes. Originals are requested when accepted, and will be returned after published.

• Proofread all aspects of your manuscript for accuracy. Then read it again!

2. Illustrations, Photos, Slides and Your Dolls

• We are happy to do the photography of your dolls in our studio. Dolls will be returned (at our expense) as our production process nears completion, usually a three-month period.

• If sending your dolls is not possible we require high-quality transparencies, slides, disk images (TIFF, high resolution, 300 dpi, CMYK color, Mac format) or clear, crisp photos to accompany your manuscript. They should be of excellent quality, particularly in regards to focusing, lighting and complete view of subject with a contrasting background.

• Please number each image and type the captions at the end of your manuscript numbered to correspond. Label the individual images with a stick-on address label.

• If you are sending digital images, title them to match your caption title.

• If there are not usable images to go with your manuscript, it may render your submission unacceptable.

Mailing address: Send submissions to Vicki Steensma, *Doll World*, 306 E. Parr Rd., Berne, IN 46711.

Contracts and payment

If your submission is accepted, you will be notified and will be sent a contract at the "manuscript deadline" listed on the editorial calendar. Payments vary depending on length (1000-1200 words are preferred), graphic images, form of submission (e-mailed submissions as a Word document are preferred), adherence to the guidelines and experience of the writer. We purchase all rights, however first rights contracts are available for a lower fee. Payment is made within 45 days after receipt of your signed contract.

If you have any questions, contact Vicki Steensma.

jkn02/02

Categories: Nonfiction—Arts—Biography—Collectibles—Crafts/Hobbies—Entertainment—Family—Fashion—Hobbies—Interview—Photography—Technology—Trade: Dolls

CONTACT: Vicki Steensma, Editor
Material: All
House of White Birches
306 East Parr Rd.
Berne IN 46711
Phone: 206-589-4000
Fax: 206-589-8093
E-mail: Vicki_Steensma@whitebirches.com
Website: www.whitebirches.com

The Dollar Stretcher

Who we are:

The Dollar Stretcher is a group of publications dedicated to "Living Better...for Less". The goal is to provide readers with ways to help them save time and money. Occasionally we will also include material on ways to make money at home.

The monthly print version of the newsletter made it's debut in January 1998. We offer it with different covers and lengths for use by private organizations. So, in effect we're creating more than one newsletter with the same content. Our online newsletters go out weekly with a circulation of 200,000. We also have a web site <www.stretcher.com>.

Compensation:

Monthly Print Version. Payment is at the rate of $0.10 per published word. We are buying the rights to use the article in the different formats of our newsletter.

Payment is made at the time of publication and will be sent to the address provided. Payment will be by check in US$. At present we are only able to pay for material that appears in the monthly hardcopy version of the newsletter.

Online Version & Website. At this time we are unable to pay for material that's used in the online newsletter and website. However, it can provide an excellent opportunity to showcase your talents. We do have a large audience and send out press releases to newspapers, radio, TV and online media regularly. Recently the site has been mentioned in The Chicago Tribune, Washington Post, Yahoo! Internet Life and other publications. Our authors have been contacted by various media outlets including the Rosie O'Donnell Show.

Rights:

Monthly Print Version. We are purchasing first time rights including reprint rights. Reprints will be provided free of charge to non-profit organizations and may also be used for promotional purposes. Non-profits may be asked to cover the cost of production and shipping. Any other potential sale will be negotiated seperately with the author or referred to the author.

Online Version & Website: We are obtaining the one time rights to include a story in the online newsletter and website. No further rights are implied. Any inquiries on usage are referred back to the author.

Writer's Qualifications:

You need not be a professional in the area being discussed. But you must be knowledgeable. Knowledge is more important than literary skill. Personal, hands-on, experience is valued. Unpublished authors are welcome.

Article Length:

We are interested in articles up to 1,100 words in legnth. The majority of articles that will be used will be in the 750 to 900 word range.

Type of Material Used:

• how to articles based on personal or professional experience

• profiles of people who are successfully living the frugal lifestyle

• time and space saving techniques

• creative ways to save on food, housing, auto and clothing

• stage-of-life material for babies, children, teens, college students, singles, couples, the divorced, single parents, empty nesters and retirees.

• Material targeting different levels of experience with frugal living is welcome. We are looking for articles for the newcomer as well as the experienced tightwad.

• Material on dealing with non-frugal partner, children or significant others

Interviews:

We are also interested in interviews with people who have successfully found ways to save time and money. An emphasis is put on those who have found new and creative ways to accomplish the frugal lifestyle and who can share ideas that can be imitated by our readers.

Book Reviews:

When reviewing a book, include:

• book title in Capitals

• author, publishing company, year of publication, soft or hard cover, number of pages and price.

• suggestions for discussion

• general description

• who would it appeal to

• author's goal in writing the book

• author's qualifications

• merits of the book

• any weaknesses of the book

• quality of indexes, recipes or financial aids

Your Article:

The article should be submitted either in the body of an email or on 3.5 inch diskette in ASCII text file format (.txt). We cannot be responsible for returning diskettes. If you're mailing your submission please include a diskette with the article. Our typist is too busy already! Please make sure that your email and postal addresses, as well as your daytime phone number, are included in the email or on the disk label.

Please include a brief one or two sentence bio statement with your text, and any title suggestions that you may have.

If your article includes resources, please make sure that you provide the necessary addresses and phone numbers. And that they are correct!

Please make sure that your lead 'hooks' the reader. In a newsletter dedicated to saving time and money our readers are very quick to skip to the next article.

How to Submit:

• email to: gary@stretcher.com with the article included in the body of the email. Please do not send attachments. Please indicate hardcopy submission in the subject of the email. We also publish material in the online newsletter without paying the writers. Neither one of us would be happy if your work was used without payment!

• by mail to: The Dollar Stretcher, PO Box 23785, Ft. Lauderdale, FL 33307.

A Final Note:

As you would expect, the monthly print version has limited space. We can be much more generous in the online and web versions. Since the online version is a weekly, we'll use about 7 times more material online than in the print version. But, remember that we're not able to pay for that material except to get your work displayed before a sizeable audience. Please mark your submission "Print Version" or "Online Version". If a submission is not marked we need to go back to you before we can begin to review it.

Categories: Nonfiction—Children—Consumer—Ecology—Education—Environment—Family—Marriage—Money & Finances

CONTACT: Submissions Editor
Material: All
PO Box 23785
Ft. Lauderdale, FL 33307
E-mail: gary@stretcher.com
Website: www.stretcher.com

The Door Magazine

OK, this is serious. That's because *The Door Magazine*, at its most basic, is serious. Beneath the brilliant humor, the wicked satire, the jaw-dropping interviews, the witty bon mots, we've got an actual purpose for putting out the magazine. We're the guys and gals who shout, "The emperor's got no clothes!" We're the people who are all about busting idols. We're folks who are interested in holding a mirror before the Church.

Why? Because we love the Church of Jesus Christ. We expose venal televangelists not because we're opposed to Christians, but because we're opposed to people who make a mockery of the Cross. We do it because we're called to do it.

That means we generally don't run straight-ahead slapstick humor. We like our humor to reflect one of those points. And that's why we don't do attack-styled ambush interviews OR softball touchy-feely interviews — because we're trying to make a point.

The absolute best place to see what we're trying to do is in past issues of *The Door*. (Sample issues are $5.95 from 5634 Columbia Avenue, Dallas, Tex, 75214.) We have a very definite style, a distinctive approach, a certain elan that belies the fact that our editor lives in Waco, Texas.

We love hearing from freelance writers. We're still 90% freelance written and proud of it — proud in a modest, life-affirming sort of way, of course. Alas, we rarely commission articles or interviews. But if you'd like to tackle former President Jimmy Carter or Stone Cold Steve Austin, by all means go for it. Just let us know ahead of time so you won't waste your time interviewing someone we've already interviewed (Steve Allen or Garrison Keillor) or someone we've already interviewed who is dead (Sam Kinison or Anton LaVey).

As for the legendary *Door* humor articles, they too are written on spec.

Here are some dos and don'ts for the prospective Door writer:

• Don't send us first person, mildly humorous essays or re-hashed sermons.

• Don't send us poetry, unless it is in the form of a howlingly funny song or hymn parody.

• Don't send us funny true-life stories, jokes, funny filler, articles with a moral to the story type ending. Aesop we ain't.

• Don't send us satire without humor.

• Don't send us humor without satire.

• Don't send us humor that's not somehow redemptive (and we can be very subtle on the redemptive stuff if we need to be).

• Don't send us articles that are only mildly amusing in a Steve Canyon suck on your pipe and gently smile sort of way. Be bold. Be funny.

• Do ... Well, I can't think of any dos.

If you've got an article or interview (or even a cartoon — and we pay $50 for each published 'toon) that meets the above criteria, then by all means send it.

If you want to e-mail an article, send it in WORD format to dooreditor@earthlink.net

We look forward to hearing from you, oh Keeper of the Faith!

Categories: Nonfiction—Christian Interests—Religion—Spiritual—Humor

CONTACT: Robert Darden, Editor
Material: Religious Humor & Satire
PO Box 1444
Waco TX 76703-1444
E-mail: dooreditor@earthlink.net
Website: www.thedoormagazine.com

Dovetail
A Journal by and for Jewish/Christian Families

Thank you for your interest in *Dovetail: A Journal by and for Jewish/Christian Families.* We have no denominational affiliation or agenda. Articles may reflect any of a variety of approaches and strategies (e.g. conversion of one partner and maintaining both religions), but should not have a proselytizing or negative tone. Personal experiences are welcome, as are articles based on research, but remember that Dovetail readers tend to be knowledgeable on this topic: avoid trite observations or broad generalizations. Each issue is geared to a particular theme.

We pay $25 plus 2 copies for 800-1000 word article; $15 plus 2 copies for a 500-word book review. Note: we occasional post published articles on our website. Since we receive no income from these postings, there will be no further compensation to authors above the original sum. Submission of an article to *Dovetail* constitutes your agreement to these terms. We prefer electronic submission as unformatted text file. It should be sent to DebiT4RLS@aol.com. I look forward to hearing from you.

Categories: Family—General Interest—Parenting—Relationships—Religion

CONTACT: Deb Tenner, General Editor
Material: All
45 Lilac Ln.
Hamden, CT 06517
E-mail: DebiT4RLS@aol.com
CONTACT: Carol Weiss Rubel, Review Editor
Material: All
310 Tulip Circle
Clarks Summit, PA 18411-0213
Phone: 502-549-5499
Fax: 502-549-3543
Website: www.dovetailinstitute.org

Downstate Story

We publish each November, and decide what to use in the fall. The deadline is always on June 30 for the issue coming out in the fall.

We aim to present a variety of work so every reader who looks at *Downstate Story* will find something fascinating.

Copies cost $8, postpaid in the USA. We encourage writers to buy a copy so they will be familiar with our publication.

Story guidelines, in general: short fiction or narrative written to the standards of fiction, under 2,000 words, never published before. Shorter is better. We prefer some connection with Illinois or the Midwest. We also need illustrators. All contributors are paid $50 on acceptance for their work. We buy first rights only. Anyone can submit work. Simultaneous submissions are OK with us. Just let us know if the story is accepted elsewhere.

Always enclose a SASE both for a resonse, and for the mss. itself, if you want it returned.

We prefer disposable mss. for the postage savings, as well as Internet correspondence. But no Internet submissions, please.

Categories: Fiction—Short Stories

CONTACT: Submissions Editor
Material: All
1825 Maple Ridge
Peoria IL 61614
E-mail: ehopkins@prairienet.org
Website: www.wiu.edu/users/mfgeh/dss

Dramatics
The Magazine for Students and Teachers of Theatre

The magazine and its readers

Dramatics is an educational theatre magazine published since 1929 by the International Thespian Society, a nonprofit honorary organization dedicated to the advancement of secondary school theatre. (In 1989 the Educational Theatre Association was formed to operate the Society as well as a separate professional association for teachers.) *Dramatics* is published nine times a year, September through May. It has a circulation of about 42,000. Approximately 80 percent of its readers are high school theatre students; about 10 percent are high school theatre teachers. Other subscribers include libraries, college theatre students and teachers, and others interested in educational theatre.

The primary editorial objectives of the magazine are: to provide serious, committed young theatre students and their teachers with the skills and knowledge they need to make better theatre; to be a resource that will help high school juniors and seniors make an informed decision about whether to pursue a career in theatre, and about how to do so; and to prepare high school students to be knowledgeable, appreciative audience members for the rest of their lives.

Opportunities for contributors We buy four to eight articles for each issue, ranging in length from 800 to 4,000 words.

Articles are accepted on any area of the performing arts, including film, video, and dance. A typical issue might include an interview with someone who has made a significant contribution to the theatre; an article describing some innovative approach to blocking, costume design, or set construction; a survey of leading theatre schools describing what they look for in students; and a photo spread, with copy, on some ground-breaking performer or theatre group.

Short news items, book reviews, and humor pieces (provided they're actually funny) are also part of the mix.

The test we apply, in deciding whether to accept an article, is whether it would engage an above-average high school theatre student and deepen his or her understanding and appreciation of the performing arts. We also look for pieces a theatre teacher might use in the classroom, studio, or rehearsal hall, although articles of this kind are more likely to be published in our quarterly journal *Teaching Theatre* (see separate guidelines).

Plays We print seven one-act and full-length plays a year. We occasionally reprint plays, but prefer that they be unpublished. Plays should be performable in high schools, which places some restrictions on language and subject matter; however, we tend not to publish children's theatre pieces, teen angst dramas, and overtly didactic "message" plays.

We buy one-time, non-exclusive publication rights to plays. The playwright retains all other rights.

Graphics Photos and illustrations to accompany articles are welcomed, and when available, should be submitted at the same time as the manuscript. Acceptable forms: color transparencies, 35mm or larger; color or black and white prints, 5 x 7 or larger; line art (generally used to illustrate technical articles); JPEG and TIFF files of high-quality scans. Unless other arrangements are made, payment for articles includes payment for photos and illustrations.

We occasionally buy photo essays.

Rights and returns

We buy first publication rights (unless we make other arrangements with an author), pay on acceptance, report in six weeks (or notify authors if a longer period is needed for review), and return all material that is accompanied by a self-addressed stamped envelope.

Queries and sample copies We prefer to see a finished manuscript but will respond to queries by letter or e-mail.

Phone queries are discouraged. Sample copies of the magazine cost $2.50. Subscriptions cost $20 a year.

Payment

Honorariums of $25 to $400 are paid for accepted work. Payment is based on quality of work, amount of editing or rewriting needed, length of work, and inclusion of photos or graphics. Contributors also receive five free copies of the issue in which their piece appears and may obtain additional copies at a minimal charge.

MS specifications

We edit manuscripts to conform to the Chicago Manual of Style. Manuscripts should be typed double-spaced on a sixty-character line. Photocopies are acceptable as long as they are clearly legible. Contributors should keep an exact copy of any manuscript submitted. Once articles are accepted, authors can score big points with the editorial staff by supplying their work electronically via e-mail (our address: dcorathers@edta.org; jpalmarini@edta.org) or on diskettes, sent to *Dramatics* magazine, 2343 Auburn Avenue, Cincinnati, OH 45219. We work on Windows-based computers; MS Word is the text program of choice.

All submissions are subject to editing, and we try to involve authors in that process as much as possible.

Whenever time allows, we send galley proofs to authors for review—usually by fax.

A CONTRIBUTORS CHEAT SHEET:

What makes us cranky

• Writers who are too lazy or careless to do basic reporting and research. Very few articles are complete with only one quoted source.

• Writers who represent themselves as experts when they're not.

• Writers who are not up front about if and where a piece has been previously published.

• Submissions that ignore or misunderstand our audience; articles that either talk down to our readers or are way over their heads. (If a piece has footnotes, it's probably too academic for us.)

• Contributors who create an impression of conflict of interest by writing about an organization in which they themselves are involved (although we do sometimes publish first-person accounts).

• Would-be playwrights who do not understand the basic conventions of the stage.

• Writers who are impossible to get ahold of, or who do not return messages.

What makes us happy

• Writers who really understand our audience.

• Writers who bring lots of strong, specific article ideas to the table, and keep abreast of topics recently covered by the magazine.

• Contributors who submit written queries or complete articles, rather than interrupting our work to make a sales pitch by phone.

• Writers who understand the need for editorial input, and can make and/or accept necessary changes gracefully.

• Writers who can provide good quality photography to go along with their pieces (snapshots are not publishable). Illustration ideas are also appreciated.

• Writers who include student voices in their pieces when appropriate, as well as a variety of other sources.

• Writers whose work is well organized, factual, and clean.

• Writers who are willing to work cheerfully for what we can afford to pay.

Categories: Nonfiction—Careers—Drama—Education—Entertainment—Film/Video—Teen—Theatre—Acting—Playscripts—Theatre Education

CONTACT: Don Corathers, Editor
Material: All
2343 Auburn Ave.
Cincinnati OH 45219

Phone: 513-559-1996
Fax: 513-559-0012
E-mail: dcorathers@edta.org
E-mail: jpalmarini@edta.org

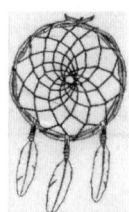

Dream Network
A Quarterly Journal
Exploring Dreams & Myth

The *Dream Network* invites articles, interviews, news items, photographs and artwork which will, in some way, inspire, inform or otherwise encourage our readers to value their dreams. Recommended are dream and myth related experiential articles, accounts of a personal/transformative nature and/or educational information that will empower readers in learning to understand the symbolic and metaphoric language of dreams and mythology. Our writers and readers consist of lay persons, students & professional dreamworkers. It is our goal to unite individuals who respect their dreams, to demystify dream work and to integrate dreamsharing into our culture. We also publish a few short poems in each issue.

Strictly promotional material is discouraged, since this is best addressed through advertising, also available in the Journal. (Send for publicity packet.)

Articles which attack, demean, or otherwise negate other people, organizations, philosophies, or systems are not accepted. Intelligently written articles which analyze or disagree with issues are welcomed as such material helps us understand one another better.

One section in each issue revolves around questions that were asked in the previous issue, i.e., our theme. Please contact us directly, by phone or mail, if you wish to be made aware of upcoming questions/themes. Other special sections are The Art of Dreamsharing and The Mythic Connection.

If you are not familiar with *Dream Network*, we ask that you avail yourself of several back issues so as to experience the texture and purpose of our mission.

LENGTH OF ARTICLES & FORMAT

If you enter your submission on a personal computer, please send copy of the article via email to Publisher@DreamNetwork.net or on computer disk, ideally with complementary illustrations and/or photographs. Include a one-sentence biographical statement and address at the end of each article submitted.

A page consists of approximately 900 words with room for title and a 2-5/8"x2-5/8" illustration and/or photograph of yourself. Preferred length, 2 to 3 pages, including photos &/or illustrations. Maximum length of articles, 1,800 words or approximately 3/4 pages, including illustrations/photos.

Please indicate copyright preference and date on submissions. DNJ reserves the right to edit all materials submitted for publication.

ART MATERIAL & PHOTOGRAPHS

Reproducible black and white original artwork and photographs are preferred. We use one color (black and white) graphics of many types—line drawings with washes, and photographs. Graphics need to be of high quality and camera ready. Art/graphic submissions can also be transmitted via email as .jpg file/300dpi or as .pdf files to Publisher@DreamNetwork.net

TIMING

Once an article is accepted for publication, we do our best to publish it in the next available issue. However we are routinely blessed with more material than we can publish. If you do not see your article in print immediately, please be patient. If you want us to consider your material for a specific issue, please indicate and/or advise us. We should be in receipt of the article no later than six weeks prior to the publication "Lifeline" and preferably much sooner. We do not promise any particular publication date for articles.

PAYMENT

In appreciation, we offer a free one year subscription and several complimentary copies of the issue in which your submission appears.

We do not pay money for articles nor do we give free advertising in exchange. If you are in business, we will also print a brief (no more than 40 words) statement of who you are and how people can reach you.

The reason we do not pay for articles is based on philosophical as well as financial considerations. The *Dream Network* exists to provide a community forum in which we learn from one another as well as a place for us to dialogue with one another. Once acceptance of articles is based upon financial remuneration, a certain segment of the population is denied access. Those denied such access would be those whose ability to express themselves well enough in writing is not such that they can earn a fee, i.e., only professional writers would be heard. Obviously, we encourage well-written articles and professional writers do write for us out of a desire to share with the dream community.

Approximate 'Lifelines' (formerly 'deadlines'):

All Saints Day/Halloween (Winter); Valentine Day (Spring); Memorial Day (Summer) Labor Day (Autumn)

Approximate Distribution Dates: January (Winter); April (Spring); July (Summer); October (Autumn)

Thank you for your interest in dreams & the *Dream Network*.

Categories: Fiction—Nonfiction—Arts—Children—Culture—General Interest—Health—Inspirational—Interview—New Age—Paranormal—Parenting—Psychology—Self Help—Senior Citizen—Spiritual—Mystery in the true sense

CONTACT: Submissions Editor
Material: All
PO Box 1026
Moab UT 84532
Phone: 435-259-5936
Website: DreamNetwork.net

Drum Business

Drum Business is designed exclusively for individuals involved in the sale of acoustic and electronic percussion and related equipment. The primary objective is to help the dealer run his or her operation more effectively by delivering relevant information on other successful operations. Other editorial will consist of manufacturer profiles, industry news, and in-depth coverage on new product information. While it is not crucial that all of our writers have worked in a drum shop or drum department, it is necessary that they know enough about drums, drum retailing, and retailing in general to be able to write about managing, merchandising, advertising, sales tips, and other topics associated with running a retail establishment.

Additionally, DB is looking for journalists who can present information in an objective manner so as to avoid making value judgements. Therefore, keep all articles as objective as possible. We are interested in how and why a particular store owner or manager operates a certain way; the reader can make their own decisions about whether or not they can adapt it for use in their own store.

Before you attempt to write an article for *Drum Business*, you should ask yourself the following questions: Will this article help a substantial numbers of retailers improve their operations? Will it enlighten them on a particular phase of retailing? Will it save them time, money, or effort? Is the topic interesting enough to attract a large number of readers? Will the article help them arrive at a decision or draw a conclusion? Will the article help retailers do their jobs better or run their

stores more efficiently? Not every article will do all of those things, but if the article does not do any of them, the DB will probably not be interested in it.

Please query us on lengthy material before you begin writing. This helps us avoid receiving articles we cannot use, and it will help you avoid having your articles returned. Send us a brief outline of the subject matter and your angle on the story. The editors will then be able to guide you in tailoring the material to the exact needs of the magazine. Also, if your idea has already been assigned or covered, we can notify you before you begin working. If you are writing for DB for the first time, or if your idea is somewhat out of the ordinary, you will be asked to submit your piece on speculation.

The above information should guide you in submitting material to *Drum Business*. If you need any further information, please write to us. We are always interested in acquiring good editorial material and in finding talented, competent writers.

PAYMENT

Drum Business pays upon publication. Rates vary depending upon the length of the story after editing, whether the article will be used as a feature article or column, and, to some extend, the length of the writer's association with *Drum Business*.

GENERAL RATES

Feature article: $250 - $350. Buys all rights.

Column: $100 - $200. Buys all rights. (Receipt of payment generally occurs three to six weeks after publication.)

OPEN COLUMNS

Retailing Columns – Column material can be technical, conceptual, or philosophical in nature.

Topics should be very specific, and we encourage the use of drawings, photos, or illustrations where applicable. (750 – 1000 words)

Progressive Management: Insightful management techniques for everything from computer usage to hiring and firing.

Effective Merchandising: Tips and practical ideas on merchandising drum and related equipment store layout, displays, etc.

Sales Seminar: Tips on retail sales techniques.

Advertising Basics: How to run cost-effective ad campaigns.

Studio Insights: Setting and running a teaching program.

Retailer Profile: A look at the management of successful drum/music shops.

A Closer Look: A look at one vertical aspect of a particular company and how it relates to over-all operation of the company.

Site Seeing: Everything about drums, drummers, and retail on the Web.

Manuscripts are edited to conform to style policies, as well as for consistency and readability.

This may involve condensing, rearranging, retitling, and, to some extent, rewording the article.

Please refer to the DB Style sheet for specific style preferences. Final decisions regarding style, grammar, and presentation are the right of the editorial staff of *Drum Business* magazine.

STYLE SHEET
Manuscript Layout

Margins: First page—three-inch margin at top, one-inch margin at bottom and sides. Subsequent pages—one-inch top, bottom, and sides.

Type specs: Copy must be typed and double spaced. Pica preferred, elite acceptable, no script.

For those using computers, manuscripts should look at much like typewritten manuscripts as possible, i.e., double spaced, margins as specified above, common typeface.

For those submitting articles on disk: Modern Drummer Publications, Inc., utilizes Microsoft Word 98 for Macintosh. If using DOS or PC Windows based, save your file as a text file, and please specify on the label what software was used. If we are unable to read files submitted on disk, they will be returned to the author. Use three and one-half inch (3 1/2") disks only. If submitting article on disk, please include hard copy as well.

E-mail submissions are acceptable. Please attach Word or text file to email document and send to kevk@moderndrummer.com.

COPY LENGTHS

Feature material should range from 2,500 to 3,000 words.

Column material should range from 750 to 1,000 words.

PUNCTUATION

Album, film, and book titles, as well as periodicals, should be underlined. Trademarks and model names should also be underlined, e.g. Tama Titan hardware, Paiste Rude crash cymbal, Remo Pinstripe head, Pro-Mark 5A drumsticks, Ludwig Black Beauty snare drum. Do not hyphenate words at the end of lines.

Dashes should be typed as a double hyphen with a space before and after (-). The initial letter of each word in album, film, and book titles, and in the names of periodicals, should be capitalized.

GEOGRAPHIC TERMS

Specific locations should be capitalized, e.g., Midwest, East Coast, West Coast. General directions should be in lowercase, e.g., east, west, north, south.

MUSICAL GENRES

Capitalize Gospel, Latin, and Dixieland. All other musical genres should be lower case, e.g., rock, jazz, etc. R&B or rhythm & blues; C&W or country & western; rock 'n' roll.

STYLE NOTES

Use words for number most of the time, except in a list of measurements or specific scientific measurements. '70s, '80s, 90s when dealing with decades. Forties, fifties, and sixties when dealing with age. LP (LPs), 45 (45s) CD (CDs)

PARAGRAPHING

The first paragraph of an article should be aligned entirely with the left margin. The first line of subsequent paragraphs should be indented one tab when using a computer, with subsequent lines aligning with the left margin. Do not insert line spaces between paragraphs.

INTERVIEWS

A. For question and answer format, introduction should follow paragraph format described in VII above. Uppercase initials of interviewer (followed by a colon) should precede questions, and initials of interviewee (also followed by a colon) should precede responses.

B. Interviews that follow narrative format should follow paragraph rules outlined in VII above.

PREFERRED SPELLINGS

A. Okay

B. Alright, Tom-tom, Hi-hat, Drumset, Drumkit, Drumheads, Drumsticks, Mic' (microphone), (noun) plural—mic's, e.g., I use three mic's. Miking, miked, mike (verb), e.g., I mike my sound room. Setup (noun), e.g., The article describes my store setup. Set up (verb), e.g., I will set up the new display. " (inch), e.g., 2" x (by), e.g., 5x4

LANGUAGE

A. Do not use gonna for going to, gotta for got to, or 'cause for because. In general, stay away from contracting verbs by omitting the ending "g," e.g., sayin' or playin'.

B. Language should be reasonably "clean." Obscenities should be kept to a minimum, or avoided, if possible.

Categories: Nonfiction—Arts—Business—Money & Finances—Music

CONTACT: Kevin W. Kearns, Associate Publisher/Editor
Material: All
12 Old Bridge Road
Cedar Grove NJ 07009-1288
Phone: 973-239-4140
E-mail: kevk@moderndrummer.com

THE ENVIRONMENTAL MAGAZINE

E Magazine
The Environmental Magazine

As the largest independent environmental magazine on the newsstand today, with a circulation of 50,000, E serves an important role as the voice for the environmental movement and as a vital information source on national and international coverage of environmental issues. Founded in 1990, E is sponsored by Earth Action network, a nonprofit organization located in Norwalk, CT. In an attempt to stay consistent with our values and goals, we print our magazine on recycled paper and screen our advertisers carefully.

1. We request that writers send an e-mail (preferred) or written query when first contacting E with a story idea. FAXed queries are acceptable. Please indicate approximate article length and which section of the magazine you are targeting, allowing a three-month lead time. We will contact you on acceptance of an article and assume no responsibility for unsolicited manuscripts. Please include writing samples and a self-addressed, stamped envelope (SASE) with your submission. We do not send free issues to potential freelancers.

2. Payment: E pays 30 cents per word upon publication. We do not usually pay for product or book reviews. Please submit an invoice upon acceptance.

3. Articles should be submitted on deadline in typed form with an approximate word count indicated. E-mail transmissions are preferred, although IBM-compatible disks are also acceptable. Please include a few sentences about yourself for the brief "author bio" we include at the end of many articles.

4. Articles for E should be written in a journalistic style in order to be easily understood by those not immersed in the environmental movement. Unfamiliar terms, scientific language and jargon should be avoided or explained for the benefit of the lay reader. We are not interested in strident, opinionated writing. We want a balanced tone that will not alienate the casual reader; E is an "advocacy" magazine that aims to broaden the base of the environmental movement, not to preach to the converted.

5. We are interested in articles dealing with environmental issues, currents of environmental thought and action and the dynamics of the movement (see "Section Guidelines" below). We are also interested in articles that explore the connections between environmental and other social change/humanitarian issues. We like articles which suggest ways to become involved and include places to write letters of support or protest, contact names and addresses, resources to tap, etc.

6. If photos and/or artwork are available, please indicate so in your query. PLEASE DO NOT SEND ANY ART MATERIALS UNTIL THEY ARE REQUESTED. We are not responsible for unsolicited artwork. Rates for images are negotiable.

7. We reserve the right to edit for grammar, brevity, clarity and tone. We prefer gender-neutral phrasing—i.e., "humankind" instead of "mankind."

8. We do not publish poetry, fiction or nature writing.

9. E's "Green Living" section features regular departments: Your Health, Eating Right, House and Home, Going Green, Money Matters, Consumer News and Tools for Green Living. These articles individualize the environmental movement and discuss ways readers can implement environmental practices into their homes and family lifestyles.

Section Guidelines

E seeks submissions for the following sections, with word lengths as indicated. Please examine back issues of E to get an idea of the style, tone and content of articles we publish.

Features: In-depth articles on key national and international environmental issues. i.e., population, transportation, children's environmental health, biotechnology, environmental education and energy. Length: 3,200 to 4,200 words.

Currents: News articles. i.e., environmental racism, cloning controversies, Maine forests for sale, cactus poachers, profiles of key organizations/campaigns. 1,000 words; five per issue.

In Brief: Short news articles. i.e., garbage art, AmeriCorps, sea cucumber conservation. 400 words; four to five per issue.

Money Matters: Information, resources and tips on greening personal finance and investments. i.e., eco-friendly stocks, saving money with community supported agriculture, shareholder activism. 750 words.

Going Green: This section follows the fast-growing eco-tourism industry and highlights notable trends and destinations. i.e., Costa Rica Rainforest Eco-Lodges, Alaska ANWR Experience and vegetarian vacations. 750 words.

Consumer News: Examines green consumer products and trends. i.e., recycled or "tree-free" paper, natural cosmetics, and "smart" wood. 1,200 words.

House & Home: Looks at services and products beneficial in the creation of a green home. i.e., eco-paints, home energy-saving tips, organic cotton bedding. 750 words.

Your Health: Explores environmental aspects of personal health. i.e., autism and the environment, antibiotic-pumped livestock, endocrine disruptors, mercury poisonings. 1,200 words.

Eating Right: Discusses the environmental implications of food choices. i.e., organic cereals, sustainable seafood. 1,2 00 words.

Tools for Green Living: Brief introductions/reviews of new green products and services. i.e., Nature's Way Feline Pine cat litter and eco-friendly shoes. 100 words; unpaid. The Books section profiles new publications. i.e., Earth Odyssey. 100 words; unpaid.

Categories: Conservation—Ecology—Environment—Politics

CONTACT: Jim Motavalli, Editor
Material: All
PO Box 5098
Westport CT 06881
Phone: 203-854-5559 ext. 109
Fax: 203-866-0602
E-mail: jimm@emagazine.com
Website: www.emagazine.com

Early American Life

Early American Life (formerly *Early American Home*) is a bimonthly magazine about the details of the American domestic past. Our time period ranges from the Pilgrim Century to 1850 and extends later if the subject warrants.

Our readers are interested in material and social history. They value what this information adds to their own lives and surroundings. They want to know more, in-depth, about the history inherent in objects—houses, gardens, textiles, painted decoration, furniture, pottery, food—indeed every element that was commonplace to early America. They like to see, and read about, the details.

This magazine is about reproductions as well as antiques. Fine craftsmanship—the work of someone who lived and worked at a certain time in a particular place—is integral to the value of objects past and present. We feature new houses, textiles, furniture, ceramics and other decorative objects and techniques made with attention to their historic precedents. Projects our readers can try themselves are also appealing, provided they, too, have an early American background.

We're receptive to articles that explore travel to historic places, discuss preservation issues, the antiques and reproductions market, journals, diaries, and inventories. We are always interested in articles that examine the human dimensions of American history; in the regular department called Life in Early America we explore what went on

day to day in a particular place in a certain period. Academic writing and images of past grandeur do not appeal.

Photographs accompanying article queries are helpful to us; their quality need not be professional, just informational. We do return them. We pay for articles on acceptance.

Virginia P. Stimmel, Editor

Categories: Antiques—Architecture—Arts—Biography—Collectibles—History—Travel

CONTACT: Virginia P. Stimmel, Editor
Material: American life, social history, and arts before 1850
207 House Ave., Ste. 103
Camp Hill PA 17011

East Bay Monthly

The *East Bay Monthly*, as you might have guessed, is a magazine published monthly and distributed throughout the East Bay (Oakland, Berkeley and environs). The Monthly's circulation—80,000—is the largest in the East Bay.

The Monthly's editors welcome queries from freelance writers. You should know that our first commitment is to fine writing. We appreciate the passionate essay, the deft parody, the tale well-told, first-person narratives, historical pieces, personality profiles, as well as carefully reported features and in-depth investigative articles. Just about the only genres we are not interested in are poetry and fiction.

We aim to be a forum for distinctive, intelligent, individual voices on every conceivable topic of interest to our audience. We like stories about local people and issues. We are generally only interested in topics outside the East Bay's borders if, a) the writer is a recognized East Bay writer, or b) the article idea can still be tied to East Bay history or culture.

We suggest you spend some time looking over recent issues of The Monthly to get a sense of what we publish and what might appeal to us.

To propose an article, send us some recent writing samples, a self-addressed stamped envelope and a cover letter with the following information: your story idea, how you will approach it, your point of view, whom you will interview, a proposed length, and why you think your idea will make our readers sit up and take notice.

Expect to receive a reply from us in four to six weeks. Please note that if you do not send us an SASE, we are not responsible for the fate of your submission.

The Editors

Categories: Culture—Lifestyle

CONTACT: Kira Halpern, Editor
Material: Any
CONTACT: Kate Rix, Associate Editor
Material: Any
1301 - 59th St.
Emeryville CA 94608
Phone: 510-658-9811
E-mail: THE MONTHLY@aol.com

East End Lights
The Quarterly Magazine
for Elton John Fans

WHAT ARE WE LOOKING FOR?

Anything, so long as it is related to Elton John. We want the voice of the fans to be heard, whether it be in a story, photos, original artwork, fan letters, ramblings, ravings... you get the idea.

You could write a deep piece about a personal experience related to a song, or a funny story about how your co-workers make fun of you for listening to Elton's music. Close encounters with EJ, the first song which turned you on to his music, lyric analysis, album critique, an outstanding concert experience, and so on.

Be creative. Write what you like. Use your own voice. As editors we try to keep our influence to a minimum. But if you should have questions, or even writer's block, we're just an email away.

East End Lights is not an Elton John love-fest. We do not subscribe to the "artist can do no wrong" policy. Be objective. *East End Lights* provides readers with historical accounts and interviews with Elton band members and associates and does not lend itself to "gossip" type stories and articles. Just the facts.

East End Lights has an open-door policy regarding submissions. You don't have to be a seasoned journalist — just a fan!

WHAT FORMAT DO I SUBMIT MY WRITTEN WORK IN?

Very simply. Electronic. You can email it to us at eel@accessthemusic.com. It can be any just about any word processing program out there (Word, Quark Epress, Simple Text, etc). Please send the file as an attachment and not embedded into your message window.

PHOTOS & ARTWORK

We accept photos and original artwork. Copyright laws are applicable; if you are not the original photographer or author of the work, we cannot accept your submission.

We accept 35mm prints only — color laser copies and inkjet prints are generally not acceptable. Photos mailed to use are not returned, so don't send anything you cannot part with.

You may also send photos via email. Scanned images should be 300dpi at 100% scale, and saved as a JPEG with a high quality setting.

Be sure to include the pertinent details about the photo, such as the date it was taken and a brief description of the subject. When submitting original artwork, include the medium used, and perhaps your inspiration for the work.

If you have any questions about submitting your photos or artwork, please contact eel@accessthemusic.com.

HOW DO I SUBMIT?

There are two kinds of submissions: unsolicited, and comissioned. The short story is, if you don't care about getting paid for your work, you can simply send it in as an unsolicited submission. However, if you would like to be paid for your efforts, you must begin with a query letter to let us know about your ideas.

UNSOLICITED SUBMISSIONS

An unsolicited submissions is a piece which, regardless of size or content, is sent to us without first being assigned to you. To get a story assignment, you must first send us a query letter. *East End Lights* is not obligated to use, nor do we pay for, unsolicited submissions.

WHAT IS A QUERY LETTER?

A query letter is simply the starting point... if you have an idea for an article, let us know what you have in mind before you before you put pen to paper.

We do not have a "standard format" for query letters. Just tell us who you are, what you want to write about, and how we can contact you. Samples of your previous works are helpful. Just drop us a line at eel@accessthemusic.com.

COMMISSIONED WORK

If your idea is accepted, we will contact you with further details on what we need for your story. If you accept the assignment, it becomes a commissioned piece.

If you write your piece before we have commissioned it, you do so at your own risk. *East End Lights* is not obligated to use, nor do we pay for, unsolicited submissions.

WHAT'S IN IT FOR ME?

Apart from international exposure and the joy of seeing your name in print, *East End Lights* will actually pay you for your commissioned work!

$50 for features and columns
$20 for fillers*
$20 kill fee**
pays on publication
byline given
does not pay expenses*** of writer on assignment
author usually handles major revisions

accompanying photos are appreciated, but not required

All authors who receive payment for their work will receive a Tax Form 1099 for the IRS if applicable.

For material which isn't time-sensitive, we may hold an article for use in a future issue due to space constraints.

GET IT RIGHT

We're pretty relaxed as far as content, but we do ask that you follow some basic tenets of writing. Proper grammar and accurate spelling are as important as the story itself.

Fact checking is equally important. If you quote a lyric, get out the liner notes and make sure you get it right. Check dates, verify quotes, and in general try not to leave holes in your work.

Edit thyself. If the story is about the EJ concert you attended, make sure that is the story. Skip the details of the sumptuous meal you ate before the show, the lovely hotel you stayed in the night before, the screaming child behind you on the plane, or the three hour delay at the airport. Focus. Tell the story you set out to tell.

And above all, have fun!

NOTES

Generally speaking, fillers are much shorter than features and columns. *East End Lights* will determine whether a piece constitutes a filler, feature, or column, and will inform you of this at the time of the assigment.

The kill fee is the amount paid for commissioned work which, for reasons beyond our control, is never published.

We will never ask you to spend any money for the sake of a story, so there will never be any expenses as a result of an assignment. If you choose to jet off to see Elton John in concert, you do so at your own expense.

Categories: Fiction—Nonfiction—Arts—Biography—Entertainment—Gay/Lesbian—Music

CONTACT: Mark Norris, Editor
Material: All
Access Entertainment, LLC
PO Box 621
Joplin MO 64802-0621
Phone: 417-782-9911
E-mail: eel@accessthemusic.com

East Texas Historical Journal
Stephen F. Austin State University

The *East Texas Historical Journal* is published in the Spring and Fall of each year. It includes articles and reviews of recently published books, mainly on Texas history, especially East Texas history. Submission must be on disk (3.5) or via email as an MS-Word attachment as well as hard copy. Notes should be placed at the end. Articles that do not exceed twenty-five to thirty pages, notes included, are preferred. We also welcome new book reviewers. Potential book reviewers should email a brief statement of their fields of expertise.

Categories: Nonfiction—History

CONTACT: Archie P. McDonald, Director and Editor
Material: All
Box 6223, Stephen F. Austin State University
Nacogdoches TX 75962
Phone: 936-468-2407
Fax: 936-468-2190
E-mail: amcDonald@sfasu.edu
Website: www.easttexashistorical.org

Ebony

Does not accept unsolicited submissions.

Education in Focus

Education in Focus is a 6-page newsletter that enlightens readers to urgent concerns in education in a fundamental way. All material must maintain a humane premise, rationally defended, and be suitably documented. Length is limited to about 3,000 words (more in exceptional cases). Please don't submit articles that support the failures of the education system or that lack sensible solutions to urgent problems. Payment is modest. Comp copy available (provide SASE—#10, one stamp).

Categories: Education

CONTACT: Joe David, Editor
Material: All
PO Box 202
Warenton, VA 20188
Phone: 540-428-3175
E-mail: staff@bfat.com
Website: www.bfat.com

Education Week

Guidelines for *Education Week* Commentary Writers:

Education Week considers unsolicited manuscripts for inclusion in the Commentary section, provided they follow the guidelines below.

Essays should run approximately 1,200 to 1,500 words (five to six double-spaced pages) in length.

Submissions should treat issues in precollegiate education or child development. In organization and tone, the piece should take the form of an opinion essay rather than a scholarly paper or research report.

Our audience includes elementary and secondary teachers, principals, superintendents, school-board members, education-school faculty members, chief state school officers, education researchers, and others. Most of our readers are already aware of basic issues in education; for this reason, we usually accept only essays that treat specific topics in a detailed and analytical way.

If your submission is accepted for publication in the Commentary section, you will be contacted about possible publication dates and the amount of your honorarium; payments are made within two weeks of publication.

Because *Education Week* has specific style rules, it is likely that we will make at least a few changes to your essay. Please provide us with daytime and evening/weekend phone numbers where you can be reached to approve any changes or answer any questions we might have.

We often receive requests from other publications to reprint Commentaries. Our procedure is to grant permission. Our credit line and the date of publication must also be printed with the essay. The person making the request is asked to contact the author of the essay. If you are contacted, it is up to you to give final permission and to discuss the subject of your payment. If you receive the initial call from someone who wants to reprint your piece, please tell the caller he or she must contact *Education Week*.

Please submit a hard copy of your manuscript as well as a copy on a computer diskette, or if you prefer, e-mail the submission to Amy E. Conrad at aconrad@epe.org. Please include a mailing address where the contract, honorarium, and other materials can be sent.

Manuscripts and diskettes cannot be returned.

Categories: Nonfiction—Child Development—Education

CONTACT: Amy E. Conrad
Material: All
6935 Arlington Rd.
Suite 100
Bethesda, MD 20814-5233
Phone: 301-280-3100
E-mail: aconrad@epe.org
Website: www.edweek.org

Educational Leadership

Educational Leadership is the official journal of the Association for Supervision and Curriculum Development (ASCD). Its contents are intended for all persons interested in curriculum, instruction, supervision, and leadership in education. Each issue contains articles by leading educators, reports of effective programs and practices, interpretations of research, book reviews, and columns.

Issues are organized around themes. In general, the more appropriate your article is for a theme issue, the more likely we will be able to publish it. We also accept articles on "Special Topics" if the subject is of great interest but not related to a theme. In addition, we invite international contributions all year long, but especially for those three to four issues designated as having an International Section.

Other important information: ASCD offers no remuneration for articles by professional educators.

Decisions regarding publication are made by the Editor and the editorial staff. ASCD reserves the right to reject material, whether solicited or otherwise, if it is considered lacking in quality or timeliness.

WHAT WE LOOK FOR...

The editors look for brief (1,500-2,500 words) manuscripts that are helpful to practicing K-12 educators. We are not looking for term papers or reviews of literature, and we rarely publish conventional research reports. We prefer articles in which the writer speaks directly to the reader in an informal, conversational style. The treatment of the topic should be interesting, insightful, and based on the writer's experiences. Practical examples should be used to illustrate key points. When reporting their own research, writers should emphasize explanation and interpretation of the results, rather than the methodology. We usually don't find query letters helpful; we prefer to read the manuscript.

HOW TO PREPARE YOUR MANUSCRIPT...

To prepare your manuscript, number all pages and show your name, address, phone number, fax number, and e-mail address on the cover sheet only. We prefer manuscripts that look like manuscripts, not like typeset articles from desktop publishing. On page one, just above the title, please indicate the number of words in the manuscript, including references, figures, and the like.

Cite references in the text like this (Jones 1988), and list them in bibliographic form at the end of the article; or use citations in the form of numbered endnotes. See a recent issue of *Educational Leadership* for examples of citations. Authors bear full responsibility for the accuracy of citations, quotations, figures, and the like.

For other matters of style, refer to *The Chicago Manual of Style and Webster's Collegiate Dictionary.*

HOW TO SUBMIT YOUR MANUSCRIPT...

Send two copies. It is not necessary to send unsolicited manuscripts by overnight mail-our deadlines are target dates, not factors in selection. You can expect to receive a postcard telling you that the manuscript has arrived; a response from an editor should arrive within eight weeks.

If you discover a small error after mailing your manuscript, please do not send a correction; small errors can be corrected in the editing process.

WHAT HAPPENS NEXT...

If your manuscript is accepted, even provisionally, we will ask you to send a computer disk or a letter-quality original of your article. Then your manuscript enters the pool of manuscripts on hand for a particular theme issue (or for use in "Special Topics"). When the editors assemble a particular issue, they review all manuscripts to make selections for the table of contents. All manuscript selections are tentative until we go to press.

When we select articles for each issue, we consider many factors, such as the balance of perspectives, locations, grade levels, and topics. If your manuscript becomes a contender for the final table of contents, you will be notified, and we'll ask you to send a computer disk or a letter-quality original. During the editing and layout process, however, we may have to make last minute adjustments, with resultant disappointments to authors.

WHAT TO DO ABOUT COMPUTER DISKS...

We edit on computer, so we'd like you to submit your manuscript on disk as well as on paper. We can use IBM-compatible or Mac disks but not Apple. Write on the disk both the kind of computer and the name of the word processing program you used-and be specific: include version numbers where applicable. If your disk has been formatted high-density, indicate this, too. And please indicate on the disk your last name and the file name of your manuscript.

If you cannot send a disk, we will use an electronic scanner to transfer your manuscript to a disk. We can only scan it, however, if it's a high-quality (clear and sharp) typewritten text or print-out.

We will also accept articles scheduled for publication sent to us via the Internet. Our e-mail address is shown below.

HOW TO SURVIVE THE EDITING PROCESS...

If your manuscript becomes a contender for the issue's table of contents, it is assigned to a staff editor, who shepherds it through all the editing and layout processes. Once your manuscript is edited, you will receive an edited version for your review, correction, and approval. At this time you will have a chance to correct errors, answer our queries, and update any outdated information. The style requirements of *Educational Leadership*—as well as space limitations—dictate heavy editing, and we appreciate collaboration with the authors in the process.

One more word about correcting your edited manuscript:

Please do not retype it! Just mark your corrections directly on the manuscript, and mail or fax it back to us. If you have insertions, please type or write them on separate pieces of paper; and indicate on the manuscript where they are to be inserted.

When you receive the edited version of your manuscript, you should also receive a transfer of copyright form, which includes permission to record your article (in case the editors select it for EL on Tape), and permission to use your article online. Please indicate your preferences on these forms, and return them by first-class mail or fax as soon as possible.

ABOUT ARTWORK AND PHOTOGRAPHS...

The editors like to have photographs and artwork related to the manuscripts, but these do not influence editorial selection. We appreciate having the opportunity to see your artwork-photos (black and white or color) or slides, and student papers and artwork. Send artwork when you are notified that your manuscript has been accepted or when the editors request it. Send photos to us by overnight mail.

Authors are responsible for ensuring that all persons in each photograph have given their permission for the photograph to be published; they are also responsible for ensuring that they have permission to use all other artwork, such as student work. Please include the name of the photographer or the source so that we may give proper credit; and, on the back of each item, tape a small piece of paper with your name and address. (Do not write directly on the back of the photo.) And please add a note to explain what's happening in each photo, including the name and location of the school, or a note to explain the artwork. This information helps us when it's time to write captions.

WHEN YOUR ARTICLE COMES OUT...

As soon as the issue is off press-about the first of each month of issue-we'll send your complimentary copies. Article authors receive five copies; column authors, two copies; book reviewers, one copy. We'll also send an "Author's Feedback Form" to gather your comments about our work. Fill that out quickly, and it's time to arrange your autograph party.

Categories: Nonfiction—Education

CONTACT: Marge Scherer, Editor
Material: All

ASCD, 1250 N. Pitt St.
Alexandria VA 22314-1453
E-mail: el@ascd.org
Website: www.el@ascd.org

Educators Edition
Teachers Magazine
Please refer to Metro Parent/Metro Baby.

The Electron
Cleveland Institute of Electronics and World College

How to write for *The Electron*

Articles in *The Electron* have "news value." We cover recent developments and trends in electronics and high technology. Because *The Electron* is published every other month, the editors and writers can't report breakthrough immediately when they occur. However, any items covered must be timely to justify its publication in our newspaper.

Cover Stories

The Electron's front page features must be written in the journalistic style, have news value, and contain quotes based on interviews with one or more sources.

Other elements the editors look for are strong lead paragraphs, a good angle, descriptive language and general readability.

You may use news releases as source material, but a manuscript that reads like a sales pitch will be rejected. Avoid an obvious slant toward a particular product or company. (An exception to this would be a "corporate profile," in which activities of a company in the forefront of electronics technology are examined. AT&T Bell Laboratories is a good example of one organization we have covered.)

You should have the ability to write about electronics/high technology in a manner the layperson can understand. Define terminology with a brief line of explanation set off with dashes or parentheses, or with a concise one or two line paragraph. Practical examples are helpful:

"Requirement at startup will be 75 kilowatts—enough to power a small radio station..."

Acronyms or terms common in everyday usage—IC, LCD, semiconductor, solid-state—do not require an explanation.

Suggested length for a cover story is 800 words.

The above guidelines also apply to articles written for *The Electron*'s various departments. However, we do not necessarily require that you interview sources or include quotes. If you are well-versed in an area (computers, broadcasting, avionics, etc.), you may rely upon your knowledge of, or expertise in that field to write your article.

Main Features

The Electron's main (photo) feature covers in depth a broad area in electronics/high technology. Examples of topic areas we have already covered include: Artificial Intelligence; Medical Electronics; Robotics; and Telecommunications.

The main feature, run on a semi-regular basis, reflects that issue's editorial theme. Other articles in the issue will relate to the main feature, particularly the cover stories.

You should follow the cover story guidelines for style, content and readability. Remember, this is a photo feature. Ask about the availability of photographs when interviewing sources for facts and quotes.

Due to the length of the main feature (2,000 words), we recommend that you take the following approach. Break down the topic area by writing a main/overview article and one sidebar. In the main article, review trends and developments relating to the general topic. For the sidebar, you may write a retrospective of the technology, or interview a prominent person in the field.

We will consider your suggestions for alternative approaches to the main feature.

Technical Features

The Electron's technical articles focus on a timely topic in technology. The preferred writing style here is "tutorial" (essay form is best). Thus, technical articles in *The Electron* have news and educational value.

Most of your readers will be the students of The Cleveland Institute of Electronics and World College. Knowledge of electronics in relation to *The Electron*'s readers range from an electronics technician (associate degree level) to an electronics engineer (bachelor's degree level.) As a technical writer for *The Electron*, you are a teacher. Help the readers understand difficult points and concepts by providing illustrations. Supplement text discussion with tables and figures. These may be submitted as clean freehand drawings or sketches.

Your choice of topic should relate to the issue's editorial theme, if possible. Suggested length for a technical feature is 1,000 words.

Categories: Education—Electronics

CONTACT: Ted Sheroke, Advertising Manager
Material: All
1776 E 17th St
Cleveland OH 44136
Phone: 216-781-9400
Fax: 216-781-0331

Electronic Servicing & Technology

These writers' guidelines describe the kinds of articles published in *Electronic Servicing & Technology*, give some idea of the recommended length, and suggest a format for manuscripts.

Also included is a list of possible article subjects as well as a list of vocabulary words that we would like to define in depth in the magazine. These are meant as idea starters, and are not intended to exclude from consideration subjects that are not on the lists.

Also included are specific guidelines for preparing materials for publication in the SYMCURE and Troubleshooting Tips departments.

Sincerely, Conrad Persson

Editor

Electronic Servicing & Technology is written primarily for servicing technicians who sell, install, and service home electronics equipment.

Articles for *Electronic Servicing & Technology* should be technical in nature and be about an electronics or electronics-related subject. *Articles published in ES&T ordinarily fall into the following general categories:*

• Specific servicing procedures for specific electronic products.
• General troubleshooting/servicing procedures.
• Theory/operation of specific items of test equipment.
• Reports of new electronics technology of interest to electronic servicing technicians.
• Tutorial articles on electronics theory.
• Symptom/cure type brief articles.
• Troubleshooting tips.
• Articles on business, as related to consumer electronics servicing.

ES&T article coverage is not limited to these subject areas, however, and we welcome inquiries from prospective authors.

We use drawings, schematics, and photos, both B&W and color. For color photos, we prefer transparencies, although we can work from prints. We have access to artists who can create finished art, so don't be hesitant to include rough hand drawings. We can put them in final form.

We especially welcome articles that are on computer disk. We use IBM format, and can accept either 3½" or 5¼" disks. Preferred format is ASCII, but we can usually accept output from any word processor. Please be sure to include information that tells us what word processor you used to create the document.

Article length for a feature article should ordinarily be between three and fifteen typewritten pages. That's just a rough guide, though, not a hard and fast rule. Articles should be as long as they have to be to cover the subject thoroughly. Other manuscripts like Symcure, Troubleshooting Tips and others may be very brief.

It might be to the writer's advantage to submit a query beforehand, outlining a proposed article. That would allow the editors to comment specifically on whether an article is appropriate and/or needed, as well as to suggest to the writer information that should be included.

In any case, do not hesitate to write or call the editors to request comments and guidance on writing for ES&T.

Symcure

The term Symcure is a contraction of the two words: Symptom/cure. Problems that are published in ES&T in the Symcure department are those that have occurred more than once.

This is the kind of problem that you can solve without even a second thought because you've already seen so many of that particular brand and model of set with those symptoms and in almost every case it was the same component that had failed, or the same solder joint that had opened.

Because of the manner in which we publish Symcure, submissions, if they are to be considered, must follow these rules:

1. Each submission must consist of seven individual symptom/cure units on a single brand and model of television set. Seven are requested so we may choose the most appropriate for publication.

2. We must have the following information about the set:
• Manufacturer's name
• Model and chassis number or ID
• Sams Photofact number if you know it
• A rough sketch of the schematic where the fault was found. Each sketch should contain a major component such as a transformer, a tube, a transistor or an IC to provide a landmark for the ES&T staff.

3. Because the very nature of Symcure is based on schematics, if for any reason there is no Sams Photofact on the unit, we cannot accept the submission.

Troubleshooting Tips

A troubleshooting tip is a description of the procedure used by a servicing technician to diagnose, isolate and correct an actual instance of a specific problem in a specific piece of electronic equipment. Its value to readers, however, lies in the general methods described rather than its applicability to the repair of the specific piece of electronic equipment.

A good, useful troubleshooting tip has the following elements:

• A brief but complete, accurate and concrete description of the problem symptoms.

• A complete identification of the set, including manufacturer's name, model and chassis number and the Sams Photofact number, if known.

• A rough, simplified, schematic sketch of the area where the trouble occurred. Include some major component such as a transformer, tube or transistor, to serve as a landmark to the ES&T staff.

• A detailed step-by-step description of the procedure used to track down the cause of the problem. This should include the thinking process used—for example, "the absence of B+ voltage led me to believe...etc." • A mention of any symptoms that misled you and perhaps caused you to follow false trails.

• A narrative telling why the defect was suspected and how it was determined to be the cause of the problem (e.g., tested open, shorted, etc.).

• A description of how the repair was performed, including any precautions about possibility of damage to the set or injury to the servicing technician, if applicable.

The characteristics of a good candidate for troubleshooting tips are as follows:

1. The cause of the problem should be relatively uncommon.

2. The diagnosis and repair should not be obvious, and preferably should present something of a challenge to a competent servicing technician.

Article Ideas

This is a list of ideas for articles for *Electronic Servicing & Technology* that readers have suggested, and that the editorial staff has added to. It is not meant to limit articles in *Electronic Servicing & Technology* to these subjects, merely to serve as a list of possible articles and idea starters.

• One type of article that many readers have requested is the article, or more usually a series of articles, that examines a relatively new model of TV set from end to end, describing all of the circuitry, and especially dwelling on any new type of circuitry.

Other article subjects:

• Power conditioning
• Troubleshooting HV and LV circuits and how they work
• Understanding and servicing TV shutdown circuits
• Understanding TV startup circuits
• Understanding TV voltage regulator circuits
• Troubleshooting horizontal circuits
• Troubleshooting vertical circuits
• Troubleshooting TV power supply circuits
• Servicing cellular telephones
• Specific troubleshooting procedures for specific brands and models of TV
• Dealing with newer, more exotic TV
• Understanding the NTSC waveform
• Preventive maintenance for printers
• Understanding electronic tuners and tuning
• DC motor control
• Servicing two-way radio
• IBM PC computer servicing
• The personal computer as a servicing tool
• Servicing CB radio
• Personal computer servicing: general and product specific
• Servicing compact disc players
• Servicing VCRs
• Understanding and servicing VCR control systems
• Servicing TVRO: downconverters, LNAs, actuators
• Understanding new circuitry: SAW filters, phase-lock loops, comb filters
• Using a spectrum analyzer in troubleshooting
• Fundamentals of electronics
• Fundamentals of electronic servicing
• Servicing projection TV
• Servicing video cameras/camcorders
• Test equipment use and operation
• Do-it-yourself circuit construction
• Diagnosing antenna problems
• Servicing consumer electronic instruments: keyboards, organs, etc.
• Troubleshooting older TVs
• Servicing microwave ovens
• Servicing, repair and calibration of test equipment
• Inexpensive test equipment/accessories
• Testing methodology
• Suggested general troubleshooting techniques/tips/hints
• Servicing audio equipment
• Detailed descriptions of how circuits work
• New methods of soldering/desoldering for new soldering technology
• Suggestions on finding/tailoring general replacements when exact replacements are no longer offered by manufacturer
• Lightning and surge protection
• TV tuner repair

• Understanding digital circuit design and operation
• Troubleshooting/repairing digital circuits
• Signal injection/signal tracing
• CIB calculations for MATV
• Identifying sources of TV interference and correcting problems
• Electronics in home appliances: what they are, how to fix
• Test equipment for personal computers
• Servicing mechanical components
• Understanding wire and cable
• Sources of replacement parts
• Description of the evolution of consumer electronic servicing
• The new multistandard TVs
• A step-by-step approach to troubleshooting: using the senses, what's the next step, etc.
• Equipping a test bench
• Troubleshooting logic circuits with logic probes, pulsers, etc.
• Training/studying
• Multichannel TV sound
• Understanding digital circuit test equipment
• Component testing: resistors, capacitors, inductors, diodes, transistors, ICs
• How switching power supplies work, and are there a lot of TVs or other consumer electronics with switchers in them
• Something like SYMCURE and Troubleshooting Tips for computers/VCR
• Information on electronics societies, organizations
• ESD protection
• Servicing the new Sanyo power supplies
• What is "HQ" circuitry in VCRs
• One reader would like to see a shop hints department showing better ways to make repairs faster in the shop.
• How about a mini course in relay and control logic for such purposes as microwave oven controls?
• Here's an idea I've toyed with from time to time: Would it be possible to start with a bare bones TV receiver and add colored overlays showing how TV has evolved from its inception to today?
• Troubleshooting using an oscilloscope
• Understanding electronics math
• Logs, R/C time constants, Kirchhoff's laws, Trigonometric functions, math primer
• Finding schematics is a problem, but is it possible in some instances to recreate the schematic by tracing the wiring and doing your own drawing?
• How does detection actually work?
• Math Cad review
• Remote control cable converters
• How does AGC work?
• How does AFC work?
• How does a VCO work?
• Discuss filters: high pass, low pass, band pass, active. And how about the word "filter"? Is it really a good word? In one sense, a filter is used to pass a band of frequencies while rejecting others. In another it is used to "smooth" a pulsating dc after rectifying an ac waveform. How should a tech think about filters?
• Why do we use Q to identify a transistor, CR or Y to identify a diode, etc.?
• What does sampling rate mean when we're talking about, for example, a digitizing oscilloscope?
• Why not a primer on transistors, explaining, among other things, why the base, emitter and collector are so called, why use a and ß for amplification, getting into PNP and NPN to a certain degree. That, then, gets into another interesting question: should bipolar transistors and FETs in fact be both called transistors? What are the similarities that get them both the name "transistor" (transfer/resistor), and what are the differences?
• Modulation: among other things, we call the modulating waveform the "carrier", when in fact it can be suppressed before transmitting the signal. It seems like it's a poor choice of terminology.

• An article on antique radio, phono, etc. What the rewards are. What the equipment is. What people, organizations, companies are involved, etc.

• The organizations that ES&T readers belong to, or that might be able to help readers: NESDA, ETA, FIA, etc. What is a CET from the point of view of NESDA and ETA, etc.

• What is a "waveform analyzer"? Is it simply an oscilloscope with some other features like a built in DMM, etc.?

• How about an article on reading manufacturers model numbers: do the numbers mean anything?

• Correcting VCR loading problems

• Correcting VCR speed selection circuit problems

• One thing I'd like to do if possible is to track and publish information on companies that seem to disappear: like Symphonette, Bohsei, etc. I'd welcome any thoughts on how to do that.

• An article that looks at herringbone on screen, and describes what problem causes it and examines the circuits involved and the mechanics of the problem.

• We frequently talk about a two-port or three-port device. How about an explanation of what we mean by that?

• Ways to deal with intermittent problems

• Sorting out all of the transistor and IC part numbers

• How about an article on closed-captioning circuitry for TVs for the hearing impaired?

• What is an "eye" pattern on an oscilloscope? What is it used to measure and how is it used?

• What is a parametric amplifier and where is it used?

• What do ferrite beads do, what are they made of, when were they introduced, etc.?

• What books, catalogs, etc. are essential to a servicing technician's library?

• Warranties, manufacturer's and extended

• Satellite TV scrambling and descrambling

• Such things as active high, active low, Vdd, Vss, etc.

• Charge pump?

• Swallow counter

• Prescaler

• How to go about estimating a job

• Reading a schematic diagram

• Technical support from manufacturers. Tech help phone lines and price and availability of service literature.

• Frequency synthesis and frequency division—what do we mean by these?

• What are servos used for and how do they work?

• On a digital multimeter, why is there a 1/2-digit, and what does "an accuracy of "2% + 2 digits (or whatever) mean?

• Bar-code scanners. Bar codes are now being used to program VCRs

• This one was suggested by a reader who sent in a Reader Service card. An article on a complete sales/service center management software package.

• I'd like to see us do an article on transformers. Describe line isolation transformers, variable transformers, autotransformers, variable isolation transformers, discuss trademarks like Variac, step up, step down, coupling.

• How about a rundown of the safety related components in a consumer electronics product? What are their special characteristics, and why can't they be replaced with universal replacements.

Vocabulary

Here are some words that we would like to define in the magazine at some convenient time. One possible way would be for a writer to write an article on a subject to which several of the words relate, and define the terms in the article. Most vocabularies or glossaries provide just a brief definition of the word. I would like to include in-depth definitions.

Something to keep in mind, is that where the term is not particularly apt, this should be pointed out. For example, I'm not sure that the terms "active" and "passive" are really descriptive of the characteristic they describe, although they come fairly close. Another example is

the term "carrier" in regard to electromagnetic transmission. If you can transmit without the "carrier", then it really isn't a carrier, is it?

• Here's another term I have a hard time with - Injection, as of a signal or a voltage? What does "injection" mean, and is it apt?

• Slew rate

• Synchronous/asynchronous

• Prescaler

• Preemphasis

• PWM

• How about an article on abbreviations concerning computers, like MS-DOS, etc.

• Ramp up

• Bio of Lord Kelvin

• Why do we use U followed by a number to designate an IC?

• Scan-derived

• It would be interesting to delve into why the elements of a transistor: base, emitter and collector are so called.

• Why do we call certain portions of a TV circuit a driver?

• A to D and D to A conversion

• What is heat sink grease made of?

• In cable TV, what is meant by head end?

• What is a balun?

• What is meant by the term "leaky" in conjunction with electronic components? For example, transistors can be leaky, or capacitors. Anything else?

• Piecrusting

• Motorboating

• Barkhausen lines

• Turbo (in connection with computers)

• Servo

• WWV

• Alignment: TV, FM, VCR, Disc drive, other?

• Bias (There's forward and reverse bias on semiconductor junctions, and a bias used on magnetic tape). Any others?

• What do we mean by sampling rate when it comes to A to D conversion?

• Where does the term "capacitor" come from.

• What does "peak reading" mean when it comes to capacitors?

• Why not do a simple article to reveal the difference between "linear" and "nonlinear"? You could use actual resistors and diodes to do the research and suggest the readers do the same experimentation to find out what's going on.

• What is meant by "dynamic range"?

• There seems to be more than one meaning of "saturation": one, for example when talking about a circuit current condition, and one when talking about tape recording. What do they mean? Are there other meanings?

• Describe modulation: AM and FM. Come to think of it, why not include PCM, and any other Ms that come to mind?

• Define "harmonics".

• Dropout

• Retrace: Is this a good term, or is it misleading?

• Damper

• Keystoning

• Explain abbreviations like BNC, DIN, etc.

• Active filters

• Data communications "protocol"

• algorithm

• excursion

• Why is the supply voltage (in some cases the "scan derived" voltage) called a B+ voltage

• The term "flyback" would be one worth exploring at some time.

• Coupling, decoupling

• Neutralization as regards transistor amplifiers

• Countdown, as in TV output circuits

• Parasitic, as in parasitic oscillations.

It saves us a great deal of time, not to mention typographical errors, if writers who submit articles to ES&T are able to submit a floppy disk containing the text along with the manuscript. All of the computers used by the ES&T editorial staff are IBM compatible, and we can handle either to 5¼" or 3½" floppy disks formatted at any density.

Our preferred formats for articles that are submitted on disk are ASCII, or Word Star format, but we can work with files created on most word processors. If you submit an article on disk in any format other than pure ASCII, please include information that tells us what word processor you used to create the file.

There really are few stringent requirements for preparation of manuscripts for ES&T, but *here are a few suggestions for writers who submit manuscripts on computer disc, that will make it easier for the editors.*

1. If you feel that a term, or some kind of description requires emphasis, make a note of it on the manuscript, with your suggestion of the type of emphasis: italic, boldface, etc. Please don't include such things as underline or all caps, because we don't do that kind of emphasis in the magazine. And don't include that kind of emphasis in your document if you're submitting it on disc, because we would have to eliminate those imbedded commands and change to our typesetting codes for that emphasis.

2. Don't leave large open spaces in the text to show where figures go. Simply refer to the art in the text, for example "see Figure 1." The art department will try to put the art in the right place.

3. Don't put the caption at the point in the article text where the art goes. At the end of the article type in the word Captions, leave a couple of line spaces, and type in the captions, like this:

Figure 1. Connect the probe of the oscilloscope to

4. If you're submitting hand drawn art to be prepared in final form by the ES&T artist, it would be very helpful to the editors if you could type the callouts for all of the art on a separate sheet of paper, as well as writing them in on the hand drawn diagram, in all capitals. This has to be done by someone before the callouts can be sent to the typesetter.

Categories: Electronics—Technology

CONTACT: Conrad Persson, Editor
Material: All
PO Box 12487
Overland Park KS 66282-2487
Phone: 913-492-4857
Fax: 913-492-4857
E-mail: cpersedit@aol.com
Website: www.electronic-servicing.com

The Elks Magazine

The Elks Magazine is published 10 times a year for the 1.1 million members of the Benevolent and Protective Order of Elks. In addition to our mission of being "the voice of the Elks," we carry features of general interest. Articles should be fresh, provocative, thought provoking, well researched, and well documented. A thumbnail profile of the average reader would be a person over 40, with some college, an above-average income, and living in a town of 500,000 or less.

What We Can Use: Each year we buy 20 to 30 articles. We're looking for informative, upbeat, entertaining writing on a variety of subjects, including technology, science, sports, history, and seasonal items.

Articles should be authoritative (please include sources) and geared toward the lay person. Articles should run between 1,500 and 2,500 words.

Not Needed: Fiction, travel, business, health, political or religious articles, humor, filler, or poetry. We usually do not publish first-person pieces.

Editorial Requirements
Rates: We prefer to see complete manuscripts. We review articles on speculation and pay 20 cents a word on acceptance.

Format: Articles should be typewritten and double-spaced in a 12-point type size. Do not send computer disks nor e-mails with attachments, as we are sensitive to viruses. Please include your telephone number or the best method to contact you. If we wish to buy your manuscript, we'll contact your for your Social Security number so that we can begin the payment process.

Photos: If we use any of your photos in the article, we pay $25 per photo. We take responsibility for securing illustrations/photographs for the article, but appreciate any assistance you might give.

Rights: First North American serial rights in print only. The author retains all other rights. Upon publication, all print rights revert to the author, and we forward all reprint queries to the author.

Response time: We read you manuscript within a day or so of receipt and either hold it for further consideration or reject the article. Basically, the longer (up to 6 weeks) it is until you hear from us, the greater the probability is that your work will be purchased.

SASE: YES. *The Elks Magazine* cannot accept responsibility for manuscripts sent without a self-addressed, stamped envelope.

Categories: Nonfiction—Associations—Aviation—Biography—General Interest—History—Rural America—Science—Sports/Recreation

CONTACT: Anna L. Idol, Managing Editor
Material: All
425 W. Diversey Pkwy.
Chicago IL 60614-6196
Phone: 773-528-0433
Fax: 773-755-4792
E-mail: annai@elks.org
Website: www.elks.org/elksmag

Elle

Formal guidelines not available. Please read a number of issues to ascertain the publication's style and needs.

Send queries to address below.

Categories: Fiction—Beauty—Diet/Nutrition—Entertainment—Fashion—Health—Lifestyle—Women's Issues

CONTACT: Submissions Editor
Material: All
1663 Broadway, 4th Floor
New York NY 10019
Phone: 212-767-5800
Website: www.elle.com

ELLERY QUEEN
THE WORLD'S LEADING MYSTERY MAGAZINE

Ellery Queen's Mystery Magazine

Ellery Queen's Mystery Magazine welcomes submissions from both new and established writers. We publish every kind of mystery short story: the psychological suspense tale, the deductive puzzle, the private eye case—the gamut of crime and detection from the realistic (including the policeman's lot and stories of police procedure) to the more imaginative (including "locked rooms" and "impossible crimes"). We need hard-boiled stories as well as "cozies," but we are not interested in explicit sex or violence. We do not want true detective or crime stories. With the exception of a regular book review column and a mystery crossword, *EQMM* publishes only fiction. We are especially happy to review first stories by authors who have never before published fiction professionally. First-story submissions should be addressed to *EQMM*'s Department of First Stories.

EQMM has been in continuous publication since 1941. From the beginning three general criteria have been employed in evaluating submissions: We look for strong writing, an original and exciting plot, and professional craftsmanship. We encourage writers whose work meets these general criteria to read an issue of *EQMM* before making a submission. *EQMM*'s range in the mystery genre is extensive: Almost any story that involves crime or the threat of crime comes within our purview. However, like all magazines, *EQMM* has a distinctive tone and style and you can only get a sense of whether your work will suit us by reading an issue. To receive a sample copy send a check or money order for $5.00 to the address below.

EQMM uses stories of almost every length. 2,500-8,000 words is the preferred range, but we occasionally use stories of up to 12,000 words and we feature one or two short novels (up to 20,000 words) each year, although these spaces are usually reserved for established writers. Shorter stories are also considered, including minute mysteries of as little as 250 words. Our rates for original stories are from 5 to 8 ¢ a word, sometimes higher for established authors. *EQMM* does not accept stories previously published in the United States.

It is not necessary to query *EQMM* as to subject matter or to ask permission to submit a story. All manuscripts should be printed on one side of the paper and double-spaced. If you would like the manuscript returned in the event that we cannot use it, please enclose a SASE of suitable size. If you do not want the manuscript returned, please indicate this and enclose a SASE for a reply; if you live outside the U.S., please use International Postal Reply coupons for return postage.

We regret that we cannot provide criticism with returned stories. Response time is up to three months.

Categories: Fiction—Literature—Mystery—Short Stories

CONTACT: Janet Hutchings, Editor
Material: Mystery Fiction
475 Park Ave. South
New York NY 10016
Phone: 212-686-7188
Website: www.themysteryplace.com

Employee Benefit Journal
Employee Benefit Digest

Please refer to *Benefits & Compensation Digest.*

Endless Vacation RCI

Endless Vacation is a magazine for vacation travelers. It is not for business travelers or armchair travelers. *Endless Vacation* shows readers where to go and what to do on vacation, and perhaps most important, why. *Endless Vacation* also addresses the issues of timeshare ownership and timeshare exchange and offers travel information geared to increasing the enjoyment of our readers who own a timeshare condominium.

Freelance writers contribute three to five features of 1,200 to 2,200 words in each issue. In addition, there are several departments of 800 to 1,000 words each.

Our features focus primarily on domestic vacation travel, with some mainstream international vacation articles. Features should cover new and interesting vacation options and should have a solid angle. Topics range from Colorado resorts in the fall to Civil War steamboating. Al-

though limited, the international features cover easily accessed areas of Europe, South America, Africa, and the Pacific. We are not looking for Nepalese mountain treks or hiking the wilds of Vietnam-however, the romantic towns of Bavaria or shopping in Singapore might turn our heads.

Department topics for which *Endless Vacation* accepts some freelance contributions include weekend travel destinations, health and safety on the road, short travel service and news-oriented pieces, and hot news tips and trends in travel.

Before You Write Your Manuscript or Query

1. The editors strongly suggest that you read the magazine thoroughly to get an understanding of our style and approach. Reading the magazine may also prevent you from querying us on a topic that has recently been covered.

2. Because our readers are doers, not dreamers, your article should cover destinations they can visit and activities in which they can participate.

3. Features should have a narrow focus but not be so limited as to have a parochial appeal. An article on the renaissance of a city is good; an article on a common event or festival in a city usually is not.

4. Articles should provide a fast read, packed with anecdotes, examples, and mini-stories. We are not looking for guidebook material, but finely written, well-constructed travel stories. Personal observations and experiences, interviews with other vacationers or local guides, and solid facts are elements we look for. Many, many publications are competing for our readers' time. Brevity, clarity, and conciseness should be hallmarks of your article.

5. Audience (based on 1994 demographic study by MRI)
• Sex: 42 percent male; 58 percent female
• Median age: 42.3
• College graduates: 32 percent
• Married: 65 percent
• Income: $57,000 median
• In addition, other research shows that 99 percent own a timeshare condominium and rank their most important activities while on vacation (in descending order) as: leisure time, visiting local tourist attractions, dining, shopping, swimming, sports activities, cultural activities, and entertaining.

For more information, *Endless Vacation*'s media kit, which includes a copy of the magazine and an 18-page demographic profile of readers, is available for $10. Single copies of the magazine are $5 each, and subscriptions are available to freelance writers for $33.50 (standard subscription rate is $67). Please mail requests to the attention of Myra Bibert.

How to Submit Manuscripts and Queries

Our editorial calendar is booked many months in advance, and currently we have extremely limited space for freelance submissions. We will review manuscripts on speculation, and for a writer who is unfamiliar to us, this may be the best entrée to our publication. The lead is crucial. If the first sentence does not catch our attention, we may never get to the second one.

If you are Interested in submitting a query for a specific issue, please submit your query as early as possible. A year in advance is suggested.

Query letters should include three to four concise paragraphs indicating the focus and tone of the proposed article. Please include samples of your travel writing so that we may give your query full consideration. Materials will be returned only if you include a self-addressed, stamped envelope. We generally respond to queries by letter in 30 days.

Please do not telephone us with your query. It is necessary for us to have queries in written form.

Photography

Photographers should submit a stock list and printed samples to the photo editor. (We cannot guarantee the return of unsolicited slides and transparencies.) The photo editor will contact you if your portfolio matches our needs.

If you are asked to submit materials, please make sure that your name and some form of ID number are on each 35mm slide and color transparency. Photos must be identified on the slide mount or with a caption sheet.

Payment for photos generally ranges between $100 and $500 per photo used, depending on size. Cover photos earn more.

Model releases are required.

If a writer submits slides with a story, they will be considered by the photo editor, and if selected, payment will be negotiated separately from the article. We do not, however, encourage writers to submit photos.

Manuscript Payment

Payment is negotiated upon assignment and tendered upon acceptance. The following ranges will give you an idea of our rates:

- Feature articles (including sidebars): $500 to $1,000
- Departments: $300 to $800
- News Briefs: $75 to $100

Expenses are not guaranteed and are negotiated individually.

If you are assigned an article, you will be sent a contract with a brief description of the topic, terms, and payment. Sign the contract and return it immediately. We cannot send payment without a signed contract on file.

Assigned deadlines are absolute. Failure to meet them may result in the cancellation of the assignment.

Categories: Nonfiction—Travel

CONTACT: Julie Woodard, Senior Editor
Material: All
North America Office
9998 N. Michigan Rd
Carmel IN 46032
Fax: 317-805-9507
E-mail: evletters@rci.com
Website: www.rci.com

The Engineering Economist

The Engineering Economist is a quarterly, refereed publication published jointly by the Engineering Economy Divisions of the American Society for Engineering Education (ASEE) and the Institute of Industrial Engineers (IIE). *The Engineering Economist* publishes articles, case studies, readers' comments, and reviews that represent current research and practice involving problems of capital investment. Opinions expressed in *The Engineering Economist* are those of the authors and do not necessarily represent those of ASEE or IEE.

Submissions

Manuscripts are to be sent in quadruplicate.

Style Requirements

Electronic submission of manuscripts accepted for publication is required and must meet the following criteria.

Submit the manuscript in an IBM PC-compatible format on a diskette in Microsoft Word format.

Word process the entire manuscript double-spaced in 10-point Times Roman type.

Submit a hard copy of the manuscript, including Figures.

Number figures, tables, equations, references, and end notes, and make sure these numbers match those cited in the text.

All Tables and Figrues must be submitted in a form ready to reproduce without further modification, enlargement, or reduction, and fit within a space no larger than 4.5 x 7.5 inches, including the title of the Table or Figure. List Table and Figure captions on a separate page.

Tables must be typed using the Microsoft Word Tables feature.

Minimize table rules. Use horizontal rules above and below the column headings, inside the table body to show totals and at the table bottom. Use vertical rules only when necessary for clarity. Do not use side rules.

Photocopies of illustrations will not be accepted.

Figures submitted in electronic form must be compatible with Microsoft Word; otherwise, they must be submitted in hard copy form. In eithe rform, Figure captions must be separate - not within the Figures.

Equations, both in-line and displayed, must be typed using Microsoft Word Equation Editor.

Abstract

Manuscripts must include a nonmathematical abstract of 50 - 100 words.

Mathematical Notation

Make mathematical expressions as simple as possible. Lengthy mathematical derivations should be placed in an Appendix. Number equations; put the equation number in parentheses, flush with the right margin of the page. Authors should restrict themselves to the English alphabet and standard Greek symbols. For interest factors, follow the functional format of ANSI Standard Z94.5-1990, "Symbology Manual of Standard Notation for Engineering Economy Parameters and Interest Factors".

Tables and Figures

Tables are lists of numbers. All other illustrations are Figures. Tables should be numbered with Arabic numerals and provided with titles at the top. Figures should be numbered with Arabic numerals and numbered and titled at the bottom.

Footnotes

Footnotes should be avoided because they disrupt the readers' train of thought and create confusion with the references. If the material is important enough for the reader to seek it out, it is important enough to be included in the text.

Acknowledgments

If any, these should be made in a separate section following the Conlusion or Summary and prior to References.

References

Use the alpabetical numbering method. References should be numbered, enclosed in square brackets (e.g., [1]) and listed in alphabetical order in the list of references. Only references cited in the text should be listed. (If material is removed or added, be sure to revise numbering.)

Biographical Sketch

A biographical sketch of 200 or fewer words for each author should be submitted on a separate page with the manuscript.

Categories: Nonfiction—Engineering

CONTACT: Latha S. Bhavnani, Managing Editor
Material: All
Dept. of Industrial and Systems Engineering
Auburn University AL 36849-5346
Phone: 334-844-1419
Fax: 334-844-1381
E-mail: bhavna1s@eng.auburn.edu
Website: www.eng.auburn.edu/~park/journal

Enrichment
A Journal for Pentecostal Ministry

Enrichment is a quarterly journal for Assemblies of God ministers and other Pentecostal, charismatic leaders. It carries articles and feature material on a wide range of ministry-related topics. It exists for the purpose of enriching and encouraging Pentecostal ministers to equip and empower Spirit-filled believers for effective ministry.

Its Free-Lance Market

Free-lance material is accepted on a limited basis in the following areas:

- Slanted to ministers on preaching, pastoral practice, and any ministry-related subject (1,200-2,100 words).
- How-to Features
- Program and ministry ideas for ministers/church leaders (200-500 words)

Sermon Illustrations

Original and previously published material with the original source indicated if the material has been previously published.

Rate of payment

Up to 10 cents per word for first rights; payment on publication.

Categories: Nonfiction—Religion—Spiritual

CONTACT: Rick Knoth
Material: All
The General Council of the Assemblies of God
1445 N. Boonville Ave.
Springfield MO 65802
Phone: 417-862-2781, ext. 4095
E-mail: fhamilton@ag.org
Website: www.enrichmentjournal.ag.org

Entrepreneur Magazine

Our Mission

Business ownership is not what it used to be. *Entrepreneur* helps entrepreneurs thrive in today's fast-paced environment, offering actionable information and practical inspiration that successful business owners can use to achieve their vision of growth.

Our Readers

Our readers are energetic entrepreneurs who are not content with the status quo. They're risk-takers who thrive on growth and innovation, constantly seeking cutting-edge ideas to improve their businesses. They're the thinkers shaping the new face of entrepreneurship.

Our Content

Entrepreneur reports on innovative methods and strategies to help readers improve their business operations. We also cover current issues and trends that affect entrepreneurial companies, as well as new business ideas and opportunities. We provide detailed how-to information in an entertaining, intriguing and evocative fashion, with a writing style that is punchy, sophisticated and chatty.

What We're Looking For

Don't give us the obvious, or merely touch on the surface of a subject. Our readers are not beginners, and they don't have time to waste reading what they already know.

We're looking for in-depth reporting, with information culled from many sources to give readers a broad perspective on a topic. Can you offer a fresh angle on a familiar subject? Can you convey atmosphere and personality when interviewing entrepreneurs and experts? Can you elicit interesting quotes from people, and find sources who don't say the same old thing in the same old way? Can you write about business with authority and passion? Then you're the kind of writer we're looking for.

Features

Features are 1,800 words, plus sidebars, charts and boxes. Types of features we are seeking include:

In-depth articles examining how a current business issue, such as the tight labor market or the health-insurance crisis, affects small businesses.

Psychological topics, such as "Can you have a business and still have a life?" or "What is the line between taking advantage of opportunities and being an opportunist?"

How-to articles, such as how to get your product into Wal-Mart, how to bounce back from a business failure, how to market to a certain demographic group (such as teens) or how to sell your product to the U.S. government.

Columns

Entrepreneur's upfront section, "Smarts," features news, trends and how-to information in a brief, punchy format. We purchase short (300 words) articles for $1 per word in the following topic areas:

• *Snapshots* — quick profiles of interesting entrepreneurs with innovative or unusual ideas or inspirational stories. This can be something readers can learn from, or just an entertaining profile.

• *Money Smarts* — business financing, financial management and personal finance issues

• *Marketing Smarts* — sales and marketing issues

• *Web Smarts* — Internet news, trends and ways to get the most from the Web

• *Tech Smarts* — technology news and trends affecting business owners; ways to get the most from technology

• *Management Smarts* - management and operations issues

• *Viewpoint* — thought-provoking, controversial first-person essay on some aspect of entrepreneurship. Could cover politics, ethics, personal life and more.

• *Miscellaneous* — We also purchase short (300- to 600-word) articles for the Smarts section that do not fall into the above categories, but simply report on interesting entrepreneurs, trends or ideas. For example: Why pork rinds are suddenly a hot snack item; what your sleeping position says about you as an entrepreneur; how the Internet is revolutionizing the crafts industry.

Other columns are not open to freelancers. However, if you have an idea for a new column—or you think you could write better than one of our existing columnists—query us and prove it.

Be Your Own Boss

Targeted at start-up entrepreneurs, "Be Your Own Boss" is a mini-magazine within a magazine; it appears in newsstand copies only. The monthly feature within "Be Your Own Boss" is open to freelancers. It is 1,800 words long and covers how-to topics of interest to start-up entrepreneurs—for example, what it's really like to launch a business from an incubator; the best places to find start-up capital; how to overcome the mental roadblocks that keep you from starting a business.

Where to Start

Please read several issues of the magazine before querying us. Pay particular attention to the columns. We have dozens of columns on topics including management, sales and marketing, business ideas, technology and finance. Many of the queries we receive are rejected because they duplicate topics covered in our columns. Only a topic that is too extensive to be covered in one of our columns warrants feature coverage.

Submit queries only. Full-length manuscripts are discouraged.

If submitting queries via regular mail, send them to the attention of Peggy Reeves Bennett, Articles Editor, at 2445 McCabe Way, Irvine, CA 92614. Enclose a self-addressed stamped envelope and a few clips of past articles you've written. Queries may also be e-mailed to pbennett@entrepreneur.com.

Queries should describe the topic clearly and succinctly. Avoid vagueness and generalities. Be as specific as possible about what aspects of the subject you will cover, people you will interview, how the story will help our readers and why you're qualified to write it.

Allow a minimum of 6-8 weeks for a response. No phone calls, please.

Include a return address and both day and evening phone numbers on all correspondence.

Entrepreneur Media buys first worldwide rights and pays upon acceptance.

Entrepreneur Media assumes no responsibility for unsolicited manuscripts, photos or tapes.

Sample copies

You can find *Entrepreneur* at most newsstands and bookstores, or you can order the magazine by sending $7.20 ($4.00/issue + $3.20 shipping) to: Entrepreneur Media, PO Box 432, Newburgh, NY 12551.

Categories: Business

CONTACT: Peggy Reeves Bennett, Article Editor
Material: Queries
Entrepreneur Media, Inc., 2445 McCabe Way
Irvine CA 92614
Phone: 949-261-2325
Fax: 949-261-0234
E-mail: pbennett@entrepreneur.com
Website: Entrepreneur.com

Entrepreneur.com

People who visit or are members of *Entrepreneur.com* are seeking a variety of accessible, easy-to-digest information. *Our readers consist of four primary groups:*

• They may be small-business owners (those with fewer than 20 employees) who have been in business for several years and are seeking innovative methods and strategies to improve their business operations but are also interested in new business ideas and opportunities as well as current issues that affect their companies.

• They may be people who are either dreaming of starting their own business or have a business that's less than 2 years old. These individuals don't necessarily have a lot of money, so they're looking for businesses that don't require mountains of start-up cash. In addition to start-up ideas, they're looking for how-to advice to help them run and grow their businesses, articles that keep them on top of business trends, and motivational articles to get (and stay) psyched up.

• They may be individuals who already run or want to start a homebased business. Like the entrepreneurs described above, they're seeking information that will help them run their businesses better.

• Finally, they may be people interested in purchasing a franchise or business opportunity. They want accurate, reliable, unbiased information from a company they can trust. They want to know what they need to know before plunking down any cash—as well as where to find the cash to plunk down. Before pitching a story to us, be sure to read a variety of the articles on our site so you can tailor your pitches to meet our content needs. Many of the queries we receive are rejected because the subject matter in no way matches what we're looking for.

Submission Guidelines

• Submit queries or queries with clips only. Full-length manuscripts are discouraged.

• If you're querying an article about a successful entrepreneur, you must include his/her age and some indication of the company's sales.

• Include your day and evening phone number, return address and e-mail address on all correspondence.

• Please send queries in writing via e-mail to Karen Spaeder, Editor, or via snail mail (include a self-addressed, stamped envelope) to 2445 McCabe Way, Irvine, CA 92614. Allow a minimum of eight weeks for a response—no phone calls, please.

• Entrepreneur Media Inc. assumes no responsibility for unsolicited manuscripts or photos.

• Entrepreneur Media Inc. pays upon acceptance.

Editorial Voice

We want our articles to sound as if they were written by people who are on the same level as—or maybe just a step above—our readers, people who are part of the community, not above the community. We want you to sound experienced, so you can point our readers in the right direction. We don't want our editorial copy to sound as if we're talking down to our readers or patronizing them. We're here to help; we want to be their mentors.

No matter what the topic or audience is, the articles you provide us should be informative yet entertaining. The style should be lively and relaxed—never dry or boring. In addition, the voice of our articles needs to be inviting. We want to involve the community. We need to inform them, but we also want to promote thought and discussion.

If you've received a writing assignment from us, we have a few helpful hints about mechanics:

• Articles should be concise and specific. They need to communicate information quickly: We can't be long-winded, or we'll lose our Web readers. Columns should be approximately 600 words long. Features, approximately 1,000.

• Headlines should concisely convey the basic information in the article. They should not be obtuse or clever for the sake of being clever. *Examples:* Advertising on the Cheap; Beat Those Wintertime Blahs; E-Promotions Done Right; Decks should also be concise. They may or may not be full sentences that briefly convey the essence of the article.

Examples: Think advertising is beyond your means? Not with these low-cost and no-cost options; Follow these 10 steps to stave off the cold-weather blues; How to promote your online business on a shoe-string budget.

• Where appropriate, articles should include real-life examples of entrepreneurs—more than one example is better—as well as information from an expert. Before including a specific entrepreneur, clear it with Karen Spaeder.

• Bulleted or numbered lists are always a plus. Web readers like information they can digest easily, and bulleted/numbered lists seem to go over well.

• Additional resources should be included with each article. This information could be from the *Entrepreneur.com* site, such as related articles or tools, an appropriate message board or link to an expert, or links to related areas of the site, such as the Franchise Zone or a specific area of Your Business. You could also include non-*Entrepreneur.com* resources, such as related books or Web sites. This information should be set off at the end of the main article with a note to include it in a box.

• Specific information must be included in every article, where appropriate. This information includes: full names and titles of all individuals mentioned or quoted in article; names of all partners or co-founders of companies; complete names and brief descriptions of all companies, organizations or associations (including Inc., Corp., and Co.); city and state where companies are located; the year a company was founded; current annual sales of companies; Web site addresses of all companies, organizations and associations; and street prices of any products mentioned.

• Contact information for all individuals mentioned in the article must be included at the end of the article so we can easily complete our fact checking.

This should include each person's name, phone number, e-mail address and Web address.

If you are not a regular contributor, please provide a brief writer's bio.

• We like to include a bio at the end of every article. And if you wouldn't mind, please provide a way for readers to contact you if they'd like to. An e-mail address would be just fine.

Categories: Nonfiction—Business

CONTACT: Karen Spaeder, Editor
Material: Queries
Entrepreneur Media, Inc., 2445 McCabe Way
Irvine CA 92614
Phone: 949-261-2325
Fax: 949-261-0234
E-mail: kspaeder@entrepreneur.com
Website: Entrepreneur.com

Environment

Environment welcomes manuscripts and proposals that make an original contribution to the public's understanding of global and regional *Environment*al issues. The award-winning magazine, now in its 44th year of publication, has a broad audience that includes world-renowned scientists, researchers, and policymakers; university professors and high school teachers (who read the magazine for themselves as well as assign it to their students); and concerned citizens. The peer-reviewed magazine offers readers extended articles on key Environmental issues, shorter articles that explore parts of these issues, reviews of major governmental and institutional reports, commentaries that provide different points of view than those in the articles, book recommendations, pointers to the best *Environment*al web sites and other digital media, and staff-written news briefs. Readers enjoy thought-provoking articles that provide balanced, authoritative analyses written in an accessible way. The goal, similar to that of a policy "white paper," is for those interested in but not necessarily familiar

A-E

with the topic (including undergraduate and graduate students, faculty members in other disciplines, and the educated public) to be able to easily grasp the key science and policy issues without wading through jargon or overly technical material.

Environment's executive editors review all submissions and may request other experts, including contributing editors, to review manuscripts and proposals. The executive editors may accept the piece as submitted, accept it pending revision, or reject the manuscript. *Final publication decisions rest with them on the five types of manuscripts:*

• Main article submissions (between 2,500 to 4,000 words) should expose readers to the major scientific and policy issues surrounding a significant topic. Articles must be concise, objective, technically accurate but free of jargon, and factually supported. They should also give appropriate weight to alternative points of view. We encourage authors to include endnotes that offer readers suggestions for further reading and document more technical information or controversial points (an average number of references is 30). We also encourage the use of maps, tables, graphs, and sidebar boxes to illustrate key points, describe relevant case studies, or provide background information for readers unfamiliar with the topic discussed. The introduction and conclusion are especially important. The introduction should entice the reader to read further as well as provide a solid foundation for understanding the article. Conclusions must follow logically from the facts and analyses presented, must give the reader an idea of what is likely to happen in the future, and must indicate the implications for both research and policy. This section is more detailed than that of the typical magazine or journal article.

• "Departments" (1,000 to 1,700 words) focus on special topics such as education, energy, economics, and public opinion. These manuscripts should elucidate a small portion of a larger issue. Though not as comprehensive in coverage as the main articles, these manuscripts should also be objective, free of jargon, factually supported, technically accurate, and well referenced. As examples of the appropriate scope, one piece presented a geographic breakdown of U.S. membership in Environmental organizations while another explored the Environmental implications of local currencies.

• The "Report on Reports" section provides lengthy reviews (1,500 to 2,000 words) of institutional and governmental reports. The reviews subject new research reports produced by government agencies and private institutions to the same scholarly scrutiny usually given to an individually authored book or monograph. Topics of recently reviewed reports include the constitutionality of the Clean Air Act, the role of pesticides in U.S. agriculture, acidic deposition, and dams and development.

• "Commentary" (maximum of 750 words) seeks to broaden the debate on various topics by providing thoughtful alternative points of view to those expressed elsewhere in the magazine.

• The "Books of Note" section provides short (100 to 150 words) notices of recent print publications to call readers' attention to a wide range of important books rather than provide detailed critical evaluations. Reviewers and books to be reviewed are selected by the magazine's contributing editors, executive editors, and managing editor. A book's relevance to *Environment*'s general themes and its accessibility to a nonspecialist audience are crucial.

More detailed guidelines for these sections are available from the editorial offices.

Editing and Style References

Once a manuscript is accepted for publication, it is edited thoroughly by the editorial staff for style, substance, and clarity. Because the magazine brings complex and technical analyses to a broad audience, we edit more extensively than do most journals or magazines. Articles that exceed the specified length may be shortened. We compose titles and subheads without consultation but query authors concerning any substantive editorial changes. We offer rapid publication of timely material, so we require a rapid turnaround when we send authors typescripts of the edited manuscript. The staff works closely with authors to ensure a mutually satisfying product.

Environment follows the 14th edition of *The Chicago Manual of Style*, published by the University of Chicago Press, and the *American Heritage Dictionary* for spelling.

Manuscript Submission and Technical Requirements

1. Send three clean copies of your manuscript to Barbara T. Richman, Managing Editor, *Environment*, Heldref Publications, 1319 Eighteenth Street, N.W., Washington, DC 20036-1802. Manuscripts can also be sent via e-mail, with a cover letter, to env@heldref.org. The preferred format is Microsoft Word 6.1 for Macintosh; DOS-based formats are also acceptable.

2. Double space everything, including endnotes and tables. Use 1-inch or greater margins and confine the page length to 10 inches or less. Sidebar boxes, tables, and figures must be on separate pages at the end of the manuscript.

3. Authors' names, positions, titles, places of employment, mailing addresses, and telephone numbers must appear on the cover page. Include fax numbers and e-mail addresses.

4. It is extremely helpful to submit figures electronically. The preferred program is Illustrator 8.0 or lower (Mac versions) with Postscript fonts (no Truetype). Colors must be in CMYK format, not RGB. Tiff and EPS files are also acceptable. Each figure should be sent as a separate e-mail. Authors must also send print-outs of the figures.

5. Authors are encouraged to submit photographs and original artwork of professional quality to accompany the text. Authors are responsible for obtaining permission to use such materials. Captions and a credit line identifying the photographer must accompany each photograph. The editorial and graphics staffs determine use of all photographs based on relevance, aesthetic value, and space availability. Maps and figures are also useful and may be redrafted to match *Environment*'s style.

6. Authors are responsible for the accuracy of endnotes, and all references and quotations must be checked against the original sources by the author. Authors are also responsible for securing permission to use material quoted from copyrighted publications as well as for use of tables and figures from other sources.

7. Do not use the endnote function in your word-processing program. All endnotes must be double-spaced and placed at the end of the article. Do not use endnotes in headlines or author affiliations or use more than one per sentence. Provide enough information to allow the reader to retrieve the referenced material from the most available source. Provide specific page numbers for general reference to articles (e.g., "For more on this topic, see…"), quotations, or references to specific facts or arguments. Where possible, include a printed source along with Internet references. *Environment uses the following styles:*

Book:

1. D. Scheberle, *Federalism and Environmental Policy: Trust and the Politics of Implementation* (Washington, D.C.: Georgetown University Press, 1997), 95-98.

Book with more than five authors:

1. G. Atkinson et al, *Measuring Sustainable Development: Macroeconomics and the Environment* (Cheltenham, U.K.: Edward Elgar Publishing, 1997), 95-98.

Chapter in a book:

1. L. White Jr., "The Historical Roots of Our Ecologic Crisis," in L. Gruen and D. Jamieson, eds., *Reflecting on Nature: Readings in Environmental Philosophy* (New York: Oxford University Press, 1994), 5-14 at 12.

Scholarly journal:

Monthly or less frequently:

1. S. T. Phillips, *"Lessons from the Dust Bowl: Dryland Agriculture and Soil Erosion in the United States and South Africa*, 1900-1950." *Environmental History* 4, No. 2 (1999): 245-66.

Weekly:

2. G. Hardin, "Extensions of 'The Tragedy of the Commons'," *Science.* 1 May 1998, 683-83.

Magazine:

Popular magazine:

1. C. Gordon, "The Warm Lessons of the Ice Storm '98," *Macleans.* 16 February 1998, 14.

Newspaper or regular newsletter:

1. K. Schneider, "New Breed of Ecologist to Lead EPA," *New York Times*. 17 December 1992, B20.

Interview or personal communication:

1. Robin L. Rivett, attorney, Pacific Legal Foundation, letter to Robert Burford, director, Bureau of Land Management, 2 February 1993.

2. Simon Smith, manager of regulator innovations, New South Wales *Environment*al Protection Authority, personal communication with the authors. Beijing, 23 November 1997.

Additional references to a previous note:

5. Lundgren, note 1 above, page 7.

Reference to an immediately preceding note:

6. Ibid., page 17.

Government report:

1. U.S. General Accounting Office, EPA and the States: *Environmental Challenges Require a Better Working Relationship*. GAO/RCED-95-64 (Washington, D.C., 1995).

International treaty:

1. "Protocol on Substances That Deplete the Ozone Layer," Montreal, 1987, in *International Legal Materials* 26 (1987): 1550.

U.S. federal law:

1. Endangered Species Act of 1973, U.S. Code, vol.16, sec. 1531(1973).

Congressional bill where title of bill appears in the text of the manuscript:

1. H.R. 3055, 94th Cong., 2nd sess., Congressional Record, 122, no.5, daily ed. (15 July 1976): H16,870.

Congressional bill where title of bill does not appear in the text:

1. Food Security Act of 1985, 99th Cong., 1st sess., H.R. 2100, Congressional Record, 131, no.132, daily ed. (8 October 1985): H8461-66.

Press release:

1. U.S. Bureau of Land Management, "BLM Announces Major Policy Change," press release (Washington, D.C., 1 November 1997).

Unpublished discussion papers:

1. F. Butera and U. Farinelli, "Lessons of Technology Transfer from Developing World Experience (paper presented at the Royal Institute of International Affairs Workshop on International Technology Transfer. London, March 1991).

For other types of notes, refer to the 14th edition of the Chicago Manual of Style or to a recent issue of *Environment*.

Updated January 2002

Categories: Nonfiction—Agriculture—Animals—Ecology—Environment—Science—Environmental Science & Policy—Energy

CONTACT: Barbara T. Richman, Managing Editor
Material: All
1319 - 18th St. NW
Washington DC 20036-1802
Phone: 202-296-6267
Fax: 202-296-5149
E-mail: env@heldref.org
Website: www.heldref.org

Equal Opportunity

Please refer to Equal Opportunity Publications, Inc.

Equal Opportunity Publications, Inc.

WRITER'S GUIDELINES

Thank you for your interest in writing for our *career-guidance magazines*, which provide college-level and professional women, members of minority groups, and people with disabilities with information on how to find employment and develop their careers.

Since 1968, Equal Opportunity Publications, Inc. (EOP) has led the way from affirmative action to diversity recruitment by publishing career-guidance and recruitment magazines for women, members of minority groups, and people with disabilities. "First in diversity, best in results" is the slogan that summarizes EOP's successful record of helping job-seekers from under represented groups find employment and in aiding companies and government agencies eager to recruit from this diversified workforce.

Our Publications

Lana D'Amico is the Senior Editor for the following magazines:

• *Woman Engineer*: Aimed at advancing the careers of women engineering students and professional engineers.

• *Workforce Diversity For Engineering And IT Professionals*: Addresses workplace issues affecting technical professional women, members of minority groups, and people with disabilities.

• *African-American Career World*: Focused on the careers of African-American students and entry-level professionals in a variety of industries, including insurance, government and military, computer science, and transportation.

• *Hispanic Career World*: Focused on the careers of Hispanic students and entry-level professionals in a variety of industries, including health care, banking, retail, hospitality and travel, and information technology.

James Schneider is the Editor for the following magazines:

• *Careers & the disABLED*: Developed to promoting the personal and professional growth of individuals with disabilities.

• *Equal Opportunity*: Dedicated to advancing the professional interests of blacks, Hispanics, Asians, and Native Americans.

• *Minority Engineer*: Focused on advancing the careers of minority engineering students and professional engineers.

GUIDELINES

• First North American serial rights are owned by EOP, Inc. Previously published articles are also acceptable. Please note that we may choose an excerpt of a published article for our Website.

• The rate for articles is ten cents per word paid within 6 weeks after publication. The rate for each photograph used is $15.00; cartoons, $25. All manuscripts are submitted on speculation.

• Articles may be submitted via E-mail. Please include social security, address, and telephone number.

Forward your query electronically to: Lana D'Amico (*Woman Engineer, Workforce Diversity For Engineering And IT Professionals, African-American Career World*, and *Hispanic Career World*), E-mail: Ldamico@eop.com.

Mail your query to James Schneider (*Equal Opportunity, Minority Engineer, Careers & the disABLED*) at 445 Broad Hollow Road, Suite 425, Melville, NY 11747.

Categories: Nonfiction—African-American—Asian-American—Associations—Careers—College—Disabilities—Education—Engineering—Health—Hispanic—Multicultural—Native American—Women's Issues—Ethnic—Technology

CONTACT: James Schneider, Director, Editorial & Production (ext.12)
Material: Submissions for Equal Opportunity, Minority Engineer, and Careers & the disABLED
CONTACT: Lana D'Amico, Editor (ext.17)
Material: Submissions for Woman Engineer, Workforce Diversity For Engineering And IT Professionals, Hispanic Career World, and African-American Career World
Editorial Department
445 Broad Hollow Rd, Ste 425
Melville NY 11747
Phone: 631-421-942
Fax: 631-421-0359
E-mail: JSchneider@eop.com (James Schneider)
E-mail: *Ldamico*@eop.com (Lana D'Amico)
Website: www.eop.com

Equine Journal

Freelance

The *Equine Journal* welcomes freelance submissions. Following are the basic guidelines we suggest.

1. Submissions should be neatly typed double-spaced. We do accept e-mailed submissions, however they must not be in the form of attachments (simply paste all text into the body of the e-mail message).

2. Most of our features run approximately 2,000-3,000 words in length. Occasionally, a topic is such that it cannot be adequately covered within this range; two-part features are arranged in this instance.

3. Photographs, if available, are welcome. It is better to note their availability rather than enclose them.

4. An Editorial Calendar listing each month's primary topics is available.

Depending on length and complexity of the topic, features pay between $75-$100. Photographs used receive an additional $10/photo.

We do our best to respond to each submission. However, if after four to six weeks you have not heard back on an article you sent, please follow up with a phone call to our editor, Kathleen Labonville, at 800-742-9171.

Solicited

The *Equine Journal* requests the following guidelines be followed when submitting event coverage.

1. Coverage must have been pre-approved and assigned by the editor or assistant publisher of the *Equine Journal*.

2. Submissions should be neatly typed and double spaced. Mail, fax and e-mail (editorial@equinejournal.com, no attachments please) are all accepted.

3. Articles must run approximately 600 words in length; photographs, a minimum of two, should also be mailed to our office.

4. The writer is asked to request from the show secretary the show results. They should be forwarded to the Journal at the Keene, New Hampshire, address or faxed to 603-357-7851. Show results are not accepted via e-mail.

5. The writer is also requested to distribute Journals at the show, which will be shipped to them via UPS. Or, you may provide us with the show's address and we will send issues directly there.

6. To ensure proper payment, an invoice (needn't be formal) should accompany the submission addressed to the editor's attention.

7. Payment will be a flat fee of $50, unless otherwise agreed to. Checks will be mailed within 30 days of the cover date of the issue bearing the write-up.

8. Write ups must be submitted within 10 days of the show unless otherwise pre-approved by the editor.

Should you have any questions, please call the editor, Kathleen Labonville, at 800-742-9171.

Spotlight

1. Spotlight articles are intended to highlight a business, farm, individual or program within the equine industry. Its primary intent is to inform our readers of what the business has to offer, by. The article should be centered around the writer's telephone or personal interview with the subject being spotlighted. Topics covered may include but are not limited to a history of the business, what they have to offer, where they plan to go in the future, etc.

2. Submissions should be neatly typed and double-spaced, then mailed or faxed to our office. We welcome e-mailed submissions, however they must not be in the form of attachments (simply paste all text into the body of the e-mail message).

3. Spotlights should be roughly 1,000 words in length and pay $50 each. If a telephone interview is conducted, please submit your phone bill for reimbursement.

4. Please request that the spotlight subject send two photographs to the *Equine Journal* office.

If you have any questions, do not hesitate to call Kathleen Labonville, editor, at 800-742-9171.

Categories: Nonfiction—Animals—Trade—Horses

CONTACT: Kathleen Labonville, Managing Editor
Material: All
103 Roxbury St.
Keene NH 03431-8801
Phone: 603-357-4271
E-mail: editor@equinejournal.com
Website: www.equinejournal.com

Equities Magazine

Formal guidelines not available. Please read a number of issues to ascertain the publication's style and needs.

Send queries to address below. No submissions by email.

Subscription Terms
1 Year $12 (Seven Issues)
3 Years $36 (Twenty One Issues)
We Accept Visa, MasterCard, American Express, Discover.
Categories: Nonfiction—Business—Economics

CONTACT: Robert J. Flaherty, Editor
Material: All
Equities Magazine, LLC
PO Box 130H
Scarsdale NY 10583
Phone: 914-723-6702
Website: www.equitiesmagazine.com

Erased, Sigh, Sigh

Erased, Sigh, Sigh is VDP's literary journal. It was formed in late 1994 to print the more serious poetry and fiction submissions we received for our early magazine *In Ravens' Eyes*. Since that time, *ESS* has become the premier journal for what we refer to as "death poets and suicide writers." Quite a few of the writers who submit their poems and stories to *ESS* go on to become authors published through Via Dolorosa Press.

If you are interested in submitting to this journal, you should use the same guidelines that are listed in the VDP section. However, we do not accept non-fiction pieces. We mostly print poetry, though we will consider very short stories. We do not charge reading fees, and we accept both simultaneous submissions and previously-published work (as long as you currently hold the rights to it). There is no limit to the number of items you may submit to us at one time. But, if you want rejected work returned, you must enclose enough return postage.

Payment for accepted work is a contributor's copy for each issue in which the writer's work appears.

Send all ESS submission to the attention of Ms. Hyacinthe L. Raven at: *Erased, Sigh, Sigh*, at the address below.

Queries are not necessary, but we do appreciate cover letters. We print bylines for accepted work, so please feel free to include one.

Enclose a SASE (or SAE with IRC) with your submission for our response. We do not respond by email and will not acknowledge submissions without a SASE enclosed.

Categories: Fiction—Nonfiction—Literature—Poetry

CONTACT: Ms. Hyacinthe L. Raven, Editor
Material: All
701 E. Schaaf Rd.
Cleveland, OH 44131-1227

Eros: Erotic Anthology
The Best Gay & Lesbian Erotic Fiction & Poetry by Today's Writers

Published: Annually

Book Formats: Anthology is a book-zine (eclectic like a magazine but in book form) and will be published in one or more of the following, traditional paper (either hardback or paperback), electronic (ebooks and/or audio).

Publishes: Short erotic fiction. Light to more in depth erotica. Also considers erotic poems.

Lengths: Open for erotic short fiction and erotic poetry. Manuscripts of all lengths will be considered.

The deadline: We read manuscripts all year for this annual anthology publication in book-zine format.

Rights: One-time use in book form (all formats). Considers reprints if author owns rights.

Poets and writers should send a bio to accompany their writings in the anthology.

Please note: Writers and poets with books and other publications or venues (i.e. a website) can submit information, website address, etc. for inclusion in the anthology to accompany their bio information. This will give writers added exposure for themselves and their books, websites, etc.

Contributors must send note (email or by regular mail) stating that he/she would like the writing(s) included in the published anthology. Submit up to 5 manuscripts, either by email or regular mail (see below). Please enclose SASE with regular mail submissions.

Contributors will receive one copy of the finished anthology.

Categories: Fiction—Erotica—Poetry

CONTACT: Editor
Material: Erotica short fiction; erotic poems iSoft c/o RSVP Press
Clinton TN 37716
E-mail: SofteBooks@yahoo.com
iSoft c/o RSVP Press
129 Thurman Lane
Website: www.geocities.com/isoftebooks

Erosion Control

Please refer to Forester Communications.

Erotique
Erotic Anthology

Please refer to *Eros:* The Best Erotic Fiction & Poetry by Today's Writers.

ESPN
The Magazine

Does not accept unsolicited submissions.

Esquire

In all correspondence with us:

1. Please consult a recent issue of the magazine for content and style and consider carefully before making your submission.

2. Materials sometimes get lost in the mail or in the great wave of submissions we receive daily. We cannot track down wayward or unanswered manuscripts.

For fiction:

1. It is best to send the finished manuscript. We will consider short stories only; please do not send full-length novels.

2. We do not accept query letters for fiction.

3. Please send one story at a time; we will not read entire collections.

4. We do not publish pornography, science fiction, poetry or "true romance" stories.

5. We receive so many manuscripts that it is impossible for us to comment individually on them.

For nonfiction:

1. While we rarely publish unsolicited manuscripts, all submissions are read and answered within four to six weeks

2. We prefer receiving a query letter together with some published feature samples, rather than receiving a finished manuscript.

3. Suggested length for nonfiction manuscripts is 1,500 to 4,000 words.

4. Fees vary. We pay upon acceptance of an article.

Categories: Men's Issues

CONTACT: Adrian Miller
Material: Fiction
CONTACT: Andrew Ward
Material: Nonfiction
250 W. 55th St.
New York NY 10019

Essence

Thank you for your interest in writing for ESSENCE, the magazine for African-American and Caribbean women. We feature personal-growth articles, celebrity profiles, and well-reported pieces on political and social issues. We are also looking for how-to pieces on careers, money, health and fitness, and relationships. And we run short items on people in the arts and community activists. Word length is given upon assignment.

Please send a query letter rather than submitting a completed manuscript. The only exceptions are for the Interiors, Our World, Brothers and Back Talk columns. Essays submitted for these pages should run no longer than 600 words and should be clearly addressed to the editor of the column.

We cannot discuss story ideas over the telephone, nor can we respond to queries that come by fax or e-mail.

Give us a clear outline of your story; one page is sufficient. It would also help to include a brief biography that describes your writing experience, and some clips. If you would like to submit more than one idea, write a separate query for each topic. Check our masthead in the current issue for the names of the appropriate editors.

If we think your subject is of interest to our readers but you are a writer new to ESSENCE, you may be asked to submit the completed manuscript on speculation. Payment will be made if the article is accepted for publication.

All manuscripts must be typed and double-spaced. (We suggest that you keep a copy of your original manuscript.) We cannot be responsible for unsolicited material. Be sure to include your name, address and daytime phone number, and include a self-addressed stamped envelope. Allow six to eight weeks for review.

We look forward to hearing from you!

WRITER'S GUIDELINES FOR "Interiors"

We are looking for short personal essays that delve into the emotional lives of African-American women and/or explore issues that are of general concern to women from the writer's viewpoint. The essay should be well-written, clearly focused and help the reader understand herself and the world better. We welcome essays relating to women's lives on a broad range of subjects.

Manuscripts should be approximately 700 words, typed, double-spaced and submitted with a S.A.S. E. (self-addressed-stamped-envelope). Be sure to include a phone number where you can be reached during business hours. Mail manuscripts to Interiors, ESSENCE, 1500 Broadway, New York, NY 10036. Please allow six to eight weeks for review.

WRITER'S GUIDELINES FOR "Brothers"

We are looking for personal essays that explore and reveal aspects of men's feelings and concerns from the writer's subjective viewpoint. We'd like to be able to look inside the writer's heart and hear about his feelings and experiences, rather than just hear his opinions. Our readers want Brothers to help them understand what Black men are experiencing, how they are perceiving their world and how this might impact on their relationships with women, other men, children, their families and friends.

If you have an essay that meets our specifications, we'd love to see it.

SUGGESTED BROTHERS TOPICS:

- Being single
- married
- divorced
- a father
- incarcerated
- unemployed/underemployed
- homosexual
- celibate
- politically active
- Growing older
- Sports—meaning/importance
- Interacting with family
- Friendship with men/women
- Cross-cultural experiences

And please suggest topics of your own!

Manuscripts should be approx. 800 words, typed, double-spaced and submitted with a S.A.S.E. (self-addressed-stamped-envelope). Be sure to include a phone number where you can be reached during business hours.

WRITERS GUIDELINES for "Our World"

"Our World" is a column in ESSENCE magazine written by people of varied ethnic and cultural backgrounds. These essays should transport our eight million readers across cultural and/or racial boundaries and provide insight into the lives of other people.

Using a first-person approach, writers should feel free to use anecdotes, phrases in her native language and descriptions of rituals and customs. But we hope you will go beyond mere descriptions to express how they feel about cultural references. "Our World" pieces should be written from the heart.

We prefer to read query letters rather than completed manuscripts. (A manuscript can be sent on speculation with the understanding that it will not be returned.) If an assignment is made, manuscripts should be no more than 800 words, typed and double-spaced. Be sure to include your name, address and daytime telephone number, and a self-addressed stamped envelope. Please allow eight weeks for review. Thank you for your interest in writing for ESSENCE.

WRITERS GUIDELINES for "Back Talk"

Think of this column as a forum page; it's your chance to make a point, deliver an opinion, build a case — or even pick a bone. Whether it revolves around an incident that happened to you, a trend or attitude you think is worth shedding light on or some timely issue of the day, it's important that you give us a concrete, distinctive perspective or new insight. Most Back Talk essays are persuasive; they exhort readers to think a certain way or do something. Others, however, simply highlight, celebrate or analyze some part of the human condition. As you write your Back Talk, or select a topic, the overriding concern should be whether or not your statements are important, relevant or of interest to Black women, Black people, or any social thinker.

Keep the language and tone of your essay as conversational or personable as possible. The most popular and effective Back Talks have been those that did not set up a large distance between the author and reader. So think of yourself as having a chat with someone, rather than giving a speech to masses. Avoid academic jargon or aimless rhetoric at all cost. As you're pulling your essay together, ask yourself questions such as: Does each point I make move toward or relate to the main theme? Have I included any examples or illustrations to make my point? Does the whole piece hold together or revolve around one major statement or theme?

Remember, what we're looking for in a Back Talk essay is clarity, unity, and substance. Whether your essay's tone is humorous or alarmist, realist or visionary, the readers should come away with her mind made up or changed: she should come away feeling resolved, enlightened , amused, provoked or encouraged.

Manuscripts should be 7-800 words, typed, double-spaced and submitted with a S.A.S.E. (self-addressed-stamped-envelope) and a color photograph that reflects the tone of your essay. Be sure to include your name and a phone number where you can be reached during business hours atop each page. Please allow four to six weeks for a written response.

Categories: Fiction—Nonfiction—African-American—General Interest—Health—Relationships—Self-Help

CONTACT: Submissions Editor
Material: All
1500 Broadway
New York NY 10036
Website: www.essence.com

Et cetera
A Review of General Semantics

The International Society for General Semantics, founded in 1943, publishes articles, essays, fiction, and correspondence related to general semantics. Our publications include a quarterly journal, *ETC: A Review of General Semantics*, and numerous books and anthologies.

General semantics, a science-oriented, educational discipline first formulated by Alfred Korzybski, applies to a wide range of human activities: communication, evaluating, perception, problem-solving, inference-making, critical thinking, to name a few.

As a writer, you communicate. You communicate your view of the world, based on your assumptions, observations, inferences, and conclusions. General semantics offers a wealth of material for the writer because it helps you understand some of the processes underlying thinking, evaluating, and communicating.

Our publishing covers many areas, including:

- Humor
- Multi-Media
- Effective Writing
- Comment
- How to Apply General Semantics
- Book Reviews
- Self-Esteem
- Fiction
- Language & Behavior
- Education
- Research Results
- Self-improvement Through General Semantics

- Metaphor
- The Media
- Problem-Solving with General Semantics
- Popular Culture
- Critical Thinking
- Communication
- Science & Language
- The Press
- Psychology
- Folklore
- History of Thought
- Computers & Networks

We produce books on using and teaching general semantics, including a number of anthologies of original material and reprints from *ETC: A Review of General Semantics*. We use material from published and unpublished writers.

Preparing to Write

Read about general semantics. Before making submissions, study *ETC: A Review of General Semantics* in order to familiarize yourself with content and style.

Read some of the recent general semantics books, such as Thinking and Living Skills: General Semantics for Critical Thinking, To Be or Not: An E-Prime Anthology, and More E-Prime: To Be or Not II. The latter two books have examples of general semantics fiction.

Our anthologies now in print also include: Classroom Exercises in General Semantics, Bridging Worlds Through General Semantics, Teaching General Semantics, Enriching Professional Skills Through General Semantics.

Manuscripts Needed

We need material for a forthcoming anthology of general semantics-related fiction. We also need submissions for *ETC: A Review of General Semantics*. As we have done in the past, we may select material from *ETC: A Review of General Semantics* for reprinting in future anthologies.

The Society, a nonprofit educational organization which exists to disseminate information related to general semantics, pays for publication with contributor's copies.

You may have noticed that we wrote these guidelines without to be verbs: is, was, am, were, be, being, been, etc. We call this variant of English E-Prime. Perhaps you heard about E-Prime on National Public Radio's All Things Considered or read about it in *The Atlantic Monthly* (February 1992). You may wish to find out how E-Prime can help improve your writing.

Preparing Submissions

When submitting your manuscript, please use standard ms. preparation: Submit two copies. We cannot accept handwritten submissions. Put your name, address, and phone number on the first page at top left. Keep length of ms. below 4,000 words. Include a biography of up to thirty words. For reference style, see copies of *ETC: A Review of General Semantics*. Please advise us if you have a word processing disk available.

If you would like a sample copy of *ETC: A Review of General Semantics*, please let us know.

Meanwhile, do the important thing—keep on writing!

Categories: Education—General Interest—Language—Literature—Psychology—Writing

CONTACT: Jeremy Klein, Editor-in-Chief
Material: All
CONTACT: Paul D. Johnston, Managing Editor
Material: All
PO Box 728
Concord CA 94522
Phone: 925-798-0311
Fax: 510-798-0312
E-mail: isgs@generalsemantics.org
Website: www.generalsemantics.org

Evangel

Evangel a publication of light and life communications, is printed quarterly and is geared toward adults. All submissions should reflect the needs, interests, and struggles of adults striving to maintain a vital relationship with Christ in the midst of everyday experiences—or seeking to know Christ in these same experiences. (In general, stories should be aimed at young to middle-aged adults.)

We accept both fiction and nonfiction work. Material can range from first person stories to Christian growth and living articles to devotional articles. Material should not be preachy or overly predictable. First-time rights are preferred, although second rights and reprints will be considered.

Materials should be limited to 1,200 words or less. We can use a larger quantity of short articles compared to long ones.

Short anecdotes and humor articles are welcome, although use is less frequent. Poetry is used on a very limited basis.

SUBMISSIONS

In the upper left-hand corner of the first page, include your name, address, phone number and social security number. In the upper right-hand corner, specify the number of words in the manuscript, what rights you are offering and if the piece is fiction or nonfiction. One-third of the way down the page, give the manuscript title and your name. All subsequent material must be double-spaced, with one-inch margins. Number your pages.

Always include a word count, and a cover letter which introduces yourself and your work.

If we accept your article, we may ask you to provide the manuscript in a computer format by email. When preparing computer manuscripts:

- Do not justify margins.
- Use single spaces after periods and colons.
- Use tabs to begin paragraphs (not 5 spaces).

Allow six to eight weeks for response. Send seasonal material at least 9-12 months in advance.

PAYMENT

Rate of pay is four cents per word as published. Minimum payment is $10.00. Your check and complimentary copy are sent on publication.

PHOTOGRAPHY

Good-quality black-and-white or color photographs relating to your article are welcome. Rate of pay is $10.00 per selected photo. Include photo credit.

COMPLIMENTARY

If you would like to examine the style and content of *Evangel*, sample issues are available when [requests are] accompanied by a self-addressed, stamped envelope (business size).

MISSION STATEMENT

The *Evangel*, a weekly adult publication, seeks to increase the reader's understanding of the nature and character of God and the nature of a life lived under the lordship of Christ. Devotional in character, it directly and unashamedly lifts up Christ as the Source of salvation and hope.

Hints:
- *Evangel* is limited in space.
- Don't ramble, stick to your thesis or theme.
- Don't be unnecessarily redundant.
- Brevity and simplicity of content makes for a more readable piece.
- Material not accompanied by a self-addressed stamped envelope is not returned and may not receive a reply.
- Rhyming poetry is seldom seriously considered.

Categories: Fiction—Nonfiction—Christian Interests—Inspirational

CONTACT: Julie Innes, Editor
Material: All
PO Box 535002
Indianapolis IN 46253-5002
Phone: 317-244-3660

Fabricator

Ornamental & Miscellaneous Metal

Fabricator

National Ornamental & Miscellaneous Metal Association

Articles can be from 800 to 2,000 words on topics related to the Ornamental and Miscellaneous Metal Industry.

These guidelines provide general tips on producing high-quality, easy-to-read articles for *Fabricator* magazine.

Tip #1: Articles should be written in a clear, concise, easy-to-read format. When writing, put yourself in the shoes of the reader and ask yourself such questions as, "Does this make sense?," "Is this interesting?," "Would I read this article if I were a *Fabricator* subscriber?"

Tip #2: Make sure the "Five W's" are included in the story: Who, What, When, Why, Where. Do not assume the reader knows what you're talking about. Explain highly technical terms in plain English.

Tip #3: As a writer, remember your goal is to benefit the reader. Whether your article is to educate, entertain, or inspire, always keep your reader in mind.

Tip #4: Place emphasis on things of special interest about your topic: Trivia, facts about the project's history, anecdotes, etc. Feel free to throw in humor and consider approaching your topic in a creative manner.

Tip #5: Once you have received an assignment, give yourself a couple of days to think about how to approach the story and what to include. If you are excited about the article, and it flows out easily, then chances are you have a great story. If a story must be forced out, line for line, then you may want to take a step back and consider another angle.

Tip #6: Always try to come up with artwork for a story—either drawings or photos. An illustrated article will catch the reader's eye, while a gray article will usually turn a reader off. If you can't find suitable artwork, then consider including a mug shot or photo of your business (all photos and artwork will be returned unharmed in about four weeks).

Tip #7: If you are a supplier, never make your articles sound like an "advertorial" or free advertisement. The purpose of the article is to provide helpful and interesting information as a valuable industry service—not to be self-serving. No "puff" pieces, please.

All articles published must be original material (i.e. you must control the copyright). If you use published information, it must be done in accordance with U.S. copyright laws. The article should not infringe on any existing copyrights.

When writing the article, you must honor any agreements on publicity that may have been signed with owners, architects, primary contractors, or other fabricators. As a matter of fairness, please credit subcontractors, partners, or employees when credit is due.

Transmission Methods

1) U.S. Mail—All stories will be scanned into our computer. Thus, they should be printed in dark ink on plain white paper.

2) Floppy Disk—Any PC format, including ASCII, Microsoft Word, or WordPerfect. Either 3½" or 5¼" disk is OK.

3) E-mail—Either as e-mail or as an "attached file."

4) Fax—You can fax directly into our computer. When faxing, please set your machine on the highest-quality setting.

Editing: All articles in *Fabricator* are subject to editing. Stories are typically edited for grammar, style, clarity, transition, voice, and length. If a story is edited, the editor will make every effort to preserve the author's original idea and intent. If a story requires complete rewriting, the editor will contact the writer. If a story is highly technical in nature, with lots of figures, the editor will likely send a proof after editing.

Statement of Purpose: *Fabricator*'s mission is to inform, educate, and inspire the industry. The magazine's long-term goal is to strengthen both the industry and NOMMA by fostering the free flow of information and knowledge.

For Freelance Writers: *Fabricator* welcomes unsolicited articles and photos.

Categories: Nonfiction—Trade—Metalworking

CONTACT: Fabricator Magazine Editor
Material: All
532 Forest Pkwy., Ste. A
Forest Park GA 30297
Phone: 404-363-4009
Fax: 404-366-1852
E-mail: fabricator@nomma.org

Faces
The Magazine About People

General Information

Lively, original approaches to the subject are the primary concerns of the editors in choosing material. Writers are encouraged to study recent back issues for content and style. (Sample issues available at $4.95. Send 7 ½" x 10 ½" (or larger) self-addressed stamped envelope.) All material must relate to the theme of a specific upcoming issue in order to be considered (themes and deadlines given below). FACES purchases all rights to material.

Procedure

A query must consist of all of the following information to be considered:

• please use non-erasable paper
• a brief cover letter stating the subject and word length of the proposed article,
• a detailed one-page outline explaining the information to be presented in the article,
• an extensive bibliography of materials the author intends to use in preparing the article

Writers new to FACES should send a writing sample with the query.

If you would like to know if your query has been received, please also include a stamped postcard requesting acknowledgment of receipt.

In all correspondence, please include your complete address as well as a telephone number where you can be reached.

Manuscripts should be typed double-spaced and include final word count. Authors are requested to supply a 2- to 3-line biographical sketch.

Articles must be submitted on disk using a word processing program (preferably Microsoft Word - MAC). Text should be saved as ASCII text (in MS Word as "text only"). Disks should be either MAC - (preferred) or DOS - compatible 3 ½ ".

GUIDELINES

Feature Articles
(about 800 words)
Includes: in-depth nonfiction highlighting an aspect of the featured culture, interviews, and personal accounts.

Supplemental Nonfiction
(300-600 words)
Includes: subjects directly and indirectly related to the theme. Editors like little-known information but encourage writers not to overlook the obvious.

Fiction
(up to 800 words)
Includes: Retold legends, folktales, stories, and original plays from around the world, etc., relating to the theme.

The above three pay 20 to 25 cents per printed word.

Activities
(up to 700 words)
Includes: crafts, games, recipes, projects, etc., which children can do either alone or with adult supervision. Should be accompanied by sketches and description of how activity relates to theme.

Poetry

(up to 100 lines)

Clear, objective imagery. Serious and light verse considered. Must relate to theme.

Puzzles and Games

Crossword and other word puzzles using the vocabulary of the issue's theme. Mazes and picture puzzles that relate to the theme.

The above three pay on an individual basis.

Photo Guidelines

To be considered for publication, photographs must relate to a specific theme. Writers are encouraged to submit available photos with their query or article. We buy one-time use.

See our website for suggested fee range for professional quality photographs.

• Please note that fees for non-professional quality photographs are negotiated.

• Cover fees are set on an individual basis for one-time use, plus promotional use. All cover images are color.

• Prices set by museums, societies, stock photography houses, etc., are paid or negotiated. Photographs that are promotional in nature (e.g., from tourist agencies, organizations, special events, etc.) are usually submitted at no charge.

• If you have photographs pertaining to any upcoming theme, please contact the editor by mail or fax, or send them with your query. You may also send images on speculation.

Note

Queries may be submitted at any time before the deadline, but queries sent well in advance of deadline MAY NOT BE ANSWERED FOR SEVERAL MONTHS. Go-aheads requesting material proposed in queries are usually sent at least seven months prior to publication date. Unused queries will be returned if a SASE is supplied.

Categories: Children—Culture—Juvenile—Multicultural—Young Adult

CONTACT: Elizabeth Crooker Carpentiere, Editor
Material: All
Cobblestone Publishing
30 Grove Street, Ste C
Peterborough NH 03458
Phone: 603-924-7209
Fax: 603-924-7380
E-mail: www.cobblestonepub.com
E-mail: facesmag@yahoo.com

Family Circle

Writers are sometimes surprised to find out that most of the articles *Family Circle* publishes are written by freelancers. We are always looking for new contributors.

If you want to submit an article proposal to *Family Circle*, please pay careful attention to the following points:

• Take a close look at *Family Circle* for some knowledge of format and an understanding of the subjects we have tackled in the past, remembering that we are a general interest women's magazine which focuses on the family. We are looking for true stories with strong plot lines and characters, or newsworthy reports on social issues and trends that affect American families. We are especially interested in women who make a difference in their community, news and information on health, child care, relationships, finances and other matters of concern to today's family; as well as dramatic personal experiences.

• Submit a detailed outline first, and include a brief cover letter describing your publishing history and two representative clips.

• Manuscripts should be typed, double-spaced, on letter-size paper. Handwritten submissions will be returned.

• Maximum length for articles is usually 2,500 words.

• *Family Circle* does not consider multiple submissions.

• Submissions must be accompanied by self-addressed stamped envelopes of sufficient size or, if mailed from abroad, by International Reply Coupons, which are available at post offices throughout the world.

• *Family Circle* takes good care of submissions; however, owing to the fact that mail is sometimes mislaid by the U.S. Post Office, we cannot assume responsibility. Be sure to have a copy of every submission you send to us.

Categories: Nonfiction—Children—Family—General Interest—Health—Money & Finances—Relationships—Personal Experiences

CONTACT: Appropriate Editor from Masthead
Material: As appropriate
375 Lexington Ave.
New York NY 10017-5514
Phone: 212-499-2000

The Family Digest

"The joy and fulfillment of Catholic family life"

Family Digest

Submission Guidelines for *Family Digest* magazine & Web site.

Publisher's note: In a world that has ignored, demeaned, devalued and berated the Black family, we stand forth to celebrate and empower Black mothers, fathers, husbands and wives. Come join us in this movement!

What's In It For Our Readers? "Smarter, Healthier, Happier Black Families."

Family Digest magazine is a magazine for Black Moms/Female heads-of-household; helping them get more out of their roles as wife, mother, home-manager - with special emphasis on areas of interest to Black Americans.

Editorial coverage includes parenting, health, love & marriage, family finances, recipes, and beauty & style,... all designed to appeal to Black Moms/Female heads-of-household. Most of our readers are married with kids.

Please note: Articles published in *Family Digest* are positive in nature and focus on providing information and solutions, not just analysis. The articles are conversational, factual and authoritative. When the reader reads *Family Digest* it is as if she is having a discussion with a friend who is an expert in a particular field.

Important: We love it when you can deliver photos appropriate for the article.

Family Digest's Interest Areas include:

1. Family: Articles in this section help parents help their children in a variety of areas, such as: how to effectively discipline their child, how to talk to kids about drugs, how to build their kids self-esteem, etc.

2. Family Travel: This is a section that we're really excited about. The key to this section is affordable, interesting vacation destinations for the family. This could be: cruises in the Caribbean, auto travel to destinations in the U.S., Club Med, Skiing, Hawaii, trips out West, air/land packages, etc. We want the trips to be accessible.

3. Auto Review: We're interested in this piece (to run in every issue) that reviews various family vehicles... This piece should always be written from the standpoint of, and the benefit of, what a Mom with kids would like in a family vehicle.

4. Enjoy Life!: This section focuses on articles that strengthen moms so that they can be better people. Articles in this section are uplifting and leave the reader feeling they can do anything. Example topics include: how to get negative people out of your life, job strategies, networking tips.

5. Love & Marriage: The articles that appear in this section allow readers to strengthen their relationship with their spouse. Features in

this section focus on: improving communication between partners, tips on how to have a strong relationship and pleasing your partner (these articles can include information on healthy sexual relations).

6. Health: The focus here is on health and medical issues of particular interest to Black women. Topics include breast cancer, fibroids, diabetes, sickle-cell, cystitis, etc... These articles should offer factual information regarding available treatments and resources.

7. Family Finances: These are tips regarding saving money and investing. Articles should provide immediately usable information and how-tos. Examples include how to save on groceries, how to choose life insurance, how to develop an investment strategy, saving for the kids' college, ...

8. Beauty & Style: This section provides information on the latest in hair and skin care, as well as relevant fashion trends. Examples might be: best skin care products for busy moms, how to effectively moisturize African-American skin, taking care of particular hair styles, the age at which it is safe to do certain things to children's hair (for instance, at what age is it safe to perm a child's hair), ...

9. Meal Time!: This section features recipes and information on food. Articles should feature foods that are easily found in a typical grocery store. Also, meals should be relatively easy to prepare.

10. Horoscope: This section should be written about adult females, in a tone that is relevant to the female head-of-household.

Submission Guidelines:

1. Please submit story ideas, and your thoughts on the angle you'd like to take to editor@familydigest.com . Ideas will be judged according to their fit with the information outlined above.

2. If you have not written for us before, please submit 3 writing samples that are representative of your work. These should also be sent to editor@familydigestbaby.com via EMail.

3. Length: Generally, articles should be 1,000 to 2,000 words.

4. Article Approach: We encourage a mix of approaches including narratives, profiles, how-tos and Q&As. Please indicate the direction you would like to take along with each story idea (see #1 above).

5. Deadlines: Inquire

6. Completed story submission: All work must be submitted by EMail to editor@familydigest.com (unless other arrangements agreed to).

7. Rewrites: If retooling is necessary, we will contact you within 3 weeks of article submission to discuss.

8. Send photos to: Angel Morning at the address below. Include your name and story title with all photos.

9. We pay upon publication. Writing fees vary based on budget and need. We will contact you with rate at time of initial contact.

Please feel free to contact editor@familydigest.com with any questions or comments.

Categories: Nonfiction—Children—Culture—Family—Parenting—Relationships

CONTACT: Submissions Edito
Material: All
Family Digest Media Group
696 San Ramon Valley Blvd., Ste. 349
Danville CA 94526
Phone: 925-838-4800
Fax: 925-838-4948
E-mail: editor@familydigest.com
Website: www.familydigest.com

Remember: Editors change jobs and publishers change addresses. It is wise to invest in a phone call for the current information before submitting.

FamilyFun

Family Fun

Thank you for inquiring about freelance opportunities at *FamilyFun*, the country's number one magazine for families with children ages three to twelve. Founded in 1991 and with a circulation now exceeding 1.45 million, our publication celebrates all the fun things families can do together, from throwing parties and making crafts to taking trips and cooking great food. Our goal is to inspire families to spend time together by providing the sure-fire ideas and activities that will make that time a success. In other words, we take fun seriously. Please note that our heavy emphasis on activities and ideas distinguishes us from other parenting and family magazines (as one of our descriptive slogans points out, we provide "100% activities for 100% fun"). This format means that we are always looking for freelancers who are experts in the art of being a fun-loving, creative parent.

We accept submissions by standard mail from published writers. Queries should describe the content, structure, and tone of the proposed article. Since we receive many queries on the same topics, please be as specific as possible about what makes your idea unique and your qualifications to write it. If appropriate, include photographs or sketches of the finished project, food, or craft. Also, with each query, please enclose two or three relevant clips for our review. Unfortunately, we no longer accept unsolicited manuscripts for feature stories. *We will continue to accept manuscripts for the following departments:* Family Traveler, Family Almanac, Family Ties, and My Great Idea (please note department on envelope). Unless otherwise indicated below, articles are scheduled and assigned at least five months in advance of their publication date. We generally take at least four to eight weeks to respond and regret that we cannot, under any circumstance, consider queries over the telephone, via email, or fax. Please enclose a self-addressed stamped envelope with correct postage for our response to your query.

FEATURES

Our features present activities that are entertaining for the whole family, relatively inexpensive, and easy to do. The specific topics include food, crafts, parties, holiday celebrations, sports, games, creative solutions to common household problems, and educational projects. Our travel features highlight moderately priced destinations, generally within the United States, that offer an exceptional value and specifically cater to the needs of families. Similarly, our food features present recipes that have a proven track record with families, dishes that are fun both to make and to eat. In all our articles, our style is upbeat, personal, and straightforward. Features generally run 850 to 3,000 words and pay $1.25 per word upon acceptance. We consider ideas in query form only.

DEPARTMENTS

Family Almanac provides readers with simple, fun, practical, and inexpensive ideas and projects (outings, crafts, games, nature activities, learning activities, kid-friendly recipes, and so on). Its tone is direct and cheerful. We read both freelance manuscripts and queries for Family Almanac. Pieces are assigned from 100 to 300 words; we pay $1 per word upon acceptance. We also pay $50 to $75 for ideas in the event that we decide to use a staff writer. We consider ideas in query or manuscript form.

Family Ties is a first-person column that lets our writers speak parent-to-parent to our readers about the distinctive pleasures, humor, frustrations, and struggles of family life. The topics vary from column to column, but at the heart of each essay is insight into the emotional relationship between the writer and his or her children. Family Ties runs 1,300 words and pays $1,500 upon acceptance. We consider ideas in query or manuscript form.

Family Traveler consists of brief, newsy items about family travel — what's new, what's great, and especially, what's a good deal. We cover festivals, civic and cultural events, museum exhibits, family hotel packages, state and national park programs, and more. We also present longer (up to 1,500 words), highly formatted articles on road trips, city weekends, and roundups of themed attractions or destinations. Because we are budget-conscious, we rarely cover international travel or expensive American resorts or programs. We read freelance manuscripts for Family Traveler and pay $100 upon acceptance for 100- to 125-word pieces. We pay $1.25 per word upon acceptance.

Traveler articles. We also pay $50 for ideas in the event that we decide to use a staff writer. We consider ideas in query or manuscript form.

My Great Idea showcases a practical, innovative idea that the writer used to solve a common household problem: a chart that got the kids excited about doing chores, say, or a trick that persuaded some reluctant letter writers to keep up their correspondence with Grandpa. Each essay also presents the story of how this Great Idea changed or inspired the family. The column runs 800 to 1,000 words, and pays $1250 upon acceptance. We consider ideas in query or manuscript form.

My Great Idea: From Our Readers

In addition, following the column we publish My Great Idea: From Our Readers, which consists of ideas and solutions from writers and readers. These too showcase simple, clever ideas that solve common household problems, but they are presented in an abbreviated format with less narrative detail. My Great Idea: From Our Readers runs 100 to 150 words and pays $50 upon publication.

Subscriptions ($14.95 for one year) can also be ordered through the above address, online at https://commerce.cdsfulfillment.com/FAF/subscriptions.cgi or by calling 800-289-4849.

If you would like to receive a sample copy of our magazine, send a check for $3 made out to *FamilyFun* to:

FamilyFun
PO Box 37032
Boone, IA 50037-0032
Categories: Nonfiction—Family

CONTACT: Features Editor
Material: Features, Food, or Travel Editor
CONTACT: Nicole Blasenak, Assistant Editor
Material: Family Almanac Submissions
CONTACT: Kathy Whittemore, Senior Editor
Material: Family Ties Submissions
CONTACT: Jodi Butler, Assistant Editor
Material: Family Traveler Submissions
CONTACT: Dawn Chipman, Senior Editor
Material: Great Idea Submissions
244 Main St.
Northampton MA 01060
Phone: 413-585-0444
Fax: 413-586-5724
Website: www.familyfun.com

The Family Handyman

Does not accept unsolicited submissions.

Family Safety and Health

About Us
This publication rarely uses freelance submissions.
Writing Style
• Keep your writing positive, upbeat and simple. Write at a 9th-grade reading level and be creative. We would rather have to tone down your writing than spice it up.

• Write creative lead paragraphs to draw readers into the article. Stick to your word count. Write tight, clear sentences.

• Write in the active voice with present-tense attribution. (Passive example: Skin cancer can be treated easily if caught early, Smith said. Better: It's easy to treat skin cancer if you catch it early, Smith says.)

• Minimize gerunds and participles. An overuse of these -ing words usually occurs when action is taking place in the writing without any actor. When no actors perform the action, less concrete writing results and readers lose interest. Example: "Keeping a healthy and safe home is not an easy initiative." Better: "It isn't always easy to keep your home healthy and safe."

• Avoid sexist language. Usually, you can avoid the "he or she" problem if you structure the sentence to use the plural "their."

• Use the Associated Press Stylebook for journalistic style.

• If you refer to somebody and don't refer to them again for at least four paragraphs, re-reference that person. Example: "Healthy Medical College's Smith says that...."

• Put parentheses around area codes in phone numbers. Example: (630) 775-2286 or (800) 775-2286.

• It's the National Safety Council on first reference and the Council on second reference. (Unless it's four paragraphs away or more.)

• Capitalize people's titles only when you put them before their name. Examples: National Safety Council President John Smith. Or, John Smith, National Safety Council president.

• Use commas in a series only in complicated phrases. Simple-series example: I like dogs, cats and all animals. Complicated-series example: I like dogs who chew on grass that people grow, cats that grew up on the city's south side, and all types of animals that come from small rural towns.

• Italicize the names of books, journals, magazines and other publications.

• We send all articles and departments to in-house or outside experts for technical review. We might ask you to follow up on technical-review questions or concerns.

• Refer to doctors on second reference by their last names only. First reference example: Dr. John Smith of Healthy Medical College. Second reference: Smith. If the two references are four paragraphs away or more, re-identify the person on second reference.

Sources
• Interview expert sources and non-experts with varying views, such as real people who have experience with a certain topic. This offers different perspectives and helps create a multidimensional article.

• Source review: Our policy is to allow sources to review their quotes before publication if they so request. You don't need to volunteer that service if a source doesn't request it.

• Document all statistics. Use National Safety Council statistics when possible.

Use of Quotations
• Try not to overquote a single source. Rule of thumb: More than two or three direct quotes from one source is usually too much.

• Make indirect quotations of statements that are not truly quoteworthy. For example, it would not be quoteworthy to state: She said, "I don't agree." Better: She said she didn't agree.

Library Resources
• Feel free to contact the National Safety Council Library at (630) 775-2199. Let them know you are writing an article for FAMILY SAFETY AND HEALTH. The librarians can do a computer search of background information and send you a printout.

• After you receive the printout, you can ask the librarians to send you copies of the articles listed, within reason.

Format
• Please supply three headlines with your article.

• To add variety to the magazine, FAMILY SAFETY AND HEALTH offers readers a variety of article formats. Follow the format outlined in your assignment letter.

• Include catchy subheads within the text body to draw readers in. Use verbs in your subheads when possible.

• When you write a sidebar, assume that readers might not read the main article. Therefore, refer to all sources with their full titles. Insert "boiler" paragraphs to explain terms or concepts that appear in the main article.

• Provide a list of addresses for sources quoted in the article. That way, we can send all sources a copy of the published article.

• Please don't indent your paragraphs—this confuses our computer program. Separate each paragraph with an extra return. Single space between lines. Use only one space after periods.

• Submit work on an IBM-compatible disk in WordPerfect (any version) or in ASCII. If you use a Macintosh, please save your file in ASCII. Or you can e-mail to the address below.

Artwork

• Solicit free art or photography from sources. Ask sources for color transparencies, slides or high-quality prints. We will add $50 to your final payment for each photo or other artwork you provide that is printed with the article.

Invoice Procedures

• Payment is made on acceptance. Typically, it takes approximately 60 days for our Accounting Department to process your payment.

• Please send an invoice directly to the editor who assigned you the article. Provide an invoice number, the issue the article is for (e.g., Fall 1997 FAMILY SAFETY AND HEALTH), the purchase-order number and the date that you turned in your article.

• Bill us for the minimum amount for the article. Articles must be on time and be of superior quality (as determined by the editors) to be eligible for an incentive.

• We reimburse writers for reasonable phone and fax expenses. Include this amount to your total bill. If your expenses exceed $50, submit your phone bill to your editor as documentation. We will determine if the excess is reasonable and make payment accordingly.

If you have any questions, please give us a call.

And good luck with your article!

Categories: Nonfiction—Family—Health

CONTACT: Laura Coyne, Editor
Material: All
1121 Spring Lake Dr.
Itasca IL 60143
Phone: 630-775-2276
Fax: 630-775-2285
Website: coynel!nsc.org or www.nsc.org

Family Therapy
The Journal of the California Graduate School of Family Psychology

The editor welcomes succinct, well-written papers within the broad field of family and marital therapy. Clinical articles devoted to techniques, and richly endowed with illustrative dialogue, are most highly regarded.

MANUSCRIPTS, REFERENCES AND REPRINTS: Manuscripts must be type-written in duplicate. All manuscripts must include an abstract of 100-150 words and typed on a separate sheet of paper. Footnotes, charts, tables, graphs, etc. should be kept to a minimum and submitted in the original, camera-ready copy. (We prefer that, when practical, the information contained in this material be incorporated into the text instead.) References to books and articles should appear at the end of the manuscript under the heading "References," with items listed alphabetically by name of author.

Authors will be furnished galley proofs which must be returned to the editor within two days. Corrections should be kept to a minimum. A schedule of reprint costs and an order blank for reprints will be sent with galley proofs.

SUBSCRIPTIONS: All business communications, including subscriptions, renewals, and remittances should be addressed to:

Libra Publishers, Inc.
3089C Clairemont Dr., Suite 383
San Diego, CA 92117
SUBSCRIPTION RATES

Individuals-U.S.A.: One year $62; Two years $122; Three years $182 Other countries: One year $69; Two years $136; Three years $203

Institutions-U.S.A.: One year $70; Two years $138; Three years $206 Other countries: One year $75; Two years $148; Three years $221

Copies of current or back issues are available at $22.00 each from Libra Publishers.

Categories: Nonfiction—Counseling—Family—Marriage—Psychology—Relationships—Family and Marital Therapy

CONTACT: Martin G. Blinder, M.D., Editor
Material: All
50 Idalia Rd.
San Anselmo CA 94960
Phone: 858-571-1414
Fax: 858-571-1414

Fantasy&ScienceFiction
Fantasy & Science Fiction

The Magazine of Fantasy & Science Fiction, founded in 1949, is the award-winning SF magazine which is the original publisher of SF classics like Stephen King's *Dark Tower*, Daniel Keyes's *Flowers for Algernon*, and Walter M. Miller's *A Canticle for Leibowitz*.

Each 160 page issue offers: Compelling short stories and novellas by writers such as Ray Bradbury, Ben Bova, Ursula K. Le Guin, Esther M. Friesner, Terry Bisson and many others. The science fiction field's most respected and outspoken opinions on Books, Films and Science (samples are available via our Departments link)

Writer's Guidelines

We have no formula for fiction. We are looking for stories that will appeal to science fiction and fantasy readers. The SF element may be slight, but it should be present. We prefer character-oriented stories. We receive a lot of fantasy fiction, but never enough science fiction or humor. Do not query for fiction; send the entire manuscript. We publish fiction up to 25,000 words in length. Please read the magazine before submitting. A sample copy is available for $5 (to NJ address).

We do not accept simultaneous or electronic submissions. Please type your manuscript on clean white bond, double spaced, with one inch margins. Put your name on each page, and enclose a self-addressed, stamped envelope. Writers from abroad are encouraged to send recyclable manuscripts with a letter-sized SASE and an International Reply Coupon or 80 cents in US postage (60 cents to Canada and Mexico).

Allow 8 weeks for a response. Please write and enclose a self-addressed stamped envelope if you have any questions.

Payment is 5-8 cents per word on acceptance. We buy first North American and foreign serial rights and an option on anthology rights. All other rights are retained by the author.

Our columns and non-fiction articles are assigned in house. We do not accept freelance submissions in those areas.

Since we use so little art—just eleven covers a year, no interiors— we have no separate artist's guidelines. Please send art samples to Gordon Van Gelder at the address below.

Categories: Fiction—Fantasy—Horror—Science Fiction

CONTACT: Gordon Van Gelder, Editor
Material: Story submissions, cartoon queries and art samples
PO Box 3447
Hoboken NY 07030

Phone: 201-876-2551
E-mail: fsfmag@fsfmag.com
Website: www.sfsite.com/fsf

Farm & Ranch Living

Unlike other farm magazines, *Farm & Ranch Living* does not tell readers how to grow crops or raise animals. Instead, F&RL is a lifestyle magazine for and about farmers and ranchers. We aren't interested in yields, costs, trends or topical issues. We are interested in stories about people and how they live. Ours is the magazine folks read not for profit, but for pure pleasure.

Our kind of story might be about a farmer who has collected dozens of antique tractor and implement seats and hung them in neat rows on his barn wall…or about a farm wife who, between chores, picks and dries wildflowers, then sells them in beautiful wreaths and arrangements. We recently ran a story about a 73-year-old dairy farmer who, in more than 50 years of farming, has spent only $15 to buy cattle! Back in 1937, when he was a teenager, that $15 purchased a heifer for a 4-H project. Later, he started his herd by breeding the heifer…and today, all his cows are descended from her!

We've also had stories about a Louisiana dirt farmer who put nine kids through college…an Indiana farmer who is an expert on American Indian history…and a Utah turkey raiser who is that state's "Cook-out King." Feature stories should focus on folks who farm or ranch under interesting or unusual circumstances or have out-of-the-ordinary crops or sidelines. Stories should be a celebration of living and working on the land and can be upbeat…poignant…lighthearted–even inspirational.

Like the other magazines we publish, F&RL carries no advertising, has full-color throughout and appears six times a year. *The ideal time for freelance submissions* is 4 or 5 months before the issue date. We are happy to consider either *queries or actual submissions*. Often, even with a query, we will ask the contributor to submit on speculation. We prefer photos to be included with submissions and usually buy a package of text and photos.

Typically, *payment is upon publication*, but exceptions can be made. Payment varies according to quality of text and photos and to space used in the magazine. Rates range from a minimum of $25 for a filler to a maximum of $300 for a package of text and photos. We use color photos only…unless, of course, the story is nostalgic or recollective and calls for old black and white photos. We accept *color prints, slides and large-format transparencies*.

Potential contributors are encouraged to obtain a *sample copy* of the magazine to better understand our needs. Because we carry no advertising and rely solely on subscription revenue, we must charge freelancers $2.00 for a sample copy (to cover the cost of postage). Contributors receive a complimentary copy of the issue in which their work appears.

Each issue of F&RL contains a special feature called *"Prettiest Place in the Country."* Writers/photographers interested in contributing to this feature should first obtain a copy of the magazine, then query the editors. "Prettiest Place" is a photos-and-text "tour" of a particularly attractive farm or ranch, including the home. Payment for this feature is negotiated with the editors.

Send query or submission, along with SASE, to Nick Pabst, Editor. Queries and manuscripts may be sent via E-mail to *editors@farmandranchliving.com*. Please remember, however, that we seldom, if ever, accept something for publication unless we can also see photos. There are instances when photos are not available (such as in the case of a personal essay), and we will illustrate the story if need be.

(We also buy scenic *farm photos without text*. For Photo Guidelines send a stamped, self-addressed, business-size envelope to: Trudi Bellin, Photo Coordinator, Reiman Publications, 5400 S. 60th St., Greendale, WI 53129.

Thanks for your interest!

Categories: Nonfiction—Agriculture—Lifestyle—Rural America

CONTACT: Submissions Editor
Material: All
Reiman Publications
5400 S. 60th St.
Greendale WI 53129
Phone: 414-423-0100
E-mail: editors@ farmandranchliving.com
Website: www.farmandranchliving.com

Farm Times
Beef Times

Farm Times is a regional, monthly publication established in 1987, which is "dedicated to rural living" and to farmers, ranchers and agriculture. *Farm Times'* primary circulation area includes Idaho, Oregon, Nevada, Utah, Wyoming, Washington and Montana.

Farm Times is an "agriculture-friendly" publication. *Farm Times* strongly supports livestock producers, farmers and the industries involved in producing ag commodities by recognizing American agriculture's role in maintaining our high standard of living in the United States. *Farm Times'* ag-related articles depict ranching and farming in a positive way.

Farm Times recognizes that world affairs, as well as public opinion, affect agriculture. *Farm Times* strives to inform its readers through the reporting of both sides of the issue using an "ag-friendly" slant. Readers' views, both pro and con, are encouraged in the form of letters to the editor and guest editorials.

Farm Times' main focus is articles involving the Intermountain and Pacific Northwest. However, articles reflecting the global issues affecting agriculture are strongly encouraged. Because *Farm Times* is "dedicated to rural living," we also accept non-agricultural article submissions of interest to farm and ranch families. Examples include historical, humor, crafts, travel (both day-trip and vacation), gardening, farm and ranch family profiles, and rural religion, to name a few.

***Farm Times* features regular sections each issue, including Rural Life (women's pages), horse and dairy.**

1. Rural Life: contact—editor. This section each month includes recipes and humor (staff written); one feature with photographs on a topic of interest to women or about women (freelance writers, but requires unique, timely or imaginative slant, i.e. home-based businesses, widows dealing with farming responsibilities, etc. People profiles should be of regional interest). Buys 12 per year. Crafts (freelance writers) - require how-to instructions and good quality photographs or drawings. Buys 6-12 per year. Query with craft article (especially holiday related) three months in advance.

2. Horse Section: contact–editor. This section each month is freelance written and features articles of interest to both working and show horse enthusiasts, including breeds, events, facilities, people, trends, rodeo, shows, etc. Photographs, both b&w and color, are encouraged.

3. "B" Section Cover: contact–editor. No ads on this page leaves room for "photo stories" of general interest.

Article length - 400-650 words, 3 or more photographs are often used.

4. Spring, summer & fall - B cover articles in the past have included 200th Anniversary of the Circus, hopes and fears of high school graduates and parents, raising unusual herds (alligators and frogs), Mormon Trail Sesquicentennial, etc.

5. Winter - B cover articles have included travel pieces for "Winter Wanderlust" features. Generally, winter is the travel season for people involved in agriculture. Articles in the past have varied from world-wide to regional get-aways (London, Puerto Vallarta, Oregon's northern coast, Disneyland and Disney World. Non-travel photo articles also are used during the winter months.

Query 3 months in advance with B Cover articles and photographs.

Farm Times does not accept fiction or first person accounts of life on the farm or rural life. (Our readers send them in as "Rural Reflections.")

Farm Times does not accept anecdotes, facts and gags from freelance writers. They are handled in-house. Some cartoons are accepted.

Farm Times editors appreciate articles that are well-written and edited by the author to desired length (400-750 words or 1,000-1,200 words for technical articles). Write tight, be sure of facts and name spellings.

Farm Times relies on its regional appeal to readers. Although news articles will have global datelines, most of the general articles center around Idaho, Oregon, Washington, Montana, Utah, Wyoming and Nevada.

If you have an article idea generated from another part of the country, find a way to "regionalize" it for us. For example, an interview with a pottery maker from South Carolina would have appeal to us if he/she sells the pottery in Sun Valley, Idaho, or Jackson Hole, Wyoming.

Or, an article on antiques would have appeal if your sources came from the Pacific Northwest as well as the New England states.

An article on seed potatoes from Maine or Canada would have appeal if you compared them with seed potatoes from Idaho.

Or, an article about the pitfalls or windfalls of gambling in Atlantic City would have appeal if you compare it with Reno, Las Vegas or elsewhere in Nevada.

Farm Times Payment Schedule

Farm Times also publishes *Beef Times*, a monthly publication, and several specialty publications dealing with agriculture.

Farm Times and *Beef Times* buy approximately 200 articles per year. Pays on publication. Editorial lead time (1 month or less for timely, late-breaking articles; 2 to 3 months for all other articles). Your social security number will be requested for payment to be issued.

Article lengths: 400-750 words for general articles; 1,000 for technical articles. *Farm Times* editors reserve the right to edit articles to length. If extensive work is required to edit to length, the article will be returned.

Payment: $1.50/column inch. Byline given. Photos used on inside pages - $7/each. Color prints are used for the issue front cover and Section B. Payment for the issue front cover photo or photos is $35/each (does not include Section B front cover). Captions, model releases and subject identification are required. Buys one-time rights. Photos may be e-mailed in a PC format as a jpeg or tiff file. *Farm Times* can resize and final print photos at 600 dpi. Photos should be in focus with strong contrasts.

Cartoons: $8/each. Buys several at a time when needed. Topics range from farming, ranching and editorial to family relationships, hunting and winter sports.

Note from the Editors: At this time, *Farm Times* is not a freelance market for "Me and Joe" first-person accounts or for articles detailing memories of farm life. Our readers, however, send in these types of stories for the "Rural Reflections" section we run occasionally.

Categories: Nonfiction—Agriculture—Business—Lifestyle—Rural America

CONTACT: Submissions Editor
Material: All
504 6th Street
Rupert ID 83350
Phone: 208-436-1111
Fax: 208-436-9455
Website: www.farmtimes.com

Farwest Magazine

Please refer to *Digger Magazine*.

Fast & Fun Crochet

General Information

Fast & Fun Crochet is a full-color digest-size 48-page quarterly magazine published by House of White Birches, a Dynamic Resource Group (DRG) publishing company.

The magazine features creative crochet patterns that use popular stitches and readily available yarns (either in yarn shops, craft stores or mail order). Yarn and thread designs include, but are not limited to, apparel, home decor, winter accessories, bazaar items, doilies and afghans.

SUBMISSIONS

Project submissions or manuscripts: Send us your completed project, a photo or proposal sketches and swatches. IMPORTANT: Label your project! Write your name, address and project name on a tag and attach it to your project.

Instructions: Send typed, double-spaced, step-by-step instructions following the *Fast & Fun Crochet* format and stitch abbreviations. Keep a copy of all instructions, diagrams and graphs.

Garment instructions must include a minimum of three sizes.

Materials list must include types of materials, quantities used and ordering information if available. If design materials were supplied free of charge, indicate which materials should be credited and to whom.

Send complete and labeled graphs, diagrams and color keys all correctly labeled. If you send preliminary sketches, it is not necessary to include the finished graphs, material amounts, etc., at this time.

Include your name (as you prefer to have it in print) address, telephone number and e-mail address.

Project review: We will review submissions according to our editorial calendar. We return items that we do not accept within two weeks of the review. See the Editorial Calendar for specific issue deadlines. Please do not call to check on the status of your design until at least two weeks after the review date.

Return of published projects: Published projects will be returned to the designer (unless otherwise arranged) after the issue is published. All manuscripts, diagrams, etc. remain the property of HWB.

Contracts and payment

If the editor accepts your project for publication, we will send you an agreement with HWB's payment offer and a business-reply envelope. If the agreement is acceptable, sign it and return it in the postage-paid envelope. Keep a photocopy of the agreement for your records and return the original to us.

Payment will be made within 45 days of acceptance. Amount will be determined by accuracy, creativity, workmanship, skill level, overall quality and instruction format. Average fees range from $50 to $400. Because HWB purchases all rights to designs unless otherwise arranged, designers should not sell the purchased design or one very similar to it to another publisher.

If you have any questions, contact Vicki Blizzard by phone or e-mail, or write to the address at the left. If you have a question about the status of a design or payment, contact Cathy Reef at HWB.

We look forward to working with you in the coming months!

Categories: Nonfiction—Crafts/Hobbies—Hobbies

CONTACT: Vicki Blizzard, Editor
Material: Completed project, photo or proposal sketches and/or swatches
House of White Birches, Publications
306 East Parr Rd
Berne IN 46711
Phone: 260-589-4000
E-mail: Vicki_Blizzard@whitebirches.com
Website: www.whitebirches.com

Fast Company

Our Mission

Launched in November 1995 by Alan Webber and Bill Taylor, two former Harvard Business Review editors, *Fast Company* magazine was founded on a single premise: A global revolution was changing business, and business was changing the world. Discarding the old rules of business, *Fast Company* set to chronicle how changing companies create and compete, to highlight new business practices, and to showcase the teams and individuals who are inventing the future and reinventing business.

Today, the business world continues to change, and *Fast Company* continues to evolve as well. In this note from the founding editors, Alan Webber and Bill Taylor discuss how the magazine continues to serve its readers:

Submissions

Does not accept unsolicited manuscripts. However, if you have a person, company, product or any other story idea, please email a pitch to content@fastcompany.com.

Or, feel free to mail or fax proposals.

Categories: Nonfiction—Business—Computers—Education—Entertainment—Lifestyle—Technology—Travel

FC World Headquarters
77 N. Washington St.
Boston MA 02114-1927
Fax: 617-973-0393
E-mail: content@fastcompany.com
Website: www.fastcompany.com

Fate
True Reports of the Strange and Unknown

Thank you for your interest in writing for FATE. We've prepared these guidelines to show you what we look for in a manuscript. Please know that we cannot accept every good article we receive; we simply don't have room.

If possible, please submit your article both on computer disk and in hard-copy form.

Because of the volume of submissions we receive, you can expect to wait one to several months for a response. If you want to be sure your submission has arrived here, include a self-addressed, stamped postcard.

FATE does not publish book-length manuscripts.

TOPICS

FATE magazine reports a wide variety of strange and unknown phenomena. We are open to receiving any well-written, well-documented article. (FATE does not publish poetry or fiction.) Our readers especially like reports of current investigations, experiments, theories, and experiences. *Here is a partial list of typical FATE topics:*

• Psychic Phenomena Dreams, prophecies, telekinesis.

• Recent Fortean Phenomena Strange creatures, mysterious events, unexplained coincidences.

• *Life After Death* Near-death experiences, mediumship, spirit contact, reincarnation, astral travel, and other proof of life after death.

• *Healing Alternative* healing systems and experiences, including acupuncture, herbalism, and psychic techniques.

• *Ghosts and Hauntings Experiences* and investigations of ghosts, hauntings, and poltergeists.

• *Scientific Breakthroughs* Including free energy, new discoveries about matter, lost continents, ley lines, and mind machines.

• *Recent UFO Occurrences* UFO sightings, encounters, abductions, activity, investigations, and disclosures.

• *How-To Healing*, divination, mediumship, dowsing, ghost hunting, astrology, dream analysis, graphology, visualization, and the like.

• *Sacred, Mystic, and Historic Sites* Modern archaeological discoveries and reinterpretations of old ones, the true stories behind myths and folklore, and ancient religions and cultures.

• *Alternative Spirituality*

DEPARTMENTS

True Mystic Experiences and My Proof of Survival

Articles for "True Mystic Experiences" and "My Proof of Survival" departments should be fewer than 500 words. They should recount personal mystic or psychic experiences of the writer. All details must be true. If your account is accepted for publication, you will be required to send a notarized affidavit attesting that the incident described is true.

Contributors should include a photo of themselves, at least 3" x 5", either color or black and white. We will return photos unharmed after publication.

Many photos we receive are poor quality. Make sure your picture has good contrast and detail. A plain background is best. Make sure your face shows and is not shadowed by hats or trees, and that glasses don't create a glare. Photocopies, color printouts, pictures cut from larger photos, large group shots in which you are one tiny face among many, and I.D. cards are not acceptable. Our graphics designer will "cut you out" electronically.

Payment is $25, including photo use.

PHOTOS AND ARTWORK

We want FATE to be as visually appealing as possible. Articles with accompanying photographs and illustrations are more likely to be accepted and published faster.

Articles, illustrations, and photos must be legally reproducible. If you are using illustrations, photos, or text from other published sources, they may fall under copyright law. You are responsible for obtaining permissions for use from either the publisher or copyright holder before the manuscript is accepted for publication. We cannot assume items are in the public domain unless you tell us so and give the source and year of publication.

Attach a slip of paper to the back of photos and illustrations, with your name, the story title, and captions.

Keep copies in case of loss.

STYLE

Write to Entertain and Inform

Articles should be lively, personal, and informative. They should play up the wonder of the subject matter and/or develop practical benefits. Avoid academic-style writing, and please be aware that we rarely publish theoretical articles.

Although FATE publishes relatively brief articles, we look for depth of content. We rarely want round-ups that merely list a variety of sightings or events. In general, it is best to focus on one event or type of event, or one time period, and provide convincing detail. Let the reader feel what it was like to be at the event.

LENGTH

• Features run 1,500 to 3,000 words.

• Briefs are 500 to 1,000 words.

• Fillers are less than 500 words. Short fillers of 150 words or less are particularly welcome.

TRUTHFULNESS

FATE is non-fiction. All articles should be documented in these ways:

• Personal experience articles should include full details of names, dates, times, and places. Although some of this material may be withheld from publication if you specifically request it, we must have it all correctly documented for our files.

• You may be asked to provide contact information for all participants. You may be asked for a sworn and notarized statement from yourself and other participants or witnesses verifying facts described. You will be reimbursed for this cost after publication if you provide a copy of the receipt.

- Sources for quotes and unusual information must be included.
- Articles that are not based on personal experience should include references.

FORMAT

- We encourage email submissions (fate@fatemag.com) and submissions on 31&Mac218;2" Macintosh or PC disks. Label disks with your name, article title, whether the disk is Macintosh or PC, and the software used. If you are using an unusual word processing program, save it as a plain text or ASCII file. Include a printed copy of the article.
- Use 81&Mac218;2" x 11" white paper, a standard typeface, and do not use all caps. Please double space.
- On the first page, include your full name, address, and phone number.
- Place identification at the top of each page. Include your name, the article's title, and page numbers.
- Include a cover letter with your submission.
- Whether you use a typewriter, word processor, or computer, output should be letter quality. Faxed articles are not acceptable.
- Keep a copy of your manuscript in case of loss. We do not accept responsibility for materials sent to us.
- Include a self-addressed, stamped envelope with enough postage to return your article if it is not accepted. (From outside the United States, send several International Reply Coupons, available at any post office.) If return postage is not included and your submission is not accepted, you will receive notification but your article will be discarded.

PAYMENT

Standard payment for feature articles is 10 cents per word, payable after publication. FATE does not pay kill fees if an article is not used, except for contracted, assigned articles where an arrangement has been specified, in writing, in advance.

Contributors who live outside of the U.S. may choose to avoid currency conversion costs by opting to be paid in kind with a FATE subscription or with other FATE merchandise.

Payment for "True Mystic Experiences" and "My Proof of Survival" is $25, including the use of the photograph, which will be returned.

Photos and illustrations that accompany news and feature articles will be paid for after publication, at a rate of $10 per item. (We do not pay for the use of contributor's photos in "True Mystic Experiences" and "My Proof of Survival.") Photo use will be determined by the graphics designer.

We will send you three copies of the issue in which your article appears, with a coupon enabling you to buy additional copies at a discount price.

POLICIES

FATE normally purchases the right to assign copyright and all rights, literary, electronic, and otherwise, to all articles and photos we accept. FATE generally retains all rights to the articles, illustrations, and photographs that we publish. This entitles FATE to use the article again, in print or in any other media, including but not limited to radio, film, and electronic media. It does not prevent you from sending a substantially different article on the same subject to another publication.

We like to see our writers published! If you are having a book published that includes material from an article you have published in FATE, write to us, giving details, and we will send you written authorization to use the article at no charge as long as FATE is credited as the original source (month and year of issue).

If you have questions about this policy or about re-selling your work elsewhere, please write to us with your specific question and we will send a detailed reply.

Original manuscripts, photographs, illustrations, documentation, etc., that are published will remain FATE's property.

FATE looks for new writers and encourages them. We hope that your inquiry is the beginning of a long and mutually beneficial relationship!

Phyllis Galde, Editor-in-Chief

Categories: Nonfiction—Folklore—General Interest—New Age—Occult—Paranormal—Spiritual

CONTACT: Llewellyn Worldwide
Material: All
PO Box 460
Lakeville MN 55044-0460
Phone: 952-431-2050
Fax: 952-891-6091
E-mail: phyllis@fatemag.com
Website: www.fatemage.com

FBI Law Enforcement Bulletin

GENERAL INFORMATION

The FBI Law Enforcement Bulletin is an official publication of the Federal Bureau of Investigation and the U.S. Department of Justice.

Frequency of Publication: Monthly

Purpose: To provide a forum for the exchange of information on law enforcement-related topics.

Audience: Criminal justice professionals, primarily law enforcement managers.

MANUSCRIPT SPECIFICATIONS

Length: Feature article submissions should be 2,000 to 3,500 words (8 to 14 pages, double-spaced). Submissions for specialized departments, such as Police Practice, Case Study, and Sound Off, should be 1,200 to 2,000 words (5 to 8 pages, double-spaced).

Format: All pages should be numbered, and three copies should be submitted for review purposes. When possible, an electronic version of the article saved on computer disk should accompany the typed manuscript.

References should be used when quoting a source exactly, when citing or paraphrasing another person's work or ideas, or when referring to information that generally is not well known. Authors should refer to *A Manual for Writers of Term Papers, Theses, and Dissertations*, 6th ed., by Kate L. Turabian, for proper footnote citation format.

Research papers, reports, and studies should be revised to reflect the editorial needs of *The Bulletinn*. Subheadings and lists should be used to break up the text and provide direction to readers.

Writing Style and Grammar: Articles generally should be written in the third person. (Point of View and Sound Off submissions are exceptions.) *The Bulletinn* follows *The New York Public Library Writer's Guide to Style and Usage*. Potential authors should study several issues of the magazine to ensure that their writing style meets *The Bulletinn*'s requirements.

PHOTOGRAPHS AND GRAPHICS

A photograph of the author(s) should accompany the manuscript. Other suitable photos and illustrations that support the text and enhance reader comprehension also should be furnished. Black-and-white glossy prints of a moderate size (3"x5" to 5"x7") reproduce best. Prints are preferred over negatives or slides.

PUBLICATION

Basis for Judging Manuscripts: Material that has been published previously or that is under consideration by other magazines will be returned to the author. Submissions will be judged on the following points: Relevance to audience, factual accuracy, analysis of information, structure and logical flow, style and ease of reading, and length. Generally, articles on similar topics are not published within a 12-month period. Because *The Bulletinn* is a government publication, favorable consideration cannot be given to articles that advertise a product or service.

Query Letters: Authors may submit a query letter along with a detailed 1- to 2-page outline before writing an article. Editorial staff members will review the query to determine suitability of topic. This is intended to help authors but does not guarantee acceptance of any article.

Author Notification: Receipt of manuscript will be confirmed. Notification of acceptance or rejection will follow review. Articles accepted for publication cannot be guaranteed a publication date.

Editing: The Bulletinn reserves the right to edit all manuscripts for length, clarity, format, and style.

Categories: Crime—Government—Law—Law Enforcement

CONTACT: Editor
Material: All
Madison Bldg. Rm. 206, FBI Academy
Quantico VA 22135
Phone: 703-632-1952
Fax: 703-632-1968
E-mail: leb@fbiacademy.edu
Website: www.fbi.gov

Feed-Lot

Feed-Lot is published 6 times per year. Circulation is approximately 11,000. A subscription costs $29.95 (foreign $50).

Feed-Lot is a trade publication for large feedlots and their related cow and calf operations and 500-plus head and stocker operations. The magazine covers all phases of production from breeding, genetics, animal health, nutrition, equipment design, research through finishing fat cattle-serious articles with information readers can use. Writers need to have knowledge of the industry and good sources of information for research.

Editorial content is reviewed by the Editor.

Categories: Agriculture—Cattle Feeding

CONTACT: Robert Strong, Editor
Material: All
PO Box 850
Dighton KS 67839
Phone: 316-397-2838
Fax: 316-397-2839

Fellowship
a magazine of peacemaking

Thank you for your interest in submitting work to *Fellowship* magazine.

In lieu of payment, *Fellowship* offers a 2-year subscription (or gift transfer) to the magazine and 3 free copies of the issue containing the author's article.

For specific themes/issues please query several months in advance of the deadline for assurance that your article will be considered. *Fellowship* is published six times a year: January/February, March/April, May/June, July/August, September/October, November/December.

Manuscripts can vary in length from 800 to 3,200 words.

Always keep a copy of your work, and include an SASE with your submission if you want it returned. We cannot be held responsible for unsolicited manuscripts, photographs, or artwork.

Please ensure that photographs and artwork are marked with a brief description (caption) and the name of the photographer/artist if credit line is desired.

We reserve the right to edit those articles accepted for publication for length and clarity.

Deadline:

For articles and reviews, deadline is two months prior to the first day of the first month of the issue. Accompanying photographs and graphics six weeks prior to that date.

Maximum length:

For articles: 3,200 words
For book reviews: 500 words.

Format:

Hard copies must be typed, double-spaced, and clean (i.e. free of italics, corrections, white-out, or pen or pencil markings). Late changes may be indicated on another copy–we will incorporate them.

Computer diskettes (3.5") are acceptable in either PC or Mac format, with the documents saved as text files or made otherwise readable by Microsoft Word 6.0 for Macintosh. We cannot be responsible for returning your diskettes. If possible, include multiple formats of the article to ensure our computer will be able to read it, particularly if you send something in PC format (we use a Macintosh). Please also send a hard copy, if possible.

E-mail submissions, with the article attached in the format specifications listed above or included in the body of the e-mail, are preferable.

Note: Do not send faxes for submission! Faxes do not scan well. They are useful for reference, but cannot be used for publication.

Book Reviews–Additional Guidelines:

At the top of your review, include the full title and subtitle of the book, full author listing, full publisher's address, year of publication, and number of pages. Please note whether the book is paperback or hardcover, or both, and the prices in either case. We must have this information in order to publish the review.

Example:

The Challenge of Shalom: The Jewish Tradition of Peace and Justice
Murray Polner and Naomi Goodman, editors.
New Society Publishers, 4722 Baltimore Avenue, Philadelphia, PA 19143.
1994, 278 pages, (paper) $18.95.

For all submissions, please include your mailing address and two lines of biographical information to serve as an author's note.

Categories: Nonfiction—Book Reviews—Politics—Religion—Spiritual—Peace—Justice —Nonviolence

CONTACT: Submissions Editor
Material: All
Fellowship of Reconciliation
PO Box 271
Nyack NY 10960
Phone: 845-358-4601
Fax: 845-358-4924
E-mail: editor@forusa.org
Website: www.forusa.org

Feminist Studies
University of Maryland

Guidelines for Contributors

Feminist Studies is committed to publishing an interdisciplinary body of feminist knowledge that sees intersections of gender with racial identity, sexual orientation, economic means, geographical location, and physical ability as the touchstone for our politics and our intellectual analysis. Whether work is drawn from the complex past or the shifting present, the pieces that appear in *Feminist Studies* address social and political issues that intimately and significantly affect women and men in the United States and around the world.

We invite submissions that are not presently under consideration elsewhere and that fall under or integrate the following categories.

Research and Criticism

FS publishes research and criticism that address theoretical issues and offer analyses of interest to feminist scholars across disciplines. We encourage scholars to pursue truly interdisciplinary research and research methodologies that not only showcase but integrate contributions from multiple disciplines. Authors should submit two (2) typewritten, double-spaced copies of their manuscripts plus a disk copy.

Author's name should appear only on a separate title page. Submissions should not exceed 10,500 words, approximately 35 pages, including endnotes. Authors should also submit a 200-word (or less) abstract. Please include a mailing and e-mail address with cover note.

Creative Submissions

We welcome all forms of written creative expression, which may include but is not limited to poetry, short fiction. Authors should send a hard copy of their work, along with a disk version to the Feminist Studies office. Deadline for these submissions is May 1 and December 1. At that point all work will be reviewed by our creative writing editor. Her recommendations will then be read anonymously by our editorial collective. Authors will receive notice of the collective's decision by mid-July and mid-February.

Art Submissions

We are always interested in displaying contemporary women artists and have done much in recent years to promote their work in the journal. The collective accepts art work three times a year at our board meetings. Artists are therefore encouraged to submit images that reflect the range and scope of their portfolio. Please submit art in digital format (as TIFF files at 300 dpi, preferably, or high quality JPEG files). We also accept prints, slides, or negatives. Do not send original works of art or anything that must be returned. For electronic submissions send e-mail attachments to: art@feministstudies.org. We also publish an artist's statement or an essay written either by the artist or another author along with art work. Feel free to submit a statement with your work; if you have suggestions of someone who could write an accompanying art essay, please include their curriculum vitae and writing sample (or essay).

Book Review Essays

The *Feminist Studies* collective selects a few books each year for review on the basis of their scholarly merit and their implications for feminist scholars and activists. Due to space limitations we do not publish reviews of individual books, but rather review essays of clusters of important books on the same general theme. Although the collective commissions most essays, we also accept unsolicited review essay proposals. Such proposals should identify the books to be reviewed, state why these books are important and deserve consideration as a cluster, and briefly present the concepts or questions that will be developed in the article. Authors should also send a curriculum vitae and a writing sample.

Other Forms of Written and Visual Work

We are actively seeking political and social commentaries, activist reports from the field, political manifestos, interviews, and other forms of writing that are not easily categorized. To this end, we encourage authors and artists to submit individual or collaborative projects that cross established boundaries of scholarship, activism, visual culture, memoir and creative writing. Through such work we hope to ensure that *FS* continues to engage, challenge, and reevaluate standard domains of inquiry to create new forms and objects of knowledge. Please send a disk and hard copy to our editorial office along with an extensive cover note explaining your project.

Graduate Students

Feminist Studies offers an annual *Feminist Studies Award*, a prize of $500, to honor the best article submitted by a graduate student and accepted for publication. With this prize we aim both to encourage and to learn from a new generation of feminist scholars. There is no deadline for submission; articles will be eligible for consideration in the year they are accepted. Although graduate students who finish their doctoral work before their article is accepted are still eligible for the prize, they must be a graduate student when they originally submit their work.

Citations and References

Scholarly articles should follow *Chicago Manual of Style* (15th ed.). *Feminist Studies* articles use endnotes, limited to only essential material and specific textual citation. We will not publish discursive notes. We may ask for full revision of manuscripts that do not follow *CMS* requirements for documentation.

Examples of Work Cited

Notes

1. Sarah Franklin and Helena Ragone, *Reproducing Reproduction: Kinship, Power, and Technological Innovation* (Philadelphia: University of Pennsylvania Press, 1998), 9.

2. Rosalind Petchesky, "The Body as Property: A Feminist Revision," in *Conceiving the New World Order: The Global Politics of Reproduction*, ed., Faye Ginsburg and Rayna Rapp (Berkeley: University of California Press, 1995), 394.

3. Mary Poovey, "The Abortion Question and the Death of Man," and Vicki Schultz, "Women 'before' the Law: Judicial Stories about Women, Work, and Sex Segregation on the Job," in Feminists Theorize the Political, ed. Judith Butler and Joan Scott (London: Routledge, 1992), 239-56.

4. Natalie Zemon Davis, "Women on Top," in her *Society and Culture in Early Modern France* (Stanford: Stanford University Press, 1975), 124.

5. Luce Irigaray, *This Sex Which Is Not One*, trans. Catherine Porter (Ithaca: Cornell University Press, 1985), 209.

6. William Farmwinkile, *Humor of the American Midwest*, vol. 2 of Survey of American Humor (Boston: Plenum Press, 1983), 132.

7. Phyllis Turnball, "The Politics of Toys: Politicization of Child Development" (Ph.D. diss., University of Hawaii, 1978), 134.

8. Memorandum to Bill, 6 June 1942, Lillan Wald Papers, reel 94, Columbia University.

9. Pepe Karmel, "Behind Folk Forms, Classical Modes," *New York Times*, 27 Oct. 1995, sec. C, 25.

10. James B. Jacobs, introduction to *Drunk Driving: An American Dilemma* (Chicago: University of Chicago Press, 1989).

11. Carla Williams, "Naked, Neutered, or Noble: Extremes of the Black Female Body and the Problem of Photographic History," www.carlagirl.net.

Further Inquiries

Questions on submissions policy can be directed to Managing Editor Sharon Groves at sgroves@feministstudies.org or submission@feministstudies.org.

Categories: African-American—Culture—Feminism—Gay/Lesbian—History—Literature—Women's Fiction—Women's Issues

CONTACT: Feminist Studies
Material: All
0103 Taliaferro, University of Maryland
College Park MD 20742
Phone: 301-405-7415
Fax: 301-405-8395
E-mail: submissions@feministstudies.org
Website: www.feministstudies.org

Fencers Quarterly Magazine

About Us

Founded in 1996 by Bruce Darling as *Veteran Fencers Quarterly*, *FQM* underwent its formal name change to *Fencers Quarterly Magazine* with the June, 2000, issue.

Our purpose is to keep the fencing enthusiast informed about some of the issues that affect you, to illuminate the history and art of fencing, and to provide a forum for your thoughts and ideas.

We are eager to read reports about your tournaments, schools, individuals, special programs, or other unique features of your group. We are also especially interested in your opinions and personal experience of fencing—today or in the past.

Feel free to send us any articles of interest to the fencing community, including local newspaper clippings, your photos, or even your own stories and comments.

We reserve the right to edit for length and clarity.

FQM is published quarterly in March, June, September, and December for a measly $19.95 annual subscription cost. We think this is awfully cheap for the quality articles, superior writers, and wide-open forum that *FQM* represents!

Want to write for *FQM*?

Great! We want to read your writing! We are interested in articles, stories, poetry, and fiction related to all aspects of fencing.

What are the basics?

First, even though you've heard it a thousand times, read a couple recent issues of the magazine — that'll give you the best examples of what we buy, the style of writing, and how we approach fencing issues.

Next, decide what you want to say to the thousands of dedicated fencers who read our magazine. Remember, you will be speaking to young beginners, mature fencers, current and former Olympians, classically trained or sport-oriented, members of re-creation groups, and people interested in the history of swordplay. We don't expect your work to appeal to ALL of them — but it must be of interest to SOME of them!

Finally, what we look for is logical progression in your writing (i.e., make a point in an orderly manner!), good command of language, spell-checked writing, and a length that fits the magazine.

What are the specifics?

Length: typically, 250-2000 words. Average article is about 1,000 words. When published, this works out to 1-2 magazine pages. We have gone as high as 4,000 words and serialized the work — but this was material from one of the top people in the discipline.

Publication: usually within 3 months of acceptance, though it can run longer.

Payment: "modest". We pay a flat rate, varying from $15 to $60, depending on how much we like the piece — pretty subjective, but that's how we do it. Occasionally, we've gone as high as $200, but this is RARE! You'll also receive 5 copies of the issue in which your piece is published. Sometimes, we trade a published article for advertising space, so if you have a product to sell and an issue you'd like to write about, please contact us to discuss the matter.

Tips: We use fiction and poetry very rarely, so it better be concise, well written, and strongly fencing-related. Most past rejections were because material was WAY too long or lacked an understanding of fencing. We like controversial material as long as it is logically presented — use the language of fencing and explain your point so that a beginner would understand.

We like new writers, and fully understand how anxiety-producing it can be! We will make every effort to help you create material that will work for *FQM*. And, if we don't use your stuff, we'll explain why!

E-mails: We prefer email submissions, in .RTF format.

Photographs: We love them! Must be clear and show proper form. $5 to $10.

Categories: Nonfiction—History—Recreation—Sports

CONTACT: Anita Evangelista, Managing Editor
Material: All
848 S. Kimbrough
Springfield MO 65806
Phone: 417-866-4370 (No phone queries)
E-mail: editor@fencersquarterly.com
Website: www.fencersquarterly.com

FIBERARTS
Fiberarts Magazine

Our readers are professional artists, textile students, fashion designers, museum curators, gallery owners, collectors, and non-professional fiber aficionados. Our editorial policy is that the magazine must provide professional and non-professional textile enthusiasts with in-spiration, support, and direction to keep them excited, interested, and committed to the field.

FIBERARTS' readers are interested in a broad range of textile-related subjects. Among these are fiber sculpture, surface design, weaving, quilting, needlework, papermaking, basketry, clothing, and mixed media art. Historical and ethnic textiles, technical information, and eccentric tidbits about the above are also of interest.

Regarding submissions, I prefer to receive a brief outline and a prose synopsis of the proposed article, together with color transparencies (35mm slides or larger formats) or black-and-white photos that might accompany the article. (We return visuals whether or not we publish.) If I'm interested, I will be back in touch to arrange specifics such as word length, payment, and deadline for the article.

While I cannot guarantee publication of unsolicited manuscripts, I will carefully consider all submissions.

Cordially,

Sunita Patterson, Editor

Editorial Policy Regarding Submissions

1. Submissions should be in the form of an outline and a prose synopsis of the proposed article. All proposals must be accompanied by good quality 35mm slides or black and white photos, representative of the subject of the article. (We prefer publication quality 2"x2" or 4"x5" transparencies.)

2. All articles must be cleanly typed, double spaced, with one-inch margins and 25 lines per page (approximately 250 words per page). Manuscripts may also be submitted via email. Please include a short bioline. An additional photocopy would be helpful. Please keep one copy of your submitted transcript, in case we need to confer about it.

3. Writers are responsible for accuracy of facts and correct spelling of names, places, titles and works. We do not have the resources to check all of this information, so we must be able to depend on the writer's accuracy.

4. Unless other arrangements are made with the editor, authors are responsible for collecting all visual material to illustrate their articles, and for providing all caption information on a separate, number-keyed sheet. Complete caption information includes artist's name, title of work, dimensions, materials and techniques used, year of execution, in whose collection and where, name of photographer, and designation for top of work shown. Authors must also provide appropriate names and addresses of artists and/or photo sources, for correct return of visuals.

5. The editor may request revisions of the article, and final editing of the material is at the editor's discretion. Writers are responsible for abiding by the word limit established for the article; manuscripts that substantially exceed the word count will be returned to the writer for shortening.

6. Deadlines are serious. All manuscripts, illustrations, and caption information are due by the date indicated, unless specifically discussed with the editor prior to that time. The editor reserves the right to kill any piece that is not submitted on time.

7. No kill fee will be paid if the material is not acceptable and if, in the editor's opinion, revisions will not make it so.

8. Payment for articles is made after publication. The signed author's agreement is confirmation of total amount due. Additional expenses must be discussed with the editor prior to submission of the completed manuscript.

Content for feature articles:

We are seeking feature-length articles of 1,000-2,000 words that communicate in an informal tone the work and personality of an artist or a concept. The latest work of a mid-career artist is appropriate for a feature-length article, as is that of a promising new talent. Also appropriate are articles that compare the work of two or three artists, discuss the work and workings of textile groups, present an important technique, explore textile history, or present ethnic textiles. Articles might also focus on a particular aspect of an artist's work, a folk artist, an innovative organization, a visionary collector, or a personal technique. Bear in mind that the readers have a fairly sophisticated knowledge of the field. At the same time, please be clear in your writing and explain specific techniques. Payment: $300-$400.

Content for Upfront, Profile, and Review articles:

Upfront covers such topics as new ideas for fiber, unusual or offbeat subjects, continuing ed, work spaces, resources, notable events, and marketing fiber art. In addition, we are looking for articles on technique, new materials and equipment, design, and trends. These articles are typically 450 words in length. Payment: $115.

A profile article focuses on one artist and is 450 words in length. The article and one photo must fit on one page. Payment: $115.

Review articles are 500 words in length and include three to five photos. Payment: $125.

Photos:

Visuals must accompany every article. A feature includes four to eight photos. Send a selection of 35mm slides (larger formats are preferable). The more photos to choose from, the better; all will be returned. We depend on quality visuals to complement your writing and to present the subject as attractively as possible. Full photo captions are essential. Please include a separate, number-keyed caption sheet. The names and addresses of those mentioned in the article or to whom the visuals are to be returned are necessary.

Manuscripts:

Refer to *The Chicago Manual of Style* or *The New York Times Style Manual*. Manuscripts should be double spaced with no less than one-inch margins. A one-sentence author's bioline should be included at the end of the manuscript, together with address and telephone/fax numbers.

Our philosophy is to preserve the author's voice, while still monitoring clarity, grammar, usage, etc. Minor revisions are made at the editor's discretion; major revisions are made in conference with the author.

Exhibition Reviews

What to Include: In about 500 words, you should provide a summary of the overall quality, significance, and focus of the show, and then evaluate selected pieces. The choice of what to select might be based on what is most outstanding, unusual, trend-setting, and/or appealing to you. Aesthetic quality, content, and technique are all valid criteria for evaluation. Not all work deserves praise; we prefer honest and thought-provoking criticism.

Keep in mind that we have an international readership. Because many of the artists you will be presenting may be known only on a local or regional level, brief biographical information or pertinent quotes within the review might be necessary.

What to avoid: The "laundry list" approach (a list of artists' names, titles of work, and short descriptive phrases) is unacceptable. Also, we find that a list of award winners has little value. In addition, you are not eligible to review a show in which you have participated as an artist, organizer, curator, or juror.

Photographs: Publication quality visuals must accompany the review. We require 35mm slides (larger format transparencies are preferable) or black-and-white glossy photos, 5"x7" or 8"x10" inches. Visuals must be clear and sharply focused to be acceptable. Often visuals are available from the show organizers, or even the artists themselves. Installation shots are usually "iffy" in print.

Please do not cite works for which visuals are not available. A number-keyed caption sheet with the following information must accompany the visuals: artist's name, title of work, dimensions, materials and techniques, year of execution, in whose collection, name of photographer, and top designated.

Format: Include a working title and sub-title. Be sure to list title, show dates, gallery, city and state, and touring schedule. Please send the show's catalog.

On a separate sheet, include addresses and phone numbers of artists whose visuals accompany the review.

We welcome submissions from artists and writers.

To submit your own artwork for consideration, send a selection of slides or transparencies, resumé, and artist statement, if available, to:

FIBERARTS
67 Broadway
Asheville, NC 28801

To submit an idea for an article, send a one-paragraph synopsis of your proposed article, writing samples, and slides or transparencies for the article to the address above. Proposals must be accompanied by appropriate visuals.

Digital images may be acceptable if they are TIFF format, at least 300 dpi in resolution, and at least as big as the size at which they would be printed in the magazine.

Please do not submit artwork or proposals by email.

Categories: Nonfiction—Arts—Crafts/Hobbies—Hobbies—Trade—Textiles

CONTACT: Sunita Patterson, Editor
Material: All
CONTACT: Susan Kieffer, Assistant Editor
Material: All
50 College St.
Asheville NC 28801
Phone: 828-253-0467
Fax: 828-236-2869
E-mail: assedttor@fiberartsmagazine.com
Website: www.fiberartsmagazine.com

Field
A Journal of Contemporary Poetry and Poetics

Field, A Journal of Contemporary Poetry and Poetics, is published twice annually, spring and fall. It emphasizes the best in contemporary poetry, poetry in translation, and essays by and about poets on the craft. We read submissions year-round and usually reply within six weeks. Enclose a SASE for response, send only poetry, and do not send simultaneous submissions. Translations should include proof of permission to translate. Electronic submissions are not accepted.

Sample issues are available for $7.00 (check or money order payable to FIELD).

Categories: Poetry

CONTACT: Submissions Editor
Material: All
Oberlin College Press
10 N. Professor St.
Oberlin OH 44074
Phone: 440-775-8408
Fax: 440-775-8124
E-mail: oc.press@oberlin.edu
Website: www.oberlin.edu/ocpress

Field & Stream

FIELD & STREAM is a tightly focused magazine. All material is related to hunting and fishing, with the articles ranging from basic how-it's-done pieces to carefully crafted features with a philosophical edge. There are many opportunities for freelancers, including:

• Short pieces (500 to 750 words) on hunting and fishing tactics and techniques, natural history relating to hunting and fishing, and DIY [Do-It-Yourself] projects with a hunting/fishing slant.

• Longer how-to features (1,500 words maximum) on hunting and fishing.

Freelancers can also score in categories like humor, mood, nostalgia (see "Perspective," in particular), and Sportsman's Notebook—word count is flexible, but shorter is better.

Writers are encouraged to submit queries on article ideas. These should be no more than a page, and should include a summary of the idea, including the angle you will hang the story on, and a sense of what makes this piece different from all others on the same or a similar subject. Many queries are turned down because we have no idea what the writer is getting at. Be sure that your letter is absolutely clear. We've found that if you can't sum up the point of the article in a sentence or two, the article doesn't have a point.

Pieces that depend on writing style, such as humor, mood, and nostalgia or essays often can't be queried and may be submitted in manuscript form. The same is true of short tips. All submissions to FIELD & STREAM are on an on-spec basis.

Before submitting anything, however, we encourage you to study, not simply read, the magazine. Many pieces are rejected because they do not fit the tone or style of the magazine, or fail to match the subject of the article with the overall subject matter of FIELD & STREAM. Above all, study the magazine before submitting anything.

FIELD & STREAM does not pay by the word. Payment ranges from $100 to as much as several thousand dollars, depending on the quality of the work, the experience of the author, and the difficulty of obtaining the story.

All queries and completed manuscripts submitted to FIELD & STREAM must be typed and double spaced. The magazine also accepts 3.5" disks, but does not accept e-mail or fax submissions.

FIELD & STREAM needs an accurate word count for every submission. Estimates based on the old system of 250 words per page have proven inaccurate. Please make your word counts accurate and include them at the top of the first page of every submission.

Categories: Fiction—Nonfiction—Conservation—Environment—Fishing—Outdoors—Sports/Recreation—Hunting—Animals (big game)

CONTACT: Kimberly Hiss
Material: All Submissions
2 Park Ave.
New York NY 10016-5295
Phone: 212-779-5000
Fax: 212-779-5114
E-mail: FSLetters@time4.com
E-mail: kimberly.hiss@time4.com

Filipinas

Mission Statement
Filipinas magazine — The magazine for all Filipinos aims to provide Filipino Americans with a sense of identity, community and pride through accurate, fair and sensitive coverage of the second largest immigrant population in the United States. It is the chronicler of the Filipino American experience. It showcases pioneers, role models and future leaders. It presents the struggles that bring about the change and successes in the community. It presents issues that affect Filipinos in North America. It is the source of knowledge about Filipino culture and the Philippine social, economic, and political state. *Filipinas* magazine aims to be the close friend who will inform, entertain, include and invigorate the Filipino in North America.

Audience
Filipinas magazine targets Filipinos in North America — immigrants and native-born; the old and the young; the ones still searching for cultural identity and the ones who take pride in their culture and heritage.

Fees
• Upon publication, writers will be paid $50-$100 depending on length and complexity

• We pay $15 for each black and white published (non-stock) photos, and $25 for each colored published photo taken by the author. Publicity shots and personal album photos are not subject to payment.

• Payment is mailed on the 15th of the month the article or photo is published.

• Unsolicited materials are not subject to payment. The writer assigns titles, rights and all interests to the story to Filipinas Publishing, Inc.

Departments
Entree (recipe and restaurant reviews), Cultural Currents (Filipino traditions, beliefs), Travel (destinations in the Philippines or other places with a Philippine slant, e.g. Spain), "Here and There" (150 words or less profile with photo of a noteworthy Filipino personality).

Non-Fiction Articles
Expose; general interest; interview/profiles of prominent Filipinos and non-Filipinos who are important to the Filipino community or the Philippines; Filipino recipes and reviews of Filipino restaurants; travel articles; "how-to" articles, e.g. making a parol (Philippine Christmas lantern) or tips on starting an export/import business or other small business; personal experience.

Word count on articles: Cover story 1,500-2,000; long profiles 1,200-2,000; short profiles 900-1,200; reviews and other features 600-1,200; "Here & There" 50-150.

Photos
Color photos should be 35mm slides or 120mm transparencies or 4 x 5 transparencies or 4 x 6 prints. Black and White prints: 5" x 7" or 8" x 10", captions, photo credits and model releases required. Electronic photos should be sent as 300 dpi, 4x5 or final size, scanned as tiff or jpeg file. Captions and photo credits are required.

Terms
We require that a writer send a query letter along with a resume and three writing samples of preferably previously published work. *Filipinas* Publishing has exclusive rights to any solicited articles. (Unsolicited manuscripts are not subject to payment even if published. They will not be returned.) Once published, the article may be reprinted with permission and credit to *Filipinas* magazine. Writer agrees to a one-time rewrite, if necessary.

Submission
Articles and queries may be electronically sent. We also accept hard copy submissions with 3.5 computer diskette, preferably using Microsoft Word. Diskettes will not be returned.

Categories: Nonfiction—Asian-American—Multicultural

CONTACT: Mona Lisa Yuchengco, Publisher
Material: All
Filipinas Publishing, Inc.
1486 Huntington Ave, Ste 300
South San Francisco CA 94080
Phone: 650-872-8650
Fax: 650-872-8651
E-mail: mail@filipinasmag.com
Website: www.filmagazime.com

Film Quarterly

In preparing material for submission to *Film Quarterly*, keep in mind that while many of our contributors are academics, not all of our readers are. By the standards of the commercial magazine world, *Film Quarterly* is quite specialized and its circulation is small-about 7,000, which means perhaps 8,000 to 10,000 readers (since library copies have multiple readers). But by the standards of the narrower academic journals, this is very large. Since its inception in 1958, *Film Quarterly's* mission has been to bring intelligent, original, and rigorous thinking about film to as large a readership as possible (including filmmakers, incidentally). The journal is sold about two-thirds by subscription and one-third by retail sales in bookstores. We also have numerous subscribers scattered throughout the world.

The English-language film journal universe includes several publications whose contents are aimed at scholars, such as *Cinema Journal*, *Screen*, and *The Quarterly Review of Film and Video*, among others. Popular magazines, such as *Film Comment* and *Sight & Sound*, seek a wide audience of moviegoers. *Film Quarterly*, somewhat like *Cineaste* and *Framework*, occupies a middle ground, making specialized ideas accessible to literate and "cinemate" readers. It is, however, peer-reviewed by academics, like other scholarly journals, and has over the years published the work of some of the most distinguished film studies scholars-and continues to do so to this day. We aim at the whole community of educated readers seriously concerned with film (and, to an increasing degree, video and television) and are particularly interested in the work of emerging writers both within and outside the academy.

Careful study of back issues is imperative for new writers hoping to have their work accepted by *Film Quarterly*. (If your library does not subscribe, you might wish to call the journal to the attention of the periodicals librarian.) We like to surprise our readers with unusual material, but we have certain emphases and do not publish certain kinds of writing: we never use personality or reportage pieces, for instance, nor do we cover festivals. We are interested in important theoretical developments, but when we run theoretical articles they include treatments of films and thus demonstrate a connection between theory and practice. We publish pieces on older films that are readily available on video or DVD, and more wide-ranging historical articles. Documentaries, experimental and avant-garde works, national cinemas, reassessments of classic works, Hollywood, the business world, foreign filmmakers, new works and new filmmakers-all these are included in our pages. We also encourage submissions on television and video. We often run interviews, mostly with film- and video-makers, but occasionally with writers, directors of photography, etc. (Interviews are best done by someone who knows the interviewee's work thoroughly, can obtain the time and attention for an extended conversation, and can prepare a solid introduction.)

We welcome communications and submissions from writers. There is no closed group of contributors to the magazine, and many now well-known writers and scholars published their first articles or reviews with us. We are eager to find innovative approaches deployed with energy, and we relish making unknown or esoteric films accessible to American audiences. We also welcome commentary and critiques on the journal and any particulars of its contents.

II. MANUSCRIPT SUBMISSION

Send in one hard copy copy of your manuscript only. You should always submit the completed manuscript, since the Editor and the Editorial Board read and assess all submissions and cannot accept anything on the basis of a query or an outline. You may, of course, check with the Editor to make sure your article idea or film review is not already in the *FQ* pipeline. Book reviews are assigned separately; if you are interested in writing a review of a particular book, check with the Book Review Editor (see below).

Our working rule of thumb for article length is that it should not exceed 25 double-spaced manuscript pages, or about 6,500 words, although we occasionally run longer pieces and can certainly consider shorter ones. If you contemplate a really long manuscript, it may be helpful to query the Editor before setting to work. Film reviews ideally amount to around ten pages, but we do run longer pieces if the issues involved seem sufficiently substantial. We seek reviews with analytic treatments that (1) give readers (who may not have seen the film) a clear idea of what it is like, in stylistic as well as plot/narrative terms; (2) provide some implicit or explicit "theory" to account for what the film seems to be trying to do-structurally, emotionally, politically, etc.; and (3) offer an estimate of its success and general quality. We are more impressed with analytic power than by vehemence or charm of

opinions, and we are always searching for that elusive ideal, the "definitive" review-essay that treats a film so intelligently and substantially that the review will remain readable in ten or even twenty years.

When submitting a manuscript, please include your name, home and work addresses, phone numbers, and email address at the top, and a brief biographical description at the end. Should you want to have your manuscript returned if it is not accepted, include a self-addressed stamped envelope. If you happen to possess stills or photos relevant to your topic, please mention this, but do not send them; they will be required only if your piece is accepted. Everything in the manuscript should be double-spaced, including quotations and notes (which should be formatted as endnotes); film titles should be italicized, TV titles in quotes. If you need guidance on detailed points of manuscript preparation, you should follow the *Chicago Manual of Style*. Printouts should *not* be right-hand justified. We do not use disks or attachments at first submission, but if your manuscript is accepted, we will then need a digital version.

Manuscripts are discussed by our editorial board at quarterly meetings (in early February, May, August, and November-deadlines for submission are one month before the meeting dates). Decisions about acceptance take about a month to reach the writer. We always have some backlog of manuscripts, and you should count on it taking about a year from acceptance to publication. Payment for a published manuscript is slightly above the magnificent sum of two cents per word, plus two gratis copies.

III. BOOK REVIEWS

Book reviews are assigned to individual writers by the Book Review Editor. If you are interested in contributing, or have a specific book you want to review, please contact Matthew Bernstein, Film Studies Department, 109 Rich Building, 1602 Fishburne Drive, Emory University, Atlanta, GA 30322 (email: mbernst@emory.edu). Send him a brief outline of your credentials, your areas of interest, and any sample book reviews you may already have written.

Categories: Film/Video—Television/Radio

CONTACT: Ann Martin, Editor, Film Quarterly
Material: All
University of California Press
2000 Center St., Ste. 303
Berkeley, CA 94704-1223
E-mail: ann.martin@ucpress.edu

Financial Planning

It's best to submit a query prior to sending your article. Your query should include whether you have written or been quoted in other articles on the same or similar subjects in any financial services publication, and the date of that publication. Please submit all inquiries to jennifer.liptow@thomsonmedia.com

Articles should be approximately 2000 words, and contain no footnotes.

Articles should be written for practicing financial professionals (readable, not excessively academic) and have a "how to" or strategy and tactics approach.

When possible, articles should contain case studies and/or examples.

There are no deadlines for unsolicited manuscripts. These are generally reviewed within six to eight weeks of submission, and published within two issues of acceptance. Seasonal stories should be submitted at least three months in advance.

Unsolicited manuscripts are not accepted for use as editorial calendar stories.

Pay for industry professionals (non-professional writers) is generally a small honorarium ($250-$500) and a brief bio with the published article. Professional writers receive $1 per word (determined by published price). Payment is made upon publication.

If you have questions, please contact Jennifer Liptow at jennifer.liptow@thomsonmedia or (212) 803-8693. E-mail is preferred. Thanks.

Categories: Nonfiction—Business—Money & Finances

CONTACT: Jennifer Liptow, Group Assistant Managing Editor
Material: All
One State St. Plaza, 26th Floor
New York NY 10004
Phone: 212-803-8693
E-mail: jennifer.liptow@thomsonmedia
Website: www.financial-planning.com

Fine Gardening

Fine Gardening is a bimonthly magazine for enthusiastic landscape and ornamental gardeners. Filled with practical information and innovative ideas, *Fine Gardening* seeks to inform, assist, and inspire gardeners of all skill levels. What makes *Fine Gardening* unique is that all articles are written by home gardeners, horticulturists, or landscape professionals based on their own experience and knowledge-whether it be about a plant, gardening technique, design approach, or project.

Style

All of our stories are written in first person, based on first-hand experience. The tone should be friendly, yet informative. The style should be casual, that of one gardener sharing information with another as they walk through the garden together.

Features

Fine Gardening features ornamental plants and home landscaping ideas. Most of our feature stories fall into the following categories: design, techniques, plants, or garden structures. Most stories are how-to or instructional in nature; many are projects. We often include other related stories, such as those on tools or garden pests and diseases. While we do not publish general garden profiles, we illustrate most stories with photographs taken in our authors' gardens. Content should appeal to both beginning and experienced gardeners. Accurate botanical names, USDA Hardiness Zones, and cultural information must be provided for all plant profiles.

Departments

Tips, Q&A, Regional Reports (6), Lawn Talk and Tool Hound are all reader-written departments. Of these, we pay for published tips.

Plants to Know and Grow, Reviews, and Container Gardening are most often assigned to horticulture professionals, but we welcome queries. Last Word features gardening essays; humorous, insightful, or sentimental; that are selected from among unsolicited manuscripts.

Most of the photography in *Fine Gardening* is taken by our editors. We occasionally use professional photographers or accept photography supplied by the author. Additional fees are paid for any published photographs not taken by staff members.

Copyright and Payment

At *Fine Gardening*, we generally purchase the following rights:
• The right to be the first magazine to publish the article.
• The right to reprint the article in one or more of our anthology books.
• The right to use portions of the article in materials promoting *Fine Gardening* or The Taunton Press.
• The right to publish the article on our *Fine Gardening* web page.

We pay for all stories on a project basis. Payment runs from $200 - $1,000 per story, depending upon its length and complexity. A portion of this fee is paid upon acceptance of a publishable manuscript and signed copyright agreement. The balance is paid upon publication. Please note that by signing a copyright agreement with you, we do not guarantee publication of your article. We reserve the right to decide later not to publish it. This doesn't happen often, but if it does, you are entitled to keep your advance as a kill fee.

We pay $35 - $50 per published tip. For individual photographs, we pay $75– per published photograph, depending upon size and use. For assignment photography, we pay day rates, plus reasonable expenses.

Submitting a Query

If you would like to propose a story, please send a brief query explaining why the subject would be of interest to our readers. Be sure to highlight key points that would be covered in the story, and enclose any snapshots, sketches, or other materials that will help us evaluate story potential.

With the exception of Last Word, we prefer that a proposal precede the development of any manuscript.

All queries, tips, and reader contributions should be sent to the address below. Please submit only one story idea per query and allow 4-6 weeks for a response. If your proposal is accepted, an editor will be assigned to work with you. If at any time you have a question regarding the status of your proposal or story, please contact our editorial secretary at 800-926-8776, ext. 509.

Categories: Nonfiction—Gardening

CONTACT: Todd Meier, Editor
Material: All Features
CONTACT: Virginia Small, Associate Editor
Material: Last word
PO Box 5506
Newtown CT 06470
Phone: 203-426-8171
Fax: 203-426-3434
E-mail: fg@taunton.com
Website: www.taunton.com

Fine Homebuilding

Submitting an article proposal to *Fine Homebuilding* is simple. You don't need to write a manuscript or take professional photographs. We ask that you mail us a cover letter and photos introducing your project. Tell us what makes the project interesting and briefly explain the problems, challenges, solutions and results. The photos should be comprehensive. We recommend that you shoot interior and exterior, before, during and completed photos. If drawings or blueprints best illustrate the project, please include them in your presentation. If we decide to pursue the article an editor will be assigned, and will contact you. If not, we will return all of your material. Please include a self addressed stamped envelope. Good luck.

Categories: Nonfiction—Carpentry—Home

CONTACT: Submissions Editor
Material: All
The Taunton Press
63 South Main St.
PO Box 5506
Newtown, CT 06470-5506
Phone: 800-309-8919
E-mail: fh@taunton.com
Website: www.taunton.com/fh

Fine Woodworking

Fine Woodworking is a bimonthly magazine for all those who strive for and appreciate excellence in woodworking, veteran professional and weekend hobbyist alike. We have always been a reader-written magazine, relying on skilled woodworkers to share their practical experience and knowledge about the best methods of work, tools, construction and design.

We're looking for good articles on almost all aspects of woodworking from the basics of tool use, stock preparation and joinery to specialized techniques and finishing. We're especially keen on articles about shop-built tools, jigs and fixtures or any stage of design, construction, finishing and installation of cabinetry and furniture. Whether the subject involves fundamental methods or advanced techniques, we look for high-quality workmanship, thoughtful designs, safe and proper procedures.

We do not require our readers/writers to be professional authors. Our staff of editors are woodworkers themselves and are experienced with standard woodworking practices, as well as in working with first-time authors. We'll do everything we can step by step to make the writing process a smooth and pleasurable experience.

• **Start with a proposal**—If you'd like to write an article for *Fine Woodworking*, start by sending us a proposal. Summarize your topic and point of view in a paragraph or so and include an informal outline of the material you plan to cover in the article. Include a paragraph about yourself and your woodworking background. The better the quality of the visual information you can supply—especially photographs of actual work in progress—the better we will be able to appreciate your ideas. But don't worry if the images are not publishable quality, we'll reshoot photos if we decide to develop your article. Finally, please include a self-addressed stamped envelope large enough to hold all the materials you send. We'll take good care of everything, and we'll return it all at the appropriate time.

Once we receive your proposal, we'll send you a letter to let you know everything arrived. You'll hear from us again within a month, with a decision about whether we want you to go ahead with the article. If we do, you'll be assigned a staff editor to work with you. This editor will be your primary contact with the magazine. You and the editor will discuss and agree on an outline for the article, as well as a deadline for a first draft. Remember though, that final acceptance of your article depends on whether we can use your manuscript.

• **Preparing the manuscript—What** makes *Fine Woodworking* special is that most of our articles are written by people who actually do the work they write about. Therefore, we're more interested in your experiences, point of view and technical expertise than in your writing style or ability to provide grammar-perfect English. But even so, there are a few things to keep in mind when writing for us. First, stick to the outline that you and your editor agreed upon. If you want to reorganize it or add new information, let your editor know what you're up to.

As far as the writing goes, it's best to adopt an easy, conversational style, as if you were describing something to a friend in a letter. Be sure to define any terms you think might be obscure or specialized; not everyone will have a specialized knowledge of your subject. Note any particular tools, hardware or materials that played a part in your operation or project. And be sure to provide us with the product name, along with the manufacturer's name, current address and telephone number.

Strive to explain technical procedures in clear, simple sentences, and organize your flow of ideas logically. If you're trying to describe parts, operations or assemblies that are hard to verbalize, don't hesitate to use a drawing. Sketches should be clear, but don't have to be works of art; an artist will redraw anything that we decide to use. Drawings should be supplied with dimensions and labeled so that the visual information is correct and complete. If appropriate, include sources of supplies (complete with up-to-date addresses) or a list of books for further reading. We'll also need your Social Security number for payment purposes, so please send it along with your manuscript.

We'd prefer to receive your manuscript in typed, double spaced pages. If you work on a computer, tell your editor; it's likely that we'll be able to translate from your word processing program to ours, in which case we'll ask you to send a floppy disc as well as the printed pages.

• **Photography**—To assure that an article will be accompanied by high quality images, our editors usually visit authors and take most of the photographs. Since our editors are trained photographers, this assures us of getting photos that accurately support the processes and projects described in the text. A visit also gives authors a chance to meet their editor and work out any details involved in preparing the article. For project articles that involve building a piece of furniture, we rarely will ask you to build the piece from start to finish. We will work with you to select and stage certain process shots, to visually convey the most important operations described in the article. By the way, don't worry about writing photo captions—your editor will prepare those when the article is edited.

While we may occasionally photograph finished pieces during a visit, we more commonly hire a professional, as it's much more complex to shoot finished work than just process photos. We may ask to borrow small finished pieces (such as a jewelry box, a turning, jigs and fixtures) or tools to photograph at Taunton's photo studio. If you already have high quality (or professionally shot) photos of your work, we'll naturally want to consider using them. original color transparencies (slides) are best for magazine reproduction, but we can work from black and white or color negatives, if need be. Unless you tell us otherwise in writing, we assume that any photographs and drawings you supply with your article belong to you, and can be covered in a copyright agreement for our use. If a professional photographer owns the copyright to photos of your work, we'll need to sign a copyright agreement with the photographer separately, in which case you'll need to supply the address and phone number.

• **Payments and copyrights**—Our basic rate is $150 per published magazine page. We'll also reimburse you for out-of-pocket expenses, such as for film purchases and photo processing (only if we approve the project before you begin shooting). We'll also reimburse you for shipping or courier charges and for materials purchased for making samples or building projects specifically for the article. All requests for reimbursement must be accompanied by a photocopy of your dated receipts (the IRS says you should keep the originals). Any other reimbursements must be cleared with us in advance.

Once your editor has a manuscript that's ready for editing, we'll send you a copyright agreement to sign. The agreement constitutes our acceptance of the article for publication. It's not a difficult document to understand, and simply states that we are buying three things:

1. The right to be the first North American magazine to publish your article.

2. The right to reprint your article in one or more of our anthology books, such as the *Fine Woodworking on...* series.

3. The right to use portions of the article, including photographs and drawings, in materials promoting the magazine or The Taunton Press.

As author, you retain all other rights, including the right to publish the article elsewhere after it has appeared in *Fine Woodworking*. If photographs were taken by a professional photographer, we'll ask the photographer to sign a similar copyright agreement. Once you sign the copyright agreement and return the original to us, we'll send you an advance of $150. We'll pay the balance at time of publication. We'll also send you two complimentary copies of the issue in which your article appears.

• **Publication and scheduling**—We don't usually schedule an article for publication until we have an acceptable manuscript in hand. And because we have to schedule our issues almost a year in advance of publication, it may seem as though we're asking you to hurry up and deliver you material only to have you wait to see it in print. Putting together the best possible magazine from available material often means juggling the mix of articles for a given issue, often right up to our publication deadline. We think the results are worth waiting for and we appreciate your understanding and patience in the meantime. You're always welcome to call your editor to find out how things are going.

Please note that by signing a copyright agreement with you, we do not guarantee publication of your article. Even if we schedule the article for a specific issue, our editorial needs and direction sometimes change. Therefore, we reserve the right to decide later not to publish your article, but that rarely happens. If it does happen, the advance will serve as a "kill fee." The material would be returned to you and released from the copyright agreement, freeing you to sell it to another magazine.

• **Editing and author corrections**—Once your manuscript is accepted and scheduled for publication, we'll assign a sponsoring editor to work closely with you throughout its production, which can take anywhere from a week to a month. The editor may ask you to supply additional information, or to rewrite or revise sections of your manuscript. The editor will try to be sensitive to your individual writing style and retain as much of the character of the original writing as possible. If any major changes are warranted or if we have any doubts about changes we're considering during the editing process, your editor will call you to discuss the matter. Remember that changes to your writing made by the sponsoring editor are done in the interest of making your writing more effective and accurate, to make for the best possible presentation of your ideas.

After your manuscript has been edited, we'll mail you a galley—a computer printout of the edited version of the text—so that you'll have a chance to review it before it goes to press. Read it carefully and check the text for technical accuracy, typos and errors in facts. Make sure your editor hasn't inadvertently misinterpreted your original material. Also, answer any questions the editor has included on the printout. Please try to limit your changes to repair of facts; this isn't the time for rewriting the entire article. If your article includes complex drawings, you may also receive the artist's pencil drawings for corrections; please check these for accurate dimensions and labels as well.

Mark any corrections directly on the printouts and drawings and call your sponsoring editor at 1-800-926-8776 to discuss changes as soon as possible. Also, please mail us back the marked-up galley and drawing, so we can later refer to them if necessary. Small additional changes are typically made by the editors after author's corrections. These changes are typically minor, and are necessary to fit the manuscript into the page layout.

• **Contributing to departments**—In addition to our articles, *Fine Woodworking* features a number of regular departments, including "Methods of Work," "Q & A," "Books," "Tool Forum," and "Notes and Comments." We invite you to contribute to these sections of the magazine as well. Be sure to address all submissions to the appropriate department, in care of *Fine Woodworking*. "Methods of Work" submissions, which include "Quick Tips," don't require a proposal first; just send us your idea about an innovative jig, shop device, tool design or mode of operation, including rough sketches and photos. We'll pay $35 for each method we accept, $10 for quick tips.

The "Books" department includes reviews of new books and videos on woodworking and related topics (e.g. upholstery). Reviews should be concise and informative as to the content and quality of information in the item reviewed. We discourage unsolicited reviews; if you have a book in ming, contact us first. If we're interested, we'll arrange to have a copy sent to you. Payment is $35 per review, plus you get to keep the book. "Tool Forum" features short reviews of new woodworking tools and gadgets. We prefer that you first contact us with ideas for tools to review and then let us make the arrangements. Payment for "Tool Forum" reviews is prorated from our standard page rate of $150/page. Articles for "Notes and Comments" are generally less than 500 words and may include one or more photos. Subjects may include reports on woodworking-related current events, trade shows, gallery shows, woodworking seminars or school programs, personal profiles or humorous essays. Payment is prorated from our standard page rate.

• **Extra copies and reprints** —If you need more copies of the issue your article is in, authors are entitled to purchase additional copies at a discount of 50% off the cover price of the issue (plus shipping). Reprints of an individual article are available only by request, are run on heavier paper than the issue and can be produced any time after the issue has been printed. Reprints are fairly expensive to produce (you must order a minimum of 500 copies), and they take about a month to complete. If you'd like more information about reprints, contact *Fine Woodworking's* editorial secretary.

• **Questions?** —Thank you for your interest in *Fine Woodworking* magazine. If you have any further questions, feel free to call us toll free at 1-800-926-8776 and ask for the *Fine Woodworking* editorial department.

Categories: Nonfiction—Crafts—Hobbies

CONTACT: Editorial Department
Material: All
The Taunton Press
63 South Main St., PO Box 5506
Newtown, CT 06470
Phone: 203-426-8171
Fax: 203-270-6753
E-mail: jdeeds@taunton.com
Website: www.taunton.com

FineScale Modeler

FineScale Modeler

How you can contribute to *FineScaleModeler*

Most *FineScaleModeler* (FSM) articles are contributed by modelers, not professional writers. This means that if you have a modeling story to tell, you can be an FSM author! In evaluating manuscripts we look first at the quality of your photos and illustrations, second at how you present your how-to information, and only third at your writing style.

If you have a modeling technique that FSM readers would like to learn about, our editors can rework your writing to the magazine's format and style. Most FSM feature articles concern how-to-do-it technique: How to build a kit into a more accurate or more representative model; how to make parts you can't buy or parts that are better than what you can buy; how to paint a model or how to paint a particular color scheme; how to build a display or diorama; and so on.. Virtually every how-to aspect of modeling, including hints, tips, and workshop techniques, is a worthwhile subject for an FSM article.

By far, the best way to learn what FSM needs is to study how stories are presented in current issues. However, we don't consider articles that are submitted simultaneously to other modeling publications, or articles previously published in other magazines.

Preparing a manuscript

We prefer typed manuscripts, and if you can also send your manuscript on a computer disk, that's even better. Almost any format will work. Be sure to enclose a paper copy even if you send a disk. In the upper right corner of the first page of your text, type your name, address, home and work telephone numbers, e-mail address if you have one, and the date you submit the article. In addition to the main text, provide captions for all photos you submit. Provide these on a separate sheet, and please make sure you describe everything shown in each photo.

Writing style

Keep your writing simple and direct, but give lots of detail. Our readers need a clear description of what you did to the model, how you did it, and what tools and materials you used. Be specific. Did you use sheet or tube styrene? Tell us the sizes. What brands and colors of paint — exactly — did you use? What sort of putty — epoxy, acrylic — did you use? Don't simply say "I scratchbuilt the transmission from sheet, tube, and rod styrene." Tell us how you did it, step by step. The best way to do this is to write as if you were telling a friend how to duplicate your modeling project. The best method for organizing your text is in chronological order, from the start of the project to its completion. Be sure to provide a complete list of materials you used and a list of references, if applicable.

Articles should be brief; most range from 750 to 3,000 words. While big features such as "How I Scratchbuilt the Hughes Spruce Goose in 1/24 Scale" are used occasionally, FSM has a greater need for short articles. Such reports usually cover only a single aspect of a project — like just the painting, or just the conversion, or just the detailing. Your best chance for breaking into print is to contribute a short article that focuses on a single modeling technique.

For first-time FSM contributors, we often run a "meet the author" box with a three- or four-paragraph biography (please concentrate on your modeling interests) and a photo showing you engaged in some modeling or research activity. Please include these with your first article.

Before you mail…

We strongly recommend that you send a written inquiry to the Editor describing your proposed article, and ask for comments or interest before preparing a complete article package. We prefer letters or e-mail, but sometimes clear up our requirements in a brief phone call.

Payment and copyright

FSM pays for feature articles upon acceptance — when we accept a complete feature for publication, you get a check. We normally purchase all rights to the material. We pay based on the estimated length of the published story, and if we underestimate the space your article requires, we issue a second payment upon publication.

Our payment rates vary; they're highest when an author does a particularly good job, or when the material is especially timely or interesting. Articles that include camera-ready scale drawings or how-to artwork also qualify for special rates.

Publishing your photographs in FSM

Photography makes or breaks most FSM articles, and by far our most common reason for rejecting a story is poor photos.

We need color slides or glossy prints from 35mm or larger film. Black-and-white photos usually are acceptable if color is not available, such as with historical photos. How-to shots should be taken against a plain background.

In-progress, how-to-do-it photos are especially important for selling your article to FSM. We often have to reject excellent material simply because it does not include photos taken while the model was being built. Showing the model before painting tells a lot about what you did to it.

In addition to the main text, provide captions for all photos you submit. Provide these on a separate sheet, and please make sure you describe everything shown in each photo.

Taking better model pictures

If you haven't taken pictures of models before, it can be a little tricky. Here are some tips from a September 1999 FSM article, "Great model photos are a snap," in case you're not pleased with your initial results. A free copy of the complete article is available from FSM on request.

Depth of field. The amount of depth of field (how much of the model is in focus) in a photo is controlled primarily by the lens aperture, or opening. The smaller the aperture, the more of your model from front to back will be sharp and in focus. Shoot your photos using the smallest aperture possible; it's usually f22 or f23 on most lenses.

Use a tripod. Small apertures mean long exposure times. Placing the camera on a tripod and using a cable release will keep camera motion from blurring your photos.

Show the whole model. Although close-up lenses make detail shots easier to take, don't forget to take a few shots showing the whole model!

Background check. A cluttered background draws attention away from your masterpiece. A poster-sized piece of colored art paper, curved up behind the model, makes a simple backdrop and helps concentrate the viewer's attention on the subject model.

Choose the right film. Use daylight-balanced film outdoors or with electronic flash; use tungsten-balanced film indoors with incandescent light. Films with "slow" speeds (ASA 50 or 100) produce sharper images than "fast" films (ASA 200, 400, or higher).

Digital photography

At this time, we need conventional transparencies, slides, or color prints. Consumer-quality digital cameras don't have the resolution that film provides, so except in special circumstances, we cannot use digital images in FSM.

If you send snapshot-quality 4 x 6 prints and negatives we can make reproduction-quality prints in our photo lab. Please include the negatives regardless of the quality of your prints. Negatives and 4 x 6 prints can be sent in a standard business size envelope, inside the larger envelope of your manuscript, to help keep them from being bent or scratched in transit.

Scale drawings and how-to illustrations

Please include sketches, patterns, templates, or plans with your article. Our artists can work from rough sketches. Draw the roughs as carefully and neatly as you can. If you can furnish reproduction-quality artwork your article will qualify for higher rates of payment. We often include arrows, circles, and words in photos to point out what's going on. You can suggest such pointers by attaching a tracing-paper flap to your photo and writing on the flap.

Payment and copyright

FSM pays for feature articles (but not Gallery images) upon acceptance. See payment and copyright information above.

Gallery, Portfolio, and Showcase stories

FSM pays on publication for photos published in the Reader Gallery, and buys all right. Published Gallery photos will not be returned. Portfolio and Showcase articles feature photos of a modeler's completed work, and usually are two magazine pages long. FSM pays on acceptance for these staff-written articles, and will follow up via questionnaire to get information needed for the text.

Categories: Nonfiction—Hobbies

CONTACT: Mark Thompson, Editor
Material: Any
CONTACT: Dick McNally, Managing Editor
Material: Any
21027 Crossroads Circle
Waukesha WI 53187
Phone: 414-796-8776
Fax: 414-796-1383
E-mail: RMCNALLY@finescale.com
Website: www.finescale.com

Firehouse Magazine
Firehouse.com

Firehouse is the world's largest publication devoted exclusively to the fire service. Our primary editorial objectives are to educate, inform and entertain our audience of 1.5 million career and volunteer firefighters and thousands of fire buffs.

Generally, we are interested in all incidents, innovations, controversies and trends that affect the fire service world. *Specifically, we concentrate on the following areas:*

• MAJOR FIRES AND DISASTERS: detailed accounts and technical analyses of firefighting operations at major incidents (see "On the Job" specifications).

• APPARATUS AND EQUIPMENT: innovations in fire apparatus and other equipment (including protective gear), advice on purchasing, new and best uses of equipment, converting and repairing equipment, analysis/critique of equipment.

• COMMUNICATIONS: equipment, dispatch systems and dispatchers, command centers, fireground communications systems.

• TRAINING: methods and tools, new, successful courses, training simulations.

• HAZARDOUS MATERIALS: incidents, training, equipment, command, protective equipment.

• ARSON: investigation, prevention, analysis, trends.

• LAW: fire-related legislation at local and national levels.

• FIRE SAFETY: new and successful ways of educating the public.

• MEDICINE: health concerns, fitness of firefighters.

• LEADERSHIP: improving command skills and systems on the fireground, interviews with high-ranking fire service personnel (commissioners and chiefs of major fire departments).

• RESCUE: unusual incidents, successful methods and tools.

• EMS: major events involving EMTs, concerns of medical technology in the fire service.

• FIREFIGHTING HISTORY: great fires of the past, collectibles and memorabilia, fire museums, old-time equipment.

• HEALTH AND SAFETY: issues pertaining to firefighter health and safety.

• PUBLIC RELATIONS: improving relations with the community, fundraising.

• HUMAN INTEREST: lifestyles, profiles of firefighters with unusual hobbies and interests.

Query us first so we can give you more specific guidance, required length of the manuscript and deadlines. *Firehouse* does not accept multiple submissions; that is, the material submitted must be an exclusive to *Firehouse*. The writer must verify, in writing, that the material submitted is his original work, it has not been published previously and that it is not under consideration at another publication.

Submissions

We would appreciate receiving manuscripts that are submitted on computer disk accompanied by a printed copy. *Firehouse* uses Macintosh computer systems. However, we can convert almost any format and application. Please indicate the system (MS-DOS, Macintosh, etc.), program used (Word Perfect, MS Word, etc.) and how it was saved (ASCII, text, etc.). For those writers who do not yet have word processing capability, clean, original typewritten pages are required. Please use a Courier 10-point typeface (the standard issue of typewriters) or comparable with one-inch margins throughout the document. If you make corrections, apply White-Out and retype. Do not handwrite corrections on typewritten copy, as our electronic scanning equipment cannot read it. Handwritten, dot matrix-printed (without floppy disk) or xeroxed manuscripts will be returned.

Please keep in mind that you are writing a magazine article. Most magazine readers, including those of *Firehouse* , want to be able to learn the important aspects of a given topic without having to read through numerous paragraphs of background information. The average length of each article in *Firehouse* is between two and three pages including visuals. In the past, we have received manuscripts that would be suitable for the first chapter of a book. Making these stories fit in the allocated space requires a great deal of editing on our part. More importantly, we may be cutting material that you would rather have included. A good rule of thumb is that one typeset page in *Firehouse* is equal to about four double-spaced, typewritten pages.

Please include a daytime telephone number and Fax number if you have one. If we have any questions regarding copy or additional information is needed, we will contact you directly. If you have any stories ready to send prior to deadline dates, please send them along. We appreciate early arrivals.

Photos

Firehouse is a visually-oriented publication. Please include photographs (color preferred) with captions (or a description of what is taking place in the photo), illustrations, charts or diagrams that support your manuscript. The highest priority is given to those submissions that are received as a complete package. Please keep a copy of all your material, including visuals. *Firehouse* makes every effort to ensure that all material is returned to the writer, whether it is published or not; however, we cannot guarantee the return of unpublished material. Enclose a stamped, self-addressed envelope with all submissions. Submissions lacking the necessary SASE will not be returned. Please make sure that the ruturn envelope is large enough to house your material. Also, please make sure the envelope has sufficient postage; do not include payment (checks or cash) for postage.

Rates

Firehouse makes payment only upon publication of written and photographic material. Once accepted, articles are published depending on timeliness and space availability. Hence, we cannot guarantee a publication date. Please include your social security number so that payment is not delayed.

• If you have any story ideas, questions, hints, tips, etc., please do not hesitate to call. We appreciate and thank you for your assistance, enthusiasm and promptness.

About *Firehouse.com*

For information on submitting to Firehouse.com, please visit our Online Content Submission Information Page.

Categories: Nonfiction—Health—Hobbies—Law—Lifestyle—Technical—Trade—Emergency Response—Fire-related

CONTACT: Firehouse Magazine, Editorial
Material: All *Firehouse Magazine* Submissions
445 Broad Hollow Rd.
Melville NY 11747
Phone: 516-845-2700
Fax: 516-845-7109
E-mail: new@Firehouse.com
CONTACT: Firehouse.com, Editor
Material: All *Firehouse.com* Submissions
9658 Baltimore Ave, Ste 350
College Park MD 20740
Website: www.Firehouse.com

First for Women

First for Women provides today's busy, on-the-go woman with a wealth of information packed into quick-reading articles. We are looking for service pieces on health and fitness, relationships and sex, happiness and parenting. We also feature real women's stories, stories of inspiration or life-changing events. Before submitting a query, please read the magazine to familiarize yourself with our style and editorial needs.

Please send a query letter rather than a completed manuscript. Clips are welcome. We regret that we do not accept email submissions, and we do not accept unsolicited fiction or poetry. Payment for articles is made upon acceptance for publication.

Please include your name, address, and daytime phone number with your query. Material not accompanied by a self-addressed stamped envelope will not be returned. *First for Women* accepts no obligation to return any material.

Categories: Nonfiction—Beauty—Cooking—Fashion—Food/Drink

CONTACT: Barbara Moff
Material: Fashion, Beauty
CONTACT: Kate Keating
Material: Food
CONTACT: Linda Moore, Features Editor
Material: All Other
Bauer Publishing Co., L.P.
270 Sylvan Ave.
Englewood Cliffs NJ 07632
Phone: 201-569-6699
Fax: 201-569-6264
Website: www.ffwmarket.com

First Things
A Monthly Journal of Religion and Public Life

FIRST THINGS does accept unsolicited manuscripts. Guidelines are as follows:

Opinions: 800-1,500 words. Honorarium of $400.

Articles: 4,000-6,000 words. Honorarium of $1000.

Book Reviews: 800-1,500 words. Honorarium of $400.

Review Essays: 4,000-6,000 words. Honorarium of $1000.

Manuscripts should be typed, double-spaced and on one side of the page. Submit manuscripts with a SASE and $2.25 postage.

Categories: Nonfiction— Book Reviews—Christian Interests—Culture—Education—General Interest—Government—Jewish Interest—Law—Politics—Religion—Spiritual—Philosophy—Public Policy

CONTACT: James Nuechterlein, Editor
Material: All
156 Fifth Ave., Ste. 400
New York NY 10010
Phone: 212-627-1985
Fax: 212-627-2184
E-mail: ft@firstthings.com
Website: www.firstthings.com

A MidWest Out(
Publication

Fishing Facts

Fishing Facts Magazine has been teaching people how to fish for the past 40 years. Every issue features stories on how-to and where-to fish at some of the hottest spots in the United States.

1) Every article submitted should be between 750 and 1,500 words.

2) They should contain color photos and/or charts, graphs and maps.

3) Clearly outline the techniques used to fish successfully.

4) Clearly outline where the author was fishing, either the specific body of water or the area.

5) Articles must be submitted in the following forms:
- via e-mail, e-mail address: info@midwestoutdoors.com
- on a 3½" diskette (We use Microsoft Word for word processing.)

Please remember, the tone of Fishing Facts Magazine is positive and upbeat.

Important checklist before sending in material:
- You have included your name, address and social security number.
- Your name is on all pages and photos.
- You have indicated what issue the material is for.
- You have written a headline and sub-headline.
- You have written a caption for each photo.

Please read: If we do not plan on using your material, it will be returned to you within 10 days of receipt. The best check you have for knowing if we have used your material, is if you receive payment from Fishing Facts. Payment for each article published is $30 paid upon publication.

Categories: Nonfiction—Fishing—Recreation—Sports/Recreation

CONTACT: Dena Kollman, Assistant Editor
Materials: All
111 Shore Drive
Burr Ridge IL 60527
Phone: 630-887-7722
Fax: 630-887-1958
E-mail: info@midwestoutdoors.com.
Website: www.fishingfacts.com

Fitness Management
Issue & Solutions to Fitness Service

Stories in *Fitness* should appeal to an educated, nationwide audience of women (median age: 30) who are interested in their health, fitness and general well-being. Front-of-the book short features cover news items, health and fitness trends, new products and workout videos. Articles cover a range of topics, including exercise (for mind, body and/or spirit),sports, trend and news-driven special reports, beauty, fashion, sex and relationships, health, nutrition, food, first person profiles and *Fitness* makeovers.

It would be helpful to look at a copy of the magazine before submitting a query. Sample copies are available from our offices for $3.50 or may be purchased at supermarkets and newsstands.

Query letters should give a sample of the style of the proposed article, tell us your angle or perspective on the subject, and specify what material you would like to cover. Please include samples of published writing, preferably consumer-magazine work, and an appropriate-size, self-addressed, stamped envelope with all submissions. *Fitness* assumes no responsibility for unsolicited material.

Acceptance and Payment: If we assign an article, you will be notified of our decision to accept it within six weeks. We do not commit to a publishing date.

We pay within 60 days of acceptance of a completed manuscript. The fee is negotiated when an assignment is made. A written agreement must be signed before payment can be made. We pay a 20% kill fee for assigned manuscripts that are not acceptable for publication.

Categories: Health—Fitness

CONTACT: Ronale Tucker, Editor
Material: Feature Articles
CONTACT: Anne B. McDonnell, Senior Editor
Material: New Products
4160 Wilshire Blvd.
Los Angeles CA 90010
Phone: 323-964-4800
Fax: 323-964-4835
E-mail: edit@fitnessmgmt.com
Website: www.fitnessmanagement.com

Flesh & Blood
Tales of Horror and Dark Fantasy

Flesh & Blood is a multi award-winning dark fantasy fiction magazine published 3-4 times/year. It is a 50+ page, full-color digest featuring a variety of the strange and offbeat.

Fiction: We will look at fiction up to 6,000 words (anything longer, query). Stories must possess a strong sense/feel of the strange, offbeat, and/or surreal. We will not consider stories without at least one or more of these elements. Fiction that deals with serial killers, stereotypical plots (zombies, vampires, cats, etc), revenge, blatant gore, and sex will not be the proper match for F&B magazine. Contrary to the magazine's title, we'd rather steer clear of the "flesh" and "blood" in fiction and place a bigger emphasis on the subtle and strange. Nevermind sending a proposal/synopsis. Instead, send the complete manuscript with mention of your background (if any) in the cover letter. We accept electronic submissions in the body of email and as MS Word attachments.

Poetry: Same guidelines for fiction apply to poetry: strange, unnatural, and plain old weird is what we want. Keep poems down to at least one typed page or less, and please send no more than five poems at a time. Poems that rhyme will have very little chance at being bought; poems with themes about love, desire, heartache, vampires, etc will also not be considered.

Artwork & Non-Fiction: We are currently fully staffed with artists and columnists.

Payment:
- Fiction—$.04 to $.05 cents/word
- Poetry—$10 to $20/poem
- Plus one contributor's copy.

Response time is 2-6 weeks. If you have not heard back from us within 60 days, query.

We will read both paper and email submissions. Please include a SASE with all paper submissions. All stories must abide by "proper manuscript format." Please send only one submission at a time and wait for a reply before sending another. All email submissions should be sent to the attention of Jack Fisher only and emailed to the appropriate address below. If you have any additional questions in any regard, please contact either Robert Swartwood or Meghan Fatras, assistant editors.

E-mail submissions to HorrorJackF@aol.com

Categories: Fiction—Horror—Paranormal—Poetry—Short Stories—Dark Poetry—Supernatural

CONTACT: Jack Fisher, Senior Editor
Material: All Fiction/Poetry
CONTACT: Robert Swartwood, Assistant Editor
Material: All Fiction
Flesh & Blood Press
121 Joseph St.
Bayville NJ 08721
E-mail: HorrorJack@aol.com
Website: zombie.horrorseek.com/horror/fleshnblood/main.htm

Florida Hotel & Motel Journal

Market: Our magazine is a reference tool for managers and owners of Florida's hotels, motels and resorts—circulation 8,000+. It is mailed on the first of each month, except Dec. & Aug.

Editorial content: Nonfiction only. Preference is given to articles that include references to mem- ber properties and general managers affiliated with the Florida Hotel and Motel Association. Since the association acquires new members weekly, queries may be made prior to the scheduling of interviews. This does not preclude the use of materials or ideas based on non-member properties, but member property sources are preferable.

Approach: Queries are encouraged. Unsolicited manuscripts must be accompanied by SASE with sufficient postage for first class return. Articles submitted for an issue with a specific theme must be received two months in advance of the publication date.

Format: Length is determined by nature and import of subject matter, not to exceed 2000 words unless specified by the editor. Shorter articles with accompanying sidebars are preferred. Manuscripts should be typed, double-spaced.

Attributions: All opinions, quotations and statements used should be attributable to a creditable source, i.e., a person in the lodging industry, a footnoted quotation from texts or clearly identified as the personal viewpoint of the author.

Writing and editing: Clarity and organization of content are essential. The editor reserves the right to edit for grammar, punctuation and simplification of subject matter, as necessary, without changing the author's intent.

Photos and Artwork: Submissions accompanying an article should be of professional quality and authorized in advance by the editor. Color slides and/or b&w glossy prints are acceptable.

Rates and Rights: Payment is $.10 per word upon publication for first U. S. A. rights. Travel and/ or telephone expenses must have the editor's advance approval. Three complimentary copies of the issue in which a commissioned article appears will be mailed to the author. Additional copies may be purchased.

Categories: Nonfiction—Business—Trade—Hotel & Motel Management

CONTACT: Lytha Belrose, Editor
Material: All
200 W. College Ave.
Tallahassee FL 32301
Phone: 850-224-2888
Fax: 850-222-3462
Website: www.flahotel.com

Florida Leader
For College Students

Please refer to Oxendine Publishing, Inc.

Florida Leader
For High School Students

Please refer to Oxendine Publishing, Inc.

Florida Wildlife

In response to Florida Wildlife Magazine's funding being eliminated, the Wildlife Foundation of Florida has started the Florida Wildlife Magazine Newsletter. In the future, we would like to resume magazine production in a printed format. Our interim solution is to distribute the newsletter as an online magazine. The newsletter will feature the same diverse content and high-quality photographs.

Submit Articles for the Florida Wildlife Newsletter

If you would like to contribute an article, artwork, photographs or recipes to the Florida Wildlife Newsletter, you must first accept the following agreement:

By transferring this image and/or text file to the Wildlife Foundation of Florida, Inc.(WFF), I hereby attest and affirm the file is not copyrighted and I have authority to release this file and its contents to the WFF. I understand by transferring the file, I am giving all rights to the property to the WFF.

Categories: Animals—Boating—Conservation—Ecology—Environment—History—Native American—Nature—Outdoors—Recreation—Travel—Bass Fishing—Habitat—Wildlife

CONTACT: Editor
Material: All
Wildlife Foundation of Florida, Inc.
Post Office Box 11010
Tallahassee, FL 32302
Phone: 850-922-1066
E-mail: Foundation@wildlifefoundationofflorida.com
Webstie: www.wildlifefoundationofflorida.com/home.htm

Fly Fisherman

NOTES TO CONTRIBUTORS

Fly Fisherman is the nation's first and largest consumer magazine devoted solely to the sport of fly fishing. We don't assume that all of our readers are expert fly fishes, nor do we assume that they are all novices. We select material for publication that, educates accomplished fly fishers, beginners and even non-fly fishers. Similarly, we provide geographic coverage that meets our responsibility as an international publication.

Our contributors are avid readers of the magazine, and their submissions reflect a familiarity with the style and content of material used in the magazine. Potential contributors should likewise familiarize themselves with the kind of material *Fly Fisherman* uses by looking over recent issues.

Over Eighty percent of *Fly Fisherman*'s readers are college educated, and ninety percent are male. However, the magazine is regularly read by other members of the household—including non-fly fishers. Our readers fish in fresh or salt water for almost any species of fish that will take a fly.

Editorial Format

The types of articles that we publish include:

1. Main features of 2,000-3,000 words, illustrated with black-and-white prints or

color transparencies (slides) and illustrations. These articles embrace a wide variety of subjects, including major destinations (where to fish), instruction about fishing techniques, and how to tie flies. Fiction, humor and personality profiles are seldom used.

2. Short features of about 750-1,500 words, usually illustrated in black-and-white or color. These articles highlight a specific aspect of the sport; most are short destination or how-to-do-it articles. The short feature is an important component of our magazine. It allows us to present a wide variety of information and topics to our readers.

3. Destination features of about 2,000-3,000 are feature articles that highlight a particular stream or the waters of a specific region. These features include good photos of fish from the waters discussed and anglers fishing in scenic surroundings. They also may include a hatch chart, a map with each water clearly indicated, local fly shop information, lodging information, and any other details that can make it easy to plan a trip to the area. The text should inform the reader about the area and techniques and flies needed to catch fish there. It should not be an account of your trip to a particular destination.

4. Technical feature articles of about 2,000 words, illustrated in black-and-white or color, deal with subjects that lend themselves to presentation in the Improving Your Skills, Fly Tier's Bench or Tips From The Experts departments. Sometimes these are used in the main feature section of the magazine. The text usually includes step-by-step instructions (such as fly-tying instructions), and if such instructions are included, appropriate photos, illustrations, or diagrams should accompany the text.

All submissions to *Fly Fisherman* containing factual information must be thoroughly and carefully documented. Double-check stream or lake locations and names (especially spelling); if you're unsure of any factual detail and can't document it, leave it out. When referring to insects or fish by their Latin names, consult a standard college text for correct spelling and nomenclature.

Photographs and Artwork

We can't overemphasize the importance of quality illustrations to accompany submissions. See the attached Artist/Photographers

If you don't have photos, send the article anyway—we may have the appropriate photos and illustrations on file. However, good photos often sell an article that is less than complete. Quality color or black-and-white art is always welcome. All photographic submissions should be accompanied by a caption sheet.

Maps and diagrams should be submitted with articles when called for by the text. When submitting fly-tying articles, drawings or photographs showing tying steps should be included when appropriate.

Submissions of cartoons are welcome.

Preparation of Material and Submission Procedures

Manuscripts must be typed and double-spaced. We do not accept handwritten manuscripts. Computer printouts are acceptable. If possible, send the manuscript on computer disk (3-1/2" disk in Microsoft Word text or ASCII format). The name, address and phone number of the author should be on the first page of the manuscript. The name of the article, the name of the author and the page number should be on each ensuing page of the manuscript. The author's name (or appropriate credit line) should be marked on each piece of photographic material or artwork submitted. Care should be taken to package all material properly before mailing. Please enclose a self-addressed envelope and attach or enclose sufficient postage for return of material.

An excellent, concise and handy guide to style is *The Elements of Style* by William Strunk, Jr. and E.B. White (2nd ed., Macmillan Publishing Co., New York, 1972, $1.95) and we recommend it highly.

Queries

We strongly recommend that you query us in advance on a specific article or article idea. A query allows us to suggest a slant on the article, or at least to inform you in advance of our interest in your proposed story idea.

Acknowledgment of Submissions

Upon receipt of a submission we'll send an acknowledgment; within six to eight weeks after receipt, material will either be returned or purchased. Sometimes we may ask for a rewrite. Article queries will be answered within four weeks, and queries concerning the status of submissions (after our reply deadline of six to eight weeks) will be answered immediately.

Payment

Payment is made within 30 days of publication or acceptance of material. *Fly Fisherman* buys First Time World Publishing Rights and all nonexclusive World Publishing Rights (for use on our internet site, www.flyshop.com). *Fly Fisherman* does not accept simultaneous submissions or previously published material. Shortly after publication, all photos, illustrations, diagrams, maps, etc. will be returned. Original manuscripts will be kept here on file. (Writers who regularly make submissions to any publication should familiarize themselves with the current copyright laws.)

Fees to contributors vary according to the manuscript's professional level, frequency of accepted contributions, and length of article. The same applies to photographs and artwork. Fees range from $400 to $700 for main features, from $100 to $300 for short features, from $200 to $300 for technical features. We pay $100 for book reviews. Contact us before writing the review.

Fees are paid for complete packages, which include manuscript, artwork, and photographs. Payment for photographs and artwork purchased without manuscripts is determined by the size and use inside the magazine and ranges from $50 to $300. We pay $600 for a photograph used on the cover of the magazine.

Publication Schedule

Fly Fisherman magazine is published six times per year. The editor usually purchases manuscripts one year in advance.

Please advise us of any change in your address or telephone number so that we may keep our files up-to-date and ensure that your submissions are returned safely. Include both home and office phone numbers as well as any seasonal addresses and e-mail.

Style Guide for Potential Contributors

1. Indent the first line of each paragraph.

2. Show the end of a story by writing End, The End, 30, #, or similar mark.

3. Use standard scientific nomenclature when referring to insects: Consult standard references, such as "Mayflies of North and Central America," Edmunds et al, for correct spellings.

4. The common names of insects are lower case, the proper names of fly patterns are capitalized: The black gnats were a nuisance that night, but I caught four trout on a Black Gnat dry fly.

5. The common names of fish are lower case unless the name includes a proper noun: I like to fish for coho salmon, Chinook salmon, Atlantic salmon and brown trout.

6. Some preferred spellings: caddisfly, drys (dry flies), fish-for-fun, fly-fishing, fly-fishing-only, fly rod, fly-rodder, fly tier, fly-tying, Matuka, marabou, mayfly, mylar, no-kill, Opening Day, snowmelt, snowpack, stonefly, whip-finish.

Guidelines

Color photographs should be in the form of 35mm slides or 2 1/4" x 2 1/4" transparencies, as color prints do not reproduce satisfactorily. The preferred format for black-and-white photographs is 8" x 10" glossy prints. Articles are best accompanied by both black-and-white and color, giving us the option of using one or the other or both to illustrate your work.

Categories: Nonfiction—Fishing—Recreation—Sports/Recreation

CONTACT: The Editor
Material: All
6405 Flank Dr.
Harrisburg PA 17112-2753
Website: www.flyshop.com

Fly Fishing in Salt Waters

Formal guidelines not available. Please read a number of issues to ascertain the publication's style and needs.

Send queries to address below

Categories: Fishing—Sports/Recreation—Travel

CONTACT: David Ritchie, Editor
Material: All
2001 Western Ave., Ste. 210
Seatlle WA 98121
Phone: 206-443-3273
Fax: 206-443-3293
Website: www.flyfishinsalt.com

Flyfisher

We're looking for writing and photography that help us reinforce our mission to conserve, restore and educate through fly fishing.

Founded in 1965, the Federation of Fly Fishers (FFF) is the nation's largest, oldest and most influential fly-fishing organization. The *Flyfisher*, first published in 1968, is the Federation's flagship publication and this country's oldest fly-fishing magazine.

Circulation of each issue is a minimum of 12,500 copies. More than 10,000 copies are delivered by mail to FFF members. The balance is distributed by the FFF to its nearly 200 affiliated local fly-fishing clubs around the country, to retail fly shops, at fly-fishing shows and expositions and in FFF promotions.

Mirroring the FFF's mission to "conserve, restore and educate through fly fishing," each issue of the *Flyfisher* takes a hard look at resource issues affecting cold-water, warm-water and saltwater game fish and their habitats.

The magazine also serves as an educational tool for the FFF and its International Fly Fishing Center, providing practical information focusing on fly fishing techniques—including emphasis on fly tying, which many FFF members enjoy. *Flyfisher* editorial also aims to attract and support new constituencies for the sport, particularly women and youths.

Feature stories

We carry features that have been the hallmark of the *Flyfisher* for nearly 30 years. We're particularly interested in how-to and technique features, fly-fishing history and tradition, personality profiles and interviews, personal narratives, fly-fishing trends, conservation profiles, fly tying and, on rare occasions, fiction. We'll run occasional where-to-fish stories that feature a fishing destination, but feel these types of stories predominate in the for-profit magazines and are less reflective of the FFF mission. Length should be from 750 to 1,500 words. Payment: $50 to $150.

Conservation stories

We run conservation-oriented stories as short news stories of not more than 400 words, or as longer stand-alone features not exceeding 1,500 words. At various times the *Flyfisher* will also feature a longer story or package of stories focusing on a conservation issue of national concern that impacts the quality of freshwater or saltwater fishery habitats or resources. We're looking for top-notch environmental journalism that 1) gets *Flyfisher* readers interested in the topic and concretely demonstrates how it affects the sport of fly fishing; and 2) provides easily assimilated information that will further reader knowledge. Length should be from 750 to 1,500 words for an individual story, or up to 2,500 words for a package of stories. If querying a conservation package idea, please suggest possible sidebar subjects and visual support. Payment: $20 to $40 for short conservation stories; $50 to $150 for stand-alone feature stories; or $150 to $250 for a package of stories.

Photography

We're always interested in photography to accompany writing, and good photos make a story more attractive to us. Although we assign very little photography, we use several stock images per issue. We encourage interested photographers to submit a list of subjects in stock and a resume of credits. If you wish to submit photos for consideration, the *Flyfisher* staff responds within one month of receiving materials with an Acknowledgment of Receipt and will hold materials with potential for use for up to 90 days.

Solicited material will be returned via Postal Service certified mail.

We use black-and-white photos which should be submitted as 5"x7" or 8"x10" prints, or as negatives with proof sheets. For color, we use 35mm or larger format transparencies. We may wish to reproduce a color photograph in black-and-white; if you object to this, please specify when submitting. Payment: $10 to $25 for black-and-white usage, $15 to $50 for color, $100 for cover. Credit line is given on all photographs. Model release is required when subject is easily identifiable and potential for litigation exists.

General guidelines

Although we'll look at unsolicited manuscripts, we encourage writers to submit query letters. If you are simultaneously submitting your story or photos elsewhere, please specify this. We also like to see one or two clips or writing samples from authors with whom we are unfamiliar.

Accuracy is of paramount importance. Writers are responsible for the accuracy of their stories, and for ensuring names and proper nouns are correctly spelled. For some subjects we may require writers to send us background material and a source list to help us perform fact checking.

Keep the length of your story within the guidelines set forth above. We strongly favor concisely written stories. Also, remember the *Flyfisher* is published in February, April, July and November; bear in mind our seasonal needs and query at least 120 days prior to the season for which your story is appropriate.

The first page [of your manuscript] should include your name, address, phone number and social security number. We use a Macintosh computer system and welcome submissions on disk in any word processing program. If you write on an IBM compatible, simply save in ASCII (text only) format on a 3.5" floppy. If you do send a disk, be sure to send along a hard copy, too.

We may also receive your story via e-mail. At this time, however, we prefer that queries be sent by regular U.S. mail, rather than as e-mail.

The *Flyfisher* buys first North American serial rights, and payment is made on publication. Writing is done on speculation unless a kill fee is agreed to in advance.

Categories: Nonfiction—Conservation—Ecology—Education—Environment—Fishing—Nature—Sports/Recreation

CONTACT: Nick Amato, Editor
Material: All
Frank Amato Publications
PO Box 82112
Portland OR 97282
Phone: 503 653-8108
Fax: 503 653-2766
E-mail: nick@amatobooks.com
Website: www.fedFlyfishers.org

Flyfishing & Tying Journal
A Compendium for the Complete Fly Fisherman

Publisher: Frank Amato
Editor: Dave Hughes
Managing Editor: Kim Koch

Writer's and Photographer's Guidelines

Flyfishing & Tying Journal (FTJ) is a quarterly *fly-fishing* magazine with issues designated Winter, Spring, Summer, and Fall. As its name implies, the magazine has two major focal points of interest, *fly fishing* and *fly tying*, that reflect the interests of its readers.

The majority of FTJ readers, 98%, fly-fish for trout, most of them many days each year. 60% also fly-fish for steelhead and salmon. 50% fly-fish for bass and panfish. 30% go after bonefish, tarpon, permit, and other saltwater species at least once a year. A high percentage of our readers tie their own flies. Three-quarters are over 40 years old, 90% have education beyond high school, and most have been fly-fishing five years or more, though we can never forget that many readers of every issue have more eagerness than they have experience.

More than half of our readers, 60%, live in the West: the Pacific coast states and Rockies. 15% live in New England and on the East Coast. 15% live in the Midwest and Great Lakes region. Many in all regions travel to other areas to fish.

Articles accepted for publication in the magazine will be balanced to reflect the above preferences for species and areas in which readers live and fish. Article selection will also reflect a balance between the two focal points of the magazine: fly fishing and fly tying. Each issue is divided into two cores, the major one the fly-fishing core toward the front and the fly-tying core toward the back. Articles for each core are very different from those for the other, and must be tailored to one or the other to fit our requirements.

Fly-fishing core feature articles. The fly-fishing core of each issue will consist of 4 to 6 feature articles, each from 1,200 to 2,000 words long, on a specific fishing technique, an insect hatch or natural food form and the flies and methods that work to take fish, a range of methods to solve a specific situation or type of fishery, or any other subject deemed by the editors to be of sufficient interest to our readers. Each feature should include one or two short sidebars, 100 to 250 words each, that illuminate or enlarge the subject. One sidebar should almost always deal with the flies used in the fishing featured. The dressing for each fly should be given in the sidebar, and a finished sample of each fly should be furnished for our photographer. If a fly pattern is written about in an article, its dressing should be given in a sidebar, and a copy of the fly, tied, should be provided for our photographer. Please use barbless hooks, or de-barb them.

Our desire is to publish informative articles that our readers can have fun reading, learn from, and put to use in their own fishing. We rarely buy articles in which a destination itself is the subject; we commonly buy articles about solutions to fishing problems with the supporting anecdotes set in a specific destination. If a destination is dealt with in any article, the article should be about the fishing, not the destination, and all high praise not directly related to the fishing should go into a sidebar along with contact information: address, phone number, e-mail address, and website.

Each fly-fishing feature will require enough high-quality color slides to illustrate it attractively. Twenty to forty slides should be submitted with any full feature. Slide selection should include lead shots to set the scene for the article, action shots, fish shots, scenery, flies, and peripheral flora and fauna.

The formula is often denigrated in outdoor writing, but it dates back to the 1500s and Montaigne's highly regarded essays, and is to this day a very fine format to follow for any feature. If you don't have a better outline, and you should rarely write an article without an outline in mind, use it:

Introduction: the fishing problem to be solved.
Part 1. the first part of the solution (e.g. recognizing an insect).
Part 2. the second part of the solution (e.g. choosing the right fly to match it).
Part 3. (optional) the third part of the solution (e.g. using the right presentation).
Conclusion: summation of the solving of the problem.
Sidebar 1. The flies used (dressings listed and flies provided for photographer).
Sidebar 2. Some peripheral part of the solution, or contact info for a destination.

This has been summed up as: tell them what you're going to tell them, tell them, tell them, tell them, then tell them what you told them. That's not far from wrong. Brief anecdotes, set on the water in the midst of the action, should be used to enliven at least one or two parts of each article. These give an immediacy to the problem and its solution, and in general makes an article more fun to read. Your editors strongly prefer first person past tense, and are known to frown on second or third person present tense.

Fly-tying core feature articles. The fly-tying core of each issue will consist of 4 to 6 features ranging from 400 to 800 words long, about a fly or fly style, and specifically instructive for tying the fly or style. These articles can focus on individual patterns, pattern styles, new tying techniques, new and innovative tools, new materials, new uses of old materials, specific imitations, or any other fly-tying subject deemed of sufficient interest to our readers. Emphasis should be on usefulness of the flies; all patterns should be related to an actual fishing situation.

Each tying feature should include a short introduction to the fly and the problem it solves, then should list one or at most two dressings with the materials listed in the order they'll be tied to the hook, followed by numbered tying steps. Steps should usually be limited to from 4 to no more than 8; captions for each step should be 25 to 75 words long. Look at previous issues of the magazine to see how these articles are laid out. Please use barbless hooks, or de-barb them.

Chances of acceptance of a fly-tying feature will be enhanced by the inclusion of handsome slides of the fishing situation the flies solve. If the flies imitate an insect, include a shot of the natural if possible, though we can often find an appropriate picture in our files.

Unless you're an expert at step photography, tie a hook to the level of each numbered step, leave the thread attached, and include these-one hook for each step, plus two finished flies-for our staff photographer to shoot. If you're an expert, include the hooks tied to each step, along with your photos of each step and the finished flies, so our photographer can shoot them if we deem this necessary.

Query letters. Each issue is planned from six months to a year in advance. Queried and approved articles, delivered on time and at the quality expected, find secure seats in the slot to which they've been assigned. Articles submitted without a query cannot be planned, though they might be accepted and then either assigned to a slot or to the waiting list for the next open slot. Your editors prefer to work from query letters, though if your work is not known to us, you can send it in, and we'll give it full consideration.

Each query should cover the following: subject of the proposed article, whether it's for the fly-fishing or fly-tying core, tentative title, brief outline, projected word count, sidebar ideas, and the extent of your expertise-tell us why you're the one to write this article. Keep queries to one page, at most two. If you have photos, send them and they'll help us make our decision. Always include a self-addressed stamped envelope (SASE).

E-mail queries will be considered, but they often print out awkwardly and therefore become strikes against you. Always send e-mail queries as a Word attachment. However, give yourself the best chance by submitting queries in an envelope, with an SASE. E-mail is becoming very undependable; with all the spam received by your editors, it's becoming a 50/50 chance, or even less, that we'll be able to sort out your message as important and open it. If you send us an e-mail and don't hear back, don't assume we've ignored you. Send us the same message by mail, and we'll be sure to get it and read it.

F-L

Round-Up. This news section of FTJ includes short conservation notes, legislative problems, regional issues, happy or unhappy news events, or any other news item related to fly-fishing and fly-tying. Word count is 200 to 800 words, depending on the demands of the subject. Round-Up pieces can be queried or submitted with an SASE. Photographic support makes a stronger presentation; please provide color slides, or call to discuss electronic files.

Photography. With each fly-fishing feature submitted, we'll be looking for one or two strong lead photos, plus several supporting shots. It's wise to submit photos from different views: wide angle, normal, telephoto, and close-up, in both vertical and horizontal formats. The better the lead photos and the mix of photos, the better your chance of acceptance. Use of a tripod is usually beneficial.

Use color slide film, 35mm or 2-1/4", the slower the film speed the better. We cannot use prints. Most pros use 100 ASA Fuji slide film as their standard. A selection of 20 slides with an article is minimal; 40 to 60 is better. Slides should be submitted in 20-slide plastic sheets, numbered consecutively, and captioned at the end of the article. Each caption can reinforce material covered in the article, or better yet mention new information. If people, fly patterns, fish, or insects are in the photo, please identify them by name, and if appropriate, Latin name.

We rarely use photographs submitted separate from articles, unless they are vertical shots sent for cover consideration. Always send an SASE with any photos.

Illustrations. We occasionally use artwork with articles. We'd like to know who is out there and willing to work on somewhat short notice. If you're interested, send a brief portfolio with SASE. We will return the portfolio, but will keep a file of artists to call when the need arises.

Manuscript preparation. Articles should be submitted in both hard copy-printed on paper-and on a 3-1/2" disk or a CD in Microsoft Word. The hard copy should have your name, address, phone, FAX, and e-mail address on the front page. The title of the article should start ten spaces down. **The hard copy must be double-spaced.** Your name, article title, and page number should be on the top of each subsequent page. At the end of each piece, add a short 2- 4-line bio about yourself.

The computer disk label should have your name, title of the piece, the program you've worked in, and whether you use a PC or Mac. **Place all information-text, bio, sidebars, captions, notes-in one file.**

Do not vary your text, headings, or anything: use one type size and style for everything from one end to the other, preferably Times New Roman 12 or Courier New 12. No bold, no underlining, nothing to make it pretty. Simplicity, please!

The package. Every submission, queried or not, should arrive as a neat and orderly package containing the following: cover letter, hard copy of text and captions, disk, SASE, and stiffener to protect the photos and disk.

Payment. FTJ buys one-time rights and pays as soon as possible after publication of the issue that includes your work. Payment rates vary with length and quality of the piece, and the amount of work we have to do on it, or the photos we must buy to support it.

Fun. Please remember in your queries and submissions that fly-fishing is fun or should be, and that we'd like the magazine to reflect that important fact. Direct queries and submissions to the address below.

Categories: Fishing—Outdoors—Recreation

CONTACT: Dave Hughes, Editor
Material: All
CONTACT: Kim Koch, Associate Editor
Material: Any
Frank Amato Publications, PO Box 82112
Portland OR 97282
Phone: 503-653-8108
Fax: 503-653-8108
E-mail: dave@amatobooks.com or kim@amatobooks.com
Website: www.amatobooks.com

Food & Wine

Formal guidelines not available. Please read a number of issues to ascertain the publication's style and needs.

Send queries to address below.

Categories: Nonfiction—Cooking—Entertainment—Food/Drink

CONTACT: Submissions Editor
Material: All
1120 Ave of the Americas
New York NY 10036
Phone: 212-382-5618

The Food Channel

Does not accept unsolicited submissions.

Footsteps
A Cobblestone Publication

General Information

FOOTSTEPS is a 52-page magazine that focuses on African American history and culture for young people ages 8 to 14. We are looking for articles that are lively, age-appropriate, and exhibit an original approach to the theme of the issue. Cultural sensitivity and historical accuracy are extremely important. Authors are urged to use primary sources and up-to-date scholarly resources for their research. And don't forget to make it interesting! FOOTSTEPS purchases all rights to material.

Procedure

Writers may propose an article for any issue. The idea must be closely related to the theme of the issue. Please include a completed query and a SASE. Each query must be written separately.

Feel free to include published writing samples with your query. Do not begin writing your proposed article until you have heard from the editor.

After the deadline for query proposals has passed, the editor will review all submissions and assign articles. We may suggest modifications to your original proposal or assign an entirely new idea. Please, do not begin work until you have received a detailed assignment sheet from the editor.

GUIDELINES

Feature Articles:
600 - 750 words
Includes: in-depth nonfiction, plays, interviews, and biographies.

Supplemental Nonfiction:
300 - 600 words
Includes: in-depth subjects related to the theme. Editors like little-known or offbeat information but encourage writers not to overlook the obvious. Especially interested in the "stories behind the stories".

Fiction:
Up to 700 words
Includes: authentic retellings of historical and biographical fiction, adventure, and legends related to the theme.

Activities:
Up to 600 words.
Includes: crafts, recipes, puzzles, games, and other creative projects that children can do alone or with adult supervision. Query should be accompanied by sketches and detailed descriptions of how activity works and relates to the theme. Approximately 20 to 25 cents per word and payable upon publication.

Photo Guidelines

To be considered for publication, photographs must relate to a specific theme. Writers are encouraged to submit available photos with their query or article. We buy one-time use.

Please note that fees for non-professional quality photographs are negotiated. Cover fees are set on an individual basis for one-time use, plus promotional use. All cover images are color.

Prices set by museums, societies, stock photography houses, etc., are paid or negotiated.

Photographs that are promotional in nature (e.g., from tourist agencies, organizations, special events, etc.) are usually submitted at no charge. If you have photographs pertaining to any upcoming theme, please contact the editor by mail or fax, or send them with your query. You may also send images on speculation.

Note

Write a brief description of your idea, including unusual sources you plan to use, your intended word length, and any unique angle or hook you think will make your article irresistible to our audience (children 8 to 14 years old and their parents and teachers). Queries may be submitted at any time before the deadline, but queries sent well in advance of deadline MAY NOT BE ANSWERED FOR SEVERAL MONTHS. Go-aheads requesting material proposed in queries are usually sent at least several months before publication date. Unused queries will be returned with SASE. Hard copy queries ONLY, no email.

Categories: Nonfiction—African-American—Culture—History—Juvenile

CONTACT: Charles F. Baker, Editor
Material: All
Cobblestone Publishing
30 Grove Street, Ste C
Peterborough NH 03458
Phone: 603-924-7209
Fax: 603-924-7380
Website: www.footstepsmagazine.com

Forester Communications

OUR PUBLICATIONS
• *MSW Management*
• *Erosion Control*
• *STORMWATER, The Journal for Surface Water Quality Professionals*
• *Grading & Excavation Contractor*

MSW Management—OUR AUDIENCE
MSW Management - selected in 1999 by the Solid Waste Association of North America as its official journal - has grown to become the preeminent journal focusing on public-sector municipal solid waste issues. It is well known throughout the industry and at all levels of government, looked upon by all as a fair and viable forum for ideas. Its departments and feature articles are informative, to the point, and readable, even when dealing with highly technical subjects.

ABOUT OUR AUDIENCE
MSW Management's audience is composed of solid waste professionals employed by local municipal governments (city/county/township), regional solid waste management authorities, and their engineers (both outside, independent, consulting engineers and those employed by the municipality). Our readers are responsible for all aspects of integrated solid waste management (source reduction, composting, recycling, incineration, landfilling, etc.). Over 20% of our readers are engineers and since the audience is made up entirely of working professionals in the field, you must assume that they have a high level of expertise and familiarity with your subject matter.

The prevailing perspective and the bulk of interviews, ascriptions, and quotes should belong to MSW managers and staff, or to private sector affiliates performing solid waste tasks. If you find yourself writing about non-municipal activities or people, take another look at the assignment and see if you're headed in the right direction

GENERAL GUIDELINES
Think like your audience. Put yourself in an MSW manager's boots. What makes this subject important enough that you would take

time out from your busy schedule to stop and read the article? Where's the hook? How best to bait it, cast it, troll it, and sink it? When you've satisfied yourself on those scores, you're ready to write.

Engage your reader. Leave no doubt in anyone's mind who you are writing to and why it is important. Rivet your full attention on your readers and drag them into the middle of your subject, address them directly and personally.

Don't shy away from technical aspects of your subject. Make your readers "reach," but never "write down" to them. Aim high in your expectations of the reader's knowledge and expertise.

Also assume that your readers appreciate sound use of language or grammar. If the article is too simple or basic, we can't use it.

Identify yourself as a writer on assignment for MSW Management and conduct yourself and the interview in an open, friendly manner. Think about the article's appearance as you conduct your interviews. How might graphics underscore an important point? What may entice a browser to take the plunge? Gather as much graphic material as possible (photos, charts, illustrations, etc.). The more options our art director has, the better.

As far as rules are concerned, follow the latest version of The Chicago Manual of Style. We have a set of conventions of our own (see the Forester Style Guide), however, we'll apply them as appropriate leaving you to concentrate on more important matters.

If it is your intention to write for Forester Communications, please sign and date where indicated, acknowledging that you have read and understand the contents of this guide.

Name:_____
Date:_____

The above general guidelines have applicability to *Erosion Control*, *Grading and Excavation Contractor* and *Stormwater* magazines

Erosion Control—OUR AUDIENCE
Erosion Control is the premier journal for erosion and sediment control professionals. The official journal of the International Erosion Control Association since 1994, it is the most widely read and highly respected magazine in its sector.

Our audience is composed of planning, engineering, construction, development, operations, and regulatory professionals employed in activities involving erosion and/or sediment control. As the audience is made up entirely of working professionals in the field, you should assume a high level of expertise and familiarity with your subject matter.

The prevailing perspective and the bulk of interviews, ascriptions, and quotes should belong to direct participants in erosion or sediment control activities. If you find yourself writing about nonparticipants, take another look at the assignment and see if you're headed in the right direction

GENERAL GUIDELINES
Think like your audience. Put yourself in an erosion control professional's boots.

Identify yourself as a writer on assignment for Erosion Control and conduct yourself and the interview in an open, friendly manner.

For further information, please refer to the General Guidelines for *MSW Management*.

STORMWATER
Around the world, awareness of the importance of surface water quality is rapidly increasing. The impacts on surface water quality made by society have been made abundantly clear, and you are the person with primary responsibility for complying with the increasing rules and regulations addressing these issues. In the United States, you are probably the person responsible for NPDES Phase 2 compliance and the other significant regulatory and business changes that impact us all.

Before *STORMWATER, The Journal for Surface Water Quality Professionals*, there has been no single publication written specifically for you - the professional involved with surface water quality issues, protection, projects, and programs. Regardless of whether you work for the government, a watershed protection agency, or a private business, a single professional publication written to assist you in your day to day work has not existed before. The need or such a magazine has never been stronger.

STORMWATER, the Journal for Surface Water Quality Professionals. If you're in stormwater, this is your magazine. Each issue, each article, each dot of ink on each page (and each pixel on your monitor) is put there specifically to meet your professional needs. We don't write for all engineers, or every municipal official, or all contractors, or the entire environmental industry. Just those with specific surface water quality responsibilities.

Every interview, every article, every news item, every facet of editorial is focused on various aspects of stormwater programs and surface water quality improvement or protection operations and is edited for that specific reader. This is a practical business journal, edited for professionals with an increasingly complex job to do. We endeavor to assist you in meeting your day-to-day professional responsibilities. With technology advancing rapidly and legislation changing almost daily, the need for STORMWATER is stronger than at any time in the past.

STORMWATER, the Journal for Surface Water Quality Professionals, is available on a complimentary basis for qualified readers.

Grading & Excavation Contractor—OUR AUDIENCE

Grading & Excavation Contractor focuses on the management of grading, excavating, site preparation and earthmoving projects, as well as the equipment and tools involved. Topics include Business Management Methods & Practices, Equipment Acquisition & Maintenance, Regulatory Updates, Insurance & Financial Matters, and other relevant issues. As our audience consists of working professionals in the field, you should assume a high level of expertise and familiarity with your subject matter.

The prevailing perspective and the bulk of interviews, ascriptions, and quotes should belong to participants in grading and excavation activities. If you find yourself writing about nonparticipants, take another look at the assignment and see if you're headed in the right direction.

GENERAL GUIDELINES

Think like your audience. Put yourself in an grading or excavation contractor's boots.

Identify yourself as a writer on assignment for Grading & Excavation Contractor and conduct yourself and the interview in an open, friendly manner.

For further information, please refer to the General Guidelines for *MSW Management.*

Categories: Nonfiction—Business—Environment—Trade: Construction

CONTACT: MSW Management Editor
(msweditor@forester.net)
Material: Submissions for *MSW Management*
CONTACT: Erosion Control Editor (eceditor@forester.net)
Material: Submissions for *Erosion Control*
CONTACT: STORMWATER Editor (sweditor@forester.net)
Material: Submissions for STORMWATER
CONTACT: Grading & Excavation Contractor Editor
(geceditor@forester.net)
Material: Submissions for *Grading & Excavation Contractor*
5638 Hollister Ave., Ste 301
Santa Barbara CA 93117
Phone: 805-681-1300
Fax: 805-681-1311
E-mail: msweditor@forester.net
Website: www.forester.net

Fourteen Hills
The SFSU Review

About Us

Since its inception in 1996, *Fourteen Hills* has held an impressive reputation within international literary magazines for publishing the highest-quality innovative poetry, fiction, short plays, and literary non-fiction. Representing a culmination of one of the best-known Creative Writing departments in the United States, the bi-annual journal is committed to presenting a great diversity of experimental and progressive work by emerging and cross-genre writers, as well as by award-winning and established authors.

Proud of (and part of) the vibrant literary heritage of the west coast and the San Francisco Bay area, *Fourteen Hills* is honored to be an active participant in the contemporary creative community. As a nonprofit press, its staff, editors, and contributors bring readers of the journal some of the most exciting offerings of independent literature-from the postmodern to the traditional, *Fourteen Hills* is a testimony to the fact that independent, innovative, experimental literature is not only alive and thriving, but also overflowing with ebullience, energy, and an irresistible embrace of what comes next.

Submissions

We accept submissions of fiction, short-shorts, poetry, short drama, and creative non-fiction in traditional and experimental styles, as well as camera-ready artwork to be considered for upcoming issues. The editors especially encourage new and emerging writers, while continuing to publish award winning poets and established writers. Writers may submit up to five selections of poetry, and up to three selections of prose or drama; word count may not exceed 4,000 words per piece. Artwork should be camera-ready, and fit the dimensions of our cover design. Manuscripts and artwork MUST be accompanied by a self-addressed, stamped envelope. We accept simultaneous submissions; however, please note that we do not accept unsolicited electronic submissions at this time. The deadline for the Fall issue is around September 1, and February 1 for the Spring issue; please contact us for precise dates. We do not read unsolicited manuscripts from March through July. Response time can be anywhere from two weeks to four months. The Editors strongly suggest that writers interested in submitting familiarize themselves with our editorial style and vision.

Categories: Fiction—Nonfiction—Drama—Gay/Lesbian—Literature—Poetry—Short Stories—Women's Fiction

CONTACT: Editor-in-Chief
Material: All Other
CONTACT: Poetry Editor
Material: Poetry
CONTACT: Fiction Editor
Material: Fiction
CONTACT: Drama Editor
Material: Drama
Dept. of Creative Writing
San Francisco State University
1600 Holloway Ave.
San Francisco CA 94132-1722
Phone: 415-338-3083
Fax: 415-338-7030
E-mail: hills@sfsu.edu
Website: mercury.sfsu.edu/~hills

Freelance Philosophy

Prospective contributors should submit a concise self-explanatory query summarizing the article and describing its highlights. Successful queries include a description of sources of information and suggestions for color and black-and- white photography or artwork. The likelihood that an article can be effectively illustrated often determines its ultimate fate. Photocopies of suggested illustrations with sources are extremely helpful. Telephone queries are not acceptable.

Completed manuscripts will be reviewed; however, they must be double- spaced and accompanied by an SASE. The author's name, mailing address, day and evening telephone numbers and social security number must appear on the title page of the article. Manuscripts must be typed or printed in letter-quality type, double-spaced on one side of standard white 8 1/2 x 11, 16 to 30-pound paper-no onion skin or dot-matrix printouts. Staple or paperclip the manuscript- manuscripts in binders are not acceptable. Authors should include a brief biography, a description of their expertise in the subject matter and suggestions for further reading. Relevant clips are also helpful. Inclusion of an IBM or Mac compatible disk copy of the manuscript increases its chance of acceptance and should accompany a hard copy of the article. Your IBM or Mac compatible disk will be returned to you.

The best way to break into our magazine is to write an entertaining, informative and unusual story that grabs the reader's attention and holds it. We favor carefully researched, third-person articles or firsthand accounts that give the reader a sense of experiencing historical events. We do not publish fiction, poetry or reprints. Manuscripts with misspelled words, poor grammar, weak leads, partial names, unsupported statements or unattributed quotes are rejected out of hand.

Categories: Nonfiction—History

CONTACT: Submissions Editor
Material: All
PRIMEDIA HISTORY GROUP
741 Miller Drive, SE, Ste D-2
Leesburg VA 20175-8920

Freelance Writer's Report

Since its first issue (March 1982), FWR's main purpose has been to help serious, professional freelance writers — whether full-time or part-time — improve their earnings and profits from their editorial businesses.

The bulk of our content is market news and marketing information — how to build a writing/editing business, how to maximize income. But we don't need the basics, like how to write a query letter. It's critical to remember our target audience.

Our target readers — members of Cassell Network of Writers — are established writers. Many of them have published hundreds of magazine articles, several books, and/or worked for dozens of business clients. We are interested only in information these writers can learn from and put to immediate use.

Because FWR is a newsletter and not a magazine, we do not use lengthy, magazine-style articles. We also do not use jumps, so our length is restricted to one page — and shorter than that is even better. Our readers are busy professionals; they hardly have time to read a newsletter at all. So we try to provide only the meat of the information, none of the fat. For example, we like bulleted copy and lists. Because our format is so specific, most of our freelance material is written by our readers—— they know what we've already covered recently and how we want information presented.

We pay 10 cents per edited word; a check is sent along with a copy of the issue in which the item appears. We lease only one-time rights. Because we use outside material for "filling in" the empty columns after our regular market columns and in-house material is laid out, it can be several months before a spot the right size becomes available for an outside piece.

Queries — e-mail or regular mail with SASE — are OK, but because we have more use for shorter material, it usually makes more sense to send in the completed piece. E-mail here is preferred because we don't have to rekey it or scan it. We usually respond within a few days.

For a sample back issue, e-mail your name and address; for a current issue, send $4 to CNW Publishing, PO Box A, North Stratford NH 03590 (the $4 can be applied toward a subscription if you decide to join CNW within 30 days of receiving the isssue).

E-mail queries or manuscripts to submission@writers-editors.com.

Contributor Guidelines for writers-editors.com
We have not yet purchased outside material, but plan to begin doing so sometime over next several months. See our website for guidelines, payment policies, and other pertinent details.

In the meantime, if you have an article or tips of interest to freelance writers or book authors, and would like us to consider posting some or all of them in exchange for mention of your book or website or other item of interest to our visitors, plus links to where people can learn more about your products and services, email Dana Cassell at contributor@writers-editors.com

Categories: Writing

CONTACT: Dana K. Cassell, Editor
Material: All
CNW Publishing
PO Box A
North Stratford NH 03590-0167
E-mail: contributor@writers-editors.com (writers-editors.com submissions)
E-mail: submission@writers-editors.com (Queries or manuscripts)
Website: www.writers-editors.com

The Freeman
Ideas on Liberty

We welcome the opportunity to consider thoughtful articles exploring the principles underlying a free society: private property, the rule of law, voluntary exchange,

individual rights, morality, and responsibility, and limitations on power. We publish both scholarly and popularly written nonfiction articles.

Although a necessary part of the literature of freedom is the analysis of collectivist and interventionist errors, we emphasize the positive case for freedom. We advocate self-improvement rather than compulsory reform of others. We avoid name- calling and partisan, electoral politics. We do not advocate political action as a cure for problems caused by government intervention.

Preparation
• Query before submitting articles and book reviews.
• Articles should be submitted via e-mail, in Word (or WordPerfect) format. Include the author's name, address, telephone number, e-mail address, Social Security number, and a sentence or two that we may use to identify the author to our readers. (If electronic submission is impossible other arrangement may be made.)
• Suggested manuscript length: 1,200-2,000 words.
• Facts and quotations must be fully documented.
• We prefer to purchase full rights to an article, but we will withhold reprint rights at the author's request. By submitting an article, the author warrants that he has unencumbered rights to it and that it has not been submitted, accepted, or published elsewhere. Authors are paid on publication.

Send manuscripts and queries by snailmail or email to the address below. —December 1, 2003

Categories: Nonfiction, Biography (of entrepreneurs)—Economic (Free-market)— Theory—Economy—History—Libertarian—Politics (public-issue analysis)

CONTACT: Sheldon Richman, Editor
Material: All
Foundation for Economic Education
Irvington-on-Hudson, NY 10533
E-mail: freeman@fee.org

Freeskier

FREESKIER is a magazine for, about, and by skiers who love the sport of skiing and the skiing lifestyle. Our editorial focus is everything new school: freeskiing, moguls, terrain park, halfpipe skiing and anything else that is young, hip and fun in skiing. From features on the best ski-town brewpubs to the hottest mountain outerwear, we emphasize the skiing lifestyle as well as the sport itself fin our editorial mix. Readers are skiers ages 18-29, about three-quarters male and dedicated skiiers.

FREESKIER provides user-friendly, service-oriented editorial that speaks directly to our readers — informing them about the sport, inspiring them to get out on the mountains, enticing them to get involved in the new school of skiing.

Most features run about 2,000 — 3,000 words. Departments include Cliff Notes, the front-of-the-book section covering news, issues, humorous anecdotes and anything else related to the skiing lifestyle. Try anything new, funky and short for this section.

Most stories are 250 words or less. We are always looking for humorous, newsy pieces here. Savoir Faire, a regular 1,500 word feature, explores how to do ski towns like a local. Writers must know the towns inside and out. Untameable Terrain highlights some of the most difficult lift-serviced terrain in the nation.

Queries should present a clear, original and well-conceived focus, and stories must be tailored specifically for our audience and the tone of our magazine. While we are always willing to review people's ideas, new/unpublished writers have the best chance by writing for one of our departments. Queries will be accepted by mail or email. Phone queries will be hung up on. If you want a reply, include a SASE — period.

Please include at least two relevant clips with queries. Unsolicited manuscripts are welcome. Payment is negotiable. For a copy of the magazine, send us a check for $3.50 made out to Storm Mountain Publishing.

Categories: Nonfiction—Lifestyle—Recreation—Sports/Recreation—Travel

CONTACT: Patrick Crawford, Senior Editor
Material: All
1630 30th St.
Boulder CO 80302
Phone: 877-LIVE2SKI or 877-548-3275
Fax: 303-449-2427
E-mail: patrick@freeskier.com
Website: www.freeskier.com

French Forum

French Forum is a journal of interest to all scholars and students of French and Francophone literatures. It accepts articles of all critical persuasions on all periods and genres of French and Francophone literary production. Founded by Virginia and Raymond La Charite, French Forum is produced by the French Section of the Department of Romance Languages at the University of Pennsylvania. All articles are peer reviewed by an editorial committee of external readers. The journal has a book review section which highlights a selection of important new publications in the field.

French Forum is available electronically through Project MUSE.

Subscription Information
Triannual
ISSN 0098-9355
Individuals $30.00
Institutions $60.00
Single issue $25.00

For foreign subscriptions please add $15.00. Payment must accompany order. Make checks payable to University of Nebraska Press and mail to:

University of Nebraska Press
233 N 8th St
Lincoln, NE 68588-0255
or call: 1-800-755-1105 U.S. Orders and customer service.

Submission Information
French Forum is a journal of French and Francophone literature. It publishes articles in English and French on all periods and genres in the field and welcomes a multiplicity of approaches. Submissions must meet the following requirements:

4,000 to 6,000 words submit
3 copies (a word count should be included)
Prepare according to Chicago Manual of Style, 14th edition.
Please do not send diskettes

French Forum observes a "blind reading" policy. The author's name should not appear on the manuscripts. Receipt of articles will only be acknowledged if a post-card or an e-mail address is included.

Send a self-addressed envelope and sufficient postage to permit the return of your article.

Categories: Fiction—Nonfiction—Book Reviews—History—Language—Literature

CONTACT: Editors
Material: Articles and books
Dept. of Romance Languages
University of Pennsylvania
Philadelphia PA 19104-6305
Website: www.nebraskapress.unl.edu/journals.html

Fresh Cut
The Magazine for Value-Added Produce

Editorial Focus: Fresh Cut magazine is written for people in the food business who manufacture, sell, use or distribute packaged salads or cut and packaged fresh fruits and vegetables. Articles can be written for actual produce processors as well as retail grocers, restaurant or food service operators, and others who handle or distribute these products.

Article Length: No more than 1,200 to 1,500 words, 1,000 words for guest opinion.

Suitable Articles

Feature stories: Again, fresh-cut processors can be the focus of such articles, but retailers who have had success with specific items or with their fresh-cut section in general and food service operators who use fresh-cut products successfully can also be feature material.

New Technology: Articles can include new equipment, packaging, supplies, processes or other advances which make the world a better place for processors or users of fresh-cut products.

Eating Trends: Time is the commodity of the 90s and articles illustrating how consumers are turning to convenient, healthful fresh-cut produce items are meat for Fresh Cut magazine. Any new and exciting fresh-cut product is fair game. Reports on health and nutrition as they relate to fresh fruits and vegetables and the 5 A Day Program are also of interest. Even information from other magazines can be reported or quoted in Fresh Cut.

Meeting Reports: Speakers who address topics related to fresh-cut produce often relate important news for our readers. Reporting their messages makes excellent copy.

Food Safety: Articles could include sanitation techniques, sanitary plant and equipment design and even keeping the "cold chain" intact to assure optimum product shelf life.

Categories: Nonfiction—Business—Food/Drink—Technology—Produce & Processing

CONTACT: Submissions Editor
Material: All
417 N. 20th Ave.
Yakima WA 98902
Phone: 509-248-2452
Fax: 509-248-4056
E-mail: brent@freshcut.com
Website: www.freshcut.com

Frontiers
A Journal of Women Studies

About Us

Frontiers: A Journal of Women Studies began publication in 1975. The original Editorial Collective chose the title to symbolize the new territories of feminist scholarship and accomplishment the journal planned to explore. Since 1975, however, understandings of "frontiers" have changed. The current editorial staff of Frontiers completely rejects any one-sided, expansionist, and racist use of the term. What we mean by "frontiers" are zones of interaction between two or more different cultures. Following Gloria Anzaldúa, we revision "frontiers" from boundary to borderlands, a concept especially suitable to our interdisciplinary and multicultural feminist purpose. With this definition in mind, Frontiers encourages submissions in all areas of women's studies that cross and/or reexamine boundaries, and that explore the diversity of women's lives as shaped by factors such as race, ethnicity, class, sexual orientation, and region.

Frontiers: A Journal of Women Studies invites you to submit articles, personal essays, photo essays, art, short stories, and poetry Submissions should be sent blind, in triplicate, with a cover letter.

Submission Guidelines

Frontiers is published three times a year at the University of Nebraska Press under the editorship of Sue Armitage and the Frontiers Editorial Collective of Washington State University, Pullman, Washington. The Frontiers Editorial Collective includes Delia D. Aguilar, Mary Bloodsworth, Jo Hockenhull, Linda Kittell, Yolanda Flores Niemann, Marian Sciachitano, Shawn Michelle Smith, Noël Sturgeon, Karen Weatherman, and Amy Wharton. The Collective is joined by a distinguished roster of contributing editors. Frontiers has published feminist scholarship and literary works since 1975.

Frontiers: A Journal of Women Studies is a juried publication committed to the discussion of the full variety of women's lives as they are shaped, for example, by such factors as gender, race, class, and sexual orientation. We seek papers that explore this variety through interdisciplinary scholarly work as well as literary and artistic contributions. We encourage unsolicited submissions. We are especially interested in work that places its topic within a broader literary, historical, political, social, or cultural framework and that argues a thesis encompassing more than a single text or event.

All textual submissions must be word-processed, double-spaced, unstapled, and accompanied by a title page with the author's name. No other page in the manuscript should identify the author. Two copies of the text should accompany the original. One set of visual materials is sufficient and slides are preferred. Art should be identified only by title, medium, and number. A list of all work sent, which includes the artist's name and address, should accompany the submission. Artists are responsible for insuring work, and only copies of originals (35mm slides or black and white photos) should be submitted for editorial review. Most published work will be in black and white.

If you want your submission returned, please provide a self-addressed, stamped envelope with correct postage. Scholarly articles must follow *The Chicago Manual of Style*, 14th edition, for text and endnotes. Permissions are the responsibility of the author.

Rights and Payment

Manuscripts are judged by the members of the Editorial Collective and by readers who have competence in the applicable field(s). This initial process usually requires three months. If the article is accepted for publication, we reserve the right to edit and/or revise it, in consultation with the author, in accordance with our space limitations and editorial guidelines. Contributors receive two copies of the issue in which their work appears.

Copyright for published material belongs to the Frontiers Editorial Collective, Inc. We do not consider previously published material or work under consideration by other journals.

Correspondence regarding editorial matters should be sent to the address below.

Categories: Nonfiction—Alternate Life-style—Feminism—Gay/Lesbian—Hispanic—History—Multicultural—Women's Fiction—Women's Issues—Scholarly

CONTACT: Managing Editor
Material: All
Women's Studies Program
PO Box 644007
Pullman WA 99164-4007
Phone: 509-335-7268
Fax: 509-335-4377
E-mail: frontier@wsu.edu

Fun for Kidz

Every *Fun For Kidz* contributor must remember we publish only six issues a year, which means our editorial needs are extremely limited.

It is obvious that we must reject far more contributions than we accept, no matter how outstanding they may seem to you or to us.

With that said, we would point out that *Fun For Kidz* is a magazine created for boys and girls from 6 to 13 years, with youngsters 8, 9, and 10 the specific target age. The magazine is designed as an activity publication to be enjoyed by both boys and girls on the alternate months of *Hopscotch* and *Boys' Quest* magazines.

Our point of view is that every child deserves the right to be a child for a number of years before he or she becomes a young adult.

As a result, *Fun For Kidz* looks for activities that deal with timeless topics, such as pets, nature, hobbies, science, games, sports, careers, simple cooking, and anything else likely to interest a child Each issue revolves around a theme. You may request a theme list by sending in a self-addressed, stamped envelope.

Writers

We are looking for lively writing that involves an activity that is both wholesome and unusual. We are looking for articles around 500 words as well as puzzles, poems, cooking, carpentry projects, jokes, riddles, crafts, and other activities that complement the theme. Articles that are accompanied by good photos are far more likely to be accepted than those that need illustrations.

We will entertain simultaneous submissions as long as that fact is noted on the manuscript. Computer printouts are welcome if they are (as all submissions should be) double-spaced.

Fun For Kidz prefers to receive complete manuscripts with cover letters, although we do not rule out query letters. We do not answer submissions sent in by fax or e-mail. All submissions must be accompanied by a self-addressed, stamped envelope, with sufficient postage.

We will pay a minimum of five cents a word for both fiction and nonfiction, with additional payment given if the piece is accompanied by appropriate photos or art. We will pay a minimum of $10 per poem or puzzle, with variable rates offered for games, carpentry projects, etc.

Fun For Kidz buys first American serial rights and pays upon publication. It welcomes the contributions of both published and unpublished writers.

Sample copies are available for $4.00 within the US & $5.00 outside the US. All payment must he in US. funds. A complimentary copy will be sent each writer who has contributed to a given issue.

Photographers

We use a number of black and white photos inside the magazine, most in support of articles used. Payment is $5-10 per photo.

Artists

Most art will be by assignment, in support of features used. We are anxious to find artists capable of illustrating stories and features and welcome copies of sample work, which will remain on file. Our inside art is pen and ink. We pay $35 for a full page and $25 for a partial page.

There's one more thing.

Fun For Kidz is a new publication. It is the companion to Boys' Quest, and Hopscotch. Like Hopscotch and Boys' Quest, the issues each revolve around a them. We often choose new themes as the result of a submission on a topic we haven't covered. We work far into the future. If you don't receive a quick response on your submissions, we are holding it and giving it serious consideration. We strive to treat all of our contributors and their work with respect and fairness. We are always in need of cute and clever recipes, well-written and illustrated crafts, riddles, and jokes.

Categories: Fiction—Nonfiction—Animals—Children

CONTACT: Marilyn Edwards, Editor
Material: Any
CONTACT: Virginia Edwards, Associate Editor
Material: Any
PO Box 227
Bluffton OH 45817-0227
Phone: 419-358-4610
Fax: 419-358-5027
Website: www.funforkidz.com

Funny Times

Dear Writer/Cartoonist Person,

Thanks for your interest in the *Funny Times*. We are currently looking for material and welcome your submissions. We are especially interested in written humor columns, interviews, book reviews, stories, and 1-2 page comics.

Here are some guidelines:

• Your submissions should be funny. If it isn't funny, don't bother sending it to us.

• Most of our material is reprinted from other sources or syndicated. We welcome submission of previously published material.

• Our pay rates vary, but in all cases are pitifully small. We pay upon publication. Figure about $25 for a single panel cartoon and $60 for a humor essay.

• We buy one-time rights; all other rights stay with the copyright holder.

• Send copies only, no originals. We cannot promise you will ever receive back anything you send us.

• Include a SASE; if not, you can simply assume you've been rejected unless we call or write you.

• There are only two of us reading these, and sometimes it takes a long time to get through it all. Don't expect a lightning-fast response and don't bug us.

• Send only complete work. No query letters.
Now get to work! Make us laugh!
Sincerely,
Raymond Lesser and Susan Wolpert, Co-editors
Categories: Cartoons—Humor—Satire—Humor

CONTACT: Submissions Editor
Material: All
2176 Lee Rd.
Cleveland Hts. OH 44118
Phone: 800-811-5267
Fax: 216-371-8696
E-mail: FT@funnytimes.com
Website: www.funnytimes.com

Remember: Editors change jobs and publishers change addresses. It is wise to invest in a phone call for the current information before submitting.

Fur-Fish-Game

For more than 70 years, FUR-FISH-GAME has been a monthly magazine dedicated to serious outdoorsmen of all ages. We purchase 150 manuscripts a year. Topics include hunting, trapping, freshwater fishing, predator calling, camping, boating, woodcrafting, conservation and related outdoor topics.

We mostly buy feature articles of a "how-to" or informative nature. We also purchase real-life tales of wilderness adventure and survival. Stories of historic or nostalgic value are also considered, as are unique personal experiences and an occasional personality profile. We buy few "where to" stories and no book, video or product reviews.

We prefer articles with a specific slant or theme that explain how to hunt, trap or fish for species that are popular with the everyday outdoorsman. Articles about trapping, especially those of an instructional nature, are used throughout the year and are very popular with our readers. Other recommended topics include hunting dogs, living off the land, and do-it-yourself outdoor projects. *No fiction*, but will consider humor pieces based on real experiences. It is strongly recommended that writers familiarize themselves with the magazine before querying article ideas.

NO phone queries, please. Written queries need to explain the specific slant or angle that sets the story apart; unsolicited manuscripts may be reviewed at the editor's discretion. All manuscripts submitted on a speculation-only basis, unless otherwise agreed.

Solid photo or art support greatly enhances the value of a manuscript. Photos or slides should be submitted with manuscript and are purchased as a package (although we do buy some photos separately). We prefer color slides, black-and-white or color prints sized 5x7 or 8x10. A variety of photos is preferred, especially closeup shots that illustrate a particular aspect of the manuscript, and overall shots that set the "scene." Hand drawings may help to illustrate aspects that cannot be adequately shown photographically. These illustrations may be redone by our staff artist. All photos and artwork should be accompanied by caption information and the name of the photographer or artist. We do hold free-lance photos for separate use, paying $25 for each use.

Feature manuscripts should be 2,000-3,000 words. Shorter how-to, humor, and human interest articles also needed. All submissions should be typed and double-spaced, with page numbers and author's name on every page. If you prepare your manuscript on a computer and can enclose a 3.5 floppy disk in ASCII format, please do. If you want your manuscript or photos returned, they MUST be accompanied by a self-addressed stamped envelope.

Payment for feature length articles usually falls between $100 and $150, depending upon length, quality of photo support, quality of writing, originality, and importance to the magazine. We may pay more for manuscript packages of particular interest to our readers. Shorter articles generally pay less. FUR-FISH-GAME buys one-time rights to photos and first North American Serial Rights to all manuscripts–no manuscripts reprints or secondary rights considered. Payment is made upon acceptance, and bylines are given. All correspondence should be directed to Mitch Cox, editor.

Categories: Nonfiction—Animals—Ecology—Environment—Fishing—Outdoors—Recreation—Sports/Recreation

CONTACT: Mitch Cox, Editor
Material: All
2878 E. Main St.
Columbus OH 43209-9947

Futures Mysterious Anthology Magazine

FMAM considers itself a stepping stone for many younger writers as well as a magazine with tremendous variety and creative power for seasoned writers and artists. Please consider that many proudly show their family the content and use appropriate language. When in doubt, feel free to inquire. We nominate for the Pushcart Prize Award each year and are honored to do so; profanity will exclude a Pushcart nomination by their own rules.

We accept submissions via email *only*. Save your story in plain text and then insert it into the body of your email message. Do not use attachments - often they cannot be opened at this end. Please get into the habit of checking back here for any new guidelines or just to refresh yourself. Keep in mind that even if you have been featured in FMAM we expect all the information *each* time.

NOTICE: FMAM will be closed to story submissions from June1st to August 1st and November 1st to January 10th each year. This closure is for story submissions only and does not include contests.

FOR ALL WORK Submitted:

Don't rely on your spellchecker; proofread your work! Give your name, address, email address, word count, along with the genre or subgenre at the TOP (we realize it is difficult to categorize many stories, but we want to give YOUR STORY the best chance by assigning it to editors who enjoy the kind of writing you do—and later, if accepted, tempt the readers!). "Include a brief tagline (twenty words or less) telling what your story is about." List these things, one under the other like an address, *not* in paragraph formation.

Under the title of your story please put YOUR NAME as you would like to see it in print.

Include a short third person bio. Limit your bio to 50 words or less (count them). The bio is a flash synopsis of your writing career. For example:

"Mary Writer teaches Physics at Arizona State University and writes fantasy tales in her spare time. Her stories have been printed in many prestigious magazines, including…"

IN ADDITION:

Use single spaced lines. One space between sentences, not two.

After each paragraph, skip one line. This includes dialogue. To let us know that you would like a one line scene BREAK, leave two lines.

To indicate italics, use the asterisk, thus: *word/sentence*. Again, use plain text, no underlining, bold print, accent marks, etc. These look nice on paper, but we are not looking at paper. Type THE END at the end of your story. This enables us to verify that your entire manuscript was received.

Fiction:

Send the entire story. We publish up to 10,000 words on a regular basis.

Non-fiction:

We seldom print non-fiction. If you feel your article fits with the tone of the magazine, send a query telling us about your idea. An example of what we are not using would be how to articles about writing, remember that we want *readers* who are not writers to read your stories, too.

Poetry Submission Guidelines:

Because our editors are scattered around the world, we can no longer accept submissions via regular mail. Please submit electronically to: RCHildebrant@mwsc.edu .Write Poetry Submission on the subject line and paste your poems into the message box. Mark line breaks with a slash / at the end of the line since email programs can distort line breaks. Double space between stanzas. If your formatting is somewhat complicated, please send the poem as an attached file in Rich Text Format. You can save most word processed documents as .rtf by choosing it from the "Save" menu. If I have trouble reading your attachment, I will let you know. See website for poetry guidelines.

Artist Guidelines:

FMAM is constantly looking for new creative people to illustrate our great fiction. If that's you, submit samples of your artwork to: babs@suspenseunlimited.net

You may send hard copies to the address below. DO NOT SEND ORIGINALS. Please always send SASE with proper postage, send a note telling us what you are interested in doing. We can give you a story to illustrate as a trial, just ask if you'd like this opportunity to show us your work.

I will accept email jpeg's if you send me a letter first and I agree to it.

Cover Artwork Guidelines:

All artwork for covers must be done up as CMYK 300 dpi/ppi tif/tiff images only. (DO NOT use RGB at all as this creates a problem with the rich black part of the image). Since we will be using two color covers (RED and BLACK), it is recommended, (by the printer), that you place the design elements on the black and magenta channels only.

Please contact Ardy at ardy@fantaseeworks.net for more information on the process we require.

CARTOONIST Guidelines:

We are actively in search of cartoon artists. Political especially! Life in the modern world, anything to do with mystery. Those and other areas.

Send a query letter first to: babs@suspenseunlimited.net

We want cartoons in a small format: black and white; maximum 300 dpi/ppi jpg; no larger that 5 inches x 5 inches; we will generally want them with a border but there are exceptions; put the artist's name on the left outside vertical line of the border. Please do not use fancy fonts/text as they do not print well.

Ask Babs about payment when you query.

Categories: Fiction—African-American—Alternate Life-style—Arts—Asian-American—Cartoons—Crime—Drama—Entertainment—General Interest—Government—Graphics—Horror—Human Rights—Language—Lifestyle—Literature—Men's Fiction—Mystery—Native American—Paranormal—Poetry—Politics—Satire—Science Fiction—Senior Citizen—Short Stories—Theatre—True Crime—Women's Fiction

CONTACT: Babs Lakey, Publisher
Material: Cartoons
CONTACT: Earl Staggs Fiction Editor
Material: Fiction
CONTACT: Andy Scott, Art Director
Material: Illustrations
3039 38th Ave South
Minneapolis MN 55406
Phone: 612-724-4023
E-mail: babs@fmam.biz
Website: www.fmam.biz

FUTURIFIC

Futurific Magazine

Futurific Inc., Foundation for Optimism, is a not-for-profit research and educational organization reporting its findings every month in *Futurific Magazine*. We highlight positive developments in all subject areas—everything from international affairs, science, technology, and finance, to all aspects of human interest. Emphasis is on accurately forecasting the future. Material submitted, text and/or graphics, should provide realistic forecasts and/or analysis of what the future will be.

FUTURIFIC welcomes book, software, CD-ROM, hardware, magazine, movie, theater, or other reviews, short stories, interviews and poetry providing they follow the guidelines listed above. Copy

F-L

should be appropriate to the subject. Art work accompanying the submission, graphics, cartoons and illustrations are all useful.

Typically, writers retain full rights to their work and receive a number of copies of the issue in which their work appears under their byline. Based on the importance of their story, writers occasionally receive payment for their expenses. These conditions are negotiable.

FUTURIFIC accepts no responsibility for unsolicited queries, articles, photographs, short stories or poetry.

Submissions accepted on 3½" diskettes or hard copy.

Categories: Nonfiction—Agriculture—Architecture—Automobiles—Aviation—Business—Computers—Economics—Education—Electronics—Engineering—General Interest—Internet—Military—Money & Finances—New Age—Politics—Science—Society—Television/Radio—Energy—Public Policy—Technology

CONTACT: Submissions Editor
Material: All
305 Madison Ave.
New York NY 10165
Phone: 212-297-0502
Fax: 212-297-0502
E-mail: Key To NYC@aol.com

The Gaited Horse

Thank you for your interest in *The Gaited Horse*: The ONE Magazine FOR ALL Gaited Horses. We appreciate your efforts and offer these tips to help you in preparing your work for publication. Our mission is to promote gaited horses to the 'rest of the horse world'. Your work is vital in accomplishing this goal, so know that you are important to us.

Since most of our 'writers' are horse people first, and not professional writers, we encourage you to participate in TGH on the basis that you have something valuable to offer your fellow horsemen, and not to worry about dotting the 'i's or crossing the 't's. That's our job!

Again, thank you for considering TGH for your work. We consider that an honor. Should we have to decline your work, we will be as frank and clear as possible in explaining why. Should we accept your story, we will work with you in polishing it to the very best version possible.

Follow these suggestions to present a clear and intriguing story and we will do the rest.

Warmest Regards, RjHart-Poe, Editor

Writers: All gaited horse enthusiasts are welcome to submit articles or ideas to *The Gaited Horse*. We are most concerned with accurate, lively content from those with first hand experience. If you have a good story to tell we can help you turn it into a great article!

Submission: We encourage you to query through e-mail (editor@thegaitedhorse.com). If you do not get an acknowledgment within three working days, please send us a brief note. Occasionally, e-mail messages wind up in space.

Include a brief overview and an outline of the article within the body of an e-mail. State availability of photos. Please do not send attachments. Full manuscripts are also considered. We do not return submissions (or photos) sent by regular mail unless accompanied by a S.A.S.E. (Self-addressed, stamped envelope) ALLOW 2 WEEKS FOR RESPONSE.

Focus: We are looking only for material that relates directly to GAITED horses. Submissions must deal exclusively with one aspect of gaited horses, i.e. adding toe-weight to correct paciness, or on a broader topic that involves gaited horses as the central focus, i.e. evaluating yearlings, including how to pre-determine their gait of choice once under saddle. If you have an idea that seems appropriate, we are happy to help you develop it to fit our needs.

Style: Articles should sound professional and authoritative, yet engaging and conversational. Since we expect you, the author, to be the authority, quotes from other sources are not usually necessary. (The obvious exceptions being profile type stories, or interviews.) Begin with a catchy lead. Divide your story into digestible segments, usually 3 - 4, that can be sub-headed, either chronologically, according to climaxes in the story, or by increments in training, medical treatment or other natural breaks in the article. Conclude, with a paragraph or two that pulls it all together. It is very effective to enter a 'problem' in your opening lead, and show how the content of the article 'solves' it in the conclusion.

Length:
Newsbits /Short news flashes: Approximately 50-300 words.
Departments: 500 to 1000 words.
Features: Full-length features run from 1500 to 2500 words.
Fillers: Brief bits of interest, from one to a few lines.

Photos: Most articles require accompanying photos. Providing these often affects acceptance of a story. TGH requires EXCELLENT photos. Consider these tips:

Unless the story concerns dirt, mistreatment, or some other angle that warrants it, horses should not appear unkempt. Among other things, TGH promotes the BEAUTY of gaited horses, so bear that in mind when choosing or preparing a subject for photographs.

Be aware of the setting of the photo, the background, color and lighting contrasts. The photo must first be high quality and attractive, and secondarily, illustrate some point of the story. No fence posts emerging from the horses belly, no extra legs, no cutting off ears, tail ends, or feet.

If possible, send more photos than you anticipate being used. A good selection, utilizing different angles, backgrounds, etc. is preferable.

Obtain a written statement from anyone in your photos giving permission to reproduce their photo in TGH. Exceptions are shows, public places, public trail rides, etc. where a 'reasonable expectation' of privacy does not apply. *The following is adequate:*

I NAME OF SUBJECT give my permission for YOUR NAME to release my photo for publication in *The Gaited Horse* magazine. Be sure it is signed by the subject and dated.

PLEASE NOTE: TGH does not offer compensation for photo subjects. Rarely do we pay for photos separate from manuscripts. It is the author's responsibility to arrange with subjects any compensation for their photos. Except for professional models, it is very unusual for photo subjects to demand compensation.

Originals: Never, never, NEVER send your only copy of a manuscript or photo to any magazine or publisher for consideration! Sometimes they cannot be returned to you, they may even be lost in the mail. If you do require photos be returned, please enclose a S.A.S.E. and we will make every effort to get them back to you promptly.

Liability and compensation: Submission of material infers that you are the sole legal owner of the material with all inherent rights to it, including the right to allow us to publish it. TGH shall not be held liable for any material which is misrepresented to us. Since many writers are more concerned with promoting their ideas or horses, than in monetary profit for their articles, compensation varies. When payment is required, we offer between $50 and $300 for full manuscripts, including any accepted photos.

Thank you for your interest in *The Gaited Horse*. We look forward to seeing your work!

Categories: Nonfiction—Animals—Outdoors

CONTACT: Submissions Editor
Material: All
4 Cadence, LLC
PO Box 3070
Deer Park WA 99006-3070
Phone: 509-276-4930 -or- 866-320-2233
Website: www.gaitedhorse.com

Game Developer

Game Developer magazine is by game developers, for game developers. No one in this industry can afford to develop in a vacuum. When we share our individual knowledge and experience, the whole industry benefits. *Game Developer* is constantly seeking out articles on cutting-edge game development techniques in the areas of graphics, AI, or network programming, audio design and engineering, art and animation, game design, quality assurance, and project management, written by those who know your challenges best: professional game developers.

Feature articles

Features are generally technical, on subjects ranging from programming, design, project management, art/animation, quality assurance, sound effects, and so on. The length of these articles is approximately 4000 words. Submit an article idea to the editors.

Postmortem

The Postmortem column is a look at a recently finished game you just worked on. Like a real-life postmortem, you talk about the goals of the game, and explain what went right and wrong during the development and roll out of the game. The length of this column is approximately 4000 words.

Soapbox

The Soapbox column, on the last page of the magazine, is your chance to rant on a topic relevant to the game development industry. Don't mince words when you talk about broken technologies, harmful industry trends, bad business practices, and so on. Just remember that there are libel laws! The length of this column is approximately 800 words.

Product Reviews

Game Developer reviews game development tools on a regular basis. It does not review games. If you are interested in writing product reviews, follow this link to get more information. Important: we do not accept unsolicited product review submissions. The length of product reviews is approximately 600 (for short reviews) to 1300 (for long reviews) words.

Also we gladly accept Letters to the Editor

Any views or opinions are solely those of the author and do not necessarily represent those of CMP Media.

The information transmitted is intended only for the person or entity to which it is addressed and may contain confidential and/or privileged material. If you are not the intended recipient of this message please do not read, copy, use or disclose this communication and notify the sender immediately. It should be noted that any review, retransmission, dissemination or other use of, or taking action or reliance upon, this information by persons or entities other than the intended recipient is prohibited.

Categories: Nonfiction—Arts—Computers—Engineering—Games—Graphics—Technical

CONTACT: Jennifer Olsen, Editor in Chief
Material: All
600 Harrison St.
San Francisco CA 94107
Phone: 415-947-6000
Fax: 415-947-6090
E-mail: jolsen@cmp.com
Website: www.gdmag.com

Gardening How-To

About *Gardening How-To*

Gardening How-To is the bimonthly publication of the National Home Gardening Club, headquartered in Minnetonka, Minnesota. As the primary benefit of membership in the Club, the magazine is available by mail only to Club members and not sold on the newsstands. The magazine aims to provide timely, informative, and inspiring editorial content that will appeal to avid home gardeners across the United States and Canada. Our audience of more than 570,000 paid subscribers is 78 percent female, average age 51, intermediate skill level.

Queries

Most GHT articles are written by staff or assigned to writers previously published in the magazine. However, we encourages potential experienced writersfirst-time writers for *Gardening How-To* to submit strong story ideas with a broad, practical appeal to our readers and with an emphasis on the "how-to" approach to gardening. We do not accept simultaneous submissions or unsolicited manuscripts, and we do not encourage telephone queries. Please query first in writing (see below).

Familiarize yourself with the content and focus of the magazine before querying. To obtain a copy of the magazine, write to Sample Copy, *Gardening How-To*, 12301 Whitewater Drive, Minnetonka, MN 55343.

When suggesting seasonal material, keep in mind that issues are planned approximately 9 months prior to publishing.

Submit a one-page query including: a brief summary describing the article idea, purpose of the piece, and its value to readers; your qualifications to write the piece to write the piece and nonreturnable published clips when appropriate writing samples; suggested length and date it could be finished; scouting slides or snapshots (need not be publication quality) if applicable; your mailing address, and daytime phone number, and e-mail address. (if e).

Manuscripts

All manuscript submissions from accepted queries are received on speculation. An accepted query does not guarantee purchase of the manuscript. We reserve the right to reject any manuscript at any stage.

We will respond to queries and manuscripts in four to six weeks. Please allow six to eight weeks for response. Include a self-addressed, stamped envelope (SASE) of correct size if you wish your manuscript returned for return of manuscript.

All manuscript submissions from accepted queries are received on speculation. An accepted query does not guarantee purchase of the manuscript. We reserve the right to reject any manuscript at any stage.

Manuscript Manuscript Format Format

Submit manuscripts in typed form, double-spaced Manuscripts should be double spaced and typed or computer printed. We encourage submission of either a Microsoft Word 97 for Windows file or text file via e-mail attachment (also pasted into the body of the e-mail), in addition to a hard copy via fax or regular mail. First page should Writers must include theirlist your Social Security number, address, and daytime telephone number, and word count. Last page should with all materials submitted to *Gardening How-To*. Please include a list of all resources, sources, and interviewees, including telephone numbers and e-mail addresses, when available.

Payment Terms

We pay $500 to $1,000 for full-length features (750 to 1500 words); $300 to $500 for columns or departments (500 to 750 words). Fees are based on the nature of individual articles, assigned length, and amount of research required. Payment will be made is made upon acceptance of completed article and receipt of an invoice and signed purchase agreement.

Rights

Freelance writers are asked to sign a purchase agreement stating that North American Media Group, Inc., publisher of *Gardening How-To*, purchases First [North?]North American Rights for all works, unless both parties agree to alternate arrangements (i.e., all rights, work for hire) set forth in the assignment letter. No agreement will be considered is final until a signed copy of the purchase agreement is returned to the attention of Mary Pestel, Senior. Editorial Assistant, *Gardening How-To*, 12301 Whitewater Drive, Minnetonka, MN 55343.

Photographs

In general, the *Gardening How-To* staff does not solicit photographs from story writers, as we regularly work with top professional photographers across the country. However, writers should mention the availability of photos they own the rights to at the time of their query or during discussion of story assignment with the editor. Photographers must include their Social Security or Federal Tax I.D. number, address, and daytime telephone number with all materials submitted to *Gardening How-To*.

Guidelines for Botanical Description

In dealing with plant names and descriptions, *Gardening How-To* expects writers to follow these guidelines: The American Horticulture Society's *Encyclopedia of Garden Plants* is the primary reference source for botanical (Latin) names and common names (as well as for plant heights and hardiness ratings). If a plant is not listed in AHS, cite which sources you use. If you prefer a source other than AHS, contact the assigning editor to discuss options.

Unless specified otherwise, include USDA Plant Hardiness Zone ratings for all plants mentioned, preferably stated in a range of Zones: (hardy in Zones 4 to 8). This and other descriptive information (color, height, bloom time, et al.) may be presented outside of text in a separate box, sidebar, or other listing, as determined by the assigning editor.

Following standard nomenclature, italicize the botanical name (*Acer ginnala*). Do not italicize parentheses. Use initial capitals for genus names. Use Roman type for cultivar or variety names, and enclose them in single quotation marks (*Acer ginnala* 'Flame'). Place all other punctuation marks outside of the single quotes.

When referring to a genus with multiple species, use plural: "A low-maintenance border of daylilies (*Hemerocallis* spp.)."

When requested by assigning editor, include other Zone system ratings, for example AHS Plant Heat-zone ratings or ratings instituted by Agriculture and Agri-Food Canada/Natural Resources Canada.

When requested by assigning editor, include metric equivalents of measurements. Measurements should be listed with the U.S. Customary Unit first, then its abbreviated metric equivalent: 10 inches (25cm).

When providing sources for plants and seeds, list correct company name, address, customer phone number, Web site, and other pertinent information as needed. Include at least one Canadian source. GHT editors reserve the right to add or delete sources.

As much as possible, doublecheck that sources will carry the plants or seeds at issue date. Also, ascertain that plants or seeds will be readily available to consumers. Consult the assigning editor when you have any questions concerning botanical description or nomenclature.

Categories: Nonfiction—Gardening—Hobbies

CONTACT: Justin Hancock, Horticulture Editor
Material: Queries
CONTACT: Mary Pestel, Sr. Editorial Assistant
Material: Queries
North American Media Group
12301 Whitewater Dr.
Minnetonka MN 55343
Phone: 952-936-9333
Fax: 952-988-7486
E-mail: Justin@gGardeningclub.com
Website: mpestel@namginc.com

Gateway Heritage

Thank you for your interest in *Gateway Heritage*, the quarterly magazine of the Missouri Historical Society. Please send one copy of your manuscript to the address below. A Macintosh or PC disk with your manuscript and the name of the word processing program you used to prepare it is also requested. Though the magazine no longer publishes endnotes, if notes are necessary they should be supplied and prepared in accordance with *The Chicago Manual of Style*, as we keep them on file and in our library for those who are interested.

Gateway Heritage publishes articles on St. Louis and Missouri cultural, social, and political issues, both historical and contemporary.

Submissions for full-length essays ideally run 3,500 to 5,000 words (not including notes). Gateway also publishes shorter essays in its departments. Submissions for these departments should run approximately 1,500 to 2,500 words.

The Missouri Biographies department features essays focusing on individual Missourians. Submissions to this department often can not (and should not) cover a subject's entire life. Some of the most successful biographical sketches choose one particular aspect of their subject on which to focus.

Literary Landmarks includes sketches of literary figures with a Missouri background.

Our Gateway Album department features excerpts from diaries and journals from the Missouri Historical Society's collections and other collections.

Missouri Memories highlights firsthand accounts of Missouri's historical personalities and events.

In the Collections focuses on the Missouri Historical Society's artifacts.

Finally, At the Society spotlights events and the work of the staff at the Missouri Historical Society.

Not all articles submitted to *Gateway Heritage* are subject to a referee process, but some articles may be sent to scholars or other experts for advice and guidance. In addition, if you are affiliated with a university or college that requires your article be submitted for peer review, such review will be arranged. In any case, you will be notified if your article will be sent out for review.

In general, the editor will let you know within four weeks from the date your submission is received in the office if it will be accepted for publication; if there will be a delay longer than four weeks, you will be notified. Should you have any other questions on our submissions policy, feel free to contact us by mail or by telephone.

Categories: History—Regional

CONTACT: Josh Stevens, Editor
Material: All
PO Box 11940
St. Louis MO 63112-0040
Phone: 314-746-4557
Fax: 314-746-4548

Genealogical Computing

Formal guidelines not available. Please read a number of issues to ascertain the publication's style and needs.

Please query by mail with SASE or email to gceditor@ancestry.com.

Categories: Computers—Family—History—Genealogy

CONTACT: Elizabeth Kerstens, Managing Editor
Material: All
My Family.com, Inc
360 W. 4800 North
Provo UT 84604
E-mail: gceditor@ancestry.com
Website: www.myfamilyinc.com

General Aviation News
The Southern Aviator

Thank you for your interest in writing for *General Aviation News* and *The Southern Aviator*. We do accept freelance submissions for feature stories. All news stories are handled in house, except in rare instances. If you would like to send us news tips, that would be great. Queries for feature stories are preferred and will receive greater consideration than unsolicited manuscripts.

We prefer our writers to be pilots or in pursuit of their private pilot's license.

Stories that work best for us are features on pilots and aircraft owners, restoration articles, Living With Your Plane articles, interesting destinations for aircraft owners/pilots, different ways pilots are using their planes (business, personal, charity, etc.), careers in GA, etc.

What we don't want: Anything to do with airlines or military flying.

Format

We prefer stories to be submitted via email in a word document. Stories should be single spaced with no space between the paragraphs. Do not indent paragraphs. Also, do not double space between sentences.

Space is quite limited in our publication. We prefer stories to be between 700 and 1,000 words. Longer stories will be very difficult to schedule for publication. In that vein, we also prefer short sentences. For example: If you are in the habit of using semi-colons, just put the idea into two sentences. I will probably do it any way.

Put your name as you would like it to appear in a byline at the top of the story in all capitals:

example: By JANICE WOOD

If you have a nickname and would like to use it in the byline, you can put it in quotes:

example: By MARCIA 'SPARKY' BARNES

Do not put your address, word count or anything else on the top of the story. Instead, include your snail mail address in the email that accompanies the story. If the story is used, I will eventually need your Social Security Number for payment purposes. You can submit this to me in the email, or if you prefer, you can call me and give it to me in person or leave it on my voice mail: 888-333-5937.

Payment is around the 15th of the month, following publication (For example, if your story appears in the October 10 issue, you can expect payment to be sent about November 15). We do not pay per word. Each story is negotiated separately. Fees start at $75 and increase as the complexity of the story increases. For example, pilot reports start at $250. However, it is quite uncommon for us to assign a pirep to a writer we are unfamiliar with. I would have to have a track record with the writer before assigning one.

All feature stories require art. Please obtain the art yourself. We run into problems when the subject of the story is charged with sending us art. They usually don't understand the importance of art and/or meeting deadlines.

We prefer to receive digital photos at least 300 dpi. However, prints and slides are acceptable. They can be sent directly to our layout designer, Russell Kasselman, Flyer Media, P.O. Box 39099, Lakewood, WA 98439. Be sure you identify which story the photos go with. Also, if you want the photos returned, let Russell know. It would aid greatly if you send a stamped, self-addressed envelope for the return.

Obviously in the varied world that is GA there are going to be stories and circumstances that aren't covered by these guidelines. Feel free to call or email me at any time to discuss ideas. I will endeavor to get back to you as soon as I can. However, do NOT fax or mail me unsolicited manuscripts. I cannot guarantee a quick response on these.

It is acceptable to email me with a story idea. If I'm interested in reviewing the story, I'll let you know. Once I review it, I will try to give you an answer as to whether we'd like to publish it or not. If the answer is no, the most likely reason would be that the subject matter or style do not fit our publication. If the answer is yes, the story will go into a backlog and will be used as space is available.

Categories: Aviation

CONTACT: Janice Wood, Editor
Material: All
PO Box 39099
Lakewood, WA 98439
Phone: 253-471-9888
E-mail: janice@generalaviationnews.com

Website: www.flyermedia.com
Website: www.generalaviationnews.com
Website: www.southern-aviator.com

Genre

About us

Sexy, Stylish, Compelling Editorial.

The first glossy, mainstream gay publication, GENRE has led the industry by providing an upscale perspective on lifestyle for the gay consumer. Awarded numerous honors by mainstream and gay media outlets, GENRE continues to provide an editorial format of style and substance that is friendly to national advertisers. GENRE's loyal market base of affluent gay consumers has subscribed an average of 5+ years, according to MRI market research.

OUR Mission

GENRE is about how we live. It's a full perspective on living a better life for gay men everywhere, from those in the urban metropolis to those in small towns. Through exciting photography, interviews, fashion, fiction and design, we offer lifestyle choices and stories that encapsulate the options for today's gay consumer. GENRE is "an upfront, upscale and unashamed celebration of gay lifestyle" according to USA Today. We are committed to providing our readers with stylish editorial content as informative and entertaining to the world at large as it is to the broad range of gay men in America today.

Editorial Content

From home design to sports, we write about the things that matter to our unique and loyal readership. We cover celebrities – gay, straight and undecided - but we're much more than a star-chasing glossy. GENRE appeals to a niche segment of the community, the gay male consumer, and we are committed to connecting with that consumer on personal and aesthetic levels. Our focus is on the advance and celebration of the individual. In each issue we present fresh, stylish fashion as well as architecture and interior design through the homes and public spaces of gay men across the country. We cover media and entertainment, health and fitness, the latest gadgets and products, grooming and hot cars from informative, humorous and enlightening points of view. Our travel section features unparalleled coverage of not only exotic international destinations, but of U.S. cities and local regions of interest to the gay consumer. Along with portfolios on artists and photographers, we provide editorial fiction that has won 3 Maggie awards from the Western Publishers Association. GENRE's first rate design, photography and cutting-edge editorial content by the pacesetters in gay culture continues to appeal to a loyal gay readership interested in style, substance and better living.

Genre. Definitive culture and lifestyle for gay men.

Categories: Nonfiction—Alternate Life-style—Book Reviews—Fashion—Gay/Lesbian—Lifestyle—Men's Fiction—Men's Issues—Sexuality—Short Stories

CONTACT: John Mok, Associate Editor
Material: Any
CONTACT: Andy Towle, Editor-in-Chief
Material: Any
7080 Hollywood Blvd., Ste 818
Hollywood CA 90028
Phone: 323-467-8300

The Georgia Review

Published quarterly by The University of Georgia since 1947, The Georgia Review features an eclectic blend of essays, fiction, poetry, graphics, and book reviews. Appealing across disciplinary lines, The Review draws its material from a wide range of cultural interests-including, but not limited to, literature, history, philosophy, anthropology, politics, film, music, and the visual arts.

Essays: We are seeking informed essays that attempt to place their subjects against a broad perspective. For the most part we are not interested in scholarly articles that are narrow in focus and/or overly burdened with footnotes. The ideal essay for The Georgia Review is a provocative, thesis-oriented work that can engage both the intelligent general reader and the specialist.

Poetry & Fiction: We seek the very best work we can find, whether by Nobel laureates and Pulitzer Prize-winners or by little-known (or even previously unpublished) writers. All manuscripts receive serious, careful attention; we try to respond within two or three months, but sometimes the ebb and flow of manuscripts causes delays. We have published stories ranging in length from less than one of our pages to more than 60, and we have run poems of less than ten lines and more than 1,000. Ordinarily we do not publish novel excerpts or works translated into English, and we strongly discourage authors from submitting these. In recent years we have been able to accept less than one-half of one percent of the poetry and fiction manuscripts received.

Book Reviews: In most cases, selection of titles to be reviewed and assignments to specific reviewers are made by the editors, so unsolicited reviews should not be submitted without a prior query. However, we are quite willing to entertain proposals from reviewers concerning assignments they might like to undertake. (Separate, more detailed guidelines for book reviewing are available upon request.)

Artwork: We publish reproductions (color or black and white) of a wide range of artwork: paintings, photography, woodcuts, ink drawings, sculpture, and more. Usually we feature one work on the cover plus an interior layout of 6 to 16 additional works, and our editorial preference is for groupings that display an engaging variety within some overall thematic unity. Submissions should include 15 to 20 original slides or sharp, glossy, black-and-white 5" x 7" photographs.

SUBMISSION OF MANUSCRIPTS:

1. Every submission to The Georgia Review should be accompanied by a postage-paid and self-addressed return envelope. Work previously published in any form or submitted simultaneously to other journals will not be considered. Submissions should be limited (except under unusual circumstances) to one story or one essay or three to five poems. All prose manuscripts should be double spaced. We do not accept submissions via fax or e-mail. If a submission is known to be included in a book already accepted by a publisher, please notify us of this fact (and of the anticipated date of book publication) in a cover letter.

3. Unsolicited manuscripts will not be considered from 15 May through 15 August; all such submissions received during that period will be returned unread. (Our offices are open year around, but our staff is small and needs the summer months to complete evaluations of the manuscripts already received.)

4. Scholarly documentation, if appropriate, should adhere to the format outlined in the MLA Stylesheet (2nd edition).

5. The Georgia Review does not consider book manuscripts. Please direct all such works or queries about them to The University of Georgia Press, 330 Research Drive, Athens, GA 30602.

OTHER CONSIDERATIONS

1. The Georgia Review pays all contributors; the current standard rates are $40 per printed page for prose and $3 per line for poetry.

2. We try to avoid having an extended backlog of accepted works awaiting publication; if accepted, your work would almost always be printed within a year-and often sooner.

3. We are capable of printing high-quality illustrations to accompany essays.

4. The Georgia Review buys first North American serial rights only. All other rights revert to the author at publication, but we offer formal, written reassignments upon request. We ask that whenever an author reprints a work that first appeared in our pages, The Georgia Review be given acknowledgment for the specific work(s) involved.

5. The Georgia Review is produced with the greatest care: we offer a well-designed format, printing on book-quality stock, and durable perfect binding of each issue's 200-plus pages. Our paid circulation is over 5,000, making The Review one of America's most widely read journals of arts and letters.

The best way to become acquainted with any publication is to read its recent issues. We invite you to enjoy and study our pages at your library or-even better-to subscribe yourself (for only $24 per year for four issues-with sample copies available for $7).

Recent contributors include: Lee K. Abbott, David Baker, Will Baker, Kim Barnes, Eavan Boland, Frederick Busch, Rita Dove, Stephen Dunn, Louise Erdrich, Carol Frost, Albert Goldbarth, Mary Hood, Yusef Komunyakaa, Ted Kooser, Maxine Kumin, Philip Levine, Barry Lopez, M. Scott Momaday, Pattianne Rogers, Reg Saner, Charles Simic, Dave Smith, James Tate, John Edgar Wideman, Robert Wrigley.

Categories: Fiction—Nonfiction—Arts—Book Reviews—Poetry

CONTACT: Editors
Material: All
The University of Georgia
012 Gilbert Hall
Athens GA 30602-9009
Phone: 706-542-3481
Fax: 706-542-0047
E-mail: garev@uga.edu
Website: www.uga.edu/garev

German Life

German Life is a bimonthly magazine is written in English for all interested in the diversity of German culture, past and present, and in the various ways that the United States has been shaped by its German element. The magazine is dedicated to solid reporting on cultural and historical events as well as travel information.

Queries/Manuscripts

To suggest a story, send us a query letter (3 or 4 paragraphs) with backup clips of your idea. Keep in mind that we receive numerous solicited and unsolicited manuscripts. Due to the large volume of unsolicited materials received by the editorial office, only queries of interest will be acknowledged. If you wish to verify receipt of your materials, we suggest scheduling them via certified mail or other traceable means. We schedule articles for our editorial calendar approximately a year and a half in advance of publication. *German Life* assumes no responsibility for the return or condition of unsolicited manuscripts, photographs or art.

Each issue of *German Life* is bound by our editorial calendar and seasonal events. Given scheduling restraints, we prefer that you submit your work several months prior to the appropriate issue. Deadlines will be given when the article topic is accepted.

Manuscripts

Your manuscript should not exceed 1,200 words. Longer pieces will be considered solely at the Editor's discretion. Smaller pieces appropriate for a sidebar or one of the magazine's departments should range between 300 and 800 words. Book reviews average 250 to 300 words.

Please ensure that we are the sole recipients of your manuscript. Also, please guarantee your work's originality. Give proper credit for any other author's ideas that you may use. If your article recounts only firsthand experiences, references are seldom necessary. In all other cases, cite the direct source on a separate sheet of paper, following *The Chicago Manual of Style*. Check the accuracy of your items carefully!

Please include: author's name, mailing address, daytime telephone, fax number and e-mail address. Please submit manuscript both on disk (IBM-compatible 3.5 inch) and as hard copy or they can be e-mailed as a Word document attachment. Photographs may be sent in digital form They must be scanned at 300 dpi and can be TIFF or EPS files. We prefer them to be sent on a CD-R, but they can also be sent on a floppy, Zip or Jaz disk. Be sure to convert all colors to CMYK. Please check first before e-mailing any graphics, especially large files. Submit the original(s) (including photos, slides, and/or illustrations), to the address below.

Most manuscripts are published from nine months to two years after acceptance. Manuscripts requiring revision are either returned in original form or first edited and then sent to the author for approval.

Please be advised that all manuscripts at the acceptance stage, including solicited works, are considered on speculation. You will be duly alerted when your accepted manuscript/photo/illustration has been scheduled into an upcoming issue. Payment is upon publication and ranges from $300 to $500 for feature articles, from $100 to $130 for reviews and short pieces, and up to $80 for fillers. In exchange for remuneration, *German Life* retains first English/German language serial rights.

All manuscripts are edited for style, consistency, and clarity. The final title of the published article, subheads, captions, photographs and illustrations, and other elements that attract attention to an article or contribute to the tone and appearance of the magazine are the Editor's prerogative.

Photographs / Illustrations

With or without manuscript, feel free to submit photographs, transparencies, or illustrations that are in accordance with the magazine's direction and style. We look for pictures that capture and/or detail the diversity of German or German-American life and culture, including images of everyday life, landscapes, people, architecture, art, festivals, and so on.

Photos should be black-and-white or color glossy prints, 4x6 or larger, with excellent focus, fine grain, and clear contrasts. Label the back of each photo with your name and caption information. Do not write directly on the back of photos, or ink stamp, or paper clip labels to them. Identify slides by writing your name, the location, and the subject on the margins.

For illustrations, any medium is acceptable. With four-color art, please send 35 mm transparencies. Computer illustrators may submit four-color laser printouts of their work (e.g., maps, charts, and graphs) for consideration. In the case of black-and-white art, we prefer to first see photocopies. However, unless you are (have) a professional artist (available), submit only rough sketches for figures and diagrams. Type captions on a separate sheet of paper, along with any credit lines.

Please note that every photograph or illustration with an article must be credited. A release must be signed by the person or party responsible for object(s) not open to public photography such as special museum items. In addition, to avoid legal complications and embarrassing situations, please alert us to any purchase of your work by other publications.

Include with each submission all relevant contact information, such as the artist's name, mailing address, daytime telephone, fax number, and e-mail address if available. For each photograph, include a description and photo credit on a label on the back of the photo. Please do not submit more than 20 glossies or transparencies at a time. On a separate sheet of paper, include a description and photo credit for each and key to the slides/transparencies. Place slides in individual plastic protectors and in a plastic slide sleeve fit for 20 slides. Send all submissions to the address below.

We rarely purchase photographic material without manuscripts. Please inquire before sending any original materials. CDs or photocopies should be sent if unsolicited. With your permission, we will keep visual materials of appropriate quality and interest for our files. Photographs, slides, illustrations, and sketches are returned only upon request. (Please include a SASE.) Publication of photographs/illustrations depends on need and topic. Effective March 18, 2002.

Categories: Nonfiction—Culture—History—Travel—Special Interest (German)

CONTACT: Editor
Material: All
1068 National Hwy
LaVale MD 21502
Fax: 301-729-1720
E-mail: editor@germanlife.com
Website: www.germanlife.com

Get Up & Go
A Magazine For Active & Involved Grandparents

Please refer to United Parenting Publications.

The Gettysburg Review

Guidelines for Submissions

Published quarterly, *The Gettysburg Review* considers unsolicited submissions of poetry, fiction, essays, and essay-reviews from September 1 through May 31 (postmark dates). New submissions received from June 1 through August 31 are returned unread. We welcome submissions of full-color graphics year round.

The main criterion for selection is quality, but the best way to determine what might be accepted by *The Gettysburg Review* is to read what has already been published. Sample copies are available at $7 each; one-year subscriptions (4 issues) are $24. We strongly encourage all potential contributors to read several issues before submitting.

In the genre of poetry, both short and long poems are of interest, including longer narrative poems. Fiction is generally in the form of short stories, although lengthier pieces are sometimes accepted and serialized, and excerpts from novels have been published. Essays can be on virtually any subject, so long as it is treated in a literary fashion—gracefully and in depth. *The Gettysburg Review* does not reprint previously published material.

Poetry submissions should be typed either single- or double-spaced on one side of the page. Prose manuscripts should be typed double-spaced on one side. Visual artists interested in having work considered should submit a selection of slides with a cover letter. Simultaneous submissions are tolerable so long as authors indicate in their cover letters that a manuscript is under concurrent consideration and notify us immediately upon acceptance elsewhere.

Address all submissions to Peter Stitt, Editor, *The Gettysburg Review*, Gettysburg College, Gettysburg, PA 17325-1491. *The Gettysburg Review* does not accept unsolicited submissions via fax or e-mail.

No manuscript or artwork will be returned, nor any query answered, unless accompanied by a self-addressed, stamped envelope. Expect three to six months for a decision. Please do not query us about a manuscript's status until five months have passed. If you do inquire, we prefer that you send us a note with an S.A.S.E. rather than contact us via phone or e-mail. *The Gettysburg Review* accepts no responsibility for the delay, damage, or loss of unsolicited manuscripts.

Payment is upon publication: $2 per line for poetry and $25 per printed page for prose. Published authors also receive two copies of the issue containing their work and a one-year subscription.

Categories: Fiction—Nonfiction—Arts—Book Reviews—Literature—Poetry—Short Stories—Writing

CONTACT: Peter Stitt, Editor
Material: All
Gettysburg College
Gettysburg PA 17325
Phone: 717-337-6770
Website: www.gettysburgreview.com

Girlfriends MAGAZINE

Girlfriends Magazine

Girlfriends Magazine is America's fastest-growing lesbian magazine. Our mission is to provide its readers with intelligent, entertaining, and visually pleasing coverage of culture, politics, and sexuality—all from an informed and critical lesbian perspective.

The sections for which we encourage freelance submissions are:

Parenting: 600 words from a first-person perspective. Anecdotal, controversial, and challenging pieces encouraged. Tell us what is different about your parenting experiences, your children, or your family structure. Give us examples. Must include two or more photos of you and your child(ren)/family.

Travel: 800 words in main text; 180 word sidebar on "best-of" the profiled area. You must tell us something unique about the area; tell us something no one else could tell us.

Fiction: 1,300 words maximum. All styles considered.

Humor: 800 words; must have some relevance to lesbian readers.

Sports: 800 words; action-oriented profile of a particular athlete, team or group involved in a sport that has some interest among lesbians. Tell us what is unique about this particular athlete.

Spirituality: 600 words; profile-oriented piece on a religious leader or activist that has some relevance to lesbians. Profiles of unusual or underrepresented religions also encouraged if they have some particular meaning for lesbians.

Health: 600 words; essay or how-to article on socio-political health issue (is Prozac good?) or on a particular ailment that affects lesbian women (breast cancer; yeast infections).

Authors are encouraged to query the editorial staff via letter or e-mail before they submit unsolicited material. Please make sure you study the magazine's style and previous articles before you send us unsolicited work. (Note: some book, video, movie, music & multimedia reviews may also be written on assignment; query with clips of work.)

Fees: *Girlfriends Magazine* pays ten cents per word for all written contributions.

Please keep in mind that we use *The Chicago Manual of Style* in considering the editorial clarity of our contributions. It is strongly encouraged that you read an issue of the magazine before you send material in for consideration.

For editorial submissions, we would like copy to arrive on floppy disc, formatted in Microsoft Word for the Macintosh. Traditional and express mail are acceptable. Please allow six to eight weeks for a response.

Categories: Nonfiction—Culture—Entertainment—Feminism—Gay/Lesbian—Politics—Sexuality

CONTACT: Jennifer Phillips
Material: All
3415 Cesar Chavez, Ste. 101
San Francisco CA 94110
Phone: 415-648-9464
Fax: 415-648-4705
E-mail: staff@girlfriendsmag.com
Website: www.girlfriendsmag.com

Girls' Life

1. *Girls' Life* does not accept unpublished fiction or poetry from adults.

2. *Girls' Life* accepts unsolicited manuscripts on a speculative basis only. Send query letters with descriptive story ideas. Please include a detailed resumé and published writing samples.

3. All stories will be assigned by the editors. Once assigned, a memorandum of agreement is to be executed by both parties before payment is made.

4. Every story should have a headline, by-line, introduction, lead, body and conclusion. Author's full name, address and phone number must be provided. Referrals for art sources are appreciated.

5. *Girls' Life* conforms to *The Associated Press Stylebook and Libel Manual.* Please submit in MS Word or similar program on disk. Manuscripts can also be e-mailed.

6. All research must rely on primary sources. Manuscripts must be accompanied by a complete list of sources, telephone numbers and reference materials.

7. Queries are responded to within 90 days if submitted with a self-addressed, stamped envelope. If material is not returned in due time, it has been placed in a file for possible future consideration. *Girls' Life* cannot be held responsible for the return of any unsolicited material.

8. Unless submission is stated to be a possible work for hire, submission will be considered property of *Girls' Life* magazine.

Categories: Children—Crafts/Hobbies—Ecology—Entertainment—Film/Video—Music—Outdoors—Relationships—Sports/Recreation—Teen—Young Adult

CONTACT: Sarah Cordi
Material: General
4517 Harford Rd.
Baltimore MD 21214
Phone: 410-426-9600
Fax: 410-254-0991
E-mail: sarah@girlslife.com

Gist Review

About *GIST Review*

GIST Review is a spin-off of *INK Literary Review*, which was published from September 1995 until September 1998. We decided to abandon traditional publishing in favor of electronic publishing because we believe that the latter allows us to reach more readers and it is also cheaper. Thus, *GIST Review* was born.

SUBMISSION GUIDELINES

GIST Review is a non-paying e-review and we are committed to promote electronic literary arts in America. *We publish all types of works including the following:*

• Book Reviews (between 500 - 2000 words)
• Fiction (between 1000 - 5000 words)
• Poems (maximum 100 verses per poem)
• Literary essays, critiques on culture/society/technology, academic or non-academic (between 1000 - 5000 words)
• Fresh interpretations of great works (between 1000 - 3000 words)
• Artwork/Photography
• Photographic journalism (maximum 1000 words)
• Non-English works are encouraged (especially in Spanish and French)... and whatever else you think we should publish!

We will only accept electronic submissions. Paper submissions will automatically be trashed.

If your works can be found in your personal webpage, we need your permission to copy and paste an accepted work into our own website. The same policy applies for artworks and photos.

Academic essays must follow the writing guidelines of *MLA Handbook for Writers of Research Papers* by Joseph Gibaldi (4th edition).

All submissions are subject to editorial trimming.

We will not publish unnecessary obscene, pornographic or unsavory material that we think may offend our readers.

Publication Frequency: *GIST Review* is published annually.

Send your comments, questions and submissions to: GISTREVIEW@aol.com

Categories: Fiction—Arts—Book Reviews—Literature—Photography—Poetry

CONTACT: Submissions Editor
Material: All
E-mail:GISTREVIEW@aol.com
Website: www.geocities.com/Broadway/Stage/8861/GIST/Home.htm

Glamour

Most of our readers are women between the ages of 18 and 45, and articles that are slanted to our older readers must work for the younger ones as well. As a rule, we do not publish unsolicited short stories or poems. Although we want timely articles, we steer away from subject matter that will seem dated by the time of publication: Stories generally take two to six months to get into print.

We do review manuscripts; however, we usually prefer to see a story proposal first, as we may already have assigned or published articles on the same subject.

"Hear Me Out," our opinion page, is approximately 1,000 words, for which we pay $500-$1000. As the name implies, "Hear Me Out" works best when the writer has a strong point to make about a newsworthy subject. Manuscripts or queries should be typed and double-spaced.

Categories: Nonfiction—Book Reviews—Careers—Cooking—Entertainment—Fashion—Food/Drink—Health—Lifestyle—Physical Fitness—Psychology—Relationships—Society—Travel—Women's Issues—Beauty—How-to

CONTACT: Manuscripts
Material: Queries and Manuscripts
Condé Nast
4 Times Square
New York NY 10036-6593
Phone: 212-880-8800
Fax: 212-880-6922
E-mail: glamourmag@aol.com
Website: www.glamour.com

Glimmer Train Stories

What will readers find in *Glimmer Train Stories*?

Great short stories by established and emerging writers, ten in every quarterly issue. A feast of fiction for the mind and heart, these stories are both beautifully written and emotionally affecting.

What We Are Looking For

Glimmer Train Stories welcomes the work of established and up-coming writers.

We especially appreciate work that is both well written and emotionally engaging. Please let us read yours! If it is chosen for publication in *Glimmer Train Stories*, you will be paid upon acceptance. Your story or poem will be prepared with care, and presented in a handsome, highly regarded literary journal to readers all over the country (even a few in Ireland, England, and Australia). If you've seen *Glimmer Train Stories*, you know that we go to some lengths to honor our contributors and their writing.

See our website for submissions categories (other than standard submissions), which provides specific details on when you can submit work for each category, when you can expect to hear results, how much (if any) is required for reading fees, how much we pay for accepted pieces, and if there are particular restrictions, such as word count limitations. *In all cases*: We are interested in original, unpublished pieces. We don't publish stories for children, and we don't publish novels. Multiple submissions are okay. (You can send more than one submission per competition, if you like, or submit the same story for different categories, if it qualifies). Simultaneous submissions are not okay, I'm sorry. (It breaks our hearts to fall for a story we can't publish.)

We are happy to consider your stories whether they are submitted as competition entries or standard submissions. There are no read-ing fees for standard story submissions. On the other hand, the monetary award paid to competition winners is more substantial than the already tidy $500 payment for accepted standard submissions. All stories are read and appreciated and considered for publication by the same diligent readers either way. So relax and choose the category that suits you.

Note: In an effort to save our backs from heavy mail buckets, we ask that you send all work via our online submission procedure (See our website). It's easy, and will save you postage and paper.

Standard Submissions

Welcome in January, April, July, and October.

We are interested in reading your original, unpublished stories. (We don't publish stories for children, and we don't publish novels.) No simultaneous submissions, please. When we accept a story for publication, we are purchasing first-publication rights. (Once we've published your story, you are free to, for instance, include it in your own collection.)

Dates: January, April, July, and October. Response within 12 weeks.
Reading fee: None.
Payment for accepted stories: $500 for first-publication rights.
Other considerations:
• Open to all writers.
• Stories should not exceed 12,000 words.
• Okay to submit up to three stories per reading month.
We look forward to reading your work!
Categories: Fiction—Literature—Short Stories

CONTACT: Submissions Editor
Material: All
Glimmer Train Press, Inc.
710 SW Madison Street, Ste 504
Portland OR 97205
Phone: 503-221-0836
Fax: 503-221-0837
E-mail: info@glimmertrain.com (for submission questions)
E-mail: eds@glimmertrain.com (for all other questions)
Website: www.glimmertrain.com

Go Magazine

Stories are submitted on spec and publication is not guaranteed. However, should we decide to use an article, our rates are $150 per story, paid after the story runs. There is no kill fee.

We prefer stories to be approximately 750-1,000 words, focusing on travel in North Carolina, South Carolina and surrounding states.

We also request that color photographs or slides accompany a story.

If you are interested, please send us your previously unpublished story to review.

Categories: Nonfiction—Automobiles—Consumer—Travel

CONTACT: Sarah Davis, Associate Editor
Material: All
Carolina Motor Club
6600 AAA Dr.
Charlotte NC 28212
Phone: 704-569-3600

Going Places
Magazine for Today's Traveler

Style: We prefer lively, upbeat stories that appeal to a well-traveled, sophisticated audience. Negative travel experiences are not acceptable. Articles must be original, accurate and up-to-date. An article should appeal both to readers who will travel to the destination and to those who will only "experience" it through reading the story. Only AAA-approved vendors may be mentioned in articles.

Inquiry: We will review your query letter or finished manuscript with equal interest. We cannot comment on each submission, but we will notify you if your material is being considered for future use.

Art: Do not send original slides, unless we agree to publish your article, at which point, original, color slides of good quality are preferred. Please write photo credits on each slide and, to protect them, insert in slide sleeves which have been clearly identified with your name, address and phone number. High-resolution digital images are also acceptable.

Payments and Rights: We pay upon publication. AAA does not accept responsibility for unsolicited manuscripts and photography. Although we do not pay extra for photography, knowing that slides are available may help in the determination of using your story.

Please submit your articles or queries to the attention of Sandy Klim at the address below. If you have any questions, please direct them to the following email address: submissions@aaagoingplaces.com.

Categories: Travel—Group Publishing Services

CONTACT: Submissions Editor
Material: All
AAA Auto Club South
1515 N. Westshore Blvd.
Tampa FL 33607
Phone: 813-289-1391
Fax: 813-288-7935
E-mail: submissions@aaagoingplaces.com

Golf Digest

Rarely accepts unsolicited manuscripts.
Categories: Nonfiction—Physical Fitness—Recreation—Sports/Recreation—Golf

CONTACT: Michael O'Malley, Exec. Editor
Material: All
PO Box 395
Trumbull CT 066113
Phone: 203-373-7240
Fax: 203-373-2162

Golf Journal Magazine

We appreciate your interest in *Golf Journal*, the official publication of the United States Golf Association. We purchase articles from freelance writers on a wide variety of subjects: history, players of the game (both past and present), course architecture, the environment, equipment (of a historic nature), profiles and humor. We do not generally publish instruction or equipment (new product) stories, nor can we publish any stories that could be construed as an endorsement by the USGA, one of the game's governing bodies. Fictional stories are also welcome.

Articles and stories should range from 1,200 to 2,800 words. Payment is negotiated on an individual basis at the editors' discretion.

All manuscripts are submitted on speculation at the author's risk. We accept no responsibility for unsolicited manuscripts, but will make every effort to return them. Stories must be typewritten and accompanied by a stamped, self-addressed envelope large enough to hold the manuscript. Queries should also include a stamped, self-addressed envelope. Manuscripts are usually read and processed within three to four weeks, although processing can take slightly longer during our busy championship season (summer months). If desired, writers may first send inquiries as to the suitability of their subject and approach.

Categories: Fiction—Nonfiction—Short Stories—Sports/Recreation—Golf

CONTACT: Brett Avery, Editor
Material: Any
CONTACT: Cathrine Wolf, Managing Editor
Material: Any

Golf House, PO Box 708
Far Hills NJ 07931-0708
Phone: 908-234-2300
Fax: 908-781-1112
E-mail: golfjournal@usga.org
Website: www.usga.org

The Golfer

These departments are open to freelance contributions:
Sports Fitness: Written with an authority on some aspect of fitness. These stories are usually written with the "we" voice (i.e. We should avoid dehydration.), mixed with references to "players" or "athletes" and maybe the very occasional "you." The goal of this section is to inform, hopefully about something "cutting edge" while trying to avoid making things sound dry and scientific. Usually about 1,400 words.

Chip Shots: Personal experiences are great, but beware the fact that at one time or another most golf writers believe that they have written the first story about someone who has a real passion for the game. Look for the offbeat.

Destinations: First-person travel stories. Approximately 1,000 to 2,000 words.

Categories: Health—Physical Fitness—Sports/Recreation—Travel

CONTACT: Lisa Maxbauer, Editorial
Material: All
21 E. 40th St. 13th Floor
New York NY 10016
Phone: 212-696-2484
Fax: 212-696-1678
E-mail: thegolfer@walrus.com

Good Housekeeping

Good Housekeeping addresses 24 million married women, most of whom have children (anywhere from newborn to college age) and who work outside the home.

Areas of interest covered include consumer issues, human interest, social issues, health, nutrition, relationships, psychology and work/career.

Several sections are especially well suited to freelancers: Better Way, which is comprised of 300 to 500 word how-to pieces; Real Lives, 400 to 600 word features on people involved in inspiring, heroic or fascinating pursuits; and "My Story," a first person or as-told-to format, in which a woman (using her real name) relays how she overcame an especially difficult impasse in her life.

It's best to familiarize yourself with the tone and content of *Good Housekeeping* before you query us. (Back issues will likely be available at your local library.) The most successful queries or manuscripts are those that are timely, appropriately researched, engagingly written, freshly angled, and tailored to *Good Housekeeping* readers in particular.

Manuscripts and queries submitted on speculation should be typed, and when possible, should have clips of previously published articles attached. Please allow 2 to 3 months for a response due to the large volume of unsolicited queries we get.

Categories: Fiction—Crime—Diet/Nutrition—Family—General Interest—Health—Lifestyle—Marriage—Short Stories—Women's Fiction—Women's Issues—Human Interest (dramatic narrative)—Humor—Profiles (inspirational, real people)

CONTACT: Submissions Editor
Material: All
959 - 8th Ave.
New York NY 10019
Phone: 212-649-2260
Fax: 212-265-3307

Good Old Days
Good Old Days Specials

Guidelines:

Manuscripts should be typed (preferably double-spaced) with the author's name, address and phone number in the upper left-hand corner. We prefer to buy all rights, but will negotiate. If you cannot offer all rights, you must specify the type of rights you are offering when submitting your manuscript. Please submit only one manuscript at a time. We do accept e-submissions via e-mail, but treat them as unsolicited manuscripts without SASE; you will only hear from us if we offer a contract for your story.

Our preferred word length is 500-1500 words. Please indicate whether or not photos are available. You may include photocopies or duplicates of your photos with your manuscript, but please do not include your originals. If we need the originals or photographic copies, we will ask for them. Do not send scanned or laser-copied photos; the quality isn't high enough for use. Identify the backs of photos with your name, address and story title. Manuscripts should include captions of complete information concerning the photographic material you are submitting.

Payment

Payment generally ranges from $15-75 and is dependent on how much of the manuscript will actually be used (don't assume that your 3,000 word document will be paid on the basis of pre-edited weight), how much editing will be required and what photographic support you have. Please enclose an SASE if you want your material returned. Sample copies: $2.00 and a self-addressed stamped manila envelope.

Good Old Days tells the real stories of the people who lived and grew up in "the good old days" (about 1900-1955). We like stories to sound conversational, as if you're sitting around the fire and Grandpa's telling you about the time he and Grandma got shivareed. However, we are open to any way you choose to write your story, as long as it is true and falls within our targeted period of time.

Subject Matter

These regular departments are in each issue: *Good Old Days* on Wheels (transportation: auto, plane, horse-drawn, train, bicycle, trolley, etc.), *Good Old Days* in the Kitchen (favorite foods, appliances, ways of cooking, recipes), Home Remedies (herbs and poultices, hometown doctors, harrowing kitchen table operations) and Looking Hollywood Way (this feature is written by a regular columnist and pretty much fulfils the quota of movie related features).

If your story is about how you remember Mom boiling handkerchiefs with her homemade lye soap, include how she made the soap! If Grandma's secret recipe for baking powder biscuits made you drool at the very thought, include the recipe!

We accept seasonal stories year 'round, from holidays to harvest, shivarees to maple-sugaring. We look for real stories; happy, sad, the good, the bad. Humor is always a plus. Good, clear, interesting old photos are a definite plus. We also purchase interesting old photos alone, with about a paragraph of caption material describing what is pictured.

Most of our writers are not professionals. We prefer the author's individual voice, warmth, humor and honesty over technical ability. Successful stories tend to stick with one subject (i.e.: how my brother and I got caught skipping school one day and faced the consequences...how I love to cook on a wood-burning stove, etc.). We also publish an occasional biography, as well as stories on memorable events, fads, fashion, sports, music, literature, entertainment, etc. Many people write a story "as told to" by the person who actually experienced it. But never, never try to pull the wool over our eyes with fiction or non-authentic manuscripts.

Good Old Days Specials

Good Old Days Specials is a bimonthly publication with basically the same story requirements of *Good Old Days*.

We receive about 200 manuscripts a month and can only offer contracts on a limited number. Therefore, we must return a lot of good stories. The mark of a good free-lance writer is persistence; be sure to keep trying! Thank you for your interest in contributing material to *Good Old Days* and *Good Old Days Specials*.

Categories: Automobiles—Cooking—Film/Video—Food/Drink—Health

CONTACT: Ken Tate, Editor
Material: All
House of White Birches
306 East Parr Rd.
Berne IN 46711
Phone: 260-589-4000
Website: www.goodolddaysonline.com

The Good Red Road

Our Focus: Our primary goal is to support and assist teachers and the American Public in their understanding and portrayal of the Native American peoples of North America. We are interested in articles that explore the beliefs, history or political concerns of these people.

Submissions: We need articles, interviews, book reviews, stories, poetry, artwork, black and white photos, my stories, self-help and how-to articles, humorous pieces and other interesting works.

Lead articles should be 800-2000 words and all other pieces should be under 1500 words. The shorter the better. We love how-to articles and interviews of authors. ALWAYS INCLUDE A WORD COUNT! If mailing in the submission, include a SASE or your material will not be answered or returned. Include research citations.

We only ask for one-time rights and will accept reprints if you write verifying where the piece was published and what rights they purchased. If your work is published in the print newsletter, you will receive contributor copies as payment. At this time we cannot pay for print or web work.

The newsletter does accept advertising. Write to the below address for advertising information.

Categories: Fiction—Nonfiction—Arts—Book Reviews—History—Interview—Native American—Poetry—Politics—Religion—Spiritual

CONTACT: Terri J. Andrews, Editor
Material: All
PO Box 1127
Athens OH 45701-1127
Phone: 614-664-3030
E-mail: tuqbutfy@hotmail.com
Website: fly.to/turquoisebutterfly

Gourmet

Formal guidelines not available. Please read a number of issues to ascertain the publication's style and needs.

Send queries to address below.

Categories: Nonfiction—Cooking—Entertainment

CONTACT: Shannon Rodgers, Editorial Dept.
Material: All
4 Tiems Square
New York NY 10036
Phone: 212-286-2860

Government Executive

Government Executive, a publication of National Journal Group Inc., is a monthly business magazine serving executives and managers in the federal government. Our 60,000 subscribers are high-ranking civilian and military officials who carry out the laws that define the government's role in our economy and society.

Government Executive aspires to serve the people who manage these huge agencies and programs much in the way that Fortune, Forbes and Business Week serve private-sector managers.

Editorial goals include:

Covering news and trends about the organization and management of the executive branch; Helping federal executives improve the quality of their agencies' services by reporting on management innovations; Explaining government problems and failures in ways that offer lessons about pitfalls to avoid; Creating a greater sense of community along the elite corps of public servants to whom the magazine circulates; Improving the image of the public service by teaching our non-government readers about the challenges federal officials confront.

Government Executive has twice won the Gerald R. Ford Prize for Distinguished Reporting on National Defense, in 1990 and 1995.

TYPES OF ARTICLES WE PUBLISH

Feature Stories

These usually range in length from 1,500 to 4,000 words. Any sidebars must be figured into the total word count. Feature stories fall into these general categories:

Management issues

These focus on topics of broad interest and include reporting from several agencies. Topics could include downsizing of agencies; reinventing government; recruitment and retention; ensuring that computers succeed in improving productivity; and upgrading training.

Agencies

These stories often focus on one agency with an eye toward finding generally applicable lessons for federal managers. For example, one story assessed the change in NASA's culture as the agency handed off operation of the space shuttle to a private firm.

Government people

Some articles are organized around certain professions within government. For example, we've written about the influence of economists on policy-making, how to make the best use of agency lawyers, and how to recruit and retain a good clerical work force.

Civil service issues

These include articles about pay, executive training, ethics, politicization of the civil service and the impact of technology on the workplace.

Guest Columns

Our Management and Viewpoint columns are good forums for members of our audience to share an opinion or their experiences. Management columns should include advice that would be useful to managers in a variety of fields. Viewpoint columns express opinions on issues relevant to civil servants. These columns are usually about 1,000 words long.

Other Departments

These are usually 1,000 words or 1,700 words, except as noted. Monthly departments for which we sometimes use freelance contributions include: Executive Memo: A series of short news items, 100-200 words each. Travel: On government/business travel. Information Technology: government applications of computer technologies.

OUR CONTRIBUTORS

Following are some guidelines for different categories of would-be contributors:

• Professional journalists
• These may be full-time freelance writers or employees of other publications. We look for people who have expertise in civil-service issues or the management of federal agencies.
• Current or former federal employees
• We publish personal reflections on the problems and opportunities of public service, as well as analytical articles on the causes and solutions of real-life agency problems. However, we often prefer to assign stories suggested by government officials to writers outside of government. We think independent reporting and analysis often lends credibility to an article.
• Consultants, corporate executives, public relations representatives
We shy away from articles that seem to be aimed at promoting the fortunes of any individual, product, or program. We almost never publish articles submitted by or on behalf of companies or trade associations.

HOW TO GET AN ASSIGNMENT

We prefer to receive queries about possible assignments in the form of a one- or two-page letter that lays out the subject you want to write about, the angle you will take and the sources you will interview. The letter should also detail any relevant experience you have. If you do send us a completed manuscript, be warned that deadline pressure often prevents us from considering or returning unsolicited manuscripts in a timely manner. We do not object if you submit a piece to other publications simultaneously. We do not return unsolicited manuscripts.

STORY SUBMISSION CHECKLIST

Stories may be submitted via e-mail or on floppy disk. Along with your manuscript, please include:

Art memo

Your written list of ideas for graphics may include portraits of your major sources, other photographs, cartoons and illustrations. We especially like to run charts, tables and graphs, so keep any eye out for information relevant to your story that could be presented that way. Please provide us with the contacts we need to arrange to shoot or obtain photographs.

Author bio

At the end of the story, please include a one to two sentence description of your professional background.

Contract

The first time you write for us, you must sign a contract stating that you will pay income taxes on your fees. If you have never signed such a contract, please request one when you submit your story.

WHAT HAPPENS NEXT?

Rewriting

We may ask for a second draft of a story, particularly if you haven't written for us before.

Accuracy checks

We expect you to check all names, titles, dates and facts for accuracy before your story is submitted. However, we always send an edited version of the story back to you so that you may check that no errors have crept in during the editing process.

Payment

We pay upon acceptance, which means after you have completed any requested rewriting or additional billtracker to our satisfaction. Please submit an invoice for the amount agreed upon at the time the story was assigned.

Copyright

Government Executive holds all rights for publication (including publication on the World Wide Web) and all reprint rights.

Categories: Nonfiction—Business—Government—Politics

CONTACT: Timothy Clark, Editor and Publisher
Material: All
1501 M St. NW Ste. 300
Washington DC 20005
Phone: 202-739-8500
Fax: 202-739-8511
E-mail: govexec@govexec.com
Website: www.govexec.com

Grading & Excavation Contractor

Please refer to Forester Communications.

Grain

*A choice Canadian
literary magazine since 1973*

Grain's Beginnings

Grain magazine published its first issue in June 1973, a gestetner edition with stapled, taped bindings, and with cover art on a card-stock cover by a then new artist Joe Fafard. The first edition, edited by Ken Mitchell, Anne Szumigalski, and Caroline Heath included writings by Robert Kroetsch, George Bowering, Robert Currie, and John V. Hicks, and cost $1.00. A subscription cost $2 a year, or $5 for three years. This was the first of a series of semi-annual issues.

Grain is a quarterly publications.

Throughout all these years, *Grain* has published the best new writing from Canada and abroad, approximately 2000 pieces of writing and over 220 art images, many of them from Saskatchewan. *Grain* editors over the years have been: Ken Mitchell, Caroline Heath, E.F. Dyck, Brenda Riches, Mick Burrs, Geoffrey Ursell, J. Jill Robinson, and currently, Kent Bruyneel.

Grain has grown up with a generation of literary magazines, and is proud to be alive and flourishing after nearly 30 years of life. This flourish is due to the readers, and contributors, but also to primary funding sponsors: Saskatchewan Writers Guild (publisher-in-chief), Sask Lotteries, Saskatchewan Arts Board, The Canada Council and The Canada Magazine Fund.

Submitting to Grain

Grain Magazine is an internationally acclaimed literary journal, publishing the freshest poetry and prose from Canada, the US, and abroad.

If you are interested in submitting your work to *Grain*, take a look at the following

Submission Guidelines. If possible, read back issues of our magazine before submitting. Sample issues of *Grain* are available for $9.95 (plus GST in Canada) or $12.00 US for American and International orders. If you'd like to order a copy, go to the go to the Subscription section of our web site.

Grain has a ten-month reading period. During June and July manuscripts will be automatically returned to writers.

E-mail submissions are not accepted. *Grain* will respond to submissions via e-mail, if submittors provide us with an e-mail address, but submissions must be sent via snail-mail.

The Manuscript

Send typed, unpublished material only. The simultaneous submission to *Grain* of material submitted to other publications is not acceptable.

Poetry: You may submit a maximum of 8 poems.

Fiction: Submit a maximum of 2 stories, or up to 30 pages of a novel-in-progress.

Other: Although fiction and poetry are the main focus of *Grain*, the editors will also consider creative non-fiction, and drama.

Do not send your only manuscript copy. A good quality, fully-legible duplicate copy is fine. Use 8 1/2 x 11 paper, one side only. Poetry may be single-spaced; fiction, double spaced; plays, standard play format. All copy must be typewritten.

Type your name and full address on the title page or first page of each work. On subsequent pages, type your last name and the abbreviated title of the piece.

Number every page of a poem or story other than the first page. Use paper clips only. No staples.

Please do not send a second submission until the *Grain* editors have completed consideration of your first one.

Grain receives more than 150 submissions a month. The editors need 2 to 4 months to consider your submission.

Submit Art Work

Artwork submissions should consist of:
- 12 to 20 slides, and black & white prints if available
- A short artist's statement (up to 200 words)
- A brief resume.

The Covering Letter

Indicate the number of poems, stories, or visual images submitted. Include your full address, postal code and phone number (with area code).

Mailing

A stamped, self-addressed envelope (SASE) is required for any response. We will not consider or return any material without this.

Submissions from outside Canada require sufficient International Reply Coupons to cover return postage. Foreign stamps are not valid in Canada for mailing out.

NEW: Save your IRC's and stamps! Provide an e-mail address, and we will respond to your submission electronically, as long as you don't need your manuscript returned. (But we still don't take e-mail submissions—sorry!)

Payment

Poetry: $40 to $175 (depending on number of pages published).
Fiction, and Other: $ 40 to $175.
Front Cover Art: $100.
Other Art: $30 per image.

Rights

Grain purchases first Canadian serial rights only. Copyright remains with the author or artist.

If you have any further questions about our Submission Guidelines, don't hesitate to contact us at: grainmag@sasktel.net.

Categories: Literature—Poetry

CONTACT: Kent Bruyneel, Editor
Material: Grain Submissions
CONTACT: Gerry Hill, Poetry Editor
Material: Poetry
CONTACT: Joanne Gerber, Prose Editor
Material: Prose
PO Box 67
Saskatoon Saskatchewan, Canada S7K 3K1
E-mail: grainmag@sasktel.net
Website: www.grainmagazine.ca

Grand Times

Does not accept unsolicited submissions.

Gray Areas

We do not print fiction, poetry or short stories. We have no word count limits and prefer depth to fluff.

We explore gray areas of law and morality in the fields of law, music, technology, sociology and popular culture.

We print all points of view and run articles by active criminals, academics, victims, law enforcement, psychiatrists and ordinary citizens.

We also review books, movies, computer software, video games, concerts, comics, catalogs, music CDs, small press magazines and more.

Categories: Alternate Life-style—Book Reviews—Crime—Culture—Film/Video—Internet—Law—Music—Society

CONTACT: Netta Gilboa, Publisher
Material: All
PO Box 808
Broomall PA 19008
Website: www.grayarea.com

F-L

The Green Hills Literary Lantern
Truman State University

Fiction

The *Green Hills Literary Lantern* is published annually, each summer, by Truman State University. Website: http://ll.truman.edu/ghllweb. It includes poetry, fiction, reviews, and interviews. The publication runs 200-300 pages. It is printed on good quality paper with a glossy 4-color cover. For the past several issues, it has received grants from the Missouri Arts Council.

We respond to work in 3-4 months. When submitting manuscripts, please send a short bio listing publications (50 - 100 words). We accept simultaneous submissions but discourage multiple submissions, though 2 - 3 "short shorts" are acceptable. Please send an SASE for return of manuscript or for reply only. Please include a phone number on manuscript where we can reach you.

This magazine is open to the work of new writers as well as more established writers. We are interested in stories that demonstrate a strong working knowledge of the craft. Avoid genre fiction or mainstream religious fiction. Otherwise, we are open to short stories of various settings, character conflicts, and styles, including experimental.

Above all, we demand that work be "striking." Language should be complex, with depths, through analogy, metaphor, simile, understatement, irony, etc. - but all this must not be overwrought, or self-consciously literary. This does not mean that in rare cases, style itself cannot be center stage, but if so, it must be interesting and provocative enough for the reader to focus on style alone. "Overdone" writing surely is not either.

We tend to be interested in stories with strong character, with conflicts that matter (where the stakes are fairly high), and with stories that do not have simple resolutions. Stories that go nowhere, that get blurred in focus, or that seem thin in idea have little chance of being accepted for publication.

We accept short stories, short shorts, and excerpts from novels. Our maximum length is 7,000 words. In rare cases, we'll accept a longer story. There is no absolute minimum.

If work is accepted, author will receive prepublication galleys. Publication is copyrighted. We purchase one-time rights.

Poetry

Submit 3-7 poems, typed, one poem per page. There are no restrictions on subject matter, though pornography and gratuitous violence will not be accepted. Obscurity for its own sake is also frowned upon. Both free and formal verse forms are fine, though we publish more free verse overall. Poems of under six lines or over two pages are unlikely to be published. A genuine attempt is made to publish the best poems available, no matter who the writer. First time poets, well-established poets, and those in-between, all can and have found a place in the GHLL. A cover letter is appreciated but not required. We try to respond within 3-4 months, if not sooner. We try to supply feedback, particularly to those we seek to encourage.

Categories: Fiction—Book Reviews—Interview—Poetry

CONTACT: Joe Benevento, Co-Editor
Material: All Poetry
Truman State University, Division of Language & Literature
Kirksville MO 63501
Phone: 660-785-4513
Fax: 660-359-2211
E-mail: Jbeneven@truman.edu
E-mail: JackGHLL@earthlink.net
CONTACT: Jack Smith, Co-Editor
Material: All Fiction
PO Box 375, Trenton, MO 64683
Website: ll.truman.edu/ghllweb

Green Mountains Review
Johnson State College

The GREEN MOUNTAINS REVIEW is an international journal publishing poems, stories, and creative nonfiction by both well-known authors and promising newcomers. The magazine also features interviews, literary criticism, and book reviews.

The editors are open to a wide range of styles and subject matter as is apparent from a look at the short list of writers who have published in its pages: Julia Alvarez, John Ashbery, Hayden Carruth, Billy Collins, Stephen Dobyns, Mark Doty, Stephen Dunn, Carol Emshwiller, Linda Gregg, Donald Hall, Maxine Kumin, Denise Levertov, Larry Levis, Phillip Lopate, Dionisio D. Martinez, William Matthews, Naomi Shihab Nye, Lynne Sharon Schwartz, Ntozake Shange, Reginald Shepard, Alix Kates Shulman, David St. John, Walter Wetherell, and Meredith Sue Willis.

Past issues have included interviews with writers such as Galway Kinnell, Grace Paley, and Derek Walcott, as well as literary essays such as David Wojahn's on memory narrative poetry and David Mura's on multicultural writing.

There have been several special issues: one devoted to Vermont fiction writers, a second called "Women, Community, and Narrative Voice" featuring short stories by women, a third filled with new writing from the People's Republic of China, a fourth devoted to multicultural writing in America, and another featuring contemporary comic poetry.

The editors read manuscripts between September 1 and March 1. During that period they will make every attempt to respond within three months. Manuscripts received outside the reading period will be returned unread.

Categories: Fiction—Nonfiction—Literature—Poetry

CONTACT: Neil Shepard, General Editor
Material: Poetry, Essays, Interviews
CONTACT: Tony Whedon, Fiction Editor
Material: Fiction
Johnson State College
Johnson VT 05656
Phone: 802-635-1350

Greensboro Review
University of North Carolina—Greensboro

• No previously published works, works accepted for publication, or dual submissions are eligible.

• Poetry may be any length; maximum length for fiction is 7,500 words.

• All manuscripts must be typed and accompanied by a self-addressed, stamped envelope for return.

• All manuscripts must arrive by September 15 to be considered for the Spring issue (acceptances in December) and February 15 to be considered for the Fall issue (acceptances in May). Manuscripts arriving after those dates will be held for the next consideration.

Categories: Fiction—Poetry

CONTACT: Poetry Editor
Material: Poetry

CONTACT: Fiction Editor
Material: Fiction
UNCG English Department
134 McIver Bldg., PO Box 26170
Greensboro NC 27402-6170
Phone: 336-334-5459
Fax: 336-256-1470
E-mail: jlclark@uncg.edu

GRIT

Grit Magazine

WHO WE ARE

Grit, America's family magazine since 1882, is dedicated to ringing the joy bells of life for its readers. We publish items about ordinary people doing extraordinary things, accounts of interesting places or events, and real-life stories about others in the GRIT family.

We tailor our magazine to provide an informative, yet entertaining, look at life in America, past and present. GRIT explores values, lifestyles and traditions important to those concerned about themselves, their families and their communities.

GRIT focuses not on age or abilities, but on attitude—taking a positive approach to the goodness of life. GRIT celebrates our readers' courage, dedication and determination to make a difference.

GRIT gladly accepts reader contributions and freelance materials appropriate for publication. See tips below. The best inside tip is to read several issues of GRIT. Copies are available by subscription, or by requesting a sample copy directly from GRIT at the address shown below.

The best inside tip is to read several issues of GRIT. Copies are available by subscription, 800-678-4883, or by requesting a sample copy from address below. For single copies, please enclose $4 for postage and handling, plus a stamped, self-addressed 9"x12" envelope. Writers guidelines are free with a SASE.

FEATURES

GRIT publishes feature-length articles (1,200-1,500 words) about topics important to today's families: American values and quality of life; outstanding people and interesting places; parenting and grandparenting; home and garden; arts and crafts; American history and traditions; family lifestyles; community involvement or service; family-oriented media and movies; Americana and nostalgia; antiques and collectibles, and travel. Submit manuscripts to the editor-in-chief on speculation, for review, color photos (original negatives and slides preferred) or black-and-white nostalgia photos. Photos are required for manuscripts to be considered. We buy only upon publication, therefore, no updates or advance commitments can be given.

FICTION & POETRY

GRIT regularly publishes historical, mystery, Western and romance serials (up to 15,000 words in 1,200-word installments with cliffhangers) and short fiction (1,000-2,000 words). Stories should emphasize the positive aspects of American life. Paid on acceptance.

GRIT prints unpublished free verse, light verse, traditional, nature and inspirational poems that are easy to read, with down-to-earth themes. Limit poetry submissions to batches of five or less, length 4-16 lines each. $10 or $15, paid on acceptance.

PHOTOS

GRIT expects professional quality color and black-and-white negatives, slides, transparencies or prints. Original negatives and slides are preferred. Be sure to label each submission with your name, address and telephone number and include caption information. Photos are required for manuscripts to be considered.

SUBMISSIONS & PAYMENT

Payment is on publication. No assignments or guarantees of publication are expressed or implied. GRIT assumes no responsibility for any material that is not returned or is lost or damaged.

Generally, the standard rate of payment for nonfiction feature-length articles, upon publication, is 15 to 22 cents per published word and $35 to $50 per original published photograph. However, when articles are used in departments or department features, the author is paid a discretionary flat rate according to length, placement and overall value to the magazine.

TIPS FOR CONTRIBUTORS

The best education is reading several issues of GRIT for types and subjects of stories we use, and our style;

Include the names and telephone numbers of all sources for fact-checking. Identify sources fully, including their credentials, titles or reasons they are qualified to comment, and provide full references for any publications used as sources.

Articles should have national appeal. Information in sidebar or graph form is appropriate for many stories: lists of tips, resources or questions to help readers better understand the subject. For travel stories, include tips such as prices, how to get there, where to stay, etc.

HOW DO I SUBMIT SOMETHING TO GRIT?

• Include your full name, address, telephone number, social security number and submission title on each page. Also send a brief synopsis of your submission, a short personal biography and several clips of any previously published works in your dated cover letter.

• Manuscripts must be accompanied by suitable photos to be considered.

• Submit double-spaced, typed manuscripts. If possible, submit the same material on a 3.5-inch Macintosh disk. Keep a copy of your work and send only completed, proofread manuscripts, including photos. GRIT is not responsible for the return of any materials. GRIT does not consider submissions made simultaneously to other publications.

• Include a return envelope with adequate postage for acceptance/rejection correspondence and for possible return of unused photos. We usually do not return full manuscripts, only the front page.

• All material should be mailed to the editor-in-chief. If writing for a particular department, please note department's name on the envelope and in your cover letter.

• Volume prohibits individual acknowledgments and status updates. No advance commitments are made nor implied. No phone calls, please. Rejected submissions are returned immediately after reading; others may be held for further consideration.

• No calls or queries. E-mail submissions or queries will not be accepted.

Categories: Fiction—Nonfiction—Agriculture—Animals—Arts—Biography—Children—Civil War—Collectibles—Conservation—Cooking—Crafts/Hobbies—Culture—Ecology—Family—Fishing—Folklore—Gardening—General Interest—Health—History—Hobbies—Inspirational—Lifestyle—Music—Mystery—Outdoors—Parenting—Poetry—Recreation—Recreation Vehicles—Regional—Religion—Romance—Rural America—Senior Citizen—Short Stories—Society—Travel—Western

CONTACT: Ann Crahan, Editor-in-Chief
Material: All
1503 SW 42nd St.
Topeka KS 66609
Phone: 785-274-4300
Fax: 785-274-4305
E-mail: grit@cjnetworks.com (no submissions)
Website: www.grit.com

The Growing Edge

The Growing Edge magazine and Web Site provide the latest news & information for indoor & outdoor growers, including hobbyists, educators, researchers, and commercial growers. A moderate to high level of experience and knowledge is necessary for successful articles. Some research may be necessary. *The Growing Edge* is actively seeking writers and photographers to cover hydroponics, aquaponics, greenhouse growing, and other related subject areas. Freelance article inquiries are encouraged.

General Information

The Growing Edge magazine is published bimonthly, four color, and 96 pages.

Manuscript format: double-spaced typed or word-processed; final, accepted manuscript must be on computer disk (include hard copy); e-mail is acceptable.

The Growing Edge and New Moon Publishing, Inc., purchase first world serial ($0.10/word), first anthology ($0.05/word), and nonexclusive electronic rights ($0.05/word) for a total of $0.20/word.

The Growing Edge and New Moon Publishing, Inc., purchase print and nonexclusive electronic photography rights (see below for rates).

Editorial Guidelines

Articles should be directly related to high-tech indoor or outdoor soilless cultivation, including hydroponics, aquaponics, greenhouse growing, and other related subject areas. Traditional, soil-based gardening articles will not be considered for publication.

All content-related queries should be addressed to the editor. New contributors should include two writing samples (preferably published) and a resume.

Include an SASE with sufficient postage for return of unsolicited photos or manuscripts.

By-lines are given, except where extensive rewriting makes them inappropriate. Please include a suggested author biography of one to two sentences.

Payment for articles is based on published word count and is made upon publication ($0.20/word).

Photography Guidelines

Photos should be related in some way to the indicated general subject areas. Most photography is submitted by the author of accepted articles.

Color negatives, slides, and prints are preferred. Photos should be numbered. Include a brief suggested caption for each photo.

Include a photographer by-line if different than the author's by-line.

Include a model release for any included human subjects.

Picture-Taking Tips:

• Check focus and depth of field carefully, especially in close-ups.

• Photographing under artificial lighting can be difficult with automatic cameras; use manual control and bracket exposures under and over the meter's setting.

• Never write on the backs of prints in ink—it can rub onto other photos.

• Payment for photos is based on published usage and is made upon publication. Payment for photos published in the interior of the magazine is $25 each. Payment for a photo published on the cover is $175.

• High-quality, high-resolution color digital images are sometimes accepted. Digital images need to be at least 300 dpi at a reasonably large physical size.

Other Artwork

Diagrams and charts may be submitted but will not be purchased and will probably be redone.

The Growing Edge and New Moon Publishing, Inc., do not assume responsibility for unsolicited photos or manuscripts.

Digital Photos

Top 3 rules for digital photography:

• You can always "size-down" an image, but you can never "size-up" an image without sacrificing image quality.

• In digital cameras, as in most other products: You get what you pay for.

• If you take poor pictures with a regular camera, you will probably take bad pictures with a digital one.

• Image size, resolution, and actual print size

• Digital cameras are still in their infancy. Even the most expensive models are just starting to be able to capture an 8.5 x 11 inch image at 300 dpi quality. Scanners follow along the same rule, but a mid-range priced scanner (with the right settings) should be able to scan your prints into digital form at an acceptable size and resolution.

• For more information—There are many Web sites that offer basic tutorials on photography. *Here are a few links to check out:* www.photocourse.com, www.shortcourses.com and scantips.com.

Categories: Nonfiction—Agriculture—Education—Gardening—Hobbies—Science—Hydroponics

CONTACT: Douglas J. Peckenpaugh, Editor
Material: All
New Moon Publishing Inc
341 SW 2nd St.
Corvallis OR 97333
Website: www.growingedge.com

Gryphon Doubles

Please refer to Gryphon Books in the publisher's section.

Guide

Guide is a Christian story magazine geared for young people, ages 10-14. The 32-page four-color publication is published weekly by the Review and Herald Publishing Association. Our mission is (1) to point young people to Jesus and (2) to show Christian character-building principles in practice.

Stories

Each issue includes three to four true stories. Although adventure continues to be the staple product of *Guide*, we do need stories in all categories. Preferred word count is 800-1,200 words. Payment is 7-10 cents per word upon acceptance for first serial rights.

Adventure

Guide adventure stories allow the reader to vicariously experience the excitement of making new discoveries while seeing character-building principles in action. These stories can take place anywhere (outdoors or even in an urban setting). Try to incorporate mystery, action, and discovery (MAD).

Personal Growth

The *Guide*-age years (10-14) can be turbulent on many fronts. Young people often struggle with friendships, self-esteem, family members, peer acceptance, body changes, etc. Stories in the personal growth category are aimed at providing guidance from a Christian perspective.

Christian Humor

Stories in this category use a lighthearted story line that goes beyond one-liners to expose a character-building principle. The key is to write what's funny to kids and keep it believable. Also let the reader decide if something's funny rather than tell that a character is "doubled over in laughter."

Inspiration

Possible topics in this category include answers to prayer, biblical narratives, mission stories, and Bible study. However, don't limit yourself to "traditional" themes. Show God at work in both the common and unusual circumstances of life.

Biography

In today's society, as much as ever, young people need good role models. Some stories we have printed in *Guide* feature Martin Luther King, Jr., Johannes Gutenberg, and Anne Frank.

Story Series

We also run continued stories (five to 12 parts, with each chapter about 1,200 words in length). The story line should maintain some degree of spirituality throughout. An adventurous slant always captures our interest—and the reader's. Please query first.

Nature

We suggest that you carefully study our bimonthly Creation Station feature and other nature stories before submitting. We are looking for creative approaches to nature, not an encyclopedia-style rendition of facts. Please include a spiritual application in the article or as a sidebar. Documentation necessary.

Games and Puzzles

We are interested in fresh game concepts for *Guide*-age readers. We see far too many word search and crossword puzzles, though of course we need some of those, too. Check out puzzles in current puzzle books and Web sites to find something new that could work for *Guide*. Payment is $35-40 for first serial rights.

Reprints

We accept submissions for reprints, but payment is less. Please let us know when and where the story or game first appeared.

10 Writing Tips

1. Be sure to study at least three issues of the magazine before submitting any of your work.

2. Before writing any *Guide* story, we encourage you to ask for the Holy Spirit's involvement.

3. Think true. We no longer use fiction.

4. Choose a story line that hasn't been beaten to death.

5. Keep your protagonists *Guide* age. Regularly spend time around 10- to 14-year-olds. This includes working to understand ethnic singularities.

6. Use lots of dialogue and word pictures. Show, don't tell.

7. Bring out a spiritual or character-building principle that the reader can put into practice in his or her life. Make the story make a difference.

8. Put a twist on the ending. Don't make the story line an exercise in predictability. Be creative.

9. Look for places to boost the energy level of your piece.

10. After you've finished your story, set it aside for at least a few days. Then give it a final editing before sending it to us. We prefer receiving final drafts.

Categories: Nonfiction—Children—Christian Interests—Inspirational—Juvenile—Religion—Spiritual

CONTACT: Randy Fishell, Editor
Material: All
Review and Herald Publishing Association
55 W. Oak Ridge Drive
Hagerstown MD 21740
Phone: 301-393-4038
Fax: 301-393-3292
Website: www.guidemagazine.org

Guideposts

Guideposts Editorial Guidelines

Guideposts magazine is a monthly inspirational, interfaith, non-profit publication written by people from all walks of life. Its articles present tested methods for developing courage, strength and positive attitudes through faith in God. Our writers express viewpoints from a variety of Protestant, Catholic and Jewish faith experiences.

A typical *Guideposts* story is a first-person narrative written in simple, dramatic, anecdotal style with a spiritual point that the reader can "take away" and apply to his or her own life. The story may be the writer's own or one written in the first person for someone else. Even our short features, such as "His Mysterious Ways," "What Prayer Can Do," "Angels Among Us" and "The Divine Touch" use this format Writing a short feature is often the easiest way of making a sale to *Guideposts*.

Please observe the following in writing your Guideposts story:

Don't try to tell an entire life story in a few pages. Focus on one specific happening in a person's life. The emphasis should be on one individual. Bring in as few people as possible so that the reader's interest stays with the dominant character.

Decide what your spiritual point, or "takeaway," will be. Everything in the story should be tied in with this specific theme.

Don't leave unanswered questions. Give enough facts so that the reader will know what happened. Use description and dialogue to let the reader feel as if he were there, seeing the characters, hearing them talk. Dramatize the situation, conflicts and struggle, and then tell how the person was changed for the better or the problem was solved.

Most important: Study the magazine.

Payments:

Full-length manuscripts (750-1500 words): $250 - $500, occasionally higher.

Shorter manuscripts (250- 750 words): $100 - $250.

Short features and fillers (under 250 words): $25 - $100. These include "What Prayer Can Do" and heavenly encounters such as "His Mysterious Ways," "Angels Among Us" and "The Divine Touch"

We do not use fiction, essays or sermons, and we rarely present stories about deceased or professional religious people. We do not evaluate book-length material.

We receive thousands of unsolicited manuscripts each month, so allow two months for a reply.

At this time we cannot accept electronic submissions.

Categories: Nonfiction—Christian Interests—Inspirational—Religion—Spiritual

CONTACT: The Editor
Material: All
16 E. 34th St.
New York NY 10016
Phone: 212-257-8100
Website: www.guideposts.com

Guideposts for Kids

About Your Manuscript: Make it good. Interactive, if possible. Relevant, playful, punchy. Tight, tight text, to reflect the quick click mentality of our Internet readers. Lots of links (at least possibilities) provided, lots of subheadings. And please, no preachy stories about Bible-toting children. *Guideposts for Kids* on the Web is not a beginner's market. Some areas of interest to freelancers:

Feature Stories: 700 words, including sidebar(s) that may include links to other cool stuff on the site, or other appropriate, reliable online materials or outside resources. Make it timely. Something kids not only need to know, but want to know as well. Recent examples include "Are You on Homework Overload?" (included sidebar linking kids to homework help sites) and "Is My Family Normal?" (included a quiz on "What is Normal?"). Topics for stories include animals, school issues, friendship, current events, sports, and any other creative, kid-friendly topic you may think of. Query.

Secondary Features: 350 words, including sidebar(s). More playful. Recent examples include "How Columbus Kept Track" (article on how Christopher Columbus measured the distance he sailed), "Dip, Dip, Goose" (story about the origin of ink pens, including a recipe for invisible ink and a sidebar on the gel pen craze), and "A Gooey New Pet," (piece on the popularity of jellyfish as pets in Japan, with a sidebar on jellyfish facts). Query.

Tips from the Top: 500 words, including "tips" (advice) from celebrity athletes who are also good role models for kids. Main piece should be a kid-friendly look at the sports star's background and rise to the top, and must include direct-from-the-source quotes. (In other words, make sure to interview the celebrity yourself!) Tips should include practical advice on how to play the game rather than simply intangible directives like "Reach for your dreams." Query.

Cool Kids: Profiles of kids (150-300 words) ages 6-11 doing great volunteer work in their communities. "Finder's fee" for clippings used. Include suggestions on how to get started helping others, point to sites and other resources that can offer kids volunteer opportunities. Query with lead/slant.

Fiction: 900 words maximum. Stories featuring conflicts our readers will respect, resolutions our readers will accept. Problematic. Tight. Filled with realistic dialogue and sharp imagery. No stories about "good" children always making the "right" decision. If present at all, adults are minor characters and do not solve kids' problems for them. Always interested in short short stories—500-700 words. Also stories that have a craft or recipe tie-in. If so, include.

Trivia: Amusing, unusual, informative. On animals, school, sports, holidays, books, music—whatever!

Quizzes: Humor works best. Be clever. No more than 10 questions, with scoring and feedback included. Can be true/false or multiple choice. Avoid sermonizing. Strive for copy that lets kids discover something about themselves.

Poetry: Original work only. Fresh language; strong imagery. (Every other line may rhyme just fine and it will still be less than a shining piece of work.)

Crafts: Original work only. Creations should showcase easy-to-follow instructions that need minimal adult supervision. Include samples.

About the Money: There is some. We buy electronic and non-exclusive print rights and pay higher rates for stories exceptionally well-written or well-researched. Regular contributors get bigger bucks, too.

Closing Comments and Parting Advice: Study our Web site. Think like a kid! Neatness does count. So do creativity and professionalism. SASE essential.

Categories: Animals—Children—Christian Interests—Crafts/Hobbies—Education—Family—Games—General Interest—Inspirational—Juvenile—Poetry—Short Stories—Sports/Recreation

CONTACT: Submissions Editor
Material: All
1050 Broadway, Ste. 6
Chesterton IN 46304
E-mail: rtolin@guideposts.org
Website: www.gp4k.com

Guns & Ammo

Editorial Profile

GUNS & AMMO is edited for the sportsman with a keen interest in the practical applications of sporting firearms always emphasizing their safe and proper use. For more than 40 years, the magazine has met the needs of recreational shooters by reflecting every aspect of shooting and firearms. It is the primary source of information for shooters, hunters and collectors.

As active participants themselves, the editors of GUNS & AMMO share the interests of their readers, and each issue of the magazine delivers a well-balanced editorial mix that includes hunting, shooting, reloading, antique and modern arms, ballistics and arms legislation. Natural resource protection and environmental preservation issues, and new products and new trends also receive regular in-depth reporting.

GUNS & AMMO attracts an audience of 5.8 million readers every month, and our appeal covers a vast spectrum of gun owners and users from the competitive shooter of rifles, handguns or shotguns, to the weekend plinker, hunter, reloader and collector. Our readers are true shooting and outdoor enthusiasts and they consider their avocation to be of paramount importance.

Submissions

Guns and Ammo rarely accepts unsolicited submissions. It is mostly a staff written publication. Queries must be submitted by snail mail. Both hard copy and digital text (any format) must be provided upon submission. The Editor will contact you, if your submission is accepted for publication.

Photos: Must be color transparency.

Categories: Nonfiction—Consumer—History—Hobbies—Outdoors—Recreation—Sports/Recreation—Firearms/Hunting/Shooting—Profiles—Opinion

CONTACT: Kevin E. Steele, Editor
Material: All
6420 Wilshire Blvd.
Los Angeles CA 90048
Website: www.gunsandammomag.com

Hadrosaur Tales

Hadrosaur Tales is a literary journal currently published every four months by Hadrosaur Productions.

Hadrosaurs, from which *Hadrosaur Tales* takes its name, are commonly called duck-billed dinosaurs. Many had tall head crests of hollow bone and looked remarkably like early depictions of unicorns. We chose this blending of the creature of science and fantasy as the symbol of our magazine and press devoted to publishing the finest quality speculative fiction.

Needs: Science Fiction and Fantasy short stories to 600 words and poems to 50 lines. Send only complete manuscripts. Electronic mail submissions okay–if sent as an attachment, please use Rich Text Format; otherwise, please send the story as the text of the e-mail. We also need science fiction and fantasy artwork: Send sample artwork and letter of interest. Artwork will be assigned based on need.

Tips: Let your imagination soar to its greatest heights and write down the results. Above all we are looking for thought-provoking ideas and good writing. Speculative fiction set in the past, present, and future are welcome. Contemporary or historical fiction is welcome as long as it has a mythic or science fictional element. Psychological or character-oriented horror will be considered as long as there is no graphic violence.

Do not send: Stories with graphic violence. Please avoid cliché-fantasy (e.g. a lone knight has gone on a quest to slay the evil dragon–unless you have a new and unique twist to this idea). Do not send stories with essentially no science fictional or fantasy elements. Do not send stories with copyrighted characters unless you are the copyright holder.

Rights: We buy one-time rights for all material except for cover art. Please inform us if the story would be a reprint. For cover art we do request limited advertising-use rights in addition to the one-time rights.

Payment: We pay $6.00 per published story and $2.00 per published poem or equivalent in trade from the Hadrosaur Productions catalog. Contributors also receive two copies of the issue in which their work appears.

Submission periods: We now read stories from May 1 through June 15 and November 1 through December 15.

Response time: Approximately 4 weeks.

Sample copies: Sample copies are available for $6.95 (includes shipping and handling). A one-year subscription (two issues) is available for $11.00. Make checks payable to "Hadrosaur Productions."

Categories: Fiction—Fantasy—Literature—Poetry—Science Fiction

CONTACT: David L. Summers, Editor
Material: All
PO Box 2194
Mesilla Park NM 88047-2199

Phone: 505-527-4163
E-mail: hadrosaur@zianet.com
Website: hadrosaur.com

Handwoven

Handwoven is devoted to the interests of hand weavers at all skill levels. Material submitted for publication should display in-depth knowledge based on experience and research. Even when the material is technical, the tone of all articles should be informal and accessible. If you are not familiar with the content and style of *Handwoven*, please request a complimentary copy.

Manuscripts

If your article is already written, enclose a copy of the manuscript with relevant graphics (photographs, slides, drawings, drafts, etc.) and a brief, informal personal biography. Your article should be typewritten or computer- generated, double-spaced, on 8½" x 11" paper. Include your name, address, and telephone number (and fax number and e-mail address if available) at the top of the first page. Write your name on all remaining pages and number each page. Do not write any notes on the copy (other than name and page numbers). If you send your article on disk, send hard copy as well. If using Microsoft Word, save files in any format; if using other word-processing programs, save as "text only." Please do not use any bolds, all caps, bullets, tabs, multiple columns, or other desktop publishing goodies - just straight text. Do not embed graphics. Do not send articles by fax. If you e-mail text, also send hard copy by mail. If fractions appear in the text, write them as 1/2, 12 - 3/4, etc. not as a superscript/subscript (1½). Keep a copy of everything. Enclose a self-addressed envelope with sufficient return postage.

Photographs and drawings

Photographs must be sharp and clear with good contrast and a simple background (please do not send digital photos as e-mail attachments). Make sure each photo is numbered and identified with your name. Do not write on the back of the photo; type the identifying information on a separate piece of paper and tape to the back. Drawings and diagrams should be prepared in black ink on white paper (or on white graph paper with blue lines) ready for redrawing by a staff artist. Include a list of all graphics with explanatory information about each on a separate sheet.

All materials will be returned. We also request a photo of you to include with your biography as part of the article.

Projects

When project articles have been accepted for publication, we usually request that authors send the projects to Interweave for photography. You will not be reimbursed for these shipping costs. We will need to keep the items on hand during photography and production (usually about four months). All projects are returned after publication of the article.

Contracts and payment

A contract is sent when an article is accepted for publication in a designated issue of *Handwoven*. The contract indicates the fee paid for the article and specifies that Interweave Press is purchasing first serial rights (in North America) for publication in *Handwoven* and subsequent non-exclusive rights for use in other Interweave Press publications and promotions. The author verifies that the article is original work and that it has not been published previously. The author retains the publication rights for the original materials.

Interweave Press reserves the right to edit the material as necessary to fit the style, format, or other requirements of *Handwoven*. A copy of the edited manuscript is submitted to the author for corrections before publication.

Tips for preparing project articles

Easy-to-understand instructions are an important feature of the projects shown in *Handwoven* and the Design Collections. For clarity and continuity, we have standardized some of the calculations and methods we use. Before writing your project directions, familiarize yourself with the project format in a recent issue.

Measuring. Take accurate measurements throughout the project.

Take-up and shrinkage. Technically, take-up is loss due to the interlacement process and shrinkage is loss due to the finishing process, but handwoven combines them in calculations. Measure the finished width and length after the fabric has gone through the finishing process but before it has been cut or hemmed.

Steps for calculating width-wise shrinkage and take-up
Method:
a. subtract finished width from width in the reed
b. divide a. by width in the reed
c. multiply b. by 100
Example:
a. 40" width in reed - 36" finished width = 4"
b. 4" 40" width in the reed = .1
c. 100 x .1 = 10% shrinkage and take-up in width

Steps for calculating lengthwise shrinkage and take-up
Method:
a. subtract loom waste and finished length from warp length
b. divide a. by warp length minus loom waste
c. multiply b. by 100
Example:
a. 118" warp length - 36" loom waste - 73" finished length = 9"
b. 9"82" (82" is 118" warp length - 36" loom waste) = .10976"
c. 100 x .10976 = 11% shrinkage and take-up in length

Yarns. Use readily available yarns, not mill-ends or odd lots. If the project has already been woven using yarns that are no longer available, find a suitable substitute and list it in the project directions (and send the substitute for the yarn sample) instead of the original yarn. Give complete information about each yarn (yds/lb, color numbers, manufacturer's name, etc.) and exact amounts required. To calculate warp yardage, multiply the number of warp ends by the warp length and add 5%. To calculate weft yardage, multiply the number of picks per inch by the woven length in inches; multiply the result by the width in the reed; and add 10% for weft take-up. Include with your article a 10" sample of each yarn used, in white if possible. Include floating selvedges in the total warp ends required by the project.

Include in your text any special features of the project, your design process, how the project was inspired, and how it evolved. If you have ideas for changes, variations, or different color schemes, mention them also.

All project articles must be accompanied by a project information sheet (Project at-a-glance) that includes attached yarn samples (request a copy of this form from Liz or Madelyn).

When you receive a copy of the edited article prior to publication, check the copy for accuracy, completeness, and inclusion of all important details.

Categories: Nonfiction—Arts—Crafts/Hobbies—Hobbies—Trade—Textiles

CONTACT: Madelyn van der Hoogt, Editor
Material: Articles or proposals for Handwoven
Interweave Press
PO Box 1228
Coupeville WA 98239
Phone: 360-678-6225 (Questions for Madelyn)
E-mail: mvdh@whidbey.net
CONTACT: Liz Gipson, Assistant Editor
Material: Submissions for Communiqué
Interweave Press
201 NE 4th St.
Loveland CO 80537
Phone: 800-272-2193, ext 629 (Questions for Liz)
E-mail: LizG@interweave.com
Website: www.interweave.com

Remember: Editors change jobs and publishers change addresses. It is wise to invest in a phone call for the current information before submitting.

F-L

Hanging Loose

About Us It doesn't sound flippant, we hope, if we say that the most meaningful guide is the magazine itself. We've published it continually since 1966 so, to some extent, past is prologue. While we hope we will always be open to new ideas, it seems unlikely that we will develop an interest in formula romance or sing-song verse. Sample copies may be ordered directly from us ($9.00 including postage) and are also available at many bookstores and libraries. Writers who send work to publications they've never seen are usually wasting time, money and effort, theirs and ours.

Magazine Submissions

As a rule, send up to six poems or one story at a time. We rarely publish non-fiction, but there are exceptions. We do not publish reviews. Manuscripts must be legible and be sure that includes your name and address. Enclose a stamped, self-addressed envelope of adequate size or we cannot reply. If you don't want your work returned, please make that clear. Cover letters are welcome if they contain pertinent information, but they are hardly a requirement. Because we read all submissions carefully, please allow up to three months for an answer. That's also why we will not consider simultaneous submissions. We also cannot accept submissions by fax or e-mail. We never have contests or theme issues. We do have a regular section of work by high school writers: special guidelines for high school writers. All contributors receive checks on acceptance and copies of the issue containing their work.

Artwork and book manuscripts are by invitation only, without exception. We cannot be responsible for unsolicited work.

High School Submissions

Hanging Loose magazine welcomes high school submissions. As with other writers, we reply within three months, and high school authors whose work we publish receive the same small fee and two copies of the issue in which their work appears. We feel a special responsibility to those young writers who look to us not only for possible publication but sometimes also for editorial advice, which we are always happy to give when asked. Our work as editors is of course time-consuming, but we feel a strong commitment to give as much time and attention as possible to the work we receive from high school age writers. We urge writers of high school age to follow these guidelines, in order to help us respond to their work.

Send all work to High School Editor, *Hanging Loose*, 231 Wyckoff Street, Brooklyn, NY 11217. Please also send us a note identifying yourself as a high school age writer, and telling us your age, and be sure to include a self-addressed stamped envelope with sufficient return postage. Send 3 to 6 poems, or 1 to 3 short stories, or an equivalent combination of poetry and prose. This enables us to get a good idea of what your work is like. All work should be neatly typed. High quality photocopies or readable computer-generated hard copies are acceptable. A brief biographical statement is welcome. We are always interested in knowing how you found out about us, what school you attend, and so forth.Please Note: We prefer to receive submissions from young writers themselves, rather than from their teachers. We strongly discourage teachers from submitting samples of work from members of their classes. Similarly, we discourage teachers from asking students to submit their work as a class assignment. We prefer teachers to encourage students who take themselves seriously as writers to write us directly.

Hanging Loose has long been known for its special interest in new writers. We read manuscripts throughout the year and we look forward to reading yours.

Categories: Nonfiction—Teen

CONTACT: Editor
Material: All
CONTACT: High School Editor
Material: High School Submissions
231 Wyckoff St.
Brooklyn NY 11217

Phone: 212-243-7499
E-mail: print225@aol.com
Website: omega.cc.umb.edu/~hangloos

Happy Times Monthly
The Good News Newspaper

About Us
Brigitte Lang, Publisher
The *Happy Times Monthly*/The Happy Herald Newspaper.
Over 200, 000 Readers of Happy and Good News.
Florida Coverage: Delray Beach, Boca Raton, Deerfield Beach, Pompano Beach, Ft. Lauderdale, Jupiter, Tequesta, and Palm Beach Gardens.

The *Happy Times Monthly*, the good-news newspaper, is a forum to spread positive ideas everywhere, and contains what people like you send us or tell us about. It provides the community with education, humor, wisdom, inspiration, and awareness of what's good in the news, and highlights people, businesses, social groups and events that can give a positive lift to our readers.

Does one of these categories bring a Happy Times story to mind?

- What I'm thankful for
- Random Acts of Kindness
- Tribute to an amazing friend
- Successful people in business, life, health, or love
- People who care
- Good deed stories
- Positive events
- Everyday heroes
- People helping people
- Tragedy turned positive
- Outstanding students/teachers
- Funniest thing that ever happened to you
- The best time of your life
- Gratitude and thank you's
- Nature & environment stories
- Unusual, funny or cute pet or animal stories
- Humorous relative stories
- Someone that really inspired you!

Write about the person and the experience and send in one or two photos with it

Word Count: 150 to 500 word articles with 1 or 2 photos (place name and address on back of photos). Encourages human interest, feature-type articles about people, organizations, or animals on a good news theme. Stories need to be expressed from the heart. For more writer guidelines or information or suggestions on articles, go to our Web Site. Pays in copy. SASE for sample issues. Subscriptions $20.

The *Happy Times Monthly* pays $50 for Cover Pages stories accompanied by color pictures.

Categories: Nonfiction—Adventure—Animals—Business—Careers—Cartoons—Children—Comedy—Cooking—Entertainment—Environment—Family—Fishing—Games—Gardening—General Interest—Hobbies—Inspirational—Lifestyle—Marriage—Men's Issues—Outdoors—Parenting—Photography—Physical Fitness—Recreation—Relationships—Romance—Senior Citizen—Short Stories—Teen—Writing—Good Deeds—Good News—Heartfelt—Humor—Philosophy

CONTACT: Sue Elmore, Submissions Editor
Material: All
Star Publications, Inc.

PO Box 7253
Boca Raton FL 33431
Phone: 561-394-7466
Fax:E-mail: HappyHeroal@aol.com
Website: www.thehappytimes.com

Hard Hat News

I am looking for two types of articles–1) original reporting of events (i.e. conferences, seminars, equipment promotional events, major legislation, 2) feature stories on heavy construction projects (i.e. roads, bridges, major structures, etc.) Where possible, articles should be less than 800 words and should include both facts AND human-interest elements.

In general, we won't pay for more than 800 words. However, if you have a story that justifies the space, break it into two (or more) sections, with pictures appropriate to each section.

If you think a story might be more suitable for one of the other publications, send it to me and I will see that it is delivered to the correct person.

I look forward to hearing from you.

Holly Reiser, Editor, *Hard Hat News*

General Freelance Information

We pay $2.50 per column inch (it works out to be about $.11 per word), $15.00 per photo used and $60.00 for a cover photo. A story printed in another publication (not another edition of the same publication) pays $1.25 per column inch and $7.50 per picture for each additional publication. Occasionally we will suggest an article. Should you choose to follow up, we will reimburse mileage at $.20 per mile, telephone, film and developing, and postage expenses as they relate to the article.

Lee Publications prints: Hard Hat News (heavy construction), Grower (greenhouse, turfgrass, nursery, vegetables and fruits), Farm Chronicle (general agriculture for mid-Atlantic states), Country Folks (general agriculture for the Northeast and Pennsylvania), Quarry News (quarry and mining, aggregates and asphalt), Waste Handling News (solid waste).

If you have an idea for an article, you might speak with me before you begin. I'll guide you as to what we are looking for. I can be reached at 518-673-3237, ext. 231. Or, preferably, via email at the email address listed below

Stories should be emailed as attachments. Word documents are preferred.

Payment Policy for Photographs, Illustrations, Graphics and Artwork.

Payment is for original work only; specifically: photos, illustrations, graphics and artwork produced or created by the person submitting the work.

Payment DOES NOT include:

1. any form of photography, graphics, illustrations or artwork copied from any source such as books, manuals, clip art disks or other publications. If you feel your article needs these illustrations, obtain permission to use the materials (second sources are almost always copyrighted) and show proof of permission when submitting the materials with your article.

2. graphics, photos, illustrations or artwork copied from the Internet. If you feel your article needs these materials, obtain permission to use the work if it is from a copyrighted site and submit the website address for the graphics along with your article.

Please note: Photos, artwork, graphics and illustrations are very important to feature stories and we encourage all freelance writers to ask interviewees if those materials are available. To save time and expenses, whenever possible please have the person submitting materials send them directly to Lee Publications.

Categories: Nonfiction—Trade—Heavy Construction

CONTACT: Holly Rieser, Editor
Material: All

Lee Publications
PO Box 121
Palatine Bridge NY 13428
Phone: 518-673-3237
E-mail: hrieser@leepub.com
Website: www.leepub.com

Hardboiled

Please refer to Gryphon Books in the publisher's section.

Harper's Bazaar

Formal guidelines not available. Please read a number of issues to ascertain the publication's style and needs.

Send queries to address below.

Categories: Fiction—Nonfiction—Beauty—Fashion—Sexuality

CONTACT: Submissions Editor
Material: All
The Hearst Corp.
1700 Braodway, 37th Floor
New York NY 10019
Phone: 212-903-5000
Website: www.harpersbazaar.com

Harper's Magazine

Harper's Magazine welcomes reader response. Short letters are more likely to be published, and all letters are subject to editing. Volume precludes individual acknowledgment.

Harper's Magazine does not accept editorial submissions via e-mail (please see our submission guidelines for more information), though suggestions for the magazine's Readings section are welcome. Please send those to: readings@harpers.org.

Harper's Magazine will neither consider nor return unsolicited nonfiction manuscripts that have not been preceded by a written query. Harper's will consider unsolicited fiction. Unsolicited poetry will not be considered or returned. No queries or manuscripts will be considered unless they are accompanied by a self-addressed, stamped envelope. Submissions to the Readings section (readings@harpers.org) are welcome and are encouraged, though volume precludes individual acknowledgment.

Categories: Fiction—Nonfiction—Arts—Business—Crime—Culture—Literature—Poetry—Politics—Science—Society—News—Essay—International Affairs—Humor—Humanities—Memoirs

CONTACT: Submissions Editor
Material: Queries
CONTACT: Letters Editor
Material: Reader response letters
666 Broadway 11th Floor
New York NY 10012
Phone: 212-420-5720
Fax: 212-228-5889
E-mail: letters@harpers.org. (Reader response letters only)
E-mail: readings@harpers.org (Reading Section only)
Website: www.harpers.org

Remember: Editors change jobs and publishers change addresses. It is wise to invest in a phone call for the current information before submitting.

Having a Baby Today

Please refer to *Midwifery Today.*

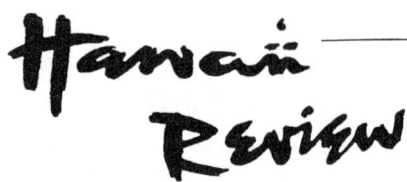

Hawaii Review

Hawaii Review publishes all forms of literature, including–but not solely–works which focus on Hawaii and the Pacific. *Hawaii Review* accepts solicited and unsolicited works of poetry, fiction, literary nonfiction, and visual art; including plays, short-short stories, reviews, translations, essays, humor, songs, and chants.

All manuscript submissions must be typed, double-spaced, crisp originals/copies on 8½" x 11" paper and must include: the writer's name, address, phone number, and number of words (prose) or lines (poetry) at the top right-hand of the first page; numbered pages; and a SASE with proper postage for reply. Manuscripts may also be submitted as Microsoft Word documents on a Macintosh- or IBM-formatted diskette. Please indicate whether you would like the manuscript returned and include enough postage on the SASE for the manuscript.

Fiction: Please submit no more than one manuscript with a maximum length of 7,000 words (28 double-spaced pages) per submission. More than one manuscript for short-short fiction or chapters from novels are acceptable if they do not exceed 7,000 words total.

Poetry: Please submit no more than five double-spaced poems per submission. Longer poems, up to 500 lines (20 double-spaced pages) will be considered; however, space limitations are more likely to be taken into account.

Nonfiction: Please submit no more than one manuscript at a time, up to 7,000 words (28 double-spaced pages) per manuscript. All nonfiction manuscripts must include complete documentation conforming to the *MLA Handbook of Style.* For book reviews, please submit no more than two manuscripts, each between 500 and 1,500 words (2 to 6 pages) long. Manuscript reviews must include at the top of the first page the title of the literary work being reviewed, the names of the authors and writers of introductions/forewords/afterwords, publisher's information, publication date, number of pages, and price of cloth/paper/hardcover copies.

Translations: Please include a copy of the original piece, and indicate the copyright status of the original.

Visual Art: Submissions of photography, and photographs of non-photographic artwork (paintings, three-dimensional art, etc.), must be printed on 8" x 10" glossy black-and-white photos. Black-and-white drawings and paintings may be submitted on 8½" by 11" paper. Artwork may also be submitted on slides. Artists may submit up to 10 pieces of art per submission. Include, in clear print, on the back of each piece: the artist's name, address, phone number, title, date, and medium. Include SASE with proper postage for return of art with response.

Allow two to three months response time.

Categories: Fiction—Nonfiction—Poetry

CONTACT: Submissions Editor
Material: All
University of Hawaii
c/o Board of Publications
1755 Pope Rd., Bldg. 31-D
Honolulu HI 96822
Phone: 808-956-3030
Fax: 808-956-9962

E-mail: hi-review@hawaii.edu
Website: www.hawaii.edu/bop/pubindex.html

Hawaii Westways

HAWAII WESTWAYS, the bimonthly member publication for AAA Hawaii, has a circulation of over 52,000 and is published by the Automobile Club of Southern California. In each issue we celebrate Hawaii's culture and traditions. We report on current Island happenings, and provide information about dining, car care, and financial matters. We also cover local, domestic, and international travel. Our lead time is four to six months. We create our editorial calendars in spring and early summer for the following calendar year.

Major features typically run 1,500-2,000 words, but we also run 300- to 500-word articles. We look for writers with sound research and reporting skills, a strong voice, and good storytelling ability.

Our departments include:

Holoholo (going on excursion): 700-word articles about places in the Islands that would make a good day-trip or weekend destination. These might be an entire neighborhood, such as Oahu's North Shore or Maui's Wailuku; a specific excursion or attraction; or even a specific hotel or resort.

Celebrity Secret Spots: 600-word stories about a noted Island resident and his or her favorite place in Hawaii. Recent stories have featured Honolulu Symphony conductor Samuel Wong, chef Sam Choy, and entertainer Jim Nabors.

We pay $1 a word, plus agreed-upon expenses, upon manuscript acceptance. We buy first North American rights. If we reuse an article in another of the six publications produced by the Auto Club, we pay up to 33 percent of the original fee for second-use rights.

Samples of previously published work must accompany your query. We do our best to respond within eight weeks. Phone, fax, and e-mail queries are not encouraged. We do not accept unsolicited or previously published manuscripts. We use professional, high-quality photographs or slides with our articles, so if you are also a published photographer, please let us know. Thanks for your interest in HAWAII WESTWAYS. We look forward to reading your proposal.

Categories: Nonfiction—Associations—Automobiles—Consumer—Regional—Travel

CONTACT: Robin Jones, Editor
Material: Queries and clips
3333 Fairview Rd., A-327
Costa Mesa CA 92626
Phone: 714-885-2376
Website: www.aaa-calif.com/westways

Hayden's Ferry Review
Arizona State University

Hayden's Ferry Review, Box 871502, Arizona State University, Tempe, AZ 85287-1502, (480) 965-1243. Sample issues are $7.50. Yearly subscriptions are $14.00 (two issues).

Hayden's Ferry Review is a nationally distributed magazine publishing quality literary and visual art. Produced twice a year at Arizona State University, *HFR* promotes the work of emerging and established visual artists and writers of fiction, poetry, and creative nonfiction. Writers are urged to read the magazine before submitting. Editors serve for two issues (Fall/Winter, Spring/Summer).

Deadlines (postmark):

Fall/Winter, February 28

Spring/Summer, September 30

Submissions received after the deadline will be held for the next issue. Response time is 8–12 weeks after the deadline. Payment is $25.00 per page/ maximum of $100.00 (cover art payment—$100.00), two copies of the magazine, and a one-year gift subscription to *HFR*. Authors/artists receive page proofs for review prior to publication.

Manuscripts must be typed or letter-quality printed; clean photo-copies are acceptable. Prose must be double spaced and printed on one side of paper. Send poetry and prose separately, limiting submissions to six poems or one story or essay per submission. Please send one manuscript per genre at a time, and wait for response before you submit additional work. We do not respond to manuscripts unless they are accompanied by a SASE. **We are not able to accept electronic submissions.** Art submissions should be standard 2" x 2" slides, clearly labeled with title, artist, medium, size, date, and arrow or dot to indicate orientation. Submit slides (limit: ten per artist) in a clear slide sheet. No reading fee.

SPECIAL SECTION: "Metafiction": (n) fictional objects that self-consciously pose questions about the relationship between illusion and reality. *Hayden's Ferry Review* seeks groundbreaking prose for an upcoming special section highlighting experimental flights of the imagination. Postmark deadline: June 15, 2004.

Categories: Fiction—Poetry

CONTACT: Fiction Editor
Material: All Fiction
CONTACT: Poetry Editor
Material: All Poetry
Arizona State University, PO Box 871502
Tempe AZ 85287-1502
Phone: 480-965-1243
Fax: 480-965-2191
E-mail: HFR@asu.edu
Website: www.haydensferryreview.org

Health

Health's focus is not on illness, but rather on ideas, events, and people. Our stories are written to inform decisions and compel action-in effect, giving readers more control over their own health. Each issue of the magazine presents some of the most important developments in health in its broadest sense-physical, emotional, even spiritual-in readable stories written with warmth, wit, and authority.

The audience for *Health* is predominantly college-educated women, age 30 through 50, who, by reason of their intellectual curiosity or practical interest, want both a dependable source of useful health information and a perspective on the rapidly changing face of personal health.

Health is published 10 times a year, with a nationwide circulation of approximately 1.4 million. The magazine relies heavily on staff writers and contributing editors. We usually assign features to regular contributors or to experienced writers whose work we know-and only after extensive discussion. Departments are more open to freelance writers new to us. Practical, service-oriented ideas are more likely to receive consideration. First-time contributors should propose stories for our front-of-book departments.

Departments usually run about 1,200 words. Fees are paid on acceptance. We pay research and travel expenses that have been agreed upon with the assigning editor.

HOW TO QUERY

All writers must submit written proposals before sending manuscripts, regardless of the planned length or nature of the story. *Health* does not accept unsolicited manuscripts.

Proposals should be sharply focused with the style and sources clearly defined. Send proposals, along with a legal-sized, self-addressed stamped envelope, resume, and copies of no more than two published stories to:

Categories: Nonfiction—Cooking—Diet/Nutrition—Family—Food/Drink—Health—Marriage—Physical Fitness—Psychology—Relationships—Self Help—Medicine

CONTACT: Amanda Storey, Editorial Assistant
Material: All
2100 Lakeshore Dr.

Birmingham AL 35209
Phone: 205-445-5123
E-mail: health@timeinc.com
Website: www.health.com

Heartland USA

Heartland USA

HEARTLAND USA is a general-interest, bi-monthly magazine with a BPA-guaranteed circulation of over 1,200,000 and a readership exceeding 2.7 million. Targeted primarily at active, outdoors-oriented blue-collar working men, the publication regularly includes an eclectic mix of short, easy-to-read articles on hunting and fishing, spectator sports (motorsports, football, basketball and baseball), how-to, country music, human interest, and wildlife.

Please keep in mind that our average reader is a high school graduate who sees himself as hard working, traditional, rugged, confident, uncompromising and daring. We have consciously chosen not to "write down" to our readers, but rather to pursue an editorial voice that reflects a relaxed, jocular, street-smart familiarity, with just a hint of attitude. The liberal use of anecdote or compelling quotations—anything to breathe some life into a piece—is looked upon favorably.

The target length for feature articles is 1,200 words, with payment varying from $250 to $950. Feature-length pieces must lend themselves to strong photographic support.

Department-length articles (generally 550-1,200 words) pay from $140 to $950.

We pay on final acceptance (i.e. when we're certain the piece will appear in an upcoming issue), offer a 20% kill fee on assigned work, purchase the first or second North American serial rights, and copyright our publication. Hard-copy submissions must be sharp, legible, and include an SASE. E-mail queries and submissions are welcome and should be sent to us at husaedit@att.net. Simultaneous, photocopied, and reprint submissions are okay. Response will usually be within 4-6 weeks. A free sample copy is available on request. Clips of published work should accompany hard-copy queries.

Categories: Nonfiction—Adventure—Animals—Automobiles—Aviation—Biography—Boating—Cartoons—Civil War—Conservation—Crime—Disabilities—Ecology—Environment—Fishing—Gardening—General Interest—Inspirational—Men's Issues—Military—Music—Outdoors—Recreation—Rural America—Sports/Recreation—HuntingMartial Arts—Technology

CONTACT: Brad Pearson, Editor
Material: All
100 W. Putnam Ave.
Greenwich CT 06830
Phone: 203-863-7279
E-mail: husaedit@att.net

The Hellenic Calendar

Tabloid newspaper (17"x11") presenting news and features of special interest to the Greek-Americans of Southern California and the Great Southwest. Circulation 10,000.

Needs: Articles on prominent Americans of Greek descent, also on trends or issues of special interest to Greek-Americans. 500-2,000 words. We're not interested in a story about your trip to Greece or the best gyro you ever ate. Mail or e-mail complete manuscript.

Reports in two weeks.

Payment: Varies, usually ranges from $25 to $100.

F-L

Categories: Nonfiction—Culture—Multicultural—Regional—Ethnic

CONTACT: Steve Pastis, Publisher/Editor
Material: All
2747 N. Grand Ave. PMB 250
PMB 250
Santa Ana CA 92705
Phone: 714-550-9933
Fax: 714-550-9696
E-mail: greekpaper@aol.com
Website: www.helleniccalendar.com/news.html

HerbalGram

About Us

HerbalGram is a publication of the American Botanical Council and the Herb Research Foundation. ABC and HRF are non-profit, educational and research organizations which focus on herb and medicinal plant research, regulatory issues, market conditions, native plant conservation, and other general interest aspects of herb use.

All articles published in *HerbalGram* are peer reviewed by some of the leading authorities in the field of phytopharmaceutical research, including James A. Duke, Ph.D., U.S. Department of Agriculture, retired; Varro Tyler, Ph.D., Lilly Distinguished Professor of Pharmacognosy, Purdue University; Norman Farnsworth, Ph.D., Professor of Pharmacognosy, University of Illinois Medical School, and Dennis V. C. Awang, Ph.D., MediPlant, Ottawa, Canada.

Submissions

We welcome proposals and finished manuscripts in hard copy form, preferably accompanied by a computer disk. We prefer Microsoft Word for Macintosh, but can interpret from Word for Windows. If neither of these programs are possible, then please save your text in rich text format (.rtf), a universal style which retains any italics or other individual formatting. Do not send manuscripts formatted in WordPerfect. If you have any questions about rich text format, please contact the editorial office at the number below. You may also send articles to our e-mail address.

We also prefer that you send straight text, with little or no formatting except when necessary for presentation of charts or diagrams. The common name of all botanicals mentioned must be followed by the Latin binomial. References must be complete, with title of the article cited as well as author/s names, publication, pages, and dates. Example—Smith, Maurice I., and E. Elvove, with the cooperation of P.J. Valaer, Jr., William H. Frazier and G. E. Mallory, "Pharmacological and Chemical Studies of the Cause of So-Called Ginger Paralysis: A Preliminary Report," Pub. Health Rep., 45 (1930): 1703-1716 (especially p.1704).]

Our stylistic authority is *The Chicago Manual of Style* and our botanical reference is *The Plant Book* by D. J. Mabberly.

Photos

If you have excellent quality color or black and white slides or photographs to illustrate your article we are interested in seeing them and will, of course, return them to you. Please include a proper description of such materials and label your photos/slides with your name and the name of the subject.

Payment

We do not pay for manuscripts, but will send you six copies of the issue in which your material appears.

We strongly suggest that you obtain a sample copy of at least one of the latest issues in order to familiarize yourself with our subject matter, journalistic style, and general focus. If you have any questions, please contact Barbara Johnston, Managing Editor.

Categories: Nonfiction— Conservation—General Interest—Health—Nature—Science—Herbal Medicine —Herbs—Medicinal Plants

CONTACT: Submissions Editor
Material: All
Herb Research Foundation
1007 Pearl St. Ste 200
Boulder CO 80302
Phone: 303-449-2265
Fax: 303-449-7849
E-mail: info@herbs.org
Website: www.herbs.org

High Technology Careers

Ceased publication.

Highlights for Children

We appreciate your interest in *Highlights for Children*. Highlights is published monthly for children 2 to 12. Circulation is 2.5 million.

Please note:

• We do not pay persons under age 16 for contributions.

• We buy all rights, including copyright, and do not consider material previously published.

• We prefer to see a manuscript rather than a query.

• All material is paid for on acceptance.

• We do not accept submissions by email or fax.

• We accept material year round, including seasonal material.

FICTION should have an engaging plot, strong characterization, and lively language. Stories for younger readers (ages 3-7) should be 400 words of fewer Stories for older readers (8-12) should be 800 words or fewer and be appealing to younger readers if read aloud.

• We prefer stories that teach by positive example, rather than by preaching.

• Suggestions of crime and violence are taboo.

• Frequent needs include humor, mystery, sports, and adventure stories; retellings of traditional tales; stories in urban settings; and stories that feature world cultures.

• We seldom buy rhyming stories.

Payment: $150 and up.

REBUS STORIES are a monthly feature for beginning readers, featuring a variety of familiar words that can easily be shown as pictures. Rebuses should be 120 words or fewer.

Payment: $100 and up.

NONFICTION includes biography, autobiography, and various approaches to the arts, science, history, sports, and world cultures. All articles should be 800 words or fewer.

• Focused articles are more successful than broad factual surveys.

• We prefer research based on consultation with experts or first-hand experience.

• Writers with an extensive background in a particular field are encouraged to share their experiences and personal research.

• Articles about cultural traditions and ways of life should reflect a deep understanding of the subject.

• Biographies of individuals who have made significant artistic, scientific, or humanitarian contributions are strengthened by the inclusion of formative childhood experiences. We prefer biographies that are rich in anecdotes and place the subject in a historical and cultural context.

• Nonfiction articles geared to our younger readers (ages 3-7) are especially welcome. These should not exceed 500 words.

• References or sources of information must be included with submissions.

• Color 35mm slides, photos, or art reference materials are helpful and sometimes crucial in evaluating submissions.

Payment: $150 and up.

CRAFTS should appeal to a wide age range of boys and girls and should have clear, numbered directions, typically not more than five steps.

• A well-made sample should be submitted with each craft idea. If this is not feasible, then a photo or a detailed illustration would help.

• Projects must require only common household items or inexpensive, easy-to-obtain materials.

• Projects should result in attractive, useful gift items, decorations, toys, and games.

• Crafts that celebrate holidays or religious traditions are welcome. Crafts from world cultures are a frequent need, as are crafts that result in games and crafts that appeal to boys.

Payment: $25 and up.

FINGER PLAYS/ACTION RHYMES should have plenty of action and minimal text. They must be easy for very young children to act out, step-by-step, with hands, fingers, and body movements.

Payment: $25 and up.

PARTY PLANS should give clever, original party ideas organized around a single theme, clearly described in 300 to 700 words. Plans should include invitations, favors, decorations, refreshments, and a mix of quiet and active games. Materials used should be inexpensive. Include drawings, photos, or samples of items. Payment: $50 and up.

VERSE is purchased sparingly. It is rarely longer than 16 lines and should be meaningful for young readers.

Payment: $25 and up.

Categories: Children

CONTACT: Manuscript Submissions
Material: All
803 Church St.
Honesdale PA 18431
Phone: 570-253-1080
Fax: 570-251-7847
E-mail: eds@highlights-corp.com

Highways

Thank you for your interest in *Highways*, the official publication of the Good Sam Club. *Highways* is published 12 times a year by TL Enterprises Inc. and is a sister publication of *Trailer Life* and *MotorHome.*

Highways is a specialty magazine for RV enthusiasts and has a circulation of more than 960,000. We suggest that interested contributors study recent issues before sending us queries. All queries must be submitted via e-mail to goodsam@goodsamclub.com. **We do not accept unsolicited manuscript submissions.** The response time to queries is generally three weeks. Our staff works considerably with freelancers, but primarily on assignment. If you receive an assignment, the text of your story must be e-mailed to us. We do not accept disks or typed stories.

Payment is on acceptance for publication. *Highways* buys first North American serial rights and electronic rights. The editors reserve the right to edit and even rewrite any article in order to make it suit the theme or space limitations of a specific issue. Major alterations will be discussed with the author when possible.

TRAVEL FEATURES

The easiest way to sell your work to *Highways* is to query us on an interesting and tightly focused RV travel story. We need features that evoke the sights, sounds, smells and even tastes of specific travel destinations. Consequently, we d much rather have a tight 1,200 words on traveling to Anchorage in the spring than on all of Alaska.

We are also looking for short 800 words first-person stories written in a smart and breezy style. These could be about your RV travels or about how a Good Sam Club benefit proved of particular value to

you. Again, submit a query, not the entire feature. Fees for full-length travel features with photos start at $300. Higher fees are negotiable. Short travel features start at $75.

If you are assigned a story by the editorial staff, please keep in mind that you now represent the magazine. Be conscious that if you receive information or materials about the subject/area you are covering, you must still write an ethical, objective story.

MAINTENANCE AND TECHNICAL

Highways publishes several types of technical stories, all of which are assigned. If you have an idea for a technical feature maintenance, how-to, RV safety send a query.

VEHICLE TESTS

Highways does not publish vehicle tests, though we do print previews of new rigs. However, they are staff written.

SPECIAL INTEREST *Highways* editorial focus also includes hobbies, crafts and other recreational activities that are popular among RVers. Recent stories have covered dominoes, a shelter for cats that could be affixed to the outside of an RV, computers and other hobbies. Special-interest features should be 1,000 words. Please do not send a manuscript send a query.

RV HUMOR

In each issue of *Highways*, we try to include a humorous vignette on some aspect of the RV lifestyle. Humor stories should be directly related to the RV experience. Maximum length for humor stories is 1,000 words. Do not send photographs. All humor stories are illustrated by line drawings. Humor stories are the only genre that *Highways* will accept without first receiving a query

COLUMNS

All *Highways* columns are assigned. If you have a column idea, send us your idea along with several sample columns and we will consider them. Columns are a tough sale and we do not foresee a need to add any new columns to the magazine in the near future.

HUMAN INTEREST

Highways publishes personality features about Good Sam Club members. If you come across a good story and know that the person/couple is a member of the Good Sam Club, please send a query

POETRY AND FICTION

Highways does not publish poetry or fiction.

PHOTOGRAPHY

All stories (excluding humor) should be accompanied by a minimum of 15 color transparencies, all originals. All transparencies should be numbered with an accompanying caption sheet identifying each subject. Digital images are accepted in TIF format and sent via e-mail or on a CD. When possible, images should feature RVs against a scenic backdrop. Also, think cover shot (vertical) when taking these photos and remember lighting is crucial to the overall effect. Focus your photography on scenic or panoramic views for the opening layout and points of interest, local color and activity shots for the carryover pages. Photos and slides supplied by someone other than the manuscript author should be clearly identified for photo credit. All photos and slides will be returned after publication when possible. Please include a self-addressed, stamped envelope for this purpose.

Neither *Highways* nor TL Enterprises Inc. assumes any responsibility for unsolicited material. —*Revised 01/04*

Categories: Associations—Lifestyle—Outdoors—Recreation—Recreation Vehicles—Senior Citizen—Travel—Camping

CONTACT: Dee Reed, Managing Editor
Material: All
2575 Vista Del Mar Dr.
Ventura, CA 93001
Phone: 800-765-1912, Ext. 609
Fax: 805-667-4009

Hispanic Career World

Please refer to Equal Opportunity Publications, Inc.

The Hollins Critic
Established in 1964

The Hollins Critic

Poetry editor Cathryn Hankla reads poetry from September to December 15th each year. Submissions received at other times will be returned unread.

Poetry submitted to *The Hollins Critic* should be typed or word processed. There are no rules about style or subject. One to five poems should be submitted to Cathryn Hankla, Poetry Editor, PO Box 9538, Hollins University, Roanoke, VA 24020. *The Hollins Critic* cannot reply without a self-addressed stamped envelope. We do not accept e-mail submissions.

The Critic pays $25.00 per poem, upon publication. All rights revert to the author following publication, but if the poem is reprinted elsewhere, *The Hollins Critic* should be credited.

Besides poetry, *The Hollins Critic* publishes an essay on a contemporary author in each issue, and book reviews as space permits. *The Hollins Critic* does not accept unsolicited essays. Rarely do we accept unsolicited book reviews. When a review is published, the author receives a copy of the issue, and two copies are sent to the book's publisher.

Thank you for your interest in *The Hollins Critic*.

Categories: Nonfiction—Literature—Poetry

CONTACT: Cathryn Hankla, Poetry Editor
Material: Poetry
Hollins University
PO Box 9538
Roanoke VA 24020
Phone: 540-362-6275
Fax: 540-362-6642
E-mail: acockrell@hollins.edu (No Submissions)
Website: www.hollins.edu/grad/eng_writing/critic/critic.htm

Home Business Journal

HOME Business Journal's purpose is to arm the reader with the best advice available to help those in home business, or seriously interested in such work, thrive and enjoy working at home.

Articles must be submitted in conventional style, word-processed or typed, with title, contributor's name, address and telephone/fax number on first page. Approximate word count and rights offered should also be displayed on first page. Feature articles should be approximately 1000 words. Filler materials are items of 300 words or less. Articles may also be submitted via E-Mail to Kim@HOME BusinessJournal.net. Submissions made by E-Mail should be included in the text. Phone ideas are not acceptable.

Contributors must warrant that all work submitted is original and that no Copyrighted material is used within contribution without permission in writing. Such permission must accompany contribution. If article or contribution that has been requested does not meet editor's approval, contributor may or may not be asked to edit material and resubmit. No additional payment will be made for such re-submissions. All photos or illustrations that include persons must be accompanied by permission to use and complete captions to explain the artwork.

HOME Business Journal is not responsible for contributions submitted to the magazine and cannot be responsible for the return of such materials.

HOME Business Journal may provide contributing writers with a byline upon publication of article. *HOME Business Journal* welcomes the submission of quality articles and news pertaining to home based businesses. Gratis submissions are welcome. Base pay of $75 is offered upon acceptance to authors seeking compensation for their original article. All other requested submissions are negotiated by the editor on a per-piece basis. Payment for requested submission is made upon publication.

HOME Business Journal is able to issue payment only to writers in the United States and Canada at this time.

HOME Business Journal recently expanded what was formerly the Entrepreneur Spotlight section of the magazine. Now labeled "The Neighborhood CEO," there are four to six of these home biz profile articles in each issue. *The specs for these articles are as follows:*

1. The profile must be on a business that is currently home based.

2. I am looking for articles that provide the story behind the business owner as opposed to an "advertorial" for the home business. Articles written from a personal, inspirational angle are preferable: ie. a senior starting over, friends combining talents, young entrepreneur, unique business, unique reason business was begun, etc.

This column was designed to provide proof that home business opportunities are not limited to MLM's, franchises, or other Business-In-A-Box type deals. In essence, I am looking for articles that leave readers saying "I could do that."

3. Neighborhood CEO articles may not exceed 700 words.

4. The home business name, address, and phone number (if applicable) must be supplied. These will be published in an inset within the article. A clear, head-shot photo of the business owner is also required. Color photos sent electronically (TIF,EPS,JPG) need to be at least 300 DPI when viewed at a 2 x 2 size.

4. Writers will be paid $75 - payable upon publication - and will receive byline credit.

Categories: Nonfiction—Business—Money & Finances

CONTACT: Editor
Material: All
9584 Main Street Holland Patent
Holland Patent NY 13354
Phone: 315-865-4100 Ext: 223 (No queries by phone)
Fax: 315-865-4000
E-mail: Kim@HOMEBusinessJournal.net or
Kim@SteffenPublishing.com
Website: www.HOMEBusinessJournal.net

Home Cooking

General Information

House of White Birches publishes Home Cooking magazine, a 96-page, bimonthly, newsprint issue.

Submissions

1. Queries or manuscripts:

• Query and manuscript reviews are held approximately every eight weeks. Check the editorial calendar for themes and dates. Your query or manuscript must be in our office by this scheduled date to be considered for inclusion in the issue.

• Queries should include an opening or summarizing paragraph, along with a list of six to 10 recipes with brief descriptions (previously published recipes are not acceptable). Completed manuscripts may also be submitted. Keep a copy of all materials.

• We will contact you within three weeks after the review date if we accept your query or manuscript. Responses to accepted queries will request the complete manuscript on speculation; no articles will be assigned. All others will be returned within four weeks after the review date when an appropriate SASE or e-mail address is provided.

2. Manuscript guidelines:

• Type and double-space all manuscripts on white paper in our magazine style, following a current publication.

• Pay special attention to ingredient lists. Spell out amounts, such as tablespoon, teaspoon, cup, ounce, etc. List ingredients in order used.

• Include temperatures, cooking times, container sizes and all other pertinent information in the directions.

• Give number of servings.

• Follow an introduction of 200 to 750 words with six to 10 recipes.

• Be certain that the subject matter has nationwide appeal.

• Include your name, address, telephone/fax number and e-mail address as appropriate in the upper left-hand corner of the first page. The upper right-hand corner must include the word count.

• Note a simultaneous submission as such. Simultaneous submissions are not encouraged.

3. **Departments:** Only "Kitchen Know-How" and "Pinch of Sage" are open to freelancers. Check current issues for style.

4. **Photographs.** Do not send.

5. **Mailing address:** Send queries and completed manuscripts to Shelly Vaughan James, Home Cooking, House of White Birches, 306 East Parr Road, Berne, IN 46711 or Editor@HomeCookingMagazine.com. If you e-mail, send a text message only; do not send attached files.

Contracts and payment

Following the manuscript deadline, we will send you a contract, a copy for your records and a business-reply envelope. Sign the contract and return it in the postage-paid envelope. Keep the copy of the contract for your records.

Payment will be made within 45 days of the time we receive your contract. Amount will be determined by length, overall quality, accuracy and adherence to guidelines. Average fees range from $25 to $250. HWB purchases all rights to manuscripts. Contributors should not sell the purchased manuscript or one very similar to it to another publisher.

If you have any questions, contact the editor. We look forward to working with you.

Categories: Nonfiction—Cooking—Entertainment—Food/Drink

CONTACT: Shelly Vaughan James, Editor
Material: Queries and completed manuscripts
House of White Birches
306 East Parr Rd
Berne IN 46711
Phone: 260-589-4000
E-mail: Editor@HomeCookingMagazine.com
Website: www.whitebirches.com

Home Education Magazine

Home Education Magazine is for families who enjoy living and learning together. If you're not familiar with homeschooling please study our publication before submitting. If you are familiar with homeschooling you might want to study it anyway, as we do take an active political stance for empowering individual families.

The current issue will be sent for $6.50 postpaid.

We offer selected articles and columns from each issue at our website.

There is also an excellent collection of reading from our magazine, sorted by topic, in the Homeschooling Information Library at our website.

TOPICS

Any topic of interest to homeschooling families will be considered. Please be aware that we have the most widely diverse readership in the homeschooling community, and our content reflects that diversity. We generally prefer completed articles to query letters. We welcome articles from inexperienced writers, especially mothers with homeschooling experience. Regardless of what you were taught in high school English classes, writing is nothing particularly mysterious. It's only another form of communication. If you can clearly explain your

ideas to a friend, you can write a good article for our magazine. Please see the article at the end of these guidelines for tips and information on writing for *Home Education Magazine*.

DEADLINES

Please feel free to submit an article on any topic at any time, and we'll schedule it appropriately. Please note that articles are often selected 4-6 months ahead of an issue.

SUBMISSIONS

Submissions via email are the preferred format (see Suggestions below), please send to HEM-Editor@home-ed-magazine.com (when submitting via email please remember to include your postal mailing address). Our computers are Macintoshes, and we have many filters so we can read most submissions, but sometimes files will need to be reformatted and special formatting (bolds, italics, etc.) will be lost. Please refer to "Suggestions for E-mail Submissions" below.

We do accept typed or handwritten articles, which you can mail to Articles, *Home Education Magazine*, Post Office Box 1083, Tonasket, WA 98855-1083. When submitting articles via postal mail, please remember to include a self-addressed, stamped envelope with sufficient postage for the return of your work. If you don't need your article returned, a stamped reply postcard or an email address will be fine.

General article length is 900 to 1,500 words, but we do occasionally run longer articles.

Please include a 40-60 word biographical credit (in third person) with your submission. If you prefer, we can run only your name and city/state. We will also accept pen names.

SUGGESTIONS FOR EMAIL SUBMISSIONS (from our Articles Editor, Kim O'Hara)

1. Start your subject line with "HEM:" or include the word "article" or "submission" in the subject header to help me sort them out from other email.

2. Include the article in the text of your email so I can look it over quickly and send you a response.

3. Also attach the article as an RTF file, which seems to be the most universal format for all different computer systems, and retains bolding and italics.

4. If you have any footnotes, be aware that RTF files don't include those; make sure they are included in the email text.

5. Include your name, regular-mail address (where we can send payment and a copy of the magazine if your article is accepted), and a short 40-60 word bio (written in third person).

PHOTOS

We always need sharp, clear photos for inside editorial use. Regular B/W print sizes work fine for inside use (images are printed at 200 dpi, 100 lpi). Covers (133 lpi, 300 dpi) require a very sharp, clear image. Color enlargements are best (8 by 10 min.), but please sent an image for review first. We prefer photos showing children and families doing everyday things, not necessarily posed educational-type shots. We advise studying our magazine before attempting photo submissions. Please include information about the photo, including names of anyone in the pictures, and the name of the photographer. Please make sure photos are clearly marked with your name so if they become separated we can still tell whose they are. Also include a SASE with sufficient postage for the return of your photos. This should be a separate SASE from the SASE or postcard you send for return of your article or editorial response.

Electronic submissions of photos are accepted. Please arrange to send low resolution (72 dpi) for review. If your low resolution image is accepted, you can send the full-sized version at the resolutions noted above for inside and cover photos. For more information write to Mark Hegener at HEM@home-ed-magazine.com.

RIGHTS

Home Education Magazine buys First North American Serial Rights (print and electronic) to all articles, columns, artwork and photos.

We upload selected articles and columns from each issue to our website: http://www.home-ed-magazine.com/ Rights purchased include our right to reproduce your work in CD-ROM format as well as in any other formats of *Home Education Magazine* in which your work appears, or in an anthology or collection of articles, columns, artwork and photos which have appeared in *Home Education Magazine*. All rights not stated here, or not directly related to *Home Education Magazine*, including Second Serial, or reprint rights, remain yours.

PAYMENT

Feature articles — $50.00-$100.00 each. We occasionally pay more for articles we've requested, or which require special expenses or considerations. Photos for inside use $12.50 each. Cover color photos $100.00 each. Contributors always receive at least one free copy of the issue in which their work appears. Up to three additional copies are available free on request.

Categories: Children—Christian Interests—Education—Family—General Interest—Parenting—Home Schooling

CONTACT: Helen Hegener, Managing Editor
Material: All
PO Box 1083
Tonasket WA 98855-1083
Phone: 509-486-1351
E-mail: HEM-Editor@home-ed-magazine.com
Website: www.home-ed-magazine.com

Home Furnishings Retailer

Home Furnishings Retailer is the official publication of National Home Furnishings Association (NHFA). NHFA is a national trade organization serving the interests of the nation's home furnishings retailers. Home Furnishings Retailer is published monthly with the exception of December. The magazine's primary audience comprises the top executives of retail stores specializing in furniture, decorative accessories and other products for the home.

Home Furnishings Retailer is owned by retailers, targeted to retailers and its editorial content focuses on issues that impact the retail community. On-going objective of all articles is to provide inrely heavily on home furnishings industry experts to author articles. Some freelance material is used. However, the NHFA Board of Directors, which provides direction for the publication, requires that writers have credentials that include specific knowledge of the industry and extensive experience in writing about it. Freelancers are compensated based on subject matter and the amount of research required.

Suggestions for freelance articles relating to the business interests of retailers will be reviewed. When submitting a query or requesting a writing assignment, include a resume, writing samples and credentials. Generally, only writers with experience within the home furnishings industry will be considered.

When articles are assigned, Home Furnishings Retailer will provide general direction along with suggestions for appropriate artwork. The author is responsible for obtaining photographs or other illustrative material.

Assigned articles should be submitted via email or on disc along with a list of sources with telephone numbers, fax numbers and email. Fees will be set upon assignment and payment made upon acceptance.

Categories: Nonfiction—Home—Woodworking

CONTACT: Submissions Editor
Material: All
3910 Tinsley Drive, Ste., 101
High Point, NC 27265
Phone: 336-886-6100
E-mail: info@nhfa.org
Website: www.nhfa.org

Home Improver Magazine

STYLE & POLICY GUIDELINES

The goal of *Home Improver* is to provide readers with concise information reported in a responsible manner. Individual style is encouraged, but not at the cost of good journalism techniques, proper word usage and grammar. Our purpose is to be informative, educational and entertaining.

It is strongly recommended that all writers read and consult *Strunk & White's Elements of Style* with particular regard for those sections detailing punctuation and sentence structure. Originally published in 1935, this small text is neither outdated nor a fundamental primer. Its contents are the foundation of skillful written communication. A writer's personal style develops from the proper creative use of the basic writing tools. It's inexpensive, a quick read and an invaluable writer's companion.

FREELANCE SUBMISSIONS

We want our editors to be known throughout the Home Improvement Industry and *Home Improver* encourages you to submit articles for publication in other periodicals. The only exceptions, of course, are submissions to our direct competitors. If possible, try to include your title of Contributing Editor, *Home Improver* as byline information.

FAX TRANSMISSIONS

Please double space all copy transmitted by fax service. Our fax machine is open 24 hours, 7 days a week.

As a backup, please have a printed copy available so it can be resent if possible.

E-MAIL TRANSMISSIONS

Files must be transmitted in ASCII.txt format. They should be sent to LouKojak@aol.com

FRACTIONS

You may write fractions in either decimal (1.75 pounds) or fraction (1 3/4 pounds) format. For modem transmissions only, please prefix fractions with a hyphen (-) as in 1 - 3/4 pounds. As with italic notations, this cues our computer to alter the printing style.

NUMBERS

Unless the reference is to a weight or measure (as above) numbers from zero to ninety-nine should be written. Numbers of 100 and above should be numerical.

JARGON

We face the use of slang and colloquialisms everywhere in the home improvement industry and we face the urge to emphasize such jargon words with quotes and italics. To do so tends to exclude the reader and makes it appear as if the reader is on the outside of a clique that knows better. Avoid emphasizing jargon words whenever possible.

PROPER NAMES

There are many ways individuals choose to spell their names and many ways to spell various location place names around our region. Without exception, we will defer to the spelling that you provide so double-check your copy.

BLOCK THAT METAPHOR

Be judicial in your use of metaphors and in your use of words that may be offensive to readers. When in doubt, don't write it.

©Home Improver Publications, Inc., 1998

Categories: Nonfiction—Architecture—Consumer—Gardening—Lifestyle—Home Improvement—Remodeling

CONTACT: Susan Luft, Editor
Material: All
©Home Improver Publications, Inc
11 Virginia Rd.

White Plains NY 10603
Phone: 914-328-1992
Fax: 914-328-1993
E-mail: himprover@aol.com
Website: www.himprover.com

Home Times Family Newspaper

Home Times is a monthly tabloid newspaper, distributed locally and nationally by U.S. Mail to paid subscribers and requestors, covering world & national news & views, home & family, arts & entertainment, and religion, all with a Biblical worldview. It is pro-Christian and pro-Jewish—but not religious.

We are a NEWSpaper, so content is generally keyed to current events and hot issues of the day. It is aimed squarely at the general public and written for them, though it receives most of its support from Christian readers. The news articles are often what we call "virtual exclusives," stories unpublished or under-published in the regular news media, often reporting on trends months, even years before they find their way into the regular press. Features on family, education, parenting, entertainment (movies, books, TV, videos) are practical, not preachy, related to issues and values.

Home Times is non-denominational and non-doctrinal, free of religious cliches or churchy or preachy perspectives. It tries not to moralize but to just be positive and Biblical in perspective. Our goal is to publish godly viewpoints in the marketplace, and to counteract the culturally elite of media and politics who reject Judeo-Christian values, traditional American values, true history, and faith in God.

Home Times is different from all other "Christian" publications— we strongly suggest you read these guidelines AND sample issues. Once you understand our slant, and if this is your kind of writing— you'll enjoy writing for *Home Times*!

We make it easy for you to "test ride" *Home Times*: send $3 to receive the next 3 issues when published (no SASE). Or as a freelance writer, subscribe at $12 for 12 issues ("Writer's Sub").

We encourage new writers at *Home Times*. We do not pay much— but it is a great opportunity for writers, especially new writers, to hone their skills. The editor has even written a 12-chapter report for new writers entitled "101 Reasons Why I Reject Your Mss"—which is an effective training course for new freelancers, easy to understand and written with lots of humor.

General Requirements: We want complete manuscripts—no multiple submissions and no queries please. Photos and illustrations may enhance a story if appropriate. No slides, negatives, computer disks, faxes or e-mail please. Pay is upon publication and ranges from $0 to $25 ($0 to $10 for reprints—which are accepted). PHOTOS if used are paid at $5 each. SEASONAL materials: 6-8 weeks in advance. LENGTH: as brief as possible, 700-800 words. Major stories up to 1200 words are accepted but not as readily. We reserve the right to shorten your story and edit it somewhat to fit our slant and style. REPLIES: we're understaffed and overworked so sometimes we get back to you in a few days, sometimes in a month. Holler if you don't hear in six weeks.

Special Opportunities: We want personal features in these categories: Human Heroes, true-to-life stories 600-800 words with photo(s), generally about ordinary people who do extraordinary things, or about the goodness of God in our lives; Light One Candle: little people who do something to change our world for the better; Sports Essays, brief (300-600 words) on the values or issues side of sports. These pay the usual rate.

Local Opportunities: Local People Stories, local events; local calendar, local issues and news events of importance to the family; usually with a slant that is of interest to families everywhere. These kinds of stories are often assigned, or suggested to the editor by phone if you are local; not available if you are not local (SE Florida). Quite frankly, we need some volunteers in this area too.

Some Non-Cash Opportunities: We generally pay for the following with a six-issue subscription: We want Briefs of all sorts, Anecdotes

in various categories such as: Family Life (funny stories from Parents & Kids), Tales Out Of School (funny incidents from teachers & students, all grades through college), In The Pew (funny things that happened in church or synagogue), First Grade Jokes (clean corny kid stuff), America! (funny stories about Americans), and Good News Only sharing faith in God and Jesus Christ; ALSO: Great Shots! (photos of babies, kids, family, pets, action, news events that are cute, funny or unusual); and Letters to the Editor (to 200 words) and OpEds (to 400 words).

Some Do's & Don'ts:
• Don't preach. No devotionals.
• We do accept poetry (traditional or light verse to 16 lines) and short fiction (up to 800 words) but it's best to read "HT" samples to see what we like.
• The Religion section is more spiritual and wants articles on prayer, unity, revival and harvest
• We run Special Emphases but they are usually tied into current events and rarely planned ahead.
• Internships/volunteers: We will talk to students interested in a career in our kind of journalism, about summer or school-year internships. We also have a small corps of volunteers who help with writing, layout, distribution, mailings, phone work, etc. "HT" is more than a business—it is a ministry to our nation, seeking to restore our godly roots—please call if interested!

Categories: Fiction—Nonfiction—Adventure—African-American—Arts—Book Reviews—Business—Cartoons—Children—Christian Interests—Comedy—Culture—Economics—Education—Entertainment—Family—Film/Video—General Interest—Government—Health—History—Human Rights—Inspirational—Interview—Jewish Interest—Lifestyle—Literature—Marriage—Money & Finances—Music—Parenting—Physical Fitness—Poetry—Politics—Psychology—Recreation—Relationships—Religion—Rural America—Satire—Science—Self Help—Senior Citizen—Short Stories—Singles—Society—Spiritual—Sports/Recreation—Teen—Television/Radio—Theatre—Women's Fiction—Women's Issues—Writing—Young Adult—Current Events—Current Issues

CONTACT: Dennis Lombard, Editor & Publisher
Material: All
3676 Collin Dr. Ste. 16
W. Palm Beach FL 33406
Phone: 561-439-3509
E-mail: hometimes2@aol.com

HomeLife

Thanks for your interest in writing for *HomeLife* magazine. We are always looking for qualified Christian writers who deliver professional Christian journalism. These guidelines will help you understand more about who we are, what we're looking for, and how we work with writers.

WHO WE ARE

The mission of *HomeLife* is to equip and challenge families to experience dynamic, healthy, Christ-centered lives.

All articles submitted should be consistent with the vision and doctrinal statements of our publisher, LifeWay Christian Resources:
• **LifeWay Vision:** As God works through us, we will help people and churches know Jesus Christ and seek His Kingdom by providing biblical solutions that spiritually transform individuals and cultures.
• **Doctrinal Statement:** We believe that the Bible has God for its author; salvation for its end; and truth, without any mixture of error, for its matter and that all Scripture is totally true and trustworthy. The 2000 statement of "The Baptist Faith and Message" is our doctrinal guideline (available online at www.sbc.net/toc.html).

FIRST CONTACT

HomeLife does not accept unsolicited queries or manuscripts. We do not accept reprints and offer nonexclusive license contracts.

In your initial contact with our editors, we ask that you provide the following:

1. **Resume.** Emphasize your formal writing training (such as a degree in journalism, communications, English, and so on); writing experience; and recent published works. List your qualifications as a writer (such as experience in researching and interviewing or particular areas of expertise).

2. **Clips.** Send recently published pieces, including your original drafts as available. Include articles that are similar to what you might write for our publication.

3. **Biographical Form.** Available upon request, this form allows you to tell us your areas of interest/expertise, as well as a brief description of your journey with Christ. (As a Christian magazine, we desire to have writers who are Christ followers and are growing spiritually.)

Please send the requested information to HomeLife, New Writer, One LifeWay Plaza, Nashville, TN 37234-0175 or fax them to HomeLife, New Writer at 615.277.8272.

Writers will be evaluated on their ability to produce articles that fit within the tone and mission of *HomeLife* and their ability to produce articles that offer our readers practical ways to live out their faith in everyday family life.

You may contact *HomeLife* with any questions through e-mail at homelife@lifeway.com.

WORKING WITH WRITERS

HomeLife's method of working with writers is by article assignment. Typically, the *HomeLife* team develops the concepts for articles in each issue. We then assign articles to freelance writers. Occasionally we accept queries from writers we have a working relationship with.

OUR EDITORIAL VOICE

In developing our editorial voice, we emphasize:

• **Practical help.** We want to offer our readers articles that offer takeaway value. As a Christian family magazine, we print articles that address matters of faith, marriage, parenting, and the practical issues of daily living.

• **Authenticity.** We want to address real-life needs and issues.

• **Quality research.** We want to offer readers information that is fresh, not stale. We look for research of primary sources and interesting slants that offer help unique to HomeLife.

• **Scriptural integrity.** Our goal is to help families experience Christ-centered life, so all of the articles in the magazine should line up with and be supported by the truths of Scripture. However, we are looking for practical magazine articles, not devotionals or Bible studies.

We follow The Associated Press Stylebook and Libel Manual. All Scripture quotations should be from the Holman Christian Standard Bible (HCSB) or New International Version (NIV), unless you have a compelling reason to use a different translation.

Categories: Nonfiction—Health—Lifestyle—Parenting—Relationships

CONTACT: Submissions/Copy Editor
Material: All
One LifeWay Plaza
Nashville TN 37234-0175
Phone: 615-251-2011
Fax: 615-277-8272
Website: www.lifewayonline.ocm/mags

Hope Magazine

Editorial Mission Statement

Hope magazine is edited to inspire a sense of hope among readers: that the world can be made a better place, and that we can better know our place within it. The editorial and photography focuses on individuals, businesses, and organizations working hard to make a difference, especially the ordinary and unsung who are doing extraordinary and inspiring things, yet whose stories are rarely heard. It reports on individuals helping others in myriad ways, individuals overcoming adversity of varying nature and degree, and businesses and organizations acting to make a difference in their communities and their world. It also seeks to share, with an unblinking, yet compassionate eye, the dignity in those human beings whose stories we are so often inclined to overlook: individuals who have not yet found their place in the world, or whose place we cannot easily comprehend from the vantage of our own lives. And yet, even in this darker and more challenging focus, *Hope* seeks to provide a much-needed balance and depth to the unrelenting bad news that abounds from nations to neighborhoods.

A magazine without religious, political, or new age affiliation, *Hope* strives unabashedly to explore and celebrate the most enduring human values, and to help us glimpse our common bonds as we move together toward the 21st century, concerned about our elderly, our youth, and ourselves. It hopes to awaken the impulse we all have—however hidden or distant—to make our world a little better, to make ourselves more responsive to it, and to better understand our place and purpose here. Without proselytizing, preaching, or asking certain action of us, *Hope* reacquaints us with much more of humanity, even in its flawed beauty, than we find in the mass media. It is not about the trappings of wealth and glamour, nor the powerful and influential. It is about us. The real us. And though the picture will not always be pretty, it will endeavor to be compelling.

Carefully designed to be attractive, inviting, and accessible, *Hope* is an intimate magazine which goes directly to the heart while engaging the mind; a welcome antidote to the fast-paced, de-personalizing way of life in which so many of us find ourselves immersed.

Published for a readership of diverse ages and interests, *Hope* appeals to the curious and the concerned, the thoughtful and the educated, the active and impassioned among us, from idealistic teens to mindful septuagenarians. There is no magazine quite like it, and yet elements of others will be found here: *Hope* aspires to the intellectual ideals of *Atlantic Monthly, Harper's,* and *The New Yorker,* as well as the emotional instincts of *The Reader's Digest, People,* and *Life.* It will be as surprising and unpredictable as *The Utne Reader, Vanity Fair,* and *Colors,* and yet thoroughly inviting and embracing in style and content. It will be as timeless, as honest, and compelling as the once-ubiquitous book The Family of Man.

Hope is a magazine whose mission is to gently alter the ways in which its readers see the world by honoring values worth pursuing, traditions worth preserving, and futures worth changing for the better. It will touch our hearts and inspire our minds, and given time, it could change the way we see the world and ourselves; given time, it could change the way we respond to the world and each other. Given time, it could help us change the world.

Guidelines for Writers and Photographers

These guidelines should combine with *Hope* magazine's editorial mission statement to provide insight for writers and photographers whose work might advance or enlighten its mission, and we welcome queries.

The myriad good news/bad news agendas of *Hope* might seem at first glance to be in contradistinction to one another, and to the objective of inspiring a sense of hope among readers. Why, after all, would such a magazine publish articles on the volatile and violent subculture of the inner city? Or the haunted world of the homeless mentally ill? Or the unfathomed mind of the rapist and murderer? On the other hand, why is a magazine determined to avoid the institutions of religion so interested in individuals whose lives are inspired by it? What are we doing saluting the efforts of those working to change political systems while steering clear of politics itself? Where, exactly, is our focus? The short answer is that our focus is broad.

Hope will be consistent only in its intention to awaken, inform, educate, and entertain, and in its determination to avoid cynicism as an overarching form. Beyond that, it is a magazine searching all corners, all surfaces—the dark and the light—for aspects of humanity too precious to avoid or ignore. Its mission is to convey good news—hopeful and inspiring news—but it is also to convey perspectives on overwhelming negative truths, and on the shifting realities that weave lives through the margins of good and bad, of failure and success. These are domains where hope itself often fades and fails, and where inspiration and action must be catalyzed. Our responsibility is to find these stories, and to reflect an honest light upon their most intricate elements.

If *Hope* is to be an effective magazine, it must foil preconception. It must be different from the journalistic norm, ever unpredictable, and yet embracing and respectful of readers. To some extent, it must seduce the wary and cynical beyond the title, for its mission is to be a catalyst for individual change by touching readers as directly and deeply as possible. So it must surprise, engage, inform, unnerve, and inspire with fine and honest writing and compelling photography and illustration. It must find exciting and artful ways of sharing good news, for we can be easily bored without intellectual and emotional tension, without a recognition of the fragility of individual goodness. It must weave humor into its sensitivity, for *Hope* cannot become melancholy.

In the darker subjects, our writing must be no less artful, and it will require courage to look into the maw, imagination to uncover the detail, and compassion to honor that which deserves it. We may struggle with the line between empathy and sympathy, but our objective is empathy: the sense we need most to increase our awareness, and to become, as it were, allies of one another, even as we preserve our individualism. We may also struggle, in the writing and the photojournalism, with the fine line between what is relevant to our missions, and what is prurient or exploitative.

We are not here to shock our readers, but we must be committed to awakening them to largely unheard cries, largely unseen faces, and largely unknown realities. We may, in fact, be searching for new definitions of terms as we attempt to share stories that move, rather than lull us. We're in this together; the world needs work, as do we all, and humor, tolerance, and optimism will be as critical to the context of our missions as unblinking honesty. The more voices heard, the more visions shared, the more effective *Hope* can be. Empathy is our ultimate objective. All the writing, all the photography, and all the illustration should create, sustain, or inform our empathy in some way, no matter what the subject.

Our occasional essays on varied subjects run from 800 to 2,000 words in length. Our features run from 1,000 to 3,000 words, depending on subject, and we're happy to integrate sidebar material where it adds substance. *In addition to the core features, we run regular departments, in which different aspects and expressions of hope are included and explored:*

• Signs of Hope: notes and dispatches, generally ranging from 300 to 500 words, in which good and great works and ideas are reported.

• Book Reviews: Devoted primarily to nonfiction works in widely diverse subject areas relevant to struggle and triumph, and to hope in general.

Hope is a strongly visual magazine. While our covers are printed in color, our editorial photography and illustration is printed in high-quality black & white. Our sensitivity to the technical and aesthetic aspects of the illustrative material is very keen, and we are always interested in seeing examples of photographers' and illustrators' works. We obtain the best results in color by utilizing transparencies, but we can work from reflective art, as well. Black & white images may arrive for examination in contact-sheet form, as long as they're accompanied by a couple of 5"x7" prints from the sheet, which allow us to better appreciate focus and contrast in the images.

We tend to favor prints that are rich in detail and balanced in contrast—in short, very readable, very detailed. As for content, we seek to evoke a sense of access and intimacy, of art and honesty. The closer the photographer can bring us to the reality of the human being,

or to the experience and the circumstance, the better we like it. Uninhibited emotion, from joy to contentment, from rage to despair, from loneliness to love, is what we want to share and convey. In this regard, we're also very interested in feature-length photo essays.

We invite and welcome samples and portfolios, asking only that return postage accompany unsolicited material. All materials furnished for publication by photographers and illustrators will be returned upon publication of the issue in which they're used.

We purchase serial rights for one-time use of text and images, except in cases of prior agreement by the parties, and all published material is protected under the umbrella copyright of *Hope* magazine. Our rates of payment are rather modest at this formative stage, and we look forward to the time when we can raise them, for it will mean that *Hope* is succeeding as a venture. For the time being, however, we are limited, and can only offer the following by way of inspiration and rationalization:

"Beyond their pride in being a part of *The New Yorker*, about the only thing the magazine's fiction and nonfiction writers had in common, at least for the first fifteen or twenty years, was dissatisfaction with their pay, which ranged from the merely inadequate to the execrable. In its later years, The New Yorker's rates would become among the highest in the business, but through adolescence its penury was almost a point of pride."

—*From Genius in Disguise: Harold Ross of The New Yorker* by Thomas Kunkel (Random House, 1995)

There is no pride in low rates for us, but we couldn't resist sharing this passage, under the circumstances. *Our basic rates are:*

• Currently $.50 per word
• Cover (color) rate: $500.
• Editorial (B&W) $300/full page and down.

We welcome queries via U.S. Mail. We prefer responding to brief descriptions and detailed outlines, which tend to receive more careful attention.

We look forward to hearing from you.

With best wishes,

Jon Wilson, Editor-in-Chief (jon@hopemag.com)

Kimberly Ridley, Editor (kimr@hopemag.com)

Categories: Arts—Associations—Education—Family—General Interest—Human Insight/Interest/Spirit

CONTACT: Deborah L. Ramirez, Editorial Assistant
Material: All
PO Box 16
Brooklin ME 04616
Phone: 207-359-4651
Fax: 207-359-8920
E-mail: info@hopemag.com
Website: www.hopemag.com

Hopscotch for Girls

Every HOPSCOTCH contributor must remember we publish only six issues a year, which means our editorial needs are extremely limited. An annual total, for instance, will include some 30 to 36 nonfiction pieces, 9 or 10 short stories, 18 or so poems, six cover illustrations, and a smattering of puzzles, crafts, and the like.

It is obvious that we must reject far more contributions than we accept, no matter how outstanding they may seem to you or to us.

With that said, we would point out that HOPSCOTCH is a magazine created for girls from 6 to 12 years, with youngsters 8, 9, and 10 the specific target age.

Our point of view is that every young girl deserves the right to be a young girl for a number of years before she becomes a young adult.

As a result, HOPSCOTCH looks for articles, fiction, nonfiction, and poetry that deal with timeless topics, such as pets, nature, hobbies, science, games, sports, careers, simple cooking, and anything else likely to interest a young girl. We leave dating, romance, human sexuality, cosmetics, fashion, and the like to other publications. Each issue revolves around a theme. You may request a theme list by sending in a self-addressed, stamped envelope.

Writers

We are looking for lively writing, most of it from a young girl's point of view—with the girl or girls directly involved in an activity that is both wholesome and unusual. Examples have included girls in a sheep to shawl contest, girls raising puppies that are destined to guide the blind, and girls who take summer ballet lessons from members of the New York City Ballet.

While on the subject of nonfiction—remembering that we use it 3 to 1 over fiction—those pieces that are accompanied by black and white photos are far more likely to be accepted that those that need illustrations.

The ideal length of a HOPSCOTCH nonfiction piece is 500 words or less, although we are not about to turn down a truly exceptional piece if it is slightly longer than the ideal. We prefer fiction to not run over 1,000 words.

We will entertain simultaneous submissions as long as that fact is noted on the manuscript. Computer printouts are welcome if they are (as all submissions should be) double-spaced.

HOPSCOTCH prefers to receive complete manuscripts with cover letters, although we do not rule out query letters. We do not answer submissions sent in by fax or e-mail. All submissions must be accompanied by a self-addressed, stamped envelope, with sufficient postage.

We will pay a minimum of 5 cents a word for both fiction and nonfiction, with additional payment given if the piece is accompanied by appropriate photos or art. We will pay a minimum of $10 per poem or puzzle, with variable rates offered for games, crafts, cartoons, and the like.

HOPSCOTCH buys first American serial rights and pays upon publication. It welcomes the contributions of both published and unpublished writers.

Sample copies are available for $4.00 within the US & $5.00 outside the US. All payment must he in US. funds. A complimentary copy will be sent each writer who has contributed to a given issue.

Photographers

We use a number of black and white photos inside the magazine, most in support of articles used. Payment is $5-10 per photo, and $5 for color slides.

Artists

Most art will be by assignment, in support of features used. The magazine is anxious to find artists capable of illustrating stories and features and welcomes copies of sample work, which will remain on file. Payment is $25 for partial illustrations and $35 for full-page illustrations.

Incidentally

Although we are working far into the future, we occasionally have room for one or two pages.

One More Thing

We are always in need of cute and clever recipes, well-written and illustrated crafts, riddles, and jokes.

Categories: Fiction—Nonfiction—Animals—Cartoons—Children

CONTACT: Marilyn Edwards, Editor
Material: All
CONTACT: Virginia Edwards, Associate Editor
Material: All
PO Box 164
Bluffton OH 45817-0164

Phone: 419-358-4610
Fax: 419-358-5027
Website: www.hopscotchmagazine.com

Horror Tales
Short vampire-related horror fiction

Published: Annually

Book Formats: Anthology is a book-zine (eclectic like a magazine but in book form) and will be published in one or more of the following, traditional paper (either hardback or paperback), electronic (ebooks and/or audio).

Poetry, short fiction and other writings about the macabre (horror of all types), including ghost stories, spooky tales, ironic horror, etc.

Lengths: Open for all short fiction, poems, articles manuscripts of all lengths will be considered.

The deadline for submissions: Editor read submissions year-round.

Rights: One-time use in book form (all formats). Considers reprints if author owns rights.

Poets and writers should send a bio to accompany their writings in the anthology.

Please note: Writers with books and other publications or venues (i.e. a website) can submit information, website address, etc. for inclusion in the anthology to accompany their bio information. This will give writers added exposure for themselves and their books, websites, etc.

Contributors must send note (email or by regular mail) stating that he/she would like the writing(s) included in the published anthology. Submit up to 5 manuscripts, either by email or regular mail (see below). Please enclose SASE with regular mail submissions.

Contributors will receive one copy of the finished anthology.

Categories: Fiction—Entertainment—Horror—Short Stories

CONTACT: Eugene Boone
Material: All
RSVP Press
129 Thurman Lane
Clinton TN 37716
E-mail: rsvppress@yahoo.com

Horrorfind

Here at *Horrorfind*, we are willing to work with both new and seasoned authors. If you write horror stories, chances are that we're willing to look at it. We have published the latest from best-selling authors alongside the first story from high school students. We don't accept names. We accept stories. Our fiction section is updated regularly, and stories appearing here have gone on to be nominated or recommended for several genre awards, including the prestigious Bram Stoker Award and the Year's Best Fantasy & Horror.

We want horror fiction and all of its sub-genres. Quiet, extreme, dark fantasy, cross-genre (horror blended with sci-fi, sword & sorcery, etc.), weird western, dark crime, surreal, occult, splatterpunk, supernatural, magic realism, bizarre, erotic, HORROR. Yes, we will look at vampires, werewolves and serial killers. We love them. Just make sure you know your history and aren't repeating something that's already been done to death.

We don't want straight science fiction, fantasy or mystery. We won't consider stories without horror content. No gore for gore's sake. No sexual or extreme violence toward children. No poetry. No copyrighted characters (i.e. Jason, Freddy Krueger, Conan, etc.) unless you either own the copyright to those characters or have legal permission to be writing about them. Permission must be documented.

Fiction to 3,000 words. Anything longer, query first. We will accept reprints as long as you have obtained the rights. Simultaneous submissions okay, but please have the courtesy to inform us. Absolutely no multiple submissions at any time. Multiple submissions will be deleted unread. Include a brief bio.

Electronic submissions only. Send as either an attached Microsoft Word Document or pasted directly into the body of the email. You may also use the submission board here at Horrorfind and paste directly into that. If your story is accepted, you will be asked to follow it up with an attached Word Document or disc.

Horrorfind requires the assignment of Electronic Rights for a period of four (4) months. You retain all other rights. After 4 months, Electronic Rights revert back to you as well. You may choose to leave the story archived at the website, or may request to have it removed at any time, providing 24 hours notice is given. We reserve the right to remove the story from publication at any time after the 4 month period.

Payment for solicited submissions will vary on an individual basis, beginning at a professional rate of three (.03) cents per word. Payment for unsolicited submissions is in exposure. Stories published at Horrorfind may also be considered for future volumes of the *Best of Horrorfind* anthology. If selected, a separate contract would be negotiated for print rights.

Our response time will vary. We receive an average of 10 to 30 submissions a week. If you haven't received a response within 5 weeks, feel free to query.

Categories: Fiction—Erotica—Fantasy—Horror—Paranormal—Science Fiction—Short Stories—Western

CONTACT: Brian Keene, Fiction Editor
Material: All
E-mail: fiction@horrorfind.com

Horse Illustrated
The Magazine for Responsible Horse Owners

WRITER'S GUIDELINES

Thank you for your interest in HORSE ILLUSTRATED. We hope you find the following guidelines helpful in preparing any future submissions. Address all correspondence to Moira C. Harris, Editor, HORSE ILLUSTRATED, PO Box 6050, Mission Viejo, CA 92690. Enclose a self-addressed stamped envelope with all materials, and please allow six to eight weeks for a response.

Magazine Focus: *Horse Illustrated* is a general-circulation magazine, directed to horse owners and riders of English and western disciplines. The magazine espouses responsible horse ownership, from providing tips to owners on better horse care and training, to alerting horse lovers about pertinent issues in the equine community. We direct our articles to the adult audience.

Suggested Articles: The best way to decide what type of article to submit is to look over a sample copy of the magazine, available at newsstands, tack stores or book stores nationwide. You may obtain one by sending in a check for $5 to HORSE ILLUSTRATED, Attn: Sample Issues, at the address above. Look over several issues, if possible. Past issues posted on our web site (www.horseillustratedmagazine.com) list the types of articles we have used in the last year.

We need informative, in-depth, upbeat articles (limited to 2,000 words) that will help readers better care for and enjoy their horses. They may be about such topics as training (for both horse and rider), management or horse-related activities. We also accept shorter articles (approximately 500 words) that are news-oriented for our "Horseman's World" department. We do not publish fiction or personal accounts told in the first person. We do not accept tributes to deceased horses or poetry. Please do not send breed profiles; this monthly feature is always assigned.

HORSE ILLUSTRATED receives dozens of unsolicited manuscripts and queries every week. The magazine accepts only a small fraction of what is submitted. Due to the high volume of unsolicited

work, we cannot review or respond to any material sent to us by fax, or material that isn't accompanied by a self-addressed stamped envelope.

Manuscript Requirements: Manuscripts should be typewritten and double spaced with wide margins. Along with a hard copy, please send a 3 ½-inch floppy disk containing the text, and indicate the operating system and word processing program used (PC-based programs are preferred), or send the file in ASCII text. We prefer that manuscripts be accompanied by art appropriate to the story. This can be either professional-quality color transparencies (preferred), photographs or illustrations. Additional guidelines are available for artists and photographers.

Reviewing Material: We prefer to review manuscripts on speculation. If you would like to query us before preparing an article, you must include a detailed outline of what the proposed article will cover and sample paragraphs, or clips that demonstrate your writing style. We do not accept simultaneous submissions, but may accept reprint material from noncompetitive publications. We require first North American serial rights in the equine industry. We appreciate knowing if your material does not need to be returned. Otherwise, include an appropriately sized SASE with each submission.

Payment: Articles are paid upon publication. Rates of payment are based on quality, not length. We pay between $200 and $400 for feature articles. Horseman's World manuscripts receive $50 to $100 per piece. Articles accompanied by high-quality photographs or illustrations earn the highest rates.

Responsibility: We cannot assume responsibility for material submitted, but reasonable care will be taken in the handling of your work.

PHOTO GUIDELINES

HORSE ILLUSTRATED is a magazine directed toward adult horse owners. Safety and responsible care are the keynotes of our editorial content. Therefore, photos must depict healthy horses (unless submitting photos for a particular article on unhealthy horses), well-appointed riders (no shorts, bare feet or other inappropriate riding attire) and horses, and handlers using safe practices. Whenever possible, riders should be wearing safety helmets (or western hats), and adult riders should be shown. Photos should also depict the whole horse or person (no cut off ears, tails, noses, hooves, etc.).

Cover submissions: We want unique and outstanding photos of horses for use on the magazine's cover. The cover horse does not have to be of the same breed as the month's featured breed, but photos submitted for cover consideration should depict the horse as an excellent representation of its breed. The cover horse is always impeccably groomed (clean eyes, ears and nose is a must), and if the horse is wearing any tack, it should be fitted correctly and be appropriate for the activity of the horse (i.e., a western show halter should not be worn by a Thoroughbred).

We are looking for spectacular cover photos that depict the beauty, versatility and action of the horse. We have moved away from the traditional head shot, and are focusing on photography that portrays the "horse lifestyle," and the bond that people have with their horses. This means that people can be included in the shots. Full-body, action shots are best, but we may still consider an exceptional head shot.

The cover photo is usually related in some way to either that month's theme (the vacation issue or the foaling issue, for example) or to a feature included in that issue (but not necessarily the featured breed). If you are shooting for a particular article, or around a particular theme of the month, please indicate that a particular photo is for cover consideration. For example, if we are running a "caring for the older horse" article, you may want to submit a photo of an owner walking with an older horse. Cover photos must have a clean uncluttered background, and be vertically formatted with room along the left side of the photo for type and at the top for our logo. Very fast-speed film is usually too grainy for the quality we need for the cover.

Stock Photography: We have an increasing need for sharp, 4/C prints and transparencies to hold in our stock photography file. We draw from this file for every issue. If you do not have anything to submit for a specific article or issue, you may still submit for our stock files. If you do so, please include a letter stating this purpose. If the photos meet our standards, you will be sent a contract detailing which shots we are holding. Stock photos are held for an indefinite period of time, and are usually not returned until after they are used or until the photographer requests their return, which can be done at any time. Photos not selected for the stock photography are returned. Please note: We are constantly in need of quality photos of problem behaviors of horses and medical ailments; in addition, if a rider is not photographed at a public venue, e.g., on private property, you must submit a model release with the photos.

When photos are submitted for a particular use or article, they are reviewed during the production schedule for that issue. Contracts are written for the photos selected, and are usually sent to the photographer along with those photos not selected. Photos used in the magazine are returned during the month that the magazine appears in print.

Rates:

$200 - cover photo; centerspread; two-page spread

$ 90 - Full page color

$ 60 - Partial page color

$ 40 - full page black and white

$ 25 - partial page black and white

$ 25 - if a photo used in a feature is also included on the Table of Contents

Payment is made upon publication. Our rates are paid according to the format that the photo appears in the magazine, not the format in which the photo was submitted. For example, a 35mm color photo on the cover is paid $200, while a 35mm color photo used in a smaller format on a black and white page is paid $25. We buy first North American serial rights on an exclusive basis; the non-exclusive right to use the photos in electronic media; and the non-exclusive right to use the photos, as well as your name, image and biographical data in advertising and promotion.

We cannot accept duplicate slides, since we cannot reproduce from them. And we rarely use black and white prints. Our magazine is digitally produced, and all photographs are electronically scanned. Therefore, it is extremely important that all photos be sharp, with well-balanced contrast.

With each submission, please include correspondence that details what article your work should be considered for. Please include your social security number (or taxpayer ID) on your correspondence to expedite payment. Each shot should be labeled with your name, address and phone number. Information about the subject (breed, event) should also be included.

Please mail submissions to us at:
HORSE ILLUSTRATED
PO Box 6050
Mission Viejo, CA 92690-6050
For UPS or overnight deliveries:
HORSE ILLUSTRATED
3 Burroughs Drive
Irvine, CA 92618

Always include a self-addressed stamped envelope with enough postage for your photo's return. We cannot be responsible for lost or misdirected mail.

Categories: Animals

CONTACT: Moira C. Harris, Editor
Material: All
Fancy Publications, Inc.
PO Box 6050
Mission Viejo Ca 92690-6050
Phone: 949-855-8822
Website: www.horseillustratedmagazine.com

Remember: Editors change jobs and publishers change addresses. It is wise to invest in a phone call for the current information before submitting.

Horticulture

Published: 6 times per year
Circulation: 210,000
Query response time: 8 to 10 weeks
Number of articles purchased: About 10 a year from the approximately 400 unsolicited queries and manuscripts received
Rights purchased: One-time, first North American serial; all rights purchased for some departments
Expenses: Reasonable expenses paid if previously arranged with editor
Kill fee: Depends on final fee
Rates:

Type of article	Word length	Payment
Features	1,200-2,000	$600-$1,000
Departments	200-1,500	$50-$600

The Magazine

Horticulture, the country's oldest gardening magazine, is designed for active amateur gardeners. Our goal is to offer a blend of text, photographs, and illustrations that will both instruct and inspire readers. While we place great emphasis on good writing, we also believe that every article must offer ideas or illustrate principles that our readers can apply in their own gardens. No matter what the subject, we want articles to help our readers become better, more creative gardeners.

We assume that our writers have an interest in and some experience with gardening. We look for and encourage personal experience, anecdote, and opinion. At the same time, an article should place its subject, to whatever degree appropriate, in the broader context of horticulture.

Query Letters

Tell us why—as succinctly as possible—you think your idea belongs in *Horticulture* and give us the general outline of your piece. Please let us know your personal involvement with the subject. If the article will require research or reporting, give us a brief description of the work you'll need to do.

We appreciate receiving any background material you may have that will help us assess the appropriateness of your idea. Proposals for garden profiles, in particular, should be accompanied by photographs or transparencies. We would also like to see a sample of your writing.

Queries with a seasonal angle should be submitted at least ten months in advance of the proposed publication date.

Manuscript Submissions

We prefer that a query precede any manuscript. Manuscripts should be neatly typed and accompanied whenever possible by a computer disk. Include your name at the top of each page.

Categories: Nonfiction—Gardening

CONTACT: Thomas Fischer, Executive Editor
Material: All
98 N. Washington St.
Boston MA 02114
Phone: 617-742-5600
Fax: 617-637-6364
E-mail: horticulture_editorial@primediamags.com

House Beautiful

Thank you for your interest in *House Beautiful's* writer's guidelines.

We are primarily interested in service articles dealing strictly with the home. We use no fiction or poetry.

Be sure to study the style and contents of a few recent issues before submitting any proposals or articles. With your submission, please include some samples of your published work.

We prefer receiving queries rather than finished manuscripts. This will save you time. If we are interested in an idea, we will ask you to send in the article on speculation.

Rates, payable on acceptance, are determined by the length of the article. Most of our articles run 400 to 1000 words.

Please label with complete name and address every page, caption, photo, etc. that you submit. We receive many articles and queries and it is very easy for material to become separated.

Any submissions sent without a stamped, self-addressed envelope will not be returned.

Address all articles, queries and related correspondence to the address below. No phone calls or e-mails, please.

Thank you again for your interest in *House Beautiful*.

Categories: Architecture—Home—Lifestyle

CONTACT: Features department
Material: All
1700 Broadway, 29th Floor
New York NY 10019
Phone: 212-903-5084

House, Home and Garden

House, Home and Garden, a bimonthly publication, publishes articles related to the home, gardening, cooking and entertainment. We reach a diverse audience whose interests include various aspects of home life. We would like to see more submissions with information, new product, decorating and pet themes.

About three quarters of what we publish is written by non-staff writers (approximately 50 manuscripts per year). If you are new to us, please send for a sample copy of our magazine before submitting your work ($3.50 and 9" x 12" SASE with four first class stamps). Doing so will help you to better understand our style and content requirements.

We will accept queries or complete manuscripts. Computer printouts are fine.

Word length varies for both articles and department/columns. When thinking about an article for us, think about real estate, practical decorating ideas, house and home, antiques, travel, leisure and crafts. For departments/columns, think about home management, beauty, new products and travel.

We will negotiate rights and pay $0.10 per word up to 1,500 words on publication, plus one contributor's copy.

Thank you for your interest in writing for *House, Home and Garden*. We look forward to hearing from you.

Categories: Adventure—Animals—Antiques—Architecture—Arts—Children—Collectibles—Computers—Cooking—Crafts/Hobbies—Diet/Nutrition—Electronics—Entertainment—Family—Fashion—Feminism—Food/Drink—Gardening—Health—Hobbies—Money & Finances—Outdoors—Poetry—Real Estate—Self Help—Short Stories—Travel—Pets

CONTACT: Earl D. Unger, Editor
Material: All
809 Virginia Ave.
Martinsburg WV 25401-2131
Phone: 304-267-2673
Fax: 304-262-0676

> *Remember: Editors change jobs and publishers change addresses. It is wise to invest in a phone call for the current information before submitting.*

THE FAMILY MAGAZINE FOR AMERICAN HOUSEBOATERS

HOUSEBOAT

Houseboat

Writer and Photographer Guidelines

Houseboat is a family-oriented publication for Houseboaters of all types across the United States and Canada. Readers of *Houseboat* includes houseboating families, couples, and retired couples; houseboat renters; houseboat manufacturers; boaters; full-time and part-time liveaboards; water-sport enthusiasts; fishermen; travel enthusiasts and so on.

Within our pages, readers will find features on new boats, destination pieces, new products, how-tos, service tips, industry news, houseboater profiles, special events and vintage houseboat articles. We also publish an annual buyer's guide and an annual Family Vacation Guide, as well as cover fishing and secondary water sports on occasion. If a topic can be tied into houseboating, there may be a place for it in our publication.

Queries: Query first with story ideas either by e-mail or snail mail to the addresses listed below. Include one or two paragraphs that briefly outline your idea and tell us why your story is timely, unique, new or of special interest. What qualifies you to write the story? Do you have photos to accompany the article?

Manuscripts: Features should run between 1,000 and 1,200 words. In addition, we like to run sidebars with features when appropriate that may run a few hundred words.

Use a third-person, reporter's viewpoint in how-to stories unless your experience in the boating industry qualifies you to write from a first-person perspective (please clear this with the editor beforehand). Our tone is a light and fun, as we want our readers to feel they can kick their feet up on their houseboats and enjoy the magazine from cover to cover.

Style: All submitted material should be consistent with the Associated Press style guide. Please pay particular attention to the use of numerals and measurements, as well as the abbreviations for states.

We prefer to receive manuscripts electronically as Microsoft Word attachments. Articles pasted into the body of the e-mail message are also acceptable if Word is not available. Include author's name, address and phone number on the top of the article. Harris Publishing reserves the right to edit submitted material as required.

Photos: We work with color slides or transparencies only. We prefer E100SW by Kodak, or Velvia by Fuji. Good contrast and sharp focus are a must. Submit 10 to 15 different photos to illustrate a feature thoroughly.

Involve people in every photo if possible. Show action and movement and attempt to do so from a fresh perspective. Utilize dawn and dusk lighting for dramatic photos.

Note: If you submit photos that belong to another person, you are responsible for splitting payment with him/her. We purchase manuscripts and photos as one package and pay only one fee.

Captions: All photo submissions must be keyed to a numbered caption sheet. Captions should be detailed enough to require little or no rewriting by our editorial staff.

Please identify people in your photos. Obtain a signed, model release if necessary and submit with the photos. Your name and address should be on each photo or transparency for proper credits, payment and photo returns.

Payment: Rates vary according to several factors including length, quality of the material, quality of the photos, and how much editing or rewriting is required. We work with professionals to maintain a certain level of quality for our readers. Therefore, we expect copy and photos to be of high quality.

Payment for features (including photos) range from $150 to $300. Columns, departments, mini-features and fillers (including photos) are worth $50 to $175. Payment is made after publication. *Houseboat* buys first North American serial rights to manuscripts and photos.

Revised 7/00

Categories: Nonfiction—Boating—Fishing—Lifestyle—Recreation

CONTACT: Steve Smede, Editor
Material: All
Harris Publishing
360 B St.
Idaho Falls ID 83402
Phone: 208-524-7000
Fax: 208-522-5241
E-mail: hbeditor@harrispublishing.com

The Hudson Review

The Hudson Review publishes fiction, poetry, essays, book reviews; criticism of literature, art, theatre, dance, film and music; and articles on contemporary cultural developments.

We read unsolicited submissions. Prose manuscripts should be under 10,000 words; if you have a novel, please make an excerpt of a section that stands well by itself. Please do not submit more than seven poems at one time; again, it is very helpful to us if you make a selection of your best work. We do not publish work that has already been printed elsewhere or that is due to appear in book form in the near future. We do not consider simultaneous submissions, and we do not accept electronic submissions.

If you are interested in writing reviews for our magazine, please note that we consider first-time review submissions on an "on approval" basis only.

Please allow up to three months for decisions on unsolicited manuscripts. Notification of decisions on manuscripts will be made only by postal mail; telephone and email inquiries cannot be answered. Manuscripts will not be returned, nor will inquiries be answered, unless accompanied by a stamped, self-addressed envelope. No responsibility is assumed for their loss or injury.

Unsolicited manuscripts are read according to the following schedule:
• Poetry: April 1 through June 30
• Fiction: September 1 through November 30
• Nonfiction: January 1 through March 31
• Unsolicited manuscripts received at other times will be returned unread. Manuscripts submitted by subscribers who so identify themselves will be read throughout the year.

As noted on the masthead, the Editors are responsible for the entire contents of the magazine. *The Hudson Review* does not have special "Poetry," "Fiction," "Articles," or "Book Review" editors. Unsolicited manuscripts should be addressed to: The Editors, *The Hudson Review*, 684 Park Avenue, New York, NY 10021.

We do not specialize in publishing any particular "type" of writing; our sole criterion for accepting unsolicited work is literary quality. The best way for you to get an idea of the range of work we publish is to read a current issue.

Thank you for your interest in *The Hudson Review*.

Categories: Fiction—Nonfiction—Arts—Book Reviews—Dance—Drama—Film/Video—General Interest—Literature—Poetry—Short Stories

CONTACT: The Editors
Material: All
684 Park Ave.
New York, NY 10021
Phone: 212-650-0020
Website: www.hudsonreview.com

Humpty Dumpty

Please refer to Children's Better Health Institute.

Hurricane Alice

We want every issue of *Hurricane Alice* to reflect the variety of women's lives and works. We welcome all feminist work, and are especially interested in work by women of color, lesbians, working class women, older women, disabled women, and young women. We will not publish work that we think demeans women.

In general, it takes about three months from date of submission to date of response, and about three more months from acceptance to publication. We do not consider work already published. Simultaneous submissions should be clearly marked as such, and should be sent with the understanding that the editorial board will consider them only as time allows.

Send at least a first-class SASE for our correspondence to you even if you do not want the entire manuscript returned, as we operate on a tiny budget. We cannot accept electronic submissions.

If you would like a sample copy of *Hurricane Alice* send $2.50 to the address below.

Guidelines for Writers
• Submit manuscripts clearly labeled with your name and address on the first page, and your name and page number on each succeeding page.
• After the title, identify the genre of the piece so that it gets sent to the appropriate review committee.
• Fiction and nonfiction should be a maximum of 3,500 words.
• Please submit no more than three pieces at one time.
• We do not accept unsolicited book reviews; if you are interested in reviewing books, contact Meg Carroll at the address below for reviewers' guidelines.
• We do accept unsolicited reviews of other cultural productions, including films, television programs, and the like.

Guidelines for Artists and Photographers
• Label drawings and photographs on the back with title, your name, and your address.
• We will accept photocopies rather than originals, but need originals if your work is accepted.
• All photographs should be black and white, 5"x7" or 8"x10".

Categories: Fiction—Nonfiction—Culture—Feminism—Gay/Lesbian—Literature—Multicultural—Short Stories—Women's Fiction—Women's Issues

CONTACT: Joan Dagle, Submissions Manager
Material: All
Dept. of English, Rhode Island College
Providence RI 02908
Phone: 401-456-8377

I Love Cats

We will not be accepting any new material in 2004.

I am always interested in new ideas for *I Love Cats* and request that you either send a paragraph or two about your idea or the finished piece. ALWAYS include a self-addressed, stamped envelope with a return address.

If accepted, I will request the story be sent via e-mail or on a disc in a format compatible with Windows.

I am now accepting email queries and completed stories at yankee@izzy.net. If you prefer, completed manuscripts to be delivered by mail to *I Love Cats*, c/o Lisa Allmendinger, Editor, 16 Meadow Hill Lane, Armonk, NY 10504.

I do not want poetry (as I seldom publish it) but I am interested in feature stories about cats and their owners, (no talking cats, please), interesting or odd happenings with cats, tips for cat owners, health issues, nonfiction pieces, behavior problems, that sort of thing. Please do not send stories about cats that live outdoors.

I'm looking for a story—preferably with photos or drawings— that is 1,000 words, tops, ideally 500-700 words. I buy all rights, since we copyright all stories. You also must sign a consent form, which spells out all resale questions. I pay between $40-$100. **Payment is upon publication.**

Nonfiction pieces can be longer and the price varies, but starts at $50-$100. Color slides are always a plus as I am usually in need of color photos.

Short fillers are also welcome and payment is $25.

I have quite a backlog at the moment and we go to press about four months ahead of the publication date. If your story were accepted today, the earliest publication date would be the end of 2004, so please keep that in mind when submitting stories, especially seasonal ones.

I am no longer returning photographs, so please do not send your only copy.

Please do not send any stories that have been published in other cat magazines or competing animal publications.

I will return any unused manuscripts provided there is a SASE with your submission. I do my best to report back in 1-2 months. I hope this answers all of your questions.

Sample copies are $4. If you would like one, please send a check or money order to *I Love Cats* Publishing c/o Hochman Associates, 900 Oak Tree Road, Suite C, South Plainfield, NJ 07080 and write sample copy of *I Love Cats* on the outside of the envelope. It may take up to 30 days to receive your copy.

PHOTO GUIDELINES FOR *I Love Cats*

We will not be accepting any new material in 2004.

I thank you for your letter regarding photo guidelines. I require 33 mm slides or color prints and buy all rights. I pay $50 for black-and-white or color inside photos, $150 for a cover. I will preview photos as .jpegs, but will need the actual print or slide for publication.

Covers may have props in them, but the cat must dominate the image. We love sweet eyes that beg the reader to "pet" the cover. To be considered for the cover, slides must be shot vertically.

Please send copies of your slides/photos to the above address and not the originals. Always include an SASE. Please do not send photos with a signature required as there is seldom anyone in the office to sign for a delivery.

Payment is upon publication and I am usually working 4-5 months ahead of the cover date. You will be required to sign a copyright contract.

Thank you for thinking of *I Love Cats*. Lisa M. Allmendinger Editor

Categories: Fiction—Nonfiction—Animals

CONTACT: Lisa Allmendinger, Editor
Material: All
16 Meadow Hill Lane
Armonk, NY 10504
E-mail: yankee@izzy.net
Website: www.iluvcats.com

> **Remember: Editors change jobs and publishers change addresses. It is wise to invest in a phone call for the current information before submitting.**

ICONOCLAST

The Iconoclast

F-L

Mission: To provide an imaginative alternative for readers and writers of original work bypassed by corporate and institutional publications. To ignore fads, movements, fashions, styles, current events, politics, mass media, and agendas–except for the purposes of satire. To support reflection, emotion, thought, and humor. To search for wisdom, accept delight, smile at wit, and admire craft. To have fun.

Appearance: Journal-sized (5½ x 8½), 44-64 pages. 70 lb. Wt. b/w cover. Professionally photocopied, double-stapled, and folded. Some issues may differ.

Needs: Poetry and Prose from writers more interested in the creation, sharing, and transmission of ideas, imaginings, and experiences than in career advancement or ego gratification. We are not here to be anyone's one-night-stand. This is not your ticket to fame and fortune– although you may form several gratifying professional relationships. Impress us with clarity and sincerity of thought, not lists of credits, hobbies, awards, and degrees. We are iconoclasts: just show us you care, that you can write.

Prose: To 3500 words (occasionally longer), prefer 2000-2500. Subject matter and style completely open. No zealotry, militancy, cruelty, or intolerance–unless in the service of the story–and then there should be some sort of redemption. Needless profanity/crudity is annoying. For whatever reason, every taboo has been broken–now let's move on.

We like work to have a point (or more). We don't care for the 'slice of life' type of story–or any other sort in which characters are unable or unwilling to change their own condition. Most stories of alcoholism, incest, domestic and public violence are best left to the mass media. Anything topical has probably already been overdone–and usually has a short shelf-life; limited socio-geographical appeal.

Simple storytelling usually wins over slickness of style. We never look down our noses at a plot. Nor are we immune to the power of a master's use of literary style. Anything done well and conscientiously has a chance. Humor and science fiction are hard sells, but we publish a fair share of both. We don't solicit mysteries. Killing a character(s) off in the end is usually the mark of a lazy or unimaginative beginner. Are you sincere–or cynical?

There is no need to explain the story in a cover letter (usually, there's not much need for one at all–especially if it's only a form letter.) As iconoclasts, we're not too interested in author bios (try the internet). Either the story can plead its own case–or we're too dumb to get it. A good writer can make us interested in something we didn't think we were interested in. It would be wonderful to get more essays that weren't mere undocumented opinion pieces.

Please don't send preliminary drafts–rewriting is half the job. If you don't truly believe in the story–or are unenthusiastic about the subject, then please don't send it. This is not a lottery–luck has nothing to do with it.

One submission per person per month is all we can handle. We no longer accept simultaneous submissions or reprints (we tried it–it didn't work: too many people abused the privilege, thinking they'd never be caught). We almost always respond to material well within a month– which we think is a fair amount of time to both writers and editors who are serious about what they do.

Please include a sufficiently stamped self-addressed envelope with all submissions or correspondence from which you expect a reply–and make it plain whether or not you want the manuscript returned. Everything counts.

Poetry: To 2 pages. Everything above applies. Try for originality; if not in thought, then expression. No greeting card verse or noble religious sentiments. Look for the unusual in the usual, parallels in opposites, the capturing of what is unique or often unnoticed in an ordinary, or extraordinary moment. What makes us human–and the resultant glories and agonies. Rhyme isn't as easy as it looks. Simple cleverness just doesn't go as far as it used to. Poets and editors would both benefit from reading and studying more good poetry of any style.

Art: We're always seeking line drawings for covers or spot illustrations. Existential, literary, philosophically relevant comics or cartoons are ok.

Payment: Generally: Prose, 2 contributor copies (40% discount for additional) and a penny a word for First North American Serial Rights on publication; Art and Poetry, 1 contributor copy per published page–2 copies for cover art (40% off for extras) and $2-5 per poem for First Rights. Occasional payment for art.

Reality Check: People who buy, read, and subscribe to The Iconoclast keep it alive and available to those who seek publication. This is not a government program or a non-profit scam, but an abstract community of people interested in a freewheeling approach to life. No interest, no 'zine. If the Iconoclast is good enough to send your work to, is it good enough to buy and read?

Single/Sample copy: $2.50–Subscription: $15/8 issues (Canada: $17, Other: $18)

Categories: Fiction—Nonfiction—Adventure—Arts—Biography—Cartoons—Culture—Drama—General Interest—Humor—Interview—Literature—Poetry—Satire—Short Stories

CONTACT: Phil Wagner, Editor & Publisher
Material: All
1675 Amazon Rd.
Mohegan Lake NY 10547-1804

IDEA Health & Fitness Source
IDEA Personal Trainer
IDEA Fitness Manager
IDEA Fitness Edge

The IDEA publication editors are interested in publishing articles that serve the needs of fitness and health professionals. Articles include practical application as well as theory.

IDEA *Health & Fitness Source* and IDEA *Personal Trainer* magazines are both published 10 times per year. IDEA *Fitness Manager* and IDEA *Fitness Edge* newsletters are published five times each per year on a rotational basis. Our readership includes personal trainers, health club and fitness staff, fitness instructors, program directors, business owners, and managers and other health and wellness professionals. These readers have a broad range of educational backgrounds, from high school diplomas to doctoral degrees in health- and fitness-related fields.

We encourage readers to submit articles for consideration by our editorial committee. If we are not able to accept your idea, we hope you will understand that the decision is a multifaceted one, not a negative judgment of your unique skills or talents. Each year, we receive hundreds of queries by mail, fax and email. We produce a limited number of issues, and we have a limited number of articles that we can assign. Current trends, previous or planned articles on related subjects, and numerous other factors also determine our ability to accept submitted ideas.

Whether or not we are able to accept your query, we appreciate your interest in IDEA and your initiative in submitting your idea to us.

Magazines:
IDEA *Health & Fitness Source*
IDEA *Personal Trainer*
IDEA *Fitness Manager*
IDEA *Fitness Edge*

The editors are interested in publishing articles that serve the needs of fitness and health professionals. Articles include practical application as well as theory. An article must be an original piece of work that has not been published elsewhere.

In order to determine if an idea is appropriate for IDEA's publications, ask yourself the following questions:

1) Would this article directly address the needs of fitness and health professionals (not just fitness and health consumers)?

2) Am I qualified to write this article? Why?

3) Would this article include practical, how-to application?

4) Would the general topic area and length of this article be appropriate for the IDEA newsletters, or would it work as a feature or column for IDEA *Health & Fitness Source* or IDEA Personal Trainer? Please review the following descriptions.

Publication — IDEA *Health & Fitness Source*

*Mission:*To provide fitness and health professionals with up-to-date industry information and comprehensive research on topics such as exercise physiology, weight management, nutrition, health promotion, wellness, sports conditioning, industry and programming trends, and career enhancement.

FEATURES

Each issue of IDEA *Health & Fitness Source* magazine includes several feature articles, which are approximately 10 typed, double-spaced manuscript pages and cover larger topics, such as industry issues and research reviews.

COLUMNS

In addition to features, the magazine includes the following rotating columns, which are approximately six to eight typed, double-spaced manuscript pages:

Specialties. This column provides detailed, practical information for fitness professionals who work with a specific group (e.g., the mature market, children or water fitness exercisers). Target groups are rotated every issue.

Food. This column may focus on a particular nutrient (such as iron) or category of food (such as sports drinks), or describe eating behaviors, dietary plans or nutrition myths. Written by dietitians or nutritionists, articles are designed to help readers both personally and professionally.

Exercise. Articles in this column provide detailed analysis and guidelines for proper exercise performance. They may also discuss specific biochemical considerations—e.g., an article might compare stretching techniques or teach ways to prevent injury. Appropriate educational background is required.

Wellness. This column explores the larger health and fitness picture, including psychological and physical realms and their interrelationship in topics of current interest. Motivation and adherence, mind-body modalities, active living, stress management, communication, motor learning and imagery are examples of relevant topic areas.

Careers. This column offers practical career and business information for fitness and health professionals. Topics include current and future career opportunities, job skills and strategies, mentoring, start-up ventures, networking and developing successful specialty programs.

Industry Watch. What's new on the fitness, health, nutrition and international fronts. Brief items of interest about current research, companies, legislation and innovative programs are included.

Publication — IDEA *Personal Trainer*

Mission: To be the source of professional information for personal trainers so they can operate successful businesses, plan prudent exercise programs and motivate their clients to adopt a fitness lifestyle.

Each issue contains one or two feature-length articles and two to four columns.

FEATURES

Sample topics include business standards and practices, client motivation and counseling techniques, industry growth, health care integration and nutrition. Research, exercise technique and program design topics that require more space are also included here.

COLUMNS

Exercise Rx. This column emphasizes the application of exercise theory. These articles are geared to the intermediate/advanced trainer who is familiar with training variables and needs information on how to manipulate them.

Target populations include clients with special conditions, such as diabetes or back injuries, or clients with special goals, such as running a 5K or conditioning for golf. The column also includes program design applications. Past articles in this category are: when to change sets, loads and reps; using manual resistance.

Profit Center. Articles give specifics on marketing the business, retaining clients, payment schemes, finance and administration, and career options. Profiles of operating businesses give information on the administration and strategies that have helped them.

What's New? Very short reports on nutrition, equipment and ideas trainers have for growing their businesses and their clients.

Publication — IDEA *Fitness Manager*

Mission: To provide the management information that program and fitness directors and club owners need to effectively plan program choices, supervise staff and attract and retain clients.

FEATURES

Focused on a theme, including program planning, personnel, time management, customer service, financial management

COLUMNS

Benchmarks. Research data to help managers compare their programs to the industry.

Staff Bulletin. One-page handout that managers can photocopy and give to their staff. Emphasizes customer service, sales, interstaff communication, motivation.

Best Practices. Three or four short articles on successful business ideas bulit around a theme.

Publication — IDEA *Fitness Edge*

Mission: To provide the detailed information instructors need to effectively develop and teach fitness programs in a group setting.

FEATURES

Sample topics include movement skills, effective use of music, programming for special populations, and job skills and strategies.

COLUMNS

Movement. The fine points of teaching skills, including what works and doesn't work for specific formats, from stretching through weight training or group cycling.

Jobs/Career Skills. How instructors can best work with management and their peers, communicate with customers, and find ways to grow their careers.

Problem Solver. Reader questions on relationships, teaching techniques and career moves are answered by peers and experts in the field.

Submission Procedure

Before you write an article, send us a query letter of one or two pages outlining the proposed topic and the questions you will try to answer, and tell us:

• why this idea is important to fitness and health professionals

• why you are the person to write the article (A resume or biography listing your credentials is helpful.)

• the general topics or points you will cover with this article (List a few, or include a rough outline.)

• how you will include practical how-to information in your article

The editorial committee will consider your idea on the basis of timeliness, relevance to our audience and your credentials or experience. Written queries are preferred. Unsolicited material must be accompanied by a self-addressed, stamped envelope if you wish it returned.

All these written ideas, as well as those generated by the editors, circulate through an editorial board of instructors, exercise physiologists and business experts who determine the ideas' relevance and timeliness.

The review process takes six to eight weeks. After this time, you will receive notification as to whether or not your article may be used. When an idea is tentatively approved but cannot be immediately slated for a specific issue, it may be held for a period of time for additional consideration. If an idea is approved, it is placed on the "go" list for inclusion in an upcoming issue. When the article is definitely placed in an issue, it is formally assigned to the author.

Preparing the Manuscript

Once your idea has been accepted for publication, the assigning editor will establish manuscript length and payment. Manuscripts vary in length from five to 12 double-spaced pages. We pay within 60 days of final acceptance and purchase all rights.

Remember as you begin to write that submissions should be targeted toward the professional, not the consumer. Authors are responsible for the accuracy of all data and must be able to document their information with firsthand experience, interviews with experts and/or references to published sources. You will be required to include this backup documentation with your manuscript. Writing should be in a clear, concise and easy-to-understand style.

Categories: Nonfiction—Cooking—Food/Drink—Health—Physical Fitness

CONTACT: Editors
Material: All
IDEA Publications
6190 Cornerstone Court. East, Ste 204
San Diego CA 92121-3773
Website: www.ideafit.com

IIE Solutions
Institute of Industrial Engineers

IIE Solutions welcomes feature articles and letters to the editor. Please use the following guidelines to help you develop your article.

Feature Articles

Try to focus on the most current industrial engineering issues, problems, and solutions, or recent developments and research that may have a significant and positive impact on today's industrial engineer. While every submission will be considered for publication, emphasis will be placed on the article's practical value and analytical approach. Highly theoretical or statistical articles are discouraged. Articles based on experience and actual "hands-on" operating situations, or those that have valuable applications in a working environment will be favored. Authors are encouraged to include supporting graphics and/or color photographs with articles.

Submission

Articles submitted to *IIE Solutions* should be offered on an exclusive basis and limited to 3,500 words or less. In addition to printed copy, please include a Microsoft Word or ASCII version of the article on a PC-compatible or Macintosh disk. Charts, graphs, and other non-photo artwork should be sent separately or included as individual files (BMP, JPEG, or TIFF) on the same disk. Articles are subject to normal review and editing procedures by the editor.

Additional Tips

The following hints may also assist in preparing an article for publication:

• Number each page.

• Photographs: High-quality transparencies/slides or prints are best. Provide identification and caption material with all photos, and do not attach with paper clips or staples. Also, please don't write on the back of photos. Specify whether the photo should be returned.

• Include a short biographical paragraph about the author and co-authors of the article.

IIE Solutions holds the copyright of all published articles. For permission to use the article for personal or educational purposes, please contact the Permissions Department at the Institute of Industrial Engineers (IIE).

Categories: Engineering—Ergonomics—Facilities Planning—Logistics—Industrial Engineering—Production & Inventory Control—Technology—Warehousing

CONTACT: Monica Elliot, Managing Editor
Material: All
3577 Parkway Lane Ste 200
Norcross GA 30092
Phone: 770-449-0461
Fax: 770-263-8532
Website: www.iienet.org

Illinois Beverage Guide
Michigan Beverage Journal
Wisconsin Beverage Guide

Submission Format: All articles must be submitted in typewritten form. All submissions should adhere to AP style. Articles should be based on in-depth, behind-the-scenes reporting. Material is subject to editing for length, style and format. Seasonal articles should be submitted three months in advance to allow for editorial planning. We pay after accepted work is printed in any of the magazines and purchase only one-time rights. We will respond to all submissions within 2 months.

What we are looking for: We are in need of a freelance writer for a monthly column about bartending. Freelance writers interested in taking up this 500 word column should contact the editor directly. We also are looking for articles about recent trends in employment, alcoholic beverages, and non-alcoholic beverages. We also need articles profiling successful or unique restaurants, bars, taverns or liquor stores and new items or promotions available in the industry. We have a strong need for writers to cover the legislative and grassroots scenes in all three states.

Tip: Our magazines are tailored to fit the needs for liquor licenses in the states of Illinois, Michigan, and Wisconsin. As you write, please keep in mind that bar and restaurant owners are your audience–not patrons. This is the biggest problem we face. If you are unsure of what we are looking for, please contact the editor for free copies of the magazine.

Categories: Nonfiction, Business, Food/Drink.

CONTACT: Submissions Editor
Material: All
Michigan Licensed Beverage Association
PO Box 4067
East Lansing MI 48823-4067
Phone: 877-292-2896 or 517-374-9612/9611
Fax: 517-374-1165
Website: www.mlba.org

Illinois Entertainer

Does not accept unsolicited submissions.

Implement & Tractor

Implement & Tractor magazine is directed primarily at tractor and agricultural implement dealers across North America. *We are interested in articles that address one or more of the following:*
1. Business issues that can/do affect profitability of dealerships
2. New technology in the agricultural implement field
3. New and/or unusual applications of products
4. New products introduced to the marketplace
The product lines we cover include: tractors (lawn/garden, compact, agricultural, construction); combines and other haying/harvesting equipment; sprayers; planting/tillage equipment; irrigation equipment; precision farming/GPS technology; outdoor power equipment; turf management equipment; ATVs/utility vehicles; office automation/management and inventory control.

We generally pay about $200 for first and second rights (we have a sister publication—Seed & Crops Digest—that may use an article if pertinent). Photos and/or other graphics are welcome.

Preferred length is 1,000 to 1,500 words.

Our magazine is bimonthly—mailed at the end of January, March, May, July, September and November. A current editorial calendar can be forwarded, or questions answered by contacting Bob Van Voorhis, editor, at rvanvoorhis@cfu.net. Editorial queries should be submitted two to four months ahead of publication date. Payment is issued upon publication.

Categories: Nonfiction—Agriculture—Business

CONTACT: Bob Van Voorhis, Editor
Material: All
Freiberg Publishing
2302 West First St.
Cedar Falls IA 50613
Phone: 319-277-3599
E-mail: rvanvoorhis@cfu.net

In the Family
The Magazine for Queer People and Their Loved Ones

GUIDELINES FOR SUBMITTING WORK

Thank you for your interest in writing for In the Family, the award-winning magazine for queer couples, single people and families. We use a psychology lens to explore the variety and complexity of our intimate relationships. We strongly recommend that you read a copy of the magazine to get an idea of the kinds of pieces we publish. To order a copy, send $6.50 to the address below.

We invite submission of feature articles, personal essays and case presentations on all aspects of queer family life, and particularly seek submissions from mental health professionals on fresh, new aspects of their clinical work or research with lesbian, gay, trans and bisexual families, couples and individuals.

We also invite submissions of original, unpublished fiction and poetry that fits with our theme of queer life. No erotica and no harlequin romance stories, please.

Submit one double-spaced copy, including your name, phone number, email address and mailing address on the first page, and an SASE. Please do not submit work by fax or by email.

We pay on publication: $35 for essays, $35 for short stories and $35 for poetry. All contributors received 5 free copies of the issue in which their work appears.

Because of the volume of material we receive, we do not give detailed feedback on pieces we are not able to use.

If you have further questions about submitting your work, please email us at LMarkowitz@aol.com

Categories: Fiction—Nonfiction—Alternate Life-style—Family—Gay/Lesbian—Human Rights—Multicultural—Psychology—Relationships—Sexuality—Society

CONTACT: Laura Markowitz, Editor
Material: All
Family Magazine, Inc.
7850 N. Siverbell Rd., #114-188
Tucson AZ 85743
Phone: 520-579-8043
Website: inthefamily.com

Remember: Editors change jobs and publishers change addresses. It is wise to invest in a phone call for the current information before submitting.

In Touch
Indulge

Emphasis is on the light-hearted, romantic, erotic, provocative and entertaining. There are no limits on sexual content or explicitness in fiction, although safer sex must be depicted. Please refrain from submitting stories involving fantastical characters (i.e. vampires, ghosts, Tarzan).

All individuals must be 18 years of age or older whether they are models or characters in fiction. All submissions are subject to editing.

Sample issue is $6.95/postage paid. Please indicate which magazine (*In Touch* or *Indulge*) you are requesting a copy of.

Erotic fiction to be between 3,200 to 3,800 words, typed, double-spaced. Fiction may also be submitted on Mac formatted computer disk or via e-mail to: michael@intouchformen.com. A requirement of acceptance is the ability to send a final version of the material electronically.

In Touch magazine features smooth, fresh young men between 18 to 24 years old. Indulge magazine features more mature, aggressive, muscular men in their late twenties and thirties. It is recommended that a writer create a story targeting the audience of the magazine they are submitting to. Serials, for either magazine, are not under consideration.

The fee paid is $75 for one-time usage, first North American rights and limited electronic rights (for use on the web site). Payment is issued upon publication. A copy of the magazine is sent with the payment.

Please include a SASE for response. Thank you.

Categories: Fiction—Erotica—Gay/Lesbian—Men's Fiction

CONTACT: Alan W. Mills, Editor
Material: All
13122 Saticoy St.
North Hollywood CA 91605
Phone: 818-764-2288
Fax: 818-764-2307
E-mail: alan@intouchformen.com
Website: www.intouchformen.com

Inc.

Formal guidelines not available. Please read a number of issues to ascertain the publication's style and needs.

Send queries to address below.

Categories: Nonfiction—Business—Lifestyle—Money & Finances—Technology

CONTACT: Micheal Hoffman, Submissions Editor
Material: All
38 Commercial Warf
Boston MA 02110
Website: www.inc.com

Independent Business

Please refer to Group IV Communications, Inc.

Indiana Review

Indiana Review is published semiannually in May and November. We read manuscripts year round, and reporting time is 2 - 4 months. IR accepts less than 1% of manuscripts submitted. Payment for publication is $5.00 per page ($10.00 minimum), two contributor's copies, and the remainder of a year's subscription. Rights revert to author upon publication.

Needs

IR publishes 6-10 stories, 40-60 pages of poetry, 1-2 nonfiction pieces, and 6-12 book reviews per issue, as well as art inserts when funding allows. All work must be previously unpublished. We look for poems, stories, and nonfiction that are well-crafted and lively, have an intelligent sense of form and language, assume a degree of risk, and have consequence beyond the world of their speakers or narrators. We also welcome interviews with established writers.

Stories

Send only one story per submission, up to 40 double-spaced pages. Translations are welcome.

Poems

Send only 4-6 poems per submission. Do not send more than 4 poems if longer than 3 pages each. Do not fold poems individually or staple poems together. Translations are welcome.

Nonfiction

Send only one essay per submission, up to 30 double-spaced pages.

Book Reviews

Reviews should be of recent fiction, poetry, nonfiction, and literary criticism (publication date within two years). Small press titles are preferred. Reviews must be 1,000 to 1,500 words, double-spaced, and include complete publication information (press, ISBN, price). Send a maximum of two reviews per submission.

Graphic Arts

Paintings, photographs, comics, and drawings are welcome. In lieu of originals, please send slides or digital images of work. DO NOT send only copy of work. Indiana artists are preferred. Send up to five pieces that are up to 6 x 9" in dimensions or may be later reduced to this size. Visual works must also be publishable in black and white, but, when funding allows, may be published in full color.

There is no need to query editors about submitting work. Submission status may be queried by mail or email, but please allow 4 months before querying.

All submissions and correspondence MUST include a self-addressed stamped envelope. We cannot respond to submissions otherwise. Include additional postage if work is to be returned. Simultaneous submissions are okay, but we must be promptly notified of acceptance elsewhere.

Clearly mark envelope to the appropriate genre editor's attention (e.g. "Fiction Editor"). Include cover letter listing work titles, previous publications and awards, and a SHORT bio. For receipt confirmation, please include email address. Explanations of manuscript meaning, theme, or technique are not necessary.

No handwritten, faxed, emailed, or poorly copied/printed manuscripts will be considered. Further, IR cannot consider work (other than book reviews) from anyone currently or recently affiliated with Indiana University.

Sample Issues: Sample copies of IR are available for $9. Add $6 per issue for postage outside of the United States ($3.50 for Canada).

Categories: Fiction—Nonfiction—Book Reviews—Literature—Poetry—Writing

CONTACT: Esther Lee, Editor
Material: All other
CONTACT: Kyle Dargan, Poetry Genre Editor
Material: Poetry
CONTACT: Will Boast, Fiction Genre Editor
Material: Fiction
Indiana University
Ballantine Hall 465
1020 E. Kirkwood Ave
Bloomington IN 47405-7103
Website: www.indiana.edu/~inreview

Indulge

Please refer to *In Touch* magazine.

Industrial Management

Industrial Management welcomes feature articles that focus on current management issues, developments, challenges, problems and solutions. The material should offer significant insight or assistance to the readers of *Industrial Management*, who are executives, department heads, operating managers, industrial engineers, and those aspiring to management positions.

While every submission will be considered for publication, articles based on experience and actual hands-on operating situations or case studies, or those that have valuable applications in a working environment will be favored. Highly theoretical or statistical articles are discouraged. Articles should be clearly written and readily understandable, though authors may assume that readers have some knowledge of basic industrial engineering concepts and have management experience.

Sample topic areas include:

Benchmarking—Budgeting—Change Management—Competitiveness—Concurrent Engineering—Continuous Improvement—Costing and Cost Control—Cycle Time Reduction—Ergonomics and Human Factors—Environmental Management—Facilities Management—Forecasting, Planning, and Scheduling—Human Resource Issues—Incentive Programs—Inventory Management—Labor Relations—Lean Manufacturing—Logistics Management—Maintenance Management—Management of Technology—Manufacturing Strategies—Materials Management—Organizational Behavior & Change—Performance Measurement—Product Development—Production Control—Productivity—Quality—Reengineering—Return on Investment—Safety—Simulation—Statistical Process Control—Strategic Planning—Supply Chain Management—Systems Integration—Teams—Technology Transfer—Theory of Constraints—World Class Strategies.

Submission

Articles submitted to *Industrial Management* should be offered on an exclusive basis and limited to 3,500 words. Articles will be edited for publication, and all editorial changes will be made solely at the discretion of the editor. Members of the editorial staff may contact authors for clarifications of fact or intent. The editor makes the final decision about whether to accept or reject an article.

Please note that IIE publishes several other periodicals. If the editor determines that your submission is more appropriate for another of our periodicals, your article may be published in a periodical other than *Industrial Management*. Under these circumstances, the editor will attempt to obtain your permission before publication, though this is not always possible. Authors are encouraged to include supporting illustrations (graphs, charts, tables, and/or photographs) with articles.

Article Checklist

Include a suggested title for the article. You may give alternate titles, as well. Titles should not be overly wordy or technical.

Include a brief overview of the article. Summarize your article in two or three clear sentences.

Use subheads where appropriate. This will help organize and communicate your information.

Bulleted and numbered items or lists are acceptable, though excessive use is discouraged.

Do not include specific references within the body of the work. Do not include footnotes or endnotes. Vital material or appropriate references should be incorporated into the narrative of the article itself. An optional list of suggested reading or reference works should be included for the "For further reading" section at the end of your article.

Include a very brief biography (one paragraph) about the author or authors. Please indicate if you are a member of the Institute of Industrial Engineers or other professional societies and, if so, whether you are a senior member, Fellow, or other distinguished member. Indicate your professional title, employer and, if appropriate, the type of business, as well as your educational background.

Materials Checklist

Please include:

- A printed copy of your article.
- An electronic file of your article. If possible, save your file as a Microsoft Word document; otherwise, save it in ASCII format. You may send the file either on a 3.5" PC-compatible or Macintosh disk, or as an e-mail attachment to editor@iienet.org.
- Relevant charts, graphs, illustrations, and photographs. Photos should be submitted as color slides, prints, or transparencies rather than electronic images. If you must send photos electronically, the following formats are acceptable: EPS, PICT, GIF, TIFF, JPEG, Photoshop, BMP, PCX, and SCITEX CT. Electronic photos must be at least 300 DPI at actual size. Other artwork such as illustrations, charts, and graphs may be submitted electronically and accompanied by a hardcopy print out. These electronic images should be saved in separate files from the text of the article. Send the images in one of the following original program files, if possible: Macromedia Freehand, Adobe Illustrator, Microsoft Word, Microsoft PowerPoint, or Quark XPress.
- Identification and caption material for all illustrations and photos. Please do not attach items to photographs with paper clips or staples, as this may damage your material and render it unusable. Do not write on the back of photos. Specify if photos should be returned.

For each article we publish, we must have a signed copyright release form on file. One will be sent to you upon receipt of your article. *Industrial Management* holds the copyright of all published articles. For permission to use the article for personal or educational purposes, please contact the Permissions Department at the Institute of Industrial Engineers.

If your article is an opinion or commentary piece, please submit a color photograph of yourself.

Categories: Technology—Industrial Engineering

CONTACT: Jane Gaboury, Editor
Material: All
CONTACT: Monica Elliot, Managing Editor
Material: All
IEE Solutions: Institute of Industrial Engineers
25 Technology Park/Atlanta
Norcross GA 30092
Phone: 770- 449-0461
Fax: 770-263-8532
Website: www.iienet.org

Inside Texas Running

INSIDE TEXAS RUNNING is a tabloid magazine issued monthly, except June and August, and is published primarily for Texas runners. Each issue averages 40-52 pages and includes race reports, a "Texas Roundup" of news from around the State, in-house columns on sports medicine and nutrition, the over-40 runner ("Concerning Masters") and articles on unusual running events, training, etc. All but the columns require freelance input. We also are seeking good photos. General guidelines are as follows:

ARTICLES: We need profiles, travel tips, unusual races, historic pieces or almost anything that would interest our readers. If you are not sure about a subject, try us anyway—especially if it's Texas-related. General topics about running are usually handled by our columnists. Unique slants are wanted.

Our audience includes beginning runners as well as veteran marathoners, so the subject matter may reflect the varying abilities of our readers. Since ability varies so widely, we might be interested in a five-hour marathoner, for example, if there is something unique about that marathoner that would inspire or intrigue. Controversy is welcomed, but not faddish or dangerous nutritional or training pieces; observing the common sense rules of running, etc. is necessary. Training articles should be written by or with the help of experts such as reputable coaches (always state experience and background) and elite athletes.

Anecdotes, examples and quotes are very much appreciated.

Payment ranges from $25 for fillers of less than 500 words up to $75 for 1,000 to 1,500 words. Higher fees are available for established writers. Byline is provided.

RACE REPORTS: We contact race directors from around the state for race reports and results and cover many major races. Any unusual happening (odd weather, lost runners, unique course layout, etc.), along with a brief account of the race, will find eager acceptance here. Results listing the top finishers (minimum top 10 overall male and female, top 3 age division winners) should accompany the write-up. The report should include the proper name of the race, the date, the distance, weather conditions, number of participants, and, if possible, quotes from participants reacting to some aspect of the race. Payment: $25 for report, one usable photo and results. Length: 100-250 words max.

CORRESPONDENTS: We are looking for regular correspondents from around the state to cover races, do interviews, report races, take photos and keep us informed of upcoming races. These regulars will be listed on the masthead of the publication and receive the publication complimentary.

FICTION: Some fiction accepted. Please contact with article.

BEST WAY TO BREAK IN: Our Texas Roundup Section includes short items of one to several paragraphs long that include news about races-unusual themes, celebrity runners, prize money, and other information above and beyond its basic calendar listing-as well as human interest, records set, and miscellaneous tidbits. We are looking for items across the state, particularly outside the Houston area.

PHOTOS: We accept digital images and prints. Please don't send snapshots of runners where features are undefinable and figures are miles away.

Human interest subject matter is desired, as well as our always necessary race photos. Articles profiling runners should be accompanied by photos of the subject training, at work, with his family or whatever else will illustrate the piece appropriately. Similarly, travel pieces might have figures running past recognizable landmarks. Payment: $15 per photo, $50 for color photo on cover. More for outstanding shots.

CARTOONS: Like everything else in INSIDE TEXAS RUNNING, cartoons are about runners, etc., but the subject matter might overlap into medical concerns, diet, non-running spouse, general fitness. Payment: Contact us to arrange.

ON SUBMISSIONS: Complete manuscripts only; no queries. Please do not send photo negatives. We will pay on publication and will report on all submissions received as above within several weeks. Please indicate whether ms is simultaneous submission.

THANK YOU FOR YOUR INTEREST IN INSIDE TEXAS RUNNING.

Lance Phegley, Editor

Categories: Nonfiction—Cartoons—Outdoors—Physical Fitness—Recreation—Regional—Sports/Recreation—Travel

CONTACT: Lanc Phegley, Editor
Material: All
PO Box 19909
Houston TX 77224
Phone: 281-759-0555
Fax: 281-759-7766
E-mail: rtnews@ix.netcom.com
Website: www.insidetexasrunning.com

Insider Magazine

Publication Definition:

INsider magazine is a national general interest publication published 5 times per year. *INsider* has a minimum 200,000 circulation and over 1.6 million readers every other month. It is distributed directly to 445 colleges and direct mailed to over 1,500 college newspapers and 600 college radio stations. There are over 15 individualized local editions of the magazine targeting various campuses and metropolitan markets. Our target audience is 18 to 34 year olds. *INsider* is also available as a national publication at many major newsstands and Borders & Barnes and Noble Bookstores.

Editorial Sections:

INsider magazine is a publication designed and written by twentysomethings from all over America. We have graduated, per se, from just focusing on the college market and your stories should reflect our new readership. Monthly surveys conducted in the magazine show that 18 to 34 year olds have tremendously varied habits and interests.

They love music and buy numerous CDs.

They are concerned about their health and appearance.

They are very active socially, going to nightclubs, bars and concerts several times a month and are constantly pursuing relationships and meeting new people.

They love to see movies both at the theater and at home on video tape.

They are very aware of current events, actively vote in major elections and are very active as volunteers for causes dealing with the environment, political issues, etc.

A majority have credit cards that they use on a regular basis.

INsider entertains our readers' interests while developing a unique editorial impression that celebrates the exclusivity of being a young adult today. One thing is true for all college-age consumers; they do NOT like to be referred or spoken to as college students. We want to emphasize what is unique about this demographic without exposing its limitations (ie: their age, where they are in their careers). Any quantitative observation makes students recoil from fear of being labelled a "member of the pack"!

ENTERTAINMENT:

Guest Editor — Each issue of *INsider magazine* is hosted by a guest editor that interacts with several of the on-going featured columns. Guest editors are featured on the cover of the magazine; there is a two page interview with the guest editor; we note their birthday on the horoscope page; the guest editor assists in reviewing music and products in the issue; and anything else we can think of related to our bi-monthly theme. The guest editor is generally a notable actor, actress or musician.

INmusic — Examines the hottest music and trends in the so-called alternative market. From Smashing Pumpkins to R.E.M. to the Dave Matthews Band, readers look to *INsider* first, to find out what they should be listening to.

In-depth features and interviews from the music industry should be from 1,000 to 1500 words. These may be considered for cover stories.

Shorter profile pieces or band reviews should be between 400 to 750 words.

CD or concert reviews should be no more than 400 words.

INsider will feature a guest entertainer (music, film, or TV), who will appear on the cover of his or her specific issue and will be tied-in to that issues' theme by way of product reviews, horoscopes, and a question and answer session focusing on the integral sections of the magazine (movies, TV, video, books, travel, careers, and sports).

INfilm — *INsider* focuses on up-and-coming actors and directors as well as established stars who appeal directly to our readership. Recent profiles include everyone from new faces such as Kevin Smith, the director of Clerks and Michael Rapaport, star of Kiss of Death, to Hollywood fixtures like Sara Jessica Parker and Ethan Hawke. *INsider* gets the celebrities to tell all about their lives, careers, and details of upcoming movies.

In-depth articles, usually featuring personality profiles or interviews, should be 750 to 1,500 words. These are often the cover story.

Movie reviews and guides featuring upcoming releases should be 300 to 500 words. Satirical or research-based retrospectives on a genre or person should be 500 to 1,200 words.

If Walls Could Talk — The movie editor writes a monthly movie-industry buzz column that tells all about soon to be released movies and the people who star in them.

INvideo — A round-up of the latest videos for rent. Readers look to *INsider* for the newest releases and the greatest classics on the market.

Video reviews and feature should be 250 to 350 words.

INtv — From MTV and cable access, to the latest Friends episode, television is a predominant source of entertainment for our readers. In TV features profile of today's TV stars like Friends' David Schwimmer, Seinfeld's Julia Louis-Dreyfuss, and JonStewart, or humorous articles on the latest trends in television. Profiles should be between 750 and 1500 words. Satirical or humor pieces should be between 600 to 750 words.

INbooks — *INsider* attracts a highly literate audience. They enjoy engaging stories about a wide and diverse range of authors and writers. Profiles should be 800 to 1500 words. Short reviews on books of interest to our readers, from fiction to career and travel guides should be 200-500 words.

FEATURES:

INsider brings readers the latest information about what is happening in the world and how it directly affects their lives. Bimonthly, *INsider* offers two to four national features covering current issues including alcohol/drug use, 'Aids and Sex in the 90s,' environmental issues and interviews with famous personalities. Features are 750 to 2500 words, often with accompanying sidebar. These are usually the cover stories with national slant.

CAREERS:

INsider gives our readers an edge on how to get ahead, from writing their r sum , to tips on how to interview and stories on workplace issues like sexual harassment. Past features have included advice from recent graduates, job and salary demographics and the do's and dont's of job interviews. *INsider* helps prepare readers for the job market with success. Informative/resource articles pertaining to job or career issues should be 400 to 750 words with a national slant.

THEMES:

Each issue of INsider revolves around a theme. Consider these themes when submitting:

November: Annual Travel Guide/Spring Break Issue

March: Automotive Issue/March Madness Preview

May: Outdoor Adventure Issue

September: Technology/ Computer Softwear/College Football Preview

October: Annual Ski Issue

LIFESTYLE:

INtravel — This section features stories on destinations popular with our readership. *INsider* will also consider humorous travel stories, travel tips and travel round-ups. Stories should be 500 to 1,500 words, often with accompanying sidebar.

INsports — This section features stories on participatory sports popular with our readership like ultimate frisbee or rugby. Also consider profiles of professional or amateur athletes. Stories and profiles should be 500 to 1,500 words. The reader that *INsider* is trying to capture is the active young adult who is interested in personal excellence and commitment to bettering their community. *INsider* wants to position itself as a proactive publication, deadicated to actve endeavors.

INteractive — The latest in happenings and issues on the info superhighway and in the world of technology. We also review the latest CD-ROMS and video game. Stories and profiles should be 500 to 1,500 words. Reviews should be 200 to 400 words.

IN View — In-depth explorations of political issues. Personal essays on issues effecting our generation. Profiles of leaders or people making a difference. Stories and profiles should be 500 to 1,500 words.

Relationships — Guest authors, specializing in relationship-counseling give advice on how to deal with the problems many readers face in their relationships. This section also features first person narratives and research based articles concerning relationships in '90s. Articles often take a humorous slant. Should be 500 to 1,200 words.

INsider Choice — Features the newest products on the market appealing to our readership. From mountain bikes to backpacks to beers, this section previews the latest trends. *INsider* is a key source of information for readers looking to buy the best products for the most reasonable price. *INsider* reviews the latest products on the market for quality, versatility and affordability. The top selections are given the *INsider* Choice Award.

Anywhere from four to eight products are previewed with graphics and accompanying descriptions including any outstanding qualities, where they can be found and the cost.

FORMAT:

Submissions — on Macintosh disk with Microsoft Word 5.0 or earlier version preferred, otherwise a clear, double-spaced copy that can be scanned is acceptable. Fax stories or queries to *INsider* at 847.329.0358 or e-mail to INsideread@aol.com

Computer Functions — Often, a great deal of our time is spent correcting minor formatting errors in the text that should, ideally, be fixed on your end. Please adhere to the following guidelines:

AP Punctuation Guide:

Space: MAKE SURE THERE IS ONLY ONE SPACE BETWEEN EACH WORD, INCLUDING THE BEGINNING OF SENTENCES. When copy editing, run the "Find" program. FIND every double-space and REPLACE it with a single space. THIS IS VERY IMPORTANT!

Brackets: cannot be transmitted over news wires. Use parenthesis. Colon: USE AT THE END OF A SENTENCE to introduce lists, text, etc.

: Can be used for EMPHASIS.

Comma: Do not use a comma before the final item in a series. When in doubt refer to an AP Style book.

Dash: Use dashes to denote an abrupt change in thought in a sentence or emphatic pause: Smith offered a plan — it was unprecedented — to raise revenues.

PUT A SPACE ON EITHER SIDE OF DASH. TO MAKE A DASH ON A MACINTOSH: HIT <opt> <shift> <->.

Ellipsis: An ellipsis is the "..." punctuation that indicates a break in thought or an omitted part of a direct quote. Instead of using the period key: to make an ellipsis on a Macintosh, hit <opt> <;>.. AN ELLIPSIS DOES NOT NEED A SPACE IN FRONT OF IT BUT IT DOES NEED A SPACE BEHIND IT.

Titles: A rule of thumb to decide if a title should be in italics or quotes: IF A WORK CAN STAND ALONE IT SHOULD BE IN ITALICS, IF IT IS A PART OF A LARGER WORK , IT SHOULD BE IN QUOTES. For example: use quotes around song titles, newspaper articles, chapter titles, article names, etc. Use italics for album names, poems, works of art, book titles, magazine names, newspapers, etc. Parentheses: USE AS SPARINGLY AS POSSIBLE! Parentheses are jarring to the reader and is often a clue that a sentence is becoming contorted. Try to write it another way. If a sentence must contain incidental material, commas or dashes are usually more effective.

Semicolon: In general, use a semicolon to indicate a greater separation in thought then a comma can convey but less then the separation that a period implies.

Indentation — The computer can automatically space and indent paragraphs, this is done by recognition of individual character returns. Therefore when typing, only put ONE RETURN at the end of every paragraph. Also, DO NOT PUT ANY SPACES OR TABS at the beginning of the next paragraph. Any marks of this nature have to be removed by us.

Smart Quotes — There are smart quotes and dumb quotes. Smart quotes curve toward the text, dumb quotes don't. Smart quotes are a preference setting on most word processing systems. If you don't have this option they can be typed manually: hit the (opt) and ([) key for opened quotes, and (shift) (opt) ([) for closed quotes.

To make single quotes: hit (opt) (]) for an opened single quote, and (shift) (opt) (]) for a closed single quote.

State Abbreviations — Are not the same as postal abbreviations. See AP stylebook.

Emphasis — to convey emphasis use italics, do not capitalize, bold or underline.

Numbers — Spell out through nine, use figures for 10 and above. Do not start a sentence with a figure. For years, use closed single quote ('94, mid-'70s). Do not make years possessive (the roaring 20s). Any Doubts? REFER TO AP STYLE GUIDELINES! It is imperative that you proof for these style errors before submitting articles.

Setting Story Headings:
Set text for SINGLE SPACE.
Set font on 12 point Helvetica.
PLACE TITLE on first line, capitalizing all principal words. Do not use all caps, bold, or underlining, and do not skip any extra spaces. Use no more then 25 characters.

Place sub-title on next line capitalizing all principal words. Use no more than 50 characters. BYLINE goes on the next line. Do not type the word "Byline," only the writer's full name should appear. SKIP ONE LINE.

DO NOT INDENT and start typing article.

If submission is on disk, write text in one block, do not skip lines between paragraphs. If hard copy only is submitted, text should be double spaced.

Hard copy should be submitted with or without a disk.
ALWAYS remember to spell check and proof all work!
Always use AP style guidelines!
ALWAYSmake sure your article is no longer than it is suppose to be!

Deadlines — 45 Days prior to issue unless otherwise specified by editorial director.

Compensation — There are several classes of writers and each is compensated differently. The associate publisher and editorial director are in charge of all class promotions.

Contributing writer: 1¢ per word
Staff Writer: 2¢ per word
Senior Writer: 3¢ per word
Featured Columnist: To Be Negotiated

Costs of article are included in payment. Any other costs associated with the production of an article must be approved in advance by the Editorial director.

Assignment

Most stories are by assignment, however suitable submissions are considered. Queries and story ideas are strongly encouraged. There is no guarantee that unsolicited articles will be returned, even with SASE. If interested in writing, please send a resume and writing samples, published or otherwise, with any story ideas or area of interest.

Categories: Nonfiction—Adventure—Arts—Automobiles—Careers—College—Computers—Conservation—Consumer—Culture—Economics—Entertainment—Environment—Feminism—Film/Video—Food/Drink—General Interest—Government—Internet—Interview—Law—Men's Issues—Music—Outdoors—Politics—Regional—Relationships—Sexuality—Society—Sports/Recreation—Theatre—Travel—Women's Issues—Public Policy—Technology

CONTACT: Jon Erchell, Senior Editor
Material: Entertainment
CONTACT: Rita Cook, Senior Editor
Material: Theme
CONTACT: Mark Jansen, Senior Editor
Material: Issues
4124 W. Oakton
Skokie IL 60076-3267
Phone: 847-673-3703
Fax: 847-329-0358
E-mail: info@incard.com

Insight

What's Insight?

• It's a weekly 16-page magazine for high school and college students.

• It's published by the Review and Herald Publishing Association and is a ministry of the North American Division of the Seventh-day Adventist Church.

• It's distributed to youth at church, at church schools, and through home sub-scriptions.

Who Reads Insight?

• Insight's audience is primarily American and Canadian youth and young adults of the Seventh-Day Adventist Church.

• The readers are diverse in gender, ethnicity, school experience (public school, private day school, boarding academy, home school, college), church experience (large, small, formal, informal, "liberal," "conservative"), interests, and spiritual maturity.

What to Write

• Insight needs: true inspirational stories, profiles of Adventist celebrities, profiles of outstanding Seventh-day Adventist youth and young adults, and general spiritual articles.

• Insight doesn't need: fiction, sermons, puzzles, and parables.

HOW TO WRITE

Writing a Story

A series of events doesn't make a story. A story has three basic elements:

1. a beginning, which provides factual details such as who, where, when;

2. a conflict or crisis, which builds suspense;

3. a resolution (physical or mental),
which shows character growth.

All Insight stories must be true, and should be told from a high school or college student's point of view. They should include element of good storytelling, such as realistic dialogue, believable characters (not "perfect" or "terrible"),sensory impressions (show—don't tell), and a strong spiritual conclusion.

Writing a Profile

When interviewing an outstanding youth or adult, look for a current "story" (see previous section). Find a time of conflict or crisis they've encountered recently (or if an adult, in their younger years). Then describe the experience as well as how the subject has grown through it.

Profiles shouldn't be a resume of what a person has done. Rather, they should show how a person has faced tribulation and how God helped them persevere and grow. Profiles should also include quotations from the subject, but they should be only the most powerful statements and should be used sparingly. Some leading interview questions might be: "What was the most difficult time of your life? How did God help you? How did the experience change you? When did you first begin to trust Christ? When you blow out the candles on your eightieth birthday cake, what do you want to look back on?" Good profiles also benefit from interviewing other people who know the subject, such as parents, close friends, siblings, etc. After asking factual questions ("How did you meet the person? How long have you known him/her?"), ask such questions as: "How have you seen God work in this person's life? What hard times have they been through? What character growth have you observed? How has this person changed your life?"

Writing an Article

Articles should address topics of interest to today's teenagers and young adults from a Christian perspective. An article should begin with a story or several anecdotes to introduce the topic. The story or anecdotes should be true and involve youth or young adults. (See section "Writing a Story" for tips.)

The article should include a Biblical perspective. (We prefer Scriptural quotations in the New International Version.) Most articles benefit from one or two sidebars, which might provide "how to" steps, resources, definitions, a self-quiz, or other information related to the subject.

Editing Checklist

When checking over your piece, make sure it includes:
• an opening that will grab the reader
• active verbs rather than "be" (is, was, were, etc.) or passive verbs
• dialogue
• description that is concrete rather than abstract, specific rather than general
• true examples and anecdotes
• simple, current language in a conversa-tional tone
• unpredictable details and fresh insights
• a strong spiritual message

How to Submit a Manuscript

• Manuscripts must be typed, doublespaced.
• With each manuscript please include: your name; mailing address; phone number; church name, city, and state; social security number (necessary for payment); gender and ethnicity(for illustrative accuracy); and biographical facts (such as age, job title, school attending, major, etc.).
• Include a stamped, self-addressed envelope for return of your manuscript.

Send manuscripts by mail or e-mail.

Categories: Nonfiction—Christian Interests—Religion—Teen

CONTACT: Editor
Material: All
Review & Herald Publishing Association
Insight Magazine
55 W. Oak Ridge Dr.
Hagerstown, MD 21740
Phone: 301-393-4038
Fax: 301-393-4055
E-mail: insight@rhpa.org
Website: www.insightmagazine.org

Instructor

Writer's Guidelines for Teachers of Grades K–8

Instructor publishes more teachers' bylines each issue than any other educational magazine. We would love to hear from you!

Our editors are waiting to hear from you!

Features: Feature stories of approximately 800 to 1,200 words on timely, relevant topics of interest to K–12 teachers. Articles may cover classroom management and practice, education trends and issues, suggestions for professional development, and in-depth lesson plans. Please send the completed article or a query letter in which you describe the article you'd like to write. To get a clear idea of the feature articles we publish, read the features found in three or more recent issues of Instructor.

Ready-to-Use Activities & Tips: Do you have an activity that's particularly effective with your students? A great tip for classroom management, organizing your time, or building classroom community?

Please share it with us-we're always looking to hear about your classroom successes! Maximum 250 words; color snapshots or samples of students' work that clarify your ideas are helpful.

Ready-to-Use Lesson Units: 400–800 word lesson-planning units on a specific curriculum area or theme. Examples might include a cross-curricular unit on sunflowers, a series of educational activities to celebrate Grandparents' Day, or an extended science lesson on bugs. We particularly seek units that you have tried with success in your own classroom. Again, samples of student work or photographs are helpful.

E-Activities: Tech-based activities for the classroom. The same information applies as for the Ready-to-Use Activities, above.

End of the Day: 400–500 word personal essays about a teacher's poignant, revelatory, even humorous experiences with kids.

General Tips

• Read the magazine so you are familiar with our style and our needs. If you would like to order an issue, send $3.00 in the U.S. or $6.00 plus $3.50 for shipping and handling elsewhere to Instructor, PO Box 53896, Boulder, CO 80322-3896, or call 800-544-2917.
• As you write, think: How can I make this article most useful for teachers?
• Write in your natural voice. We shy away from wordy, academic prose.
• Let us know what grade/subject you teach and the name and location of your school.
• Send seasonal material at least six months in advance.
• Make sure your manuscript is typewritten, double-spaced; send only one copy to the appropriate department.
• Print your name and address on the manuscript and on all photos and samples. Include your phone number.
• Enclose a self-addressed stamped envelope.
• Expect a reply from us within 8-12 weeks only if you have enclosed a SASE. Please note that due to the volume of mail we receive, we regret that we cannot reply to "Ready-to-Use" submissions, and materials will not be returned. You will be contacted if we decide to use your activity or tip.

Thank you! We can't wait to hear from you.

Categories: Nonfiction—Children—Education—Juvenile—Teen

CONTACT: Manuscript Editor
Material: All
555 Broadway
New York NY 10012
Phone: 212-343-6100
Website: www.teacher.scholastic.com/products/instructor

Interior Design

Needed for publication:

Set of original 4 x 5 transparencies illustrating the project.

Camera-ready floor plans and other drawings needed to explain the job. These should be 8 x 10 glossy prints of ruled ink drawings or high quality black and white laser prints. Please put all necessary legends, notes and dimensions on tracing paper overlay, not on the drawing; we will have them set in type. Please be sure your name and address are on all pieces submitted including the people biographies.

A brief professional biography of the principal team. A brief description of the project, noting the clients program, your design solution, total square footage and the project cost. If total project cost not available, give cost per square foot.

Please note that *INTERIOR DESIGN* is adamant about exclusivity; we make no publishing commitments without seeing original 4x5' transparencies (their quality being a factor in our decision) and that we look for photography in which the lighting detail is clear: fabric patterns, chair legs, etc. Some other magazines prefer dramatic shadows, but we prefer visual information.

The project submitted must not have been published in any magazine as a feature layout in the United States or Canada. It is acceptable that a project may have been mentioned as a news item.

We hope this information will help you and we look forward to seeing your presentation.

Categories: Arts—Home

CONTACT: Cindy Allen, Editor-in-Chief
Material: All
360 Park Ave. South, 17th floor
New York, NY 10010
Phone: 646-746-6400
Website: www.interiordesign.net

International Midwife

Ceased publication. Please refer to *Midwifery Today.*

The International Railway Traveler

The *International Railway Traveler* (IRT) is the official newsletter of The Society of International Railway Travelers, an international organization of sophisticated travelers who prefer going by rail. IRT provides exclusive and up to-date information on rail travel worldwide for both prospective and armchair railway travelers.

Information about international rail-travel possibilities geared to the general traveler, as opposed to the train fan, is available from no other single source.

While IRT concentrates on Europe and N. America, it also covers more exotic rail travel destinations. IRT conveys both the romance of rail travel as well as practical information vital to making successful rail trips.

IRT's full-length features and other articles are referenced to the world-famous Thomas Cook European and Overseas Timetables, making trip-planning easy.

IRT is not limited to intercity passenger trains. It covers regional passenger trains, suburban passenger trains, mountain trains, as well as trams and "light rail." In short, if it runs on rails, IRT is interested in it.

In 21 years of its existence, IRT has become recognized as the leading publication on international railway travel.

WRITERS

In general, IRT needs reports that are timely, detailed, and, above all, scrupulously accurate. All story submissions should include appropriate photos and/or graphics (i.e., items with a railroad's logo, etc.)

IRT seeks the following kinds of reports:

1) **News Shorts** no more than 100 words long. These appear in the regularly featured column "Sidetrack."

2) **Short Features** of around 500-900 words in length. These stories report on new equipment, services, routes, fares, package deals, dining and sleeping car services, stations and anything else of interest to the railway traveler.

3) **Travel Features** consist of the main story and a detailed, informational ("If You Go...") sidebar, which together should run no more than 1,200 words. (Lengthier submissions will be returned.)

Main Story

IRT's travel features should convey the romance, wonder and excitement of rail travel for the newsletter's sophisticated, well-traveled readership. The stories should be lively, personal and, above all, not dull. Also, where it is appropriate, they should be opinionated. Writers are encouraged to dwell on any aspect of their journey that appeals to them: unusual food in the dining car, interesting people met, unusual places visited, etc.

Sidebar

The following information must be included in a separate sidebar (except where otherwise noted) if the story is to be considered for publication.

Stories will be returned if this information is not included:

a) Prices for major portions of trip described, such as air and rail fares, hotel, restaurant, public transit, major attractions, etc.

b) Specific advice on amenities from the rail traveler's point of view.

That is, hotels, restaurants, museums, etc., accessible to the main railroad station or public transit, or those facilities which cater specifically to the rail traveler through special packages, promotions and/or fares.

c) Phone, fax, Internet address, Web page URL and mailing addresses of travel providers/attractions mentioned in story as well as contact information for the national tourism office in the U.S. of the country or countries described. The writer is responsible for the accuracy of this information. Please double-check these numbers and addresses.

d) Any other pertinent traveler's information, such as visa requirements, health news, political updates, etc.

e) Relevant Thomas Cook Timetable numbers.

f) Date the trip was taken.

Unless prior arrangements are made, IRT retains the right to publish "The Society of International Railway Travelers" as the sole contact for more information and booking of travel connected with stories published in IRT.

4) Spotlight **Features** cover the following topics on an occasional basis:

a) STATIONS - A detailed look at railway stations around the world from the point of view of facilities and services of interest to the railway traveler (i.e., restaurants, shops, information booths, hotels, access to city center and public transport, etc.). These stories also give something of the "aesthetics" of the station—its architecture, denizens, and overall "mood."

b) DINERS - This is an appreciation of dining cars from around the world, with an emphasis on the type of food served, prices, method and quality of service, as well as a physical description of the dining car, inside and out.

c) SLEEPERS - As with "Diners," "Sleepers" stories feature a
detailed description of the cars' physical appearance/quality of service, comfort, amenities, etc., as well as their overall character.

d) DESTINATIONS - As the term implies, these are short descriptions of places of aesthetic, cultural or historical interest which can be reached by train and which are of special interest to the enthusiastic railway traveler (railway museums, for example). Please include directions for reaching these places by public transport.

PHOTOGRAPHERS

Trains may be fascinating to look at and a joy to ride. But pictures of them tend towards monotony if they are taken from the same dull perspective (i.e., on the station platform, with the train describing an oblique, diminishing line). Include people with train shots wherever possible.

Also, IRT likes train photographs which include something of the country's native scenery, photographs which emphasize the word "international" in IRT's name. (The Japanese "Shinkansen" racing past Mt. Fuji is the classic example.)

We prefer photos submitted digitally as TIFF files for Macintosh computers, either via email or ZIP disk at a resolution not below 300 dpi. Digital files should be submitted in a compressed format (i.e., as "zip" or "sit" files).

If digital submission is not possible, we prefer black-and-white glossy photos, although color prints or transparencies are also acceptable. Photos should be high contrast, and in focus, preferably 8 x 10 inches, although 5 x 7's will be accepted. IRT uses no color.

SUBSIDIZED TRAVEL

IRT recognizes that professional travel writers must accept subsidized travel. However, writers for IRT must acknowledge receipt of any subsidized travel and promise to remain scrupulously objective in their reporting. Further, unless prior arrangements are made, writers must understand that IRT retains the right to publish "The Society of International Railway Travelers" as the sole contact for more information and booking of travel connected with stories in IRT.

PAYMENT

IRT pays for stories and photos within one month of the cover date of the issue in which the writer's story appears. IRT buys first N. American serial rights and all electronic publishing rights to stories and photos.

In the event a story requested or accepted by IRT is unsuitable for publication, IRT will pay its author a 25 percent "kill fee."

Payment is $.03 per word plus $10 for each photo used ($20, if the photo is the main page-one art). Payment is in U.S. dollars. To receive full payment, photos should be submitted as digital files with a resolution of at least 300 dpi. Digital files should be submitted in a compressed format (i.e., as "zip" or "sit" files). Costs associated with converting photographic material to digital format are deducted from payment.

Sample copies of The *International Railway Traveler* cost $6 each.

SUBMISSIONS

IRT encourages submissions by email. Submissions may also be made on computer disk (3 1/2-inch disks OR ZIP DISKS for IBM or compatibles, or Macintosh, with Microsoft Word preferred. Use ASCII file format if Microsoft Word is not available.

Although IRT welcomes the submission of unsolicited material, it can assume no responsibility for its return unless a self-addressed envelope with sufficient postage is enclosed. Query letters with published clips are strongly encouraged.

IRT editorial office: Gena Holle, Editor; P.O. Box 3747; San Diego, CA 92163. Telephone: (619) 260-1332; FAX: (619) 296-4220; E-mail: IRTTRS@aol.com or irt.trs@worldnet.att.net.

The Society of International Railway Travelers business and tour office: Owen C. Hardy, Publisher/CEO; Eleanor Flagler Hardy, President; 1810 Sils Ave., Suite 306B, Louisville, KY 40205. Telephone: (502) 454-0277; FAX: (502) 458-2250; E-mail: tourdesk@irtsociety.com.

(Updated 7/2/:4)

Categories: Nonfiction—Travel— Rail Travel

CONTACT: Gena Holle, Editor
Material: All
PO Box 3747
San Diego, CA 92163
Phone: 619-260-1332
Fax: 619-296-4220
E-mail: IRTTRS@aol.com or irt.trs@worldnet.att.net.
Website: www.irtsociety.com

International Sports Journal
University of West Haven

The *International Sports Journal* welcomes both empirical and theoretical articles that can be applied or be pertinent to current sports issues and practices or contribute to academic research in the international sports community.

Authors' articles should not exceed 25 double-spaced typewritten pages, and footnotes should appear on a separate page and follow A.P.A. style. References should be listed separately corresponding to the body of the manuscript. The author should send three copies of his/her manuscript plus a short biography. Include also an abstract of not more than 100 words summarizing the paper.

All articles are anonymously reviewed by the editorial board entirely in terms of scholarly content. Previously published articles cannot be accepted.

Categories: Nonfiction—Health—Physical Fitness—Recreation—Sports/Recreation

CONTACT: Thomas Katsaros, Ph.D., Editor
Material: All
University of New Haven
300 Orange Ave.
West Haven CT 06516
Phone: 203-932-7118
Fax: 203-931-6084
E-mail: mharvey@charger.newhaven.edu

Interweave Knits

Interweave Knits is a quarterly publication of Interweave Press for all those who love to knit. In each issue we present beautifully finished projects accompanied by clear step-by-step instruction. The projects range from quick but intriguing projects that can be accomplished in a weekend, to complex patterns that may take months to complete. The magazine includes feature articles from around the country and around the world about people who knit. *Interweave Knits* readers want to know where each kind of knitting comes from, how it was and is done, who did and does it, and why. Striking examples of the technique are important.

Our knitters want to know how to employ any new techniques they encounter in our magazine today. Therefore, each article will have an associated knitting project that uses the technique to produce a high-quality item that they will want to keep or give away.

Submissions

We invite written queries and submissions of manuscripts, photographs, and artwork related to all aspects of hand knitting. Material submitted should display in-depth knowledge of the subject matter and, when appropriate, careful, documented research, with all sources acknowledged.

Keep a copy of everything. If the submission is unsolicited and/or you wish any part of it to be returned, include a self-addressed envelope with sufficient return postage. *Interweave Knits* is published quarterly-press dates are last week of January for Spring, first week of April for Summer, first week of June for Fall, and last week of September for Winter. Issues are planned six to twelve months in advance; if you have materials intended for a particular issue, please submit them six months before the month of publication.

Manuscripts

Technical accuracy is essential, but the tone should be personal and informal. If your article is historical, use primary resources, such as letters and diaries, wherever possible to make information accessible and arresting to the reader. Strive for clear organization as you convey information, including subheads where appropriate.

Please include a sketch and yarn sample for the project that will accompany your article. The project must include clear step-by-step directions and precise diagrams wherever the reader will need visual direction on where fingers, yarns, tools, or other materials go. Highlight techniques that the knitter will learn and/or employ to complete the project successfully. Include any information you have on where to get necessary supplies and what they will cost. A unique feature of *Interweave Knits* is that for each project, we will suggest yarn substitutions and alternate colorways. We aim to accommodate the knitter who needs to start your project today, so it is important to propose readily-available yarns.

We expect that the article you ask us to consider has not been published nor is it presently submitted elsewhere. If any part of your submission has been published previously, please let us know when and by whom. If the article is still in the idea stage, send a detailed proposal-complete outline, written description, sample pages, or sketches-sufficient to give us a clear idea of what to expect in the finished piece. Once we've made any adjustments to the project concept and agreed on the details, you would begin work on the project instructions. It is possible to provide the design and written instructions and have us outsource the actual knitting.

The manuscript should be computer-generated and submitted on a 3 /12-inch disk. Include a hard-copy of the manuscript as well; it should be double-spaced, on 8 1/2-by-11-inch white bond paper with at least a 1-inch margin all around. Our production is done on MS-DOS computers with Microsoft Word software, but we can accept and convert generic (ASCII) text files created with other MS-DOS software and most Macintosh computers. Label the disk with your name and phone number as well as program used to create the manuscript. Any special instructions or charts may be included on a separate sheet of paper. We will accept typewritten manuscripts if you do not have access to a computer.

Visuals

When you submit a manuscript in which you plan to include photographs of historical or other items, please send photocopies of those items with your manuscript. When you are providing visuals for an accepted article, please send samples of finished, publication-quality photographs (color transparencies or black-and-white glossies, please) or artwork. On occasion, it may be best for you to send actual garments and tools for us to photograph. We will work together to choose what will best suit the story and make sure all pieces are transported safely. All photographs, artwork, and other materials will be returned promptly and appropriately insured. If you are knitting or supervising the knitting of the project that will accompany your article, please send the article to us for photographing. Projects will be photographed and retained by Interweave Press unless other arrangements are made.

Acceptance, Editing, and Payment

Receipt of your submission will be promptly acknowledged, but we may not be able to make a decision about its use right away. Please be patient.

When we pay for accepted material, we purchase first North American serial rights for publication in *Interweave Knits* and subsequent nonexclusive rights for use in other Interweave Press publications and promotions. The author retains the publication rights for the original materials. Payment for manuscripts is at the rate of approximately $100 per published page (approximately four manuscript pages or 1000 words) and is made upon publication unless other arrangements are made. Project instructions are contracted for separately. Before your work is published, we'll send you an agreement stating the terms of acceptance and payment for your approval.

We reserve the right to edit your material as necessary to fit the style, format, or other requirements of *Interweave Knits*. For feature articles and projects, a copy of the edited manuscript will be submitted to you for review before publication. Unfortunately, it is sometimes necessary to make further edits due to space limitations, and we may not always have the opportunity to appraise you of these changes.

Categories: Nonfiction—Crafts/Hobbies—Hobbies

CONTACT: Editors
Material: Queries or submissions
Interweave Press
201 East Fourth Street
Loveland CO 80537
Phone: 970-669-7672
Fax: 970-613-4667
E-mail: knits@interweave.com
Website: www.interweave.com

IR World

IR World (formerly *Compressed Air*) does not accept unsolicited submissions.

Iris
A Journal about Women
University of Virginia

Submissions

iris offers feature stories, fiction, art and photography, poetry, book reviews, news, and personal essays focusing on feminist issues for young women. We appreciate the diversity and activism found in fine writing, whether it be critical or creative. We are a nonprofit organization, staffed by undergraduate student interns and women interested in making a difference in the world around them. The magazine appears twice yearly, and each issue has a particular theme.

Call for Submissions!

Spring 2005, Issue #50

Milestones: The 25th Anniversary Issue

Iris is celebrating 25 years in print-what's your excuse to party? Dig deep to your roots and reveal the tantalizing tales and amazing achievements that have grounded your feminism. How, when, and where did the "f" word enter your life? What are your milestones? Reminisce about a long sought graduation, an unorthodox wedding, a valiant act of social protest, or the birth of your child. These are and have always been your pages-join us in writing iris's next chapter.

Final Deadline: December 1, 2004

Directions for Submissions:

For all nonfiction submissions, please submit two typed, double-spaced, clean copies of all material, and use language inclusive of differences in gender, sexual orientation, and race. Use short endnotes as needed, and provide a short bibliography at the end of the article when it is appropriate. Please use MLA style. Send an SASE for response; if you'd like your submission returned, be sure to include sufficient postage.

Feature stories and personal essays should run between 1500 and 2500 words. We are looking for timely, well-written pieces of political import or intellectual concern. These pieces generally fit into an issue's theme, so determine upcoming themes before you submit. Address submissions to Abby Manzella, Coordinating Editor.

Short news items should run 500 to 1000 words. We seek coverage of issues not generally addressed in the mass media, that relate to our theme, and fit into our twice-yearly publishing schedule. Address submissions to Abby Manzella, Coordinating Editor.

Film, book, music, exhibit, and other reviews generally run about 900 words for a single item and 1500 for a combined review. Address submissions to Abby Manzella, Coordinating Editor. **Fiction submissions** should run between 2000 and 6500 words-we rarely publish long pieces-and be typed and double-spaced. Please submit only one story at a time unless they are "short shorts." We prefer a point of view that reflects the diversity of women's experiences. We are seeking fiction that takes risks and that is not necessarily of the sort found in mainstream publications. While we always keep the theme in mind while selecting pieces, it is not our deciding factor for acceptance. Above all, the writing must be fresh and imaginative. Please address submissions to the Fiction Editor.

Poetry decisions are made with the goal of showcasing quality work from a variety of women's viewpoints. We seek vivid and surprising poems that take risks and teach us to see things in a new way. Though we do keep the theme in mind when making final selections, it is not our deciding factor in acceptance. Send no more than three poems at once, and please be patient as turnaround times can be up to four months. Please address submissions to the Poetry Editor.

Art submissions can include line drawings, cartoons, photography, or slides of other media. All work will be returned with an SASE. We are looking for original pieces that reflect the many facets of women's lives and stories. Please address submissions to the Art Editor.

Upon acceptance, please submit a copy of your piece, preferably as an e-mail attachment, in a format able to be read by Word for Windows. We also may ask you to submit a copy on an IBM-formatted computer disk. Additionally, we require a brief biography (two or three sentences). Upon acceptance of artwork, we will provide specifications for scanned images to be submitted on zip disk. You will be paid with five copies of the magazine in which your work appears.

iris acquires one-time rights to the printed work we publish. Accepted pieces may also appear in iris online. If you subsequently sell the piece to a reprint publication, remind the editors to forward a standard permission form to us and to acknowledge that the piece first appeared in our journal.

send all submissions to the address below.

We do not accept e-mail submissions, but you may reach us at iris@virginia.edu if you need information.

Categories: Fiction—Nonfiction—Book Reviews—College—Feminism—Gay/Lesbian—Multicultural—Poetry—Short Stories—Women's Fiction—Women's Issues—Writing

CONTACT: Submission Editor (specify genre)
Material: All
The Women's Center, PO Box 800588, University of Virginia
Charlottesville VA 22908
Phone: 434-924-4500
Fax: 434-982-2901
E-mail: iris@virginia.edu

Islands

Thank you for your interest in ISLANDS. The most useful thing a prospective contributor can do is read the magazine, which is available on newsstands or in bookstores. If the magazine is not available locally, we'll mail you one for $6 ($11 for non U.S.). Subscriptions cost $24 per year ($33 for non U.S.).

ISLANDS (8 times a year) is a travel magazine that focuses on islands around the world: urban, rural, tropical or windswept, well-known or virtually undiscovered. We strive for geographical and topical diversity and encourage articles with a well-defined focus and point of view. Our purpose is, in effect, to take the reader to the island. To that end, we seek informative, insightful, personal pieces that reveal the essence of the place.

In every issue there are usually several feature articles, ranging from 2,500 to 4,000 words. There are also occasional shorter features of about 1,500 to 2,000 words.

Front-of-the-book sections include Art Beat (columns on the arts), with brief book and record reviews (staff written), short profiles, and Q & As with artists and writers, as well as short pieces on museums, films, and other arts topics. Crossroads includes regular columns by contributing editors on the Caribbean and Hawaii, as well as department-length pieces (750-1500 words) on slices of island life. These can be essays or narrative experiences - profiles or topics that range from sports to nature to encounters with islanders.

The Guide is our back-of-the-book section of service information. Within The Guide, Bearings relates specifically to the features and is staff-written. Insider (850 words) is a Top 10 list of not-to-be-missed (but not overly obvious) things to do in on-the-beaten track island destinations. IslandWise pieces (up to 500 words) showcase a great place to stay, eat, or hike; a tour to take or a new thing to do; even a whole island experience. For a hotels or restaurant to be an appropriate subject, it must be more than something new or luxurious. There must be a good story behind it, something that links it inherently to the island.

Prospective authors should submit material on speculation or send a detailed proposal of each article idea (no laundry lists, please), including an estimate of travel expenses (for features only) and samples of previously published work. Do not send query letters without samples

of writing. In general, we look for accomplished feature writers with many assignments to their credit. Less experienced writers may have better luck submitting articles on speculation or proposing shorter pieces — Horizons, Crossroads, or IslandWise columns.

Be sure to enclose a self-addressed envelope with adequate postage to ensure the return of your material. Allow at least two months for a response. We receive a large volume of inquiries and need time to consider each thoughtfully. You may also send queries or articles on speculation via E-mail to editorial@islands.com. (We may request writing samples via regular mail.)

ISLANDS pays $.50 and up per word for articles. The fee is paid within 45 days of acceptance of the manuscript. If an assigned article is rejected, a kill fee of 25% is paid within 45 days of rejection. Contributors receive three complimentary copies of the magazine in which their article appears.

We hope you continue to enjoy the magazine.

HORIZONS Column

The "Horizons" section is great for writers and photographers with creative ideas, especially those relating to idiosyncratic events, people, activities, customs, news, oddities, etc. from islands anywhere. It's also a great place to break into the magazine.

This section is light, punchy, and varied. We often accompany the stories with humorous illustrations. Some pieces may be purely photographic.

Horizons is the place to use the stuff that didn't quite fit into a feature story; it's a home for intriguing and amusing items you happen to find. The scope is as wide as the horizon, so while the headings below are useful as guidelines let them be your outer limit.

Features: Solid short subjects of up to 200 words, with lively leads and headlines. *Sample subject:* The nation's top private security expert has moved to Fiji to study this peaceful society and bring its lessons home to the U.S. The headline could be: "Peace and Love Man." Subhead: "Why is the world's smartest bodyguard (Madonna, etc.) living in Fiji? To find out why a society needs no bodyguards."

Other elements: These range from creative visual presentations to text pieces of 25-150 words. You can submit ideas and concepts, and/or write the finished products. Imaginative graphic suggestions can "sell" an idea. Example: "Lipstick Sunset," an illustration of a tropical sunset done in hot shades of lipstick - with a chart showing the SPFs and skin-moisturizing benefits of various brands.

Reader Interaction: Designed to get readers involved. Examples: Contests (e.g., writing a caption for a desert-island cartoon). Island travel tips. Responses to editorial queries (the most romantic island you've visited?). All ideas welcome (and paid for if used).

Celebrity Connections: Film or TV star, director, writer, musician, architect, fashion designer, explorer, chef, journalist, politician, etc.

Formats Ideas: Q & A. On a Desert Island: What a celebrity castaway couldn't live without ? and could. Top-five list John LeCarre's favorite London bookstores, surfing champ Kelly Slater's top island surf spot. On location: about a movie or TV show being filmed on an island (note: should have genuine story value in addition to celebrity angle). We also want newsy leads; e.g., Don Johnson bought an island in Vietnam and recently honeymooned there (we'd need details) and a way to verify the facts. Or maybe a celebrated person was on an island you visited, and you can supply information, island contacts, and great quotes. Editorially, this might be fashioned into an "island postcard" with a photo and a quote.

Photo features: A photo that conveys an intriguing "visual factoid" about an island. Format might be a single illuminating photo with a caption. A small group of photos on a theme: Pacific islander tattoos, London clubgoers, Japanese Elvises. A photo quiz: What in the world is this? preferably offbeat and revealing of an island culture, not a scenic. Humor and the unexpected are welcome in all categories.

Island Classics: A single "iconic" product, such as the perfect beach chair. Arrows and blurbs point out its features (e.g., "alloy frame weighs less than a Tom Wolfe novel"). Or a text-and-graphic exploration of a classic island subject. Examples: The Pineapple. The Volcano A-Z. A Perfect Zombie (i.e., the tropical rum drink).

PEOPLE:

Island Character: Photo and text that create a brief encounter with a worthy, funny, offbeat, or colorful personality.

Culture-Gram: Manners, customs, etiquette in an island culture. Several factoids that can be illustrated. Example: When visiting a village in Fiji, bring the chief a gift. Usually it's yangona, the root used to make kava, the national drink.

Locals Rule: Insiders' tips from island residents. Examples: Beach where a Waikiki beachboy goes on his day off. This could be verbatim, capturing a local voice.

Island Health: Health issues, prevention, remedies for island travelers. Could be a short item (see Briefings, below) or a more developed piece. Better as positive tips than frightening hypotheticals.

Life's a Beach: Highlights of a great island beach, with highlight noted.

Short-shorts: Tidbits that multiply the information and entertainment value of Horizons: Web sites for island travelers (with a brief review of what's special). Lingo (how the locals talk; lingo translator). Jokes (heard any good ones lately? must be island oriented). Factoids (quirky, fun items). Statistics (illustrating or ironic, as in *Harper's*). Verbatim (quote from writer, comedian, island character, etc. From the sublime to the ridiculous, but must be memorable). How an island got its name (e.g., why "Santorini"? what does it mean?) Briefings: News and updates on islands around the world. Can be almost anything: environmental news, quirky museum or attraction opening, natural-history update, money saver, travel tip , health news, or…

PAY

Ideas and leads: $25. These are ideas, graphic concepts, or leads that Horizons develops and uses.

Short-shorts: $25. About 20-50 polished words. You can send finished ones on spec., or just the idea for a go-ahead.

Non-feature pieces: $50-150. These are developed midsize pieces of 50 to 200 words (such as a celebrity Q & A, Culture-Gram, Life's A Beach). Please send a brief query.

Features: $150-200 for 250 words. Please send a query.

Photos: Standard rates, plus $25 if suggested concept is used.

Categories: Nonfiction—Travel

CONTACT: Mancy Maul, Editorial Assistant
Material: All
CONTACT: Allison Joyce, Senior Editor
Material: Art Beat, Islandwise
Islands Media Corporation
PO Box 4728
Santa Barbara CA 93140-4728
Phone: 805-745-7100
CONTACT: Jerry Camarillo Dunn, Jr.
Material: Horizons Submissions
6309 Carpinteria Ave.
Carpinteria CA 93013
E-mail: jdunn@islands.com (for Jerry Camarillo Dunn, Jr.)
Website: www.islands.com

Italian Cooking and Living

General Guidelines

Italian Cooking & Living is aimed at an audience that is not necessarily well informed about Italian food and culture but is interested in learning more. Our readers have little time for cooking, but they want to glean all they can and learn easy tips for impressive entertaining and dining. IC&L is overall a "guide"-type magazine that provides a savvy introduction to Italian cuisine and culture for the busy professional.

We are looking for qualified contributing editors to submit articles and accompanying photographs on relevant subjects. We only seriously consider articles that include photographs.

Main Article Subjects

1. TRAVEL to various locations in Italy, highlighting their most distinctive and significant features: the mountains, lakes, rivers, big cities (one or more of their aspects), towns. We usually make a distinction between a city article and a region article.

    a. In 70-80% of the cases, the photos must contain people. We try to present Italian cuisine and culture with the people that make it interesting. In other words, if the article is about Herculaneum, the images should show people in front of the ruins, walking around, holding interesting objects, eating (even someone enjoying a sandwich if there is nothing else), and perhaps selling souvenirs. The rest of the pictures should show the surrounding places and perhaps some from your arrival and any typical modes of transportation. A personal voice in the article is encouraged.

2. Articles on an INGREDIENT such as a cheese, meat product, or other ingredient specific to Italy and Italian cooking. These articles should have some of the aspects of a trip article and some of a purely food feature. These articles are to be 1000-2000 words, with 12-16 images (3 or 4 of which must be of dishes). The recipes must be included.

3. Articles on a cellar or producer of WINE, or on a specific wine. In addition to the images outlined above, you must also provide images of vines, vineyards, cellars, bottles, and labels. These articles are to be of 1000-2000 words with 10-14 images. The article must refer to a production zone (or IGT wine).

Photographs

Pictures of food must have natural coloring and succeed in capturing the beauty of the dish and its composition. They should be done with a large-format camera, or if of very high quality, with 35 mm film (100 ASA). We do not accept postcard-type photos.

The publisher reserves the right to examine services not specifically requested, whether photographs or complete texts, and will return them only if requested and provided with a SASE.

Conditions and Procedures

Any agreement made will be confirmed in writing and will outline the topic, images, price, and deadline to be signed by both parties.

The articles must be sent either by mail, fax, or e-mail to the managing editor, accompanied or preceded by the photographic images. The material must be unpublished. The author will be informed of the outcome of the manuscript in the shortest time possible. For the first submission, we would like a short biography of the author as well.

If the submission is accepted, it will be edited (or edited, translated, and edited again) and when possible, sent to the author for approval before publication.

The images that are accepted will be held from when they are received until after the publication of the article.

The payment of a fixed price for the service will be sent immediately after publication.

Categories: Cooking—Culture—Food/Drink—Lifestyle—Travel

CONTACT: Editorial Office
Material: All
230 Fifth Ave., Ste 1100
New York NY 10001
Phone: 212-0725-8764, ext.24
Fax: 212-889-3907
E-mail: stella@italiancookingandliving.com

Jack and Jill

Please refer to Children's Better Health Institute.

Jakes Magazine

Please refer Turkey Call.

Jam Rag

MISSION STATEMENT

Jam Rag exists to promote our local community of independent, creative musicians. *Jam Rag* strives to foster a creative environment, draw attention to talented independent artists in our area, and invigorate our local music economy.

We are not interested in major label bands or artists, even from Detroit. *Jam Rag* is about independent musicians.

We are not interested in bands from other areas. *Jam Rag* is about the independent music being created in our own home town.

For the most part, we aren't interested in cover bands. *Jam Rag* is about creative artists.

As a *Jam Rag* writer, you are allowed to set your own pace and your own direction. You work as hard as you want, as much or as little as you like. You can turn in stories every week, every month, or once a year if you like. You set your own deadlines. You write when it's convenient for you and when you feel like it.

And you choose your own stories. Unless you request guidance, we will never give you assignments. You decide which bands you want to cover, and how you want to cover them. You (for the most part) decide how long your article needs to be, and how it should be written.

Not only is this approach intended to make the job more fun, we also want *Jam Rag* to reflect a wide variety of personalities and backgrounds. Thus, by giving our writers this freedom, each brings their own unique character to the mix.

We try to give our writers as much freedom as possible. However, at the same time, we try to stay closely focused on local independent, creative music.

We're looking for stories on local bands, musicians and songwriters. We're looking for bands with an interesting story to tell, bands who are particularly talented, bands who've played a key role in our local community, etc. Who decides if a band is interesting or talented enough to deserve story in *Jam Rag*? You do.

We're not interested in articles on music in general, musical instruments or stereo gear, etc. We're not looking for how-to articles. We're not trying to teach local musicians how to play their guitar or how to make it in the music business.

We don't want potential readers to pick up *Jam Rag* and think, "This is a magazine for wanna-be musicians." We want them to pick up the magazine and realize there is a huge and fascinating world of creativity blossoming right in their own back yard. We interview local bands as if they are already stars—because, in our eyes, if they are contributing something new and creative to our collective cultural stew they are stars.

We are also interested in articles about local music-related businesses: studios, music stores, labels, clubs, etc. However, these articles should not serve as a plat-form for the subject to pitch their business. These articles should not appear to be a glorified ad. Instead, you might want to cover things like how the person got into the business, their opinions about local music, predictions for the future, etc.

Call or write for a complete copy of our guidelines.

Categories: Arts—Entertainment—Music—Politics—Society

CONTACT: Tom Ness, Owner/Publisher
Material: All
PO Box 20076
22757 Woodward Ste 240
Ferndale MI 48220
Phone: 248-336-9243
E-mail: jamrag@glis.net

Japanophile
Evoking the old and the new Japan

CONSIDER:

Japanophile takes the culture of one country as its only subject. Other literary magazines try to cover everything, everywhere.

Japanophile covers not only Japan, but Japanese culture as it's found throughout the world. One article may be about zen in New York City, another about a Japanese garden in Vancouver.

WHO'S IT FOR?

It's not just for the initiated few who are studying Japanese or who like to write haiku or who are taking classes in Japanese flower arranging or in judo or karate or for those who wonder about travel in Japan ... or any of hundreds of other approaches that may bring one to an interest in Japan. It's for virtually everyone who is interested in Japan and isn't satisfied with the snippets given on television and the press during a Presidential visit or an Imperial wedding.

JAPAN'S CULTURE

Japan culture is not a narrow, limited subject. Here are lively articles about a wide range of subjects: education, sports, literature, religion, art, architecture, international relations, politics, economics, painting, crafts, flower arranging, science, technology; and not just as they affect Japan, but the world.

***Japanophile*'s GUIDELINES FOR WRITERS**

Short stories may be up to 5,000 words and should involve at least one Japanese and one non-Japanese. Most stories used in the magazine are only 3,000 words.

We need:

1) Color or b&w photos with good contrast. 5x7 is large enough. We need drawings and cartoons. These can be simple drawings. We also like to see sumi-e.

2) Articles about Americans or other non-Japanese who are interested in Japan and its culture. A Michigan naturalist who is also a haiku poet was the subject of one article. Other examples: an Ohio man who collects netsuke, a North Carolina woman who has become a bunraku performer in Osaka, a Virginia potter who was an apprentice potter in Japan.

3) Poems in a Japanese form such as haiku. These may be about America or any place in the world. If a poem is not in a Japanese form it must be about Japanese culture. For example: a comic poem about a Kentucky man who rides a Honda motorcycle, a serious poem about racism as it has affected Japanese-Americans. A haiku about New York City may work for *Japanophile*.

4) Scholarly articles with authoritative quotes or a first person account of living or traveling in Japan may be acceptable if it has literary merit.

If you can write a column about a particular part of the United States or some other country as it relates to Japanese culture, you can become a columnist for *Japanophile*. For example: Japanese culture in London or San Francisco or Chicago. We already have a column called TOKYO TOPICS. Your sources include your local newspapers.

Payment for stories is $20 and sometimes an article gets that much, usually less. We pay $1 for haiku and the same for a funny filler. Cartoons and other art fetch $15 and up. All are payment for one-time rights and rights revert to the author.

A reading fee of $5 must accompany short stories entered in our annual contest. Payment for each published short story is $25 and rights revert to the author. A prize of $100, plus an attractive certificate, is awarded to the author of the best short story each year. This is in addition to $25 paid for one-time publication of the story.

It's best to study the magazine. Subscriptions are $14 for four issues and a single issue is $4.00. Add one dollar for a single issue sent abroad; foreign subscriptions are $20.

Include a short bio, i.e., "Ralph Smith taught English to Tokyo businessmen for two years. His poems have appeared in *Ploughshares* and *The Iowa Review*." (A list of credits is not required.) Also, a disk (DOS or Mac format) of a text file or MS Word file is greatly appreciated, but not required.

Categories: Fiction—Nonfiction—Asian-American—Book Reviews—Poetry—Short Stories

CONTACT: Submissions Editor
Material: All
PO Box 7977, 415 Main St.
Ann Arbor MI 48107
Phone: 734-930-1553
Fax: 734-930-9968
E-mail: jpnhand@japanophile.com
Website: www.japanophile.com

Jet Magazine

Does not accept unsolicited submissions.

Jewish Action

Thank you for expressing an interest in our publication.

Submissions should cover topics of interest to an international Orthodox Jewish audience. Articles related to current ongoing issues of Jewish life and experience, human-interest features, poetry, art, music and book reviews, historical pieces and humor are all acceptable. Because the magazine is a quarterly, we do not generally publish articles dealing with specific timely events.

Articles should be double spaced, typewritten and should average 1,000-3,000 words, including notes. If used, notes should follow the article as endnotes. E-mail submissions are preferred. Mailed or faxed submissions are also acceptable. The author's name, address and daytime telephone number should be enclosed with the article. If mailed, a self addressed, stamped envelope is appreciated.

Authors will be informed of a decision within six-eight weeks of submission.

Jewish Action is published by the Orthodox Union, a non-profit organization based in New York City. See our web site at www.ou.org. Nechama Carmel is the editor of Jewish Action. The assistant editor is Diane Chabbott.

Categories: Jewish Interest—Religion

CONTACT: Submissions Editor
Material: All
11 Broadway
New York NY 10004
Phone: 212-613-8146
Fax: 212-613-0646
E-mail: ja@ou.org

> **Remember: *Editors change jobs and publishers change addresses. It is wise to invest in a phone call for the current information before submitting.***

Jewish Currents

JEWISH CURRENTS prints articles, reviews, fiction and poetry pertaining to Jewish subjects or presenting a Jewish point of view on an issue of interest. Pieces submitted should ideally be about 3 magazine pages in length, but in any case, should not exceed 4 such pages. (A magazine page contains approximately 600 words.) Submissions must be typed and accompanied by a SASE and a brief biographical note including the author's publishing history. We do not accept simultaneous submissions, nor do we reprint material already published elsewhere.

Finally, JEWISH CURRENTS is unable to pay its contributors beyond a year's free subscription plus six copies of the issue in which they appear.

Categories: Jewish Interest

CONTACT: Editorial Board
Material: All
22 E. 17th St. Ste. 601
New York NY 10003
Phone: 212-924-5740
Fax: 212-414-2227

Joiners' Quarterly

Thank you for thinking of *Joiners' Quarterly*. While our basic interest lies in timber framing, we also pursue several topics that are relevant to natural and traditional building. We look for new enclosure systems such as straw bales, straw/clay and wood chips/clay, rammed earth, wheat straw panels, or any other new products that would be suitable for enclosing a timber frame.

We also look for articles on mechanical systems such as heating, air conditioning, solar, plumbing and electrical and how they can be applied to timber frame structures, whether it is an article about new innovations, historical uses, or simply installation techniques and precautions. We're always looking for articles on joinery techniques, timber frame design, CAD programs compatible with timber framing, engineering aspects whether modern or historical. Natural house building and whole house building systems also appeal to us.

Other topics: historical building techniques (especially if they are still viable today), hand-hewing, thatch, historic paints, barns, outbuildings, boats, innovative projects, new materials or equipment that would pertain to any of the above, green building. We also desire book and video reviews on any of the above subjects. The more relevant your articles are to timber framing and sustainable construction, the more likely we are to be interested in publishing them.

Payment is generally $50 per published page including photos and/or diagrams.

Manuscripts should be typewritten. Each page should have a page number, title of article, and author's name. Photos should be developed "glossy" and should be labeled with a suggested caption and ID info on back. We do not pay for cover photos.

Diskettes need to be Mac formatted in Microsoft Word.

Call for e-mail submissions.

Thank you,

Editorial Staff at JQ—Steve Chappell, Laurie LaMountain, Jim Marks, and Janot Mendler

Categories: Nonfiction—Architecture—Engineering—Environment—Sustainable Building—Technology—Timber Framing

CONTACT: Steve Chappell, Editor/Publisher
Material: All
PO Box 249
Brownfield ME 04010
Phone: 207-935-3720
Fax: 207-935-4575
E-mail: foxmaple@foxmaple.com
Website: www.foxmaple.com

The Journal of Adventist Education

The *Journal of Adventist Education* is the professional publication of Seventh-day Adventist teachers and educational administrators, worldwide, and should address topics of interest to that group.

The target audience may be teachers: elementary, secondary, or college/university level; or educational administrators. The Journal's constituency is international, a fact writers should keep in mind as they explore the implications or applications of a given topic. Special attention, where applicable, should be given to the concerns of minorities and students with special needs. Writers should define their target group precisely and address its concerns in a specific manner.

Articles by free-lance authors are welcome. Please submit an inquiry or summary of the article before sending a finished manuscript. The *Journal of Adventist Education* purchases first North American rights for each article it prints. Authors are paid upon publication of their articles. Amount varies, depending on length and other factors. Authors also receive two copies of the finished magazine in which their article appears. Articles may be translated and printed in the international edition of the *Journal* (French, Spanish, and Portuguese), and/or posted on the *Journal*'s Web site.

Articles may deal with educational theory or practice, although the *Journal* seeks to emphasize the practical. Articles dealing with the creative and effective use of methods to enhance teaching skills or learning in the classroom are especially welcome. Whether theoretical or practical, such essays should demonstrate the skillful integration of Seventh-day Adventist faith/values and learning.

Periodically, issues will deal extensively with a single topic or issue. Articles representing various approaches or the in-depth discussion of aspects of the issue will be welcome.

Topics Preferred for *Journal of Adventist Education*:
• Call for action on some problem (drug use, need for physical activity, lack of computer access, minority graduation rates, violence, sexual harassment, teacher burnout and morale, hazards at school); with suggestions about how to solve it
• Addressing the needs of students with special needs-learning disabilities, physical handicaps
• New methods and approaches; applying educational research in the classroom
• Church projects related to education
• Classroom climate, interpersonal skills; counseling; discipline
• New methods and approaches, such as cooperative learning, multiple intelligences, individualized instruction, thematic instruction, etc.
• Educational administration
• Extracurricular activities
• Ideas for professional enrichment, staff development, teacher training
• Ideas for worships, religious activities
• Inspirational articles related to the task of the teacher, goals of Adventist education
• Integration of faith and learning
• Issues relating to multigrade and multicultural classrooms
• Legal issues in schools
• Marketing, promoting Adventist education
• Personal experience or inspirational articles (school-related)
• Pro and con on a controversial topic
• Relations with boards, parents, administrators

• Reports on innovative programs and projects or research on Adventist education
• School libraries
• Service and outreach activities
• Teaching techniques, innovative and practical methods of presenting specific topics and subjects
• Testing and assessment
• Use of technology in the classroom
• Clear, sharp, black-and-white photographs and appropriate charts and graphs are a welcome adjunct. Photos can be submitted as prints, slides, or in electronic format such as high-resolution scans or digital photos (300 dpi).

The *Journal of Adventist Education* is published five times yearly, with approximately eight articles appearing in each issue. Due to space limitations, many articles will not be published immediately. Articles should be submitted at least five months before publication date. The editorial staff reserves the right to edit all manuscripts as they deem necessary.

Please call, fax, or write the Editor before submitting an article, to be sure that the topic is usable and that the *Journal* has not printed anything recently on the same subject.

If the article has already been printed elsewhere, please include information regarding publisher, source, and date of issue.

When sending materials to the *Journal*, include the following: your name, employer, position as an educator or status if a student; Social Security number and home address if employed in the United States; and other contact information such as E-mail address and fax number. Please include a photo of yourself.

The following manuscript form is preferred:
• Articles should be six to eight pages long, with a maximum of ten pages in length, including references.
• Two-part articles will be considered.
• Material should be double-spaced, using a 70-character line and standard paragraph indention.
• Subheads should be inserted at appropriate intervals.
• Articles submitted on disk or by E-mail as attached files are welcome.
• Please store in IBM WordPerfect or Word format.
• If you submit a disk, be sure to include a printed copy of the article with the disk.
• Quotations should be clearly indicated. Please follow the instructions in *The Chicago Manual of Style* for bibliography and endnotes. Endnotes, in numerical order, should include complete bibliographic information: full name of author, title of work, volume and number if applicable, city of publication, publisher, year of publication (include month if a periodical), and page number(s). Please enclose photocopies pages to verify facts and quotations. The information to be photocopied is as follows: the page(s) on which the fact or quotation occurs, the title page of the book or journal, and copyright information. Authors should obtain permission for reprints of charts, graphs, and photos.

Writers are paid upon publication of their articles. In addition to financial remuneration, they will receive two copies of the issue in which their article appears, and may purchase additional copies (a discount will be offered on orders of ten or more copies).

All of the magazine's articles are copyrighted, and may not be reproduced without permission of the editor.

The *Journal* purchases first North American rights to all articles published, unless other arrangements are made. Articles published in the English edition may be translated into French, Spanish, and Portuguese for the *Journal*'s international edition, and may be featured on the *Journal*'s Web site.

Categories: Nonfiction—Christian Interests—Education

CONTACT: Submission Editor
Material: All
12501 Old Columbia Pike
Silver Spring MD 20904-6600

Phone: 301- 680-5069/5075
Fax: 301-622-9627
E-mail: 74617.1231@compuserve.com
E-mail: CookeC@gc.adventist.org
Website: www.education.gc.adventist.org

The Journal of Asian Martial Arts

MESSAGE FROM THE EDITOR

There are more aspects related to Asian martial arts than commonly meet the eye. Most publications have focused on this subject only to satisfy the interests of the mass market, while other scholarly writings limit themselves to a highly specialized audience. Our journal spans both types of readership. *How?*—Although the journal treats the subject with academic accuracy, we believe that writing styles need not lose the reader! *The Journal of Asian Martial Arts* offers a mature, well-rounded view of this uniquely fascinating subject, attracting a readership that has a close affinity to Asian history and culture.

Our journal logo stylizes the tips of a sword and pen—symbolic of the martial and the cultured. Entwined, they represent an embodiment of balanced characteristics that is necessary for individual and social welfare. Viewed in this perspective, the field of Asian martial arts offers a broad range of interrelated material to cover. Therefore, being both general and specific, our journal offers a unique display case for works by artists and writers. We appreciate your interest and thank you for considering our journal as a medium for your work. Feel free to contact me personally, the editor, regarding any aspect of the journal.

EDITORIAL POLICY

The Journal of Asian Martial Arts is a cover perfect bound 8.5" x 11" quarterly journal. We publish three types of materials: (1) scholarly articles based on primary research in recognized scholarly disciplines, e.g., cultural anthropology, comparative religions, psychology, film theory, and criticism, etc.; (2) more informal, but nevertheless substantial interviews (with scholars, master practitioners, etc.) and reports on particular genres, techniques, etc.; and (3) reviews of books and audiovisual materials on the martial arts. These three types of materials are organized in separate sections of the journal. In order to ensure the quality of all submissions in terms of scholarship as well as writing, each submission will be reviewed by at least two members of our editorial board. We look forward to making the journal accessible to all readers while establishing and maintaining a high quality of scholarship, writing, and graphics.

EDITORIAL CONTENT

Interview/profile—art/aesthetics—philosophic—announcements—cross-cultural—translation—media—reviews—comparative—geographic—technique—scientific—legal—weaponry—reports—social—historical—literary—health.

Article length: 2,000 to 10,000 words for feature articles.

Review length: 1,000 or less for news items, reviews and reports.

Buys: First World Rights with Reprint Rights.

Pays: For articles, $150-500 on publication, plus 2 copies. Payment in copies for reviews.

Audience: Although the *Journal* is targeted for college-level readers, it is distributed to persons of varied backgrounds, ages and occupations. For this reason, articles are written in a clear style for those who may not be totally familiar with the subject and its particular vocabulary.

Internationally distributed: practitioners, scholars, schools, libraries, bookstores, and institutes.

Reports: 2-4 weeks on queries; 1-2 months on manuscripts.

Bionote: Given. Include a short summary of your background and credentials (academic and martial) in your cover letter.

STYLE DETAILS FOR WRITERS

Writers should have martial arts experience and be very knowledgable in Asian culture. Query letters should tell of the writer's qualifications, provide a clear outline of the intended article, and state if

illustrations are available. We pull our hair out when submissions arrive that simply rehash old material or are geared to the wrong audience! Articles are published for knowledgeable readers and must offer special information and insights not available elsewhere.

It is not necessary to provide clips, but a self-addressed stamped envelope (SASE) is appreciated, especially if you want your materials returned. We like to work with writers and are happy to provide suggestions on how to improve any materials that do not meet all criteria the first time through our office door. If you decide to submit a manuscript, have a martial artist and/or Asian scholar critique it first. Of course, the best guide for suitability is the *Journal* itself.

Reviews all articles on speculation. Double-spaced typed manuscripts or letter-quality computer printout acceptable. If possible, also provide text on computer disk in any basic word-processing program (Macintosh formats preferred). Articles must be historically and technically accurate with a list of references at the end. Keep footnotes at a minimum.

Romanization: Provide Chinese and Japanese characters when possible for important names, terms, and places mentioned in the article. Give personal names in the Asian order with family name first. We use Pinyin Romanization for Chinese.

DETAILS FOR PHOTOGRAPHERS & ARTISTS

We expect the quality of article illustrations to be of equally high quality as the articles we publish. The talents of a professional photographer should be utilized in order to meet the proper standards for printing. Most photographs and other illustrations should emphasize what is important to the text.

Special note must be taken when photographs are used to illustrate technical aspects of a martial art. Please do not include distracting backgrounds, such as school insignia or busy geometric patterns! A simple, plain background works best in these cases. We want to view the martial art, not studio decor or geographic scenery. However, we do encourage photographers to be creative whenever appropriate. Photos showing movement, a mood enhancing environment, or a particular social aspect are welcome whenever they portray a significant insight, feeling, or thought that relates to martial arts.

Material Requirements: We will only consider good quality black-&-white glossy prints, negatives, and color transparencies. Color photography is reproduced in black-&-white inside the *Journal*, but in full color if used on the cover. Contact sheets and photocopies of hand art can be submitted for preliminary review purposes.

Acceptance & Payment: Reviews art work on speculation. In the case of computer generated art, we prefer Macintosh formats, such as Quark-Express, Adobe Illustrator, or Photoshop. Rates vary, but are competitive with other publications of similar standards.

Model Releases: Photo model releases and captions are required for all photos.

Categories: Nonfiction—Arts—Asian-American—Culture—Health—History—Literature—Mass Communications—Military—Multicultural—Philosophy—Physical Fitness—Science—Sports/Recreation—Martial Arts

CONTACT: Michael A. DeMarco, Publisher
Material: All
Via Media Publishing
821 West 24th St
Erie PA 16502
Phone: 814-455-9517
Fax: 814-455-2726
E-mail: md@goviamedia.com
Website: www.goviamedia.com

F-L

JCN

Journal of Christian Nursing

The *Journal of Christian Nursing* strives to help Christian nurses view nursing practice through the eyes of faith. It is a professional journal by and for nurses. Topics covered include Christian concepts in nursing, professional issues, spiritual care, ethics, values, healing and wholeness, psychology and religion, personal and professional life, patient/client experiences which include a faith dimension (including case studies), and stories of nurses who have stepped out in faith to care for others in new or unusual ways in the U.S. or overseas. Articles must be relevant to Christian nursing and consistent with the purposes and statement of faith of Nurses Christian Fellowship (available on request). Priority will be given to nurse authors, although some articles by non-nurses will be considered.

Preparing Your Manuscript

1. *Style.* Scan a recent copy of JCN. You will see that the style is popular, not academic. Articles should be written to communicate clearly to staff nurses. Avoid (or define) technical jargon and abbreviations (these may differ in other clinical settings). Use lively illustrations. Give practical examples. Share; don't preach. Academic papers may have some good content which JCN readers would appreciate, but they must be rewritten in article format. See "Avoiding the 'School Paper Style' Rejection," by Suzanne Hall Johnson, Nurse Author & Editor; Summer 1991, for help in revising an academic paper. Style is governed by *The Chicago Manual of Style*, 13th edition (Chicago/London: University of Chicago Press, 1982).

2. *References.* Limit your references to only those necessary to document your point. Avoid presenting a review of the literature. As the author of the article you are the expert. Endnotes must contain the full name of authors (not just initials of first name) and be listed as they appear in article, not alphabetically. Be sure to include page numbers. See back issues of JCN for examples. You are responsible for accuracy in citation and interpretation of resources. Check spelling of authors' names carefully. If a reference has more than one author, list them in the correct order.

3. *Length.* Most articles range from 6 to 12 double-spaced, type-written pages. Essays on "Why I Love Nursing" should be about 600 words. Use one-inch margins.

4. Number your pages and put your name on each page.

Submitting Your Manuscript

1. *Query letter.* If your article fits these guidelines, we prefer to receive the manuscript without a query letter. However, if you are uncertain about the suitability of your topic, please query either by letter or phone. Most articles by non-nurse freelance authors are rejected unless they have outstanding insights valuable to nurses. We will work with nurses who have significant information to communicate but need help with writing style.

2. *Manuscript.* We prefer email submissions.

3. *Review process.* Manuscripts with significant professional content will be sent to several review panel members for evaluation. If your manuscript is reviewed you will receive copies of the reviewers' comments. We may ask you to revise an article based on reviewers' suggestions. Names of authors and reviewers are kept confidential in the review process.

4. *Illustrations.* Good candid photos can bring an article to life. Do not write on photos or use paper clips. Include captions or explanatory material with each illustration.

Note: Identify all persons in photos and include a signed, written release for each. Suggested release format: I hereby give (author's name) permission to submit this photo of (subject's name) for possible use in the *Journal of Christian Nursing*.

5. *About the Author.* Give a brief description of yourself including your nursing credentials, where you work, your church and community involvement, and any other information you think readers might like to know—especially anything that would enhance your credibility in the topic covered in your article.

6. *Remuneration.* Ranges from $0 to $80. We do not pay for book reviews, but reviewers may keep the book reviewed.

7. *Rights.* JCN usually buys first rights. We occasionally purchase reprint rights. If your article has been published before, please indicate where and when. Never submit an article to two publications at the same time. We retain the right to grant permission to photocopy articles for educational purposes.

8. *Poetry.* JCN no longer accepts poetry.

Categories: Nonfiction—Children—Christian Interests—Disabilities—Education—Family—Feminism—General Interest—Health—History—Inspirational—Interview—Multicultural—Music—Physical Fitness—Psychology—Relationships—Religion—Spiritual—Women's Issues—Humor— Nursing—All categories only as they pertain to Christian nursing

CONTACT: Cathy Walker, Managing Editor
Material: All
PO Box 7895
Madison WI 53707-7895
Phone: 608-846-8560
Fax: 608-274-7882
E-mail: jcn.me@ivcf.org

Journal of Information Ethics
St. Cloud State University

Manuscripts dealing with any aspect of information ethics are welcome. The *Journal of Information Ethics* deals with ethics in all areas of information or knowledge production and dissemination. This includes, but is not limited to, library and information science, education for these professions, technology, government publication and legislation, graphic display, computer security, database management, disinformation, peer review, privacy, censorship, cyberspace, and information liability approached from sociological, philosophical, theoretical, and applied perspectives. The *Journal of Information Ethics* publishes letters to the editor, brief notes (4-6 pages), essay (10-25 pages), and book or topical journal issue reviews. Upon publication, authors will receive an honorarium and two copies of the issue.

General Instructions: When preparing a manuscript, please double-space on one side only, leave generous margins, avoid right-hand justification, number pages consecutively, and use good white paper. Two copies of the manuscript are sufficient. If a computer disk is available, please enclose it. Include your name, affiliation, address (which will be printed with your article), and phone number. On a separate sheet of paper, provide a biographical statement of 75 words or fewer, which will be edited and published in the "About the Contributors" section.

Content: All submissions must deal with some aspect of information ethics. Scholarship does not have to be mind-numbing, tedious, or pedantic; try to create stimulating, controversial, and enticing pieces.

Style: This is a scholarly journal. Therefore, develop paragraphs fully; use neither contractions nor first or second person pronouns; avoid repetition, jargon, sexist language, and awkward syntactical constructions; do use a limited number of succinct headings and subheadings; and underline or italicize when required.

Carefully honed, mellifluous prose is as important as substantive content. A good way to achieve these objectives is to show the manuscript to a colleague whose writing you respect. All accepted material is subject to editorial emendation.

Documentation: Use current APA (American Psychological Association) style. Do not number references. Avoid footnotes. Follow the style manual carefully; attend to the details of order, punctuation, inversions, upper and lower cases, and the precise method of parenthetical documentation.

Query or send manuscripts directly to the editor, Robert Hauptman, *Journal of Information Ethics*, Learning Resources & Technology Services, 720 4ᵗʰ Ave. So., St. Cloud State University, St. Cloud, MN 56301. Please include a self-addressed, stamped envelope. Thank you.

Categories: Nonfiction—Internet—Ethics—Information Science—Library Science—Philosophy—Public Policy—Technology

CONTACT: Robert Hauptman, Editor
Material: All
Learning Resources and Technology Services
720 - 4th Ave. S
St. Cloud State University
St. Cloud MN 56301
Phone: 320-255-4822
Fax: 320-255-4778
E-mail: hauptman@stcloudstate.edu

Journal of Modern Literature
Temple University

The editors welcome submissions of research-based studies of modern literature as well as critical studies based on scholarship. Papers should conform to the 1977 MLA Style Sheet. See recent issues for House Style variations. We require a disk in WordPerfect format for accepted articles. Essays will not be returned unless they are received with return postage.

Submit two copies of your manuscript.
Categories: Literature—Academic

CONTACT: Dr. Morton Levitt, Editor-in-Chief
Material: All
Temple University
921 Anderson Hall
Philadelphia PA 19122
Phone: 215-204-8505
Fax: 215-204-9620
E-mail: dmcmanus@nimbus.temple.edu
Website: www.muse.jhu.edu/journals/jml

Journey
Meeting Life's Challenges

Ceased publication.

jubilat

jubilat welcomes submissions of poetry, as well as essays and other forms of writing on poetry, poetics or—especially—subjects that have nothing to do with "poetry" but capture, in some way, a quality of poetic thought. Past issues have included work by Dean Young, Caroline Knox, Michael Burkard, Mong-lan, Matthew Rohrer, Jane Miller, Nathaniel Mackey, Paul Celan, James Tate, Claudia Rankine, Killarney Clary and Odysseus Elytis among many others. Please visit www.jubilat.org for complete submission guidelines, features from recent issues and other information.

Mail three to five poems and/or one prose piece at a time (mail genres separately). Poems should be individually typed either single- or double-spaced on one side of the page. Prose should be typed double-spaced on one side and be no longer than twenty-five pages. We do not publish short stories. All manuscripts and correspondence regarding submissions should be accompanied by a self-addressed, stamped envelope (SASE) for a response.

jubilat considers manuscripts year around.
Categories: Poetry, Short Stories

CONTACT: Lisa Olstein, Managing Editor
Material: All
Bartlett 482
Dept. of English
University of Massachusetts
Amherst MA 01003-0515
Website: www.jubilat.org

Junior Swimmer

Please refer to *Swimming World* magazine.

Kaleidoscope
Exploring the Experience of Disability through Literature & Fine Arts

KALEIDOSCOPE Magazine has a creative focus that examines the experiences of disability through literature and the fine arts. Unique to the field of disability studies, this award-winning publication is not an advocacy or rehabilitation journal. Rather, KALEIDOSCOPE expresses the experiences of disability from the perspective of individuals, families, healthcare professionals, and society as a whole. The material chosen for KALEIDOSCOPE avoids stereotypical, patronizing, and sentimental attitudes about disability. Although the content always focuses on a particular aspect of disability, writers with and without disabilities are welcome to submit their work

The criteria for good writing apply: effective technique, thought-provoking subject matter, and in general, a mature grasp of the art of story-telling. Works should not use stereotyping, patronizing, or offending language about disability ("uses a wheelchair" not "confined to a wheelchair" or "wheelchair bound"). KALEIDOSCOPE uses person-first language ("person who has cerebral palsy" not "cerebral palsied').

KALEIDOSCOPE is published twice a year, in January with a submission deadline of August 1, and in July with a submission deadline of March 1.

KALEIDOSCOPE accepts:

Nonfiction—Articles relating to the arts, both literary and visual, interviews, or personal accounts.

Fiction—Short stories with a well-crafted plot and engaging characters—5,000 words maximum.

Poetry—Poems that have strong imagery, evocative language—six poems maximum.

Book reviews—Reviews that are substantive, timely, powerful works about publications in the field of disability and/or the arts. The writer's opinion of the work being reviewed should be clear. The review should be a literary work in its own right.

Visual arts—Art of all media, from watercolor and charcoals to collage and sculpture; three to six works maximum. We accept art in 5"x7" or 8"x10" black and white glossy photos or 35mm slides, or color photos. The photos should have minimal background with the art as the main focus. Include captions on the photos stating the size, medium, and title of work.

Publishing information
• Considers unsolicited material
• Accepts simultaneous submissions
• Publishes previously published work
• Acknowledges receipt in two weeks
• Rejects or accepts within six months
• Accepts photographs or illustrations complementing work

• Reserves right to minor editing without author's approval; substantive editing with approval

Payment information

• Payment is made upon publication, and varies from $10 to $125.
• Contributors receive two complimentary copies of the magazine.
• Copyright reverts to author upon publication.

Subscription rates:

Individual—$10 per year
Institutional—$15 per year
Sample copy—$6, prepaid
Single copy—$6

Add $8 for international, $5 for Canadian (U.S. funds only) for postage and handling.

Categories: Arts—Disabilities—Literature

CONTACT: Gail Willmot, Editor-in-Chief
Material: All
701 S. Main St.
Akron OH 44311
Phone: 330-762-9755
Fax: 330-762-0912
E-mail: mshiplett@udsakron.org
Website: www.udsakron.org

Kalliope
a journal of women's art

Kalliope
A Journal of Women's Literature and Art

Kalliope is recognized as one of the best women's literary journals in the U.S.A. 2003 marks *Kalliope*'s twenty-fifth anniversary, which makes us one of the oldest feminist literary journals in the U.S.! Please support *Kalliope* in our effort to ensure that women's works will continue to be seen and heard.

Kalliope publishes poetry, short fiction, interviews, reviews, and visual art by women. We are open to experimental forms. Please submit poems in groups of 3-5; submit short fiction under 3,500 words.

Visual art should be sent in groups of 4-10 works. We require B&W professional quality glossy prints made from negatives. Please supply photo credits, date of work, title, medium, and size on the back of each photo submitted. Include artist's resume and model releases where applicable. We welcome an artist's statement of 50-75 words.

Please include SASE and a short contributor's note with all submissions. Foreign contributors must send U.S. postage or International Reply Coupons. Manuscripts without SASE will be neither read nor returned. Payment is usually in copies; a grant sometimes permits a small stipend. Copyright reverts to the author upon request. Because each submission is reviewed by several member of the *Kalliope* Writers' Collective, response time may be 3-6 months.

Thank you, in advance, for your patience.

Categories: Fiction—Arts—Biography—Literature—Poetry—Women's Fiction—Women's Issues—Writing

CONTACT: Submissions Editor
Material: All
3939 Roosevelt Blvd.
Jacksonville FL 32205

Remember: Editors change jobs and publishers change addresses. It is wise to invest in a phone call for the current information before submitting.

Kentucky
MONTHLY

Kentucky Monthly

1. Query first, either e-mail, mail or fax. We try to respond within one month to queries. E-mail query to Stephen M. Vest at Steve@kentuckymonthly.com or Michael Embry at membry@kentuckymonthly.com.

2. We publish stories about Kentucky and Kentuckians, including those who live elsewhere. Among the subjects are history, fashion, art, profiles, travel, politics, bed and breakfast, restaurants, religion, and humor. Most cover stories run in the 1,500-2,500 word range.

3. We prefer a minimum editorial lead time of three months, but chances for publication are enhanced with longer lead time.

4. We publish fiction and poetry by Kentucky writers or Kentucky-related subjects. Fiction usually runs from 1,000-3,000 words.

5. State availability of photos with query.

6. Sample copy available at www.kentuckymonthly.com.

7. *Kentucky Monthly* is also listed in *Writer's Market.*

Categories: Nonfiction—Arts—Biography—Book Reviews—Campus Life—Civil War—Collectibles—College—Conservation—Consumer—Cooking—Crafts/Hobbies—Crime—Culture—Dance—Drama—Ecology—Education—Entertainment—Environment—Fashion—General Interest—Government—Health—History—Inspirational—Lifestyle—Literature—Music—Outdoors—Poetry—Politics—Regional—Short Stories—Sports/Recreation—Television/Radio—Theatre—Travel—Women's Fiction—Women's Issues

CONTACT: Michael Embry, Editor
Material: All
CONTACT: Stephen Vest, Publisher
Material: All
PO Box 559
Frankfort KY 40602-0559
Phone: 502-227-0053

The Kenyon Review

The Kenyon Review

Thank you for your interest in *The Kenyon Review.*

We consider submissions of poetry (up to ten pages), short fiction and essays (up to 7,500 words), and proposals for book reviews. Plays, or excerpts from plays, should be under 35 double-spaced pages.

All manuscripts must be double-spaced, and accompanied by a stamped, self-addressed envelope. We do not accept simultaneous submissions.

Our basic payments to contributors are as follows:

Prose	$10.00 (per printed page)
Poetry	$15.00
Book Reviews	$10.00
Drama	$10.00
Translations	$10.00 to translator and $5.00 to author

Payment, plus two copies of the issue in which the material appears, will be mailed upon publication. Additional copies of the issue are available to authors at $5.00 each.

The Kenyon Review will read unsolicited manuscripts only from September 1 through March 31.

We discourage "blind" submissions from writers who have not read—or seen—a recent issue of the magazine. We hope your interest in The Kenyon Review will extend to ordering a sample copy or subscribing if you don't already.

Categories: Fiction—Nonfiction—Arts—Drama—General Interest—Language—Literature—Multicultural—Poetry—Short Stories—Writing

CONTACT: David H. Lynn, Editor-in-Chief
Material: All
Kenyon College
104 College Drive
Gambier OH 43022
Phone: 740 427-5208
Fax: 740 427-5417
E-mail: kenyonreview@kenyon.edu
Website: www.kenyonreview.org

Kids' Ministry Ideas

Managing Editor: Tamara Michalenko Terry. Contact: Editor. 95% freelance written. "A quarterly resource for those leading children to Jesus, *Kids' Ministry Ideas* provides affirmation, pertinent and informative articles, program ideas, resource suggestions, and answers to questions from a Seventh-day Adventist Christian perspective."

Estab. 1991. Circ. 5,000. Pays on acceptance. Publishes ms an average of 3 months after acceptance. Byline given. Offers variable kill fee. Buys first North American serial, electronic rights. Editorial lead time 3 months. Submit seasonal material 3 months in advance. Accepts queries by mail, e-mail, fax. Responds in 3 weeks to queries; 3 months to mss. Sample copy and writer's guidelines free.

Nonfiction: Inspirational, new product (related to children's ministry), articles fitting the mission of Kids' Ministry Ideas. Buys 40-60 mss/year. Send complete ms.

Length: 300-1,000 words. Pays $30-$100 for assigned articles; $30-$70 for unsolicited articles.

Photos: State availability with submission.

Buys one-time rights. Captions required.

Columns/Departments: Buys 20-30 mss/year. Query. Pays $30-$100.

Tips: "Request writers' guidelines and a sample issue."

Categories: Nonfiction, children, inspiration, religion, spiritual

CONTACT: Tamara Michalenko Terry, Managing Editor
Material: All
Review and Herald Publishing Association
55 W. Oak Ridge Dr.
Hagerstown MD 21740
Phone: 301-393-4115
Fax: 301-393-4055
E-mail: kidsmin@rhpa.org

Kitplanes

Welcome to KITPLANES magazine's website and the fascinating world of homebuilt aircraft, currently the most dynamic segment of sport aviation. (Compared to factory-built certified light airplanes, many times more homebuilt aircraft are registered with the Federal Aviation Administration [FAA] every year.)

Now in its 18th year, KITPLANES is the premier periodical for people interested in the most dynamic segment of sport aviation: homebuilt airplanes, rotorcraft, ultralights and other special-interest, do-it-yourself flying machines.

The magazine features pilot reports on the best kitbuilt and plansbuilt aircraft, builder surveys on the most popular projects and annual directories of hundreds of current kit aircraft, plus homebuilder supplies and aviation electronics.

Every issue contains a wide range of topics from understanding aerodynamics to humor. Our objective with this website is to introduce the subject of building your own aircraft and provide enough information to help you decide whether to investigate this possibility further.

Writers Guidelines
Read this first.

Thank you for your interest in KITPLANES magazine. Before submitting material, we suggest that you obtain a copy to the magazine and acquaint yourself with its style and content. Back issues are $6 postpaid. Call 800/358-6327 or 413/662-2610 (International). Your queries and submissions are welcome, but they may be in our hands for several weeks before we can evaluate them. We cannot assume responsibility for material submitted, but be assured that reasonable care will be taken.

Submission Format
First choice: PC- or Mac-compatible ASCII (text) files on a 3.5-inch floppy with a hard copy included as a backup. We routinely use Microsoft Word, so files in this format are also acceptable. We encourage articles via e-mail (address to editorial@kitplanes.com). An attached text file works well.

Color photos are preferred, but black-and-white photos are acceptable. Do not send negatives. High-resolution digital images can be used in some cases, but those need to be discussed in advance. Please send only sharp, professional-quality photos.

Necessary artwork (usually photos) and captions must accompany manuscripts. Technical artwork must be sharp and clear, drawn with black ink or drafting pencils. Drawings may be submitted in EPS, PICT or TIF file formats. Include versions both with and without text.

Please include your daytime phone number.

Payment

Payment depends on the length of the article as published, including artwork. Thus the more and better the art, the more we pay. The budget for first-time KITPLANES writers is $70 per page as printed in the magazine (this includes illustrations/photos). Thus an average feature that runs four pages will pay about $280. After your first KITPLANES appearance, the rate increases to $100 per page.

A photo used on the cover brings an additional $300. For covers, 35mm slides, vertical format, are the usual medium.

Categories: Nonfiction—Aviation

CONTACT: Dave Martin, Editorial
Material: Submissions or queries
8745 Aero Dr., Ste. 105
San Diego CA 92123
Phone: 858-694-0491
E-mail: editorial@kitplanes.com
Website: www.kitplanes.com

THE **KIWANIS** MAGAZINE

The Kiwanis Magazine

KIWANIS magazine is a monthly publication, except for combined June/July and November/December issues. It is distributed to the 275,000-plus members of Kiwanis clubs in North America, as well as to clubs in more than seventy overseas nations. Though KIWANIS is the official magazine of Kiwanis International and is responsible for reporting organizational news, each issue also includes five or more feature articles geared to other interests of Kiwanians and their families and friends.

Kiwanis club members are business and professional persons who are actively involved in community service.

Freelance written materials submitted to KIWANIS may deal with almost any topic of interest to an intelligent readership. Editorial need primarily is for articles on current business, international, social, humanitarian, self-improvement, and community-related topics. Other subjects of continuing appeal include health and fitness, family relations, young children's needs, recreation, consumer trends, and education.

The magazine has a special need for articles on business and professional topics that will directly assist readers in their own businesses and careers.

Some of KIWANIS magazine's recent titles have included: "Operation Zero-Defect Marketing," "Shots for Tots," "The Downsizing Myth," "Withstanding the Coastal Crunch," "One's Quest for Self-Renewal," "Farming Fields of Dreams," "Preventing Lead's Poisonous Legacy," and "Organ Donations: A Thin Harvest."

DEMOGRAPHICS

To help you identify the audience to which you are writing, here are some statistics on KIWANIS magazine readers:

- Median age 56
- Graduated high school 98%
- Attended/graduated college 87%
- Post-graduate degree 29%
- Median household income $57,100
- Married 90%
- Manager 61%
- Professional 29%
- Owner/Partner 15%
- Own a home 88%
- Market value of home $142,000
- Median size of company/business employees 26

Articles published in KIWANIS magazine are of two general types: serious and light nonfiction. (No fiction, poetry, filler items, jokes, opinions, or first-person accounts are used.) Manuscripts should be between 1,500 and 2,000 words in length (five to eight pages, typed doublespaced). Payment is on acceptance, ranging from $400 to $1,000 depending on current editorial need, depth of treatment, appeal to the magazine's readership, and other factors. Queries are preferred to manuscript submissions.

Proposed articles are tested against two major criteria: (1) be about an overall subject rather than an individual person, place, event, or organization, and (2) have applicability in the lives and concerns of KIWANIS magazine's readership.

In addition, an article, when feasible, should be international in scope, providing information from various world regions. Writers should be aware that KIWANIS magazine is not an exclusively US magazine; it has readers in Canada, Europe, Central and South America, Australia, Africa, and Asia as well. Terms such as "our nation" and "our president" must be avoided. Articles on global topics, particularly if they have a strong bearing on current US developments, could be ideally suited for KIWANIS magazine.

In all manuscripts, a writer's treatment of a subject must be objective and in depth, and each major point should be substantiated by illustrated examples and quotes from persons involved in the subject or qualified to speak on it. The question "why?" should be as important as "what?" and perceptive analysis and balanced treatment are valued highly. Serious articles should not contain intrusions of the writer's views. Writing style should not be pedantic but rather smooth, personable, and to the point, with anecdotes, descriptions, and human detail where appropriate.

Treatment of light subjects must be as authoritative as serious topics, but humorous examples and comparisons and a lighter writing style are valued where needed.

An article's lead must be strong, drawing the reader's attention and setting the tone of the piece. It should be followed by a clear statement of the article's central thesis: Readers quickly should know what they are going to read about and why.

Manuscripts also should contain pertinent background and historic information, as well as a balanced presentation of issues. Firsthand interviews as well as research of published sources are essential. All information should be the most current available on the subject. And the article's conclusion should summarize the consequences of what has been said.

Photos are not essential, but they are desirable when they are high quality and add substantially to the impact of the text. Color transparencies and color slides are preferred. All photos should be captioned and are purchased as part of the manuscript package.

Writers are encouraged to study a recent issue of KIWANIS magazine for a better understanding of the writing styles and story subjects used in this publication. To receive a sample copy, send a self-addressed, stamped (five first-class stamps) large envelope to the address shown below.

Your interest in KIWANIS magazine as a market for your work is appreciated.

Categories: Associations

CONTACT: Submissions Editor
Material: all
3636 Woodview Trace
Indianapolis IN 46268
Phone: 317-875-8755
Fax: 317-879-0204
E-mail: Kiwanismagazine@kiwanis.org
Website: www.kiwanis.org

Knitting Digest

Knitting Digest
Please refer to *Creative Knitting* magazine.

Knives Illustrated
The Premier Cutlery Magazine

As the title implies, what we are looking for at *Knives Illustrated* magazine are factual, well-researched, knowledgeable articles about knives-preferably leaning toward a large quantity of photos showcasing a large number of knives.

The most important item above everything else is that what you write about knives must be INTERESTING!

1. It must interest you in writing about it because that will show in the story.

2. It must interest me to the point that I believe it will interest our readers.

3. Most important it must have the potential to interest our readers.

If you have not read *Knives Illustrated* or other knife magazines and are not familiar with the desires of knife readers, then you're probably not going to sell us an article. If you have a different approach, we're eager to see it and eager to publish it-but you do have to understand the world of knives as a base from which to start your new approach.

How to contact us: If you have a story idea, query first. E-mail will get you the quickest response.

Technical stuff: We can take your article electronically, but we strongly prefer PC-based articles. Do not attach as an automatically opening file via E-mail. If you send it on a floppy disk, make sure you have the floppy within a rigid container, and be sure you print out a hard copy of the EXACT file on the floppy (and note on the hard copy the exact name of the file on the floppy). E-mail me first that you are sending an article and attach as a download. My E-mail address is bruce@jbrucevoyles.com

Article Length: Use every word it takes to tell the story and not one word extra. If you use a lot of adverbs that end in "ly" you can often find another word. Note: We have no place for words proclaiming any knifemaker as to their ranking among other knifemakers. Everyone is "one of the best" and "one of the top makers" in someone's opinion. We don't pay by the word, so don't get crazy with the keyboard thinking you'll get more money. It might actually get your story turned down completely.

Photos: I know you may have a scanner, but I prefer to see the photos themselves as hard copies rather than electronic for a number of reasons, most importantly I can spread them all out at one time on a table-which I can't do with a computer image. If I

have a hard copy print or transparency, I can control more aspects of the photos. Color photos are preferred. (If I want it in black and white I can convert it that way, if it's sent in as black and white I can only run it in black and white.) No Polaroids! We need clear, crisp, in focus photos of the knives in full frame (don't cut the tip off). We only want shots of the knife. It would be seriously worth your while to pick up a copy of KI and see the types of photos we use.

General articles: Choose strong, dramatic subjects with a lot of photos. When possible, if the article is centered around a group of knives based on older versions (such as Bowie reproductions), photos of original Bowies etc. included adds more interest. We can supply some of those and on vintage knives as well, but be aware of that as a potential sidebar when writing such an article.

Profiles/Shop Tours: What we do not want is to be Knife People Illustrated. We do publish three to four profiles/shop tours per issue, but understand that just because someone makes knives doesn't mean they will merit a profile.

Again, and I can't stress this enough-it has to be interesting. It is possible for a knifemaker who is not making the best knife in the world to be the subject of a published profile provided he and his approach to knifemaking is interesting. SPECIFICS: On any shop tour we want to know the equipment the makers uses: brand specifics, speed and types of, belts, anything special or a different approach, steels, etc. However, this information is boxed and should not be included in the text of the story; use the words in the story to say something interesting about the maker or his methods.

Ethics: Do not use a profile as an excuse to get free knives. If we find that was a condition of the article we will kill it automatically. If a maker gives you a knife that's his business. If a knife is a condition of a profile or your writing about him that is our business, and will end in a rejection if we find out about it.

Also in your selecting subjects for profiles, the fact that they advertise in *Knives Illustrated* is a minor factor in whether a profile is accepted or rejected. At KI we do appreciate our advertisers, they are one of the things that keep us in business. However, from the editorial side our first obligation is not to our advertisers but to our readers. We produce quality editorial that attracts and keeps readers. Advertisers pay us for access to those readers. If we let advertisers direct our editorial we are letting the tail wag the dog, and in the long term we lose readers because of it, because we are not producing the editorial that the readers want. Magazines are edited for readers not advertisers. We must always use that as the first criteria.

We can break down the decision to publish into a scale as follows:
Out of 100 points:
- Is the article interesting?   60 points
- Is the subject newsworthy or significant   25-30 points
- Advertiser   5 points
- Other intangibles   5-10 points

Payment: Payment is upon publication, as all article payment vouchers are submitted to bookkeeping on the same day and issued at

one time. If your story is accepted for publication, you will be sent a contract to fill out. No payment can be sent to you until the contract is filled out completely, so it is very important that you provide, when submitting your story, your entire contact information (full name, address, phone number, fax number, E-mail address) so we can contact you later. If you do not provide adequate contact information, and we can't locate you, payment may be delayed or you may not receive payment at all.

Categories: Nonfiction—Collectibles—Consumer—Fishing—General Interest—Men's Issues—Outdoors—Hunting

CONTACT: Bruce Voyles, Editor
Material: All
CONTACT: Jeff Howe, Managing Editor (send to the California address)
Material: All
265 S. Anita Dr. Ste. 120
Orange CA 92868
Phone: 714-939-9991, ext. 202
Fax: 714-939-9909

Kung Fu Tai Chi

Thank you for your interest in submitting your work to *Kung Fu Tai Chi* magazine and KungFuMagazine.com. Much of the magazines' contents are freelance-written. All submissions are reviewed for publication for either media, print magazine or web 'e-zine', unless you specify that your work is designated only for one or the other. However, our editorial board may opt to accept any given piece for one specific media only, and not the other. On occasion, unabridged versions of longer print magazine articles are accepted for the e-zine.

In general, we accept more experimental 'edgy' submissions for the e-zine. First person narratives such as travel logs, tournament reviews, media reviews such as recent films and articles that are over 2500 words are also directed towards the e-zine. Many authors find the print magazine to be more prestigious, but in fact, a well-written article can find a larger readership on the web since it is free access and does not fall victim to shelf life.

Topics:
Topics should be of interest to advanced, traditional Chinese Martial Arts aficionado as well as the rank beginner of any style. We welcome articles on martial arts history, weapons, training, techniques, philosophy, well-known martial artists, and notable individual experiences. We are not accepting any fiction, poetry, personality profiles, comics or cartoons, or articles for or about children at this time.

Query Letters:
If you have not written your article already, it is advised that you call, write or email to discuss your topic. This will save your time of writing an article on a topic which may not be right for the magazine or has already been covered.

Simultaneous Submissions:
Simultaneous article submissions are not accepted. You may submit simultaneous queries.

Focus:
Rather than generalizing about a topic in a superficial way, narrow your subject, find an interesting angle, and write an in-depth, information-packed piece. For example, instead of trying to fit your style's entire history into an article, you might write about how one incident changed the course of your martial art. Rather than writing about various kicks, for instance, one writer angled a recent story to explain how kicks can set the opponent up for grappling maneuvers. General topics such as "What is martial arts?" have been narrowed to a more specific focus, such as "10 Questions to Determine if You're Learning True Wing Chun".

Point of View:
Most articles should be written in the third person. The second person form is sometimes appropriate for instructional articles. Use

the first person only if the focus of the whole article is an incident from your life.

Attribution:

If quotes or information are attributable to other sources, cite them within the story; do not use footnotes or end notes. Do not add "thank you to..." at the end of the article; if another person was an integral part of writing or researching the story, you may share the byline either as "by Jane Smith and John Jones", or "by Jane Smith with John Jones".

Author Information:

Please provide brief information about yourself for "About the Author" section at the end of the article. This could include your martial arts style and rank, education, profession, city of residence, school, and teacher. Contact information is permissible. This is subject to editing. If no material is provided, it will be determined by our editorial board without your consultation.

Foreign Words and Phrases:

Please italicize all foreign words and phrases throughout the text. On the first reference place a concise definition in parenthesis following, such as jian (straight swords), and provide the Chinese characters. All mandarin words should use modern pinyin Romanization. Other dialects such as Cantonese, Hakka, etc., can be preserved in their original spelling along with the Chinese characters. Chinese characters are mandatory.

Capitalize proper names of systems, but not the martial art itself, such as Fut Gar, Bak Mei Pai, White Crane kung fu. Words that appear in the English dictionary such as "kung fu, "tai chi," "karate" need not be capitalized or italicized. Capitalize names of organizations, ie: United States Kung Fu Association. Do not capitalize the names of weapons such as guandao, gun, qiang.

These rules may be disregarded for organizations and names that have previously established spellings in English, such as Jun Fan Gung Fu, but do not change the spelling within the text of the article, such as "Gung Fu," instead of "kung fu."

Photo Quality:

All articles must be accompanied by at least eight photos or illustrations. Photos must be in sharp focus, well-lit, and composed so that the main subject is not too small or cut off. Shoot against a neutral, contrasting background such as wall for techniques shoot. Do not shoot subjects against a background of trees, mirrors, equipment, signs, etc. All photos must be done with a matte finish, no glossiness. Digital photos must be submitted at full size with a minimum of 300 dpi for print.

Letters, News and Promotional articles:

Letters, News and Promotional articles are not contracted or compensated. They are subject to editing.

Captions:

Please provide a separate caption for each photo or illustration, including a separate caption for each photo in a sequence. Clearly identify people present in the shots, and clearly mark the photo order and which captions go with which photos. Photo credit should be included for each photo as well, either "courtesy of ..." or "photo by...".

Physical Guidelines:

Articles should be between 1500 to 2500 words for print. There is no limitation on the word count for web submissions. Insert subheads where appropriate. Please avoid using the subheads "introduction" and "conclusion" within your article. That may be fine for technical or scientific writing, but is inappropriate for a popular newsstand magazine.

Technical Guidelines:

All text submissions must be sent in a format that is readable by Microsoft Word for IBM. All photo submissions must be sent in a format that is readable by Adobe Photoshop for IBM. Both text and photos may be submitted by email, however separate the photos into separate emails, or compress them appropriately. E-mail submission is highly recommended. If submitting via regular mail, please include a hard copy of the article and the photos. Digital submissions are preferred.

Categories: Nonfiction—Asian-American—Culture—Health—Physical Fitness—Sports/Recreation

CONTACT: Article Submissions
Material: All
40748 Encyclopedia Circle
Fremont, CA 94538
Phone: 510-656-5100
Fax: 510-656-8844
E-mail: editor@kungfumagazine.com
Website: www.kungfumagazine.com

Kungfu Qigong Magazine

Please refer to *Kung Fu Tai Chi* magazine.

Kuumba

POETRY

Kuumba seeks previously unpublished verse of the highest quality. Your work should be well written and feature themes related to the experience of being black and in the life. You may submit up to five original poems at one time, but no more than one poem per page. All poetry should be typed, with line and stanza breaks clearly delineated. Include your name and mailing address. Tell us if you wish to use a pseudonym.

ILLUSTRATIONS

Kuumba also seeks line-art illustrations related to the experience of being black and in the life. These are typically images of two women or two men, but we are open to other possibilities. Acceptable media include pen-and-ink, pencil line, linoleum cut, woodcut, and computer-generated or digital illustrations that mimic these styles. We are less interested in illustrations that include tonal graduations such as watercolor or airbrush. We are not accepting photographs at this time. Submit photocopies of your work. Do not send originals.

DEADLINES

While we accept submissions year-round, submissions should be postmarked no later than February 1 to be considered for publication in the spring/summer issue, October 1 for consideration in the fall/winter issue.

RIGHTS

Kuumba secures first North American rights and the right to anthologize accepted work. You retain all other rights to your work. Payment is in four copies of the issue in which accepted work appears.

DELIVERY

Submission may be mailed to Editor, *Kuumba*, PO Box 83912, Los Angeles, CA 90083-0912. Please include a self-addressed, stamped envelope with adequate postage if you want your work returned. Submissions may be faxed to the Editor at 310-410-9250. Submissions may be emailed to: reggieh@blk.com. We usually respond within a month.

ACCEPTANCE

Individuals whose works are accepted for publication must provide *Kuumba* with a brief biographical sketch. Accepted poetry should, whenever possible, be provided on diskette in either PC or Macintosh format. You should provide the original or a reproduction-quality duplicate of accepted artwork.

LEGALESE

The Editors do not assume responsibility for loss of or damage to submitted materials. Publication of the name, photograph or likeness of any person or organization in articles or advertising in *Kuumba* is not to be construed as any indication of the sexual orientation of such persons or organizations. The opinions of *Kuumba* are expressed only in editorials. Other opinions are those of the writers and do not necessarily represent the opinions of *Kuumba*.

Categories: African-American—Gay/Lesbian—Poetry

CONTACT: Reginald Harris, Editor
Material: All
PO Box 83912

Los Angeles CA 90083-0912
Phone: 310-410-0808
Fax: 310-410-9250
E-mail: reggieh@blk.com
Website: www.kuumba.net

LA Architect
The Magazine of Design in Southern California

LA Architect is interested in articles on art, architecture and design topics with a Southern California connection. This includes all design disciplines including architecture, graphics, interiors, set design, etc. Articles normally emphasize design innovation or culture as opposed to technical or how-to. Our focus is contemporary and modern design.

Submit proposals electronically to laura@balconypress.com or mail to address below.

Proposals should include the following:
• Brief summary of the content.
• Proposed length of mss. and approximate quantity of illustrations, photos, etc.
• What is unusual about the topic and has it been published previously (if published, what was the slant?)
• 100-word author bio.
• DO NOT SEND MATERIAL WITH THE PROPOSAL YOU WANT RETURNED.

In general:
• Authors are responsible for providing all photos and permissions to be used.
• No advances or expenses are offered.
• Fees are negotiated.
• Proposals will be responded to within 1 month.
Categories: Nonfiction—Architecture

CONTACT: Laura Hull, Editor-in-Chief
Material: Projects, Features
CONTACT: April Eckfeld, Editorial Assist.
Material: Products, News
512 E. Wilson, Ste 306
Glendale CA 91206
Phone: 818-956-5313
E-mail: laura@balconypress.com

The Labor Paper
Serving Southern Wisconsin

Columns are 200-500 words.
Submit by email.
Payment varies by piece.
Categories: Nonfiction—Business—Careers—Consumer—Economics—Interview—Technical—Trade—Labor

CONTACT: Mark T. Onosko, Editor/Publisher
Material: All
Union-Cooperative Publishing
3030-39th Ave., Ste 110
Kenosha WI 53144
Phone: 262-657-6116
Fax: 262-657-6153

Lacunae

Lacunae publishes comics, fiction, poetry, prose, reviews of independent music, film, fiction, comics and web sites. We are always open to new ideas and pride ourselves on versatility.

Please pay attention to the guidelines. They are important. And, if you are not familiar with the publication, take the time to read a copy to see if your work suits our needs.

Lacunae offers some of the writing and comics industry's best information, art, reviews and fiction. *Lacunae* is a great market for professional and never-before-published writers and artists. Published bimonthly by CFD Productions, *Lacunae* is distributed internationally, features full color covers and at least 32 interior b/w pages. Standard cover price is $2.50 USA.

Lacunae is for mature readers (not adults only). We don't publish full nudity, but we do present some mature themes. There is no requirement to submit mature or provocative manuscripts or illustrations.

SUBMISSIONS
Short stories, poems, columns, reviews, comics, illustrations, photography, among other forms of work are generally considered for publication year-round.

Fiction and poetry may be almost any genre (humor, horror, sci-fi, etc.), except no romance. Lengths vary upon submission and space availability. Generally, the cap on word count is 3,500. Please Note: *Lacunae* is overwhelmed with poetry submissions and is cutting down on the amount of poetry featured each issue.

Illustrative submissions should consist of a clean photocopy, and should be mailed, not e-mailed.

Reviews (of old and new media) must always include price, ordering address (if applicable), ISBN or other identification and other standard information (page count, media type...)

Submissions must be typed in a serif font (preferably Courier). Usual response time is 3-6 weeks, but this time may vary during certain seasons, depending on the influx of submissions. If you have not received a response in 12 weeks, feel free to alert us.

When making a submission, be sure to include full name and address on the first page of any manuscript, name on subsequent pages; full name and address on each page of poetry or artwork. A cover letter is required. When making an e-mail submission, include text as an e-mail message. *Lacunae* does not accept uploads of submissions.

PAYMENT
Lacunae pays in copies according to work (usually 5 to 25 copies) and great recognition in the comics and writing markets. Copies of each issue are sent to major publishers and agents in the industries. Writers and artists retain all rights to their work and *Lacunae* contracts allow for creators to republish their work in other publications after such works appear in *Lacunae*. Previously published works are OK, provided there is no buying of second rights on *Lacunae*'s part. No work may be published in *Lacunae* without a contract (provided by *Lacunae*).

REVIEWS
Lacunae accepts other publications—magazines, comics, books, albums, videos, etc. for review. These will not be returned, but offered as giveaways to our readers. The creators or publishers of reviewed works will receive a tearsheet, but will be required to purchase an entire issue at a discount cost if desired.

COPIES
If there are questions as to whether your work(s) meet our specifications, we, as all publishers, recommend you review a copy of our latest issue. Those requesting guidelines may purchase the latest issue at $3.25 (standard cost, includes postage).

Anyone published in *Lacunae* requesting additional copies will be able to purchase them at a discounted rate.

QUESTIONS?
Just ask!
THE CFD E-MAIL LIST
CFD Productions periodically notifies those interested of upcoming projects, calls for submissions and publishing schedules. To be included on the CFD e-mail list, send us your e-mail address.

Categories: Fiction—Entertainment—Horror—Interview—Music—Mystery—Writing

CONTACT: Pamela Hazelton, Editor
Material: All
PO Box 827
Clifton Park NY 12065
E-mail: judy@mediasi.com
Website: www.mediasi.com

Ladies' Home Journal

Thank you for your interest in writing for the Journal. While we do not have specific guidelines about subject matter or writing style, we do offer these suggestions:

Read Back Issues: We do not publish an editorial calendar, so familiarizing yourself with our editorial content and style will help you decide if your work fits our needs. Back issues can be found in the periodicals section of your library or purchased from our customer service department for $3 each (Call 800-678-2699). Do not send payment to our editorial offices.

We Have a Four Month Lead Time and seasonal material is usually assigned six months in advance.

Submit Queries Rather than Manuscripts: Keep your query brief - one to two pages - citing your lead and describing how you will research and develop your story. Be specific, and always direct your query to the appropriate editor, as listed on the masthead of the magazine. If you have been published before, send clips, your credits and a resume.

Always Include a Self-Addressed, Stamped Envelope: We will not respond unless an SASE is enclosed (with adequate postage for return of the manuscript, if so desired). We are not responsible for returning unsolicited material, so do not send original copies or photographs.

Payment, Story Length and Deadlines are discussed upon assignment and writers are paid upon acceptance. Average story length is 2,000 words.

We particularly welcome reader submissions for the following column: "First Person": Submissions should be approximately 1,500 words, written in the first person and typed double spaced. These must be true, personal stories about dramatic events. Enclose a self-addressed, stamped envelope and mail to *Ladies' Home Journal* at our New York address.

Submit Fiction Only Through a Literary Agent
We Do Not Accept Poetry of Any Kind

Please Do Not Call to Query or Follow up on a Submission: We read every query carefully, and do our best to respond as promptly as we can. It may take up to three months to receive a response.

We Cannot Provide Comments on Unaccepted Material: Due to the large volume of manuscripts we receive, we are unable to evaluate each writer's work personally.

Categories: Fiction—Nonfiction—Arts—Biography—Children—Consumer—Cooking—Crafts/Hobbies—Diet/Nutrition—Education—Entertainment—Family—Fashion—Food/Drink—Gardening—Health—Hobbies—Marriage—Parenting—Psychology—Relationships—Self Help—Sexuality—Society—Travel—Women's Issues—Beauty—Medicine—Interior Decorating—Celebrities—How-to

CONTACT: Editor
Material: All
125 Park Ave. 20th Floor
New York NY 0\10017-5516
Phone: 212-557-6600
Fax: 212-455-1313

Ladybug Parent's Companion

To view a sample of *Ladybug Parent's Companion* visit www.cricketmag.com. Ladybug, a magazine for young children ages 2 to 6 published by Cricket Magazine Group, is accompanied by *Ladybug Parent's Companion* on the World Wide Web. Each issue of *Ladybug Parent's Companion* includes articles by recognized authorities in the field of child development or early childhood education, profiles of authors and artists, suggested parent-child activities, and recommended book lists for children and adults. We hope that the following information will be useful to prospective contributors.

Published 12 months a year, Ladybug welcomes original submissions for *Ladybug Parent's Companion*. PLEASE DO NOT QUERY FIRST. Send complete manuscript and enclose a resume and/or statement of contributor's qualifications for writing on the topic. Enclose a self-addressed stamped envelope for a reply; submissions without a SASE will be discarded. Electronic submissions are not accepted. Usual response time is 6 to 12 weeks.

Articles: 700 to 1000 words on issues of interest or concern to parents of children age 2 through 6. Our subscriber base is primarily upscale, educated parents who want to go beyond the basics of child rearing. Treatment is practical and tone is conversational, but suggestions must be based on a thorough, up-to-date understanding of child development.

Book Lists: 10 to 12 recommended children's books related to the topic of the article. Include complete citation, appropriate age range, and a 10- to- 20-word annotation for each title. Adult books for the parent to read may be mentioned. Books must be in print or readily available at public libraries. Ladybug editors will not recommend any book without reading it first.

Activities: Games, crafts, adventures, and learning activities; simple, enjoyable things a parent and child can do together using materials found around the house. Our readers appreciate new ideas they have not already seen in other parenting guides.

Profiles: By assignment only.

Payment: Up to 25¢ per word ($25 minimum), on publication. Rights vary.

Categories: Arts—Children—Education—Interview—Literature—Parenting

CONTACT: Paula Morrow, Editor
Material: All
Ladybug Parnets Companion
PO Box 300
Peru IL 61354
Website: www.cricketmag.com

Ladybug
The Magazine for Young Children

About Us

For a sample issue of Ladybug, please send $5.00 to: Ladybug Sample Copy • PO Box 300 • Peru, IL 61354. NOTE: Sample copy requests from foreign countries must be accompanied by International Postal Reply Coupons (IRCs) valued at US $5.00. Please do NOT send a check or money order.

Ladybug, a magazine for young children ages 2 to 6, is published by Cricket Magazine Group. *Ladybug* features original stories and poems written by the world's best children's authors, illustrated in full color by the best children's artists from around the world. *Ladybug* measures 8" x 10", is full color, contains 36 pages plus a 4-page activity pullout, and is staple-bound. We hope that the following information will be useful to prospective contributors.

Published 12 months a year. Price is $35.97 for 1-year subscription (12 issues).

Manuscripts

Fiction: read-aloud stories, picture stories, original retellings of folk and fairy tales, multicultural stories. Length: up to 800 words. Rebuses focus on concrete nouns. Length: up to 250 words.

Nonfiction: concepts, vocabulary, simple explanations of things in a young child's world. Length: up to 400 words. (Be prepared to send other backup materials and photo references—where applicable—upon request.)

Poetry: rhythmic, rhyming; serious, humorous, active. Length: up to 20 lines.

Other learning activities, games, crafts, songs, and finger games. See back issues for types, formats, and length.

An exact word count should be noted on each manuscript submitted. Word count includes every word, but does not include the title of the manuscript or the author's name.

Rates

Stories and articles: 25¢ per word; $25 minimum
Poems: $3.00 per line; $25 minimum
Payment upon publication

Art

• *By assignment only.* Artists should submit review samples of artwork to be kept in our illustrator files. We prefer to see tear sheets or photo prints/photocopies of art.

• If you wish to send an original art portfolio for review, package it carefully, insure the package, and be sure to include return packing materials and postage.

• Author-illustrators may submit a complete manuscript with art samples. The manuscript will be evaluated for quality of concept and text before the art is considered.

• *Rates:* $500/spread ($250/page)

• Payment within 45 days of acceptance. We purchase all rights; physical art remains the property of the illustrator and may be used for artist's self promotion.

Comments:

• *Ladybug* would like to reach as many children's authors and artists as possible for original contributions, but our standards are very high, and we will accept only top-quality material. Before attempting to write for *Ladybug*, be sure to familiarize yourself with this age child.

• In evaluating manuscripts, we look for beauty of language and a sense of joy or wonder.

• PLEASE DO NOT QUERY FIRST.

• We will consider any manuscripts or art samples sent on speculation and accompanied by a self-addressed, stamped envelope. Submissions without a SASE will be discarded.

• Please allow 8 to 10 weeks response time for manuscripts, 12 weeks for art samples.

• We do not distribute theme lists for upcoming issues.

Ladybug normally purchases the following rights:

For stories and poems previously unpublished, *Ladybug* purchases all rights. Payment is made upon publication. For stories and poems previously published, *Ladybug* purchases second North American publication rights. Fees vary, but are generally less than fees for first publication rights. Payment is made upon publication. Same applies to accompanying art.

For recurring features, *Ladybug* purchases the material outright. The work becomes the property of *Ladybug* and is copyrighted in the name of Carus Publishing Company. A flat fee per feature is usually negotiated. Payment is made upon publication.

For commissioned artwork, *Ladybug* purchases all rights plus promotional rights (promotions, advertising, or in any other form not offered for sale to the general public without payment of an additional fee) subject to the terms outlined below:

(a) Physical art remains the property of the illustrator,
(b) Payment is made within 45 days of acceptance,
(c) Illustrator may use artwork for self promotion.

Categories: Fiction—Children—Crafts/Hobbies—Fantasy—Games—Music—Poetry—Short Stories

CONTACT: Submissions Editor
Material: Manuscripts
CONTACT: Suzanne Beck, Art Director
Material: Art Samples
CONTACT: Mary Ann Hocking, Permissions Coordinator
Material: Questions about rights
Ladybug Magazine
PO Box 300
Peru IL 61354
Website: www.cricketmag.com or www.cobblestonepub.com

Lake Michigan Travel Guide

Who We Are

LAKE MICHIGAN TRAVEL GUIDE is an annual magazine focused on Lake Michigan and its bordering states: Wisconsin, Michigan, Indiana and Illinois. LMTG features articles on unique travel opportunities and the interesting destinations that await readers, as well as that which will enhance their travel experiences along the lakeshore. From history, nature and adventure to culture, events, family fun, unique lodgings and restaurants serving fine and regional cuisine, this is the ultimate Lake Michigan traveler's guide. LMTG is produced by the editors of *Wisconsin Trails* magazine, and owned and published by Trails Media Group Inc., publisher of regional magazines, guidebooks and other publications.

Subjects

We're interested in the out-of-the-way and the popular (even widely traveled destinations hold surprises). The articles are meant to entertain and provoke readers' desires to travel to the featured destinations. *The LMTG format:*

• an upfront department on various subjects (see "The Lake Effect" guidelines)

• a full-length feature per state, focused on some aspect of that state

• a short feature, map/attractions page, lodging department, dining department and events department for each tourism region.

*The tourism regions within each st*ate:

• **Michigan**
Upper Peninsula: Menominee to Mackinac Island
Northwest: Mackinaw City to Ludington
West Central: Pentwater to Grand Haven
Southwest: Holland to New Buffalo

• **Indiana**
Michigan City to Whiting

• **Illinois**
Chicago to Winthrop Harbor

• **Wisconsin**
Southeast: Kenosha to Milwaukee
East Central: Port Washington to Manitowoc
Northeast: Two Rivers to Marinette, including Door County

Style

We are committed to stories of the highest quality, and expect lyrical, engaging magazine-style writing that takes you beyond just the nuts 'n' bolts of an experience or place. First-person is appropriate only for essay submissions. We appreciate a moderate use of the verb "to be" and welcome fresh, descriptive approaches. It is important that you write in an engaging, active tense and style that lets the reader join you in the experience. We expect that a story convey a sense of place-history, geography, environment, which all help set the scene. After reading your story, readers should know what they can expect from a visit to the highlighted destination or event-and what they will come away with. For example, if you're camping by a stream, we'd like to hear about the last thing you saw at night or the first thing you heard in the morning. What kind of creatures inhabit this place? If you're visiting the dunes, tell us what sort of impact the area and setting have on a person, what makes it special enough to send your friends there. If it's a piece on canoeing, biking, hiking, etc., we want a sense of the action-not a dull blow-by-blow rundown, but a vital account of the experience that lets readers join in the adventure. If you're writing about people, ethnic festivals or community events, we're interested in the spirit and interaction of people, place and culture, and what makes these events unique and exciting.

Currently we prefer stories on specific destinations near the shoreline-a great sand dune or state park, as opposed to a roundup of several great dunes or state parks. Sidebars accompany each story. They serve two purposes: to share specific trip details-how readers can make the same trip-and share other great similar destinations (i.e., roundup sidebars).

Length, Contract and Payment

Features vary from 1,000 to 2,000 words.
Payments: $300-$650.
Departments range from 75 to 1,000 words.
Payments: $50-$350.

We expect and accept only original work. We purchase first, one-time rights that last through 160 days after publication (the magazine will be on newsstands April to September). Flat-fee and by word payments are based on $.30/word and story length and difficulty. Expenses as discussed with and approved by the editors are reimbursed upon submission; receipts and an invoice detailing the expenses are required. (Unfortunately, there are no reimbursable expenses for the 2003 issue).

Submissions One-page written queries, with enclosed SASE, are preferred over manuscripts. Writers new to the magazine should enclose a letter of introduction outlining their writing, editing and publishing backgrounds and topics of interest. Published writers should include a resume detailing their writing, editing and other pertinent backgrounds, as well as nonreturnable published clips of their work (photocopies are acceptable). Please: We prefer printed material, so no e-mailed clips or referrals to Web sites. SASE required for return of any submitted materials. No telephone queries; we prefer written materials and/or e-mails we can share at editorial planning meetings. Response time is one to three months. Accepted stories must be furnished on computer disk or via e-mail as attached files in Microsoft Word or RTF; a double-spaced hard copy must also be supplied. A source list including names, addresses and contact phone numbers for sources is required, as are copies of background material used to research and write about the assigned topic.

LMTG Departments

Lodging (100-200 words per locale)

We feature up to five unique lodgings per region. Text should describe the lodgings what's unique about it, its amenities and setting, and who it's best suited to (families vs. couples only). Include price ranges for room rates, address, phone and e-mail.

Events (100-200 words)

We highlight two to five major events per region, plus a calendar of other notable events. Events must occur some time from April through August. Unusual festivals, places, exhibits, classes, heritage events and sites are of particular interest. The writing should be lively, capture the spirit of the event and invite the readers into a fun experience.

Restaurants (100-300 words)

These minireviews offer a glimpse into up to five of the region's restaurants. From cafes and diners offering down-home or ethnic fare, to fine dining establishments, each offers readers a worthwhile dining opportunity-whether it's just about a place that's the spot for cherry pie or an establishment that's the perfect place for a special occasion. These reviews are tightly written; describe the setting, atmosphere and fare; and mention any other notable aspects about the restaurant (for example, an interesting owner or noteworthy chef). Include price ranges for entrées, phone number, address, credit cards accepted, and whether reservations are required and if the restaurant is wheelchair accessible.

Previous restaurant reviewing experience preferred.

"The Lake Effect"—the upfront department

(100-1000 words per item)

An upfront department about other general travel opportunities within each of the four states. *For example:*
• a piece on the history of lighthouses on Lake Michigan with a sidebar on those open to tourists in each of the four states.
• a short piece on a great scenic drive in each of the four states
• a short piece on cruising, ferry and sailing opportunities on Lake Michigan.

Categories: Nonfiction—Adventure—Culture—Food/Drink—Nature—Regional—Travel

CONTACT: Knick Wood, Editor
Material: All
LMTG Trails Media Group Inc.
PO BOX 317
1131 Mills St.
Black Earth WI 53515
E-mail: nwood@wistrails.com
Website: www.wistrails.com

Lake Superior Magazine

Lake Superior Magazine is a bimonthly full-color consumer magazine which focuses exclusively on the Lake Superior region — history, current events, life styles, environment, tourism. Our long suit is outstanding photography accompanied by well-written and relevant editorial. We like to surprise our readers, and therefore will try to present an unexpected slant to the stories they'll receive in each issue. The magazine was established in 1979 and has since become the authority on Lake Superior living and travel. All submissions should support that concept.

As a regionally focused publication with national distribution, we are highly selective, considering only quality material. However, each year we accept a number of offerings from new writers and photographers. The strongest advice we can give is to read the magazine to understand our approach before submitting. Sample copies are not free. Send cover price ($3.95) plus $4.00 shipping and handling.

Categories (not all inclusive):
• *Photographs* — Our hallmark! As a complete picture essay or as illustrations for articles.
• *Illustrations* — Normally assigned, although freelance submissions will be considered.
• *Cartoons* — Must be pertinent to the region and humorous.
• *Nonfiction* — Persons, places and events in the Lake Superior region (contemporary; historic with current tie).
• *Fiction* — Pertinent to the region or theme of an issue. (Only about two published per year.)
• *Departments* — Shorter articles on specific topics of interest (Nature, Wilderness Living, Chronicle, I Remember, Superior Science, Wild Superior, Haunted Shores, Heritage).
• *About the Boat* — Short articles and photographs about boats, ships or watercraft of note, and their crews.
• *Around the Circle* — Significant short items and photographs of interest concerning the condition of Lake Superior and the events and highlights from the region.
• *Destinations* — Short articles or features about places of particular interest to travelers.
• *Life Lines, Lake Superior's Own, Making It In the North* — Short articles about individual people who work and play in our region, their life styles and impact. "People who make a difference in our lives."
• *Lake Superior Living* — Articles about homes, life styles and construction.

Written Submissions

Lake Superior Port Cities Inc. receives many queries on duplicate subject matter. We reserve the right to accept or reject a specific query based upon quality, appropriateness and editorial subjectivity. We prefer manuscripts, although short queries, naming possible sources, will be considered. Submissions must be in writing. Please do not FAX queries or unsolicited manuscripts. DO NOT CALL. Do not send queries or manuscripts. Send a sample of your work. We do not purchase from queries. Submissions will be acknowledged, expect an opinion in three to four months following review by our Editorial Review Board. Although we plan a year or more in advance, articles are not earmarked for a specific issue of the magazine until they have been accepted. We cannot return material that is not accompanied by a self-addressed, stamped return envelope. You should retain a copy of all submitted material.

Persons whose manuscripts are accepted for publication must be able to assume responsibility for permission to publish photos and names of individuals and places. Secure written permission to protect yourself when appropriate. Short biographical information on the writer should always accompany the submission. If accepted, a black-and-white photo of the writer may be requested. When accepted, we may edit, abridge and condense the material as we may consider appropriate. As a rule, Lake Superior Port Cities Inc. does not consider material previously published.

Payment for Writing — We may pay up to $600, according to length, importance of story and writer's experience. Top dollar is earned by a well-written and researched manuscript-photo package. The average feature runs 1,600 to 2,200 words. Departments and Columns average 900 to 1,400 words and usually pay from $65 to $125.

Assignment — Lake Superior Port Cities Inc. publications are copyrighted. You will be asked to sign a standard agreement assigning some rights to your work. We generally ask for First North American serial rights and electronic rights and some Second serial rights in the case of reprints of our special publications. You will be notified before reprinting. First serial rights are reserved for 90 days following the first month of the publication. Payment is made upon publication. You will receive at least one copy of the publication in which your work appears, with additional copies available at wholesale cost.

Submission Appearance — Please double space and leave reasonable one-inch margins! Dot matrix computer printouts are acceptable if dark ribbon is used. MS-DOS ASCII, Windows95/98 and MAC disk submissions are acceptable if they are submitted with a legible printout, preferred when a submission is accepted. Most word processing formats can be accommodated, although software neutral files are preferred. Disks cannot be returned unless accompanied by proper postage. Place name, address and telephone number in the upper left-hand corner of every page of your manuscript with the total number of words on the first page in the upper right-hand corner. Social Security number is required prior to publication.

Photographic Submissions

When you query, we suggest you send duplicates of good quality, if available. Lake Superior Port Cities Inc. will assume a maximum insurance liability of $10,000 per submission, so we advise sending duplicates only for approval. Please identify these as duplicates. However, only originals are used for final publication. Full name of photographer must appear on each photo or slide, or they will be returned without consideration. We will not apply your name to your material for you. Complete photographic identification must be on each photo or on an accompanying cutsheet, which includes subject ID, location and date taken. Photos must be numbered to coincide.

Lake Superior Port Cities Inc. cannot accept responsibility for material damaged during transit to or from the publisher. Enclose a self-addressed, stamped return envelope or box. Unless specified, material will be returned by the mode received to the extent covered by your postage, or by an insured mode convenient to us.

Formats

• *Black and White* — 5" x 7" or 8" x 10" glossies.

• *Color* — 35mm, 2 1/4," 4" x 5" or 8" x 10" transparencies preferred, although color-corrected glossy prints are accepted.

• *Digital* — at this time, size, resolution and quality limit use of digital photography. Considered on a case-by-case basis. Photographer has sole responsibility for rights of accessibility and acquisition, proper attribution and release for use of each photograph. Written permission may be necessary from the subject of the photograph, and at the very least should be held by the photographer for personal protection.

• *Payment* — Payment is made to originators of photographic works. We pay $50 for each usage, not based on size of use or number of pages. Cover photo pays $150. Additional use within the same publication, such as on the title page, at no additional payment. Combination writer/photographer stories may be negotiated as a package. Payment is made upon publication.

• *Assignment* — As with editorial material, you will be asked to sign a standard agreement assigning some rights to your work. We prefer photography being published for the first time. We ask for 90-day protection and electronic rights for all photography and illustrations used in magazines, 18-month protection for use in calendars or books. To protect our investment in color separations, we also ask for pre-assignment of republication rights. You will be notified before reprinting. You will receive at least one copy of the publication in which your work appears, with additional copies available at wholesale cost.

• *Ancillary Categories* — Lake Superior Port Cities publishes many additional products which require photography and artwork. Although photographic material submitted to the magazine is primarily considered for that publication, we also look for other uses. Some of the other products we produce are calendars, note cards, Christmas cards and books. We accept submissions for all.

All submissions MUST include an address, daytime and evening phone numbers, fax number, website and e-mail address as applicable.

Categories: Nonfiction—Adventure—Consumer—Regional

CONTACT: Konnie LeMay, Editor
Material: All
Lake Superior Port Cities Inc.
P.O. Box 16417
Duluth MN 55816-0417
Phone: 218-722-5002
Fax: 218-722-4096
E-mail: edit@lakesuperior.com
Website: www.lakesuperior.com

Leadership Journal
Writing for Leadership

How To Submit A Query

Leadership is written by our readers, so we welcome your ideas. Please send a brief query letter describing your idea and how you plan to develop it. We will respond as quickly as possible—almost always within two weeks.

To send a query: Put your name, address, and telephone numbers, and your church name and address, and your position at the top of the e-mail. Please put your query in the body of the e-mail. Please do not send a file attachment. We do not open attachments.

Or you may send queries by snail mail.

Core Qualities of a *Leadership* Article

Each article describes real experiences, painting vivid scenes that those in ministry can identify with. Readers can see what went wrong and what went right—valuable lessons they won't have to learn the hard way. Writers must show they understand the complexities, joys, and pain of local-church ministry. Then they can offer right-to-the-point counsel on the practical issues: the conflicts, temptations, mistakes, and successes.

A fuller explanation of writing a "*Leadership* article" follows this list of article-starters. Be sure to scroll down and read the Writer's Guidelines.

What Kinds Of Articles Is *Leadership* Looking For?

Leadership has two major sections and three departments.

1. Theme section. Half of each issue focuses on a single theme. Upcoming themes are listed below.

2. Non-theme section. Each issue has several non-theme articles of general interest. We look for articles on leading volunteers and staff, developing disciples, the pastor's personal life, solutions to church problems and problem people, true stories from personal experience.

3. Currents: a section on trends in ministry and ideas for ministering in the local church setting. We especially welcome "Ideas that Work," short accounts telling how a new idea worked in your church.

4. Sunday's Comin': a department on preaching and worship ideas, and illustrations. Short items are welcome.

5. Growing Edge: book reviews and new resources.

Upcoming Themes And Article Ideas

Half of each issue is devoted to a particular theme. *Our upcoming themes include:*

• Growing Generous Givers: stewardship and money matters
• Integrity, Ethics, & Tough Calls: making right choices
• Emerging Leaders: training and welcoming younger people

• To spark your creativity, here are some ideas, but don't limit your thinking to these suggestions. Your experience and interests provide the best material for your article.

Non-Theme, Anytime Ideas

• *Docudrama:* the story you wouldn't believe if it hadn't happened to you. What happened? Tell it drama-style, and let the scenes tell us what you learned along the way.

• *Homelife:* Stories from the fishbowl. Tell the ministry episode that affected your family life and how you grew from it. Or, perhaps how your family life is affecting your ministry.

• *Turning Point:* A moment that changed my ministry. There was a moment when a relationship changed, an antagonist became a friend, the church grasped your vision, the momentum shifted. What was it? What did you do to bring it about? What have you learned from it?

• *Learning to Lead:* What I've learned about leadership recently. Did your latest plan work well or did it bomb? Is the vision you cast three years ago finally coming about? Tell us the transferable principles from your leadership experience that other pastors can use.

• *Managing conflict.* A church member blew up at you. She said she's just being honest. You said she's rude and out of control. Suddenly, everybody was taking sides. So what did you do?

• *Team building:* Training leaders and future leaders. How are you training deacons or team members or new staff members? What are you teaching them and in what setting. Tell how you're enabling others to use their spiritual gifts.

• *The Pastor's Heart.* Give us fresh insight into your ministry, something new you've discovered about preaching or pastoral care. What happened in a member's long illness or the crisis involving the youth department that made you love the calling even more?

Theme Ideas

• *Growing Generous Givers:* Stewardship And Money Matters
• *Preaching, Teaching, and Modeling Stewardship.* How do you do it? Tell us a story about how you're growing generous givers.

• *Pastor as Fundraiser.* Tell us about a campaign that really worked. How did you feel aout being the lead money raiser?

• *Debate: The Pastor Should Know Who Gives and How Much.* Which side are you on? Why? Tell us your experience.

• *What to Do When Times Are Tough.* When you're not making budget, what should be your first response? If you do decide to cut expenses, what should get trimmed and why?

• *Pastoring with the "Pay as You Go" No-Debt Thinkers.* Some congregations are populated with a few influential people convinced that churches should never assume a loan. How do you handle situations where that creates a severe financial pinch?

• *Debt is a Good Thing.* Your church took on a big project, and it grew their faith, their unity, and their effectiveness in ministry.

• *Our Church Changed Our Community.* The fundraising campaign supported a new ministry, not just a new building. Tell us about it. What worked? The 50/50 Church. We give away half of every dollar we take in.

Integrity, Ethics, & Tough Calls: Making Right Choices

• *Personal Motivation.* You realized you were in the right job but for the wrong reasons. Or you did the right thing, and it turned out okay, but your heart wasn't right. What were the signs? Who did you tell? What did you do?

• *An Affair Forgotten.* A staff member confesses sexual sin. It's been over for a while. What action do you take? Do you tell the church?

• *When Your Lay Leaders Won't Confront Troublemakers.* Everyone knows who's causing the conflict. But because of their long history together in the church, lay leaders won't confront those stirring things up. How does a pastor work to handle the conflict constructively?

• *My Job Is on the Line.* Church growth is often motivated by a pastor's real need for providing adequately for his/her family. How do you keep a right attitude when your financial security is on the line?

• *Including Sinners in Ministry.* In a society with rising divorce rates, children born out of wedlock, and co-habitation, fewer people qualify for leadership positions under our old standards. Who will lead when everybody has a past (and many have a present)? How has your church responded?

• *Preaching Other People's Sermons.* With the Internet making it ever-easier to copy others' material and plop it into our sermon notes, what's fair/unfair in using other people's stuff?

• *My Most Profitable Mistake.* What's one episode in your life in which you made a mistake or lapse in judgment, but it turned out to have positive long-term results because of what you learned?

Emerging Leaders: Training And Welcoming Younger People

• *Spotting Leadership Potential.* Who's got it? How can you tell? Especially when they have little or no experience? Tell us your success story (or failure).

• *Chad and Jeremy and Hazel and Irving.* Who is the youngest person you've brought on your board? How did you get older, perhaps entrenched members to accept young leaders.

• *That's the Craziest Idea I've Ever Heard!* Young leaders bring new ideas. Some are great and some are stupid. How do you know when to let younger leaders pursue an idea you don't think will work?

• *A Mentoring Program that Works.* If you have one, we want to hear about it.

• *Inductive Leadership.* Sometimes the best leadership comes from asking the right questions. How do you help other leaders come to their own conclusions?

• *The Young Leader Who Failed But Got Up and Tried Again...*and eventually succeeded because that's how young leaders learn.

• *The Youth-Sensitive Church:* Developing a Youth-Friendly, but not Youth-Dominated Church Culture. How did your church do it?

Writer's Guidelines

Who reads *Leadership*? Who doesn't?!

Although a select group, *Leadership* readers represent a broad spectrum of denominations, degree of education, background, experience, and expertise. Pastors, church staff members, and lay leaders read *Leadership*.

What Is *Leadership*'s Personality?

Practical, thoughtful, and (we hope) fun.

Every article in *Leadership* must provide practical help for problems that church leaders face. *Leadership* articles are not essays expounding a topic or editorials arguing a position or homilies explaining biblical principles. They are how-to articles, based on first-person accounts of real-life experiences in ministry. They allow our readers to see "over the shoulder" of a colleague in ministry who then reflects on those experiences and identifies the lessons learned.

As you know, a magazine's slant is a specific personality that readers expect (and it's what they've sent us their subscription money to provide). Our style is that of friendly conversation rather than directive discourse—"what I learned about local church ministry" rather than "what you need to do."

Our readers expect our articles to be fresh and candid, to reflect the honesty of the writer—describing disappointments and struggles as well as triumphs. Each article must balance "what went well" and "what didn't go so well." We find this allows our pastor/readers to identify more readily with the situation and gives the writer more credibility.

How Do I Write A "How To' Article?

Since *Leadership* articles help church leaders with pressing problems, they often take a how-to format. Here's how to structure the article in that format:

1. Select one problem that you and many church leaders have—and you've made progress in dealing with. You'll know you've gotten a topic defined when you can express it as "How to…" For example, "How to help a congregation want to reach out" or "How to preach about hell to postmodern people" or "How to restore your soul on Monday morning."

2. Identify 2-7 principles, practices, and/or understandings that have helped you in addressing this problem.

3. For each principle, tell a story, from your experience or someone else's, that shows the principle at work.

Does *Leadership* Prefer A Particular Style?

Yes. Content makes an article worthwhile; style makes it readable. Unlike some journals that don't make the effort to develop compelling and lucid writing, we believe *Leadership*'s impact is enhanced through fine and fascinating writing. We want to produce such a well-written, practical journal that the reader will always approach *Leadership* with a sense of anticipation.

Have you read *The Elements of Style* by Strunk and White? We recommend this widely read little paperback as a guide for style.

• Use action verbs. Forms of the verb "to be"—is, was, were, etc., make for dead writing. In every possible case, pick forceful verbs.

• Use anecdotes. Each point in a *Leadership* article needs a carefully chosen illustration, colorfully written. By basing principles in specific experiences, we show how to minister effectively amid the complexity and ambiguity of real life.

• Use short sentences whenever possible. Variety of length, of course, contributes to good style, but writers err more often with too many long sentences than short ones.

• Use long words only when necessary. Some critics claim scholars and professionals purposely write to obfuscate meaning, to cover fuzzy thinking, or to sound intellectual. Of this *Leadership* writers will never be guilty!

• Assume your reader bores easily. Remember, if he flips the page from lack of interest, you've lost! Keep asking yourself, "What grabs my attention? An illustration? A fresh insight? A well-turned phrase?" Keep the reader with you by introducing a constant stream of interesting material.

After writing your manuscript, go through it and see how many action verbs you have. Mark each noun you can taste, hear, see, smell, or feel. You can see hubcaps, handkerchiefs, coffee mugs, and lightning bugs. Good writers fill their prose with objects you literally see in your mind's eye. Be as specific as possible. For instance, "Toyota" is better than "car" for conjuring up an image.

We don't want to put a straitjacket on anyone; styles do differ. We are not looking for a formula type of writing in *Leadership*. But we are looking for a readable, commanding, and fluent style.

How Should I Submit A Manuscript?

After your query has been accepted, write the article. We welcome electronic submissions. When sending your manuscript electronically, you should include it as part of the body of your email and not as a separate attachment. Be sure to include full name, address, and phone number, plus church name, address and phone number, and your position.

If you submit a manuscript by mail, we prefer to read typed, double-spaced material submitted on 8 1/2 X 11 inch paper (one side only). The full name, address, and phone number of the author should appear on the first page of the manuscript with the last name appearing near the number on each succeeding page. If we decide to publish your material, we will contact you for a copy of your article on disk.

Thanks for your interest in writing for *Leadership*. Send us a query, and let's get started.

Categories: Nonfiction—Christian Interests—Religion—Spiritual—Leadership

CONTACT: Marshall Shelley, Executive Editor
Material: Queries
Christianity Today Publications
465 Gundersen Dr.
Carol Stream IL 60188
Phone: 630-260-6200
Fax: 630-260-0114
E-mail: LJeditor@LeadershipJournal.net
Website: www.christianitytoday.com

The Leather Crafters & Saddlers Journal

What we at *The Journal* are always looking for from our subscribers are how-to, step-by-step leatherworking articles of projects for all skill levels. Here is our suggestion for article guidelines. *We call our article guideline the "Triple Four" formula.*

1. Text
2. Patterns
3. Photos

Each of these three steps is divided into four parts.

1. *Text*: Please type in lower case, not in all capital letters. Save text on disk and include a print out.

    a. Short autobiography about yourself in leatherwork

    b. List of materials

    c. List of tools

    d. A step-by-step description of what methods work best for you in completing this project.

2. *Patterns*: Draw pattern(s) using black ink on white paper, not on disk. (camera ready)

    a. The overall pattern(s)

    b. Carving designs and patterns

    c. Alternative design pattern (where possible)

    d. Show sequence of tooling and/or coloring

3. *Photos*: Digital camera photos need to be in pdf, jpeg or tiff format. Preferably set at 300 dpi.

    a. Submit good contrast photos (no slides)

    b. Photos of project pieces

    c. During-construction photos (or illustrations)

    d. Photos of completed project

How to E-Mail the Article: Type article in simple text only–not all capital letters, cursive or layout. E-mail digital photos as separate, jpeg attachments. Include your full name, phone number, and e-mail address.

These are guidelines only, and it is hoped they will help you in preparation of your manuscript. The better the article is prepared, the better the consideration that it will be printed.

We want only articles that include hands-on, how-to, step-by-step information of a *project oriented* nature. *These pay $20.00 to $250.00 depending on several factors:*

• How "camera-ready" is it?

• How complete is the article?

• Are patterns finalized in ink?

• Are disks, photos and hardcopy provided?

• Over-all necessary length.

• Are alternate patterns provided?

• Is the writer also a subscriber?

These and perhaps other considerations are used in determining the price. We buy first North American serial rights.

Categories: Nonfiction—Consumer—Crafts/Hobbies—Hobbies—Trade—Leather

CONTACT: WR Reis, Editor
Material: All

331 Annette Court
Rhinelander WI 54501-2902
E-mail: tworjournal@newnorth.net

The Ledge Magazine

1. Reading period for regular submissions: September through May.
2. Submit 3-5 poems with SASE.
3. Reporting time: 3 months.
4. We recommend that you read a copy of *The Ledge* before submitting. The current issue is $8.95. A subscription is $15 for 2 issues, $28 for 4 issues.
5. No restrictions on form or content. We publish a wide range of work by poets of all backgrounds and persuasions. We seek exciting poems, compelling poems, poems with purpose, poems we can empathize with, powerful poems. Excellence is the ultimate criterion.
6. We consider simultaneous submissions but not previously published poems.
7. Contributors receive a copy of the issue in which their work appears. We send typeset copies of all poems to contributors for proofreading before going to press.
8. Send submissions, inquiries and orders to: *The Ledge*, 40 Maple Ave., Bellport, NY 11713.
9. Thank you for your interest in and support of *The Ledge*. We look forward to reading your work.

The Ledge **announces its 2005 and eleventh annual poetry awards competition.**
First prize: $1,000 and publication in *The Ledge*.
Second prize: $250 and publication in *The Ledge*.
Third prize: $100 and publication in *The Ledge*.
Complete guidelines:
1. No restrictions of form or content. Excellence is the only criterion. Unpublished poems only. Simultaneous submissions are acceptable.
2. Entry fee: $10 for the first three poems; $3 for each additional poem.
3. $15 subscription to *The Ledge* gains free entry for the first three poems.
4. All poems will be considered for publication in *The Ledge*.
5. Postmark deadline: April 30, 2005.
6. Include name and address on each poem. Include SASE for contest results or manuscript return. Winners will be announced.
7. Send entries to *The Ledge* 2005 Poetry Awards at address below.

The Ledge **announces its 2004 and eleventh annual poetry chapbook competition.** Winner will receive a cash award of $1,000, chapbook publication and 50 copies of typeset, perfect-bound, professionally printed chapbook.
Complete guidelines:
1. Submit 16-28 pages of original poetry with title page, bio and acknowledgments, if any. The title page should include name, mailing and e-mailing addresses (if applicable). Simultaneous submissions are acceptable and poets may enter as many manuscripts as they wish.
2. There are no restrictions on form or content. Excellence is the only criterion.
3. Entry fee: $15. All entrants will receive a copy of the winning chapbook upon its publication in the Fall of 2005. Sample chapbooks: $7 postpaid.
4. Please include a SASE for contest results or manuscript return. Winner will be announced in February 2005 and in the September/October issue of *Poets & Writers*.

5. Postmark deadline: November 1, 2004.
6. Send entries to: The Ledge 2004 Poetry Chapbook Contest, 40 Maple Ave., Bellport, NY 11713.

The Ledge **announces its 2005 fiction awards competition.**
First prize: $1,000 and publication in *The Ledge*.
Second prize: $250 and publication in *The Ledge*.
Third prize: $100 and publication in *The Ledge*.
Complete guidelines:
1. No restrictions of form or content. Excellence is the only criterion. Stories should not exceed 7,500 words Unpublished stories only. Simultaneous submissions are OK.
2. Entry fee: $10 for the first story; $6 for each additional story.
3. $15 subscription to *The Ledge* gains free entry for the first story.
4. All entries will be considered for publication in *The Ledge*.
5. Postmark deadline: February 28, 2005.
6. Include SASE for competition results or manuscript return. Winners will be announced in June.
7. Send entries to *The Ledge* 2005 Fiction Awards Competition at 40 Maple Ave., Bellport, NY 11713.

Categories: Poetry

CONTACT: Timothy Monaghan, Editor and Publisher
Material: All
40 Maple Ave.
Bellport, NY 11713

LEFT CURVE

Left Curve

Editorial Statement: *Left Curve* is an artist-produced critical journal that addresses the problem(s) of cultural forms, emerging from the crisis of modernity, that strive to be independent from the control of dominant institutions, and free from the shackles of instrumental rationality. In general we are interested in any form of work that can be readily reproduced within a 7"x9" format. We encourage open, critical, defetishized work that attempts to unravel, reveal contemporary (inner/outer) reality.

Articles: We publish fiction (traditional or experimental) and non-fiction texts (critical social, cultural, historical, philosophical essays, as well as reviews, interviews, journalistic pieces, etc.) that are concerned with issues that deal with our general editorial thrust. Length can be roughly up to 5,000 words, though most are about 2,500. Illustrations to accompany texts (photos, graphics, etc.) are welcomed.

Poetry: Most of our published poems are one page length, though we have published longer poems of up to 8 pages. We will look at any form of poetry, from experimental to traditional.

Visuals: We are interested in any form of visual work (reproducible painting, line drawings, traditional as well as electronic graphics, photography, visual/verbal art, etc.) that fit into our general editorial thrust.

Other Information: We make a serious attempt to personally respond to all submissions. Please allow at least 3 months response time. Our issues are published irregularly. For accepted work, we will let you individually know when to expect the work to appear. In general, payment for published work will be 5 copies of the issue in which the work appears for longer pieces, 3 copies for short works. In the event that we receive funding specifically for honorariums (which has happened once so far), payments will be determined on an individual basis depending on available funds. Sample copies of the current issue are $10, $10 for back issues. A list of published issues will be sent upon request with a SASE.

For accepted longer work we prefer submission of final draft on a floppy disk. E-mail submissions are also acceptable.

Categories: Arts—Culture—Literature—Multicultural—Poetry—Politics—Society—Cultural Critique

CONTACT: Csaba Polony, Editor/Publisher
Material: Fiction and Nonfiction
CONTACT: Jack Hirschman, Associate Editor
Material: Poetry
PO Box 472
Oakland Ca 94604
Phone: 510-763-7193
E-mail: editor@leftcurve.org

Legacy
A Journal of American Women Writers

Legacy is the official journal of the Society for the Study of American Women Writers. It is the only journal to focus specifically on American women's writings from the seventeenth through the early twentieth century. Each issue's articles cover a wide range of topics: examinations of the works of individual authors; genre studies; analyses of race, ethnicity, gender, class, and sexualities in women's literature; and historical and material cultural issues pertinent to women's lives and literary works. In addition, *Legacy: A Journal of American Women Writers* regularly publishes profiles of lesser-known or newly recovered authors, reprints of primary works in all genres, and book reviews covering current scholarship in the field. Periodically, the journal publishes conversations on provocative issues in the field and presentations of previously unpublished archival material.

Legacy: A Journal of American Women Writers is available electronically through Project MUSE.

Subscription Information
Semiannual
ISSN 0748-4321
Individuals $25.00
Institutions $40.00
Students $17.00
Single issue $13.00

For foreign subscriptions please add $15.00. Payment must accompany order. Make checks payable to University of Nebraska Press and mail to:

University of Nebraska Press
233 N 8th St
Lincoln, NE 68588-0255
or call: 1-800-755-1105 U.S. Orders and customer service.

Submission Information
Legacy: A Journal of American Women Writers welcomes essays on texts and contexts of U.S. women writers from the seventeenth through the early twentieth centuries. The journal seeks articles on individual authors' works; genre studies; implications of race, ethnicity, class, and sexualities in women's (con)texts; and historical and material culture issues pertinent to women's lives and literary productions. *Legacy: A Journal of American Women Writers* also publishes sections on "Profiles" of lesser-known authors and "Reprints" of notable works in all genres, as well as book reviews. The journal accepts articles for its "From the Archives" section, which focuses on letters and other previously unpublished archival materials.

Legacy: A Journal of American Women Writers accepts submissions that meet the following requirements:
• 10,000 words or less
• profiles no more than 2,500 words
• submit 2 copies accompanied by a self-addressed envelope with sufficient postage for return of the article
• prepare according to the latest *MLA Style Manual* .

Legacy observes a "blind reading" policy. The author's name should appear only on the title sheet, and references to the author's previous work in the text or the notes should be in the third person. Permissions and copyright fees, if any, are the responsibility of the author and should be arranged for and paid before submitting the article. Individuals whose works are accepted for publication must supply them in both paper and electronic form (IBM compatible, Microsoft Word, or WordPerfect).

Categories: Fiction—Nonfiction—Book Reviews—History—Literature—Multicultural—Society—Women's Fiction—Women's Issues

CONTACT: Prof. Sharon M. Harris (Texas Address)
Material: Manuscript
Department of English
Texas Christian University
TCU Box 297270
2800 South University Ave
Fort Worth TX 76129
CONTACT: Prof. Karen Dandurand (Pennsylvania Address)
Material: Profiles and Reprints
Dept. of English
Indiana University of Pennsylvania
Indiana PA 15705
CONTACT: Prof. Martha Cutter
Material: Book Reviews
Department of English
Kent State University
PO Box 5190
Kent, OH 44242-0001
Website: www.nebraskapress.unl.edu/journals.html

Leisure Group Travel
Please refer to Premier Tourism Marketing, Inc.

Leisure Travel Directories
Please refer to Premier Tourism Marketing, Inc.

Letter Arts Review

Letter Arts Review magazine (formerly *Calligraphy Review*) began publication in 1982 as a focal point for the exchange of calligraphic information. Published quarterly, *Letter Arts Review* has evolved into its current status as the primary international publication of record for the lettering arts. As such, *Letter Arts Review* actively encourages and welcomes submissions from practicing calligraphers, graphic designers, and lettering artists, as well as from professional writers, photographers and others with an interest in the related arts.

Audience
Letter Arts Review readers include calligraphers, lettering artists, graphic designers, teachers, students and individuals who appreciate the best in lettering.

Objectives
The only magazine in the field, *Letter Arts Review*'s objective is to serve the lettering community on many levels: *Letter Arts Review* offers the amateur and the professional informative articles on topics ranging from historical manuscripts to contemporary trends; *Letter Arts Review* presents thought-provoking viewpoints which stimulate inquiry into related topics; as well as quality reproductions which provide the serious student and the art lover with a valuable visual resource.

Format
Each 64 page issue (except for the Annual Review) has 4-6 feature articles plus up to 4 other columns.

Feature articles should be between 1,500 and 3,500 words unless otherwise agreed upon. Contents should be of lettering interest or related in nature. For instance, many of the book arts would be of interest to practicing calligraphers. Practical and conceptual treatments are welcomed, as are learning and teaching experiences. Third person is preferred, however first person will be considered if appropriate. Contributors should read current issues of *Letter Arts Review* prior to submitting queries or materials.

Topics of particular interest to our readers include:

• Profiles of past and present leaders in the field-this can be written in interview form, or third person. Several examples of the artist's work should be included;

• Manuscripts-reproductions of both contemporary and historical manuscripts appear in this section. Advanced and beginning calligraphers should be able to refer to this section as a resource. Color reproductions are often used;

• Creative process pieces;

• Ethical issues of specific interest to the lettering audience.

Columns should generally be between 500 and 1,000 words.

Topics include:

• Viewpoints: this department contains feedback from readers as well as input of new ideas and personal opinions on all aspects of lettering.

• Reviews: Reviews of books, exhibitions, or new type designs. Some reviews can be in-depth, others can be noteworthy.

• Other topics and new ideas will gladly be considered.

Guidelines for submitting work to be reproduced in full color in *Letter Arts Review*:

1. For best lighting and color-and to avoid the "Keystone" effect that usually results from using standard lenses and equipment—have your work shot by a professional.

2. When interviewing a photographer, look for one who is skilled not only in lighting and technology, but who also understands the limitations of printing. Look at their printed portfolio, not just their transparencies and color prints.

3. Whenever possible, submit transparencies (slide format, 2¼", 4"x5", etc.).

4. When shooting 35mm, use Kodachrome rather than Ektachrome for sharpness and color quality. When possible, use Kodachrome 25 because of its absence of grain.

5. When shooting 2¼" or 4"x5", use as low a speed Ektachrome film as possible—or Fujichrome films.

6. Open up dark shadow areas (even when shooting outdoors) by using fill-in flash.

7. Shoot at the correct exposure—as well as one f-stop underexposed and one-half and one f-stop overexposed. Indicate the one which best represents the color as you see it-but submit all transparencies to provide for the best reproduction at the separation and print stages.

Submission Requirements

Queries for all submissions are preferred. Unsolicited manuscripts and artwork will be considered.

Photography and artwork: Photographs and artwork/illustrations are an integral part of each issue. Considerable space is devoted to illustrative material. Black and white photographs, and color transparencies are preferred. Good quality 35mm slides are acceptable. Please arrange with our editor as to what would be required specifically. Captions indicating artist, title, medium, size and date must be included for each piece.

Payment: Manuscript rates range from $100-250 for feature articles depending on length and quality. Review rates are $50. Photography and artwork rates must be agreed upon.

All payments are mutually agreed upon in advance of commitment to publish. Payments are made upon publication.

Assignments: Assignments are made by written agreement. If for any reason *Letter Arts Review* does not accept an assigned feature after completion and submission on deadline, the contributor will be paid a "kill fee" of 25% of the mutually agreed upon payment. All materials will be returned to the contributor with all rights. When schedules permit, contributors will be given an opportunity to resubmit.

Sample Copies: A sample copy of *Letter Arts Review* is available upon request accompanied by a self-addressed 9"x12" mailing envelope with seven first class postage stamps.

Categories: Nonfiction—Arts—Graphics—Photography—Calligraphy—Lettering

CONTACT: Rose Folsom, Editor
Material: All
212 Hillsboro Dr.
Wheaton MD 20902
Phone: 336-272-6139
Fax: 336-272-9015
E-mail: lar@johnnealbooks.com
Website: www.johnnealbooks.com/lar

LIBIDO
The Journal of Sex and Sensibility

Libido
The Journal of Sex and Sensibility

Does not accept unsolicited submissions.

Life

Special Editions publication only. Does not accept unsolicited submissions.

Lifeglow

Due to a current over abundance of manuscripts, *Lifeglow* will not be accepting additional manuscripts until 2009. Please keep us in mind and submit your manuscripts then.

Target Audience

Lifeglow is a quarterly magazine for visually impaired adults over the age of 25. It is published four times a year in large print for an interdenominational Christian audience.

Purpose

Lifeglow seeks to draw the reader into a relationship with God and, from a Christian perspective, to provide wholesome reading material that brightens, inspires, and entertains. It is a positive-living journal that includes a "Vitality Plus" section dealing with current health-related topics. As sight-impaired adults face today's challenges, it is important that *Lifeglow* assist in stimulating their thinking, in dealing with their feelings, and in maintaining their role in today's society.

Types of Material

We select manuscripts for publication from the following categories: adventure, biography, camping, career opportunities, devotion/inspiration, handicapped (experiences involving them), health (both physical and mental), history, hobbies, holidays, marriage, nature, nostalgia, relationships, self-help, and travel.

We do not accept fiction. The story must be based on a true incident.

Writing Tips

Whether for a story or an article, the narration and description should be:

• specific rather than general.

• concrete rather than abstract.

- active rather than passive.
- The ending should be clear, bringing into sharp focus the purpose for which the manuscript was written.
- Devotional/inspirational articles: a personal story illustrating your point is much more effective than sermonizing or moralizing.
- Informative articles should be carefully documented. Please secure permission to use any copyrighted material.
- Whenever possible, good quality photos should accompany the manuscript.
- Feature stories and articles should not exceed 1400 words.

Payment/Publication

We pay 4 cents per word, on acceptance.

When we publish your material (a minimum of two years after acceptance), we will send you two complimentary copies of the issue containing your article.

Manuscript Preparation

Manuscripts must appear professional. *Please:*

- use standard 8½ x 11 inch white opaque paper.
- use double-spaced typing.
- use one-inch margins.
- use correct page numbering.
- use proper spelling and punctuation.
- place your name and address in the upper left corner of page 1.
- place the word count in the upper right corner of page 1.
- begin title and body of the manuscript about 5 inches from the top of page 1.

If the material has been submitted to or published by another publication, the words "Second Rights" should appear below the word count. Also please indicate if the manuscript is a simultaneous submission.

We are a non-profit organization and cannot return your manuscript(s) unless accompanied by a self-addressed, stamped envelope (SASE), with sufficient postage to cover the cost of returning all manuscripts included.

Even if you don't wish to have your manuscript(s) returned, an envelope with one first-class stamp attached will help facilitate sending your payment check, should we accept your manuscript.

Categories: Nonfiction—Adventure—Biography—Careers—Disabilities—Hobbies—Inspirational—Marriage—Nature—Outdoors—Relationships—Self-Help—Travel

CONTACT: Gaylena Gibson, Editor
Material: All
Christian Record Services
PO Box 6097
Lincoln NE 68506

LifeWayonline.com

LifeWayonline.com will consider freelance articles, but does not pay for unsolicited content. If you are interested in having your work appear on *LifeWayonline*.com, please e-mail a brief summary to Lifeway@*LifeWayonline*.com. If we choose to use your submission, we can provide a hyperlink back to your Website, as well as a brief author bio. When *LifeWayonline*.com does pay for content, it is for specific assignments that we have commissioned.

About *LifeWayonline.com*

For many of you, the name *LifeWayonline* represents the brand name of our popular filtered Internet Service, and that will not change. You will still be able to find all the information you need at *LifeWayonline*.com to continue to benefit from our first class, family-safe Internet service provider. But, after listening to our customers, it became clear that there was so much more that we could offer. Thus, we are now offering our *LifeWayonline*.com subscribers and guests some of the best lifestyle content on the Web, in the form of articles from LifeWay's many family magazines, as well as in moderated online message boards and chats.

What makes *LifeWayonline*.com different from other online destinations? Unlike similiar Web sites, nearly all of the content you will read at *LifeWayonline*.com has been developed and published by the seasoned editorial teams here at LifeWay. When looking for "biblical solutions for life," it is important to find sources you can trust. LifeWay has been writing and publishing magazines, devotionals, and teaching guides for over 100 years. Where else on the Web will you be able to find over 100 years of trust? Nowhere else, but at *LifeWayonline*.com.

LifeWayonline.com is wholly owned by LifeWay Christian Resources.
Categories: Nonfiction—Christian Interests—Religion—Spiritual

CONTACT: Submissions Editor
Material: All
One LifeWay Plaza
MSN 123
Nashville TN 37234
Phone: 615-251-2000 (Main LifeWay operator)
Fax: 615-251-5881
E-mail: Lifeway@lifewayonline.com
www.lifewayonline.com

Light

LIGHT is the only magazine available in this country devoted exclusively to light verse, satire, cartoons, parodies, and word-play. Published quarterly, each issue contains thirty-two pages of the best of well-known and new writers. (Our contributors include John Updike, William Stafford, Donald Hall, Michael Benedikt, J.F. Nims, Tom Disch, W.D. Snodgrass, and William Matthews, among others.)

- What's unique in this magazine is that it prints not only funny, topical, satiric and witty verse (both free-form and metrical), but that this verse is understandable by a literate reader, and enjoyable as well. Its pages are accessible, with large type-faces and elegant graphics. It also features light and literate essays and articles, gossip, prose satire and letters, and puzzles that are guaranteed to sharpen your mind and blunt your pencil.

Guidelines for contributors:

NO HALLMARKS—unless stamped out of the same aery yet durable material as that of Rochester, Swift, Pope, Calverley, Byron, Praed, W.S. Gilbert, Beerbohm, Belloc, Shaw, Chesterton, Benchley, Coward, Dorothy Parker, Ogden Nash.

LIGHT seeks to continue the tradition established by the *Punch* of the eighteen-nineties, the Vanity Fair of the twenties, and the New Yorker of Ross and Shawn, of De Vries and Nabokov, of Thurber and E.B. White. Slang and superciliousness, epigrams and aphorisms, parodies and satire, cartoons and line drawings, nonsense and spoonerisms and absurdist clippings from the daily press: If it has wit, point, edge or barb, it will find a home here.

Verse written for an occasion, private or public, is particularly welcome.

Reviews and essays are encouraged, in the spirit (if not the words) of Stevenson, Beerbohm, Chesterton. Any topic, from Light Verse or its antecedents to ephemeral or everyday objects, may suit; in lengths from brief apéritifs to lengthy meditations. Write with proposals or for further details.

Please be neat, submit letter-quality typescripts or clean photocopies, and a stamped self-addressed business (#10) or manila-sized envelope (no post cards). There should be only one poem on each page, and each page should have your name and address on it. Works that extend over several pages should be numbered. Submissions of more than one page should be folded once; that is, do not fold each sheet of paper separately. Payment is in copies (two for domestic contributors, one for foreign) of the issue your original contribution appears in. Foreign submissions should include sufficient U.S. postage for their return.

Cartoons and line drawings are also solicited, from those solicitous of the honorable and corrosive tradition laid down by Rowlandson, Daumier, Hogarth, Lear, Steinberg, Beerbohm, and Thurber; or continued in the acid-dropping work of Trudeau, Larsen, L.J. Barry, R. Crumb, Robt. Williams, and S. Clay Wilson. The dimensions of your work should normally be no larger than 3.75"x6". This is so that they can be scanned into the computer. Once scanned, the size can be adjusted to be larger or smaller. Line drawings only; no washes or halftones. Send only clean photocopies on good heavy-weight white paper. Submissions should be in black and white.

If you wish to connect with a vital tradition, subscribe to the magazine *USA Today* described as "...much like *The New Yorker* without the annoying hubris." Subscriptions are $16/yr. (four issues), $28/2 yrs. (eight issues), $24 International; single copies $5, and back issues/sample copies $4. For domestic First Class postage, add $2.00 per copy. Send checks (drawn on a U.S. bank) to the address below. Or call toll-free (VISA or MASTERCARD): 1-800-285-4448.

If you're not completely satisfied for any reason, we'll be happy to give you a full refund.

Categories: Fiction—Nonfiction—Cartoons—Comedy—Literature—Native American—New Age—Poetry—Short Stories—Writing—Humor

CONTACT: Submissions Editor
Material: All
PO Box 7500
Chicago IL 60680

Light of Consciousness
A Journal of Spiritual Awakening

Light of Consciousness is in its 16th year of publication. We welcome submissions of articles and poetry inspiring and interesting to spiritual seekers in today's world. A universal message or meaning is preferred but writing may derive from or illustrate a particular tradition. Contributions should be reader-friendly (non-academic), uplifting (not derogatory), and from the heart as well as the intellect. These can range from personal accounts to epic passages and include non-fiction, fiction, poetry and "how-to" in spiritual practice or living.

Departments include Featured Articles plus The Spiritual Journey, Spirit and Nature, Spiritual Practice, The Eternal Wisdom, Spirituality and Science, Saints and Sages, Spirituality and Art, Healing, "Lightlines," Poetry.

Please send clean documents (spell-punctuation checked), 1,000-4,500 words, if possible on a disk in MAC format. Photographs and artwork are also welcome.

Currently, *Light of Consciousness* has a national circulation of 20,000, appealing to readers interested in spiritual unfoldment, meditation, personal growth, music, books/magazines, healing, environment, nature, the arts and travel.

Light of Consciousness is a not-for-profit service; we make no profit on it nor do any of us take salaries. As such, we rely upon and are deeply grateful for the generosity of writers and artists; full credit to

the contributor (and contact information if desired) is published; copyright remains with the creator of the work.

Categories: Fiction—Nonfiction—Arts—Biography—Inspirational—Native American—New Age—Poetry—Religion—Spiritual

CONTACT: Submissions Editor
Material: All
Desert Ashram
3403 W. Sweetwater Dr.
Tucson AZ 85745-9301
Phone: 520-743-8821

Ligourian

LIGUORIAN is a leading Catholic magazine written and edited for Catholics of all ages. Our purpose is to lead our readers to a fuller Christian life by helping them to better understand the teachings of the gospel and the Church, and by illustrating how these teachings apply to life and the problems confronting them as members of families, the Church, and society.

1. Articles and stories should not exceed 2,000 words. Style and vocabulary should be popular and readable. Use an interest-grabbing opening, state Wily the subject is important to readers, use examples, quotes, anecdotes, make practical applications, and end strongly.

2. LIGUORIAN does not consider simultaneous submissions or articles previously accepted or published.

3. Topical articles should be submitted six months in advance.

4. Manuscripts should be typewritten, double spaced, and should include name, address, and social security number. (No check may be issued without a SS#.)

5. Please allow six to eight weeks for our response.

6. We pay 10 to 12 cents a published word on acceptance. 7. Authors are advised to read and study several issues of LIGUORIAN before submitting articles.

8. LIGUORIAN receives over two hundred manuscripts each month. Your manuscript stands a better chance of acceptance if it is neatly presented, carefully polished, and on a topic of special interest to our readers.

Good luck and we hope to be hearing from you soon.

The editors of Liguorian

Categories: Christian Interests—Family—General Interest—Parenting—Relationships—Religion—Senior Citizen—Spiritual—Young Adult

CONTACT: Allan Weinert, .SS.R., Editor-in-Chief
Material: All
One Ligouri Dr.
Ligouri MO 63057
Phone: 314-464-2500
Fax: 314-464-8449
E-mail: aweinert@liguori.org
Website: www.liguori.org

Lilith
The Independent Jewish Women's Magazine

Lilith, the independent Jewish women's magazine, publishing since 1976, welcomes high quality, lively writing: reportage, opinion pieces, memoirs, fiction, and poetry on people and issues of concern to Jewish women.

Content:

• Features (1000-2000 words approximately) can include: autobiography (testimony, letters, journals, memoirs); biographies of women living or dead; interviews; social analysis; sociological research; oral history; new rituals; reviews; investigative reporting; coverage of local, national, international conferences and grassroots projects; opinion pieces.

• *Lilith* welcomes: Letters to the Editor, news briefs (500 words or less), and resource listings of new organizations, projects or upcoming events.

Editorial Specifications:

• Author's bio: one to two sentences, written in the third person, should accompany the manuscript.

• Footnotes: None! Sources should be incorporated into the story, in parentheses if necessary. Larger digressionary remarks or information should be submitted on separate pages for use as possible "boxes" or "sidebars" (companion pieces to the main feature).

• Translations: All non-English (including Hebrew or Yiddish) words or phases must be followed by English translation the first time they are used in a non-fiction piece and should appear in italics.

• Form: Manuscripts should be submitted in hard copy, double spaced with author's name, address and phone number and e-mail address on the first page. Name and email address or phone number on each successive page. If an article is accepted for publication, author will usually then be asked to submit an electronic version, preferably in Word software. Queries may be sent by e-mail to Lilithmag@aol.com.

Procedures:

Receipt of manuscripts cannot be acknowledged unless a stamped self-addressed postcard is enclosed. Manuscripts will be returned only if *Lilith* **receives a self-addressed envelope with suffi-cient postage. Allow 12-16 weeks for editorial decisions.** All artwork and photographs accompanying articles that need to be returned should be labeled (lightly on back). Letters to the Editor cannot be acknowledged or returned and must include the writer's name, address and daytime phone number, though these can be withheld from publication at the writer's request.

We encourage you to read our magazine to judge whether *Lilith* is the appropriate vehicle for your work. The enclosed subscription flyer gives examples of topics we have covered. You may order a sample copy of *Lilith* for $6.00 (includes postage). One-year subscriptions are $21. Orders accepted by mail, e-mail, fax or phone.

Categories: Fiction—Nonfiction—Biography—Drama—Film/Video—Jewish Interest—Lifestyle—Music—Poetry—Women's Issues

CONTACT: Submissions Editor
Material: All
250 W. 57th St., #2432
New York, NY 10107-0172
Phone: 212-757-0818
Fax: 212-757-5705
E-mail: lilithmag@aol.com
Website: www.lilithmag

Linn's Stamp News

General

The goal at *Linn's Stamp News* is to create a weekly publication that is indispensable to stamp collectors.

Everything we do, from the broadest editorial policy to the most trivial stylistic idiosyncrasy, is thought out in the light of this one overriding goal.

We try to achieve indispensability in various ways:

Every collector, from the beginner to the most sophisticated, wants to know the news. Our aim is to provide all the news, as conveniently and as accessibly as we can. In this regard, we feel we are the *New York Times* of philately.

In stamp collecting, the news is not just club and show announcements, new issues and auction realizations.

New discoveries are constantly being made, sometimes involving material that is decades or even centuries old. We cover this news too, relying on the worldwide network of columnists and correspondents who contribute to our pages.

Of course, we rely on these contributors for much more than hard news. Many of the feature items in *Linn's*, which make up the bulk of our editorial content, originate with free-lance contributors in the collector community.

Here *Linn's* performs an important educational function, by bringing to the attention of approximately 55,000 subscribers (and many more thousands of readers) a diverse selection of facts, thoughts and observations about stamps, postal markings, covers and stamp-related subjects.

Writing in *Linn's*, the free-lance contributor has the opportunity to share his specialized knowledge with the largest stamp collector audience of any periodical in the world.

It should go without saying, then, that *Linn's* features are aimed at a broad group of relatively novice collectors, whose average level of sophistication, on any given subject, is less than that of the specialist author.

Linn's writers should keep this general interest level of the audience uppermost in mind. Advanced or more sophisticated collectors, as many of our columnists tend to be, must also avoid writing down to the reader.

The goal in writing for the *Linn's* audience is to provide information that makes stamp collecting more interesting to more people. Ideally, every feature we run promotes the hobby.

A *Linn's* article is not the appropriate place to showcase everything the author knows, nor is it a lofty podium from which to speak over people's heads.

The *Linn's* writer must strive to reach out and embrace the reader, to invite him in, even to hold his hand along the path. This attitude of friendliness and openness in one's prose is difficult to articulate, but it's extremely important. It is very much a part of our desire to make *Linn's* accessible to all collectors, and to help them grow as philatelists.

Without condescending, the *Linn's* writer should assume that the reader knows little or nothing about the specific subject at hand. Complicated terms or unfamiliar words should be defined, even if they might be familiar to the more advanced philatelist.

The *Wall Street Journal* is a good model here: Every time its uses the phrase "short sale," it defines what a short sale is. *Linn's* strives to be similarly introductory in its approach to the jargon of philately.

The ideal *Linn's* feature would contain enough new (or newly presented) information to instruct even the specialist in the field, written in a way to capture the attention (and hold the interest) of the beginning collector.

While the scope of our editorial interest ranges as widely as philately itself, many of our features focus on U.S. and U.S.-related material. No matter what his collecting specialty, the *Linn's* reader still maintains an interest in the stamps and postal history of his own country. Week after week, *Linn's* offers the most complete coverage of the U.S. philatelic scene available anywhere.

This is not to say that we ignore the philately of the rest of the world—quite the contrary. We have regular columns in many non-U.S. areas; we record and notice the new issues of the entire world; and our feature writers routinely range the globe, writing on subjects from classic to contemporary.

Linn's is also big enough to accommodate a wide range of writing styles.

Many of our columnists have individual voices, and we don't discourage this.

We will always try to preserve a writer's style, if it is a style worth preserving.

F-L

Terms

We purchase first worldwide periodical rights plus a non-exclusive right to anthologize or otherwise reuse on a proportionate royalty basis, and to use the artwork online.

We want to be the first periodical to publish the work. The author is subsequently free to resell the work elsewhere, 60 days after we've published it; but here we'd like to be credited. We reserve the right to reuse all works published in *Linn's* (in our almanac or in an anthology, for instance), and we will pay an appropriate royalty for such print reuses.

The specific legal details of our purchase are spelled out in the "Standard terms governing acceptance of original material" section at the end of this guideline.

Articles submitted should be exclusive to *Linn's*. We are not interested in material that is simultaneously submitted to other publications (except press releases, of course, which are not part of this discussion).

Thus, we want to see original e-mail files, faxes or typescripts.

We reserve the right to edit, cut or reject anything submitted. Unsolicited materials will be returned only if accompanied by an addressed envelope, suitably franked.

Articles accepted may not appear immediately. Please be patient. The acceptance/rejection process is fairly quick (about four weeks), but accepted pieces sometimes sit for months before publication.

Payment for features and columns is made upon publication. Checks are mailed monthly, shortly after the 5th of the month. Thus, in the ordinary course of events, writers should have received, by the middle of the month, our check for whatever of their works was published in the issues of *Linn's* cover-dated the previous month.

Rates vary, generally between $25 and $100 per feature. We do strive to pay every contributor who produces original work for us. This is more by way of saying "thank you" than providing a livelihood, because the economics of newspaper publishing don't sustain magazine rates.

Payment varies according to quality, craft, degree of difficulty, previous work done for *Linn's*, number and quality of visuals, and length.

We do not pay by the word. Longer is not necessarily better. In fact, the longer a feature, the less likely we'll have room for it.

We usually have a large inventory of half- to full-page features (over 750 words) and a screaming need for shorter items (200-500 words).

Illustrations

Include illustrations wherever possible: stamps, covers, postmarks or whatever other visual material supports your text.

Many would-be contributors seem to break down here. For *Linn's*, a picture is indeed worth, if not 1,000 words, at least 250. More frequently than we would prefer, we find ourselves returning otherwise publishable work because it lacks the necessary visual support.

As a general rule, the best way to write an article on almost any philatelic subject is to have the photos, scans, stamps or covers in front of you before you begin. That way you are sure to properly illustrate your subject, and your text is fairly certain to explain what's in its pictures.

Conversely, an easy way to get into trouble is to write an article with no visual support, in the expectation of finding a photo after the article is done. Nine times out of 10, the result is a text that lacks illustrations or doesn't connect to them.

On the other hand, bear in mind that in final page make-up there must be a balance between illustrations and text. Too many illustrations can overpower a skimpy text and make it difficult (sometimes impossible) for us to lay out the words.

We prefer separate (not embedded) jpg or tif scans at 300dpi twice the size of the original item. Crisp, sharp-focus, high-contrast glossy black and white photos can still be used, but here no color is possible, of course. Each of our weekly issues includes approximately three to five pages with color editorial news or columns.

A few items that have no tonal gradations, postmarks or surcharges for instance, can be reproduced adequately from photocopies. Stamps and covers cannot.

If you can't provide decent photos, send us the stamps or covers and we'll make the scans or photos here. (Clear this with us first if the value is substantial.)

Please don't expect us to seek out your visuals for you; we don't have the time or the resources.

Our typical purchase includes the acquisition of the illustrations. If you want any photos returned, we should discuss this beforehand. Include your name and full address on the reverse of each photo.

Along with illustrations, we expect you to provide captions. Please provide captions on a separate sheet of paper, not embedded within your manuscript.

The ideal caption should explain what the picture shows and make the reader want to read the accompanying text. At the very least, a caption should explain what's in the picture. Identify all people and everything else that would provoke reader curiosity. "Figure 1" with no explanation is not an acceptable caption. All information in a caption must also be in the text of the article.

Don't paste visuals or captions onto your manuscript. Don't embed scans into a text document. Keep them separate.

Copy Preparation

Copy should be prepared in a standard electronic format, such as Microsoft Word or similar software, and submitted on a disk with a paper copy. With the managing editor's permission, it can be submitted by e-mail.

If typewritten, it should be double spaced with ample margins, on one side only of sheets of white 8 1/2-inch by 11-inch bond paper. Put your name and the page number in the upper-right corner of each page.

Those still using a typewriter should avoid typewritten strikeovers, especially with figures. Better to cross it out and say it again. Clarity is more important than neatness.

Footnotes and bibliographies are not appropriate to our newspaper style. If attribution or citation is essential, then it's important enough to be worked into the text.

Refer to illustrations as Figure 1, Figure 2, etc. Avoid eye directions such as above and below, which might be contradicted by page makeup.

For similar reasons, charts in the text should be avoided. They typically run wider than one column width, and cause difficult (sometimes impossible) make-up problems. If you must include a chart, prepare and discuss it separately, as if it were a photo.

Submit articles to Managing Editor, *Linn's Stamp News*, Box 29, Sidney, OH 45365.

Style: General

Linn's is a weekly magazine in newspaper format. Our editorial style is designed to communicate information as quickly and as clearly as possible.

Stylistic quirks that hinder rapid communication are discouraged. Our basic reference in matters of editorial style is *The Associated Press Stylebook*, available from AP at 50 Rockefeller Plaza, New York, N.Y. 10020.

Even though your subject might be specialized, write it understandably.

Always explain terms. Remember that *Linn's* is read by tens of thousands of readers who don't know your subject as well as you do. Reach out and help them.

Avoid lengthy paragraphs. One typewritten line makes two lines of type in *Linn's*. Our newspaper style calls for very short paragraphing. This also aids readership.

Don't use lengthy sentences. Two or three short sentences are easier to read than one long one. Never use parentheses or dashes when commas or separate sentences will serve the same end. Never use a comma when a period will do.

Avoid cliches. Don't try to be cute. Reread your sentences to see if you can express the same thoughts in fewer words.

Check and double check all facts, especially names, addresses, catalog numbers and other critical bits of information. We rely on you for the accuracy of your prose.

Don't be afraid of the first person. We'll be publishing your work under your name. "We" or "this writer" are pedantic and often confusing. Say "I" if it's appropriate. Use a dictionary or a spelling guide. Frequent misspellings suggest a lack of attention to detail that is inappropriate to the craft of journalism. The back pages of Webster are useful regarding punctuation and grammar. Avoid jarring repetition of the same words or phrase. There are many ways to say the same thing.

Style: *Linn's*

Never refer to a stamp by Scott number only. Describe it first and then add the Scott number if needed.

As an example: "The U.S. 10¢ 1869 stamp (Scott 116) . . ." In a series, it's Scott 51-58; 233-37.

Spell out numerals one through nine, then use figures for 10 and higher.

Don't use decimals after an even number of dollars (we say $20, not $20.00). For large numbers, insert the comma beginning with 1,000.

Generally, figures are used in ages; always in percentages.

No comma after a month without a day (March 1983); adding the day requires the comma (March 13, 1983). The reverse "13 March 1983" takes no comma, but is difficult to read and should be avoided.

We abbreviate months when used with days (Aug. 12, 1869) but not without days (August 1869). We never abbreviate the five short months: March, April, May, June, July.

We never use italics or quotation marks for emphasis. If you want to emphasize a word or a point, write emphatically. Don't use quotation marks to indicate anything other than a quotation. Periods and commas go inside the quotation marks; semicolons go outside.

Abbreviations: We use the old style state abbreviations. We don't abbreviate Alaska, Hawaii, Idaho, Iowa, Maine, Ohio, Texas, Utah. Two-word states are abbreviated with no space: W.Va. We only use the two-letter postal abbreviation when an address is given.

Mr. is used only with Mrs. or when the man is dead. Mrs. and Miss are generally unnecessary. We never use Ms.

We don't use periods with most well-known organizations: USSS, APS, UPU, USPS, UNPA, APO, GPO, etc. However, we do use periods with country initials as an adjective: U.S., U.N.

Postal administrations and other organizations take the singular: APS will stage its spring meeting, UNPA will announce its 2003 stamps.

Note the punctuation and separation of the following: American Stamp Dealers Association, Citizens' Stamp Advisory Committee, price list. The following are all one word: mailcoach, handcancel, handstamp, datestamp, semipostal, multicolor, steamship.

Our general style is lowercase. When in doubt over whether a word should be capitalized, leave it down.

STANDARD TERMS GOVERNING ACCEPTANCE OF ORIGINAL MATERIAL

Linn's Stamp News, a division of Amos Press Inc. (the publisher), accepts original copy and/or artwork subject to the following terms and conditions:

1. *First Worldwide Periodical Rights and Electronic Rights.* The contributor grants to publisher the exclusive right to be the first to publish the article and supporting artwork in whole or edited fashion (sometimes referred to collectively as the "work" in *Linn's Stamp News* and to use said work in advertising and/or promotion.

The contributor also grants to the publisher the non-exclusive right to publish in electronic form, on any Internet web site created or maintained by *Linn's Stamp News*, any and all stories and/or photos that *Linn's* has purchased, or will purchase, from the writer.

This authorization for electronic publishing may be terminated at any time by written notice to *Linn's Stamp News*, which notice shall be effective with respect to such stories and/or photos received by *Linn's* after receipt of the written notice.

2. *Subsequent Use.* The contributor retains the right to sell the work elsewhere provided such subsequent sale occurs no sooner than sixty (60) days after publication by *Linn's* Stamp News. The contributor agrees that any subsequent reprint will appropriately reference *Linn's Stamp News* copyright.

The contributor grants to publisher a right to reuse said work in any print publication of the publisher, subject to publisher's payment of an appropriate fee to the contributor.

3. *Copyright.* The contributor grants to the publisher the right to obtain copyright on the work in the publisher's name in the United States and any other country, subject to the contributor's retained non-exclusive right to reuse as set forth above.

4. *Indemnity.* The contributor warrants and guarantees that he is the sole proprietor of the work; that said work violates no existing copyright, in whole or part, that it contains no libelous or otherwise injurious matter; that the work has not heretofore been published; that he is the sole and exclusive owner of the rights granted herein to the publisher; and that he has not heretofore assigned, pledged, or otherwise encumbered said work. At his own expense, the contributor will protect and defend said work from any adverse claim of copyright infringement, and shall indemnify, defend and hold the publisher harmless from asserted claims of whatever nature, damages, costs and expenses that the publisher may incur as a result of the publication of said work and/or subsequent reuse.

5. *Payment.* The contributor accepts such amount as is tendered by separate check from the publisher as payment in full for the rights in the work granted herein to the publisher; provided, however, that it is agreed that additional monies may be due only as a result of subsequent reuse as set forth in paragraph 2 hereof.

6. *Rights Reserved.* All rights in the work not specifically granted to the publisher are expressly reserved to the contributor.

7. *Applicable Law.* The agreement between the contributor and publisher shall be governed by the law of Ohio and shall be deemed to have been entered into at Sidney, Ohio, as of the date of the issuance of publisher's check in payment of the amount due to the contributor pursuant to paragraph 5.

8. *Arbitration.* Any claim, dispute or controversy arising out of or in connection with the agreement between the contributor and publisher or any breach thereof, shall be arbitrated by the parties before the American Arbitration Association under the rules then applicable of that association. The arbitration shall be held in the city of Sidney, Ohio.

9. *Successors and Assigns.* The agreement of the contributor and publisher shall be binding upon, and inure to the benefit of each of their respective heirs, successors, administrators, and assigns.

10. *Entire Agreement.* It is understood by the contributor and publisher that these Standard Terms And Conditions and publisher's check tendered in payment in accordance with paragraph 5 set forth the parties' entire agreement regarding this work and may not be varied except by an additional writing signed by the contributor and the publisher. Copyright 2001

Categories: Nonfiction—Hobbies—Stamp collecting only

CONTACT: Fran Pfeiffer or Michael Schreiber
Material: All
PO Box 29
Sidney OH 45373
Phone: 937-498-0801
Fax: 888-304-8388
E-mail: fpfeiffer@linns.com
Website: www.linns.com

The Lion Magazine

The Lion Magazine welcomes freelance article and photo submissions that depict the service goals and projects of Lions clubs on the local, national and international level.

Contributors may also submit general interest articles that reflect the humanitarian, community betterment and service activism ideals of the worldwide association or family-oriented, humorous essays.

Lions Clubs International is the world's largest service club organization, with a membership composed of more than 1.4 million men and women in 178 countries and geographical areas. Lions are recognized globally for their commitment to projects that benefit the blind, visually handicapped and people in need.

The Headquarters Edition of *The Lion Magazine*, produced in Oak Brook, Illinois, is published 10 times yearly; December/January and July/August are combined issues. The circulation of the Headquarters Edition reaches approximately 600,000 readers.

Article length should not exceed 2,000 words, and is subject to editing. No gags, fillers, quizzes or poems are accepted. Photos should be at least 5"x7" glossies; color prints are preferred. *The Lion Magazine* pays upon acceptance of material.

Advance queries save your time and ours.

Categories: Nonfiction—Associations

CONTACT: Robert Kleinfelder, Senior Editor
Material: All
Lions Clubs International
300 W. 22nd. St.
Oak Brook IL 60523
Phone: 630-571-5466

Liquid Ohio

Format: Our format is 8.5 X 11, 32 pages, B&W.

Poetry: Try not to go over 60 lines, but a good epic is fine.

Short stories: Between 2000-3000 words.

Photography/artwork: Color or b/w, but they will appear in B&W.

Genre: The best idea is probably to order a sample copy and get a feel for what we're all about.

All written work sent in via e-mail should either be pasted into the letter itself or in MS *Word.* Any work sent via postal mail should include a SASE if you would like a response. If you would like your work returned, please indicate this with your submission.

Sample copies are available for $4.00. Subscription rates are $15.00/year for 4 issues. Please make checks payable to Amber Goddard.

Categories: Fiction—Arts—Cartoons—College—Feminism—General Interest—Photography—Poetry

CONTACT: Submissions Editor
Material: All
PO Box 60265
Bakersfield CA 93386
Phone: 661-871-0586
E-mail: info@liquidohio.net
Website: www.liquidohio.net

STIMULATING PROSE, POETRY & ART

Literal Latte

Literal Latte is the stimulating Literary Arts Magazine of fiction & Poems from known & emerging writers around the world

It's brewed in New York City and is brimming with stories, poetry, essays & art. *LL* is in its ninth year of publishing the best words around.

LL features fiction, poetry and essays by established and emerging authors:

Ray Bradbury, Michael Brodsky, Robert Olen Butler, Stephen Dixon, Harlan Ellison, Allen Ginsberg, Daniel Harris, Phillip Lopate, Carole Maso, Nancy Milford, Carol Muske, Lynn Sharon Schwartz, Gloria Steinem, Frank Stella, John Updike, Jerry Uelsmann & exciting new talents.

MIND STIMULATING PROSE, POETRY & ART

It's Not Who You Know or Where You've Been...It's What You Write 98% of what we publish comes from the so-called slush pile.

We take submissions 365 days a year.

We accept work for publication on a continual basis, not just for the upcoming issue, and publish

within one year of acceptance.

Most issues contain someone who has not been published before.

GENERAL GUIDELINES

• Send unpublished stories or personal essays, up to 6,000 words.

• Short plays or poems up to 4,000 words.

• Art—from cover art to literary cartoons. Photographs, paintings, drawings in B&W or Color (slides or copies, not originals)

• Styles range from classical to experimental.

• Include biography and SASE or email for response or return of work. Or include email for response only.

• Simultaneous submissions welcome, let us know if a piece is accepted elsewhere.

• It takes us approximately 3-6 months to respond.

• E-mail submissions are NOT accepted.

SUBSCRIPTIONS

1 year/6 issues: Only $11 ($25 international, must be in US dollars). 2 Year/ 12 issue subscription Only $20.

SAMPLE ISSUE, $3

Include Check or Money Orders made out to *Literal Latte*

Or Visa/MC/American Express #, & Expiration Date (you may call in your credit card order to

1-888-8-LitLat)

Categories: Nonfiction—Arts—Poetry

CONTACT: Submissions Editor
Material: All
61 East 8th Street, Ste 240
New York NY 10003
Phone: 212-260-5532
E-mail: LitLatte@aol.com
Website: www.literal-latte.com

Literary Magazine Review

UW-RF's English Department is now home to a nationally circulated journal, the *Literary Magazine Review* (LMR). LMR is a twenty-year-old quarterly that reviews periodicals that publish mostly poetry and creative prose. It began at Kansas State University where the editor was able to establish an exchange program bringing over 60 new titles of literary magazines to the library. Later LMR moved to the University of Northern Iowa, where it has resided until its recent move to UW-RF.

LMR is an excellent resource for both writers seeking publishing outlets and readers searching for the best contemporary literary magazines to read. Its audience includes writers, academic libraries, and the editors of literary magazines. Its reviews are often quoted in other national magazines such as Poets and Writers and American Poetry Review, as well as in advertisements for the literary magazines it reviews. The most recent promotional information for New England Review, for example, quotes LMR.

The opportunities for UW-RF students and benefits to the UW-RF campus are numerous. LMR provides excellent opportunities for English, Business Communication, and Journalism majors to serve as editorial assistants and interns, while the entire campus can look forward to readings by prominent writers interested in reading at the home of LMR. The University will have the prestige of housing a 20-year-old national magazine. Its publication will be a teaching opportunity for instructors. The journal will help to foster strong working relationships with other universities by establishing a network of contributors, and by encouraging a continuing interchange between LMR and literary magazines housed on other campuses. LMR will generate new titles for the library through an exchange program much like the one set up at Kansas State University. It may initiate a UW-RF conference stemming from the magazine and new outreach opportunities, such as extension courses for adult learners. It will be an excellent opportunity for good university publicity and add interest for other possible publication ventures.

Jenny Brantley, Editor; Brian Fitch, Assistant Editor, Univ. of Wisconsin-River Falls, English Dept., 410 S. 3rd Street, River Falls, WI 54022, email: jennifer.s.brantley@uwrf.edu, web site: http://www.uwrf.edu/lmr/. Founded in 1981. Articles, criticism, reviews. LMR is devoted to providing critical appraisals of the specific contents of small, predominantly literary periodicals for the benefit of readers and writers. We print reviews of about 1.5M words that comment on the magazines' physical characteristics, on particular articles, stories, and poems featured, and on editorial preferences as evidenced in the selections. Recent contributors include John Pennington, D.E. Steward, Phil Miller, Kevin Prufer, Steve Heller, Maria Melendez, Stella Pope Duarte, and John McNally. We would be happy to entertain queries offering disinterested reviews and omnibus notices and pieces describing, explaining, or examining the current literary magazine scene. Subscription exchange inquiries are welcome. Circ. 300. 4/yr. Pub'd 4 issues 2003; expects 4 issues 2004, 4 issues 2005. sub. price $16; per copy $5; sample $5. Back issues: $7 an issue. Discounts: 10% to subscription agencies. 48-52pp. Payment: copies. Copyrighted, rights revert on author's request. Pub's reviews: 70 in 2003. Literary magazines. We are interested in magazines that publish at least some fiction, poetry, literary nonfiction, or all three. Ads: none. Subjects: Criticism, Literary Review, Magazines, Reviews.

Categories: Literature—Poetry

CONTACT: Dr. Jenny Brantley, Editor
Material: All
University of Wisconsin
English Department
410 S. Third St.
River Falls WI 54022
Phone: 319-273-2821
Fax: 319-273-5807
E-mail: jennifer.s.brantley@uwrf.edu
Website: www.uwrf.edu/lmr

The Literary Review
Fairleigh Dickinson University

MAJOR INTERESTS: TLR has an international focus and welcomes work in translation.

CONTENT: Original poetry, fiction, work in translation, essays, review essays on contemporary writers and literary issues. Review essays should include a group of works of common interest rather than a single title.

LENGTH: We have no length restrictions for fiction or poetry; however, long works must meet an exceptionally high standard of excellence. In general, essays should be under 5,000 words and reviews from 1,500 to 2,500 words.

STYLE: We accept work in any format or style, ranging from traditional to experimental. We expect our contributors to have a strong understanding of technique and a wide familiarity of contemporary writing, but editorial decisions are based on quality alone.

NUMBER: We read only one story, essay, or review-essay by an author at one time, and no more than six poems.

PRESENTATION: Clear photocopies and dot-matrix printouts are permissible.

TIME: We try to advise of our decision within 12 to 16 weeks of receiving a manuscript. Accepted manuscripts usually appear within 18—24 months, often sooner, depending upon our commitment to special issues.

COMPENSATION: Contributors receive two copies of the issue in which their work appears and are eligible to compete in our annual Charles Angoff cash award.

COPYRIGHT: All material appearing in TLR is copyrighted. Authors are granted reprint rights as TLR only holds one-time rights to their work.

SAMPLES: Sample copies are available for $5.00 U.S., $6.00 foreign, prepaid.

Categories: Fiction—Nonfiction—Book Reviews—Interview—Literature—Poetry—Short Stories

CONTACT: Rene Steinke, Editor-in-Chief
Material: All
285 Madison Ave.
Madison NJ 07940
Phone: 973-443-8564
Fax: 973-443-8364
E-mail: tlr@fdu.edu
Website: www.theliteraryreview.org/

Live Wire

Does not accept unsolicited submissions.

The Living Church

Formal guidelines not available. Please read a number of issues to ascertain the publication's style and needs.

Send queries to address below.

Categories: Nonfiction—Christian Interests—Religion—The Episcopal Church

CONTACT: Submissions Editor
Materials: All
Living Church Foundation
PO Box 514036
Milwaukee WI 53203
Phone: 414-276-5420

LIVING WITH
Teenagers

Living With Teenagers

Living With Teenagers is a Christian monthly magazine for parents of teenagers. It focuses on the practical aspects of parenting, as well as informs, educates, and inspires parents to be aware of issues and understand their teenagers as they grow into responsible young adults.

Content: The editorial staff will evaluate articles dealing with any subject of interest to parents of teenagers.

Preparation: Cover page should include suggested title and blurb, by-line, author's full name, address, social security number, and rights offered (all, first, one-time reprint).

Submit manuscripts 600-1,200 words in length.

Queries with writing sample are preferred.

Disk submissions must be accompanied by a hard copy. Prefer disk on a Macintosh word processing program, but can convert most IBM programs.

Writing Tips: Quoted material must be properly documented (publisher, location, date, and page numbers), along with permission verification.

Include Bible references and thoughts when appropriate.

Remember readers are parents of teenagers.

Use brief, clear sentences.

Construct paragraphs logically.

Sidebars helpful.

Payment: Payment is negotiable and on acceptance.

Publication: Writers will receive, without cost, 3 advance copies of the issue in which their manuscripts are published. Extra copies can be ordered from the Customer Service Center (MSN 113 at address below, or 800-458-BSSB).

• For a sample copy, send a 9"x12" manila envelope with your address and return postage.

• I have prayed about and reread my submission, and it reflects a Christian worldview that will help distinguish the magazine from other secular parenting magazines.

• I have included a cover page with this information: article title, a short writer bio; total word count; my full name, address, phone number, email address (if available), and Social Security number.

• I am submitting the manuscript in one of the following ways:

1. I am submitting the manuscript in hard-copy form through regular mail, and I agree to submit it electronically if it is purchased through a contract.

2. I am submitting the manuscript by disk, and I am also sending it in hard-copy form. I have indicated on the disk which word processing program was used. (Microsoft Word is preferred.)

3. I am submitting the manuscript by email. I am sending it to parentlife@lifeway.com or to lwt@lifeway.com. I am also sending this checklist by regular mail.

• I have secured necessary permission for quoted material and have properly documented all quotations (source, publisher, date, and page number). I have also enclosed a photocopy of the original quote as well as a photocopy of the title page and copyright page of the source from which the quote is taken.

• I have verified all statistics and factual information (anything that is not considered common knowledge among the general public). I have properly documented this information (source, publisher, date, and page number), and I have enclosed a photocopy of the source (including a copy of the title page and copyright page).

• I have verified any Scripture that I have quoted, and it is quoted from NIV. (LifeWay has permission to quote from the NIV, and photocopies are not necessary.)

• I have included at least two blurbs or pull quotes that will quickly draw the reader into the article.

• I have included at least one and possibly up to three sidebars. The sidebar provides valuable information for the reader (quick tips, ministry ideas, lists, Web sites, books, phone numbers, addresses, and so on).

• I have used headings and subheadings throughout the article, and they relate to the suggested title.

Please provide a two or three sentence writer bio that we can use as a standard for you.

Please check the topics or subjects which interest you most as a writer:

College—communication—cults—education—entertainment/media/music—exceptional teens—finance—food/nutrition—health issues—recreation—religion—technology—teen physical development—teen emotional development—teens and spiritual issues—discipline—siblings—sports—learning styles—sex education—peer pressure—drugs/alcohol—problem solving/conflict resolution—family issues (for example: single parent, blended family)—other

As a Christian parenting magazine, we desire to have writers who have a growing commitment and relationship to Jesus Christ. Please tell us briefly how you became a Christian and about your present journey with Christ.

Other biographical information we would like to have: birth date, current vocation (if retired, previous vocation), place of employment, church membership, current church or denominational leadership positions, educational background, spouse's name, children's names and ages, articles and books you have had published, special interests and hobbies.

Categories: Christian Interests— Teen—Young Adult

CONTACT: Editor
Material: All
One LifeWay Plaza
Nashville TN 37234-0140
Phone: 615-251-2229
Fax: 615-251-5008
E-mail: lwt@lifeway.com
Website: www.lifewayonline.com/mags

Llewellyn Journal

Thank you for your interest in *The Llewellyn Journal*. For more than 100 years Llewellyn has published books on metaphysics, astrology, magic, spirituality, alternative healing, and associated topics. *The Llewellyn Journal* is our on-line presentation of in-depth articles on these and similar subjects.The following Guidelines include the information you need to send us an article for consideration.Purpose:

There are two major purposes for *The Llewellyn Journal*:First, *The Llewellyn Journal* will give authors published (or soon to be published) by Llewellyn a chance to present practical ideas and concepts from their writings. *The Llewellyn Journal* also gives these authors a chance to share some of the results of working with those ideas and concepts. These may include new concepts based on their writings or expand upon ideas presented in one of their Llewellyn books. Second, *The Llewellyn Journal* will give voice to a selection of high-quality writers who have not yet been published by Llewellyn. If a submitted article is intelligent, well-written, has documentation for any references, and can be seen to comment upon, build interest in, or in some way add to a current Llewellyn title, it will be considered for publication.We are providing *The Llewellyn Journal* as a free service to the community. However, the costs of design, editing, maintenance, articles, artwork, etc. are considerable. Further, unlike magazines you might obtain by subscription or buy at a store, *The Llewellyn Journal* receives no money from outside advertisers and no money from subscriptions or newsstand sales. It's free. In return for this free service, we hope readers will support the Journal by purchasing Llewellyn books which they read about here. It is only through such reader support that we will be able to maintain *The Llewellyn Journal* as a free service. Articles that further this end are most likely to be published.

Length:

We are seeking articles of 2,500 words or less.Subjects:

The Llewellyn Journal considers for publication substantive, indepth articles that discuss metaphysical topics. For Llewellyn, the metaphysical category is broad and inclusive as can be seen in the wide subject range of books that we publish. If you have a topic in mind for *The Llewellyn Journal*, please email us and ask if it is appropriate before writing and submitting an actual article. *The Llewellyn Journal* seeks to publish powerful, practical, even life-changing techniques (including necessary background), based on Llewellyn books. *The*

Llewellyn Journal may also carry articles that are thought provoking, philosophical, and theoretical as long as they are focused toward a specific Llewellyn book. *The Llewellyn Journal* will include articles that are between popular and academic styles. Including bibliographic references to concepts and ideas are encouraged but not required. References to any quoted material are required (see below). For an article to be accepted for publication in *The Llewellyn Journal*, it must be clear and unambiguous in content. We are not looking for beginners' guides. For example, if you are a Llewellyn author with a book on the Tarot, we would prefer to see an article on ""Working with The Tower Card to Improve Your Life"" as opposed to ""Your First Tarot Deck.""

HOW TO SUBMIT AN ARTICLE TO THE LLEWELLYN JOURNAL

Things to consider before you submit:

1) Are you sure we would be interested in your article's subject? Does it clearly and directly relate to a book published by Llewellyn? E-mail the editor (TLJEditor@llewellyn.com) and ask first. 2) We only accept new, previously unpublished articles. By that we mean your article cannot have previously appeared in a book, magazine, on a web site, on a CD, or in any printed form whatsoever.3) *The Llewellyn Journal* is an online only publiation. Therefore, we only accept email submissions.4) We accept complete articles only. We do not accept partial articles.5) Although we primarily support authors who are published by Llewellyn, we will also consider thoughtful, well-written articles by other writers if they discuss a Llewellyn title or focus on a Llewellyn topic. We do not work with agents.

Specifications:

For the article itself, we require the following:1) If you send the article as an attachment, use a standard, easy-to-read font (Times, Palatino, Helvetica, Arial, etc.).2) Do not justify the page. Right margin should be ""ragged.""3) Do not use the return or enter key (or make a ""hard break"") at the end of each line. You should only use the return or enter key at the end of a paragraph.4) Do not indent paragraphs.5) Do add an extra line space between paragraphs.6) Date your title page.7) Include your name, address, email address, and phone number in the article.8) Keep a copy of your article and all correspondence for reference and to protect against loss. NEVER SEND US YOUR ONLY COPY.

Submission:

We accept email submissions only. They must be in one of two forms:1) Within the body of the email.2) As an attachment. Under no circumstances will we accept any ""executable"" file (.exe). No matter what word processor you use, please send us a ""text only"" (ASCII or .txt) file.2a) If you are sending an attachment be sure to include your name, address, email address, and phone number in the attachment as well as in the body of the email.

What is Unacceptable:

1) As mentioned above, if a topic does not fit our broad metaphysical field or support a Llewellyn title, it will not be considered.2) We will not accept writing that is sexist or racist; writing that ""bashes"" any group; or writing that shows intolerance toward groups, organizations, or individuals.3) Words that are popularly considered to be obscene or defamatory are unacceptable. Writing containing these words will not be considered for publication.4) Decisions of the editors on what will be published are final.

Permissions and Fair Use:

The Llewellyn Journal seeks fresh, original approaches to metaphysical topics; we don't want ""retreads"" of what's already out there. We strongly discourage quoting or paraphrasing of books or articles not published by Llewellyn.If you cite concepts from other sources, *The Llewellyn Journal* requires proper attribution and documentation. When citing an outside source in your text, include the complete publishing information for the reference (title, author(s), publisher, date and city of publication, and page number) in the body of the article or in your endnotes. For more information on citation and documentation, we recommend the Chicago Manual of Style.

Illustrations:

As a journal that is focused on text, the use of illustrations and photographs is limited — and frankly discouraged. However, if you feel that an illustration or photo is necessary for your article, you may send a .gif, .jpg, or .tif attachment file along with your article. Indicate in ALL CAPITAL LETTERS where the image should be placed within the text of your article. Please be aware that *The Llewellyn Journal* reserves the right to omit any graphics.If you include a photo, you must either have taken the photo yourself or have written permission from the copyright holder to use the photo. If there are any people in the photo besides yourself, you must have written permission from them to use their image for any purpose.If you are using illustrations or photographs from other published sources, you must obtain permission and suitable reproductions from the copyright holder. Do not assume anything is public domain, no matter how old. You are responsible for obtaining all art clearances, and will be held responsible if permissions are infringed upon.

Llewellyn's Editing Process:

If we decide to publish your article and you agree to the terms of the agreement, your article will be edited. *The Llewellyn Journal* reserves the right to edit all or any part of the article submitted by the author, and to make the final decisions in terms of editing.

Payment:

1) Payment for articles is $75 per article, regardless of length.2) The Article is a Work For Hire. Llewellyn will own and copyright in its name.3) You will be paid no more than 30 days after your article is posted on our site and during a regular Llewellyn payment cycle.4) You will always receive credit as the author of the article.5) Llewellyn will grant the Author, as well as any other person, permission to post the first 250 words of your Article on their own websites so long as the following is printed with the article: ""Permission to post this article granted by *The Llewellyn Journal*"" followed by the Internet address of *The Llewellyn Journal*(www.llewellynjournal.com).6) Llewellyn employees will not receive payment for Journal articles, unless they are written off the clock.

Policies:

We want to keep *The Llewellyn Journal* free so as many people as possible can see it. We even encourage websites to post portions of our articles, including your name as author. In order to do these things, we maintain the following policies:1) Articles purchased for use by *The Llewellyn Journal* are considered ""Works for Hire."" This means that the payment you receive gives *The Llewellyn Journal* the right to use it in any way.2) If you are having a book published that includes material from an article you have published in *The Llewellyn Journal*, write to us at TLJEditor@llewellyn.com giving details, and we will send you written authorization to use the article at no charge as long as *The Llewellyn Journal* is credited as the original source.3) Neither *The Llewellyn Journal* nor Llewellyn Worldwide, Ltd. are responsible for any actions of the readers of *The Llewellyn Journal* or the Public at Large who may copy all or parts of your article or even make changes to it with or without your permission.4) If you have questions or concerns about this policy, please write to us with your specific question and we will send a detailed reply.

Personal Information

In order to publish your article in *The Llewellyn Journal* we must have the following information:

• Your name, mailing address, phone number, and email address.
• Your pseudonym, if you wish to use one.
• Your social security number or tax ID number.

If you are not comfortable sending this information to the Journal editor via e-mail at TLJEditor@llewellyn.com, please send it via post to the address below:

Categories: Nonfiction—Health—Metaphysics—New Age—Spiritual

CONTACT: The Editor
Material: All

Llewellyn Worldwide
PO Box 64383
St. Paul, MN 55164-0383
Phone: 612-291-1970
E-mail: TLJEditor@llewellyn.com
Website: www.llewellynjournal.com

Log Home Living
Timber Frame Homes

Description

Log Home Living is a monthly magazine for people who own or are planning to build contemporary log homes. It is devoted almost exclusively to modern manufactured and handcrafted kit log homes. Our interest in historical or nostalgic stories of very old log cabins, reconstructed log homes, or one-of-a-kind owner-built homes is secondary and should be queried first.

Readership

Our audience comprises primarily married couples between 30 and 45 years old. They are generally well-educated and very individualistic do-it-yourselfers.

Specifications

Log Home Living welcomes new talent and strives to develop long-term relationships with those contributors who consistently deliver quality work. We buy two to four bylined feature articles of 1,000 to 2,000 words per issue. These articles should reflect readers' lifestyles and interest in log homes as follows:

• *Log Home Owner Profiles.* Articles about people who have built modern log homes from manufactured or handcrafted kits. In a conversational tone, describe the home as it is and tell how it came to be. Emphasize the elements that make this home special—intent, design, solutions to unique problems, features, furnishings, interior design and landscaping. Every story must include feature photos. Floor plans of the completed home, construction costs and schedules are a plus.

• *Design and Decor Features.* Photo stories on various architectural features of log homes. Stories can focus on a particular home or the same architectural feature on different homes.

• *Historical Features.* Articles about historical log structures in North America or abroad and restorations of same. As mentioned before, we have a limited need for this material.

• *Technical Articles.* How-to advice about specific aspects of log home construction or pre-construction. Examples are scheduling a construction project, selecting wood preservatives, installing flooring, decorating log homes, dealing with subcontractors and innovative financing programs. Writers of these articles should be experts or able to interview experts and convey the information for a lay audience.

Submissions

Manuscripts should be typed, double or triple spaced with wide margins, on white bond paper. Computer printouts are acceptable, but we prefer they be unjustified (ragged right) and letter quality. We will read unsolicited manuscripts but prefer an outline or a detailed query letter first. Enclose a SASE.

Photos

Stories must be accompanied by extensive professional-quality color photographs of log home interiors, exteriors or construction shots as appropriate. See our Photographers Guidelines for specific requirements. If you are not a professional photographer, advise us in your query. Also tell us if you know a professional photographer who can work with you on an assignment; otherwise, we will locate one to accompany you.

Payment & Rights

Payment for features ranges from $250 to $500 (without and with photos), depending on their length, the nature of the work and the amount of editing required. We acknowledge receipt of submissions immediately and try to provide an editor's response within thirty days. Payment is made within 30 days of acceptance.

Cancellations

If we determine that a submitted article requires substantial rewriting, we will pay a $100 research fee for the information supplied. If we decide not to use an assigned accepted article, we will pay a $100 kill fee.

Rights & Conditions

Log Home Living buys first North American rights and nonexclusive reprint rights. Upon publication, authors will receive two complimentary copies of the issue with their work.

We cannot accept responsibility for the personal safety or property of any freelancer while on assignment for the magazine. Writers and photographers are urged to have their own insurance in place while on assignment.

We assume that all contributed manuscripts are original and that all facts and quotes have been verified. Articles that have been published or submitted elsewhere must be so identified; in such cases, the author is responsible for obtaining permission to reprint previously published materials prior to submission to *Log Home Living*.

Expenses

Reasonable expenses will be covered, provided that travel plans and all anticipated costs are discussed beforehand with the editor. A complete expense report, including receipts for all claims, should accompany the contributor's work. Expense reimbursement is made with payment for an accepted article.

Sample Copy

If you would like a sample copy of *Log Home Living* magazine, please send your check or money order for $4.00 to HBPI, Attn: Sample Copy, PO Box 220039, Chantilly VA 20153.

Timber Frame Homes

Timber Frame Homes magazine uses the same guidelines as *Log Home Living*.

Categories: Nonfiction—Architecture—Lifestyle—Real Estate—Trade—Home Construction—Travel

CONTACT: Kevin Ireland, Executive Editor
Material: All
PO Box 220039
Chantilly VA 20153
Phone: 703-222-9411
Fax: 703-222-3209
E-mail: editor@loghomeliving.com
E-mail: editor@timberframehomes.com
Website: www.loghomeliving.com/loghomeliving
Website: www.loghomeliving.com/timberframehomes

Long Island WOMAN

Long Island Woman

ABOUT THE PUBLICATION

We are a monthly tabloid magazine of special interest to Long Island women, with a free distribution of 40,000 copies throughout Long Island, NY.

TYPES OF ARTICLES

Articles of special interest to women. Topics would include news, humor, lifestyles & family, mental & physical health, sports & fitness, nutrition & dining, fashion & beauty, business & finance, home decorating & gardening, entertainment & media, travel & leisure, books, interviews with interesting or inspiring women and women celebrities. No poetry or fiction, please.

MANUSCRIPTS

Submissions and queries will be accepted via mail and email.

No submissions or queries will be accepted by telephone.

All manuscripts and queries should be typed and double-spaced.

Please include suggested headlines, subheadlines, and a brief biography (up to 20 words) that may appear at the end of the article.

Include any photographs or artwork that may enhance the presentation of your article.

Include your name, address, telephone number, fax number, email address.

If we publish your article we will need your social security number.

Submissions will be returned only if accompanied by a self-addressed, stamped envelope.

Allow 6–8 weeks for a response.

DEADLINES

The last week two months preceding publication date (ie – deadline for February issue is the last week of December)

RIGHTS

Long Island Woman buys one-time rights to articles that will appear in print and on our website (liwomanonline.com) and will not appear in other publications on Long Island, NY within one year of publication.

PAYMENT

Invoice us for our agreed amount plus include your name, address and social security number. Payment will be made within 30 days of publishing of article.

RATES

300–500 words	$35
501–700 words	$50
701–900 words	$65
901–1,100 words	$75
1,001–1,300 words	$100
1,301–1,600 words	$120
1,601–1,800 words	$150

Kill Fee: 33%

Categories: Nonfiction—Antiques—Arts—Book Reviews—Business—Careers—Cooking—Crafts/Hobbies—Diet/Nutrition—Economics—Family—Fashion—Food/Drink—Gardening—Health—Law—Marriage—Money & Finances—Physical Fitness—Psychology—Relationships—Senior Citizen—Sexuality—Singles—Sports/Recreation—Women's Issues

CONTACT: Arie Nadboy, Managing Editor
Material: All
PO Box 176
Malverne NY 11565
Phone: 516-897-8900
E-mail: editor@liwomanonline.com

THE LONG TERM VIEW

The Long Term View
Massachusetts School of Law

Editorial Philosophy

The *Long Term View* is a public policy journal which devotes each issue to a balanced discussion of a single topic or question. We provide a forum where academics, professionals, and other knowledgeable persons can make their information available to lay persons m a direct and readable manner.

To achieve this objective, we welcome submissions in many forms, including essays and analytical articles. Whatever the format, we want unambiguous, economical prose. We discourage the extensive use of footnotes: main points should be made in the text. Authors are responsible for the accuracy of all citations and data.

Manuscripts will be edited for clarity, brevity, and style. Topics for future issues of LTV are printed at the end of each issue.

Manuscript Guidelines

Authors are asked to include an electronic version of their manuscript, via e-mail (vietzke@mslaw.edu) or disk.

Any footnotes should appear at the end of the manuscript.

Please include a separate cover page with your name, affiliation, title of manuscript, and a brief biographical note.

Categories: Nonfiction—Government—Law—Politics—Academia

CONTACT: Holly Vietzke, Editor
Material: All
500 Federal St.
Andover MA 01810
Phone: 508-681-0800
Fax: 508-681-6330
E-mail: vietzke@mslaw.edu

The Lookout
For Today's Growing Christian

Our Magazine

• THE LOOKOUT is a 16-page, full-color weekly magazine from Standard Publishing with a circulation of 100,000.

• THE LOOKOUT is written and designed to provide Christian adults with true-to-the-Bible teaching and current information that will help them fulfill their desire to mature as individual believers, develop godly homes, and live in the world as faithful witnesses of Christ. In short, we went to help our readers understand and respond to the world from a biblically based viewpoint.

• THE LOOKOUT publishes from a theologically conservative, nondenominational, and noncharismatic perspective. It is a member of the Evangelical Press Association.

Our Readers

• We have a diverse audience with readers in every adult age group, but we aim primarily for those aged 35 to 55.

• Most readers are married and have older elementary to young adult children. But a large number come from other home situations as well.

• Our emphasis is on the needs of ordinary Christians who want to grow in their faith, rather than on trained theologians or church leaders.

Our Needs

• As a Christian general-interest magazine, we cover a wide variety of topics—from individual discipleship to family concerns to social involvement. We value well-informed articles that offer lively and clear writing as well as strong application. We often address tough issues and seek to explore fresh ideas or recent developments affecting today's Christians.

• Our annual theme list is available on request (send a self-addressed stamped envelope). *Query for theme-related articles.* **Please note.** We publish strictly according to our theme for the year. All major articles we purchase will address one of the 52 themes we have scheduled for the year. We continue to purchase non-theme articles for occasional features (Word Windows, Salt & Light, Faith Around the World, and Outlook).

• Please do not submit poetry or fiction.

• Please do not submit previously published material.

We usually publish six kinds of nonfiction articles:

• *Teaching articles* (1,200-1,600 words): Help readers *practically* apply Scripture to present-day needs or show them fresh ways to grow in their Christian walk. Your article should provide either solid principles to help readers better understand your subject or skills to help them effectively respond.

• *Informational and journalistic articles* (1,200-1,600 words): We are looking for timely, well-researched articles, interviews, profiles, or essays dealing with topics of current concern. (List sources when applicable.)

• *Human-interest stories* (1,200-1,600 words): Let your unique experiences and observations help our readers see God at work in the world. Better yet, show us the experiences of others. Become a reporter and tell our readers about Christian individuals or families with extraordinary stories. Humor and inspiration articles are welcome.

• *"Outlook"* (500-800 words): We publish reader-written opinion essays addressing current issues that concern Christians. Address your submission to "Outlook."

• *"Salt & Light"* and *"Faith Around the World"* (500-800 words): These articles inform our readers about Christians—in America and other parts of the world—who are living out their faith and reaching out to their communities. We're looking for exciting true stories about people who are making a positive difference.

• *Word Windows* (250 words): Every other week we publish a lively, reader-friendly illustration—a short story that sheds light on a specific verse of Scripture. No canned illustrations, please. We want true-to-life stories that will touch our readers' hearts.

Your Submission

• Please query six to nine months in advance for theme-related articles and nine to 12 months in advance for seasonal articles. Your query letter should concisely describe the article you propose to write. Enclose a legal size, self-addressed, stamped envelope. If we are interested, we will ask for the article "on speculation," which means we are willing to examine the article, but cannot promise to publish it.

• Submit your typed manuscript, double-spaced, on one side of 8½" x 11" paper. Enclose a legal size, self-addressed, stamped envelope. (Self-addressed, stamped reply postcards are also acceptable.) Do not send more than one manuscript per SASE.

• Suggest a subhead for every 300-350 words of the article and a pull quote for every 600-700 words.

• Secure permission from the appropriate publishing house when quoting songs, hymns, or poetry in the article.

• Legible photocopies and letter-quality printouts are acceptable.

• We do not accept unsolicited submissions by fax.

• We accept queries by e-mail, but we do not accept unsolicited submissions by e-mail or on disks.

• With your submission, please provide your name, address, daytime telephone number, social security number, and word count.

• Allow up to 10 weeks for reply.

• THE LOOKOUT pays up to nine cents per word for first rights on unsolicited articles and up to 15 cents per word for first rights on assigned articles. We pay on acceptance.

• Simultaneous submissions to non-competing markets are acceptable.

• THE LOOKOUT does not publish poetry or fiction.

• To receive a theme list, send a self-addressed stamped envelope with your request.

• To receive a sample issue, send $1.00 and your mailing address with your request.

Categories: Christian Interests—Family

CONTACT: Submissions Editor
Material: All
8121 Hamilton Ave.
Cincinnati, OH 45231
Fax: 513-931-0950
E-mail: lookout@standardpub.com

Lost Treasure
Treasure Cache

Lost Treasure, Inc. reviews manuscript submissions for two treasure magazines as follows: 1) *Lost Treasure*, a monthly publication, accepts lost treasure, folklore, personal adventure stories; legends; and how-to articles. 2) *Treasure Cache*, an annual publication, accepts only documented treasure cache stories with a sidebar from the author telling the reader how-to search for the cache highlighted in the story. Additional tips and guidelines on writing for *Treasure Cache* are sent on request (be sure to include an SASE).

SUBMISSIONS

1. Original Stories with photos, maps, and documentation are what we want! No rehashes of well known treasure stories.

2. Queries: *Lost Treasure*—not required. *Treasure Cache*—required. Queries should be typed, one page or less, and may be faxed, mailed, or emailed. Queries are answered as quickly as possible, usually 2-4 weeks.

3. Source Documentation: *Lost Treasure* and *Treasure Cache*—require source documentation. Articles dealing primarily with personal how-to information does not require source documentation unless the author makes reference to information outside of the realm of his/her personal experience. Then documentation is required. For source documentation requirements, see Source Documentation, #15.

4. Format, Disk: Manuscripts must be typed, caps and lower case (not all capital letters) and accompanied by a readable 3½" floppy disk in ASCII or Microsoft Word. If a disk is not available, typewriter copy must be of scannable quality (clean, clear, sharp black ribbon). See #8 below.

5. Page Identification: Your name, address, telephone number (including area code) and social security number should appear on each manuscript page in the upper right hand corner, and on the backs of all slides, photos, maps, or other accompanying material. Photos should also be numbered on the back (see # 9 below).

NOTE: Do not rubber stamp nor write information on the backs of photos, maps, etc., as damage may result making them unusable.

TIP: Type information on a sticky back label and affix or, type on a piece of paper and tape to the back of the photo.

6. Word Count: An approximate word count should appear in the upper right hand corner on the first page of your manuscript.

7. Page Numbering: Manuscript pages should be page numbered.

8. Sequence: Manuscripts should be typed in the following sequence: 1) Article. 2) Sources. 3) Captions (photo, map, art) and should appear on your disk as well as hard copy.

9. Identification—Photos and Captions: All photos should be assigned an identification number (i.e., 1, 2, 3, etc.). Accompanying captions should be typed and numbered to correspond to photo I.D. numbers and, appear at the end of the article. If you are submitting a computer disk, captions must appear on the computer disk at the end of the article.

10. All or Nothing: All photos, maps, documentation, other pertinent information and floppy disk (if available) should accompany your manuscript at the time of submission.

11. Article Lengths: *Lost Treasure*—500-1,500 words. *Treasure Cache*—1,000-2,000 words. Occasionally two-part articles are published. These are accepted by query only.

12. Issue Themes: *Lost Treasure* articles should coordinate with an issue's theme if possible (editorial calendar available on request. Send SASE with [one first class stamp]). Stories deviating from the theme are always considered and used whenever possible. How-to articles are used in each issue. *Treasure Cache* is documented stories.

13. Caution: Stories should not read like ads for particular products. It is acceptable to name products in your story, but refrain from consistently repeating the detector's name or the name of other equip-

ment unless you are submitting a field test story or the product did something unusual.

14. Don't Fold Them: Submissions should be mailed unfolded in 9"x12" (or larger) envelopes.

15. SOURCE DOCUMENTATION: At least two sources (preferably more) are required with each submission. Exception: personal experience stories.

• Newspapers: List newspaper name, issue date, article title. If newspaper clippings have no identification or date, note this fact in your sources.

• Magazines: List magazine title, publication date (month and year), article title, article's author.

• Books: List by author, title, publisher, publication date.

• National Archives, Library of Congress, etc.: List title, document number.

• Historical Societies, Museum Files, etc.: List organization name, location (city, state), and other identifying information as applicable.

• Personal experience stories:

• Yours: Identify yourself as the source, telling this is a personal experience, where it happened and when.

• Others: Identify whose experience it is, where it happened and when. Tell how you learned of the experience (examples: interview, letters, other).

TIP: Write down source information as you work. This insures accuracy and eliminates the necessity of backtracking.

16. PHOTOS: (Remember to identify them. See #'s 5 and 9 above.)

• Cover Photos: Accepted with or without accompanying story. Only 35mm color slides (vertical shots) are accepted.

• Article Photos: Black and white or color photos, any size smaller than 5"x7" accepted. No Polaroid shots. All photos must have sharp focus with good contrast.

17. MAPS: May be hand drawn or copied. They should indicate where the lost treasure is located and contain specific directions to lost treasure sites. (Remember to identify them. See #'s 5 and 9 above.)

18. PICTURES, BLACK AND WHITE LINE ART (not created by you): May be used only if you have received permission to do so and, credit is given to the source (museum, Library of Congress, illustrator's name, etc.). Exception: Newspapers—permission is not required but, credit must be given to the newspaper if a picture is copied. (Remember to identify them. See #'s 5 and 9 above.)

19. CARTOONS: As a rule we do not use cartoons in our magazines. Occasionally a cartoon accompanying a story is used.

20. SAMPLE ISSUES OF OUR MAGAZINE: Available on request. Write to: Managing Editor, Lost Treasure, Inc., at the address shown below. Enclose SASE with $1.47 postage.

21. NON ACCEPTANCE: We do not accept foreign manuscripts. Writers must reside in the U.S.A.

22. CONTRACT: We required a signed contract (our Magazine Rights Agreement form) from each writer giving us ALL rights to all material used (manuscripts, photos, art, etc.). No exceptions.

23. PAYMENT: Cover shots—$100.00. Articles—4¢ per word. Photos, hand-drawn maps, artwork—$5.00 each used. Payment is made on publication, not acceptance.

We appreciate your interest and hope to receive a submission from you soon.

Janet Warford-Perry
Managing Editor
Categories: Treasure Hunting

CONTACT: Janet Warford-Perry, Managing Editor
Material: Metal Detecting/Treasure Hunting
PO Box 451589
Grove OK 74344
Phone: 918-786-2182
Fax: 918-786-2192
E-mail: Managingeditor@losttreasure.com

Lucky Magazine

Formal guidelines not available. Please read a number of issues to ascertain the publication's style and needs.

Send queries to address below.

Categories: Nonfiction—Beauty—Fashion—Literature

CONTACT: Submissions Editor
Material: All
4 Times Square, 8th Floor
New York NY 10036
Phone: 212-286-2860

The Lutheran Digest

The Lutheran Digest, published quarterly, accepts a limited number of original manuscripts. Approximately 70 percent of the magazine's content is reprinted from other publications. The Digest's goal is twofold: To entertain and encourage believers and to subtly persuade nonbelievers to embrace the Lutheran-Christian faith. Distribution is free to participating Lutheran churches through the proceeds of business advertising.

ARTICLES WE WOULD LIKE TO SEE:

Articles should be no more than 7,000 characters in length. Articles of less than 3,000 characters are encouraged. Stories frequently reflect a Lutheran-Christian perspective, but are not intended to be "lecturing" sermonettes. Popular stories show how God has intervened in a person's life to help solve a problem. Also needed are seasonal and special interest stories and stories reflecting God's presence in nature. Seasonal stories should be submitted at least 6 months in advance of possible publication date. Payment is $25-$50 on acceptance, plus a complimentary copy upon publication.

ARTICLES WE WOULD RATHER NOT SEE:

• Stories with premises such as: "I was walking my dog (watering the lawn, washing the dishes, etc.) when I suddenly thought about how God takes care of my daily needs (gives us nourishment, washes away our sins, etc.)"

• Personal tributes to deceased relative or friend are seldom used unless the subject of the article is well known.

• Stories about the moment when an individual personally accepted Christ.

BIBLICAL QUOTATIONS:

Scripture references, which should be included for any Biblical quotations, should be inside the final quotation mark. [Example: "God so loved…life (John 3:16)."] Also, the first letter of all pronoun references to God and/or Jesus should be capitalized.

MANUSCRIPT MECHANICS:

Front page—In the upper-left corner include your name, address and phone number. In the upper-right corner, note the character count (not word count). Title should be centered and printed in upper- and lower-case lettering, 1/3 down the page, followed by your byline. Manuscripts should be typed, double-spaced, with paragraph indentations and spacing between paragraphs. A short, one-line biographic sketch should follow the article. Please do not submit more than three items at a time.

MANUSCRIPT RECEIPT PREFERENCES:

The Lutheran Digest prefers to receive manuscripts in hardcopy format via conventional mail. Response to, and return of, manuscripts that are not accepted will occur only if accompanied by a self-addressed, stamped envelope. We take no responsibility for lost or damaged manuscripts. Our preference is to not receive simultaneous submissions, but they will be considered. Please notify us of the manuscript's simultaneous submission status.

Manuscripts submitted by fax or email should comply with the Manuscript Mechanics section above. We regret that the number of unsolicited submissions we receive makes it impossible to respond to everyone. Therefore no responses to manuscripts submitted by fax or email will be made unless a manuscript is accepted for publication. E-mailed manuscripts should come as separate attachments and not be included in the body of the email text. Acceptable email attachment formats are Microsoft Word documents or .pdf (portable document format) files suitable for viewing with Acrobat Reader.

REPRINTS:

Authors are encouraged to submit previously published articles for which they have retained reprint rights. Content should be similar to that described in Article above. Payment is $25-$50 on acceptance plus a complimentary copy upon publication. [Note: As a professional courtesy, the last publication to feature the article will be acknowledged via a credit line. Be sure to include the name & date of that publication.

POETRY:

The Lutheran Digest accepts a limited number of short poems each issue. We're most likely to accept poems of one or two stanzas that will fit into a single column of the magazine. Only two full-page poems are used each issue. Subject matter is open. There is no payment for poetry, however, a complimentary copy is sent when the poem is used. Each poem should be typewritten on a separate sheet of 8 ½" x 11" paper. We are interested also in seeing poems that can be sung to the melodies of familiar hymns. Please do not submit more than three poems at a time.

FILLERS:

Items such as "Recipes Lutherans Digest" and jokes may be submitted. A Complimentary copy of the magazine will be sent on publication.

RIGHTS PURCHASED:

The Lutheran Digest buys one-time rights for original material or one-time reprint rights for previously published items. We also ask that authors allow us to grant limited reprint permission to individual churches for use in their congregations. (Commercial inquires are referred to the author.) Articles accepted for print may also be considered for our website: (www.lutherandigest.com). If we include your article on our website an additional payment will be made.

Categories: Nonfiction—Animals—Cartoons—Children—Christian Interests—Comedy—Confession—Conservation—Consumer—Diet/Nutrition—Family—Gardening—General Interest—Health—Hobbies—Inspirational—Marriage—Money & Finances—Music—Outdoors—Parenting—Poetry—Recreation—Relationships—Religion—Rural America—Senior Citizen—Spiritual—Teen—Confession—Humor

CONTACT: The Editor
Material: All
PO Box 4250
Hopkins MN 55343
Phone: 952-933-2820
Fax: 952-933-5708
E-mail: tldi@lutherandigest.com
Website: www.lutherandigest.com

Lynx Eye

LYNX EYE is a quarterly literary magazine of short stories, poetry, essays, social commentary, and black-and-white art. "Lynx-eyed" means sharp-sighted, and each issue showcases the work of visionary writers and artists. Familiar formats are combined with the experimental; experienced contributors appear alongside new voices. The opening feature, Presenting, introduces a previously unpublished artist.

The pages of LYNX EYE take you on imaginative journeys in the company of colorful characters. You may visit a Baltimore diner, the Indiana state fair, or a Tuscan village. Meet the world's greatest fishing dog, a forgetful vampire, and the queen of jingle junk. From pastoral odes to biting commentary, each issue of LYNX EYE offers thoughtful and thought-provoking reading.

Along with the pleasure of the written word, visual treats are plentiful. Original cover art invitingly presented—occasionally in eye-opening color—greets the LYNX EYE reader. Graphic designs, pen-and-ink drawings, and astute cartoons are scattered throughout the publication.

LYNX EYE is a journal-sized magazine; average page count is 120. It is published every February, May, August, and November. With a steadily growing readership, the lynx has been spotted worldwide: Paris, Kharkov, Bangkok...and Whidbey Island. Shouldn't your address be listed too?

In the U.S.
• One-year subscription (4 issues): $25.00
• Two-year subscription (8 issues): $48.00
Outside the U.S.
• One-year subscription (4 issues): $32.00
• Two-year subscription (8 issues): $60.00
Sample Issue: $7.95 within the US.
                  $10.95 outside the US
Please make checks payable to ScribbleFest Literary Group.

ScribbleFest Literary Group is a nonprofit organization dedicated to the promotion and development of the literary arts. With a mission to encourage excellence in writers and artists, founders Pam McCully and Kathryn Morrison began publishing LYNX EYE in November, 1994. ScribbleFest plans to expand its activities by sponsoring special events, readings, and support services vital to the development of the literary arts.

"From our humble beginnings over tepid cappuccino in a Westwood coffeehouse, our love of literature compelled us to provide a forum for uncommon ideas and unheard voices."

—Pam and Kathryn
Writer's Guidelines

Each issue of LYNX EYE includes fiction, essays, poetry and black-and-white artwork. Prose should be between 500 and 5,000 words, Poetry should be 30 lines or less. Our format is journal size; artwork should be 6"x4" (or something that will reduce to that size). If you have an excellent piece of work that falls outside of our requirements, send it.

Each issue opens with the feature, Presenting, in which a writer or artist makes his or her print debut.

LYNX EYE accepts never-before-published work only. We acquire first North American serial rights to your work. All other rights remain with you. We pay $10 per piece upon acceptance. You also receive three complimentary copies of the publication.

Manuscripts must be typed. Artwork should be camera-ready. We will respond within eight to twelve weeks.

Creativity is the antithesis of prejudice: having an open mind in the most complete sense of the word-non-judgmental, open to possibilities, open to new ideas, open to one's own feelings, open to others' feelings and needs.

Creativity is not-stopping too soon. How many creative ideas are squelched, and how many creative possibilities are never approached because someone gave up? But the creative person has to know when to "change gears": on arriving at an idea you really believe in, determination becomes necessary to follow through with it and to not be discouraged by others. Creative people work hard.

—From Cognition to Creativity
LYNX EYE

We are committed to the written word and eagerly await reading yours.

Categories: Arts—Poetry—Short Stories—Essays—Social Commentary

CONTACT: Pam McCully, Co-editor
Material: All
PO Box 6609
Los Osos CA 93412-6609

The MacGuffin

The MacGuffin is a national literary magazine from School-craft College in Livonia, Michigan. Our journal is a 160 page 6" x 9" perfect bound collection of the best poetry, short fiction, and creative non-fiction that we receive. We also have artwork including black and white photos, prints, and drawings. We publish two issues yearly. Our Spring issue always has a special theme.

If you are interested in good works by both new and well established writers, you are invited to get a sample or to subscribe.

If you write, we have provided you information on how to submit your work.

You will also find out about special issues, competitions like the National Poet Hunt, and Schoolcraft College literary events.

We hope that you will contact us.

Guidelines for Submitting Manuscripts

The MacGuffin publishes the best new work in contemporary poetry, prose, and visual art. Although the editorial staff of *The MacGuffin* pride themselves on the fact that every submission is considered, the following guidelines are highly suggested for a thorough examination and prompt reading of your material.

For All Submissions

Please enclose a self-addressed, stamped envelope (SASE) or sufficient International Reply Coupons for reply only.

Submissions may be made electronically to macguffin@schoolcraft.cc.mi.us

Please submit each work as a separate, Word or Word Perfect document attachment. Submissions made in the body of an email will not be considered.

Please include name, email address, and address on every page.

List titles and brief bio in cover letter.

We do accept simultaneous submissions if informed. We expect prompt notification if the work is accepted elsewhere.

Do not send revisions unless our editors have requested them.

All inquiries about submissions must be made via electronic or US Mail.

Allow eight to 16 weeks for a response. We thank you in advance for your patience.

Translations are welcome and should be accompanied by a copy of the original text. Translators are responsible for author's permission.

Manuscripts may be withdrawn until issue enters the typesetting process.

The MacGuffin is copyrighted. Upon publication all rights revert to authors. We appreciate acknowledgement as first place of publication.

Authors and artists receive two copies of the issue in which their work appears. Additional copies may be purchased at substantial savings.

We prefer easy to read, standard typeface.

Poetry

We consider traditional, formal, free verse, and experimental poetry. Poems can be up to 400 lines.

There are no subject biases.

Please do not submit more than five poems at one time.

Poems should be typed, single-spaced, and one per page

Fiction and Creative Non-Fiction

We have no subject biases. Maximum length is 5,000 words. Portions of longer works are acceptable if they can stand-alone. All prose should be typed and double-spaced.

Images

Submit the best quality image available; i.e., original photographs, slides, or artwork. Photocopies or laser output scan unevenly and leave streaks across the image.

If you want an image cropped, indicate the cropping on a photocopy of the image. Do not cut photos or artwork. We size and crop the image on the computer.

Electronic images should be EPS or TIFF files saved at 300 dpi for photos and 600 dpi minimum - 1200 dpi maximum for line art. Embedded images are not accessible to the page layout software.

Categories: Fiction—Nonfiction—Literature—Poetry—Short Stories—Writing

CONTACT: Anne Hutchinson, Senior Editor
Material: All Other
CONTACT: Carol Was, Poetry Editor
Material: Poetry
CONTACT: Elizabeth Kircos, Fiction Editor
Material: Fiction
Schoolcraft College
18600 Haggerty Road
Livonia MI 48152-2696
Phone: 313-462-4400 ext. 5292
Fax: 313-462-4558
E-mail: macguffin@schoolcraft.cc.mi.us
Website: www.schoolcraft.cc.mi.us/macguffin

Maelstrom

1. For poetry submissions please send no more than 4 pieces with name and address on each page.

2. Short Fiction must be 3,000 words or less.

3. Every submission should include address, cover letter, 2-3 line bio and a SASE or they will not be returned. While not required, submissions accompanied by a $1.00 donation will be answered immediately.

4. No attachments in e-mail submissions will be accepted. Please paste your text into the body of your e-mail.

5. Previously published and simultaneous submissions O.K.

6. Also seeking black and white art and book reviews.

7. Pay is 1 copy.

8. Pornography is not acceptable.

9. Staff writes short reviews of chapbooks and magazines, materials can not be returned.

10. Subscriptions are available for $20.00/4 issues or single copies may be purchased for $5.00 current or $4.00 sample. Check or money order made payable to *Maelstrom*. Copies also may be purchased online through Paypal at our web site, IMaelstrom@ aol.com

11. Response time at least 3 months*

*Submissions accompanied by a $1.00 donation will be answered immediately.

Categories: Fiction—Book Reviews—Cartoons—Poetry—B/W Art—Humor

CONTACT: Christine L. Reed, Editor
Material: All
PO Box 7
Tranquility NJ 07879
E-mail: IMaelstrom@aol.com
Website: www.geocities.com/~readmaelstrom

The Magazine of La Cucina Italiana

General Guidelines

The Magazine of La Cucina Italiana is unique in its authoritative approach to Italian cuisine, travel, wine, and culture. Readers rely on our publication to provide them with in-depth, accurate information concerning Italian regional foods, dining establishments, places and people of interest, and Italian specialty food shops in Italy and around the world. The *Magazine of La Cucina Italiana* is aimed at an audience that is well-to-do (with incomes around $150,000 per year) who "know" Italy, its food, and culture. They love cooking and good eating, as well as the cultural subjects that we write about. This magazine is fit for coffee table display.

Our editorial mission is to attract and educate the public about the many pleasures of Italian gastronomy, wine, culture, art, tradition, and tourism.

We are looking for qualified contributing editors to submit articles and accompanying photographs on relevant subjects. We only seriously consider articles that include photographs.

Main Article Subjects

1. TRAVEL to various locations in Italy, highlighting their most distinctive and significant features: the mountains, lakes, rivers, big cities (one or more of their aspects), towns. We usually make a distinction between a city article and a region article.

In 70-80% of the cases, the photos must contain people. We try to present Italian cuisine and culture with the people that make it interesting. In other words, if the article is about Herculaneum, the images should show people in front of the ruins, walking around, holding interesting objects, eating (even someone enjoying a sandwich if there is nothing else), and perhaps selling souvenirs. The rest of the pictures should show the surrounding places and perhaps some from your arrival and any typical modes of transportation. Every article must contain at least one element that suggests "luxury" or "richness" in the presentation of the object or items being sold. For example, a restaurant, café, or hotel that is clearly upscale and luxurious in appearance or a place that is open to the public (a monument or gallery) that has the same qualities. Stores that sell gifts or elegant items are also acceptable. It would be ideal to have enough pictures to contrast the typical with the luxurious. For our readers, this lavishness could be Baroque, Rococo, or contemporary, as long as it is obviously upscale.

2. CHEFS/RESTAURATEURS, their kitchens/restaurants, (inside and out), personalities, their context and training, two or three dishes, typical ingredients, and customers.

Occasional Topics for The *Magazine of La Cucina Italiana*:

1. Articles on an INGREDIENT such as a cheese, meat product, or other ingredient specific to Italy and Italian cooking. These articles should have some of the aspects of a trip article and some of a chef article (and must have some element of luxury). These articles are to be 1000-2000 words, with 12-16 images (3 or 4 of which must be of dishes). The recipes must be included.

2. Articles on a cellar or producer of WINE, or on a specific wine. In addition to the images outlined in points "a" and "b" above, you must also provide images of vines, vineyards, cellars, bottles, and labels. These articles are to be of 1000-2000 words with 10-14 images. The article must refer to a DOC or DOCG wine.

The Article Breakdown

For every issue, there are 2 or 3 travel articles (of which at least one must be on an urban environment) and 1 article about a famous chef or restaurateur. The breakdown is as follows:

• 1 travel article of 2500-3000 words and 12-14 images; and 2 travel articles of 1500-2000 words and 8-12 images.

• 1 chef article of 1500-2000 words and 12-16 images (more images and fewer words). Images of at least 2 or 3 dishes and their recipes.

The mix of articles in each issue showcases different regions of Italy.

Photographs

Pictures of food must have natural coloring and succeed in capturing the beauty of the dish and its composition. They should be done with a large-format camera, or if of very high quality, with 35 mm film (100 ASA). We do not accept postcard-type photos.

The publisher reserves the right to examine services not specifically requested, whether photographs or complete texts, and will return them only if requested and provided with a SASE.

Conditions and Procedures

Any agreement made will be confirmed in writing and will outline the topic, images, price, and deadline to be signed by both parties.

The articles must be sent either by mail, fax, or e-mail to the managing editor, accompanied or preceded by the photographic images. The material must be unpublished. The author will be informed of the outcome of the manuscript in the shortest time possible. For the first submission, we would like a short biography of the author as well.

If the submission is accepted, it will be edited (or edited, translated, and edited again) and when possible, sent to the author for approval before publication.

The images that are accepted will be held from when they are received until after the publication of the article.

The payment of a fixed price for the service will be sent immediately after publication.

Categories: Nonfiction—Cooking—Food/Drink—Life-style—Travel

CONTACT: Marie Dalby, Managing Editor
Material: All
230 Fifth Ave. Ste. 1100
New York NY 10001
Phone: 212-725-8764, Ext. 14
Fax: 212-889-3907
E-mail: piacere@earthlink.net
Website: www.italiancookingandliving.com

The Magazine of Speculative Poetry

MSP was founded in 1984 by Mark Rich and Roger Dutcher. Mark published one the first speculative poetry magazines, "Treaders of Starlight." Roger published "Uranus," another speculative poetry magazine. Finding themselves in the same city, they naturally founded a new magazine. MSP went 13 issues with both as editors when Mark, having moved and found success in his writing, decided to "move on." MSP has been edited by Roger since then.

Basics:
3 cents a word, $5.00 minimum, $25.00 maximum on acceptance.

First North American rights.

All rights revert to the author(s) upon publication, except for permission to reprint in any "Best of" or compilation volume. Payment will be made for such publication.

Poets receive a copy of the issue in which their poem(s) appears.

Return time of 1 to 8 weeks. Usually 1 to 2 weeks.

No simultaneous submissions; we do not use reprints.

What MSP wants:

I want more than just images. I want a poem to take me someplace I haven't been before. Have a fresh look at an old trope. I am more concerned with a good poem first, then a speculative poem.

Speculative poetry: Speculative poetry may be described as the equivalent in poetry to speculative fiction, that interesting confluence of post modernism and science fiction in the late sixties and early seventies of Britain and America. Authors associated with this movement include: J.G. Ballard, James Sallis, Pamela Zoline, Keith Roberts, Brian Aldiss, Samuel Delaney, Thomas Disch, and the poets George MacBeth and D.M. Thomas.

Speculative poetry can result from several approaches. One might be called projection: we imagine ourselves viewing from other perspectives than our own or simply being another being—for instance, we might be a tree, an alien sentience, perhaps ourselves five years from now. A second approach is simply that of the extended metaphor: science fiction has created a rich vocabulary of images and ideas, many of

which might be utilized in generating poetry. Other approaches may be used and the poems themselves may range from the meditative to the narrative to the lyric. What is most important to remember is that speculative poetry is a species of imaginative literature, and that it is a new species. Each poem in part defines the field as it is written.

I will leave it to others (or to another place) to argue whether speculative poetry is separate from or inclusive of, yet more than, science fiction poetry and the other identifiers we use, fantasy and horror. "Slipstream" seems to be a term that is similar. Literary has been used to describe the type of poetry we use.

Science fiction poetry: Based on science (soft or hard) and speculating on or exploring that science for an outcome we, in our current world, have not discovered yet. How do we react to, manage in, the world you have constructed. Was it Ray Bradbury who said SF doesn't predict the future, it tries to prevent it.

Science poetry: Read Diane Ackerman and Loren Eisley for an idea. The poem should still convey a sense of wonder. Not just nature poetry. Astronomical poetry with an edge perhaps. Speculation on contemporary science perhaps.

Fantasy poetry: I don't see enough fantasy poetry. What does MSP want? Fantasy from the realm of myth, fairy tales, and contemporary fantasy like Tolkien, Susan Cooper's "Dark is Rising" series, Le Guin's "Earthsea," McKillip's "Riddle Master" series, etc. Jim Dorr "Flight From the Tower" in a previous MSP fits the bill. I don't mean horror, dark fantasy or sword and sorcery. Once in awhile MSP sees Beowulf "like" poems, usually epic in length, no, I don't mean these, either, and not just because of the length. Just because there is an elf doesn't make it fantasy. I don't particularly like elves with motorcycles and assault weapons fantasy. In contemporary settings I enjoy the prose of James Blaylock and prose and poetry of Charles de Lint.

Horror or Dark Fantasy poetry: I am hard to please in this area. There is a lot of poetry written in this area. There are a lot of markets in this area. It is going to take a poem that grabs me to be accepted. It is not likely to be a vampire, werewolf or zombie poem. I do seem to have a penchant for mummies. It is most likely to be psychological horror that I will look at more closely. I am not likely so take a "splatter" poem.

Concrete and prose poetry: OK, I have not seen a lot of concrete poetry I have liked that was speculative, but then again, it seems the field should be able to produce some interesting visions. I would probably ask for a disc copy of any poem I might accept.

I won't try to define prose poetry. Shorter will be better. Have more than images.

Essays and reviews but query first with general idea/outline.

Not much help? If you feel it is a good poem and you want to spring for the postage, try me out. MSP would publish good poems in any of the areas above. I would rather read, enjoy and accept a poem than not have it sent because of any strictures inferred or implied above.

I have sent back good poems that are: mainstream, love, nature or political in content, but are not speculative. I have taken some I have liked because they are "on the edge."

Length, style, etc.:

A number of editors are very strict about how they want everything. You should pay attention to those details if you are submitting to them. Although we have always been pretty easy going, there are some general guidelines that make it easier for me.

We are a small magazine, we can't print epics, yet they still arrive now and again. We have printed some poems that run two or three pages, but it is rare to do anything longer. If you have something you feel is your best and it is longer, go ahead and send it.

No simultaneous submissions. We do not use reprints.

I am not persnickety about the number of poems you send. Send as many as you want to spring for postage on. Your acceptance is based on your poem, not on the number. Be reasonable though, not twenty or thirty. There does seem to be a correlation between a poet sending large numbers and my not liking the poetry, but that could be illusion. But, it seems a waste to send one, unless it is long, so send what you want. Three to five seems to be the most common number.

I have read poems that are hand written (usually prisoners or young people), single-spaced, double-spaced, with a regular font, with hard to read fonts, etc. I am not persnickety here either, but double-spaced (on smaller poems) is better, and a "regular old font" is best. I don't recall ever accepting a poem that was handwritten, in a hard to read font or something out of the ordinary. Not because of the handwriting but because of the poem; again, there seems to be a correlation. My eyes do seem to require more focusing of late, so double-spacing is best.

Cover letters: I like 'em. But they aren't necessary. If you do include a cover letter, make it more than "here are my poems, I hope you like them." A practical matter is to include the names of the poems you are submitting, if the poems get separated from your cover letter, then it helps to find them. Tell me where you have been published before (you don't have to have been) if you want, it may help trigger a memory of a poem you have done. You don't need to send a complete list of every poem you have ever published, just some high spots. Tell us where you have heard of us, it helps us know which market sources produce the best results. You can tell me a bit about yourself if you like.

Your name and your address should appear somewhere on each poem, your name on each page if it is a longer poem. This is practicality, if your poems get separated from your cover letter or return envelope, I am not likely to recall whose they are. Including the number of lines/words in each poem, usually in the corner opposite your name and address, is useful as well.

Postage: You should include an appropriate amount of postage for the return of your mss., if it cost you 37 cents to mail them to me it is going to cost you 37 cents to mail them back. If you are submitting from a country other than the US, remember, I can only use US stamps. Send loose US stamps (see USPS website for current rates to your country) or an IRC. I have yet to meet a USPS employee who has treated an IRC the same as another. Most of the time I have good luck with them. However they do require you and me to stand in line and to have the employee figure out what to do with them. If you can arrange a stamp swap with someone, that is nice. In the case of non-US poets only, if you don't want your mss. returned, send me your e-mail address and I will let you know. My e-mail address is a work address and seriously limited re: non-work related mail.

If you send me your poems in an 8"x10" envelope and a #10 envelope for their return, I am going to stuff them all in the #10 envelope. This can result in an envelope which is overweight for the postage on it. I don't put on extra postage, you are liable to get a postage due return.

If you don't want your mss. returned, please state this clearly in your cover letter and/or on the mss. itself. If you don't, you will get your poems back in whatever envelope you send me.

If your submission comes to me postage due you are very likely to get it returned to you as "refused."

Submissions without an SASE or postage/IRC are held for about 2 to 3 months. If I haven't received an SASE in that time the poems are recycled.

Electronic submissions: Yes, it is the world of the Internet and e-mail, no, I don't have a computer (believe it or not.) I do have an e-mail address but it is for work and I have to limit the amount of non-work e-mail I receive. I am not open to electronic submissions. With the exception of non-US poets noted above, I can not e-mail a poet about their submission.

At the moment I am not requiring or requesting submissions on disk.

MSP does not want:

Prose. Plays. Art work.

Nature poetry, animal/pet poetry, religious poetry, love poetry unless they have some correlation to one of the genres we publish. We get a fair amount of the type of poetry completely unrelated to speculative poetry, some of it is good, most of it bad, but none of it accepted.

An Organization of interest:

Science Fiction Poetry Association, now in its 25th year. Send $18 to John Nichols, 6075 Bellevue Dr, North Olmsted, OH, 44070. The

SFPA publishes Star*Line, a newsletter, six times a year and the association administers the Rhysling Award for best science fiction poems of the year. You also receive the Rhysling Anthology, which publishes the nominated poems, with your membership.

Categories: Fantasy—Horror—Literature—Poetry—Science—Science Fiction

CONTACT: Roger Dutcher, Editor
Material: All
PO Box 564
Beloit WI 53512

Magical Blend

Thank you for your interest in *Magical Blend* magazine. We are always interested in reviewing focused, well-written nonfiction articles and interviews. The best way of assessing our style is to look at copies of our magazines, which are available in most major bookstores and on the internet at www.magicalblend.com. Our Statement of Purpose, located in the beginning each issue, is a good places to start. You might also examine *A Magical Universe: The Best of Magical Blend Magazine* (Swan Raven, 1997) and *Solstice Shift: Magical Blend's Synergistic Guide to the Coming Age* (Hampton Roads, 1997) for samples of the kind of writing we publish in *Magical Blend*.

We do not respond to query letters, and we only consider final products.

We prefer that you submit your article by email. If you do submit a hard copy, please include a self-addressed, stamped envelope or email address for our reply. Allow up to six months for a response. We don't send back submissions, so do not send us your only copy. We no longer publish poetry or fiction. Writing in the form of a sermon is discouraged.

Submissions should not have already appeared in other publications or on the web.

Magical Blend is the leading magazine for metaphysics, cultural trends, indigenous spirituality, and more. Now in its third decade, Magical Blend tracks the changes in society, always holding true to the vision that, together, we can co-create the best possible reality for our world and ourselves. Our readers are primarily interested in personal and planetary growth and change, with an emphasis on spiritual and social subjects that are well researched. It is not news to our readers that alternatives to the Western medical paradigm or to conventional consciousness exist. They want innovative techniques for living life more fully, articles that show where magic, miraculous healing, and esoteric philosophy meet Main Street, and information that sheds light on the process of global and personal transformation. They are curious about alternative technologies, health, the environment, and the significance of the internet. Their musical tastes range from inspirational to world beat to fusion jazz. Light-hearted pieces with a point to make about the human condition are welcome.

FORMAT: Feature articles range in length from 1000 2000 words. E-mailed

versions are preferred (in Rich Text Format or text-only format, or in MSWord 98 or earlier), though hard copies can be mailed to Magical Blend, PO Box 600, Chico, CA 95927-0600. E-mail us at editor@magicalblend.com. Work that has been edited for length and clarity is more likely to be considered. Payment is considered strictly on an individual basis.

Artwork for our Creativity section or to accompany articles may be submitted digitally or on slides or color prints. Do not send us originals! SOME ARTICLE IDEAS *Magical Blend* MAGAZINE CONSIDERS:

• Sacred Travel
• Health & Alternative Healing
• Music
• Better Tomorrow
• Personal Transformation
• UFOs/Paranormal
• How-To
• Sexuality & Intimacy
• Celebrities
• Women's Empowerment
• Men s Empowerment
• Traditional Spirituality
• Notes & Quotes
• Money, Work, & Technology
• Culturally Diverse Spirituality Children s Spirituality
• Nature & Spirit
• New Ideas & Innovations
• Animals as Spiritual Teachers
• Humor
• Ancient Mysteries
• Practical Spirituality
• Astrology/Astronomy/The Stars
• Environmentalism/ Gaian Spirituality
• Fairies
• Conscious Death & Dying
• Divination
• Love
• Mythology/Archetypal Tales

We look forward to reading submissions that show your passion!

Categories: Nonfiction—Alternate Lifestyles—Animals—Book Reviews—Conservation—Culture—Diet/Nutrition—Ecology—Environment—Feminism—Health—Inspirational—Internet—Interview—Lifestyle—Men's Issues—Multicultural Music—Native Americans —New Age—Outdoors—Paranormal—Psychology—Relationships—Religion—Science—Self Help—Sexuality—Society—Spiritual—Travel—Women's Issues

CONTACT: Susan Dobra, Editorial Director
Material: All
PO Box 600
Chico, CA 95927-0600
E-mail: editor@magicalblend.com
Website: www.magicalblend.com

The Maine Organic Farmer & Gardener

The Maine Organic Farmer & Gardener is the newspaper of The Maine Organic Farmers and Gardeners Association (MOFGA). It is published four times a year (March-May, June-August, September-November, December-February) and accepts about three articles from freelancers per issue.

Some areas of concentration are:
• Rural skills and rural development
• Livestock care and management
• Farming, gardening and forestry practices and techniques
• Agricultural and biological research (soil-plant relationships, biochemical interactions...)
• Profiles of individual plants (edible and ornamental) and pests
• Agricultural economics, politics, and issues--international, national, regional, community
• Agricultural agencies, organizations and groups; influential individuals within agriculture
• Agricultural resources, their efficient use and ecological management
• Tools, equipment and machinery for small, diversified or organic farming and gardening

- Energy use, production and conservation
- Farmers and gardeners, preferably organic, with interesting farms, gardens, viewpoints or techniques. Also, first-person farming and gardening experiences
- Businesses related to agriculture, food or natural resources
- Agricultural marketing
- Environmental issues
- Nutrition

Sample copies of The MOF&G are available for $2 each from the MOFGA office at PO Box 170, Unity ME 04988; Phone (207) 568-4142; Fax (207) 568-4141; email: mofga@mofga.org. Some articles from our paper are on our website, www.mofga.org, as well. Unsolicited manuscripts are welcome when accompanied by SASE or sent by email. Queries are also welcome.

Accompanying photos and/or illustrations are a plus.

We pay about $20 to $200 for articles, depending on length (250 to 2500 words, usually) and quality. Payment is on publication. We buy first or one-time rights. We do not pay a kill fee. Glossy b&w photos earn $10. Deadlines for final drafts of articles are January 15, April 15, July 15 and October 15 for the respective issues.

We look forward to working with you on educational and entertaining, ecologically-oriented articles that will help people enjoy farming, gardening and healthful eating.

Categories: Nonfiction—Agriculture—Alternate Life-style—Animals—Associations—Book Reviews—Conservation—Consumer—Cooking—Culture—Diet/Nutrition—Ecology—Food/Drink—Gardening—Health—Hobbies—Lifestyle—Regional—Rural America—Organic Foods

CONTACT: Jean English, Editor
Material: All
Maine Organic Farmers & Gardeners Association
662 Slab City Rd.
Lincolnville ME 04849
E-mail: jenglish@midcoast.com

Mama's Little Helper Newsletter

Our Focus: Our primary goal is to support and assist parents and teachers of ADD/ADHD children with guidance, concrete information, tried and tested tips and medical information. Topics include (but are not limited to:) Ritalin (positive and negative), diet, positive discipline, alternative discipline, parental stress, childhood stress, mental focus, genius information alternatives to standard medication, tips for those outside of the family, social stigmas, adult ADD/ADHD, resources, peers, schooling, restaurants, vacationing, and any accurate information or personal stories relating to this disorder.

Submissions: We need articles, interviews, book reviews, stories, poetry, artwork, black and white photos, my stories, self-help and how-to articles, humorous pieces and other interesting works. Stories from children are especially appreciated.

Lead articles should be 800-2000 words and all other pieces should be under 1500 words. The shorter the better. We love how-to articles and interviews of authors and doctors. In desperate need for medical updates. ALWAYS INCLUDE A WORD COUNT! If mailing in the submission, include a SASE or your material will not be answered or returned. Include research citations.

We only ask for one-time rights and will accept reprints if you write verifying where the piece was published and what rights they purchased. If your work is published in the print newsletter, you will receive contributor copies as payment. At this time we cannot pay for print or web work.

The newsletter does accept advertising. Write to the below address for advertising information.

Categories: Nonfiction—Arts—Book Reviews—Children—Education—Interview—Parenting—Poetry

CONTACT: Terri J. Andrews, Editor
Material: All
PO Box 1127
Athens OH 45701-1127
Phone: 614-664-3030
E-mail: tuqbutfy@hotmail.com
Website: fly.to/turquoisebutterfly

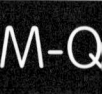

Manoa
A Pacific Journal of International Writing

What We Are Looking For

Fiction, poetry, essays, and interviews need not be related to Asia, the Pacific, or Hawaii'i, nor be by writers from the region. We are not interested in genre or formalist writing for its own sake, or Pacific exotica and picturesque impressions of the region.

Translations are usually commissioned by a guest editor, who is responsible for the portion of the issue featuring writings from a country or region of Asia or the Pacific. The rest of the issue is usually reserved for North American writing. We may occasionally run translations other than those selected by the guest editor, but you might want to query us first.

Submissions

We do not have specific length, subject-matter, or style requirements. We do prefer to see five or six poems at a time, depending upon the length. Like most literary magazines, we suggest reading a copy of the magazine to get an idea of what we like to publish. To order a sample copy, please visit our ordering page.

Please also note that we do not accept submissions by e-mail.

MANOA is published twice a year, summer and winter, and accepts submissions throughout the year. Please include a self-addressed, stamped envelope with each submission for the return of the submission and/or our reply. Submissions should be originals or good photocopies; handwritten manuscripts, dot-matrix printouts, and originals typed on onion-skin sheets are not acceptable. Please allow about four weeks for reply on poetry manuscripts, essays, and reviews, and about six months for reply on fiction manuscripts.

Reviews

Reviews are on recent books in the arts, humanities, or natural sciences; usually, these books are related to Asia, the Pacific, or Hawaii, or are published in these places. Separate guidelines are available for reviews.

Questions

If you have further questions, we'll be glad to answer them. Just drop us a note. We try to reply promptly.

July 2002

Categories: Nonfiction—Asian-American—History—Literature—Multicultural—Nature—Poetry—Short Stories—

CONTACT: Submissions Editor
Material: All
English Dept. University of Hawaii
Honolulu HI 96822
Phone: 808-956-3070
Fax: 808-956-3083
E-mail: mjournal-l@hawaii.edu
Website:www.hawaii.edu/mjournal

> **Remember:** Editors change jobs and publishers change addresses. It is wise to invest in a phone call for the current information before submitting.

MARINE CORPS GAZETTE

Marine Corps Gazette:
The Professional Journal of U.S. Marines Since 1916

Our basic policy is to fulfill the stated purpose of the *Marine Corps Gazette* by providing a forum for open discussion and a free exchange of ideas relating to the U.S. Marine Corps and military capabilities.

The Board of Governors of the Marine Corps Association has given authority to approve manuscripts for publication to the editorial board and editor. Editorial board members are listed on the Gazette's masthead in each issue. The board, which normally meets once a month, represents a cross section of Marines by professional interest, experience, age, rank, and gender. The board reads and votes on each manuscript submitted as a feature article. A simple majority rules in its decisions. Other material submitted for publication is accepted or rejected based on the assessment of the editor. The *Gazette* welcomes material in the following categories:

• **Commentary on Published Material:** Submit promptly. Comments normally appear as letters (see below) 3 months after published material. Be brief.

• **Feature Articles:** Normally 2,500 to 5,000 words, dealing with topics of major significance. Ideas must be backed up by hard facts. Evidence must be presented to support logical conclusions. In the case of articles that criticize, constructive suggestions are sought. Footnotes are not necessary, but a list of any source materials used is helpful.

• **Ideas and Issues:** Short articles, normally 500 to 2,000 words. This section can include the full gamut of professional topics so long as treatment of the subject is brief and concise.

• **Letters:** Limit to 300 words or less and double-spaced. As in most magazines, letters to the editor are an important clue as to how well or poorly ideas are being received. Letters are an excellent way to correct factual mistakes, reinforce ideas, outline opposing points of view, identify problems, and suggest factors or important considerations that have been overlooked in previous Gazette articles. The best letters are sharply focused on one or two specific points.

• **Book Reviews:** Prefer 300 to 750 words. It is a good idea to check with the editor in advance to determine if a review is desired. Please be sure to include the book's author, publisher (including city), year of publication, number of pages, and cost of the book.

The best advice is to write the way you talk. Organize your thoughts. Cut out excess words. Short is better than long. Submissions should include one copy of the manuscript and, if possible, a disk in ASCII Text format and author's name clearly indicated. All electronic correspondence can be sent to our Internet address. Any queries may be directed to the editorial staff by calling 800-336-0291, extension 344.

Note: Honorariums are no longer paid for articles. Exceptions are made for enlisted personnel on active duty and in some cases for students and faculty at designated military schools. Consult editor for details.

Categories: Military

CONTACT: Col. Jack Glasgow, USMC (Ret.), Editor
Material: All
PO Box 1775
Quantico VA 22134
Phone: 800-366-0291
Fax: 703-630-9147
E-mail: gazette@mca-marines.org

Marlin
The International Sports Fishing Magazine

1. *Marlin* accepts freelance-written articles on a query basis for both features and departments. Please send written queries for any articles you may have for *Marlin* with your name, address, phone number, social security number and an SASE. Queries should be concise and pertain to offshore fishing, destinations, personalities and related topics only. For detailed information regarding *Marlin*'s scope, direction and editorial needs, call editor David Ritchie at (407) 628-4802.

2. All features will be edited as necessary, usually to a length of 1,500 to 2,500 words. If an assigned article is unacceptable as submitted, the author may be given one opportunity at a rewrite. If an article is accepted by the editor, but is not used for reasons out of the author's control, a one-third kill fee will be paid to author.

3. *Marlin* gladly accepts "over the transom" submissions, but accepts no responsibility for the return of such materials. In all cases, though, the editors will attempt to respond to such materials in a timely fashion.

4. Very often, one of the key determining factors in our decision-making process regarding submitted queries and manuscripts is the amount and quality of available photography on the subject in question. See the Photographer's Guidelines in the following section for more information on this subject.

5. One of the easiest ways to begin publishing your material in *Marlin* is by contributing to the smaller departments:

Send short news items which directly relate to offshore fishing, fishery regulations, the boating industry or other related topics to the attention of "Blue Water Currents." Keep the items short and to the point, and provide photography or illustration support when possible.

The "Tips & Techniques" section is the place for you to submit short briefs on offshore fishing techniques, tackle innovations, boat handling advice, etc. Keep the items under 250 words, and provide photo or illustration support.

"Lines In" is *Marlin*'s section for tournament reports. Call editor David Ritchie at (407) 628-4802 to discuss possible event coverage. Keep "over the transom" reports short, make sure all names and boats are spelled correctly, detail the "Keys to Victory" that led to the winning catch, and provide a photo of the winners when possible. No hanging fish photos, please.

PHOTOGRAPHER'S GUIDELINES & POLICIES

Marlin continues to emphasize the finest saltwater fishing photography to be found in any magazine. Most of that comes from freelance professionals. *Marlin* provides bona fide international exposure for photographers' best work.

RETURN POLICY: It remains our fundamental goal to review and send out images not selected within a few days of receipt. We do NOT ordinarily hold photos at all unless we have a projected possible use. A tracking sheet will be included with images returned showing which slides are being kept and for what purpose.

SHIPPING: If we call and request photography quickly, we'll reimburse for shipping. Otherwise, the photographer pays to ship. We'll take care of returns, usually via Certified Mail unless otherwise specified.

OVER-THE-TRANSOM SUBMISSIONS: When in doubt, ship it out. We're always happy to review images, whether solicited or unsolicited (and since we won't hold those for which we see no specific, possible use, there's little to lose and much to gain).

WHAT TO SEND

FILM TYPE: We prefer Velvia 50 or equivalent for non-action shots in bright light; High shutter speeds for fast moving fish (1/1000+); Bracket where possible and try for both horizontals and verticals; Compose to keep fish main focus of most shots and to avoid extraneous objects in frame (also avoid clothing with nasty/racist/sexist inferences).

DUPES OR ORIGINALS?: We run originals, not dupes. You may send in duplicate slides for review purposes, but only if the originals are available. Also, there is always a better chance of selection for an original slide simply because it offers better definition and color than subsequent generations.

SUGGESTIONS

DON'T SEND US FUZZY SHOTS!!!

Instead, give us photos that are, by any measure, "tack sharp." Every day I see otherwise great shots precluded from use by being too "soft." There's just not much point in sending any images that are not crystal clear.

AVOID INANIMATE "GRIN & GRAB" SHOTS.

Send us images of people animated as they hold fresh (preferably lively) but not bloody fish. Counteract the dreaded Zombie Stare Syndrome. Have subject interacting with someone else if available. (Have 'em hold fish together and look at/talk to each other—while forgetting the camera even exists—anything to get subject loose, happy, natural.) If subject alone, suggest interaction with the fish—hook removal, lifting from deck, even admiring it (looking at it, not you). Avoid dead fish in such photos—take 'em quick when the fish is in the boat and lively, before it's clubbed or languishes to a pale, glassy-eyed state of rigor mortis.

Finally, do keep the angler's tackle in the shot!

AVOID KILL SHOTS OF BILLFISH AND BLUEWATER SHARKS!

Send us exciting, in-focus shots of leaping, tailwalking, greyhounding fish; of fish being wired for tagging or being released or admired at the boat. Skip the traditional dead stuff— hanging at the dock, draped over the transom, bleeding on deck—or anything with a gaff in it.

"Kill" shots of other, food fish okay if—you should pardon the expression—tasteful. Sport, not carnage, is what we're after.

AVOID SHADOW-DARKENED SHOTS.

Give us shots liberal with use of fill flash under high sun or backlit conditions.

DON'T LIMIT SUBMISSIONS TO FISH/FISHING ALONE.

Have an eye to all things related to fish/fishing, viz: rigging, technique (gear/action), baits, lures, equipment, diving birds, weather, water (color/rips/ weedlines), feeding schools, schools of baitfish (and catching them), other boats fishing/running, Bimini starts, etc, etc. Also, don't hesitate to photograph any/all near shore/offshore species, gamefish or others, including those that are unusual.

COVERS

Marlin covers emphasize fish, boats and fish action—fish leaping, underwater, at the surface, on a line out of the water and so on. That may include anglers interacting with fish—fighting fish, releasing or tagging fish and the like. Other offshore pelagic gamefish may occasionally qualify. Remember: 35 mm focus must be laser-sharp to retain its quality when enlarged 1,200 percent. The dominant image must fill most of the frame to minimize blow-up necessary (e.g. a jumping fish that's a dot on the horizon won't make it).

WHEN PACKAGING SUBMISSIONS

1. Make sure that every image has—at the very least—your name on it. Otherwise, return can't be guaranteed. Words of description (area, species, etc.) written right on the slide can be of great help.

2. If sending slides/other images in one package targeting two or more articles, please places slides in a separate sheet (or sheets) for each different article and mark the sheet accordingly.

3. If brief captions are written on each image, a page with extended captions is helpful; if no information is written on images, a sheet of captions is essential.

4. Make sure your social security number is included somewhere, unless you are certain we have it (or unless you have no interest in remuneration).

5. Payment will be issued to the first name on the slide (stock agency or photographer) unless other payment arrangements are specified.

COMMUNICATIONS

Don't hesitate to call Editor David Ritchie or Managing Editor

Scott Leon at (407) 628-4802 anytime you have any general or specific questions about photo needs, submissions or payment.

Categories: Nonfiction—Adventure—Boating—Conservation—Consumer—Fishing—Outdoors—Recreation—Sports/Recreation

CONTACT: David Ritchie, Editor
Material: All
PO Box 2456
Winter Park FL 32790
Phone: 407-628-4802
Fax: 407-628-7061
E-mail: editor@worldpub.net
Website: www.marlinmag.com

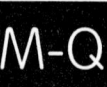

Marriage Partnership

Description & Philosophy

Marriage Partnership seeks to provide realistic, challenging, and practical insights into healthy Christian marriage. We offer hope and help to our readers through practical how-to pieces; interviews with experts; humorous articles; true-life, dramatic stories of couples dealing with major life challenges; thoughtful essays; and couple profiles.

We begin with the premise that marriage is a life-enhancing gift from God. We are solidly rooted in biblical truth, but our approach to sharing that truth is somewhat different from other Christian magazines. The principles we communicate—lifelong commitment, sexual fidelity, mutual sacrificial love, mutual respect—are taken from Scripture, but we use everyday language to communicate those principles. We recognize that there are a number of legitimate models for successful and God-honoring marriage; therefore, we avoid dogmatic, legalistic advice. While we want to show how God's grace and redemptive power can work in our readers' lives, we also recognize that staying married in today's culture can be a difficult and complex challenge. The answers aren't always easy—but God sees us through.

Our Readers

We want our readers to "see" themselves in the articles we publish. The majority of our readers are middle-class, college-educated Christians in their 20s, 30s, and 40s (median age 36). They are busy raising kids and juggling jobs (about two-thirds of our women readers work outside the home). Our readers are concerned with finances, communication, church involvement, time management, parenting, sex, conflict management–everyday, nitty-gritty issues. Rather than presenting an idealized portrait of marriage and family, we work hard to present a realistic image of life that makes our readers say, "Yes, that's how it is in my house!"

Our Writers

We do not accept unsolicited manuscripts or simultaneous submissions. Rather, we welcome well-thought-out and well-written query letters that include: a thorough summary of the article, the purpose of the piece and its value to readers, the author's qualifications to write the piece, suggested length and deadline, and a stamped, self-addressed envelope.

Writers who can communicate with freshness, clarity, and insight will receive serious consideration. We are looking for writers who are willing to candidly speak about their own marriages. We strongly urge writers who are interested in contributing to *Marriage Partnership* to read several issues to become thoroughly acquainted with our tone and slant.

With some exceptions, we pay on acceptance of completed articles and buy first rights. All submissions are received on speculation. An accepted query does not guarantee purchase of the manuscript. Editors reserve the right to reject any manuscript at any stage. We try to respond to queries and manuscripts within 8 to 10 weeks. Manuscripts should be typed double-spaced. Send queries and other editorial correspondence to the address below.

Categories: Nonfiction—Christian Interests—Consumer—Family—Lifestyle—Marriage—Relationships

CONTACT: Ginger Kolbaba, Managing Editor
Material: All
Christianity Today International
465 Gundersen Dr.
Carol Stream IL 60188
Phone: 630-260-6200
Fax: 630-260-0114
E-mail: mp@marriagepartnership.com
Website: www.christianitytoday.com

Martha Stewart Living

Does not accept unsolicited submissions.

The Massachusetts Review
University of Massachusetts

Thank you for your interest in *The Massachusetts Review*, a quarterly of literature, the arts and public affairs. We represent no stylistic or ideological coterie. The Editors seek a balance between established writers and artists and promising new ones, and material of variety and vitality relevant to the intellectual and aesthetic life of our time. We aspire to have a broad appeal; our commitment, in part regional, is not provincial.

"Inspired pages are not written to fill a space, but for inevitable utterance; and to such our journal is freely and solicitously open." (Emerson)

ARTICLES & ESSAYS of breadth and depth are considered, as well as discussions of leading writers; of art, music, and drama; analyses of trends in literature, science, philosophy, and public affairs. No reviews of single books.

FICTION: We consider one short story per submission, usually up to 25-30 pp.

POETRY: A poetry submission may consist of up to six poems. There are no restrictions in terms of length, but generally our poems are less than 100 lines. Please write your name on every page.

Fiction and Poetry manuscripts should be submitted separately. No mixed submissions, please.

MR no longer considers plays for publication.

In addition:

Please include your name and address on first page of manuscript.

Please do not send mss. from June 1st through October 1st.

Please do read a copy of MR before sending work.

The Massachusetts Review is a nonprofit journal and it is impossible for us to acknowledge receipt of the many manuscripts we receive or to honor requests made for sample copies. You may order an issue for $9.00 (incl. Postage) or begin a subscription. Subscription rates:

Individuals, USA: 1 year, $22; 2 years, $34; 3 years, $52
Outside USA: 1 year, $30
Libraries: 1 year, $30
Categories: Fiction—Poetry—Essays/Articles—Memoirs

CONTACT: Ellen Watson
Material: Poetry
CONTACT: Editors
Material: Fiction
South College, University of Massachusetts
Amherst MA 01003
Phone: 413-545-2689

Massage & Bodywork
Nuturing Body Mind & Spirit

Massage & Bodywork is a specialty magazine, published six times per year, for professional practitioners of massage, bodywork, somatic and esthetic therapies, as well as members of the general public with an interest in the field. Unsolicited submissions are accepted. We suggest that potential writers study recent issues before sending queries or manuscripts. All manuscripts should be submitted (single space) on a 3.5 inch diskette (ASCII or text format), and typed, double spaced, on standard white paper. Photocopy submissions are acceptable.

If accepted, *Massage & Bodywork* negotiates for North American rights and electronic rights. The editor reserves the right to edit or rewrite any article in order to make it suit the theme, style or space limitations of a specific issue. Major alterations will be discussed with the author. It is always acceptable, even beneficial, to include photographs and/or illustrations with the submission. Authors are compensated on a case-by-case basis once submission is accepted.

Modality/Technique Articles

Massage & Bodywork looks for interesting, tightly-focused stories concerning a particular modality or technique of massage, bodywork, somatic and esthetic therapies. The editorial staff welcomes the opportunity to review manuscripts which may be relevant to the field of massage, bodywork and esthetic practices, in addition to more general pieces pertaining to complementary and alternative medicine. This would include the widely varying modalities of massage and bodywork (from Swedish massage to Polarity therapy), specific technique articles and ancillary therapies, including such topics as biomagnetics, aromatherapy and facial rejuvenation. Reference lists relating to technical articles should include the author, title, publisher and publication date of works cited. Word count: 1,500 to 4,000 words; longer articles negotiable.

Technical/Research Articles

For an audience eager to explore the scientific aspects of massage and bodywork, writers are encouraged to submit technical articles relating to the field. Pieces specific to anatomy, medical conditions and contraindications are welcome. Research-related articles and accounts of formal and informal case studies are of interest. Word count: 1,500-4,000 words; longer articles negotiable.

Professional/Practice-building

Other articles of interest to *Massage & Bodywork* magazine include those relating to legalities/legislation, business or practice-building, success stories, politics of the profession, health care and insurance. Word count: 500-2,000 words; longer articles negotiable.

Travel Related to the Profession

Accounts of travel to places that help expand knowledge of techniques particular to certain areas of the world are welcome. Exploration of other cultures' views of the healing arts, historical considerations and similarities are areas of interest. Word count: 800 to 1,200 words.

Human Interest

Articles about people who have had an impact on the fields of massage, bodywork, somatic therapies or esthetics are welcome. The story should relate the person's connection with the particular field, why their contribution is important, how their students or clients have been affected by their work, etc. Photographs of the person in action or posed photos should accompany the article. Personal accounts, successful community interactions, volunteer events, etc. are also of interest. Word count: 800 to 1,200 words.

Columns

All *Massage & Bodywork* columns are assigned. If you have a column idea and wish to discuss it with us, explain your proposal, write a sample column and submit for consideration.

Fiction

We do not accept fiction.

Note: If your topic is not mentioned here, but you feel it would be of valid interest to the readers, please feel free to discuss it with our editor.

Photo Requirements

Features should be accompanied by color transparencies, high quality prints or slides, or high resolution electronic images. All photos should be accompanied by a caption sheet identifying each subject.

Artwork supplied by someone other than the manuscript author should be clearly identified for credit, along with necessary releases. All photos, slides and illustrations will be returned after publication. Please include a self-addressed, stamped envelope for this purpose, and allow 45 days after the mail date of the publication for return.

Lead Time

Because this is a bimonthly publication, it may be a matter of months before your article appears in print, although the decision as to whether or not the article will be used is generally made promptly. We assume no responsibility for material submitted, but every effort will be made to return original artwork. Please enclose a self-addressed stamped envelope if return of items is requested.

Liability

Neither *Massage & Bodywork* nor Associated Bodywork & Massage Professionals assumes any responsibility for unsolicited material.

Demographics

80% of our readers are female, average age of 42, with an average household annual income of $56,833.

Categories: Nonfiction—Health

CONTACT: Leslie A. Young, Editor
Material: All
Associated Bodywork & Massage Professionsals
1271 Sugarbush Drive
Evergreen CO 80439-9766
Phone: 800-458-2267
E-mail: leslie@abmp.com
Website: www.messageandbodywork.com

Massage Magazine

About Massage Magazine

Massage Magazine is an internationally circulated trade publication for massage therapists and allied health professionals. We have been in publication since 1985, have a readership of about 80,000, and publish six times per year.

We strive for comprehensive coverage of the art and science of massage therapy and related healing arts, with the goal of supporting our readers as they work to promote the benefits of healing touch.

About our readers

Most of our readers are professional therapists who have been in practice for several years. About 80 percent are self-employed; 95 percent live in the United States.

The vast majority of our readers have completed formal training in massage therapy. The techniques they practice include Swedish, sports and geriatric massage, energy work and myotherapy, among many others. Our readers work in settings ranging from home-based studios to spas to integrated clinics.

What we're looking for

Our readers seek practical information on how to help their clients, improve their techniques and/or make their businesses more successful, as well as feature articles that place massage therapy in a positive or inspiring light.

Since most of our readers are professional therapists, we do not publish articles on topics like "how massage can help you relax."

Before preparing a query or manuscript for us, read at least one issue of the magazine, as this is the best way to get a feel for the topics we cover and the tone they're presented in.

Types of articles

FEATURES. We publish six to 12 full-length feature articles per year. Topic examples: the use of massage in a particular setting (such as corporate or hospital); projects that provide massage therapy to disadvantaged populations; accounts of how massage helped a person overcome or deal with a physical condition; descriptions of types of massage used in non-Western cultures; and trends of national significance, such as the incorporation of complementary techniques into the mainstream medical system, among others. Submissions should be 1,500 to 3,000 words.

BUSINESS. We publish at least six articles per year that describe, in detail, to grow or improve a massage therapy practice. Topic examples: increasing or retaining clientele; setting goals; marketing techniques; new business ventures; and money management, among others. General business-related articles written for small-business owners will be considered. Submissions should be 500 to 3,000 words, depending on the complexity of the topic.

NEWS BRIEFS. We publish up to 15 news articles per issue. These articles must display concise, fact-checked reporting and direct or paraphrased quotes, and must focus on current events or trends in the massage and/or spa industries. News briefs can be on anything newsworthy, particularly those situations that impact therapists on a national or North American level. Submissions should be 200 to 800 words.

IMPRINTS. We publish one article per issue that details an experience which has left an imprint on the client and/or therapist: a new realization, a reason for entering the health care field, a poignant or humorous remembrance, etc. Submissions should be 500 to 1,000 words.

PROFILES. We publish two to six profiles per year. Profiles must highlight why a particular therapist's story is compelling; describe a particular clientele; or serve as an example of how the therapist solved an ongoing business- or clientele-related situation. Submissions should be 1,000 to 2,500 words.

MIND/BODY/SPIRIT. We publish two to six articles per year on the topic of the relationship(s) between mind, body and spirit, with a specific focus on how massage therapy impacts clients' emotions or spirituality, and how therapists can address or respond to this during sessions. Submissions should be 1,000 to 3,000 words.

SELF-CARE. We publish three to six articles per year which describe techniques that help the therapist care for her/himself. Topics range from exercises to relieve repetitive stress injuries, to ways to relax. How-to articles must be accompanied by photos or illustrations. Submissions should be 1,000 to 3,000 words.

GUEST EDITORIALS. We publish one guest editorial per issue. These may be written by either a practicing therapist or student of massage/bodywork who is passionate about a particular issue facing the field, who has a challenge to present to massage and bodywork practitioners, or who has a unique perspective on the role of massage/bodywork in the greater society. Guest editorials must be accompanied by a professional-quality head shot of the author. Submissions should be 750 to 1,500 words.

TECHNIQUE, GENERAL DESCRIPTION. We publish three to six articles per year that describe a particular, well-established system of bodywork. These articles must be written to a specific guideline, available by contacting our editorial department.

TECHNIQUE, HOW-TO. We publish three to six articles per year that tell readers, through both text and photos/illustrations, how to perform a massage technique or stroke. These articles must be written by a professional therapist with several years' proven experience in the application of the technique, and must be written to a specific guideline, available by contacting our editorial department.

Categories: Nonfiction—Health—Self Help

CONTACT: Karen Menehan, Editor
Material: Queries and manuscripts

200 Seventh Ave., #240
Santa Cruz CA 95062
Phone: 831-477-1176
Fax: 408-477-2918
E-mail: edit@massagemag.com
Website: www.massagemag.com

Mature Living
Christian Magazine For Senior Adults

Mature Living, a Christian-oriented, leisure-reading magazine designed for senior adults, has a lead time of approximately 10 months. We are interested in unique, creative manuscripts that are characterized by human interest, Christian warmth, and humor. Manuscripts should be written with simplicity and clarity. Writers should provide documentation for quotations, titles, facts, figures, or other information taken from other sources for verification by the *Mature Living* staff.

Mature Living **only purchases all rights.** Writers who want to continue to sell a manuscript after publication in *Mature Living* can receive a non-exclusive perpetual license to publish the work in whole or in part, allow others to publish the work in whole or in part, and receive payment from other publishers. However, *Mature Living* retains all rights to the manuscript in these situations.

Mature Living claims the editorial privilege of editing, abridging, and condensing purchased manuscripts. Purchase of a manuscript is an intent, but not necessarily a commitment, to publish. The magazine staff further retains the right to illustrate manuscripts as deemed appropriate.

QUERIES
Do not send queries (letters, e-mail, or telephone).
GUIDELINES FOR SUBMITTING MANUSCRIPTS
• With the exception of manuscripts for "Grandparents' Brag Board" and "Cracker Barrel," all manuscripts must be accompanied by a self-addressed, stamped envelope (not just stamps). Allow at least 2 months for a reply from the editors. Writers who submit manuscripts without a self-addressed, stamped envelope will not receive a response. NOTE: Manuscripts for "Grandparents' Brag Board" and "Cracker Barrel" features are not returned.

• Although *Mature Living* does not accept responsibility for photos and slides that may get lost or damaged in the publication process, all reasonable care will be taken to ensure their safe return. If pictures are old and rare, please have them professionally reproduced locally and send the reproductions with the manuscript.

• Do not submit previously published manuscripts or simultaneous submissions.

• Keep a duplicate copy of the manuscript for your files.

• Do not write or call to inquire about which issue an accepted manuscript will appear. Manuscripts originally intended for one issue might be moved to another issue or, on rare occasions, discarded.

• Send manuscripts via postal mail to the address listed here. Do not send articles via

e-mail. If your article is accepted for publication, you may be contacted to then send an electronic copy via e-mail.

Mature Living
One LifeWay Plaza
Nashville, TN 37234-0175
SPECIFICATIONS
Manuscripts should be typed and double-spaced. Include word count, your name, address, telephone number, e-mail address, and Social Security number on the top of the first page and your name on every page. If you use a pen name, please indicate that clearly on the first page. Correct all spelling, document unique material, and conform to preferred lengths.
TYPES OF ARTICLES DESIRED
General: Articles may deal with a variety of subjects related to senior adult life, such as current issues, problems, and life adjustments; humor; or seasonal emphases. Preferred length is 600 to 1,000 words.

Nostalgia: Articles of 600 to 1,000 words may be about personal memories or historically based.

Travel: Articles should have general appeal to senior adults that includes descriptive information. Preferred length is 800 to 1,200 words with 4 to 8 color slides or photographs.

Fiction: High-quality fiction, relating to senior adults, should have a strong story line, underscore a biblical truth, and provide enjoyable leisure reading. Preferred length is 800 to 1,200 words.

Cartoons: Cartoons should relate to senior adults and their interests.
DEPARTMENT FEATURES
Cracker Barrel: Each issue includes a page of brief, humorous, original quips and verses. Payment: $15 after publication.

Food: Recipes should be of special interest to senior adults. Include an introduction and 4 to 6 recipes. Payment: $50 after publication.

Game Page: Crossword or word-search puzzles and a variety of quizzes are used. Please include solution. Payment: $40 after publication.

Grandparents' Brag Board: Accounts of something said or done by your grandchild or great-grandchild (humorous or insightful) should be brief, accurate, and original. Payment: $15 after publication.

Inspirational: Each issue includes devotional articles (125 words or less each) and poetry (12 lines our less) for "Communing with God" section. Items should be Bible-based, insightful, unique, and slanted to senior adults. Payment: $25 after publication.

Over the Garden Fence: Informational articles of 300 to 350 words should relate to vegetable or flower gardening on a year-round basis. Payment: $40 after publication.

Poetry: We accept a limited amount of brief (12 lines or less), quality poetry that has a direct relationship to senior adults. Payment: $25 after publication.
PAYMENT
Except for Department Features (see above), the payment rate for all rights ranges from $75 to $105 per manuscript accepted. Exceptional quality may be rewarded above the base rate. Payments are made after publication. A Social Security number is required for all payments.

Payment of $25 for the use of each original photograph or slide is paid after publication. These will be returned after publication. Please include your name and address on the back of every photograph submitted.

Writers will receive, without cost, 3 copies of the issue in which their manuscripts are published. Extra copies can be purchased from LifeWay Church Resources Customer Service Center, One LifeWay Plaza, Nashville, TN 37234-0113; or call 1-800-458-2772.

Categories: Christian Interests—Lifestyle—Religion—Senior Citizen—Spiritual

CONTACT: Editorial
Material: All
One LifeWay Plaza
Nashville TN 37234-0175
Phone: 615-251-2000
Fax: 615-277-8272
E-mail: matureliving@lifeway.com (no submissions)

Mature Years

So You Want Your Work in *Mature Years*
Mature Years magazine is published by Abingdon Press, an imprint of the United Methodist Church. The audience comprises persons of retirement age and beyond (55 years plus), and the magazine's purpose is to help persons understand and use the resources of the Christian faith in dealing with specific opportunities and problems related to aging.

We publish quarterly with 112 pages, trim size 8.5 x 11 inches, full-color, 12 point New Century Schoolbook typeface. Pages are two-column. The publication is perfect bound. Circulation is approximately 70,000, and is entirely paid subscription. The magazine is mailed throughout the United States, and through the Protestant Church-owned Publishers Association, it is available in some military base chapels around the world.

Writers are not restricted to being older adults. Unsolicited manuscripts are welcomed.

Reader Description

Our readers like to see themselves in what they read. Writers should acknowledge the readers' maturity and use illustrations that reflect older adult lifestyles, which are varied. Some older adults are employed; some are retired. Some of our readers are active; some are not. Some are married while others are widowed or never married. Housing arrangements may be in their own homes, living with adult children, or in congregate housing of varied types. Most older adults are in good health, but many are ill. They have a variety of educational backgrounds, but writers should assume that they are intelligent and not treat them as forgetful, mindless individuals. Financial status is also greatly varied among our readers.

Mature Years magazine readers do not want to see only older adults in their stories, poems, and articles. They are fearful of being shut up in an "old age ghetto." Inter-generational pieces score great successes with our audience.

Guidelines for General Editorial Content

Quoted Material—You must include photocopies of any material quoted from other sources and give a complete citation.

Subheads—You may include subheads in your text. The editor may or may not use them. If there are multiple levels of subhead, make them plainly distinguishable.

When we review manuscripts we look for the following:

Appropriate Subjects—Popular articles address current issues in aging; including health and fitness, housing, financial conditions, social and emotional needs, security, family life, self-help, and so on. Articles should provide practical aids for older adults: what to do, how to, when to, where to. Especially important are opportunities for older adults to read about service, adventure, fulfillment, and fun. Items of entertainment, like hobbies and crafts, are also popular.

Positive Approach—Articles should be upbeat, picturing older adults who are enjoying living and finding fulfillment in this period of their lives. If articles are about the problems of living as an older adult, they should demonstrate the power of faith for difficult times and offer possible solutions and/or sympathy and comfort.

Active Subjects—Persons featured in articles should be active, creative, involved with their family, church, community, nation, and world. While many of our readers are inactive, they do not want to read about people sitting and doing nothing with their lives.

Varieties of Approaches—Articles can be serious or humorous. They may be based on memories or current experiences. Fiction may be for the purpose of pure entertainment, or stories may explore a social justice issue or concern of aging.

Christian Orientation—When appropriate, articles should demonstrate faith in God as a resource for life in all circumstances, both good and bad. Persons featured should be older adults with a vital lifestyle. For instance, when they travel it will be for educational purposes or to engage in ministry or service to others. Articles and stories should reflect the joy of living out one's Christian faith.

Absence of Stereotypes—Older adults should be freed from the stereotypes of age, gender, nationality, and race. Examples of aging stereotypes are frailty, memory loss, illness, sedentary lifestyle, being socially inflexible, and being unstylish. Be supportive of persons and groups rather than poking fun at them.

Guidelines for Cartoons and Photographs

Cartoons—Cartoons may either have a religious theme or relate to aging as outlined in the "Guidelines for General Editorial Content" above. While bringing some humor to older adult situations, cartoons should never trivialize circumstances and should never demean anyone or their circumstance.

Photographs—If photographs accompany articles, color prints or transparencies are required. If photos are historical, black and white prints or negatives are accepted. Photographs of recognizable people must be accompanied with model releases.

Unsolicited professional studio photos are reviewed and returned. If the quality of the work is acceptable, the studio will be added to the approved list for future assignments.

Be certain that captions are clearly matched with photographs to guarantee proper placement with the photographs.

Guidelines for Poetry

Poetry—Poems are limited to sixteen lines of up to fifty characters. Content should conform to the "Guidelines for General Editorial Content" detailed above. Free verse is allowed. When using rhymes and meter, make sure they are accurate. Seasonal poems are accepted according to the "Seasonal Acceptance Schedule" below. Accompanying photography and graphic designs are never accepted.

Guidelines for Departments

Daily Meditations and Bible Study—This department is a part of the Uniform Series of the National Council of Churches of the USA and is written by invitation only to professional Bible study writers.

Fragments of Life—This department uses short glimpses of everyday life (cuddling with grandchildren, a humorous moment at church, a sweet memory) to inspire and to illustrate the joys, sorrows, and poignant moments of living. It may or may not overtly mention God, but it never preaches. (250 to 600 words)

Going Places—Travel articles must:

a) feature some location or travel aspect particularly appropriate to older adults, such as special activities or facilities planned for the age group. Seniors hiking or snorkeling are examples. Tours for grandparents and grandchildren is another.

Or, b) reflect the predominantly Christian character of the magazine by taking our readers to Bible lands or on a pilgrimage, discussing the historic sites of Christian believers, or showing the countryside or towns of different Christian groups. Typical articles might feature cathedrals of Europe, monasteries or retreats in the United States, Amish communities, or Roman Christian catacombs. (1,000 to 1,500 words)

Health Hints—Health problems and fitness opportunities for older adults are found in this department. Description of a health problem and solutions for alleviating or eliminating conditions should be discussed. Other articles might tell about exercises and activities designed to help older adults keep fit. We never promote pharmaceutical companies or their products. Medicare and Medicaid are not acceptable subjects. (900 to 1,500 words)

Media Shelf—This department reviews books, audio recordings, and computer software of special interest to older adults. Review copies of these items are welcome, but articles are by invitation only.

Merry-Go-Round—This page features cartoons, jokes, and 4-6 line humorous verses. The subject of all these items must conform to the "Guidelines for General Editorial Content" and "Cartoons" printed above. We publish two cartoons in every issue.

Modern Revelations—Overtly religious and inspirational, this department deals with contemporary understanding of the Christian faith. While it is often an essay relating the Bible to modern life and quotes Scripture, it is not a Bible study. It may give advice for spiritual living as an older adult. (900 to 1,500 words)

Money Matters—All economic issues of importance to older adults are acceptable; including banking, investing, wise purchasing, savings instruments, consumer frauds and scams, cost of health care, and insurance. All articles must be written with a personal finance point of view. (1,200 to 1,800 words)

Puzzle Time—Many different forms of puzzles and quizzes are published; including cross words, word-finds, anagrams, and unique formats. Subjects must either have biblical or religious themes or have older adult interest such as great dance bands, grandparenting, or reminiscence. Puzzles and quizzes must be challenging.

Social Security Questions and Answers—This department is furnished by a regional office of the Social Security Administration.

Seasonal Acceptance Schedule

Mature Years magazine closes manuscript purchases for individual issues approximately one year before publication. We are looking for seasonal articles and poems in the following time frames:

Spring—December, January, February

Summer—March, April, May

Fall—June, July, August

Winter—September, October, November

Because *Mature Years* has such a long lead-time, we are not able to publish hard news or anything with specific upcoming dates. The exception to this rule is annual events.

Several departments (Going Places, Health Hints, Media Shelf, and Money Matters) have a news briefs sidebar with a four-month deadline. Information about upcoming events and products and services introduction is included.

Guidelines for Manuscript Preparation

Maximum Word Limit—Specific departmental lengths are printed above. For all other articles no more than 2,000 words are published.

Electronic Submission—Electronic submissions are preferred. They may be sent as a Word attachment to an e-mail or the text may simply be printed in the e-mail. All submissions must be accompanied by your name, address, telephone number, and social security number. We automatically decline submissions without this essential information.

Our e-mail address is matureyears@umpublishing.org.

Hard Copy Format—All manuscripts must be typed double-spaced on 8.5 by 11 inch white paper. Do not send computer disks. Hand written manuscripts will be automatically returned.

Hard Copy Submission—Send manuscripts printed with your name, address, telephone number, and social security number along with a required SASE to the address below.

Rights

Mature Years requests a variety of rights depending upon the material offered. Our most common request is for one-time North American serial rights. We do accept a limited number of Reprint Rights. For work-for-hire we require All Rights.

Payment Schedule

Payment is made upon acceptance of any text or cartoon. We pay 5 cents per word for articles and $1.00 per line of poetry. Verses and fillers used in the Merry-Go-Round department are paid a flat $5.00.

Payment for photos accompanying stories is $20.00 for each one inside publication. Payment for cover publication is negotiable. Payment for photos follows final selection during the design stage. Payment for professional photography to accompany articles is negotiable.

Miscellaneous

Response Time—Replies to unsolicited manuscript submissions come within eight weeks of receipt. We do not acknowledge receipt of manuscripts at the time they are received. Because of the tremendous volume of submissions, it is not possible to make comments in the replies.

Letters of Inquiry—Inquiries are permissible with a required SASE; responses come within two weeks of receipt of the proposal. Permission to submit an article does not guarantee publication.

Samples—Sample copies are available for $5.00 each including shipping and handling.

Columns—*Mature Years* magazine is not interested in adding new regular columns.

Categories: Fiction—Nonfiction—Christian Interests—Family—Health—Inspirational—Money & Finances—Poetry—Relationships—Religion—Senior Citizen—Short Stories—Spiritual—Travel

CONTACT: Marvin W. Cropsey, Editor
Material: All
201 Eighth Ave. S
Nashville TN 37202
Phone: 615-749-6292
Fax: 615-749-6512

MB Media

Please refer to *Magical Blend*, *Natural Beauty & Health*, and *Transitions magazine*s.

Meetings East
Meetings South
Meetings West

Please refer to Stamats Meetings Media.

The Melic Review

The *Melic Review* seeks poems, essays, and fiction of the highest quality. To get a better idea of what we mean, read C.E. Chaffin's essay "On Modulation."

With accept previously print-published material, but not previous net publications as yet. We discourage simultaneous submissions, as we take our work as editors seriously. All work should be sent in the body of the e-mail. Attachments will be accepted for formatting reasons, but only if accompanied by plain text versions in the body of the e-mail.

Submissions are always open, but the cut-off date for inclusion in a new issue is the tenth of the month preceding the issue. Thus, for our March 1 issue, submissions received after February 10 will be carried over for consideration in the next issue. Our response time is less than or equal to three months. If you haven't heard by then, please write us.

We prefer fiction under a thousand words and poetry under fifty lines but will make exception for longer works of exceptional merit. 5000 words is the absolute limit for fiction of exceptional merit, two hundred lines for poetry. Only one fiction piece of this length has made it into the magazine, and no poems of this length have yet been accepted. Please send no more than five poems or one prose piece per submission.

We do not pay contributors, nor are we a publishing house for chapbooks or books. We are simply a literary e-zine.

Copyrights revert to the authors upon publication. All work published is with the express consent and permission of the author, who may withdraw it at anytime before we go online with a new issue.

We also offer a one-on-one online tutorial in poetry taught by Dr. Chaffin, including an extensive syllabus. Cost is $250 and the course lasts six weeks. Please send a query if interested.

All submissions and queries should be e-mailed to melicreview@hotmail.com. We do not accept snail submissions.

Categories: Fiction—Poetry—Short Stories

CONTACT: C.E. Chaffin M.D.
Material: All
700 E. Ocean Blvd. #2504
Long Beach CA 90802
E-mail: melicreview@hotmail.com
Website: www.melicreview.com

Memory Makers
The First Source for Scrapbooking Ideas

Dear prospective writer,

Thank you for your interest in *Memory Makers*. As a short introduction to our editorial content, let us explain that in addition to feature articles we have several departments that appear in each issue. These departments, including Keeping It Safe and Scrapbooking 101, deal with topics that are of continued importance and interest to our scrapbooking audience. The following editorial guidelines are offered to help you as you develop story ideas for us.

Our Writers

We have in-house writers who are responsible for many different features and departments. However, we are looking for talented freelance writers who possess knowledge or new insights on scrapbooking. Material is aimed at scrapbookers of all levels and age groups.

Our Content

Editorial content for *Memory Makers* features is typically driven by actual scrapbook page ideas submitted by our readers. However, we also consider article queries covering related topics (Pages That Heal, Scrapbooking Around the World). Editorial is finalized six months in advance of newsstand date, so plan appropriately for timely or seasonal article topics. Our "voice" is conversational and friendly. We look for detail-oriented writing that captures people's personalities and experiences. When applicable, we prefer articles that include at least two expert sources.

Features

We typically run five features in each issue. The two longest are usually about 1,500 words in length and deal with a scrapbook theme (such as scrapbooking about yourself or everyday inspiration for pages) or technique (such as using vellum). Our inspirational feature (1,000-1,200 words) tells the personal story of how someone's life has been impacted by scrapbooking. It is often written in the first person, from the perspective of the person featured in the article. The two other features (about 800 words each) are designed to motivate readers to try a new technique, craft or product in their albums. Our craft features include a short introduction and step-by-step instructions. Strong instructional writing skills are necessary. Material for these articles is typically generated from reader-submitted ideas.

Keeping It Safe

This section covers all issues surrounding the safe preservation of your albums and photographs. It includes one topic per issue. Previously published articles include The Safety of Computer Inks, The Stability of Color Copies, The Safety of Crayons. (500-700 words)

Scrapbooking 101

Here, we offer how-to instructions and tips for the beginning scrapbooker as well as a basic review of techniques for the pro on various scrapbook-related topics. Previous articles include Design Basics: Creating Focal Point and Five Things Every Scrapbook Page Should Have. (about 800 words)

Photojournaling

This department gives readers new and useful ideas for improving their journaling techniques. Past articles have dealt with calendar-style journaling, creative ideas for adding journaling to finished pages and self-esteem journaling. (600-800 words)

Modern Memories

In this department, we address computer and modern technology issues as they relate to scrapbooking. Past issues have included articles on sharing pages via Internet and e-mail, using your computer for scrapbook layouts and choosing genealogy software. (600-800 words)

Ask *Memory Makers*

This department is written in question/answer-style, based on questions our readers send us. If you are writing an Ask *Memory Makers* article, we will assign you one to three questions to research and write the response. Let us know if you'd like to be considered for this section of the magazine. (600 words)

Our Deadlines

Deadlines for articles will be assigned when the editor initially contacts the writer about an article. Articles can be submitted by e-mail or Macintosh-formatted disk (using Microsoft Word or Quark Xpress) on or before the deadline that the writer has been given. Computer disks should be clearly marked with the author's name (and address if they want the disk returned), magazine department and article's title. Along with the finished article, please include information for verifying all sources used in the article. Freelancers are responsible for providing some means of verification for names, titles and other pertinent information used, such as a phone number, business card or e-mail address.

Payment

Memory Makers purchases first world serial rights for the one-time use of articles. Payment will vary on a per-assignment basis. We will not reprint articles previously published in other scrapbooking publications. *Memory Makers* Writer's Contract outlines all agreement details. The contract must be signed and returned by the author, accompanied by a numbered invoice. Authors will be paid approximately 30 days after completion of the project.

Advice to New Writers

Familiarize yourself with *Memory Makers*. Then send or e-mail a query letter to the attention of our copy editor, Amy Partain, with the idea you feel may interest our readers. Include samples of your previous work and an outline of your writing experience. We are also willing to look at completed manuscripts. Be sure to include your phone number and enclose a stamped return-reply postcard. We are unable to return unsolicited manuscripts.

We look forward to working with you in the future!

Editorial Guidelines 2004

Categories: Nonfiction—Computers—Crafts/Hobbies—Hobbies—Inspirational—Internet—Interview—Photography—Software—Technical—Scrapbooking

CONTACT: Sarah Kelly, Editorial Assistant
Material: Any
F&W Publications
12365 Huron St., Ste. 500
Denver CO 80234
Phone: 303-452-1968
Fax: 303-452-2164
E-mail: editorial@memorymakersmagazine.com
Website:www.memorymakersmagazine.com

Men of Integrity

OUR PURPOSE

Men of Integrity is a pocket-sized daily bible devotional guide that encourages regular Scripture study and applies biblical truth to the specific gritty issues men face.

Men of Integrity, published in association with Promise Keepers, also seeks to encourage men in their Christian walk to better fulfill their commitment to godly service in Christ by reminding them of the Seven Promises of a Promise Keeper:

1. Commitment to honoring Jesus Christ through worship, prayer and obedience to God's Word in the power of the Holy Spirit.

2. Commitment to pursuing vital relationships with a few other men, understanding that he needs brothers to help him keep his promises.

3. Commitment to practicing spiritual, moral, ethical and sexual purity.

4. Commitment to building a strong marriage and family through love, protection and biblical values.

5. Commitment to supporting the mission of his church by honoring and praying for his pastor and by actively giving his time and resources (I Thessalonians 5:12-13).

6. Commitment to reaching beyond any racial and denominational barriers to demonstrate the power of biblical unity.

7. Commitment to influencing his world, being obedient to the great Commandment (Mark 12:30-31) and the Great Commission. (Matthew 28:19-20)

OUR READERS

Men of Integrity readers are usually men between the ages of 30 and 50 working in business, or a specialized trade, such as sales or engineering. They are not likely to be a pastor or teacher, and have attended at least some college. About 30 percent of our readers are using the guide as part of a men's group or Bible study. Often, they are new Christians and not readers of a "traditional" Bible devotional. *Men of Integrity* serves as an introduction to regular Bible study for these men.

OUR WRITERS

Typically, our writers are Christian men fairly established in their walk with Christ. We look for stories that illustrate biblical principles, written by men who draw from their everyday experiences and lives. Personal experiences that caused you to grow in your faith, or stories about areas of struggle where God has challenged your thinking and encouraged a change in behavior, are the types of stories that fit best into the *Men of Integrity* format.

Men of Integrity seeks to regularly publish African-American, Hispanic, Native American, and Messianic Jewish writers.

THE ARTICLES

Men of Integrity gets its point across by telling gripping stories rather than by exhorting or commenting on Scripture passages. We are looking for easy-to-read pieces built on narrative. The narrative should clearly illustrate a biblical principle around a certain theme.

Generally, we choose themes that will help men cultivate healthy "horizontal" (human) relationships—with their wives, children, co-workers, and friends. Themes also address the "vertical" relationship—relationship with God. Articles should offer practical advice and personal insights that support growth in both these areas.

Themes used in past issues include: caring for others, loving your wife, spiritual accountability, prayer, self-discipline, God's love, dealing with failure, sexual purity, spiritual warfare, handling anger, fatherhood, hearing God, loving Jesus, wise decisions, boldness, commitment, truthfulness, and enriching your wife. This is not meant to be an exhaustive list but to give you examples of what we have used in the past.

Men of Integrity seeks a mix of articles, from both individuals known in the evangelical community and from ordinary laymen.

Men of Integrity uses the New Living Translation for all Scripture References.

Should you wish to obtain a sample issue, please send $5.00 with your request to Men of Integrity, 465 Gundersen Drive, Carol Stream, IL 60188. *Men of Integrity* also appears in online form at www.christianity.net/menofintegrity.

MANUSCRIPTS

Men of Integrity accepts unsolicited manuscripts. They can be sent in hard copy format or via e-mail. Submissions should be sent to the attention of the editor, 465 Gundersen Drive, Carol Stream, IL 60188 or, via e-mail, to: moimail@christianitytoday. com.

Men of Integrity will report only on those manuscripts received via e-mail or sent with a self-addressed, stamped envelope (SASE). We will respond in 3-5 weeks. Please include your name, address and telephone number on all manuscripts.

Devotionals are no more than 200-300 words each. We will accept longer pieces, but you should expect them to be condensed to about 200 words. We like a tight, punchy style and prefer condensing a slightly longer piece to make it fit to receiving a more loosely constructed 200-word piece.

Men of Integrity will pay $50 for each original piece accepted ($25 for reprints and excerpts). (4/04/01)

Categories: Nonfiction—Christian Interests—Family—Lifestyle—Men's Issues—Parenting—Religion—Spiritual

CONTACT: Harry Genet, Editor
Material: All
Christianity Today International
465 Gundersen Dr.
Carol Stream IL 60188
Phone: 630-260-6200
Fax: 630-260-8428
E-mail: mail@menofintegrity.net;
moimail@christianitytoday.com
Website: www.christianitytoday.com

Men's Fitness

Men's Fitness magazine is a total-service publication for healthy, active men. It contains a wide range of features and monthly departments devoted to all areas of health, fitness and an overall active lifestyle.

Editorial fulfills two functions: entertainment and information, with special attention paid to accuracy.

Manuscript tone: The editorial voice must be friendly, speaking directly to the healthy, active man. Academic-journal composition is not acceptable. Please read the magazine for an understanding of its style.

Manuscript length: 1,000 to 1,250 words for departments; 1,500 to 1,800 words for features.

Response time: Four to six weeks.

Writers' contracts/kill fees: Contracts are required for all work. Kill fees (paid if we find the work unacceptable for any reason after a contract is signed) are 1/3 the original payment amount.

Payment rates: $500 (or less) for departments; $1,000 (or less) for features. All fees are negotiated individually. Payment made within six weeks of final acceptance.

Fact checking: Accuracy is the responsibility of the author. Manuscripts should be accompanied by the telephone numbers of sources quoted within the article, so editors can verify their names, titles and educational credentials. Products or services mentioned in the articles should also be accompanied with contract names and phone numbers. Books should be cited by complete title, publisher and price. Include photocopies of both covers and the title page in the article's backup. Include a copy of the abstract of any studies cited. If the information cited comes from a secondary source, include a copy of the newspaper or magazine article.

Queries: One-page summary of idea or ideas. Send recent clips with bylines. Please send only clips that reflect your own writing style along with a SASE.

Unsolicited manuscripts: We prefer queries. Please do not send manuscripts.

Sample copies: Unfortunately, we cannot offer sample issues.

Categories: Nonfiction—Consumer—Diet/Nutrition—Health—Inspirational—Physical Fitness—Psychology—Science—Self Help—Sexuality

CONTACT: Dean Brierly, Managing Editor
Material: All
21100 Erwin St.
Woodland Hills CA 91367
Phone: 818-884-6800
Fax: 818-704-5734

Men's Health

Men's Health

It's not easy to break into *Men's Health*. Don't even try if you haven't been published in a major magazine. Still with us? Okay, study a back issue or two, then consider the following: Most unsolicited queries fail because they don't address the Men's Health reader.

The *Men's Health* Reader

Our circulation is 1,625,000+; 85 percent of our readers are men. Our average reader is 35 years old and is a well-educated urban or suburban professional. He's active in a number of sports and exercise pursuits.

What We Cover

As you'll see, we're an authoritative source of information on all aspects of men's physical and emotional health. We rely on writers to seek out the right experts, and to either tell a story from a first-person vantage or to get good anecdotes. We carefully fact-check all quotes and health information contained in the magazine.

Tone

Most of our articles have the tone of a peer who happens to have spoken to a few authorities on the issue at hand. Imagine you're relating that information to the reader, one on one, over a beer or at dinner.

Length, Payment, Rights

The best place to break into the magazine is "Malegrams" or one of our one-page columns. For "Malegrams," we seek submissions of about 200 words. We pay $25 to $50 upon completion of fact-checking. Other than that:

Departments run 1,500 words and pay $500-$2,000

Features run 1,200-4,000 words and pay $1,000-$5,000

We usually buy all rights, but this is negotiated on an individual basis. We will consider buying second rights, if your published piece has not appeared in another national magazine, in another health magazine, or in another magazine written primarily for men. When we pay: For departments and features, following acceptance, upon completion of the fact-checking process.

The Departments

Malegrams: Short takes relevant to men. Clinical and research advances in health, medicine, psychology, sports performance, work and relationship issues, the offbeat.

Training: We cover what's tried and needs to be tried again (i.e., calisthenics revisited), as well as the trends.

Nutrition: What to eat and when.

Working: How to succeed. How to fail. How to know the difference.

Couples: New takes on major relationship issues.

Self-Care: What to do so that you don't have to call a doctor.

Looks: Practical and health aspects of grooming, dressing, etc.

Man-to-Man: Simple, well-told stories about manhood, manliness, machismo, momentary lapses. The wiser you are, the more of a wiseguy you can be.

Mind/Body: The psychology of men, and how that relates to health, exercise, performance.

Clips

We don't assign anything without seeing published clips. Photocopies are a good idea, as we may not return clips. Send your best. One or two will do. They don't all have to be about health or medicine. We want to see how well you report, write and interpret stories.

How to Query *Men's Health*

Structure an article proposal this way:

• Start with the lead you expect to put on the piece.

• Write a summary of where you'll go from there.

• Give specifics on whom you plan to interview, what types of real-life anecdotes you'll include, what research sources you plan to go to and what conclusion the story might reach. Queries shouldn't run longer than one page, single-spaced. We'll get back to you in two-four weeks. (Be sure to enclose a SASE.)

Manuscripts

If you send a manuscript, it must be typed double- or triple-spaced, with margins of at least 1 inch. Send a copy of your original, just in case. We report on manuscripts in four to eight weeks.

Back Issues

Call our customer service department at (800) 666-2303 to order back issues.

Please send article submissions by regular mail to me at the address below. No phone calls please!

Categories: Nonfiction—Careers—Diet/Nutrition—Fashion—Health—Physical Fitness—Recreation—Relationships—Sports/Recreation—Travel

CONTACT: Pamela Brinar
Material: All

Rodale, Inc.
33 East Minor St.
Emmaus PA 18098-0099
Phone: 610-967-5171
Fax: 610-967-8963
Website:www.menshealth.com

Men's Journal

Men's Journal is a men's lifestyle magazine for 25- to 49-year-old active men. Its editorial emphasis is on travel, fitness, adventure and participatory sports, but it is also open to a wide range of topics of interest to contemporary American men.

Front-of-the-book articles cover a wide range of general interest topics and news, and are between 400-1,200 words. Feature articles and profiles run between 2,000-7,000 words. Articles for the equipment and fitness sections are 400-1,800 words. These are service-oriented articles meant to provide sporting and leisure reviews for the active man.

One-page queries, accompanied by one or two applicable clips, should be sent to the address below. Do not submit queries by fax.

Categories: Adventure—General Interest—Men's Issues—Physical Fitness—Sports/Recreation—Travel

CONTACT: Submissions Editor
Material: All
1290 Avenue of the Americas
New York NY 10104
Phone: 212-484-1616
Fax: 212-484-3434
E-mail: letters@mensjournal.com
Website:www.mensjournal.com

Mercury

Mercury
The Journal of the
Astronomical Society of the Pacific

Thank you for agreeing to write for *Mercury, the Journal of the Astronomical Society of the Pacific.* In its original incarnation, *Mercury* was first published by the ASP in 1925. It is now read by 5,200 ASP members and at 800 academic libraries, observatories, and other institutions in 71 countries. The ASP is the largest general astronomy society in the world. Our members include professional astronomers, amateurs, educators, and motivated lay people.

Fees

Alas, because the ASP is nonprofit and impoverished, we are unable to pay for submissions. Writing for *Mercury* is a labor of love and good exposure for your ideas. We do have a limited capacity to reimburse expenses, such as postage or photo reproduction. We send four free copies to all contributors and can provide more, within reason.

Queries

We are unequipped to review unsolicited manuscripts; if you have article ideas, please write or e-mail the editor. In your letter, please discuss the basic idea for the article, its general content, its relevance to our readership, and the relationship of the prospective writer to the subject matter. The editor tries to respond to all correspondence within two weeks, although it may take somewhat longer or shorter depending on other deadlines we must meet.

Level of Articles

We encourage writers to read past issues to get a sense of our style. *Mercury* assumes that its readers are motivated and informed about basic astronomy. In our 1994 survey of readers, 49 percent of the respondents said they were involved in amateur astronomy, 29 percent in astronomical research, and 86 percent in astronomy education at some level. *Mercury* articles are roughly at the same level as *The Sciences*: between a mass-market science magazine such as *Discover* and a more scholarly magazine such as *Scientific American*.

We think of *Mercury* as the *Atlantic Monthly* of astronomy, giving informed perspectives on salient issues in research, education, history, and public policy. An article should not focus solely on the research or history of any particular individual, unless it is of unusual importance. Articles should appeal to readers' personal experiences and draw broader conclusions about how science is conducted. We encourage writers to be innovative and forceful, to devise clever metaphors, to go out onto a limb. The ASP does not endorse anything our contributors say, but we believe in challenging readers and making *Mercury* a vigorous part of the marketplace of ideas.

Length of Articles

Regular departments are one magazine page, or 1,000 words. Book reviews are one page, 800 words. The standard feature is eight magazine pages, 3,000 words plus illustrations and a sidebar.

Rights

The ASP asks that contributors transfer their copyright to the ASP in order to facilitate electronic distribution and academic photocopying, which we allow free of charge. In return, we grant writers the non-exclusive right to reuse any part or all of their work. We have found that this arrangement avoids hassles, but if contributors prefer to retain copyright, we have no problem with that. Our concern is simply to protect ourselves legally. The minimum we can accept is worldwide first appearance, non-exclusive print and electronic rights.

Submission

To avoid transcription errors, we require electronic submission. We prefer rich text, (.rtf) or Microsoft Word 5.1 format, but will accept plain-text, MacWrite, or WordPerfect formats. You can e-mail the document to the address below or send us a 3½" low-density Macintosh diskette. If you send a plain text file, we ask that you fax or mail a formatted version as well.

Deadlines

First drafts are due 10 weeks before the cover date; final drafts, eight weeks before.

Editing

Mercury rarely rejects a manuscript. When you submit an article, we assume that you agree to work with the editor in preparing it for publication. The *Mercury* editor is an active one who enjoys bouncing ideas back and forth and who takes pain to ensure readability and interest. Most writers realize that every manuscript benefits from careful, respectful critiquing.

Editing occurs in two stages. First, the editor reads the submitted draft and makes suggestions for a revised draft. On occasion, the editor may ask an anonymous outside reviewer for advice. Typical issues include: making sure readers know where the article is heading and why they should be reading it; making sure that the article does not present readers with too much information too quickly; checking that concepts are defined as naturally as possible; identifying and highlighting particularly enlightening ideas; and anticipating and addressing readers' questions.

Second, the editor copy-edits the revised draft for grammar, spelling, flow, style, and so forth. We make every reasonable effort to show writers the final version of their articles while there is time to make changes. There is one exception: During layout, the editor sometimes must condense in order to fine-tune length, eliminate widows, or correct errors noticed at the last minute. Usually such changes are vanishingly minor. We cannot inform writers of such changes.

Titles, abstracts, subheads, and captions are our domain, although we generally work from writers' suggestions and include these elements in the drafts we return for writers' approval.

House Style

Mercury is somewhere between a magazine and an academic journal. In most cases, it adheres to Associated Press style, with concessions to Chicago style. Exceptions are detailed in the *Mercury* stylebook and are routinely made during copy-editing.

Mercury does not have footnotes or formal bibliographies. If acknowledgment has to be given, work it into the body of the article or the biography. Articles should not include a bibliography unless it is interesting in itself. Such bibliographies should be short and annotated.

Mercury uses SI units, with English equivalents given in parentheses. Spell out the names of measurement units. Take care not to overstate precision. Normally, two significant figures suffice.

Acronyms intimidate readers. Use only abbreviations likely to be recognized outside a specialty. Do not define an abbreviation in parentheses on first reference: If the abbreviation is not obvious enough to be recognized on second reference, it shouldn't be used to begin with.

Biography

Following every article is a one-paragraph biography of the writer, written in third-person, including research interests, a personal anecdote or factoid, and an e-mail address.

Illustrations

We ask the writer to obtain, help to obtain, or at least suggest illustrations. This ensures that the illustrations are what the writer intends; in any event, most writers have better access to illustrations than we do. We prefer photographs in print form and can reimburse reproduction expenses. We can also accept GIF, JPEG, and TIFF files. *Mercury* is published in two colors.

Categories: Education—Science

CONTACT: Submissions Editor
Material: All
390 Ashton Ave.
San Francisco CA 94112
Phone: 415-337-1100
Fax: 415-337-5205
E-mail: rnaeye@astrosociety.org

Message Magazine

Thank you for your interest in MESSAGE Magazine. MESSAGE is the oldest and most widely circulated African-American religious journal addressing ethnic issues in the USA. We work hard to preserve our unique role interpreting current events through a Black Christian perspective. We're happy you want to be a part of this powerful ministry. Here is how you can participate in writing the message.

Getting to know MESSAGE

• Published: Bimonthly, in a 32-page format, by the Review and Herald Publishing Association. Sponsored by the Seventh-day Adventist Church. Circulation: 125,000; primary readership based in the United States.

• Audience: Predominantly Black, though increasingly multi-cultural. MESSAGE is a missionary journal tailored to the unchurched.

• Lead time: When submitting seasonal material, remember our production schedule requires us to work four to six months ahead.

• Payments: MESSAGE pays upon acceptance.

• Rights: MESSAGE purchases first North American publishing rights to all submissions. This also includes first electronic publishing rights. Each article published first in MESSAGE should carry a line attributing credit to MESSAGE magazine.

WHAT TO WRITE

• MESSAGE publishes: informational, devotional, inspirational, doctrinal, profile, interview and self-help articles that have wide appeal to people of many backgrounds. Feature articles should never exceed 1,200 words unless otherwise specified.

• MESSAGE does not accept: sermons, outlines, poetry, reprints, or anything that is not in an article format.

• Hot topics include: biblical exposition, celebrity and humanitarian profiles with distinct ministry perspectives, family, health, education, worship, news and current events, religious freedom and racial reconciliation. Feel free to query us by phone or e-mail about article ideas.

Departments
• MESSAGE also accepts freelance submissions for the following magazine departments:

Minding Your Business: This 600-word column addresses work-related issues such as personal development and finance, stress control, and workplace politics. Pieces should include a distinctive biblical Christian response or perspective on these issues.

HealthSpan: This 600-word column—sidebar excluded—covers a variety of health topics of interest to our audience. It is typically accompanied by a sidebar or chart.

Message Jr.: Our column for children, ages 5 to 8, is no longer than 500 words. We prefer Bible-based stories, but stories with a clear-cut moral are also accepted.

HOW TO GET PUBLISHED:
Here are Nine Ways to Woo Our Editors:

1. Make sure your article is biblically sound and offers spiritual perspective and insight.

2. Support your material with facts, statistics and quotes from experts.

3. Invite the reader to read your whole story by writing an interesting lead.

4. Sharpen your focus. Sometimes writing a title, subtitles and subheadings helps.

5. Look for interesting, fresh, insightful twists on old topics. Say something new.

6. Write about timely topics and events.

7. Answer the underlying, heartfelt questions a reader may have about your topic.

8. Include anecdotes or illustrations to make your writing come alive.

9. Carefully follow all directions you have read in these guidelines or those given by editors.

How to submit a manuscript
• Submit only typewritten, double-spaced articles no longer than 1,200 words, unless otherwise specified.

• Enclose your name, address, phone number, e-mail address, Social Security number, and a self-addressed, stamped envelope. Without this information your manuscript will not be reviewed.

• Enclose a one-sentence bio at the end of your article. Example: "Jane Doe is…"

• We prefer manuscripts on computer disk (MS Word for MAC or PC) or e-mailed (MS Word for MAC or PC) to Message@ rhpa.org. Articles submitted via regular mail should be accompanied by a typewritten, double-spaced copy.

• You will be notified by postcard that we have received your manuscript. If your article is accepted, you will be notified within six to eight weeks. If your manuscript is not accepted, we will return it to you only if you have enclosed a SASE.

Categories: Fiction—African-American—Christian Interests—Consumer—Inspirational—Religion—Spiritual

CONTACT: Ron Smith, Editor
Material: All
55 W. Oak Ridge Dr.
Hagerstown MD 21740
Phone: 301-393-4099
Fax: 301-393-4103
E-mail: Message@rhpa.org or ronsmith@rhpa.org
Website: www.Messagemagazine.com

The Messenger

Ceased publication.

Metro Baby

Please refer to *Metro Parent* magazine.

Metro Parent
Metro Baby
African American Family
Best of Times
Educators Edition
The Party Book

Guidelines
Query by email to: sdemaggio@metroparent.com
Feature stories are 1500-2500 words. Columns are 750 words.
Categories: African-American—Children—Culture—Education—Family—Parenting—Regional—Senior Citizens—Teen

CONTACT: Susan DeMaggio, Managing Editor
Material: Parenting, Women's Health, Family, Travel
CONTACT: Denise Crittendon, Editor
Material: Black lifestyle
Metro Parent Publishing Group
24567 Northwestern Hwy., Suite 150
Southfield MI 48075
Phone: 248-352-0990
E-mail: dcrittene@metroparent.com
Website: www.metroparent.com

MetroKids
MetroKids Pennsylvania, MetroKids South Jersey, MetroKids Delaware

General Information: In business for more than 13 years, *MetroKids* Magazine has become an indispensable family tool. *MetroKids* distributes 125,000 copies of our magazines, *MetroKids Pennsylvania, MetroKids South Jersey* and most recently, *MetroKids Delaware*, each month to over 1,500 locations in eleven counties throughout the Tri-State Area.

We distribute to public libraries, museums, schools, childcare centers, community centers, retail stores, malls, hospitals, doctor's offices, bookstores, tourist centers, and many other locations.

Mission statement: *MetroKids* is the resource for parents and children in the Delaware Valley. Our objective, in monthly publications, special issues, and special events, is to help Delaware Valley families take advantage of the vast resources—both educational and recreational—available in the culturally rich and diverse community in which we live.

MetroKids, through its editorial, advertising and promotional outreach offers options to Delaware Valley families.

Submissions: Submit at least 6 weeks ahead of publication. 800-1200 words. No first-person accounts. Delaware Valley (Philadelphia and suburbs, Delaware, Southern New Jersey) sources preferred. Send via e-mail.

Topics: Health, practical parenting, women's issues, technology for the family, children's fashion, home décor, special needs, education, nutrition and activities.

Categories: Nonfiction—Children—Culture—Education—Family—Food/Diet—Health—Home—Parenting—Regional—Teen—Women's Issues

CONTACT: Tom Livingston, Executive Editor
Material: All

1080 Delaware Ave., Ste 102
Philadelphia PA 19125
Phone: 215-291-5560
Fax: 215-291-5563
E-mail: editor@metrokids.com
Website: www.Metrokids.com

METROPOLIS

Metropolis

WHAT IS METROPOLIS?

Metropolis examines contemporary life through design—architecture, interior design, product design, graphic design, crafts, planning, and preservation. Subjects range from the sprawling urban environment to intimate living spaces to small objects of everyday use. In looking for why design happens in a certain way, *Metropolis* explores the economic, environmental, social, cultural, political, and technological context. With its innovative graphic presentation and its provocative voice, *Metropolis* shows how richly designed our world can be.

EDITORIAL SUBMISSIONS

Send query letters—not complete manuscripts—describing your idea and why it would be good for our magazine. Be concise, specific, and clear. Also, please include clips and a resume. The ideal *Metropolis* story is based on strong reporting skills and includes an examination of current critical issues. A design firm's newest work isn't a story, but the issues that their work brings to light might be. We do not cover conferences or seminars. Please send these announcements to the general magazine address or email.

DESIGN WORK SUBMISSIONS

Design professionals: keep us apprised about projects as they are awarded, in progress, and completed. We are especially interested in projects that illustrate innovative design approaches or unconventional responses to typical problems in:
• Single-family (though we publish few in this category) and multi-family interiors and exteriors
• Public work, such as schools and health facilities
• Graphic design
• Product design
• Commercial work.

Each year we cover the evolving workplace, educational buildings, and new or forgotten materials or technologies.

Include a brief description of the goals of the project and snapshots, renderings, floorplans, color copies of professional photos, or digital images—tiffs, jpegs or other formats that can be opened on a Mac. Please do not send irreplaceable art.

Digital images intended for use in the magazine are best in jpeg, tif, or eps format in the final print size or larger, and with a resolution of at least 300 dpi. Zipped and stuffed files are fine; compressed images are unacceptable.

Categories: Nonfiction—Architecture—Arts—Consumer—Culture—Environment—General Interest

CONTACT: Julien Devereux
Material: All
61 West 23rd St. 4th Floor
New York NY 10010
Phone: 212-722-5050
Fax: 212-627-9988
E-mail: edit@metropolismag.com (queries); kira@metropolismag.com (submission questions)

Metropolitan Home

Writing for *Metropolitan Home* requires expertise in the field of home design and associate lifestyle matters. It is not enough to be a good writer. You must be able to speak with authority about interior design, architecture, cooking, gardening, or whatever other subject you wish to cover. It is not a market for beginners or those new to the world of interior design.

In most cases, you must query before submitting. The only exception is the first-person experiential essay.

No previously published work will be considered. No home will be considered for publication if it has previously been published in a competing national magazine. If you are proposing a location that has appeared in local newspapers and/or magazines, we need to see copies of the articles to consider the story.

All queries and/or submissions must be written. We do not accept telephone calls or fax submissions. We prefer that you submit by mail or courier service.

Proposals should be approximately 250 words long and must include basic reportage. Remember: *MET HOME* is a timely journal of contemporary design. We do not generally cover antiques, restorations or anything that is not newsworthy. We do not generally use seasonal material (i.e. December holidays, Mothers Day, etc.); our lead time is six to twelve months. We are a consumer publication with a highly educated, affluent audience, not a "ladies magazine" or a "how-to" magazine. Forty percent of our readers are men.

Most proposals must be submitted with visuals: We prefer 35mm slides. We cannot consider any proposal about any aspect of design without seeing pictures.

If you have not already written for *MET HOME*, please include no more than three clips with your proposal. "Clips" means published stories in a related field.

We are not seeking travel stories of any kind. "My House" stories are normally written by widely published writers at the invitation of the editors of *MET HOME*. We generally do not accept unsolicited "My House" pieces.

What we need most are front-of-book stories about issues of contemporary housing, about "good works" relating to design and architecture, about ecological issues, financial aspects of home owning, apartment living, etc.—in other words, thought pieces that involve expertise and research.

Please know the magazine before submitting. We are not able to offer free copies of the magazine. If you cannot find *Metropolitan Home* on your local newsstand or in a nearby library, you may order back issues from 201-451-9420.

Categories: Architecture—Cooking—Gardening—Interior Design

CONTACT: Kate Walsh, Associate Editor
Material: All
1633 Broadway
New York NY 10019
Phone: 212-767-6000

MHQ, The Quarterly Journal of Military History

Please refer to Primedia History Group

Michigan Beverage Guide

Please refer to *Illinois Beverage Guide*.

Michigan Historical Review
Central Michigan University

The *Michigan Historical Review* publishes articles on Michigan's political, economic, social, and cultural history, and those on American, Canadian, and Midwestern history that explore important themes related to Michigan's past. All manuscript submissions receive a double-blind peer review, but final decisions about publication rest with the editorial staff. The MHR does not accept manuscripts under consideration elsewhere.

Prospective authors are requested to use the following guidelines:

1. Manuscripts should not exceed 10,000 words; endnotes must be used and are to be double spaced.

2. Authors should submit three paper copies of the manuscript and a copy on an IBM-compatible diskette (preferably in MS Word). To permit anonymous reviewing, the author's name should appear on a separate title page. Articles may also be submitted electronically.

3. *The Chicago Manual of Style*, 15th edition, should be followed in matters of style and for endnote format. The MHR uses open punctuation and standardizes spelling of Native American tribal names.

4. Authors are requested to use bias-free language that is sensitive to race, ethnicity, gender, religion, age, ability, and sexual orientation. We recommend *Guidelines for Bias-Free Writing*, by Marilyn Schwartz and the *Task Force on Bias-Free Language of the Association of American University Presses* (Bloomington: Indiana University Press, 1995).

5. We encourage the inclusion of photographs, illustrations, and graphs within articles. Photographs should be in 8" x 10" black-and-white glossy format. It is the author's responsibility to secure permission to publish when necessary.

6. For additional information, please contact the editorial staff via telephone or e-mail.

Categories: Michigan and Great Lakes History

CONTACT: Editor
Material: All
Clarke Historical Library, CMU
Mt. Pleasant MI 48859
Phone: 989-774-6567
Fax: 989-774-2179
E-mail: MIHISREV@cmich.edu

Mid-American Review
Bowling Green State University

Stories, poems, and articles will generally be returned or accepted within one to four months. Please include an SASE. Sample copies $5.00, current issue $7.00, rare back issues $10.00. Payment is $10.00 per page (pending funding) for fiction, poetry, translations, and nonfiction, with a maximum payment of $50.00; contributing authors receive two complimentary copies. All rights revert to the author upon publication. MAR does not consider work which has previously been published in any form..

Fiction Editor: Michael Czyzniejewski
Assistant Fiction Editor: Lisa DeCook

Mid-American Review considers work that is character- and/or language-oriented without sacrificing narrative. We are open to submissions from new and established authors, both traditional and experimental work, including short-shorts, but discourage genre fiction. Basically, we want to read something well writen and original.

MAR considers pieces up to 6,000 words; authors wishing to submit longer manuscripts or novel excerpts should query first with SASE.

Nonfiction Editor: Dustin Parsons

Mid-American Review seeks creative nonfiction, literary essays, and critical articles which focus on contemporary authors and topics of current literary interest. Contributions should generally not exceed 5,000 words and should follow standard MLA style. We also seek short (400-word) book reviews of current works of poetry, fiction, and nonfiction prose, published within six months of our publication (Apr. & Nov.).

Poetry Editor: Karen Craigo
Assistant Poetry Editor: Abigail Cloud

Poems should emanate from textured, evocative images, use language with an awareness of how words sound and mean, and have a definite sense of voice. Each line should help carry the poem, and an individual vision must be evident.

We encourage new as well as established writers. There is no length limit on individual poems, but please send no more than six at one time.

Translation Editor: George Looney

All submissions must include the original as well as the translated work. Chapbooks (approx. 10-15 poems) are designed to provide readers with an introduction to a single contemporary poet or a group of poets. An introductory essay of 300-500

words outlining the historical context of the poetry is encouraged.

Translations of contemporary fiction are also welcome and should follow these guidelines as well as those listed under Fiction.

Categories: Fiction—Nonfiction—Book Reviews—Poetry—Translations

CONTACT:
Karen Craigo, Assoc. & Poetry Editor
Material: Poetry
E-Mail: karenka@bgnet. bgsu.edu
CONTACT: Michael Czyzniejewski, Fiction Editor
Material: Fiction
E-Mail: mikeczy@bgnet.bgsu.edu
CONTACT: Dustin Parsons, Nonfiction Editor
Material: Non-fiction and reviews
E-Mail: djack@ bgnet.bgsu.edu
CONTACT: George Looney, Translation Editor
Material: Translation-related queries
E-Mail: gol1@psu. edu
Dept. of English
Bowling Green State University
Bowling Green OH 43403
Phone: 419-372-2725
Website: www.bgsu.edu/midamericanreview

MidWest Outdoors

MidWest Outdoors' Philosophy

MidWest Outdoors is in business to help people enjoy the outdoors, so we print only positive stories about outdoor experiences. MidWest Outdoors does not dwell on pollution, poaching, bad manners, etc. Please do not be critical of lakes, products or services. If you do mention a product, service or resort, please give us a contact name for possible advertising.

MidWest Outdoors' Editorial Requirements

MidWest Outdoors is interested in where to go and how to do it stories on outdoor recreation in the Midwest – an area encompassing a 10- to 15-hour drive from Chicago. Material should provide information the outdoorsman can use in his immediate vicinity and in areas he can travel to on weekends or a short vacation.

The accent in MidWest Outdoors is on:
• FISHING • HUNTING • CAMPING.

Related subjects are hunting dogs, archery, boats, snowmobiling, shooting, outdoor cooking or wild game cooking and canoeing.

Remember, you are writing for publication one or two months in advance, and your subject matter should reflect that time lapse. Spring fishing articles should be submitted in January, February and March; fall hunting articles in July and August. Illinois turkey hunting, for example, is in April, but turkey stories should be printed as early as February because that's when hunters must apply for permits. We never want to lose sight of our primary goal which is to provide useful information for the reader.

Any material accepted is subject to such revision as is necessary to meet the requirements of this publication. Manuscripts and photos not used will be returned if a stamped, self-addressed envelope is provided, but we assume no responsibility for lost materials.

Please include a title of the article on each page. Also include an overline or subtitle (example: Walleye Hotspot – Fox River Spring Madness). Include a byline and page number on each page and please include your social security number. If you submit a timely item, please indicate the month for suggested use.

Main Vs. State Section Requirements

Main section editorial should be general in tone, not area specific. The Main section is seen and read by people throughout the Midwest. Please keep facts such as fishing regulations or opening dates out of your material or specify the areas such rules are intended for. Example: readers in Iowa or Illinois would be confused by length requirements for Wisconsin northern pike. *MidWest Outdoors'* editors are particularly interested in where-to and how-to articles.

State section editorial should focus on one state exclusively or be written for one particular region. Example for a good state story: bass fishing on the Illinois River for the Illinois section. Example for a good regional story: fishing Wisconsin's southern lakes for the Wisconsin and Illinois sections. First time writers are encouraged to first write for state sections.

MidWest Outdoors' Special Sections

You are invited to submit material for any or all of these special sections:

• IceBreakers: The most comprehensive ice fishing annual in the Midwest. Deadlines: October 1st plus expanded ice fishing coverage in Nov., Dec., Jan. and Feb. issues.

• Canada Fever: The only two months *MidWest Outdoors* features Canadian editorial. Deadlines: Nov. 1st, Dec. 1st and Jan. 1st

MidWest Outdoors' Acceptance Policy – PLEASE READ BEFORE CALLING

If you make an editorial submission to *MidWest Outdoors* and it is not returned in 30 days, you can assume we do plan to use it. However, we do keep some material for as long as 12 to 18 months before using it. Your best way of knowing if we have used your editorial is if you receive payment from *MidWest Outdoors*. Payment will be issued promptly after a submission has run in the magazine.

MidWest Outdoors Magazine receives a very large volume of editorial submissions daily. Therefore, a call to our office asking about the status of an article will not receive an immediate response. Again, your best check if you have made a submission that has not been returned is to wait for payment. After you receive payment, you know the article has been used.

MidWest Outdoors' Web Site Permission Form

The *MidWest Outdoors* web site, www.midwestoutdoors.com, currently features a sampling of articles found in the magazine. These articles are chosen at random from the current issue. If your article appears in *MidWest Outdoors* and you do not wish to see it on the web page, please indicate below. The use of an article on the web site involves no additional compensation from *MidWest Outdoors*. Even if you would like to see *MidWest Outdoors* use your submission(s) on the internet, please return this form so we have a record for our files.

_____ Yes, I want to be part of *MidWest Outdoors* promotions on the website. I understand that there is no additional compensation for the use of my articles.

_____ No, I do not want my material used on the *MidWest Outdoors'* website or any other promotional material.

Signed_____Date _____

Please Print Name Clearly

Please return this form to:

Gene Laulunen, *MidWest Outdoors* • 111 Shore Drive, Burr Ridge, IL 60527-5885 • info@midwestoutdoors.com

MidWest Outdoors' Deadline Schedule

Main Section: 35 Days Preceding Publication. Example: April 25th for the June issue. Subscribers receive the issue the 28th and newsstand sales start the 1st.

STATE SECTIONS:

Illinois Sections (Southern/Northern): 5th of the Month Preceding Publication. Example: May 5th for the June issue.

Iowa, Michigan, Minnesota, Wisconsin and Indiana Sections: 1st of the Month Preceding Publication. Example: May 1st for the June issue.

Specific Requirements for *MidWest Outdoors* STORIES...

• Should be accompanied by black and white or color photos or slides.

• Should be between 600 and 1,500 words – with shorter stories preferred. The story's focus should be on where to and how to. Stories should impart information in an entertaining fashion, and not in a text book or preachy tone.

• Should be prepared with the top sheet as illustrated below.

• Can be submitted in the following forms:

• via e-mail. We have had best results with files that are attached to e-mail.

• e-mail address: info@midwestoutdoors.com

PHOTOS...

• *MidWest Outdoors* can accept color or black and white photos or color slides. Photos may also be e-mailed. A good photo is usually one that catches the action of some outdoor pursuit.

• Please send no more than 3 to 4 photos per story.

• You must place your return address on the back of the photo if you want it returned. Caption sheet, with the title of the story it accompanies should be taped to the back of the photo. There is no better way to insure that your photo will not be used with another writer's story.

E-MAILING PHOTOS:

This is what we need. Minimum 5" x 5"; 200 pixels per inch; 1000 pixels x 1000 pixels from input device—scanner, digital camera etc. and not from a graphics program. Any questions contact Jesse Saenz (our Graphic person) 888-666-8878 x116 or email jsaenz@midwestoutdoors.com.

MAPS...

• are a great way to visually tell where the lake, pond or river is located and where the fish are located in the body of water. DEFINITELY A PLUS FOR FIRST TIME WRITERS.

IMPORTANT CHECKLIST BEFORE SENDING IN MATERIAL

• Your name is on all pages and photos.

• You have included your social security number.

• You have indicated what month the material is for.

• You have written a headline and subheadline.

• You have written a caption for each photo.

PLEASE REMEMBER: If we do not plan on using your material, it will be returned to you within 10 days of receipt. The best check you have for knowing if we have used your material, is if you receive a check from *MidWest Outdoors*.

Categories: Nonfiction—Fishing—Outdoors—Regional—Sports/Recreation—Travel

CONTACT: Submissions
Material: All
111 Shore Dr.
Burr Ridge, IL 60527
Phone: 630-887-7722
Fax: 630-887-1958
E-mail: info@midwestoutdoors.com

Midwest Traveler

About Us

Founded: April 1971. Name magazine changed from *The Midwest Motorist* to *AAA Midwest Traveler* in January 1999.

Frequency: Mailed bi-monthly, Jan./Feb. through Nov./Dec.

Circulation: 435,000. Mailed to AAA households in Missouri, southern Indiana, Southern Illinois and Eastern Kansas

Readership: 870,000

Source: Mediamark Research, Inc., New York, NY / February 2000

AAA Midwest Traveler features articles on regional, national and international travel opportunities. Area history, auto safety, highway and transportation news also are featured. The South is often the focus of travel articles.

As the official publication for AAA members in Missouri, southern Illinois southern Indiana and eastern Kansas, we reach an audience that travels throughout the year. AAA, America's premier travel organization, serves more than 40 million members nationally.

The magazine's goal is to provide members with a variety of useful information on travel, auto safety, and other topics that appeal to the motoring public. The magazine carries on average six articles per issue and buys 20-30 manuscripts per year.

How to contact us: Send queries rather than finished manuscripts. In addition, please send a list of credits or published clips when you query us for the first time. We will not take phone queries and prefer not to see a laundry list of story ideas. In general, we try to reply within four weeks of receipt. We will consider a previously published article if it appeared in a non-competing publication. Simultaneous queries are acceptable, but tell us the idea is being considered elsewhere.

Assignments: We work from an editorial schedule and assignments are usually made at least six months in advance. Sometimes the calendar is assigned by July for the following year. Usually purchase first North American rights. A story assignment is always made by letter. The writer signs an outline-agreement and returns one copy to the editor. We do not pay any expenses in conjunction with the article (travel expenses, phone bills, etc.). Payment for an article is made upon acceptance. Our rates range from $50 to $350. It helps to send photos/slides (color only) with manuscripts. While we do not pay for photos, we consider it in payment for the manuscript. To assist with fact-checking, please send copies of materials used to research the article.

Style: We use the *AP Stylebook*. Third-person voice usually works best, but in some cases first-person description is appropriate. A copy of a current magazine will be sent with assignment so our editing style can be observed. A story will not be drastically changed without discussing this with the writer. Send the manuscript on floppy disk, saved either in Microsoft Word 5.1 or a lower version, or as an ASCII text file. Always include hard copy with the disk.

Taboos: Humor, satire, fiction, poetry, cartoons. Technical and safety articles usually are written by staff. Departments (e.g. "Travel Treasures, Day Tours") also are written by staff.

Categories: Associations—Automobiles—Consumer—Travel

CONTACT: Deborah Reinhardt, Editor
Material: All
AAA Auto Club of Missouri, 12901 N. Forty Drive
St. Louis MO 63141
Phone: 314-523-7350
Fax: 314-523-6982
E-mail: dreinhardt@aaamissouri.com
Website: www.ouraaa.com/traveler

Midwifery Today

Mission Statement

Midwifery Today, (a 72-page journal that includes International Midwife) and The Birthkit (a 12-page newsletter) are quarterly publications for birth practitioners. We emphasize natural childbirth, breastfeeding, networking and education. Our aim is to foster communication between practitioners and families, and to promote responsible midwifery and childbirth education around the world.

We seek a balance between scientific or technical material and "softer" personal and/or philosophical articles, including birth-related art, poetry and humor. We consider submissions on all aspects of pregnancy and childbirth. The professional and business aspects of midwifery and childbirth education are also of interest to our readers.

Concise material that clearly expresses your knowledge, experience, feelings or findings will receive consideration. If you are submitting an instructive article aimed at midwifery procedure or practice, please be accurate and factual. Identify and credit your sources of information. Proofread your work. We reserve the right to edit for clarity, content, and length, but whenever possible, we ask you to approve all edits.

E-mail your article, if possible, to: editorial@midwifery today.com, or include a disk if mailing. (See guidelines for e-mail at end of this document.) We prefer articles that are typed and double-spaced, although neatly written articles are also accepted. Include your name, address and telephone number, as well as your FAX number and e-mail address on the opening page. Your name, article title, and page number should appear on each following page if you are mailing. Please include a biographical sketch of no more than 40 words. If you wish to withhold your name, please indicate this; instruct us whether you prefer an anonymous citing, your initials, or a pseudonym.

Photography and Artwork

Overall guidelines: We prefer that images come to us in the highest resolution format possible, closest to the original picture. Thus, it's best to have prints of film images and original digital files of digital camera output. We have difficulty working with digital versions of film images and printed versions of digital camera pictures. It is not impossible, in most cases, but it is substantially more difficult. The results are rarely the best they could be. In all cases, cameras and pictures should be handled with care. If you keep your lenses free from dust and scratches, handle prints gently to avoid fingerprints and dust, and avoid re-sampling digital files, we've got a better chance of being able to work easily with your pictures.

We generally pay $15 per inside shot, $25 for full bleed and HABT cover, $50 for MT cover. We will also trade for magazine subscriptions or advertising space in the magazine. Advertising space is generally only traded when we use a large number of photos over a long period of time (i.e. Patti Ramos or Harriette Hartigan) or for special photos (for example, the cover of our conference program, book covers, etc.)

We like pictures of mothers and babies together, babies alone, siblings with babies, etc. We prefer pictures of babies for our cover, with or without parents/siblings/etc. We prefer pictures of families for HABT, though with everything it depends on the subject of the article, etc. Photos which involve midwives, doulas, midwifery students, and specific procedures/positions/equipment are also helpful.

Glossy prints are preferable. Color is fine. We can use either color or black and white easily. 5x7 is ideal, but we can work with smaller snapshots, too.

In general, we recommend the following when taking pictures:

• Make sure your lens is free from dust and grime.

• Take lots of photos

• Film is more likely to make it onto our cover than digital...only the newest digital cameras are capable of capturing enough information to present a quality 9x11 ½ print at 300 dpi (the resolution we need for our cover). Film is continuous tone, and so resolution is not such an issue. See the sections below on each type of photography for more information.

Take care to keep your focus on the important parts of a picture. It is easy to accidentally blur a face by setting focus on a collar, or blur a baby by focusing on a mama's breast.

• Get more information than less. That means that you shouldn't try to crop the picture before it's taken. For example, if you're shooting in a bathroom, don't try to eliminate the top of the shower curtain for style if that means also eliminating the top of the subject's head... We manipulate images heavily in production, which means that the entire shower curtain may be "digitally cut" from the image... but we can't put the top of someone's head back on very convincingly.

• At the same time, don't be afraid to get as close as your camera will tolerate and still be focused.

• Remember that we have great flexibility once a picture is taken to adjust colors, lighting and fix minor flaws and dust... If you're not sure about a picture, send it anyway.

Digital Manipulation

We're used to getting photos in all sorts of states of disrepair... we enhance, tweak, edit, etc. almost every photo that comes in. That said, we greatly prefer to do that enhancement in-house. We've got good eyes for "diamonds in the rough" and don't mind working with a rough print.

We generally do all digital artwork in house. I don't believe we've ever used a photographer's digital artwork, particularly not printer output of digital files. There is just no good way for us to get a high enough quality, high resolution scan of printer output. Printers are not "continuous tone" the way that photos are, and it just doesn't work well. Photoshop has nifty and neat filters, but they work best at 72 dpi. Because our output (halftoned greyscale) is so radically different from the format most pictures come to us (continuous tone color), many effects get lost completely in the translation. It is best, when filters are needed, for them to be applied with a mind to the end result, not just in overall appearance, but in terms of the printing process. This is why we prefer to do such manipulation in-house.

Film images

We can work with a wide variety of prints. Our preferred photo format is 5 x 7 glossy prints. We can work with just about any size print, but 5 x 7 seems to be the ideal compromise between detail and graininess for cover or full-page images. Larger film prints tend to be grainier than scanned enlargements, while smaller film prints can lose detail or get blurry on scanning enlargement. For anything smaller than a full-bleed photo such as the cover or center image, size of the original photo is much less important. Anything from 2 x 3 up to 8 x 10 will usually work. Larger images get down sampled, improving sharpness, and smaller pictures are simply scanned at their original size, which avoids the problem of enlargement blur.

Please avoid sending matte photos. A glossy finish will scan much better, the irregular surface of a matte photo will cause distortions on a scanner. With many photos this is not terribly significant, but for anything that will be enlarged, glossy finish is vitally important.

Color or black and white images are acceptable. We have no preference in either direction. Although our final output is black and white, our photo-manipulation capabilities are such that we can convert a color photo into a higher-contrast black and white image with very little difficulty at all. We do occasionally have use for color images (such as on book covers, catalog, Web site).

About composition and picture quality:

Dust, lines, etc. are not a reason to scrap a photo. We have a lot of tools for "erasing" dust and lines without losing detail.

Background: Ditto. Half the time we don't use the background at all. Much of the time we will "blur out" the background. When we do leave it in, we edit liberally—we've been known to erase oddly placed light switches, remove the ring and bar from a shower curtain, etc. Cropping is trivially easy, so is vignetting.

Even poor lighting can be fixed. We've managed to pull shadows off of faces or out of the background when necessary. As long as there aren't overexposed places where all definition is lost, we can usually compensate for just about anything else.

Digital cameras

Digital photos will work with the following caveats:

• We will be altering resolution to make the photo 200 dpi in most cases, and we will do that without altering the total pixel resolution. That means that if a photo is designed to be viewed in a reasonable size on the screen, we'll probably reduce it down to a fairly small picture, less than half of the "screen size".

• There is no "lossy" compression. This means that image quality must be "best," not a compressed .jpg. Uncompressed .jpg is okay in most cases. Compression creates all manner of weirdness in a .jpg— fine for viewing on screen and absolutely rotten for printing. Otherwise we will have to make the photo much smaller to compensate and still get a good print.

To give you a sense of what we can do with different digital cameras:

• To print a cover photo at proper resolution, a photo must be 9 inches wide by 11.25 inches tall, at 266 dpi minimum resolution. That is the equivalent of an 8 MP camera. 8 MP cameras are not currently available at prices mere mortals can afford.

• To print a full-bleed image inside the magazine, a photo must be 9 inches wide by 11.25 inches tall, at 200 dpi minimum resolution. That is well within the range of a 5 MP camera.

For photos inside the magazine, digital cameras are much more practical. Even a 2 MP camera will make a reasonable sized photo which can be easily used in the magazine at 200 dpi. We often use a 1.3 MP camera to do small images within the magazine.

Another limitation of digital cameras is picture format. If pictures are taken with .jpg compression used, they will often have to be down sampled to smooth out the compression artifacts generated by the format. That is, when you save a jpeg, it averages out blocks of color to make a smaller save file, and those blocks can sometimes lead to distortions and "fuzzy" images. This can be minimized on most cameras by using "best quality" or "no compression." You will get fewer pictures per disk, but we're more likely to be able to use them. Some cameras will allow you to save in .tif format. This is preferred, because it does not degrade the image quality.

With any digital photo, we prefer that you send the photo without any alterations or edits. Every time you edit, re-save as a .jpg, rotate, adjust color, etc. you reduce the amount of information available in the picture. We edit photos as needed, but we can't usually put back information that isn't there. Repeat saving as a .jpg is a good way to trash a photo completely. The ideal is to keep your original photos as they come off the camera, and make edits and changes on copies of those photos for your own use. For our use, we want the originals, not even opened and re-saved. This allows us the greatest latitude for getting the end result we need.

Scanned pictures

We prefer that any picture we receive come to us as a copy of the original, in the same format. If your pictures are taken with a digital camera, we want you to copy the original files and send those to us. If your pictures are taken with a film camera, we want you to make duplicate prints from the original negatives and send the duplicates to us. We prefer that if at all possible, we be allowed to do the scanning from film. If you want to e-mail us low-resolution scans (72 dpi jpgs) before having prints made and snail mailed-to be sure we're interested in the photos-you may do that. But we try to avoid having other people do the scanning for our final output.

Photo Submission Guidelines

We prefer that prints be sent by post for all film-based photo submissions.

If you are sending photographs or artwork via e-mail, it must be saved in the TIFF standard (.tif).

Send only one attachment per e-mail (.zip and .sit packages are okay.) E-mail all photos to layout@midwiferytoday.com ONLY.

• Do not send photos to jan@midwiferytoday.com.

We cannot guarantee return of material submitted.

Submit high quality copies of your work and retain a copy of your photography or artwork.

Editorial Columns and Features

Full Length Articles: All pregnancy, birth and postpartum subjects directed toward midwives, doulas, childbirth educators or their clients. Technical, objective (or journalistic reporting), or instructive, as well as personal experience. References are encouraged where appropriate, and suitable photographs, charts, diagrams and other graphics may clarify or enhance your article. Although quarterly themes are useful for our editorial plan, please do not feel constrained by them.

Please note the following topics *Midwifery Today* emphasizes in its publications: birth insights—birth stories told in a way that shares the author's insights or information learned; formulary-submit recipes for tinctures, hot packs, herbal treatments, salves, teas, as well as nutrition-packed recipes for pregnancy and labor; her story (hers, his and kids', too)—birth stories that are powerful, poignant, challenging, entertaining and educational, related by mothers or other family members, with the specific intent of helping birth practitioners gain knowledge and understanding; improving your practice—specific information, systems, and suggestions to help midwives and childbirth educators improve their practices; meet the practitioner—an autobiographical or biographical portrait: how and why did you or someone else enter the birthing field; your training, practice(s), goals, family, non-birthing interests and insights; midwifery and the law—news, litigation, information and advice, pending legislation, insurance issues concerning the practice of midwifery in your area; opinion pieces.

Abstracts: Synopses of full-length scientific articles or manuscripts. Accuracy is essential; restricted to objective review of scientific reports or studies. Credit source, include name(s) of original author(s), date, title of piece, name of journal/book/magazine it appeared in, page numbers, volume/issue numbers.

Media Reviews: Each publication features media reviews. Be sure to include the following information: authors/editors, name of book/video/cassette, cost, pages/length, format, publisher/producer name, address, phone. Keep in mind the item should be useful to birth practitioners or parents; explain why it is or isn't helpful and give readers a feel for what the product is like. Topics covered? Clearly covered? References included? Photos or illustrations included?

Networking: Air formal and informal comments and opinions, share news, ask questions, critique articles in past issues, and give technical advice or spiritual support. Two to five paragraphs, or in letter form.

Question of the Quarter: Reader's insights, comments, arguments, and instruction in response to a query posed in each issue. Questions are published two issues in advance.

Tricks of the Trade: Information you won't find in a textbook. Share practical wisdom and helpful hints from your practice.

We welcome additional contributions to any of the following columns:

International Midwife, a section of *Midwifery Today*: Midwifery from around the world:

All feature articles should emphasize pregnancy, birth and postpartum subjects, customs, traditions, remedies, cultural roles, legal issues, challenges and triumphs from a global perspective. How can midwives weave a global future? What are some opportunities for working abroad? Tell readers about your experience working in a country other than your own. Or, list current opportunities you are aware of. Explain how work abroad can be accomplished.

International Midwife will enable all readers to share and learn more about each other, and share ideas and practices for midwifery care from other countries. This is more than a cultural exchange; it's a place where we can explore and expand. Submission of photos is strongly encouraged.

Cards and Letters: We welcome your letters, opinions, updates on your international practice, submissions from midwives in all corners of the globe, descriptions of the joys and challenges as you practice in your own country, information on your country's midwifery organizations, etc. Limit length to two to five paragraphs.

News and Views: News and information presented in a journalistic style about pregnancy, birth, breast-feeding, and midwifery, in all countries of the world.

Media Reviews: See description in *Midwifery Today* section. Review publications and productions from countries other than the United States.

The Birthkit

Full-length articles submitted to *Midwifery Today* are also considered for *The Birthkit*. We look for birth stories with an eye toward imparting midwifery knowledge; short practice articles; articles about the business of midwifery, childbirth education or doula practice; articles that can serve as handouts for midwifery clients; motivational pieces; pregnancy, birth and midwifery poetry; related line drawings. Remedies: Choose a favorite herb, aroma or homeopathic that you use for pregnancy, birth, postpartum or lactation and describe its preparation and use. Or, choose a topic or condition to frame your article, then describe a variety of remedies. In either case, be specific about amounts.

Having a Baby Today

Having a Baby Today (HABT) is a quarterly, 16-page newsletter directed toward parents in the childbearing year and beyond. Emphasizing the miracle of birth, HABT is the voice of the experienced midwife sitting down with a mom and having a talk over tea. We are looking for short articles (400-1200 words) covering topics such as: breast-feeding tips; herbal and natural remedies for moms and babies; good nutrition and how to have a healthy baby and mom; birthing options; getting dads/partners involved in birth; and exercises for the pregnant and postpartum mom. We also welcome suitable, high-quality photographs. Please query HABT editor at editorial@midwiferytoday.com or PO Box 2672, Eugene, OR 97402.

HABT is not a paying market. Contributors receive one to two copies and authors of full-length articles receive two copies plus a year's subscription.

Midwifery Today E-News

A free weekly online publication for all childbirth practitioners and interested parents. Our intention is to reach beyond our print capabilities as well as expand our already existing Internet capabilities by offering a modern, quick and timely way to inform, network and support those who work with women during their childbearing years. E-News features convenient links to other appropriate and helpful sites, and an eventual link to the *Midwifery Today* articles database. It is also a springboard to other *Midwifery Today* Internet projects.

E-News guidelines: All material must be e-mailed. Please send to this address: mtensubmit@midwiferytoday.com. Your e-mailed submission must be received in the form of a standard e-mail message, not an attachment. Include your full name and city/state or country.

We do not accept graphics at this time. Photography and art are always considered for our print publications, however.

Feature Articles: We are striving for brevity so that busy birth practitioners may receive valuable information, comments, techniques and so forth that are highly useful yet quickly read. Please limit yourself to one to seven paragraphs. Longer submissions will be considered for either of our print mediums, *Midwifery Today* magazine or *The Birthkit* newsletter.

Please also consider the following areas for submissions:

News Items: Practical, timely, informative, factual; please cite your sources

Abstracts: Very brief synopses of current published articles; please cite source and author(s)

Commentary: Your view on a subject germane to birth

Art of Midwifery: Techniques that have worked for you

My Story: Your opportunity to teach by using storytelling

Switchboard: Ask questions, make comments, respond to material in past issues of E-News, sound off.

From the Garden: Share your favorite herbal treatments or remedies, or related therapies such as aroma therapy or homeopathy, in a paragraph or two per treatment.

Media Reviews: Let readers know what you've read or viewed about midwifery, pregnancy, birth, postpartum, breast-feeding, childbirth education; please cite all pertinent information to help readers easily find the book, tape, CD Rom or video.

Educating the Public: Tell how you inform your community about midwifery and natural birth.

Cultural Exchange: Information, techniques, history, news, stories from diverse cultures.

We will not consider multiple submissions or previously published articles for publication in *Midwifery Today*. Exceptions are made for *The Birthkit*. We also reserve the right to publish articles in other forms, such as theme booklets and electronic sources, including World Wide Web pages.

Please Note: All submissions are reviewed by the editors and are considered for the upcoming editorial year.

Payment

Midwifery Today and *The Birthkit* are nonpaying markets. Contributors receive two copies, and authors of full-length feature articles receive a complimentary one-year subscription to either *Midwifery Today* or *The Birthkit*, depending on placement.

How to Submit Via E-Mail

First, save your article in one of the following formats:

.rtf (Rich Text Format)

.doc (Microsoft Word)

.txt (Plain Text)

Send only one attachment per e-mail. E-mail your document to BOTH of the following addresses (using the "cc" function):

jan@midwiferytoday.com

editorial@midwiferytoday.com

We reserve the right to edit for clarity, content, and length, but whenever possible, we ask you to approve all edits.

Important: We reserve the right to refuse any advertisement.

Categories: Nonfiction—Education—Trade—Birth Practitioners—Women's Issues—Childbirth—Midwifery—Nursing

CONTACT: Editor (editoral@midwiferytoday.com)
Material: Articles
CONTACT: Photo Editor (layout@midwiferytoday.com)
Material: Photos
PO Box 2672-350
Eugene OR 97402
Phone: 541-344-7438
Fax: 541-344-1422
E-mail: editorial@midwiferytoday.com
Website: www.midwiferytoday.com

Military History

Please refer to PRIMEDIA History Group.

Military Officer

General

• Publisher: Military Officers Association of America, a nonprofit organization.

• Editor: Col. Warren S. Lacy, USA-Ret.

• Audience: Commissioned and warrant officers, families, and surviving spouses of the seven uniformed services: Army, Marine Corps, Navy, Air Force, Coast Guard, Public Health Service, and National Oceanic and Atmospheric Administration—both actively serving and retired.

• Circulation: 390,000 monthly. Sample magazine on request with 9x12 SASE.

Editorial Requirements

• Topics: Current military/political affairs; recent military history, especially Vietnam and Korea; travel; financial planning; health and fitness; military family; retirement lifestyles; and general interest. No fiction, poetry, or fillers. Original material only; no reprints.

• Format: MS Word-compatible file or typed, double-spaced manuscript. No footnotes.

• Deadlines: Feature articles normally are scheduled six months in advance.

• Queries: Submit detailed query before sending manuscript. Enclose copies of published clips and résumé. Unsolicited manuscripts are rarely accepted.

• Style: Active voice, nontechnical, with direct quotes. Optimistic, upbeat theme. Use *The Associated Press Stylebook and Libel Manual*.

• Length: Features, up to 2,500 words; minifeatures, up to 1,400 words.

• Terms: First rights, to include Internet and reprint rights.

• Payment: Features, up to $1,800; minifeatures, up to $1,000. Payment on acceptance.

• Submit to: Managing Editor, The Retired Officers Association, 201 N. Washington St., Alexandria, VA 22314-2539. Enclose SASE for return of submissions.

• Response time: Three months. No phone calls, please.

Photographs

Original color transparencies suitable for color separation preferred. $75 for one-eighth page, $125 for one-fourth page, $175 for one-half page, $250 for full page. 5x7 or 8x10 black-and-white glossies occasionally acceptable. $20 for each black-and-white photo used. Prefer captions and credit line on separate sheet. Include SASE for return of photos.

Categories: Family—General Interest—Health—Lifestyle—Military—Money & Finances—Physical Fitness

CONTACT: Managing Editor
Material: All
MOAA
201 N. Washington St.
Alexandria VA 22314-2539
E-mail: editor @ moaa.org
Website: www.moaa.org/magazine

Miniature Quilts

Please refer to *Traditional Quiltworks*.

Minnesota Memories

Minnesota Memories accepts prose stories from current and former Minnesota residents. The books, which are compilations of stories and accompanying photos, are published at least once a year and marketed mainly in Minnesota. Stories may be funny, sad, heroic, historical, mysterious, reflective, inspirational or unusual, but they must be true. *Minnesota Memories* will not accept commercial endorsements for products or services, nor will it accept self-congratulatory testimonials. Published stories usually range from 300-2000 words. Storytellers receive a copy of the book and a chance to become part of published Minnesota history via the *Minnesota Memories* project.

E-mail or snail mail stories. Include a 25 word bio of the writer, which will appear at the end of your published story.

Categories: Nonfiction—Biography—Regional History—Personal History

CONTACT: Submissions
Material: All
439 Lakeview Blvd.
Albert Lea, MN 56007
Phone: 507-377-1255
E-mail: Minnmemory@aol.com

Remember: Editors change jobs and publishers change addresses. It is wise to invest in a phone call for the current information before submitting.

the minnesota review

The Minnesota Review
University of Missouri, Columbia

Regarding submission guidelines for *The Minnesota Review*, please note the following:

We have a long tradition of publishing politically engaged work, whether it be Marxist, socialist, feminist, etc. In particular, we would like to publish the work of committed younger writers.

We will continue to publish poetry and fiction on a variety of topics that need not relate to our special topics. In each issue, our editor's aim is to present writing that is cutting-edge, both stylistically and conceptually.

As for technical matters, we ask that essays and reviews be submitted in duplicate and that they adhere to the form specified in the MLA Handbook. We also ask that your manuscript, whether poetry or fiction, be double-spaced. Clear photocopies are acceptable. Simultaneous submissions are also acceptable. Our reading period is usually about two to six months. Please enclose SASE; manuscripts submitted without postage will not be returned. If we do accept your work for publication, we will request the article as an MS Word file on a Macintosh-formatted disk. We will also need a few sentences for Contributors Notes.

Sample issues are available for $12 each. Past issues include n.s. 52-54 (Academostars); n.s. 50-51 (Activism and the Academy); n.s. 48-49 (The Academics of Publishing); and n.s. 47 (The White Issue). Send check to the address below.

Spring 2002

Categories: Fiction—Nonfiction—Culture—Feminism—Film/Video—Gay/Lesbian—Literature—Multicultural—Philosophy—Poetry—Politics—Short Stories

CONTACT: Editorial Submissions
Material: Correspondence, submissions, and subscriptions
Department of English, 107 Tate Hall
University of Missouri
Columbia MO 65211
Phone: 573-882-6421
E-mail: williamsjeff@missouri.edu
Website: www.theminnesotareview.org

Minority Engineer

Please refer to Equal Opportunity Publications, Inc.

MISSISSIPPI
Magazine

Mississippi Magazine

Mississippi Magazine is a bimonthly publication that celebrates the positive points of our state—from interesting people and places to homes, gardens, food, history, culture, special events, and more. All topics that appear in the magazine must have a direct and obvious link to Mississippi.

Many of our articles are written by freelance contributors, and because our magazine is only published six times each year, we must choose each story very carefully. We often develop story ideas ourselves and assign them to freelancers. To be considered for such assignments, send at least three clips of your recent work, along with a letter detailing your writing specialities. We also welcome article proposals from freelance writers themselves. Follow these tips to ensure that your idea will be promptly considered.

Developing a Story Idea

Before submitting a query, study at least one recent issue of *Mississippi Magazine*. Familiarize yourself with our editorial style and the types of articles we generally include. Sample copies are available for $5 each; mail a check (Memo: Sample Copy) to Mississippi Magazine, 5 Lakeland Circle, Jackson, MS 39216.

Consider whether your idea will fit well in our publication. Try to place your story within one of our current issues and see if you can visualize it, illustrations and all. Chances are, if you can't see the story in the magazine, you will have a hard time convincing the editorial staff to use it.

We are always looking for unusual subjects that still manage to fit within our editorial scope. Find a unique perspective that you can use to make your story out of the ordinary. A general story on a well-covered topic (like the Natchez Trace, the city of Oxford, or Eudora Welty) is not likely to be accepted. We are looking for unique topics or fresh angles on familiar ideas.

Keep in mind that we strive to be original, so don't propose an article on something you've recently seen in another statewide publication unless you have a very different perspective or new information.

We do not accept fiction; poetry; articles relating to politics, business news, or controversial topics; or previously published articles.

Suitable Topics

Subjects that we regularly cover include interesting people, places, or events; unique historical subjects; great gardens or gardening topics; beautiful and unique homes or interior design; and party or recipe ideas.

For new writers, departments—rather than features—are often the best places to break into our magazine. These include:

Southern Scrapbook—Short (100- to 600-word) articles on a variety of topics. See recent issues for examples. Due to the brevity of these articles, we prefer to consider **full manuscripts** instead of queries.

Culture Center—800-1,200-word articles on a specific artist or any aspect of the arts, culture, theater, or music in Mississippi.

Gardening—800-1,200-word articles on specific planting topics or profiles of individual gardens.

Home Pages—400-800-word reviews of new books that directly relate to Mississippi.

On Being Southern—The last page of each issue is a personal essay written by someone with a Mississippi connection. These essays may be humorous, are often nostalgic, may be related to a specific season, and should always have an upbeat, positive tone. Full manuscripts must be submitted for consideration and must be 500-800 words. Send these stories by email (no attachments, please) or by U.S. mail on a disk in text-only format, along with a printed hard copy and cover letter containing your name, address, social security number, daytime phone number, and a short biographical sentence.

Submitting a Query Letter

With a few exceptions (noted above), we prefer preliminary query letters to unsolicited full manuscripts. Queries allow us to more easily review your idea and potentially suggest how to tailor it for our audience before you begin writing. Due to the large volume of queries we receive, **we cannot accept story ideas by phone**. And no simultaneous submissions, please.

Because we are a bimonthly publication, keep in mind that we plan each issue several months in advance. Seasonal topics should be submitted well in advance of the intended issue date.

Query letters must be typed and must include the following information:

• Name, address, daytime phone number, and email address.

• The subject of story, along with (if applicable) the intended department or specific issue for which it would be appropriate.

• Your proposed lead, followed by a short but thorough summary of the story's content—noting potential interviewees, sources, and other highlights—and a conclusion. Also note any ideas for sidebars.

• Details about why you think this story would be of interest to the readers of *Mississippi Magazine*.

• Any photographs you have to illustrate the article. This is crucial for–this is crucial for home, garden, or art-related story ideas. For consideration purposes only, snapshots are fine. If you have strong photography skills and would like us to consider using your photographs along with the article, please submit high-quality prints or 35mm color transparencies. For articles on subjects other than home, garden, and art, it's okay if you don't have photos, but please briefly describe how the article will lend itself to visual presentation.

• Brief information about yourself and your writing experience.

• A few recent clips or samples of your work.

All queries must also include a self-addressed stamped envelope for a reply and for the return of any materials you would like to have back. Always make a copy of any original materials before submitting. *Mississippi Magazine* assumes no responsibility for the return of unsolicited materials.

Queries sent by U.S. mail are preferred, but emailed queries are acceptable if you follow a few special guidelines: Type or paste the entire text of the proposal in the body of the email rather than include an attached document. Compose an email query just as you would one that is sent by regular mail, being sure to include all of the details mentioned above. Please do not send large picture files as attachments. E-mail queries will not be answered any more quickly than those submitted by mail.

Our Response

The editor will respond to your letter within eight weeks in one of the following ways:

• Acceptance for publication. If your idea is accepted, you will receive a letter detailing word count, payment information, specifics of the article, deadline, and tentative publication date. You will also receive a writer's contract, which should be signed and returned immediately, and a format sheet, which you should follow carefully in preparing your article.

• Request for more information. Sometimes the staff needs photographs or more details about your idea in order to make a decision. If we request more information, we are still considering your idea.

• We would like to file your idea. Sometimes we have an overflow of ideas for a particular kind of story and need to wait a while to see if and when the story will fit into our editorial plans. With permission from contributors, we also like to keep selected "On Being Southern" essays on file indefinitely for potential use in future issues.

• This story does not fit into our magazine. We want each issue to possess a distinct style and continuity from story to story. Many good ideas simply do not fit into the current editorial plans, or a similar story may have recently been done.

While waiting for a response, your patience is appreciated. Please do not call to check on the status of your submission until at least eight weeks have passed. We receive hundreds of freelance queries each year, and with a small staff, it takes a while to go through each inquiry and respond accordingly.

Submitting an Article

After writing an article you have been assigned, take time to confirm and double-check all facts and figures, quotations, spellings of names and places, phone numbers, addresses, etc. Please consult *The Associated Press Stylebook* for all style questions.

Include two or three suggested headlines (usually 2-6 words) and subheads (can range from a short phrase to a couple of sentences), but please note that these elements are selected at our discretion.

Send the completed piece on a disk in text-only or Microsoft Word format. On the first page, include your name, address, phone number, social security number, and the number of words in the article. Also send a hard copy of the article, printed on high-quality paper by a laser or inkjet printer. Attached to your article, please include a list of refer-

ences used and people interviewed or included in the article, along with their phone numbers. Articles may also be submitted by email if prior arrangement is made with the editor to do so.

Mississippi Magazine buys only previously unpublished manuscripts. We buy first publication rights and pay on publication. We assume no responsibility for unsolicited manuscripts, and we request a self-addressed stamped envelope for the return of any materials. We reserve the right to edit any article for space, grammar, and content. Author proofs are generally not provided. All articles submitted will remain in the custody of *Mississippi Magazine* until publication, unless a rewrite is necessary.

Payment

Feature articles: $200-$400

Southern Scrapbook: $25-75

On Being Southern: $150

Other department articles: $150-$250

Expenses: $35 limit

Categories: Nonfiction—Culture—Food—Gardening—History—Regional

CONTACT: Kelli L. Bozeman, Editor
Material: All
5 Lakeland Circle
Jackson, MS 39216
Phone: 601-982-8447
Fax: 601-982-8447
E-mail: editor@mismag.com
Website: www.mississippimagazine.com

The Mississippi Review
The Mississippi Review online
University of Southern Mississippi

The Mississippi Review online is posted quarterly. Each issue has a guest editor and to submit work you should contact the guest editors directly. The guest editors for upcoming issues will always be listed on the home page of the magazine. If you can find no editor and issue listed there, then the magazine is not reading new work for the moment. Usually, however, you will find the names of editors who have issues in progress, often with notes about what kinds of things these editors are looking for--please contact these editors directly with queries and submissions.

Submissions should be sent as attachments preferably in Microsoft Word or RTF format, or in ASCII text in the body of an email message.

Our so-called mission?

Mississippi Review is a national literary magazine published twice yearly in print, and quarterly on the web. Among the writers MR has published in recent years are Jamaica Kinkaid, Derek Wolcott, Tom Drury, John Barth, Rick Bass, Padgett Powell, Barry Hannah, Martin Amis, Roddy Doyle, Will Self, Margaret Atwood, Robert Olen Butler, Susan Minot, Thom Jones, Paul Auster, Kazuo Ishiguro, Tomaz Salamun, William Gibson, and hundreds of others. While we continue to publish well-known writers, we are also committed to finding new work in fiction and poetry by emerging writers.

Categories: Fiction—Poetry—Regional—Essay

CONTACT: Frederick Barthelme, Editor
Material: Fiction
CONTACT: Angela Ball, Poetry Editor
Material: Poetry
Center for Writers
The University of Southern Mississippi
Box 5144
Hattiesburg MS 39406-5144

Phone: 601-266-5600
Fax: 601-266-5757
E-mail: rief@netdoor.com
Website: www.mississippireview.com

The Missouri Review

The editors invite submissions of poetry, fiction and nonfiction of general interest (no literary criticism). Please clearly mark the outer envelope as fiction, poetry or essay. Do not mix genres in the same submission.

Previously unpublished material only. Manuscripts will not be returned unless accompanied by a stamped, self-addressed envelope. Standard response time is from 10-12 weeks. Manuscripts are read year round. Sample copies are available for $7.95.

Simultaneous submissions are okay as long as you notify us if accepted elsewhere.

POETRY

MR publishes poetry features only—6 to 14 pages of poems by each of 3 to 5 poets per issue. Please keep in mind the length of features when submitting poems.

The Tom McAfee Discovery Feature in poetry is an ongoing series, awarded at least once a year at the discretion of the editors, to showcase the work of an outstanding new poet who has not yet published a book. This award is chosen from among the regular submissions. There are no deadlines and no application process. This feature carrries an additional cash award beyond the regular payment schedule and has been funded by the family and friends of Tom McAfee.

FICTION

All fiction manuscripts should be double-spaced. While there are no length restrictions, "flash fictions" are rarely accepted. We recommend writers familiarize themselves with fiction from previous issues before submitting.

The William Peden Prize of $1,000 is awarded annually to the best piece of fiction to have appeared in the previous volume year. The winner is chosen by an outside judge from stories published in MR. There is no separate application process.

ESSAYS

Nonfiction of general interest only. All submissions should be double-spaced and addressed to "nonfiction editor." There are no restrictions on length or topic, but we suggest that writers familiarize themselves with nonfiction from previous issues. Queries are welcome. Excerpts from book-length nonfiction manuscripts will be considered, but must be able to stand alone.

EDITORS' PRIZE & LARRY LEVIS PRIZE

MR sponsors an annual Editors' Prize Contest in fiction and essay and the Larry Levis Editors' Prize in poetry, with a winner and 3 finalists named in each category. Length restrictions are 25 pages for fiction and essay, 10 pages for poetry. Winners will be published in the following spring issue plus each will receive a cash prize: $2,000 each for fiction, poetry, and essay. Postmark deadline is October 15. A $15 fee per submission includes a one-year subscription to MR.

The Larry Levis Editors' Prize is to honor the memory of MR co-founder and distinguished poet, Larry Levis and is partially funded by his family, friends, students and colleagues.

SUBMISSIONS

Send all submissions by snail mail.

Categories: Fiction—Nonfiction—Book Reviews—Interview—Poetry

CONTACT: Editor
Material: Indicate genre or contest category
1507 Hillcrest Hall, University of Missouri
Columbia MO 65211
Phone: 573-882-4474
Fax: 573-884-4671
Website: www.missourireview.org

Model Railroader

Thanks for your interest in contributing to MODEL RAILROADER. Before you prepare and submit any article, you should write us a short letter of inquiry describing what you want to do. We can then tell you if it fits our needs and save you from working on something we won't want.

We publish articles on all aspects of model railroading and on prototype (real) railroading as a subject for modeling. Here's a general list of our requirements:

TEXT: Present your subject simply and directly in plain English. Keep it brief-most of our articles are one-third text and two-thirds illustrations.

PHOTOGRAPHS: For color we need original 35mm slides or larger transparencies; or glossy color prints 5"x7" or larger. Be sure to include a caption for every photo.

Photography makes or breaks most of the articles we see, so here are six pointers on color photography:

1. Load your 35mm (or larger format) camera with slow-speed indoor color film such as Fujichrome 64T (RTP) or Kodak Ektachrome 64T (EPY).

2. Use at least three photo floods matched to your color film. Floodlights rated for 3200K match the Fuji RTP and Kodak EPY films.

3. Stop your camera down as far as it goes; f22 is good for a 35mm camera, f32 is best. Mount your camera on a tripod so you can make long exposures.

4. Position your lights for even lighting with no harsh shadows. Always light the background first, then the foreground.

5. Bracket your exposures by time, and make lots of bracket exposures over a wide range. You're bound to get a couple of good exposures.

6. Select what you think is the best exposure for each shot, along with one lighter and one darker for insurance. The best exposure for magazine reproduction is the "perfect" exposure.

DRAWINGS: Clean, neat pencil drawings are fine for how-to illustrations, electrical schematics, track plans, and maps-these will be redrawn by our art staff for publication. Track plans must be to scale. If you are a draftsman and want to contribute prototype drawings, write for information on our style and standards.

Send everything for one article at one time, if possible all in one package, and with your name and address on every item. Address your package to "TO THE EDITOR, MODEL RAILROADER MAGAZINE," and mark it "MANUSCRIPT ENCLOSED." We'll send you a card acknowledging receipt of your article, and try to review it within 60 to 90 days. We'll return articles that we can't use if you include return postage.

If we can use your article, we'll pay you for it upon acceptance. Our standard rate is $30 per column, or $90 per page, including drawings and photos. Our standard acceptance agreement specifies that we are buying all rights to the article.

The soonest an article can appear in MODEL RAILROADER is usually four months after acceptance, and we try to use most articles within a year. Our initial payment will be based on a space and color estimate, and we'll make an additional payment upon publication if the article exceeds our estimate. We'll return photos and other material that we don't publish, but we usually keep everything that is used in MODEL RAILROADER.

Thanks for your interest in MODEL RAILROADER.

How-to checklist

The how-to article you send to MODEL RAILROADER should include the following items:

1. TEXT: Tell how you did the project, or tell the reader how to do it, in simple, clear, and direct language. Keep it as brief as possible—most MODEL RAILROADER stories are no longer than six magazine pages. Use photos and drawings extensively, and put details, dimensions, and part numbers in the illustrations. Use active description or instruction, such as "I painted the roof black" or "Paint the roof black," and avoid the passive, "The roof was painted black."

2. LEAD PHOTOGRAPH: Show the model or project at its best, to get the reader's attention and encourage him to read and follow the article. The lead photo should be in color. Usually it's best to show the subject of the article in a finished model scene, with the photo composed so the article subject is the dominant element. Alternately, show the subject against a plain, untextured backdrop of a neutral color—seamless photo backdrop paper is ideal.

3. HOW-TO ILLUSTRATIONS: Use drawings and photos to show the project under construction. Number each as a figure, i.e., fig. 3, and refer to them by the corresponding number in the text. Neat, legible pencil drawings are adequate, as our art staff will prepare finished ink drawings for publication. Drawings need not be to scale unless scale is important, as with exact-size templates, for example.

4. BILL OF MATERIALS: Give a detailed list of items needed to build the project. Include manufacturers' names, part numbers, part names or descriptions, and quantities required. Be sure your information is current. Explain if the reader will have to substitute for items which are no longer available. If you doubt that the reader will know where to find some item, include the manufacturer's address.

5. PROTOTYPE INFORMATION (where applicable): Use photos and/or drawings to show the reader the prototype you followed. Photos may be color, black-and-white, or both. If you have drafting skills and would like to prepare prototype drawings, write for information about our requirements.

Categories: Nonfiction—Crafts/Hobbies—Hobbies

CONTACT: Submissions Editor
Material: All
PO Box 1612
Waukesha WI 53187-1612
Phone: 262-796-8776
Fax: 262-796-1142
E-mail: mrmag@mrmag.com
Website: www.modelrailroader.com

Model Retailer
Resources for Successful Hobby Retailing

The magazine pays for one-time print and electronic publication rights to freelance manuscripts and images. Freelance stories generally are assigned in advance, but we welcome proposals for feature articles and columns, or the submission of articles sent on speculation. Payment is made upon acceptance of the material for publication. Feature material generally should be limited to 1,500 or fewer words. Illustrative materials—including but not limited to photographs, graphics, charts and graphs—are welcome and will be judged on their own merit. The material must be original and, where needed, referenced as to the source.

Please send freelance material in hard copy or disk format.

You also may send the manuscript as a e-mail attachment to msavage@modelretailer.com, or fax it to 262-796-1383.

Categories: Business—Cartoons—Collectibles—Computers—Hobbies—Money & Finances—Retail

CONTACT: Mark Savage, Editor
Material: All
Kalmbach Publishing
21027 Crossroads Circle
PO BOX 1612
Waukesha WI 53187-1612
Phone: 262-796-8776
Fax: 262-796-1383
E-mail: msavage@modelretailer.com
Website: www.modelretailer.com

Modeler's Resource

Modeler's Resource is the only bi-monthly magazine that brings you 408 pages of modeling overdrive each and every year! We represent what we feel is modeling at its best and most diverse. Page after page of techniques, reviews and show coverage, not to mention our in depth brand of "how-to" articles with the emphasis on quality, in-progress pictures, which allows you to recreate what our writers accomplish!

Do We Need Articles?
Our regular staff of writers keeps us pretty stocked up on articles that we publish in the magazine. However, many have called or written to find out if we're interested in accepting articles from those who are not staff writers. The following FAQ should provide most of the information you need.

Who's Eligible?
Anyone who builds models and/or reports on the modeling industry.

What Are We Looking For?
We're mainly looking for quality "how-to" articles which include taking a kit right out of the box and building it, painting it or customizing it. Articles that take us behind-the-scenes or onto the main floor of a model-related show are also desired.

Your Article
Your article can be submitted to us in any number of ways:
Save it to disk (ASCII, Plain Text or RTF) and send a printed copy of the article with it in case we encounter difficulties opening your disk. Your article can also be submitted in Microsoft Word format.

E-mail it to us! Create it in your computer, then copy the entire text to your clip board, then paste it into a "new message." You can also e-mail it with an attachment (Microsoft Word, for instance). This is probably the easiest way for us because we can then simply import it directly into our computer and go from there.

The Best Way to Write
Keep things as simple as possible, but be as precise as you can be with the details. If you're already a writer, then you've undoubtedly developed your own style. If you're just starting to pick up pen in hand, your style will come to the fore soon enough.

Length of Article
Optimal length is between 2000 and 2500 words. Most articles in the magazine run between 2 to 3 pages in length and 2500 words allows you to say what you need to say and allows us to keep your photos larger. This enables the reader to get the full benefit of your article. If you keep your article succinct, we can keep the photos larger. In some cases, we will edit an article to make it flow better and fit into our guidelines and we reserve the right to edit any and all articles we choose to publish.

Photos
This is the area that will undoubtedly make or break your article. We need good quality photos or slides (either in black and white or full color) with good contrast. Your article might be phenomenal but without equally rewarding photos, your article won't make it into one of our issues. If you're not good with a camera, find someone who is or start learning about it yourself. It's important that correct lighting is used to avoid harsh shadows or a washed out look.

We also need quality in-progress shots for our readers. It doesn't do any good to describe some marvelous technique without seeing how you accomplished it. It simply can't be stressed enough: Pictures are the most important aspect of the article.

Photo Captions: When photos are submitted, it's important that captions go with them wherever necessary. These can be typed on a label and affixed to the back of the photo or simply place a numeral 1,

2 or 3, etc. or a letter from the alphabet on the back discreetly in a corner and then place the information about the photo on a separate paper. Try not to mark directly on the back of the photo if you can help it though, because those marks can sometimes come through when scanning the photo in.

Drawings or Illustrations

While you don't need to be a professional artist (though it helps!), any final drawings for your article should be done with black ink and as a finished drawing. At times, if we feel the article warrants it, we will have one of our artists create drawings to go with your article.

Payment

The best news is that you will receive payment for all articles we publish! Rate is $25.00 per published page for unestablished writers for the following types of articles: model or sculpting how-tos and/or reviews, interviews or company profiles, etc. Articles dedicated to show/convention coverage are paid out $20.00 per page. (Final page count is determined by the layout and design team at *Modeler's Resource*). If you'd prefer, we will trade your article for the same value in ad space if you have product you'd like to advertise in our magazine. Payment is made upon actual publication of your article and checks are printed and mailed out on the 15th of the month that the issue is published.

Article Inquiries

The best way to find out whether or not we're interested in your article(s) is to send us a note or e-mail describing the proposed article as opposed to simply sending in the entire article with pictures. We may already have an article similar to yours in the wings waiting for publication.

When Will Your Article Be Published?

The appearance of your article(s) in *Modeler's Resource* could be anytime between six months up to a year from our acceptance. It may appear sooner but in most cases, the time frame listed above is what you can expect.

Returning Your Article/Photos

Articles that we ultimately do not use will be sent back if you provide postage and packaging.

Restrictions

We ask that you do not send us an article that you are planning on sending or have already sent to another model-related magazine.

Categories: Nonfiction—Crafts/Hobbies—Hobbies

CONTACT: Fred DeRuvo
Material: All
4120 Douglas Blvd, #306-372
Granite Bay CA 95746-5936
Phone: 916-784-9517
Fax: 916-784-8384
E-mail: modres@modelersresource.com
Website: www.modelersresource.com

Modern Bride

1. We are a consumer bridal publication. All articles must be of direct interest to the engaged or newly married couple.

2. Send query letter with a brief outline of areas to be covered or complete manuscript. Enclose a stamped self-addressed envelope for response or return of material.

3. If you are a published author, send two clips with your query.

4. Queries usually are answered within four weeks of receipt.

5. Article lengths range from short features, 500 to 800 words, to main features, 1,500 to 2,000 words.

6. Prefer typed, double-spaced manuscript or computer letter-quality print-out.

7. Assignments may be made on speculation or with a 25 percent kill fee provision depending on circumstances.

8. Purchase first periodical publishing rights. Payment on acceptance.

Categories: Nonfiction—Consumer—Crafts/Hobbies—Family—Fashion—General Interest—Health—Hobbies—Marriage—Money & Finances—Physical Fitness—Psychology—Relationships—Self Help—Travel—Home-Beauty—How-to—Personal Experience

CONTACT: Susan Schneider, Executive Editor
Material: All
4 Times Square
New York NY 10036
Phone: 212-286-6285
Website: www.modernbride.com

Modern Drummer

Modern Drummer is dedicated to helping drummers in all areas of music, and

at every level of ability. It is important to understand that MD is not a "fan magazine" for people who like drummers; it is a professional magazine for drummers themselves. In fact, many of our columns are written by top professional drummers and drum teachers. While it is not crucial that all of our writers be drummers, it is necessary that they know enough about drums and drumming to be able to write about such topics as technique, equipment, style, and musical philosophies.

A certain amount of biographical information is good, as long as it serves to provide background or put things into perspective. But remember: There are any number of magazines providing biographical and lifestyle information; MD is read by people who want information about drumming, so do not get too far away from our main focus.

Additionally, MD is looking for music journalists rather than music critics. Our aim is to provide information, not to make value judgements. Therefore, keep all articles as objective as possible. We are interested in how and why a drummer plays a certain way; the readers can make their own decisions about whether or not they like it.

Before you attempt to write an article for *Modern Drummer*, make sure you are familiar with the magazine. You should have read at least three recent issues to acquaint yourself with our general style and tone. (Sample copies are available upon request for $7 each at mdrm@kable.com.)

In addition, when considering writing an article, you should ask yourself the following questions: Will this article help a substantial group of drummers improve their abilities? Will it enlighten them on a particular phase of drumming? Will it save the reader time, money, or effort? Is the topic interesting enough to attract a large number of readers? Will the article help the reader arrive at a decision or draw a conclusion? Will the article help drummers do their jobs better? Not every article will do all of

those things, but if the article does not do any of them, then MD will probably not be interested in it.

Please query us on lengthy material before you begin writing. This helps us avoid receiving articles we cannot use, and it will help you avoid having your article returned. Send us a brief outline of the subject matter and your angle on the story. The editors will then be able to guide you in tailoring the material to the exact needs of the magazine. Also, if your idea has already been assigned or covered, we can notify you before you begin working. If you are writing for MD for the first time, or if your idea

is somewhat out of the ordinary, you will be asked to submit your piece on speculation.

The above information should guide you in submitting material to *Modern Drummer*. If you need any further information, please contact Bill Miller or Rick Van Horn at the address listed above. We are always interested in acquiring good editorial material, and in finding talented, competent writers.

PAYMENT

Modern Drummer pays upon publication. Rates vary depending upon length of the story after editing, whether the article will be used as a feature article or column, and, to some extent, the length of the writer's association with *Modern Drummer*.

General Rates

Feature article: $300: $500. Buys all rights.

Column: $75: $150. Buys all rights.

(Receipt of payment generally occurs three to six weeks after publication.)

OPEN COLUMNS

Music Columns: Column material can be technical, conceptual, or philosophical in nature. Topics should be very specific, and we encourage the use of musical examples where appropriate, as well as photos or illustrations.

Rock Perspectives: Mainstream or commercial rock

Rock 'N' Jazz Clinic: Progressive rock and fusion

Jazz Drummers' Workshop: Mainstream, bebop, or avant-garde jazz

Driver's Seat: Big band

Strictly Technique: Technical studies that could be applied to any area of drumming

Shop Talk: How-to's on maintaining, customizing, and restoring drums

Latin Symposium: Latin and reggae rhythms as applied to drumset

Teachers' Forum: Articles dealing with teaching and education

The Jobbing Drummer: Freelance drumming: casuals, weddings, etc.

In The Studio: All facets of recording

Show Drummers' Seminar: Broadway, Vegas, theater, resorts, circus, ice shows, etc.

Basics: Primarily beginner-oriented material

Rock Charts: Complete transcription of the drum part to a classic track or current hit

Drum Soloist: Transcriptions of current or classic drum solos

Health & Science: Health matters of importance to drummers

Rudimental Symposium: Technical material pertaining to rudimental technique, drum corps, etc.

Taking Care Of Business: Legal and/or business matters relevant to drummers

Profile Columns: These columns are similar to feature interviews, but shorter in length, and can include popular contemporary drummers, those who have recently come to national attention, or historical drummers from all areas of music (1,500 to 2,500 words).

EDITORIAL POLICY

Manuscripts are edited to conform with style policies, as well as for consistency and readability. This may involve condensing, rearranging, re-titling, and, to some extent, rewording the article. Please refer to the MD Stylesheet for specific style preferences. Final decisions regarding style, grammar, and presentation are the right of the editorial staff of *Modern Drummer*.

STYLESHEET

I. MANUSCRIPT LAYOUT

A. Margins

1. First Page: 3" margin at the top, 1" margin at bottom and sides

2. Subsequent Pages: 1" margin top, bottom, and sides

B. Type Specs

1. Copy must be double-spaced

2. Text must be typed as a Word document, and either emailed or printed & mailed to us. Type should be 12 point, double-spaced. Typewritten manuscripts are acceptable, as long as they are clean and easy to read.

3. Preferred font for computer-printed articles: Geneva

C. Page Numbering-consecutive

D. Paper

1. 8 1/2 x 11 only

2. Original manuscript or clear Xerox copy

E. Bylines

1. Top of first page under title at left margin "by" (lowercase) followed by name of author.

2. Author's address, phone number, and social security number should also appear on manuscript

II. COPY LENGTHS

A. Feature material should range from 2,000 to 4,000 words

B. Column material should range from 350 to 1,500 words

III. PUNCTUATION

A. Album, film, book, and periodical titles should be underlined.

B. The initial letter of each word in album, song, book, and periodical titles should be capitalized.

C. Song titles should be in quotation marks.

D. Dashes should be typed as double hyphen with a space before and after (—).

E. Do not hyphenate words at ends of lines.

F. Periods and commas should be placed before quotes; colons and semi-colons come after quotes.

IV. MUSICAL GENRES: Preferred spellings (note capitalization)
Afro-Cuban

ambient; trance; chill-out; alternative rock; college rock; indie rock; alternative country; alt-country; Americana; y'alternative; avant-garde; avant-garde jazz; bebop; hard bop; big band; bluegrass; blues; the blues; blues-rock; Cajun; classic rock; classical; 20th-century classical; C&W or country & western; country; country-rock; dance music; disco; Dixieland; doo-wop; drum 'n' bass; dub; dub reggae; electronic music; electronica; emo; folk; funk fusion; jazz-rock; garage rock; glam; Gospel goth; goth rock; hard rock; heavy metal; metal; death metal; nüü metal; dark metal; grind; (grind-core); thrash; hip-hop; house; industrial; jam bands; jazz; jump blues; klezmer; Krautrock; laptop; glitch; Latin; Latin jazz; lite jazz; lo-fi; lounge; minimalism; new age; new wave; synth-pop; opera; pop; pop-rock; post-punk; power-pop; progressive rock; prog rock; psychedelia; psychedelic; pub rock; punk; punk rock; hardcore punk; hardcore; rap; rap-rock; reggae; R&B or rhythm & blues; rock 'n' roll; rockabilly; roots; contemporary roots music; ska; skiffle; soul; soundtrack music; southern rock; surf-rock; swing; techno; Tejano; Tex-Mex; world music (specific styles generally lower-case: samba, afro-pop,; polka, etc.); zydeco

V. STYLE NOTES

A. Spell out numbers one hundred and below. Use numerals for numbers over one hundred. Exceptions include: 8th note, 16th note, and 32nd note; dimensions of gear (drum sizes, shell plies, etc.); and instances where many numbers are used throughout an article that's technical in nature.

B. '60s, '70s, '80s when dealing with decades.

C. Twenties, thirties, forties, etc. when dealing with age.

D. LP (LPs), 45 (45s), CD (CDs).

E. A.M. and P.M. should be typed in small caps.

F. Specific times should be expressed in numerals, with minutes: "The gig ended at 2:00 A.M."

VI. PARAGRAPHING

The first paragraph of an article should be aligned entirely with the left margin. The first line of subsequent paragraphs should be indented with a standard tab, with subsequent lines aligning with the left margin. Make sure your preferences do not automatically indent the first line of paragraphs. New paragraphs should be manually tabbed in.

VII. INTERVIEWS

A. For question & answer format, introduction should follow paragraph format described in VII above. Uppercase MD (followed by a colon) should precede questions, and first name of interviewee (also followed by a colon) should precede responses. MD and interviewee's name should be boldfaced.

B. Interviews that follow narrative format should follow paragraph rules outlined in VI above.

VIII. MISCELLANEOUS PREFERRED SPELLINGS

musical terms; backbeat; bandleader; bandmember; barline; butt plate; China cymbal; China-type; drum & bugle corps; drumhead; drum key; drumkit; drum pad; drumset; drum shell; drum shop; drumstick; EQ; EQ'd (past-tense verb); footboard; freelancer (noun); freelance (verb, adjective); hi-hat; lineup; mic' (microphone) (noun); plural: mic's; midrange; miking, miked, mike (verb: I mike my drumset.); multitrack; odd time (noun); odd-time composition (adj); onstage; on stage (my onstage sound when I'm on stage); overdub; rimclick; rimshot; setup (noun), set up (verb); sight-read; single strokes; single-stroke roll; soundcheck; throwoff; timekeeper; timekeeping; tom-tom; upbeat

Miscellaneous terms alright; email; okay; T-shirt; Web site, World Wide Web; " (inch), for instance: 2"; x (by), for instance: 5x14

IX. LANGUAGE

A. Do not use gonna for going to, gotta for got to, or 'cause for; because. In general, stay away from contracting verbs by omitting the ending; "g," for instance: sayin' or playin'.

B. Language should be kept reasonably "clean." Profanities should be; kept to a minimum; obscenities should be avoided.

Categories: Nonfiction—Music

CONTACT: **Submissions Editor**
Material: **All**
Modern Drummer Publications
12 Old Bridge Rd.
Cedar Grove NJ 07009
Phone: **973-239-4140**
Fax: **201-239-7139**
E-mail: **sueh@moderndrummer.com**
Website: **www.moderndrummer.com**

Modern Haiku

Modern Haiku is a journal devoted to English-language haiku, book reviews and articles on haiku. Publication is three times a year: February, June and October. It has an international circulation and is widely subscribed to by university, school and public libraries. *Modern Haiku* has been cited by the International Division of the Museum or Haiku Literature in Tokyo as: "The best haiku magazine in North America." Issues have from 90 to 136 pages.

Material submitted to *Modern Haiku* should meet these guidelines:

1. Haiku should by typed or clearly printed. They may all be on one sheet of paper or may be on separate sheets of any size, but each sheet must contain the contributor's name and full address in the upper left corner.

2. A self-addressed, stamped envelope must accompany each submission of material.

3. It is advisable to submit several haiku at a time.

4. All material submitted to *Modern Haiku* must be the original, previously unpublished work of the contributor, and no material must be currently under consideration by any other publication.

Normally, contributors will receive a report on their material in two weeks.

Modern Haiku does not give copies of the magazine to contributors whose work has been accepted, as it pays $1 for each haiku that is accepted and $5 a page for articles and essays.

Since *Modern Haiku* refrains from carrying advertising and depends on subscriptions to meet publication, mailing, payments and all other costs, we would sincerely appreciate your subscription. If you enter a gift subscription a card in your name will be sent at your request to the recipient with the first issue.

A one-year subscription (three issues) is currently $23 bulk rate. Payment should be made in U.S. currency. A sample copy is $8.

Thank you for your support of *Modern Haiku*,
Lee Gurga, Editor
Categories: Poetry—Haiku

CONTACT: **Lee Gurga, Editor**
Material: **All**
PO Box 68
Lincoln IL 62656
Phone: **217-732-8731**
Website: **www.modernhaiku.org**

Modern Maturity
AARP, The Magazine

Please Note:
Modern Maturity is now known as AARP, The Magazine.
General Editorial
Most *AARP, The Magazine* features are assigned to writers whose work is known to us and who have an established reputation in journalism. We rarely assign a major feature as the result of an unsolicited query.

The magazine does, however, encourage query letters for specific features and departments. These should be one-page in length and accompanied by recent writing samples. We expect proposers to be familiar with the magazine and its departments.

AARP, The Magazine discourages the submission of unsolicited manuscripts and assumes no responsibility for their return.

Features and departments cover the following categories:
• Finance, investments, legal matters
• Health
• Food (including recipes; emphasis on healthy eating)
• Items of regional interest - 150 to 300 words
• Travel (domestic and international)
• Consumerism (practical information and advice)
• General interest (new thinking, research, information on timely topics, etc.)

Rate of Payment
AARP, The Magazine pays on acceptance at the minimum rate of $1.00 per contracted word. A kill fee of 25% will be paid for assigned articles that are not accepted for publication.

Categories: Nonfiction—Careers—Cooking—Food/Drink—Health—Money & Finances—Relationships—Senior Citizen—Society—Travel—Retirement—Medicine

CONTACT: **J. Henry Fenwick, Editor**
Material: **All**
601 E St. NW
Washington DC 20049
Phone: **202-434-6880**
Fax: **202-434-6883**
E-mail: **310-496-4124**

Mom Guess What Newspaper

CONTENT: General and Political News, Book, Film, Restaurant, Theater Reviews, Entertainment, Interviews, Art Profiles, Advertising, Sports, Features, and Financial.

AUDIENCE: A newspaper for gay men, lesbians and their straight friends in the State Capitol and the Sacramento Valley area. Founded in 1978. First and oldest gay newspaper in Sacramento.

FORMAT: Deadlines: 8th and 23rd. 60%, 40% advertising. Tabloid, 34". Newsprint. Trim size 17"x11¼". Body copy is 9/10 points. 85 line screen photographs. Free and/or 50¢ donation. Published every 2 weeks since 1978. 21,000 copies. $30 subscription. Sample issue $1.00. 32+ pages each issue.

NEEDS: Freelance articles on People, Politics, Trendsetters, Features, Health, Artists, Photography, Artwork. Material is not limited to the gay & lesbian lifestyle. 1,500-2,500 words. No Poetry.

TERMS: MGW is published primarily from volunteers. Payment is in copies. Byline appears with each published article; photos credited. Editors reserve right to edit, crop, touchup, revise, or otherwise alter manuscripts, and photos, but not to change theme or intent of the work. Enclose SASE postcard for acceptance or rejection.

MECHANICAL REQUIREMENTS: Author's name, address, phone should appear on first page with approximate word count. Photo captions should be typed on a separate page. Black & white glossy preferred. 5"x7" or 8"x10". No negatives or slides. Label all photos.

DISKS: Label each diskette with:
1. Headline/Filename
2. Your name
3. Program and version you used
4. Type of computer: PC-IBM compatible or Macintosh
5. Date you're submitting the disk
6. Your phone number

Send printed copy with disk. We use Quark.

CARTOONS: Pen & Ink. High contrast. PMT/stats, velox preferred. Do not send originals.

Categories: Computers—Feminism—Film—Food—Gay/Lesbian—Lifestyle—Men's Issues—Politics—Relationships—Sexuality—Sports

CONTACT: Submissions Editor
Material: All
1103 T St.
Sacramento CA 95814
Phone: 916-441-6397
Website: www.mgwnews.com

Moment
America's Premier Independent Jewish Magazine

Stories for MOMENT are usually commissioned, but unsolicited manuscripts are occasionally selected for publication. We look for analytical, colorful, thought-provoking features and essays on Jewish life in the United States, Israel, and elsewhere.

MOMENT's feature articles run from 2,500 to 4,000 words. Successful features offer our readers an in-depth journalistic treatment of an issue, phenomenon, institution, or individual-a treatment that is characterized by solid and accurate reporting, that draws upon multiple sources, that makes lively and abundant use of quotations, and that offers visual color through accurate observation. The more the writer can follow the principle of "show, don't tell," the better for our readers.

A fresh perspective on an issue, or a national or global take on an otherwise local affair, is also an important editorial consideration. Also, a writer must be familiar with other works on the same topic, and with articles published in previous issues of MOMENT.

In addition to major features, MOMENT runs regular departments. Olam (the Jewish world) contains a selection of first-person accounts, colorful reportage, and humor pieces of 800 to 1,500 words each. 5760 contains snappy pieces of not more than 300 words each, including news items, ideas to improve Jewish living, and coverage of quirky events in the Jewish community. MOMENT also reviews fiction and nonfiction books, but these 250- to 800-word pieces are generally assigned to regular contributors.

We receive many more articles than we are able to publish, particularly about certain subjects, such as the Holocaust and Israel. We're more likely to use an article if it is not on these subjects.

Payment for articles is determined on an individual basis, depending on the nature of the piece, its length and complexity, and the writer's experience.

Best of luck!

Categories: Nonfiction—Jewish Interest—Religion—Spiritual

CONTACT: Submissions Editor
Material: All
4710 41 St., NW
Washington DC 20016
Phone: 202-364-3300
Fax: 202-364-2636
Website: www.momentmag.com

Money

Does not accept unsolicited submissions.

Monitoring Times

Style and Content

Stories accepted for publication in *Monitoring Times* have two things in common: first, the story is a "good read" and second, it is of utility to the radio monitor.

This means that your story should have broad appeal in a *Reader's Digest* or *National Geographic* sort of way. Anyone, radio enthusiast or not, should find the story fascinating. Those that are radio enthusiasts, on the other hand, should find within the article information of value—especially specific frequencies—that they can use to participate in the topic you have addressed.

We encourage the use of vivid imagery and lively anecdotes, especially for the opening and closing paragraphs. It's important that you convey a sense of excitement and enthusiasm for the topic you are covering. You are, in effect, "selling" people on the radio monitoring hobby.

K-I-S

No matter what topic you've decided to write about, *Keep It Simple.* The vast majority of MT readers are beginners. Believe it or not, there are hundreds of millions of people out there to whom shortwave is a mystery and UTC absolutely mind-bending. Thus, it is unlikely they'll understand a passing mention of something like propagation or synchronous detection circuitry. K-I-S!

Always define abbreviations and acronyms on first use (FCC, NASA, USB, etc.) and always provide a source (company address or publisher) for any business, equipment, or book you recommend. Though writing on a basic level, if you explain your terms as you go along, your article will bring the beginner along with you.

If your article is a basic one, you can provide those who wish to pursue the topic further with suggestions of where to go for more information or experience. If your article is more complex or technical, it would be appropriate to suggest sources for more basic background information.

Keep in mind the time factor while writing; your article must still be valid six months from now. We appreciate your willingness to check the article for accuracy if significant time passes before publication.

Homework

We do not suggest topics for potential authors. Rather, we rely on your creativity and experience to suggest articles. We strongly advise prospective authors to review past copies of the magazine to get an idea of what kind of articles we generally run. While we hope you don't try to mimic what you see, it does give you some idea of where it is we are headed editorially.

The most general ideas include profiles of radio systems, "how-to" articles ranging from "how to hear a broadcast or transmission" to listening tips such as "how to make the best use of loggings, DX Latin America, where to find military communications, etc...."

Technical articles and reviews are hardest to place, so be sure to check first before investing a great deal of time. We do accept them, but our regular columnists also cover these topics, so check with us to avoid duplication.

Common Courtesies

Check your facts; don't expect the editor to catch errors. If they're someone else's facts, check for obvious mistakes.

Credit your sources and your graphics (individuals, publications, clubs). It's their only payment for making your material look good!

Provide a current contact address or phone number for any companies whose products or services are mentioned in your article.

Query Us

Although we do accept unsolicited manuscripts, if you have an idea for an article, we recommend you query us in advance of completing a manuscript. And when you do query us, do not be afraid to give

us your best pitch. Give an overview of the article, highlight some of the things you want to cover, perhaps providing an anecdote or two from the article, and tell us why we would want to buy the article and how it might appeal to the reader. Don't hesitate to follow up the written query with a phone call to the editor after at least six weeks have passed.

All queries, questions and comments, along with manuscripts submitted on approval, must be accompanied by a self-addressed stamped envelope. Direct your query or manuscript to the editor, Rachel Baughn, at *Monitoring Times*, 7540 Hwy 64 West, Brasstown, NC 28902, e-mail mteditor@grove-ent.com, or you may fax your request to (828) 837-2216. The editor is not available by phone, but a call-back may be arranged by leaving a message at 828-837-9200.

The Next Step

If your idea sounds good and there is a reasonable chance the article will be published, you will be invited to submit a manuscript. We ask that in addition to submitting your manuscript in hard copy form that you also include it on IBM-formatted disk or via email, if possible. Be sure to include the following information at the top of your manuscript: Name, address, daytime phone number, date, and your social security number. Once received, the manuscript will be accepted, returned for modification, offered hold status, or rejected.

Payment and Rights

We receive more articles worthy of acceptance than we can publish or pay for in a month. Our practice is as follows: after an article is accepted, it remains in file, and payment is made when the manuscript is published. If this arrangement is not acceptable, other terms may occasionally be negotiated with the editor. If you live in the U.S., we must have your Social Security number on file before payment is made.

Payment for most full-length (1800-3000 words) feature articles accompanied by at least three suitable illustrations is around $50 per laid-out page: $i.e., $150-$200. A one-year subscription to the magazine is complimentary (limited to one per year). The inclusion of appropriate illustrations, in the form of photos, slides, or line art, and your proven reliability will help guarantee this payment.

On occasion, a manuscript will be offered "hold" status. These are manuscripts which, perhaps because of the writing, information, or subject matter, have less guarantee of being published. If you are offered hold status, your manuscript will remain at the editorial office under the same conditions as "accepted" articles.

Monitoring Times purchases First North American Serial Rights (we will be the first to publish your article in North America), and limited reprint rights as follows: single photocopies of your article if the back issue is no longer available, its inclusion in single issue sales of the magazine in digital format, and inclusion in the yearly compilation of all twelve issues on a compact disk.

Until you receive payment, you may retract an article or *Monitoring Times* may return an article for any reason.

Once Published

Once published, you are welcome to give or resell your article elsewhere with the proviso that it contain the line "(Name of article) was previously published in *Monitoring Times*, Brass-town, NC 28902." It is your responsibility to ensure that this line appears in all subsequent publications.

Text Preparation Guidelines for *Monitoring Times*
STYLE

Type your article in a simple, straightforward style; do not do any formatting or layout on your disk. For example, long lists of frequencies should be typed in a single column, even though it may end up as three columns in a finished layout. If you wish to provide a suggested layout on your hard copy, that's okay.

Use subheads to break up your work; it helps you, the editor, and the reader to follow the flow of logic throughout the article. Type subheads in upper and lower case.

Indent paragraphs with a tab, not spaces

Do not insert blank line between paragraphs

Use one tab, not spaces, to separate columns in tables

Single space (hit space bar once only) between sentences.

Use upper and lower case, never all caps, even in tables, if possible

MT/ST customary usage of some commonly confusing punctuation/spellings:

- Hz / kHz / MHz / GHz / kW / am-pm / AM-FM
- Comma is used before and AFTER state when giving city and state .
- Periods and commas go inside ending quotation marks.
- Comma is used preceding the word "and" when used in a series (example: red, white, and blue).

WORD PROCESSOR

MS Word, Word Perfect, or Rich Text Format preferred.

Use minimal formatting, and NO TABLES.

Recommended: Provide file in ASCII as well in case it does not convert correctly.

MODE OF TRANSMISSION

Best: On disk (IBM 3½" HD disk), accompanied by graphics and hard copy.

OK: Sent as email attachment.

Typed, high contrast paper copy for scanning.

Worst: Faxed copy (okay as advance copy only).

Note: Unless this is a rush job, provide back up hard copy whenever possible.

Graphics

Best: Glossy prints, especially for cover art (Matte, velvet, or textured surfaces do not scan well); high quality line art (please avoid super thin lines and shading screens); digital vector graphics (anything that can be imported by Aldus PageMaker, such as Aldus -FreeHand EPS, Adobe Illustrator EPS, Corel Draw placeable EPS, etc.); and digital bitmap graphics (Tiff, jpg, gif and pcx with resolutions of at least 200 dpi at the approximate size of final reproduction).

OK: Pen and ink drawings; already published pictures if they are not copyright protected and exhibit good contrast and very fine dot screens.

Worst: Pencil sketches; dot matrix graphics; low resolution digital files that exhibit "stairstepping" or "jaggies"; no graphics at all!

Send digital illustrations in a separate file, not imbedded in text file.

Please provide photo captions on disk; a list of graphics and captions should appear at the head of your article. DO caption your pictures, even if it's just a simple identification.

CONTACT: Rachel Baughn, Editor
Material: All
7540 Hwy 64 West
Brasstown NC 28902-0098
Phone: 828-837-2216
E-mail: mteditor@grove-ent.com

The Montana Catholic

The Montana Catholic newspaper serves the Roman Catholic community residing in western Montana. Tabloid in format, it is published 16 times per year—usually every three weeks—and is mailed directly to some 9,200 homes for an estimated readership of 21,000. Some parishes and institutions make free copies available on their literature stands. Total printed circulation is 9,400.

Nearly all recipients of *The Montana Catholic* are paid subscribers. All contributors to the Diocesan Offertory Program—the annual appeal of the Catholic Diocese of Helena—receive a one-year subscription to the newspaper as part of their contribution. Individuals who do not contribute to the DOP may subscribe separately. Provision is made for free subscriptions for persons who wish to receive the paper but cannot afford it.

Our predominant editorial focus is to report news and develop feature stories which relate directly to the activities and concerns of the Catholic community in western Montana.

News and Feature Articles

We buy a limited number of news and feature articles from freelance writers. The majority of these are articles which originate with or are assigned to established freelance writers who reside in western Montana. However, several articles each year are purchased from freelance writers outside the area who write more general feature stories relating to seasonal or special supplement topics.

Seasonal topics include Thanksgiving, Advent, Christmas, Lent, and Easter. Supplement topics have been scaled back recently, but two that will remain will be Religious Vocations (January and early Spring) and Respect Life (October).

Submissions are also welcome for an ongoing series on the coming of the Third Millennium.

In general, however, our emphasis is on the local church; therefore, we look primarily for Catholic-oriented material with a tie-in to western Montana.

We buy one-time rights; reprint rights and simultaneous submissions are accepted. We prefer full disclosure of where else submitted or previously printed.

Commentaries

At present, our only regular columns are by local writers. However, we often allow space for occasional commentary by other local, non-local, or syndicated writers. Thoughtful commentaries on issues of current or seasonal concern to the Catholic church are welcome.

Photos/Illustrations

Original photos and illustrations which help highlight news and feature stories are encouraged. All pertinent subjects appearing in the photo must be identified and, where necessary, permission for use must be granted.

Poetry

Please do not submit poetry. We have published perhaps three poems in the last eight years, only one of which was written by a freelance writer.

Length

News and feature articles can range from 400 to 1,200 words, although most successful writers keep their work in the 600- to 900-word range. We reserve the right to edit all manuscripts accepted for publication.

Payment

For original news and feature articles assigned to local freelance writers, we pay up to $0.10 per word based on the final, edited word count, up to the maximum word count assigned.

For other news, features and commentaries, we generally pay $0.05 per word, based on the final, edited word count.

Rarely, a different fee or rate can be negotiated for first rights on a particularly outstanding piece.

We do not guarantee publication of assigned articles, and publication may be advanced or delayed for space or editorial reasons.

Kill fee on assigned articles is 50%. If writer has been informed that article is "accepted for publication" but the article is later killed, kill fee is 25%. No kill fee will be paid if articles are delivered after deadline or if the author fails to comply with requests for revisions or additional research.

Payment for photos varies from $5 to $20 per photo published.

Style

Please observe the following writing guidelines:

Although there are exceptions, avoid writing in the first person, except perhaps for commentary pieces.

Maintain a positive, uplifting tone—but avoid Pollyannaism.

Avoid "preachiness," including excessive quotation of scripture or other church documents. When scripture citation is appropriate, use the *New American Bible* or the *Revised Standard Version.*

Check all facts and quotations. One error will cast suspicion upon the accuracy of the entire manuscript.

Also check spelling and grammar carefully; leaving fundamental writing errors is the fastest way to make an editor lose interest in a writer.

Do not inject subjective language into news pieces; limit its use in feature stories.

We value strong leads, a body of the article which develops and delivers on the lead, and a definitive conclusion.

Manuscript Preparation

Please do not use a dot-matrix printer. For submissions on disk, IBM-compatible format is required, preferably using Microsoft Word or ASCII. Use a standard indent for paragraphs and a one-inch margin on every page.

Title page should include writer's name, address, and telephone number in the upper left corner; word count in the upper right corner; and article title with writer's byline centered in the middle of the page. Subsequent pages should have a running head in the upper right corner with the writer's surname, article title (abbreviated if necessary), and page number.

Underline titles, italicized words or phrases, and foreign words for emphasis.

Handwritten corrections and changes should be few and legible.

Queries and Submissions

For news and feature stories pertinent to the Catholic community in western Montana, query or send completed manuscripts. Writers should familiarize themselves with our style and format prior to submitting a query. Each query should include the primary focus of the proposed article, the main point of discussion, and a list of any authorities who would be consulted in the article. No phone calls except from freelance writers in western Montana who have an established relationship with us.

Categories: Regional—Religion—Rural America—Catholic—Montana

CONTACT: Editor
Material: All
Diocese of Helena, PO Box 1729
Helena MT 59624
Phone: 406-442-5820
Fax: 406-442-5191
E-mail: MontanaCatholic@DioceseHelena.org
Website: www.diocesehelena.org/pages/montanacatholic.htm

Montana Magazine

Montana Magazine is published bimonthly, in January, March, May, July, September, and November. Please read our publication so you have a good grasp of our style and content. Back issues are available for $5 each, postpaid. Subscriptions cost $23 per year. We assign work, and also consider freelance material. Please query in writing. We read every query and try to respond within two months. Queries by e-mail are accepted, but go into the queue along with all the snail-mail ones.

Overview

Montana Magazine varies from 100 pages to 132 pages. We are noted for excellent photographs and entertaining, informative writing about Montana. The magazine contains about five feature articles of 1,800 to 2,500 words, and four to six departments of 800 to 2,500 words. The issues are four-color throughout.

Focus

Montana Magazine subscribers include lifelong residents, first-time visitors, and "wanna-be" Montanans from around the nation and the world. Readership is estimated at 120,000. We publish articles on Montana recreation, contemporary issues, people, natural history, cities, small towns, humor, wildlife, real-life adventure, nostalgia, geography, history, byways and infrequently-explored countryside, made-in-Montana products, local businesses, and environment—in short, anything that will inform and entertain our readers. We avoid commonly-published topics so Montanans won't ho-hum through more of what they already know. If it's time to revisit a topic, we look for a unique slant. We are strictly a Montana-oriented magazine. Articles of generic Western flavor will not make it. We're ill-disposed toward stories of wild-animal trapping, gory hunting tales, or "me & Joe" adventures. No poetry or fiction, please.

Queries

We accept written queries and unsolicited manuscripts. Please be patient—eventually all submissions are reviewed and responded to. Telephone queries are heartily discouraged. If we like your proposal, we may ask to see it on speculation. Acceptance for review does not imply that the article will be published. Queries should include a thorough outline of the proposed article. Start with the lead, then write a short summary of content, including specifics on whom you plan to interview, research sources, highlights, anecdotal information, and conclusion. Provide several samples of your writing if we are unfamiliar with your style. Include a return envelope and postage. Manuscripts must be typed, double- or triple-spaced. Do not send your original copy. We can convert almost any commercial software word processing program from 3.5" or 5 1/4" disks. Include a return envelope and postage if you want your material returned. We are not responsible for unsolicited material of any kind.

Rates

Montana Magazine's basic rate is approximately 15¢ per published word. Higher payment for assignments involving extra expenses may be arranged before publication. Whenever possible, include illustrative material for the article, such as snapshots or portraits supplied by the subject of the article. Please identify all such artwork with the name of the photographer (if known) or studio. Artwork in that category is credited in the magazine as "Courtesy of XXXX." Payment for assigned, published photographs is additional. Full-page $125; larger than half-page $100; half-page or smaller $50. Payment, returnable materials, and a complimentary copy of the magazine are sent to each author within thirty days of publication.

Rights

Montana Magazine buys one-time-rights to your article, which may include both print and electronic versions. This does not require the written exchange of copyright from freelancers to the magazine. Occasionally, we are asked for permission to reprint an article. These requests are generally from an educational institution or a hobby club. We cannot grant permission, and will forward such requests to the author. Most material is purchased on a one-time-rights basis, which does not require the written exchange of copyright. We reserve the right to edit and rewrite to comply with our style. Author proofs are generally not provided.

Categories: Nonfiction—History—Outdoors—Recreation—Regional—Travel

CONTACT: Beverly Magley, Editor
Material: Queries
PO Box 5630
Helena MT 59604
Phone: 406-443-2842 (no phone queries)
Fax: 406-443-5480
E-mail: editor@montanamagazine.com
Website: www.montanamagazine.com

Montana
The Magazine of Western History

Submitting Your Manuscript

Montana: The Magazine of Western History, published quarterly by the Montana Historical Society, welcomes authentic articles on the history of Montana and the American and Canadian wests.

Montana is a scholarly journal, which means that articles are submitted to peer review and must show evidence of original research, through footnotes or bibliography, on significant facets of history or provide a new interpretation of historical events that changes the way we view a particular historical topic. A rewriting of standard incidents generally available in other sources will not be accepted.

Manuscript length should run between 3,500 and 6,500 words, or about 14 to 25 double-spaced pages, plus endnotes. Because we are an illustrated journal, photographs of acceptable quality assist in our judgments.

In reviewing articles, if your article is judged appropriate for *Montana*, we will submit it to anonymous review; that is, a blind copy of your manuscript will be sent out-of-house for evaluation, usually to two experts in the field. Upon receiving their comments, we will forward a summary of the readers' reports to you with our determination. The process usually takes six to eight weeks.

The best guide to style for *Montana* is a recent issue of our magazine, but generally we follow the latest revised edition of *Chicago Manual of Style*.

We prefer receiving two copies of your manuscript for review and end notes instead of footnotes. No computer disk is necessary at first, although we will request to have your manuscript on a 3.5 disk if accepted. At that time, endnotes should be made a separate document from the text.

Categories: Nonfiction—History—Regional—Western—Western History

CONTACT: W. Clark Whitehorn, Editor
Material: All
225 N. Roberts St.
PO Box 201201
Helena MT 59620-1201
Phone: 406-444-4708
Fax: 406-444-2696
E-mail: cwhitehorn@state.mt.us
Website: www.his.state.mt.us/departments/magazine

Moody Magazine

WHO WE ARE

Published six times a year, *MOODY* magazine exists to encourage and equip Christians to live biblically in a secular culture. *MOODY* seeks practical, popular-level articles that focus on the application of scriptural principles in daily life, as well as some that examine current events and issues from a scriptural perspective.

OUR READERS

Conservative, evangelical laity of all denominations, with a target age of 35-54 years. Most of our readers are married, college graduates, and active in their church. The male-female ratio is 41-59.

WRITING FOR MOODY

Because we assign each issue's package of cover articles—and because we seek to present a variety of topics in each issue—we do not offer an editorial theme list. Instead, we look for free-lancers to query us about individual article proposals.

FEATURE ARTICLES

Feature Articles cover a broad range of topics, but have one common goal: to foster application—by a broad readership—of specific scriptural principles. Many authors use a personal narrative style, but we are also open to articles that take an anecdotal reporting approach. Typical Length: 1,200 to 2,400 words.

MOODY especially seeks narrative accounts showing the process of one's realization and application of specific, scriptural principles in daily life—that others can also apply in their own situations. In generating ideas for such articles, we recommend a writer consider:

What have you been learning that Scripture calls you to do in some key area?

What difficulties have you encountered as you've sought to put those insights into practice?

What effect has this ongoing application had on you and those around you?

Looking beyond your own experience, what could others learn—and apply—from this?

SOME ARTICLE CATEGORIES

- discipleship
- innerlife
- church
- outreach
- issues/culutre/society
- family/marriage
- workplace/finances

DO's AND DON'Ts

How-To's: Rather than directive how-to's, we prefer articles that show how you (or other believers) have learned to approach a situation scriptural and the difference that has made.

Exhortations: Similarly, we do not seek articles declaring a certain issue is a problem Christians should address. We prefer a journalistic approach that shows examples of believers who are already taking a positive, scripturally based response.

Inspirationals: Our goal for narratives is not simply to describe a dramatic or inspirational event, but to show the process of one seeing the need to apply the truth of God's Word to an aspect of everyday life—and then following through with that application.

No biographies, historical articles, or studies of Bible figures.

COMPELLING WRITING

Remember the last time you glanced at an article—then flipped the page because it just wasn't interesting. Now remember that other article you couldn't stop reading. Afterward you clipped it out, made copies for a friend, and told others about it. That's the kind of writing MOODY seeks. An article has perhaps 10 seconds to grab a reader's attention. We want articles that grab readers—and then keep them grabbed all the way to the end. Great topics alone aren't enough. Ask yourself, "Would I want to read my article if someone else had written it?" We know your mom, your spouse, or your best friend would read it. We look for articles that everyone else wants to read, too. We want writing that breathes life into a topic—but not melodramatic or jargon-filled prose. We look for accounts that find the human dimension, apply God's Living Word, and then convey that information in simple, powerful, straightforward language.

OUR PROCEDURE

MOODY does not accept unsolicited manuscripts. Writers must first write a query letter and secure permission to forward their manuscripts. Our usual response time is eight weeks. Do not query by telephone, fax, or e-mail unless urgent subject matter requires an immediate editorial response.

QUERY LETTERS

In you letter, which should be only one page, include your article's:

- title
- topic (what it is about)
- takeaway/purpose/application/audience (what and whom it is for)
- treatment (its style of writing, such as narrative or journalistic) and length

It should also include types of support materials, such as:

- anecdotes
- personal observation
- interviews
- Scriptures
- statistics
- quotations/citations

If possible, include a representative sample paragraph. In addition, please let us know briefly about your writing experience and your qualifications to write on this subject. Always include a self-addressed stamped envelope. Please, no simultaneous or reprint queries.

DEADLINES

MOODY begins editing each issue five months prior to the date of publication and plans each issue several months in advance of that. For seasonal material, query nine months in advance.

POETRY AND FICTION

MOODY does not print poetry. Although we print little fiction, we will consider well-written contemporary stories. Rather than inspirational accounts, we seek one that, like our non-fiction, are rooted in biblical truth. Dialogue, action, and descriptions must be crisp and believable. Avoid clichéd salvation accounts, biblical fiction, parables, and allegories. Typical Length: 1,200 to 2,200 words.

MANUSCRIPT FORMAT

Print-outs must be double-spaced. Include a 3.5-inch floppy disk in any popular word-processing format. Include on the first page the approximate article length, your name, address, day phone, e-mail address, and Social Security number. Always include an SASE for the return of your materials should your manuscript not meet our needs.

PAYMENT AND RIGHTS

MOODY buys First North American Serial Rights. Once the work has been published in an issue of *MOODY* magazine, we retain the non-exclusive right to re-publish that work in electronic form, without further compensation. *MOODY* may authorize electronic "readers" worldwide to print a copy of the work for personal use; however all requests for commercial reprints shall be referred to the author. All other rights return to the author once the article has been published.

MANUSCRIPT POLICY

We examine all manuscripts on speculation. A positive response to a query does not guarantee purchase. The author grants *MOODY* the right to edit and abridge the manuscript and warrants that it has not already appeared in print and that it has not been simultaneously submitted to other publications. Further, the author warrants that nothing in the article infringes the copyright ownership of any person, firm, or corporation, and that he is its sole and true author.

Categories: Nonfiction—Christian Interests—Evangelical Christianity

CONTACT: Managing Editor
Material: All
820 N. La Salle Blvd.
Chicago IL 60610
Phone: 312-329-2164
Fax: 312-329-2149
E-mail: MoodyEdit@moody.edu
Website: www.moody.edu/MOODYMAG

Mopar Muscle

Formal guidelines not available. Please read a number of issues to ascertain the publication's style and needs.

Send queries to address below.

Circulation: 69,621

Frequency: monthly

Mopar Muscle is dedicated to Chrysler performance. Its primary emphasis is on musclecar-era Dodge, Plymouth and Chrysler vehicles, with technical and feature articles oriented toward functional restoration and street/race performance.

Categories: Nonfiction—Automobiles

CONTACT: Geoff Stunkard, Editor-in-Chief
Material: All
3816 Industry Blvd.
Lakeland FL 33811
Phone: 863-644-0449
Website: www.moparmusclemagazine.com

More

Thank you for your interest in writing for MORE. While we do not have specific guidelines about subject matter or writing style, we do offer these suggestions:

READ BACK ISSUES: We do not publish an editorial calendar, so familiarizing yourself with our editorial content and style will help you decide if your work fits our needs. Back issues can be found in the periodicals section of your library or purchased from our customer service department for $3 each (call 888-699-4036, then press #1). Do not send payment to our editorial offices.

WE HAVE FOUR MONTH LEAD TIME: Keep in mind that *MORE* is targeted at women ages 45-64, so we will be looking for stories that both involve and appeal to women in that age group. If we feel that a submission to *MORE* is more appropriate for *Ladies' Home Journal*, we will consider it for publication in that magazine. Please do not send simultaneous submissions to both magazines.

SUBMIT QUERIES RATHER THAN MANUSCRIPTS: Keep your query brief-one to two pages-citing your lead and describing how you will research and develop your story. Be specific, and always direct your query to the appropriate editor, as listed on the masthead of the magazine. If you have been published before, send clips, your credits and a resume.

ALWAYS INCLUDE A SELF-ADDRESSED, STAMPED ENVELOPE: We will not respond unless a SASE is enclosed (with adequate postage for return of the manuscript, if so desired). We are not responsible for returning unsolicited material, so do not send original copies or photographs. Our editorial offices are located at 125 Park Avenue, New York, NY 10017. We regret that we cannot reply to submissions sent by fax or E-mail.

PAYMENT, STORY LENGTH AND DEADLINES: are discussed upon assignment and writers are paid upon acceptance. Average story length is 2,000 words.

SUBMIT FICTION ONLY THROUGH A LITERARY AGENT. WE DO NOT ACCEPT POETRY OF ANY KIND.

PLEASE DO NOT CALL TO QUERY OR FOLLOW UP ON A SUBMISSION: We read every query carefully, and do our best to respond as promptly as we can. It may take up to three months to receive a response.

WE CANNOT PROVIDE COMMENTS ON UNACCEPTED MATERIAL: Due to the large volume of manuscripts we receive, we are unable to evaluate each writer's work personally.

Categories: Nonfiction—Culture—Entertainment—Fashion—General Interest—Health—Money & Finances—Travel—Women's Issues

CONTACT: Barbara Brody, Associate Editor
Material: All
Meredith Corp.
125 Park Ave
New York NY 10017
Phone: 212-455-1303
E-mail: bbrody@mdp.com

Mortgage Banking

• Feature articles should run between 3,000 and 4,000 words in length. Columns should run between 750 and 1,000 words.

• Please e-mail a Word (any version) or text file of the article and e-mail or fax hard copies of any accompanying charts/graphs in advance of sending the article (all graphics are recreated from scratch in Quark by a typesetter). Article should be in text-only format (no graphics embedded in text). The text-only file may be e-mailed to janet_hewitt@mbaa.org. Hard copies of graphics can be faxed to (202) 721-0245.

• Do not use footnotes. Include subheads to help set off transitions from one subject to another throughout the article. Spell out ac-

ronyms and use trademark or service mark symbols on first reference ("Fannie Mae's Desktop Underwriter (DU)," and thereafter, "DU"). Use full names/ titles of people being quoted and full names of companies/company locations on first reference.

• Clearly label the hard copies of accompanying charts/graphs (Figure 1, etc.), and be sure all graphics are referenced in text where appropriate ("see Figure 2," etc.). All charts and graphs must include a title and source, even if the source is the company or person submitting the article.

• Include brief biographical information for each author at the end of the article. This should include the author's name, title, company name and location. A brief description of the company is permitted. The editor reserves the right to condense biographical information as necessary.

• Should your article be selected for publication, an edited version will be faxed back to you prior to publication. This version will include, embedded in the text, queries from the editor. You will be asked to write your answers onto this faxed copy and to then fax it back to us within a short period of time—generally one to two days. (If you prefer, we can e-mail to you an edited Word document of your article, which you can make changes to with the Tracking function active so that it is clear where alterations to text have been made.)

• Two author's copies of the magazine will be mailed to you as soon as they are received from the printer. A reasonable number of additional copies may be requested by contacting the editor.

• Please submit your invoice as soon as possible after sending your article. Include your full name and address, Social Security No. or tax identification number and our full address on the invoice.

Please note that we can only accept an original hard copy or e-mailed invoice—faxed invoices are not acceptable. Payment will be mailed within 7-10 days of receipt of your invoice. Please send invoice to: Lesley Hall, Mortgage Banking magazine, 1919 Pennsylvania Ave. N.W., Washington, DC 20006, or e-mail it as a Word document to lesley_hall@mbaa.org.

Thank you for your interest in submitting an article to *Mortgage Banking* magazine.

Categories: Nonfiction—Business—Economics—Money & Finances—Real Estate

CONTACT: Janet Hewitt, Editor-in-Chief
Material: Real estate finance, mortgage banking
Mortgage Bankers Association of America
1919 Pennsylvania Ave, NW
Washington DC 20006
Phone: 202-557-2856

Mother Earth News

INFORMATION FOR POTENTIAL CONTRIBUTORS

Mother Earth News is a bimonthly magazine dedicated to presenting information which will help readers become more self-sufficient, financially independent and environmentally aware. Readership age ranges from the early teens to over 90. The magazine is distributed to 350,000 people across the United States and Canada.

WE USE ARTICLES ON:
Organic gardening—Renewable energy—Living well cheaply—Self-sufficiency—Building projects—Alternative Housing/Green Building—Holistic Health—Wild foods—Wildlife/Wildlands Conservation—Crafts—Herbal remedies—Energy conservation tips—Small farm livestock—House and garden tips—Hand tools—Homesteading techniques (If at all possible, accompany articles with diagrams and/or photos. Please include your return address on all materials, including slides and photos. As we cannot guarantee return of items submitted, please retain a copy of all materials you send.)

WE DO NOT USE: Poetry, memoirs or fiction.

MANUSCRIPT PREPARATION PRINCIPLES: Work should be double spaced, typed (or word processed) in a standard serif black font (e.g., Times New Roman, 12 pt.) on one side of white 8½" by 11" paper. We prefer manuscripts to be submitted via e-mail (in either Microsoft Word or WordPerfect) to the appropriate editor.

PAYMENT will be negotiated between writer and editor. The writer will receive payment upon publication.

Mostly written by staff and team of established freelancers. Bimonthly magazine emphasizing living wisely. Resourceful living and country skills for rural residents and for urbanites who aspire to a more independent lifestyle. *Mother Earth News* is dedicated to presenting information that helps readers be more self-sufficient, financially independent and environmentally aware. Circ: 400,000. Pays on publication. Byline given. Submit seasonal material 5 months in advance. No handwritten manuscripts. Responds within 6 months. Sample copy for $5. Writer's guidelines for #10 SASE with one first-class stamp.

Non-fiction: How-to, alternative energy systems, organic gardening, home building, home retro-fit and maintenance, energy-efficient structures, seasonal cooking, home business, living "off the grid." Buys 35-50 mss. a year.

Query: "A brief, focused paragraph or two will generally do the trick. If the idea intrigues us and seems appropriate for our readers, we'll ask to see the whole piece. No fiction and no telephone queries, please."

Length: 300 to 3,000 words. Payment negotiated. Publishes non-fiction book excerpts.

Photos: "Although not essential, we very much encourage contributors to send good, usable photos with their mss." Send prints or transparencies. Use 8 x 10 b&w glossies or any size color transparencies. Include type of film, speed and lighting used. Total purchase price for mss includes payment for photos. Captions and photo credits required.

Columns/Departments: For those with little writing experience, submissions to Country Lore or Reports from the Field (personal accounts of the *Mother Earth News* lifestyle) are a good entry point. Other departments include Natural Remedies and Mother's Natural Kitchen.

Tips: "Read our magazine. Read our magazine. Read our magazine. Readers of *Mother Earth News* comprise one of the most thoughtful, curious, industrious and engaging magazine audiences in the country. Since 1970, *Mother Earth News* has been an exemplary source of information about homesteading, rural skills, environmental consciousness and natural health. It is North America's leading publication for people interested in contemporary rural lifestyles, and we are committed to providing hands-on, useful information for real people who want to take charge of their own lives. Practicality is the key. Articles should be well-documented and tightly written."

Categories: Nonfiction—Agriculture—Conservation—Cooking—Crafts/Hobbies—Food/Drink—Gardening—Health—Home

CONTACT: Submissions Editor
Material: All
Ogden Publications Inc.
1503 SW 42nd St.
Topeka KS 66609-1265
Phone: 785-274-4300
E-mail: letters@motherearthnews.com
Website: www.motherearthnews.com

The Mother is Me
Profiling the Cultural Experience of Motherhood

Ceased publication.

MOTHERJONES
Mother Jones

Who we are:

Mother Jones, with a paid circulation of 140,000, is one of the largest progressive publications in the country. The national bimonthly magazine is known for its investigative journalism and exposes, and its coverage of social issues, public affairs, and popular culture. Most of the articles we print are written by freelancers.

What we're looking for:

Hard-hitting, investigative reports exposing government cover-ups, corporate malfeasance, scientific myopia, institutional fraud or hypocrisy, etc.

Thoughtful, provocative articles which challenge the conventional wisdom (on the right or the left) concerning issues of national importance.

Timely, people-oriented stories on issues such as the environment, labor, the media, health care, consumer protection, and cultural trends.

How to query us:

Send a letter proposing your story idea(s).

Explain what you plan to cover and how you will proceed with the reporting. The query should convey your approach, tone, and style; and should answer the following: What are your specific qualifications to write on this topic? What "ins" do you have with your sources? Can you provide full documentation so that your story can be fact-checked?

Keep in mind that our lead time is three months and submissions should not be so time-bound that they will appear dated. If we, or another publication, have run a similar story in the last few years, explain how your story will differ.

If you have not contributed to *Mother Jones* before, please send two or three photocopies of previously published articles along with your query. We do not accept unsolicited manuscripts or fiction. Mother Jones assumes no responsibility for unsolicited queries or manuscripts and will only respond to those accompanied by a self-addressed, stamped envelope. Therefore, please do not query us by phone or fax.

Back issues are $6.00 and can be ordered through Reader Services at the address below.

Categories: Nonfiction—African-American—Asian-American—Culture—Economics—Environment—Film/Video—General Interest—Government—Interview—Money & Finances—Multicultural—Politics—Investigative Reporting

CONTACT: Queries and Manuscripts
Material: All
731 Market St. Ste. 600
San Francisco CA 94103
Phone: 415-665-6637
Fax: 415-665-6696

E-mail: query@motherjones.com
Website: www.motherjones.com

MotorHome

Please refer to *Highways magazine.*

Motor Trend

Formal guidelines not available. Please read a number of issues to ascertain the publication's style and needs.

Send queries to address below.

Categories: Nonfiction—Automobiles—

CONTACT: Matt Stone, Exec. Editor
Material: All
Petersen Publishing Co.
6420 Wilshire Blvd.
Los Angeles CA 90048
Phone: 323-782-2220
Website: www.motortrend.com

Mountain Living
Mountain Living

1. SUBJECT

Subject will be determined following discussion with editor, who will provide resource materials, contact names and suggestions for research when possible. Editor prefers written queries.

2. LENGTH

Department articles usually run 300-1,500 words. Feature articles run 1,200-2,000 words.

3. DEADLINES

All assignments are due on the morning of the date assigned. If an agreed-upon deadline can't be met, please contact the editor a minimum of two weeks beforehand to renegotiate an appropriate date.

4. SIDEBARS

As discussed with editor. Department articles may require a sidebar with information such as reference-book listing, ingredients, facts and figures, and addresses.

5. PHOTOGRAPHS

For all department articles and some features, we ask that you speak with your sources about obtaining photographs. Slides or transparencies are preferable. When possible, mail the photos with your completed article. Otherwise, include a list of photo resources. We will return all artwork after the issue has been published.

6. RESOURCE LIST

Each home feature must be accompanied by a list of interior designers, architects, landscape planners, contractors, builders, etc., who have contributed to the project, as well as their company names, addresses and phone numbers. Each feature must also be accompanied by a list of design resources, for all furnishings, fabrics and materials (available retail or wholesale) used in the project. Only antiques are excluded—custom pieces should be identified as such, with credit to the designer and manufacturer. The interior designer or other professionals who contributed to the project are usually willing to help put together this list.

7. COMPLIMENTARY COPIES

Include a list of photo, research and interview resources, their addresses and phone numbers, so we can send a complimentary copy of the magazine.

8. DELIVERY

Printed submissions should be accompanied by a disk. Speak with the editor about sending articles on-line.

9. PAYMENT

As discussed with the editor and stipulated in the contract. Checks are usually mailed two to three weeks after the material is accepted. A 15 percent kill fee is paid for unacceptable material.

Categories: Antiques—Architecture—Arts—Conservation—Cooking—Culture—Ecology—Environment—Fishing—Gardening—Lifestyle—Travel

CONTACT: Editor
Material: All
7009 S. Potomac St.
Englewood CO 80112
Phone: 303-397-7600
Fax: 303-397-7619
E-mail: irawlings@mountainliving.com
Website: www.mountainliving.com

MSW Management

Please refer to Forester Communications.

Muscle & Fitness

Thank you for your interest in writing for *Muscle & Fitness.*

Of note, we generally don't assign articles to new freelancers but rather ask that you pitch us a detailed query. Please try and narrow in on a specific topic(s) of interest and the points you will bring up. If relevant, cite research, experts you will speak with and any pro bodybuilders that will help fill out the article. As we are a bodybuilding publication, M&F likes to include quotes from exercise/nutrition researchers and bodybuilders whenever possible to bring in an "in the trenches" perspective.

Please contact me if you have any further questions.

Sincerely,

Bill Geiger, Editor

Editorial Guidelines

MUSCLE & FITNESS is a bodybuilding and fitness publication for healthy, active men and women. It contains a wide range of features and monthly departments devoted to all areas of bodybuilding, health, fitness, injury prevention and treatment, and nutrition.

Editorial fulfills two functions: information and entertainment, with special attention to how-to advice and accuracy.

Assignments: All features and departments are written on assignment (including those written on speculation). Writers must be cognizant of deadlines, article length, outline approval and technical requirements. Writers should check assignment confirmation forms for details, and contact assigning editor if necessary.

Queries: Contact us in writing with your article ideas. Your query should be a short summary (one page or less) of your idea or ideas, along with potential sources and your own qualifications to write the article. Send recent clips with bylines. Please send only clips that reflect your own writing style.

Manuscript tone: The editorial voice must be friendly, speaking directly to the healthy, active man or woman. Academic journal composition is not acceptable. Please read the magazine for an understanding of its style.

Manuscript length: As specified with assignment. Generally 500-800 words for departments; 1,500-1,800 words for features.

Writer's contracts/kill fees: All manuscripts from first-time contributors are read on speculation only. Contracts specifying kill fees and author rights are available to repeat contributors.

Payment rates: $360 (or less) for departments; $400-800 (or less) for features. All fees are negotiated individually. Writer must sign M&F contract before any payment can be made.

Fact checking: Accuracy is the responsibility of the author. Manuscripts should be accompanied by the telephone numbers of sources quoted within the article, so editors can verify names and titles, pro-

fessional associations and any related product prices. If a book is referred to in the article, you must include the author's name, the book publisher, year of publication and the book's price if it's still in print. For scientific journal citations, full references are required (and photocopies requested).

Unsolicited manuscripts: We require queries. Please do not send manuscripts.

8 STEPS TO WRITING A BETTER ARTICLE FOR M&F

The following guidelines are intended to remind all writers on those elements that make for great copy. They include:

1) Focus your article. What's your special angle? Why is it important to readers? What new do you have to add to the volumes already printed on the subject?

2) Be clear on where you are going. What questions will you answer? What controversies are there? What research supports the question? What relevant bodybuilders and experts can provide insight? Get an outline together and talk to your assigning editor about it.

3) Get quotes. Unless you are THE one and only expert, it's better to quote those who really are. This adds credibility. Dissenting quotes also offer balance. Quotes from bodybuilders are also good because these are the people who've done it "in the trenches."

When you quote a "doctor," like a physician, dentist, chiropractor or university professor, do not precede the name with "Dr.," but rather give their degree after the name (like MD, DC, PhD, etc.) Also affiliation if applicable (i.e., from the University of Pittsburgh School of Medicine) and its location.

When you introduce anecdotal persons, provide more than just name. Also include city, state, age, maybe profession.

4) Leave out filler. Too many articles come in over 3,000 words that must be returned to be cut. (Or would you rather have a copy editor unfamiliar with your material cut it for you?) Make your points succinctly and don't repeat yourself.

5) Pull the reader into the article. Know why the reader is going to be interested in reading your piece. What's she learning that she can use? Provide solutions and how-to information. How-to articles work well in the second person: for example, "Keep your arms by your sides at all times as you curl the weight."

6) Use subheads to break up long sections of copy and to organize ideas. Use sidebars for background that slows the flow of the main copy, like tangential but relevant topics, technical information, a summary of tips, relevant diagrams or charts, background information, or related information that doesn't insert into the text well but is important to the article.

7) Make sure you're on schedule. Talk to your editor in advance if you need an extension. Don't turn in a half-baked article just to meet deadline; it will be coming back to you for a rewrite.

8) Review your article. Double check the spelling of all names, titles and facts. Also do a spell check.

How to send: Completed manuscript should be e-mailed, sent via dial-in modem connection to M&F at 818-348-1195 (we use PC Plus, 9600 baud, settings are N,8,1). By mail, send 3.5" disk. We prefer IBM Microsoft Word for Windows 6.0 (saved as a document); other software users should save as ASCII text files. Don't forget a clean manuscript as well.

Categories: Diet/Nutrition—Health—Men's Issues—Physical Fitness

CONTACT: Vince Scalisi, Editor
Material: All
21100 Erwin St.
Woodland Hills CA 91367
Phone: 818-884-6800
Fax: 818-595-0463
E-mail: vscalisi@earthlink.net

Muscle & Fitness Hers

Thank you for your interest in writing for *Muscle & Fitness Hers.*

Of note, we generally don't assign articles to new freelancers but rather ask that you pitch us a detailed query. Please try and narrow in on a specific topic(s) of interest and the points you will bring up. If relevant, cite research, experts you will use that will help fill out the article. As we are a fitness publication, *M&F Hers* likes to include quotes from exercise/nutrition researchers and fitness competitors whenever possible to bring in a "real world" perspective.

Please contact me if you have any further questions.
Sincerely,
Carey Rossi Walker, Executive Editor
Editorial Guidelines

Muscle & Fitness Hers is a publication for healthy, active women who are enthusiastic about the fitness lifestyle. It contains a wide range of features and monthly departments devoted to all areas of weight training, health, fitness, injury prevention and treatment, and nutrition.

Editorial fulfills two functions: information and entertainment, with special attention to how-to advice and accuracy.

Assignments: All features and departments are written on assignment (including those written on speculation). Writers must be cognizant of deadlines, article length, outline approval and technical requirements. Writers should check assignment confirmation forms for details, and contact assigning editor if necessary.

Queries: Contact us in writing with your article ideas. Your query should be a short summary (one page or less) of your idea or ideas, along with potential sources and your own qualifications to write the article. Send recent clips with bylines. Please send only clips that reflect your own writing style.

Manuscript tone: The editorial voice must be friendly, speaking directly to the healthy, active woman. Academic journal composition is not acceptable. Please read the magazine for an understanding of its style and its audience.

Manuscript length: As specified with assignment. Generally 750-1000 words for departments; 1,500-2,000 words for features.

Writer's contracts/kill fees: All manuscripts from first-time contributors are read on speculation only. Contracts specifying kill fees and author rights.

Payment rates: $400 (or less) for departments; $400-800 (or less) for features. All fees are negotiated individually. Writer must sign *M&F Hers* contract before any payment can be made.

Fact checking: Accuracy is the responsibility of the author. Manuscripts should be accompanied by all backup material and the telephone numbers of sources quoted within the article, so editors can verify names and titles, professional associations and any related product prices. If a book is referred to in the article, you must include the author's name, the book publisher, year of publication and the book's price if it's still in print. For scientific journal citations, full references and photocopies are required.

Unsolicited manuscripts: We require queries. Please do not send manuscripts.

8 STEPS TO WRITING A BETTER QUERY FOR M&F HERS

The following guidelines are intended to remind all writers on those elements that make for great copy. They include:

1) Focus your article query. What's your special angle? Why is it important to readers? What new do you have to add to the volumes already printed on the subject?

2) Be clear on where you are going. What questions will you answer? What controversies are there? What research supports the question? What relevant competitors and experts can provide insight?

3) How will you pull the reader into the article? Know why the reader is going to be interested in reading your piece. What's she learning that she can use? Provide solutions and how-to information.

4) Review your query. Double check the spelling of all names, titles and facts. Also do a spell check.

Categories: Physical Fitness

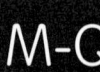

CONTACT: Carey Rossi Walker, Executive Editor
Material: All
21100 Erwin St.
Woodland Hills CA 91367
Phone: No phone calls please.
E-mail: Carey.Rossi-Walker@weiderpub.co
Website: www.muscleandfitnesshers.com

Muscle Mustang & Fast Fords

About Us
Circulation: 135,000
Frequency: 12 times per year
Published by the PRIMEDIA Enthusiast Group.

Muscle Mustangs & Fast Fords is written by and about enthusiasts of high performance Fords, with special emphasis on late-model 5.0L and 4.6L Mustangs. It features editorial on the latest factory aftermarket and performance parts and services for the street and strip, as well as how-to tech articles on making a great car even better. Regular features include inside stories on Ford racing, new car news, plus ways to make a Mustang run faster and handle better.

Ninety-three percent of *Muscle Mustangs & Fast Fords'* readers drive a late model Mustang. *Muscle Mustangs & Fast Fords* offers these enthusiasts a practical guide to making their vehicles perform at peak level. Superchargers, nitrous oxide systems, any and all aftermarket parts and accessories currently manufactured to increase performance are presented in the magazine, usually in the context of a highly readable tech piece. In addition, we bring to our avid readers the hottest industry news, the latest products and complete coverage of shootouts and races.

Submissions

Editorial submissions are welcomed, but the editor recommends that contributors query first. All contributions must be accompanied by a self-addressed, stamped envelope. Solicitations for editorial coverage, including car feature articles, should be submitted via US mail. Please include a photograph of the vehicle/project, a quick reference sheet and a few paragraphs detailing the editorial significance of your work. Due to busy travel and work schedules, the editor is not able to field calls related to potential editorial coverage. We assume no responsibility for loss or damage of any unsolicited materials.

For more information, visit the magazine's Web site at: www.musclemustangfastfords.com.

Categories: Nonfiction—Automobiles—Technical

CONTACT: Jim Campisano, Editor/Editorial Director
Material: Editorial Feedback, Submissions
299 Market St.
Saddle Brook NJ 076636
Phone: 201-712-9300 ext. 611
E-mail: jimc@mcmullenargus.com
Website: www.musclemustangfastfords.com

Muse Magazine

About Us: From the publishers of *Smithsonian* and *CRICKET* magazines.

In October 1996, the Cricket Magazine Group, in conjunction with *Smithsonian Magazine*, launched a new publication entitled MUSE, a nonfiction magazine for children ages 9 to 14. MUSE is published 10 times a year for a subscription price of $32.97. It is 48 pages long.

Mission: The goal of MUSE is to give as many children as possible access to the most important ideas and concepts underlying the principal areas of human knowledge. It takes children seriously as developing intellects by assuming that, if explained clearly, the ideas and concepts of an article will be of interest to them. Articles should meet the highest possible standard of clarity and transparency aided, wherever possible, by a tone of skepticism and humor.

Queries: Articles for MUSE are commissioned. Authors interested in being considered for commissioned work should send a resume, writing samples, and detailed story ideas. We cannot respond to a query that doesn't include story ideas. It is also important to describe any relevant areas of expertise. Please allow 16 weeks for a reply.

Terms: For commissioned articles, MUSE pays inexperienced writers 25 cents a word for all rights. Higher rates are negotiated on the basis of experience. Authors will receive three complimentary copies of the issue in which their article appears.

Commissioning Procedures: Once commissioned, authors are required to submit as many drafts as are necessary. Articles will be assigned at between 1,000 and 1,500 words, and drafts should be sent by e-mail. Authors are also required to provide MUSE with a bibliography that lists all resource material (including names, addresses, and telephone numbers of key persons interviewed for an article). Please note that because of the unique mission of MUSE, extensive rewrites are often necessary.

Criteria for an Acceptable Article: Each article must be about a topic that children can understand. The topic must be a large one that somehow connects with a fundamental tenet of some discipline or area of practical knowledge. The treatment of the topic must be of the competence one would expect of an expert in the field. On the other hand, MUSE does not want articles that could be mistaken for chapters in a textbook. Instead we prefer the author visit the scientist or research site and report on what he or she sees or hears there. An article must be interesting to children, who are under no obligation to read it.

Categories: Nonfiction—Children—Education—Juvenile—Teen

CONTACT: Submissions Editor
Material: Queries
CONTACT: Art Director
Material: Art Samples
332 S. Michigan Ave., Ste 1100
Chicago IL 60604
Website: www.cobblestonepub.com or www.cricketmag.com

Mushing
The Magazine of Dog-Powered Sports

CONTRIBUTOR GUIDELINES

Mushing works with experienced freelance writers and photojournalists as well as first-time authors and photographers. These guidelines are intended to provide an idea of the kinds of submissions we are looking for as well as how our submission process works. Please feel free to contact us if you have questions or if you would like to discuss an idea for submission.

Editorial Profile *Mushing* is distributed in 49 states and 25 countries. Readers include both recreational and competitive mushers with a wide range of experience, from beginners to veterans. In addition, some of our readers are "armchair mushers," who enjoy reading about or watching the sport but are not mushers themselves.

We urge contributors to study the magazine before submitting material. Samples are $5 in the United States, $6 (U.S. funds) to Canada and $8 (U.S. funds) overseas.

ARTICLES

We prefer detailed queries but also consider unsolicited manuscripts. Please make proposals informative yet to the point. Spell out your qualifications for handling the topic. We like to see clips of previously published material but are eager to work with new and unpublished authors, too.

An affirmative response to a query proposal does not necessarily mean the resulting article will be accepted. Tentative scheduling does not necessary guarantee publication.

Content Each issue of *Mushing* includes a mix of information, features and columns. We consider articles on canine health and nutrition, sled dog behavior and training, musher profiles and interviews, equipment how-to's, trail tips, expedition and race accounts, innovations, sled dog history, current issues, and humor, including cartoons. We consider personal experience when the experience illustrates information that is useful to mushers and generally do not when the focus is the personal experience itself. See Editorial Schedule below for current special issue focuses.

All articles should be well researched, logically organized and readable. Appropriate photo support and/or illustrations are encouraged.

Mushing also publishes news, stories, poems, artwork and puzzles by junior contributors. See Junior Mushers Page.

Style and Length

We prefer clear, informative, straightforward writing. We generally follow Associated Press style, although we have our own style guide as well. We reserve the right to edit all submissions.

Features generally run between 1,000 and 2,500 words. Longer articles are considered if well written and of particular interest. Columns and departments usually run from 500 to 1,000 words. Short news pieces run from 150 to 500 words.

Submission Format

Contributor phone number, social security number, name, address and the article's approximate word count should appear at the top. Include a two- to four-sentence author's biography. Do not send originals, and always keep a copy of your work. We treat submissions with care but cannot be responsible for loss or damage.

E-mail: Send as enclosures, as part of the message or both.

Computer Disks: Send Mac or IBM disks, but include a hard copy of the article.

Hard Copies: These need to be clearly typed/word-processed, doublespaced, with a minimum of 1-inch margins all around. Number pages. Photocopies OK if good quality.

PHOTOGRAPHS AND ARTWORK

Mushing uses both color and black-and-white photographs. All photos and slides to be considered must be clean, sharp and accurately exposed. Potential subjects include dogs working, playing and resting as well as expedition and racing events, recreational Mushing, skijoring, winter camping, freighting, mushing equipment and mushing personalities. We use a variety of horizontals and verticals.

We work at least three months ahead of each publication date, so we need summer photos beginning in February and winter photos in June. We are always looking for good cover photographs. These should be strong, sharp, uncluttered vertical photographs with enough open area at the top for the *Mushing* banner.

Black-and-white images account for about 50 to 80 percent of the art in any given issue. Contributors of color images agree to have their images published in black-and-white format unless a specific written agreement is made with *Mushing* in advance of submission.

All photos and artwork must be clearly marked with the contributor's name and address. If you are concerned about the safety of your work, keep the original and send prints, duplicate slides, digital images or photocopies of artwork as long as originals are available for final printing. All photos, slides and original artwork are returned after consideration or use unless other arrangements are specified.

Photo Prints

Black-and-white photos should ideally be 8-by-l0-inch glossy prints, or negatives accompanied by a contact sheet. High-quality prints on semi-matte paper are acceptable but not preferred.

Color prints should be high-quality and be submitted on glossy paper. We prefer slides.

Slides

Ideally submit color photos in 35-mm or 120-mm Kodachrome transparencies. Submit slides in protective slide sheets.

Digital Photos

Send by e-mail for preview at low resolution. JPEG format preferred. For final printing, we need high resolution digital images but prefer original slides or prints.

Artwork

Mushing occasionally uses black-and-white illustrations and drawings—mostly simple images of sled dogs running, howling, sleeping, eating, playing, etc. We have used color artwork on the cover. Sled dog-related cartoons are considered.

Artwork and cartoons can be sent digitally in TIFF or EPS formats. Some artists submit work that *Mushing* can keep on file and use as the need arises.

RATES, RIGHTS, AND PAYMENT

We purchase first serial rights and second (reprint) rights. Please advise us if submitted work has been published elsewhere, including on the Internet, and where and when that publication took place.

Article rates average $.09 per published word.

Photograph and artwork payment rates run from $15 (small black/white) up to $165 (cover).

We also purchase the right to publish some articles and photos on our Internet site for one year following the print publication date. An additional fee of $10 per photo and $20 per article is paid for work used in this way.

Payment within 60 days of publication. Unless a written agreement is made between *Mushing* and a writer or photographer, exact rate of payment for articles and photographs will be determined by the editorial staff of *Mushing*.

Categories: Nonfiction—Animals—Outdoors—Recreation—Sports/Recreation

CONTACT: Deirdre Helfferich, Managing Editor
Material: All
PO Box 149
Ester AK 99725-0149
Phone: 907-479-0454
Fax: 907-479-3137
E-mail: editor@mushing.com

Mustang & Fords

About Us
Circulation: 98,657
Frequency: bi-monthly

Mustang & Fords is dedicated to performance enthusiasts who have a passionate interest in vintage Fords, Mercurys and Lincolns. The primary editorial focus is on 1965-73 Mustangs with an emphasis on Ford musclecars like Fairlanes, Galaxies and Falcons.

Mustang & Fords does not have any written formal guidelines. For more information, visit *Mustang & Fords* on-line at www.mustangandfords.com.

Categories: Nonfiction—Automobiles—Technical

CONTACT: Submissions Editor
Material: All
3816 Industry Blvd.
Lakeland FL 33811
Website: www.mustangandfords.com

Mustang Monthly

About Us
Circulation: 58,122
Frequency: monthly

Mustang owners turn to *Mustang Monthly* for advice on making their distinct cars look and perform better. The title's specialized editorial package covers everything from do-it-yourself recommendations to the history of Mustang; it is the only magazine on the market that caters strictly to the Mustang hobby, from vintage to late-model vehicles.

Submissions

Mustang Monthly does not have formal guidelines. Send submissions to the address below.

For more information, visit *Mustang Monthly* on-line at www.mustangmonthly.com.

Categories: Nonfiction—Automobiles—Technical

CONTACT: Submissions Editor
Material: All
3816 Industry Blvd.
Lakeland FL 33811
Website: www.mustangmonthly.com

Muzzle Blasts

Thank you for your interest in our magazine. Enclosed is a set of writing guidelines to help you prepare your manuscript. If you have any further questions, please don't hesitate to call.

SELECTED TOPIC INFORMATION

Many of our members are knowledgeable in various fields of our muzzleloading sport and the era we represent. Our magazine publishes articles with topics on the history of the muzzleloading era, on hunting with a muzzleloading rifle, and on technical aspects of muzzleloading firearms. If you would like to write an article on any given topic related to muzzleloading, the following will provide needed information in submitting your manuscript.

If your article deals with the history of the muzzleloading era or a muzzleloading firearm, please include detailed information about all references used in developing the article. Articles will not be accepted without proper source documentation in footnote or endnote form. If quoting from a book, please include the author's name, title of book, city and state of publication, publisher's name, year of publication, and page references. If periodicals (such as magazines) are sources, include the author's name, title of periodical, volume and issue numbers, cover date, and page references. If extensive quotations are used, submit photocopies of the pages from which the quotations came.

If hunting is your forte, precede your article with a short descriptive background of the hunting area so the reader can better envision the hunt. Give full details of the firearm used-include the manufacturer or gunmaker, bullet make and caliber, and powder type and load. (Beware of blackpowder overloads; do not exceed manufacturer's recommended maximums.) Pay attention to the details of the hunt, and try to relay humorous situations that occurred, or the imminent danger that was present.

If your article is technical or instructional ("how-to"), be sure to mention the equipment used and describe the procedures step-by-step. Relate the reasons why the subject matter works. Be especially accurate in measurements. Include all charts, photographs, and tables necessary to give a complete description of the process. Remember to include all relevant manufacturer information, especially if the article involves a product evaluation.

In whatever topic you are writing, do not be wordy. Simple and direct writing enhances your subject matter. On the other hand, be sure you provide all necessary information.

TO SUBMIT AN ARTICLE

First, know your topic. Know that the subject matter conforms to the standards of our association and that it has been researched thoroughly.

Be aware of all safety measures (see photo requirements) when writing technical, instructive, or hunting articles.

Present a manuscript on DOS format computer diskette, preferably in one of the WordPerfectTM formats, MicrosoftTM Word©, LotusTM Ami Pro©, or in ASCII. If that is not possible, please submit the typewritten manuscript.

Six to eight typewritten pages, double-spaced, provide the editor with an average-sized article. Longer manuscripts will be considered if the topic warrants the length. Please number manuscript pages.

All manuscripts accepted for publication are subject to editing. This will ensure that they conform to *MUZZLE BLASTS'* format, style, and space limitations.

Be sure your name, address, telephone number, and social security number are included in a cover letter accompanying your manuscript. Please note: We require your social security number for payment and taxation purposes only.

Manuscripts will be acknowledged upon receipt.

ILLUSTRATIONS

All submissions should include high-contrast black-and-white or color photographs and/or well-defined diagrams. Black-and-white or color prints are preferred and must be of good quality. Photos will be reviewed and selected by the editor. On the back of the photo(s) submitted, print your name, address, and title of the article. Use a very soft lead pencil or a typed label. Ink pens, especially felt pens, can bleed through the backing paper. Include a separate sheet of paper with captions, and key the captions to the photos.

All mechanical art, line drawings, and tables must be submitted in black and white. If necessary, ink the drawings for clean-cut reproduction. Submit on a separate sheet of paper. Mechanical art and line drawings produced on IBM-compatible computers can be submitted on a diskette in PCX or TIFF formats, among others. Contact the editor for more information.

REQUIREMENTS FOR PHOTOS AND MECHANICAL IL-LUSTRATIONS

Photos should be 5" x 7" or 8" x 10". However, a good, sharply contrasting 3" x 5" photograph is acceptable. All submissions should be black-and-white or color prints. The submission of color slides with a document may be the cause for its return.

Mechanical artwork, including charts, may be lettered in pencil; such text will be typeset and sized to fit the illustration. Identify the manuscript location of illustrative work on the back of the sheet.

When submitting cover art, recognize that 3" x 5" transparencies are preferred; sharply-contrasting 35mm color slides are acceptable if the subject is unusual or exceptionally deserving of attention, but acceptance is extremely rare. Submissions for cover art must be in portrait (vertical) format.

BE AWARE OF SAFETY WHEN SUBMITTING PHOTOS

Do not submit photos that depict firearms used in an unsafe manner (such as with a blocked muzzle, pointed in an unsafe direction, cocked or half-cocked, and so forth). When submitting photos for technical articles, be aware of and demonstrate all safety measures; for example, if the topic is a review of a new rifle, all shooters who are photographed should be wearing hearing and eye protection.

WRITER/ARTIST RESPONSIBILITIES

Liability for copyright-law compliance of submitted materials (such as artwork or text), as well as the procurement of all model-release forms, is the responsibility of the submitter and not the NMLRA or its affiliates. When submitting materials that have been reproduced whole or in part from other sources, include with the materials copies of permission letters from the appropriate person or persons.

Upon receipt, articles will be reviewed for MUZZLE BLASTS publication by the editor, the publications committee, and technical advisors as deemed necessary. Payments will be made for articles that deal with muzzleloading firearms or firearms with historical value, and for those that provide good instructive subject matter. If there are questions on an accepted article, the editor will contact the writer.

ELECTRONIC RIGHTS

The National Muzzle Loading Rifle Association also publishes on the World Wide Web. This electronic magazine is focused primarily for a nonmember audience. From time to time the editor will contact a writer if he feels that a submission is appropriate for the Web publication. Writers and photographers are free to accept or reject this use of their work, and statements regarding this issue can be enclosed with your submission. Payments for electronic rights are made in addition to regular rates for the paper publication.

MUZZLE BLASTS Writers' Pay Schedule
(All payments made upon publication.)

Special-Purchase Photos

Black and white, up to $30 maximum

Four-color (for covers), up to $300 maximum

Product Reviews

All reviews, $100-$300, depending on the amount of research and tests necessary and the number of photos submitted.

Columns and Articles

All standing columns, $50-$150, depending on the amount of research and tests necessary and the number of photos or illustrations submitted (if any).

All features, $100-$400, depending on the amount of research and tests necessary and the number of photos or illustrations submitted.

Electronic Use

Standing columns, $50 paid in addition to standard scale above.

Feature articles, $100 paid in addition to standard scale above.

Categories: Associations—Education—Hobbies—Outdoors—Recreation—Sports/Recreation

CONTACT: Terri Trowbridge, Director of Publications
Material: Any
CONTACT: Eric A. Bye, Editor
Material: Any
PO Box 67
Friendship IN 47021
Phone: 812-667-5131
Fax: 812-667-5137

My Legacy

My Legacy is for short stories only, and the guidelines are short and sweet. Just remember 2,500 words maximum (sometimes a bit longer is OK). Please submit work in good taste…with no bad language (think of a better way to say it). Stories on any subject are read but must catch my eye to be accepted. The "Editor's Choice Award" of $5 goes to my favorite story in each issue.

USA Rates for Subscription/Single Copy: $16/4 issues; $4.50 next issue only.

Categories: Fiction—Adventure—Animals—Children—Christian Interests—Civil War—Crime—Culture—Family—Fantasy—Inspirational—Mystery—Native American—New Age—Rural America—Science Fiction—Senior Citizen—Short Stories—Spiritual—Western—Writing—Ethnic

CONTACT: Kay Weems, Editor/Publisher
Material: All
207 Willow Wind Dr.
Artemas PA 17211-9405
Phone: 814-458-3102

The National Enquirer

An *Enquirer* story requires fast, extremely detailed, accurate work. It's not particularly complex, but it has to be done. On the other hand, The *Enquirer* pays enough money to make the work worthwhile. A number of freelancers are making better than $1,500 a week right now and there is room for twenty more like them.

You get $360 or $180 just for providing a story idea, plus source information, even if you do nothing more on the story. If you go ahead and cover the story, you get another $720 or $450. So that's either $1,080 or $630 a story—the difference being whether it's used as a "T" (top page) or a "D" (down page). You should aim for twenty leads and one or

two stories each week and don't worry about the high attrition rate of story suggestions. Everyone faces the same situation and it's worth it if you can get one out of ten.

The lead fees and story rates I've just mentioned are the best in the country for newspaper stories. What do you have to do to get them? Well, you have to do a couple of things differently from the way they are done on most newspapers.

First, the writing: the difference here is that we want you to over-write substantially. We want a basic magazine structure: lead, backup (with anecdotes), conclusion. But forget about stylistic tricks—everything is rewritten, you are supplying a basic file, like *Time* reporters do—and you write at least five to seven double-spaced pages. Just put on a straight introduction covering the points raised in the lead sheet and follow it mostly with quotes—the more that's in direct quotes the better, far more than you'll see in the finished story. And get this point clear in your mind—even a small story has to start out this big. We need to cover all the bases.

Your report will be read for the quality of the reporting, not the writing. I know this is frustrating, but it is an essential part of the system and you will be highly regarded for doing it. I might add that, since you don't have to worry about tight writing, style and paraphrasing, an *Enquirer* piece tends to go a lot quicker than a magazine yarn.

Second, there will be questions and call backs. Please don't feel put down if I come back and ask for clarifications. There are three levels of people beyond me whose job it is to nitpick—we strive not just for accuracy but for proof of accuracy. So almost everyone gets called back, though not on every story, and has to check back sources. Just do a thorough reporting job and callbacks will be minimal. We know it is tedious. One of the reasons we pay more than other publications is to compensate you for this occasional necessity.

Here's how to avoid callbacks:

1. Don't state anything in your copy unless you have it in quotes or have other adequate proof that it is true. Don't leave any unanswered questions.

2. Each assignment will have a story number. Mark this number on your copy and add a 'contact sheet' with names and phone numbers of interviewees (they won't be called back if you don't want it, but we need them for our files).

3. Get backup for any substantial claims from other reputable sources. A medical breakthrough, for instance, needs details of test results proving its efficacy, plus a statement by some other authority (often the original source will refer you to others in the file) that the discovery is valid and significant.

4. Avoid dull copy by including anecdotes where at all possible (and appropriate).

5. Follow the lead sheet exactly. If the lead says something is an incredible breakthrough, then you can't quote someone as saying it may be a breakthrough. *Enquirer* stories are black and white—there are no gray areas. We don't do balanced stories. If we decide to run a story, it's because we believe in it. Negative or questioning comments by anyone quoted—either in the file or in the tape recording of interview—will lead to the story being killed.

To ease the shock of all of this, think of this—you can get as much as $2,780 for one story in the *Enquirer*. That's $360 for the lead, $720 for the reporting—and $1,700 if your story makes Page 1. That bonus is paid twice every week and each week we use eighty to ninety stories about half from non-staffers.

Okay, so where do you get these stories? The basic starting points are the newspapers—all the newspapers. Next comes the TV and radio talk shows, then the magazines, general and special interest; then the trade papers and specialist journals, abstracts, and so on. Offbeat books also tend to be good sources. There are also your personal contacts in the various fields—show biz, the universities, hospitals, politics, newspapers and so forth. Also stories you have worked on, are now working on, often have aspects that make an Enquirer angle.

Here's how to recognize an *Enquirer* story and how to write a lead that'll grab us. First, you can pretty much rule out stories that

have been picked up by the wire services, unless you find a completely fresh angle. Second, look for stories that have mass appeal to about half the population. Third, look for the significant things the daily press tends to miss—the story behind the story: a case in point was the disastrous Kentucky nightclub fire some years ago, where *Enquirer* reporters discovered that the reason so many people died was that the management was trying to collect customers' checks before opening the doors.

In writing your lead suggestion, try always to indicate a clear, fresh angle to the story. But be awfully careful you don't write anything in the lead that you can't back up. This is a major reason for stories being killed. In fact, it is a very good idea to do some investigation of your story before submitting it. This will enable you to spell it out with concise facts, figures and examples and give you a much better chance of getting it accepted.

Here's what happens to your idea when you submit it. If I like it, I send it to the Editor. He either okays the lead or kills it. He marks it a "T" or a "D" if approved. I have the approved ones typed on lead sheets. We then give it a story number and check the computer to see that we haven't already done the story in the last five years or that no one currently is working it. When I get the lead sheet back, I assign the story to you or someone else if you can't or don't want to do it.

When you send in your copy—always with the story number on it, I check that it's all there and then I send it to an evaluator. His job is to assess how big the story should finally run and he writes this opinion, along with a summary of your file for the writers to then re-write to the length decided. The written article then goes to the researchers, who check it. You can see that there are quite a few steps here and this is why it's important that your file be complete—otherwise any or all of these people will ask for clarification and this causes delays.

What kind of stories? Please read the paper. Browse through some back issues. They will tell you more than I could. The requirements haven't changed, except perhaps that stories pertaining directly to women are more popular now than before. A general test is—would this story interest 50% of our readers?

Here are some suggestions and reminders you should tape to the wall over your desk:

1. Scandals, big news breaks, exclusives of all kinds—especially untold angles on major stories.

2. Anything about major personalities, especially TV—romances, breakups, illnesses, interviews with them. Almost any interview is usable if the star is big enough but always look for a fresh angle.

3. Medical breakthroughs, especially concerning cancer, heart disease, arthritis, diabetes, and other maladies a broad spectrum of the public has or is worried about. Important scientific discoveries—especially involving common substances.

4. Interesting new diets.

5. Beauty ideas that people can use.

6. Dramatic new fashions, good news and self-help for women.

7. Success stories, people overcoming adversities.

8. Miracle escapes, great rescues, adventures, survival.

9. Ghosts, exorcisms, physics, ESP, UFOs.

10. New self-help ideas—five steps to a new you (especially getting smarter or more successful).

11. Great ripoffs.

12. New light on famous unsolved mysterious (e.g. Amelia Earhart, Bermuda Triangle, etc.)

13. The Kennedys, Reagans, Clintons—their fads, dirty linens, new interests, etc.

14. New information on major controversies—saccharine and cancer, butter and cholesterol, etc.

15. 'Fringe Medicine'—acupuncture, graphology, reflexology, healing—studies that appear to show they have scientific validity. Dreams that come true. But there must be good backup on all these offbeat claims.

16. Governmental misbehavior—officials ripping off funds, unnecessary trips, putting relations on payrolls, misuse of government plans,

FDA keeping valuable drugs off the market, CAB keeping airlines unsafe, etc.—major sources are government auditors, congressional committee staffs and investigators (and equivalents on state and city levels) and ambitious 'out' politicians. Also good are consumer and special interest groups and wayout publications.

17. Sins against the community by other major power blocks—business lobbying and ripoffs, oil depletion, unions costing people their jobs by feather-bedding that kills the firm, stealing pension funds. Labor rackets like the wholesale organized stealing on waterfronts.

18. Public health—good and bad news—e.g., plague still a threat, cancer 'epidemic' in Rutherford, New Jersey, polio is dead.

19. Where are they now? Film star Betty Hutton is a cook in a rectory, etc.

20. New info, especially with pics, on childhoods of famous people or hidden episodes in their lives.

21. Delicately handled sex stories like 'How to Put New Life Into Your Marriage,' 'Why Husbands Lose Interest,' etc.

22. Stories of great wealth—like the custom-made aircraft of the rich.

23. Every kind of 'How To' story especially ten ways to variety.

24. Significant new gadgets and scientific devices, like attaching magnets to your fuel line to increase gas mileage 30 to 40%.

25. News about computers—especially development of artificial intelligence, computer crimes and means of combatting the privacy issue, 'the government has your number' sort of thing.

26. Wacky stunts, such as those of having an *Enquirer* reporter check the waiting time in hospital emergency rooms across the country or taking the Encyclopedia Britannica sales course and reporting all the sales tricks they teach.

27. Human interest. This can be anything that people like to read and talk about. But it's got be good. If it's a dying child who miraculously survives, I want quotes that make me cry, ones that will really touch my heart. If it's a handicapped man who's climbed Mount Everest, I want quotes in the story that will make me cheer. Human interest stories are obviously 'people' stories, but don't forget their pets too.

28. Any happening or development that will cause readers to exclaim, 'Gee Whiz!' or 'How Dare They?' or similar expressions of amazement, joy or anger.

29. There is one other story source—a most important one. It's what we refer to here as 'off the top of your head.' This source can be tapped single-handedly by sitting back, putting your feet on the desk and just thinking in headlines. Think of the sort of headline you've seen on the front page of the *Enquirer*, on the cover blurb of *Reader's Digest*, on the TV ads for this and other publications. Then mentally write a few yourself. All you have to do then is figure out where and how and from whom you can get a story that would fit such a headline. And there you have it—the $1,700 front page bonus. Joint assaults on the top of the head also work; sit around with some of your favorite friends and favorite substances and bounce a few 'what-ifs' around. You'll be amazed how they blossom in mid air. As often as not, this sort of process is the source of our big 'production numbers,' and they're the stories we like best and that will score best for you.

Samples of the sort of thing I mean.
- What if there is one best diet?
- How to find your roots
- 100 easy ways to save money
- Harvard docs reveal simple plan to beat stress
- Lose weight on fast food diet
- TV shows that reduce stress
- Simple no-drug headache cure
- Live up to 20 years longer

Each one of these made a front-page banner headline. Of course, the slight catch to it is that the reporters who thought of those leads also came up with ideas on how to do them.

I am also sending along a couple of other idea ticklers: one is an alphabetical listing of *Enquirer*-type subjects, the other is a list of

Enquirer 'category' stories.

You may choose to specialize in one or two of these areas; it can be a good strategy. But be aware of them all. There's money in every one. Good luck and stay in touch.

Enquirer Category Stories:
- Card & Letter Appeal: for the very sick/lonely/courageous.
- Celebrity Fantasies: The *Enquirer* can make come true.
- Contests: see those we publish to spark your imagination.
- Court Watch: shocking examples of injustice.
- Diet
- Education
- *Enquirer* Impact: how an *Enquirer* article has changed a reader's life for the better.
- Escape From the Rat Race: focusing on somebody successful who's given it all up for a less stressful, preferably wayout, life.
- Good Samaritan Award
- Government Waste or Bureaucracy Run Wild: self-explanatory examples of red tape, incompetence, bureaucratic waste that will make our readers hot under the collar.
- Hero Award: potential recipient must have risked own life.
- Honest Person Award
- How To: self-improvement, etc.
- How To: improve your marriage.
- How To: beat loneliness.
- Incredible World of Animals: each feature concentrates on fascinating attributes of a particular creature.
- Medical: general—breakthrough, new treatments, techniques, etc. We have sub-categories recognizing readers' special interests in cancer, arthritis and heart problems.
- My Most Embarrassing Moment: (celeb)
- My Most Frightening Moment: (celeb)
- Occult
- Rags to Riches: subjects must have started in straitened circumstances and now be verifiably wealthy.
- Recipe for a Happy Marriage: (celeb)
- Reveal Personality: interesting how mannerisms, habits, etc. show us what we're really like.
- Success Without College: subject must be well-known or be associated with a well-known venture.
- Woman at the Top: must be well known.
- Women's Interest: fashion, beauty, etc.
- Young Achiever: kids, preferably under 20, who've achieved fame or fortune through their own endeavor (not showbiz).
- Quiz: relatively light—often psychological (such as "How Brave Are You?") or general knowledge ("How Much You Know About Such and Such?")

Categories: Nonfiction—Adventure—Alternate Lifestyles—Animals—Arts—Biography—Diet/Nutrition—Education—Entertainment—Fashion—Government—Health—New Age—Physical Fitness—Relationships—Science—Self Help—Sexuality—Women's Issues—Celebrities—Astrology—Medicine —UFO Experiences/Research—How-to—Human Interest

CONTACT: Charlie Montgomery, Articles Editor
Material: All
5401 Broken Sound Blvd.
Boca Raton FL 33487
Phone: 800-628-5697, ext. 2216
Fax: 800-336-3973
Website: www.nationalenquirer.com

National Geographic

Does not accept unsolicited submissions.

National Geographic Traveler

Thank you for your interest in contributing to *National Geographic Traveler*, which is published eight times a year by the National Geographic Society. *Traveler*'s publishing goals are to find the new, to showcase fresh travel opportunities, to be an advocate for travelers. *Traveler*'s tag line is "Where the Journey Begins," and accordingly, a *Traveler* story must capture a place's essence in a way that inspires readers to follow in the writer's footsteps—and equip them to do so with useful destination information.

What Types Of Stories Does *Traveler* Publish?

Each issue of the magazine contains five or more features, roughly balanced between U.S. and foreign subjects. Generally, we are interested in places accessible to most travelers, not just the intrepid or wealthy. The types of destinations we cover vary widely, from mainstream to adventure travel.

Traveler features are usually narrow in scope; we do not cover whole states or countries. Subjects of particular interest to us are national and state parks, historic places, cities, little-known or undiscovered places, train trips, cruises, and driving trips. Service information is generally given separately at the end of each feature in a section that includes how to get to the destination, things to see and do there, and where to obtain more information. The writer is expected to send along as much service information as possible with the manuscript to help us prepare this section.

We also publish several regular service-oriented departments, with the emphasis on meaty, practical information. Subjects include photography, food, lodgings, ecotourism, adventurous learning experiences, and short getaways. Essays offering reflections on the travel experience round out the department mix.

What Kinds Of Proposals Is *Traveler* Looking For?

We accept freelance queries for most of our departments. Ideas for features are generated both by the *Traveler* staff and by freelance contributors. We do assign features to writers we have not used but only to those whose published clips demonstrate the highest level of writing skill. We do not accept phone queries from writers, and we discourage the submission of unsolicited manuscripts for feature articles. We do not accept proposals about trips that are subsidized in any way.

How Should An Idea Be Proposed?

If we have to sell readers to consume our magazine, then writers must sell us with more than just notions and place-names, so please do not send us any unfocused wish lists of multiple queries. Restrict each submission to one or two well-developed proposals that have been crafted especially for us. A carefully considered proposal combines support for doing a particular destination with some premise or hook. A good query has a headline that suggests what the story is, a deck that amplifies on that, a strong lead, and not much more than a page that clearly sets out the premise and approach of the piece. The query should represent the writer's style and should answer these questions about the story: Why now, and why in *Traveler*?

Check the *Traveler* index to make sure we have not recently run a piece on the topic you are proposing. Please include your credentials, relevant published clippings and a SASE to ensure that the requested materials are returned. Mail your proposal to Query Editor, *National Geographic Traveler*, 1145 17th St NW, Washington DC 20036. Prospective contributors doing preliminary research for a story must avoid giving the impression that they are representing the National Geographic Society or *Traveler*. They may use the name of the magazine only if they have a definite assignment. When *Traveler* gives an assignment, the terms are clearly stated in a written contract.

How Long Are Traveler Feature Stories And Departments?

Most *Traveler* features range from 1,500 to 2,500 words, depending on the subject. *Traveler* departments generally run from 750 to 1,500 words. Compensation varies depending on the type of feature or department but is competitive with other national magazines. Payment is made upon acceptance. We buy all rights to manuscripts, although copyright is returned to the author 90 days after publication.

What Does *Traveler* Look For In Writing Style?

There are no limitations on style, as long as the writing is lively and interesting, although a sense of discovery should be at the heart of every *Traveler* story. We want our writers to project a curious and knowing voice that captures the experience of travel—the places and personalities, the insights and idiosyncrasies. Writers who work for us must see destinations with fresh eyes and real insight. We place a premium on surprise and good storytelling—the compelling anecdote, the colorful character, the lively quote, the telling detail. And we prefer that our readers be allowed to experience a destination directly through the words and actions of people the writer encounters, not just through the writer's narrative.

Beyond being strongly evocative of place, our articles attempt to speak to the soul of traveling. Every traveler, no matter how seasoned, wonders what awaits at a new destination. This goes beyond weather and accommodations and language and scenics and museums. There's a certain frisson of expectation: How foreign is this destination? What new experience will I have? This is travel as texture—the feel of a place, its essential differentness, its look, its flavor. We seek that texture in every story we publish.

Categories: Nonfiction—Consumer—Ecology—Economics—Education—Food/Drink—Health—Money & Finances—Photography—Recreation—Regional—Sports/Recreation—Travel

CONTACT: Submissions Editor
Material: Queries
National Geographic Society
1145 17th Street N.W.
Washington DC 20036-4688
Phone: 202-775-6700
Fax: 202-828-6640
Website: www.nationalgeographictraveler.com

The National Pastime

Please refer to the Society of American Baseball Research.

National Review

NR isn't a likely place to break in; virtually all our contributors are established writers and/or experts in their fields. In our articles section we publish reports on aspects of the current political or socioeconomic scene—opinionated reporting, not pure opinion. We prefer articles of not more than 2,000 words, and we suggest writers new to NR try a shorter piece, from 900 to 1,500 words.

NR is different enough from other magazines that new writers generally need to read a few issues to understand what we're looking for. It's best to send the articles editor a query by mail before writing an article. (Queries about book reviews should be addressed to the literary editor.)

Categories: Nonfiction—Politics—Public Policy

CONTACT: Andrew Oliver, Articles Editor
Material: All
215 Lexington Ave.
New York NY 10016
Phone: 212-679-7330
E-mail: letter.nationalreview.com
Website: www.nationalreview.com

Native Peoples

Native Peoples strives to offer a sensitive portrayal of the arts and lifeways of the Native peoples of the Americas. We seek writers and photographers—Native and non-Native—who have a unique expertise about their subject. If you are Native, please let us know. Competition is stiff: The magazine receives numerous unsolicited manuscripts and hundreds of queries a year.

Native Peoples is a high quality, bimonthly magazine of nonfiction feature articles and departments. We do not publish fiction, photo essays or reprints. Poetry is only published in context with an accompanying nonfiction article. Most feature stories run 1,200 to 2,000 words, but the subject should dictate your story length. The only departments open to freelancers are our travel section, "Pathways," opinion section "Viewpoint" and artists mini-profile section "Discovering."

The magazine seeks stories reflecting Native life throughout the Americas, from the Arctic Circle to the southern tip of Chile, though our prime focus is on subjects set in the United States. We strive to include a diverse mix of topics, from serious to entertaining, including artist and other personality profiles, events and issues reflecting today's Native peoples. We value stories that help bring an understanding of Native culture—its past, present and future. We write for a diverse audience—about one-third of our subscribers are Native and two-thirds are non-Native. Powerful, descriptive, clear and concise prose is essential. Accuracy and sensitivity are paramount. The readership wants to know and we want you to show them— not just tell them—the Native point of view on any given subject matter.

Stories need to be illustrated with high quality photography. Writers are asked to suggest, or work with, professional photographers.

To have a story considered for publication, please submit a brief outline of your proposed subject via mail or e-mail (e-mail is preferred). Please do not submit original manuscripts, art or photography unless solicited by the magazine. The magazine cannot accept responsibility for unsolicited original materials. A biography or resume, and writing sample(s) are encouraged. We try to respond to queries within 30 days. We work a minimum of six months in advance. We plan a year in advance, so the more lead time you give us about a time-sensitive story, the better the chances are that we will be able to respond and get it published in the most appropriate issue. If an unsolicited story is accepted, the editing process begins. Backup material and rewrites may be requested.

Our standard rate is 25 cents per published word, payable upon publication. (First publication rights only—you own the story).

Categories: Nonfiction—Arts—Book Reviews—Consumer—Culture—Food/Drink—History—Literature—Multicultural—Native American

CONTACT: Daniel Gibson, Editor
Material: All
5333 North Seventh St, Ste 224
Phoenix AZ 85014-2804
E-mail: dgibson@nativepeoples.com

MBMEDIA

Natural Beauty and Health

Thank you for your interest in *Natural Beauty & Health*. We are always interested in reviewing focused, well-written nonfiction articles and interviews. The best way of assessing our style is to look at copies of our magazines, which are available in most major bookstores and on the internet at www.nbhonline.com. Our Statement of Purpose, located in the beginning each issue, is a good place to start.

We do not respond to query letters, and we only consider final products. We prefer that you submit your article by email. If you do submit a hard copy, please send a self-addressed, stamped envelope or email address for our reply. Allow up to six months for a response. We don't send back submissions, so do not send us your only copy. We no longer publish poetry or fiction. Writing in the form of a sermon is discouraged.

Submissions should not have already appeared in other publications or on the web.

Natural Beauty & Health inspires people who take personal responsibility for their mental, physical, and spiritual health and who seek alternatives to the standard paradigm such as yoga, meditation, nutritional discoveries, organic living, holistic healing, and an awareness that beauty comes from inside out. *Natural Beauty & Health* is almost fully devoted to holistic health issues and information. It is not news to our readers that alternatives to the Western medical paradigm exist. They respond to significant discoveries and research into alternative therapies, revised ideas of health and beauty, cultural mythologies, and spiritual disciplines.

FORMAT: Feature articles range in length from 1000 2000 words. E-mailed versions are preferred (in Rich Text Format or text-only format, or in MSWord 98 or earlier), though hard copies can be mailed to MB Media, PO Box 600, Chico, CA 95927-0600. E-mail us at editor@magicalblend.com. Work that has been edited for length and clarity is more likely to be considered. Payment is considered strictly on an individual basis.

Artwork to accompany articles may be submitted digitally or on slides or color prints. Please do not send us originals!

SOME ARTICLE IDEAS *Natural Beauty & Health* MAGAZINE CONSIDERS:

- Herbal Remedies
- Homeopathy
- Ayurveda
- Aromatherapy
- Flower Essences
- Nutrition
- Bodywork/Yoga
- Spiritual/Paranormal Healing
- Self-Improvement
- Alternative Ideas of Beauty Well-Known Health Experts/Celebrities
- Parenting
- Food/Healthy Recipes
- Detoxification/Cleanses
- Organic, non-GMO Foods
- Personal Transformation
- How-To
- Natural Childbirth/Pregnancy
- Men s/Women s Health
- Senior Health

We look forward to reading submissions that show your passion!

Categories: Nonfiction—Alternate Lifestyles—Careers—Children—Comedy—Conservation—Consumer—Cooking—Culture—Diet/Nutrition—Education—Family—Food/Drink—Gardening—General Interest—Health—Interview—Lifestyle—Marriage—Men's Issues—Money and Finances—Parenting—Physical Fitness—Politics—Psychology—Recreation—Relationships—Self Help—Sexuality— Society—Sports/Recreation—Spiritual—Travel—Womens Issues

CONTACT: Susan Dobra, Editorial Director
Material: All
PO Box 600
Chico, CA 95927-0600
E-mail: editor@magicalblend.com
Website: www.nbhonline.com

NATURAL HISTORY

Natural History

We are a magazine of nature, science, and culture published monthly by the American Museum of Natural History. We are seeking new research on mammals, birds, invertebrates, reptiles, ocean life, anthropology, astronomy, preferably written by principal investigators in these fields. Articles for *Natural History* are written by scientists and scholars. Scientists may write about their own research findings or report upon new findings in their field. Straight environmental reportage is not in our purview, but related issues are. Our slant is toward unraveling problems in behavior, ecology, and evolution. In every case, the highest standards of writing and research apply. All submissions are subject to review by experts in the field and to rigorous fact-checking.

The most important thing to do before submitting a proposal to *Natural History* is to look closely at the magazine. We run a range of columns and features. While many are written by staff or regular contributors, we do welcome new submissions. Columns run from 800 to 1,500 words and include "Journal," a short piece of reporting from the field on a subject of scientific interest or debate; "Findings," a summary of new or ongoing research that poses some new questions, usually written by a scientist about his or her own work; "Naturalist at Large," a medium-length essay usually tied to field experience; and "Endpaper," a short essay. We also publish essays, profiles, and commentaries on current events in science.

Features run 1,500 to 2,500 words and are usually accompanied by photographs. Writers may submit photographs, but most photography for *Natural History* is obtained from professional photographers. Occasionally a photographer will be commissioned to work directly with a scientist or writer.

Article proposals may be submitted at any time. Our article schedules are set at least six months in advance. Please consider this in proposing articles with a time-critical or seasonal connection. (We are glad to work with scientists who would like a general article on their research to appear in *Natural History* the same month their research paper appears in *Nature*, *Science*, or other peer-reviewed journal. We will develop the article ahead of time and, if necessary, hold it until the research paper appears.)

Article proposals should be brief. Scientists should accompany their proposals with samples of their published work in the field and/or in general publications. Unless arranged beforehand, we do not accept proposals or submissions by phone, fax, or email. Editorial decisions are usually made within three to four months. Because of the number of submissions we receive, we are unable to supply comments on the reasons for rejection. Payment for articles ranges from $500 to $2,500 depending upon length.

Categories: Nonfiction—Environment—Science—Anthropology—Natural History

CONTACT: Board of Editors
Material: All
American Museum of Natural History, 79th St. at Central Park West
New York NY 10024
Phone: 212-769-5500
Fax: 212-769-5511
E-mail: NHMag@amnh.org
Website: naturalhistory.com

Natural Home

Natural Home offers today's health-conscious, environmentally concerned homeowners the information they need to practice earth-inspired living. Since our first issue in May 1999, *Natural Home* has brought together the best in home design, earth-friendly décor and natural living. Our bimonthly magazine and dynamic website feature sustainable, healthy homes, decorating tips, and the latest green products and services.

Natural Home's readers are educated, eco-savvy home-owners whose values and purchasing patterns mirror the Cultural Creatives, a growing market of 50 million individuals who care deeply about healthy living, natural products, and a sustainable economy. Join us!

Writers' Guidelines

Natural Home is a bimonthly magazine devoted to health-conscious, earth-conscious readers who are concerned with the quality of their personal environment.

Natural Home is published six times a year in January, March, May, July, September, and November. Issues are planned six to twelve months in advance; queries should be sent at least eight months before an issue's publication date. Material submitted for publication should display in-depth knowledge of the subject matter based on experience and thorough research.

Keep a copy of everything. If the submission is unsolicited and/or you wish any part of it to be returned, include a self-addressed, stamped envelope with sufficient return postage.

Manuscripts

If you aren't familiar with the content, style, and tone of *Natural Home* magazine, we suggest you read a few issues.

Although we prefer to assign our own stories, if the article is already written, please enclose a copy of the manuscript, accompanying photos or drawings if any, and a brief informal personal biography. (These illustrations are for editing purposes and will not necessarily be published as part of the article.) If any part of your submission has been published previously, please tell us when and by whom. If the article is still in the idea stage, send a detailed proposal—complete outline, written description, sample page(s), or sketches—sufficient to give a clear idea of what to expect in the finished piece.

The manuscript should be computer generated and submitted on disk or via email. A hard copy of the manuscript should be double-spaced on 8½ x 11 white bond paper with at least one-inch margins. Manuscript length may range from three to sixteen typewritten pages depending on the subject matter. Put your name, address, and telephone number at the top of each page.

We will accept Microsoft Word documents or text files (.txt) created with MS-DOS or Windows-based software and most Macintosh software. Any special instructions may be included on a separate sheet of paper.

Visuals

If you wish to provide your own visuals, please send samples of finished publication-quality photographs (35mm, 2¼ or 4x5 transparencies, please) or artwork; we will determine what best suits the material and our design requirements. All artwork and photographs will be returned promptly and appropriately insured.

Acceptance and Payment

Receipt of your submission will be promptly acknowledged, but we may not be able to make an immediate decision about its use. Please be patient.

Natural Home pays on publication unless other arrangements are made with the editor. Articles range in length from 250 to 1,500 words. Fees are based on a rate varying from $.33 to $.50 per word.

We reserve the right to edit your material as necessary to fit the style, format, or other requirements of *Natural Home*.

Categories: Nonfiction—Environment—Health—Home

CONTACT: Maren Bzdek, Managing Editor
Material: Queries and submission

201 E. Fourth St.
Loveland CO 80537-5655
Phone: 970-613-4660
E-mail: editor@naturalhomemag.com
Website: www.naturalhomemagazine.com

Naturally

Please refer to Travel Naturally.

Nebo: A Literary Journal
Arkansas Polytechnic University

Submissions are preferred from August through February. Themes vary according to the current editor.

Please enclose a cover letter with author's name and address, brief bio, a short list of published works, and a SASE. Indicate for return of manuscript if necessary, and use the required amount of postage.

We do not accept simultaneous submissions or previously published material.

Poetry: We accept blank verse, free verse, sonnets, dramatic monologues, etc. No more than five poems per submission.

Fiction: Short-short (up to 750 words) and short stories are the stuff of life and we appreciate all such submissions. Due to space restraints, please limit stories to 2,000 words.

All works must be typed (single-spaced for poetry is acceptable). Please include an approximate word count for short prose fiction.

Advice to Writers

We are interested in quality poetry and fiction by new and established writers. In fiction we are open to a wide range of styles, but ask that the length be kept to 2,000 words (750 for short-shorts). We seek poems whose content is convincing and whose rhythms are as compelling and memorable as their diction and images.

Thank you for your interest in our journal!

Categories: Fiction—Poetry

CONTACT: Dr. Michael Karl Ritchie
Material: Any
English Dept. Arkansas Tech. University
Russellville AR 72801-2222
Phone: 501-968-0487

Nebraska Review
The University of Nebraska-Omaha

Quality, well-crafted literary fiction, creative nonfiction and poetry. No restrictions on content, style, or length, although fiction generally should not exceed 7,500 words. Longer pieces of exceptional merit will be considered. Response in 3 to 6 months, sometimes sooner.

Please note these submissions deadlines:
Open submission of original fiction and poetry
January 1 - April 30

Fiction manuscripts should include the writer's name and address on the first page.

Poetry may be single-spaced, and should include the writer's name and address on each poem. Standard submission is three to six poems.

Subscriptions: $15.00 per year (2 issues); $18 for two years. Individual copies: $8. Back issues and sample copies: $4.50 when available.

Categories: Fiction—Nonfiction—Literature—Poetry—Short Stories—Writing

CONTACT: Coreen Wees, Poetry Editor
Material: Poetry
CONTACT: James Reed, Fiction Editor
Material: Fiction

CONTACT: John Price, Nonfiction Editor
Material: Creative Nonfiction
Program in Creative Writing, University of Nebraska-Omaha
Omaha NE 68182-0324
Phone: 402-554-3159

Nevada Magazine

Nevada Magazine is constantly searching for stories and photographs that tell the story of Nevada.

Stories and photos are accepted on speculation. Recommended subjects include Nevada's people, history, recreation, entertainment, events, towns, and scenery. If you have another Nevada topic you'd like to write about, we'd be happy to hear your suggestion. However, if your article is about a Nevada character in Europe, or a recreational article that takes place half the time in California, it probably won't work. Keep in mind that the magazine's purpose is to promote tourism in Nevada and that the majority of readers live out of state. Payment is on publication and varies with article length and the size and quality of photographs. We encourage you to submit photos with your stories. Most stories range between 500 to 1,800 words. Fees range from 25 to 30 cents per word and $30 to $150 for photos and illustrations. The magazine buys first North American rights. Manuscripts should be double-spaced with a suggested title, byline, and writer's credit. Your name, address, phone(s), and email address should be on the first page of the manuscript, and be sure to leave ample margins on the sides and bottom of each page.

You can e-mail queries and stories to the editors below. We are Mac-based. Our software program, Microsoft Word, can convert most Macintosh and IBM programs. If you submit a disk, please include a hard copy. For color photographs, we prefer transparencies (35mm sides and larger) to color prints, although sharp color prints can be used. With black-and-white photos, we prefer 8" x 10" glossies. Write your name, address, and identification of the subject on each slide or photograph. You can also e-mail images to us at denise@nevadamagazine.com. Send 72 dpi jpeg images to us to evaluate and 300 dpi tiff or jpegs for publication. To receive a copy of the magazine's Photo Alert, a list of current photo needs, contact Art Director Denise Barr or Production Assistant Melissa Loomis.

The editors reserve the right to edit all material and cannot guarantee against damage to, or loss of, any materials. However, we will make every effort to handle submissions as if they were our own and to work with writers and photographers. You can help by sending a self-addressed, stamped envelope with your material to ensure its safe return. Please allow four or five weeks for reply. We look forward to hearing from you.

—The Editors

Nevada Magazine is designed to promote tourism in Nevada and educate the public about the state's recreation, people, places, history, events, entertainment, and other attractions. Since the state publication first appeared in 1936, readers have relied on *Nevada Magazine* for informative and entertaining features on the Silver State. The magazine's circulation (bimonthly) is approximately 80,000 (for the NEVADA EVENTS & SHOWS center section, nearly 200,000), and 70 percent of the magazine's readers are from out of state. Readers are active travelers and Nevada enthusiasts who take frequent Nevada vacations.

DEVELOPING STORY AND PHOTO IDEAS

When developing your ideas, consider *Nevada Magazine*'s audience and how your story would work in the magazine's format. For example, these kinds of stories appear in every issue:

Places and Travel

Destinations: Focusing on locales such as Wendover, Laughlin, Lake Tahoe. Roadside Attractions: Intriguing things to do, places to go. Side Trips: Excursions to unique places. Dining Out: Unusual eateries.

Hotel-Casinos
People stories.

Trends in gaming, dining, and other hotel offerings.
Vacation ideas.
Recreation
Guides to golf, fishing, skiing, boating, and other sports. First-person stories on outdoor adventures.
History
People, places, and events in old-time Nevada.
People
Nevadans, Nevada Characters, People Page, Artists.
Photography
Photo features.
Annual photo contest, the Great Nevada Picture Hunt.
Nevada Events & Shows (the magazine's center section)
Lead story on seasonal event(s) or entertainment.
Show People.
Show Review.
Event and show listings.
Nevada Travel Update (newsletter to travel agents)
Hotels, destinations, sightseeing, adventure tours.

SUBMITTING ITEMS AND IDEAS TO *Nevada Magazine*

Please write, email, or give us a call if you have a story or photo idea that you think might work in *Nevada Magazine*:

Categories: Nonfiction—History—Outdoors—Recreation—Regional—Travel

CONTACT: David Moore, Editor
Material: All
CONTACT: Joyce Hollister, Assoc. Editor
Material: All
401 N. Carson St., Ste 100
Carson City NV 89701
Phone: 775-687-5416
Fax: 775-687-6159
E-mail: jhollister@nevadamagazine.com
E-mail: dave@nevadamagazine.com
Website: www.nevadamagazine.com

The New Centennial Review
Interdisciplinary Perspective on the Americas

About CR (Formerly *The Centennial Review*)

CR: The New Centennial Review is devoted to comparative studies of the Americas. The journal's primary emphasis is on the opening up of the possibilities for a future Americas which does not amount to a mere reiteration of its past. We seek interventions, provocations, and, indeed, insurgencies which release futures for the Americas. In general, CR welcomes work which is inflected, informed, and driven by theoretical and philosophical concerns at the limits of the potentialities for the Americas..

Such work may be explicitly concerned with the Americas, or it may be broader, global and/or genealogical scholarship with implications for the Americas. CR recognizes that the language of the Americas is translation, and that therefore questions of translation, dialogue, and border crossings (linguistic, cultural, national, and the like) are necessary for rethinking the foundations and limits of the Americas.

For forty-five years, CR has been a journal committed to interdisciplinarity, and we continue to encourage work which goes beyond a simple performance of the strategies of various disciplines and interdisciplines, and which therefore interrogates them. This journal is a member of the Council of Editors of Learned Journals.

Submission Guidelines

CR is a refereed journal. We take approximately 2-3 months to read and comment on unsolicited manuscripts. When submitting an article for consideration, please enclose three (3) copies and an e-mail address where you may be reached.

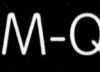

M-Q

In preparing your submission, use *The Chicago Manual of Style* with the following modification: you may cite page numbers interlinearly once a text has been referenced in the notes. Please use endnotes rather than footnotes.

We do not accept electronic submission of articles at this time. Unsolicited manuscripts are returned to authors only when accompanied by a stamped, self-addressed envelope.

Please e-mail one of the editors if you would like to write a book review for CR.

Categories: Nonfiction—African-American—Agriculture—Architecture—Arts—Biography—Careers—College—Culture—Drama—Ecology—Economics—Education—Electronics—Engineering—Feminism—Government—History—Language—Literature—Multicultural—Politics—Psychology—Society—Theatre—Philosophy—Public Policy—Technology

CONTACT: Scott Michaelsen (smichael@msu.edu)
Material: All
CONTACT: David E. Johnson (dj@acsu.buffalo.edu)
Material: All
Department of English
201 Morrill Hall, Michigan State University
East Lansing MI 48824-1036
Phone: 517-355-9543
Fax: 517-353-3755
E-mail: David E. Johnson (dj@acsu.buffalo.edu)
Website: www.msupress.msu.edu/journals/cr

New England Review
Middlebury College

New England Review is published four times a year: winter, spring, fall, and summer. However, our reading period is September 1 through May 31 (postmark dates) only. Any submissions that arrive during the summer must be returned unread.

All editorial and business correspondence should be mailed to *New England Review*, Middlebury College, Middlebury, VT 05753. All correspondence must have a return address written or printed clearly on the outer envelope. Mail received without a legible return address will not be opened and will be discarded.

We consider short fiction, including shorts, novellas, and self-contained extracts from novels, and we consider a variety of general and literary nonfiction: long and short poems; speculative, interpretive, and personal essays; book reviews; screenplays; translations; critical reassessments; statements by artists working in various media; interviews; testimonies; and letters from abroad. We are committed to exploration of all forms of contemporary cultural expression in the United States and abroad. With few exceptions, we print only work not published previously elsewhere.

We suggest that you peruse a copy of NER to see what our standards and preferences are. The current issue is available for $8.00 from the better bookstores or post paid (add $2 for overseas surface delivery, $3 for air mail.

Prose: maximum of thirty pages in length (except novellas, of course), double-spaced with one-inch margins. Please send just one piece at a time, unless the pieces are very short. Poems: send no more than six at once, please. All manuscripts should be typed in standard type on one side only of white 8 1/2" X 11" paper. Good photocopies are acceptable. Never send your only copy; we cannot be responsible for lost or damaged manuscripts. Very brief cover letters are useful. Please note that we cannot accept submissions via electronic mail.

Please address your submission to Prose, Fiction, or Poetry Editor, and write your full name and address on the front of the manuscript envelope. Enclose a self-addressed, stamped envelope (SASE) that is large enough and carries enough U.S. postage to return your manuscript and our reply. If you don't need your manuscript returned,

enclose a letter-size SASE (not a postcard, please). Overseas contributors should include international reply-paid coupons. Be sure to send an SASE with any query.

Please do not send another submission until hearing about the first. We cannot accommodate changes, revisions, or forgotten SASEs. Additional manuscripts must be returned unread. We will consider work that has been offered simultaneously to other publications, but we do ask that you indicate simultaneous submissions in your cover letter and withdraw your submission immediately upon acceptance elsewhere.

NER will respond to your submission within twelve weeks. After twelve weeks have passed, you may query as to the status of your submission by mail or electronic mail, supplying your name, address, phone number, and the postmark date of your submission.

A contract is sent upon acceptance, and payment is $10.00 per page, $20.00 minimum, plus two copies of the issue in which your work appears. Authors proof the galleys. Copyright reverts to the author upon publication. NER retains the right under Copyright Law to reprint your work only as part of a whole volume in a *New England Review* anthology or re-issue, for example, or in publicity materials.

Thank you for your interest in NER.

Categories: Fiction—Nonfiction—Literature—Poetry—Essays

CONTACT: Stephen Donadio, Editor
Material: Fiction, Poetry, Literary Essays
Middlebury College
Middlebury VT 05753
Phone: 802-443-5075
E-mail: NEREVIEW@middlebury.edu
Website: www.middlebury.edu/~nereview

New Letters

Dear Writer,

Thanks for your interest in *New Letters*. Although we do not have any formal writers' guidelines, here are a few suggestions:

• We prefer that you send no more than six poems or one short story per submission.

• We prefer shorter stories to longer ones. An average length is 3,500 words.

• We have no rigid preferences as to subject, style or genre, although "commercial" efforts tend to put us off. Even so, our only fixed requirement is on good writing.

• We discourage multiple submissions, but appreciate knowing if you're sending your work to us and someone else simultaneously.

• Like most literary magazines, our staff is small, so our reporting time varies from 6-18 weeks. Sorry.

• We do not read submissions between May 1 and October 15.

Sample copies are available from this office for $7.00. We pay the postage if you prepay.

I hope this information is helpful.

Cordially,

James McKinley, Editor

Categories: Fiction—Nonfiction—Arts—Culture—Literature—Poetry—Short Stories

CONTACT: Robert Stewart, Editor
Material: All
University House, 5101 Rockhill Rd.
Kansas City MO 64110
Phone: 816-235-1168
Fax: 816-235-2611

New Mexico Journey

Texas Journey and *New Mexico Journey* are the bimonthly magazines for members of AAA Texas and AAA New Mexico, with **608,000**

and 80,000 readers respectively. Editorially focused on regional, travel, and automotive topics, we strive to present creative, intelligent, and helpful stories.

In each issue, we publish three to four feature articles between 1,000 and 2,000 words each. Items for our Travel News and Auto News columns are 75 to 250 words each. We assign stories based on writers' proposals, and, as a rule, do not accept already completed manuscripts. We assign most often to established writers with a solid knowledge of Texas, New Mexico, and the surrounding states, and value writers with a strong voice, storytelling ability, and sound research and reporting skills.

We pay $1 a word, plus agreed-upon expenses on acceptance of a manuscript, and $50 each for story ideas. We buy first North American rights.

We seek stories that uncover a fresh angle on the people and places in and around Texas and New Mexico. Generally speaking, we're most interested in features about the outdoors, cultural travel, consumer travel, and personality profiles. We periodically cover the states of Colorado, Arizona, Louisiana, and California. Non-U.S. destinations include Mexico, Europe, and Canada.

We usually respond to queries within two months. Phone and fax queries are not encouraged. To be considered for an assignment, please mail queries, clips, and a self-addressed stamped envelope to the address below. Thank you for your interest in our publications. We look forward to reading your proposal.

Categories: Nonfiction—Associations—Automobiles—Consumer—Regional—Travel

CONTACT: Nina Elder, Features Editor
Material:3333 Fairview Road, A-327
Costa Mesa CA 92626
Phone: 714-885-2376
E-mail: www.aaa-calif.com/westways

New Mexico Magazine

New Mexico Magazine covers the people, culture, arts, history and landscape of New Mexico for a highly educated readership from every corner of the world. Monthly magazine, 84 to 132 pages. Established 1923. Circulation: 117,000. Pays on acceptance for manuscripts, on publication for photos. Buys first North American serial or one-time rights for photos and artwork. Query first. Buys few manuscripts on speculation. Plans issue six to 12 months in advance. SASE. We reply in four to six weeks. Sample copy $3.95.

Articles

Profile, travel, archaeological, historical (examining little-known facets of New Mexico history or shedding new light on major events and personalities of the past), humor, Southwest lifestyles (food, fashion, homes, gardens), arts and crafts, cultural topics (traditional ways of life, customs, unusual celebrations, social trends), photo features, offbeat science, business stories—anything involving an aspect of New Mexico. Buys seven to 10 manuscripts/issue. Send published writing samples with query. Length: 250-2,000 words. Pays 30 cents a word, $100 minimum.

Style

Use AP style for writing guidelines. Type name, address (including E-mail if available) and phone number in the upper left corner of each page of correspondence and manuscript. Double- or triple-space text. Number pages. Prefer letter-quality printout, typed manuscript or computer diskette.

What We Need From You

Tag Line—Include a short paragraph about yourself and your experience for the end of the story. This lets the reader know who you are.

Contact Information—(A) If there is any way the public can contact and/or interact with the subject of your story, include it. Telephone numbers, addresses, locations to sites, galleries where art is shown or sold, etc.—we want to involve the reader if at all possible. (B) Though it may be the same as above, editors need the names and contact information for subjects interviewed or mentioned in your story. Sometimes we hold onto a story for up to a year and need to make sure nothing has changed in your story. If you interview a national park superintendent, we need to be able to easily call and confirm that person is still there. If not, we can easily edit the story to bring it up-to-date, saving us all embarrassment.

Think Art—We almost always run photos or artwork to illustrate stories. While you may not be a photographer, we encourage your suggestions as to what images would enhance your story or how to contact subjects regarding photos. Also, consider if your story is seasonal. If an outdoor story is scheduled to run next summer, we need to shoot images this summer. Shooting gardens in the winter doesn't work too well. If your story is a timely event, it is best to do the photography at that time. Let us know in advance so we can arrange for a photographer to cover these events as well.

Develop Queries—We sometimes receive the "shotgun" approach to queries, where the writer gives only a sentence or two of explanation for a story idea and then moves on to the next. We usually reject all the proposals, as we get 20 ideas with no good information. Your best bet is to pick one or two strong ideas and develop these into at least a half-page pitch. If the idea isn't interesting enough to at least write this much in a query, it's probably not interesting or detailed enough for a story. Always include your contact info on each page of the query. Often, pages of queries are separated. It's hard to make assignments if we can't get in touch with you. We do not accept e-mail or fax queries.

Be Familiar with the Magazine—This isn't a ploy to sell more magazines. The best way to find out what we're after is to read *New Mexico Magazine*, know the departments, style and what we have already covered. Many libraries catalog the magazine. With any writing, know your audience.

Makin' Tracks

Makin' Tracks focuses on outdoor recreation in New Mexico's backcountry. While all fitness and experience levels should be considered and addressed, the idea is these are places you can't just drive to—you have to get out, explore and enjoy. The text is 750 words. Two quality slides are needed, at least one horizontal. Relevant information such as ranger district contacts and maps to use are required. The text pays $300; photos are paid based on our stock rates. Query with writing samples first.

Makin' Tracks Notes:

• The point of the trips should be to have fun, learn about and enjoy New Mexico's backcountry, not to prove you can power hike 30 miles in a day.

• All destinations should be completely open to the general public. List all restrictions and necessary permits, if any.

• Be very clear and honest about the physical level needed for the trip. Can you be in average shape to do the hike or should you work up to it? Is altitude a factor to consider? If you have to be an Olympian athlete to make the hike, we're probably not interested.

• Avoid lingo without explanation. Write in such a way a general audience will understand you.

• List special considerations of the trip. Is water available? Are the trails marked? Where, if anywhere, can people go for help? Is the area open to hunting at certain times of the year?

• State what makes this trip unique. No generic strolls in the woods—there should be something special about this place. Note flora, fauna, archaeological sites, anything to look out for.

• Keep in mind the health of the environment. If a section of a trail is receiving too much pressure, make people aware so they can reroute. Many people don't willingly harm areas, they're just unaware they're doing so. We want to tell people about these great areas, but we also want to help protect them. State the rules so people can follow them.

• Know your subject. Anyone can look at a map and some U.S. Forest Service brochures and get a general feeling for what's there. Write about the details you can only experience by going there.

Así Es Nuévo Mexico (This is New Mexico)

This department is a fun mixed-bag of short stories from all over the state with a strong New Mexico angle—things you can only find here. Text should not exceed 350 words. One quality slide or illustration to accompany the story is needed. Asis pay $100 upon acceptance; the photographer or artist is paid $60 upon publication of the story and artwork. Query with writing samples first. Así's cover, but are not limited to, these categories:

• **Human interest stories**—Examples: A grandmother who has sent homemade tamales to troops overseas during the holidays for the past 40 years; an individual who is for no pay helping communities restore their churches. We're looking for New Mexicans who inspire and deserve recognition.

• **Unique artists, crafts and business people**—New Mexico has no shortage of quality artists and it's impossible to feature them all, so we look for those who stand out, either in their work or in the way they live. This could mean they have donated work to the public, use an unusual process to create their work, use a cave as a studio—anything out of the ordinary. Artwork must be publicly displayed.

• **Quirky, fun subjects**—Anything of interest the public can visit or participate in that's out of the ordinary. If you enjoyed checking it out, readers may also.

Some Así requirements:

• **General public should be able to interact with the subject of the story.** Examples: An artist's work needs to be on public display or available in a gallery; an event needs to be open to the public; unique objects and places need to be accessible to the general public and not located on restricted property. Contact and additional information should be clearly noted in the Así story.

• **Short and Sweet.** Though many Así subjects could justify a book, we just don't have the space. The objective is to pique the readers' interest with fun, active, informative writing and tell them how to pursue learning more about or interacting with the subject.

• **Make sure it's interesting.** You should be able to express in a sentence or two why this subject stands out, even if you think it's obvious. Also, if it is boring to write, it's probably boring to read.

• **Make sure it's New Mexico.** Enough said.

Categories: Arts—Book Reviews—Culture—History—Regional—Society—Travel—Western

CONTACT: Steve Larese, Assoc. Editor/Photo Editor
Material: All
495 Old Santa Fe Trail
Santa Fe NM 87501
Phone: 505-827-7447
Fax: 505-827-6496
E-mail: Submissions@NMMagazine.com (Proposals, articles and queries)
E-mail: Photos@NMMagazine.com (Photo submissions)
Website: NMMagazine.com

New Mexico Woman

Thank you for your interest in writing for *New Mexico WOMAN* magazine. Please see our Editorial Calendar for 2004. The calendar outlines the proposed theme and industry focus for each issue in 2004.

Our primary readership is working women between the ages of 25 and 55 who are interested in reading about successful New Mexico women and women-owned businesses. The majority of our readers are professionals, and many are business owners. (Detailed readership demographics are available from our advertising department.)

The editor currently accepts queries for article ideas via FAX, e-mail or mail only. Please request an Editorial Query Form to be sent to you by e-mail or by FAX if the form is not included in this packet. Duval Publications Inc., is not responsible for unsolicited manuscripts or photographs.

The majority of our contributors are experienced, professional writers. *New Mexico WOMAN* magazine currently pays writers new to the magazine a minimum of .05 per published word, unless otherwise negotiated. While all support the mission of our magazine, each writes for different reasons. Our magazine is an excellent way to break into the freelance market, or to have a continuing voice in women's activities.

Guidelines for manuscript submission:

1. Submit an Editorial Query Form to the editor.

2. Receive acceptance for your query and suggestions for story angle from the editor.

3. Submit your article by deadline to the editor via e-mail attachment in this format:

a. Microsoft Word .doc file-OR-.rtf file (If a Mac user, please submit .rtf)

b. Times New Roman or similar serif font in 12-point type.

c. Single spaced. ALSO: Please only one space after a period.

d. Each paragraph indented (NO double space between paragraphs).

e. Writer's name, phone number, and e-mail address attached.

4. Please follow AP style (outlined in the Associated Press Stylebook) with this exception:

Include the serial comma before the and in a series.

Example: cats, dogs, and horses

NOT: cats, dogs and horses

Guidelines for photograph submission:

1. Preference: e-mail photos. Compress file attachments (.zip) or send separately. Max file size: 800K.

2. If sending prints, include SASE for return. Send copies only; we cant guarantee return of originals.

3. Label on all prints (or include in all photo filenames) the article title for easy identification.

4. Always include captions/cutlines and photo credits for all photos.

5. Best formats for photos that are e-mailed as attachments: High-res JPEGs, PDFs, or TIFs.

Categories: Business—Women's Issues

CONTACT: M.T. Hyatt, Editor
Material: All
Duval Publications, Inc
PO Box 12955
Albuquerque, NM 87195
Phone: 505-247-9195
Fax: 505-842-5129
E-mail: heygals@nmwoman.com
Website: www.nmwoman.com

New Millennium Writings

Now accepting submissions for *New Millennium* Awards for Fiction, Poetry and Nonfiction

$2,000 in Cash Prizes, Plus Publication ($1,000 for best story; $500 for best poem; $500 for best nonfiction).

Twenty-five runners-up received Certificates of Honorable Mention and were named in the Fall '97 Issue of NMW.

1. All winners and selected finalists will be published in the Fall issue, which will feature interviews, new and noteworthy writings, photographs and illustrations. All contestants receive a copy.

2. There are no restrictions as to style, content, format, or number of submissions. Keep entries to no more than 25 typed, double-spaced pages of prose or five pages of poetry (three poems). No previously published material accepted.

3. Deadlines are June 16 (postmarked by then) and January 16 (twice annually).

4. Send a $10 check payable to NMW with each submission.

5. Each piece of fiction or nonfiction prose (essay, article, interview, etc.) is counted as a separate submission. Each Poetry submis-

sion may include up to three poems. Simultaneous and/or multiple submissions welcomed.

6. Include name, phone number, address and category (Fiction, Poetry, or Nonfiction Prose) with each submission. Paper clips preferred, but staples O.K.

7. Manuscripts will not be returned except in hardship cases (printer broken? no computer? Include SASE in such instances). We do recycle. Winners and finalists will be notified in August. Enclose business-size SASE for list.

Judges and editorial advisors include: Novelists and short story writers Jon Manchip White and Allen Wier; Poets Lisa Coffman and Marilyn Kallet; Journalists and essayists Fred Brown, David Hunter and Don Williams, editor.

To subscribe only, send $12.95 to "Subscribe" at the address below. For pre-contest sample copy, send $8; Phone for more information.

Categories: Fiction—Nonfiction—Arts—College—Comedy—Education—Environment—Experimental Fiction—Literature—New Age—Poetry—Public Speaking—Sexuality—Short Stories—Spiritual—Women's Fiction—Writing—Trade - Writing/Publishing

CONTACT: Dan Williams, Editor
Material: All
NMW Contest Room 101, P. O. Box 2463
Knoxville TN 37901
Phone: 423-428-0389

New Moon
The Magazine for Girls and Their Dreams

Objectives of *New Moon*:

New Moon portrays girls and women as powerful, active and in charge of their own lives—not as passive beings who are acted upon by others. *New Moon* celebrates girls and their accomplishments. *New Moon* supports girls' efforts to hold onto their voices, strengths and dreams as they move from being girls to becoming women. *New Moon* is a tool for a girl to use as she builds resilience and resistance to our sexist society, moving confidently out into the world, pursuing her unique path in life.

***New Moon* strives to:**

• be an international, multicultural magazine which connects girls and celebrates diversity by providing a place for girls to express themselves and communicate with other girls around the world.

• portray strong female role models of all ages, backgrounds, and cultures now and in the past.

• encourage pursuit of interests in which girls are often discouraged, e.g. math, science, and physical activity.

• acknowledge the difficulties and celebrate the joys of being female in the world.

• understand that respecting girls, attending to their needs and giving them voice and power means upsetting the fabric of society.

Therefore, we seek high-quality literary and artistic work which has a diversity of cultural and stylistic influences, and represents real connection with girls.

General Guidelines:

All material should be pro-girl and focus on girls, women, or female issues. *New Moon* was created by girls and women for girls who want their voices heard and their dreams taken seriously. It is

edited by and for girls ages 8-14. *New Moon* takes girls very seriously; the publication is structured to give girls real power. The final product is a collaboration of girls and adults. An editorial board of girls aged 8-14 makes final decisions on all material appearing in the magazine.

Submissions:

Please read a copy of *New Moon* to understand the style and philosophy of the magazine. Writers and artists who comprehend our goals and philosophy have the best chance of publication.

Include your name, address and phone number on the title page of each submitted work or query.

New Moon is not able to acknowledge or return unsolicited manuscripts. Please do not send originals.

New Moon prints original works, except under special circumstances. If your work has been published previously, note the date and publication. If you are sending this work simultaneously to another publication, please let us know this, too.

For Writers:

New Moon edits manuscripts for style, length, clarity and philosophical considerations.

We prefer e-mail submissions. All other work must be typed, double spaced with one-inch margins. Your name and address should appear on each page.

Submit only copies of your work, not originals. We do not acknowledge or return unsolicited submissions.

Non-fiction articles are between 300 and 600 words. Non-fiction profiles of women are preferred. Feel free to send us ideas of girls to profile. We prefer to have those written by the girls themselves. Non-fiction has better chance for publication when it focuses on one of our editorial themes. We regularly publish adult non-fiction in our Body Language, Herstory and Women's Work sections.

New Moon publishes about three adult-written, short fiction pieces (900-1200 words) annually.

Please keep the original of your work for your own files. Submissions from girls and women only, please.

For Artists:

New Moon has a four-color cover and two-color interior (inside colors change from issue to issue).

For cover guidelines, send us a SASE or go to www. newmoon.org. Proposals for covers should be sent as drafts, and include examples of earlier, finished artwork. Several drafts may be required in the multi-step process by which the Girls Editorial Board chooses a cover. Cover art submissions from girls and women only, please.

To be considered for editorial illustration work, please send samples to the address below. Samples will not be returned. New Moon Publishing, Inc. is not responsible for unsolicited material.

Categories: Fiction—Nonfiction—Children—Feminism—Teen—Women's Fiction—Women's Issues—Young Adult

CONTACT: Submissions Editor
Material: All
34 E. Superior St., Ste 200
Duluth MN 55802
Phone: 218-728-5507
Fax: 218-728-0314
E-mail: girl@newmoon.org
Website: www.newmoon.org

the new renaissance

At *the new renaissance* (**tnr**), we're looking for writing that has something to say, says it with style and grace, and, above all, speaks in a personal voice.

FICTION: Contemporary, literary, off-beat, translations, humor, satire, prose/poems and, occasionally, experimental fiction. We don't want to see popular or slick writing, overly academic or sentimental fiction, or strictly commercial pieces. No pornography. One story per submission unless stories are four pages or less, then two stories are allowed.

We are interested in fiction that offers a revelation or illumination on the human condition. Although we stress substance, style is important, and we pay close attention to diction, phrasing, and personal vision.

Approximations in language are not good enough. Since we accept only one ms out of every 125 submissions, we ask writers to read tnr closely and to send in stories that are at least as good, however different, as those we've been publishing. Mss. can be two to 36 pps. although we will occasionally accept a longer work. We are interested in translations (send originals). Allow 4-5 months for a decision.

POETRY: Contemporary, lyrical, narrative, humorous and satirical poems. No pornography or obscenity. Eroticism will be considered. We are especially interested in poetic imagery ground in experience, but accept all styles

Mss. of 3-6 one-page poems or 2-4 two-page poems are preferred,; we occasionally publish the long poem, but only one long poem per submission. We are especially interested in translations (send originals). Allow 3-4 months for a decision.

FICTION/NON-FICTION ONLY SUBMITTING PERIODS: [1997] January through May; and September and October.

HOW TO SUBMIT: All fiction and poetry submissions are tied to our award programs: The Louise E. Reynolds Memorial Fiction Award and the **tnr** Poetry Award. These awards have been established in order to honor **tnr**'s Founding Manager, Louise E. Reynolds, "to reward **tnr**'s writers," and to promote quality writing. Only writers published in a three-issue volume are eligible. Entry fee required.

Independent judges determine winners. All published writers will receive our regular, nominal rates of payment as well as a copy of the issue containing their work. There are three awards in each category: Fiction: $500.00, $250.00, and $125.00. Honorable Mention $50.00. Poetry: $250.00, $125.00, and $50.00, with three to four honorable mentions for poetry ($20.00 each).

Current subscribers: Send ms. with SASE or IRC, and $11.50 entry fee ($13.50 foreign). Each discipline and each submission requires an entry fee. You may extend your subscription or receive two back issues or a recent issue.

All others: Send ms. with SASE or IRC, and $16.50 entry fee ($18.00 foreign). You will receive two back issues or a recent issue. Each discipline and each submission requires an entry fee.

Categories: Fiction—Nonfiction—Culture—Film/Video—General Interest—Interview—Literature—Multicultural—Music—Poetry—Politics—Short Stories

CONTACT: Louise T. Reynolds, Editor-in-Chief
Material: All
26 Heath Rd. Ste. 11
Arlington MA 02474-3645
Website: www.tnrlitmag.net

THE NEW TIMES

The New Times

We welcome your interest in contributing to *The New Times*, your monthly resource for authentic living. Our purpose is to provide inspiration and resources for wellness, personal growth, and spirituality and to empower positive choices for the natural and social environments, and we look for articles, interviews, news items, and art that support that purpose.

The New Times is distributed free to over 50,000 readers at 500 locations throughout the Pacific Northwest, and there are paid subscribers throughout the United States and Canada.

Please read and follow these guidelines before submitting your article.

CONTENT

Besides the quality of the writing, acceptance or rejection of an article submitted to *The New Times* is essentially based on the answers to four questions:

Will it benefit readers? Will the article provide our readers with new, unique, or relevant insights or information that will be useful to them regardless of whether they follow up by buying a book or CD, attending a workshop, etc.?

Does it stand alone? Will readers benefit from the material whether or not this is the only article by you or on your topic they ever read?

Is it original? We do not accept articles excerpted from published works or ones previously published in or simultaneously submitted to other publications.

Is it consistent with our purpose? Will the article encourage readers to be more spiritually aware, happy, and healthy, and to actively carry these values into the world?

We do not base our decisions on whether or not advertising is being placed, whether we like or dislike the author or whether she or he is famous, or whether we agree with the material.

We accept articles that analyze or disagree with issues, but do not print ones that attack, demean, or negate other people, organizations, philosophies, or systems. Unless the topic being discussed is gender-specific, articles must be written in gender-inclusive language. We do not print press releases or any other strictly promotional material.

APPEAL TO OUR READERS

Our readers have told us that they are looking for practical, grounded, and succinct editorial content; they look to us for useful, "how-to" information and inspiration they can apply to their own lives. Here are just a few examples of the types of articles we're looking for:

• Memoirs that follow the author from a vividly and artfully described concrete experience to a breakthrough or some other deeply significant—preferably life-changing—and universally appreciable insight.

• Pieces designed to awaken awareness of what Thomas Moore and others would call "the soulful approach to living," inspiring one to look at small details of life anew; fresh contemplations of "ordinary" daily tasks and personal exchanges.

• Articles that deal with difficult-to-talk-about or controversial subjects. You should be well versed in the subject and acknowledge and respectfully address at least one other side of the question.

• Pieces that give readers fresh, practical ways to renew their experience of relationships and communication.

• Articles on parenting targeted toward guiding the smallest among us to understanding, even as we seek to better understand our world and ourselves.

• Short, inspiring, hands-on pieces with one clear spiritual theme. Examples include pieces that inspire and uplift readers' experience of work as well as thoughtful pieces on aging and the elderly, beauty, health, and longevity, especially focusing on how spiritual disciplines support these, with compelling examples from ancient times to the present.

M-Q

TAKE RESPONSIBILITY

Speak in "I" or "you," not "we," statements. Our readers are anxious to learn about—and from—your experiences, feelings, and thoughts, but are put off by generalizations like "When we experience such-and-such, we feel so-and-so."

We do not accept submissions consisting solely of channeled material.

All quotations must be accompanied by a cited source. Partial quotations, as a single word or phrase, must be treated according to the context in which they originated, and entire quotes (at least entire sentences) are preferable in every case.

WORD COUNT

The quality of the writing determines the maximum length we will accept: the longer the submission, the more stringent the acceptance criteria. We will consider outstanding articles of up to 1800 words if they need very little editing; otherwise, the absolute maximum word count is 1500 (and the recommended maximum 1200). Articles of fewer than 1200 words are adjudicated equally.

HOW TO SUBMIT

Always include a cover letter with your article submission. It should contain your name, address, and telephone number, a brief statement of how you feel your article supports our purpose, and your assurance that the article has not been and will not be submitted elsewhere unless we do not accept it.

Whenever possible, send your article as an e-mail attachment (doc, rtf, or wpd) to: editor@newtimes.org, using "article submission" as the subject line. We will send you a form letter indicating either that a) we successfully opened your attachment, b) we were unable to open it, or c) your article was in the body of your e-mail rather than in an attachment and therefore not eligible for review. If you don't receive one of these letters within a week, it means that we didn't get your message and that you should try again.

If you cannot e-mail your submission, we prefer it on disk, but ask that you enclose a hard copy of your article in case we are unable to open the electronic version. If you cannot supply a disk, make sure your paper copy is double-spaced and free of markings, and use a sans-serif font (such as Arial) 11 points in size or larger.

ADD GRAPHIC INTEREST

We encourage writers to send photos or relevant art with their articles. Your submission has a better chance of being considered for a feature position (front page or lead article in our "In Harmony" or "Education" section) if you provide a compelling and pertinent image to accompany it. We are especially interested in photos and illustrations that relate to the theme of the article, but are always happy to have a head shot of the author, too. Graphics can be e-mailed with your submission; if you mail them, they must be 8.5 by 14 inches or smaller, black and white or high-contrast color (no photocopies, please). We'll return your photo with the notification of your article's acceptance status.

We are also always looking for distinctive art and photos to use on our front page, and make every effort to correlate cover art and cover story. While we cannot pay for images selected, we will be happy to publish up to 150 words on the contributor and the work. Contact us for information on how to have your work considered.

DEADLINES, ACCEPTANCE, AND TIMING

Articles are generally due the last Friday of each month (see calendar for specific dates), and acceptance/rejection letters are sent out within a few days of the deadline. Articles received after one deadline will be held for the following one.

If you submit by mail, include a stamped, self-addressed envelope for notification of your article's acceptance status; if you submit by e-mail, you will be notified by return e-mail. These notifications usually go out within a week after the article deadline.

Because we routinely receive more material than we can print each month, we are not able to promise any particular publication date for articles accepted. Once an article is accepted for publication, we publish it in the timeliest manner possible, but articles are generally held over for several months before they appear in print.

EDITING

We edit every submission for punctuation, spelling, grammar, clarity, and compliance with our conventions. If substantial editing is required, we will either reject the article or return it with some suggestion as to what is needed.

Attention-grabbing headlines that convey the article's content are a must; we reserve the right to re-title accepted submissions as needed.

CHANGES

Any changes to an article must be made in writing prior to the deadline date. If changes are made after that date, we will hold the article until the next deadline.

PHONE CALLS

We do not discuss articles over the phone. If you have not heard back from us regarding your article, drop us a postcard or e-mail.

MULTIPLE SUBMISSIONS

Space restrictions preclude us from running more than one article by any one writer at a time. Do not submit again until one accepted article has been published.

COMPENSATION

You receive a free one-year subscription upon acceptance of your article (up to a maximum of three years from the one most recently accepted). We do not pay for articles, nor do we exchange advertising for them. At the end of the article, you may, if you wish, include a short (up to sixty-word) statement of who you are and how people can reach you.

RIGHTS

The New Times retains the rights to all articles published within its pages. There is an exception: we will consider excerpts from unpublished manuscripts. If we accept yours, we will return rights to you once we have published it, provided that you 1) specifically state that you are submitting an excerpt from a book scheduled for publication and are granting us first North American serial rights and 2) let us know when the book is due to be published.

If you would like to have your article reprinted elsewhere, contact us first for the wording of the short statement of acknowledgment to add at the end. If others request reprint rights from us, we will not grant them without first obtaining your permission and any revised closing paragraph about yourself you may wish to provide.

We reserve the right to publish your article as a reprint in response to readers' requests. Some articles also appear in *The New Times'* Internet edition. We assume that we have your permission to use accepted material on our Web site unless you specifically let us know when you submit that we do not.

Please note: While we have made our writers' guidelines as comprehensive as possible, we reserve the right to accept or reject submissions for any reason we deem appropriate.

Categories: Nonfiction—Diet/Nutrition—Ecology—Environment—Feminism—Gay/Lesbian—Health—Inspirational—Interview—Lifestyle—Men's Issues—Native American—New Age—Paranormal—Religion—Spiritual—Women's Issues

CONTACT: Charles Alkire, Editor
Material: All
PO Box 51186
Seattle WA 98115
Phone: 206-320-7788
Fax: 206-320-7717
E-mail: editor@newtimes.org
Website: www.newtimes.org

Remember: Editors change jobs and publishers change addresses. It is wise to invest in a phone call for the current information before submitting.

New Witch

Please refer to *SageWoman* magazine.

New York Runner

NEW YORK RUNNER is the official quarterly magazine of NYRR. The magazine is written by runners, for runners, with the strong belief that running is great exercise, great fun, and a good, healthy thing to do.

Consequently, we consider it our job to keep the magazine a perpetual source of interest and joy by:

1. Addressing current and topical issues in the sport
2. Reporting the interesting happenings at recent and upcoming NYRRC events
3. Finding insights and information related to the sport that is useful, relevant, and entertaining
4. Finding ways for you to keep your running interesting and finding ways for you to use your running and fitness to keep your life interesting
5. Providing training, nutrition, and injury information that will keep you feeling and running your best

Categories: Nonfiction—Diet/Nutrition—Lifestyle—Recreation—Sports/Recreation

CONTACT: Gordon Bakoulis, Editor
Material: All
New York Road Runners
9 East 89th St
New York NY 10128
Phone: 212-423-2260

New York Stories

Guidelines for Submission

New York Stories is seeking short fiction and non-fiction.

Stories should have strong characters, fresh voices and distinctive angles of vision. We are open to the best work we can find from around the world. The stories do not need to be set in New York, but we do welcome stories that explore the city's diversity. Stories above 5,000 words have less chance due to space constraints. We publish six to eight an issue.

Non-fiction pieces should focus on life in New York City—the magic moment, history unlayered, the familiar, the off-beat, the marginal illuminated. We've published pieces as diverse as a profile of Ludlow Street and an account of a job in a bagel factory. At least one appears in each issue.

We publish interviews with major literary figures or film directors: E.L. Doctorow, Grace Paley, James Gray. Query us on these.

Competition is intense. We pay for your work on publication at rates competitive with major literary magazines.

Please include a cover letter listing prior publications or relevant background and an SASE. No need to provide a synopsis of your story or reasons why we should publish it: the work will speak for itself. Multiple submissions okay.

We are keen to discover new talent and have published first-time stories as well as the John Updikes of the literary universe. We generally respond within two months. Stories that excite interest among our editors are, alas, occasionally held longer. We publish three times a year: March, June and November. Sample copies available at $5.95.

Categories: Interview—Literature—Regional—Short Stories

CONTACT: Daniel Caplice Lynch, Editor in Chief
Material: Manuscripts
English Dept. E-103, LaGuardia College
31-10 Thomson Avenue
Long Island NY 11101
Phone: 718 482-5673

E-mail: NYSTORIES@lagcc.cuny.edu
Website: www.newyorkstories.org

The New Yorker

Submissions should be sent by e-mail to the appropriate department, as indicated below. We cannot accept submissions that are sent as attachments, so please send your work as part of the body of an e-mail. No more than one story or six poems should be submitted at one time. We prefer to receive no more than two submissions per writer per year, and generally cannot reply to more.

The New Yorker does not accept unsolicited submissions by mail or by fax, and we cannot be responsible for the loss or return of unsolicited pieces. We do not consider simultaneous submissions or material that has been previously published. We try to respond to all submissions, but, due to volume, we may take up to eight weeks to respond.

Categories: Fiction—Antiques—Arts—Book Reviews—Cartoons—Culture—Entertainment—Film/Video—Food/Drink—Music—Poetry—Politics—Theatre—Travel

CONTACT: fiction@newyorker.com
Material: Fiction Submissions
CONTACT: talkofthetown@newyorker.com
Material: The Talk of the Town Submissions
CONTACT: shouts@newyorker.com
Material: Shouts & Murmurs Submissions
CONTACT: poetry@newyorker.com
Material: Poetry Submissions
The New Yorker, Inc., 4 Times Square
New York
NY 10036-6592
Website: www.newyorker.com

Newsweek

My Turn Column

Submissions for *My Turn* columns must be original, unpublished essays, approximately 850 and 900 words. If your piece is a time sensitive subject, it's probably not appropriate for the column.

Please, do not submit any photographs, but be sure to include your full name, address and phone number.

Responses take 8-10 weeks. We receive about 500 essays a month. It takes time to read them and make decisions. We will send you a letter, if your piece is not accepted.

All submissions should be emailed to: myturn@ newsweek.com.

Do not send your essay as an attachment. The article *must* be included as text within the email.

Categories: Nonfiction—Current Affairs—Politics—News—Opinion

CONTACT: Submissions Editor
Material: All
Phone: 212-445-4000
E-mail: myturn@newsweek.com

Nimrod
International Journal of Prose and Poetry (University of Tulsa)

Annual Sales: 4,000 copies

Subject: Quality poetry and short fiction and essays. Two issues annually. Awards Issue (fall publication)—no designated theme. Winners and finalists of yearly competition. Thematic Issue (spring publication): Previous themes have included the following: Writers of Age; American Indian; The City; and numerous issues devoted to emerging writers from several countries including China, India, Latin America, Russia, Canada, Australia, Eastern Europe.

Format: Each issue 160 pp.; perfect bound; 4-color cover.

Titles in print: 84

Alternate formats: Audio + portions on Web

Subscription: $17.50/1 year (outside USA $19); $30.00/2 years (outside USA $33)

Sample copies: $10.00 each

Publication: Always pays with two copies.

Annual Contest: $2,000 First Prize; $1,000 Second Prize in poetry and fiction. Send SASE for contest guidelines. Deadline April 30 of each year.

Categories: Fiction—Nonfiction—Arts—Culture—Poetry—Writing—Philosophy

CONTACT: Francine Ringold, Editor-in-Chief
Material: Poetry, Fiction, Essays
The University of Tulsa, 600 S. College
Tulsa OK 74104-3189
Phone: 918-631-3080
Fax: 918-631-3033
E-mail: nimrod@utulsa.edu
Website: www.utulsa.edu/nimrod

Nine
A Journal of Baseball History and Culture

NINE studies all historical aspects of baseball, centering on the societal and cultural implications of the game wherever in the world it is played. The journal features articles, essays, book reviews, biographies, oral history, and short fiction pieces.

NINE is available electronically through Project MUSE.

Subscription Information
Semiannual
ISSN 1188-9330
Individuals $35.00
Institutions $35.00
Single issue $20.00

For foreign subscriptions please add $15.00. Payment must accompany order. Make checks payable to University of Nebraska Press and mail to:

University of Nebraska Press
233 N 8th St
Lincoln, NE 68588-0255
or call: 1-800-755-1105 U.S. Orders and customer service.

Submission Information

NINE will seek to promote the study of all historical aspects of baseball and will center on the cultural implications of the game wherever in the world baseball is played. The journal will reflect an eclectic approach and will not foster a particular ideological bias. *NINE* accepts submissions that meet the following requirements:

• between 2,000-5,000 words
• submit 3 copies
• prepare according to *Chicago Manual of Style*, 14th edition
• include a short personal bio (no more than three sentences)
• footnotes and author date systems are not acceptable
• simultaneous submissions are not accepted
• accepted works must supply manuscripts in both paper and electronic form (RTF, Microsoft Word or Word Perfect)
• all figures and tables must be submitted in camera-ready format and will be printed as is
• book reviews are by invitation only

Authors will be asked to sign a declaration that the submitted work is not being considered for publication elsewhere. No major revisions will be allowed after acceptance. The editor will attempt to have all manuscripts reviewed by two umpires and will respond to the au-

thors within three months of receiving the manuscript.

Submissions can be e-mailed to bkirwin@ualberta.ca or snail mailed.

Categories: Fiction—Nonfiction—Biography—Book Reviews—Culture—History—Short Stories—Society—Sports/Recreation

CONTACT: Bill Kirwin, Editor
Material: All
The University of Calgary in Edmonton
Faculty of Social Work
#444, 11044-82 Ave.
Edmonton, Alberta Canada T6G 0T2
E-mail: bkirwin@ualberta.ca
Website: www.nebraskapress.unl.edu/journals.html

Nineteenth-Century French Studies

Nineteenth-Century French Studies provides scholars and students with the opportunity to examine new trends, review promising research findings, and become better acquainted with professional developments in the field. Scholarly articles on all aspects of nineteenth-century French literature and related fields are invited. Published articles are peer-reviewed to insure scholarly integrity. The journal has an extensive book review section covering a variety of disciplines.

Nineteenth-Century French Studies is published twice a year in two double issues, fall/winter and spring/summer.

Beginning with volume 29, *Nineteenth-Century French Studies* can be consulted on-line, by subscription, through Project MUSE of the Johns Hopkins University Press.

Subscription Information
Semiannual
ISSN 0146-7891
Individuals $45.00
Institutions $60.00
Single issue $18.00

For foreign subscriptions please add $15.00. Payment must accompany order. Make checks payable to University of Nebraska Press and mail to:

University of Nebraska Press
233 N 8th St
Lincoln, NE 68588-0255
or call: 1-800-755-1105 U.S. Orders and customer service.
1-800-526-2617 U.S. Fax orders and customer service.
1-402-472-3584 Foreign orders and customer service.
1-402-472-6214 Main fax line.
Telephone and fax orders must be prepaid.

Submission Information

Nineteenth-Century French Studies accepts submissions that meet the following requirements:

• should not exceed 5,000 words (20 pages, 25 lines per page, double-spacing, and ample margins), including endnotes
• submit 3 copies
• footnotes are not acceptable
• original typescript, plus an electronic copy in Word Perfect, IBM format, will be requested for accepted works
• abstracts will be requested for accepted works
• book reviews need only be submitted in a single copy
• suggested length for book reviews is between two and three type-written pages (double-spaced) and without endnotes

Anonymous submission

NCFS subscribes to the policy of anonymous or "blind" submissions. Readers will not know the identity of the authors whose articles they are asked to evaluate. Authors must therefore omit references that would allow them to be identified. They should include a separate, unnumbered page giving the essay's title along with their name, postal and e-mail addresses, and telephone and fax numbers. The first page of the manuscript paper should be numbered and the title repeated one inch from the top of the page (in capitals). Articles not retained for publication will be destroyed.

For further information contact:
Professor Marshall Olds, Editor
molds2@unl.edu
Categories: Nonfiction—Book Reviews—Culture—Language—Literature

CONTACT: Editors
Material: Submissions in English or French
PO Box 880319
University of Nebraska-Lincoln
Lincoln NE 68588-0319
E-mail: molds2@unl.edu
Website: www.nebraskapress.unl.edu/journals.html

The North American Voice of Fatima

Introduction

The North American Voice of Fatima is a quarterly magazine of Catholic spirituality, published by the Barnabite Fathers, North American Province at the National Shrine Basilica of Our Lady of Fatima in Lewiston, NY. The Barnabite Fathers, through this little publication, wish to share the joy and challenge of the Gospel and to foster devotion to Our Lady, the Mother of the Redeemer and Mother of the Church, who said at Cana: "Do whatever He tells you." *The Voice* publishes articles of a spiritual and inspirational nature. It is a Catholic magazine, and will be faithful to the Magisterium of the Roman Catholic Church and its Tradition. We however welcome contributions from those of other Christian confessions in the spirit of the Second Vatican Council Document Unitatis redintegratio, and even from those of other faiths. The magazine is published quarterly according to the liturgical calendar: Advent/Christmas; Lent/Easter; Pentecost and a Marian issue published in late summer.

Submissions

Manuscripts prepared for submission should be from 500 to 1200 words. Double or 1½ line spacing is preferred. Hard copy manuscripts should be sent by mail to the Editor at the address below. Electronic submissions may be made by sending a disk to the address below or by electronic mail to Voice@fatimashrine. com. MS-Word formatted documents are preferred, but other common word processor software formats may be used. Related photos may accompany submissions.

Voice also publishes a few poems in each issue. Poetry submissions may be traditional or free verse but always of a spiritual or inspirational nature.

Original drawings may also be submitted. Our publication process prefers monochrome artwork with sharp contrast.

Manuscripts are not returned; photographs will be returned upon request if sent with SASE.

Remuneration

Articles are paid for at a rate of $0.05/word. Payment made at time of publication. Generally, no additional fee is paid for photographs. Poems and drawings receive a fee ranging from $10.00 to $25.00, depending on length and location in the magazine. All contributors will receive a copy of the magazine in which their work appears.

Categories: Nonfiction—Christian Interests—Inspirational—Religion—Spiritual

CONTACT: Rev. Peter M. Calabrese, CRSP, Editor
Material: All
The Barnabite Fathers
PO Box 167
Youngstown NY 14174-0167
Phone: 716-754-7489
Fax: 716-754-9130

E-mail: Voice@fatimashrine.com
Website: www.fatimashrine.com

NORTH DAKOTA horizons

North Dakota Horizons

North Dakota Horizons is a quarterly, non-profit magazine with circulation in all 50 states and several foreign countries. The mission of *Horizons* is to discover and showcase North Dakota's resources and people. The magazine promotes North Dakota's many virtues: a clean environment, open spaces, friendly and creative people, and interesting things to see and do. Stories that encourage people to travel to state places and events are of prime importance.

Unsolicited contributions are welcome; however, written or e-mail inquiries are preferred. *Horizons* seeks short, nonfiction stories (1,000 to 1,500 words) and major in-depth feature articles (1,500 to 3,000 words). Whenever possible, manuscripts should be accompanied with illustrations, black and white photographs, color slides or color prints. *Horizons* strives to be a visual publication. Sketches, maps, artwork or illustrations available and appropriate should be submitted for ideas.

When submitting written material, please double-space the manuscript. Work may be submitted on Macintosh or PC compatible discs, zip disks or 3½ inch diskettes. On the disk cover, please indicate your word processing software. Your name, address and telephone number should be clearly marked. Identifications for illustrations and photos should be clearly marked and as complete as possible. Stories may also be submitted by e-mail to lyle_halvorson@gnda.com.

Horizons reserves the right to edit all material submitted. We cannot provide proofs to authors or photographers before publication. If you wish your material returned, please provide a self-addressed, stamped envelope of appropriate size. We are not liable for unsolicited materials sent to us. We cannot guarantee against loss or damage to any materials while in our possession, but we make every effort to handle the material carefully.

Short articles and essays average $50 to $150. Feature length articles average $150 to $300 depending on subject matter, timeliness and available illustrations.

Horizons also encourages the submission of photographs that relate to life in North Dakota, which may include people, places and events. Payment for a front cover photo ranges up to $150 and up to $50 for a back cover photo. Generally, photo rates are based on a one-time use. Photographs and original artwork are returned by mail to the photographer or illustrator after publication unless other arrangements are made with the editor in advance.

Horizons requires writers and photographers to sign an agreement specifying agreed upon compensation as well as deadlines. Payment will be made after publication unless other arrangements are negotiated with the editor in advance.

Categories: Nonfiction—Consumer—Culture—Regional—Rural America—Society—Travel

CONTACT: Lyle Halvorson, Editor
Material: All
PO Box 2639
Bismarck ND 58502
Phone: 701-222-0929
Fax: 701-222-1611
E-mail: lyle_halvorson@gnda.com
Website: www.ndhorizons.com

Northwest Family News

Northwest Family News strives to provide its readers with informative, educational, entertaining and locally-focused articles which emphasize positive parenting. Our readership is largely comprised of educated parents, ages 25-45, with an upper-level income. The editorial emphasis is uplifting, positive and practical, focusing on the importance and pleasures of family life.

Our publication is tabloid-sized on newsprint with a circulation of 50,000. We are distributed at 1,200 locations from Seattle/Tacoma through the Puget Sound region to the Canadian border.

SPECIFICATIONS

Submitted articles via email to nwfamilysubmissions@earthlink.net as plain text in the body of the email. Submissions should include the authors name, address, phone number, email address for reply and word count. If you don't have email access, we request submissions be submitted on a Macintosh Compatible disk in Microsoft Word or plain text. Query via email or phone is appreciated, but not necessary for email or electronic submissions.

Submissions may also be on letter quality paper, typed (upper/lower case), double spaced, one side only, on 8-1/2 x 11 white paper with word count noted. Please query before submitting paper copy. We usually don't have time to consider unsolicited paper submissions. The first page should include the writer's name, address, phone number, email address (if applicable) and article word count. Subsequent pages should include the writer's name and page numbers.

Photos to accompany the article are encouraged and may be submitted for us to scan or as digital images. File size of digital images should be no smaller than 350Kb. Please indicate whether photos are available to accompany the article in your email or in your written or electronic submission. Photos submitted to us can be returned at your request at our expense if used in an issue. Unsolicited photos will not be returned unless sent with a stamped, self-addressed envelope or mailer.

Please advise as to whether you're offering electronic rights for our website at www.nwfamily.com.

Local content and local writers are given priority. Human interest stories of local families dealing successfully with challenges such as natural disasters, health or education.

We accept both previously unpublished articles and reprints (our standard rate is $25-40). Payment is made within 30 days after an article has been published. Reimbursement for photos is in addition to the rate for articles and reports and is based on the size of the image used. A tear sheet will be mailed to the writer along with a check. Please note, we do not use much poetry, even as filler. However, poetry by children will be considered if a query is sent.

Categories: Book Reviews—Children—Family—Juvenile—Parenting—Recreation—Teen—Travel

CONTACT: Rick Adair, Features Editor
Material: All
16 West Harrison St., Ste. 204
Seattle, WA 98119
Phone: 206-281-8015, 800-494-3025
E-mail: nwfamilysubmissions@earthlink.net
Website: www.nwfamily.com

Northwest Fly Fishing

Thanks for your interest in *Northwest Fly Fishing* magazine. To receive consideration for publication you should read and follow these guidelines closely.

ABOUT THE MAGAZINE

Northwest Fly Fishing magazine is a destination specific publication to be viewed as an inspiring, collectible reference of Northwest angling destinations. The staff at *Northwest Fly Fishing* takes pride in our editorial content. Our writing is refreshing, our photography, captivating. *Northwest Fly Fishing* is issued quarterly each Spring, Summer, Fall, and Winter.

FEATURE ARTICLES

Our goal is to give an inspiring and complete report on specific Northwest angling destinations. Angling destinations include both the famous and the lesser know waters, and include all species found in our diverse geographical region. If more than one species is found in any given water, writers should cover each species, as well as every season that water is fishable. In short, feature articles should be concise, and leave no holes. Our goal is to cover specific angling destinations as no other publication has done in the past. The best way to get a feel for what we want is to study one of our magazines.

Photography is very important. *Northwest Fly Fishing* has set high standards for all images used in our magazine. Writers have a much better chance of being published if articles are accompanied by stunning photography. We will not publish dead fish, poorly exposed or composed shots.

The area of coverage for our features includes Washington, Oregon, Northern California, Idaho, Montana, Wyoming, Alberta, British Columbia, Alaska, Yukon Territory, and Northwest Territories.

Feature Article Requirements

• Provide practical traveling and angling information to specific destinations, including personal anecdotes
• Included should be pertinent angling history and thorough description of the fishery
• Detailed description of angling techniques, tackle and flies, and local perspectives
• Articles should be thorough and specific so as to sufficiently inform and give the angler confidence to effectively fish the presented water
• Included with each article should be any applicable hatch chart and detailed map of the coverage area
• Conservation issues and future considerations should be addressed
• Selection of 35mm (or larger) slides (captioned)
• Three popular flies of the fishery should be included for us to photograph, as well as a material list for each pattern
• Feature article length should be 2,500 to 3,500 words

DEPARTMENTS

Most department material is staff-written. Exceptions are as follows:

Northwest Fly Tying

This department covers one Northwest fly pattern each issue. New, unusual and exciting patterns are encouraged, but we will also represent the time-proven standards. Flies for any Northwest species can be considered. Articles should include a little history and use of the fly, as well as step-by-step photos of the tying sequence, shot against a neutral-colored background. Two finished flies should accompany the article for photographic purposes.

Notes, News & Reviews

This department covers news events, and mini destinations (200 to 500 words). As with all material submitted, query first.

Conservation

Any conservation issue concerning the Pacific Northwest. Maximum length 850 words.

Exposure

Photo essay of 8 to 10 images depicting Northwest angling.

MANUSCRIPT SUBMISSIONS AND PAYMENTS

Initial contact with the editor by e-mail is preferred. A formal query letter, outlining the proposed article, should be sent to the editor before making a submission. A selection of slides MUST accompany the formal query. Unsolicited manuscripts must include a self-addressed, stamped envelope (S.A.S.E.) for their return. *Northwest Fly Fishing* is not responsible for submissions in transit to and from our editorial office.

Text and photos are purchased as a package. Manuscripts accepted without the appropriate photographic support will warrant less money for their use. *Northwest Fly Fishing* buys first North American serial publication rights. We reserve the option to edit all articles, however, we will make every effort to minimize editing to avoid changing the style or content of manuscripts.

All manuscripts should be submitted in typewritten form, double spaced. The author's name, address, phone number and manuscript word count should appear on the first page of the manuscript. A 3½" computer disk needs to be included, and your work saved in Microsoft Word, Word Perfect, ClarisWorks or AppleWorks.

Payment is made approximately one month prior to publication, and the pay rate varies with the length and completeness of the submission. Inclusion of high-quality slides has a major impact in determining the pay rate for any given article. Our pay rate is as follows:

- Feature Articles $400 to $600
- Northwest Fly Tying $250
- Notes, News & Reviews $25 to $100
- Conservation $25 to $100

PHOTO SUBMISSIONS, ARTWORK AND PAYMENTS

Northwest Fly Fishing usually buys text and photos as a package. There are exceptions, however, and additional photography may be purchased on occasion. Contributors must query first.

We accept 35mm (or larger) transparencies only. Slides should be shipped in a clear sleeve, with concise captions. The pho-tographer's name and address should appear on each slide mount. Payment varies for size used and impact. Our pay rate is as follows:

- Cover $500
- Exposure $600
- Inside use $25 to $300
- Illustrations & artwork $25 to $300

Categories: Nonfiction—Conservation—Fishing—Nature—Photography—Recreation—Sports/Recreation—Travel

CONTACT: Steve Probasco, Editor
Material: All
PO Box 708
Raymond WA 98577
Phone: 360-942-3589
E-mail: probasco@nwflyfishing.net

Northwest Palate

Our editorial mission

Founded in 1987, *Northwest Palate* is a bimonthly magazine devoted to food, wine, travel, and lifestyles in the Pacific Northwest. Our readers are well-read, well-traveled, and knowledgeable about food and wine. We strive to educate and entertain them by profiling the places, products, and people that exemplify this region's extraordinary bounty and quality of life.

Submitting a story

We rely on freelancers for the majority of our stories and departments. All wine reviews, special tastings, and book reviews are handled in-house or on assignment only. Please review these guidelines and recent issues of the magazine in order to familiarize yourself with our format and subject matter. Bear in mind that we plan our editorial calendar as much as a year in advance, and we follow the seasons closely.

Submit a written query before sending a finished piece. If you have not written for us before, please enclose samples of your writing, preferably work that has been published. Queries are accepted by mail at *Northwest Palate*, PO Box 10860, Portland, OR 97296, or email (you may call us first if you like) and will be answered within three months. Materials will be returned only if you provide a stamped, self-addressed envelope.

Departments

Our "Department" stories range from 650-1200 words. Our most frequently assigned departments include the following:

"Inns & Lodges"—Profiles of inns, lodges, resorts, hotels, and B&Bs in the Pacific Northwest. These are often accompanied by recipes from the inn's restaurant or chef.

"Wine"—Includes profiles of Northwest wineries, discussions of particular varietals, round-ups of good value wines, stories about wine and food pairing, and more.

"Artisans"—Profiles of artisans in the food and wine world, from bread-bakers to wine-label artists.

"Flavors"—Focusing on a particular cuisine, dish, or ingredient. Usually includes recipes.

"In Our Kitchen"—In which a rising or renowned Northwest chef visits our Portland kitchen and prepares a dish or demonstrates a technique. These stories include recipes.

"Excursions"—Outings in the Pacific Northwest that emphasize outdoor activities.

"Last Course" An essay or article of no more than 700 words, on any subject within our normal editorial scope. This is an opportunity to offer personal or humorous reflections, or to describe, with brevity and flair, an interesting phenomenon, person, activity, or place.

Features

Feature stories range from 2000-2500 words, and offer more in-depth treatment of the subjects mentioned above. Some of our most common topics are "destination" stories, in which the writer explores the lodgings, wineries, eateries, and other attractions of a Pacific Northwest destination.

More Specific Guidelines

For a complete set of writers' guidelines, including rates and rights, email or call us.

Categories: Nonfiction—Cooking—Entertainment—Food/Drink—Lifestyle—Regional—Travel

CONTACT: Submissions Editor
Material: All
PO Box 10860
Portland OR 97296-0860
Phone: 503-224-6039
E-mail: editorial@nwpalate.com

Northwest Regional Magazines

OUR PUBLICATIONS

Oregon Coast and *Northwest Travel* magazines

WRITERS:

We prefer a clear, crisp writing style. We publish family magazines—no four-letter words or off-color references. We do not want stories of limited interest or any that are exceedingly technical. We do not publish fiction or poetry.

Thoroughness, accuracy, and logical organization are crucial. We respond best to articles that are rich in anecdotes, quotations, and personal experiences. Be perceptive—but not flowery.

Writing must be accurate. Check and double-check spelling—especially proper names—and any numbers before submitting an article. Be wary of details that may change between writing and publication.

We cannot emphasize enough the importance of accuracy of all material submitted for publication. We subject manuscripts to a fact checking process, but it is the primary duty of the contributor to provide accurate, up-to-date information. Stories containing errors or out-of-date information may be returned, and stories that require excessive editing may receive less than the standard rate of pay.

Include current addresses and phone numbers of your key sources of information and photocopies of references to aid in editing and fact checking. Brochures are helpful.

Brief information, if applicable, should include how to get to a featured destination, places of interest nearby, opening and closing times of attractions, whether they are wheelchair-accessible, when roads are open and if they are suitable for RVs, and where to obtain more information.

In general we consider any article submitted to Northwest Regional Magazines for use in any of our magazines.

We buy first North American serial rights with an understanding that the article will not be offered to a similar publication for at least six months following its appearance in one of our magazines. Similar publications include *Cascades Fast*, *Western Living*, *Sunset*, *Travelin'*, and *Beautiful B.C.*

We don't want stories written from travel brochures. Bring your story alive with quotes and anecdotes.

QUERY LETTERS

Please do not telephone us about story proposals. Send us a query letter, with clips of your work, that briefly outlines the ideas (no more than three at once) being proposed. If we like your idea, we will ask to see your story on speculation, set a story length, and give you a deadline. A go-ahead on spec does not constitute an assignment or guarantee publication.

We prefer not to receive queries or manuscripts via fax.

ARTICLES SUBMITTED ON SPEC

Features, usually supported by some black-and-white or color photos, maps, or art, from 1,250 to 2,000 words (5 to 9 double-spaced typed pages): $100 to $250 total.

Features of special interest requiring special research or with heavy photo or art content, from 1,250 to 2,000 words (5 to 9 double-spaced typed pages): $200 to $350 total.

Restaurant reviews (*Oregon Coast*) should be about 1,000 words and include prices of foods mentioned and a recipe (if possible). A menu, brochure, or something with the restaurant's name or logo should accompany the review. Payment for restaurant reviews is $125, and we do not reimburse for the meal.

Do not announce you are doing a review or do anything that would obligate you to give a favorable review or create an expectation in a proprietor's mind that a story will be published. Interview a restaurant owner, resort manager, or B&B proprietor after your meal or stay or make a follow-up phone call.

ASSIGNED ARTICLES

We occasionally assign an article. Payment will be agreed upon at the time of assignment. Such assignments will be made in writing. If an assigned story is not run for any reason, a kill fee of 1/3 the agreed upon price will be made.

EDITING

We reserve the right to edit all material submitted for publication.

PAYMENT SCHEDULE

Payment is made after publication, and the amount is dependent on quality, not length. Most photos supporting submitted articles will be considered part of the editorial package.

You must return a completed W-9 form to us. Your name as shown on the form must exactly match the name on your federal income tax return. We cannot issue payment without this form.

Typical news-release items, such as chamber of commerce reports of coming events or local club news, will be accepted on a no-fee basis. We are pleased to receive such articles and will publish as many as space permits.

DEADLINES

Copy and accompanying photographs should be in our office at least four to five months prior to desired date of publication. Stand-alone color photographs should arrive at least three months prior to publication.

PHOTOGRAPHERS (COLOR SUBMISSIONS)

We prefer to work with positive transparencies 35mm to 4" x 5"

but can use color negatives. It is sometimes necessary to cut negatives. If you object to this, please send duplicates.

We do not send out want lists but would be happy to review your work. Please send 20 to 40 seasonal scenic shots in mostly vertical format.

Payment for magazine cover photo, $325; for photos used in calendars (including the cover), $100; for full-page photos used inside the magazine, $75; for less than full-page $25-$55. Payment is for one-time rights, with the understanding that no pictures will be printed in any similar magazine within two months. We reserve the right to use photographs of the magazines and calendars in which your work has been published in our own promotional material. Unless we are informed otherwise, we reserve the right to use color photos in a black-and-white format to accompany editorial features.

We publish two annual four-color calendars. One calendar needs photos of the Oregon Coast and the other one needs photos of the Northwest. Submissions should be horizontal rather than vertical and be in slide or other transparency format. Any size up to 4" x 5" is acceptable. Deadline for calendars is May 15.

We prefer scenic photos for calendar and full-page use. We also have a need for humorous, unusual, or animal photos for features in both magazines.

We take every precaution with photographic submissions, but we cannot be responsible for damage in processing, loss in mailing, or normal wear. If a transparency is damaged beyond repair, we will pay up to three times our normal one-time use fee.

PLEASE NOTE: We do not sign personal delivery memos and agree only to the terms stated herein.

GENERAL INFORMATION

If your submission includes slides, negatives, or historical photos, add $1.90 (beyond the cost of postage) to cover cost of return by certified mail. We do not guarantee return of submissions unless you include return postage. Label all photographs with a number and your name and address.

Be sure to provide a complete caption and credit for each photo on a separate typed sheet. If your manuscript is on disk, include the captions on the disk also. Send slides or negatives in plastic sleeves or protectors, not loose or in plastic boxes. Check accuracy and spelling on captions. Advise us of any change in your address.

If art is needed for a story, send a photocopy. Usually color prints or slides are satisfactory.

We accept 5¼" or 3½" IBM-formatted diskettes in Word-Perfect 5.1 or ASCII text. Enclose a hard copy. Leave at least 1½" margins on all sides of copy. Your manuscript should be typed or printed using 10- or 12-point type with name, address, and phone number on the first page. Allow one character space between sentences. Don't use tabs. Use hard returns at ends of paragraphs only.

Portions of our magazines may be used on the Internet at www.northwestmagazines.com. Before any writer's or pho-tographer's work appears on the Internet, permission will be obtained. The fee will be negotiated and paid afterwards.

Oregon Coast and *Northwest Travel* magazines are published bi-monthly.

Sample copies are available for $4.50, which includes shipping and handling.

Send all mail to the address below.

OREGON COAST

Oregon Coast publishes articles of interest to residents, visitors, and anyone else who loves the coast. Some suggested topics to develop are:

- Historical items
- Beachcombing adventures
- Special happenings
- Backroads and byways

- Favorite camping and picnicking spots
- Nature and everyday science
- Popular one-day driving tours
- Community profiles
- Walking tours
- Restaurant reviews
- Profiles of notable coastal residents

NORTHWEST TRAVEL

Northwest Travel regularly covers Washington, Oregon, British Columbia, Idaho, and occasionally covers adjacent areas and Alaska.

Northwest Travel emphasizes places to visit. Some suggested topics to develop are:

- Special happenings in the Northwest
- Community profiles
- Popular one-day tours
- Profiles of notable Northwest residents
- Adventure stories
- Backroads and byways
- Restaurant features
- Weekend getaways
- Historical (prefer to have museum, park, or other present-day connection)
- Eye-catching photo (slide) and brief text (100 words) for back page (Include camera type and lens, film, and F/stop used.)
- B&Bs, country inns, or other small lodging establishments
- Photo essays
- Nature and wildlife stories (prefer to have travel connection)

The Worth a Stop department features bylined 300-500 word stories on unusual destinations that are worth a stop—$50 payment. Photos are occasionally used.

PROFILE FOR WRITERS AND PHOTOGRAPHERS

Please provide a 30- to 50-word summary of appropriate information. (Please note we reserve the right to edit.) See samples below for style.

Return of this form indicates that you have read and understood the writers and photographers guidelines.

Samples of typical profiles:

- Norman Hesseldahl is the Public Affairs Staff Officer for the Siuslaw National Forest. He and his family are regular visitors to the Oregon Coast, where they have discovered many special places.
- Melissa Livingston, a native Oregonian, has lived in France and traveled extensively throughout the United States. She returned to Oregon after living in New Jersey while attending Rutgers University. Currently she is writing a children's book.
- Karen Keltz is a nationally published poet, essayist, and freelance Writer-photographer. An English teacher at Tillamook High School, she has written a novel and accompanying writing textbook for the upper elementary grades.

Categories: Nonfiction—Outdoors—Regional—Travel

CONTACT: Submissions Editor
Material: All
4969 Hwy 101, North Ste #2
Florence OR 97439
Phone: 541-997-8401
Website: www.northwestmagazines.com

NORTHWEST REVIEW

Northwest Review
University of Oregon

NORTHWEST REVIEW is published tri-annually, and invites submissions of previously unpublished poetry, fiction, essays, interviews, book reviews and artwork. Artists are encouraged to query before sending their work. Manuscripts are considered year-round.

1. The only criterion for acceptance of material for publication is that of excellence.

2. No simultaneous submission will be considered.

3. If submitting both poetry and fiction, please send in separate envelopes.

4. There are no length restrictions.

5. The author's name and address should appear on each poem and on the cover page of each story submitted. The author's name should appear on each page of his or her story.

6. We try to respond within ten weeks. Payment (unless grant money comes available for this purpose) is in contributor's copies. Potential contributors are encouraged to subscribe to any magazine that they admire enough to want their work to appear therein. Magazines such as *Northwest Review* depend for their survival on subscriptions.

7. We encourage you to study a recent issue of *Northwest Review*, available to authors at the discounted price of $4.00.

Subscriptions:
One year (three issues) at $22.00.
Two years (six issues) at $40.00.
Three years (nine issues) at $58.00.
Students: $20.00/year; $36.00/two years.
Foreign subscribers please add $5.00/year for handling.
Special Bonus: Subscribe for two years and receive free our 30-Year Retrospective issue, a $10.00 value.

Subscribe for three years and receive the Retrospective plus our six-color Morris Graves/Northwest Review poster, a $30.00 value.

Categories: Fiction—Arts—Literature—Poetry

CONTACT: John Witte, General Editor
Material: Essays, Artwork, Interviews, Book Reviews
CONTACT: John Witte, Poetry Editor
Material: Poetry
CONTACT: Jan MacRae, Fiction Editor
Material: Fiction
369 PLC, University of Oregon
Eugene OR 97403
Phone: 541-346-3957
Fax: 541-346-1509

Northwest Travel

Please refer to Northwest Regional Magazines.

Northwoods Journal

Please refer to The Conservatory of American Letters in the Book Publishers section.

Northwoods Press

Please refer to The Conservatory of American Letters, in the Book Publishers section.

Nostalgia Nostalgically

Please refer to *Secondwind*.

Now What? E-Zine

Please refer to the *Bible Advocate*.

Oblates

OBLATES is a bimonthly publication of the Missionary Association of Mary Immaculate—24 pages. Circulation 500,000. One poem and one inspirational articles freelance per issue. All photos and features done in-house. No fiction, fillers, or book reviews.

AUDIENCE

We write mainly for a mature adult Catholic audience. Our readers are looking for encouragement, comfort, and, most of all, a sense of positive Christian direction applicable to their lives.

EDITORIAL NEEDS

We need poems and nonfiction articles which inspire, uplift, and motivate through expressions of positive Christian values as they relate to everyday life.

Nonfiction Articles 500-600 words. We use well-written, tightly edited articles with pertinent and well-developed themes. First person approach seems to work best. Keep tone positive. A Christian slant or Gospel message should be apparent, but subtle. Avoid topical and controversial issues.

Poems 12 line average. We use well-written, perceptive, inspirational verse. Avoid obscure imagery, allusions, and irreverent humor. Make sure rhyme and rhythm flow without strain.

TERMS

All manuscripts are submitted on speculation and must be the original work of the writer. We consider completed manuscripts only. Do not query. No reprints purchased. Simultaneous submissions accepted if so noted. Submit seasonal material 6 months in advance. Manuscripts must be typed, with a self-addressed, stamped envelope enclosed (2 FIRST CLASS STAMPS). Response within 6 weeks. Payment upon acceptance for first North American serial rights. Three complimentary copies sent on publication.

Categories: Christian Interests—Inspirational—Poetry—Religion

CONTACT: Submissions Editor
Material: All
9480 N. De Mazenod Dr.
Belleville IL 62223-1160
Phone: 618-398-4848
Website: www.oblatesusa.org

Obsidian III
Literature in the African Diaspora

Obsidian III: Literature in the African Diaspora, a non-profit organization hosted by North Carolina State University, is a semiannual journal of contemporary poetry, fiction, drama, and non-fiction prose from within and concerning the African Diaspora. All bibliographies should follow the *MLA Handbook for Writers of Research Papers*. Manuscripts should be submitted in hard copy and on disk in PC compatible format. Files are preferred in Microsoft Word; otherwise, RTF.

Poetry should be single spaced. All other submissions should be double spaced. Poetry submissions are limited to five poems totaling no more than eight pages. Fiction wind essays are limited to twenty pages. Playwrights should submit scenes or short plays of no more than twenty pages in the Samuel French format.

Reviews should be no more than 1500 words. All writers should include cover sheets bearing the author's name, contact information, and the contents of the submissions. All decisions of the editorial staff are final.

We do not accept simultaneous submissions or previously published works. Copyright reverts to authors upon publication. Poets and fiction writers should allow three months for a response. Scholars and critics should allow four months for a response.

Obsidian is published twice a year (Spring-Summer and Fall-Winter).

Subscription Information:
Individuals
One year: $22 (US); $25 (Outside US)
Two years: $37 (US); $40 (Outside US)
Institutions
One year: $28 (US); $30 (Outside US)
Two years: $45 (US); $48 (Outside US)
Send check or money order to:
Obsidian III
Department of English
Box 8105
North Carolina State University
Raleigh, NC 27695-8105

Categories: Fiction—Nonfiction—African-American—Book Reviews—Culture—Drama—Interview—Language—Literature—Men's Fiction—Multicultural—Poetry—Reference—Short Stories—Theatre—Women's Fiction—Writing—Ethnic

CONTACT: Submissions Editor
Material: All
North Carolina State University
Dept of English, Box 8105
Raleigh NC 27695-8105
Phone: 919-515-4153
Fax: 919-515-1836
E-mail: obsidian@social.chass.ncsu.edu
Website: www.ncsu.edu/chass/obsidian

Odyssey Magazine

General Information

ODYSSEY is interested in articles rich in scientific accuracy and lively approaches to the subject at hand. The inclusion of primary research (interviews with scientists focusing on current research) are of primary interest to the magazine. Keep in mind that this magazine is essentially written for 10- to 16-year-old children. Writers are encouraged to study recent back issues for content and style. (Sample issues are available at $4.95. Send 10" x 13" self addressed $2.00 stamped envelope.) All material must relate to the theme of a specific upcoming issue in order to be considered. *ODYSSEY* purchases all rights to material.

Procedure

A query must consist of all of the following information to be considered:

• a brief cover letter stating the subject and word length of the proposed article,

• a detailed one-page outline explaining the information to be presented in the article,

• a bibliography of sources (including interviews) the author intends to use in preparing the article,

• a self-addressed stamped envelope.

Writers new to ODYSSEY should send a writing sample with the query. If you would like to know if your query has been received, please also include a stamped postcard that requests acknowledgment of receipt. In all correspondence, please include your complete address as well as a telephone number and/or email address where you can be reached.

A writer may send as many queries for one issue as he or she wishes, but each query must have a separate outline, bibliography, and self-addressed stamped envelope. Telephone queries are not accepted unless the material is extremely time-sensitive to a specific issue. Please type all queries.

Articles must be submitted on disk using a word processing program (preferably Microsoft Word-MAC). Text should be saved as ASCII text (in MS Word as "text only"). Disks should be either MAC- (preferred) or DOS-compatible 3½".

GUIDELINES

Feature Articles:

750 - 1200 words

Includes: in-depth nonfiction articles. (An interactive approach is a definite plus!) Q & A interviews, plays, and biographies are of interest, as well.

Supplemental Nonfiction:

200-500 words

Includes: subjects directly and indirectly related to the theme. Editors like little-known information but encourage writers not to overlook the obvious.

Fiction:

Up to 1,000 words

Includes: science-related stories, poems, science fiction, retold legends, etc., relating to the theme.

Department Features:

400-650 words

Includes: "Far out"; "Places, Media, People to Discover"; "Fantastic Journeys." Not a bad idea to consult back issues for direction of these departments that are also theme-related.

The above four pay 20 to 25 cents per printed word.

Activities:

Up to 750 words.

Includes: critical thinking activities, experiments, models, science fair projects, astro-photography projects, and any other science projects that can either be done by children alone, with adult supervision, or in a classroom setting. Query should be accompanied by sketches and description of how activity relates to theme. The above pays on an individual basis.

Photo Guidelines

To be considered for publication, photographs must relate to a specific theme. Writers are encouraged to submit available photos with their query or article. We buy one-time use.

Please note that fees for non-professional quality photographs are negotiated.

Cover fees are set on an individual basis for one-time use, plus promotional use. All cover images are color.

Prices set by museums, societies, stock photography houses, etc., are paid or negotiated.

Photographs that are promotional in nature (e.g., from tourist agencies, organizations, special events, etc.) are usually submitted at no charge.

If you have photographs pertaining to any upcoming theme, please contact the editor by mail or fax, or send them with your query. You may also send images on speculation.

Note

Queries may be submitted at any time, but queries sent well in advance of deadline MAY NOT BE ANSWERED FOR SEVERAL MONTHS. Go-aheads requesting material proposed in queries are usually sent four months prior to publication date. Unused queries will be returned approximately three to four months prior to publication date.

Categories: Nonfiction—Children—Juvenile—Science—Teen

CONTACT: Elizabeth Lindstrom, Editorial Dept
Material: All
Cobblestone Publishing
30 Grove Street, Ste C

Peterborough 03458
Phone: 603-924-7209
Fax: 603-924-7380
E-mail: bethlindstrom2000@cobblestone.mv.com
Website: www.cobblestonepub.com

Office Number One
Office Number One

ONO is an 8.5"x11", 12 page zine set in 10 pt times, printed virtually randomly and distributed to approximately 1,800 of the most fortunate people on the planet. Sample copies are $2 and SASE. Subscriptions are $8.82/6 issues (note this is by the issue, not by the year).

Guidelines

Articles should be in the 200 word range or less (few exceptions). Stories should be no longer than 400 words. Poetry should be technically perfect. All should satisfy one or more of the following conditions:

Know who you are addressing and why. Writing should create a change in the person reading it. Be aware of the kind of change you create in who.

A Shock of Liberation: A very special shock can create freedom. The shock can be subtle. It can have a time fuse. No genre of writing is excluded. The shock is a paradox because it seems to come from elsewhere, yet it is here.

Satire: Satire should address something that should be changed intrinsically, not merely based on personal likes or dislikes. For example, many people protest violence, yet their solution is violent. They are prime targets for satire. Not because being passive or violent is politically correct, but because one of their aims must fail.

Provide an unusual angle, be up beat and humorous. Bear in mind, humor is a funny thing. It doesn't have to be funny to be humorous. "Up beat" means liberation for tortured souls.

Be short and to the point. No fair having the point be there is no point or some other non-sense. If your idea gets too long, break it into several short pieces each of which can stand on their own. Try to say it in 200 words or less.

Do not substitute slapstick absurdity, non-sequiturs or gimmicks for humor, satire or shock. If you don't enjoy the issue of ONO you received, then you'll probably have a hard time writing for it.

Articles should be written in one of the following styles:
News Report
Interview
EssayLimerick (technically perfect)
Super Short StoryHaiku (5-7-5 or 3-5-3 only)
Quiz or TestQuatrain (consistent rhyme & meter)
Review (Imaginary theater or book)
Cartoon
Of course, I'm open to something else if it works.
Carlos B. Dingus, Editor
Categories: Fiction—Horror—Paranormal—Poetry—Satire—Short Stories—Humor—Philosophy

CONTACT: Carlos B. Dingus, Editor
Material: All
1708 S. Congress Ave.
Austin TX 78704

Offshore
Northeast Boating at Its Best

Offshore is a monthly full-color magazine for boaters—both power and sail—in the Northeast. Our territory reaches from Maine to New Jersey. The majority of our readers own cruising and fishing boats from 20 to 40 feet.

With our features we cover destinations (both ports of call and narrowly defined regions), cruising trips, fishing, people involved in boating (from harbormasters to maritime artists), boat design, seamanship, maritime history and the environment. Most of our features are about things that take place in or are particular to the Northeast. Some topics, however, are universal (such as seamanship) and can be handled as such, but local references are desirable where appropriate. Every month we also publish two to three marina reviews (staff- and freelance-written), about six regular columns, and short news briefs.

Our typical reader is an experienced boater, so articles on the basics are usually not our fare. Freelance writers themselves need a certain level of boating knowledge to handle most assignments.

Our features range from 1,500 to 3,000 words. Our news briefs and marina reviews are shorter. We buy first-time North American publishing rights and pay on publication or within 60 days of acceptance, whichever is first. We pay between $100 and $500 for articles, with exceptions made for more involved work. We also pay extra (stock photo rates) for writer-submitted photography, but we need very high-quality slides.

Interested writers should submit a detailed, written query outlining the story, their angle on the story and why they are a good choice to write it. They should also submit a written summary of their writing experience, a writing sample and a photography sample (if applicable).

Categories: Nonfiction—Boating—Environment—Fishing—History—Travel

CONTACT: Editorial Dept.
Material: All
Offshore Communications Inc.
500 Victory Rd, Marina Bay
Quincy MA 02171
Phone: 617-221-1400

Ohio Magazine

Ohio Magazine Guidelines for Writers

Ohio Magazine is in the process of increasing its pool of freelance writers, and we are particularly looking for writers in Southeast, Southwest and Northwest Ohio. If interested, please send a resume, clips, an SASE and any story pitches to: *Ohio Magazine*, Attn: Nicole Gabriel, Managing Editor, 62 E. Broad St., Columbus, OH, 43215. In your cover letter please tell us where your writing interests and strengths lie (i.e. travel, profiles, living, general features, etc.). Please note: only those resumes that include writing samples—or a link to a web site with samples—will be considered. Also note: submitting great story pitches with your packet is another way to stand out of the crowd. Here's what we look for:

First and foremost, *Ohio* publishes stories that "celebrate Ohio"—stories that celebrate its people, its rich culture and heritage, and especially, its wonderful travel spots. Our audience is educated, active, affluent and very loyal to Ohio. We know they expect the best. Because our readership is drawn from the entire state, each of our stories must possess a statewide appeal.

Features

Feature stories in *Ohio* should meet all the above criteria. Typically, our feature well contains stories about interesting Ohioans, top travel destinations, Ohio's arts and cultural institutions, as well as trend pieces and service pieces that provide readers with a statewide set of options on a particular topic. All features should have the potential for wonderful art to accompany it, so the story has a strong visual impact on our readers.

Profile pieces typically focus on an individual who can claim an impact—large or small—on the entire state, or whose actions would be of interest to our statewide audience. A recent piece profiled the new ambassador to Switzerland who hails from Cincinnati. Similarly, emerging trends should be pitched with the same attention to statewide appeal. A story about a man with an impressive private wine collection is interesting, a story on Ohio's first master sommelier (professional wine taster) has much better appeal (this story was in our October, 2001, issue).

Trend stories can vary greatly, ranging from home decorating, gardening and food. But all must be proven emerging trends in our back yard. A trend toward massive renovations of old hotels was the cover story in the September issue of *Ohio Magazine*. Food trends are also important and in the last few months, we've covered an emerging taste for imported specialty cheese and blended teas.

We are often pitched service pieces, but choose very few. Service, or "roundup" stories typically cover one topic by providing localized, statewide information on the topic. A piece on Ohio's best colleges, or the state's best boutique shopping are good examples of excellent service pieces. A good service piece is one that provides hard-to-find information that readers would otherwise not have. So, while a guide to Ohio's biggest shopping malls isn't very crucial to readers—they could easily discover them on their own—a guide to Ohio's specialty clothing boutiques would be valuable.

Travel

While *Ohio* has evolved somewhat in recent years, we still remain dedicated to bringing our readers the best travel information in the state—where to go, what to do and what to see all over our great state. Each month, *Ohio* dedicates well over 50 percent of its pages to covering travel destinations in the state. *Ohio* readers are interested in discovering new inns and B&Bs in which to stay, finding off-the-beaten-path destinations where they can immerse themselves in local culture, and exploring excellent outdoor parks and recreation areas where they can relax and play. Almost every story provides readers with an itinerary that includes a place to stay, highlights a mixed variety of things to do and suggests local venues for dining and shopping. The key to the success of any travel pitch is the words "local" and "unique." We have files filled with information about museums and major attractions in every area of the state—we rely on contributors to tell us what's new, unique or different about each destination.

The travel section of *Ohio* contains a number of running features. Main Street stories profile a small town in Ohio that has big appeal. Typically, these are charming, old-fashioned downtown streetscapes where a reader could spend a day shopping, eating and perhaps taking in a local museum or attraction. Weekend Itinerary pieces provide readers with just that, an itinerary for an entire weekend in one location, complete with a locally owned inn or B&B, a series of options for what to do that include both well-known and not-so-well-known local attractions, and suggestions on the best locally-owned restaurants. Borderland departments cover a destination just outside of Ohio. Destination stories explore one specific destination—a new museum, a historic site, or a place worth visiting for a day or an overnight trip. These are all places that an Ohioan could drive to with ease, and have the same appeal described in the sections above.

Story Pitches

Too many writers send us pitches without ever having looked at a copy of the magazine. We encourage all potential freelance writers to do some research—go to the library, look at our archives on our web site, go to the bookstore and pick up this month's issue. Story pitches should be well thought out and offer, in a few paragraphs, a brief outline of the topic. Be specific about your subject and provide details on elements of the story that you plan to write about. Take care to note those elements of the story that you feel we might not know about—new destinations, updated attractions, and newly opened restaurants always help a pitch.

It is essential that you also provide a resume, at least three clips of your work and a SASE. Links to your web site are also welcome and e-mails with your resume and attached clips are also fine. Phone queries are discouraged. Pitches and clips should be forwarded to the address below.

Guidelines for Photographers

Send samples of your work in slides or as printed clips along with any proposed photo idea(s) to Rob McGarr, Art Director, 1422 Euclid Ave. Suite 730, Cleveland, 44115. If you have an electronic portfolio, e-mail a few examples to the attention of rmcgarr@glpublishing.com. If you're on the Web, even better. Point us in the direction of your site. If you do send samples via the mail and would like your materials returned to you, please include a self-addressed, stamped envelope and be sure to include your telephone number and e-mail address. Telephone queries are discouraged.

Please remember that our editorial calendar is established three to six months in advance. For queries related to a timely event or seasonal events, allow nine month's to a year's notice. If we're interested in your work, we'll contact you to discuss a potential assignment.

Payment

For writers and photographers, we pay on publication, buy first-time rights (and, sometimes, electronic rights), but may reassign second serial (reprint) or one-time rights.

Thanks for your interest in *Ohio Magazine*.

Categories: General Interest—Regional

CONTACT: Nicole Gabriel, Managing Editor
Material: Articles
CONTACT: Rob McGarr, Art Director,
E-mail: rmcgarr@glpublishing.com
Material: Photo samples and proposals
62 E. Broad St.
Columbus OH 43215-3522
Phone: 614-461-8723
Website: www.ohiomagazine.com

Ohio Writer

We are looking for nonfiction articles that deal with any area of writing, including how-to, profiles and interviews with Ohio writers, poets and journalists. *Ohio Writer* is read by both beginning and experienced writers and hopes to create a sense of community among writers of different genres, abilities and backgrounds. We want to hear a personal voice, one that engages the reader. We're looking for intelligent, literate prose that isn't stuffy.

Focus articles should be approximately 700–1,500 words. Payment: $25 on publication. Reprinted articles: $15 on publication.

Feature articles should be approximately 2,000-2,500 words. Payment: $25–$50 on publication.

Reviews are accepted of any publication or book by an Ohio writer or Ohio press. Include title, author, press, city where published, year of publication, number of pages and price. Occasionally we use reviews of events: conferences, readings, bookstores, etc. Length: 400-600 words. Payment: $5-$10.

Include short biographical statement with all submissions.

Unsolicited manuscripts and book reviews will be accepted.

Reporting time: Four to six weeks.

We suggest writers unfamiliar with the magazine order a sample copy. Back issues are available for $2.00 plus 50 cents postage.

We buy one-time rights, plus the right to reprint. Any editing, except copy editing, will be done with author's approval.

We also accept announcements or notes concerning writing, writing opportunities, and the writing life in Ohio for publication in our "Notes, Previews and Announcements" column. Suitable calendar listings are published without charge.

Categories: Fiction—Nonfiction—Literature—Poetry—Short Stories—Writing

CONTACT: Mark Kuhar, Editors
Material: All
c/o Poets' and Writers' League of Greater Cleveland
PO Box 91801

Cleveland OH 44101
Phone: 216-421-0403

Oildom Publishing

Writer's guidelines for these Publications:
• *Underground Construction*
• *Pipeline & Gas Journal*
• *Power & Gas Marketing*
• *Pipeline News*
• *Rehab Technology*
Submissions
• Always query first—1200 to 1500 words per query.
• Article rate includes basic telephone work. However, extensive long distance phone work and/or faxes, along with other relevant expenses may be paid by Oildom Publishing.

Significant expenses (generally defined as over $25 per story) should be pre-approved. Payment upon final article approval by the magazines' editors. Always submit invoice with final story draft/disk.

• We prefer stories submitted on disk. Oildom Publishing is PC based. Sometimes stories written on a Mac can be imported via special programs we have; often times they can't. The word processing software we support for PC is WordPerfect Windows, Microsoft Word for Windows 6.0, or generally any program in ASCII or ANSI formats. To circumvent any software incompatibilities, a clean, clear hard copy should accompany all submissions. We can then scan the story into our system.

For specific questions on formats and compatibility issues, contact Maxine Witcher, in the Houston office, (713) 558-6930, ext. 221.

• Whenever possible, all stories should be accompanied by artwork: Slides, color photographs and/or graphics. For specific graphic formats and compatibility inquiries, contact Elizabeth Bailey, for *Underground Construction*, (713) 558-6930, ext. 216, or Sheri Biscardi, (713) 558-6930, ext. 214 for *Pipeline & Gas Journal*.

• We like to break out all significant manufacturers, vendors and/or contractors with reader service numbers so interested readers can easily obtain information. Please include contact names, address, phone and fax numbers whenever possible.

• We buy exclusive rights. We prefer story queries, but cold submissions are considered. We generally will respond within 30 days.

• As a rule, we follow the *Associated Press Stylebook*. Exceptions include certain industry-accepted terms and abbreviations, and two-letter state abbreviations.

• Our readers tend to be management personnel from both contractors and owning companies. Technical material is acceptable only to a moderate level. Our readers are responsible for dollars. Always try to include economic considerations when applicable and practical.

• Kill fees are addressed on a case-by-case basis.

Categories: Trade—Underground Construction (gas, sewer, water, cable)

CONTACT: Robert Carpenter, Editorial Director
Material: Underground Construction
CONTACT: Jeff Share, Editor
Material: Pipeline & Gas Journal
CONTACT: Rita Tubb, Managing Editor
Material: Underground Construction/Pipeline & Gas
Journal and all other
Executive Offices
PO Box 941669
Houston TX 77094-8669
Phone: 281-558-6930
Fax: 281-558-7029
E-mail: rita@oildompublishing.com
1160 Dairy Ashford Rd., Suite 610
Houston TX 77079
Phone: 281-558-6930

Fax: 281-558-7029
Website: www.oildompublishing.com

Oklahoma TODAY

Oklahoma Today Magazine

About *Oklahoma Today* Magazine

Oklahoma Today is a regional bi-monthly magazine with a circulation of 45,000 and an estimated readership of 153,000. Stories, essays, columns, etc. focus on Oklahoma's people and places. We strive to give our readers a sense of what Oklahoma is all about.

People figure strongly into all of our stories. We believe the best way to write a story is not to just tell it, but to show our readers through anecdotes, quotes, and experiences of past and present people.

The magazine likes to give the readers information on not only the regular "hot spots" to visit, but places that are "off the beaten track" as well.

About Your Story

When deciding on a subject, you need to think "Could the reader see or do what the article talks about?" or "Will the story expand the knowledge of the readers' Oklahoma cultural knowledge?"

The history behind the person or place also should be included. It lets the reader know why a particular thing is happening, but the focus needs to be on today.

Considering A Story For Publication

Some of the questions we ask when considering a story are, "Does the writer answer all the questions about the subject?," "Who and what are the source materials?," "Does the writer surprise the reader with something?," and "Could anything else be included in the story?"

Topics in *Oklahoma Today* have a wide range. Some of the successful stories from the past include: Oklahoma cowboy poet roundup, profiles—hamburger joints, and a photo essay on the Tallgrass Prairie.

Oklahoma Today is always looking for a fresh editorial perspective to complement the seasoned writers we already use. While we appreciate and encourage a distinct voice, we usually do not publish opinion pieces. The best way to get in is to send us a story with a fresh angle on an old subject or person, or a new idea that goes along with our style of covering Oklahoma's people and places.

How To Get In

Read our magazine. Read Oklahoma newspapers and any other Oklahoma publication you can get your hands on. Keeping up with what goes on in our state is the best way to write stories that we can use. Include a biography of yourself and clips of previous work, so we can see what experience you have. Realize that the editors receive many manuscripts and that yours will be reviewed as soon as time allows. Don't necessarily expect your first piece in the magazine to be a feature; start small and suggest items for departments such as Across the Range. Even Letters to the Editor are good ways to "get some ink."

1. Deadlines

Oklahoma Today is usually planned a year in advance, so stories submitted in March may not appear until next January. We produce an issue two months ahead of time (in September, we are in production for November/December), so submit timely stories well before the production deadlines. *Oklahoma Today* is published seven times a year.

2. Story Guidelines

Stories will range in length from 250 words for regular department articles to 3,000 words for major features. We prefer to be queried in advance, but will review unsolicited manuscripts and photos "on spec."

Submission of transparencies and black-and-white photographs are welcome. We prefer scenic photographs that may or may not include people. However, we reserve the right to reject photographs submitted with the story, even if we accept the story itself.

3. Rates/Payments

Rates start at $50 for shorter pieces, $75 and up for department and feature stories, and $300 and up for major profiles or stories.

Payment will be upon publication.

We pay for quality, not quantity.

We do not pay for expenses, but do take into account the demands of story assignment when negotiating payment.

Terms of the agreement for stories on both assignment and bought "on spec" are confirmed with a standard editorial contract.

4. Policies and Procedures

Oklahoma Today takes no responsibility for unsolicited manuscripts, artwork, or photography.

Articles need to be e-mailed or submitted on disk, preferably in Microsoft Word, and with an accompanying printout.

Never send an original, uncopied manuscript.

Rejected material will not be returned unless sent with a SASE.

REPORTING STANDARDS

Oklahoma Today requires its writers to conduct their reporting according to the magazine's high standards of truth and accuracy. To that end, we have adopted the following guidelines. Of course, all stories are unique. Editorial judgment is always the final arbiter and will be exercised on a case-by-case basis by *Oklahoma Today*'s editors.

Our Guidelines

1. *Oklahoma Today* won't publish any statements that haven't been documented to its satisfaction.

2. *Oklahoma Today* requests primary sources for all previously unreported facts and for all other facts important to the story.

Any fact that might be contested should ideally have at least two primary sources.

Although *Oklahoma Today* typically does not publish controversial material, the more controversial a fact, the higher a standard of sourcing will be required. Countervailing opinions should be weighed by the writer and brought to the editor's attention if appropriate. An example of a primary source is a credible person in a position to know the fact in question. A properly filed public document is also a primary source. Other documents uncovered in reporting may be considered primary sources.

3. *Oklahoma Today* discourages reporting that relies too heavily on secondary sources.

However, we accept that certain facts—mostly, minor facts that serve as background for a story—may be established via secondary sources. Newspapers and magazines will be accepted as secondary sources on a case-by-case basis. Common sense and skepticism will be our guides. In the field of medicine, for example, the *New England Journal of Medicine* would likely be accepted as authoritative. In most cases, *Oklahoma Today* will regard the following publications as acceptable secondary sources:

- *Daily Oklahoman*
- *Tulsa World*
- State dailies (Lawton, Muskogee, Enid, Stillwater, Norman)
- *Dallas Morning News*
- *New York Times*
- *Washington Post*
- *Wall Street Journal*
- *Time*
- *Newsweek*

Why these particular publications? Because they're journals of record, widely available and widely read, with a good record for correcting mistakes. We don't necessarily believe they are more accurate than other publications. But we do believe it's reasonable to assume that if one of these publications reports something and it's not corrected, it's accurate. Reports in publications that aren't deemed acceptable secondary sources by your editors should be verified with a primary source—or more that one primary source, if appropriate.

4. *Oklahoma Today* believes in giving credit to other publications for original reporting

We don't think it's right to rely on other publication's work without acknowledging the debt. Even if we re-establish the facts first reported by another publication, we give credit if credit is due. The guidelines here are common sense and generosity.

5. *Oklahoma Today* expects its writers to take responsibility even for so-called common knowledge.

For matters of general and historical background, we rely on established encyclopedic reference and other general sources. But we will accept citation to any source that, in our opinion, can reasonably be called authoritative.

6. *Oklahoma Today* requires its writers and editors to keep unpublished drafts of assigned articles confidential.

We believe sharing any unpublished version of your article with the subject matter or a source—a big journalistic no-no—is inappropriate. Soliciting approval from your subject or source compromises the editorial integrity of the piece and thus the magazine. Many sources will ask you to share with them a printed version of your draft. Please explain the magazine's policy and refer those sources to your editor. If you feel you need feedback on a draft, please contact your assigning editor.

7. *Oklahoma Today* requires its writers to supply an annotated fact-checking manuscript that reflects these guidelines.

Writers and editors will work together to decide which sources should be cited in final copy and how they should be cited. Meanwhile, writers must submit material that provides appropriate documentation of their reporting. Usually, such material will be requested shortly after a story has been accepted.

8. Here's what we need, specifically:

- Any notes, transcripts, or tapes of interviews
- All magazine or newspaper stories used in reporting
- All other supporting material, with relevant parts clearly marked
- Phone numbers for sources
- The annotated manuscript

Please be understanding of the fact checkers' work and cooperate fully with their efforts. Highlighting quotes and supplying page numbers helps enormously—and reduces the amount of time you'll spend on the phone with a fact checker. Any questions about these guidelines? Ask your editor.

In keeping with the intent of these "Reporting Standards," *Oklahoma Today* would like to acknowledge Worth for creating the original version of this document.

Categories: Nonfiction—Consumer—History—Native American—Regional—Travel

CONTACT: Editor
Material: All
PO Box 53384
Oklahoma City OK 73152
Phone: 405-521-2496
Fax: 405-522-4588
Website: oklahomatoday.com

The Old Farmer's Almanac

The Old Farmer's Almanac is the oldest continuously published periodical in North America. Since 1792, it has provided useful information for people in all walks of life: tide tables for those who live near the ocean; sunrise tables and planting charts for those who live on the farm or simply enjoy gardening; recipes for those who like to cook; and forecasts for those who don't like the question of weather left up in the air. The words of the *Almanac*'s founder, Robert B. Thomas, guide us still: "Our main endeavor is to be useful, but with a pleasant degree of humor."

An almanac, by definition, records and predicts astronomical events (the rising and setting of the Sun, for instance), tides, weather, and other phenomena with respect to time. In recent years, we've expanded the *Almanac* content—but always with an eye on Mr. Thomas's wise words about keeping things fun and practical.

We encourage you to study back issues of our publication to gain an idea of what we publish. Some of our content is also available on our Web site, www.almanac.com. Keep in mind that we attempt to create a sort of time capsule with each issue: We cover the current year with articles that reflect current events, trends, and interests, and we commemorate past people and events with "anniversary" stories that shed new light on the subject and update the subject as is appropriate. (An anniversary year is typically one that is divisible by 5.) The "big picture" goal is to produce a "snapshot" of the issue year so that readers in 2, 20, or 200 years will understand and appreciate what is topical today.

These are among the general story categories we look for: pertinent articles on science and weather; nature, including insects, animals, and the outdoors (fishing, for example); plants, gardening, and farming; history, including events, people, and inventions; natural health, folklore, and traditional ways (herbal remedies, for example); geography and climate; amusements; food and recipes. We regularly feature a "special report" on a topic of broad general interest. Recently those have included romance, superstitions, and wedding traditions past and present. We especially encourage humor of all kinds: the fanciful, the bizarre, the ludicrous, and the offbeat.

Our readership spans the generations: In age, they range from 9 to 90; they live in the cities, the suburbs, and out in the country.

We publish both a U.S. and a Canadian edition. For the Canadian edition, we substitute six to eight stories that are uniquely and specifically about life in Canada, based on the topic areas cited above.

The *Almanac* comes out every year on the second Tuesday in September. Payment is made on acceptance; rates vary. We prefer to buy all rights.

If you have a story idea, send us a query with a brief outline via regular mail (email only if an editor has invited you to do so). Please include a self-addressed, stamped envelope for our reply. If you have been published—especially in the proposed topic area—a sample of clips would be appreciated (photocopies only, and an SASE if you would like clips returned).

Categories: Nonfiction—Agriculture—Associations—Biography—Children—Consumer—Cooking—Crafts/Hobbies—Culture—Ecology—Folklore—Gardening—General Interest—History—Outdoors—Reference—Rural America

CONTACT: Janice Stillman, Editor
Material: All
PO Box 520
Dublin NH 03444
Phone: 603-563-8111
Website: www.almanac.com

Old West

Please refer to *True West* magazine.

Omnific

Are you guilty of storing your poetry in the closet? Do you say that contests are not for you because you would waste your money? Do deadlines make you nervous? If you answered "yes" to any of these questions, then this publication is for you.

Get those poems out of the closet and dust them off because OMNIFIC is now accepting 4 poems per person, per year, for publication in this well-known quarterly. Just think of it. Each issue could feature one of your poems. This is your chance to become published and stay published.

Poems are attractively displayed in alphabetical order according to your state, along with complete address of author. Readers vote on their favorites, and for now we have small prizes to be awarded. The top three entries receiving the most votes receive the next issue free. There is also an "Editor's Choice Award" of $5, and the poem(s) in the "Lucky No. 7" spot will receive a small award. As interest builds and subscriptions come in, prizes will be increased. (Not to mention the contact and awards furnished by some of our readers.)

Each author's complete name and address will be published with his/her poem. This encourages reader/writer contact, and also the awards given by our readers may be mailed directly to YOU. (However, if you wish your address to remain anonymous, I will accept your awards and forward them on to you. But YOU must let me know this at the time you send in your poetry, or upon receiving your acceptance letter.)

You will be proud to see your work published here and I can also promise that you will enjoy reading each issue, along with voting for your favorites. And the excitement builds from one issue to the next, because after reading OMNIFIC and casting your vote, you will want to know who the winners will be—and that information will be disclosed in the next issue.

OMNIFIC means "all creating" and as poets and writers, isn't that what we're doing?

COME...join our family today. Don't you be the one to miss out on the fun that's in store for everyone.

Wouldn't YOU like to be published in this exciting, fun-filled quarterly and have your poem appear in the next issue?

There is no entry fee and due to the weight involved, no payment in copies. Poetry to 40 lines (sometimes over), and in any style or format. Submission does not guarantee publication. Only work in good taste is accepted.

1 Year Subscription (4 issues) $16.00/Overseas $20 (US Funds)

Single issue—$4.50/Overseas $5.00 (US Funds). Payable to Weems Concepts.

This publication is habit-forming and good for your morale. Read at your own risk.

Categories: Poetry

CONTACT: Kay Weems, Editor/Publisher
Material: Poetry
207 Willow Wind Dr.
Artemas PA 17211-9405
Phone: 814-458-3102

On Mission

Flagship magazine of the North American Mission Board, SBC.

On Mission's primary purpose is to help readers and churches become more on mission in the areas of personal evangelism and missions. Effective articles will always include elements that move readers toward spiritual growth, evangelism and missions. On Mission is approximately 50 percent freelance written. Articles are 600-1,200 words. Payment is 25 cents/word—35 cents/word for cover stories (usually assigned). On Mission's readership is 100,000.

Here is a checklist of some points to consider as you match your work with On Mission's objectives:

Spiritual – Each article should move readers toward a deeper walk with God and a commitment to sharing Christ with others. On Mission articles must maintain an eternal, "big picture" perspective.

Practical – Each article should include "take away" value readers will find helpful. Will they gain insights into how they can grow in sharing their faith or gain strength in their own relationship with Jesus Christ? Will they learn more effective ways of relationship building or communication? In what specific ways will your article encourage, provide hope or show "how to?"

Personal – On Mission wants readers to feel connected with the people featured on its pages. Articles should quote and describe the people in ways that not only convey meaning, but also give readers a glimpse into the hearts and minds of those being featured.

Approachable – Readers might be intimidated if those featured appear to be "super Christians" who seem to live on a higher spiritual plane. Try to introduce subjects as "three dimensional, real" people. Include anecdotes or examples of their fears and failures, including ways they overcame obstacles. In other words, take the reader inside the heart of the on mission Christian and reveal the inevitable humanness that makes that person not only believable, but also approachable. We want the reader to feel encouraged to become on mission by identifying with people like them who are featured in the magazine.

Believable – The Bible clearly explains the basics for the Christian walk. These points are non-negotiable. However, working out an approach to evangelism and missions can take many forms. On Mission will look for different insights on this topic, but we will not be afraid to admit that we don't know everything on the subjects of evangelism and missions.

Hopeful – Sharing Christ is an intimidating prospect for many readers. Without increasing fear, On Mission wants to acknowledge that reality while at the same time giving readers encouragement and hope. We can do this by holding up as models of the successful on mission lifestyle those people who are willing to share their struggles with the reader – as well as their success stories.

Knowledgeable – Without conflicting with these last two points, On Mission strives to be a source of information and knowledge, as well as a helpful resource. On Mission will help readers do their homework on these issues. We want to provide accurate information and up-to-date knowledge. Research your article. Document your sources. Depend on the most trustworthy, factual sources you can locate.

Submission Format:

Articles may be submitted by postal mail or email. If you send a document electronically, please ensure that your document is in a Microsoft Word format and double spaced. We prefer electronic submissions, with the article included as an attachment to the email or embedded into the body of the email. Material is subject to editing for length, style and format.

On Mission is primarily an "on assignment" magazine, meaning that editors first develop story ideas and then locate writers whose expertise and interests fit the articles. However, we do accept queries and manuscripts. If you have a story idea, please send a query letter and/or manuscript along with your resume and clips. It takes about 8-16 weeks to respond to query letters and manuscripts, so allow time for event-related and seasonal story ideas. Payment is made on acceptance. Send queries with SASE or manuscript.

Categories: Nonfiction—Christian Interests—Religion

CONTACT: Carol Pipes, Managing Editor
Material: All
North American Mission Board
4200 North Point Pkwy.
Alpharetta GA 30022-4176
Phone: 770-410-6382
E-mail: cpipes@namb.net
Website: www.onmission.com

Onion World

Onion World is written for commercial onion growers, packers and shippers. Hence, any free-lance material accepted for publication must be informative and specifically addressed to this audience.

The following types of articles represent subject matter that normally would be acceptable:

Educational pieces: Articles focusing on various disease, insect and production challenges and what is being done to resolve them. Such articles must be based on solid research from reputable industry sources.

Feature articles: Focus should be on onion growers and/or onion packer/shippers, what they are doing, what kinds of equipment they are using, the benefits, etc.

Health-related articles: Articles pointing out the health benefits of eating onions. Again, solid research is a must.

Onion Meetings/Field Days: Reports on special onion educational meetings/seminars are acceptable and are encouraged.

Taboos:

1. General interest articles with no particular focus on onions.
2. Articles designed for the home gardener.
3. Fiction pieces.
4. Poetry

Length:

1. Articles should not exceed 1,200 to 1,500 words.
2. Shorter articles are acceptable and are often preferred.

Photos:

1. Avoid the canned pose.
2. Involve people.
3. Colored jps or prints preferred.
4. Color prints and/or jpgs considered for covers.
5. Writers should submit prints or jpgs, along with appropriate captions.

Remuneration:

Dependent upon length of and quality of submission. Price range: Up to $150, including photos.

Categories: Nonfiction—Agriculture—Business—Education—Health

CONTACT: Editor
Material: All
Columbia Publishing
417 N. 20th Ave.
Yakima WA 98902
Phone: 509-248-2452
Fax: 509-248-4056
E-mail: carrie@freshcut.com
Website: www.onionworld.net

Orange Coast Magazine

Orange Coast Magazine and *Orange Coast Online* (www. orangecoastmagazine.com) are published for the educated and affluent residents of Orange County, California. Priority is given to well-told stories that have strong local interest, always with an emphasis on stylish writing and clear thinking.

GUIDELINES

To propose a story, writers should send a detailed query with published writing samples, or a completed manuscript. Proposals that arrive with a stamped, self-addressed envelope will be returned if the manuscript is not usable. Others will not be returned. Manuscripts should be saved in ASCII, or text-only, format and sent by e-mail. Writers should include their name, address, phone number and social security number.

WRITING TIPS

1. Read previous issues of *Orange Coast* to gauge the range of story ideas and how they were handled.

2. Give stories a hard, narrow focus. Rather than a story about the Pacific Symphony Orchestra, tell us the story of the lead cellist who scoured the world for the perfect cello, then mortgaged his house in order to buy it.

3. Once the story is focused, broaden the perspective. A story focused on our cellist should raise much larger questions: Why would a musician take a huge financial risk to get an instrument that to an untrained ear sounds pretty much like any other cello? What does the musician hear that the rest of us don't?

4. Narrative stories work best, with scenes, characters and situations developed in the writer's own words. But the editors also encourage writers to experiment with style—there is no right formula. Ask yourself what's the best way to tell this particular story. The story should dictate the style and the style never should dominate or obscure the story.

5. Show, don't tell. Instead of telling readers the room was cold and drafty, give them the details that show the cold: a character puffing clouds of vapor, a flickering candle, the butler wearing mittens. Effective details let the reader see; useless details clutter the story.

6. Avoid newspaperese. In the economy of newspaper writing, a man who dedicated his life to police work, who built a career during weekends and midnight shifts and who faced countless dangers for inadequate pay becomes a "28-year police veteran." In magazine writing, you can create real characters for the reader. There is no need to boil the elements of a personality into such efficient language.

7. But don't overwrite. If the subject isn't compelling enough to carry the story without embellishment, the value of the story immediately comes into question.

8. When appropriate, draw conclusions and interpret what you have seen and learned. If the most powerful banker in town has a pencil-thin mustache and dresses in hand-painted Niagara Falls ties, white bucks and loud sports jackets, provide the reader with those details. Then, if you think he looks like a used-car salesman, you're certainly free to say so. Just make sure the image is precise and accurate.

9. Save your notes in case additional material is needed for the story.

10. Remember that you are writing for an audience that generally is literate, wealthy and sophisticated, but avoid dry intellectual discourse.

11. Write about real people in real situations; let their stories crystallize the broader issues.

RATES

• *Orange Coast* pays between $300 and $700 for main features, which generally range between 1,200 and 2,500 words. The amount of the payment ultimately depends on the amount of reporting involved and the quality of the writing, and it includes the writer's expenses. Monthly travel features pay $210. Short Cut stories pay between $50 and $75.

• Payment is made on publication. Editorial payments are processed on the 20th of each month and checks are mailed out within one week. No additional payments are made for photographs or accompanying artwork

• For stories done on speculation, no kill fee is paid if the submission is unsuitable for use. For stories assigned by the editors, the kill fee will not exceed 20 percent of the agreed-upon publication price.

• *Orange Coast* buys one-time rights. If the submitted article has appeared elsewhere, writers should let the editors know when and where, and verify in writing that they have not relinquished their rights to it.

Categories: Nonfiction—Regional

CONTACT: Nancy Cheever, Editor
Material: Any
CONTACT: Anastacia Grenda, Managing Editor
Material: Any
3701 Birch St. Ste. 100
Newport Beach CA 92660
Phone: 949-862-1133
Fax: 949-862-0133
E-mail: agrenda@orangecoastmagazine.com

Remember: Editors change jobs and publishers change addresses. It is wise to invest in a phone call for the current information before submitting.

Oregon Business

Dear Prospective Contributor:

Our purpose is to produce a useful, compelling and indispensable monthly magazine that will serve our business readers and help us earn our motto: "Indepth, intelligent, inspiring,." In addition we hope we can help you in your professional development. We understand that contributors are the editorial engine of Oregon Business.

Gillian Floren, Publisher

Readership

Our subscribers include owners of small and medium-sized businesses, government agencies, professional staffs of banks, insurance companies, ad agencies, attorneys and other service providers. The typical reader earns more than $100,000 a year, is college educated and owns a home. Circulation is 21,000, although readership reaches 53,000.

Coverage

About 50% of the magazine's content is written by freelancers, including standing section stories and cover features. Although freelancers most commonly pitch general profiles, we rarely cover a company just because it's there. An *Oregon Business* story must meet at least two of the following criteria:

• Size and location: The topic must be relevant to Northwest businesses. Companies (including franchises) must be based in Oregon or Southwest Washington with at least five employees and annual sales above $250,000.

• Service: Our sections (400-800 words) are reserved largely for service pieces focusing on finance, marketing, management or other general business topics. These stories are meant to be instructional, emphasizing problem-solving by example: "Building a Business Plan: Company X broke the rules and succeeded."

• Trends: These are sometimes covered in a section piece, or perhaps a feature story (2,000 to 4,000 words). We aim to be the state's leading business publication, so we want to be the first to spot trends that affect Oregon companies. If we can't be first, we'll be best. That means going deeper than the typical coverage, offering fresh perspectives and challenging assumptions: "Are Employee Incentives on Their Way Out?" "The New Oregonians: They came, they stayed, get used to it."

• Exclusivity or strategy: Usually a feature or cover story offering a insider's account of an event, whether it's a corporate merger, a dramatic turnaround, a marketing triumph or a PR disaster. The rare breaking news story will focus on the "what"; the more common piece analyzing strategy will talk about the whys and the hows: "Two CEOs. One Golf Game: How the courtship between U.S. Bank and West One led to marriage."

• Compelling figures: A personality profile of a business leader whose style or accomplishments merit an in-depth look. The subject must be interesting, complex, visionary or controversial: "High Volume, High Pressure. How Scott Thomason turned a single dealership into an auto empire."

Standards

Oregon Business adheres to the highest journalistic standards of fairness, diligence and accuracy and expects our contributors to do the same. Stories must be authoritative, which requires thorough reporting using several sources. They must be clearly organized with a well defined theme. And they must be illustrated with real-life examples, because, above all, business is composed of people.

We expect smart and elegant writing in the best of magazine traditions. This means telling—or more accurately, showing—the story from the players' perspectives: the executives who did the deal, the middle manager who got laid off, the line workers who changed the manufacturing process. Industry analysts and statistics are necessary to support a point, but they should be used sparingly.

Writers are responsible for making sure their submissions are error-free; this includes fact checking in final draft form. Editors will return for a rewrite stories that are sloppily put together or underreported. Poor rewrites requiring extensive editing may result in a fee reduction.

Submissions

We do not accept unsolicited material, but we're happy to receive query letters in writing (no phone calls). If we like your idea we'll give you a written assignment along with a word length and deadline, usually 45 days before publication.

• Format. Send material via e-mail with plain text attachments. Use fax or snail mail sparingly.

• Compensation. We pay an average of $360 for a section story and between $700 and $1,500 for a feature story, depending on length and complexity. Submissions should include an invoice. Payment is shortly after publication.

• Rights. We buy first publication rights, which include the contributor's agreement not to sell the story or photo to another publisher within four months after publication in *Oregon Business*.

Photography

Oregon Business is recognized for its artful and unusual pictures. A successful contributor will have an eye for turning the mundane into the interesting and the drab into the colorful. We encourage creativity, which sometimes means puffing together elements from disparate locations or asking subjects to travel off site. The more our magazine's reputation grows, the more our subjects are willing to go along with the photographer's vision.

We like candid shots as much as portraits, so please include both to give us a variety. We do not accept grip-and-grin shots, gimmicky set ups or "class picture" poses. If we receive photos that do not meet our standards, we may request a reshoot at no extra charge.

• Format: Color slides, either 2¼" or 35mm. To avoid confusion, stamp each frame with your name, address and phone number and encase the slides in plastic sleeves. Attach the subject's business card and always include written caption information.

Although we like a variety of shots, one roll of film is usually enough and not more than two.

• Compensation: We pay $125 plus film and processing for photos inside the magazine and a flat $450 for covers. Include an invoice with your submission. We return the slides along with a copy of the issue on publication. Payment is sent 30 days after invoicing.

• Loss/damage. We will not be liable for any lost or damaged slides, negatives or prints if the photo was assigned by the magazine. Photographers submitting stock photos must obtain written loss/damage protection in advance.

What you can expect from us

We will do our best to treat you fairly and professionally. If we need you to turn around work for us quickly, we will try to remember that you write or shoot for other publications, too. If your story requires substantive editing, we'll go over the changes with you before the piece goes to press.

We want to create steady, long-term relationships with our contributors. The best will be given frequent assignments and projects.

We look forward to working with you to make a good magazine even better.

Categories: Business—Regional

CONTACT: **Mitchell Hartman, Editor**
Material: All
CONTACT: Christina Williams, Managing Editor
Material: All
610 SW Broadway Ste. 200
Portland OR 97205
Phone: 503-223-0304
Fax: 503-221-6544
E-mail: Christinaw@oregonbusiness.com

Oregon Coast

Please refer to Northwest Regional Magazines.

Oregon Quarterly
The Magazine of the University of Oregon

Oregon Quarterly is the successor to *Old Oregon*, the University of Oregon's alumni magazine founded in 1919. Although our 110,000 readers consist predominantly of UO alumni, our editorial approach has evolved in the past few years from a traditional alumni magazine to a regional magazine of ideas. To highlight this change, we now describe ourselves as "The Northwest Perspective from the University of Oregon."

Unlike a traditional alumni magazine, the majority of our features are not about the UO, as such. Instead, we generally address topics of state and regional interest (ideas, issues and personalities) using the resources of UO faculty and alumni. The UO benefits from its involvement in these stories, not as their subject matter. Our goal is to reach a broad, well-educated regional audience, whether or not they have ties to the UO. As a magazine, we want to be recognized for the quality of our writing.

Good magazine stories should have shape and depth. They are closer in conception and execution to a thoughtful essay than to a newspaper feature. They should involve the reader, awaken the imagination. They require some effort to write, but they are much more a pleasure to read.

Although our departments are staff-written, most of our features and short subjects are contributed by free lancers. If the topic has a contemporary regional interest, and if UO involvement can be demonstrated (through faculty or alumni participation), we'd like to hear about it. We prefer brief query letters that show the flavor of the proposed article and your writing style. Submit clips that demonstrate your ability. If you don't have a story idea but would like to be considered for assignments, submit clips with a cover letter explaining your interests and experience.

We invite queries for features, which generally run 2,500-3,000 words. We pay 20 cents a word on acceptance (after requested revisions), plus reasonable expenses (with receipts), provided they are cleared by us in advance. For contracted stories we do not accept, we pay a kill fee of 20 percent the contracted amount. We generally follow *The Chicago Manual of Style*.

Recent Freelance Features

"Oregon's Miracle?" by Lisa Cohn (Winter 1995): What the boom of high-tech manufacturing in the region may mean to Oregon's future.

"New Voices" by Alice Evans (Autumn 1995): How the UO Creative Writing Program emerged from a period of turmoil to become nationally renown.

"The Resurrection of Knowles Creek" by Lucy Vinis (Summer 1995): How saving Oregon's salmon runs may involve not only hard work, but a close reading of Aristotle as well.

Categories: Nonfiction—College—Culture—Education—Regional

CONTACT: Submissions Editor
Material: All
5228 University of Oregon
Eugene OR 97403
Phone: 541-346-5048
E-mail: gmaynard@oregon.uoregon.edu
Website: www.oregon.edu

The Other Side

Our Mission and Focus:

The Other Side is an independent ecumenical magazine that seeks to advance a broad Christian vision that's biblical and compassionate, appreciative of the creative arts, and committed to the intimate intertwining of personal spirituality and social transformation. We weave together first-person essays, insightful analyses, biblical reflection, interviews, fiction, poetry, and an inviting mix of visual art. We strive to nurture, uplift, and challenge readers with personal, provocative writing that reflects the transformative, liberating Spirit of Jesus Christ.

How to Submit:

Articles should be sent with a stamped, self-addressed return envelope to the attention of our fiction, nonfiction, or poetry editor (as appropriate) at the address below. Articles without return postage will not be returned. Although we do not require queries or purchase articles on speculation, if you want to query about our potential interest in an article, you may call 215-849-2178 and ask to speak to someone on the editorial staff. We do not currently accept unsolicited manuscripts by fax or e-mail.

Prospective authors should review current issues of the magazine—or at least examine the material on our website at www.theotherside.org—before submitting. Sample issues are available for $6.00; Subscriptions are $27 per year. Send payment to Subscription Office, 300 W. Apsley St., Philadelphia, PA 19144—or order by credit card by calling 1-800-700-9280 or visiting our subscription page.

Submission Guidelines:

NONFICTION pieces range from 400 to 4,000 words, with most running 2,000 words or less. Payment for nonfiction ranges from $50 to $300, depending on the piece. Less than 3 percent of submitted manuscripts are accepted. We publish reflective essays, personal journeys, biblical analysis, spiritual explorations, interviews with unusual people, theological explorations, investigative reporting, and creative thinking.

We are looking for articles addressing contemporary social, political, and economic issues (especially those revealing an awareness of race, class, gender, and other dynamics). We have a strong interest in the arts, cultural change, and creative expression. And we are always interested in writing that makes connections between spiritual and social renewal, reflecting God's longing that our world—and each of our lives—might be made new. All authors should keep in mind *The Other Side*'s commitment to social and economic justice, peace and nonviolence, the liberating power of Scripture, and the compassionate, inclusive ways of Christ.

POETRY submissions should include strong imagery, fresh viewpoints, and lively language, while avoiding versifications of religious instruction or syrupy piety. Poems should be no more than 50 lines in length, and no more than three submissions will be considered at any one time from the same author. Payment for poems is generally $25. Less than one-half of 1 percent of all poems submitted are accepted.

FICTION should be between 500 and 5,000 words in length, the shorter the better. Payment is between $75 and $250. We're looking for strongly crafted fiction that deepens our readers' encounter with the mystery of God and the mystery of ourselves.

We normally report on submissions in four to eight weeks, depending on the timeliness of the piece. We buy first serial and additional associated rights. We will not consider previously published material.

In addition to financial payment, authors receive complimentary copies of the issue in which their material appears and a free two-year subscription (or subscription extension). Payment is on acceptance.

Categories: Fiction—Nonfiction—African-American—Arts—Christian Interests—Environment—Feminism—Gay/Lesbian—Human Rights—Inspirational—Poetry—Politics—Religion—Spiritual

CONTACT: Deborah Good, Editorial Associate
Material: Nonfiction, Fiction

CONTACT: Jeanne Minahan, Poetry Editor
Material: Poetry
300 W. Apsley St.
Philadelphia PA 19144-4285
Phone: 215-849-2178
Website: www.theotherside.org

Other Voices
University of Illinois-Chicago

Fiction Guidelines

1. OV reads unpublished, unsolicited manuscripts between October 1 and April 1, only.

2. Short stories and self-contained novel excerpts only

3. One story at a time, please!

4. 5,000 word maximum preferred, but not mandatory.

5. Writer's name on each page of mss.

6. Save a tree—the Editors suggest a letter-size SASE for reply only (and promise to recycle your mss.).

7. 10-12 week reply

8. No taboos, except ineptitude and murkiness.

Send Us Your Best Voice/Your Best Work/Your Best...

Categories: Fiction—Literature—Short Stories

CONTACT: Gina Frangello, Executive Editor
Material: Fiction
CONTACT: JoAnne Ruvoli, Assistant Editor
Material: Fiction
University of Illinois at Chicago
Dept. of English, 601 S. Morgan
Chicago IL 60607
Phone: 312-413-2209

Outdoor America

About Our Magazine and Parent Organization

Founded in 1922, *Outdoor America* is the quarterly publication of the Izaak Walton League of America, one of the nation's oldest and most respected conservation organizations. The League's 40,000 members and 300-plus chapters, are the heart of its grassroots mission to defend America's soil, air, woods, waters, and wildlife for future generations. *Outdoor America* seeks to keep this membership informed of the latest conservation issues, as well as spread word of the League's work to prospective members and policy makers. The magazine is published in January, April, July, and October.

Article Submissions

• Manuscripts

Although *Outdoor America* is primarily staff written, we publish several freelance articles per issue. These include 2,500-3,000 word features, 1,500-2,000 word essays, and 600-800 word "department" pieces. With the exception of essays, we rarely accept unsolicited manuscripts.

Queries and submissions: Letter queries must be brief and accompanied by clips and a SASE. Although we accept e-mail queries and submissions, we do not accept phone or fax queries. We do our best to respond within 60 days. We assume no responsibility for lost or damaged manuscripts. Send materials to *Outdoor America* Editor, IWLA, 707 Conservation Lane, Gaithers-burg MD 20878-2983; oa@iwla.org.

Style: We prefer articles that have a conversational tone, speak directly and concisely, and provide fresh perspectives. We urge journalists to employ scene, characterization, narrative, and other tools of literary nonfiction.

Audience: IWLA members are grassroots conservationists from all walks of life—salt-of-the-earth environmentalists with a strong interest in outdoor recreation, especially hunting and fishing. They are also very politically active. A 2001 survey of League members found that 91% of them voted in 2001, with 41% percent identifying themselves as Republicans, 39% as Independents, and 19% as Democrats.

What we don't want: Poetry, fiction, unsubstantiated opinion pieces, travel writing, and articles about local conservation issues that do not have national implications.

Tip: *Outdoor America* is first and foremost the membership magazine of the Izaak Walton League. Therefore, we strive to publish stories that involve IWLA members at the local, state, regional, and/or national level(s). Members and chapters should be included as sources and in anecdotes whenever possible. If you need to find a source, visit the chapter section of our Web site or call the Editorial Director at (301) 548-0150, ext. 228.

Photography

Outdoor America is always looking for exceptional, professional photography. Principal subjects are wildlife shots (particularly game species); outdoor recreation subjects (fishing, hunting, camping, or boating); and scenics (especially of the Chesapeake Bay and Upper Mississippi watersheds). We also like the "unusual" shot—new perspectives on familiar subjects—for use on covers.

Color work can be 35mm, but we prefer 2¼ x 2¼ or larger format. (Front cover shots must be cropped to fit a vertical format.)

Submitting material: Send only tearsheets of published work or nonreturnable samples. Do not send original material, unless requested. Mail to *Outdoor America* Art Director, IWLA, 707 Conservation Lane, Gaithersburg, Md. 20878-2983. Include SASE if you would like a response to your query. Allow 8–10 weeks.

Payment

Articles: We generally pay between $0.25 and $0.35 cents per word, as well as agreed-upon expenses. The fee grants *Outdoor America* first North American serial rights, exclusive to us for the 30 days following publication. If the writer wishes to sell subsequent rights, he or she must credit *Outdoor America* as the first publisher. Kill fees are determined at the editor's discretion, and are generally between one-third and one-half of the original rate.

Photos:
• Front cover: $500
• Back cover: $250
• Inside pages: $75-$200

Front-cover fee grants IWLA the non-exclusive use of the photo in the *Outdoor America* cover format for publication on our Web site, media guide, and other promotional materials. Any other appearance of the photo in non-cover format would be considered an additional use and would be subject to the normal rates and guidelines listed above.

Contracts and invoices: When *Outdoor America* contracts a writer or photographer, the magazine will send a contract outlining the terms of the assignment. To process payment, this contract must be signed and returned to the editor, and must be accompanied by an invoice noting the contractor's full name, mailing address, Social Security number, amount due, article or photo title, and publication date.

Categories: Nonfiction—Conservation—Environment—Fishing—Outdoors—Sports/Recreation—Hunting

CONTACT: Jason McGarvey, Editor
Material: All
Izaak Walton League of America
707 Conservation Lane
Gaithersburg MD 20878
Phone: 301-548-0150
Website: www.iwla.org/oa

Outdoor Life

WHAT DOES *Outdoor Life* BUY?

Outdoor Life serves the active sportsman and his family with primary emphasis on hunting, fishing, outdoor adventures and game conservation.

• We do not buy: poetry, fiction, backpacking, kayaking, cycling or adventure travel stories. If you are interested in writing for *Outdoor Life*, study the magazine. What we publish is your best guide to the kinds of material we seek.

• We accept very few unsolicited manuscripts. The best advice is to query first. Write a crisp, concise (one-page) query letter that clearly outlines your idea in a few paragraphs. Include a few sentences about how the story might best be illustrated, e.g. with photographs, illustrations, technical drawings or cartoons. Please include a self-addressed, stamped envelope to expedite replies. Electronic queries are also acceptable (OLMagazine@ aol.com).

• Do you have something new to offer the reader that will help him or her enjoy hunting and fishing more? How do you think it will help? How would you present it? All of our columns and features include a wide use of interesting sidebars, charts, graphs, pull quotes, pictographs and subheads to provide multiple points of entry for readers into stories. How might you incorporate these to engage readers?

• Our Snap Shots, Private Lessons and Regional sections are three places where writers who have never worked with us before can break in. Please note the section in which you are interested on the outside of your envelope to ensure that your query reaches the right editor for that section.

You are better off being early—even considerably early—with a query than to be even a little late. Right now, we are thinking about what will be in *Outdoor Life* a year from now. Writers and photographers should be thinking the same way. Though we have millions of readers, we never forget that we reach them one at a time. A reader who picks up a copy of *Outdoor Life* is asking, "What's in it for me?" You are writing for intelligent readers who are eager to learn more about the sports they are most passionate about. Your job is to make it clear and interesting.

• Please be advised that we are free at any time to use story ideas that are the same or similar to yours and that we shall be under no obligation to you unless we enter into a written agreement with you with respect to your story.

• We pay on acceptance.

PREPARING MANUSCRIPTS AND PHOTOS

• Manuscripts must be typed, double-spaced and you must include a copy of your manuscript on a 3½-inch computer disk either as a Word document or MS-DOS file. Number the pages, and type your name and the story title at the top of every page. Leave wide margins. Do not staple or bind manuscript pages. Paper clips are fine.

• Please do not send photographs until your query has been accepted and a formal assignment made.

• Photographers desiring to make "photo-only" submissions should request our photographer's guidelines before sending photos.

We take every possible precaution in handling unsolicited materials. However, we are not responsible for their damage or loss. Submissions not accompanied by a properly stamped, self-addressed envelope WILL NOT be returned.

Categories: Nonfiction—Adventure—Animals—Book Reviews—Conservation—Consumer—Cooking—Crafts/Hobbies—Ecology—Fishing—Health—History—Hobbies—Interview—Outdoors—Photography—Physical Fitness—Recreation—Regional—Sports/Recreation—Travel—Hunting - How-to - Nostalgia—Essay—Personal Experience—Nature

CONTACT: Collin Moore, Exec. Editor/Manuscript Review
Material: All
CONTACT: Joi Harvey, Senior Assistant to the Editor-in-Chief
Material: All
Time4 Media, Inc. /Time, Inc.
Magazine and Publishing Division
Two Park Ave., 10th Floor
New York NY 10016-5695
Phone: 212-779-5257
Fax: 212-779-5366

E-mail: olmagazine@aol.com
Website: www.outdoorlife.com

Outdoor World

Subjects. *Outdoor World* covers all aspects of hunting and fishing from spring gobbler hunting to trolling for walleyes to bow-hunting monster whitetails. It strives to keep readers aware of all aspects of the outdoors by mixing serious conservation issues with informational articles and light-hearted stories.

Length. Features range from 1,000 to 3,000 words.

Contract and Payment. We buy one-time rights, and a signed contract is required. Payment is $250 to $600 for features.

Submissions. Queries accompanied by a SASE are preferred over manuscripts. Published writers should include a resume and nonreturnable clips of their work. Other materials will not be returned without a SASE. Written queries are preferred over phone queries. E-mail is also acceptable. Response time is three to four months. Accepted stories should be sent by e-mail or on a computer disk, if possible, and should be accompanied by typed hard copy. Address correspondence to Brian Lovett, editor.

Photos. *Outdoor World* requires a variety of photography and is very dependent on contributions. We are always in need of good vertical shots with cover potential. Cover images are generally of animals, and should be sharp and vibrant. Each cover relates to the theme of the issue, i.e. white-tailed deer for the bow-hunting issue or elk or mule deer for the big-game issue. Inside photo possibilities are endless. A photography needs list is available upon request. Contact Jennifer Pillath, managing editor.

Outdoor World purchases one-time rights for photography, and payment varies according to the size of the photo used in the magazine.

Photography Rates:
• Front Cover - $500
• More than 1.5 pages - $250
• Full to 1.5 pages - $150
• Half-page to full - $100
• Less than half-page - $75
• Black and white - $50

Categories: Nonfiction—Fishing—Outdoors

CONTACT: Brian Lovett, Editor
Material: All
CONTACT: Jennifer Pillath, Managing Editor
Material: All
Krause Publications
700 E. State St.
Iola WI 54945
Phone: 715-445-2214
Fax: 715-445-4087
E-mail: lovettb@krause.com
Website: www.outdoorworldmag.com

OVER the BACK FENCE

Over the Back Fence

For written submissions used in *Over the Back Fence* or in other publications produced by Panther Publishing, LLC, the following rates and guidelines apply:

Over the Back Fence is a regional magazine serving over thirty-five counties in Southern Ohio. Our approach can be equated to a friendly and informative conversation with a neighbor about interesting people, places and events.

Panther Publishing, LLC purchases one-time North American print publication rights from freelance writers as well as makes assignments for specific articles. We reserve the right to reprint written submissions and will make payment for any additional usage—negotiable, but not to exceed original payment. If a submission has been previously published elsewhere, the date and name of the other publication must accompany text.

QUERIES: It is good to send queries or proposals for stories. This allows Panther Publishing, LLC the opportunity to work with writers in developing the most appropriate stories for our publications. However, you may send samples of your writing style, or may send existing stories for consideration.

SUBMISSIONS: Your manuscript should include your name, address and daytime phone number on the top right corner of the first page. And your name must appear on every page thereafter. Submission on disk is appreciated, but not required for initial consideration.

If on disk, submissions should be saved in an ASCII text format or in a Word file. This disk should be labeled with your name, address, daytime phone number, name of format and name of file. Always send a cover letter with your name, address, daytime telephone number and a brief description of your submission.

Feature stories are usually 1,000 words after editing. A byline will appear in the publication for writers of published submissions, except in the case of paid advertisements, where it may or may not appear.

Our magazine is published quarterly—each February (spring issue), May (summer issue), August (fall issue) and November (winter issue). Please make submissions at least six months to one year before the intended issue. Please consider the season for which your work is submitted.

RATES: Rates begin at 10 cents per word, but may be negotiated depending upon experience. A minimum fee of $25 will be paid in the case of pieces shorter than 250 words. Payment is upon publication (net 15 days).

ASSIGNMENTS: Writers may be selected to complete writing assignments that match their writing styles, interests, specializations, or location and ability to travel to neighboring counties.

TEXT/PHOTO PACKAGES: For writers who want to supply photographs (or illustrations) along with their submissions, please request our Photographers' and Illustrators' Rates and Guidelines.

Rates and guidelines are subject to change without notice. Sample copies of the magazine may be obtained by sending $4.00. For questions or to obtain a subscription, call the number shown below or 800-718-5727

Categories: Fiction—Nonfiction—Arts—Family—General Interest—History—Outdoors—Recreation—Regional—Rural America—Short Stories—Travel

CONTACT: Sarah Williamson, Editor-in-Chief
Material: General
PO Box 756
Chillicothe OH 45601
Phone: 614-772-2165
Fax: 614-773-7626
E-mail: backfenc@bright.net

Overland Journal
Oregon-California Trails Association

The *Overland Journal* is always in need of articles, and all articles received are appreciated and given careful consideration. There are three general requirements for an OJ article:

(1) TOPIC: The focus of an article must be on some aspect of the emigrant trails or the overland migration in western America;

(2) ORIGINAL RESEARCH: An article must reflect some form of original research or interpretation. It should not be just a compilation of information from modern authors' articles or books (i.e., secondary sources.) Original research would include any one or combination of the following:

a) Articles that are based substantially on primary written source material, both published and unpublished, such as diaries, journals, reminiscences, letters, contemporary newspapers, government reports and other archival materials. It is understood that articles of original research can and usually will make use of and have reference to secondary sources, but the main supporting evidence should be taken from primary sources. An exception to this requirement would include articles that interpret, evaluate or analyze secondary sources and published primary sources of published emigrant trail literature;

b) Articles that are based on non-literary evidence drawn from areas of archaeology, technology, geology, geography, cartography, field research, statistics or personal interviews;

c) Articles that are themselves primary sources and are supported by primary and secondary sources, such as an unpublished emigrant diary edited and annotated especially for the *Overland Journal.*

The requirements on documentation and original research are not to imply that the OJ is a scholarly publication primarily written for academic specialists. Quite the contrary, it is a history magazine primarily designed for the lay reader who is interested in the western overland trails and the migration experience. Nevertheless, even with this lay emphasis, there is a need for original ideas and interpretations that are convincingly documented.

Articles submitted for consideration must not be submitted to other publications concurrently;

(3) DOCUMENTATION: All significant evidence, references, assertions, data and facts not commonly known must be well documented. The appropriate form of documentation will depend on the type of evidence used.

The OJ uses endnotes rather than footnotes. Text and notes are based for the most part on *The Chicago Manual of Style.* However, the best reference to use when preparing a manuscript is a copy of the OJ itself. If you do not have a copy, please write to OCTA headquarters to obtain a sample copy.

Endnotes should include author of publication cited, editor if appropriate, exact title (including unusual spelling, capitalization or punctuation), city and state of publisher, publisher's name, date of publication of the source you used and page numbers of text to which you have referred. When quoting from a diary, please give the present location of the diary and whether it has been published. If it has been published, all of the above information about annotation of books would apply.

MANUSCRIPTS

Manuscripts, both text and endnotes, should be typed and DOUBLE-SPACED and average approximately 35 double-spaced pages in length. We also welcome shorter submissions for special use. Lengthy studies of more than 35 to 40 pages will be considered for serialization, but editorial contraction or re-writing to a more focused subject is preferred. We suggest authors give attention to illustration materials and maps to accompany their articles and advise the editor regarding same at the time of submission.

When directly quoting from another source, PLEASE triple check for exact accuracy of spelling, wording and punctuation as the author wrote it. Some sources are difficult for us to obtain for verification. This is of utmost importance when quoting from a diary. When a diarist has not bothered with punctuation, we use four spaces to indicate we think this is the end of a sentence. We do not improve upon spelling, punctuation, etc.

COMPUTER DISKETTES

We prefer original submission of material in printed format, but appreciate your advising us regarding availability of the manuscript in electronic format on diskette. We accept 3.5 inch diskettes from either PC or Macintosh platforms and in a variety of programs.

Submission of the electronic files in the original program format is fine, but we request that the author also save the file a second time in "text only" or "ASCII" format, and send both formats to us on the disc. If illustrations are to be sent in electronic format, please contact the editor regarding scanning requirements.

When submitting manuscripts in electronic format, please keep the copy as clean of codes, hidden or shown, as possible. Avoid any manual or automatic hyphenation of words. Do not use the paragraph return to break lines, only to end paragraphs. If your computer has an endnote code which enables you to move back and forth from body copy to endnotes (microsoft word commonly uses this feature), PLEASE DO NOT USE IT! Prepare your notes in a separate file.

BIOGRAPHY

Please include with your manuscript a brief biography, one to three sentences about yourself that can be used to accompany your article.

Categories: Nonfiction—History—Western

CONTACT: Robert Clark, Editor
Material: All
PO Box 14707
Spokane WA 99214
Phone: 509-928-9540
Fax: 509-928-4361
E-mail: bob@anclark.com

Oxendine Publishing, Inc.

The mission of Oxendine Publishing is to teach college and high school students to be more effective and ethical leaders of the future. We believe that it is vital to help students understand why it is important to be fair, conscientious, and moral leaders in their future careers in business, politics, and government.

Through magazines, related books, newsletters, seminars, and on-line services, Oxendine Publishing strives to be an information source with our staffers viewed as experts in the area of leadership development.

WRITER'S GUIDELINES—The Publications

Oxendine Publishing produces three four-color, glossy magazines for high school and college students, two of which are distributed in Florida and one nationally.

Florida Leader for college students, the company's flagship publication launched in 1983, is read by students at 86 colleges and universities around the Sunshine State. In 1990, Oxendine Publishing started an edition of *Florida Leader* for college-bound high school *Student Leaders*, which is now read at more than 550 public and private high schools statewide.

In October 1993, America's premier leadership-development magazine, *Student Leader*, was unveiled as a forum for the top five percent of active students at nearly 1,400 colleges and universities across the nation.

Primarily produced by Oxendine Publishing staff, *Florida Leader* for college students (see www.floridaleader.com) is published in March, April, and September with a circulation of 25,000. Each issue has a unique theme, and queries for general content are considered for the September issue only. Readers of the college version of *Florida Leader* are above-average college students who likely are involved in several campus activities and may hold one or more leadership positions.

In March, the "Best of Florida Schools" issue is a 48-page annual review that highlights more than 100 outstanding and unusual accomplishments by students and campus organizations. The issue also pro-

files the winners of the hotly contested "Best Student Government" and "Best College Newspaper" Awards.

The 24-page "Student of the Year" issue published in April features the profiles of the 20 winners of the annual Florida College Student of the Year Award, a scholarship and leadership-development program founded by *Florida Leader* (see www. floridaleader.com/soty).

Each fall, *Florida Leader* releases the results of the "What Florida Students Think" survey in the 24-page September issue. General content makes up about half of this issue, and queries from freelance writers are considered. Recent stories include "Nurturing Young Leaders" and "Homecoming Traditions."

The high school edition of *Florida Leader* is published in January, June, and October with a circulation of 44,000. Each 24-page issue includes the following departments: College Life, The Lead Role, Florida Forum, and In Every Issue (a pop quiz and brief "FYI" columns).

Student Leader, a national leadership-development magazine, is published in October, and March with a circulation of 50,000 per issue at 1,400 schools, most of which pay to get the magazine (see www.studentleader.com). *Student Leader* provides practical information and leadership news to help Student Government officers, Greek leaders, resident assistants, honor society leaders, volunteer coordinators, programming staffers, and other campus decision-makers lead more ethically and effectively. Queries are accepted for both issues. See www.studentleader. com for sample articles.

In addition to student readers, *Student Leader* and Oxendine's regional magazines are read by college and high school guidance counselors, career faculty, public relations directors, deans of students, directors of campus activities, college and corporate recruiters, as well as members of the media and legislators statewide.

EDITORIAL FOCUS

Both *Florida Leader* magazines feature academic-major and career articles, current financial aid and admissions information, and stories on other aspects of college life for current or prospective college students.

•Note: *Florida Leader: For High School Students* and *Florida Leader: For College Students* have the same guidelines.

Oxendine Publishing's national magazine *Student Leader* focuses on helping veteran and developing campus leaders become more effective and ethical campus decision-makers, and student government leaders. Typical articles include advice on motivating and organizing students, recent leadership and management strategies, how to balance school, work and extracurricular activities, and news about service and fund-raising projects and achievements nationwide.

WRITER'S TIPS FOR PRINT

Full-length articles (about 900 words) should include five to nine sources, quoting student and collegiate leaders, as well as appropriate sources. For the four Florida publications, primary sources, for the most part, should be from colleges, high schools and businesses within the state. For *Student Leader*, college and corporate sources should be varied geographically and demographically. Writers may query ideas for articles or discuss possible assignments already on the calendar. If possible, state availability of photos with query.

Longer stories (more than 1,000 words for 1-page article) can be placed in their entirety at the website and cut for print for the publication. Sidebar information can also be included at the web or in print.

Copy should be double-spaced and follow AP style. When students are mentioned by name, first reference should include year in school, institution they attend, and if relevant, their major. The full names, titles, addresses, and E-mail addresses of all interview subjects should be included separately with each submission. Articles may be edited for space and content. Writers are responsible for the accuracy of all information in the article. Articles by first-time writers may be used, but only experienced writers will receive payment, which varies from $35 to $75 per piece for Florida publications and from $50 to $200 for *Student Leader*. Payment is made within 30 days after publication. All writers will receive at least one full-color copy of their article. Unsolicited manuscripts or art will not be returned unless accompanied by

M-O

sufficient postage. Send a SASE envelope to receive query response, writer's guidelines, or an editorial calendar, or $3.50 for guidelines and a sample issue.

WRITER'S TIPS FOR WEB

Articles for the *Student Leader* website fall under two categories, Featured Articles and Trendsetters. Featured Articles cover broad topics with a variety of different sources. Trendsetter articles cover outstanding groups and people on specific campuses and highlight their accomplishments. Often, Trendsetter articles are written by the person or group that is involved. Both Featured Articles and Trendsetters are exclusive to the web. Trend-setters should be 500-1,000 words and Featured Articles should be around 1,000.

WHAT SHOULD A QUERY INCLUDE?

A one-page query should include all personal contact information, such as a name, address, phone number, and E-mail address along with a SASE. Include a detailed idea for the article, demonstrating major themes and reader need, as well as key point the article will cover and types of sources to be used. Also, give past writing credits and one or two sample pieces of work. You may include suggestions for the article's format as well as information regarding photo options and artwork. Please include suggestions for titles and subheads also. Direct *Florida Leader* queries to Stephanie Reck and Student Leader queries to John Lamothe.

The query should give a sense of your writing style, not just important information.

Oxendine DOES NOT ACCEPT...

No previously published work will be accepted. Oxendine buys first rights only. Poetry, trivia, puzzles, or straight humor pieces are not accepted for publication. Focus on trends and how students are adapting them to their organizations. Current happenings are too timely for a magazine that publishes three times a year. The information should be practical, not philosophical.

HOW TO CONTACT US

For *Florida Leader*: Stephanie Reck, stephanie@student leader.com
For *Student Leader*: john@studentleader. com
Categories: Teen—Young Adult—College

CONTACT: Submissions Editor
Material: All
PO Box 14081
Gainesville FL 32604-2081
Phone: 352-373-6907
Fax: 352-373-8120
E-mail: info@studentleader.com

Pacific Fishing

GUIDELINES FOR WRITERS AND PHOTOGRAPHERS

For Writers: *Pacific Fishing* is a trade magazine for the U.S. and Canadian West Coast commercial fishing industry. Our audience is primarily commercial fishermen from San Diego to Alaska, and secondarily seafood processors, distributors and brokers. Circulation is around 10,000.

We view fishermen as small businessmen and professionals who are innovative and success-oriented. To appeal to this reader, *Pacific Fishing* offers four basic features:

1. Technical, how-to articles that give fishermen hands-on tips that will make their operation more efficient and profitable;

2. Practical, well-researched business articles discussing the dollars and cents of fishing, processing and marketing;

3. Profiles of a fisherman, processor or company with an emphasis on practical business and technical areas;

4. In-depth analysis of political, social, fisheries management and resource issues that have a direct bearing on West Coast commercial fishermen.

Features usually range between 2,000 and 3,000 words, specific length to be assigned by the editor. For most assignments, we pay $.10 to $.15 per word on publication.

Before sending unsolicited manuscripts, contributors should query the editor with a brief written proposal outlining the article idea and noting whether photographs are available. Contributors should also include samples of their writing unless it is already familiar to the editor. All first-time contributions are submitted on a speculative basis. All proposals will receive our immediate attentions, but please allow 2-3 weeks for a response. Note: Any expression of willingness to consider material from a freelancer does not constitute an assignment, nor does it in any way indicate that the contribution will be purchased. A kill fee of 10% will be paid for assigned articles that are deemed unsuitable.

Only original, previously unpublished manuscripts are solicited. Manuscripts may be submitted digitally; hard copy should be double-spaced on one side of the paper only. Unsolicited manuscripts, photographs or illustrations will not be returned unless accompanied by a self-addressed stamped envelope.

For Photographers: We need high-quality photography, especially color, of West Coast commercial fishing. In general, shots showing people and action (e.g. fishing activity, running boats) are more useful than scenics. We prefer 35mm color slides and usually consider prints for inside use only. Our rates, payable on publication, are:

- Cover: $200
- Inside Color: $100 for full page and larger
- $75 for one-half page up to full page
- $50 for spot photo less than one-half page
- Black and White: 75 for full page and larger
- $50 for one-half page up to full page
- $25 for spot photo less than one-half page
- Table of Contents: $10

Unsolicited photos can be sent to the attention of the art director if they are for general use and not accompanying a written submission. Salient information should be included with the photos, including: location of shot, fishery, year, vessel name, and, if possible, names of people featured prominently in the photo. Name of photographer should be printed on each individual slide.

Clear indication of how to contact the photographer should be included in the submission.

Unless otherwise stipulated by the photographer, photos will be kept on file here if it is perceived that they may be useful within the year to illustrate relevant stories; photos deemed not usable will be returned. A self-addressed stamped envelope is appreciated for this purpose. Photos on file will be returned anytime upon request from the photographer. If preferred, dupe slides or scans may be submitted for our files with the understanding that the original photo could be obtained from the photographer when needed.

Pacific Fishing is the prestige publication of the fishing industry and our editorial and photographic standards are high.

Further inquiries are welcome.

Categories: Nonfiction—Fishing—Recreation—Sports/Recreation

Salmon Bay Communications
4209 21st Ave W, Ste 402
Seattle WA 98199
Phone: 206-216-0111
Fax: 206-216-0222
Website: www.pfmag.com

Pack-o-Fun

If you would like to submit a craft idea for possible publication, we ask that you follow these guidelines:

- Send us a photo of the item or items and a telephone number where you can be reached during the day.
- Write complete, accurate instructions (typed and double-spaced, please). Explain everything someone would need to know to complete the project. Use a current issue of the magazine as a guide.
- Include all patterns. Suggest any illustrations you feel neces-

sary to make things clear. A quick line drawing may save many words of instruction.

• If drawing a cross-stitch or needlepoint chart, draw one symbol for each color, using a black grid and black ink. DO NOT color in chart squares.

• Please include a source for hard-to-find supplies. if a brand name is given, indicate whether a ™ or ® is used with the name. (Look on the packaging.)

We will contact you if we are interested in your project. If the design is accepted for publication, you will be asked to send the item to be photographed.

We are looking forward to seeing your original designs and hope that we will be able to work with you sometime soon!

POLICIES

Final Acceptance

• When you are notified that your design has been accepted for publication, you will be asked to send the completed design to us. We reserve the right to ask you to rework your design or the right to return it if we do not feel that your completed design meets our necessary standard for publication.

Contracts

• Contracts are sent to the designer on the Design-In date, provided the completed design and instructions are in our office. Check the schedule card. The design and instructions must be in our office before we send the contract.

• Payment will be sent 30 days after Design-In date, provided the signed contract is in our office by the due date stated on the contract. Otherwise, payment will be sent within 30 days of the date contract is received.

• You may send your completed design to us earlier than the Design-In date; however, the contract will not be sent until the Design-In date.

Design Fees

• The design fees we pay are based on quality, originality, craftsmanship, complexity, and appeal of the design. We also consider the accuracy and completeness of the instructions.

• All fees quoted are for all rights to the design. Fees are discounted 10% for first rights.

• Six complimentary copies of the issue in which your design appears will be sent to you shortly after the On-Sale date. Additional copies are available to designers at a discounted rate.

Rights

• We buy all rights to the design, which means that you grant us all rights to the design/article, including the right to publish the article in printed form and to publish video productions and other derivative works.

• If you would like to print your original article in another publication after we have purchased all rights, please let us know which publication and the publication date; we will be happy to grant you permission whenever possible.

• You must warrant that you are the sole owner of the design/article, that it is original and does not infringe upon the copyrights or rights of anyone else, and that it has never been published in any form.

• We will buy first rights upon special request, paying 10% less than the originally quoted design fee.

Issue of Publication

• When a design is accepted, we will notify you of the magazine issue in which your design is scheduled to appear. If we move your design to another issue before the Design-In date, we will let you know the new deadline. If we move your design after the Design-In date (after the contract has been signed and payment processed), we will let you know that it has been held-over for another issue, and we will keep you informed of its status.

Manufacturer/Product Names

• We will list manufacturers' names only when use of their specific products are vital to the successful completion of the design.

Completed Designs

• We ask that you send us your completed design so we can photograph it in our studio; the completed design also helps us edit

instructions accurately. We will keep your design until the magazine is published. We will return the design to you shortly after the On-Sale date. If for some reason you need your design returned before then, please let us know in advance, and we will try our best to comply.

Categories: Children—Crafts/Hobbies—Recreation—Skits

CONTACT: Billie Ciancio, Editor
Material: All
2400 Devon Ste. 375
Des Plaines IL 60018
Phone: 847-635-5800
Fax: 847-635-6311

Paddler
World's No. 1 Canoeing, Kayaking and Rafting Magazine

So you want to write for *Paddler*? Great. We'd love to have you. Here's all we ask: Send us stories that are both informative and entertaining. If your article only has one of these two ingredients, then try again before sending it to us. For example, if your destination piece tells us everything there is to know about a particular place to paddle, but does so in a boring manner, then you've only achieved half your goal. Also, to paraphrase Steve Martin (In Planes, Trains and Automobiles): "If you're going to tell a story, have a point—it makes it so much more interesting for the reader."

Paddler is published six times a year and is written by and for knowledgeable paddlers. We cover the whole spectrum—whitewater, flatwater, canoeing, sea kayaking, rafting, sit-on-tops—if you do it with a paddle in your hand, we're all over it. Our core audience is the intermediate to advanced paddler, yet we strive to cover the entire range from beginners to experts. If you're the type of contributor we're looking for, you already know this because our first requirement is that you be familiar with *Paddler* magazine. We ask that you not just read the magazine before querying us, but that you know it. Check out a few issues and think about querying for one of the departments first—that's the easiest way to break into the magazine and those are often the stories we are most in need of—particularly the Hotlines department. Being able to include photos with the piece is also a huge plus, as it means one less step for us.

After sending in your query, please allow up to an eternity for a response, but feel free to bug us along the way—email is best. A SASE must accompany all material if it is to be returned. We assume no responsibility for unsolicited manuscripts, photographs or other material or for loss due to postal negligence, natural disasters or dogs carrying envelopes off to parts unknown. We prefer to receive queries by e-mail or snail mail and we prefer to receive manuscripts by e-mail or 3.5-inch, IBM-compatible disks. Include typed, double-spaced hard copy with each submission, as well as your name, address, telephone number, e-mail and a word count.

We prefer queries, but will look at manuscripts on speculation. No phone queries please. Make your ideas unique. Think creative—not outlandish but original. Remember, we don't know exactly what we're looking for—if we did, we'd simply assign it or write it ourselves. Show us something we haven't seen, not a boring, "Me and Joe" story.

Features: *Paddler* publishes at least three features per issue, trying to give equal representation to all disciplines. They should be between 2,000 and 3,000 words and be accompanied by high-quality photos—preferably slides.

Departments: Submissions should include photos or other art. Again, consider submitting to departments first, especially as a first-time contributor, and be creative.

• *Hotlines*—timely news, exciting developments or humorous happenings relating to the paddling community. Stories should be lively and newsworthy. (150-800 words)

• *Paddle People*—unique individuals involved in the sport. (600-800 words)

• *Destinations*—places to paddle, plain and simple. We often follow regional themes and cover all paddling disciplines. Submissions should include map, photos and all pertinent information. (800-1000 words) Marketplace Review—new boats, paddles, clothing, etc. Paddling Schwag includes gadgets, Into the Wild includes other equipment paddlers use—like headlamps, tents and water purifiers. (250-800 words)

• *Paddle Tales*—short, generally humorous anecdotes. (75-300 words)

• *Different Strokes*—two opposing viewpoints from the world of paddling. Must be first-person and opinionated—no fence-sitting. (600-800 words)

• *Skills*—a "how-to" forum for experts to share their knowledge, from playboating techniques to backcountry safety. (250-1,000 words)

• *Eco*—issues related to the paddling environment, from dam updates to pollution and access issues. (150-800 words)

• *First Descents*—doesn't have to be a river. Any exploratory journey qualifies. But remember, we don't just want good stories, we want good story-telling. Include photos and a map if possible. (700-1,500 words)

• *Innuendos*—essays, generally first-person. Can be humorous or serious and introspective. But should be non-fiction. (800-1,500 words)

• *Book and Video Reviews*—current reviews of interest to a large number of Paddlers—'nuff said. (500-700 words)

Paddler pays 15 to 25 cents per published word 30 days after publication. Rates are based on the experience of the writer and the amount of work we put into the piece. Letters to the Editor ("Eddylines") are unpaid. *Paddler* buys First North American Serial Rights and one-time electronic rights. All subsequent rights revert back to the author.

Photographer's Guidelines: Photo submissions should be 35mm transparencies and/or glossy prints. Dupes are acceptable. Call for details about digital submissions. Photos for "Frames" can be scenic or action but need to be exceptional; photos for "Ender" and "Flip Side" are humorous. Originality and quality count. Feel free to suggest captions. Place name, address, phone number or e-mail on each image. We give one photo credit per image and pay 30 days after publication. Please allow eight weeks for return of photos. Photo Rates: $200-$300 for cover; $100 for full page; $50-$75 for a half-page to full-page; $35-$50 for less than a half-page.

Correspondence: Address all submissions to appropriate department or e-mail.

Categories: Nonfiction—Adventure—Associations—Boating—Conservation—Environment—Fishing—Lifestyle—Outdoors—Physical Fitness—Recreation—Regional—Short Stories—Sports/Recreation—Travel—Paddlesports

CONTACT: Editorial
Material: All
PO Box 775450 • 735 Oak St.
Steamboat Springs CO 80477
Phone: 970-879-1450
Fax: 970-879-1450
E-mail: bieline@paddlermagazine.com
Website: www.paddlermagazine.com

PanGaia
Creating an Earthwise Spirituality

Please refer to *SageWoman magazine.*

Pangolin Papers

PANGOLIN PAPERS is published tri-annually by Turtle Press.

1. We publish literary fiction from short-shorts up to 7,000 words, including novel extracts. We do not publish poetry or genre fiction such as science fiction and romance.

2. We generally respond within two months, or sooner.

3. Simultaneous submissions not considered, but please advise if your ms. has been previously accepted for publication.

4. We can only pay in copies for now. Turtle Press retains first North American serial rights. Copyright reverts to the author on publication.

5. We like crisp copy. Laser prints are fine. Stories on IBM-compatible PC disks using Microsoft Word™ format are acceptable. Disks can be returned on request. E-mail submissions are not acceptable.

6. We follow *The Chicago Manual of Style* and the *American Heritage Dictionary.*

PANGOLIN PAPERS is published summer, winter, and spring by Turtle Press.

Single copies $7.95 + $1.00 postage. Subscription rates one year $20.00, two years $35.00. Canadian subscribers add $5.00 per year in U.S. funds.

Categories: Fiction—Literature—Short Stories

CONTACT: Submissions Editor
Material: All
PO Box 241
Nordland WA 98358
Phone: 360-385-3626

Paperback Parade

Please refer to Gryphon Books in the publisher's section.

Parabola
The Magazine of Myth and Tradition

Parabola is a quarterly journal devoted to the exploration of the quest for meaning as it is expressed in the myths, symbols, and teachings of the world¹s religious traditions, with particular emphasis on the relationship between this store of wisdom and modern life.

Each issue of *Parabola* is organized around a theme. Examples of themes we have explored in the past include Rites of Passage, Sacred Space, Dreams and Seeing, Ceremonies, Addiction, The Sense of Humor, Language and Meaning, The Hunter, and Prayer and Meditation.

TYPES OF SUBMISSIONS

• Articles and Translations

Parabola welcomes original essays and translations. We look for lively, penetrating material unencumbered by jargon or academic argument. We prefer well-researched, objective, and unsentimental pieces that are grounded in one or more religious or cultural tradition; articles that focus on dreams, visions, or other very personal experiences are unlikely to be accepted. All articles must be directly related to the theme of an issue.

All material should be written in clear, grammatical, and fluent English. We are willing to consider submissions by authors for whom

English is not a primary language, but they should be checked carefully by a reader who is fluent in English before they are sent to us.

• Poetry and Short Fiction

We rarely consider original fiction, and then only if directly related to the theme of an issue. We do not accept submissions of poetry.

• Book Reviews and Epicycles

Separate guidelines for book, video, and audio reviews and for retellings of traditional stories are available upon request.

• Readers Forum

The Forum is an expansion of our letters column, in which we invite readers to share their thoughts about the topic of the forthcoming issue (Forum contributions on past issue themes are also welcome, but will only appear on our web site). Contributions to the Forum should be brief, but can be more personal and informal than article submissions. There is no payment for Readers Forum contributions.

SUBMISSION GUIDELINES

1. Length

• Articles run 1000-3000 words

• Book Reviews run 500-1500 words

• Retellings of traditional stories run 500-1500 words

Forum contributions should be no longer than 500 words

2. Query Letter

Please send us a one-page letter describing what you propose to write about and how it relates to a given theme. We will let you know if we are interested, or we may suggest a different approach or subject. If the idea fits into our editorial plans, you will be given a deadline to submit a finished manuscript. Assignment of a deadline does not guarantee acceptance or publication of the article; it only means that we are interested in your idea and would like to pursue it.

Brief queries may be sent via e-mail to editors@Parabola.org. We prefer electronic queries to be included in the body of the message, rather than as attachments.

Our acceptance of a query serves as permission to submit material electronically.

3. Preparation of copy

Typewritten, double-spaced, on standard white letter-size paper (8 ½" x 11"), with wide margins at top and bottom. No onionskin or erasable bond. In the upper left-hand corner of the first page of your article, please type the following information:

1. Your Name

2. Your Address and Telephone Number

3. Your Social Security Number

4. Word Count

If endnotes are used, they should be as complete as possible: include the author's name, book or article title, translator or editor (if applicable), city of publication, name of publisher, date, and page numbers.

4. Electronic submissions

Parabola will accept material submitted on disk or via email, providing we responded positively to a prior query. *Our acceptance of a query serves as permission to submit material electronically.* We prefer to receive attached documents, and can open most Macintosh and IBM-compatible applications. If you include your article in the body of an email message, please use only ASCII text. Your biographical information should be included in the same document as the article; do not send it as a separate attachment. It is very easy for bios to get lost or mixed up if sent as separate attachments. Include your last name in the file name (ie, "smith.doc"), not our name (ie, "parabola.doc").

Do not use "netspeak" either in your query or submission. Upon acceptance we will request your disk or transmission. Parabola will not accept any articles via e-mail without a prior query. If you are sending us a word processing file or disk copy, please try to keep the formatting as simple as possible. In particular, we prefer manually created endnotes to automatic footers.

5. Biographical Information

On a separate page, include a brief (2—3 sentence) biographical description of yourself. Fit the description to the subject matter of the article, e.g., for an article on Tibetan Buddhism, "Smith spent three years travelling in Tibet." Or, a publication credit: "Smith is the author of Pilgrimage in Tibet (W. W. Norton, 1987)." Always include your publisher. When submitting material electronically, please note that "separate page" does NOT mean "separate document."

6. Return Envelope/Postage

All submissions must be accompanied by a stamped, self-addressed return envelope, #10 or larger. Manuscripts without SASE will not be returned.

7. Rights

Parabola purchases the right to use an article in all substantially complete versions (including non-print versions) of a single issue of our journal. We also request the right to use the piece in the promotion of Parabola, and to authorize single-copy reproductions for academic purposes. All other rights are retained by the author.

8. Payment

We do not have a fixed pay rate for articles, but pay each author a portion of a set issue budget, depending on the length of each article and the number of total articles accepted. If an issue includes a few long articles, each author will receive a larger payment; if there are a larger number of shorter articles, each author will receive a smaller amount. Article payment generally ranges from $150 to $400. The payment for epicycles and book reviews is $75. Forum contributions are unpaid. Payment is made upon publication. Publication is not guaranteed.

Categories: Nonfiction—Folklore—Religion—Spiritual—Philosophy

CONTACT: The Editors
Material: All
656 Broadway
New York, NY 10012
Phone: 800-560-MYTH
E-mail: parabola@panix.com
Website: www.parabola.org/

Parade

Thank you for your interest in *Parade*. The following guidelines should help prospective writers tailor and present article ideas for editorial consideration.

Give us a unique perspective on the news.

Parade covers topics as diverse as the 81 million readers we reach each Sunday. Many stories involve news, social issues, common health concerns, sports, community problem-solving or extraordinary achievements of ordinary people. We seek unique angles on all topics-this is especially important for subjects that have already received national attention in newspapers and other media.

Topics must appeal to a broad audience.

• Your subject must have national scope or implications. For example, a story about first-year interns at a Dubuque hospital might have limited appeal, but the subject of job opportunities or work conditions in hospitals across the nation would be of widespread concern.

• Reporting must be authoritative and original, based on interviews that you conduct yourself. Health for example, should quote medical experts rather than simply relating a personal tale.

• Choose a topic that you care about deeply. If your story does not make you happy or sad, angry or elated, excited or curious, chances are that *Parade* readers won't care that much either.

Do not propose spot news, fiction or poetry, cartoons, regular columns, nostalgia or history, quizzes, puzzles or compilations of quotes or trivia. We almost never assign unsolicited technical-science queries or unsolicited queries for interviews with entertainment celebrities, politicians or sports figures.

You should be able to write your article concisely.

Parade has room to publish only the most tightly focused story. Topics that will be compelling and complete at 1,200 to 1,500 words are the only ones worth proposing.

How to submit your proposal to *Parade*:

Assignments are based on query letters of one page-three or four paragraphs should be sufficient. Propose only one topic per query.

The query should include:

• Your central theme or point in no more than a few sentences. If you cannot state the theme in this way the article surely lacks focus.

• Your sources on all sides of the issue. Whom will you interview?

• The story's general trajectory. Briefly, how will you organize it?

• A summary of your most important writing credits.

• Attach one or two writing samples and a self-addressed, stamped envelope and send to the address below.

Parade is not responsible for unsolicited materials. Do not send any valuable or irreplaceable items. Though many queries have merit, because of great volume we can only assign those few that precisely meet our needs and standards.

Again, thank you for your interest, and best of luck in your efforts.

Categories: Nonfiction—General Interest

CONTACT: Sharon Male, Articles Editor
Material: All
711 Third Ave., 7th Floor
New York NY 10017
Phone: 212-450-7000
Fax: 212-450-7284

Parameters
US Army War College Quarterly

Subject: *Parameters* is a refereed journal of ideas and issues, providing a forum for mature thought on the art and science of land warfare, joint and combined matters, national and international security affairs, military strategy, military leadership and management, military history, military ethics, and other topics of significant and current interest to the US Army and the Department of Defense. It serves as a vehicle for continuing the education and professional development of USAWC graduates and other senior military officers, as well as members of government and academia concerned with national security affairs.

Style: Write clearly and simply. Clarity, directness, and economy of expression are the main traits of professional writing, and they should never be sacrificed in a misguided effort to appear scholarly. Avoid especially Pentagonese and bureaucratic jargon. Humdrum dullness of style is not synonymous with learnedness; readers appreciate writing that is lively and engaging. Theses, military studies, and academic course papers should be adapted to article form before submission. In the interests of length, security, clarity, and conformity with the stylistic standards of *Parameters*, the editor reserves the right to edit all manuscripts; however, substantive changes are provided to the author for approval.

Length: Articles of 4,500-5,000 words (18-20 double-spaced pages) are preferred.

Concurrent Submissions: Do not submit a manuscript to *Parameters* while it is being considered elsewhere. Also, do not submit a manuscript if it has been published elsewhere or if it is available on the internet.

Submitting Your Manuscript: Unsolicited article manuscripts are welcome; book reviews are by assignment only. Authors are encouraged to submit their manuscript by e-mail, as an attachment, to Parameters@carlisle.army.mil. Manuscripts also may be mailed to the address below; in that scase include one paper copy and a disk containing the computer file. Paper copies should be double-spaced and printed on one side of the sheet only. Carefully edit your text before submitting it. Include your name, address, daytime phone number, and e-mail address. Indicate whether the disk is Windows or Mac format, and tell us what word processing program you used. Do not submit your manuscript by fax.

Documentation: Documentation is placed in endnotes; a bibliography is not necessary. Indicate all quoted material by quotation marks or indentation. Reduce the number of endnotes to the minimum consistent with honest acknowledgment of indebtedness, consolidating notes where possible. Lengthy explanatory endnotes are discouraged. Endnotes must contain complete citation of publication data; for internet citations, include the date accessed. *Parameters* generally uses the conventions prescribed in Kate L. Turabian, *A Manual for Writers*, 4th ed. (Chicago: Univ. of Chicago Press, 1973).

Biographical Sketch: Include a brief biographical sketch of four to six lines, highlighting your expertise.

Illustrations: Charts and graphs should be used only if they are absolutely essential to clarify or amplify the text. Photos are seldom used, but illustrative black-and-white photos (preferably 5" x 7") are considered.

Clearance: Manuscripts by US military personnel on active duty and civilian employees of the Defense or service departments may require official clearance (see AR 360-1, ch. 6). *Parameters* will assist authors on request.

Honoraria: Upon publication, *Parameters* extends a modest honorarium to eligible contributors.

Review Process: We send an acknowledgment to the author when the manuscript is received. Submissions not forwarded to our referees for further consideration are generally returned to the author within three to four weeks. For submissions sent to our referees, the review process can take from six to eight weeks from date of receipt, sometimes longer.

Our Website: To familiarize yourself with our journal, and to gain a better understanding of our current editorial scope, visit our website.

Categories: Nonfiction—Military—Politics—Public Policy

CONTACT: Col Robert H. Taylor (USA Ret.), Editor
Material: All
US Army War College
122 Forbes Ave.
Carlisle PA 17013-5238
Phone: 717-245-4943/DSN 242-4943
Fax: 717-245-4233
E-mail: Parameters@carlisle.army.mil
Website: www.carlisle.army.mil/usawc/Parameters

Parenting

Parenting addresses readers who are considering pregnancy or expecting a child, as well as parents of children from birth through age 12. The magazine covers both the psychological and practical aspects of parenting.

The magazine is largely freelance written. Fees for articles depend on length, degree of difficulty, and the writer's previous experience. Generally, feature articles run between 1,000 and 3,000 words in published form.

For writers new to *Parenting*, the best opportunities are the departments, which are comprised of pieces that range from 100 to 800 words. Queries for each of these departments should be addressed to the appropriate editor (such as Parenting Reporter Editor, or Ages & Stages Editor).

Put all queries in writing (no phone calls, please), and enclose a stamped, self-addressed envelope for a reply and the return of any materials you submit. Allow about two months for a response, due to the large volume of unsolicited queries we receive. We will not consider simultaneous submissions. In addition, we do not publish poetry.

The best guide for writers is the magazine itself. Please familiarize yourself with it before submitting a query—read several issues if possible. The most successful queries and manuscripts are timely, appropriately researched, well-written, and geared to PARENTING in particular.

Categories: Nonfiction—Book Reviews—Children—Consumer—Education—Family—Folklore—Health—Marriage—Parenting—

Physical Fitness—Psychology—Relationships—Humor—Personal Experience

CONTACT: Submissions Editor (Specify Dept.)
Material:All
530 5th Ave., 4th Floor
New York NY 10036
Phone: 212-522-8989
Fax: 212-522-8699
Website: www.parenting.com

ParentLife
BabyLife

Thank you for your interest in writing for *ParentLife*. We are interested in finding Christian writers who are able to deliver professional journalism. By following these guidelines, you enable us to get to know you, your writing style, and how carefully you can craft an article that will impact parents. At the same time you will have less frustration trying to figure out what our editorial team is really looking for when we evaluate manuscripts.

WHO WE ARE
Our Vision

All articles submitted should be consistent with the vision for our publisher, LifeWay Christian Resources, as well as our magazine.

ParentLife vision: To encourage and equip parents with biblical solutions that will transform families.

LifeWay vision: As God works through us ... we will help people and churches know Jesus Christ and seek His kingdom by providing biblical solutions that spiritually transform individuals and cultures.

Our Audience

Our readers are primarily parents of babies through 12-year-olds. Most of our readers are women, although we are making a concentrated effort to impact more fathers throughout our entire magazine. Our audience is a mixture of stay-at-home moms and dual-income families. We also have a mixture of home school, Christian school, and public school families. We also are sensitive to the needs of single parents, adoptive families, blended families, grandparents, and families with special needs.

HOW TO ESTABLISH A WRITING RELATIONSHIP

We currently accept few unsolicited manuscripts. At the same time, we know that God may have a message that we might overlook if we don't at least glance at the submissions that do come into our office. In your initial contact, we suggest the following:

1. Guidelines

Be familiar with our writer's guidelines and our magazine. If necessary, request a current issue of our magazine by sending us a 10-by-13-inch manila SASE.

2. Bio Form and Resume

In the writer packet we also will send a bio form that must be completed and returned with the rest of the requested information. We will ask you to share about your personal salvation experience and how you are currently serving in your church or community. A current resume is not required, but it will help us identify your formal writing training, experience in feature writing, and recent publishing credits. You will be able to identify topics and subjects which interest you most as a writer on your writer bio form. We do accept Christian writers from various denominational backgrounds. Return the bio form to William Summey, MSN 172, One LifeWay Plaza, Nashville, TN 37234-0172.

3. Clips, Published Pieces, Queries, and Manuscripts

We prefer writers to submit queries you believe of value to parents rather than articles or completed manuscripts. Articles are not returned without a SASE. Journalists will be evaluated on their ability to convey the tone and editorial voice of our magazine and on their ability to write in a clear, concise, and grammatically correct manner.

Please submit these at any time to william.summey@lifeway.com or when you return your bio form.

4. Contracts and Payment

Be patient. We have been known to keep an article for 6 to 12 months before stepping out to invite a new writer to write for us. If you want an immediate yes or no as soon as we receive the article, the answer will be no in most cases. If we decide to accept your article, we will contact you to discuss payment and ask you to sign a non-exclusive rights contract. To process your payment, you will need to verify your social security number, address, and phone number on your contract. You will receive, without cost, one complimentary copy of the issue in which your article is printed. The complimentary copies are processed outside our department, so if you do not receive your copy, you can contact our editorial team and we will be happy to send you some copies.

5. Extra Copies of Magazines

You can order extra copies of the magazines by writing LifeWay Customer Service Center, MSN 113, One LifeWay Plaza, Nashville, TN 37234-0113, sending a fax to Customer Service at (615) 251-5818, or e-mailing customerservice@lifeway.com. Churches can buy our magazine in bulk (five or more copies to one address) for $1.40 per issue by calling (800) 458-2772. Please encourage your church or parenting groups to order our magazines.

6. The Quick Tips

You will find an enclosed tip sheet that will give you an overview of what we are looking for when your article arrives. We suggest that you use this sheet as your guide and make sure that you are writing to our specifications with our mission and target audience in mind.

The Quick-Tip Reference Page For Queries and Submissions

(Please use this sheet as a reminder when sending in your manuscript.)

• I have prayed about and reread my submission, and it reflects a Christian worldview that will distinguish the magazine from other secular parenting magazines.

• Cover page includes title of article; a short writer bio; total word count; writer's full name, phone number, e-mail address (if available), and social security number.

• The article is being submitted in one of the following ways:

1. If the article is being submitted in hard copy form through regular mail, the writer agrees to submit it electronically at the time of contract.

2. If the article is being submitted by e-mail. The attachment can be sent to William Summey at william.summey@lifeway.com.

• Quoted material must be properly documented (source, publisher, date, and page numbers) along with permission verification and a photocopy of the original quote.

• Statistics or factual information which the public would not normally know need to be properly documented along with a photocopy of the information.

• Quoted Bible references must be from the Holman Christian Standard Bible® (HCSB) and do not need to be photocopied.

• Include two blurbs or pull quotes that will quickly draw the reader into your article.

• Include at least one and possibly up to three sidebars that could impact the reader. The sidebar provides helpful information that the reader will value (quick tips, ministries, suggestions, Web sites, books, phone numbers, addresses, and so on).

• Headings and subheading are used throughout the article and relate to the suggested title.

The Quick-Tip Reference Page For Contracted Assignments

(Please use this sheet as a reminder when sending in your manuscript.)

• I have prayed about and reread my submission, and it reflects a Christian worldview that will distinguish the magazine from other secular parenting magazines.

• Cover page includes title of article; a short writer bio; total word count; writer's full name, phone number, e-mail address (if available), and social security number.

• The article is being submitted in one of the following ways:

1. By disk. (If the article is being submitted by disk, a hard copy must also accompany submission. Indicate word processing program on the disk. Microsoft Word is preferred.)

2. By e-mail. (If the article is being submitted by email. *ParentLife* articles may be sent to William Summey at william.summey@lifeway.com. Editors will verify receipt of articles through e-mail.)

• Quoted material must be properly documented (source, publisher, date, and page numbers) along with permission verification and a photocopy of the original quote.

• Statistics or factual information which the public would not normally know need to be properly documented along with a photocopy of the information.

• Quoted Bible references must be from the Holman Christian Standard Bible® (HCSB) and do not need to be photocopied.

• Include two blurbs or pull quotes that will quickly draw the reader into your article.

• Include at least one and possibly up to three sidebars that could impact the reader. The sidebar provides helpful information that the reader will value (quick tips, ministries, suggestions, Web sites, books, phone numbers, addresses, and so on).

• Headings and subheadings are used throughout the article and relate to the suggested title.

Categories: Nonfiction—Christian Interest— Diet/Nutrition— Education—Family—Parenting—Spiritual

CONTACT: William Summey, Editor in Chief
Material: All
One LifeWay Plaza
Nashville, TN 37234
Phone: 615-251-2021
Fax: 615-277-8142
E-mail: william.summey@lifeway.com.
Website: www.lifeway.com

Parents Magazine

We are interested in:

• Articles which offer professional and/or personal insights into family and marriage relationships.

• Articles that help women to cope with our rapidly changing world.

• Well-documented articles on the problems and successes of pre-school, school-age, and adolescent children-and their parents.

• Good, practical guides to the routines of baby care.

• Reports of new trends and significant research findings in education and in mental and physical health.

• Articles encouraging informed citizen action on matters of social concern.

We prefer a warm, colloquial style of writing, one which avoids the extremes of either slanginess or technical jargon. Anecdotes and examples should be used to illustrate points which can then be summed up by straight exposition.

Articles vary in length from 1,500 to 3,000 words. Payment is on acceptance.

We recommend that writers query us by mail, fax or email (no phone calls please) about the article idea before submitting a completed manuscript. Manuscripts should be typed, double-spaced, and must be accompanied by a stamped, self-addressed envelope.

Please allow three to four weeks for a reply.

The Editors/*Parents Magazine*

Categories: Nonfiction—Beauty—Children—Family—Fashion—Health—Marriage—Physical Fitness—Relationships—Women's Issues—Retirement

CONTACT: Wendy Schuman, Executive Editor
Material: All

375 Lexington Ave.
New York NY 10017
Phone: 212-499-2083
Fax: 212-867-4583
Website: www.parents.com

Parents' Press

Who We Are

Parents' Press is a monthly newspaper for parents and expectant parents in the San Francisco Bay Area counties in Alameda, Contra Costa, Marin, San Francisco and Solano. Our circulation is 75,000. Our readers have children ranging from infancy to high school.

What We Buy

Our focus is on practical, down-to-earth articles. We use very little academic, theoretical or personal-experience pieces. No political material, fiction or poetry. Please study the newspaper before submitting ideas. We do not mail out sample copies, but free copies are available at most Bay Area Safeway stores, libraries and children's stores. Back issues are available at some local libraries, or by mail from us for $3 per issue.

Writers

We use up to 3 freelance articles per issue. All manuscripts must be typed, double-spaced and accompanied by a stamped, self-addressed envelope. (If you do not accompany your manuscript with an SASE, we will not return it. We do not respond to query letters that are not accompanied by an SASE.) You may e-mail queries and/or submissions to us at ParentsPress@aol.com. Please include material in the body of the e-mail; we do not download attachments. We do not download or review unsolicited e-mail manuscripts.

Articles on health, education and child development are usually written by professionals in those fields. Good possibilities for non-specialist writers include interviews with well-known Bay Area figures who have young children; places to go with children; parent resources (e.g., crisis hotlines): "how-to" articles on every day aspects for childrearing (e.g., giving a birthday party, buying play equipment, dealing with peer pressure). We seldom use articles that focus on a single organization. Round-up articles should cover the five counties named above. Popular past articles by freelances have included: "Skates and Blades: Bay Area Youths' Hot New Pastimes," "How To Set Up A Parent Co-op," "Air Travel with Children," "Choosing the Right School for Your Child" and "Are You Spoiling Your Child?"

Parents' Press generally buys all rights, including web/electronic publishing (certain rights may be assigned back to the author upon written request). Other rights we occasionally purchase include First North American Serial Rights with a provision for perpetual exclusivity in Northern and Central California. This means that an article that appears in *Parents' Press* cannot be sold without our written permission to any publication whose primary circulation area is in Northern or Central California. We will occasionally buy reprint rights or simultaneous submissions, but pay considerably less for such material and require the same territorial exclusivity. We do not buy material that has been simultaneously submitted to other Northern or Central California publications. You must accompany previously printed or syndicated submissions with a statement of their publishing history.

Payment

Payment ranges from $50 to $500, depending upon the complexity of the material, quality of writing, amount of research and length. Articles generally run from 300 to 1,500 words, occasionally up to 2,500 words. We usually pay within 45 days of publication. If we accept an article that we think may be delayed in getting published, we will pay on acceptance. If you accompany an article with photos, the fee we negotiate with you will include payment for them.

Photographers

We use 10 to 20 black-and-white photos of children per issue. Preferred form is glossy, professional quality 5x7 or 8x10 prints. We encourage the submission of photos of children of different ethnicities, abilities and ages. We require written parental permission for any child whose face is identifiable in a photo, as well as model releases for similarly identifiable adults.

Payment is $15 per photo, paid within 6 weeks of publication; one-time rights. Call Ann Skram at 510/524-1602 to show photos. (You may submit photos by mail, accompanied by an SASE, but we cannot guarantee a quick response.)

We usually purchase one-time rights to one full-color photo for our cover each month. Contact Ann Skram to discuss rates and requirements and to show photos. Slides accompanied by prints or color photocopies are preferred. Model releases are required. Photos showing professional models are seldom used and require special arrangements.

Expenses

Parents' Press will pay certain expenses (mileage, phone, photocopies, film) within limits stated in writing at the time we commission an article. No expenses are paid for articles submitted on spec.

Categories: Nonfiction—Children—Juvenile—Parenting—Teen

CONTACT: Dixie Jordan, Editor
Material: All
1454 Sixth St.
Berkeley CA 94710
Phone: 510-524-1602
Fax: 510-524-0912
E-mail: ParentsPrs@aol.com
Website: www.parentspress.com

Parnassus
Poetry in Review

Thank you for your interest in *Parnassus*. We consider unsolicited poetry and prose year round, and usually respond within two months. However, you should know that virtually all our material is solicited; while we try to give unsolicited work close scrutiny, we almost never publish it. On poetry, we place few restrictions of length, form, or style. As for prose, though, we have no interest in reading academic or "theoretical" work, only criticism that is colorful, idiosyncratic, and written with verve.

Categories: Literature—Poetry

CONTACT: Ben Downing, Managing Editor
Material: Poetry, Poetry Criticism
205 W. 89th St. Apt. 8F
New York NY 10024-1835
Phone: 212-362-3492
Fax: 212-875-0148
Website: www.parnassuspoetry.com/about.htm

Parnassus Literary Journal

Parnassus Literary Journal is a tri-yearly (spring, summer, fall-winter).

We welcome well constructed poetry in any form, but ask that you keep it uplifting and free of language that might offend one of our readers. We have no regularly scheduled contests, but a contest is sometimes sponsored by one of our subscribers. All rights are returned to our authors after publication.

Due to the ever increasing expense of publishing and mailing, we are now asking our subscribers to either subscribe or purchase a copy of the issue in which their work appears. Subscribers are guaranteed a by-line in each issue. I regret this change in our procedure, but it is necessary for survival. We receive no grants and we sell no advertising.

Type your poems on a single sheet of 8½x11 bond (haiku excepted) and enter your name and address at the upper left corner of each page. No carbon copies or onion skin. Clear xerox ok, simultaneous submissions and previously published ok. Haiku on a single sheet of bond,

please. No poetry on half-sheets, 3 x 5 cards, and never more than 3 poems at one time. We do not publish stories, reviews, or articles.

Submit your work in a number 10 envelope with an SASE of like size folded in thirds and sufficient postage for return if necessary. If you do not wish your work returned, so state.

Important: I do not acknowledge submissions, request for guidelines, or queries unless accompanied by a SASE. Nor do I accept work that arrives here with postage due.

Our last issue contained over 145 poets from the beginner to the well known, including Eugene Botelho, Matthew Louviere, David Hay, and many others. Ours is one of the oldest and most respected literary journals in the business. We recommend you purchase a sample copy.

Categories: Poetry

CONTACT: Denver Stull, Editor
Material: All
PO Box 1384
Forest Park GA 30298-1384
Phone: 404-366-3177

The Party Book
Celebrations Magazine

Please refer to Metro Parent/Metro Baby.

Parting Gifts

Please refer to March Street Press, in the Book Publishers section.

Party & Paper Retailer

Formal guidelines not available. Please read a number of issues to ascertain the publication's style and needs.

Send queries to address below.

Categories: Trade—Parties & Paper—Retail

CONTACT: Submissions Editor
Material: All
107 Mill Plain Rd., Ste. 107
Danbury CT 06811-6100
E-mail: editor@partypaper.com

Passages North
Northern Michigan University

Passages North, a biannual literary journal, has been publishing since 1979. The journal features poetry, short fiction, creative nonfiction, and interviews.

General Guidelines

All work submitted should:

• Include your name and address on the top right corner of each page.

Additional Poetry Guidelines

• Poems need not be double-spaced.

• Please submit 3-6 poems only.

Additional Prose Guidelines

• We accept prose up to 5,000 words.

Hints for Writers

• Brief cover notes help.

• Editors review work only from the beginning of September through April.

• Simultaneous submissions are considered.

• If you wish, please include your phone number and/or e-mail address.

• We seldom publish poems over 100 lines.

Payment for accepted work is one copy of *Passages North*.

Subscriptions

Passages North, a voice of the nation from the shores of the Great Lakes, publishes one issue annually. Like all literary journals, *Passages North* is entirely dependent upon its subscribers, occasional grants, and donations. We invite you to take this opportunity to subscribe or renew your subscription. Please make checks payable to *Passages North*.

2 years (2 issues): $23/US, $30/Foreign

1 year (1 issues): $13/US, $16/Foreign

Sample (current issue): $7/US, $9/Foreign

Back issue: $3/US, $5/Foreign

Categories: Fiction—Nonfiction—Arts—General Interest—Interview—Literature—Poetry—Short Stories—Writing

CONTACT: Kate Myers Hanson, Editor

Material: All

Dept. of English, Northern Michigan University, 1401 Presque Isle Ave.

Marquette MI 49855-5363

Passport

Passport

Passport is no longer accepting freelance submissions. We will begin accepting them again in 2007.

Categories: Fiction—Nonfiction—Adventure—African-American—Asian-American—Cartoons—Children—Christian Interests—Crafts/Hobbies—Family—Games—Jewish Interest—Juvenile—Multicultural—Mystery—Religion—Short Stories—Teen—Humor

CONTACT: Submissions Editor

Material: All

6401 The Paseo

Kansas City KS 64131-1284

Phone: 816-333-7000

Fax: 816-333-4439

E-mail: mwonch@nazarene.org

Website: www.nazarene.org

Pastoral Life
Magazine for Today's Ministry

Purpose

Pastoral Life is a religious monthly review designed to focus on the current issues, needs and practical activities related to pastoral ministry and life. It avoids merely academic treatments on abstract and too controversial subjects. It features pastoral homilies for Sundays and Holydays.

Manuscript Requirements

Articles average between 1600-2000 words and shouldn't be longer than 3,500 words. Articles for our Reflections section are between 600-1000 words. Articles should be typed single-spaced and enclosed with a self-addressed return envelope. Articles submitted be e-mail or disk using or translating into Microsoft Word. Long articles should be broken with proper subheadings. Queries are appreciated before submitting manuscripts. New contributors are expected to accompany their material with a few lines of personal data.

Additional Information

Payment of four cents per word. Receipt of manuscripts acknowledged within 14 days. Rejected manuscripts are returned unless otherwise specified. Publishers retain exclusive rights between acceptance and publication. Contributors receive 50% of honoraria when their material is reprinted. Free copies available to contributors.

The editors of *Pastoral Life* invite you to submit manuscripts on any topic similar to the following suggestions (simply meant to be a basis for a wider development of ideas):

Communications

• Parish Outreach through a Media Approach

• Impact of TV/Movies on Faith Values

• Communication within the Diocese/Parish

• New Approach in Home Visitation

• Providing Reading Material for Parishioners

• Liturgy and the New Media

• Improving Public Relations in Your Parish

• How do Parents and Children Communicate?

Counseling

• Counseling the Alcoholic

• Premarital Counseling

• Counseling Victims of an Addiction

• Counseling Youth

• Counseling Servicemen and Veterans

• Counseling Single Parents

• Counseling Divorced, Singles or Widowed

• Counseling the Aged/Homeless

• Counseling Vocations

• Counseling the Depressed

• Counseling in Hospitals

• Counseling in Jails/Detention Centers

• Counseling Victims of Tragedy

Education

• School Crisis— Old and New

• Adult Education

• Continuing Pastoral Education

• Teaching the Catechism

• Sex Education

• OCD Programs

Liturgy and Sacraments

• Options in Sacramental Rights

• Effective Paraliturgies

• Conducting Funeral Services

• Role of Music in Liturgies

• How the Choir Saves the Parish

• Power of the Word in Liturgies

Categories: Education—Inspirational—Religion—Spiritual

CONTACT: Bro. Joshua Seidl, SSP, Managing Editor

Material: Religion

CONTACT: Fr. Arthur J. Palisada, SSP, Associate Editor

Material: Religion

Society of St. Paul, PO Box 595

Canfield OH 44406-0595

Phone: 330-533-5503

Fax: 330-533-1076

E-mail: plmagazine@hotmail.com

PC Magazine

Formal guidelines not available. Please read a number of issues to ascertain the publication's style and needs.

Send queries to address below.

Categories: Computers, Technology

CONTACT: Submissions Editor

Material: All

28 E. 28th St.

New York NY 10016

Phone: 212-503-5100

Remember: Editors change jobs and publishers change addresses. It is wise to invest in a phone call for the current information before submitting.

PC World

What kind of magazine is *PC World*?

PC World is a monthly magazine providing real-world reviews, advice, feature stories, news, and how-to support to people who buy manage, and use IBM and compatible computer systems for professional productivity. It is geared to a consumer audience of business decision makers who are responsible for making their personal computers work on the job. *PC World*'s circulation exceeds 1,000,000 copies per month.

Who Writes for *PC World*?

We look for writers who have a clear writing style and a degree of technical knowledge appropriate to a knowledgeable PC user audience. This combination of talents can make it difficult to break into our pages. Freelance writers contribute to all sections of the magazine.

We pay varying amounts depending on the author's experience, the quality of the writing, and the length of the piece. The fee is negotiated with a staff editor whose specialties include the subject area under consideration. At every stage of every article, editors work closely with writers to generate the best work possible.

Though most of our regular writers are people we're familiar with, we do welcome queries from those who are new to us. One way we discover new talent is by assigning short tips and how-to pieces.

What's the Best Way to Proceed?

Our first suggestion is to be familiar with the magazine. Read some issues, understand the editorial focus (why particular topics are covered, what level of knowledge is imparted), and learn what the magazine's sections are and what goes into each one.

Once you're familiar with *PC World*, you can write us a query letter if you have an idea for a review, how-to, news item, or feature. Your letter should answer the following questions as specifically and concisely as possible:

- What is the problem, technique, or product you want to discuss?
- Why will *PC World* readers be interested in it?
- Which section of the magazine do you think it best fits?
- What is the specific audience for the piece (e.g. database or LAN users, desktop publishers, and so on)?

PC World editors ask these questions when considering ideas for every piece in the magazine, and we expect you to do the same. So send us a letter with your ideas, but please do not send unsolicited manuscripts, clips, or any disks: We will not be able to return them. If we're interested in your query, we'll contact you for more information and proceed from there.

Thanks again for your interest in *PC World* magazine. We hope this information is useful. Feel free to write us.

Categories: Nonfiction—Computers—Technology

CONTACT: Proposals
Material: Queries
501 - 2nd Ave.
San Francisco CA 94107
Phone: 415-243-0500
Fax: 415-442-1891
E-mail: letters@pcworld.com
Website: www.pcworld.com

Pearl
A Literary Magazine

SUBMISSION GUIDELINES

Pearl is a 96-128 page, perfect-bound magazine featuring poetry, short fiction, and black & white artwork. We also sponsor the Pearl Poetry Prize, an annual contest for a full-length book, as well as the Pearl Short Story Prize, an annual ficiton contest. Our annual poetry issue contains a 12-15 page section featuring the work of a single poet, and our annual fiction issue features the winner of our short story contest, as well prose poems, "short-shorts," and some of the longer stories submitted to our contest. Submissions are accepted September through May only. Manuscripts received in June, July or August will be returned unread. We do not read email submissions. We report back in 6-8 weeks. Work accepted for publication appears 6-12 months from date of acceptance. Please send submissions and correspondence to:

POETRY

Send 3-5 previously unpublished poems with cover letter and SASE. Simultaneous submissions must be acknowledged as such. We prefer poems no longer than 40 lines, though we occasionally consider longer ones. Our format and page size, however, will not accommodate lines of more than 10-12 words. So unless you're Walt Whitman or Allen Ginsberg, please consider your line breaks.

FICTION

Send previously unpublished stories with cover letter and SASE. We only consider short-short stories up to 1200 words (about 5 manuscript pages). Longer stories (up to 4000 words) may be submitted to our short story contest only. All contest entries are considered for publication.

ARTWORK

Send camera-ready, black & white artwork spot-art (either photocopies or originals) and SASE. Accepted artwork is kept on file and used as needed.

BOOK-LENGTH MANUSCRIPTS

We do not consider unsolicited book and chapbook manuscripts for publication.

PAYMENT

Contributors receive a copy of the magazine as payment. Additional copies may be purchased at a 50% discount.

SAMPLES

We recommend reading our magazine before submitting. For a sample copy, send $7 check or money order payable to: *Pearl*, 3030 E. Second St., Long Beach, CA 90803. If you wish to receive a copy of the all-fiction issue, please specify.

Categories: Fiction—Poetry—Short Stories

CONTACT: Joan Jobe Smith or Barbara Hauk, Poetry Editors
Material: Poetry
CONTACT: Marilyn Johnson, Fiction Editor
Material: Short Fiction
3030 E. Second St.
Long Beach CA 90803
Phone: 562-434-4523
Fax: 562-434-4523
E-mail: PearlMag@aol.com
Website: www.pearlmag.com

A Premier Online Literary Magazine

The Pedestal Magazine

As editors of *The Pedestal Magazine*, we intend to support both established and burgeoning writers. We are committed to promoting diversity and celebrating the voice of the individual. We are currently receiving submissions in the following areas:

- **Poetry:** We are open to a wide variety of poetry, ranging from the highly experimental to the traditionally formal.
- **Pay Rate:** $30-$60 per poem
- **Fiction:** We are receptive to fiction of all sorts, including literary, experimental, science fiction, and fantasy; however our interests do lean towards works that cross genres, works that do not readily fall into one specific category.
- **Pay Rate:** $.05 per word
- **Non-Fiction:** We are open to academic/scholarly works, as well as works that focus on issues of aesthetics, psychology, philosophy, and religion.
- **Pay Rate:** $.05 per word
- **Length:** up to 6,000 words

The Pedestal Magazine does not accept previously published work, unless specifically requested; however, we will accept simultaneous submissions. At the time of publication, all rights revert back to the author/artist; however, *The Pedestal Magazine* retains the right to publish your piece in any subsequent issue or anthology, whether in print or online, without additional payment. Should you decide to republish the piece elsewhere, we ask that you cite *The Pedestal Magazine* as a place of previous publication and provide *The Pedestal Magazine*'s web address.

Due to the number of submissions we are currently receiving, *The Pedestal Magazine* has implemented reading periods. We accept submissions according to the following schedule: Our new issues are released bimonthly on the (give or take a day or two) 21st of the month. During a month in which an issue of the magazine is released (February, April, June, August, October, and December), we close submissions beginning a week prior to the release date, and reopen submissions a week after the release date; for example, we close submissions on August 14 and reopen them on August 28. In addition, during the odd month (January, March, May, July, September, and November), we close submissions for one week, from the 12th to the 19th. We will receive submissions at all other times. Here is a clear breakdown of our submission cycle:

Closed

January 12-19	July 12-19
February 14-28	August 14-28
March 12-19	September 12-19
April 14-28	October 14-28
May 12-19	November 12-19
June 14-28	December 14-28

Submissions

Online submissions only at: www.thepedestalmagazine.com

We will be open to submissions at all times other than those periods listed above.

We thank you for your incredible support of *The Pedestal Magazine* and look forward to receiving your work.

Categories: Fiction—Nonfiction—Poetry

Website: www.thepedestalmagazine.com

Pediatrics For Parents

Pediatrics For Parents emphasizes an informed, common-sense approach to childhood health care. We stress preventative action, accident prevention, when to call the doctor and when and how to handle a situation at home. We are also looking for articles that describe general, medical and pediatric problems, advances, new treatments, etc. All articles must be medically accurate and useful to parents with children—prenatal to adolescence. *Pediatrics For Parents* is not a general parenting magazine and will not consider such material.

Professional Submissions by Medical and Dental Authorities: We will consider articles previously published in professional journals if rewritten for our lay audience. All articles must be in an active voice, avoiding medical language while adhering to our strict standards of factual accuracy. Explanatory articles on body functions, disease processes and treatment approaches would be on target. We are also looking for articles on wellness, prevention, and modes of interaction between children, parents and medical and dental professionals.

Submissions by Non-Medical and Dental Authorities: We are interested in original, well researched, factual, and informative articles on topics described above. Articles must be authoritative and specific with reference citations accompanying each article. We are not particularly interested in "first person stories" unless they are extremely moving or contain a large amount of information.

Submission Requirements: All articles must be typed, single spaced, and have 1 inch margins. Use block paragraph style as exemplified by this page. Don't use proportional spacing or full justification. Capitalize the first letter of titles, subtitles, etc. Use single space to separate sentences, etc. Put your name, address and phone number on a title page only and not on subsequent pages. Don't number your pages. Please staple the pages of your articles. Copies are acceptable.

Submission Format-Electronic: We prefer to receive articles via email. We can read most formats, but prefer Word. We do not publish photographs, although drawings and diagrams may be used. If you wish to have your article, diagrams and drawings, please send a self-addressed stamped envelope. Otherwise, articles cannot be returned. Articles will be returned within 6-8 weeks if not accepted. We will consider reprints.

Fillers and Short Articles: We do not accept these items.
Length: 150-2000 words.

Payment: Our pay schedule varies depending on the type of article, its length, and our needs. Payment is also influenced by the quality of expression, importance of topics, amount of research and/or expertise involved. We generally pay between $5 and $50 per article. Payment is on publication.

Sample Copy: We strongly recommend you read a couple issues of the newsletter the get a flavor for our publication. Sample copies are available free for downloading on our website at www.pedsforparents.com or for $3 each, postage paid.

Categories: Nonfiction—Children—Health

CONTACT: Submissions Editor
Material: All
Pediatrics For Parents, Inc.
PO Box 63716
Philadelphia PA 19147
Website: www.pedsforparents.com

Pen America
A Journal for Writers and Readers

Unfortunately, due to extremely limited staff and other resources, at present we are unable to review unsolicited submissions except from members of PEN.

As you may have noticed, almost all of the content to date has been drawn from PEN events or from books that received awards from the organization. We hope that as the journal's circulation and reputation grow, we will soon be able to attract enough funding to sustain a more inclusive editorial process. Until then, however, I'm afraid it's PEN all the way. Our calls for submissions are distributed as needed via e-mail or membership mailings, so we have no prepared guidelines for you to include.

Categories: Nonfiction—Politics—Writing

CONTACT: Bridget Cross, Managing Editor
Material: All
568 Broadway, Ste 401
New York NY 10012
Phone: 212-334-1660 Ext.115
E-mail: journal@pen.org
Website: www.pen.org/journal

Pennsylvania Magazine

WHO ARE WE? *Pennsylvania Magazine* is a privately owned, bimonthly publication produced by a team—our staff and people like you, the freelance contributors throughout the state who have contact with the topics that our subscribers will enjoy. Since our name is Pennsylvania, all topics we cover must have an obvious link to someone, something, or some event within our borders. And, since our subscribers live in all parts of the state, your topic must also have an interest to this widespread audience.

THE SUBSCRIBERS OF *Pennsylvania Magazine* expect the magazine to be a source of timely articles about interesting people, unique places, fun festivals, and fascinating history. When our readers exclaim, "I didn't know that about Pennsylvania," we have succeeded and they are likely to renew their subscription.

WE RELY ON FREELANCERS. Therefore, we've included more advice and comments in our guidelines than you may find in others'. We've found that when we begin with a contributor who knows how we work, much time is saved in queries, rewrites, photographs, and other aspects of the publishing routine. So please take the time to review these guidelines thoroughly.

Begin With a Query Letter

WE LIKE TO WORK FROM QUERIES. This simple letter that briefly explains your idea saves time and effort for both of us. Within four weeks of our receipt of your query, you'll receive one of the following responses:

1. Go ahead with your idea. Guidance as necessary for completion of your article will be provided.

2. We need more information to make a decision. You will be asked to supply illustration samples for your topic, provide more information about your topic, or supply something else so that we can determine if our subscribers will find your topic of interest.

3. Send this idea to another publication. This idea is not what our subscribers look for in our magazine. If possible, we will direct you to another publication that may be interested in your topic.

Hints for Your Query

1. If you are sending a multiple query, use a separate sheet of paper for each topic. This helps us respond faster.

2. Explain how you would cover the topic and give an estimated word count.

3. Consider these topics first:
- Historical events (past).
- Travel with a historical interest (specific theme, i.e. hex signs, steeples or geographic area—county, region).
- Vacation/weekend trip ideas within the state.
- People/family success stories—see Panorama.
- General interest subjects that are related to happenings in Pennsylvania.
- Statewide roundups of attractions, resources, happen-ings, etc.

4. We usually avoid these topics: Hunting, skiing, fashions, exposes and scandals, film and product reviews, government/church/borough/institution anniversary-related events.

Template for Your Query Letter to *Pennsylvania Magazine*

Today's date
Your name/address
City/State/Zip Department/Feature
Phone Number Estimated word count
If seasonal, when the article should run

RE: Article subject

Introduction paragraph—who you are, why you suggest this topic now to *Pennsylvania Magazine*, why the subject would be of interest to our readers.

Explain what types of photos you can supply to illustrate your subject. Enclose photocopies of existing illustrations for your topic, or of photos similar to the ones you will supply.

What is your expected timeline for completion? Is this a simultaneous submission? Has this been printed previously elsewhere? Have you seen coverage of this topic in other publications?

Your name
List any enclosures

Tips

1. In your query, send photocopies of available illustrations or tell how you will provide them.

2. Do not send original slides at any time.

3. Do not send originals or anything valued by you or the owner (such as an old photo or certificate). Send a photocopy when you query.

4. We want people-related photos. With few exceptions, we do not want photos of building/structures (such as, "This is the house William Penn built.") or rooms/an empty field/etc. as the only illustration.

5. We prefer to begin with a written query, but if you already have a ms, you can send us a photocopy (include how you will handle illustrations).

6. Tell us if your material has been printed or is being considered elsewhere.

7. Do not send samples of previously published work.

8. Send your ideas often. The wider the choice, the more likely of a go-ahead.

9. We strongly suggest you send for a sample copy ($2.95 prepaid) if you are not already familiar with the magazine.

When an Article Is Submitted

SUBMITTING MATERIALS: Send your article and its illustrations together. Do not have an illustrator or photographer send illustrations to us under separate cover. We can wait for you to assemble all components of an article package before sending it to us. Provide names and addresses of photographers or artists whose work is used. You will need to supply written permission for our use of photos/illustrations from owners/copyright owners) and their names so we can provide credit.

EDITING: All written materials submitted to us are subject to editing for style, clarity, flow, and organization. This editing is intended to keep a cohesive, familiar style for readers of the magazine.

STYLE NOTES: We use the Associated Press Stylebook. Do not use the terms first, only, or unique unless you can prove it. Include a citation with your text.

Write in the active voice. Location of a person, place or event should usually be cited in the first paragraph and include the county—Terry Smith of Camp Hill in Cumberland County. Omit county references for the following: Erie, Harrisburg, Lancaster, Philadelphia, Pittsburgh, Scranton, Allentown, Bethlehem, and York.

DEADLINES: We operate without rigid deadlines for most stories. If your item is appropriate for an upcoming issue, and we expect that you are able to complete it for that issue, we'll give you a deadline. Otherwise, articles are scheduled in the magazine when we have a suitable text/illustration package and the subject/geographical location fits a niche in the content of a specific issue.

ASSIGNMENTS: When we respond favorably to a query from a potential contributor who has not worked with us before, this does not constitute an assignment (and we will not pay a kill fee if the materials are not acceptable).

A contributor new to us submits only on speculation.

Payment for accepted materials is usually made upon acceptance. It may sometimes follow editing if the writer has exceeded the word limit.

Unless we specify otherwise, we purchase first, one-time use rights of your original materials. We then own our edited, published version.

You can resell your original copy elsewhere after our publication of your material.

Payment Information
RATES: We pay 10 to 15 cents a word, depending on the amount of editing required. (Payment for reprinted articles is five cents per word.)

We pay $15 to $25 for each photo you take, depending on the number we use. For a cover, we pay up to $100. Photos you obtain from a subject's file: $5 each. We may suggest a flat package fee for an article with illustrations.

MINIMUM RATES: We pay a minimum of $50 for each item (copy and one photo) appearing in the PANORAMA and MUSEUM departments—more if two photos and/or copy exceeding 350 words are used.

EXPENSES: We seldom pay expenses. The only expense that we usually pay is for the reasonable fee for reproduction of a photo or illustration provided by a museum, library or historical society.

Quick Reference
CREDITS: In the author credit at the end of the article, we like to mention your hometown, county, and any related interest you may have in the subject of your article.

COPIES: Upon publication, we will return your materials with two copies of that issue. Additional copies can be purchased for $2.50 each, plus a shipping charge, prepaid.

COPYRIGHT: We copyright each edition of the magazine with the Lbrary of Congress.

Specifics Regarding Content Features
ALMANAC AND GENERAL: Usually range between 1,000 to 2,500 words in edited form and cover historical items (places, people, and events), travel with a people focus, and topics of current interest. GENERAL FEATURES must be illustrated with a majority of color photos; ALMANAC ITEMS should have period photos or appropriate illustrations. Published articles range from two to six pages.

Departments: Usually range between 250 to 900 words.

PANORAMA items cover people and organizations involved in noteworthy projects/festivals, unusual activities, or significant achievement.

MUSEUM items usually cover collections in the state that are open to the general public on a regular (not appointment) basis.

AMERICANA PHOTO JOURNAL includes one to four interesting photos and a lengthy (250 words) caption about a single topic.

PHOTOGRAPHY ESSAY highlights our annual Photo Contest entries. The contest is announced in the first two issues of the year, and winners are announced/published in the fourth.

Details on Photography
WE ALWAYS ASK OUR CONTRIBUTORS TO supply photographs with articles. If you don't own or are not familiar/comfortable with a camera, we suggest that you join a photography club in your area to refine your skills. We believe that you will sell more material to us and other publications when you can supply the illustrations as a package.

We prefer people to be in photographs for articles and department items. This is for scale and personality. In close-up shots, we should have people's names and addresses (if their photo is used, we'll send a copy of that magazine).

People should be doing something or talking to one another to give the photograph vitality. Objects important to the article can be in the foreground or background, and people can also be shown looking slightly off camera. The best way to show people in a natural setting is to ask them questions and shoot as they respond, remembering to direct their attention away from you and the camera. A flash on the camera should not be used unless the background wall is at least 10 feet away.

We do not want original slides and will not be responsible for them. We prefer color prints (4" x 6" to 5" x 7") and can use duplicate slides. We have found that Kodacolor, if shot in a contrasting setting (sunshine and dark areas in the same scene) will result in either over- or under-exposure. Seek shade or all sun in a scene. If faces are in shade or backlit, use flash for fill-in.

Articles about resorts, parks, etc. should have a people focus, with them in the fore- or background of shots. We don't need model releases. But if a person notices you taking a picture and objects, do not take or use it. Do not send us photos of Amish people. We need to identify people when appropriate. For example, staff in a museum or attraction photo.

We may hold your submission for some time, so do not send us your only copies of original illustrations. Make and send a copy.

Categories: Nonfiction—History—Regional

CONTACT: Matthew K. Holliday, Editor
Material: All
PO Box 576
Camp Hill PA 17001-0576
Phone: 717-697-4660

Pentecostal Evangel

Please note: About 95 percent of our material is done by assignment. Only a small percentage of free-lance articles are accepted. Before submitting an article, please adhere to the guidelines below.

What Articles We Use
Christian living. How to better understand the Bible, develop a richer prayer life, live more victoriously, overcome personal problems, etc.

Soul winning, conversions and answers to prayer. Often written in the first person or "as told to."

Doctrinal. The baptism in the Holy Spirit, the Second Coming (premillennial in viewpoint) and divine healing. Physical healings must be endorsed by a minister acquainted with the case.

Salvation appeal. Strong evangelistic appeal targeted to the unsaved (250 to 500 words).

Home and family. Helps for building Christian homes. Include illustrations from life. Avoid preachiness.

Seasonal. New Year's, Easter, Pentecost Sunday, Mother's Day, Father's Day, Thanksgiving, Christmas. Submit at least six months in advance.

Current issues. Adhere to doctrinal positions of the Assemblies of God.

News. News pieces and photographs from free-lancers are printed in the News Digest, occasionally. If you can report on a major event connected in some way with the Assemblies of God or with religious issues, please call our office. Generally, stories written about a church, Bible college or some religious institution do not receive payment. If the story requires independent research, payment can be negotiated.

Human interest. To glorify God for what He is accomplishing through individuals, groups or churches. People like to read stories about sacrifice, courage, victory, etc.

Regular features. Send material for "etc.," "Talk-back" and "Letters."

Poetry. Poetry is not being accepted at this time.

To Help You Meet These Needs
Read the *Pentecostal Evangel*. Study current issues for slant, content and style.

Be thorough. Give attention to sentence structure, spelling and word selection. When quoting a Scripture passage, check the Bible for wording, spelling and punctuation. Please indicate which version is used.

Keep the reader in mind. The *Pentecostal Evangel* is the voice of the Assemblies of God and is read by both Christians and non-Christians.

Pray. The *Pentecostal Evangel* goes into homes, prisons, public libraries and many other places. Pray that your article, if published, will bless many.

If your manuscript is returned, it does not mean the work is of poor quality; it may mean we already have similar material. We are unable to give reasons for rejection of manuscripts because of time constraints; however, each manuscript is carefully read and appraised.

Mechanics of Preparation

Manuscripts. Should be typewritten or printed on a letter-quality or near letter-quality printer (preferably not dot matrix), double spaced, with your name, address and social security number in the upper left-hand corner of the first page. The approximate number of words should be in the upper right-hand corner. Keep a copy in your personal file; we cannot be responsible for safekeeping of manuscripts.

Postage. Your manuscript must be accompanied by a self-addressed envelope and sufficient postage, if you need it returned.

Article length. From 500 to 1,200 words.

Multiple submissions. No multiple submissions, please. Do not submit a manuscript to the *Pentecostal Evangel* and some other publication at the Assemblies of God Headquarters at the same time.

New writers. Please tell something about yourself.

Queries. Submit your manuscript without query.

Rate of payment. We pay up to 6 cents a word for first-rights articles by free-lance writers. Payment is made upon acceptance. Writers will receive complimentary copies of the *Pentecostal Evangel* in which the article appears. Second rights are paid at approximately half of first-rights material.

Rights. We purchase first or second North American serial rights, plus nonexclusive reprint rights, which includes electronic reproduction.

Photos. Guidelines are available upon request for free-lance photographers.

Developing an Article

1. Organize and outline.
- Make a preliminary selection of the content.
- Determine purpose and scope.
- Choose a working title.
- Make a preliminary outline (whether or not it appears in the finished manuscript).
- Conduct necessary research. Use personal experiences. Get information through interviews and conferences. Study published and written materials.

2. Write the first draft.
- Interest the reader with a strong lead.
- Make the writing flow smoothly. Bridge gaps with good transition. Use relationship-showing devices. Write clear and concise paragraphs. Introduce new ideas with topic sentences.
- Make the writing colorful. Use illustrations. Incorporate dialogue. Integrate anecdotal and illustrative material. Leave the reader with a strong takeaway.

3. Check your writing style.
- Does the article move? Give background that is interesting and needful, but don't bore the reader.
- Is it understandable? Use words that are familiar to the reader. Avoid technical jargon.
- Is it lively? Use concrete words. Choose active verbs. Don't overwork adjectives.
- Is it readable? Watch grammar and spelling. Avoid long, involved sentences. Cut down on number of parenthetical and qualifying expressions. Avoid cliches.

4. Rework your manuscript.
- Appraise it for content and approach. Does it say what you want?
- Edit your own material.
- Check spelling, grammar and Scripture references

Categories: Nonfiction—Christian Interests—Family—Home—Religion—Spiritual

CONACT: Submissions Editor
Material: All
1445 N. Boonville Ave.
Springfield MO 65802
Phone: 417-862-2781 ext 4109
Fax: 417-862-0416
E-mail: pentecostalnews@ag.org
Website: www.pentecostalevangel.ag.org

Penthouse

1. The best way to discern the material *Penthouse* might be interested in is to look at the magazine. Articles are usually related to current affairs or topics that would appeal to our readers (predominately male, aged 18-49). Subjects might include celebrity or sports figure profiles, exposes on government or corporate affairs, and analyses of trends in lifestyle or sexuality. Interviews should be exclusive queries on personalities who are obviously of interest to a diverse audience.

2. Queries should include a detailed description of your article, who or what your sources will be, and how you plan to present the material. Queries should demonstrate an in-depth knowledge of the subject. Proposals for photo essays should be accompanied by slides or suggestions for sources of art.

3. Please submit any credits, clips or other examples of your published writings, if available. A stamped, self-addressed envelope is essential for a reply or return of material.

4. Features run 3500 to 5000 words and shorter articles for our "View From The Top" section are 600-700 words.

5. Writer's fees and expenses are negotiated when an assignment is made. Features pay from $2,500 to $5,000, depending on length and complexity of subject. Shorter pieces pay $250. Payment is made on acceptance. There is a 25% kill fee on assigned articles.

6. Forum letters should carry name and address, though these will be changed by the editor. All letters become the property of *Penthouse*. We do not pay for letters but your submissions are welcome.

7. All letters should be sent to address below. Designate Editorial Department and appropriate editor (i.e., features, fiction, sports, forum).

Bedtime Stories, Women's Erotic Fiction Section Writer's Guidelines: Thank you for your interest in "Bedtime Stories," *Penthouse*'s women's erotic fiction section. Stories for the column should be well-developed, well-plotted, erotic in nature, written by a woman, and between 2,000-2,500 words in length. The main character or voice should be female. We request that the stories contain no bondage/discipline, S/M, painful anal sex, fist fucking, excessive come on the face, or minors (which includes reflections on adolescence—no one even thinking about being younger than 19). We also request that the material be unpublished, and that it not be submitted to any of our associate publications during the time we are reviewing it. If it is being considered elsewhere, please make note of that in your cover letter.

The manuscript should be double spaced, with 1" margins, on white paper. Please make sure the pages are numbered, and that your name, address, phone number, and social security number appear on the first page. The fees vary per author and individual story. We do request that writers use their own names, not pseudonyms; if this is a problem for you, please consider it before submitting material.

We will return submissions which arrive with envelopes large enough to accommodate them. If not, they will be discarded.

We look forward to hearing from you soon.

Categories: Fiction—Nonfiction—Entertainment—Erotica—Fashion—Food/Drink—Government—Humor—Interview—Lifestyle—Recreation—Sexuality—Society—Sports/Recreation

CONTACT: Barbara Rice
Material: Bedtime Stories
CONTACT: Peter Bloch
Material: All
1110 Pen Plaza Floor 12
New York NY 10001
Phone: 212-702-6000
Fax: 212-702-6279
Website: www.penthouse.com

Remember: Editors change jobs and publishers change addresses. It is wise to invest in a phone call for the current information before submitting.

Penthouse Variations

Thank you for expressing interest in *Penthouse Variations* magazine.

Contributions to *Variations* should be neatly typed and double-spaced with one-inch margins. Proper grammar should be used as well as the kind of language you would be proud to share with a good friend. If you are making a professional freelance submission to be published as one of our featured stories, be sure to clearly indicate this in a cover letter to the editor. *Variations* publishes 3000-word, first-person narratives of credible erotic experience, squarely focused within a specific category. *Variations* does not accept electronic story submissions or pay for material sent to the editorial office via e-mail. For your material to be considered for publication as a lead story, you must send a manuscript to the editorial office with your legal name and mailing address printed on the first page. Payment for an accepted, fully revised manuscript is up to $400.00. One contributor's copy is mailed to each author of a featured story upon publication. *Variations* does not publish poetry of any kind.

Manuscripts take six to eight weeks to be read. They are rejected usually because of the quality of the writing or because the category described is unsuitable or oversold to us. We strongly recommend that you read several issues of the magazine to become familiar with our categories, style and vocabulary.

Variations is proud of its reader-generated letter sections and less experienced writers should feel free to make submissions to the editor on this basis, either by surface mail or e-mail. Letters to *Variations* magazine are assumed intended for publication and republication in all media, in whole or in part, edited or unedited. All letters become the property of *Variations*. We do not make payments for letter material. We guarantee confidentiality of all material, both letters and articles. In fact, we choose pseudonyms in order to avoid writers libeling themselves in choosing their own.

Categories: Fiction—Alternate Life-style—Erotica—Gay/Lesbian—Sexuality

CONTACT: Submissions Editor
Material: All
11 Penn Plaza, 12th Floor
New York NY 10001
Phone: 212-702-6000
E-mail: variations@generalmedia.com
Website: penthouse.com

Perdido
Leadership with a Conscience

Editorial description & audience

Perdido is a magazine devoted to examining organizational life in all its forms. "Leadership with a Conscience" means that we are concerned with what's happening in organizations that are mission-oriented—as opposed to merely profit-oriented. *Perdido* is focused on helping conscientious leaders put innovative ideas into practice. We seek articles on management techniques as well as essays on social issues. Perdido publishes feature articles, interviews/profiles, book excerpts, and book reviews. The common thread is being the questioning of easy answers and examining issues from a socially-aware, progressive perspective.

Our readers are managers, CEOs, executive directors, vice presidents, and program directors of nonprofit and for-profit organizations. We try to make the content of *Perdido* accessible to all decision-makers, whether in the nonprofit or for-profit world, government, or academia. *Perdido* actively pursues diverse opinions and authors from many different fields.

Writer's guidelines

In general, follow *Associated Press Stylebook and Libel Manual* guidelines. Humor, opinion, and innovative insights into management, leadership, and organizational issues are sought-after qualities in writers. *Perdido* is interested in new management trends, concepts, practices, philosophies, business leaders, and authors. Articles should use stories and anecdotes to put these ideas into a useful context.

Any article submitted to *Perdido* should possess a strong (i.e., humorous, compelling, shocking, thought-provoking, perplexing, enigmatic) lead.

In terms of writing style, *Perdido* favors clear, concise, active writing that tries to entertain the reader. Jargon, unnecessarily big words, passive constructions, and italicized, foreign phrases like zeitgeist or mise en scène (unless used ironically) are heartily discouraged. Journal articles belong in journals and research papers belong wherever it is they are published. Dry, excessively technical, or just plain dull articles will be handled with steel tongs and placed in the appropriate receptacle. Strunk and White's *The Elements of Style* and William Zinsser's *On Writing Well* are excellent guides to the kind of engaging, accessible prose we strive for at *Perdido*.

Offensive speech is a particular no-no for *Perdido* in that many of our readers work in human services. Sexist, bigoted, and stereotypical language is obviously not welcome—nor is speech offensive or insensitive to minority groups and people with disabilities. The *Publication Manual of the American Psychological Association* is a good reference for using language that is not unnecessarily offensive. Common sense is probably the best guide.

Queries and submissions...

We accept queries with published clips for feature articles. If you are interested in writing a book review, please send a sample book review (published or unpublished) and your resume. We usually respond in about four weeks to queries and submitted manuscripts. Articles should be submitted via mail or e-mail. If submitting the article by mail, please include a double-spaced printout of the file. If an article is accepted for publication, you will be required to provide a digital file. Files in Microsoft Word for Mac or Windows, WordPerfect for Mac or DOS/Windows, or any word processing application are acceptable.

Every article should include a title, author, submission date, and word count.

Deadlines...

Perdido is published quarterly—Winter, Spring, Summer, and Fall. Deadline for copy, photographs, and artwork is always 45 days prior to the publication date, i.e.; Winter: Nov. 15; Spring: Feb. 15; Summer: May 15; Fall: Aug. 15.

Articles and queries should be directed to: Mary Rundell-Holmes, Editor, *Perdido* Magazine, 3650 W. 183rd Street, Homewood, Illinois 60430. E-mail and computer files can be sent to: editor1@hightidepress.com.

DEPARTMENTS...

Fast Foreword

This one-page (500-750 words) article comes at the beginning of the magazine and usually relates a story from personal experience that imparts some insight or lesson in leadership or management. It is always written by *Perdido*'s editor-in-chief, Art Dykstra.

Points of Interest/Voices Carry

News items/quotes, culled from a variety of sources by *Perdido* editorial staff.

Book Reviews

Perdido always features one main and one alternate book review per issue. This is normally two pages (750-850 words) and covers a new or recently-published book important to the fields of management, leadership, business, technology, trends, self-improvement, or psychology. Usually this a book that we want to recommend to our readers. However, if the book warrants a negative review and it's an important title, we will run it.

One alternate book is usually reviewed following the main selection. These are shorter (650-700 word) reviews of similar books that are determined to be less significant than the main selection.

Perdido Puzzler

Usually a crossword puzzle written by staff, the Puzzler is open to anyone who can originate a good management/leadership-related puzzle (not necessarily a crossword puzzle, but something challenging).

Rewind

A companion to Fast Foreword, Rewind is usually on the last page or two pages of the magazine and is similar in form to Fast Foreword. It is created by *Perdido* staff.

Features...

1500-5000 word articles on a wide variety of subjects. Investigative reports, interviews, and profiles of businesses, programs, and individuals in a variety of fields are all desirable story formats for *Perdido*. The focus of any article should always relate in some way to the issues surrounding leadership, management, human resources, current events that impact organizational life, technology as it applies to the workplace, and/or psychology. Current trends in business, new ways of doing things, new concepts and models should always be sought out.

Pay rates for submissions...

Features of 1500-5000 words are paid at the rate of between $0.05 and $0.07 per word upon publication. Book reviews are paid a flat rate of $75.00 upon publication.

For samples of *Perdido*'s content, visit us on the Web at: www.perdidomagazine.com.

E-mail us at editor1@hightidepress.com to request a sample issue.

Categories: Nonfiction—Business—Leadership

CONTACT: Mary Rundell-Holmes, Editor
Material: All
High Tide Press, 3650 W. 183rd St.
Homewood IL 60430-2603
Phone: 708-206-2054
Fax: 708-206-2044
E-mail: managing.editor@hightidepress.com

PEREGRINE
The Journal of Amherst Writers & Artists

Peregrine
The Journal of Amherst Writers & Artists

Peregrine has provided a forum for national and international writers for twenty-four years, and is committed to finding exceptional work by beginning as well as established writers. We seek work that is unpretentious and memorable. No work by or for children. Peregrine features poetry, fiction, and short personal essays. Each work is read by several readers. Final decisions are made by the editors. Published annually, designed by Barbara Werden, cover art by Barry Moser, Peregrine is professionally printed, perfect-bound with glossy cover. No unsolicited manuscripts for our AWA Chapbook Series.

FICTION: 3,000 word limit. Double space. Indicate word count on first page.

POETRY: 3-5 poems, each poem limited to 70 lines (and spaces). Indicate line count for each poem.

PERSONAL ESSAYS: 1,200 word limit. Double space. Indicate word count.

• we accept manuscripts postmarked October 1 to April 1
• original, typed/word processed, unpublished work
• no electronic submissions
• up to 3 manuscripts a year; simultaneous submissions OK.
• cover letter with name, address, day/evening phone numbers, 40 word bio (max).
• If you use a pseudonym, provide legal name for mailing purposes.
• #10 self-addressed stamped envelope (SASE) for our response.
• for manuscript return: affix sufficient postage. (otherwise, we'll recycle)

• for acknowledgment of manuscript receipt: self-addressed stamped postcard (SASP)

Submission Deadline: April 1 (postmark)

The editors make decisions after reading ALL incoming manuscripts. Send submissions and all other correspondence to the address below.

Current copy of Peregrine: $12. Sample copy, $10 (ppd). Check payable to AWAPress

3-year subscription $25, 5-year subscription $35, Lifetime Subscription $250.

• Subscriptions and Gifts are fully tax deductible. Friends of Peregrine ($100 or more).

Names listed in Peregrine & receive 5% discount on all AWAPress books.

Categories: Fiction—Poetry—Short Stories—Writing

CONTACT: Submissions Editor
Material: All
Amherst Writers & Artists Press
190 University Dr.
Amherst, MA 01002
E-mail: awapress@aol.com (e-mail contact preferred)
Website: www.amherstwriters.com
Phone: 413-253-3307
E-mail: awapress@aol.com
Website: www.amherstwriters.com

Persimmon Hill

Persimmon Hill magazine is published quarterly by the National Cowboy and Western Heritage Museum for an audience interested in western art, history, ranching, and rodeo. Circulation approximately 15,000. Buys first North American rights; byline given. Accepts no reprints. Pays on publication. Query with clips and self-addressed, stamped envelope. No phone, Fax, or E-mail queries are accepted. Allow a minimum of six weeks for a response from the editor and editorial board. Sample copy $10.50, including postage and handling. Annual subscription $30.00.

Non-fiction:

Historical and contemporary articles on notable persons connected with pioneering the American West; western art, rodeo, cowboys, western flora, animal life, or other phenomena of the West of today or yesterday. Articles must be historically accurate. Sources must be documented. We require lively, top-notch writing for a popular audience. Length: no more than 1,500 words. Pay ranges from $100 to $250, including illustrations.

Regular Departments:

• Around the Western States—Short features (500 to 750 words) on events in the West or interesting places to visit.

• Great Hotels of the West—historic lodges, hotels or inns, 1000 words or less.

• Western Entrepreneurs—contemporary craftsmen who are keeping traditional western gear and trappings alive, 1000 words or less.

• Western Personalities—contemporary western men/women who are making a positive contribution to the western lifestyle, 1,000 words or less.

Photos:

Black and white glossy prints or color transparencies, submitted and purchased with the manuscript. Captions required. *Persimmon Hill* will not be responsible for any loss or damage to original or historic photographs or documents. If materials are of heirloom quality, copies should be made.

Format for Submissions:

All manuscripts must be typed, double spaced, using front side of paper only. Computer discs accompanied by a letter quality print-out are required. Discs must be in a software program that is compatible with Word Perfect 6.1. Software program information must be provided with the manuscript. Discs will not be returned. We prefer not to receive E-mail manuscripts.

Tips:

Send us a story that captures the spirit of adventure and individualism that typifies the Old West or reveals a facet of the western lifestyle in contemporary society. The availability of superior illustrations or photographs strongly influences the sale of an article to us.

Categories: Nonfiction—Adventure—Animals—Antiques—Architecture—Arts—Biography—Book Reviews—Careers—Collectibles—Conservation—Cooking—Entertainment—Environment—Fashion—Folklore—History—Lifestyle—Literature—Native American—Outdoors—Regional—Rural America—Travel—Western

CONTACT: M. J. Deventer, Editor and Director of Publications
Material: Western Themes
National Cowboy and Western Heritage Museum
1700 N.E. 63rd Street
Oklahoma City OK 73111
Phone: 405-478-6404
Fax: 405-478-4714

Personal Branding Magazine

The only publication on Personal Branding.

Peter Montoya's *Personal Branding* magazine is the only source for the critical secrets you need to become a Personal Branding scholar and develop the skills to achieve the success you desire.

• Each full color issue is a power-packed user's manual of insights, how-to tips and real-world branding stories:
  • Profiles of some of today's hottest Personal Brands
  • Personal Branding basics
  • Practical brand strategies for entrepreneurs
  • Career advancement tactics for corporate professionals
  • Ideas on using Personal Branding in sales, financial services and more

Personal Branding Press

For Personal Branding Press, please refer to their listing in the Book Publisher section of this directory.

Categories: Business—Careers—Money & Finances—Advertising, Sales

CONTACT: Peter Montoya, Publisher
Material: All
Personal Branding Press
1540 S. Lyon St.
Santa Ana CA 92705
Phone: 714-285-0900
Fax: 714-285-0929
E-mail: info@petermontoya.com
Website: www.petermontoya.com

Phantasmagoria

Guidelines for Submission

1. Send previously unpublished short stories or poems of literary merit, and include SASE for return of your work.

2. Fiction—typed and double-spaced short stories of 4,000 words or less. Send only one story at a time.

3. Poetry—typed poems of 100 lines or fewer. Send no more than six poems at a time.

4. Faxed or emailed submissions will not be read.

5. As payment, contributors will receive two copies of the issues in which their work appears.

6. *Phantasmagoria* acquires First North American Serial Rights. All other rights revert to the author upon publication.

Categories: Fiction—Literature—Poetry—Short Stories

CONTACT: Abigail Allen, Editor
Material: All
English Dept.
Century Community and Technical College
3300 Century Ave. North
White Bear Lake MN 55110

Phi Delta Kappan

Phi Delta Kappan, the professional journal for education, addresses policy issues for educators at all levels. An advocate for research-based school reform, the *Kappan* provides a forum for debate on controversial subjects. The annual PDK/Gallup Poll is published in September. Published since 1915, the journal appears monthly September-June. A volume index is published in the June issue. The *Kappan* is also indexed in Education Index and in Current Index to Journals in Education; available on microfilm, University Microfilms, Inc., Ann Arbor, Mich.

Following are brief answers to the more common questions asked by persons interested in publishing in the *Phi Delta Kappan*.

What makes an article acceptable to the editors?

We look primarily for two qualities: educational significance and readability. There is no easy formula for achieving these goals, since there are many kinds of significance and many different styles that are readable. However, we believe that to be significant an article must in some way be usable by our readers—to enlarge their knowledge, to improve their practice, to influence their decisions. We want it to deal with real problems. We want it to be factual, logical, and well focused. To be readable, it should avoid the use of jargon, it should include concrete examples, it should not waste words, and it should display—if at all possible—some wit and erudition.

What are the procedures for submission of manuscripts?

Very simple: type your manuscript, double-spaced, and send one copy to the editor. If YOU want your manuscript to be returned if it cannot be published, enclose a stamped, self-addressed envelope. In your cover letter, give us sufficient information about yourself for a standard author-identification paragraph.

If you wish, send a letter of inquiry first, describing the article and perhaps including an outline. We must balance our coverage; sometimes we can tell you, on the basis of an outline, whether an article will fit in with our editorial plans.

Who makes the decision to publish?

The editor. Often, she will consult with the other editors or with other members of the Phi Delta Kappa professional staff. Sometimes, if she is undecided, she will solicit the opinions of several of the editorial consultants listed on the *Kappan* masthead.

What is the ideal length?

We like some very short pieces. For example, the manuscripts we use in the Prototypes section and our occasional humorous pieces tend to run 1,000 words or less in length. Feature articles vary between 1,500 and 5,000 words.

What editorial style is used?

Kappan style is based largely on *The University of Chicago Manual of Style*. For footnote style, see past issues of the *Kappan*.

What about diagrams, tables, graphs, photographs?

We use graphic material quite sparingly. The rare diagram, table, or graph that we find indispensable will be reset to our specifications. We will consider photographs, either black and white or in color, but they should be of professional quality. Amateur photography is seldom usable.

Do you pay for manuscripts?

Very seldom. Usually we pay an honorarium only when we solicit an article from a well-known authority or from a professional writer.

How can I contribute to one of the special sections?

Special sections are generally planned by the editors and/or a guest editor many months in advance, and most of the articles are solicited from individuals who have published original work on the topic. We do not announce special sections in advance, largely because we wish to preserve some flexibility. But special sections never fill entire issues; thus we are always seeking good manuscripts on a variety of topics.

Who holds copyright on *Kappan* articles?

Phi Delta Kappa, Inc., generally does. Each issue is fully copyrighted. But an author may give permission for one-time use and retain all other rights.

How long does it take for the editors to make a decision?

We acknowledge all unsolicited manuscripts immediately upon receipt. We try not to hold a manuscript longer than two months without returning it, accepting it, or in some way communicating with the author. But in the months when more than 100 unsolicited manuscripts come in, we sometimes fall behind schedule. If two months pass and you have not heard from us, please feel free to phone our office.

ILLUSTRATOR GUIDELINES

Phi Delta Kappan is a journal for professional educators—school superintendents, teachers, school board members, state and federal education department staff. The journal has been published since 1915; our current circulation is about 100,000.

A few articles in each issue are illustrated on an assignment basis by freelance artists from around the country. Artists are selected to receive assignments based on the samples they submit to us and their previous experience as professional illustrators.

Most of the illustrations we require are color. Many types of media are appropriate—pencil, graphite, acrylic, gouache, wash, ink, paper collage, construction—but most illustrations are now submitted as digital art and are sent on CD or via e-mail.

Illustrators are expected to work from the original manuscript, concept notes, or the design director's sketches to come up with rough or thumbnail sketches to show a choice of concepts and compositions. These may then be selected, refined, or altered by the editors or design director.

Further, we would like to remind everyone that we would prefer to choose from (and are more likely to approve) illustrations that feature diverse people in a variety of roles. Remember—not all elementary teachers are women—not all people are white—not all school administrators are men—and school children reflect our nation's history as the melting pot of the world.

To be considered for freelance assignments, please send printed samples (or e-mails) of your work that can be kept on file. Be sure to include samples of both color and black and white work. Generally three to ten samples are acceptable. Please label each sample with your name, address, and telephone number. If the sample was published, please include the name and date of the publication and any information you wish to include about the nature of the assignment.

We pay on acceptance of the final art and receipt of invoice. Payment is for one-time use. The artist retains copyright. Original art is returned to the artist after publication and any reprint requests are forwarded. We provide a number of tearsheets (usually about 90) of the printed piece. We do not pay for incomplete or unacceptable work.

The general time frame for assignments is two to three weeks from the assignment to the final deadline.

Address samples to: Design Director, *Phi Delta Kappan*, PO Box 789, Bloomington, Indiana 47402-0789. Or send samples via e-mail (or your portfolio web address) to cbucheri@pdkintl.org. Please do not send original work or telephone with inquiries.

CARTOONIST GUIDELINES

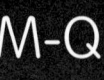

Phi Delta Kappan is a journal for professional educators—school superintendents, teachers, school board members, state and federal education department staff. The journal has been published since 1915; our current circulation is about 100,000.

We prefer to receive original cartoons in print format so that all of our editors and designers can easily review them. Please include an SASE of sufficient size and with sufficient postage to return your work. We recommend submitting 8 to 20 cartoons in a packet.

If you choose to submit copies rather than originals, please send the original immediately when we notify you that we will be purchasing the work. Also, please note any cartoonist guild or association memberships you hold. Be sure that your name, address, and phone are on the back of each cartoon, and that your artwork is signed. Cartoonists retain copyright to any cartoons that we publish. Reprint requests will be forwarded. Please be sure that we have your current contact information.

Cartoons must deal with some aspect of the issues in education to be considered for purchase. (Editorial cartoons should deal with issues that will continue to be newsworthy for a few months.)

Further, we would like to remind everyone that we would prefer to choose from (and are more likely to purchase) cartoons that feature diverse people in a variety of roles. Remember—not all troublemakers are boys—not all principals are men—not all elementary teachers are women—not all people are white—not all elementary teachers who are women are mean—and just once in a great while—could the cat beat the dog to the homework ? (We haven't heard from the cat lobby yet, but I'm expecting a letter any day.)

We've had the great good fortune to work with many terrific cartoonists over the years. They have always provided the most enjoyable moments of our days. We welcome you to join their ranks, but please understand that the competition is pretty fierce—we review many hundreds of cartoons every month and can publish only a tiny fraction of them. We will do our best to review your work within six to eight weeks.

Categories: Nonfiction—Arts—Cartoons—Education

CONTACT: Pauline B. Gough, Editor
Material: All Other
CONTACT: Design Director
Material: Illustrations
CONTACT: Cartoon Editor
Material: Cartoons
CONTACT: Cartoons
408 N. Union
PO Box 789
Bloomington IN 47402-0789
Phone: 812-339-1156
Fax: 812-339-0018
Website: www.pdkintl.org

PHOEBE
A JOURNAL OF LITERARY ARTS

Phoebe
A Journal of Literary Arts

Phoebe seeks to publish quality writing. Do not send formulaic writing, romance fiction, or greeting card poetry. We welcome experimental writing.

All submissions must be typed. Address submissions to Poetry or Fiction Editor. Enclose an SASE with sufficient postage for return of manuscript. Submissions without an SASE will not be returned. If you want your manuscript to be recycled, please tell us. Keep a copy of your work, as *Phoebe* cannot be responsible for lost or damaged manuscripts.

Reporting time can be up to three months, though it is usually sooner. We do not read during June, July, and August.

Contributors receive two copies of the journal upon publication. *Phoebe* also sponsors poetry and fiction contests each year.

Categories: Fiction—Literature—Poetry—Writing

CONTACT: Poetry Editor
Material: Poetry
CONTACT: Fiction Editor
Material: Fiction
MSN 2D6
George Mason University
4400 University Dr.
Fairfax VA 22030-4444
Phone: 703-993-2915
E-mail: phoebe@gmu.edu
Website: www.gmu.edu/pubs/phoebe

PieceWork
Needlework and History, Hand in Hand

PieceWork is a bimonthly magazine with high visual impact focusing on the historical aspects of needlework around the world. *PieceWork* readers are passionate about and do needlework; they value the role needlework has played, and plays, in the ongoing human story. Well-researched feature stories explore the historical traditions of needlework, including needlepoint, embroidery, cross-stitch, quilting, knitting, crocheting, basketry, beadwork, lace making, and surface design. *PieceWork* readers want to know the origin of the various needlework techniques, how they were done, who did them, and why. Striking examples of the technique are important. Readers also want to know how they might use a technique today. Therefore, several articles in each issue have associated projects that use the technique to produce a high-quality finished item that readers will want to keep or present as a gift.

SUBMISSIONS

Features: We invite submissions of complete manuscripts related to most aspects of historic needlework, textiles, and fiber arts. Stories focusing on a particular person in needlework history are encouraged. Material submitted for publication should display in-depth knowledge of the subject matter and carefully documented research with all sources acknowledged. Visuals are critical; manuscripts should include a list of appropriate visuals and where each may be obtained.

Projects: We invite submissions of design sketches and/or color charts for hands-on projects in any of the techniques mentioned above. Projects should display technical expertise in the technique. Include an outline for the instructions, along with a list of diagrams and/or illustrations, necessary to complete the project.

Keep a copy of everything. If the submission is unsolicited and/or you wish any part of it to be returned, include a self-addressed envelope with sufficient return postage. *PieceWork* is published six times a year in January, March, May, July, September, and November. Issues are planned six to twelve months in advance, and we prefer to have materials intended for a particular issue at least six months before the month of publication.

MANUSCRIPTS

If you are not already familiar with the content, style, and tone of the magazine, we suggest you read a few issues. Historical and technical accuracy are essential but the tone should be personal. Use primary resources such as letters and diaries whenever possible to make the story arresting to the reader. Strive for clear organization as you convey information, but also include vivid detail and engaging quotations to give readers a sense of people, place, and meaning: you are telling a story. Please include a brief informal personal biography. A list of sources for "Further Reading" is very helpful.

We expect that the article you ask us to consider has not been published nor is it presently submitted elsewhere. If any part of your submission has been published previously, please let us know when and by whom. If possible, submit copies of the manuscript electronically either via email (piecework@interweave.com) or on a disk in addition to sending a hardcopy. All manuscripts not produced on a computer should be typewritten and double-spaced. Manuscript length may vary from 1,000 to 5,000 words depending on the subject matter.

VISUALS

Please include all the information you have about supporting visual materials you think will enhance the story. Museum photographs are preferable; if citing a piece in a museum collection as a supporting visual, please include the accession number of the object whenever possible. Some visuals (such as a family photograph showing a vintage piece of clothing) can only be provided by you. When you submit your manuscript, however, photocopies of such will be acceptable. If an article is accepted, arrangements for receiving publication-quality color transparencies, black-and-white glossies, color prints, or color slides will be made by the *PieceWork* staff. You also may be required to ship actual pieces and tools to the *PieceWork* office for photography. We will work together to choose what will best suit the story and make sure all pieces are transported safely. All photographs and other materials will be returned promptly and appropriately insured.

ACCEPTANCE, EDITING, AND PAYMENT

Receipt of your submission will be promptly acknowledged, but we may not be able to make a decision about its use right away. Please be patient. We are primarily looking for manuscripts that fit within the issue themes outlined on the editorial calendar. All unrelated manuscripts are considered on an issue-by-issue basis depending on the available space in the magazine. When we pay for accepted material we purchase first North American serial rights for publication in *PieceWork* and subsequent non-exclusive rights for use in other Interweave Press publications and promotions. The author retains the publication rights for the original materials. Payment rate is $100 per printed page based on a two-column galley of the edited text without visuals or illustrations (approximately four manuscript pages or 800 words) and is made upon publication unless other arrangements are made. Projects are contracted for separately. If a project design is accepted, most materials for completing the project will be supplied to you and the finished item will be retained by *PieceWork*. Before your work is published, we will send you an agreement stating the terms of acceptance and payment for your approval. We reserve the right to edit your material as necessary to fit the style, format, or other requirements of *PieceWork*. Thank you for your interest in *PieceWork*. We look forward to hearing from you.—Jeane Hutchins

Categories: Nonfiction—Crafts/Hobbies—History—Hobbies

CONTACT: Editor
Material: All
Interweave Press
201 East 4th St.
Loveland CO 80537-5655
E-mail: piecework@interweave.com
Website: www.interweave.com

Pig Iron Series

Formal guidelines not available.

Send queries or book proposals to below address.

Categories: Fiction—Nonfiction—Adventure—Arts—Experimental Fiction—Family—History—New Age—Poetry—Religion—Short Stories—Spiritual—Western—Writing

CONTACT: Heather Krygowski, Administrative Assist.
Material: All
Pig Iron Press
PO Box 237
Youngstown, OH 44501

The Pinter Review
The University of Tampa Press

The Pinter Review Prize for Drama will recognize an original work of contemporary drama with hardcover book publication by the University of Tampa Press, a $1,000 cash award, a public reading in Tampa, and royalties on sales of the published book.

Guidelines

1. Manuscripts may consist of one original full-length play or two or more shorter plays. Entries should be typed, with pages consecutively numbered (suggested length 85-150 pages). Clear photocopies are acceptable. Portions of the manuscript may have previously appeared in print, provided this is clearly acknowledged and that the work has not previously appeared in its entirety

2. Please submit your manuscript as loose pages held only by removable clip or rubber band and enclosed in a standard file folder. Do not staple or bind your manuscript.

3. Entries should include two title pages, one with author's name, address, phone number, and e-mail address (if available), and one with no author information. A one-page summary of the play should also be included. Author's name should not appear within the manuscript.

4. Include a nonrefundable handling fee of $20 for each manuscript submitted. Make check or money order payable to "University of Tampa Press."

5. The winner will be announced by Spring of each year, with publication scheduled for the Fall. Enclose a stamped, self-addressed postcard for notification of receipt of manuscript, and a stamped, self-addressed envelope for notification of contest results. No manuscripts will be returned. All paper entries become property of University of Tampa Press and those not chosen will be recycled. All contestants enclosing SASE will be notified following the final selection.

Deadline for submissions:

Must be postmarked by December 31 of each year.

CONTACT: Submissions Editor
Material: Manuscripts
The Pinter Review Prize for Drama
The University of Tampa Press
401 West Kennedy Blvd.
Tampa FL 33606

Pipeline & Gas Journal

Please refer to Oildom Publishing.

Pipeline News

Please refer to Oildom Publishing.

PITTSBURGH

M-C

Pittsburgh

It's your town. Make the most of it.

Mission: PITTSBURGH magazine is the monthly community publication for Western Pennsylvania, Eastern Ohio, Northern West Virginia and Western Maryland. PITTSBURGH presents issues, analyzes problems and strives to encourage a better understanding of today's community to more than 75,000 readers.

Style: Each issue features a mix of stories that includes a "people" profile, in-depth news and a service piece, plus feature and lifestyle stories for our target reader: primarily 30ish, professional, with children. Without exception-whether the topic is business, travel, the arts or lifestyle—each story is clearly oriented to Pittsburghers today and the greater Pittsburgh region of today. We have minimal interest in historical articles. PITTSBURGH does not publish fiction, poetry, advocacy pieces or personal reminiscences.

Scheduling: Seasonal story ideas should be submitted at least six months in advance. Each issue is fully scheduled at least four months in advance; feature ideas that do not fit that timeframe cannot be considered. Short (under 200 words) timely items for UpFront can be considered as late as six weeks before publication.

Payment & rights: Features vary from $300 up, depending upon length and complexity of story, and experience of writer. Feature fees are negotiated separately. UpFront items start at $50, up to $150. Most feature stories and service pieces range from 1,200 to 4,000 words, in-depth news features up to 4,000. We purchase first North American serial rights; second rights, only when the article has not appeared in the same geographic market.

Submission: Address all queries to the executive editor. PITTSBURGH prefers to receive a brief query with a sample lead and one-page outline, not completed manuscripts. We will, however, review manuscripts on spec. Writers should enclose samples of their writing when submitting queries. We do not assign stories to new freelancers. All queries will be answered within two months. We do not respond to unsolicited email, fax, or phone queries. Manuscripts and other materials will be returned only if the writer includes a self-addressed stamped envelope, or can be picked up at the office. The writer guarantees that the piece is his or her own work and is not plagiarized.

After acceptance: Once a story is accepted, we will review the first draft and, possibly, ask for changes and a second draft. The writer is responsible for completing all research deemed necessary by the editors. We also need a list of sources and their phone numbers for fact-checking.

Categories: Regional

CONTACT: Michelle Pilecki, Executive Editor
Material: All
4802 Fifth Ave.

Pittsburgh PA 15213-2918
Phone: 412-622-1360
Fax: 412-622-7066

The Plain Truth

OUR PURPOSE

The goal of *The Plain Truth* is to inform, inspire and encourage. Our biblically based insight is fresh and relevant, offering hope in a world of shattered lives, corrupted values and meaningless existence. We stand for the renewal of faith and values, seeking to reach those who have given up on Christianity and God.

OUR READERS

Circulation of The PT is approximately 60,000 in the United States and Canada. Our average reader is 54 years of age. The female-male ratio is 52-48.

WRITING FOR THE PT

If you are interested in writing for us, here's what we look for in a standard article:

Personal interest: Material should offer biblical solutions to real life problems. Both first person and third person illustrations are encouraged.

Creative thinking: Articles should take a unique twist on a subject. Material must be insightful and practical for the reader, moving him or her toward a closer relationship with Jesus.

Biblical accuracy: All articles must be well-researched and biblically accurate without becoming dry and boring. We seek to make the Bible plain to our readers by bringing the Scriptures to life.

Compelling logic: Use convincing arguments to support your Christian platform. Make it clear to the reader where you are going, and make it difficult for him or her to turn down your invitation to follow.

Colorful personality: Use vivid word pictures, simple and compelling language. Avoid stuffy academic jargon and Christian "inspeak." Captivating anecdotes are vital.

OUR PROCEDURES

Query letters: *The Plain Truth* does not accept unsolicited manuscripts. Please first submit a query letter or e-mail (managing.editor@ptm.org) and secure permission to forward manuscript.

Queries/manuscripts will not be responded to unless accompanied by a SASE. A positive response to a query does not guarantee a purchase.

Your query letter should include the following information:

• Your specific subject and working title

• An outline of your ideas, enumerating your main points

• A profile of your experience and qualifications, as well as any other personal information that lets us know why you are the person to write this article)

Manuscript format: Once accepted, manuscripts are required in electronic form, preferably in Microsoft Word. Manuscripts should be double-spaced with 1.5 inch margins. Include your name, address, daytime phone and Social Security number in the upper left hand corner of the first page.

Payment and rights: Payment is at the rate of 15 cents a word for reprint material, and 25 cents a word for first-rights material. Payment is for one-time nonexclusive world all-language rights for publication in *The Plain Truth* and its affiliated international publications, and posting on the Plain Truth Ministries website as part of our archives. We reserve the right to use a portion or description of your article with your name in our promotional materials. We reserve the right to grant reprint requests of up to 500 copies that are intended for educational use only. The author retains all rights once the article has been published. We will place your copyright notice at the end of the article only if specifically requested. All manuscripts are examined on speculation. If you have submitted the manuscript to another magazine before ours, please advise.

The author, by submitting the manuscript, grants *The Plain Truth* the right to edit and abridge the manuscript and warrants that he or she is the sole and true author of the submitted material.

Categories: Nonfiction—Christian Interests—Inspirational—Religion—Spiritual

CONTACT: Submissions Editor
Material: All
300 W. Green St.
Pasadena CA 91129
Phone: 626-304-6077
Fax: 626-304-8172
E-mail: manager.editor@ptm.org
Website: www.ptm.org

Plastic Canvas Today

GENERAL INFORMATION

Plastic Canvas Today is a full-color, 32-page, bimonthly, House of White Birches plastic canvas publication. *Plastic Canvas Today* features innovative plastic canvas designs worked in a variety of styles and on 7-count, 10-count, 14-count and 5-count plastic canvas.

SUBMISSIONS

Project submissions or manuscripts:

Your completed project or photo.

Typed, double-spaced, step-by-step instructions following our format.

Complete and labeled graphs, diagrams and color keys.

Materials list including types of materials, quantities used and ordering information if unavailable at most craft stores. If design materials were supplied free of charge, please indicate which materials should be credited and to whom.

Your name (as you would like published), address, telephone number.

Accepted projects or manuscripts:

We will review submissions on the dates given on our editorial calendar, after which we will issue agreements and return all designs we are unable to use. Please see our Editorial Calendar for specific deadlines.

Published projects will be returned to the designer (unless otherwise arranged) after all photography is complete. All manuscripts, diagrams, etc. remain our property.

Since we purchase all rights to designs unless otherwise arranged, designers should not sell the purchased design or one very similar to it to another publication.

Mailing Address: Send submissions and completed projects to *Plastic Canvas Today*, 306 East Parr Rd., Berne, IN 46711.

CONTRACTS & PAYMENT

If your project is accepted for publication, we will send you an agreement with our payment offer and a pre-addressed envelope. If the agreement is acceptable, you should complete it with your signature, phone number and Social Security number. Please sign and keep the photocopy of the agreement in your records and return the original to us in the pre-addressed envelope. Payment will be made within 45 days of acceptance. Amount will be determined by creativity, workmanship, skill level and overall quality.

If you have any questions, contact Vicki Blizzard or Kelly Keim.

Categories: Nonfiction—Crafts/Hobbies—Hobbies

CONTACT: Submissions Editor
Material: Submissions and completed projects
House of White Birches

306 East Parr Rd.
Berne IN 46711
Phone: 260-589-4000
Website: www.whitebirches.com

Playboy

Playboy regularly publishes nonfiction articles on a wide range of topics—sports, politics, music, topical humor, personality profiles, business and finance, science and technology—and other topics that have a bearing on our readers' lifestyles.

You can best determine what we're looking for by becoming familiar with the nonfiction we are currently publishing. We frequently reject ideas and articles—many of high quality—simply because they are inappropriate to our publication. We have a six-month lead time, so timing is very important.

Your brief query should outline your idea, explain why it's right for *Playboy* and tell us something about yourself. Handwritten submissions will be returned unread. Manuscripts should be typed, double-spaced and accompanied by a self-addressed, stamped envelope. Writers who submit manuscripts without a stamped, self-addressed return envelope will receive neither the manuscript nor a printed rejection.

The average length for nonfiction pieces is 4,000 to 5,000 words, and minimum payment for an article of this length is $3,000. We do not accept unsolicited poetry. *Playboy* buys first North American serial rights only—no second serial rights are considered. *Playboy* does not accept simultaneous submissions.

A bit of advice for writers: Please bear in mind that *Playboy* is not a venue where beginning writers should expect to be published. Nearly all of our writers have long publication histories, working their way up through newspapers and regional publications. Aspiring writers should gain experience, and an extensive file of by-lined features, before approaching *Playboy*. Please don't call our offices to ask how to submit a story or to explain a story. Don't ask for sample copies, a statement of editorial policy, a reaction to an idea for a story, or a detailed critique. We are unable to provide these, as we receive dozens of submissions daily. Our response time is approximately four weeks.

We appreciate your interest in *Playboy*. We hope these guidelines will assist you in submitting work that is suited to *Playboy*'s high standards.

Categories: Nonfiction—Business—Culture—Entertainment—Fashion—General Interest—Interview—Money & Finances—Music—Politics—Recreation—Science—Sexuality—Sports/Recreation—HumorProfiles—Technology

CONTACT: Articles Editor
Material: Nonfiction
680 North Lake Shore Dr.
Chicago IL 60611
Phone: 312-751-8000
Fax: 312-751-2818
E-mail: articles@la.playboy.com
Website: www.playboy.com

Playgirl

PLAYGIRL addresses the needs, interests and desires of women 18 years of age and older. We provide something that no other American women's magazine provides: an uninhibited approach to exploring sexuality and fantasy that empowers, enlightens, and entertains.

We publish feature articles of all sorts: interviews with top celebrities, articles on sex, love, and romance and dating, how-to features, and erotic fantasies. PLAYGIRL's common editorial thread besides good, lively writing and scrupulous research, is a fresh, open-minded, inquisitive attitude.

Freelancers MUST read a few issues before submitting their article ideas. Query letters with published clips are preferred, but completed, unsolicited manuscripts will be considered. Payment rates vary. All submissions must include a self-addressed, stamped envelope, and a telephone number at which you can be contacted.

Freelance writers may contribute to any of the following PLAYGIRL department:

Nonfiction features are 1600-2500 word (may vary) articles. we ask that you send us outlines and descriptions of projects (with documentation) rather than completed pieces.

Celebrity features are in-depth interviews with today's hottest stars that ask questions that only PLAYGIRL can get away with asking. If you have a professional relationship with a celebrity that you know you can approach, we'd love to hear about it. You MUST supply a transcript and a tape recording of these interviews.

Q&A is a quick, 500-word question and answer interview with a celebrity or a well-known entertainer. You must include documentation (tape recording and transcript).

Fantasy Forum features first person, steamy erotic fiction. This column is devoted to female pleasures of the flesh, must be written from a female perspective and is the best opportunity for unpublished writers to write for PLAYGIRL. Please mark envelopes with "Fantasy Forum." All submissions become PLAYGIRL's property and will not be returned.

PLAYGIRL does not publish poetry, jokes (or short humorous blurbs), or features that do not pertain to women's issues.

We regret that all submissions cannot be acknowledged or returned.

Entries must include your name, address, telephone number (e-mail address is optional).

Categories: Fiction—Nonfiction—Erotica—Fantasy—Fashion—Feminism—Music—Relationships—Romance—Sexuality—Short Stories—Television/Radio—Women's Fiction—Women's Issues—Confession

CONTACT: Michelle Zipp, Editor-in-Chief
Material: All
Playgirl Magazine
801 Second Ave, 9th Floor
New York, NY 10017
Phone: 212-661-7878
Fax: 212-697-6343
E-mail: editorial@playgirlmag.com
Website: www.playgirl.com

Pleiades
A Journal of New Writing
Central Missouri State University

Pleiades publishes fiction, poetry, essays and reviews by writers from around the world. The editors read manuscripts year-round. When submitting to *Pleiades*, please observe the following guidelines:

• Submit manuscripts with a SASE for response or manuscript return.

• Prose should be double spaced with reasonable margins. Poetry should be single spaced, with the author's name on each page.

• Do not send your only copy of any manuscript.

• *Pleiades* accepts simultaneous submissions. We ask, however, that you note if a piece has been sent to another magazine.

• Do not fax or email submissions.

• Submit in only one genre at a time.

• Poetry should be addressed to Kevin Prufer and Wayne Miller.

• Fiction should be addressed to Susan Steinberg.

• Non-fiction should be addressed to Eric Miles Williamson.

• We accept queries for book reviews. Please send query and clips of previously published reviews to Kevin Prufer. No unsolicited reviews will be accepted.

• Cover art is solicited directly from artists. We do not accept unsolicited submissions of art.

• Send submissions to the appropriate editor.

Categories: Fiction—Nonfiction—Book Reviews—Drama—Literature—Poetry—Short Stories—Personal Essays

CONTACT: Kevin Prufer, Editor-in-Chief
E-mail: kdp8106@cmsu2. cmsu.edu
Material: Poetry
CONTACT: Susan Steinberg, Fiction Editor
E-mail: ssteinberg@ usfca.edu
Material: Fiction
CONTACT: Eric Miles Williamson, Essays Editor
E-mail: guniter@ earthlink.net
Material: Essays
Dept. of English, Central Missouri State University
Warrensburg MO 64093
Phone: 660-543-4425/8106
Fax: 660-543-8544
E-mail: kdp8106@cmsu2.cmsu.edu
Website: www.cmsu.edu/englphil/pleiades

Ploughshares
The Literary Journal of Emerson College

Ploughshares welcomes unsolicited submissions of fiction and poetry. We consider manuscripts from August 1 to March 31 (postmark dates). All submissions sent from April to July are returned unread. We adhere very strictly to the postmark restrictions. Since we operate on a first-received, first-read basis, we cannot make exceptions or hold work.

Ploughshares is published three times a year: usually mixed issues of poetry and fiction in the spring and winter and a fiction issue in the fall, with each guest-edited by a different writer.

In the past, guest editors often announced specific themes for issues, but we have revised our editorial policies and no longer restrict submissions to thematic topics. In general, if you believe your work is in keeping with our standards of literary quality and value, submit it at any time during our reading period.

We do not recommend trying to target specific guest editors unless you have a legitimate acquaintance with them. Our backlog is unpredictable, and staff editors ultimately have the responsibility of determining for which editor a work is most appropriate. If a manuscript is not suitable or timely for one issue, it might be considered for another.

Please send only one short story and/or one to three poems at a time (mail fiction and poetry separately). Poems should be individually typed either single- or double-spaced on one side. Prose should be typed and no longer than twenty-five pages. Although we look primarily for short stories, we occasionally publish personal essays and memoirs. Novel excerpts are acceptable if they are self-contained. We do not accept unsolicited book reviews or criticism, nor do we consider book-length manuscripts of any sort.

Please do not send multiple submissions of the same genre for different issues/editors, and do not send another manuscript until you hear about the first (no more than a total of two submissions per reading period). Additional submissions will be returned unread. Mail your manuscript in a page-size manila envelope, your full name and address written on the outside, to "Fiction Editor," "Poetry Editor," or "Nonfiction Editor." Unsolicited work sent directly to a guest editor's home or office will be discarded. We suggest you enclose a business-size SASE with a [first class] stamp and ask for a reply only, with the manuscript to be recycled if unaccepted (photocopying is usually cheaper than return postage).

Expect three to five months for a decision (sometimes faster, depending on the backlog). We cannot respond to queries regarding the status of a manuscript until five months have passed. To query at that time, please write to us, indicating the postmark date of the submission, instead of calling. Simultaneous submissions are amenable to us as long as they are indicated as such and we are notified immediately upon acceptance elsewhere.

We cannot accommodate revisions, changes of return address, or forgotten SASEs after the fact. We do not reprint previously published work. Translations are welcome if permission has been granted. Payment is upon publication: $25 a printed page, with a $50 minimum and a $250 maximum per issue, plus two copies of the issue and a one-year subscription.

More information about *Ploughshares* is available on the Web.

Sample copies are available to writers at a discount: $8.50 (regularly $10.95). Writers also receive a discounted subscription rate: $21 (regularly $24) for one-year (3 issues).

Thank you for your interest in *Ploughshares*.

Categories: Fiction—Poetry

CONTACT: Submissions Editor
Material: All
120 Boylston St., Emerson College
Boston MA 02116
Phone: 617-824-8753
E-mail: Pshares@emerson.edu
Website: www.pshares.org

We Weren't Born Yesterday

Plus Magazine

PLUS welcomes submissions from freelance writers.

Our ideal story or article length is 900-1,200 words.

We are interested in profiles of unusual or notable people, nostalgia, unique hobbies, men and women in second careers, health, physical fitness, humor (if handled deftly, not heavy-handed), travel and reviews of current books.

We pay $1.50 per published column inch and $10-$15 for photos we use with the article or story. We prefer black and white photos.

We receive many more submissions than we can publish. If you would like a query answered or an article returned if we can't use it, enclose a stamped, self-addressed envelope with the query or submission.

For a sample copy of the magazine send $2.00 in postage and a large self-addressed stamped envelope.

We try to respond to queries and submissions within two weeks after receiving them.

Categories: Nonfiction—Biography—Collectibles—Comedy—Diet/Nutrition—Entertainment—Gardening—Health—Recreation Vehicles—Television/Radio—Travel

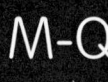

CONTACT: Anne Stubbs, Health Editor
Material: Health & Fitness
CONTACT: George Brand, Editor
Material: All Other Submissions
3565 S. Higuera
San Luis Obispo CA 93401
Phone: 805-544-8711
Fax: 805-544-4450

Pockets
A Devotional Magazine for Children

What is *Pockets*?

Designed for 6- to 12-year-olds, *Pockets* magazine offers wholesome devotional readings that teach about God's love and presence in life. Each page of *Pockets* affirms a child's self-worth. Included are fun and exciting puzzles, games, stories, poems, recipes, colorful pictures, and scripture readings. The magazine is published monthly (except in February) and includes a wide variety of materials.

The purpose of *Pockets* is to open up the fullness of the gospel of Jesus Christ to children. It is written and produced for children and designed to help children pray and be in relationship to God. The magazine emphasizes that we are loved by God and that God's grace calls us into community. It is through the community of God's people that we experience that love in our daily lives.

What should I write about?

Each issue is built around a specific theme with material that can be used by children in a variety of ways. Scripture stories, fiction, poetry, prayers, art, graphics, puzzles, and activities are included. Submissions do not need to be overtly religious. They should help children experience a Christian lifestyle that is not always a neatly wrapped moral package but is open to the continuing revelation of God's will. Seasonal material, both secular and liturgical, is appropriate. We welcome submissions from children.

Themes are set each year in December. They are available with an SASE or online.

Pockets is ecumenical, and our readers include persons of many cultures and ethnic backgrounds. These differences should be reflected in the references that are made to lifestyles, living environments (suburban, urban, rural, reservation), families (extended families, single-parent homes), and individual names. Stories should show appreciation of cultural differences and not leave the impression that one way is better than another.

What ages are *Pockets* readers?

The magazine is for children of ages six through eleven, with a target reading age of eight through eleven. Though some may share it with their families, it is designed primarily for the personal use of children.

What type of material should I write?

Fiction and scripture stories should be 600 to 1400 words. Our primary interest is in stories that can help children deal with real-life situations. We prefer real-life settings, but we occasionally use fables. We do not accept stories about talking animals or inanimate objects. Fictional characters and some elaboration may be included in scripture stories, but the writer must remain faithful to the story.

Stories should contain lots of action, use believable dialogue, be simply written, and be relevant to the problems faced by this age group in everyday life. Children need to be able to see themselves in the pages of the magazine. It is important that the tone not be "preachy" or didactic. Use short sentences and paragraphs. When possible, use concrete words instead of abstractions. However, do not "write down" to children.

It is no longer common practice to use such terms as "man," "mankind," "men," in the familiar generic sense. Substitute non-sexist terms that are inclusive of everyone (e.g., "humankind," "persons," "human beings," "everyone").

Poems should be short, not more than 24 lines.

Non-fiction articles should be 400 to 1,000 words. These should be related to a particular theme which has been projected (a list of themes and due dates is available from the editorial office). We also seek biographical sketches of persons, famous or unknown, whose lives reflect their Christian commitments and values. These may be either short vignettes (a single incident) or longer and more complete biographies. Articles about various holidays and about other cultures are included.

We particularly desire articles about children involved in environmental, community, and peace/justice issues.

How should I submit my writing?

Contributions should be typed, double-spaced, on 8½" x 11" paper, accompanied by a SASE for return. Writers who wish to save postage and are concerned about paper conservation may send a SASP for notification of unaccepted manuscripts, and we will recycle the paper the submission is printed on. Please list the name of the submission(s) on the card. We do not accept manuscripts sent by FAX or e-mail.

Will *Pockets* pay to use my writing?

Yes, payment will be made at the time of acceptance. We will make an initial response within one month after receiving the manuscript. We often place manuscripts on long-term hold for specific issues. Authors are free to request that their manuscripts be returned to them at any time during the long-term hold. We purchase newspaper, periodical, and electronic rights, and we accept one-time previously published material.

Stories and articles: 14 cents a word
Poetry: $25.00 and up
Activities, games: $15.00 and up
Categories: Children—Christian Interests—Family—Religion—Spiritual—Devotional

CONTACT: Lynn W. Gilliam, Editor
Material: Manuscripts
The Upper Room
PO Box 340004 • 1908 Grand Ave.
Nashville TN 37203-0004
Phone: 615-340-7200/7333
E-mail: pockets@upperroom.org
Website: www.upperroom.org

Podiatry Management

Podiatry Management is the national practice management magazine for podiatrists.

A sample of the current issue is posted at the Internet address shown below.

We invite articles to be submitted via e-mail. Articles can also be mailed along with an IBM formatted disk to the address below.

You may telephone us.

Articles should be of interest to the practicing podiatrist. Articles which feature quotes from podiatrists or are about DPMs are preferred.

Categories: Nonfiction—Business—Health—Management—Podiatry

CONTACT: Barry Block, Editor
Material: All
PO Box 750129
Forest Hills NY 11375
Phone: 718-897-9700
E-mail: bblock@prodigy.net; copy to: bblock@prodigy.net
Website: www.podiatrym.com

Poem
Huntsville Literary Association

Poem, published in spring and fall, has been in continuous publication since 1967.

We equally welcome submissions from established poets as well as from less known and beginning poets. We publish both traditional forms and free verse. We want poems characterized by compression, rich vocabulary, significant content, and evidence of "a tuned ear and practiced pen." We want coherent work that moves through the particulars of the poem to make a point. We do not want "greeting card verse" or proselytizing or didactic poems.

The editor and two assistant editors individually read all submissions. At each editorial conference, all preliminary selections are read aloud and discussed. Then final selections are made. We sometimes accept a poem upon the condition that the poet agree to a suggested change. We do not comment on rejections.

We do not accept translations, previously published works, or simultaneous submissions.

Poem is perfect bound, digest-sized, professionally printed on good stock paper with a clean design and a matte cover. It is about 90 pages and contains over 60 poems and notes on contributors. Press run is 475. Copies go to all Huntsville Literary Association members, to individual out-of-town subscribers, to subscribing libraries throughout the United States and in Canada, and to the contributors.

Poem is a member of CLMP and indexed in the Index of American Periodical Verse.

Submissions: Submit 3-5 poems, preferably with a cover letter. Include a self-addressed envelope with sufficient postage. Submissions are read throughout the year. We generally respond in 1-3 months. We normally wait several issues before again publishing a contributor, especially if several poems were accepted for an issue.

Copyright and payment: *Poem* acquires first serial rights. Because we are a non-profit organization, we can pay only in copy to contributors. We pay 2 copies to each contributor.

1. Subscriptions and sample copies: Subscriptions for out-of-towners are $20 per year. Sample copies and back issues are $7. Send to *Poem*, Huntsville Literary Association, P.O. Box 919, Huntsville, AL 35804.

Categories: Poetry.

CONTACT: Rebecca Harbor, Editor
Material: All
PO Box 2006
Huntsville, AL 35804

Poetic Realm

Poetic Realm is for poetry only. The guidelines are easy. Poems to 36 lines on any subject, in good taste. No reading fee...and my favorite poem in each issue will receive the "Editor's Choice Award" of $5.00.

Please help keep this publication afloat by either becoming a subscriber or purchasing the copy you are published in.

Thank you.
Rates: $16/yr; $14 for a single issue
Categories: Poetry

CONTACT: Kay Weems, Editor/Publisher
Material: All
207 Willow Wind Dr.
Artemas PA 17211
Phone: 814-458-3102

Remember: Editors change jobs and publishers change addresses. It is wise to invest in a phone call for the current information before submitting.

Poetry

SUBMISSION GUIDELINES

All submissions and inquiries regarding submissions must be made by mail. Your return address must appear on the outside of the envelope. Always include a self-addressed return envelope for our reply. We do not consider, and will not respond to submissions made by email and fax.

Poetry has no special manuscript needs, no special requirements as to form or genre: we examine in turn all work received and accept that which seems best. We can not consider anything which has been previously published or accepted for publication, anywhere, in any form, either in the United States or abroad. We do not consider simultaneous submissions. We regret that the volume of submissions received and the small size of our staff do not permit us to give individual criticism.

Submissions should be limited to four poems or fewer, typed single-space. Manuscripts are usually reported on within 16 to 20 weeks from the day of receipt. All manuscripts must be accompanied by a stamped, self-addressed envelope. Stamps alone are not sufficient. Writers living abroad must enclose a self-addressed envelope together with enough postage in validated international reply coupons for air mail return.

Manuscripts should have the author's name and address on every page. Avoid oversized envelopes. Do not send revisions unless they have been specifically requested by the editors. Inquiries about the status of a manuscript should be avoided, but when necessary must be made in writing and should include a self-addressed stamped return envelope for our reply.

Payment is made on publication at the rate of $6.00 per line, $150.00 per page of prose. All prose contributions are commissioned.

Poetry is copyrighted for the protection of its contributors. The author, the author's agents or heirs, and no one else, will be given transfer of copyright when they request it for purposes of republication in book form.

Several prizes, awarded annually, are announced each December for the best work printed in *Poetry* during the preceding year. Only poems already published in the magazine are eligible for consideration, and no formal application is necessary.

The Ruth Lilly Poetry Prize is also given each year to a poet whose published work merits special recognition. The selection is made by a panel of judges and no applications are accepted.

Two Ruth Lilly Poetry Fellowships are awarded annually to students who have not yet received the M.A. or M.F.A. degree, based on work submitted. Students must be nominated by their program directors or department chairs.

Anyone contemplating a submission is encouraged to examine the magazine before sending a manuscript. Sample copies cost $3.75 plus $1.75 for postage and handling.

Categories: Nonfiction—Book Reviews—Poetry

CONTACT: The Editor
Material: All
1030 N. Clark St., Ste 420
Chicago IL 60610
Phone: 312-787-7070
Fax: 312-787-6650
Website: www.poetrymagazine.org

Points North
Serving Atlanta's Stylish Northside

Points North was created to provide a first-class lifestyle magazine for affluent residents of suburban communities in north metro Atlanta. We place editorial emphasis on leisure activities for our readers, with articles that cover travel, dining and shopping; interior and landscape design; cultural, community and sporting events;

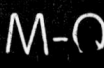

as well as profiles of interesting people and places with ties to Atlanta's north side.

Our magazine currently runs three to four features (including a profile) per issue, along with one or two travel and recreation pieces, one or two home and garden articles, a shopping column, and a wine column. We also print three to five short restaurant reviews each month, which are substituted once a quarter for a full-length feature on a "special occasion" restaurant. Currently, we are accepting articles in all areas of the magazine except the wine column. (Please see article specifications for more information.)

Points North, a free publication with a circulation of 50,000 copies per month, is distributed to many of the Atlanta area's most prestigious ZIP codes including Buckhead, Dunwoody, Sandy Springs, East Cobb, Roswell, Alpharetta, Windward, South Forsyth, John's Creek, Duluth and other neighboring areas at more than 400 retail businesses. *Points North* is also available at several locations within North Point Mall, Perimeter Mall and Phipps Plaza, and is distributed via direct-mail each month to 15,000 north Atlanta homeowners with properties valued in excess of $400,000.

Submitting Queries

If you are interested in submitting an existing article, or if you have an idea for an article, please submit a written, one-page Query Letter to include:

• **Personal information.** Your name, address, an e-mail address and a daytime phone number (or a number where you can be reached in the evenings if you cannot be contacted during the day).

• **Article description.** Describe the subject of your article or the story idea in enough detail for us to get a clear picture. If it's an existing piece, you might want to include the opening paragraph(s) to show us how this article will grab our readers' interest. How many words is or will the article be? What direction did or will you take with it (e.g., a humorous look at average commute times for morning rush hour in Atlanta, filled with anecdotes and quotes from north side residents). Tell us where in the magazine you think the article should appear (as a feature or profile, or in Food & Entertainment, Travel & Recreation, North-side Shopper or Grand Designs).

• **Article relevance.** Explain why you think *Points North* readers will find this article interesting, or why it's specifically significant to them. What elements does or will your piece contain that makes it relevant to the north side of Atlanta or its residents? What questions that our readers might have about the subject does or will your article answer? Why is now (or at a certain time in the future) a good time to publish this story?

• **Writer's sources.** What sources have you used or will you use for the article? What are their connections to our readership or to Atlanta's north side? If the article is not yet written, how do you know your sources are available to you? In addition, let us know if you have photographs available for an existing story, but please do not send photos with your Query Letter.

• **Writer's qualifications.** Why are you qualified to write about this subject? What experience or particular interest do you have in the subject matter, or what contacts do you have available to you that make this a subject that "fits" you? We prefer that Queries and/or existing articles be sent via e-mail (as attachments only please—not within the body of an e-mail message) to managingeditor@ptsnorth.com.

If you're not Internet-active, you can mail your Query and articles to Managing Editor, *Points North*, 568 Peachtree Pkwy, Cumming, GA 30041.

Important:

Please do not send originals of any kind, including manuscripts, photographs, etc., to our offices. We assume no responsibility for any materials sent unsolicited to *Points North*. Copies sent by mail to our offices will not be returned unless accompanied by a written request and a self-addressed envelope suitable for mailing the materials in, with proper postage affixed.

We will respond to your submission, normally within six to eight weeks of receipt, by e-mail or form letter. Due to time constraints we regret that we cannot respond individually to questions about materials or Query Letters sent to the editor.

If your article is one we intend to pursue further, or if we are interested in talking with you about writing a story for an idea you've submitted, we'll be in touch by telephone within six to eight weeks.

Editorial Content

Popular regular columns appearing in *Points North* include:

• **Travel and Recreation.** Most issues include our "Here" column, which highlights day trips or weekend getaways within a few hours of north metro Atlanta by car. Past columns have included Calloway Gardens, Big Canoe, Lake Hartwell and the Asheville area. The column "There" includes destinations for three-or four-day weekend getaways within a few hours by car or less than three hours away by plane, such as Charleston, The Cloister at Sea Island, Colonial Williamsburg and The Greenbrier in Virginia. Length of articles: 1500-2000 words.

• **Food and Entertainment.** Three issues per quarter include short reviews on three to five restaurants, usually done with a style, theme or location in mind. We've spotlighted groups of restaurants specializing in Italian and southern cooking; pubs and sushi bars; as well as establishments in Duluth, Roswell and the Perimeter Mall areas.

We are looking for restaurants in or close to north Atlanta that demonstrate a passion for pleasing their clientele through preparation, presentation and outstanding service.

Length of articles: 500-750 words.

Once per quarter we present a more in-depth overview of a "special occasion" restaurant. These pieces contain not only a review of the food and the restaurant in general, but might also include topics such as banquet facilities, an interview with the chefs and/or owners, and highlights of special amenities the restaurants have to offer when the reader is looking for that very special place to celebrate. Length of articles: 1500- 2000 words.

• **Grand Designs.** This department consists of one or two articles each month; "Home" covers interior matters such as painting, decorating and basement remodeling, while "Garden" spotlights exterior subjects like garden pests, spring planting and coping with summer droughts. Some of the north side's best interior, exterior and landscape designers have demonstrated and discussed aesthetic improvements for both the dwelling and the yard including Feng Shui, grand landscaping and home wine storage.

Length of articles: 1500-2000 words.

• **Northside Shopper.** Added in August 2001, each month this column will look at a particular shopping area or a specific group of specialty stores or unusual items. We've featured the North Georgia Premium Outlet Mall in Dawsonville, Ga. and The Avenue shopping center in East Cobb, along with Halloween costumes for our October issue and holiday shopping for December. Some brainstorming from our editorial staff came up with suggestions for 2002 such as china, crystal and silver, elegant linens for bed and bath, and high-end children's clothing as examples of group items; one-of-a-kind art pieces, unusual collectibles and rare book sellers; jewelry stores, Christmas boutiques and those great places where you can design your own gift baskets. Come up with your own ideas! Length of articles: 1200-1500 words.

• **Indulgence.** Added in January 2002, Indulgence is a column that will provide readers with options for fulfilling desires (or maybe just dreams!) for that perfect larger-than-life experience: The Perfect Valentine's Day, the Essential Guy's Weekend, Learning to Race at Panoz Racing School or a Truly Romantic Anniversary.

The focus of these columns should be experiences people have always wanted to have but have hesitated to spend the time and money to indulge themselves. Length of articles: 1200-1500 words.

The best way for a freelance writer who is interested in being published in *Points North* to get a sense of the types of articles we're looking for is to read the magazine. The current issue is available in many locations free of charge, and we will mail one or more back issues to you upon receipt of your check for $3.00 per issue (to cover shipping and handling).

Additionally, most features from each issue published to date are available for viewing at our Web site: ptsnorth.com.

ARTICLE SPECIFICATIONS

In general, successful articles will be clear, concise and well organized, with an effective introduction, sufficient information presented in a way that's easy to understand and makes us want to read more, and a strong conclusion to the piece that leaves us satisfied or eager to find out more on our own. Basically, when you're deciding if an existing or proposed article achieves a "fit" with *Points North* magazine, please keep these things in mind:

• **Composition.** Your piece should have just one central theme and an effective lead-in which attracts our attention, then lets us know what the article is about and piques our curiosity regarding what's to come and why we're going to be interested.

The body of the article should give us the information we need about the subject—in a logical order—and be organized in a few individual sections (with appropriate sub-headings) which together present, support and substantiate the theme. The summary and conclusion should close the article, bringing the readers full-circle and, hopefully, leaving them happy that they read to the end.

• **North Atlanta connections:** anecdotes, quotes and details. *Points North* readers pick up our magazine because they know the articles will have relevance to them as north side residents. We feel that the use of as many anecdotal stories and details related directly to the people, places and things in our circulation area, as well as quotes from experts on the subject being written about or from North Atlanta residents and businesses, is crucial to a successful *Points North* article. Whenever possible the article should have a connection with the people, places and businesses in north metro Atlanta, or relate to issues of concern to our readership.

• **Personal observations.** As we read your article, we want to know your opinion about why the topic is something we should be interested in; why you liked what you wrote about and why the readers won't be sorry if they take the time to read the piece. That being said, remember that most articles should have more than just the author's voice. That can be done with quotes, anecdotes and descriptive details as mentioned above, written in a narrative style that allows us to picture in our mind's eye what you are writing about.

• **Negative and controversial elements.** Articles don't have to be 100% objective; however, negativity in any form has no place in an article published in *Points North*. This will generally be a stopper to the article getting published, as will a subject considered to be controversial. (At the very least, negative and controversial elements will be edited out.) We realize this makes an article about a subject such as out-of-control development or the traffic in north Atlanta a bit difficult, but you are a writer after all!

• **Summary/conclusion.** Leave the readers with a lasting impression of your topic. For example, why did you find this subject interesting or worth writing about, and how did the points you made, along with the examples and expert quotes you used, fit together to bring you to this conclusion? Give the readers something to think about—perhaps challenge them to redirect their thought processes regarding the topic by posing a question, or answer a question you posed in your introduction. Offer a strong opinion, use a significant quote, or include something from the intro to bring the topic full circle.

• **General information.** Before submitting your article, please take a moment to spell-check and self-edit to the best of your ability; then re-read what you've written with a mind toward the following things:

—**Using Web sites as resources.** Research pulled from a Web site should be incorporated into the article, in the author's voice, and not submitted as a "listing" of items (and of course, cutting and pasting information directly from a Web site is not acceptable). As with all facts, information and statements presented within an article, the author is responsible for insuring that the Web information is current and accurate.

—**Sidebars.** We like the use of sidebars in an article if they genuinely enhance the presentation. The information presented in this manner should be a definite highlight to your story, as opposed to being simply pieces of data pulled from the article for the sake of a sidebar. Sidebars shouldn't contain information on how a reader can contact a source or listings of local events; these go in that issue's Resource Guide or Calendar of Events.

—**Advertorial.** The current policy of *Points North* is that we don't do paid "advertorial." What is or isn't advertorial is subjective—so we let our publisher decide.

We do like to support our advertisers and the merchants in our distribution area with a plug when we can—this is a lifestyle magazine and we don't take ourselves too seriously (and our salespeople gratefully accept all the help they can get!). So any time you can use a current or prospective advertiser for *Points North* as a resource or as an expert reference in your article, you should certainly do so.

—**Sources.** We generally require a minimum of three sources for each feature article. A writer's first choice for all sources should be, as much as is possible, people, businesses and experts with a connection to our circulation area.

In addition to information required for the Resource Guide (see below), the author is responsible for submitting a full name and phone number for any person quoted or referred to within the article so the editor can contact sources when the author is unavailable. When a book, article, professional paper, etc. is referred to, please provide the name of the source and the author's name. We'll also need addresses for all sources used in each article who would like a copy of the magazine mailed to them.

—**Resource Guide.** In lieu of resources detailed within an article itself or in sidebars, *Points North* includes a monthly Resource Guide to provide a central place for all information contained in that issue. Information for the Resource Guide must be complete on all sources including correct business names and addresses, local (and if available, toll-free) telephone numbers, along with e-mail addresses and Web site information when applicable.

—**Fact-checking requirements.** Authors are responsible for the accuracy of all information used within their articles. Submission of any printed materials available about your subject (e.g., brochures or other advertising materials, business cards, etc.) are extremely helpful, and we require menus or business cards to be submitted for all restaurants reviewed.

—**Photographs.** We do not expect our authors to provide photographs for the articles they submit. Please do, however, ask your sources if they have professional-quality photos that might be used in the article. 35mm color slides are preferred; we also may be able to use 4"x6" color prints and digital images of 270 dpi or better (TIF or EPS format) submitted on CDs, JAZ or ZIP disks. (CDs must be formatted for Macintosh; all other disks accepted in PC or Mac format.)

FINANCIAL AND LEGAL INFORMATION

• **Story rights.** In most cases, terms for story rights can be negotiated with the publisher but generally, *Points North* buys first serial rights in the Southeast with a six month moratorium, along with electronic rights. That means your article hasn't been previously published anywhere in the southeastern US, and that you will not sell it for publication in the southeastern US for a period of 6 months after its *Points North* publication. Electronic rights enable us to publish your article as part of the issue it originally appeared in on our Web site for an indeterminate period of time, and are not normally negotiable.

• **Bylines.** Our authors receive a byline for all published articles.

• Fees and payment for articles. Fees for unsolicited articles and assigned features begin at $350, and may be negotiable at the publisher's discretion depending upon such factors as the author's experience with *Points North*, article content and the complexity of research required, the amount of editing required after submission, and other circumstances. Fees for assigned restaurant reviews are $75.00 plus reimbursement for the cost of the meal up to but not exceeding $100.00 and, for legal liability reasons, exclusive of alcohol. Receipts with menu items detailed are required for all meals before payment will be made.

Points North does not pay expenses, and writers are encouraged to consider this before accepting an assignment.

Once an article is accepted for publication, payment will be processed on the first of the month after the deadline date for the current month's issue, regardless of whether the article is actually published in that issue or not. For example, an article accepted for the October issue, with a deadline date of August 1 will be paid on September 1.

Categories: Nonfiction—Culture—Food/Drink—Gardening—Home—Lifestyle—Regional—Sports/Recreation—Travel

CONTACT: Submsissions Editor
Material: All
568 Peachtree Pkwy .
Cumming GA 30041
E-mail: managingeditor@ptsnorth.com
Website: www.ptsnorth.com

POLICE and SECURITY NEWS

Police and Security News

The target audience for *Police and Security News* consists of middle and upper management, including top administration, in a variety of law enforcement entities comprised of city, county, state and federal agencies. Our goal is to provide information of a contemporary, educational and/or entertaining nature. We strive to offer our readers information that can be of assistance by explaining how to do their jobs better or easier, how to save money (very important), how to avoid problems, etc. Basically, we try to provide "news they can use." We also endeavor to present subjects that can be, at times, complex in nature in a manner that is easily understood, but not oversimplified. In other words, we try to edit for the expert in a way the nonexpert can understand. Articles that are directed towards helping the smaller municipal department or agency are especially desirable, since nearly eighty percent of the municipal departments in this country have ten or fewer employees.

In terms of article length, they can run anywhere from 500 to 3000 words. Past that limit, please advise me regarding specific plans.

We typically pay ten cents per published word for articles and ten to twenty dollars per published photo or illustration. Payment is issued upon publication of your material.

Categories: Nonfiction—Law—Trade—Law Enforcement

CONTACT: Al Menear, Assoc. Publisher
Material: All
CONTACT: James Devery, Editor
Material: All
DAYS Communications, Inc
1208 Juniper St.
Quakertown PA 18951
Phone: 215-538-1240
Fax: 215-538-1208
Website: www.policeandsecuritynews.com

Police Times
The Voice of Professional American Law Enforcement
The Chief of Police Magazine

M-Q

Dear Writer/Photographer:

Police Times is the official journal of the American Federation of Police and Concerned Citizens. We seek articles on speculation regarding all areas of law enforcement, with special emphasis on stories involving smaller police departments or individuals who have made a special place in law enforcement…past or present. *Police Times* is published quarterly. *The Chief of Police Magazine*, published bi-monthly, is the official journal of the National Association of Chiefs of Police. For *The Chief of Police Magazine* we seek articles that would be of particular interest to command rank American law enforcement personnel. If accepted, we may elect to publish a particularly interesting piece in both publications. Allow 90-180 days for publication, which is at the editor's discretion, and may include publication on our website as part of our magazine's contents.

We pay from $25 to $100 for articles including photographs. Photos may be submitted in b&w or color. Fillers and short articles are also considered. Length of articles may vary, but usually range up to 2,500 words for *Police Times*; 5,000 words for *The Chief of Police Magazine*. Payment is made upon acceptance. A complimentary copy of the issue in which the article appears is provided to the writer.

If you are using a personal computer for typing articles, please send them on IBM compatible 3½" disks as well as a hard copy.

Sample copies: For *Police Times* $2.50, for *The Chief of Police Magazine* $3.00. Include SASE with all submissions.

Assigned Articles: Articles specifically assigned by the editors are paid at double scale. These are reserved for writers who we have previously published in our publications.

Faxed proposals: Accepted by faxing short proposal to: Jim Gordon, Executive Editor, *Police Times* (305) 573-9819. Allow ample time for reply. If corresponding via E-Mail, please provide hard copy address for reply.

Categories: Nonfiction—Law—Trade—Law Enforcement

CONTACT: Jim Gordon, Executive Editor
Material: All
3801 Biscayne Blvd.
Miami FL 33137
Phone: 305-573-0070
Fax: 305-573-0070
E-mail: policeinfo@aphf.org
Website: www.aphf.org

Polo Players' Edition

About The Magazine

POLO Players' Edition is an approximately 6,000-circulation magazine published 12 times a year by Rizzo Management Corp. for Westchester Media. Our readers are polo players and fans from the United States and abroad who come from diverse social and economic backgrounds and share a passion for polo.

First and foremost, *POLO Players' Edition* is a sports magazine that offers readers profiles of the game's personalities, professional advice on everything from horse care to playing techniques and strategy, and coverage of important tournaments. It is also an "insider's" magazine for those who want to follow polo people and their lifestyles.

We go behind the scenes at Palm Springs, West Palm Beach, Boca Raton, Saratoga, Dallas, St. Moritz, Buenos Aires, Windsor Park and other places where polo people live and play.

Our readers are an affluent group. Most are well educated, well read and highly sophisticated. They're well enough established in the business world to be able to afford the game. A general knowledge of polo and of horses is necessary for some of the more technical stories in *POLO Players' Edition*. For profiles and other features, we don't demand that you know what an offside foreshot means or how long a chukker lasts, but you'll find it helpful in communicating with people who are devoted to the game.

Writing Opportunities with *POLO Players' Edition*

The best entree for a first-time writer in POLO Players' Edition is to query us on a personality profile or a general-interest feature. Full-length features run from about 1,500 to 4,000 words; short profiles, columns and departments run from 800 to 1,200 words. *POLO Players' Edition* pays on acceptance a minimum of $200 for full-length features and a minimum of $50 for columns, departments or short profiles. Some expenses are paid if arranged at the time of assignment. A 10 percent bonus is offered to writers who can provide visuals to accompany their articles. While we prefer to receive submissions by computer modem in ASCII format, legible typed manuscripts, computer printouts and Apple Macintosh or IBM-compatible disks are acceptable.

Submitting A Manuscript

In addition to staff-written articles, POLO Players' Edition publishes work by freelance contributors who have been assigned or who have suggested articles are submitted on speculation, which means the author is guaranteed payment only if the material is accepted for publication. Fees and rights purchased are specified at the time of acceptance and all acceptances are made in writing.

In the case of manuscripts or queried articles assigned in writing by the magazine, POLO Players' Edition will pay all fees stipulated at the time of assignment if the manuscripts is accepted and published. If an assigned manuscript is not accepted for publication, the author will be paid a percentage of the agree-upon fee as compensation for his time and effort. Unless otherwise specified, the magazine purchases first North American rights..

Categories: Animals—Hobbies—Recreation—Sports/Recreation

CONTACT: Gwen D. Rizzo, Editor and Associate Publisher
Material: All
Rizzo Management Corp.
3500 Fairlane Farms Rd, Ste 9
Wellington FL 33414
Phone: 561-793-9524
Fax: 561-793-9576

Poptronics

Dear Author:

If you have a story or a story idea centered around electronics, I'd like to have the chance to read it, and consider it for purchase and use in *Poptronics*. To improve the probability of your story being published, I have placed some suggestions in this guide to help you prepare your article.

What type of article is *Poptronics* seeking? I've always sought first-rate stories covering communications, computers, test equipment, audio, video and virtually every other electronics subject. Good construction, tutorial, informational, and how-to articles are always in demand. If they are timely, their appeal and chances of acceptance are further enhanced.

Articles about new technology or the theory behind new devices are particularly valuable and make for interesting reading. The key to writing such an article with authority is thorough research and accuracy. A poorly researched article can lose its author some respect among the editors, as well as lose the sale. Make sure of your facts, and make them complete.

How-to-do-it features are among the most interesting types of articles that you can write. Show a reader ten new ways to use his oscilloscope or sweep generator or an easy way to make printed-circuit boards, and your story will be enjoyed by our readers.

Troubleshooting and service manuscripts, on the other hand, require an experienced author. Nothing falls apart as thoroughly as a troubleshooting article written by someone who knows little about the subject.

Construction articles must show readers how to build electronic projects. The devices discussed must be of practical use in the field of electronics, in hobby pursuits, or around the house or in the car. The cost of parts is important; the cost of assembling a project should be justified by what it does. I seek construction stories at different levels, some for neophytes and some for those who have the training to carry out complex building instructions. In general, easier projects take preference.

Construction manuscripts need special care. Schematics must be complete and detailed. Show all IC pinouts, power connections, bypass capacitors, parts designations and values, etc. If a printed-circuit board is used, a clear, reproducible, full-size foil pattern must be included. Parts-placement diagrams should be shown from the component side of the board and the parts should be identified by part number, not values. Completely describe all construction methods and techniques that are not common knowledge.

Include calibration and adjustment instructions in all construction articles that require them. Include debugging information: How long did it take to get the device working? To build it? The reader may experience some of the same difficulties. Place critical voltages on schematic diagrams; those help the project builder check the operation of the finished project.

Include a complete list of parts, manufacturers, type numbers, and electrical/electronic specifications and ratings where appropriate. Make sure that the list agrees with the information presented in the text and on schematic diagrams. Accuracy is absolutely necessary! Avoid hard-to-get items or those that are one-of-a-kind. If you must use an uncommon part, you must give two sources for that part. Where values are not critical, say so and give approximate tolerances. Where special parts are required, be precise in the Parts List by including all the specifications. Do not merely say "5,000-ohm relay" if contact spacing or armature tension is critical. Tell us (in the text) why a particular part is chosen over others like it. Failure to make the parts list complete may mean some reader can't make the project work and will blame the magazine or author.

Check and double check your work. Be sure that the schematic agrees with the Parts List, the parts-placement diagram, other illustrations, and the text. Your reputation as an author, as well as the reputation of this magazine, can be damaged by inaccurate or sloppy work.

Commonly used abbreviations such as AC, DC, IC, Hz, etc., may be used freely. However, the use of less common abbreviations should be limited except when their use promotes clarity. All such abbreviations must be defined in the article the first time they are used.

Do not dismantle your equipment or change it after sending us your manuscript. Before the article is finally accepted, the editors must compare it to its description to check for accuracy.

Finish the job! Don't send half-done manuscripts. "Photos to come" or "material to be added here" are flags of incompleteness. I can't judge the manuscript without seeing all of it. Incomplete articles will be rejected as they cannot be properly evaluated.

MECHANICS:

Use standard 8½-inch by 11-inch paper. Print on one side only. Double-space between lines. You must have your name and address in the top left corner of the first page; some authors use a rubber stamp to put their name and address on the back of each succeeding page. Also include a telephone number where you can be reached during the day in case my editors have a question that requires immediate attention.

If you are working on a computer, submit your story with text pages printed on a letter-quality, laser, inkjet or dot-matrix printer and include a floppy disk of the manuscript in the following IBM-compatible formats: ASCII, WordPerfect, or MS Word (the latter is preferred). Label the disk, indicating what word processor you used. Please include photographs and images for the article on the disk. Photographs should be saved as JPEGs. Resolution should be at least 300 dpi. A disk of your article will save input time and eliminate typing errors at this end.

Mail the manuscript flat. Include a self-addressed envelope and return postage. Save a copy of your manuscript until you see it in print. It is often necessary for us to ask questions about it so having access to a copy is important. Furthermore, a copy helps protect your work should it get lost in the mail. Do not send Xerox copies of the manuscript or the illustrations. Send the original and keep the copy for your own files.

ILLUSTRATIONS:

If any of your illustrations are smaller than 8 by 10 inches, fasten them to standard-size sheet of paper.

Photographs should be 5 by 7 inches, or larger, black-and-white glossy prints, and in good focus all over. Avoid using color prints. All details should be easy to see, not hidden in dark areas or "washed out" in overexposed or too-bright areas. Don't mark or write on prints; you simply spoil them for reproduction. If you need to identify sections of a photograph, put a piece of tracing paper over the print and make the identification on it, or send an extra print.

Put an asterisk or the figure number in the margin of your text when you refer to an illustration or figure. Try to scatter illustrations throughout the story so they're not all bunched.

Diagrams must be clearly drawn in pencil or ink, but need not be finished artwork, as all art is redrawn here in Poptronics style. To enhance accuracy, we request that you adopt *Poptronics* parts designations and symbol conventions where possible. Contact us for a sample issue if needed.

Draw each diagram on a separate page. Use standard-size paper or sheets that can be folded to standard size. Drawings must be accurate. Check each one carefully; it is almost impossible for the editors to catch all errors.

RATE OF PAYMENT:

My payment calculations are more complex than a simple page rate, since I consider such variables as reader interest, illustrations, text, photography, how much editing my staff will have to do, accuracy of research, and originality of approach.

The payment rate currently ranges from $100 to $500. Manuscripts that need practically no editing, are complete, that hit precisely the slant we want, that are written in the easy-reading style of *Poptronics*, and that are thoughtfully and imaginatively illustrated will command the highest payment rate. Payment is issued upon publication of the manuscript.

The staff members are trained in writing, researching, and editing. As you are developing your story, I will gladly work with you. After I buy your manuscript, your help is often needed to fill gaps in your story, check a doubtful connection on a schematic diagram. etc. The editors take every possible step and precaution to make sure that your article is authoritative, easy-to-read, and interesting, but much of the responsibility must, of course, rest with the author.

I'll look forward to reviewing your manuscripts.

Chris La Morte, Managing Editor

Categories: Nonfiction—Automobiles—Electronics—Engineering—Internet—Science—Software—Technical—Television/Radio—Robotics

CONTACT: Chris La Morte, Managing Editor
Material: All
Gernsback Publications, Inc.
275-G Marcus Blvd.
Hauppauge NY 11788
Phone: 631-592-6720

Popular Mechanics

We are always in the market for good free-lance articles, and invite your queries. Because our magazine is divided into departments according to subject matter, you should direct editorial queries to the departmental editor m your area of interest. The editors are listed at the end of this guide. Since we do not print fiction, please don't submit any fiction articles. Because of the workload of our editors, queries are best handled by a short paragraph and perhaps a photo or drawing, via mail. Before you submit a query, do a little homework. Check with the *Reader's Guide To Periodic Literature* and/or our own indexes to editorial features. Chances are, we've already published an article similar to the one you are about to propose. Don't waste your time unless you can give us something new that we haven't run before. Our typical reader is male, about 37 years old, married with a couple of kids, owns his own home and several cars, makes a good salary and probably works in a technically oriented profession. Keep this in mind before proposing articles. In any article query, you should be specific as to what makes the development new, different, better, interesting or less expensive.

Submission Format: All articles must be submitted to us typewritten, double spaced on one side of the page only. All manuscripts must include a self-addressed, stamped envelope with sufficient return postage in case we do not accept your submission. All how-to articles must be accompanied by well-lit, clear, black-and-white photos or rough artwork that we can use to produce finished art for publication. Photos should be either 5x7 or 8x10 in size, glossy finish. If we like an idea, we may also ask you to supply color photos. These should be 35mm or larger transparencies. We pay anywhere from $300 to $1000 and more for features. We pay on acceptance and purchase all rights. If we pay for your submission, we are under no legal obligation to run the piece, but will make our best effort to get it into print. Material is subject to editing for length, style and format Here is some specific information from each of our areas of editorial interest:

Automotive: We do all of our own road testing and conduct our own owner surveys. Please don't query us about submitting driving reports on specific models, or articles about what it's like to own a specific car.

Home Improvement: We buy how-to-do-it articles on home improvement, home maintenance, energy-saving techniques, and shop and craft projects. These must be well illustrated with drawings and photos. Finished drawings suitable for publication are not necessary. Rough, but accurate, pencil drawings are adequate for artist's copy. Topnotch photos are a must, shot during construction of the project as well as after construction. Photos should be taken with a background that is not cluttered or distracting from the main action.

Science/Technology/Aerospace: We are interested in long and short pieces that cover the latest developments in science, technology, aerospace, industry and discovery. We stress newsworthy items here. An old subject can be interesting if new facts have recently become known. Accuracy is paramount. Check your facts and sources before submitting queries. As a rule, we are not interested in machines or inventions applicable to a very limited field or industry, ordinary industrial processes, informative material without a news angle as found in textbooks or encyclopedias, or items that deal with accidents or freaks of nature. We publish articles on sport aviation, homebuilt aircraft, net commercial aircraft, new combat aircraft, etc. Also, we are interested in restoration projects on older collectible aircraft and other hands-on type articles that involve planes.

Boating/Outdoors: Testing of new boats, recreational vehicles or outdoor gear is conducted by our own staff. We publish articles on new equipment in the boating and outdoors areas, as well as articles on how to maintain and/or repair boats, boat engines, camping equipment, motorcycles, recreational vehicles, etc. We are interested in articles covering new types of outdoor recreational devices, such as paraplanes, balloons, all-terrain vehicles and campers.

Electronics/Photography/Telecommunications: We publish articles on new types of equipment in the audio, video, computer, telecommunications, photographic and optical fields, but our staff does most of these. We also publish technique articles, such as how to take trick photos, new developing techniques, how to hook up stereo equipment and telephones in the home, etc. Check some back issues for specific areas of our coverage.

General Interest Articles: We occasionally publish general interest articles. We look for pieces with a strong science, exploration or adventure emphasis.

Departmental Editors: If your query doesn't fit into any of the department, send it to the editor-in-chief.

Categories: Nonfiction—Automobiles—Aviation—Boating—Business—Computers—Consumer—Crafts/Hobbies—Electronics—Engineering—Environment—Military—Outdoors—Photography—Recreation—Science—Home—Technology—How-to—Audio—Telecommunications

CONTACT: Don Chaikin
Material: Automotive
CONTACT: Steven Willson
Material: Home Improvement
CONTACT: Tobey Gumet, Tech Editor
Material: Electronics/Photography/Telecommunications
CONTACT: Jim Wilson
Material: Science Editor
CONTACT: Cliff Gromer
Material: Boating/Outdoors
CONTACT: Joe Oldham, Editor-In-Chief
Material: All other material
810 7th Ave. 6th Floor
New York NY 10019
Phone: 212-649-2000
E-mail: popularmechanics@hearst.com
Website: www.popularmechanics.com

Popular Photography & Imaging

Do you have a story idea or photos that you think are perfect for *Pop Photo*? Here's how to submit your ideas to us.

We are primarily interested in articles on new or unusual phases of photography which we have not covered recently or in recent years. We do not want general articles on photography which could just as easily be written by our staff. We reserve the right to rewrite, edit, or revise any material we are interested in publishing.

Anyone wishing to write for us is advised to send a query letter, not a finished manuscript. The query should briefly describe the purpose of the proposed article, and give a sense of your writing style.

Queries should be accompanied by a sampling of how-to pictures (particularly when equipment is to be constructed or a process is involved), or by photographs which support the text. Please send duplicates only; do not send negatives or original slides. We are not responsible for the loss of original work.

All written materials should be typed double-spaced. The sender's name and address should be clearly written on the back of each print, on the mount of each slide, watermarked on digitally sent sample images, and on the first and last pages of all written material, including the accompanying letter.

Technical data should accompany all pictures, including the camera used, lens, film (or image format if digital), shutter speed, aerture, lighting, and any other points of special interest on how the picture was made.

Material mailed to us should be carefully wrapped or packaged to avoid damage. All submissions must be accompanied by a stamped, self-addressed return envelope. We assume no responsibility for safe return, but will make every effort to handle and return it with care.

The rate of payment depends upon the importance of the feature, quality of the photographs, and our presentation of it. Upon accep-

tance, fees will be negotiated by the author/photographer and the editors of the magazine.

E-mail submissions are also welcome. Samples of your work in attached Microsoft Word files are OK (sorry, no other word processing formats can be accepted). A small selection of sample photos under 75K each in JPG format are OK. If we are interested we will request high-resolution files and hard copy versions of prints for color matching purposes.

Please note: we are unable to accept individual portfolios for review. However, we do welcome samples of your work in the form of promotional mailers, press kits, or tear sheets for our files. These shoud be sent to the attention of Mason Resnick, Managing Editor, at the above address or via email at mresnick@hfmus.com.

Categories: Arts—Photography

CONTACT: Jason Schneider, Editor-in-Chief
Material: All
1633 Broadway
New York, NY 10019
E-mail: popeditor@aol.com
Website: www.popphoto.com

Popular Science

Submitting article ideas or product information :
What's New

What's New Editors: Suzanne Kantra Kirschner and Jenny Everett
The following information is required for consideration:

• Color photograph, transparency, or slide(unsolicited materials will not be returned).

• Date when product will be available to the public or date when product was first sold if available.

• Description of the product's unique features and how the product works Suggested retail price of the product.

Newsfronts

Newsfronts are broken down into content areas. Article queries should be addressed to the appropriate editor.

Computers & Software Newsfront Editor: John Quain / john.quain@time4.com@popsci.com

Electronics Newsfront Editor: Suzanne Kantra Kirschner / kantra@popsci.com

Home Technology Newsfront Editor: Charles Wardell / charles.wardell@time4.com

Sci-Tech Newsfront Editor: Dawn Stover / stover@popsci. com

Medicine & Health Newsfront Editor: Gunjan Sinha / gunjan.sinha@time4.com

Feature Story Proposals

Please send your short (one- to two-page) pitch to: features@popsci.com . Proposals should include the story's suggested angle, timing, and length. Ideas about illustrations and a short list of potential sources are also helpful. If you have not written for *Popular Science* before, please also include two or three clips. Due to the volume of queries,only materials accompanied by a SASE can be returned.

WRITER'S GUIDELINES

Popular Science covers new and emerging technology in the areas of science, automobiles, the environment, recreation, electronics, the home, photography, aviation and space, and computers and software. Our mission is to provide service to our readers by reporting on how these technologies work and what difference they will make in our readers' lives. Our readers are well-educated professionals who are vitally interested in the technologies we cover.

We seek stories that are up-to-the-minute in information and accuracy. We expect the writer to interview all sources who are essential to the story, as well as experts who can provide analysis and perspective. If a hands-on approach is called for, the writer should visit critical sites to see the technology first-hand—including trying it out when appropriate.

We publish stories ranging from hands-on product reviews to investigative feature stories, on everything from black holes to black-budget airplanes. We expect submissions to be, above all else, well written: that is, distinguished by good story-telling, human interest, anecdotes, analogies, and humor, among other traits of good writing. Stories should be free of jargon, vague statements, and unconfirmed facts and figures.

We seek publishable stories written to an agreed-upon length, with text for agreed-upon components such as sidebars or how-to boxes. The writer is responsible for the factual content of the story and is expected to have made a systematic checking of facts. We require that the writer file with his story contact numbers for all important sources and subjects in the story.

We expect our authors to deliver a complete package. The *Popular Science* Art department requires illustrations, photographs, and diagrams/sketches pertaining to stories submitted. These may be in the form of copies, but we prefer camera-ready artwork. We accept the following formats: four-color or black and white photography, illustration and digital files (tiff or eps). We track and log all artwork and, if indicated on the original, we will return artwork. We also require more than one piece of reference material. This allows for more accurate and original artistic interpretations.

A story should come with a headline for each story element and captions for photos. The complete package will include background material and documentation used by the author.

Freelance contributions to *Popular Science* range from feature-length stories to shorter "newsfront pieces" and shorter-yet stories to accompany What's New products.

We respond promptly to queries, which should be a single page or less and include an SASE. The writer should submit a tight summary of the proposed article and provide some indication of the plan of execution. Samples of the writer's past work and clips concerning the emerging story are helpful.

Categories: Nonfiction—Automobiles—Aviation—Computers—Electronics—Environment—General Interest—Photography—Science—Technology—Home

CONTACT: features@popsci.com
Material: Feature Story Proposals
CONTACT: John Quain, Computers & Software Editor
E-mail: john. quain@time4.com@popsci.com
Material: Computers & Software
CONTACT: Suzanne Kantra Kirschner, Electronics Editor
E-mail: kantra@popsci.com
Material: Electronics
CONTACT: Charles Wardell, Home Technology Editor
E-mail: charles.wardell@time4.com
Material: Home Technology
CONTACT: Dawn Stover, Sci-Tech Editor
E-mail: stover@ popsci. com
Material: Sci-Tech
CONTACT: Gunjan Sinha, Medicine & Health Editor
E-mail: gunjan. sinha@time4.com
Material: Medicine & Health
2 Park Ave.
New York NY 10016
Phone: 212-779-5000
Fax: 212-481-8062
Website: www.popsci.com

© *Popular Woodworking Woodworking Magazine*

Writer's Guidelines

Popular Woodworking is published seven times a year. This magazine invites woodworkers of all levels into a community of experts who share their hard-won shop experience through in-depth projects and technique articles, which helps the readers hone their existing skills and develop new ones. Related stories increase the readers' understanding and enjoyment of their craft. Any project submitted must be aesthetically pleasing, of sound construction and offer a challenge to readers.

Features

On the average, we use four features per issue that are written by freelancers, usually professional woodworkers. Our primary needs are "how-to" articles on woodworking projects, and instructional features dealing with woodworking and techniques. We do not publish features about woodworkers and their particular work. The tone of articles should be conversational and informal, as if the writer is speaking directly to the reader. Word length ranges from 1,200 to 2,500. Payment for features starts at $150 per published page, depending on the total package submitted, including its quality, and the writer's level of woodworking and writing experience. Submit your best work. Submissions must include three-view construction drawings and professional slides or digital images to be considered (see "Illustrations"). We receive and look at many great submissions each month. If you want your work to be considered for publication, you must put your best foot forward.

Columns

• Out of The Woodwork: This one-page article, averaging about 700 words, reflects on the writer's thoughts about woodworking as a profession or hobby. The article can be either humorous or serious. Payment starts at $150. This is a good entry-point for first-time freelancers. We purchase six of these columns a year. The writer does not need to be a professional woodworker.

• Tricks of the Trade: Each issue we publish woodworking tips and tricks from our readers that we think are useful. Tricks should be two to three paragraphs long. Brevity is important. Sketches are helpful. In each issue, the author of the best trick receives a prize. All other tricks' authors each receive a check for $75. Send your tricks to David Thiel at david.thiel@fwpubs.com or Tricks of the Trade, *Popular Woodworking*, 4700 E. Galbraith Road, Cincinnati, OH 45236.

Queries

All submissions, except Out of the Woodwork columns and Tricks of the Trade, should be preceded by a query. We will accept unsolicited manuscripts and artwork, although they must be accompanied by a self-addressed stamped envelope to be returned. We will try to respond to all queries within 60 days.

Queries must include:

• A brief outline of the proposed article.

• A summary of the techniques used to complete the project. Include step-by-step illustrations if possible.

• A short biographical sketch, including both your woodworking and writing experience and accomplishments. Also provide your address and daytime telephone number.

• A color photo or transparency of the completed project.

• A list of all materials needed.

Manuscript Submissions

Send your manuscript via U.S. mail or e-mail to Kara Gebhart,

Popular Woodworking, 4700 E. Galbraith Road, Cincinnati, OH 45236 or kara.gebhart@fwpubs.com.

For project articles, include the following:

1. Introduction: Describe an important point about your project or subject. What made you develop or design it? Also note any unusual qualities.

2. Preparation: Explain any work needed to be done before starting the project.

3. Instructions: Go step-by-step through the process, explaining each point without excessive detail. Include only necessary information, and write in a conversational style. When writing, keep in mind that there may be multiple ways to do any one step. Offering these options to the reader makes your manuscript more flexible and appealing. Clarify any technical words. NOTE: Brand names should only be included when they are critical to the construction or finishing process.

4. Finishing: Give complete instructions on how to finish the project.

5. Closing: Close your article with a brief paragraph that ties everything together.

6. Materials: Please provide the list of all materials used in the project, including types and sizes (thickness, width & length). Also, if materials are hard to find, include the supplier's address and telephone number (with the price of the product & shipping, if available).

7. About the Writer: Provide a brief biography on your experience and interests.

Illustrations

Visual aids are a vital part of instruction, and essential to both projects and articles. Whenever possible, PW prefers to show through photography and diagrams how a step is done rather than tell through text. Many queries are rejected on photo quality alone.

• All projects must include professional photos. We only accept slides and digital images. We don't accept prints. The opening photo for the article is almost always shot in medium (2-1/4") format to account for the enlargement in the magazine.

• All projects must include a fully detailed three-view construction drawing with an accurate cut list.

• If a complex technique is necessary for the project, make a suggestion for a special "sidebar" demonstrating it. Sidebars also can be used as an important source of additional information, such as suggesting alternative methods or tools.

• All artwork, photographs and drawings will be returned upon request.

Originality and Rights

All material submitted must be original and unpublished. *Popular Woodworking* purchases first world rights for one-time use in the magazine, and all rights for use of the article (both text and illustrations) in any F&W Publications Inc. promotional material/product or reprint, and in non-fee paying areas of our web site. You always retain the copyright to your work, and are free to use it in any way after it appears in the magazine. We request, however, that you do not publish the same material for at least six months from the time it appears in our publication.

Popular Woodworking's Guide to Writing and Style

• Write as if you're standing beside the readers as they follow your instruction. Use second person (ex: Cut the wood size). Only use first person when talking specifically about yourself (ex: I chose oak, but any wood will do.).

• Writing should be concise and straightforward.

• Watch redundancies and get rid of unnecessary words, such as that, all, rather, in order, very, etc.

• Avoid repeating the same word within the sentence or in the following one. For example: The board should be sanded on the board's right side. Include a pronoun instead: The board should be sanded on its right side. Don't be afraid to use pronouns, unless they hinder comprehension.

• Replace passive voice with active voice to avoid redundancies and increase clarity. Hint: Watch for words like was, were, is and are—they usually indicate passive voice. Passive: The project was a success. Active: The project succeeded.

• Possessive apostrophes also can cut back on your word count. For example, the side of the board can become the board's side. As a side note, remember it's is a contraction of it is, while its shows possession.

• For measurements, *Popular Woodworking*'s style is: 7" x 8", 7", 7"-thick board. Take note of the difference between measurements: The 7"-thick board should be cut 2" wide. The hyphenated version is used as an adjective of an object, while no hyphen denotes a measurement itself.

• Generally, a comma does not separate the last series member from a verb. For example: You will need shellac, sandpaper and wood. However, if the omission of commas becomes too confusing, leave them in: You will need shellac and stain, sandpaper and steel, and pine and maple wood.

• When using and, but, so, nor, or, remember the comma precedes them when it introduces a complete sentence. Never use the phrase and then. Only then is necessary.

• Parentheses should be used sparingly and only for information that needs understatement. For example, note the distinction between the use of dashes and parentheses in this sentence: For 10 hours—but only 10 hours—let the glue dry (yellow carpenter's glue works best) so your project will not come apart while you are working.

• Always have punctuation follow parentheses, unless a complete sentence is within it: This book is excellent for beginners (zero to one year experience), but only a handy guide for more advanced levels.

I cut the wood according to size. (I later found out I had used the wrong materials.)

Final Checklist

Although the following reminders are simple, they've been neglected by writers in the past. So make sure your manuscript meets these requirements when you read it over a final time:

• Make sure you're getting your point across to the readers. Look at the article through their eyes—not your own experienced ones.

• Double check all measurements and facts to make sure they're correct. Error-plagued manuscripts will not be published.

• Watch the overuse of you and I. It does make the piece more personable, but use sparingly. Often you can get the same point across after omitting them.

• Make sure all punctuation is used correctly.

Categories: Nonfiction—Crafts/Hobbies—Hobbies—Technical

CONTACT: Kara Gebhart
Material: All manuscripts
Contact: David Thiel
Material: Tricks of the Trade articles
F&W Publications Inc.
4700 E. Galbraith Rd.
Cincinnati, OH 45236
Phone: 513-531-2690 ext. 1348
Fax: 513-891-7196
E-mail: kara.gebhart@fwpubs.com
E-mail: david.thiel@fwpubs.com
Website: www.popularwoodworking.com

Potluck Children's Literary Magazine

The magazine for the serious young writer

Potluck is an international, non-for-profit, quarterly magazine for and by writers/artists 8 to 16, though we have published works from writers as young as four. Young writers from around the world fill each issue with an array of poetry, short stories, book reviews and artwork. *Potluck* provides informative articles to expand one's writing abilities and knowledge on the business of being a writer. We want your experience with *Potluck* to be one of accomplishment and new understanding. Welcome to the world of *Potluck*.

Guidelines

1. Work should be typed Roman or Arial, and in black ink.

2. Your name, age, address, email address, and word or line count should be in an upper corner.

3. #10 (large) self-addressed stamped envelope (SASE) must be included for reply. E-mailed work will receive reply by email. Work without a SASE or an email address will not be considered.

4. Do not send your only copy, it will not be returned. Proper postage and envelope must be included for return of original artwork.

5. Profane, sexual, or violent works are not accepted.

Poetry (30 line max.) All forms; double space between stanzas.

Short Stories (1500 word max.) Any subject. Double space between paragraphs.

Book Reviews (250 word max.) Title, author, awards the book may have received. Tell us about the book, what made it worth reading, do you recommend it, and for what age level.

Artwork (8½" x 11"). All styles. A color photocopy is acceptable.

Potluck pays one copy and responds 3 weeks after deadline. All work must be original, unpublished, and not submitted elsewhere.

By submitting to *Potluck* you give *Potluck* permission to publish your work online as well as in print format. Work will remain online for 3 months. *Potluck* acquires first rights. All rights return to author/artist upon publication.

Submission Deadlines (Work received after deadline will be considered for the next issue.)

Spring Issue - December 1

Summer Issue - March 1

Fall Issue - June 1

Winter Issue - September 1

Subscriptions: US: $21.99 one year (4 issues), single issue $5.80 prepaid

Canada: $31.00 one year, single issue $9.80 prepaid (US dollars)

Elsewhere: $41.99 one year; single issue $14.80 prepaid (US dollars)

Visa, MasterCard, Discover and American Express accepted.

Categories: Children—Juvenile—Literature—Poetry—Short Stories—Teen—Writing—Young Adult

CONTACT: Susan Napoli Picchletti, Editor-in-Chief
Material: All
Box 546
Deerfield, IL 60015-0546
Phone: 847-948-1139
Fax: 847-317-9492
E-mail: submissions@potluckmagazine.org
Website: www.potluckmagazine.org

Potomac Review

• Poetry: up to three poems/five pages at a time.

• Prose: (fiction/nonfiction) up to 5,000 words.

• Art: bookplates/line art/photographs; inquire first.

Include SASE, brief bio, e-mail address or phone number.

Response within three months. Spring/summer issue due out in May, fall/winter in November.

Reading periods: May-July, Nov.-Jan.

Simultaneous submissions accepted, but not for contests (see below).

Complimentary copy for contributors; discount for extra copies.

Potomac Review explores the topography and inner human terrain of the Mid-Atlantic region and beyond for a growing readership. Would your work provide content that educates, challenges or diverts in fresh ways?

A vivid, individual quality is prized, with ethical depth and, as Flannery O'Connor said, "the vision to go with it."

The 8th annual fiction/poetry contest open Jan.-Apr. 15, 2003. Results for 2002 in fall/winter issue.

Sample issue $10. Year's subscription (2 double issues) $18, two years (4 double issues) $30.

See our Web site at www.montgomerycollege.edu/potomacreview

"Writers are notorious for failing to support their own. How many...buy or even read literary magazines?" —Thomas E. Kennedy

Categories: Fiction—Nonfiction—Arts—Children—Culture—Ecology—Environment—Literature—Poetry—Regional—Short Stories—Writing

CONTACT: Submissions Editor
Material: All
Montgomery College
51 Mannakee St.
Rockville MD 20850

Potpourri

Ceased publication.

Power & Gas Marketing

Please refer to Oildom Publishing.

POWER & MOTORYACHT

Power & Motoryacht

EDITORIAL PROFILE

Power & Motoryacht is edited and designed to meet the needs and pleasures of owners of powerboats 24 feet and larger, with special emphasis on the 35-foot-plus market. Launched in 1985, the magazine gives readers accurate advice on how to choose, operate, and maintain their boats as well as what electronics and gear will help them pursue their favorite pastime. In addition, since powerboating is truly a lifestyle and not just a hobby for these experienced readers, PMY reports on a host of other topics that affect their enjoyment of the water: chartering, sportfishing, and the environment, among others.

Some of the regular article themes are:

• CRUISING—places readers can take their own boats for a few days' enjoyment

• PROFILES—stories about interesting and even quirky boaters, craftsmen, etc.

• MAINTENANCE—tips on upkeep and repair

• LEGISLATION—how pending or recently enacted laws will affect readers' lifestyle

• TECHNOLOGY—advances that are improving construction/ engineering and performances

WRITING STYLE

Since PMY readers have an average of 35 years' experience boating, articles must be clear, concise, and authoritative; knowledge of the marine industry is mandatory. Include personal experience and information from marine industry experts where appropriate. Also include a list of the people and organizations (with phone numbers) contacted during your research.

All manuscripts must be e-mailed or sent on disk (Microsoft Word). Articles should run between 800 and 1,400 words. If a travel story is being submitted, 35-mm color slides must accompany the manuscript.

PAYMENT POLICY

Depending on article length, compensation is between $500 and $1,200; this fee includes photography if it is part of an assignment. Payment is upon acceptance; if an assigned article does not meet with our guidelines, a one-third kill fee will be given.

SUBMISSIONS

Query first; unsolicited manuscripts and photography are not accepted and will not be returned.

Send a one-page query with a self-addressed, stamped envelope to the address below or via email. No phone inquiries.

Categories: Boating—Environment—Fishing—Outdoors— Sports/Recreation—Travel

CONTACT: Diane M. Byrne, Executive Editor
Material: All
260 Madison Ave., 8th Floor
New York NY 10016
E-mail: diane.byrne@panix.com
Website: www.powerandmotoryacht.com

Prairie Schooner
University of Nebraska Press

Thank you for your interest in our magazine. *Prairie Schooner* publishes short stories, poems, interviews, imaginative essays of general interest, and reviews of current books of poetry and fiction. Scholarly articles requiring footnote references should be submitted to journals of literary scholarship.

Prairie Schooner's intention is to publish the best writing available, both from beginning and established writers. In our seventy years of publication, we have printed the work of Eudora Welty, Octavio Paz, Tennessee Williams, Weldon Kees, Joyce Carol Oates, and Rita Dove, Richard Russo, Reynolds Price, Julia Alvarez, Sharon Olds, Cornelius Eady, plus scores of others.

All submissions to *Prairie Schooner* should be typed, double-spaced (except for poetry), and on one side of the paper only. Use margins of at least one inch, and be sure to put your name on each page of the manuscript. A self-addressed envelope, with adequate return postage on it, must accompany the submission. For poetry, we prefer a selection of 5-7 poems; for fiction, essays, and reviews, we prefer you send only one selection at at time. Send submissions to the attention of the editor at the address below.

Please allow 3-4 months for reply. *Prairie Schooner* does not read simultaneous submissions, and submissions must be received between September 1 and May 31. All manuscripts published by *Prairie Schooner* will be automatically considered for our annual prizes.

Subscription Information

We encourage you to read *Prairie Schooner* before submitting work.

Subscribe now to one of the oldest and most prestigious of the campus literary magazines in America. *Prairie Schooner* is published quarterly by the University of Nebraska Press.

Subscription rates
$26.00 for one year
$45.00 for two years
$60.00 for three years
Prairie Schooner accepts Visa and Mastercard.

If you do not wish to charge online, please send a check or money order to:
Prairie Schooner
201 Andrews Hall
Lincoln NE 68588-0334

The *Prairie Schooner* Prize Series

The *Prairie Schooner* Prize Series, an annual book series competition publishing one book of short fiction and one book of poetry each year through the University of Nebraska Press.

The *Prairie Schooner* Prize Series welcomes manuscripts from all writers, including non-US citizens writing in English, and is open to all writers, including those who have previously published volumes of short fiction and poetry.

Award winning manuscripts will be published by the University of Nebraska Press under the Press's standard contract. Winning authors will receive $3000 (including a $500 advance from UNP).

Guidelines:

Stories and poems previously published in periodicals are eligible for inclusion. Novels are not considered. Xeroxed copies are acceptable. Writers are welcome to enter both contests. No application forms are necessary. All entries will be read anonymously. Please send two cover pages: one listing only the title of the manuscript, and the other listing the author's name, address, telephone number and email address. The author's name should not appear on the manuscript. A $25 processing fee must accompany each submission, payable to *Prairie Schooner*. No past or present paid employee of *Prairie Schooner* or University of Nebraska Press or current faculty or students at University of Nebraska will be eligible for the prizes. Please include a self-addressed postage-paid postcard for confirmation of manuscript receipt. A stamped, self addressed business size envelope must accompany the submission; the manuscript will be recycled.

Any questions, please contact Kelly Grey Carlisle, Managing Editor (kgrey2@unl.edu).

Categories: Fiction—Poetry—Creative Nonfiction

CONTACT: Hilda Raz, Editor
Material: All, except Prairie Schooner Prize Series
CONTACT: Kelly Grey Carlisle, Managing Editor
Material: Prairie Schooner Prize Series
201 Andrews Hall
University of Nebraska
Lincoln NE 68588-0334
Phone: 402-472-0911
Fax: 402-472-9771
E-mail: kgrey2@unl.edu
Website: www.nebraskapress.unl.edu/schooner.html

Premier Tourism Marketing, Inc.

Writers' Agreement For Premier Tourism Marketing Publications

Premier Tourism Marketing Inc. publishes three publications: *Leisure Group Travel*, *Travel Tips* and *Leisure Travel Directories*. Each is published six times per year. *Leisure Group Travel* and *Travel Tips* each usually contain four to five feature stories per edition. Story lengths are usually 1500-2500 words. All stories are specifically aimed at helping our readership, travel planners for group travelers, who use the information when planning and booking interesting day and longer trips for their groups. We include details about attractions and interesting stops like festivals, events, cultural attractions, historic and scenic spots, etc. We include information and details about seasonality, distances between destinations, suggested gateways or hubs, and transportation options. Local convention and visitors bureaus or other travel information sources are included, with phone

numbers and Web sites. The demographics of the travelers themselves skew toward the more mature traveler, therefore stories should take this into consideration.

Our stories typically feature a specific country or region or part of a state or states, such as Southern California or the Great Lakes states. We do cover major cities within a featured region and occasionally feature specific cities as a stand-alone story. Theme stories use senior and group friendly examples from several destinations with topics like excursion railroads, live theater, cruise lines' booking policies for groups, city packages, etc.

Photos: We ask writers to request CDs, photos or color slides from contacts during story research and we credit photos as noted. We sometimes use maps or other illustrations. Stories will not be accepted without ample accompanying photographs.

Contacts: We will provide some contacts that writers should use while researching a story and expect the writer to find other appropriate contacts and verify information for accuracy.

Rights & Payments: We pay upon publication (generally $.12 per assigned word) or as agreed upon. Kill fee is usually $25. It is mutually agreed that one revision is included in the contract, not including any revisions necessitated by the word count varying more than 10% from the contracted story length. It is further agreed that Premier Tourism Marketing Inc., by making payment to writer, has the unlimited right to republish all stories in electronic format. Writers will be paid one half the original fee for any stories republished in any other of its magazines.

Format: We ask that stories be submitted via e-mail attachment in Microsoft Word for Windows format. Alternatively, we can accept a Word diskette. We prefer photo images on CD.

Time: Feature stories are assigned to writers at least one month in advance. Premier Tourism Marketing Inc. reserves the right to kill stories without payment if the copy deadline is missed.

Notes to writers: We welcome query letters and are willing to consider story ideas and angles, but rarely accept stories directly from queries, as our editorial calendar is prepared a year in advance. We like to see writing samples and are happy to send a sample issue upon request.

Categories: Regional—Travel

CONTACT: Editor
Material: All
4901 Forest Avenue
Downers Grove IL 60515
Phone: 630-964-1431
Fax: 630-852-0414
E-mail: johnk@premiertourismmarketing.com

Presbyterians *Today*

Presbyterians Today

Presbyterians Today is a magazine for members of the Presbyterian Church (U.S.A.). It is published 10 times a year, with combined January/February and June/July or July/August issues. Circulation is about 60,000.

The target audience for *Presbyterians Today* is laypeople. Readers are quite diverse in age, sex, education, theological viewpoints, and involvement in the life of the church.

Presbyterians Today seeks to:

• Report in a fair, accurate and balanced way on the activities of the Presbyterian Church (U.S.A.) and of its members, leaders and mission partners.

• Uphold the mission of the Presbyterian Church (U.S.A.).

• Illuminate the faith and heritage that bind Presbyterians together.

• Express the rich diversity within the denomination.

• Challenge readers to grow in their commitment to Jesus Christ as Lord.

• Provide a Christian perspective on contemporary issues.

• Be a source of inspiration, spiritual direction and practical tools for life and ministry.

• Reflect the denomination's priorities: evangelism, justice, spiritual information and leadership development.

FEATURE ARTICLES

Presbyterians Today welcomes contributions from free-lance writers. Stories vary in length (800-2,000 words; preferred, 1,000-1,500). Appropriate subjects: profiles of interesting Presbyterians and of Presbyterian programs and activities; issues of current concern to the church; ways in which individuals and families express their Christian faith in significant ways or relate their faith to the problems of society. Most articles have some direct relevance to a Presbyterian audience; however, Presbyterians Today also seeks well informed articles written for a general audience that can help individuals and families cope with the stresses of daily living from a Christian perspective.

Presbyterians Today almost never uses fiction or short fillers, and poetry only occasionally. Original manuscripts are preferred. Reprints are occasionally used, but submission of reprints and multiple submissions are not encouraged.

Authors are asked to submit only one article at a time. Manuscripts are read by at least two editors, and a reply given normally within one month after receipt.

Presbyterians Today pays for articles upon acceptance. With the author's permission, the magazine may hold a manuscript for future consideration (which does not preclude the author from submitting the article elsewhere), and payment will be offered at the time the article is scheduled for publication—if publication rights are available to Presbyterians Today at that time. Authors receive complimentary copies of issues in which their articles appear.

SHORT FEATURES

Presbyterians Today also accepts short features (250-600 words) about interesting people, programs, events and congregations related to the Presbyterian Church (U.S.A.), for the "SpotLight" department. The editors may suggest that a full-length feature article, because of timeliness, space limitations or content, would be more appropriate as a "SpotLight" feature.

HUMOR

Presbyterians Today uses jokes or short humorous stories for the "LaughLines" department. Credit will be given to contributors, but the material should be in the public domain, not copyrighted. Preferred length: 150 words or less.

"AS I SEE IT"

Presbyterians Today's op-ed department, "As I See It," on its Web site (www.pcusa.org/today), is primarily for *Presbyterians Today* readers—an opportunity for them to express views or opinions on current topics of interest to Presbyterians. Normally only one submission will be posted each issue. Preferred maximum length, 500 words. No payment is offered for "As I See It" articles. Because of planning and production schedules, specific responses to material in previous issues of Presbyterians Today should be made in shorter form as letters to the editor for the "Readers Write" department.

QUERIES

Queries are not required, but may save effort and postage if a subject proposed is clearly inappropriate or if similar articles have fairly recently been used or are currently in the works. Manuscripts are received on speculation.

SUBMISSIONS

Manuscripts should be typed, double-spaced, on 8 1/2" X 11" paper. The author's name and address, including zip code, and Social Security number should be typed on the manuscript as well as the cover letter. Postage or a self-addressed, stamped envelope should be enclosed for the return of a manuscript if it is not accepted. Manuscripts may also be submitted by E-mail.

Photos accompanying a manuscript should be of good quality for reproduction. Black-and-white or color prints, transparencies, or contact sheets are acceptable. They should be identified as to content and credit line. Photos may be sent after an article is accepted, but it is helpful to know whether or not they are or could be available.

Facts, quotations and the spelling of proper names should always be checked for accuracy. *Presbyterians Today* normally uses the New Revised Standard Version for Biblical quotations; if another version of Scripture is used, this should be indicated. If copyrighted material is quoted, the author should secure permission in writing from the copyright holder and cite the work, author, publisher and date of copyright.

RULES FOR WRITING

Writer's Digest has suggested 20 rules for good writing:

1. Prefer the plain word to the fancy.
2. Prefer the familiar word to the unfamiliar.
3. Prefer the Saxon word to the Romance.
4. Prefer nouns and verbs to adjectives and adverbs.
5. Prefer picture nouns and action verbs.
6. Never use a long word when a short one will do as well.
7. Master the simple declarative sentence.
8. Prefer the simple sentence to the complicated.
9. Vary the sentence length.
10. Put the word you want to emphasize at the beginning or end of your sentence.
11. Use the active voice.
12. Put the statements in a positive form.
13. Use short paragraphs.
14. Cut needless words, sentences and paragraphs.
15. Use plain, conversational language.
16. Avoid imitation. Write in your natural style.
17. Write clearly.
18. Avoid gobbledygook and jargon.
19. Write to be understood, not to impress.
20. Revise and rewrite. Improvement is always possible.

To these *Presbyterians Today* adds one more:

Reporting is preferred to reflection. Your chances of having your article accepted for publication increase to the extent that you write in the third person, not the first person. Most stories can be told better without the use of "I."

Before you begin to write, ask yourself: "What do I want to say?" "Why?" "To whom?" "How do I plan to say it?" If your article is geared to a Presbyterian audience, make sure it is clear how and why the subject relates to that audience. Assemble and organize your material. An outline may help. After you have written your first draft, it is good practice to leave it for a time. When you return to it, read it aloud, making sure its language flows freely and comfortably.

Categories that pertain to our publication: Non-fiction relevant to the Presbyterian Church (U.S.A.)—not essays, but articles about unusual Presbyterian individuals, creative ministries.

Categories: Nonfiction—Christian Interests—Religion

CONTACT: Eva Stimson, Editor
Material: All
100 Witherspoon St.
Louisville KY 40202-1396
Phone: 502-569-5637
Fax: 502-569-8632
E-mail: today@pcusa.org
Web site: www.pcusa.org/today

> *Remember: Editors change jobs and publishers change addresses. It is wise to invest in a phone call for the current information before submitting.*

Presentations
TECHNOLOGY AND TECHNIQUES FOR EFFECTIVE COMMUNICATION

Presentations
Technology and Techniques for Effective Communication

Presentations Magazine accepts three kinds of articles for publication: columns, product reviews, and features. Many of our contributors are unpaid. As a rule, we pay only for pieces by professionals with whom we have contracted ahead of time, and with whom the fee is negotiated in advance.

For all manuscripts, it will increase your chances of acceptance if you bear the following stylistic guidelines in mind:

• We generally use the present tense ("say," not "said"), the active voice, and the familiar "you" when appropriate ("you find," not "it is found"). We discourage unsolicited first-person pieces.

• We do not describe situations or scenarios that did not happen without explaining to the reader that the event is fictional.

• We use the Associated Press stylebook as our chief reference in matters of editorial style.

• We encourage writers to interview end users of technology (not just vendors and manufacturers) whenever possible.

• Word counts in our magazine amount to about 800 words (just over three double-spaced typed pages) per printed page. Thus 800 words is the target length for "Speaker's Notes" and other one-page columns.

• For features, we expect writers to interview four to eight sources, chosen with an eye to their geographical disbursement as well as their expertise. We are a national magazine, not a regional one, and we expect our sources to reflect this.

• Most of our stories are accompanied by pictures of products, which we generally expect the writer to supply via the manufacturer. Many columns—"Speaker's Notes," for example—also require a head shot of the author. We welcome high-quality photographs, which we are happy to get electronically (by diskette or e-mail), although good prints, 35mm slides or 4 x 5 transparencies are also acceptable. Our software supports a variety of file formats, including EPS and TIF (300 dpi or higher); digital files are accepted on Iomega Zip and Jaz disks, as well as floppies, CDs and via e-mail. *JPEG and GIF file formats tend to degrade image quality and are strongly discouraged.* If your article is illustrated with screen captures, they should be 640 x 480 in the highest color resolution possible.

• Your manuscript should include a headline and subhead (with the understanding that editors may choose another one for the article once it appears in print). You should also provide captions for any pictures or images you submit with your story. Any book or article you cite should have a complete bibliographic reference (author, publication date, publisher); any product you mention should include the exact product name and number, together with the full company name and location (including the manufacturer's phone number and e-mail address). Please also provide a list of the names and phone numbers for all your article's sources. (This last information won't be printed, but it will be very helpful to your editors.)

• We insist on exclusive, first-time publication rights to all accepted manuscripts, which means we don't reprint articles that have appeared in other publications. We may consider an author's original adaptation of material from a previously published (or about-to-be-published) book, however.

Queries from writers new to our magazine are considered for feature articles only, not for columns (excluding Speakers Notes submissions). For full manuscripts, we accept paper copies, but we encourage writers to submit articles electronically—by diskette or e-mail. Allow 30-60 days for response. Special formatting (other than bold, italic and underline) is strongly discouraged. **E-mailed articles *must* include the contributor's snail-mail address and telephone number.**

E-mail **features or columns** to: jhill@presentations.com

(If you are submitting an article that has been previously assigned to you, please e-mail it to your assigning editor—and call to tell him or her you sent it.)

Categories: Nonfiction—Business—Computers—Education—Government—Internet—Presentations—Technology

CONTACT: Julie Hill, Managing Editor
Material: All
VNU Business Media Inc.
50 South Ninth St.
Minneapolis MN 55402
Phone: 612-333-0471
Fax: 612-333-6526
E-mail: jhill@presentations.com
Website: www.presentations.com

Prevention Magazine

Dear Writer:

Thank you for your recent request. Unfortunately, we do not have writers' guidelines to send you because we use very little freelance material. If you are interested in submitting material, we suggest sending a query with full details.

If the piece is already written, you may send a nonreturnable copy if you wish.

We appreciate your interest in our publication.

Best wishes!

Sincerely yours,

Readers' Service

Categories: Nonfiction—Cooking—Diet/Nutrition—Food/Drink—Health—Physical Fitness—Medicine

CONTACT: Denise Foley, Features Editor
Material: All
33 E. Minor St.
Emmaus PA 18098
Phone: 610-967-7650
Fax: 610-967-7654
Website: www.prevention.com

Primavera

IN GENERAL

Primavera publishes original fiction, poetry, and art that reflects the experiences of women. We interpret this theme as broadly as possible. We select works that encompass the lives of women of different ages, races, sexual orientations, social classes, and locations. We will consider work by male writers but it must not require a male perspective to be understood or enjoyed.

Address all submissions to the editors at the address below. All submissions without an SASE will be discarded—illustration or manuscript.

Primavera pays both writers and artists in contributors' copies: two for each published item. If your work is accepted, we will send you a form to assign us the first rights to its publication. After publication, the copyright reverts to you, and you may reprint your work as long as *Primavera* is credited with its initial publication.

Do not send previously published work or simultaneous submissions.

We are happy to offer artists and writers a special discount on copies of *Primavera*! Back issues, usually $7.00 each, are only $5.00 when you mention this offer; current issues, usually $9.00, cost only $7.00. We pay for shipping.

WRITING

Poetry should be single-spaced, with stanza and line breaks clearly indicated. Computer printouts are fine, as long as the type is legible.

Primavera is published by a small staff of volunteers who meet biweekly (less often in summer), and it often takes several weeks, even months, before a manuscript completes the review process. Please be patient with us! We will respond to you, although unfortunately our staff is too small, and the volume of manuscripts we receive too large, for us to comment on each submission.

We edit poetry and fiction. If your work is selected, we may write to you with proposed changes, or ask you to rewrite troublesome sections. We always send you the edited version for your approval before publication.

We are interested in all writers, published and unpublished. We judge each work on its merit and not on the author's reputation (or lack of one).

ART

Primavera publishes black-and-white art inside the magazine: line and continuous-tone drawings, paintings, and photographs. Infrequently, we publish color illustration. We accept submissions on approval and do not commission work. We review work by women artists only.

For review, please send slides or photocopies. If we select your work for publication, we will ask you to send us the original or a professional-quality transparency. Write us if you aren't sure of the best way to represent your work

Categories: Fiction—Poetry—Women's Fiction

CONTACT: Board of Editors
Material: All
PO Box 37-7547
Chicago IL 60637
Phone: 733-324-5920

Primedia History Group

Guidelines apply to the following periodicals:

American History   *America's Civil War*
Aviation History   *British Heritage*
Civil War Times   *Military History*
MHQ: the Quarterly Journal of Military History
Vietnam   *Wild West*
World War II

PRIMEDIA History Group, a division of PRIMEDIA Enthusiast Publications History Group in Leesburg, Va., publishes ten bimonthly historical magazines: *America's Civil War, American History, Aviation History, British History, Civil War Times, MHQ: The Quarterly Journal of Military History, Vietnam, Wild West*, and *World War II*. Prospective contributors should be familiar with the individual magazines before querying.

Historical accuracy is imperative. We do not use fiction or poetry. We do not publish reprints.

STYLE: The two paramount considerations in all PRIMEDIA History Group publications are absolute accuracy and highly readable style. Give proper attribution in the manuscript when using another author's work and cite your major sources for our review. We like to see action and quotes where possible to heighten reader interest.

QUERY: Submit a short, self-explanatory query summarizing the story and its highlights. Also state your sources and expertise. Cite any color and black-and-white illustrations and primary sources of illustrations (museums, historical societies, private collections, etc.) you can provide. Please put complete name on every photo submitted. Photocopies of suggested illustrations are extremely helpful. Illustration ideas are an absolute must. The likelihood that articles can be effectively illustrated often determines the ultimate fate of manuscripts. Many otherwise excellent articles have been rejected due to a lack of suitable art. All submissions are on speculation and must be accompanied by an SASE if you want your submission returned. Sample copies cost $5 each. Xerox copies of articles cost $2 each.

FORMAT: We expect authors to submit with manuscripts computer disks that are IBM or Macintosh compatible. The disk will be returned to the sender. We also accept e-mail submissions. Manuscripts must be typed, double-spaced on one side of standard white 8½ x 11, 16 to 30-pound paper. Name, address, telephone number and Social Security number must be on the first page of your article. Indicate sources and suggested further reading at the end of your manuscript. Include a 1-2 paragraph autobiography. Address your submission to the appropriate magazine, Attention: Editor, c/o PRIMEDIA History Group at the address listed below.

LENGTH: Feature articles should be 3,000-4,000 words in length and should include a 500-word sidebar. Departments should be 2,000 words or less. PRIMEDIA History Group retains the right to edit, condense or rewrite for style.

PAYMENT: Payment, which is made 30 days after publication, varies by magazine and ranges from $300 for features (including sidebar) and $150 to $200 for departments. We also use book reviews, payable at a per-published-word rate, with a minimum payment of $40. PRIMEDIA History Group buys exclusive worldwide publication rights, and the right to reprint the article in all languages, in hard copy or through electronic means, at no additional cost on TheHistoryNet.com.

REPORTING TIME: Please allow six months' response time for queries and manuscripts. If you want immediate verification that a submission has been received and is being considered, please enclose a stamped, self-addressed postcard containing the title of your submission.

PRIMEDIA History Group Editorial Philosophy

PRIMEDIA History Group is committed to creating accurate, entertaining, and informative magazines, books, and products. It is our responsibility to ensure the loyalty and confidence of our customers by maintaining the highest editorial standards. To this end, our editorial content is never used as a sounding board for political partisanship, religious points of view, or social agendas. Our mission is to present an undistorted view of history and to encourage understanding and appreciation for the events, personalities, and artifacts of the past.

Just as writer's guidelines provide the mechanical requirements for submission of a manuscript, the following tips are intended to provide more subjective guidance for the preparation of copy that is editorially "clean" and enjoyable to read.

• Please give the reader a little excitement, some sense of being there, with lively, but always factual, anecdotes. Lead with one of these, if possible, to foster the reader's interest in seeing more of your story and to let him or her know that here is an article that is worth reading.

• Know what the reader expects from the publication in terms of subject matter and style of writing. Be very careful to keep technical terminology in the proper context.

• Start most paragraphs with a simple, active sentence—so many begin with As, When, Because, After, or other passive openers. Active writing keeps readers' eyes open. Our aim is to bring life to history, not to use it as a bedtime soporific. The same goes for "…ing" verbs; use them sparingly, as you do sleeping pills, to which their effects are related.

• Provide each paragraph with more than one sentence, except to make an occasional emphatic point. Break a paragraph before it runs on and takes up half a page.

• Keep to your story, and tell one story at a time. If there is a related aside, put it into a sidebar rather than break the flow of the main story.

• Maintain a smooth flow of information. It's fine to begin with an attention-getting action lead and a flashback, but from then on proceed straight through the story rather than jump around chronologically. If you make it difficult for the reader to follow your story, he will desert you; if you do that to the editor, he will protect his readers from a similar experience.

• Watch your spelling and grammar. You may be an expert in your subject, but your credibility can be shattered by sloppy copy.

• When you—either in exhaustion or exultation—finish the last keystroke, never, never rush the manuscript into the mail in an I'm-so-glad-to-be-finished dismissal. Put the manuscript aside and out of your mind at least overnight; then get back to it in a day or two and play editor. Go through the entire manuscript slowly, thoroughly and critically and correct all spelling errors. Question the spelling of every name—person, thing, company—all of them. Make sure you have included full name and rank/title for every person mentioned. Read through the manuscript as if you were the reader who has never seen it before and does not know what you are trying to get across. Does it flow smoothly? Does it say what you want it to say? Does it proceed logically through a basic beginning, middle and end? Is it simple and clear rather than flowery and hobbled by descriptive adjectives? Are your facts straight? Check how presentable the final, assembled package is. Make it professional, not pretty. Do not dress it in fancy folders or tie it with ribbons. Keep your manuscript straight, neat and clean.

• What you are doing here is just what the editor will do when he receives your material. His job is to select quality material that will hold the interest of his readers. If your submission is unprofessional, it may be returned unread with a standard rejection letter. A professional presentation of a well written and researched manuscript has a better chance of being reviewed and seriously considered. From then on, the appropriateness of the subject, the writing and the facts will influence whether the editor believes your manuscript will please the reader—and will determine its acceptance.

• Keep your facts straight.

For *Aviation History* Magazine

Aviation History is a bimonthly subscriber and newsstand magazine published by PRIMEDIA History Group that aims to make aeronautical history not only factually accurate and complete, but also enjoyable for our varied subscriber and newsstand audience. We always seek well-written, non-fiction writing about traditional and unique aviation history articles, plus excellent illustrations. We like an entertaining, informative and unusual story that grabs the reader's attention and holds it. We favor carefully researched third-person articles or firsthand accounts that give the reader a sense of experiencing historical events. We do not publish reprints. Manuscripts with misspelled words, poor grammar, weak leads, passive sentence structure, partial names, unsupported statements or unattributed quotes are rejected without further consideration.

Categories: Nonfiction—Aviation—Civil War—History—Military—Western

CONTACT: Phil George, Editor
Material: *American History* Submissions
CONTACT: R. Vance, Editor
Material: *British Heritage* and *Civil War Times* Submissions
CONTACT: Jon Guttman, Editor
Material: *Military History* Submissions
CONTACT: Richar Latture, Editor
Material: *MHQ* Submissions
CONTACT: Art Sanfelici, Editor
Material: *Aviation History* Submissions
CONTACT: Greg Lalire, Editor
Material: *Wild West* Submissions
CONTACT: Dana Shoaf, Editor
Material: *American Civil War* Submissions
CONTACT: David T. Zabecki, Editor
Material: *Vietnam* Submissions
CONTACT: Chris Anderson, Editor
Material: *World War II* Submissions
741 Miller Drive SE, Suite D-2
Leesburg VA 20175
Phone: 703-779-8318
Fax: 703-779-8310
Website: www.thehistorynet.com

Progressive ENGINEER

Progressive Engineer

Progressive Engineer celebrates the accomplishments of forward-thinking engineers using a journalistic style that goes beyond describing the technology they work with and delves into their personal background. Published monthly on the Internet, the online magazine reaches engineers of all disciplines in all types of jobs.

How to Approach Us

The best way to to get a feel for our editorial style and content is to read a sample issue of the magazine on our website. Then send us a query letter outlining your idea.

Types of Articles We Use

Features: These cover projects that entail significant amounts of engineering with broad implications and describe the technology used and profile the engineers involved. Length: Approximately 2000 words (including sidebars). Payment: $300.

Short Profiles: These describe engineers or inventors who accomplish something significant in the course of their jobs and careers and tell of engineers applying their skills in unusual and innovative ways. These are often average people who do something out of the ordinary either on the job or off. Length: 1000-1500 words. Payment: $150.

Company Profiles: Describe companies that employ engineers, such as engineering firms, manufacturing companies, and construction companies, focusing on engineering work the company does as well as its scenario for hiring engineers. The latter includes the types of engineers the company uses, current hiring status, and what they look for in engineers. 1000-1500 words. Payment: $150-$175

Style

Progressive Engineer covers engineering in an easy-to-read style devoid of equations, jargon, and long words found in many technical journals. When applicable, we expect authors to use several sources in researching an article to maintain balance and objectivity. Obtain quotes from experts, principles involved in projects, and subjects of profiles. Feel free to use first person if appropriate. Features often use sidebars (generally 300-500 words) to complement the main body, often covering the technical content involved. Profiles should be written around a theme, such as a particular development or characteristic of the individual, and shouldn¹t just list credentials and accomplishments.

Manuscript Requirements

All manuscripts should include name, address, phone number, social security number, e-mail address, and word count at the top of the first page. Submit them by e-mail.

Photos

When possible, supply photos (and diagrams, if helpful) with your manuscript or tell us where we can obtain them. We can use digital images as well as B&W and color prints and 35mm or larger transparencies—originals or duplicates. Include a list of captions keyed to numbers on the photos. If you didn't take a photo you send us, tell us who did so we can give proper credit. We accept photos from companies and PR firms but don¹t pay for them. Payment: $25 per photo used in an article.

Rights and Payments

We consider reprints and simultaneous submissions if the markets don¹t compete; for reprints, payment is 50 percent of normal rates. Many times, we can use previously published material modified for our slant, in which case we pay full rate. Payment for all work is on publication.

Categories: Nonfiction—Engineering—Regional—Technology

CONTACT: Tom Gibson, Editor
Material: All

2049 Crossroads Dr.
Lewisburg PA 17837
Phone: 570-568-8444
E-mail: progress@jdweb.com
Website: www.ProgressiveEngineer.com

Protooner

In *Protooner*, you will find many things of interest to Cartoonists and to Gagwriters, Professional and Amateur alike.

CARTOON COVERS

• **Slant:** Generals pertaining to the fields of cartooning, for the cartoonist/gagwriter receiving acceptance of sales or rejection slips; humorously themed.

• **Avoid:** Generals not containing the slant requested above. Medicals, profanity, gender slandering, racial digs, un-coded submissions or originals.

• **Submit:** B&W line drawings—single or double panel. Clear photocopies are preferred. Limit of ten (10) per batch—with or without gaglines—caption less preferred. Seasonal Cartoons—3 months in advance.

• **Pays:** $25.00/cover art. *Protooner* will not be responsible for original artwork.

CARTOON SPOTS (by assignment only):

• We accept samples for our files.

• **Pays:** $15-20/O.A.

SHORT HUMOR

• **Themes:** Related to cartooning, gagwriting, Internet.

• **Avoid:** How-to articles

• **Submit:** Query letter/SASE/Typed and double-spaced

• **Length:** 2,000-5,000 words

• **Pays:** Negotiated/O.A.

Categories: Cartoons—Comedy—Humor

CONTACT: Ladd A. Miller, Art Director
Material: All
PO Box 2270
Daly City CA 94017-2270
Phone: 650-755-4827
Fax: 415-755-3005
E-mail: protooner@earthlink.net
Website: protooner.lookscool.com

Psychology Today
MIND BODY SPIRIT

Psychology Today

Thanks for your interest in *Psychology Today*! As you know, PT explores every aspect of human behavior, from the cultural trends that shape the way we think and feel to the intricacies of modern neuroscience. Although many psychologists and mental health professionals read PT, most of our readers are simply intelligent and curious people interested in the psyche and the self. Think of us as a health magazine for the mind!

WHAT WE NEED: Good, clearly articulated feature ideas and writers with the talent to bring those ideas to life. Nearly any subject related to psychology is fair game. We value originality, insight, and good reporting; we're not interested in stories or topics that have already been covered ad nauseam by other magazines unless you can provide a fresh new twist and much more depth. Although our articles are aimed at an intelligent mainstream audience, rather than specifically at psychologists, the ideas and claims made in the stories should be backed up where appropriate by good, solid scientific research. We're not interested in simple-minded "pop psychology."

While our readership is two-thirds female and largely college-educated, it is also diverse. There is no typical PT reader—and no typical PT story.

HOW TO GET AN ASSIGNMENT: Please don't send us complete manuscripts—our desks are already overflowing with journals, faxes, books, and articles awaiting editing. Instead, send a one- to two-page query letter explaining:
- what you want to write,
- why you want to write it now, and
- why you should be the one to write it.

Tell us why and how your story will affect people's lives, if applicable, and mention sources you might contact. If your work has been published before, feel free to attach a clip or two. Address the query to executive editor Lybi Ma or senior editor Carin Gorrell. We greatly appreciate an enclosed SASE.

We highly recommend that you read some recent back issues of the magazine to get a feel for what we publish and what topics we've covered lately. If we've written about topic X in a recent issue, chances are we won't want to run another feature on that subject for at least a year or two.

Many of the news stories in our Insights section are written in-house, but we do run pieces by freelancers. Topics include work, education, health, nutrition, relationships and neuropsychology and are directly linked to the most recent scientific findings. Address your queries to news editor Kaja Perina.

WE DON'T PUBLISH poems or short stories; we do consider first-person accounts of facing and overcoming psychological adversity for the one-page "My Story" column.

PLEASE NOTE: that we receive a lot of queries, and sorting through all that mail takes time, particularly for a tiny staff. We usually answer queries within six to eight weeks, but if your letter arrives as deadlines approach we may not get to it for awhile. Please be patient.

MISCELLANY: We pay on publication and payment will be negotiated between the writer and editor. We'll also reimburse you for minor necessary expenses (phone calls, yes; plane tickets, no). Of course you'll also receive some contributor's copies.

If your article has a seasonal or timely aspect, keep in mind our production schedule: our editorial deadline for an issue is nearly three months before the issue hits newsstands. Count on a five-month lead-time to get an assignment.

If you have any further questions, feel free to call executive editor Lybi Ma (ext. 130).

Thanks again for your interest, and we look forward to hearing from you!

Categories: Nonfiction—Health—Psychology—Science

CONTACT: Carin Gorrell, Senior Editor
Material: All
49 E. 21st St. 11th Floor New York NY
10010
Phone: 212-260-7210, ext. 105
Fax: 212-260-7445

Quarterly West
University of Utah

Thank you for your interest in our magazine.

Quarterly West is a semiannual publication. Sponsors a biennial award for novellas. Work published in *Quarterly West* has been selected for inclusion in *Best American Short Stories, Best American Poetry, Best American Travel Writing*, and the Pushcart Prize anthology. QW publishes literary, experimental, and formal poetry, fiction and creative nonfiction as well as translations and reviews. Submit 3-6 poems, 2-3 short shorts, or 1 short story/essay/book review. Brief cover letters welcome. Send SASE for reply or return of ms. No fax or email submissions. Responds in up to 8 months; sooner when possible. Sample copies are available for $7.50. Pays $15-50 and two contributors copies on publication for all rights.

You may wish to know the following information:

1. *Quarterly West* expects the standard format for fiction or essays: typed, double-spaced, author's name and title on the first page. Poetry should be single-spaced.

2. Each manuscript must be accompanied by an SASE for response and return.

3. Editors will consider simultaneous submissions, but expect to be informed. Authors must notify editors immediately of simultaneously submitted work accepted elsewhere.

4. We read submissions between September 1 and May 1 only. Submissions received between May 2 and August 31 will be returned unread.

5. Submit only one story or essay, or three to five poems at a time. Writers may submit up to two short-shorts (less than five pages each).

6. Contributors receive two copies of the issue in which their work appears, as well as a small honorarium.

7. *Quarterly West* sponsors a biennial novella competition. Please send an SASE for complete guidelines.

8. We ask that former contributors wait at least one year after publication before submitting new work to *Quarterly West*.

Categories: Fiction—Nonfiction—Book Reviews—Interview—Literature—Poetry—Short Stories—Writing

CONTACT: David C. Hawkins, Editor
Material: All, except poetry
CONTACT: Poetry Editor
Material: Poetry
200 S. Central Campus Dr., Rm 317
University of Utah
Salt Lake City UT 84112-9109
Phone: 801-585-5167
Website: www.utah.edu.quarterlywest
or www.webdelsol.com/Quarterly_West

Quick & Easy Quilting
Quilt World

General Information

House of White Birches publishes *Quick & Easy Quilting* and *Quilt World* magazines, two quilting hardcover books a year, patterns for e-PatternsCentral.com and quilt pattern books.

Project submissions or manuscripts:

Begin each submission with a sentence or two about the topic/project (a personal anecdote or historical information about the project).

Each publication has its own style. Look through recent copies of each one to familiarize yourself with that style and the type of project that has been published recently. Pattern your submissions after those in the publication to which you are submitting your designs.

Quilt World is a general quilting publication. We accept articles about special quilters, techniques, coverage of unusual quilts at quilt shows, special interest quilts and patterns. We include 5–8 patterns in every issue.

Quick & Easy Quilting fills the need of the quilter wanting to make quality quilts in less time. We print patterns (traditional or contemporary) and technical articles on machine piecing, quilting and quick-cutting techniques.

Quilt Pattern Books feature the work of one quilter and include several projects with a specific theme. They are usually 8 to 32 pages in length.

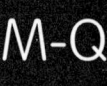

Quilt Hardcover Books feature the work of many quilters. They include 30 to 60 projects around a general theme. Designer suggestions for specific hardcover books are sent to quilters in our database, but can also be requested.

Include a list of materials needed to complete the project using generic names. Brand names can be listed beneath the Materials List in the form of a credit. If you do so, provide exact names of products and a current address for the company.

Mark whether patterns/templates are with or without seam allowances both on templates and in cutting instructions.

Be sure the instructions are accurate.

Diagrams/drawings should be numbered (using Figure 1, Figure 2) and clear and easy to understand.

Mailing address: Send submissions and completed projects to Sandra Hatch, Magazine Name, RR #3 Box 930, Sweet Rd., Lincoln, ME 04457, or for books and pattern books to Jeanne Stauffer, Book Name, House of White Birches, 306 East Parr Road, Berne, IN 46711.

Writing guidelines:

Query letters with photos are encouraged. Unsolicited manuscripts should be typewritten, easy to read and accompanied by return postage

The author/designer's name and complete address and page number should appear in the upper left-hand corner of all pages

Submissions may be made on disk. We use Macintosh computers with Microsoft Word. We also need a hard copy of the manuscript.

Photos

Color slides or clear photographs are accepted. Please provide photo captions for all photographs.

Label each slide/photograph with your name and address and a number. List the numbers with photo captions as part of your manuscript.

Return of published projects: Projects will be returned to you after publication with your complimentary copy. This may be 6–8 months for magazines or 10–12 months for hardcover books and pattern books.

Contracts and Payment

When we receive the completed project, instructions and all related materials, we will send you an agreement and a business-reply envelope. Sign the agreement and return it in the postage-paid envelope. Keep the photocopy of the agreement for your records and return the original to us.

Payment will be made within 45 days of the time we receive your contract. Amount will be determined by accuracy, creativity, workmanship, skill level, overall quality and instruction format. Average fees range from $50 to $550. Because HWB purchases all rights to designs unless otherwise arranged, designers should not sell the purchased design or one very similar to it to another publisher.

If you have any questions, contact Jeanne Stauffer or Sandra Hatch. If you have a question about the status of a book design, contact Dianne Schmidt, Associate Editor, (260) 589-4000, Dianne_Schmidt@whitebirches.com.

We look forward to working with you in the coming months!

Categories: Nonfiction—Crafts—Hobbies

CONTACT: Sandra Hatch, Editor, hatch@link.net
Material: Submissions and completed projects (Send to Maine address)
RR #3 Box 930
Sweet Rd.
Lincoln ME 04457
Phone: 260-589-4000
CONTACT: Jeanne Stauffer
Material: Books and pattern books
House of White Birches
306 East Parr Rd.
Berne IN 46711
Website: www.quilt-world.com

> *Remember: Editors change jobs and publishers change addresses. It is wise to invest in a phone call for the current information before submitting.*

Quilt World

Please refer to *Quick & Easy Quilting.*

Quilting Arts Magazine®

***Quilting Arts Magazine®* is actively seeking the following queries for publication:**

- Art Quilt and Mixed Media Artists to be profiled
- Fiber-altered books
- Quilts with a landscape theme
- Unique embellishment and surface design techniques
- Quilting with mixed media including found objects
- Pictorial quilts
- Art dolls made of cloth
- Narrative quilts (quilts that depict a story)
- Working with interesting mixed media
- Quilts with image transfers
- Beaded embellishments
- Interesting uses of silk ribbon
- Bobbin thread embroidery
- Wearable art techniques
- One-of-a-kind garments
- Abstract quilts
- Fiber journals
- Working with transfer inks
- Embossing on fabric
- Unique fabric painting and dyeing methods

Guidelines for Submissions: *Quilting Arts Magazine®* is interested in articles concerning contemporary art quilting, wearable arts, embellished quilting, mixed media, surface design, and crazy quilting.

Copyright Issues: No submissions which may violate copyright laws will be accepted. If your artwork could be perceived by Quilting Arts, LLC as a potential copyright violation, please provide written consent by the party which may have standing with regard to the copyright issue. Thank you for cooperation.

Query first, please. Editors will consider articles submitted on speculation, but prefer that you query first MAIL ONLY (no emails, please) with an idea or brief proposal describing the idea, explaining how you'd handle the story, and summarizing your writing experience. If you'd like to see sample queries, click here.

What we are looking for? We like an enthusiastic, inspiring and elegant approach whenever possible. For how-to articles, we ask that they be user-friendly.

The length of the articles we publish varies greatly depending on subject and treatment. Feature articles range from 800-2500 words; briefer articles are usually 400-1,000 words.

Quilting Arts Magazine is most interested in receiving queries regarding the following:

Previously unpublished how-to articles that cover unique embellishing, quilting, and wearable arts techniques geared for either the beginner or advanced quilter.

Feature articles that explore motifs and methods of interest to art and embellished quilters; for example, different types of threads and their common (or uncommon) uses.

"In the Spotlight" pieces — Quilts with brief explanations of how the work was accomplished.

Rates of Pay: *Quilting Arts Magazine®* pays for feature articles only. Rates of pay depend on length of article, depth of subject matter, and quality of writing. Payment occurs within 45 days after publication.

For All Submissions: Please include your address, telephone number and a brief biographical paragraph that specifies the way you prefer your byline to appear, your title, your affiliation, and/or any relevant experience.

Materials submitted—written or photographed—cannot be returned unless a SASE (Self Addressed Stamped Envelope) is provided.

Categories: Arts—Crafts/Hobbies—Hobbies

CONTACT: Patricia Bolton, Editor in Chief
Material: All
PO Box 685
Stow, MA 01775
Phone: 978-897-7750
E-mail: editorial@quiltingartsllc.com (no submissions
please)
Website: www.quiltingartsllc.com

Quilting Today

Please refer to *Traditional Quiltworks*.

Rack
Adventures in Trophy Hunting

Rack magazine is published six times a year, from July through December, and is available only by subscription. Inside each issue are between 20 and 25 stories (averaging 1,000 words apiece) detailing the hunts behind world-class big game animals. Approximately 75 percent of the stories concern white-tailed deer, which MUST be scored on the Buckmasters (BTR) measuring system. By this yardstick, whitetails must score at least 160 as "typicals" or a minimum of 175 as "irregulars" to qualify. Other big game animals must simply qualify for any of the record books (B&C, P&Y, SCI, Rowland Ward or Longhunter).

Two-thirds of the stories that appear in *Rack* are either first-person accounts furnished by the hunters or written by the editors. The rest are bought from freelancers. An unpublished 1,000-word article with at least two accompanying photographs will fetch $250 upon publication; half that for second-time rights. A cover photo (always hunters with their whitetails) could garner an extra $500.

Queries and/or manuscripts should be sent to the managing editor via e-mail (mhandley@buckmasters.com). We prefer color prints or slides to be sent by regular mail. Please do not bother submitting queries or stories that stray beyond actual hunting tales. We do not publish how-to or destination stories; no gear-related features; no columns; and no personal profiles or human interest pieces.

Categories: Nonfiction—Adventure—Outdoors—Hunting

CONTACT: Mike Handley, Managing Editor
Material: All
Buckmasters Ltd., PO Box 244022
Montgomery AL 36124-4022
Phone: 800-240-3337

Radio World
The Newspaper for
Radio Managers & Engineers

Why should I contribute to *Radio World*?

Radio World is the newspaper for U.S. radio station managers and engineers, with more than 12,000 readers. Our readers are the people who own, manage and operate FM and AM stations as well as the suppliers and other organizations that serve this audience. These readers are radio professionals: engineers, corporate managers, general managers, owners, production people, IT managers, news reporters, show hosts, educators, regulators and more. We have a technical pedigree but have evolved into a publication covering a broad range of news and feature topics.

Your article will reach a nationwide audience of important radio people. Exposure in *Radio World* can increase your stature in the industry and help you build a valuable network in our business. In addition to the satisfaction they feel in taking part in this forum, many of our contributors benefit professionally from the exposure that their articles give them.

What topics does *Radio World* seek?

Our readers want to know about radio in the United States: how to use new technology, how to keep or find a job, what the latest business trends are. We write about books, education, industry news, public radio, satellite radio, the Internet and more. You can help them by bringing your expertise on a given topic to an article, or by writing about other people involved in these trends. Our sister publication, *Radio World International*, pursues a similar mission abroad.

Radio World is divided into sections: News, Features, GM Journal, Studio Sessions, Buyer's Guide, Reader's Forum.

News: Goal: to provide news and in-depth analysis. *Radio World* articles are more in-depth than those found in other trade publications, many of which are not devoted strictly to radio. Radio World articles

also address the important technical side of these issues, which is lacking in other trades. This section includes breaking industry developments, regulation, important technology, convention coverage, obituaries, format trends.

Features: Goal: to provide a broad range of engineering and general-interest articles, including technical how-to tips, personality interviews, history of radio, unusual new programming, ideas on finding or keeping a job, product news, humor.

GM Journal: Goal: to help the radio manager understand our medium and make his or her station more profitable or successful at meeting its mission. Station promotional ideas, radio business trends, station profiles, advertiser profiles, station services. This section also looks at Internet radio: how to stream, how to run a profitable Web site and more.

Studio Sessions: Goal: to provide a resource for on-air and production personnel. Product reviews, how-to articles, profiles of successful production people and voice-over talent, humor.

Buyer's Guide: User Reports by consumers of these products. Goal: to assist equipment buyers in making their decisions. Every other issue of RW contains a Buyers Guide category (e.g., Microphones, FM Transmitters, Live Assist and Automation).

Reader's Forum: Goal: to give readers a place to air their views. Letters to the editor and Guest Commentaries.

How should I submit my article?

Submit your article in electronic form, preferably in MS WORD, via e-mail to radioworld@imaspub.com; or if typed, mail to the address at the top of this document. Your editor will specify the story length (usually between 600 and 1,200 words).

On questions of style, refer to the *Associated Press Stylebook and Libel Manual* (published by The Associated Press, 50 Rockefeller Plaza, New York, N.Y. 10020). From time to time, *Radio World* will provide a list of industry-specific style points to complement the AP Stylebook.

If sending hard copy, mail text and photographs so that they reach us by the deadline. If possible, please send a floppy disk or CD with the story saved in MS WORD or as an ASCII file.

Although headlines frequently are reworked to comply with our format and to fit the allotted space, please give your article a title of 28 to 32 characters, using a clearly defined subject and an active verb.

Include your name as you want it to appear in the byline. Include your title, address and phone number.

Radio World often includes a brief bio at the end of stories, usually a sentence or two. ("The author is a freelance writer and former production manager for Smith Broadcasting. Reach her at (703) 998-7600 or via e-mail at carrot@aol.com.") Please let us know whether we can print your phone number for use by our readers.

Should I submit photographs? In what format?

Writers are responsible for providing artwork to illustrate articles. Please do not overlook this important part of your story. Visual elements help pull the reader into your story and make it more informative.

Artwork can be a picture of a piece of equipment, a studio snapshot, a "headshot" photo of your subject, company logos, a copy of the book you are reviewing, charts and graphs, or any other visually interesting art that pertains to the story. Use your imagination. No one knows the topic like you do.

We can accept a print, slide or electronic file of the image. Electronic JPG or TIF images should have resolution of at least 300 dots per inch for publication at 5 inches wide. The most common mistake made by contributors is that electronic images sent to us are of insufficient resolution.

RW publishes images in both color and black-and-white.

If you wish to have artwork returned to you, please include a note to that effect with your article.

Most RW writers find that they can obtain artwork for their stories at no cost. For example, if you are writing about AM antenna monitors, call manufacturers of such equipment and request photos to illustrate your story. Most will be happy to oblige you and will ask only that you include a photo credit. If you are writing about a radio station group owner, ask for a headshot of the company president, a photo of their headquarters, a studio picture, a logo, a copy of the company's annual report, or any creative photos from recent station events. With the spread of digital cameras, many subjects now can take photographs at your request and e-mail them to you.

If you expect to incur expenses related to artwork (for instance, if you plan to shoot your own pictures), please call your editor first to make arrangements.

I need more info. I still have questions.

Call your editor with any questions. We would rather hear from you ahead of time, than discover later that we and you had different expectations about your article.

Each section of our newspaper has its own demands and guidelines. If you are uncertain where your article will appear and would like help in targeting your article, don't hesitate to call your editor.

Categories: Nonfiction—Business—Education—Engineering—Internet—Mass Communications—Technology—Television/Radio

CONTACT: Paul McLane, Managing Editor
Material: All
PO Box 1214
5827 Columbia Pike, First Floor
Falls Church VA 22041
Phone: 703-998-7600
Fax: 703-820-3245
E-mail: radioworld@imaspub.com

The Ragged Edge

What we publish:

The Ragged Edge examines current and emerging public issues from a disability perspective: civil rights, politics, culture, humor, sexuality, art, technology. We publish freelance journalism, essays, poetry and fiction.

Nonfiction:

The Ragged Edge accepts very few new freelance submissions. Nonfiction essays and articles should be between 750 and 1500 words and must focus on issues of interest to the disability rights movement. Analysis, criticism and journalism are acceptable approaches; we publish very few first-person accounts. We are not interested in inspirational accounts. Freelancers are urged to familiarize themselves with the subjects we cover and our style and approach by reading back issues, available in the archives on our website at http://www.raggededgemagazine.com.

Fiction/poetry:

We seek work of high literary quality which explores the social and political aspects of disability. We'd love to see work from writers exploring the intersections of ethnicity and disability, sexual identity and disability, writing that's experimental; work in which it's clear that the writer has thought about disability culture and aesthetic practice. Since space is limited, short poems and short pieces of fiction have a better shot at getting published.

Terms/Rights purchased:

We do not pay freelancers; we provide two copies of issue with your article. We also publish your article online at http://www.raggededgemagazine.com.

Query first for nonfiction, please!

Please send a short (2-3 paragraphs) query first that opens with a possible lead for your story. Send your query by e-mail only to: editor@raggededgemagazine.com.

Submitting your article: formats

Once we accept your query, you will need to submit your article by e-mail. Our e-mail address is: editor@raggededge magazine.com..

ALL Submissions by e-mail only, to: editor@raggededge magazine.com.

Also, please note that we expect queries first for nonfiction.

Sample issues:

A sample issue of *The Ragged Edge* is available for $4 . Or browse our website at http://www.raggededgemagazine.com to read our archives.

Categories: Disabilities

CONTACT: Mary Johnson, Editor
Material: General
CONTACT: Anne Finger, Poetry/Fiction Editor
Material: Poetry and Fiction
PO Box 15
Louisville KY 40201
Website: www.raggededgemagazine.com

Rain Crow

Ceased publication.

Rainbow Review
gay & lesbian poetry, fiction, and nonfiction

Poetry, fiction and articles about being gay, experiences, coming out, reactions of family and others, love, relationships, abuses, rights, discrimination, anything that is important, influences or affects gay and lesbian people today.

Published: Annually

Book Formats: Anthology is a book-zine (eclectic like a magazine but in book form) and will be published in one or more of the following, traditional paper (either hardback or paperback), electronic (ebooks and/or audio).

Publishes: Poems, short fiction, and nonfiction.

Lengths: Open for all manuscripts - poetry, short fiction, nonfiction. Manuscripts of all lengths will be considered.

The deadline: We read manuscripts all year for this annual anthology publication in book-zine format.

Rights: One-time use in book form (all formats). Considers reprints if author owns rights.

Poets and writers should send a bio to accompany their writings in the anthology.

Please note: Writers and poets with books and other publications or venues (i.e. a website) can submit information, website address, etc. for inclusion in the anthology to accompany their bio information. This will give writers added exposure for themselves and their books, websites, etc.

Contributors must send note (email or by regular mail) stating that he/she would like the writing(s) included in the published anthology.

Submit up to 5 manuscripts, either by email or regular mail (see below). Please enclose SASE with regular mail submissions.

Contributors will receive one copy of the finished anthology.

Categories: Alternate Life-style—Gay/Lesbian—Lifestyle

CONTACT: Eugene Boone
Material: All
RSVP Press
129 Thurman Lane
Clinton TN 37716
E-mail: rsvppress@yahoo.com

Ranger Rick

Does not accept unsolicited submissions.

Reader's Digest

Reader's Digest, headquartered in Pleasantville, N.Y., 45 minutes north of Manhattan, has been published monthly since February 1922. From that first issue, founders DeWitt Wallace and Lila Acheson Wallace built a mass-interest magazine that is now bought by more than 16 million people in the United States and nearly 31 million around the world—reaching 100 million readers every month.

What is the market for original material at *The Digest*? Roughly half the 30-odd articles we publish every month are reprinted from magazines, newspapers, books and other sources. The remaining 15 or so articles are original—most of them assigned, some submitted on speculation. While many of these are written by regular contributors—on salary or on contract—we're always looking for new talent and for offbeat subjects that help give our magazine variety, freshness and originality. Payment, on acceptance, is $3,000, plus reasonable expenses. For a "Drama in Real Life" or "Unforgettable Character," we pay $3,500. This rate covers all world-wide periodical rights—including condensation, adaptation, compilation and anthology rights—for all forms of print and electronic publishing media. *Reader's Digest* also reserves the right of first refusal on all remaining rights. For assigned articles that don't work out, our kill fee is $500. There's one other important market: fillers and short department items. We pay up to $400 for true, unpublished stories used in our departments; for original material that runs as a filler, we pay $30 per *Reader's Digest*, two-column line, with a minimum payment of $50. To the first contributor of an item we use from TV, radio or a published source, we pay $35. For more on this market, check the front of the magazine, where we solicit reader contributions each month.

How should an original article be proposed to *The Digest*? Don't send us unsolicited manuscripts. We no longer read them. Just send a letter to *The Digest*, briefly describing the article you'd like to do and, if you're new to us, listing your writing credits. If the idea sounds right for us, we'll check our article index, our assignment list and our inventory of original and reprint material for overlaps. If there are none, we'll ask to see a manuscript on speculation, or, if the idea is assignable, we'll request a detailed outline—not a formal A-B-C outline, but a structured, reasonably polished piece of writing that sells not only the article but also you-the-writer and what you bring to your subject. In three or four double-spaced pages, give us a lead that could sit on top of your finished article, and show us where you plan to go from there. Above all, we want a sharp, crisp focus and viewpoint. Here is how Patricia Skalka opened a proposal about a flood that threatened Fort Wayne, Ind., and how Fort Wayne's children helped save the city:

"'I can't feel my fingers anymore,' the young girl sobbed. 'Don't stop. Don't stop,' the others cried. With hands bloody, backs sore and eyes bloodshot from exhaustion, they continued to pass bag after bag of heavy sand down the line. Nearby someone told a joke. In the distance, a rhythmic chant began. The lines of volunteers knew the words from days of marching with schools bands to victory, from evenings spent sitting around Scout camp fires. 'One-two. Sound off. Three-four. Once more…' Now in the eerie dark, rain-soaked from head to foot and mired ankle-deep in mud, they joined the chant.

"Along a 32-mile network of water-logged earthen dams, they sang. They sang to keep going, to keep the sand bags moving. They sang for themselves, for their city. They sang to protect the lives and homes of total strangers. They sang because it is the nature of youth to face danger with bravado, innocence and good spirit. They sang to win one of the country's most awesome battles against the forces of nature. This is the story of Fort Wayne, Ind., and last month's 'Great Flood,' a disaster of such proportions that it literally threatened to destroy the city. Nearly one third of Fort Wayne's populace fought to save the city from the flood waters that poured over the banks of the St. Mary, St. Joseph and Maumee Rivers. Of the estimated 50,000 volunteers who joined in the effort, 30,000 were students. Some were as young as eight years old. Some were in college. Most of them were teenagers. When it was all over, their valor reduced Fort Wayne's mayor to tears and brought them credit for saving the city."

How soon, after assignment, does *The Digest* expect to see a completed manuscript? We seldom set deadlines, because our magazine is geared toward articles of lasting, rather than passing or topical, interest. Such material can usually run anytime. But as a rule, writers deliver two to three months after assignment.

How long should a manuscript run? Only as long as it take to tell your story. The average manuscript length on straight, reportorial journalism is 3,000 to 3,500 words. Some manuscripts run much longer, some shorter. Only after an article is purchased and scheduled do we start thinking about its final length in the magazine. So don't try to write to *The Digest* length—almost certainly, you'd exclude some top-notch material. Leave the condensation to us. This is a meticulous process in which article length is reduced by a third to a half or more—while preserving the style, flavor and integrity of the original manuscript and, more often than not, heightening the effect. The author, of course, reviews the edited version before publication.

How does a writer get his previously published material reprinted in *The Digest*? If your article has appeared in a major American magazine or newspaper, the chances are it's already been considered. In our search for article pickups, fillers and department items, our reading staff screens more than 140 publications each month, along with 2,000 books a year. If in doubt, simply submit tear sheets of your article. For reprinted articles, we pay $1,200 per *Reader's Digest* page for world periodical rights. This is split 50-50 between the original publication and the writer.

What kinds of articles is *The Digest* looking for? The best advice: read and study the magazine. You'll find our subject matter as varied as all human experience. Here are some titles from a single typical issue: "Beirut Under Siege," "Why Our Weather Is Going Wild," "Help Keep Your Teen-Age Driver Alive," "Are You a Man or a Wimp?", "The Real 'Lessons of Vietnam,'" "The Day Jessica Was Born," "Troubled Waters for Our Coast Guard," "Dancing Ground of the Sun," "Top Secret: Is There Sex in Russia?," "Trapped in a Sunken Ship," "New Ways to Buy and Sell Houses," "From Cuba With Hate: The Crime Wave Castro Sent to America." The common thread that weaves through all these articles is reader involvement. When we deal with major concerns—child abuse, government waste, Mideast tensions, breast cancer—we want a constructive approach that goes beyond the problem itself and points the way toward solution or hope. In the same way, we want profiles that go beyond merely "interesting" or "successful" people; we want to celebrate those who inspire by their example. "Chi Chi Rodriguez: Golf's Ace with Heart" was typical. Here's how Jolee Edmondson opened her article:

"It was another tournament town, another cardboard hotel room, another evening spent staring at the too blue, too orange TV images atop the Formica-covered bureau. Juan 'Chi Chi' Rodriguez, vying for the lead at the 1967 Texas Open in San Antonio, was practicing putts on the carpet and thinking about the birdies that had got away that afternoon. The drone of the evening news suddenly riveted his attention: a reporter was interviewing a distraught woman whose home in Illinois had been destroyed by a tornado. All she had left were the clothes she had on. Rodriguez was so moved that he made a pact with himself. If he bagged the trophy the following day, he would send the tornado relief fund $5,000. The next day he won—and so did the tornado victims."

A prime article category is the personal happening or awakening. In "Lure of the Winter Beach," Jean George stumbled onto one of nature's many magical surprises and had an experience everyone can readily share and appreciate. She opened her article this way:

"After a storm several winters ago, a friend asked me to check on her Long Island beach house. So one bright, windy day I bundled against the cold and drove out to the edge of the Atlantic Ocean. I imagined a dreary scene—an abandoned cottage set among pines, stirred by mournful winds. But the instant I climbed from my car my senses came awake. The air smelled clean as I looked out on a brilliant waterscape. The sea was a violet-blue, the sky turquoise, and the beach, which last summer had sloped gently, was no steep, scooped-out and luminous. Crabs scurried for burros and gulls spiraled down on them, like paper airplanes against the sky. At the water's edge, empty shells that whisper when summer waves turn them now made shrill, whistling sounds."

What does *The Digest* look for in writing? Clarity. Straight, simple sentences in simple, direct language. We also want the writer to show us, through solid example or anecdote—not just tell us—through general statements without anything to back them up. The best writing evokes an emotion and gets the reader to experience what the writer experienced—whether shock, affection, amusement. When he wrote his hard-hitting article on "Auto Theft Turns Pro," Thomas R. Brooks combined fact, viewpoint, emotion and anecdote in a deceptively simple, straightforward lead:

"Every 28 seconds, somewhere in the United States, a car is stolen. That's 1.1 million vehicles a year. If your turn is next, chances are you will never get your car back. If you do, it possibly will have been stripped for parts. When Connecticut police showed a West Hartford owner his new Buick Riviera—minus fenders, hood, doors and wheels—he wept."

Above all, in the writing we publish, *The Digest* demands accuracy—down to the smallest detail. Our team of 83 researchers scattered through 19 cities around the world scrutinizes every line of type, checking every fact and examining every opinion. For an average issue, they will check 3,500 facts with 1500 sources. So watch your accuracy. There's nothing worse than having an article fall apart in our research checking because an author was a little careless with his reporting. We make this commitment routinely, as it guarantees that the millions of readers who believe something simply because they saw it in *Reader's Digest* have not misplaced their trust.

How to Submit Brief Anecdotes to *Reader's Digest*: Have you read—or heard—something interesting or amusing you would like to share? Although *Readers' Digest* does not read unsolicited article-length manuscripts, it welcomes short contributions. Payment is made on publication:

$400 for Life in These United States. Contributions must be true, unpublished stories from your own experience, revealing adult human nature and providing appealing or humorous sidelights on the American scene. Maximum length: 300 words. Address: Life in U.S. Editor.

$400 for true, unpublished stories used in Humor in Uniform (experiences in the armed services), Campus Comedy (life at college), Tales Out of School (highschool anecdotes), and All in a Day's Work (humor on the job). $35 to the first contributor of each item from a published source used in any of these departments. Maximum length: 300 words. Address: Humor in Uniform, Campus Comedy, Tales Out of School or All in a Day's Work Editor.

$50 for an original item for Toward More Picturesque Speech. $35 for the first contributor of a published item. Address: Picturesque Speech Editor.

For items used in Laughter, the Best Medicine, Notes From All Over, Personal Glimpses, Points to Ponder, Quotable Quotes and elsewhere: $35 to the first contributor of an item from print or electronic media; $30 per *Reader's Digest* two-column line for original material. Original poetry is not solicited. Address: Excerpt Editor.

Original contributions—which become our property upon acceptance and payment by *Reader's Digest*—should be typewritten. Previously published material must have the source's name, date and page number. Please address your submission to the appropriate features editor; for electronic mail, put feature name under Subject. Include your name, address, phone number and date; in e-mail, make this part of your Message.

Contributions Cannot Be Acknowledged or Returned

Categories: Nonfiction—Education—General Interest—Health—Inspirational—Interview—Physical Fitness—Society—Medicine—HumorHuman Interest—Profiles—Opinion—Personal Experience

CONTACT: (Appropriate Feature) Editor
Material: All
Reader's Digest Rd.
Pleasantville NY 10570-7000
Phone: 914-238-1000
Fax: 914-238-6390
E-mail: readersdigest@notes.compuserve.com
Website: www.readersdigest.com

Rearview

Rearview is constantly looking for submissions of all styles of poetry, black and white artwork and photography, and very short stories and vignettes. We suggest before you submit that you read these guidelines carefully and look over back issues of *Rearview* to get the feel of what we're looking for. All contributors receive one complimentary copy. Accepted work will appear in the print edition and may appear in the edition highlights online as well.

Poetry

We are currently looking for poetry of all styles, with a special emphasis on narrative poetry. We acquire First North American Serial Rights. We accept simultaneous submissions and previously published works, if the situation is noted in the submission.

All submissions should be made via email to rearview quarterly@yahoo.com. Submissions should include three to seven poems in the body of the email, along with your name and e-mail address. A cover letter is optional. We will respond within three months. If accepted, you will be asked for a brief biography.

Short Stories

We will occasionally publish very short stories of exceptional quality. Short stories must be less than 1.000 words and relate to our central theme of memoir and narrative works.

All submissions should be sent in the body of an email to rearviewquarterly@yahoo.com. Please include your name and email address, along with a cover letter if you wish. We will respond within three months, but if accepted the work may be held for publication in future issues.

Art and Photography

We accept black and white photography and line drawings for the front and back covers, as well as several places within, *Rearview Magazine*. We acquire One Time Rights on artwork. Submissions should be fairly small in size. Please send submissions to rearviewquarterly@yahoo.com; we accept attachments or urls. In your email, please include a title to your artwork, your name, and your email address.

• The individual authors retain all rights to their work.
Categories: Arts—Photography—Poetry—Writing

CONTACT: rearviewquarterly@yahoo.com
Material: All
PO Box 486
Sudbury MA 01776
E-mail: rearviewquarterly@yahoo.com
Website: rearview.domynoes.net

Red Rock Review

Manuscripts must be mailed flat in a large manila (clasp-style) envelope. Do not fold pages into a letter-sized envelope.

Submissions must include a cover letter and a self-addressed, stamped envelope for return of manuscripts.

Manuscripts must be legibly typed or computer-generated on 8½" x 11" white bonded paper. Use standard fonts or typefaces (Courier, Helvetica, or Times) and standard font sizes (10 point for typing, 12 point on computers).

Freshly typed or printed manuscripts or clear, fresh photocopies are required.

Fiction must be no more than 7,500 words; essays must be no more than 5,000 words; poems must be no more than 80 lines.

Short Fiction and Essay Submissions (Suggested):

One-inch margins all around each page. Indent new paragraphs five spaces or ½"; justify left margin. Justification of right margin is not necessary.

Name, address, and phone number appear single-spaced in the top left corner of page one.

Approximate word count appears in the top right corner of page one.

Title (in CAPS) and byline (including name) appear single-spaced and centered 1/3 of the way down the first page.

A header including last name, key word from title, and page number appears on subsequent pages. The header appears in the left corner ½" down from the top of the page and 1" in from the left edge.

Text is double-spaced. Do not add extra blank lines between paragraphs unless creating section breaks.

Poetry Submissions (Suggested):

Left and right margins are set at the discretion of the poet; top margin (and bottom if necessary) should be 1".

Name, address, and phone number appear single-spaced in the left corner of every page.

Include key word from title and page numbers (top right corner of page) if a poem goes over one page.

Lines of text may be single- or double-spaced.

Send all correspondence and submissions to *Red Rock Review*, Richard Logsdon, Editor, Department of English J2A, Community College Southern Nevada, 3200 East Cheyenne Avenue, North Las Vegas, Nevada 89030.

We do not consider general submissions between June 1 and August 31.

The *Red Rock Review*, a literary journal published twice annually by the Community College of Southern Nevada and edited by Dr. Richard Logsdon, is dedicated to the publication of fine contemporary literature. We invite submissions of poetry, fiction, and creative non-fiction as well as book reviews. We do not publish literary criticism.

Red Rock Review Homepage:

If you have questions about the material on this web page, please contact Todd Moffett at todd_moffett@ccsn.nevada.edu.

Categories: Fiction—Poetry—Short Stories

CONTACT: Dr. Richard Logsdon
Material: All
English Dept. J2A
Community College of Southern Nevada
3200 East Cheyenne Ave.
North Las Vegas NV 89030

Redbook

Redbook is targeted to young married women between 25 and 44 who define themselves as smart, capable and happy with their lives. *Each issue is a provocative mix of features geared to entertain and inform them, including:*

• News stories on contemporary social issues that strike a universal chord and reveal the emotional ramifications

• First person essays about dramatic pivotal moments in a woman's life

• Marriage articles with an emphasis on strengthening the relationship

• Short parenting features on how to deal with universal health and behavioral issues

• Reporting exciting trends in women's lives

Writers are advised to read at least the last six issues of the magazine (available in most libraries) to get a better understanding of appropriate subject matter and treatment.

We prefer to see detailed queries, rather than completed manuscripts, and suggest that you provide us with some sources/experts. Please enclose two or more samples of your writing, as well as a stamped, self-addressed envelope.

The *Redbook* Short Story Contest has been discontinued, but we continue to welcome high quality, accessible short stories.

Writer's Guidelines for Fiction: Thank you for your interest in *Redbook*. We publish approximately 15 short stories a year, and we welcome unsolicited short story manuscripts. Our fiction has received such prestigious honors as the National Magazine Award for Fiction and inclusion in *Prize Stories/The O. Henry Awards* and *The Best American Short Stories*.

Redbook's target reader is a woman between the ages of 25 and 45 who is or was married, has children, and generally is employed outside the home. Because she's a bright, well-informed individual with varied interests, she's not solely concerned with fiction that reflects her own life—although most of our stories deal with topics of specific interest to women: relationships, marriage, parenthood, relatives, friendships, career situations, financial problems, and so forth.

All submissions should be typed and double-spaced and accompanied by a self-addressed, stamped envelope. (If you do not send an SASE, you will not hear from us unless we are interested in buying the story.) Our reply time is usually 8 to 10 weeks. We receive approximately thirty-five thousand submissions per year and take every care in handling them, but we cannot be responsible for the receipt or the condition of the manuscript. (In the interest of protecting the original manuscript, you may submit a legible photocopy.)

Redbook publishes short stories 25 manuscript pages or fewer; the average length is 15 pages. Payment for a short story begins at $1,000. *Redbook* buys First North American Serial Rights and pays on acceptance. Most stories are scheduled within a year of purchase, and prior to publication, short story galleys are sent to the author. Please note that we do not consider unsolicited poetry and novels.

Sorry, but we are unable to provide complimentary copies.

Categories: Fiction—Nonfiction—Arts—Beauty—Biography—Book Reviews—Business—Children—Cooking—Crime—Entertainment—Fashion—Food/Drink—Health—Interview—Marriage—Mass Communications—Money & Finances—Parenting—Psychology—Sexuality—Society—Women's Fiction—Women's Issues

CONTACT: Lisa Lombardi, Fiction Editor
Material: Fiction
CONTACT: Patty Curtis, Health Editor
Material: Health
CONTACT: Andrea Bauman
Material: All except fiction and health
224 W. 57th St.
New York NY 10019
Phone: 212-649-3450
Fax: 212-581-8114
Website: www.Redbookmag.com

Referee

The Style Guide is developed for the convenience of our writers and editors. When we receive an article from a freelance writer, the editor will consider it for publication.

Rates vary from five to 10 cents per published word, depending on how we use the text. We may decide to hold your submission on file until space opens up or we will pick a month to run it. Scheduled articles need standard contracts that will be sent to the writer to sign and return for payment.

We accept submissions on speculation, but appreciate direct queries, either by mail or e-mail. No phone calls, please.

Thanks again for your interest.

WHAT WE ARE LOOKING FOR

Referee publishes three main types of articles: features, sport specific columns and regularly appearing articles ("Profiles," "Law," "Back To Basics," etc.).

Features

We want articles that speak to our readership—sports officials. The content must focus on officiating. We are interested in articles that help our readers improve an aspect of their officiating, articles about unique or very successful officials, articles dissecting the major issues that officials face and articles that delve into certain officiating "philosophies." *Referee* also publishes several "Banner Features." Examples of these are:

• **You Are There**: Two-page features that focus on a famous sporting event through the eyes of an official. It is almost always necessary to interview one or more of the officials from whatever game or event is being covered.

• **Basic Training**: Two-page features that focus on a single aspect of officiating and give a "basic" how-to lesson on that topic, including tips and expert opinions from several officials in a variety of sports and levels.

Sport-Specific Columns

Sport-specific columns may pertain to rules, mechanics or officiating philosophy. Rules columns must include parenthetical rulebook, casebook or approved ruling references to the pertinent rules. In all cases, the NFHS reference should be listed first, followed by the NCAA reference. Other rulebook references may follow in any order. Use semicolons to separate codes. Here is and example of correct referencing:

(NFHS 6-3-1A, 7-4-1 THROUGH 3, 6.2.2C; NCAA 6-2-1; Pro 6-5).

Following are the required references for each sport: Basketball—NFHS, NCAA men's and NCAA women's; Baseball—NFHS, NCAA, pro; Football—NFHS, NCAA; Soccer—NFHS, NCAA, FIFA; Softball—NFHS, NCAA, ASA, USSSA.

Regular Appearing Articles

To get a better feel of articles that appear monthly in *Referee* and that are not sport specific, request a sample issue at submissions@referee.com.

PAYMENT

You will receive a contract soon after your article is received, accepted and edited. Payment will be sent within 30 days of the date we received the signed contract or the completed writing effort. Our standard rate varies from 5 to 10 cents per published word. Return your contract as soon as possible.

SCHEDULES

The due dates have been carefully selected, so we need your help in staying on the schedule provided. Obviously, we work well ahead of the publication date in this business. Early due dates allow us ample time to edit your work and work with you on any potential changes. **We welcome early submissions!** If you feel like cranking out two or three articles, go ahead and do so. If an emergency threatens a deadline, let us know immediately. Adjustments can be made if we know early enough.

SIZE AND SPECULATIONS

All sport-specific articles should be around 500-1,000 words; features vary from 1,000-3,000 words. Items must be typed and double-spaced. Please use our on-line style sheet, found at submissions@referee.com, when writing your material.

SUBMITTING MATERIAL

The best way to submit your work is via e-mail. Our e-mail address is submissions@referee.com.

We also accept mailed articles on high-density computer disks.

Categories: Nonfiction—Law—Sports/Recreation—Sports Officiating

CONTACT: Andrew Greene, Features Editor
Material: All
Referee Enterprises, Inc.
PO Box 161
Franksville WI 53126
Phone: 262-632-8855
Fax: 262-632-5460
E-mail: submissions@referee.com
Website: www.referee.com

Rehab Technology

Please refer to Oildom Publishing.

Remembrance
A Celebration of Life

REMEMBRANCE ANTHOLOGY GUIDELINES:

A tribute to lives lived well—people who are so memorable, they will never be forgotten.

Publication date: Anthology in book-zine format, published annually.

Book Formats: one or more of the following, traditional paper (either hardback or paperback), electronic (ebooks and/or audio).

Poetry and other writings (articles, prayers, etc.) about loved ones, their lives, and how they touched us and others while they were alive.

Lengths: Open for all poems, articles, prayers, etc. Manuscripts of all lengths will be considered.

Contact us for the next deadline for submissions for *Remembrance*.

Rights: One-time use in book form (all formats). Considers reprints if author owns rights.

Poets and writers should send a bio to accompany their writings in the anthology.

Contributors must send note (email or by regular mail) stating that he/she would like the writing(s) included in the published anthology. Submit up to 5 manuscripts, either by email or regular mail (see below).

Contributors will receive one copy of the finished anthology.

Categories: Family—Lifestyle

CONTACT: Eugene Boone
Material: All
RSVP Press
129 Thurman Lane
Clinton TN 37716
E-mail: rsvppress@yahoo.com

Reminisce Magazine

Reminisce helps readers "bring back the good times" through true stories and vintage photographs. Any appropriate photo or memory is welcome, as long as it originated from 1900 through the 1960s.

We also publish a sister magazine to *Reminisce* called *Reminisce EXTRA*. It's similar in format and is available by a separate bimonthly subscription—mailed on alternating months. This lets subscribers choose whether to receive a magazine every month or every other month. Neither magazine contains any paid advertising.

Our editorial style is relaxed and conversational, so please write your memory the way you'd relate it to a friend. We invite "regular" people like you to tell their own stories. As a result, most of the issue is written by our readers who are eager to share their memories. We rarely use freelance-written material.

Because our features don't often run more than 700 words, we cannot take the time to read lengthy submissions or books. We especially like short items with a first-person "I remember when" angle.

An exception is an interesting article describing the origin of a certain product or business with a nostalgic tie.

Before you send anything:

Be sure the first page of your submission contains your name, mailing address, phone number and E-mail address, if available. Don't forget to include the year or decade (can be approximate) in which your memory took place.

Write your name and address on the back of each photo, preferably with soft pencil or marker, and identify any information you know regarding who, what and when. You're welcome to send a photocopy of an original photo (for reference only, since photocopies cannot be reproduced for publication). Or, we recommend that you first have a reprint made of cherished family photos before sending them. If we're able to use the story, we'll ask to borrow the original or a sharp reprint. We are also able to use high-resolution scans sent via E-mail. Photos are returned upon publication.

We do not publish fiction. Instead, we invite folks to tell their own true-life stories—personal reminiscences of years gone by...memorable people who affected their lives...interesting descriptions of trips, adventures and family anecdotes...seasonal or holiday memories (these may be submitted at any time of the year)...recollections of now-famous people they knew "back when"...little-known historical items, etc. We're especially glad to get humorous anecdotes. We will accept previously published material, as long as the story had minimal exposure and appeared in a "non-nostalgia" publication.

• Due to the high volume of submissions we receive, and in an effort to involve as many contributors as possible in this "reader-written" magazine, we often edit or excerpt longer stories to fit within one of our "short memory" departments.

Any submission may also be considered for publication in a *Reminisce* or Reiman Publications book or related product, promotional piece or on our web-site.

Reminisce pays only for "feature" stories. Photos and shorter memories earn contributors a unique gift they can display on a bookshelf or coffee table—a Classic Red '57 Chevy car bank. This popular keepsake car identifies them as a "Reminisce Staffer." We normally pay $50 per full-page feature, plus the tabletop Chevy.

If you would like a response regarding your submission, or if you're sending photos you'd like to have returned, be sure to enclose a self-addressed return envelope, with the proper return postage. Due to postage costs and our limited amount of staff, we cannot respond to submissions that do not have an SASE.

After you send us photos or articles, and if you've included an SASE for a response, please be patient. We receive an awful lot of material, and often it takes us a while to catch up.

Professional/stock photos: Separate guidelines and payment rates are available upon request. Write to Trudi Bellin at the address below.—Revised Jan 2001

Categories: Nonfiction—Photography—Short Stories

CONTACT: Submissions Editor
Material: All
5927 Memory Lane
Greendale WI 53129
E-mail: editors@reminisce.com
Website: www.reminisce.com

Renaissance Magazine

Renaissance Magazine accepts unsolicited manuscripts related to the Renaissance and Middle Ages, including but not limited to: historical articles, martial arts, recipes/culinary arts, travel, interviews with artisans, articles on the SCA and related re-enactment groups, etc. Before pursuing any topic, please query first to confirm our need for it.

Average article is approx. 3,000 words in length although longer work will be considered. Sidebar information is also encouraged, as well as graphics, including copyright-free logos, illustrations and pho-

tographs (finder's fee: $7.50/image). *Renaissance Magazine* takes full North American serial rights on all work accepted.

Those interested in writing for *Renaissance Magazine* on a regular basis as a staff writer must query first, and include a brief bio/resume and sample article. If accepted, a writing contract will be mailed to that individual and this person will be expected to contribute articles on a regular basis.

All submissions should be set up in the standard manuscript format (title, name, address, phone number, approx. word count on title page, and every subsequent page fully numbered). Cover letter should include a brief bio and credits, where you heard of *Renaissance Magazine*, and any other pertinent information. An SASE must be included with your submission to be considered. We encourage writers to e-mail their articles directly, to save on mailing and paper costs. E-mail all queries and submissions to the address below.

Work may receive a written critique and editorial suggestions. All work will be edited to some degree, to match our editorial format. No one need submit articles who is not willing to have their work edited. Allow 3-6 weeks for a response.

Although all writers will be notified of acceptance within a few weeks of submission, we cannot guarantee a publication date. However when the article is scheduled for an upcoming issue, we will attempt to notify the writer before publication. We reserve the right to reject previously accepted work at any time and for any reason.

Book Reviews: We accept unsolicited reviews of Renaissance and Medieval-related books, including fiction and nonfiction (500 words max.). Please include the original cover of the book or a GOOD photocopy of the book jacket along with review. Authors of Renaissance and Medieval-related books (fiction or nonfiction) are encouraged to submit a review copy of their book to Kim Guarnaccia, Editor, at the address below.

Editorial Suggestions: We encourage all readers and writer to make suggestions on what kind of articles should be published in *Renaissance Magazine*. To do so, call, write or e-mail Kim Guarnaccia, Editor.

PAYMENT

Payment of $.08 per published word is made upon publication. Two (2) contributor copies will also be given to each contributor, and more copies are available upon request. Direct your queries to Kim Guarnaccia, Editor.

SAMPLE ISSUES

Sample issue: $9; 1 year subscription (6 issues) $29; 2 year subscription (12 issues) $56. To order, make checks payable to Renaissance Magazine and mail to SFS, PO Box 82, Vandalia, OH 45377, Attn. Renaissance. US funds only. Overseas orders, please add an additional $4 per year to order. Back issues are available; please query first for prices.

Categories: History

CONTACT: Kim Guarnaccia, Editor
Material: As Above
13 Appleton Rd.
Nantucket MA 02554
Phone: 508-825-8864
Fax: 508-325-5992
E-mail: editor@renaissancemagazine.com
Website: www.renaissancemagazine.com

The Retired Officer's Magazine

Please refer to Military Officer.

Reunions Magazine

American mobility intensifies a desire to reunite with people/places to recapture what seem to be simpler times. Reunions touch everyone and can be with family, friends, classmates, associates, buddies, neighbors, survivors.

Reunions magazine is primarily for those actively involved in organizing reunions. Readers refer to us for practical ideas about searching, researching, planning, organizing and attending reunions, along with good stories.

Read *Reunions* magazine to discover our tastes. We welcome your queries.

Please address our readers. They are people organizing family, class, military and other reunions; or are searching (lost loves, friends, ancestors).

Give our readers what they want. They want to learn the nitty gritty of organizing successful reunions. Give help, suggestions, smashingly fresh new ideas, reunion advice and inspiration. What's special about your reunion? Where was it and why? Who was invited and why? What made attendees happy and wanting to come back?

Ease organizers' challenges, answer questions they don't know how to ask, solve problems before they know about them. Our readers ideas about getting people engaged, involved, enchanted by the idea of being part of a special group.

We highlight and examine ways to be a savvy reunion consumer. We point readers to wonderful places to stay and why they're special for reunions. They want products and services that make reunions special. Family reunions want ways to entertain kids, not just theme parks and video games but active play and exploring, involving all generations, grounding them with family, history, pride, strength, and fun.

Titles. Please be creative. Avoid using: Reunion, Reunions, The Reunion, A Reunion, Our Reunion, My Reunion. In fact anything with any of the foregoing titles is rarely read with eagerness.

Say it with "humor, expertise, passion, perseverance, creativity, a fresh approach"

Comments. We appreciate constructive feedback. If you have a complaint, tell us. If you have praise, tell others—though we'd not mind hearing praise too!

CONTENT GUIDELINES

Features are written mainly by readers and roughly fall into these categories.

• How-to articles about organizing reunions usually address single issues of relevance to many reunion groups. Examples include early decisions, how to formulate and follow through with plans, how to use convention and visitors bureaus, document reunions, plan games, make invitations and newsletters, etc.

• Personal stories. These articles encourage and inspire others initiating similar reunions. Articles elaborating on the reunion organizing process or search are preferred. We're partial to triumph stories. Many readers have similar stories to share, so unusual or heartwarming stories with unique aspects, twists or universal insights are more likely to be published. Topics include family, class and military reunion stories with humorous or poignant narratives, military buddies returning to the scene or genealogical searches with surprising results. When appropriate, feature articles should include additional sources, names, addresses, emails, websites, publication title, author, publisher, etc.

Departments

Reviews. Reunion books, movies, TV programs, computer software, videos or plays to be reviewed by persons with proven subject-matter expertise. Bio must accompany reviews. We welcome materials with requests for review.

RSVP: Inviting Examples. Share reunion invitations, include original sample (flat), its use, distribution and why it was effective.

Scrapbook. We accept clipped articles (recipes, cartoons, fliers) about reunions. Sources and dates must be identified. Credit is given (and a small fee paid) to the first contributor of material that is used.

Photos can accompany articles or be independent with a caption. They must be well-focused, tell a reunion story and identify name, address, phone number of owner, names of persons in the picture (unless it's a large group) and a signed publication permission release. Vertical photos are all considered for covers. Self-addressed, stamped envelopes (SASE) must accompany photos you wish returned.

Hot Spots. Tell us about exciting or unusual reunions places. Tell us where, how to get there, what's special, what they did for your reunion and why you'd go back.

Regular columns highlight single issues or current trends and must educate reunion organizers. Submissions about 1,000 words with universal and timeless appeal.

SPECIFICATIONS. All mailed submissions must be typed and double-spaced. Indicate if your submission is available on 3.5" disks formatted for PC or Macintosh. Send articles and queries to address below. E-mail is our preference. Please attach it in Microsoft Word and send to reunions@execpc.com.

Payment. We are able to pay very little for unassigned work but are generous with extra copies of the issue.

Replies in up to two years. Possible 12-month delay between acceptance and publication.

Categories: Nonfiction—African-American—Consumer—Family—General Interest—Lifestyle—Military—Travel—Reunions

CONTACT: Submissions Editor
Material: All
PO Box 11727
Milwaukee WI 53211-0727
Phone/Fax: 414-263-6331
E-mail: reunions@execpc.com

Rhino

Annual Reading Period: April 1-October 1
Sorry, no electronic submissions at this time!
Basic Guidelines

Send 3-5 poems, typed, single-spaced, along with a short cover letter telling us a little bit about you, how you heard about *RHINO*, and/or your past publications, if you have any. Always include a SASE (self-addressed stamped envelope), and let us know whether we should use it for return of the poems or just for our response. (We can recycle unused poems, if you prefer. If you want them returned, be sure to put sufficient postage on the SASE.) Please also include your name, address, and phone number on each poem, for ease in contacting you. Send submission by first-class mail to RHINO, PO Box 591, Evanston, IL 60204.

Etiquette Note:

Please do not send more than one submission during our reading period, April 1 to October 1, unless we request to see more via your first SASE. We will return extra submissions unread.

Sample Copy

As with any literary publication, it is always best to read the magazine first. You can read sample poems here at our website, and you can obtain a hard copy by sending a check or money order for $10 for the current issue or $5 for a back issue before 2001 and $8 for a back issue from 2001 on to RHINO, PO Box 591, Evanston, IL 60204. You can also purchase copies of RHINO at our workshops, readings, and at some bookstores and galleries in Chicago, its suburbs, and in central Illinois. We are our own distributors for now.

RHINO is looking for excellent poetry, translations, and short short fiction in any style. We also publish the occasional short essay on poetry. (See RHINO 2000 for an essay on the poet Martin Espada by John Bradley.) Send 3-5 poems OR 1-3 short prose pieces. Please note that we only read very short prose—pieces of 250-650 words—no novel excerpts, no long academic essays. (See RHINO 2002 for exemplary short fiction by Geoffrey Forsyth.)

Submissions are read by multiple editors with various tastes, all looking for quality work. We have published formal poems, free verse, very accessible poems, wild experimentations with language, visual poems, prose poems, poems of stark beauty, and even funny poems. Sometimes we call ourselves "eclectic" in the best sense of the word. We are very proud of the content of RHINO and of the variety of the work we publish.

Annual Awards

Modest cash prizes are now awarded annually through our Editors' Prizes (no special application necessary) and through our READERS-WRITERS Contest, open to readers of RHINO. Details about the latter appear on the website when the new issue is pending or available, and on the inside back cover of the magazine.

Art

We are pleased to have added art to our pages. (See RHINO 2000 for the photographs of Roger Pfingston and RHINO 2002 for the photographs of Liz Chilsen and Joanne Warfield.) Interested photographers should submit a group of 8x10 black and white photos for distribution throughout the magazine, or a possible center section. Again, enclose a SASE with sufficient postage for return of the photographs.

Acceptances

If we accept your work, we will ask you to sign a contract allowing us to publish it and ensuring that it is not previously published. We want first serial publication rights only, and the copyright reverts to you. Please credit RHINO with first publication if you republish your work in a book or anthology or on a website. On our contract, you can say yes or no about electronic publication of your work (or an excerpt of it) here on our website. We will also ask for a brief bio, a contributor's note, and a list, if you like, of people who might want to hear about the issue you are in. These names will not be added to our general mailing list. We will request a new clean copy of the accepted work and a diskette with your work in both MS Word and ASCII format for ease in typesetting. The diskette helps avoid typesetting errors, but please send it in appropriate packing to avoid damage, or we can't use it, anyway. We do not permit any revision of accepted work after this stage, though we may suggest slight revisions upon acceptance or during the proofreading process. We generally provide you with a proofing copy in late fall or early winter.

Rejections

When we reject submissions, please know that we have read your work with care. If we have brief comments that we think could help you, we will write them on the rejection slip. If you don't receive comments, then perhaps this particular work just wasn't right for us. Just do more market research, revise, write something new, and move on! Don't let it get you down! Occasionally we make pencil notations to alert you to typos or glitches in the manuscript you sent us. Etiquette Note: Such errors are a turn-off for some editors, and not a big deal for others, but do realize that errors can damage your credibility as an artist. Readers, like writers, do pay attention to small details; what if you get them wrong? So it's best to send us a carefully proofread manuscript, but don't worry too much if a small error slipped by your personal or technological spell check or grammar check. It happens. We'll do our best to edit/proofread your work if we publish it! Because of the volume of submissions, we cannot respond personally to most writers, but we do wish you well! Keep writing, and keep trying!

Categories: Fiction—Arts—Language—Literature—Poetry—Short Stories—Writing

CONTACT: Alice George, Editor
Material: Any
CONTACT: Alice George, Deborah or Nodler Rosen, Editors
Material: Any
PO Box 591
Evanston IL 60204
Website: www.rhinopoetry.org

River Town Gazette
Rockland County's Lifestyle Publication

At the *River Town Gazette*, our focus is on Entertainment and Information of interest to residents and tourists in the Historic River Towns of New York's Hudson Valley area.

Featuring Columns and Articles about: Automotive, Boating, Restaurants and Food, Home Improvement, Real Estate, Personal Improvement, Alternative Healing, Commuter Information, Cultural Events, Social Events, Style and more.

Categories: Nonfiction—Antiques—Architecture—Arts—Automobiles—Boating—Book Reviews—Business—Campus Life—Cartoons—Children—Collectibles—Comedy—Computers—Consumer—Crafts/Hobbies—Culture—Diet/Nutrition—Disabilities—Ecology—Entertainment—Family—Fashion—Film/Video—Fishing—Folklore—Food/Drink—Games—Gardening—General Interest—Health—Hobbies—Internet—Jewish Interest—Juvenile—Lifestyle—Marriage—Men's Issues—Money & Finances—Music—Mystery—Native American—New Age—Outdoors—Parenting—Photography—Politics—Psychology—Real Estate—Recreation—Regional—Relationships—Self Help—Senior Citizen—Singles—Society—Sports/Recreation—Teen—Television/Radio—Travel

CONTACT: Mark Kalan, Publisher
Material: All
PO Box 808
Nyack NY 10960
Phone: 845-353-0000
E-mail: info@rivertowngazette.com
Website: www.rivertowngazette.com

RiverSedge
The University of Texas-Pan American

RiverSedge is published twice yearly by The University of Texas-Pan American Press, under the direction of Professor Sandra Cararas, The University of Texas-Pan American, Edinburg, Texas. The contents of the journal do not necessarily represent the viewpoints of the University.

RiverSedge welcomes submissions of art, photography, poetry, short stories and essays. Works may be submitted in either traditional or electronic media, but must be accompanied by postage and packaging if return is desired. Artwork should be reproducible in black and white. Please include telephone number. Payment is in copies. Rights revert to artists and writers.

Submission deadlines: Fall issue, November 15; Spring issue, April 15. Please remember to include a short bio with each submission. Address submissions to the address below or contact the editors by e-mail.

FICTION GUIDELINES

RiverSedge, a journal of arts and literature, seeks quality mainstream literary and experimental fiction, emphasizing that prose which has a regional Southwestern flavor or locale, but not excluding voices from other areas. Characters should be memorable and plots believable within the story's setting and context.

Our audience is educated and largely academic, but we are interested in work that transcends the campus and explores the real world in language and contexts accessible to lay readers.

Because of limited space, stories should not exceed 2,500 words. Payment is two copies upon publication. Short biographical sketch should accompany submission.

Submissions should be accompanied by SASE, or clear instructions not to return. Simultaneous submissions should be identified, although they are not prohibited. Computer disks in Macintosh format preferred.

Notification time is usually within 3 to 4 months, but may be sooner.

POETRY GUIDELINES

RiverSedge seeks quality mainstream literary and experimental poetry, emphasizing regional Southwestern flavor or locale, but not excluding voices from other areas. Any variety is welcomed, although most of the poetry we print is modern free verse. There are really no limitations on themes, topics, or language.

Our audience is educated and largely academic, but we are interested in work that transcends the campus and explores the real world in language and contexts accessible to lay readers. Poetry should be foolishly simple, but divinely insightful.

Because of limited space, poems of 25 or fewer lines are preferable, although longer ones are used on occasion, since quality and interest are more important than length.

Payment is two copies upon publication. Short biographical sketch should accompany submission.

Submissions should be accompanied by SASE, or clear instructions not to return. Simultaneous submissions should be identified, although they are not prohibited.

Notification time is usually within 3 to 4 months, but may be sooner.

Subscriptions: $12.00

Categories: Arts—College—Directories—Family—Literature—Multicultural—Poetry—Short Stories—Textbooks

CONTACT: Director
Material: All
The University of Texas-Pan American
1201 W. University Dr. CAS 266
Edinburg TX 78539
Phone: 956-381-3638
Fax: 956-381-3697
E-mail: Bookworm@panam.edu

The Roanoker

The *Roanoker* magazine is a city magazine accepting stories relating to the Roanoke and New River Valley areas of Virginia. The magazine covers lifestyles, dining, history, homes, events, arts/culture and business and is geared towards an upscale readership. Queries are accepted for feature-length stories in these topics and also for departmental shorts (150-300 words); contact the editorial department for more information.

Special annual features and issues:
• Education and schools (fall)
• Retirement in western Virginia (Sept/Oct)
• Technology in western Virginia (spring/summer)
• Roanoke-area Almanac/visitor and newcomer guide (Jan/Feb): Education, retirement, technology, real estate, arts and culture

Every-issue sections:
• Dining in Roanoke area
• Festivals and special events
• Short news/cultural/human interest pieces (The Skinny)

Categories: Nonfiction—Arts—Business—Culture—Education—Entertainment—Food/Drink—General Interest—Interview—Lifestyle—Regional—Society

CONTACT: Kurt Rheinheimer, Editor in Chief
Material: Lifestyle, Profile, Dining, Business
CONTACT: Cara Ellen Modisett, Associate Editor
Material: Events/Arts/New Business
Leisure Publishing
PO Box 21538
Roanoke VA
540-989-7603

ROCK & ICE
AMERICA'S #1 CLIMBING MAGAZINE

Rock and Ice

Rock and Ice, established in 1984, celebrates the high-energy sports of rock climbing, bouldering, mountaineering, ice climbing, and aid climbing. We are proud to be the industry's leading venue for world-class adventure writing, training and technical tips for climbers of all levels, hard-hitting gear reviews, and stunning photography. Our readers look to *Rock and Ice* as the authentic source of climbing information and inspiration, so their expectations for accuracy, detail and talent from our contributors are very high. Below are some suggestions on crafting your work to fit our needs.

Editorial Submissions

Rock and Ice is published nine times a year, or roughly every six weeks. Please submit all article proposals in a one-page query letter, preferably via email, to editor@bigstonepub.com. If this is your first time submitting to *Rock and Ice*, it's helpful if you can include clips of previously published work. Please be sure to read several issues of *Rock and Ice* to familiarize yourself with the voice and content of the magazine before submitting queries.

We pay $.35/word for published work.

Features

Rock and Ice features focus primarily on: profiles, destinations, current outdoor/climbing-related issues, survival stories and, occasionally, fiction. Features are 1200 to 3500 words in length, and require in-depth research, quotes, and talented writing. We do not publish trip reports.

Departments

These are good places for writers to begin a relationship with *Rock and Ice*. The departments have a specific focus and format, and are generally shorter than features.

Breaking News—short (100 to 500 words) write-ups of the latest feats, events, controversies, and access issues in the climbing world. Strong photos are a big plus when we are considering a piece for publication.

Spotlight—a 700-word profile or Q&A featuring an up-and-coming climber, or noteworthy person in the news.

Milestones—obituaries, generally 250 to 300 words in length, of well-known climbers.

Road Trips—covering the finest destinations in North America for rock and ice climbing. This department currently includes SuperTopos, highly accurate and featured topos by SuperTopo.com founder Chris McNamara.

Famous Faces—a 500- to 800-word article opening with a stunning photo of a legendary North American alpine face (e.g. the North Face of the Grand Teton, the North Ridge of Mount Assiniboine) and highlighting a memorable story or adventure from the peak's history. A sidebar includes detailed Nuts and Bolts information, including a topo of the route(s) mentioned. You don't have to supply the photo, we can solicit that separately.

Performance—the latest training tips and techniques, presented in a detailed, easy-to-digest format for beginner and advanced climbers alike. We like to see the article focused around one or two top climbers and their training strategies. This section also includes Nutrition, dedicated to eating strategies for more power, endurance, etc, and generally ties into the training tips. Alternating positions with Nutrition every other issue is Field Medicine, focusing on, for example, how to treat a sprained ankle in the field or preventing heat stroke.

Scene—photos and brief, 100-word accounts of the latest gatherings, festivals, and events. This department also includes our Happenings calendar of upcoming events.

Field Tested Gear—our equipment reviews are a signature item of the magazine, and require expert (and exhaustive) field testing of gear in a certain category (i.e. two-person portaledges, ultra-light waterproof/breathable shell jackets). Writer/testers must be objective, honest, hard-working, and capable of writing catchy, detailed reviews.

What's New—our new-products section, featuring field-tested reviews of the latest gear and cragwear. Reviews are roughly 200 words long, sometimes only 100 words. Our reviews section also include Book of the Month, a 150-words review of a book or video.

PHOTOGRAPHY

Rock and Ice places a strong emphasis on stunning, cutting-edge photography. Please feel free to submit photos for any of the above departments as well as for our Exposed section, featuring the staff's picks of their favorite images each issue.

Rock and Ice is not responsible for unsolicited submissions. Please address all submissions to photo editor David Clifford, Big Stone Publishing, 1101 Village Road Ste UL D4, Carbondale CO 81623 USA. You must include a self-addressed, stamped envelope for their return. We accept original slides and black-and-white prints; color prints are NOT acceptable for our Exposed section. You can also email David Clifford low-res samples at: dclifford@bigstonepub.com.

Below are *Rock and Ice*'s photo rates:

Cover:	$700
Two-page spread:	$400
Full Page (and Exposed):	$300
2/3 Page:	$200
1/2 Page:	$150
1/3 Page:	$100
1/4 Page and Spot:	$75

Table of Contents: paid at standard space rates, or $50 per photo as a second use if published elsewhere in a department.

Categories: Nonfiction—Health—Photography—Physical Fitness—Recreation—Sports/Recreation—Rock Climbing

CONTACT: Tyler Stableford, Editor-in-Chief
Material: All
BIG STONE PUBLISHING
1101 Village Rd., Ste UL D4
Carbondale CO 81623
Phone: 970-963-4965
Fax: 970-704-1442
E-mail: editor@bigstonepub.com
Website: www.rockandice.com

Rockford Review

The Rockford Writers' Guild was formed originally in 1947 and now has over 130 members nationwide. A non-profit, tax-exempt corporation, the Rockford Writers' Guild exists to encourage, develop and nurture writers and good writing of all kinds and to promote the art of writing in the Rockford area.

The Guild provides an environment for writers to develop ideas, improve their craft, and share their writing experiences and marketing techniques. We seek to increase community interest, support and appreciation for the literary arts by providing a forum for discussion, conducting workshops and encouraging local talent.

Three times a year, we publish the *Rockford Review*, which has been praised for the quality of its content and its production values. Its poetry, short stories, essays, art and photography represent the best works submitted from all parts of the world.

The *Rockford Review* is a 50-page literary arts magazine published by the Rockford Writers' Guild each winter, spring, and fall. The spring issue is devoted to Guild members who are invited to publish any one piece of their choice.

Review seeks experimental or traditional poetry of up to 50 lines (shorter works are preferred). Short fiction, essays, and satire are welcome in the 250 to 1,300-word range. We also publish one-acts and other dramatic forms (1,300 words). *Review* prefers genuine or satirical human dilemmas with coping or non-coping outcomes that ring the reader's bell. We are always on the lookout for black and white illustrations and glossy photos in a vertical format.

If your work is accepted, you will receive an invitation to be a guest of honor at a Contributors' Reading and Reception in the spring and a complimentary copy of the *Review*. Your work also will be considered for the $25 Editor's Choice Prizes. We award six prizes each year.

Try us with up to three pieces of your best unpublished work at a time. We read year-round and try to report within eight to 12 weeks. There is no reading fee. Simultaneous submissions are okay.

Good luck!

Categories: Fiction—Drama—Poetry—Satire

CONTACT: David Ross, Editor
Material: All
Rockford Writer's Guild
PO Box 858
Rockford IL 61105

Rocky Mountain Sports

Thank you for your interest in *Rocky Mountain Sports*. rocky is about the cutting-edge attitudes and athletic lifestyles that thrive in the Rocky Mountain region. Our mission is to inspire, inform and entertain through provocative profiles, reviews and where-to/how-to writing. Blow-by-blow news reporting applies only if it has an angle, a twist, an insight that a newspaper wouldn't dream of printing.

There are several hard and fast rules for prospective ROCKY writers:

• QUERY ALL stories in writing or via e-mail; don't submit a manuscript.

• DON'T send us a query without first reading ROCKY.

• DON'T send us a personal essay—we use "how-to, where-to" guides, profiles and news formats almost exclusively.

• DON'T ask for your own column—we don't have the space.

Your best bet for getting published with us is to target one of these sports: running, mountain biking, road racing, snowboarding, both alpine and nordic skiing, kayaking, hiking, climbing, mountaineering or other individual sports.

Incorporate humor but avoid cornball. Think fun. On a final note, feel free to go ballistic, be weird or provocative. Don't be afraid to try something new. We like new.

The following goes into more detail on what we're looking for.
—Rebecca Heaton, Editor

Here are some general rules of writing for *Rocky Mountain Sports*:

• You should try to make it fun. We like to see anecdotes, great quotes and vivid descriptions.

• We try to keep a conversational tone to most of the stories in the magazine. You can get away with using the first person if it works in your story. For the most part, we follow the Associated Press Stylebook, although we use the present tense in attribution. ("People want to be like me," Michael Jordan says.)

• Your story should be thoroughly edited, spell-checked and fact-checked when submitted.

• Stay away from technical jargon. Keep the tone conversational.

• Quote Colorado people as often as possible. If that's not possible, try to stick to the Rocky Mountain region or people with Rocky Mountain connections.

• Avoid relying too heavily on PR people and manufacturers. They obviously have a bias for their product or company. Getting their input is fine, just make sure you have others to confirm what they say.

• Whenever you quote someone, get their age, where they live and the correct spelling of their name. You should never invent quotes, but it is legitimate to clean up people's grammar or put in a word for clarity's sake.

• Every story should have multiple sources. If you need additional sources, please ask.

• Make sure that your story isn't quote heavy. Quotes are vital to a good story, but they shouldn't dominate it.

• All claims involving statistics or scientific research should be attributed to a source, such as the League of American Bicyclists, The Environmental Protection Agency or a professional (doctor, nutritionist, personal trainer).

Include the following with your copy:

• A headline. If you can't write a good, concise headline, your story may lack focus. It's a good test to be sure that your story accomplishes what you set out to do.

• Photos. Always try to include a graphic element with your story. Ask your subjects for photos. (We can convert color photos to black and white, and we can use slides. We will return them if asked.) Also interesting with stories are graphs, charts and cartoons—keep your eyes open. If you are unable to come up with any photo ideas, let your editor know early.

• A bio. In about three sentences, tell our readers about yourself, including your involvement in sports or anything relevant to the subject of the article.

• A bill. Send the editor an invoice with your name, address, telephone number and social security number. Payment will follow upon publication.

Categories: Nonfiction—Adventure—Diet/Nutrition—Health—Outdoors—Physical Fitness—Recreation—Sports/Recreation

CONTACT: Rebecca Heaton, Editor
Material: All
Windy City Publishing
2525 15th Street, #1A
Denver CO 80211
Phone: 303-477-9770
Fax: 303-477-9747
E-mail: rheaton@rockymountainsports.com
Website: www.rockymountainsports.com

Rosebud

Thank you for your interest in *Rosebud*. We are open to outside submissions and we review material throughout the year. Although there are a few pointers below, the best way to get a feeling of what we do is to read an issue or two. You can either visit your local bookstore (we are available in Borders and Barnes & Noble), or better yet—subscribe or buy a sample copy directly from us at www.rsbd.net.

ROSEBUD'S SUBMISSION POLICY:

Rosebud, Inc. is a nonprofit organization staffed by volunteers. To handle the growing thousands of submissions we receive every year, we are launching the Rosebud Fast-track Initiative (RFI) to streamline submission processing. To achieve this we will be charging a handling fee of one dollar. For a guaranteed response to your submission in 30 days from the date of receipt, along with some reasons for our response, please:

• Put the letters RFI on the outside of the envelope, and circle it!

• Include a one-dollar fee or check for $1 made out to ROSEBUD.

• Include no more than three stories or five poems per envelope.

• Include a self-addressed stamped envelope for our reply and manuscript return (or, if you specify, we will recycle the manuscripts).

• Send fiction, essays, and/or poetry with SASE and $1.00 handling fee included.

The Rosebud Fast-track Initiative (RFI) offers advantages to authors at a reasonable cost:

• Approximate 40 day response from date of manuscript receipt.

• An acceptance notice or, where appropriate, some indication of why a given piece was not a match for *Rosebud*, and/or how you might better target future work (for prose pieces only).

• Periodic reports on *Rosebud* writing contests with $1000 prizes.

A $1 handling fee (cash or check) must be included with all mailed submissions. Unsolicited materials unaccompanied by a $1 fee will no longer be considered for *Rosebud*.

We must be able to easily contact you by phone, e-mail or regular mail. Fiction and non-fiction submissions must be typed, double-spaced; poetry must be typed, single spaced. The writer's name should be at the top of each page. Send only hardcopy at this time. If your piece is accepted be prepared to send an electronic file by e-mail or on disk. We use *The Chicago Manual of Style* and *Webster's Dictionary* (10th Edition) as editorial guides.

WHAT WE ARE LOOKING FOR IN PROSE:

We publish short stories and an occasional essay. The ideal length for prose is 1,200 to 1,800 words. Send one to three of your strongest pieces. We like good storytelling, real emotion and authentic voice. On rare occasions we publish essays, but we do not publish conventional travel, political, or religious material, sentimentality, "inspirational" essays or nostalgia. Most of the stories we receive read like stories submitted to journals 50 years ago, and often are too generic and predictable to publish. Many start too slow and spend too much time up front telling us what the story is about. Get us interested first, then weave in exposition as you go.

WHAT WE ARE LOOKING FOR IN POETRY:

Send three to five one-page poems representing your best work. If you send an SASE and sufficient postage we will return the poems. Otherwise the paper will be recycled. You should be well-read in contemporary poetry and criticism. Avoid excessive or well-worn abstractions, not to mention clichés. Present a unique and convincing world (you can do this in a few words!) by means of fresh and exact imagery, and by interesting use of syntax. Explore the deep reaches of metaphor. But don't forget to be playful and have fun with words. Never tell the reader what to think.

IF WE PUBLISH...

Rosebud purchases one time rights of original or previously published pieces; this means you are free to sell that same piece to another publication. Selected writers may be contacted later for publication in *Rosebud* anthologies. For stories or articles, *Rosebud* currently pays a flat fee of $25.00, and three issues. *Rosebud* pays for poems in issues only: the amount is generally three, depending on supply. (For those published, the RFI fee will be returned.) Aside from compensation, however, the benefit of publishing in *Rosebud* can be enormous. Your piece will be read across the U.S., Canada, and to some extent, around the world. Literary agents often ask us about writers they have seen in *Rosebud*, and sometimes we can make connections. A significant number of *Rosebud* writers later publish collections or novels elsewhere.

HOW TO SUBSCRIBE:

Subscribe or purchase issues online at The Rosebud Store. Or you can send a check or money order payable to *Rosebud*. A 3-issue subscription is $20; a 6-issue subscription is $35. Sample copies are $7.95 each + $2 shipping/handling. For subscriptions, renewals, and sample copies contact:

SUBSCRIPTIONS or SAMPLE ISSUE:
c/o Roderick Clark
N3310 Asje Rd.

Cambridge, WI 53523

WHY YOUR SUBSCRIPTIONS AND SUBMISSIONS ARE IMPORTANT:

As writers, all of us are dependent upon magazines which publish our work. And, these magazines depend upon us. If we don't buy, read and promote them, they cease to exist. This is particularly true of periodicals like *Rosebud* that are open to submissions from new voices. We are a non-profit organization with no outside affiliation, grants or subsidies. Send in your manuscripts, but also send in your subscription. Let us work together to create a new kind of writing/publishing success.

Categories: Fiction—Nonfiction—Arts—Biography—Consumer—Drama—Erotica—Family—Fantasy—Feminism—General Interest—Humor—Language—Literature—Men's Fiction—Men's Issues—Music—Mystery—Native American—New Age—Poetry—Rural America—Science Fiction—Short Stories—Theatre—Women's Fiction—Women's Issues—Writing

CONTACT: Roderick Clark, Editor
Material: Prose
CONTACT: R. Virgil Ellis, Poetry Editor
Material: Poetry
Send Prose to: N3310 Asje Rd.
Cambridge WI 53523
Phone: 608-423-9609
Send Poetry to: PO Box 614
Cambridge WI 53523
Website: rsbd.net

Rug Hooking

Make your *Rug Hooking* article the best it can be by following these guidelines. Adhering to them will save time and eliminate frustration for both you and the editorial staff.

1. To help you with the arrangement of information in your article, begin with an outline and refer to it often throughout the writing of the story.

2. Please use complete sentences.

3. Use proper punctuation.

4. Answer within your article all the questions listed in your contract.

5. Double-space your article.

6. Make sure your article contains the number of words that are stipulated in your contract. Your word processing software should include a word counting feature. If you do not have this feature, do a rough estimate by counting the average number of words per line of type and multiplying it by the number of lines on a page. Then multiply that figure by the number of pages you have written.

7. Check your spelling. Refer to a dictionary and use the spellcheck feature included in your computer's word processing software.

8. Double check the spelling of all names, addresses, phone numbers, and any other piece of information that you incorporate into your article.

9. When you have finished your story, read it aloud—hearing your story often alerts you to poorly constructed sentences or sections that don't make sense.

10. If you are including art, such as slides of rugs, list for each image the following caption information: the name of the rug, its dimensions, its cut of wool and backing, the designer's name, the hooker's name, the location of the hooker, and the year the rug was hooked.

11. Submit your article on a computer disk as well as on paper. Let us know which word processing software you used to create the file.

Categories: Nonfiction—Antiques—Arts—Collectibles—Crafts—Hobbies—Recreation

CONTACT: Virginia P. Stimmel, Editor
Material: All
Stackpole Magazines
1300 Market St., Ste. 202
Lemoyne PA 17043-1420
Phone: 717-234-5091
Fax: 717-234-1359

Ruminator Review

As a theme-based magazine, we are rarely able to use unsolicited essays and reviews. If you are interested in joining our group of reviewers and want to grab our attention, the best way to do so is by sending a query letter that outlines your writing experience and reviewing interest, along with three or four published clips (book reviews preferred.) If it looks like your writing and interests are a good fit, we'll try and assign a review your way.

What to Expect

We're a very small staff, so it usually takes us a month or two to respond to queries. (Don't worry, though, we will.) Writers are paid on publication; queries and other unsolicited material will not be returned unless sufficient postage is included.

Where to Go to Find Out More

If you'd like a sample issue to see for yourself the quality and style of writing in *Ruminator Review*, e-mail review@ruminator.com to find out how to obtain one. General questions and queries can be addressed to mjk@ruminator.com or mailed to:

CONTACT: Matt
Material: All
1648 Grand Ave.
St. Paul, MN 55105
Phone: 651-699-2610
Fax: 651-699-7190
E-mail: review@ruminator.com
Website: www.ruminator.com

Runner's World

We're providing the following information to help you tailor materials for publication in *Runner's World*. It should go without saying that the best way to understand RW, and what we're looking for from freelancers, is to read several recent issues of the magazine closely.

In addition, you should understand that most RW articles are written by staffers, senior writers or experts (podiatrists, nutritionists, etc.). In other words, it's not easy to be published in *Runner's World*. We don't need and won't publish general articles on the benefits of running, fitness and the like. We may agree with your sentiments and advice but that alone isn't enough to make an article publishable.

Our columns and departments offer the best opportunities for freelancers, in particular: Finish Line, Women's Running and Human Race. It's not necessary to query when contributing to these sections of the magazine; all submissions are on speculation.

Finish Line is our back-of-the-magazine essay. Topics defy descriptions, ranging from humor to life and death. Finish Line is about the running experience and all the variety it brings to our lives. The successful Finish Line essay should strongly identify you as a runner and at the same time relate an experience that other runners can identify with. No fiction. Approximately 750 words. Pays $300 on acceptance. Address all materials to "Finish Line."

Women's Running is an essay page written by and for women. There's no formula for success here, but the best essays tend to describe emotional experiences that have been colored by the writer's running. Pays $300 on acceptance. Address all materials to "Women's Running."

Human Race tells the everyday, inspirational and humorous stories of typical middle-of-the-pack runners. Almost anyone can be a Human Race story so long as you find out something interesting about the person's running or lifestyle. Pay's $50 plus a photo space rate. Photos essential. Address all materials to "Human Race."

Other Departments and Features: Other parts of the magazine are more difficult to break into. An exception is "Warmups" which mixes international running news with human interest stories. If you can send us a unique human interest story from your region, we'll give it serious consideration.

We receive hundreds of first-person stories every year, most from people describing how they ran their first marathon. These are never publishable unless they contain something highly unusual or emotional.

We are always looking for "Adventure Runs" from readers—runs in wild, remote, beautiful and interesting places. These are rarely race stories but more like backtracking/running adventures. Great color slides are crucial.

Photos. Nearly all our photos are taken by professionals. The exception would be the photo that you managed to capture that no one else in the world got, i.e., Madonna running in Central Park, a scenic wilderness photo, a photo of an elephant chasing a runner in India.

We hope the above answers many of your questions.

Happy writing and running.

The Editors

Categories: Nonfiction—Health—Physical Fitness—Recreation—Sports/Recreation

CONTACT: Adam Bean, Managing Editor
Material: All
33 E. Minor St.
Emmaus PA 18098
Phone: 610-967-5171
Fax: 610-967-7725
Website: www.runnersworld.com

Running Times
The Runner's Best Resource

Running Times, The Runner's Best Resource, is the national magazine for the experienced running participant and fan. Our audience is knowledgeable about the sport and actively participates in running and racing. All editorial relates specifically to running: improving performance, enhancing enjoyment, or exploring events, places, and people in the sport. Please read recent issues to learn the type of material we seek.

Three principles that guide our editorial section are:

1) We go beyond basic, beginner information: presenting the "why" as well as "how-to," digging for principles, exploring contexts, analyzing and drawing conclusions from the facts.

2) We present honest content that accurately reflects the runner's experience and inspires trust.

3) Good writing is a priority; writing aimed at an intelligent, informed and discriminating audience.

We assign approximately 40% of our editorial material to freelance writers. We are willing to work with unpublished writers. Although we consider unsolicited manuscripts, we prefer to see a written query which describes in two or three paragraphs your idea, the article's proposed length and scope, why *Running Times*' readers would find the material interesting, and what qualifies you to write about it.

We close each issue three months ahead of on-sale date, and assign well in advance of our printing deadlines. Payment is made upon publication.

We publish editorial material in the following categories:

• Features (1,500 to 3,000 words). Training, Athlete Profiles, Travel, Current Events and Issues

• Columns (400 to 1,000 words). Nutrition, Sports Medicine, Training.

• Fiction (1,500 to 3,500 words). Any genre, related to running and runners.

We request that all writers submit their articles via e-mail. Send your proposal via email or with an SASE.

Categories: Fiction—Nonfiction—Health—Recreation—Sports

CONTACT: Jonathan Beverly, Editor
Material: All
CONTACT: Marc Chalufour, Managing Editor
Material: All
Fitness Publishing, Inc.
213 Danbury Rd.
Wilton CT 06897-4006
Phone: 203-761-1113
Fax: 203-761-9933
E-mail: editor@runningtimes.com
Website: www.runningtimes.com

RURAL HERITAGE
Rural Heritage

RURAL HERITAGE was established in 1975 as a link with the past, not for nostalgic reasons, but to help preserve a way of life for future generations. Our readers are commonsense country folks who enjoy doing things for themselves. Many of them have always farmed with horses, mules, or oxen; others are returning to the practice for economic and/or environmental reasons. Our editorial policy is guided by the philosophy that the past holds the key to the future.

Subjects: We publish hands-on how-to stories covering the broad spectrum of rural skills and creative problem solving, with emphasis on draft animals used in the field or wood lot. We are especially seeking technical details on specific pieces of horse-drawn equipment, how it was obtained/restored, how much it cost, how it's put together, how it works, problems encountered, and how they were solved. We do not publish religious material or non-relevant political or social topics.

Submission: If you are unknown to us, please either submit your material on speculation or else query (outline what you intend to cover and how you'll handle it) and if possible include clips of three previously published pieces. Be sure you know your subject—our savvy readers are quick to notice errors in terminology, breed identification, and similar details.

Format: Disk, CD, or via email. Please include a two or three sentence bionote describing your non-writing interests and qualifications for your subject.

Length: Minimum is 650 words with at least one illustration (850 words without illustration); features run 1,200 to 1,500 words; special subjects occasionally run longer.

Illustrations: Please include detailed captions identifying breed(s), equipment, and visible people, and indicate the name of the photographer or artist to whom we should give credit. Put your name and address on the back of each piece and send a self-addressed stamped envelope for the return of your material.

Payment: Payment for first English language rights is 5 cents per published word and $10 per illustration, paid on publication, and two copies of the issue bearing your work.

Sample copy: If you are not familiar with RURAL HERITAGE and would like a sample issue, please send $8.00 (US $9.00 to Canada or US $10.00 overseas). Subscriptions to the bimonthly are $26.00 per year (US $32.00 to Canada, US $37.00 overseas).

Categories: Nonfiction—Rural America—Draft Animals—Farming—Livestock—Logging

CONTACT: Gail Damerow, Editor
Material: All
281 Dean Ridge Ln.
Gainesboro TN 38562-5039
Phone: 931-268-0655
E-mail: editor@ruralheritage.com
Website: www.ruralheritage.com

Russian Life

Russian Life has as its fundamental editorial mission telling the story of Russia. It is a primary looking glass into Russia for some 40,000+ Americans and covers Russian culture, travel, history, politics, art, business and society. As a bimonthly magazine, *Russian Life* focuses on current issues and events facing Russia and Russians. The majority of *Russian Life* content is feature articles, most of which are not time-sensitive, but all of which are current.

The majority of *Russian Life* articles are also written by freelance Russian journalists and writers. The role of contributions by freelance Western or expat writers is to provide a unique "outsider" perspective. While no one knows Russia like Russians, sometimes it takes the view of foreigners to help shape a message that resonates with foreign readers.

Russian Life's writing style is frank, terse and incisive. The model is good American journalism style (and spelling) on the lines of the AP Stylebook—i.e. third person reportage. We seek to provide coverage of Russia that is free of illusions (but not blemishes) and full of hope (but not ideology or agendas). We adhere to the belief that Russia is a land of endless fascination and opportunity, but a place that, like many others, is fraught with its own problems, risks and dangers. Our job is to present a realistic, truthful and independent view that balances these realities, providing enjoyable, insightful reading. It is also helpful to remember that *Russian Life* is a very visual magazine; few stories do not include photographs.

Persons interested in either submitting articles (or photos) to *Russian Life* or being assigned stringer work should first contact *Russian Life* editorial offices to discuss the parameters of such work with our editors. While we welcome unsolicited manuscripts, we feel that it is most productive to work with writers ahead of time—to hone story ideas to fit the *Russian Life* mold. Manuscripts are returned only if accompanied by a self-addressed stamped envelope. Submissions may also be made electronically, with prior approval. Fees for freelance work is agreed upon on a individual basis, depending on the scope, difficulty and nature of the story being written. Payment is upon publication. Most stories will be between 2000-4000 words in length.

Categories: Nonfiction—Culture—History—Travel—Russian Topics

CONTACT: Paul Richardson, Editor
Material: All
RIS Publications
PO Box 567
Montpelier VT 05601
Phone: 802-223-4955
Fax: 802-223-6105
E-mail: info@rispubs.com

Remember: Editors change jobs and publishers change addresses. It is wise to invest in a phone call for the current information before submitting.

Website: www.russian-life.com -or- www.rispubs.com

S & T Magazine

Please refer to *Space & Time Publishing*.

Safari

SAFARI Magazine was founded in 1971 as the official publication of Safari Club International. SAFARI Magazine is bi-monthly; is focused on big game hunting and conservation; and, includes editorials, feature stories and columns about SCI national, international and chapter activities, affiliated organizations and members' hunting reports from around the world. Circulation is 27,000-30,000, mailed nationally and internationally to the SCI membership list and to selected other individuals or organizations. Send submissions to SCI, at the address shown below.

EDITORIAL CONTENT
The magazine scope of interest is:
• Outdoor recreation with special emphasis on big game hunting around the world
• Ethnic and traditional hunts of particular regions around the world
• Current or historical hunting and conservation
• Philosophy and heritage of hunting
• Background on a particular species
• Conservation and environmental affairs relevant to big game or hunters

We buy first rights manuscripts. Queries prior to submissions are encouraged; no fiction or poetry accepted. Avoid sending simple hunting narratives that lack new approaches. Features run 2,000-2,500 words and should be informative, accurate, designed to appeal to sportsmen and women as well as others who enjoy out-of-doors. Rate for a full-length story with illustrations submitted by a professional writer is $300 paid upon publication. Short stories or non-pro contributions by SCI members rate an honorarium of $25. (Professional photographers are paid up to $100 for each color photo used, depending on size, up to $45 each B&W-all on if published/when published basis.)

News briefs are welcomed and will include bylines, but are not bought by SAFARI.

MANUSCRIPT PREPARATION
Submitted manuscripts should fit these specifications in order to be reviewed.
• Original: typed or laser jet printout, no photocopies.
• Consecutive-number all manuscript pages.
• Computer disks: ASCII language accepted with hard copy. (Mac 3½" or IBM 5¼")
• Double-spaced or 1½-spaced text OK.
• All pages: 1½" left margin, 1" right and base.
• Title page (first page): Author name, address, telephone in upper right corner, title halfway down first page, followed by text. Author name on all pages following.
• Pica-sized, sans-serif type preferred.
• Spell-check for proper names, animals, places.
• Do not staple manuscript pages.
• We have prepared an editorial style sheet for information and use on any manuscript.

PHOTOGRAPHY SUBMISSION
We are interested only in huntable big game subjects of trophy quality in a natural setting.

Color photographs, slides or transparencies are preferred. (Prints accepted for color or black-and-white uses. In all cases, use will depend on the reproduction quality of submitted materials.)

All photos must be captioned. Type caption information on a separate sheet of paper and number to match slide or print being described. We prefer to receive more photos than we may be able to use, in order to have a choice. Send SASE. All photos will be returned following publication unless otherwise directed.

• Color Slides: use plastic sheets to hold slides or transparencies; do not ship unprotected. Label each slide with name stamp or label.

• Black-and-White: 35mm contacts, glossy or semi-gloss prints; added minimum of ½" white border on four sides preferred.

• Slides or transparencies preferred for color and should be sharp and well-exposed. (Prints are OK, glossy preferred. If 35mm: double-sized, or 5"x7" or larger).

• Print sizes 5"x7" or 8"x10" preferred; others considered based on quality and story needs.

• Do not write on prints. Attach label with pre-typed information or use grease-pencil only.

Categories: Conservation—Outdoors—Hunting

CONTACT: Steve Comu, Director of Publications
Material: All
Safari Club International
4800 W. Gates Pass Rd.
Tucson AZ 85745
Phone: 520-620-1220
Fax: 520-618-3555
E-mail: scomus@safariclub.org
Website: www.safariclub.org

SageWoman
PanGaia
The Blessed Bee
New Witch

SageWoman is a quarterly magazine of women's spirituality. Our readers are people who identify positively with the term "Goddess." Our readership includes women of a variety of religious faiths, ranging from Roman Catholic to Lesbian Separatist Witch and everywhere in between. What our readers have in common is summed up in the statement "Celebrating the Goddess in every woman." If you feel a connection with our subject matter, we welcome your contributions to our pages. The majority of every issue is created from the contributions of our readers, so your creativity and willingness to share is vital to *SageWoman*'s existence! We welcome material from women of all races, ages, sexual orientations, and socio-economic backgrounds. Our editorial staff is English-speaking only, so we ask that written contributions and letters to us be submitted in English, but we encourage submissions from non-American women and women for whom English may be a second language. We also strongly encourage contributions from women of color. SageWoman offers the following guidelines to help you in submitting your work to us.

1. Subject matter

a. All submissions should focus on issues of concern to Pagan and other Goddess-friendly women. We accept non-fiction prose related to women's spiritual experience. We accept very modest amounts of poetry and receive far more poetry than we can publish. We also accept photographs and graphic artwork (drawings, painting, prints, etc.) suitable for publishing in a magazine format. We do not accept fiction, screenplays, long narrative poems, erotica, or press releases/advertorial.

b. *SageWoman* is dedicated to helping women explore their spiritual, emotional, and mundane lives in a way that respects all persons, creatures, and the Earth. We encourage women of all spiritual paths to send writings and artwork, but our focus is on material, which expresses an Earth-centered spirituality. Our editorial style focuses on personal experience; please write in the first person! Please don't limit yourself because you aren't a "professional" writer or artist—most of our published material is from previously unpublished writers. If you haven't

seen a copy of *SageWoman*, please send for a sample copy ($7) or look at our sample articles at our website before submitting material; this will enable you to understand the kind of material we publish and will save both you and us a lot of time!

c. *SageWoman* accepts material created by women only. (Male contributors are encouraged to contact our co-ed publications *Pan Gaia*, *The Blessed Bee*, or *New Witch*, at the same address; these titles accept submissions from both men and women.)

2. Written Submissions

a. All written submissions should be the original work of the author. We prefer receiving submissions via email sent to editor@sagewoman.com or on computer disk accompanied by a double-spaced paper manuscript. (Please don't just send a disk—sometimes compatibility problems prevent us from reading disks which are submitted to us, and without a manuscript, we won't be able to evaluate your submission!) We are Windows based and prefer ASCII compatible or Word files attached to your email or if email is not an option by 3.5" or Zipdisks. We may be able to translate Macintosh based disks as well. Disks sent to us will not be returned unless you send an SASE with adequate postage with the submission. If computer-based submission is not possible, typed, double-spaced manuscripts are also acceptable, as well as neatly handwritten pieces if no other method is possible. Please do not send us your only copy of your manuscript; accidents can happen and material sent to us is occasionally lost or damaged.

b. Articles should be between 800 and 5000 words in length, and written manuscripts should contain the author's name, pen name (if appropriate), address and phone number on each page.

c. We are aware that you have worked hard on your writing, it is personal and special to you, and contains your unique voice. Nonetheless, we often find it necessary to edit for length, clarity and grammar, sometimes at the last minute before publication. Therefore, we CANNOT guarantee that your article will appear precisely as you submitted it. If you do not want your material edited in any way, please do not submit your writing to us. (Also, please inform us of deliberate uses of non-traditional spelling so the tone of your work will not be accidentally altered.)

3. Graphic Art

a. All graphic art submissions should be the original work of the artist. Clear, black and white drawings are best, but penciled or colored works may be acceptable in some cases. Please be aware that all artwork will be reproduced in black and white only, except for pieces used on our outside covers. Our covers are usually commissioned works, but you may feel free to submit color photocopies or slides of your color work for possible use on the cover. Please send us clean copies of your artwork only—we cannot be responsible for your original artwork! We encourage the submission of artwork which celebrates the Goddess and women in all of our many guises; different skin colors, cultures, ages, sexual orientations, body types, sizes, and shapes, and levels of ableness.

b. We are always looking for new artists to share their creativity in our pages. If you have a portfolio of your work, feel free to send it; when sending a body of work, please inform us if any of the pieces have been previously published or are not available for publication. We do commission special pieces of artwork for the magazine; however, the majority of artwork we publish has been sent by artists on spec. We keep files of artwork, by artist, and when an issue is in production we find the pieces of artwork on file that fit each article, and then inform the artist in question that we have decided to publish their work. For this reason, your artwork maybe on file for months, or years, without being used—if this is a problem for you, please inform us so we can work out other arrangements with you.

4. Photography

a. All photographic submissions should be the original work of the photographer. If persons other than the photographer are shown, a signed release from said person(s) must be included in order for us to

publish the photo. Please send standard black and white or color prints, negatives or slides.

All photographs will be reproduced in black and white only. Our use of photography is similar to that of graphic art; please see guidelines above.

5. General Information

a. Please send a self-addressed, stamped envelope with your submission. If you wish for us to return your submission, please ensure that the SASE has adequate postage to return your manuscript, artwork, or other submission. If you do not wish for your submission to be returned, please write "Do not return" on it, and simply send an SASE or stamped postcard for us to respond to your submission. Please put your name, address and phone number with area code on each page of your manuscript.

b. Your submission will be acknowledged when we receive your material; we cannot guarantee exact publishing dates but will attempt to keep you up-to-date on the status of your work. We prefer to accept material which has not been previously seen or published—please inform us of multiple submissions or previous publications.

c. *SageWoman* publishes quarterly. All material should be sent to the attention of the Editor at the address (either e-mail or U.S. mail) given below.

6. Compensation and Rights

a. *SageWoman* offers modest cash payments for unsolicited artwork, photography, and articles.

Articles are compensated at approximately $.01 per word for unsolicited material, with a minimum of $10. (No payment is made for *Rattle* letters or networking information printed in *Weaving the Web*.) Artwork and photography are compensated on a piece-by-piece basis, depending on the size, complexity and usefulness of the piece. Artists and photographers are paid a minimum of $15 per piece for their work. We are often able to pay more in cases where the article, artwork, illustration or photograph is commissioned especially for *SageWoman*; please contact us if you are interested in working with us on commission. We realize how very modest these payments are; we offer them not as full compensation for your creativity, but as a "thank-you" for sharing your gifts with us. If you are a business or craftsperson who would benefit from advertising in our pages, please inform us that you are interested in trading advertising for your contributions; we are able to be substantially more generous in trading for advertising space than we can be in our cash payments!

b. If your material is accepted, you will also receive a free copy of the issue in which your work appears. Payment will be sent to you within 30 days of your return of our contributor's form, which is sent out to all contributors shortly after an issue goes to press. *SageWoman* requires first worldwide serial rights, and prefers (but does not require) all rights for one year, and the right to reprint in future *SageWoman* collections as well as non-exclusive electronic rights (for use on the "sample" page of the *SageWoman* Website.) All remaining rights will revert to you.

When you submit work to us, we will assume your work is available for the purchase of these rights at the compensation level specified above, unless you state otherwise.

If there are any questions that these guidelines do not answer, please feel free e-mail, call or write to us for more information, or simply to try out your ideas on us! Our usual office hours are 9-4 Pacific Time, Monday-Friday, but feel free to leave a message if you don't reach us.

We will return your call! Thanks again for your interest in *SageWoman*. We look forward to hearing from you soon. Submissions may be sent by e-mail, fax or postal mail. An FTP site is available for graphics files call for details, 707-882-2052.

Special Note

The above guidelines apply to all four magazines listed at the top: *SageWoman Magazine, PanGaia, The Blessed Bee* and *New Witch.*

Categories: Feminism—Religion—Spiritual—Women's Issues

CONTACT: Submissions Editor
Material: All

PO Box 641
Point Arena CA 95468-0641
Phone: 707-882-2052
Fax: 707-882-2793
E-mail: editor@sagewoman.com
Website: www.sagewoman.com

Sailing Magazine

20% freelance. Sailing Magazine *is for the sailor committed to the sport. All kinds of sailing are featured on big pages full of pictures and text complemented by technical articles. Welcomes new writers. Circ. 40K. Monthly.*

Pays on publication. Publishes ms 6 months after acceptance. Buys one-time rights. Rarely accepts reprints. Responds 2 months. Sample for written request and $5.

Needs: Features with pictures. Pays $250-500 for 800-2,500 words. Submit complete ms with cover letter by mail with SASE.

Photos/Art: Pays $50-800.

Categories: Nonfiction—Boating—History—Outdoors—Recreation—Sports/Recreation

CONTACT: Greta Schanen, Managing Editor
Material: All
PO Box 249, 125 E. Main St.
Port Washington WI 53074
Phone: 262-284-3494
Fax: 262-284-7764
E-mail: editorial@sailingmagazine.net
Website: www:sailingonline.com

Sailing World

Guidelines for Writers

Prospective contributors to *Sailing World* should study recent issues of the magazine to determine appropriate subject matter. The emphasis here is on performance sailing: keep in mind that the *Sailing World* readership is relatively educated about the sport. Unless you are dealing with a totally new aspect of sailing, you can and should discuss ideas on an advanced technical level; however, extensive formulae and graphs don't play well to our audience. When in doubt as to the suitability of an article or idea, submit a written query before time and energy are misdirected. (Because of the volume of queries received, editors cannot accept phone calls.)

All mss. should be typewritten and double-spaced. Unless specific arrangements have been made ahead of time with *Sailing World*, submissions must include all necessary artwork and photos. (See SW's Photographer's Guidelines.) Materials should bear the contributor's name, address and phone number. Unsolicited articles should be sent as queries via e-mail. If the article idea is accepted, the full text can then be sent as a text or Microsoft Word document on a floppy disk (Mac or Windows format). The disk should be sent with a self-addressed, stamped envelope.

Most writing for *Sailing World* falls into one of several categories. Articles on one-design or offshore sailing can be presented as any of the following:

1. Feature (B&W or color)
   - Instructional
   - Event-oriented

- Personality profiles
2. Race Report
3. Starting Line
4. Finish Line

Non-racing features may be either instructional or narrative; in the latter case, suitability for SW will be determined by the quality of writing and ideas, or by the value of lessons learned.

"Gee-whiz" impressions from beginning sailors are generally not accepted.

Payment for article is upon publication, and varies with the type of article, its placement in the magazine, and the amount of editing required. Average payment is $400 for up to 2000 plus words.

Thank you for your interest in contributing to *Sailing World*.

Guidelines for Photographers

Prospective contributors should study recent issues of the magazine to determine photographic style. Preference is given to color slides; our Art Department recommends shooting with Fuji VELVIA film. Other submissions should be 5x7 or larger B&W or color glossy prints— no negatives, please. Name and address of contributor should be attached to each submission or slide, and the delivery should be accompanied by a memo covering the details of the submission. Return method should be specified if other than Certified Mail. Please also include a street address for Express return services, as well as any account information with FedEx or other courier services. Returns typically take 3 months, unless an expedited return is requested by the photographer. Payment for photos is upon publication, and varies with photo size and type according to *Sailing World* rates.

Generally, all photos are story related. While *Sailing World* does not discourage the submission of other photos, it is unlikely that they will be used in feature stories. We do, however, encourage submissions of competitive, current events taking place throughout the world for use in our monthly columns which examine the local and global racing scene. In addition, we will enter your name in our contributors file to receive periodic mailings regarding our needs.

Photos usually fall into one of the following categories:

1. Cover: Always color, usually related to an inside story. Preferably vertical. Feature Or Photo 2. Feature: Color slides. Usually covers a specific topic (instructional or technical) or event. Most is commissioned work. Assignment ideas accepted in writing only (or fax).

3. Finish Line: One shot per story. Exciting event action preferred.

4. General: General sailing photography welcomed (new boats, interesting people, spectacular wipe-outs, unusual rigs). Please send all photos to the attention of Elizabeth Carroll. Thank you for your interest in contributing to *Sailing World*.

Digital Photo Guidelines

Digital photos must be 300 dpi: 6 by 8 inches for standard (half-page or less) photos, 11 by 16 inches for spreads. Please include a labeled contact sheet or an additional folder containing 72 dpi thumbnails of your photos.

Please send files in one of these formats, listed in preference order:
- Photoshop compressed TIFF
- Photoshop EPS
- Photoshop BMP
- Photoshop JPEG

We cannot accept these formats: GIF, PCX, PDF, PNG, PIXAR, RAW, SCITEX, EXE.

Please send a disc, again in order of preference:
- CD
- Zip
- floppy

Categories: Boating—Outdoors—Sports/Recreation

CONTACT:
David Rud, Managing Editor
Material: All
5 John Clarke Rd.
PO Box 3400
Newport RI 02840-0992
Phone: 401-847-1588
Fax: 401-848-5048
E-mail: editor@sailingworld.com
Website: www.sailingworld.com

Salmon-Trout-Steelheader

No formal guidelines. However, we do accept unsolicited articles. Our general focus is on fishing and the out-of-doors.

Categories: Fishing—Outdoors—Recreation—Sports/Recreation

CONTACT: Nick Amato
Material: All
PO Box 82112
Portland OR 97282
Phone: 503-653-8108
Website: www.amatobooks.com

Salon

Salon welcomes article queries and submissions. The best way to submit articles and story pitches is via e-mail.

We ask that you please send the text of your query or submission in plain text in the body of your e-mail, rather than as an attached file, as we may not be able to read the format of your file. If you wish to contribute, please spend some time familiarizing yourself with *Salon*'s various sites and features. Please put the words "EDITORIAL SUBMISSIONS" in the subject line of the e-mail. You can find the editor's name on our *Salon* Staff page. And please tell us a little about yourself — your experience and background as a writer and qualifications for writing a particular story. If you have clips you can send us via e-mail, or Web addresses of pages that contain your work, please send us a representative sampling (no more than three or four, please).

We do our best to respond to all inquiries, but be aware that we are sometimes inundated. If you have not heard back from us after three weeks, please assume that we will not be able to use your idea or submission.

Also please note that *Salon* does not solicit fiction or poetry submissions and will not be able to respond to such submissions

Categories: Nonfiction—Arts—Book Reviews—Business—Current Affairs— Entertainment—Lifestyle—Politics—Sexuality—Technology

CONTACT: Kerry Lauerman, Editor
E-mail: klauerman@Salon.com
Material: Arts & Entertainment
CONTACT: Andrew O'Hehir, Editor
E-mail:aoh@Salon.com
Material: Books
CONTACT: The Editor, Life
E-mail: life@Salon.com
Material: Life
CONTACT: Geraldine Sealey, Senior Editor
E-mail: gsealey@Salon.com
Material: News/Politics
CONTACT: Karen Croft, Editor
E-mail: kcroft@Salon.com
Material: Sex
CONTACT: Andrew Leonard, Editor
E-mail: aleonard@Salon.com
Material: Technology & Business
22 4th St., 11th Floor,
San Francisco, CA 94103
Phone: 415-645-9200

Fax: 415-645-9204
Website: www.*Salon*.com

San Francisco

We do not have formal writer's guidelines. We accept queries. Ouor advice to new writers: First, read a few back issues of *San Francisco* to get a feel for what we publish. Then send us a query letter.

Categories: Culture—General Interest—Lifestyle—Regional
CONTACT: Lisa Trottier, Managing Editor
Material: All
243 Vallejo St.
San Francisco CA 94111
Phone: 415-398-2800

Sandlapper
The Magazine of South Carolina

Editorial Philosophy

Sandlapper is a quarterly magazine focusing on the positive aspects of South Carolina. We look for articles and phot-essays about South Carolina's interesting people, places, activities, heritage and cuisine. No political/controversial issues, except as they relate to history. *Sandlapper* is intended to be read at those times when people want to relax with an attractive, high-quality magazine that entertains and informs them about their state.

Article Content & Style

We consider for publication nonfiction articles and photo-essays. No fiction or poetry, at this time. We occasionally buy reprints.

Simultaneous submissions are not accepted; we presume an article submittal is for our exclusive consideration, subject to terms under the "Payment & Rights Acquisition" section, below.

The editors consider articles of variable length, from approximately one to six magazine pages (500-3,000 words). Any approach the author chooses to take—standard third-person, first-person, Q&A format, impressionistic, etc.—may be accepted, provided it works. We look for top-quality literature. Humor is encouraged. Profanity is discouraged. Good taste is a standard. Unique angles are critical for acceptance. Dare to be bold. But not too bold. ! (Napoleon, or whoever)

Topics to avoid:
• Politics
• Topical/controversial issues
• R-rated subjects
• Commercial enterprises
• First-person nostalgia

Articles should not be submitted incomplete or subject to change/correction/addition. Late changes can create major problems. If you elect to let your sources review your m;anscrtipt draft, then YOU deal with them; please complete all discourse with them before submitting the manuscript for publication.

The editors reserve the right to change the title of a submitted article and to alter, condense, expand and otherwise edit the text of the article without approval by the author.

Photographs & Illustrations

Sandlapper buys black-and-white prints, color transparencies and art. Digital photography will be accepted in the following format only: JPEGS at minimum 300 dpi, at 8½ x 11-inch size. Please provide digital images on CD or IBM-compatible disk, accompanied by proof or laser print. Photographers should submit working cutlines for each photograph. Unused photos will be returned to the photographer if adequate return postage is provided. Photographs for accepted articles will be returned after publication. Please put your name on each slide or print so they can be properly credited and returned.

Our guidelines for accepting digital photography:
• First and foremost, all digital photos used by *Sandlapper* have to have been taken in South Carolina.
• Next, if you are simply submitting in hopes of being published, rather than for an assignment we have handed out, consider this: There are four issues a year—Spring, Summer, Fall and Winter—so we shoot photos that represent those seasons and you might just find your photo on the cover. A date reference on your submissions would help. In the past we have selected what we thought was a beautiful spring flower shot, but upon further research found that the plant actually blooms in fall. If we had only known we might have used that photo two issues earlier. But we missed that chance, as well as the Spring issue!
• Always take pictures on the highest settings your camera allows. The higher the resolution the sharper and clearer the image will reproduce. The larger the file, the less photos you can get on your camera's disc—invest in a 64 MB or larger disk for your camera!
• When taking photos remember that magazines are vertical. Do you want to get the cover shot? Do you want to see your photo as a full page in an article? Remember to take some vertical shots!
• Please do not direct us to Ofoto or a similar internet site to review your submissions—we need a CD or Zip disk containing your photos and a printout of each photo to do our job effectively. The printout of each photo should be *100% size*. This can be as simple as a black and white laser printout. Only digital photos *with* printouts will be considered! If you sorted through thousands of great images each issue, you would understand how important it is to keep each article and its corresponding images together in one envelope! The internet doesn't fit in an envelope.
• Please be sure that your Zip disk or CD is not formatted exclusively for PCs. Our photo editors work on Macs and you may get bumped out of the photo selection if we can't open your submissions. Want to submit your photo on a floppy disk? Think twice! A general rule is that if the photo will fit on a floppy, it's probably not a large enough file!
• JPG or TIF formats are preferred.
• RGB color modes is preferred.
• Please submit lo-resolution files as well as hi-resolution files—and label them as such. We handle thousands of photos each issue and it would be wonderful if your hi-res and lo-res files were named exactly the same name, but with the addition of LO on the lo-res files and HI on the hi-res files names. For example: RedBarnLO.jpg and RedBarnHI.jpg.
• Do not try to make the file sizes or image sizes larger AFTER you have taken the digital image. The information is not there—don't force it or the images will look pixilated.
• Before submitting photos, please do a little editing. We trust that you can edit from the 300 shots you took last week down to 10 you are really, really proud of! Please send your best, not your entire portfolio. Please give us a call of email if you have any questions about *Sandlapper* digital image submissions: Elaine Gillespie, 803-779-2126, elaine@thegillespieagency.com.

Queries, Assignments & Article Submittals

Unsolicited manuscripts will be considered, but we strongly recommend that you query in writing with a brief description of the article topic you have in mind. Several ideas maybe described in one query. (Please don't send further query letters until we've responded to your first one.) One or two (maximum) clips of your previously published work would be helpful. Telephone queries are DISCOURAGED; we will not be able to give you an immediate decision on the phone, and we prefer that you submit your own typed description rather than make us scribble a description based on telephone notations.

Seasonal article ideas should be suggested at least six months in advance.

Article topics are discussed at regular editorial staff meetings. We try to report on queries withn one month. If we like an idea, we will invite the author to submit the article ON SPECULATION; we will not guarantee purchase of an article in advance of submittal. No kill fees.

Text should be TYPED, DOUBLE-SPACED, on standard 8½ x 11-inch white paper. Article submittals on microcomputer diskette are STRONGLY encouraged but not required. Acceptable disk systems are PC Windows or DOS. The diskette should be accompanied by a hard-copy print-out of the text, double-spaced. Electronic submissions encouraged.

DO NOT submit an article that is incomplete, is pending approval or revision by your sources, or is otherwise subject to change before we go to press.

All correspondence, including query letters and article/photography submittals, should be accompanied by an SASE with adequate return postage. *Sandlapper* accepts no responsibility for unsolicited material.

Payment & Rights Acquisition

Payment for articles and photographs varies, based on a freelance budget of approximately $50-$100 per published magazine page (including combined text and photography/art). We typically pay $25-$75 per photograph and artwork; maximum $100 for a cover or centerspread photo.

Payment normally is made approximately one month after publication.

The author/photographer will retain the copyright. *Sandlapper* will acquire a) the right of first publication of the article and photographs (in the magazine and in the on-line editions of *Sandlapper*), b) subsequent, multiple reprint rights, including electronic media of the article and photographs in *Sandlapper*-related reprints, and c) the right to grant access to the article, photographs, and other bibliographic citation material stored electronically in public databases, and to furnish printed copies thereof requested through such public databases. If the author/photographer subsequently grants reprint rights to another publication, *Sandlapper* requests but does not require that the subsequent publication include credit to *Sandlapper* as the original publisher. *Sandlapper* requires a current issue embargo on subsequent publication; the article must not appear in print elsewhere until after the dateline period of its *Sandlapper* appearance has ended.

By submitting an article, the author warrants and represents that a) the author has included no material in the article in violation of any rights of any person or entity, and b) the author has disclosed to *Sandlapper* all relationships of the author to any person or entity featured in the article, and all relationships to any person or entity producing or marketing any product or providing any service referred to in the article.

A Note about Idea Submittals...

Before the start-up of the magazine was announced formally, the editors began building a database of article ideas (several hundred, initially). Most of these were the editors' ideas; some came from prospective freelance writers. we immediately discovered many suggestions were duplicates—as many as five different writers suggested the same article topic almost simultaneously. In the ensuing weeks, as more freelancers got word of pending publication, the duplicity of certain article topics quickly became a *multiplicity*.

We try to be fair. Whenever we receive a good article suggestion, we enter a brief description of it in a computer database, noting the name of the original proposer. However, we make no pledges. If you suggest an article idea to us and you see an article on the subject published later in the magazine under another writer's byline, it probably will be because a) that writer submitted the idea first or b) we believed that writer had better credentials to prepare that particular article.

Where to Send Queries, Articles and Photographs

Please correspond to: Aïda Rogers, managing editor. Please enclose a self-addressed, stamped envelope. Or, E-mail her at aida@sandlapper.org.

Thank you for your interest in *Sandlapper*! We wish you the best with your writing, photography and art, and we hope to work with you in the future.

Categories: Nonfiction—Adventure—Arts—Biography—Business—Children—Civil War—College—Conservation—Cooking—Culture—Education—Entertainment—Environment—Family—Fishing—Folklore—Food/Drink—Gardening—General Interest—History—Hobbies—Humor—Interview—Lifestyle—Outdoors—Photography—Recreation—Regional—Rural America—Senior Citizen—Sports/Recreation—Travel

CONTACT: Aïda Rogers, Managing Editor
Material: All
PO Box 1108
Lexington, SC 29071
Phone: 803-359-9941
Fax: 803-359-0629
E-mail: aida@sandlapper.org
Website: www.sandlapper.org

The Saturday Evening Post

Guidelines for Submitting Work Writers & Cartoonists

Before submitting work to *The Saturday Evening Post*, please take the time to read our guidelines

For Writers

Before sending us a manuscript or query, we hope you will look over past issues of *The Post* to get an idea of the range and style of articles we publish. You will discover that our main emphasis is health and fitness. Although there are many specialty publications in this field, the *Post*'s goal is to remain unique by presenting not only cutting-edge news but by combining this with information of practical use to our readers.

Major freelance contributions in recent years include: "Hats On For Health: A Skin-Cancer Warning from Down Under," about the advanced skin-cancer-prevention program in Australia, and "Munchausen by Proxy The Deadly Game," about a little-understood but prevalent psychological disorder that can be devastating to children.

In addition to health-related articles, *The Post* buys humor and anecdotes suitable for "Post Scripts," as well as cartoons, illustrations, and photos. Payment ranges from $15 for Post Scripts to $25-$400 for most feature articles.

Our nonfiction needs include how-to, useful articles on gardening, pet care and training, financial planning, and subjects of interest to a family-oriented readership. For nonfiction articles, indicate any special qualifications you have for writing about the subject, especially for technical or scientific material. Include one or two published clips with your query. We prefer typed manuscripts between 2,500 and 3,000 words in length. We generally buy all rights.

Although we seldom publish new fiction, our readers enjoy upbeat stories that stress traditional relationships and family values. A light, humorous touch is appreciated. We are also always in need of straight humor articles. Make us laugh and we'll buy it. We respond quickly to queries, normally within three weeks. If you do send the whole manuscript, either (1) include a sufficiently stamped and sized SASE for its return should we decide not to use it; or (2) indicate you do not want the material returned and include an SASE with appropriate Postage for a reply. Please send typed, double-spaced copy. We normally respond to manuscript submissions within six weeks. You are free to submit the article simultaneously elsewhere.

Feature articles average about 2,000 words. We like positive, fresh angles to *Post* articles, and we ask that they be thoroughly researched.

For Cartoonists

• Objective: We aim to please all readers and insult or offend none.
• Audience: All ages, average age 50+, male/female evenly split.
• Payment: *The Post* buys all rights for $125, payable upon publication.

• Size Requirements: 8 1/2" x 11" or half that size is fine.

• SASE: Return envelopes are required because you will get a response letter; business envelopes are OK if you send in Xerox copies that don't need to be returned. Response Postcards are not helpful.

• Copies or Originals: Either is acceptable. We are careful with originals, and they are easier for us to pick.

• Lines: We tend to only use cartoons we can typeset captions at the bottom. Avoid dialogue balloons. Please print or type your captions in dark blue or black ink only.

• How Many?: Feel free to send up to a dozen submissions per mailing. Please submit one mailing to *The Post* at one time. *The Post* publishes every two months, so expect an 8-10 week turnaround.

• Original Ideas Only: We like to buy never-published material. That's what our readers expect.

• Ideas to Avoid: Vices,such as smoking, drinking, adultery. People you would not like or trust. Don't ridicule doctors, lawyers, or politicians.

• Ideas that Work: Kids, pets, family, twists of fate. Doctor and medical situations are always needed.

Categories: Fiction—Nonfiction—Animals—Cartoons—Family—Gardening—Health—Humor—Money and Finances—Physical Fitness—Travel

CONTACT: Cory SerVaas, M.D.
Material: Medical/Fitness
CONTACT: Holly Miller
Material: Travel
CONTACT: Fiction Editor
Material: Fiction
CONTACT: Steve Pettinga.
Material: Post Scripts
Saturday Evening Post
1100 Waterway Blvd.
Indianapolis, IN 46202
CONTACT: Post Toons
Material: Cartoons
Post Toons
Box 567
Indianapolis, IN 46202
Phone: 317-634-1100
Website: www.satevepost.org

Saveur
Savor a World of Authentic Cuisine

Formal guidelines not available. Please read a number of issues to ascertain the publication's style and needs.

Send queries to address below.

Categories: Nonfiction—Cooking—Food/Drink

CONTACT: Submissions Editor
Material: All
World Publications
304 Park Ave, South
New York NY 10010
Phone: 212-219-7400
E-mail: saveur@worldpub.com
Website: www.saveur.com

School Mates

Please refer to *Chess Life* magazine.

Remember: Editors change jobs and publishers change addresses. It is wise to invest in a phone call for the current information before submitting.

SchoolArts

SchoolArts is a national magazine for elementary and secondary art and classroom teachers as well as for others who are active or interested in art education. We encourage anyone involved in the field of art education to submit articles for publication.

What our readers want:

Art educators look to *SchoolArts* for inspiration, information, and ideas. Think about what excites them, what worries them, and what they need to know in order to do what they do better. We're most interested in articles on:

• successful and meaningful units, lessons, or activities

• safe and economical applications of art techniques, equipment, or materials; low-budget tips

• how to integrate art with other subjects

• how to organize artrooms or classrooms; tips for teaching from a cart

• exemplary art programs (in school, after school, museum, summer or community)

• how to teach, and assess learning in, art history, art production, art criticism and aesthetics

• teaching art to special populations

• effective public relations efforts related to art (exhibitions, open houses, newsletters, advocacy)

• art curriculum development (pre-K-college)

• staff development programs for art teachers

• parent involvement and community partnerships

Writing your article

1. Before you begin, review recent issues of *SchoolArts*. Notice the balance of photographs and text in feature articles. Remember that teachers spend about an hour reading an issue. Try to keep your ideas focused and your article concise.

2. Outline your ideas. If your article describes an activity or process, think about these questions:

• How and why was the activity developed? What will students learn?

• What equipment, materials, and resources are needed?

• For what grade level(s) is the activity intended?

• What skills, concepts or attitudes can be improved by the activity?

• How is learning assessed?

• Can other disciplines be incorporated?

• What problems might teachers encounter when attempting this activity?

3. When you begin to write, remember to:

• Tell more than just the facts. Share the human element in your experiences: sights, sounds, unexpected events, humorous situations. Don't be afraid to mention the hard parts or disasters.

• Take a friendly, casual tone.

• Break complex processes into simple steps.

Special reminders

Avoid presentations of school projects that trivialize the sacred arts of cultural groups.

If you use hazardous, volatile, or toxic materials in your activity, say so. Explain what precautions and safety measures teachers and students must take while using these materials.

Include suggestions to adapt your article for different grade levels.

Include references and helpful resources.

Submitting your Manuscript

Electronic submission along with a hard copy is preferable. Submit a double-spaced, typed manuscript, preferably using Helvetica (Mac) or Arial (PC) fonts, with one-inch margins on all sides. Number each page. Please avoid using any script-type fonts and or all capital letters. On a cover page, suggest a title and type your name, position, school, home mailing address, home telephone number, and e-mail address. All but your home mailing address and home phone number will be included in your credit line, so that readers can contact you if they have questions or comments about your article. Most manuscripts are about four pages, not counting the title or captions.

Captions

Provide captions for each photograph on a separate captions page. Number each caption with a corresponding number marked on the back of the photograph or on the top of the slide. If the photograph is of student artwork, the caption should, at least, identify the name of the student, grade level, age, school, media, and title. If the student has described the work or made a personal statement about the work, include that as part of the caption.

Electronic Submissions

We accept digital files on:

- 1.44MB HD floppy disks (3 1/2")
- Zip disks--100MB or 250MB
- CD ROM
- Jaz disks--1GB
- Imation SuperDrive 120MB disks
- E-mail attachments—stuffed or zipped only.

Photographs and artwork

Let your illustrations tell your story! Illustrations are as important as the text of an article, and they should accompany any submission to *SchoolArts*. Include as many illustrations as necessary. If your article describes a process or technique, photograph each step. Submit slides and photographs in plastic sleeves. Do not mount prints. Do not write directly on front or back of photographs: Use self-adhesive labels on backs. Number each illustration and provide the student's name, your name, and any other relevant information on a separate caption sheet. Indicate the top of image. Supply photographs that are in focus and carefully composed. Avoid busy backgrounds or foregrounds. Photograph sculptures or three-dimensional works against a plain background. If the subject is colorful, use color slide film. Slides reproduce best. Color prints and digital files are also acceptable. We cannot use digital print-outs without the actual digital files or color photocopies. Note: Turn off the date mode on your camera. If photographing under fluorescent lighting, use a flash or Tungsten 160 film. If black-and-white film suits the subject, send high contrast black-and-white prints.

Permissions:

If students appear in the photographs, send signed permission forms for each student.

When submitting electronic images, please remember:

- Images must be scanned at 300 dpi or higher. Any image less than 300 dpi will not print well. Please do not convert images from a lower resolution to 300 dpi; it does not change the poor quality of the image.
- In order to be able to provide you with the best designed article, scan images to approximately 4 x 6" or larger.
- Save images in the following formats: TIFF (.tiff) EPS (.eps) Quark 3.3 or greater* Illustrator 6.0 or greater* Photoshop 5.0 or greater* (*Mac applications only)
- All images should be submitted as CMYK or grayscale.
- Always submit laser copies of all images on the disk. If you are concerned about color, please submit color copies for color correction.

We prefer:

- clear photographs of finished artwork.
- step-by-step photographs illustrating a process.
- photographs of individual students or small groups creating art, especially views that focus on the artwork.
- photographs of teachers working with students.

We prefer not to use:

- photocopies of drawings.
- photographs of students holding their artwork.
- Polaroid™ photographs.
- color photocopies or low resolution computer printouts

Line Drawings

If line drawings best illustrate your article, label, caption, and number them as you would photographs. Line art should be drawn with black ink or felt-tip markers. Protect art with a tissue overlay and pack between cardboard for protection.

Return of your submissions:

For return of your submissions, please enclose a self-addressed stamped envelope with sufficient postage. If you submit original artwork, *SchoolArts* cannot be responsible for its return.

Categories: Nonfiction—Arts—Children—Education—Juvenile—Teen

CONTACT: Eldon Katter, Editor
Material: All
Davis Publications, Inc.
464 East Walnut St.
Kutztown PA 19530
Website: www.davis-art.com

Science of Mind

Science of Mind magazine accepts query letters only. Include a brief description/outline and word count. We publish several types of articles that teach, inspire, motivate, and inform. Editorial content addresses the concerns, interests, and problems of readers, offering thoughtful perspectives on how they can experience greater self-acceptance, empowerment, and meaningful living. Achieving wholeness through applying Science of Mind principles is the primary focus.

The basic requirements of good, clear writing apply to all material used in the magazine. In addition, these special guidelines should also be noted:

First-Person Articles—These articles concern individuals who have experienced a significant, often dramatic, event in their lives. The theme of the article should inspire readers to make a similar change in their own lives. The article may also recount a deep spiritual experience or the way in which Science of Mind principles have been applied to create a positive inner change. Queries only. Length: 1,000-2,000 words. Payment: $25 per printed page.

Interview—Each month an interview with a notable spiritual leader is featured. These articles are usually assigned, but queries are welcome. Refer to previous issues of *Science of Mind* for typical interview subjects and style to be followed. Bio, lead-in and photo required. Length: 3,500 words. Payment: $350.

Daily Guides—Inspirational meditative readings for each day of the month are based on SOM teachings and include a quotation from scripture as well as THE SCIENCE OF MIND by Ernest Holmes. A sample set of six Daily Guides may be submitted. These are usually written by Science of Mind ministers or practitioners, but not always. Refer to previous issues of *Science of Mind* for length, style, and sample content. Payment: $250-$300.

Poetry—A limited number of poems are accepted and should be inspirational in theme and characterized by an appreciation for SOM principles. Average length: 8-12 lines. Max. length: 25-30 lines. (Not necessary to submit a query for poetry). Payment: $25.00. Payable within 30 days of publication.

1. Carefully check punctuation, spelling, and sentence structure before submitting your article. ELEMENTS OF STYLE by William Strunk is an excellent source book for basic writing practices.

2. Make a concerted effort to use language that is inclusive and gender neutral.

3. All accepted articles should be typed and preferably accompanied by Macintosh or IBM disc.

4. Type the number of words in the upper right corner of the first page. Be sure to include your name, address, and telephone number.

REMINDERS

- Ensure quality printout.
- Double-space everything, including quotations.
- Do not try to imitate the typeset copy using different styles of type. Simply type everything normally using lower-case letters, capitalizing in accordance with standard practice.
- Represent the quotations accurately and be sure they are sourced correctly.

• Be sincere.

SOM Photo Guidelines

Images for use in *Science of Mind* magazine should reflect the contemporary, creative, and empowering message of the Science of Mind philosophy. From conceptual to artistically literal, photographic materials should convey a thoughtfulness and originality which will enhance editorial content.

SOM magazine accepts duplicate transparencies or prints only. Please do not send original images. All photographic material must have the photographer's name clearly printed on each image. Credit line is given. On acceptance, images will be filed in the *Science of Mind* Stock Library by subject matter. Upon usage, the photographer will be notified. Always include a 6"X9" SASE when submitting images for consideration.

Payment is $300 for cover, $100 inside. For other publications, i.e., books, brochures, flyers, advertising, product, etc., payment will be determined on a per project basis. Advertising usage is limited to the instance per advertisement and does not reflect the number of times the advertisement is run.

Payment will be made within 30 days of the masthead date. For example, photographs used in the June issue will be paid by June 30. We buy one-time rights unless otherwise specified. Simultaneous submissions and previously published work are accepted.

Include a SASE for safe return of images. Again, please send only duplicates.

Categories: Nonfiction—Inspirational—Poetry—Religion—Spiritual—New Thought

CONTACT: Randall Friesen, Publisher
Material: All
3251 West Sixth Street
Los Angeles CA 90020-5096
Phone: 213-388-2181
Fax: 213-388-1926
E-mail: rfriesen@scienceofmind.com
Website: www.scienceofmind.com

Scouting

The magazine is published by the Boy Scouts of America six times a year. It is mailed to about one million adult volunteer and professional Scout leaders (Scouters). Subscription is included as part of each Scouter's annual registration fee.

Scouting magazine articles are mainly about successful program activities conducted by or for Cub Scout packs, Boy Scout troops and venturing crews. We also include features on winning leadership techniques and styles, profiles of outstanding individual leaders, and inspirational accounts (usually first person) of Scouting's impact on an individual, either as a youth or while serving as a volunteer adult leader.

Because most volunteer Scout leaders are also parents of children of Scout age, *Scouting* is also considered a family magazine. We publish material we feel will help parents in strengthening families. (Because they often deal with communicating and interacting with young people, many of these features are useful to a reader in both roles as parent and Scout leader).

We also feature an occasional general-interest article geared to our adult audience. These include subjects such as nature, social issues and trends, historical topics and humor.

Many of our best article ideas come from volunteer and professional Scouters, but most stories are written by staff members or professional writers assigned by us. We seldom publish unsolicited manuscripts (the exception being inspirational accounts or successful program ideas by individual Scouters). We rely heavily on regional writers to cover an event or activity in a particular part of the country.

A query with a synopsis or outline of a proposed story is essential. Include a SASE to insure a reply. We respond to queries within three weeks. We buy short features of 500 to 700 words; some longer features, up to 1,200 words, usually the result of a definite assignment to a professional writer. We do not buy fiction or poetry.

We pay on acceptance. We purchase first rights unless otherwise specified (purchase does not necessarily guarantee publication). Photos, if of acceptable quality, are usually included in payment for certain assignments. (We normally assign a professional photographer to take photographs for major story assignments). Payment rates depend on the professional quality of the article. Payment is from $300 to $500 for a short feature, $500 to $800 for a major article.

Writers or photographers should be familiar with the Scouting program and *Scouting* magazine. A sample copy will be sent if you provide a SASE and $2.50.

Categories: Nonfiction—Children—Conservation—Crafts/Hobbies—Ecology—Education—Environment—Family—Fishing—Health—Outdoors—Parenting—Physical Fitness—Recreation—Sports/Recreation—Teen—Travel—Young Adult

CONTACT: Magazine Division—Editorial
Material: All
Boy Scouts of America
1325 W. Walnut Hill Lane
PO Box 15207
Irving TX 75015-2079
Phone: 972-580-2367
Fax: 972-580-2079
Website: www.bsa.scouting.org

Scr(i)pt Magazine

scr(i)pt magazine is a bi-monthly publication that examines the film industry through the eyes of the screenwriter. The magazine serves as both a resource for the craft of screenwriting and source of inspiration from professionals in the field. We have featured interviews with such talented screenwriters as: Ron Bass, Frank Darabont, Robert Duvall, Randall Wallace, Les and Glen Charles and Richard LaGravenese. Each issue of *scr(i)pt* offers writers information about writing, marketing and selling screenplays throughout the industry. Having been established in the industry since 1989, *scr(i)pt* magazine offers writers the edge they need to break into the screenwriting community.

EDITORIAL GUIDELINES

scr(i)pt is currently seeking writers presently working in the industry to contribute meaningful articles on the craft and business of screenwriting.

SUBMISSION GUIDELINES
TYPES OF ARTICLES

We are interested in articles written by or dealing with currently working screenwriters, agents and producers. Any articles submitted should be timely, in-depth and of interest to screenwriters in particular. We accept articles about both the craft and business of screenwriting, with an emphasis on writing excellent screenplays and managing a successful career. We are interested in both feature articles and interviews. We do not accept comparative book or software reviews, or film or festival reviews in the print magazine. We do, however, consider those types of pieces for the web site. Please do not submit fiction, poetry, cartoons or reviews. We publish only original, previously unpublished material. IF YOUR ARTICLE PERTAINS TO OR PROMOTES SOMETHING YOU ARE SELLING—WE WILL NOT PUBLISH IT. NO EXCEPTIONS.

SENDING A QUERY

We ask that all potential writers send a query letter proposing your article before sending a complete manuscript. Please do not telephone our editors, as we only accept proposals in writing. All unsolicited and assigned articles are on speculation unless prior arrangement is made. You should receive a response in four to six weeks (please enclose a SASE). For a faster response, feel free to send queries via e-mail , being sure to supply a return e-mail address.

ARTICLES AND STYLE

All articles must be between 2,000 and 3,000 words unless other arrangements are made with the editors. Please consult the General Style Guidelines for further information.

SUBMISSION FORMAT

Accepted articles can be either e-mailed or sent on a Macintosh compatible disk in Microsoft Word, RTF or Text Only format. All submissions should be neatly typed and double spaced, include a title, your byline and a suggested deck. Please place an asterisk around any italicized words or movie titles, (i.e. *Raging Bull*). For interviews, please list contact information for the interviewee(s). Additionally, a list of any photo stills or illustrations that you feel would best illustrate your article would be helpful. Please check with the editors before submitting photos.

REVISIONS

Depending on the number of revisions that need to be made, we may either return the article to you with suggestions for changes, or make minor changes before publication. Any articles which are significantly longer than the assigned length will be returned to the sender to be edited. Writers who provide us with a fax number will be faxed a designed copy of his article.

PAYMENT

An invoice must accompany all articles accepted for publication. Writers are responsible for submitting invoices! Payment will be made 30 days from receipt of the article and invoice (no exceptions). Rate is $0.05 to $0.08 cents per word based on edited word count, amount of research and style of the article and is for first-time reprint rights. An additional $25 may be paid should the editors decide to print all or part of the article on the web site. Invoices must be submitted on a separate piece of paper, hard copy, and must include the date, your name, address, contact information, social security number, article title, intended print issue and amount due. A kill fee of 50% of the agreed upon fee may be paid for materials originally solicited by the editors.

ISSUES

Sample issues of *scr(i)pt* are available for $8 per issue plus postage. Send check or money order to: *scr(i)pt* magazine, 5638 Sweet Air Road, Baldwin, Maryland, 21013. Issues are also available at most major bookstore chains, or purchase a back issue or subscription online.

ONLINE ARTICLES

Scriptmag.com accepts a wide range of articles for the e-articles. Film, book, software, video, and seminar reviews are accepted. Payment is between $25 and $50 per article. Please contact editor@scriptmag.com with your article ideas.

Categories: Nonfiction—Business—Screenwriting—Writing

CONTACT: Editor-in-Chief
Material: All
5638 Sweet Air Rd.
Baldwin, MD 21013-0007
Phone: 888-245-2228, ext. 202
Fax: 410-592-8062
E-mail: editor@scriptmag.com
Website: www.scriptmag.com

Sea
The Magazine of Western Boating

Sea is four-color, monthly publication for active West Coast boat owners. It was founded in 1908, and is published by the Duncan McIntosh Co. Circulation is approximately 50,000.

Sea is read by power boaters and sportfishing enthusiasts from Alaska to Mexico, and across the Pacific to Hawaii. *Sea* contains articles on Western cruising and fishing destinations, new boats and marine electronics, safety, navigation, seamanship, maintenance how-to, consumer guides to boating services, marine news and product buyer's guides.

Readers of *Sea* are experienced boaters: • 89.4% own a boat • 91.5% own a power boat • 58.8% have been boating 20+ years • 63% sportfish from their boat. —Source: Simmons Market Research

EDITORIAL FOCUS

Feature articles generally are between 1,200 and 1,600 words. Other articles range between 250 and 750 words. First-time contributors are encouraged to pitch articles on:

• West Coast cruising destinations—especially those in Baja California, Southern California, Puget Sound and British Columbia.

• Boating news from your Western home port.

• Western boating trends and issues.

• Seamanship (power boating only).

• Boat maintenance and repair.

Another good avenue for freelancers is *Sea*'s West Coast Focus section. It is comprised of brief news stories or isolated bits of information about Western boating and sportfishing. Focus stories are about 250 words each, and stand the best chance of running if they are accompanied by a color slide.

Focus story topics include: new marinas and boating projects; new fishing regulations; boat parades, festivals or owner rendezvous; and boating legislation updates. Preview stories are preferred over post-event reports, so readers who wish to participate may do so.

WHAT NOT TO SEND

Sea is not the market for stories about: boardsailing, canoeing, kayaking or surfing; power boat racing; wetlands restoration; party boat fishing; commercial fishing; boating accident reports; fiction; poetry; yacht club-oriented social activities; marine mammals; ferry boats, steamships, military ships, cruise ships, river boats or any boat or ship that is not a pleasureboat; and boating events on the East Coast of the United States or abroad.

SUBMISSION GUIDELINES

Submit written queries.

• Please allow 4 weeks for review of unsolicited manuscripts.

• Assigned stories should be sent via e-mail or on 3.5" computer disk, single spaced in ASCII format or Microsoft Word. Enclose a hard copy of the story with the disk.

• Include your address, daytime phone number and social security number on the first page of the manuscript.

• *Sea* buys first-time North American rights. Please notify us if your query or manuscript is a simultaneous submission or has been previously published.

PAYMENT

• Rates are based on length of the article, amount of research required and complexity of the assignment. A rate will be quoted by the assigning editor prior to commencement of work.

• Payment for articles and photographs used is made on publication. Checks are sent out in the first week of the issue month.

• Quoted rates may change if a story does not meet the criteria of the assignment. If major revisions are required, we will return the manuscript to the author to revise prior to final editing or rate adjustment.

• Some expenses, such as telephone calls or mileage, may be reimbursed by the assigning editor only if approval for such expenses is requested in advance. An invoice itemizing the expenses must be submitted within 10 days of the article.

• Approved overnight mail charges are reimbursed. We do not accept C.O.D. packages and do not have an account with a mailing service.

• *Sea* retains reprint rights via print and electronic media. The contributor retains all other rights for resale, re-publication, etc.

• It may be necessary to reschedule the publication date of the author's accepted work as editorial space dictates.

FOR MORE INFORMATION

Individual guidelines are available upon request for:

• West Coast Focus, SoCal Focus, Boat Reports and Cruising Destination Features.

Thank you for your interest.

Categories: Nonfiction—Boating—Recreation—Sports/Recreation—Travel

CONTACT: Eston Ellis, Managing Editor
Material: Any
17782 Cowan
Irvine CA 92614
Phone: 949-660-6150
Fax: 949-660-6172
E-mail: editorial@goboatingamerica.com

Sea Kayaker

We prefer contributions from experienced kayakers with some writing experience. You may submit articles on speculation or contact our editorial department for feedback before you begin work on an article.

Submission Requirements Contributions may be submitted via email with text pasted into the body of the email message or as an attachment using one of the following formats: plain text (.txt), rich-text (.rtf), or Microsoft Word (.doc). Please include complete contact info (name, address, phone number and alternate email address, if applicable). Submissions may also be sent via regular mail to our office on CD (previously listed file formats are acceptable) with a hard-copy print-out. Clearly label all materials with your name, address, phone number and email address (if applicable).

Features

We recommend submitting an outline of your proposed feature along with a short writing sample from the story (approx. 500 words) to give us an idea of your writing style, ability and story direction (see our Writer's Tips for additional suggestions).

Destination Articles

Destination articles provide our readers with information about interesting places to paddle. They are usually based in North America, as the majority of our readership resides in this area. The area described should be large enough to provide several paddling itineraries and numerous overnight options.

If you'd like to write a Destination piece, you should have longstanding experience with the area: numerous trips and experiences throughout the location's paddling season. One or two trips to an area will not provide enough personal knowledge of the place.

Destination authors are required to provide information about launch sites, camping/overnight options, permits and other requirements for the area, along with tips on weather and water conditions to advise paddlers on paddling safely.

Destination articles include a map of the area (original provided by the author) and a short "Trip Planner" sidebar listing contact information for outfitters and other resources that our readers would find useful. Word count for Destination articles should be in the range of 2,500-3,000 words. See our Photography Guidelines for information about Destination photography.

Journey Articles

These are narratives about kayaking trips that take place over a minimum of 4 or 5 days. (Articles about trips organized by a 3rd-party touring company pose some special challenges and should be discussed with the editorial department.) The focus and length of Journey articles vary, but you'll need to do more than recount your trip: You must create an experience for the reader.

To give Journey continuity and a sense of progress, it helps to develop a theme or relate a personal goal or expectation specific to the trip. Whether your experience was a harrowing adventure, a trip to an exotic or unique setting, or a journey during which you experienced some transformation or learned something valuable, a theme will help drive your story.

Journey stories usually range from 2,500 to 5,000 words. See Photography Guidelines for information about Journey images.

Other Features

Other acceptable feature formats include essays, race stories, event coverage (from a non-commercial standpoint) and more. We will consider short-format Journey stories (if the duration of the trip is too short for a regular Journey) or narratives of kayaking experiences that don't fall into Destinations or Journeys. This category is flexible. Contact the editorial staff for feedback.

Departments

We recommend that all Department ideas are approved by the editor before articles are written. Regular Departments include:

• **Daytrippers**—These are "mini-Destinations" that provide information on one-day paddling itineraries in urban, densely populated, or frequently visited areas. Authors must be well-versed in the area. Contact the editors for complete guidelines.

• **Technique**—Techniques cover a wide range of topics: paddles strokes and braces, rolling, navigation, group dynamics, rescues, etc. We prefer authors to be experienced paddlers or instructors. Articles include: a brief intro explaining the technique's usefulness and, if relevant, history; instruction in an appropriate order; precautions about any risks; and images, usually photos, illustrating each step and demonstrating the technique in a "realistic" setting. Length varies from 500 words for a single technique to 3,000 words for a range of techniques.

• **Do-It-Yourself**—D-I-Y articles are complete sets of instructions for projects useful to kayakers. Supplied instructions must be clear and complete, and materials must be available from independent sources. Projects must be within an average skill range and require tools that readers are likely to own or can easily afford to purchase. We require photos of the finished project as well as photos or drawings of the parts and critical phases of the work in progress. A list of materials, sources and costs should be supplied. D-I-Y articles lengths vary in relation to the complexity of the project.

• **Off the Water**— Short tips (200 words or less) for the workshop or on shore that enhance kayaking-related experiences or solve problems typically encountered while camping or maintaining kayaking equipment.

• **Gear Reviews**— Equipment reviews are usually assigned articles. Reviewers must be free of any relationship with the manufacturer that would compromise an objective review or suggest a conflict of interest. Authors must have experience or credentials to make a thorough and fair evaluation of the gear.

• **Safety**— Safety articles primarily cover kayaking accidents. Their main purpose is education to enable readers to learn from and avoid the misfortunes of others. Safety articles have two sections: a description of the incident and an analysis underscoring the significant factors and discussing how to better handle similar situations. We encourage readers to inform us about accidents they've heard of or been involved in, and we make every effort to be sensitive to the needs of those involved.

• **History**— Our History section covers everything from Aboriginal kayaking to events in past decades. Articles must reflect a thorough knowledge of the topic or extensive research. Old photographs or drawings are useful. Image sources must be identified, as we may need permission to publish them.

Submitting Content to Sea Kayaker All content submitted should be previously unpublished unless special permission is given from Sea Kayaker's editor. For examples of acceptable writing style, see our current issue, available through many bookstores and newsstands. To obtain a current or back issue, click here, or phone 206-789-9536.Please contact Sea Kayaker's editorial department with questions or for more information at 206-789-1326. Materials can be sent via USPS to: Sea Kayaker Editorial Dept.; P.O. Box 17029; Seattle, WA, 98127 (if a physical address is needed, send to: 7001 Seaview Ave. NW, Suite 135; Seattle, WA 98117), or emailed to: gretchen@seakayakermag.comSea Kayaker magazine is not responsible for any unsolicited materials received. To ensure return of your materials, enclose a self-addressed envelope with correct postage.

Photography Guidelines

Feature Articles For Journey and Destination articles, we prefer approximately 40 images to choose from. If you have significantly more, we suggest eliminating those of poor or questionable quality. A minimum of 20 images will be considered if the shots are directly in keeping with the guidelines below. Requirements for "Other" features vary. Sea Kayaker will assign accompanying illustrations as necessary. If interested, keep our Cover Photography Guidelines in mind while taking photos for feature articles.**Accepted Image Formats**1. High-quality 35mm film color slides (SK's preferred format) or negatives (larger format transparencies OK)NOTE: Duplicate slides may be submitted initially for approval, but we'll request originals for final scanning2. High-resolution digital photographs (TIFF format on CD preferred; JPEG acceptable for email)3. High-quality print photographs**Image Quality/Composition**• Sharp focus and good, clear composition—subjects should be attractively framed and easy to "read" by viewers• Good contrast with rich, vivid color• Proper exposure (no overexposed or underexposed images)• Interesting subject matter• A dynamic quality (for example, an active paddler versus one who appears to be posing)• An interesting perspective or angle (we rarely use bow shots; often, the best photos are taken from a different eye level than that of sitting in a kayak or standing on shore)• Photos that support the article (there should be a good selection of images to match locations mentioned in the text)• A portrayal of safe, correct kayaking practices (PFDs should be worn in most cases)**Destination Articles**In order of importance (meaning, the categories from which we'd like the most photos to choose from), here is what we look for in Destination photography:1. On-the-water shots of paddlers actively paddling, with a scenic backdrop unique to the paddling location.2. Panoramic or scenic shots that don't necessarily show paddlers, but that give a feel for the geography of the area.3. Medium-focal-length shots of paddlers doing things like reading charts, setting up camp, launching, fishing, exploring caves, or something specific to the area.4. Shots of flora, fauna or scenery particular to the area paddled.**Journey Articles**Same guidelines as for Destination articles but including shots that capture moments in the narrative and any images describing an area's unique culture as discussed in the text: the people, their dwellings, handicrafts, etc.**Departments**See Writer's Guidelines for descriptions of individual Departments. General photo quality should be good and easy to "read." Contact editorial staff for more information.**Last Glance**The last page of Sea Kayaker magazine features a single photo or photo series providing an unusual perspective, along with a text-based description. Send your unique, humorous and/or thought-provoking sea kayak–related images in the following formats: 35mm slide or negative, good-quality print photo, print-resolution digital image.**Cover Guidelines**Vertical orientation required for cover images**Accepted Image Formats**1. High-quality 35mm color slides (SK's preferred format) or negatives (larger format transparency OK) 2. Digital images:• Most consumer-quality digital cameras cannot achieve a high enough resolution for a cover

image. If you have a professional-quality digital camera (6 megapixels or higher), the following specs must be met for digital files: High-quality digital images must be a minimum size of 9" x 12" at 300 dpi• Large-format digital photography is still a new area for us, so please feel free to educate or enlighten us as necessary.**General Comments**Following are general guidelines for Sea Kayaker cover images; however, we are always willing to consider other possibilities. Be creative!1. Cover theme should tie into kayaking; images should include a striking central subject that is very clear, well-lit and easy to "read" by the viewer.2. Color and contrast should be rich and well-defined.3. Pictures taken from unique angles or perspectives are generally more visually interesting than standard eye-level "landscape" images taken with a mid-frame horizon line.4. Faces are good. Not all potential cover images have to include faces, but readers like being able to "connect" with a cover subject.5. A cover image should include background area simple enough that the magazine logo and cover text can be clearly read over it (not too much texture and/or color variation). Keep this in mind when framing your pictures—it's always a good idea to include some space around your subject.Note: The Sea Kayaker logo always appears on the top portion of the cover, covering approximately the top 1/5 of the image; cover text generally appears in the area below the logo, particularly on the left side, but is not limited to this space. We may also put additional text over the bottom of the image or elsewhere on the page.(Cover images must not appear to endorse a particular product or products by way of including company logos or product names. To comply with this policy, our production department may alter final digital files as necessary to remove logos appearing on kayaks, clothing and equipment.)

Submitting Images to Sea Kayaker All images should be previously unpublished unless special permission is given by Sea Kayaker's editor. For examples of appropriate images, see our current issue, available through many bookstores and newsstands. To obtain a current or back issue, click here, or phone 206-789-9536.Please contact Sea Kayaker's editorial department with questions or for more information at 206-789-1326. Images can be sent via USPS to: Sea Kayaker Editorial Dept.; P.O. Box 17029; Seattle, WA, 98127 (if a physical address is needed, send to: 7001 Seaview Ave. NW, Suite 135; Seattle, WA 98117). Low-resolution sample digital files can be sent in JPEG format via email to: gretchen@seakayakermag.com..Sea Kayaker is not responsible for any unsolicited materials received. To ensure return of your materials, enclose a self-addressed envelope with correct postage.

Top 10 Tips for Writers—Feature Articles

1. **Appeal to the senses.**During your paddling experience, the world around you came to you through your eyes and ears. To put the reader in that same place, focus the writing on the same sensory information. For example, "The wind was blowing very hard," doesn't describe the scene, it only analyzes it. Write vividly, describing what you saw in enough detail for the reader to picture the same image: "The waves crested in white streaks of foam, and the spray coming over the bow stung my skin and eyes. I shouted to John, who was no more than a boat length ahead of me, but he never even turned his head." The readers can feel that they are a part of the scene and will come to the same conclusion: It's blowing hard.2. **Avoid unnecessary language.**Avoid vague descriptors: Words like "glorious," "incredible," "awesome" and "magnificent" have no real content. What is an enormous wave? Is it as big as a boxcar? A split-level house? What color is the "colorful" fish?Avoid words you wouldn't use in conversation: An "ursine interloper" is still just a bear that wandered into your camp. If you interrupt the flow of the story to send a reader to the dictionary, the word should be worth the trip.Avoid pathetic fallacy/anthropomorphism: The sea may seem cruel, but it's just a bunch of waves, none of them malicious. In describing animal behavior, focus on what you see and hear, and steer clear of what you think the animal is thinking or feeling.3. **Write economically and selectively.**William Faulker said, "Writing consists of killing your little darlings." In other words, be your own editor, and be ruthless. The writing should not draw undue attention to the writer. We want articles filled with great description,

yet short enough to be read in one sitting. Eliminate extraneous words and passages. **4. Develop a theme.** It helps to develop a theme or relate a personal goal or expectation specific to your paddling experience. Whether your story was a harrowing adventure, a trip to an exotic or unique setting, or a journey during which you experienced some transformation or learned something valuable, a theme will help drive your story. **5. Cover the important stuff.** Focus on the highlights and the most significant moments of your story. We can include section breaks in the article to signify gaps in time. If it's important to describe regular routines, pick a specific representative instance. Describe events as they unfold, not as you are looking back on them. **6. Keep to the point.** Tangents must take readers somewhere worth going. If you need to take a detour to bring some interesting information to readers, make sure you bring them back to the story. Don't lead them down a dead end, only to pick up the narrative again where you left off. **7. Maintain flow.** Read your story aloud. Better yet, have someone read it aloud to you. You'll get winded if your sentences are consistently too long and hyperventilate if they're too short. Vary the length and structure of sentences as the content dictates to keep the pace of the story lively. **8. Use the appropriate tense.** Although there are exceptions, the past tense is the best choice for most narrative stories. Don't confuse readers by switching back and forth between present and past tense. **9. Create an interesting chronology.** Nothing puts readers to sleep faster than a story that starts at Day One of a trip and trudges on through Day Two, Day Three, etc. If your story is a harrowing adventure, you may want to start with the most harrowing moment, whether it's in the middle or at the end of your trip, then take the reader back through the events leading up to that point. If your story is more reflective, lead off with your central theme and follow it through to the end. **10. Be clear.** Put yourself in the reader's seat. Be aware that others will not be as familiar with your subject as you are, and write accordingly. Develop a sense of continuity throughout. We (editors and readers) don't want to work too hard at deciphering your meaning.

Categories: Nonfiction—Boating—Kayaking—Recreation—Sea Kayaking—Sports

CONTACT: Karin Redmond, Executive Editor
Material: All
PO Box 17029
Seattle WA 98107-0729
Phone: 206-789-1326
Fax: 206-781-1141
E-mail: editorial@seakayakermag.com
Website: www.seakayakermag.com

SEATTLEHOMES
AND LIFESTYLES™

Seattle Homes and Lifestyles

Seattle Homes and Lifestyles is published eight times a year. Sixty percent of the content is written by freelance writers on assignment for the magazine. Writers are paid between $125 and $375 per article, depending on the assignment.

We always welcome inquiries from experienced freelance writers, with special consideration given to those living in the Puget Sound area. Interested parties should submit a resume and photocopies of three published articles to Fred Albert, Editor, at the address below. Please do not e-mail or fax your submission, or follow up with a phone call. We regret we cannot return writing samples or unsolicited photos.

Although we will review story proposals, such queries are not encouraged, and should be limited to Seattle-focused lifestyle topics, consumer pieces and personality profiles, or stories on US or international travel. (Travel stories should focus on a region, not a hotel or resort.) Food, wine and garden stories are written by regular columnists and are not assigned to outside freelancers.

Thank you for your interest in *Seattle Homes and Lifestyles*. We look forward to hearing from you.

Categories: Nonfiction—Architecture—Gardening—Lifestyle—Regional

CONTACT: Fred Albert, Editor
Material: All
Wiesner Publishing LLC, 1221 East Pike St., Ste. 204
Seattle WA 98122-3930
Phone: 206-322-6699

Second Wind

Formerly *Nostalgia*.

Poetry: Modern prose poetry preferred. Payment in copies. Submissions returned if SASE included. Author retains all rights. If material previously published, please advise. Please do not e-mail submissions.

Categories: Poetry

CONTACT: Connie L. Martin, Editor
Material: All
Nostalgia Press
2003 Broughton St.
Orangeburg SC 29115
E-mail: secondwind@sc.rr.com

The Secret Place

The Secret Place was begun over sixty years ago by a woman who wanted to provide a way to draw Christians closer to Christ and to one another. It's now a quarterly devotional magazine with a worldwide readership of over 150,000 and editions in regular print, large print, Braille, and cassette. Produced by Educational Ministries of the American Baptist Churches in the U.S.A. and the Christian Church (Disciples of Christ), Christian Board of Publication.

How to Submit Devotions, Poems, and Photographs

The Secret Place is written solely by freelance writers, and anyone may submit original, unpublished meditations for consideration. Each submission should be typed (if possible), double-spaced, and contain:

• your name, address, and phone number in the upper left-hand corner of each devotion.

• a title.

• a suggested Scripture passage to be read.

• a "Thought for Today," usually a Scripture verse (cite full reference and Bible version) but may also be a pertinent thought. We use the New Revised Standard Version unless you specify otherwise.

• an original meditation of 100 to 200 words that relates to your Scripture reading and "Thought for Today." (Do not quote others at length unless you include written permission to do so.)

• a brief concluding prayer.

• your name, city, and state as you would like them to appear in print.

We are especially interested in devotional meditations that:

• are original, creative, and spiritually insightful.

• are concise and focused on one theme.

• explore less familiar biblical passages and themes.

• address urban/suburban as well as rural/nature experience.

• appeal to young adults as well as older adults.

• encourage outreach, mission, and service.

• are written by men as well as women, young adults as well as older adults.

• reflect racial and cultural diversity and use inclusive language.

We retain the right to edit submissions as necessary for clarity, brevity, and inclusivity of language. Original poems (thirty lines maximum) and clear, high-quality photographs (eight-by-ten-inch color prints for the cover, four-by-six-inch or larger black/white or color prints for inside, verticals preferred) are also welcome. We pay $15 for each submission printed and purchase first rights to the use of original, unpublished material in *The Secret Place* and on our website (www.judsonpress.com). We work nine to twelve months ahead of schedule, so please plan any seasonal submissions (maximum six at a time) accordingly. Include a stamped, self-addressed envelope for the return of your submissions and notification of any rejections. Due to the volume of material we receive, we are unable to give updates on the status of individual submissions. Please allow up to nine months for notification of publication. Send your meditations, poems, and photographs to the address below.

Categories: Nonfiction—Poetry—Religion—Spiritual—Devotional

CONTACT: Kathleen Hayes, Senior Editor
Material: All
PO Box 851
Valley Forge PA 19482-0851

Seek the abundant life

For Your Information…

SEEK is a colorful, illustrated weekly take-home or pass-along paper designed to appeal to modern adults and older teens. *SEEK* first appeared in its present form in 1970, expanding a four-page Sunday school lesson leaflet, which was published for ninety-five years, into a new concept for personal spiritual enrichment. Its use ranges from the classroom of the Sunday morning Bible class to group discussion and light inspirational reading for individuals and the family.

Materials Accepted for Publication…

ARTICLES—400 to 1,200 words in length. Usual rate of payment is about 5¢ per word. Articles for publication in SEEK should be in one of the following categories:

1. Inspirational, devotional, personal, or human interest stories.

2. Controversial subject matter, timely religious issues of moral or ethical nature.

3. First-person testimonies of Christian life or experiences, true-to-life happenings, vignettes, emotional situations or problems, examples of answered prayer.

Articles should not he preachy or patronizing. They must be wholesome, alive, vibrant, current, relevant for today's reader, and have a title that demands the article be read. No poetry, please!

Articles are purchased for SEEK as early as one year before the date of publication. Complimentary copies of articles are mailed to writers immediately following publication.

PHOTOGRAPHS—Good human interest pictures of professional quality to accompany articles. We prefer 8"x10" glossy photos with sharp black-and-white contrast. Rate of payment is about $25.

May We Suggest…

Please type manuscripts on 8" paper. Write name, address, and social security number in upper left-hand corner of the first page. Also indicate approximate number of words in the manuscript at the upper right-hand corner of the first page. Number all pages in center top.

Because of the large volume of correspondence involved, we are unable to critique or offer suggestions in regard to contributions that are not acceptable. You may best determine our needs by a careful study of issues of the magazine. Write for free copies. Self-addressed stamped envelope appreciated.

Categories: Fiction—Nonfiction—Christian Interests—Inspirational—Religion—Short Stories

CONTACT: Eileen Wilmoth, Senior Editor
Material: All
8121 Hamilton Ave.

Cincinnati OH 45231-2396
Phone: 513-931-4050
Website: www.standardpub.com

Self

Formal guidelines not available. Please read a number of issues to ascertain the publication's style and needs.

Send queries to address below.

Categories: Beauty—Food/Drink—Health—Physical Fitness

CONTACT: Submissions Editor
Material: All
4 Times Square
New York NY 10036
Phone: 212-286-2860

Seneca Review

Seneca Review reads manuscripts of poetry, translations, essays on contemporary poetry, and lyric essays between September 1 and May 1 annually. We do not publish fiction. Manuscripts received during the summer months are returned unread. We recommend submissions of 3-5 poems and essays up to 20 pages. We generally respond to submissions within twelve weeks.

Due to the great number of manuscripts we receive, we ask that you limit yourself to just one submission during our annual reading period (September 1-May 1). We can then give all submissions the attention they deserve.

Please note that we do not accept manuscripts electronically and that we do not wish to receive simultaneous submissions. All submissions must be accompanied by a self-addressed, stamped envelope in order to be returned. If you don't wish to have your manuscript returned, please indicate that in a cover letter and supply a stamped envelope or postcard for our reply.

Although we cannot pay authors for work published, we provide two copies of the issue in which your work appears and a complimentary two-year subscription. Copyright is held by Hobart and William Smith Colleges until publication, at which time rights revert to the author.

To get a sense of our editorial interests, we suggest you read a recent issue of the magazine. Sample copies are available for $7 each on our website or at the address below.

Seneca Review is published twice yearly, spring and fall.

Categories: Poetry—Lyric Essay
CONTACT: Deborah Tall, Editor
Material: All
Hobart and William Smith Colleges
Geneva NY 14456
Website: www.hws.edu/SenecaReview

Senior Living

About *Senior Living* newspapers: *Senior Living* newspapers has a circulation of 50,000 plus. Papers are published monthly with distribution in Arkansas, Missouri, Kansas, and Oklahoma. Editorial slant is directed to mid-life and retirement lifestyles and offers a positive and upbeat look at the 50 + reader.

Senior Living readers are primarily well-educated and affluent retirees, homemakers, and career professionals—most of whom enjoy a very active lifestyle.

Topics: *Senior Living* publishes feature articles, personality profiles, and timely articles on travel, health, finance, relationships, nostalgia, consumer issues and retirement. We do very little poetry and no fiction. Staff writers and columnists do most of our writing, but we welcome queries and unsolicited manuscripts.

Query & Cover Letters: A query letter is not necessary, but should you choose to send one, make it short and to the point. Indicate the focus and tone of your proposed article. We prefer that you send a cover letter with your manuscript informing us about your experience or qualifications as a writer. If you don't have any experience, tell us that too. Perhaps we will be able to help you get a much needed byline. No need to tell us what the article is about, we'll know that when we read it.

Manuscripts: Preferred length is 400-600 words. They should be typewritten and double-spaced on 8 1/2 X 11 inch paper, with 1 inch margins. Place name, address and Social Security number in upper left corner and word count in upper right corner. Computer discs are acceptable, but you still need to send hard copy. Absolutely no manuscripts or photographs will be returned without a SASE with ample postage to cover their return.

Style: Keep it clear, simple and to the point. Originality, concrete details, short paragraphs and strong words are essential. Avoid flowery prose in articles. Accuracy is a must.

All articles are submitted on a speculative basis unless assigned.

Payment of ($5 to $35) will be decided according to timeliness of article, content, clarity and neatness. Fillers and Poetry, if accepted pays $1 to $5. Checks are mailed 30-45 days post publication. Beginning writers who need a byline may stand a chance with *Senior Living*. We welcome articles and poems that require no compensation. Please state if payment is, or is not required. Unpaid writers may obtain a paper containing their work by request.

Categories: Nonfiction—General Interest—Health—History—Inspirational—Physical Fitness—Poetry—Recreation—Senior Citizen—Sports/Recreation—Retirement—Essay—Nostalgia—Personal Experience—Humor

CONTACT: Joyce O'Neal, Managing Editor
Material: All
318 E. Pershing
Springfield MO 65806
Phone/Fax: 417-862-9079
Website: www.seniorlivingnewspaper.org

The Server Foodservice News

Ceased publication.

Seventeen

Seventeen accepts articles of interest to teens and young adults, roughly ages 13-21. Please read 6-12 back issues of the magazine (not just the fiction) before submitting your work. Include a SASE for our response. Correspondence should include the writer's name, address and phone number. We regret that we cannot offer individual comments or criticism. We read all stories and will respond as quickly as possible. Generally, allow six to eight weeks for consideration of your manuscript. No follow-up phone calls, please.

GUIDELINES

My Story and Real Deal Stories

Do you have an experience you'd like to share? Tell us what you're thinking. Real Deal and My Story sections of the magazine are devoted to first-person essays, and we welcome all original contributions. We are looking for true stories on interesting, unusual, life-altering or inspiring events, struggles or challenges overcome, and reflective essays on significant personal decisions.

Real Deal and My Story is a chance for you to speak about what matters to you in your individual style and voice.

Your article should be typed, double-spaced, and about 1,200 words. Be sure to include a brief cover letter with your name, age, address and telephone number (with area code), as well as a SASE for our reply. With few exceptions, authors should be 23 or younger.

Fiction Stories

We're looking for great short fiction. The stories we want should deal with issues that are familiar and important to our readers (roughly ages 13-21), but they should also challenge the reader and make them think.

Seventeen publishes between six and twelve short stories each year that run from 1,000 to 3,500 words and possess the quality and integrity of today's very best literary short fiction.

Aspiring writers, especially those in M.F.A. programs, are encouraged to submit. We also hold an annual Fiction Contest for writers between 13-21 years old; guidelines appear in the December issue.

All fiction submissions should include a brief cover letter listing prior fiction publication credits, if any. Only completed manuscripts will be considered.

Non-Fiction Stories

Seventeen gives assignments and guarantees a fee only to writers who have been published in the magazine or whose work is known to the editors. Writers whose work has not appeared in *Seventeen* should include published clips when submitting. Inexperienced writers may be asked to write on speculation, with no guarantee of payment. Work is paid for on publication, and rates vary depending on quality, length and placement in the magazine.

Queries are preferred for all sections, except Voice, Fiction and Quizzes, where only complete manuscripts are considered. Please read the additional guidelines for Voice and Fiction, and see past issues for the tone and style of Quizzes. Simultaneous submissions are considered, although not preferred. Seasonal material should be submitted at least six months in advance. *Seventeen* does not accept filler.

We recommend that writers target queries to the appropriate section to speed the consideration process:

• Features: Tamara Glenny, Deputy Editor. Maximum 2,500 words.
• Quiz: Margaret Magnarelli, Assistant Editor. See past issues.

Categories: Nonfiction—Beauty—Fashion—Health—Relationships—Sexuality—Women's Issues—Young Adult

CONTACT: Real Deal Editor
Material: Real Deal submissions
CONTACT: My Story Editor
Material: My Story submissions
CONTACT: Darcy Jacobs, Fiction Editor
Material: Fiction
CONTACT: Tamara Glenny, Deputy Editor
Material: Non-Fiction Features
CONTACT: Margaret Magnarelli, Assistant Editor
Material: Non-Fiction,Quiz
1440 Broadway, 13th Floor
New York NY 10018
Phone: 212-204-4300
Website: www.seventeen.com

Sew News

Who We Are

Sew News magazine is a monthly, national consumer magazine for the sewing enthusiast, whether novice, expert or somewhere in between. The magazine expresses the fun, creativity, excitement and rewards of sewing though "how-to" and feature articles, as well as monthly columns. It is sold by subscription, in retail fabric and sewing machine stores and on many newsstands.

What We Want

Articles should teach a specific technique; inspire the reader to try a project; introduce the reader to a new product or company related to sewing, textiles or fashion.

Although *Sew News'* primary emphasis is fashion-sewing for women, secondary interests include home decor sewing, sewing for children and men, and sewing for specialty groups like senior citizens, large sizes, petites and the handicapped. In addition to sewing, Sew

News also peripherally covers the areas of machine embroidery, monogramming and fabric painting. *Sew News* does not normally cover "artisan" areas like hand weaving and hand needlecrafts or "crafty" areas like cross stitch, crochet, macrame and tole painting.

Acceptance/Payment

At the time an article is assigned, you will be sent a succinct form letter detailing what is expected of you for the assignment and the intended payment (from $50 to $1,000, depending on the length and complexity of the subject, and the garment(s), photography, illustrations or sources to be supplied).

However, all articles, including those specifically assigned, are written "on speculation." Payment will be made only on acceptance. To be accepted at the full payment suggested in the assignment letter, the article must:

• be submitted by the deadline specified.
• include all elements detailed in the assignment letter.
• be of acceptable quality (to be determined by the *Sew News* editorial staff).

Payment may be decreased for late arrival, missing elements or poor quality. *Sew News* reserves the right to return articles for rewriting or clarification of information and, in extreme cases, to return them without payment.

In all cases, *Sew News* reserves the right to edit, rewrite and cut articles where necessary.

Any extraordinary writing expenses (fabric, notions, travel, telephone bills, etc.) will be reimbursed only by previous agreement between you and *Sew News*.

The Contract

Sew News, as part of the Primedia Enthusiasts Group, requires an "all rights" contract to be signed before publication of any article. "All rights" means *Sew News* purchases complete rights to the manuscript and art covered in the contract and that they may not be used in conjunction with any other article in another publication.

These rights apply to specific projects, but not to individual techniques. For example, when a writer signs a *Sew News* "all rights" contract for an article on a machine-embroidered jacket, he/she may not allow the particulars (step-by-step how-tos) of that project to be published anywhere else. However, he/she may publish another article on machine embroidery, including an article on a machine-embroidered jacket, as long as it's neither the same jacket nor the same embroidery designs.

Submissions

We would appreciate receiving your work via e-mail, CD-Rom, or on a 3 1/2" PC or Mac disk.

To submit by e-mail:
• Attach a text file to your e-mail and send it to Linda. Griepentrog@primedia.com.
• You may also include the text in the body of your e-mail.
• Send how-tos separately via regular mail.

To submit by CD Rom or disk:
• If you use Microsoft Word 5.5 or higher software, simply print a hard copy, save the article on the disk as you normally would and send us both the hard copy and the disk.
• If you use any other software program, print a hard copy, save the article on the disk as a text file (in ASCII; see your manual for details) and send us the hard copy, the disk and a note telling us which software you used. We'll take it from there.

Please do:
• Computer-generate or type your article on 8½"x11" nonerasable paper.
Use approximately 1" top and bottom margins and a 55-character line, and double-space between lines.
• Begin your article approximately halfway down the first page.
• Keep an article under eight pages, unless otherwise specified.
• Include your name, address, phone number(s) and social security numbers on the last page and paper clip all pages together. Mail together with your disk (in the disk mailer for grotection).
• Follow the *Sew News* Style Guide (sent to new writers upon acceptance of a query) for style matters and specific punctuation prefer-

ences, referring to *The Associated Press Stylebook* (revised edition), *Webster's New Collegiate Dictionary* and Chilton's *Grammar For Journalists* for matters not covered in the guide.

• Submit sources and resources of products and publications noted in your article, as well as information on how Sew News readers can contact the businesses of people interviewed. Be sure all information is current.

• Submit sketches of how-to drawings to accompany your article, drawing only one or two on one page and supplying appropriate cutline and label information. Label the illustrations Figure 1, Figure 2, etc. and refer to them as such within the copy.

• Label all photographs submitted with an article with descriptions and information on where they should be returned.

• Assume nothing. Check and double-check all spellings (especially those of proper names) and all facts. In the case of how-to articles, the writer bears responsibility for testing techniques.

• Include a short biography and photo for use with your story.

• Submit your article on or before the due date, allowing time for mailing to: Editor Linda Griepentrog, Sew News, 741 Corporate Circle, Suite A, Golden, CO 80401.

• If mailing projects, please pack them carefully and send via UPS, keeping the appropriate information for tracing in the event of loss. Second-day air and overnight mail also are acceptable, but not required unless necessary for your project to arrive on time. Send projects (with the related article enclosed, if possible) to: Sew News Editor, 741 Corporate Circle, Suite A, Golden, CO 80401. If agreed in advance, *Sew News* will return the project via UPS after publication.

• Keep a copy of your completed article and all of your notes for at least six months after the date of the article's publication.

• Read your published articles and compare them to your originals for feedback.

Please don't:
• Deviate from the *Sew News* style.
• Change an article's focus without approving it with *Sew News* first.
• Submit any article containing facts or techniques of which you are unsure.
• Copy material directly from any other source.
• Make excuses about missed deadlines. Legitimate reasons will be accommodated if possible. Questionable and recurring ones will not.
• Hesitate to give *Sew News* feedback. A better product is always our goal!

Sample query

Ours is a small staff. Therefore, we request you query by letter; do not send finished manuscripts. Your query should consist of a brief outline of the article, a list of the types of illustrations or photographs you envision with it, an explanation of why your proposed article would be of interest to the *Sew News* reader and, when applicable, why you are qualified to write it. Consider the season and timeliness of your suggestions, keeping in mind *Sew News* works on a six-month lead time.

The *Sew News* staff considers queries and makes story assignments quarterly. At that time, all queries are considered and, within a few days, you will either receive an assignment, a request to hold the query for further consideration, or a rejection. If more than three months have passed without a reply to your query, feel free to write a note requesting its status.

Categories: Nonfiction—Accessories—Consumer—Crafts/Hobbies—Fashion—Hobbies—Home Decor

CONTACT: Linda Griepentrog, Editor
Material:Primedia Enthusiast Group
741 Corporate Circle #A
Golden CO 80401
Phone: 303-278-1010

Sewanee Review

For matters of spelling and usage, consult the *The Chicago Manual of Style*, 15th edition; *Merriam-Webster's Collegiate Dictionary*, 11th edition; and *Webster's Third New International Dictionary*. Unsolicited submissions should be original double-spaced typescripts mailed to the editor at 735 University Avenue, Sewanee TN 37383-1000. No electronic submissions are accepted at this time. A self-addressed stamped envelope must be supplied for reply. Rejected submissions without sufficient return postage will be discarded. No responsibility can be assumed for loss or damage. Only unpublished original work (no translations) can be considered.

Queries are suitable for essays (7500 words or less) and reviews (unsolicited reviews are rarely accepted). Send fiction and poetry without writing in advance. Poems (40 lines or less) should not exceed 6 per submission; stories (3500-7500 words; no short short stories, please) should be sent individually. For each poem published, roughly 250 poems are considered here; for each story, 150 stories.

The average time to reply to a submission is four to six weeks. We do not accept simultaneous submissions. When you have sent one submission, please do not send another before you have received a reply to the first. Unsolicited works should not be submitted between June 1st and August 31st. A response to any submission received during that period may be greatly delayed.

The *Sewanee Review* awards four prizes annually to the best short fiction, poetry, essay, and book reviewing of the previous year. The Aiken Taylor Award in Modern American Poetry is presented annually to established poets. Winners of these awards are determined by the board of editors and a prize committee; one cannot apply for any of them.

For information about literary magazines see the current editions of the *International Directory of Little Magazines and Small Presses*, *Literary Market Place*, *Magazine Industry Market Place*, and *Ulrich's International Periodicals Directory*.

The *Sewanee Review* is America's oldest continuously published literary quarterly. Only erudite work representing depth of knowledge and skill of expression is published here. We urge you to read at least one issue of the magazine before submitting any work. Sample copies cost $8.50 ($9.50 foreign). Individual subscriptions cost $24 per year ($29 foreign). MasterCard and VISA are accepted, as well as checks payable in U.S. dollars drawn on U.S. banks. Further information about the magazine is available on our Web site: www.sewanee.edu/sreview/home.html.

Thank you for your interest in the *Sewanee Review.*

Categories: Fiction—Nonfiction—Book Reviews—Literature—Short Stories

CONTACT: The Editors
Material: All
University of the South
735 University Ave.
Sewanee TN 37383-1000
Website: www.sewanee.edu/sreview/home.html

Shape Magazine

Queries/Pitches/Story Ideas

When submitting a query or pitch to *Shape*, please follow the guidelines below regarding tone and style. For further information, see a recent issue of the magazine. *Shape* is not responsible for and does not accept unsolicited material. Story ideas and query letters should be on suitable topics and reflect *Shape*'s philosophy (see below).

Shape's Mission Statement

We seek to help women 18-34 years old create better lives. Each issue provides immediately useful information in the areas of exercise, nutrition, psychology, beauty and more — to help the reader improve her health and to stimulate a deeper understanding of fitness.

Submissions

We recommend that writers who haven't been previously published in the magazine submit story ideas in the form of a one-page letter. We do not accept completed, "spec" articles.

Please identify your story pitch as either a feature or column. If you are suggesting a story for a particular column, please tell us which one.

When pitching a story, please be sure to include the names and qualifications of your resources, the reasons they are viewed as experts in their fields and/or why you chose them for your direct quotes.

Be sure to include your contact information with your pitch, including your e-mail address, if you have one.

If you want your materials returned, please include a stamped return envelope.

Tone

The "voice" of a story should always reflect *Shape*'s service role and embody the magazine's mission as a positive, empowering force in its readers' lives. Toward that end, we eschew derogatory physical descriptions or characterizations of women's bodies. The desired tone is affirming and helpful.

We do not publish:
Celebrity question and answer stories
Celebrity profiles
Profiles of anyone (other than Success Stories that have a specific format)
Menopausal or hormone replacement therapy stories
Categories: Nonfiction—Cooking—Diet/Nutrition—Fashion—Food/Drink—Health—Interview—Physical Fitness—Recreation—Sports/Recreation—Travel—Women's Issues—How-to —Profiles—Medicine—Beauty

CONTACT: Anne Russell, Editorial Dept.
Material: All
21100 Erwin St.
Woodland Hills CA 91367
Phone: 818-595-0593
Fax: 818-704-7620
Website: www.shapemag.com

Shenandoah
The Washington and Lee University Review

For over half a century *Shenandoah* has been publishing splendid poems, stories, essays and reviews which display passionate understanding, formal accomplishment and serious mischief.

Founded in 1950 by a group of Washington and Lee University faculty members and students, including Tom Wolfe and William Hoffman, *Shenandoah* has achieved a wide reputation as one of the country's premier literary quarterlies and has been praised by *USA Today* as "a 'little' magazine notable for not being little in its aspirations." Recent issues have featured work by Stephen Dunn, Mary Oliver, Rodney Jones, Alyson Hagy, Erin McGraw and Chris Offutt.

Please type (double space for prose) your manuscript on one side of the page only. Number pages consecutively and use margins of at least one inch. Place your name and address in an upper corner of the first page. Address the outer envelope to the Editor and write your name and address on the upper left corner of the envelope. Enclose a self-addressed stamped envelope (SASE) with your manuscript; we will not return manuscripts or disks not accompanied by an SASE. E-mail and simultaneous submissions are not considered.

We read previously unpublished poetry, fiction and critical as well as personal essays, and we prefer that work submitted to us not be simultaneously submitted elsewhere. Manuscripts are read between September 1 and May 30. We adhere strictly to postmark dates; manuscripts received outside that period will be returned unread provided an SASE accompanies the manuscript.

You are encouraged to read *Shenandoah* to acquaint yourself with the material we publish. Single copies are $8.00 each and are available from this office or your local bookstore. Subscription rates are 1 year (4 issues) / $22; 2 years / $40; 3 years / $54.

Contests

• THE JEANNE CHARPIOT GOODHEART PRIZE FOR FICTION—$1,000

• THE JAMES BOATWRIGHT III PRIZE FOR POETRY—$1,000

• THE THOMAS H. CARTER PRIZE FOR THE ESSAY—$500

Each prize is awarded annually to the author of the best story, poem and essay published in *Shenandoah* during a volume year.

Categories: Nonfiction—Book Reviews—Poetry—Short Stories

CONTACT: Lynn L. Leech, Managing Editor
Material: All
Troubadour Theater, 2nd Floor
Washington and Lee University
Lexington VA 24450-0303
Phone: 540-458-8765
Fax: 540-458-8461
Website: shenandoah.wlu.edu

Shofar

Shofar, a quarterly, interdisciplinary journal of Jewish Studies, is the official journal of the Midwest and Western Jewish Studies Associations. *Shofar* ranges far and wide thematically in a multi-disciplinary world that spans four thousand years. It publishes scholarly articles, opinion pieces, readers' forums, pedagogical essays, and book reviews. Articles are peer reviewed for scholarly rigor but at the same time are written with a minimum of professional jargon and are accessible to a diverse and general readership.

Frequent special thematic issues are also published under guest editorships. Topics for recent and forthcoming special issues include Jewish feminism, Jewish-Christian dialogue after the Shoah, Judaism and Asian religions, Jewish music, Jewish studies in Latin America, and Jewish studies in Germany.

Shofar is available electronically through Project MUSE.

Subscription Information

Quarterly
ISSN 0882-8539
Individuals $34.00
Institutions $55.00
Single issue $14.00

For foreign subscriptions please add $20.00. Payment must accompany order. Make checks payable to University of Nebraska Press and mail to:

University of Nebraska Press
233 N 8th St
Lincoln, NE 68588-0255
or call: 1-800-755-1105 U.S. Orders and customer service.

Submission Information

The aim of *Shofar* is to promote the exchange of ideas and information among teachers and scholars in the area of Jewish Studies. *Shofar* favors material written for the general reader rather than a subgroup of specialists. Of particular interest is the area of teaching Jewish Studies at colleges and universities. *Shofar* publishes scholarly papers (5,000-15,000 words), book reviews, and review essays. All papers are reviewed by invited readers; other materials are evaluated by the editorial board. *Shofar* accepts submissions that meet the following requirements:

• submit 3 copies

• clearly identify the title of the paper on the cover letter and do not write your name on the paper itself

• prepare according to *The Chicago Manual of Style*, 14th edition

• include a one-sentence personal bio typed double-spaced (including quotations and endnotes)

• papers may be submitted via e-mail to the Managing Editor

If you wish your manuscript to be returned, enclose a stamped, self-addressed envelope. Letters to the editor are normally limited to 500 words; the editors reserve the right to edit letters.

Categories: Nonfiction—Book Reviews—Culture—Feminism—Jewish Interest—Literature—Music—Religion—Spiritual

CONTACT: Submissions
Material: All
Purdue University
Jewish Studies Program
1363 Liberal Arts & Education Bldg.
West Lafayette IN 47907-1363
E-mail: nlein@sla.purdue.edu
Website: www.nebraskapress.unl.edu/shofar.html

Short Stuff Magazine

Short Stuff Magazine (for grown-ups) is 8½" x 11", 32-40 pages, bond paper, enamel cover, black & white illustrations and photographs.

Fiction and humor can be any genre, any subject. We are designed to be a *Reader's Digest* of fiction. Nonfiction must be regional, pertaining to Colorado and the adjacent states (Wyoming, Nebraska, Kansas, New Mexico, Arizona, Utah). We are found in professional waiting rooms (doctors', dentists', lawyers' offices, etc.) Bimonthly.

Needs: Adventure, contemporary, historical (general), humor/satire, mainstream, regional, romance (contemporary/historical), science fiction, senior citizen/retirement, suspense/mystery. Some poetry accepted, preferably humorous. We always need clean jokes. We receive 300 mss/month, but use 9-12 mss/2 months. Length: 1,500 words maximum (no exceptions).

How to Contact: Send complete manuscript with cover letter telling about the author. Put full name, title of submission, address and telephone number on the first page. Must include self-addressed stamped envelope–otherwise the manuscript will be destroyed. If the manuscript is dated, indicate this on the envelope (e.g., if the story is related to the Christmas holiday season, put CHRISTMAS). We are seasonal. We report in roughly three to six months. Photocopied submissions OK. No reprints or simultaneous submissions. We do accept computer printouts. For a sample copy send $1.50 plus a self-addressed, 9" x 12" envelope with $1.85 postage (or five 37-cent stamps).

Payment: We pay $10-$50, at our discretion, with free subscription to magazine for stories. Fillers (500 words or less) $1-$5. We do not pay for single jokes or poetry but do give free subscriptions.

Terms: Acceptance and pay at publication for first North American serial rights.

Advice: We seek a potpourri of subjects each issue. A new slant, a different approach, fresh viewpoint. Prefer third person, past tense. Be sure it is an actual story with a beginning, middle and end. It must have dialogue!

Categories: Fiction—Nonfiction—Cartoons—Comedy—Family—Folklore—General Interest—Humor—Lifestyle—Literature—Mystery—Romance—Rural America—Satire

CONTACT: Donnalee Bowman, Editor
Material: Fiction
CONTACT: Greg Palmer, Copy Editor
Material: Non-Fiction
Bowman Publications
712 West 10th St.
Loveland CO 80537
Phone: 970-669-9139
E-mail: shortstf89@aol.com

Shuttle Spindle & Dyepot
Handweavers Guild of America, Inc.

Background

Published by the Handweavers Guild of America, Inc., *Shuttle Spindle & Dyepot* magazine features emerging artists and craftspeople, highlights innovative techniques and events, and honors established fiber artists and textile traditions. SS&D is a magazine for artists and craftspeople. As an international forum for weavers, spinners, dyers, basketmakers and felters, it is a visually appealing, in-depth publication that promotes excellence in fiber art through articles that inform, enlighten, instruct and inspire.

Articles

We are interested in articles that present ideas and concepts related to textile arts; articles on textile history and preservation, artists' profiles and guild related projects. We feature in-depth reviews of museum, gallery and textile shows, as well as examine current issues relative to textiles.

Targeting all levels of experience, we look for articles on weaving, spinning, dyeing, felting, weaving with beads and basketmaking that examine a technique or tradition. Our emphasis is on developing design skills, understanding techniques, marketing and craftsmanship.

Manuscripts

We invite written proposals that summarize the subject and point of view of the article. Complete articles, not exceeding 1200 words, are also welcomed.

Please present your article or ideas in the following format:
- Use 8½" x 11" white bond paper.
- Type and double space.
- Provide a disk with the hard copy. Indicate Macintosh or IBM format.

Save the document:
1. in Microsoft Word (as Word 2)
2. in Word Perfect (as WP 5.1)
3. or as an ASCII file

Label disk with your name, file name, and indicate MAC or IBM disk format.

- Place your name, address and phone number in the upper right hand corner of each page.
- Indent paragraphs.
- Use two inch margins at the top and bottom and one inch on the sides.
- If the article is unsolicited, please include a brief outline of the article, hard copy only (no longer than one page).
- Include the bibliography at the end of the manuscript on the hard copy and disk.
- Include photo captions on the hard copy and disk.
- Include a list (hard copy) of enclosed illustrations (photographs, slides, drawdowns, graphs, line drawings) with an accompanying descriptive note of each illustration.
- Include a brief autobiographical note.

Illustrations

Use clear, good quality original slides, 4" x 5" transparencies and/or black and white glossy prints to illustrate articles. All slides and photographs should be sharp and clear without background clutter.

Photographs should be included on the list of illustrations with a brief description. All illustrations/photograhs/samples should be keyed to the text and captioned. Do not write on the back of photographs but tape a piece of paper on the back of the photo. People in the photograph should be identified.

All illustrations should be labeled with the following information:
- Name of artist and/or author
- Address of author (or artist if different)
- Name of piece, dimensions, fiber content and other pertinent information
- Name of photographer to be given photo credit
- How the piece is keyed to the text for example (Illustration 1)
- An arrow on the right side indicating the top of the slide/photograph/sample

When it is necessary for the author/artist to send in the actual piece for in-house photography, the item must be tagged with:
- Owner's name and shipping address
- Title of the piece
- An indication of the right side
- Insurance value
- The piece must be keyed to the text

We will return the piece/s postage paid, insured via the same transport service used for delivery.

Drafts

In order to keep drafts uniform all drafts will be redone on a computer software program to our specifications.
- Draw drafts on graph paper.
- Use numbers to mark the threading draft.
- For the rising shed (jack loom) tie-up draft, number the harnesses, with the highest number on top and the lowest on the bottom, and indicate it as a rising shed.
- For the sinking shed (counter balance) tie-up draft, use X.
- Use short vertical dashes for the treadling draft.
- For the drawdown, fill in the squares where appropriate.
- Be sure to label the threading and the treadling.
- Indicate tabby by using a and b.

The publication process

Once a manuscript is chosen for publication, the copy is read for content, clarity, conflicts and duplications. Then it is sent to the copy-editor.

The copy-editor checks spelling, punctuation and grammar. She also corrects awkward sentence structure. She edits and checks that names and places are spelled correctly. Whatever appears on the original copy from the author is considered correct. For example, if a person's last name is Smith and the author spells it Smythe, we have no way of knowing that it should be Smith.

The copy is then set in a three column format and a draft or galley proof is printed. The galley proof or draft copy is returned to the author for verification and author comments. It is extremely important to check the spelling of names and places at this time.

Authors, members and guilds love to see their name in print, especially in their national organization's magazine, but only if it is spelled correctly!

Check: photo, illustration and diagram captions; author's biographical note, illustrations and diagrams.

Comments from the author should be forwarded (faxed, if possible) to the editor as quickly as possible with errors, misspelled names or misplaced diagrams noted on the returned copy.

Review

The manuscript will also be reviewed by a specialist. For example, an article that includes formulas for mixing dyes will be reviewed by a chemist. Once the consultant's and author's comments have been implemented, the page layouts are designed.

Proofreader

The proofreader inspects all final copy and photo captions.

Honoraria and Publication Agreement

The Handweavers Guild of America, Inc., provides a small honorarium, upon publication of an article. In exchange, the author agrees to convey First English Language publication rights, Anthology (reprint) rights, electronic publication rights, and rights to photocopy or otherwise reproduce the work to the Handweavers Guild of America, Inc./*Shuttle Spindle & Dyepot*. In addition, the author agrees not to sell, assign or transfer any remaining rights in and to the article until six months after publication in SS&D, unless otherwise agreed with the editor.

Occasionally we may request electronic publication rightswork will be watermark protected—to include on HGA's Web site: www.weavespindye.org.

References

All references must be documented.

Bibliography:

Please use this format for a book:

Atwater, Mary M. *The Shuttlecraft Book of American Hand-Weaving*. New York: Macmillan Publishers, 1928.

Use this format for a magazine article:

Guy, Sallie. "Twill 2-Double Width Afghans." *Shuttle Spindle & Dyepot*, Winter 1983, 34.

Citations:

Parenthetical references are used to clarify (in the body of the text) when documenting research or when reference should be made to a particular book, page or section of a book. For examples see below.

Example 1: author date method (Atwater 1928) or

Example 2: author, date, page method (Atwater 1928, p. 178)

An example of citations used in an article can be found in the following:

Duncan, Kate. "The Kutchin Baby Carrying Strap." *Shuttle Spindle & Dyepot*. Spring 1992, 38.

Book reviews

Book reviews follow general manuscript instructions. Please begin your book review with this format:

BOOK TITLE IN CAPITALS, by Author's Name. Publishing Company, Street, City, State, Zip. Year of Publication. Soft or Hard Cover. Number of pages. Price.

Do not exceed 500 words.

Suggestions for discussion:

- general description
- to whom it would appeal
- author's purpose in writing the book
- author's qualifications
- merits of the book
- any weakness
- quality of illustrations and/or diagrams

Reviewed by Your Name, City and State or Province

Categories: Arts—Associations—Crafts/Hobbies—Culture—Education—Fashion—General Interest—Hobbies—Reference—Trade—Textile & Fiber Arts

CONTACT: Submissions Editor
Material: All
Two Executive Concourse, Ste. 201
3327 Duluth Hwy.
Duluth GA 30096-3301
Phone: 770-495-7702
Fax: 770-495-7703
E-mail: weavespindy@compuserve.com
Website: www.weavespindye.org

SIERRA

Sierra
The Magazine of the Sierra Club

PUBLISHED SINCE 1893

Sierra is a bimonthly national magazine publishing writing, photography, and art about the natural world. Our readers are environ-mentally concerned and politically diverse; most are active in the outdoors. We are looking for fine writing that will provoke, entertain, and enlighten this readership.

Though open to new writers, we find ourselves most often working with authors we have sought out or who have worked with us for some time. We ask writers who would like to publish in *Sierra* to submit written queries; phone calls are strongly discouraged. If you would like a reply to your query or need your manuscript returned to you, please include a self-addressed stamped envelope. Prospective *Sierra* writers should familiarize themselves with recent issues of the magazine; for a sample copy, send a self-addressed envelope and a check for $3 payable to *Sierra*; back issues are included on the Sierra Club's Web site, www.sierraclub.org/sierra/.

Please be patient: Though the editors meet weekly to discuss recently received queries, a response time of from six to eight weeks is usual.

Please do not send slides, prints, or other art work. If photos or illustrations are required for your submission, we will request them when your work is accepted for publication.

We greatly prefer queries by U.S. Mail to e-mail. Please include clips if possible.

Feature Articles

Sierra is looking for strong, well-researched, literate writing on significant environmental and conservation issues. Features often focus on aspects of the Sierra Club's conservation work. For more information about issues the Club is currently working on, visit our web site at www.sierraclub.org. Writers should look for ways to cast new light on well-established issues. We look for stories of national or international significance; local issues, while sometimes useful as examples of broader trends, are seldom of interest in themselves. We are always looking for adventure travel pieces that weave events, discoveries, and environmental insights into the narrative. Nonfiction essays on the natural world are welcome, too.

We do not want descriptive wildlife articles, unless larger conservation issues figure strongly in the story. We are not interested in editorials, general essays about environmentalism, or in highly technical writing. We do not publish unsolicited cartoons, poetry, or fiction; please do not submit works in these genres.

Feature articles in recent years that display the special qualities we look for are "Salmon's Second Coming" by David James Duncan (March/April 2000), "One Man's Wilderness" by Joe Kane (March/April 2000), "Where the Caribou Roam" by Reed McManus (July/August 2000), "The New Gold Rush" by Rebecca Solnit (July/August 2000). "Circling Back to the Sierra" by Daniel Duane (January/February 2004); "Old Europe's New Ideas" by Samuel Loewenberg (January/February 2004)

Feature length ranges from 1,000 to 3,000 words; payment is from $800 to $3,000, plus negotiated reimbursement for expenses.

Departments

Much of the material in *Sierra*'s departments is written by staff editors and contributing writers. The following sections of the magazine, however, are open to freelancers. Articles are 100-1500 words in length; payment is $100 to $1500 unless otherwise noted. Expenses up to $50 may be paid in some cases.

"Food for Thought" is concerned with what we eat and its connection to the environment. Topics range from drying food for backpacking to bovine growth hormones to the consequences of buying imported produce.

"Good Going" succinctly describes a superlative place, including fascinating environmental and cultural facts, in about 300 words.

"Hearth & Home" offers information and advice on how we can live our environmental principles in our own homes; topics have ranged from composting with worms to building with straw to energy conservation. Articles for this department should be accurate, lively, and helpful (750-1500 words).

"Body Politics" discusses relations between health and environment, often with practical advice on how to avoid health hazards. Articles should be carefully researched (750-1500 words).

"Lay of the Land" focuses on environmental issues of national or international concern. Regional issues are considered when they have national implications. At 500 to 700 words, "Lay of the Land" articles are not sweeping surveys, but tightly focused, provocative, well-researched investigations of environmental issues. Payment varies according to length.

"Mixed Media" features 750-word essays on how media, the arts, and other cultural topics relate to the environment, and also offers short (200-300) word reviews of the books and videos on environmentalism and natural history. (Payment per review is $50).

"Profiles" are 3,000-word biographical sketches of people doing important work to protect the environment. We try to broaden our readers' understanding of the environmental movement with subjects they haven't read about elsewhere: for instance, a pig farmer in Mississippi or an outfitter in Wyoming.

"One Small Step" features the first-person accounts of ordinary folks doing extraordinary things. We publish a 100-150 word quotation from an interview that explains the person's actions, motivations, and impact.

Payment for all articles is on acceptance, which is contingent on a favorable review of the manuscript by our editorial staff, and by knowledgeable outside reviewers, where appropriate. Kill fees are negotiated when a story is assigned. 03/17/03

Categories: Conservation—Ecology—Environment—Travel

CONTACT: Bob Schildgen, Managing Editor
Material: All
85 Second St., 2nd Floor
San Francisco, CA 94105-3441
Phone: 415-977-5572
Fax: 415-977-5794
E-mail: sierra.letters@sierraclub.org
Website: www.sierraclub.org/sierra

Signs of the Times®

Signs of the Times® is a 32-page, monthly outreach magazine published by Pacific Press, a Seventh-day Adventist publisher, for the Adventist church in North America (both the United States and Canada). It has been in continuous publication since 1874 and is thus one of the oldest religious magazines in North America. The mission of Signs is to share the gospel with those who are not of our faith, both Christians and non-Christians.

Sample copies.
You may receive a sample copy of *Signs of the Times®* by sending a self-addressed, stamped envelope to us at P. O. Box 5398, Nampa, ID 83653-5398. The envelope will need postage for three ounces.

Queries.
We use a significant number of free-lance articles. You may query us if you wish. However, we prefer to see the completed manuscript. We will consider simultaneous submissions but request that you let us know you have submitted your manuscript to other publications.

Manuscript preparation and submission.
You can submit your manuscript as either hardcopy or by e-mail. Our response to your submission can take up to two months.

• **Hardcopy submissions.** If you submit your manuscript as hardcopy, it should be typed, double spaced, on white paper. If you are submitting on speculation, do not send the article on a disk with your manuscript. If we accept it, we will request an electronic copy. You should include a self-addressed, stamped envelope if you want a response.

• **E-mail submissions.** If you submit your manuscript by e-mail, please send it as a copy and paste rather than as an attached file. Our company has given us strict instructions not to open attached files because of the problem of viruses that so often come with these files. If you send us an article as an attached file only, we will return it with the request that you send it as a copy and paste.

Payment
Signs of the Times® pays on acceptance. For first North American serial rights we pay 10 cents a word for articles sent on speculation, half that for reprints. Since some articles are posted on our Web page, we request electronic rights as well. When accepting an article for publication, we send the author a contract specifying the rights we are purchasing and the amount of the payment. The contract also requests a photograph of yourself, the author, preferably a mug shot. We will mail you a check after we receive your signed contract and photograph.

TYPES OF ARTICLES
Signs of the Times® publishes articles in the following categories that are of interest to free-lance authors submitting on speculation: Gospel, Christian lifestyle, God's Amazing Grace, and first-person stories. Also needed are fillers of 450 or 750 words. Following is a description of what we are looking for in each of these types of articles.

Gospel
Gospel articles deal with salvation and how to experience it. This includes articles on salvation by faith, how to cultivate a devotional life (Bible study, meditation, prayer), how to experience victory over temptation and sin, how to trust God in trial, etc. Stories that share what others have learned in these areas are also welcome. While most of our gospel articles are assigned or picked up from reprints, we do occasionally accept unsolicited manuscripts in this area. Gospel articles should be 1,000 to 1,200 words. We like sidebars that give additional information on the topic wherever possible. Sidebars should be included in the word count.

Christian lifestyle
Lifestyle articles deal with the practical problems of everyday life from a biblical and Christian perspective. Recently published titles in this category include "Taming the Strong-willed Child," "Emotional Abuse: What It Is and Why It Hurts," "When Kids Are Home Alone," and "How to Comfort a Grieving Friend." Lifestyle articles are typically 1,000 to 1,200 words. We request that authors include sidebars that give additional information on the topic wherever possible. Sidebars should be included in the word count.

God's Amazing Grace
The emphasis in this department is on spiritual growth. We want to hear readers' stories about their walk with God—conversion stories, answers to prayer, victory over temptation, and other ways in which God's leading in their lives has helped them to be more spiritual persons. These articles should be your own experience written in the first person. Length should be 650 to 1000 words. We always put the author's picture with God's Amazing Grace articles, so please enclose a recent photograph of yourself when you send your article. Our payment for these articles is a fixed $75.00.

First-person stories
These articles must be written in the first person. Authors who are writing about someone else's experience should use "as told to" in the by-line. First-person stories must illuminate a spiritual or moral truth that the individual in the story learned. We especially like stories that hold the reader in suspense or that have an unusual twist at the end. First-person stories should be 800 to 1,000 words.

Short fillers
Often a one-page article is needed to fill an empty spot in a particular month's layout. These fillers can be inspirational/devotional, Christian lifestyle, stories, comments that illuminate a biblical text—in short, anything that might fit in a general Christian magazine. Fillers should be 450 to 750 words.

SUGGESTIONS FOR WRITERS

Audience

The audience for *Signs of the Times*® includes both Christians and non-Christians of all ages. However, we recommend that our authors write with the non-Christian reader in mind, since most Christians can easily relate to articles that are written for the non-Christian reader, whereas many non-Christians will have no interest in an article that is written from a Christian perspective. Also, writing for readers who are in the 25- to 45-year age span will probably attract adults of nearly all ages.

Religion versus spirituality

In today's world, "spiritual" is in and "religion" is out, as are also "church" and "denomination." Thus, unless religion, church, or denomination are an essential part of the article or story, we prefer that these be left out. While Signs® is published by Seventh-day Adventists, we mention even our own denominational name in the magazine rather infrequently. The purpose is not to hide who we are but to make the magazine as attractive to non-Christian readers as possible. Also, please avoid denominational jargon and stained-glass piety. These are almost guaranteed to cause non-Christians to stop reading the magazine.

Solutions to problems

We are especially interested in articles that respond to the questions of everyday life that people are asking and the problems they are facing. Since these questions and problems nearly always have a spiritual component, articles that provide a biblical and spiritual response are especially welcome. A good rule of thumb is to write at least two words of solution for each word stating the question or problem. Write about benefits! What benefit will the reader get from reading your article?

Reprints

If you have written an article that you feel meets our criteria but that has already been published elsewhere, feel free to submit it to us with a notation that you are offering us second rights. Photocopies of previously published articles are acceptable. And, according to current U.S. copyright law, unless you sold all rights to the previous publisher, neither you nor we need to request the first publisher for permission to reprint. The copyright reverted to you once the article appeared in the previous publication.

Sidebars

Any time you can provide us with one or more sidebars that add information to the topic of your article, you enhance your chance of getting our attention. Sidebars can vary in length from a short paragraph to a column. Two kinds of sidebars seem to be especially popular with readers: Those that give information in lists, with each item in the list consisting of only a few words or at the most a sentence or two; and technical information or long explanations that in the main article might get the reader too bogged down in detail. Whatever their length, sidebars need to be part of the total word count of the article.

Introductions

We like the articles in *Signs of the Times*® to have interest-grabbing introductions. One of the best ways to do this is with anecdotes, particularly those that have a bit of suspense or conflict.

Illustrations and authorities

We find that it also helps to include one or two more anecdotes later in the article. Readers also like to know that someone who is an authority on the topic supports the author's point. Thus we encourage authors to do a bit of research to find some authorities they can quote in their article. Quotations of a paragraph or two are considered to be "fair use," and you need not obtain permission from the original author. However, even a couple of lines from a song or poem can constitute such a large percentage of the total work as to violate copyright law. It is the author's responsibility to obtain any permissions that are required and to pay for those permissions where that is necessary.

Religious affiliation

It is not necessary to be a Seventh-day Adventist in order to be published in *Signs of the Times*®. However, you may find it helpful to know something about our beliefs, which we will be glad to share with you in a booklet called Let's Get Acquainted, available free on request. Please include a self-addressed, stamped envelope (6-1/2 x 9-1/2) with postage for three ounces.

Categories: Nonfiction—Religion

CONTACT:
Material:
P. O. Box 5398
Nampa, ID 83653-5398
Phone: 208-465-2579
Fax: 208-465-2531
E-mail: signs@pacificpress.com
Website: www.signstimes.com

Skating Magazine

Thank you for your interest in writing for SKATING magazine. Without your help, we would not have the informative, interesting and compelling articles that make up SKATING magazine. This is a list of guidelines that we like to follow in SKATING magazine.

Who We Are:

SKATING magazine, with a paid circulation of about 45,000, is the official publication for the United States Figures Skating Association, the national governing body for the sport of figure skating. The magazine is published 10 times a year (June/July and August/September issues are combined), and freelancers write the majority of articles. The magazine's mission is to communicate information about the sport to the USFSA membership and figure skating fans, promoting USFSA programs, personalities, events and trends that affect the sport. Over half of our membership is under 17 and active in the sport of figure skating and the vast majority is female.

What We're Looking For

There are three main types of stories that we usually run in *SKATING* Magazine:

Competition Reviews.

Features: (on athletes of all levels—elite, adult, synchronized skaters; also judges and other USFSA members).

Remember that SKATING focuses on U.S. eligible athletes. We occasionally print an article on a foreign skater(s) or coach.

Columns: i.e. sports medicine; On the Lookout (dealing with young athletes working their way up the ranks); Athlete Programs (showcasing USFSA athletes who have succeeded due to USFSA programs).

Stories for SKATING magazine are evaluated on an individual basis, but in general, should fit more than one of the following criteria:

1. Accurate
2. Interesting and entertainin—appeals to the majority of our readers
3. Newsworthy—should have value and affect and/or impact our readers
4. Representative of the USFSA
5. Timely
6. Relevant to the figure skating audience
7. Educational
8. Has not appeared in any other publication

How to Query Us:

Send a letter or e-mail proposing your story idea to the address below.

Explain what you plan to cover and how you plan to proceeding with the reporting. The query letter should discuss your qualifications and knowledge of figure skating and convey the tone and style you plan to use for the story. If you are a first-time writer for SKATING, copies of published samples would be appreciated. If you are an unpublished writer, any sample of your writing would help. SKATING magazine wants quality writers with an imaginative style and the courage to seek out the interesting and unusual in a story, regardless of how often a writer has been published.

SKATING Magazine will occasionally accept unsolicited manuscripts, but a query is preferred. SKATING assumes no responsibility for unsolicited queries or manuscripts and will only respond to those accompanied by a self-addressed, stamped envelope. SKATING does not accept articles and stories that have appeared in other skating publications.

Photos are an important part of submitting a story idea. In your query, please note what kind of photos you plan to provide for the article.

Submitting an Article

• As you go through and edit your article, it is important to do a fact check. Consult second sources and make sure everything in your article is verified.

• If you are writing a sports medicine article, please clearly state your qualifications for writing the article. All outside sports medicine articles will be reviewed by the USFSA Sports Medicine Committee for accuracy before publication.

• Under no circumstances should you feel compelled to advance a copy of the entire story to your sources.

• Before submitting an article, make sure it has been spell-checked and edited for grammatical errors.

• SKATING also has a style guide for writers for the magazine. Please adhere to this guide when you are writing for SKATING. It makes our editing work much easier!

• E-mail submissions are preferred. Payment upon publication. Payment varies.

Photography

SKATING pays $35 per color photo used; $15 for black and white. A color photo on the cover is paid $50. All payment is on publication. SKATING will accept prints, slides and transparencies or electronic images. Electronic images must be scanned at 300 dpi, at least 100 percent of the original image, if the image is scanned from a print. Other details about electronic images can be determined when a photo is "purchased."

Quality prints and high quality scans are preferred.

For more details about photography, please contact Laura Fawcett at lfawcett@usfsa.org.

Categories: Diet/Nutrition—Physical Fitness—Sports/Recreation

CONTACT: Amy Partain
Material: All
20 First Street
Colorado Springs CO 80906
Phone: 719-635-5200
Fax: 719-635-9548
E-mail: apartain@usfigureskating.org
Website: www.usfigureskating.org

Ski
The Magazine of the Ski Life

SKI focuses on accuracy and timeliness. And we need your help. SKI's authority is contingent on the accuracy of your submission. While we do as much fact-checking as possible, you must provide us with accurate information. That includes everything from general facts to quotes to spellings.

Writers are paid upon acceptance. They will not be paid until manuscripts are complete—and that includes all TKs.

Please review the following list of guidelines. If you have any questions, contact your assigning editor.

Thank you.

WRITER GUIDELINES
I. SOURCES AND FACT CHECKING

You are responsible for providing a source list A) names and phone numbers of all your contacts and B) phone numbers for each individual quoted.

Hold onto your notes and research materials. If we have questions during the editing process, we will come back to you for clarification or more information.

II. TRAVEL INFORMATION

Authors submitting travel/feature stories that focus on particular resorts or regions must provide a standard information box with the following information: Contact address and phone and fax numbers (including tourist boards and airlines when applicable); Acres of skiable terrain (including off-piste for European destinations); Ticket prices—weekday and weekend; Snow report number; Nearest city; How to get there.

Lodging and dining information must offer at least two options in three categories—budget, moderate, luxury. If a resort has SKIwee or NASTAR programs, these should be mentioned as well.

III. STYLE

For grammar, please follow *The Associated Press Stylebook.* You are responsible for correct spellings (names included) and word usage.

IV. FORMAT

All stories must be submitted by the deadline indicated, on computer disk (please specify what software) or via e-mail and in hard copy format. NOTE: *SKI* will not pay for overnight delivery of stories or materials.

V. WORD COUNT

Stories that are grossly above (or under) the specified word count will be returned to the writer and considered incomplete.

VI. EXPENSES

An itemized list of expenses, with receipts attached must be received no later than 45 days after the assignment is completed. Expenses received later than this may not be reimbursable.

Categories: Nonfiction—Adventure—Lifestyle—Recreation—Sports

CONTACT: Submissions Editor
Material: All
Times Mirror Magazine
929 Pear St.
Boulder CO 80302
Phone: 303-448-7600
Fax: 303-448-7638
Website: skimag.com

Skiing Magazine

SKIING readers are smart, curious and passionate about the sport. For them, every ski trip is a modern adventure. They might ski, snowboard, or telemark; they will seek out the best clubs, parties, and restaurants. They want to know about the biggest expeditions, the most exotic locations, the latest first descents. Studying several past issues of the magazine should help you determine whether a query is appropriate, and whether we've covered a given subject before. While a large portion of SKIING is written by regular contributors and staff members, including nearly all features, we welcome freelance writers to send us your ideas. Scene, the Hot List, and Trail Run are all good entry-level sections for your first assignment.

In general, we look for the following attributes:

• Skiing. Although we cover other winter sports, such as snowshoeing, mountaineering, and nordic skiing, SKIING primarily sticks to its title—with some exploration into resort telemarking, backcountry, AT, and even snowboarding.

• Trends. Whether it's new gear, an up-and-coming resort, or a hot destination, we want to be the first to reveal it.

• Service. Virtually every SKIING story contains useful information, something practical that the reader can learn.

FEATURES

Most SKIING features focus on gear, instruction, destinations—both nearby and far-flung, big and small—and personalities. The voice can range from objective reporting and service to humorous first-person narrative, but it needs to be unique and descriptive. All stories have some component of service (how to get there, where to stay, what to buy), whether it's a sidebar, a box, or a more central focus of the piece. Our regular contributors usually pitch fantastic stories (China, Morocco, Iran, Turkey) and popular destinations (heli-skiing in Alaska, Chamonix, summer in Chile), so it may help to consider less obvious subjects: smaller ski areas, local ski cultures, and colorful personalities.

Every year, we publish a Best Of, a gear guide/ski test, a travel guide, and regular Private Lessons (instruction). These are generally written and produced in-house with the participation of experienced testers and skiers.

DEPARTMENTS

Scene: Often defined by art, these are short shapshots that inspire readers and reveal what's really going on in skiing: rumors, weirdness, athletes, trends, techniques. It's our most timely section. 70-150 words per item.

Hot List: Hottest new innovative products, techniques, books, trends, with a quick description about why it's the latest, greatest thing on the market, and price/contact info.

The Inside Line: These are essentially pocket guides to skiing resorts with a map and short paragraphs that deliver hardcore service.

Face Shot: A profile of someone in the ski world, with a range from an Olympic downhill racer to an up-and-coming freeskier to a world-class mountaineer, who has recently done something notable.

Outfitter: This section shows readers how to outfit themselves for adventure, whether it's a comprehensive look at the basics, a rundown of techie accessories, or the gear you need for hut trips or pre-season training. We try to uncover trends in the industry and give round-ups on products in categories. Examples: soft shells, AT gear, helmets, hydration packs.

Trial Run: We rank a certain gear category (glasses, altimeter watches, packs) for three price points—Race Stock, Retail, and BroDeal—with brief descriptions of the product and its functionality.

Be Strong: Legitimate, scientific and timely information about how to get and stay strong and fit. Each issue includes a 3-5 page short feature about a certain exercise program or trend, smaller boxes that highlight recent studies and charts to compare new products, and a sidebar or two with short new/product/website blurbs.

East/California Regional: We publish an extra section in these two regions with limited distribution, and each one has an Inside Line section, a Deal Monitor, and short news items. (The Underground, Deep Thoughts, and Dropping In are written by our columnists.)

ACCURACY

We are committed to providing reliable information, so it is important that all contributors check facts and figures, provide contact information for sources, and provide extra copies of maps, catalogs, brochures, or other primary sources when the story is submitted.

QUERIES

We prefer queries to completed works. With your initial query, please send examples of your published work and a brief cover letter explaining your background and past experience. Include a SASE if you would like your materials returned. We're not responsible for returning unsolicited artwork, photos, and manuscripts, so don't send originals.

ASSIGNMENTS AND PAYMENT

SKIING assignments require a signed contract, which specifies rights, payments, and deadline in order to be valid. We pay $.75-$1.00 a word, depending on the experience of the writer.

Categories: Nonfiction—Adventure—Consumer—Outdoors—Recreation—Sports—Travel

CONTACT: Perkins Miller, Editor-in-Chief
Material: All

929 Pear St., Ste 200
Boulder CO 80302
Phone: 303-448-7600
Fax: 303-448-7676
E-mail: editors@skiingmag.com
Website: www.skiingmag.com

Skin Inc. Magazine:
The Complete Business Guide for Face & Body Care

Manuscripts are considered for publication that contain original and new information in the general fields of skin care and makeup, dermatological, plastic and reconstructive surgical techniques. The subject may cover the science of skin, the business of skin care and makeup establishments or of an individual esthetician, or treatments performed by estheticians, dermatologists and plastic surgeons on healthy (i.e., non-diseased) skin. Subjects may also deal with raw materials, formulations and regulations governing claims for products and equipment.

A manuscript must be written exclusively for this publication, that is, not submitted to any other publication, and contain significant material not previously published elsewhere. Publication rights for reprints and other republication purposes is normally granted on request.

Acceptance for publication is in the hands of our Editorial Committee. A decision will be given to an author within one month.

TECHNICAL DETAILS

A manuscript must be submitted in English, although perfect grammar and style are not required. We reserve the right to edit all manuscripts accepted for publication. Any editing required will be done by our editorial staff. Whenever possible, please submit your manuscript to us on a 3E" DS/DD PC disk. Manuscript file must be submitted in Microsoft Word or ASCII format. Manuscripts also can be e-mailed.

All product trade names for product lines, drugs, equipment, etc. must be credited to their manufacturers including the city and state of manufacture. All facts quoted or used in the manuscript text from other literature sources must be properly referenced. References must be submitted according to the style sheet below.

Illustrations should be provided as black and white glossy photographs. Original charts and graphs should be in black ink on white paper. They will be returned at the author's request. Photocopies of illustrations are most often not clear enough to be reproduced in a publication.

Two copies of the manuscript should be supplied.

The usual scheduling of manuscripts is done four to eight months in advance of publication. This will be the usual time between acceptance of a manuscript for publication and its appearance in the magazine.

In the case of original material written exclusively for this magazine, an honorarium will paid to the author upon publication. This will be a cash payment.

Style Sheet for References and Footnotes

REFERENCES

Magazines, Journals, and Periodicals

Please number the references. Start with the author's name(s), article title, journal or magazine name, volume number, issue number, starting page number, month and year of publication.

1. Science of beauty: High tech products: form meets function. Elle IV (2), 252 (October 1988)

2. C Duhe, Powder is back: The return of delicate dustings. Elle IV (2), 276 (October 1988)

Please note that the author's initials precede the surname, that there is very little punctuation, that only the first letter of the article title is capitalized, that the first number is the volume number, followed by the issue number, followed by the page numbers, followed by the year. The page number and issue month and year must be included with each reference.

Books

Start with the book's author(s), chapter name and number if appropriate, book name, editor's name(s) if any, publisher's city and state, publisher name, year of publication, and page number(s)

2. L Schorr and SM Sims, The need for skin care, Ch 6, in Lia Schorr's *Seasonal Skin Care*, New York, NY: Prentice Hall Press (1988) p 87

FOOTNOTES

Retin-A (Ortho Pharmaceutical Corporation, Raritan, NJ)

Please footnote all trade names (e.g. drugs, product lines) used in the text. Include the full name of the manufacturer, its city and state.

Please contact the editor if you have any questions on this style sheet.

Categories: Nonfiction—Health—Skin Care

CONTACT: Melinda Taschetta-Millane, Associate Publisher
Material: All
362 S. Schmale Rd.
Carol Stream IL 60188
Phone: 630-653-2155
Fax: 630-653-2192
E-mail: skininc@allured.com

Slipstream

For Magazine

Submit poetry, short fiction (under 15 pages), black & white photographs, graphics, and illustrations (better to send photocopies of artwork rather than originals).

We prefer contemporary urban themes—writing from the gut that is not afraid to bark or bite—and shy away from pastoral, religious, and rhyming verse.

If you're unsure, the editors strongly recommend that you sample a current or back issue of *Slipstream*. Submitting blindly to any magazine may result in wasting your time, money, and effort.

If you desire a response, please include a SASE. Payment is in copies.

For Annual Chapbook Contest

$1,000 prize plus 50 professionally printed copies of your chapbook.

Deadline for entries: Dec. 1 every year.

Send up to 40 pages of poetry—any style, format, theme (or no theme), plus a SASE with correct postage for the return of your manuscript, and a $10 check, bank draft, or money order for reading fee.

Simultaneous submissions are okay as long as you keep us informed of status. Previously published poems with proper acknowledgement and photocopies which are easy on the eyes are also acceptable.

All entrants receive a copy of the winning chapbook plus one issue of *Slipstream* magazine.

A winner is selected in the spring, at which time manuscripts are returned.

The winner is featured on the Grants & Awards page of *Poets & Writers Magazine* as well as *Slipstream*'s web site, and will also receive exposure in *Slipstream* catalogues, press releases, and promotional materials.

Past winners include: Gerald Locklin, Kurt Nimmo, Sherman Alexie, Serena Fusek, Matt Buys, Robert Cooperman, Richard Amidon, Katharine Harer, David Chorlton, Leslie Anne Mcilroy, Renny Christopher, Alison Pelegrin, Laurie Mazzaferro, Ronald Wardall, J.P. Dancing Bear, Nikki Roszko, and most recently, Beth Anne Royer.

Categories: Fiction—Literature—Poetry—Short Stories

CONTACT: Editor
Material: Poetry, fiction and chapbook entries
Box 2071
Niagara Falls NY 14301
Website: www.slipstreampress.org

Small Farm Today

Small Farm Today magazine is dedicated to preserving and promoting small farming, rural living, community and agri-preneurship. We use a "can-do," upbeat, positive approach and all articles submitted should reflect this attitude.

We need "how-to" articles (how to grow, raise, market, build, etc.), as well as articles about small farmers who are experiencing success through diversification, specialty/alternative crops and livestock, and direct marketing. *Small Farm Today* is especially interested in articles that explain how to do something from start to finish citing specific examples involved in the process or operation being discussed. It is important to include data on production costs, budgets, potential profits, etc. See the list of topics at the end of these guidelines for ideas. We do not usually use fiction, poetry or political pieces.

REPRINTS: If your manuscript has been printed in another publication, please list the publications and dates published. We prefer to publish original articles.

WE PREFER:

• 1,400-2600+ word articles, typed or on a 3.5" disk in text format.

• Accompanying captioned photographs with SASE for photo return.

• The article should be "how-to," describing how to raise the crop or animal and how it is marketed. It should list the address of the farm examined or other resources to contact for more information.

• Please include data on production costs, budgets, profit information, and marketing methods.

• Articles which meet these preferences and the other standards listed herein (in the opinion of the editors) will be paid a half-cent bonus per word published. Contact the Managing Editor for more information.

MANUSCRIPTS

We welcome both completed manuscripts and queries, but recommend you query your idea before sending in a manuscript.

Manuscripts submitted for consideration become the property of Missouri Farm Publishing, Inc. and will NOT be returned unless accompanied by a self-addressed, stamped envelope. Please type manuscripts, allowing at least 1/3 page at the top of the first page for editing notes. We also accept articles on disks compatible with a Macintosh computer. Length, depending on subject, should probably be between 800 and 3,000 words (we usually prefer 1,200-2,600 words). We prefer manuscripts with accompanying photos (see Photos, below).

Because we use an image scanner to transfer most hard copies of manuscripts onto the computer, we would prefer an original copy of your manuscript or a very clean photocopy.

It is important to include the addresses and phone numbers of your primary sources/interviewees. We usually include this information at the end of the article so the readers can contact them for more information. Please specify if the source or interviewee does not wish to have their phone number or address listed at the end of the article.

If you have charts, diagrams or sources for additional information on your subject matter, we will try to use them as sidebars with the article.

ALTERATIONS

Small Farm Today reserves the right to alter your manuscript for readability or space considerations. There will be no deliberate changes in the meaning of the text. Although every effort is made to avoid error, *Small Farm Today* does limit its responsibility for any errors, inaccuracies, misprints, omissions, or other mistakes in the article content.

SPECIAL SECTION: OUR PLACE

Small Farm Today features a special section called Our Place. This section is written by farmers/landowners about their own property. We prefer it to be written in first person form (I, we, our). It should include a description of your farm and what you raise. Some "how-to" tips on what you have learned from dealing with your crops/livestock would be appreciated. Other things that can be mentioned are: how you got started, plans for the future, what makes your property unique, and marketing strategies you employ.

Several people have expressed concern about their writing abilities—don't worry. The story will be edited for publication, but will still contain your own unique voice. Payment for Our Place is a box of magazines of the issue featuring your story. You can pass it out to family, friend, and customers.

HOLDING POLICY

After the article is received, it is submitted to the editor for review. If approved, it will be slated for publication. There is a long waiting period for articles to be published, often close to a year. This is due to limited space (only 6 issues) and a multitude of interested writers. Please bear with our slow publishing times. If we have not published the issue after one year, we will return the story to you (if you included an SASE). If you would prefer not to have your story held, please send notification of this with your manuscript.

PAYMENT

Unless otherwise arranged with the publisher, Missouri Farm Publishing, Inc. buys first serial rights and nonexclusive reprint rights (the right to reprint article in an anthology) for both manuscripts and photos. Missouri Farm Publishing, Inc. reserves the right to edit the story for publication. (See Alterations, page 2.) Rate of pay for reprints may be less than our standard rate of pay.

Payment for articles:
- 3.5 cents per word for each word published (see above paragraph) for first serial rights and nonexclusive reprint rights.
- There is a half-cent per word bonus for quality articles. (See We Prefer, above.)
- 2 cents per word for each word published for reprinted articles.
- We do not pay for book reviews

Payment for photos:
- $6.00 each for b&w or color prints
- $10.00 for photo used on cover
- $4.00 each for negatives or slides

Payment for line art, graphs, charts, and cartoons:
- $5.00 each

Payment is made 30-60 days after publication. Sorry, no exceptions.

PHOTOS, LINE ART, GRAPHS, CHARTS, & CARTOONS

Please send color or black and white prints of photos and include information about each photo for use in captions. Only color photos can be used on the cover. If you do not have prints, we can use negatives or slides. All photos sent to us will be returned if you include a SASE for photo return.

Cartoons, line art, graphs and charts are also welcome.

SUBJECT MATTER

Here is a list of some of the topics we cover regularly:
- Money-making alternatives for the small farm
- Exotic animals (ostriches, buffalo and elk are some we have covered)
- Minor breeds (Jacob sheep, Dexter cattle and red wattle hogs are some we have covered)
- Draft horses (using them on a small farm; also other draft animals)
- Small stock (sheep, goats, rabbits, poultry)
- Direct marketing (farmers markets, subscription marketing, roadside stands, U-pick)
- Gardening
- Wool and other fibers (production, processing, and marketing)
- Specialty crops
- New uses for traditional crops (ethanol and plastic from corn, for example)
- New sustainable farming methods
- Rural living (particularly how-to)
- Small fruits (grapes, berries, exotic new fruits)
- Tree fruits
- Sustainable agriculture (organic, reduced-input, agro-ecology)
- Horticulture (herbs, ornamentals, wild flowers, vegetables, other opportunities)
- Aquaculture (catfish, crawfish, fee fishing, tropical fish)
- Home-based business (crafts, food processing)
- Small-scale production of livestock (cattle, hogs, poultry)
- Equipment appropriate to small-scale acreage work

Be warned that stories may have a long lead time. As of this writing, we have 80 stories in stock. We do not limit ourselves to the topics on this list. If you have an idea for a story, drop us a note outlining your idea. If you are not familiar with *Small Farm Today*, we can send you a sample copy for $3.00.

Thank you for showing an interest in *Small Farm Today*!

If you have any other questions, please write or call.

Categories: Nonfiction—Agriculture

CONTACT: Paul Berg, Managing Editor
Material: All
3903 W. Ridge Trail Rd.
Clark MO 65243-9525
Phone: 573-687-3525
Fax: 573-687-3148
E-mail: smallfarm@socket.net
Website: www.smallfarmtoday.com

Smithsonian Magazine

Thank you for contacting *Smithsonian Magazine*. Starting Monday, May 3, 2004, we are no longer accepting unsolicited email or postal mail article proposals. We are now using a web submission form which can be found online by going to www.smithsonianmag.com, clicking the "Feedback" link on the navigation menu, and then clicking the black button labeled "Submissions."

This new system will ensure that we get all of the information we need to evaluate your query, and it will allow you more direct, timely access to our editors.

The web page also contains updated Writer's Guidelines and a list of Frequently Asked Questions.

CHECKING STATUS OF YOUR QUERY

If you are contacting us regarding the status of a proposal you sent prior to May 3, 2004, send an email to articlesdept@si.edu and be sure to include the word "status" (without the quotation marks) in the SUBJECT line of the email. Or you may call 202-275-7225 and press option (2).

Categories: Nonfiction—Arts—Conservation—Culture—Ecology—History—Humor—Nature—Science—Society—Technology—Travel—Archaeology

CONTACT: Marlane Liddell, Senior Editor
Material: All
Smithsonian Institution
MRC 951, PO Box 37012
Washington DC 20013-7012
Phone: 202-275-2000
E-mail: articles@simag.si.edu
Website: www.smithsonianmag.si.edu

Smoke Magazine
Life'sBurning Desires

Formal guidelines not available. Please read a number of issues to ascertain the publication's style and needs.

Send queries to address below.

Categories: Nonfiction—Automobiles—Crime—Fishing—Food/Drink—Men's Issues—Recreation—Recreation Vehicles—Sports

CONTACT: Allyson Boxman Levine, Editor-in-Chief
Material: All
Lockwood Publications, 26 Broadway, Floor 9M
New York NY 10004
Phone: 212-391-2060

Snake Nation Review

Snake Nation Review appears four times a year:
We welcome submissions throughout the year.
Fiction: 5,000 word limit
Poetry: 60 line limit
Essays: 5,000 word limit
Art: pen & ink drawings, photographs,
Payment $100 for art
Subscriptions are $20; sample copy $6 (includes mailing)
Institutions $30
Subscription includes the contest poetry book.

All well-written submissions on any topic in any form will be considered.

Simultaneous submissions are allowed with prompt notification if the piece places elsewhere.

Editors' Choice wins $100 for each category.

Categories: Fiction—Arts—Culture—Poetry—Science Fiction—Sexuality—Writing

CONTACT: Jean Arambula, Editor
Material: Poetry
110 West Force St.
Valdosta GA 31601
Phone: 229-244-0752

Soap Opera Digest

Does not accept unsolicited submissions.

Soap Opera Weekly

Does not accept unsolicited submissions.

Society of American Baseball Research
The Baseball Research Journal
The National Pastime

SABR's membership publications are written mainly for members. We're interested in hearing from any member who wants to share a piece of research on any baseball topic that would interest a portion of the membership. If you're interested in working up a piece for a SABR publication, here's some information that should help.

Queries

For your own sake, don't go to all the trouble of writing an article before you touch base with the Publications Director, who is the editor of most SABR publications. Query first. E-mail your proposal, an outline or both, setting out your idea for an article to Publications Director Jim Charlton at binswanger@aol.com. SABR will give you an honest appraisal of your idea, perhaps some suggestions, and will tell you whether or not we'd like to see a complete manuscript.

This doesn't necessarily mean that your article will be published. We may find that it doesn't stick to the point that your query advertised, or even (heaven forbid) that it is just poorly written. But querying does prevent you from doing a lot of work on something that we simply don't think will work for the publication in question.

Computers

You don't have to submit your manuscript on a computer disk, but if you do, you save SABR both time and the expense of having your article keyboarded.

We produce SABR publications on a MAC, using Microsoft Word and PageMaker. We can handle most Mac or MS-DOS word-processing programs, but not CP/M, Apple II, Amiga, Atari, et al.

Even if you do submit your article on disk, please send along a hard copy as well. It's easier to read that way, so we can make a judgment on it and get back to you more quickly.

Format (For Hard Copy)

Please double-space your manuscript. Please give us a word count. Leave generous margins all around—a roughly 60 character line (if using Pica or Courier type) and 25 lines or so per page is about right. This makes your manuscript easy to read and leaves room for notes in the margins.

Start typing manuscript about halfway down the first page. This leaves space for even more notes at the top of your copy. Make sure the top of every page carries your last name and the page number. If you are using a computer, please don't set your word processing program to justify text (this means making every line the same length as in a book). Your manuscript should be ragged right, as in standard type-written documents. The reason? It's much easier for the editor working with the hard copy to roughly verify your word count for a non-justified manuscript.

Photos, Graphics, Tables, and Charts

If you have photos, sent them (or copies of them) along, so we know what we've got to work with. Sometimes, researchers come up with wonderful cartoons or drawings. We'd like to see those, too. If your article requires tables or charts, build them carefully, and make sure they make their point clearly (A surprising number don't). Tables will be re-keyboarded and set up to fit the publication. Charts, on the other hand, should be "camera ready"—clear enough to be shot and printed.

Copyright

If we accept your article, we will send you a letter of agreement, which will make a few points clear. the two main ones are these: (1) you retain copyright, (2) you grant us First Serial Rights and the right to use the article in any future SABR compendiums.

How Long Should You Wait For Response?

We try to get back to you within a few days of receiving any sort of communication. But, the office is small, the work is large, and occa-

R-U

sionally something falls through the cracks. If you don't hear from us in three weeks or a month, give a call or write an indignant note.

Authors' Galleys

We will send you an edited, typeset of your article before it goes in press. If you have any serious problems with it, you must get back to your editor by phone within two weeks so we can work them out.

Which Publication

SABR puts out four membership publications a year. Not meant to be commercial publications, these are for the most part by SABR members, for SABR members.

Of these four publications, *The Baseball Research Journal* (BRJ) and *The National Pastime* (TNP) are annuals, and the two others are "specials" often created by one of SABR's committees. The two annuals are open to all SABR members, but there's often some confusion over how they differ. Here's a short description that might help you decide which one your article best suites.

The Baseball Research Journal is the repository for SABR members' "hard" research. Virtually all statistical studies belong here, and although we don't want to turn it into an academic journal, you should include notes, bibliographies, etc., where appropriate. Short articles focused on long-passed historical figures or events are okay here, but they must have a strong analytical approach. This is also the place for articles focusing technically (as opposed to historically) on the business of baseball, or on playing techniques.

The National Pastime is just what John Thorn's original subtitle calls it—"A review of baseball history." Articles don't require that strong analytical edge, and are usually more anecdotal than those in BRJ. This doesn't mean that we don't require solid research on historical subjects for TNP, just that there's more room here for speculation, opinion, nostalgia, humor, poetry and a certain amount of writing culled from non-SABR resources.

There's some overlap between the two publications. Some articles can go either way, and if that's the case with yours, your editor will make a suggestion.

Timely Publication

When we accept an article for publication, we usually tell you where and when we want it to run. Sometimes we get so much good material that we're forced to tell you when we accept it that we may have to hold onto you manuscript until the next year's edition.

Occasionally, we learn as we get into the editorial process and start assembling an issue that we have to roll one or more articles out and over to the next years' edition. This is sometimes a matter of space, and it's sometimes a matter of editorial balance (too much National League 1950's, not enough 19th Century). It's never a signal to you that we really don't like your article. (If we accepted it, we want to run it!) We never do this casually, because we know how hard you've worked and how eager you are to see your article in print. And we never do it without notifying you apologizing for the disappointment we know we're causing, and offering to free you from your Letter of Agreement (although we hope you stick with us).

Categories: Nonfiction—History—Humor—Poetry—Sports/Recreation

CONTACT: Jim Charlton, Publications Director
Material: Queries
James Charlton Associates
680 Washington St.
New York NY 10014
Phone: 212-691-4951
E-mail: binswanger@aol.com
Website: www.sabr.org

South American Explorer

South American Explorers is a non-profit organization. With clubhouses in Quito, Ecuador, and Lima and Cusco, Peru and U.S. headquarters in Ithaca, New York, the SAE collects and makes available to its members up-to-date, reliable information about Latin America.

Aims and Purposes

South American Explorers is dedicated to:
• Furthering the exchange of information among travelers and researchers
• Promoting responsible travel through the publication of pamphlets, information packets, the internet, and our magazine, the *South American Explorer*
• Publicizing projects aimed at improving social and environmental conditions in Latin America and collecting funds for their activities
• Awakening greater interest and appreciation for the welfare of endangered peoples, wildlife protection, and wilderness conservation
• Collecting information on volunteer and research opportunities
• Fostering ties between non-profit organizations, NGO'S, and conservation groups

General Membership Services:

Members of the South American Explorers receive:
• A one-year subscription (four issues) to the *South American Explorer* magazine.
• Access to our clubhouses in Quito, Lima and Cusco—trip reports, luggage storage, book exchange, mail and e-mail service etc.
• Discounts at a number of lodges, hotels, travel agencies, language schools, and guides in Peru and Ecuador.
• Help and advice from the friendly, knowledgeable club staff when planning trips and expeditions. Members can do their own information searches at any one of our clubhouses or solicit information by phone, mail, e-mail. It helps if we know when you plan to travel, the size of your budget, your interests, the number of people in your group, your preferred type of transportation, and anything else that will guide us in providing you with the most useful and detailed information possible. As a rule, the more specific your questions, the better our answers.
• Discounts on books, tapes, maps, and other goods available from the club's store.
• Access to the club's libraries, map collections, scientific reports, magazine and newspaper articles, theses, and books.
• Networking, the art of bringing like-minded people together. Members looking for travel companions or who wish to contact experts in various fields can post notices to the SAE electronic bulletin board, or on the bulletin boards in the Lima, Quito and Cusco clubhouses. They can also place classified ads in the *South American Explorer* (For the first 25 words: Members—(noncommercial) $10, (commercial) $30. Non-members—(noncommercial) $20, (commercial) $40. Each additional word is 50 cents).
• Additionally, members can call upon the SAE staff for help when emergencies or other problems arise.

The club will receive donations of money or goods for research and allocate these to worthy projects. Gifts by donors are tax deductible.

SAE Membership Categories

• Regular ($50 individual, $80 couple): Benefits include a subscription to the *South American Explorer*, the quarterly journal of the club, discounts on items in our catalog, a laminated rabid-bat-spittle-proof membership card, use of our information and trip planning services, storage for equipment and supplies at the Lima and Quito lubhouses, and much more. A complete list of membership services is available upon request.
• Contributing ($80): Contributing Members, as the name indicates, contribute immeasurably to the general cheer and goodwill of their club. In addition, they receive a free t-shirt.
• Supporting ($150): As the name implies, these Members are virtual pillars, generously supporting their club in its heroic efforts. Our honored Supporting Members receive a free t-shirt. And, because we know that Supporting Members always welcome a thoughtful token of our appreciation, we offer these discerning individuals a book from the catalog. Finally, a Supporting Member may also bestow two free gift subscriptions to the *South American Explorer* at any time during the period of their Membership.

• Life ($750): Our most worthy Life Members receive all the benefits of club Membership during their mortal tour of this planet. These esteemed Life Members are encouraged to choose any one of the large selection of items from our catalog. As a final gesture of gratitude, Life Members will be sent a complete set of South American Explorers still in print, and ten free gift subscriptions upon request.

• Afterlife ($7,500): As an Afterlife Member you will, of course, receive all the benefits bestowed upon Regular, Contributing, Supporting, and Life Members. In addition, when you pass into the realm beyond, you will face eternity with serenity, assured of your club's perpetual gratitude. You will know the true meaning of immortality as you return each year to preside at the annual club bacchanal held in your honor. Imagine the envy of your fellow spirits when they witness this outpouring of affection and devotion to your revered memory, a blessed dividend of immortality that might have been theirs had they but followed your sublime example and shown but a mote of your greatness of heart during their brief and pointless jigs upon the stage of life.

Rough Writer's Guidelines for the *South American Explorer*

If you're a famous, frequently published writer commanding tens of thousands of dollars for your breathless prose, calmly disregard the following. On the other hand, if you're a humble quill-pusher like the rest of us, peruse these not necessarily hard-and-fast guidelines.

Generally we like pieces that run about 3-5,000 words.

Even wretched and awful submissions are greeted with cries of joy and read in the most favorable light if they arrive on an IBM-compatible diskette. Preferably in WordPerfect 6.1. However we can read any IBM-compatible word-processing program. Please put your diskette in a protective mailer. If mailing from abroad, inscribe "Do Not X-Ray" on the package. Yes, we know it's not a photographic plate, but do it anyway.

The inclusion of dramatic photographs in focus is appreciated. Ideally we like color or black-and- white glossy photographs. If you send copyrighted slides, include a release so we can have them made into prints. Please label (your name and address) and caption all photos and slides. Also include biographical info on yourself, and a sketch map (it can be rough, we'll redraw it anyway) where appropriate.

Content and style? Ay, there's the rub. Need we say the article should be readable. This is a magazine, after all. Style helps. Lengthy extracts from a dreary diary don't hack it. "Got up at 7:00, breakfast ham & eggs, boat in at 7:30, blah, blah." No Inca trail articles unless they're fantastic. Personal accounts fine, provided they reveal the wonderful and fascinating you. Best of all are articles by knowledgeable authors about their specialty.

To get a better idea of what we want, read Mark Mardon's *In Search of Elusive Metaphors: The Art of Travel Writing*.

Remuneration? Ah yes, well…Best of all, there's vanity indulged. Then too, the Club pays, albeit reluctantly, a munificent (if you happen to live in Bangladesh) $50, and even sweetens the deal by conferring a one-year membership, or extending your existing membership one year. You also get any amount (within reason) of free magazines featuring your article, a free T-shirt (we choose the color), and if you visit us briefly in Ithaca, we will treat you to a sumptuous, though modest, meal at a local beanery.

Boot up and write on.

Categories: Nonfiction—Associations—Conservation—Ecology—Nature—Travel

CONTACT: Don Montague, Editor
Material: All
126 Indian Creek Rd.
Ithaca NY 14850
Phone: 607-277-0488
Fax: 800-274-0568
E-mail: explorer@saexplorers.org (digital format is preferred)
Website: www.saexplorers.org

South Florida History

South Florida History

Purpose of the Magazine

To engage readers in stories about the history of South Florida and the Caribbean in a manner that is both educational and entertaining and is illustrated with both historic and contemporary images.

History

The Historical Museum of Southern Florida began publication of the magazine in 1974. In 1988, the name was changed to *South Florida History Magazine*, and in 2000 it became *South Florida History*.

Presentation Style

Articles should be suitable for general audiences with interest—but not necessarily with a great deal of background—in our region's history. The editors strive for variety and balance so that each issue contains at least one article of interest to each reader.

Style Authority

The Associated Press Stylebook and Libel Manual should be consulted on matters of style as this is the guide used by the editors of the magazine. Webster's first choice is used when multiple spellings of a word are acceptable. Exceptions are made when the presentation form warrants.

Content

Articles should recall, retell and explore historic events, people, places and themes pertaining to southern Florida and the Caribbean. The magazine covers Florida south of Lake Okeechobee, coast to coast, and all countries in the Caribbean. Articles are generally presented as non-annotated narratives in third person or first person, and can include quotations from historic records, diaries and other documents. Exceptions are made when material warrants. Bibliographies and footnotes will not be published.

Book reviews are also accepted. Reviews are encouraged for publications relating to southern Florida and the Caribbean. It is suggested that potential reviewers inquire about a specific book they would like to cover to see if a review is already in the works.

Photographs

Photographic illustration is very important in *South Florida History*; authors are encouraged to identify available accompanying visual material whenever possible and provide copies of such images when submitting manuscripts. Original documents and photographs that must be returned to their owners will be copied by the Historical Museum of Southern Florida and handled according to the highest level of curatorial standards. Materials will be returned via certified delivery systems after publication of the magazine.

Submission of Articles and Book Reviews

• Articles should be 2,500 to 5,000 words, and book reviews should be approximately 300 words in length. Submissions may be edited for clarity or to meet space requirements.

• Articles may be submitted via e-mail or on a disk or cd (IBM or Macintosh), saved in a word processing format. Label disk/cd with author's name and article's title.

• Photographs and other illustrative materials, if identified, should be submitted with the manuscript (copies acceptable). Scanned photographs and images may be sent electronically as well, but prints will be required upon acceptance of the article for production.

• A brief biographical sketch of the author should accompany the article.

• Articles related to the published editorial calendar must be submitted prior to the submission deadline; any other articles may be submitted at any time.

• All articles are subject to review by *South Florida History* editorial staff. Submission of an article does not guarantee publication. Articles will be accepted based on appropriateness of subject and quality of writing.

The editorial staff of *South Florida History* strives to respond in a timely fashion to writers who have submitted manuscripts. When we receive your article we will notify you that it is under consideration for publication. If acceptable, the article becomes part of the pool of material undergoing production steps to ready them for publication. Articles are pulled from the pool and assigned to specific issues on an ongoing basis. The editors at the Historical Museum of Southern Florida maintain the right for flexibility in deciding publication dates as geographical, thematic and seasonal concerns are considered.

Due to our non-profit status, we cannot pay our contributors, but the Historical Museum of Southern Florida will send you our most sincere appreciation and ten (10) copies of the magazine.

Standards

The editorial staff of *South Florida History* strives for the highest level of accuracy and fairness possible when presenting the past. Standard journalistic and research practices and principles should be adhered to at all times.

The Historical Museum of Southern Florida disclaims any responsibility for errors in factual material or statements of opinions expressed by contributors.

A Word to Contributors

You are the lifeblood of *South Florida History*. Your time, energy and thoughtfulness in submitting a contribution are sincerely appreciated as we strive to spread interest in and understanding of our region's rich past.

Thank you.

Editor, *South Florida History*

Categories: Nonfiction—African-American—Arts—Asian-American—Biography—Conservation—Culture—Hispanic—History—Jewish Interest—Lifestyle—Multicultural—Native American—Regional—Ethnic

CONTACT: Editor
Material: Any
Historical Museum of Southern Florida
101 W. Flagler Street
Miami FL 33130
Phone: 305-375-1492
Fax: 305-375-1609
E-mail: publications@historical-museum.org
Website: www.historical-museum.org

Southern Accents

No formal guidelines.
Categories: Antiques—Architecture—Arts—Book Reviews

CONTACT: Julie Gillis, Managing Editor
Material: All
Southern Progress Corp., 2100 Lakeshore Dr.
Birmingham AL 35209
Phone: 205-445-6000

The Southern Aviator

Please refer to *General Aviation News*.

The Southern California Anthology
University of Southern California

We read all fiction and poetry that comes to us, whether traditional or non-traditional, and publish a variety of forms and styles. The *Southern California Anthology* selects manuscripts for publication using literary merit as the sole criteria.

All manuscripts should be typed. Poetry should be single-spaced within stanzas; double-spaced between stanzas.

Fiction submissions and interviews should be no longer than twenty-five pages. Please limit prose submissions to one.

Please limit poetry submissions to no more than five. Place only one poem per page.

We appreciate cover letters. They give us not only a sense of the writer, but are also helpful if they include sufficient information for the editors to compose a brief biography in the event of acceptance.

Categories: Fiction—Poetry—Short Stories

CONTACT: Dr. James Ragan
Material: All
Master of Professional Writing Program
University of Southern California
WPH 404
Los Angeles, CA 90089-4034
Phone: 213-740-3252
Fax: 213-740-5775
E-mail: mpw@usc.edu
Website: www.usc.edu/dept/LAS/mpw

SHR *Southern Humanities Review*

Southern Humanities Review
Auburn University

Always include a self-addressed stamped envelope, or a self-addressed envelope with international reply coupons, even for a reply only. Queries are welcome. Simultaneous submissions are NOT accepted. E-mail submissions are NOT accepted. Submit poetry, fiction, and essays separately, as different editors will consider them. Do not submit a second manuscript if we already have one from you under consideration. With the exception of translations, we do not consider material that has been published elsewhere. In prose submissions use one-inch margins and double line spacing. Prepare manuscripts using the MLA Handbook. Use at least a 10-pt. font. If you use an ink printer, make sure the print is dark. Payment is two contributors' copies; copyright reverts to author upon publication. Response time usually varies from two weeks to three months, depending on the editors' other responsibilities, but might be a bit slower in summer. Please do not assume from our name that we're interested in Southern literature or research topics only; any setting or subject matter is acceptable, but do avoid excessive vulgarity, profanity, and jargon (medical or military, for example).

Poetry Send three to five poems at a time. It is wise to submit no more than four times per year unless the editors ask to see more of your work. We rarely print a poem longer than two pages. Translations are encouraged, but please include the original AND written permission from the copyright holder for you to publish a translation.

Fiction Send only one story per submission. Manuscripts should be between 3,500 and 15,000 words, double-spaced. It is wise to submit no more than four times per year unless the editors ask to see more of your work. Translations are encouraged, but please include the original AND written permission from the copyright holder for you to publish a translation.

Essays Send only one essay per submission. Manuscripts should be between 3,500 and 15,000 words, double-spaced (including notes). Be sure to direct your essay to a general humanities audience, avoiding specialist jargon. Translations are encouraged, but please include the original AND written permission from the copyright holder for you to publish a translation.

Book Reviews The review should be no more than 1200 words in length. About two thirds of the review should be devoted to a summary of the content of the book, and about one third to your evaluation. Please pay particular attention to the forms illustrated below for the heading and closing of your review. Do not use footnotes or cite page numbers in your review.

A SAMPLE REVIEW HEADING:
Your Name
Your Address
Contemporary Literary Theory. Edited by G. Douglas Atkins and Laura Morrow. Amherst: University of Massachusetts Press, 1989. xiv + 249 pp. $40.00, cloth; $12.95, paper.

(If the price of the book is not listed, please use the abbreviation "Npl." as follows: xiv + 249 pp. Npl. For non-university presses in unfamiliar cities use the city and state as follows: Port Townsend, Washington: Copper Canyon Press, 1994.)

A SAMPLE REVIEW ENDING:
Your University or Your City and State   Your Name
                                  (Please note italics here.)

Categories: Fiction—Nonfiction—Arts—History—Literature—Music—Poetry—Short Stories—Criticism—Humanities—Philosophy

CONTACT: Editors
Material: All
9088 Haley Center
Auburn University, AL 36849-5202
Phone: 334-844-9088
Fax: 334-844-9027
E-mail: shrengl@auburn.edu
Website: www.auburn.edu

Southern Living

Thank you for your interest in submitting articles to *Southern Living*. However, with the exception of our Southern Journal column, the articles and photography are produced by members of our staff.

For Southern Journal, we don't have a rigid set of guidelines; however, there are some characteristics of a typical Journal that you might find interesting. Above all, it must be Southern. We need comments on life in this region—written from the standpoint of a person who is intimately familiar with this part of the world. It's personal, almost always involving something that happened to the writer or someone he or she knows very well. We take special note of stories that are contemporary in their point of view.

We require that the piece be original and not published. We need about 600 words, typed and double spaced. The writing must have an essay quality—as opposed to a reporting, interpretive, or editorial approach. Finally, it must be of exceptionally high quality.

We can't guarantee acceptance of any piece for publication, but if we do decide to use it, we require complete ownership rights. If interested, send your manuscript to the address below. If we are interested, we will contact you directly.

Again, thanks for considering *Southern Living*. Good luck in placing your work.

Categories: Nonfiction—Book Reviews—Cooking—Diet/Nutrition—Food/Drink—Gardening—Regional—Travel—Home

CONTACT: Sara Askew Jones, Associate Features Editor
Material: All
2100 Lakeshore Dr.
Birmingham AL 35209
Phone: 205-445-6000

Southern Lumberman:
The Sawmill Magazine

The Magazine: SOUTHERN LUMBERMAN is The Sawmill Magazine and is edited for owners and managers of sawmills in North America. Articles explore sawmill equipment and management issues. Sawmill operations include primary breakdown of logs, production of lumber, dimension parts, treated wood, chips, pallets and boxes, and other wood by-products. Subjects featured include marketing, economics, kiln-drying, computerization, and processing of products.

In its 124th year, the magazine targets an average reader who is the owner or manager of a small- to medium-sized sawmill operation. Circulation is 15,000 and growing. An average issue presently is 48 pages. Regular features are: calendar, industry news, dateline news, new products, lumber market trends, species of the month, and value added opportunities. We also include at least one theme article each month, frequently an equipment-themed piece. Two features, Lumbermen and Installations, are particularly suitable for freelance writers' queries and submissions.

What We Want: We're interested primarily in articles about sawmill operations across the country—we're strongest east of the Mississippi, but we are a national publication. Articles might include: sawmill operations (or who is doing what better) and how-to or technical pieces dealing with the lumber industry. Sawmill operation stories should be about those that are doing something different—better marketing, venturing into a new market, installing new facilities to change or improve production, and so forth.

Sawmill operation stories should include information about the mill's history, the owner/manager's insights into changes in the industry, and of course what it is that is being done that is different/better than other mills. We're always interested in stories about sawmills branching out into value-added opportunities or success stories tied to installation of a particular piece or pieces of equipment. Stories should be 500-900 words long and accompanied by publication quality color photographs.

To Query or Not: We welcome queries or manuscripts. A query should describe author's qualifications, the article's focus and probable length, and describe pictures that will accompany the article. Writers will find the editor most helpful in giving direction to an article of interest to SOUTHERN LUMBERMAN's readers.

Payment: Payment, upon publication, is for first North American serial rights—$100-$150 for most stories. Color images to accompany stories are included in this price. Other color photographs may be considered for purchase (payment on publication) depending on subject matter (coverage of national lumber association meetings, for example) at $10 each. Slides and transparencies of attractive lumber-related scenes (woods, logging, sawmills, etc.), preferably tied to some event, are also welcome on a submission basis (enclose SASE for return). Payment is negotiable.

Don't Forget: All manuscripts should include the writer's phone number so the editor can contact the writer with whatever questions arise.

Categories: Sawmills

CONTACT: Nanci P. Gregg, Managing Editor
Material: All
PO Box 681629
Franklin TN 37068-1629
Phone: 615-791-1961
Fax: 615-591-1035
E-mail: ngregg@southernlumberman.com
Website: www.southernlumberman.com

The Southern Review
Louisiana State University

The Southern Review publishes fiction, poetry, critical essays, interviews, book reviews, and excerpts from novels in progress, with emphasis on contemporary literature in the United States and abroad, and with special interest in southern culture and history. Poems and fiction are selected with careful attention to craftsmanship and technique and to the seriousness of the subject matter. Although willing to publish experimental writing that appears to have a valid artistic purpose, *The Southern Review* avoids extremism and sensationalism. Critical essays and book reviews exhibit a thoughtful and sometimes severe awareness of the necessity of literary standards in our time.

Minimum rates to contributors are twelve dollars a printed page for prose and twenty dollars a page for poetry. Payment is made on publication. Two complimentary copies of the issue in which the work appears are sent to each contributor; no reprints are available. Manuscripts must be typewritten, double-spaced, and accompanied by self-addressed, stamped envelopes with sufficient postage to cover return. We cannot accept e-mail submissions, nor can we respond to manuscripts unaccompanied by self-addressed, stamped envelopes, and manuscripts will not be returned without adequate return postage. Only previously unpublished works will be considered. Allow at least two months for editorial decisions.

Poetry lengths preferred are one to four pages; fiction, four to eight thousand words; essays, four to ten thousand words. All book reviews are on a commissioned basis. Do not send fillers, jokes, plays, feature articles, or artwork. Queries are not necessary. First American serial rights only are purchased. Manuscripts will not be considered during the months of June, July, and August.

Sample copies are $8.00 payable in advance. For style information, see *A Manual of Style*, published by the University of Chicago Press. Use a minimum of footnotes. Send, on a separate sheet, citations for quotations used in essays. *The Southern Review* and Louisiana State University do not assume responsibility for views expressed by contributors.

Categories: Fiction—Nonfiction—Interview—Literature—Poetry—Short Stories

CONTACT: The Editors
Material: All
43 Allen Hall, Louisiana State University
Baton Rouge LA 70803-5005
Phone: 225-578-5108
Fax: 225-578-5098
E-mail: bmacon@lsu.edu

Southern Traveler

Founded: January 1998
Frequency: Mailed bi-monthly, Jan./Feb. through Nov./Dec.
Circulation: 175,000. Mailed to AAA households in Arkansas, Louisiana and Mississippi
Readership: 350,000
Source: Mediamark Research, Inc., New York, NY / February 2000
AAA Southern Traveler features articles on regional, national and international travel opportunities. Area history, auto safety, highway and transportation news also are featured. The South is often the focus of travel articles. As the official publication for AAA members in Arkansas, Louisiana and Mississippi, we reach an audience that travels throughout the year. AAA, America's premier travel organization, serves more than 40 million members nationally.

The *Southern Traveler* magazine's goal is to provide members with a variety of useful information on travel, auto safety, and other topics that appeal to the motoring public. The magazine carries on average six articles per issue and buys 20-30 manuscripts per year.

How to contact us: Send queries rather than finished manuscripts. In addition, please send a list of credits or published clips when you query us for the first time. We will not take phone queries and prefer not to see a laundry list of story ideas. In general, we try to reply within four weeks of receipt. We will consider a previously published article if it appeared in a non-competing publication. Simultaneous queries are acceptable, but tell us the idea is being considered elsewhere.

Assignments: We work from an editorial schedule and assignments are usually made at least six months in advance. Sometimes the calendar is assigned by July for the following year. Usually purchase first North American rights. A story assignment is always made by letter. The writer signs an outline-agreement and returns one copy to the editor. We do not pay any expenses in conjunction with the article (travel expenses, phone bills, etc.). Payment for an article is made upon acceptance. Our rates range from $50 to $350. It helps to send photos/slides (color only) with manuscripts. While we do not pay for photos, we consider it in payment for the manuscript. To assist with fact-checking, please send copies of materials used to research the article.

Style: We use the AP Stylebook. Third-person voice usually works best, but in some cases first-person description is appropriate. A copy of a current magazine will be sent with assignment so our editing style can be observed. A story will not be drastically changed without discussing this with the writer. Send the manuscript on floppy disk, saved either in Microsoft Word 5.1 or a lower version, or as an ASCII text file. Always include hard copy with the disk.

Taboos: Humor, satire, fiction, poetry, cartoons. Technical and safety articles usually are written by staff. Departments (e.g. "Travel Treasures, Day Tours") also are written by staff.

Categories: Nonfiction—Associations—Automobiles—Consumer—Culture—History—Regional—Travel

CONTACT: Robin Jones, Editor
Material: All
12901 N. Forty Drive
St. Louis MO 63141
Phone: 314-523-7350
Fax: 314-523-6982
Website: www.ouraaa.com/traveler

Southwest Fly Fishing

Thanks for your interest in *Southwest Fly Fishing* magazine. To receive consideration for publication you should read and follow these guidelines closely.

ABOUT THE MAGAZINE

Southwest Fly Fishing magazine is a destination specific publication to be viewed as an inspiring, collectible reference of Southwest angling destinations. The staff at *Southwest Fly Fishing* takes pride in our editorial content. Our writing is refreshing, our photography, captivating. *Southwest Fly Fishing* is issued quarterly each Spring, Summer, Fall, and Winter.

FEATURE ARTICLES

Our goal is to give an inspiring and complete report on specific Southwest angling destinations. Angling destinations include both the famous and the lesser know waters, and include all species found in our diverse geographical region. If more than one species is found in any given water, writers should cover each species, as well as every season that water is fishable. In short, feature articles should be concise, and leave no holes. Our goal is to cover specific angling destinations as no other publication has done in the past. The best way to get a feel for what we want is to study one of our magazines.

Photography is very important. *Southwest Fly Fishing* has set high standards for all images used in our magazine. Writers have a much better chance of being published if articles are accompanied by stunning photography. We will not publish dead fish, poorly exposed or composed shots.

The area of coverage for our features includes Colorado, Utah, Nevada, New Mexico, Arizona, Texas, Central to Southern California, Mexico, and Central America.

Feature Article Requirements

• Provide practical traveling and angling information to specific destinations, including personal anecdotes

• Included should be pertinent angling history and thorough description of the fishery

• Current regulations for the fishery

• Detailed description of angling techniques, tackle and flies, and local perspectives

• Articles should be thorough and specific so as to sufficiently inform and give the angler confidence to effectively fish the presented water

• Included with each article should be any applicable hatch chart and detailed map of the coverage area

• Conservation issues and future considerations should be addressed

• Selection of 35mm (or larger) slides (captioned)

• Three popular flies of the fishery should be included for us to photograph, as well as a material list for each pattern.

• Feature article length should be 2,500 to 3,500 words

DEPARTMENTS

Most department material is staff-written. Exceptions are as follows:

Southwest Fly Tying

This department covers one Southwest fly pattern each issue. New, unusual and exciting patterns are encouraged, but we will also represent the time-proven standards. Flies for any Southwest species can be considered. Articles should include a little history and use of the fly, as well as step-by-step photos of the tying sequence, shot against a neutral-colored background. Two finished flies should accompany the article for photographic purposes.

Notes, News & Reviews

This department covers news events, and mini destinations (200 to 500 words). As with all material submitted, query first.

Conservation

Any conservation issue concerning the Southwest. Maximum length 850 words.

Exposure

Photo essay of 8 to 10 images depicting Southwest angling.

MANUSCRIPT SUBMISSIONS AND PAYMENTS

Initial contact with the editor by e-mail is preferred. A formal query letter, outlining the proposed article, should be sent to the editor before making a submission. A selection of slides MUST accompany the formal query. Unsolicited manuscripts must include a self-addressed, stamped envelope (S.A.S.E.) for their return. *Southwest Fly Fishing* is not responsible for submissions in transit to and from our editorial office.

Text and photos are purchased as a package. Manuscripts accepted without the appropriate photographic support will warrant less money for their use. *Southwest Fly Fishing* buys first North American serial publication rights. We reserve the option to edit all articles, however, we will make every effort to minimize editing to avoid changing the style or content of manuscripts.

All manuscripts should be submitted in typewritten form, double spaced. The author's name, address, phone number and manuscript word count should appear on the first page of the manuscript. A 3½" computer disk needs to be included, and your work saved in Microsoft Word, Word Perfect, ClarisWorks or AppleWorks.

Payment is made approximately one month prior to publication, and the pay rate varies with the length and completeness of the submission. Inclusion of high-quality slides has a major impact in determining the pay rate for any given article. Our pay rate is as follows:

• Feature Articles	$400 to $600
• Southwest Fly Tying	$250
• Notes, News & Reviews	$25 to $100
• Conservation	$25 to $100

PHOTO SUBMISSIONS, ARTWORK AND PAYMENTS

Southwest Fly Fishing usually buys text and photos as a package. There are exceptions, however, and additional photography may be purchased on occasion. Contributors must query first.

We accept 35mm (or larger) transparencies only. Slides should be shipped in a clear sleeve, with concise captions. The photographer's name and address should appear on each slide mount. Payment varies for size used and impact. Our pay rate is as follows:

• Cover	$500
• Exposure	$600
• Inside use	$25 to $300
• Illustrations & artwork	$25 to $300

Categories: Nonfiction—Conservation—Fishing—Nature—Photography—Recreation—Sports—Travel

CONTACT: Steve Probasco, Editor
Material: All
PO Box 708
Raymond WA 98577
Phone: 360-942-3589
E-mail: probasco@nwflyfishing.net

Southwest Review
Southern Methodist University

Published: Quarterly.

Subscriptions: 1 yr. $24; 2 yrs. $42; 3 yrs. $65; sample issue $6. VISA and Mastercard accepted on our secure web site. (Please add $6 per year for each subscription outside of the U.S.)

Begun in 1915 and with a circulation of approximately 1500, the *Southwest Review* is the fourth oldest, continuously published literary quarterly in the U.S. We try to discover new writers and publish them beside those of more established authors. All submissions should be typed neatly, on white paper. Manuscripts must be accompanied by a stamped, self-addressed envelope for reply, and will not be returned unless SASE includes sufficient postage. *SWR* prefers not to receive simultaneous, email, or fax submissions, and does not consider work that has been published previously. If you so choose to submit simultaneous submissions, we must be informed immediately if the work is accepted elsewhere. Manuscripts will not be accepted during the months of June, July, and August.

Our articles embrace almost every area of adult interest: contemporary affairs, history, folklore, fiction, poetry, literary criticism, art, music, and the theatre. Material should be presented in a fashion suited to a quarterly that is not journalistic and not terribly overloaded with academic apparatus or jargon. It should not be too specialized, after the manner of papers that appear in learned journals of different fields of study.

In each issue the *Southwest Review* publishes two or three stories, which must be of high literary quality. We have published fiction in widely varying styles. We prefer stories of character development, of psychological penetration, to those depending chiefly on plot. We have no specific requirements as to subject matter. Some of our stories have a southwestern background, but even more are not regional. We prefer, however, that stories not be too strongly regional if the region with which they deal is not our own.

The preferred length for articles and fiction is 3,500 to 7,000 words.

It is hard to describe *SWR*'s preference in poetry in a few words. We always suggest that potential contributors read several issues of the magazine to see for themselves what we like. But some things may be said: We demand very high quality in our poems; we accept both traditional and experimental writing; we place no arbitrary limits on length; we have no specific limitations as to theme.

The McGinnis-Ritchie Memorial award is given to the best works of fiction and non-fiction that appeared in the magazine in the previous year. The two awards consist of cash prizes of $500 each. Robert F. Ritchie, who died in 1997, was a long-time generous supporter. In 1960 he established the John H. McGinnis Memorial Award to honor the man who edited the Review from 1927 to 1943. With a bequest in his will, Mr. Ritchie enabled us to maintain the tradition of his generosity. Please note that manuscripts are submitted for publication, not for the prizes themselves.

The Elizabeth Matchett Stover Memorial award was established in 1978 by Jerry S. Stover of Dallas in memory of his mother, who was for many years a key member of the *Southwest Review*. The award consists of a $250 cash prize and is given to the author of the best poem or group of poems published in the magazine during the preceding year. Please note that manuscripts are submitted for publication, not for the prizes themselves.

Thanks to the generosity of Marilyn Klepak of Dallas, the *Southwest Review* gives an annual award of $1000 to a poem by a writer who has not yet published a first book. Ms. Klepak has endowed the prize in honor of her father, Morton Marr. Contestants may submit no more than six poems in a traditional form (e.g., sonnet, sestina, villanelle, rhymed stanzas, blank verse, et al.). A cover letter with name, address, and other relevant information may accompany the poems which must be printed without any identifying information. Contest entry fee is $5 per poem. Submissions will not be returned. Entry deadline is November 30, 2004. The poem (or poems) will be published in the *Southwest Review*.

The *SWR* is published quarterly. We make a nominal payment upon publication and send author three gratis copies of the issue in which the work appears.

Categories: Fiction—Nonfiction—Arts—Culture—Interview—Literature—Multicultural—Poetry—Essays

CONTACT: Submissions Editor
Material: All
Southern Methodist University
307 Fondren Library West
PO Box 750374
Dallas TX 75275-0374
Phone: 214-768-1037
Fax: 214-768-1408
E-mail: swr@mail.smu.edu
Website: www.southwestreview.org

Space and Time

We are currently reading, very selectively, for #94. Because of our cash flow situation, even if we love your stuff, we can't pay until just before publication.

Space & Time is a bi-annual magazine of science-fiction and fantasy. We publish supernatural horror, hard s-f, swords and sorcery, and our favorite: that-which-defies-categorization. If you're not sure your manuscript is right for us, send it in and let us decide.

For fiction, we prefer under 10,000 words; more than that has to be very good indeed. Poetry of any type is fine, as long as it falls within the sf/fantasy genre; strong narrative poems are welcome here. We're generating pretty much all the non-fiction we want right now, so hold off on that. Payment is 1 cent per word ($5.00 minimum) for First North American Serial Rights, with a non-exclusive option on subsidiary rights, plus two copies on publication and a 40% discount on additional copies. Normally we pay on acceptance; because of our current cash-flow problems, though, we probably can't issue checks until we're ready to start work on the issue for which you are scheduled.

Manuscripts must be typed double-spaced, with your full name and address in an upper corner of the first page. Legible photocopies are okay; also dot-matrix of near-letter quality with a dark ribbon. We prefer no simultaneous submissions.

We do not take electronic submissions at present, although if we accept your work we will ask if it is available in that form. You must include a self-addressed envelope with sufficient return postage (or IRCs outside of the U.S.), or use disposable manuscripts and a stamped business-size envelope for our response. Address fiction to Gerard Houarner (or any associate editor), and poetry to Linda D. Addison. Mixing poems and stories delays our response.

You needn't read our magazine before submitting material, but we're not about to discourage you from trying to psyche us out or ingratiate yourselves. We could use the sale, especially now. A sample issue is $5.00 plus $1.50 handling charge (Canada $2.00; all other countries $3.00). Order from: *Space & Time*, 138 West 70th Street (4B), New York NY 10023-4468. Outside U.S., please use U.S. postal money order or check payable against any U.S. bank.

Categories: Fiction—Fantasy—Horror—Science Fiction

CONTACT: Gerard Mouarner, Fiction Editor
Material: Fiction
CONTACT: Linda D. Addison, Poetry Editor
Material: Poetry
CONTACT: Faith L. Justice, Features Editor
Material: Nonfiction
Space & Time Publishing
138 West 70th Street, 4B
New York NY 10023-4468
Website: www.cith.org/space&time.html

Specialty Retail Report

Specialty Retail Report is a full-color, quarterly trade magazine that serves the specialty-retail industry. We're an established, quality publication with a strong and growing readership.

Our readers

Independent specialty-retail entrepreneurs (including temporary and seasonal retailers) selling from carts, kiosks and stores in malls and other shopping venues; mall management and developers; product entrepreneurs (manufacturers, distributors, turnkey companies).

Our editorial

Features (three to five per issue; 2,500 words and up, depending on subject): Topics include new products/product categories, market profiles, location opportunities/profiles, consumer trends. Recent features include "The Power of Color" (color trends), "A New Sense of Calm" (massage/spa products), "Shades of Cool" (sunglasses), "Show Time! 12 Top Gift Shows"; **Entrepreneur Profile** (two per issue; 1,800-2,000 words): The success stories of individual specialty-retail entrepreneurs; **Departments** (include Money Matters, Business Builders, Marketing Matters, Selling Points; three or four per issue; 1,200-1,500 words): Retail business strategies, management and how-to on topics such advertising, hiring, visual merchandising, purchasing. Recent articles include "Nine Secrets of Yellow Pages Ads," "Finding a Bank You Can Bank On" and "Merry Ideas for Great Holiday Sales."

Nearly all of our editorial is freelance-written. All of our features and Entrepreneur Profiles are by assignment only. We do buy reprints for Department articles.

Note to writers

Always query first, and include your bio or résumé with clips and/or links to your work online. We're an upbeat publication that speaks to a unique, knowledgeable audience, so please become familiar with SRR's scope and target readers before querying. Feel free to visit our Web site for more about us, and call or e-mail to request a sample copy of the magazine plus our "Writers' Guide to Formatting."

Categories: Business—Trade—Retail/Gifts

CONTACT: Gerard Mouarner, Fiction Editor
Material: Fiction
293 Washington Street
Norwell MA 02061
Phone: 800-936-6297 or 781-659-7675
Fax: 781-659-4394
E-mail: info@specialtyretail.com
Website: www.specialtyretail.com

SPECIALTY TRAVEL INDEX

Specialty Travel Index

Specialty Travel Index (STI) is the number one magazine and web site about worldwide adventure travel. Our readership is a combination of consumers and travel trade professionals (travel agents, etc). Our print circulation is 50,000 (45,000 travel agents, 5,000 consumers). The accompanying web site is mainly accessed by consumers and is receiving up to 30,000 hits a day.

The magazine is semi-annual, published in January (Spring/Summer issue) and August (Fall/Winter issue). The web site is updated frequently with home page articles on a weekly rotation. In addition to a directory-type listing of over 600 adventure tour operators, the magazine and web site run approximately 11 special-interest travel stories per issue.

Our editorial requirements are:

• Length—1,250 words
• Rate—$300 (payable upon receipt of completed manuscript)
• Lead time—Six months
• Web site use—Writers receive 10% of the Original Fee when story appears on the STI web site.

We consider both written queries (accompanied by clips and writer bio) plus finished manuscripts ON SPEC. ABSOLUTELY NO SUBMISSIONS BY PHONE OR FAX. Story may not be written by employee of tour operator being featured in the piece. STI will not accept articles that have been picked up by any major wire service (i.e. Copley, AP).

Stories should deal with special-interest, adventure-type travel—from soft adventures (cycling through French wine country) to daring exploits (an exploratory river-rafting run in Pakistan). A variety of styles work for us: first-person, descriptive, etc. In general, STI does not like articles written in the present tense.

Articles should have a lively immediacy, not just relate facts that readers might know already. Since the readership includes both travel agents and consumers, avoid using "you" in the articles (i.e "You'll walk through flower-filled meadows…"). Instead, say: "Travelers (or trekkers or participants) can walk through…"

For submission of materials, we require:

• Hard copy and 3.5" disk--IBM compatible (ASCII) or Word document sent via e-mail plus color transparencies or digital images (high-rez—at least 300 dpi). We pay $25 per contributor photo used.
• Upon assignment or acceptance of story, writers will receive a contract which must be signed and returned to *Specialty Travel Index*.
Categories: Nonfiction—Adventure—Culture—Travel—Specialty Travel

CONTACT: Submissions
Material: All
CONTACT: Risa Weinreb, Editor
Material: Any
PO Box 458
San Anselmo CA 94979-6458
Phone: 415-455-1643
Fax: 415-455-1648
E-mail: info@specialtytravel.com
Website: www.specialtytravel.com

Remember: Editors change jobs and publishers change addresses. It is wise to invest in a phone call for the current information before submitting.

Speedway Illustrated

Speedway Illustrated is a monthly, full-color magazine sold at newsstands and by subscription. It covers stock car racing exclusively. Our audience is deeply committed to the sport. Many own, drive or crew race cars. Typical readers attend 30 or more races per year. Therefore, stories we buy must be written for the relatively sophisticated.

Story Needs:
Study the magazine before attempting to write for us. We want the story behind the story in stock car racing, from backyard street stock garages to the biggest events in the sport. We buy interesting technical articles, offbeat features and shorts, interviews, personality pieces and issues-oriented features. Most of the stories we run are short. Most issues have no more than four full length features but carry many one- or two-page items. We buy dozens of photos that have one or two paragraphs of support copy, but very few 10-page articles.

Support Graphics:
A separate photo guideline sheet is available. In some cases, we can provide support photography. However, it's always wise to be sure that if we can't provide pictures, you can. If the story's about an active big-league racer, or if we can illustrate it with generic images, we can probably help. But if the story is about a weekend racer from your area, you must be able to supply quality support photography (snapshots won't do) or we can't publish it.

Rights:
We purchase first-time rights. Material purchased for the magazine may also be used on our internet site but without additional payment.

Credentials/Press Cards:
We do not issue credentials–only speedways can do that. We can, however, write to speedways requesting credentials for those working on stories and shorts for *Speedway Illustrated*.

Payment:
We pay on publication. Tech features pay most. Photos are paid separately. Payment varies with story quality, length, and interest value.

Method of Submission:
We prefer receiving work on computer disc with a hard copy backup, or via e-mail. If an SASE is included with a submission, we'll do our best to return your submission if we fail to accept it. However, we can take no responsibility for lost or damaged manuscripts, art, photography, etc. It's always best to include support photography with written submissions since judging is always based not only on the story but its support art as well.

Exclusivity:
We expect that all materials submitted to us are exclusive and have not been previously published. In some cases, we will publish material that has already been published or will be published elsewhere. If you are making a simultaneous submission here and elsewhere, please tell us.

Story Ideas:
The most important part of any story is the idea behind it. Our goal is to publish stories that are so interesting that people will buy the magazine to read them. Therefore, interest value—the story behind your story—is absolutely critical. We rarely call an author to offer a story idea. Editor Rob Sneddon prefers that you query story ideas either by e-mail, conventional mail or by fax. Phone queries are our least favorite method, since it's difficult to judge a person's writing ability based on a phone call. Interest value counts. If a short or feature is of high interest value to people deeply involved in stock car racing, it appeals to us.

Categories: Nonfiction—Automobiles—Recreation—Sports/Recreation

CONTACT: Karl Fredrickson, Technical Editor
Material: Technical Material, New Products
CONTACT: Rob Sneddon, Editor-in-Chief
Material: All other materials
Performance Media, LLC
107 Elm St.
Salisbury MA 01952
Phone: 978-465-9099
Fax: 978-465-9033
E-mail: rsneddon@speedwayillustrated.com

Spider
The Magazine for Children

About Us

For a sample issue of SPIDER, please send $5.00 to: SPIDER Sample Copy • PO Box 300 • Peru, IL 61354

NOTE: Sample copy requests from foreign countries must be accompanied by International Postal Reply Coupons (IRCs) valued at US $5.00. Please do NOT send a check or money order.

In January 1994, Cricket Magazine Group of Carus Publishing Company launched SPIDER, a magazine for children ages 6 to 9. SPIDER publishes original stories, poems, and articles written by the world's best children's authors. Occasionally, SPIDER publishes reprints of high-quality selections. SPIDER is full color, 8" x 10", with 34 pages and a 4-page activity pullout. It is staple bound. We hope that the following information will be useful to prospective contributors.

Published: 12 months a year

Price: $35.97 for 1-year subscription (12 issues)

Categories

Fiction: realistic fiction, easy-to-read stories, humorous tales, fantasy, folk and fairy tales, science fiction, fables, myths.

Nonfiction: nature, animals, science, technology, environment, foreign culture, history.

(A bibliography is required for all nonfiction articles, and copies of research material will be required for all accepted articles. Be prepared to send other backup materials and photo references—where applicable—upon request.)

Poetry: serious, humorous, nonsense rhymes.

Other: recipes, crafts, puzzles, games, brainteasers, math and word activities

Length

Stories: 300 to 1,000 words. Poems: not longer than 20 lines

Articles: 300 to 800 words

Puzzles/Activities/Games: 1 to 4 pages. An exact word count should be noted on each manuscript submitted. Word count includes every word, but does not include the title of the manuscript or the author's name.

Rates

Stories and articles up to 25¢ per word (1,000 words maximum)

Poems up to $3.00 per line

Payment upon publication

Themes

There is no theme list for upcoming issues. Submissions on all appropriate topics will be considered at any time during the year.

Comments

SPIDER would like to reach as many children's authors and artists as possible for original contributions, but our standards are very high and we will accept only top-quality material. PLEASE DO NOT QUERY FIRST. SPIDER will consider any manuscripts or art samples sent on speculation and accompanied by a self-addressed, stamped envelope. For art samples, it is especially helpful to see pieces showing children, animals, action scenes, and several scenes from a narrative showing a character in different situations. SPIDER prefers to see tear sheets or photo prints/photocopies of art. If you must send original art as part of a portfolio, package it carefully and insure the package. SPIDER will also consider submissions of photography, either in the form of photo essays or as illustrations for specific nonfiction articles. Photographs should accompany the manuscript. Color photography is preferred, but black-and-white submissions will be considered depending on subject matter. Photocopies or prints may be submitted with the manuscript, but original transparencies for color or good quality black-and-white prints (preferably glossy finish) must be available upon acceptance. Please allow 12 weeks to receive a reply to submissions.

SPIDER normally purchases the following rights: For stories and poems previously unpublished, SPIDER purchases all rights. Payment is made upon publication.

For stories and poems previously published, SPIDER purchases second North American publication rights. Fees vary, but are generally less than fees for first publication rights. Payment is made upon publication. Same applies to accompanying art.

For recurring features, SPIDER purchases the material outright. The work becomes the property of SPIDER and is copyrighted in the name of Carus Publishing Company. A flat fee per feature is usually negotiated. Payment is made upon publication.

For commissioned artwork, SPIDER purchases all rights plus promotional rights (promotions, advertising, or in any other form not offered for sale to the general public without payment of an additional fee) subject to the terms outlined below.

(a) Physical art remains the property of the illustrator.

(b) Payment is made within 45 days of acceptance.

(c) Illustrator may use artwork for self promotion.

Categories: Fiction—Nonfiction—Animals—Children—Crafts/Hobbies—Culture—Environment—Fantasy—Games—History—Humor—Nature—Poetry—Science—Technology—Puzzles

CONTACT: Submissions Editor
Material: Manuscripts
CONTACT: Sue Beck, Art Director
Material: Art Samples
CONTACT: Mary Ann Hocking, Permissions Coordinator
Material: Questions about rights
Spider Magazine
PO Box 300
Peru IL 61354
Website: www.cricketmag.com

Spinning Jenny

Spinning Jenny is an open forum for poetry, fiction, and drama. We are pleased to consider experimental writing and work by unpublished authors. However, writers are strongly encouraged to review a recent issue of the magazine before submitting their work.

Please send up to six poems or ten pages of fiction or drama for consideration. We prefer to receive no more than three submissions per writer per year, and generally cannot reply to more. We do not consider simultaneous submissions or material that has been previously published in any format. Note that we are not considering full-length manuscripts for book publication at this time.

Submissions and correspondence may be sent via post or email (see below). Postal submissions must include a self-addressed stamped envelope if a reply is desired; we will not reply to postal submissions via email.

We accept submissions all year and make every effort to respond to all correspondence within twelve weeks. Because of the volume of mail we receive, we regret that it is not possible for us to provide comments on returned submissions, nor can we provide critiques. We cannot be responsible for the loss or return of unsolicited pieces.

Spinning Jenny does not charge reading fees. Payment to authors is made in complimentary contributor copies. The magazine is copyrighted; rights to pieces revert to the authors upon publication.

E-mail Submissions

We cannot accept submissions that are sent as attachments, so please include your work in the body of an email.

Categories: Fiction—Drama—Poetry

CONTACT: The Editor
Material: All
c/o Black Dress Press
PO Box 1373
New York NY 10276
E-mail: submissions@blackdresspress.com

Spin-Off

Thank you for requesting contributor's guidelines from *Spin-Off* magazine.

Spin-Off is a quarterly magazine devoted to the interests of handspinners at all skill levels.

Informative articles in each issue aim to encourage the novice, challenge the expert, and increase every spinner's working knowledge of this ancient and complex craft. If you are not already familiar with the style and tone of the magazine, please read a few issues before submitting a proposal. We review both proposals and full manuscripts. If you'd like to get our thoughts before you start, please write us a letter and tell us about your project or idea.

• If you are not a spinner, it will be difficult for you to write effectively for this magazine.

• If you are a spinner whose idea interests us, but you're an inexperienced writer, we will work with you on presenting your thoughts.

• Your projects and/or samples must contain handspun yarns as an essential component; commercial yarns may be used only in supporting roles.

• *Spin-Off* is many things—as a contributor think of it as a forum where you can share your experiences and knowledge with your community. Consider how your contribution will serve the reader.

Articles in a typical issue may include the following subjects.
• Spinning and preparation techniques
• Tools for spinning and preparing fibers
• Information on fibers: how to choose them, how to use them
• Ideas for using handspun yarn in a variety of techniques (knitting, weaving, rug hooking, lace—anything spinners can think of)
• Profiles of people who spin: why and how
• A gallery of contemporary work, complete with instructions or just as inspiration
• Tips on blending fibers
• The history and/or cultural role of spinning
• Something a little bit surprising
• Methods of dyeing, with natural and chemical dyes
New approaches to familiar topics are welcome.

Technical matters

You should display a thorough command of your topic—technical accuracy is a must. Make your information accessible to the reader. Strive for a personal and informal style of presentation. We prefer double-spaced computer-generated manuscripts presented both as hard copy and disk, but we read everything that's legible.

If you include references to other published sources or if your idea is based on or was inspired by someone else's work, please provide a complete bibliography. You can photocopy the title and copyright pages of each book for us, or make a list. For a book, we need full title and subtitle, complete names of author(s), publisher's name, place of publication, date of publication, and pertinent page numbers. For a magazine article, we need full title and subtitle, complete names of author(s), magazine title, volume number, issue number, and pertinent page numbers.

We reserve the right to edit material as necessary to fit the magazine's style and available space.

Submitting manuscripts or ideas

If you have already written an article, enclose a copy of the manuscript, supportive photos or drawings, and a brief personal biography. If you are at the idea stage, send a detailed proposal of your subject, with any sketches or photos you have. Clear snapshots are always useful. If you send the actual handspun item(s), we like to see them but may need to keep them for longer than you'd wish. Keep a copy of everything you send. Please include your name, address, e-mail address, and telephone and fax numbers in your cover letter.

Rights, scheduling, and payment

We purchase first North American serial rights, paid upon publication, and we give byline credit.

We occasionally arrange to reprint an article that has appeared in a local or regional publication.

You retain all other rights to your material.

We schedule articles several issues in advance, and we'll let you know the issue your article is scheduled for as soon as we know. Before we go to press, we will send you a copy of your edited article for review. About a month before the publication date, we'll send you an Author Agreement form to sign.

Payment for articles is $50 per published page, based on the edited version. If you provide images, we pay you $10 per published photograph.

Deadlines

Spin-Off is published four times a year, in March, June, September, and December.

Once we have scheduled your article, we will contact you to make sure that the deadlines for the completed manuscript, projects, and photography are agreeable to you.

Format

Ideally, your article will be computer generated, double spaced, and printed on 8½" x 11" white paper. Please include hard copy and a disk labeled with. the program you used to create the file.

Titles, headings, and subheadings, if appropriate, should be included in your article.

Captions for photos, with all people clearly identified, are very useful.

Simultaneous submissions

Simultaneous submissions are generally not acceptable. Please tell us if you are submitting your material elsewhere.

Length

Length depends on the subject; most articles contain between 200 to 2,700 words.

Visuals

Good, solid visual information is an important feature of *Spin-Off*. If you can provide clear photos or drawings, we may be able to use them directly; even if we choose not to use them, they will help us produce finished artwork. Snapshots and sketches are wonderful resources. Feel free to send us several versions.

Photographs: Please send color transparencies (slides) or color prints for your article.

Photographs must be sharp and clear, with good contrast, clear focus, and a simple background.

Make sure to include the photographer's name with the image.

Put captions on a separate sheet of paper, with a sticky note on the back of each photo number-coded to the caption list. Include your name on each photo or slide. Do not write on the back of any photograph. Sticky notes or taped strips of paper will not harm the image. All photographs will be returned to you.

In many instances, we photograph items, materials, and tools here. We'll schedule photography sessions and then ask you to send the objects. We will usually need to have them on hand for between four and twelve weeks, although we will do our best to get them back to you as quickly as possible. If you need an item at a particular time, call us before shipping it to make special arrangements.

Drawings and diagrams should be created in black ink on white paper; use white paper with blue graph lines if the grid is helpful. We nearly always re-render drawings here to be sure they will reproduce consistently. Any type of sketch is helpful, even if it's not in the ideal format.

Please provide any necessary labels, captions, or explanations.

Swatches, yarn, and fiber samples should be included whenever possible.

Swatches should be a minimum of 4" x 4" (10 x 10 cm), and yarn samples at least two yards (2m) long.

Remember: Handspun yarns should be the critical part of your samples.

Please enclose a self-addressed, stamped envelope to return your materials.

Receipt of your submission will be promptly acknowledged with a postcard that lists everything we received.

You may also email your submission to SpinOff@ Interweave.com. Visuals can be submitted electronically as jpeg, tiff, or GIF files. Expect a response to your submission within two months.

Please call us if you have any questions about the submission process or the status of your submission at (970) 669-7672. Thank you for your interest in contributing to *Spin-Off.*

We look forward to hearing from you.

Categories: Nonfiction—Crafts—Hobbies

CONTACT: Amy C. Clarke, Editor
Material: All
Interweave Press
201 East Fourth St.
Loveland CO 80537-5655
Phone: 970-669-7672
E-mail: SpinOff@interweave.com
Website: www.interweave.com

Spoon River Poetry Review

The Spoon River Poetry Review is a journal of fine poetry from both established and emerging poets from the United States and around the world (in translation). Its publication base is located in the heart of the midwest but its soul aspires toward something more transcendent, having, like Borges' circular book, everywhere for its center and nowhere for its circumference. Each issue features a selected Ilinois poet alongside others from around the nation and the world. In both open and closed forms, from the traditional to the avant-garde, the journal publishes poems written on the edge, in language that takes risks. The journal has been published without a break since 1974 and features review articles that engage some of the most compelling poetry you'll read.

The Spoon River Poetry Review is published twice a year by the Spoon River Poetry Association. The editors read submissions of fine poetry from all over the nation and the world from September 1 to May 1 each year. Manuscripts postmarked between May 1 and September 1 are returned unread. Send 3-5 poems to the address below. Submissions to *The Spoon River Poetry Review* Illinois Poet feature should contain 12-18 pages of mostly unpublished poems by poets who have an Illinois connection. Reviews of contemporary poetry and poetic theory should address texts and issues in a balanced and intelligent way. All submissions should be accompanied by a SASE (self-addressed stamped envelope).

Categories: Poetry

CONTACT: Dr. Lucia Getsi
Material: All
4240 English Dept., Illinois State University
Normal, IL 61790-4240
Website: www.litline.org/Spoon/

> *Remember: Editors change jobs and publishers change addresses. It is wise to invest in a phone call for the current information before submitting.*

Sport Fishing Magazine

BACKGROUND: *Sport Fishing* is geared to serious saltwater fishing around North America. That means bluewater, reefs, inlets and inshore (bays, flats and backcountry). It's published nine times per year (monthly January-June; bimonthly July-December). Our readers: several-hundred thousand (over 130,000 paid circ nationally) are generally well-educated and quite affluent. Nearly all are men who own boats, often both a large offshore boat and skiff as well.

EDITORIAL CONTENT: Material in *Sport Fishing* should provide useful information about saltwater fishing which is (1) new/fresh/different; (2) specific/in-depth and (3) accurate. Concepts behind all queries should meet these criteria. Please don't submit an idea which has been written about by us and/or similar publications. FIND A FRESH IDEA OR A FRESH ANGLE TO AN OLD IDEA; like most publications, we too are looking for subjects that will have our readers saying, "I never knew that!" Examples of material that could be of interest: a new, effective technique for a species or type of fishing that has wide applicability; an area recently opened up to sport fishing; or a new look at conservation concerns regarding a particular fishery or species/group. As with any magazine, our very specific needs are best understood by studying recent issues.

FEATURES: We strive for a mix of genres including fishing how-to, where-to and conservation. Remember that our readers are not beginners; they're seeking to advance their knowledge, not rehash basic saltwater fishing. We cannot use material related to pier/jetty/surf fishing; a boat must be involved if an idea is to work for *Sport Fishing.*

DEPARTMENTS: We're always looking for good material for several departments, particularly Sportfishing News, Rigging and Techniques and Fish Tales. Unlike short items that fit the format of the first two departments, Fish Tales can be 800 to 1,200 words. Except for the humorous Fish Tales (for which a cartoonist draws art), these columns are illustrated. Clear photos or even a good hand sketch from you will do; we'll have it professionally drawn for publication.

QUERIES & SUBMISSIONS: We'll look at over-the-transom submissions, but your efforts are much more likely to bear fruit if you query us first. First choice is e-mail, but we'll accept queries sent via fax or (with SASE) via post. They should be directed to the attention of Jason Cannon. He'll will pass along queries to the appropriate editor. "Laundry list" written queries are a welcome initial step. If a query warrants a speculative submission, then communication between editor and writer becomes the key to making things work. The editor will send a feature proposal to reiterate exactly what we expect in terms of substance, slant, style, length, sidebars, maps/charts and of course deadlines and request a written/emailed response. Most *Sport Fishing* editors request some sort of outline from the writer. Generally, this step is an invaluable way to (1) make sure the writer doesn't waste his/her time on something not right for us and (2) in general maintain close communication between writer and editor to make sure what the writer thinks the editor wants is in fact what the editor really wants. Often the outline will be reworked; so when the writer actually begins writing the feature he'll be on the right track. Finally, if questions develop as you work, give the editor a call to discuss it. We welcome the opportunity to work with new/unestablished writers who know their stuff—and how to say it.

SUBMITTING FEATURES/DEPARTMENTS: Most features, after editing as necessary, run 1,500 to 2,500 words including sidebars; rarely longer. Payment (see below) is for edited length. Please try to keep length of your features under 3,000 words; avoid submitting rambling 8,000-word manuscripts. If extensive rewriting is necessary, we like to work with the writer to resubmit the feature rewritten to meet our needs. However, again, writer-editor communication before and during the time the feature's written should minimize the chances of any major rewrites.

TIPS FOR *Sport Fishing* CONTRIBUTORS:

1. Meet or beat deadline dates. We like to work regularly with writers we can count on. Also that gives us time to ask you to rewrite if necessary.

2. Send photos. They may be yours or those of other photographers (remember: photo payment is additional to payment for manuscript. Separate photo guidelines are available upon request).

3. Quotes the experts. When possible, interviewing one or more professionals (skippers, mates, tournament experts or the like gives a subject great credibility. Also, wherever appropriate, contact fishery managers/biologists regarding status of species/fisheries. (Often they can provide tables, graphs, charts, etc. to help illustrate a topic.

4. Balance information with readability. Anecdotes can impart information while lending human interest. These are safest in third person but there are times when first-person narrative, if not overdone, is useful. Avoid talking down to our informed readership, but also avoid sounding ponderous or using $10 words when 5-cents' worth says it clearly.

5. Include sidebars where appropriate. In any feature that has to do with a destination include information on travel, lodging, charters/guides etc. We also like to see a seasonal availability chart for species (a hand sketch is acceptable). See recent issues for examples of required format. If a feature has to do with a genre of product, include a sidebar listing manufacturers.

FORMAT FOR SUBMISSIONS: These days, it's generally unnecessary to bother with hardcopy or floppy disks; simply email your text as Word, ASCII or text files. Of course you need to make sure your header contains your address (email, post), phone and social security numbers. Send maps, illustrations, charts/diagrams as well as photos separately.

PAYMENT: Payment is initated once the manuscript has been reviewed for acceptability. All features and columns are submitted on speculation. For features we pay $500. You'll be paid $75 to $300 for each of your photos used to illustrate a manuscript. Other payment schedules: Rigging/Techniques or Sportfishing News shorts, $25-75; Fishtales, $250.

Categories: Nonfiction—Boating—Conservation—Fishing—Recreation—Sports

CONTACT: Jason Cannon, Managing Editor
Material: All
460 N. Orlando Ave., Ste. 200
Winter Park FL 32789
Phone: 407-628-4802
Fax: 407-628-7061
E-mail: do1@worldzine.com
Website: www.sportfishingmag.com

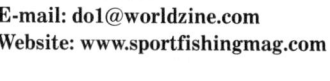

Sports Afield

Sports Afield is America's original outdoor magazine, founded in 1887. The magazine is devoted to people who share a passion for high-end sporting pursuits, especially North American and African big-game hunting. Our focus is on species such as sheep, elk, caribou, moose, trophy whitetails and mule deer, bears, African plains game, and dangerous species such as Cape buffalo, lion, and leopard. Coverage of fine guns, optics, clothing, and equipment is an essential part of the magazine. To a more limited extent, we also feature stories on upland hunting and big-game hunts outside North America and Africa.

While most of our departments are written by regular contributors, we are continually looking for fresh feature ideas. The majority of our coverage consists of big-game hunting destination pieces and exciting, well-written hunting adventure stories. Please do not send "hunt-payback" pieces; we do not run stories that are blatant advertisements for a particular outfitter. We are interested in stories about guns and gear that are appropriate to the type of hunting we cover. Features should be no more than 2,500 words in length. We also accept short items (100-400 words) for our Almanac section. These items can include hunting tips, travel tips, and unusual facts about wildlife or outdoor lore.

The best way to sell to *Sports Afield* is to first query the editor. Queries should clearly explain what you'd like to write about, show the editor why the subject is relevant, and why you're qualified to write the piece. Each feature concept should be accompanied by sidebar suggestions that support the main subject of the feature.

Specific Guidelines

All manuscripts should be submitted on 3.5-inch disk or CD-ROM; both Mac and PC disks are acceptable. Microsoft Word files are preferred; otherwise, save your article as a text-only file. Please include a hard copy of the article. Please include a self-addressed, stamped envelope with all queries or manuscript submissions. Articles should not be submitted via email unless requested in that format by the editor. We will not review any simultaneous submissions or stories that have been previously published elsewhere.

Photographic support is very important. Every article submission should be accompanied by a good selection of high-quality color slides. Package slides and transparencies carefully, for the magazine will not be responsible for photos damaged or lost in shipment. All editorial submissions should be accompanied by a variety of supporting images ranging from scenic/landscapes to action and portraits. Photos of hunters posing with their trophies should be tasteful, free of blood, and show the animal to best advantage. We cannot accept black-and-white photos or color prints. In some cases we can accept digital photos, but they must be of exceptionally high quality, with a resolution of 300 dpi at the size they will be used in the magazine, and taken with a camera of not less than 4 megapixels.

Include a photo release form for all recognizable people pictured in your photographs, and submit clear captions for each photograph that include: names of people depicted, location, date, activity, and relevance to the story subject.

Unless they were assigned by the editor, all submissions are reviewed "on speculation." If your work is accepted for publication, you will be sent a freelance contract. We purchase first worldwide rights for all features and departments; we buy all rights to Almanac items. Payment will be made after we receive your signed copy of the contract.

Categories: Nonfiction—Adventure—Environment—Outdoors—Recreation—Sports—Travel

CONTACT: Diana Rupp, Editor in Chief
Material: All
15621 Chemical Ln.
Huntington Beach, CA 92649-1506
E-mail: Editorinchief@sportsafield.com
Website: sportsafield.com

Sports Illustrated

Does not accept unsolicited submissions.

Sports Illustrated for Kids

Freelance writers may query *Sports Illustrated For Kids* with specific story ideas. Completed articles, submitted on the basis of speculation, will be read. But such articles are not encouraged. Be advised that most *SI For Kids* articles are staff written. Fewer than 20 freelance proposals are accepted each year.

Sports Illustrated For Kids reaches sports fans ages 8 to 15. The magazine strives to be informative and fun, presenting exciting personalities and insightful stories from the world of sports. Freelance writers should note that editors expect extensive reporting and research on all stories. The following are categories in which the editors might accept freelance material:

• Cover/Bonus Stories—Articles about interesting topics and trends in sports, 1,000-1,500 words, $1,000-$2,000.

• Athlete Profiles—Articles about top pro, college, high school, or kid athletes, 400-1,500 words, $500-$1,500.

• Puzzles and Games, $500-$700.

Kids are encouraged to submit letters, drawings, and poems to *SI For Kids*. These submissions are unpaid.

Please note that *SI For Kids* does not run general fiction or fillers.

Categories: Nonfiction—Children—Games—General Interest—Inspirational—Interview—Juvenile—Recreation—Sports/Recreation—How-to—Humor—Profiles

CONTACT: Bob Der
Material: Pro Football
CONTACT: John Rolfe
Material: Pro Baseball
CONTACT: Erin Egan, Ellen Cosgrove or Andrea Whittaker
Material: Pro Basketball
CONTACT: Nick Friedman
Material: Action Sports, Kid Sports, Pro Hockey
CONTACT: Ellen Cosgrove
Material: College Sports
CONTACT: Andrea Whittaker
Material: Puzzles and Games
135 West 50th St., 4th floor
New York NY 10020-1393
Phone: 212-522-1212
Fax: 212-467-4247

Sports Spectrum
A Christianity Today Publication

Basic Purpose of Sports Spectrum
a. Help lead people to faith in Jesus Christ.
b. Help Christians to grow in their walk with Him.

Our primary reason for existing is to reach non-Christians with the gospel. We do this through looking at key issues in life through the testimonies and experiences of sports figures. At the same time, we want to give Christian readers what they want and need.

Dual Audience

Although our primary focus in *Sports Spectrum* is evangelistic (to lead people to faith in Jesus Christ), we also must appeal to people who are already Christians.

Christians should see the athletes in *Sports Spectrum* as people mature enough to teach them biblical principles that apply to their lives. As the athletes tell about their victories and setbacks, they should *reflect a Christian world-and-life view.* We want Christian readers to feel at home with the magazine, and we also want them to give the magazine to their friends who don't know the Lord.

Sports Spectrum *Athletes*

It is essential that the athletes featured in *Sports Spectrum* demonstrate a strong Christian testimony. The fact that they occasionally talk about God or attend chapel is not enough to go on. *What we mean by Christian is that a person has accepted Jesus Christ as his/her Savior, trusting that through Jesus' death on the cross, his/her sins can be forgiven.*

SS athletes should be respected by their peers for their stand, willing to articulate their faith, and unashamed of the gospel of Jesus Christ. We talk to chaplains, teammates, and others in sports to verify an athlete's testimony.

In addition, we are generally interested in sports people and sports stories that either have national importance or we think will have as their careers develop.

Sports Spectrum *Writers*

We are looking for writers who are followers of Jesus Christ. We may ask prospective writers to testify of their faith in Jesus. Our purpose is to lead people to Christ, so we want writers who share our vision.

We are not about writing about good people just for the sake of telling interesting stories. *Our goals are Christ-centered—leading the reader to know and understand the importance of faith in Christ and true Christ-like living.* Writers who do not understand the gospel and the importance of trusting Christ as Savior cannot possibly share our mission.

In addition, we are looking for experienced sports writers. It is important to us that our writers understand sports and that they know how to obtain and conduct an interview with an athlete. We are looking for writers who are creative in their approach to putting an article together—not afraid to be clever, emotive, humorous, cutting edge.

Sports Spectrum already has a large stable of freelance writers developed over the past 15 years. It is becoming increasingly difficult to break into the freelance group.

It is essential that a prospective Sports Spectrum writer know and understand the magazine. We would hope that before a person suggests an article for *Sports Spectrum* that he or she will have already read the magazine and perhaps be a subscriber. It helps our communication with the writer if he or she is familiar with the magazine.

Approach

Our feature articles are intended to allow Christian athletes to tell how their faith and their knowledge of God's Word help them as they face difficult issues. These issues should be things all people can relate to. The articles must be both nondenominational and noncharismatic. In fact, we prefer not to mention any denomination or specific church unless it is absolutely essential.

Whenever pertinent, the article should detail the athlete's salvation testimony unless there's a good reason not to. However, there should be a clear indication of the athlete's faith and its impact on his or her life. We like for the athlete to tell about coming to faith in his or her own words instead of having the writer tell about it.

Keeping the intended audience in mind, the writer should understand that he is not addressing Christians specifically, but telling the athlete's story in a way that both Christians and non-Christians would enjoy.

Because we want to talk to non-Christians with our articles, we don't want to scare them off with a lot of religious-sounding words, nor do we want to start the article off with Bible verses or other "Christian talk." Those will come into the story as it is told, but the lead should be nonreligious.

Also, since this is a sports magazine, our writers must include plenty of sports information in the articles. Let the reader find out about the sport the athlete plays.

We also want to emphasize the aspect of storytelling. As much as possible, we like the life of the athlete to be revealed through anecdotes—either from him or from supplementary interviews.

What To Do

If you are an experienced, Christian freelance writer who has a sports writing background and would like to inquire about writing for *SS*, send an email to Dave Branon at dbranon@rbc.org.

Along with that introductory email, attach some samples of your published writing that reflect your ability to profile sports figures.

Do not send unsolicited articles of any kind. We do not operate on this basis. Instead, we operate on an assignment-only basis. Feel free to send story ideas and topic ideas and names of sports people you think we should consider.

If you have any ideas for future articles, please email them to the editor at the address listed above. We get many of our article ideas from our freelance writers. First, though, make sure you have read the magazine and understand the kind of articles we're looking for.

Once we receive your ideas, we will get back to you. We keep all ideas on file, but we cannot make decisions on them immediately. We have six planning times each calendar year, and those are the times we decide what articles to assign.

What Not To Do

Please do not use the name *Sports Spectrum* in obtaining credentials or other press privileges without prior approval of this magazine. Also, do not tell a sports person (athlete, coach, etc.) that you are doing an article on him or her for *Sports Spectrum* unless that article has already been assigned, and do not interview athletes for *Sports Spectrum* unless we have given our approval. (Exceptions could be longtime SS writers who have been told they can do articles on speculation.)

Features

If we assign you a feature article, we will pay you at least 21 cents per word, plus any reasonable expenses (phone calls, local travel are considered reasonable and don't need prior permission; plane fares, hotels, etc. are paid only on rare exceptions and do need permission). We prefer face-to-face meetings with the athletes. Also, we do not want research articles for personality features. The sports personality must be interviewed subsequent to receiving the assignment unless other arrangements are made with the editor.

These articles generally run from 1,500 to 2,000 words plus one or two sidebars, which run generally 150 words.

Payment is made according to assigned word count. For instance, if you are assigned an 1,800-word article and send an article with 3,400 words, you will be paid for 1,800. Keeping to the assigned word count helps us tremendously in fitting the articles into the magazine.

Schedule

Generally, we assign our issues 5 months before the cover date. Therefore, to present article ideas in season, you need to submit them far in advance. In other words, by the time May rolls around, we are starting to assign articles about football and basketball. When an idea is submitted during a sports season, it is generally too late for us to consider that idea until the next sports season.

Audience

Sports fans, predominantly male (75 percent), between 20 & 55 years of age. We realize that we have many younger readers, but we don't target teenagers with our writing style.

Bible Versions

We suggest that our writers use the New International Version of the Bible.

Rights

All rights for all articles purchased. We do not use reprints of previously published articles. All articles in *Sports Spectrum* must be offered to us for first use, and they become the property of *Sports Spectrum*. All permissions questions should be addressed to Debbie Miller at 616-974-2718.

What We Don't Do

Poetry, Reprints, Fiction, or Profiles of sports ministries, chapels, etc.

Queries

Please make all queries about potential articles by E-mail rather than by phone. Do not submit unsolicited articles. Please allow sufficient time for a response.

If You Get An Assignment

Follow these guidelines.

• Start early in securing the interview. Let the managing editor know if you are having a problem getting the interview. *Please do not wait until the article is due before letting us know you are experiencing problems.*

• Unless the assignment is a straight interview, talk to *at least* two other key people about the person you are profiling for a feature article.

• If you have a face-to-face interview, make sure the athlete understands what *Sports Spectrum* is all about. Give him or her a copy of the magazine. To get copies for that purpose, call Debbie Miller at 616-974-2718 or E-mail her at dmiller@rbc.org.

Categories: Christian Interests—Religion—Spiritual—Sports/Recreation

CONTACT: Dave Branon, Managing Editor
Material: All
Box 3566
Grand Rapids MI 49501
Phone: 616-957-2711
Fax: 616-957-5741
E-mail: dbranon@rbc.org
Website: www.sports.org or www.sportspectrum.com

Springfield! MAGAZINE

Springfield! Magazine

Springfield! Magazine is a monthly publication now in its 26th year. The magazine is 85% free-lance written, and the magazine works with talented but unpublished writers along with veteran writers from a variety of backgrounds. The best approach to selling material to this magazine is to study copies of the magazine to determine its style and approach before submitting material for publication. A sample copy of the magazine is available by mail for $5.30, and a one-year subscription is only $16.99.

Springfield! Magazine is very provincial. Query in writing first, and be sure that the query includes a clear "hook" to Springfield, Missouri, to be sure that the article will fit in with the magazine's local slant. If the query includes a Springfield "peg" the query will be answered within two weeks.

Springfield! Magazine buys approximately 150 manuscripts each year. Payment ranges between $35 and $250 for manuscripts and payment is made upon publication. Both by-line and photo credits are given. Magazine buys only first serial rights. Publication ranges from three months to three years after acceptance. Photos of subjects and subject's family should accompany the manuscript and originals will be returned after publication. Captions, model releases and full identification of persons appearing in photos are required.

Springfield! Magazine publishes no fiction, and non-fiction material sought includes in-depth profiles (with more quotes from others than subject) on men and women of distinction, personal experiences, local photo features, travel within a day's drive of Springfield for most part, humor (if strong local angle), historical/nostalgic pieces (if photos available) and book reviews and/or excerpts (by Springfield authors only). Features on Springfield couples are a strong priority right now.

Springfield! Magazine prefers both queries and manuscripts be typewritten, double spaced, with your full name and address (plus social security number) on first page. Editors will read unsolicited manuscripts (allow six months). Unsolicited manuscripts should be accompanied by stamped, self-addressed envelopes if return is expected.

Categories: Nonfiction—Adventure—African-American—Animals—Architecture—Arts—Asian-American—Associations—Biography—Book Reviews—Careers—Children—Civil War—College—Comedy—Confession—Crime—Culture—Drama—Directories—Ecology—Education—Environment—Erotica—Family—Fashion—Feminism—Film/Video—Fishing—Folklore—Food/Drink—Gardening—Government—Health—Human Rights—Inspirational—Interview—Jewish Interest—Juvenile—Language—Law—Lifestyle—Literature—Marriage—Mass Communications—Men's Issues—Military—Money & Finances—Multicultural—Music—Native American—Outdoors—Parenting—Photography—Psychology—Real Estate—Reference—Relationships—Religion—Romance—Satire—Science—Self Help—Sexuality—Singles—Sports/Recreation—Teen—Television/Radio—Textbooks—Theatre—Travel—Women's Issues—Writing—Young Adult

CONTACT: Robert C. Glazier, Editor & Publisher
Material: All
Springfield Communications, Inc.
PO Box 4749
Springfield MO 65808-4749
E-mail: pub@sgfmag.com

St. Anthony Messenger

St. Anthony Messenger is a general-interest, family-oriented Catholic magazine. It is written and edited largely for people living in families or the family-like situations of Church and community. We want to help our readers better understand the teachings of the gospel and Catholic Church, and how they apply to life and the full range of problems confronting us as members of families, the Church and society.

Types and examples of the kinds of articles we publish:

• Church and Religion: "The Incarnation of Jesus," "10 Lessons on the Beach," "Spirituality for the New Millennium," "Corpus Christi: Feast of the Eucharist," "Faith and Works: Catholics and Lutherans Find Agreement."

• Marriage, Family and Parenting: "Brendan's Song: A Father's Day Story," "Eight Ways to Pray With Your Kids."

• Social: "The Arch: A House Full of Love," "Adult Day Programs: New Trend in Holistic Care," "I'd Like to Say: It's Time to Rethink Our Criminal Justice System."

• Inspiration: "A Bed to Lie On: Fran Heitzman's Mission," "Oklahoma City Bombing: Two Fathers and Forgiveness."

• Psychology: "The True Meaning of Contemplation," "Faith and Medicine: A Growing Practice."

• Profiles and Interviews: "Blessed Pope John XXIII: An Ordinary Holiness," "Martin Sheen: Catholic President on Prime Time," "Madeleine L'Engle: An Epic in Time."

• Fiction: "Weeds," "Tree Lights," "Walter Makes a Fourth," "Sophia's Cat," "The Art of Love."

THE BEST WAY TO KNOW WHAT WE PUBLISH IS TO READ AND STUDY SEVERAL RECENT ISSUES OF *St. Anthony Messenger*. Text of two articles per month are posted at www.AmericanCatholic.org.

GUIDELINES FOR WRITING, PREPARING AND SUBMITTING AN ARTICLE

Query in advance. State proposed topic, sources, authorities and your qualifications to do the article. Library research does not suffice. Fresh sources and interviews with experts or people in the field will be necessary. Reporting articles are more needed than opinion pieces. Seasonal material (Mother's Day, Lent, Christmas, etc.) should be submitted six or more months in advance.

We do not publish filler material—anecdotes, jokes, thoughts to ponder.

We do not publish articles or stories in installments or serial form. And we very rarely reprint materials first published by other publishers.

We do not use essays or personal reminiscences. Articles about historical events or people no longer living need a current news peg.

We do not consider articles submitted simultaneously to other magazines.

Manuscripts should be typed double spaced. Mark your submission fact or fiction. Place your name, address, phone number and Social Security number on the first page. Number the pages.

Articles should not exceed 3,000 words. Preferred length is 2000-2500 words.

Keep the vocabulary simple. Avoid jargon, technical and theological language. Keep sentences short. Ask, "Would my grandmother understand this?"

An attention-getting introduction is important! Use anecdotes, examples, quotes from real people. Make practical applications. End strongly.

For return of manuscripts, enclose a self-addressed stamped envelope.

We assume no responsibility for lost manuscripts, accompanying photos or slides. Keep copies or insure against loss. Protect photos against cracking.

Please allow up to eight weeks for return or purchase of publication rights. Hardly any manuscript is published without review by eight or more staff members. Phoning the editor for a progress report invites aborting review process and returning the manuscript immediately to avoid more phone calls.

Payment for articles and fiction is 16 cents a published word—upon acceptance and return of signed author-publisher agreement form. Authors receive 2 copies of published work.

Payment for photos accompanying an article is $25 for each photo used. Photos should be documented with any necessary releases from photographers or persons in the photos. Payment for photos is made after photos have been selected and the issue laid out and printed.

Articles sent after a positive response to a query are received on a speculation basis.

If no article is received within two months after a positive response to a query, we feel free to consider a query on the same subject from another author.

We buy first worldwide serial rights to publish and republish "the work" in any and all forms or formats, including all electronic formats.

INFORMATION FOR FICTION AUTHORS

Besides these guidelines, freelance authors submitting fiction pieces should read our general information sheet for all freelance writers. Note the audience for whom we publish and the purpose of *St. Anthony Messenger*. Most of our readers live in families. The greater part are women between 40 and 70 years old.

Preferred word length for short stories is 2,000 to 2,500 words.

Manuscripts must be typed and should be double-spaced with wide margins.

We cannot accept responsibility for undelivered, lost or damaged manuscripts. Authors should always keep a copy of their stories.

Please do not phone to ask if your manuscript has been received. Allow six to eight weeks for response or return of your manuscript. Any story that is accepted will have had at least six or eight readers. And many that are returned may also have had as many readers.

We receive over 1,000 short story submissions a year. We publish 12 at the most—one an issue. Man: stories must be returned—even stories that may be well written and have merit.

In submitting a short story please clearly label it as fiction. Number the pages. Include a self-addressed, stamped envelope and your Social Security number (information we must supply the I.R.S. when issuing a purchase check).

We pay 16 cents a word on acceptance for first Worldwide Serial Rights and do not consider stories submitted to other publications at the same time or reprints.

We are interested in stories about family relationships, people struggling and coping with the same problems of life our readers face. Stories that show people triumphing in adversity, persevering in faith, overcoming doubt or despair, coming to spiritual insights. Stories about people that offer hope. Characters and resolutions must be real and believable. Sudden realizations, instant conversions and miracle solutions won't do.

Stories that sound more like essays or monologues, stories that are straight narratives with no dialogue or interaction on the part of characters will not succeed.

Dialogue should contribute to moving the story forward, It should sound real—the way people talk to each other in real life. Conversation should not be artificial or sound stilted.

We are not interested in retold Bible stories or stories overly sentimental or pietistic.

Seasonal stories (Christmas, Easter, etc.) should be submitted at least six months in advance.

INFORMATION FOR POETRY WRITERS

St. Anthony Messenger is a general-interest, family-oriented Catholic magazine. It is written and edited largely for people living in family situations or the family-like situations of Church and community. We want to help our readers better understand the teachings of the gospel and Catholic Church, and how they apply to life and the full range of problems confronting us as members of families, the Church and society.

The poetry we publish attempts to reflect the philosophy stated above. Poetry is subjective, for the most part, but we do require that the poems we publish have most or all of these characteristics:

• originality
• creativity in word choice, images and overall thought/idea
• each section of the poem fitting together well with other sections
• subject matter somewhat universal in nature
• a religious (in a broad sense, not theological) or family dimension

Both rhyming and non-rhyming materials are considered. We do not consider previously published poetry, or poetry submitted at the same time to other publications.

Each poetry submission should be typed, double-spaced on a separate piece of paper. Your name, address and Social Security number should be typed at the top.

PLEASE DO NOT SUBMIT POEMS LONGER THAN 20-25 LINES—the shorter, the better. Due to space limitations, the poetry section does not appear every month. When space is available for it, there is room for only one page of poetry (four to five poems at the most). Therefore, OUR POETRY NEEDS ARE VERY LIMITED.

As we like to give as many people as possible the chance to be published poets, we do not buy "collections" of poems for publication (that is the role of a poetry book publisher), nor do we usually buy more than a few works from each poet a year. And while we pay on acceptance, publication may not follow for a considerable length of time. When a poem is published the poet receives two complimentary copies of the issue it appears in.

WE PAY $2 (two dollars) PER LINE for each poem purchased. We try to return poems not accepted within FOUR TO SIX WEEKS. Please do not write or phone to ask if your poem has been received until that amount of time has passed. Poetry WILL NOT BE RETURNED UNLESS ACCOMPANIED BY A SELF-ADDRESSED STAMPED ENVELOPE. We assume no responsibility for material damaged or lost, and advise poets to keep a copy of any poem submitted.

Due to the poetry editor's time constraints, poetry critiques will not be given. Thank you very much for your interest!

Our Mission

St. Anthony Messenger Press and Franciscan Communications seeks to spread the Word that is Jesus Christ in the style of Saints Francis and Anthony. Through print and electronic media marketed in North America and worldwide, we endeavor to evangelize, inspire and inform those who search for God and seek a richer Catholic, Christian, human life. Our efforts help support the life, ministry and charities of the Franciscan Friars of St. John the Baptist Province, who sponsor our work.

Our Books

We seek to educate and inspire Catholic Christians, not to challenge church authority. We try to identify trends surfacing in the Catholic world (for example, the need for RCIA materials, the needs of the baby-boom generation). In programs, we look for universal applicability, not just the story of how a program worked in a single parish or classroom, and we look for tried and tested programs. Our style is popular: easy to read, practical, concrete, filled with examples. We do not publish fiction, poetry, autobiography, personal reflections, academic studies, art books.

We publish approximately 20 to 30 books per year.

Most of our books fit into one of the following categories:

—Aids for liturgy, sacraments: The Ministry and Mission of Sung Prayer • A Child's Journey: The Christian Initiation of Children • The Sacraments: How Catholics Pray • Why Go to Confession? Questions and Answers About Sacramental Reconciliation • Your Child's Baptism • When Your Child Becomes Catholic: What Parents and Sponsors Need to Know

—Aids to prayer, spirituality: A Retreat With... series • On-the-Job Spirituality: Finding God in Work • Remarkable Women, Remarkable Wisdom: A Daybook of Reflections • Hope Against Darkness: The Transforming Vision of Saint Francis in an Age of Anxiety • Praying the Gospels through Poetry: Lent to Easter • God Is with You: Prayers for Men in Prison • Prayers for Feasts • Harvest Us Home: Good News as We Age • The Blessing Candles: 58 Simple Mealtime Prayer-Celebrations • Armchair Mystic: Easing Into Contemplative Prayer • Saint of the Day • Mary's Flowers: Gardens, Legends and Meditations

—Catholic teaching and identity: 100 Names of Mary: Stories and Prayers • Twelve Tough Issues and More: What the Church Teaches and Why • People of God: The History of Catholic Christianity • Lost and Found Catholics: Voices of Vatican II • Practicing Catholic • Conscience in Conflict: How to Make Moral Choices • What It Means to Be Catholic • Believing in Jesus: A Popular Overview of the Catholic Faith

—Scripture: Healing Plants of the Bible: Legends, Lore and Meditations • Woman, You Are Free: A Spirituality for Women in Luke • Live Letters: Reflections on the Second Readings of the Sunday Lectionary • Bible Stories Revisited: Discovering Your Story in the Old Testament • Pray the Bible • Reading the Gospels With the Church: From Christmas Through Easter • Jesus' Plan for a New World: The Sermon on the Mount • Breaking Open the Gospel of Matthew, Mark, Luke, John

—Parish ministers/pastoral ministry resources: Handing on the Faith series • Practical Catechesis: Visions and Tasks for Catechetical Leaders • Called to Preside: A Handbook for Lay-people • God Is Close to the Brokenhearted: Good News for Those Who Are Depressed • Prayers for Caregivers • Visiting the Sick: A Guide for Pastoral Ministers

—Franciscan resources: The Sun and Moon Over Assisi: A Personal Encounter With Francis and Clare • To Live as Francis Lived: A Guide for Secular Franciscans • Francis: The Journey and the Dream • Clare, A Light in the Garden • Day by Day With Followers of Francis and Clare • Swimming in the Sun: Discovering the Lord's Prayer With Francis of Assisi and Thomas Merton

—Children: People of the Bible: Life and Customs • Francis of Assisi: Activities and Coloring Fun for Children • Can You Find Jesus? Introducing Your Child to the Gospel • Can You Find Bible Heroes?

Introducing Your Child to the Old Testament • Can You Find Followers? Introducing Your Child to Disciples • Friend Jesus: Prayers for Children • Saints and Heroes for Kids

—**Family-based religious education:** God Is Calling: Together Time for Families • The Table of the Lord • The Forgiveness of the Lord • Holy Bells and Wonderful Smells: Year-round Activities for Classrooms and Families

Our Market

Reading Catholics, mostly adults; priests and religious directors of religious education, catechists, teachers; people who are actively involved in parish life and ministry; small-group leaders; people seeking inspiration for their spiritual life or help with special problems; parents.

We look for books that will sell in bulk quantities to parishes, teachers, pastoral ministers, etc. About 65 percent of our books are sold in bookstores. We expect to sell at least 5,000 to 7,000 copies of a book.

Your Idea

Address your book idea to our editorial director of books, Lisa Biedenbach. Send a brief (500 words) description and an outline. Tell us about your subject, the approximate length of your book, the intended audience, what makes your idea unique, your background or credentials for writing. In response, we may ask for an introduction and a sample chapter or for the entire manuscript. It may be six to eight weeks before you hear from us. We do not consider anything submitted to another publisher at the same time. We do not accept responsibility for lost manuscripts; always keep a copy of anything you send to us.

Categories: Fiction—Nonfiction—Christian Interests—Family—Inspirational—Interview—Marriage—Parenting—Poetry—Psychology—Religion—Short Stories—Society—Spiritual—Catholics—Profiles

CONTACT: Pat McCloskey, O.F.M., Editor
Material: Articles, Fiction
CONTACT: Poetry Editor
Material: Poetry
28 W. Liberty St.
Cincinnati OH 45210
Phone: 513-241-5615
Fax: 513-241-0399
E-mail: St.Anthony@AmericanCatholic.org
Website: www.americancatholic.org

Stamats Meetings Media
Meetings West, Meetings South and Meetings East

Stamats Meetings Media publishes three regional monthly trade magazines—*Meetings West, Meetings South*, and *Meetings East*—targeted at a controlled circulation audience of meeting and convention planners. All three magazines focus on the meeting, convention, conference, tradeshow, and retreat industry.

Freelance coverage includes: features and site inspections (4 to 6 full-length city/state/regional roundups per issue)

We RARELY take stories on query; the vast majority of our assignments are based on our editorial calendar.

(Editorial calendars are available at: www.meetings411.com/editorialcal_main.asp)

If you're interested in writing for us, please send a resume and two or three "relevant" clips covering meetings/conventions topics to the address below, along with the list of localities in which you are expert. We typically pencil in story assignments in the fall for our upcoming calendar year's coverage, although some last-minute assignments may occur.

We strongly favor writers who are local to their subject matter.

Categories: Nonfiction, Business

CONTACT: Tyler Davidson, Editor
Material: All
Stamats Meetings Media
550 Montgomery St. #750
San Francisco CA 94111
Phone: (no calls, please)

Standard

Thank you for considering *Standard* for your free-lance submissions.

Standard is published 52 times a year by Beacon Hill Press of Kansas City and has a circulation of more than 150,000. Based on biblical truth and the Wesleyan-Arminian tradition, *Standard* seeks to present quality Christian material for a diverse audience of adults.

Standard uses about 200 manuscripts and 100 poems per year. We publish a variety of material, including:

• Short stories (1200 words maximum)
• Christian poetry (30 lines maximum)
• Puzzles

In *Standard* we want to show Christianity in action, and we prefer to do that through stories that hold the reader's attention. We seldom use how-to articles, sermons, and devotionals, unless they are written in our preferred style.

Standard purchases the right to publish material one time, either first rights or reprint rights. After publication, copyrights to the material revert to the author. *Standard* does not purchase first rights on simultaneous submissions. Due to our lead time, we assume that the story will appear elsewhere before *Standard* goes to press. Payment is made on acceptance as follows:

• First Rights: 3½ cents per word
• Reprint and simultaneous submissions: 2 cents per word
• Poetry: 25 cents per line (minimum payment $5.00)

Manuscripts can be submitted by e-mail.

(We can only work with Microsoft Word or WordPerfect attached documents in PC formats. If you use any other word-processing programs or a Mac computer, please put your manuscript in the body of the e-mail.)

We will respond within 90 days. Material accepted for publication will appear in *Standard* approximately 18 months after acceptance. Contributors will receive three complimentary copies at time of publication.

• Include a SASE with every mailed submission, and please indicate if the manuscript is disposable. If you submit via e-mail, we will respond within our usual review time frame (90 days) to the e-mail address on your submission.

• We need the following information on the first page of the manuscript:

1. Your name
2. Mailing address (and e-mail address, if available)
3. Telephone number
4. Social Security number
5. Number of words in manuscript or number of lines of poem
6. Whether first or reprint rights are being offered
7. If reprint, where previously published

• Please put your name on second and subsequent pages you send via regular postal service, because sometimes pages get separated during handling.

• Do not submit any manuscript which has been submitted to or published in any of the following: *Vista, Wesleyan Advocate, Holiness Today, Preacher's Magazine, World Mission, Women Alive*, or various teen and children's publications produced by WordAction Publishing Company. These are overlapping markets.

• Since we accept unsolicited manuscripts, query letters are unnecessary. Please submit only complete manuscripts.

• Be conscientious in your use of Scripture; don't overload your story with quotations. When you quote the Bible, quote it exactly and cite chapter, verse, and version used. (We prefer the NIV.) *Standard* will handle copyright matters for Scripture. Except for quotations from the Bible, written permission for the use of any other copyrighted material (especially song lyrics) is the responsibility of the writer.

• Keep in mind the international audience of *Standard* with regard to geographic references and holidays. We cannot use stories about cultural, national, or secular holidays.

• Do not mention specific church affiliations. *Standard* is read in a variety of denominations.

Categories: Nonfiction—Christian Interests—Poetry—Religion—Short Stories—Spiritual

CONTACT: Submissions Editor
Material: All
6401 The Paseo
Kansas City MO 64131
E-mail: Evlead@nazarene.org
E-mail: Cyourdon@nazarene.org

Stock Car Racing

Circulation: 257,296
Frequency: monthly

Stock Car Racing remains the largest and best-selling automotive racing magazine in the United States. From NASCAR to the local dirt track scene, the title's respected journalists and photographers mix inside stories of special interest with basic how-to technical information for racing fans, enthusiasts and competitors.

Formal guidelines not available. Please read a number of issues to ascertain the publication's style and needs. Or visit *Stock Car Racing* on-line at www.stockcarracing.com

Send queries to address below.

Categories: Automobiles

CONTACT: David Bourne, Editor-in-Chief
Material: All
3816 Industry Blvd.
Lakeland FL 33811
Phone: 863-644-0449
Website: www.stockcarracing.com

Stone Soup
the magazine by young writers and artists

Stone Soup
The Magazine by Young Writers and Artists

Stone Soup welcomes submissions by young people through age 13!

What to Include: Include your name, age, home address, phone number, and e-mail address if you have one. Please do not include a self-addressed stamped envelope. Send copies of your work, not originals. If we need the original, we will request it. You do not need to include a photo of yourself.

Where to Send Your Work:
Stone Soup
Submissions Dept.
PO Box 83
Santa Cruz, CA 95063
USA
(Please send your work by regular mail; do not send it by Certified Mail or Registered Mail. Thank you.)
E-mail Address: (for foreign contributors only)
editor@stonesoup.com

A Word About E-mail Submissions: We do not accept e-mail submissions from the U.S. or Canada. Because we are a very small company we're concerned that if we allowed e-mail submissions, we'd be

flooded with material and we wouldn't be able to handle it all. We like to think that serious young authors would be more than willing to polish their work, print it out in a nice format, and mail it to us. We hope you'll understand.

What Happens Next: We only respond to those submissions we are considering for possible publication. If we are considering your work, you will hear from us in four to six weeks. If you do not hear from us, it means we were not able to use your work. Don't be discouraged! Try again!

General Information: Stone Soup is made up of stories, poems, book reviews, and art by young people through age 13. Although all the writing we publish is in English, we accept work from all over the world. To get an idea of the kind of writing and art we like, please look through our highlights from past issues.

Writers: Send us stories and poems about the things you feel most strongly about! Whether your work is about imaginary situations or real ones, use your own experiences and observations to give your work depth and a sense of reality. Writing need not be typed, as long as it is legible. If you type your work, please type it double-spaced in a plain, medium-sized font. We can consider writing in languages other than English; include a translation if possible. The maximum length we can publish is about 2500 words; we have no minimum length. It's OK to send more than one piece of writing in the same envelope. Please don't send us work you are also sending to other magazines. Send your work to one magazine at a time.

Illustrators: If you would like to illustrate for Stone Soup, send editor Gerry Mandel some samples of your art work, along with a letter saying what kinds of stories you would like to illustrate. Although we sometimes use simple line drawings in Stone Soup, we are especially interested in artists who can draw or paint complete scenes. Send us samples that fill the entire page with detail, including the background. Please include your name, age, birthdate, address, telephone number, and a self-addressed stamped envelope for our response to you.

Book Reviewers: If you are interested in reviewing books for Stone Soup, write Ms. Mandel for more information. Tell her a little about yourself, why you want to be a book reviewer, and what kinds of books you like to read. Be sure to include your name, age, birthdate, address, telephone number, and a self-addressed stamped envelope for our response to you.

Payment: All contributors whose work is accepted for publication receive a certificate, two complimentary copies, and discounts on other purchases. In addition, contributors of stories, poems and book reviews are paid $40 each; illustrators are paid $25 per illustration.

Note: We're always looking for new writers and artists, and we really want to encourage all our young readers to send us their work. However, please keep in mind that we receive an average of 250 submissions a week; we are only able to publish a small percentage of the work we receive. Send us your work with a spirit of adventure, and try not to be too disappointed if we can't use it.

Categories: Arts—Book Reviews—Children—Education—Juvenile—Literature—Poetry—Short Stories—Writing—Young Adult

CONTACT: Submissions Dept.
Material: All
PO Box 83
Santa Cruz, CA 95063 USA
Phone: 831-426-5557
Fax: 831-426-1161
E-mail: (for foreign contributors only)
editor@stonesoup.com
Website: www.stonesoup.com

Stormwater
The Journal for Surface Water Quality Professionals

Please refer to Forester Communications.

R-U

Strategic Health Care Marketing

Editorial Profile

Twelve-page monthly newsletter, covering all areas of marketing and business development in a wide range of health care settings—hospitals, medical group practices, home health services, HMOs. Editorial focus is on strategies and techniques employed within the health care field and on relevant applications from other service industries. No photos or artwork. Byline on longer articles.

Kinds of Articles/Style

News, interviews, profiles, opinion and commentary, advice and how-to. Preferred format for feature articles is the case history approach to solving marketing problems. Crisp, almost telegraphic style...most articles range from 500 to 2,000 words in length.

Reader Profile

Directors/Vice Presidents of Marketing, Public Relations, Planning in hospitals. Administrators in small hospitals, medical groups, and in other types of delivery systems. Marketing and advertising consultants and agencies serving the service sector of the health care industry. Pharmaceutical and medical device sectors are not represented.

Rights

All articles must represent original unpublished work. First North American serial rights; Publisher also retains rights to use work in subsequent editorial reprints, collections, advertising and promotion, and in any other Health Care Communications publications.

Payment

Upon publication. Payment runs $100-$400+, depending on complexity of assignment, length, and writer's credentials. Articles normally published within two months of manuscript acceptance. Two revisions if necessary.

Kill Fee

25% for specifically commissioned material.

Out-of-Pocket Expenses

For commissioned material will reimburse long-distance telephone and out-of-pocket travel expenses, provided documentation submitted. Prior approval required for expenses (individual or in total per article) that will exceed $50.

Query First!

Many articles are written by marketing authorities and practitioners in the health care field. You should be familiar with either marketing or the industry—preferably both.

Categories: Health Care Marketing

CONTACT: Submissions Editor
Material: All
11 Heritage Ln.
Rye NY 10580
Phone: 914-967-6741
Fax: 914-967-3054
E-mail: healthcomm@aol.com

Student Lawyer
The Magazine of the Law Student Division

INFORMATION FOR AUTHORS

Award-winning *Student Lawyer* magazine is published each month from September through May by the American Bar Association's Law Student Division. It circulates to approximately 38,000 readers, most of whom are law student members of the ABA.

Student Lawyer is a legal-affairs features magazine, not a legal journal, that competes for a share of law students' limited spare time. The articles we publish, therefore, must be informative, lively, well-researched good reads. We do not accept poetry, fiction, or footnoted academic articles or briefs. These guidelines are for paid submissions only. For letters to the editor, reviews, opinion essays, and student/school news, please refer to our guidelines for unpaid submissions.

Each issue of *Student Lawyer* includes feature articles by paid freelance writers that range in length from 2,500 to 4,000 words apiece. We are looking for features on societal trends that affect the law, trends in the legal profession or law of interest to law students and young practitioners, possible careers—legal or otherwise—for lawyers, and legal education issues. Writers should provide thorough reporting, lively writing, and insightful analysis. They should expect to work extensively with the magazine's editor to provide missing or additional information, to clear up the unclear, and to polish any rough edges.

Columns also offer publication possibilities for freelance writers. Most are prepared by regular columnists, but we're open to new talent. "Briefly" consists of short news items of interest to law students. "Coping" helps law students deal with the unique challenges of law school. "Legal-ease" offers tips for readers to improve their writing and communications skills. "Jobs" helps readers market themselves to potential legal employers. "Online" is *Student Lawyer's* computers-and-the-law column. And "Esq." profiles lawyers who are doing something out of the ordinary with their careers. Columns should be about 1,500 words. If you'd like to propose a new column on a topic that would serve law students, please send us your résumé, three clips, and your ideas for possible columns.

We don't make assignments to writers with whom we're unfamiliar. If you're interested in writing for us, mail us a double-spaced hard copy of an actual story or a detailed query with three previously published clips. We are always willing to look at material on spec, but we don't accept such material via e-mail or fax. Sorry, we don't return manuscripts. Please include your e-mail address if you'd like a quick response.

The best way to find out what *Student Lawyer* is all about is to read an issue. They're available for $8 apiece (plus postage and handling) from the ABA Service Center, 800-285-2221.

Questions? Call editor Ira Pilchen at 312-988-6048 or e-mail studentlawyer@abanet.org.

Submissions

Student Lawyer welcomes unpaid submissions from readers as well as paid features and columns from professional writers. *Student Lawyer* is a legal-affairs features magazine, not a legal journal. We do not accept footnoted academic articles or briefs, poetry, or fiction. For feature articles and columns that require lively writing and extensive reporting and analysis, please see our guidelines for paid submissions.

• Letters to the editor. Brief, to-the-point letters that respond directly to a *Student Lawyer* article are preferred.

• Opinion essays. Readers may submit 600-word essays for *Student Lawyer's* Opinion department. To be accepted for publication, Opinions should pertain to issues relevant to our nationwide readership and have a clear introduction, body, and conclusion. We can accept an essay previously published (for instance, in a law school newspaper) if the writer provides contact information for the previous publisher and if we're able to secure reprint permission.

• Reviews. *Student Lawyer* accepts 600- 1,500-word reviews of books, films, and other media that have a connection with the law or unique perspective of law students. Submissions will be evaluated for writing quality and relevance to our readers.

• Student/school news. Please keep *Student Lawyer* and our Division Dialogue section in mind when issuing news releases, photos, and other material about student bar association events and accomplishments. We also want to know about interesting students to profile in our Spotlight department—all we need are their name, phone number, and brief description of why they deserve to be featured. Photos, preferably, should be in color and clearly shot. (For digital submissions, we require 266 dpi resolution.)

• General submission requirements. Editorial contributions are evaluated by the editor and student editor and are subject to review by a committee of the Law Student Division. We reserve the right to edit for clarity and space, and to reject any unsolicited item. Because of our production schedules, an item may not appear until several months after submission.

We cannot guarantee publication of any particular contribution, but we will acknowledge receipt upon request if an e-mail address is provided. You may enhance your chance at publication by discussing approaches beforehand with the editor, by e-mail (studentlawyer@abanet.org) or phone (312-988-6048).

All contributions must include the writer's name, school and year, address, daytime phone number, and, if available, an e-mail address.

E-mail submissions should have "Letter to the Editor," "Opinion," "Review," or "Student News" in the subject line. *Student Lawyer*'s e-mail address is abastulawyer@abanet.org. Word or WordPerfect attachments are preferred.

You may also mail or fax your submissions.

Authors of accepted Opinion essays, reviews, and other bylined articles will be required to sign a standard publication agreement granting copyright to the American Bar Association.

Categories: Nonfiction—Careers—Education—Law

CONTACT: Ira Pilchen, Editor
Material: All
American Bar Association—ABA Publishing
321 N. Clark St.
Chicago IL 06010
Phone: 312-988-6048
Fax: 312-988-6081
E-mail: studentlawyer@abanet.org
Website: www.abanet.org/lsd/studentlawyer

Student Leader
The Forum for America's Emerging Leaders

Please refer to Oxendine Publishing.

Studies in American Jewish Literature

Studies in American Jewish Literature (SAJL), the official journal of the Society for the Study of American Jewish Literature, publishes peer-reviewed scholarly articles, book reviews, occasional poetry, and short stories dealing with aspects of the Jewish experience in literature. Published annually, SAJL has issues featuring one writer, such as "Bernard Malamud: In Memoriam" and "The World of Cynthia Ozick," and issues that cut across various authors, subjects, and themes, such as "New Voices in an Old Tradition." Future issues will focus on new American Jewish voices, including Myla Goldberg, Thane Rosenbaum and Allegra Goodman.

Subscription Information
Annual
ISSN 0271-9274
Individuals $20.00
Institutions $30.00

For foreign subscriptions please add $6.00. Payment must accompany order. Make checks payable to University of Nebraska Press and mail to: University of Nebraska Press, 233 N 8th St, Lincoln, NE 68588-0255 or call: 1-800-755-1105 U.S. orders and customer service; 1-800-526-2617 U.S. fax orders and customer service.

Submission Information
Studies in American Jewish Literature accepts submissions that meet the following requirements:

• between 10-20 pages
• prepare according to the MLA Style Manual
• should contain endnotes rather than footnotes
Categories: Nonfiction—Book Reviews—Culture—Feminism—Jewish Interest—Literature—Music—Poetry—Religion—Short Stories—Society—Spiritual

CONTACT: Daniel Walden, Editor
Material: All
116 Burrowes Building
Penn State University
University Park PA 16802
Website: www.nebraskapress.unl.edu/journals.html

Succeed
The Magazine for Continuing Education

SUCCEED Magazine is designed to provide its readers with information about postgraduate and continuing education programs. The magazine's editorial content includes information of interest to adults recommitting themselves to education and provides insight on making such a transition easier.

Published four times a year to coincide with the fall, winter, spring, and summer academic semesters, SUCCEED Magazine is distributed to colleges and universities, career and planning centers, corporations, and public library branches throughout the New York, New Jersey, and Connecticut area.

SUCCEED Magazine is comprised of both regular departments and full-length feature articles. We typically pay $50 to $75 for department inclusions and $75 to $125 for feature articles. Departments run approximately 300-600 words. Features should be 1,500-2,000 words in length. We usually buy first rights to a piece. We will consider buying second rights if your published piece has not appeared in a national magazine, continuing education-oriented publication, or any other magazine written primarily for adults returning to the classroom. For all departments and features, you will receive payment upon publication.

Please query us by structuring an article proposal in the following matter:
• Begin with the lead you expect to put on the article–grab our attention!
• Write a summary of your intended areas of coverage.
• Give specifics about who you plan to interview, what types of real-life anecdotes you'll include, which resources you plan to utilize, and what conclusion the story might reach.

(With your query, please send us two or three published clips. Please send photocopies; we do not return writing samples.)

Familiarize yourself with SUCCEED Magazine. Get to know what kinds of articles interest our readership of over 155,000 professionals.

Departments:
• Memo Pad—Consists of short, newsworthy items about cutting-edge trends and tips that relate to today's changing job market and continuing education endeavors. (100-225 words)
• To Be…—Profiles career-changers and lifelong learners with captivating stories. How were they inspired? What sorts of contacts did they utilize to "get where they are now?" What advice do they have to offer others interested in pursuing careers or study in a similar field? (500-700 words)
• Financial Fitness—Advises readers how to keep their money in tip-top shape—even after they've signed their tuition check! Consists

of interviews with financial experts, explorations of money-saving strategies and suggestions, etc. (200-350 words)

• Job Talk—Provides cutting-edge career resource news, often in the form of short feature articles. Recent issues have included an in-depth look at on-line job sites, tips for managing a bad boss, a "job search refresher," etc. (700-900 words)

• Tech Zone—Offers objective reviews of software, CD-ROMs, Web sites, and other techno-advancements that assist with educational and professional advancement endeavors. (200-450 words)

• Sold Success—Includes entrepreneurial advice for readers who've chosen to "do it on their own," including professional profiles and recommendations of related resources. (200-400 words)

• School@Home—Features a cutting-edge look at news and advances affecting adults' capabilities to advance their education via distance learning and technology-enhanced academic and career services. (200-500 words)

Recent Feature Topics:
• Finding A Career That Fits
• A Week in the Life of an Online Learner
• Sharpening Your Emotional Intelligence
• Preparation Is the Cure to Exam Anxiety
• Turning Techie: Clicking Into E-Commerce
• Submit your intelligent, thought-provoking ideas. To us, a winning article presents useful information with creativity!
• Keep in mind that our response time to manuscripts and queries is approximately four to five weeks.

Categories: Nonfiction—Business—Careers—Education

CONTACT: Gina LaGuardia, Editor-in-Chief
Material: All
1200 South Ave., Ste. 202
Staten Island NY 10314
Phone: 718-761-4800
Fax: 718-273-2539
E-mail: editorial@collegebound.net
Website: www.classearch.com

The Sun

We're interested in essays, interviews, fiction, and poetry. While we tend to favor personal writing, we're open to just about anything—even experimental writing, if it doesn't make us feel stupid. Surprise us; we often don't know what we'll like until we read it.

We pay from $50 to $200 for poetry, from $300 to $500 for fiction, and from $300 to $750 for essays and interviews, the amount being determined by length and quality. We may pay less for very short works. For photographs we pay from $50 to $200, depending on placement. We'll consider photographs of any size, but we can use only black-and-white prints. For drawings and cartoons (which, be forewarned, we rarely publish), we pay up to $75. We also give contributors a complimentary one-year subscription to *The Sun*.

We're willing to read previously published works, though for reprints we pay only half our usual fee. We discourage simultaneous submissions. We rarely run anything longer than seven thousand words; there's no minimum word length. Don't bother with a query letter, except perhaps on interviews; the subject matter isn't as important to us as what you do with it.

We try to respond within three months. However, with more than seven hundred submissions a month, our backlog of unread manuscripts is often substantial. Don't let a longer wait surprise you.

Submissions should be typed. Your work will not be returned without sufficient postage, and we cannot respond unless a return envelope is provided.

Thanks for your interest in *The Sun*.

Sy Safransky, Editor

P.S. To save your time and ours, we suggest you take a look at *The Sun* before submitting. Sample issues are $3.50 each.

Categories: Fiction—Nonfiction—Interview—Literature—Photography—Poetry—Short Stories

CONTACT: Sy Sanfransky, Editor
Material: All
107 N. Roberson St.
Chapel Hill NC 27516
Phone: 919-942-5282

Sun Valley Magazine

Articles should relate specifically to the Wood River Valley, Idaho, or environmental in nature. Almost all stories are assigned to local authors. We will consider articles of a more general nature as they relate to life in the mountains. Examples of articles we've purchased from freelancers:
• Reviewing ski movies
• Humor article on the plight of the salmon

Query with article

(Departments average 1,200-1,500 words), or fully developed idea (including opening paragraph, brief outline, and conclusion).

We begin developing our storyline a year in advance. Send SASE with $1.49 postage for sample copy of magazine.

Categories: Nonfiction—Environment—Nature—Outdoors—Recreation—Regional—Sports

CONTACT: Karen Oswalt, Managing Editor
Material: All
12 E. Bullion St., Ste. B
Hailey ID 83333
Phone: 208-788-0770
Fax: 208-788-3881
E-mail: info@sunvalleymag.com
Website: sunvalleymag.com

Sunday School Ministries

Does not accept unsolicited submissions.

Sunset Magazine

Freelance travel articles

Sunset is Western America's largest-circulation regional magazine, with monthly issues devoted to four subject areas: travel and recreation; garden and outdoor living; food and entertaining; home design, remodeling, and projects.

Sunset is looking for well-written travel stories that offer our readers reliably satisfying travel experiences that can be successfully accomplished in a day or weekend outing, or included as part of a vacation.

Submission Procedures: No responsibility is assumed for unsolicited manuscripts. Writers must submit a query letter to the editor in advance. The letter should explain and outline the proposed story idea, and suggest an appropriate month or season. E-mail queries are preferred. Send them to travelquery@sunset.com. You also may send your query letter along with a return SASE to Editorial Services, *Sunset*, 80 Willow Rd, Menlo Park, CA 94025. It will be forwarded to the appropriate editor.

Once an editor approves an idea for a story, the writer will be issued a Story Contract assigning an approximate word length and due date for the text. The contract specifies the terms of the agreement between the writer and *Sunset* Publishing Corporation.

Writers must have computer capabilities to submit stories by e-mail. The assigned text should be submitted with the resource material specified in the contract.

Following submission of the text, the writer may be asked to revise the manuscript for publication or to supply further information or answer questions posed by the editor.

Payment will be made upon acceptance of the text with submission of an invoice in the amount specified in the contract.

After acceptance, the text will then be processed by staff copy editors and fact checkers. Writers will be credited with a byline if the manuscript is not substantially altered before publication in *Sunset Magazine*.

Word Length: One-page stories usually run from 300 to 400 words, depending on the number of color photographs or other illustrations such as maps.

Regional Editions: Some of *Sunset's* travel stories offer close-to-home outings for readers in *Sunset's* five regional editions: Northern California; Southern California (Los Angeles, Santa Barbara, Ventura, San Diego, and western parts of Riverside and San Bernardino counties, and also, Hawaii); Northwest (Oregon, Washington, Alaska, and British Columbia); Southwest (Arizona, New Mexico, and Clark County, Nevada); Mountain (Colorado, Idaho, Montana, Nevada except Clark County, Utah, and Wyoming).

Take-action Magazine: *Sunset* is not an armchair magazine. While each story ought to be entertaining to read, it must also take a how-to approach so that readers can actually participate.

Accuracy & Readability: Every story must be correct, clear, and interesting. *Sunset* is proud of its reputation for accuracy and dependability.

Style: Stories should be written using the active voice. The tone should be informative but friendly, intelligent but not intimidating. Write as if you were giving travel guidance to a friend or family member. Writers may want to address the reader in the familiar (you) form ("You've probably never heard of a calf blabber, a chain-gang persuader, or a frozen Charlotte. Even if you have, you'll enjoy a stop at the Frontier Relic Museum.").

Sense of Place: Travel writers should strive to convey a sense of place: the characteristics that set a place apart and make it a worthwhile destination.

The writer's personal insight into a place or event can help the reader to more thoroughly enjoy a travel experience ("Upon arrival, honk your horn") or to avoid an unpleasant one (crowds, sunburn, dangerous terrain, etc.).

Insight and local flavor also can be expressed through the judicious use of a quote or two from an expert source ("I've traveled the world, and always come back. There's a lot of hype about Malibu but also an intangible magic.").

Logical Order: Establish a logical order for topics, categories, and listings: alphabetical, chronological, geographical (north to south, near to far, etc.). Begin with an arresting lead that clearly establishes a reason for reading on.

Straight Facts: Basic travel facts are essential—directions for getting to a destination, distances, addresses, dates, hours of operation, costs, and telephone numbers for further information.

Freshness: Look for news pegs and fresh angles on familiar destinations or events. Often a single destination offers multiple opportunities for readers to visit related attractions such as art galleries, specialty shops, or restaurants.

Variety: Look for activities that would appeal to a wide range of readers, from families to empty-nesters. Here are some subjects regularly treated in *Sunset's* stories:

OUTDOOR RECREATION: Bike tours; bird-watching spots; camping and hiking in state and national parks; cruising; fishing; hiking; skiing (downhill and cross-country); walking or driving tours of historic districts, fruit- or wine-producing areas.

INDOOR ADVENTURES: New museums and displays; art exhibits with unique Western themes; living history programs dealing with Western lore; hands-on science programs at institutions such as aquariums or planetariums; specialty shopping (Western art, crafts, antiques).

SPECIAL EVENTS: Festivals that celebrate a region's unique social, cultural, or agricultural heritage (examples: Oktoberfest, jazz festival, strawberry festival).

SURPRISE US: Look for great weekend getaways, backroad drives, urban adventures, culinary discoveries (ethnic dining enclaves).

Photography: Writers are encouraged to submit the names of prospective sources of color photographs (35mm or medium-format transparencies preferred) to illustrate stories. However, *Sunset* will arrange for all photo submissions and/or assignments to photographers.

Freelance garden articles

Sunset is Western America's largest-circulation regional magazine, with monthly issues devoted to four subject areas: travel and recreation; gardening and outdoor living; food and entertaining; and home design and decorating.

Sunset is looking for thoroughly researched, well-written stories and Garden Guide items that describe home gardening projects that can be successfully accomplished in a day or over a weekend or growing season.

Submission Procedures: No responsibility is assumed for unsolicited manuscripts. Writers must submit a query letter to the editor in advance. The query letter should explain and outline the proposed story idea, and suggest an appropriate month or season and the intended edition. Snapshots showing gardens or plants may be submitted with the query letter; include a self-addressed, stamped envelope for their return. Send query to Editorial Services, *Sunset*, 80 Willow Rd., Menlo Park, CA 94025. It will be forwarded to the appropriate editor.

Once an editor approves an idea for a Garden Guide item or story, the writer will be issued a Story Contract assigning an approximate word length and due date for the text. The contract specifies the terms of the agreement between the writer and *Sunset* Publishing Corporation.

Writers must have computer capabilities to submit stories by e-mail. The assigned text should be submitted with the resource material specified in the contract.

Following submission of the text, the writer may be asked to revise the manuscript for publication or to supply further information or answer questions posed by the editor.

Payment will be made upon acceptance of the text with submission of an invoice in the amount specified in the contract.

After acceptance, the text will then be processed by staff copy editors and fact checkers. Writers will be credited with a byline if the manuscript is not substantially altered before publication in *Sunset Magazine*.

Word Length: One-page stories usually run from 300 to 400 words, depending on the number of color photographs or illustrations such as charts or drawings.

Items for *Sunset's Garden Guide* currently run from 150 to 300 words.

Take-action Magazine: *Sunset* is not an armchair magazine. While each item or story ought to be interesting to read, it must also take a how-to approach so that readers can use the information to duplicate the activity in their own home gardens.

Climate Zones: In the West, the kinds of gardening people do, and the seasons in which they garden, are determined by the climate and topography of the area in which they live. The *Sunset Western Garden Book* identifies 24 different plant climate zones in the West, and it is to these zones (not USDA zones) that stories in *Sunset Magazine* refer. These climate zones dictate different planting times, gardening seasons of varying lengths, and, in most cases, different plants. For this reason, *Sunset's Garden Guide* items and many of the garden stories are published in regional editions.

Regional Editions: Garden Guide items are tailored to meet the home gardening needs of readers of *Sunset's* five regional editions: Northern California; Southern California (Santa Barbara to San Diego; also Hawaii); Pacific Northwest (Alaska, Oregon, Washington, and British Columbia); Southwest (Arizona, New Mexico, Clark County, Nevada/Las Vegas) and West Texas (Amarillo to El Paso); Mountain (Colorado, Idaho, Montana, Nevada except Clark County, Utah, and Wyoming).

Seasonality: *Sunset* times the publication of its garden stories to coincide with the periods during which plants are planted, in bloom, or ready for harvest.

Plant Availability: Every plant *Sunset* describes must be readily available in nurseries or from mail-order suppliers of plants or seeds. For plants not commonly available, be sure to list sources, including complete mailing addresses, telephone numbers, and prices for plants or seeds.

Accuracy: Every *Sunset* article must be correct. *Sunset* is proud of its reputation for accuracy and dependability. Writers are urged to verify their information by consulting with several expert sources such as botanists, horticulturists, Certified Nurserymen, extension agents, commercial growers, Master Gardeners, and landscape architects and designers. Writers are also urged to check botanical and common names for plants as listed in The *Sunset Western Garden Book* or another widely respected reference such as Hortus Third.

Style: Stories should be written using the active voice. The tone should be informative but friendly, intelligent but not intimidating. Write as if you were giving gardening guidance to a friend or family member visiting your backyard. Writers may want to address the reader in the familiar (you) form. Begin with an arresting lead that clearly establishes a reason for reading on.

Logical Order: Establish a logical order for topics, categories and listings: alphabetical (by common name), chronological (step-by-step technique), physical characteristics (plant size or flower color), sun to shade, etc.

Straight Facts: Basic gardening facts are essential: plant form and size; leaf color and shape; flower color, shape, size, and scent; fruit or vegetable size, flavor, and texture. Give clear directions for planting, fertilizing, harvesting, pruning, etc.

Variety: *Sunset* publishes Garden Guide items and stories that address a wide range of gardening subjects, including the following:

PLANTS: Flowering plants (annuals, bulbs, perennials); landscape plants (deciduous and evergreen trees, shrubs, vines, ground covers, ornamental grasses); fruits (berries, citrus, grapes, nuts, pome and stone fruits); vegetables and herbs. Emphasis is on what's new, rediscovered, or otherwise noteworthy.

GARDENS: Borders (mixed and formal); containers (pots, hanging baskets, window boxes); country-style (informal or old-fashioned Western look); raised beds; small spaces (narrow yards, rooftops); specialty gardens (antique roses, cooks' gardens, herbs, native plants, rock gardens, wildflowers).

LANDSCAPING: Drought-tolerant landscapes; garden remodels; outdoor "rooms" (spaces defined by plants, decks); privacy screens using plants; steep-slope landscaping solutions; water features (ponds). Timeliness is important: for example, a story on landscaping in fire-prone areas of California might be most appropriate for summer when there is the greatest chance of wildfires.

INDOOR GARDENING: Houseplant care, culture, and display; greenhouses, lighting techniques.

TIPS AND TECHNIQUES: *Sunset* looks for new and better solutions for familiar gardening problems, including soil preparation, planting, transplanting, propagation (cuttings, grafting), irrigation, mulching, fertilizing, harvesting, composting, pruning, plant disease and pest control using environmentally safe methods, lawn care, and flower arrangement (fresh and dry).

HOMEMADE DEVICES: Tools and other devices that help gardeners achieve success while saving time and effort. These devices must be tested and their usefulness proven.

PHOTOGRAPHY: Writers are encouraged to submit the names of prospective sources of color photographs (35mm or medium-format transparencies preferred) to illustrate stories. However, *Sunset* will arrange for all photo submissions and/or assignments to photographers.

Categories: Nonfiction—Architecture—Cooking—Crafts/Hobbies—Family—Food/Drink—Gardening—Outdoors—Recreation—Reference—Regional—Travel—Western

CONTACT: Editorial Services
Material: All
80 Willow Rd.
Menlo Park CA 94025
Phone: 650-321-3600

Supervision

Supervision is a monthly magazine for supervisory and middle management personnel. Its primary objective is to provide informative articles which develop the attitudes, skills, personal and professional qualities of the supervisory staff, enabling them to use more of their potential to increase productivity, reduce operating costs and achieve personal and company goals.

CONTENT: *Supervision* usually contains five or six feature articles each month, plus several regular columns prepared by our contributing editors. Most of the articles are contributed by people with practical experience in business and industry. We will also use question-and-answer interviews with people in industry and in-depth third-person features about how foremen and supervisors are doing their jobs in innovative ways. No advertising is used in this publication.

NEEDS: We are interested in articles addressing the following: time management, planning, delegating authority and assigning responsibility, building morale, empowering their staff, goal setting, quality management, motivating staff, teamwork, discipline, safety/accident prevention, cost cutting and new innovative management concepts.

We can use articles that deal with human relations and communication, such as specific ways in which people in business and industry can deal with each other more effectively; ways the supervisor can aid in the development of an individual employee; specific methods of supervision that produce results such as improved morale, lowered turnover, reduced absenteeism; ways to improve the communication of facts and feelings both upward and downward. How product costs and product quality affect the company's competitive position; topics that will stimulate the supervisor to broaden his/her perspective, develop personally and thus make an increasing contribution to a company.

SUBMISSION OF ARTICLES: We work in advance. Therefore, articles may be retained over a year. NRB buys all rights. A signed release is required before publication. Finished articles should contain from 1,500 to 1,800 words. We pay 4 cents a word. Payment is made according to the release date of the issue in which the manuscript appears. A sample is mailed to the free-lancer.

Manuscripts should be high quality typed (suitable for scanning—do not submit articles on low quality dot-matrix printers), double-spaced and on only one side of the paper. *The Associated Press Stylebook* is followed for editing. Please list the approximate number of words on each manuscript. The author should indicate address, current by-line containing background employment, company affiliation and educational degrees listing alma mater. Send a black-and-white glossy author photo to accompany credit line upon acceptance.

Your experience and your ideas are valuable. Through the pages of *Supervision*, your message may become helpful to thousands of supervisors.

Categories: Business—Careers—Cartoons—Money & Finances—Relationships—Personnel

CONTACT: Teresa Levinson, Editor
Material: All
320 Valley St.
Burlington IA 52601-5513
Phone: 319-752-5415

Remember: Editors change jobs and publishers change addresses. It is wise to invest in a phone call for the current information before submitting.

Supply Chain Systems Magazine

About Us

Supply Chain Systems Magazine, the automation/collaboration resource, is published 12 times a year. This publication was formerly known as *ID Systems: The Magazine of Automated Data Collection*. *Supply Chain Systems Magazine* writes about the software and hardware used by companies to improve efficiencies and cut costs in their business. These products include extended ERP, Warehouse Management Software, Advanced Planning and Scheduling, Customer Relationship, distribution, e-business, and bar code labeling on the software side. On the hardware side, we cover RFID, wireless local and wide area networks, mobile handheld devices, portable data terminals, ruggedized PCs, printers, media, smart cards, biometrics, and bar code scanners and readers. In addition to the magazine, ID Systems also publishes an annual hardcopy Buyer's Guide, which is also available in an online, interactive format on the Web at www.idsystems.com. We also publish news on our Website, and a weekly email with headline links called Supply Chain NewsLink.

Supply Chain Systems Magazine's readers are professionals involved in the design, specification, and approval of supply chain and asset management solutions. According to *Supply Chain Systems Magazine*'s June 2000 BPA statement, 29 percent of readers' primary function is IT professional, 23 percent corporate management, 18 percent warehouse or manufacturing, 15 percent engineer, and 15 percent, Other Supply Chain management.

Submissions

If you write a feature story for *Supply Chain Systems Magazine*, you are required to submit a source list with contact information of each person interviewed for the story, and a summary of attempted contacts with sources that the author and editor deemed appropriate for the story.

Supply Chain Systems Magazine has several types of feature stores. Most of our features require the author to interview multiple (at least 10) sources. For example, the Vertical Industry Overview requires the author to interview vendors and users in a given industry about a wide variety of new and emerging technologies and practices used in that industry's supply chain. The same is true for our TechEdge (focus on a particular emerging technology) and TechFocus (focus on a particular product category such as CRM) feature tracks. Additionally, the author needs to work with the editor to help provide ideas for and sources for graphical artwork.

Graphics & Photos

Supply Chain Systems Magazine's graphics are often technical diagrams that show the relationships and data flow between various integrated systems. We will also accept screen shots, photos, and other types of graphics, provided they advance the text of the article by relaying additional information. The author doesn't need to create these graphics, but instead should work closely with the editor to provide ideas or rough drafts of graphics that *Supply Chain Systems Magazine*'s professional designers can re-do in a professional format. We can accept Illustrator, PhotoShop, PowerPoint, JPG, EPS, TIFF, GIF, and PDF file formats. Electronic images must be at 266 Dots Per inch at 100 percent size to be used in the magazine.

Solutions Focus

Supply Chain Systems Magazine also publishes every month a case study on manufacturing and one on warehousing called Solutions Focus. If you are writing a case study for a vendor, and submit it to *Supply Chain Systems Magazine*, you should expect the article to be rewritten, and that the *Supply Chain Systems Magazine* editor will need to follow up with a source who works for the customer to ask additional questions. We also require technical figures to show data flow between various integrated systems in the particular solutions focus.

For information visit this year's editorial calendar in our Media Kit on our website.

Categories: Nonfiction—Business—Computers—Technology

CONTACT: David Andrews, Publisher
Material: All
PO Box 874
174 Concord St.
Peterborough NH 03458
Phone: 603-924-9631
Fax: 603-924-7408
E-mail: editors@idsystems.com
Website: www.idsystems.com

Surfer

Surfer gives surfers of all levels spectacular photos, informative and impassioned articles, insightful interviews and ground-breaking travel features. For more than four decades, it has been internationally recognized as a leading publication and trendsetter for the surfing community.

Visit *Surfer* on-line at www.surfermag.com.

We do not have formal writer's guidelines, but we do accept unsolicited material on a highly discriminatory basis. This publication is very subject specific, therefore, few freelance articles are published in our magazine. Please read a number of issues or visit us online to ascertain the publication's style and needs.

Send queries to address below.

Categories: Nonfiction—Interview—Lifestyle—Photography—Recreation—Sports—Travel

CONTACT: Sam George, Editor-in-Chief
Material: All
33046 Calle Aviador
San Juan Capistrano CA 92675
Website: www.surfermag.com

Swank
Erotic Fiction

All of the fiction currently used by SWANK is erotic in some sense—that is, both theme and content are sexual. Most of the stories (The Mysterious Stranger, The Bawdy Birthday Present) have been done before, so familiarity with previous tales of this type—in SWANK and elsewhere—is recommended. New angles are always welcome.

• Canadian restrictions: SWANK is distributed in Canada and the censors there practice their own strict standards regarding sexual material. To avoid problems, we generally shy away from material we know they'll object to or edit out any offensive references. Thus, we cannot consider stories about, or containing, the following: 1) S&M (including light bondage and mild humiliation); 2) Sex involving, or between, minors; 3) Unconscious, or dead, participants in sex; 4) Incest; 5) Bestiality.

Other Fiction

The magazine's format is currently flexible, and we will consider stories that are not strictly sexual in theme (humor, adventure, detective stories, etc.). However, these types of stories are much more likely to be considered if they portray some sexual element, or scene, within their content.

Nonfiction

1) Sex-related: Although dealing with sex and sexually related topics, these articles should be serious and well researched without being overwritten. Examples: "Sexaholics Anonymous," "Dream Programming," and "Voyeurism." Advice-type articles are also regularly featured. Examples: "How To Pick Up Girls At The Beach," and "How To Make The Man Shortage Work For You."

2) Action-oriented: We will consider non-sexual articles on topics dealing with action and adventure. The availability of photos to illustrate the articles is crucial to their acceptance—frequently, we will buy a package that includes both the article and transparencies. Recent

features include such diverse topics as mercenaries, dangerous occupations and off-road racing. Automotive features run monthly.

3) Interviews: Although SWANK has not been running interviews lately, we will consider conversations with entertainment, sports and sex-industry celebrities.

Procedure

In most cases we respond to article queries within three weeks and manuscripts within five weeks. Due to the volume of material we receive, we discourage phone calls.

Terms

Payment is upon publication. You will be notified of the publication date after acceptance. A sample copy is available for $7.99 postpaid; please make checks or money orders payable to Swank Publications.

Categories: Fiction—Nonfiction—Adventure—Entertainment—Erotica—Horror—Men's Issues—Paranormal

CONTACT: Jeremy McSandal, Editor
Material: All
210 Rt. 4E, Ste. 401
Paramus NJ 07652
Phone: 201-843-4004
Fax: 201-843-8636

Swim Magazine

Established 1984. *SWIM Magazine,* "the world's foremost authority on adult swimming," is an internationally recognized swimming magazine dedicated to adult fitness and competitive swimmers. *SWIM Magazine* has a circulation of over 50,000 subscribers and is the official magazine of United States Masters Swimming (USMS). Subscribers are about 50% male and 50% female. The average reader is a college-educated professional in his or her mid-30's to mid-40's; almost 17% of our readers have "terminal" (i.e., professional) degrees, such as M.D., Ph.D., etc. Swimmers subscribe to our magazine for entertainment, instruction and inspiration. Masters swimmers range in age from 19 to 103+. Articles must be well written and appeal to a broad audience. Query first.

SPECIFICS

Bimonthly. Pays approximately within one month after publication, generally 12 cents per word. Publishes ms. an average of four months after acceptance. Buys all rights. Byline given. Negotiates payment for artwork and photos. Photo credit given. Query first. Reports in two months on queries. Sample copy for $3.95 prepaid and 9" x12" SASE with $1.67 for postage.

EDITORIAL

Training Tips, Interview profiles, inspirational stories, new products, medical advice, dryland exercise, swim drills, nutrition, fitness, competition and exercise physiology make *SWIM Magazine* the #1 source worldwide of information for adults about the sport of swimming.

COPY

All submissions must include a brief background about the author. If possible, send a disk or an e-mail attachment as well (Word preferred). *SWIM Magazine* accepts freelance articles on a continuing basis. Articles range in length from 500-3,500 words. *SWIM Magazine* reserves the right to make any editorial changes.

Categories: Nonfiction—Diet/Nutrition—Health—Lifestyle—Physical Fitness—Recreation—Sports—Swimming

CONTACT: Phillip Whitten/Editor-in-Chief
Material: All
90 Bell Rock Plaza, Ste 200
Sedona AZ 86351
Phone: 928-284-4005
Fax: 928-284-2477
E-mail: swimworld@aol.com
Website: www.swiminfo.com

Swimming Technique

Established 1964. *Swimming Technique* magazine is the leading magazine for coaches and self-coached adult swimmers. Subscribers are primarily swim coaches, technical directors and self-coached adult swimmers. Articles must be well written and authoritative. Query first.

Specifics

Quarterly. Pays approximately one month after publication, generally 12 cents per word. Publishes mss an average of two months after acceptance. Buys all rights. Byline given. Negotiates payment for artwork and photos. Photo credit given. Query first. Reports in two months on queries. Sample copy for $5.50 prepaid and 9x12 SAE with $1.80 for postage.

Editorial

Technique, stroke analysis (especially through the use of underwater photography), training methods and tips, training programs of leading swimmers and swim clubs, interview profiles, new products, medical advice, dryland exercise, swim drills, nutrition, exercise physiology and discussion of new ideas, techniques and theories make *Swimming Technique* the #1 source worldwide for swimming coaches and self-coached adult swimmers.

Copy

All submissions must be typed, double-spaced and include a brief bio of the author. If possible, send a disk or an e-mail attachment as well (Word preferred). *Swimming Technique* accepts freelance articles on a continuing basis. Articles range in length from 500-3,500 words. *Swimming Technique* reserves the right to make any editorial changes.

Categories: Nonfiction—Health—Interview—Sports/Recreation

CONTACT: Dr. Phillip Whitten, Editor-in-Chief
Material: All
CONTACT: Bob Ingram, Managing Editor
Material: All
Sports Publications, Inc., 90 Bell Rock Plaza, Ste. 200
Sedona AZ 86351
Phone: 928-284-4005
Fax: 928-284-2477
E-mail: swimworld@aol.com

Swimming World Junior Swimmer

Swimming World & Junior Swimmer magazine

Established 1960. *Swimming World* magazine, acknowledged as "the Bible" of competitive swimming, is internationally recognized as the foremost authority on all aspects of competitive swimming. Circulation is 59,000. Subscribers are about 60% female and 40% male. Though readers include top competitive swimmers in their teens and twenties, and coaches, technical directors and officials from around the world. However, the average reader is a 14 year-old American girl. Swimmers subscribe to our magazine for information, instruction and inspiration. Articles must be well written and appeal to at least one (and preferably, several) of the major segments of our readership. Query first.

Specifics

Monthly. Pays approximately one month after publication, generally 12 cents per word. Publishes mss an average of two months after acceptance. Buys all rights. Byline given. Negotiates payment for artwork and photos. Photo credit given. Query first. Reports in two months on queries. Sample copy for $4.50 prepaid and 9x12 SAE with $1.80 for postage.

Editorial

Training and technique tips, meet stories and results, insider information, interview profiles, inspirational stories, new products, medical advice, dryland exercise, swim drills, interview profiles, inspirational stories, new products, medical advice, dryland exercise, swim drills, nutrition, fitness, competition and exercise physiology make

Swimming World the #1 source worldwide of information for competitive swimmers. The "Junior Swimmer" section of each issue includes articles and interactive features written by and for kids.

Copy

All submissions must be typed, double-spaced and include a brief bio of the author. If possible, send disk or e-mail attachment as well (Word preferred). *Swimming World* accepts freelance articles on a continuing basis. Articles range in length from 500-3,500 words. *Swimming World* reserves the right to make any editorial changes.

Categories: Nonfiction—Children—Health—Physical Fitness—Recreation—Sports/Recreation—Teen—Young Adult—Swimming

CONTACT: Phillip Whitten, Editor-in-Chief
Material: All
Sports Publications Inc
90 Bell Rock Plaza, Ste 200
Sedona AZ 86351
Phone: 928-284-4005
Fax: 928-284-2477
E-mail: swimworld@aol.com

Sycamore Review
Purdue University

1) The editors aim to publish the new writer alongside the established writer; in all cases we look for exceptional writing. Please send us only your very best work.

2) *Sycamore Review* accepts original poetry, short fiction (stories or novel excerpts), creative nonfiction (e.g., personal essays), short drama and translations. We generally do not accept genre pieces (conventional science fiction, romance, horror, etc.) or critical essays. All graphic artwork, interviews and book reviews in the magazine are solicited or staff work. Aside from translations, we do not publish material that has already appeared in another publication.

3) Poetry manuscripts should be typed single-spaced, one poem to a page. All other submissions should be typed double-spaced. We do accept simultaneous submissions, though we expect prompt notification if the work is accepted elsewhere.

4) *Sycamore Review* reads manuscripts from September 1 through March 1. Manuscripts received during the summer months will be returned if accompanied by a SASE.

5) As a general rule, *Sycamore Review* will not publish creative work by any student currently attending Purdue University. Former students of Purdue University should wait one (1) calendar year before submitting a manuscript to the magazine. (This rule does not apply to book reviews or otherwise solicited work.)

7) Purdue University acquires first-time North American rights to work published in *Sycamore Review*. After publication, all rights revert to the author.

8) The artist shall receive two (2) copies of the issue in which his or her work appears.

9) Subscriptions to the *Sycamore Review* are $12.00/year ($14.00 foreign) in U.S. funds for two issues/year (Winter/ Spring and Summer/Fall). A sample copy of the latest issue is available for $7.00. Back issues of volumes 1-7 of the magazine are available for $4.00 each; back issues of volume 8 and all subsequent volumes are $5.60 each. Please make checks payable to Purdue University. Indiana residents add 5% sales tax.

This document is subject to change without notice.

Thank you for your interest in our magazine.

The Editors

Categories: Fiction—Nonfiction—Arts—Drama—Interview—Literature—Men's Fiction—Photography—Poetry—Short Stories—Women's Fiction—Writing

CONTACT: Poetry Editor
Material: Poetry

CONTACT: Fiction Editor
Material: Fiction
CONTACT: Editor-in-Chief
Material: All other submissions
Dept. of English, Heavilon Hall, Purdue University
W. Lafayette IN 47907
Phone: 765-494-3783
Fax: 765-494-3780
E-mail: Sycamore@purdue.edu
Website: www.sla.purdue.edu/sycamore

symploke

symploke supports new and developing notions of comparative theory and literature, and is committed to interdisciplinary studies, intellectual pluralism, and open discussion. The editors are particularly interested in scholarship on the interrelations among philosophy, literature, culture criticism and intellectual history, though we will consider articles on any aspect of the intermingling of discourses and disciplines.

The journal takes its name from the Greek word *symploke* which has among its various meanings interweaving, interlacing, connection and struggle. The journal's editors believe that continuing change in the humanities is contingent upon the interweaving, connection, and struggle between traditionally independent domains of discourse. One of our broader goals is to contribute to the opening of alternative academic frontiers by providing a forum for scholars of varying disciplines to engage in the intermingling of ideas in innovative ways.

symploke is published and distributed in association with the University of Nebraska Press.

Submissions

Submissions of any length which are appropriate to the aims of *symploke* will be considered, although those between 4,000 and 6,500 words (approximately 16-26 typed, double-spaced pages) are preferred. Please keep in mind that submitted manuscripts need not be intended for an upcoming special issue; general submissions of high quality are encouraged. The editors reserve the right to make stylistic alterations in the interest of clarity. Authors will receive two complementary issues of the journal. All submissions must strictly follow the guidelines for copy preparation listed below. Articles not conforming to these guidelines may be sent back to the author for revision.

Preparation of Copy

1. All submissions must provide a complete listing of references and use footnotes rather than endnotes.

2. Footnotes should generally consist only of references and are to be consecutively numbered throughout the manuscript.

3. References must include the names of publishers as well as places of publication. Also include full names and a complete listing of translators and editors.

4. The format of the manuscript must conform to the current *MLA Style Manual*.

5. All manuscripts must be submitted in duplicate. If the manuscript was word-processed, include a copy of your IBM- or Macintosh-compatible disk. Microsoft word or ASCII files are preferable.

6. All quotations, titles, names and dates must be checked for accuracy.

7. All articles must be written in English.

8. This journal has a policy of blind peer reviewing; thus the author's name should not appear on the manuscript and a separate title page must be provided.

9. Material not kept for publication will be returned if accompanied by a stamped, self-addressed envelope.

All materials published in this journal are copyrighted by *symploke*. Submission of an article to this journal entails the author's agreement to assign copyright to *symploke*. Articles appearing in *symploke* may be reproduced for research purposes, personal reference, and classroom use without special permission and without fee payment. This permission does not extend to other kinds of reproduction such as copying for general distribution, for the creation of collected works or anthologies, for advertising or promotional purposes, or for resale. These and all other rights are reserved.

Categories: Culture, History, Literature, Philosophy

CONTACT: Jeffrey R. Di Leo, Editor-in-Chief
Material: All
University of Houston—Victoria
3007 N. Ben Wilson
Victoria TX 77901
E-mail: editor@symploke.org (send submissions as attachments)
Website: www.symploke.org

Syracuse New Times

Every year more than half the editorial matter published in the *Syracuse New Times* comes from people not on our full-time staff. Cover stories, interviews, What's Shakin' items, arts and entertainment features, sports stories, book reviews and cartoons are all occasionally generated by free-lancers. It's fair to say *The New Times* would have a tough time surviving without them.

As a result, we look forward to reading, editing and eventually publishing free-lance material.

This being said, you should be aware that for every 10 unsolicited manuscripts we receive, only one is likely to be published in *The New Times*. To ensure that you waste neither our time nor yours, here are some guidelines.

Substance

Generally speaking, what most impresses us is thoughtful, clear writing. The subject matter is almost secondary. It is crucial that the piece be lively, interesting and appealing to the uninterested reader—in the way that a well-written piece on boxing can appeal to a reader who hates the subject. We tend to avoid journalism that is abstract and generalized and to favor writing that deals with specifics and, in so doing, suggests the universal. We generally turn down stories written in the first person.

With good writing of paramount importance, we then give preference to the stories that fit our format. Take a look at recent copy of *The New Times* to see what we make room for and what we don't really have. Cover stories are often news stories of features of considerable length. The What's Shakin' section is shorter, newsier items, other sections contain art and entertainment stories, human-interest pieces, food and lifestyle articles and reviews.

Since *The New Times* is a Syracuse newspaper, we generally run stories that are about the metropolitan area, or at least relevant to Central New York readers.

Now that we've laid down the rules, remember that rules are made to be broken. A story, no matter how it may deviate from these guidelines, may be published in *The New Times* if it is well written and strikes our fancy.

Process

If you have an idea for an article, send us a brief explanation of the story and how you expect to put it together, including possible sources and key questions. If this is your first query to us, please include some kind of resumé. (Sorry about the formality, but we like to know with whom we're dealing.)

If you're already written an article and would like us to look at it, we are happy to look at unsolicited manuscripts. Most of the articles we use are between 600 and 1,000 words (three to six typed pages). Cover stories and longer features sometimes run two to three times that length.

Generally speaking, the shorter the better, but you should write what you're comfortable with. We can always adjust it later.

Odds and Ends

The New Times purchases first publication rights only; all other rights revert to you.

The New Times' libel insurance does not cover free-lance writers. You must assume full responsibility for the legal consequences that may occur as the result of your reporting.

NEVER say you are writing a story for this newspaper without first getting permission from the editor.

Manuscripts should be triple-spaced, on erasable paper. If you can furnish us a floppy disk created an IBM-compatible word processing program, so much the better.

Do not send us your only copy. We do not return manuscripts unless they are accompanied by a stamped, self-addressed envelope. Please allow us up to a month to respond to your submissions.

A Final Note

You may mail, e-mail or fax your query to us or leave it in person at our front desk. Please don't make an editor's life any more difficult by asking to see him or her. The time to discuss a story is after we have read it, not when you first bring it in.

Categories: Nonfiction—Alternate Life-style—Arts—Book Reviews—Campus Life—Culture—Entertainment—Food/Drink—Human Rights

CONTACT: Molly English, Editor-in-Chief
Material: All
A. Zimmer, Ltd.
1415 W. Genesee St.
Syracuse NY 13204-2156
Phone: 315-422-7011
Fax: 315-422-1721
E-mail: menglish@syracusenewtimes.com
Website: www.syracusenewtimes.rway.com

T'ai Chi

Types of Articles

Generally speaking, an article should take into account the special needs and desires of the readers of *T'ai Chi*. Many are beginners or thinking about starting classes. Many are serious students, and have studied and even taught for years.

They are interested in many aspects: self-defense, internal skills, health, meditation, fitness, self-improvement, ch'i cultivation, Traditional Chinese Medicine (acupuncture, herbs, massage, etc.) and spiritual growth.

More specifically, articles may be a feature or interview about a style, self-defense techniques, principles and philosophy, training methods, weapons, case histories of benefits, or new or unusual uses for T'ai Chi Ch'uan. Try to avoid profiles of teachers that focus just on their many skills and accomplishments. Interviews with teachers or personalities should focus on their unique or individual insight into T'ai Chi Ch'uan, internal martial arts, qigong, or Traditional Chinese Medicine rather than on their personal achievement or ability, although their background can be woven into the article.

Examples of the uses could be teaching the disabled, teaching of T'ai Chi Ch'uan in a corporate or medical environment, or martial techniques. New approaches to teaching or practice or the basic principles are almost always of interest as long as it doesn't promote a particular teacher or school. When planning and writing the article ask yourself: Is the material new or fresh? Is it useful to practitioners? Is it interesting?

An examination of past issues is one of your best guides to what we publish.

Present the information clearly, fairly, and objectively. Quotations, anecdotes, examples, and parallel references help make an article more readable and interesting. Writing that is simple and direct is understood best. If organization of the article is a problem, try a question and answer format.

If you want to discuss a story possibility first, please feel free to contact me by phone or with a note or by e-mail at taichi@ taichi.com.

Please do not send articles that are simultaneously sent to other publications, unless it specifies on the first page that it is a news release or that it has been submitted elsewhere, too.

Also, please do not send articles that you have put on your web site or plan to put on your web site. We pay for articles and do not want to have to pay for an article that you are giving away free on your website. Our subscribers should not have to pay to read articles that are available free on a website.

We appreciate that many people now have their own websites and want to include good articles to attract visitors. But it is best that you create your own material for your website that is distinct from whatever you submit to us.

Manuscript Specifications

Manuscripts should be typed, double-spaced, with a margin not more than 80 characters wide. Put a tentative title on the front page. Put the title abbreviated on each subsequent page with a page number. At the end of the article write "-30-" to indicate it is complete. Include your name, address, and phone number on the first page and the best times to reach you by phone. Include a paragraph about yourself and also about the subject if it is an interview with someone else. Articles can be from 500 to 3500 words long or more. Payment can range from $75.00 to $500.00, depending on the length and quality of the article. This includes payment for photos. Payment is for first North American Serial rights only. Payment is on publication. Payment is usually within 30 days of publication.

If possible, include one or more 4 x 6, 5 x 7 or 8 x 10 glossy black and white prints. Color photos can be used but may print a little dark, red colors in particular. Indicate if you want them returned.

Do not send photos over the internet. If you plan to send them on a CD, they should be scanned as RGB at 300 dpi and saved as Tiff files.

The photos should have identification of the individuals in the photo written on a separate piece of paper sent with the photos or on a post-it on the photo. If the photo is of a posture, the name of the style and posture should be given. Don't write on the back of the photo. Model releases are required. Releases authorizing use of the photos should be dated and witnessed.

Categories: Nonfiction—Asian-American—Health—Physical Fitness—Sports/Recreation—Martial Arts

CONTACT: Marvin Smalheiser, Editor/Publisher
Material: All
PO Box 39938
Los Angeles CA 90039
Phone: 323-665-7773
Fax: 323-665-1627
E-mail: taichi@tai-chi.com
Website: www.tai-chi.com

Take Pride! Community

Take Pride! Community is a weekly publication that promotes education and economic empowerment for all people. Topics must pertain to the following categories: Education, Economics/Finance, Business, Technology, Health Arts/Culture, Politics, Religion, Family/Society, History, or Seasonal pieces. Article length: 250-800 words. Writers are paid upon publication of their articles, which must be submitted one month in advance of publication. Byline given. All paid articles must be requested and approved by the president/CEO. Responds in two weeks on queries. (Include SASE for postal response.) Every article must include photograph(s); exceptions within discretion of the editor. Photo payment negotiated individually. Model releases and identification of subjects required. *Take Pride! Community* buys unlimited rights, makes work-for-hire assignments and accepts queries by mail and e-mail.

Categories: Arts—Business—Culture—Economics—Education—Family—Health—History—Money & Finances—Politics—Religion—Society

CONTACT: Ryan D. Arnold
Material: All
1014 Franklin St SE, Ste. 4969
Grand Rapids MI 49507-1327
Phone: 616-243-4114
E-mail: gdesigns@oneblood-onerace.org
Website: www.oneblood-onerace.org/TakePride/Contact.html

Tampa Review
Literary Journal of the University of Tampa

1. *Tampa Review* is the faculty-edited literary journal of the University of Tampa. We publish two issues a year, one in the Fall and one in the Spring. Our editorial staff considers submissions between September and December for publication in the following year. Manuscripts received prior to August will be returned unread. We maintain this policy so that works submitted to us are not held for an unduly long time.

2. We suggest you submit 3 to 6 poems and/or one or more prose manuscripts of up to 5,000 words. We do not print book-length poetry, and rarely publish excerpts from larger works of either poetry or prose.

3. Poetry may be submitted single-spaced. Clearly indicate any space breaks within stories, and stanza breaks in poetry, especially when they occur at the end of a page, so that these breaks will be obvious to our editors.

4. Please do not send us work which is also being submitted elsewhere. We do not consider simultaneous submissions. This policy saves our editors from reading work which is not actually available for first North American publication, and it saves authors the embarrassment of having to withdraw a manuscript.

5. The writer's name and complete address should appear on the first page of each manuscript. For multiple-page submissions, subsequent pages should be numbered and should include the author's name and short title at the top of each page. We also appreciate receiving a telephone number and/or e-mail address.

6. Fiction and nonfiction submissions should state a total word count at the top of the first page (upper right-hand corner). For poetry manuscripts, a line count is useful.

7. Translations must be submitted in original language as well as translated versions. Please also include a short biographical note on the translated author and the author's permission to translate.

8. A reporting time of approximately 12 weeks can be expected.

9. Our payment is ten dollars per page for both prose and poetry, payable upon publication, one free copy of the review in which the work(s) appears, and a 40% discount on additional copies.

Suggestion: It is sometimes helpful to get an idea of the kinds of work a magazine is publishing; sample copies are available for that purpose. *Tampa Review* sample copies are $5.00, including postage.

Categories: Fiction—Nonfiction—Literature—Poetry—Creative Nonfiction

CONTACT: Donald Morrill/Martha Serpas, Poetry Editors
Material: Poetry
CONTACT: Lisa Birnbaum/Kathleen Ochshorn, Fiction Editors
Material: Fiction Editor
CONTACT: Elizabeth Winston, Nonfiction Editor
Material: Nonfiction
University of Tampa Press, 401 W. Kennedy Blvd.
Tampa FL 33606
Phone: 813-253-6266

Teacher Magazine:

Thank you for contacting *Teacher Magazine*. *Teacher Magazine* was founded in 1989 by Editorial Projects in Education, which also publishes Education Week. Teacher is an independent, nonprofit publication that covers education issues, school culture, and the profession in general. It is published eight times a year and goes to about 130,000 readers nationwide.

Guidelines for submitting STORY IDEAS:

Articles in *Teacher Magazine* are split into several sections: Current Events, which are shorter and newsier; Front of the Book, mid-length features about different facets of educational life; and full-length features, which run 3,000 to 6,000 words and are more narrative in style.

The editors of Teacher welcome ideas from new sources, though the large number of unsolicited pitches received makes it impossible to respond personally to each one. An editor will be in touch if an article is to be considered for an upcoming issue. Please do not follow up with phone calls, e-mails, or letters to check the status of a submission. Future submissions will be considered independently.

Guidelines for submitting COMMENT PIECES:

The editors of Teacher encourage submissions for the magazine's "Comment" section. The magazine aims to challenge, provoke, connect, and entertain teachers. To do this, we must hear from a variety of voices in "Comment."

Articles generally fall under two headings. "Viewpoint" submissions should address issues in pre-collegiate education that are of particular interest to classroom teachers. In organization and tone, these articles should take the form of opinion essays rather than scholarly papers, research reports, or lesson plans. The essays may touch on local or state issues, but they must not solely focus on regional matters.

"First Person" submissions should describe a particularly meaningful or moving personal experience. These articles are generally school-related, and they are often lighter in tone than "Viewpoint" essays.

Submissions should run at most about 1,200 words (roughly four to five double-spaced pages). Shorter stories are also accepted and often run under a separate heading, "Voices." If your submission is accepted for publication, you will be contacted about its publication date by phone or mail. An honorarium will be paid upon publication.

Essays can be submitted at any time. Note clearly on your submission your name, phone number, fax number, address, and e-mail address.

Categories: Nonfiction—Education

CONTACT: Features Editor
Material: Story Ideas
CONTACT: Comment Editor
Material: Comment Section
6935 Arlington Rd., Ste. 100

Bethesda, MD 20814
Phone: 301-280-3100
Website: www.teachermagazine.org

Teachers of Vision
A Publication of Christian Educators Association International

Teachers of Vision is a magazine for Christian educators in public and private education. Its articles inspire, inform and equip teachers and administrators in the educational arena. In the words of Forrest Turpen, executive director of CEAI, "It is an extended faculty room, a place of refreshment, dialogue, encouragement and guidance." The guidance often deals with the legality of living out one's faith in the workplace.

Our Readers

Teachers of Vision is a membership and limited subscription publication. Readers look for educational articles that inspire and provide practical ideas they can use in their profession. Our audience is primarily public school educators.

Our writers are:

• Able to integrate secular and spiritual insights
• Faithful to the teachings of Scripture
• Up-to-date on trends in contemporary education

Our Editorial Needs

We invite writers to submit the following types of manuscripts:

Feature articles between 1000-2500 words, dealing with specific issues of interest to Christian educators. These may be written as how-to articles, personal experience pieces, educational philosophy, methodology, or documented reports.

Our Editorial Needs

Mini-features between 400-750 words that: highlight a holiday or special event and its classroom relevance; describe a successful teaching technique; or update readers on newsworthy happenings in education; or share an inspirational personal experience.

Interviews of 500-750 words with outstanding Christian educators.

Classroom resource reviews between 100-200 words. These may be on books, curriculum, videos, visual aids, games or other items related to teaching.

Payment issued upon publication $20-$40 and copies.

IMPORTANT: Please submit articles via email to: judy@ceai.org or send a floppy disk (WordPerfect 6.1 , WORD or RTF format) to the mailing address below. Request permission to send photographs.

When you submit manuscripts, remember:

• Include a 2-3 sentence byline with your article (we may also request a color photo if your work is accepted for publication).

• Due to limited staff, it may take several weeks to respond to your submission. You are welcome to inquire about the status of your manuscript after four weeks.

• We cannot guarantee your article will be accepted.

• We reserve the right to edit material for length and content.

• We maintain the right to reprint your article in other CEAI publications and CEAI's website.

• We accept previously published articles, provided you inform us of where the article appeared and verify ownership of reprint rights.

• You are welcome to query us with article ideas to avoid submitting material we cannot use (send a brief description of the article, detailing its main points).

• Seasonal material must be received at least four months in advance.

• If you wish to have your manuscript returned, you must enclose a self-addressed, first-class stamped envelope.

• If your article is accepted for submission, it may take 4-6 issues before final publication. We do appreciate your patience.

• For a hard copy of these guidelines and samples of our publications, please send a 9x12 SASE with five first class postage stamps.

Teachers of Vision **Magazine Theme:**

Keep in mind that our articles need a distinctively Christian viewpoint. However, please avoid even the appearance of preaching and cut all religious jargon! We need writers who are able to present topics naturally and who portray issues of faith as an integrated part of teaching.

Categories: Nonfiction—Education—Religion

CONTACT: Judy Turpen, Contributing Editor
Material: All
Christian Educators Association Int'l
PO Box 41300
Pasadena CA 91114
Phone: 626-798-1124
Fax: 626-798-2346
E-mail: judy@ceai.org

Teaching Theatre

Teaching Theatre is a quarterly educational theatre journal published by the Educational Theatre Association, a professional association for theatre educators and artists. *Teaching Theatre*, available to EdTA members and libraries only, has a circulation of approximately 3,200. The majority of the journal's readers are high school theatre teachers. Subscribers also include elementary, middle school, and college theatre teachers, school administrators, libraries, and others interested in educational theatre.

Opportunities for contributors

Teaching Theatre is an even blend of advocacy, how-to, and theory. If an article can be of use to a theatre teacher—either by presenting a model, an innovative idea, or a specific teaching methodology—we're going to be interested in taking a look at it. *Teaching Theatre*'s readers are a well-educated and experienced group, for the most part; general interest essays on the value of educational theatre aren't going to be of much interest to them and, therefore, not to us either.

We buy twelve to fifteen articles a year, general length 750-4,000 words. A typical issue might include an article on theatre curriculum development, a profile of an exemplary theatre education program, a how-to teach piece on acting, directing, or play writing, and a news story or two about pertinent educational theatre issues and events.

Graphics

Photos and illustrations to accompany articles are welcomed, and when available, should be submitted at the same time as the manuscript. Acceptable forms: black and white prints, 5 x 7 or larger; line art. Unless other arrangements are made, payment for articles includes payment for the photos and illustrations.

Rights and returns

We buy first publication rights (unless we make other arrangements with an author), pay on acceptance, report in four to six weeks, and return all material that is accompanied by a self-addressed stamped envelope.

Queries and sample copies

We prefer to see a finished manuscript but will respond to query letters. Sample copies are available for $2.

Payment

Honorariums of $50 to $350 are paid for accepted work. Payment is based on quality of work, amount of editing and rewriting needed, length of work, and inclusion of photos or graphics.

Manuscript specifications

We edit manuscripts to conform to *The Chicago Manual of Style.* Manuscripts should be typed double spaced on a sixty-character line. Photocopies are acceptable as long as they are clearly legible. Contributors should keep an exact copy or computer file of any manuscript submitted.

Once articles are accepted, authors are asked to supply their work electronically via e-mail (jpalmarini@edta.org) or on IBM compatible diskettes, sent to Teaching Theatre, 2343 Auburn Avenue, Cincinnati, OH 45219.

All submissions are subject to editing, and we try to involve authors in that process as much as possible.

Whenever time allows, we send galley proofs to authors for review—usually by fax.

A Contributor's Cheat Sheet:
What makes us cranky

• Writers who are too lazy or careless to do basic reporting and research. Very few articles are complete with only one quoted source.

• Writers who misrepresent themselves as experts, or are not up front about if and where a piece has been previously published.

• Submissions that ignore or misunderstand our audience; articles that either talk down to our readers or are way over their heads. (If a piece has footnotes, it's probably too academic for us.)

• Contributors who create an impression of conflict of interest by writing about an organization in which they themselves are involved—although we do sometimes publish first-person accounts.

• Writers who are impossible to get a hold of, or who do not return messages.

What makes us happy

• Writers who really understand our audience.

• Writers who bring lots of strong, specific article ideas to the table, and keep abreast of topics recently covered by the journal.

• Contributors who submit written queries or complete articles, rather than interrupting our work to make a sales pitch by phone.

• Writers who understand the need for editorial input, and can make and/or accept necessary changes gracefully.

• Writers who can provide publishable photography to go along with their pieces (snapshots are not publishable).

Illustration ideas are also appreciated.

• Writers who include student voices in their pieces when appropriate, as well as a variety of other sources.

• Writers whose work is well organized, factual, and clean.

Categories: Drama, Education

CONTACT: James Palmarini, Editor
Material: All
Educational Theatre Association
2343 Auburn Ave.
Cincinnati OH 45219
Phone: 513-421-3900
E-mail: jpalmarini@edta.org
Website: www.edta.org

TEACHING
TOLERANCE

Teaching Tolerance

The semiannual magazine *Teaching Tolerance* is dedicated to helping preschool, elementary, and secondary teachers promote tolerance and understanding between widely diverse groups of students. It includes articles, teaching ideas, and reviews of other resources available to educators. Our interpretation of "tolerance" follows the definition of American Heritage Dictionary: The capacity for or the practice of recognizing and respecting the beliefs or practices of others.

In general, we want lively, simple, concise writing. The writing style should be descriptive and reflective. Writers should show the strength of programs dealing successfully with diversity by employing clear descriptions of real scenes and interactions, and by using quotes from teachers and students. We cannot accept articles that employ jargon, rhetoric, or academic analysis. We ask that prospective writers study previous issues of the magazine to see our style and content. Then submit a query letter and writing samples.

Features: 1,000-3,500 words. Should have a strong classroom focus, with national perspective where appropriate. Usually accompanied by sidebars of helpful information such as resources, how-to steps, short profiles. Writers are typically free-lance journalists with knowledge of issues in education or educators with experience writing for national non-academic publications. Fees range from $500 to $3,500 depending on length and complexity. The freelance fee and reasonable expenses are paid on acceptance. If a solicited story is unacceptable as submitted, we may assist in preparing a publishable manuscript, but sometimes, despite the best intentions of both author and editor, a manuscript will be judged unacceptable. In such instances, a kill fee in the amount equal to one-half of the agreed-upon fee will be paid to the writer.

Essays: 400-800 words. Personal reflection, description of school program, community-school program, classroom activity, how-to. Writers are typically teachers, counselors, parents or other educators. "Between the Lines" essays describe how literature can be used to teach tolerance. Fees range from $300-$800 upon publication.

Idea Exchange: 250-500 words. Brief descriptions of classroom lesson plans, special projects, or other school activities that promote tolerance. These are usually submitted by teachers, administrators or parents who have successfully used the technique or program. Fee: $100-$200 upon publication.

Student Writing: Poems and short essays dealing with diversity, tolerance and justice. Printed when appropriate to magazine content. Fee: $50 upon publication.

If you have any questions concerning submissions, please contact Cynthia Pon.

Categories: African-American—Arts—Asian-American—Associations—Book Reviews—Cartoons—Children—Christian Interests—College—Crime—Culture—Dance—Drama—Directories—Disabilities—Education—Entertainment—Family—Feminism—Film/Video—Folklore—Gay/Lesbian—General Interest—Government—Hispanic—History—Human Rights—Internet—Jewish Interest—Juvenile—Language—Law—Lifestyle—Men's Issues—Multicultural—Music—Native American—Parenting—Poetry—Psychology—Reference—Relationships—Religion—Rural America—Short Stories—Society—Spiritual—Teen—Television/Radio—Textbooks—Theatre—Women's Issues—Writing—Young Adult

CONTACT: Submissions Editor
Material: All
400 Washington Ave.
Montgomery AL 36104
Phone: 334-956-8200
Fax: 334-956-8484
E-mail: cpon@splcenter.org
Website: www.teachingtolerance.org

Technical Analysis of Stocks & Commodities

These guidelines are provided to acquaint you, as a *Technical Analysis of Stocks & Commodities* artist or prospective artist, with our needs and requirements, as well as to provide you with some basic information about submitting art to STOCKS & COMMODITIES for publication.

WHAT IS TECHNICAL ANALYSIS?

Technical analysis is a form of financial market analysis that studies demand and supply for securities and commodities. This analysis is based on studies of price and trading volume. Using charts and modeling techniques, technicians attempt to identify price trends in a market.

Charting is the most common method of analysis for technical analysts. Traders chart price movement in various markets either by

hand or by computer. Because charts are such a basic component of technical analysis, most illustrations for articles will incorporate some chart elements. Below is a typical price chart that a technical analyst or investor might study:

Technical Analysis of Stocks & Commodities is a monthly magazine for traders and investors who trade or invest in securities, commodities, options, mutual funds or other tradables. Our readers include institutional as well as individual investors. The magazine is an educational, how-to publication that covers a variety of subject categories in each issue. Some of those categories are trading techniques and methods, computerized techniques, statistical and mathematical analysis, artificial intelligence, psychology of trading, and product reviews.

ART CONTENT, STYLE & USE OF COLOR

We are looking for art that is relevant to technical analysis and trading as well as to the article for which the art piece is assigned. The Art Director, Christine Morrison, assigns art monthly for an upcoming issue. Each art order will list the specifications and other important information about each art assignment, including art dimensions, deadlines and ideas for content. A summary of an article scheduled to be published is sent with an art assignment to help establish a theme for the art. However, because the editorial content of any issue may change without notice at any time, art submitted may be used with another article in the same issue instead.

COVER ART

For cover art, we require two elements to be present: first, that the content of the art is generically representational of technical analysis and trading; and second, that colors used are bright enough to stand out on the newsstand.

The cover art for any given issue is usually used inside the magazine as well to introduce one of our articles. Therefore, the concept used for the cover art will usually be based on an article.

COPYRIGHTS

Upon acceptance, Technical Analysis, Inc. acquires one-time rights to the artwork plus reprint rights. Reprint rights include the right to reuse an image whenever a page of the magazine or magazine cover is reprinted, such as in book form, on computer disk or other media. Your material must be an original work that has not been previously published and is not currently under consideration by any other publication.

PAYMENT

Payment is made upon publication. Payment for art varies depending on the art budget for that issue and art specifications, such as whether the piece will be color or black and white and whether the piece is for the cover or inside the magazine. Payment information for each art assignment will be included in the art order.

To receive payment, we need the following information: Artist's name, address, telephone number and Social Security Number (SSN). You can include all this information in an invoice sent to us based on your art order.

Payment is mailed along with a tearsheet or copy of the STOCKS & COMMODITIES issue in which the art appears. Artists wishing additional copies of the issue in which their work appears may order them from the main office (currently $3.50 per copy). Large quantity orders should be arranged prior to publication. Reprint rates are available for quantities of 100 or more.

Categories: Nonfiction—Money & Finances

CONTACT: Jayanthi Gopalakrishnan, Editor
Material: All
4757 California Ave. SW
Seattle WA 98126
Phone: 206-938-0570
Fax: 206-938-1307
E-mail: www.traders.com
Website: www.traders.com

The Tennessee Magazine

Does not accept unsolicited submissions.

Tennis Magazine

Formal guidelines not available. Please read a number of issues to ascertain the publication's style and needs.

Send queries to address below.

Categories: Nonfiction—Physical Fitness—Recreation—Sports—Travel

CONTACT: Submissions Editor
Material: All
79 Madison Ave., 8th Fl.
New York NY 10016
Phone: 212-636-2700
Fax: 212-636-2730
E-mail: editors@tennis.com
Website: www.tennis.com

Tequesta

Purpose of the Journal

To present articles about our region's past in a scholarly format that is informative and, when possible, illustrated with historic images.

Distribution

3,000 copies of the journal are printed, reaching an estimated readership of 7,700, not including users in libraries and at other institutions receiving the journal in their collections.

History

The Historical Association of Southern Florida began publication of the journal in 1941, and it has been published annually since its beginning. *Tequesta* has become one of the most authoritative journals on Florida's history.

Presentation Style

Articles should be suitable for academic audiences with interest in our region's history. The editors strive for variety and balance so that each issue contains at least one article of interest to each reader.

Style Authority

The Chicago Manual of Style should be consulted on matters of style as this is the guide used by the editors of the journal. Webster's first choice is used when multiple spellings of a word are acceptable. Exceptions are made when the presentation form warrants.

Content

Articles should recall, retell and explore historic events, people, places and themes pertaining to southern Florida and the Caribbean. The journal covers Florida from about Lake Okee-chobee on down, coast to coast, and all countries in the Caribbean. Articles are generally presented as annotated narratives in third person or first person, and must include citations from primary research material, such as historic records, diaries and other documents. Exceptions are made when material warrants. Footnotes are required; bibliographies are optional.

Photographs

Photographic illustration is helpful but not necessary in *Tequesta*. Authors are encouraged to identify available accompanying visual material whenever possible and provide copies of such images when submitting manuscripts. Original documents and photographs that must be returned to their owners will be copied by the historical Museum of Southern Florida and handled according to the highest level of curatorial standards. Materials will be returned via certified delivery systems after publication of the journal.

Submission of Articles

A typed manuscript is requested with accompanying computer disk or CD copy of the article whenever possible. Manuscripts are also accepted via e-mail. Photographs and other illustrative materials, if identified, should be submitted with the manuscript (copies acceptable). Scanned photographs and images may be sent electronically as well, but prints will be required upon acceptance of the article for production. Articles may be submitted at any time throughout the year and should be 2,500 to 6,000 words in length.

The editorial staff of *Tequesta* strives to respond to writers who have submitted manuscripts in a timely fashion. Writers are asked to call if a timely response has not been made. The first response back will generally be an indication of whether the material is of interest for the publication and subsequent correspondence will indicate whether any additional research or writing is requested. If acceptable, the article becomes part of the pool of material undergoing production steps to ready them for publication. Articles are pulled from the pool and assigned to specific issues on an ongoing basis. The Editors at the Historical Museum of Southern Florida maintain the right for flexibility in deciding publication dates as geographical, thematic and seasonal concerns are considered.

Payment to authors for articles used includes the Historical Museum of Southern Florida's most sincere appreciation and 10 copies of the journal.

Standards

The editorial staff of *Tequesta* strives for the highest level of accuracy and fairness possible when presenting the past. Standard journalistic and research practices and principles should be adhered to at all times. Please refer to the *Associated Press Stylebook and Libel Manual* and *The Chicago Manual of Style* for any questions or doubt.

The Historical Association of Southern Florida disclaims any responsibility for errors in factual material or statements of opinions expressed by contributors.

A Word to Contributors

You are the lifeblood of *Tequesta*. Your time, energy and thoughtfulness in submitting a contribution are sincerely appreciated as we strive to spread interest in and understanding of our region's rich past.

Thank you. The Editors, *Tequesta*

Categories: Nonfiction—African-American—Arts—Asian-American—Biography—Civil War—Culture—Hispanic—History—Jewish Interest—Multicultural—Native American—Regional—Ethnic

CONTACT: Managing Editor
Material: Any
CONTACT: Dr. Paul S. George, Editor
Material: Any
101 W. Flagler St.
Miami FL 33130
Phone: 305-375-1492
Fax: 305-375-1609
E-mail: publications@historical-museum.org

Texas Gardener

TEXAS GARDENER is interested in articles containing practical, how-to information on gardening in Texas. Our readers want to know specific information on how to make gardening succeed in Texas' unique growing conditions. All articles must reflect this slant.

Our bimonthly magazine reaches over 25,000 home gardeners and covers vegetable and fruit production, flowers and ornamentals, landscape and trees, technique and features on gardeners.

We will accept both technical and feature articles. Technical articles should explain how to do some aspect of gardening (like graft pecans or plant bulbs) in a clear, easy-to-follow manner, and must be accurate. All technical articles should refer to experts in the field. Accompanying artwork such as photographs, illustrations or diagrams are essential.

Feature articles, including interviews or profiles of Texas gardeners, new gardening techniques or photo features should relate specifically to Texas. We will not publish general gardening essays. Personality profiles may be on hobby gardeners or professional horticulturists who are doing something unique.

In-depth articles should run 8 to 10 double-spaced type pages (approximately 1,400 to 1,750 words) though we encourage shorter, concise articles that run 4 to 6 typed pages (700 to 1,050 words). All articles are reviewed on speculation. Writers should submit a query and outline of a proposed article first, unless they wish to send a manuscript they have already completed. We accept articles on PC disks written in Microsoft Word for Windows or WordPerfect 5.0. Writers should include a list of areas of expertise and a writing sample or copy of published work.

Rights negotiable. We pay $25 for submission to Between Neighbors and $50 to $200 for feature articles. Payment is made upon publication and includes two copies of the issue in which the author's article appears. We respond to queries within 6 weeks. Please—no duplicate submissions.

We accept only high-quality color and clear black-and-white photographs. Slides are preferable, but prints, transparencies and contact sheets may be acceptable. Model releases and identification of subjects are required. Rights negotiable.

Categories: Nonfiction—Gardening

CONTACT: Chris S. Corby, Publisher, Editor
Material: Any
CONTACT: Linda Filgo, Managing Editor
Material: Any
PO Box 9005
Waco TX 76714
Phone: 254-848-9393
Fax: 254-848-9779
E-mail: suntex@calpha.com
Website: www.texasgardener.com

Texas Highways,
The Travel Magazine of Texas

Subscribe to *Texas Highways*...Discover the Lone Star State!

Take a monthly page-by-page journey with Texas' top travel writers and photographers as they explore the best of Texas. A one-year subscription includes 12 issues of *Texas Highways* magazine. As a special gift, you'll receive the Texas Highways Travel Discount Card FREE with your paid order. You can use it for travel savings around the state.

There's not another magazine like it anywhere. It's *Texas Highways*—the state's official travel magazine.

FREELANCE PHOTOGRAPHY PROCEDURES AND RATES
Submission Guidelines

Want to write or photograph for *Texas Highways*? The magazine always seeks new creative talent, and the links below will download guidelines that spell out how we work.

For a copy of our photographic wants list, please write, call or email Mike Murphy, photo editor, at PO Box 141009, Austin, TX 78714-1009.

Freelance Photographer's Guidelines:

The Travel Publications Section publishes all travel literature distributed by the Texas Department of Transportation. This includes *Texas Highways* magazine; the Texas State Travel Guide, state maps, various brochures; and ancillary products such as posters, calendars, and cards. Photographers submitting photography to the magazine automatically have the work considered for ancillary products as well. The following guidelines should help you understand how the travel publications section utilizes photographs.

Magazine Guidelines

Submit a query letter outlining your suggested picture-story topic or theme before sending actual photographs and captions, unless you're submitting work in response to our photographic wants list. The magazine is not responsible for unsolicited photographic materials! The magazine works at least three months in advance, and generally has an editorial calendar planned 18 to 24 months ahead.

1. After being notified of our interest, submit original color slides or transparencies (no color prints, negatives, or digital files) in 35mm or larger format. There should be enough images to fully illustrate the topic.

2. Photographs should depict an interesting Texas event, theme, site or activity. They also may depict interesting shopping, dining, or entertainment in the border areas of Mexico adjacent to Texas.

3. Your name and an identification number must be printed clearly on the mount of each slide or on the sleeve of each transparency. Each photograph must have its own unique number (not number 1, sheet 4 or top right, sheet 10). If you submit 100 slides in five sheets, they should be numbered from 1 to 100. If they have been numbered differently for some other purpose, they will be acceptable if each has a unique number keyed to the caption information. (Slides with neatly labeled mounts are okay, too.)

4. Include a caption sheet with the photographs, listing by identification number the location of each image, names of objects, identities of recognizable people (unless crowd or distance shots) and date taken. Send us the telephone number where we can reach you during office hours in case we have questions. The more information you send us the better. (Accuracy is very important, too.)

5. All photographs are submitted for speculation only. The magazine may choose to retain certain images for publication at a future date. In this case we would return the photographs in two parts—the "outtakes" right away, and the "selects" after publication.

6. If you include a delivery memo with your submission, please note we do not accept work "for examination only," nor do we pay holding fees. If you use a standard ASMP-style delivery memo that specifies holding fees, "for examination only," "negotiated fees," "payment before use," or other similar clauses, please alter and initial each one. If you can't do this, we can't consider your work.

Space Rates (Paid upon publication)
• $60 for individual photograph used less than 1/4 page.
• $80 for individual photograph used 1/4 to 1/2 page.
• $120 for individual photograph used 1/2 to 3/4 page.
• $150 for individual photograph used 3/4 to full page.
• $170 for individual photograph used full page.
• $300 for back cover
• $350 for two-page spread
• $400 for front cover
• $550 for wrap-around cover
• $15 additional for electronic usage on TexasHighways.com (low-res)
• $25 additional for use in Table of Contents

Usage Rights

Texas Highways purchases one-time use of photographs for the magazine, but reserves the right to use the same images for promotional purposes and/or reprints without additional compensation. Re-use of images for other purposes such as prints or calendars will be compensated separately—see rates below. *Texas Highways* expects six months' exclusivity for all work. (This means the same or like images must not appear in other publications distributed in Texas for six months—three months before magazine publication and three months after.)

Should we electronically reproduce an image we used in the magazine on our *Texas Highways* website, we'll pay $15 in addition to our normal space rates.

R-U

Ancillary Products Guidelines

Ancillary Products include calendars, posters, greeting cards, and other items. All of the guidelines stated above apply, with the exception of exclusivity. All work must come with 12 months of exclusivity—six months before scheduled publication and six months after.

Image Format

Transparencies submitted for *Texas Highways*' calendar must be horizontal. We prefer medium and large format images. Vertical and horizontal images will be considered for print and greeting card use.

Rates

(The following rates apply for each individual photograph)

Item	Rate	Quantity	Reprint Rate:
• Calendar cover	$350	20,000	
• Calendar, full page	$250		
• Poster	$250	1,000	$125
• Greeting card	$200	1,000	$100
• Other products are negotiated on an individual basis.			

Photographers must agree to reprints or work submitted will not be accepted. (Reprinting means printing additional copies in excess of the original quantity.) Photography used in producing ancillary products will be paid for upon publication.

All photographs will be returned after publication. The above rates include the right to reproduce the photograph in any related promotions. (Photographs will be used to advertise the products for sale.)

Image Content Considerations

1. All of the department's publications are meant to showcase Texas as a premier travel destination. Consequently, we are seeking photography taken under the best possible circumstances, whatever the topic. Given the choice of two images of the Alamo, one taken on a nice, sunny day, the other shot in gloomy, overcast weather; the sunny day image will have a greater chance of being used.

2. Litter (discarded cups, bottles, cans, scraps of paper) is unacceptable in any photo.

3. Models—when and where possible, involve people in photographs meant for use in travel literature. This generally enhances travel aspect of the imagery, allowing viewers to think "That could be me." Find and utilize people, of all races, that represent an American family image, including children and senior citizens. Models should be engaged in activity appropriate to the subject, and definitely not posing for the camera. Smiles are important—the people should look like they are enjoying themselves. Spontaneity is what we're seeking, not stilted, posed shots of someone pointing at some distant attraction. Model (and property) releases are not required, but are always good protection for any photographer.

4. When automobiles are in a scene, attempt to use late-model vehicles. Older cars, unless antiques or classic cars, make fresh photos seem dated. Avoid large trucks, but pickups, RVs, and trailers are fine.

5. Technique should be appropriate for the subject. For landscapes, use the largest format and/or slowest film available. When shooting indoors, light areas so they will look natural; and balance your light with existing light. On-camera flash by itself won't do the job. High-speed film is okay for dimly lit events with lots of action, but otherwise we prefer the slower films such as Fuji Velvia and Provia, Kodachrome, and Kodak's newest E-6 films. Film should be balanced to the light to render natural appearing color—don't shoot daylight film under tungsten lights and expect natural color. Also, when shooting under overcast conditions it is appropriate to use a warming filter on daylight film.

6. Regional diversity—for travel promotion purposes, Texas is divided into seven regions: Big Bend Country, Panhandle Plains, Prairies and Lakes, Piney Woods, Gulf Coast, South Texas Plains, and Hill Country. We seek images that showcase the best of each region, and take care not to over-emphasize any one region. When we select images for the calendar, we include at least one photo from each region and won't use more than three photos from any one region. Please help us highlight the state's geographic diversity by sending us compelling images from every region.

Work will be reviewed promptly for potential usage in any of the department's travel publications. All photographs will be returned by Certified Mail.

WRITERS' GUIDELINES AND RATE INFORMATION

Texas Highways, the official travel magazine of Texas by designation of the Texas Legislature in 1974, "encourages travel within the state and tells the Texas story to readers around the world." The magazine, which is published by the Travel Division of the Texas Department of Transportation, has gained wide respect, as well as numerous awards, for its stories and outstanding photography. The magazine has a circulation of approximately 280,000, with subscribers in every state in the nation and more than 100 countries. Surveys tell us that a majority of our readers are 60 and older, and that they especially like coverage of Texas scenery, history, small towns, and out-of-the-way places.

Approximately 80% of our stories and photographs come from freelance contributors.

Query Guidelines:

1. Submit a query letter outlining your proposed feature with a brief description of the scope and slant. The letter should give us some idea of the style and tone you propose to take in the story. Do not send the completed story until requested to do so. It helps to include copies of previously published articles to show your writing style. Keep in mind, however, that *Texas Highways* never approves a story idea based on how much or where you may have published. The subject matter, slant, and style must be right for us.

We are not responsible for unsolicited material. We do not accept queries over the telephone or by email. We do not publish poetry or fiction.

2. Before you query, review the indexes found in the December issues of the magazine (the 1980 index is in the January 1981 issue). You can find back issues of *Texas Highways* at most libraries. Since we do not publish two features on the same subject within five years, the indexes are useful in identifying previously published subjects.

3. Subjects should focus on things to do or places to see in Texas. Include historical, cultural, and geographic aspects if appropriate. Text should be meticulously researched. Include anecdotes, historical references, quotations, and, where relevant, geologic, botanical, and zoological information.

4. We do not commission articles. Material is submitted on speculation only. The author warrants that the work is his or her original creation.

5. *Texas Highways* purchases first North American serial rights, and may reproduce the work in printed and/or electronic form.

6. Include a SASE, and allow up to eight weeks for a reply.

Manuscript Guidelines:

1. After we notify you of our interest, submit manuscripts typed, double-spaced, standard six-inch line on white paper. Length will vary according to topic (generally 1,200-2,000 words), but we prefer too much rather than not enough. Again, material is submitted on speculation only. If you use a computer to write your story, submit a hard copy along with a CD or e-mailed copy. (We use Microsoft Word.)

2. Good research is imperative. Get everything right the first time. Check and doublecheck facts, dates, spellings, directions, distances, heights, all matters of historical record, telephone numbers—check and recheck everything. Assume nothing: Ask individuals how to spell their names. Do not rely on friends, relatives, telephone books, newspaper articles, or programs for an event. Put a small check mark in ink over names, addresses, times, numbers, etc. (first occurrence only), so that we know that you have verified them beyond a doubt.

3. Read a few back issues of *Texas Highways* before submitting your story. The approach should be informal, with a polished, readable quality. Write a strong lead and ending. Use active constructions and strong verbs. Avoid the passive voice. Avoid the "to be" verb form as much as possible. We welcome a sense of humor when and if appropriate.

4. Include the names and phone numbers of all persons quoted or used as information sources for your article. Check the spelling of all names in your story, then check again. Include a list of published sources, as well. *Texas Highways* customarily fact-checks all aspects of every story. We need a telephone number where we can reach you between 8 am and 5 pm.

5. If, in the course of researching an article, you find interesting illustrations on the subject such as old photographs, period engravings, maps, or paintings, please make a note of what they are, what publication they're in, and who owns the copyright, if any. Please include this information with your feature.

6. If you write about a place, please send us the most recent descriptive literature. If you write about an event, send us the latest program.

7. Send information for the "When Where How" box with your manuscript. Include dates, times, locations, prices, and instructions on how to get to a place or event. Be sure to include information on facilities for the handicapped. If you prepare a historical feature, furnish names or descriptions of sources (books, old letters, museum displays, etc.). Refer to recent issues of the magazine for the format and type of facts needed.

8. Please submit a brief biographical sketch that we might edit and use with your story.

9. Please submit two or three title suggestions with your story.

10. We expect you to write to the editors' specifications. When necessary, we expect you to rewrite an article at least once.

11. Except for certain in-house preferences, we use *The Random House Dictionary of the English Language*, Second Edition Unabridged as our standard reference.

12. When your article is scheduled, an editor will work with you to resolve ambiguities and answer questions. The editor may request that you add material or rewrite portions of the text to prepare the story for publication. We cannot promise that an article will be published when scheduled.

Rates (We pay on acceptance.):

1. *Texas Highways* pays approximately 40 to 50 cents per word. After we accept your manuscript, we will ask you to send us an invoice that includes the subject matter of your article, and your name, address, a unique invoice number, and social security number. Payment takes about four weeks.

2. Please type your name, address, and telephone number on the front of your manuscript. Let us know immediately if your address or phone number changes.

Remember:

—Submit a list of your sources, including names, addresses, and telephone numbers. If you have used published sources, provide that information as well. *Texas Highways* customarily fact-checks every aspect of every story.

—Submit brochures, maps, charts, or other information that will help us verify what you have written or help us in illustrating your material.

—Keep a copy of your article. Manuscripts may get lost in the mail or in our office.

—Always check and double-check your information. *Texas Highways* strives to be accurate on all counts, including spelling of names, historical facts, highway numbers, directions, place names, and caption details. Because we do not have the staff to retrace the steps of every author, we depend on YOU for much of that accuracy. Please take the time to ensure that you have included all the information we need to keep your feature correct. Thank you.

Writing for Texas Highways

By Jack Lowry, Editor

The first thing we think of when we review a query is our readership: Is the proposed subject of interest to our readers? Familiarize yourself with the magazine, with the kinds of stories we publish, and with topics we have covered recently.

Work on your writing. We like strong leads that draw in the reader immediately. We look for writing that is accurate, clear, and concise. Think about ways to tighten your writing.

For example, use adjectives and adverbs sparingly; opt for nouns instead. Favor the concrete over the abstract. Get to the point. Specify. Avoid passive constructions and the "to be" form as much as possible. When appropriate, use anecdotes, quotes, wordplay, examples, and contrast. In general, your writing should help information and ideas flow smoothly for the reader.

Keep our production cycle in mind. Queries frequently arrive too late for us to consider. For most features, we must work at least a year in advance, primarily because we schedule seasonal photography one year for publication the following year.

Expect anything you send us to be edited and possibly returned (at least once) for a rewrite.

What do we not want? Avoid superlatives that sound like advertising copy. Don't use words whose meanings you don't really understand. Avoid words whose meanings have become distorted through general (over)usage: "Unique" is perhaps the most common example in travel writing.

Don't forget the basics—who, what, when, where, why, and how.

Categories: Nonfiction—Culture—History—Photography—Regional—Travel

CONTACT: Jack Lowry, Editor
Material: All
CONTACT: Jill Lawless, Managing Editor
Material: All
CONTACT: Michael A. Murphy, Photo Editor
E-mail: mmurph1@ dot.state.tx.us
Material: Photos
PO Box 141009
Austin TX 78714-1009
Phone: 512-486-5858
Fax: 512-486-5879
E-mail: editors@texashighways.com
Courier: 150 E. Riverside Drive
Austin TX 78704
Website: www.texashighways.com

Texas Journey

Please refer to *New Mexico Journey*.

Texas Parks & Wildlife

Texas Parks & Wildlife, the Outdoor Magazine of Texas, is a monthly magazine published by Texas Parks and Wildlife. We are looking for strong, well-researched and eloquently written stories on all aspects of the Texas outdoors. *Texas Parks & Wildlife* covers state park destinations, conservation issues, trends, and such outdoor activities as fishing, hunting, camping, bicycling, canoeing and hiking. Keep in mind that we publish many features that don't necessarily fit into the categories listed below.

Departments

• Scout—This front-of-the-book department is a collection of short (100-700 words), lively articles covering news and trends in the outdoors across the state. We particularly welcome submissions from freelancers for this department.

• Skill Builder—How do you tie fishing knots? Train your dog to avoid rattlesnakes? Pack a first-aid kit? These authoritative how-to lessons (700 words) brief readers on a variety of outdoor skills.

• Legend, Lore and Legacy—As the title indicates, this award-winning department (1,000 words) encompasses a wide range of stories. We've run profiles of people who've left a legacy on the Texas outdoors (wildlife artist Orville Rice, duck hunting guide and conservationist Jimmy Reel); legends (tales of the Big Thicket), and Lore (the horned lizard and other natural history pieces).

Features

• State Parks—These destination pieces (1,500-2,500 words) cover a Texas state park in a compelling way that would make readers consider visiting it. Recent stories have included "Glorious Goliad," bass fishing at Possum Kingdom and hiking in Pedernales. Stories should convey a strong sense of place, weave in the natural history of the park and describe the primary activities. Include a sidebar on facilities, how to get there, and reservations phone number.

Hunting and Fishing stories

• Conservation stories—Recent assignments have included "Crabbers Sing the Blues: A Losing Season for Blue Crab" and a feature on the fate of the prairie dog. These pieces must be informed by good science and reflect a balanced approach. Include quotes from experts at TPW, reliable research universities or elsewhere.

General Tips

• We prefer that stories be written in an active rather than passive voice.

• Use present tense when possible.

• Use good quotes. Quotes from experts, whether from inside or outside TPW, add much to the reliability of a story. A pithy quote is also an excellent way to help paint a picture for the reader. Sidebars, subheads and other devices for breaking up copy are welcome.

Hunting/Fishing Writers' Guidelines

Be aware of the magazine's audience. Hunting and fishing stories should emphasize the challenges, pleasures and rewards of the entire outdoor experience rather than simply the taking of game. Many of our readers are neither hunters nor anti-hunters, and we want to build as many bridges as we can with that group, showing them that hunters share many of their interests. Readers love to learn about a hunter or fisher who is passionately interested in wildlife-viewing, wildflowers or other outdoor-related activities. Such experiences can be included either in the main body of the story or in a sidebar, as appropriate. If you enjoy watching neotropical migratory birds while spring turkey hunting, you could do a sidebar on what species you saw and that can probably be seen in the area covered in the story, and give birding tips. Other ideas for sidebars include:

• Information about requirements for hunting or fishing on public lands the best places to hunt or fish for a particular species on public or private lands tips on the best hunting or fishing methods (unless that is the main thrust of the story) conservation programs or successes related to the species in the article (TPW and others) threats to the continued survival of the species in the article and what is being done about them, especially if hunter/fisher groups or funds generated by hunters and fishers are helping fund the effort experiences related to introducing someone to the outdoors recipes for preparing wild game or fish.

Harvesting of Game—Since TPW magazine is a general-interest, family-oriented magazine, hunting and fishing stories, while dealing honestly and matter-of-factly, with the fact that game is harvested, should take care to avoid emphasizing body count and killing. It is usually not necessary to give details on the methods used to harvest animals. It is sufficient to say that the animal was shot, or boated, or released or that the hunt ended with the successful taking of the game (or not). Naturally, articles dealing with specific hunting or fishing techniques will go into considerable detail of this type, but it should be done tastefully. If you provide photos, no pictures of mounted animals, please see photo guidelines.

Use care in dealing with issues that affect conservation. Hunters and fishers are as concerned as anyone with caring for game and the habitat where it lives, and this needs to come through in articles in the way we show respect for game and the environment, not to mention the sensibilities of our readers. Avoid graphic descriptions of blood and gore while being honest about the fact that game is harvested. Show respect for the game in both text and photographs. Some examples of ways to handle this follow:

• Example 1:

No: Among the five of us, we had 50 dead geese piled up on the ground.

Yes: Each of us took our limit of geese.

(The body count is not important, but the way you treat harvested game is.)

• Example 2:

No: On the way to my blind, I killed a rattlesnake.

Yes: On the way to my blind, I was startled by a rattlesnake.

(You may indeed kill a rattlesnake while hunting, but we don't want to hear about it, nor do we want to rile readers who object to such behavior.)

• Example 3:

No: I cut a limb from a tree to probe for hidden obstacles in the water.

Yes: I used a stick to probe for hidden obstacles in the water.

(Harming vegetation is forbidden on most public land, and many private landowners don't appreciate it, either.)

Photography/Artwork Guidelines

Transparencies in any format 35mm or larger are acceptable. Photographers may submit duplicate transparencies for consideration, provided that originals can be furnished on request. Each transparency must be labeled, stamped or marked with the photographer's name and address. A caption or description of each transparency must be included with every submission. All transparencies will be returned if this is not done.

Properly exposed transparencies are preferred. One-half stop overexposed is better than underexposure. Do not underexpose for deep color saturation.

Make it your goal to submit transparencies that are as good or better than those you see in our magazine. Edit your photos carefully before submitting. More is not better. Submit no more than 80 transparencies per story. Use separate slide file pages for each story submission so slides can be reviewed and those selected can be placed in the respective story folder. Those rejected will be returned.

Photographs of a location such as a state park should evoke a sense of place. Photos should show an intelligent selection of subject and time of day. For hunting stories, no pictures of mounted animals, please.

Artwork to be published will be on assignment to illustrate a specific story. Contact the magazine art director for size and medium limitations. Payment to be determined. We occasionally use previously published photos in departments such as the letters page. Payment for use of the photos will be one-half the original payment.

Payment photo schedule:

• Front cover: $500
• Wraparound and gatefold: $400
• Other covers: $250
• Inside color—rate per individual picture
• More than a full page: $180
• Three-quarters to a full page: $165
• One-half to three-quarters of a page: $125
• Less than one-half page: $80
• Black and white: $50 for all sizes

Payment is upon publication. The magazine retains possession of color separations for all photos and art published. No original separations leave the magazine, but duplicates are available at cost. Occasionally, other publications request the use of *Texas Parks & Wildlife* separations. No freelance material will be released without the permission of the contributor, but it will be the responsibility of the contributor to arrange for compensation from the requesting publication.

Texas Parks & Wildlife will exercise care in the handling of all material received, but the department will not be responsible for loss

R-U

or damage. Color separator is responsible for the care of color photos and art while in his possession.

Submitting

Please submit assigned articles typed and double-spaced. Submit e-mailed as an attachment or pasted in as text. Or submit on a 3 1/2-inch disk, either Mac or DOS format. Be sure your name, address, and phone number are on your manuscript. Please submit queries with published clips.

Please address your submissions to the appropriate editor, listed below:

Categories: Nonfiction—Adventure—Boating—Conservation—Environment—Fishing—Outdoors—Regional—Travel—Camping—Hiking—Hunting—State Parks—Wildlife

CONTACT: Larry D. Hodge, Senior Wildlife Editor
Material: Fishing and hunting stories
CONTACT: Bill Reaves, Photo Editor
Material: All Photos
CONTACT: Susan L. Ebert, Publisher and Editor
Material: All Other
CONTACT: Mary-Love Bigony, Managing Editor
Material: All Other
3000 S. IH-35, Ste. 120
Austin TX 78704
Phone: 512-912-7000
Fax: 512-707-1913
E-mail: magazine@tpwd.state.tx.us
Website: www.tpwmagazine.com

THEMA

Thema

SUBMISSIONS

Schedule: See our website for upcoming premises and deadlines for submission.

The premise must be an integral part of the plot, not necessarily the central theme but not merely incidental. Fewer than 20 double-spaced pages preferred. Indicate premise on title page.

Because manuscripts are evaluated in blind review, do NOT put author's name on any page beyond the title page. Indicate target theme in cover letter or on first page of manuscript. Include self-addressed, stamped envelope (SASE) with each submission. Rejected manuscripts unaccompanied by an SASE will not be returned. Response time: 3 months after premise deadline.

Payment: short story, $25; short-short piece (up to 1000 words), $10; poem, $10; artwork, $10. Copyright reverts to author after publication.

SHORT STORIES

All types welcome-both traditional and experimental.

What we like: A carefully constructed plot; good character delineation; clever plot twists.

What we don't like: bedroom/bathroom profanity.

Why we object to bedroom/bathroom profanity: It's boring! Writers should be more creative than to depend on the same tired and dubious language crutches to express surprise, disdain, shock, bemusement, anger, sadness, and other emotions.

Such profanity, used in excess, often serves as a camouflage for a weak plot.

If the plot is good, the story can be told much more effectively in nonscatologic language even though a character in the story may be sleazy.

Stories of lasting quality rarely need it.

POETRY

All types of poetic form welcome. Submit no more than three poems per theme, please.

What we like: poems that are thoughtfully constructed and carefully distilled.

What we don't like: sexually explicit wording. Subtlety is more creative.

ART

MUST FIT THEME—Cover: color illustration/photograph; inside art: black and white (pen and ink; computer-generated; photograph) Submit xerographic copy or 5" x 7" photograph of artwork.

SAMPLE COPIES

Sample copies of THEMA are available at $8.00 per copy. Subscription rate: $16.00 per year for three issues ($20.00, foreign addresses). Make check payable to "THEMA Literary Society" and mail to the address below.

NOTE

For all submissions, include SASE and indicate premise.

Categories: Fiction—Arts—Cartoons—Literature—Poetry—Short Stories

CONTACT: Virginia Howard, Editor
Material: Short Stories and/or Art
CONTACT: Gail Howard, Poetry Editor
Material: Poetry
PO Box 8747
Metairie LA 70011-8747
Phone: 504-887-1263
Website: members.cox.net/thema

Thoughts For All Seasons
The Magazine of Epigrams

Thoughts for All Seasons:
The Magazine of Epigrams

The guidelines for writing epigrams published in Vol. 5 of TFAS (2000 issue) are still applicable.

1) Is the statement (or question) original, or have we heard it somewhere before?

2) If the stem of the statement (question) is an old saw, has the author put an interesting twist on it?

3) Is the statement (question) intelligible, or are we uncertain about the author's intentions?

4) Is the statement (question) succinct, or is it overly wordy?

5) Is the statement (question) funny, or is it preachy?

6) If it is not funny, is it a profound and original truth?

7) If the statement (question) is silly, is it at least a good play on words?

8) Is it a dancing thought, or a sinking thought?

9) Is it sour grapes, or is it wine?

10) Is it outrageous, or is merely tasteless?

Volume 6 (2005) will mark the centennial of *Devil's Dictionary* by Abrose Bierce. Other themes (volume 6) will include satirical trips for good health, and new lyrics for old songs.

Poetry Guidelines

Suggestions: rhymed quatrains, original limericks, and longer poems including nonsense verse with good imagery. Tone may be serious or humorous. (We do not accept Haiku.) For more detail, consult any back issue of TFAS.

Readers who are interested in a more technical analysis may wish to refer to "A Taxonomy of Epigrams" by M. P. Richard in the Autumn 1989 issue of *Verbatim: The Language Quarterly*.

Categories: Language—Poetry—Satire—Society—Writing—Humor

CONTACT: Prof. Michel P. Richard, Editor
Material: All
86 Leland Rd.
Becket, MA 01223
Phone: 413-623-0174

Threads

Threads is a bimonthly, how-to magazine celebrating garment sewing, design and embellishment, machine and hand embroidery, and related crafts. We're always looking for new authors to help us bring fresh, exciting ideas, techniques, and information to our readers. If you've never written anything before, don't worry. We work with many first-time authors and are far more interested in your excellence in your craft and your innovative ideas than in your ability to spell or punctuate a sentence (that's where our editors come in).

We're interested in articles about construction and embellishment techniques, materials, tools, and design. We want the magazine to include both classic and innovative techniques, which produce the best results in the most streamlined manner possible. In particular, we're interested in articles on dressmaking, tailoring, patternmaking and alteration, fabrics, fitting, and embellishment. We're also looking for related articles on making interesting closures and buttons, and making unusual fabrics, as well as on intriguing ways of finishing edges and hems.

Our readers span the gamut of skill levels, from those just turning—or returning—to sewing, to those with advanced skills who may even be earning a living at their craft. To accommodate this broad range of readers, as well as those who work in or outside the home and have very little time for their favorite pastime, *Threads* includes articles geared toward several skill levels and degrees of complexity.

Threads has a paid circulation of about 150,000 readers. The magazine is four-color throughout, and its feature articles are uninterrupted by advertising.

Our Point of View

Our emphasis is on teaching techniques, developing skills, understanding finishing details, and providing ample inspiration to help readers begin to create their own uses for this information. We focus on providing the basic information readers need in order to sew successfully.

We are a reader-written magazine (we don't use freelance writers) that looks at techniques and processes from the viewpoint of the curious, practical craftsperson who wants to know how and why things work. We want to know, for example, how and why you make a bound buttonhole or set in a sleeve the way you do, whether or not your method conforms to a classic technique. We're interested in the full range of technical information, from what you've discovered in your own workroom to the methods used in the garment industry to produce high-end, ready-to-wear and couture clothing. Our goal is to give home sewers the knowledge they need to create professional-looking garments and projects and have fun in the process.

Threads presents casually elegant, beautifully constructed, wearable garments and accessories. We're interested in exceptional examples of the techniques we present, whether their design is classic or cutting-edge. Because we feel that inspiring our readers is key, we work hard to create lively photography, illustrations, and layouts that enhance the technical information presented and make the magazine both accessible and a pleasure to read.

Article Proposals

If you would like to write an article for *Threads*, start by sending us a proposal. Here's what to include: a brief one- or two-paragraph summary of the article you have in mind; an outline of the ideas and points you'll cover; sample photographs of work illustrating the topic (quick snapshots are fine) or supporting fabric swatches if you have them. The idea is to give us an overview of what you're proposing with enough details and supporting information to help us carefully consider your proposal.

Manuscripts

When we decide to pursue the article you're proposing, we'll contact you by phone or mail to clarify any questions and further explore the outline that you provided and discuss a timeline for the article delivery. Authors are not expected to provide photography or illustrations.

Payment

Once we accept your article and have all of the necessary materials in hand, we'll agree upon a fee and send you a contract. We are buying exclusive first publication rights, the right to republish all or part of the article in print, electronic or other media, the right to use it on the *Threads'* Web site if we choose, and the right to excerpt it in promotional pieces for The Taunton Press. We have the right to edit, revise, and adapt the article as we deem appropriate. Once the contract has been signed and we receive your manuscript, we usually advance a partial payment to you. We pay the balance when we've completed the editorial process, and you have sent us all samples (if they were agreed upon in initial discussions). We'll also send you two complimentary copies of the issue when it has been published.

We would be happy to discuss article ideas with you. If you have questions, feel free to call us at 800-309-9262 (from outside the United States, call 203-426-8171). If you are ready to submit a proposal, you may send it via postal mail or email, whichever you prefer, using the addresses printed on the reverse.

We appreciate your interest in *Threads*.

Categories: Nonfiction—Crafts/Hobbies

CONTACT: Articles Editor
Material: All
The Taunton Press
63 South Main St.
PO Box 5506
Newtown, CT 06470-5506
Phone: 203-426-8171
Fax: 203-270-6753
E-mail: th@taunton.com
Website: www.taunton.com

The Threepenny Review

1. At present *The Threepenny Review* is paying $200 per story or article, $100 per poem or Table Talk piece. In addition, each writer gets a year's free subscription and may buy extra copies of the issue in which his or her item appears at a discounted rate ($3.00 each, including postage).

2. All manuscripts should be submitted with a stamped, self-addressed envelope.

3. All articles should be double-spaced, with at least one-inch margins. Critical articles should be about 1500 to 3000 words, stories and memoirs 4000 words or less, and poetry 100 lines or less. Exceptions are possible.

4. Xeroxes and computer-printed copies are acceptable (letter quality preferred to dot matrix). We will not, however, consider simultaneous submissions.

5. Critical articles that deal with books, theater, films, etc., should cite these occasions at the front of the article in the following form:
   • Theater Piece by Playwright.
   • Theater, City
   • Season 19
   • Book Title
   • by Author's Name, Publisher, Year Published, Price (cloth) (paper).

Remember that *The Threepenny Review* is quarterly and national; therefore each "review" should actually be an essay, broader than the specific event it covers and of interest to people who cannot see the event.

6. Writers will be consulted on all significant editing done on their articles, and will have the opportunity to proofread galleys for typographical errors.

7. Response time for unsolicited manuscripts ranges from three weeks to two months.

8. It is recommended that those submitting work for the first time to *The Threepenny Review* take a look at a sample copy beforehand. Individual copies are available from the publisher for $12.00 each (cover price plus $5.00 postage/handling).

9. We do not review manuscripts September through December.

Categories: Fiction—Nonfiction—Arts—Book Reviews—Dance—Drama—Film/Video—General Interest—History—Literature—Music—Poetry—Politics—Short Stories—Essay—Personal Experience—Memoirs

CONTACT: Wendy Lesser, Editor
Material: All
PO Box 9131
Berkeley CA 94709
Phone: 510-849-4545

Tikkun

Bimonthly magazine covering politics, culture and society. 95% freelance written. Established in 1986. Circulation 20,000. Publishes manuscripts an average of six months after acceptance. Byline given. Kill fee varies, buys first North American serial rights. Editorial lead time two months. Submit seasonal material four months in advance. Reports in six months. Sample copy for $8.00.

Nonfiction: Book excerpts, essays, general interest, historic/nostalgic, humor, opinion, personal experience, photo feature, religious, political analysis, media and cultural analysis. Prints 25 manuscripts/yr. Send complete manuscript. Length: 2,000 words maximum.

Photos: State availability of photos with submissions. Reviews contact sheets or prints. Negotiates payment individually. Buys one-time rights.

Fiction: Contact Thane Rosenbaum, fiction editor, 60 W 87th, NY, NY 10024. Ethnic, historical, humorous, novel excerpts, religious, romance, slice-of-life vignettes. Prints 6 manuscripts/yr.

Poetry: Avant-garde, free verse, Haiku, light verse traditional. Submit a maximum of five poems. Long poems cannot be considered. *Tikkun* does not pay for poetry.

Tips: Internships are available. Write to *Tikkun* for information. Enclose a résumé and a self-revealing letter. Read magazine as writer's guidelines.

Telephone Contact: Jodi Perelman, Assistant to the Editor

Categories: Fiction—Nonfiction—Culture—Economics—Education—Environment—Feminism—Government—Jewish Interest—Literature—Poetry—Politics—Psychology—Religion—Sexuality—Society—Spiritual—Writing—Humor

CONTACT: Michael Lerner, Editor
Material: All
CONTACT: Thane Rosenbaum, Fiction Editor
Material: Fiction (to address above)
CONTACT: Josh Weiner, Assistant Poetry Editor
Material: Poetry
2107 Van Ness Ave. Ste. 302
San Francisco CA 94109
Phone: 415-575-1200
Fax: 415-575-1434
E-mail: magazine@tikkun.org

Timber Frame Homes

Please refer to *Log Home Living* magazine.

Time Magazine

Does not accept unsolicited submissions.

Timeline

TIMELINE is an illustrated magazine published bimonthly by the Ohio Historical Society. TIMELINE's editorial content embraces the fields of history, prehistory, and the natural sciences, and is directed towards readers located in the Midwest.

Each issue features lively, authoritative, and well-illustrated articles, photo essays, and occasional reviews, and special departments.

Since its inception in 1984, TIMELINE has received numerous local, state, and national awards. Among them are Printing and Publishing Executive's Gold Ink Award, American Association of Museums Award of Merit, Ohio Museums Association Award of Excellence, Ohioana Award for Editorial Excellence, Printing Association of America Award of Merit, and American Association for State and Local History Award of Merit.

TIMELINE is distributed to subscribers, to members of the Ohio Historical Society, and to public libraries throughout Ohio. Single copies may be obtained from the Ohio Historical Society or from selected retail outlets.

Manuscripts

The editors are accepting manuscripts of 1,500 to 6,000 words related to the history; prehistory; and natural history of Ohio and to the broader cultural and natural environments of which Ohio is a part. Articles with a regional or national focus also will be considered. Suitable topics include the traditional fields of political, economic, military, and social history; biography; the history of science and technology; archaeology and anthropology; architecture; the fine and decorative arts; and the natural sciences including botany, geology, zoology, ecology and paleontology.

In addition to full-length feature articles, shorter, more sharply focused vignettes of 500 to 1,000 words will be considered.

Both feature-length manuscripts and short submissions should be susceptible to high-quality black-and-white or color illustrations and will be evaluated, in part, on that basis. Authors are encouraged to include photographic prints, transparencies, or photocopies concurrently with submission of manuscripts and will be expected to supply the editors with suggestions for supplementary illustration.

Unless otherwise specified, the publishers will purchase one-time North American serial rights to both manuscripts and illustrations. Manuscript fees are negotiable and will be paid upon acceptance. Photographs and transparencies will be purchased separately. The editors reserve the right to edit all accepted manuscripts to conform to the style and usages of TIMELINE. For further information in this regard, please refer to the guidelines.

Manuscript Guidelines

• Articles are intended for the lay person, not the specialist.

• Writing style should be simple and direct. Vary the arrangements of sentence elements, paragraph length, and sentence length. Avoid one-sentence paragraphs.

• Avoid jargon and non-standard English. Limit use of technical terms to those necessary for clarity and accuracy.

• Although formal documentation will not be reproduced, manuscripts should be accompanied by a list of sources and suggestions for further reading. Limit internal documentation.

• Graphics should be accompanied by captions that do not duplicate textual information. Authors are expected to provide suggestions for illustrations.

• Avoid first-person narratives except in special cases where the first-person point-of-view is an essential element of the manuscript.

• Avoid extended direct quotations and parenthetical materials. TIMELINE does not accept fiction, fictionalizations, or poetry.

• Where questions of style or usage arise, refer to *The Chicago Manual of Style*.

• Manuscripts should be 1,500 to 6,000 words in length. Longer manuscripts will be considered if suitable for serialization.

• If unsure of a manuscript's suitability, authors are encouraged to submit outlines in advance.

• If your manuscript is prepared on an IBM-compatible, Apple II, or Macintosh computer system, please indicate this in your submission letter.

Illustrations

TIMELINE features photo essays related to the subject areas described. In addition, some freelance photographic contracts for article illustration may be offered from time to time. Photographers and illustrators are encouraged to submit portfolios to the editors for consideration. Proposals for photo essays should be submitted in advance. Appropriate model releases are required.

Categories: History—Regional

CONTACT: Christopher S. Duckworth, Editor
Material: All
1982 Velma Ave.
Columbus OH 43211-2497
Phone: 614-297-2360
Fax: 614-297-2367

Times News Service

Thank you for your interest in writing for the *Times News Service*, which serves Army Times, Navy Times, Marine Corps Times and Air Force Times, with a combined worldwide circulation of approximately 250,000. We are always interested in receiving freelance articles that are informative, helpful, entertaining and stimulating to a military audience. We prefer that you first send a query, describing your purpose and goal. If you have an idea with a military angle and aren't sure whether we would be interested, don't hesitate to write us.

WHAT WE WANT: We are looking for articles about military life, its problems and how to handle them. Keep in mind that our readers come from all of the military services. For instance, a story can focus on an Army family, but may need to include families or sources from other services as well. You do not have to be in the military, or part of a military family, to write for us. But the stories we publish reflect a detailed understanding of military life. We also buy articles dealing with hunting and fishing, automobiles and motorcycles, and travel.

WHAT WE DON'T WANT: We don't publish fiction or poetry. We cannot use historical essays or unit histories. We don't want articles that have nothing to do with the military. They are our audience, and it must affect their lives in one way or another.

RIGHTS: Articles will be a work made for hire under the U.S. copyright laws. That means we buy exclusive publication rights in our newspapers, as well as the exclusive rights to reproduce, edit, adapt, modify, perform, transmit and otherwise use the work, including any derivative works created therefrom, in any manner or medium throughout the world in perpetuity without additional compensation.

PAYMENT: Payment for articles is made upon acceptance. Remember that once we purchase an article, it might be several months before we publish it. When we do publish it, the article will appear simultaneously on the electronic service Military City Online, a division of Army Times Publishing Co. Your acceptance of payment is acceptance of these conditions.

PHOTOS: We pay for use of original photographs. Color slides or prints are acceptable. By original, we mean photos that you own either because you took them or because you bought the rights to them. We do not pay for photos bought at a souvenir stand, for example. Fees are negotiable.

SPECIAL SECTIONS: The *Times News Service* also publishes regular supplements to *Army Times*, *Navy Times*, *Marine Corps Times* and *Air Force Times*. Topics include careers after military service, travel, personal finance and education. Stories generally should include military people.

Categories: Nonfiction—Adventure—Careers—Civil War—Entertainment—Film/Video—Military—Money & Finances—Television/Radio—Travel

CONTACT: Phillip Thompson, Editor
Material: All material except material for supplements
CONTACT: Donna Peterson
Material: Material for Supplements
Army Times Publishing Co.
6883 Commercial Dr.
Springfield VA 22159
Phone: 703-750-7479
Fax: 703-750-8781

Tiny Lights
A Journal of Personal Essay

Since 1995, *Tiny Lights* has been celebrating the power of personal voice with a biannual journal devoted to short essay. The annual essay contest, which offers $1000 in prizes, provides the material for the summer issue, while the winter issue is by invitation only.

Regarding unsolicited manuscripts: At present, we are only considering material submitted to the annual essay contest and to two Lights Online columns mentioned below. See also: www.tiny-lights.com.

Guidelines for our annual Essay Contest:

We can only consider unpublished work, or previously published material for which the author holds rights. Rights revert to author after publication in *Tiny Lights*.

Each essay must be accompanied by an entry fee. $15 for first essay, $10 each additional essay.

SASE (self-addressed, stamped envelope) with sufficient postage required for contest notification and/or manuscript return. Multiple submissions OK.

Essays must be no longer than 2,000 words.

Entries should be typed and double-spaced.

Cover letters are optional, but the first page of the manuscript should include author's name, complete address, e-mail (if one exists), phone number, and essay word count.

Personal essay requires writers to communicate the truth of their experiences to the best of their abilities. While no theme restrictions apply to this contest, we will not consider essays that celebrate brutality or pornography. *Tiny Lights* does not accept poetry, short stories, or material written for children. Entry fees for inappropriate submissions may not be returned.

Entries must be postmarked by deadline date in February (see website.)

Prizes are awarded as follows:

First Place: $300 // Second Place: $200 // Third Place: $150 // Two Honorable Mention Prizes: $100. Awards will be determined by a panel of judges. Final authority rests with the Editor-in-Chief.

Winners will be posted at www.tiny-lights.com by April following contest deadline.

Winning essays may be edited before publication. Final copy must be approved by writer. No essays published without author's permission.

All contestants will receive *Tiny Lights'* contest publication featuring the winning entries.

The online component of *Tiny Lights* (www.tiny-lights.com) is designed to catch what can't be contained in the pages of the newsstand editions. Lights Online provides a venue for additional voices, information about *Tiny Lights* and resources for writers of personal essay.

Lights Online has two columns of particular interest to writers seeking publication. Searchlights & Signal Flares is a monthly writer's exchange which features answers to questions like, "What inspires you?" and "What's the best writing advice you ever got?" Flash in the Pan, for those brief bursts of first person genius, is posted quarterly. Detailed guidelines are posted at www.tiny-lights.com.

All business with Lights Online is conducted via email. All material submitted for these columns will be considered for use on Word by Word, a Sonoma County, CA, literary talk show on KRCB radio (www.krcb.org). Participation constitutes permission to use and/or edit your work. Writers whose work is chosen for the radio will be notified, although air dates are not guaranteed.

Subscriptions to *Tiny Lights*: $10 per year (3 issues)

Current issues: $5 each; Back issues: $3 each. Checks payable to *Tiny Lights* Publications, P.O. Box 928, Petaluma, CA 94953

Categories: Nonfiction—Personal Essay

CONTACT: Submission Editor
Material: All
PO Box 928
Petaluma, CA 94953
Website: www.tiny-lights.com

The Toastmaster

Circulation

Toastmasters International, a nonprofit educational organization, publishes *The Toastmaster* monthly for approximately 180,000 members in 9,000 clubs worldwide.

Toastmasters are people who recognize the need for self-improvement in communication, especially in their own oral presentations, and for developing their leadership potential. Members give at least one speech each month. An average Toastmaster will stay with his or her club for about eighteen months and completes the basic educational manuals. But many remain members longer to take advantage of more specialized programs, such as advanced speaking and leadership programs, community involvement and leadership development. The average member is 35 years old and has a college degree.

Payment

Toastmasters International will buy all serial rights for $100 to $250; payment is on acceptance. Payment for reprint rights depends on how valuable the material is to us. One-time and/or first serial rights are available on request.

Article Guidelines

Send a query letter first. Article length should be from 600 to 2000 words, double-spaced. Include a brief author biography and a word count.

To speed up publication of your article, send it on a 3.5" disk in either Microsoft Word or ASCII text. (Please do not format the text of the article.) If you do not have access to the above programs, send your article in a text only format and we will try and convert it. Please include a typed, double-spaced manuscript along with your disk and indicate the article's word count. Please note: We prefer not to receive unsolicited article submissions via e-mail.

We need articles related to the fields of communication and leadership, on topics members can use in their self-improvement efforts. Use anecdotes and examples to present your ideas and write with a "how to" approach, giving readers practical tips for improving their communication and leadership skills. Appropriate topics include speaking techniques, leadership development, language use, club management principles, and profiles of famous speakers in history.

Book reviews, exposes, personality profiles, articles with obvious political and religious slants, poems and speeches will not be accepted for publication.

Categories: Nonfiction—Associations—General Interest—Trade—Public Speaking

CONTACT: Submissions Editor
Material: All

Toastmasters International
PO Box 9052
Mission Viejo CA 92690-9052
Phone: 949-858-8255
Fax: 949-858-1207
E-mail: pubs@toastmasters.org
Website: www.toastmasters.org

Today's Catholic Teacher

Today's Catholic Teacher is a nationally circulated magazine for K-12 educators concerned with private education in general and Catholic education in particular. Issued six times during the school year, it has a circulation of about 50,000 copies and an estimated total readership of about 200,000. Although that readership is primarily classroom teachers, *Today's Catholic Teacher* is read also by principals, supervisors, superintendents, boards of education, pastors, and parents.

Articles: *Today's Catholic Teacher* aims to be for Catholic educators a source of information not available elsewhere. Subject matter may be any topic of practical help, concern, or interest to educators in Catholic schools. Examples include:

• Developments in curriculum, testing, technology, school relationships, creative teaching, school and community needs, classroom management, and administration as it affects the classroom

• National issues and trends which are of concern to Catholic educators

• Suggestions on the teaching of curricular subjects, including all academic areas as well as religion

Audience: The focus of articles should span the interests of teachers from early childhood through junior high. Articles may be directed to just one age group yet have wider implications. Preference is given to material directed to teachers in grades 4 through 8.

Style: The desired magazine style is direct, concise, informative, and accurate. Writing should be enjoyable to read, informal rather than scholarly, lively, and free of educational jargon.

Length: Feature articles fall into three general categories: 600-800 words, 1,000-1,200 words, and 1,200-1,500 words. Photographs: Prints, slides, or transparencies in color or black and white are helpful. Write identifying information on back or accompanying paper. Photos will not be returned unless requested.

Payment: Paid on publication, payment for features is generally $100 to $250, depending on length and quality of writing. Photos or other illustrations may increase payment.

Sample Issue: Send $3 for mailing and handling.

Contact: Query letters are encouraged. Write, call, fax, or e-mail the editor for editorial calendar, current editorial plans, and specifications for computer submissions.

Categories: Nonfiction—Education—Religion

CONTACT: Mary C. Noschang, Editor
Material: All
2621 Dryden Rd., Ste. 300
Dayton OH 45439
Phone: 937-293-1415
Fax: 937-293-1310
E-mail: mnoschang@peterli.com

Today's Christian

Today's Christian accepts fewer freelance articles than many other magazines since most of our articles are reprints or staff-written. But in each issue (6 per year), we feature several outstanding original pieces. While competition is keen (we receive an average of 40 unsolicited manuscripts a week), you can tailor your submissions to meet our needs by observing the following guidelines.

The *Today's Christian* audience is truly a general interest one, including men and women, urban professionals and rural homemakers, adults of every age and marital status, and Christians of every church affiliation. We seek to publish a magazine that people from the variety of ethnic groups in North America will find interesting and relevant.

We welcome both original and reprint materials on a wide range of subjects (see topics below), though first-person nonfiction stories are our staple. We do not accept juvenile material. Fiction is almost never used. Poetry only occasionally. Payment is made upon acceptance for original material; upon publication for reprint material. *Today's Christian* retains the right to edit material for length or content.

While query letters are accepted, article manuscripts are preferred. In general, they should be no longer than 1,300 words and should be computer-generated (no disks, please) or typed. *A cover letter or entry at the top of the manuscript should provide the following information:*

- Your name
- Date
- Phone number (day and evening)
- Fax number (if available)
- Rights offered (first rights preferred; if reprint, give publication and date)
- Type of submission (non-simultaneous strongly preferred)

Note: Enclose a self-addressed, stamped envelope if you wish to receive an acceptance/rejection letter. (If you want the manuscript returned, indicate that and enclose appropriate return postage and envelope size.) Or, you can send your manuscript in the body of an e-mail (no attachments, please). We respond to most submissions within two weeks, but please allow up to two months processing time. E-mail: TCeditor@christianity.com.

TYPES OF ARTICLES SOUGHT BY *Christian Reader*

Stories

- *Action Drama:* real-life; also missionary; first or third person
- *Character Drama:* conversions, recovery, relationships, etc.
- *Lessons from Life:* winsome, poignant, but not moralistic
- *Real-Life Parable:* a short true story with an implicit moral lesson
- *Fiction:* TC almost never uses fiction
- *Humor:* quality humor is hard to write and highly valued by TC editors
- *Celebrity Profile:* Christian and "cross-over" personalities
- *Seasonal:* Christmas, Easter, Mother's/Father's day, etc.; best if submitted at least nine months in advance

Interesting & Artsy Stuff

- *Poetry:* We are no longer soliciting for poems.
- *History/Archaeology/Science:* written factually and popularly with a Christian angle
- *Trivia:* fun, quirky, or interesting facts about life and Christian culture

Topics

- *Family:* stories, how-to's
- *Romance & Marriage:* stories, how-to's
- *Sex:* Christians' perspectives and benefits of purity
- *Social Issues:* compelling, informative, and fresh perspectives on cultural, moral, social issues such as gambling, euthanasia, abortion, racial injustice, etc.–written for the popular audience, usually with statistics or personal accounts that illustrate the subject

Spiritual Reflection

- *Church Life:* no yawners, please
- *Evangelism/Missions:* stories, how-to's
- *Meditation/Devotional:* shorter than most articles; must be fresh, contemporary, personable
- *Prayer:* stories, how-to's
- *Personal Growth:* stories, how-to's
- *Other:* general articles on spiritual living

Categories: Nonfiction—Christian Interests—Drama—General Interest—Inspirational—Religion—Spiritual

CONTACT: Editor
Material: All
465 Gundersen Dr.
Carol Stream IL 60188
Phone: 630-260-6200
Fax: 630-260-0114
Website: www.todayschristian.com

Today's Christian Preacher

The focus and frequency of these magazines will be changing in the near future in response to changing marketplace conditions. For this reason, we will no longer be accepting unsolicited submissions.

We apologize for any inconvenience these changes may cause you. Of course, we wish you all the best as you submit your material to other publishers.

Sincerely,
Elaine Williams, Asst. Editor

Today's Christian Senior

Does not accept unsolicited submissions.

Today's Christian Teen

The focus and frequency of these magazines will be changing in the near future in response to changing marketplace conditions. For this reason, we will no longer be accepting unsolicited submissions. We apologize for any inconvenience these changes may cause you. Of course, we wish you all the best as you submit your material to other publishers.

Sincerely,
Elaine Williams, Asst. Editor

TODAY'S CHRISTIAN
Woman

Today's Christian Woman

Our Purpose

Today's Christian Woman is a practical magazine geared for women in their 20s, 30s, and 40s. It seeks to help women deal with the contemporary issues and hot topics that impact their lives, as well as provide depth, balance, and a biblical perspective to the relationships they grapple with daily in the following arenas: family, friendship, faith, marriage, single life, self, work, finances, and health.

Our Readers

The TCW reader represents a broad spectrum of familiarity with what it means to have a vital faith in Jesus Christ. Readership includes those who are knowledgeable about the Bible and are involved in a church, as well as those who either are still investigating Christianity or are relatively new believers.

Almost 83 percent of TCW readers are married; 17 percent are single, widowed, divorced, or separated; 66 percent are employed (49 percent full-time), and 57 percent have children living at home.

Our Tone

TCW articles should be personal in tone and utilize real-life anecdotes as well as quotes/advice from noted Christian professionals or related resources. Articles should be practical and contain a distinct evangelical Christian perspective. While TCW adheres strictly to this underlying perspective in all its editorial content, articles should refrain from using language that assumes a readers's familiarity with Christian or church-oriented terminology. Bible quotes and references should be used selectively. All Bible quotes should be taken from the New International Version if possible.

Our Writers

• TCW does not accept unsolicited manuscripts. Please query first (see below).

• TCW will report on queries and manuscripts in 8 weeks. Include a SASE of correct size, if you wish your manuscript returned.

• All submissions are received on speculation. An accepted query does not guarantee purchase of the manuscript. Editors reserve the right to reject any manuscript at any stage.

• Payment on acceptance of completed articles, 20 cents per printed word, first rights.

• TCW does not accept simultaneous submissions.

• TCW does not issue kill fees.

Query letters should include:

1. A summary describing the article idea
2. The purpose of the piece and its value to readers
3. The author's qualifications to write the piece
4. Suggested length and date it could be finished
5. A self-addressed stamped envelope for reply

Address query letters to The Aquisitions Editor, at the address below. Include your mailing address and daytime phone number. No query should be sent without a thorough knowledge of TCW's audience.

For a sample copy, writers' guidelines, or subscription information, write:

Today's Christian Woman
PO Box 37060
Boone, IA 50037-0060.

Please include a self-addressed, stamped #10 envelope for writers' guidelines.

For a sample copy, please send $5.00.

Manuscripts

Manuscripts should be typed double-spaced. In addition to the author's address, the first page should include his/her phone number, social security number, and the word length. Also include a SASE for possible return of the manuscript. Manuscripts may also be e-mailed (but not as attached files) to: tcwedit@ christianitytoday.com.

Our Editorial Needs

Freelance submissions are accepted for the following: 1,000- to 1,800-word articles that help women grow in their relationship to God as well as provide practical help and a biblical perspective on these topics: family/parenting, friendship, marriage, health, self life, single life, finances, and work. TCW is also interested in practical spiritual living articles.

We do not accept poetry, fiction, or Bible studies.

Our magazine is also always on the lookout for:

• **Humor:** light, first-person pieces that exaggerate a real-life occurrence instead of focus on a hypothetical situation, giving a fresh twist and a subtle spiritual distinctive to topics the majority of women can relate to. Length: 1,000-1,500 words.

• **Issues/Hot Topics:** reports that tackle the topics that impact women's lives today, such as infertility, homosexuality, ADHD, or pornography. These articles need to avoid a preachy or clinical tone; fully develop the scope of the specific issue and provide authoritative research and/or up-to-date statistics; incorporate real-life illustrations from women our readers can relate to; present a distinct Christian perspective. Sidebars of accompanying first-person stories and/or resources are welcome. Length: 1,800-2000 words.

• **My Story:** a first-person, true-life dramatic narrative that describes how you worked through a difficult situation, event, or traumatic turning point in your life (can be written as an as-told-to).

• **Length:** 1,500 words. Payment: $300 upon purchase.

Regular Features

We pay $25 for the following features, and regret submissions cannot be acknowledged or returned:

• Faith in Action—a true story of how you've recently shared your faith with someone on the job. Length: 300 words. Please include a

quality photo of yourself.

• Readers' Picks—a short review of your current favorite cd or book, and why. Length: 200 words.

• Small Talk—the funny things kids say. Length: 100 words. Please include a quality color photo of your child.

Categories: Nonfiction—Children—Christian Interests—Family—General Interest—Inspirational—Interview—Marriage—Parenting—Relationships—Religion—Self Help—Singles—Spiritual

CONTACT: Jane Struck, Editor
Material: Queries
CONTACT: Camerin Courtney, Managing Editor
Material: "My Story" submissions
Christianity Today International
465 Gunderson Dr.
Carol Stream IL 60188-2498
Phone: 630-260-6200
Fax: 630-260-0114
E-mail: tcwedit@christianitytoday.com
Website: www.todayschristianwomen.com

Today's School
Shared Leadership in Education

Contributor's Guidelines

Today's School: Shared Leadership in Education is a nationally circulated magazine for K-12 administrators who participate in the shared decision making that distinguishes many of our nation's public and private schools. Issued six times during the school year, it has a circulation of about 50,000 copies. Although that readership is primarily principals, *Today's School* is read also by school board members, teachers, parents, and other staff members who seek to promote quality decision making in their schools.

Articles: Subject matter may be any topic of practical help, concern, or interest to administrators in site-based schools. Areas of special focus are:

• Administration, including curriculum trends and instructional materials; the decision-making process, NCLB.

• Technology, including the tools of technology (hardware, software, Internet, networking); training and staff development to make optimal use of these tools.

• Facilities, including budgeting and management of the school site; safety and security for staff and students.

Style: The desired magazine style is direct, concise, informative, and accurate. Writing should be enjoyable to read, informal rather than scholarly, lively, and free of educational jargon.

Length: Feature articles fall into three general categories: 700-1000 words, 1000-2000 words, and 2000-3000 words.

Photographs: Color prints, slides, or transparencies are helpful. Write identifying information on back or accompanying paper. Photos will not be returned unless requested.

Payment: Paid on publication, payment for features is generally $100-$300, depending on subject, length and quality of writing. Photos or other illustrations may increase payment.

Sample Issue: Send $3 for mailing and handling.

Contact: Query letters are encouraged. Write, call, fax, or e-mail (soconnor@peterli.com) the editor for editorial calendar. Articles may be submitted as hard copy; submission by e-mail or on disk with accompanying hard copy is preferred.

Categories: Nonfiction—Education

CONTACT: Shannon O'Conner, Editor
Material: All
2621 Dryden Rd., Ste. 300
Dayton OH 45439
Phone: 937-293-1415, ext. 134

Fax: 937-293-1310
E-mail: soconnor@peterli.com

Town&Country

Town & Country

If you are interested in proposing an article for *Town & Country*, please send a query letter and samples of your published work to the appropriate editor and department at the address below. Be sure to include an e-mail address or self-addressed stamped envelope so we may reply. Please do not submit article queries by e-mail.

Send query letters to *Town & Country*, 1700 Broadway, New York, NY 10019.

Regarding writer's guidelines, we do no make available any such listings. The magazine itself serves as the best guide possible to the kinds of stories we're looking for, so please consult recent issues for content and style before making your submission.

Also, in the case of already completed manuscripts, please keep in mind that we rarely publish work we have not originally commissioned.

Thank you for your interest in *Town & Country*.

Categories: Nonfiction—Antiques—Architecture—Arts—Beauty—Fashion—General Interest—Health—Home—Literature—Society—Travel—Women's Issues

CONTACT: Melissa Biggs Bradley, Travel Editor
Material: Travel
CONTACT: Sarah Medford, Director of Design & Architecture
Material: Luxury Homes, Estates
CONTACT: Janet Carlson Freed, Director of Beauty & Health
Material: Health & Beauty
CONTACT: Tom Farley
Material: "On the Town" and "Social Graces"
CONTACT: Tony Freund
Material: "In the Country" and "Connoisseur's World"
The Hearst Corp.
1700 Broadway, 30th Floor
New York NY 10019
Phone: 212-903-5000

Toy Cars & Models

Unsolicited manuscripts are welcome but should include a self-addressed, stamped envelope (SASE) with sufficient return postage. Query letters are appreciated with samples of the author's writing.

Content

Toy Cars & Models is published monthly and includes feature stories, news items and columns in each issue. Articles are of general interest to toy car and model car collectors, focusing mainly (but not exclusively) on newer items from the 1960s-present. Stories should focus on the collectibility of specific toys or manufacturers' lines. Features should not be too narrow but rather hit the highlights of a particular line or type of toy/model. Smaller features may focus on more specific topics.

Features generally run 750-900 words for a short piece and 1,000-1,250 for a longer feature. All stories are subject to editing for accuracy, clarity, conciseness and space considerations. Current values of toys/models and other pricing information should be incorporated into features or placed in an accompanying sidebar. Readers want to know not only the historical information about toys/models, but also what is available and how much the items are worth.

Other ideas for stories may include histories of prominent toy/model companies, interviews with collectors, model reviews of new or old releases and features on topics that affect and interest those in the toy car and model hobby.

Rights and Payment

Krause Publications purchases exclusive rights. Krause Publications also maintains a license to reproduce the material and distribute it by all means and media now known or hereafter discovered, including, without limitation, print, microfilm and electronic media as well as the right to display and transmit the work publicly online.

Authors must warrant that each contribution is original work that has not been in the public domain or previously published, unless noted otherwise, and that each is free of unauthorized extractions from other sources, copyrighted or otherwise. Payment for accepted articles is decided on a per-story basis at the editor's discretion. Payment is upon publication. Contact editor Merry Dudley for specific and current rates.

Manuscript Format

Hard copy submitted must be typewritten on white paper with the author's name, address and phone number at the top. Please leave at least a one-inch margin on all sides of the page. Computer submissions should be in Microsoft Word format to be followed by hard copy.

Electronic submissions are accepted only for solicited or assigned stories. No unsolicited manuscripts via e-mail, please. Send e-mail submissions to editor Merry Dudley.

Style

We follow the basic journalistic style guidelines in *The Associated Press Stylebook*. Consult Strunk & White's *The Elements of Style* for additional considerations.

Photographs

Authors are encouraged to submit color photographs (slides, prints or transparencies) to accompany their submissions. Photos should be identified on a separate sheet or with a Post-It note on the back of the photo. Do NOT use ink on the backs of photos. If desired, photo credits will be given, and photos will be returned upon publication if requested.

High-resolution images sent via e-mail or on disk in TIFF format are acceptable, but please call for more information if you choose to use this method.

Publication

Authors will not be notified prior to publication and will be sent one copy of the issue containing their story.

Please note: Publication time may be anywhere from 3 months to 12 months following acceptance.

Sample Copy

For a sample copy of *Toy Cars & Models* or other titles published by Krause, call 800-258-0929.

Categories: Automobiles—Hobbies

CONTACT: Merry Dudley, Editor
Material: Query
Krause Publications
700 East State St.
Iola WI 54990-0001
E-mail: dudleyMCkrause.com (no manuscripts)
Website: www.collect.com

Toy Farmer

Copy should be as legible and accurate as possible. Please type and double space. If you use a dot-matrix printer with your word processor, please make sure it is on 1½ or double space when printing.

Please submit copy as early as possible ahead of copy deadlines. If we have questions or need additional information, We will have plenty of time to refer back to you.

Copy submitted on disk is preferred but do enclose a hard copy of your article, in case we have problems with your disk.

Photos should be accurately identified and labeled on back with your name or name of owners of photos. If you have several photos with your article, please label back of your photo with an identifying number to make sure we correctly position photos with cutlines.

R-U

Please call if you have questions or problems getting copy in before the deadline.

Agreement Rights

You grant us the following rights:

A. Exclusive periodical publication rights for a period of 60 days from first publication of the contribution.

B. Nonexclusive reprint rights without fee, when reprinted for reader convenience.

C. Promotional and publicity rights, including the right to use your name, biography and likeness in connection with publication and promotion of the contribution.

D. The right to edit, revise, condense, abridge, augment and re-title the contribution to suit our requirements.

E. We pay you the sum of ten cents per word, plus agreed-upon expenses.

*The above guidelines apply to both *Toy Farmer* and *Toy Trucker & Contractor.*

Categories: Nonfiction—Business—Collectibles—Hobbies—Trade—Farm Toy Collecting/Construction Toy Collecting

CONTACT: Cheryl Hegrik, Editorial Assistant
Material: All
Toy Farmer Publications
7496 - 106th Ave. SE
LaMoure ND 58461
Phone: 800-533-8293
Fax: 701-883-5209
E-mail: zekesez@aol.com

Toy Shop

Submissions

Unsolicited manuscripts are welcome, but should include a self-addressed, stamped envelope (SASE) with sufficient return postage. Query letters are appreciated with samples of the author's writing.

Content

Toy Shop is published bi-weekly (twice a month) and includes feature stories, news items and columns in alternating issues. Articles are of general interest to toy collectors, focusing mainly (but not exclusively) on toys from the 1940s to present. Stories should focus on the collectibility of specific toys or manufacturers' lines. Features should not be too narrow, but rather hit the highlights of a particular type of toy—such as board games, Marx play sets, action figures, Barbie dolls or construction sets. Smaller features may focus on more specific topics. Auction coverage is also welcome.

Features generally run around 500 to 750 for a short piece to 1,000 to 1,500 for a longer feature. All stories are subject to editing and re-writing for accuracy, clarity, conciseness and space considerations.

Current values of toys and other pricing information should be incorporated into features or placed in an accompanying sidebar. Readers want to know not only the historical information about toys, but also what is available and how much it's worth.

Other ideas for stories may include histories of prominent toy companies, interviews with collectors or features on particularly unique, unusual, or large toy collections.

Rights and Payment

Krause Publications purchases exclusive rights to manuscripts for *Toy Shop*. For more details on our editorial contract, contact Editorial Director Sharon Korbeck.

Authors must warrant that each contribution is original work that has not been in the public domain or previously published, unless noted otherwise, and that each is free of unauthorized extractions from other sources, copyrighted or otherwise.

Payment for articles accepted is based on a per-story basis at the editor's discretion.

Payment is upon publication, unless other arrangements have been agreed upon. Contact Editorial Director Sharon Korbeck for specific, current rates.

Manuscript Format

Hard copy submitted must be typewritten and double-spaced on white paper with the author's name, address and phone number at the top. Please leave at least one-inch margins on all sides of the page. Computer submissions should be on a DS/HD disk in ASCII (text) format with accompanying hard copy.

Electronic submissions are accepted only for solicited or assigned stories. No unsolicited manuscripts via e-mail, please. Send e-mail submissions to korbecks@krause.com.

Style

We follow the basic journalistic style guidelines in *The Associated Press Stylebook*. Consult Strunk & White's *The Elements of Style* for additional considerations. Please proofread stories carefully before submitting them.

Photographs

Authors are encouraged to submit color or black-and-white photographs (slides, prints or transparencies) to accompany their submissions. Photos should be identified on a separate sheet or on a Post-It note on the back of the photo. Do NOT use ink on the backs of photos. If desired, photo credits will be given, and photos will be returned upon publication.

Photos sent via in TIFF or JPG format electronically or on disk are acceptable. Resolution must be 170 dpi or greater.

Publication

Authors will not be notified prior to publication and will be sent one copy of the issue containing their story.

Please note: Publication time may be anywhere from two months to 24 months following acceptance.

Contact

Interested free-lance writers should query Editorial Director Sharon Korbeck at 715-445-2214, ext. #468, via mail at 700 E. State St., Iola, WI 54990-0001 or or via e-mail at korbecks@ krause.com.

For a sample copy of *Toy Shop* magazine or other Krause publications, call 800-258-0929.

For more information about our company's books and magazines, visit our Web site at www.collect.com.

Categories: Collectibles—Consumer—Hobbies

CONTACT: Sharon Korbeck, Editorial Director
Material: All
700 E. State St.
Iola WI 54990-0001
Phone: 715-445-2214, ext. 468
Fax: 715-445-4087
E-mail: korbecks@krause.com
Website: www.collect.com

Toy Trucker & Contractor

Please refer to *Toy Farmer*.

Tradition

Only accepts articles that deal with traditional, acoustic music. Pays in copies of our publication. Otherwise, there are no formal guidelines.

Categories: Nonfiction—Arts—Dance—Entertainment—Folklore—Music—Recreation—Rural America

CONTACT: Robert Everhart, Editor
Material: All
Nat. Trad. C.M.A.
PO Box 492
Anita IA 50020
Phone: 712-762-4363

Traditional Home

Does not accept unsolicited submissions.

Traditional Quiltworks
Quilting Today
Miniature Quilts

We offer complete directions and diagrams for completing quilt projects, as well as interesting and instructional articles concerning all aspects of quilting. Articles should be informative to quilters, presenting new ideas or techniques. Upon submission of your manuscript, please allow six to eight weeks for a response. Articles are scheduled for publication up to a year in advance. Publication hinges on the quality of the photos or the availability of quilts for photography.

Submissions

We seek articles with one or two magazine pages of text and quilts that illustrate the content. (Each page of text is approximately 750 words, 6500 characters, or three double-spaced typewritten pages.) Please submit double-spaced manuscripts with wide margins. Ideas need to be logical, sequential and fully developed. We may ask you to revise or clarify your manuscript to make it publishable. We prefer original material accompanied by 35mm slides or 2¼" transparencies. Please include detailed photo captions and photo credits. You may send suggestions for a one-line subhead after the title, a pull quote and a cover line of three or four words if you wish, but these are generally written by our editors. Send the name and addresses of your subjects in case we need to contact them for more information. Please include the following information in the upper right-hand corner of the first page: your name, address, telephone number, Social Security number and the estimated number of words in your article.

Magazines are published six times per year. Specific guidelines for each follow:

• *Traditional Quiltworks* is a pattern magazine offering a variety of instructional features and directions for up to a dozen full-size projects. "What If...Design Challenge" is a regular column which encourages quilters to creatively use one pattern in many different ways. "Featured Teacher" is a profile about a quilting teacher accompanied by photos of his/her work. It is followed by "Private Workshop" which contains the teacher's instructions for completing a specific project. We occasionally feature one-page human interest/personality profiles accompanied by quilt slides/photos.

• *Quilting Today* offers feature articles on quilt history, techniques, tools and quilters sharing their knowledge with readers. Articles are accompanied by color slides/photos and sidebars containing helpful tips. The pattern section offers six quilt patterns. Patterns are written according to the established magazine format. Other features include book and product review, a calendar of quilt events, a guest editorial and "The Sampler," a news column. Fictional pieces are rarely accepted.

• *Miniature Quilts* offers dozens of patterns for small quilts with block sizes 5" or less. Also included are how-to articles, profile articles about quilters who make small quilts and photo features about noteworthy miniature quilts or exhibits.

Editing

We reserve the right to edit and/or rewrite for style, clarity, length and adherence to format. When an article is ready for publication, a press copy is provided as a courtesy to ensure that all facts are accurate.

Photos

Clear 35mm slides or 2¼" or larger transparencies can be used. Photos should be professional quality. Quilts should be straight shot-on so they do not appear distorted. Include your name and address on all photos. Write "TOP" on all slides. Include the photographer's name for the photo credit if required. Send photos in plastic sleeves or cardboard to protect them. If you want your photos returned, include a self-addressed, stamped envelope.

Payment

Upon preparation of your manuscript for publication, you will be asked to sign a contract stating that your submission is not an infringement on the rights of others. Payment is made approximately 6 weeks after the on-sale date. Payment varies, depending upon the amount of work required to prepare the article and whether or not the article promotes your business. Payment averages $75 per 800 published words, without photos. If your photo is used for a feature article or a pattern quilt, payment is $20. Payment varies for multiple photos. No payment will be made to you for quilts photographed by Chitra Publications. No payment is made for photos shown in the "letters" column.

Regular Columns

If you would like us to consider your idea for a regular column, please use the following guidelines:

• Submit a description of the proposed feature, indicating its philosophy or goals and indicating why readers would benefit from reading it in sequential issues.

• Submit an autobiography of about 100 words, with an emphasis on quiltmaking, along with a professional-quality photo.

• Submit an outline of one year's columns (six).

• Submit two sample columns, including snapshots of projects or to-scale diagrams, if applicable. Patterns must be written to our format.

Upon acceptance of the feature, we require submission of one year's worth of manuscripts (six) before publication of the first installment. Upon receipt of the installments, we will edit the material and issue a contract. Payment for each installment is made approximately six weeks after the on-sale date. Should we desire the column to continue, a new contract will be issued at the proper time.

Categories: Nonfiction—Crafts—Hobbies

CONTACT: Connie Ellsworth, Production Manager
Material: Articles & Reviews
CONTACT: Jack Braunstein, Senior Editor
Material: Books
Chiltra Publications
2 Public Ave.
Montrose PA 18801-1220
Phone: 570-278-1984
Fax: 570-278-2223
E-mail: chitra@epix.net
Website: www.QuiltTownUSA.com

Trail Runner
The Magazine of Running Adventure

Author Submissions

First, be sure to read about *Trail Runner* on our website. When pitching story ideas to *Trail Runner*, please include information regarding the availability of images to illustrate the article. Send your queries with published clips.

Photo and Art Guidelines

Trail Runner pays $250 per page with a minimum of $50 per spot usage. A two-page spread pays $375 and covers pay $500. A submission of images to *Trail Runner* implies acceptance of these rates. We also ask that you notify us when making simultaneous submissions to other magazines. If we decide to publish one of your images, we request that you do not submit the image to any other publication for six months from the on-sale date.

R-U

We are happy to consider original art—photos, illustrations, cartoons, etc.—with or without accompanying text. For photos, we prefer original color slides or black-and-white prints. We are also willing to review a representative sample of your work; a stock list would be a useful reference. All slides should be clearly labeled with the photographer's name, address and telephone number. Include a caption sheet that indicates the location of the photo and, if applicable, the trail name and names of the people in the photo.

Shooting Trail Running: A few notes for photographers planning to shoot images for *Trail Runner*. Trail running is a fun activity, but most people aren't smiling with perfectly clean clothes and looking directly at a camera out on the trail. Please do not shoot runners wearing brand-new clothes and shoes with smiling faces looking right at the camera. Even if shots are staged, there are ways to get more authentic shots. Use real runners, not pretty models. Also, let the runners run for 30 to 45 minutes before shooting. (Sweat, mud, blood and other elements of trail running make good pictures.) And, make sure runners have proper hydration equipment (either water bottle pouches or proper hydration reservoir packs), especially if photos are taken in the mountains or in the desert.

Off the Beaten Path: The last editorial page of *Trail Runner* will feature an Off the Beaten Path photo. This will consist of a stunning photo (in crispness, color, subject matter, location) and run at least two-thirds of the page. A brief caption will be included, as well as details of the photographer, camera and film.

SUBMISSIONS

All materials sent to *Trail Runner* should be accompanied by a self-addressed, stamped envelope suitable for return of all of your submitted work. If you would like your work returned certified or registered, please include sufficient postage. Please include your name, address, telephone number, Social Security number and email address for billing purposes.

Categories: Nonfiction—Health—Physical Fitness—Sports/Recreation

CONTACT: Brian Metzler, Editor/Associate Publisher
Material: Features and departments, except Wanderings,
Off the Beaten Path and Training
E-mail: editor@trailrunnermag.com
CONTACT: Monique Cole, Senior Editor
Material: Training, Wanderings
E-mail: monique@ trailrunnermag.com
CONTACT: Jeff Cloud, Photo Editor
Material: Photo submissions and queries, plus
Off the Beaten Path
E-mail: photo@rockandice. com
North South Publications
5455 Spine Rd., Mezzanine A
Boulder CO 80301
Phone: 303-499-8410
Fax: 303-530-3729
E-mail: www.trailrunnermag.com

Trailer Boats

EDITORIAL PROFILE: As the name implies, *Trailer Boats* is written for owners and prospective buyers of trailerable powerboats—generally under 30' with no more than an 8'6" beam (no sailboats). Most of our readers are seasoned boating veterans who use their boats and equipment frequently.

Regular features include reports and evaluations of products useful to trailerboaters, including boat tests on current-model cruisers, runabouts, skiboats, fishing boats, pontoon/deck boats, etc. Related topics such as maintenance, seamanship, towing, navigation, electronics, repairs, watersports, etc., are also regularly covered, often in either a technical or how-to format. Each issue also includes travel destinations and a high-performance (racing oriented) article.

SPECIFICS: Boat tests, comparisons, and product evaluations are generally staff written. Technical articles are always in demand, wherein experts in the field either write them or are consulted for accuracy. When consulting "experts" it is best to go to more than one source—our readers catch errors. How-to articles should be explained in simple, easy-to-follow terms, but should not be superficial in content. Travel articles on destinations in and around the continental U.S. and its Canadian and Mexican borders, as well as Alaska, are welcome.

We prefer a hands-on boating approach to travel pieces, rather than a simple travelogue. The boating theme must permeate the story.

We don't want redone news releases from local chambers of commerce. The high-performance story in each issue is generally presented as race coverage, a personality profile, or a how-to, although general-interest pieces on new developments run occasionally.

Fishing articles should center around the boat—its special design, equipment and accessories, etc.—more than on fishing techniques. How to install downriggers or how to choose the right electronics are examples. An occasional fishing oriented destination story is also acceptable.

SUBMISSIONS: Study the magazine first. (Sample copies are available for $1.25.) Then query. Please allow 4-6 weeks for a response. We prefer submissions on computer disk (WordPerfect 5.1 or ASCII), accompanied by a type written hard copy of the manuscript. We also accept transmissions via modem. We desire complete packages, including headline, subhead, photos (and/or artwork) and captions. Travel articles should also include a map of the area.

PHOTOGRAPHY: *Trailer Boats* is a visually oriented magazine that uses photos with virtually all stories. We want sharp—no dupes, please—color slides or medium-format transparencies. First-time travel articles are usually assigned after we've seen the quality of photos. Please identify all photos with a tag line or caption. Photos are usually included as part of the editorial package, but when submitted separately, we will negotiate price. That includes the cover. Technical and how-to articles often utilize 5"x7" or 8"x10" glossy B&W photos, but it's wise to verify with the editor first.

PAYMENT: We pay on acceptance except for departments, which are paid on publication. Payment ranges from $100 for short fill pieces, to between $300 and $700 for features, depending on length, nature of assignment and quality of product.

Categories: Automobiles—Boating—Outdoors—Recreation Vehicles—Travel

CONTACT: Mike Blake, Managing Editor
Material: Any
CONTACT: Randy Scott, Editor
Material: Any
20700 Belshaw Ave.
Carson CA 90746-3510
Phone: 310-537-6322

Trailer Life

Please refer to *Highways* magazine.

Remember: Editors change jobs and publishers change addresses. It is wise to invest in a phone call for the current information before submitting.

Transaction Publishers Rutgers
The State University of New Jersey

Please see this listing in the book publishing section.

Transitions

Thank you for your interest in *Transitions*. We are always interested in reviewing focused, well-written nonfiction articles and interviews. The best way of assessing our style is to look at copies of our magazines, which are available in most major bookstores and on the internet at www.transitionsmag.com. Our Statement of Purpose, located in the beginning each issue, is a good place to start.

We do not respond to query letters, and we only consider final products. We prefer that you submit your article by email. If you do submit a hard copy, please include a self-addressed stamped envelope or email address for our reply. Allow up to six months for a response. We don't send back submissions, so do not send us your only copy. We do not longer publish poetry or fiction. Writing in the form of a sermon, research paper, or personal narrative is discouraged. Submissions should not have already appeared in other publications or on the web.

Transitions reassures readers over the age of 50 that "It s still our time!" *Transitions* addresses the wide range of issues that confront society today politics and aging, sex and entertainment, and everything in between. It s fun, challenging, thought provoking, sometimes controversial...but never boring!

FORMAT: Feature articles range in length from 1000 2000 words. E-mailed versions are preferred (in Rich Text Format or text-only format, or in MSWord 98 or earlier), though hard copies can be mailed to MB Media, PO Box 600, Chico, CA 95927-0600. E-mail us at editor@magicalblend.com. Work that has been edited for length and clarity is more likely to be considered. Payment is considered strictly on an individual basis.

Artwork to accompany articles may be submitted digitally or on slides or color prints. Please do not send us originals!

Some article Ideas *Transitions* magazine considers:
• Health & Fitness over 50
• Retirement
• Estate Planning
• Aging
• Travel
• Celebrities
• Humor
• Families & Grandchildren
• Eating for Longevity
• Optimism and Quality of Life
• Dealing with the Loss of Loved Ones Dating/Sex after 50
• Interviews
• Health and Life Insurance
• Gardening/Pets
• Assisted Living/Home Care
• Volunteering
• Leisure
• Learning New Things Late in Life
• Anecdotes
• Age-Related Mental Illness and Depression
• Book Reviews

Categories: Nonfiction—Animals— Biography—Book Reviews—Careers—Comedy—Culture—Crafts/Hobbies—Disabilities—Education—Entertainment—Environment—Family Food/Drink—Gardening—General Interest —Health—History—Hobbies—Inspirational—Interview—Lifestyle—Marriage—Men's Issues—Money and Finances—Outdoors—Parenting—Physical Fitness—Politics—Psychology—Real Estate—Recreation—Relationships—Religion—Science—Self Help—Senior Citizens—Sexuality—Society—Sports/Recreation—Spiritual—Travel—Women's Issues

CONTACT: Editorial Director
Material: All
PO Box 600
Chico, CA 95927-0600
E-mail: editor@magicalblend.com
Website: www.transitionsmag.com

Transitions Abroad

Transitions Abroad is a bimonthly magazine guide to practical information on affordable alternatives to mass tourism: living, working, studying, or vacationing alongside the people of the host country. Circ. 12K , 95% freelance. Editorial Calendar is available on the Transitions Abroad web site under Writers[1] Guidelines (se URL below). Lead-time is six months prior to issue date. Pay is $2.00 per column inch. Photography $25 per use ($10 each if part of an accompanying article.) Read a copy of the magazine. *Transitions Abroad* is the "alternative" to standard travel magazines for traditional kinds of travel. Emphasis is on actually getting to know the people and place by living, working, studying or vacationing alongside the people who live there. Readers like to think of themselves as travelers and not tourists. Preferred method of query is e-mail.

Who We Are

After over a quarter of a century of publication, Transitions Abroad remains the premier magazine for independent travelers, especially for those seeking to extend their time abroad through employment, study, and/or finding the best bargains. (It's also great for those of us who want to keep their overseas experiences alive by discovering and sharing ways that overseas culture can be kept alive in our lives at home through music and other creative arts and activities.) The magazine's title, Transitions, suggests the personal discoveries and changes in perception and understanding—not just in place—that result from immersion in another culture, even for a short time. Its purpose is to provide readers with the practical information and ideas they need to make their own plans. Readers are most interested in learning about the culture by meeting the people and value for money.

Features and Departments Overview
What We Are Looking For

The magazine's four major departments—Travel, Work, Study, and Living—are all devoted to immediately usable practical information and ideas (the "nuts and bolts"). Contributors write from personal knowledge, usually from first-hand experience, and stress ways to avoid the cultural isolation of a tourist. The more useable information presented in a concise manner, the greater the likelihood of publication. As the editors are unable to check sources, current and accurate information is essential. Sidebars include details that are not in the body of the article: relevant names and addresses, web sites and email addresses, telephone numbers, costs, and other options similar to the ones described in you submission. Well-researched supporting material in sidebars greatly increases the likelihood of publication.

Information Exchange Departments

Since Transitions Abroad is primarily a place for travelers to share information, your contribution need not take the form of a full-length article. Be as brief as possible (250 words maximum). The editors will sometimes shorten material submitted for other departments for inclusion in Information Exchange, which leads off each issue. Payment is a free one-year subscription or subscription extension.

Submissions that otherwise fit our guidelines but are simply too lengthy to include in the magazine (or to shorten for Information Exchange) may be published on our web site. Please tell us if you do not wish your material to be considered for web publication.

What We Do Not Want in Features or Departments

Sightseeing or "destination" pieces that focus exclusively on what to see rather than on the people and culture;

Personal travelogues or lengthy descriptions of personal experiences (unless readers can use the practical details in your account to make their own travel plans);

Articles that represent travel as a form of consumption and objectify the people of other countries;

Information that is readily available in guidebooks or from government tourist offices.

Featured Articles

Length and Format of Feature Articles

Maximum length: 1,500 words. Average length: 1,000 words. For the magazine we must edit tightly because of space limitations. Four feature-length articles are used in each issue: one each on Travel, Work, Study, and Living. Their content, which must be information-based and not a travelogue or narrative description of a personal, should correspond to those of the shorter articles for departments described below.

Departments

The Independent Traveler

In this major section of the magazine the emphasis is on value for money, avoiding superficial tourist routines, and engaging with local people and culture. Articles may involve finding and selecting such things as a home stay or a rural bed and breakfast, a 1- or 2-week language study course, or pursuing a hobby or activity like cooking, music or mountain hiking. The length of the articles vary: If you have a lot of useful information to share, put it all in (1,000 words maximum if possible). The editors will decide whether your submission can run as a full-length feature or under the heading of one of the shorter features described below.

(Note: Because of space limitations in the magazine an abbreviated version may sometimes run in print and an extended version on the web site. This is true of all submissions.)

Best Travel Bargains

500 words maximum. Current information on good value for money options (not necessarily the cheapest). Be specific about dates, contacts, etc. in the text (no sidebars). Several used each issue.

The Learning Traveler

500 words maximum (longer pieces will be considered for the Education Abroad section). Usually first-hand reports on a travel-study program or an independently organized learning experience such as a language-learning vacation.

Itineraries

500 words maximum. Readers who travel on their own like to learn about detailed itineraries that will take them off the tourist trail—whether to the less-visited areas of Europe or to remote regions of the rest of the world.

Alternative Tours and Activities (Responsible Travel)

500 words maximum. Ways to combine a vacation abroad with a rewarding activity that travelers would find difficult to organize on their own. Several used each issue.

Solo Woman Traveler

500 words maximum. More and more women are traveling solo or with other women. Submissions should emphasize the advantages of independent solo travel and precautions regarding health and safety.

The Gay or Lesbian Traveler

500 words maximum. The increasing numbers of our gay and lesbian readers are seeking details on gay-friendly destinations abroad.

The Working Traveler
International Careers

1,000 words maximum. Submissions should focus on securing long-term jobs abroad and discuss the experience. Emphasize practical information and insights based on experience in an international career (which may include international work in the U.S.).

Short-Term Work

1,000 words maximum. Your experience in finding and maintaining a short-term job abroad (from crewing a yacht to teaching English) is of great interest to our readers, especially as a way to extend your stay. You should include resources and practical information for how readers can find a similar work experience. Working Traveler Editor Susan Griffith, an authority on short-term work abroad, supplements your own articles with her own expert reports on topics such as the pros and cons of particular jobs around the world, and tips on how to make the most of your job abroad. Several used each issue.

Volunteering

1,000 words maximum. Another very popular, fascinating and rewarding way to extend a trip abroad is to exchange work for free room and board (and sometimes a stipend). First-hand reports on how to do this are welcome. Several used each issue.

Community-Based Travel and Ecotours

1,000 words maximum. Department editors Ron Mader and Deborah McLaren welcome information on how local communities abroad organize and profit from eco-tourism, plus details on responsible ecotour organizers.

Living Abroad

1,000 words maximum. The best way to learn about a country and its culture is to live there (or short of that to travel like a local). For longer stays nothing beats exchanging your home for a comparable home abroad or renting or buying a vacation home. Share your first-hand experience and practical information on assimilating into the local culture and getting to know the people.

Abroad at Home

1,000 words maximum. The opening of borders between people and cultures through art and other forms of expression (music, film, literature, art, craft work, cuisine, etc.) is a bridge to other countries and cultures. Submissions should provide insights on the creative arts of another culture that may be embraced in our day-to-day life while not physically abroad. Resource sidebars may include web sites related to the subject and contact information for relevant groups, clubs, and organizations.

Education Abroad

Articles in this department provide practical information and advice for readers planning a "study abroad" experience, travel abroad for specifically academic purposes, or travel to gain experience in preparation for an international career. Columns include: Study Abroad Adviser, Student to Student, Work Abroad Adviser, and Disability Travel Adviser. (See Education Abroad Guidelines and Student Writers Guidelines. Columnists appreciate your feedback and suggestions, and guest columnists are welcome. 1,500 words maximum.

Program Notes

250 words maximum. News of newly organized programs and tours—work, study, or study/travel—or changes in existing programs. Several used each issue.

Submission Procedures
Articles

Maximum length: 1,500 words. Average length: 1,000 words. We edit tightly for length. Manuscripts should be sent electronically and addressed to editor@transitionsabroad.com. Include your contact information. Please attach only Microsoft Word documents: if you use another format, please cut and paste your article into the text portion of your email message. We prefer that you do not send photos electronically until your article has been accepted for publication. If you do not submit your article via email (not recommended), you must provide an electronic version of your manuscript on disk (Macintosh platform) via regular mail. The author's name, address, phone and fax number, and email address should appear on at least the first page of the manuscript.

Photos

We strongly recommend that you let us know whether photos are available with your article. However, if you are submitting an article electronically, please do not submit photos electronically until your article has been accepted for publication. It is fine to send prints, slides, or digital photos on disc or standalone photos via postal mail at any time. It is also fine to send electronic standalone photos at anytime. See Photographic Guidelines for all information on sending photos.

Other Submissions Considerations

Regular mail should be accompanied by a business-size SASE. If sending by mail please include your email address! All material is submitted on speculation. We purchase one-time rights only; rights revert to writers upon publication. However, we reserve the right to reprint published articles in part or whole on our web site. We will consider reprinted material from publications outside our primary circulation area. Since ours is not the usual travel publication, writers may want to browse the back issues of our web site or review a recent issue of Transitions Abroad for style and content (See order form).

Contact Information

Electronic Submissions: Editor@TransitionsAbroad.com.
Our postal address is below.

Include a short biographical note at the end of each submission, including your email address. We include these on all published articles so that readers can contact you directly with their feedback.

Include your name, address, telephone numbers (day and evening), and email address on at least the first page of your manuscript.

If sending the manuscript in postal mail, include an envelope of adequate size and with the correct postage for return. We do not return material unaccompanied by SASEs.

Initial response time to manuscripts is about four weeks. We often request permission to hold a submission longer pending final decision shortly before publication. We record and file each submission and take great care with material "on hold" awaiting the appropriate issue. Unless you need your manuscript or photographs returned immediately, please do not telephone. We cannot provide status reports by phone.

Payment

Payment is on publication, approximately $2 per column inch (50-55 words), sometimes more for repeat contributors. For the most part our contributors are not professional travel writers but people with information and ideas to share; we are much more interested in usable first-hand information than in polished prose. We are always looking for experienced writers to become regular contributors or contributing editors. Fees for regular contributors are by agreement. Two copies of the issue in which your story appears will be included with payment.

Categories: Nonfiction—Adventure—Conservation—Education—Language—Multicultural—Travel

CONTACT: Ms. Sherry Schwarz, Editor
Material: All
PO Box 745 • 314 Silver St. (for UPS or FedX)
Bennington, VT 05201
Phone: 802-442-4827
Fax: 802-442-4827
E-mail: editor@transitionsabroad.com
Website: www.TransitionsAbroad.com

Travel & Leisure

Travel & Leisure is published monthly and has a ratebase of 1,000,000 subscribers, plus limited newsstand distribution. Our readers are sophisticated, active travelers who look to us for planning both pleasure and business trips.

About 95 percent of the magazine is written by freelance writers on assignment . Every assignment is confirmed by a contract. We buy only the first-time world rights, and request that the work not be published elsewhere until 90 days after it appears in T&L. We pay upon acceptance of the article. Neither editors nor contributors may accept free travel.

How to Proceed:

1. Look at several issues of the magazine and become familiar with the types of articles published in the various sections, and the two Regional editions, whose page numbers carry letters that indicate the region—E(East), W (West).

Please note that a place is not an idea, and that editors are looking for a compelling reason to assign an article: a specific angle, news that makes the subject fresh, a writer's enthusiasm for and familiarity with the topic.

Service information is important to every destination article: when to go, how to get there, where to stay, where to eat, what to see and do. The reader must be able to follow in the author's footsteps, and the articles are scheduled withat in mind—i.e., before the season in question. We have a three-month lead time.

Please do not telephone us about story proposals. Instead send a query letter that briefly outline the ideas (no more than three at once) being proposed. Please enclose recent clips of your work and a SASE. Query letters can also be via e-mail. The address is tlquery@amexpub.com. In most cases, e-mail queries will receive the fastest responses.

It is rare that we will assign a feature article to a writer with whom we have not worked. The best section to start with are departments in the front and back of the magazine and the regional editions.

Photography Portfolio Submission Guidelines

If you mail your portfolio, include a stamped, self-addressed package for its safe return. Or you can send it by messenger Monday through Friday between 11 A.M. and 5 P.M. We accept work in book form exclusively—no transparencies or loose prints. Send Xerox copies or photo prints, not originals, as we aren't responsible for lost or damaged images in unsolicited portfolios. We do not meet with photographers if we haven't seen their book. However, please include a promo card in your portfolio with contact information, so we may get in touch with you if necessary. You do not need to call ahead to ask to retrieve your portfolio. Simply come to the 10th Floor reception area at Travel & Leisure Monday through Friday between 11 A.M. and 5 P.M. and the receptionist will notify the Photo Department to bring out your book. You may also get this information by visiting our website at www.travelandleisure.com or by calling 212-382-5856. Thank you.

Categories: Nonfiction—Consumer—Fashion—Food/Drink—Lifestyle—Recreation

CONTACT: Editorial Dept.
Material: Queries
CONTACT: Photography Dept.
Material: Photography portfolios
1120 Avenue of the Americas (address to the 10th Floor for photo portfolio submissions)
New York NY 10036
Phone: 212-382-5600
Fax: 212-382-5877
E-mail: tlquery@aexp.com
Website: travelandleisure.com

Travel Naturally
(Formerly known as Naturally)

Overview: For the average American, a vacation is a period of travel and relaxation when you take twice the clothes and half the money you need. And for nude vacationers? Well, the latter may still hold true, but the places where you spend that money can be oh-so-different! *Travel Naturally* looks at why millions of people believe that removing clothes in public is a good idea, and at places specifically created for that purpose with good humor, but also in earnest. *Travel Naturally* takes you to places where your personal freedom is the only agenda, and to places where textile-free living is a serious commitment. *Travel Naturally* invokes the philosophies of naturism and nudism, but also activities and beliefs in the mainstream that invoke nudity: spiritual awareness, New Age customs, pagan and religious rites, alternative and fringe lifestyle beliefs, artistic expressions and many individual nude interests. Our higher purpose is to help restore our sense of self. *Travel Naturally*'s parent company, Internatually, Inc., is a marketing-publishing firm that came out of the naturist movement — a non-membership-based organization with distribution access to the public. Internatually, Inc. also publishes and distributes other educational materials about nude recreation; its attractive Internaturally catalog is known worldwide and on the Internet at www.Internaturally.com. *Travel Naturally* seeks mainly informational articles that showcase nude resorts, nude parks, and other nude recreation organizations. Their success assures future clothes-free vacations for everyone. We support public nude beaches, volunteer groups and even private nude homes, because their successes increase public awareness and participation. It's obvious that nudity or nude activities are not philosophies in themselves but, rather, the products of certain philosophies and ideologies some of which are deeply rooted in history and social ritual like nude public bathing and skinny-dipping, meditation and celebration through dance. For most nudist and naturist organizations social nudity, and its benefits, is a serious philosophy and lifestyle commitment that is their main purpose for existence. Other alternative lifestyle groups include nudity ritually, peripherally, or spontaneously, as one of many ways to express cleansing, a celebration of life, and personal freedom. Although the term "nude recreation" may, for some, conjure up visions of sexual frivolities inappropriate for youngsters which can also be technically true these topics are outside the scope of *Travel Naturally* magazine. Here the emphasis is on the many varieties of human beings, of all ages and backgrounds, recreating in their most natural state, at extraordinary places, their reasons for doing so, and the benefits they derive. *Travel Naturally* exists to explore these notions of higher personal freedom and recreational possibilities, worldwide. This is our purpose and your invitation to submit your story, articles and pictures.

Photography: Travel Naturally's photo policy is liberal. We encourage photography at all clothes-free events by courteous and considerate photographers. Although Travel Naturally publishes primarily the work of nudist and naturist (amateur and professional) photographers, we believe strongly that all who are interested in taking pictures at nude events should be free to do so without extraneous restrictions for purposes of protecting anonymity. Unreasonable photo restrictions discourage openness and sabotage the depiction of genuine, and sincere nude recreation. Of course, we do respect the rights of nudist and naturist clubs to set the rules as hosts. Travel Naturally will honor imposed publishing restrictions placed upon some photos by a host. Photographs taken on public land or in establishments open to the public, do not require photo releases unless intended for commercial use (e.g., in an advertisement, to sell something). However, common courtesy and consideration prevails. Photographs acquired surreptitiously or by insensitive methods are not accepted for publication. Photographs taken in closed private areas, not generally thought of as public should have releases from all recognizable persons when the photo is not of a newsworthy situation. For a legitimate newsworthy photograph, Travel Naturally magazine does not require photo releases, even when the picture is taken on private property. Again, common courtesy and consideration prevails, and photographs acquired by insensitive methods are not accepted for publication. Photo releases are the responsibility of the photographer. Photographs may be submitted in color or b & w, as prints, negatives, or slides. Slides or negatives yield the highest reproduction quality. It is preferred, but

not required, that selected photos for publication are retained as file copies for possible future use. Unpublished photos are returned as a matter of procedure, unless there is a likelihood for future publication in Travel Naturally magazine or other books and magazines published by Events Unlimited.

Illustrations and Poetry: Thematic renderings, paintings, poems, and other art submissions are welcomed. We document the theme of all submissions and attempt to combine the art with relevant articles, poems, and stories, which are available to the magazine. Please submit only copies or photos of the art so that they can be filed. Do not send originals.

Cartoons: Cartoon illustrations can generally stand on their own, although we may combine them with relevant editorials or other text. The topics are wide open, but the cartoonist should avoid any sexual connotation or innuendo. Payment ranges from $15 per small spot, to $70 per full page. Compensation for full-color cartoons and more elaborately illustrated plates are negotiable.

Organizations: We support most naturist and nudist groups and organizations in their endeavor to educate the mainstream about nude recreation. Toward this endeavor, we have chosen a less political and more lighthearted approach. However, articles and/or photos submitted by nudist/naturist organizations, to inform, to promote an event or political agenda, are accepted and appreciated. Fund-raising appeals are accepted for publication from naturist and nudist organizations. Brevity is requested. We accept event schedules for publication if open to all-comers and dated sufficiently ahead (preferably 5-6 months) to be useful to our readers for at least up to one month after publication.

Paid Participation (at time of publication): All contributors receive copies of Travel Naturally magazine in which their material appears. Travel Naturally pays $70 per published page (text and/or visuals). Fractional pages or fillers are pro-rated. Frequent contributors and regular columnists, who develop a following through Travel Naturally, are paid from the Frequent Contributors Budget. Payments increase on the basis of frequency of participation, and the budget is adjusted quarterly as Travel Naturally grows. We purchase news items that are creatively combined and submitted as one major news article. Blurbs or short news write-ups are graciously accepted as contributions to the cause (see unpaid participation).

Unpaid Participation & Contributions: Published materials, submitted with a commercial agenda, such as product releases, news releases, resort news, etc. are not paid. Published articles intended to promote a commercial entity, resort or nudist park, organization, group, etc. are not paid. It is generally understood that Travel Naturally publishes this material as free promotional/publicity support. Short news (current events) items and clippings are also appreciated as contributions to the cause of promoting the benefits of clothes-optional freedom. Opinion pieces are accepted as contributions only when adequately researched.

Exclusivity: We accept articles and photos that have been previously published elsewhere, when submitted by the original authors or photographers. However, the value of the material is diminished as a non-exclusive submission. We deduct 50% from previously published submissions if accepted for publication.

Assignments: When all-expense-paid assignments are awarded, Travel Naturally magazine will provide paid travel and accommodation expenses. Food and other routine daily living expenses are not paid for. Additional payments are made for the published article(s) and/or photo(s), based upon the above-stated "Paid Participation" criteria. Articles and photos resulting from assignments are for Travel Naturally magazine's exclusive use.

Categories: Nonfiction—Alternate Life-style—Lifestyle—Travel

CONTACT: Submissions Editor
Material: All
PO Box 317
Newfoundland NJ 07435
Phone: 973-697-3552

Fax: 973-697-8313
E-mail: naturally@internaturally.com
Website: www.internaturally.com

Travel Tips

Please refer to Premier Tourism Marketing, Inc.

Treasure Cache

Please refer to *Lost Treasure.*

Troika Magazine

Formal guidelines not available. Please read a number of issues to ascertain the publication's style and needs.

To submit your work to *Troika* for consideration please e-mail your submissions to submit@troikamagazine.com.

You will be contacted by the editors within approximately 90 days.

Categories: Nonfiction—General Interest—Lifestyle—Literature

CONTACT: Submissions Editor
Material: All
PO Box 1006
Weston CT 06883
Phone: 203-227-5377
Fax: 203-222-9332
E-mail: submit@troikamagazine.com
Website: www.troikamagazine.com/home.html

True Romance

True Romance was formerly *Modern Romance. True Romance* features first-person narratives written for the average, high school educated woman. She is juggling family and work responsibilities, but family comes first. After a long day, she wants to read compelling, realistic stories about other women and how they have overcome obstacles. Stories must be set in towns, cities, and neighborhoods where hardworking Americans live.

Emotionally charged stories with a strong emphasis on characterization and well-defined plots are preferred. Our suspenseful stories deal with romance, families, marital problems, tragedy, peril, mystery, and Americana. The plots and characters should reflect the average American's values and desires.

Do not send query letters. Send completed manuscripts. Seasonal material should be sent six months in advance. Mark the outside of the envelope: seasonal material. We do not accept simultaneous submissions. We buy all rights of our published materials.

Manuscripts should be double-spaced. Typewritten and letter-quality inkjet or laser printer manuscripts are acceptable. A dot-matrix manuscript is only acceptable if it is letter quality. Please send your submission on disk, along with a paper copy. If you want your manuscript and/or disk returned, you must send a self-addressed, stamped envelope. Unfortunately, the editorial staff cannot critique each manuscript.

Tips: Writers should read three or four issues of *True Romance* before sending submissions. Do not talk down to our readers. Timely,

first-person stories told by a sympathetic narrator are appreciated. Dramatic stories and stories featuring ethnic characters are always needed, but stay away from stereotypical plots and characteristics.

Greatest Needs: Stories between 5,000 and 10,000 words.

Terms: We receive a vast number of submissions, and each one is given careful consideration; therefore, we ask for your patience in receiving replies. *True Romance* reports back to writers in eight to twelve months. The editor reads all stories. We pay three cents per word a month after publication. Again, please do not send simultaneous submissions.

Columns: "That's My Child" pays $50 for a photo and up to 50 words about your child. Only the parents of the child may submit his or her picture. "Loving Pets" pays $50 for a photo and up to 50 words about your pet. Photos must be in focus and no other people should be in the picture. "Cupid's Corner" pays $100 for a photo and up to 750 words about you and your spouse. "That Precious Moment" pays $50 for 1,000 words about a unique personal experience.

Poetry: Look at poetry published in three or four issues before submitting. Poetry should be no longer than twenty-four lines. Payment is $10 to $30.

Good luck with your writing,
The Editors

Categories: Fiction—Inspirational—Romance—Rural America—Short Stories—Women's Fiction—Confession

CONTACT: Pat Vitucci, Editor
Material: All
The Sterling/Macfadden Partnership
333 Seventh Ave., 11th Floor
New York NY 10001
Phone: 212-979-4894
Fax: 212-979-7342

True West

TRUE WEST magazine publishes nonfiction articles on the history of the American West from 1800 to the early 20th Century. More recent topics may be used if they have a historical angle or retain the Old West flavor of trail dust and saddle leather.

Our readers are predominantly male, forty-five years of age or older, from rural areas and small towns. Nearly all have graduated from high school, and slightly more than half have attended college. They are knowledgeable about Western history and ranching and want articles to be informative and entertaining.

We cover all states west of the Mississippi and all areas of western history—Native Americans, trappers, miners, cowboys, ranchers, farmers, pioneers, the military, ghost towns, lost mines, women, and minorities. We especially need good western humor and stories on lesser-known people and events. If widely-known topics are used, the article should include newly discovered information or take a fresh approach to the subject.

Historical accuracy and strict adherence to the facts are essential. We much prefer material based on primary sources (archives, court records, documents, contemporary newspapers, and first person accounts) to those that rely mainly on secondary sources (published books, magazines, and journals). We occasionally use first person reminiscences, but proper names and dates must be accurate and double-checked by the author. We do not want dialogue unless it can be documented, and we do not use fictionalized treatments of historical subjects. Manuscripts other than first person recollections should be accompanied by a bibliographic list of sources.

TRUE WEST prefers one-page queries with one subject per query. Please provide information regarding the availability of photographs and/or illustrations. We usually need from four to eight photos for each story, and we rely on writers to provide them. We respond to submissions in a timely manner.

To judge our needs, consult our 2003 back issues.

TRUE WEST is published 10 issues per year. 2004 is the 51st anniversary of the magazine.

Categories: Nonfiction—History—Lifestyle—Western

CONTACT: R.G. Robertson, Editor
Material: All
True West Publishing, LLC
PO Box 8008
Cave Creek AZ 85327
Phone: 888-687-1881
E-mail: editor@truewestmagazine.com
Website: www.truewestmagazine.com

Turkey Call
Women In The Outdoors
Wheelin' Sportsmen
The Caller
Jakes Magazine

National Wild Turkey Federation Contributors' Guidelines

Welcome to the exciting world of the wild turkey! The National Wild Turkey Federation (NWTF) is a nonprofit conservation/education organization dedicated to the conservation of the North American wild turkey and the preservation of the hunting heritage. Established in March 1973, the NWTF has 500,000 members throughout the United States, Canada and 11 foreign countries.

The NWTF has five publications: *Turkey Call*, *Women In The Outdoors*, *Wheelin' Sportsmen*, *The Caller* and *Jakes Magazine*. All of our publications are available exclusively through membership in the NWTF.

Turkey Call

Turkey Call, the flagship publication of the NWTF, is dedicated to the interests and entertainment of wild turkey enthusiasts everywhere—people who hunt, study and actively support the restoration and conservation of the North American wild turkey.

Turkey Call is published bi-monthly and includes articles that focus on the hunting, history, restoration, management, biology and distribution of the American wild turkey. We also purchase short items and illustrative materials sent separately. They can be turkey related such as unusual hunt experiences, historical vignettes, the wild turkey in art or literature, biographical sketches, tips, anecdotes, humor or other appropriate outdoor subjects.

Turkey Call articles must be written for wild turkey "experts," except when specifically addressing the neophyte, and the articles should appeal to a national readership. Wild turkey management and restoration material should be meticulously researched. Dates, figures and the names and titles of agencies and persons involved must be correct.

Women In The Outdoors

Women In The Outdoors is the quarterly magazine of the NWTF's Women In The Outdoors program. The mission of this program is to provide outdoor learning opportunities for women, ages 14 and over, that are hands on and exciting.

Similarly, *Women In The Outdoors* magazine is dedicated to inform and entertain outdoorswomen of all skill levels who aspire to become more involved in a variety of outdoor sports and activities including camping, fishing, hiking, shooting, hunting, canoeing, boating and bird watching. The publication also relays information about the Women In The Outdoors program and the NWTF.

Women In The Outdoors feature articles average 1,800 words and cover a wide variety of outdoor activities and subjects. We also run shorter articles that average 800 words, depending on the specific department. Regular departments include:

• outdoor-related book reviews,
• game and fish recipes,
• wildlife profiles,
• stories of notable outdoors-women,
• outdoor health issues,
• outdoor gear and backyard habitat enhancement.

Most articles are geared toward the novice outdoors enthusiast, including information on where to go, necessary equipment and how to find out more on a specific activity. Articles should treat women as independent outdoors enthusiasts, depict outdoor activities in a positive/encouraging manner and appeal to a national audience.

Wheelin' Sportsmen

Wheelin' Sportsmen, is the quarterly magazine of the Wheelin' Sportsmen NWTF program. The mission of this program is to deliver, and in some cases re-introduce, the beauty and excitement of the the outdoors to thousands of disabled people.

Wheelin' Sportsmen magazine also is dedicated to bringing the outdoors to disabled outdoors enthusiasts who enjoy all kinds of hunting, fishing and recreational shooting, as well as a variety of other outdoor activities. The publication is also a tool for able-bodied sportsmen and women to learn more about sharing the outdoors with their disabled peers and relays information about the Wheelin' Sportsmen NWTF program and the NWTF.

Wheelin' Sportsmen feature articles average 1,500 words. Most articles are targeted to people with disabilities that range from "how to enjoy" to "where to enjoy" the outdoors. We're also interested in stories about disabled people who enjoy the outdoors and ways able-bodied individuals can help the disabled participate in outdoor fun. Articles should depict outdoor activities in a positive/encouraging manner and appeal to a national audience.

Jakes Magazine

Jakes Magazine is the NWTF's publication for members of its youth program, JAKES (Juniors Acquiring Knowledge, Ethics and Sportsmanship). The magazine is dedicated to informing, educating and involving youth in wildlife conservation and the wise stewardship of our natural resources.

All stories need to be fun and keep the interest of our readers (mean age of 10 years old). Feature criteria for *Jakes Magazine* should be either documentary or fictional with the emphasis on the outdoors, conservation, hunting, hunter safety, hunting ethics or heritage. Historical fiction must be accurate, including cultural and social accuracy. Stories should be between 800 and 1,200 words.

The Caller

The Caller is the official newsletter of the NWTF, which is comprised of more than 1,800 local chapters. The primary purpose of *The Caller* is twofold: one, to communicate to the membership news related to hunting, wildlife habitat management and the programs available to them through the national office of the NWTF; and two, to give the membership an outlet to publicize the work of local chapters.

News to the membership is supplied by members who volunteer their time to write about their chapters' efforts to fulfill the NWTF's hunting and conservation mission. No payment is issued for publication.

Editorial Information

• We purchase first North American serial rights, and in some cases, all electronic rights, to articles.

• All written material should be original and unpublished and must consist of accurate information that appeals to our special interest readership.

• We do not publish poetry, but we do accept fiction that contributes to the education, enlightenment or entertainment of our readers in some special way.

• We enjoy articles that are easy to read, which can mean supplemental text including sidebars, bulleted lists, graphic elements, etc. We also welcome copy that comes with subheads and pull quotes already written.

Article Submissions
• **Submitting Queries**

A query is a letter that first introduces the writer to the editor, then offers an idea for an article and tells the main points of the article. A query letter may include a "laundry list" of article ideas.

Always include possible graphic aids and sidebar ideas. Remember, your query should exemplify your writing talent.

We recommend that you submit written queries to save time for both you and our staff.

Even though you may have a fantastic article idea, we may have recently published a similar story or have one in our files. Queries allow us to assign specific articles according to our needs. This way, your time and ours is well spent.

All queries are kept in our files and reviewed at the time of assignment. Our editor will contact you with assignment specifications if your idea is accepted.

If you don't hear from our office, this in no way means that your query has been rejected. Our office will send you a notice if your query is rejected.

• Submitting Over-The-Transom Articles

Over-the-transom articles are complete manuscripts with all graphic aids, photo captions and sidebars, which are submitted for review and possible publication.

These submissions are accepted for review, but are not preferred. When submitting complete manuscripts, keep in mind that your article may remain in our files for a long time before being reviewed.

If accepted, our editors or publishing assistants will contact you. If rejected, all materials will be returned promptly to you. (Enclose a SASE for prompt return.)

Article ideas also can be submitted by email to the individual editor. (See Article Submission Mechanics).

Timelines
• *Turkey Call*

Our production schedule allows us to work four to 12 months ahead of each issue, and most issues are planned a year in advance. If you want to send a query or article suitable for the November/December issue, August is too late to send it.

• *The Caller, Jakes Magazine, Wheelin' Sportsmen* and *Women In The Outdoors*

Our editorial coverage for *The Caller, Jakes Magazine, Wheelin' Sportsmen* and *Women In The Outdoors* is prepared three months or more ahead of each issue's release date. They are quarterly publications with winter, spring, summer and fall issues each year.

Article Submission Mechanics

• Articles must be saved to either a 3.5" double-sided, double density or a high-density diskette.

• We prefer that articles and cutlines be written in Microsoft Word for the Macintosh or the PC, Word Perfect 6.0 or lower version.

• Article text should be single-spaced, with only one space after periods and no tabs or indents on the first line of paragraphs.

• There should only be one "hard" return at the end of each paragraph.

• Send a printed hard copy with the disk.

• Articles can be sent via email. Please send the text as a compatible attachment and in the body of your message. Check with the editor to see if email is appropriate for sending a particular assignment.

• We follow *The Chicago Manual of Style, Associated Press (AP) Stylebook and Libel Manual* and the *Outdoor Writers Association of America (OWAA) Stylebook*.

Editor's Expectations For Articles

• Articles must fulfill the promise of the author's query and, more importantly, the editor's assignment.

• A familiarization with the publications is beneficial in submitting an article that is compatible with the magazine's format or needs.

• Articles must be free of spelling errors, grammatically correct and, above all, accurate.

Photo Submissions

We look for quality-clarity, sharpness, composition and correct exposure. Each photo should have a written caption with a description of the shot and the names of any people shown.

• *Turkey Call*

For *Turkey Call*, we are looking for various wild turkey subspecies in their natural habitats, turkey hunting scenes, colorful scenics of wild turkey habitat, vintage turkey hunting scenes, etc.

• *Women In The Outdoors*

For *Women In The Outdoors*, we accept shots that illustrate wildlife, conservation, colorful scenics, women participating in various outdoor activities and families participating in hunting and outdoor pastimes together.

• *Wheelin' Sportsmen*

For *Wheelin' Sportsmen* magazine, we accept shots that illustrate wildlife, conservation, colorful scenics, individuals with a variety of disabilities participating in hunting, shooting, fishing and other outdoor pastimes, as well as able-bodied and disabled people enjoying the outdoors together.

• *Jakes Magazine*

For *Jakes Magazine*, we accept shots that illustrate wildlife, conservation, colorful scenics, families participating in hunting and outdoor pastimes together and youth and their involvement in hunting.

Please contact the individual editor for the specific, immediate photo needs of each publication.

Mailing Photography Submissions

Please be certain to carefully package your photographs. Remember that those who handle the mail may not have our same consideration for the value of your photographs, and if not packaged correctly, your photos risk being damaged. The NWTF is not responsible for photos not received.

Return of your photos is very important to us. Each photo should have the photographer's name, address and phone number on it, as well as an attached cutline identifying the subject matter, and, if possible, a photographer's code number for identification of each slide.

Pay Rates
• Articles

All NWTF publications pay upon acceptance of assigned articles or publication of over-the-transom articles.

• *Turkey Call*

We pay $100 for short pieces having 600-700 words $200-$275 for articles having 700-1,100 words; $300-$375 for up to 1,500 words; and $400 for up to 2,000 words.

• *Jakes Magazine*

Article payment is negotiable, starting at $100.

• *Wheelin' Sportsmen*

We pay $100 for short pieces having 600-700 words; $200-$275 for articles having 700-1,100 words; $300-$375 for up to 1,500 words; and $400 for up to 2,000 words.

• *Women In The Outdoors*

We pay $200-$275 for articles having up to 1,100 words; $300-$375 for up to 1,500 words; and $400 for up to 2,000 words.

• Photos

We will pay $35 minimum for one-time rights on black & white photos and simple art illustrations. We will pay $75-$200 for inside color.

Pay rates will depend on size, quality and placement in the magazine. Payment for cover photos is $400.

In color, we need the original (not duplicates) transparencies; 35mm is the most common, although medium format, 4x5 or 5x7 transparencies have a better chance of being selected for cover use.

Electronic Rights

The NWTF does occasionally purchase all electronic rights on original and reprint articles, as well as color photos. Payment and terms are negotiated at the time of assignment.

Payment Information

Please include the following information with your query, photo or article submission: your name, mailing address, contact number and your Social Security number or Federal I.D. number.

You can contact all members of the NWTF's editorial staff at the following addresses and numbers:

Categories: Fiction—Nonfiction—Recreation—Sports—Hunting (turkeys, all aspects of hunting)

CONTACT: Doug Howlett, Editor
E-mail: dhowlett@nwtf.net
Material: *Turkey Call* Submissions
CONTACT: Jason Gilbertson, Managing Editor
E-mail: jgilbertson@nwtf.net
Material: *The Caller* Submissions
CONTACT: Karen Lee, Editor
E-mail: klee@nwtf.net
Material: *Women In The Outdoors* or *Wheelin' Sportsmen*
Submissions
CONTACT: Matt Lindler, Editor
E-mail: mlindler@nwtf.net
Material: Jakes Magazine Submissions
National Wild Turkey Federation
PO Box 530 • 770 Augusta Rd.
Edgefield SC 29824
Phone: 803-637-3106
Fax: 803-637-0034
Website: www.nwtf.org

Turtle

Please refer to Children's Better Health Institute.

Twins
The Magazine for Parents of Multiples

TWINS, *The Magazine for Parents of Multiples*, is a bimonthly, international publication that provides informational and educational articles regarding parenting twins, triplets and more.

TWINS magazine consists of four to six features and 10 departments per issue. Features are 1,100 to 1,500 words and departments are 750 to 950 words including sidebars and additional materials. Please limit your manuscripts to these lengths.

Because our readers are very busy, articles must be written in an easy, conversational style. Please study our format before starting an article. To make articles more readable, please break up long copy with subheads. TWINS conforms to AP style.

All department articles must have a happy ending, as well as teach a lesson or provide a moral that parents of multiples can learn from.

TWINS accepts queries for feature articles. For departments, we accept either queries or manuscripts sent on speculation. Submissions must tell stories that teach lessons about family life with multiples. Subjects of interest include perspectives on being or parenting multiples, as well as child-rearing, family and social issues.

Please send queries by mail or e-mail to the contact listed below, along with a resume and samples of your work. Please indicate if you are interested in us contacting you for feature assignments.

Submit assigned articles by mail or e-mail. When mailing assigned articles, please include a hard copy as well as the file saved on a 3.5" floppy disk. To ensure our computers can read the file, save it as an ASCII or "text only" file. If you would like your disk back, please enclose a self-addressed, stamped envelope. When e-mailing articles, please embed the story in the body of the message and attach the word processing file at the end of the message.

Please also include your signed contract, an invoice and a two-sentence biography for the story tag line. We cannot publish an article without a signed contract and cannot pay a you without an invoice. The invoice must have your name, address, payment amount and social security number.

Fees are negotiated prior to publication and payment is made within 30 days following publication. A contract is sent after assignment is made.

A byline is supplied, and one complimentary copy of the magazine is sent to each contributor following publication.

TWINS magazine purchases first North American serial rights.

Categories: Family—Parenting

CONTACT: Sharon Withers, Managing Editor
Material: All
5350 S. Roslyn St. Ste. 400
Englewood CO 80111
Phone: 303-290-8500
Fax: 303-290-9025
E-mail: twins.editor@businessword.com
11211 E. Arapahoe Rd., #101
Centennial CO 80111

Two Rivers Review

Founded in 1998, *Two Rivers Review* is a biannual journal of quality contemporary poetry and fiction. Our goal is to present the best writing we can find, with a special interest in writing that gives pleasure to the reader. To that end, we have published authors as respected as Billy Collins, Lee Upton and Naomi Shihab Nye, alongside lesser-known but equally astonishing poets like Robert Bense, Myrna Stone and Daniel Donaghy. Each issue of TRR is 40-48 pages long. Work is printed in a clear, easy-on-the-eyes format. TRR mostly prints contemporary poetry, along with a small amount of short fiction, and occasional translations. TRR also publishes an annual poetry chapbook, selected through a national competition.

Poetry Guidelines

TRR welcomes submissions of original, unpublished poetry. Please follow the following guidelines when sending your work.

• All submissions must include an SASE.
• Submit no more than four poems per submission.
• All poems must be previously unpublished.
• No handwritten submissions.
• No e-mail submissions, please.
• Please do not submit more than three times per calendar year.

Poets should keep in mind that TRR is extremely competitive. We receive approximately 5,000 poems per year, and accept about 25 per issue. Of those 25, 5-10 are from manuscripts solicited by the editor. This is not to discourage anyone, of course; merely a reminder that all poets, regardless of reputation or prior publication, should submit only their best work for consideration at TRR. We strongly suggest that poets read an issue of *Two Rivers Review* before submitting work.

All poetry submissions (as well as subscriptions and other business correspondence) should be sent to:

Two Rivers Review
PO Box 158
Clinton, NY 13323

Fiction Guidelines

Beginning with issue #7, TRR will print short fiction along with poetry. Please follow the following guidelines when submitting fiction.

• All submissions must include an SASE.
• Submit no more than one story per submission.
• All stories must be previously unpublished.
• Simultaneous submissions acceptable, provided that you tell us in your cover letter.
• All submissions must be typed and double-spaced.
• No e-mail submissions, please.
• Stories may be submitted ONLY during the following reading periods: June 1 - July 15, and January 1 - February 15. Fiction received outside of these reading periods may be returned unread.

Categories: Fiction—Poetry

CONTACT: Carole Burns
Material: Fiction
CONTACT: Submissions Editor

Material: Poetry
PO Box 158
Clinton NY 13323
Website: trrpoetry.tripod.com

THE UKRAINIAN WEEKLY

Published by the Ukrainian National Association

The Ukrainian Weekly

We greatly appreciate the materials—feature articles, news stories, press clippings, letters to the editor, and the like—we receive from our readers. In order to facilitate preparation of *The Ukrainian Weekly*, we ask that the guidelines listed below be followed.

• News stories should be sent in not later than 10 days after the occurrence of a given event.

• All materials must be typed and double-spaced.

• Photographs (originals only, no photocopies or computer printouts) submitted for publication must be accompanied by captions. Photos will be returned only when so requested and accompanied by a stamped, addressed envelope.

• Full names (i.e., no initials) and their correct English spellings must be provided.

• Newspaper and magazine clippings must be accompanied by the name of the publication and the date of the edition.

• Information about upcoming events must be received one week before the date of *The Weekly* edition in which the information is to be published.

• Persons who submit any materials must provide a daytime phone number where they may be reached if any additional information is required.

• Unsolicited materials submitted for publication will be returned only when so requested and accompanied by a stamped, addressed envelope.

Categories: Ethnic newspaper
CONTACT: Roma Hadzewycz, Editor-in-Chief
Material:Ukrainian National Association
2200 Route 10
PO Box 280
Parsippany NJ 07054
Phone: 973-292-9800

Underground Construction

Please refer to Oildom Publishing.

Unique Opportunities

EDITORIAL PHILOSOPHY

Unique Opportunities is a national bimonthly magazine for physicians looking for their first or next practice opportunity. Its goal is to educate the reader about how to evaluate career opportunities, negotiate the benefits offered, and plan career moves. It also provides information on the legal and economic aspects of accepting a position and running a practice.

AUDIENCE

Unique Opportunities is distributed to 80,000 physicians who are interested in new practice opportunities or who are in their final years of residency.

QUERY

Submit article ideas via mail or e-mail. The editors prefer to assign articles from queries rather than receive complete article submissions.

TYPES OF ARTICLES

Unique Opportunities publishes feature articles that cover the economic, business, and career-related issues of interest to physicians who would like to relocate or change practices. Feature articles range in length from 1,500 to 3,500 words. Previously run stories include:

• Paving the Way for Employee Terminations—Firing the smart way.
• Logged on to the Future—On-line CME gets easier and better.
• The Road to Private Practice—A roadmap to entering private practice.
• What's That, Doc?—Physician-inventors.

FORMAT FOR SUBMISSIONS

Submit articles via e-mail as ASCII text file attachments or as the body of an e-mail message. Articles may also be submitted on a 3.5" diskette as ASCII text or other files compatible with Microsoft Word from either a Macintosh or MS-DOS computer.

PAYMENT

Unique Opportunities pays within 30 days of acceptance and receipt of an invoice. Standard rate for feature articles is $.75 a word plus expenses up to $75. (Any expenses incurred over $75 must be approved at the Louisville office, 502-589-8250.)

Rights: First North American print rights, exclusive for 90 days after publication, and rights to publish electronically on UO's Web site with no time limit. Will not consider duplicate submissions.

Categories: Nonfiction—Careers—Trade—Physicians Career Opportunities

CONTACT: Bett Coffman, Associate Editor
Material: All
214 S. 8th St., Ste 502
Louisville KY 40202
Phone: 502-589-8250
Fax: 502-587-0848
E-mail: tellus@uoworks.com
Website: www.uoworks.com

United Parenting Publications

United Parenting Publications publishes these periodicals in the San Francisco Bay Area:

• *Bay Area Parent* magazine is a regional monthly parenting magazine with distribution of 180,000 copies through four zoned editions, covering San Francisco, Silicon Valley, the East Bay, and the North Bay, including Sonoma and Marin Counties.

• *Get Up & Go, A Magazine For Active & Involved Grandparents*, is published in March, June and October.

• *Bay Area Parent's B.A.B.Y.* (The Best Advice For Baby & You) is published two times a year, with distribution of 60,000 copies to new and expectant parents all over the Greater San Francisco Bay Area.

• *Bay Area Parent of Teens* is no longer published.

To receive a free copy of one of these magazines, please send a self-addressed envelope (at least 8½ x 11) stamped with ten stamps. Indicate which publication you want to receive.

Most of the editorial for these publications is written by freelance writers on assignment. A few unsolicited articles are run. The information most likely to BE used is local, well-researched and geared to parents of newborns to early teens.

Poetry or fiction is not accepted. Timeliness is critical, e.g., swimming in June and snow skiing in December. Editorial content is planned 3 to 6 months in advance, so articles pertinent to a particular season should be proposed or submitted well in advance.

We appreciate submission of appropriate photographs with a story. We pay upon acceptance. Rates are based on the nature and scope of the piece.

United Parenting Publications was formerly known as Bay Area Publishing Group.

Categories: Children—Family—Juvenile—Parenting—Teen

CONTACT: Regional Editor
Material: All
11076 Coloma Rd., Ste. 7
Rancho Cordova CA 95670
Phone: 916-635-1655
Fax: 916-635-4262
Website: parenthood.com

The Upper Room

You can write for *The Upper Room*.

The meditations in each issue are written by people just like you, people who are listening to God and trying to live by what they hear. *The Upper Room* is built on a worldwide community of Christians who share their faith with one another.

The Upper Room is meant for an international, interdenominational audience. We want to encourage Christians in their personal life of prayer and discipleship. We seek to build on what unites us as believers and to link believers together in prayer around the world.

Literally millions of people use the magazine each day. Your meditation will be sent around the world, to be translated into more than 44 languages and printed in over 65 editions. Those who read the day's meditation and pray the prayer join with others in over 100 countries around the world, reading the same passage of scripture and bringing the same concerns before God.

Have God's care and presence become real for you in your interaction with others? Has the Bible given you guidance and helped you see God at work? Has the meaning of scripture become personal for you as you reflected on it? Then you have something to share in a meditation.

Where do I begin?

You begin in your own relationship with God. Christians believe God speaks to us and guides us as we study the Bible and pray. Good meditations are closely tied to scripture and show how it has shed light on a specific situation. Good meditations make the message of the Bible come alive.

Good devotional writing is first of all authentic. It connects real events of daily life with the ongoing activity of God. It comes across as the direct, honest statement of personal faith in Christ and how that faith grows. It is one believer sharing with another an insight or struggle about what it means to live faithfully.

Second, good devotional writing uses sensory details—what color it was, how high it bounced, what it smelled like. The more sensory details the writing includes, the better. Though the events of daily life may seem mundane, actually they provide the richest store of sensory details. And when we connect God's activity to common things, each encounter with them can serve as a reminder of God's work.

Finally, good devotional writing is exploratory. It searches and considers and asks questions. It examines the faith without knowing in advance what all the answers will be. It is open to God's continuing self-revelation through scripture, people, and events. Good writing chronicles growth and change, seeing God behind both.

What goes in a meditation?

Personal experiences described in meditations must be true accounts. Each day's meditation includes a title, a suggested Bible reading, a scripture text, a personal witness or reflection on scripture, a prayer, a "thought for the day" (a pithy, summarizing statement), and a suggested subject for a prayer during the day (usually tied to the content of the story). Including all of these elements, the meditation should be about 250 words long. Indicate what version of the Bible is quoted in the text, and give references for any scripture passages mentioned.

Use clear, simple words, and develop one idea. Think about how you can deepen readers' Christian commitment and nurture their spiritual growth. Encourage readers to deeper engagement with the Bible.

Include your name, address, and social security number on each page you submit. Please include a guide for pronouncing your name as our meditations are recorded for an audio edition. If possible, please type your meditation, double-spaced. Always give the original source of any materials you quote. Meditations containing quotes or other secondary material that cannot be verified will not be used.

What should not go in a meditation?

• Fiction.

• Previously published material cannot be used.

• Hymns, poems, and word plays such as acrostics or homonyms make meditations unusable because the material in *The Upper Room* is translated into many languages. Translation cannot do justice to these forms.

• Also, very familiar illustrations ("The Touch of the Master's Hand," stories like George Washington cutting down the cherry tree) have little impact and should not be used. Remember that your personal experience provides unique material—no one is exactly like you.

How do I get started writing a meditation?

When you find yourself in the middle of some situation thinking, "Why—that's how God is, too!" or, "That's like that story in the Bible…," that can become a meditation. Excellent ideas come from reading and meditating on scripture, looking for connections between it and daily life. When you see such a helpful connection, here's a simple formula for getting it on paper:

Retell the Bible teaching or summarize the passage briefly.

Describe the situation that you link to the Bible passage, using a specific incident. Write down as many details of the real-life situation as you can. For example, if you write about an incident when people were talking, write down what each person said.

Tell how you can apply this spiritual truth in days to come.

After a few days, look carefully at what you have written. Decide which details best convey your message, and delete the others. Ask yourself whether this insight will be helpful to believers in other countries and other situations. If you feel that it will, add any elements that are necessary to *The Upper Room*'s format. Then you are ready to submit your meditation for consideration for possible use in *The Upper Room*.

When will I know if my meditation is going to be used?

If your work is being considered for use, we will send you a postcard. If your meditation is chosen for publication, you will receive a copyright card. Please fill it out and return it to us as soon as possible. It may be as much as a year before a final decision is made; seasonal material may be held even longer. If you wish to be notified if your work is eliminated from consideration, include a stamped, self-addressed postcard FOR EACH MEDITATION. We are unable to give updates on the status of individual meditations. All published meditations are edited. We buy the right to translate your meditation for one-time use in our editions around the world, including electronic and software-driven formats. We pay $25.00 for each meditation, on publication.

Meditations cannot be returned, so please keep copies of what you submit. If you wish to know that we have received your work, include a stamped, self-addressed postcard (in addition to the one above). We will use the postcard to notify you that your work has reached us. Meditations submitted through e-mail should be sent individually and should not contain attachments. Always include your complete postal address with each meditation.

Subscriptions

Individual subscriptions of *The Upper Room* are available for $7.95 per year (large print, $8.95). To order, call 1 (800) 925-6847. You can also place your order online.

Categories: Nonfiction—Christian Interests—Inspirational—Religion—Spiritual

CONTACT: Managing Editor
Material: All
PO Box 340004
Nashville TN 37203-0004

Phone: 615-340-7200
E-mail: TheUpperRoomMagazine@upperroom.org
Website: www.upperroom.org

The Urbanite
Surreal & Lively & Bizarre

First of all, my apologies to anyone who has been waiting longer than usual for a reply from *The Urbanite: Surreal & Lively & Bizarre*. For some time now, I have been trying to figure out the next step in the magazine's evolution. I considered many possibilities—Webzine? CD? Some sort of electronic book? I did some research and discussed the various options with different folks.

Eventually talks began with an exciting new publishing firm, and I am happy to state that *The Urbanite: Surreal & Lively & Bizarre* has been reborn as an annual paperback anthology, published by Catalyst Books. I'll still be editing it, so manuscripts should still be sent to the usual Urbanite address. Still snail-mail only—I do most of my manuscript reading in coffee shops.

The Urbanite will be an annual paperback anthology of dark fiction. There will be no themes—except of course, quality. I'll still consider poetry, but probably won't be accepting as much. Payment for fiction: three cents a word. Payment for poetry: $10 per poem.

Categories: Fiction—Poetry

CONTACT: Mark McLaughlin, Editor
Material: All
PO Box 4737
Davenport IA 52808

U.S. Kids

Please refer to Children's Better Health Institute.

US News & World Report

Does not accept freelance submissions.

USA Cycling

Please send summary of your article to Kelly Walker by fax, email, or snail mail with a SASE. Editor will respond within 2 weeks. Articles will run no sooner than two months of acceptance. Feature articles are at least 1,000 words. Payment depends on length and quality and usually ranges from $50-$100.

Categories: Nonfiction—Outdoors—Sports/Recreation

CONTACT: Kelly Walker, Editor
Material: All
TPG Sports, Inc.
One Olympic Plaza
Colorado Springs CO 80909
Phone: 719-866-3360, Ext 3360
Fax: 719-866-4628
E-mail: kwalker@usacycling.org
Website: www.usacycling.org

Remember: Editors change jobs and publishers change addresses. It is wise to invest in a phone call for the current information before submitting.

Vacation Industry Review

Editorial Policy: *Vacation Industry Review* is a quarterly trade magazine published by Interval International, a global vacation-exchange company. The readership of VIR consists of people who develop, finance, market, sell, and manage timeshare resorts and mixed-use projects such as hotels, resorts, and second-home communities with a vacation-ownership component; and suppliers of products and services to the vacation-ownership industry. Interval International operates The Quality Vacation Exchange Network, and resorts featured in VIR should be part of that network.

We assign practically every article in VIR. Most ideas originate with us, although we make some assignments based on detailed queries. We accept practically nothing "over the transom" because few such submissions meet our very specific and specialized needs. VIR is not a consumer travel magazine.

We want articles about the business aspects of the vacation-ownership industry: entrepreneurship, project financing, design and construction, marketing and sales, operations, management—in short, anything that will help our readers plan, build, sell, and run a quality vacation-ownership property that satisfies the owners/guests and earns a profit for the developer, marketer, and management entity. We're also interested in owners associations at vacation-ownership resorts (but not residential condos).

Articles in VIR typically range in length from 800 to 1,500 words. Queries should include a suggested length.

To Break In: By way of introduction, write a letter to tell us about yourself and enclose two or three (non-returnable) samples of published work that show you can meet our specialized needs.

Photo Requirements: We don't pay extra for photos, but we may require them as a condition of purchase. Resort and destination photos must be in color (transparencies 35mm or larger, or prints 5" x 7" or larger). We prefer people photos in color, though black-and-white prints are acceptable. Images must be esthetically effective and must reproduce well in print. We will reject photos that are grainy or poorly focused.

Rights and Payment: Unless otherwise specified, we buy all rights to original material, on a work-for-hire basis. When we accept an article, we will ask you to sign a letter of agreement that confirms your understanding of these terms.

Upon written request, we may allow you to reprint your material without compensation to us, providing that you require any subsequent user to identify this material as having been reproduced from *Vacation Industry Review.*

We pay on acceptance at the rate of 30 cents a word (calculated at a flat rate on assignment).

Categories: Timeshare—Timeshare Resorts

CONTACT: Matthew McDaniel, Editor-in-Chief
Material: All
6262 Sunset Dr.
Miami FL 33143
Website: ResortDeveloper.com

Vampire Tales

Short vampire-related horror fiction
VAMPIRE ANTHOLOGY PUBLICATION GUIDELINES:
Publication date: Published annually. Manuscripts are read year-round.

Book Formats: *Anthology* is a book-zine (eclectic like a magazine but in book form) and will be published in one or more of the following, traditional paper (either hardback or paperback), electronic (ebooks and/or audio). Poetry, short fiction and other writings about vampires.

Lengths: Open for all short fiction, poems, articles Manuscripts of all lengths will be considered. The deadline for submissions: Editor read submissions year-round.

Rights: One-time use in book form (all formats). Considers reprints if author owns rights. Poets and writers should send a bio to accompany their writings in the anthology.

Please note: Writers with books and other publications or venues (i.e. a website) can submit information, website address, etc. for inclusion in the anthology to accompany their bio information. This will give writers added exposure for themselves and their books, websites, etc.

Contributors must send note (email or by regular mail) stating that he/she would like the writing(s) included in the published anthology.

Submit up to 5 manuscripts, either by email or regular mail (see below). Please enclose SASE with regular mail submissions.

Contributors will receive one copy of the finished anthology.
Categories: Fiction—Entertainment—Horror—Short Stories

CONTACT: Eugene Boone
Material: All
RSVP Press
129 Thurman Lane
Clinton TN 37716
E-mail: rsvppress@yahoo.com

Vanity Fair

Formal guidelines not available. Please read a number of issues to ascertain the publication's style and needs.

Send queries to address below.
Categories: Arts—Biography—Culture—Film/Video—Literature—Politics—Society—Theatre

CONTACT: Submissions Editor
Material: All
4 Times Square
New York NY 10036
Phone: 212-286-2860

Veggie Life

GENERAL REQUIREMENTS

• All articles must be credible and authoritatively written. We're not interested in personal opinion (product/company bashing), dogma, or religious beliefs. Provide us with clear, upbeat, concisely written information and you'll have our attention. Writing resume and related published clips are a plus! Please do not send us any articles on why you became vegetarian or any related spin-off on the subject.

• All articles making specific health claims for foods and ingredients must be accompanied by pertinent reference material for our verification. Reference information must include full names, phone numbers, email, and any other necessary information. No article will be considered without sufficient fact-verification information.

• Queries are preferred to completed manuscripts. If possible, send us a couple of clips or copies of previously published work. We do not accept phone queries. Materials will not be returned unless accompanied by a self-addressed envelope with sufficient return postage.

Allow at least 12 weeks for response–no phone calls please. E-mail OK (VeggieEd@egw.com).

• Manuscripts should be submitted in a typed format with proper identification. Include a few sentences about yourself for your author bio. For Macintosh or PC users, you may include a digital copy of the manuscript on a 3½" disk, along with a hard copy of the file. For online writers, e-mail text to VeggieEd@ egw.com.

• Payment rate is per article, at approx. $.35/ed, $35.00/recipe, $25.00/photo (if applicable). Payment is made half upon acceptance of the completed manuscript, and half upon publication. EGW Publishing buys all rights to manuscripts and art on a work-for-hire basis only. One-time unpaid photographic agreements are also made in certain cases.

FEATURES

• Food features include a 200 to 300-word article land 7 to 8 recipes, each with a short introduction. Please observe the *Veggie Life* recipe style and write your recipe in that manner. (See below.)

• We're looking for a wide variety of delicious seasonal vegetarian recipes. Exciting regional, ethnic, special occasion, everyday, and down-home cooking are our favorites, but we're open to your original ideas. Quick and tasty recipes are always welcome. We do not publish food travel articles.

• All recipes accepted for publication will undergo editing, testing, and nutritional analysis. With some exceptions, most recipes in *Veggie Life* should have 30% or fewer calories from fat—ideally no more than 10 grams of fat per serving. Some of our meatless recipes may contain dairy and/or eggs, but vegan options are regularly included.

DEPARTMENTS

• Healing Foods—A 1000-word article followed by 3 to 5 recipes focusing on improving health and preventing disease by eating certain known health-enhancing whole foods (like garlic, nuts, tomatoes, beans, olive oil, etc.).

• Readers' Recipes—Send us your favorite vegetarian recipes. Please include a few words about why the recipe is special to you, along with your name, address, and telephone number. Readers whose recipes are selected for publication will receive a $50 honorarium.

• On the Table—An 1800 to 2500-word comparison article on nutritious plant-based packaged foods. This article needs to provide the reader with a descriptive analysis of the nutritional components of a particular packaged food group. We're looking for nutritional analyses, comparison charts, and solid scientific information written in a lively and dynamic style. For example, past articles have included a descriptive analysis of the nutritional characteristics of different types and brands of flours, alternative sweeteners, tofus, soy yogurts, and veggie meats, giving readers valuable information for making informed buying decisions. Articles must include 4 to 5 recipes using the featured packaged food.

• People Profile—1800-2500 word feature on a pioneering, exuberant individual or group who has made a difference in the world of vegetarian cooking, natural healing, responsible farming, and public awareness. This may include a vegetarian chef, writer, responsible farmer, natural healer, artist, or an inspirational person who has made a difference in the community. The article involves an interview but should not be written in a question and answer format. Celebrity profiles are welcome but not necessarily preferred. Examples of people profiled in *Veggie Life*: Mollie Katzen, Deborah Madison, Sarah McLachlan, Dean Ornish, and Bradley Ogden. Profile articles generally include 2 to 4 recipes.

VEGGIE LIFE RECIPE GUIDE

RECIPE TITLE: The recipe title should be descriptive and creative.

RECIPE INTRO: This is a good place to mention variations, special tips, or food facts. Give one or two descriptive phrases about the recipe's taste, compatibility with other foods, etc.

INGREDIENTS:

• The ingredients should be listed in the order in which the steps refer to them, larger amounts first.

• For clarity, preparation method should follow whole ingredients (i.e., 1 large onion, chopped; 1 16-oz. can kidney beans, drained). They should precede prepared ingredients (i.e., ½ cup chopped onions; 1 cup cooked kidney beans).

• Spell out measurements (i.e., tablespoon or ounce, not Tbs or oz.).

• List ingredients in the easiest unit of measure (i.e., ¼ cup, not 4 tablespoons).

• When possible, use the entire unit (can, package, carrot, or apple) in the recipe.

• Provide can and package sizes–(1 15½ ounce can kidney beans).

• If an ingredient is optional, follow the ingredient with the word (optional) in parentheses.

INSTRUCTIONS:

• Instructions for preheating the oven generally should be the first step.

• Keep the steps simple. Be sure to note the size and type of mixing bowls, cookware, and bakewear used (In a large skillet; a 9x13-inch baking pan).

• Use phrases that create a picture of the procedure or result in the reader's mind (Chill until syrupy; beat until frothy; mixture thickens to the consistency of sour cream).

• Name each ingredient as it is to be combined saying, for example, "Add parsley, thyme, salt, and pepper," rather than just saying, "Add spices."

• Try to foresee questions, problems, or doubts. For example, if you have developed a cake recipe and the batter is unusually thin, say so.

• Give specific and descriptive cooking or baking times. For example, "Bake 20 minutes, or until puffed and golden."

SERVINGS:

List how many cups, cookies, slices, etc. per recipe and/or state how many servings per recipe.

WATCH THOSE FATS:

Our definition of a low-fat recipe is one that derives 30% or less of its total calories from fat or has no more than 10 grams of fat per serving. While we strive to keep fats to a minimum, we are mindful that using the right fat is even more important. When possible, keep to healthy fats like olive and canola oils and avoid saturated fats.

All of our recipes undergo a nutritional analysis and will be tested for this criteria before they are accepted. There are some exceptions, however. Optional ingredients are not included in analyses.

Low-fat cooking tips:

• Cut back on nuts, oils, cheese, and eggs.
• Sauté vegetables in vegetable stock, wine, or water instead of oil.
• Use pan sprays instead of oils or margarines.
• In many recipes, 2 egg whites can be substituted for one whole egg.
• Use non- or low-fat dairy and soy products.

SAMPLE RECIPE:

Pasta Fagioli Soup

Makes 6 servings

"Fagioli" is the Italian word for beans—and there are plenty more good things to be found in this hearty meal-in-a-pot.

1 large onion, chopped
6 cups vegetable stock or water
1 28-ounce can crushed tomatoes
1 15-ounce can cannelloni or navy beans, drained
1 cup diced carrots
1 cup sliced celery
2 cloves garlic, chopped
1 teaspoon each, dried oregano and basil
4 ounces ziti or penne pasta
6 ounces prepared veggie burgers, crumbled
Salt and pepper
Chopped parsley (optional)
Parmesan cheese (optional)

1. In a large pot over medium heat, cook onion in ½ cup vegetable stock or water until softened, about 4 minutes. Add tomatoes, beans, carrots, celery, garlic, oregano, basil, and remaining vegetable stock or water. Bring to a boil, reduce heat to low, and simmer, partially covered, until vegetables are tender, about 15 minutes.

2. Add pasta and cook until almost tender, 7 to 10 minutes. Stir in crumbled burgers. Add salt and pepper to taste. Cook until heated through, about 3 minutes. Sprinkle with chopped parsley and grated Parmesan cheese, if desired.

Categories: Nonfiction—Consumer—Cooking—Diet/Nutrition—Gardening—Health—Physical Fitness—Herbs—Remedies

CONTACT: Shanna Masters, Editor
Material: All
1041 Shary Circle
Concord CA 94518
Phone: 925-671-0692
Fax: 510-671-0692
E-mail: VeggieEd@egw.com

Verses Magazine

Verses Magazine is a quarterly publication dedicated to publishing both new and experienced poets, essayists and short-story writers. *Verses* is designed as a learning, teaching and publishing tool for writers, students and teachers alike.

In each issue of *Verses* we include poetry, prose and short stories from authors all around the world. We will also include information on poetry competitions, awards programs, workshops, seminars, writing groups and other educational programs. We will publish book reviews, articles on copyright, publication, etc. Receive a sample back issue of *Verses* be sending a 9" x 12" self-addressed envelope and $2.00/issue to cover shipping and handling. A one-year (4 issue) subscription is only $21.00.

THE LAUREATES PROGRAM
QUARTERLY LITERARY COMPETITIONS
General Guidelines

The *Verses Magazine* competition, the Laureates Program, is running continuously. There are three (3) categories of competition: Poetry, Short Prose and Short Story. Each issue will feature a "Poet Laureate," "Prose Laureate," and "Short Story Laureate."

• Each quarter, a winner will be picked in each of the categories and awarded one (1) complimentary copy of the issue of *Verses* in which he/she was published.

• In addition, the winners will receive a handsome, personalized "Laureate" award certificate.

• In consideration of publication, each published writer will receive one complimentary copy of *Verses*.

• All published contributors in the magazine can purchase additional copies of the magazine at $3 while supplies last.

Judging

Entries will be judged by the editorial staff appropriate to each genre, based upon content, style, clarity, meter, ability to hold the reader's interest, aesthetic appeal and subject matter. All decisions are final.

Poetry Competition

• There are no line-limits or style limitations for the Laureates Program.

• Selected, non-winning entries will be published in *Verses*.

Prose Competition

• Prose pieces arc limited to 575 words.

• Selected, non-winning prose will be published in *Verses* at the discretion of the editors.

Short Story Competition

• Short stories may range from 600 to 2,500 words.

• Selected, non-winning short stories will be published in *Verses* at the discretion of the editors.

Submission Procedures

• Please send entries with the entry form below. Use a separate entry form for each of the three categories, (i.e., do not send both prose and poetry on the same form).

• Be sure to put your name and address in the upper right-hand corner of each entry. Write the name of the contest below your name and address, (i.e., "Poet Laureate," "Prose Laureate," "Short Story Laureate"). Improperly addressed and/or labeled entries will be disqualified.

• Send only copies of your works, not originals. Entries cannot be returned.

• If you would like confirmation that your entry has been received, either send your submission certified mail, return receipt requested, or enclose a self-addressed, stamped post card, and we'll drop the post card in the mail when we receive your submission(s).

• Submit with the appropriate reading fees if necessary.

Reading Fees & Number of Allowable Submissions

• Lifetime Members of the National Authors Registry may submit an unlimited number of Laureates Program entries in any combination of categories.

• Regular NAR members and Associate Members may submit up to 10 entries per quarter.

• Subscribers to *Verses* may submit up to three (3) entries per quarter.

• Contestants who are neither subscribers nor members must submit a reading fee of $2 per entry with every entry.

• Entries submitted may be in any single category, or any combination of categories.

• The fourth and subsequent entries in a calendar quarter must be accompanied by a $2 reading fee per entry.

ARTICLE/BOOK/REVIEW/FILLER GUIDELINES

There are no reading or submission fees for articles, book reviews or fillers. We pay on publication at the rate of 2 cents per word for articles and book reviews. Other fillers, quotes and comics may be published at the editors' discretion. All published authors will receive as consideration, a complimentary copy of the issue of *Verses* containing his/her work. We do not pay kill fees.

Submission Guidelines

• Send copies and not originals. Your submissions cannot be returned.

• Send your submissions certified, return receipt requested, or, include two self-addressed, stamped post cards with your submission. We will drop the first post card in the mail upon receipt to confirm that we have, in fact, received your submission. We will return the second post card when your work has been accepted or rejected. Please do not call to inquire whether or not we have received your submissions. Please allow three to six months for notification of acceptance/rejection.

• Be sure to put your name and address in the upper left-hand corner of page 1 of each article/review. Write "Article," "Book Review," or "Filler" below your name and address. Improperly addressed and/or labeled submissions cannot be considered for publication.

This form may he reproduced.

VERSES LAUREATES ENTRY FORM

Please enter the attached poems/essays/stories in the Laureates Program. I grant Cader Publishing, Ltd permission to print all listed/attached entries in *Verses*. If my entry(ies) are selected for publication, I will receive one (1) complimentary copy of Verses.

Name
*Age
Address
City
State, Zip

*If you are under age 21 and your work appears in the "Youthful Voices" section, your age will be published.

[ ] Yes, include my name and full address in Verses if I am published. Check category of work submitted. One entry form required per category.

[ ] POETRY [ ] PROSE [ ] SHORT STORY

Check one of the following:

[ ] I am a subscriber to *Verses* [limit 3 entries]
[ ] I am an Assoc. NAR member [limit 10 entries]
[ ] I am a regular NAR member [limit 10 entries]

[ ] I am not a subscriber or member. I have enclosed $2.00 per entry as a reading fee.

I have read, understood and agreed to the guidelines for regular submission to *Verses*.

Contestant's Signature

Parent or guardian must sign if author is under 18 years of age.

All entries must be accompanied with this form. The Verses Laureates Entry Form may be reproduced. Failure to submit entries with this form properly filled out will result in disqualification of entries.

Categories: Fiction—Literature—Poetry—Writing

CONTACT: Sharon Derderian, Executive Editor
Material: Poetry, Prose, Short Stories, Articles
36923 Ryan Rd.
Sterling Hts. MI 48310
Phone: 810-795-3635
Fax: 810-795-9875

VFW Magazine

VFW Magazine is published by the Veterans of Foreign Wars at national headquarters in Kansas City, Mo. VFW is the nation's 29th largest magazine in circulation. It is published monthly (the June and July issues are combined), and has a readership of some two million.

Subscription is largely through VFW membership, which is restricted to honorably discharged veterans who received an officially recognized campaign medal. Founded in 1899, the VFW is the oldest major veterans organization in America.

TOPICS

Recognition of veterans and military service is paramount at the VFW. Articles related to current foreign policy and defense along with all veterans issues are of prime interest. Topics pertaining to American armed forces abroad and international events affecting U.S. national security are particularly in demand.

Some national political and social issues also qualify for inclusion in the magazine, especially if covered by VFW resolutions. New resolutions are passed each August at the VFW national convention and priority goals are subsequently established, based on these formal issue positions.

And, of course, we are always looking for up-to-date stories on veterans' concerns. Insight into how recent legislation affects the average veteran is always welcome. Anything that contributes to a better understanding of how the Department of Veterans Affairs operates is useful to fellow veterans. Positive, upbeat stories on successful veterans who have made significant contributions to their communities make for good reading, too.

Also, interviews with prominent figures are of interest if professionally done. No first-person accounts or personality profiles accepted.

We do not accept poetry , fiction, reprints or book reviews.

MANUSCRIPTS

Manuscripts should be no longer than five double-spaced typewritten pages (or about 1,000 words), depending on the subject. Simultaneous submissions and reprints are not considered. Changes are often required to make copy conform to editorial requirements. Absolute accuracy is a must. If little-known facts or statistics and quotes are used, please cite a reference.

Quotes from relevant individuals are a must. Bibliographies are useful if the subject required extensive research and/or is open to dispute. Submit manuscripts on 3½" diskette, and please include a hard copy. E-mail submissions are acceptable.

STYLE

Clarity and simplicity are the two cardinal virtues of good writing. Originality, concrete detail, short paragraphs and strong words are essential. Write in the active voice, and avoid flowery prose and military jargon. Please feel free to suggest descriptive decks (sub-titles) and use sub-heads in the body of the copy. Consult *The Associated Press Stylebook* for correct grammar and punctuation.

PHOTOGRAPHS

Photos of exceptional interest are considered for publication. Payment is arranged in advance. Captions must accompany photos, including a separate caption sheet. Pictures accompanying manuscripts are generally for one-time use only. Please send along all relevant sketches, maps, charts and photos. Sources of additional artwork are also most helpful. Color transparencies (35mm slides or 2¼"x2¼") are preferred. But we can always use color as well as black and white prints (5" x 7" or 8" x 10").

PAYMENT

Payment generally ranges up to $500 per article, depending on length and writing quality. Commissioned articles are negotiable. Payment is made upon acceptance, and entitles *VFW Magazine* to first North American serial rights. Kill fees are paid if the writer is working on assignment and the article is not published.

QUERIES

Do not query over the telephone. A one-page outline (theme, scope, organization) of the proposed article will save the author and editor valuable time and effort in determining the suitability of a piece for *VFW Magazine*. Articles are submitted on a speculative basis for first-time contributors unless commissioned. Topics that coincide with an anniversary should be submitted at least four months in advance.

Use the query letter to demonstrate your knowledge and writing ability. Send along published examples of your work. Familiarize yourself with *VFW Magazine* before writing full-length features.

BIOGRAPHIES

Finally, please enclose a brief biography describing your military service and expertise in the field in which you are writing. Three sentences is generally sufficient. If you are a VFW member, let us know.

VFW Magazine looks forward to receiving submissions from members and freelancers alike.

Categories: Nonfiction—Associations—History—Military—Public Policy

CONTACT: Richard K. Kolb, Editor-in-Chief
Material: Any
CONTACT: Tim Dyhouse, Senior Editor
Material: Any
CONTACT: Robert Widener, Art Director
Material: Any
406 W. 34th St. Ste. 523
Kansas City MO 64111
Phone: 816-756-3390
Fax: 816-968-1169
E-mail: jcarter@vfw.org

Via

Via (formerly *Motorland*) is the magazine of the California State Automobile Association (AAA). It is published bimonthly and goes to almost 2.5 million members in northern and central California, Nevada, and Utah. It is primarily a service magazine, with articles on travel, events, leisure activities, and matters of interest to the motoring public—car care, insurance issues, consumer information, legislation, and transportation.

Although most of our content is staff-written, we do buy a few freelance articles each year, almost all of them on travel. The purpose of our travel stories is two-fold: first, to encourage members to use the free-with-membership services of the CSAA, such as maps, trip-planning, reservations for hotels, tours, car rental, air and train travel. Second, we also consider the magazine a service in itself, and giving our readers ideas about places to go is part of that service. Our emphasis is on close-to-home travel in our territory and nearby western states, although we do occasional stories on foreign travel.

Competition is very keen; we receive between 1,200 and 1,500 freelance queries and manuscripts each year, and can buy only 12 to 20 of these (in other words, a little over one percent of stories submitted). Because our small staff is perpetually occupied with writing and editing, it may take us a very long time to respond to queries. In fact, most of our freelance stories are purchased from, or assigned to, writers already known to us for excellent, accurate, and dependable work.

If you are still interested, here are some guidelines: We are always looking for excellent writing. We like our stories to be personal, original, and literary, not the usual dry guidebook recounting of where-and-what. We want to sense the magic and wonder—or even squalor—of a place, to know what it means to go there, to know how the visitor might be changed by the journey. We urge you to read our magazine to get a sense of what we're looking for. We also need the service details which will help our readers go, too.

At this time, we are not giving firm assignments for features to writers new to us—even if they have an impressive portfolio of clippings. We prefer to see a finished manuscript. You may, of course, query to see whether we'd consider a story on a certain subject.

Our articles are short—between 250 words for our travel columns and 1,500 words for a feature. We pay from $150 to $700, depending on the research required, length and quality of the writing. We illustrate our articles with freelance photography, and you're welcome to submit your finest color transparencies with your story. We pay separately for any photography published.

We are unhappy with writers who get their facts wrong. Because of our small staff, we don't have the facilities for extensive fact-checking. We are also unhappy with writers who do not send SASE's with their queries and manuscripts. Also, we do not buy stories from writers who do any kind of public relations work with travel, automotive, or other suppliers which might be covered in the magazine.

Thank you for your interest in *Via*.

Bruce Anderson, Editor

Categories: Nonfiction—Automobiles—Consumer—Travel

CONTACT: Bruce Anderson, Editor
Material: All
150 Van Ness Ave.
San Francisco CA 94102-5292
Phone: 415-565-2451
Fax: 415-863-4726

Vibe

Formal guidelines not available. Please read a number of issues to ascertain the publication's style and needs.

Send queries to address below.

Categories: African-American—Arts—Culture—Entertainment—Fashion—Lifestyle—Multicultural—Music—Politics—Society

CONTACT: Writer's Submissions
Material: All
215 Lexington Ave., 6th Floor
New York NY 10016
Website: www.vibe.com

Vietnam

Please refer to PRIMEDIA History Group.

Virginia Quarterly Review

1. For results only, include a #10 SASE. You will not be notified otherwise.

2. No simultaneous submissions are accepted.

3. Submissions per envelope are limited to two stories or five poems.

4. Articles, essays, memoirs, and short stories are usually reviewed within three weeks, but, due to the large number of poems we receive, results for these may be delayed three months or longer.

The Emily Clark Balch awards for fiction and poetry are made annually for the best short story and best poem published in the *Virginia Quarterly Review* during the calendar year. There are no specific guidelines except that submissions be of reasonable length (fiction: 2,000-7,000 words; no length restrictions on poetry).

Categories: Fiction—Nonfiction—Literature—Poetry—Politics

CONTACT: Submissions Editor
Material: All
One W. Range
Charlottesville VA 22903
Phone: 434-924-3124
Fax: 434-924-1397

Visions-International Arts

How to Send & Submit Poems to Magazines

As an editor and active poet I've learned a lot about the mistakes you can make in submitting poems. It's important to know the simple courtesies that make an editor not feel like trashing your work or returning it unread. It pays to check what the requirements are. One source for this information is the *International Directory of Little Magazines and Small Presses*. Among the things it will tell you are: 1. If they accept unsolicited mss. 2. Are copies acceptable. 3. Are there certain times when they don't read mss. 4. What are the length and number limits. 5. Usually it will also tell the kind of work they're looking for, how long the response time is, and if there's any payment (some don't even give copies, a questionable policy in this editor's opinion).

Most editors appreciate a brief vita (half a page or less) and don't want to see another submission from a rejected author within a year (unless asked).

Before selecting poems try to review a sample of the magazine to see what they like (a sample of *VISIONS-International* is only $4.95). Here are some of our own policies:

1. We like to see 3-6 poems (rarely more than three double-spaced pages each).

2. We don't accept old fashioned, sentimental stuff. On the other hand we don't like the obscure, ultra-modern, often emotionless pap published by some well known academic type journals. (We don't mind rhyme but it's hard to do well.)

3. We like to see vita but don't let it influence our judgement and a "big name" means nothing to us.

4. If you don't want us to make editorial comments on your poems tell us ahead of time. If we do it's a compliment (means it was worth the bother).

Also don't forget that if you're going to get published the magazines have to survive (believe it or not most editors are poor and their magazines don't make money), so subscribe to at least a couple (*VISIONS-International* is only $12.00 per year for 2 issues).

Good luck, B.R. Strahan
Categories: Poetry

CONTACT: Bradley R. Strahan, Editor
Material: Poetry
CONTACT: Jerry Minor, Editor
Material: Art
1007 Ficklen Rd.
Fredericksburg VA 22405

Vogue

Thank you for inquiring about *Vogue*'s writers' guidelines.

Articles for *Vogue* are written in an upbeat, engaging manner to appeal to a broad-based, well-educated audience. Ranging in length from 500 to 2,500 words, stories are informative and thoroughly researched. Payment depends on source, length and use.

Writers are welcome to direct article ideas and writing samples for consideration to the appropriate editor listed on the masthead.

We appreciate your interest in *Vogue* and hope that this brief outline of *Vogue*'s editorial standards is helpful.

The Editors
Categories: Culture—Fashion

CONTACT: Laurie Jones, Managing Editor
Material: All
4 Times Square, 12th Floor
New York NY 10036
Phone: 212-886-6910
Fax: 212-880-8169
E-mail: talkingback@vogue.com
E-mail: stylefeedbac@CONDENT.com
Website: condenet.com

Volleyball Magazine

Formal guidelines not available. Please read a number of issues to ascertain the publication's style and needs.

Send queries to address below.

Categories: Nonfiction—Health—Physical Fitness—Recreation—Sports

CONTACT: Dennis Steers, Editor
Material: All
774 Marsh St., Ste. C
San Luis Obispo CA 93401
Phone: 805-541-2438
E-mail: letters@volleyballmag.com
Website: www.volleyballmag.com

VOYAGEUR

Voyageur
Northeast Wisconsin's Historical Review

Voyageur: Northeast Wisconsin's Historical Review is a nonprofit magazine about the history and prehistory of a twenty-six-county region of greater Northeast Wisconsin. Its coverage area extends from the Sheboygan and Fond du Lac areas northward to the Michigan border and westward from Lake Michigan to the Wausau and Stevens Point areas.

Voyageur is cosponsored by the Brown County Historical Society, University of Wisconsin-Green Bay, and St. Norbert College in De Pere. Submissions may focus on social, economic, political, technological, in-

stitutional, religious, environmental, educational, legal, archeological, architectural, transportation, health, sports, recreational, or other historical issues and themes.

Manuscripts are blind-reviewed by *Voyageur*'s Editorial Committee and will be returned upon request. Authors will be notified within three months of submission whether a manuscript has been accepted for publication. *Voyageur* does not accept creative nonfiction or fictional accounts of people, places or events based on the historical record.

Submissions

1. Format & Length. *Voyageur* is produced on Macintosh computers using Microsoft Word 5.1. Authors are encouraged to submit their works on a DOS-based or Macintosh disk and specify the word-processing program used. Authors should also submit at least one typed or computer-processed, double-spaced copy of their manuscripts.

Manuscripts should be no longer than 5,000 words, not including notes and tables. Only with the author's approval, longer manuscripts may be edited down or split into parts as a multi-part series. Please indicate word count on your manuscript. Original manuscripts are preferred, although exceptions on occasion are made to publish previously published works in Voyageur if appropriate permission is given.

2. Style. Use *The Chicago Manual of Style* (14th edition) guidelines for all manuscripts. Do not use in-text references, i.e., (Weston, 1972). In ordinary text, whole numbers from one through ninety-nine are spelled out. However, when normally spelled numbers cluster in a sentence or paragraph, use figures. Use % instead of percent in reference to statistics; for rounded percentages write the words. Underline or italicize names of cities when using newspaper names, i.e., New York Times.

3. Sources. *Voyageur* strongly urges endnotes and/or a bibliography or sources consulted list to help readers evaluate information presented in a manuscript. See the *The Chicago Manual of Style*.

4. Photographs and Other Images. Voyageur also urges authors to submit images or photocopies of images that could be used with their texts. Images may include photographs, drawings, maps, artwork, and reproductions of documents.

5. Tables. Do not duplicate material in text and tables. Tables and figures are helpful when they aid the reader in clarifying complicated or voluminous information or data.

6. Headings. The use of headings is encouraged to organize information and to break up long blocks of text. First-level headings should be typed in bold and centered. Second-level headings, if used, should be flush left and typed in bold italic. Third-level headings, if used, should be flush left and typed in italic.

7. Abstract. Please include an abstract of no more than 150 words.

8. Deadlines. Deadlines for manuscripts submitted to Voyageur are June 1 and November 1 of each year.

9. Copyright. The contents of *Voyageur* are protected by copyright in the name of the Brown County Historical Society. Permission is freely granted by Voyageur and the Society for authors to have their submissions published elsewhere if proper credit is given to *Voyageur*.

10. Remuneration. It is not possible at this time for the nonprofit Voyageur to pay authors or other contributors for publishing their work. However, *Voyageur* does pay image reproduction fees.

If your manuscript is accepted, please submit the final copy on a 3½-inch disk in WordPerfect or Microsoft Word for IBM Compatible or in Microsoft Word 5.1 for Macintosh. Please submit images to accompany the story and include appropriate captions on a separate piece of paper.

Also indicate the source of your images on the same sheet. Finally, please write a 100-word biography and include a photograph of yourself (head shot).

Thank you for your time and effort and for considering *Voyageur*.

Book & Video Reviews. Anyone who wishes to review books or videos for *Voyageur* or to propose a book or video review should contact *Voyageur* at the address below hereafter.

Categories: Nonfiction—History—Regional

CONTACT: Victoria Goff, Editor
Material: All

PO Box 8085
Green Bay WI 54308-8085
Phone: 920-465-2446
Fax: 920-465-2890
E-mail: voyageur@uwgb.edu
Website: www.uwgb.edu/voyageur

Wall Fashions

Formal guidelines not available. Please read a number of issues to ascertain the publication's style and needs.

Send queries to address below.

Categories: Fashion—Reference—Trade—Wall Products

CONTACT: Kate Lundquist, Managing Editor
Material: All
G & W McNamara Publishing
4215 White Bear Parkway, Ste. 100
St. Paul MN 55110-7635
Phone: 651-293-1544

Washington Monthly

Writers' Guidelines

The *Washington Monthly* is a DC-based publication covering politics, government, culture and the media. Before you pitch a story to us, we recommend you read through a few of our back issues online or in print to get a feel for the type of investigative, system-analysis journalism we value and promote.

The magazine is published 10 times a year and includes investigative and opinion-based feature articles (2,000 to 5,000 words), occasional short news items and humorous sidebars (500 to 1,000 words), and book reviews of recent political and cultural titles (usually about 800 words). We occasionally print excerpts from forthcoming political books. We never publish fiction, poetry, or celebrity profiles.

Our editors welcome story pitches that suit our editorial mix. We ask freelancers to submit query letters or articles in writing by either emailing us at: editors@washingtonmonthly.com or mailing submissions to 733 15th Street, NW, Suite 520, Washington, DC 20005.

All freelance pieces are submitted "on spec"; we don't pay kill fees. The pay rate for published articles is 10 cents per word.

Complimentary copies of the magazine in which their articles appears are mailed to freelancers. Published articles are also available online.

Thank you for your interest in *The Washington Monthly*.

Categories: Nonfiction—Culture—Government—Politics—Media

CONTACT: Submissions Editor
Material: All
733 15th Street, NW, Ste 520
Washington DC 20005
Phone: 202-393-5155
Fax: 202-393-2444
E-mail: editors@washingtonmonthly.com
Website: www.washingtonmonthly.com

Watercolor

Please refer to *American Artist* magazine.

Watercolor Magic

If you'd like to see your work featured in a national magazine specializing in watermedia, here are a few secrets from the editors of *Watercolor Magic*:

CHOOSE THE TYPE OF ARTICLE

Watercolor Magic is open to submissions for feature articles, columns and short essays. Features, which typically amount to four to six pages, should focus on teaching a watermedia technique (many artists showcase a signature technique), and most often will include a step-by-step demonstration. We also are looking for artists to contribute to several columns, including "The Working Artist" (a column that focuses on the business and marketing side of making art), "Swipe File" (a forum for homemade solutions and tips), and "Picture This" (a short essay on the artist's take on a phrase or technique associated with watercolor that is also illustrated).

SEND A QUERY LETTER

Submitting your work for an article in *Watercolor Magic* is much like entering a juried show, but with a few extra steps. The first thing you should do is send a query letter to the editorial staff. This letter should explain what you are interested in writing about and why it would appeal to *Watercolor Magic*'s readers. Your query letter also should explain your background in watermedia, including any awards or instructional experience you have. Most importantly, include at least eight samples of your work by photographing them on slides or larger transparencies.

WAIT FOR A RESPONSE

If the editorial staff is interested in publishing your work, you will receive an assignment letter that outlines how your article should be structured. While taking your ideas and information into account, the editor will suggest a theme, introduction, body and conclusion for your article, as well as work out the details such as your deadline, payment and the issue your work is scheduled to appear. (Please note this may change due to space limitations.) Once you have your assignment, keep in mind that you should stay focused on the technique you are teaching. We'll supply more details on how to put your article together at this point.

SUPPLY FIRST-RATE PHOTOGRAPHY

Photography is a very important element in your article. Please remember that your color slide or transparency will be magnified in size, so any flaws in color or lighting from the photography will also increase. You may want to put your slides in a projector to see how they will look. You also can get photo tips from "Photographing Your Paintings," a reprint from *The Artist's Magazine*. (To order with your Visa or Master Card, call 513-531-2690, ext. 1328, or you can write to Photographing Your Paintings, F&W Publications Inc., Attn: Terri Boes, 4700 E. Galbraith Rd., Cincinnati, OH 45236.) Remember, the better the photography, the better your work will reproduce.

Once your article and photography has been sent to us, an editor will make it fit the magazine's style and "clean it up." After it is edited, you will be sent an author's galley, which is a copy of the article that you can review before publication. You will also receive your payment (negotiated individually) around the same time. Then your article will be ready for the magazine.

You can expect a reply within four to six weeks. Good luck!

Categories: Arts—Painting—Watermedia

CONTACT: Submissions Editor
Material: All
4700 E. Galbraith Rd.
Cincinnati OH 45236
Phone: 513-531-2690
Fax: 513-531-2902
E-mail: wcmedit@fwpubs.com
Website: www.watercolormagic.com

Weatherwise Magazine
The Magazine about the Weather

Guidelines for writers and photographers

Weather is one of the common denominators of our lives. It helps shape our culture, character, conduct, and health. It frequents the pages of our history and can change its course. It colors our conversations, folklore, and literature; it rains on our parades, awes us with its power and beauty, frightens us, and sometimes kills us. *Weatherwise* magazine shares this force of nature with engaging features and breathtaking photography. *Weatherwise* articles are anecdotal, analytical, and illuminating. They take a creative look at everyday occurrences and are accurate, authoritative, and easily understood by a large, non-technical audience that includes teachers, students, and farmers.

Generally

Please initiate your interest in writing for *Weatherwise* by sending a query letter and SASE (or e-mail) to Lynn Elsey, Managing Editor, Weatherwise, 1319 18th St. NW, Washington, DC 20036-1802.

Your letter should outline the direction of the article, give an indication of your writing style and perspective, tell us why or how you're qualified to write the article, list potential sources and illustration possibilities, and include clips of your published work. (If you have not been published, please send a sample of your writing suitable for magazine-style work.) We will consider research topics, but do not publish academic papers. Authors are expected to write (or rewrite) in a conversational, magazine style suitable for a popular audience. Look for the story within the story, and emphasize the human element. Tell us about the triumphs, failures, and other anecdotes of the people you meet while researching your article.

Be aware of the *Weatherwise* production schedule and submit your story ideas and photos accordingly. We begin planning an issue at least six months before the cover date (i.e. September/October in March). In other words, think hurricanes in January and blizzards in July. We try to respond to queries within two months.

Unsolicited manuscripts are discouraged, and may be held indefinitely without response. Please remember that queries and manuscripts under consideration at *Weatherwise* should not be submitted to other publications concurrently.

Payments to established authors are at the discretion of the managing editor and are made upon publication.

Manuscripts

Feature articles are relatively short (900 to 2,000 words) and well-illustrated. Departments—including software, video, and book reviews; and essays on topics ranging from folklore to personal experiences—should be between 600 and 1,000 words. Short news fillers (200 to 500 words) about noteworthy people, events, or trends will also be considered. Where appropriate, include a list of sources, both published materials and personal interviews.

Include your name and phone number on everything you submit. Also, include other ways we can contact you—preferable an e-mail address—and a SASE large enough for the return of your materials if necessary. Once an article is accepted, it must be submitted in an electronic format, as a word file. On the first page, include a word count. Our preferred format is Microsoft Word 5.1 for Macintosh.

Illustrations

Published articles are often chosen as much for the quality and impact of the photographs as for editorial excellence. Authors must at least provide sources, leads, or ideas on illustrating an article. We will gladly research photo leads or commission artwork for an author whose article is worthy of publication. On the other hand, photos are rarely accepted without supporting text, even if that's just a short but enlightening discussion of the circumstances under which the photos were taken. We maintain a file of stock weather photos and prefer photos of recent events or unique treatments of familiar sights. Great photos that stand alone may be considered for our annual Photo Contest with permission and a signed entry form from the photographer.

We do not publish cartoons.

Photographs may be submitted as prints, slides, or electronic files. Color is preferred. Please provide captions on a separate sheet of paper. Do not write on the backs of photos. Other illustrations (i.e. maps, graphs, charts, tables, etc.) should be submitted as finished, camera-ready art or on disk with hard-copy back-up that need not be camera-ready. Many software formats are acceptable.

Categories: Environment—Hobbies—Science—Meteorology

CONTACT: Lynn Elsey, Managing Editor
Material: All
1319 - 18th St. NW
Washington DC 20036-1802
Phone: 202-296-6267
Website: www.weatherwise.org

Weavings

General Guidelines

Weavings seeks to promote informed, committed spiritual growth with attention to the corporate dimension of the spiritual life. Such growth, to which laity and clergy alike are called, embraces all those expressions of discipline and discipleship that mark the Christian's response to God's work of weaving together the torn fabric of life.

Weavings invites participation in the spiritual life, seeking to provide a forum in which our life in the world and the spiritual resources of the Christian heritage can encounter and illuminate one another. The journal strives to create a space in which contributors and readers can converse on important matters of common concern. Published bi-monthly and organized by themes, each issue presents a broad range of materials dealing with:

• significant topics in Christian spirituality visible in personal, congregational, and public life;
• practicing spiritual disciplines;
• the role of non-discursive communication in spiritual formation (e.g. art, music, architecture, dance);
• linking individual and corporate renewal in the church;
• relating personal and social transformation;
• integrating contemporary experience and classical wisdom.
• These and similar themes may be explored through articles, stories (fiction and non-fiction), meditations on scripture, sermons, or poetry.

Readership

The journal is for clergy, lay leaders, and all thoughtful seekers who want to deepen their understanding of, and response to, how God's life and human lives are being woven together in the world. The journal seeks to move beyond the dichotomy between pulpit and pew by probing the depths of the spiritual life in ordinary language common to both clergy and laity.

Format and Length

Articles should be 1250 to 2500 words in length. Our main interest is in writing that perceptively examines the spiritual issues that arise when Christian faith and present-day cultures meet. Articles should help readers see that the spiritual life leads to the very heart of the world, and that there is no issue in the personal, congregational, or political sphere that is without spiritual significance.

Sermons and meditations on scripture may vary in length from 500 to 2500 words. At the center of the Christian spiritual life is the practice of listening attentively to God's word in scripture. Contributions should exemplify the rich variety of insights and incentives to action that flourish when we begin to see the connections between the biblical story of God's redemptive love and our own life story. These guidelines also apply to spiritual autobiographies and biographies.

Stories (fiction or non-fiction) in the form of short vignettes or longer narratives (up to 2500 words) should strive to depict the movements of God's Spirit in the very midst of ordinary human life. Humor is welcome, as are poems and profiles of "ordinary saints."

Book reviews should be approximately 750 words.

Style

Contributions may take several forms. Hard copy should be typed, double-spaced, on 8.5" x 11" paper and should be accompanied by a self-addressed stamped envelope (SASE). Electronic files should be compatible with Microsoft Word 6.0 or higher or Word for Mac 6.1.0. Please include proper documentation for all direct quotations or other references to published works. Copyright law allows for quoting up to two lines of poetry. If more than two lines are quoted, we ask that an author secure permission to do so. When citing passages from the Bible, kindly indicate which translation is being used. Writers should include their Social Security number.

Weavings is neither a popular devotional guide nor a technical scholarly journal. We are looking for material that has spiritual depth expressed in simple, even poetic, prose. We hope authors will show our readers the subject rather than simply describe or explain it. That is to say, we encourage authors to offer readers an experience of the subject itself. For example, we would hope that an article on prayer would be prayerful in style, and that readers would be likely to experience reading this article as a prayerful event. Reading the article might even lead a reader into a time of prayer. We seek material for *Weavings* that is meditative in tone, drawing on the rich metaphors of scripture and everyday life to help readers see and respond to God at work in their lives and in the world.

Weavings readers may be assumed to share a real interest in the spiritual life, while differing significantly in their knowledge and experience of Christian tradition. Therefore, writing should be simple, authentic, and inclusive.

Simplicity in the structure and language of contributions places the spiritual life where it belongs—at the center of life as such. Simplicity shows that spirituality is not only for the select few.

Authenticity accents the integrity of the spiritual life. Authentic writing expresses what the writers themselves have sought, experienced, and struggled with in their own lives. The best guidance for authentic spiritual writing is still to be found in the First Letter of John: "It was there from the beginning; we have heard it; we have seen it with our own eyes; we looked upon it, and felt it with our own hands; and it is of this we tell. Our theme is the word of life" (1:1, NEB).

Inclusiveness means, among other things, sensitivity to gender-specific language, openness to the many traditions of historic Christianity, and attention to the manifold wisdom of various cultures and ethnic groups. Such inclusiveness affirms that the spiritual life is not merely a special province of life, but the whole of life lived under the authority of the One whose claim upon humanity is universal in scope.

Payment

We buy first periodical rights for a variety of media, including print, electronic, software-driven, and other media formats. We accept previously published material.

Payment is made when the final content of an issue is determined.

Articles, stories, sermons, book reviews, and reports: 11 cents a word and up.

Poetry: $75 and up.

We will notify contributors of manuscript status within three months of receipt. Unusable material will be returned if an SASE was sent with the manuscript.

Additional copies of our writer's guidelines and a list of themes for future issues will be sent free upon receipt of SASE. If you would like a sample copy of *Weavings*, please send SASE of at least 7.5" x 10.5" with postage (approximate weight is 5 oz.).

Categories: Fiction—Nonfiction—Arts—Christian Interests—Poetry—Religion—Spiritual

CONTACT: Editor
Material: All

1908 Grand Ave., PO Box 340004
Nashville TN 37203-0004
E-mail: weavings@upperroom.org
Website: www.upperroom.org/weavings

Weight Watchers Magazine

Weight Watchers Magazine has no formal guidelines.

Weight Watchers Magazine is the proven authority on motivating self-improvement, self-image, nutrition, fitness and healthy, active living with an emphasis on weight loss and weight maintenance. Our readers are affluent, sophisticated, well educated, professional, and interested in living healthy lives.

Send submissions/queries with a SASE. Be sure to include a your resume and clips.

Categories: Nonfiction—Diet/Nutrition—Fashion—Health—Inspirational—Physical Fitness—Self Help

CONTACT: Editor
Material: All
747 Third Ave
New York NY 10017
Phone: 212-207-8800
Website: www.weightwatchers.com

Weird Tales

Some of what follows may be terribly basic to you — but will be new to someone else. And some of what you already know (especially in matters of format) may be wrong, and you may have been irritating various editors for years by — for example — using italics in on-paper manuscripts instead of underlining or even *gasp* leaving your snail-mail address off the first page of manuscripts. So:

There are only three **Rules** for writing; all else is commentary.

Rule One: You must seize, then hold, your readers' and your editor's interest and attention, then repay the readers' time and the editor's money by having something to say.

...and the Awful Truth of the matter is (as Rear Admiral Pinney once put it) "If you don't get the reader's attention in the first paragraph, the rest of your message is lost." This applies even more to fiction than to U.S. Navy correspondence; you must capture the reader's attention on the first page (or better, in the first few words).

These **Rules** apply both to poetry (discussed throughout these Guidelines) and to prose.

Rudyard Kipling wrote: "There are nine and sixty ways/ of constructing tribal lays,/ and every single one of them is right!"

What follows is commentary, not rules. These suggestions may help, but what's important is the result — your selling an *interesting* story to our magazine.

The archetypical plot consists of a *Situation* (the protagonist meets a problem), *Complication* (the problem makes the protagonist do something about it in a series of actions/reactions of rising intensity), *Climax* (the protagonist must solve the problem or be broken by it), *Resolution* (the problem unwinds, the protagonist succeeds or fails), and an *Anticlimax* (left-overs are carted off or explained away). Many (but not all) stories follow this pattern.

One of those nine and sixty ways to construct your story is based on suggestions from the science-fiction writer and teacher, James Gunn:

• Begin with an idea: What would happen if…? And then work out its logical, believable consequences.

• Create a background, colorful enough to hold interest; but don't overwhelm the story. Remember background is *back*-ground; write a story, not a gazetteer nor a history text.

• Select characters who will best dramatize the conflict you've plotted. Observe real people, and model your cast on them. show them in action from the start; show their characters by what they say and do. Write a story, not a set of résumés.

• Pick the best viewpoint for telling this story (almost always the most important decision made when writing fiction). Put the reader so firmly into that viewpoint that as he reads, he *is* that character. Do not pull the reader out of a viewpoint character to describe what he looks like or to present his biography. Get on with the story. If your protagonist's appearance is important to him, he'll think about it or act on it soon enough, showing the reader that facet of character without telling the reader about it; if it's not that important, get on with the story.

• Begin your story where and when things become interesting. Homer began the Iliad right in the middle of a war ("Sing, Godless, of the anger of Achilles…") and Homer sings to us still! Backtrack to explanation or flashback only when it's so relevant to the story that the viewpoint character and the reader, still *being* that character, remember what happened before this story began. You'll be surprised how few flashbacks you really need!

• Write in scenes, dramatizing everything possible. In every scene, put your characters — and readers — firmly into the time and place of that scene. Appeal to the senses — go beyond how things look, go on to the sound and smell and *feel* of the setting. But don't overdo it; omit everything that doesn't advance the story.

• Don't lecture; exposition is all dead matter. Avoid clichés like the plague! Learning to avoid triteness in word and phrase and in ideas, plots, characters, and backgrounds is easily half of becoming a good writer.

Mark Twain wrote, in his famous essay, "Fenimore Cooper's Literary Offenses," that:

1. A tale shall accomplish something and arrive somewhere.

2. The episodes of a tale shall be necessary part of the tale, and shall help to develop it.

3. The personages in a tale shall be alive, except in the case of corpses, and always the reader shall be able to tell the corpses from the others.

4. The personages in a tale, both dead and alive, shall exhibit a sufficient excuse for being there.

5. When the personages of a tale deal in conversation, the talk shall sound like human talk, and be talk such as human beings would be likely to talk in the given circumstances, and have a discoverable meaning, also a discoverable purpose, and a show of relevancy, and remain in the neighborhood of the subject in hand, and be interesting to the reader, and help out the tale, and stop when the people cannot think of anything more to say.

6. When the author describes the character of a personage in his tale, the conduct and conversation of that personage shall justify said description.

7. When a personage talks like an illustrated, gilt-edged, tree-calf, hand-tooled, seven-dollar Friendship's Offering in the beginning of a paragraph, he shall not talk like a Negro minstrel in the end of it.

8. Crass stupidities shall not be played upon the reader by either the author or the people in the tale.

9. The personages of a tale shall confine themselves to possibilities and let miracles alone; or, if they venture a miracle, the author must so plausibly set it forth as to make it look possible and reasonable.

10. The author shall make the reader feel a deep interest in the personages of his tale and in their fate; and shall make the reader love the good people in the tale and hate the bad ones.

11. The characters in a tale shall be so clearly defined that the reader can tell beforehand what each will do in a given emergency.

12. The author shall *say* what he proposing to say, not merely come near it.

13. He shall use the right word, not its second cousin.

14. He shall eschew surplusage.

15. He shall not omit necessary details.

16. He shall avoid slovenliness of form.

17. He shall use good grammar.

18. He shall employ a simple, straightforward style.

Elsewhere, he wrote: "The difference between the right word and the almost-right word is the difference between the lightning and the lightning bug." Also: "Truth *is* stranger than fiction, because fiction is obliged to stick to possibilities. Truth isn't."

But these just are commentary, not **Rules**.

Rule Two: You must put your story into a format the editor can read, the copy-editor can edit, and the compositor can set into type.

Ursula Le Guin, in her *The Language of the Night*, writes: "Your story may begin in longhand on the backs of old shopping lists; but when it goes to an editor, it should be typed, double-spaced, on one side of the paper only; with generous margins — especially the left-hand one — and not too many grotty corrections per page.

"Your name and its name and the page number should be on the top [right corner] of every single page; and when you mail it to the editor it should have enclosed with it a stamped, self-addressed envelope."

Typed (or **machine-printed**) means just that. If you use ribbons, have a supply of new ones on hand; change to a new ribbon when you start the final draft of a story. When you make a xerographic copy, make sure that all pages are copied clearly. The printing must be black, not grey. But do not overdo that; be sure no letter looks like a black blob. The typesetter must follow copy to the letter. To do this, he must be able to read, without guessing, every letter on every page. It's best to use a simple font that looks like the output of a typewriter, like 12-point Courier type, which is ideal; the closer to that, the better. Never change typefaces within your manuscript; if you want the editor to make such a change, say so in a penciled, marginal note. Avoid typefaces that confuse "i," "I," "1," and "l," or which confuse the comma "," with the period "."

Modern computers offer an astonishing variety of type-faces and type-sizes. Keep in mind, however, that editors are not asking you to typeset your stories; we merely want to see which words you picked, which punctuation you picked, and the order that you put them on paper. Do not use all-italic, all-capital, or script or other fancy fonts. We strongly prefer what's called a "mono-spaced" font, like 12-point Courier.

Do not use type smaller than 12-point. This should give you about 10 letters, spaces, and punctuation marks per horizontal inch of text.

Double-spaced means double-*line*-spacing: leaving a full, blank line after every typed line; it does not mean putting extra space between words! On a typewriter, set the line-feed control to advance the paper two full lines at a time; on a printer, set the line spacing at 24 points. Either should give you about three typed lines per vertical inch. Do not use the on-&-a-half-line setting some typewriters have; do not reduce the line spacing anywhere in the manuscript.

Indent every paragraph five spaces, including every paragraph of dialog. (And remember that it is customary to start a new paragraph wherever the speaker changes from one character to another.) Leave extra space between paragraphs only where you want to mark a shift in scene or a lapse of time.

On one side of the paper, which should be white, 8.5 by 11 inches (or European equivalent), inexpensive 16 or 20 pound bond. Do not use "erasable" paper.

With generous margins, about an inch, all the way around. Margins much larger than one inch waste paper and postage. If you use a word processor, check its manual, and then turn *off* the right-justification and the hyphenation; do *not* let it suppress "widows & orphans" (that is, do *not* let the word-processing program keep the first line of a paragraph from appearing at the end of a page nor keep the last line of a paragraph from appearing at the top of a page.) Do *not* break words at the end of lines. Editors (all editors!) Prefer ragged right margins with even spacing between words, and we prefer the same number of lines on every page but the first and the last. Keep in mind that the people who write word-processing programs do not have the remotest idea what proper manuscript format is.

And not too many grotty corrections per page. Neither editors nor compositors are grading for neatness; we don't demand letter-perfect-the-first-time typing. We *do* object to erasures. If you use a typewriter, XXX-out or line out your deletions, and type or legibly hand-print any corrections above the place each is to be inserted. If you are using a word-processor and printer, proofread, proofread, and proofread again before you print the submission copy. Watch out for mistakes that spell-check programs are blind to, like "it's" for "its," "breath" for "breathe," "hoard" for "horde," and all the many possible mistakes involving "lie" and "lay."

Identify your story. Type (or machine-print) your full real name, yur social security number, **and your address** (make it easy for us to send you money!) At the upper left-hand corner of the first page, an inch inside the top and left edges of the page. If you use a cover letter, put your address on that too. Your story's title is *your* responsibility (editors don't buy nameless stories) goes about a quarter of the way down the first page, with your name (or your pen name, if you use one) directly under that title. (Two suggestions: Avoid cutesy pen names; your own real name, especially an unusual one, is far better. But if a well-known writer has the same name as yours, change yours in some say, such as spelling out your middle name instead of an initial, or the like.) Use paper clips, not staples, to hold manuscripts together.

Pages sometimes do go astray in an editor's office. Therefore, a glance at any page in the manuscript should reveal the story title, its author, and the page number. So: type or print your last name (plus initials if your name is a common one), a word or two from the title, and the page number on the upper right-hand corner of every page, starting with page 2, like: **XmasCarol/Dickens/pg 26**, or **Cujo/S. King/7**. (If you use a separate title page, page numbering starts with the first page of text.)

And when you mail it to the editor, it should have enclosed with it a stamped, self-addressed envelope. Editors much prefer a new, 9-by-12, *non*-clasp envelope to carry the story to the editor, with a second envelope of the same size, folded once, paper-clipped to the back of the manuscript. (The Post Office and editors do not like clasps, those brass things that stick through holes in envelope flaps; and non-clasp envelopes are cheaper.) Please do not use padded envelopes or envelopes larger than 9 by 12. Address the return envelope to yourself. Both the outgoing and return envelopes should be addressed by typewriter or printer; if the envelope won't fit, type or print addresses on labels. Please *affix* U.S. postage stamps (foreign postage is useless to us, and you do us no favors by sending loose stamps!); do not use binders or stiffeners; do not use registered or certified mail, because these make editors go to the post office and stand in line, which makes them grumpy and eager to reject you and all your works. Your only protection against loss is to keep a good copy of anything you send out. need U.S. postage? See below.

The more standard your format, the less editors are distracted from what is really important: *the story itself.* Manuscript format is not a place to innovate.

To find out how long the story is, do not actually count the words. Instead, take an average-length, mid-paragraph line. Count the letters and spaces and punctuation in that line (with 12-point monospace type, this will be around 60; if it's much large, you are using type that is too small). Divide by six. Multiply by lines per page. Multiply by pages (correcting for partly blank pages at beginning and end). Put this "word" count in the upper right corner of the first page.

Call for italics by underlining; do not use an italic typeface in the manuscript itself (but it is okay to use underlined italics); do not use the e-mail convention of putting one underline before and one after the "underlined" word. Distinguish between the hyphen, as in "mother-in-law" and the dash — which should be typed like this — with a space before and a space after.

Proofread: Spell-check programs do not catch errors like its for it's; remember that you're responsible for proofreading your manuscripts.

We say, "You must punctuate, paragraph, and indent carefully and correctly."

"How about in dialog? You ask.

"Especially in dialog," we say. "If in doubt, you must look up how to do it properly. Note that when two or more consecutive paragraphs are spoken by the same speaker, all have quote marks at the beginning, but only the last has quote marks at the end.

"Also," we suddenly, excitedly expostulate unto thee, "when you're writing dialog, do not reach for substitutes for 'say' or 'said,' as we did in this paragraph, nor hang unnecessary adverbs on 'say.' doing so will soon get silly; worse, it distracts from the story. Notice how we punctuated and capitalized all through this conversation."

You look puzzled. "Can I identify the speaker without using 'said' or a synonym for 'said'?"

"You just did." We smile reassuringly. "Just don't overdo it. Identify the speaker often enough that the reader always knows who is speaking. Don't let pronouns run wild as in: 'He saw him look at him.' Since 'ten foot long sticks' can mean 'ten sticks a foot long' or 'sticks ten feet long,' use commas or hyphens ('ten foot-long sticks' or 'ten-foot-long sticks') to tell the reader which."

Cover letter? No more than one page long, and only if you really want to; remember that editors don't buy cover letters; they buy stories. Don't spoil the suspense with a synopsis; and don't include your bibliography or resume. You may cite two or three earlier sales, especially if they are to markets as good or better than our own (do mention if you've sold something to *The New Yorker*. Don't bother to mention selling something to *The Bee-Keeper's Gazette* unless your story involves bees); then get out of the way and let the story sell itself.

However, if the editor has seen the story before, a cover letter is necessary, to remind her what she said about the story before and to tell her exactly what you've done about her suggestions. Use a cover letter to explain anything unusual about the rights offered — for example, if the story is part of a novel to be published by [insert name] on [insert date]. Put your typed name and address, and your story's title on every cover letter. But if you don't need a cover letter, omit it.

If it's cheaper to send a disposable copy (and it usually is), mark the manuscript "disposable" so the editor can throw it away if she doesn't buy it. Provide a business-letter-sized return envelope, what stationers call a number 10 envelope (not a postcard!), with letter-postage affixed, for the editor's reply.

If you are sending us stories from outside the U.S., remember that only U.S. stamps can be used for return postage. Since international postage is so expensive, we strongly recommend that you send a disposable manuscript (so marked0 and a return envelope at least 10 by 230 centimeters in size, for the editor's reply. You can send International Postal Reply Coupons to pay for the return postage; each is worth about U.S. $0.80 to us. To send a one-ounce (28 gram) letter to Canada costs us U.S. $0.60; to an overseas address, U.S. $0.80. Reply Coupons cost you a lot, but you can buy U.S. postage by sending a postal money order, payable in U.S. funds, to cover the cost of 10 stamps or more, to Postmaster, Bridgeport, PA 19405, U.S.A. (or to the Postmaster of any other U.S. city). Include your own address. Explain what stamps you want, and how many of each.

When a reply envelope is to be mailed in the U.S. for delivery to another country, put the name of that country at the *end* of the *last* line of the address.

Dot-matrix printing is acceptable only if one cannot tell at a glance that the print is dot-matrix. Do not use draft mode, do not use seven- or nine-pin dot-matrix machines.

Submissions to us must be on paper in the format described above, not on disk and not by e-mail. (We have a system for handling on-paper submissions; having two systems — one for snail-mail and another for e-mail — is more than we can cope with.) Unless an editor announces otherwise, assume this is so for all publications. an editor who buys your story will almost certainly want to know if you can supply it by disk — and if so, which word processor and which kind of computer: PC, Apple, or MacIntosh — or by e-mail. Put these data on the manuscript's first page. (We use a PC, XyWrite, and Ventura; we can also cope with Word, plain-text, and .rtf formats.)

Again: format is not the place to innovate; do not divert the editor's attention from the story! Instead, your format should be as invisible as possible.

Rule Three: You must put your story before an editor who might buy it.

Parents, siblings, spouses, offspring, teachers, and friends don't count; neither do closets or desk drawers. You simply must send your story to editors (one editor at a time). Remember that editors do not reject people, nor do they predict careers. At worst, editors reject pieces of paper that you typed on; at best, editors send you money. The only opinion that really counts is that of someone who might pay to publish your story.

We call your attention to the chorus in the opening song of The Music Man: "But ya gotta know the territory!" Read your target publications. See what kind of stories they use; note what kinds of stories they use. Ask for guidelines, always including a return envelope (with postage affixed) for the reply.

In the short-story market, it is almost always better to send a complete manuscript rather than a "would you like to see?" letter. If you fear that a particular market might not be open for submissions at all, write to the editor and ask if it's open now; and if it's not open, when will it be, with a postcard (addressed to you, with postage affixed) for the editor's reply.

How does the "who might buy it" part of the Rule apply to *Weird Tales*? Please keep in mind our magazine's title. We almost never buy a story or a poem which has no fantasy content; we hardly ever buy science fiction which lacks fantasy elements; we never buy stories in which the weird elements turn out to be nothing but a dream. But this leaves room for an extraordinary range of fiction — and poetry: Robert E. Howard's Conan the Cimmerian and modern swordplay-&-sorcery were born in Weird Tales. H. P. Lovecraft's Cthulhu Mythos, Miskatonic University and all, are welcome to our pages, as are stories set in fantasy-worlds of your own invention. We're looking for the best in fantasy-based horror, heroic fantasy, and exotic mood pieces, plus the occasional "odd" story that won't fit anywhere else. We want to please our readers with superior writing and to surprise them with new ideas. To this end, we will occasionally publish a story in which the ominous, eldritch, and/or squamous horrors waiting to pounce turn out to be quite harmless. We almost never use material already published in the U.S.

Most stories we buy are shorter than 7,000 words. We may serialize novellas in two parts; we do not serialize novels. We have no minimum length. Short-short stories (less than 1,000 words or so) are very hard to write, but they are easy to sell.

WT does use humor, but the humor should touch on fantasy or horror themes. We find that humor works best when structured like other fiction, with high points and low, tension and relief, building to a climax and (usually) a very quick anticlimax or none at all. Do not try to make every line screamingly funny.

Remember that printed fantasy stories (and science fiction, for that matter) are usually years — even decades — ahead of movie and TV versions of the same themes. Especially beware of building a story (*any* kind of story) on current newspaper headlines, which may well be forgotten by the time the story could be printed. As an example: spousal and child abuse, and schoolyard shootings are real-life problems, yes — but they're perhaps too familiar to our readers to work as fiction just now.

To know our territory ("…ya gotta know the territory!"), look at what we publish in *Weird Tales*. Then try to do even better. (Back issue of Weird Tales ((and *Worlds of Fantasy & Horror*, our title for four issues)) are available from the address below: single copies, $6 each, including postage; in Canada & Mexico, $7; and elsewhere, $10. Make back-issue and single-copy payments by checks or money orders payable to Weird Tales, all prices in U.S. dollars.)

We respond as fast as we can, and we write an individual letter almost every tme. In return, we expect that your submission is not now being seen by any other editor (that is, no simultaneous submissions), and we hope you will not get too upset if we tell you why *we* don't want to use it. Ours is only one opinion, but it *is* possible for us to be right, and our comments might help you to do better with your next story. Again: we reject pieces of paper; we cannot and will not reject *you*. We pay about 3¢ per word on publication.

Problems we see too often:

No return address on the first page of the manuscript, and no return address on the cover letter. Do you really want to make it hard for editors to send you money?

No return envelope with postage affixed. We couldn't possible afford to pay postage to return comments on all the manuscripts we get — and why put editors in a bad mood before they even start reading?

Format so far removed from professional standards that we did not or could not read your story at all.

Writing which is simply not of professional quality — which includes awkward writing, using not-quite-right words, using too many adjectives (there isn't an adjective built that is as effective as the exactly right noun!), or failing to stay in a chosen viewpoint character for the duration of a scene.

Stories that don't catch the reader's attention by the middle of the first page.

Stories and poems which have no supernatural or fantasy content. (Remember, though, that some of our best stories have been about apparently supernatural elements that turn out to have a non-supernatural explanation; we don't use many like that, but will run a few such stories that have exceptional merit.)

Stories with characters we cannot bring ourselves to care about.

Stories and poetry which try to make up for uninteresting content by "going for the gross-out," as by using shock-value instead of real story-telling and innovation.

Stories with disappointing endings, or whose resolution is too obvious too soon (some as early as half-way through the first sentence!), or that do not resolve at all. We don't object to corpses nor to tragic endings, but protagonists who exist only to wallow in mundane woes and then succumb quietly to an undeserved doom really don't belong in *Weird Tales*. Your protagonists must at least *try* to cope, and must try to change *some*thing, even if the outcome is tragic.

Stories whose only point is that the world is a dreadful, dreadful place tell our readers what they already know; people read *Weird Tales* to escape everyday futility, not to be splattered with more.

More description of a horror is not as effective as telling a story about people trying to cope with one, successfully or not. Believable, often sympathetic people make horror stories scary; but standard-issue, cardboard villains rented by the yard from Central Casting and who come to a (usually predictable) bad end do not.

The pseudo-Medieval never-never land, overrun with generic swords-persons, wizards, and dragons has been sword-played (and ensorcelled) into the ground by now. But *your* imaginary-world setting, characters, and plot elements can be fresh, and new, and *interesting*. Look at real histories; get a feel for just how complex the pre-industrial world was. Don't base your characters or your magic on a role-playing game; invent your own.

Although there's nothing inherently wrong with stories about classical vampires, deals with the Devil, formalities of the Hereafter, and people eating people (or vice versa), our readers have already read stories based on these ideas. If you wrap a story around an old, familiar idea, then add something new and different! A story seldom surprises readers if all it does is reveal, as "surprise" ending, that the protagonist is a vampire, or that he just noticed he's been dead snce page 1.

R-U

Please remember that *Weird Tales* is a fiction magazine; the Real Inside Truth About The Occult belongs elsewhere, as do real-life ghost sightings and anything about airborne crockery and alien abductions.

To sum up:

Most manuscripts rejected by any fiction editor are rejected for one or more of these flaws:

Text that is too hard to read comfortably.

Lack of a clear, consistent point of view.

Failure to establish the characters' identity (including gender) and setting, in both time and place, early in the story.

Too much exposition and too little narration, especially at the beginning.

Characters so uninteresting, unpleasant, or unconvincing that the readers don't *care* whether or not those characters get eaten alive (or worse) on stage.

Characters who don't even try to cope with their problems (your protagonists should protag!)

Plots that fail to resolve (tragically, happily, or otherwise) their problems or conflicts, but just present them. Plots with neither problems nor conflicts. Plots based on ideas so old and tired that the ending is obvious half-way down page 1. Plots that cheat readers by holding back information for a "surprise" ending.

Writing so flowery and so filled with sesquipedalian prose that the basic story is lost under too many adjectives, adverbs, and not-quite-right words.

Writing which feels as if the author were being paid by the word (well, you are, but don't let the readers notice that).

Writing too murky or opaque to decipher and decode.

Writing so filled with errors in spelling, punctuation, and grammar that no editor wants to wade through the mess.

Something you must read:

The Elements of Style by William Strunk, Jr., and E. B. White, third edition, published by Macmillan, is widely available from good bookstores in hard covers and soft. Absolutely essential. Get hold of a copy, and you better believe it!

Something we'd merely *like* for you to read:

On Writing Science Fiction: The Editors Strike Back! By Scithers, Schweitzer, and Ford — we wrote it, so of course we recommend it. In it, we discuss fantasy as well as science fiction; you can order it from Owlswick Press, 123 Crooked Lane, King of Prussia, PA 19406-2570, for $19.50, postpaid. (In Pennsylvania, please add 6% sales tax.)

Categories: Fiction—Fantasy—Horror—Poetry—Science Fiction—Short Stories

CONTACT: Submissions Editor
Material: All
123 Crooked Lane
King of Prussia, PA 19406-2570
E-mail: weirdtales@comcast.net

Westchester Magazine

Westchester and lower Fairfield's premier upscale lifestyle publication, *Westchester Magazine* focuses on the hot issues, the innovative trends, the people on the scene, what to do and where to go in two of the wealthiest counties in the U.S. Departments focus on area people in the news, regional events, travel, gift ideas, education, shopping, restaurants and theater, health and fitness, among others.

Editorially, *Westchester Magazine* tries to reflect the values of the strongest magazine journalism: objective reporting, lively writing and trenchant analysis. We are interested in the news of the area—the creative idea, happening, the important concern, the entertainment the unusual place or "find"—delivered in sophisticated, crisp and punchy fashion.

Westchester Magazine accepts queries and clips from all writers. Manuscripts should be accompanied by a self-addressed stamped en-

velope, cover letter, resume and any applicable clips. The annual subscription rate for writers is $15, the professional rate.

Articles are accepted on speculation as well as assigned. Optimum length for articles is 800-2,000 words. If you have photographs relating to your story, please include them.

Thank you for your interest in our magazine.

Categories: Lifestyle—Regional

CONTACT: Esther Davidowitz, Editor-in-Chief
Material: All
100 Clearbrook Rd.
Elmsford NY 10523
Phone: 914-345-0601
Fax: 914-345-8123

WestCoast Magazine

Thank you for your interest in submitting articles to *WestCoast Magazine.*

We receive articles from seven cities, crossing three county lines every month. So that we may process your submission in a timely manner, articles are due no later than the 10th of each month for consideration in the upcoming issue. To be considered for publication, articles will be accepted in the following format:

• Name and phone number on front page, upper left hand corner
• Typed, double-spaced
• Preferred font: Times Roman, 12 point
• Length: 375 words maximum
• Preferred method of submission:
E-mail to editorial.wcmedia@mindspring.com
• May fax to: 909-390-9590
• Hard copy or computer disk may be walked in or mailed to address listed below

WestCoast Media strives to uphold excellent standards to educate, entertain and inform our readers with a balance of local and general articles in our community magazine. We are always looking for fresh, innovative and inspiring articles of interest for our readers; however, publication is not always guaranteed. Publication is based on appropriateness of the article, quality of writing and available space in the magazine.

Your ideas are always welcome. We look forward to hearing from you.

Categories: Book Reviews—Cooking—Diet/Nutrition—Education—Entertainment—Family—Fashion—General Interest—Health—Inspirational—Money and Finances—Parenting—Physical Fitness—Psychology—Real Estate—Relationships—Self Help—Short Stories

CONTACT: Elizabeth Cohn, Publisher
Material: All
800 S. Rochester, Ste. B.
Ontario, CA 91761
Phone: 909-390-5727
Fax: 909-390-9590
E-mail: editorial.wcmedia@mindspring.com

Western Humanities Review

We do not publish specific writers' guidelines, because we feel that the magazine itself conveys the most accurate picture of our requirements.

Writers may wish to obtain a sample copy from us or to look for a recent copy at their local university or college library. (Poets may want to check out a recent issue of the more widely distributed *Paris Review,* with which we share our poetry editor, Richard Howard.)

Submissions

Submissions are read from September 1 through May 1 of every year. Submissions received outside of this time frame may be returned unread. Electronic submissions or queries are not accepted. Please be sure to include an SASE, or we will not respond to your submission. We accept simultaneous submissions with notification of such.

Categories: Fiction—Nonfiction—Literature—Poetry

CONTACT: Paul Ketzle, Managing Editor
Material: Fiction, Non-Fiction
CONTACT: Richard Howard, Poetry Editor
Material: Poetry
Dept. of English
The University of Utah
255 S. Central Campus Dr., Rm. 3500
Salt Lake City UT 84112-0494
Phone: 801-581-6070
Fax: 801-585-5167
Website: www.hum.utah.edu/whr

Western Publications

Please refer to *True West* magazine.

Western RV News & Recreation

The goal of *Western RV News & Recreation* is to further the RV lifestyle.

Editorial is aimed at active RVers, both seasoned experts and fresh newcomers, providing them with practical information on the proper use and care of their vehicles, unusual and exciting destinations, from metropolitan to remote, unique uses of RVs and the latest news of the RV world.

Western RV News accepts both submissions and queries, through email or hard-copy. An electronic copy, emailed as an attachment or submitted on disk (in format acceptable for Word 2000) is preferred with hard copy. Articles must be well-written in an informative and interesting manner. Destination pieces should include, usually in a sidebar, clear directions, information regarding nearby RV parks and facilities with addresses, and contact information. A length between 800-1,400 words is acceptable. Articles should be written from the third party point of view (avoid: I, we, they, you, etc.). Technical articles must be thoroughly researched and accurately written in a clear and easily read style. Short fillers, humorous anecdotes, cartoons, and RV tips are also encouraged.

Photographs add much to a story. High quality color slides are preferred, but color and/or B&W prints are also accepted. Digital photos must be a minimum resolution of 300 dpi at printed size (generally 5" x 7" is adequate) and can be emailed or included on a high-capacity disk (CD-R or Zip Disk). Include captions and releases. While every effort is made to return photo material in original condition, *Western RV News & Recreation* will not be responsible for lost or damaged material. Generally, the greater the number of photos submitted, the greater the number of photos published.

If material has been published previously, indicate when and in what publication it appeared. If possible, include a copy. Responses are usually made within six weeks. Include a postage-paid envelope for return of materials and $0.83 of postage for each copy requested in which article appears. Publication is normally within 6 to 12 months of submission.

Editorial material is due three months prior to the first day of the month of publication. Payment is made upon publication. We pay $.08 per published word for first rights. Second rights are $.05 per *Western RV News* published word. Photos are $5.00 per published photo.

Website links that are helpful to the article will included, at the editor's discretion, and paid $2.00 per published link up to a maximum of $10.00. Permission for web-publishing rights are encouraged as well.

Western RV News is a monthly publication. While an editorial calendar is used, we count on freelance material to work into the planned editorial. We leave adequate room in our publication for additional material to capture timely and unique pieces for our readers. Articles specific to the Northwest and Southwest are a key component of our content, but articles focusing on other North American destinations are also included and appreciated from time to time—RVers do like to travel!

Categories: Nonfiction—Adventure—Automobiles—Lifestyle—Outdoors—Recreation—Recreation Vehicles—Senior Citizen—Travel

CONTACT: Justin Snyder, Editor
Material: All
64470 Sylvan Loop
Bend OR 97701
Phone: 541-318-8089
Fax: 541-318-0849
E-mail: editor@westernrvnews.com
Website: www.westernrvnews.com

R-U

Westways
Southern California Lifestyle Magazine

Westways, the bimonthly magazine for Auto Club of Southern California members, has a circulation of 3.2 million. Our editorial focus is Southern California popular culture, travel, and automotive topics.

In each issue, we publish several feature articles ranging from 1,000 to 2,500 words in length. We assign stories based on writers' proposals and rarely accept completed manuscripts. We look for writers with sound research and reporting skills, a strong voice, and good storytelling ability. In early summer, we create our editorial calendars for the following calendar year.

Before you submit article ideas, we strongly encourage you to read several issues of *Westways* to familiarize yourself with our requirements. Please send samples of your published work with your proposal; otherwise, we rarely make an assignment.

Sections that are most open to new writers include: What's New (Travel, Automotive, and Lifestyle), Day-Tripping, Roads to Roam, and After Dark. What's New items are typically between 150 and 250 words in length; the other departments vary from 750 to 1,500 words.

We pay $1 a word upon acceptance, plus agreed-upon expenses, for first North American rights. We use high-quality photographs or slides with our articles, so if you are a published photographer, please let us know. (Photographers may submit their books to the Art Director.)

We usually respond to queries within two months, but do not respond to queries submitted without an SASE, nor do we respond to follow-up calls regarding queries. In addition, we do not accept queries via fax, phone or e-mails.

To be considered for an assignment, mail queries and clips to the address below. We look forward to reading your proposal. Thank you for your interest in *Westways*.

Categories: Nonfiction—Associations—Automobiles—Consumer—Regional—Travel

CONTACT: Robin Jones, Copy Editor
Material: All
PO Box 25222
Santa Ana CA 92799-5222
Phone: 714-885-2376
Website: www.aaa-calif.com/westways

Wheelin' Sportmen

Please refer to *Turkey Call*.

Whole Life Times

Calling All Freelancers!

Whole Life Times relies almost entirely on freelance material to fill its pages every month. We have only a few "regulars," so the field is wide open to all who wish to submit. We depend on freelancers like you!

What Kind of Articles Should I Submit?

As a Cultural Creative lifestyle publication, *Whole Life Times* is open to articles on a wide variety of topics. Our main focus of coverage includes new approaches to: health, food, social justice and social responsibility, conscious business, the environment, spirituality and personal growth; in short, anything that deals with a progressive lifestyle. The important words to remember when writing for WLT are information and narrative style: We strive to provide leading-edge editorial that is not only entertaining, but also directly usable by our readers—information that the mainstream media often abridges, is unaware of or is unwilling to print.

Whole Life Times' content is predominantly local. We publish stories about issues, events and people in southern California. In generic stories (e.g. health-related), we use local sources for quotes and backup information.

Whole Life Times accepts up to five long (1,500-2,200 words) and short features (800-1,000 words) per issue, covering the areas mentioned above.

In addition, we have several short features we run regularly:

Spotlight focuses on an individual in our community who is generously giving of self to those less fortunate in some way. Subjects of this feature are our local heroes and sheroes.

Conscious Business highlights a local business that is operating with a consciousness of the triple bottom line: In addition to being a profit-making venture, it has environmentally-friendly business practices and treats its employees and customers with integrity.

BackWords is a short feature that highlights a personal event or moment in the life of the writer. It could be characterized as an "aha" moment or event. Ideally it inspires, educates or informs our readers.

Uncommon Healer profiles a health provider in our community.

Manuscript Format

Typed, double-spaced submissions are best, and we also accept in MicrosoftWord format via email. For best results with completed stories, please attach a Word file, and also copy and paste in the message section of your email. Queries may be sent via e-mail to Editor@wholelifetimes.com.

If including graphs, charts or other original art, please send a hard copy in addition to a disk, or e-mail us for digital art submission guidelines. Original photos and illustrations are welcome and may be submitted along with your article for consideration.

Notification of Acceptance or Rejection

Ah, the life of an editor—deadlines, deadlines and more deadlines! Every time we look up from our desks, it seems there's another deadline to meet. So, we set aside time to look at submissions during our precious, limited "quiet time," that late time of the month just after we've completed the last issue. Sometimes our response rate to submissions is probably not as rapid as you'd like it to be.

If we do not immediately accept or reject your article or pitch, we may set it aside for a rainy day. If you are uncomfortable with ambiguity or are in a hurry because you want to submit it to other publications, be sure to make note of it on your submission.

No matter what, be sure to include a self-addressed, stamped envelope for notification of acceptance or rejection. Articles will not be returned unless specifically requested, so be sure to keep a duplicate.

Query Letters

If you have not written for us before, please be sure to include your bio and up to three published clips. Alternatively, you may submit a completed manuscript. If your article addresses the categories described above, your treatment of the issue, the timeliness of the article and the quality of your writing are the main keys to getting published.

General tip: Keep in mind that *Whole Life Times* readers are more sophisticated than the average Joe or Joan when it comes to health, personal growth, social justice and metaphysical issues. We prefer thoughtful, well-researched articles with an informed and upbeat tone. We favor a narrative approach in which "story-telling" is emphasized. We welcome investigative reports and personal interviews, but outside of BackWords, rarely publish pov. Please include reference material for fact verification, and avoid using anecdotal claims to support your thesis or argument.

Deadlines

We accept articles any time. If you want your article to be considered for a specific issue, we should have it in hand three to five months before the month of publication.

Pay

Our rates vary dramatically from $35-$800 based on our experience with the writer, the writer's professional experience, and type and length of story.

In the event that the magazine decides not to publish your assigned story, a kill fee of 50 percent of the original fee is offered. However, no kill fee is offered if this is your first assignment with *Whole Life Times*; you are free to publish the work elsewhere. If we do print your work, we customarily pay within 30 days of publication.

We ask for one-time print rights and non-exclusive perpetual Web site publishing rights. In addition, we request the right to reprint your article in other Dragonfly Media publications at the rate of 33% of the original fee.

AlterNet (www.alternet.org) also picks up our articles, and we pay the writer a fee equal to half of any payment we receive.

Please join *Whole Life Times* in our endeavor to make our world a healthier, happier place!

Categories: Nonfiction—Conservation—Consumer—Cooking—Diet/Nutrition—Ecology—Environment—Feminism—Food/Drink—General Interest—Government—Inspirational—Interview—Lifestyle—Marriage—Men's Issues—Money & Finances—Multicultural—Music—New Age—Outdoors—Paranormal—Parenting—Physical Fitness—Politics—Psychology—Regional—Relationships—Sexuality—Spiritual—Sports/Recreation—Travel—Women's Issues—Holistic Health—Humor—Philosophy—Technology

CONTACT: Andrea Sercu, Associate Editor
Material: All
PO Box 1187
Malibu, CA 90265
Phone: 310-317-4200 x208
Fax: 310-317-4206
E-mail: editor@wholelifetimes.com
Website: www.wholelifetimes.com

The Wild Foods Forum

The Wild Foods Forum is a quarterly publication with articles on wild edible foods, rare or poisonous plants, book reviews, upcoming events, trip reports, forager feature stories, herbal folklore, and survival skills. Articles are accepted from large pool of contributing writers. A few are regular, but most are occasional. Informative or unusual topics based on personal experiences are preferred.

Articles

Length: Recipes-24-50 words. Book reviews: 50-100 words. Trip reports: 200-5 words. Informative or How-to Articles: 500-1,200 words.

Format: E-mail or as an attached document in Microsoft Word preferred; otherwise, Typed, single spaced. Each page should contain author's name, address, phone number.

Subject: See topics listed above.

Deadline: Articles should be submitted at least 2 months before the publications date.

If it is an article that would be better suited for another time period, it will be held until that time.

Art, Illustrations, Photography

Original line drawings with captions and artist's name, address, and phone number. Color or black-and-white photos or slides are accepted. Identification, including scientific names, should accompany each photo or slide. Duplicates should be used for irreplaceable slides, photo, or artwork. All artwork and photos or slides will be returned to the contributing artist or photographer.

Payment

Contributing writers and artists receive a free subscription. Additional payments are not always possible and depend on the length, amount of research and uniqueness of the article.

Editing

All work is subject to editing, depending on space and the quality of writing. When possible, editing is reviewed with the author. Please indicate with your submission if you wish to be notified of editorial changes or if you feel strongly about keeping the article intact.

Categories: Nonfiction—Cooking—Diet/Nutrition—Food/Drink—Gardening—Health—Nature—Outdoors—Recreation

CONTACT: Vickie Shufer
Material: All
PO Box 61413
Virginia Beach VA 23466-1413
Phone: 757-421-3929
Fax: 757-421-3929
E-mail: wildfood@infionline.net
Website: wildfood.home.infionline.net

Wild West

Please refer to PRIMEDIA History Group

Wildlife Art
The World's Foremost Wildlife Art Magazine

Wildlife Art is the recognized journal about contemporary and historical art and artists, depicting wildlife and nature. *Wildlife Art* strives to present informative, thought-provoking features on wildlife and art topics, while providing a forum for news and events of the wildlife art industry. We also include articles about conservation, as habitat preservation is essential to the survival of wildlife. Themes (e.g., sporting art, conservation, landscapes, Western) provide special writing opportunities. *Wildlife Art* has more than 33,000 subscribers worldwide and about 18,000 copies of each issue are sold on newsstands, at art shows and in galleries in the United States and Canada. Our target audience includes art collectors, wildlife art enthusiasts, publishers, galleries and artists.

Topics of Articles

Many of our feature stories spotlight artists. These articles define artists' skills and techniques, share details of artists' personalities and experience, and provide insight into their art. We also publish authoritative and thematic pieces in art history or current art trends, and about groups of artists who share similar medium, location, style, nationality, etc. Read a current issue of the magazine and scan back issues to learn about the range of subjects we cover, what we have addressed recently and typical topics and lengths of articles.

Writing for *Wildlife Art*

You must query us to gain an assignment. Articles must be original, accurate, timely, educational, memorable and entertaining to our readers. We seek dynamic articles that cover new artistic treatments or familiar issues from a new angle. Good writing is essential. We want to take our readers on a journey of words and images that reveals the thoughts, techniques, and styles of present-day and historical artists who depict nature.

You should be able to describe works of art with clarity and perception, and use insight to assess the place of the artists in the field—but we don't want academic criticism. We want lively, knowledgeable writing that places art and artists in context and helps readers judge for themselves. Biographical highlights can be included, but should not be overemphasized—the art should be core. In-depth articles should examine what artists are communicating and their techniques. When possible, include appropriate assessment and evaluation from recognized experts.

Query and Assignment Procedure

The best way to query is with a letter containing:

A title and topic heading for your article.

A one- or two-paragraph outline of the content, and structure, indicating why *Wildlife Art* should publish it.

Several sentences about your qualifications to write this article. Send photocopies of writing samples (writing samples will not be returned).

Examples of the artist's/artists' work(s) in the form of photographs, slides, or transparencies—we must see the art to give proper consideration to the idea.

Mail or e-mail your query to the editor—if you elect to fax it, send your art samples by mail. Allow a minimum of 8-10 weeks to hear from us. If accepted, you may be asked to sign a writer's agreement. Deadlines are arranged at the time of story assignment, but the general editorial deadline is four months in advance of the publication month (e.g., March 1 for the July/August issue). *Wildlife Art* magazine assumes no liability for unsolicited material.

Submissions

Articles must be typed, double-spaced, with wide margins, on numbered pages. Final page should include a brief biographical statement about the writer (see samples in magazine), an artwork courtesy line, if possible, and a listing of the captions for the accompanying artwork. Feel free to make headline and subhead suggestions when appropriate. Send the article by e-mail to mnelson@wildlifeartmag.com as a text or Word file. Include full contact information. All submitted manuscripts are subject to approval/acceptance.

Fundamentals that increase your article's chances of acceptance:

A snappy, creative lead, a well-crafted structure and a strong close.

Incorporate specific examples, descriptive details and quotations.

The ability to capture the artist's vision and to elicit anecdotes about experiences.

Verify accuracy, especially of quotations and proper names. Do your research thoroughly.

Judicious use of expert opinions from gallery owners, collectors, museum curators, other artists, etc., will bolster the credibility of your evaluation. (*Wildlife Art* may be able to assist you with contacts.)

Assure that you have checked with the artist(s) about art availability. (Do not focus your article on one or two works without being certain that reproduction-quality transparencies or slides are available for possible use in the article.)

Use the *Associated Press Stylebook* and *Webster's New World College Dictionary* (fourth edition) as authorities.

All articles are edited by the magazine's editorial staff. We reserve the right to edit the manuscript as necessary for our publication. Manuscript acceptance does not guarantee publication.

Submit background materials and a source/contact list with your article(s) to aid us in checking facts. This material may also be used to create a "Read More About It" sidebar. Authors are responsible for obtaining any necessary permission to quote from other publications and to reproduce copyrighted photographs or artwork. Enclose permission letters with submitted materials (see *The Chicago Manual of Style* for sample permission requests).

Artwork and Captions

Do not send original art. Photographs are adequate for querying, but unacceptable for reproduction. Professionally photographed medium- or large-format transparencies (preferred) or high-quality, professional 35mm slides will provide the best four-color reproduction.

Send us the transparencies or a source/phone number where we can obtain them. Captions must accompany art submissions, including complete and accurate title, dimensions in inches (height x width x depth), medium(s), year completed, and artist's name. Be sure to code the slides or transparencies to the caption list and label all slides and transparencies with title, artist, "top," and "front." Artwork will be returned only if you request it at the time of submittal and only if accompanied by a self-addressed envelope large enough to accommodate the art and sufficient postage. Delays in requested returns can result from the review process and/or the production process.

Rights and Requirements

All articles must be exclusive to *Wildlife Art* magazine as submitted, and the content must be original and essentially exclusive. A manuscript (or parts of a manuscript) that appeared in other, noncompeting publications may be considered, but only if the author makes *Wildlife Art* magazine aware of this previous publication at the time of submittal. By submission, contributing artists, writers and advertisers agree to indemnify and protect the publisher from any claim or action based on unauthorized use of any person's name, photography or copyrighted material.

Wildlife Art magazine purchases rights to the article for a period of ninety (90) days from the date of publication and has an unlimited right to use the article for other purposes (reuse in special issues) and to authorize reprints. If *Wildlife Art* magazine authorizes a reprint of the article, writer will receive $100 for reprint rights. If *Wildlife Art* magazine is able to negotiate a "larger press run" or if the reprint is for special purposes, every effort will be made to obtain a larger fee. After 90 days, all rights to the article, except for use by *Wildlife Art* magazine for promotional, advertising (including our Internet Web page), historical, anthology or reprint purposes, revert to the writer. Any subsequent appearances of the article elsewhere must indicate the article first appeared in *Wildlife Art* magazine. If *Wildlife Art* magazine reprints the article in a separate magazine or book published by Pothole Publications, a flat $150 fee will be paid to the writer.

Payment

Material submitted for publication is considered on speculation; we are not obligated to buy an article until we have approved it, even if we assigned it. Payment is made upon acceptance. If your story is accepted, submit an invoice that includes your Social Security number. We do not usually pay a kill fee, although this can be negotiated at the time of assignment. Basic phone expenses are reimbursed. Other expenses must be authorized prior to expenditure.

How to Reach Us

Submit written queries by mailing.

Categories: Animals—Arts—Collectibles—Conservation—Environment—Outdoors

CONTACT: Mary Nelson, Editor
Material: All
PO Box 22439
Eagan MN 55122-9439
Phone: 952-736-1020 (Writers on assignment only)
Fax: 952-736-1030
E-mail: Publisher@winternet.com
Website: www.wildlifeartmag.com

William and Mary Review
College of William and Mary

The *William and Mary Review* is published annually by the College of William and Mary. The *Review* is dedicated to publishing visual arts, fiction, nonfiction, poetry and innovative literary works by established artists and authors in addition to introducing those by new and vital talents.

When submitting, it is best to send no more than one or two fiction or nonfiction works, unless they are under 1,000 words; length should not exceed 7,000 words in any case. For poetry, five to eight poems is a good size selection. All work must be typed; visual arts must be submitted in color slide format. We do not acknowledge receipt of work, and decisions are usually reached within four months. Please note that staff members are not available during the summer months; all material received then will be considered beginning in September.

As the *Review* is published in April of each year, the deadline for each issue is January 15. Back issues of the *Review* are available from the above address at $5.50 including postage. Direct all inquires to Fiction, Poetry, Nonfiction, Art or Managing Editors, whichever is most applicable.

PAST CONTRIBUTORS TO THE REVIEW INCLUDE

Douglas Crase, Amy Clampitt, Julie Agoos, W.S. Penn, Debbie Lee Wesselmann, John Allmann, Dana Gioia, W.D. Snod-grass, David Ignatow, Cornelius Eady, A.R. Ammons, Barnie K. Day, Paul Wood, Carolyn Harris, Geneva Beavers, Michael Mott, William Logan, Debora Greger, Ron Smith, David Acker, Jane Hirschfield, Judson Jerome, and Richard Kostelanetz.

Categories: Fiction—Nonfiction—Arts—Literature—Poetry—Short Stories

CONTACT: The Editor
Material: All
CONTACT: Elizabeth Lathrop, Fiction Editor
Material: All
Campus Center, PO Box 8795
Williamsburg VA 23187
Phone: 757-221-3290

Willow Springs

Willow Springs is published twice a year—in January and June. We consider manuscripts between September 15 and May 15. All submissions not postmarked within those dates are returned unread.

We publish poetry, short fiction and non-fiction of literary merit. We suggest you familiarize yourself with our journal before submitting. We value poems and essays that transcend the purely autobiographical, and fiction that conveys a concern for language as well as "story." Translations are always welcome if publication permission has been acquired from the author of the original work. We are happy to receive book reviews as long as the books reviewed have not been in print more than two years.

Please submit prose and poetry in separate envelopes. All manuscripts must be accompanied by an SASE with postage sufficient to return the submission or a response. We ask that you DO NOT send the same manuscript elsewhere while we are considering it. You may expect a response from us in four to eight weeks. We offer a year's subscription and two complimentary copies for work we publish.

Categories: Fiction—Nonfiction—Adventure—African-American—Alternate Life-style—Arts—Asian-American—Book Reviews—Civil War—Culture—Dance—Drama—Entertainment—Environment—Experimental Fiction—Folklore—General Interest—Hispanic—History—Human Rights—Interview—Literature—Men's Fiction—Multicultural—Music—Native American—Outdoors—Poetry—Regional—Satire—Short Stories—Society—Theatre—Women's Fiction—Writing

CONTACT: Christopher Howell, Editor
Material: All
Eastern Washington University
705 W. 1st Ave.
Spokane WA 99201
Phone: 509-623-4349

WINES&VINES

Wines & Vines

About Us

Since 1919, *Wines & Vines* has been the Authoritative Voice of the Wine and Grape Industry. From prohibition to phylloxera, we have covered it all and our paid circulation reaches all 50 states and 40 foreign countries. Because we are intended for the trade, including growers, winemakers, winery owners, retailers, wholesalers, restaurateurs and serious amateurs, we do not accept "gee whiz" type articles on the "wonders of wine," the romance of the grape, etc.

Wines & Vines magazine has been published every month since December, 1919. Issues include the latest industry news, editorial columns on politics, legal and regulatory opinions, the world wine market, health, vineyard management, a variety of pertinent articles, profiles of industry people and businesses and a calendar of upcoming events. Each month we also devote a portion of the magazine to one particular focus.

Submissions

All articles should be summated on typed pages (e-mail is fine too) and the cover page should include your name, address, phone and fax. We encourage you to send photos with your article but we cannot guarantee the return of unsolicited manuscripts and photos.

Our January issue is our trade show issue. In February, we focus on the Vineyard: An overview of last year's harvest; crop size; quality by regions and by states. Other editorial covers pest control, vineyard management and much more. In March we zero in on International issues. April is our Hot Topics issue. In May we focus on Packaging. Wine Marketing. June is the Annual Open Meeting of the Society for Enology and Viticulture (ASEV) and Enology issue. We supply our readers with extensive convention information and the most accurate floor plan available. Exhibitors are given an opportunity to tell our readers what they will be displaying at the show. This issue is given out at the convention so our advertisers are seen even if they can't attend. July is our Import/Export issue. August is the Wine Marketing issue, in which we cover such things as electronic wine marketing, the top retail players and their markets, interviews with marketers, designers, those who create the new campaigns and those who pay for them.

September, our State-of-the-Art issue, is just that. It covers the new, the innovative and the future, throughout the grape and wine industry. October is set aside for what we term Management. It's a compilation of what is going on within the industry; how companies are being run; how problems are being tackled and solved. In this issue we focus on the business of wine. November is primarily reserved for Equipment, Supplies and Services. In this big issue we list the suppliers, contact information and descriptions of new products and services.

In the December issue we look at Champagne. We visit wineries and cover the new and the not so new but always fun side of champagne.

Payment

Our current rate for articles accepted for publication is $.15 per word and $10 per photo.

If you have any questions please call me.

Categories: Nonfiction—Agriculture—Business—Careers—Diet/Nutrition—Food/Drink—Government—Health—Interview

CONTACT: Tina Caputo, Managing Editor
Material: All
1800 Lincoln Ave.
San Rafael CA 94901
Phone: 415-453-9700
Fax: 415-453-2517
E-mail: tina@winesandvines.com
Website: www.winesandvines.com

WIN-Informer

Writers Information Network is celebrating 20 years of providing a link for professional writers, editors, publicists, and others trying to keep in touch with the expanding and changing climate of the Christian publishing industry.

Articles We'd Love to Receive

• UP-TO-DATE MARKET INFORMATION: Anything that is news-worthy that will tell our writers what today's religious editors seek.

• INDUSTRY NEWS AND TRENDS: hot tip, trends, announcements of CBA magazines and book publishers. If you can quote editors/publishers, agents or other industry insiders, all the better.

• WRITING HELPS, CONNECTIONS, HOW-TO ADVICE and CHALLENGING ARTICLES: short, pithy ideas of what works; the best suggestions that you've picked up at conferences; practical advice to advance writing/speaking careers; devotional/inspirational material and quotes with "take-away value" from successful Christian authors. Subjects we'd love to see: working with your agent, hot tips for the "business" end, keeping tax records, effective radio or TV appearance, contract negotiation, and more.

• WRITERS CLUBS/FELLOWSHIP GROUPS/AND CONFERENCE ANNOUNCEMENTS: news of conferences, meetings, events of interest to Christian writers and speakers. Send a press release.

• BOOK REVIEWS: Books of special writing/speaking interest; books by WIN members; bestselling books that show popular trends, current issues, what people are talking about, what's important in our world; books by authors writers should be reading.

Your Submission

Your article must encourage and challenge professional Christian writers, editors, and publicists. Give us btye-sized information in reader friendly 800 words or less. For longer feature articles, interviews, personality profiles, query first via e-mail. Please submit all news, press releases, and articles in the body of an e-mail. No attachments! Articles received any other way will not be considered. Payment varies, $20–$50 depending on length and quality, or often a one-year subscription ($40) to WIN. Accepts first rights only.

Sample copies: $5.00. Send 9" x 12" envelope with 6-stamps, and check payable to WIN.

Categories: Associations—Book Reviews—Christian Interests—Inspirational—Religion—Writing

CONTACT: Elaine Wright Colvin, Editor/Publisher
Material: All
Writers Information Network
PO Box 11337
Bainbridge Island WA 98110
Phone: 206-842-9103
Fax: 206-842-0536
E-mail: WritersInfoNetwork@juno.com
Website: www.ChristianWritersinfo.net

Wired

The purpose of *Wired* is to illuminate the roots, issues and possible destiny of the emerging digital culture. *If you want to write for us, here are some things to keep in mind:*

Amaze us.

• We know a lot about digital computers and we are bored with them. Tell us something about them we've never heard before, in a way we've never seen before. If it challenges our assumptions, so much the better. *Wired* is a multimedia event on paper. Fiction, non-fiction, semi-fiction; essay, how-to, expose; picture story, profile, interview—all in one issue.

• We seek young and new voices—voices that are passionate and involved.

• Events drive the news of television and newspapers. "Ideas"—conceptual reporting—drive the news in *Wired*. It shouldn't matter too much if someone rereads your piece next month or next year. Poet Ezra Pound calls this kind of information "news that stays news." It's rare. We'll go out of our way to find it and publish it.

• If you care deeply about something that's inextricably tied to digital technologies, chances are we cover it. If the topic is just cresting the digital horizon, it's perfect.

• Write it well—long, if the material demands. Take chances. Sweep, color, scene, and strong character anecdotes are imperative. If there's no conflict—moral, institutional, cultural—there's no story.

• The piece must be definitive.

• We are re-inventing paper as a communication tool for the digital era. Send us an example of what a re-invented magazine article would be like.

• We don't want anything that duplicates what you can read elsewhere.

• We print complaints.

• How to review a product, book, or item: Write your review. Then write us a letter explaining why we should devote space to your item. Throw away your review and send us the letter.

• Give it to us in digital, or analog form. We'd prefer you send it on Mac diskette, Word ready. Don't send us the only copy of anything. Via E-Mail—send it to (submissions@wired.com). If it's a long piece, (over 7500 words) we'd prefer you first send an under-300 word synopsis of what it's about.

Thanks for your interest in *Wired*.

Categories: Fiction—Nonfiction—Computers—Electronics—Interview—Lifestyle—Software—Technology—Communication—Essay—Opinion—How-to—Profiles

CONTACT: Editor
Material: All
520 Third St. 3rd Floor
San Francisco CA 94107-1815
Phone: 415-276-5000
Fax: 415-276-5150
E-mail: editpress@wiredmag.com
Website: www.wired.com

Wisconsin Beverage Guide

Please refer to *Illinois Beverage Guide*.

Wisconsin Trails

Who We Are *Wisconsin Trails*, a privately owned bimonthly magazine, turns 45 in 2005. As the "Magazine of Life in Wisconsin," it features articles on Wisconsin people, history, nature, adventure, lifestyle, arts, sports, recreation and business. We're interested in the out-of-the-way (ever been to Blueberry Bog, known for its bluegills and blueberries?) and the popular (even widely traveled places hold surprises). Nearly 80 percent of our readers are Wisconsin residents, while most of the other 20 percent are frequent visitors here.

Subjects *Wisconsin Trails* magazine gives readers experiences of all kinds. Some articles are meant to entertain, some to provoke readers' desires to participate in an adventure, others to educate or enlighten. It is important that you write in a style that lets the reader join you in the experience and conveys a sense of place. If you're camping by a North Woods stream, we'd like to hear about the last thing you saw at night or the first thing you heard in the morning. What kind of creatures inhabit this place? Tell us what sort of impact the area has on a person, what makes it special enough to send your friends there. If it's a piece on canoeing, biking, hiking, etc., we want a sense of the action—not a blow-by-blow rundown, but a vital account of the experience that lets readers join you in the adventure. If you're writing about

people, ethnic festivals or community events, we're interested in the spirit and interaction and what makes them unique and exciting.

Style Many *Trails* stories have a strong sense of voice and place. We always appreciate a moderate use of the verb "to be" and we welcome fresh, descriptive approaches. Typically, our stories are written in the present tense, and published in the appropriate season.

LengthDepartments range from 75 to 300 words. Features vary from 800 to 2,500 words.

Contract and Payment We expect original work. We buy one-time rights that last through 60 days after publication. Payment, made upon publication, is 25 cents a word, based on assigned word count.

SubmissionsOne-page written queries via snail mail, with a SASE, are preferred over manuscripts, with one exception: we need to see a complete manuscript of a "My Wisconsin" essay submission. Please include two or three nonreturnable writing clips that showcase stories and/or approaches similar to the one you're pitching. Other materials will not be returned without a SASE. No phone queries, please; we prefer written materials we can share at editorial planning meetings. Response time is three to four months. Accepted stories must be furnished via e-mail. We do not subscribe to clipping services or pay for clippings.

Tips

Familiarize yourself with the magazine: We publish only six issues each year, so we choose our stories carefully. We also prepare our stories carefully, so be ready to work with the editorial staff. Please direct department submissions to the appropriate editor.

General Wisconsin stories we're always looking for:

• outdoor activities; family-oriented travel; romantic couples getaways; adventure travel

• history

• natural history and environmental pieces—our readers love both

• hidden or out-of-the-way places

• unknown and quirky people for profiles

• unique homes, gardens, vacation homes and cottages

• suggestions for the photography portfolio in each issue

• the offbeat—we're looking to fun things up

• unique Wisconsin businesses

• new happenings—in everything from the arts to medicine

Wisconsin Trails *Departments*

Editors' Finds

Editor: Laura Kearney

"Editors' Finds" should share with readers new places they might like to visit while traveling around the state, or items they might like to purchase. The spectrum is pretty broad: "Editors' Finds" includes everything from reviews of books written about Wisconsin subjects or by Wisconsin authors to Wisconsin-made products. Maybe you've found a new adventure outfitter, specialty garden store or even an antiques shop, bakery, art gallery or jumpin' swing club. If you have, our readers would like to hear about them.

What doesn't fit: theater or other performance reviews; events and happenings; items that do not have a Wisconsin connection.

Style: These are minireviews that capture the charms of the item reviewed, tell readers what the item offers them and make clear why the place or item is worth a visit or their money. We prefer that quotes from owners, authors, etc. not be included, as they often make the copy seem promotional. We do not run negative reviews.

Each issue, we feature approximately four finds. Word count: 100 to 150 words. Payment: $40, flat fee. Send in written reviews for consideration. Also let us know if a visual is available.

Profile

Editor: Harriet Brown

Wisconsin is filled with interesting people of all ages, and not all of them are high-profile. They may be business or community leaders, artists, craftsmen, educators, entrepreneurs, athletes. We'd like to know more about these individuals, from the award-winning 80-year-old gardener to cutting-edge artist to the innovative business leader. Who are they? What makes them interesting to a wider audience?Word count: 500 to 750 words. Payment: $0.25/word.

My Wisconsin

Editor: Harriet Brown

Each issue we spotlight a personal essay—a first-person vignette or slice of life in Wisconsin. "My Wisconsin" is an opportunity to recollect, philosophize, be humorous about a wide range of topics: people, places, events, nature, history, the environment, seasonal reflections—just about any Wisconsin subject is an opportunity for "My Wisconsin." As with any well-written essay, "My Wisconsin" submissions should transcend the experience and take the reader somewhere beyond—the meaning behind the experience, lessons learned, etc. Simple recountings or regurgitations will not do; we want essays that are poignant, intelligent, probing, observant or just plain fun. Word count: 800 to 1,000 words. Payment: $0.25/word.

News & Views

Editor: Tom Davis, c/o Editor: Harriet Brown This department is a compendium of news, quips, quotes, facts and quirks from across Wisconsin that is fun, intelligent and sometimes, slightly irreverent. Word count: 50 to 125 words. Payment: $40, flat fee.

Discover / Calendar

Editor: Laura Kearney Each issue we highlight about 10 events or places for readers to attend or visit. They must fall within the two calendar months the issue covers. We are always looking for unusual festivals, places, exhibits, classes or other events. The writing should be lively and invite the readers into a fun experience. Word count: 75-125 words. Payment: $40, flat fee.

Gone for the Weekend

Editor: Harriet Brown

"Gone for the Weekend" is a standing department of 1,200 to 1,500 words that appears in each issue of Wisconsin Trails. Your mission, when writing a "Gone for the Weekend," is to give the reader a "you are there" feel while offering fun suggestions for making an enjoyable weekend escape to the destination you're writing about. Weekend adventures come in many shapes and forms—think of the many ways a visit to Milwaukee can be cast. Though each piece must satisfy a basic formula, each trip should have its own unique flavor. Good travel pieces convey a sense of place. They are immediate, intimate without being too personal, and rich with details, and are written in a flowing (but not long-winded) style that focuses on the writer's actual experiences while visiting the destination. Keep in mind during your weekend and as you write:

- Unique people who made your visit memorable.
- Unexpected places worth visiting. Don't overlook the obvious, but don't dwell on it either. You've probably encountered the unusual along the way—include those remarkable people, places and things in your story.
- Information for the "details" sidebar at the end of the piece: necessary phone numbers, addresses and other details that would get in the way if placed in your story. (Some appropriate sidebar subheads include: "Lodging," "Special Events" and "Eating Well."
- Are you able to photograph your weekend?

You should not:

- write a blow-by-blow of your weekend.
- make your piece so personal readers can't glean helpful information for their own trip-planning needs.

The bottom line: Show us, don't tell us. Have fun! Payment: $0.25/ word, plus pre-approved expenses.

Echoes: Wisconsin History

Editor: Harriet Brown Every issue includes at least one substantial story devoted to the people, places, and events that have enriched our past, shaped our present, and continue to influence our future. We're interested in stories that we haven't heard before: the lost, the forgotten, the overshadowed, the unrevealed. It could be an individual whose name is unfamiliar but whose deeds had a lasting impact. It could just as easily be a little-known episode in the life of a famous person, or an obscure aspect of a pivotal event. It might be a place that seems unremarkable today, but was once a prominent landmark; it might be a contribution to art, science, commerce, or culture that Wisconsinites would be proud of—if they only knew about it. All realms of human endeavor are fair game, as are all the men and women who, for better or worse, made their marks on the Badger State. We want your best ideas, the ones that will grab the reader's attention and keep it, the ones that are the most fascinating, the most compelling, the most surprising. Keep your queries short and sweet, and be sure to indicate how and where we can access photographs, artwork, or other materials for illustration purposes.

Payment: $0.25/word.

Categories: Nonfiction—Adventure—Conservation—Culture—Ecology—Entertainment—Environment—Food/Drink—General Interest—History—Lifestyle—Outdoors—Recreation—Regional—Travel

CONTACT: Harriet Brown, Editor
Material: All
Trails Media Group, Inc.
PO Box 317
Black Earth WI 53515
Phone: 608-767-8000
Fax: 608-767-5444
E-mail: hbrown@wistrails.com
Website: www.wistrails.com

With
The Magazine for Radical Christian Youth

With is published six times a year for Mennonite and other Christian youth, ages 15 to 18, in the U.S. and Canada. Each issue focuses on a theme such as peer pressure, peacemaking, or devotional life. A list of upcoming themes is available for a #10 SASE. *With* has a reputation for tackling tough social issues other Christian magazines won't touch.

WHAT WE NEED

FIRST-PERSON STORIES: (800 to 1,800 words): We like to lead off with a Christian teen's first-person story of a life-changing experience. Such a story usually involves the teen's faith, and the lesson the teen learned must be one readers can apply in their lives. We sometimes use a how-to sidebar (100 to 600 words) with a personal experience article.

These stories are usually written on an as-told-to basis. You interview the teen then write his/her story in first-person. You receive an as-told-to byline unless you prefer not to. We also welcome stories from adults describing such experiences from their own teen years. We consider stories of any Christian youth, but give preference to stories of youth involved in Mennonite, Mennonite Brethren, or Church of the Brethren congregations.

We prefer a query on this kind of story. Detailed guidelines for first-person stories available for a #10 SASE. We pay $100 for first rights on first-person stories written on assignment and pay extra for photos. Usual rates for reprints.

HUMOR: (prose 100 to 1,500 words; poetry up to 50 lines): We're hungry for more well-written humor—fiction, nonfiction, light verse, or cartoons. When it comes to humor, it doesn't have to be religious, just wholesome. If your writing makes teens laugh, we want to hear from you.

REALISTIC FICTION: (800 to 2,000 words): Most issues include a short story with many of the same elements we look for in the first-person stories described above, except that fiction can be either first- or third-person. Fiction must have strong elements of conflict and change, and the message must be one readers can apply to their lives. We look for fiction that is believable and engages the readers' emotions. We're interested in occasional fiction with an "unreliable narrator."

HOW-TO ARTICLES: (800 to 1,500 words): Most issues include a how-to article with practical teaching on the issue's theme. Examples: "How to Help a Friend Who's Suffering" and "How Not to Be a Witless Witness." How-to articles need a strong opening hook (usually a true anecdote from the author's teen years), a clear step-by-step outline, anecdotes to illustrate at least most outline points, and a satisfying conclusion. To avoid sounding preachy, tell how you learned through your mistakes or from another's example. Detailed how-to guidelines available for a #10 SASE. We pay $75 for first rights on an assigned how-to. Query to receive an assignment.

SPECULATIVE FICTION: (500 to 1,800 words): We like parables, allegories, and fantasy that communicate spiritual truth with symbolism, but the symbolism must be clear. Subtle writing goes right by some of our younger readers.

POETRY: (up to 50 lines): We consider poetry of any style. While most poetry has a spiritual theme, we also use short nature poems (often seasonal), and light verse (just because it's funny). We look for strong sensory images, fresh insight or perspective, and language that pleases the ear. We use about six poems a year.

MEDITATIONS: (100 to 1,200 words): We use meditations that inspire wonder, awe, or reflection in the reader. These can be based on personal experience, a biblical event or symbol, or even a dream or imagined scene. We occasionally publish prayers (up to 200 words).

PHOTOS, CARTOONS, ILLUSTRATIONS: Photographers' guidelines available for #10 SASE. For cartoons, see "HUMOR" above and check recent issues for samples. If you wish to illustrate on assignment, send samples of your work.

OUR WRITER-FRIENDLY APPROACH

Because we have a small circulation (about 6,000), we can't pay top dollar, yet we expect top-quality writing. So we try to make it worthwhile for good writers to work with us through favorable policies on rights, prompt replies and payments—in general, lots of TLC. Here are the specifics:

RIGHTS AND PAYMENT: We pay on acceptance 5 cents a word for simultaneous rights (unpublished manuscripts you are free to submit elsewhere simultaneously) and 3 cents a word for reprint rights. We pay $10 to $25 for poetry (one-time rights) depending on length and how it is used. We pay more for first rights to assigned work (see "First-Person" and "How-To" articles). We sometimes offer a 30%-50% kill fee for assigned articles. You get two author's copies upon publication.

REPLY TIME: We respond to most submissions within four to six weeks. If we want to hold a manuscript longer, we'll ask your permission.

SAMPLES: For a sample copy, send a self-addressed stamped 9"x12" envelope ($1.24 postage). For two issues, affix $1.93 postage. For three, $2.62.

SUBMISSIONS AND QUERIES: Make seasonal and theme-specific submissions at least 6 months before publication date. All manuscripts except poetry should be double-spaced. Type your name, address and phone in the upper left corner of the first page, and the approximate word count and rights offered in the upper right corner.

Queries should be no more than a page and a half, accompanied by published clips if you haven't written for us before. Include your phone number. Don't phone us with a query without prior invitation from an editor.

Categories: Fiction—Nonfiction—Cartoons—Christian Interests—Fantasy—Inspirational—Religion—Teen—Humor

CONTACT: Carol Duerksen, Editor
Material: All
PO Box 347
Newton KS 67114
Phone: 316-283-5100

Woman Engineer
An Equal Opportunity Career Publication for Women and Experienced Professionals

Please refer to Equal Opportunity Publications, Inc.

woman's touch

Woman's Touch
An Inspirational Magazine for Women

Do You Write?
Woman's Touch is looking for submissions!
About *Woman's Touch*

Woman's Touch is a bimonthly inspirational magazine for women published by the Women's Ministries Department of the Assemblies of God. We are committed to providing help and inspiration for Christian women, strengthening family life, and reaching out in witness to others. *Woman's Touch* is the voice of Women's Ministries across the nation.

The editors of *Woman's Touch* seek original articles written from a perspective that includes God or spiritual laws and is geared specifically for women. The following is a list of topics that may be covered in upcoming issues.

• Aging gracefully—inner beauty / outer beauty / character / health / wisdom / planning ahead
• Blended families
• Careers—your life in the workplace or in the home
• Character—the goal of our Christian walk
• Compassion—developing true compassion like Jesus had
• Crafts/décor—unique, relatively simple ideas for home décor
• Depression—combating on spiritual/mental/emotional/physical levels
• Forgiveness
• Health / fitness / exercise—informative, practical advice
• Humor
• Kindness—making the world a better, friendly place by our behavior and presence
• Knowing God intimately and discerning His will
• Loving our neighbors—unchurched around us/those hit by disaster; etc.
• Marriage/family—Positive testimonies as well as dealing with various difficulties
• Ministering to others—personal ministry to various groups/needs
• Profiles of born-again women who are leaders or entrepreneurs in their own particular sphere: Finance, education, research, medicine, politics, music, finance, law, the arts, journalism, etc.
• Recipes—tested, well-loved recipes for food features
• Staying committed to Christ through all kinds of trials/good times/hard times
• Temptation—avoiding/being victorious in
• Volunteering—touching those around you with practical love and godly lifestyle
• Witnessing—through relationships with unchurched; methods for, etc.

Query Letters
• *Woman's Touch* does not accept manuscripts.
• *Woman's Touch* does welcome query letters. We prefer queries sent via e-mail to womanstouch@ag.org. Writers who have no access to e-mail can mail queries to: Woman's Touch, 1445 North Boonville Avenue, Springfield, MO 65802-1894.
• Do not enclose a self-addressed stamped envelope or postage-paid postcard.
• All queries will be evaluated.
• Specify whether you own photographs related to your proposed article, but do not send photographs. E-mail queries may include scans.
• Due to the large volume of materials received, writers are urged to refrain from contacting *Woman's Touch* for status reports regarding queries. If your query is of interest to our editorial team, you will be contacted.

• A request to see your manuscript does not guarantee that *Woman's Touch* will accept or print the article.

• Study our style and content to learn what type of articles we use. Subscribe to the magazine or purchase a single copy of *Woman's Touch* by contacting Gospel Publishing House at GPH@ ag.org or 800-641-4310.

• Seasonal queries should reach us 9 to 12 months prior to the holiday or season described.

Important Details

• We purchase electronic rights and one-time print rights. Payment will be made on publication. You will receive two complimentary copies of the issue in which it appears.

• The editors of *Woman's Touch* reserve the right to edit your manuscript for clarity and space, and to reject any article at any stage of our editing/production process.

Thank you for considering *Woman's Touch*!

Categories: Nonfiction—Christian Interests—Inspirational—Women's Issues

CONTACT: Submissions Editor
Material: Queries
1445 North Boonville Ave.
Springfield MO 65802-1894
Phone: 417-862-1447, Ext. 4066
E-mail: womanstouch@ag.org
Website: www.womanstouch.ag.org

Woman's World
The Woman's Weekly

If you can write for—and about—the average woman, we want to hear from you! *Woman's World*, a weekly magazine reaching women in the United States and Canada, publishes heart-tugging feature articles about ordinary women's real-life experiences.

Our magazine caters to a cross section of the female population—from women in their twenties to lively senior citizens, from homemakers to harried mothers juggling home and job. What we strive to do through our feature stories is provide our readers with a brief escape into someone else's life—to let them experience another woman's drama, turning point or happy ending.

Articles must be thoroughly researched, not only providing pertinent facts but also revealing the innermost thoughts and feelings of the women profiled. We seek to unfold a story that gets the reader involved with the subject and makes her care about the heroine.

To get to know *Woman's World*, read several issues from cover to cover; the magazine (which you can find at supermarket checkout counters) is your best guide. We suggest you carefully study our style and the types of stories we publish.

Woman's World pays approximately 50 cents a word for feature stories.

Fiction Guidelines

Mini Mysteries: We purchase whodunnits or howdunnits of 1,000 words. Stories should be cleverly plotted, entertaining, and conclude with a startling, totally unexpected twist. The villain may be male or female, and it must be clear by the end that he or she will not get away with the crime.

We are not interested in the grotesque or bizarre, extreme violence, ghost stores, science fiction or fantasy.

We pay $500 per mystery and retain First North American Serial Rights for six months after publication.

Romantic Short Stories: We buy contemporary romances of 1,100 words. Stories must revolve around a compelling, true-to-life relationship dilemma; may feature either a female or male protagonist; and may be written in either the first or third person. Characters may be married, single, divorced, or widowed; should be down-to-earth (no yuppies or jetsetters); and their dilemma should be poignantly or humorously conveyed. Please think carefully about a story's setting, mood and plot, and tell the story with interesting action and dialogue. (Every sentence, paragraph, and scene of the story should deliver more information about your characters and their situation and/or briskly advance the storyline.)

We are not interested in stories involving life-or-death matters, nor are we interested in fluffy, flyaway-style romance. When we say romance, what we really mean is relationship—whether it's just beginning or is about to celebrate its 50th anniversary. The emphasis in our stories is on real life—which is why we do not buy science fiction, fantasy or historical romance.

We pay $1,000 per romance and retain First North American Serial Rights for six months after publication.

Important Notes!

Manuscripts should be double spaced in legible size type.

Where to send manuscripts: Fiction Editor at address below. Indicate Mini Mystery or Romance on the envelope.

How to send manuscripts: (1) You must include a Self-Addressed Stamped Envelop to receive a reply. Manuscripts not accompanied by a SASE will be discarded. Note: A #10 SASE is necessary not just for a response, but for your contract if we purchase your story.

(2) Please DO NOT fax or e-mail manuscripts—because such submissions do not include SASEs, we have no means of responding to your submission.

Get to know us: Please familiarize yourself thoroughly with our romances and mini mysteries before submitting your work.

Be patient: Because we receive a tremendous volume of manuscripts, our turnaround time may range from one to six months. If you still have not heard from us after that time, feel free to re-submit your manuscript. Please do not call or write us to inquire about a manuscript's status.

Our feature articles are divided into categories. A brief description of each is listed below. Keep in mind that some of the categories overlap and that a story may fit into more than one classification. Don't worry if you're not sure which category would suit a particular story or even if it doesn't fit an established category—we always have room for a compelling story.

Emergency!: Gripping, minute-by-minute accounts of heart-pounding dramas are told as they unfold, so the reader can feel as if she is an actual witness to the event. Written in the third person, dramatic quotes and splashes of colorful detail (but no gore!) should give the reader a vivid mental picture of what occurred. The focus is on a true story of a woman (or child) overcoming a life-threatening crisis, such as a disaster or a dangerous situation.

• Examples: (1) A four-year-old girl calls 911 and saves her diabetic mother. (2) Three strangers appear as if by fate to save a woman's life. (3) When a teenager falls through the ice, a woman braves frigid water temperatures to save him. (4) When a sudden storm overturns their boat, a couple spends seven terrifying hours in the water until they're rescued. (5) While walking to school one morning, a teenager notices smoke billowing out of an apartment building. She heroically risks her life to save the 13 elderly people living there. (6) When a little boy wanders into the woods and gets lost, his dog saves his life by keeping him warm through the night until searchers find him. (7) When flood waters reach her doorstep, a grandmother risks her life to save her grandchild.

Happy Ending: These third-person stories may resemble those in other categories, but here the emphasis is on the joyous resolution, which comes almost as a surprise considering how bleak the situation appeared.

• Examples: (1) After he finds his birth mother, a young man asks her to help him find his birth father. She does, and after they reunite, love blossoms again. They marry and live happily ever after. (2) A 40-year-old woman wants to have a baby but is told she's in the early stages of cervical cancer and must have a hysterectomy. By chance, she finds a woman who wants to give a baby up for adoption—two weeks after the surgery, she's holding a baby in her arms. (3) A handicapped man nobody really notices discovers a town full of friends after his bike is stolen. (4) After an on-again, off-again romance, a cop at last recognizes true love in his girlfriend as she helps him recover from a gunshot wound.

Helping Each Other: Heartwarming tales of good Samaritans who reach out to someone in need. These are third-person stories, told from a female point of view—either the good Samaritan, the person in need or someone (spouse, daughter, or the like) close to the story. Lots of emotion, vivid descriptions and strong quotes are needed. We need to know how grateful the recipients are, and how terrific the do-gooders are.

• Examples: (1) When a young mom gives birth to triplets, 25 members of her church volunteer to change, feed and play with the babies. (2) When they learn a little boy needs a bone-marrow transplant, friends, neighbors and even caring strangers turn out in droves to become possible donors—and one is found. (3) A young man's dreams are shattered when his 20-year-old fiancee is diagnosed with terminal cancer. Friends and neighbors give the couple a wedding. The rings, gown, cake—even the reception—are all gifts to the couple, who can't believe so many people care. (4) When a four-year-old girl suddenly goes into kidney failure and isn't expected to live, the people in her hometown start a prayer chain. Almost as suddenly as she was stricken, the little girl recovers. Her doctors can't explain why—but everyone else knows it's a miracle. (5) A homeless family of six gets a fairy godmother when a woman reads a newspaper article about their plight. She moves them into her own home until they can get back on their feet.

Medical Miracle: A third-person retelling of a recovery, birth or the like that defied all odds or was made possible by a new medical procedure.

• Examples: (1) Almost seven months into her pregnancy a woman suffers two heart attacks. An emergency angioplasty saves her and her unborn child. (2) When a brain aneurysm nearly kills a 22-year-old student, her doctors worry, is her identical twin in danger too? They find that she, too, has an aneurysm, and clamp it before it bursts. (3) After battling cystic fibrosis her whole life, a 29-year-old mom is told only a lung transplant can save her life. She's put on a transplant list, but when her condition worsens, her sister donates a lobe from one of her own lungs, giving her a second chance at life. (4) After trying for 10 years to have a baby, in vitro fertilization makes a couple's dream of conceiving come true. They feel triply blessed to learn they're having three babies, but when she goes into premature labor the woman fears for the lives of her unborn children. After delivering one baby, her doctors are able to stop her labor, giving the other two more time to grow. Sixteen days later, the other two are born. All are healthy.

My Guardian Angel: Told in either the first or third person, My Guardian Angel tells the story of a woman facing a crisis or situation she doesn't think she can overcome. At her darkest moment, help appears. It can be a good Samaritan in the form of a friend, family member or perfect stranger. Or fate can step in, leaving the woman with a strong feeling that someone is watching over her.

• Examples: (1) Although she was never able to have a child, a woman loves her teenage nephew as her own. When he dies in a car accident, she thinks she'll never get over her grief. Then one day, she hears a bluebird chirping in her yard. She remembers that, as a young boy, her nephew promised that if he died before her, he'd come back as a bluebird and sing to her. Realizing that the love they shared could never die, her heart begins to heal. (2) A young mom is struggling to raise her two young children when her four-year-old is diagnosed with a brain tumor. She wonders how she'll cope with a sick child and pay the mounting hospital bills. Just when she feels she's all alone, a friend offers her a job that allows her to work from her daughter's hospital room. (3) After her abusive husband's beating leaves a woman visually impaired, she leaves him. But she feels worthless and alone until a service dog helps her reclaim her life and her happiness. (4) While in a coma, a young woman waits for death until she's "visited" by her deceased sister. Told it isn't her time to die, the young woman finds the will to live again and makes a full recovery. (5) A mother is heartbroken over her daughter's infertility. Desiring her child to know the happiness she's known as a mom, she prays that her daughter will have a baby. Miraculously, the daughter and son-in-law are soon blessed with an adopted baby. A few years later, knowing her daughter aches for another adopted baby, she prays again. It works! Sure that God hears her prayers, the mom asks once more for a blessing of a child for her daughter. This time—against all odds—the daughter finally conceives! (6) After years in an abusive marriage, a woman feels so trapped and alone she doesn't think there's a way out. But one night, a stranger in a parking lot sees the pain in her eyes and hands her a card with her name and phone number on it. Telling her she isn't alone, the stranger asks the woman to call if she needs to talk. She does, and the kind stranger becomes her lifeline, helping her find the strength to leave her abusive marriage and build a new life for herself and her children.

My Story: A first-person narrative that reveals one woman's thoughts and emotions as she comes to terms with a major life problem. We must be able to sympathize with the woman and her plight: Her hopes, fears and aspirations must be candidly exposed. On occasion a man's story is told, but only as it relates to his wife's, daughter's or girlfriend's situation. Sometimes a child's story is told. No matter what the age or gender of the subject, the story must be moving.

• Examples: (1) When her baby girl tragically dies, a young mother's grief is so deep it tears her marriage apart. Just when all seems lost, she realizes she's pregnant. Although she could never forget her firstborn child, the new life growing inside her helps her realize life must go on. Her heart and her marriage are healed. (2) When an 18-year-old girl is diagnosed with breast cancer and undergoes a mastectomy, she faces a mountain of fear. Afraid she'll feel like a victim for the rest of her life, she takes on the challenge of joining a mountain-climbing expedition to raise money for breast cancer research. The grueling 19,000-foot hike teaches her she's stronger than she realized. At the end of the climb she realizes she's no longer a victim but a survivor. (3) After living her whole life hiding the fact that she has AIDS, an 11-year-old girl wants to share her secret in the hopes that her teachers, friends and the kids at school will understand why she's often tired and sick. She bravely stands before her class and tells her story. To her great joy, she wins understanding and acceptance. (4) A young mother's life turns into a nightmare when, just days after giving birth, she experiences severe mood swings that have her laughing one minute and crying the next. Things go from bad to worse when she becomes obsessed with cleanliness and begins hallucinating. She's diagnosed with postpartum psychosis and is hospitalized. Medication, therapy and her desire to be a mother to her child help her reclaim her life. (5) When her teenage daughter is diagnosed with anorexia, a heartbroken mother is determined to make her well. But her loving intentions turn their home into a battleground. As her daughter withers away before her eyes, the mom realizes her daughter will only get better when and if she decides she wants to live. She lets go, and the daughter chooses life and makes a full recovery. (6) After battling her weight all her life, a wife and mother decides that being happy and healthy is more important than being thin. Once she stops hating her reflection in the mirror, she feels freer and happier than she imagined possible.

One Woman's Battle: (runs in the magazine as Courage, Triumph, Victory, Justice or Success) One Woman's Battle is a third-person account of how a woman meets a challenge, injustice, poverty or other setback. The cause she takes up can be her own or one taken up on behalf or in memory of a loved one. Whenever possible, the piece should have strong quotes reflecting both sides of the story, and some sort of resolution. Take care not to approach it like a newspaper account—we don't want a list of facts. If legal proceedings are part of the story, include them as a springboard that gives us insight into how the situation has affected the woman and her family. As with any Woman's World story, we need to share her experience.

• Examples: (1) A teenager beseeches a high school to posthumously award an honorary diploma to her younger sister who, at the time of her death, was just a few credits short of graduation. (2) A woman sues her ex-husband on behalf of her young children because he's a deadbeat dad. (3) An emergency room nurse fights to get a law passed enabling doctors and nurses to notify the police when drivers responsible for DWI accidents are brought in for medical treatment. (4) A mom fights for anti-stalking laws after her teenage daughter is stalked. (5) Told she'll never walk again, a stroke victim refuses to give up hope for a complete recovery. With nothing but faith and her family's love to sustain her, she undergoes painful physical therapy for 10 years until, one day on the beach; she realizes she can wriggle her toes in the sand! Eventually she regains the use of her legs. (6) After her hairdresser gives her a bad perm, a woman sues the salon. (7) After she's told her pet pig must go, a woman fights her condominium association and wins the right to keep her beloved pet. (8) A woman whose little boy is diagnosed as learning disabled designs computer programs to help him—and winds up starting a successful business helping kids learn. (9) A woman left struggling after a layoff decides to become her own boss and launches her own construction business.

A Woman's Story: A third-person account of real, undying love—a moving piece about the bond that exists between a parent and child, a husband and wife or friends, or even a pet and owner. It can also be about the love that blossoms between a man and woman. The story should leave the reader with a warm, wonderful feeling. It has to be filled with tender, loving quotes and anecdotes.

• Examples: (1) An 11-year-old is in a coma after a car accident and nothing can rouse him until his dog Rusty gives him a kiss, waking his young master. (2) Although she's never had a child of her own, a single woman keeps a promise to her dying friend and raises her teenage daughter. (3) When their stepdad is diagnosed with terminal cancer, the kids he selflessly helped raise return his love a hundred fold. Telling their mom to quit her job so she can spend all her time with Dad, they make sacrifices to pay the bills—moving back home to pay rent, getting second jobs to cover the mortgage payments. They cook meals, cut the grass and take care of repairs. He tearfully thanks them—but they tell him he's the one who deserves the thanks for giving them the fatherly love, understanding and guidance they needed growing up. (4) A grandma donates her kidney to her critically ill granddaughter and saves the little girl's life. (5) An adoptive mom finds her son's birth mother to fill an empty place in his heart. (6) A dying dad leaves his two-year-old daughter a legacy of love by writing her letters for her to open on all the important days of her life—the first day of school, her graduation, wedding, birthdays, days when she's feeling sad.

Woman's Best Friend: We run real-life stories in our pets column.

• Examples: (1) A family's cat wakes a mom just in time for her to get help for her son, who was having seizures while the family slept. (2) An ailing cat receives a kidney transplant, and the owners adopt the donor cat, a stray who would have been euthanized at the shelter. (3) A family is heartbroken when their dog has a stroke. They can't bear to put her to sleep, so they give her lots of tender loving care, and against all odds, she walks again and makes a full recovery.

Send your story idea/synopsis typed and double-spaced, with the original newspaper clip, if any, along with a self-addressed, stamped envelope (SASE) and your name, address and day and evening phone numbers to the address below. Please be sure to include which category you think your article is appropriate for and write it on the envelope. Or fax to Features. Sorry, we can only return your submission if you provide an SASE.

Categories: Nonfiction—Beauty—Business—Children—Consumer—Cooking—Crafts/Hobbies—Diet/Nutrition—Economics—Entertainment—Family—Fashion—Food/Drink—Gardening—Health—Hobbies—Home—Marriage—Mystery—Nature—Physical Fitness—Romance—Short Stories—Women's Issues—How-to

CONTACT: Fiction Editor
Material: Fiction
CONTACT: Fred Gioffre, Research Editor
270 Sylvan Ave.
Englewood Cliffs, NJ 07632
Phone: 201-569-6699
Fax: 201-569-3584
E-mail: DearWW@aol.com

Women Alive!

We are especially interested in articles which encourage spiritual growth such as those on prayer, praise, and Bible reading.

Other topics of interest to our readers:
• Living as a Christian in the workplace
• Mothering—helps in discipline and in rearing spiritual children
• Improving marriage
• Discouragement—especially in ministry
• Self-consciousness/shyness—relating to new people
• Improve communication in family and marriage
• Help with handling finances
• Do retired women still have a place of service?
• Temptations known only to the singles
• Reinforcement techniques for single mothers
• How can I reach the unsaved?

We are interested in articles which show Scripture applied to daily living. Most Christian women understand what they should do but need godly role models, so we prefer that you use examples of your obedience rather than your failures.

To receive a sample magazine please send $1.25 or a 9 x 12 envelope with four first-class stamps.

Editors of Women Alive! *evaluate a manuscript using the following criteria:*
1. Can the focus of the article be supported by Scripture?
2. Does it meet our purpose of helping women who are intent on spiritual growth?
3. Is the focus maintained throughout the article?
4. Is it well developed and illustrated?
5. Does it have a unique approach to the subject?
6. Is it written in a natural style (avoiding triteness and clichés)?
7. Will it have impact?
8. Will the reader's interest be maintained throughout the article?

Women Alive! pays from $15 to $50 for each article depending on length and quality of article. Women Alive! purchases either first rights or reprints but with payment we purchase the right to allow the articles to be translated into other languages by nonprofit missionary organizations.

We look forward to receiving your articles!

Categories: Nonfiction—Christian Interests

CONTACT: Aletha Hinthorn, Editor
Material: All
PO Box 480052
Kansas City KS 64148
Phone/Fax: 913-402-1369

Women and Music

Women and Music, an annual journal of scholarship about women, music, and culture, is a publication of the International Alliance for Women in Music. Drawing on a wide range of disciplines and approaches, the refereed journal seeks to further the understanding of the relationships among gender, music, and culture, with special attention being given to the concerns of women.

R-U

Subscription Information

Annual

ISSN 1090-7505

Individuals $55.00

Institutions $55.00

Single issue $40.00

For foreign subscriptions please add $6.00. Payment must accompany order. Make checks payable to University of Nebraska Press and mail to:

University of Nebraska Press

233 N 8th St

Lincoln, NE 68588-0255

or call: 1-800-755-1105 U.S. Orders and customer service.

1-800-526-2617 U.S. Fax orders and customer service.

Submission Information

Women and Music *accepts submissions that meet the following requirements:*

- submit a brief abstract
- submit 3 copies, two without identifying information and one with
- prepare according to *The Chicago Manual of Style*, 14th edition
- typed double-spaced (including quotations and endnotes)
- 8½" x 11" paper
- footnotes are not acceptable
- Microsoft Word and Word Perfect formats accepted
- obtain and provide necessary copyright permission

Authors whose articles are accepted will be asked to provide camera-ready, publication-quality musical examples. Submissions received after 30 November will be considered for the following year's issue.

Categories: Nonfiction—Culture—Music—Women's Issues

CONTACT: Catherine J. Pickar, Editor (The George Washington University)
Material: Manuscript
CONTACT: Fred Everett Maus (University of Virginia)
Material: Books for review
The George Washington University
Washington DC 20052
CONTACT: Department of Music
Material: For Book Submission
University of Virginia
Charlottesville VA 22903
Website: www.nebraskapress.unl.edu/journals.html

Women Artists News Book Review

Please refer to Midmarch Arts Press, in the Book Publishers Section.

Categories: Arts—Literature—Poetry—Women's Issues—Women Artists

CONTACT: Submissions Editor
Material: All
300 Riverside Dr.
New York NY 10025

Women In Business

Women in Business, the American Business Women's Association bimonthly national magazine, updates members on Association events and members' activities and accomplishments, in addition to featuring informative articles covering a range of topics of interest to business women. Besides previous articles about appropriate office gift giving and the health benefits of chocolate, past articles also have featured job hunting hints in the new millennium, considerations in starting a business, tax relief for women business owners, how to motivate your employees and hints on managing a career with motherhood.

Women in Business also includes excerpts from today's powerful business books, which can be used by members for credits in the ABWA contact hours program. Magazine subscription is free for members (dues include a one-year subscription), non-member subscriptions are $20 a year; $24 foreign, plus taxes.

Categories: Nonfiction—Associations—Business—Careers—Computers—Consumer—Diet/Nutrition—Government—Health—History—Internet—Self Help—Women's Issues

CONTACT: Kathleen Isaacson, Editor
Material: All
American Business Women's Association
9100 Ward Pkwy.
Kansas City, MO 64114
Phone: 816-361-6621
Fax: 816-361-4991
Website: www.abwahq.org

Women in the Outdoors

Please refer to Turkey Call.

Women Today

Women Today Magazine offers the women of the world information about the issues that affect us every day: relationships, career, health and beauty, spirituality, fitness, parenting, marriage, finances, and more. This information, while broad-based, is offered from a Christian perspective.

Seeking

We select articles that will appeal to a global audience. These articles must be uplifting, informative and pertinent to modern women. With the exception of Life Stories, articles do not need to have specific Christian content; however, the tone and content of every story will reflect a Christian viewpoint. We believe that every woman's life is a gift from God and that a personal relationship with Him will provide them with meaning, purpose and significance.

We publish journalistic, nonfiction items only and therefore do not accept photography, cover art, poetry, short stories, or product endorsements. We welcome unpublished and first time writers. Excerpts from books that can stand alone are considered.

Readership

Statistics indicate that our visitors tend to be engaged in a career, are moderately to highly computer-literate and are usually over the age of eighteen. Many of our visitors log on from the workplace and many find us as a result of commercial women's networks and search engines.

Publishing

Women Today Magazine is published monthly online. We are currently seeing over 1.5 million hits a month with an impressive average user session of just over 8 minutes. Close to 60% of the magazine is free-lanced.

NB: There is also a print magazine called *Women Today* that is loosely associated with the online version. The print version is printed annually, published in-house and does not accept submissions.

Rights & Compensation

We are seeking One Time Rights. All copyright remains with the author. Any reprint requests we receive will be directed to the author if a contact address has been provded for this purpose. The copyright you designate will accompany all text online. *Women Today Magazine* is part of a non-profit organization and as such cannot offer compensation for articles. We also do not carry advertising for revenue. Publication on our site offers contributors international exposure and we are always happy to add a link to the website of your choice along with author contact information.

Queries & Submissions

E-mail queries and submissions are preferred. Queries sent by email receive a response approximately three times faster than those sent by mail. Please do not fax queries or submissions. All submissions must be preceded by a query letter that states the title of the article, a brief synopsis, the department you are submitting it to, length (approx) and author contact info (an email address is sufficient). The departments are as listed below. Simultaneous submissions are permitted within reason.

E-mail submissions should be in standard manuscript format (exactly the same as the format for print submissions) and sent as an attachment. WordPerfect 8 or higher is preferred, however most word processing programs are accepted. Please do not cut and paste submissions into the body of your email as we do not have time to format your submission for you. Use the subject line of the email carefully. Do not label it "submission" – make it easy for me to find you. Last name and abbreviated title of the article is preferred. HTML coding is not required as we will format the final version to meet our specifications.

Departments & Columns

Departments

Articles for the different departments should range 1000 to 1200 words (approx) and be in a format suitable for Internet readers. Again, we are seeking non-fiction journalistic articles. Assignments are occasionally given to writers we have worked with previously. If you wish to be considered for further assignments, please indicate this in your query. Writing for the Internet audience entails the use of subtitles, bulleted lists where possible and concise writing. Paragraphs are usually shorter than those in a print article and must not contain more than one idea. Simply submitting the same article as written for print is not effective. If you need assistance to format for an Internet audience we can help you, however articles in the proper format will always be given precedence.

Career Focuses on any aspect of the working woman in the new millennium. Includes, but not limited to, using technology, office protocol, stress, working moms, tele-commuting, career switching, continuing education, the glass ceiling, balancing home and office, effective interviewing and goal setting.

Family Seeks to provide women with the information they need to nurture and maintain positive, meaningful family relationships. Includes parenting, children of all ages, schooling, step-families, dealing with bereavement, home management, stress, spending quality time and the ever changing role of women in the modern household. Does not include marriage (see Relationships below).

Life Stories Life Stories are the true autobiographical account of one woman's personal encounter with Jesus Christ and the resulting positive changes in her life. All life stories will be edited to include a sample prayer and invitation. Please not that the same word count applies for life stories. We receive many life story submissions that far exceed the length guidelines. We are unable to use these lifestories as we do not have the time to edit them down for you.

Money Approaches finance from an international perspective. Articles must be applicable outside of North America. Sample topics include household budgeting, use of credit, starting your own business, insurance, investing, the need for retirement savings, and teaching kids about responsible use of resources.

Relationships Focuses on healthy relations between the sexes. Sample topics include marriage, couples, dating, singleness, online dating, marriage building, dating your spouse, mutual devotion, encouraging your spouse, dealing with stress, marital expectations and heartbreak.

Columns

All columns should range 600 to 1000 words and deal with a practical application of the topic. Columns tend toward, but are not limited to, "how-to" articles.

Beauty Any aspect of fashion, make up, hair, nails, spa treatments, bath necessities or personal grooming.

Health and Fitness Nutrition, (please note that we rarely print diets) exercise, healthy living, well being are all covered.

Food and Cooking Recipes, kitchen tips, exotic food, preparation tips, seasonal, time savers, plan ahead and freezer meals. For recipes nutritional information including Food Exchange values are appreciated, but not mandatory.

Advice The advice column is written by a professional, licensed therapist and does not accept submissions.

Specifics

All articles will be accompanied by the byline and the biography specified by the author. Author bios should be one to three lines of type (approximately 50 words). A contact email and / or URL will be included if provided and deemed appropriate. *Women Today* reserves the right to refuse URLs that link to sites that are in conflict with the mandate of the magazine. A photograph of the author is not necessary. Published clips are also optional. If all the requested information appears in your query a cover letter is not necessary.

Lead time is at least one month in advance of publication date (publication date is the last week of the previous month) for regular submissions, two months in advance for seasonal pieces.

Reviewing takes approximately four to six weeks – please do not inquire about your work before this time as it slows down the process for everyone. If we have not responded to you by the end of the fifth week, feel free to send an email enquiry. Please note that we are unable answer phone enquiries in regard to submissions.

Categories: Nonfiction—Beauty—Biograohy—Career—Christian Interest—Cooking—Family—Food/Drink—Health—Marriage—Money and Finances—Parenting—Physical Fitness—Relationships—Spiritual

CONTACT: **Claire Colvin, Editor**
Material: All
Campus Crusade for Christ
Women Today Magazine
Box 300 Stn A
Vancouver, BC V6C 2X3
E-mail: editor@womentodaymagazine.com (preferred)
Website: www.womentodaymagazine.com

Wonderful Ideas for Teaching, Learning, and Enjoying Mathematics!

1. Manuscripts should focus on a successful teaching idea, lesson, strategy, project, problem, or program for teaching, learning, and enjoying mathematics. While the readers of WI cover a wide range of ages and abilities, we generally publish ideas geared to grades 2 through 8. We prefer hands-on, classroom-tested ideas.

2. Manuscripts should be typed and not more than 900 words in length. Manuscripts submitted on 3.5" Macintosh format (Microsoft Word preferred) are welcome and appreciated. If sending a disk, please also send a printout of your article.

3. There are different types of articles that appear in *Wonderful Ideas*:

• Puzzlers: double-sided, problem-solving cards to be passed out directly to students. Featured every month.

• Kids' Corner: monthly "brain teaser" problems for students to solve. Each month, we include at least six problems and solutions.

• Wonderful Materials: occasional feature reviewing worthwhile math materials of many kinds, such as manipulatives, books, or games. In the past, reviews have included Fraction Bars and NCTM's Addenda Series.

• Make-It Math: occasional feature showcasing a puzzle or activity that requires students to make something. Past Make-It Math articles have included tessellations, Tangrams, and Pentominoes.

• Wonderful Ideas: general category for all other activities, games, and lessons.

4. Manuscripts should include the following information: topics involved, appropriate grade levels, materials needed, type of activity, description of the idea, and extensions or variations. If appropriate, include discussion questions, student responses, or samples of student work. Also, include author's name, address, phone number, current position, and school name.

5. Oftentimes in WI, text is accompanied by a reproducible page featuring worksheets, charts, game boards, problems or other graphics. We encourage you to include graphics with your article. Graphics must be black and white. Photographs are not acceptable. Examples of student work are welcome.

6. We reserve the right to edit and rewrite articles without prior author approval.

7. Payment is rendered upon publication. Rates of pay are modest and vary according to the material sent. Authors receive one copy of the newsletter in which the material is published.

8. Manuscripts are normally evaluated within ten weeks of receipt.

9. If you have an idea, but dislike writing, we will be happy to talk to you about your idea. If it matches our needs, we will write it up for publication and credit you for the idea. However, no payment is offered.

10. All submissions must be original and not previously published.

11. Samples of previously published articles are available upon request.

WI is always pleased to receive manuscripts and to talk to teachers about their ideas. Please call us with any questions you might have.

Note: Payment is not provided for students and/or teachers who send in names and solutions for Kids' Corner Problem Solvers. In addition, payment is not provided for contest entries that are published.

Multiple authors share the standard pay.

Categories: Nonfiction—Children—Education—Juvenile—Mathematics

CONTACT: Julie Wilder
Material: All
235 McCullough Hill Rd.
Mont Pellier VT 05602
Phone: 800-924-3327
Fax: 973-376-9386
E-mail: jwilder@math.tv

Woodall Publications, Corp.

Thank you for your interest in Woodall Publications, Corp. We publish seven regional titles, which are distributed at RV campgrounds, dealerships, tourism centers and Camping World stores across the United States.

Following is a list of our publications and the states in which they are distributed:

• *Woodall's Camperways* (Delaware, Maryland, New Jersey, Central and Northern New York, Pennsylvania and Virginia)

• *Woodall's Northeast Outdoors* (Connecticut, Maine, Massachusetts, New Hampshire, Central New York, Rhode Island and Vermont)

• *Woodall's Midwest RV Traveler* (Illinois, Minnesota, Indiana, Michigan, Ohio and Wisconsin)

• *Woodall's Southern RV* (Northern Florida, Georgia, North Carolina, South Carolina and Alabama)

• *Woodall's Florida RV Traveler* (Florida)

• *Woodall's Texas RV* (Texas)

• *Woodall's Southwest RV Traveler* (California, Nevada)

• *Woodall's Sunny Destinations* (annual snowbird publication)

Each Woodall publication is a specialty magazine for RV and camping enthusiasts and has a circulation of approx. 35,000 for a combined circulation of more than 200,000. Articles may appear in only one title, in multiple titles or in all titles at the discretion of the editorial staff. We suggest that interested contributors study recent issues before sending us queries.

You should hear from a member of our staff within four to six weeks for queries. We do not encourage unsolicited manuscript submissions. Our staff works considerably with freelancers, as well as on assignment. Manuscripts must be submitted on a 3.5 inch diskette (most word processing programs are acceptable) and typed on standard white paper. We accept queries via email at editor@woodallpub.com.

Payment is on acceptance for publication and ranges between $100 and $400. Woodall Publications Corp. buys first North American serial rights and electronic rights. The editors reserve the right to edit and even rewrite any article in order to make it suit the theme or space limitations of a specific issue. Major alterations will be discussed with the author when possible.

Travel Features

The easiest way to sell your work to Woodall's is to query us on an interesting and tightly focused RV travel story. Please do not send us travel logs of attraction lists. We need features that evoke the sights, sounds, smells and even tastes of specific travel destinations. We are looking for articles that have a unique approach, provide history and are relevant to RV travel or camping in the regions we serve. Articles should run about 1,200 words in length. The maximum length for travel features, unless cleared by the editorial staff, is 2,000 words.

All stories (excluding humor) should be accompanied by a comprehensive selection of clear, color transparencies with interesting captions and credits. Digital images are not accepted. Think cover shot when taking these photos and remember lighting is crucial to the overall effect. Focus your photography on scenic or panoramic views for the opening layout and points of interest, local color and activity shots for the carryover pages.

Campground Spotlights

Each issue highlights a campground in our "Stopping Points" department. These articles run between 800 and 1,000 words and should include information on location, facilities, recreation, local attractions and camping fees. Interviews with campers and campground personnel, as well as transparencies or photos of the grounds are essential. Articles submitted by campground personnel will not be considered. "Stopping Points" articles pay $150.

RV Humor

We accept humorous vignettes on some aspect of the RV lifestyle. Humor stories should be directly related to the RV experience. Maximum length for humor stories is 1,200 words; minimum, 800 words. Do not send photographs. Pay range is between $75 and $150.

Maintenance and Technical

Woodalls publishes a variety of technical stories. It is important that we maintain a balance of articles for both the novice and the veteran RVer.

• Maintenance: RV maintenance stories should be 1,100 to 1,500 words long. Color transparencies showing the maintenance procedure are essential.

• How-to: These features for handy RVers should be 1,100 to 1,500 words and include step-by-step instructions, diagrams and transparencies.

• RV Safety: Stories should be 800 to 1,200 words and be accompanied by a selection of transparencies.

• Gadgets & Gear: This department highlights RV accessories and maintenance products, as well as products that are pertinent to the RV lifestyle.

• Product Evaluations: Woodall's does not cover product evaluations.

Vehicle Tests

The editorial staff assigns Road Test articles. If you are interested in writing such a story, query the editorial staff and include pub-

lished clips of similar work. Evaluations must be fair and unbiased. Queries by any representative of the product's manufacturer or distributor will be rejected and all product claims must be independently substantiated. No writer is to contact a manufacturer or distributor as a representative of Woodall's Publication, without explicit permission from the editorial staff.

If you are assigned a story by the editorial staff, please keep in mind that you now represent the magazine. Be conscious that if you receive information or materials about the subject/area you are covering, you must still write an ethical, objective story.

Special Interest

Woodall's editorial focus also includes hobbies, crafts and other recreational activities that are popular among RV-ers. Special-interest features should be 800 to 1,500 words.

Columns

All Woodall's column are assigned. If you have a column idea, send us your idea along with several columns and we well consider them. Columns are a tough sale and we do not foresee a need to add any new columns to the magazine in the near future.

Poetry and Fiction

Woodall's does not publish poetry or fiction.

Photo Requirements

Travel features should be accompanied by a minimum of 10 color transparencies, all originals. All transparencies should be numbered with an accompanying caption sheet identifying each subject. Photos and slides supplied by someone other than the manuscript author should be clearly identified for photo credit. All photos and slides will be returned after publication when possible. Please include a self-address, stamped envelope for this purpose.

Revised 08/00

Categories: Nonfiction—Crafts/Hobbies—Hobbies—Humor—Outdoors—Recreation—Recreation Vehicles—Regional—Travel

CONTACT: Jennifer Detweiler, Managing Editor
Material: All
2575 Vista Del Mar Dr.
Ventura CA 93001
Phone: 805-667-4204
Fax: 805-667-4122
E-mail: editor@woodallpub.com
Website: www.woodallspub.com

Woodworking Magazine

Please refer to Popular Woodworking.

The Worcester Review

The Worcester County Poetry Association, Inc. was founded in 1971 and incorporated as a non-profit organization in 1972. Over the years it has sponsored readings by nationally and internationally-known writers, providing a forum for local poets and students, and celebrating the rich literary history of Central Massachusetts.

The Association prints and distributes original poetry broadsides and publishes *The Worcester Review*, an annual literary magazine.

SUBMISSIONS

The Worcester Review invites submission of previously unpublished poetry, fiction, literary articles, photography, and graphic art.

Guidelines are as follows:

POETRY: Submit 3-5 poems, typed on 8½"x11" paper. The author's name should appear in the upper left-hand corner of each page.

FICTION: Submit 4,000 words maximum on 8½"x11" paper. Author's name should appear in the upper left-hand corner of each page. Pages must be numbered in sequence.

LITERARY ARTICLES: Submit scholarly and critical articles with a New England connection (10 typed, double-spaced pages maxi-

mum using MLA guidelines) on 8½"x11" paper.

PHOTOGRAPHY: Submit black and white glossy prints (minimum size 5"x7").

GRAPHIC ART: Submit black and white graphic art on white paper (5"x7").

All submissions must be accompanied by a cover letter indicating author, materials submitted, and return address.

The Worcester Review reserves first publication rights for all submissions chosen for publication. Payment will be two copies upon publication plus a small honorarium.

Response time is six-12 months so multiple submissions are acceptable if you note that.

Categories: Fiction—Literature—Poetry

CONTACT: Rodger Martin, Editor
Material: All
6 Chatham St.
Worcester MA 01609
Phone: 508-797-4770
Website: www.geocities.com/paris/leftbank/6433

Workforce Diversity For Engineering and IT Professionals

Please refer to Equal Opportunity Publications, Inc.

Working Mother Magazine

Thank you for your interest in *Working Mother*. The magazine is looking for articles (700 to 1500 words in length) that help women in their task of juggling job, home, and family. We like tightly focused pieces that sensibly solve or illuminate a problem unique to our readers. Topics of particular interest include: time, home, and money management; family relationships; and job-related (work/family) issues. Pieces dealing with travel, food, beauty, and fashion are usually staff-written.

It's best to familiarize yourself with the tone and content of *Working Mother* before you query us. The most successful queries are those that are timely, appropriately researched, engagingly written, and tailored to *Working Mother* readers.

Manuscripts and queries should be typewritten and double-spaced. If possible, please enclose clips of your previously published materials. Materials will not be returned. We prefer to receive proposals for pieces rather than completed work. Then, if we find the subject suitable, we can discuss the best way to handle the material. Due to the large volume of unsolicited queries we receive, we are, unfortunately, unable to respond to every proposal. Therefore, if you don't hear from us within three months, please assume that we are not interested in that particular idea.

Categories: Nonfiction—Beauty—Careers—Children—Cooking—Diet/Nutrition—Family—Fashion—Food/Drink—Home—Humor—Marriage—Money & Finances—Parenting—Relationships—Travel—Women's Issues

CONTACT: Editorial Dept.
Material: All
260 Madison Ave., 3rd Floor
New York NY 10016
Phone: 212-351-6400
Fax: 212-351-6487
E-mail: jculbreth@womweb.com
Website: www.workingmother.com/writers.shtml

The World & I

The World & I is a multifaceted monthly publication that presents a broad range of thought-provoking reading in the areas of politics and current affairs, the arts, cutting-edge science, international cultures, the latest in literature, the most talked-about issues in the academe, and popular culture.

The World & I is intended primarily for a thoughtful, educated audience. We accept articles from journalists but also place special emphasis on scholarly contributions. It is our hope that the magazine will enable the best of contemporary thought, presented in accessible language, to reach a wider audience than would normally be possible through the academic journals appropriate to any given discipline.

Below is a list of guidelines pertaining to all writers submitting manuscripts to *The World & I*.

One-Page Proposal

• All initial inquiries should be a one-page typewritten proposal that outlines the idea and is addressed to the appropriate editor and/or section (see magazine masthead). Completed articles will be considered on speculation only. (Please do not send photographic images with uncommissioned articles or proposals or attach images to an unsolicited submission. We are not responsible for unsolicited images.) If your proposal is accepted, please adhere to the following guidelines.

Format

• Please submit the article on a 3.5" disk or E-mail to your editor or to: input@worldandimag.com. In addition, please send in a double-spaced manuscript.

• If you don't have access to a computer or E-mail, please send us a clean, double-spaced manuscript on white, standard 8.5" by 11" paper of normal weight (i.e., not "onion skin" paper).

• We do not accept manuscripts printed on dotmatrix printers lower than 24 pin or from typewriters that do not type legibly.

• Information for sidebars should not be included in the body of the text but should be in a separate manuscript, clearly identified.

• The manuscript should be headed by a short literary title and should include short subheadings at appropriate intervals (preferably every 1.5 pages). (Exception: The "Nature Walk" feature of the Natural Science section does not require subheadings.)

• Please include a bibliography or an additional reading list when appropriate.

• Footnotes, where needed, should follow Style A (also called the Humanities Style) in the Chicago Manual of Style (see section 17 of the 13th Edition or section 15 of the 14th Edition).

Style

• *The World & I* generally follows the Chicago Manual of Style (and Merriam Webster's Tenth New Collegiate Dictionary for spelling).

• The first reference to an organization or any other term with an abbreviation should give the full name followed by the abbreviation in parentheses. Subsequently, you may use the abbreviation alone.

• Because *The World & I* is circulated in many nations, the article should be clear from any reader's perspective (e.g. "the government" may need to read "the U.S. government" or "the French government").

• Be sure to write such that the article is comprehensible to people outside your area of expertise.

Content

• We encourage articles that make an original contribution to the subject area.

• The content should be representative of current trends in the subject area.

• The information should be accurate, and the scholarship and research must be sound and verifiable.

• The overall coverage of the topic should be adequate; be sure that no important points are omitted.

Miscellaneous

• Please double-check facts obtained from primary or secondary sources; do not rely on the research of others.

• Include your home address when signing the contract (if you are an American citizen, also include your Social Security number).

• For the length of the article or other particulars, please refer to the contract accompanying the assignment.

Photographs

• If you wish to submit photographs with your manuscript, please refer to the "Photographer's Guidelines."

Items to Accompany the Manuscript

• Writer's name as it should appear in the byline.

• Summary sentence (20-25 words maximum) to be used in the table of contents.

• An author's biography indicating qualifications—including academic background, published works, and any special life experience—for writing in the subject area.

Payment

• *The World & I* pays on a per-article basis that varies according to the length of the article, the complexity of special research required, and the experience of the author.

The World & I consists of eight colorful editorial sections .

Current Issues

Covers national and world affairs—through analysis, commentary, and special reports—and presents foreign perspectives on timely issues through its "World Views" and "Global Forum" subsections.

The Arts

Presents current and lasting achievements in art, poetry, music, dance, film, design, architecture, theater, and more. Includes "Gallery," a 10-page color feature of the work of a particular artist.

Natural Science

Illuminates the world of science from its historical underpinnings to the latest cutting-edge discoveries.

Life

Focuses on the enrichment of our daily lives by highlighting personalities, food, travel, health, sports, humor, and more.

Book World

Excerpts recent releases, with insightful commentary, and reviews important new fiction and nonfiction, including some foreign-language titles.

Culture

Surveys the world through a historical and an anthropological perspective. Includes "Patterns," a 10-page photographic study of a chosen culture.

Currents in Modern Thought

Presents diverse points of view on education, philosophy, history, political science, sociology, and economics by leading authorities throughout the world.

Special Section

Originally conceived as an occasional section to treat important subjects from a number of perspectives, it includes our 16-month, ongoing "Millennial Moments" series surveying the achievements of the past 1,000 years.

Categories: Nonfiction—Arts—Book Reviews—Culture—Current Affairs—Economics— Education—Lifestyle—Literature—Philosophy—Politics—Science

CONTACT: Submissiosn Editor
Material: All
The Washington Times Corporation
3600 New York Ave., NE
Washington, DC 20002
Phone: 202-635-4000
Fax: 202-269-9353
E-mail: editor@worldandimag.com
Website: www.worldandimag.com

Remember: Editors change jobs and publishers change addresses. It is wise to invest in a phone call for the current information before submitting.

World War II

Please refer to PRIMEDIA History Group

The Writer

The Writer is dedicated to helping and inspiring professional and aspiring writers. We do this by producing a magazine that provides information, instruction and motivation. We hope to foster the idea of a writers' community in which writers share their experiences, expertise, struggles, successes and suggestions on our pages.

About 80 percent of our articles are by freelance writers. The best way to get an assignment is to send a query letter with clips of previously published work. It helps to include the lead and an outline of the proposed article. We do not accept fiction or poetry.

Feature articles run 1,600-3,000 words, including how-to articles that address issues of interest to writers in the areas of fiction, nonfiction, poetry, and children's and young-adult literature. Recent articles include: "The role of fact in fiction," "Tips for writing a humorous mystery," "Mining family gold for fiction," "What makes a good short story?," "In whose voice should you write?," "Is it good enough for children?," "Adventures in travel writing" and "Writing issue-oriented articles."

We encourage a roundup approach for articles on market or publishing trends, such as the changing youth market, the growing interest in inspirational writing, the best of the small presses, how to get your manuscript past the first reading, what small press editors want, how to find an agent. In addition, we run profiles of writers who have a unique story to tell—a first-time author, an unusual background, a unique approach to marketing, someone who breaks new ground in style or content.

Columns and departments run 800 to 1,200 words. Our columns and departments include:

• Bottom line: How-to articles on the business of writing. Recent articles include: Organizing your accounts for taxes, balancing your assignments, tools that help writers make the most of their time.

• Ethics: Ethical questions related to writing or freelance business.

• Market focus: Reports on specific market areas such as trade journals, alumni magazines, parenting, sports and travel.

• Net//working: The Internet and e-publishing.

• Off the cuff: Personal essay on the writing life.

• Poet to poet: Specific aspects of writing poetry, such as imagery, revision or poetic forms. Contributors are asked to include hands-on exercises for readers.

• Syntax: Language and grammar usage. Should be light but informative.

• WriteStuff: Reviews of books and other products of interest to writers.

• Breakthrough: Short, formatted first-person articles about a writer's experience in "breaking through" to publication (with an article, book, etc.).

• Get started: Short articles specifically angled toward instructing the beginning writer. Most of these are assigned by an editor but queries are accepted.

Basics

All queries should be submitted in writing. Include a SASE for a response and the return of materials. We do not take queries by telephone but we do accept electronic queries. You may electronically e-mail your submission to queries@writermag.com. Query for features about six months in advance; columns and departments, four months.

Assignments are acknowledged by a contract. Generally, we buy first rights. Payment varies, depending on length and complexity of the material covered. In general, our rates for articles range from $50 for book reviews to $100 to $400 for columns and $300 to $500 for features, depending on length, complexity and the research required. We are also looking for writing-related cartoons ($50) and photos ($50 to $100). Payment is made on acceptance. We pay only those expenses agreed upon in advance.

We prefer articles to be submitted electronically as a Word attachment or on a Mac disk. Otherwise, send a double-spaced printed manuscript (and a SASE, if you want it returned). Be sure to include your name, address, phone number, e-mail address and a list of contacts used for the article, along with their phone numbers. To help us fact-check, we ask that you include any printed background materials you used for the piece. Photo suggestions are appreciated. Be sure your name appears on each page of the manuscript. Please do not send original manuscripts, artwork or slides, as we cannot be responsible for their return. You may e-mail your submission to queries@writermag.com.

Categories: Fiction—Nonfiction—Poetry—Children's and Young Adult Literature—Writing

CONTACT: Submissions Editor
Material: All
21027 Crossroads Circle
PO Box 1612
Waukesha WI 53187-1612
Phone: 262-796-8776 (No queries by phone)
E-mail: queries@writermag.com
Website: www.writermag.com

The Writer Gazette

The Writer Gazette is a writer's resource site that provides tips, techniques, resources, articles, job postings, and more to help induce, improve, and promote your writing career. We've also got online Writer Statistics, Freebies for Writers, and more!

We provide a free weekly newsletter that is sent out every Thursday and includes the following:

• Articles and Interviews
• Courses for Writers
• Resources for Writers
• Freebies for Writers
• Writer-Related Classified Ads
• Call for Submissions Listings
• Freelance Job Listings
• Contest Listings for Writers
• Books and Software for Writers...and more!

Submission Guidelines

Writer Gazette welcomes submissions from experienced and/or new writers. *We look for:*

• Informative articles pertaining to the craft of writing
• Tips & Techniques on the craft of writing
• Book Reviews on the craft of writing
• Product Reviews (such as writing programs, etc.)
• Course Reviews (Such as writers conferences, classes, etc.)

We are not looking for personal experience stories at this time. We want how-to or step-by-step, informative articles that will teach writers how to enhance and increase their writing skills. Articles are to be between 300-1,500 words. At this time we can offer you a full byline, bio, photo, two links to the website(s) of your choice, and a contact email address (optional).

All stories must be true and about you or someone you know. Reprints are acceptable but please tell us when and where your story was printed.

Submissions must be between 750-1,500 words. Any submissions that do not meet the word count requirement will be deleted immediately.

Please include the following with your submission:

• your full name (or pen name—please specify)
• address
• email address

R-U

- phone number
- story title
- word count
- your bio
- the book title you are submitting to

Send your submissions to: *writersguide@yahoo.com*.

Please make the subject line match the book title that you are submitting to. All submissions must be pasted into the body of your email—absolutely no attachments. E-mails with attachments will be immediately deleted.

Please note: it may take up to 2-3 months for us to respond to your submission. Thank you for your patience with us as we review submissions. There is no deadline to submit for these books at this time.

Payment Upon Acceptance:

At this time we can pay $10 (Canadian) per submission with full bio and a free copy of the book. It is our desire to raise the payment amount in the future.

Rights:

We require one time rights and editing rights (if needed). You retain all copyrights. Upon acceptance of your submission, we will send you an agreement form. This form will include the final proof of your submission and must be signed and returned in order for your submission to be published in our series. Upon acceptance of your submission, you hereby grant Topzone Publishing the right to publish and reproduce your submission in book form or any other media form that may result from publication worldwide.

Disclaimer:

We have the right to refuse any and all submissions that we believe will not fit with the theme of our books.

About Us:

Krista Barrett and Michelle Froese are the running force behind this new book series. Books will be published through Topzone Publishing and will be available in electronic format and POD.

Our Mission for this book series:

- To provide encouragement and inspiration to writers worldwide.
- To provide a new market for writers worldwide.

Special Call for Submissions:

Writer Gazette is currently seeking 750-1500 word submissions for the following upcoming writing inspiration books: Rejection Lessons, Writer Calamities, and Writer Inspiration. Payment upon acceptance. Online guidelines: http://www.writer gazette.com/insidewritersguide.shtml

Categories: Nonfiction—Computers—Interview—Writing

CONTACT: Submissions Editor
Material: All
E-mail: writersguide@yahoo.com
Website: www.writergazette.com/insidewritersguide.shtml

Writer's Digest

General Focus

Writer's Digest is a monthly handbook for writers who want to get more out of their writing. That means every word we publish must inform, instruct or inspire the reader. Our readers want specific ideas and tips that will help them succeed, whether success means getting into print, finding personal fulfillment through writing or building and maintaining a thriving freelance career.

Our style is informal and personal. We try to speak with the voice of a compassionate colleague, a friend as well as a teacher. But that doesn't mean we shy away from explaining the difficulties of getting published today. To the contrary, keeping informed on industry trends is essential to our readers' success, so it's essential for our editorial to address timely issues. WD is infused with a belief in anyone's potential to succeed as a writer. Our goal is to provide our readers with the inspiration, how-to instruction and insider information to fulfill their writing potential.

Our Readership

You can best understand our philosophy by being intimately familiar with *Writer's Digest*. Reading several issues of the magazine will help you understand the types and tone of the articles we publish.

We are a monthly publication founded in 1920 with a circulation of more than 180,000. Our readers are of all ages and are scattered throughout the US, Canada and several other countries. Each year we buy about 60 major articles and about 75 shorter items. Be aware that at least one-third of those articles are assigned by staff, and seldom result from unsolicited queries.

To obtain sample issues of *Writer's Digest*, send $5.25 per copy to Lyn Menke, *Writer's Digest*, 4700 E. Galbraith Road, Cincinnati, Ohio 45236. You also may purchase copies via our Web site, www.writersdigest.com. A helpful index of each year's contents is published in the December issue. You can also turn to our Web site for issue previews and the current table of contents.

How to Submit

Freelance submissions are accepted for features and Markets. For features, *Writer's Digest* editors prefer queries over unsolicited manuscripts. Queries allow us to review your article ideas and to suggest how to tailor them for our audience before you begin writing. Queries also save you time and energy should we reject your idea.

Queries should include a thorough outline that introduces your article proposal and highlights each of the points you intend to make. Your query should discuss how the article will benefit our readers, why the topic is timely today and why you are the appropriate writer to discuss the topic.

Although we welcome the work of new writers, we respect success and believe the selling writer can instruct our reader better and establish more credibility. Make sure to include your publishing credentials related to your topic with your submission. We like to see published clips. For writers with whom we haven't previously worked, we prefer fully developed queries sent by mail with clips. Writers who have been published in the magazine may contact their previous assigning editor via e-mail.

Please submit only one query at a time and allow us 6-8 weeks to review your proposal. If we like your proposal, we may either assign the article to you or ask to see a more detailed query before we make a final decision. Each submission must include your name, address, daytime telephone number and e-mail address. Please wait for a response before sending another submission.

All submissions must include SASE—self-addressed, stamped envelope. We are not responsible for, and will not respond to, queries and manuscripts not accompanied by SASE—unless an e-mail address is included. If an unsolicited query or manuscript is rejected and an e-mail address is included, a rejection note will be sent via e-mail and the submission will be destroyed. If you don't enclose SASE or an e-mail address and we aren't interested in your query, it will be destroyed without acknowledgment; calls to check on the status of such queries will not be returned. E-mail queries should be addressed to wdsubmissions@fwpubs.com; again, give us 6-8 weeks to review your proposal and respond.

All accepted freelance articles must be submitted in electronic form, either by e-mail or on disk, in text-only or Microsoft Word 6.0.

Finally, we expect writers to double-check all facts included in their stories and to submit documentation to support the information included in their stories.

Submission Don'ts

If you want us to read your query—and take it seriously—then here are a few pointers to keep in mind:

We do not accept queries made over the phone or via fax.

We do not accept unsolicited illustrations, artwork, cartoons or photos.

We do not use poetry, fiction or scripts; we do not buy newspaper clippings and we handle book and software reviews in-house.

We do not buy reprints of articles previously published in other writing magazines.

We do not accept unsolicited proposals for columns.

We do not accept simultaneous submissions.

We do not accept freelance submissions for the Calendar, Poetry, Fiction, Nonfiction, Business, Scripts, Writing for Kids, E-Publishing, Zine Scene, Freelance Success, Global Writing, Tools of the Trade, Careers, Trademarks, Literary Trails and Your Assignment columns and departments; WD and First Success interviews; and Writing Clinic critiques. For information on how to submit a manuscript for a Writing Clinic critique, please go to the end of these guidelines.

Payment and General Terms

For manuscripts, we pay 30-50 cents per word, on acceptance, for first world rights for one-time use and non-commercial electronic use. Should we want to reprint anything we've purchased from you, in other than electronic format, we'll pay you 25% of the original purchase price for each use. Contributor copies are sent to writers and artists whose work appears in that issue.

Tone

In general, don't shy away from the word I in your articles. The first-person perspective is important to establishing your credibility. But don't overdo it. We want instructive articles, not articles based solely on your own writing experience (what we call "And then I wrote..." articles). Round out your experiences with those of other writers and with information from editors, when appropriate.

We use a friendly, informal—but not lackadaisical or cutesy—style. We demand lively writing. Use anecdotes, examples, samples and quotes to strengthen the message of the article. Also consider using sidebars and subheads in your writing. Look at the magazine for clues on how to do this effectively.

WHAT WE WANT—LONG STUFF
How-To Articles

How-to articles are our mainstay: How to write better, enjoy your writing life more, market successfully, recycle and resell ideas, maintain records and more. These articles present a common problem or goal, offer the appropriate solution, and give an example of how that solution has worked. Articles generally run 800-1,200 words. Pieces that can cover a topic completely in 500 words or fewer are of particular interest to us. Actual length will be discussed when the article is assigned.

In general, we're looking for timely articles, and we work on a five-month lead time. That's why, if you send us a proposal for a topic that was just covered on Oprah, it's too late.

Topics for features vary widely. Categories for which we seek material include writing inspiration and technique, trends in publishing, and how to write for specific genres. We're also interested in marketing opportunities and money-making ideas; tools, equipment and supplies; and marketing mechanics.

Writing Technique Articles

These pieces highlight an often misunderstood or poorly utilized writing method and detail how to use it precisely, appropriately and successfully. Examples include how to write an effective lead, how to use dialogue to establish character, how to brighten your prose or how to use suspense effectively.

Articles may cover fiction, nonfiction, poetry or script writing techniques, but must be accessible to all writers and offer advice that can be applied directly or indirectly to all forms of writing. Writers should have a proven track record of publication in the area about which they are writing. How a particular piece is structured depends on the complexity of the subject, but every piece will need to:

• Define the technique and its importance.

• Outline how to use the technique. The best explanations break the technique down into distinct parts and deal with each part individually. When appropriate, use a step-by-step explanation.

• Give recent examples of its usage. Be in touch with current literature relevant to your topic and apply it. Using examples is a vital part of your article; give us more than you think necessary—and then add two more. Illustrate every point with examples—either from your own writing or from well-known works. On major points, readers can benefit from "right" and "wrong" or "before" and "after" examples, showing writing before the technique is applied or when it is used inappropriately, followed by the corrected version.

• If appropriate, give readers tips on incorporating the technique into their writing. For example, an article on using anecdotes might give tips on how to collect anecdotes to use.

As with all how-to articles, instruction is the key to making the article work. Analyze your own writing to determine what gives it power, what makes it successful. Then give our readers a thorough guide to using that technique powerfully and successfully, too.

WHAT WE WANT—SHORT STUFF
Genre and Market Reports

These pieces are very timely. Market reports are generally 750 words, highlight general article or book trends and offer instruction on how any writer might break into a particular market. Genre reports detail what's changing or hot in fantasy, mystery or romance and keep writers up-to-date on how to write and sell effectively to their genre market. An example is the growth in romance mini-series books.

You'll want to cover several essential elements in genre and market reports. This isn't a formula—only a checklist. Remember, anecdotes, specific examples and quotes are important here, too. Establish the market. It must be current and have a growing need for manuscripts. Quote editors. Emphasize specific sales and payments, either your own or other writers'.

Describe the market. Detail the differences from and similarities to other markets and types of writing. Give an idea of the people who read these types of articles so readers will know if this is a market that appeals to them.

Explain how to find ideas for the market. What kinds of topics and treatments does the market use most? Point out how writers can generate ideas that are salable. Provide tips on matching ideas to publications.

Explain how to write for the market. Detail the process of turning ideas into salable stories. What are the special requirements of writing for this market or writing this type of article or book? Point out common pitfalls and how to avoid them.

Chronicle

Writer's Digest accepts submissions to the online-only monthly contest, Chronicle. Read the complete rules found at www.writersdigest.com/contests/your_chronicle_display.asp before submitting. Chronicle submissions should be personal essays on writing challenges and triumphs. Entries must be no more than 500 words, including title and byline, and may not have appeared elsewhere in print or online. Submissions will be accepted until the 25th of each month. Each month the winning entry will be posted for 30 days beginning the business day closest to the 5th of the following month. All winners will be contacted in advance to sign a contract giving F&W Publications first world electronic rights and non-exclusive electronic archiving rights. More than one entry by the same author may be entered for the same month and essays may be re-entered in different months. Send entries only via e-mail to wdsubmissions@fwpubs.com with Chronicle-Month as the subject line. Paste the entry directly into the e-mail message (no attachments) and include your name, e-mail address, and daytime phone number at the end so we may contact you if your essay is selected. All winners receive $100.

Writing Clinic

Each month, *Writer's Digest* offers an expert critique of an unpublished manuscript or poem. If you have a manuscript you'd like to submit, please print a copy of our release agreement, available at our Web site (www.writersdigest.com) and mail it along with your work to Writing Clinic, *Writer's Digest*, 4700 E. Galbraith Road, Cincinnati, OH 45236. Alternatively, send SASE requesting a release to our address before submitting your manuscript. Manuscripts are not accepted by e-mail or by fax; any manuscript submitted without a signed release will be destroyed. All critiqued manuscripts also appear in our online discussion forum for moderated public critique; we also post additional manuscripts each month for online critique that do not appear in the magazine. The writer of the work being critiqued receives no payment.

R-U

Categories: Writing

CONTACT: Kate Dumont, Exec. Editor
Material: All
4700 E. Galbraith Rd.
Cincinnati OH 45236
Phone: 513-531-2690, ext. 1483
E-mail: wdsubmissions@fwpubs.com
Website: www.writersdigest.com

Writer's Guidelines & News

We consider ourselves "The Friend of the Writer" and so, as a friend, we are very flexible in our guideline policy. We will consider anything that is well-written and informative with a writing slant. However, short interview articles with photos on authors and news items about writers or the writing profession have the best chance of acceptance here. The same is true for short interview articles with photos about small press publishers. Other categories include: general interest, historical articles on writers, how-to, profile pieces, personal experience, my first sale, opinion, motivational, humor, desktop publishing news and related fillers are needed. Length: 750-1000 words. pay ranges from $5 to $50 per article. (*Photos or artwork accompanying submissions has the best chance of acceptance.) Payment is upon publication. Buys First North American Serial Rights. Poetry, short pieces, opinions, news items, fillers receive payment in copies.

Submissions for THE YOUNG WRITER (ages 8-18) prose, poetry and/or artwork receive $5-10, plus copy. Send complete manuscript. No E-mail or fax submissions at this time. Must include proper SASE for a reply.

FICTION pieces should be no more than 2,000 words and have a writing slant. Pays $15, plus copy.

As is true with any market, it is best to study a copy of WG&N first. A sample copy (56+ pages, w/glossy cover) is $5; one year subscription, $19.95, or 2 years at $29.95. Make checks payable to INDEPENDENT PUBLISHING COMPANY.

Thanks, Ned

Categories: Fiction—Nonfiction—General Interest—Poetry—Writing—How-to

CONTACT: E.P. "Ned" Burke, Editor
Material: All
PO Box 18566
Sarasota FL 34276
Phone: 941-924-3201
Fax: 921-925-4468
E-mail: WritersGN@aol.com
Website: www.fiber-net.com

Writers' Journal
The Complete Writer's Magazine

ABOUT US

Writers' Journal (originally named "The Inkling") was founded in 1980 as a four-page newsletter for writers. Through a period of several owners, it has been transformed into a full-fledged, professional writers' journal. We are a bi-monthly publication, with a circulation of around 26,000 aspiring writers whose love of writing has prompted them to take the next step—attempting to become published.

We try to give such writers the tools and information necessary to get their work in shape for publication. Articles are geared to those at all levels of experience, from beginning writers to those who are already professionals. We cover techniques for improving writing style—punctuation, grammar, structure, vocabulary, etc.—as well as helpful advice on how to develop various types of writing, in both fiction and nonfiction categories.

We offer writers guidance in selling and publishing their work and advice on desktop publishing, E-publishing, and publishing-on-demand. Our columnists deal with various creative forms, such as photography, poetry, and screenwriting.

Our readers also get the chance to put into practice what they learn by entering our short story, poetry and photography contests. We publish the winners of these contests.

The scope of Writers' Journal information makes the magazine a valuable tool for all types of writers, freelancers, screenwriter, editors, teachers and poets.

GUIDELINES

Although most of the columns in the *Writers' Journal* are staff written, articles from freelance writers are always welcome. Send either complete manuscripts or query with clips. Several feature articles, running 1200-2200 words, are published in each issue. Some of the topics we are looking for include:

• *The Business Side of Writing:* Tips, techniques, record keeping tactics on how to increase writing production, taxes, financial matters.

• *Self/Independent Publishing:* Practical advice on all aspects of independent publishing. Particularly wanted are success stories that impart solid information on book design and production, distribution costs, marketing, profits, etc.

• *Skills of Writing:* The how-to of writing style, punctuation, sentence structure, story composition, interviewing, and research.

• *Income Venues:* Unique and unusual income-producing methods. Past articles include: Juvenile craft writing, ghostwriting, church/business histories, technical manual writing, city web site writing, and specialty dictionaries.

• *Other Nonfiction Topics:* Photography, travel writing, screenwriting, technical writing, newspaper, corporate/business writing.

• *Fiction:* Although we publish staff-written articles on writing fiction, we welcome articles on the subject, covering technique, plotting, marketing, character development, or any of the other aspects of writing fiction. We do not publish fiction except for the winning entries of our various contests.

• *Poetry:* This is adequately covered by the *Writers' Journal*'s poetry editor, although an authoritative "guest editorial" may be considered.

• *Poetry Submissions:* The *Writers' Journal* buys about 25 poems a year, which we use for fillers. We welcome light verse, preferably about writing. Short, lively, exciting, witty and imaginatively written poems will stand a better chance of acceptance than "run-of-the-mill" pieces. We do not respond to submissions without a SASE. Author will be notified by mail if a poem is accepted. Unpublished poems only. (No vulgarity or pornographically explicit pieces considered.) Maximum length—10 lines. All other poetry submissions must follow poetry contest guidelines available with SASE or see our web site.

• *Style and Focus:* We want to see highly informative articles of an advisory nature that feature a positive and practical approach to the topic being covered, with a narrow focus, in a tightly written style, and with good use of basic elements of article construction. No dull writing, please. Appropriate touches of humor are always appreciated.

Mail submissions with SASE for editor's response, however, manuscripts will not be returned. Submissions may also be emailed—Text only. For overseas contributors, this option is welcomed.

Pay Rates and Rights:

• *Articles and Columns:* Writers' Journal pays on a variable scale, depending on budget. We ask for one-time rights. We print previously unpublished work only.

• *Poetry:* $5.00 per poem, for one-time rights.

• *Contest:* Writers' Journal sponsors a short story contest, a travel article contest, a romance contest, two photo contests and three poetry contests each year. Writers' Journal pays cash for first, second and third place. These and selected honorable mentions are published. All winners will be kept for possible future publication. Send SASE for current contest guidelines or see our web site.

A sample issue of the *Writers' Journal* is available for $5.00. Annual subscription is $19.97. Canada—$34.97. Europe—$49.97. Others—$54.97.

Categories: Nonfiction—Writing

CONTACT: Leon Ogroske, Editor
Material: All
Val-Tech Media
PO Box 394
Perham MN 56573
Phone: 218-346-7921
Fax: 218-346-7924
E-mail: writersjournal@lakesplus.com
Website: www.writersjournal.com

Yachting

Overview

Yachting is edited for experienced, affluent boat owners—power and sail—who don't have the time or the inclination to read sub-standard stories. They love carefully crafted stories about places they've never been or a different spin on places they have, meticulously reported pieces on issues that affect their yachting lives, personal accounts of yachting experiences from which they can learn, engaging profiles of people who share their passion for boats, insightful essays that evoke the history and traditions of the sport and compelling photographs of others enjoying the game as much as they do.

They love to know what to buy and how things work. They love to be surprised. They don't mind getting their hands dirty or saving a buck here and there, but they're not interested in learning how to make a masthead light out of a mayonnaise jar.

If you love what they love and can communicate like a pro (that means meeting deadlines, writing tight, being obsessively accurate and never misspelling a proper name), we'd love to hear from you. We prefer written queries. Include a self-addressed, stamped envelope.

A few pointers: Don't bother sending us anything about sailboarding or hydroplane racing. Translation: Read the magazine. We have a great desire for good powerboat stories and we kill for great first-person stuff, especially when our readers can learn something from it. Don't bother us with queries about sailboat racing. We have the scene covered. Send your fiction and poetry to *The New Yorker*.

If you have an idea you want to pitch to us, make sure it is focused and well-evolved. For instance, don't send us a query for a piece on "Cruising the Virgin Islands." Propose a lead. Make us love it. Share your enthusiasm. It wouldn't hurt to send some clips with your query.

Boat reviews and technical articles on navigation, electronics, engines, materials, etc., are mostly written by experts we know. However, if you have expertise in these areas, we'd be happy to review a resume and sample manuscript—submitted on speculation.

Payments

Generally, we pay $300-$500 for short pieces (columns) and $750-$1000 or more for longer stories (features).

Photos

Most photographs in *Yachting* are shot on assignment by professionals we know. However, we would be happy to review your portfolio. We can't be responsible for unsolicited material.

For photos we pay:
- Cover: $500
- Four-color inside $350/page; $200 1/2 page;
- Black and white $75 for spot art. Up to $250 for full page (rarely used).

For assignments we pay $450 a day against page rate (whichever is greater). In most cases a cap is agreed upon beforehand. We pay all reasonable expenses (to be discussed beforehand).

Whom to query:

Art Director: Rana Bernhardt
Executive Editor: Kim Kavin

If You Have an Assignment From Us

This is a guide written for the *Yachting* contributor or freelancer who has received an assignment from the magazine or is sending in an article on spec. All queries and copy submissions should follow these forms unless negotiated with the editor in charge beforehand.

Columns

These should contribute much toward defining the personality and authority of the magazine. They should inform, entertain and stimulate the reader to think beyond the surface of an issue, product, event, personality or how-to concept.

Whenever possible, columns should build upon, or launch from a news event, new product or emerging trend. They should have a narrow subject focus—not be "a column about sails" or "a column about depth sounders"—and should reveal the unique perspective of the writer.

They should be meticulously factual and the writer should indicate somewhere in the text that his point of view is based on experience or interviews with other experts in the field.

While *Yachting* hires columnists and contributors more for their expertise in a given field, we expect copy that is tight and reasonably polished. Word count is important. If we ask for 350 words, we expect 350, not 600.

The editing process often involves queries to authors and may sometimes include requests for rewrites. We may send unsatisfactory material back to the author for rewrites, more than once if necessary.

Columnists and contributors are expected to be our eyes and ears in the field. We expect them to provide briefs each month and keep us informed on developments in the field.

Features

Features are the heart of the magazine. They generally contain the greatest amount of space for copy and visual elements.

They should follow the classic feature model: they should have a beginning, preferably an anecdote involving someone using a boat or equipment that illuminates the "theme" or lead of the story which follows close behind; a middle that contains evidence to back up the lead; and an end that ties back into the lead.

Because we are a four-color magazine and visually driven, writers should work to obtain the best possible photos to accompany the story. Whenever possible, photos should illustrate the "theme" of the story, not just be a running shot of the boat and a shot of the interior. As with columns, writers should expect queries from editors and editors may request rewrites.

Categories: Boating

CONTACT: Refer to Guidelines
18 Marshall St., Ste. 114
Norwalk CT 06854
Phone: 203-299-5900
Fax: 203-299-5901
E-mail: editor@yachtingnet.com
Website: www.yachtingnet.com

The Yalobusha Review

The Yalobusha Review, founded in 1995, is an annual journal of fiction, poetry, creative non-fiction, and black-and-white artwork and photography.

We are open to submissions from students, writers in the Oxford community, the region, and across the country. Its sixth issue in 2002 featured a new story from Dan Chaon, an interview with Tom Franklin, and an introductory essay from Barry Hannah. It is published in April of each year by the University of Mississippi with an approximate distribution of 500 copies.

Single issue copies are available for $10.00 including postage.

Multiple-year subscriptions are available for $8.00 per year.

Send checks made payable to The Yalobusha Review to the address below.

Submission Guidelines:

We are looking for primarily short prose (up to 25 pages), poetry, and black-and-white artwork.

There is no preferred or restricted subject matter or theme; we just want work.

Submit a maximum of one piece of prose, 10 poems, or 5 pieces of 8"x10" artwork.

Submit only previously unpublished work.

We do not accept simultaneous submissions.

We pay two contributor's copies.

Cover letters and SASE are required.

Submit by regular mail only.

No submissions will be returned.

Categories: Fiction—Nonfiction—Literature—Poetry—Writing

CONTACT: Non-fiction Editor
Material: Non-fiction
CONTACT: Fiction Editor
Material: Fiction
CONTACT: Poetry Editor
Material: Poetry
CONTACT: Art Editor
Material: Art
The University of Mississippi
PO Box 1848
University MS 38677-0186
Phone: 601-232-7103
E-mail: yalobush@olemiss.edu (inquiries only)
Website: www.olemiss.edu/depts/english/pubs/
yalobusha_review.html

Yankee
The Magazine of New England Living

Guidelines for Writers and Photographers

It is to your advantage to read several current issues of *Yankee* before sending us a query or a manuscript. We prefer to receive queries and manuscripts by U.S. mail, with SASE. Manuscripts will not be returned without an SASE.

The editors are always open to receiving story ideas and reviewing short nonfiction manuscripts from established writers. Freelancers are welcome to query us on ideas; please send recent clips of your published work. Our staff and well-established freelancers who have worked with us before write most of our stories and articles, and provide photography and art.

We are no longer accepting submissions for fiction, poetry, cartoons, or book reviews. We do not use fillers or serial articles/stories.

New England Today: Every issue includes 6 pages of very short, factual, and sometimes humorous stories up front. Our editors write these stories but occasionally accept an item from freelance writers.

Submissions should be no longer than 400 words, and in most cases much shorter. We enjoy the occasional submission in the form of charts or graphs.

Home, Food, and Garden including House for Sale: Staff-written or assigned to established writers who have worked with us. If you would like us to consider writing about your house, send a letter describing the house, with the selling price and including photocopies of photographs, if available, to House for Sale at the address above.

Feature Articles: This is the most difficult kind of story for a first-timer to sell to us, but it is not without precedent. Study the magazine and query us first. Payment based on content and length. Send to Editorial.

Photography and Art: Assigned to experienced professionals. If you would like to work with us, show us a portfolio of your best work. We prefer 35 mm 2-1/4" or 4"x5" color transparencies.

Before sending work, please contact Leonard Loria, Art Director, at extension 115.

Travel: We may purchase short stories about favorite inns, restaurants, tourist attractions, historical sites, or an area of natural beauty in New England. Articles should not exceed 500 words, and you should query us first. Send query to Travel Editor.

Rights, deadlines, etc.: We buy all rights and pay upon acceptance by an editor. If a story relates to a holiday or season (e.g., Christmas, baseball season), ideas or manuscripts should be submitted one year earlier, so that there is time to get seasonal photographs. Our normal editorial deadline is 6 months prior to publication.

Payments: Upon acceptance of the editor, based on the length of the piece.

A self-addressed envelope with appropriate postage must accompany unsolicited manuscripts, art, or photos. We do not assume responsibility for the return of unsolicited material, so if it is priceless or irreplaceable, don't send it! It is always a good idea to query us first and send clips of previous work. Allow at least 8 weeks for reply or return of manuscripts.

E-mail note: Please always include at least your name and phone number. We have found that our server cannot always locate your sender address.

"Dear Yankee": Letters to the editor can be e-mailed to dearyank@yankeepub.com (please include your name, address, and phone number).

Categories: Nonfiction—Cooking—Food/Drink—Gardening—General Interest—Interview—Travel—Essay—Personal Experience—Home

CONTACT: Micheal Carlton, Editor
Material: Manuscripts
CONTACT: Mel Allen, Exec. Travel Editor
Material: Travel
CONTACT: Amy Traverso, Food Editor
Material: Food
Yankee Publishing Inc.
PO Box 520
1121 Main St.
Dublin NH 03444-0520
Phone: 603-563-8118, ext. 157
Fax: 603-563-8252
E-mail: queries@yankeepub.com
Website: www.yankeemagazine.com
www.almanac.com

Yoga Journal

Yoga Journal covers the practice and philosophy of yoga. We define yoga broadly to encompass practices that aspire to union or communion with some higher power, greater truth, or deeper source of wisdom, as well as practices that tend to increase harmony of body, mind, and spirit.

In particular we welcome articles on the following themes:

1. Leaders, spokespersons, and visionaries in the yoga community
2. The practice of hatha yoga
3. Applications of yoga to everyday life (e.g., relationships, social issues, livelihood, etc.)
4. Hatha yoga anatomy and kinesiology and therapeutic yoga
5. Nutrition and diet, cooking, and natural skin and body care.

We encourage a well-written query letter outlining your subject and describing its appeal. Query before submitting an article, and please include a SASE (self-addressed, stamped envelope).

We encourage you to read an issue of *Yoga Journal* carefully before submitting a query. Please keep in mind our editorial department's three E's: Articles should be enlightening, educational, and entertaining. Please avoid New Age jargon and in-house buzz-words as much as possible. Features run approximately 3,000 to 5,000 words. Departments run 1,000 to 2,500 words. Centering runs about 750 words. We do not print unsolicited poetry or cartoons. We consider everything except a direct assignment to be submitted on a speculative basis. When an article has been assigned, we will send you a contract specifying terms, kill fee, and deadline.

Remember to indicate the availability of photos or artwork in your query letter or with your article. (Pertinent, high quality photos or illustrations can greatly enhance an article's desirability.)

Payment varies, depending on length, depth of research, etc. We pay within 90 days of final acceptance: $800 to $2000 for features, $400 to $800 for departments, $25 to $100 for Om Page and Well-Being, and $200 to $250 for book reviews.

All manuscripts should be typed, double spaced, and clean. Include your name, address, phone number, and word count on the title page, and your name and page number on each subsequent page. Also include a concise, two-sentence tagline identifying yourself to our readers. Always keep a copy of your work, and include a SASE with your submission if you want it returned.

If possible, please also send your work on a computer floppy disc. We strongly prefer submissions in Microsoft Word 5.1 for Macintosh. However, we may also be able to translate files from the following applications: (for Mac) ClarisWorks, FrameMaker, MacWrite, Macwrite II, MacWrite Pro, Nisus, Microsoft Works, RTF; Text, WordPerfect, WriteNow; (for PCs) Ami Pro, ClarisWorks, DCA-RFT, FrameMaker, Microsoft Word, Microsoft Works, MultiMate, OfficeWriter, Professional Write, RTF, Text, WordPerfect, WordPerfect Works, WordStar, XYWrite. Please do not send us files written in other applications.

We cannot be held responsible for loss or damage to unsolicited manuscripts or artwork. We do not accept unsolicited manuscripts by e-mail or fax. Make sure all photos are marked with a brief descriptive caption and the photographer's name and address.

Categories: Health—New Age—Philosophy—Physical Fitness—Spiritual

CONTACT: Editor
Material: All
2054 University Ave., Ste. 600
Berkeley CA 94704
Website: www.hogajournal.com

Young & Alive

Due to a current overabundance of manuscripts, *Young and Alive* will not be accepting additional manuscripts until 2009. Please keep us in mind and send in your manuscripts then.

Target Audience
Young & Alive is a quarterly magazine for visually impaired adults between the ages of 16 and 25. It is published in braille and large print for an interdenominational Christian audience.

Purpose
Young & Alive seeks to draw the reader into a relationship with God and, from a Christian perspective, to provide wholesome entertaining material for our readers. It also seeks to stimulate the thinking, feelings, and activities of blind or legally blind people.

Types of Material
We select manuscripts for publication from the following categories: adventure, biography, camping, careers, handicapped (experiences involving them), health (both physical and mental), history, hobbies, holidays, marriage, nature, practical Christianity, relationships (parents, siblings, peers, dating, etc.), and sports.

We do not accept fiction. The story must be based on a true incident.
Writing Tips:
Whether for a story or an article, the narration and description should be:
- specific rather than general.
- concrete rather than abstract.
- active rather than passive.
- The ending should be clear, bringing into sharp focus the purpose for which the manuscript was written.
- Devotional/inspirational articles: a personal story illustrating your point is much more effective than sermonizing or moralizing.
- Informative articles should be carefully documented. Please secure permission to use any copyrighted material.
- Whenever possible, good quality photos should accompany the manuscript.
- Feature stories and articles should not exceed 1400 words.

Payment/Publication
We pay 4 cents per word, on acceptance.

When we publish your material (a minimum of two years after acceptance), we will send you two complimentary copies of the issue containing your article.

Manuscript Preparation
Manuscripts must appear professional. *Please:*
- use standard 8½ x 11 inch white opaque paper.
- use double-spaced typing.
- use one-inch margins.
- use correct page numbering.
- use proper spelling and punctuation.
- place your name and address in the upper left corner of page 1.
- place the word count in the upper right corner of page 1.
- begin title and body of the manuscript about 5 inches from the top of page 1.

If the material has been submitted to or published by another publication, the words "Second Rights" should appear below the word count. Also please indicate if the manuscript is a simultaneous submission.

We are a non-profit organization and cannot return your manuscript(s) unless accompanied by a self-addressed, stamped envelope (SASE), with sufficient postage to cover the cost of returning all manuscripts included.

Even if you don't wish to have your manuscript(s) returned, an envelope with one first-class stamp attached will help facilitate sending your payment check, should we accept your manuscript.

Categories: Nonfiction—Adventure—Animals—Biography—Campus Life—Careers—Cartoons—Christian Interests—Civil War—College—Comedy—Computers—Cooking—Crafts/Hobbies—Diet/Nutrition—Family—Games—General Interest—Health—History—Hobbies—Inspirational—Interview—Money & Finances—Outdoors—Physical Fitness—Recreation—Relationships—Rural America—Science—Self Help—Spiritual—Sports/Recreation—Travel

CONTACT: Gaylena Gibson, Editor
Material: All
Christian Record Services
PO Box 6097
Lincoln NE 68506

Youth Update

Ceased publication.

R-U

Zoetrope: All-Story

Zoetrope: All-Story is a quarterly literary publication founded by Francis Ford Coppola in 1997 to explore the intersection of story and art, fiction and film.

Submission Guidelines

Zoetrope: All-Story considers unsolicited submissions of short stories and one-act plays no longer than 7,000 words. Excerpts from larger works, screenplays, treatments, and poetry will be returned unread.

Simultaneous submissions are accepted, and first serial rights are required. Please do not submit more than one story or one-act play at a time for consideration.

Only submissions with a return address clearly marked on the outside envelope will be opened. Submissions accompanied by a self-addressed stamped envelope (SASE) will receive a response within five months. We regret that we are unable to respond to submissions without a SASE.

Zoetrope: All-Story does not accept submissions via email. We do, however, provide the Virtual Studio as a way to submit online.

Categories: Fiction—Arts—Film/Video—Short Stories

CONTACT: Tamara Straus, Editor-in-Chief
Material: Any
CONTACT: Michael Ray, Senior Editor
Material: Any
916 Kearny St.
San Francisco CA 94133
Phone: 415-788-7500
Website: all-story.com

paintings or sculpture, please. Self-addressed stamped envelope required.

If you would like to volunteer to work on ad sales, circulation, distribution, or editorial, please send a cover note and resume.

If you would like a sample copy, send us a check for $7 ($4 off the cover price).

Categories: Fiction—Nonfiction—Poetry—Short Stories—Nostalgia—Humor—Personal Experience

CONTACT: Howard Junker, Editor
Material: All
Po Box 590069
San Francisco CA 94159-0069
Phone: 415-752-4393
E-mail: zyzzyvainc@aol.com
Website: www.zyzzyva.org

ZYZZYVA

ZYZZYVA

the journal of west coast writers & artists

West Coast writers and artists only. This means currently living in AK, HI, WA, OR, or CA.

Submissions by mail only; do not phone. O.K. to query by e-mail. Do not submit manuscripts by e-mail. Snail mail only. Double-spaced. Self-addressed stamped envelope required for a reply.

We respond promptly, but do not offer comments or suggestions. We do not read simultaneous submissions, that is, material submitted at the same time to other editors.

We pay on acceptance an honorarium of $50, plus two author's copies, for first North American serial rights (and *ZYZZYVA* anthology rights) only. We reserve the right to put your piece up on our Web page.

We do not commission work.

We are committed to reflecting the full range of talent in our neighborhood—many genres, many generations, many schools. We have published a wide range of poetry, fiction, and nonfiction. Take your best shot.

We do not do interviews, reviews, or criticism. We do do translations, especially of Latin American and Asian writers.

ZYZZYVA is published in March, August, and November.

Photographers and graphic artists: submit copies or slides only. Only of work originally done in black & white on paper. No photos of

Book Publishers' Guidelines

29th Press

Duke Communications International, publisher of 29th Press books, *Windows NT Magazine*, NEWS/400, and *Controller Magazine*, maintains its corporat e headquarters in Loveland, Colorado, with regional sales offices in New York, Chicago, and San Francisco. Duke Communications currently employs about 100 people in Colorado, plus a staff of technical editors and reporters throughout the U.S. Duke Communications began publishing a newsletter, NEWS 34/38, in 1982 when founder and president David A. Duke, a former IBMer, recognized the need for information about the proliferating IBM midrange systems entering the market.

About 29th Press

In January 1991, the 29th Press division of Duke Communications published its first book for 3X/400 professionals. Currently, 29th Press maintains a list of about 50 titles in print, including reference books and textbooks. Target audiences are AS/400 professionals, and Windows NT users, administrators, and developers.

29th Press strives to publish practical, easy-to-read books that present clear, complete explanations of underlying concepts needed by readers. Practitioners who can communicate their technological expertise in a down-to-earth manner are the mainstays of the 29th Press publishing tradition. Many of our authors are technical editors for or contributors to leading technology journals, as well as pioneers and entrepreneurs in their respective fields.

Check our Web site for new Windows NT and AS/400 books, as well as an online catalog of our entire product line.

How to Submit a Proposal

If you are interested in submitting a proposal to 29th Press, you should send us the following information about your project and yourself:

• An overview that describes the type of book, its approximate length, and any special features or accompanying materials (diskette, CD, and so forth)

• A description of the intended audience

• A content outline or proposed Table of Contents

• A sample chapter or several pages from a typical chapter

• An estimate of the length of time to complete the final manuscript

• Information about competing products and market potential

• Personal information about your background and writing experience, including such items as a resume, a list of previously published works, and a writing sample.

Categories: Nonfiction—Computers—IBM AS/400—Windows NT

CONTACT: Katie Tipton, Acquisitions Editor
Material: All
CONTACT: Dave Bernard, Publisher
Material: AS/400
221 E. 29th St.
Loveland CO 80538
Phone: 970-663-4700
Fax: 970-203-2756
E-mail: kmptipton@aol.com
Website: www.iseriesnetwork.com/store

Abbott, Langer & Associates

We do not have a formal set of guidelines for manuscripts. Initially, just the title and table of contents would help us decide whether to reject a manuscript or investigate further.

Categories: Nonfiction—Associations—Business—Computers—Reference—Security & Loss Prevention—Human Resources Management

CONTACT: Dr. Steven Langer, President
Material: All
548 First St.
Crete IL 60417
Phone: 708-672-4200
Fax: 708-672-4674
E-mail: slanger@abbott-langer.com
Website: www.abbott-langer.com

ACTA Publications
Assisting Christians to Act

1. If you are not familiar with our products, please request our current catalog. Read it carefully and see if your book or tape seems to fit. You might even want to order one or two items to get a feel for the kind of material we publish.

2. If you truly feel we would be the best publisher for you, then send a proposal with three parts:

    a. A cover letter that explains your proposal and tells a little bit about yourself and why your proposed work fits our product line.

    b. A table of contents for your proposed work.

    c. One chapter of a book or one segment from a proposed tape. (We will not read entire manuscripts.)

3. Be sure to enclose a self-addressed, stamped envelope with your proposal, indicating whether you want the entire proposal returned or just our answer. Your proposal will not receive a response without this.

4. Upon our receipt of your proposal you will receive either an immediate rejection or a letter indicating that it has been received and when you can expect an answer (usually six weeks).

5. At the end of that time period, you will receive another letter either giving the reasons why we are not interested in your proposal or indicating that we are interested and asking for additional information or samples.

6. Upon our receipt of that requested material you will receive another letter indicating when you can expect a response.

7. At the end of that time period, we will contact you either with a final rejection or with an offer of a contract.

8. If a contract is signed, then a timetable will be set up for the completion and publication of your work.

9. We do not offer advances to any of our first-time authors.

10. We will accept proposals that have been sent to other publishers simultaneously. You must, however, indicate this on your initial proposal. If not, your proposal will be automatically rejected at the point this fact becomes known—no matter how far along we are in the process.

Categories: Religion—Spiritual

CONTACT: Gregory F. Pierce, Acquisitions Editor
Material: All
4848 N. Clark St.
Chicago IL 60640
Phone: 773-271-1030
Fax: 773-271-7399
E-mail: actapublications@aol.com

Addicus Books, Inc.

Addicus Books, Inc. is based in Omaha, Nebraska. An independent publisher, we publish ten quality nonfiction titles a year. Our focus is consumer health. We publish only nonfiction; we do not publish poetry or fiction.) We're seeking titles on: health, self-help, and psychology, however will also look at titles on, how-to, business, economics, investing, and books of regional interest — true crime, histories, and profiles.

Submission Guidelines

We prefer first a one-page query, outlining the nature of your work, who your market is and information about your background. If we're interested in taking a closer look at your book, we'll ask for a proposal.

Note: when querying electronically, send only a one-page email, giving an overview of your book and its market. Please do not send attachments unless invited to do so.

Book Proposals should include:
- A one-page overview of the book
- Two or three sample chapters
- A chapter-by-chapter outline
- Number of photos or illustrations
- Author's background/credentials
- Target completion date
- Market/audience information
- Word count/number of pages

Audience / Market information should include:
- Who is the audience?
- What is the market for your book and how many potential buyers?
- Who wants this book? Why do they want it? Why do they need it?
- Do you have specific marketing ideas in mind?
- Does your book help the reader?
- How will this book benefit the buyer? How will it help them?
- What need does it fill for your target market?
- What makes your book special?
- What makes your book different from other such books? (Are there other such books?)
- Does your book have more information? Is it more comprehensive, easier to use? What advantages does it have over the competition? Why will people buy it instead of something else? Note: Please do a data base search for competing titles through Amazon.com — the largest online book store with more than one million titles in its data base. Report your findings in your proposal.
- Market niches/ Special markets (Please be thorough here.)
- List any special markets your book may have outside regular trade book channels (book stores).
- Could sales result from your contacts— associations, organizations, corporations, groups, hospitals, treatment centers, workshops, seminars or speaking engagements?
- Which magazines or professional/trade journals may review your book or print articles by you which in turn promotes the book?
- Do you have specific ideas for marketing your book?
- How willing are you to be active in marketing your book?

True Crime Submissions

We'd like a synopsis with a clear layout of the story line, how the plot unfolds. Also, give us a sense of the book's structure as well as its scope. Why does this book need to be written?

Note: We are seeking manuscripts that have good stories behind the crimes. Unfortunately, heinous crimes happen everyday, but crimes alone do not make a book. We're looking for twists and turns in the story behind the crime — a plot with rising action. And, we want the author to get us inside the minds of the main characters so we know what makes them tick. Characters' motivation must be established. As you can see, we're looking for many of the devices used in fiction. We also prefer fairly recent, high-profile cases. We publish high quality, trade paperbacks and do extensive promotion within the given region.

Submission of Text (for all genres)
- All materials should be clearly printed on white, 8 1/2 x 11 paper, double-spaced, with at least 1" margins on all sides.
- No more than 250-300 words per page.
- Do not staple, clip or otherwise bind pages in the submission.
- All submissions should include an SASE. Materials will not be returned unless accompanied by an SASE.

NOTE: Do not send by Certified Mail or Return Receipt Requested.

Categories: Nonfiction—Business—General Interest—Health—True Crime—Health Relationships

CONTACT: Acquisitions Editor, Addicus Books
Material: All
PO Box 45327
Omaha, NE 68145
Phone: 402 330-7493
Fax: 402 330-1707
E-mail: Addicusbks@aol.com

Aegis Publishing Group, Ltd.

We specialize in telecommunications books for non-technical end users such as small businesses (small office/home office) and entrepreneurs. We do not publish anything that does not fit this niche.

Categories: Nonfiction—Business—Technology—Small Business—Telecommunications

CONTACT: Robert Mastin, President
Material: All
796 Aquidneck Ave.
Newport RI 02842
Phone: 401-849-4200
Fax: 401-849-4231
E-mail: Aegis@aegisbooks.com
Website: www.aegisbooks.com

Aeronautical Publishers

Our Mission

"Our mission is to help people learn more about aviation and model aviation through the written word. We want to help youth get started and enhance everyone's enjoyment of the hobby." Guidelines for #10 SASE with 2 first-class stamps.

Nonfiction: How-to and historical. Subjects include radio control, free flight, indoor models, electric flight, rubber powered flying models, micro radio control, aviation history, homebuilt aircraft, ultralights and hang gliders.

Recent Non-fiction Title: *Those First Magnificent Flying Machines.*

Tips: Our focus is on books of short to medium length that will serve the emerging needs of the hobby.

Categories: Nonfiction—Automobiles—Aviation

CONTACT: Michael A. Markowski, Publisher
Material: All
One Oakglade Circle

Hummelstown PA 17036-9525
Phone: 717-566-0468
Fax: 717-566-6423

Alaska Northwest Books

Please refer to Graphic Arts Center Publishing Company.

Alba House

Alba House is the North American publishing division of the Society of St. Paul, an International Roman Catholic Missionary Religious Congregation dedicated to spreading the Gospel message via the media of communications.

As such it welcomes for consideration manuscripts which contribute, from a Roman Catholic perspective, to the personal, intellectual and spiritual growth of individuals in the following area:

- Scripture
- Theology and the Church
- Saints–Their Lives and Teachings
- Spirituality and Prayer
- Religious Life
- Marriage and Family Life
- Liturgy and Homily Preparation
- Pastoral Concerns
- Religious Education
- Bereavement
- Moral and Ethical Concerns
- Philosophy
- Psychology
- No fiction
- No children's books
- No poetry
- No simultaneous submissions
- No personal testimonials or autobiographies

We prefer that manuscripts be submitted in full, typewritten and double-spaced along with a brief curriculum vitae of the author. Please include a self-addressed stamped envelope for the return of the manuscript if you wish to have it sent back to you in case it is not accepted.

If accepted for publication, we find it helpful if the work can then be submitted on floppy disk (IBM or Macintosh) from any of the more popular Word Processing programs: e.g., Word Perfect, Microsoft Word, Word for Windows, Wordstar, Ami Pro, etc.

We thank you for considering Alba House and look forward to reviewing your work with an eye to its possible publication. You can expect to hear from us within six weeks or less of our submission.

Categories: Nonfiction—Family—Marriage—Philosophy—Psychology—Religion—Spiritual

CONTACT: Father Victor Viberti, S.S.P., Aquisitions Editor
Material: All
2187 Victory Blvd.
Staten Island NY 10314-6603
Phone: 718-761-0047
Fax: 718-761-0057

Algora Publishing
Imprint: Agathon Press

Due to the large volume of inquiries we receive, Algora Publishing is unable to respond to queries by telephone and cannot answer or acknowledge receipt of query letters. Materials cannot be returned unless accompanied by a stamped, self-addressed envelope. Do not send original manuscripts, artwork, photographs or documents, as we cannot be responsible for their return.

Inquiries and complete proposals may be sent via email to Editors@algora.com or (on paper) by mail to the address below. We aim to respond to all proposals, if you include a self-addressed stamped envelope or your email address. Responses are usually sent within 1–3 months of receipt.

Algora Publishing is an independent publisher of serious nonfiction books featuring top American and international authors on questions of global scope. The perspectives our authors bring can help readers sharpen their own analyses of issues in the areas of international relations as well as human relations, politics, history, philosophy, sociology, economics, current events, criminology, mind & spirit, literature, and education and reference topics. No children's books, no fiction or poetry, self help, religious works or personal memoirs. Please visit our website at www.algora.com to familiarize yourself with the type of books that Algora publishes.

First-time authors are welcome. We can sometimes offer guidance in the final shaping of a work, and we sometimes provide considerable editing, but we give preference to authors with professional qualifications, academic credentials, endorsements by established professionals in the field, and to works that reflect an extensive level of research.

Suitable manuscript length is generally 75,000-125,000 words.
What to submit:
- Include a one-page synopsis of the book (the subject matter and the approach taken), and an outline or table of contents, and a sample chapter or two
- Describe your qualifications for writing this book.
- Identify your intended audience: for what readers is the book written?
- Explain how your book is different from others on related topics. What unmet need does your book fill?
- Indicate how your position, circumstances, skills, abilities, or commitments would help to market the book.

Categories: Nonfiction—Business—Culture—Economics—Government—History—Philosophy—Politics—Relationships—Society

CONTACT: Martin DeMers, Editor
Material: All
222 Riverside Dr., 16th Floor
New York NY 10025-6809
Phone: 212-678-0232
Fax: 212-666-3682
E-mail: Editors@algora.com
Website: www.algora.com

Allworth Press

Manuscript Submission Guidelines

Allworth Press publishes business and self-help books for artists, designers, photographers, film and performing artists. The press also publishes classic and contemporary critical writing on art and graphic design.

Please review our catalog of books on our Web site, which should give you an idea of the kind of titles we are accustomed to publishing. We do not publish picture books, fiction, poetry, or full-color books.

We prefer to see a one- or two-page outline of a proposed book, even if the book has already been written. The outline should give a chapter-by-chapter summary of the book's contents. It should also indicate the author's background, the intended audience for the book, any books that might be considered competitive, and why this book will compete successfully with those books. If the book has been written, please include two sample chapters with the outline.

Categories: Nonfiction—Architecture—Arts—Crafts/Hobbies—Dance—Drama—Film/Video—Money & Finances—Music—Photography—Self-Help—Theatre—Graphic Design

CONTACT: Nicole Potter, Editor
Material: All

10 East 23ʳᵈ Street, Ste. S10
New York, NY 10010
Phone: 212-777-8395
Fax: 212-777-8395
E-mail: PUB@allworth.com
Website: allworth.com

Alpine Publications

If you excel in breeding, training or other aspects of dog or horse care, you may have something to write about and there is an audience thirsty for your knowledge. If you are searching for a publisher, let us help you decide whether Alpine Publications is right for your book.

We Offer:

As a small, specialized publisher concentrating on nonfiction animal books, you can count on us for:

• Personalized attention during both writing and production stages
• Targeted, specialized marketing plan
• Quality production resulting in a book you can take pride in
• Guidance and supervision that leads to award winning titles whether you are a professional author or writing your first book

We Are Interested In:

• Training or behavior books with a unique approach
• Semi-technical subjects for professionals or breeders
• Animal stories for youth.

We Favor These Approaches:

• Subjects covered in depth and well documented
• An unbiased, well-researched presentation of facts and opinions
• Inclusion of numerous photos or illustrations
• Breed books.

We Are Not Interested In:

• Fiction
• Books on small pets, fish, birds, or reptiles
• Books of poetry
• Photographic essays

We Create These Types Of Products:

• Hardbound books in various formats
• Trade paperbacks
• Workbooks
• Video or audio tapes

Our Audiences Are:

• Purebred owners, breeders, trainers, exhibitors
• Pet owners
• Students

We Sell Via These Channels:

• Direct to the consumer through magazine advertisements and direct mail
• Book, pet, tack and specialty retail stores
• Book and pet supply wholesalers in the U.S., Canada, Europe, Scandinavia, Britain, Australia, and other foreign markets

Should You Query First?

Yes, queries with an outline are encouraged. Queries are accepted by mail and by email to alpinepubl@aol.com

With All Submissions Include:

• Outline and up to three complete sample chapters
• Your credentials for doing this book
• Who is the intended audience?
• What your work will offer that audience
• What other books are available on the subject
• Why your work is unique

Complete manuscripts are also accepted. Specify if manuscript is being submitted simultaneously to other publishers. Submit only by mail; email submissions will not be accepted

What Writing Style Should You Use?

Use *The Chicago Manual of Style* (13th Edition).

Manuscript Requirements:

• Double-spaced on 8 1/2 x 11 white paper with margins of at least one inch on all sides pages numbered consecutively

• Photocopies are accepted
• Average length is 45,000 to 80,000 words

Photographs and Art

• Send samples only with initial query

Proper Submission Speeds Response Time

• Query first
• Include all materials mentioned above
• Enclose an SASE or adequate postage if you want the manuscript returned. Allow 12 weeks for a reply

Categories: Nonfiction—Animals

CONTACT: Betty McKinney, Publisher
Material: All
225 South Madison Ave.
Loveland CO 80537
Phone: 907-667-9317
E-mail: alpinepubl@aol.com

Alyson Publications, Inc.

QUERY SUBMISSIONS

Alyson Publications is the leading publisher of books by, for, and about lesbians, gay men, and bisexuals from all economic and social segments of society and of all ages, from children to adults. In fiction and nonfiction format, Alyson books explore the political, legal, financial, medical, spiritual, social, and sexual aspects of gay, lesbian, and bisexual life and the contributions to and experiences in society of our community.

We are happy to consider book queries. We only consider solicited manuscripts. Please note the following before submitting a query:

INQUIRY: Please send a query letter detailing your novel's plot or your nonfiction idea. Give a summary of the book, a chapter outline if you have it, approximately how many words, and what qualifies you to write this particular book. We do NOT want to see sample chapters at this stage.

MANUSCRIPT: Unsolicited manuscripts will not be considered and will be returned if accompanied by appropriate SASE. They will be destroyed if not accompanied by appropriate SASE.

OTHER: Nonfiction should be written in a popular (i.e., nonacademic) style. We do not consider individual short stories or poetry. At this time, we do not have a service referring individual short stories to any anthologies we will be publishing. We prefer manuscript length to be around 100,000 words. If you would like to see what Alyson has previously published, our books are available at all gay and lesbian bookstores as well as larger chains.

DECISION TIME: We try to give serious consideration to each query we receive. Each query mill be reviewed and a response sent to you within one month of its receipt. Please do not call to check on the status of your submission.

Categories: Fiction—Nonfiction—Alternate Life-style—Gay/Lesbian

CONTACT: Acquisitions Editor
Material: All
PO Box 4371
Los Angeles CA 90078-4371
Phone: 213-871-1225
Fax: 213-467-6805
E-mail: alyson@advocate.com
Website: www.advocate.com

American Book Publishing

American Book Publishing's mission is to support, document, and disseminate, through book publication, great works and teachings of talented authors, scholars, and professionals. We publish both nonfiction and wholesome fiction books. We prefer books with an identifiable target market that has a reachable audience. We do not publish cookbooks, coffee table books, poetry, erotica, hate or books with obscenities or disrespectful use of the names of deity, or children's books with color illustrations.

We review unsolicited manuscripts within 30 days of submission, when submitted by e-mail to acqeditor@american-book.com when accompanied by answers to our submission questionnaire (ask info@american-book.com for that info and then send it with the manuscript as an attachment to e-mail. (**No snail mail submissions**).

We favor proposals that best fit the imprints of American Book Publishing. These imprints are divided into five distinct divisions, each focusing on a particular genres. American Book Classics, American University & Colleges Press, American Book Business Press, Millennial Mind Publishing, and Bedside Books.

For more information please read our web site at www.american-book.com we keep it updated and have daily book publishing news and about a hundred articles for writers about publishing.

Categories: Fiction—Nonfiction

CONTACT: Submissions Editor
Material: All
E-mail: acqeditor@american-book.com
Website: www.american-book.com

American Correctional Association (ACA) Book Publishing

Publishing With ACA

Enhance Your Contribution to the Field of Corrections by Publishing Your Book with the American Correctional Association For more than 13 years, the American Correctional Association has been serving the needs of corrections professionals by providing them with the resources, support, and services they need to excel in the fields of corrections and criminal justice.

Whether you come from professional work in a prison, jail, probation, parole, juvenile, or from a counseling background, our members need your expertise. We are seeking submissions on topics that would enhance and contribute to the field of corrections.

What better way to contribute your knowledge, research, and insight to this dynamic field than by authoring a publication which can be used by your colleagues.

Our current titles discuss the following topics:
- Anger Management
- Boot Camps
- Law/Legal Issues
- Career Development
- Management Issues
- Cognitive Behavioral Therapy
- Community Corrections
- Restorative Justice
- Counseling
- Security
- Facility Design
- Sex Offenders
- Female Offenders
- Special Needs Offenders
- Gangs
- Staff Training and Education
- Health Care
- Substance Abuse
- History Suicide
- Issues, Policy, and Research Women Working in Corrections
- Jails Youthful Offenders

Where Do I Start?

If you are interested in publishing a book with the American Correctional Association, please start by completing the Author Proposal Form (see our website). *Send the completed form to:*

Alice Heiserman, Manager of Publications and Research
American Correctional Association
4380 Forbes Boulevard
Lanham, MD 20706-4322
Phone 301-918-1894; Fax 301-918-1886
e-mail: aliceh@aca.org

We are seeking practical, how-to books based on professional experience. Our audience includes correctional practitioners. We also have texts suitable for college students taking courses in corrections, criminal justice and social work. If your proposal appears to have potential for inclusion in our publishing program, we will ask you to submit a full proposal. A full proposal includes an outline and a summary plus one or two sample chapters. You may submit a full proposal along with your Author Proposal Form. Full manuscripts also may be submitted.

Information About Our Authors

Many of our authors are first-time writers. Others have been published with major publishing houses but choose to work with ACA because of the personal attention we provide. Other authors choose ACA because they see an opportunity to make a significant contribution to corrections through our books.

We do not publish fiction, poetry or materials from offenders.

The Review Process

Your proposal will be reviewed by the core management of ACA. It also will be sent out for a blind review to your peers for their opinion. If the submission is deemed to have merit, and market potential, we then will ask you to submit your entire manuscript for review. At this point, you will need to submit one paper copy of the full manuscript plus an electronic copy in WordPerfect or Microsoft Word format. The review process usually takes four months.

As a result of the review process, ACA may make suggestions for modification of the original manuscript, or we may accept it as is. If you agree to make the revisions or changes, we will review your changes to see if they meet the recommendations of the reviewers. If they do, ACA will extend a contract. Once we have your signed contract and your manuscript, we can begin the processes of editing and typesetting your manuscript into a book. This stage generally takes between four and seven months.

The ACA Publishing Team

Our editorial department will review your manuscript to ensure that it meets our standards for clarity, punctuation, grammar, and style. We work closely with our authors to insure our books are readable and look inviting. During this time, we select a title and in conjunction with our graphics team, design the cover and interior pages.

Throughout this process, the marketing department will meet to discuss the format, price, and marketing strategies for your book. We will ask you to complete an Author Questionnaire. This will give us additional information on how and where to market your book. Marketing will include announcements to the criminal justice media, direct mailings, exposure at annual and regional ACA meetings, and at other criminal justice conferences and meetings. We are happy to provide you with materials to self-promote your book.

Additionally, we will look for partnerships outside the organization as ways to promote your book. These may include bulk sales to bookstores or other organizations that wish to distribute your title. We look forward to your active participation in the promotion of your book.

The American Correctional Association also publishes *Corrections Today* and *Corrections Compendium* magazines. Refer to the magazine section of this directory, for their writer's guideines.

Categories: Nonfiction—Careers—Crime—Disabilities—Juveniles—Psychology—Reference—Senior Citizens—Corrections—Criminal Justice—Sociology—Women's Issues

CONTACT: Alice Heiserman, Manager
Material: Book submissions
CONTACT: Susan Clayton, Editor, Corrections Today and Corrections Compendium
Material: Magazine submissions
ACA Book Publishing
4380 Forbes Boulevard
Lanham MD 20706-4322
Phone: 301-918-1894
Fax: 301-918-1886
E-mail: aliceh@aca.org
Website: www.aca.org

American Literary Press

American Literary Press, Inc.
Noble House

Typed or laser printed, unbound 8.5"x11" pages, upper and lower case letters. Title page should include authors name, address, work and phone numbers with complete page count. Forwarding a 2-3 paragraph synopsis of your manuscript would be helpful to our staff. Please be aware that we will keep your work in our files for three months only.

Categories: Fiction—Adventure—Children—Cooking—Feminism—Health—History—Horror—Juvenile—New Age—Poetry—Religion—Romance—Science Fiction—Short Stories—Sports/Recreation—Western—Women's Fiction—Young Adult—Humor

CONTACT: Acquisitions Editor
Material: All
8019 Belair Rd. Ste. 10
Baltimore MD 21236
Phone: 410-882-7700
Fax: 410-882-7703
E-mail: amerlit@erols.com

The Americas Group

The Americas Group has no specific guidelines for writers submitting manuscripts for possible publication. While not wishing to restrict writers as to style or format, we do not accept any material to review outside of the field of public policy. We also always ask authors to identify the specific audience they think will not only be interested in their writing, but are likely to spend their money to buy and own their work.

Categories: Nonfiction—Public Policy

CONTACT: Godfrey Harris, Director
Material: All

9200 Sunset Blvd., Ste 404
Los Angeles CA 90069-3506
Phone: 310 278 8037
Fax: 310 271 3649
E-mail: hrmg@aol.com
Website: www.americasgroup.com

AMG Publishers

Before an actual book proposal is submitted, I would like to see, via e-mail a query letter for your manuscript.

This letter should:
• Be one page in length, no longer
• Include a brief, tantalizing description of the book that you propose
• State who and how large the market or audience is for your book-be specific
• Give the proposed page count of your book
• Include a few words about yourself, the author-why you are expertly qualified to write the book.

Then, at that point, I can inform you if your proposed book fits into our current publishing plan. If your query letter indicates a possible fit with AMG Publisher's focus, we will then ask you to submit an actual book proposal following the guidelines that I will then send you.

Please note:
AMG Publisher's focus is on books that:
1. Help the reader get into the Bible, directly or indirectly.
2. Facilitate confrontation and interaction with Scripture toward a positive change in thought or action.
3. Give a hunger to studying, understanding, and applying Scripture.
4. Encourage and facilitate one's personal growth in such areas as personal devotion and a skillful use of the Bible.

We have a broad interest in biblically oriented books, including Biblical Reference, Applied Theology and Apologetics, Christian Ministry, Sermon and Illustration Books, Bible Study Books in the Following God series format, Christian Living, Women/Men/Family Issues, Single/Divorce Issues, Devotionals, Inspirational, Prayer, Contemporary Issues, and so on.

Our interests, though, do not include Fiction, Poetry, Children/Youth books, Personal-experience stories, and Autobiographical stories.

Categories: Nonfiction—Religion—Spiritual

CONTACT: Dan Penwell, Director of Product Development/ Acquisitions
Material: All
6815 Shallowford Rd.
Chattanooga TN 37421-1755
Phone: 423-894-6060

Amherst Media

Amherst Media is always looking for photographers interested in sharing their vision and experience with others. If you feel that there is a book inside of you, please contact us.

Keep in mind that Amherst Media only publishes instructional books on photography, but don't let that discourage you if you're interested in seeing your images in print. Our books are distributed across the globe and have been translated into three different languages. Most Amherst Media titles run up to 128 pages, with 15,000 to 30,000 words and anywhere from 25 to 300 images.

Please send an outline, small sample of your photographic work and contact information.

Categories: Photography

CONTACT: Submissions Department
Material: All
Amherst Media, Inc.
155 Rano St., Ste. 300

Buffalo, NY 14207
Phone: 716-874-4450
Fax: 716-874-4508
E-mail: submissions@amherstmedia.com.
Website: www.amherstmedia.com

Anchorage Press Plays, Inc.
International Agency of Plays for Young People

Anchorage Press Plays, Inc. (formerly Anchorage Press) publishes theatrical plays for a youth and family audience. Submissions should be appropriate in subject, theme and language to a universal norm of juveniles and adolescents: fantasy, fable, adventure, quest, journey, unfolding maturity, self discovery, etc.

1) Manuscripts must be typed or computer printed,

2) Submitted by mail with a SASE adequate for the postage return of the manuscript. No email or fax submissions accepted.

3) Please send play script only after it has gone through testing of productions and rewrites. We cannot accept play scripts for consideration that have not been produced.

4) Adaptations of books beloved by young people require proof of authorization to create a dramatic adaptation, and permission to submit for publication.

Several months are required for response to a submission.

Creative Education/Theatrical text books: Anchorage publishes a limited number of text books relating to theatrical design, production, education for the youth drama teaching field and producing plays.

Send one page inquiry describing text proposal, plus biographical/professional credentials relating to the specialty of the text. Initial inquiry in this short format is accepted by mail or email.

Categories: Fiction—Nonfiction—Arts—Children—Drama—Juvenile—Theatre

CONTACT: Submissions Editor
Material: All
PO Box 2901
Louisville KY 40201
Phone: 502-583-2288
E-mail: applays@bellsouth.net (inquiries only)
Website: www.applays.com

Angel Bea Publishing

Mission Statement: Angel Bea Publishing produces top-quality books featuring true stories about real animals. Through full color illustrations and factual text Angel Bea delivers compelling information with an artistic flare.

Angel Bea is only interested in nonfiction for ages 8-12.

Categories: Nonfiction—Animals—Children—Christian Interests—Short Stories

CONTACT: Kat Shehata, Publisher
Material: All
9504 Bainbrook Court
Cincinnati, OH 45249
Phone: 513-683-8592
Fax: 513-683-9523
Website: www.angelbea.com

Anhinga Press

Anhinga Press publishes full-length volumes of poetry. For thirty years we have sought out the best writing available and brought it to the public in attractive and reasonably-priced editions. The Anhinga Prize for Poetry contest, which runs from February 15th through May 1st, draws about six hundred entries each year from around the world.

Interested in publishing your work with Anhinga? The best place to start may be the Contest page mentioned above; entries are blind-judged, which (at least in theory) puts relatively unknown and beginning poets on an equal footing with those who have been publishing their work for years. For non-contest entries, please first visit our GUIDELINES page.

Anhinga Press publishes only full-length collections of poetry (usually 60-80 pages), no individual poems or chapbooks. We are always open to reading manuscripts. There is nothing that we are inherently prejudiced toward or against; we are looking for the best poetry out there.

However, for the sake of your peace of mind (and perhaps your sanity), you should do some homework first. Start by reading some of the poems from the books here on our Web site to see if your work is comparable in quality, and perhaps style, to some of the poetry we have published. Read the biographical and other notes about each poet, and compare that information with your own. We are probably not a press for beginners (in the sense of "never had any poetry published before," regardless of how long you may have been writing it), for subjects of local or limited interest, or for private and/or overly sentimental work.

You should know that the odds are not good. We usually publish five books a year:

one is the winner of the Anhinga Prize for Poetry;

one is a volume of the Florida Poetry Series; and

For this reason, we reject far, far more unsolicited manuscripts than we accept. In fact, we reject about 98% of the work that is submitted to us.

If all of these dire warnings have not daunted your spirit, and if after looking at some of the poems on our Web site, you think that Anhinga Press might be interested in your manuscript, please send us a query letter and a ten-page sample (not the full manuscript!). No e-mail samples please.

CONTACT: Submission Editor
Material: All
PO Box 10595
Tallahasse, FL 32302
Phone: 850-442-1408
Fax: 850-442-6323
E-mail: info@anhinga.org (no submissions)
Website: www.anhinga.org

Apage4You Book Publishing

We accept all submissions (except those in the children's genre) without reading fees. Our primary interest is in Non-Fiction, Controversial and religious books, although each manuscript is carefully reviewed and considered for mainstream publication.

Additionally, unlike most other publishers, we also offer subsidy, self and e-book publication.

Many have inquired of Apage4You Book Publishing which genres have the best chance of receiving mainstream publication. *While each and every manuscript submitted is considered, we have extreme interest in the following:*

• Non-Fiction
• Fiction
• Novels
• Religious
• Political
• Lifestyle
• Historic
• Controversial
• Current Events

Reason being, mainstream publication is usually reserved for works appealing to a wide market. Works with limited public appeal are rarely accepted for mainstream publication, while many are offered alternative publishing options.

NOTE: submissions in the children's genre will not be accepted for mainstream publication until further notice. Children's books will however be evaluated for subsidy, self and e-book publishing if requested.

Submit Your Manuscript to Apage4You Book Publishing.

We've made it very easy to get you started. Just follow the instructions below and you'll be well on your way to seeing your book in print.

Step by Step Instructions:

1. Make certain your work is complete, fully edited, and ready for publication

2. Submit your manuscript for evaluation .

STEP ONE - Submit your Manuscript/Standard Submission FREE

Use your book title in subject line

1. Do NOT embed photos within your manuscript - Submit each photo as a separate file and advise page, paragraph and line where photo should appear.

2. Submit Manuscript as an attachment in RTF or Microsoft Word, or if unable to provide your manuscript as an attached file using your e-mail system, you may:

  a. Copy and paste the entire document into the body of your e-mail, and e-mail to acquisitions@apage4youpublishing.com -or-

  b. Send Complete Manuscript together with photos, graphs, illustrations, etc (remember do not embed in manuscript) by postal service to the address below.

Categories: Fiction—Nonfiction—History—Lifestyle—Religion

CONTACT: Manuscript Submissions
Material: All
2025 Balla Way, Ste 200
Grand Prairie TX 75051-3907
E-mail: info@apage4youpublishing.com
Website: www.apage4youpublishing.com

Arbenteuer Books

Please refer to Black Forest Press.

Arden Press, Inc.

Arden Press publishes nonfiction books, including women's titles (women's history, biography, general guides), popular how-to books, directories, guides, and film titles. We sell primarily to bookstores and to public and academic libraries. Many of our titles are adopted as texts for college courses. We do not publish fiction, poetry, or personal memoirs.

We prefer to receive manuscript proposals rather than complete manuscripts. If we believe that your project might fit our publication profile, we will request the manuscript.

What To Include In Your Manuscript Proposal

1.) Tentative Title: A descriptive title for the purpose of identifying the particular manuscript.

2.) Scope/Purpose: Describe in one paragraph the intended purpose of the book, the scope of coverage, and primary and secondary audience.

3.) Outline: A preliminary outline should show all chapters and key subsections. The outline should be accompanied by written chapter summaries that explain the main theme and scope of each chapter.

4.) Methodology & Presentation: Summarize the search plan that is to be used in locating necessary data. List the types of sources to be consulted. Indicate the need for illustrations, maps, appendixes, indexes, etc.

5.) Sample Section: A sample chapter or section in preliminary form should be submitted to demonstrate the organization, content, writing style, and documentation to be used.

6.) Similar or Related Works: Identify books on the same topic or on similar or related topics. Explain the need for the proposed book and how it will fill a specific gap in coverage or take a unique approach to the subject.

Thank you for your interest in Arden Press.

Categories: Nonfiction—Biography—Film/Video—General Interest—History—Reference—Women's Issues—College Course Adoptions

CONTACT: Susan Conley, Publisher/Editor
Material: All
PO Box 418
Denver CO 80201
Phone: 303-697-6766
Fax: 303-697-3443

Art Direction Book Company, Inc.

Want to see a Table of Contents and a chapter; not an introduction. Please list your various positions.

Categories: Arts—Advertising Art

CONTACT: Don Barron, Publisher
Material: Ad Art
456 Glenbrook Rd.
Glenbrook CT 06906
Phone: 203-353-1441
Fax: 203-353-1371

Arte Público Press
The University of Houston

Arte Público Press, affiliated with the University of Houston, specializes in publishing contemporary novels, short stories, poetry, and drama based on U.S. Hispanic, Cuban American, Mexican American, Puerto Rican, and other themes and cultural issues. Arte Público also is interested in reference works, non-fiction studies, especially of Hispanic civil rights, women's issues and history.

Manuscripts, queries, synopsis, outlines, proposals, introductory chapters, etc. are accepted in either English or Spanish; the majority of our publications are in English. All submissions must be typed, double-spaced, and include a self-addressed, stamped envelope (SASE) to return those not selected for publication. Address all submissions to: Arte Público Press, SUBMISSIONS, University of Houston, 452 Cullen Performance Hall Houston, Texas, 77204-2004. *Manuscripts not accompanied by an appropriately sized SASE will not be returned. Queries and proposals take 2-4 months and manuscripts take 3-6 months to respond. We are NOT responsible for any damages or loss of any manuscript.*

Please be advised that we do NOT accept, review or respond to any submissions via Internet. Please take time to familiarize yourself with our current and previous titles, as well as specialized fields, and send only the material relevant to our publishing needs. Due to the overwhelming amount of submissions we get each year, we would advise that the writer take time to distinguish whether or not his/her work is appropriate for APP so that response time is diminished. We recommend that writers include a one-page cover letter specifying relevant information and brief description of the manuscript, and an introductory sample of the manuscript instead of sending the manuscript in its entirety first. We do not accept digital files of the work until it has been accepted for publication. For further information of our previous publications, please visit our website.

Accepted manuscripts should be accompanied by a digital file of the work on disk. (Microsoft Word v.6.0 or later, for Macintosh or Windows.)

Piñata Books

Piñata Books is Arte Público Press' imprint for children's and young adult literature. It seeks to authentically and realistically portray themes, characters, and customs unique to U.S. Hispanic culture. Submissions and manuscript formalities are the same as for Arte Público Press.

Illustrators

Guidelines for illustration submissions, for the most part, remain the same as stipulated above for Arte Público Press' and Piñata Books with the following exceptions: we will not return any submissions; so please do **NOT** send originals. All artworks, photos, slides, etc. will be kept in separate illustrator files for future consideration. These files may be updated by submitting new art samples. Our Managing Editor will contact you once it is determined that your work is suitable for our publishing needs; so please be sure to include your current address, phone number(s) and e-mail address.

Recovering the U.S. Hispanic Literary Heritage

The Recovering the U.S. Hispanic Literary Heritage series publishes recovered literature written by Hispanics between the colonial period and 1960 in the geographic area that has become the United States. For further details, contact Dr. Nicolás Kanellos, Director, at this address.

Categories: Fiction—Nonfiction—Hispanic—Juvenile—Literature—Multicultural—Women's Issues—Young Adult

CONTACT: Marina Tristán, Assistant Director
Material: All
University of Houston
452 Cullen Performance
Houston, TX 77204-2004
Phone: 713-743-2846
Fax: 713-743-3080
E-mail: submapp@mail.uh.edu
Website: www.artepublicopress.com

Aslan Publishing

Our Mission

Aslan Publishing offers readers a window to the soul via well-crafted and practical self-help books, inspirational books, and modern day parables. Our mission is to publish books that uplift one's mind, body, and spirit.

Living one's spirituality in business, relationships, and personal growth is the underlying purpose of our publishing company, and the meaning behind our name Aslan Publishing. We see the word "Aslan" as a metaphor for living spiritually in a physical world.

Aslan means "lion" in several Middle Eastern languages. The most famous "Aslan" is a lion in *The Chronicles of Narnia* by C. S. Lewis. In these stories, Aslan is the Messiah, the One who appears at critical points in the story in order to point human beings in the right direction. Aslan doesn't preach, he acts. His actions are an inherent expression of who he is.

We hope to point the way toward joyful, satisfying and healthy relationships with oneself and with others. Our purpose is to make a real difference in our reader's everyday lives.

We invite you to submit a query of 1-3 pages for any work related to our mission statement including; self-help; relationship; business-related, humor, autobiographical and so on.

We are not interested in text books, poetry books, or channeled books. Include your full name, mailing address, email address, and phone numbers.

Please Do Not send query letters via email. Please include a letter- sized, self-addressed stamped return envelope.

Categories: Nonfiction—General Interest—Inspirational—Lifestyle—Relationships—Self Help—Spiritual

CONTACT: Barbara Q. Levine, Publisher
Material: All
2490 Black Rock Turnpike, #342Q
Fairfield CT 06825
E-mail: barbara@aslanpublishing.com (no submissions)
Website: www.aslanpublishing.com

Aspect

Please refer to Time Warner Book Group.

ATHENEUM
BOOKS FOR YOUNG READERS

Atheneum Books

Atheneum Books publishes original hardcover trade books for children from pre-school age through young adult. Our list includes picture books, chapter books, mysteries, science fiction and fantasy, and middle grade young adult fiction and nonfiction. The style and subject matter of the books we publish is almost unlimited. We do not, however, publish textbooks, coloring or activity books, greeting cards, magazines or pamphlets or religious publications. Anne Schwartz Books and Richard Jackson Books is a highly selective line of books that are part of the Atheneum imprint. The lists of Charles Scribner's Sons Books for Young Readers have been folded into the Atheneum program.

General Submission Guidelines

Atheneum accepts only letters of inquiry describing your work, regardless of length or type (picture books, novels, non-fiction). Should the work seem to be in line with our current publishing needs, we will then request the complete picture book manuscripts or outlines and sample chapters of longer works.

With your submission, you may also wish to include a brief resume of your previous publishing credits.

Please allow twelve weeks for your material to be considered. Although it often takes less time, it can take even longer than we would like because of the many thousands of submissions we receive and because every submission is carefully considered.

Picture Book Submissions

Atheneum publishes 15-20 picture books each year. You may include illustrations with your manuscript submission. It is the prerogative of the publisher to choose illustrators. If you yourself are a professional artist, you might wish to send samples (no larger than 8½"x11") to our art director, Ann Bobco. Drop-off portfolios are accepted only on Thursdays at 10 a.m. and will be left at the reception desk for pick up at noon. No manuscripts will be read or considered at this time.

Questions frequently asked:

"What are you looking for?"

The most common answer each editor gives to this question is simply, "Nothing specific—just good writing." Atheneum puts less emphasis on particular trends, fads and gimmicks and more on quality of craftsmanship—fine writing and artwork. This and originality are the most important things we look for in a manuscript.

"Why did you turn my manuscript down?"

Although it is easy to understand a writer's desire for a critique of his work, the constant heavy influx of submissions makes it impossible to offer evaluations of work that has been declined. Form rejection letters are not meant as an insult, but simply are the only way publishers can handle the number of submissions received. A writer can expect feed-back on his work by taking one of the many excellent writing courses offered by local colleges and universities—some of them specifically geared to children's books. Another source of evaluation can be found in oining a local writers group. Such groups commonly critique members' work in progress. THE SUBJECT GUIDE TO BOOKS IN PRINT by R.R. Bowker Company also lists helpful books on writing for children and the Children's Book Council (568 BROADWAY, NEW YORK NY 10003) has a pamphlet on the subject available on request. But perhaps the simplest and cheapest way of finding out what publishers look for is to go to your local public or school library and read.

Categories: Fiction—Nonfiction—Children—Juvenile—Literature—Teen—Young Adult

CONTACT: Ginee Seo, Editorial Director
Material: Any not assigned below
CONTACT: Anne Schwartz, V.P., Editorial Director
Material: Anne Schwartz Books
CONTACT: Richard Jackson, Editor
Material: Richard Jackson Books
CONTACT: Caitlyn Dlouhy, Executive Editor.
Material: All other material
1230 Avenue of the Americas
New York NY 10020
Phone: 212-698-2715
Fax: 212-698-2796

ATL Press
Science Technology

1. We are interested in many science and non-fiction areas, including astronomy, biochemistry, biomedicine, biotechnology, chemistry, computers, earth science, foods, medicine, nutraceuticals, pharmaceuticals and polymers. We publish monographs, edited volumes and conference proceedings. However, ATL Press also welcomes submissions on other topics, including fiction titles. Our interests include non-book products, such as software, CDs, audiovisual materials, etc. Your submission will be particularly appealing to us, if it is unique or of special topical interest. Examples of such titles include leading edge research results, topics with broad public appeal, and areas of major scientific discoveries with notable impact on society.

2. Before you send us the completed manuscript or work, we prefer to receive an introductory letter that describes your proposed project, together with an outline, estimated length, expected completion date, nature (that is, line drawings, color, B&W photos, etc.) and number of any illustrations, and, if available, perhaps a few sample chapters (please include a SASE with your submission).

3. A very essential point to consider in your submission is the ultimate customer: who are your target readers, why should they be interested in your book, what makes your book unique, which other titles do you know of on your topic, and how does your book differ from these? A visit to one of the major bookstores or libraries in your neighborhood may help you answer some of these questions, if you look up the section that is most relevant to your topic.

4. Can you suggest individuals who can review and comment on your manuscript? If so, please provide a list with the relevant contact information.

5. Please tell us also about yourself: your educational background, professional credentials, any achievements, awards, etc. (a resume and a list of publications—if applicable—are acceptable).

6. We generally accept only manuscripts prepared with word processing software. Please indicate in your submission the word processor used, and the platform (PC or Mac). Detailed information on submitting camera-ready manuscripts is available upon request.

7. Last, and not least: if you have not embarked on this venture yet, be prepared to spend a substantial amount of time and effort. At the same time, it can be an extremely enjoyable undertaking. On our part, we work very closely with our authors to produce and market their projects.

Categories: Business—Computers—Juvenile—Science—Technology

CONTACT: Editorial Office
Material: All
PO Box 4563 T Stn.
Shrewsbury MA 01545
Website: www.atlpress.com

Avalon Books

Under its Avalon Books imprint, Thomas Bouregy & Co., Inc. publishes hardcover secular romances, mysteries, and westerns for the library market. Our books are wholesome adult ficiton, suitable for family reading. There is no graphic or premarital sex in any of our novels; kisses and embraces are as far as our characters go. It is the author's responsibility to heighten the romantic atmosphere by developing love scenes with tenderness and emotion. There is never any profanity in any of our books.

We publish sixty books a year in bimonthly cycles of ten. A cycle consists of: four contemporary romances, two historical romances, two mysteries, and two westerns. The mysteries and contemporary romances are all set in the present day; all the westerns are historical. Books range in length from a minimum of 45,000 words to a maximum of 60,000 words (usually about 160 to 210 manuscript pages.) However, if the manuscript is exceptional, we will accept somewhat larger books.

Romances

We do not want old-fashioned, predictable, formulaic books. We are looking for contemporary characters, fresh plots, and story lines. Supporting characters and subplots should be interesting and realistic, and they should add an extra and interesting dimension to the book.

Heroines: She should be an independent young woman with an interesting profession or career. She is equal to the stresses of today's world and can take care of herself, yet she remains feminine and loyal to traditional values; when he comes along, the man she loves will take priority in her life, just as she will be a priority in his.

Heroes: He should be warm, likable, realistic, sympathetic, and understanding. He should treat the heroine as an equal. With respect for her intelligence and individuality. The rude, overbearing, patronizing, egotistical, brooding, macho men are not welcome in our romances; they make very poor role models for husbands—and men—in today's world.

Historical Romances

The manuscripts should be between 50,000 and 70,000 words. Time period can range from medieval times to World War I. No time travel romances. Period, place and cultural events are vital to creating a historical feel. The historical romances will maintain the high level of reading expected by our readers.

Mysteries

The element of suspense is very important, but it is equally important to have a tight, well-researched, believable story line. Avoid contrived, predictable, mechanical plots and clichés. We are now looking for longer (50,000 to 70,000 words), gritty, more mainstream mysteries. Murders, of course, is often a necessary part of a mystery, but avoid gory descriptions. Sexual violence of any kind is not acceptable. The protagonists should not be drinkers, although it is acceptable if the villains drink. The occasional profanity is fine as well.

Westerns

All westerns are historical novels, and it is important that they be placed in the past and that the background be carefully researched. Avoid using words and phrases that were not part of the language at the time your western is set. Plots should be suspenseful and action-packed, but vivid descriptions of the gory details of violence should be avoided.

It is fine to you the occasional "hell" or "damn", but limit the use of profanity. Though it is important for flavor and authenticity to use some westernisms in dialogue ("pardner" and the dropping of the final "g" in present particles, for example), overuse of the dialect is to be avoided; it slows down the reader's pace and, as a result, the narrative pace too. The use of alcohol is allowed, but should not be overdone.

General Submission Guidelines

You must include with you submission:
- Query letter addressed to: The Editors (no specific editor's name is required)
- Synopsis (2-3 pgs.)
- First three chapters
- Self-Addressed, Stamped Envelope

S.A.S.E. (See requirements below*) Or note in your query letter that you do not want the partial returned.

Keep in mind, we do accept unagented work and multiple submissions. Multiple submissions are when authors send their manuscript to multiple publishing houses. Please indicate if it is a multiple submission in your query letter.

You should hear back from us anywhere between two weeks and a month from when we receive your submission. If we think that your novel may be suitable for our list, we will contact you and request that you submit the entire manuscript. After we receive your manuscript, the response time is typically 4- 6 months.

- The envelope must be large enough for the partial, with sufficient postage for its weight. Only first class and priority stamps allowed. No media mail, Fed Ex, or metered mail. Also, we cannot return partials or manuscripts to areas outside the U.S. No international Reply Coupons, please, except for letter-sized SASE's. Any material that does not meet these requirements will be recycled.

Categories: Fiction—Mystery—Romance—Western

CONTACT: The Editors
Material: All
Thomas Bouregy & Co. Inc.
160 Madison Ave.
New York, NY 10016
Phone: 212-598-0222
Fax: 212-979-1862
E-mail: editorial@avalonbooks.com
Website: www.avalonbooks.com

B. Klein Publications

Formal guidelines not available.

Send queries or book proposals to the below address.

Categories: Nonfiction—Business—Directories—Military—Money & Finances—Native American—Psychology—Reference

CONTACT: Submissions Editor
Material: All
PO Box 6578
Delray Beach FL 33482
Phone: 561-496-3316
Fax: 561-496-5546

Back Bay Books

Please refer to Time Warner Book Group.

The Backwaters Press

THE 2005 BACKWATERS PRIZE
Submission Guidelines:

General: This contest is open to anyone writing in English, whether the poet has previous book publications or not. This is not a first-book contest. Full-length ms., (between 60 & 85 typewritten pages, not including credits, title page, contents page) original poetry in English (no translations). No Collaborations. May be a collection or a single long poem. Standard poetry format. Typescript or clear dot matrix OK. No identification of poet anywhere in MS, including in the text of the poems. Mss. in which poet's name is included in the text will be disqualified. If the poet needs to refer to or uses his/her own name in poems, a pseudonym must be used in the text. Winner will be allowed to make changes to text. Do not include photos or drawings in the manuscript. Winner will be able to work with press to include such items in finished book. Do not send manuscript corrections-winner will be allowed to make manuscript changes. Send two title pages, one with writer info: Name, address, evening phone, e-mail address; one with title only of ms. Include a short cover letter with bio. Single poems or group of poems may have been previously published in magazines or chapbooks but the manuscript as a whole may not have been previously published in book form, including self-publication.

Simultaneous submissions: OK, but please so state in your cover letter. You must inform The Backwaters Press immediately if your ms. is accepted for publication elsewhere. Include a SAS postcard for notification of receipt of ms. by the press, if desired.

- Entry fee: $25 must accompany each ms. You may submit more than one ms., but each must be accompanied by the $25 entry fee. Mss. received without entry fee will be recycled. Personal check OK, please make them out to The Backwaters Press.
- Notification of Winner: All entrants will receive a copy of the winning book, so you do not need to send an envelope for notification of prizewinner. OK to send an SASE for earlier notification.
- Returns: All manuscripts will be recycled. Do not include a return envelope or return postage.
- Submission Deadline: Postmarked no later than June 4th, 2005. Send the cheapest way if you want to. Just get it postmarked before midnight, June 4th, 2005.
- Prize: $1000.00 and ten copies of the book to the winning poet; publication in an edition of at least 500 copies, perfect bound. Promotion and distribution by The Backwaters Press. Prizewinner announced in P&W and AWP Chronicle. The Press will enter the winning book in book contests for the year and send review copies to respected literary journals. Prizewinner will be able to purchase copies of the winning book if desired, for resale at half price.
- Judging: The decision of the Judge is final. Judge for 2004 is Philip Levine. Philip Levine was born in 1928 in Detroit and was educated there, at the public schools and at Wayne State University. After a succession of industrial jobs he left the city for good and lived in various parts of the country before settling in Fresno, California. The Names of the Lost won the Lenore Marshall Award for the best book

of poetry published by an American in 1976. Three of his books have been nominated for the National Book Critics Circle Award, and two of them, Ashes and 7 Years from Somewhere, have received it. Ashes also received the Ruth Lilly Poetry Prize "for distinguished poetic achievements," awarded by Poetry magazine and The American Council for the Arts. What Work Is received the National Book Award in poetry for 1991. The Simple Truth won the Pulitzer Prize in poetry for 1995. The Mercy was published in 1999. Judges in past years have included: Greg Kosmicki, Greg Kuzma, Ted Kooser, CarolAnn Russell, Hilda Raz and Hayden Carruth.

Check our website to read poems and parts of novels we've published, see author and book cover pictures, or download contest information.

Previous Winners

1998 Kevin Griffith Paradise Refunded Judge: Greg Kosmicki

1999 Sally Allen McNall Rescue Judge: Greg Kuzma

2000 David Staudt The Gifts and Thefts Judge: Ted Kooser

2001 Susan Firer The Laugh We Make When We Fall Judge: CarolAnn Russell

2002 Ginny MacKenzie Skipstone Judge: Hilda Raz

2003 Michelle Gillett Blinding The Goldfinches Judge: Hayden Carruth

Winner of the 2003 Backwaters Prize

Michelle Gillett for her manuscript *Blinding The Goldfinches,* Chosen by Hayden Carruth from among 15 Finalists

Mr. Carruth's statement:

What one finds in these poems is the truth. It's as simple as that. No frills from the workshop, no ostentatious diction or imagery, but only the firm, quiet enterprise of authenticity. In a world increasingly crude, cruel, and repulsive what could be more pleasing, more useful? Not that these poems shun our actual history. Violence and dislocation are the clearly stated context here. But the accurate vision of a committed imagination prevails, and does so in language as flawless as language can be. I recommend these poems for their wisdom and insight, but even more for their steadfast initiative and independence, their refusal to be fashionable. —Hayden Carruth, November, 2003

About the Poet

Born in New York City, Michelle Gillett is an editor, columnist, and teacher. She holds an MFA in writing from the Warren Wilson program. As well as the 2003 Backwaters Prize, Michelle has won the 1998 Billy Murray Denny Poetry Award and the MacGuffin Poet Hunt in 2001. Her magazine publications include Poetry Northwest, the Owen Wister Review, Passages North, and many others. She has also won numerous poetry fellowships from the Massachusetts Cultural Council. Her chapbook, Rock and Spindle, was published by Mad River Press in 1998.Gillett currently lives in Stockbridge, Massachusetts, with her husband and their two daughters.

About The Readers' Choice Award

The readers are in process of re-reading the Finalist manuscripts to chose the two winners of The Readers' Choice Awards for 2003. The awards will be announced on the website at www.thebackwaterspress.homestead.com as soon as the determination is made. The winners will be notified personally, as usual. Sadly, the editor has decided to discontinue The Readers' Choice Award after this year because it is more than the press can handle with its limited resources.

The Backwaters Press Announces The Weldon Kees Prize

Before his disappearance in 1955, Beatrice, Nebraska native Weldon Kees became noted not only as a poet, but also as a fiction writer, director, artist, musician, composer, art and literary critic, playwright and photographer. In 1954, his car was found at the entrance to the Golden Gate Bridge, and Kees has not been seen since.

A great site to learn more about Kees is at: http://mockingbird.creighton.edu/NCW/kees.htm

To honor Kees' name, The Weldon Kees Award for a chapbook of poetry has been established by The Backwaters Press. Three winners will be chosen and published annually. $125 cash prize to each winner.

• Guidelines: Submit 20-30 pages of original poetry by a single poet. This is not including Title and Contents page. No style/content restrictions. $20 entry fee. You may enter as many manuscripts as you like, but each must be accompanied by the $20 entry fee. Deadline: POSTMARK Dec 31st, 2004 Send SASE for ms. return. Judging by editors of the Press. Please follow the usual precautions in protecting the poet's identity on the manuscript.

Further questions—please e-mail to gkosm62735@aol.com. Submit all manuscripts to the address below.

Categories: Poetry

CONTACT: Greg Kosmicki
Material: All
3502 North 52nd Street
Omaha NE 68104-3506
E-mail: Gkosm62735@aol.com
Website: www.thebackwaterspress.homestead.com

Books A-L

Baen Books

Dear Author:

We publish only science fiction and fantasy. Writers familiar with what we have published in the past will know what sort of material we are most likely to publish in the future: powerful plots with solid scientific and philosophical underpinnings are the sine qua non for consideration for science fiction submissions. As for fantasy, any magical system must be both rigorously coherent and integral to the plot, and overall the work must at least strive for originality.

Those manuscripts which survive the "first cut" as outlined above are then judged primarily on plot and characterization.

Style: Simple is generally better; in our opinion good style, like good breeding, never calls attention to itself.

Payment rates: very competitive.

Preferred length: 100,000 - 130,000 words Generally we are uncomfortable with manuscripts under 100,000 words, but if your novel is really wonderful send it along regardless of length.

SUBMISSION PROCEDURES:

Query letters are not necessary. We prefer to see complete manuscripts accompanied by a synopsis. We prefer not to see simultaneous submissions.

Electronic Submissions: Electronic submissions are strongly preferred.

Send to slush@baen.com . No disks unless requested.

Attach the manuscript as a Rich Text Format (.rtf) file. Any other format will not be considered.

Send the manuscript as a single file (do not break it into separate chapter files).

Your submission must include your name, email address*, postal mailing address, and telephone number. *[If you have an alternate permanent email address, please include it, in case your primary account goes out of service.] Include a plot outline if possible.

Minimal formatting, please. Indent paragraphs; center chapter headers and scene break indicators (###, ***, etc.); use page breaks only at the end of chapters. For emphasis, choose underline or italics and use it throughout. Try to avoid bold face, as it tends not to show up. Also avoid non-standard fonts, and unnecessary changes in font face, size, etc. Make it readable, or we won't read it. If something needs special formatting—e.g., small caps for a certain entity's dialog—explain it in a cover letter.

Include, if you like, your ideal cover treatment, including cover copy, a teaser page, and whatever else you would like. (But don't try to "sell" the story in a cover letter. It will stand or fall on its own merits.)

NOTE: Any viruses attached to your submission will send your manuscript straight into the bit-bucket.

Hardcopy Submissions: (for those who cannot submit electronically)

Standard manuscript format only: double-spaced, one side of the page only, 1 1/2" margins on all four sides of the page. We will consider photocopies if they are dark and clear.

Font must be readable, or we won't read it. This means seriphed or at least semi-seriphed, 12-point or greater. Publisher likes Omega and Lucida. Typesetter likes any standard bookface, Times Roman or Courier.

Title, author (last name only is okay), and page number at the top of each page are mandatory. Include your name, mailing address, and telephone number on the first page.

All submissions should be accompanied by a stamped return envelope. Submissions from outside the U.S. should be accompanied by sufficient International Reply Coupons.

Reporting time: usually within 9 to 12 Months. (Sorry, we get lots of manuscripts.)

Thank you for thinking of Baen Books.

The Editors

P.S. Baen will be maintaining offices in New York after the move so continue to use this address.

Categories: Fiction—Fantasy—Science Fiction

CONTACT: Submissions Editor
Material: All
PO Box 1403
Riverdale NY 10471
E-mail: jimbaen@baen.com
Website: www.baen.com

Baker Publishing Group

About Us

Baker Publishing Group is a leading evangelical publisher offering more than 200 releases per year in its six separate divisions.

Mission Statement

The mission of Baker Publishing Group is to publish writings that promote historic Christianity, irenically express the concerns of evangelicalism, and reflect the diversity of this movement. Its books are well conceived, competently written, and handsomely produced. They furnish resources to all—from individuals to families, from laypeople to pastors, from collegians to seminarians—who seek to live for the Lord and worship him.

Submission Policy

Baker Books, Fleming H. Revell, Chosen Books, and Brazos Press (imprints of Baker Publishing Group) do not accept unsolicited manuscripts. All manuscripts received will be returned to the sender without review.

We will consider unsolicited work only through one of the following avenues: Materials sent to our editorial staff through a professional literary agent will be considered. In addition, our staff attend various writers' conferences in which prospective authors can develop relationships with those in the publishing industry.

If you are interested in having an editor at Baker view your work, we recommend submitting it to one of two writing services: The Writer's Edge, available both online and in print, or First Edition, an online service of the Evangelical Christian Publishers Association. We subscribe to both these services and regularly review the proposals which appear there, as do many other Christian publishers. *These organizations can be reached at the following addresses:*

• First Edition
On the web: www.ecpa.org/FE
E-mail: FirstEdition@ECPA.org
• The Writer's Edge:
On the web: www.writersedgeservice.com
E-mail: info@WritersEdgeService.om
Mailing address: P.O. Box 1266
Wheaton, IL 60189

Preparing a Proposal — Baker Academic Books Only

1. Book proposals, which are always welcome at Baker Academic, vary in form from a one-page description to an extensive prospectus including sample chapters.

2. We prefer to see a proposal before you complete the manuscript. This enables you to obtain from us guidelines for the project, which increases the likelihood that we will publish the manuscript.

3. Even if you finish your manuscript before approaching us, we ask that you submit a proposal instead of the manuscript. This helps us to control the flow of manuscripts, knowing that we can conscientiously review only so many at one time. We do not promise to examine unsolicited manuscripts; we return them only if you have sent return postage.

4. The proposal you submit initially may range from a brief query letter to an extensive proposal. As a rule, the shorter it is, the more quickly we answer; the longer and more promising it is, the more definitive our response.

5. A fully developed proposal consists of the following:

a. The proposed book's purpose.

b. The primary audience for the book; its secondary audiences. If it has potential as a textbook in institutions of higher education, identify: (i) specific courses for which it might be used as a primary text (if any), then those for which it could serve as a supplementary text; (ii) the educational level of the book; and (iii) pedagogical aids, such as exercises, discussion questions, glossaries, and bibliographies, to be included in it.

c. Books with which it will compete, and the uniquenesses and strengths that set it apart from them; or reasons why no book of its kind exists.

d. The estimated date for the manuscript's completion.

e. An annotated outline, with paragraph summaries or brief outlines of each chapter.

f. The approximate length of each chapter, in words. (See appendix below.)

g. Kinds and quantities of illustrative material (such as photographs, line drawings, maps, charts, tables) that need to be included. (Remember that, on the one hand, illustrations can make a good book a great one; and on the other, they can increase the book's price to the point of inhibiting its sale.)

h. Some sample chapters. These should include a chapter that represents the book's distinctive contribution and, if possible, an introduction that explains such things as the book's background, purpose, distinctives, approach, thesis, and contents.

i. A full vita, one that shows your qualifications to write the proposed volume.

j. Letters from others in your field who testify to the need for such a volume and, if you are new to publishing, your ability to write it.

6. Put your proposal in the most refined form you can. We will judge your ability to craft a well-written and accurate manuscript by the quality of your proposal.

7. We naturally prefer that you submit your proposal to us first. If you choose to submit it simultaneously to other publishers as well, we only ask that you say as much in your cover letter.

8. After evaluating your proposal, we will either advise you to send it elsewhere or we will commit to publishing your project and issue a contract.

Appendix: Estimating Length

Word processing programs make it easy to estimate the length of a project. Using the word count feature you can obtain an accurate word or character count.

As a rule of thumb, our standard trim-size academic book has 2700 characters (including spaces) or 450 words per typeset page. Footnotes are included in the character/word counts.

Add an additional 10-25 pages for front matter and indexes. Thank you!

Categories: Christian Interests—History—Religion—Spiritual

CONTACT: Submissions Editor
PO Box 6287
Grand Rapids MI 49516
Phone: 616-676-9185
Fax: 616-676-9573
Website: www.bakerpublishinggroup.com

Baker Books

Please refer to Baker Publishing Group.

Balcony Press

Balcony Press is interested in manuscripts on art, architecture and design topics with a preference for west coast or southwest subject matter. Books normally take a historic or cultural slant as opposed to technical, biographical or how-to.

If you are planning to submit an idea for a photography book please be sure there is a strong cohesive idea, that it is unique, and that you have a qualified writer lined up to do accompanying text.

Submit proposals via e-mail or snail mail.

Proposals should include the following:
• Book title and brief summary of the book's content
• Proposed length of manuscript and approximate quantity of illustrations, photos, etc.
• Description of the audience for the book and any ideas you have for promoting it
• What is unusual about the book and what is the competition?
• Author biography or resume
• Suggested table of contents
• Sample chapter and introduction
• SASE for anything you want returned—MANDATORY
In general:
• Authors are responsible for providing all photos, illustrations and permissions to be used in the book
• No royalty advances or expenses are offered
• Royalties are 10% of net revenues from book sales
• Proposals will be responded to within 1 month
• Full manuscript will be responded to in 3 months.
Categories: Nonfiction—Architecture—Arts

CONTACT: Ann Gray
Material: All
512 E. Wilson St., Ste. 213
Glendale CA 91206
Phone: 818 956-5313
Fax: 818 956-5904
E-mail: editor@balconypress.com (submissions)
Website: www.balconypress.com

Remember: Editors change jobs and publishers change addresses. It is wise to invest in a phone call for the current information before submitting.

Ballantine Books

We do not accept unsolicited submissions, proposals, manuscripts or submission queries at this time.

If you would like to have your work or manuscript considered for publication, we recommend that you work with an established literary agent.

Barbed Wire Publishing

Barbed Wire Publishing is a regional publisher that prefers to publish Southwestern, children's, and bi-lingual books. However, almost any subject that strikes our fancy is a potential candidate for publication. Novels, histories, political and religious manuscripts have been published by the company. Yucca Tree Press is an imprint of Barbed Wire Publishing.

The company has three publishing tracts: traditional publishing, Keepsake Publishing, and Pardner Publishing. Because we are a small company, our traditionally published books are limited (25% to 30% of our books). Keepsake Publishing is a process that is designed for family histories, generational stories and mementos where a limited number of copies (25-50 books) are produced reasonably for distribution to family and friends. Pardner Publishing is our form of vanity publishing in which the author participates financially in the production process, Barbed Wire provides full editorial, design, composition, and printing/binding services as well as sales, marketing, and distribution of the books. The author can expect 50% of net book sales after full return of his/her investment.

We aggressively market all of our books and distribute through B&T, Books West, Amazon.com, Borders.com, and BN.com. We submit all of our books to the major bookstore chains' Small Press Divisions and we actively sell into independent bookstores and defined niche markets.

E-mail query letters are encouraged. Manuscripts can be submitted electronically or as hard copy. A synopsis, a few representative chapters, a potential market analysis, and a brief author bio will help our evaluation of the MS.

Categories: Nonfiction—Children—History—Language—Politics—Regional—Religion—Southwestern

CONTACT: George Stein, Publisher
Material: All
270 Avenida de Mesilla
Las Cruces NM 88005
Phone: 505-525-9707
888-817-1990 (toll free)
Fax: 505-525-9711 (fax)
E-mail: thefolks@barbed-wire.net
Website: www.barbed-wire.net

Barricade Books

For starters, Barricade Books publish virtually no fiction. Furthermore, we do not publish poetry or children's books.

We do look for non-fiction, mostly of the controversial type. We look for books that we can promote with authors who can talk about their topics on radio and television, and to the press.

Please review the books on our web site. Given the above stipulations, if you believe your material fits our list send an outline and one or two chapters together with a self-addressed, stamped envelope to Carole Stuart. Please let us know if you want your material returned.

As of now, we do not accept proposals on disk, nor do we accept them via email.

Categories: Nonfiction—African-American—Biography—Entertainment—Gay/Lesbian—Mass Communications—Regional—Relationships—Sexuality—Humor—Martial Arts

Books
A-L

CONTACT: Carole Stuart, Publisher
Material: All
185 Bridge Plaza North Ste 308-A
Fort Lee NJ 07024
Phone: 201-944-7600
Fax: 201-944-6363
E-mail: customerservice@barricadebooks.com (no submissions)
Website: www.barricadebooks.com

Barrons Educational Series, Inc.

Publishers of Elementary, High School, College and General Books.

Submission Guidelines

For initial consideration of your project, query letters are recommended.

NOTE: We do not accept e-mailed or faxed proposals.

Include a self-addressed postcard if you desire notification of receipt of material.

Include a large, *self-addressed, stamped envelope* to accommodate the return of your material should it be determined unsuitable for our needs.

Indicate if the material being submitted is in response to a positive reply to a query letter previously sent to Barron's; also, write **"Requested Material"** on the package.

Simultaneous submissions are welcomed.

It is not necessary to have a literary agent in order to submit material.

Due to the large volume of unsolicited submissions received, complete evaluation of a proposal may take up to eight months. A system for tracking the status of unsolicited material does not exist. Therefore, *we do not accept telephone inquiries regarding the status of individual proposals.*

When submitting a work of juvenile fiction:

• Include the manuscript in its entirety.

• Artwork is not necessary. If artwork is available, include a sample.

• Include author's credentials.

When submitting a work of adult or juvenile nonfiction:

• Include a table of contents and two sample chapters.

• Include a brief description of the work. This overview should cite the market being targeted (e.g., children, ages 2-4; secondary school teachers; etc.).

• Include author's credentials.

We will contact you if additional information or material is needed in order to properly evaluate your project. *Do not send additional material unless specifically requested to do so. It will be discarded.*

Thank you for your adherence to the above guidelines.

Categories: Nonfiction—Animals—Business—Careers—Children—College—Cooking—Crafts/Hobbies—Diet/Nutrition—Education—Gardening—Health—Juvenile—Language—Parenting—Reference—Textbooks—Young Adult

CONTACT: Mr. Wayne Barr, Acquisitions Editor
Material: All
250 Wireless Blvd.
Hauppauge, NY 11788-3917
Phone: 631-434-3311
Fax: 631-434-3723
E-mail: info@barronseduc.com (no submissions)
Website: barronseduc.com

Battelle Press

Battelle Press publishes both science and management books for engineers, scientists, and researchers. Battelle Press is looking for management, project management, and communication titles specifically targeted to these technical readers. To review current Battelle Press titles, visit our web bookstore at battelle.org/bookstore.

Categories: Management

CONTACT: Joe Sheldrick, Aquisitions Editor
Material: All
505 King Ave.
Columbus OH 43201-2693
Phone: 614-424-6393
E-mail: press@battelle.org
Website: battelle.org/bookstore

Bay Tree Publishing

Bay Tree is a small, independent, nonfiction publisher of business, psychology, current affairs and science. We are looking for manuscripts that appeal to an educated but nonprofessional audience. We do not publish fiction, poetry or personal memoirs. Recent and forthcoming titles include, *Taking the War Out of Our Words: The Art of Powerful Non-Defensive Communication, Get Slightly Famous, and Bring in More Business with Less Effort*, and *The Wrong Way Home: Uncovering the Patterns of Cult Behavior.*

Please do not send entire manuscripts. Query with a one-page synopsis, table of contents and author bio.

Categories: Nonfiction—Business—Psychology—Science

CONTACT: Acquisitions Editor
Material: All
721 Creston Road
Berkeley CA 94708

Baywood Publishing Company, Inc.

Baywood Publishing invites authors to forward proposals for publications in counseling, death & bereavement, psychology, and gerontology, health policy and technical communication. We welcome submissions in these areas from authors who desire to publish with a scholarly professional press. These guidelines are provided to expedite the submission process.

The Proposal Package:

1. Cover Letter introducing yourself, the title of your proposed publication, a concise description of the purpose and scope of the book, and an indication of whom the audience will be.

2. Curriculum Vita for each author(s)/editor(s) involved. This should include: Names, titles, addresses, and phone/fax numbers.

3. List of Contributors, if applicable. Please indicate the total number of contributors and provide their names, titles addresses, and phone/fax numbers.

4. Table of Contents, to include chapter titles and paragraphs describing those chapters.

5. Introduction or Preface, and at least one chapter for the proposed publication.

6. The primary specialty and any areas of subspecialization for the author/editor.

7. Status of the manuscript: Is it in the idea stage? Is it less than 50% complete? More than 50% complete? Has any of the material been previously published?

8. Probable date that the manuscript will be completed.

9. Mechanical dimensions including: Number of typed double-spaced pages; number of charts; number of tables.

10. Potential Markets. Describe the primary and any secondary professional and/or student markets for which this book is intended and the level of readership at which it is aimed.

11. Timeliness. Please try to estimate how long, in years, the content of the book will remain current and useful.

12. List of Competing Titles. Please include the author, title, publisher, year, pages, price of each competing publication.

13. Uniqueness. How does this book differ from competing titles? List any special or unique features your work contains

Categories: Nonfiction—Counseling—Health—Psychology—Technical—Textbooks—Gerontology—Public Health—Death & Bereavement

CONTACT: Stuart Cohen, Managing Editor
Material: Proposals
26 Austin Ave
P.0 Box 337
Amityville NY 11701
Phone: 631-691-1270
Fax: 631-691-1770
E-mail: baywood@baywood.com
Website: www.baywood.com

Bee-Con Books

BEE-CON BOOKS is a new publishing company (est. 2001) that concentrates on fiction. It has published *The Parcel Express Murders and Damaged!* by author Bernadette Y. Connor. Romance, mystery, children's fiction and general fiction submissions will be considered. Submit a query letter and synopsis. Manuscripts will be returned only if self-addressed-stamped mailers are included.

Categories: Fiction—Children's—Mystery—Romance—Teen

CONTACT: Erica L. Watts
Material: All Submissions
PO BOX 27708
Philadelphia PA 19118
Website: www.bee-conbooks.com

> *Remember: Editors change jobs and publishers change addresses. It is wise to invest in a phone call for the current information before submitting.*

Bella Books

Bella Books specializes in fiction by and about lesbians. We publish general lesbian fiction, romance, mystery / thriller, some sci-fi / fantasy, and some erotica. Bella is interested in novels with a solid plot and engaging, fully-realized characters. The main characters must be lesbians and the story must be credible. The manuscript should be between 50,000 and 80,000 words.

Bella Books does NOT accept unsolicited manuscripts. Your manuscript should be completed before sending your query to us. We are not interested in manuscripts that have been submitted simultaneously to multiple publishers.

To make sure that your manuscript is considered, please follow these instructions carefully. Send a cover letter, précis and a self-addressed, stamped envelope to:

Bella Books
P.O. Box 10543
Tallahassee, FL 32302

The cover letter should very briefly describe your book, including the title and word count. It should also include a brief biographical sketch of the author.

Make sure you include your address, phone numbers where you can be reached, and your email address. The précis should include an outline of the plot (please keep this to one or two pages) and some information about all of the main characters.

If we are interested in reading the manuscript, we will contact you. Please understand that we receive many queries each day, and it may take up to 30 days for us to contact you.

If we ask to see your manuscript, please send it typed (double-spaced) with one-inch margins. Remember that you are trying to woo a publisher for your book. Make it as clean (no typos, pages in correct order, etc.) as you can to the best of your ability. Your manuscript must be available by email or on disk if we need it. (Microsoft Word preferred.)

For more information on Bella's Manuscript Formatting Mechanics and the books we publish, please visit our website at www.bellabooks.com. Thank you for your interest in Bella Books.

Categories: Fiction—Erotica—Gay/Lesbian—Myster—Romance—Science Fiction

CONTACT: Acquisitions Editor
Material: All
PO Box 10543
Tallahassee, FL 32302
Phone: 800-539-5965
Website: www.bellabooks.com

BenBella Books

BenBella specializes in science fiction and pop culture. In the area of science fiction and fantasy, BenBella publishes both original works and classics. For our line of original science fiction and fantasy, BenBella is looking first and foremost for "great reads" - exciting plots, engaging characters and mind-blowing ideas. For our line of science fiction and fantasy classics, BenBella is looking for great works of fiction that should never have fallen out print, that remain accessible and relevant to today's readers.

In the area of popular culture, BenBella will be publishing a broad range of titles, from smart celebrity biographies to current trends to critical analyses of hit movies. The books in this line, however different, will share a common intelligence, accessibility and sense of fun.

BenBella will occasionally publish works of exceptional potential outside of our specialization.

SUBMISSION GUIDELINES:

BenBella Books welcomes submissions from authors and their agents. *Our guidelines are as follows:*

Pop Culture

Have you written or are planning a non-fiction work that you'd like to submit to us, please send the following information:

• Description of the book — Describe, in a page or two, the essence of the book. This description should give us a good understanding of the book and should position the book as favorably as possible — think of this as the back cover/inside flap description of the book.

• High-level table of contents — Provide your thinking on the overall flow of the book. This should be only a page or two.

• Target market for the book — Who is the target market for this book? "Everyone" is not a good answer. The target market should be specific and clear. Explain why this book will have great appeal to the target market.

• Relationship of the book to the competition — What are the main competitors to this book and how will this book distinguish itself from the competition? Every book has competitors, so you will need to do the legwork to find your competition, review the books, and assess how you will effectively differentiate your book against theirs.

• Useful endorsements — If you have personal relationships that are likely to result in endorsements for the book from qualified/well-known individuals, please let us know.

• Resume and qualifications — Your expertise is a critical selling point for the book. So tell us why you are uniquely qualified to write this book. Also list your publishing credits, if any.

This entire package should just be 5-10 pages. If we like what we see we'll ask for a detailed table of contents and a sample chapter. Please do not send a manuscript until we ask for one. We prefer exclusive submissions and will respond quickly to them.

Science Fiction

BenBella publishes original works and republishes great sci-fi works that never should have fallen out of print.

To submit an original work, please send the manuscript to us, along with a 1-2 page letter describing the work.

To submit a great work for republication, please send a manuscript or copy of the published book, along with a 1-2 page letter describing the work.

The proposal should be printed in 12-point type, double-spaced on letter-sized unlined white paper. The Internet is great, but we prefer to review crisp proposals on paper so, please, no fax or e-mail submissions. We get a lot of these and they need to be easy to read and take notes on.

Please send only copies of your materials, no original manuscripts or artwork. We will not be held liable for materials lost or destroyed in the mail.

If you want your work returned, please enclose a properly sized self-addressed, stamped envelope with your proposal. If you don't include a self-addressed, stamped envelope, we'll assume you want us to keep your proposal on file.

Categories: Culture—Science Fiction—Pop Culture

CONTACT: Editorial Submissions
Material: All
P.O Box 601389
Dallas TX 75360
Phone: 214-750-3600
Fax: 214-750-3645
E-mail: info@benbellabooks.co
Website: www.benbellabooks.com

Berkshire House Publishers

We specialize in a series of guides, the Great DestinationsTM Series, about specific destinations around the U.S. that are of unusual charm and cultural importance—destinations such as Berkshire County, Santa Fe and Taos, Napa and Sonoma, the coast of Maine, the Adirondacks, the Chesapeake Bay area, the Hamptons on Long Island, Newport and Narragansett Bay in Rhode Island, the central coast of California, Aspen, the Gulf Coast of Florida, and the Texas Hill Country. Our greatest interest would be in writers who reside in U.S. destinations that are particularly attractive to upscale visitors. Writers must be willing to write in the Great Destinations format—comprising chapters on the history, lodging, dining, culture, recreation, shopping, etc., of each area.

We also specialize in books about our own region (the Berkshires in Western Massachusetts) and the various recreational activities that can be enjoyed here. We occasionally publish cookbooks that are related to New England or to country living/country inns in general. We have a line of books on Shaker crafts and artifacts, but we are not currently seeking to add to it. We offer books of historical interest in our American ClassicsTM series, notably books by Alice Morse Earle—*Home Life in Colonial Days* and *Child Life in Colonial Days*—but have no immediate plans to add to this series.

Categories: Nonfiction—Cooking—History—Travel

CONTACT: Jean Rousseau, Publisher
Material: All
CONTACT: Philip Rich, Managing Editor
Material: All
480 Pleasant St. Ste. 5
Lee MA 01238
Phone: 413-243-0303
Fax: 413-243-4737
E-mail: Berkhouse@aol.com

Berrett-Koehler Publishers

Berrett-Koehler Publishers' publishing mission is to publish books that support the movement toward a more enlightened world of work and more free, open, humane, effective, and globally sustainable organizations. *With this in mind, please prepare a proposal that covers the following topics:*

• Need: Why is a new publication on this topic needed at this time?

• Purpose: How is the publication designed to meet the need? What are the primary and secondary purposes of the publication?

• New Contribution: What new does the publication offer? What are the five to ten most competitive or similar publications, and how—specifically—does the proposed publication differ from and go beyond each of them? Please describe the publication's new contribution in considerable detail—this is a central issue.

• Audiences and Uses: Who are the intended audiences and how will they be able to use the publication? Be specific and realistic, rather than claiming that people or managers in general will be interested. Distinguish between primary and secondary audiences. Identify specific professional associations that are audiences.

• Knowledge Base: Describe the publication's knowledge base of experience, research, theory, and/or literature review. Attach your vita or other biographical information.

• Outline: Attach a detailed chapter-by-chapter outline of the publication's planned contents.

• Manuscript Length and Special Materials: How many pages (assuming 250 words per page) do you expect that the manuscript (not the book) will be? What special materials (drawings, tables, figures, exhibits, and so on) do you anticipate will be included?

• Timetable: What is your schedule for completing the manuscript?

• Sample Chapters: Please submit two to four sample chapters with the publication proposal. Indicate if more of the draft manuscript is available, or when it might be available.

• Marketing Support: In what ways (speaking, articles, media contacts, etc.) will you as author be able to support the publisher's marketing of the book? Attach any interviews with you, stories about you, or articles by you that have already appeared in local or national media.

Categories: Nonfiction—Business—Careers—Consumer—Economics—Government—Human Rights—Inspirational—Self Help—Spiritual

CONTACT: Jeevan Sivasubramaniam, Managing Editor
Material: All
235 Montgomery St., Ste. 650
San Francisco, CA 94104
Phone: 415-288-0260
Fax: 415-362-2512
E-mail: bkpub@bkpub.com
Website: www.bkconnections.com

Bethany House Publishers

WRITER'S GUIDELINES FOR ADULT NONFICTION

Bethany House is an evangelical publisher of books in a broad range of categories. Non-fiction bestsellers include *Becoming A Vessel God Can Use* by Donna Partow, *I'm Too Young To Be This Old* by Poppy Smith, *The Subtle Power of Spiritual Abuse* by David Johnson & Jeff VanVonderen, *Telling Yourself the Truth* by William Backus & Marie Chapian, *Where Does A Mother Go to Resign?* by Barbara Johnson and *The Kingdom of the Cults* by Walter Martin. (BHP publishes no poetry or music.) *We are seeking unique, well-targeted, and thought-provoking books in the following categories:*

Christian Living

Books which help the lay person apply biblical truths to everyday life. (e.g. *Walking in Total God-Confidence* by Donna Partow, *12 Steps for the Recovering Pharisee* by John Fischer)

Devotional

Unique, stimulating approaches geared to specific audiences. (e.g. *The Perfect Catch* by H. Norman Wright, *Sweet Persecution* by Ron Brackin, *Becoming Friends with God* by Leith Anderson)

Contemporary Issues

Information and answers on cults, abortion, euthanasia, evolution, humanism, divorce, etc. (e.g. *Legislating Morality* by Dr. Norman Geisler & Frank Turek, *The New Absolutes* by William Watkins, *When Someone You Love is Dying* by David Clark & Peter Emmett, *Truth About Rock* by Steve Peters & Mark Littleton, *The Death of Truth* by Dennis McCullum)

Marriage and Family

Biblical principles for roles and relationships which will nurture love and communication. (e.g. *The Power of Believing in Your Child* by Miles McPherson, *Daze of Our Wives* by Dave Meurer, *Coaching Your Kids in the Game of Life* by Ricky Byrdsong & Dave and Neta Jackson)

Women's Issues

Books written by women, for women on various topics of concern to today's Christian woman. (e.g. *Where Does a Mother Go to Resign* by Barbara Johnson, *Sanctuary* by Marsha Crockett, *Be Still* by Elizabeth Hoekstra, *Shop, Save and Share* by Ellie Kay)

Spirituality

Experiencing a deeper walk with God through quiet time, Bible reading, and prayer. (e.g. *Contemplating the Cross* by Tricia Rhodes, *Quiet Places* by Jane Rubietta, *Into the Depths of God* by Calvin Miller)

Cults

Information and answers on cults and world religions. (e.g. *The Compact Guide to World Religions* by Dean Halverson, *Is The Mormon My Brother?* by James White, *The Dark Side of the Supernatural* by Bill Myers & Dave Wimbish)

Applied Theology

Theological topics investigated and explained for the lay person with practical application. (e.g. *The King James Only Controversy* by James White, *Chosen But Free* by Dr. Norman Geisler, *The Forgotten Trinity* by James White)

Once a contracted manuscript satisfies our editorial requirements, we assume all costs of production and distribution (the author is responsible for expenses incurred on inside art or photos, indexing, etc.). The author receives a royalty on each book sold, comparable with rates from other publishers in the CBA industry.

Our books are promoted through our trade catalog, dealer mailings, and ads in booksellers' journals and leading Christian magazines. The books are sold to bookstores, both Christian and general-market outlets, by a nationwide network of sales representatives, by major American and Canadian distributors, and by distributors in over twenty foreign countries.

WRITER'S GUIDELINES FOR ADULT GENERAL FICTION

Bethany House is the leading publisher of Christian fiction. Bestsellers include *The Meeting Place* by Janette Oke and T. Davis Bunn, *The Shunning* by Beverly Lewis, and *Legend of the Celtic Stone* by Michael Phillips. *We are seeking unique, carefully developed books in the following categories:*

Historical Fiction

This category features stories in any historical setting prior to 1950. Some examples include *The Widow of Larkspur Inn* by Lawana Blackwell, *Texas Angel* by Judith Pella and *The Dark Sun Rises* by Denise Williamson. Most of our historical fiction is developed in series.

Contemporary Fiction

This category features both stand-alone novels and series whose primary setting falls within the past 50 years. Examples include *The Redemption of Sarah Cain* by Beverly Lewis, *Some Wildflower in My Heart* by Jamie Langston Turner, and *A Son Comes Home* by Joseph Bentz.

Successful Bethany House fiction will generally include the following characteristics:

• An intriguing, well-written story with well-developed characters, a compelling plot and authentic description.

• A coherent, identifiable theme and/or particular characters who reflect biblical values or teachings.

• Historical/geographical/social accuracy.

• Relationships that portray the true meaning of love-commitment and responsibility rather than merely emotional and physical attraction.

• Adult manuscripts should be 75,000 words or longer. Typical Bethany House novels range up to 125,000 words.

WRITER'S GUIDELINES FOR CHILDREN'S AND TEEN BOOKS FICTION

Bethany House is an evangelical publisher of books in a broad range of categories, from preschool to adult. As the premier publisher of youth fiction in the Christian market, our list contains many bestselling series, including Three Cousins Detective Club, Mandie Books, Girls Only, and Bloodhounds, Inc. We also partner with Focus on the Family to bring their KidWitness Tales, The Christy Miller Series, and other youth books to the marketplace.

We do not accept unsolicited proposals for full-color picture books, nor do we publish cartoons, biographies, poetry, or short stories. Also, please note that we publish only series fiction, no stand-alones.

Bethany Backyard (imprint for ages 0-10)

Bethany Backyard comprises a variety of fun-to-read fiction and nonfiction books for young children ages 0-10. Some examples include Janette Oke's Animal Friends, *The Wonderful Way Babies Are Made*, *Glow-in-the-Dark Fish and 59 More Ways to See God Through His Creation*, and the For Me! Books. (For more information on our nonfiction books, please see the reverse side of this page.)

Early reader and first chapter book series are designed for children who are ready for the challenge of reading books divided into short chapters on their own. Books for early readers should be written for 5- to 8-year-olds and be about 3,000 words long. First chapter books are aimed at 7- to 10-year-olds and should be between 6,000 and 7,500 words in length. Stories should be exciting and fun, with a kid's view of the world. Each should integrate easy-to-understand biblical lessons that develop children's Christian faith. Examples: AstroKids, Three Cousins Detective Club, The Cul-de-sac Kids.

Middle-Grade Readers (ages 8-13)

Bethany has several strong-selling series for middle readers. Although our list is full, we will consider unique, imaginative stories (20,000 to 40,000 words) with believable characters who grow and change as a result of the events in the story. A Christian theme should be delicately woven into each book. Examples: Girls Only (GO!), Promise of Zion, and Bloodhounds, Inc.

Teens (ages 12 and up)

Fiction manuscripts for preteens and teens should be at least 50,000 words and should contain believable characters with real-life appeal; contemporary issues woven into a strong plot; and circumstances with which young adults identify. Scriptural themes should be skillfully crafted into the story in a way that is not preachy or tacked on. We are looking for suspenseful stories with strong take-away value. Successful series include Passport to Danger, Jennie McGrady Mysteries, SummerHill Secrets, and High Hurdles.

Before You Send Your Fiction Manuscript:

- Is the language appropriate for the intended age group?
- Have you checked your facts?
- Is the plot too complex? too simplistic?
- Is the theme realistic and meaningful to today's youth?
- Are there books in the market similar to your idea? If so, what makes yours unique?
- Does your main character have a clearly defined goal he or she is trying to achieve?
- Does your story build to a natural, effective climax?

Nonfiction

Bethany House has a history of publishing strong, relevant nonfiction for children and teens of all ages. A sampling of bestselling titles includes *Could Someone Wake Me Up Before I Drool on the Desk?*; *Hero Tales*; and *God's Will, God's Best*. We are seeking well-planned and thoughtfully developed books with an outstanding ability to communicate with youth.

Bethany Backyard

Backyard nonfiction includes a variety of books to be used for personal and family devotions, homeschooling, Christian education, and Sunday school. Books should teach key faith lessons in a way that is accessible to children. Representative titles are *Christmas Is...For Me!*; *The Wonderful Way Babies Are Made*; *Glow-in-the-Dark Fish and 59 More Ways to See God Through His Creation*; and *Fins, Feathers, and Faith*.

Devotional/Personal Growth

We're looking for unique, stimulating tools for middle readers and early and late teens to use in their personal quiet times or in youth group settings. Titles include *You're Worth More Than You Think!*; *Wise Up*; *Bad to the Bone*; and *Was That a Balloon or Did Your Head Just Pop?*

Contemporary Issues

Information on and answers to the issues most relevant to today's youth. *What Children Need to Know When Parents Get Divorced*; *What's With the Mutant in the Microscope?*; *If I Could Ask God One Question*; and *Find Your Fit* are examples of topics we've published in the past.

Nonfiction manuscripts should fall between 20,000 and 40,000 words for middle readers, and 30,000 and 40,000 words for teens.

FOR ALL SUBMISSIONS

(Adult Fiction, Non-Fiction, and Children and Teen Fiction)

Do your homework: Familiarize yourself with our company and what types of books we publish. Study our catalog and your local Christian bookstore shelves to determine where there might be a need. (To obtain a copy of our catalog, send an 11" x 14" self-addressed envelope with five first-class stamps affixed.)

Submitting Your Fiction or Nonfiction Proposal:

In light of current security concerns, Bethany House Publishers is no longer able to accept unsolicited manuscripts and book proposals. Material that does not come from a recognized source will be stamped Refused/Return to Sender when there is a return address.

We will accept one-page only facsimile proposals directed to Adult Nonfiction, Adult Fiction, or YA/Children editors. Faxes of interest will be responderd to in 4 to 6 weeks. Check our website for the current number.

Bethany House Publishers will continue to accept queries, proposals, and manuscripts through established literary agents, recognized manuscript services, and writers' conferences attended by BHP editorial staff.

Literary agents

Sally Stuart's annual publication, *The Christian Writers' Market Guide* (Harold Shaw) provides a list of literary agents who work with Christian publishers.

Manuscript services

First-time authors may find the following services valuable:

First Edition, a service of Evangelical Christian Publishers Association (www.ECPA.org), posts proposals on its Web site for review by ECPA member publishers.

Writer's Edge Manuscript Service (see information at www.writersedgeservice.com) evaluates manuscripts and provides information to subscriber publishers.

Writers' Conferences

Representatives of BHP and other Christian publishers attend various writers' conferences throughout the U.S. For a conference near you, consult The Christian Writers' Market Guide or www.billyates.com/cww/links.html.

Categories: Fiction—Nonfiction—Children—Family—Juvenile—Parenting—Relationships—Religion—Sexuality

CONTACT: Editorial
Material: All
11400 Hampshire Ave. South
Minneapolis MN 55438
Fax: 952-996-1304 (one-page queries)
Website: www.bethanyhouse.com

Beyond Words Publishing

Every book we publish must fulfill our mission: Inspire to Integrity. Beyond this, our titles aren't easy to collectively characterize, and we are always on the lookout for innovative ideas. *Currently, our list comprises the following categories:*

- Living Well: art, science, new learning, new thought, home, and community
- Vital Women: women 40 and up, women's health, creativity, intuition, spirituality
- Kinship with Nature: animals, nature, interactions with humans, nature's energy

• Inspired Parenting: early parenting, nurturing, raising teens, new ways of educating

• Cultural Activism: volunteering, philanthropy, spirituality in action

• Children's Books: picture books, young adult personal-improvement, nonfiction by kids for kids (for more specific guidelines, please refer to Kids By Kids, in the book publishing section of this directory).

• Coffee Table Books: highly selective trade titles, corporate and organizational histories, tie-ins with movies and shows

We do not publish poetry, autobiographies, adult fiction, or children's fiction by children. We are not currently publishing books that would be shelved in a bookstore's self-help section; if your book is self-help, try to find an additional sales angle for it. To get more familiar with our list, please visit our Web site.

We receive close to 4,000 proposals, and only publish 20-25 books, each year. As submissions are typically handled by only two people, we regret we are not able to respond to requests about the status of proposals. Please note we handle absolutely no submission-related correspondence by e-mail. To determine if your work has reached our office, enclose a self-addressed, stamped postcard and we will mail it back to confirm receipt. If you follow these guidelines, you will hear from us within six months. We thank you for your patience and for considering us as a possible publisher of your work.

Manuscript Submission Guidelines

Note we don't accept submissions by e-mail. Please indicate on the envelope whether your manuscript is for the adult or children's department. *All submissions should include:*

1. A cover or query letter, with the following information:

A clear, concise description of your book, including the intended market (children, preteens, teens, adults, parents, women, etc.), where it would be shelved in a bookstore (inspiration, women's studies, parenting, or other area), and approximate word count.

The purpose of the book. What is your vision for it? How will it benefit the reader? Can you distill the essence of the book and how it is unique and necessary into a few key phrases that could be used as back jacket copy, for example, or to pitch the book to booksellers?

Your motivation and qualifications for writing this book. What inspired you? What in your professional or personal experience qualifies you to write on the subject? Why will readers want to read this book?

Information about your credentials as an author. What else have you written? (Note that we publish many first time authors, so having previously published work is not a prerequisite.)

Indicate whether it is a multiple submission.

2. A market analysis that provides:

The names, authors, and publishers of similar books on the market. Check Bowker's Books in Print at your local library for comparative titles less than ten years old and still in print.

A detailed discussion of how your proposed book differs from the competitive titles.

Sales information for these titles. Note bestseller lists, ranks, or awards. Check Amazon.com to determine sales rank for each book. (Note: This rank is just a snapshot of a book's rank on any given day.) Refer to the book's copyright page to get the number of times it has been reprinted.

Research on potential alternative markets for the book. What places, besides retail booksellers, could your book be sold to? We sell our books to gift stores, catalogs, museums, and book clubs, to corporate clients and the U.S. government for formal gifts, and translations to overseas markets. What catalogs or book clubs carry books in the same genre? Are you a member of any organization through which the book could be marketed? Are you an acknowledged expert who is asked for advice, or who leads seminars at which you could market the book or use it as a program or resource material?

The skills and resources you could bring to collaboratively market your book with us. Where and how would you feel most comfortable promoting your work? How much time could you devote to publicity? What media experience do you have? What contacts could you use to market your book? We look for authors who have a continuing commitment to market their book, long after our in-house marketing team has moved on to the next season's new titles.

3. A proposed table of contents and detailed outline of the book.

4. Two to three sample chapters, if they have been written, double-spaced, on plain paper.

5. A SASE with sufficient postage to either return your entire proposal and manuscript or for us to simply send a one page reply. We cannot return your work without sufficient postage.

Please do not send us the only copy of your work. Beyond Words is not responsible for lost or misdirected manuscripts, photos, or artwork.

Categories: Nonfiction—Children—Christian Interests—Conservation—Culture—Ecology—Family—Feminism—General Interest—Inspirational—Native American—New Age—Paranormal—Parenting—Photography—Relationships—Religion—Self Help—Teen—Women's Issues—Young Adult

CONTACT: Jenefer Angell, Editor
Material: All
20827 NW Cornell Rd. Ste. 500
Hillsboro OR 97124
Phone: 503-531-8700
Fax: 800-284-9673
Website: www.beyondword.com

BkMk Press
University of Missouri-Kansas City

1. Send a sample of your work: approximately 10 pp. poetry; or 50 pp. prose.

2. Typed and paginated. Prose should be double-spaced.

3. Please include a cover letter indicating your name and address and the title of your submission.

4. Please also send a self addressed stamped envelope for our reply (with sufficient postage for the manuscript's return, if applicable). Please indicate whether you want your manuscript returned or recycled.

5. BkMk publishes quality poetry, short fiction collections, and creative non-fiction essays. We do not currently publish novels.

5. DO NOT SUBMIT MANUSCRIPTS VIA E-MAIL OR OTHERWISE THROUGH THE INTERNET

7. We try to reply to your submission in two to six months.

Note: It is highly unusual for us to accept a novella or anything aspiring to novel-hood, preferring instead to publish short fiction collections. We will not consider mystery, western, or romance novels.

Categories: Fiction—Nonfiction—Literature—Poetry—Regional—Short Stories—Creative Nonfiction

CONTACT: Ben Furnish, Managing Editor
Material: Poetry, Short Fiction, Creative Nonfiction
University of Missouri-Kansas City
5101 Rockhill Road
Kansas City MO 64110-2499
Phone: 816-235-2558
Fax: 816-235-2611
E-mail: bkmk@umkc.edu (no submissions)
Website: www.umkc.edu/bkmk

Black Forest Press
Arbenteuer Books, Dichter Books and Kinder Books

Black Forest Press is a self-publisher. What we do is of interest to authors who want to see their book in print, but cannot get traditional publishing editors to read their manuscript. Black Forest Press is for authors who have considered the alternative to traditional or subsidy publishing and have decided to financially invest in their own work. These authors maintain 100% of their profit, and pay no book sale royalties to the publisher. That right! All profits and book sale royalties belong 100% to the author (that's you). Self-publishing with the experts makes much better sense.

Black Forest Press is now pleased to offer Print on Demand (POD). Black Forest Press (BFP) offers author's special terms, pricing and printing options with our Print on Demand (POD) Program. The POD option has different parameters than our traditional publishing program, and part of those parameters are limitations which many prevent some authors from choosing the POD approach to successful and quick publishing. Let's look at the benefits and drawbacks.

Drawbacks (Not for every book published; limited by size dimensions and short runs)

1. All books must meet a minimum of 108 pages and cannot go over 740 pages.

2. All books can only be 5 X 8, 5½ X 8½, 6 X 9, 7½ X 9¼, or 8¼ X 11.

3. Only a maximum of 500 books can be printed. POD is almost exclusively short runs.

4. Only two options of marketing are available: The almost nonexistent plan, or the plan which covers considerable and significant basic features. Option two is the best choice. See Benefits below. Call us to discuss our POD Marketing package.

5. Books are listed in all important book availability data bases as POD books. This carries an unfair stigma of being not as good or acceptable as most standard published books. Yet POD books are as good as any book we've seen printed. The only difference is that POD books are digitally generated...and that is technology at its best. You won't believe how good the quality really is. We defy you to tell us the difference.

6. An author is limited to only so much production time: copy and online editing, a couple of covers, proofs or manuscript (book form) galleys and other individual needs are outlined in the POD Publishing Contract. Call BFP for an opportunity to find out exactly what the contract spells out.

Benefits (Save thousands of dollars if a book qualifies and meets the correct criteria)

1. The cost is terrific! Call us for a quote, each book has to be figured differently; however, the difference in publishing costs is affordable to almost everyone.

2. There is no set amount for how many books you want to publish. Publish and print one copy, ten copies, 100 copies or whatever amount you desire and the price of your publishing is mostly predicated on the size of the printing run plus production work. Marketing is separate.

3. The marketing plan is designed to meet all of the most necessary features for getting a POD book in front of the eyes of the book buyers, as well as notifying all the right book entities about the existence of a POD book.

4. All books are digitally generated and digitally stored. This means there are no warehousing fees and no chance of a book getting damaged. Why? Because a book is not printed until there is a need to print it. For example: no orders, no printing. If we get an order for five books, the books will be printed, bound and shipped within 48-72 hours! If the order is for one book or 330 books, it doesn't matter, they all get printed and shipped as they are requested or sold.

5. We also do hardback books with or without stamped covers. For example: a Kivar cloth-style cover with gold foil or a four color cover, or a dust jacketed cover is available. Unit prices for hardback books are more expensive, but not by much. Request a specific quote.

6. All books are drop shipped as orders come in; handling and shipping prices are very low.

7. If an author decides to revise his or her book, all we need are the changes or revisions to do the production work and make a new set up for print.

8. Most books can be finished within six weeks; sometimes certain books take longer due to unexpected or unscheduled author delays in the publishing process.

Note: There are no discounts when doing POD publishing with Black Forest Press.

POD Publishing Contract and POD Marketing Contract

Both of these contracts may be discussed or reviewed by another, prior to an agreement for publishing an author's book. A review may be requested by simply contacting BFP and asking for the contract of interest, Publishing, Marketing or both, to be emailed with a contract attachment. BFP does not send out hard copies of contracts until a publishing agreement has been reached and a serious negotiation has been decided upon.

Most vanity/ subsidy presses will charge an author thousands of dollars to publish his or her work. The break down is simple: production, printing and promotion equal MEGA- dollars; at Black Forest Press we've learned how to cut costs throughout the publishing process. This includes all phases of production and printing. Lastly, our book-marketing efforts to sell and promote an author's work are separate. Black Forest Press has a special contract, which covers several significant items which are done in marketing an author's book. The cost of this contract is low, while getting an author started on the right foot towards a successful sales endeavor. There are a few good book marketing companies in the United States and each of these companies has their own cut on what should be done in marketing and what should have to be done. An author must carefully choose the book marketing company to handle his or her work. Black Forest Press will coordinate and/or assist with the efforts of the marketing professionals hired by the author.

Our book publishing process is very easy to understand. Initially an author sends his or her non-returnable manuscript, which must be double spaced typed, preferably a laser printed copy, and a 3.5 inch MAC or PC computer disk or CD with the manuscript in Word Perfect 6.1 or a newer version. If there are difficulties in converting the text sent to Black Forest Press, the author will be contacted and arrangements will be made to secure a workable copy of the book. We then copy edit, line edit, and proofread the manuscript. During the entire publishing process, the author's manuscript will be edited and proofed between 12 and 14 times. Galley prints are then sent to the author for changes and approval. When the galleys are returned, they are typeset into Quark Xpress 4.1 and then once again the text is proofed and necessary content or format changes are made. An author can see his or her blue lines, but that takes more time and any new changes are additional charges. The author is sent and Authorization to Print form to be signed and returned giving approval to go to press.

Early in the editing process, Black Forest Press graphic cover designers begin working on the author's book cover. The author will receive drafts of the covers for approval. Authors do have input as to the design of their covers. An author is assigned an artist who will design the cover or dust jacket. Each author will see his or her cover design prior to Black Forest Press printing it. If an author desires his or her picture on the back cover, it will be necessary to send either a black and white or color picture and a short personal biographical sketch. Any endorsements will be placed inside or on the back of the book cover; they must come from the author. An author can have a color portrait printed on the back cover instead of a black and white one, because all book covers are full color, unless specified otherwise by the author. Any special artwork requested, like metallic ink, colored foils, or embossed lettering will be an additional charge. All these charges are totaled and a final figure is given to the author by Black Forest Press, and agreed upon in the formal written author contract.

Unlike most subsidy or vanity presses, Black Forest Press will provide an author open and ongoing communication with production and printing staff members working on his or her book. You'll be one telephone call away, eight hours a day, five days a week; from knowing how your book is maturing and progressing on schedule. This is a plus when an author self-publishes with guidance, direction, instruction, awareness and confidence.

As previously mentioned, the promotion of an author's book is also done by Black Forest Press. Although we do have several marketing packages we can also give authors choices of various book-marketing companies that will package, distribute, and sell their books. Promotion is a separate cost from publishing (production and printing). When and author's book is printed, the majority of the books (along with 150 free copies of the author's book cover) will be shipped directly to the promoter, or a specified amount to the author's residence with the remainder of the books, perhaps, going to the promoters warehousing facility. If BFP is the promoter, a specified amount of books will be kept with BFP. If BFP is the promoter, a predetermined and specified amount of author books will be kept in the BFP storage unit. Black Forest Press will only stock or warehouse books for up to three months at no extra cost. We do, however, request a sample copy of an author's book for each contributing member of our production team. This should never exceed ten copies; two of those copies go into our archives and two copies go the Registrar of Copyrights.

Indexing is also available for an extra modest, reasonable fee. Most authors who desire indexing will provide Black Forest Press with a list of the subjects, names or various entries they wish to have indexed. This is also true of a working Bibliography and a Footnote section. Black Forest Press recommends an author use either The Chicago Manual of Style or Form and Style to properly construct these sections.

The normal time for book production is 90 to 110 days. Much of that time depends on how long the author takes to review the galley copies and return them to Black Forest Press. On occasion, some extra requested author changes may also hold up the production schedule of the book, such time delays are not the responsibility of Black Forest Press. Once the author's book goes to press, an author should allow no more than four weeks for perfect bound books, or two to three months for hardback/case bound books, to be printed and packaged for shipment. Color page inserts are very expensive and are usually done in groups of four pictures. Full color books, especially children's books, will take about three to four months for printing, because the printing department brokers color printing with the Hong Kong facility. This is fairly standard printing time for any reputable quality color printer. Printing overruns are not calculated into the contract cost, nor are they an extra charge to the author: Overage charges: if an author requests a desire to purchase the overruns, the overages will be offered at Black Forest Press cost. Overruns can be used by promoters to effectively market an author's book along with or inside of press kits or promo packages, etc. To reiterate, Black Forest Press provides each author with an additional 150 covers, for promotional purposes, at no extra cost. This is a service where a necessary product is supplied to the author for free.

Common sizes for books are 5 ½ x 8 ½ and 8 ½ x 11 inches. Books which are

6 x 9 or 4 ½ x 6 inches are considered special cuts which cost the same as the next larger size. Printing runs of 1,000, 2,000, 2,500 or 3,000 books are usual for an author. Remember: although the cost of printing more books goes up, the unit cost per book will decrease drastically. For example, 1,000 books may have a unit cost of $3.00 per copy, but 2,000 books may drop the price to $2.00 or less per book. The unit price goes down with larger printing runs and prices vary with the size and page count of each book. With full color insides, the prices may vary or increase. Unless an author sells most of his or her books directly, without any middle men, distributors, wholesalers or libraries being involved in the sales process and/or taking a healthy percentage out of the actual sales price, an author may possibly clear a respectable profit from printing 1,000 books. Otherwise, depending upon the cost of publishing, the retail price at which the book is sold, and including the calculations of third party percentages, and author should consider printing upwards of over 1,350 to break even or make only a negligible profit. Serious profits begin with a minimum printing of 1,500 or 2,000 books, if the book is promoted properly and sells. Early in the publishing process, the marketability of each book should be discussed with the publisher and the promoter. Presale fliers would also be a wise decision to consider. Such fliers are designed and sent out early in the

publishing process in order to get a feel for the potential sales of a book. A healthy result in presales may well determine the amount of extra books an author might want to have printed. An author may then want to consider increasing the amount of books to be printed for which he or she initially contracted. Black Forest Press will gladly renegotiate the printing amount with an author. The publishing process must be a win-win effort. There are no losers when working with Black Forest Press.

If you are interested in self-publishing with Black Forest Press, please write us and let us know the specifics of your book. You may also view our price graph. Only then can we give you a realistic cost for the publishing of your book. Read the Black Forest Press Production Procedure Steps for Processing Author Manuscripts very carefully. It details the most important specifics of the Black Forest Press publishing process. Personal inquiry should give a prospective author a good idea of what it costs to self-publish with Black Forest Press. If another publisher will not furnish you with similar detailed information, you should carefully consider what they may be keeping from you, like hidden cost or not so comprehensive work. For authors who are serious about publishing with Black Forest Press, the names and telephone numbers of other Black Forest Press authors can be provided, upon request, prior to contract signing, for your convenience. Call them and chat about their publishing experiences with Black Forest Press and the published product they each received. Because Black Forest Press does the job right, we are proud of our publications, all of them. You select authors with whom you wish to speak; we will not provide a prescreened list of authors. Individual choices are yours without Black Forest Press input or suggestion.

Payments are usually made in two parts: one payment is to be made at the beginning of production; the second payment must be made just prior to press time. An author may also pay everything down, or divide his or her payments into three parts: one third down, one third due at the time the first galleys are returned, and the last one third, prior to press time. No book will be printed until all author payments have been made in full. Black Forest Press does not do co-op publishing, nor does it sponsor and subsidize books for authors who suggest that Black Forest Press receive their manuscript for free, publish it at our cost and then take the first profits as repayment after the book sells. Black Forest Press will subsidize select books, which are felt to be within our realm of financial capability. However, we solicit those types of books and we only schedule them at our publishing convenience.

Personal blue line changes will result in an extra cost to the author who will be billed separately for his or her blue line changes. All payments should be a cashier's check or money order and made out to Black Forest Press Productions. We accept credit cards, however there is an additional charge. Black Forest Press will wait until your check clears our bank before we begin production or printing work. When you receive our contract, you may have an attorney review it for approval. You will feel better and have less worry. An author's trust and cooperation are paramount to us. This process can't be made much easier than what it is already.

We accept only good books worthy of being sold and read by the public. No obscene, racist, sexist, overly violent, blasphemous or discriminating manuscripts will be accepted by Black Forest Press. The materials we accept are totally at our own discretion; decisions are made without prejudice or bias. We reserve the right to refuse work. Black Forest Press chooses only works of good taste, offensive to no one.

If an author has suffered permanent physical disabilities, is 65 years of age or older, a United States Armed Forces veteran, ore receives social security benefits, a 5% deduction of production costs will be given. However, Black Forest Press request substantiating evidence or legal documentation for that claim. Keep claim submissions simple. Send no original documents or personal paperwork, only photocopies. This information must be presented to Black Forest Press prior to negotiating the contract or receiving the initial cost work up. We will not be surprising you, so please extend us the same courtesy and don't surprise us by expecting a discount after you've been give the contract amount.

Black Forest Press will serve you in a timely, efficient, and friendly manner. Prior to considering Black Forest Press as your publisher, we do suggest that you get at least four or five vanity/subsidy press or other self-publishing quotes for publishing your book. You will see the difference we make when the bucks hit the table. Black Forest Press will show you where we can save you money and probably time. Keep in mind, most vanity presses will only do a limited marketing or promotional campaign for your book; a book marketing company will cost you extra, but it should get the job done correctly. You can judge for yourself what they do. Black Forest Press has no ownership in any book marketing companies we recommend, we prefer our own. We can only direct you and give your our best advice. You will know a good deal when you see it. For further information, call or fax us your questions. If you do not choose Black Forest Press to do your work, we wish you good fortune and success elsewhere. There are many decent, fair and honest publishers around.

Black Forest Press hours of operation are Monday through Friday, 9:00am to 5:30pm Pacific Standard Time. No weekend or collect telephone calls are accepted. You can E-mail Black Forest Press at the following: dahk@blackforestpress.com or at bfp1@cox.net.

Categories: Fiction—Nonfiction—Adventure—Biography—Business—Careers—Children—Christian Interests—Civil War—College—Cooking—Culture—Drama—Disabilities—Education—Family—Fantasy—General Interest—Government—Health—Hispanic—History—Inspirational—Literature—Military—Multicultural—Mystery—Native American—Poetry—Politics—Psychology—Reference—Religion—Romance—Science Fiction—Short Stories—Society—Spiritual—Sports/Recreation—Textbooks—Western—Writing—Ethnic—Philosophy

CONTACT: Julie Knox, Chief Administrative Acquisitions Officer
Material: All
PO Box 6342
Chula Vista, CA 91909-6342
Phone: 800-451-9404
Fax: 619-482-8704
E-mail: inquiries@blackforestpress.com
E-mail: bfp3@cox.net
Website: www.blackforestpress.com

Bloomberg Press

Bloomberg Press publishes basic and advanced investing books, books for financial professionals and planners, and money-related books for the general public. We seek leading authors and experts recognized in their professional circles.

Overview: Bloomberg Press publishes topical books focused essentially on finance and business, written by experts in their fields. Books for:

• Financial Professionals
• Topics for money-makers and money-movers
• Guides to basic investing techniques and specialized interests for more sophisticated investors

Books Published: 15 to 20 books published annually domestically

Marketing: Bloomberg Press books are sold and distributed to the book trade by W.W. Norton, one of the leading independent publishers in America, and works with leading distributors worldwide. Bloomberg Press has won numerous design awards for its catalogues, as well as awards for its books. We can give our authors worldwide exposure through various media, including but not limited to our own TV, radio, magazines, international news service, and the BLOOMBERG PROFESSIONAL service (the company's proprietary global network of business news and financial information terminals).

Global Presence: Books available in countries throughout the world and many are published in multiple languages, including: Complex and Simplified Chinese, Japanese, Italian, German, Spanish, Portuguese, Korean, Arabic, Thai, Bulgarian, Polish, and Russian.

Categories: Business—Investing—Institutional Investing—Professional Finance

CONTACT: Acquisitions Editor
Material: All
100 Business Park Dr.
PO Box 888
Princeton NJ 08542-0888
E-mail: kpeterson@bloomberg.net
Website: www.bloomberg.com/books

Blue Mountain Arts®

We are interested in reviewing poetry and writings suitable for publication on greeting cards and in books. We are looking for original, heartfelt poetry and prose on love, friendship, family, special occasions, positive living, aspirations, self-help, and other similar topics. We strongly suggest that you familiarize yourself with Blue Mountain Arts products before submitting material. The following guidelines are for our books and poetry card lines and do not apply to card lines created specifically for niche or specialized markets.1. Greeting card submissions should communicate a message that one person would want to express to or share with another person. Writings on special occasions (birthday, anniversary, graduation, etc.) as well as the themes listed above are also considered. Poetry and writings should be about real emotions and feelings written from your personal experience. We suggest that you have someone in mind (a friend, relative, etc.) as you write. The majority of the poetry we publish DOES NOT RHYME.

*Important note: Because of the large volume of poetry we receive written to mothers, sons, and daughters, we are accepting only highly original and creative poetry that expresses new thoughts and sentiments on these themes.*2. Book manuscripts and proposals in typewritten form are also accepted. We are particularly interested in receiving books that fall under the self-help, family, gift, inspiring young adults, relationships, self-improvement, and motivational categories. We do not wish to receive poetry chap books.

3. Your work need not be copyrighted prior to submission. However, to obtain a copyright, you may contact the Copyright Office (address: United States Copyright Office, Library of Congress, Washington, DC 20559).4. If you are submitting via postal mail, we prefer that manuscripts be typewritten; one greeting card submission per page please. Your name should appear on every page. You may submit as many poems at one time as you wish.5. If you are submitting your work by postal mail and would like a response and/or to have your work returned, you must enclose a self-addressed, stamped envelope (SASE) of adequate size, with the correct postage. While we always try to respond to your submission as quickly as possible, please allow 2 to 4 months for a reply. Please be sure to include your name, address, and telephone number with your submission, and please keep us informed of all address and telephone number changes.

6. E-mail greeting card submissions are welcome. Send to editorial@spsstudios.com. PLEASE DO NOT SEND ATTACHMENTS. Type or paste the text of your work into the body of the e-mail. If you are submitting more than one poem at a time, please include all of them in one e-mail message. Be sure to include your name, address, and telephone number. Please do not send book proposals or manuscripts by e-mail.

7. E-mail submissions will receive a reply only if the work is selected for further review for possible publication. Selected submissions

will receive a response by postal mail within 2 to 3 months. We are unable to respond to e-mail submissions that are not selected for further review.

8. We pay $300 per poem for the worldwide, exclusive rights to publish it on a greeting card and other products, and $50 per poem for one-time use in a book. Book submissions are negotiated on an individual basis. Publication procedures will be explained in detail prior to actually publishing your work. 9. Manuscript submissions and questions concerning your work may be directed in writing to the addresses below. Please do not telephone.

Categories: Poetry

CONTACT: Editorial Department
Material: All
PO Box 1007
Boulder, CO 80306
E-mail: editorial@spsstudios.com
Website: www.spsstudios.com

Blue Poppy Press, Inc.

If I had an idea for a book, what would I need to send in the way of a proposal?

First of all, Blue Poppy Press only publish books about acupuncture and Chinese medicine. Secondly, we only publish books by professional practitioners who have been in practice A) not less than five (5) years, and B) read at least one Asian language. We prefer our authors to be native English-speakers, but this is not a hard and fast rule.

What we like to see in the way of a proposal are the following:
• A query letter stating the concept of the book, why its needed, and identifying its target audience.
• The book's outline or Table of Contents
• At least two sample chapters, usually the introduction and at least one technical chapter.
• The author's resume or curriculum vitae
If the book is a translation, then we also need:
• The name and author of the source text
• Date and place of publication and original publisher's name
• Some description of copyright status, e.g. public domain
• Several sample pages of the original language text for comparison
• A description of translational methodology, whether denotative, connotative, or functional.

Categories: Nonfiction—Health—Acupuncture—Chinese Medicine

CONTACT: Bob Flaws, Editor in Chief
Material: All
5441 Western Ave, #2
Boulder CO 80301
Phone: 303-447-8372
Fax: 303-245-8362
E-mail: bob@bluepoppy.com
Website: www.bluepoppy.com

Blue Water Publishing, LLC

Please refer to Granite Publishing Group.

BNA Books

Discover the advantages of teaming up with a highly respected leader in legal publishing. *BNA Books welcomes inquiries from established, talented professionals who seek a publisher for their manuscripts in the following subject areas:*
• Labor and Employment Law
• Labor Relations
• Legal Practice
• Health Law
• Employee Benefits Law
• Arbitration and ADR
• Intellectual Property Law
• Occupational Safety and Health Law

BNA Books gives its authors an extraordinary combination of editorial support and marketing resources, backed by The Bureau of National Affairs, Inc., one of the largest private information-gathering organizations in the world.

If you have an idea, outline, or manuscript that would complement the BNA Books publishing program, we would like to hear from you.

Please use the form below to describe your project's subject, purpose, content, intended market, and estimated length. An outline or table of contents will show us how the subject matter is organized. In addition, please send us a current curriculum vitae or description of your credentials. Be sure to include your current telephone and fax numbers.

All suggestions you send will be kept in confidence and given our full consideration. We will contact you in three to six weeks to discuss your proposal.

If you prefer to submit your proposal by mail.

Categories: Nonfiction—Law

CONTACT: Acquisitions Manager
Material: All
BNA Books Editorial Offices
1231 25th St. NW
Washington DC 20037
Phone: 202-452-4110

Bonus Books, Inc.

We publish primarily nonfiction trade books.

If you would like to submit a manuscript or proposal for our review, please follow these guidelines.

1. The material must be typed and double-spaced.

2. Please include a self addressed, stamped business-size envelope for a reply. Because of the large volume of submissions we receive, if you don't include an SASE, you will not receive a reply. If you would like any of your material returned, please enclose an SASE large enough to do so.

3. If you are submitting your work electronically, please send it as an attachment in either Word or Rich Text Format.

4. If you are submitting a proposal, please include an outline or summary of your book and a few sample chapters.

5. Allow six to eight weeks for a response.

Thank you for the opportunity to consider your work.

Categories: Nonfiction—Business—Cooking—Games—Sports/Recreation—Textbooks—Textbooks (Medical, Health)

CONTACT: Erin Kahl, Acquisitions Editor
Material: All
160 East Illinois St.
Chicago IL 60611
Phone: 312-467-0580
Fax: 312-467-9271
E-mail: Webmaster@bonus-books.com
Website: www.bonus-books.com

Book Peddlers

For parenting, household hints books and Christmas titles, we do not have any guidelines. That is because we are NOT looking for new manuscripts in these areas. Please save your submissions for others. If and when our policy changes, we will post it here.

We are able to entertain submissions for our !NK gift books, however. These are small 5-1/2"x 5-1/2" books that are created to be bought and given as a gift for specific situations. They are 500-800 words in length. Please read one of the current ones to understand the format and tone. Send query, copy and a SASE to the address below:

Categories: Fiction—Nonfiction—Lifestyle

CONTACT: !NK Submissions
Material: All
15245 Minnetonka Blvd
Minnetonka MN 55345
Phone: 952-912-0036
Fax: 952-912-0105
E-mail: vlansky@bookpeddlers.com
Website: www.bookpeddlers.com

Bookhaven Press LLC

Bookhaven Press LLC, founded in 1985, is an independent publishing house dedicated to producing award winning business and career books. Owned and operated by Dennis V. Damp, the author of the Benjamin Franklin Awards finalist for "Best Career Book" The Book of U.S. Government Jobs - 8th edition, 1996 and 2001.

Bookhaven publishes for a select group of experts and our titles include:
- The Book of U.S. Government Jobs - 8th edition
- Post Office Jobs - 2nd edition
- Health Care Job Explosion, 3rd edition
- Dollars and Sense
- How to Raise A Family and a Career Under One Roof
- Applying For Federal Jobs
- Air Conditioning & Refrigeration Technician's EPA Certification Guide

Manuscript Submission Guidelines:

Writers must send a query with SASE. The query must include the following:
1) A comprehensive outline of the book
2) A draft table of contents
3) A copy of the first chapter
4) Detailed author bio, credentials, affiliations, etc.
5) Computer system that you work with, wordprocessor, IBM/Apple, etc.
6) Target marketing perspective (who would buy this book)

All authors that we publish are computer literate and submit the final manuscript on IBM formatted disks in WordPerfect or Microsoft Word.

Bookhaven replies within 8 weeks if an SASE is included with your material or via email if an email address is provided.

We do not accept files via the internet. Submit copies as noted above by snail mail.

Categories: Nonfiction—Business—Careers—Family—Government—Lifestyle—Money & Finances—Technical

CONTACT: Submissions
Material: All
PO Box 1243
Moon Township PA 15108
Phone: 412-494-6926
Fax: 412-494-5749
E-mail: Bookhaven@aol.com
Website: members.aol.com/bookhaven

Branden Publishing Company

Branden Publishing Company is always interested in publishing new books and finding new authors. If you wish to contact Branden regarding the publishing of your work, please mail your query (one or two paragraphs) with a self-addressed, stamped envelope to the address below; no other form accepted.

Due to the high volume of publishing requests, we will not accept phone calls, e-mails, or faxes.

Categories: Fiction—Nonfiction—African-American—Arts—Aviation—Biography—Business—Children—Civil War—Consumer—Culture—Drama—Disabilities—Education—Entertainment—Family—General Interest—Government—Health—History—Internet—Jewish Interest—Language—Law—Literature—Military—Multicultural—Poetry—Politics—Regional—Religion—Society—Sports/Recreation—Teen—Textbooks—Theatre—True Crime—Western—Women's Issues—Young Adult—Ethnic

CONTACT: Adolph Caso, Editor
Material: All
PO Box 812094
Wellesley MA 02482
E-mail: Branden@branden.com
Website: www.branden.com

Brassey's, Inc.

If you are interested in submitting a manuscript for publication, please refer to the following guidelines:

Proposals should consist of a half-page synopsis, a table of contents or rough outline of the book's structure, 1-2 sample chapters (double-spaced), reviews of any previous books, and a biographical sketch or vita.

No email submissions, please.

Please include a self-addressed, stamped envelope so we can respond and return the materials if we decide not to proceed.

Categories: Nonfiction—Aviation—Biography—Civil War—Government—History—Human Rights—Military—Politics—Regional—Sports/Recreation—Textbooks—Defense—Foreign Policy—Intelligence—International Affairs

CONTACT: Donald Jacobs, Aquisitions Editor
Material: Proposals
22841 Quicksilver Drive
Dulles VA 20166
Phone: 703-661-1548
Website: www.brasseysinc.com

Brassey's Sports

Proposals should consist of a half-page synopsis, a table of contents or rough outline of the book's structure, 1-2 sample chapters (double-spaced), reviews of any previous books, and a biographical sketch or vita.

No email submissions, please.

Please include a self-addressed and stamped envelope so that we can return the material if we decide not to proceed.

Send proposals to Chris Kahrl, Aquisitions Editor.

Categories: Nonfiction—History—Sports/Recreation

CONTACT: Chris Kahrl, Acquisitions Editor
Material: Sports
Brassey's Inc., 22841 Quicksilver Dr.
Dulles VA 20166
Phone: 703-661-1548
Website: www.brasseysinc.com

Brazos Press

Please refer to Baker Publishing Group.

Bridge Works

Bridge Works is a small house, an imprint of the larger Rowman & Littlefield Publishers. We receive 2-3,000 queries per year, including unsolicited mss. However, of the 12 new titles we publish a year, 60% are agented. We publish general trade fiction (including some ss collections and mystery novels) and non-fiction, although 75% of our titles are fiction. Our non-fiction includes biography, public policy and essays. Because we receive so many submissions and publish so few titles, our standards are high, and we require fresh, original material in both categories. We no longer publish poetry. We ask that all unagented material be first vetted by a freelance editor. We will review every proposal, but will not reply or return mss unless they are accompanied by an SASE.

We prefer to receive the first fifty pages of a ms with a query letter, outlining the author's qualifications and the scope of the ms. We reply to the 50 pages within one month. We do not read computer disks or any other electronic medium, only hard copies.

As to what we DO NOT publish, the following applies: no genre material except mysteries, no YA or children's books, art books, cookbooks, romance novels.

Categories: Fiction—Nonfiction—Adventure—Asian-American—Civil War—Comedy—Crime—Drama—Feminism—General Interest

CONTACT: Barbara Phillips, Editorial Director
Material: All
PO Box 1798
Bridgehampton NY 11932

Bright Mountain Books, Inc.

Bright Mountain Books, Inc., was founded in 1985 as a Southern Appalachian regional publisher. We have published manuscripts written by area writers, republished books originally self-published, and have secured reprint rights for regional out-of-print books. While our major emphasis is on nonfiction, we have published some creative nonfiction, i.e., fictionalized histories based on factual events. We have not published poetry, textbooks, novels, self-help manuals, religious texts, or family histories.

If you already have your work on computer, please send a disk of the entire manuscript plus a printout of the first several pages. If the manuscript exists only in typed form, please do not send the entire manuscript; three sample chapters and an outline are sufficient. Photos or artwork should be submitted in the form of photocopies or computer printouts, not the originals.

Send your materials to the address below. We will acknowledge their receipt, but since our procedure is to have at least two readers evaluate each submitted manuscript, a process which can be as short as a day or two or take several weeks, please be patient during our evaluation. If we feel that yours is a book we have a definite interest in publishing, we will request the entire manuscript.

If we cannot consider publication, we will return your manuscript to you only if you supply an appropriate postage-paid envelope. We will be happy to recommend other publishing avenues for you to consider if we can do so.

Categories: Nonfiction—General Interest—Native American—Outdoors—Regional

CONTACT: Cynthia F. Bright, Editor
Material: All
206 Riva Ridge Dr.
Fairview NC 28730
Phone: 828-628-1768
Fax: 828-628-1755

Bristol Fashion Publications, Inc.
The World's Largest Nautical Publishing House

You will find we are very cooperative when dealing with freelance contributors. Our CEO and Publisher, John Kaufman, and our COO and Editor-in-Chief, Bob Lollo, were both freelance photographers and writers long before Bristol Fashion Publications, Inc. came to be in 1993. They still retain the memories of the "difficult years" getting started. This is one of the reasons we are interested in submissions from new authors and photographers.

All of our titles are nautical themes, aimed at the new or seasoned boater. All our titles cover restoration, repair, maintenance, cruising, living aboard, cruising, etc.

Boating is a fast changing industry. Therefore, we rarely project more than six months in advance. Always include a SASE for any submissions you would like returned. Include your telephone number with any correspondence or submissions. Sample books are available at a 40% discount.

Photography Submissions

COVERS: Color glossy prints. Prints should be 3-1/2 x 5 to 5 x 7. Digitized images (300 DPI) in a JPG or GIF file are preferred for final use.

All covers depict the theme of the book. Use deep saturation, vivid colors and good contrast to bring out the main subject matter. This is NOT the type of cover you will see on a boating magazine. Send several sample copies of your work for consideration. Mark each copy with your name, address and phone number.

INTERIOR: Digitized images (300 DPI) in a GIF or JPG file are the only images we consider for use.

Presently, we use line drawings for the bulk of the interior art work. We would rather use photos if more were available for our use. Photos should show hands using tools, when appropriate, the steps involved in completing a project and the finished results. These are the photos we most often need, however, other photos of boats and boating may be needed for a current title. Good contrast, lighting and subject matter is necessary. Send several hard copy samples of your work for consideration. Mark each copy with your name, address and phone number.

Simultaneous submissions are fine. Notify us if a photo we have on file becomes unavailable. Model and property releases are preferred if the person or vessel is identifiable. All submissions should be non-returnable disks or prints. If we can keep copies of your work on file, we are more likely to call you when the need arises. We will notify you within one month, whether or not we feel we can use your work. Assignments may be given at the same rate of pay, as noted below.

We purchase book/reprint rights as a one time buy. Cover prices range from $50.00 to $300.00 depending on the project. Interior B & W prices range from $10.00 to $25.00. Credit line given. One copy of the book will be given to each contributor.

Writer's Guidelines

Considering what we have read on the shelves, it appears we are the only publishing company that writes for the non-handy boater. Our books use simple to understand and follow processes, for the person who knows which end of the wrench to hold, but little else about boating. Each subject should take the reader from the very basics, through each step, until the complete subject matter is discussed.

As an example: Start by describing the steps involved in replacing a damaged receptacle and work up to wiring an entire boat. As the project expands and becomes more complicated, each new phase or technique should be described. If a friend, who knows nothing about boats, can read, understand and feel comfortable doing the work you have described, you have written what we want to publish.

Non-How-To titles should be extremely interesting to read. Cruising related books should speak of the culture and events more than the "what I did" topics. Live aboard topics are always well received. How-To topics are the most marketable with a wider audience. We are always seeking new ideas and topics for our books.

Simultaneous submissions are not accepted. Submit a few chapters for review, along with the table of contents. All submissions must be hard copy. Include your past credits, tear sheets, state if photos or line art is available and the state of completion of your manuscript. We will report in two weeks of receipt, often sooner.

If you have never been published or have not yet stated the manuscript submit a short sample (1000 words), outline, completion date and photo/line art availability.

We pay royalty of 8% to 11% based on the retail price of the book. Average retail price is $20.00 to $30.00. Photos and line art submitted by the author will be considered as part of the manuscript and the percentage adjusted accordingly. Follow the photography submission guideline above. We will purchase worldwide book/reprint rights.

WRITERS TIPS: Know or research the industry, boat owners and technical knowledge. Use the proper nautical language and terms. A well-written manuscript is useless if the knowledge of the writer is lacking. If you are not familiar with a given subject, talk to a tradesman who has been around boats for many years. Do not use unwarranted technical jargon to explain a subject. Use simple terms and an easy to understand and follow, step-by-step writing style. When we have to choose, we are more likely to use poor writing and good knowledge, than good writing and poor knowledge.

PREPARING YOUR MANUSCRIPT: Never use an exclamation point for emphasis except in a direct quotation. We! and! the! reader! don't! care! what! startles! you!

Don't double-space, regardless of what you were taught in typing class.

Don't use the Tab key or Space bar to indent a paragraph.

Boat names should be in italics, not quotation marks.

A boat's name is a proper name, therefore, the word The should not precede the name. It is not The Sea Cow it is Sea Cow. They don't call you The Bob, do they?

Don't attempt to make your manuscript look as you'd like your book to appear. Just write. Converting your manuscript into a book is what we do.

Don't use "Captain Bob," Captain Bob, Capt. Bob and CAPTAIN BOB—pick one and stay consistent.

Trust us. We have a combined experience of more than 300 years in the boating and publishing industries. We will edit your manuscript to suit its intended market. The better your work reads, the better it sells, and that benefits all of us.

Please understand this—You will not retire from the book sales of any single nautical title. Specialty titles simply do not sell that well in any market. A very successful nautical title may sell 20,000 copies over a five year run. A very few sell more. Most sell one quarter or less of that number and are considered a successful book. Our successful boating authors often have three or more books published with us and they started by reading this very same letter.

After preparing your submission, following the above guidelines, you may submit it by land mail (hard copy only, do not include a disk) or by email. To submit by email, attach an ASCII text or MSWord file to the email—DO NOT paste the text into the body of the email or include graphic files with this submission. Send the email to jpk@bfpbooks.com. Include only one manuscript with each email submission. Our best tip—Visit our web site to view our current titles.

Imprints

Motorcycling and Railroading are listed alphabetically in the book publisher section.

Categories: Nonfiction—Boating—Recreation—Sports/Recreation

CONTACT: Submissions
Material: All
P. O. Box 4676
Harrisburg, PA 17111
Phone: 772-559-1379
Fax: 800-543-9030
E-mail: jpk@bfpbooks.com
Website: www.bfpbooks.com

Bristol Publishing Enterprises
Nitty Gritty Cookbooks

Greetings: We currently have no specific manuscript guidelines but are primarily interested in cookbooks.

Our Nitty Gritty cookbooks are 5¼"x8¼", bound on the short side, and include approximately 100 to 120 recipes. We are looking for authors with a proven history of success in the food industry: dietitians, professional chefs or bakers, teachers or others. Topics must be of interest to the mass market and must have an expected term of interest of at least 5 years.

Rather than submit an entire manuscript, we prefer that you send an initial proposal (an outline is also recommended), a resume and a sample of your published writing.

Sincerely,

Aidan Wylde, Managing Editor

Categories: Cooking—Food/Drink—Gardening—Home—Trade—Cookbooks

CONTACT: Aidan Wylde, Managing Editor
Material: All
PO Box 1737
San Leandro CA 94577
Phone: 510-895-4469
Fax: 510-895-4459

Broadman & Holman Publishers

Broadman & Holman actively seeks to enlist both new and established authors to work with us in producing the finest books in Christian publishing. We have been publishing books since 1934, and we bring a commitment to traditional Christian values and beliefs to everything we do.

OPPORTUNITIES

Broadman & Holman publishes books for adults, youth, pastors, church staff, and lay ministers. *We are currently accepting submissions in these general categories:*

• Bible Study Helps—Books in the Bible Study Helps Series help ministers and lay leaders communicate biblical truths to others.

• Christian Living—Books in the Christian Living Series are designed for adults ages twenty-five and older. These books apply sound, biblical principles to issues and concerns that face Christians, enabling them to grow in their faith.

• Inspirational—Books in the Inspirational Series are designed to inspire adults to grow in their Christian faith and relationships with others. Biographies, inspiring stories of faith and courage, and devotional books are included in this series.

• Ministry—Books in the Ministry Series are designed to equip laypersons with ministry and relational skills.

• Parenting/Leadership—Books in the Parenting/Leadership Series are designed for parents or adult leaders of children from birth through college. These books assist readers in dealing with children, teenagers, and college students as they face issues and develop as persons and Christians.

• Practical Theology—Books in the Practical Theology Series are designed for adults, ages twenty-five and older. These books apply timeless truths from the Bible, Christian theology, and church history to real-life situations, enabling believers to understand their faith and communicate the gospel clearly.

• Professional—Books in the Professional Series are designed to equip ministers for their work.

• Youth/Juvenile—Books in the Youth/Juvenile Series are designed for older children through college students. These books introduce readers to a relationship with Christ in an age-appropriate manner; offer guidance as they face questions, issues, and decisions; and encourage them to grow in their Christian faith and share that faith with others.

Please Do Not Send:

• Poetry
• Articles or short stories
• Adult fiction or Juvenile fiction
• Tracts or Pamphlets
• Exposés of prominent persons or organizations
• Art books
• Children's picture books

GETTING OUR ATTENTION

One of the secrets to catching our attention is helping us see the marketability of your idea. The following questions are commonly asked by our editorial, sales, and marketing staffs as we consider products.

• What other books or articles have you published?

• Have you read other books in your subject category? What makes your idea unique? What features or reader benefits have you included to make your book attractive to potential customers?

• Is your topic timely?

• How can you help market your book? Do you lead conferences or speak frequently in public? Do you have access to radio or television? Are you a recognized authority in your field?

• Are there prominent people who could give endorsements for this book?

OUR PROPOSAL FORMAT

While Broadman & Holman accepts ideas in several forms, we prefer that you query first. If sample chapters are available, please include at least two with your submission. *We ask that you use this format for your query:*

I. Content

A. Premise: a one-paragraph description of what the book is about.

B. The manuscript:

1. Status (Is it complete? When do you expect to complete it?)
2. Special features (epigraphs, charts, illustrations, lists, index, bibliography, etc.)
3. Anticipated length
4. Outline
5. Competition. List other recent titles in your subject area and compare the features and benefits of your manuscript to each title.

II. Audience

A. Target audience: age, sex, special interests or needs

B. Motivation: Why will readers want to purchase this book?

III. Author

A. Background

B. Previous writing

C. Resumé: include address, phone number, birth date, and social security number

D. Opportunities you have to market and promote the book

IV. Chapter synopsis: a one paragraph summary of the premise of each chapter.

V. Sample chapters (two)

Broadman & Holman receives over fifteen hundred unsolicited trade book submissions each year. We try to respond within two months. If you haven't heard from us within that time, please feel free to ask about your submission.

GENERAL GUIDELINES

• Do not bind or staple your submission.

• If you're submitting to several publishers, please tell us.

• Be open to editorial guidance.

• Provide suggestions for charts, graphs, photographs, illustrations, or other features that would make your idea attractive to readers.

• Final proposal submissions and finished manuscripts must be available on computer disk.

A FINAL WORD

Thanks for thinking of Broadman & Holman Publishers. If you're as committed as we are to being a leader in Christian publishing, you may be the type of author we're looking for; we may be the kind of publisher you need. If you have an idea for a book that will meet needs and change lives, we want to hear from you. Please write to the address below.

We look forward to hearing from you!

Sincerely,

Broadman & Holman Editorial Staff

Categories: Nonfiction—Christian Interests—Family—Inspirational—Humor

CONTACT: Acquisitions Editor
Material: All

127 - 9th Ave. N
Nashville TN 37234
Phone: 615-251-3638

Brookline Books

The trade and professional lines of Brookline Books publish titles in education, disabilities, psychology, parenting, and other related topics. Our selection includes workbooks for teachers and students, scholarly texts for teachers and health professionals, and trade books for students, parents, and a general audience. Please call and request a catalogue to get a better sense of our selection.

We look for well-written, well-organized manuscripts with a clear and original focus. We primarily consider texts based on solid research or professional experience. Books based solely on personal (vs. professional) experience are considered only if they display exceptional writing quality, provide original insights, and do not attempt to offer advice on parenting, self-help or education. We do accept multiple submissions, with notification. We rarely accept a book without first seeing the entire manuscript, and never accept one without at least seeing several chapters.

Categories: Fiction—Nonfiction—Animals—Disabilities—Education—Hispanic—Jewish Interest—Literature—Parenting—Poetry—Psychology—Short Stories—Travel—Writing

CONTACT: Sadi Ranson, Series Editor, Lumen
Material: Fiction, Literature, Writing
CONTACT: Michael Beattie, Assistant to the Publisher
Material: Disabilities, Education, Psychology, Parenting
PO Box 97
Newton Upper Falls MA 02464
Phone: 617-558-8010
Fax: 617-558-8011
E-mail: milt@brooklinebooks.com

Browser Press

Does not accept unsolicited submissions

Bulfinch Press

Please refer to Time Warner Book Group.

The Business Group

We publish for the small business market. My cornerstone book is *How to Grow Your Business without Driving Yourself Crazy*—just out.
Other titles include:
• *Success Tips From Small Business Owners*
• *The Magic Chain of Marketing*
• *Pay Yourself First*
• *Finding and Keeping Good Employees*
• *Hiring Your First Employee*
• *Promote Yourself to CEO*
• *Recapture Your Time*

Up to now we have distributed exclusively through our own seminars and workshops, but are now entering the wider book market—via Amazon, Baker&Taylor, Publisher's Marketing Assn.
We will consider manuscripts with the following qualities:
• "How to" books for owners of small businesses. Practical, useful, nuts and bolts topics, like our titles above.
• Tested on real people; not just good ideas.
• Friendly, easy to read style; not academic or pedantic. Lots of examples and illustrations. All our materials are judged by one of the world's toughest audiences—small business owners.
• Short. Our workbooks are a max of 96 pages. Our "big book" is 304 pages.
• Has a demonstrable market.

I will consider products that include computer templates for CDs or electronic distribution. For example, a book on how small business owners can ever afford to retire that includes a CD template with a spreadsheet that helps readers calculate how much they need and how they will generate it, using different scenarios.

We cannot take on the role of a standard publisher; however, for the right submission, we will work with the author to help produce and distribute an excellent book.

An interested author should contact us via email with a proposal, table of contents, and sample chapter, along with the author's background and a marketing plan for the book. Send via Word (Office 98) or PDF. Mailed material will be returned only with SASE.

Contact info is below. My personal email is mvh@businessgroup.biz. Problem solving groups for business owners.
Mike Van Horn
Categories: Nonfiction—Business—Money & Finances

CONTACT: Mike Van Horn, President
Material: All
135 Paul Drive, Ste. 300
San Rafael CA 94903
Phone: 415-491-1896
Fax: 415-491-1855
E-mail: mvh@businessgroup.biz.
Website: www.businessgroup.biz

Bye Publishing

Established 1996. We publish books by authors whose writings might otherwise be missed by many readers. We seek manuscripts from writers who write about experiences that will assist readers with achieving a higher level of awareness. We publish books that focus on self-development, empowerment, spirituality, ethnic studies, education, male and female relationships, and some specialized ethnic poetry. We publish 1-2 novels a year. No author advances. Pays royalty on retail price. Report in 30 days on queries.

Submit query letters only, which describe the project briefly, the author's writing and professional credentials, and promotional ideas.

Recent nonfiction title(s): *The Life and Confessions of a Black Studies Teacher*, by Dr. Cecelia Louise Hatshesput Arrington. *Let There Be Life*, by Malcolm Kelly.
Categories: Nonfiction—Education—Inspirational—Poetry—Relationships—Religion—Self Help—Spiritual

CONTACT: Malcolm Kelly, Publisher
Material: All
BYE PUBLISHING SERVICES
5245 College Avenue Ste 333
Oakland CA 94618
Phone: 510-272-0101
Fax: 510-336-3230

Remember: Editors change jobs and publishers change addresses. It is wise to invest in a phone call for the current information before submitting.

Calyx Books

CALYX Books is a nonprofit feminist publisher particularly interested in fine literature by women. We are committed to publishing work by women of color, working class women, lesbians, and other women whose voices need to be heard. We publish three to four books each year: novels, collections of short fiction, poetry, translations of writers (poetry and fiction), nonfiction works of exceptional literary merit, and special anthologies.

Follow the guidelines below for submitting manuscripts. If we are interested in the manuscript, after the initial review we will request the complete manuscript for further consideration.

ALL MANUSCRIPTS

All manuscripts should include page numbers, the manuscript title, and the author's name and address. Submit a resume, a biographical statement, and an SASE with the manuscript.

POETRY

In addition, submit only up to 10 poems (not to exceed 20 pages of poetry), a table of contents, and a one-page description (synopsis) of the book manuscript.

FICTION

In addition: for novels, submit three chapters, a table of contents (if appropriate), and a synopsis; for short story manuscripts, submit three short stories, a table of contents, and a synopsis.

TRANSLATIONS

In addition: follow the above guidelines for poetry and fiction and include the same parts of the manuscript in the original language as well as the English translations. Include biographical data on both the translator and the author. Include the information on who holds the English translation rights on the author's work. Include a letter showing permission to translate from the author or the author's estate by the translator. Include the address for the author or the author's estate and any appropriate information on the publisher of the original edition or editions of the author's work.

NONFICTION/ANTHOLOGIES

In addition: for nonfiction, submit three chapters or sections, a table of contents, and a synopsis; for anthologies, submit three samples of the work included, an introduction and/or synopsis, and a table of contents.

Manuscripts submitted that do not follow the guidelines above will not receive consideration. Allow six to nine months for response from the editorial board. We are currently closed to book mss. until further notice.

Categories: Fiction—Nonfiction—African-American—Asian-American—Feminism—Hispanic—Humor—Jewish Interest—Literature—Native American—Poetry—Self Help—Senior Citizen—Women's Fiction—Women's Issues

CONTACT: Margarita Donnelly, Director
Material: Any
CONTACT: Micki Reaman, Managing Editor
Material: Any
PO Box B
Corvallis OR 97339
Phone: 541-753-9384
Fax: 541-753-0515
E-mail: Calyx@proaxis.com

Capital Books

Capital Books publishes non-fiction titles in the following areas of interest: self-help, personal and career development, business, lifestyles, travel, parenting and family, and memoirs.

We seek authors who are, or who have the potential to become, the preeminent spokesperson in the field and whose professional affiliations can provide a potentially large additional distribution channel to augment the traditional bookstore and retail channels.

We expect to collaborate with our authors in actively marketing their books using their contacts as well as those our marketing team provides. We offer a substantial author discount for the authors affiliated organizational sales.

We evaluate proposals using the following criteria:
• The subject matter is in one of our core areas
• The writing and literary style is compelling
• The author will actively participate in the marketing process
• The project is financially viable for both parties

While we prefer to review a finished manuscript, we will accept proposals that contain sample chapters. *All submissions should include:*

1. *A one page synopsis of the project comprised of:*
• Description of the book
• Definition of the target audience
• Statement of why you are uniquely qualified to write this book
2. Table of Contents or an outline of the structure of the book
3. One or two sample chapters or a manuscript (double spaced)
4. Biographical sketch or resume

Categories: Business—Careers—Family—Lifestyle—Parenting—Self Help—Travel

CONTACT: Acquisitions Editor
Material: All
22841 Quicksilver Drive
Sterling VA 20166
Phone: 703-996-1020
Fax: 703-661-1547
Website: www.capital-books.com

Carolrhoda Books
A division of Lerner Publishing Group

Please note: Our submission policy has changed. Effective immediately, we will only accept submissions during the month of November. Submissions received in any other month will be returned to the sender unopened. Thank you for abiding by our policy and please be patient—it can take up to 8 months to read and respond to each submission.

All submissions must contain a sufficiently posted SASE (we will not respond to or return manuscripts that do not have a SASE) and a one-page cover letter that briefly describes the project and includes the writer's name and previous publications, if any.

For nonfiction, we prefer to receive a complete manuscript. Please send a brief outline/synopsis and a recently updated résumé. Nonfiction submissions should be clearly marked as such.

For picture book submissions, we prefer to receive the whole manuscript. Dummy books are not necessary. For longer fiction, please send a brief outline/synopsis and a few sample chapters not exceeding fifty pages.

Our fiction department publishes about ten picture books each year geared to ages 5 to 8. We also publish longer fiction for ages 7 and up, including chapter books and middle-grade and YA novels. We like to see unique, honest stories that stay away from unoriginal plots, moralizing, and religious themes. We're also interested in seeing science fiction/fantasy for young readers.

In both fiction and nonfiction, we are especially interested in new ideas, fresh topics, and well-crafted, polished writing. Make sure your manuscript avoids racial and sexual stereotypes. The best way to know whether your work fits our company is to familiarize yourself with our books. Study our catalog, find our books in the library, or browse our website. For a catalog, send a self-addressed 9x12 envelope with $3.85 in postage. Address the request to CATALOG REQUEST. We do not publish alphabet books, textbooks, workbooks, songbooks, puzzles, plays, or religious material.

Thank you for your interest in Carolrhoda Books—and good luck!

Categories: Fiction—Nonfiction—Biography—Children—Fantasy—History—Juvenile—Science Fiction—Young Adult

CONTACT: Jennifer Zimian
Material: Nonfiction
CONTACT: Zelda Wagner
Material: Fiction
241 First Ave., North
Minneapolis, MN 55401
Phone: 612-332-3344
Fax: 612-332-7615
Website: www.lernerbooks.com or
www.carolrhodabooks.com

Carson-Dellosa Publishing Co., Inc.

SUBMISSION GUIDELINES FOR
PRODUCT IDEAS AND MANUSCRIPTS

Carson-Dellosa Publishing Company, Inc. welcomes manuscripts and product ideas from teachers and writers. We primarily publish supplemental educational materials for PK–8th grades, such as teacher resource and activity books, student workbooks, bulletin board sets, charts, and other decorative classroom items. Works of fiction, including children's storybooks, are generally not considered for publication. *If you are interested in having Carson-Dellosa review your work, please observe the following guidelines:*

PROPOSAL FORMAT:

A proposal for a product idea or manuscript should consist of:
• A brief cover letter introducing yourself or your company.
• A summary of the product idea containing its objectives, how it compares to other products on the market, how it would stand out from the competition, and the intended audience/grade level for the product.
• A mock-up of the product, depending on size
• A résumé listing experience relevant to the submission.
For manuscript proposals, please also include:
• A tentative table of contents including chapter titles and a three-to four-sentence summary of each chapter.
• The status of the manuscript explaining how much of the manuscript is complete, how long you think it will take to complete, and what length the book should be.
• 1–3 sample chapters to provide us with an introduction to the material and a representation of your writing style.

NO ORIGINALS: Do not send us the only copy of your manuscript or product idea. It is also very important that you do not send us original artwork. We cannot be responsible for lost or damaged materials.

A SELF-ADDRESSED, STAMPED ENVELOPE: If you wish to have your materials returned, please include a SASE or the appropriate postage for shipping.

DURATION OF REVIEW: Some proposals are sent to reviewers who have expertise relevant to the subject matter or grade level of the proposals. Due to reviewers' schedules and the quantity of submissions, the duration of in-house review varies. On average, it takes 6–8 weeks for materials to be reviewed.

IF WE FEEL WE CAN USE YOUR MATERIAL, WE WILL
CONTACT YOU. PLEASE NOTE THE FOLLOWING:

Carson-Dellosa Publishing prefers to purchase the idea or manuscript from you for a flat fee, but we will consider paying royalties in some cases.

Once your materials are purchased, the copyright becomes the property of Carson-Dellosa Publishing Company, Inc.

All artwork will be the responsibility of Carson-Dellosa unless agreed upon otherwise.

IF WE CANNOT USE YOUR MATERIALS,
PLEASE NOTE THE FOLLOWING:

Consideration of your proposal depends upon the quality of the material, the marketability of the project, economic feasibility, and the nature of other Carson-Dellosa projects that we have in progress or in our catalog.

We are unable to provide a critique of materials we do not plan to publish.

We may already have projects similar to or the same as yours in production. We will notify you when we have received your submission.

Thank you for following these guidelines and considering us as a publisher. We look forward to reviewing your ideas.

Categories: Nonfiction—Education

CONTACT: Wolfgang Hoelscher, Acquisitions Editor
Material: All
PO Box 35665
Greensboro NC 27425-5665
Phone: 336-632-0084
Fax: 336-632-0087

Catbird Press

No longer publishing books.

Caxton Press

CAXTON PRESS has a long tradition of publishing Western works of timeless appeal. We always are looking for new material. We ask that you follow our guidelines when submitting so that we may give your manuscript the attention it deserves.

Suggested Topics: Caxton publishes nonfiction trade books for general audiences. Although we may consider a manuscript on any subject, we prefer to publish western or frontier history, travel, pictorials, or narratives: nonfiction with a western theme. We will consider historical fiction if it deals with the West. We do not publish poetry.

Topics to avoid: "How I spent my years on the farm, on the mountain, in the city, etc." or "My family history."

Standards: We prefer to receive a query letter first that outlines your topic. If we feel it has possibilities, we'll usually request some sample chapters and an outline before requesting the complete manuscript.

We only accept manuscripts that are typewritten on one side of the page. Everything must be double-spaced: text, notes, bibliography, etc. Do not bind, staple, paper clip, or attach the pages together in any way. Send the pages loose and numbered, preferably in a box. We will accept sample chapters, and in some cases complete manuscripts, via e-mail. Please check in advance on format requirements.

Use active rather than passive verbs, and vibrant, colorful prose.

The piece must be responsibly researched. Your sources must be thoroughly documented and not infringe on existing copyrights. It is your responsibility to provide all photographs, illustrations, and graphics for your book. If your manuscript is accepted, the final version must be delivered to us on computer disk or via e-mail (WordPerfect or Microsoft Word format preferred). Some of our books include indexes, and we may ask the author to assemble the index at the appropriate time.

Style: We request our authors to follow *The Chicago Manual of Style* (14th edition).

Equipment: If possible, prepare your manuscript on Macintosh, Windows or MS-DOS compatible word processing systems. Letter quality is required —dot matrix is not acceptable. Do not send your disk unless we ask for it.

Proposals: Submit a cover letter addressed to the editorial department with your proposal. Introduce yourself and the theme of your manuscript. Tell us about your target audience, and why you think Caxton should publish your book. Include either an outline or a table of contents, a sample of the manuscript (usually one or two chapters), photocopies of artwork samples, and a SASE for return of your materials.

We handle every manuscript we receive carefully. But prudence dictates that you keep a copy of everything you send us. Don't send original documents, photos or artwork unless we request them.

Please allow 8-12 weeks for our response. We receive many manuscripts every year and evaluate each for readability, literary merit, accuracy, research, and sale-ability.

Categories: Nonfiction—History—Native American—Western

CONTACT: C. W. Cornell, Editor
Material: All
312 Main St.
Caldwell ID 83605-3299
Phone: 208-459-7421
E-mail: wcornell@Caxtonpress.com
Website: Caxtonpress.com

CCC Publications, LLC

1. CCC Publications is currently interested in reviewing Humor and How-to.

2. Our decision to publish a book is based on two criteria: the quality of writing and marketability. Both qualifications must be met before we will offer a contract.

3. For best results, send a query letter first, briefly explaining your book idea and your background (if it relates to the book). If we then solicit your ms. it has a much better chance of receiving priority in getting reviewed by an editor.

4. We prefer to see a complete manuscript—not chapter samples or outlines—submit photocopy or good quality computer printout.

5. Most of the books we do require some cartoon art or illustrations. Providing art or illustrations is the responsibility of the author. We will make an exception only in the case of an unusually well-written ms. If your book requires illustrations and you do not have them available at this time, include a list of your "proposed art" (short description and placement in the text).

6. As we receive approximately 200-300 submissions per month, our response time may be up to three months (shorter for query letters). Feel free after sixty days to inquire about the status of your submissions.

7. All manuscripts and correspondence that do not include a SASE receive low priority.

We thank you for your interest in CCC Publications and look forward to reviewing your manuscript for possible publication.

—Editorial Department

Categories: Fiction—Nonfiction—Comedy—Humor—Self Help—How-to

CONTACT: Mark Chutick, Publisher
Material: Humor
9725 Lurline Ave.
Chatsworth CA 91311
Phone: 818-718-0507

Celestial Arts

Please refer to Ten Speed Press.

Centerstream Publishing

Hello Writers,

We really don't have any formal guidelines. Since we only publish music history, music instructional books, and videos, our guidelines are simple: Just send it in.

We use Macs and request a hard copy and disk if we decide to do the project.

Thanks for considering Centerstream Publishing.

Ron Middlebrook

Categories: Music—Music History

CONTACT: Ron Middlebrook
Material: All
PO Box 17878
Anaheim Hills CA 92807
Phone: 714-779-9390
Fax: 714-779-9390
E-mail: Centerstrm@aol.com
Website: centerstream-usa.com

Century Press

Please refer to The Conservatory of American Letters, which can be found in the Book Publishers section.

Champion Press, Ltd.

Champion Press, Ltd. was established in 1997 in response to a need. With consolidation, change of ownership and attrition thinning the ranks of large publishing houses in New York and elsewhere, too many good books were going unpublished. Books providing valuable information, books telling stories that transport readers, books filled with imagery and imagination borne of the soul and capable of touching that in readers all of these works representing talented voices that would not be heard were it left to publishers dependent on minimum sales figures to cover overhead allocations and returns on equity. These books need to be published. They need to be printed and shipped and sold so that they may find their audiences, and do so without the added weight of supporting a corporate infrastructure so elaborate that product must constantly flow outward in massive quantities just to keep the lights on. We ask many things of our stable of authors at Champion Press, Ltd., but we demand only one: write a good book. When they do so (and they do with remarkable consistency), we'll work to get that book to its audience. No good book should fall like a tree in the forest, with no one there to hear its sound. Of our readers, we ask only that they trust our intent. The tastes of our editorial staff will not always mesh with their own, but our readers can rest assured that if a book bears the Champion Press, Ltd. imprint, it was deemed to be of quality, to be of value and to be deserving of presentation. We would rather work harder to find new sales for our existing books of quality than release a marginal title for financial requirements. Take a chance with our books. Try something that may not normally be your cup of tea. If we published it, it captured our fancy and it might just do the same for you. Then, if you like one of our books, let us know. Let us know if you didn't. We're easy to find, by both e-mail and traditional mail. If you keep letting us know who our audience is, we'll keep finding authors and titles that push you, thrill you, inform you and uplift you. Champion Press, Ltd. has been founded on these goals. We look forward to this century as one of the most exciting and challenging times in the history of humankind fully aware in the knowledge that no matter where peoples of this planet may reach, succeed, fail and endeavor; there will always exist the human need to occasionally look inward. There, we can hone improvement of self and mind. We can lose ourselves in lands and stories distant from our own existence. We can let our spirits dance with words and images. We can meet the very needs that make us human. Current Guidelines for Writers: NEEDS: Nonfiction: We are looking for cookbooks and fitness titles that are especially geared toward a busy woman's lifestyle. We are also interested in new and innovating home management topics. We publishing a limited number of education and homeschooling titles. We also publish self-help titles. We are no longer seeking submission in fiction, poetry or parenting. Please send ONLY a proposal, including market analysis, marketing plan and ideas (VERY IMPORTANT), your credential and bio, first 3 chapters and a SASE. Submissions without a SASE will not be returned. DO NOT PHONE OR E-MAIL. We get too many solicitations this way and thus do not reply. Please follow our guidelines and be familiar with the types of books we publishing prior to sending your project our way. WHAT TO SEND: Submission guidelines: A query letter summarizing the project. o A detailed proposal including an overview, a summary of market competition, a chapter by chapter outline, author bio and marketing approaches (for nonfiction); for fiction—send the first three chapters instead of the chapter by chapter outline and market summary. o A self-addressed, stamped envelope with sufficient postage to ensure the return of all materials desired by author, or explicit instructions informing that author does not wish the return of materials. Submissions made without sufficient return postage will not be returned or acknowledge. Under no circumstances should an entire manuscript be submitted without express written request from Champion Press, Ltd. All manuscripts submitted without request by Champion Press, Ltd. will be discarded. Submissions should be made to the following: The Editors Champion Press, Ltd. 4308 Blueberry Road Fredonia WI 53021 WHEN WILL I HEAR BACK? Champion Press holds four editorial meetings per year for manuscript submissions. These occur in early January, April, July and October. If you would like your proposal considered at these sessions, please make sure it arrives by the 15th of the previous month. You can expect to hear back within 8 weeks of the meeting. I.e. for the January meeting, you would have a response by end of February—if proper postage or reply is enclosed. We will not response otherwise. Please do not e-mail queries or materials. Please follow the procedures outlined above. Any deviation from these procedures and the material will not be considered for publication.

Categories: Nonfiction—Cooking—Education—Health—Lifestyle—Self Help—Women's Issues

CONTACT: The Editors
Material: All
4308 Blueberry Rd.
Fredonia WI 53021
E-mail: info@championpress.com
Website: www.championpress.com

Charles River Media

WHAT IS THE BOOK OR CD-ROM ABOUT? (Be as descriptive as possible.)

The proposal should convey the ideas that motivate your work and present the essential features that will set your book or CD-ROM apart. Describe in two or three paragraphs the purpose and importance of the project.

Include an outline of topics to be covered or a tentative table of contents.

WHAT TECHNOLOGIES WILL BE COVERED?

What product or technology is discussed and why. Where do you think the technology is headed in the next 12-18 months, or what is the schedule for new releases of the product?

AUDIENCE

Describe as specifically as possible the primary audience(s) for your project, e.g. graphics programmers, multimedia developers. Are there any secondary audiences for the project? What topics in your project will be of the greatest interest to each of these audiences?

Would your project be appropriate for professional-level short courses? If so, please describe.

Optional: Would your project be appropriate as a textbook or as a supplement for a course? If so, please list the name of the course(s) which could use it.

DESCRIBE WHAT IS ON THE CD-ROM.

If your book includes a CD, please describe what will be included on it. If your project is a standalone, this will be covered above.

LIST 5 TO 10 SIGNIFICANT SELLING POINTS.

Please list the selling points that you think are the strengths of your books on its own and as it compares to the competition.

COMPETITION

With which other products will your project most closely compete in terms of style, level and coverage? How will yours be better or different? Please be specific.

PRODUCTION CONCERNS

Please provide a rough estimate of the page length of the book and an estimated completion/delivery date. How many illustrations do you expect to include (roughly)? Will any of the illustrations need to be redrawn by Charles River Media?

Please provide the exact hardware and software used to prepare the manuscript. If this is for a CD-ROM, please list any software/authoring tools necessary to create the product and any licensing fees which may be necessary.

THE AUTHORS

Have you ever written a book or magazine article? Please include a current resume with your proposal.

Categories: Nonfiction—Technical

CONTACT: Aquisition Editor
Material: All
20 Downer Ave., Ste. 3
Hingham MA 02043
Fax: 781-740-8816
E-mail: info@charlesriver.com
Website: www.charlesriver.com

Charlesbridge Publishing

The Charlesbridge Trade Department publishes a unique variety of illustrated picture books for children from one to ten years old. Our nonfiction books focus on appealing and educational nature, science, social studies, and multicultural books as well as other nonfiction subjects. Our lively, fiction/plot-driven books feature strong, engaging characters and meaningful themes. We also publish cozy, fun stories, in whimsical verse or prose, for young children and parents to share at bedtime, quiet time, in the car, or any time at all.

Charlesbridge accepts unsolicited manuscripts submitted exclusively to us. "Exclusive Submission" must be written on all envelopes and cover letters. We prefer to see complete manuscripts, rather than query letters. At this time, we do not publish chapter books, books with audio tapes or CD-ROM, coloring or activity books, and we are not actively seeking alphabet books or board books.

Manuscripts should be typed and double spaced, but illustrations are not necessary. Please make a copy of your manuscript before sending it. We cannot be responsible for submissions lost in the mail. Please be sure that your name, address, and telephone number appear on the first page of your manuscript and in your cover letter. Be sure to list any previously published works or relevant writing experience. Enclose a self-addressed, stamped envelope (SASE) large enough and with sufficient postage (not a check or cash) to return all submitted material, or a small SASE if the work need not be returned. Material submitted on a computer disk or website, by email, or by fax will not be reviewed or returned.

Please submit only one or two manuscripts at a time. We make every effort to respond in three months, but cannot guarantee that we will be able to do so due to the volume of submissions we receive. To find out if your project reached us, enclose a self-addressed, stamped postcard for us to return upon receipt of your submission. If after three months you have not received a reply, you may wish to check on the status of your submission by writing to us at the address above. "Manuscript Status Query" should appear on the outside of your mailing envelope. Regretfully, we are unable to respond personally to every submission. Although we must sometimes resort to a form letter response, we carefully consider every manuscript we receive.

It is not necessary to copyright your work. Copyright is understood upon creation of a work, and formal registration is completed by the publisher upon publication. Like most trade publishers, we pay royalties or a flat fee to the author in the event a manuscript is accepted.

To become better acquainted with our publishing program, we encourage you to review some of our published books through a library or bookstore or to take a look at our website (www.charlesbridge.com) where you will find our complete catalog, the latest version of our guidelines, and tips from our editors. If you would like to request a printed catalog, please send a 9" x 12" self-addressed stamped envelope with postage (contact us for the postage).

For more information about Charlesbridge and other publishers, we recommend R. R. Bowker's *Literary Market Place* and the Children's Book Council's membership list. The latter may be obtained by sending a self-addressed stamped envelope with $.78 postage and a $2.00 fee to Children's Book Council, 568 Broadway, Suite 404, New York, NY 10012.

Categories: Fiction—Nonfiction—Biography—Children—Ecology—Environment—Family—Fantasy—Food/Drink—History—Juvenile—Music—Outdoors—Parenting—Science

CONTACT: Submissions Editor, Trade Editorial Department
Material: All
85 Main St.
Watertown MA 02472
Phone: 617-926-0329
Fax: 617-926-5720
Website: www.charlesbridge.com

Chatoyant

Chatoyant publishes high quality poetry and literature. We presently do not accept unsolicited submissions. All unsolicited materials will be recycled. Please see our website for more information: www.chatoyant.com.

Thanks,
Susana Wessling
Categories: Literature—Poetry

CONTACT: Submissions Editor
Material: All
PO Box 832
Aptos CA 95001
Website: www.chatoyant.com or www.poetrysantacruz.org

Chelsea Green Publishing Company

Chelsea Green is an independent publisher located in Vermont. We specialize in authors and books exploring contemporary environmental issues—ecology, renewable energy, self-sufficiency, and sustainable ways of living. We look for books that are comprehensive, fluent, and practical books on the politics and practice of sustainable living.

We are not presently considering fiction and poetry.
We appreciate submissions that include:
• A brief proposal summarizing your idea, with a table of contents.
• A representative sample chapter. Please do not send a copy of the complete manuscript unless we request one.
• A description of your previous experiences as an author and your qualifications for completing the project you propose.
• A self-addressed, stamped business envelope for our response to your query, and a self-addressed, stamped mailer if you would like your materials returned. Please do not send original art work or irreplaceable documents as we cannot assume responsibility for these.

Please allow 2-4 weeks for a response.

Please let us know if you would like to see our current catalog, and if you would like to be on our mailing list to receive semi-annual announcements of new Chelsea Green titles.

Categories: Nonfiction—Ecology—Environment—Gardening—Energy—Politics

CONTACT: Ben Watson
Material: All
PO Box 428
White River Junction VT 05001
Phone: 802-295-6300
Fax: 802-295-6444
E-mail: bwatson@chelseagreen.com

Chess Enterprises

Chess Enterprises only publishes books on the game of chess: instruction, game collections, analysis.
Categories: Nonfiction—Games—Chess

CONTACT: Submissions Editor
Material: All
107 Crosstree Red.
Moon Township PA 15108-2607
Phone: 412-262-2138
E-mail: bgdudley@compuserve.com

Chitra Publications

The following elements need to be included in a book proposal. Please address each as a separate item in your submission packet.

- Statement of the book's purpose.
- Identification of the book's subject.
- Description of your intended audience.
- Statement of what makes your book different from or superior to competing books.
  - Outline or table of contents.
  - Sample chapter(s).
  - Layout and graphics plan including number of pages, illustrations and photos (both color and/or black and white) per page. How do you "see" each page of your book? This can be an actual size "dummied up" version of the book or a thumbnail sketch noting what's on each page.
  - Sample photos or slides, preferably in color, and any illustrations you may have.
  - Desired publication date.
  - Biography of one page or less with emphasis on your credentials.
  - Your ideas on how your book should be marketed.

Books published by Chitra Publications are how-to books with plenty of support for the reader: clear directions, appealing projects, illustrative photos and diagrams, including patterns for ten to twelve projects. Books are approximately 32 pages in length. We prefer to use color photographs, generally eight-page or sixteen-page sections. Placing color sections in the middle of the book helps keep production costs down, so you may want to consider this in planning. Your illustrations must be accurate, so the graphic designer can make them camera-ready.

We will look over your proposal and advise you of our interest within 4 to 6 weeks.

We may invite you to submit your manuscript for further consideration.

Categories: Nonfiction—Arts—Crafts/Hobbies—Hobbies—Recreation—Quilts/Quilting

CONTACT: Connie Ellsworth, Production Manager
Material: Books, Articles, Reviews
CONTACT: Jack Braunstein, Senior Editor
Material: Books
2 Public Ave.
Montrose PA 18801-1220
Phone: 570-278-1984
Fax: 570-278-2223
E-mail: chitra@epix.net
Website: www.QuiltTownUSA.com

Chosen Books

Please refer to Baker Publishing Group.

Christian Ed. Publishers

All writing is on assignment only. Please review guidelines carefully.
1. When submitting a manuscript to us:
   a) That is a sample assignment – write SAMPLE ASSIGNMENT in lower left-hand corner of mailing envelope
   b) That is by assignment – write ASSIGNMENT in lower left-hand corner of envelope.
2. The Kinds of Material We Publish
(all handled by our assigned free-lance writers only)
- Curriculum for children and youth, including program and student books
- Church-wide special event program kits
- Bible-teaching craft kits
3. The Kinds of Writers We Seek
- Those who love the Lord
- Those who relate well to the age group written for
- Those who have hands-on experience with the children or youth they want to write for

- Those who are active members of a Bible-believing church
- Those who write well, whether published or unpublished
- Those who are able to meet deadlines, and consistently submit manuscripts on time

4. How to Contact Us
If interested in writing by assignment for us, request a free-lance writer application. Include a SASE. Address all submissions to Carol Rogers, Managing Editor, at address below.

5. The Assignment Process
   a) Contact us to receive a free-lance writer application. Include a SASE.
   b) Return the completed application and a resume of your Christian experience with the age group you want to write for, and your writing background (including clips).
   c) We send you a sample assignment for the age group you indicated.
   d) After reviewing and accepting your returned sample assignment, we add you to our list of available writers.
   e) We make an assignment to you based on our scheduled needs.

6. Payment Policy
   a) Our payments are made upon acceptance within 90 days after an assignment is submitted, reviewed, and approved. We do not pay for sample assignments unless we are able to publish them.
   b) Regular assignments receive 100% of the agreed rate of payment, upon acceptance, whether we are able to use the assignment for the particular project assigned, or use it in a future project.
   c) We pay 3¢ a printed word, or a fixed a mount for certain projects.

7. Additional Information for Writers
Make sure your typewriter ribbon or printer cartridge is not worn. Do not submit on onion skin or erasable paper. Always make a copy of anything you submit to us. Include a computer disk, if possible. (Let us know which software you use.) Neatness and legibility is a must. Carefully proofread before submitting anything.

We are always eager to locate writers of top quality who can have a part in our ministry for Christ. If interested in requesting an application, please include a SASE.

Christian Ed. Publishers is an independent, non-denominational, evangelical publishing company. We produce Christ-centered curriculum based on the Word of God. We provide these curriculum materials to thousands of churches of different denominations throughout the world. Our mission is to introduce children, teens, and adults to a personal faith in Jesus Christ and to help them grow in their faith and service to the Lord. We publish materials that teach moral and spiritual values while training individuals for a lifetime of Christian service. Spiritually dedicated writers and employees assist in this ministry.

Categories: Fiction—Nonfiction—Christian Interests—Religion—Spiritual

CONTACT: Carol Rogers, Managing Editor
Material: All
PO Box 26639
San Diego CA 92196
Phone: 858-578-4700, ext.114
E-mail: cgast@cepub.com

Christian Publications, Inc.
OWNERSHIP AND DOCTRINAL POSITION OF THE PUBLISHING HOUSE:

Christian Publications, Inc. (CPI) is the official publishing house of The Christian and Missionary Alliance Church. CPI adheres to the same evangelical doctrinal position as its sponsoring denomination. A copy of the leaflet, "Statement of Faith," is available free of charge to all who request it.

BOOK SUBJECTS CONSIDERED:

Christian Publications, Inc. publishes both for the denomination and for the general Christian public. To be considered, all manuscripts must be compatible with our doctrinal position. CPI will consider book manuscripts dealing with theology, the church, pastoral helps, Bible studies, the Christian home, devotional studies, Christian living and deeper life. Manuscripts NOT accepted are: poetry, short stories, children's, fiction, unsolicited Bible commentaries and reference works. A complete proposal must be submitted, as detailed below. Proposals will not be returned unless accompanied by sufficient return postage.

PREPARATION OF MANUSCRIPTS:

A complete proposal should include the following:

1. A query/cover letter explaining what you envision for the manuscript

2. An overview of the concept for the book, including a description of the intended audience

3. A chapter-by-chapter synopsis.

4. Two sample chapters, including Chapter One.

5. A biographical sheet or resume of the author(s), spelling out why you are qualified to write this book and/or what your unique perspective is.

6. A review of competitive titles currently in print on the same or similar topics.

7. A review of marketing possibilities available to the author(s).

An alternative submission method is to fill out the submission form on our web site: www.christianpublications.com.

All submissions should meet the standards of *The Chicago Manual of Style*. All submissions must be a copy of your original materials. We will not accept responsibility for lost text or artwork.

Proposals should be on 8 1/2" x 11" white bond paper. No glossy paper please. Pages should be numbered consecutively from the beginning to the end of the manuscript rather than by chapters.

The author is responsible to obtain permission to use any copyrighted material. Please allow up to four months for your manuscript to be evaluated by our review committee and editors. If your manuscript is accepted for publication, CPI prefers manuscripts on standard computer disks in a word processing format convertible to WordPerfect. Each chapter should be self-contained in an individual file.

FINANCIAL ARRANGEMENTS FOR BOOK MANU-SCRIPTS:

Contract arrangements are made upon final acceptance of the book by the publisher. While a flat rate is paid for some books, most are contracted on a royalty basis.

Please note that although we will consider ONE-PAGE queries by fax or email, we DO NOT appreciate receiving sales pitches for a manuscript over the phone.

Categories: Christian Interests—Inspirational—Religion—Spiritual

CONTACT: Editorial Department
Material: All
3825 Hartzdale Dr.
Camp Hill PA 17011
Phone: 717-761-7044
Fax: 717-761-7273
E-mail: editorial @christianpublications.com
Website: www.christianpublications.com

Chronicle Books LLC

Adult Trade Division—Submission Guidelines

Chronicle Books LLC publishes approximately 175 books a year. We specialize in high-quality, reasonably priced books for adults and children. Our titles include best-selling cookbooks; fine art, design,

photography, and architecture titles; full-color nature books; award-winning poetry and literary fiction; regional and international travel guides; and gift and stationery items. We will accept unsolicited manuscripts in each of these subject areas. To gain a better understanding of our publishing program, please examine our books in a bookstore, library, a Chronicle Books catalog, or visit our web site: www.chroniclebooks.com.

When submitting a proposal, initial query letter, or completed manuscript, please remember that it may take up to three months for the editors to review it. (Please note, we do not accept proposals on disks, over the Internet, or by fax.) Outlined below is the basic procedure for submitting manuscripts and proposals. While by no means are all of the steps mandatory, bear in mind that it is your vision you are presenting to us, so the more information you give us to visualize your project, the better. Please send us copies of your material and keep the original for your records.

A nonfiction proposal could include:

1. Cover letter giving a brief description of the project and what is included in the package.

2. Proposal, including outline, introduction, illustrations list, sample captions, and text/sample chapters (approximately 30 pages of text). If you are submitting a cookbook proposal, include a list of recipes plus at least ten sample recipes with headnotes in addition to the information described above.

3. Sample illustrations or photographs (duplicates rather than originals).

4. A market analysis of the potential readership for the book, including title, publisher, and date of all similar books, with an explanation of how your book differs from each.

5. Author/illustrator/photographer biography, including publishing credits and credentials in the field.

6. A self-addressed, stamped envelope for return of the material. If desired, include a self-addressed, stamped blank postcard for acknowledgment of receipt of manuscript.

If you are submitting fiction (a novel or a short story collection), submit the complete manuscript to Adult Trade — Fiction and include a self-addressed, stamped envelope for its return. Please note that Chronicle Books does not publish romances, science fiction, fantasy, westerns, or other genre fiction.

Do not submit original material (either art or manuscript) and please keep a copy of your project. Please note that material unaccompanied by a SASE will not be returned. Also, please do not contact President Jack Jensen or Chairman/CEO Nion McEvoy directly with your query. Instead, direct your proposal to our editorial department at the address below.

Thank you for your interest in Chronicle Books.

Children's Division—Submission Guidelines

Chronicle Books LLC publishes an eclectic mixture of traditional and innovative children's books. We are interested in projects that have a unique bent to them — be it in subject matter, writing style, or illustrative technique. We are looking for books that will contribute to our lists a distinctive flair. Primarily we are interested in fiction and nonfiction picture books for children ages up to eight years and non-fiction books for children ages eight to twelve years. We are also interested in early chapter books, middle grade fiction, and young adult projects. To gain a better understanding of our publishing program, please examine our books in a bookstore, library, a Chronicle Books catalog, or visit our web site: www.chroniclebooks.com.

Picture books may be submitted without query first. Projects for older children and/or young adult, should be submitted by query (synopsis and three sample chapters) and SASE first. When submitting, please be sure to include a self-addressed, stamped envelope large enough to hold your materials. Projects submitted without an appropriate self-addressed, stamped envelope will be recycled. Do not send checks or cash for postage; only US postage and international reply coupons will be accepted. If you would like confirmation that your materials have been received, please include a self-addressed, stamped

Books A-L

postcard. (Such confirmation cannot be given over the telephone. Also note that we do not accept proposals by fax, via e-mail, or on disk.) If your proposal is a simultaneous submission, please indicate this in your cover letter.

When submitting artwork, either as a part of a project or as samples for review, do not send originals. If you would like your work kept on file, please indicate which work we may keep. And please, always keep a copy of your project because we will not be responsible for the loss or damage of unsolicited material.

All materials received are reviewed and will get an official response, but due to the enormous number of children's projects Chronicle Books receives each year, we are unable to respond to each project personally. Our response time varies, but generally you should expect to wait from four to eighteen weeks.

Please note that due to postal regulations, SASE packages weighing a pound or more require special handling and therefore will be delayed by as much as 30 days.

Thank you for your interest in Chronicle Books.

Gift Division—Submission Guidelines

Chronicle Books LLC publishes approximately 175 books a year. We specialize in high-quality, reasonably priced books for adults and children. Our titles include best-selling cookbooks; fine art, design, photography, and architecture titles; full-color nature books; award-winning poetry and literary fiction; regional and international travel guides; and gift & stationary items.

The Gift Division of Chronicle Books publishes a wide assortment of quality gift items, including calendars, note cards, address books, journals, and postcard collections. We will consider unsolicited proposals and manuscripts.

To gain a better understanding of our publishing program, please examine our books in a bookstore, library, a Chronicle Books catalog, or on our web site at www.chroniclebooks.com.

When submitting a proposal, initial query letter, or completed project, please remember that it may take the editors up to three months to review it. (Please note that we do not accept proposals on disk, by fax, or via email.) The deadline for calendar submissions is 18 months prior to the year you wish to publish. Outlined below is the basic procedure for submitting proposals and manuscripts. While by no means are all of the steps mandatory, bear in mind that it is your vision you are presenting to us, so the more information you give us to visualize your project, the better.

A proposal could include:

1. Cover letter giving a brief description of the project and what is included in the package.

2. Samples of illustrations or photographs (i.e., duplicates rather than originals).

3. Where appropriate, a proposal including outline, introduction, illustrations list, sample captions, and text/chapter samples.

4. An analysis of the potential market for the project, including title, publisher, and date of all similar projects, with an explanation of how your proposal differs from each.

5. Author/illustrator/photographer biography that includes publishing credits and credentials in the field.

6. A self-addressed, stamped envelope for return of the materials. If desired, include a self-addressed, stamped blank postcard for acknowledgment of receipt of the materials

Do not submit original material (either art of manuscript) and please keep a copy of your project. Please note that material unaccompanied by a SASE will be recycled. Direct your submission to our Gift Department at the address below.

Note

These guidelines are for informational purposes only and do not constitute a solicitation of any manuscript, artwork, transparencies, or other material. Submission of any unsolicited materials shall be done at the author/illustrator's own risk of loss or damage.

Thank you for your interest in Chronicle Books.

Categories: Fiction—Nonfiction—Animals—Architecture—Arts—Cooking—Crafts/Hobbies—Culture—Entertainment—Film/Video—Food/Drink—Gay/Lesbian—General Interest—Lifestyle—Literature—Music—New Age—Parenting—Photography—Travel—Young Adult

CONTACT: Gift Division
Material: Gift Division Submissions
CONTACT: Editorial Dept, Adult Trade Division
Material: Adult Trade Division Submissions
CONTACT: Children's Division
Material: Children's Division Submissions
85 Second St., 6th Floor
San Francisco CA 94105
Phone: 415-537-4200
Website: www.chroniclebooks.com

Chrysalis Books

Please refer to the Swedenborg Foundation, Inc.

Clarity Press, Inc.

Human rights and social justice issues viewed in the context of universally recognized human rights norms.

Dear Writer:

Clarity's writer's guidelines are as follows:

Nonfiction only: visit Website for editorial purview. Please send query letter first, with brief bio, table of contents, synopsis and endorsements. SASE unnecessary; due to volume of queries, we will respond only if interested. Manuscript should be available on disk in Microsoft Word.

Sincerely,

Diana G. Collier, Editorial Director

Categories: Nonfiction—African-American—Asian-American—Government—Human Rights—Law—Multicultural—Native American—Politics

CONTACT: Diana G. Collier, Editorial Director
Material: All
3277 Roswell Rd. NE
Atlanta GA 30305
Phone: 877-613-1495
Fax: 877-613-7868
E-mail: claritypress@usa.net
Website: www.claritypress.com

Clover Park Press

Clover Park Press, publisher of great books about life's wonders and wanderings, is seeking book-length manuscripts for its current publishing interests. We are looking for fresh ideas and superior writing in the following categories:

Non-Fiction in the areas of:

• California (history, natural history, travel, culture or the arts).

• Biography of extraordinary women.

• Acts of Courage (Please request further information before submitting in this category.)

• Nature, the environment or place.

• Other cultures.

• Travel, exploration, adventure.

• Scientific/medical discovery.

No fiction, poetry, children's, photography, true crime, diaries or journals, new age, or books about alcoholism or addiction.

Submission guidelines:

• Query with letter summary of one page; author's prior publications and background relevant to the subject; outline; and two strong sample chapters including the first chapter.

• Manuscript should have font between 10-12 pt, be paginated and secured with a clip (not stapled).

• If you have any questions, do inquire by mail or e-mail (preferred) before sending submission. Because of our heavy volume of e-mail, begin your subject line with "A-Query."

• No phone calls.

• Include your phone and e-mail address.

Categories: Nonfiction—Adventure—Biography—History—Multicultural—Regional—Travel—Women's Issues

CONTACT: Martha Grant, Acquisitions Editor
Material: All
PO Box 5067
Santa Monica CA 90409
E-mail: cloverparkpr@earthlink.net
Website: home.earthlink.net/~cloverparkpr/

Collectors Press, Inc.

Thank you for your interest in Collectors Press, Inc. Please note we do not publish novels, poems, children's books, or short stories.

To expedite a response to your inquiry, please send the following:

• A clean, typed, completed manuscript or three sample chapters clipped together or in booklet form. Do not send computer diskette.

• A table of contents (without page numbers).

• If illustrations/photographs are used, send high-quality examples, with an estimate of total images in the completed work.

• Include a post-paid mailer with your mailing label affixed if you want your manuscript returned. Include a SASE (self addressed stamped envelope) if you only want a reply.

Please help us learn more about you and your book by providing the following (if applicable):

• Brief explanation of the book.

• Why the subject is worthy of a book.

• What other published books does your work compare to?

• What will you do to promote the book on an on-going basis?

• Have you written other books?

• Do you have other books planned or in the works?

• Any media experience and/or contacts?

• Quotes of recognized authorities for your work. Do you have a published author or celebrity to write an introduction/foreword?

Please allow one to two months (including mailing time) for us to review your material and reply back to you. If you would like to know the date your submission was received, include a post-paid postcard or SASE with the request.

We look forward to reviewing your submission!

Categories: Nonfiction—Arts—Collectibles—Cooking—Food/Drink—History— Nostalgia—Pop Culture— Science Fiction

CONTACT: Jennifer Weaver-Neist, Editorial Manager
Material: All
PO Box 230986
Portland, OR 97281
Phone: 503-684-3030
Fax: 503-684-3777
Website: www.collectorspress.com

Commonwealth Editions

Commonwealth Editions publishes nonfiction books about the history and beauty of New England. We do not publish fiction or poetry.

If you have a manuscript or book idea that fits this description, please feel free to send a short e-mail to publisher Webster Bull, explaining the book you have in mind.

If you like, instead, you may send a proposal and a writing sample of no more than twenty pages to the address below.

If you do send an outline and writing sample, please provide a stamped self-addressed envelope to assure the return of these materials.

Categories: Nonfiction—History—Regional—New England

CONTACT: Webster Bull, Publisher
Material: All
266 Cabot St.
Beverly, MA 01915
Phone: 978-921-0747
Fax: 978-927-8195
E-mail: websterb@commonwealtheditions.com
Website: www.commonwealtheditions.com

COMPANION
★ P ★ R ★ E ★ S ★ S ★
Naked Cinema Books
The Companion Press

The Companion Press Writing Contest
Please read carefully before submitting a story.

Companion Press publishes creative non-fiction SHORT STORY ANTHOLOGY BOOKS ONLY! Stories are selected from winning entries in our regular WRITING CONTESTS.

CONTEST RULES

LENGTH: Stories must be non-fiction, ranging in length between 300-1500 words.

ORIGINAL AND PREVIOUSLY PUBLISHED STORIES: All entries must be the original work of the writer. Stories be previously published or unpublished. Writer agrees to be legally responsible for submitting any plagiarized material.

JUDGING: Stories are judged by publisher and author Steve Stewart, along with rotating staff editors. The judges decisions are final.

COPYRIGHT: Copyright remains with the author but Companion Press reserves the right to publish the winning and runner-up stories in book format, on our web site and to use to promote the book and/or contests in newspapers, magazines and any other media.

FIRST TIME AND UNPUBLISHED WRITERS: We welcome first-time writers as well as professional writers. We also welcome short stories from writers worldwide.

DEADLINES: If, after the contest deadline has passed we haven't received enough winning stories to fill a book, the deadline may be extended until we do. If we still don't receive enough stories, contest entry fees will be returned and publication of the book will be cancelled.

DATE OF PUBLICATION: Once the winner and runners-up have been selected, it can take three to six months or more for an anthology to be published and distributed to bookstores. Sometimes, in rare instances, it may take a year or even longer. Please be patient, and feel free to check our web site for the planned date of publication of all upcoming books.

EDITING: We reserve the right to edit stories for length and style.

YOUR BIO: A bio, a short paragraph (of about 50 words or less) about you must be included with your story. Feel free to promote your latest book, service, etc. Our books are sold nationwide and worldwide, so in addition to your story being published, your brief bio can be great advertising and promotion for you.

RETURNING YOUR STORY: We do not return submissions, so please don't send the original. If you e-mail your story we will send you a return e-mail confirmation that we have received it. Please send a SASE if you wish confirmation of mailed submissions, otherwise your cancelled check or credit card statement will serve as your confirmation.

NOTIFICATION: If your story wins First Prize or is a runner-up you will be notified. However, if your story is not chosen, you will not receive a rejection letter due to the fact that there are future books for which it will be considered at no additional fee.

LEGALITIES: Entering this competition implies your acceptance of all guidelines and rules.

HOW TO SUBMIT A SHORT STORY

BY E-MAIL E-mail: sstewart@companionpress.com

Entries must be e-mailed as text only (NO ATTACHED FILES) and must be written in English only. Stories must be contained within the body of the e-mail and not sent as attachments. Please ensure that your name, address, phone number and all other relevant contact information is included. Your entry fee must be sent at the same time.

BY SNAIL MAIL: If you don't have access to the Internet, print the entry form and mail it along with your story. Type it on plain white 8 1/2" x 11" paper, in 12-point Times New Roman font. Then send your story with the entry fee to Contest, Companion Press, Box 2575, Laguna Hills, CA 92564. Mail your submissions in a flat, 9x12 envelope. Do not fold. Your entry fee must be included.

ENTRY FEE: None

HOW TO SEND PAYMENT: We accept Visa, MasterCard, Check or Money Order (U.S. currency only).

To mail in your entry fee: See our website to print out an entry form to mail in your entry fee. Make check or money order payable to Companion Press.

HOW TO CONTACT US

We hope this answers all of your submission guideline questions. If not, please feel free to write or e-mail us. We do not open attached files. Send text files only.

Categories: Erotica—Film/Video—Gay/Lesbian—Sexuality

CONTACT: Steve Stewart, Publisher

Material: All

PO Box 2575

Laguna Hills CA 92654

Phone: 949-62-9726

Fax: 949/362-4489

E-mail: sstewart@companionpress.com

Website: www.companionpress.com

The Conservatory of American Letters

Dan River Press, Northwoods Press and Century Press

The Conservatory of American Letters is a non profit tax exempt literary educational foundation. *The IRS requires we publish our purpose:*

• To conserve and make public literary works of exceptional merit without regard to commercial potential.

• To encourage and develop literary talent.

• To offer the reading public an alternative to mass marketing mediocrity.

In order to accomplish this objective, we own and operate the following companies and plans. Northwoods Press, the poet's press, publishes poetry, local and family histories and works about them. It does offer a teacher's custom publishing arm. Northwoods Press also publishes the quarterly *Northwoods Journal*, a magazine for writers.

Dan River Press publishes only fiction and biography. Dan River Press also publishes the annual (since 1984) Dan River Anthology.

Century Press publishes in all areas.

Perhaps most importantly (at least used by more writers than any other service) is our Personal Publishing Program (PPP) where you act as your own publisher. We believe that if you can't get a royalty contract this is the best way to go for most writers.

Notes to Authors: Don't waste time and postage by submitting before you've read guidelines. If you want to submit a book length work, query first with SASE. Do not send complete manuscript until query has been answered. There is a lot of money being wasted on postage. Do not send anything express mail, or overnight, it is a waste of perfectly good money. I recently received an express mail piece ($3.50 postage) that could have been sent for .74 postage (or maybe .57) for a deadline that is eight weeks away. If you've that kind of money to throw away, throw some at the Conservatory. It's deductible on all tax forms. Believe me, there is nothing we're that eager to see. When submitting your work, please adhere to the appropriate submission guidelines. To receive guidelines through the mail, send us a #10 self-addressed stamped envelope and tell us which guidelines you want. Do not submit anything electronically or on disk unless requested to do so. **Do not fax manuscripts!**

Dan River Press

Dan River Press was created in 1976 in Meadows of Dan, Virginia. It has become the fiction and biography arm of the Conservatory and publishes the ever popular (since 1984) Dan River Anthology.

Guidelines For Submissions: Dan River Press

As always, we suggest writers read our books to determine if Dan River Press is an appropriate place for your work.

We may offer a minimum advance of $250 against royalties of 10% of the amount we receive on the first 2,500 copies, 15% of the amount we receive on all additional copies. Royalties are paid each March for the prior year, or by request. Quality book production is in hardcover and paperback with a guarantee of in-print status for two full years and as long thereafter as our sales total only $250 annually.

Everyone gets the same discount: 1 copy none; 2-24 copies, 2% X number of books ordered. (10 books X 2%=20%); 25 or more copies 50%. Hardcovers are usually produced in extremely limited numbers. Multiple copy discounts are not offered on hardcover books.

Send self addressed stamped envelope for return of materials and additional SASEs for answers to questions, confirmation, and so forth.

Do not submit electronically, by fax, or by e-mail. Do not submit with disk. If we accept, we will ask for a disk, but we don't want one with the first read. Simultaneous submissions are not encouraged, but they are not forbidden. Because we are a conservatory, and publishing = conserving, we don't consider previously published work.

Dan River Press considers work from all. Membership in the Conservatory is not required. If accepted, however, membership will be required over the life of the publication. Members always receive preference when all else is equal, as we seek to support those who support us.

Dan River Press accepts chapbooks for publication. A chapbook is defined as a book of 64 or fewer pages, self covered, saddle stapled in the spine. We will accept chapbooks from 4 to 64 pages (always a multiple of 4). This is an ideal way to promote the longer short story (up to about 10,000 words), with no payment (or anything else) required of the author. Authors are paid a royalty of 10% of the amount we receive on all sales after the first 100. Publications will be attractively and professionally produced. In keeping with our stated purpose, virtually all excellent, fundable manuscripts will be accepted.

Dan River Anthology, 2004

You are not required to buy a copy!

We pay a non-refundable advance on acceptance and offer opportunities to earn more.

The anthology is not overpriced and is actually sold (Multiple Copy Discounts up to 50%). The 2002 number actually sold out and by February a second printing was ordered.

Nothing is required of the author except proofing his/her own galleys.

Listed in the top 50 fiction markets in the land by *Writer's Digest*. (In spite of the fact that we consider our small advance but token payment.)

Nothing previously published can be considered. We can not accept simultaneous submissions. Do not submit anything electronically, on disk, or by fax, unless specifically requested. All rights returned to author on publication.

Guidelines for typing: Since we use a scanner, manuscripts must be typed. If you own an old typewriter be sure that the ribbon is fresh and the keys are clean. Some old typewriters cannot produce scannable copy and that earns a rejection, no matter how great the work. Please forget what you learned in typing class. Do not justify, do not use hyphens at the end of lines. One hypen means a hypen, two hyphens mean a dash. Be careful about spaces before and/or after dashes. Scanner will give what you send. Changing will generate an AA charge. Avoid strange spacing in poetry. It usually only detracts from the poem anyway, and it's a good way to guarantee rejection. Titles of entires are bold and italic. Titles of parts are only italic. Foreign words should be italicized. Indicate italics by underling, bold italics by all caps and underling. We can produce most accented letters, but are not multi-lingual, so we can accept no responsibility for errors. Stanza break, or paragraph break, at the end of a page must say so.

We only receive work from January 1 to March 31 each year. We accept work by May 15 of each year and send proofs by June 15. Assuming all proofs returned in 24 hours we release the paperback edition about the first of December, and the hardcover in Mid-January of its date/title.

There is a reading fee of $1 per poem and $3 per 2,500 words, or any part, of fiction. Reading fee must be paid in cash, no checks, no money orders, no credit cards. The reading fee goes directly to the first reader of your work, the company gets none of it and bookkeeping such small amounts would be impractical, and costly.

SASE if you want your work returned. Others if you want acknowledgement or other correspondence.

Paperbacks sell for $15.95 and are subject to all discounts.

Hardcovers sell for $39.95 and are not subject to multiple copy discounts, but do qualify for CAL member discounts and do earn royalties. Normally only as many hardcovers as are sold in advance are produced. Almost always fewer than 25. Last year we produced 12 full-color dust jackets.

The only possible charge to authors is for Author's Alterations. If you change something from your original you will be billed at $52 per hour with a $25 minimum. Any change, even a comma to a period, will activate the charge. Proofreading after typesetting can be very expensive. Of course all errors that we make are corrected without charge of any kind.

The Dan River Anthology, 2005 will feature a full color cover and professional production.

Order a recent copy, see what we're like, then submit. Order from our bookstore or call us with a credit card at 207/354-0998.

Northwoods Press

The Poet's Press

Northwoods Press was created in Bigfork, Minnesota in 1972.

Any excellent poet with even a very small following may be able to have her/his chap book published with royalty contract. We may actually be able to publish with prospects of as few as 25-50 sales.

Over the years the company has changed and evolved. Currently it publishes poetry, local and family histories, and plays. Northwoods Press is available to academia for custom publishing books for classroom use under its University Press division. Northwoods Press seeks to provide a companion CD for every book published. The CD is usually recorded by the author and may/should include readings, and/or other comment deemed appropriate by author and publisher. Northwoods Press seeks to acquire three poetry books per year from its on-going poetry contest, plus any other excellent works which can be published. Northwoods Press can not receive direct subsidy from authors.

The University Press division requires advance sales of only 80 books. Books for classroom use are limited to poetry, local histories and related themes.

Northwoods Press publishes the annual Northwoods Anthology. Use the same guidelines as Dan River Anthology. Deadline is October 30th.

Northwoods Press is a royalty publisher and may pay an advance against royalties.

American History Press, a division of Northwoods Press, publishes histories, including family and church histories, and geneology. American History Press works extremely well in the Northwoods Press chapbook publishing program.

You should send poetry manuscript exactly as you would have your book to appear, including all front matter (front matter means: title page, copyright page, dedication, acknowledgements, contents, forward, and whatever else you feel appropriate.) front and back covers (We want full color covers, or at least a clear idea as to what you want if you can't provide the artwork or photography.). If you have no cover design, we can acquire one, using color photography, for a $250.00 charge. You should paginate, using not more than 44 lines per page (40 is better) (remember, a line is a line is a line, no matter what is/isn't written in it) . Include an SASE or clear instructions to discard manuscript if rejected. We regret we will not be able to comment on rejected manuscripts. Because we are tax exempt and a conservatory, we can not spend money on already conserved works (Published = Conserved), therefore no more than 10% (by line count) of any book or chapbook can be previously published in any form. You may submit in any hardcopy form, but prior to publication you may be required to provide a compatible disk.

Rhymed poetry has little chance.

Typewriter poetry has even less.

We have bias against poetry about poetry, and poetry about and writing poetry.

We may offer an advance against royalties of 10% of the amount received on the first 2,500 copies sold, and 15% on all copies sold after 2,500. Royalties are payable each March for the prior year.

We provide bar codes, ISBN, a listing in *Amazon.com, Baker & Taylor, Ingram, Books In Print, Small Press* record of books in print, the copyright, and so forth.

Most books of 64 pages or larger are produced in hardcover and paperback.

Books are promoted to libraries, bookstores, individual poetry buyers, and areas where the author has influence.

We don't accept simultaneous submissions, electronic submissions, faxed submissions, submissions on disk, (Once accepted you will be asked to provide disk.) or previously published material.

Include an SASE for return of material, plus an SASE or SASP for receipt confirmation or for other correspondence. Writers who are interested in submitting to Northwoods Press should check out our current offerings.

Northwoods Journal: A Magazine for Writers

Northwoods Journal, a magazine for writers, has been listed in *Writer's Digest's* Best 50 Fiction Markets.

Northwoods Journal offers writers an excellent chance to be published. We receive a small number of submissions. Publication "credits" help build a writer's career. We have lots of room in our pages for career building. If you submit good work, you're likely to sell to the Journal. More than 90% of work submitted to major publishers is never read by anyone, but this small press publisher reads every submission.

Most small presses pay nothing, but a couple of copies they can't sell anyway. We, on the other hand, do not pay in copies. We actually sell what we print. Our circulation runs 200 to250—SOLD each issue. Most small-press magazines don't sell half that many. Many don't actually "sell" any.

Submit to the Journal. Your manuscript will actually be read by an editor with the authority to accept. While the *Northwoods Journal* is a magazine for writers, it is not a how-to (though it may contain a few how-to elements), it is a showcase. Writers get to show off their finest works through legitimate, paid publication. Everything published in the *Northwoods Journal*, a magazine for writers, is paid for on acceptance.

The Journal does not require any purchase, subscription, or membership. Send an SASE.

Century Press

Century Press was formed in 1997. Its purpose is to offer writers an alternative to the extremely high prices of large subsidy presses.

Century Press accepts any type of book, and discourages subsidy publications.

Personal Publishing Program

In keeping with its purpose to encourage and develop literary talent, CAL offers a Personal Publishing Program (PPP) where the author becomes his/her own publisher.

This program is designed to make authors of writers. No acceptance is needed. (We don't even read the manuscripts.) All profits accrue to the author.

CAL will serve as your printer, your typesetter, your cover artist, your editor, your fulfillment office, your bookkeeper, your webmaster, anything you wish. All on a fee-for-services basis. We can provide things like bar codes, ISBNs, copyright services, and more.

Most writers hire us as printers and/or typesetters. A smaller number buy other services of creation or promotion. We've printed more than 2,000 (and counting) titles for writers. References on request.

Cost of printing is $200, plus cost of books ordered.

Categories: Fiction—Nonfiction—Adventure—Biography—Civil War—Conservation—Drama—Erotica—Fantasy—Fishing—History—Literature—Men's Fiction—Mystery—Outdoors—Paranormal—Romance—Rural America—Science Fiction—Short Stories—Sports/Recreation—Textbooks—Western—Writing—Hunting

CONTACT: Century Press
Material: Century Press submissions
CONTACT: Dan River Press
Material: Dan River Press submissions
CONTACT: Dan River Anthology
Material: Dan River Anthology submissions
CONTACT: Northwoods Press
Material: Northwoods Press submissions
CONTACT: Northwoods Journal
Material: Northwoods Journal submissions
CONTACT: Northwoods Anthology
Material: Northwoods Anthology submissions
PO Box 298
Thomaston ME 04861
Phone: 207-354-0998
Fax: 207-354-8953
E-mail: cal@americanletters.org
Website: www.americanletters.org

Contemporary Books
A Division of McGraw-Hill Companies

Project Submission Guidelines

McGraw-Hill is committed to maintaining the highest standards of quality in all areas in which we publish. If you have an idea for a book that you would like us to consider, please simply provide the information requested below. This will assist us in evaluating your proposal. Summarize your material concisely and accurately, being as specific as possible. Remember, the quality of the proposal you submit may be our only guide to the quality of the book that you plan to write.

Rationale

Why do you feel compelled to write this book? Why will someone want to read it? Is there a particularly timely nature of the subject area? What are the specific benefits of your book? These will be key selling points, so be precise.

Subject

Describe the contents of your book in commonly understood language. Be as precise as possible, providing both a general overview and a rundown of subjects treated in detail. Indicate how in-depth your coverage will be.

Market

Who will be the audience for this title? Try to avoid falling into the "all things for all people" trap. Specify who will need to read this book, citing job titles, and identifying industries. Include information on professional associations, potential courses, and any other items that may help us reach your audience.

Competition

List other books on the same or related subjects that have been written for the same market. Include all pertinent information (author, title, publisher, date published, price, and number of pages). Then provide a sentence or two to explain how your book is different from (and of course, better than) each.

The Book

Describe your ideas about the physical book: How many pages do you estimate it being? Approximately how many illustrations will be included? Can these be black and white, or is color necessary? How long will it take you to complete the entire manuscript? Is this tied to any software release? Will the work require any add-ons such as a disk or CD-ROM?

Your Curriculum Vitae

We'd like to get to know you. Please include a recent resume, as well as a list of professional affiliations. Are you a member of any Associations related to the subject matter of the book?

Suggested Reviewers

While we may not use them, at times we find it helpful to have the names of one or two people whose expertise or reputation in your field will facilitate our evaluation process. These should not be close colleagues or friends, but peers whose opinions you would appreciate having. Please provide names, addresses, and phone numbers if possible.

Rough Outline, Book Materials

Ideally, we'd love to see a finished manuscript. Therefore, please include as much material as you have already prepared, including Table of Contents and any Chapters you may have. If pertinent, it's also a good idea to enclose some illustrations if you can.

Thank you for your time and effort in compiling this information. We hope that the preparation of this proposal has helped you think about your book, and increased your awareness of publishing requirements.

Categories: Nonfiction—Business—Careers—Diet/Nutrition—Education—Health—Language—Money & Finances—Parenting—Physical Fitness—Recreation—Reference—Relationships—Self Help—Sports/Recreation

CONTACT: Submissions Editor
Material: All
130 E. Randolph St., Ste. 900
Chicago IL 60601
Phone: 312-233-7500
Fax: 312-233-7570
Website: books.mcgraw-hill.com

Contemporary Drama Services

Please refer to Meriwether Publishing Ltd., in the Book Publishers section.

Cornell Maritime Press, Inc.

Thank you for thinking of Cornell Maritime Press/Tidewater Publishers as a prospective publisher for your book. The topic of your proposed book must fall within our current areas of interest. As specialized publishers, we undertake only the following kinds of projects:

1. pragmatic works for the merchant mariner,
2. practical works on the maritime industry and maritime law,
3. books for boaters (also of a practical nature),
4. nonfiction for adults about Maryland, the Delmarva Peninsula, and the Chesapeake Bay, and
5. regional fiction and nonfiction for children.

Our publishing focus excludes personal narratives, adult fiction, and poetry for adults.

To determine our interest in your book, please submit to us the items listed below. These guidelines apply whether you are proposing a book for publication or have a completed manuscript.

1. A letter that answers these questions:
   a. What is the book about?
   b. Who is its audience?
   c. How large is that audience and in what ways might the audience be reached?
   d. If you had to market your book to your audience, what major selling points would you emphasize?
   e. Are there any special marketing opportunities for the book of which you are aware?
   f. In what ways are you qualified to write the work?
   g. What other books are in print about the topic and how does the proposed work differ from them?
   h. How many pages do you anticipate will make up the final manuscript?
   i. What additional elements are to be included: illustrations (drawings, photographs, or other), appendices, bibliography, index?
   j. When do you think the manuscript will be ready for submission?

2. An outline or a detailed table of contents to indicate the scope of the work.

3. A sample chapter or two to demonstrate the basic qualities of your written work. Please be sure that the sample you submit is something with which you are completely satisfied. Do not send something that is incomplete, needs "polishing," or is not your best work.

All submissions should be double-spaced (with ample margins) on one side of 8½" x 11" white paper. The pages should be consecutively numbered, and they should not be stapled or bound into a folder.

Although we will take all reasonable care, we cannot be responsible for material submitted. Do not send unique documents or artwork; rough copies or photocopies of photographs or sketches will convey your intention adequately.

Please include a self-addressed, stamped envelope if you would like the material returned to you. For questions regarding submission, please email the managing editor at address below. We look forward to receiving your submission.

Categories: Nonfiction—Boating—Regional—Maritime

CONTACT: Managing Editor
Material: All
PO Box 456
Centreville, MD 21617 (if using the post office)
101 Water Wy.
Centreville, MD 21617 (for delivery by UPS or other carrier)
Phone: 410-758-1075

Fax: 410-758-6849
E-mail: cornell@crosslink.net

Cottonwood Press, Inc.

Cottonwood Press is always looking for fresh material for our customers—English and language arts teachers, grades 5 - 12.

We like to use material that is clever, requiring thought and creativity from students—not mindless busy work. Many of our books have both ideas for teachers as well as ready-to-use activities designed for the teacher to photocopy and pass out to his or her students.

We are not interested in variations of the same old games and ideas you see everywhere. (If we see one more game on homonyms, for example, we may scream.) We also do not use word search (word find) puzzles. We love to use materials with a humorous, light-hearted, offbeat or down-to-earth approach, the kind of material that real teachers can use with real kids.

A careful look through our catalog will help you better understand our products. We strongly suggest that you also familiarize yourself with some of the activities in our books. It is impossible to write for Cottonwood Press without understanding how our books are different from similar products on the market.

We try to get a response to the author within two to four weeks after receiving a manuscript.

Sincerely,
Cheryl Thurston, Editor
Categories: Education—Textbooks

CONTACT: Acquisitions Editor
Material: All
109-B Cameron Dr.
Fort Collins CO 80525
Phone: 970-204-0715
Fax: 970-204-0761
Website: www.cottonwoodpress.com

Books
A-L

Council for Indian Education

Council for Indian Education will not be accepting manuscripts for the next 2 years (until June 2006).

Countrysport Press

Please refer to Down East Books.

Craftsman Book Company

Books on the following subjects would sell well to Craftsman customers. The book should be loaded with step-by-step instructions, illustrations, charts, reference data, diagrams, forms, pictures, samples, cost estimates, rules of thumb, man-hour estimates and examples that show how work should be done on the construction site or that solve actual problems in the builder's office. The book must cover the subject completely, become the owner's primary reference on the subject, and have a high utility-to-cost ratio. This list is by no means complete, and is subject to changing trends in the marketplace. Any reference manual that will help construction tradespersons, builders, remodelers, construction estimators or adjusters make a better living in their profession is a good candidate for publication by Craftsman Book Company.

• How to Estimate Sitework (or Concrete, Steel, Masonry, Roofing, HVAC, Demoliton, Mold Remediation)
• Man-hour Estimates for Residential, Commercial, and Industrial Construction
• Cost Estimates for Commercial and Industrial Construction

• Estimating Remodeling and Renovation Costs (With Man-hour Estimates)
• Demolition Methods & Estimating (With Man-hour Estimates)
• How to Take-off Construction Material Quantities
• Estimating Building Losses and Damage Repair Costs (With Man-hours)
• Construction Scheduling, CPM and Project Control
• Set Up and Run Your Subcontracting Business
• How to Design and Build Homes and Apartments
• How to Get the Insurance and Bonds You Need at the Right Price
• Field Supervision for Construction Contractors
• How to Get Lucrative Government Construction Projects
• How to Remodel and Renovate Commercial and Industrial Buildings
• Operating Excavation and Grading Equipment (all types)
• Start and Run an Excavation and Grading Contracting Business
• General Excavation Methods (Earth, Rock, Hauling, Placing, Banks)
• Concrete Formwork: Designing, Installing and Estimating
• Simplified Design of Reinforced Concrete for Builders
• Installing and Estimating Concrete Reinforcing
• Modern Masonry (Block, Brick, Tile, Terrazzo—With Man-hour Estimates)
• Estimating and Erecting Structural Steel and Fabricated Metals
• Modern Cabinet Making and Installation Manual
• The Complete Manual of Roof and Stair Layout
• How to Install and Replace Flooring: Hardwood, Resilient, Carpet, and Tile
• Painting and Decorating Commercial and Industrial Buildings
• Plumbing Repair and Renovation Manual (With Troubleshooting Guide)
• Practical Guide to the Uniform Mechanical Code
• Plumber's Vest Pocket Reference Book
• Low Voltage Electrical Guide: Design, Installation, Estimating
• Electrician's Vest Pocket Reference Book
• Footing & Foundation Construction & Estimating
• Computer Applications Tutorial for Contractors
• Construction Estimating for Beginners
• How to Get Insurance Repair Work
• Specifications for Construction Plans
Categories: Business—Engineering—Reference—Construction

CONTACT: Laurence Jacobs, Managing Editor
Material: Professional Building Books
PO Box 6500
Carlsbad CA 92009
Phone: 760-438-7828
Fax: 740-438-0398
Website: www.craftsman-book.com

Creative Publishing International, Inc.
NorthWord Press

As an imprint of Creative Publishing International, NorthWord Press is a publisher whose primary commitment is to wildlife, habitat, and natural history topics of the world for adults and children.

The following topics may be considered, but generally stand little chance of acceptance: "how-to" titles, collections of magazine stories or articles, journal memoirs, essays about travel, and manuscripts dealing with limited regional subject matter.

We publish: Non-fiction wildlife and nature topics, including substantial species natural history information.

Our books generally focus on the species with little human interaction; we typically do not publish stories involving animals in domestic situations.

We do not publish these kinds of books: fantasy, adventure novel, rhyme/poetry, biography, memoir/journal books.

We do not publish books with ecology or "green" themes. Nor do we particularly emphasize endangered species.

Our children's list does not include "relationship" or growing-up stories.

Please include the following details when submitting a book proposal:
• Author background, credentials, writing experience
• Brief synopsis of the book being proposed
• Detailed outline or table of contents
• Sample chapters (generally 2 or 3 on hard copy)
• Samples of art, photos, or transparencies intended for use in the book (duplicate photos or transparencies only, please)
• Bibliography (if appropriate)

If the proposal is accepted, manuscripts should be submitted on 3½" floppy disks or CDs formatted in Macintosh or DOS word processing program. A hard copy (double spaced) should accompany the disk.

Proposals submitted to NorthWord Press are reviewed for style, content, appropriateness, conceptual integrity, author expertise, and marketability. Therefore, a rejection does not necessarily reflect any judgment regarding the literary merit of an author's work.

NorthWord uses a standard author contract, which may be modified upon mutual agreement by the author and publisher. Advances against royalties are negotiable, and royalties are paid semi-annually.

Categories: Nonfiction—Animals—Outdoors—Nature—Wildlife

CONTACT: Submissions Editor, Adult Books
Material: All
CONTACT: Submissions Editor, Juvenile Books
Material: All
18705 Lake Drive East
Chanhassen MN 55317
Phone: 952-936-4700
Fax: 952-933-1456

Cricket Books

Does not accept unsolicited submissions.

Cross Cultural Publications, Inc.

Submit book proposal in summary, with table of contents and resumé of author. If we are interested we will invite the author for more details and completed manuscript.

Categories: Asian-American—Biography—Christian Interests—College—Conservation—Culture—Ecology Economics—Education—Entertainment—Environment—Family—Feminism—General Interest—Government—History—Inspirational—Jewish Interest—Literature—Multicultural—Native American—New Age—Politics—Religion—Society—Spiritual—Women's Issues—Ethnic—Philosophy—Public Policy

CONTACT: Acquisitions Editor
Material: All
PO Box 506
Notre Dame IN 46556
Phone: 219-273-6526
Fax: 219-273-5973

The Crossing Press

The Crossing Press is accepting book proposals in the following areas: Natural health; Spirituality; and Empowerment/self-help. We no longer publish fiction, poetry or calendars.

Please submit as much of the following information as possible in your book proposal. We find this information essential in evaluating the project for publication consideration.

Description of the book. Includes text content, style, number of manuscript pages, and how you envision the published book (physical attributes).

Definition of the market. Who is the intended audience? What need is this book fulfilling? What is the book designed to accomplish? How is the topic of increasing rather than declining or passing interest? How does it compare with other books on the market (please list)?

Outline and description of contents. Provide a few sentences about the purpose and contents of each chapter, giving specific details and examples as well as general statements. Explain the logic of the book's organization.

Introduction and sample chapters. If complete, please submit 1-2 sample chapters as well as an introduction to the manuscript.

Timetable. Is the manuscript complete? If not, provide a schedule for submitting sample chapters (if not already included), and the complete manuscript.

Author information. Include your resume, vita, or biography detailing your professional and educational background, including prior publications and publicity materials, and any other relevant information.

We look forward to reviewing your proposal.

Categories: Nonfiction—Cooking—Diet/Nutrition—Health—New Age—Spiritual—Empowerment—Natural Healing

CONTACT: Acquisitions Editor
Material: All
1201 Shaffer Rd. Ste B
Santa Cruz CA 95060
Phone: 408-722-0711
E-mail: Crossing@aol.com
Website: www.crossingpress.com

Crossway Books

A Division of Good News Publications

Crossway Books does not accept unsolicited submissions. Items sent without permission will not be returned. This policy went into effect June 1, 2003.

Crossway Books does review selected manuscripts submitted to:

First Edition
www.ecpa.org/FE
4816 S. Ash, Suite 101
Tempe, AZ 85282
(800) 600-4592

The Writer's Edge
www.writersedgeservice.com
PO Box 1266
Wheaton, IL 60189
No phone number is available.

Both these organizations offer very fine services at modest rates that allow your work to be reviewed simultaneously by more than forty-five other Christian publishers. We will contact the author if we see a proposal that will fit within our publishing program. Proposals sent by agents will still be considered.

tian perspective. The best way to understand what type of books we publish is to review our current catalog. We provide the following information as a general reference.

Areas of Interest
We are interested in reviewing submissions in the areas listed in Category A, and are not accepting submissions for anything from Category B and Category C.

Category A—Of Interest
Nonfiction
• Issues Books. These books typically address the critical issues facing Christians today in our personal lives, families, communities and the wider culture.

• Books on the deeper Christian life. In general, these books seek to provide a deeper understanding of Christian truth and its application to daily life. Many of these involve the exposition of Scripture; others are more topical and systematic. Books in this category could include biblical teaching, the application of the Bible to Christian growth, evangelism, devotions, and so on.

• A select number of academic and professional volumes. These books tend to reflect the same general approach mentioned above under issues books and books on the deeper Christian life, but are directed more toward the academic and professional audience. These would include books in theology, biblical studies, church history, preaching, critical issues in specific academic disciplines, and so on.

Fiction

We do not accept or respond to e-mail queries or proposals.
We are interested only in books written from an evangelical Chris-
• Historical
• Adventure/Action/Intrigue/Thriller
• Contemporary/Christian Realism

Category B—Selectively Publish
Fiction
• Mystery
• Western
• Supernatural

Category C—NOT Interested
Nonfiction
• End-time or prophecy books
• Collected sermons
• Missionary biographies
• Contemporary/popular biographies
• Exposés of well-known Christians
• Personal experience stories
• Art books

Fiction
• Children's picture books
• End-time or prophecy novels
• Short stories or anthologies
• Biblical novels (set in Bible times)
• Fantasy/science fiction
• Horror novels
• Romance

The following information is ONLY for those who have been given permission to submit a manuscript to Crossway Books.

Format
Please do as thorough a job of research and writing as possible before submitting your manuscript. If possible, have a professional proofreading service look over your manuscript for grammar, punctuation and spelling errors.

Requirements for a submission are: A synopsis of one or two pages as well as a chapter-by-chapter synopsis and two sample chapters. Please do not send outlines or tables of contents only. These will tell the reviewer little about the manuscript's content, nor will it give the reviewer any knowledge of your writing skills.

All submissions must be neatly typed and double-spaced. Send a photocopy, not the original. On the first page of the submission, please include your name, address, telephone number, and an approximate total word count for your entire manuscript.

We do not accept submissions of entire manuscripts. We are not accepting submissions on disk or by e-mail at this time.

Categories: Fiction—Nonfiction—Adventure—Christisn Interest—Education—History—Juvenile—Mystery—Paranormal—Religion— Western—Young Adult

CONTACT: Jill Carter, Editorial Administrator
Material: All
1300 Crescent St.
Wheaton, IL 60187

Daily Guideposts

Guideposts Books creates inspirational, faith-filled books to help our family of readers live fuller, richer lives. As we continue to expand and develop our publishing program, we'll let you know here about ways you can share in this ministry. Our devotional, Daily Guideposts, published annually since 1977, now brings more than a million readers closer to God through prayerfully sharing in the personal experiences of its writers. If you'd like to audition for Daily Guideposts, please read the guidelines below.

Auditioning for Daily Guideposts

Daily Guideposts devotionals are first-person anecdotes, told in an informal, conversational style, which make a single spiritual point. They open with a Bible verse related to the theme of the devotional, and end with a prayer. At their best, they are like short-short stories, using vivid description and dialogue to draw the reader into the spiritual insight the writer has gained from the experience described.

The challenge of writing a Daily Guideposts devotional is to tell a compelling story, convey something of your personality to the reader, and communicate an uplifting spiritual insight, all in the space of 200 to 350 words. *The following do's and don'ts in mind should help you get started:*

• *Be concise.* A devotional should be no more than 350 words, including Scripture and prayer. One typewritten page, double-spaced, is preferable.

• *Make a point.* Each devotional should have one clear spiritual point to convey, a point that grows naturally out of the story.

• *Tell a story.* Use setting, dialogue, and a dramatic situation to get the reader involved.

• *Be specific.* Tell us the names of the people and places in your story. Use the senses: give the reader sights, sounds, smells, and tastes. Concrete details make the story live.

• *Be practical.* Show us how you were changed in some specific way. Giving examples of how you changed or did something differently will help the reader to identify with you, and give him or her something to apply in his or her own life.

• *Show us how your faith is part of your daily life.* Your story should be an occasion of spiritual growth for yourself and your reader. Although showing your faith in action may involve worship, prayer, and talking about spiritual things in the context of the everyday aspects of your life, it's not necessary to confine yourself to explicitly religious topics. Find a unique angle of vision. Look for a point or application that isn't obvious, that takes the story or situation out of the realm of the routine and provides new insight for the reader.

• *Tell us about yourself.* We are looking for writing that has personality, so the more your devotionals reveal about your lifestyle, work, family and hobbies, the better. Be selective—you can't tell us everything in only a few devotionals, so consider what details will be most revealing.

How to Audition for Daily Guideposts

Please submit three to five sample devotionals for consideration. Previously published material is not acceptable. Submissions should be typed, double-spaced, and accompanied by a stamped, self-addressed envelope. Please include your name, telephone number, and Social Security number. Please allow two months for our reply.

Categories: Nonfiction—Christian Interests—Inspirational—Religion—Spiritual

CONTACT: Daily Guideposts Editor
Material: All
Guideposts Book Division
16 East 34th Street
New York NY 10016
E-mail: www.guideposts.org

Dalkey Archive Press

Although we have returned to publishing original fiction, we are only publishing 2-4 original works each year, and our main focus is still on reprints. If you would like to submit a manuscript, you should be familiar with our list and the types of books we publish in order to determine whether your book is appropriate for our list. Please keep in mind we publish primarily literary fiction, and rarely publish poetry, criticism, or non-fiction. Additionally, we place a heavy emphasis upon fiction that belongs to the experimental tradition of Sterne, Joyce, Rabelais, Flann O'Brien, Beckett, Gertrude Stein and Djuna Barnes.

Also, keep in mind:

A query letter with contact information should accompany your submission.

Without an SASE we can't respond to or return unsolicited submissions.

In general, we respond within 2-4 months of receiving a submission.

We do not accept queries or submissions via e-mail.

Categories: Fiction—Experimental Fiction

CONTACT: Acquisitions Editor
Material: All
Dalkey Archive Press
ISU Campus Box 8905
Normal, IL 61790-8905
Phone: 309-438-7555
Fax: fax: 309-438-7422
E-mail: contact@dalkeyarchive.com
Website: www.centerforbookculture.org

Dan River Press
Dan River Anthology

Please refer to The Conservatory of American Letters, in the Book Publishers section.

David R. Godine, Inc.

David R. Godine, Inc., is a small publishing house located in Boston, Massachusetts, producing between twenty and thirty titles per year and maintaining an active reprint program. The company is independent (a rarity these days) and its list tends to reflect the individual tastes and interests of its president and founder, David Godine.

At Godine, quality has remained foremost. Our aim is to identify the best work and to produce it in the best way possible. All of our hardcover and softcover books are printed on acid-free paper. Many hardcovers are still bound in full cloth. The list is deliberately eclectic and features works that many other publishers can't or won't support, books that won't necessarily become bestsellers but that still deserve publication. In a world of spin-offs and commercial "product," Godine's list stands apart by offering original fiction and non-fiction of the highest rank, rediscovered masterworks, translations of outstanding world literature, poetry, art, photography, and beautifully designed books for children.

Our submissions policy:

Authors should note that Godine does not accept unsolicited manuscripts or proposals. Due to the large number of submissions, we will not be able to return any materials not accompanied by a self-addressed, stamped envelope. Any materials sent that do not include sufficient postage to cover the expense of their return will be held for 90 days and then destroyed. Please note that while we do reply to queries via email that we prefer queries and submission to be submitted by regular mail. Authors are advised to have their agent contact us if they would like us to consider a project. We strongly advise against sending original artwork or unreplacable documents; while all reasonable care will be taken with such materials, we cannnot be held responsible in the event of damage or loss.

Editorial, Publicity, Marketing, and Production are handled through our Boston office.

Categories: Fiction—Nonfiction—Architecture—Arts—Biography—Boating—Children—Cooking—Crime—Feminism—Food/Drink—Gardening—Gay/Lesbian—History—Jewish Interest—Juvenile—Literature—Men's Fiction—Mystery—Outdoors—Photography—Poetry—Religion—Rural America—Short Stories—Women's Fiction—Writing—Young Adult

CONTACT: David R. Godine, Publisher
Material: All
9 Hamilton Place
Boston MA 02108-4715
Phone: 617-451-9600
Fax: 617-350-0250
E-mail: info@godine.com
Website: www.godine.com

DAW Books

Thank you for your inquiry concerning our requirements. We hope the following information will answer your questions:

We publish science fiction and fantasy novels. We do not want short stories, short story collections, novellas, or poetry. The average length of the novels we publish varies but is almost never less than 80,000 words. (To estimate the length of your manuscript, you may want to use the technique mentioned below.)

Please do not submit handwritten material. Manuscripts must be typewritten or letter-quality computer generated. Use a dark ribbon. Clear photocopies are acceptable. The manuscript should be on 8" x 11" good white paper, double-spaced, with at least 1" wide margins all around. Please use only one side of the page, number your pages consecutively, and put the title of your novel at the top of each page.

Very important: Please type your name, address and phone number in the upper right hand corner of the first page of your manuscript. Right under this, please put the length of your manuscript in number of words.

We publish first novels if they are of professional quality. A literary agent is not required for submission. We will not consider manuscripts that are currently on submission to another publisher.

Be sure to include a postage paid envelope for the return of the manuscript, if it is not found acceptable. You are entitled to Fourth Class rates for literary manuscripts—ask at your local post office. If you prefer to send your work by First Class Mail and wish it returned the same way, be sure to include sufficient postage, or a check or money order to cover the postage costs. Canadian return postage can only be sent via Canadian Postal Money Order in US$. If you are mailing your manuscript from outside the U.S.A. or Canada, postage payment may only be made via American Express Money Order in US$, or by a check in US$ payable from a New York City bank. (Please do not enclose International Postal Coupons, except as postage for a single letter. IPCs cost approximately $3.50 each, but are only valid for 55 cents postage). Never send cash through the mail.

It may require up to three months or more for our editors to review a submission and come to a decision. If you want to be sure we have received your manuscript, please enclose a stamped, self-addressed postcard which we will return when your manuscript is logged-in.

It is not necessary for you to register or copyright your work before publication—it is protected by law as long as it has not been published. When published, we will copyright the book in the author's name and register that copyright with the Library of Congress.

ADDITIONAL INFORMATION FOR NEW WRITERS:
HOW TO GET THE WORD COUNT OF A MANUSCRIPT

1. Count the words in 10 lines and divide the total number of words by ten.

2. Count the lines on an average page.

3. Multiply the total number of lines for the sample full page by the approximate word count for one line. This gives you the word count for one page.

4. Then multiply this total count for the words on one page by the total number of pages in your manuscript. This is the total length of your manuscript in words. Please put this number on page one of your manuscript, right under your name address.

5. To check the accuracy of your count, please repeat this process twice.

6. Please send manuscripts to Peter Stampfel, Submission Editor.

7. Free DAW Books catalog available upon request.

Categories: Fiction—Fantasy—Science Fiction

CONTACT: Peter Stampfel, Submission Editor.
Material: All
DAW Books
375 Hudson St.
New York, NY 10014
Website: us.penguingroup.com/

Dawn Publications

Thank you for your interest in Dawn Publications. We accept unsolicited manuscripts. DAWN is primarily a nature awareness publisher for adults and children. In part the company grew out of the enthusiastic public response to the now-classic *Sharing Nature With Children* by Joseph Cornell, the eminent naturalist and nature educator. Increasingly our goal is to teach children the wonders of nature and of themselves through high-quality picture books, including trade books suitable for use in the classroom.

Dawn generally does not publish material which:
• contains animal dialogue or other highly anthropomorphic material;
• merely explains nature;
• is a fantasy;
• is a retelling of a legend with supernatural elements;
• is centered primarily on human situations or foibles.

The best way to get a sense of Dawn's publishing mission is to examine some of our books. Our complete catalog is available online at www.dawnpub.com.

Many of our publications come from unsolicited submissions and first-time authors. Please be aware, however, that we are a small company: we receive thousands of queries or manuscripts annually and accept only half a dozen or fewer for publication. Please observe the following mechanics of submission:

Please enclose a cover letter with the manuscript describing your work, the intended age of the audience, your other publications if any, your motivation for writing, and relevant background.

Be aware that most picture books are 32 pages. Indicate where you want your page breaks to be-don't send 32 separate sheets. (However, if you have a mockup that meaningfully enhances appreciation of the work, send it. Be sure to enclose an SASE if you want it returned.)

If you are presenting us with artwork, please let us know whether the art and text are a package. Usually we want to retain the option of selecting the artist.

Always enclose an SASE! If an SASE is not enclosed, we will not necessarily respond.

Address manuscript submissions to the attention of the editor, Glenn J. Hovemann. Although we try to be reasonably prompt, please allow at least two months for response.

If you are an illustrator please address your work to the art director, Muffy Weaver.

Categories: Nonfiction—Children—Nature—Science

CONTACT: Glenn Hovemann, Editor
Material: Manuscripts
CONTACT: Muffy Weaver, Art Director
Material: Illustrations Samples
12402 Bitney Springs Rd.
Nevada City, CA 95959
Phone: 530-478-0111
Website: www.dawnpub.com

The Denali Press

The Denali Press publishes books on multiculturalism. We emphasize reference and scholarly books with a strong appeal to the library and institutional market. Selected titles include: *Hispanic Resource Directory*; *Refugee and Immigrant Resource Directory*; *Judaica Reference Sources*; and *Lives Between Cultures: A Study of Human Nature, Identity and Culture.*

The Denali Press would like to see queries, proposals, summaries, and outlines rather than full manuscripts. If the substance of the work cannot be fully communicated in this manner, a couple of chapters may be included. We encourage queries with full descriptions both of the proposed work and of the author's background and interests, since from them we may be able to identify ideas for books other than the one proposed. *Specifically, proposals should discuss:*

• the book's subject matter and approach
• the audience, i.e., the size of the market and how it can be reached
• how the book differs from similar books currently in print, and
• author qualifications

We are pleased to sponsor the American Library Association's The Denali Press Award. This award is presented to recognize achievement in creating reference works, outstanding in quality and significance, that provide information specifically about ethnic and minority groups in the United States.

Categories: Nonfiction—College—Culture—Directories—Environment—Hispanic—Human Rights—Jewish Interest—Multicultural—Native American—Politics—Reference

CONTACT: Sally Silvas-Ottumwa, Editorial Associate
Material: All
PO Box 021535
Juneau AK 99802
Phone: 907-586-6014
Fax: 907-463-6780
E-mail: denalipress@alaska.net

Denlinger's Publishers, Ltd.

SUBMISSIONS AND RETURNS

Genre: We do not publish poetry, illustrated works, erotica or textbooks.

Length: Maximum: 100,000 words. Prefer: 70,000 to 80,000 words. Minimum 100 pages.

Note: All authors are required to read our contract BEFORE submission:

Go to: thebookden.com/agree.html. We DO NOT change the contract.
Query
Query should contain the following:
• Title of Manuscript.
• Genre(s).
• Target audience, add age range for Juvenile and Young Adult.
• Estimated number of words.
• Brief synopsis (single paragraph).
• Author's statement that they have read and agree to our contract if the work is accepted.
• **Manuscript via email attachment or on disk:**

Disks must be a standard 3.5 inch floppy disk in a PC, NOT Mac or ASCII, word processing format. HTML format is OK, but view it first utilizing latest versions of Internet browsers. View it on several computer monitors to verify correct format.

Do not zip (AOL does that automatically if multiple attachments).

Word processing software should be equal to or less than Microsoft Word 2000 or Word Perfect 8. MS Works 4.0 or Lotus WordPro 96 are acceptable, but less desirable.

Word processing format must be single spaced - 1" margins without visible headers, footers, or page numbers.

Manuscript must be formatted as a single running file, not multiple files, i.e. by pages or by chapters.

Spell and grammar check is a necessity, possibly an outside edit. Over 5% errors equals reject, no matter how good a book. Scene breaks must be marked by two or more asterisks.

Optional

If you wish verification that we have received your material via regular mail, ship your materials with a return receipt requested.

Inquiries regarding the status of your manuscript may be made by email only. Note: Please be patient. We handle hundreds of manuscripts and it can easily be six months or longer before yours is reviewed.

Returns: Since we no longer request hard copy submission during the evaluation phase, no return postage is required. If you do send any hard copy material or disks and wish to have them returned, you must send adequate postage and packaging for return shipping.

Categories: Fiction—Nonfiction—Adventure—History—Horror—Mystery—Memoirs—Self Help—Western

CONTACT: Elizabeth-Anne Rogers
Material: All
PO Box 1030
Edgewater, FL 32132-1030
Phone: 386-424-1737
Fax: 386-428-3534
E-mail: editor@thebookden.com
Website: www.thebookden.com

Dial Books for Young Readers

A Division of Penguin Putnam Books for Young Readers

We accept unsolicited picture book manuscripts and query letters for longer works. A query letter should briefly describe your manuscript's plot, genre (i.e. easy-to-read, middle grade or YA novel), the intended age group, and your publishing credits, if any. You may send an entire picture book manuscript and a maximum of 10 pages for longer works (novels, easy-to-reads). Do not send more than the specified amount; any excess will not be read. Never send cassettes, original artwork, marketing plans, or faxes. Manuscript pages sent will be returned only with a self-addressed stamped envelope. In response, you will receive a form letter either requesting the longer manuscript or letting you know that the manuscript isn't right for Dial. Please allow four months for a reply.

Due to the large volume of mail we receive, we can only read longer manuscripts specifically requested through the query system. In addition, we can only keep track of these requested manuscripts; we do not track unsoliciteds. Never call or fax to inquire about the status of an unsolicited submission; instead write a letter only if the reply time has exceeded four months. We will not reply to anything that is sent without a self-addressed stamped envelope. If you do not live in the United States, you must send an international reply coupon. We recycle all letters and manuscripts sent without sufficient postage.

We do not supply specific guidelines, but we will send you a recent catalogue if you send us a 9x12 envelope with four 37-cent stamps attached. Please do not send cash or checks. This is one way to become informed as to the style, subject matter, and format of our books, as is a trip to your local library or bookshop. Art samples should be sent to Attn: Dial Design and will not be returned without a self-addressed stamped envelope. Never send original art. Please do not phone to inquire about your submission. Questions and queries should be made only in writing to Submissions Coordinator.

Categories: Fiction—Nonfiction—Adventure—Biography—Family—Folklore—Teen

CONTACT: Submissions Coordinator
Material: Queries
CONTACT: Dial Design
Material: Art Samples
Penguin Putnam Inc.
345 Hudson St., 3rd Floor
New York NY 10014

Dimi Press

DIMI PRESS is a small, independent book publisher. At present we have published 21 books. We welcome your query letter if you are a serious author with a non-fiction book manuscript or well-conceived outline for a book you want to write. At this time we are looking for non-fiction manuscripts about unusual natural phenomena. DIMI PRESS *has published six books of this type:*

(1) *The Running Indians,* an account of the Tarahumara Indians of north Mexico and the huge canyon in which they live. The Tarahumara may be the world's greatest long-distance runners and the canyon in which most of them live is bigger than the Grand Canyon.

(2) *Komodo, The Living Dragon* is an account of the world's largest lizard, its habits and habitat. Although not a scientific tome, this work is accurate and has been very well received by the herpetologist community.

(3) *Komodo, The Living Dragon* (Revised Edition) further extends information about this magnificent beast, specifically to include an account of the first successful breeding outside of its native Indonesia.

(4) *Hidden Amazon* encourages readers to visit the Amazon and thus help support the local economy and the study/preservation of the rain forest.

(5) *Across African Sand* is an account of an incredible 3000 mile bicycle trip across the deserts of southern Africa. It includes information about the author's life while teaching in a rural village in Botswana as well as information about the cultures of this region.

(6) *Patagonia, At the Bottom of the World* relates the author's impressions during a trip there and then covers detailed facts about its history, wildlife, climate, terrain, extinct native groups, and current situation.

Because of our interest in nature and the environment, we have decided to focus on books like these. Thus, we are currently soliciting ONLY manuscripts about unique things in nature or fascinating adventurous trips.

Some suggested topics are huge disasters, such as a volcanic eruption or earthquake. A book about the coelacanth fish or the tuatara lizard might be something we would be interested in. It should include

information on how to travel to observe the rare wildlife (or whatever) written about. We want books that, in a bookstore, would categorize as nature/travel.

But we do not want travel guides, although accounts of interesting trips are a possibility. If the title could be marketed other than solely through bookstores that would be a plus. Example: a subject that would be of interest to bird-watchers or some other specific interest group. Your initial contact with us should be a one or two page query letter accompanied by a SASE. Unsolicited manuscripts will not be read. Letters without a SASE will not be returned or answered. Simultaneous submissions are fine.

Authors, in their query letter, must address the marketing of the book. Who is going to buy this book? How can they be reached? The author should have the poise and ability to be a good interviewee on radio and TV.

Royalties to the author will generally be 10% on net revenues. Advances are not given. (We are a small company and need all the cash possible for promotion.)

It is best that the title and subject of the book be of such general interest that it can be marketed through bookstores, libraries, and sold in other countries. We prefer previously published authors, but do not insist on this.

If we like your query letter (and we'll try to tell you in four weeks) we will ask to see the manuscript. The manuscript review may well take more than four weeks, but if we're reading the manuscript you can be sure that we are very serious about it.

DIMI PRESS feels that a book is a joint project of the author and publisher and we need to have a good feeling about working with you. In other words, we're not looking for an adversarial relationship.

Categories: Nonfiction—Animals—Ecology—Environment—Nature—Travel—How-to—Nature

CONTACT: Dick Lutz, President
Material: All
3820 Oak Hollow Ln. SE
Salem OR 97302-4774
Phone: 503-364-7698
Fax: 503-364-9727
E-mail: dickbook@earthlink.net

Dichter Books

Please refer to Black Forest Press.

Diogenes Publishing

As an alternative press, we are primarily interested in nonfiction pieces that challenge mainstream views. We will consider a variety of genres, including satire, humor, psychology, philosophy, and social criticism. Please do NOT send us self-help, spiritual, and inspirational material. We do not publish books with these themes.

If you believe your word fits our list, send a query letter or outline and one chapter with an SASE to Mary Gillissie. Please let us know if you want your submission returned. Currently, we are not accepting proposals on disk, though we are accepting them by email (Microsoft Word).

Categories: Nonfiction—Comedy—Culture—Family—Psychology—Satire—Society

CONTACT: Mary Gillissie, Editor-in-Chief
Material: All
PO Box 40
Sutter Creek CA 95685
Phone: 209-296-6082

Books A-L

Do-It-Yourself Legal Publishers

We publish general, non-academic, non-fiction. The proposed work should address some aspect of American law—should have a simplistic, practical, self-help, how-to orientation.

Send the following:
1. A brief letter of inquiry
2. An outline of the proposed book
3. One or two complete sample chapters
4. One paragraph synopsis of each of the other chapters.

In the letter, include the following information:

What is the book's subject matter? For whom is the book primarily written and for what segments of society would it appeal? What needs or purposes do your book fulfill? Your general background and qualifications for writing the book? Why is your book appropriate for the kinds of books done by Do-It-Yourself Legal Publishers? Are you familiar with other books previously published on the same subject? And what distinguishes your work from others previously published or in the market today?

Provide us with a brief (1 or 2 pages), separate summary of the work, namely, the substance of the work and its' essential theme and essences.

Proposals should be submitted in this format: Unbound book (paper) format.

Thank you for your cooperation in respect to our above-outlined general policies for submission to Do-It-Yourself Legal Publishers, as we receive scores and scores of proposals each year.

Categories: Nonfiction—Law—Money & Finances—Self Help—Self Helper

CONTACT: Submissions Editor
Material: All
Law Press of America
60 Park Place, Ste 1013
Newark NJ 07102
Phone: 973-639-0400

Dorchester Publishing Co., Inc.

THE FOLLOWING ARE THE ONLY CATEGORIES OF ORIGINAL FICTION WE ARE CURRENTLY ACQUIRING.

HISTORICAL ROMANCE—Sensual romances with strong plots and carefully thought out characterizations. Spunky heroine whose love for the hero never wavers; he's the only one she makes love with and she's as passionate as he, although he may have to instruct her in the ways of love, since she's almost invariably untouched before she falls in love with the hero. Hero is often arrogant, overbearing; heroine often can't stand him at first, but discovers that beneath the surface lies a tender, virile, and experienced lover. It helps if both the heroine and hero have a sense of humor—a certain amount of wit leavens the heavy-breathing passion. Hero and heroine are separated by emotional conflict or the twists and turns of the plot, but in the end they overcome the barriers between them and live happily ever after.

We don't want a heroine who sleeps around, or a hero who's sadistic, although if there's a villain or villainess, he or she can be as nasty as possible.

Historical background, details of costume, etc., should be accurate; however, we don't want endless descriptions of battles, the political climate of the period, or a treatise on contemporary social history. Our readers are much more interested in the trials, tribulations, and love life of the heroine than in how many men Napoleon lost at the Battle of Waterloo.

Historical Romances should be approximately 120,000 words.

FUTURISTIC ROMANCE—Futuristic Romances contain all the elements of Historical Romances—beautiful heroine, dashing hero, some conflict that separates them, a happy ending, etc.—but they are set in lavish lands on distant worlds.

Avoid science-fiction-type hardware, technology, etc.

Finished manuscripts should be 120,000 words.

TIME-TRAVEL ROMANCE—A modern-day hero or heroine goes back in time and falls in love. Traditional guidelines for Historical Romances apply. The challenge here is to maintain credibility during the transition between the present and the past. The fun is seeing history and another way of life through the eyes of someone from our own time. The conflict and resolution of the romance arise from the fact that the hero and heroine are from different eras.

Beware of a lot of philosophizing about fate, the meaning of time, and how the past affects the present. No time machines please.

Finished manuscripts should be 120,000 words.

PARANORMAL ROMANCE—Either historical or contemporary romance with magic, witches, ghosts, vampires, etc., as a subsidiary element. Must have a happy ending.

Finished manuscripts should be 120,000 words.

OTHER CATEGORIES

WESTERNS—Exciting novels set in the Old West (before 1900 and west of the Mississippi River) with three-dimensional characters and strong plots. Historical accuracy is important, but should not eclipse the story. In addition to traditional heroes, Native Americans, women, African Americans, etc. are fine as protagonists.

Finished manuscripts should be 70,000 - 90,000 words.

HISTORICAL FICTION—Sweeping sagas set primarily in the Old West, containing all of the general elements of Westerns, but with a larger scope and greater cast of characters.

Finished manuscripts should be 90,000 to 115,000 words.

HORROR—Suspenseful, terrifying novels in a contemporary setting. Supernatural horrors (ghosts, vampires, demons, monsters, etc.) are strongly preferred, although psychological suspense and killers on the loose can work if well-handled and original. Please avoid science fiction.

Finished manuscripts should be 80,000 – 115,000 words.

TECHNOTHRILLERS—Action-filled, contemporary or near-future thrillers with emphasis on cutting-edge technology, frequently featuring advanced jets, submarines, weaponry, etc. Conflict should be on a large, usually international, scale.

Finished manuscripts should be 90,000 - 115,000 words.

GUIDELINES FOR SUBMITTING MATERIAL TO LEISURE BOOKS AND LOVE SPELL

Please query or submit synopsis and first three chapters only—no complete manuscripts unless specifically requested.

Synopsis, sample chapters (and manuscript if requested) must be typed, double-spaced. Word processors are okay, but letter quality only.

For a free catalogue of Leisure Books, please send a self-addressed, stamped envelope (#10) to the address below.

The best way to learn to write a Leisure or a Love Spell romance is to read a Leisure or a Love Spell romance.

Categories: Fiction—Horror—Romance—Western

CONTACT: Ashley Kuehl, Editorial Assistant
Material: Romance, Horror, Western
CONTACT: Leah Hultenschmidt, Editorial Assistant
Material: Romance, Horror, Western
276 Fifth Ave. Ste. 1008
New York NY 10001
Phone: 212-725-8811
Fax: 212-532-1054
Website: dorchesterpub.com

Down East Books

Imprint: Countrysport Press

Although Down East Books is the largest book publisher in Maine, we are still a relatively small, regional publisher specializing in books with a strong Maine or New England theme. Current subject areas include general interest nonfiction, art and photography, regional attractions and travel guides, biography and memoir, gardening, cooking, crafts, history, nature and ecology, nautical books, and fiction. Please note that a fully developed regional connection is critical in our fiction titles, too, and we do not as a rule publish collections of family lore or family recipes.

We also publish children's books, and here also the regional subject and setting are highly desirable. Note that the New England setting must be integral to the work; a story that with little or no change could be set in another region would not meet our requirements. We are not interested in stories about a writer's own children or pets.

Under the Countrysport Press imprint, we publish sporting titles on hunting, fishing, target shooting, dog training, cooking, and fine guns and fishing tackle. These titles include both "how-to" books and memoir and sporting literature.

New Media

Down East Books also distributes CD-Roms, videos, DVDs, and tapes. If you are looking for a distributor, contact us if you have a title that would fit well with our subject preferences. Please note that we distribute only professionally produced videos/CDs/DVDs/cassettes.

We have not yet published e-books, but we are always open to new ideas! If you'd like to discuss Web publishing on our sites or reprinting an article from one of our books or yours, send an email to: info@downeastbooks.com.

The Manuscript Submission Process

If you believe your project meets our requirements, we will be glad to evaluate its potential for our list. A query letter is a good place to start. Your letter should describe the subject and theme of the book and specify its intended audience. It should also include some information about your knowledge of the subject and your previous publications, if any. Providing a synopsis of the book is critical, as is including a sample chapter. A table of contents is helpful, too. There is no need to send the entire text at this stage, unless your manuscript is very short. If the synopsis and sample chapter look promising, we will ask to see the rest of the text (see Preparing Your Manuscript for Submission). Do keep a copy of anything you send us. We handle all submissions with care, of course, but accidents can happen, particularly when your manuscript is in transit.

If you wish to recommend a particular illustrator or photographer, please include samples of his or her work. Do not, however, go to the trouble and expense of having an artist or photographer prepare an art program until you know what your publisher wants. And unless you are a professional artist or photographer, it is best not to attempt to illustrate your book yourself. Keep in mind, too, that many of our books are not illustrated.

Please note: We do not accept electronic submission of proposals or manuscripts due to the large number we receive and difficulties tracking them and printing them out to be circulated.

What Happens Next?

A book proposal that is a good candidate for Down East Books's list will be reviewed by our editorial board, who will discuss your proposal's merits and marketability. From time to time, we will ask an outside authority to read and comment on a manuscript. (If you are a novice author, it's a good idea to have a professional in your field critique your work before submitting it to a publisher. Doing so could prove to be extremely valuable to you.)

Remember that sometimes a genuinely interesting title just isn't suitable for the markets we serve or would be too expensive to publish. Occasionally we partner with an organization or author who bears part of the costs or guarantees a certain number sold in order to publish a title we are interested in but that doesn't work financially. In general this is not the case, however; we are not a "vanity publisher."

If we accept your manuscript for publication, we will contact you about drawing up a contract. If we decide that your proposed book doesn't fit our current needs, we will let you know. With almost a thousand manuscript submissions every year between Down East Books and Countrysport Press, we obviously have to say no to most of them. Sometimes it is difficult to turn down a particular book idea, but please, unless we request that you revise a manuscript and resubmit it to us,

consider our answer to be final. Sometimes we offer suggestions that might help you place the manuscript with another publisher, but if we want you to make revisions specifically for us, we will make that clear.

Allow up to eight weeks for a reply, and be sure to enclose a sufficiently large, self-addressed, stamped envelope for return of your materials in case we decide that your manuscript does not fit needs.

Categories: Fiction—Nonfiction—Arts—Biography—Children—Cooking—Crafts/Hobbies—Ecology—Fishing—Gardening—General Interest—History—Outdoors—Photography—Recreational—Regional (New England)—Sports/Recreation—Travel

CONTACT: Michael Steere, Editor
Material: All
PO Box 679
Camden, ME 04843
Street Address for delivery:
680 Commercial St.
Rockport, Maine 04856
Phone: 207-594-9544
Fax: 207-594-0147
E-mail: msteere@downeast.com
Website: www.downeastbooks.com/

Dutton Children's Books

Please include a self-addressed stamped envelope (SASE) to cover the full weight of all materials submitted or a business-sized SASE for a reply only.

Please supply a cover letter with the following information:
• Titles and publishers of any published children's books• names of magazines and/or newspapers in which any work has appeared
• Whether manuscript is simultaneous submission (will not disqualify)

Picture books may be sent in their entirety. Unless author is also the illustrator, publishers usually select suitable illustrators for manuscripts chosen for publication. We do not require or encourage authors to seek out illustrators for materials they plan to submit.

For longer manuscripts, please send synopsis and up to 10 pages. Author's full name and address must appear on title page of manuscript. Last name should be typed on each page of manuscript.

Authors who wish to confirm that Dutton has received their materials may include a "return receipt requested" (available at the post office) or a self-addressed stamped postcard with the work's title on it.

We recommend that authors send their materials via first class or fourth class manuscript rate. Costly overnight letters draw no attention to manuscripts.

Manuscripts are read as soon as possible and are returned to the author (if a SASE is enclosed) or discarded. Some are held for further consideration.

Unfortunately, the volume of manuscripts makes it impossible for us to write a critique of every submission. We do, however, give all materials a fair and extensive reading.

While we take reasonable care of all items we receive, we can assume no responsibility for loss of or damage to submissions. We discourage the submission of costly or irreplaceable items.

Categories: Fiction—Nonfiction—Adventure—Animals—Children—Literature—Middle Grade Fiction—Picture Books—Young Adult Novels

CONTACT: Submissions Editor
Material: All
345 Hudson St.
New York NY 10014
Phone: 212-414-3495

Remember: Editors change jobs and publishers change addresses. It is wise to invest in a phone call for the current information before submitting.

Eclipse Press

Non-Fiction: We are looking for prospective books on all equine and equine-related subjects, including Thoroughbred racing, breeding, handicapping; English sport horses and disciplines; Western sport horses and disciplines; horse health care and management; and horse people.

Fiction

Eclipse Press does not yet publish fiction.

To consider your non-fiction book for publication, we need your proposal to include the following:

- A brief synopsis of your book
- Author resume or bio
- Detailed outline or table of contents
- Sample chapters
- A list of competing or comparable titles and how your book differs

Do Nots

Do not send queries or proposals to the editor via e-mail. Please allow sufficient time for proper review of your proposal. If it is not accepted, we will return your materials to you. It could take longer to hear from us if your book comes under consideration for publication.

Do not send original materials or artwork. Eclipse Press will not be held liable for any materials lost or destroyed in the mail.

Categories: Nonfiction—Animals—Lifestyle—Sports/Recreation—Western

CONTACT: Jacqueline Duke, Editor
Material: All
PO Box 4038
Lexington KY 40544-4038
Phone: 800-866-2361
Fax: 859-276-6868
E-mail: editorial@eclipsepress.com

Edupress, Inc.

1. Manuscript submissions and all rights are purchased outright by Edupress, Inc. Edupress, Inc. does not pay royalties. Manuscript must not include any material that has been previously copyrighted.

2. Manuscript may be presented in any reasonable form. It does not have to be complete; outlines and sample pages are acceptable. Proposals are also acceptable; good ideas often generate usable products.

3. Original manuscripts should not be sent; send photocopies or other facsimile. If you would like your manuscript returned, please enclose a self-addressed, stamped envelope.

4. Receipt of the manuscript will be acknowledged immediately, but expect that a response to the submitted materials may take 3 to 5 months.

5. Manuscript must be accompanied by a cover letter that includes an outline or synopsis, as well as the author's name, address, and any curriculum information that is relevant. Please provide a résumé, if available.

6. Information regarding knowledge of different formats (Microsoft Word, Quark Xpress, etc.) should be included.

7. Edupress, Inc. uses its own staff of artists, but will consider any artwork that accompanies the manuscript.

Categories: Fiction—Nonfiction—Children—Education

CONTACT: Amanda Meinke
Material: All
208 Avenida Fabricante, Ste 200
San Clemente CA 92672-7536

Elderberry Press, LLC

Remember when publishers considered more than profit? …fiction had a moral dimension? …books had something real, something vital to say? …agents and editors actually read submissions and made it their goal to encourage writers in their craft? We do.

At Elderberry we judge each submission by one standard:

Either a MS leaves the reader a better person and the world a better place, or we don't publish it. Period.

Tough standard…Does your writing meet it? If so, we'd like to read your MS.

Submission Guidelines

There's nothing new here, and nothing that's not common sense. Editors are just people, after all, and those of us who actually read what is sent us must be able to read it.

Submit your MS in hard copy printed on a single side, large enough to read, unbound, double spaced, with name, and page number on each page. I read in a leather chair by the fire, not at my monitor, so please don't send me a disk to read.

Please include a short author bio and one page synopsis. (Nothing formal, just for my information. And don't spend more than ten minutes writing the synopsis as I am well aware how frustrating it can be to try and condense 500 pages into one and make it sound anything but a Danielle Steel novel. And Dear God, we don't need any more of those, do we.

Don't bother sending your MS express or overnight. I'm stacked up two weeks out with submissions anyway. Save your money and send it MEDIA MAIL. I'll get it in a week anyway.

I'm looking forward to seeing your MS.

What We Publish

We Publish politically incorrect, Christian, conservative/progressive, iconoclastic fiction and nonfiction off all genres including memoir, military history, political, scripture and satire.

Categories: Fiction—Nonfiction—Cartoons—History—Military—Politics—Satire

CONTACT: David W. St.John, Executive Editor
Material: All Queries
1393 Old Homestead Dr, 2nd Floor
Oakland OR 97462
Phone: 541-459.6043
Fax: 541-459-6043
E-mail: editor@elderberrypress.com
Website: www.elderberrypress.com

Emerald Ink Publishing

Dear Author,

Our submission guidelines are fairly simple.

We prefer electronic submission or on disk, PC readable (simply access our Website to begin communications, or send files). You should not send files larger than 300-400KB by attaching to e-mail. If files are larger, arrange transmission via ftp. Word, WordPerfect, text or ASCII files, .pdf or .rtf file formats are fine. However, if you wish to send us a manuscript, query first with a stamped, self-addressed envelope or include a return postage postcard.

We always answer inquiries.

Sincerely,

Chris Carson

Categories: Nonfiction—Business—Health—Inspirational—Energy

CONTACT: Chris Carson, Owner
Material: Business, Energy
CONTACT: Patrick Zale, Editor
Material: Health, Inspirational
16630 Imperial Valley Dr., Ste 149

Houston, TX 77060
Phone: 832-598-9808
E-mail: emerald@emeraldink.com
Website: www.emeraldink.com

Empire Publishing Service

Send query letter with SASE—ONLY—for response. Gaslight—Sherlock Holmes, only. Health Watch—Health and Nutrition, only. Empire—Entertainment, History.

Categories: Diet/Nutrition—Entertainment—Mystery

CONTACT: Submissions Editor
Material: All
PO Box 1344
Studio City CA 91614-0344
Phone: 818-784-8918

Emquad International, Ltd.

EMQUAD was founded in 1988 as a publisher of specialty advertising and has

more recently turned to books. In September we shall publish "Ao Dai: My War, My Country, My Vietnam" by Xuan Phuong and Daniele Mazingarbe, which Robert MacNeil, author and former coanchor of The NewsHour on PBS, calls "one of the most extraordinary memoirs I have ever read." ISBN 0-9718406-2-8. More at www.emquad.com/aodai.html.

In general, we shall be pleased to consider any book of exceptional merit,

regardless of category. Any book considered for publication will be in good

taste.

Unsolicited manuscripts will not be returned without an SASE.
Categories: Fiction—Nonfiction

CONTACT: Jon Myers, Publisher
Material: All
PO Box 60
Great Neck, NY 11022
Phone: 516-829-3456
E-mail: emquad@att.net
Website: www.emquad.com

ETC Publications

Our guidelines are *The Chicago Manual of Style* (the book).
Categories: Nonfiction—Christian Interests—Education—Textbooks

CONTACT: Acquisitions Editor
Material: All
700 E. Vereda Del Sur
Palm Springs CA 92262
Phone: 760-325-5352
Fax: 760-325-8844

Evergreen Press

Please refer to Genesis Communications, Inc., in the Book Publishers section.

Excelsior Cee Publishing

Publishes nonfiction, general interest books. Simultaneous submissions accepted. Reports in one month. Does not accept electronic submissions.

Categories: Nonfiction—Biography—Family—General Interest—Inspirational—Writing—Genealogy—How-to

CONTACT: Acquisitions Editor
Material: All
PO Box 5861
Norman OK 73070
Phone: 405-329-3909
Fax: 405-329-6886

Faber & Faber, Inc. Publishers

Please refer to Farrar, Straus and Giroux, Publishers, Inc.

Face to Face Press

About Us

FACE to FACE is a community independent press devoted to publishing all genres of written works that explore the mixed race, interracial, transracial and, more broadly, the multi cultural experience. Founded in 1999, F2F Press published its flagship book *Voices of Brooklyn: Writings from The Women of Color Writer's Workshop*, an anthology of 14 women of color writers, in September 2000. F2F Press seeks to build ties and coalitions across marginalized communities; give under-represented writers a forum for expression and access into the publishing industry; and advocate that communities of color create and maintain their own media.

Submissions

Preparing a proposal is the first important stage in developing a project. In order for us to assess the merits of the idea and arrive at a careful publishing decision, *we recommend your proposal include the following key elements:*

• THE MARKET—Describe the market, customers, any relevant organizations, academic segments, etc.

• UNIQUE SELLING PROPOSITION—How is the book unique and different from other books in the same market?

• COMPETITION—What are the competing books? What are their strengths and weaknesses?

• CONTENT—Describe the project in as much detail as possible, with a description of the book's key features.

• FORMAT—Provide an estimate on the number of manuscript pages and illustrations and in what format. Please specify any design considerations.

• SAMPLE MATERIAL—Please submit 1-2 sample chapters and table of contents, if applicable.

• BIOGRAPHY—Please include your biography or resume.

If you have any questions, contact us by mail, phone or email.

Categories: African-American—Alternate Life-style—Lifestyle—Multicultural—Relationships—Society

CONTACT: Editorial Dept.
Material: All
16 West 32nd St., Ste 10A
New York NY 10001
Phone: 212-494-9143
Fax: 419-828-4684
E-mail: publisher@face2facepress.com
Website: www.face2facepress.com

Fairleigh Dickinson University Press

Established in 1967, Fairleigh Dickinson University Press has published over 1,400 titles in a variety of scholarly fields, including literature, history, art, and the social sciences.

Authors wishing to submit work to FDU Press should write a query letter that describes the manuscript and the contribution it will make to its scholarly field. If the Director and Editorial Committee believe the project is suitable for us, we will ask that the manuscript be submitted. Because of the costs associated with evaluation, FDU Press requires that we be the only press considering the work during the time we have it under review.

Manuscripts considered for publication by FDU Press are subject to internal review and external evaluation by specialist readers. The identity of evaluators is kept confidential, unless they specifically permit us to reveal their names. Authors may suggest possible evaluators, but should note any previous connection they may have had to the project.

The editorial committee of FDU Press, composed of university faculty in a variety of disciplines, meets every two months to select manuscripts for publication.

The typical run for FDU Press is 400-800 copies. Time from delivery of the final manuscript to publication averages between 14-18 months.

FDU Press discourages submission of unrevised dissertations. It does not publish textbooks or original fiction, poetry, or plays. It does, however, publish scholarly editions of literary works, in English or in translation.

FDU Press welcomes inquiries about essay collections. It requires, however, that the majority of the material in a collection be previously unpublished; that the essays have a unifying and consistent theme; and that the editor provides a substantial scholarly introduction. The press holds festschrifts to the same standards we would any other collection of essays.

Decisions of the Editorial Committee of FDU Press are based on the scholarly merit and value of manuscripts under consideration. FDU does not require subsidies or subventions for publication. Where such support is available, it will be employed in a manner mutually acceptable to the author, the press, and the subsidizing organization or individual.

Manuscripts must be submitted in "hard" copy for evaluation. However, once a manuscript has been accepted for publication, the press requests authors send a disk of the work.

Books accepted for publication by the FDU Press Editorial Committee are published by Associated University Presses, 2010 Eastpark Boulevard, Cranbury, NJ 08512, which has similar arrangements with the University of Delaware, Bucknell University, Lehigh University, and Susquahanna University. Only in exceptional cases will manuscripts rejected by one of the above mentioned presses be considered by one of the others.

For documentation, FDU Press books follow *The University of Chicago Stylebook*, 15th edition. MLA format is not accepted. Bibliographies are required. For spelling, the press follows *Webster's Third New International Dictionary* and the *Tenth New Collegiate Dictionary*. The press very strongly recommends that translations be provided for all foreign language extracts. As stated in *The Chicago Manual of Style*, the original language quotations should be retained only when the original language itself is of scholarly significance. For example, in a work of Racine, quotations from Racine's plays should be given in French, followed by English translations. Quotations from critical works on the plays, however, should be given in English translation only.

Fairleigh Dickinson University, founded in 1942, has campuses in Florham-Madison, NJ, Teaneck-Hackensack, NJ, and Wroxton, England.

Members of the Editorial Committee of FDU Press are: René Steinke, Walter Cummins, Kalman Goldstein, Martin Green, Samuel Raphalides, Irene Taviss-Thomson. Ex Officio member: J. Michael Adams.

A complete catalogue of FDU Press books is available online at www.fdu.edu/newspub.

Categories: Nonfiction—African-American—Architecture—Arts—Asian-American—Biography—Civil War—Drama—Government—History—Jewish Interest—Literature—Native American—Poetry—Politics—Psychology—Sports/Recreation—Theatre—Western—Women's Issues—Ethnic—Philosophy—Public Policy

CONTACT: Harry Keyishian, Director
Material: All
Fairleigh Dickinson University, 285 Madison Ave.
M-GH2-01
Madison NJ 07940
Phone: 973-443-8564
Fax: 973-443-8364
E-mail: fdupress@fdu.edu
www.fdu.edu/newspub

Fairview Press

At this time we are particularly interested in acquiring manuscripts on the following topics: grief and bereavement; aging and seniors; caregiving; palliative and end-of-life care; health, medicine (including complementary medicine), and patient education. But we will also consider proposals on other topics of broad interest to families.

We do not publish fiction, and, although our audiences include adults, teens, and children, we are not currently acquiring children's picture books.

Please take the time to study our catalog and the guidelines before submitting a proposal. We prefer that you mail your proposal rather than submitting it by phone, fax, or e-mail.

Fairview Press is not responsible for lost or damaged submission and will not respond to any submissions that do not include a self-addressed, stamped envelope (SASE).

Submissions should include:
• Cover letter
• Outline of book
• Sample chapter(s)
• Marketing plan for the book
• Self-addressed, stamped envelope

Categories: Nonfiction—Diet/Nutrition—Disabilities—Family—Health—Inspirational—Parenting—Physical Fitness—Psychology—Reference—Relationships—Self Help—Family Issues—General Issues—Gift—Humor

CONTACT: Stephanie Billecke, Editor
Material: All
2450 Riverside Ave. South
Minneapolis MN 55454
Phone: 612-672-4180
Fax: 612-672-4980

Falcon Guides

Please refer to Falcon Publishing.

FALCON™

Falcon Publishing
Falcon Guides, Two Dot, Three Forks

About *Falcon*

Falcon Publishing, an imprint of The Globe Pequot Press, specializes in outdoor guides, high- quality photographic gift books on regional or natural history themes, general interest nonfiction books with Western Americana or environmental themes, and regional cookbooks.

We publish about sixty new titles a year and have more than three hundred titles currently in print.

Imprint of The Globe Pequot Press

Falcon Guides, Two Dot, Three Forks

We Publish:

Outdoor recreation guidebooks (FalconGuides):
• Birding
• Camping
• Fishing
• Hiking (regions and statewide)
• Mountain Biking (cities and statewide)
• Rock climbing
• Rockhounding
• Paddling
• Scenic Driving
• Touring/Historic Traveling
• Walking
• Wild Areas
• How-to camping/wilderness/outdoor guides
• Field guides (wildflowers, wildlife, etc.)
• TwoDot Books: Western Americana, History, Biography,
• General non-fiction with Western/wilderness/Rocky Mountain regional themes
• Large format photo gift books (coffee table books)
• Cookbooks (with outdoor or regional themes)
• Some children's and young adult books (with environmental education or historical themes)

We Don't Publish:
• Poetry
• Coloring books
• New Age texts
• Religious texts
• Self-help books
• Scientific treatises

Submitting a Book Proposal to Falcon Publishing

Do not send us a complete manuscript. Instead, your proposal should include the following materials only:
• A letter explaining your proposal, its sales potential, and a description of its competition.
• A resume and/or list of publishing credits.
• An outline or annotated table of contents.
• One, or at most two, sample chapters.
• Sample copies of any illustrations or photographs. Do not send original materials (transparencies, original art, original copy of manuscript)!

The above materials should be organized, self-explanatory, and succinct. Address all queries to the Acquisitions Editor .

Considering Your Book

Our primary criteria are accuracy, lively and readable prose, and a new angle on natural history, regional, or environmental topics. We will analyze your proposal for editorial value, marketability, and projected costs, as well as for how well it fits with our existing line and publishing plan.

We will respond to queries within eight to ten weeks of their receipt. If your proposal is a likely candidate for a Falcon book, one of our editors may contact you for further writing samples or other materials. Once again, do not submit original materials-clear and readable photocopies are acceptable and preferred.

What You Can Expect From Falcon

Should Falcon decide to publish your book, you will be contracted and paid on a negotiated royalty basis, although we occasionally pay a flat fee. Once we have a contract with an author, we will invest in every necessary resource to produce an attractive, high-quality product and market it effectively.

Thank you for considering Falcon as a possible publisher for your book.

Categories: Nonfiction—Cooking—Environment—Fishing—History—Outdoors—Recreation—Regional—Rural America—Sports/Recreation—Travel

CONTACT: Acquisitions Editor: Falcon
Material: All
The Globe Pequot Press
246 Goose Lane
Guilford CT 06437
Phone: 203-458-4500
Fax: 203-458-4604
E-mail: info@globe-pequot.com

Books A-L

Farrar, Straus and Giroux, Publishers, Inc

Books for Young Readers
Northpoint Press
Hill and Wang
Faber & Faber, Inc

TRADE PUBLISHING

Farrar, Straus and Giroux was founded in 1946 by Roger W. Straus. The firm is renowned for its international list of literary fiction, nonfiction, poetry and children's books. Farrar, Straus and Giroux authors have won extraordinary acclaim over the years, including numerous National Book Awards, Pulitzer Prizes, and twenty-one Nobel Prizes in literature. Nobel Prize–winners include Knut Hamsun, Hermann Hesse, T. S. Eliot, Pär Lagerkvist, François Mauriac, Juan Ramón Jiménez, Salvatore Quasimodo, Nelly Sachs, Aleksandr Solzhenitsyn, Pablo Neruda, Eugenio Montale, Isaac Bashevis Singer, Czeslaw Milosz, Elias Canetti, William Golding, Wole Soyinka, Joseph Brodsky, Camilo José Cela, Nadine Gordimer, Derek Walcott, and Seamus Heaney.

Poetry has always played a pivotal role on the Farrar, Straus and Giroux list, which boasts some of the greatest names in modern verse, ranging from Elizabeth Bishop, Ted Hughes, and Philip Larkin to John Ashbery, Thom Gunn, and Les Murray.

Fiction has an even greater international reach, distinguished by Rosellen Brown, Jim Crace, Michael Cunningham, Jonathan Franzen, Carlos Fuentes, Peter Høeg, Jamaica Kincaid, Bernard Malamud, Alice McDermott, Péter Nádas, Walker Percy, Richard Powers, Susan Sontag, Scott Turow, Mario Vargas Llosa, Tom Wolfe, and Lois-Ann Yamanaka.

History, art history, natural history, current affairs and science round out a strong list in nonfiction represented by Thomas Friedman, Philip Gourevitch, Roy Jenkins, Gina Kolata, Ben Macintyre, Louis Menaud, Giles Milton, and John McPhee, among others.

IMPRINTS of FARRAR, STRAUS and GIROUX:

Northpoint Press, Hill and Wang, Faber & Faber, Inc, FSG Juvenile Program.

Hill & Wang and North Point Press
Guidelines for Submission

Query letters should be approximately one page long. Fiction submissions should include one chapter and a synopsis or summary of the book. Authors of nonfiction books should send a proposal which includes a rationale for the book, and a description of proposed chapters. We do not encourage the submission of unsolicited poetry manuscripts due to the size of our list. All submissions must be accompanied by a stamped, self-addressed envelope; manuscripts will not be returned without one. The review process will take approximately two months.

We recommend that an author considering submitting his or her work to us look in a bookstore or library to see which publishers produce what kinds of books and then submit to houses that publish books with some similarity to their own. Narrowing down the field of potential publishers this way can save both the author and the publisher a great deal of time and work.

Books For Young Readers (FSG Juvenile Program)
Guidelines for Submission

Especially in the case of longer manuscripts, it is a good idea to send a letter of inquiry before submitting the entire manuscript.

Manuscripts should be typed, double-spaced. Make sure to keep a copy of your submission-publishers make every effort to safeguard a manuscript, but they cannot be held responsible in the event of its loss.

If you would like confirmation of the receipt of your submission, include a self-addressed, stamped postcard.

Include a cover letter containing any pertinent information about yourself, your writing, your manuscript, etc.

Be sure that your name and address are on the manuscript itself, as well as on the cover letter. ALWAYS include the right-sized, self-addressed, stamped envelope for reply and the return of your material. Clearly indicate the mail class by which you would like your manuscript returned.

If you have illustrations, please send only two or three samples. Do NOT send original artwork.

The length of story depends on the age of the reader for whom it is intended; there are no fixed lengths. Do not expect an editor to give you specific comments. We receive far too many manuscripts for this to happen.

We suggest familiarizing yourself with various children's publishers to get a sense of which company would be most receptive to your type of work. Most publishers will send their catalogue if you write a letter requesting it and provide a self-addressed, stamped manila envelope for it. (Please send us a 9 X 12 envelope, with $1.87 postage.)

THE LITERARY MARKETPLACE, published by R.R. Bowker, contains a list of all publishers; a list of children's book publishers can be obtained from the Children's Book Council, 568 Broadway, New York, NY 10012.

Send submissions to: Children's Editorial Department, Farrar, Straus & Giroux, 19 Union Square West, New York, NY 10003.

• Please do not submit more than one manuscript at a time.

• Please note: Response time for queries and manuscripts is generally within three months.

• Please do not call to query about the status of your manuscript before three months have passed, at which point we may ask that you write us regarding your submission.

Categories: Fiction—Children—Juvenile—Young Adult—Hardcover fiction

CONTACT: Children's Editorial Department
Material: Children's Literature

CONTACT: Editors
Material: All other
19 Union Square W
New York NY 10003
Phone: 212-741-6900
Fax: 212-633-9385
E-mail: fsg.editorial@fsgee.com
Website: www.fsgbooks.com

Fiesta City Publishers

Before submitting material send a query letter.

Query should include brief description of work to be submitted.

With music or song submissions 1.) a lead sheet or complete manuscript and 2.) a cassette must be included.

Fiesta City Publishers will consider unique, unusual and well-constructed material in the fields of fiction, nonfiction (how-to books especially) and music and/or songs.

Categories: Fiction—Nonfiction—Music—How-to—Songs

CONTACT: Frank E. Cooke, President
Material: all
PO Box 5861
Santa Barbara CA 93110
Phone: 805-681-9199

Fleming H. Revell
A Division of Baker Publishing Group.

Please refer to Baker Publishing Group.

Fordham University Press

About Us

2002 marks the 95th anniversary of Fordham University Press, making it one of the oldest presses in the nation.

Fordham University Press, a member the Association of American University Presses (AAUP) since 1938, was established in 1907 not only to represent and uphold the values and traditions of the University itself, but also to further those values and traditions through the dissemination of scholarly research and ideas.

The press publishes primarily in the humanities and the social sciences, with an emphasis on the fields of philosophy, theology, history, classics, communications, economics, sociology, business, political science, and law, as well as literature and the fine arts. Additionally, the press publishes books focusing on the metropolitan New York region and books of interest to the general public.

Guidelines

Formal guidelines not available.

Send queries or book proposals to below address.

Categories: Nonfiction—Civil War—Economics—Education—Film/Video—Government—History—Law—Regional—Religion—Television/Radio—Philosophy—Theology

CONTACT: Anthony Chiffolo, Managing Editor
Material: All
University Box L
2546 Belmont Ave.
Bronx NY 10458-5172
Website: www.fordhampress.com

Forge Books

Please refer to Tom Doherty Associate, LLC, in the Book Publishers section.

Forum Publishing Company

Established in 1981, *Forum Publishing Company* specializes in business-related titles of all types. We are especially interested in 'how-to' start & run business books. We openly welcome unsolicited manuscripts. SASE for return of manuscript.

Categories: Nonfiction—Business—Trade

CONTACT: Submissions Editor
Material: All Directories
383 E. Main St.
Centerport NY 11721
Phone: 631-754-5000
Website: www.bizbooks.org

Frank Amato Publications, Inc.

No formal guidelines. However, we do accept unsolicited manuscripts. Our general focus is on fishing and the out-of-doors, but we are also looking for Non-fiction manuscripts. *Please send non-fiction only.*

Categories: Fishing—Outdoors—Recreation

CONTACT: Frank Amato, Publisher
Material: All
PO Box 82112
Portland OR 97282
Phone: 503-653-8108
Website: www.amatobooks.com

Franklin, Beedle & Associates, Inc.
Publishing for the Computer Sciences

We seek proposals for books and online products. The primary areas of interest are operating systems, computer programming, software applications, and the Internet and the World Wide Web. The intended market for your project should be either professionals in these fields or undergraduate students majoring in one of these disciplines.

Your submission should include the following: a prospectus, a topical outline, a sample of the proposed work, and a personal resume. The prospectus should identify the market the project is intended for, explain why it is unique, identify any existing competitors, cover any special features, provide a brief description of the end result, and offer an estimate of the schedule for completing it. The topical outline should explain the coverage and organization. If your publication will be a book, provide chapter titles and any important subtopics covered in the chapters. Sample material should be two to three chapters for books, or a runtime demo for online products.

Categories: Nonfiction—Computers—Internet—Software—Technology

CONTACT: The Editor
Material: All
Franklin, Beedle & Associates, Inc.
8536 SW St. Helens Dr., Ste. D,
Wilsonville, OR 97070
Phone: 800-322-2665
E-mail: jimleisy@fbeedle.com
Website: www.fbeedle.com

> *Remember: Editors change jobs and publishers change addresses. It is wise to invest in a phone call for the current information before submitting.*

Frederick Fell Publishers, Inc.

Frederick Fell Publishers, Inc is formerly known as Lifetime Books, Inc.

Thank you for your interest in Frederick Fell Publishers, Inc. *Our submission guidelines are as follows:*
1. Proposal Letter
2. Two sample chapters (optional)
3. A Table of Contents for the book
4. Author Bio/Credentials
5. Market Analysis: Tell us what books are your competition and why yours is better than the others. What makes it unique?
SASE for return of manuscript.
Good Luck and Good Writing!

Categories: Nonfiction—Business—College—Cooking—Diet/Nutrition—Entertainment—Food/Drink—Health—Hobbies—Inspirational—Jewish Interest—New Age—Sexuality

CONTACT: Don Lessne, Senior Editor
Material: All
2131 Hollywood Blvd. Ste. 303
Hollywood FL 33020
Phone: 954-925-5242
Fax: 954-925-5244
E-mail: info@fellpub.com
Website: www.fellpub.com

Free Spirit Pubishing

How to Become an Author
See if any (or all) of the following describe you:
• Educator
• Mental-health professional
• Self-help expert
• Youth worker
• Parent
• Childcare professional
• Experienced writer
• Someone who cares deeply about children and teens

Our mission is to provide children and teens with the tools they need to succeed in life and to make a difference in the world. We publish high-quality nonfiction books for children and teens, parents, teachers, counselors, and others who live with or work with young people.

Look through our books and study our latest catalog.

You'll find Free Spirit books at your local bookstore, library, or schools. To request a copy of our Parent's Choice Approved catalog, call (612) 338-2068, send us an email, drop us an online note, or view our catalog online right now.

Founded in 1983 by author and educator Judy Galbraith, Free Spirit was the first publisher to offer self-help materials for young people. Today we continue to be the leader in providing positive, practical, solution-based information that meets the needs of children at home, at school, and in their communities.

Decide if you have an idea that would enhance our award-winning list.

We publish books and creative learning tools in three main areas: (1) self-help for children and teens, (2) enrichment activities for classroom teachers and youth workers, and (3) successful parenting and teaching strategies. Our award-winning books are recognized and respected for their creative, practical, jargon-free, and solution-based focus. *We are looking for strong proposals in these topic areas:*

- Mental and emotional health issues
- Bullying, conflict resolution
- Social skills
- School success
- Creative teaching and learning
- Gifted and talented youth
- LD (learning differences)
- Family issues
- Social action
- Violence prevention
- Healthy youth development
- After-school programs

We do not publish the following:
- Fiction or picture storybooks
- Books with animal or mythical characters
- Books with religious or New Age content
- Single biographies, autobiographies, or memoirs

Mail your proposal.

Include the following information:
- Your relevant background and subject of expertise.
- A brief overview, an outline or table of contents, and at least two sample chapters. Do not send originals. (Query before sending full manuscript. Queries only, not full proposals, are accepted by email: help4kids@freespirit.com.)
- Intended audience (include age ranges and audience description).
- How your idea is different from existing products on the topic.
- To be certain your materials have reached us, enclose a self-addressed, stamped reply postcard. • For return of your materials, include a self-addressed return envelope with sufficient postage.

Please be patient! Reply time is one to four months.

Your idea might be precisely what we're looking for. Or we might request revisions to your proposal. If you're a subject-matter expert in need of a writer, we can suggest a good match for you. We can also put professional writers together with credentialed coauthors.

You Might Like to Know That
- We publish 16–22 new titles and creative learning tools per year.
- We offer an advance plus royalties.
- You can expect a high level of personal attention from our editors and our promotions and sales departments.
- Our strong backlist ensures that your book will have a long life in print.
- Our 95 authors have published more than 120 titles with Free Spirit to date.
- Our books are available through major trade and library distributors (Ingram and Baker & Taylor) and can be found in independent and national bookstores (Barnes & Noble and Borders), at Amazon.com and other online booksellers, and in select catalogs.

Our books and other products are also available through our own widely distributed consumer catalog and here on our Web site. In addition, we attend and sell our books at 45–50 regional and national conferences per year.
- Our books have been translated into 15 languages.
- Our best-sellers include *What Kids Need to Succeed* (550,000 in print), *The Gifted Kids' Survival Guides (For Ages 10 & Under* and *a Handbook For Teens)* (274,000), *Fighting Invisible Tigers: a Stress Management Guide For Teens* (185,000), TEACHING GIFTED KIDS IN THE *Regular Classroom* (178,000), *Stick up for Yourself! Every Kid's Guide to Personal Power and Positive Self-esteem* (137,000), and *How Rude! The Teenagers' Guide to Good Manners, Proper Behavior, and Not Grossing People out* (70,000).

Our books have been reviewed by KLIATT, School Library Journal, and Publishers Weekly.

Our books have been featured in the Los Angeles Times, Washington Post, Boston Globe, and USA Today.
- Awards include Learning magazine's "Teachers' Choice," Early Childhood Education's "Directors' Choice," Parents' Choice, Parent Council®, Voice of Youth Advocates (VOYA), American Library Association's "Quick Picks," New York Public Library's "Books for the Teen Age," Parent magazine's "Book of the Year," and many more.

Categories: Nonfiction—Children—Education—Family—Health—Juvenile—Parenting—Psychology—Self Help—Teen—Young Adult

CONTACT: Acquisitions
Material: All
217 Fifth Ave., North, Ste. 200
Minneapolis, MN 55401-1299
Phone: 800-735-7323, 612-338-2068
Fax: 612-337-5050
E-mail: help4kids@freespirit.com
Website: www.freespirit.com

Front Row Experience

Perceptual-Motor Development Movement Education

We are only interested in "Movement Education" activities for pre-school to sixth grade teachers. Send a one-page letter of inquiry with proposal. If we are interested, we will request more information, sample activities, manuscript, etc. Do not send unsolicited manuscripts! Call us for more information.

Categories: Physical Fitness—Movement Education

CONTACT: Frank Alexander, Editor
Material: All
540 Discovery Bay Blvd.
Discovery Bay CA 94514
Phone: 510-634-5710

Front Street, Inc.

GUIDELINES FOR SUBMISSIONS

Front Street is an independent publisher of books for children and young adults. Please visit our web site at www.frontstreetbooks.com to see the types of books that we publish.

OUR SUBMISSIONS POLICY

Front Street is willing to consider unsolicited manuscripts. It is our policy to consider all submissions in the order they are received. This is a time consuming practice and we ask you to be patient in awaiting our response. We understand the reasons for multiple submissions, although we discourage them. We feel it is important for you to know in advance that if our decision is negative, you will receive a form rejection letter. This procedure enables us to reduce the time it takes to respond to submissions, time we can devote to reviewing more submissions.

Picture Books

We are not currently accepting unsolicited picture book manuscripts.

Fiction

If under 100 pages, submit the complete manuscript. If over 100 pages, submit one or two sample chapters, and a plot summary. We will request the balance of the manuscript if we are interested.

Poetry

Please send a selection of no more than 25 poems that are representative of your work. We will request more if we are interested.

Anthologies

We will only consider anthologies of work by various authors if accompanied by a detailed proposal and permissions budget.

Nonfiction

A detailed proposal and sample chapter will suffice.

Whatever it takes to give us a sense of the project.

Please enclose a dated cover letter so that we have your name and return address.

We are unable to return materials unless you provide us with a self-addressed, stamped envelope. If there is no SASE included, we will assume the materials can be discarded.

We are unable to return manuscripts to destinations outside of the US.

Do not send submissions as e-mail attachments. Submissions sent in this manner will be automatically deleted from our computers.

Categories: Fiction—Nonfiction—Children—Juvenile—Literature—Poetry—Teen—Writing—Young Adult

CONTACT: Joy Neaves, Editor
Material: All
20 Battery Park Ave., #403
Asheville NC 28801
Phone: 828-236-3097
Fax: 828-236-3098
E-mail: neaves@frontstreetbooks.com
Website: www.frontstreetbooks.com

FSG Juvenile Program

Please refer to Farrar, Straus and Giroux, Publishers, Inc.

Future Horizons

Future Horizons, Inc., relies on a combination of personal relationships within the autism community and unsolicited manuscripts in order to offer unique, quality books and products that serve the autism community. Our goal is to offer parents, professionals caregivers, and individuals with the disability fun, creative, practical information that will help them focus on the ability rather than the disability in autism, Asperger's Syndrome and other related disorders. We welcome all submissions written with this goal in mind, but due to limited time and the great number of manuscripts we receive, please do not submit proposals that are not related to the subject of autism and other pervasive developmental disorders.

In order to properly evaluate a publication proposal we need to receive certain essential information. All works are carefully reviewed for their quality, suitability, originality, and current information. Please include a cover letter, author resume, book synopsis, chapter-by-chapter outline, and at least three consecutive chapters. We do not accept hand-written manuscripts. We encourage authors to provide any relevant artwork, tables, charts or graphs that will enhance the quality of your submission. Please refer to the following guidelines for more information on our expectations.

Cover Letter
Be sure to include the following:
• Your name
• Your current mailing address
• The titles, publishers, and publication dates of any previous books, journal articles or presentations you have authored or co-authored
  • A suggested book title
  • The estimated length of the book
  • Proposed artwork, tables, charts and/or figures
• A description of any special features of the book. For example, each chapter contains suggested readings or a "Coping Strategies" section.
  • Your assessment of the book's main selling points
• A description of the book's unique qualities (how it differs from other books in its category and why there is a need for a book of its nature)
  • An explanation of your intended readership
Author Resume
Be sure to include the following:

• Educational credentials, including degrees earned, awards, research projects and other information that would lend to your credibility and an expert on your chosen topic.
• Positions held within the autism community and a short description of your duties (Outreach centers, schools, medical practices, volunteer organizations)
• Speaking experience (if any), including a list of specific engagements
  • General career timeline
  • Interests and activities
Book Synopsis
Please include a typed summary of your book not to exceed 750 words.
Chapter Outline
This is a brief summary of each chapter. Please keep it to less than 500 words per chapter.
Three Consecutive Chapters
Send three chapters that express your originality, subject matter, and writing quality. You may send us a complete manuscript, but we ask that you recommend three chapters.

Keep a copy of your manuscript for your files as we may not return submissions. We know that you have spent months and possibly years crafting your work and we will do our utmost to do your submission justice by reviewing it thoroughly. However, please be aware that we receive many proposals and that it is not unusual for the process to take many months. We appreciate your patience in this lengthy process.

We notify all authors upon receipt of material, so there is no need to follow up.

Categories: Nonfiction—Disabilities

CONTACT: Victoria Ulmer, Editor Coordinator
Material: All
721 W. Abram St.
Arlington TX 76013
Phone: 817-277-0727
Fax: 817-277-2270
E-mail: Victoria@futurehorizone-autism.com
Website: www.FutureHorizons.com

Garth Gardner Company

For Authors: How to Submit a Book Proposal
GGC/Publishing is always looking for great book proposals! We accept submissions directly from authors (including first time authors) and also from literary agents.

Your book proposal should include the following:
• A description of the intended market for the book
• An explanation of why someone would want to buy the book
• A summary of the author's background
• A table of contents, as detailed as possible
• A sample chapter. Do not send in the whole manuscript.

We are not accepting electronic submissions at this time. We will contact you only if we are interested in your proposal. If you wish to have any material returned, include a self-addressed and stamped envelope.

We accept no responsibility for proposals and manuscripts. The volume of submissions does not allow us to accept phone calls or e-mail or other inquiries, or to provide comments or feedback on unsolicited manuscripts.

Thank you for your interest in Garth Gardner Company.

Categories: Nonfiction—Careers—Cartoons—College—Computers—Film/Video—Graphics—Reference—Textbooks

CONTACT: Anthony Mason, VP of Marketing
Material: Animation, Computer Graphics
GGC/ Publishing
5107 13th St. NW
Washington, DC 20011
Phone: 202-541-9700

Books A-L

Fax: 202-541-9750
E-mail: anthony@ggcinc.com
Website: www.gogardner.com

GATFPress

Please refer to Graphic Arts Technical Foundation (GATF).

Gazelle Press

Please refer to Genesis Communications, Inc., in the Book Publishers section.

Gem Guides Book Company

Gem Guides requests a book outline including Table of Contents and two or three sample chapters, along with examples of photos and illustrations that would accompany text. Please include information about the market for the book, how it is differentiated from competitive titles in print on the same topic, and your qualifications to produce a book on the subject.

Categories: Nonfiction—Crafts/Hobbies—Hobbies—Native American—Outdoors—Regional—Travel—Bead Crafts—Lapidary—Prospecting—Rocks and Minerals

CONTACT: Kathy Mayerski, Editorial Assistant
Material: All
315 Cloverleaf Dr. Ste. F
Baldwin Park CA 91706
Phone: 626-855-1611
Fax: 626-855-1610
E-mail: gembooks@aol.com
Website: www.gemguidesbooks.com

Genesis Communications, Inc.
Imprints: Evergreen Press & Gazelle Press

We publish books written from a biblical world view. We publish both hardcover and softcover books written from a Christian viewpoint. Our main categories of interest are: Christian business, Christian personal growth, Christian living, inspirational, true short stories, deeper life, Bible study, Christian health, Christian finance, Christian success and motivation, prayer. Above all, we are interested in books that empower people for breakthroughs in their lives.

We prefer to see the entire manuscript. We will send out author information packets and catalogs upon request.

We publish approximately 30 books per year. We have our own distribution company, plus our books are carried at Spring Arbor, and other major distributors.

Categories: Christian Interests—Health—Inspirational—Lifestyle—Money & Finances—Short Stories

CONTACT: Kathy Banashak, Senior Editor
Material: All
PO Box 19540
Mobile AL 36619
Phone: 251-973-0682
Fax: 251-973-0682
E-mail: info@evergreenpressbooks.com
Website: www.evergreenpressbooks.com

> *Remember: Editors change jobs and publishers change addresses. It is wise to invest in a phone call for the current information before submitting.*

The Globe Pequot Press

Guidelines for Globe Pequot Press titles

Thank you for your interest in The Globe Pequot Press! By perusing our website, you can see if your book idea is right for our list. You will note that our Globe Pequot line primarily publishes travel guides, with some select nature titles, cookbooks, and home-based business books. Our Falcon line specializes in outdoor recreation, both how-to and where-to, with hiking, biking, climbing, and other specialized lines, including regional history.

We welcome submissions appropriate to our publishing list. *When submitting a book proposal, please include the following:*

1. A brief synopsis of the proposed work.

2. A definition of the book's projected target audience/market and an analysis of competing titles, if any. (The latter can be found by researching *Books in Print.*) Who is the book for, and why is it better than what is already on the bookshelves?

3. A table of contents or outline of the entire book, plus a sample chapter to give us a sense of your writing style.

4. A biographical statement of your credentials. This statement should explain why you are particularly qualified to undertake the proposed project.

5. A self-addressed, stamped envelope large enough to return submitted materials. If this is not enclosed, we will not return your materials. Never send the only copy of anything!

6. To expedite the process, be sure to address your proposal to the Submissions Editor of the particular book category appropriate to your idea. For example, a proposal for a travel guide should go to Submissions Editor - Travel. A book about kayaking should be sent to the attention of Submissions Editor - Kayaking. You get the idea!

We wish you the best of luck. Please allow six to eight weeks for a response to your proposal. Again, thank you for your interest in The Globe Pequot Press.

Categories: Nonfiction—Business—Careers—Cooking—Family—Gardening—History—Outdoors—Recreation—Rural America—Sports/Recreation—Travel

CONTACT: Submissions Editor
Material: All (Specify subject category)
246 Goose Lane
PO Box 480
Guilford CT 06437
Phone: 203-458-4500
Fax: 203-458-4604
Website: www.GlobePequot.com

God Allows U-Turns Book Series

SEND US YOUR TRUE SHORT STORY

Published by Promise Press, an imprint of Barbour Publishing, Inc., in association with Alive Communications, Inc. This is a Christian inspirational book series. Each book in the series will contain up to one hundred uplifting, encouraging and inspirational true short stories written by contributors from all over the world. Stories go into a book. Multiple volumes are planned. Volumes are available in bookstores now. We are currently accepting true short stories for multiple future volumes, see web site for future volume topics. 100% freelance. Pays $50 honorarium upon publication (plus 1 copy of book). By-line and short bio. Send complete manuscript with full contact information. We will respond only if your story is selected for submission. Accepts simultaneous submissions & reprints (tell when/where appeared). Prefers submission via web site. Accepts e-mail submission (copied into message, NO attachments). Sample story appears on web site. Read a current volume in the series to understand our needs and story format. Thoroughly review web site if possible.

SPECIAL NEEDS

Open to well written, personal inspirational pieces showing how faith in God can inspire, encourage and heal. Hope should prevail. Human-interest stories with a spiritual application, affirming ways in which faith is expressed in daily life. These true stories MUST touch the emotions. Our contributors are a diverse group with no limits on age or denomination. When possible, show how a change of heart, attitude, thought, and/or behavior occurred that clearly describes a u-turn toward God. Using a "u-turn" lesson/analogy within the story is a plus.

TIPS

Read a current volume, or see the web site for a sample story. Keep it real. Ordinary people doing extraordinary things with God's help. Focus on timeless, universal themes like love, forgiveness, salvation, healing, hope, faith, etc. Be able to tell a good story with drama, description and dialogue. Avoid moralisms and preachy tone. The point of the story should be some practical spiritual help the reader receives from what the author learned through his experience. Remember our "u-turn toward God" theme.

DEADLINES

Deadlines vary and are open for future volumes, see our "Future Volumes" page on our website for specific niche titles and various deadlines. www.godallowsuturns.com.

THREE WAYS TO SUBMIT YOUR STORY

1. Via our Web Site at http://www.godallowsuturns.com (submit story directly from the site)

2. Via email at editor@godallowsuturns.com (write STORY SUBMISSION in subject line.)

3. Via the United States Post Office (aka: "snail mail") See snail mail guidelines on reverse side.)

STORY FORMAT

Submissions must be from 500-1,500 words. No formatting needed if sent via web site or email. If submitting via snail mail, you must send your story on a PC formatted disk, typed, double-spaced, one-inch margins, and 12 point "Times" font. Sorry, but we cannot accept handwritten stories.

RIGHTS

One time non-exclusive rights. Reprint rights. No returns. We will reserve full editorial rights. You will be sent a Permissions Form (contract) in the event your story is chosen for publication. This form must be signed and returned promptly.

TIMELINE

Due to the volume of material we are now receiving, we truly regret that we can no longer respond personally to every contributor. However, you can rest assured you will be contacted in the event your submission is selected for publication. Our professional team of editors is taking considerable time reading, rating and discussing all stories before final decisions are made. Feel free to submit your story elsewhere during this review process. In the event your work is chosen for inclusion in a future volume, you will be notified by mail to see if your story is still available for our use, and to obtain your written permission to edit and print your story.

SNAIL MAIL SUBMISSIONS

If you send your true short-story by good old-fashioned snail-mail, please include your contact information and send your typed submission along with a copy on a PC formatted disk.

CONTACT INFORMATION TO INCLUDE WITH YOUR STORY

• First and Last Name
• Day and Evening Telephone & FAX
• Mailing Address/City/State/Zip and Country
• E-Mail Address (if you have an email address, please send your story via email)

Triumphant Teens:

True Stories of Hope and Healing for Teens

We are in the process of compiling the fifth book in the popular God Allows U-Turns book series compiled by Allison Gappa Bottke

and published by Promise Press, an imprint of Barbour Publishing in association with Alive Communications, Inc.

While this book is being developed for Christian teens, it is our prayer that it will also be read by teens at the beginning of their U-Turn journey toward God. Stories in the God Allows U-Turns books are changing lives. People around the world tell us how the stories in previous volumes of God Allows U-Turns have touched their lives and helped them turn toward God - now the time has come to develop a collection that will impact and influence teenagers around the globe.

Please pray about writing a story that will make a difference in the lives of teenagers.

Our writers can be any age or denomination - but the story theme must involve a teenager and a teen topic. Perhaps you know a teen whose story is perfect but they choose not to write it - you may want to write that teen's story using the byline, "as told to." Here are some guidelines to help you in the process. Please read them carefully and prayerfully.

OUR AUDIENCE

The broad audience for this book is ages 12-18, but most readers will fall in the 13-15, possibly 16, age range.

TEEN VOLUME SPECIAL NEEDS

These TRUE stories MUST touch the emotions of teens. Open to well written, personal inspirational pieces showing how faith in God can inspire, encourage and heal. Hope should prevail. We want human-interest stories with a spiritual application, affirming ways in which faith is expressed in the daily life of a teen. When possible, show how a change of heart, attitude, thought, and/or behavior occurred that clearly describes a u-turn toward God. Using a "u-turn" lesson/analogy within the story is a plus.

TIPS

The God Allows U-Turns book series dares to go where many short story collections fear to tread. We touch on hard-hitting, real life topics in today's world. Read a current volume, or see the web site for a sample story. Keep it real. Ordinary teens doing extraordinary things with God's help. Focus on timeless, universal themes like love, forgiveness, salvation, healing, hope, faith, etc. Be able to tell a good story with drama, description and dialogue. Your story must have a clear beginning, middle and end. Use strong verbs - show us, don't tell us. Avoid moralisms and preachy tone. The point of the story should be some practical spiritual help the teen reader receives from what the author learned through his experience. Remember our "u-turn toward God" theme.

We are currently developing the chapter topics for this teen book and we are open to hearing feedback from you for possible chapter topics. (Join our TEEN TROUPE to help select stories - see web site.)

Perhaps the topics below will help trigger some story ideas for you.

• God's Love & God's Plan
• Faith and Forgiveness
• Prayer
• Peer Pressure
• Tales of Triumph
• Hope and Healing
• Courage
• Dare to Dream
• Heroes & Mentors
• New Direction U-Turns
• Life Lessons
• Virtue
• Trends VS Tradition
• Music & Movies
• Thankfulness
• Relationships
• Family & Friends
• Memories
• Ethics & Integrity

Books
A-L

• Trust

DEADLINES

Deadlines change and vary and we are always open for future volumes. See our "Future Volumes" page on our website for future volume titles and various deadlines. www.godallowsuturns.com.

STORY FORMAT

Submissions must be from 500-1,500 words with a few exceptions for longer ones. No formatting needed if sent via web site or email. If submitting via snail mail, you must send your story on a PC formatted disk. Sorry, but we cannot accept handwritten stories.

RIGHTS and FEES PAID

One time non-exclusive rights. Reprint rights. No returns. We will reserve full editorial rights. You will be sent a Permissions Form (contract) in the event your story is chosen for publication. This form must be signed and returned promptly. The payment rate for non-exclusive rights varies from $50-$100, depending on word count and if the story was previously published.

TIMELINE

Due to the volume of material we are now receiving, we truly regret that we can no longer respond personally to every contributor. However, you can rest assured you will be contacted in the event your submission is selected for publication. Feel free to submit your story elsewhere during this review process. In the event your work is chosen for inclusion in a future volume, you will be notified by mail or email to see if your story is still available for our use.

CONTACT INFORMATION TO INCLUDE WITH YOUR STORY

First and Last Name— Day and Evening Telephone & FAX — Mailing Address/City/State/Zip and Country — EMail Address (if you have an email address, please send your story via email)

THREE WAYS TO SUBMIT YOUR STORY

1. Via our Web Site at http://www.godallowsuturns.com (submit story directly from the site)

2. Via email at editor@godallowsuturns.com (write STORY SUBMISSION in subject line.)

3. Via the United States Post Office (aka: "snail mail") See snail mail guidelines below.)

SNAIL MAIL SUBMISSIONS

If you send your true short-story by good old-fashioned snail-mail, please include your contact information and send your typed submission along with a copy on a PC formatted disk to:

Attention Editor, The GOD ALLOWS U-TURNS Project, STORY SUBMISSION, Post Office Box 717, Faribault, MN 55021-0717 (This is the God Allows U-Turns business address.)

Thanks so much, and we look forward to hearing from you! Please share this with other writers.

Categories: Nonfiction—Christian Interests—Family—General Interest—Inspirational—Lifestyle—Marriage—Men's Issues— Parenting—Religion—Self Help—Short Stories—Singles—Spiritual— Teen—Women's Issues—Young Adult

CONTACT: Allison Gappa Bottke, Compiler/Editor
Material: True Short Stories
The God Allows U-Turns Project
PO Box 717
Faribault MN 55021-0717
Phone: 507-334-6464
E-mail: godallowsuturns.com
Website: www.godallowsuturns.com

GOLDEN WEST PUBLISHERS

Golden West Publishers

Golden West Publishers specializes in cookbooks and books about outdoor recreation (Southwest). Currently we are expanding our cookbook line and are interested in regional titles. We are creating a cookbook for each state as part of our Cooking Across America series and we also want to add regional titles of interest. We prefer buyouts as opposed to royalties. We require a query letter with sample Table of Contents and sample chapter, if possible.

Categories: Cooking—Regional—Cookbooks

CONTACT: Hal Mitchell, Editor
Material: Cookbooks
4113 N. Longview
Phoenix AZ 85014
Phone: 602-265-4392
Fax: 602-279-6901

G. P. Putnam's Sons
Books for Young Readers

Picture Books

We accept full picture book manuscripts for review. Art should not be sent until specifically requested.

Fiction (middle-grade, chapter books, young adult)

Please send a query letter before submitting fiction. Please include a synopsis and one to three sample chapters. Your query letter and sample chapters will be circulated among the editors and the entire work will be requested upon interest.

Nonfiction

Please send a query letter before submitting nonfiction. Please include a synopsis and one or two sample chapters, as well as a table of contents. Your query letter and sample chapters will be circulated among the editors and the entire work will be requested upon interest.

Submissions must include a SASE (self-addressed, stamped envelope) for our reply. If you wish to have your materials returned, your SASE must have the correct postage.

If you would like to receive a catalog, you must send a 9x12 envelope with the appropriate postage.

Categories: Fiction—Nonfiction—Children's—Young Adult

CONTACT: Putnam Children's Editorial
Manuscript Editor
Material: All
345 Hudson St., 14th floor
New York, NY 10014
Website: us.penguingroup.com

The Graduate Group

We look for manuscripts that will be helpful to high school, college and graduate students in their attempt to establish themselves in a career, manuscripts which alert students to opportunities and ways to become more effective.

Graduate Group books are distributed exclusively to career planning offices and libraries in the U.S. and abroad.

Authors are provided a liberal royalty.

Categories: Nonfiction—Business—Careers—College—Computers—Crime—Education—Environment—General Interest—Government—Health—Internet—Interview—Law—Military—Money & Finances—Reference—Law Enforcement—Nursing

CONTACT: Robert Whitman, Vice President
Material: Any
CONTACT: Mara Whitman, President
Material: Any
PO Box 370351
West Hartford CT 06137-0351
Phone: 860-233-2330

Granite Publishing Group, LLC
Imprints: Wild Flower Press and Swan-Raven & Co.

Granite Publishing through its two primary imprints, Wild Flower Press and Swan-Raven & Co., accepts only a few manuscripts per year, and those that are accepted must follow the following guidelines:

Wild Flower Press prefers work that deals with some aspect of the UFO/ET phenomena and earth changes. Swan-Raven & Co. prefers material related to, spirituality, shamanism, societal change, or a related area. All work must be non-fiction. We do not do stories, fiction, novels, novellas or poetry.

The work must demonstrate high scholarship. The work must demonstrate coherent thinking and novel insights; it must break new ground and be significantly different from other works on the market.

Writing style must be clear, interesting and effective. Spelling must be exact as specified in *Webster's Ninth Collegiate Dictionary*, and grammar must follow the *Chicago Manual of Style*. Submissions should include a chapter outline, some representative chapters and a cover letter about yourself and about why the book will be of interest to a wide audience. See *Non-Fiction Book Proposals Anybody Can Write* by Elizabeth Lyon.

Categories: Nonfiction—Environment—Inspirational—Native American—New Age—Paranormal—Spiritual—UFO Experiences—UFO Research

CONTACT: Pam Meyer, Granite Publishing Group
Material: All
PO Box 1429
Columbus, NC 28722
Phone: 828-894-8444
Fax: 828-894-8454
E-mail: Pam@5thworld.com
Website: www.5thworld.com

Graphic Arts Center Publishing Company
Graphic Arts Books
Alaska Northwest Books
WestWinds Press

Graphic Arts Center Publishing Company publishes and distributes national and regional titles through its three imprints: Graphic Arts Books, Alaska Northwest Books, and WestWinds Press. GACP is known for its excellence in publishing high-end photo-essay books.

Alaska Northwest Books, established in 1959, is the premier publisher of non-fiction Alaska books on subjects ranging from cooking, Alaska Native culture, memoir, history, natural history, reference, biography, humor, and children's books. WestWinds Press, established in 1999, echoes those themes with content that focuses on the Western States.

Categories We Publish

The rule of thumb is this: If you are proposing a photo-driven book, it would be published under the Graphic Arts Books imprint. Text-driven books that are supported with photos or illustrations–and all children's books–are published under Alaska Northwest Books or WestWinds Press. To familiarize yourself with the books that we publish, browse our website.

Editors look for the following:

• Non-fiction material that reflects life as it is or was in Alaska, the Northwest, adjacent Canada, and the Western states

• Authoritative material about the region's wildlife, plants, or other natural resources

• Material about people and places in history, especially that which provides unpublished information and fresh insights

• Arts and crafts of the region both aboriginal and contemporary

• Practical guides to cooking, gardening, travel, and recreation in Alaska and in the West

• Regionally focused children's books, non-fiction and fiction (with themes related to Alaska, the Northwest, or Western States)

• Occasional out-of-region subjects for which there is a demonstrable reader interest and market

Submission Basics

Submissions should be typewritten from a computer or typewriter, double-spaced. Author should retain a copy of the submission.

Along with your manuscript, or sample chapters, please include the following with your submission:

• A cover letter describing the project

• A complete outline of your idea/concept (include your thoughts about what would be the ideal book specifications: trim size, number of pages, number of photos, text size)

• A table of contents detailing the areas/regions/themes to be covered

• An individual bio with examples of work previously published, if any

• Discussion of the potential market for the book–i.e.: what other books similar to this book exist and how this differs in quality, style, breadth, and timelines; who the potential buyers of this book are and what access you have to any of these markets through mailing lists, membership in professional societies, media contacts; trends that lend support to your project; relevant demographics; etc.

If you are enclosing samples of art and/or photography, do not send originals. Duplicate slides and color photocopies are acceptable.

Please package all materials securely, enclose return postage, and include cost of certification if material is to be returned certified mail. We do not guarantee the return of unsolicited material. We do, however, take all possible precautions against loss or damage.

Response to Submission

Upon receiving your submission, we will send you a letter of receipt. After you have received this, please allow ample time (up to 6 months) for careful consideration of your work. We will let you know as soon as we have made a decision.

Please remember that editors base their final decisions upon numerous considerations, such as books previously published by GACPC, material already accepted and scheduled for publication, and what appears to be current reader interest.

Further Reading

We highly recommend Judith Applebaum's *How to Get Happily Published* (Fourth Edition, 1992: Harper Collins) for additional information on preparing a successful proposal for consideration by a publisher.

Books A-L

About Graphic Arts Center Publishing Company

We publish scenic calendars and photographic essay books that cover topic, region, state, sort, or specialty. The following is a list of guideline specification.

We use only full-time, professional photographers and/or *well established* photographic businesses.

Transparencies, in any format, are acceptable. They must be tack sharp and possess high reproductive quality. If you prefer, you may submit equivalent digital files.

Our books and calendars usually represent one photographer

New calendar or book proposals must have large market appeal and/or have corporate sale possibilities, as well as, fit our company's present focus.

Obtaining Permission to Submit

Contact the Editorial Department to receive permission to send a submission. An unsolicited submission will be returned unopened, with postage due.

Once permission is granted to send in a submission, please include the following: (1) an individual biography (2) samples of your work (3)20-40 transparencies that are numbered, labeled iwth descriptions, and verified in a deliver memo (4) return postage or a filled-out Fed Ex form.

You will receive a confirmation note upon arrival of your submission. Please allow 3-6 months for us to preview a book proposal.

All transparencies wil be kept in our fire-proof vault, protected by a Halon fire protected system.

We will make every effort to handle your transparencies with the utmost of care. *However, we are not liable for any loss or damage of transparencies submitted with a book proposal. In addition, we do not pay pull, research, or holding fees to preview your transparencies.*

Thank you for your interest in Graphic Arts Books.

Categories: Nonfiction—Adventure—Children—Cooking—Culture—Gardening—Native American—Outdoors—Photography—Reference—Regional—Travel

CONTACT: Timothy W. Frew, Executive Editor
Material: Submissions for Graphic Arts Books
(photo-essay books)
CONTACT: Tricia Brown, Acquisitions Editor
Material: Alaska Northwest Books or WestWinds
Press submissions
PO Box 10306
Portland OR 97296-0306
Phone: 503-226-2402
Fax: 503-223-1410
website: www.gacpc.com

Graphic Arts Technical Foundation
GATFPress

GATF's strong commitment to research and education drives its publications program—GATF*Press*—which includes textbooks, primers, reference books, training modules, CD-ROMs, and videocassettes. Many GATF publications are adopted as required texts at the high-school, college, and university levels across the country.

GATF*Press* publishes nonfiction books on most aspects of the graphic communications industry and the ancillary processes prevalent in today's rapidly changing technologies. Some of the manuscript topics in which GATF*Press* is interested include: graphic design (particularly advanced and computerized processes), electronic publishing/communications, color management, digital photography, safety, estimating, printing management, print buying, sales and marketing, desktop publishing, aspects of lithographic production, and the printer's compliance with OSHA/EPA regulations. GATF*Press* does not publish "coffee table" art books.

GATF books are not product-specific; therefore, manuscripts on specific software programs or products are not accepted. In order to gain acceptance, content must not appreciably overlap with any other GATF books in print or production.

Book proposals from both veteran and first-time authors are welcome.

Submissions Should Include:
• *A cover letter:*
This serves as your sales proposal in which you convince GATF's editorial group that your manuscript is a marketable product and that you are the right author for them.
• *A comprehensive outline/synopsis, covering:*
1. The rationale behind the book: Include a summary of what the book is about, what it will and will not cover, how it compares to similar books, why it is unique, and why it is necessary.
2. The focus of the book: Define who the target audience is and what readers will learn or gain from the text.
3. Your background: Explain why you are qualified to write this book—your professional background, expertise, and experience as a professional writer.
4. The book itself: Provide a chapter-by-chapter outline with a detailed explanation of the material to be covered in each segment. Identify chapter titles, heads, and subheads; explain each topic and segment division; and include a separate section on possible illustrations.
5. Writing samples: If you've already begun writing, include no more than two sample chapters from the manuscript.

Include a self-addressed stamped envelope (large enough and containing the proper postage) to return the materials to you. GATF is not responsible for unsolicited materials received without adequate return postage and packaging.

You can expect a response acknowledging receipt of your proposal within two weeks. Submissions are then reviewed by GATF's editorial staff, consultants, and a product planning committee for final approval. If your manuscript is accepted, it also will go through more in-depth technical review ("peer review") prior to publication. Responses are generally sent within four months. Interest in an outline does not guarantee publication of your manuscript. GATF does not pay kill fees for manuscripts for which there is no signed contract.

Categories: Nonfiction—Associations—Graphics—Technical—Textbooks—Trade—Printing

CONTACT: Amy Woodall, Managing Editor
Material: All
CONTACT: Peter Oresick, Vice President
Material: Technical Information
200 Deer Run Rd.
Sewickley PA 15143-2600
Phone: 412-741-6860

Great Quotations Publishing

Great Quotations seeks original material for the following general categories:
• Humor
• Inspiration
• Motivation
• Success
• Romance
• Tributes to mom/dad/grandma/grandpa, etc.
Generally speaking we do not currently publish:
• Children's books and others requiring multi-color illustration on the inside

- Novels and other such fiction, or text that is extremely narrative and detailed
- Manuscripts substantially consisting of poetry
- Highly controversial subject matter

Our books are often purchased on impulse. Therefore the material must be simple, concise and a light read. *They are also physically small and short in length, and comprise five different formats:*
- Paperback Books 6"x4½", 168 pp., Retail $5.95
- Comb Bound Books 4½"x6", 78 pp., Retail $7.95
- Mini-Perpetual Calendars 4"x3¾", 365 pp., Retail $6.50
- Large Perpetual Calendars 5½"x4½", 365 pp., Retail $8.95
- Hard Cover Books 4"x5½", 64 pp., Retail $6.50

The ideal submission consists of a cover letter explaining the idea and a few sample pages of text. Include two SASEs for both a response and for the return of materials if such is desired. Submissions sent without a SASE are subject to disposal without consideration. We do not respond initially by phone.

We publish new books twice a year, in January and July. Submissions are usually reviewed approximately six months prior to publishing deadlines.

As an aside, we do not hire freelance readers/editors.

Thank you, and Good Luck!

Categories: African-American—Cartoons—Christian Interests—College—Comedy—Education—Entertainment—Family—General Interest—Humor—Inspirational—Lifestyle—Marriage—Parenting—Regional—Relationships—Romance—Senior Citizen—Spiritual—Women's Issues—Ethnic

CONTACT: Ringo Suek, Editor
Material: All
8102 Lemont Road, #300
Woodridge IL 60517
Phone: 630-390 3580
Fax: 630-390 3585
E-mail: greatquotations@yahoo.com

Green Nature Books

Our guidelines are simple!

1. Inquire first with small sample;

2. We want specialty "how-to" grow and breed exotics–written by experts; and

4. Writers who promote themselves increase their royalty checks.

Categories: Nonfiction—Agriculture—Animals—Conservation—Crafts/Hobbies—Ecology—Environment—History—Hobbies—Inspirational—Photography—Science—Travel

CONTACT: Submissions Editor
Material: All
PO Box 105
Sumterville FL 33585
Phone: 352-793-5496
Fax: 352-793-6075
Website: www.greennaturebooks.com

> *Remember: Editors change jobs and publishers change addresses. It is wise to invest in a phone call for the current information before submitting.*

Gryphon Books

Small press publishing is a labor of love but it is also fraught with risk and very expensive. Therefore we must be selective in the work we choose for magazines or imprints of Gryphon Books. We receive dozens of stories and proposals each week, many are fine and quite publishable, however most are not compatible with our present publishing program. Please keep in mind that the rejection of a work can be for many reasons but is never intended to be a rejection of you as an author or of your talent.

What are we looking for? Quality material that will interest our readers.

The specifics are listed individually by publication below. Publishing today means a small outfit such as Gryphon Books must be very selective. That aside, if your work shows promise or is something that we think our readers will like, we'll work with you. We often comment on short stories that are sent for *Hardboiled* and have worked with writers to make their story publishable. In other cases, while we've rejected some stories, authors have told us that our comments allowed them to fix the story and send it to another market where it was published. We're very proud of any help we are able to give newer writers, especially when it results in that author being published.

A few things to remember before submitting any work to Gryphon Books:

- Absolutely NO submissions through email. Only hard copies to the PO Box address below will be considered. All email submissions or queries will be deleted unopened.
- We can NOT consider any work by anyone incarcerated in any prison facility. Manuscripts will be returned to sender unopened.
- We have a one-a-month rule: because of time constraints and ms volume, we can only look at one ms or query letter per month. So make it your best!
- NO multiple submissions. Only one story at a time (per envelope) and not more than one submission (envelope) per month. We don't want to open any more unsolicited envelopes with 10 or 20 stories in them. Or receive 10 separate envelopes with a story in each. That's not professional. You'll just be wasting time and postage as these will be returned unread.
- NO reprints, unless we request it. However, you may query about a reprint.
- We will look at simultaneous submissions, BUT they must be so labeled.
- Always remember to send in your ms in the standard format, which MUST be double-spaced, also don't put it in a binder or folder.

Below is a general overview of what we are interested in for Gryphon Books.

Novels: Right now we are NOT actively looking at any novels from agents or any unsolicited manuscripts for any genres of fiction. DO NOT send any complete ms or chapters. However, if you want to take a chance and run a query idea by us we will look at a short one-page query letter, and if you want an answer you must enclose an SASE. The market is tough. We do mostly classic and pulp novels in various genres, not much contemporary material in the longer lengths.

Non-fiction: We are looking for finely written and detailed articles and book-length material on any aspect of books or book collecting, especially in the paperbacks, the pulps, hard-boiled crime fiction, authors, artists, or interviews with same; articles about science fiction, fantasy, horror, pulp-related books, bibliographic material, paperback book publishers. Your best bet is to query with a short ONE-PAGE letter about yourself and your work, and qualifications, if necessary. For shorter articles see *Paperback Parade*.

Paperback Parade: For this magazine we are looking for finely written and detailed non-fiction articles from 1,000 to 5,000 words (sometimes longer) on any aspect of paperbacks; including publishing, collecting, art, authors, runs of books, much more. We're open to different types of things but it is best to query first about your idea as many topics have been done in previous articles. This way we can better di-

Books A-L

rect you to our specific needs. It is also a good idea to send for a sample copy or subscribe to *Paperback Parade* (subscriptions are $35 for 4 issues; a sample is $10 + $2.00 Media postage), and it just might open up a whole new world for your writing career. Non-fiction is a large and lucrative field. It offers many avenues for publication. *Paperback Parade* is also an excellent venue to have your work and byline seen by our many author, publisher, and editor readers. We've been publishing this magazine since 1986 and we still feel we've only scratched the surface in what this field has to offer. Payment is in copies or other arrangement depending on length and quality of your article.

Longer Stories: The *Gryphon Doubles* series contains tow short novels or novellas (generally 15,000 to 30,000 words each) published back-to-back in the format of the classic Ace Doubles. They have two illustrated covers (one for each story) and sell for $12 each. Some of the authors who have appeared include: William F. Nolan, Mike Avalione, Jack Williamson, E. C. Tubb, Jesse Sublett, Richard S. Prather. We are extremely selective here and at present the series is on hiatus, but there are new books in the hopper yet to appear and they will soon. We are looking for unique genre fiction, it can have a pulp flavor; exciting, hard-hitting stories, in all genres, but especially hard-boiled crime and noir, science fiction, pulp reprints. Pays nominal advance. ONLY query letters with an SASE considered at this time.

Short Stories: We are always looking for original short crime stories for *Hardboiled* magazine. Keep it short, hard, intense and to the point. You should become a fan of the genre you want to write in and of the magazine. Become familiar with the type of story by subscribing. No Chandler clones or cliches unless you can put a new spin on an old idea. We want quality writing, great ideas and interesting characters, mixed with hard-hitting realism. Competition is tight. We can offer only a minimal payment but your work will be published alongside giants like Mickey Spillane (latest issue #31), or Andrew Vachss, Joe Lansdale, Richard S. Prather, Ed Gorman, Richard Lupoff, Edward Hoch, Lawrence Block, Vin Packer and many other classic and contemporary crime masters. Just make it your best story and keep it under 3,000 words (longer would have to be extraordinary; anything over 4,000 words query with SASE).

Support: Lastly, as writers we need to keep our markets alive and viable and that means supporting the publishers and magazines in our field. I fervently believe that everyone who wants to sell to *Hardboiled* should subscribe to *Hardboiled* ($35 brings you 4 hard-hitting issues). Or for non-fiction writers, you should subscribe to *Paperback Parade* ($35 for 4 issues). Of course, not subscribing in no way hinders your chances for consideration. For longer fiction check out books in the *Gryphon Doubles* series ($12 each + postage). Your support keeps your markets strong. That support will also give you the opportunity to read a lot of great crime fiction or non-fiction, better than the boring newsstand magazines. You'll also get an excellent idea of the type of fiction we're looking for in the pages of *Hardboiled* and the articles we want for *Paperback Parade*. So support the magazines you want to write for with a subscription, support the publishers you want to publish your book, *by buying one of our books*. The publishing world is very competitive and you need to make your voice heard. Small publishers need your support so there will be more venues for the work *you* write, and the work we all want to read.

Submissions and Subscriptions: All story or query submissions should be sent as hard copy only (NO disks, CDs, emails) with an SASE if your want a response. International ms must use 2 IRCs. All book orders or subscriptions to *Hardboiled* or *Paperback Parade* should be sent to this address only. Send to: Gryphon Books, PO Box 209, Brooklyn, NY 11228-0209, USA.

Final Advice: What do you think is the most important quality that a writer must have? That's a tough one. Could it be great dialog? Excellent plotting? A talent for fine characterization? Friends in high places? That's all well and good but the most important quality really is *professionalism*. Remember that in all your dealings with publishers and editors, even if they may not always be professional themselves. Sometimes especially if they're not professional. You will al-

ways need to be professional in all your actions and dealings. You never know when a submission will be accepted down the line or what can come of a small seed planted months or even years before. *Now get writing!*

Categories: Fiction—Nonfiction—Book Reviews—Crime, Interviews—Fantasy—Horror—Pulp—Science Fiction—Short Stories

CONTACT: Submissions Editor
Material: All
PO Box 209
Brooklyn, NY 11228-0209

Gryphon House, Inc.

We're Always Looking for New Book Ideas!

If you have an idea for a book, we'd like to hear about it. At Gryphon House, our goal is to publish books that help teachers and parents enrich the lives of children from birth through age eight. We strive to make our books useful for teachers at all levels of experience, as well as for parents, caregivers, and anyone interested in working with children. The staff at Gryphon House cares deeply about children and about teaching them appropriately and positively. We also believe that spending time with children is a valuable and fun thing to do. Our books reflect these beliefs.

We look for books that are developmentally appropriate for the intended age group, are well researched and based on current trends in the field, and include creative, participatory learning experiences with a common conceptual theme to tie them together. Our books are essential tools for teachers. As such, the books should be ones that teachers will want to use every day. Books that cater to a particular market beyond teachers are also appealing.

We are not interested in books of paper and pencil activities, or activities that involve cutting out patterns and pasting them on paper, or ditto books, or books about computers (or worse, television) and young children. We do not publish children's books at all.

Things to Consider Before Submitting a Proposal
Competition

Find and review books similar to yours. You can find books in the library, in a book called *Books In Print*, retail bookstores, and teacher and school supply stores. Familiarize yourself with the books on your topic and then tell us how your book is different.

Market

Is there a need for another book on your topic? What makes your book unique? Is this a book that teachers will want to use every day?
Other Important Issues

Who has reviewed or tested your book? Have you led classes or workshops on the topic? What is your background? Have you published other books, articles, or other materials? If so, please tell us. How will you be able to promote your book? Can you conduct workshops at professional meetings, or do demonstrations at bookstores? Include this information in your letter of inquiry, outlined below.

Submitting a Proposal

We prefer to receive a letter of inquiry and/or a proposal, rather than the entire manuscript. That means you don't have to wait until you've completed your book to send it to us. *Your proposal should include:*

• The proposed title

- The purpose of the book
- Table of contents
- Introductory material
- 20-40 sample pages of the actual book

In addition, please describe the book, including the intended audience, why teachers will want to buy it, how it is different from other similar books already published, and what qualifications you possess that make you the appropriate person to write the book. If you have a writing sample that demonstrates that you write clear, compelling prose, please include it with your letter.

Categories: Nonfiction—Education—New Age—Paranormal—Parenting

CONTACT: Acquisitions
Material: All
PO Box 207
Beltsville MD 20704
Phone: 301-595-9500
Fax: 301-595-0051
E-mail: info@ghbooks.com
Website: www.gryphonhouse.com

Gürze Books

Dear Author,

Thank you for your interest in Gürze Books. We are a small company which publishes between 2-3 trade paperback books per year on eating disorders and related issues, including body image, size-acceptance, and self esteem. At this time, we do not publish personal stories, fiction, or poetry. Our books are sold through bookstores, our website (www.bulimia.com) and eating disorder resource catalogue, as well as other specialty markets. We have been in business since 1976.

In order to consider publishing your book, we need the following:
- Cover letter including the title.
- Table of Contents
- Provide an outline of your book, with optional 1-2 paragraph summaries of each chapter.
- The Concept Statement: In 150 words or less, explain what is unique about your book and how the reader will benefit from reading it.
- About the Author: Detail your qualifications to write the book.
- About the Market, the Competition, and Promotion: Describe your targeted reader, your market and how to reach them. Summarize the competition. Outline a plan for promoting your book.
- Sample Chapters: Send two edited chapters that best showcase the contribution your book offers to make in our field.

Please note: Allow for 1-2 months for us to get back to you. If you would like your manuscript returned, please send adequate postage.

Categories: Nonfiction—Food/Drink—Health—Self Help

CONTACT: Lindsey Hall/Cohn
Material: Manuscripts
5145-B Avenida Encinas
Carlsbad CA 92008
Phone: 760-434-7533
E-mail: gurze@aol.com
Website: www.bulimia.com

Hachai Publishing

Subject: Children Jewish Interests Religion.

Hachai Publishing welcomes unsolicited manuscripts. Children's books for the very young (2-4) and slightly older children (3-6) are our specialty.

We are looking for stories that convey:
- The traditional Jewish experience in modern times or long ago.
- Traditional Jewish observance such as Holidays and year-round mitzvos such as mezuzah, tzitzis, honoring parents etc.
- Positive character traits (middos) such as honesty, charity, respect, sharing etc.

We are also interested in:
- Biographies of spiritually great men and women in Jewish history.
- Historical fiction adventure novels for beginning readers (ages 7-10) that highlight devotion to faith and the relevance of Torah in making important choices.

Please, no fantasy, animal stories, romance, violence, preachy sermonizing.

We do not produce games, textbooks, workbooks, or books for adults.

All submissions must be typed or neatly printed, double spaced on opaque white paper - one side only.

Please include your name, address and phone number on title page of your manuscript.

You must include a self addressed stamped envelope (SASE). We will not respond to or return manuscripts sent without a SASE.

We are always looking for new artists with skill in children's book illustration. Please do not send original art. Color photocopies and tear sheets are best. Make sure your samples include a human character. SASE necessary for any response.

Categories: Nonfiction—Children—Jewish Interest—Religion—Spiritual

CONTACT: Submissions Editor
Material: All
156 Chester Ave.
Brooklyn NY 11218
E-mail: yossi@hachai.com
Website: www.hachai.com

Hampton Roads Publishing

Please send a proposal only (a synopsis, a chapter-by-chapter outline and one or two sample chapters), not a full manuscript. Please, typed or computer-printed only; we cannot and will not read handwritten manuscripts, faxed, disk, web-based or e-mail submissions. Enclose SASE with sufficient first class postage if you wish to have your submission returned. (Note that prepaid postage strips from your post office are only good for that location; our post office will not accept them for outgoing mail.) If you do not enclose postage, we will recycle your proposal after we consider it.

At the moment we are not accepting submissions for our Young Spirit Line for children.

We welcome artwork submissions, but send a small sample of your work, and please send copies, not originals.

Your cover letter should contain your complete contact information (including phone number, address, and email).

Finally, be aware that we and all publishers have an enormous number of proposals to read and that it is not unusual for the process to take many months. Your patience is appreciated

Categories: Fiction—Nonfiction—Health—Inspirational—New Age—Occult—Paranormal—Psychology—Self Help—Spiritual

CONTACT: Frank DeMarco, Chief Editor
Material: All
1125 Stoney Ridge Rd.
Charlottesville, VA 22902
Phone: 434-296-2772
Website: www.hrpub.com

Hancock House

Hancock House requires the following for reviewing prospective manuscripts:

- A brief (one or two page) synopsis of the proposed manuscript.
- An account of any miscellaneous support information, such as the writer's expertise, or any marketing advantage inherent to the manuscript.
- A sample of the writer's work, such as a chapter from the work in question.
- Enclose your phone number as well as address.

Hancock House Titles

Our titles are predominantly as follows: Pacific Northwest history and biography, nature guides, and native culture; and international natural history, biological science, and conservation biology including aviculture and animal husbandry.

Manuscript Format

We require both a computer disc, DOS format, and a hard copy.

Categories: Nonfiction—Animals—Aviation—Biography—Conservation—Outdoors—Birds—Pacific Northwest

CONTACT: Editor
Material: All
1431 Harrison Ave.
Blaine WA 98230
Phone: 604-538-1114
Fax: 604-538-2262
E-mail: hancock@uniserve.com
Website: hancockhouse.com

Hannover House

Hannover House is a multimedia company with operating activities in both the publishing and film industries. As a publisher of books, Hannover releases about six titles per year. As a distributor of feature films and videos, the Company releases about ten titles per year, to theaters, video outlets and television broadcasters. The Company is currently seeking submissions of quality manuscripts, and prefers fiction or nonfiction works that may lend themselves to production as motion pictures.

Editorial inquiries should be to the Fayetteville, Arkansas office. Please do not send fax or e-mail submissions.

Categories: Fiction—Nonfiction—Entertainment—Film/Video

CONTACT: Samantha Nichols, Director of Editorial
Material: All
1722 N. College Ave., # C-303
Fayetteville AR 72703
Phone: 479-587-0857
Website: www.HannoverHouse.com

Harbor Press

Harbor Press publishes nonfiction books only. We are best known for our self-help and health titles, especially in the area of holistic health and healing, but we have recently begun branching out into other areas of interest in non-fiction. Recent publications include *Yes, Your Teen Is Crazy!–Loving Your Kid Without Losing Your Mind* by Michael J. Bradley, Ed.D., and *Healing Back Pain Naturally* by Art Brownstein, M.D.

We consider only titles which are, in our opinion, highly promotable, written by an appropriately credentialed author, and likely to appeal to a mass audience. If your nonfiction project meets these criteria, we welcome your submission. *Please include the following:*

I. Query letter
   A. Subject
   B. Audience
   C. Need/purpose
   D. Unique approach
   E. Qualifications for writing
II. Book proposal
   A. Title page
   B. Your contact information
   C. Overview
   D. Author background
   E. Competition section–What else is out there?
   F. Marketing analysis–Who will buy your book?
   G. Promotions section–What will you do to help market your book?
   H. Table of contents
   I. Two sample chapters

For detailed information on how to write a successful query and proposal, please consult any number of good books on writing proposals for non-fiction literature, such as *Write the Perfect Book Proposal: 10 Proposals That Sold and Why* by Jeff Herman and Deborah M. Adams (John Wiley & Sons, Inc. $15.95), or *The Fast-Track Course on How to Write a Nonfiction Book Proposal* by Stephen Blake Mettee (Word Dancer Press, $12.95).

We are also interested in hearing from professional, versatile, published writers who are interested in freelance writing and ghostwriting assignments. Please send a résumé and samples of your work.

Please address submissions to Debby Young at the address below. We review and consider all submissions that we receive. You will hear from us only if we find that your project is a good fit for us. Otherwise, we are unable to respond to submissions and to follow-up inquiries, so please do not call, write, or e-mail. We will be able to return your book proposal only if it is accompanied by a stamped, self-addressed envelope.

We are able to publish only a small percentage of the book projects submitted to us, so please keep in mind, if we do not respond to your submission, it is because it does not fit our objectives and requirement at that particular time. It does not mean that your project is without merit, or that it cannot be sold to another publisher.

Thank you for your interest in Harbor Press. We wish you well!

Categories: Nonfiction—Health—Inspirational—New Age—Parenting—Psychology—Relationships—Self Help—Spiritual—Teen—Young Adult

CONTACT: Debby Young, Acquisitions Editor
Material: All
5 Glen Drive
Plainview NY 11803
Phone: 253-851-5190
Fax: 253-851-5191
Website: harborpress.com

HARLEQUIN®

Harlequin

Imprints of Harlequin
Harlequin American Romance
Harlequin Blaze
Harlequin Flipside
Harlequin Historicals
Harlequin Intrigue
Harlequin Presents (Mills & Boon Modern Romance)
Harlequin Romance (Mills & Boon Tender Romance)
Harlequin Superromance
Harlequin Temptation
Mills & Boon Historical Romance

Mills & Boon Medical Romance
Silhouette Desire
Silhouette Intimate Moments
Silhouette Romance
Silhouette Special Edition
Steeple Hill Women's Fiction
Love Inspired
MIRA
Red Dress Ink
HQN Books
Luna
Silhouette Bombshell

Please find below the editorial guidelines for Mills & Boon, Harlequin, Silhouette, MIRA, Steeple Hill and Red Dress Ink books. These pages are designed to be a guide, not a substitute for extensive reading. There is no formula for writing a publishable romance or mainstream women's fiction novel. The editors for each of the series have written guidelines that reflect their requirements. As a result, each set of guidelines "reads" differently as some are more specific than others, depending on the degree of focus the editors would like submissions to have.

What are some other things you can do to help sell your manuscript? First, we expect you to enjoy reading romance fiction. If you are already a fan, your appreciation for this type of book will be apparent in the writing. If you have not done so already, we encourage you to read many, many books from each series. The series that emerges as your favorite is probably where you should submit your manuscript.

Second, remember reading is an emotional experience. We hope you will write from the heart and we will feel touched by what you have to say. When you put pen to paper (or finger to keyboard), do so because you have something to share with other readers.

You will also find answers to some frequently asked questions. Should you require further information don't hesitate to write to us. The appropriate addresses have been included following the submission instructions for your convenience. Good luck!

Harlequin American Romance
Length: 70,000-75,000 words
Executive Editor: Paula Eykelhof
Editorial Office: Toronto

Upbeat and lively, fast-paced and well plotted, American Romance celebrates the pursuit of love in the backyards, big cities and wide-open spaces of America. These all-American stories have a range of emotional and sensual content and are supported by a colorful secondary cast, creating a sense of community within the plot's framework. In the confident and caring heroine, the tough but tender hero and their dynamic relationship that is at the center of this series, showcasing real-life love as the best fantasy of all!

Harlequin Blaze
Length: 70,000-75,000 words
Executive Editor: Birgit Davis-Todd
Editorial Office: Toronto

Harlequin Blaze is an exciting new series that has evolved out of the very successful Temptation line. It will showcase the very best writers and stars from the original Blaze program. It is also a vehicle to build and promote new authors who have a strong sexual edge to their stories. Finally, it is *the* place to be for seasoned authors who want to create a sexy, sizzling, longer contemporary story.

Blaze will feature sensuous, highly romantic, innovative plots that are sexy in premise and execution. The tone of the books can run from fun and flirtatious to dark and sensual. Submissions should have a very contemporary feel—what it's like to be young and single in the new millennium. We are looking for heroes and heroines in their early 20s and up. There should be an emphasis on the physical relationship developing between the couple: fully described love scenes along with a high level of fantasy and playfulness. The hero and heroine should make a commitment at the end.

Are you a *Cosmo* girl at heart? A fan of *Sex and the City, Ally McBeal* or *Friends*? Or maybe you just have an adventurous spirit. If so, then Blaze is the series for you! New authors should send a query and/or submit chapters and a synopsis. Agented and unagented submissions are welcome.

Harlequin Flipside
Length: 50,000-55,000 words
Editor: Wanda Ottewell
Editorial Office: Toronto

Harlequin Flipside are a delightful combination of romance and comedy. Fast-paced and plot driven, these novels depend upon the comedy building from the relationship between the hero and heroine. We are looking for a comic premise, a strong humorous voice and a great romance. A high degree of sexual tension is a must and while we encourage love scenes, they are not a requirement. So whether your story is a screwball comedy, a comedy of errors or simply the lighter side of love, we are looking for entertaining romance that would bring a smile to the face of every reader.

Harlequin Historicals
Length: 95,000-105,000 words
Editor: Ann Leslie Tuttle
Editorial Office: New York

The primary element of a Harlequin Historicals novel is romance. The story should focus on the heroine and how her love for one man changes her life forever. For this reason it is very important that you have an appealing and believable hero and heroine, and that their relationship if a compelling one. The conflicts they must overcome and the situations they face can be as varied as the setting you have chosen; but there must be romantic tension, some spark between your hero and heroine that keeps your reader interested.

We will not accept books set after 1950. We're looking primarily for books set in North America, England or France between 1100 and 1950 AD. We do not buy many novels set during the American Civil War. We are, however, flexible, and will consider most periods and settings. We are not looking for gothics or family sagas, nor are we interested in the kind of comedy of manners typified by straight Regencies. Historical romances set during the Regency period, however, will definitely be considered.

Harlequin Intrigue
Length: 70,000-75,000 words
Senior Editor: Denise O'Sullivan
Editorial Office: New York

Taut, edge-of-the-seat contemporary romantic suspense tales of intrigue and desire. Kidnappings, stalkings, women in jeopardy coupled with best-selling romantic themes are examples of story lines we love most. Whether a murder mystery, psychological suspense or thriller, the love story must be inextricably bound to the resolution where all loose ends are tied up neatly…and shared dangers lead right to shared passions. As long as they're in jeopardy and falling in love, our heroes and heroines may traverse a landscape as wide as the world itself. Their lives are on the line…and so are their hearts!

Harlequin Presents
(Mills & Boon Modern Romance)
Length: 50,000-55,000 words
Senior Editor: Tessa Shapcott
Editorial Office: London

Pick up a Harlequin Presents novel and you enter a world full of spine-tingling passion and provocative, tantalizing romantic excitement! Although grounded in reality, these stories offer compelling modern fantasies to readers all around the world, and there is scope within this line to develop relevant, contemporary issues, which touch the lives of today's women. Each novel is written in the third person and features spirited, independent heroines who aren't afraid to take the initiative, and breathtakingly attractive, larger-than-life heroes. The conflict between these characters should be lively and evenly matched, but always balanced by a developing romance that may include explicit

Books A-L

lovemaking. Harlequin Presents novels capture the drama and intensity of a powerful, sensual love affair.

Harlequin Romance

(Mills & Boon Tender Romance)
Length: 50,000-55,000 words
Associate Senior Editor: Bryony Green
Editorial Office: London

Written in third person, from the heroine's point of view, each book should focus almost exclusively on the developing relationship between the main protagonists. The emphasis should be on warm and tender emotions, with no sexual explicitness; lovemaking should only take place when the emotional commitment between the characters justifies it. These heartwarming stories must be written with freshness and sincerity, featuring spirited, engaging heroines portrayed with depth and affection—as well as heroes who are charismatic enough to fulfill every woman's dreams! Readers should be thrilled by the tenderness of their developing relationship, and gripped by romantic suspense as the couple strives to overcome the emotional barriers between them and find true happiness in the romance of a lifetime!

Harlequin Superromance

Length: 85,000 words
Senior Editor: Laura Shin
Editorial Office: Toronto

The aim of a Superromance novel is to produce a contemporary, involving read with a mainstream lore in its situations and characters, using romance as the major theme. To achieve this, emphasis should be placed on individual writing styles and unique and topical ideas.

The criteria for Superromance books are flexible. Aside from length, the determining factor for publication will always be quality. Authors should strive to break free of stereotypes, clichés and worn plot devices to create strong believable stories with depth and emotional intensity. Superromance novels are intended to appeal to a wide range of romance readers.

A general familiarity with current Superromance books is advisable to keep abreast of ever-changing trends and overall scope. But we don't want imitations and we are open to innovation. We look for sincere, heartfelt writing based on true-to-life experiences and fantasies the reader can identify with.

Harlequin Temptation

Length: 60,000 words
Associate Senior Editor: Brenda Chin
Editorial Office: Toronto

Temptation is sexy, sassy and seductive! This is Harlequin's boldest, most sensuous series, focusing on men and women living—and—loving-today! Almost anything goes in Temptation; the stories may be humorous, topical, adventurous or glitzy, but at heart, they are pure romantic fantasy. Think fast-paced, use the desires and language of women today, add a high level of sexual tension, along with strong conflicts and then throw in a good dash of "what if..." The results should sizzle!

Mills & Boon Historical Romance

Length: 75,000-85,000 words
Senior Editor: Linda Fildew
Editorial Office: London

This series covers a wide range of British and European historical periods from 1066 to approximately the Second World War. The romance should take priority, with all the emotional impact of a growing love, and should be developed over a relatively short space of time. The historical detail should be accurate, without sounding like a textbook, and should help to create a true sense of the chosen setting, so that the reader becomes immersed in that time. A query letter with a synopsis and first three chapters are advised.

Mills & Boon Medical Romance

Length: 50,000-55,000 words
Senior Editor: Sheila Hodgson
Editorial Office: London

These are present day romances in a medical setting. There should be a good balance between the romance, the medicine and the underlying story. At least one of the main characters should be a medical professional, and developing the romance is easier if the hero and heroine work together. Medical detail should be accurate but preferably without using technical language. An exploration of patients and their illnesses is permitted, but not in such numbers as to overwhelm the growing love story. Settings can be anywhere in the world. More detailed guidelines are available on request with a stamped, addressed envelope.

Silhouette Desire

Length: 55,000-60,000 words
Senior Editor: Melissa Jeglinski
Editorial Office: New York

Sensual, believable, compelling, these books are written for today's woman. Innocent or experienced, the heroine is someone we identify with; the hero is irresistible. The conflict should be an emotional one, springing naturally from the unique characters you've chosen. The focus is on the developing relationship, set in a believable plot. Sensuality is key, but lovemaking is never taken lightly. Secondary characters and subplots need to blend with the core story. Innovative new directions in storytelling and fresh approaches to classic romantic plots are welcome.

Silhouette Intimate Moments

Length: 80,000 words
Executive Editor: Leslie Wainger
Editorial Office: New York

Believable characters swept into a world of larger-than-life romance are the hallmark of Silhouette Intimate Moments books. These books offer you the freedom to combine the universally appealing elements of a category romance with the flash and excitement of mainstream fiction. Adventure, suspense, melodrama, glamour—let your imagination be your guide as you blend old and new to create a novel with emotional depth and tantalizing complexity. The novels explore new directions in romantic fiction, or mine classic plots in contemporary ways, always with the goal of tempting today's demanding reader.

Silhouette Romance

Length: 53,000-58,000 words
Associate Senior Editor: Mavis Allen
Editorial Office: New York

Silhouette Romance books require talented authors able to portray modern relationships in the context of romantic love. Although the hero and heroine don't actually make love unless married, sexual tension is vitally important. Writers are encouraged to try creative new approaches to classic romantic and contemporary fairy-tale plots. Our ultimate goal is to give readers vibrant love stories with heightened emotional impact—books that touch readers' hearts and celebrate their values, including the traditional ideals of love, marriage and family.

Silhouette Special Edition

Length: 75,000-80,000 words
Senior Editor: Gail Chasan
Editorial Office: New York

Sophisticated, substantial and packed with emotion, Special Edition demands writers eager to probe characters deeply, to explore issues that heighten the drama of living and loving, to create compelling romantic plots. Whether the sensuality is sizzling or subtle, whether the plot is wildly innovative or satisfyingly traditional, the novel's emotional vividness, its depth and dimension, should clearly label it a very special contemporary romance. Subplots are welcome, but must further or parallel the developing romantic relationship in a meaningful way.

Steeple Hill

Women's Fiction

Length: 80,000-125,000 words
Senior Editor: Joan Marlow Golan
Editorial Office: New York

This new Steeple Hill program will be dedicated to publishing inspirational Christian women's fiction that depicts the struggles the characters encounter as they learn important lessons about trust and the power of faith.

We are looking for compelling and thoughtfully developed stories that promote strong family values and high moral standards. These complex stories are character driven. They should provide readers with an uplifting and satisfying ending, and they can be written in the first or third-person narrative and can be single or multiple point of view.

The program is open to a variety of genres, ranging from contemporary women's fiction (family dramas, romance, suspense, romantic suspense) to historicals and thrillers. There should be no explicit sex in these stories, and a minimum of sensuality and sexual desire. And unless it is part of the struggle the protagonists face, there should be no premarital sex or graphic violence.

Although the faith element is central to these stories, the degree of religiousness can vary. We would prefer that specific Christian denominations not be named unless the story requires it, e.g., we prefer "Good Shepherd Christian Church" to "Good Shepherd Baptist (or Presbyterian, Methodist, etc.) Church."

Love Inspired

Length: 70,000-75,000 words
Senior Editor: Joan Marlow Golan
Editorial Office: New York

The Love Inspired line is a series of contemporary, inspirational romances that feature Christian characters facing the many challenges of life and love in today's world.

Each story should have an emotional, satisfying and mature romance; however, the characters should not make love unless they are married. These are "sweet" romances. Any physical interactions (i.e. kissing, hugging) should emphasize emotional tenderness rather than sexual desire.

Drama, humor, and even a touch of mystery all have a place in the series. Foul language, swearing and scenes containing violent content do not. Any subplots should come directly from the main story. Secondary characters (children, family, friends, neighbors, fellow church members, etc.) can also help contribute to a substantial and gratifying story.

Although an element of faith should be present in the books, it should be well integrated into the plot. And the conflict between the main characters should be an emotional one, arising naturally from the characters you've created.

Manuscript length is 70,000 to 75,000 words. The word count we are looking for is an approximate one which you can get by multiplying (the average number of words in a full line) x (the number of lines on a full page) x (the number of pages). Please don't go by the exact word count from your computer because it doesn't count the spaces in time breaks, conversation or chapter and time breaks.

MIRA

Length: 100,000-150,000 words
Senior Editor: Amy Moore-Benson
Editorial Office: Toronto

MIRA Books is proud to publish outstanding mainstream fiction for readers around the world.

As a result of the broad range of fiction published under the MIRA imprint, there are no tip sheets. MIRA publishes mainstream contemporary and historical romance, romantic suspense, thrillers, family sagas and relationship novels.

We recommend that you familiarize yourself with the wide range of books published by MIRA. Our authors include Mary Lynn Baxter, Rebecca Brandewyne, Stella Cameron, Candace Camp, Diane Chamberlain, Jasmine Cresswell, Margot Dalton, Karen Harper, Christiane Heggan, Penny Jordan, R. J. Kaiser, Debbie Macomber, Curtis Ann Matlock, Carla Neggers, Diana Palmer, Emilie Richards, Rosemary Rogers, Nan Ryan, Sharon Sala, Taylor Smith, Erica Spindler, Anne Stuart, Laura Van Wormer and Susan Wiggs.

Agented submissions only.

Red Dress Ink

Length: 90,000-110,000 words
Senior Editor: Margaret Marbury
Editorial Office: New York
We're looking for a few good women…

Women who are ready to start a new chapter in their lives by writing strong, sassy Red Dress Ink books.

Red Dress Ink books are about City Girls—urban women twenty-something and up who are discovering themselves, sharing apartments, meeting men, struggling with jobs. These books are pragmatic, relevant and have a unique tone: they show life as it is, but with a strong touch of humor, hipness and energy. Red Dress Ink books are about how single urban females *really are.* We see life in all its messy details—meddling moms, rivalries at work, unfaithful boyfriends. But driving the story is the heroine's development into a strong woman, supported by close friends. And if she finds love along the way, what a bonus! The style of writing is light, highly accessible, clever, funny and full of witty observations. The dialogue is sharp and true-to-life. These are characters you can immediately identify with in a story you just can't put down!

These books are *Ally McBeal* meets *Sex and the City, Bridget Jones's Diary* meets *The Girls' Guide to Hunting and Fishing.*

HQN Books

Length: 100,000-150,000 words
Executive Editor: Tracy Farrell
Editorial Office: New York

HQN Books is proud to publish outstanding romance fiction for readers around the world.

Debuting August 1, 2004, the new imprint will publish a broad range of romantic fiction. Because HQN Books is a mainstream imprint, there are no tip sheets.

While actual HQN Books titles will not be available until August 2004, perspective authors can familiarize themselves with the wide range of books we will be publishing by reading other books by the authors who will be writing for the imprint. These authors include Carly Phillips, Diana Palmer, Kasey Michaels, Beverly Barton, Gayle Wilson, Geralyn Dawson, Margaret Moore, Candace Mann and Rita Herron, among others.

The imprint is looking for a wide range of authors from know romance stars to first time authors. Both agented and slush submissions are welcome. Please send your projects to our New York Editorial Office.

LUNA

Length: 100,000-150,000 words
Executive Editor: Mary-Theresa Hussey
Editorial Office: New York
Editor: Kate Paice
Editorial Office: London
Powerful, alluring, mythic, elemental—magical.

Luna Books delivers a compelling, female-focused fantasy with vivid characters, rich worlds, strong, sympathetic women and romantic subplots.

Luna Books wants emotionally complex, sweeping stories that highlight the inner female power. Whether the heroine is on a quest to save the world—or someone or something important to her—discover her past or develop her own abilities, these stories are involving, gripping and sweep the reader away into a detailed, convincing world. They also contain romantic subplots that enhance the main story, but don't become the focus of the novel. They can be set in alternate historical worlds containing magic, a fantasy world or a contemporary location. Point of view can vary, but should be predominantly female. Read authors such as Mercedes Lackey, Catherine Asaro, Sarah Zettel, Barbara Hambly and Tanith Lee.

Silhouette Bombshell

Length: 80,000-90,000 words
Associate Senior Editor: Lynda Curnyn
Editorial Office: New York

Books
A-L

Each Silhouette Bombshell book is a fast-paced action adventure story featuring a heroine often in high-stakes situations. It is the heroine's ability to get out of that situation that drives the plot and ultimately provides the thrilling and unpredictable reading experience. Each book will also contain an exciting romance subplot. Though not every book needs to end in marriage, in every book there should be a commitment at the story's end to take the relationship to the next level, whether that be a first kiss or a new emotional and/or sensual awareness between the couple. First and third points of view are acceptable, however the story should be mostly from the heroine's point of view. Settings can be urban, rural, international. Time period is contemporary but we will also consider futuristic stories.

How to Prepare Your Submission to Harlequin, Silhouette, MIRA

Unless otherwise noted, we do not accept unsolicited complete or partial manuscripts, but ask instead that you submit a query letter. The query letter should include a word count and pertinent facts about yourself as a writer including your familiarity with the romance genre. Please indicate what series you think your project is appropriate for, if it is completed, what you think makes it special and previous publishing experience (if any). Also include a synopsis of your story that gives a clear idea of both your plot and characters and is no more than two single-spaced pages. A self-addressed envelope and return international postage coupons will ensure a reply. Should your manuscript be requested, please note the following information.

1. Harlequin, Silhouette, Mills & Boon and Steeple Hill publishes only category/series romance (and inspirational romance under Steeple Hill). Please do not submit any other type of fiction or non-fiction. Your manuscript should be told in the third person, primarily from the heroine's point of view. However, the hero's perspective may be used to enhance tension, plot or character development. Please see the guidelines for each series for details.

2. All material should be the author's own original work. Stories that contain scenes or plot lines that bear a striking resemblance to previously published work are in breach of copyright law and are not acceptable.

3. All material must be typewritten, double-spaced and on a reasonably heavy bond paper. No disk submissions. Computer-generated material is acceptable, but must be letter quality, and pages must be separated. Any material received on computer reams will be returned without evaluation.

4. Do not submit your material bound in binders, boxes or containers of any kind. Secure material by rubber bands. Cover sheets must have your complete name, address and phone number. Each page should be numbered sequentially thereafter. Please type your name and title in the upper left-hand corner of each page. If we ask to see your manuscript, please include a complete synopsis. Enclose a self-addressed, stamped postcard if you require acknowledgment of receipt.

5. All material will be evaluated in as timely a fashion as volume allows. Please do not call regarding the status of your manuscript. You will be notified by mail as soon as your work has been reviewed.

6. Do no send any material that is being considered by another publisher. Multiple submissions are not acceptable. A literary agent is not required in order to submit.

7. You must enclose a stamped, self-addressed envelope with all material you send in. This will ensure the return of your material. Please send an envelope large enough to accommodate your work and adequate postage in the form of international postage coupons or an international money order, where appropriate.

8. This sheet is designed as a guide to aid you in understanding our requirements and standards. However, there is no better way to determine what we are looking for than reading our books.

9. We enter into discussions about payment only when a contract is offered. This information is confidential.

10. We take every reasonable care of manuscripts while they are with us and will return any which prove unsuitable (provided return postage is supplied), but we cannot take responsibility for the vagaries

of the post office, so please be sure to retain a photocopy of your manuscript against unfortunate losses.

Submitting to Mills & Boon

Mills & Boon prefer to receive partial submissions. These should include the first three chapters and synopsis of the rest of the story.

Submitting to MIRA

At this time, MIRA Books is only accepting agented submissions. Harlequin and Silhouette published authors should contact their editor is interested in submitting to MIRA.

Submitting to Red Dress Ink

Point of view: first person/third person, as well as multiple viewpoints, if needed.

Settings: urban locales in North America or well-known international settings such as London or Paris.

Tone: fun, up-to-the-minute, clever, appealing, realistic.

If you are a city girl at heart, please submit a detailed synopsis and three sample chapters or a complete manuscript.

EDITORIAL OFFICES

• Toronto
Harlequin Books/MIRA Books
225 Duncan Mill Road
Don Mills, Ontario
M3B 3K9
Canada

• New York
Silhouette/Harlequin Books/Steeple Hill Books/Red Dress Ink
Harlequin New York
233 Broadway, Suite 1001
New York, NY 10279

• London
Harlequin Mills & Boon Ltd.
Eton House, 18-24 Paradise Road
Richmond, Surrey, United Kingdom
TW9 1SR

Check bookstores and your library for information about writers' organizations and writing. For updated submission guidelines, information about writing and tips, visit www.eHarlequin.com.

Categories: Fiction—Romance

CONTACT: Submissions Editor
**Material: Submissions for Silhouette/Harlequin Books/
Steeple Hill Books (Send to New York address, listed above)**
CONTACT: Submissions Editor
**Material: Submissions for Harlequin Books/MIRA Books
(Send to the Toronto address, listed above)**
CONTACT: Submissions Editor
**Material: Submissions for Harlequin Mills & Boon Ltd
(Send to the London address, listed above)**
Website: www.eharlequin.com

Harvard Common Press

The Harvard Common Press is a small independent publisher of quality trade books. We specialize in cookbooks, parenting and childcare books, and the occasional health and beauty book, though our backlist includes career, business, and nature titles.

Authors interested in publishing with The Harvard Common Press are asked to submit the following:

• a chapter-by-chapter outline of the proposed book
• two complete sample chapters
• a résumé or brief personal history
• an evaluation of other books available on the subject

Submissions should be typed, double-spaced, on a standard typewriter, word processor, or computer, but please avoid dot-matrix printers. We will return submissions not suited for our list if a stamped, self-addressed envelope is provided.

Categories: Nonfiction—Beauty—Busines—Career—Cooking—Health—Nature—Parenting

CONTACT: Publisher
Material: All
The Harvard Common Press
535 Albany St.
Boston, MA 02118
Website: www.harvardcommonpress.com

Harvest House Publishers

Does not accept unsolicited submissions.

Hatherleigh Press

Hatherleigh Press is a small, independent publisher focusing on health, fitness and self-help titles, with a few other titles in general non-fiction. Submissions in the fields of health and fitness are welcome; however, most of the books we publish are written by trained doctors, trainers, psychologists, and other professionals, so please be sure to include a C.V. along with the manuscript.

Please use the following guidelines when submitting your proposal:
1. Cover letter
2. Complete table of contents
3. Chapter-by-chapter summary
4. One to three sample chapters
5. Author's C.V. and qualifications (especially important for health/fitness titles)
6. SASE

Please do not send complete manuscripts.

No memoirs or personal accounts, please.

Categories: Nonfiction—Health—Outdoors—Psychology—Recreation—Relationships—Self Help—Sports/Recreation

CONTACT: Submissions Editor
Material: All
5-22 46th Ave., Ste 200
Long Island City NY 11101-5215
Phone: 718-786-5338
Website: www.hatherleighpress.com

Hay House, Inc.

Hay House publishes hardcover and trade paperback originals, and trade paperback reprints. We average 40 titles a year. We receive approximately 2,000 submissions/year. 5 percent of published books are from first-time authors. Agented submissions only. Free book cataglog. SASE required for return material from agents. No response of any kind without an SASE.

NONFICTION: Self-help, New Age, Sociology, Philosophy, Psychology, Health, Men's/Women's Issues. Subjects include social issues, current events, ecology, business, food and nutrition, education, the environment, alternative health/medicine, money/finance, nature, recreation, religion, and men's/women's issues/studies. We also publish gift books in the above subject areas.

BEST SELLING NONFICTION TITLES: *You Can Heal Your Life*, by Louise L. Hay; *The Western Guide to Feng Shui*, by Terah Kathryn Collins; *Adventures of a Psychic*, by Sylvia Browne; *Menopause Made Easy*, by Dr. Carolle Jean-Murat; *The Prodigal Father*, by Jon Du Pre; *Yoga Pure and Simple*, by Kisen.

TIPS: Our audience is concerned with our planet, the healing properties of love, and self-help principles. Hay House has noticed that our readers are interested in taking more control of their lives. If I were a writer trying to market a book today, I would research the market thoroughly to make sure that there weren't already too many books on the subject I was interested in writing about. Then I would make sure that I had a unique slant on my idea.

Categories: Nonfiction—Cooking—Diet/Nutrition—Environment—Feminism—General Interest—Health—Inspirational—Marriage—Men's Issues—New Age—Psychology—Relationships—Self Help—Spiritual—Women's Issues—Astrology—Philosophy

CONTACT: Shannon Littrell, Editor
Material: All
PO Box 5100
Carlsbad CA 92018-5100
Phone: 760-431-7695 x127
Fax: 760-431-6948

Hazelden Publishing

If you have an idea, a proposal, or a manuscript that you would like Hazelden to publish, these author guidelines will help you get started.

About Hazelden

Hazelden publishes information that helps build recovery in the lives of individuals, families and communities affected by alcoholism, drug dependency and related diseases. Hazelden publications and services are intended to meet a full range of chemical health issues for alcoholics, drug addicts, families, counselors, educators, doctors, and other professionals. Hazelden publications support Twelve Step philosophy and a holistic approach that addresses the needs of the mind, body, and spirit.

What We Publish

Hazelden publishes content in several formats: print (books, pamphlets, workbooks, leaflets, curricula), multi-media (video, audio, electronic), and live trainings. Our publications are sold to bookstores, treatment programs, hospitals, schools, churches, correctional facilities, government and military agencies, mental health and counseling agencies, and private corporations' employee-related programs.

Hazelden editors look for innovative materials that address issues relevant to substance abuse, prevention, treatment, recovery, and chronic illness. Our publications address topics related to chemical dependency, family and relationship issues, spirituality, eating disorders, gambling, nicotine cessation, mental health, and historical information on the Twelve Step movement.

What We Don't Publish

Hazelden discourages submissions of poetry, fiction, personal stories, dissertations, and art.

How to Submit a Proposal

It is not necessary to send an entire manuscript. *A complete proposal should include information on the following:*

• Overview: What is the general content and objective of your work? What do you intend to accomplish?

• Audience: Who or, what type of organization, is most likely to purchase your work?

• Market: Who, or what type of organization, is most likely to purchase your work?

• Competition: What competing publications are on the market? How is your work different?

• Contents: Include with your proposal a table of contents, a detailed chapter outline, an introduction, and two or three sample chapters.

Books A-L

• Author information: Provide information on yourself and your qualifications, including previous writing or relevant experience, and previously published works.

All submissions must be typed double-spaced. Photocopies are acceptable. If you want your submission returned, please include a self-addressed envelope with correct postage. Otherwise, your submission will not be returned.

We encourage you to review our publication catalog for information on our current titles. You may request a catalog by calling our toll-free number: 1-800-328-0098.

Manuscript Evaluation

Once received, your proposal will be screened and either forwarded to an editor or immediately rejected. If it is not immediately rejected, a card will be sent to you to inform you it has been forwarded to an editor for review.

The review process may take up to twelve weeks, during which time an editor will evaluate your proposal based on editorial, marketing, and philosophical criteria. The purpose of such evaluation is to determine whether your proposal fits with our editorial mission, market niche, and product plans.

During this period, if conditions warrant, you might be asked to submit a complete manuscript for editorial review. As soon as a final decision has been made, you will be notified by mail or phone.

Literary Agencies

Having a literary agent represent your work is not necessary; however, our editors work with a wide network of agents.

Accepted Manuscripts

Authors are offered either a royalty contract or a work-for-hire agreement, according to the type of work and the market it serves. All manuscripts are subject to editing.

Thank you for your attention to these author guidelines.

Categories: Nonfiction—Counseling—Family—Philosophy—Relationships—Self Help—Spiritual

CONTACT: Editorial Department
Material: All
Hazelden Information and Education
PO Box 176
Center City MN 55012

Health Communications, Inc.

Dear Prospective Author:

Thank you for your interest in Health Communications, Inc. For over two decades, we have enhanced our readers' lives through top-quality books promoting recovery, personal growth, and the enrichment of mind, body and soul. In that time, we have become one of the nation's leading life-issues publishers.

Seven of our over 30 national bestsellers have appeared on the New York Times bestsellers list: *Healing the Shame That Binds You* by John Bradshaw; *Adult Children of Alcoholics* by Janet G. Woititz; and five books in the Chicken Soup for the Soul series by Jack Canfield and Mark Victor Hansen—*Chicken Soup for the Soul, A 2nd Helping of Chicken So up for the Soul, A 3rd Serving of Chicken Soup for the Soul, Chicken Soup for the Woman's Soul* (co-authored by Jennifer Read Hawthorne and Marci Shimoff) and *Chicken Soup for the Soul at Work* (co-authored by Maida Rogerson, Martin Rutte and Tim Clauss).

Although we have been a forerunner in recovery publishing, we have grown in new directions. Today, recovery/addiction is only one of several categories that comprise our title base. In addition, we now publish in the following areas: self-help/psychology, health/wellness, soul/spirituality, inspiration, women's issues, relationships, and the family.

To continue our tradition of excellence in publishing, we seek high-caliber authors who produce original material that appeals to a broad readership. We are interested in nonfiction books that emphasize self-improvement, personal motivation, psychological health, overall wellness or mind/body/spirit integration. We do not publish biographies, autobiographies, poetry, children's books or fiction of any kind.

Most of our authors are established experts in their fields and, in some cases, already enjoy national recognition. Many of the authors we publish are professional speakers and consultants who conduct workshops, seminars, or training classes regionally or nationwide. Therefore, these authors are well prepared to promote their books successfully.

The publishing process at HCI begins with a book proposal, which is evaluated by our editorial department. To ensure that book proposals are evaluated on an equal basis and that all necessary information is provided, we require prospective authors to follow our submission guidelines in preparing their proposals. Material that does not conform to our guidelines is rejected.

SUBMISSION GUIDELINES

In order to consider publishing a book, we need a book proposal consisting of the elements outlined below. Do not send a complete manuscript unless asked to do so. All submissions are evaluated on the basis of content, author credentials and marketability. Submissions that do not conform to these guidelines are rejected.

I. AUTHOR INFORMATION

Send us your bio or curriculum vitae. Include information on professional credentials, current occupation, previously published works, any public speaking or promotional experience you have, and any television or radio appearances you have made.

II. MARKETING DATA

• Supply detailed information on the marketability of your book, including:
• Target Audience
• Who is it? How big is it? How do you know it exists?
• Competing Titles
• What other books on the same or a similar topic have already been published? How popular are they?
• Uniqueness Value
• What makes your book interesting and different from others already on the market? Why would readers choose your book over others currently available?
• Marketing Plan
• How do you intend to promote the book? What marketing channels can you propose? Do you have access to any special avenues for marketing the book?

III. MANUSCRIPT SAMPLE

Please send no more or less than the following:
A. Detailed outline of the book.
B. Table of contents.
C. Introduction.
D. Two sample chapters.

In preparing the manuscript sample, please observe our format requirements (these also apply if you are asked to send a complete manuscript):

• Spacing and Type Size: All text, tables and caption material must be double spaced. Use at least 12-point type.
• Chapter and Section Titles: All words in these titles should be upper- and lowercase.
• Spelling: Use the first spelling listed in the most recent edition of *Webster's New International Dictionary* or *Webster's Collegiate Dictionary.*
• Punctuation and Style: Do not use the serial comma. In running text, numbers below 10 should be spelled out; all others should be writ-

ten as numerals. Otherwise, refer to the most recent edition of *The Chicago Manual of Style.*

• Pagination (applies to complete manuscript only): Pages should be numbered continuously throughout a manuscript, not chapter by chapter.

IV. SASE

Due to new postal regulations, we can no longer use a SASE to return parcels weighing 16 ounces or more. Therefore, we no longer return any submissions weighing 16 ounces or over—even if a SASE is included. If your parcel weighs 16 ounces or more, neither your submission nor your SASE will be returned.

We are not responsible for submissions that exceed the returnable weight limit. Include a cover letter containing your name, return address and daytime phone number with your proposal. The cover letter is for our records and will not be returned to you. Send book proposals to the address below.

You should allow a minimum of six to eight weeks for a response. During periods when we receive a large number of submissions, response time can be two to three times longer. We consider all book proposals in the order received. We will notify you of our decision by mail. No phone calls, please. Calling to check the status of your submission will not expedite consideration of your proposal.

Categories: Nonfiction—Family—Health—Inspirational—Men's Issues—Psychology—Relationships—Spiritual—Women's Issues

CONTACT: Editorial Committee
Material: All
3201 SW 15th St.
Deerfield Beach FL 33442
Phone: 954-360-0909 x404
Fax: 954-360-0034

HEARTS & TUMMIES COOKBOOK COMPANY
-a Dinky Division of Quixote Press

Hearts 'N Tummies Cookbook Company

Regional cookbooks, fun cookbooks, cookbooks re specific geographic areas or historical periods, special interest cookbooks, offbeat cookbooks and cookbooks particularly suitable for sale at farmers' markets and tourist traps.

Vary in size from 120 to 500 recipes.

We would want the product, in final form, to be camera-ready...illustrated, clip art okay.

Categories: Children—Cooking—Fishing—Food/Drink—Gardening—Native American—Outdoors—Regional—Cookbooks—Hunting

CONTACT: Bruce Carlson, President
Material: All
1854 - 345th Ave.
Wever IA 52658
Phone: 319-372-7480
Fax: 319-372-7485

Hellgate Press

Please refer to PSI Research.

Heritage Books, Inc.

Heritage Books, Inc. was founded in 1978 to help Americans celebrate life by exploring various aspects of their heritage. We interpret heritage broadly to include history, biography, genealogy and related topics. Many of our publications deal with some aspect of history at the local or regional level, while others deal with some aspect of the various ethnic groups which constitute the American people. We also publish many reference works which contain the raw data used by historians, social scientists, and family historians, such as vital statistics and record abstracts.

The resources we publish are produced in traditional book format, as books and databases on CD-ROM, and/or in e-book format. In the past twenty-five years we have published over 2,500 titles and have over 1,800 in print at present. For a number of years we have published 20-30 new titles each month year round.

A free paper copy of a recent catalog describing many of our publications is available on request, and all our publications are listed on our web site: http://www.heritagebooks.com. An author information flyer is also available on request.

Submissions should include the following: 1) A cover letter which describes the nature and content of your compilation, the audience for whom it is intended and what you see as the market for it, the need that it fills and how it compares with other works on the topic, etc. Be sure to describe your experience and education as it relates to the project., i.e., your qualifications for writing the work. Also include your name, address, phone number, and email address. 2) A detailed outline or synopsis of the work and at least several sample chapters; a complete draft is preferred.

Submissions should be printed on standard bond typewriter paper; a single copy in either single or double spaced format is acceptable. Do not submit electronic media; if we decide to publish your work, we will request that later. Do not submit any originals of text or illustrations for which you do not have masters. We will not be responsible for lost materials, and will not return any materials submitted unless you provide adequate return postage. Submissions are normally accepted or rejected within four weeks of receipt by us.

Topics of interest include, but are not limited to: local and regional histories; accounts of various wars from the early Indian wars down to the present; compilations of source records of interest to historical and/or genealogical researchers; descriptions of the early settlements of various areas; studies of various aspects of the many ethnic groups found in America; biographical dictionaries, noteworthy memoirs, and family histories.

Categories: Nonfiction—Biography—Civil War—History—Native American—Reference—Regional

CONTACT: Editorial Director
Material: All

1540-E Pointer Ridge Place
Bowie MD 20716-7708
Phone: 301-390-7708
E-mail: submissions@heritagebooks.com
Website: www.heritagebooks.com

HiddenSpring

HiddenSpring, the general trade imprint of Paulist Press, publishes a broad range of non-fiction "with a spiritual twist." HiddenSpring publishes hardcover and both trade paperback originals and reprints. HiddenSpring publishes 8-10 titles a year, accepts manuscripts from both unagented and first-time authors, and offers variable advances. Please submit proposal package including outline, one (1) sample chapter, SASE; do not send complete manuscripts.

Categories: Nonfiction—Alternate Life-style—Biography—Culture—Ecology—Gardening—General Interest—History—Inspirational—Lifestyle—Multicultural—Religion—Science—Self Help—Spiritual—Travel

CONTACT: Jan-Erik Guerth, Editorial Director
Material: All
997 Macarthur Blvd.
Mahwah NJ 07430
Phone: 201-825-7300

High Tide Press

We're seeking titles on: mental health/psychology, disabilities, business, marketing, nonprofit leadership, and management. You should send us a one-page query with SASE, giving a brief overview of the book, its market, and your background. If we are interested, we will request a Book Proposal.

The Book Proposal (as described below) outlines the nature of your work, who your market is, and information about your background. If we're interested in taking a closer look at your book, we'll contact you. Please do not send a complete manuscript unless we request one.

Note: When querying via e-mail, please just give an overview of your book, its market, and your background.

Please do not send attachments unless invited to do so.

Book Proposals Should Include:
• A One-Page Overview of the Book
• Two (2) or Three (3) Sample Chapters
• A Chapter-by-Chapter Outline
• Number of Photos or Illustrations
• Author's Background / Credentials
• Target Completion Date
• Word Count / Number of Pages
• Audience / Market Information

Audience / Market Information Should Include:
1. Who Is the Audience?
What is the market for your book and how many potential buyers? Who wants this book? Why do they want it? Why do they need it? Do you have specific marketing ideas in mind?
2. Does Your Book Help the Reader?
How will this book benefit the buyer? How will it help them? What need does it fill for your target market?
3. What Makes Your Book Special?
What makes your book different from other such books? (Are there other such books?) Does your book have more information? Is it more comprehensive, easier to use? What advantages does it have over the competition? Why will people buy your book instead of something else? What existing or forthcoming titles compete with your book?
Note: Please do a database search for competing titles through Amazon.com, the largest online book store with more than four million titles in its database. Report your findings in your proposal.
4. Marketing Niches / Special Markets (please be thorough here)
List any special markets your book may have outside regular trade book channels (book stores).
Could sales result from your contacts—associations, organizations, corporations, groups, hospitals, treatment centers, workshops, seminars, or speaking engagements?
Which magazines or professional/trade journals may review your book or print articles by you which in turn promotes the book?
Do you have specific ideas for marketing your book? How willing are you to be active in marketing your book?

Submission of Text
All materials should be clearly printed on white, 8 1 2 x 11 paper, double-spaced, with at least 1" margins on all sides.
No more than 250-300 words per page.
No dot matrix print outs, please.
Do not staple, clip, or otherwise bind pages in the submission.
Manuscripts must be submitted in electronic format (3.5" diskette [Mac or PC], Zip disk, or via e-mail [as long as the file is no larger than 1mb) in addition to a printout. Acceptable file formats include: Microsoft Word, Wordperfect, QuarkXPress, most word processing programs, or plain text. For our convenience, please do not put 2 returns after each paragraph, and start new paragraphs with a tab. Also, use only one space after a period. Do not use two spaces after a period.
Categories: Nonfiction—Disabilities—Psychology

CONTACT: Diane J. Bell, Managing Editor
Material: All
CONTACT: Monica Regan, Editor
Material: Leadership
3650 W. 183rd St.
Homewood IL 60430-2603
Phone: 708-206-2054
Fax: 708-206-2044
E-mail: managing.editor@hightidepress.com
Website: www.hightidepress.com

Highlands Keep Publishing

Highlands Keep Publishing is an e-book and trade paperback press. At present, we are a niche market, and every effort will be made to acquire manuscripts with a military theme. Manuscripts should be well written and can include fantasy, science fiction, romance, history and alternative history. A major consideration for acceptance is that the manuscript must be "believable." Authors should be zealous in the accuracy of their descriptions of battle scenes, strategies, weapons, etc.

Books published by Highlands Keep Publishing include the Ragnarok Series "Song of the Valkyrie," Book 1, Episodes I and II by C. R. MacPhadrick.

Publishes three manuscripts per year. Responds within four weeks. Send a detailed synopsis and the first three chapters of your manuscript.

Categories: Fantasy—Military

CONTACT: Janet Musick, Senior Editor
Material: All
PO Box 157
Amherst VA 24521
E-mail: janetm1943@aol.com

Highsmith Press

Please refer to UpstartBooks.

Hikoki Publications

Please refer to Howell Press, Inc.

Hill and Wang

Please refer to Farrar, Straus and Giroux, Publishers, Inc.

Hillbrook Publishing Company

We focus on high quality books in spirituality, afterlife, channeled information, after-death communications, and out-of-body experiences. While we prefer nonfiction books, we will consider fiction in any of these categories.

Please send your query letter and book proposal to the attention of the Senior Editor by postal mail only. We cannot accept faxed, disk, web-based, or email submissions. Enclose a self-addressed-stamped-envelope (SASE) with sufficient postage if you wish to hear from us or want your manuscript returned. Your cover letter should contain complete contact information, including telephone number, mailing address, and email.

The chances of having your proposal considered for publication will be greatly enhanced if you include an analysis of competing books and show us how your book is different and better than others already in the market. Please be aware that we receive a large number of proposals and it may take us many months to respond. We realize it can be frustrating for an author to wait so long for a response. Therefore, we encourage you to submit your proposal simultaneously to other publishers or to consider self-publishing your work if you are turned down by several publishers.

Categories: Fiction—Nonfiction—Paranormal—Spiritual—Afterlife—After-Death Communications—Channeled Information

CONTACT: Senior Editor
Material: All
13190 Calle Caballeros, Ste. 201
San Diego, CA 92129-2916
Phone: 858-484-9850
Fax: 858-777-5459

E-mail: info@HillbrookPublishing.com
Website: www.hillbrookpublishing.com/

Hilliard & Harris

Initial Submissions for review:

Please submit a query letter identifying your manuscript and the genre that it is in. Include One (1) copy of the first 5 chapters of your manuscript or 100 pages whichever is greater. (Do not break a chapter to meet the 100 page limit.) Include a brief synopsis of your novel (as if for a jacket liner) and brief bio of the author. Also include a self-addressed, stamped mailing envelope large enough for the return of manuscript documents. If you prefer for us to shred the submission documents, please include written instructions to do so with signature.

If interested we will notify the author and request the entire manuscript. *The guidelines for submitting the entire manuscript are as follows:*

• All manuscripts must be typed, double spaced, 12 point type, in a standard font (for example, Arial or Courier New). No script fonts, please.

• Please calculate the word content of your manuscript with your word processing software and include on the upper left hand corner of the cover page. If you are submitting a manuscript from a typewriter, please estimate 250 words per page.

• Please include your name, mailing address, email address (if applicable), and phone number on the lower right hand side of your cover page. Please include your complete name, manuscript title, and page number on each page of the manuscript.

• Please include a self addressed stamped postcard for acknowledgment of receipt and return postage for the entire manuscript or instructions to shred it with signature in the event it is not accepted for publication.

Hilliard & Harris will notify authors of our progress in the evaluation process. We will correspond by mail and email as appropriate.

Hilliard & Harris will provide support from our editors for authors who are accepted for publication for final manuscript preparation, but manuscripts submitted requiring substantial mechanical or line editing will be rejected.

Categories: Fiction—Children—Mystery—Poetry—Romance—Western

CONTACT: Shawn E. Reilly, Editor-in-Chief
Material: All
PO Box 275
Boonsboro MD 21713-0275
Phone: 301-432-7080
Fax: 301-432-7505
E-mail: info@hilliardandharris.com
Website: www.hilliardandharris.com

Historical Resources Press

We are a Small Press specializing in Publishing HISTORY Made YESTERDAY and TODAY as RESOURCES for TOMORROW.

Our Mission:

Encouraging people of all ages to write, preserve and share history in published documents, small booklets and sometimes full-size books.

Our Guidelines:

Non-Fiction only, determined by the client to be accurate, true and important to those who are submitting it.

If you do not preserve this Non-Fiction, who will? What will be forever lost?

We are here to help anyone interested in Publishing HISTORY made YESTERDAY and TODAY as RESOURCES for TOMORROW.

Karin K. Ramsay, Owner & Sole Proprietor.
Categories: Nonfiction—History

CONTACT: Submissions Editor
Material: All
2104 Post Oak Court
Corinth/Denton TX 76210-1900
Phone: 940-321-1066
Fax: 940-497-1313
E-mail: historybuffs@worldnet.att.net
Website: www.booksonhistory.com

Hobby House Press, Inc.

Formal guidelines not available.
Send queries or book proposals to below address.
Categories: Nonfiction—Collectibles—Crafts/Hobbies—Hobbies

CONTACT: Editor
Material: All
1 Corporate Dr.
Grantsville MD 21536
Phone: 800-554-1447
Website: www.hobbyhouse.com

Hohm Press

Thank you for considering Hohm Press for your book proposal. Since 1975, Hohm Press has provided a venue for pioneering authors whose work promotes intellectual, emotional, physical and spiritual integrity. In response to the growing need for such work in contemporary culture, we publish books in the areas of transpersonal psychology and religious studies, herbistry, alternative health methods and nutrition. At present we are not accepting any poetry, fiction or children's books. *Please include the following in your submission:*

1. Cover letter—*start with a one or two page cover letter:*
   a. Summarize the topic of your book.
   b. State what qualifies you to write this book. Include applicable experience, education and other materials previously published.
   c. Briefly outline how you think your book could be most effectively promoted. Would you be willing to promote your book?
2. Outline and sample chapter—Provide a detailed outline and include a sample chapter. Please use white paper, double-spaced text.
3. SASE—If you would like us to return the materials that you send, please include a self-addressed return envelope large enough to hold the materials with the appropriate amount of postage.
4. Remember to be patient and allow us enough time to carefully review your proposal. We have a very small staff, and therefore this can take from eight to twelve weeks. Thank you.
Categories: Nonfiction—Diet/Nutrition—Health—Religion—Spiritual

CONTACT: Regina Sara Ryan, Senior Editor
Material: All
PO Box 31
Prescott AZ 86302
Phone: 928-778-9189
Website: hohmpress.com

Holiday House, Inc.

Holiday House is a small independent publisher of children's books only. We specialize in quality trade hardcovers from picture books to young adult, both fiction and nonfiction, primarily targeting the school and library market.

We are now especially interested in acquiring picture books, short chapter books, both humorous and serious middle-grade novels, multi-cultural stories, historical fiction, fantasy for ages 8-12, and exciting nonfiction books for all ages. We are not currently seeking folktales or fairy tales, picture books for the preschool market, or books with a religious theme other than some limited Judaica.

We do not accept unsolicited manuscripts or simultaneous submissions. We do accept query letters. However, we do request that if you are making multiple submissions, you state this in your cover letter.

If you do not include a SASE, your manuscript will be discarded. This policy is strictly enforced

We do not accept certified or registered mail.

Picture Books: Please send a complete manuscript. We do not respond to picture book queries. We do accept artwork with the text as long as they may be considered separately.

Novels: Please send a synopsis and the first three chapters.

Artwork: Please do not submit original artwork or slides; color photocopies or printed samples are preferred. Please send samples that can be kept on file.

Allow 8-10 weeks for a response. A manuscript under serious consideration may require more time. If 10 weeks have passed and you have not received an answer, follow up with a written query, including an SASE. No phone calls please.

Thank you for your interest in Holiday House.
Categories: Children

CONTACT: Acquisitions Editor
Material: All
425 Madison Ave.
New York NY 10017
Phone: 212-688-0085

Holloway House Publishing Company

Holloway House publishes African American crime, mystery, and street genre novels, along with highly provocative nonfiction such as Hollywood exposes and true crime. We welcome unsolicited submissions: please send us at least three chapters (or 30 pages) or your manuscript accompanied by a 1-3 page story synopsis. Include a SASE large enough to contain your manuscript, if you want the option of having it returned.
Categories: Fiction—Nonfiction—African-American—Crime—Mystery—True Crime

CONTACT: Leonard King, Editor
Material: All
CONTACT: Neal Colgrass, Editor
Material: All
8060 Melrose Ave.
Los Angeles, CA 90046-7082
Phone: 323-653-8060
Fax: 323-655-9452
Website: www.hollowayhousebooks.com
www.hhbookstore.com

Horizon Books

Please refer to Christian Publications, Inc.

Howell Press, Inc.

About Us

Howell Press, Inc is a book publishing company located in Charlottesville, Virginia. We specialize in books about history, aviation, transportation, food and wine, quilts, and Mid-Atlantic and Southeastern regional subjects. Selected gift items and calendars are also available.

Our books are available in retail bookstores, museum shops, and specialty stores nationwide. Retail stores interested in carrying Howell Press books should call us at our toll-free number below to discuss establishing an account.

Howell Press publishes and distributes books featuring high-quality photography and artwork. Photographers who are not familiar with Howell Press are encouraged to request a free catalog before contacting us regarding assignments. Those who request catalogs should enclose a self-addressed, 8½ x 11-inch envelope and return postage with their request.

Please use the following guidelines to help make the review process as efficient as possible. Because we receive such a high volume of materials, we cannot review submissions that do not conform to these guidelines.

Author's Guidelines

Limit query letters to a concise one- or two-page description of your proposed project, its unique qualities, and its intended audience. Be sure to include your name and address on the first page of any correspondence. Your query should be accompanied by a proposal that provides a general overview of your idea and offers a chapter-by-chapter outline of the book. Please include three to five sample chapters (including the first two chapters) to familiarize us with your writing style and the development of your ideas. State your qualifications for handling this topic, including a brief summary of your writing experience.

If the proposed title is to be heavily illustrated, please outline the content and source of the photographs and/or artwork. It is also helpful to provide sample illustrations. For color illustrations, please send 8 x 10-inch prints. Send only transparencies or prints-no originals. While we will take every precaution in the handling and safe return of transparencies and prints, we assume no financial responsibility for them.

Offer a marketing plan for your book. How would you suggest your book's publisher reach the potential audience? Are there magazines, clubs, or radio and television shows that target the same market? Be specific. If you cite a magazine or club, tell us its circulation or size.

Be sure to check *Books in Print* (available at most public libraries) to see if someone has already published a book similar to the one you propose. Include an analysis of the competition in your proposal-let us know what similar titles are out there and how your book will be different.

For those who have queried Howell Press and have been asked to submit manuscripts, we ask that you include a cover letter with your manuscript. On the front page, include your name, address, telephone number, and an accurate word count of the manuscript's length. The manuscript should be typed double spaced on 8½ x 11-inch paper and have page numbers and at least one-inch margins on all sides. On the left margin, alongside key quotations, dates, figures, or other pertinent information, pencil in brief citations (author, book, and page) to direct us to the references for fact-checking purposes. If a source is not commonly available, please photocopy the relevant material and submit it with the manuscript.

Use *The Chicago Manual of Style* as a guide for proper punctuation, capitalization, and style. Tune your presentation to the popular reader rather than the scholarly one. Because quality illustrations and photography are a hallmark of our products, suggestions for obtaining illustrations to accompany your manuscript should be included.

All book proposals should be addressed to Ross A. Howell, Jr., President. No matter what materials you send, be sure to include sufficient return postage and a self-addressed envelope large enough to contain your materials if you want them to be returned. Manuscripts not accompanied by an SASE will not be returned. Do not send a check or cash for postage. If you do not wish to have your materials returned, please include a self-addressed No. 10 envelope with $.37 return postage for our response.

We will be in touch with you as soon as possible, but please keep in mind that it could take eight weeks or longer for us to adequately assess your submission and reach a decision.

Thank you for your interest.

Photographer's Guidelines

We work individually with photographers on book-length projects. Photographers who have proposals for book projects or wish to be considered for assignments should submit a written query.

Please limit queries to a concise one- or two-page letter describing your proposed project, its unique qualities, and its intended audience. Type your query/cover letter on 8½ x 11-inch white paper. Be sure to include your name and address on the first page of any correspondence. Photography samples must accompany queries. For color illustrations, send 35 mm color transparencies; for black-and-white illustrations, please send 8 x 10-inch prints. Send only transparencies or prints-not originals. While we will take great care to ensure the safe return of your materials, we assume no financial responsibility for them.

State your qualifications for handling this topic, and be sure to include a brief summary of your photographic experience. Offer a marketing plan for your book. How would you suggest your publisher reach the potential audience? Are there magazines, radio and television shows, or clubs that target that market? Be specific. If you cite a magazine or club, tell us its circulation or size.

All proposals should be addressed to Ross A. Howell, Jr., President. No matter what size manuscript you're mailing, always include sufficient return postage and a self-addressed, stamped envelope large enough to contain your work should you want it to be returned. Work not accompanied by an SASE will not be returned. Please do not send a check or cash for postage. If you do not wish to have your materials returned, please include a self-addressed, No. 10 envelope with return postage for our response.

We will be in touch with you as soon as possible, but please keep in mind that it could take eight weeks or longer to make a decision.

Thank you for your interest.

Categories: Nonfiction—Automobiles—Aviation—Boating—Cooking—Crafts/Hobbies—History—Regional—Regional: Virginia

CONTACT: Ross A. Howell, President
Material: All
1713-2D Allied Lane
Charlottesville VA 22903
Phone: 434-977-4006 or 800-868-4512
Fax: 888-971-7204
E-mail: custserv@howellpress.com
Website: www.howellpress.com

Howells House, Inc.

We have no formal, written guidelines. Instead, we ask for a query letter giving a synopsis and description of the work and the qualifications and experience of the author. If we think we might be interested, we will request more information or samples. Ultimately, we will need sample chapters or the entire ms. on 3½" disk formatted in WordPerfect 6.0. Any necessary permissions will be the responsibility of the author.

Thank you for your interest.

Categories: Biography—Crime—General Interest—History—Military—Politics—Public Policy

CONTACT: Acquisitions Editor
Material: All
PO Box 9546
Washington DC 20016

Phone: 202-333-2182
Fax: 202-333-2184

Human Kinetics

Do you have an idea for a book?

Human Kinetics publishes approximately 100 books a year. We do review unsolicited manuscript proposals, if prepared according to our book prospectus form.

If you are interested in submitting a book proposal, you can find prospectus forms available online for both trade (Consumer) books and academic/professional books.

Human Kinetics also publishes more than 20 journals for the physical activity field. Submission guidelines for articles are found on the Human Kinetics journals Web pages.

More Information about Submitting Manuscripts to HK

How long does it take for a manuscript to become a book?

Most trade books take about one year, often less, from the time the first draft is written by the author to the time the book is in print. Academic titles, such as textbooks and large reference books, may take longer to develop. Time frames for publication vary depending on the book's complexity, length, and the timeliness of the topic. At least half of the publication time involves careful review of your manuscript by our editorial staff, author revisions of the manuscript, design of the book's interior and cover, and planning for the marketing of your book.

How many products does HK release in one year?

About 100 books

23 journals (80+ issues)

Numerous other products including kits, videos, and software

Categories: Nonfiction—Physical Activity—Physical Fitness

CONTACT: Academic Book Division or Trade Book Division
Material: All
Human Kinetics
PO Box 5076
Champaign, IL, 61825-5076
E-mail: webmaster@hkusa.com
Website: www.humankinetics.com

Hunter House Publishers

The guidelines below are in two parts: (a) the subject areas we publish in and the kind of books we do; and (1) the kind of proposals we like to see. They reflect our tag line, which is Books for health, family and community, although sometimes it is difficult to keep a clear separation between these three areas.

SUBJECT AREAS

Health and wellness, especially women's health

Our health books focus on emerging or current health issues that may be inadequately covered for the general population. We look for comprehensive, balanced and up-to-date information presented in a clear and accessible manner. The book should describe causes, symptoms, medical theories, current and possible treatments, complementary and alternative therapies, successful strategies for coping, prevention, and so on. Illustrations, sidebars, reading lists, and resource sections that provide additional information or enhance the content are desirable. We specialize in women's health, with sublists on cancer; pregnancy & childbirth; women's health reference; and women's health as a women's issue. We are currently interested in books about aging and complementary therapies. At the top of our health list are Menopause *Without Medicine*; *Women's Cancers*; *Running on Empty: The Complete Guide to Chronic Fatigue Syndrome (CFIDS)*; and *The Cortisol Connection.*

Family: Personal growth, lifestyles, relationships, sexuality

Personal growth topics that we are currently interested in are sexuality; partner and family relationships; and changing, evolution-ary lifestyles. Successful titles provide step-by-step aids or a program to help readers understand and approach new perspectives on family issues or dynamics, celebrate their sexuality, and establish healthy, fulfilling lives that incorporate a planetary perspective. Examples include: *Sexual Healing: How Good Loving is Good for You* and *Your Relationship; Helping Your Child Through Your Divorce;* and *The Pleasure Prescription—A New Way to Well-being.*

Violence prevention and intervention, social justice

We have a small but growing line of books and workbooks, often done in collaboration with nonprofits, which address community issues such as violence prevention, access for people with disabilities, and human rights. They should include clear reviews and explanations, new activities and exercises, provocative insights, and practical theory. Examples are: *Violent No More: Helping Men End Domestic Abuse; Helping Teens Stop Violence: A Practical Guide for Counselors, Educators, and Parents; Computer Resources for People With Disabilities;* and *The Amnesty International Handbook.*

Resources for counselors and educators

Resources for educators are generally specialized curricula that address violence prevention and social justice issues, including *The Uprooted: Refugees and the United States; Human Rights for Children;* and *Making the Peace: A Violence Prevention Curriculum for Young People.*

Books for counselors and helping professionals tend to offer information in new and underexplored fields, such as trauma and crisis in children. Titles include *Trauma in the Lives of Children: Crisis and Stress Management Techniques for Counselors and Other Professionals.*

We are also looking for additions to our Growth and Recovery Workbooks series. These materials are for professional or supervised use with young children who have experienced trauma, abuse, or other critical life events. It is important that they have accompanying guides for the professionals who will use them. Titles include *No More Hurt* and *Someone I Love Died.*

Audience

Our health and family books are meant to appeal to both the general reading public and health care and mental health professionals. They should be written clearly to the general reader, but include enough background explanation, theory, and resources so that they are good references for professionals. This comprehensive approach also ensures that readers can trust the authors as authorities on the topic. It is important that author have credentials and experience within the field. If you do not have this background, it is important that you have a co-author who does. It also helps if a reputable and well-known expert contributes a foreword or the introduction.

Our social issues books should be accessible to lay readers but should speak clearly to the specialized groups involved with the subject on a professional, volunteer, or community basis. Again, we look for credentialed authors with experience and a resource network in their field.

It is crucial that the authors of educational or professional books have credentials and experience within the specific areas they address. We look for a need for information within these areas, and networks through which we can reach the professionals who will use these materials. Endorsements and a preface or foreword from noted individuals within the field are important and helpful.

We do not publish fiction or illustrated books for children.

PREPARING A BOOK PROPOSAL FOR US

A good non-fiction book proposal is made up of the following components: an overview; a chapter-by-chapter outline; about the author(s); and marketing considerations.

The Overview should be a two- to three-page summary of the work: the content, and your presentation and approach. *It should include the following:*

1. The subject hook, which creates interest in the book, including the title, subtitle, the book's angle on the current market, and approximate length of the book.

2. An anecdote or example that illustrates your theme and its significance.

3. Discussion of the book's other essential ingredients—illustrations, exercises, etc.

4. A foreword, preface, or endorsements for the book written by authorities or celebrities.

The final page of your proposal should discuss the markets for your work, your experience and credibility as an author, and any other information that makes the book unique. Our editors and salespeople must understand why your book should be written. Specify the audience your book will address (women, professionals, tradespeople). Include marketing or promotional ideas you have for getting the book known to your audience. Lastly, list current books that compete with and complement yours.

The Chapter-by-chapter Outline is a 3-6 page outline, including all chapter titles and itemized lists of the major topics or contents of each chapter. Significant illustrations, appendices, and recommended reading should be listed. Work from a table of contents. You should have enough chapters to break up the topic in digestible pieces for the reader, but not so many that the material is scattered. Most books flow from an overall organizing subject or theme—the subject "hook" we ask for in the overview. For example, a book on breast cancer can be organized according to risks and detection, operations and choices involved, and recovery processes. After you complete your table of contents, go on to outline each chapter. Make a brief listing of topics which will be discussed in each chapter, or summarize each chapter in a paragraph.

About the Author: your credentials as evidence you are qualified to write on the subject, and any experience or training that qualifies you especially well for this project. A resume or short biography that includes other publishing experience and media experience is helpful. The more you can tell us about yourself, the more we understand your proposal as a whole.

Marketing and Promotion Information: We look for authors who are positive about and have access to publicity. Explain what you will do to help promote the book. Describe your speaking, mass media, TV, radio, or promotional experience and include a plan of how your work can be promoted. Do you lecture, do seminars, tour, or travel for training and business; do you belong to active organizations and have strong networks; do you teach classes or write a newspaper column; are you prepared to market your materials?

The Review Process

If we are interested in pursuing your project further, we will request sample chapters. Please send only two to three sample chapters—not the whole manuscript. Each chapter should have one concept, subject, skill, or technique. Use main headings and subheads so a reader can know at a glance where the chapter is going.

In a chapter that explains a process or teaches a technique, explain the process step-by-step in exactly the order a reader should follow to understand the process. The general and most important concepts come first, while the exceptions and special considerations come last. Any background information can be explained first or in a separate chapter.

To effectively teach an individual step of a process or technique, follow this sequence: state the rule or instruction first. Be clear and to the point. Then give an example of how someone else did this step. Finally, provide an exercise for the reader to perform. This gives the reader three ways to learn the technique: intellectually by precept, emotionally by example, and experientially by doing.

Sending Us Your Manuscript

After you have done your marketing research and written your chapter outlines, consider whether Hunter House is the right publisher for you. We do not publish fiction, autobiography, or general children's books, so those types of works get returned right away. If you do have what we are looking for, then send it on. Proposals received without an SASE that are not accepted for publication will not be returned or responded to.

We do accept simultaneous submissions and look for computer printouts of good quality, or e-mail. Please inform us if a manuscript is available on computer disk (IBM format is preferable).

Categories: Nonfiction—Diet/Nutrition—Disabilities—Family—Health—Lifestyle—Men's Issues—Multicultural—Psychology—Relationships—Self Help—Sexuality—Women's Issues—Growth & Recovery—Violence Prevention

CONTACT: Kiran Rana, Publisher
Material: Any
CONTACT: Jeanne Brondino, Acquisitions Editor
Material: Any
PO Box 2914
Alameda CA 94501
Phone: 510-865-5282
Fax: 510-865-4295
E-mail: acquisitions@hunterhouse.com
Website: www.hunterhouse.com

Hyperion

We regret to inform you that Hyperion does not accept unsolicited manuscripts for review, as per our Legal Department:

"Note to authors: please do not send unsolicited submissions. As a matter of long-standing policy, The Walt Disney Company does not accept unsolicited creative submissions. Please understand that the policy's purpose is to prevent any confusion over the ownership of ideas that the company is working on or considering. Unsolicited submissions will be deleted without being reviewed or retained in our files."

Hyperion, like most major publishing houses will only accept manuscripts for review that have been submitted via a literary agent.

Website:www.hyperionbooks.com

Iconografix, Inc.

Iconografix is a publishing company specializing in books for transportation enthusiasts. We publish in a number of different areas, including Automobiles, Auto Racing, Buses, Construction Equipment, Emergency Equipment, Farming Equipment, Railroads and Trucks. The Iconografix imprint is constantly growing and expanding into new subject areas.

Authors, editors, and knowledgeable enthusiasts in the field of transportation history are invited to contact the Editorial Department at the address below.

Categories: Nonfiction—Automobiles—Recreation Vehicles—Transportation—Railroads

CONTACT: Editorial Department
Material: All
PO Box 446
Hudson WI 54016
Phone: 715-381-9755

IHS Press

Background and Editorial Philosophy: IHS Press is the only publisher dedicated exclusively to the Social Doctrine of the Catholic Church. As such IHS Press specializes in works of Catholic Social Thought which are faithful to the Traditional Teaching of the Roman Catholic Church. As a publisher in Social Thought, IHS Press is interested in considering for publication manuscripts which apply the Social Doctrine of the Church to any and all problems within the social science disciplines: history, sociology, economics, economic thought, history of economic thought, political theory; as well as works of a generally cultural, philosophical, or literary nature.

We are also seeking manuscripts by journalists, academics, scholars, and culturalists which explore various aspects of the numerous problems, both practical and philosophical, that plague modernity (as an ideology) and the modern world (in practice). We prefer analysis of those problems from the standpoint of the Social Doctrine of the Church, but we are happy to consider any analysis of those problems which speaks from a genuinely alternative viewpoint - that is to say a viewpoint that takes the true common good of society into account, and does not speak from the sterile categories of "right" and "left," or "communist/socialist" and "capitalist."

We intend, therefore, to be a publisher which is unique for its willingness to foster frank discussions, research, and intellectual exchanges about the issues that lie at the root of the problems of the modern world, and to contribute to their solution.

Submission procedure: Before considering a manuscript, the IHS editors prefer to have an opportunity to review and discuss the topic proposed for development in a full-length manuscript. This saves both the author and the editors time and energy.

The first step is to send us via fax, e-mail, or regular mail a one-page prospectus, sketching the general topic that a manuscript would potentially cover and the manner and extent to which the manuscript will cover it. Be sure to include an extensive author's biography and detailed and correct contact information. Including a stamped, self-addressed envelope will facilitate the process of our correspondence with you.

Additionally, include with the submitted prospectus the following supplemental information: (1) author's credentials and qualifications for writing on the proposed topic, (2) potential market(s) for the proposed book, (3) suggested contacts to approach for testimonials, blurbs, and endorsements (to include professionals, academics, individuals, and associations qualified to comment on the topic in question), (4) a list of the author's access to normal channels of book publicity including contacts with relevant special or mainstream media who would be interested in reviewing the book or interviewing the author on the subject of the proposed book (include a summary of the author's previous exposure in print or other media if applicable), and (5) the author's proposals, supplemental to the publisher's standard marketing efforts, for marketing the book.

In summary: In addition to considering manuscripts that correspond with our editorial vision, we insist upon manuscripts that are well written, to the point, and accessible. No manuscript, on no matter how interesting a subject, will be considered that is poorly written.

Categories: Nonfiction, Culture, History, Philosophy, Politics, Religion, Spiritual

CONTACT: John Sharpe
Material: All
222. W. 21st St., Ste F-122
Norfolk VA 23517
Phone/Fax: 877-IHS-PRESS (447-7737)
E-mail: editor@ihspress.com
Website: www.ihspress.com

Illumination Arts Publishing Co., Inc.

Mission Statement: Illumination Arts publishes high quality, enlightening children's picture books with enduring, inspirational and spiritual values. Our aim is to touch people's lives, with illumination and transformation. We are currently seeking fiction and non-fiction stories that are 500 to 1,500 words.

MANUSCRIPTS

All manuscripts must be typed, double-spaced. Please keep a copy of your work. Be sure your name and address are on your manuscript.

Manuscripts must be accompanied by a cover letter, including author's name, address, phone number, and the word count of the story.

Please enclose a short author's bio with personal and professional background and a list of previously published material, if any.

Include a description of what makes your book special or different from others currently on the market in the same category.

Tell us how you will be able to assist in the promotion of this book.

Sample illustrations are accepted but not necessary.

Please proofread the manuscript for spelling and grammatical errors.

We make every effort to respond in one month, but because of the volume of submissions received, we may be very late responding to authors.

We suggest that you review our books, and visit our website at www.illumin.com, to determine if your manuscript is appropriate for our company.

SUBMISSIONS

We do not accept chapter, or full-length, unusually sized books, or books on disc or video.

You *must* include SASE for reply, with sufficient postage, if you wish to have your manuscript returned. Submissions without SASE are not reviewed at all.

ARTWORK

Send resume, and samples of printed artwork, or photocopies. (Do not send original artwork or slides.)

Include SASE, with sufficient postage, if you wish to have your artwork returned. Electronic submission, discs, or video tapes are not accepted for stories.

Categories: Fiction—Children—Spiritual

CONTACT: Ruth Thompson, Editorial Director
Material: All
PO Box 1865
Bellevue WA 98009
Website: www.illumin.com

ImaJinn Books
Romance, Urban Fantasy, and Silk and Magic Erotica

NOTE: We are **NOT** an electronic publisher. We publish Trade-size paperback books.

• **Romance Guidelines:** ImaJinn (pronounced Imagine) Books publishes supernatural, paranormal, fantasy, and futuristic romances. We are looking for fast-paced, action-packed romances involving ghosts, psychics or psychic phenomena, witches, vampires, werewolves, shape shifters, and futuristic in space or on other planet. All novels should be atmospheric according to the chosen subject. Make sure the supernatural, paranormal, fantasy or futuristic element is strong enough to carry the story. If the element can be lifted out of the story and a publishable story still exists, the element is not strong enough. Also, in the case of vampires, werewolves, witches, or shape shifters, the hero or heroine must be the vampire, werewolf, etc., and these storylines should have a dark, eerie overtone.

The developing romantic relationship between the hero and the heroine is the focus of the story. The stories may be told from both points of view, and the hero may be the lead character of the story. Although books written in the third person are preferred, first person will be considered. Sensuality may range from sweet to highly sensual.

The heroine must be a strong woman, capable of confronting and conquering any threats of physical and/or psychological danger she faces in the story. She is always a match for the hero who should be bold and brash—an Alpha male—and he may or may not represent danger. The ending must be a happy one, with everlasting romance the reward for triumphing over the darkness or evil faced in the story. Although we prefer Alpha male heroes, we will consider Beta heroes, but they must still be bold and a match for the heroine. However, we do not want Beta vampires, werewolves, etc. We feel these types of heroes must have a dark, dangerous edge for survival purposes, and although they may have some Beta traits, their main personality should be Alpha.

• **Urban Fantasy Guidelines:** We are also considering Urban Fantasy storylines along the order of Laurell K. Hamilton's Anita Blake series. We do expect a romance or a blossoming romance in the story, although the romance does not have to be the main focus of the story. We expect these storylines to be set up for a continuing series with the same characters, although we will consider single book storylines. The main protagonist must be a "kick ass" heroine with the same traits as our romance heroines, as listed above.

LENGTH: 70,000 to 90,000 words

SUBMISSION: You do not need an agent to submit, but you **must** query us first. All query letters should include a synopsis no longer than six double-spaced pages and may be submitted by regular mail or e-mail, although we prefer e-mail queries and submissions. If you mail your query, please include an SASE if you want the material returned. If there is no enclosed SASE, we will dispose of the material. It is recommended that you either check our web site (http://www.imajinnbooks.com) or write or call us to see what storylines we're currently looking for. We do not accept simultaneous submissions. We only consider queries with story lines that meet our current needs.

We will **not** consider previously e-published books because of print-on-demand rights conflicts. If your book has been published by an e-publisher, please do **not** query us.

Copyright 2004 by ImaJinn Books

• **Silk and Magic Erotica Guidelines:** In keeping with the nature of all books ImaJinn publishes, a story or novel appropriate for our erotica line will be, first and foremost, a romance. The main plot of the story should be the sensual development of an intimate relationship between one man and one woman, who are both heroic in stature (i.e., possessing high moral standards) and who ultimately make a commitment to each other. In general, we are not looking for multiple partner relationships, although multiple partnerships are acceptable in some storylines, such as societies where there are more men than women or vice versa, but again, these multiple partners must ultimately make a commitment to each other.

We will accept any type of erotica storyline, from contemporary to historical to paranormal, futuristic and fantasy. A successful story will be highly erotic but not pornographic. The difference is usually one of focus; erotica, like romance, seeks to involve the reader's emotions, while pornography focuses almost entirely on the physical. We expect there to be sex involved—lots of it—but it must be part of the plot, not gratuitous. Authors are encouraged to begin with a premise that, by its nature, will put the hero and heroine in sexually charged circumstances from the beginning of the story. We don't expect the couple to make love in the first chapter, although it is acceptable to have it in chapter one, but we do expect some lovemaking or sexually charged foreplay by chapter two. We expect that sexual scenes will be at least half or more of the story.

In general, we're looking for stories that turn us on, not off. We want to be excited—not disgusted or bored. We don't want stories about heavy BDSM, torture, bestiality (dogs, horses, snakes, and other real-world critters), non-sexual bodily functions ("golden showers"), pedophilia, necrophilia, cannibalism, weapons or other deadly implements being shoved into orifices, rape or anything else so kinky that it will offend our core readership. On the other hand, we understand that writing erotic stories about werewolves and aliens could lead to some interesting situations. Indeed, the paranormal element you choose could provide exactly the sort of sexual tension and eroticism these stories will require.

Regarding language, authors should think carefully about the words they use. A story doesn't automatically become erotic when "manhood" gets changed to "cock" or "feminine core" is replaced by "pussy." They're all still euphemisms, and the way they're used is what matters; indeed, it can mean the difference between erotica and pornography. So authors may use whatever words they wish to name body parts and to describe actions, but keep in mind that the goal is turn the readers on—not jar them out of the story or make them laugh at inappropriate moments. (By the way, it's perfectly acceptable to use real, official words for body parts and sex acts, too.)

LENGTH: We'd like the word count for these stories to be at least 30,000 words, and we have no limitation on word counts above 30,000, but lengthy stories must remain highly erotic from beginning to end. We will consider novellas between 15,000 to 30,000 words. However, we emphasize that even in the shorter format, it's essential that the story primarily be a romance.

Our erotica line will be available in e-book and CD format and as print-on-demand books. E-books and CDs will be sold exclusively by ImaJinn Books. Royalties will be paid at 50% of the net receipts for e-books and CD format, and royalties will be paid monthly on these sales. We will routinely combine novellas and books under 40,000-45,000 words into anthologies and offer them in print-on-demand books. Royalties on print-on-demand books will be split among authors, based on the number of stories in a book, and single title royalties will range from 6-10%. Royalties on books will be paid on a semi-annual basis.

These guidelines are subject to change as we refine this new line.

SUBMISSION: You do not need an agent to submit, but you must query us first. All query letters should include a synopsis no longer than six double-spaced pages and may be submitted by regular mail or e-mail, although we prefer e-mail queries. If you mail your query, please include an SASE if you want the material returned. We do not accept simultaneous submissions. Copyright 2004 by ImaJinn Books

Query letters or inquiries should be sent to the address below.

Categories: Fiction—Adventure—Fantasy—Juvenile—Paranormal—Romance—Science Fiction—Teen

CONTACT: Editorial Staff
Material: Silk and Magic Erotica
PO Box 545
Canon City, CO 81215-0545
CONTACT: Editorial Staff
Material: Romance and Urban Fantacy Submissions
PO Box 162
Hickory Corners, MI 49060-0162
Phone: 719-275-0060
Fax: 719-276-0741
E-mail: editors@editors@imajinnbooks.com
Website: www.imajinnbooks.com

Impact ✵ Publishers®, Inc.

Impact Publishers, Inc.

If you are a professional in the human services who's been working on—or at least thinking seriously about—a book manuscript, and wondering how to connect with the right publisher, this may help.

Impact Publishers, Incorporated

Impact is a small, family-owned and operated publishing firm which has been publishing self-help by qualified human services professionals since 1970. Impact produces up to six new books each year, and has about 40 currently active titles in its catalog. Our purpose is to make the best human services expertise available to the widest possible audience. We are recognized both in the book trade and among human service professionals as an outstanding publisher of self-help materials.

Impact's door is always open to qualified new authors. We invite your written inquiries, and ask that you follow the guidelines presented in this flyer.

Author-Publisher Relations

We believe an author-publisher relationship should be collaborative, not adversarial.

The author's job—and it is hard work—is to prepare the best possible manuscript on a subject of interest to a definable audience.

The publisher's job—it's not easy either—is to help the author "polish" that work for the marketplace, to produce it attractively and appropriately for its audiences, and to place it in the hands of as many buyers as possible through effective marketing.

Impact, like all legitimate publishers, pays royalties to authors; we do not ask authors to subsidize their books. A modest advance and a royalty of 10 to 15 percent of sales receipts are typical.

Active authors (those who do workshops, make public and professional presentations, write articles, get media exposure) almost always have the most successful books.

You need not have a literary agent. We're happy to work with your agent if you have one, but we frequently contract directly with authors.

If you're writing now, keep your audience in mind, and remember that writing self—help is like talking to clients, but it's not the same. In a book, you must spell everything out clearly, simply, and completely. You won't be there for your readers to ask questions.

Subject Fields and Author Qualifications

Impact Publishers, Inc. publishes only popular psychology and self-help materials written in "everyday language" by professionals with advanced degrees and significant experience in the human services. *The Impact list is focused in five fields:*

• Personal Growth (e.g., emotional development, self-esteem, self-expression, coping with change, individuality, life choices...)

• Relationships (e.g., intimacy, love, marriage, divorce, on-the-job, getting along with others...)

• Families (e.g., children's emotional development and self-esteem, parenting, prevention of sexual assault, child behavior management...)

• Communities (e.g., small groups, leadership, community life, non-competitive games...)

• Health (e.g., stress management, smoking, hearing loss, depression, mental health...)

The Impact Publishers catalog will give you more information about the type of books of interest to us. It will help you determine if your manuscript is likely to fit our list.

Manuscript Submission Procedures

We look at all submitted material.

Your chances of hearing from us promptly are greatly enhanced by the inclusion of a self-addressed stamped envelope.

We love to see initial inquiries which look like this:

1. A brief letter of introduction, telling us:
   a. what your book is about,
   b. the audience to whom you've addressed it,
   c. why you're the right person to have written it,
   d. why Impact is the right house to publish it, and
   e. why it's outstanding enough to have a chance when 50,000 other books will be published that year.

2. An annotated table of contents (with a paragraph summarizing each chapter)

3. A couple of sample chapters

4. A short resume or curriculum vita (we don't need your lists of publications in refereed journals and/or presentations at professional meetings—yet).

It'll take us a few weeks (from four to twelve, on average) to respond. Please don't telephone. If you want to be sure we got the manuscript, include a simple response device (postcard, or check-off letter & SASE) with your submission.

We'll be glad to send you a copy of Impact's Author Guidelines, or you may view them online at www.impactpublishers.com.

Criteria for Manuscript Selection

Since its founding in 1970, Impact Publishers has elected to publish only books which serve human development. *A manuscript we select for publication will exhibit a strong combination of the following characteristics:*

• It will present a message we believe in.

• It will be a work which, in our opinion, needs to be published.

• It will present practical ideas which an individual, family, group, organization, or community may use to improve its well being in one or more of the following realms: emotional, intellectual, interpersonal/social, physical, political.

• It will fit well into the Impact Publishers catalog of books.

• It will honor the principles set forth in the Universal Declaration of Human Rights (although it need not be a work devoted to human rights per se).

• It will be written in non-academic readable style. We're fond of the saying, "The language of truth is unadorned, and always simple."

• It will be written by person(s) whom we believe to be qualified to speak with authority on the subject.

• It will be more likely to present an integrative perspective than one which reflects a single school of thought regarding human behavior.

• It will be marketable within our means. We have an assertive and effective marketing program which emphasizes publicity, direct mail, limited advertising, and energetic author activity. We do not send authors on extensive personal appearance tours.

• It will have promise of selling enough copies—at a fair price—to pay its own way.

Categories: Nonfiction—Careers—Family—Marriage—Parenting—Psychology—Relationships—Self Help—Senior Citizen—Women's Issues—Human Services—Divorce

CONTACT: Acquisitions Editor
Material: All
PO Box 6016
Atascadero CA 93423
Phone: 805-466-5917
Fax: 805-466-5919
E-mail: info@impactpublishers.com
Website: www.impactpublishers.com

In Print Publishing

In Print publishes nonfiction books for a general sophisticated audience.

In these most difficult times of change the manuscript must be able to leave a reader with a positive message of HOPE or have impact for timely issues.

In Print does consider some metaphysical books but we will not consider any personal journey to awakening or any channeled material. Our editorial staff will only consider how-to books and other general manuscripts in the metaphysical genre.

At the present time there is no reading fee.

Submit letters of query or submissions with synopsis, three chapters and a bio of the author. In Print will respond in eight to ten weeks.

I wish you every bit of success in finding a publisher for your work.
Sincerely,
Tomi Keitlen, Publisher

Categories: Nonfiction—Biography—Ecology—Environment—Film/Video—General Interest—Health—Inspirational—New Age—Occult—Politics—Spiritual

CONTACT: Tomi Keitlen, Publisher
Material: General Interest - Eclectic
PO Box 20765
Sedona AZ 86341
Phone: 928-284-5298
Fax: 928-284-5283
E-mail: inprintpub.@aol.com

Incentive Publications, Inc.

Manuscripts

Incentive Publications, Inc. publishes *teacher resource materials*. We publish *no fiction*.

If you have a manuscript that you think would be suitable for our needs, you may send: a letter of introduction; a table of contents; a sample chapter; and a self-addressed stamped envelope. If you would like your materials returned to you, please include an envelope large enough to hold the materials and with sufficient return postage. We make every effort to reply within 6-8 weeks.

Art Guidelines

Incentive Publications looks for a whimsical, warm style of illustration that respects the integrity of the child. Black and white line art is used for the inside illustrations of our books. Four-color art in any medium is used for our cover art. Good quality Xeroxes, photostats or printed pieces are acceptable for showing line art pieces through the mail. Color photographs or printed pieces are best for showing four-color work through the mail. Please mail samples to the address below.

To show original artwork or printed pieces in person, please call 800-421-2830 to make an appointment.

Categories: Nonfiction—Children—Education

CONTACT: Patience Camplair, Editor
Material: All Manuscripts
CONTACT: Art Department
Material: Art Samples
3835 Cleghorn Ave.
Nashville TN 37215-2532
Phone: 615-385-2934
E-mail: patiencec@incentivepublications.com
Website: www.incentivepublications.com

Intercontinental Publishing
New Amsterdam Publishing

In order to be considered, please submit the following:
1. Synopsis (about 2 pages maximum) of your book.
2. At least one (1), but no more than 3 sample chapters.
Additional suggestions:

Additional material may, or may not be requested, but final manuscript should be on disk in either WordPerfect 5.1 or ASCII. Text should contain no codes other than Tab [TAB], Underline [UND][und] to indicate italics and [RETURN]. Do not load any (unnecessary) parameters at beginning of manuscript, or repeat a lot of "macros" throughout text. Do not paginate, and do NOT add "headers" and/or "footers."

Material should be original and above all, should be entertaining. Use proper English and grammar. Do not use slang, vulgarisms or contractions (I'll, you'd, we're, etc.) in narrative and/or descriptive text unless book is written in the first person.

For spoken text (i.e. text within quotation marks ("/") almost anything goes, but Publisher frowns on the gratuitous use of vulgarisms, unless it is clearly a characteristic of the person (or character) speaking (being quoted).

We (me, myself and I) are a very small publisher and we will respond to all inquiries as soon as possible, but are not bound by a specific time frame. We only publish books in the spring of each year, therefore only submissions made (and accepted) before the 4th of July, will be published the next spring.

Our books are manufactured in the United States.

Thank You and Good Luck!

Categories: Fiction—Mystery

CONTACT: H. G. Smittenaar, Publisher
Material: All
11681 Bacon Race Rd.

Woodbridge VA 22192
Phone: 703-583-4800
Fax: 703-670-7825
E-mail: icpub@worldnet.att.net

Intercultural
P R E S S

Intercultural Press

Submitting a Proposal for Publication

Intercultural Press welcomes fresh ideas and new insights in the ways people live and work with each other across cultures. If you would like to submit a proposal for consideration, please follow the guidelines below.

Note that our review process may take several weeks, and we are not able to return your materials unless you send a self-addressed, stamped envelope for that purpose. Please do not send complete manuscripts.

Guidelines for a Book Proposal

The proposal is one of the most important parts of the publishing process, designed to clarify your thoughts and the viability of your project. We find the following key pieces of information helpful in making our publishing decisions. Please include:

Working title: Suggest a title that clearly expresses the essence of your work. Include possible alternatives as well.

Estimated length: Estimate the number of double-spaced pages, in your typewritten or word-processed manuscript.

Estimated delivery date and format

Synopsis: Provide a paragraph or two that describes the subject and overall content of the work.

Need: Explain what the work intends to do for the reader and how it will accomplish that goal.

Knowledge base: What unique features of the book contribute to the field? What new insights, models or research add to current thinking and practice?

Audience: Describe the primary and secondary audiences for the book. Is the project designed for consumers, travelers, trainers, students, educators, businesspeople, government agencies or NGO's? Is the audience global, North American? European? Regional?

Competing and related works: Please list the primary competition for your work and any titles that are similar to yours. What are the major differences? How is your work useful or authoritative?

Table of contents: Provide an outline of the contents with a sentence or two summarizing each chapter or section.

Sample chapters are helpful, but not essential at the proposal stage. A single chapter that is indicative of the content and shows your writing style is extremely useful in our decision process. Please, no complete manuscripts at this stage.

Author information: Your biography, vita or resume should include relevant professional experience and your qualifications for writing this book.

Marketing opportunities: How would you be able to promote your work: within your community or professional organization, through speaking engagements, through your own mailing lists and connections, at your training sessions? Publishing is a partnership, and we would like to understand your ability to help us market the book.

Other publishers: It is helpful to know if you have submitted this work to other publishers for consideration.

Topics of interest to Intercultural Press today

These are some, but not all, of the areas of interest to our readers:

Intercultural communication, specific country and culture guides, organizational culture and diversity, diversity training, multicultural issues, intercultural training, business and culture, coaching and culture, international business-negotiation-mediation and conflict resolution, culture and counseling, culture and health care, culture and education, religion and culture, gender and culture, leadership across cultures, teams—virtual and real, across cultures.

You can get a good idea of our publishing program by viewing our complete catalogue at this website. Go to www.interculturalpress.com.

Categories: Nonfiction—African-American—Asian-American—Business—College—Culture—Education—Film/Video—Health—Multicultural—Religion—Textbooks

CONTACT: Judy Carl-Hendrick, Managing Editor
Material: All
Intercultural Press—A Nicholas Brealey Company
374 U.S. Rte. One
PO Box 700
Yarmouth, ME 04096
Phone: 866-372-2665 (toll free in U.S.), 207-846-5168
Fax: 207-846-5181
E-mail: judy@interculturalpress.com
Website: www.interculturalpress.com

International Foundation of Employee Benefit Plans

How To Submit Your Ideas for Publication

1. Send your proposal

Please send proposals to the Publications Department. We make our initial decisions based on brief outlines. If you are interested in writing a book, please submit a one-to-four page typed outline. Indicate the nature and scope of each chapter as well as significant appendixes. Also tell us:

• Your proposed title
• Anticipated length of manuscript
• Titles of any previous books or articles
• Briefly why your treatment of the subject will be unique
• Briefly where/how you will collect and verify the factual information that you will be including
• Briefly why you are particularly qualified to write a book on this subject.

Be sure to include your complete address and telephone number.

2. What happens next?

You may anticipate our initial response to your proposal within one month. We will tell you if we feel that the proposed book is appropriate for our audience. If we are potentially interested in publishing the book, we will send you an autobiographical questionnaire that will help us in preparing future promotional material. At that time, we may request samples of your previous work.

Next, we will begin our formal review process. One step of the process is to submit the proposal to our Executive Committee for final approval. We will inform you of their decision as soon as possible after their review.

3. Sign a book agreement

Our basic agreement gives the author a standard royalty from our net receipts (after discounts and refunds) from all of our sales of the book. There is also a standard royalty paid for each copy of the work distributed without charge (excluding those distributed for advertising/promotional purposes and the copies provided to the author).

We will also require you to sign a copyright transfer agreement that will enable us to disseminate the work to the fullest extent.

4. What about the manuscript?

A completion date for the final version of your manuscript will be specified in your contract. Failure to meet this deadline could result in delays in publication or production.

Please submit your manuscript as a word document. Charts and figures should be submited as tif, eps or jpg files.

After the book agreement has been signed, we will send a more detailed list of suggestions for submitting your manuscript.

5. Work with us

We will keep you informed of the schedule for publication of your book. An editor assigned to the project will keep you informed of our progress, give you suggestions for possible improvements, clear any major revisions with you, and seek your input for possible ideas for marketing and promotion of the book.

Learn about the Foundation

Since 1954 the International Foundation of Employee Benefit Plans has been recognized as the foremost educational association in the employee benefits field. The International Foundation is a non-profit organization offering educational programs, publications, information services, the Certified Employee Benefit Specialist (CEBS) Program and a student intern program.

The International Foundation continuously examines the latest issues and trends in the employee benefits field, and publishes in-depth reports, studies, survey results, periodicals and books for both the benefits professional and the general consumer.

Categories: Nonfiction—Business—Health—Employee Benefits

CONTACT: Dee Birschel, Senior Director of Publications
Material: All
PO Box 69
Brookfield WI 53008-0069
Phone: 414-786-6710 x8240
Fax: 414-786-8780
E-mail: books@ifebp.org
Website: www.ifebp.org

International Marine

Thank you for requesting manuscript guidelines for International Marine. Our slogan is "Books that take you off the beaten path."

We publish a variety of books on outdoor sports, recreation, and fitness in several categories. First, we are interested in beginning-to-intermediate level how-to manuscripts about non-competitive sports or fitness. This could include anything from archery to sport diving. We have a special interest in paddlesports, including sea kayaking, whitewater paddling, and canoeing.

We are also interested in big, serious reference books and small, gift books for outdoor enthusiasts, including adventure narratives.

To help your proposal move swiftly through our review process, please address your materials to Tristram Coburn, Acquisitions Editor, and include the following:

• Cover letter with your contact information (address, telephone and fax numbers, email address)
• Table of Contents with brief summaries of each chapter
• One or two sample chapters
• Sample photographs and/or illustrations if these are central to your proposal
• Competition analysis (a listing of similar books in print, copies of recent supporting magazine articles and newspaper clippings, etc.)
• A personal or professional biography or resume (if you feel it is relevant)
• A self-addressed stamped envelope (if you want your materials returned)

Please anticipate a four- to six-week waiting period for a response from us. Thanks again for your interest in Ragged Mountain Press. We look forward to receiving your proposal.

Categories: Nonfiction—Biography—Boating—History—Outdoors—Physical Fitness—Recreation—Reference—Sports/Recreation

CONTACT: Jonathan Eaton, Editorial Director
Material: All
CONTACT: Tristram Coburn, Acquisitions Editor
Material: All
The McGraw-Hill Companies
PO Box 220
Camden ME 04843-0220

Interweave Press
Craft Books

We at Interweave Press produce genuinely useful, informative, and aesthetically pleasing literature and related products that nurture and extend the special interests of our communities of readers. We specialize in books about handweaving, knitting, beading, handspinning, needlework, and traditional textile processes. Most of our publications have a strong emphasis on technique, including general information on how to make and do things. We publish about twenty books each year, selecting material that will instruct and inspire our readers and will not duplicate available material.

Our authors are very special to us. They tend to become friends and colleagues as we work together to produce a new book, and we do everything within our power to foster good communications and positive working relationships during this process.

We have prepared this booklet to answer some major questions that you might have as an author dealing with us. Included is information on proposal preparation and submission, general contractual terms, manuscript preparation, and the publication process. Throughout, we have tried to make clear how author and publisher interact during the joint venture of producing a book.

Of course, we cannot possibly anticipate everything. Do let us know if you have additional questions or problems that we have not addressed. We look forward to hearing from you.

—Betsy Armstrong, editorial director

SUBMITTING a PROPOSAL
Topic

A subject with which you are thoroughly familiar, perhaps through doing, teaching, or writing about, will naturally be easiest for you to develop into a book.

Of great interest to both readers and publishers will be new topics not currently in print, or a fresh approach to a particular subject. Give serious thought to the niche you hope to fill with your book. What unique contribution could your book make to the knitting, weaving, spinning, or general textile world?

When you are developing an idea for a book, be sure to research the existing literature. If, for instance, a successful inkle weaving book is currently on the market, there may not be room for another one, even if you could write about the subject better.

Keep your audience in mind. For whom are you writing? Readers at different levels of expertise will require different approaches as well as different amounts and types of information. A very narrow topic likely will have a restricted audience; a broader subject may draw a larger, less homogeneous readership.

When and What to Submit

It is perfectly acceptable to approach us with the germ of an idea. A brief statement of your intent and an outline of the information you would like to cover will give us enough common ground to begin a dialogue about the possibilities for publication, and can save both you and us time if your idea is clearly not one we can use.

However, we cannot make a definite commitment to publish a manuscript until we have seen a fairly comprehensive proposal. It should include:

- Detailed outline
- Introduction
- Sample chapter or two
- Examples of illustrative material (to show both content and technical quality of photos and drawings, if applicable.)
- Estimated number of manuscript pages and illustrations

A cover letter summarizing why you think this book should be published can be very helpful. Put yourself in our shoes, and muster facts to convince us that your idea meets our criteria for publication.

Publisher's Considerations

First, we look at the concept of the book. Does it fit within the general area of textile related information which is the specialty of Interweave Press? Does it complement our current roster of books? Is the subject matter fresh, and not currently available in print? Is the approach to the topic positive and encouraging?

Further, what is the potential audience for this topic? Will enough people be interested in buying a book on this subject to make publishing it feasible? Are any other books currently available on similar topics which afford significant potential competition for this audience?

We must also take into account the quality of writing and illustrations submitted in a proposal. Even the best ideas may never find an audience if they are not well expressed. Not only words and pictures but also general organization are important here. Even if we like an idea very much we can not undertake projects that will require major rewriting. We can sometimes provide illustrations and photographs.

Finally, what would be the estimated production costs? Would they allow a reasonable return on our investment at a reasonable retail price for the volume?

As you can see, many of these factors have nothing to do with your particular manuscript. Keep in mind that even if Interweave Press cannot publish your work at this time, it may be appropriate for another publisher or for self-publication.

Response Time

Responses to book proposals may take several months. Don't expect quick decisions from any publisher, large or small. Manuscripts are often read by several editors who then engage in a wide-ranging discussion of world affairs and the effect of your proposed book on the twenty-first century before a decision is reached. Putting out a book represents a very large investment of time, money, and personal energy on the part of both author and publisher—so commitments cannot be made hastily.

If you'd like to know what's happening, you may follow your proposal with a letter or phone call inquiring about its status. Please wait at least a month before doing this, and have patience as we thoroughly evaluate your material.

THE CONTRACT
Timing

As publisher, we generally would offer a contract to you, as author, at whatever time we feel you have created a marketable product with which we can work. Both author and publisher must also be comfortable with setting schedules for manuscript delivery and publication before a contract can be written. If you have a proven track record, we might write a contract at the outline stage; if not, we might take this step after the complete manuscript is submitted.

Terms

Our standard contract provides a negotiated royalty based on the amount received by the publisher less returns. Royalties are paid semi-annually.

An advance against future earned royalties can be negotiated to help an author cover up-front costs, such as photography, illustrations, supplies, etc. Advances from Interweave Press usually fall within the range of $500-$1,500.

Sometimes Interweave Press handles color photography, or all photography and/or illustrations. Once you have a contract in hand, please read its terms carefully, and don't hesitate to ask questions or get a legal opinion on it. Note the author's responsibility in the matter of obtaining permission to use copyrighted material from other sources. If you are quoting extensively from other material, modeling illustrative material after the work of others, or using someone else's pho-

Books
A-L

tography, you must obtain written permission from the copyright holder and give appropriate credit.

After the book is published the author receives ten courtesy copies; additional copies can be purchased at our standard retail discount schedule. However, authors should not expect resale privileges except in special cases in agreement; Interweave Press is committed to supporting its existing retail dealers.

Manuscript Preparation

These guidelines for manuscript preparation have been devised to make life easier both for you, the author, and for the staff of Interweave Press. We hope that standardization of the format for manuscripts and accompanying illustrations will allow you to concentrate on words and pictures rather than on logistics. Editing, typesetting, layout, and associated duties all go more smoothly with such a format.

Included below is information pertaining to text, captions, photos, slides, drawings, drafts, projects, permissions and acknowledgments, bibliographies and references, indices, bibliographical material, and shipping. We hope we have covered everything that you will need to know, but if we have failed to anticipate your questions, please ask.

Text

Format. Interweave Press requires submitted material to be computer generated. Print a hard copy to include with the disk. Double-spaced on 8 1/2" x 11" white paper, one side only. Indent paragraphs. Include 2" margins at top and left side of each page and 1" margins on remaining sides. Set the line spacing for double-space—do not use hard returns at the end of each line. Do not right justify the lines. Use only one space after periods.

Please do not use erasable paper or onionskin. If necessary, a paragraph can be printed on an additional full-sized sheet, clearly marked, and clipped to the appropriate page.

Number all manuscript pages consecutively, including all front and back matter such as title, page, contents, bibliography, glossary, etc.

Put name, address, and telephone number at the top of page 1, and last name at top of all subsequent pages.

Headings. Type all headings flush left. Do not underline or type in all capitals. Indicate the comparative value of each heading by keying it with a number in pencil, in the left margin, as follows:

1-Major heading (chapter title)

2-Minor heading (sub-chapter)

3-Sub-heading

Make a hard return between sections.

Style, spelling, and measurements. Interweave Press uses Webster's New Collegiate Dictionary (and Webster's International Unabridged as necessary) or The American Heritage Dictionary for spelling and hyphenation, and the Chicago Manual of Style, in general, for style and grammar. At present, Interweave Press uses both English and metric units with English being dominant and metric following in parentheses.

In editing, we work to retain the author's own wording and individual style, but it is important that whatever style is used be consistent throughout the manuscript.

Please note that we work to make Interweave Press books approachable and readable, regardless of the subject. We strive for a friendly, reasonably informal style without passive verbs, tortuous pronouns, or outlandish prepositional constructions. We also ask you to eliminate any gender-specific pronouns which do not refer to individuals; use alternative sentence constructions instead.

Captions for Illustrations. Copy for captions should be typed separately from text, with color illustrations listed separately from other illustrations. Double space captions. Number caption pages consecutively (separately for each caption list). Do not attach captions to illustrations.

Number the illustrations and captions consecutively within each chapter. Prefix the illustration number with the caption number; for instance, the illustrations in Chapter 2 would be labeled 2-1, 2-2, 2-3, etc. If there are several parts to an illustration, label them a, b, c, etc.;

for instance 2-1a, 2-1b, etc. Type the illustration number, followed by a period, before each caption.

Obtain permission from and give credit to all artists/craftspeople whose works are illustrated.

For each photo include the photographer's name, unless you give a blanket credit or acknowledgment at the beginning of the book. Examples: "Photo by John Jones", or "Photographer, Jane Smith".

Illustrations

Label all artwork with author's name, a number corresponding to the caption number, and an arrow indicating the top of the illustration. See below for specific directions on label placement.

If you have two illustrations of the same item and cannot decide between them, send both. Final choice can be based on page layout and actual size of the illustration in the book. If one or the other is your first choice, please indicate this.

Black-and-white halftones. Black-and-white photography should be submitted as 5" x 7" or 8" x 10" glossy prints. Include at least a 1/2" white margin for marking purposes. Do not crop or mount photos. If you want to indicate cropping, use tracing paper overlays. Do not send negatives.

Label all photos on the back. Do not press down heavily on the photo when labeling; use a felt- tipped marker or soft pencil, pressing lightly, or use previously marked adhesive labels.

Color illustrations. Color slides (35mm) or color transparencies (2 1/4" x 2 1/4" or larger) may be used for color illustrations. Except in special circumstances, these should be originals. Color prints are not useable. Transparencies are easily damaged—be careful not to scratch or soil them. Plastic pocket sheets will protect them in shipping and handling.

Label slides on their mounts, indicating viewing side and direction. It will also help us if you put your name and a brief identification of the subject on the slide.

Label transparencies by using adhesive labels on their protective envelopes. Do not handle transparencies any more than is absolutely necessary, and never write over them.

Line drawings. If possible, make drawings actual size or larger. Size reduction will hide flaws, while enlargement will exaggerate them. Line drawings should be rendered in India or similar black ink on heavy, smooth paper, with a separate sheet for each drawing. Protect them with tissue overlays; label them in pencil on the front.

Weaving drafts. Drafts will be typeset by Interweave Press. Write drafts clearly in dark ink on graph paper. Somewhere in your book, in text or appendix, clearly explain the format you have chosen for the drafts, then be consistent in using this format. For instance, HANDWOVEN magazine employs the following format: shaft numbers are used in the threading draft, which is at the bottom of the diagram; "O"s are used for the tie-up (indicating rising shed), which is at the bottom of the diagram; and slash marks are used for the treadling sequence (unless there are multiple repeats of that treadle in which case numbers are used, or multiple weft colors in which case symbols are used) which is above the tie-up. Threadings are to be read right to left; treadlings, bottom to top. If drawdowns are included, make completely black squares rather than using "X"s or other symbols, and note whether warp threads or weft threads are blackened.

Tables. Type tables or print very clearly in dark ink. Number tables separately within chapters (Table 2-1, Table 2-2, etc.). Include caption with each table. Consider placing large tables in appendices at the end of the manuscript. Use only one tab between column entries.

Tips on taking photographs. In general, photos and transparencies should be sharp and clear, with good contrast. If you are uncertain what film to use, check a photography book or consult your local photography shop. Indoor versus outdoor film or slow speed versus fast speed film are decisions you will have to make based on the conditions under which you will be working. (Slower speed films generally have finer grain structure, which produces better enlargements. This is particularly important when using 35mm film.)

Plain backgrounds are usually best, in a color which will set off the item being photographed. You should be careful to get a good value contrast (dark versus light) between the background and the item. This is especially important when you work in black-and-white. Watch out for small anomalous items such as electric light switches and cats, which you might not notice until they magically appear in the processed photo!

Take care to avoid distracting shadows on the surface of the item. When photographing outside on a sunny day, a good placement of the item would be completely within the shadow of a building. Inside, position your lighting to eliminate or substantially reduce shadow. An exception would be if you want to highlight the texture of a fabric; side-lighting can help to bring it into prominence.

Generally, smaller apertures (higher f-stops) with correspondingly longer exposure times will give better depth of field. In photographing textiles, this can help bring out their texture. Of course, good depth of field is particularly important for three-dimensional pieces.

Particularly when shooting at slower speeds, set your camera on a tripod or solid object and use a cable release.

Film is relatively inexpensive compared to time wasted by having to retake botched photos. To be sure you get the right exposure, take at least three shots of a given item, including one "correct" exposure, one overexposed by an *f*-stop, and one underexposed by an f-stop. Consider photographing the item in several different positions or settings, so that you can choose the best one. (Note that you do not have to make full-size prints from all your negatives. Even if you are not doing your own darkroom work you can request that a "contact sheet" of negatives be printed without enlargement. From this, you can choose the best negatives for full-sized prints—or we can.)

Last, and perhaps most important, unless you have a good deal of experience, consider using a professional photographer. Authors who have done so have frequently found it to be a good investment in the quality of the final product. It's important to realize that photographers can only *lose* quality in the printing process.

Permissions and Acknowledgments

It will be necessary for you to obtain written permission from the owners of items illustrated in your book. (Specify that they are giving rights only for photographic reproduction of their work). Written permission from the copyright owner is also required for the use of written material or illustrations from a copyrighted work. In addition, you will need to obtain written releases from people (such as models) who appear in photographs.

A simple form can be used for this purpose, for example:

The undersigned authorizes Interweave Press, 201 East Fourth Street, Loveland, Colorado 80537 to include the following material in any and all editions of the forthcoming book tentatively entitled:

_____

by _____, to be published _____

Description(s):

Signature_____Date_____

Authority of Signator (author, owner, etc.) _____

Credits for permission to use material may appear in an "acknowledgments" section. Photographic and artistic credits related to items in photographs should be included in captions.

Bibliographic and References

A "Selected Bibliography" includes only articles and books directly referred to in your manuscript; a more general bibliography may include all titles which may help the reader pursue your topic further. You may or many not choose to categorize or annotate the entries.

Double-space the bibliography, indenting every line after the first entry. Arrange entries alphabetically by author. If entries are categorized, follow the same format for these section headings as for subchapter headings.

For each entry include author, title, place of publication and publisher (in the case of books), or magazine title, and publication date. Italicize titles of books and magazines; put titles of articles in quotation marks. Be consistent in the format you choose. Here are two ex-

amples of a possible format, one for a book or pamphlet and the other for a magazine article:

Collingwood, Peter, The Techniques of Rug Weaving. New York: Watson-Guptill, 1969.

Scorgie, Jean. "A Double Weave Jacket," Handwoven IV: 4:48-49 (September-October 1983).

Except in special circumstances (such as scholarly works incorporating significant book research), do not use footnotes or numbered references. Publication usually can be cited by author within the text, avoiding the need for an additional formal system. If you do need to set up a formal reference system, choose a format and be consistent throughout the book.

Index

Indexing may be done by either the author or the publisher; this is a negotiable task. Though it may seem a daunting undertaking, indexing may be accomplished in a relatively straightforward manner.

One method is to go through the book page by page, noting key words and writing each one on a file card. Then the cards can be alphabetized and further annotated with page numbers on which these words appear. If you use a word processing program, you can key in the words with the page numbers, then sort alphabetically, and fine tune. Several decisions do have to be made; for instance, what level of detail to include (e.g., just "warping," or "warping—front to back," "warping—back to front," "warping—sectional beam," etc.), and what words are truly key (e.g. "herringbone twill" versus "twill, herringbone"). When in doubt, think of what would help you if you were looking up a topic in this book. Indexing is best done working with page proofs (see below, "The Publication Process").

Biographical Information

For the book jacket or cover, for marketing, and for Library of Congress cataloging, we will need a brief biographical sketch and a color photo of you, the author. A form will be provided with the contract. You may use other materials you have already prepared instead, if they cover the same territory.

You may send your photo(s) along with the completed manuscript.

Shipping

Be sure to keep a copy of your manuscript, including illustrations if possible.

With your manuscript, please include a summary count of all illustrations enclosed, listing black-and-white photographs, color transparencies, and line drawings and diagrams separately. All illustrations will be returned to you after your book has been published. (This will probably be around nine months to a year after submission of the completed manuscript.)

To forestall damage or loss in the mail, wrap everything very securely (include stiffening to keep the photographs from being creased) and send it Registered or Certified mail, UPS, or Federal Express.

Categories: Nonfiction—Crafts/Hobbies

CONTACT: Submissions Editor
Material: All
201 E. Fourth St.
Loveland, CO 80537
Phone: 970-669-7672
Website: www.interweave.com

Iron Horse Free Press

Formal guidelines not available.
Send queries or book proposals to below address.
Categories: Nonfiction—Biography—History

CONTACT: George R. Dreher, Publisher
Material: All
PO Box 10746
Midland TX 79702
Phone: 915-686-0397

Books
A-L

Fax: 915-570-0397
E-mail: ihfp@aol.com
Website: www.georgedreher.com/Book_Publisher.html

Island Press

THE FOLLOWING INFORMATION will help both first-time and seasoned authors understand how Island Press's publishing process works. Please read it carefully, and remember that your editor is always available for questions.

Submitting Your Idea

Island Press will be happy to consider a book at any stage of development. The earlier in the writing process we receive your proposal, the more in-depth market research we can perform and the better able we are to guide you so that your manuscript addresses the major concerns of potential readers.

In order to consider a proposal, we should have the following:

A detailed table of contents with a brief paragraph or annotation describing the topics that will be covered in each chapter.

Two sample chapters. Please be sure that your sample chapters are as typical of your writing as possible. If illustrations, graphs, or charts are important elements of your manuscript, you should provide samples of those as well. Chapters must be typed double-spaced with one-inch margins on all sides.

A detailed curriculum vitae or resume of the author(s). If you are proposing a contributed volume, please include resumes or, at least, full identifications for all chapter authors.

A prospectus. The prospectus for the book gives you a chance to explain why you are writing your book, and for whom. It explains the logic behind the project: what need the book will address, and why it should be published. It enables you to communicate the goals and function of the book to the acquisitions editor, who can then make an informed decision on how the project is to progress.

The Prospectus

The following section lists questions that your prospectus should answer:

THESE QUESTIONS are intended to help you write a prospectus that will help us make a publishing decision. Please answer all questions that apply to your book and provide any additional information that will help us in our evaluation.

• Describe the contents of the book. What is its thesis? What do you hope to accomplish in writing this book? What need does it fill? (Be very specific on this point.) Why is the subject important?

• How would you characterize the book? Is it policy analysis or practical how-to information? • • • Does it develop a theory? Is it a practical tool that professionals will use? Does it shed new light on current controversies? Does it provide historical or analytical information? On what level is it written? Does the reader require specialized knowledge to understand it? What is unique about this book?

• Who is your audience? Be as specific as possible and identify both primary and secondary markets. For professional audiences, please give job titles (city planners, wetland managers, for example). Is the book likely to be used as a primary or supplemental text for college courses? If so, please provide course titles for which it would be appropriate. (If you know how many such courses are taught nationally or how many students they involve, please include that information.) If you think it will be of interest to citizen activists, list names of organizations and membership numbers. Also provide names of newsletters or other publications that reach that audience. Are there any other groups or associations that may have a particular interest in this book? If you know of possibilities for bulk sales, through organizations or conferences, include that information.

• What topics does your book cover? Are there any topics that have not been covered before?

If you are proposing a contributed volume, please discuss the origin of the project (is it based on a conference, for example?), how much (if any) of the material has been previously published, and what you as

editor plan to do to make the book cohere. How will you work with the contributors? Will the contributors see other chapters? How much editing and/or rewriting will you do? What level of consistency of style and quality do you plan to achieve?

What other books have been published on this subject? (Include author, publisher, and date of publication.) What are their strengths and weaknesses? How will your book differ in organization, level, approach, and content? How will your book relate to other books in the field?

• What is the approximate length of the final typed manuscript? Assume 8-1/2-x-11 double-spaced pages with one-inch margins.

• *What elements will the manuscript include:* charts, graphs, tables, photographs, glossary, index, bibliography, and so on? Please be as specific as possible.

• Do you have any particular conception of the production, design, or marketing of the manuscript that we should know about?

• Has your proposal (or manuscript) been read by anyone else whose opinions would be of value to us? Can you suggest the names of three persons who would be competent to read and review your proposal or manuscript?

• When will the manuscript be complete?

Manuscript Development

MANUSCRIPT DEVELOPMENT encompasses the period of writing, reviewing, and rewriting necessary to ensure a well-organized, complete work that is attuned to the needs of its potential audience.

All proposals and manuscripts are carefully reviewed in-house. In addition, when appropriate, manuscripts are sent to several experts in the field. Reviews are conducted for two reasons. First, they help us ensure that the book offers the most complete, well-argued, and current information on the subject. Second, comments, suggestions, and quotations from the reviewers are used by our marketing department to help reach the greatest number of readers possible. In today's highly competitive marketplace, we realize that only a thoughtfully developed book can reach the highest level of success.

Expert reviewers are asked to critique the style, level of writing, organization, comprehensiveness, accuracy, and structure of the text. They evaluate the author's development of his or her argument and the thoroughness of the research. They are asked to cite strengths and weaknesses of the material and to offer suggestions for changes. They comment on the possible audiences for the book and how the book might best meet the needs of those audiences. Those comments are used to guide the authors in manuscript revision. The reviewers' comments help us to determine whether the manuscript requires further work or if it is in acceptable final form, as discussed in the publishing agreement.

We realize that if you are preparing your manuscript in collaboration with an organization you may be conducting your own reviews. In that case, we ask that you send us the names and addresses of reviewers, as well as copies of relevant correspondence. That information will help us in our marketing efforts as well as editorially.

Throughout the review process, our common goal is kept foremost in mind: to develop a book that meets the needs of its audience with cogent, well-presented information that will make a contribution to the environmental literature.

Production

ONCE YOUR EDITOR has an acceptable draft of the manuscript that includes all elements of the book-artwork, glossaries, introduction-it is ready to go into production. The production process and schedule vary for each book, depending on the format, number of pages, illustrations, complexity, and other considerations. What follows is a brief overview of the process.

Copyediting is the first step in the production process. The copyeditor edits the manuscript for grammar, typographical errors, style, consistency, and punctuation, and "marks up" the manuscript for the typesetter. The copyeditor will frequently raise questions regarding ambiguities in content, will point out or clear up discrepancies, and will make minor revisions as necessary.

You will see the copyedited manuscript for your final approval before it is typeset. We want you to review the entire copyedited manuscript to ensure that your meaning has not been inadvertently altered in the copyediting process. This is your last opportunity to make corrections.

The internal text and cover design of the book are done by professional designers who consider all elements of the text and illustrations, as well as the purpose and market of the book. The design process includes input from the editorial, production, and marketing staff.

After copyediting and design are completed, the book goes to the typesetter. The first set of proofs, either galleys or page proofs, will go to you for review, and although a copy will also be sent to a professional proofreader, you are expected to ensure the accuracy of the proofs.

Preparing Your Manuscript

ISLAND PRESS requires that final manuscripts be submitted in duplicate, accompanied by a disk of the same material. All text, including references and extracts, should be double-spaced, and paragraphs should be indented, with no extra lines of space between them. Pages must be numbered consecutively from the first page to the last. If you cannot provide a disk, Island Press can still produce your book, but your editor should be made aware that you will not submit a disk. More-detailed instructions on how to prepare your disk, organize art material, and secure permission to use previously published material can be provided by Island Press staff.

Marketing

AT ISLAND PRESS, we realize that producing a high-quality book is only the first part of a successful publication. Without proper marketing, even the best work in the field may go unnoticed.

We also recognize that you, as an expert in your field, can contribute to the marketing effort, and we encourage you to do so. Your suggestions and advice will be carefully considered, for we share the goal of reaching the largest market for your book.

Once your proposal has been accepted for publication, you will be asked to fill out an author information sheet that will help the marketing department begin its marketing plan. The information you provide will be used throughout the marketing effort.

Our individually tailored marketing plan is designed to capitalize on the strengths and uniqueness of each book and its intended market. Your editor will work closely with the marketing department to provide information and suggestions. Because we have positioned ourselves as the publisher of books for the environmental community, we have a specialized and in-depth understanding of the market for your book.

Our marketing program employs several different strategies in order to ensure that the information we develop and distribute is available to the interdisciplinary and disparate audiences that are working to solve our myriad environmental problems.

Direct mail, especially the Annual Environmental Sourcebook, is the principal marketing mechanism for our books and those of other nonprofit organizations whose work we distribute. The Sourcebook is a unique resource, distributed biannually to more than 150,000 federal, state, and local public officials, businesses, libraries, organizations, community leaders, colleges, and universities. Since 1985 we have marketed and distributed more than 150 titles published by 60 conservation and environmental organizations. The Island Press Sourcebook offers a selection of books available nowhere else. Publishers whose books are represented include nonprofit policy and research organizations, university presses, and commercial and professional publishing houses. The subjects covered include toxics, water, federal lands, wildlife, forestry, tropical forests, agriculture, community issues, business and the environment, population, and sustainable development. The books are used as manuals for citizen action, for technical training in college classrooms, for congressional and corporate offices, for environmental professionals, and for libraries. Books are selected by our editorial and marketing staff, taking into account recommendations of our Editorial Advisory Committee and other key individuals and organizations in the environmental community. The same criteria that we use to evaluate manuscripts submitted to Island Press for publication are applied to our "client line" titles.

Our direct-mail program includes not only the Sourcebook, but other targeted direct-mail pieces about books that would be of interest to particular audiences. The direct-mail program ensures that Island Press books reach key groups of environmental professionals, planners, and state and local officials.

Journals and magazines are important marketing vehicles for Island Press books. Not only do we place advertising in specialized magazines and journals, but also our books are widely reviewed. Reviews are a major source of information on these books to key audiences. In our books are widely reviewed. Reviews are a major the last two years, Island Press books have been reviewed in every major environmental periodical, and in many of the most important environmental newspapers and magazines. Reviews in Choice, Publishers Weekly, The New York Times, Library Journal, The Washington Post, Science News, Booklist, E Magazine, Environment, Garbage, Sierra, and others, including the more technical environmental periodicals, ensure that professors, professionals, librarians, and the public are made aware of Island Press books.

Course adoption. Special direct-mail promotions to professors have been extremely successful for Island Press. This is a crucial market for us because it means our information is being used for two critical purposes: to train the environmental professionals and public policymakers of the future, and to assist in current research and policy analysis.

Bookstores. Since 1988 our sales to bookstores have steadily increased, reflecting the growing interest among the general public in environmental issues. In 1989 we contracted with twenty-eight regional sales representatives; the result is that Island Press books are now marketed to bookstores throughout the United States, giving us the capacity to reach concerned citizens throughout the country.

Conference exhibitions. Our editorial and marketing staffs exhibit at professional conferences such as the North American Wildlife and Natural Resources Conference and the annual meetings of the American Institute of Biological Sciences, the American Association for the Advancement of Sciences, the American Planning Association, and the Society for Ecological Restoration. This is one of the most productive methods of introducing new titles to targeted groups of faculty and professionals.

Bulk sales. Selling books to organizations for distribution to their membership is an important channel of distribution for Island Press books. This is an effective way to reach key market segments efficiently and quickly.

Publicity and promotion. In addition to providing our authors with materials for speaking engagements, we conduct publicity campaigns to generate media coverage such as interviews on radio and television, articles in magazines and newspapers, and coverage by organizational newsletters. For selected books, we also arrange bookstore appearances by authors.

Categories: Nonfiction—Agriculture—Conservation—Ecology—Environment—Science

CONTACT: Acquisitions Editor
Material: All
1718 Connecticut Ave., N.W., Ste. 300
Washington, DC 20009-1148
Phone: 202-232-7933
Fax: 202-234-1328
E-mail: info@islandpress.org
Website: www.islandpress.org

Remember: Editors change jobs and publishers change addresses. It is wise to invest in a phone call for the current information before submitting.

Ivan R. Dee, Inc., Publisher

If you wish to inquire about our interest in a book manuscript you have prepared or are preparing, please send a query letter along with a brief description of the work, if possible a listing of contents or chapters, and at least two sample chapters. If you simply have an idea for a book, write us about it in detail.

Ordinarily you will hear from us within thirty days–sooner if the manuscript is clearly not for us, occasionally later if the work presents a difficult publishing decision.

We are publishers of serious nonfiction, in both hardcover and paperback, in history, politics, literature, biography, and theatre.

Categories: Nonfiction—Biography—History—Literature—Politics—Theatre

CONTACT: Ivan R. Dee, President
Material: All
1332 N. Halsted St.
Chicago IL 60622
Phone: 312-787-6262
Fax: 312-787-6269

Jewish Lights Publishing

Guidelines for Manuscript Submissions

Jewish Lights publishes books for people of all faiths and all backgrounds. Our authors are at the forefront of spiritual thought. They draw on the Jewish wisdom tradition to deal with the quest for the self and for finding meaning in life. Our books are non-fiction almost exclusively, covering topics including religion, Jewish life cycle, theology, philosophy, history, and spirituality. We do not publish biography, haggadot, or poetry. At this point we plan to do only two books for children annually.

Because of the tremendous number of manuscript submissions we receive, we cannot correspond individually with authors until we receive a proposal of what they would like to submit for publication.

A proposal includes:
• A cover letter
• A table of contents
• The introduction to the book
• Two sample chapters (do not send the entire book)

A self-addressed stamped envelope if the material is to be returned to the author. (Please note that without a self-addressed stamped envelope, your material will not be returned.)

If your project is a short (under 40 pages) children's picture book, you should send the entire text.

Send the material (on paper, no computer disks and no e-mail please) to the Submissions Editor at Jewish Lights at Sunset Farm Offices, Route 4, P.O. Box 237, Woodstock, Vermont 05091. Please note that we cannot accept submissions via the internet.

After sending your material, please allow approximately three months for a reply. We are very sorry that this process is slow, but it is the only way we can that all material receives proper consideration.

Thank you for considering Jewish Lights Publishing.

Categories: Nonfiction—Biography—Cooking—Crafts/Hobbies—Culture—Ecology—Family—History—Inspirational—Jewish Interest—Parenting—Religion—Spiritual—Travel—Women's Issues—Children's Picture Books—Healing/Recovery—Life Cycle—Mysticism—Philosophy—Theology

CONTACT: Submissions Editor
Material: All
Sunset Farm Offices, Route 4
PO Box 237
Woodstock VT 05091
Phone: 802-457-4000
Fax: 802-457-4004
E-mail: everyone@longhillpartners.com

Jist Works/Park Avenue

Book Proposal Guidelines

Thank you for your interest in being a JIST author. We are proud of our hundreds of products that help people help themselves find good jobs and make their lives better. If you have an idea for a book that fits with JIST's core values and markets, we will be glad to review it for possible publication. To give your proposal the best chance of being selected for publication, please make sure that it includes everything we need to determine whether your book is right for JIST.

Before You Send Your Proposal

Before sending your proposal, you need to do a little homework to make sure your book is right for us and that we completely understand what your book is about, who it is for, and how it will sell.

Familiarize yourself with JIST. Browse our Web site or request a catalog. Look at the types of books we publish and the subjects we cover. We are currently publishing books and other media (videos, software, assessment inventories, workbooks, and instructors' guides) on job search and careers. We are especially interested in products that appeal to institutional markets such as schools, colleges and universities, government agencies, and workforce-development programs. We occasionally publish books on education and training, as well as business topics; however, career and job search books get top consideration. Your book must fit our niche but not compete directly with any of our current products.

Research the competition. Go to bookstores or Amazon.com and see what other books have already been published on the subject. Think of how your book is different and better than existing books. Does it approach the subject from a different angle, include new coverage of the topic, or have some other element that will be irresistible to buyers?

Research the audience and market. Know who your book is for and how a publisher can best make these people aware of your book so that they will buy it.

Compile your formal book proposal. Put together all the items that we will need to determine whether will publish your book. See the next section for details.

Please don't call! We regret that the volume of submissions prevents us from discussing proposals over the telephone.

What Your Proposal Must Include

Your proposal should be clear and concise. It should be three to seven pages in length, not including the sample chapters and your resume or CV. Crucial elements to include are the following:

Working Title

What title do you propose for this book? Please include your first choice as well as a few alternatives. List the keywords that the title should definitely include—words that convey the essence of the book and appeal to the target audience.

Summary

Answer as many of the following questions as possible:
• In a nutshell, what is the book about?
• What led you to write it?
• What need does the book fill? What problems does it solve? Why is the information important?
• How is the topic increasing in importance rather than declining?
• How do you envision the finished product? What are its dimensions, page count, and other physical specifics? Does it include charts, worksheets, illustrations, or other special features?

Target Audience

Who is going to buy your book? Provide demographic information for your target audience, such as:

- Age
- Reading level
- Gender (if applicable)
- Education level
- Place in career (entry level, mid-career, advanced)
- Vocation or industry (blue collar, professional, clerical, etc.)
- Specific fields (medical, legal, computers, teachers, etc.)
- What magazines or professional journals do they read?
- What associations do they belong to and what conferences do they attend?

Target Markets

Besides bookstores, where is this book going to sell? Identify institutions and organizations that are likely to purchase the book. Identify the primary market and at least two secondary markets.

Competitive Analysis

Determine which existing books are the most similar to your proposed book in terms of audience, scope, and coverage. List the top 5 or more most relevant competing books and include the following information for each:

- Book title
- Year published
- Publisher
- Page count
- Price
- Trim size (6 x 9, 8½ x 11, etc.)
- Amazon.com sales ranking
- How your book is different and better than each book

Sales and Marketing Analysis

- Research the potential market for your book and give facts and figures that support the notion that significant numbers of people will buy it.
- Are there factors, such as government spending, that will affect the demand for information in this area?
- Demonstrate your ability and willingness to help promote and sell the book after it is published. Suggest ways that your publisher can partner with you to market and sell the book.
- If you have contacts within companies or organizations that would be interested in buying the book in quantity, describe them here.
- If you have previously published other books, please provide sales figures for them.

Outline

Include a full, detailed outline of the topics that your book will cover. The outline should include chapter titles, chapter subtopics, and synopses of what each chapter covers.

Sample Chapters

Include the book's Introduction, which should explain the questions the book addresses and what answers it gives. Also send at least one full chapter (preferably not the first chapter) that is representative of your writing and organizational skills as well as your knowledge of the subject.

Your Bio and Qualifications as an Author

Please send a copy of your current resume or CV. Include information on previous writing and publications you have done. Demonstrate why you are an authority on your subject and why you are the right person to write this book. Include any affiliations or associations you belong to that will enable you to help promote the book after it is published. Do you regularly speak to large audiences on topics related to your book's subject? Do you have access to specific, relevant mailing lists? Do you write a regular column for a newspaper or magazine? Are you an instructor who will use your own book as required reading in your classes?

Project Status

Is your book already written? If not, when do you expect to finish it? Have you proposed it to other publishers previously or simulta-neously? Has it been previously published and the rights have reverted to you? What type of software are you using to prepare the manu-script?

Self-addressed, Stamped Envelope

If you would like your materials returned to you, please include a self-addressed, stamped envelope. Otherwise, they will be filed or discarded after a period of time.

Where to Send Your Proposal

We accept submissions through the mail and by e-mail. If your career or job search book or assessment is intended primarily for the institutional markets or is a labor market reference book.

Categories: Nonfiction—Business—Careers—Interview—Reference

CONTACT: Susan Pines, Associate Publisher
Material: All
8902 Otis Ave.
Indianapolis, IN 46216-1033
E-mail: spines@jist.com

J.N. Townsend Publishing

J. N. Townsend Publishing has been bringing you classic animal books since 1986. We will continue to bring out reprints of past classics, as well as occasional new books that catch our fancy and will delight our readers.

No formal guidelines available
Categories: Fiction—Nonfiction—Animals

CONTACT: Jeremy Townsend, Publisher
Material: All
4 Franklin St.
Exeter, NH 03833
Phone: 603-778-9883
Website: www.jntownsendpublishing.com

Jodere Group

Jodere Group was created as a unique publishing and multimedia avenue for individuals whose mission it is to positively impact the lives of others.

Jodere Group recognizes the strength of an original thought, a kind word and a selfless act — and the power of the individuals who possess them. Jodere Group is committed to providing the support, passion and creativity necessary for these individuals to achieve their goals and their dreams.

The Jodere Group is driven by our mission statement. If you and your book fall under the umbrella of our mission statement, then we would consider publishing you. Beyond that, we are looking for creative works that push the reader to explore new areas of life or of themselves. We don't shy away from controversy — so long as it serves a higher purpose. The Jodere Group team is happiest when our work provokes good conversation, stimulates thought and, ultimately, changes lives.

The best way to submit to us is by adhering to the following loose guidelines. We're only human, so queries that are thoughtful, well written, typed and proof read make a better impression. We want to know who you are, what you've done before, and what your project is about. In terms of length, we need enough detail to be interested, but it is not necessarily a bad thing to leave us wanting more.

A good guideline to follow is a cover letter, outline or brief synopsis of the work (with word count if possible), a sample chapter or two and a stamped, self-addressed envelope for our response. Please double-space.

Since we read all submissions, it does take us a little time to get back to you. We make every effort to respond no later than four weeks from receipt.

Books
A-L

You're welcome to call and confirm that we've received your submission, but then if you could be patient we'll get back to you when we've had a chance to give it appropriate time and consideration.

If you include a SASE we will return your materials, however, we learned a long time ago not to assume responsibility for acts of God or the Post Office. If it doesn't make it back to you once it is mailed — we apologize.

We respect your work and would never deliberately lose or damage it.

We look forward to reading your work. Again, thank you for your consideration.

Categories: Nonfiction—Business—Children—Health—Inspirational—Psychology—Relationships—Self Help—Spiritual—Women's Issues

CONTACT: Submissions Editor
Material: All
PO Box 910147
San Diego CA 92191
Phone: 800-569-1002
Fax: 858-638-8170
E-mail: info@joderegroup.com
Website: www.jodere.com

John Daniel & Company
P U B L I S H E R S

John Daniel & Company

About the Press.

John Daniel and Company is a small press publisher of belles lettres. We publish only four titles a year, with print runs averaging 1,000-2,000. Our books are distributed to the trade by SCB Distributors. In addition to trade sales, we rely heavily on direct-mail sales from our website and from announcements we send out for each book we publish.

Editorial focus.

"Belles lettres" is a fuzzy term that allows us a lot of leeway, but it does exclude children's books, genre fiction, cookbooks, photography books, how-to books, and a number of other categories that are better published by the major-league publishing establishment. "Belles lettres," for us, means stylish and elegant writing; beyond that definition I should mention that we are particularly interested in essays, literary memoirs, and short fiction dealing with social issues. We publish only one poetry title a year. For economic reasons almost all our books are under 200 pages long.

Royalties.

We do not pay advances, and our royalties are based on 10 percent of the net receipts (cover price minus discount allowed to the customer).

Submission requirements.

To submit material, send synopsis plus 50 sample pages. Allow six to eight weeks for response. Manuscripts received without SASE will be discarded. We do not accept submissions in the form of disks, e-mail, fax, or phone calls.

Some free advice.

We receive over five thousand unsolicited manuscripts and query letters a year. We publish four manuscripts a year, of which fewer than half were received unsolicited. Obviously the odds are not with you. For this reason we encourage you to send out multiple submissions and we do not expect you to tie up your chances while waiting for our response.

Categories: Fiction—Nonfiction—Literature—Poetry—Short Stories—Essays—Memoir

CONTACT: John Daniel, Publisher
Material: All
PO Box 2790
McKinleyville, CA 95519
Phone: 707-839-3495
Fax: 707-839-3242
E-mail: dandd@danielpublishing.com
Website: www.danielpublishing.com

Johnston Associates International

JASI publishes nonfiction trade-format regional travel books. *The following guidelines are designed to assist you in submitting a book proposal:*

Submission Guidelines

Your proposal should consist of seven sections:

1. Important and unique features of the topic

Explain what your book is about and why it is needed. Also describe the unique features of your book and anything that makes it different from all other books of the same topic.

2. Market

Describe the audience for your book. Who are the most likely readers to buy your book? Why should they buy it, keep it or talk about it?

3. Competition

List the books that directly compete with the project you are proposing. How do they compare with your book subject in length, scope, format and visual appeal? Explain why they are not adequate to meet the need you have identified. If no such book is available for the market you're addressing, cite any books that seem even remotely comparable and explain the difference between your approach and theirs.

4. Outline or annotated table of contents

The outline of your book should be similar to a table of contents. It should include chapter titles and subheads, if any. For each chapter, include a paragraph of about 100 words summarizing the chapter's contents.

5. Publishing details

Give an estimate of how long your book will be. Do you plan to have photographs or illustrations? Maps? How many? How long will you need to complete the manuscript?

6. Author background

Please include a resume or information sheet detailing your background and areas of expertise and/or interest, including prior publications.

7. Promotion

How will you help promote your book? Do you have databases, lists of contacts?

Additional Tips

If you submit to other publishers simultaneously, please let us know.

Be sure to include phone and fax numbers and an e-mail address (if you have one) where you may be reached.

Allow 4 weeks for initial response.

Please include sample chapters. If you don't have these, the outline will suffice.

Thank you for thinking of JASI!

Categories: Nonfiction—General Interest—Outdoors—Recreation—Regional—Senior Citizen—Travel

CONTACT: Priscilla Johnston, Publisher
Material: All
PO Box 313
Medina WA 98039
Phone: 425-454-3490
Fax: 425-462-1335
E-mail: JasiBooks@aol.com

Jona Books

GENERAL INFORMATION:

Submit an introductory letter, two sample chapters and synopsis for the rest of the book. All manuscripts should be on white paper and double-spaced. Please allow two months for a reply. Floppy or CD preferred.

- Queries/proposals — please allow two weeks for a reply.
- Simultaneous submissions are ok.
- Electronic queries accepted (please put Book Submission in subject line; attachments are in Microsoft Word).
- We publish 18 months after acceptance.

GENRE

Nonfiction:
- Biographies
- Native American history
- Old West
- True crime
- Military history
- Americana

Fiction:
- Alternate history
- Science Fiction
- Military Science fiction
- Historical fiction
- Humor

Payment:
- Negotiated on an individual basis with writer.
- No advance offered at this time.

Categories: Fiction—Nonfiction—Biography—History—Humor—Military—Science Fiction—True Crime—Western

CONTACT: Tim Baker, Senior Editor
Material: Queries
PO Box 336
Bedford IN 74721
Phone: 812-278-9512
Fax: 812-278-9518

Judson Press

Guidelines for Unsolicited Manuscripts

Judson Press is a ministry of the Board of National Ministries, American Baptist Churches in the U.S.A.

First Things

Aspiring writers should proceed with confidence that even if they are virtually unknown, it is still possible to get a book published. The primary ingredients for success are (1)content that is unique and compelling, (2)identification of an appropriate target market, and (3)writing that is unusually artful and insightful.

Writers should realize, however, that because the competition is so great, getting a book published is extremely difficult. Judson Press publishes only about one book for every twenty-five ideas or proposals it receives. With larger publishers, this ratio is typically one to one hundred or even higher. Thus the importance of considering carefully the elements that go into a successful book cannot be overstated.

Content

It is the writer's responsibility to be aware of published resources similar to the book he or she has in mind and to ensure that the proposed book will be unique-substantially different from resources currently available. Not only must the book be unique, but it must also be compelling. It should contain some combination of information, analysis, perspective, or insights that a substantial number of readers will find valuable and to which they will be drawn.

Target audience

It is a rare book that can succeed if written for everyone. A writer must identify a target market and must know intimately the character traits, needs, and wants of the individuals who form that target market.

When a writer identifies "all people" or "all Christian people" as the potential audience, it usually signifies that he or she has not thought carefully enough about the target audience. It may seem advantageous for everyone to be a potential buyer of the proposed book. But generally the way the market thinks is, "If this book is for everyone, it must not be for me."

While the target market should not be too broad, neither should it be too specific. For example, recently publishers have produced devotional books for gardeners (an appropriate narrowing of the market), but not for tulip enthusiasts.

Finding the Right Publisher

Successful publishers have developed specific "niches," or areas of specialty. These niches are based on such related factors as the content and style of books, as well as their target audience(s). It is the writer's responsibility to search out and find publishers best suited for the book he or she has in mind.

To accomplish this, the writer may make use of such publications as *The Writer's Market* and *Literary Marketplace*, both of which can be found in most public libraries. Writers may consult publishers' catalogs either in printed form or on-line. Another option is to visit local bookstores in order to determine who publishes books similar to the one the author has in mind. Writers are advised not to call publishers for this information.

It is perfectly appropriate for writers to submit a book proposal to more than one publisher simultaneously. As a courtesy, the writer should inform each publisher of this simultaneous submission. Should more than one publisher be interested in the proposed book, the writer has every right to compare offers, regardless of which publisher may have been first to offer a contract.

Judson's Publishing Niches

Judson Press is currently NOT pursuing works of fiction (including children's fiction), poetry, or autobiography (books based largely or exclusively on the author's life experiences).

Following are Judson's primary areas of interest:

- Practical church resources for pastors and laity in such areas as church life, spiritual formation, discipleship, Christian education, Christian living, worship, evangelism, leadership, family life, drama, Bible study, renewal, social issues, marriage, parenting, theology, self-help, resources related to ministry to children and youth, and resources for seniors.
- Resources for the African American church
- Baptist heritage and identity resources
- Resources for Christian women
- Pastors' resources (including preaching resources)

Submitting a Book Proposal

Many writers want to avoid writing a book-length manuscript only to find out that no publisher is interested or that a publisher prefers a substantially different approach. And most publishers, including Judson Press, and would rather not receive an entire manuscript in order to make a decision. The book proposal addresses the concerns of both writer and publisher.

A book proposal submitted to Judson Press should contain the following five elements:

- A Working Title-A title and subtitle that successfully convey the book's tone and essential content indicates that the writer has thought carefully about the book's focus and target market.

• Summary of the book-Two or three paragraphs summarizing the book's content and purposes should include some reference to the book's target audience.

• Chapter descriptions-A listing of the book's proposed chapters, along with a one- or two-sentence description of each chapter, helps editors to see how the book "unfolds" and to determine if the book is organized clearly and logically.

• Sample chapters-Writers should submit twenty to thirty pages of sample writing. This typically means two or three sample chapters, but it will vary based on the nature of the book.

• Market analysis-The writer should provide information on books in print that are similar to the idea being proposed, focusing on what is distinctive about his or her idea.

Writers should also either include a resume or make reference in the cover letter to relevant qualifications (experiences, vocation, education, etc.) for writing this book.

Please do not submit proposals via e-mail or computer disk. We prefer a printed copy. Sample chapters should be double-spaced with one-inch margins and in 12-point Times New Roman font. Please include a postage-paid envelope if you would like to have your materials returned to you.

After Submitting Your Manuscript

Typically, Judson Press is able to respond to book proposals within six weeks. Generally there is no relationship between Judson's interest in a manuscript and the amount of time it takes to respond. Authors should feel free to contact the publisher by phone or e-mail every six weeks or so.

If a book proposal is approved by Judson Press, the author will receive a contract offer. In accordance with the contract, the author turns over rights to the publisher. In exchange, the publisher agrees to pay all costs associated with editing, designing, manufacturing, marketing, and distributing the book. The contract also specifies details pertaining to the length of the book, royalty payments to the author, and the author's deadline for turning in the completed manuscript.

The people of Judson Press hope the best for you as you explore the possibility of writing a book for publication. If you need more information, you may call 1-800-4-JUDSON and ask for the acquisitions editor.

Categories: Nonfiction—African-American—Children—Christian Interests—Family—Inspirational—Multicultural—Religion—Senior Citizen—Spiritual—Women's Issues

CONTACT: Acquisitions Editor
Material: All
PO Box 851
Valley Forge PA 19482-0851
Phone: 610-768-2109
Fax: 610-768-2441
Website: www.judsonpress.com

Jupiter Scientific Publishing

Company Description

Jupiter Scientific is dedicated to the promotion of science and scientific education through books, the internet, and other means of communication.

Author Submissions

Jupiter Scientific Publishing will only consider non-fiction books of the highest scientific standards. No metaphysical or philosophical books should be submitted. Historical discussions of science, if present, should play a secondary role in the book.

Authors should first send a query letter no longer than two pages, providing the subject matter for the book, the qualifications of the author(s) and the targeted market. Authors should point out features that are unique and how their book is different from those currently available. The query letter may be sent by ordinary mail or by e-mail.

Multiple submissions are permitted but must be indicated in the query letter.

Jupiter Scientific Publishing responds to query letters within 30 days. Approximately 1% of the proposals submitted to JSP are accepted for publication.

Categories: Nonfiction—Ediucation—Science

CONTACT: Stewart Allen
Material: Popular Science Books
415 Moraga Ave
Piedmont CA 94611
E-mail: admin@jupiterscientific.org
Website: www.jupiterscientific.org/science/authors.html

Just Us Books

Thank you for your interest in Just Us Books. A premier, independent publisher of Black-interest books for young people, Just Us Books has an active publishing program that produces eight to twelve new titles per year.

Just Us Books is happy to announce that we are now accepting manuscript queries. We are currently looking for chapter-book manuscripts targeted to middle readers ages 8-12 and novels for young adult readers ages 13-16.

Writers: To submit a manuscript please mail a query letter with a 1-2 page synopsis of your manuscript, a short bio or description of previously published work or writing experience, and a self addressed stamped envelope (SASE) for our reply. If we wish to review your manuscript, we will request in writing that you forward it to us for consideration. All queries that are accompanied by a SASE will receive a response, generally within 8-10 weeks. Queries that are not accompanied by a SASE will not receive a response.

Please do not send unsolicited manuscripts. Just Us Books does not accept nor will we be held responsible for unsolicited manuscripts. Just Us Books also does not respond to queries sent via e-mail, fax or phone. All queries must be sent by mail only. Due to the volume of submissions we receive, our editorial department is unable to verify receipt of a query. Receipt verification must be done via certified mail, Federal Express, or other similar services.

Artists: Please send non-returnable samples or tearsheets only. Do not send original art. All submissions will be reviewed and filed for consideration.

We encourage authors and illustrators to familiarize themselves with Just Us Books publishing program before submitting a query. Information about the company, its focus, and editorial needs is available at www.justusbooks.com. Additionally, a wealth of information about the publishing industry is available through Internet resources and trade journals such as Publishers Weekly, Quarterly Black Review and Black Issues Books Review. You may also find helpful information through the MultiCultural Education and Publishing Council's web site, www.mpec.org, the Small Press Center, www.smallpress.org, and the Children's Book Council, www.cbcbooks.org.

Please also take advantage of continuing education courses, writing workshops, and publishing seminars offered by local colleges and professional literary organizations. Just Us Books founders, Wade and Cheryl Hudson are also available for customized writing workshops. For more information, visit www.justusbooks.com.

Again, thank you for your interest in Just Us Books.

Categories: African-American—Biography—Christian Interests—Culture—Family—Juvenile—Multicultural—Teen—Trade: Children's—Young Adult

CONTACT: The Editor
Material: All
356 Glenwood Ave.
East Orange, NJ 07017
Phone: 973-672-7701

Fax: 973-677-7570
E-mail: justusbooks@aol.com
Website: www.justusbooks.com

Kali Press

Mission Statement

There are two divisions which accept queries and manuscript submissions:

Kali Press currently has five titles published which focus on specialized areas of natural health care topics. Kali Press is interested in endemic cultures, nonfiction works with emphasis on spiritual breakthroughs and/or teachings.

Submission Guidelines

Queries must precede submissions. The query must include the following: A synopsis or outline of the manuscript; a description of figures, captions, photos or illustrations together with a number count. Full manuscripts will be requested and further instructions will be provided upon approval of the book concept.

Categories: Nonfiction—Diet/Nutrition—Environment—Health—Inspirational—Native American—Parenting—Spiritual

CONTACT: Cynthia Bellini, Managing Director
Material: All
PO Box 1031
Port Townsend WA 98368
Phone: 360-385-1933
Fax: 360-385-1180
E-mail: info@Kalipress.com

Kar-Ben Publishing
A division of Lerner Publishing Group

Guidelines for Writers and Illustrators

Kar-Ben publishes about 8-10 new titles each year. All of them are books on Jewish themes for children and families. We are happy to review unsolicited manuscripts and artists' samples. These are accepted at all times of the year. If you wish a response, you must include a SASE. Please allow 3-5 weeks for a reply.

Illustrators

Please submit samples that show skill in children's book illustration. Color photocopies and tear sheets are preferred. Please do not send original art.

Writers

We consider fiction and nonfiction for preschool through high school, including holiday books, life-cycle stories, Bible tales, folk tales, board books, and activity books. We do not publish games, textbooks, or books in Hebrew.

Your story should be concise, have interesting, believable characters, and action that holds the readers' attention. Good prose is far better than tortured verse.

Manuscripts must be typed and double-spaced. Don't forget to check spelling, grammar, facts and typos.

Art is contracted for separately. It is not necessary or desirable to include art with your text.

We do not have time to critique unsolicited manuscripts. Please do not call us in this regard.

We offer both contracts based on a flat fee as well as royalty.

Thank you for your interest in Kar-Ben Publishing.

Categories: Fiction—Nonfiction—Children—Family—Jewish Interest—Young Adult

CONTACT: Submission Editor
Material: All
6800 Tildenwood Ln.
Rockville, MD 20852
Phone: 301-984-8733
Fax: 301-881-9195
E-mail: editorial@karben.com
Website: www.karben.com

Kids Books By Kids

Dear Kid Writer,

Thanks for your interest in sending your book idea to Beyond Words Publishing. We do publish books written by kids like you in our "Kids Books By Kids" series. We only publish nonfiction book ideas by kids—no fiction stories or poetry.

So far, we've published three "Kids Books By Kids": *Better Than A Lemonade Stand*, written by a 15-year-old, describes *50 Small Business Ideas for Kids*; *100 Excuses For Kids*, co-written by 10 and 11-year-old best friends, gives excuses for everything from escaping vegetables to avoiding chores; and *Girls Know Best* was written by 38 girls, ages 7-16, and gives advice and activities for girls. We are looking for unusual, practical, nonfiction book ideas for kids. If you can look at any of these three books (at a bookstore or library), they'll give you a better idea of what we're looking for.

When you send us your book idea, here's what we'd like you to include: 1 page about you, 1 page summarizing your book idea, 2-3 pages of writing from your book, 1 self-addressed stamped envelope (we call it a "SASE") so we can send back your story if we decide not to publish it. Also include 1 page of "market research" about your book idea. "Market research" is when you go to the library or a big bookstore and see if there are any other books like yours. If there are, tell us why yours is different and better. Also, tell us who you think will buy your book and why. Can you think of any places besides bookstores that will buy it?

It may take us a while to read and return your book idea, because we get so many every day. It can take up to six months. Thank you for being patient.

Thank you for thinking of us. By following these guidelines, it really helps us to see if your book idea is right for us.

We can't wait to see what you send us!

Submissions Department/Beyond Words Publishing, Inc.

Categories: Nonfiction—Children—Juvenile—Teen

CONTACT: Summer Steele, Manager Editor
Material: All
Beyond Words Publishing, Inc.
20827 NW Cornell Rd. Ste 500
Hillsboro OR 97124
Phone: 503-531-8700
Fax: 503-531-8773
Website: www.beyondword.com

Books A-L

Kinder Books

Please refer to Black Forest Press.

Kregel Kidzone

Please refer to Kregel Publications.

Kregel Publications
Kregel Kidzone

Our Mission Statement

Our mission as an evangelical Christian publisher is to provide—with integrity and excellence—trusted, biblically based resources that challenge and encourage individuals in their Christian lives.

Our Doctrinal Position

We uphold the essentials of the historic conservative, evangelical Christian faith, as reflected in the following primary doctrines: the verbal and plenary inspiration of the Bible as God's Word, inerrant in the original writings; one God existing in three persons—Father, Son, and Holy Spirit; the deity of Jesus Christ; his virgin birth, vicarious death, bodily resurrection, and personal return; the Holy Spirit who convicts the world of sin, righteousness, and judgment, and who regenerates and indwells all believers.

Submission Guidelines for Kregel Publications
Our Publications

We publish new material in the areas of:

• Biblical studies
• Contemporary Issues
• Family and Marriage
• Fiction
• Youth Fiction
• Women's
• Inspirational/Devotional

We do not publish autobiographical material, curriculum, poetry, cartoons, cookbooks, games, or privately subsidized editions for individuals, nor do we distribute private editions previously printed by individuals. Please visit www.kregelpublications.com for a complete product list. If you are submitting children's stories or material for educators, pastors, and leaders please return to the top of this page and click on the appropriate link.

Your Query Letter

Kregel Publications is accepting unsolicited query letters at this time. Your query letter should contain the following information: a summary of your proposed book, its target audience, a brief description of your qualifications to write on this subject, and your educational background. Please send your query letter to Acquisitions Editor, Kregel Publications, PO Box 2607, Grand Rapids, MI 49501-2607 (addressing it to Acquisitions Editor, rather than a name, will allow your letter to be reviewed in the most timely manner). We do not accept queries by email or phone. While we are pleased to review unsolicited query letters, we are not able to respond to every letter we receive. If your project description proves to be of interest to us, we will contact you with further instructions. Please be sure to provide adequate contact information.

We are thankful for your interest in Kregel Publications.

Submission Guidelines for Kregel Kidzone
Kregel Kidzone Publications

Kregel Kidzone is committed to publishing books and collateral materials that target both the spiritual and educational development of children by engaging their God-given creativity, imagination, and interest in the world around them. All of our children's products, whether using Bible narratives, fictional story lines, or real-life situations, must be biblically based and emphasize solid Christian principles and values. We do not publish curriculum, privately subsidized editions for individuals, nor do we distribute private editions for individuals.

Kregel Kidzone Submissions (Query Letters and Manuscripts)

Your query letter should contain the following information: a summary of your proposed book, its target age, an assessment of the manuscript's uniqueness in comparison to books currently available in the same subject area, a brief statement of special marketing/promotional considerations, if any, and a short autobiographical paragraph. We also invite you to submit your manuscript if it is 32 pages or less.

Due to heightened security measures it is no longer possible to return manuscript material. We do not retain materials once they have been reviewed. All materials should be typed, printed, or copied on white, 8 1/2" by 11" paper in a 12-point courier or roman typeface; computer printers should be letter-quality ink jet or laser printers. Please do not bind materials by any means other than a paper clip or spring clip. Staples, three-hole-punch binders, or other means of binding can be a hindrance rather than a help. Kregel Publications cannot be held responsible for materials lost or damaged during the submission process. Please send your submission to: Acquisitions Editor, Kregel Publications, PO Box 2607, Grand Rapids, MI 49501-2607.

Submission Guidelines for Kregel Academic & Professional
Our Purpose & Mission Statement

Kregel Academic & Professional Books publishes resources that enlighten the mind and enrich the heart. Our purpose, therefore, is to offer titles that are both academically responsible and spiritually nourishing. As an evangelical Christian publisher, our mission is to provide—with integrity and excellence-trusted, biblically based resources that challenge and encourage individuals in their Christian lives.

Our Priorities

Kregel Academic & Professional Books is interested in works that meet the needs of professors and students, pastors and missionaries, educators and Christian leaders. We publish new material covering a wide range of theological disciplines, including biblical languages, biblical studies, theology, church history, evangelism and missions, ethics, pastoral ministry, and Christian education. We also seek to publish Bible reference works such as commentaries, dictionaries, and handbooks. We do not publish dissertations.

Your Query Letter

Before sending a formal proposal or a complete manuscript, please address a query letter to Jim Weaver, Director, Kregel Academic & Professional Books, 1190 Summerset Dr., Wooster, OH 44691; or you may send e-mail to jweaver@kregel.com. The query letter should contain the following information: a summary of your proposed book, its target audience, a brief description of your qualifications to write on this subject, and your educational background. Please note that we cannot accept liability for materials lost or damaged during the submission process. Please keep a copy or electronic file of all submitted materials.

Your Proposal

In response to your query letter we may request a formal proposal, which includes the following elements:

• Book's purpose and contribution.
• Book's primary and secondary audiences. Please be specific. It is better to have a specific readership(s) in mind than to have a general one. If you believe the book will be used in institutions of higher learning, state which course(s) of study would use your work.
• Similar volumes. Research the books on the market and describe how your book differs from or improves upon existing works.

- Outline with chapter summaries.
- Sample chapters. This should include the introduction and at least one representative chapter. They will help us identify your writing style and the book's approach and distinctives.
- Estimated date of completion.
- Length. The ratio for a double-spaced manuscript (with 26 lines per page and 65 characters per line) and the finished book is roughly 3:2. For example, a manuscript of 300 pages translates into roughly 200 printed pages.

Illustrative items. Mention the approximate number of photographs, line art, tables, charts, graphs, and maps you envision using in your book.

- Pedagogical aids. Indicate if your book will have such items as study and discussion questions, exercises, boxes, sidebars, glossaries, chapter bibliographies, etc.
- Curriculum vita.
- Testimonials. Letters from experts in the field indicating the need for your book and your ability to write it will help us significantly in assessing the merits of your proposed book.

Send proposal to Jim Weaver, Director, Kregel Academic & Professional Books, 1190 Summerset Dr., Wooster, OH 44691. Do not send your only copy, and be sure to include a self-addressed, stamped envelope for return of your material if so desired. All materials should be typed, printed, or copied on white, 8 1/2" x 11" paper in a 12-point courier or roman typeface. Please do not bind materials by any means other than a paperclip or spring clip. Staples, three-hole punch binders, or other means of binding can be a hindrance rather than a help.

In the event we request a copy of the complete manuscript, please do not send your only copy. Include a SASE if you would like your manuscript returned. We do not retain materials sent without return postage once they have been reviewed. If we request the manuscript be sent on disk or by e-mail, directions will be provided.

Our Procedure

Your manuscript will be reviewed by our editors and/or qualified outside readers. Based upon their favorable assessment, your manuscript will be recommended to our Editorial Committee. The Committee will evaluate your manuscript based upon the reviewers' assessments, the book's creativity, quality of writing, distinctiveness, timeliness, contribution to the field of study, and consistency with the mission of Kregel Academic & Professional Books. Please allow six to nine weeks for us to complete this process. You will be notified of the Committee's decision.

Due to the large number of manuscripts we review, we unfortunately cannot provide updates on the review process. Should we decide to publish your work, a contract will be sent to you, which clearly sets forth the legal agreement to publish and distribute your book. All submissions are the copyrighted property of the author and will not be published by Kregel Academic & Professional Books without a publishing contract.

Thank you for contacting us. We welcome your interest in Kregel Academic & Professional Books.

Categories: Nonfiction—Biography—Children—Christian Interests—Education—Family—Inspirational—Juvenile—Marriage—Parenting—Relationships—Religion—Singles—Spiritual—Teen

CONTACT: Acquisitions Editor
Material: Kregel Publications and Kregel Kidzone submissions
PO Box 2607
Grand Rapids, MI 49501-2607
Phone: 616-451-4775
Website: www.kregel.com

Contact: Jim Weaver, Director, Kregel Academic & Professional Books
Material: Kregel Academic & Professional Books proposals
1190 Summerset Dr.

Wooster, OH 44691
Phone: 330-264-3600
E-mail: jweaver@kregel.com
Website: www.kregel.com

Lake Claremont Press

Where the Second City is second to none . . .
- Preserving the past
- Exploring the present
- Ensuring a future sense of place for our corner of the globe

In a highly-mobile, rootless world where places can easily lose their individual character, Lake Claremont Press books foster and reveal Chicago's special identity by sharing what's distinctive about our city's history, culture, geography, built environment, spirit, people, and lore.

In an age of giant media mergers at one end of the spectrum, Lake Claremont Press represents the alternative at the other end: a small, independent, niche publisher specializing in a subject that we know better than anyone. As such, we stand shoulder-to-shoulder with the publishing houses of that other big city.

Founded by Sharon Woodhouse in 1994, Lake Claremont Press has published 28 titles, including local bestseller Chicago Haunts: Ghostlore of the Windy City and award-winners Hollywood on Lake Michigan: 100 Years of Chicago and the Movies, The Chicago River: A Natural and Unnatural History, and Near West Side Stories: Struggles for Community in Chicago's Maxwell Street Neighborhood. We will release five new books in 2004 and are working on our first Spanish translation, two new product lines, and titles that cover aspects of Chicago sports, architecture, education, nature, music, and African-American neighborhoods.

We welcome new and established authors to submit book proposals and finished manuscripts on all things Chicago. We publish nonfiction trade paperbacks only at this time; we do not publish memoirs, coffee table books, photography, fiction, or poetry. If you have a query that fits these qualifications, we ask that you submit the following:

1. Complete proposal/cover letter
2. Book outline
3. Author credentials
4. Brief marketing analysis
5. 1-2 sample chapters (if not available send samples of previous writing)

Please do not send a full manuscript until it is requested.
Categories: Nonfiction-History-Regional-Travel

CONTACT: Sharon Woodhouse, Publisher
Material: All
4650 N. Rockwell Street
Chicago, IL 60625
Phone: 773-583-7800
E-mail: lcp@lakeclaremont.com
Website: www.lakeclaremont.com

Books A-L

Latin American Literary Review Press

The Latin American Literary Review Press is a non-profit publishing house dedicated to bringing the fiction and poetry of Latin American, Spanish, Brazilian and Portuguese authors to the English-speaking public.

Publications focus on works that were originally written in Spanish or Portuguese and translated into English.

Manuscripts are considered for publication only after the translations have been completed and received by us in their entirety.

Unsolicited manuscripts are considered.

Categories: Fiction—Hispanic—Jewish Interest—Literature—Poetry—Short Stories—Women's Fiction

CONTACT: Yvette E. Miller, Editor
Material: Any
CONTACT: Leanne Longwill, Assist. Editor
Material: Any
PO Box 17660
Pittsburgh PA 15235
Phone: 412-824-7903
Fax: 412-824-7909
E-mail: Latin@angstrom.net
Website: www.Lalrp.org

Legacy Press

Our Objective:
New acquisitions for Legacy Press are now focused on non-fiction books for children ages 2-12. Our books are evangelical Christian (non-denominational) and marketed primarily through Christian bookstores.

These books may include but are not limited to:
• Additions to our Criss Cross Collection, non-fiction books for boys or girls ages 2-12
• Devotionals
• Journals
• Activity ideas
• Books that encourage or promote Christian values
• Books that teach the Bible

We do not publish:
• Books for adults
• Academic work
• Poetry
• Stand-alone fiction
• Curricula

The kinds of writers we are looking for:
• Have accepted Jesus as Savior and are dedicated to serving Him and leading others to Him

• Relate well to the needs of the evangelical Christian market
• Are active participants in a Bible-believing church
• Write creatively, either published or unpublished

To submit your proposal:
• Send a table of contents and 2-5 chapters for our evaluation
• Enclose a resumé or statement explaining your qualifications for writing the book
• Explain the audience for your book and how your book differs from those already on the market
• Enclose a SASE for return of your material if you want it returned
• Type on 8½" x 11" paper, one-sided and double-spaced
• Keep copies of everything you submit to us
• Address to Christy Scannell, Editorial Director. We normally respond in three to six months.

After evaluating your proposal/manuscript, we will do one of the following:
• Offer you a contract. We issue both royalty and full-rights contracts, depending on the type of book.
• Seek expanded material from you
• Ask for revisions and resubmittal

Categories: Nonfiction—Children—Christian Interests—Crafts/Hobbies—Games—Hobbies—Inspirational—Juvenile—Religion—Spiritual

CONTACT: Christy Scannell, Editorial Director
Material: All
PO Box 261129
San Diego CA 92196
Phone: 858-668-3260
E-mail: rainbowed@earthlink.net

Lehigh University Press

The Lehigh University Press is a conduit for nonfiction works of scholarly interest not appropriate for the popular market. Less constrained by demands for profit than a commercial publisher, LUP bases its selection criteria on a manuscript's contribution to the world of ideas. The Press does not publish fiction, poetry, or textbooks.

Our Ever Widening Publication List
Established in 1985 and initially publishing in areas of Lehigh's established strengths in technology and society and eighteenth century studies, LUP today is moving beyond these areas in pursuing its mission to provide high quality monographs for the academic community.

The Press's increasingly wide-ranging publication list includes titles on local, national, and international history; foreign affairs, biography, film, politics, philosophy, East Asian studies, and works for bibliographical reference.

Goals
The director and editorial board have recently made the commitment to publish an increasing amount of primary source material. Titles in our current catalogue include a memoir of the holocaust, an immigrant woman's frontier diary, and the autobiography of a noted scientist. Forthcoming publications will expand the list.

How We Work
Lehigh University Press is an affiliate of Associated University Presses, Cranbury, NJ. LUP's director acquires manuscripts through submission, has them reviewed, and gives his recommendation to the editorial board, which makes the final decision to publish. Approved manuscripts are forwarded to Associated University Presses, which handles the entire production and distribution process.

Inquiries are Encouraged
The Press welcomes for submission any manuscript (or synopsis and sample text of an unfinished manuscript) which is nonfiction, intellectually substantive, and whose format conforms to *The Chicago Manual of Style*, 15th ed. A current resume should accompany all submissions.

The Road to Publication
All manuscripts must be read by one or more scholarly reviewers,

and it is rare that some degree of revision is not called for. Once favorably reviewed and revised, a manuscript must be approved by the editorial board, composed of Lehigh faculty members, which meets two or three times a year. To shorten a journey that extensive revision could make lengthy, it is wise to submit as polished a manuscript as possible. A clearly conceived, sharply focused, thoroughly researched, logically organized, fully documented, and crisply written manuscript sets the author well on the road to publication.

One Last Note

A very important point that scholars seeking to publish dissertations must remember is that dissertations and monographs address rather different audiences. Significant revision or reorganization is usually necessary before a dissertation can make the transition from research piece to scholarly publication.

For information or assistance please write or call Dr. Philip A. Metzger, Director, at the addresses given below.

Manuscript Information Sheet

• Author
• Current Position
• Title of Book

1. Has any part of this manuscript been published previously? If so, where?

2. Is this work a doctoral dissertation? From what University? Date If so, has it been revised? How?

3. Please list any previous publications.

4. Is the manuscript under consideration by any other publisher? (Please list)

5. How long is the manuscript?
Number of chapters or sections?

6. Please supply an abstract (ca. 500 words).

7. Has this manuscript been previously considered by another Associated Universities Presses member? *These include:*

Balch Institute Press
Bucknell University Press
Corning Museum of Glass Press
University of Delaware Press
Fairleigh Dickinson University Press
Folger Shakespeare Library
Lehigh University Press
Moravian Music Foundation Press
University of Scranton Press
Susquehanna University Press
Virginia Center for the Creative Arts
Western Reserve Historical Society

Categories: Nonfiction—Asian-American—Biography—Business—Film/Video—Government—History—Jewish Interest—Music—Reference—Regional—Academic—Philosophy—Public Policy—Technology

CONTACT: Dr. Philip H. Metzger, Director, LUP
Material: All
30 Library Dr.
Bethlehem PA 18015-3067
Phone: 610-758-3933
Fax: 610-758-6331
E-mail: inlup@lehigh.edu
Website: is1.cc.lehigh.edu/inlup/

> *Remember: Editors change jobs and publishers change addresses. It is wise to invest in a phone call for the current information before submitting.*

Lerner Publishing Group
Imprints: Lerner Publications, Carolrhoda Books, Kar-Ben Publishing, LernerSports, First Avenue Editions, Lerner Classroom

Author Submission Policy

Please note: Our submission policy has changed. Effective immediately, we will only accept submissions during the month of November. Submissions received in any other month will be returned to the sender unopened. Thank you for abiding by our policy—it allows us the time to give each submission adequate attention.

The nonfiction submissions editor is Jennifer Zimian; the fiction submissions editor is Zelda Wagner. A SASE, addressed to either Ms. Zimian or Ms. Wagner, is required for all submissions. Allow 8 months for a response. No phone calls please.

Lerner Publishing Group does not publish alphabet books, puzzle books, song books, textbooks, workbooks, religious subject matter, or plays. We accept request for guidelines and catalogs year-round. Do not address these requests to Ms. Zimian or Ma. Wagner. For guidelines please address to GUIDELINE REQUEST and send a business-sized SASE. To receive both a catalog and guidelines, write to CATALOG REQUEST and send a 9"x12" SASE with $3.85 for postage.

Thank you for your interest in Lerner Publishing Group.

Categories: Nonfiction—African-American—Animals—Arts—Asian-American—Biography—Children—Culture—Education—Food/Drink—Government—History—Language—Mulitcultural—Science—Young Adult

CONTACT: Jennifer Zimian
Material: Nonfiction
CONTACT: Zelda Wagner
Material: Fiction
241 First Ave., North
Minneapolis, MN 55401-1607
Phone: 612-332-3344
Fax: 612-332-7615
Website: www.lernerbooks.com

Limelight Editions

To be considered by our editors, both previously published books and manuscripts must be submitted to the address shown below.

Although every proposal is reviewed, we cannot acknowledge any submission or return any material that does not include a self-addressed stamped envelope.

Responses are generally sent within three months.

We are unable to acknowledge receipt of submissions or give status reports.

We cannot be responsible for original copies of manuscripts, photos, artwork, etc. Send only photocopies of such material.

Limelight Editions, an imprint of Proscenium Publishers Inc., is an independent publisher specializing exclusively in nonfiction related to the performing arts–primarily theater, film, music and dance–that includes biographies and autobiographies, instructional books, histories, criticism, collections of interviews, and occasionally play scripts (for adults and children), screenplays and collections of lyrics. While many of our books are adopted for college course, we publish for a general audience and do not publish textbooks as such. Nor do we publish booklets, dissertations or art books.

Submissions must include a covering letter and/or a proposal that describes the book's subject matter and approach, identifies its audience, distinguishes it from other books on the subject and explains what qualifies the author to write the book.

Books
A-L

Submissions may include up to four double-spaced chapters, representative of the book as a whole, that are not bound in any way (no staples, no looseleaf binders) and that are numbered consecutively within each chapter or throughout all the chapters.

Submissions must not include audio cassettes, computer disks or video tapes.

A proposal for a reprint of a previously published book should include a copy of that book.

Categories: Arts—Drama—History—Music—Theatre

CONTACT: Submissions Editor
Material: All
Proscenium Publishers Inc.
118 East 30th St.
New York NY 10016
Phone: 212-532-5525
Fax: 212-532-5526
E-mail: info@limelighteditions.com (for letters only)

LionHearted Publishing, Inc.

New Submission Guidelines
On May 1, 2002, we implemented a new policy

We no longer accept, review, or consider any unsolicited materials without a signed release. Check our website to see if submissions are open or temporarily closes.

Print, complete and return by email, fax, or mail the PDF Release Form or HTML Release Form (available on our website).

ALL SUBMISSIONS MUST FIRST BE EMAILED to Editor@LionHearted.com. Include:

1. A query letter with a 1 paragraph brief story synopsis
2. A 1-2 page full story synopsis.
3. An optional first chapter in the body of the email, or as an attachment, as a sample of your writing style.

An editor will respond by email, phone or mail. Please allow 2-4 weeks.

Any materials submitted without a Release Form will be held without review for 30 days pending arrival of the Release Form, then discarded, or returned if postage is provided.

We realize not everyone has email, but libraries and office supply stores are everywhere offering email, fax, and other electronic services.

Open PDF files with Adobe Acrobat Reader available for free from Adobe's web site.

If you are not able to view or print the Release Form, a PDF verson can be emailed or faxed to you.

Query Letter
E-mail submissions to: Editor@LionHearted.com. PLEASE include:

The manuscript sub-genere (ie: contemporary, historical, time-travel, paranormal, etc.)

Word count.
A one paragraph synopsis (thumbnail sketch) of the story line MUST be included.

A pseudonym if applicable.

Your phone, fax, mail and email addresses.

Synopsis
Synopsis must be included with every submission. It should be a 1-2 page, clear, concise rendering of the complete story line.

Format
Typewritten, double-spaced, minimum one inch (1") margins. Title page must include the author's real name, address, phone/fax numbers, email address, title and word count. Indicate if a pseudonym will be used. In the upper left hand corner include the author's last name and the first major word in the title, e.g., Mitchell/Gone; Woodiwiss/Flame. Include page numbering. Start chapters a third to halfway down the page to allow room for editor comments.

Agents
Unsolicited and non-agent manuscripts are welcome to follow the Submission Policy above. All manuscripts are evaluated equally at LionHearted. The contract is standard.

Postage
For manuscript return, include sufficient stamps (avoid dated postage), International Reply Coupons (IRC=$.80 USD/ea), or a check with a manuscript size self-addressed envelope.

Requested Manuscripts
Manuscripts must have a cover letter and a synopsis. Turnaround is aprox 4-12 weeks. Simultaneous submissions are discouraged.

Payment
LionHearted is not a vanity or subsidy press. Royalties are paid on paperbacks and ebooks. A market competitive advance is paid to contracted authors. LionHearted employs many avenues of distribution on a national level. No author funds are withheld for reserve against returns. All authors should promote their books.

Copyright
Copyright is in the author's name.

We Recommend:
Use two or three rubber bands in both directions to secure your pages.

Include a #10 SASE for editor's comments even if you include a large return envelope.

Send a self-addressed/stamped post card with requested manuscript if confirmation of receipt is desired.

For ease in handling we prefer return envelopes to be Priority Mail envelopes — free from any US post office. Self-address and attach return postage (if metered it must be without a date).

Mail is not delivered to the street address at Lake Tahoe.

Thank you in advance for your cooperation. We look forward to reviewing your submission.

Categories: Romance

CONTACT: Acquisitions Editor
Material: All
PO Box 618
Zephyr Cove NV 89448
Phone: 775-588-1386
E-mail: Editor@LionHearted.com
Website: www.lionhearted.com

Little Simon
An imprint of Simon & Schuster.

We are a novelty imprint that specializes in board books, pop-up books, life-the-flap books, sticker books, touch-and-feel books, and cloth books. The main focus of our list is children 6 months to age 8, and we do not publish picture books. All picture book queries should be directed to Atheneum Books for Young Readers or Simon & Schuster Books for Young Readers, attention of the Submissions Editor.

Because of the volume of submissions we receive, we ask that you follow a few guidelines when sending us a proposal. Please type all query letters and manuscripts, and be sure to include a copy of your manuscript along with your query letter. As we cannot be responsible for manuscripts that are misplaced or lost in the mail, it is advisable to always keep an original copy of your manuscript. Also, please include a self-addressed stamped envelope along with your submission. This helps us respond to you more quickly.

Categories: Children

CONTACT: Submissions Editor
Material: All
Simon & Schuster Children's Publishing Division
1230 Ave of the Americas
New York NY 10020-1295

Little, Brown Children's Books

Please refer to Time Warner Book Group.

Llewellyn Publications

Thank you for your interest in Llewellyn Publications. Llewellyn is the oldest and one of the largest publishers specializing in the New Age Sciences, and we always welcome new writers.

To save you time and effort, we have prepared these Guidelines. They explain both our subject areas and the information we need to consider a manuscript for publication. Please read the Guidelines carefully before submitting anything.

Llewellyn's subject areas include the following:

• *Alternative Realities and Technologies.* Whole food farming, organic gardening, moon gardening, herb gardening and preparation, alternative energy sources, pyramid energies, chaos theory.

• *Alternative Health and Healing.* Diet and nutrition, inner body awareness, longevity, massage and movement, herbalism, aromatherapy, visualization, energy and body work, tai chi, chi gong.

• *Astrology.* Any popular or professional aspect of astrology including natal, relationship, electional, predictive, mundane, horary, financial, medical, historical, magickal, etc.

• *Crafts.* Construction of magical tools, instruments, and objects; cookbooks.

• *Divination.* Tarot, I Ching, runes, dowsing, geomancy, numerology, cards, palmistry, graphology, and body language.

• *Fiction.* Educational and entertaining topics reflecting true "occult" principles: astrology, parapsychology, Witchcraft/Wicca, Pagan lifestyles. No "supernatural horror."

• *Magick and Shamanism.* World and folk magick; mysticism; ceremonial and high magick; use of incense, oils, candles, crystals; spells, ceremonies, and charms; invocation, evocation, and worship; animal magick; the Kabbalah.

• *Men's and Women's Studies.* New issues and approaches to gender-related spiritual, psychic, and physical concerns and needs.

• *Nature Religions and Lifestyles.* Certain aspects of mythology and folklore, solar and lunar related festivals, Paganism, Wicca, rituals, meditations, Earth energies, and ecology.

• *Paranormal.* Hauntings, psychic phenomena, mysteries, UFOs, lost continents.

• *Self-Awareness.* Dream recall, regression and past life recall, personality analysis, consciousness exploration, and occult anatomy (chakras, psychic energies, etc.).

• *Self-Development.* Meditation, personal programming, guided imagery, yoga and some martial arts, development of psychic abilities, past life therapy.

• *Self-Improvement.* Creative visualization, self-hypnosis; success principles; use of color, music, sound, dance; magick for better living; feng shui.

• *Spiritist and Mystery Religions.* Voudoun, Macumba, Huna, Shamanism, Candomble, techniques of trance, drumming, the use of masks, and body magic.

• *Spiritual Science.* Techniques for spiritual growth, prayer, mantra, worship, and the esoteric side of religious and ritual drama.

• *Tantra.* Sex magick, bio-energies, body awareness, Taoism, esoteric dance, Goddess worship, sensual enhancement.

In addition to books, we publish calendars, datebooks, almanacs, magazines, card deck kits, and audio and video cassettes. We prefer books and products that have strong mail-order potential as well as general bookstore and specialty store appeal, and we actively promote our publications, via mail order and direct mail.

Our emphasis is always on the practical: how it works, how to do it, and self-help material. We aim our products at a general audience and do not assume our readers possess previous specialist knowledge. We do not publish "about" books, collections of poetry, or biographies. We are not an academic or scholarly publisher.

PREPARING YOUR MANUSCRIPT FOR SUBMISSION

General Approach. Seeing your book in print is the reward for a long, arduous creative effort, and publishers understand and respect that. But publishing is a business, and you must regard potential publishers as you would any other professional contact. That is, be prepared, well-informed, and realistic. Use your library and any good bookstore for "How to Get Published" guides. *The Writer's Market*, updated annually, also has excellent general guidelines on preparing a submission, and there are some good FAQ (frequently asked questions) sites on the Internet.

Patience is another publishing virtue. Given the volume of submissions Llewellyn now receives, it can take six months for us to respond. If a manuscript requires a second read, it may take even longer.

Submission Package. Llewellyn accepts entire manuscripts for submission or proposals (cover letter, outline, and sample chapters). In either case, we ask you to observe some simple submission rules. *In general:*

• Inform us if this is a multiple submission, and include the number of current submissions.

• We welcome unagented authors (and actually prefer to work directly with authors), but if you do have a literary agent, provide the agent's name, address, and phone number.

• Date and sign all materials, including correspondence, manuscript title page, and diskettes.

• Complete and include the Author Questionnaire and Biographical Data & Book Info Form included with these Guidelines. These forms are essential for our acquisitions, production, marketing, and publicity departments, and your submission will not be reviewed without them.

Please see our website (www.Llewellyn.com) for more specific information on preferred formatting for submissions, marketing, etc.

Categories: Fiction—Nonfiction—Cooking—Diet/Nutrition—Gardening—Health—Inspirational—New Age—Paranormal—Psychology—Religion—Spiritual

CONTACT: Acquisitions Department
Material: All
Llewellyn Worldwide
PO Box 64383
St. Paul MN 55164-0383
Phone: 612-291-1970
Fax: 612-291-1908
E-mail: lwlpc@llewellyn.com
Website: www.Llewellyn.com

Books A-L

Loyola Press

Loyola Press is a not-for-profit publisher, owned and operated since 1912 by the Chicago Province of the Society of Jesus. Our mission is "to help people find God in all things." In that tradition, we publish books about finding God's presence in every aspect of life.

Spirituality books have grown increasingly popular in bookstores over the last five or six years. With our 1997 publication of Cardinal Bernardin's nationally best-selling memoir, *The Gift of Peace*, trade books became our growing product line.

If you are interested in submitting your book proposal to our trade department, please take a few moments to read the following frequently asked questions. Our editorial staff has provided answers. We hope this information helps you decide whether or not to submit your materials to Loyola Press.

What kinds of books does Loyola Press publish?

Loyola Press publishes religion books for the general trade. Our books are about Catholic spirituality—how to live and pray as a Catholic Christian at the turn of the millennium.

Loyola books are practical, focusing on everyday life. Their tone is conversational, not scholarly. They are written for people who live in a fast-paced, bottom-line-driven, technology-focused world—and who long for a welcoming community, deep personal relationships, and time for solitude and reflection.

What kinds of authors write for Loyola Press?

We publish only about two dozen Loyola books a year, so we are highly selective. We are looking for authors who are experts in their fields, yet who can communicate their knowledge to beginners without "talking down." We need authors who love the Catholic spiritual tradition and can open up its riches to others, not in a pedantic way, but in an adult-to-adult manner. We want authors who write simply and clearly—and with style. The winning combination, then, is expertise + experience + style. If you have all three characteristics, please come to us!

What types of manuscripts are you currently interested in?

Loyola Press is a Catholic publisher, and we develop religion books for the general trade. Within the broad areas of religion, spirituality, and Catholicism, here are some specific categories we are developing:

• *Catholic spirituality:* books that integrate spiritual wisdom with various aspects of everyday life. We have a particular interest in Ignatian spirituality for lay people

• *Catholic tradition:* books that explore the time-honored traditions of the church and show what significance they have to our lives today

• *Personal relationships:* books that recognize the spirituality of human connections and help families, friends, and colleagues relate to one another in loving and healthy ways

• *Prayer and meditation:* books of short meditations or books that explain and illustrate how to pray

• *The Seeker Series:* short, popular introductions to various aspects of Christian living

• *Scripture study:* books for nonspecialists on how to pray with or gain wisdom from the Scriptures

• *Jesuit Way:* books that focus on Jesuit life and history as well as on Ignatian spirituality and ministry

What are some of the most recent titles published by Loyola Press?

Loyola books you may have recently seen in a bookstore include *Visions, The Book of Catholic Prayer, Inner Compass, spirituality@work,* and *Bumping into God Again.*

What types of books do not interest Loyola Press?

We also do not consider proposals for academic monographs or dissertations, textbooks, multiauthored collections of essays or symposium papers, fiction, poetry, drama, music, manuscripts with no spiritual applications, or any other category not mentioned in the list under "What types of manuscripts are you currently interested in?" Please also avoid sending us argumentative, ideologically driven books.

How do I interest Loyola Press in my manuscript?

Send a copy of your proposal, not your entire manuscript, to the editorial department. *Your proposal should include the following:*

• A one-paragraph description of the book's theme

• A description of the book's intended audience. Be specific. For example: "young Catholics (aged 18–35) seeking an understanding of Catholic traditions of prayer and devotional practices" instead of "everyone who is interested in prayer"

• A summary of your book's unique features. In other words, explain what your book offers that other books do not. What does it give a reader that he or she cannot get anywhere else?

• An extended outline or chapter summary showing how you develop the theme

• One or two sample chapters

• A summary of your qualifications for writing this book

• A stamped, self-addressed mailer if you wish your materials returned

If you send materials on disk, please:

• Use a fresh 3.5" disk, straight out of the box

• Save your files in MS-Word, Word Perfect, Rich Text Format, or text only

Please do not send us originals of manuscripts, disks, photographs, illustrations, or anything else. We cannot accept responsibility for irreplaceable materials.

When can I expect a reply from Loyola Press?

Proposals are often read by several people, any of whom may be facing deadline pressure or a heavy travel schedule. Thus it can take anywhere from two weeks to three months for us to respond to your proposal. If you wish verification that your proposal was received, please include a stamped, self-addressed postcard, which an editorial assistant will return to you without comment.

Will Loyola Press return my materials?

Yes, if you include a stamped, self-addressed mailer. Otherwise we assume that you have saved the materials on your computer and do not wish us to return them.

What is your main reason for rejecting a manuscript?

In most cases, we turn down manuscripts because they are unsuitable for our list. Loyola Press serves it mission, its readers, and its authors by concentrating on those books that we know we can publish successfully. In general, these are books in the categories described elsewhere in these guidelines. We turn down many proposals not because they are unsound but because we do not think we could publish them well.

Where can I reach you?

Please do not phone. You may contact us by letter, fax, or e-mail. Thank you for your interest in Loyola Press.

Categories: Nonfiction—Christian Interests—History—Relationships—Religion—Spiritual

CONTACT: Daniel Connor
Material: All
3441 N. Ashland Ave.
Chicago IL 60657-1397
Fax: 773-281-0152
E-mail: editors@loyolapress.com
Website: www.lionhearted.com

Lumen Editions

Lumen Editions

All manuscripts submitted to Lumen Editions should be typed. We do not publish genre writing, i.e., science fiction, fantasy, horror, romance. We look for intelligent fiction and nonfiction that is original and that is, most importantly, memorable and evocative of the senses. We do accept multiple submissions, but writers should note in their cover letter that the book is under consideration at other houses. It is suggested that before submitting any manuscript to Lumen, that you telephone and request a catalogue to get a sense of what we do publish. For a catalogue, please send an SASE with two first class stamps.

Categories: Fiction—Nonfiction—Hispanic—Jewish Interest—Literature—Travel—Writing

CONTACT: Milt Budoff, Series Editor
Material: All
PO Box 120

The Lyons Press
An imprint of The Globe Pequot Press

Editorial Director: Jay Cassell

Acquisitions: Jay Cassell, editorial director (fishing, hunting, survival, military, history); Tom McCarthy, senior editor (sports & fitness, history, outdoor adventure, memoirs); George Donahue, senior editor (military history, martial arts, narrative nonfiction); Ann Treistman, senior editor (narrative nonfiction, travelogues, adventure, sports, animals, cooking); Jay McCullough, editor (narrative nonfiction, travelogues, adventure, military, espionage, international current events, fishing); Susannah Hogendorn, editor (adventure & travel, nonfiction narratives, history, memoirs, fiction*, nature, environment, self-sufficiency, woodworking, Americana); Laura Strom, editor (narrative, fiction*, memoir, self-help, Americana-including earlier social customs, ethnic customs, traditions, history, country living of yesterday and today); Lilly Golden, editor-at-large (fiction*, memoirs, narrative nonfiction); Lisa Purcell, editor-at-large (history, adventure, narrative nonfiction, cooking); Steve Price, editor-at-large (equestrian). *Fiction as related to our core categories (horses, fishing, hunting, etc.).

Established 1984: (Lyons & Burford), 1997 (The Lyons Press). Publishes hardcover and trade paperback originals and reprints. Publishes 270 titles per year: 50% of books from first-time authors; 30% from unagented writers. Pays 6-10% royalty of retail price. Offers $2,000-$7,500 advance. Publishes book one year after acceptance of ms. Accepts simultaneous submissions. Responds in 90 days to queries, proposals, and mss. Book catalog is available online.

The Lyons Press has teamed up to develop books with Orvis®, L.L. Bean, *Field & Stream, Outward Bound*, Buckmasters, and *Golf Magazine*. The Lyons Press publishes practical and literary books, chiefly centered on outdoor subjects-natural history, all sports, horses, fishing, and hunting. Currently emphasizing adventure sports, while de-emphasizing gardening, fiction, hobbies, travel.

Nonfiction: Biography, cookbook, how-to, reference. Subjects include agriculture/horticulture, Americana, animals, anthropology/archeology, cooking/foods/nutrition, health/medicine, history, military/war, nature/environment, recreation, science, sports, and travel. "Visit our website and note the featured categories." Query with SASE or submit proposal package including outline, three sample chapters (or 30-50 sample pages), and marketing description. Reviews artwork/photos as part of ms package. Send photocopies or non-original prints.

Category-related Fiction: Historical, military/war, short story collections (fishing, hunting, outdoor, nature), sports. (For more categories, see below.) Query with SASE or submit proposal package including outline and 3-5 sample chapters.

Recent Titles: *Harvest* by Nicola Smith (nature), *Faraway Horses* by Buck Brannaman and Bill Reynolds (equestrian), *The Devil in Buenos Aires* by Lily Powell (fiction), *Frontiers of Heaven* by Stanley Stewart (travel), *Embedded* by Bill Katovsky and Timothy Carlson (current events), *Why I Hate the Democrats* and *Why I Hate the Republicans*, by Randy Howe (politics), *Bitch Creek* by William G. Tapply (mystery), *Going Home Again* by Adam Lucas (sports), *The Orvis® Ultimate Book of Fly Fishing* (fishing), and *The Complete Book of the .22* by Wayne van Zwoll (hunting/weaponry).

Categories: Nonfiction—Adventure—Americana—Boating—Cooking—Fishing—Food/Drink—History—Horses—Hunting—Literature—Military—Outdoors—Pets—Health/Fitness/Recreation—Science—Sports—Travel

Books A-L

CONTACT: Submissions Editor
Material: All
The Lyons Press
Box 480
246 Goose Lane
Guilford, CT 06437
Phone: 203-458-4500
Fax: 203-458-4668
Website: www.lyonspress.com

Remember: Editors change jobs and publishers change addresses. It is wise to invest in a phone call for the current information before submitting.

Mage Publishers

Mage Publishers publishes high-quality English-language books about Persian culture, including: cookbooks, translations of literature, history, children's tales, biography and autobiography, architectural studies, and books on music and poetry. Only books relating to Persian culture are considered by the editors.

Authors interested in submitting work for consideration should send a letter or email outlining their work and a brief biographical statement to the attention of Amin Sepehri at the following address: Mage Publishers, 1032 29th St. NW Washington, DC 20007. We will usually respond to your letter within 2-4 weeks.

Categories: Fiction—Nonfiction—Architecture—Cooking—Culture—Gardening—History—Literature—Multicultural—Music—Short Stories—Ethnic

CONTACT: Amin Sepehri
Material: All
1032 - 29th St. NW
Washington DC 20007
Phone: 202-342-1642
Fax: 202-342-9269
E-mail: as@mage.com
Website: www.mage.com

The Magni Group, Inc.

Formal guidelines not available.
Send queries or book proposals to below address.
Categories: Nonfiction—Animals—Cooking—Crafts/Hobbies—Health

CONTACT: E.B. Reynolds, President
Material: All
Magnico Publishing
7106 Wellington Point Rd.
McKinney TX 75070
Phone: 972-540-2050
Website: www.magnico.com

MAISONNEUVE PRESS

Maisonneuve Press

About Maisonneuve Press: We are the publishing division of the non-profit, educational organization, the Institute for Advanced Cultural Studies. The Institute defines itself as a progressive or left-wing group and intends to promote cultural studies from that radical perspective.

Subject Areas We Publish: The Institute seeks to bring the traditional university based scholar to the forefront of political activism and likewise bring the agenda of radical politics to the university classroom and research. We are interested in books in the general areas of critical cultural studies, the arts, politics, philosophy/theory, international relations, intellectual history, and history. These may be newly written works by a single or group of authors. They may be edited collections of new or old essays. MP does not publish poetry, novels, personal narratives, crime, police, or war stories (though we are interested in anti-war materials), or self-help books.

Currently two book series are active and we are especially interested in adding books in these areas:
- Post Modern Positions
- Critical Studies in Community Development and Architecture

Audience and Market: Our books are aimed somewhere between the academic market and progressive/activist politics. When we review manuscripts, we consider what they contribute to that readership group. The research must fulfill the best of academic standards while the style and rhetoric may address a more informal audience.

Submission Process: MP is interested in relationships with authors at any stage of manuscript development. Ideally, an author would send a letter of inquiry or a proposal for publication, describing the book project and telling something about the author. These initial contacts may range from a single page to about a dozen pages. We will respond to the proposal to let you know if your project appears to be appropriate for MP. If we feel it is appropriate, we will ask you to send the whole manuscript. If your manuscript is finished (or a near-final draft), you can send it or some sample chapters and we will read and report to you. In-house editors first evaluate every manuscript. If a work is judged to be appropriate for the press and to be of significant merit, it will be sent to an outside expert for review and commentary. While we encourage letters and proposals via e-mail, we do not take whole manuscripts electronically (i.e., by e-mail or on a floppy that we must print out to read).

Length and Etc.: Ideally we seek to publish books that have a finished length of 175-300 pages (75,000 to 125,000 words). We encourage the use of photographs, illustrations, or other visual materials. Inside the book, all illustrative material will be printed in black and white, but the cover will be in full color. We follow the MLA style of documentation and manuscript formatting. We appreciate your sending return postage if you wish to have your manuscript returned. We will help you secure rights to publish photos or illustrations.

Manuscript Selection: MP is a small publisher, producing about six titles per year. For that reason, we have to be very selective. We typically receive about 200-300 book proposals each year. The selection of which book to publish is entirely the responsibility of the editors, but each decision is supported by recommendations from outside, expert readers.

Contracts and Royalties: Normally, we issue a contract on finished books. In our contract, we seek exclusive rights to publish and distribute the work all over the world. We actively seek foreign translations and/or publications in other countries. The exclusive rights extend to all formats, including the Internet or CD, but all points in the contract are negotiable. Generally, we pay a royalty of about 5% of the cover price twice each year on actual sales, but on collections of previously published essays we generally pay a flat fee rather than a royalty. We do not pay advances. We pay 50% to the author on any fees we receive from translations or foreign publications. Typically, we publish books in both hardcover for libraries and paperback for the mass market.

Categories: Fiction—Nonfiction—Arts—Culture—Feminism—Film/Video—Human Rights—Law—Literature—Politics

CONTACT: Robert Merrill, Editor
Material: All
PO Box 2980
Washington D.C 20013-2980
Phone: 301-277-7505
Fax: 301-277-2467
Website: www.maisonneuvepress.co

Marcato Books

Please refer to Cricket Books.

Remember: Editors change jobs and publishers change addresses. It is wise to invest in a phone call for the current information before submitting.

March Street Press

March Street Press
Parting Gifts

About Us

We are publisher of ground-breaking poetry and fiction in chapbooks and the semiannual magazine, *Parting Gifts.*

Guidelines for *Parting Gifts* and March Street Press

The editorial vision of *Parting Gifts* and March Street Press relies entirely on a deeply entrenched collection of prejudices. We are highly suspicious of work that turns too heavily on rhyme or meter. Look for the work of Kelly Cherry, Janet Kauffman, C.K. Williams, Jim Harrison, Charles Baxter, and Amy Hempel if you want to see the kind of writing we most enjoy and want to foster. All of these authors are published widely, so you should have no trouble finding their work.

Poetry of the kind that can be found in Ann Landers, Hallmark cards, church bulletins, or high school haiku magazines will probably never appear in our publications. We occasionally receive poems that sound like recycled song lyrics. They are always returned immediately. Even though our semiannual literary magazine has what might be considered a sad title (*Parting Gifts*), that doesn't mean that we specialize in poems written on the deaths of parents, siblings, spouses, children, or pets. Come to think of it, we've covered all those bases over the past ten years—which means that we've paid our dues, so don't send us any more of those, thank you very much.

We publish more poetry than fiction, but fiction is actually our first love. The problem is that we have such high standards and peculiar preferences that it's hard to find fiction to publish. We prefer very short fiction, between 500 and 1000 words. The language in the fiction we publish has to be as strong as the language in poetry—not a misplaced word. And it has to tell a story. No slices of life, please. We've published more than our share of "mad girl" stories—stories about neurasthenic women with cruel boyfriends and outlandish ideas about the world they're muddling through. We're tired of them. Please don't send any more.

Chapbooks should be 25–50 pages. When we accept a chapbook, we often make suggestions—sometimes strong ones—involving inclusion and exclusion of poems or specific lines or stanzas that don't work for one reason or another. That's what real editors do. If you don't think that your work needs an editor, you shouldn't be sending it to one.

We usually accept 5–7 book manuscripts per year. Selection is always made on the basis of quality, so please don't write a letter promising to buy 100 (or 200 or 1000) copies if we accept the book. We aren't a vanity press and that sort of promise doesn't sway us in the slightest. In fact, we find it somewhat insulting. We accept no government grants or loans. For that reason, we occasionally, with deep regret, have to turn away excellent manuscripts for lack of resources to publish at a particular time. We wish we could publish everything of quality that we receive. Generally, when we reject a manuscript (if it is accompanied by a full-sized SASE) we include something of value (usually a book) so you won't feel you've wasted your $20 reading fee. We can't guarantee that, but it's something we try to do as funds permit. When we accept a manuscript, we send the author ten copies of the finished book free (a $90 value at retail) and we are open to providing a limited number of review copies and promotional materials (such as postcards or posters for readings) on request, so long as the privilege isn't abused.

Now we come to an issue that has confused many people: We don't consider book manuscripts from within North Carolina. This is a political statement against the peculiar arts policies of Senator Jesse Helms. We urge North Carolina artists to work against his re-election and we will not publish books by North Carolina artists or sell our books or magazines within North Carolina or accept money from the state arts councils until this man (and we use the term loosely) has have been replaced in the United States Senate by someone who more accurately represents the views of the citizens of North Carolina with regard to freedom of expression. Some feel this is a misguided policy that hurts artists in some way, but we reject that notion because there are plenty of other publishers both inside and outside North Carolina that don't have this policy. If you need a referral, we will be glad to provide it.

Sample copies: $9.00. Subscriptions: $18.00 per year. Checks and money orders (U.S. currency only) should be made out to March Street Press. First rights are all that is claimed by March Street Press for work that appears in *Parting Gifts*. Once the magazine is published, the rights revert to the author. March Street Press requests that publication elsewhere be accompanied by a mention of *Parting Gifts.*

March Street Press is actively seeking chapbook manuscripts. Economic pressures have forced a $20 reading fee. We are sorry for this, but the expenses of this operation are incredible and even at this, we are just breaking even. We encourage authors to submit a computer disk with the manuscript in electronic form along with the paper manuscript. Include a SASE with your submission. We can't seriously consider a submission unless it is accompanied by SASE and reading fee. Please don't bother sending a selection of poems and asking us to make a decision about the book based on them.

And now a word about a writer's responsibility to his or her constitution. Currently the ACLU is involved in a desperate fight to protect our First Amendment rights. While the late Ayatollah attempted to silence one author's voice, the spirit of Ed Meese rose from the sleaze to silence a whole generation of writers. If you thought Jesse Helms as art critic was chilling, the Justice Department as literary critic will put you in the deep freeze. Literally. In the words of Kurt Vonnegut, "The Justice Department has found yet another devastating legal weapon to misuse in its war on our…right to say, show, hear, read, or see whatever we please without fear of punishment." The facts are far too complicated to cover here, but I urge you to contact Ira Glasser of the ACLU at 132 West 43rd Street, New York, New York 10036 for details. And if your right to free expression is important to you, send a check as well. Tell as many people as you can about this situation. Motivate them to contribute, too.

Another worthy cause is the National Coalition Against Censorship. The kind of harassment you might have thought only happened in Nazi Germany is commonplace in America today. Teachers, librarians, booksellers, and others to whom we owe much of our culture and education (what little of it survives) inspire fringe religious and political groups to follow their basest instincts. Write for details: National Coalition Against Censorship, 2 E. 64th St., New York, NY 10023.

Any questions? Please send email to March Street Press.

Categories: Fiction—Poetry

CONTACT: Submissions Editor
Material: All
3413 Wilshire Dr.
Greensboro NC 27408-2923
Website: www.marchstreetpress.com

Margaret K. McElderry Books
An Imprint of Simon & Schuster

Margaret K. McElderry Books publishes original hardcover trade books for children from pre-school age through young adult. The list includes picture books, easy-to-read books, middle grade fiction, poetry, fantasy and young adult fiction. The style and subject matter of the books we publish is almost unlimited. We do not publish textbooks, coloring and activity books, greeting cards, magazines and pamphlets or religious publications.

General Submission Guidelines

Margaret K. McElderry Books is not currently evaluating unsolicited manuscripts. You may send a query letter. The letter should briefly describe the nature of the book. You may also include a very brief resumé of your previous publishing credits. Query letters may be addressed to Emma D. Dryden, Vice President and Editorial Director or Karen Woityla, Senior Editor.

If we ask to see your manuscript

We do not consider submissions sent by fax or on computer disk. If you would like to insure the safe arrival of your manuscript, please enclose a self-addressed, stamped postcard which we will date and send back to you. A self-addressed, stamped envelope must accompany each submission.

Please note: Margaret K. McElderry Books publishes a limited number of picture books each year. It is the prerogative of the publisher to choose illustrators and the art director regularly interviews professional artists for this purpose.

Categories: Children's Trade—Young Adult

CONTACT: Emma D. Dryden, Vice President and Editorial Director
Material: Query Letters
1230 - 6th Ave.
New York NY 10020

Marion Street Press, Inc.

Marion Street Press, Inc. publishes books of interest to writers and journalists. We are known for practical, professional titles that help writers and journalists do their jobs better. Our books are narrow in focus - how to cover a particular beat, how to write in a particular fashion, etc. We also publish reference works of interest to writers.

Recent titles have included *The Dictionary of Concise Writing, Championship Writing, Math Tools for Journalists* and *Pen & Sword: A Journalist's Guide to Covering the Military*. Please visit our website, www.marionstreetpress.com, for more information.

Please query publisher Ed Avis at edavis@marionstreetpress.com before sending a manuscript.

Thank you.
Ed Avis, Publisher—Marion Street Press, Inc.
Categories: Nonfiction—Reference—Writing

CONTACT: Ed Avis, Publisher
Material: All
804 Harrison St., Ste. 2E
Oak Park IL 60304
Phone: 866-443-7987, 708-445-8330
Fax: 708-445-8648
E-mail: edavis@marionstreetpress.com
Website: www.marionstreetpress.com

Markowski International Publishers, Possibility Press

Established in 1976. Publishes trade paperback originals. Publishes 10 titles/year. Receives 1,000+ submissions/year. 95% of books from first time authors; 100% from unagented authors. Average print order for a first book is 5,000-50,000. Pays on royalty basis. Usually publishes book 24 months from acceptance. Accepts simultaneous submissions. Reports within 2 months. Books catalog and ms. guidelines at www.possibilitypress.com.

Nonfiction: Primary focus on personal development, self-help, sales and marketing, leadership training, network marketing, entrepreneurship, motivation and success topics. We are interested in how-to, motivational and instructional books of short to medium length that will serve recognized and emerging needs of focus topics. Query or submit outline, table of contents, and entire ms.

Recent Nonfiction Title: The Power of Having Desire?

Tips: We're intensifying our search for best-selling manuscripts. We're looking for authors who are dedicated to their message and want to make a difference in the world. We especially like to work with authors who speak and consult.

Categories: Business—Inspirational—Money & Finances—Self Help—Entrepreneurship Opportunity—Pop—Psychology—Success

CONTACT: Marjorie L. Markowski, Editor-in-Chief
Material: All
One Oakglade Circle, Ste. 222
Hummelstown PA 17036
Phone: 717-566-0468
Fax: 717-566-6423
Website: www.possibilitypress.com

Maupin House

Maupin House publishes innovative and practical supplemental professional resources for K-12 educators. Our special focus is writing workshop. Other areas of interest are language arts; reading; research; and some K-5 math. All our resources are standards-based and are founded in solid research; however, they are not theoretical advice, but instead focus on the "how to do it" aspect of instruction. Many of the resources are written by teachers, or people who have taught and now are educational consultants. Please look at our web site to first to familiarize yourself with the Maupin House publishing philosophy.

All Maupin House books reinforce our basic publishing premise of empowering teachers to do a better job in the classroom. We do not accept, or espouse formula approaches to teaching. We believe in the power of the teacher to effect classroom learning. We are always looking for the "next great thing" in instruction for our target topics. Classroom-proven techniques always score higher with us than ideas that have not been tested. Our initial response to your email will be within a week. Upon submission of an outline or other supporting materials, expect a response in about two weeks to two months.

We are not interested in poetry, general non-fiction, children's picture books, or other non-target topics. We cannot be responsible for original copies of unsolicited art, photos, or manuscript copies.

Do not submit a finished manuscript. Query by email first with your idea. If we are interested, we will reply and ask you for more specifics regarding your credentials, the marketability and positioning of the work, the competition, and the need for or purpose of the book. Maupin House authors are enthusiastic partners in publishing. They are interested in actively working to market their books through speaking engagements and/or consulting.

Categories: Education—Language

CONTACT: Julia Graddy, Publisher
Material: All
PO Box 90148
Gainesville FL 32607-0148
Phone: 352-373-5588
Website: www.maupinhouse.com

Mayhaven Publishing

When Considering a Manuscript for Mayhaven or our Co-op option: For each manuscript we require one hard copy.

ACCEPTING A MANUSCRIPT IS BASED ON
A NUMBER OF FACTORS:
- The subject
- The slant
- Writing style
- Marketing Considerations

Our Schedule

If the manuscript is a nonfiction work, we require the author's credentials and a summary of the research.

Children's books have special considerations in regard to the type of artwork required.

If a manuscript is accepted, we offer the appropriate Mayhaven or Wild Rose Agreement.

We also offer annual awards for fiction. Categories are adult fiction and children's fiction. Submissions must be in English; must be full manuscript; must not have been previously published; will be accepted from authors or their authorized agents; will not be returned. There is an entry fee of $50.

Thank you for your interest in Mayhaven/Wild Rose Publishing.

Categories: Fiction—Nonfiction—Adventure—Animals—Asian-American—Biography—Children—Civil War—Cooking—Crime—Drama—Disabilities—Family—Fishing—Folklore—Food/Drink—General Interest—Health—History—Inspirational—Juvenile—Literature—Military—Mystery—Native American—Paranormal—Poetry—Politics—Regional—Relationships—Rural America—Satire—Science Fiction—Short Stories—Spiritual—Teen—True Crime—Western—Young Adult—Awards

CONTACT: Doris Wenzel, Editor
Material: All
PO Box 557
Mahomet IL 61853
Phone: 217-586-4493
Fax: 217-586-6330
E-mail: mayhavenpublishing@mchsi.com
Website: www.mayhavenpublishing.com

MacAdam/Cage Publishing

MacAdam/Cage Publishing was founded as an independent trade publisher in 1998 by David Poindexter with the aim of publishing books of quality fiction and non-fiction and committed to bringing new and talented voices to the literary marketplace.

In 1999 MacAdam/Cage Publishing acquired MacMurray & Beck, another independent press, well known in the industry for launching authors such as Patricia Henley (Hummingbird House), William Gay (The Long Home) and Susan Vreeland (Girl in Hyacinth Blue) and heavily supported by the bookselling trade with many BookSense 76 picks as well as appearances in chainstore fiction programs aimed at highlighting new authors.

Having joined forces, and now with operations in both San Francisco and Denver, MacAdam/Cage Publishing represents independent publishing at its best. Innovative in its approach to marketing and yet committed to the time-honored style of publishing, MacAdam/Cage Publishing will continue to introduce new and exciting authors from across the nation and beyond.

Submit a cover letter including a brief synopsis and estimated word count, three sample chapters, and a brief author bio.

Include a letter-sized SASE for reply only or a larger SASE if you would like all materials returned.

We accept double-sided or bound submissions.

We do not accept electronic submissions.

No romance, sci-fi, fantasy, self-help, poetry, thrillers, religion, children's books, or cookbooks.

We report back on queries and manuscripts within 3 to 4 months.

Categories: Fiction—Nonfiction

CONTACT: Kate Nitze, Assistant Editor
Material: All
MacAdam/Cage Publishing
155 Sansome St., Ste. 550
San Francisco, CA 94104-3615
Phone: 866-986-7470, 415-986-7502
Fax: 415-986-7414
Website: www.macadamcage.com

McBooks Press

The bulk of our publishing is historical fiction, especially military and naval series. We can accept NO unsolicited manuscripts. Letters of inquiry are welcome. We publish a very few books and we make the decision to publish on the basis of both commercial potential and literary merit.

Categories: Fiction—Family—History—Military—Parenting—Regional—Sports/Recreation—Nautical

CONTACT: Alexander G. Skutt, Publisher
Material: All
ID Booth Building
520 N. Meadow St.
Ithaca NY 14850
Phone: 607-272-2114
Fax: 607-273-6068
E-mail: mcbooks@mcbooks.com

The McDonald & Woodward Publishing Company

Publishing Program

The McDonald & Woodward Publishing Company publishes nonfiction adult trade and semi-scholarly books in the areas of natural and cultural history, as broadly defined. The primary audience for these publications is the relatively curious and well informed sector of the general population. Our publishing program falls into three divisions, as described below. We rarely consider proposals which fall outside these divisions.

Manuscripts submitted for consideration should be authoritative, substantive, well organized, and written clearly at the semi-popular or sub-technical level. We are especially attracted to work by scholars or amateur authorities on their subjects that is written in a style which is accessible to the curious, informed reader. We may have any submission reviewed by at least two authorities in the subject area before a manuscript is accepted for publication.

We recommend that authors who are interested in having us consider a manuscript for publication:

a. visit our Web site at www.mwpubco.com to review our complete list of titles and

b. review a sample of titles that we have published recently. Doing so will suggest the scope of subject matter that we are interested in publishing and will demonstrate the style and level of writing that we have found acceptable.

We welcome inquiries from authors wishing to explore our interest in considering manuscripts for publication. Please feel free to contact us by telephone, fax, e-mail, or mail to discuss projects completed, under way, or contemplated. A final decision about our interest in publishing any manuscript will, however, be made only when a completed manuscript is submitted for our consideration; a complete manuscript

Books
M-Z

includes text and front matter, back matter, and illustrations as appropriate.

I. General Titles

M&W will consider for publication as a general title any manuscript that deals with a subject within natural and cultural history, as broadly defined. The length and format of general titles will vary widely.

Representative examples of published and forthcoming general titles include:

• *A Guide to Common Freshwater Invertebrates of North America*, by J. Reese Voshell, Illustrations by Amy Bartlett Wright• *Vernal Pools: Natural History and Conservation*, by Elizabeth A. Colburn• *A Mile Deep and Black as Pitch: An Oral History of the Franklin and Sterling Hill Mines*, by Carrie Papa

• *The New Patterns in the Sky: Myths and Legends of the Stars* by Julius Staal

• *The Stone Canoe and other stories* by John L. Peyton (Ojibway tales)

• *Sweetwater Sea Saga* by Virginia Soetebier (45 years of sailing on Lake Superior)

• *The Other Side of the Medal: A Paleobiologist Reflects on the Art and Serendipity of Science* by Everett C. Olson

• *The Snowflake Man: A Biography of Wilson A. Bentley* by Duncan C. Blanchard

• *Ponce de Leon and the Spanish Discovery of Puerto Rico and Florida* by Robert Fuson

II. Guides to the American Landscape

Guides to the American Landscape are specialty guides that identify, describe, and interpret themes and places of significance on the landscape of Canada, Mexico, and the United States. Each title in the series is devoted to a specific place or set of places representing a well defined theme in the natural and/or cultural heritage of North America. Books in the Guides series are designed to facilitate the reader's awareness of, visitation to, and understanding of publicly accessible sites that represent or document the theme. Our guides typically are organized into three sections which provide (1) a narrative review of the content and temporal and spatial patterns of the subject theme which provides a conceptual framework by which the subject theme can be understood clearly; (2) detailed descriptive, interpretive, and access information about publicly accessible sites related to the theme; and (3) sources of additional information about the theme, including books, articles in periodicals, maps, museum exhibits, web sites, etc. The detailed organization of each guide will vary according to the nature of the subject; a guide to a national park, for example, will differ in the details of organization from a guide to archeological sites.

Books in the Guides series are written by persons with either scholarly training or authoritative amateur experience in the subject and for that part of the general public with a defined interest in the theme. The audience is broad, ranging from interested lay persons to professionals. Representative consumer groups include tourists, students, librarians, teachers, planners, resource managers, scholars, and various special interest groups.

Manuscripts submitted for the Guides series are expected to be authoritative, versatile, up-to-date, well organized, clearly written, and extensively illustrated with tables, line drawings, maps, and photographs. Book length can vary from about 75 to about 300 printed pages. Final book format is 6" x 9", perfect bound, paperback with full color cover, and, increasingly, with color inserts.

Titles in the Guides to the American Landscape series already published or forthcoming include:

• *Indian Mounds of the Middle Ohio Valley* by Susan L. Woodward and Jerry N. McDonald

• *Indian Mounds of the Atlantic Coast* by Jerry N. McDonald and Susan L. Woodward

• *Shenandoah National Park: An Interpretive Guide* by John A. Conners

• *Old Bones and Serpent Stones: A Guide to Interpreted Fossil Localities in Canada and the United States-Western Sites* by T. Skwara

• *Homes and Libraries of the Presidents* by William Clotworthy

• *Maryland's Catoctin Mountain Parks: A Guide to Catoctin Mountain Park and Cunningham Falls State Park* by John Means

• *In the Footsteps of George Washington* by William G. Clotworthy

III. Essays on a Changing Planet

Essays on a Changing Planet is a forum by which scholarly or other professional or learned opinions and perspectives can be disseminated to a broader audience than is normally available to specialists. The Essays should be addressed to the informed sector of the general public in a style convenient to both writer and reader.

Essays should deal with ideas of current or future significance relative to mankind's impacts on and adjustments to a changing Earth. The topics addressed may be large or small, simple or complex, global or regional, but the perspective must be that of a specialist addressing a general audience about an issue or issues of current or future importance.

As the name of the series implies, an essay format should be followed. Books may range from about 50 to about 200 pages in length. Illustrations are optional, but recommended.

Final book format is 6" x 9", paperback, perfect bound.

At present we have three titles in the Essays series:

• *Ownership and Productivity of Marine Fishery Resources* by Elmer A Keen

• *Taking Stock: The North American Livestock Census* by Donald E. Bixby and others.

Preparing and Submitting Manuscripts to McDonald & Woodward

1. Please submit inquiries, proposals, or manuscripts only for titles that fit within the scope of our publishing program. Whatever form the initial submission takes, it should be addressed to Acquisitions Editor, The McDonald & Woodward Publishing Company, 431-B E. College St., Granville, OH 43023.

2. Typically, no decision will be made as to the acceptability of a manuscript until it is complete; a complete manuscript contains all text and front, back, and illustrative matter, as appropriate. The manuscript will be first reviewed in-house by the Acquisitions Department. If interest remains high, the manuscript and background survey will then be passed to a) the Pre-press Department, which will determine feasibility of production in terms of copy editing and formatting and b) the Marketing Department, which will determine sales potential. The recommendations of all three departments will be considered by the Publisher before a final determination is made. Please allow a minimum of two to three months for this process to be completed.

In general, a project will be evaluated according to the following criteria:

• How well it fits within our publishing program

• How well it fits with our publishing schedule and existing commitments

• How substantive and authoritative it appears

• How appropriate it appears in subject, style, and content to the general, well informed audience to which we cater

• How well its sales potential fits within our marketing plan

3. We will try to notify you within 2-4 weeks of receipt of your submission whether or not McDonald & Woodward has further interest in your project. If you have not heard from us in that amount of time, please feel free to inquire by telephone, letter, fax, or e-mail.

4. If you initially submit a letter of inquiry or a proposal, and if the Acquisitions Editor deems your proposal of definite potential interest to McDonald & Woodward, you will be asked to submit a complete manuscript for review.

5. If the Publisher decides to accept your manuscript for publication, you will be sent a contract which stipulates our terms. In general we provide royalties to authors of 10% of gross receipts. We do not pay advances on royalties.

6. Upon signing the contract, you should be prepared to work initially with the Acquisitions Editor in finalizing the development of the

project in terms of content and basic organization. All materials for completion of the book-illustrations, tables, appendices, bibliographies, etc. - must be assembled before the manuscript is considered final and can be referred to Pre-press for copy editing, text and page formatting, and cover design. Publication averages 6 months after the final manuscript is received.

7. The complete manuscript must be submitted as hard copy and on diskettes in PC-compatible format. DO NOT FORMAT your manuscript electronically other than to provide adequate margins, paragraph indentations, chapter breaks, and sub-heading breaks, and do not place or embed supportive materials (tables, figures, etc.) in the text. Text and page format is the responsibility of our Pre-press Department, and they will only have to spend valuable time removing unnecessary format commands and embedded elements. Please refer to our (a) Digital Manuscript Format and Content Guidelines and (b) Final Check-Off for Submitting Manuscript below for more specific guidance.

8. Generally speaking, illustrations which support a manuscript are part of the manuscript and hence the responsibility of the author. You will be expected to acquire and provide appropriate illustrative materials. The Acquisitions Editor may also recommend specific illustrations.

9. The single most important variable influencing the speed with which a manuscript can move through the review and production processes is the state of the submitted mansucript. Manuscripts which are (a) well organized and well written, (b) complete, and (c) properly formatted will become books much more quickly than will manuscripts that do not meet these criteria. We strongly advise authors to consider having their work reviewed by at least one critical reviewer or editor before submitting the final manuscript to us. Many manuscripts that we receive for consideration could benefit from more extensive pre-submission review and constructive editing.

Presubmission Checklist

Digital Manuscript Format Specifications and Content Guidelines

• Page size is formatted at 8.5" x 11".

• Text proper is submitted as a single file.

• All files have been spell-checked.

• Supporting textual material, such as captions, tables, etc., is at end of text proper or as separate files.

• Body text is set in 11- or 12-point serif font in normal face (no sans serif or cursive fonts).

• Paragraphs are formatted to indent first line, to double-space all text, and to layout as left-justified (i.e., "ragged right").

• Chapter titles, subheads, and other titles and labels are not in all-caps and not in bold or italic face.

• All necessary indents and special line positioning are achieved by formatting commands (indents, tabs, center, justify right, etc.) and not by using the space bar. Unnecessary line formatting should be avoided.

• All double spaces between sentences and after colons or semicolons have been reduced to a single space.

• All spaces preceding a hard return at the end of paragraphs have been removed. The hard return should follow immediately the final number, letter, or punctuation sign at the end of a paragraph or paragraph equivalent.

• The manuscript has been checked further for any extraneous unnecessary "noise" such as, but not limited to, consecutive hard returns, consecutive quotation marks, underlines/rules linked to hard returns, unused section and/or page breaks, etc.

• All pages are numbered, and numbering is consecutive from the beginning to the end of the manuscript.

• All headers and footers - other than page numbers, if they are inserted as headers or footers - have been removed.

• The manuscript has not been coded for computerized indexing.

• No figures, tables, footnotes, or other supportive or decorative matter has been placed in (i.e., embedded in) the manuscript.

• Automatic hyphenation has not been used, and no words have been manually hyphenated.

• Bold and italic formatting has been kept to a minimum; italic formatting has been used, where necessary, instead of underlines.

• Letters have never been used as numbers, and numbers have never been used as letters - never use "ell" for "one," and never use "oh" for "zero," and vice-versa.

• All diacritical marks have been either included during word processing or clearly marked on the hard copy of the manuscript.

• Em-dashes, preceded and followed with a single space, have been used instead of single or multiple hyphens where a "dash" is intended. But, hyphens have been used where hyphens are necessary.

• The use of parentheses has been kept to a minimum. If something is worth saying, it can usually be stated as a part of the primary narrative, not as an aside.

• Abbreviations have been kept to a bare minimum; in most cases, either spell out the word completely (Figure, not Fig.) or use its acronym equivalent (VA, not Va.; US, not U.S.). The elimination of all abbreviations is, of course, not practicable, but if an abbreviation can be eliminated without increasing the awkwardness of the presentation, then it should be eliminated.

• Sources for specific information and supportive material, such as quotations, blocks of statistical data, tables, etc., have been provided.

• Permissions for the use of copyrighted material have been obtained and are being submitted herewith.

• All illustrations are in a form suitable for publication, or for conversion to a publishable form.

• Captions are included for all supportive material, and all supportive material is clearly identified (numbered, lettered, etc.) and cross-referenced with its caption and its suggested location in the text.

• Credits for the use of illustrations have been provided.

• All supportive material is necessary and directly relevant to the text of the book.

• All captions clearly and effectively relate the captioned matter and the text of the book to each other.

• No photograph is included in which: Resolution and/or color quality are poor; The central subject is cropped - buildings without roofs, people without heads or feet, etc.; The central subject is obscured by visual distractions such as light reflections or utility lines.

• My car, family, pets, etc., are featured as adornments to the subject.

• Parallax is extreme.

• All references in the bibliography or its equivalent are presented using the same format, and all necessary information for each entry is present.

• I have made and retained a copy of the final version of the manuscript being submitted.

Final Check-Off for Submitting Manuscript

1. The author should submit two hard copies (i.e., paper copies) of each manuscript, one copy on floppy disk, and supporting graphics (preferably more than will be required in the finished book). These materials should be submitted to the Acquisitions Editor. Authors who submit a complete, well-organized package will see their manuscript processed more quickly than those manuscripts that are only partly complete or poorly organized.

2. The two hard copies of the manuscript should be double-spaced throughout and produced directly from the disk version that you submit (i.e., do not print the hard copies, then make editorial changes on the disk) - the manuscript will be edited using the hard copy, but design will be done using the disk copy. Figure captions, tables, computer graphics, boxes, and all other supplemental matter should be separated from the main text and either placed at the end of the text portion of the manuscript or as separate files. One hard copy of the manuscript should contain no markings. On the other copy indicate the preferred location of figures, tables, boxes, etc.

3. The disk copy should be complete, contain the various categories of material (main text, tables, captions, etc.), be nondefective, and be submitted in PC-compatible format in a major word processing software. M&W uses Microsoft Word as its basic word processing software.

4. Figures may be submitted either as hard copy or digital copy. Where photographs are involved, we prefer prints to color transparencies in most cases.

What to Submit

• One disk copy of all word-processed files in PC-compatible format on 3.5" floppy or 100 M ZIP portable hard drive.

• Two paper copies of manuscript produced from final version of digital text. One of the 2 paper copies should be marked with the suggested locations of tables, maps, and other supporting material.

• One complete set of non-text supporting materials (maps, photographs, etc.) in either hard copy or digital format.

Categories: Nonfiction—Biography—Conservation—Ecology—Environment—History—Travel

CONTACT: Submissions Editor
Material: All
431-B E. College St.
Granville OH 43023
Phone: 740-321-1140
Fax: 740-321-1141
E-mail: mwpubco@mwpubco.com
Website: www.mwpubco.com

McFarland & Company, Inc.

McFarland is what has traditionally been known as a scholarly and reference publisher (no fiction, poetry, etc.). Our market has seen more libraries (of all kinds, including academic, public, corporate, etc.) than bookstores, though direct-mail sales to individuals are prominent in our overall marketing picture, particularly in certain specialty lines. We publish around 275 books a year and that's headed upward.

We welcome nonfiction manuscripts on a wide range of subjects, not limited to the following: performing arts (especially film, television, and radio), pop culture, history, women's studies, black studies, sports (especially baseball), chess, art, music, international studies, automotive history, librarianship, criminal justice, environmental studies (especially chemical sensitivity), and literature. Reference books are one of our specialties.

We do not publish fiction, poetry, children's books, inspirational works, cookbooks, diet or self-help books, religious or political tracts, exposés, stories of personal triumph over adversity, or occult or New Age works.

What We Need to See

Authors may contact us with a query letter, a full proposal, or even (if the manuscript is complete and you're confident it could fit in among the books we've already published) a finished manuscript with cover letter. In a query letter you should describe the manuscript, tell us how far along you are, estimate its final length (in either word count or double-spaced typescript pages), and tell us what is unique about the manuscript (or about you!).

We answer most queries within a few days; if we're interested we'll invite you to send either the complete manuscript or a full proposal, consisting usually of the following elements: an outline or table of contents, estimates of length and completion date, a preface or introduction, comments on how the book differs from any competing works on the same topic, a summary of what you might offer in the way of photographs or other illustrations, and some samples of the manuscript (1-2 chapters or the equivalent, plus representative pages of any special parts).

How to Present the Work

The most important thing is that it be typed and submitted on paper rather than disk (though if we accept the manuscript we will later be interested in your disks for possible use in typesetting). Manuscripts must have pages numbered consecutively, and we prefer that they not be bound in any way. Valuable documents or photographs need not be sent at the proposal stage, though photocopies of them are helpful.

Because of the nature of manuscripts and of reading, we prefer to operate via old-fashioned mail (or UPS) as opposed to phone, fax, or e-mail. We won't summarily turn you down if you come to us through electronic means, but (a) you won't get a faster reply that way, and (b) a proper, easy-to-deal-with copy makes a better impression. Please do not send copies to two or more of our editorial staff. Do not send e-mail attachments.

Be sure to put your name and return address on your cover letter, and on the top page of the proposal or manuscript.

What to Expect from Us

We usually respond to proposals quickly—within two to three weeks. Our decisions are based largely on the freshness of the topic, how well it fits in with our list, how thoroughly and authoritatively you cover it, the quality of the research and writing, and the likely marketability of the book.

When we do accept a book, publication cannot occur immediately. Because we can handle only a certain number of books in a year, and publication entails time-consuming processes (editing, design, typesetting, proofreading, promotion, printing and binding, and so forth), as well as considerable advance planning, a manuscript generally must reach us complete in every way no later than fall in order to be a candidate for publication in the following calendar year.

Categories: African-American—Asian-American—Civil War—Environment—Film/Video—History—Multicultural—Reference—Sports/Recreation—Television/Radio—Theatre—Scholarly—Automotive

CONTACT: Robert Franklin, President
Material: Any
CONTACT: Steve Wilson, Executive Editor
Material: Any
CONTACT: Virginia Tobiassen, Editorial Development Chief
Material: Any
UPS: 960 Hwy. 88 W
PO box 611
Jefferson NC 28640
Phone: 336-246-4460
Fax: 336-246-5018
E-mail: info@mcfarlandpub.com
Website: www.mcfarlandpub.com

McGavick Field Publishing Co.

We are receiving about one hundred proposals a year, which is great for a small press. This leads us to ask for queries, which we will respond to within 90 days. It is not necessary to send a SASE because we feel that any author contacting us is worth a stamp.

We do accept proposals. We do not accept pictures.

Categories: E-mail: fhernan@prodigy.net for categories.

CONTACT: Anne Field
Material: All
118 N Cherry
Olathe KS 66061
Phone: 913-780-1973
Fax: 913-782-1765
E-mail: fhernan@prodigy.net

McKenna Publishing Group

Looking for nonfiction.

Send email query to: Mckennapubgrp@aol.com with a simple email query letter (no attachments please—we do not open attachments unless the author is under contract) addressed to Eric Bollinger, Publisher, McKenna Publishing Group. In your initial email query, please provide the following:

• Your name, address and email address.

• A brief synopsis of your work. Note: We do not publish children's books or poetry.

• Its length. We prefer works under 275 double-spaced pages. The reason? Book sellers provide publishers limited shelf space, and would prefer to offer two books from the publisher in that shelf space rather than one longer book. It gives them twice the opportunity for a sale. Also, shorter books keep our cost to print and the price of the book down, and that helps sell it to the book buyer.

• Your qualifications for writing this work.

• The market and audience for it.

• Other books you know written on the subject.

• Your ability to promote the work if published. We expect our authors to actively promote their works at book signings, on the radio, television and other unique events. We do not accept submissions from authors who reside outside of the United States, and who cannot actively promote their work in the United States.

If you receive an email back from us indicating we would like to give your work a read, we ask that you follow these guidelines:

• Include a cover letter to the publisher describing our email correspondence and our acceptance of your submission.

• Mail it in a US Priority pouch mailer (not a box) if possible.

• Put your name and the title of the work on the outside of the mailer.

• Include a SASE with postage affixed if you wish the work returned to you should that be necessary. Note: Do not use metered mail that is good only on the date of purchase. We will not return your ms to you if there is not sufficient and good postage included.

• Double-space the ms, and print on one side of the page only. Do not bind the ms.

• Put your last name and a key word from the title top left, and page numbers from one to the end top right.

• Always include its synopsis.

• Always include your email address with your cover letter

Categories: Nonfiction

CONTACT: Eric Bollinger, Publisher
Material: All
74-923 Hwy. 111, Ste. 173
Indian Wells, CA 92210
E-mail: Mckennapubgrp@aol.com
Website: www.mckennapubgrp.com

Meadowbrook Press

General Author Guidelines

Meadowbrook has been in business since 1975 and has grown to become one of the leading Midwest publishers of books sold nationally through bookstores and other retail outlets. We specialize in pregnancy, baby care, child care, humorous poetry for children, and children's activities. Please note that we are not currently accepting unsolicited manuscripts or queries for the following genres: adult fiction, adult poetry, humor, and children's fiction. Also note that we do not currently publish picture books for children, travel titles, scholarly, or literary works.

We take great pride in our ability to edit, design, and promote books so that they achieve their full commercial potential. Four of our books have sold more than a million copies, three books have been New York Times best-sellers, two have been #1 bestsellers, and over twenty have been on B. Dalton's and Waldenbooks's bestseller lists.

Guidelines for Submitting Manuscripts to Meadowbrook Press

Enclose a self-addressed stamped envelope. Please make sure it's large enough to allow return of all materials and has an appropriate amount of postage.

Manuscripts that lack an SASE will not be returned.

Summarize your manuscript in a cover letter. (What is it about? How is it organized? Does it have or require illustrations, charts, graphs, or photographs?)

Tell us why your book will sell. (Why do you think there is a need for this book? How large is the market? What is the precise market? What potential secondary distribution channels—outside of bookstores—exist?)

State the competition and why your book is better. Share any knowledge of the sales history of competing books.

Tell us what qualifies you to write this book. Also, if you have any promotional experience, or would be willing to promote the book, say so.

Please state your publishing history, if any. State what books you have written, when, and who published them. Please include sales figures for your books.

Be neat! Typos and sloppiness have a great negative impact.

After you have submitted your work, please allow four months for a response.

Categories: Nonfiction—Parenting

CONTACT: Submissions Editor
Material: All
5451 Smetana Dr.
Minnetonka MN 55343
Phone: 800-338-2232
Fax: 952-930-1940
Website: www.meadowbrookpress.com

Medical Physics Publishing

Medical Physics Publishing is a small, nonprofit publishing company designed to publish books by and for medical physicists. We only publish books written by authors working in the fields of medical physics, diagnostic radiology, oncology, and related areas.

We welcome manuscript proposals for technical books written by professionals working in medical physics, mammography, radiation oncology, diagnostic radiology, and related areas. We do not accept general trade manuscripts.

—Betsey Phelps, Managing Editor

Categories: Technical—Medical—Diagnostic Radiology—Mammography—Medical Physics—Radiation Oncology—Related Technical Medical Areas

CONTACT: Acquisitions Editor
Material: All
4513 Vernon Blvd.
Madison WI 53705
Phone: 608-262-4021
Fax: 608-265-2121
E-mail: betsey@medicalphysics.org
Website: www.medicalphysics.org

Mel Bay Publications, Inc.

Before submitting a work for consideration, we recommend that you examine Mel Bay's full product line as presented on our web site and in our print catalogs to get a clear idea of the type of books we publish. Please note that traditionally we have not published individual pieces of sheet music, contemporary pop vocal music, or band or orchestra music, but rather method books and solo anthologies of historically, stylistically or thematically related material. Due to high print licensing costs, our primary focus has been on original and public domain material arranged for solo instruments.

To avoid duplicating areas that we have already addressed thoroughly, we strongly recommend that you examine our catalog before mailing your submission.

To evaluate projects and manuscripts for possible publication, we require that the following materials be sent by mail:

1.) A copy, not originals, of your manuscript or proposal. It is not necessary to send a completed work, although you may if you wish. Three or four pieces from a collection or a table of contents and a couple of chapters from an instructional book will usually suffice depending on the nature of the work. (We may request a more complete submission for clarification if necessary. This does not imply acceptance of the manuscript for publication.) A professional-looking submission, printed from a one of the products in the Finale® family from Coda Music if possible, is preferred. If this is not possible, send an orderly, clean and neatly handwritten manuscript. Do not send submissions in electronic format or on disk. While we appreciate an author's ability to provide computer files once a project is accepted, we cannot evaluate submissions in this format.

2). A detailed statement of purpose showing:
   a. what the book proposes to do;
   b. what makes it unique or different from other publications;
   c. and what the author views as the market or marketability of the item.

3). A demo CD or cassette if possible

4). A bio of the author.

We do not discuss submissions until they have been received and evaluated.

Finally, we suggest that you approach a music publisher as a freelance journalist might approach a magazine editor. Don't spend a year preparing a complete manuscript only to find out that your subject matter has already been thoroughly addressed in an existing publication. Rather, send the materials listed above. These are really all we need to evaluate a project. While Mel Bay Publications, Inc. is not currently soliciting new manuscripts, we are always open to an original music publishing concept.

Categories: Nonfiction—Music

CONTACT: William A. Bay
Material: All
#4 Industrial Dr.
Pacific, MO 63069
E-mail: email@melbay.com
Website: www.melbay.com

Menasha Ridge Press

Menasha Ridge Press publishes distinctive books about the outdoors, wilderness sport, wildlife, cooking, history, dining, and travel worldwide. Before you submit a book proposal, browse through our website to see if your book idea matches what we publish. If you have a book idea you think would fit our book list, *follow the directions below:*

Provide a brief synopsis of the book

Describe the book's target audience and why would they buy it. Also, note any potential competition and describe how your book brings something new and exciting to the arena.

Table of contents for the book as well as 1 or 2 sample chapters.

A short, biographical statement noting your qualifications for writing this book.

How to Submit

Manuscripts can either be submitted via e-mail attachment or by mail. A cover letter should accompany the submission, including name, address, phone number, and e-mail address of the contributor.

If sent via mail, please include a self-addressed, stamped envelope large enough to return submitted materials. If this is not enclosed, we will not return your materials. Never send the only copy of anything!

Categories: Nature—Outdoors—Recreation—Sports—Travel

CONTACT: Acquisitions Editor
Material: All
2204 1st Ave, S.
Birmingham AL 35233
E-mail: chelms@menasharidge.com
Website: www.menasharidge.com

Mental Floss

So, you think you got what it takes to enter the Floss Factory? Well, bring it on! But before you write in with your brilliant ideas, here are some tips that might help you "wow" us.

A. Just Pitch It

Here at the Floss Factory, we don't dig people who write in to say, "Hey, look at all my clips. Can I write for you guys?" Clips don't tell us enough. We want to know that interested writers just "get it" – that they get the concept, style and wacky sense of humor that is *mental floss*. In order to prove that to us, try pitching us an article idea that you think is quintessentially *mental floss*. If we think you "get it," then we'll ask for clips/resumes and see if you're qualified to write it.

B. Give It to Us Straight

A lot of people have written into
mental floss with really fascinating article ideas that look at new theories or perspectives on old themes. And while we like these ideas on a personal level,
mental floss long ago made an editorial decision not to publish articles that "theorize." We are in the business of reporting facts — and straight facts only — in an entertaining and original way.

C. Complete the Mission

When *mental floss* first started out, we wrote up some fancy, schmancy mission statement, but I won't bore you with that now. If you want to know what we look for in our articles, all you have to know is what we want to share with our readers. Here's a quick run-down:

   • What you SHOULD have learned in school but were too hung-over to remember.
   • What they WON'T TEACH YOU in school, but you've always wanted to know.
   • What you were too INTIMIDATED to learn about because it seemed too complex.

D. Know the Editor's Pet Peeves

1. No satire! (See #2 for reason)

2. Have a column or feature spot in mind for your article: Often, submitted facts or subjects are interesting, but they are only that: short facts or topics not necessarily suitable for a 1500-word article. If you send in an article idea, include where you envision the article being published in the magazine: right_brain, left_brain, spinning_the_globe, etc. Keep in mind that our scatter_brained section and cover stories are written in-house.

3. Stay out of politics:
mental floss likes to stay as "controversy-free" as possible, so please avoid submissions dealing with political beliefs or current politicians.

4. Avoid current events:
mental floss is one of the few magazines in the world that actually avoids "timely" topics. We try to present educational information that is more timeless, so submissions focusing on current trends or social situations may be hard sells here.

E. Just Do It!

Categories: Nonfiction—Book Reviews—Education—History—Philosophy—Science

CONTACT: Neely Harris, Editor-in-Chief
Material: All
PO Box 528
Novelty, OH 44072
Phone: 440-338-1816
Fax: 440-338-6315
E-mail: neely@mentalfloss.com.
Website: www.mentalfloss.com

Meriwether Publishing Ltd
Contemporary Drama Service

School Guidelines

DRAMA:

Please include cast list, and (if required) prop list, costume information, set specifications, etc., with all play manuscripts. *Following are the types of drama we publish:*

• One-act non-royalty plays — originals or adaptations, comedies, parodies, social commentary and novelty drama. Plays with large and small casts and with many parts for women and a few plays for children's theatre.

• Full length (90 minutes) Musical Comedies — Large cast, 20 or more participants: soloists, chorus, dancers and comics. Author/composer must provide a cassette or CD of the music. Book and performance royalties paid.

• Speech contest materials — monologs for women and men, dialogs, short playlets addressing the high school experience with honest feelings and real situations of current importance.

• Full-length royalty plays — up to three acts, comedy, large casts.

• Adaptations — Shakespeare, the classics, and popular modern works (with original author's permission).

• Oral interpretations — folktales and storytelling.

• Prevention plays — drama as a teaching tool about drug abuse, pregnancy, gangs, etc.

• Readers Theatre — adaptations or originals.

BOOKS:

Our books cover a wide variety of theatre subjects from play anthologies to theatre craft. We publish books on monologs, duologs, short one-act plays, scenes for students, acting textbooks, how-to speech and theatre textbooks, improvisation and theatre games.

Send sample chapters or an outline — no complete manuscripts.

QUERY LETTER SPECIFICATIONS:

• Include a synopsis or brief statement of objectives.

• Tell us why you believe your work deserves publication. Define the market you see as the potential audience.

• Please include a list of your publishing credits and/or experience and your payment expectations.

• Include a self-addressed, stamped envelope for our response.

• Allow 4-6 weeks for response.

Church Guidelines

DRAMA:

Please include cast list, and (if required) prop list, costume information, set specifications, etc., with all plays and musicals. *Following are the types of drama we publish:*

• One-act non-royalty plays on religious themes up to 30 pages.

• Christmas and Easter chancel drama or liturgy — length 30 minutes maximum — for children's Sunday school departments and also for adults.

• Collection of short sketches on a central theme — five per collection — humorous, entertaining, Christian.

• Religious musicals for Christmas and Easter — one hour maximum. (Computer generated musical accompaniment score and cassette of performance preferred.)

• Readers Theatre scripts — 30 minutes maximum.

• Monologs.

BOOKS:

Our Christian books cover creative worship on such topics as clown ministry, storytelling, banner-making, drama ministry, children's worship, and more. We also publish anthologies of Christian sketches. We do not publish works of fiction or devotionals.

Send sample chapters or an outline — no complete manuscripts.

QUERY LETTER SPECIFICATIONS:

• Include a synopsis or brief statement of objectives.

• Tell us why you believe your work deserves publication. Define the market you see as the potential audience.

• Please include a list of your publishing credits and/or experience and your payment expectations.

• Include a self-addressed, stamped envelope for our response.

• Allow 4-6 weeks for response.

Categories: Arts—Children—Drama—Music—Religion—Spiritual

CONTACT: Editor
Material: Manuscripts
CONTACT: Editor, Contemporary Drama Service
Material: Drama Scripts
885 Elkton Dr.
Colorado Springs CO 80907-3557
Phone: 800-937-5297
Fax: 888-594-4436
E-mail: MerPCDS@aol.com
Website: www.meriwetherpublishing.com

Metamorphous Press

Dear Writer:

Thank you for inquiring about our manuscript guidelines for new works. Since we receive from 2,500-3,000 unsolicited submissions each year, we ask that you first submit a query letter with an outline of your work, and a sufficient sample of your writing style for our acquisitions staff to determine if your work fits within our editorial policy. From there, we can decide whether we need to request a complete manuscript for further review.

We cannot be responsible for returning manuscripts due to the large quantity we receive. *We encourage you to submit your work for consideration at this time:*

• It may be considered (budget allowing) for publication by Metamorphous Press

• We may offer subsidy publishing

• Or we can assist you with the details of self-publishing

In any case, we are always excited about being involved in projects that can make a positive difference.

Thank you for your interest in Metamorphous Press.

Sincerely,

Nancy Wyatt-Kelsey, Acquisitions Editor

Categories: Nonfiction—Business—Education—Health—Psychology—Self Help—Sexuality—Enneagram—Ericksonian Hypnosis—N.L.P.—Personal Development

CONTACT: Nancy Wyatt-Kelsey, Acquisitions Editor
Material: All
PO Box 10616

Portland OR 97296-0616
Phone: 503-228-4972
Fax: 503-223-9117
E-mail: metabooks@metamodels.com

Metropolis Ink

There are only two requirements to become an author published by Metropolis Ink:

• First, we have to like your book and believe in it as much as you do. We accept only well-written manuscripts with broad appeal. In fiction, we want excellence in narrative, dialogue, and plotting. In nonfiction, we want clear, distinctive, well-researched material on popular, helpful topics.

• Second, we accept only authors committed to working hard to promote their own books. We'll work hard to sell your books, but we need the assurance of your help.

We do not charge to publish the MSS we accept; neither do we offer an advance for those books.

To have your work considered by Metropolis Ink, attach at least the first several chapters of your manuscript to an email as an MS Word or Adobe PDF file and send it to the address below. In the body of your email, include a brief synopsis, and tell us something about yourself. What is your writing experience? Have you been published? What? Where? Are you able, willing and eager to promote your published book?

We'll evaluate your submission and tell you whether we are interested.

We especially encourage submission of nonfiction works, but are always open to high-quality fiction.

Thank you.

Categories: Fiction—Nonfiction

CONTACT: Kurt Florman, Partner/Editorial Manager
Material: All
PO Box 682
Yarnell AZ 85367
Phone: 928-427-0329
Fax: 928-427-9488
E-mail: submissions@metropolisink.com
Website: www.MetropolisInk.com

Michael Wiese Productions

MWP publishes a best-selling line of books for independent filmmakers and university film students around the world. Our how-to books are used in 500 film schools throughout the world and have been translated into ten different languages.

Submission

To submit a proposal, please send a Table of Contents, and two sample chapters.

Categories: Nonfiction—Arts—Education—Film/Video

CONTACT: Ken Lee (206-283-2948)
Material: All
11288 Ventura Blvd, Ste 621
Studio City CA 91604
Phone: 818-379-8799
Fax: 818-986-3408
E-mail: kenlee@mwp.com
Website: www.mwp.com

Remember: Editors change jobs and publishers change addresses. It is wise to invest in a phone call for the current information before submitting.

Midmarch Arts Press

Midmarch Arts Press publishes from two to four books a year and an annual magazine, *Women Artists News Book Review*. Our books are mostly on the arts and poetry with a focus on women artists. It is a feminist press that is neither sexist, racist, or homophobic. We seek to represent the widest possible range of feminist perspective in our books and reviews and essays in our periodical.

• Include name, address and telephone number on all manuscripts and pictures.

• Include a brief biographical note for author's blurb.

• Submit computer disk and hard copy.

• Reviews or essays for the Book Review should be 1,200 to 1,800 words.

• Provide photographs if possible.

• Book manuscripts should be queried before submission.

• Subjects: Our focus is on art, women artists, literature and poetry, and women's issues.

• Style: Avoid wordiness. Art doesn't have to be the best thing since Da Vinci to be worth writing and reading about. Gushing praise, rhetorical clichés, and overblown jargon are not interesting to read. Personal, social, historical, political, and artistic particulars are interesting—that is, information and explication.

Categories: Arts—Literature—Poetry—Women's Issues—Women Artists

CONTACT: Acquisitions Editor
Material: All
300 Riverside Dr.
New York NY 10025
Phone: 212-666-6990
Fax: 212-865-5509

Milkweed Editions
Milkweeds for Young Readers

Part of Milkweed's goal is to publish books by under-recognized and emerging authors — an important mission in a world dominated by bestsellers. As a part of that mission, we consider and respond to every manuscript that is submitted according to our guidelines.

If you have a manuscript you'd like us to consider, please read the guidelines for your type of manuscript before sending it to us. Before submitting, we request that you familiarize yourself with our current titles, and determine if your work meets our publishing program and our mission.

In addition to publication, we also offer prizes for fiction and children's fiction manuscripts; please read the appropriate guidelines to determine whether you are eligible.

Please Note: Inquiries about the guidelines or about submissions should be directed to the editorial department: editor@milkweed.org.

Please note: We are continuing to accept unsolicited manuscripts by mail. PLEASE DO

NOT SEND SUBMISSIONS VIA EMAIL. Due to changes in postal regulations, however, Milkweed can no longer return manuscripts in stamped book mailers. In the event that manuscripts are not accepted for publication, we prefer to recycle them. If you need your work returned, please enclose a check for $5.00 rather than a stamped book mailer.

For notification of the safe arrival of your manuscript, please include a stamped, self-addressed postcard. Please send a photocopy of your manuscript and/or any artwork, not the original, since we cannot guarantee the safekeeping of irreplaceable work. Our review process can take from one to six months. Please make no phone or email inquiries regarding submission status.

Thank you for your interest in Milkweed Editions, and good luck in your writing endeavors. Milkweed books are available at most fine bookstores. You can write to us for a catalog; enclose $1.50 for postage.

FICTION

Milkweed Editions is looking for fiction manuscripts of high literary quality that embody humane values and contribute to cultural understanding.

We welcome submissions from writers who have previously published a book of fiction (novel, short stories, or novellas) or a minimum of three short stories (or novellas) in nationally distributed commercial or literary journals. Novels, novellas, and collections of short stories are welcome, as are translations.

Your Manuscript Must Be:
- 150-400 pages
- typed or computer-printed on good-quality white paper
- double-spaced
- submitted with a stamped, self-addressed envelope for our reply.

CHILDREN'S

Milkweed Editions is looking for high-quality novels for readers aged 8-13 for its children's book publishing program, Milkweeds for Young Readers.

At this age, readers are ready for well-written books that range widely in subject matter, from fantasy to fiction grounded in history to books about everyday life. Manuscripts should be of high literary quality, embody humane values, and contribute to cultural understanding.

We are especially interested in fiction set in the contemporary world and in fiction that explores our relationship to the natural world.

We welcome submissions from writers who have previously published a book of fiction or nonfiction for children or adults, or a minimum of three short stories or pieces of nonfiction in nationally distributed commercial or literary journals. Translations are welcome. Please note that we do not publish children's picture books, poetry, or collections of short stories.

Your Children's Manuscript Must Be:
- 90-200 pages
- typed or computer-printed on good-quality white paper
- double-spaced
- submitted with a stamped, self-addressed envelope for our reply.

POETRY

Milkweed Editions is looking for poetry manuscripts of high literary quality that embody humane values and contribute to cultural understanding. Milkweed reads poetry manuscripts only in January and June of each year. Although poetry manuscripts are not limited in subject matter, we are particularly interested in poetry about the natural world as part of our publishing program, The World As Home: Literature about the Natural World.

We welcome submissions from writers who have previously published a book of poetry or a minimum of six poems in nationally distributed commercial or literary journals. Translations are welcome, as are bilingual books. We encourage simultaneous submissions.

Your Poetry Manuscript Must Be:
- 60 pages or more
- typed or computer-printed on good-quality white paper
- submitted with a stamped, self-addressed envelope for our reply.

NONFICTION

Milkweed is focusing its nonfiction publishing on a program called The World As Home: Literature about the Natural World and is actively seeking book-length literary essays and essay collections about the physical and natural world, as well as book-length works about community—that is, about living well and harmoniously in place, whether that is rural, urban, or suburban. We are looking for books with strong personal narratives; although we publish informed and intelligent thinkers, we do not publish academic or scientific studies.

As part of that publishing program, Milkweed is continuing its Literature for a Land Ethic series of literary books about specific endangered places by regionally committed writers. Literature for a Land Ethic supports writers, educators, and activists in defining and evolving the role of literature in furthering our culture's environmental knowledge and in articulating the possibilities for a sustainable future.

We welcome submissions from writers who have previously published a book of nonfiction (this can be a collection of essays) or a minimum of two essays in nationally distributed commercial or literary journals. Collections of essays are welcome, as are translations.

Your Manuscript Must Be:
- 150-300 pages
- typed or computer-printed on good-quality white paper
- double-spaced
- submitted with a stamped, self-addressed envelope for our reply.

Categories: Fiction—Nonfiction—Children—Conservation—Environment—Literature—Poetry—Short Stories

CONTACT: Fiction Reader
Material: Fiction
CONTACT: Children's Book Reader
Material: Children's
CONTACT: Poetry Reader
Material: Poetry
CONTACT: Editor, The World As Home
Material: Nonfiction
1011 Washington Ave. South, Ste. 300
Minneapolis MN 55415
Phone: 612-332-3192
Fax: 612-215-2550
Website: www.milkweed.org

Milkweeds for Young Readers

Please refer to Milkweed Editions.

Millbrook Press

Imprints: Twenty-First Century Books, Roaring Brook Press, Copper Beach Books

The Millbrook Press is a curriculum-oriented children's book publisher with a concentration on quality non-fiction for the school and library market. We publish approximately 130 new titles a year. Our imprints include Millbrook Press, Twenty-First Century Books, Roaring Brook Press, and Copper Beach Books.

ROARING BOOK PRESS

Roaring Brook Press is the new fiction and picture book division of Millbrook. We do not accept any unsolicited manuscripts or submissions.

Copper Beach Books

Copper Beach Books publishes works created by our affiliate in the United Kingdom. We do not accept any unsolicited manuscripts or submissions.

The Millbrook Press and Twenty-First Century Books

The Millbrook Press and Twenty-First Century Books accept only agented submissions. We do not accept unsolicited manuscripts. We are interested in works that have a strong, relevant tie to a school curriculum, such as math, science, American history, social studies, biography, etc. Proposals aimed at teachers or parents are not appropriate for us. We do not accept fiction, picture books, activity books, or other novelty submissions.

Please have your agent send a sample chapter, query letter, and outline, rather than a completed manuscript. Include a self-addressed, stamped envelope with all submissions, and allow at least six to eight weeks for our response. Manuscripts will be returned if not selected for further review by our editors—please send an appropriate-sized envelope with enough postage to handle the entire package—or you will not receive an answer of any kind.

We do not accept manuscripts over the Internet.

Categories: Nonfiction—Children—Education—History—Science

CONTACT: Editorial Assistant
Material: All
2 Old New Milford Rd .

Brookfield, CT 06804
Website: www.millbrookpress.com

Millennium Publishing Company

Established in 1998, MPC strives to produce quality literature that assists and serves a purpose that would otherwise go unnoticed by the publishing giants.

Facts

Publishes nonfiction only. Short, usually 200-400 pages. paperback only.

Publishes up to 5 titles per year.

90% first time authors. 100% unagented writers.

Responds in 1-2 months on queries, proposals and manuscripts.

Subjects

Nonfiction only. *Prefers the following:*

How To, Small Business Subjects, Career, General Reference, Travel, Medical Reference, Technical Manuals, Computer Subjects and Teen Subjects.

We consider any well-written nonfiction short book, that has a definable target market and that have not been done to death.

For example, in 2003 will publish: *Piece of Paradise: A Country by Country Guide to Foreign Ownership.* And *Entrepreneur's Guide to the Financial Section of a Business Plan.*

Does not want

Fiction, Poetry, cookbooks, personal stories and novels.

Pays

Usually buys all rights. Pays up to 30% royalty on net profits. Markets books with major retail bookstore chains and over the Internet.

How to submit

Prefers query (informal is okay) via email. State if book is already written or in progress. If written for a particular audience, explain potential market. If we are interest we will request sample chapter. E-mails can have attachments of .doc and .pdf only. Otherwise, paste directly into the body of the email.

Categories: Nonfiction—Business—Careers—Computers—General Interest—Health—Technical—Teen—Travel

CONTACT: Michele Hahn
Material: All
2307 Monaco
Mission TX 78574
E-mail: Michele@MillPubCo.com
E-mail: Submissions@MillPubCo.com (Send Queries)

Mills & Boon Historical Romance
Mills & Boon Medical Romance

Please refer to Harlequin, in the Book Publishers section.

Mira

Please refer to Harlequin, in the Book Publishers section.

Mississippi
University Press of Mississippi

The University of Mississippi Press is a nonprofit publisher that serves chiefly an academic audience. We receive approximately 600 submissions and publish an average of 60 manuscripts a year. Our editorial program focuses on the following areas:

Scholarly and trade titles in African American studies; American studies, literature, history, and culture; art and architecture; biography and memoir; ethnic studies; fiction; film studies; folklife; health; music; natural sciences; photography; popular culture; reference; serious nonfiction of general interest; Southern studies; women's studies; other liberal arts. Special series: American Made Music; Center for the Study of Southern Culture; Chancellor's Symposium in Southern History; Conversations with Comic Artists; Conversations with Filmmakers; Conversations with Public Intellectuals; Faulkner and Yoknapatawpha; Folklife in the South; Hollywood Legends; Literary Conversations; Margaret Walker Alexander Series in African-American Studies; Studies in Popular Culture; Understanding Health and Sickness; Willie Morris Books in Memoir and Biography; Writers and Their Work. Imprints: Banner Books; Muscadine Books.

If you have a manuscript appropriate to our publishing program that you would like us to consider, we ask that you first submit a proposal. *Your proposal should include the following:*

• A description of the work
• A chapter outline
• One or two completed chapters
• The total number of words in the manuscript
• The number and type of illustrations, if any
• The anticipated date of completion

It normally takes 8-12 weeks for the editorial staff to review proposals and respond.

Thank you for your interest in the University Press of Mississippi.

Categories: Fiction—Nonfiction—African-American—Architecture—Arts—Biography—Civil War—Culture—Feminism—Film/Video—Gardening—General Interest—Health—History—Literature—Music—Native American—Photography—Reference—Regional—Theatre—Ethnic—Scholarly

CONTACT: Craig Gill, Editor-in-Chief
Material: Scholarly Books, Trade Books
3825 Ridgewood Rd.
Jackson MS 39211-6492
Phone: 601-432-6205
Fax: 601432-6217
E-mail: press@ihl.state.ms.us

Moondance Publishing

Moondance Publishing, a company founded by Author/Lecturer Barry McKeown & Associates has positioned itself on the cutting edge of this revolution.

Moondance will continue to be very selective about what is published. If you have written what you feel is a work that will stand up to the high standards established by the associated network that makes up the Moondance Publishing Company we would be happy to hear from you. Please review the accompanying information and feel free to contact us about your manuscript.

Created by writers for writers, Moondance is an upscale publishing house with the highest regard for professionalism.

Submissions

Submission information and the submission form can found on our web site.

We publish mostly fiction but are not held to just that genre. Some humor and informational and if it's something really good we'll publish poetry.

Categories: Fiction—Humor—Poetry

CONTACT: Submissions Editor
Material: All
P O Box 16
Upper Black Eddy PA 18972
Phone: 610-982-5331
Fax: 610-982-5227
E-mail: caravan@moondancepublishing.com
Website: www.moondancepublishing.com

Morgan Reynolds Publishing

JUST THE FACTS

Morgan Reynolds publishes serious-minded nonfiction books for Juvenile and Young Adult readers. Our titles complement elementary and secondary school curriculums for young readers ages 10 to 18. We avoid obscure figures and "pop culture" icons (rock stars, movie stars, and sports figures). We prefer lively, well-written biographies of interesting figures for our biography series and insightful, exciting looks at critical periods for our events series. Subjects may be contemporary or historical. Past series have included: Makers of Media, Feminist Voices, Notable Americans, World Writers, Champions of Freedom, Masters of Music, American Business Leaders, and Great Events. We do not publish fiction, memoirs, pictures books, poetry, etc.

The burden is on the writer to convince us their idea is viable. To that effect, we suggest that writers wishing to make a submission first familiarize themselves with our books. Go to our website, your local public library, or favorite bookstore to obtain one or two of our books. Read our books!

A WORD ON FORM

We are looking for well-crafted biographies that present the subject's personality and development as a human being. Historical events should be treated with equal attention to detail and context. Thorough research of a subject is a prerequisite of any successful submission. The manuscript should draw from a variety of sources. Primary source quotations are a necessity. (However, secondary source quotations, such as what another biographer has written about the subject, are inappropriate.) Writers are urged to maintain chronology and to include information about the subject's childhood, youth, middle age, etc. Also important are the subject's family life, personal interests, and idiosyncrasies. Overall, manuscripts should bring the subject's PERSONALITY to the FOREFRONT, while providing a VIVID BACKDROP of CONTEXT.

Required text length is 25,000 words (exclusive of end matter) with 8-10 chapters of 2,500 to 3,000 words each. Writers provide contact information for illustration sources, a bibliography, source notes, glossary, and appendices (to be specified by the editor). Style sheets for end matter will be made available upon signing of a contract.

CHAPTERS, AN OVERVIEW

Chapter One

We prefer the first chapter to utilize a "hook," which gives the reader an idea of the subject's personality and legacy. The hook is gener-

ally a scene taken from adulthood of a particularly crucial point in the subject's life. For instance, a biography of Martin Luther King, Jr. may begin with his "I Have a Dream Speech."

Following the hook, there should be a brief discussion of the book's major theme. This theme is largely up to the writer, although it should incorporate the most notable aspect of the subject's life. The theme can be discovered by asking a few questions, such as: Why is this person or event worth writing about? What is the dominating characteristic of this person or event? Using King as an example, the theme of his biography could be: King fought to further the lives of black people in America using the tenents of nonviolence and direct action. Throughout the book, the writer should focus on the theme that is established in the first chapter.

Following the discussion of theme, the writer should begin a chronological biography starting with the subject's birth and family information, childhood, and education. In most cases, the first chapter should conclude with the subject's reaching maturity.

For books on historical events, the hook should reveal the players and circumstances at an exciting moment central to the event. The discussion of theme should isolate the focus of the book, and from there, the writer should begin a chronological discussion of the event.

Chapters Two and on

Each chapter can be thought of as mini-books, each with a beginning, middle, and end, that reflect the theme introduced in chapter one. Subsequent chapters should be centered around one or two central events, and care should be taken that the events are clearly explained with attention to their root causes and their influence. Conclude with a suggestion of what's to come.

At certain points in the book, it will be necessary to stop the chronological narrative for a discussion of historical context. Describing context will add interest and dynamism to the story. It will help young readers understand the world in which the subject lived and provide a framework for the choices the subject made. Using King as an example, a discussion of Jim Crow laws would help young readers understand segregation in the South. Pausing to discuss of the passage of the Civil Rights Act of 1964 will help young readers understand the impact of the Civil Rights movement. These discussions of context should provide enough information to embody the subject without overshadowing him.

In general, avoid ending with a summary chapter that lists why the subject was important. In some cases, a "legacy" chapter will be needed. For instance, in a biography of Martin Luther King, a short chapter at the end of the book discussing events after his assassination would be appropriate.

A WORD ON STYLE

Be concrete-use dates and outside events as yardsticks.

Although the audience is younger readers, the narrative voice should never be patronizing. Avoid speaking directly to the reader or asking rhetorical questions. Language should be concise and to the point. Strive to create reader interest by presenting the story in an exciting manner. Do not try to generate excitement with an elaborate or "cute" writing style.

COMMON STYLE CHOICES TO AVOID
• Rhetorical questions
• Subjunctive mood
• Overly-familiar tone
• Flowery language
• Extended metaphors
• Exclamation points
• Tentative language, such as "Probably," or "Perhaps"
• Passive voice

SUBMISSIONS

We suggest first-time writers query with a full manuscript. Sample chapter and an outline is admissible for experienced writers only. Mail submissions with a SASE to: Morgan Reynolds, Inc., Acquisitions, 620 South Elm Street, Suite 223, Greensboro, NC 27406. Please do not use any delivery service that requires a signature, such as registered or certified mail. Include daytime telephone number and email address

on cover letter. If you would like your manuscript returned, include correct postage and envelope. A complete listing of our books is available at our website: www.morganreynolds.com or send us $1.06 postage to receive a printed catalog.

Categories: Nonfiction—Biography—Young adult.

CONTACT: Acquisitions
Material: All
620 South Elm St., Ste 223
Greensboro, NC 27406
336-275-1311
www.morganreynolds.com

Motorcycling
An Imprint of
Bristol Fashion Publications, Inc.

Dear Colleague,

Thank you for requesting our Writer & Photographer submission guidelines. You will find we are very cooperative when dealing with freelance contributors. Our Chairman and Publisher, John Kaufman, and our COO and Editor-in-Chief, Bob Lollo, were both freelance photographers and writers long before Bristol Fashion Publications, Inc. came to be in 1993. They still retain the memories of the "difficult years" getting started. This is one of the reasons we are interested in submissions from new authors and photographers.

All of our titles are motorcycle themes, aimed at the new or seasoned rider. All our titles cover restoration, repair, maintenance, touring, etc.

We rarely project more than six months in advance. Always include a SASE for any submissions you would like returned. Include your telephone number with any correspondence or submissions.

Photography Submissions

COVERS: Color glossy prints. Prints should be 3-1/2 x 5 to 5 x 7. Digitized images (300 DPI) in a JPG or GIF file are preferred for final use.

All covers depict the theme of the book. Use deep saturation, vivid colors and good contrast to bring out the main subject matter. This is NOT the type of cover you will see on a magazine. Send several sample copies of your work for consideration. Mark each copy with your name, address and phone number.

INTERIOR: Digitized images (300 DPI) in a GIF or JPG file are the only images we consider for use.

Photos should show hands using tools, when appropriate, the steps involved in completing a project and the finished results. These are the photos we most often need, however, other photos may be needed for a current title. Good contrast, lighting and subject matter is necessary. Send several hard copy or jpg/gif (on disk) samples of your work for consideration. Mark each copy with your name, address and phone number. We will not consider e-mailed images—please do not send them.

Simultaneous submissions are fine. Notify us if a photo we have on file becomes unavailable. Model and property releases are preferred if the person is identifiable. All submissions should be non-returnable disks or prints. If we can keep copies of your work on file, we are more likely to call you when the need arises. We will notify you within one month, whether or not we feel we can use your work. Assignments may be given at the same rate of pay, as noted below.

We purchase book/reprint rights as a one time buy. Cover prices range from $50.00 to $300.00 depending on the project. Interior B & W prices range from $10.00 to $25.00. Credit line given. One copy of the book will be given to each contributor.

Writer's Guidelines

Considering what we have read on the shelves, it appears we are the only publishing company that publishes for the non-handy riders. Our books use simple to understand and follow processes, for the person who knows which end of the wrench to hold, but little else. Each subject should take the reader from the very basics, through each step, until the complete subject matter is discussed. As the project expands and becomes more complicated, each new phase or technique should be described. If a friend, who knows nothing about bikes, can read, understand and feel comfortable doing the work you have described, you have written what we want to publish.

Non-How-To titles should be extremely interesting to read. Touring related books should speak of the community, to-do's, camping, culture and events not the "what I did" topics.

How-To topics are the most marketable with a wider audience. We are always seeking new ideas and topics for our books.

Simultaneous submissions are not accepted. Submit a few chapters for review, along with the table of contents. All submissions must be hard copy with a SASE. Include your past credits, tear sheets, state if photos or line art is available and the state of completion of your manuscript. We will report in two weeks of receipt, often sooner.

If you have never been published or have not yet started the manuscript submit a short sample (1000 words), outline, completion date and photo/line art availability.

We pay royalty of 8% to 11% based on the retail price of the book. Average retail price is $20.00 to $30.00. Photos and line art submitted by the author will be considered as part of the manuscript and the percentage adjusted accordingly. Follow the photography submission guidelines above. We will purchase worldwide book/reprint rights.

WRITERS TIPS: Know or research the industry, owners and technical knowledge. Use the proper motorcycle language and terms. A well-written manuscript is useless if the knowledge of the writer is lacking. If you are not familiar with a given subject, talk to people who has been around bikes for many years. Do not use unwarranted technical jargon to explain a subject. Use simple terms and an easy to understand and follow, step-by-step writing style. When we have to choose, we are more likely to use poor writing and good knowledge, than good writing and poor knowledge.

Preparing Your Manuscript

Never use an exclamation point for emphasis except in a direct quotation. We! and! the! reader! don't! care! what! startles! you!

Don't double-space, regardless of what you were taught in typing class.

Don't use the Tab key or Space bar to indent a paragraph.

Don't attempt to make your manuscript look as you'd like your book to appear. Just write. Converting your manuscript into a book is what we do.

Trust us. We have a combined experience of more than 200 years in the publishing industries. We will edit your manuscript to suit its intended market. The better your work reads, the better it sells, and that benefits all of us.

Please understand this—You will not retire from the book sales of any single specialty title. Specialty titles simply do not sell that well in any market. A very successful specialty title may sell 20,000 copies over a five year run. A very few sell more. Most sell one quarter or less of that number and are considered a successful book. Our successful authors often have three or more books published with us and they started by reading these very same guidelines.

After preparing your submission, following the above guidelines, you may submit it by land mail (hard copy only, do not include a disk) or by email. To submit by email, attach an ASCII text or MSWord file to the email—DO NOT paste the text into the body of the email or include graphic files with this submission. Send the email to jpk@bfpbooks.com. Include only one manuscript with each email submission.

Categories: Automobiles—Lifestyle—Mechanics—Travel

CONTACT: Submissions
Material: All
Bristol Fashion Publications, Inc.
PO Box 4676
Harrisburg, PA 17111
Phone: 772-559-1379
Fax: 800-543-9030
E-mail: jpk@bfpbooks.com
Website: www.bfpbooks.com

Mountain N' Air Books

1. Forms of Submissions
• By electronic means.
• Use major word processor, or ASCII format. Store it on a Zip 100-drive, or CD-ROM.

2. Subjects
• Non-fiction.
• Personal account on outdoor activities (climbing, biking, hiking, backpacking, etc)
• Adventure Travel, Armchair Travel, or Wilderness Travel Accounts.
• How to on cooking, outdoor activities, and travel tips.

3. Photos, Illustrations
• Prefer color slides, glossy black and white
• Illustrations, drawings and charts in 8" x10" or smaller.
• If submitting by electronic means all photographs, drawings and illustrations should be set at 300dpi (150 lpi)
• Must have model release from any identifiable person appearing on any photograph, or recognizable facsimile on drawings or illustrations.

4. Miscellaneous
• Any quotes contained must have permission to print from the author of the quote or publication from which the quote came from.
• Word count not necessary.
• No simultaneous submissions please.
• All materials should be sent to Mountain N' Air Books accompanied of a signed release authorizing Mountain N' Air Books and its agents to review the materials, without any obligation or commitment to publish or distribute any or all the materials.

Materials submitted will not be returned unless requested otherwise. If some or all the materials are to be returned to sender, or forwarded to others, please enclose a correctly addressed SASE.

Categories: Nonfiction—Adventure—Cooking—Outdoors—Recreation—Sports/Recreation—Travel—Western Writing

CONTACT: Gilberto Urso, Publisher
Material: All
PO Box 12540
La Crescenta CA 91224
Phone: 800-446-9696
Fax: 800-303-5578
Website: www.mountain-n-air.com

Mountain Press Publishing Company

Mountain Press publishes nonfiction trade books for general audiences, primarily adults. We will consider proposals for projects in natural history (including field guides for birds, wildlife, plants, etc.) western or frontier history; non-technical earth science and ecology; and some horse-related topics. Mountain Press is perhaps best known for its state-by-state series on Roadside Geology and Roadside History; extended guidelines are available for these.

Other than reprints of the works of Will James, we do not publish fiction or poetry.

STANDARDS. We accept only well-written, responsibly researched manuscripts. Your composition must engage the reader with lively, colorful prose. The sources you rely on must be thoroughly documented and not infringe on any existing copyrights. Double-space everything—text, notes, bibliography, everything. You are responsible for supplying all photographs, maps, and other graphics your book may need.

STYLE. We urge authors to follow the tenets set forth in *The Chicago Manual of Style* (14th edition) and Strunk & White's *The Elements of Style*.

EQUIPMENT. Prepare your manuscript on a computer using a Macintosh, Windows, or MS-DOS compatible word-processing program. We will not accept camera-ready copy. Do not send your disk until we ask for it.

PROPOSALS. Submit a cover letter addressed to the Editorial Department with your proposal telling us who you are, what your manuscript is about, who your target audience is, and why you think Mountain Press should publish your work. Include an outline or table of contents, a sample of the manuscript (one or two chapters), a core bibliography, and photocopied examples of the artwork you plan to use. Normally we can respond to your proposal within one month. Please call first if you have any questions.

WEBSITE. For more information about Mountain Press, we encourage you to visit our Website.

Categories: Nonfiction—Biography—Ecology—History—Native American—Outdoors—Regional—Science—Geology

CONTACT: Acquisitions Editor
Material: All
PO Box 2399
Missoula MT 59806
Phone: 406-728-1900
Fax: 406-728-1635
E-mail: info@mtnpress.com
Website: www.mountain-press.com

Mountaineers Books

The Mountaineers Books produces guidebooks, instructional texts, historical works, adventure narratives, natural history guides, and works on environmental conservation. More than 450 titles from The Mountaineers are now in print. All of the books we publish are aimed at fulfilling the club's mission—to explore, study, preserve and enjoy the natural beauty of the outdoors—and, by extension, addressing the needs and concerns of like-minded outdoor enthusiasts throughout the world.

Mountaineers authors come from all over the world. Some are professional writers, while others are people who just want to share their specialized knowledge of some aspect of the outdoors.

Subject Matter:

The Mountaineers Books publishes nonfiction material about the outdoors. This includes non-competitive, non-motorized, self-propelled sports such as mountain climbing, hiking, walking, skiing, snowshoeing, and adventure travel. We also publish works on environmental and conservation subjects, narratives of mountaineering expeditions and adventure travel, outdoor guidebooks to specific areas, nature field guides, mountaineering history, safety/first aid, and books on skills and techniques for the above sports. If you plan to submit an adventure narrative, please request information about the Barbara Savage Miles From Nowhere Memorial Award. We do not publish fiction, general tourist guides, or guides dealing with hunting, fishing, snowmobiling, RV travel, horseback riding, or team sports.

Submission Procedures:

The Mountaineers is a non-profit outdoor activity club that publishes books via a paid staff. The review and approval process for a book we want to publish can take up to three months. We will make no commitment to any author until a project is approved. If you have something you think would fit in our line of books, we'd be happy to have a look and respond. If you aren't sure whether the subject of your proposal matches our interests, please send a query letter and SASE. *If you feel your proposal or manuscript fits the criteria above, then please supply the following:*

• A statement that explains the proposed project's purpose, focus, scope, and significance, including a brief summary of the text

• A detailed chapter/subject outline or a detailed table of contents.

• At least five pages of introductory material and a complete table of contents

• For narratives, at least two sample chapters (not necessarily the first in the book) or for guidebooks, two to three trip write-ups, written in the style and length of the proposed book

• Information on the number and type of any photos, artwork, maps, or other illustrations proposed, along with samples (or good photocopies) of each type

• Information on the author's background and credentials to do this particular project

• Samples of other previously published writings by this author, if any

• Three editorial references

• Data on the size and scope of the intended market/audience of the project

• Description of what you would do to promote and market your book

• Information on any competitive books now in print (list and comment on specific titles) and how the proposed book is different and better than each

Mechanics:

All manuscript materials (reading text) must be double spaced, whether typewritten or word-processed. Please do not send disks. Do not send original manuscript materials; send only legible photocopies. When sending original art or photos, use UPS or Registered Mail to prevent loss in shipping. Include your name and address on all submitted materials-not just the outside envelope!

Categories: Nonfiction—Adventure—Conservation—Outdoors—Recreation—Hiking

CONTACT: Acquisitions Editor
Material: All
1001 SW Klickitat Way, Ste. 201
Seattle WA 98134
Phone: 206-223-6303
Fax: 206-223-6306
E-mail: acquisitions@mountaineers.org
Website: www.mountaineersbooks.org

Munchweiler Press
Quality Books for Young Readers

(when we are accepting)

1. Submissions must be typewritten and double-spaced.

2. Enclose a brief cover letter with an introduction to the submission and a short bio of the author. Mention if you have anything published and by whom.

3. Enclose a self-addressed stamped envelope for feedback.

4. If you want the manuscript returned (if it's rejected), enclose a large enough envelope with sufficient postage for its return.

5. When we are accepting we are only open to picture book manuscripts for ages 4-8. No Young Readers, Middle Readers, chapter books, young adult or adult material will be considered. Stay tuned, we'll begin accepting again as soon as we can.

We normally respond within one to two months.

ARTIST'S SUBMISSION GUIDELINES

(Still accepting art samples.)

1. Artists may submit samples of their work for consideration in future projects.

2. Only copies should be sent. Please never send original art.

3. We are open to all styles, and all submissions will be acknowledged. We acknowledge receipt of materials within one to two weeks.

Categories: Nonfiction—Careers—College—Consumer—Culture—Entertainment—Family—Food/Drink—Games—General Interest—Hobbies—Lifestyle—Parenting—Recreation—Reference—Sports/Recreation—Travel—Humor

CONTACT: Rollin Riggs, President
Material: All
PO Box 770426
Memphis TN 38177
Phone: 901-684-1200
Fax: 901-684-1256
E-mail: MustangPub@aol.com

Music Sales Publishing Group

Please refer to Schirmer Trade Book.

The Mysterious Press

Please refer to Time Warner Book Group.

Narwhal Press Inc.
Narwhal Press, Inc.

Formal guidelines not available.

Send queries or book proposals to below address.

Categories: Fiction—Nonfiction—Adventure—Biography—Boating—Civil War—Collectibles—Crime—History—Law—Men's Fiction—Military—Mystery—Regional—Women's Fiction—Young Adult

CONTACT: E. Lee Spence, Editor
Material:All
CONTACT: Robert P. Stockton, Associate Editor
Material: All
1436 Meeting St.
Charleston SC 29405

Naturegraph Publishers

Please approach us first with a query letter, outline of your work, and a sample chapter or two of your manuscript.

Your query letter should tell us what is unique about your book, your qualifications to write it, how it compares and contrasts with similar books on the same subject, why there is a need for your book, and how you can help us to make it a marketing success. We will acknowledge receipt of your proposal immediately.

If we are interested in your proposal, we will send you an author questionnaire to fill out and request to see the rest of your work. Authors whose work is accepted for publication will receive a contract specifying author responsibilities, royalties, expected publication date, etc.

Proposals submitted to us for consideration by our reviewing committee should belong to one of the following general categories: natural history, Native Americans, outdoor subjects, and natural crafts. Look at our catalog on our website or write to request our free catalog to get an idea of the types of books we publish.

Thank you for considering Naturegraph Publishers.

Categories: Environment—Games—Native American—Outdoors—Nature

CONTACT: Barbara Brown, Editor
Material: All
3543 Indian Creek Rd., PO Box 1047
Happy Camp CA 96039
Phone: 530-493-5353
Fax: 530-493-5240
E-mail: nature@sisqtel.net
Website: www.naturegraph.com

Naval Institute Press

Joint and general military subjects; naval biography; naval history; oceanography; navigation; military law; naval science textbooks; seapower; shipbuilding; professional guides; nautical arts and lore; technical guides. Limited military fiction.

Submissions require a minimum of two sample chapters, chapter outline, list of sources used, and authors biography. Include a cover letter.

All submissions must be typed, unbound, and accompanied by a cover letter. Only photocopies of artwork and photographs should be sent, not originals. Do not send disks with your submission. No manuscripts in binders!

Receipt of your manuscript will be acknowledged. Evaluation may take as long as twelve weeks.

Thank you for your interest in the Naval Press Institute.

Categories: Fiction—Nonfiction—Aviation—Boating—History—Military—Reference

CONTACT: Sara Sprinkle, Acquisitions Coordinator
Material: All
291 Wood Rd.
Annapolis MD 21402-5034
Phone: 410-295-4004
Fax: 410-295-1084

Nelson Reference & Electronic Publishing

We welcome proposals for reference books that promise to serve readers well. We want to review a book proposal before receiving a completed manuscript. Reviewing and making initial publishing decisions on the basis of a proposal, rather than a completed manuscript, is almost always in the best interests of both the author and the publisher. Even if you have completed a manuscript you wish us to review, please prepare and submit a proposal first. Write the proposal as well as you can; in deciding whether or not to pursue publication, we will consider not only the merits of your proposal, but also the quality of your writing.

Do the following in your proposal:

1. State the books purpose and scope. Usually one paragraph is sufficient. The purpose statement should identify what your proposed work enables readers to do; and the statement of scope should identify your works range or depth of treatment. Keep in mind that we publish almost exclusively for the lay and general audience. We rarely publish works primarily for an academic audience. However, we do publish works that have special value for ministers and other church leaders when those works are also clearly useable by lay and general readers.

2. Describe the primary audience of the book and any secondary audiences. For us, the formula to publishing success requires books to have both merit and marketability. To determine marketability, we need to know who are the target buyers and who are the secondary ones.

Think carefully about who would benefit the most from what your work offers. Think about the situations in which your work would be used and what it assumes the target reader will already know, be able to do, and desire.

Sometimes the primary audience may be truly general. For example, the primary audience for a desktop or collegiate dictionary of American English includes all truly literate Americans—all who want help with words they find in their reading or use in their writing or speaking. But often the primary audience of a book is smaller. For example, the primary audience of our academically oriented Word Biblical Commentary differs greatly from the primary audience of our Communicators Commentary, which aims at helping preachers and teachers move from the biblical text to their contemporary listeners.

Describe your works primary and secondary audience(s) as realistically and precisely as you can.

3. Demonstrate the need for the book by analyzing the books already on the market with which it will compete. Research all books on the market that are at all similar to the work you propose. Identify and list in a comparative table the features and benefits to the reader for each; then list the features and benefits of your work. Indicate how your book will surpass what is now available. If no other books do what you propose to do, explain why that is the case. Do not overlook the importance of this step. Your proposal is your attempt to make a strong case for our publishing your work, and we need you to show us that you know what is already available and why the target audience for your work would buy it over another book.

4. Summarize the main points of each chapter with an annotated Table of Contents. Two to five sentences per chapter is usually enough. State concisely what each chapter does, as well as how each chapter benefits the reader. Some reference books are not, of course, divided into chapters. For such a work, treat each major section as a chapter.

Books M-Z

5. Provide two or three complete chapters (or representative samples of major sections if the work is not organized in chapters). Provide an introductory chapter that sets the task of the rest of the book, the chapter you believe provides the most helpful or distinctive information, and a chapter that summarizes and concludes the work. For works not divided into chapters, provide a full introduction and representative samples of each major section. For these representative samplings, include a group of continuous pages that shows all the features of that section.

6. Estimate the length of the complete manuscript (in double-spaced pages and in total words) and the date by which you could complete it.

7. Describe the kinds and quantity of non-text material to be included in the work. Such items include photographs, line art, charts, tables, graphs, and maps. Indicate which you can provide and which you expect the publisher to provide. Keep in mind that properly illustrating a book enhances its value greatly but that such illustrations usually also raise the cost of its production. Be judicious in specifying non-text material that will not be provided in camera-ready form. (For example, photographs are not camera ready, while line drawings are.)

8. Identify authorities in the subject field of your work who you believe will endorse or contribute a Foreword to your work. Especially if you are a new author, the marketability of your work increases at least partly to the extent to which you can solicit good endorsements. At the proposal stage, we must have only a list of potential endorsers. Depending on the work and the extent to which you are known as an author, we may agree to publish your work contingent on your getting enough satisfactory endorsements.

9. Indicate if you are submitting this proposal to other publishers at the same time. We prefer that you propose your work only to us; however, if you have proposed it to other publishers also, please tell us.

10. Provide information about you—the contents of a resume or vita (although not necessarily that formal), along with an emphasis on the education and/or experience that qualifies you as somewhat of an authority on the topic your work covers.

11. Allow us twelve weeks after receipt of your proposal before you call to ask about its review. We will acknowledge receipt of your proposal by letter.

Categories: Christian Interests—Reference—Religion—Spiritual

CONTACT: Nelson Reference & Electronic Publishing
Material: All
501 Nelson Pl., PO Box 141000
Nashville TN 37214(-1000)
Phone: 615-889-9000
Fax: 615-391-5225

New Harbinger Publications

We have an ongoing need for book-length manuscripts on how readers can best deal with specific psychological and health care challenges. We're looking for books that appeal to both lay and professional audiences, offering theory, step-by-step techniques, and examples.

Recent titles that we have published include:

1) Natural Relief for Anxiety: Complementary Strategies for Easing Fear, Panic, and Worry

2) Overcoming Compulsive Hoarding: Why You Save and How You Can Stop

3) Coping With Your Partner's Jealousy: Understand Why Your Partner Gets Jealous

If you have any further questions, please feel free to email me anytime. Thanks for including us in your directory.

Categories: Nonfiction—Health—Psychology

CONTACT: Aquisitions
Material: All
5674 Shattuck Ave.
Oakland, CA 94609
Phone: 510-652-0215, 800-748-6273
Fax: 510-652-5472
Website: www.newharbinger.com

New Horizons Press
Small Horizons Imprint

We are continuing the Tradition of True Stories of Uncommon Heroes. We are always looking for manuscripts about true-life heroes. If you have one, we welcome unsolicited manuscripts.

Topics and Types of Stories We Are Looking For

Topics: Manuscripts which fit into our :60 Second Series, such as grief aid and other "bandage" topics for quick remedy pain relief (*:60 Second Anger Management/:60 Second Sleep-Ease/:60 Second Stress Relief*).

• Targeted self-help topics for general and specialty audiences written by mental health and other professionals (*Older Women, Younger Men, I'm Grieving As Fast As I Can, Red Hot Relationships*).

• Hard-hitting issues with news impact and publicity value (*Swallowing A Bitter Pill Sweet Poison, Woman to Woman 2000*).

• Topics which fit into our *Small Horizons* imprint, such as those which teach crisis, coping and service skills, and which are written by mental health professionals or educators (*My Stick, Family, I Am So Angry, I Could Scream, The Empty Place*).

Types of Stories: People who change the system. The courageous individual must be one of the characters in the story and has to be the author or co-author.

• Redemption/True Crime Stories: A person goes wrong, repents and then does something incredibly good for others. Crime oriented accounts are welcome, as long as there is a hero advancing justice, but no child abuse or incest stories (*Grave Accusations, Legacy of Courage, Murder In Memphis*).

• Exploring New Frontiers Stories: People who break or dismantle social or personal barriers (*Klan-destine Relationships, A Mountain Too Far, Edgewalkers*).

• Victim Stories: Victims who fight back and refuse to be victimized and then fight for the rights of others or a good cause (*Tainted Roses, Whispers of Romance, Threats of Death, Run Jane Run*).

IF YOU HAVE A NONFICTION MANUSCRIPT THAT FITS OUR FOCUS, WE WOULD LOVE TO SEE IT.

Be Sure to Include:

• Cover letter with your name, address, phone and fax numbers and E-mail address

• Book Proposal, which includes:

• Title page

• Table of contents

• Overview

• Chapter-by-chapter outline

• Photograph of author(s)

• Bio or CV of author(s)

• Marketing or commercial outlook

• Competition

• Promotion outlets

• Full or partial manuscript (If you have been previously published in nonfiction, a partial is acceptable)

• SASE.

Categories: Nonfiction—Alternate Life-style—Children—Crime—Family—Health—Human Rights—Inspirational—Lifestyle—Multicultural—New Age—Relationships—Self Help—True Crime—Women's Issues

CONTACT: Ms. P. Patty, Editor
Material: All
US Mail—PO Box 669
Far Hills NJ 07931
Phone: 908-604-6311
E-mail: nhp@newhorizonpressbook.com
Package Delivery: PO Box 218
34 Church St.
Liberty Corner NJ 07938
Website: www.newhorizonpressbooks.com

New Society Publishers

NEW SOCIETY PUBLISHERS is a progressive publishing company that specializes in books for activists that build ecological sustainability and a just society. We pride ourselves on being the only publishing house in North America specifically committed to fundamental social change through nonviolent action. We sell our books to a North America-wide market, using trade distributors in both Canada and the United States, as well as through direct mail.

A large majority of the books we publish we either initiate ourselves or acquire through previous contact with the author, or with an organization with which the author works. We sometimes publish manuscripts that are wholly unsolicited, and we welcome queries from authors, potential authors, or organizations seeking a publisher or co-publisher.

Editorial Objectives

Our editorial goal is to publish books which help create a sustainable, more peaceful and just world through nonviolent action. We are interested in analyzing examples and situations, in developing theories and strategies of nonviolent social change, and in identifying and spreading useful skills.

Our emphasis is always inspirational, motivational, and skill-oriented. We don't publish books which merely catalog what is wrong in the world; we do publish books which show that we can take control over our lives and change the way things are — and which suggest how we can accomplish this. Although we believe that fiction and poetry can play an important role in social change, they require different expertise and different marketing, neither of which we can provide; please do not submit such works.

While we will consider any proposal which fits our broader editorial goals outlined above, *we are particularly interested in books which fall into these major (and overlapping) areas:*

• *Sustainability:* books that contribute in original ways to achieving ecological, social, and cultural sustainability; books on ecological analysis, design and planning; on forestry, urban and rural development, transportation, etc.

• *Resistance and Community:* books that help break the vicious cycle of environmental exploitation and the cultural, economic, political, and social dislocation of communities — here and in the third world — and books that help people reestablish the bonds of community, both with humankind and with nature.

• *Progressive Leadership:* resources and training manuals devoted to nonhierarchical group dynamics and democratic decision making, nonviolent action strategies and tactics, support and empowerment for leaders, activists, and organizations, etc.

• *"Conscientious Commerce":* books that focus on the "new business"—ways in which business is transforming itself to take responsibility for environmental and social concerns, etc.

• *Educational & Parenting Resources:* books that analyze our educational systems and propose alternatives; books that explore nonviolent forms of child rearing and play; and books that encourage conflict resolution, social responsibility, and democratic behavior in young people from kindergarten through young adult levels.

• *Nonviolence:* books that analyze or describe nonviolent perspectives, strategies and visions that can be applied to local, national, and international affairs;

• *Feminism & Diversity:* books that help transform oppressive attitudes and structures and encourage respect for, and celebration of, diversity in a multi cultural world.

What to Submit

The number of manuscripts we are actually able to read is finite. In order to increase the chance that your proposal will receive good attention and hence increase the chance that we'll publish it, we ask that you do not submit the entire manuscript until we ask for it, but rather send us the following:

• A table of contents
• A sample chapter
• A proposal which answers the following questions:

1. In 75 words or less, what is the book about?

2. What qualifies you, or gives you authority, to write such a book? (We are not especially interested in degrees.)

3. What other books in the field exist, when were they published, and how is yours similar or different? Trees are valuable and increasingly scarce: will the world really benefit from decreasing the number of trees in order to add another book on this subject?

4. Out of over 4,000 trade book publishers in the United States and Canada, why are you sending your proposal to New Society Publishers? How did you learn of us?

5. Whom do you imagine to be the audience for the book? What do you think are the best ways to reach them? If you could have the book serialized or reviewed, what are the 5 or 10 most important publications in which it could appear?

6. What help can you be in the promotion of the book? Organizational connections? Mailing lists? Workshops? Tours? (We are primarily interested in publishing authors who are prepared to help substantially with the promotion of their own books.)

7. We sell books back to authors at a very large discount. How many of your own books do you think you might need initially, if any?

8. Manuscripts must be submitted on disk. What platform do you work on (Mac or Windows)? What make and model of computer do you have? What word-processor and version?

9. What is the length of your manuscript? Provide a word count (many word processing programs can calculate this automatically).

10. When do you expect your book to be completed? How much do you currently have written?

NOTE: We cannot guarantee serious consideration of a proposal that does not include all of the elements above. If you want a response and/or your manuscript returned, include a self-addressed stamped envelope (or international stamp coupon of sufficient value, if you are outside Canada); we cannot either acknowledge receipt of, nor return, materials for projects we reject which come without a SASE or equivalent.

Please be patient; we are reading as fast as we can! We will ask for the whole manuscript if we wish to see it. Please understand that decisions to publish require much more time than do refusals. Please do not call us once you have sent us your proposal; we'll contact you as appropriate.

Thanks very much indeed for thinking of us!

Categories: Nonfiction—Business—Conservation—Ecology—Feminism—Lifestyle—Parenting

CONTACT: Submissions Editor
Material: All
PO Box 189
Gabriola Island
BC, Canada V0R 1X0
Phone: 250-247-9737
Fax: 250-247-7471
E-mail: info@newsociety.com
Website: www.newsociety.com

New Victoria Publishers

In 1860 women's rights activist Emily Faithful founded Victoria Press, an all-woman print shop in London, England. Her tradition was revived in New England in 1975 with the establishment of New Victoria Printers and, in 1976, New Victoria Publishers, a non-profit feminist literary and cultural organization publishing the finest in lesbian feminist fiction and nonfiction.

We are primarily interested in well-crafted fiction in all genres featuring lesbians or strong female protagonists.

The following ingredients should be present:

• Clear narrative story line.
• Well-drawn, intelligent, introspective characters.
• Accurate background locations or atmosphere.
• Issues pertinent to the lesbian community whether emotional, societal, or political.
• Humor and/or eroticism.

We are especially interested in lesbian or feminist mysteries, ideally with a character or characters who can evolve through a series of books. Mysteries should involve a complex plot, accurate legal/procedural detail, and protagonists with full emotional lives.

We prefer science/speculative fiction or fantasy with amazon adventure themes and/or detailed, well-crafted alternative realities, complete with appropriately original language and culture.

We are also interested in well-researched nonfiction on women, lesbian-feminist herstory, or biography of interest to a general as well as academic audience.

We advise you to look through our catalog to see our past editorial decisions as well as what we are currently marketing. Our books average 80-90,000 words, or 200-250 single-spaced pages.

Please send your enquiry to us with:

• A brief outline or synopsis highlighting key issues in the story, why you wrote it, and any target audience you have in mind.
• Several sample chapters or approximately 50-75 pages.

We prefer single submissions (ms. sent to one publisher only), so please let us know if you have submitted your manuscript to or are under contract with another publisher.

A partial List of New Victoria Authors: Sarah Dreher (*The Stoner McTavish Mysteries*); Lesléa Newman (*Secrets, In Every Laugh a Tear, Saturday is Pattyday, Every Womans Dream*); Kate Allen (*Tell Me What You Like, Give My Secrets Back, I Knew You Would Call*); J.M. Redmann (*Death by the Riverside, Deaths of Jocasta, Chris Anne Wolfe, Shadows of Agar, Fires of Agar*); Cris Newport (*Sparks Might Fly*); Jane Meyerding (*Everywhere House*); Lesa Luders (*Lady God*); Morgan Grey & Julia Penelope (*Found Goddesses*); Claudia McKay (*Promise of the Rose Stone, The Kali Connection*); ReBecca Béguin (*Runway at Eland Springs, In Unlikely Places, Hers Was the Sky*)

Books M-Z

Categories: Fiction—Nonfiction—Feminism—Gay/Lesbian—Mystery—Romance

CONTACT: Acquisitions Editor
Material: All
PO Box 27
Norwich VT 05055
Phone: 802-649-5297
Fax: 802-649-5297

New World Library

Manuscripts should be neatly typed and double-spaced. Please send two or three sample chapters, an outline or table of contents, a market assessment (a listing of competing books and how your book is different), and a detailed statement of author credentials/biographical information. Please do not send original artwork as we cannot be responsible for it. Instead, we recommend you only send copies of artwork, when appropriate. We do not accept email submissions. Sorry we are no longer accepting unsolicited children's book manuscripts at this time.

We presently focus on high quality books in the following categories: spirituality, self-improvement, parenting, women's studies, alternative health, religion, enlightened business, animal spirituality, and multicultural studies. Our works appeal to a large, general audience.

VERY IMPORTANT: Please include a self-addressed stamped envelope (SASE) if you wish to hear from us, and especially if you want your manuscript returned. Due to the number of queries and manuscripts we receive, we can respond only if a SASE is enclosed. Be sure the envelope is large enough to contain the manuscript and that you include sufficient postage.

Please allow us twelve weeks to respond.

Thank you.

Categories: Business—Health—Multicultural—New Age—Parenting—Religion—Spiritual— Women's Issues

CONTACT: Submissions Editor
Material: All
14 Pamaron Way
Novato, CA 94949
Phone: 800-972-6657, 415-884-2100
Fax: 415-884-2199
Website: www.newworldlibrary.com

North Point Press

Please refer to Farrar, Straus and Giroux, Publishers, Inc.

North Ridge Books

North Ridge Books will consider manuscripts in the following categories:

If you have a manuscript ready to be published, e-mail us a book proposal—which must include a detailed marketing plan—at info@nrbooks.com.

Explain to us why your book fills a need. And remember: Publishing a book requires a considerable investment. Consider North Ridge Books only if you are a top-notch writer, have something fresh and original to say, and are able to heavily promote it on radio and TV.

We are not in a position to offer advances, but we will consider new talent. We are also open to co-publishing arrangements in which we package and promote the book for you, while you keep all rights. No phone calls and no faxes please. Please, no fiction or poetry or fiction—no matter how brilliant you are. We will only consider manuscripts we know how to market.

Categories: Biography—Current Events—History—Humor—Reference—Travel

CONTACT: Submissions Editor
Material: All
PO Box 1463
Lake Forest, CA 92609
E-mail: info@nrbooks.com
Website: www.nrbooks.com

North Street Publishers

We publish fiction, nonfiction, mysteries, biographies and memoirs. To know me better, please go to our website. Also read the first chapter of *Hard Boiled Eggs and Other Psychiatric Tales*.

Categories: Fiction—Nonfiction—Biography—Mystery

CONTACT: Albert Honig
Material: All
616 North St.
Doylestown PA 18901
Phone: 215-348-2134
Fax: 215-348-2134
E-mail: albhon@earthlink.net
Website: www.dramhonig.net

Northern Publishing

We publish mostly Alaskan titles about hunting or the outdoors. Other similar topics are accepted depending on their merit. We do not publish fiction, how-to manuals are our preference. We accept manuscripts or detailed proposals targeting a specific audience. Titles with unique ideas or written by recognized authorities or experts on a subject are preferred.

Some of our titles are:

Sheep Hunting in Alaska: The Dall Sheep Hunters Guide, The Manual for Successful Hunters: Why 10% of the Hunters take 90% of the Game, The Quest for Dall Sheep: A Historic Guide's Memories of Alaskan Hunting, Bear Hunting in Alaska, Moose Hunting in Alaska.

Tony Russ, Owner, Northern Publishing

Categories: Nonfiction—History—Outdoors—Recreation—Sports/Recreation

CONTACT: Tony Russ
Material: All
PO Box 871803
Wasilla AK 99687
Fax: 907-373-6474
E-mail: tony@TonyRuss.com
Website: www.TonyRuss.com

Nova Press

We publish only books and software for, or closely related to, test preparation for college entrance exams: LSAT, GRE, SAT, GMAT, MCAT.

Categories: Nonfiction—College—Education

CONTACT: Acquisitions Editor
Material: All
11659 Mayfield Ave., Ste. 1
Los Angeles CA 90049
Phone: 310-207-4078
Fax: 310-571-0908
E-mail: NovaPress@aol.com

Remember: Editors change jobs and publishers change addresses. It is wise to invest in a phone call for the current information before submitting.

The Oasis Press

Please refer to PSI Research.

Omnibus Press

Omnibus Press is an imprint of Music Sales Corporation. Founded in 1935 by the Wise family, Music Sales is an international family of companies with interests in four main areas of music publishing: Copyright ownership and promotion of standard and popular music, classical music, printed music, and book publishing. Music Sales maintains offices in New York, London, Sydney, Copenhagen, Madrid, Tokyo, Helsinki, and Paris.

Omnibus is a leading publisher of musician biographies, with a special focus on rock & roll and pop. Most Omnibus books are commissioned in our U.K. headquarters, but the U.S. office is always interested in seeing your proposals.

We're especially keen on unofficial musician biographies (high-profile entertainers with large fan bases, as well as up-and-coming), as well as graphic novels. (See Godspeed: The Kurt Cobain Graphic and In My Skin: The Eminen Graphic.) We rarely publish books about classical music. We prefer rock & roll, folk, blues, and pop.

Send full book proposals, including: Cover letter, overview of the book, target audience, author bio, competitive titles, marketing and promotion ideas, detailed chapter-by-chapter table of contents, and a sample chapter (if available).

Categories: Nonfiction—Biography—History—Music—Reference—Performing Arts

CONTACT: Andrea Rotondo, Managing Editor
Material: All
257 Park Ave. South
New York, NY 10010
Phone: 212-254-2100
Fax: 212-254-2013
Website: www.musicsales.com

Orange Frazer Press, Inc.

In a nutshell, we specialize in highly designed, well-produced books on Ohio information, education, entertainment and sports—and every so often, cross over the borders (of Ohio) just for fun.

We cannot acknowledge any submission or return any material that does not include a self-addressed, stamped envelope.

Responses are generally sent within three months.

We are unable to acknowledge receipt of your submission or give status reports.

We cannot be responsible for original copies of manuscripts, photos, artwork, etc. Do not send these materials.

Orange Frazer Press is a small press that publishes books about Ohio that we have commissioned authors to write for us, or the authors have brought to us as finished manuscripts, that we feel suit our mission for providing lively, knowledgeable, entertaining and educational material about Ohio and famous Ohioans.

Submissions Should Include:
1. *A cover letter.*
2. An outline and a sample chapter or two.
3. A brief synopsis of each of the other chapters.

The Cover Letter Should Explain
1. The book's subject matter and approach.
2. Anticipated audience.
3. What distinguishes your book from others on the matter.
4. Your qualifications for writing this book.
5. Why do you think your book is appropriate for Orange Frazer?

Audio cassettes, computer disks, or videotapes in lieu of typed manuscripts are not acceptable. *All proposals must be submitted in the following format:*

• Unbound and without staples, paste-ups, or anything that will interfere with photocopying should multiple copies be necessary for editorial staff review.

• Consecutively numbered throughout–clean photocopies are acceptable.

• It is helpful if your name and address are on the first page of the document.

Although Orange Frazer Press does do extensive editing on many manuscripts, we do not have the staff for re-writing, so-called "ghost writing," or to serve as o-authors. (You may want to contact local universities or colleges, writers guilds, or editorial services for help.)

Additionally, we create, write, edit, design, format, and print books for companies, corporations, municipalities and organizations who wish to have a book made for one reason or another.

Categories: Nonfiction—Education—Entertainment—Regional—Sports/Recreation

CONTACT: Tammy McKay, Acquisitions
Material: All
CONTACT: John Baskins, Editor
Material: All
PO Box 214
Wilmington OH 45177
Phone: 937-382-3196
Fax: 937-382-3159

Orb

Please refer to Tom Doherty Associate, LLC, in the Book Publishers section.

Orchises Press

Orchises Press is a small literary and general publisher located outside of Washington, D. C. It publishes five to eight books a year and has a list of one hunded titles, many of them original poetry, a love of the editor, Roger Lathbury. Unlike many other presses, small and large, Orchises reads unsolicited manuscripts and tries to publish books on their merit, both literary and commercial. It prides itself on the attractiveness of its volumes, both paperback and hardcover.

MANUSCRIPT SUBMISSION GUIDELINES

Orchises is one of the few publishers that reads unsolicited freelance submissions. If a manuscript is presented in a reasonable manner, well look at it. "Reasonable" means:

1. Typed, preferably double-spaced. Photocopies are OK; they're indistinguishable from laser print anyhow.

2. A return envelope is enclosed-a self-addressed stamped envelope large enough to accommodate the manuscript if you want the manuscript returned, a size 10 or 6 3/4 envelope if a response is all that's needed. While understanding that such is not the fate writers most want, Orchises recycles all unreturnable manuscripts. In general, mail with no materials for a response will not receive a response nor will it be retained pending the arrival of a forgotten envelope.

3. A phone number is helpful for those rare occasions when we accept.

OTHER REMARKS

1. Orchises does not publish original fiction, children's books or cookbooks.

2. If you submit poetry, you may be interested to know that in one year Orchises receives 200-300 poetry manuscripts or queries accompanied by poems. Two or three such may be accepted; one year four were, another none was. Usually poetry Orchises publishes has appeared previously in magazines of national repute, e.g., *American Poetry Review, The Atlantic Monthly, Harpers, The New Republic, The New Yorker,* Poetry—as well as respected literary magazines (e.g., The Paris Review, Shenandoah, The Southern Review). These places build

audiences. Of course, publication in those magazines is not an absolute criterion. All readers, I expect, have read poems in those venues that are quite fine but also others that seem less good than poems in less prominent places. The only way to judge is to read; we'll read.

3. Reporting times vary but usually are within 1 month. Longer means closer.

4. The volume of submissions makes it impossible to provide commentary.

With thanks and good wishes,
Roger Lathbury, Orchises Press
Categories: Nonfiction—Poetry—Textbooks

CONTACT: Acquisitions Editor
Material: All
PO Box 20602
Alexandria VA 22320-1602
E-mail: lathbury@gmu.edu

Origin Media, Inc.
"Books for the Integral Age"

IMPRINTS
Origin Press—www.originpress.com
Wisdom Editions—www.wisdomeditions.com
Celestia—www.celestiapress.org

OUR APPROACH TO PUBLISHING:

Origin has won three national awards for its books, and currently enters into traditional publisher-author agreements only with previously published authors. Agents should know that we pay very low advances. We only publish a few commercial titles each year. We also have a unique arrangement for first-time authors or writers with specialized non-commercial titles who are willing to subsidize their first title—but only if their title meets high editorial standards. We also consult to self-publishers and small presses.

ORIGIN'S IMPRINTS:

The Origin Press and Wisdom Editions imprints work with authors of books on practical spirituality, psychology, self-help, global religion, philosophy, integral studies, progressive business and politics, ufology, visionary fiction, and related subjects. Celestia publishes works with authors in Urantia Book studies, esoterica, paranormal, and metaphysics. Please study the website for each imprint.

SUBMISSIONS
Prefer emails of short queries to: byron@originpress.com.
Categories: Fiction—Business—Politics—Psychology—Self Help—Spiritual

CONTACT: Submissions Editor
Material: All
PO Box 151117
San Rafael CA 94915-1117
E-mail: byron@originpress.com

Osborne/McGraw-Hill

McGraw-Hill/Osborne Media, a unit of McGraw-Hill Education, is a leading publisher of self-paced computer training materials, including user and reference guides, best-selling series on computer certification, titles on business & technology, and high-level but practical titles on networking, programming, and Web development tools. McGraw-Hill/Osborne Media is the official press of Oracle, Corel, Global Knowledge, J.D. Edwards, Intuit, and RSA Security Inc., and has a strategic publishing relationship with ComputerWorld. McGraw-Hill/Osborne Media is focusing on consumer support, emerging technologies, and innovative applications for developing future computer books.

McGraw-Hill Education is a division of The McGraw-Hill Companies (NYSE: MHP), a global information services provider meeting worldwide needs in financial services, education, and business-to-business information through leading brands such as Standard & Poor's and BusinessWeek. The Corporation has more than 300 offices in 32 countries. Sales in 2000 were $4.3 billion.

How to Prepare Your Manuscript Proposal

The following guidelines outline the major areas that you should cover in your proposal. Please be as complete as possible, as it will help us make a decision more quickly. Also, feel free to add relevant information even if we haven't specifically asked for it below.

The most important elements are:
• Why we should publish this book
• What specific skills do you bring to this book/topic
• Why will this book sell better than other similar books (or if there is no competition, what are the market conditions that make you believe that this is a book worth publishing.)

Your proposal should include the following information:
• Brief description of the book.
• Brief description of the product or technology.
• Audience: Who is the major audience for your book; for whom is your book intended? At what level is your book written; what technical background will the reader of your book need?
• Outstanding features: List what you consider to be the outstanding or unique features of your work.
• Outline: Provide a detailed outline of your book. This will give reviewers an idea of what topics you are including and how your material is organized. Your outline should include part titles, chapter headings, subheadings, and appendixes, with explanations as necessary. It should also include your estimate of the length in manuscript pages of each chapter.
• Competition: List the existing books, if any, with which yours will compete and discuss specifically their strengths and weaknesses. Spell out how your work will be similar to and different from competing books.
• The Market: Mention any factors that might have an impact (positive or negative) on the market for your work. How is the market changing? If your work focuses on particular hardware or software, and you have sales figures for the product, include these.
• Schedule: What is your timetable for completing your book? What portion of the material is now complete? When do you expect to have a complete manuscript?
• Size: What do you estimate to be the size of the complete book? (Double-spaced typewritten pages normally reduce by about one-third when set into type: for example, 300 typewritten pages equal approximately 200 printed pages).
• Resume: Include a copy of your vita, or a paragraph or two of relevant biographical information. Please include a list of hardware and software for which you have expertise.
• Writing Sample: Please include a magazine article or the introduction or chapter of the book, or other writing samples.

You can send your proposal directly to members of our Acquisitions team either through regular mail or e-mail.

Categories: Computers—Internet

CONTACT: Manuscript Proposal
Material: All
2600 10th St.
Berkeley CA 94710
Phone: 510-549-6600
Fax: 510-549-6603
E-mail: srogers@mcgraw-hill.com
Website: www.osborne.com

The Overmountain Press

If you are searching for a publisher and are considering The Overmountain Press, you need to know a few things about what we publish. Along with these guidelines, we will include our list of titles so that you may become more familiar with the type of books we publish, some of the authors we work with, and the retail prices of our books.

We are primarily a publisher of regional-interest books. Some of our titles are reprints of older historical accounts that have gone out-of-print. Below we will list some guidelines for manuscripts from different literary genres. This will list what you should provide when submitting a proposal.

In addition to these items, we would like for you to include the following: brief description of the book, your background and qualifications for writing this book, prospective market for selling the book, any other marketing suggestions you may have, and a self-addressed stamped envelope for returning. We will not return your manuscript without the self-addressed stamped envelope.

Categories of Publication

Children We have recently begun to publish titles for children. Although we have published a few exceptions, we are now accepting regional (Southern Appalachian) titles ONLY. In reviewing a children's manuscript for publication, we prefer to have copies of the illustrations at the same time we review the text. Very few publishers review in this way. Most of the larger companies with hundreds of titles prefer to find the illustrator from their database.

At an author's request we can send a list of illustrators and graphic artists who can be hired out or collaborated with in producing a children's book. At present this list is small, and we are looking for illustrators who wish to be added. This is a list of artists who have approached us. We do not recommend one over another. You can pay the artist a flat fee, or you can choose to split the royalties from book sales. This decision is between you and the illustrator. Again, please do not send the original artwork. Copies are fine, but please include a couple of color copies so we can get a feel for the artist's use of color.

The Overmountain History Series for Young Readers is a new series of books teaching Southern Appalachian history to readers on a 3rd-8th grade reading level. Books will need to have many photos or drawings - all historical. These books are strictly non-fiction. Books will have anywhere from 5000-15,000 words depending on subject matter and illustrations. Please submit the entire manuscript.

Cookbooks When accepting cookbook manuscripts, we look for a new and interesting way of cooking or organizing the recipes. A regular cookbook is hard to market without some sort of characteristic to set it apart from the others on the shelves. Your book should have a unique setup that is distinctive and obvious to the consumer.

Ghost Lore We have published several stories of "true" ghost lore. We have been successful in selling these titles and will consider manuscripts of this type. They must be Appalachian in nature and be "true" stories. For example, *The Infamous Bell Witch of Tennessee* is a "true" ghost story passed through generations and put into book form. This is extremely marketable.

Guidebooks We have published a few guide/hiking books, and we are interested in looking at others. It should be Appalachian in nature and include plenty of photographs, maps, drawings, etc.

Mystery Our new Silver Dagger Mystery series has its own set of guidelines for submission. They are available on our website at www.silverdaggermysteries.com.

Regional History / Nonfiction We would like to see either a complete manuscript or an outline plus three chapters. If the manuscript is very large, we can look at an outline with sample chapters to determine whether it will fit within our scope of titles. If, at that point, we decide to take a closer look, we will request the complete manuscript. We do not accept titles without looking at the entire work.

We like photographs! Illustrations, slides, photos, maps, etc., all enhance nonfiction works. When submitting your proposal, please send samples of illustrations for the book. PLEASE DO NOT SEND ORIGI-NALS! Photocopies are fine for review. Each photo should include a brief description. You do not need to send every photo that you plan to include in the book - just a few to let us get a feel for your collection.

Tall Tales / Folklore We have published several compilations of *Appalachian Tall Tales and Folklore*. Some of the works of Charles Edwin Price and Denvil Mullins fit into this category. In submitting, please send a proposal and a couple of sample tales along with any illustrations you may be planning.

We may have left some other categories off this list. Please do not hesitate to call with questions regarding the types of books we publish.

Categories Not Published by The Overmountain Press
- Biography
- General Fiction / Novels
- Inspirational
- Poetry
- Reminiscences

Timelines We generally take anywhere from one to three months to review manuscripts. Several people are involved in the decision-making process, and it sometimes takes time to read these manuscripts. Please do not call to find the status of your manuscript. It may take us a few weeks, but we will get back to you! After acceptance we generally plan a production schedule of approximately six months to one year. This is a huge variable depending upon what your book needs to be perfect. If your book will be hardback, this will typically add one month to the production schedule. This is annoying, but it is a fact that we cannot change. *Following is a list of pointers to take significant amounts of time off the production schedule:*

- Have the manuscript on a computer disk. Call us to see if your program is compatible with ours.
- Have several people offer editorial advice to reduce Overmountain editorial time
- Place your illustrations, photos, etc., where you want them before you submit the manuscript
- Devise some marketing strategies to share with our marketing department
- Obtain all permissions for using photos, quotes, excerpts, etc.
- Think of some possible cover ideas to share with our graphic designers
- Be receptive to changes concerning your manuscript

Questions If you are not sure of your project's suitability to our list, please call at 423-926-2691 before spending the time and postage to send it in for review.

PLEASE DO NOT EMAIL QUERIES. THEY WILL NOT BE ANSWERED!

Categories: Nonfiction—Biography—History—Native American—Regional

CONTACT: Jason Weems, Editor
Material: All
PO Box 1261
Johnson City TN 37605
Phone: 423-926-2691
Website: www.overmountainpress.com

Pacific View Press

Dear Author,

We apologize for this form letter, but we receive many queries, and cannot personally respond to those which are not within our area of publication interest.

We are a small press focusing on the Pacific Rim and its unique, growing interplay of economic and cultural forces. *We publish titles in three series:*

Contemporary Affairs, on Pacific Rim topics only, including guides for Asia-related international business; Books for a Multicultural Society; nonfiction on Asia and Asian-American themes, primarily for

Books M-Z

children [see guidelines below]; Traditional Chinese Medicine, primarily texts, for practitioners.

We do not publish travel books or travelogues, autobiographies or biographies, photojournalism, literature or fiction.

If you feel your project fits our publishing interests, you are welcome to submit a proposal, accompanied by a sample chapter, and an outline or table of contents. Please include autobiographical information. We prefer not to receive manuscripts. We do not accept typewritten material. You may wish to request a current catalog first or visit our website.

If we are interested in your proposal we will respond within 6 weeks, after your proposal has been evaluated by our editorial committee. Your material is assumed to be copyrighted and will be kept confidential.

Thank you for your interest, and good luck.

Regards,

Pacific View Press

Guidelines for Children's Book Authors and Artists

Our children's books focus on hardcover illustrated nonfiction for readers aged eight to twelve. We look for titles on aspects of the history and culture of the countries and peoples of the Pacific Rim, especially China, presented in an engaging, informative and respectful manner. We are interested in books that all children will enjoy reading and using, and that parents and teachers will want to buy. Our titles are available nationally through quality trade bookstores, museum stores, multicultural specialty catalogs, and the leading library and trade distributors. Recent titles have included *Exploring Chinatown: A Children's Guide to Chinese Culture* and *A Thousand Peaks: Poems from China.*

We welcome proposals from persons with expertise, either academic or personal, in their area of interest. While we do accept proposals from previously unpublished authors, we would expect submitters to have considerable experience presenting their interests to children in classroom or other public settings, and to have skill in writing for children.

We do not publish fiction, picture stories, or photo-picture books. At this time we are not considering natural history or biographies.

Our finished books are usually 48-96 pages, 8½"x11", with full-color illustration throughout.

You are welcome to submit proposals, accompanied by a sample chapter or unit and an outline for the entire book. Please include autobiographical information. We would prefer not to receive completed manuscripts.

If we are interested in your proposal we will respond within 6 weeks, after your proposal has been evaluated by our editorial committee. Our contracts with authors are fairly standard for small publishers and cover finances, time frames and obligations of both author and publisher. We pay royalties based on net sales, with a small advance against royalties paid upon acceptance of the final manuscript.

Categories: Nonfiction—Asian-American—Children—Multicultural—Asia—Contemporary Affairs

CONTACT: Acquisitions Editor
Material: All
PO Box 2897
Berkeley CA 94702
Phone: 510-849-4213
Website: www.pacificviewpress.com

Padlock Mystery Press

Hello! Padlock Mystery Press has published ten books since 1997 and plans to publish at least two books a year in the future. We are interested in mystery novels of 50 to 60 thousand words. No graphic sex scenes or torture. Our preference is for cozy novels, especially if they include locksmiths, key or lock themes whether present day forensic locksmiths or historical. KEY DECEPTIONS and KEY CON-

FRONTATIONS is an example. Query by email is preferred. If we are interested, we'll ask to see the entire novel.

Categories: Fiction—Mystery

CONTACT: Mary Ellen Cooper
Material: All
412 E. 9th
Stillwater, OK 74074
Phone: 405-372-2254
Fax: 405-372-8338
E-mail: Padlockmystery@aol.com
Website: www.mecooper.com

Paladin Press
Sycamore Island Books
Flying Machines Press

Paladin Press primarily publishes original nonfiction manuscripts on military science, self-defense, personal privacy, espionage, police science, action careers, guerilla warfare, and other action topics. Submissions may be outlines with 1-3 sample chapters or complete manuscripts. Allow 1 month from receipt for a reply. Paladin also produces videos on the above topics.

Categories: Nonfiction—Adventure—Crime—History—Military—Money & Finances—Outdoors—Martial Arts—Personal Freedom—Weaponry

CONTACT: Editorial Department
Material: All
PO Box 1307
Boulder CO 80306
Phone: 303-443-7250
Fax: 303-442-8741
E-mail: editorial@paladin-press.com

Paradise Cay Publications

Paradise Cay is a small independent publisher specializing in nautical books, video, and art prints. Our major market is the United States; however, we have distributors in many other countries. Our primary interest is in manuscripts that deal with the instructional and technical aspect of ocean sailing and motorboating. We also publish and will consider fiction if it has a strong nautical theme.

All submitted manuscripts will be personally considered by the publisher, Matt Morehouse. He will usually contact the author by phone or e-mail. To present in the best possible way, submissions should include a cover letter containing a story synopsis and a short biography of the author, including any plans the author may have to promote the work. The cover letter should describe the book's subject matter, approach, distinguishing characteristics, intended audience, author's qualifications, and why the author thinks this book is appropriate for Paradise Cay.

Although Paradise Cay does do extensive editing on many manuscripts, it is the responsibility of first-time or little-known authors to pay for editing. We can refer authors to an independent editing service we use and highly recommend, www.we-edit.com, or the author may secure these services locally. We emphasize that any manuscript accepted for publication must be complete and ready for print production. Manuscripts must be double-spaced on 8.5" x 11" paper. Each page should be numbered consecutively and should carry a header with the author's name and the manuscript's title. Do not send the entire manuscript unless the publisher requests it; sixty pages should be sufficient. If the author wants these pages returned, a self-addressed, stamped envelope should be included.

Paradise Cay does not normally pay advances to first-time or little-known authors. If your manuscript is accepted for publication, Paradise Cay pays all costs of printing, binding, warehousing, shipping, advertising, marketing, billing, and collection. The author has no cost beyond manuscript preparation. The author is paid a semiannual royalty, usually ten percent.

Categories: Nonfiction—Boating—Book Reviews—Cooking—Fishing—Outdoors—Recreation—Regional—Sports/Recreation—Trade—Nautical—Travel

CONTACT: Matt Morehouse, Publisher
Material: All
PO Box 29
Arcata, CA 95518-0029
Phone: 707-822-7038
E-mail: mattm@humboldt1.com
Website: www.paracay.com

Paragon House

Paragon House publishes reference and scholarly titles, in the areas of Biography, History, Philosophy, Psychology, Religion, Spiritual Health, Reference, Political Science, and International Relations.

Please include the following items to help us make a prompt decision on your project:

• An abstract of your project, which must include a summary of your premise, main arguments, and conclusions.
• A table of contents.
• A sample chapter.
• Your current curriculum vitae.
• An estimated number of diagrams, figures, pictures or drawings.
• An estimated number of double-spaced manuscript pages, in your completed project, along with the computer format (for example: PC compatible in Word Perfect).
• A tentative schedule for completion of your project.
• A list of competing books, if any, and a brief note telling how your book compares to each. Please include publisher, date of publication, page count and price, if possible.
• Any endorsements you have received.
• No email submissions
• A stamped, self-addressed, return envelope, of adequate size, and with enough postage to return your manuscript, in case of rejection. Materials submitted without adequate postage will not be returned.

Categories: Economics—Human Rights—New Age—Philosophy—Psychology—Religion—Spiritual—Textbooks

CONTACT: Rosemary Yokoi, Acquisitions Editor
Material: All
2285 University Ave. West, Ste. 200
St. Paul MN 55114-1635
Phone: 651-644-3087
Fax: 651-644-0997
E-mail: paragon@paragonhouse.com
Website: www.paragonhouse.com

Remember: Editors change jobs and publishers change addresses. It is wise to invest in a phone call for the current information before submitting.

Parenting Press, Inc.

Categories that we publish:
1. Skill building books for parents
2. Personal safety for kids
3. Emotions and social problem solving for kids

We publish:
Books that teach practical life skills to parents, children, and the people who care for them. The books are nonjudgmental in attitude, useful to people with many different value systems, and full of options rather than "shoulds." They are short, easily understood, and present material in a fresh way.

We do NOT publish:
Books with animals as main characters
Fairy tales, autobiographies, biographies
Children's illustrated story books
Religious books
Parenting books based on an author's experience with one child or one family
Academic or theoretical works
Craft or activity books, workbooks
Poetry
Illness-or disability-based books

Submission guidelines:
Please tell us about you . . .
What uniquely qualifies you to write on your subject.
What you would like to accomplish by having this material published.
What experience you have writing other books or materials and their sales history.
What kinds of book promotion you are ready to undertake.
Tell us about your idea . . .
Who is the primary audience for your material? Secondary?
In what ways will your material be helpful to the audiences you identified?
Comparing your manuscript to the competition among published books, how and why is your idea different and better?
What kinds of promotion do you think will be particularly effective for you and your book?

What we need to see in writing . . .
Send a letter of inquiry to us in which you respond to the questions above and relate any other information you think will help us make a decision about the suitability of your manuscript.

Send a paper copy, double spaced, of all or as much of the manuscript as you have ready with your letter. At a minimum, we need a detailed outline showing the organization of the manuscript, a table of contents, an introduction, and two chapters showing your best and truest writing style.

If you would like your material returned to you in the event it is not suitable for Parenting Press, also send a postage-paid reply envelope large enough to hold it.

Do NOT send your material via e-mail.
Categories: Nonfiction—Parenting

CONTACT: Carolyn Threadgill, Acquisitions
Material: All
PO Box 75267
Seattle, WA 98175-0267
Phone: 800-992-6657
Website: www.ParentingPress.com

Parkway Publishers, Inc.

We are primarily interested in regional non-fiction books. The region of our interest is Western North Carolina in particular and North Carolina and Appalachian region in general. We like to receive com-

Books M-Z

pleted manuscripts with self-addressed, stamped envelopes. We prefer manuscripts of about 200 double-spaced pages.

Thank you.
Sincerely,
Rao Aluri

Categories: Nonfiction—Regional

CONTACT: Rao Aluri, Ph.D.
Material: All
Box 3678
Boone NC 28607
Phone: 828-265-3993 (Ph & Fax)
E-mail: parkwaypub@hotmail.com
Website: www.parkwaypublishers.com

Pathfinder Publishing of California

Formal guidelines not available.

Send queries or book proposals to below address.

Categories: Nonfiction—Careers—Computers—Disabilities—Family—Health—Men's Issues—Self Help—Society

CONTACT: Bill Mosbrook, CEO
Material: All
3600 Harbor Blvd., #82
Oxnard CA 93035
Phone: 805-984-7756
E-mail: bmosbrook@earthlink.net

Pauline Books & Media

Pauline Books & Media reviews and accepts manuscripts in the areas of Scripture (biblical spirituality, pastoral biblical study), spirituality (prayer/holiness of life), catechetics (adults/children), family life (parenting, activities...), teacher resources (reproducibles, activities, games, crafts...), lives of the saints, mariology, prayerbooks and books for young people and children We generally do not accept fiction for adults, biographical or autobiographical works or poetry.

Manuscripts for adults are evaluated on:
- adherence to Gospel values
- harmony with the Catholic tradition
- relevance of subject matter
- linguistic quality and style

A query letter is preferred, accompanied by a synopsis, two or three sample chapters, which will not be returned, and a self-addressed, stamped envelope. Please allow at least two to three months for a response.

If your manuscript has not already been typed, we would like to specify:
- double spacing with paragraphs indented; no dot matrix
- exact wording and punctuation of biblical quotations with citation and Scripture translation noted
- use of inclusive language whenever this will not be awkward
- footnotes or chapter notes on separate sheets

YOUNG PEOPLE'S BOOKS

Pauline Books & Media publishes books of religious instruction, Christian stories, and books on coping for pre-teens and adolescents. Authority, self-esteem, loneliness, prayer, peer pressure, family relationships, substance abuse, suicide, grieving, pro-life issues and dating are special areas of interest, particularly in "coping" books.

All material is expected to be consonant with Catholic teaching and practice.

A query letter is preferred, accompanied by a synopsis, two or three sample chapters, which will not be returned, and a self-addressed, stamped envelope. Please allow at least two to three months for a response.

If your manuscript has not already been typed, we would like to specify:
- double spacing with paragraphs indented; no dot matrix
- exact wording and punctuation of biblical quotations with citation and Scripture translation noted
- use of inclusive language whenever this will not be awkward
- footnotes or chapter notes on separate sheets

CHILDREN'S BOOKS

Through children's literature Pauline Books & Media seeks to provide wholesome and entertaining reading that can help children develop Christian values.

We publish prayerbooks, lives of the saints, coloring books, Bible stories, Christmas and Easter stories, seasonal activity books and religious instruction titles in picture book, easy-to-read and middle reader formats. All material is expected to be consonant with Catholic teaching and practice. We generally do not accept anthropomorphic stories, fantasy or poetry.

Length of manuscript—general guidelines picture books 150-500 words easy-to-read 750-1500 words middle reader 15,000-25,000 words

A query letter is preferred, accompanied by a synopsis, two or three sample chapters, which will not be returned, and a self-addressed, stamped envelope. Please allow at least two to three months for a response.

Categories: Children—Religion—Spiritual—Catholic religion

CONTACT: Sr Madonna Ratciff, Aquisitions Editor
Material: All
Daughters of St. Paul
50 Saint Paul Ave
Boston MA 02130-3491
Phone: 617-522-8911
Website: www.daughtersofstpaul.com

Paulist Press
HiddenSpring

HiddenSpring, the general trade imprint of Paulist Press, publishes a broad range of non-fiction spirituality. HiddenSpring publishes hardcover and both trade paperback originals and reprints. HiddenSpring publishes 8-10 titles a year. Accepts manuscripts from both unagented and first-time authors, and offers variable advances. Please submit proposal package including outline, one (1) sample chapter, SASE; do not send complete manuscripts.

Categories: Nonfiction—Biography—Culture—General Interest—History—Inspirational—Lifestyle—Multicultural—Religion—Spiritual

CONTACT: Paul McMahon, Managing Editor
Material: All
997 MacArthur Blvd.
Mahwah NJ 07430
Phone: 201-825-7300

Peachtree Publishers
Peachtree Jr., Freestone

Peachtree currently publishes the following categories: children's picture and illustrated chapter books, young adult books, education, parenting, self-help, and health books, travel and recreational guides about the southeast, nature and outdoors titles, general gift books, and cookbooks and gardening books with southern orientation. We do accept original fiction with a southern flavor, but publish very few titles in this category, seldom more than one a year.

Peachtree does not publish: poetry, plays, science fiction, fantasy, romance, westerns, horror, historical novels, scientific or technical reference, or books intended specifically as textbooks. We do not publish adult fiction of any kind. We also do not publish CDs tapes, or videos.

If you would like to submit your manuscript, please send one of the following:

- For children's picture books, send full manuscript;
- For all others, send either the full manuscript or a Table of Contents plus three sample chapters.

Plus:

- Biographical material on the author(s) and
- A stamped, self addressed #10 envelope for a response.

Please do not send original artwork or original copies of manuscripts. Artwork in general is not required. The publisher reserves the right to select the illustrator.

Please do not fax or e-mail queries or manuscripts. We will not review any submission received this way. All queries and manuscripts must be sent by U.S. Mail.

Peachtree receives approximately 15,000 submissions each year, so please do not call regarding the status of your submission for at least four months. After that time, you may call on Thursday afternoons between 1:00 and 4:00 p.m. If you wish to receive a copy of our catalog, please send a self-addressed 10 x 12-1/2 envelope with $1.98 in postage attached.

Categories: Fiction—Nonfiction—Children—Health—Juvenile—Regional—Young Adult

CONTACT: Helen Harriss, Submissions Editor
Material: All
1700 Chattahoochee Ave.
Atlanta GA 30318-2112
Phone: 404-876-8761
Fax: 404-875-2578
Website: www.peachtree-online.com

Pelican Publishing Company

Pelican Publishing Company does not accept unsolicited manuscripts. All writers should send us a query letter and SASE, describing the project briefly and concisely. This letter should include a complete address and telephone number. Pelican Publishing Company does not accept queries or any other submissions by e-mail. All queries must be submitted by mail according to the following guidelines. Multiple (or "simultaneous") queries are not considered.

A query letter should discuss the following: the book's content, its anticipated length (in double-spaced pages, not in words), its intended audience, the author's writing and professional background, and any promotional ideas and contacts the author may have. If the author has previously been published by another firm, please specify why a change is being sought. A formal synopsis, chapter outline, and/or one or two sample chapters may be sent with a query letter, but these are not required. Never send the original copy of any material.

Be advised that we have certain expectations in the length of a proposed manuscript. Most young children's books are 32 illustrated pages when published; their manuscripts cover about 7 pages when typed continuously. Proposed books for middle readers (ages 8 and up) should be at least 150 pages. Adult books should be more than this. For cookbooks, we require at least 200 proposed recipes.

If necessary, brief children's books (for readers under nine) may be submitted in their entirety. Photocopies of any accompanying artwork are welcome, but again, NEVER send any original artwork.

We will respond as promptly as possible (usually one month), letting you know whether or not we feel the project is worth pursuing further. If we feel that it is worthy of consideration, we will request a partial or full manuscript. Following this procedure ensures the most expeditious treatment of all inquiries.

We do not require that writers contacting us have a literary agent representing them.

A phone call to the editor or secretary or an in-person drop off of unrequested material does not automatically imply that a project has been solicited. For this and other obvious reasons, we discourage phone inquiries and in-person drop offs. If an author we have requested additional material from is unclear as to what we're asking for, a phone call to clarify the matter is acceptable.

Solicited manuscripts are carefully scrutinized by the editor(s). On occasion, they may be examined by our sales and/or promotions departments to gauge their marketability. They are then passed on to the publisher for preliminary and final consideration. The submissions are reported on as soon as possible, but this process may take up to three months (12 weeks). If acceptance is recommended, the author(s) will be asked to sign a contract with Pelican Publishing Company.

If the three-month period for solicited manuscripts passes without the author being informed of a decision, a polite note of reminder from the author is not out of order. Phone calls on the status of manuscripts are very strongly discouraged. Never badger the editor for an instant decision or make demands or threats; this can only hurt the author's chances of acceptance. Authors who feel unsatisfied with our procedures or the amount of time being taken to reach a decision are free to request the manuscript's return at any time.

Pelican Publishing requires exclusive submission for all solicited manuscripts during the 12-week period mentioned above. This is for obvious reasons. We can only give full attention to those manuscripts which we are likely to be able to publish if accepted by us.

Books
M-Z

We also ask that authors who have solicited works under consideration please refrain from sending us other works or proposals during this time unless they are specifically requested to do so. Agreement on our part to look at a particular work does not imply blanket authorization to send unrelated materials and doing so could hurt, rather than help, an author. Materials related to the requested submission, such as favorable newspaper clippings, endorsements by qualified professionals in the field the author is writing about, or other amended data may be sent and added to the material already on file. Use careful judgment in selecting these items and be certain that they enhance the material and its chances of being accepted. Sending in later data that refutes or calls into question points made in the earlier submission may cast doubts on the whole project's veracity and damage its chances of acceptance. Always be certain to refer to the work's title, the author name under which it was submitted, and the date the original query was mailed.

Materials will not be returned unless they are accompanied by sufficient postage. Policies regarding SASE's apply to all submissions from foreign countries, including Canada. Return postage must be in stamps, checks on U.S. banks, or International Money Orders in U.S. money.

We require all submissions, including outlines, resumes, sample chapters, etc., be neatly typed on 8 ½ by 11 inch paper and double-spaced with sufficient margins (1 inch on all sides). Query letters are customarily single-spaced. Be sure that your typewriter has a well-inked ribbon and, if corrections are made, they should be "whited-out" as inconspicuously as possible. Submissions with numerous misspellings, typographical errors, and handwritten corrections reflect unfavorably on the author and may contribute heavily toward a rejection. Writers are cautioned not to rely on editors to clean up after them or interpret unclear information, regardless of how good they think their material may be. A sloppy submission is often indicative of worse problems—the type editors and publishers prefer not to deal with.

Handwritten submissions and/or queries, unless neatly printed in the absence of a typewriter, do not make favorable impressions on editors and could jeopardize your chances of acceptance. For those using computers, we strongly advise you to send us your submissions in letter-quality or near-letter-quality type—not dot matrix. Electronic submissions (discs) are not accepted. These would only be needed once a contract was signed. Never send discs, videotapes, or audio tapes without inquiring beforehand.

We accept no responsibility for original and only-copies of material. We require that all writers send us copies of their work and to retain the originals at home. We will not be responsible for misplaced or lost material.

Authors should avoid undue "hype-ing" of their work. Materials submitted with author projections of it being a "blockbuster" or "the next *Gone With the Wind*" rarely live up to these pretensions. The publisher and editor(s) are professionals who can make up their own minds on the quality and potential of a proposal without the "self-hype." Comments and/or reviews from qualified professionals or publications, as stated earlier, can be desirable in many cases. Likewise for rejection letters from other publishing companies that acknowledge a project's potential value and which base their rejections on other factors unrelated to quality of author workmanship.

We look for clarity and conciseness of expression and presentation in a synopsis/outline and we ask to see those that will most likely yield proposals fitting our list and that we feel we can market successfully. We turn down thousands of adequate proposals every year just because they have no clear "hooks" or well-defined audiences. The author should present a strong case as to why we should take on the book and who would buy it. Saying that "all children would love it" is very vague, but saying "libraries and schools in Tennessee would like this" is more informative.

All work submitted to us must be in good taste, nonlibelous, and consistent with the level of quality we have established for our company. Although many of our titles are specialized, they are all suitable for general readership and are free of gratuitous, off-color words, phrases, or references.

If an author seeking to publish an illustrated work plans to use artwork copyrighted by an author, illustrator, publication, or syndicate, permission must be obtained in writing from that source. Permission in writing must also be obtained by any author seeking to use quotes or other materials from previously copyrighted publications. We will not publish illustrations or portions of another copyrighted work without written authorization to do so.

Authors seeking to have previously published books reprinted must have, in writing from their previous publisher, a signed letter transferring all rights (including copyright) to them. This is required under the 1978 Copyright Law and must be adhered to in all such cases.

Under the revisions contained in the 1978 Copyright Law, a work is automatically copyrighted at the time of creation. If we agree to accept the work for publication, we will apply for the copyright in the author's name on publication.

TYPES OF BOOK PUBLISHED

Hardcover and trade paperback originals (90%) and reprints (10%) including hardcover, trade paperback, and mass market. We publish an average of 50 to 60 titles a year and have about 800 currently in print.

Specialties are art/architecture books, cooking/cookbooks, motivational, travel guides, history (especially Louisiana/regional), nonfiction, children's books (illustrated and otherwise), inspirational and religious, humor, social commentary, folklore, and textbooks. A very limited number of fictional works are accepted for publication, but we will consider fiction if well written and/or timely.

We seek writers on the cutting edge of ideas who do not write in cliches, or take the old, tired, unimaginative way of foul language and sex scenes to pad a poor writing effort. We strongly urge writers to be aware of ideas gaining currency. We believe ideas have consequences. One of the consequences is that they lead to best-selling books.

We do publish a limited number of posters, cards, giftware, and similar works of art. Consideration of submission of this type is based on consistency with other motifs we are marketing at the present time.

Finally, we would ask you to study Pelican's books and lists. Our latest catalog is available for free on request, and a look through it will help you understand where our interests lie. We have been called "innovative" by the *New York Times*. We will consider almost any well-written work by an author who understands promotion.

PAYMENT POLICY

Pelican pays its authors a royalty based on sales. The rate depends on the type of material and the format.

All terms are specified in the contract all authors publishing under our imprint(s) are required to sign. No book will be published by Pelican without a contract signed beforehand.

All guidelines listed above are subject to revision at any time by Pelican Publishing Company and its editorial board.

Categories: Fiction—Nonfiction—African-American—Architecture—Arts—Asian-American—Biography—Boating—Business—Cartoons—Children—Civil War—Cooking—Family—Hispanic—History—Inspirational—Jewish Interest—Multicultural—Music—Native American—Outdoors—Regional—Religion—Sports/Recreation—Textbooks—Travel—Western

CONTACT: Editorial Department
Material: All
PO Box 3110
Gretna LA 70054-3110
Phone: 504-368-1175
Website: www.pelicanpub.com

THE PERMANENT PRESS
SECOND CHANCE PRESS

The Permanent Press
Second Chance Press

Dear Writer:

We are looking for material of a high literary quality; material that is original and stimulating with an authentic point of view and a unique voice.

If you are interested in submitting a manuscript, we would prefer a short synopsis, and the first chapter. We will get back to you as soon as possible.

Please note that we publish novel-length fiction, and occasionally nonfiction. We no longer publish cookbooks, children's stories, story collections, novellas, or poetry.

The above criteria is used for both Second Chance Press and The Permanent Press. Books submitted for reprint by Second Chance Press must be at least twenty years old.

Sincerely,
Judith Shepard, Editor and Co-Publisher
Categories: Fiction

CONTACT: Acquisitions Editor
Material: All
4170 Noyac Rd.
Sag Harbor NY 11963
Phone: 516-725-1101

Perron Press

Statement of Purpose

Perron Press is a relatively new imprint at the Stellar Attractions Network specializing in non-fiction from first time or little know authors who need a professional start for their good ideas and quality manuscripts. Unlike its sister imprint, the Enneagram Consortium's narrow editorial policy, Perron Press is seeking to publish and disseminate how-to and self-helpful works that assist people in becoming more personally and professionally effective, more fulfilled, healthier, and active in life.

Perron Press works with the author to present quality titles to the trade using its network of non-exclusive distributors, trade marketing lists, and promotional channels that may be individually tailored to the type and content of the work. Books are produced in quality trade editions with traditional front and back pages and bar-codes for trade outlets.

The publishing process is a cooperative effort with the author to produce a quality edition optimized for the target audience of the work. Perron Press' mission is to give overlooked quality works a professional first opportunity at being appreciated by the buying public.

Manuscript Submission Guidelines

Thank you for inquiring about our manuscript guidelines for new works. We receive thousands of unsolicited submissions each year. To save us both time, paper, and postage we ask that you first submit a query letter, instead of the whole manuscript, along with an outline of your work, your assessment of the target audience, and a sufficient sample of your writing style for our acquisitions staff to determine if your work fits within our editorial policy. From there, we can decide whether we need to request a complete manuscript for further review.

If you want a response from us either way, please send your query along with a SASE or a working e-mail address. We cannot be responsible for returning manuscripts due to the large quantity we receive, but we make every effort to do so with what you include for that purpose.

We are actively reviewing manuscripts again and we are eager to find manuscripts we can be excited about and get behind. Unagented and first time authors, simultaneous and email submissions are all okay. We encourage you to submit your work for consideration at this time:
• it may be considered (budget allowing) for publication by Perron Press
• we may offer subsidy publishing
• or we can assist you with the details of self-publishing

In any case, we are always excited about being involved in projects that can contribute positively to people's lives. Thank you for your interest in Perron Press.

Categories: Nonfiction—Education—Psychology—Relationships

CONTACT: Nancy Wyatt-Kelsey, Acquisitions Editor
Material: All
PO Box 10826
Portland, OR 97296-0826
Phone: 503-228-4972
Fax: 503-223-9117
E-mail: perron@sa-inc.net
Website: www.sa-inc.net/perron/pr.html

Personal Branding Press

What we are looking for

Non-fiction, Personal Branding disciplines only;

1. Personal Branding Development: (Collateral: brochures, web sites, direct mail etc.), Personal Marketing: Advertising (Print & Broadcast), Database Development, Direct Response, Networking, Outdoor Advertising, Professional & Client Referrals, Sales, Seminars, Web site development & marketing, Customer Service, Public Relations, Personal Presentation, Image, Speaking.

Will accept manuscripts or proposals. Books published include The Personal Branding Phenomenon, The Brand Called You and The Brand Called You for Financial Advisors.

Peter Montoya's *Personal Branding* magazine

For Peter Montoya's *Personal Branding* magazine, please refer to the their listing in the Magazine section of this directory.

Categories: Business—Public Speaking—Advertising—Marketing

CONTACT: Peter Montoya, Publisher
Material: All
1540 S. Lyon St.
Santa Ana Ca 92705
Phone: 714-285-0900
E-mail: 714-285-0929
E-mail: info@petermontoya.com
Website: www.petermontoya.com

Perspectives Press, Inc.
The Infertility and Adoption Publisher

Perspectives Press, Inc. is a small publisher focusing narrowly on infertility issues and alternatives, and on adoption and closely related child welfare issues such as interim (foster) care or psychological services. Our purpose is to promote understanding of these issues and to educate and sensitize those personally experiencing these life situations, professionals who work with such clients, and the public at large. We invite authors whose philosophy concerning these issues agrees with ours to follow our process for submitting manuscripts for consideration, beginning with a careful examination of the many pages on our web site, followed by writing a query letter. (All communications should contain a stamped, self addressed envelope. Please refrain from querying by telephone!)

OUR POINT OF VIEW Regarding infertility and alternatives, Perspectives Press takes the position that we live in the best and worst of times to be infertile. Though research daily provides new treatment options, it has become increasingly difficult for couples to know when to stop treatment, and alternatives are becoming more and more complex: infant adoption is a shrinking alternative, surrogate parenting is in legal limbo, donor insemination's traditional secrecy is being questioned, some technical alternatives provide for as many as five "parents" for a single child, and rising costs of testing and treatment and family building alternatives stifle the dreams of many families. We believe in and actively promote adoption as a positive option for family planning and family building. We do not accept the philosophy that adoption should be eliminated, nor are we accepting of the absolutist idea that any one form of adoption is the only appropriate approach. We agree that adoption is a service designed first to benefit children, not adults, and that every adoption should be child-centered. But we believe that it is incumbent upon professionals working in this arena to treat birthfamilies and prospective adoptors with respect and sensitivity and with objective regard for their needs, which will vary widely, as each set of birthparents and each set of adoptors is unique. We believe that children deserve the permanency of family as quickly as possible after the disruption of a birth family. We believe that any societal institution, including adoption, must meet the needs of a current society, and to that end we are open to discussion and debate of a variety of approaches to and issues in adoption. Perspectives works actively to promote understanding between adoptees, adoptive parents, and birthparents. We feel that it is important that manuscripts respect the variety of feelings of and the decisions made by those who are members of the adoption triad and that they be written using realistic and neutral adoption language.

OUR EDITORIAL POLICIES Perspectives Press titles are never duplicative. We seek out and publish materials that are currently unavailable through other sources. Furthermore, because our company is small and our list of titles is kept short, we will not consider manuscripts that seriously overlap or compete with titles already on our list. After over ten years in business, we know our own subject matter and its audience very well, but we also know our limitations! We are not a general publisher. Please do not ask us to consider stretching our focus beyond infertility- or adoption-related issues or to change our stated decisions about what topics and genres we will consider as described here. Manuscripts outside our specific field are returned unread if SASE is supplied; without SASE, they are discarded. When submitting (see adult-specific and childrens-specific query/submission information which follows) we respectfully request that you NOT use registered, certified or other signature-required mail to send a manuscript to our post office box address. This necessitates a long and irritating wait in a post office line during "rush hour" or a trip back later in the day! If you would like notification of the arrival of your packet, we are indeed happy to accommodate. Simply enclose a stamped, self addressed postcard, which will be filled out and returned to you the day we open your package.

OUR AUTHORS While we do consider manuscripts from writers who are not personally or professionally involved in our field, we are more inclined to accept a manuscript submitted by an infertile person, an adoptee, a birthparent, an adoptive parent, or a professional working with these clients. Because we work most frequently with never-before-published authors, we make it a policy not to offer a contract based simply on a proposal. At a minimum we require a completed first draft. Authors are oriented before a contract is signed so that they have realistic expectations about the realities and complexities of marketing in our niche. We expect our authors to be closely involved in an ongoing way in their own title's promotion and in the full line of books from Perspectives Press, seeking opportunities to speak and write on the issue, distributing our catalog broadly, etc.

OUR NEEDS For adults we are looking for non-fiction in the form of decision-making materials, books dealing with issue-related parenting concerns, books to share with others to help explain infertility or adoption issues, special programming or training manuals. Our audience is made up of both consumers and professionals in our field. We are not an academic publisher and are disinclined toward research-oriented materials, though we are favorable toward research-based perspectives presented in consumer style. We insist that the books we publish be written in an open, engaging, and user-friendly style, free of jargon.

Manuscripts must be book length—a minimum of 40,000 words. We will not consider pamphlets or singly submitted essays, short stories, or poems.

Because in general first person, autobiographical, and journal-style books in this field have not sold well (no matter what size the publisher) we are not accepting "our infertility experience" or "how we got our child" or "the story of my search" manuscripts. The exception would be books in which the personal materials are included only to provide anecdotal color in a manuscript whose larger purpose is to offer decision-making materials or advice on developing coping skills.

We are not currently publishing novels or other adult fiction. We are a secular publisher and do not publish books rooted in a specific religious view.

After first carefully exploring our web site in order to get a sense of the kinds of books that have appealed to us for publication, writers of adult materials should *schedule a reading by querying* first with a proposal packet before sending a completed manuscript, enclosing a stamped, self addressed envelope for reply— which will follow within

about two weeks. (Unsolicited manuscripts arriving without having scheduled a reading will usually be returned unread.) Please do not query electronically. Your proposal should fully describe your topic and should include an outline and/or a table of contents. Tell us the number of typed, double-spaced pages in the full manuscript and the approximate word count. We expect those who write in this field to be familiar with the literature already being marketed. Your query should mention similarly-themed books both in and out of print and discuss how your book would differ from and be superior to them. Also include a careful description of your book's potential audience, including a researched estimate of the realistic size of that audience and a marketing proposal discussing how you think your audience could best be located and reached out to. Tell us about yourself and your qualifications for writing your proposed book. If we are interested in your concept we will give you a date for sending the full manuscript (typed, double spaced, on standard size paper, with margins at least one inch all around, SASE for return) for a scheduled reading. We will respond within two months of the scheduled reading date.

Our *children's books* are primarily fiction and non-fiction manuscripts appropriate for preschoolers and elementary aged youngsters. We encourage writers to carefully examine materials that are already available for children about the issues which we address and to avoid developing materials which compete with or overlap well regarded books already in print from any publisher. Currently we see few glaring gaps in the children's market in our field. The exceptions may be in books for families built by donor egg and embryo and all forms of surrogacy, and for the children of birthparents who have made an adoption plan for another of their children, about families in open adoptions. We are looking for manuscripts to fill these gaps, but we are picky, picky, picky!...

We encourage authors to familiarize themselves with Piagetan theories about children's cognitive development before trying to write for a particular audience. We see far too many manuscripts which really deal with parents' issues rather than childrens'. We will read nonfiction, but not fiction, for middle schoolers and young adults. Unless you are an author/illustrator submitting your own art work, we would prefer that you NOT find your own illustrator before submitting your manuscript. We ask you to recall that because this market is narrow, it is important to make such materials as inclusive as possible. We are not likely to accept, for example, international adoption stories which are country-specific. Make stories racially and ethnically inclusive, remember that some adoptees join their families as infants and some at an older age, keep in mind that not all adoptive parents adopt for reasons of infertility and that many are single parents, and speak respectfully of birthparents.

Because our children's publication program is very small, writers of children's picture books, too, should *query first before submitting.* Your submission packet should include your writing resume and pertinent information about your personal or professional connections to the field about which you are writing. It should include information which indicates that you have familiarized yourself thoroughly enough with available materials in the field to understand how and why your book fills a heretofore empty niche. Include SASE for the reply. We will reply within one month.

I look forward to hearing from you!
Patricia Irwin Johnston, Publisher

Categories: Nonfiction—Children—Family—Health—Parenting—Psychology—Infertility and Adoption

CONTACT: Acquisitions Editor
Material: All
PO Box 90318
Indianapolis IN 46290-0318
Phone: 317-872-3055
E-mail: info@perspectivepress.com
Website: www.perspectivepress.com

Perugia Press

Perugia Press publishes one collection of poetry each year, by a woman at the beginning of her publishing career. Our books appeal to people who have been reading poetry for decades, as well as those who might be picking up a book of poetry for the first time.

Awards

Perugia Press Intro Award for a First or Second Book of Poetry by a Woman

Prize: $1000 and publication

Guidelines

Manuscript Requirements

• Send between 48 and 72 pages, on white, 8.5 x 11-inch paper, with legible typeface, pagination, and fastened with a removable clip.

• Include two cover pages: one with title of manuscript, name, address, telephone number, and e-mail address, and one with just title of manuscript. No cover letter or bio required. Include a table of contents and an acknowledgments page.

• No electronic submissions.

Terms

An entry fee of $20 must accompany each submission, made payable to Perugia Press. You may submit more than one manuscript; each is considered a separate submission and must include a separate entry fee.

Simultaneous submissions are permitted. Notify Perugia Press if manuscript is accepted elsewhere.

Individual poems may have been published previously in magazines, journals, chapbooks of fewer than 48 pages, or anthologies, but the collection as a whole must be unpublished.

Translations and previously self-published books are not eligible, nor are revisions; the winning manuscript may undergo revisions before publication.

Judging

A judging panel made up of published poets, previous Perugia authors, longtime poetry lovers, booksellers, and scholars will screen and choose the winner.

Notification

Enclose SASE or email address for notification of winner. Notification will be by April 1, 2003.

Do not enclose SASE for return of manuscript; all manuscripts will be recycled at the conclusion of the competition. Please do not send your only copy.

Deadline

Annual submission period: August 1 to November 15. Check our website for current information.

Mail Manuscript and Entry Fee to: (No FedEx or UPS)

Categories: Poetry

CONTACT: Submissions Editor
Material: All
Perugia Press Intro Award
PO Box 60364
Florence MA 01062
Website: www.perugiapress.com

The Phi Delta Kappa Educational Foundation
And the Center for Evaluation, Development, and Research

Special Publications is the name given to the *Phi Delta Kappa Educational Foundation*'s publications department. When George H. Reavis established the Foundation in 1966, he expressed a vision:

The purpose of the Phi Delta Kappa Educational Foundation is to contribute to a better understanding of 1) the nature of the educative process, and 2) the relation of education to human welfare.

This vision guides the selection of manuscripts for Special Publications.

The Maynard R. Bemis Center for Evaluation, Development, and Research (CEDR), also founded in 1966, has two primary missions: 1) dissemination of research information and 2) improvement of understanding about processes of education research and evaluation. CEDR places a special emphasis on the practical applications of research, especially those findings that help teachers and administrators improve their professional skills.

The best way to understand the scope and character of works published by the PDK Educational Foundation and the Center for Evaluation, Development, and Research is to examine the annual PDK International catalog and to peruse individual publications.

Books

The books published by Special Publications and CEDR reflect a broad range of professional interests and topics. Some are sweeping in scope; a good example is John I. Goodlad's classic, *What Schools Are For*, now in its second edition. Others are more narrowly focused, such as Kenneth Chuska's *Improving Classroom Questions* and Jack Lyne's *Schoolhouse Dreams Deferred*. The principal topic areas include: education policy, philosophy, and history; curriculum and instruction; school administration; school law; international and comparative education; and education research.

Manuscript length: 40,000-70,000 words
Honorarium: $3,000-$5,000

Short Monographs

Like the books, PDK's short monographs cover a broad range of topics. Examples include: *Values on Which We Agree* (38 pages), *Your Future Career in Education* (62 pages), and the *S.A.F.E. Handbook on School Security* (53 pages). Works tend to be highly focused and practical.

Manuscript length: 20,000-30,000 words
Honorarium: $1,000-$2,000

Fastbacks

The Special Publications fastbacks were initiated in 1972 as a series of short, authoritative publications for educators at all levels. Twelve new titles are published annually, six each fall and spring. Of more than 500 titles, some 150 are currently in print. More than 8 million copies of the various titles have been disseminated.

The fastbacks have been characterized as "sophisticated primers." Many are practitioner-oriented, but the series also has room for program profiles and occasional philosophical pieces.

Manuscript length: 10,000 words

Honorarium: $500

From Inquiry to Practice

The CEDR booklets in the From Inquiry to Practice series are condensations of research on timely issues. They are designed to help educators make decisions about school management and student learning.

Manuscript length: 8,000-10,000 words
Honorarium: $500

Proposals and manuscripts for these four types of publications are accepted year-round.

SUBMISSION GUIDELINES

1. Initially, a query letter is preferred. This letter should succinctly state the purpose and audience for the publication, a proposed manuscript length, and a suggested writing timeline. Consider: Is the issue or topic "hot"? Is interest in the topic likely to be enduring? The editor responds to queries usually within 2-3 weeks.

2. The prospective author should be prepared to submit a well-developed outline, including chapter or section headings and basic content descriptions. For longer works, the editor may request a sample chapter. The editor responds to such proposals usually within two months, often sooner.

3. In most instances, an author-publisher agreement (contract) is issued on the basis of a successful proposal. However, in some cases, the editor may require a complete manuscript prior to issuing a contract to publish.

4. The editor will assist the author in developing a successful manuscript. However, in spite of the best intentions of both author and editor, sometimes a manuscript will be judged unacceptable. Authors should be aware that PDK editors reserve the right to edit extensively and, on occasion, to rewrite poorly written materials. But substantive changes are not made without the author's permission.

5. Authors are advised to avoid education jargon. Simple, straightforward prose that makes ample use of examples, anecdotes, and case studies is preferred. Any citations must be complete. The PDK style is based on *The Chicago Manual of Style*.

6. Tables, charts, and graphs should be used only when they are necessary to understand the text. Large figures are discouraged, particularly for the fastbacks, which are printed in a small format.

7. Photographs may be submitted with a manuscript. Clear, 5x7-inch (or larger) black-and-white prints are preferred. All photos must include captions. A model release must be provided for all persons who can be identified in a photograph.

8. Manuscripts must be submitted on standard size paper using a type that can be electronically scanned. CEDR also requires that manuscripts be submitted on disk and unformatted. A disk version is optional for Special Publications.

9. PDK purchases all rights by contract. Payment is made in the form of a one-time honorarium, which is paid about one month prior to publication. Royalty contracts are not provided at the present time.

10. PDK reserves the right to select the manner of publication — for example, paperback or hardcover — and how the work will be promoted and distributed. All costs of production, promotion, and distribution are borne by PDK.

Categories: Nonfiction—Education

CONTACT: Donovan R. Walling, Director of Publications & Research
Material: Queries, proposals, and other correspondence
PO Box 789
Bloomington IN 47402-0789
Phone: 812-339-1156
Fax: 812-339-0018
E-mail: information@pdkintl.org
Website: www.pdkintl.org

Piano Press

Piano Press is looking for children's songs for beginning piano songbooks, poems, short stories and/or essays on music-related topics only. Poems may be of any length and in any style, single-spaced and type-written. Short stories and essays should be no longer than five double-spaced, type-written pages.

Piano Press publishes a bi-annual anthology titled *The Art of Music — A Collection of Writings*. Inclusion in this collection may be through acceptance of submissions or by placing first, second or third in *"The Art of Music Annual Writing Contest."* Payment for accepted submissions (poems, short stories or essays) includes copies of the anthology. Payment for accepted children's songs includes one copy of the songbook/CD and the standard print music and CD mechanical royalty.

All inquiries and submissions should be sent to:
Categories: Children—Music—Poetry—Short Stories

CONTACT: Elizabeth C. Axford, Editor
Material: All
PO Box 85
Del Mar CA 92014-0085
Phone: 619-884-1401
Fax: 858-459-3376
E-mail: PianoPress@aol.com
Website: www.pianopress.com

PICCADILLY BOOKS

Piccadilly Books, Ltd.

Piccadilly Books specializes in the publication of books within two general subject categories (1) Theater & Entertainment and (2) Nutrition and Health.

THEATER AND ENTERTAINMENT

In this category we are looking for nonfiction, how-to, and activity topics suitable for children and adults. We have a strong interest in family entertainment—magic, clowning, puppetry, etc. Comedy skits, games, unique fun activities and any business topics related to these subjects are also of interest. *Samples of the type of titles we publish are:*

- Creative Clowning
- Ventriloquism Made Easy
- Clown Magic
- Tricks and Stunts to Fool Your Friends
- Humorous Dialogs
- The Birthday Party Business

NUTRITION AND HEALTH

Books in this category are published under our imprint name HealthWise Publications. We are interested in nonfiction books on any aspect of health, diet, exercise, and bodywork. Must be written from a holistic or natural health viewpoint. *Samples of the type of titles we publish are:*

- *The Detox Book*
- *The Healing Crisis*
- *The Healing Power of Rebounding*

We do not accept children's picture books, novels, or any subject outside those described above. Material from unagented and first-time authors are welcomed and encouraged.

Submissions should consist of a query letter and sample chapters of your manuscript. You may submit a full manuscript if it is completed along with a cover letter describing the contents of the manuscript. We do not return manuscripts or sample chapters, if rejected they are discarded. We review all submissions within a few days of their arrival and send responses as soon as we have made a decision. The most promising submissions take several weeks to thoroughly evaluate. Please allow up to two months for a response.

All manuscripts should include the title, your name, and your address on the first page. Following pages should be numbered consecutively.

Computer printout submissions are acceptable. Letter quality printouts are highly preferred over dot-matrix. Hand written manuscripts are not acceptable.

Be sure to obtain permission to use any quotation, illustration, or other copyrighted material. Contact the house which published the material and get their written permission.

Categories: Nonfiction—Comedy—Diet/Nutrition—Entertainment—Health—Theatre—Humor

CONTACT: Submissions Department
Material: All
PO Box 25203
Colorado Springs CO 80936
Phone: 719-550-9887

Picton Press

Our guidelines for submissions, in our categories of history and genealogy:

Picton Press publishes top quality scholarly works in these two fields, with emphasis on the 17th and 18th centuries.

Manuscripts to be submitted should show:
• 17th or 18th century subjects preferred; 19th century acceptable
• highest quality technical expertise
• comprehensive grasp of the subject matter
• new subject matter or a new approach to well-established subject matter

We will publish works with relatively limited markets, and even books which are unlikely to break even, so long as they demonstrate the items above. On a common-sense basis we give priority to works which are camera-ready and/or require only limited editing.

Categories: History—Genealogy

CONTACT: Acquisitions Editor
Material: All
PO Box 250
Rockport ME 04856-0250
Phone: 207-236-6565
Fax: 207-236-6713
E-mail: sales@pictonpress.com

Pineapple Press, Inc.

Most of our books are Florida nonfiction. We also publish a few literary novels, some nonfiction on other southern states, and some general nonfiction. Almost all of our fiction is set in Florida. We also have a line of nonfiction geared toward nonprofit organizations, and we publish books about lighthouses.

Our only children's books are on Florida topics for Florida schools. We publish a few Florida-related cookbooks. We do not publish genre fiction (mysteries, romances, science fiction, action/adventure, Westerns) unless they are strongly Florida-related.

Send submissions via US mail to our post office box. Do not send registered or certified or in any way requiring a signature. These packages will not be picked up as they require waiting in long lines at the post office. If you want confirmation of receipt, enclosed a self-addressed, stamped postcard with a place for marking that the submission was received.

Fiction
Please send:
1. query letter describing your manuscript and yourself (any previous publications, etc.). It should be brief and state specifically what you have to offer in the first paragraph (e.g., a historical novel, a mainstream love story, an experimental novel). Also please give the title. Though you may prefer not to categorize your work, please try.
2. brief (one-page) synopsis
3. sample chapters, including first
4. Self-addressed stamped envelope (SASE) for anything you want returned. Many writers are now sending SASE for the reply letter only. Paper is recycled.

Nonfiction
Please send:
1. query letter describing your manuscript and why you are qualified to write it. Please give the title.
2. table of contents
3. sample chapters, including introduction
4. proposed market for this book
5. listing of other books on or near this topic, with an explanation of how yours is different, better, targeted to a specific group, etc.
6. SASE (as above)

Please make sure that your manuscript is easy on the eyes. Manuscripts in all caps or single-spaced will not be read. We prefer manuscripts available on disk, but we do not read from computer disks until quite far into the editorial process. Please tape rather than staple your mailer. Again, please do not send anything via registered or certified mail.

We accept simultaneous submissions. We usually reply within eight weeks.

Thanks for your interest in Pineapple Press.

June Cussen, Editor

Categories: Fiction—Nonfiction—Associations—Cooking—Education—Regional

CONTACT: Submissions Editor
Material: All
PO Box 3889
Sarasota FL 34230
Website: www.pineapplepress.com

Players Press, Inc.

Players Press is continually looking for new works to publish. Send a clearly typed copy of your play, musical, or performing arts book to:

Players Press, Inc.
PO Box 1132
Studio City, CA 91614-0132
USA

Remember to enclose the following:
1. A stamped, self-addressed envelope for the return of your manuscript.
2. Two (2) stamped, self-addressed #10 envelopes for correspondence.
3. A brief biography and/or resumé of the writer.

For Plays and Musicals:
1. A copy of the flyer and program with production dates on it. **No manuscript will be considered unless it has been produced.** (Produced means: One professional production, or two amateur productions, or one award-winning amateur production. A *reading is* **not** *considered a production.*)
2. Reviews, when available. (Specify if no reviews are available.)

3. If a musical, supply a copy of the music, in text and audio cassette(s).

Performing Arts Books:

Send a query letter with synopsis, chapter contents and author's bio. We will advise if we can review the manuscript.

If accepted for publication, the script must be made available on computer disk. We prefer Mac-compatible in either Microsoft Word or PageMaker. Please advise.

Our editors will try to read your work and return it to you within 90 days (our normal reading is 30 to 365 days).

Categories: Nonfiction—Arts—Dance—Drama—Education—Entertainment—Fashion—Film/Video—Mass Communications—Military—Music—Television/Radio—Theatre—Writing

CONTACT: Robert W. Gordon, Senior Editor
Material: All
PO Box 1132
Studio City CA 91614-0132
Phone: 818-789-4980
Fax: 818-990-2477

Possibility Press

Established 1981. Publishes trade paperback originals. Publishes 5-10 titles/year. Receives 1,000 submissions/year. 90% of books from first-time authors; 95% from unagented writers. Royalties vary. Publishes book approximately 18-24 months after acceptance of ms. Responds in 2 months to queries. For response you need to send a SASE. Manuscript guidelines are obtainable from website. Imprints: Aeronautical Publishers, American Aeronautical Archives, and Possibility Press.

Nonfiction

How-to, business, self-help, inspirational. Subjects include business/economics, pop psychology, success/motivation, inspiration, entrepreneurship, sales, marketing, network marketing, and homebased business topics, success parables, and human interest success stories. Submissions need to include a one-page summary of book, contents, introduction, chapter-by-chapter synopsis, comparison with competitive books, marketing plans, and photo of author. Author needs to have completed manuscript before submission.

Recent Titles

The Power of 2 by Anthony C. Sciré, In Business And In Love by Chuck and Aprill Jones, Full Speed Ahead by Joyce Weiss, SOAR to the Top by Shawn Anderson, and What Choice Do I Have? By Michael Kerrigan.

Tips

"Our focus is on creating and publishing short-to-medium length (12,000-36,000 words) bestsellers written by authors who speak and consult. We're looking for authors who are serious about making a difference in the world."

Categories: Nonfiction—Business—Christian Interests—Psychology—Relationships—Self Help

CONTACT: Marjorie L. Markowski, Editor-in-Chief
Material: All
Markowski Int'l. Publishers
One Oakglade Circle
Hummelstown PA 17036
Phone: 717-566-0468
Fax: 717-566-6423
E-mail: posspress@aol.com
Website: www.possibilitypress.com

The Post-Apollo Press

Thank you for your interest in The Post-Apollo Press. We accept all manuscripts but are mostly interested in experimental poetry and fiction by new writers. We only ask that people send a SASE if they would like their manuscript returned to them.

The Post Apollo Press was founded in Sausalito, California in 1982, specializing in writing by women. Writers published on Post Apollo include internationally-known poets Etel Adnan and Anne-Marie Albiach, and novelists Marguerite Duras and Ulla Berke'wicz. Post Apollo books have received wide acclaim by noted writers in reviews in The New York Times Review of Books, the San Francisco Chronicle, The Nation, The American Book Review, P.M.L.A. Journal, the New England Review of Books, among others.

Categories: Fiction—Poetry

CONTACT: Simone Fattal, Editor
Material: All
35 Marie St.
Sausalito CA 94965
Phone: 415-332-7018
Fax: 415-332-8045
E-mail: tpapress@dnai.com
Website: www.dnai.com/~tpapress

Prep Publishing

Established in 1994, PREP Publishing is the publishing division of a company, PREP, Inc., founded in 1981 by graduates of Harvard Business School and Yale University. The parent company is a diversified writing/editing organization and is the country's largest resume writing organization.

The company's first title was published in 1995: Second Time Around is a mystery/romance and literary fiction by Southern writer Patty Sleem. *Library Journal* described Patty Sleem's second book, *Back In Time*, as "an engrossing look at the discrimination faced by female ministers."

In 1996 PREP Publishing launched its line of career titles with the publication of *Resumes and Cover Letters That Have Worked for Military Professionals*, a how-to guide to resume and cover letter preparation for veterans and military professionals leaving active duty. Praised by the highly respected *Booklist* as "A guide that significantly translates Veterans' experience into viable repertoires of achievement," that 256-page book contains resumes and cover letters of "real people" who used those resumes and cover letters to transition into civilian jobs. The second title in PREP's line of career titles was *Resumes and Cover Letters That Have Worked*, a 272-page how-to book containing more than 100 resumes and cover letters of "civilians" with special sections devoted to Experienced Professionals, People Changing Careers, and Recent College Graduates.

PREP's publishing interests include mysteries and other fiction and nonfiction, including biographies of famous people, business books, self-help and how-to books, and career titles. We are also developing a line of Christian fiction. Our mission is to publish quality materials, both for children and adults, that enrich people's lives and help them optimize their human experience.

PREP Publishing is listed in *Literary Marketplace* and our titles are listed in *Books in Print* and in *Forthcoming Books in Print*. PREP Publishing is a member of the American Booksellers Association, Southeast Booksellers Association, Publishers Association of the South, Publishers Marketing Association, the Christian Booksellers Association, and the Council of Literary Magazines and Small Presses. Our titles are distributed by Seven Hills Book Distributors and by Ingram Book Company, Baker & Taylor Books, Quality Books, Unique Books, and others.

There are two ways to make submissions to PREP Publishing:

1. One way is to send a cover letter and synopsis of your book. Published authors may prefer this query-first method. Address cover-letter-and-synopsis submissions to Frances Sweeney at the address below. Limit your total submission to three pages! Try to sell us on your concept; if we are interested, we will get in touch with you.

2. The other way to make a submission to PREP is to send your complete manuscript with a non-refundable reading fee of one hundred dollars payable to PREP. Because of the volume of mail received, it has become impossible for our existing staff to read all the manuscripts which authors wish to submit to us and we now employ outside readers to evaluate the book's suitability for publication and write a written "Reader's Report" which the author gets a copy of. Pre-published authors or published authors writing in a new genre may find this professional evaluation helpful.

If you wish to submit your complete manuscript, please send a hard copy (not an electronic submission) of the entire manuscript along with a check for $100 to PREP and an SASE with sufficient postage for the manuscript's return to you. Our readers are professional editors, "book doctors," and respected librarians, and our turn-around time is two weeks. Please bear in mind that our professional readers do try to identify the areas in plot, characterization, etc. which need to be "fixed" if it is the reader's opinion that author revisions are necessary. Address such submissions to Janet Abernethy at the address below.

Once a manuscript is selected for publication, payment to authors is through a royalty schedule based on final sales. Once a manuscript is accepted, publication usually takes 18 months.

Thank you for your interest in PREP Publishing.

Categories: Fiction—Nonfiction—Adventure—Biography—Business—Careers—Christian Interests—Crime—Family—Inspirational—Literature—Military—Mystery—Relationships—Religion—Romance—Spiritual—Women's Issues—Writing—Young Adult—Humor

CONTACT: Anne McKinney, Editor-in-Chief
Material: All
110½ Hay St.
Fayetteville NC 28305
Phone: 910-483-8049
Fax: 910-483-2439

Prima Publishing

PRIMA PUBLISHING, founded in 1984, publishes hardcovers and trade paperbacks in nonfiction categories including popular culture, current affairs and international events, travel, business, careers, legal topics, sports, cooking, health, lifestyle, self-help, and music. Prima is an imprint of the Crown Publishing Group, a division of Random House, and maintains a solid backlist.

The following Prima titles reflect the varied interests of the company: *Churchill on Leadership* by Steven F. Hayward, *The Wave 3 Way to Building Your Downline* by Richard Poe, *Positive Discipline A-Z* by Jane Nelsen, Lynn Lott, and H. Stephen Glenn, *The Wealthy Barber* by David Chilton, *Encyclopedia of Natural Medicine* by Michael Murry, N. D. and Joseph Pizzorno, N.D.

Please include the following when sending a proposal to Prima Publishing:

1. Brief explanation of the book. What is the manuscript about, and why would someone buy it? Like the short text written on the back cover of a book, the explanation should describe the contents of the book while also enticing the reader to know more about it. The overview is also an opportunity for the author to display his or her unique writing style. To prepare for an overview, it may be a worthwhile practice to read the back covers of several books in a local bookstore, noting the way the publisher tries to catch and hold the reader's interest.

2. Detailed table of contents and chapter outlines. Breaking the manuscript down into individual chapters, write a paragraph discussing the information in each chapter.

3. Sample chapter. The editor will need to see your best chapter in order to evaluate your writing.

4. Anticipated market for the book. Who is the target audience? Publishers are looking for profitable books, and especially if it is a new area for Prima, we need to know the size of the market and the likelihood of reaching it. What makes your book unique from others already on the market? How will you promote the book? Will it have appeal outside the usual trade bookstore channels? are there books currently on the bestseller lists that reach the same type of market?

5. Competition for the book. Are there other books currently on the market that address the same or similar subjects? How and why is your book different? Does your proposed book fill a niche presently open? Identify the competition but tell us how your book will surpass that competition because of the added material or new slant it offers.

6. Author's Qualifications. What makes you the right person to write this book? Tell us about your career experience and educational credentials as well as your experience in the area of your subject and with the media, for example, speaking and teaching experience. Also of interest is your publishing history and why you came to write this book. Do you have periodical, journal, or book writing experience?

Prima does not publish original fiction, personal narrative, or poetry.

If you are a first-time author, the book should be completed before the proposal is sent. Please do not send a manuscript unless specifically requested.

For help in preparing a proposal, refer to Prim's *The Writer's Guide to Book Editors*, Publishers, and Literary Agents by Jeff Herman.

Please allow four to six weeks for an answer.

Categories: Nonfiction—Business—Careers—Computers—Cooking—Health—Lifestyle—Self Help—Sports/Recreation

CONTACT: Acquisitions Editor
Material: All
3000 Lava Ridge Ct.
Roseville CA 95661
Phone: 916-787-7000
Fax: 916-787-7005

Books M-Z

Primer Publishers

Authors wishing to submit manuscripts should first send a brief letter stating purpose, qualifications of author on subject, and why Primer should be the publisher. We also ask that no more than 10 pages of sample text be sent at that time. Please be sure your subject matches our niche.

We publish book about the Southwestern United States, including Colorado, California, and Arizona. Our subjects are primarily about the outdoors, nature, and history of the West.

Primer Publishers imprints are Renaissance House Publishers and American Traveler Press.

Categories: History—Nature—Outdoors—Regional

CONTACT: Bill Fessler
Material: All
5738 N Central Ave.
Phoenix AZ 85012
Phone: 602-234-1574
Fax: 602-234-3062
E-mail: info@primerpublishers.com
Website: www.primerpublishers.com

Pruett Publishing Company

Pruett Publishing Company specializes in, but is not limited to, nonfiction books and guides for the Rocky Mountain West. Our subject areas include: outdoor recreation and hiking, flyfishing, travel, western history, and nature and the environment. We welcome proposals for books in any of these areas from both authors and agents. We encourage you to review our catalog to help determine whether your book is appropriate for our publishing program. First-time authors are welcome. If you are uncertain whether your topic will interest us, feel free to send a letter of inquiry.

Book Proposals should include the following:

1. A brief summary of the proposed book
2. An outline or table of contents
3. One or two sample chapters
4. Examples (or discussion about) artwork you plan to include
5. A discussion of the market you envision for the book
6. A list of other published books you know of on the topic that may compete with yours and comments on how they differ from yours
7. A biography or resume of the author

If you send a complete manuscript double-spacing will make it easier to read and comment on. If you prefer, you can query us via e-mail at pruettbks@pruettpublishing.com.

Categories: Nonfiction—Environment—Nature—Outdoors—Recreation—Regional—Sports/Recreation—Travel

CONTACT: Jim Pruett
Material: All
7464 Arapahoe Rd., Ste A-9
Boulder CO 80303
Website: www.pruettpublishing.com

PSI Research
The Oasis Press
Hellgate Press

Company History

Established in 1975, The Oasis Press was the first publishing imprint of PSI Research. In 1997 we started the Hellgate Press imprint.

Background on The Oasis Press

The objective of The Oasis Press is to give people who are considering starting a business or who already own or manage a business — especially small businesses — the tools they need to make sound business decisions and operate their companies successfully. The Oasis Press is known for our state-specific startup series, SmartStart Your (State) Business. We offer more than 80 additional business titles which round out our PSI Successful Business Library.

To be published by The Oasis Press, your book should be a step-by-step how-to guide designed for startups, business owners, or managers. The text should be solution-oriented, and focus on action plans or procedures for starting or operating a business more efficiently. To appeal to our audience of busy laypeople, the writing needs to be friendly and concise, not technical or academic.

The Oasis Press books typically include checklists, worksheets, charts, and sample documents to build on points in the text. Information should be quickly accessible.

Some of our books are accompanied by software. We don't require authors to submit software for their books. Software that compliments your book may be developed or marketed by The Oasis Press.

The Oasis Press publishes anywhere from 15 to 30 titles per year. We receive approximately 150 to 200 submissions annually. Sixty percent of these come from first-time authors. Ninety percent come from unagented authors.

We are interested in books that will supplement or complement our present Successful Business Library titles (please review our current booklist). We are especially interested in books that will address new laws, regulations, or concerns that businesses will face in the future.

Background on Hellgate Press

Hellgate Press is a new imprint that is quite diverse. Hellgate Press is named after the historic Hellgate Canyon on the Rogue River (just a few miles from our office) which was the first river in the United States to be designated as a wild and scenic river. We are looking for books that personify the adventure of the canyon: subjects that include outdoor recreation, adventure travel, history and military history. Books for the Hellgate Press need not be based in the Pacific Northwest.

Book format and style

Books for both Oasis and Hellgate are paperbacks, which are generally priced from $8.95 to $24.95 retail. Our preferred format is now 7½ by 10 inches, usually bound as a quality paperback.

Our books are distributed through a number of business associations, direct mail organizations, and catalogs, including PSI Research's own mail order catalogs. Our own in-house sales force actively promotes our publications.

Distribution

Our books are distributed nationwide to independent and chain booksellers and retailers, as well as discount houses, libraries, and book clubs. Major booksellers include Waldenbooks, Barnes and Noble, and B. Dalton Bookseller. Books are also available through Baker & Taylor, Midwest Library Services, The Bookhouse, Blackwell North America, Ingram, and Quality Books.

Calendar

June 30th and November 30th are our cutoff dates for reviewing proposals. All book proposals we have received by June 30th will usually be reviewed in July, and we will inform authors about our decision sometime in August. Similarly, all book proposals we have received by November 30th will usually be evaluated in December, and we'll inform authors of our decision in January. If our review schedule creates an unusual problem for you, please send a FAX to our acquisitions department at (541) 476-1479 describing the situation.

Steps for submission

If you want to know if we would consider a particular topic before you submit a completed proposal, please don't call to describe the book over the phone. Instead, send us a brief letter describing your book, an outline or synopsis, a proposed table of contents, and a sample chapter. We'll review your material and respond with a letter.

If your topic warrants further consideration, we may request the following information:

• Your completed manuscript. If not complete, we will need to review at least two chapters.

• A list of proposed worksheets, forms, and checklists.

• Your completed Editorial Fact Sheet. (The Fact Sheet will be included in the Author Manual which we will send to you as we work out the licensing agreement.)

• If you want us to return what you have sent, please enclose a self-addressed stamped envelope.

Once we have accepted your completed manuscript, we will include the book in our list of titles to be distributed for the following season. We must have your manuscript in double-spaced printed copy as well as on a 3½ disk, Zip disk or CD in ASCII or text file. You will be expected to provide additional details about the manuscript as well as help prepare the word/phrase list for the index.

Royalties

We pay a royalty of 10% on the net cash we receive on all sales. It is not our policy to pay advances. Once the book is in the marketplace generating sales, you will receive monthly sales status reports. Monthly royalty payments begin 120 days after receipt of your first sales report.

A Tip For Submission

Your book has a better chance of acceptance if you take the time to explain why our readership will buy and/or use your book, who your potential audience is, and what competition your book faces in the bookstores. The success of any book depends largely on how well recognized the author is or how adept at promotion. Please list ways you will promote your book.

Where To Send Your Manuscript
Simultaneous submissions are acceptable.

Categories: Nonfiction—Business—History—Military

CONTACT: Acquisitions Editor
Material: All
PSI Research
PO Box 3727
Central Point OR 97502
Phone: 541-245-6502
Fax: 541-245-6502
E-mail: eramey@psi-research.com
Website: www.psi-research.com

Puget Sound Books

Here is the simple page...no fancy type, no guarantees, no hype. We are currently searching for quality, book-length manuscripts of 70,000 words or more. We are NOT currently looking for Romance, Westerns, Religious text, science fiction, children's books or political manifestos. Poetry we accept only for our Puget Sound Stories publication.

Short stories are also only accepted for our Puget Sound Stories publication.

What we ARE looking for is the finest in:
• Action Adventure
• Mystery
• Suspense manuscripts.

We will also consider other types of general interest fiction if the story is strong and your characters are bold, complex and fascinating.

Author Guidelines:
Manuscripts must be complete-no partial works. Don't send a query - send your complete manuscript along with a self-addressed, stamped envelope. If you want your manuscript returned, enclose an envelope and postage for it also.

• Hard Copy Only - No disc or email submissions.
• Print should be double spaced, printed on one side only, 11 or 12 point type - black ink.
• Please, no fancy typestyles- simple block or Times New Roman is appreciated.
• Do not send your only copy. We are not responsible for lost items.
• Manuscripts that do not have a return envelope and have not been considered for publication will be destroyed. Allow 4 to 6 weeks for our response. We are looking at many new manuscripts, but publish only 1 book per quarter - 4 per year.

Categories: Fiction—Adventure—Mystery

CONTACT: Editor
Material: All
P. O. Box 220
Gig Harbor WA 98335
Website: www.pugetsoundbooks.com

QED Press

QED Press is a small, award-winning west coast publishing house whose vision is to publish nonfiction and fiction that inspires readers to transcend national, racial and ethnic boundaries through an appreciation of the humanities, world literature, art, and poetry.

Submission Guidelines
Manuscripts must be typed or output on a letter-quality or laser printer, double-spaced and with ample margins. A self-addressed envelope with sufficient postage to return materials should accompany all manuscripts and queries.

We do not charge a reading fee and receive too many submissions to be able to comment on any but the most striking manuscripts. We generally respond between thirty and ninety days to queries and submissions and prefer to receive completed manuscripts. Electronic submissions are not welcome.

We are interested in books for readers over the age of thirty-five, preferably non-fiction, although we will publish strong, non-formulaic fiction. Previous credits are not necessary, although we hold to high writing standards. We are also very interested in publishing paper airplane books (we are currently working on our third), and welcome any serious folder to reply. Our royalties are as high as any mainstream publisher, but since we are not a large press, we do not pay advances against royalties.

Thank you for your interest in our company and we look forward to hearing from you.

—Stephanie Rosencrans for QED Press

Categories: Fiction—Nonfiction—Arts—Human Rights—Literature—Poetry

CONTACT: Stephanie Rosencrans
Material: All
155 Cypress St.
Fort Bragg CA 95437
Phone: 707-964-9520
Fax: 707-964-7531
E-mail: qedpress@mcn.org
E-mail: stephanie@cypresshouse.com
Website: www.qedpress.com

Quality Words In Print

We are currently accepting the submission of novels and narrative non-fiction pieces for an adult literary audience. We are not accepting romances, crime novels, westerns, horror, science fiction, young adult fiction, "how-to" non-fiction, religious, children's books, or poetry. We will consider mystery, historical fiction and biography of literary quality.

Authors interested in having their work evaluated for publication by QWIP should submit the following for consideration:
• A detailed, one-page summary of the work.
• A 25-50 page writing sample, or approximately three chapters (if we have an interest based on a writing sample, a full manuscript will be requested for consideration).
• A brief statement of author background, including previous publication, or specific background relevant to the work.
• A self-addressed, pre-posted return envelope should be included with submissions if the return of samples is desired, otherwise non-accepted submissions will be discreetly recycled.

First time authors and unagented authors will be considered. We attempt to respond to prospective authors within two months of submission.

Author compensation in the form of royalties and author's copies.

Categories: Fiction—Nonfiction—Biography—History—Mystery

CONTACT: Submissions Editor
Material: All
Quality Words In Print, LLC
P. O. Box 2704
Costa Mesa CA 92628-2704
Phone: 714-436-5700
Fax: 714-668-9448
Website: www.qwipbooks.com

Quill Driver Books
Word Dancer Press

We publish nonfiction books only and if you have one that has a large, identifiable and reachable audience, we'd like to hear from you. We do not publish poetry, children's books, or fiction.

We prefer to receive a query letter along with a book proposal. Please submit to us by snail mail. We consider simultaneous submissions. Naturally, if we are interested, we will contact you; however, if you wish to hear from us in the event we are not interested, please enclose an SASE. Keep in mind that every publisher turns down projects for reasons that have nothing to do with the merit or publishability of the book. Even if we aren't interested, we encourage you to keep trying with other publishers.

We suggest you read the book *The Fast Track Course on How to Write a Nonfiction Book Proposal* by Stephen Blake Mettee, available at bookstores and libraries, and follow Mettee's instructions in preparing your book proposal. While this isn't absolutely necessary, a properly prepared book proposal will increase your chances with us as well as with other publishers. It will also help you think your project through completely.

Recent titles we have published include *Pitching Hollywood:How to Sell Your TV and Movie Ideas* by Jonathan Koch and Robert Kosberg with Tanya Meurer Norman and *If You Want It Done Right, You Don't Have to Do It Yourself!: The Power of Effective Delegation* by Donna M. Genett, Ph.D.

We are particularly interested in seeing proposals that fit the following four areas:

The Best Half of Life ™ series

The Best Half of Life books are practical, upbeat, encouraging how-to or self-help books that enhance the lives of people in their 50s and over. These titles help the reader to improve and to better enjoy his or her life. We want sound, well-thought-out, positive, focused writing. No personal *How-I-Survived (-Cancer, -Caring for a Spouse Afflicted with Alzheimer's,* etc.) essays. The book must offer something distinctly helpful to the reader. Books with the greatest chance of being published as a part of The Best Half of Life series will have life-changing potential.

Text should be for the popular market rather than the academic market. The inclusion of checklists, sidebars, real-life anecdotes, exercises and similar elements is encouraged.

Subjects may include the whole gamut of human experience, from cooking to creativity, sex to careers, recreation to finances. A recent Best Half of Life book is *Just Pencil Me In: Your Guide to Moving & Getting Settled After 60,* by Willma Willis Gore.

Writing and Getting Published

We are always interested in seeing proposals on books for writers. Here the credentials of the author are very important. If you have never published a novel, it is doubtful that we would be interested in a book from you on how to write a novel.

There are quite a number of everything-an-author-needs-to-know-about-writing books out there. Try to focus your project to a specific aspect of writing or getting published. This focus is shown in our titles *Damn! Why Didn't I Write That? How Ordinary People are Raking in $100,000 or More Writing Nonfiction Books & How You Can Too!* by Marc McCutcheon and *LifeWriting: Drawing from Personal Experience to Create Features You Can Publish* by Fred D. White, Ph.D.

California

We publish one or two regional California titles each year. Titles with a narrow focus, yet a broad appeal have the best chance of catching our interest. Examples are our *Black Bart Boulevardier Bandit* by George Hoeper, about the 1880s stagecoach robber; *California's Geographic Names* by David Durham, California's definitive gazetteer, and *From Mud-Flat Cove to Gold to Statehood: California 1840–1850* by Irving Stone. Titles may be on the history or the recreation of California, or on any other subject distinctive to the state. The availability of illustrations is often a necessity.

The Fast Track Course™ series

The Fast Track Course series features concise, clear, interestingly written books that present 90% of what a reader needs to know on the subject. FTC books can be on virtually any subject. They may be how-to or self-help, or simply informative. Word count should be 30,000 to 50,000.

Thank you for your interest, we look forward to hearing from you.

Categories: Nonfiction—Aging—Biography—Californiana—Celebrities—Directories—Fund-raising—Health—History, Western—How-to—Lifestyles—Reference—Regional—Self-help—Senior Citizens—True Crime—Western—Writing

Contact: Stephen Blake Mettee
Material: All
1831 INDUSTRIAL WAY #101
Sanger, CA 93657
Phone: 559-875-2170
Fax: 559-876-2180
E-mail: Info@QuillDriverBooks.com
Website: www.QuillDriverBooks.com

Quilt in a Day Publications

Please refer to Howell Press, Inc.

Ragged Mountain Press

Thank you for requesting manuscript guidelines for Ragged Mountain Press. Our slogan is "Books that take you off the beaten path."

We publish a variety of books on outdoor sports, recreation, and fitness in several categories. First, we are interested in beginning-to-intermediate level how-to manuscripts about non-competitive sports or fitness. This could include anything from archery to sport diving. We have a special interest in paddlesports, including sea kayaking, whitewater paddling, and canoeing.

We are also interested in big, serious reference books and small, gift books for outdoor enthusiasts, including adventure narratives.

To help your proposal move swiftly through our review process, please include the following:

• Cover letter with your contact information (address, telephone and fax numbers, email address)

• Table of Contents with brief summaries of each chapter

• One or two sample chapters

• Sample photographs and/or illustrations if these are central to your proposal

• Competition analysis (a listing of similar books in print, copies of recent supporting magazine articles and newspaper clippings, etc.)

• A personal or professional biography or resume (if you feel it is relevant)

• A self-addressed stamped envelope (if you want your materials returned)

Please anticipate a four- to six-week waiting period for a response from us. Thanks again for your interest in Ragged Mountain Press. We look forward to receiving your proposal.

Categories: Nonfiction—Biography—Conservation—Cooking—Ecology—Environment—Family—Fishing—Physical Fitness—Recreation—Sports/Recreation—Travel—Women's Issues

CONTACT: Tris Colburn, Acquisitions Editor
Material: All
CONTACT: Jonathan Eaton, Editorial Director
Material: All
PO Box 220
Camden ME 04843-0220

Railroading
An Imprint of Bristol Fashion
Publications, Inc.

You will find we are very cooperative when dealing with freelance contributors. Our Chairman and Publisher, John Kaufman, and our COO and Editor-in-Chief, Bob Lollo, were both freelance photographers and writers long before Bristol Fashion Publications, Inc. came to be in 1993. They still retain the memories of the "difficult years" getting started. This is one of the reasons we are interested in submissions from new authors and photographers.

We rarely project more than six months in advance. Always include a SASE. Include your telephone number with any correspondence or submissions.

Photography Submissions

COVERS: Color glossy prints. Prints should be 3-1/2 x 5 to 5 x 7. Digitized images (300 DPI) in a JPG or GIF file are preferred for final use.

All covers depict the theme of the book. Use deep saturation, vivid colors and good contrast to bring out the main subject matter. This is NOT the type of cover you will see on a magazine. Send several sample copies of your work for consideration. Mark each copy with your name, address and phone number.

INTERIOR: Digitized images (300 DPI) in a GIF or JPG file are the only images we consider for use.

Photos should show hands using tools, when appropriate, the steps involved in completing a project and the finished results. These are the photos we most often need.

The railroad history books' photographic needs center around railroading from the beginning of railroading to the late 1960's.

Good contrast, lighting and subject matter is necessary. Send several hard copy or jpg/gif (on disk) samples of your work for consideration. Mark each copy with your name, address and phone number. We will not consider e-mailed images—please do not send them.

Simultaneous submissions are fine. Notify us if a photo we have on file becomes unavailable. Model and property releases are preferred if the person is identifiable. All submissions should be non-returnable disks or prints. If we can keep copies of your work on file, we are more likely to call you when the need arises. We will notify you within one month, whether or not we feel we can use your work. Assignments may be given at the same rate of pay, as noted below.

We purchase book/reprint rights as a one time buy. Cover prices range from $50.00 to $300.00 depending on the project. Interior B & W prices range from $10.00 to $25.00. Credit line given. One copy of the book will be given to each contributor.

Writer's Guidelines

Our books use simple to understand and follow processes, for the person who knows little about model railroading. Each subject should take the reader from the very basics, through each step, until the complete, advanced subject matter is discussed. As the project expands and becomes more complicated, each new phase or technique should be described. If a friend, who knows nothing about model railroading, can read, understand and feel comfortable doing the work you have described, you have written what we want to publish.

Non-How-To and History related titles should be extremely interesting to read. Photographic history books should be well captioned with a paragraph or two on each photo subject. These same guidelines apply to prototype photographic reference books.

How-To topics are the most marketable with a wider audience. We are always seeking new ideas and topics for our books.

Simultaneous submissions are not accepted. Submit a few chapters for review, along with the table of contents. All submissions must be hard copy with a SASE. Include your past credits, tear sheets, state if photos or line art is available and the state of completion of your manuscript. We will report in two weeks of receipt, often sooner.

If you have never been published or have not yet started the manuscript submit a short sample (1000 words), outline, completion date and photo/line art availability.

We pay royalty of 8% to 11% based on the retail price of the book. Average retail price is $20.00 to $30.00. Photos and line art submitted by the author will be considered as part of the manuscript and the percentage adjusted accordingly. Follow the photography submission guidelines above. We will purchase worldwide book/reprint rights.

WRITERS TIPS: Know or research the industry, owners and technical knowledge. Use the proper railroading language and terms. A well-written manuscript is useless if the knowledge of the writer is lacking. If you are not familiar with a given subject, talk to people who has been around trains/modeling for many years. Do not use unwarranted technical jargon to explain a subject. Use simple terms and an easy to understand and follow, step-by-step writing style. When we have to choose, we are more likely to use poor writing and good knowledge, than good writing and poor knowledge.

Books M-Z

Preparing Your Manuscript

Never use an exclamation point for emphasis except in a direct quotation. We! and! the! reader! don't! care! what! startles! you!

Don't double-space, regardless of what you were taught in typing class.

Don't use the Tab key or Space bar to indent a paragraph.

Don't attempt to make your manuscript look as you'd like your book to appear. Just write. Converting your manuscript into a book is what we do.

Trust us. We have a combined experience of more than 200 years in the publishing industries. We will edit your manuscript to suit its intended market. The better your work reads, the better it sells, and that benefits all of us.

Please understand this—You will not retire from the book sales of any single specialty title. Specialty titles simply do not sell that well in any market. A very successful specialty title may sell 20,000 copies over a five year run. A very few sell more. Most sell one quarter or less of that number and are considered a successful book. Our successful authors often have three or more books published with us and they started by reading these very same guidelines.

After preparing your submission, following the above guidelines, you may submit it by land mail (hard copy only, do not include a disk) or by email. To submit by email, attach an ASCII text or MSWord file to the email—DO NOT paste the text into the body of the email or include graphic files with this submission. Send the email to jpk@bfpbooks.com. Include only one manuscript with each email submission.

We look forward to hearing from you.

Categories: Crafts/Hobbies—History—Model Railroads—Technical

CONTACT: Submissions
Material: All
Bristol Fashion Publications, Inc.
PO Box 4676

Harrisburg, PA 17111
Phone: 772-559-1379, 800-478-7147
Fax: 800-543-9030
E-mail: jpk@bfpbooks.com
Website: www.bfpbooks.com

Rainbow Publishers
Book for Children's Ministries

Our objective:

We publish helpful how-to books, activity books and "teaching tips" for leaders of children in both the church and home settings. Generally, our children's ministries products are reproducible books issued in series for ages 2 through grade 6. All are Bible-based and at least 64 pages.

We specifically seek:
• Classroom resources for Christian educators, such as crafts, activities and worksheets, bulletin boards and games
• Proposals for our existing series
• Manuscripts or queries for other teacher help books. All materials must be designed to help Christian educators lead ministries to children.

We do not publish:
• Poetry
• Picture books
• Fiction
• Symbolic stories
• Books that require full-color illustrations

The kinds of writers we are looking for:
• Have accepted Jesus as Savior and are dedicated to serving Him and leading others to Him
• Relate well to children and teachers
• Have hands-on experience working with children
• Are active participants in a Bible-believing church
• Write creatively, either published or unpublished

To submit your proposal:
• Send a table of contents and 2-5 chapters for our evaluation
• Enclose a resumé or statement explaining your qualifications for writing the book
• Explain the audience for your book and how your book differs from those already on the market
• Enclose a SASE for return of your material if you want it returned
• Type on 8½" x 11" paper, one-sided and double-spaced
• Keep copies of everything you submit to us
• Address to Christy Allen, Editor. We normally respond in two to eight weeks.
• If your proposal includes crafts, be prepared to send the completed crafts, if requested.

After evaluating your proposal/manuscript we will do one of the following:
• Offer you a contract
• Seek expanded material from you
• Ask for revisions and resubmittal
• Suggest you contact another publisher
Categories: Nonfiction—Children—Christian Interests—Crafts/Hobbies—Education—Games—Inspirational

CONTACT: Christy Allen, Editor
Material: All
PO Box 261129
San Diego CA 92196
Phone: 619-271-7600
E-mail: rainbowed@earthlink.net

Really Great Books

We are not accepting submissions at this time.
　　—Petra Frank, Acquisitions Editor
Categories: Nonfiction

CONTACT: Petra Frank, Acquisitions Editor
Material: All
548 S. Spring St., Ste. 320
Los Angeles CA 90013
Phone: 213-624-8555
E-mail: petra@reallygreatbooks.com
Website: www.reallygreatbooks.com

Red Dress Ink

Red Dress Ink is looking for women's fiction that is fresh and irreverent and depicts young, single, mostly city-dwelling women coping with the sometimes difficult aspects of modern life. Red Dress Ink, like our iconic red dress, can be fun and flirty, but also powerful and in-your-face. The stories are centered on the heroine as she strives to find herself and her place in life. She doesn't have to be perfect; in fact, there is always room for her to grow. There will be bumps in the heroine's journey to achieve her goals, but because of the witty, sharp tone, her "life's little curves" will be funny and relatable.

These books are pragmatic and relevant; they show life as it is, but with a strong touch of humor, hipness, energy and depth. Our brand of City Girl books are about how single urban females really are. The dialogue is sharp and true-to-life, and the style of writing is highly accessible. While a strong voice is essential, an engrossing tale—one that entices the reader to keep turning the pages to find out what will happen next—is vital. There is a happy ending, but it doesn't necessarily involve a man.

• Word Length: 90,000-110,000 words
• Point of view: first person/third person, as well as multiple viewpoints, if needed
• Settings: urban locales in North America or well-known international settings such as London or Paris
• Tone: fun, up-to-the-minute, clever, appealing, realistic
If you are a city girl at heart, please submit a detailed synopsis and three sample chapters or a complete manuscript.
Categories: Fiction—Romance—Women's Fiction

CONTACT: Margaret Marbury
Material: All
300 E. 42nd St., 6th Floor
New York NY 10017

Red Wheel/Weiser
Imprints: Red Wheel, Weiser Books, Conari Press

Red Wheel/Weiser publishes three imprints: Red Wheel, Weiser Books, and Conari Press. Red Wheel publishes Spunky Self-Help, Self-Help/Inspiration, and Spirituality/Self-Help.

Weiser Books are esoteric by nature. Categories include Magic, Wicca, Tarot, Astrology, and Qabalah.

Conari Press topics include spirituality, personal growth, parenting, and social issues.

Before submitting any materials to Red Wheel, Weiser Books, or Conari Press, please study our books in a bookstore, a library, a Red Wheel/Weiser or Conari Press catalog, and visit our web sites at www.redwheelweiser.com and www.conari.com.

When submitting a proposal, initial query letter, or completed manuscript, please remember that it may take up to three months for your material to be reviewed. Please also note that we do not accept proposals on disc, over the Internet, or by fax. Only send copies of your material and keep the original for your records.

Include a self-addressed stamped envelope with your submission. Submissions will be recycled if ample postage is not included. Canadian and any other foreign submissions must included U.S. postage—we can't use international postage coupons.

A submission in the form of a proposal could include:
• Cover letter including author information and brief description of proposal.
• Proposal, including a table of contents, three sample chapters, and a synopsis of the entire manuscript.
• Sample illustrations or photographs (duplicates, please! Not originals.)
• A market analysis including similar books and how yours differs from each.
• A self-addressed stamped envelope for a response and/or return of materials. Please include ample postage if you would like to have your materials returned.

Good luck and thank you for your interest in Red Wheel, Weiser Books, and Conari Press.

Categories: Nonfiction—Inspirational—New Age—Parenting—Self Help—Society—Spiritual

CONTACT: Ms. Pat Bryce, Editor
Material: All
368 Congress St.
Boston, MA 02210
Phone: 617-542-1234
Fax: 617-482-9676
Website: www.redwheelweiser.com

Redleaf Press

Do you have a book idea?

Whether you have an entire manuscript or just a good idea, submitting a proposal to Redleaf Press is easier than you might think. We acquire most of our books as proposals rather than as manuscripts, which means that you don't have to write the whole book before sending it to us to be considered for publication.

To submit a book proposal, just send us the following:

• A cover letter describing your book idea. As well as the content, we need to know the audience it is intended for (family child care providers, staff in child care centers, trainers, directors); how it compares to books that are already available on the same topic; and the experience that makes you the right author for the subject.

• An outline or table of contents to show us what you think the book would include and how you would organize it.

• A writing sample that shows your ability to write clear, coherent prose. This could be previously published material such as article, staff or parent handbook, brochure, or newsletter, or it could be a sample chapter from the proposed book.

• A resume showing your relevant experience and education.

Your proposal will first be considered by our editorial department. If it meets our Acquisitions Standards , it will be sent to our full acquisitions committee for review. The committee includes the director of Redleaf, the managing editor, the marketing manager, the development editor, and the acquisitions editor for our catalog. This group considers the following questions, among others:

• Is the content original and authoritative?
• Is the book needed in the field? Does it duplicate work that is already available?
• Does the content address our audience (primarily professionals in early childhood care and education)?
• Does the book fit into our editorial plan? Does it complement or compete with books we have already published or have already committed to publishing?
• Is Redleaf Press the best publisher for the book?

You can expect a response from the acquisitions committee within three months of submitting a proposal. If the proposal is accepted based on its content, we then have to determine that it is financially feasible for us to publish the book. This analysis takes an additional four to six weeks. If the proposal passes feasibility, we negotiate a contract with the author, and work on the project begins. We usually allow at least a year for an author to write a first draft and an additional three to four months for revisions before a final draft is expected. During this time, the author works closely with a development editor to shape the content and the writing style. Once we have the final draft in hand, publication takes from six to nine months.

Acquisition Standards

The mission of Redleaf Press is to improve the lives of children by strengthening and supporting the people who care for them. We publish and distribute resources to make best practice in the early childhood field accessible to people who work directly with young children. In order to be considered for publication or distribution by Redleaf Press, a resource must meet the following content standards:

1. The material must be developmentally appropriate for the age group for which it is intended. If it is intended for children from birth to eight years of age, it must take into account the Developmentally Appropriate Practice standards published by the National Association for the Education of Young Children (Bredekamp et al., Developmentally Appropriate Practice in Early Childhood Programs , revised edition [Washington, DC: NAEYC, 1997]). If the authors take issue with these standards for cultural or other reasons, the proposal or manuscript should explicitly address this difference.

2. The material must be based on sound theory and research in child development. It should demonstrate an awareness of recent developments within the early childhood field, including the work that is being done on brain development, but should be grounded in theory that has proven durable over time. If the research of others is cited to support arguments made in the material, it must be documented thoroughly and used responsibly.

3. The material must take cultural differences in child development and childrearing practices into account. Examples, stories, curriculum activities, and training exercises must give an accurate picture of human differences and must not further stereotypes or bias based on gender, race, culture, economic class, age, family structure, sexual orientation, disability, or any other facet of identity. In addition, materials must actively contribute to welcoming all children and adults in early childhood programs and must address the issue of bias wherever appropriate.

4. Materials must reflect an active, learner-centered approach to education. Curriculum materials should acknowledge that each child has his or her own pattern of development and should recognize that firsthand and hands-on experiences are vital to young children's learning. For this reason, books that contain primarily dittos, patterns, or handouts that support teacher-directed early childhood education will not be considered. Materials for trainers must demonstrate an understanding of adult development and an awareness of different learning styles.

Additional Guidelines

We also publish and distribute resources resources about the management of child care centers and family child care businesses. The material must be based on sound business practice, and the legal and financial information contained in these resources must be current.

Books M-Z

The children's books we publish and distribute are issues-oriented. We do not accept alphabet books or fairy tales.

We do not publish or distribute parenting books, unless they foster communication between parents and caregivers.

Categories: Nonfiction—Education—Child Development

CONTACT: Acquisitions Committee
Material: All
10 Yorktown Court
St. Paul, MN 55117-1065
Phone: 800-423-8309
Fax: 800-641-0115
Website: www.redleafpress.org

Renders Wellness Publishing

Renders Wellness Publishing only publishes non-fiction and would be interested in seeing manuscripts that include topics such as: Nutrition, alternative medicine and Weight loss. All manuscripts must include SASE for return, or will be unreturend. Publisher will give priority to manuscripts that include clinical research, and includes those references. Publisher pays 10% of Net Sales to author.

Allow 6 to 8 weeks for response, no phone calls please!

Categories: Nonfiction—Alternative Medicine—Diet/Nutrition

CONTACT: Editorial
Material: All
1540 Mays Landing Rd.
Egg Harbor Township, N. J. 08234

Republic of Texas Press

Republic of Texas Press was formed in 1987 to publish non-fiction books with a Texas theme. We are very interested in any book that relates to the history, humor, music, travel, especially with children, regional guidebooks and some specialized cookbooks. Please be familiar with our current book line. We will be happy to look at any idea as long as it fits our state-specific criteria. We do not, at this time, publish any fiction, poetry or novels.

To submit a proposal please include the following:
1. Proposed title and subject
2. Table of contents and a brief outline
3. Two or three sample chapters
4. Estimated number of words and/or pages
5. Manuscript completion date
6. Similar and/or competing books currently in the market
7. Target audience, author availability
8. Author experience, prior published works, subject expertise

Categories: Nonfiction—Regional—Texas related topics only

CONTACT: Ginnie Siena Bivona, Acquisitions Editor
Material: All
2320 Los Rios Blvd., Ste. 200
Plano TX 75040
Phone: 972-423-0090
Website: www.republicoftexaspress.com

Resurrection Press, Ltd.

Formal guidelines not available.
Send queries or book proposals to below address.
Categories: Nonfiction—Religion—Spiritual

CONTACT: Emilie Cerar, Editor
Material: All
Catholic Book Publishing Co.

77 West End Rd
Totowa NJ 07512-1405
Phone: 973-890-2400, ext.118
Website: www.catholicpublishing.com

Richard C. Owen Publishers, Inc.
Books for Young Learners

Richard C. Owen Publishers, Inc. seeks brief, bright, fresh stories with charm, magic, meaning, and appeal for five, six, and seven year old children that they can read by themselves. We want stories that interest, inform, entertain, and inspire children.

We are interested in publishing a variety of themes in different styles and genres.

Fiction: includes original, realistic, contemporary stories, as well as tall tales, legends, myths, and folktales of all cultures.

Nonfiction: fascinating subjects presented as a story in language accessible to five-, six- and seven-year olds. No dry facts, or encyclopedia type pieces, please.

Structure: well-developed stories with captivating beginnings, clear and energetic middles, that end with a fresh, humorous, or unexpected twist or flourish. Length: between 45 and 100 words is best.

Storyline: fresh, strong, focused, lively, and interesting to today's children.

Characters: vivid, believable, and child-appealing, whom children can relate to, identify with, and care about. Animals in stories must act authentically and not be humanized or "cute."

Sentences: complete and grammatically correct.

Language: a mix of both natural and book language. If dialog is used it must sound natural and realistic.

Please do not submit:
• Holiday or religious themes
• Lessons, morals, vocabulary lists, or language skills
• Manuscripts that stereotype or demean individuals or groups, or present violence, or hopelessness
• Stories with talking, humanized, personified animals or objects
• Stories that have been previously published, unoriginal, or imitative stories or characters
• List stories

BOOKS FOR OLDER LEARNERS

Richard C. Owen Publishers, Inc. seeks short, easy to read, high-interest pieces that will fascinate, inspire, entertain and inform eight, nine, and ten year old children in the third grade.

We want short, strong, snappy, exciting pieces that will capture a child's imagination and hold a child's interest.

Please write clearly and simply, yet with richness, and style about topics, and events that have meaning for this age group. We want tight, concise, well-structured, and well-developed strong pieces in different genres about a variety of themes.

All submissions should have the economy of words, and the vitality, freshness, energy, and impact of high quality magazine or newspaper articles.

We will publish prose and poetry, fiction and nonfiction in a variety of styles, and formats.

We seek: adventure, action, mysteries, humor, science, science-fiction, journals, diaries, photo essays current trends, sports, music, how-to, letters, nature and the environment, careers, technology, geography, architecture, travel, myths and legends, and wordless pieces.

Word length: 250—750 words is best.

Our response time is 4—8 months.

Submission procedures:
1. Manuscripts should include your name, phone number, and the page number on each page.
2. Include a short cover letter with your name, address, and the manuscript title.
3. Send photocopies, no originals please.

Requests for revisions do not in any way imply, suggest, or guarantee acceptance or publication of a manuscript.

Categories: Fiction—Nonfiction—Adventure—African-American—Animals—Asian-American—Children—Environment—Juvenile—Humor—How-to

CONTACT: Janice Boland, Director of Children's Books
Material: All
PO Box 585
Katonah NY 10536
Phone: 914-232-3903
Fax: 914-232-3977

RLN & Company

Accepting any genre, any category. (Non-fiction preferred.) Query first recommended.

Electronic submissions preferred in Microsoft Word (.doc) or Acrobat (.pdf) or plain text (.txt) files. Send electronic submissions or queries to submissions@rlnonline.com

Hardcopy submissions accepted with the provision that the manuscript cannot be returned without return postage included. Partial submission accepted only if complete manuscript is immediately available.

Expect up to 8 weeks for a response.

Categories: Nonfiction

CONTACT: Submissions
Material: All
PO Box 61219
Seattle WA 98121
E-mail: submissions@rlnonline.com
Website: www.rlnonline.com

Roadman Press
Eurail & Train Travel Guides

Are you a rail traveler? Roadman Press would like your stories for two rail guides, the "Eurail & Train Travel Guide to Europe" and the "Eurail & Train Travel Guide to the World." The books are updated annually and submissions are due in our office by August 31 for the next year's edition.

The two types of articles we want are (1) short, first-person rail experiences and tips for traveling by rail around the world, and (2) luxury train evaluations.

RAIL EXPERIENCES/RAIL-TRAVEL TIPS
Eurail & Train Travel Guides

We are seeking short (200-500-word) first-person musings about rail travel around the globe as well as tips for taking a smooth, trouble-free rail journey. Topics may include a favorite scenic trip, or an adventure-filled journey like a wild ride on a South American local train. Or it could be a fantastic dining car meal or an interesting night-train experience, or tips for making reservations and buying tickets. We're especially looking for off-beat "finds," rail trips not listed in other travel guides. Feel free to mention meeting interesting people on the rails, too. We want to give readers snapshots of the rail-riding experience and show them the infinite possibilities rail travel presents for a civilized, stress-free way to see the world. Your experiences should be current, within the last six months.

We buy one-time rights and payment is $0.07 per word. Please query first. E-mail submissions are OK, preferably pasted into an e-mail message. If you send a disk or printout, please include an SASE if you want your materials returned.

LUXURY TRAIN INSPECTIONS AND EVALUATIONS
Eurail & Train Travel Guides

For the first time, the "Eurail & Train Travel Guide to Europe" and the "Eurail & Train Travel Guide to the World," will include comprehensive information about luxury trains around the globe. The luxury train section will appear in both editions. We know of no other publication that offers this detailed level of information. To bring this information to our readers, we rely on travel writers and travel industry experts to provide us with the latest information about these luxury trains. Because our evaluation form is so complete, all you have to do is jot down notes while traveling and you'll be ready to write the short report. It's a perfect way to earn a few extra dollars while already on an assignment!

QUERY FIRST

Assignments are made upon review of a query letter. Writers should send a résumé, clips of published work highlighting relevant experience, and a self addressed stamped envelope. New reviewers submit work on spec. We will forward you an evaluation form by e-mail or by post.

ASSIGNMENTS

When you accept an assignment, you agree to cover the assigned luxury train. If you have any questions while on assignment, please contact the editor at 619.260.1332 or by e-mail, editors@roadmanpress.com. It is permissible to accept concurrent assignments on luxury trains. You may also accept complimentary transportation, meals, and accommodations if offered, but you must not enter an agreement with any train operator regarding the content of any review.

INSPECTIONS

You may identify yourself as a travel writer to railway personnel, and usually they will be accommodating. Your attire should be professional and fit in with the train's clientele. Speaking discreetly with guests can yield an unbiased opinion of the train. Also, talk with employees such as waiters or cabin attendants; they may be willing to point out the good and bad aspects of the operation. Ask the train manager if you can view a variety of compartments and suites, and obtain any pertinent printed information such as menus and gift catalogues.

You must inspect all public areas, and at least one accommodation of each type offered. On trip-related tours ask local tourism representatives or others connected with the train and the tour about the train's reputation and service, whether it's consistently excellent, good, fair or poor.

PRESS KITS

Unless advised otherwise, you should obtain the latest press kit for the train and forward it to us with your completed review. The press kit should include a fact sheet, brochure, fares, schedules and the public relation contact's business card.

WRITING THE REVIEW

When writing the review keep these things in mind:

• Give us a clear picture of the character of the train and its clientele: This is the kind of information available only from a firsthand visit. What stands out or is unique about the train? What are its strong and weak points? To whom is the train likely to appeal, and to whom will it be a turn-off? How does this train compare with other luxury rail services?

• Write in complete sentences and use strong, concrete, colorful prose. Skip vague terms like nice, pretty, some, there are, etc. Use active voice! Be creative! But also provide as much specific detail as possible.

• As you write your review please follow the order on the evaluation form. Every category is important, and failure to address even one can result in an incomplete review. Assume the editor is clueless about the train!

• Describe the reader precisely what the train is like, not just what it provides. Paint a word picture! Show us the condition and appearance of what you see. Give us a feel about the ambience of the train and the intangibles that contribute to its strengths and weaknesses.

• Tell it like it is! Don't sidestep when criticizing any aspect of an operation. Even the best luxury trains have flaws, and they must be included in your review. On the other hand, if your experience war-

rants praise, don't hesitate to report it.

• Reviews should run 200 to 500 words.

Please send your review by disk (MS Word, WordPerfect or text format for Mac) or by e-mail to editors@roadmanpress.com, preferably pasted into an e-mail message.

PAYMENT

Payment is $30 per review (this includes a postage allowance for sending us press kits, brochures, etc.). Please submit an invoice to the above address with your review, press kit and other related materials. U.S. citizens should submit their social security number. You are responsible for all your travel expenses connected with the inspection. You will receive a byline for your review, if you wish. We buy one-time rights.

Categories: Nonfiction—Travel

CONTACT: Eurail & Train Travel Editor
Material: Rail Travel
CONTACT: Luxury Train Evaluation Editor
Material: Rail Travel
PO Box 3747
San Diego CA 92163
Phone: 619-260-1332
Fax: 619-296-4220
E-mail: editors@roadmanpress.com
Website: www.roadmanpress.com

Roberts Rinehart
Imprint: Court Wayne Press

Roberts Rinehart publishes in the areas of Irish studies, National Parks, Nature, Native America, the West, and general non fiction and fiction (adult and children's works).

Submissions Guidelines

If you would like to submit a proposal, please include:

• A description of the book, what makes it unique, and why are you qualified to write it

• An analysis of competing or similar titles (include publisher and dates)

• A description of your target audience

• An indication of whether any of the material in the book has been previously published and if so, when and where

• The names of other publishers to whom you have submitted a proposal (if relevant)

• The length of the manuscript on 12 point type on double-spaced 8 ½ x 11 paper

• And, if the manuscript is not complete, an estimate of when you expect to finish

• Please also send a detailed table of contents

• Include one or two sample chapters

• If an introduction or overview is available, please include it as well

Categories: Fiction—Nonfiction—Children—General Interest—Irish Studies—National Parks—Native America—Nature

CONTACT: Rick Rinehart, Publisher
Material: All
5360 Manhattan Circle #101
Boulder, CO 80303
Phone: 303-543-7835
Fax: 303-543-0043
E-mail: No electronic submissions please.
Website: www.taylor-trade.com

> **Remember: Editors change jobs and publishers change addresses. It is wise to invest in a phone call for the current information before submitting.**

Rockbridge Publishing

Now an Imprint of Howell Press, Inc. Please refer to Howell Press.

Rodnik Publishing Co.

Areas of publishing interest:
• Foreign language phrasebooks
• Foreign language dictionaries
• Language learning materials
• Vocational ESL materials
• Titles currently in print:
• *English-Russian Dictionary-Phrasebook of Love*, 800 pp, C 2000
Guidelines for manuscripts:

Paper manuscripts for foreign-language phrasebooks, foreign-language dictionaries, and textbooks and materials for learning foreign languages and ESL may be submitted at any time for consideration. If return of the manuscript is desired, please include a stamped self-addressed envelope of suitable size.

Authors wishing to submit manuscripts on computer disks should first contact Rodnik Publishing by telephone or e-mail to discuss and arrange the submittal.

Synopses of projects may be submitted by e-mail or e-mail attachment, but please do not submit full manuscripts as e-mail attachments.

We will endeavor to review your manuscript and give you a decision on it within two weeks of receiving it. If it appears that we need more time to assess it, we will notify you.

Authors and translators with native expertise in Albanian, Amharic, Armenian, Bahasa Indonesian, Bantu, Bengali, Kinyanwanda, Somali, Swahili, Urdu and tribal languages of Africa are especially encouraged to contact us.

Categories: Nonfiction—Education—Language

CONTACT: Bob Powers, Director
Material: All
PO Box 46956
Seattle WA 98146-0956
Phone: 206-937-5189
Fax: 206-937-3554
E-mail: rodnik2@comcast.net

Ronin Publishing, Inc.

Formal guidelines not available.
Send queries or book proposals to below address.
Categories: Careers—Culture—Health—Lifestyle—Self Help

CONTACT: Beverly Poter, Publisher
Material: All
PO Box 22900
Oakland CA 94609
Phone: No Phone Calls

Running Press

Children's Proposals

For our Running Press Kids list, we specialize in publishing innovative, hands-on, educational products for children from birth through ninth grade. Our industry-leading book-plus products encourage kids to enjoy learning about the world around them. Books bearing our Kinesthetic Learning Tools™ logo help preschoolers master basic concepts through movement and activity. And our high-quality picture books include fiction from award-winning authors and illustrators.

If you would like to submit a proposal for interactive nonfiction (see our Discovery Kit™ line for examples), basic concepts books (such as letters, numbers, opposites, or shapes), or beginning reading projects, we would be happy to respond to a query letter accompanied by a brief outline or table of contents.

When submitting a picture-book proposal please send the entire manuscript. Please note that at this time we are not publishing novels or any fiction longer than picture-book length.

General Audience (All Ages) Proposals

For our general-interest lists (Running Press, Courage Books), we specialize in publishing illustrated nonfiction. We very rarely publish any new fiction or poetry and are not seeking submissions in those categories at this time. We also do not accept proposals for Miniature Editions™ of any kind.

To submit a proposal for an appropriate work of nonfiction, please send a query letter accompanied by a brief outline or table of contents to the address below.

How to Submit Your Proposal

When submitting a proposal to Running Press, please note:
We do not accept submissions or query letters via e-mail.

We are not responsible for materials sent with your proposal that become lost or damaged.

Please do not send original photographs, slides, or artwork, one-of-a-kind dummies or mock-ups, or irreplaceable items of any kind with your proposal. Running Press is not responsible for the return of such materials.

Please include a self-addressed, stamped envelop (SASE) with your submission so that we may send you a reply.

If you send materials you would like us to return to you, we ask that you enclose sufficient return postage. Once again, please do not send any original or irreplaceable materials—we receive dozens of submissions each week and cannot guarantee the return of materials, even when postage is provided.

We try to respond to all submissions within six to eight weeks.

Categories: Fiction—Nonfiction—Children—Education

CONTACT: Submissions Editor, Running Press Kids
Material: Children
CONTACT: Assistant to the Editorial Director, Running Press Book Publishers
Material: General-Interest
125 South 22nd St.
Philadelphia, PA 19103-4399
Phone: 215-567-5080
Fax: 215-568-2919
Website: www.runningpress.com

Rutledge Hill Press

In your submission letter please include such information as why you have written (or want to write) the work, what the market for your manuscript is, what it will contribute to potential readers, and what makes it unique. We are particularly interested in how you see it relating to similar or competing works already in print.

Send a synopsis of no more than three pages, an outline or table of contents, and two or three chapters (30 to 40 pages). This will let us see how well you arrange your thoughts and evaluate your writing style and writing skills.

In the case of reference works or cookbooks, include enough material to illustrate the scope and purpose of the work in detail.

All correspondence will be handled by mail. You will receive a response concerning your submission within five to seven weeks. If you would like a copy of our current book catalog, please mail us a self-addressed, stamped 9"x12" envelope.

Rutledge Hill Press will not accept manuscripts delivered in person. All materials must be mailed.

Rutledge Hill Press will not review the following:
- Autobiographies
- Children's books or short stories

- Educational and/or academic materials, including psychology and self-help
  - Fictional materials
  - Poetry
  - Religious materials

Categories: Nonfiction—African-American—Biography—Civil War—Cooking—Entertainment—Film/Video—Food/Drink—History—Inspirational—Outdoors—Sports/Recreation—Travel—Women's Issues—Humor—Quilts

CONTACT: Editorial Dept.
Material: All
PO Box 141000
Nashville TN 37214-1000
Phone: 615-244-2700, ext. 169
E-mail: tmenges@rutledgehillpress.com
Website: www.rutledgehillpress.com

Safari Press, Inc.

If you are considering submitting a manuscript (MS) to Safari Press, please read the information on this sheet carefully. Make sure the following points are included when you submit your MS to us. (This will help you get your book published either by us or other publishers.)

1. Cover letter that includes the subject matter and scope.

2. Approximate number of words.

3. Complete Table of Contents, annotated if you are submitting sample chapters.

Author information (full name, address, phone and fax numbers). Any other relevant background information on yourself. This might include a listing of books you have previously published.

5. Approximate number of photos you can provide. We like to have 10 photos per every 10,000 words. Photo copies of some photos if possible.

Manuscript Guidelines

Safari Press accepts MS only on big-game hunting, firearms, and wingshooting. Always send a copy of your MS, not the original, just in case it gets lost in the mail. Please state if the work is original or if it has been published previously. If previously published, we will need a written statement from the publisher giving you permission to reprint the work. Make sure to state if there is a co-author. We discourage autobiographies, unless the life of the hunter or firearms maker has been exceptional. We routinely reject MS along the lines of "me and my buddies went hunting for . . . and a good time was had by all."

Please do not offer a MS that is full of obscene, vulgar, or offensive language. We believe ethical hunting is sound conservation. Hunters have a duty to preserve their sport for future generations and this will only happen if the general public has a positive view of hunting. Although we recognize game laws were non-existent or widely ignored in the past, we believe that all modern-day hunters should uphold the game laws of the country in which the game was shot.

Normally, only MS over 60,000 words (we prefer 75,000) will be accepted. We make exceptions for guidebooks and "how-to" books. (Almost all word processors have a "word count" feature.)

While we will review a sample of chapters, we prefer the whole MS. Do not send a partially completed MS. Send only completed sample chapters or a complete MS.

Initial submission must be in hard copy (on paper). If your MS is accepted, you will need to put it on a PC compatible disk in MS Word for Windows (preferred), Word Prefect for Windows, and most other IBM compatible word processors. Please do not e-mail MS to us, there are all sorts of problems with e-mailed MS. Space prevents us from listing them all. In case you can not submit a MS any other way than via e-mail please contact us first for instructions before sending.

Print out We accept print outs on 8.5x11 inch paper or the A4 (210 x 297mm) format. Please leave at least one inch (25 millimeters) margins all around, NUMBER ALL PAGES. We prefer the Courier font in size 12.

Numbers: For fractions please type out the entire number as in the following example "the shotgun has a 2 1 / 2 inch chamber." Please place a space between each digit and the slash. Some word processors will make "2 1 / 2" into "2½" if the numbers are typed without spaces in between them. We find that the typesetting program does not translate these reduced size fractions making for mistakes in the typeset version.

Naming: Name your chapters clearly so that they may be put in the correct order. Opening a separate document for each chapter is very helpful and a must. Make sure your Foreword, Introduction, Captions et al are labeled.

Photos and Artwork: Manuscripts should have photos or appropriate artwork. Submit a list of illustrations, or a general idea of what kind of illustrations you have available. Be sure to include whether they are b/w photos, color photos, or drawings and how many you have.

Do not send any original art or photos unless there is an agreement to publish. Once we have a contract; the first rule is always send the best image no matter if it is a slide, black and white, or color picture. If you have a good slide but a bad black and white, send the good slide and keep the bad black and white!

Do not send dozens and dozens of pictures with a note "please select the best." We are not nearly as qualified as the author to select the best picture, and we will invariably not use pictures you want in!

Select your pictures with quality and variety of images in mind. If you have line drawings, advertisements, or other art that you want to submit, always send the original, if at all possible.

Once you have the right number of images together, please mark each with a number. We prefer the following style: For picture 1 in chapter 1 by Ernest Hemingway, the label would read: EHCH0101. This is EH (Ernest Hemingway), CH01 (Chapter 1), 01 (picture 1). Also, never write on the back of the pictures with any kind of ballpoint pen or one than can smudge!!! Use a pen from a graphic supply store (such as a "Sharpie" by Stanford Manufacturing) made for marking photos.

We cannot tell you how many countless good pictures we have received over the years that were ruined with ink smudges and marks all over them! ALL ballpoints, felt tips or fountain pens have ink that takes hours to dry on photo paper and even then will smudge. The result is ink smudging on the face of the next photo when the photos get stacked. USE A SHARPIE! We will provide a Sharpie free of charge to all authors with a contract!

Photos, slides, negatives. As stated before a good sharp, well balanced image, via ANY media is ALWAYS preferred over a bad, out of focus image, from ANY other media. OK, so you have excellent photos and slides, what do we prefer? All other things being equal slides reproduce better than anything else. Next to slides we prefer photos. We DO NOT want to take negatives UNLESS you can send the photos from the negatives with it. Why? With negatives alone it is impossible to see the quality of the image and therefore we can not choose the best image from a selection.

Digital Camera images We GREATLY prefer NOT to take digital camera images? Why? In most cases the quality can not hold a candle to a regular slide or photo. In all cases the lighter shades (such as fog or smoke etc) do not show up well at all on a digital image.

Scanning your own photos Please DO NOT attempt to scan your own photos and send these to us on a CD. However appealing this may sound the quality of the image (for all sorts of reasons) is always less than if we get the photos scanned here. Our photos are scanned on professional scanning machines that render an image quality 5 to 8 times better than a regular scanner attached to a home PC.

Captions: Number the captions with the same number as the picture to which it corresponds. Place the captions in a separate computer file titled "Captions" and place the caption number above each caption. Allow one blank line between each caption.

Spacing: Lastly, and of utter importance: When typing your MS, do not hit the Enter Key at the end of a sentence. Let your word processor program wrap sentences around. Every time you use the "Enter" key you create hidden paragraph marks in the MS. We spend an inordinate amount of time stripping paragraph marks from the MS. In most cases, we will return the MS to you and ask you to do the work. Believe us, it is time consuming! Save yourself hours of work, let the program warp the sentence! Place two spaces between each sentence.

Chapter Titles: If you are writing a reference book, or something of the sort, please write titles for the chapters and a completed a table of contents. Please make the chapter titles concise and have them reflect what the chapter is about.

Finally, we are not nearly as grumpy as this paper sounds! Please believe us when we say that in these few pages are the cumulative experiences of 40 years of publishing. By sharing this we hope to help you avoid the most common mistakes made in writing a book. The instructions are not very difficult to follow and you will have a better book for it.

Categories: Nonfiction—African-American—Animals—Book Reviews—Short Stories

CONTACT: Susan Appleby, Officer Manager
Material: All
15621 Chemical Lane, Bldg. B
Huntington Beach CA 92649-1506
Phone: 714-894-9080
Fax: 714-894-4949
E-mail: info@safaripress.com
Website: safaripress.com

Safer Society Press

Safer Society Foundation is a nonprofit organization dedicated to the prevention and treatment of sexual abuse. Safer Society Press, a program of the Foundation, publishes books, audio and video tapes that assist clinicians and professionals in the treatment of their clients and titles of interest to families, victims, survivors and organizations dealing with sexual abuse. We do not publish poetry or fiction.

Please use the following guidelines:

• Your proposal should include a brief description of the work, a complete outline of the book and 2 sample chapters. You will be contacted if additional information is needed.

• Include author's credentials.

• Enclose a stamped, self-addressed envelope for the return of your materials.

Please note evaluations can take up to three months. An acceptance or rejection letter will be sent once a decision is reached.

Thank you for following these guidelines.

Categories: Nonfiction—Health—Psychology—Self Help—Sexuality

CONTACT: Press Committee
Material: All
Safer Society Foundation, Inc.
PO Box 340
Brandon VT 05733

Santa Monica Press

Santa Monica Press is not shackled by a narrow publishing niche. Instead, we publish books across a wide variety of categories. For instance, our Arts & Literature titles include the highly acclaimed *Footsteps in the Fog: Alfred Hitchcock's San Francisco*; the cutting-edge *Dogme Uncut: Lars von Trier, Thomas Vinterberg, and the Gang That Took on Hollywood*; and the epic biographical poem *Jackson Pollock: Memories Arrested in Space*.

James Dean Died Here: The Locations of America's Pop Culture Landmarks, *Tiki Road Trip: A Guide to Tiki Culture in North America*, and *Redneck Haiku* are a few of our best-selling Popular Culture titles, which also include the one-of-a-kind *Quack!*, the now-classic *Offbeat Museums*, and the hilarious *The Butt Hello..*.

Finally, we also specialize in "How-To" and Reference titles. These books provide readers with practical guidance in a wide variety of subjects, from the two volumes of *Letter Writing Made Easy!* (over 125,000 copies sold!) to *Exotic Travel Destinations for Families* to Steve "America's Sweepstakes King" Ledoux's *How to Win Lotteries, Sweepstakes and Contests in the 21st Century*.

At Santa Monica Press, our goal is to inspire, inform, and entertain. Look for the shell!

To submit a book proposal, send us the following information:
• An outline indicating the nature and scope of each chapter
• Two sample chapters
• Photocopies of any photograph or illustrations you believe might assist us in evaluating your proposal (do not send originals!)
• A description of the book's audience
• A brief summary of similar or competitive books (including title, author, publisher, ISBN number, and date of publication—all readily available on Amazon.com and other on-line booksellers)
• An explanation of why your book is unique
• Marketing and publicity ideas or plans you may have
• The anticipated length of the manuscript
• A brief autobiographical summary or resume
• Your complete address, daytime phone number, and e-mail address

Please note that we do not accept proposals or submissions via the internet or fax. If you would like a response, you must include a self-addressed, stamped envelope. If you would like your material returned, you must include a self-addressed, stamped envelope with sufficient return postage.

Note to authors who reside outside of the United States: We do not accept International Response Coupons and therefore cannot return your material. You may, however, include your e-mail address with your material, and we will send you a response.

You can expect an initial response within two months of our receipt of your proposal. At that point, if we are interested, we will ask you to send the entire manuscript.

Categories: Nonfiction—Arts—Biography—Consumer—Culture—Drama—Entertainment—Film/Video—Folklore—General Interest—Mass Communications—Music—Reference—Television/Radio—Theatre

CONTACT: Acquisitions Editor
Material: All

Santa Monica Press LLC
PO Box 1076
Santa Monica, CA 90406
E-mail: jgoldman@santamonicapress.com
Website: www.santamonicapress.com
No phone calls, please!

Sarabande Books

As a small press, Sarabande Books can accept unsolicited manuscripts only two times each year: • The first is Open Submission Season during the month of September only. We ask that writers send a sample of ten poems, a single story, a single literary essay, a section of a novella or short novel, postmarked in September. Response time is under three months. If, during this preliminary period, we find your work of interest, we will invite you to submit your entire manuscript.

Sarabande also holds two national contests: The Kathryn A. Morton Prize in Poetry and the Mary McCarthy Prize in Short Fiction, judged by well-established writers. Guidelines and required entry form are available from November 1 through February 1 each year. You can get these guidelines and entry form by sending a business-sized, self-addressed, stamped envelope to us, or printing out everything you'll need from our Website at www.sarabandebooks.org.

Sarabande Books publishes complete manuscripts of poetry of 48 pages minimum.

We also publish collections of short stories, novellas, short novels, and literary essays that fall between 150-250 pages. We do not consider longer novels, memoirs, mysteries, westerns, children's books, chapbooks, adventure or science fiction, nor do we publish single poems or stories.

Manuscripts written by Kentucky authors (current or former residents) or with a Kentucky setting, may be submitted during July for the Woodford Reserve Series in Kentucky Literature.

Sarabande Books looks for poetry and short fiction that offer originality of voice and subject matter, uniqueness of vision, and a language that startles because of the careful attention paid to language that goes beyond the merely competent or functional. We recommend that you request our catalog and familiarize yourself with our books. Our complete list shows a variety of style and subject matter.

Categories: Fiction—Poetry—Short Stories

CONTACT: Submissions Editor
Material: All
2234 Dundee Rd., Ste 200
Louisville KY 40205
Phone: 502-458-4028
Fax: 502-458-4065
Website: www.sarabandebooks.org

Sasquatch Books

Sasquatch Books is happy to consider queries and proposals from authors and agents for new projects that fit into our West Coast regional publishing program. We can evaluate query letters, proposals, and complete manuscripts.

When you submit to Sasquatch Books, please remember that the editors want to know about you and your project, along with a sense of who will want to read your book.

Categories: Nonfiction—Children—Food/Drink—Gardening—Nature—Regional—Travel

CONTACT: The Editors
Material: All
119 South Main, Ste. 400
Seattle, WA 98104

Scarecrow Press, Inc.

Scarecrow Press publishes scholarly, professional and academic reference books on a variety of subjects. We seek proposals that represent new treatments of traditional topics, original scholarship in developing areas, and cogent syntheses of existing research. While we accept unsolicited submissions, we prefer that you submit a proposal rather than a completed manuscript. Please note that our review process normally takes between two and four months.

Guidelines for submitting a book proposal

1. Please provide a tentative descriptive title.

2. Tell us the subject matter, scope, and intended purpose of your manuscript. Include an introduction, table of contents, and chapter summaries. A completed sample chapter (so that we can gauge your writing style, organizational techniques, and documentation) would also be helpful.

3. What research methods or data sources will you use?

4. When do you estimate the work will be completed? How long do you think it will be?

5. Whom do you see as your audience? What other books exist in your subject area?

Please send your proposal, including a recent c.v., to the appropriate editor. Be sure to enclose a self-addressed envelope, stamped with sufficient postage, if you would like us to return the materials you sent in.

Categories: Nonfiction—African-American—Arts—Biography—Computers—Culture—Education—Feminism—Film/Video—Gay/Lesbian—Hispanic—History—Internet—Military—Multicultural—Music—Reference—Teen—Textbooks—Young Adult—Library Science

CONTACT: Editorial Department
Material: All
4501 Forbes Blvd., Ste 200
Lanham MD 20706
Phone: 301-459-3366
Fax: 301-459-2118
Website: www.scarecrowpress.com

Schirmer Trade Books

Schirmer Trade Books is an imprint of Music Sales Corporation. Founded in 1935 by the Wise family, Music Sales is an international family of companies with interests in four main areas of music publishing: Copyright ownership and promotion of standard and popular music, classical music, printed music, and book publishing. Music Sales maintains offices in New York, London, Sydney, Copenhagen, Madrid, Tokyo, Helsinki, and Paris.

Schirmer is committed to intelligent, educational, and entertaining books about all aspects of popular music, especially the recording arts, music business, and genre histories.

We're especially interested in books about songwriting (music and/or lyrics), musician biographies (high-profile entertainers with large fan bases, as well as up-and-coming), and gift books. We rarely publish books about classical music. We prefer rock & roll, folk, blues, and pop. We do NOT publish fiction.

Send full book proposals, including: Cover letter, overview of the book, target audience, author bio, competitive titles, marketing and promotion ideas, detailed chapter-by-chapter table of contents, and a sample chapter (if available).

Categories: Nonfiction—Biography—History—Music—Reference—Performing Arts

CONTACT: Andrea Rotondo, Managing Editor
Material: All
257 Park Ave. South
New York, NY 10010
Phone: 212-254-2100
Fax: 212-254-2013
Website: www.schirmertradebooks.com

Second Chance Press

Please refer to The Permanent Press.

Serendipity Systems
Books-on-disks

NOTE: E-mail with attachments from unknown sources will be dumped without being read or opened! Writers who violate this rule will have all their future e-mail automatically put in the trash unread.

Serendipity Systems publishes fiction and reference works related to literature, writing, and publishing.

We are only interested in seeing works which can take advantage of computer-enhanced features such as hypertext or multimedia. Except in rare cases, we do not publish works which are straight prose (no hypertext or multimedia.) We can NOT use manuscripts on paper. We may be able to use Macintosh files if they have been saved as ASCII under System 7 or higher, however, we only publish IBM-PC compatible disks. Royalties for books published under the BOOKS-ON-DISKS (tm) imprint are thirty-three percent of the retail or wholesale sales, less shipping. No advance is offered. Serendipity Systems only contracts for the electronic rights; all on-paper, movie, and similar rights are retained by the author.

We do NOT want to see:
• romance novels
• religious tracts
• sword and sorcery fantasy
• occult works
• anything "new age"
• political diatribes
• imitations of Stephen King or Tom Clancy
• "Penthouse Forum" quality materials
• children's literature (pre-teenage)
• "Academic" novels *
• non-fiction works not related to literature, writing, or publishing

We ARE interested in seeing:
• hypertext novels
• mixed-media works
• new computer-enhanced genres
• interactive fiction
• experimental works
• reference works on literature, writing, and publishing
• Windows-compatible works
• manuscripts written in HTML

Submissions should:
• be on IBM-PC compatible disks (160K, 5.25" to 1.44MB, 3.5"; 100MB ZIP disks; CD-ROMs)

• be in ASCII (unless the author has already added hypertext/multimedia features)

• have margins of 1 and less than 80 (WordPerfect users note this!)

• include the complete manuscript

• include an SASE or return postage

• include a cover letter describing the work and the author's qualifications

• send the complete manuscript by postal mail (Postal address below;) send ONLY queries by e-mail

NOTE: E-mail with attachments from unknown sources will be dumped without being read or opened!

UPDATE: December 22, 1999

Things change very rapidly in the world of electronic publishing, and we have again changed our focus to meet the new conditions.

We are now publishing Rocket Editions—electronic books that run on NuvoMedia's Rocket eBook portable "reader" device. (See our Rocket Page.)

As a result of our survey of What do Rocket eBook users want? (See the results under "Survey" at EPF29.) we will be most interested in seeing science fiction manuscripts. As always, we are looking for believable plots, credible characters, and a strong story line.

For Rocket Editions we need manuscripts in ASCII or plain HTML. Do not submit manuscripts with complex HTML—Rocket eBooks can not display tables, color illustrations, or many of the common features of the versions of HTML used on the Internet. We will also be publishing windows-compatible versions of our Rocket eBooks—same source code; different display engine.

Submit manuscripts on disk via postal mail only. E-mail with an attached file from an unknown source will be automatically dumped.

We will continue to be interested in new genres, interactive fiction, etc., however, you should keep in mind that there isn't yet much of a market for such material.

UPDATE

September 8, 2000

Existing books and future publications will be converted into Microsoft Reader format. Other formats will continue be supported as long as they are viable. (The "source code" will continue to be HTML; files will be converted to .lit format.)

UPDATE: September 27, 2001

Serendipity Systems will publish general non-fiction books (primarily reference books) under the TheInfiniteBook imprint and will launch a www.TheInfiniteBook.com Internet site.

Before submitting a manuscript, see our Writers' Manuscript Help section on our website.

If you are getting rejection slips from publishers, see this file.

Categories: Fiction—Nonfiction—Internet—Literature—Writing

CONTACT: John Galuszka, Publisher
Material: All
PO Box 140
San Simeon CA 93452
E-mail: bookware@thegrid.net

Shambhala Publications, Inc.

Imprint: New Seeds Books

If you are interested in submitting a book query, proposal, or manuscript to Shambhala for consideration, please read the following guidelines:

We suggest that you send a book proposal including a synopsis of the book, a table of contents or outline, a copy of the author's résumé or some other description of him or her, and two or three sample chapters. Be advised that we publish very few contemporary fiction, poetry, art, or children's books. Be sure to include a self-addressed envelope with sufficient postage (or an international postal money order) if you want your materials returned. We cannot be held responsible for

lost or misplaced materials if you do not include a self-addressed, stamped envelope. The manuscript should be double-spaced, in upper and lower case letters. The review process of a manuscript can take two to four months. Please send your materials to:

We do not review materials submitted via e-mail.

Categories: Nonfiction—Alternate Life-styles—Arts—Asian American—Biography— Christian-Interest—Diet/Nutrition—Native Americans—Religion—Self Help—Spiritual

CONTACT: Editorial Assistant
Material: All
Shambhala Publications
300 Massachusetts Ave.
Boston, MA 02115
Phone: 617-424-0030
Fax: 617-236-1563
E-mail: editors@shambhala.com
Website: www.shambhala.com

Sierra Club Books

Sierra Club Books is seeking nonfiction projects intended for the general reader. We are interested in great nature writing, first-person narratives, and all subjects relating to ecology and the environment. Please send an outline and a sample chapter of your proposed book and sufficient postage if you would like your material returned. We are currently not accepting any unsolicited manuscripts or proposals for children's books. For additional information, current titles, and a list of FAQ's, please visit our website at www.sierraclub.org/books. Sierra Club Books is co-published and distributed by University of California Press.

Categories: Nonfiction—Environment

CONTACT: Editorial Department
Material: All
85 Second St., Second Floor
San Francisco, CA 94105
Phone: 415-977-5500
Fax: 415-977-5792
Website: www.sierraclub.org/books

Silhouette Desire
Silhouette Intimate Moments
Silhouette Romance
Silhouette Special Edition

Please refer to Harlequin, in the Book Publishers section.

Silver Dagger Mysteries

Silver Dagger is an imprint of The Overmountain Press.

Please review the following guidelines before submitting manuscripts to us:

1. Subject matter. We publish Southern mysteries. Sub-genres such as cozies, police procedural, hardboiled, etc. will all be considered. We will consider romantic suspense only if the book is a true mystery first,

and the romance is a subplot only. Young reader (3rd-9th grade) books are published as well. The book should be set in the South or the author should have very strong ties to the South. We define "The South" as the following states: Texas, Alabama, Arkansas, Mississippi, Georgia, Tennessee, Kentucky, Virginia, North Carolina, South Carolina, Florida. Manuscripts set in states which border these MAY be considered if the author lives in a Southern state.

2. Content. We do not publish books with graphic content. This includes graphic violence, graphic sex, horror, or heavy supernatural lines. Foul language must be at a minimum and not gratuitous. Basically, if the networks get away with it on prime time television, that's fine. Most books with dead bodies tend to have police, and police tend to use hard language. No problem! Just don't go overboard. Young reader books should have NO foul language at all.

3. Length. We are currently accepting books with a 60,000 to 80,000 word count for adult novels, and 30,000 to 60,000 word count for young reader editions.

4. Authors. Silver Dagger publishes only committed, strong, active authors. As you will realize with publication, your sales depend very heavily upon your promotional activity. As you may know, Silver Dagger is not your typical publishing house; we are a consortium of authors. Everyone knows each other and talks to each other regardless of geography. Our veteran authors hand down suggestions and pointers for our first-timers. Silver Dagger is committed to the first-time author; we plan to stock our publication list with half veterans and half first-timers. Each author is carefully selected not only for his or her writing, but also for his or her willingness to promote, speak to groups, serve on panels, attend book signings, etc. If your book is selected as a candidate for publication, we will contact you with details about contracts, the publication process, and a few more details about our promotional and marketing plans.

5. The submission package. *For your initial query, include the following:*

• Cover Letter — describing you, your background, your qualifications for writing this book

• Brief Synopsis — just a couple of paragraphs about your book. Write the blurb that will be on the back of your cover. NO more than a page.

• First three chapters — send this in hard copy format. We don't care about fonts, line spacing, point size, and all that. Just put it on plain white paper and make it readable. Please do not send in computer disks.

• Marketing Outline—Put together a sample marketing plan for your book. Include the following (if applicable): any contacts in the mystery field, contacts in the media, previous publications, and (realistically) how many copies of your book do you think you can sell? We ask for this outline for a number of reasons, most notably because we want ACTIVE authors to join our consortium. Each author on the 2000 list was very carefully selected not only on the basis of the manuscript but also for his/her track record and enthusiasm for promotion. If you have published before (even if it wasn't a mystery) tell us what you did that worked. If you are a first—time author, don't worry! We have a marketing department to assist you! Just give us some ideas as to what you think will work for you and your book.

6. Manuscripts. Do not send a manuscript unsolicited. It will be returned immediately. If our reviewing editors like your first three chapters and want to read the rest of the book, we will inform you of manuscript submission guidelines and addresses.

7. PLEASE DO NOT EMAIL SUBMISSION QUERIES.

8. Timelines. Due to possible overload of submissions, we cannot guarantee these times. We hope to adhere to the following schedule:

• Initial query — 2-4 weeks response time
• Manuscript request — 1-3 months

Please do not call to check on the status of your submission. If you have not heard anything at all from us 3 months after your initial query, send an email to bethw@overmtn.com. We will check our records for your package and let you know if we have received it, and estimate a response date.

Categories: Fiction—Mystery

CONTACT: Alex Foster, Acquisitions Editor
Material: Mystery
The Overmountain Press
PO Box 1261
Johnson City TN 37605
Phone: 423-926-2691
Website: www.silverdaggermysteries.com

Skinner House Books

Skinner House Books is an imprint of The Unitarian Universalist Association.

Skinner House Books is currently seeking proposals on these topics:

• how to nurture tolerance in our children
• how to talk to children about spiritual subjects
• spirituality in the workplace
• spirituality and/or spiritual practice in everyday life
• aging and spirituality
• young adulthood and spirituality
• prayer collections
• how to become a social justice activist
• nature and spirituality
• interconnectedness; living the values consistent with our "small planet"
• collected stories for children
• cultural appropriation vs. cultural diversity: how to strike a balance
• stories about congregational life that focus on a particular theme, such as welcoming blended families, nurturing diversity, nurturing social activism, managing grief, managing conflict, nurturing intergenerational contact

To submit a proposal to Skinner House or to contact us for more information, send an email to skinner_info@uua.org.

Proposals and Queries

Skinner House Books accepts query letters and proposal packages from interested writers. A query should be 1-3 pages long. In addition to a concise summary of the proposed manuscript, it should include an explanation of why the author is qualified to write such a work and why the manuscript is appropriate for the Skinner House audience. A proposal package should include an outline or summary (2-10 pages), table of contents, introduction, and two sample chapters.

Due to the large number of submissions we receive, Skinner House is unable to comment in detail on manuscripts or proposals that are declined.

Manuscript Guidelines

The Skinner House editorial style is based on *The Chicago Manual of Style.* Please consult it for questions regarding style and manuscript preparation.

All submissions should be typed on a word-processor or computer and printed double-spaced by a laser-quality printer. Please submit manuscript in one file on a PC disk if possible. Do not set manuscripts in all caps. Serial commas should be used. Subheads should be set off from text by a line space above and below. Pages should be numbered and held by binder clips or paper clips, not stapled. Please provide a table of contents identifying manuscript pages for each chapter/unit. Manuscripts will not be returned unless a self-addressed stamped envelope is enclosed with the submission.

Skinner House Books prefers numbered endnotes, divided by chapter. Do not use footnotes, as they will require extra time and money to convert to endnotes.

The Unitarian Universalist Association is committed to gender-inclusive language. Generic use of the words "man" or "he" are widely perceived as sexist and should be avoided. We also recommend using inclusive terms for occupations or roles (i.e., salesperson, police officer, chair) and "it" not "she" for ships, cities, and countries. Advice on avoiding sexist language can be found in *The Bias-Free Word Finder* by Rosalie Maggio (Beacon Press, 1992).

Categories: Nonfiction—General Interest—Inspirational—Religion

CONTACT: Ari McCarthy
Material: All
The Unitarian Universalist Association
25 Beacon St.
Boston MA 02108
Phone: 617-948-4603
Website: www.uua.org/skinner

Smithsonian Oceanic Collection
Smithsonian Backyard
Smithsonian Let's Go to the Zoo!

Please refer to Soundprints.

Soho Press Inc
Imprints: Soho & Soho Crime

Soho Press primarily publishes fiction, with the occasional autobiography or cultural historical account. Completed manuscripts should be 60,000 words or more. While many of our published works arrive here through agents, we place a high priority on publishing quality unsolicited materials from new writers.

Though eager to accept a wide range of literary fiction, we are generally unenthusiastic about publishing formula fiction, young adult dramas, stock romances, juvenile literature, cookbooks, self-help, fantasy, westerns, and anything that might recommend itself as a "quick read." Further, we do not consider electronic submissions.

Writers may submit completed manuscripts at any time, however, a query letter accompanied by three chapters of the work (preferably the first three) and a brief outline of plot events should precede the submission of an entire novel. A cover letter listing previous publishing credits should be included with your work. Please accompany all submissions with postage and packing materials sufficient for their return.

Write well!

Bryan Devendorf, Editorial Assistant

Categories: Fiction—Nonfiction—Crime—Literature—Mystery—Women's Fiction

CONTACT: Juris Jurjevrs, President and Publisher
Material: Fiction, Nonfiction
CONTACT: Laura Hruska, Associate Publisher
Material: Mystery, Fiction, Nonfiction
853 Broadway
New York NY 10003
Phone: 212-260-1900
Website: www.sohopress.com

Solas Press

SUBMITTING A QUERY
1. INTRODUCTION

The following is a brief outline of the publishing process. It will serve as guideline for authors who think Solas Press may be of assistance to them. Just as every author is different so each publisher is different. The ideal relationship for publishing a book is when the author and publisher complement each other. However, an author should surely look for a publisher that will do a splendid job of editing his manuscript and has the resources and desire to promote the finished book.

2. WHAT IS A BOOK?

This question may sound somewhat outlandish. Does not everyone know what a book is? Six hundred years ago a book might have been so large that a person would have difficulty in removing from the shelf, where it was chained. Such a book likely took more than one man-year to copy, and consumed many expensive parchments. In Irish monasteries where the copyist art achieved a high level of perfection, the completed works were often stored in leather cases that hung from the rafters. Technology has brought a wide variety of physical types of books. This variety relates to the size and type of binding that is important in deciding on the design of a book.

More important than the physical unity of the book is the conceptual idea behind the work. Even works which are a compendium of materials must have a unifying concept.

3. WHAT IS A PUBLISHER?

The publishing industry is made up of some very large well known companies and a very large number of small entities. The basic functions of these publishers is to:

1 Acquire manuscripts suitable to the company's mission through contracts with authors.

2. Develop the manuscripts in conjunction with authors into viable products, through editing, rewrites and conceptual development.

3. Design the physical aspects of the books for production and distribution using service vendors and artists.

4. Prepare for the acceptance of the final product through galleys, press releases, opinion makers, peers, authorities in the subject area, official and semi official agencies.

5. Deal with vendors of binding, packaging, and printing.

6. Place the books into the distribution channels.

In addition the publisher needs to conduct the work as business which includes financial and fiscal responsibilities.

4. POLICIES OF SOLAS PRESS

Solas Press by the mission it has accepted works to meet two basic requirements:

1. To publish worthwhile ideas not otherwise available to the public.

2. To operate the business for profit.

To meet these two necessary conditions we follow these guidelines in working with authors

1 Initial inquiry
2. Sample materials
3. Manuscript evaluation
4.1 Initial inquiry

This is a short description of what the author intends to achieve. It should first describe the concept and uniqueness of the ideas. Secondly it should delineate the audience that will find the ideas interesting. Finally it should give the qualifications of the author in the area of interest. This final point is most important if there are any autobiographical elements.

Solas Press will respond within about a month to this initial query. A simultaneous submission of the initial query is acceptable to Solas Press.

4.2 Sample materials

If after the initial inquiry we mutually agree there is interest in proceeding the next step can be an evaluation of sample materials which shows the end quality that can be achieved.

4.3 Manuscript evaluation

Before submitting a manuscript for evaluation, the author(s) and Solas Press will complete an agreement dealing with the ownership of the materials, copyright protection, indemnity, and performance within a timeframe

One hard copy of the manuscript is required. The text should also, if possible, be submitted in electronic form. A mock-up or a description of the proposed layout of the work will generally not be needed unless it is significant for some reason.

If during the editing of the manuscript Solas Press decides that it will not proceed to publish the work it will, if requested, return all the materials supplied by the author, and not retain copies of the materials. It may retain notes generated by Solas Press.

Categories: Nonfiction—History—Religion—Spiritual

CONTACT: Acquisitions Editor
Material: All
PO Box 4066
Antioch, CA 94531
Phone: 925-978-9781

Soundprints
A Division of Trudy Corporation

Soundprints currently publishes the following series:
- Smithsonian's Backyard
- Smithsonian's Let's Go to the Zoo!
- Smithsonian Oceanic Collection
- Soundprints' Wild Habitats
- Soundprints' Read-and-Discover (early reading chapter books)
- Soundprints' Make Friends Around the World

Soundprints is primarily a publisher of wildlife picture books for children that educate as they entertain. Soundprints' stories are fiction based on fact and are rigorously reviewed for accuracy by wildlife experts. Because of the review processes, all authors are responsible for the thorough and careful research of their subject matter. None of the animals in our stories are portrayed in an anthropomorphic light. As a publisher with very specific guidelines for our well-defined series, we are not able to accept unsolicited manuscripts for publication. All of our authors are contracted on a "work for hire basis," and create manuscripts to our specifications, depending on our need. We are always interested in reviewing the published work of new potential authors. If you would like to submit some samples of your published work, we would be happy to review them and keep them on file for future reference. Please send all writing samples to the address listed.

Categories: Animals—Children—Education—Nature—Outdoors

CONTACT: Chelsea Shriver, Assistant Editor
Material: All
353 Main Ave.
Norwalk CT 06851
Phone: 203-846-2274
Fax: 203-846-1776
Website: www.soundprints.com

Sourcebooks, Inc.
Sourcebooks Casablanca
Sourcebooks Hysteria
Sourcebooks Landmark
Sourcebooks MediaFusion
Sphinx Publishing

Sourcebooks has strong distribution into the retail market—bookstores, gift stores and specialty shops whose primary product is something other than books—and provides tremendous editorial, sales, marketing and publicity support for our authors.

We follow a somewhat out-of-date model for book publishing that makes our passion for books central. In short, we believe in authorship. We work with our authors to develop great books that find and inspire a wide audience. We believe in helping develop our authors' careers, and recognize that a well-published, successful book is often a cornerstone. We seek authors who are as committed to success as we are.

Fiction:
Our fiction imprint, Sourcebooks Landmark, publishes a variety of titles. We are interested first and foremost in books that have a story to tell. We are currently only reviewing agented fiction manuscripts.

Nonfiction:
We are interested in books that will establish a unique standard in their subject area. We look for books with a well-defined, strong target market. Our Sourcebooks publishing list includes most nonfiction categories, including entertainment, history, sports, general self-help/psychology, business (particularly small business, marketing and management), parenting, health and beauty, reference, biography, gift books and women's issues.

In addition, we have several imprints focused on publishing great books into specific categories:
- Sourcebooks Casablanca publishes titles related to love and relationships
- Sourcebooks Hysteria publishes humor books
- Sourcebooks MediaFusion publishes titles that uniquely mix traditional books with integrated new media
- Sphinx Publishing is a leading consumer self-help law publisher

We are not currently publishing children's books, but we do keep an active file of artists and illustrators.

In order to consider your nonfiction book for potential publication, we will need to see a proposal that includes the following items:
- A brief synopsis in 1-2 paragraphs
- Author bio or resume specifying credentials and publication credits, if any
- A complete table of contents, plus estimated length of manuscript in words and pages
- Two to three sample chapters (not the first)
- A description of the target audience
- One page/paragraph on your book's unique advantages
- A list of competing or comparable titles and how your book differs
- Please do not send complete manuscripts unless a specific request is made for one. Queries only and simultaneous submissions are OK. We advise against the expense of sending your proposal via overnight delivery or certified mail.

While we love talking to authors, we're a bit bookish, meaning we need to actually read your proposal. That's the long way of saying it's best not to call or personally email us. If you follow the directions above (or if you even come close), your proposal will be given a fair and thorough review. For more hints, try books like *The Writer's Market*, or any number of books and magazines like it, available in bookstores and libraries. Finally, receiving proposals via email or fax may seem convenient, but isn't for us, and may actually cause manuscripts to miss the review process other proposals receive. Therefore, we advise against it.

Please send only copies of your materials. Do not send us any original manuscripts or artwork. We will not be held liable for materials lost or destroyed in the mail. Please enclose a correct size (depending on what you want returned) self-addressed, stamped envelope with your proposal. We will not return manuscripts without appropriate postage. Canadian and foreign postage coupons will not be accepted.

We usually return rejections within six to eight weeks. We may take longer if your book is being considered for publication.

Thank you again for thinking of Sourcebooks for your book. We look forward to reviewing your materials and considering your book for publication.

Categories: Fiction—Nonfiction—Biography—Careers—College—Diet/Nutrition—General Interest—Health—History—Law—Marriage—Money & Finances—Music—New Age—Parenting—Relationships—Self Help—Singles—Sports/Recreation—Women's Fiction—Women's Issues

CONTACT: Editorial Submissions
Material: All
PO Box 4410
Naperville IL 60567-4410

Phone: 630-961-3900
Website: www.sourcebooks.com

Southern Illinois University Press

Southern Illinois University Press welcomes book proposals in the fields in which we publish. To ensure timely consideration of your proposed work, please provide the information outlined below. Do not submit unsolicited complete manuscripts. Your proposal should be about 750 to 1,000 words. This statement, which can take the form of a letter, should cover:

1. the names of the author(s) or editor(s).
2. the complete title and subtitle.
3. the length or proposed length.
4. the content of the book including your aims in writing it, your primary findings or arguments, the sources used in your research, and the relationship your work has to previous studies in the field.
5. the intended audience or markets for your book, including courses for which the book might be used as a text or collateral reading and organizations or groups that might be interested in purchasing copies of your book.
6. any features in the proposed manuscript that will require special attention in the design and production of your book, such as photographs, line drawings, or other illustrations; charts, graphs, or tables; technical or foreign languages; complex mathematical or scientific data.
7. the status of your manuscript-including how much of it has been written and when you expect to finish writing it.

Please include with your proposal a copy of your current vita and those of the other author(s) or editor(s). Also enclose a copy of the table of contents of the proposed work, preferably annotated. If available, please include a sample chapter from the manuscript-please double-space the text in all sample chapters.

Your proposal will be referred to one of several acquiring editors who specialize in the fields in which we publish. Your editor may follow a variety of procedures in evaluating your proposal, but in most cases, you will hear an indication of our decision from him or her within two months.

If you have additional questions about our publishing program, please write to the acquisitions department. You may also contact the acquisitions department by phone, fax, , or by email.

Thank you.

Categories: Nonfiction—African American—Civil War—Drama—Film/Video—History—Language—Literature—Poetry—Regional—Television—Theatre

CONTACT: Acquisitions Department
Material: All
PO Box 3697
Carbondale, IL 62902-3697
Phone: 618-453-2281
Fax: 618-453-1221
E-mail: kageff@siu.edu
Website: www.siu.edu/~siupress

Spellmount Publishers

Please refer to Howell Press, Inc.

Sphinx Publishing

Please refer to Sourcebooks, Inc.

Spinsters Ink

Spinsters Ink is primarily interested in full-length novels and nonfiction works that deal with significant issues in women's lives from a feminist perspective: books that not only name crucial issues in women's lives, but—more important—encourage change and growth. We are particularly interested in creative works by women writing from the periphery: fat women, Jewish women, lesbians, old women, women examining classism, women of color, women with disabilities, women who are writing books that help make the best in our lives possible. We want well-told stories that exhibit fine writing, are lively and engaging, and treat our lives with the honesty and complexity they deserve. The main characters and/or narrators must be women or address social justice issues.

Submission requirements and procedures:

If you wish us to read your manuscript, first send a query letter, including a synopsis of the work for our review, by e-mail only (spinster@spinstersink.com). If we want to review the work in greater depth, we will send you a letter asking for two to five chapters (depending on length-should not exceed 50 pages or five chapters) of the work itself. Include a self-addressed, stamped postcard which we will return to you, letting you know that we received the material. Also, include a self-addressed, stamped envelope in which we'll respond to you when we've finished reading your materials. If the preliminary work looks suitable to us, we will ask you to send us the entire manuscript.

Please do not send anything—neither the query materials or the manuscript itself—by certified mail or return receipt requested.

Do allow at least three months to review your manuscript. Depending on our workload and availability of staff, we will get to your submission as quickly as possible and give it the thorough attention it deserves.

At the top of each manuscript page should be written the chapter number, the page number, and your last name.

If you have submitted your work to other publishers, please do us the courtesy of informing us of this and notifying us immediately if another publisher begins to give the manuscript serious consideration. We have no intention of "competing" with our publishing colleagues, so please don't put us in this position.

If you are offered a contract:

If you are offered a contract, we will go through it in detail with you. We can recommend reading resources to help you understand publishing contracts, and we encourage you to check with an attorney if you desire.

Spinsters Ink pays for all production costs of the books we publish. Because we are a small press, we cannot afford to pay advances or provide travel allowances for promoting your book. However, we do extensive publicity both prior to and after publication. Your royalties are a percentage of the sales of the books and of the sale of subsidiary rights, such as foreign translations and television and film rights.

When your contract is signed, we will determine a publication schedule for your book. This includes editing, text design, cover design, proofreading, and marketing. Generally, a book is published about 12 to 18 months after the contract is signed.

Call us with any questions you may have.

Categories: Fiction—Nonfiction—Feminism—Lesbian—Mystery—Women's Fiction—Women's Issues—Social Justice

CONTACT: Acquisitions Editor
Material: All
191 University Blvd., #300
Denver CO 80206
Phone: 303-761-5552
E-mail: spinster@spinsters-ink.com

SPS Studios, Inc.,

Please refer to Blue Mountain Arts, Inc.

Square One Publishers

Square One is an independent Long Island-based publisher of adult nonfiction trade books. Our books are aimed at people who are looking for the best place to start. We focus on providing titles that are accessible, accurate, and interesting. We look for intelligently written, informative titles that have a strong point of view, and that are authored by people who know their subjects well.

To submit your manuscript proposal to us, we ask that you include the following:

• a cover letter telling us about your book, its market, and your own background.

• a table of contents detailing each chapter in one or two paragraph summary.

• a two- or three-page introduction that provides an overview of your book's topic, its approach, and its goal(s).

• a self-addressed stamped envelope. If you wish the proposal returned, make sure the envelope is big enough to accommodate your material and that you have included sufficient return postage. If you wish nothing returned and you want a speedy reply, provide us with your email address.

Responses to submissions are generally sent within two weeks of receipt.

Before submitting your proposal, we strongly suggest you peruse our website (squareonepublishers.com) to determine if our house is truly right for your book.

Categories: Nonfiction—Collectibles—Cooking—Crafts/Hobbies—Games—Money & Finances—New Age—Paranormal—Parenting—Reference—Self Help—Singles—Writing

CONTACT: Acquisitions Editor
Material: All
115 Herricks Rd.
Garden City Park NY 11040
Phone: 516-535-2010
Fax: 516-535-2014

St. Bede's Publications

We are a small Roman Catholic publishing company owned and operated by a monastery of Benedictine nuns. Our major interests are in the areas of monastic sources and spirituality and patristics. Most of our books are in the areas of theology and philosophy, prayer and spirituality. We do not publish fiction and only rarely do we publish poetry.

Please do not send your entire manuscript unless requested. We prefer to receive an inquiry first, at which time you may submit a summary of your book, table of contents and a few sample chapters. If we are interested, we will request the full manuscript. Faxed proposals will not be considered.

Manuscripts should be formatted with at least 1½" margins on all four sides. Please use the same typewriter or printer font for the entire manuscript. All pages should be numbered consecutively. The first line of each paragraph should be indented one-half inch. Sketches, photographs and other art that is to be included must be submitted with the manuscript. Authors should submit a short biographical sketch and a précis of their book. If we accept the manuscript for publication, we will require two copies.

We prefer *The Chicago Manual of Style*, but any major style manual is acceptable as long as the manuscript is consistent. If your manuscript is accepted, we can accept, along with the hard copy, computer disks in IBM-compatible format. The computer files must be exactly the same as the printed copy.

If your manuscript is accepted, the final copy must be in perfect condition before it goes into production. Any alterations made in the text after page proofs will be charged against author royalties.

Categories: Nonfiction—Christian Interests—Religion—Spiritual—Catholic

CONTACT: Mother Mary Clare Vincent, President
Material: All
PO Box 545
Petersham MA 01366-0545
Phone: 978-724-3213
Website: www.stbedes.org

Stackpole Books

Thank you for requesting our submission guidelines. Authors send us ideas for books in lots of forms, but we especially appreciate the query, and here's why:

For you, it's a quick way to find out whether we're interested in your idea before you take the time to write a book about it. For us, it's a quick way to decide whether your idea fits among the other books already on our list and those we've planned for the future, and whether what you have in mind and what we're looking for are similar.

Even if the idea you send isn't a book for Stackpole, your query might spark one that you and we could develop together, or it could show us that you'd be able to do another book for which we've been trying to find the right author. We hope that following the suggestions we've made below not only can help you convince the editor who looks over your proposal that it's worth pursuing but also will help you hone your thoughts about your subject.

First of all, send your query to an individual editor by name rather than to the Stackpole offices or to the editors in general. Describe briefly and clearly what the book is about, who and how large your target audience is, what qualifies you to write the book (including samples of previously published work if you have them), what other books are on the market that will compete with yours, and how yours differs from them. Include a sentence outline describing the contents of the book, and describe the physical book as you envision it. We also like to see sample photographs and illustrations if you have them. If you've already written the manuscript, send only a sample chapter or two, along with the other information.

Of course, when you submit a query, you may not have all of that information. However, the more you can supply, the better, because you must sell your idea to the editor, who, if she's convinced, must in turn sell it to the other editors and the sales department.

No, it's not a simple process, for you or for us. But one of the most pleasant aspects of our jobs as editors is opening the daily mail, anticipating potential books. So we look forward to hearing from you and to seeing your work.

Categories: Nonfiction—Fishing—History—Military—Outdoors—Regional—Sports/Recreation

CONTACT: Judith Schnell
Material: Outdoor Sports and Fly Fishing
CONTACT: Mark Allison
Material: Nature
CONTACT: Christopher Evans
Material: History
CONTACT: Col. Edward Skender
Material: Military Reference
CONTACT: Kyle Weaver
Material: Pennsylvania
5067 Ritter Rd.
Mechanicsburg, PA 17055
Phone: 717-796-0411
Fax: 717-796-0412
Website: www.stackpolebooks.com

Staplegun Press
Poetry that humps your leg.

• submissions of poetry/art/photos/reviews welcome year-round. 5 total pieces or less.
• name & address on every page.
• must have sufficient return postage for reply.
• no longer accepting e-mail submissions.
• contributors will receive a free copy of the magazine and a nice pat on the ass.
• staplegun press hits about 3-4 times a year, depending on lunar cycle and drug intensity.
Categories: Poetry

CONTACT: Scott Gordon, Editor/Publisher
Material: All
PO Box 190184
Birmingham AL 35219
Phone: 205-933-4025
E-mail: staplegunp@bham.rr.com

Starscape

Please refer to Tom Doherty Associate, LLC, in the Book Publishers section.

Steeple
Hill™

Steeple Hill Love Inspired

Please refer to Harlequin, in the Book Publishers section.

Stenhouse Publishers

As you're thinking about writing a book for publication by Stenhouse Publishers, this information is designed to encourage you, and help you proceed in a manner that will increase your chances of being published.

If you've never before written a book - or even submitted a proposal to publish a book - the process and prospects may seem daunting, if not downright frightening. In fact, while you are reading this, you may be thinking of a dozen other things you need to do before you start writing. Well, washing the dishes, mowing the lawn and paying the bills can wait. This is the time to start writing. You are in fact risking rejection, but rejection isn't the worst fate in life. Even if your proposal isn't accepted or your manuscript isn't published, you will have learned some valuable lessons that you can carry forward to your next attempt. And if your proposal and manuscript are accepted, you will have accomplished something to be proud of. Linda Rief knew it was time to start writing when she found herself vacuuming her pocket book. The outcome was *Seeking Diversity*, a wonderful book about teaching language arts with adolescents.

So, where to begin? A logical starting place is the proposal. The point of the proposal is to help you figure out what you want your book to be, to say, to accomplish, and you probably will be surprised by some of the ideas that emerge. There's nothing like writing to find out what you want to say.

The proposal also has a second purpose - and a second audience. You are writing to answer basic questions likely to be asked by any publisher reviewing the proposal. *These questions include the following:*
• What is this book to be about?
• What is its intended audience?
• What writing style will you use?
• How will your book be organized?
• What books have been written on this subject, and how will yours differ?
• Who are you?
• How long do you anticipate the manuscript will be?
• How much have you already written?
• When do you expect to finish the manuscript - or a first draft?
• Will your book include samples of student writing, drawing or other work?

Of course, we understand that every proposal has its own wrinkles and specific questions; try to anticipate and pre-empt as many of these as you can. Remember that your proposal may be our first exposure to the idea you're offering. You can't assume that we understand very much. For example, you may submit a journal article that forms the basis of your manuscript; or, the article may be written in an academic style and you are intending to rewrite it as Chapter 4 of your book. We don't know; so explain exactly what you plan to do to any writing you submit, including stylistic changes you will make.

Here are a few other considerations in preparing your proposal and manuscript:
• Print everything double spaced. Your submission should be readable, not fancy. And please number the pages, either by hand or computer.
• Don't worry about submitting computer disks at this point. However, we will be interested in them later.
• If your project is accepted, you will need written permission for any student work that appears in the book. Photographs of students also require signed releases. And, if you are planning to reproduce extracts, poems, or illustrations from published books, you will need written permission from the copyright holder.
• Finally, if you are writing in detail about the classroom practices of other teachers, it is both courteous and prudent to show them what you plan to publish.
• We hope you will write the most complete proposal you can. If we are interested in your proposal but still have questions, we'll ask. For instance, if you haven't yet written any of the manuscript, we

Books
M-Z

would ask to see a sample chapter or two if we think the proposal looks promising.

• Which brings us to the next step. After you've submitted your proposal you can expect first to receive a brief acknowledgment notice. We may call or write with questions, or we may notify you that we've decided, regretfully, that your book is not what we're looking for.

• On the other hand, we may decide to send your proposal directly to one or more readers for their responses. These readers may be teachers who are familiar with your topic and/or target audience, or they may be other professionals with experience and expertise that qualifies them to assess your ideas. This stage of the process almost always takes longer than you would wish; like you, these people are trying to squeeze this project into their busy lives.

• After we receive the readers' responses, we must decide whether any particular project is a "yes," a "yes, if . . . ," a "maybe," or a "no." A request for more material is an encouraging response that falls into the "maybe" category. On the other hand, please don't consider "no" as an indication that we judge your work unsuitable; it only means that it doesn't meet our present needs as publishers. Don't give up - on us or on writing.

• Which brings us back to the beginning: Relax, give this project your best effort and get it done. The only proposals we will never accept are the ones we don't receive.

• The rest of the material in this packet consists of a sample cover letter and a sample proposal. We've included these as examples of how one author has chosen to present her material. You will see that she has written a rather detailed cover letter and a detailed chapter outline; a brief cover letter, overview, and chapter outline would also be an acceptable way to fashion a proposal. We did not want this packet to deter you with its sheer size, so we didn't include a sample chapter or vita; a brief vita can be helpful.

Enough. Now, start writing and good luck. We hope to hear from you soon.

Best wishes,
Philippa Stratton, Editorial Director, Stenhouse Publishers
Categories: Education

CONTACT: William Varner, Senior Editor
Material: All
477 Congress St Ste 4B
Portland ME 04101-3417
Phone: 207-253-1600
Website: www.stenhouse.com

Stipes Publishing, LLC

Frequently Asked Questions

1. Does Stipes finance the publication? Yes. We pay all costs involved. The author has no financial obligation. Our obligation extends for all costs involved in the manufacture and distribution of the book. All of the risk involved is ours. We also pay a royalty twice a year.

2. Does Stipes market books nationally? Yes. Our books are sold through over 2,500 bookstores throughout the world. Four of our books have over 300 college adoptions and dozens of our books have from 20 to 250 adoptions.

3. Is Stipes interested in publications which are not for national distribution? Yes. Many of our publications are designed for use by an author for a specific course at his or her school. Some of these publications are course outlines, syllabi, or specialized materials developed for a particular course. The feasibility of such an arrangement depends upon the number of students involved. It would normally require over 150 students per year. If enough students are involved, revisions can be made from year to year and in some cases even more frequently.

4. Will Stipes work with material in its developmental stage? Yes. We frequently work with an author on a preliminary edition. Our requirements for the size of a printing are small enough that such an arrangement allows for revisions and additions after a short period of time. Until the book is in final form, it is usually used at only the author's own campus or possibly a few others. After it has evolved into a final publication, it can be marketed nationally.

5. Would Stipes be interested in working on a publication which is under contract to another publisher? With the approval of the other publisher, we have worked on preliminary editions of another publisher's book. In such a case, the author is enabled to use the material in the classroom for a few years before it is released for publication in a final edition.

6. What types of formats and bindings does Stipes offer? We are in no way limited in this sense. The economy involved is the only limitation. Some of our publications are cloth, some with standard wraparound paperback binding (perfect binding), some with spiral wire and plastic binding, and some with a specially designed binding that allows for tearout sheets.

7. Will Stipes permit photographs and other illustrations? Yes. All types can be used, including 4-color illustrations. Here again, economy is the only limitation.

8. Will my publication be reasonably priced? Yes. Very few publishers have their own printing facilities. We do have our own complete facilities. On occasion, we will farm out work the way most publishers do for all of their publications. However, our prices are based on our normal costs, which do not include a "middleman" mark-up that many publishers must include.

9. What sort of manuscript preparation is required? We have no magic formula. All we require is that the manuscript is legible. We can work directly from any type of computer disk. We usually request that the author supply us with a hard copy in addition to the disk. We also frequently work from camera-ready copy provided by the author.

10. Will I get help in the preparation of my manuscript? Yes. We work closely with our authors. We are not a giant corporation, and we feel that our personal working relationship with our authors is the essence of our business. We do not presume to be expert in each of our authors' fields. However, we can give some editorial assistance and arrange for critical evaluations if the author desires us to do so.

11. Can disks or CD's be included with my book? Yes, we include these media. We usually insert them in a pocket attached to the inside front or back cover and shrinkwrap the book.

12. Will Stipes take care of obtaining permissions to use copyrighted materials which I have included in my manuscript? Yes. We will contact the copyright holder and obtain all necessary permissions. We also pay any required permission fees. When we are faced with unusually high permission fees, we consult with the author before proceeding.

13. Will my publication be copyrighted? Yes. It can be copyrighted either in our name or that of the author. In addition, all books that are marketed nationally are listed in the various publications such as Books in Print that are used throughout the country to facilitate finding and ordering a book.

14. Can I obtain references regarding Stipes? Yes. We are more than happy to refer you to any of our authors. We have authors on campuses from coast to coast and in Canada. We feel that the goodwill we have with our authors is our greatest asset. Please do ask us for references.

15. Will I lose control over my manuscript once it is turned over to Stipes? No. We do not presume to make reprintings, revisions, editorial changes, or other changes without the author's consent. No decision regarding the handling of your book, manual, syllabus, or outline will be made without your consent.

16. How quickly can my book be produced? Because we have our own facilities, we are able to rush books through our plant. Sometimes we have been able to get a book out in a matter of two to three weeks. However, normal scheduling requires that we have two to four months. This is flexible, and we will be happy to do our best to accommodate your needs.

17. How long has Stipes been in the publishing business? We have been in business for over 60 years.

18. How many titles does Stipes have? We have more than 300 titles.

19. What is the standard Stipes royalty? Our standard royalty is 15% of the list price.

20. How will my book be distributed? Stipes publications are sold through all normal publishing outlets, including your local campus bookstores.

21. What kind of information can I furnish Stipes for evaluation of the commercial potential of the material? See the "Prospectus Guideline" below.

Prospectus Guidelines

This outline is intended to provide a general frame of reference for evaluation of the commercial potential of your material. Please discuss with us any questions it may arouse, or any concerns you may have about preparing material for review.

I. MARKET CONSIDERATIONS
A. General Market
   1. What course is the text intended for?
   2. What are the prerequisites for the course?
B. Market Segment
   1. What segment of the market is your text designed for?
   2. Discuss which competing books will be closest to your text in level and appeal.

II. THE TEXT
A. Brief Description
   1. In one or two paragraphs describe the work, its rationale, approach, and point of view.
B. Outstanding Features
   1. List briefly what you consider to be the outstanding features of the work.
C. Apparatus
   1. Please outline the pedagogical elements of a typical chapter.
   2. Please discuss all the ancillary items you feel will be needed to publish a competitive text.
D. Competition
   1. Identify the leading texts and briefly discuss their main strengths and weaknesses compared to your text.
   2. What aspects of your topical coverage are similar to or different from the competition?

III. STATUS OF THE TEXT
A. Schedule for completing the text
   1. When do you expect to have a completed manuscript?
B. Length
   1. What is the goal for the page length of a bound text?
   2. What is the estimate of the length of text in manuscript pages?
C. Competition
   1. Do you intend to class-test the material?

IV. STATUS OF THE GRAPHICS
A. Layout features
   1. What special layout features (spot color, shadings, gradients, bleeds) do you plan to employ?
B. Illustrations
   1. How many illustrations, photos and line-drawings (graphs and diagrams) do you plan to include? C. How are these illustrations generated, and in what form will they be submitted?

V. ADDITIONAL MATERIALS
A. Annotated Table of Contents
   1. A detailed outline provides reviewers with a sense of how the material will be organized and developed.
B. Vita
   1. We would appreciate a current vita.
C. Sample chapters
   1. Sample chapters need not be chronological – it would be advisable to prepare the chapters you feel initially most comfortable in writing.

Categories: Nonfiction—Agriculture—Architecture—Business—Ecology—Engineering—Gardening—Music—Sports/Recreation—Technical—Textbooks

CONTACT: Robert Watts, Partner
Material: Music, Ag, Business, Horticulture
CONTACT: Benjamin H. Watts, Partner
Material: Technical, Architecture, Sports, Ecology
PO Box 526
Champaign IL 61824-0526
Phone: 217-356-8391
E-mail: stipes@soltec.net
Website: www.stipes.com

Stone Bridge Press

General guidelines for submitting proposals and manuscripts to Stone Bridge Press are listed below. These guidelines may not apply to every project; please use your best judgment as to which items are appropriate to include with your submission. If there is any question as to the suitability of your book for Stone Bridge Press, please consider sending us a detailed letter of inquiry first. If you want to make an electronic submission via e-mail, read this important information first!

IMPORTANT: Stone Bridge Press is no longer accepting original fiction manuscripts for review.

Proposals for publication ideally should include items from the following checklist:

___(1) A one-page cover letter summarizing what the book is, who it's for, and why it's useful, important, necessary, or unique.

___(2) An expanded table of contents, chapter by chapter with summaries. Indicate what will be included in the front- and backmatter (introduction, preface, bibliography, glossary, index, etc.).

___(3) For fiction or translation, at least two sample chapters. For non-fiction, an introduction and one sample chapter, or two sample chapters.

___(4) Estimated manuscript length and completion date (if it's still incomplete). Indicate how the manuscript is being prepared (typewriter? word processor? If you're using a computer, what platform and what program?).

___(5) Number of illustrations and what kind (line drawings, black and white photographs, color, etc.). Are there any special production requirements? Please provide representative samples so we can judge for quality: use high-grade photocopies for samples of line drawings, glossy prints for black and white photos, and transparencies for color photos (always send dupes, not originals, unless requested otherwise).

___(6) Information about you. Include a c.v. if you have one, and indicate your qualifications to write on your subject.

___(7) A discussion of the size of the market for your book and how the book compares to its competition. What makes it different/better? What are you prepared to do to promote the book (very important!)? Do you know others in your field who will provide reviews or testimonials?

___(8) Your financial and scheduling requirements, if any.

Mail your submission to P.O. Box 8208, Berkeley, CA 94707.

IMPORTANT!!!! If you require a certificate of delivery or are using Express Mail or a delivery service like UPS, DO NOT USE THE POST OFFICE BOX ADDRESS AND MAKE THE EDITOR STAND IN LINE; instead PLEASE use our street address: 1393 Solano Avenue, Suite C, Albany, CA 94706.

ELECTRONIC SUBMISSIONS: In principle we support use of the Internet for correspondence and submissions. However, we do NOT accept attachments from people unknown to us. So if you've got an idea you think we might be interested in, send a simple email query to us first. If you want us to see some of your work, embed a short sample within your e-mail message (that is, do not include it as an attachment). Detailed proposals with supporting information are welcome. If we do invite you to send an attached manuscript sample, you should send it as either ASCII text or as MS Word. WordPerfect? Fuggedaboutit! We prefer Macintosh files.

Please note that we are primarily interested in books with a Japan connection (however tenuous). If you have genre fiction, like science fiction, war stories, mysteries, and romances, or commercial fiction, you probably shouldn't be talking to us at all. (As of January 2003, we are no longer accepting original fiction manuscripts for review.)

No materials can be returned to you unless you provide us with sufficient return postage.

Thanks for writing. We look forward to hearing from you.

Categories: Nonfiction—Arts—Asian-American—Business—Careers—Culture—Film/Video—Language—Reference—Special Interest (Japan)—Travel

CONTACT: The Editors
Material: All
PO Box 8208
Berkeley, CA 94707
For Deliveries:
1393 Solano Ave, Ste. C
Albany, CA 94706
Phone: 510-524-8732
Fax: 510-524-8711
E-mail: sbpedit@stonebridge.com
Website: www.stonebridge.com

Storey Publishing, LCC

The mission of Storey Publishing is to serve our customers by publishing practical information that encourages personal independence in harmony with the environment. We seek to do this in a positive atmosphere that promotes editorial quality, team spirit, and profitability.

The books we select to carry out this mission include titles on gardening, small-scale farming, building, homebrewing, crafts, part-time business, home improvement, woodworking, animals, nature, natural living, personal care, and country living.

We are always pleased to review new proposals, which we try to process expeditiously. We offer both work-for-hire and standard royalty contracts.

If you have ideas for a book on any of the subjects in our line, and if you are intrigued by the philosophy expressed in our mission statement, we hope you will think of Storey Publishing.

Please include the following information:
• A Letter of Introduction.
• A one-paragraph description of your book idea. What is the "hook" for your book? Why is it unique? Examples: "Finally, a natural health-oriented body care and personal grooming book focused on the particular needs and interests of men" (*Body Care Just for Men*); "Hands-on birding: How you can attract wild birds to come and feed right from your hand?" (*Hand-Feeding Backyard Birds*).
• A brief statement explaining why you think your book is needed and describing the potential readers of the book. Answer the question, "Who will buy this book and why?"
• A list of recent books (if any) that are similar to your own, with an explanation of how yours will be different and better. Give the competition for your book by listing books published within the last three years. Include title, author, page count, retail price, publisher, and description.
• A paragraph about yourself and your credentials for writing the book you are proposing, (you may also wish to include your resume).
• A table of contents, including a brief description of each chapter.
Some of your thoughts about the length, general appearance, and photographic and illustrative requirements of the book.
• A sample of your writing from previous books or magazines.
• A sample chapter from the proposed book.
Storey is also looking for authors of our popular *Country Wisdom*

Bulletins. Each 32-page bulletin provides valuable, in-depth, how-to coverage on a single topic with in-depth information and illustrations. We have over 150 widespread topics available now, and are always pleased to review proposals for new *Country Wisdom Bulletins*. Please address inquiries and proposals to: Nancy Ringer, Bulletin Program Manager.

Categories: Nonfiction—Agriculture—Animals—Architecture—Arts—Cooking—Crafts/Hobbies—Gardening—Hobbies—How-to

CONTACT: Deborah Balmuth
Material: Building and mind/body/spirit
CONTACT: Deborah Burns
Material: Equine
CONTACT: Gwen Steege
Material: Gardening
CONTACT: Dianne Cutillo
Material: Cooking, wine, and beer
CONTACT: Nancy Ringer
Material: Animals, nature, natural health and beauty, home reference and crafts
210 Mass MoCA Way
North Adams MA 01247
Phone: 802-823-5200
Fax: 802-823-5819
Website: www.storey.com

Stylus Publishing, LLC

Stylus is an independent publisher, and the distributor of independent publishers. *We meet the needs of:*
• Teachers, faculty developers and administrators in higher education
• Trainers and HRD professionals
• Development and third world practitioners, policy makers and academics
• Teachers and researchers in the humanities and social sciences
• Teachers from pre-school through high school

A clear, well thought out proposal is the key to getting a project considered by a publisher. We recommend taking time over your proposal, to think through the guidelines and questions that follow, and to give yourself the opportunity for reflection and second thoughts. The process of refining your focus and ideas will also help smooth the writing process.

Bear in mind that the market for books and information is highly competitive, and that as authors and publishers we need to focus on filling real needs, or developing new ideas, information, solutions or concepts which have real value for our audiences.

THE PROPOSAL
The proposal should cover all the following issues, many of which overlap, in the sequence that's most logical for your project.

1. Title
A good title sends a clear signal to your intended audience about your goals. It is also a vital element in marketing and differentiating your book from others. A good final title may only emerge during the writing process, so we're happy to begin with a "working" title.

2. Description, scope and purpose
Explain your subject matter and provide a rationale for why your project is timely and why it will appeal to your intended audience. Describe the scope and topics which will be covered. What are you contributing to the subject, and how broad an interest do you envisage?

If the project is an edited collection, a coherent focus is important. Discuss how you propose to achieve the cohesion and describe individual contributors' chapters in this light.

3. Audience
Be as specific as possible in terms of academic discipline or job title, level, type of institution/company. Distinguish between primary

and secondary audiences, and consider specific geographical appeal if relevant (e.g. likely interest in specific regional or national markets). If you're proposing a textbook, specify level and courses, and give an estimate of market size.

4. Need

Define the need your book will meet or create. Why will people buy it? What does it do, or do in a new way, that meets the need of your intended audience? Will it significantly add to a body of knowledge, or significantly improve practices?

5. Competition

List competing and related works (giving author, title, publisher, year and price) and explain specifically how your book differs or improves upon the competition. Bear in mind that competition may include materials available in journal form or available electronically. State whether price, timing or format issues are critical.

6. Qualifications & related activities

Although this may duplicate information in your resume / curriculum vitae, highlight the work you've done which is relevant to this project. Also let us know if you lecture outside your institution, give presentations at meetings, are otherwise involved with information media related to the subject of your book (are you on the board of a journal; an owner of a listserv?), or active in a relevant organization or association. If you have plans to present at meetings in the next 12 months, let us know. Do you have influential contacts in your field you might be willing to give a pre-publication endorsement? Do you have contacts in relevant media?

In an environment where so much information competes for our limited time, an author's participation in publicizing his or her book can make a major difference to sales. With an edited volume, provide similar key information on contributors.

7. Table of contents

Provide a line or two of description with each chapter title. Your comments on sequence and organization may be helpful.

8. Format, length, special features

Let us know if you have specific ideas about format: traditional book? binder product? electronic component? Provide an estimate of length in terms of printed pages (approx. 360 words to a printed page). Does the book need illustrations? Are there any unusual features?

9. Timetable

Give an estimate for completion of manuscript. Are there any factors which should influence publication date? Do you have commitments which may delay delivery?

ACCOMPANYING MATERIAL

We ideally like to see proposals accompanied by:

1. A writing sample

A draft chapter or introduction, or recent article by you on the topic, but not a complete manuscript. With an edited work, are you familiar with the contributors' writings, and are you confident they will follow your guidelines as editor?

2. Resume / curriculum vitae

We look forward to hearing from you.

Categories: Nonfiction—Campus Life—Education

CONTACT: John Von Knorring, Publisher
Material: Higher Education/Training
22883 Quicksilver Dr.
Sterling VA 20166
Phone: 703-661-1504
Fax: 703-661-1501
Website: www.styluspub.com

Success Publishing

Formal guidelines not available.
Send queries or book proposals to below address.

CONTACT: Allan Smith
Material: All
3419 Dunham Rd.
Warsaw NY 14569
Phone: 585-786-5663

Sulgrave Press

Please refer to Howell Press, Inc.

Sunbelt Publications

Sunbelt Publications, incorporated in 1988 with roots in the book business since 1973, produces and distributes publications about "Adventures in Natural History and Cultural Heritage of The Californias." These include multi-language pictorials, natural science and outdoor guidebooks, histories and regional references, and stories that celebrate the land and its people.

Our publishing program focuses on the Californias, today three states in two nations sharing one Pacific shore. Sunbelt books help to discover and conserve the natural and historical heritage of unique regions on the frontiers of adventure and learning.

GUIDELINES FOR PROSPECTIVE SUNBELT AUTHORS

Thank you for your interest in publishing with us. Please review the following information, and call for clarification or further information.

Categories and Content

We specialize in regional travel and reference, guidebooks, natural science, and outdoor adventure in California, Baja California, and the Southwest U.S. Our publishing program focuses on "Adventure in the Natural History and Cultural Heritage of the Californias." A marketable non-fiction title generally includes photos and illustrations (e.g., maps, artwork, diagrams, tables), all with captions that enhance understanding of the text. Natural history and guidebooks require substantial map work.

A goal of our publishing program is to contribute to the body of knowledge about selected disciplines or

topics (e.g., San Diego region, Baja California, introductory earth science). To this end, we highly encourage you to review Sunbelt books related to your topic and cite them as appropriate in your manuscript. We will loan copies of these books to local authors or you may purchase them for research purposes at 40% off retail prices.

Quantitative Guidelines

Sunbelt titles generally have about 200 pages of main text with approximately 400 words per formatted page, not including front matter (e.g. table of contents, title page) or back matter (e.g. bibliography, index). A design guideline is to have a photo, illustration, or chapter heading every three pages.

Query Letter

Authors are advised to query first with their idea/concept before submitting the initial proposal. Queries should be short, succinct, and focus on what makes the proposed work unique, as well as publishable and marketable. Authors may query via email to jredmond@sunbeltpub.com or send a single-page query letter to Jennifer Redmond, Publications Coordinator, Sunbelt Publications, 1250 Fayette Street, El Cajon, CA 92020. Please do not query, or follow up on queries already sent, by telephone. Queries may be followed up by email or U.S. mail, if no answer has been received within 60 days. **Materials submitted will not be returned unless accompanied by SASE with sufficient postage.**

Initial Proposal

Once contacted, the author shall send the proposal. This includes the General Outline (see below), a brief discussion of the target market for the title and the author's qualifications, comments on complementary or competing titles currently on the market, and sample illustrations and/or photographs (if applicable). Include comments on author's commitment to promotion as noted below under "Teamwork." Proposals may be followed up by email or U.S. mail, if no answer has been received within 60 days. **Materials submitted will not be returned unless accompanied by SASE with sufficient postage.**

General Outline (for natural history, guidebooks, and histories)

Foreword-by the publisher or a topical authority.

Preface-to the book, its genesis, authorship and contributors, and niche.

Introduction-to the subject matter, geared to the target market.

Text-including illustrations and photos with captions.

• Natural history chapters (e.g. biology)

          b. Cultural history chapters (e.g. pioneers)

• Outdoor recreation chapters (e.g. trail logs)

References-geared to the target market (including related Sunbelt books).

Appendices-supplementary or technical material.

Glossary-May also be integrated into index or as "sidebars."

Index-every occurrence of proper names, key words and concepts (author's responsibility after final page proof).

General Outline (for literary non-fiction)

Text-synopsis and 2 sample chapters mandatory for all works of literary non-fiction and applicable fictional works (e.g. memoirs, historical fiction, regional short story collections).

Teamwork in Title Development and Marketing

The appropriate and profitable relationship between author and publisher is "teamwork" whereby both contribute to the production and promotion process. Promotional opportunities include written and online reviews, bookstore signings, author lectures, field trips (if applicable), media features and interviews (newspapers, magazines, radio and television), and brochure mailings to selected lists. Authors are expected to actively promote their book by following guidelines established for author signings and interviews, especially during the crucial 6 months after release. Authors are also encouraged to write articles for publication that will stimulate interest in the sale of their book, and to suggest promotional ideas or events. An active partnership is key to a successful sell-through of your book.

Materials Received from Author

• Once instructed to submit their full manuscript for evaluation, author supplies final text electronically together with identical hard copy. The preferred format for electronic files is Microsoft Word (Courier font). Hard copy should be double-spaced, single sided, in 11 point text. Author supplies camera-ready artwork, illustrations, and photographs at or above minimum standards of the appropriate profession (e.g. cartography).

Rights and Permissions

• Copyright is assigned to the publisher with exclusive permission to publish and distribute the work in all media and in all formats. Publisher will edit, title, price, and package the work to maximize its marketability, consistent with maintaining the essential content of the work. Excerpts printed in other Sunbelt books, with full credit to the author, facilitate promotion of the original work. Author is fully responsible for the accuracy of information presented in the work.

• Author is responsible to procure and provide written permission for use of all non-owned material including photographs and illustrations and to pay for same if required. Owners of such material are often willing to grant permission gratis if credit is given. There is generally no fee for material published by public entities although written permission is required for all but U.S. government agencies (e.g. USGS). Sunbelt-owned photo files and other materials are generally available at no cost but with full credit. Permission to reprint material from periodicals must generally be granted by original author.

Price and Royalty

• Retail price is determined by the cost of production, marketing and royalty plus the publisher's best judgement of a title's price point with respect to similar titles in the market. Royalty is a percentage of net sale receipts (less returns and promotional copies) and is paid semi-annually with a statement of sales. Typical examples of the margins for a $14.95 retail book are:

High margin direct sale to consumer (e.g. direct mail/website sales):

Retail price to consumer (100%)	$14.95
Price to buyer (100%)	$14.95
Royalty to author (10% of $12.95)	$ 1.50

Medium margin sale to bookstores:

Retail price to consumer (100%)	$14.95
Publisher price to bookstore (60% of $12.95)	$11.22
Royalty to author (10% of $7.77)	$ 1.12

Low margin sale from publisher to wholesaler for resale to bookstores:

Retail price to consumer (100%)	$14.95
Publisher price to wholesaler (45% of $12.95)	$ 8.42
Royalty to author (10% of $5.83)	$ .84

AUTHOR COPIES

Ten complimentary copes are provided to the author. The author may purchase additional copies at 60% OF or 40% OFF the retail price (same as for bookstores) plus sales tax, unless author's valid certificate of resale is on file with Sunbelt. These copies may be resold in compliance with legal requirements and not-to-compete with Sunbelt bookseller customers. Additional copies are available to the author on consignment for lectures and other sales opportunities.

PUBLISHING PROCESS

• After submission of proposal and request to submit full manuscript, author submits manuscript and accompanying materials to publisher, who may accept it finally or conditionally. Acquisition committee considers content (which may include a technical review process), marketing, and financial aspects of proposed project.

• Author is contacted and informed of Publisher interest, and signs memorandum of understanding (MOU), and/or publishing agreement.

• If conditional, author revises work until final acceptance by publisher, which will be established by written memo, and submits hard copy and disk of approved manuscript and camera-ready supplementary materials (e.g. photos, illustrations, maps). Author changes are not accepted beyond this point.

• Publisher copyedits, designs, and typesets the work including interior, cover, and title. Author reviews copyedited version.

• Publisher develops and initiates marketing plan in collaboration with author.

• Galley proof (text and layout w/o illustrations) is shared with author for comments, time permitting.

• Page proof is produced including total interior and cover. Final total proofreading.

• Printer produces blue-line for publisher approval; delivers final bound product by ship date.

• Publisher commences distribution to booksellers.

• Official publication date is peak of launch marketing campaign, several months after ship date.

• Commence on-going marketing process.

• Reprint if successful.

MARKETING MATERIALS:

• Author will complete an "Author Questionnaire" once the contract is signed.

• Author will provide the publisher a photograph and negative that can be used for promotional   purposes.

• Author will follow "Book Signing Tips" and "Interview Tips" while promoting his book. (to be supplied by Sunbelt)

• Author provides a paragraph "About the Author" and "About the Book", suitable for marketing use.

Categories: Nonfiction—History—Outdoors—Recreation—Regional—Travel—Regional History

CONTACT: Jennifer Redmond, Acquisitions Editor
Material: All
1250 Fayette St.
El Cajon CA 92020
Phone: 619-258-4911
Website: www.sunbelt.com

Swan-Raven & Co.

Please refer to Granite Publishing Group, LLC

Swedenborg Foundation, Inc.
Chrysalis Books

A. Publishing History and Mission

The Swedenborg Foundation, Inc., was organized in 1849 and incorporated in 1850 as the American Swedenborg Printing and Publishing Company. Its original purpose was to print and distribute books by Emanuel Swedenborg (1688-1772), eighteenth-century scientist and visionary.

The Foundation operates as a nonprofit, educational, literary, and charitable organization, dependent on public support. Its mission is to make available materials that "foster an affirmative and increasingly broad engagement with the theological thought of Emanuel Swedenborg, especially among persons desiring to apply spiritual principles to life." To accomplish this mission, the Foundation has established two imprints : the Swedenborg Foundation imprint, for books written by or about Emanuel Swedenborg and his philosophy, and the Chrysalis Books imprint, for books intended for the general trade market; these work also incorporate Swedenborgian philosophy. Our publications are intended for three primary audiences:

1. Serious readers of Swedenborg. These books are published under the Swedenborg Foundation imprint.

2. Thoughtful persons seeking to broaden their spiritual insights and development, who may or may not identify with traditional religious organizations. These titles are intended for the general trade audience and are published under the Chrysalis Books imprint.

3. Scholars and teachers in the fields of Bible, theology, psychology and personal transformation studies, literature, and philosophy. These books are part of the "Swedenborg Studies" series and are published under the Swedenborg Foundation imprint.

B. Publication Program

The Foundation acquires quality manuscripts written for each of its audiences.

1. Books intended for either audience 1 (serious readers of Swedenborg) or audience 3 (scholars) must directly address the works of Emanuel Swedenborg. Audience 1 books should explain the philosophy of Emanuel Swedenborg and should show how that philosophy applies to living an ethical life. Books intended for audience 3 should analyze Swedenborg's writings from a comparative, historical, biographical, religious, or philosophical standpoint and should incorporate existing and up-to-date scholarship.

2. Books intended for audience 2 (general trade) should also incorporate the philosophy of Emanuel Swedenborg in an integral way but may also include the philosophy of other spiritual traditions and may fall into one of the following categories:

    a.Social concerns (such as stewardship of the earth, service to others)

    b. Personal growth and spirituality (self-help, recovery, meditation, or lifestyle issues)

    c. The spiritual dimension of reality from the perspective of art, nature, philosophy, or natural science.

C. The Book Proposal

A first step toward publication is the development of a book proposal. The proposal, in two to three pages, addresses several important questions:

1. What is the book about? A paragraph or two should describe the subject matter and the author's approach to writing about it.

2.How is the treatment of the subject different or unique from other books available in its field? Why was the manuscript written? In what ways does it incorporate a Swedenborgian theme or perspective?

3. For what audience or market is the book directed? Is there a special-interest group or market for whom the book might have appeal?

4. What is the anticipated or finished length of the book in manuscript pages and in approximate words? When will the completed manuscript be available for review?

5. What is the author's background or credentials for writing the book?

Academic or religious professionals may wish to send a resume. Include a list of publishing credits. The Foundation is open to publishing an author's first book, so lack of publishing experience is not a serious drawback.

In addition, the proposal should include an introductory letter, a detailed chapter-by-chapter outline (another two or three pages), a completed chapter or other sample of writing, and a stamped, self-addressed envelope (for the return of materials). It may also be sent via email. The author will receive an initial response from the senior editor on whether we are declining or interested in proceeding within a month of the proposal's arriving at our office. A final decision on whether the Foundation's Publication Committee wishes to read the completed manuscript may take as long as three months. Should the manuscript be requested, the Foundation asks for exclusive reviewer privileges.

D. Manuscript Format and Evaluation

If the Foundation is interested in evaluating the manuscript, the form for submitting copy is fairly standard. Submit two, unbound manuscripts. They should be typewritten, double-spaced (including any notes, bibliography, appendices, or other matter) on good-quality 8-1/2 x 11-inch white paper, with margins of at least one inch on all sides. Sending high-quality photocopies is acceptable, as are minor, neat corrections within the text. Experienced writers keep an extra copy of the entire manuscript in the unlikely event that it may be lost in handling. The Foundation assumes no liability for any materials submitted to it. Again, please include sufficient return postage.

The Foundation follows The Chicago Manual of Style, 14th ed. (University of Chicago Press) regarding questions of style and format. In preparing the manuscript, keep these points in mind:

1. The completed manuscript includes:

    a. title page (with the author's name exactly as desired in print)

    b. dedication page, if appropriate

    c. table of contents

    d. accompanying charts, tables, maps, photos or artwork, appendices, bibliography, and other matter

2. Number pages consecutively

3. Mark and fully document all quotations

4. Place notes (endnotes) in a separate section rather than on the page where the citation occurs

5. Clearly identify all biblical references, extracts from other sacred literature, or the writings of Swedenborg

Use inclusive language in the body of the text.

Once the manuscript is received, several types of evaluations must be made. This process can be quite lengthy, typically six to eight months, sometimes longer. Generally, the Foundation asks one or more readers familiar with the subject matter to read and critique the manuscript. Financial and marketing studies are also made to determine the expected cost for producing the book, a projected retail price, and the number of copies which must be sold over a given period to break even. Sometimes a reviewer or editor may suggest that certain

structural changes or redrafted passages will make the book stronger. Favorably reviewed manuscripts are accepted according to the overall quality of the book, the suitability for the publishing program of the Foundation, and anticipated market needs over the next several publishing seasons.

If, after reviewing the entire manuscript and on the advice of its readers, the Publications Committee accepts the book for publication, authors must also submit the draft manuscript in an electronic file. For transmission of an approved manuscript, the Foundation is best prepared to received text files using the Windows 95 version of Corel WordPerfect 8.

E. The Published Book

If the Foundation accepts the manuscript, the author will be asked to sign a formal agreement, or contract. This agreement gives the Foundation the exclusive right to publish and distribute the book. Book manuscripts designed to compete in the general religious trade are usually published on a royalty basis. In royalty contracts, the author is paid a percentage of the net income from the sale of the book, typically 10 percent. Sometimes an author might be paid a cash advance against future royalty earnings. The agreement also covers when the final manuscript is due, any special formatting requirements, copyright and subsidiary rights information, the number of free copies due the author, and other such matters.

Authors are responsible for obtaining the necessary permissions to quote at length from copyright-protected materials. Permissions must be obtained in writing, usually from a publisher, and submitted with the final draft of the manuscript. Photocopies of printed material from which quotes are taken may later be used for verification. The author is also asked to proofread galleys (typeset pages), and may be asked to prepare an index. Authors may also be asked to secure appropriate illustrative materials. On occasion, the author may be asked to contact agreed-upon persons to write a foreword or promotional statement.

Categories: Nonfiction—Lifestyle—Philosophy—Psychology—Religion—Spiritual

CONTACT: Mary Lou Bertucci, Senior Editor
Material: 320 North Church St.
West Chester PA 19380
Phone: 610-430-3222, ext. 11
E-mail: editor@swedenborg.com
Fax: 610-430-7982
Website: www.swedenborg.com

Sycamore Island Books

Please refer to Paladin Press.

Talewinds

Please refer to Charlesbridge Publishing.

Taylor Trade

Imprints: Cooper Square Press, Derrydale Press, Madison Books

Proposals should be limited to a query letter; an email will generate the quickest response. If querying by email, please note in the memo box "book proposal." Send no attachments unless requested. What we look for at this stage is suitability of the proposed book to our publishing program (see categories below) as well as the author's unique qualifications for writing his or her book.

Taylor Trade Publishing is especially interested in regional gardening, nature, field guides, cooking, sports, nature, self-help, Texana/Western history, general history and entertainment. We do not publish fiction or poetry. However, proposals from institutions such as museums or galleries pertaining to their collections are strongly encouraged.

Categories: Nonfiction—Cooking—Entertainment—Field Guides—Gardening—History—Nature—Self Help—Sports/Recreation—Texana/Western History

CONTACT: Editorial Assistant
Material: All
5360 Manhattan Circle, #100
Boulder, CO 80303
Phone: 303-543-7835
Fax: 303-543-0043
E-mail: aphillips@rowman.com
Website: www.taylor-trade.com

Temple University Press

Temple University Press invites inquiries and proposals that include a project overview, a tentative table of contents, and the author/editor's resume. Proposals might also include sample chapters or writing samples, but they are not required for an initial inquiry. Prospective authors are encouraged to contact the Editor-in-Chief by phone, e-mail or letter before sending completed manuscripts. Editors prefer to see double-spaced copy with no justification on the right margin and unbound pages. We do not accept electronic versions of proposals or manuscripts.

What Should You Send?

Apart from the cover letter and collateral material, editors strongly prefer to have all material typed and double-spaced. We do not accept project inquiries or proposed manuscripts on disk, and we prefer not to have extensive proposals sent by email. Please send only photocopies of art work; the Press cannot be responsible for one-of-a-kind materials.

For projects in the early stages of development, you might begin with a written inquiry or phone call to determine whether the topic is suited to Temple's editorial program. If you decide to send the proposal you have prepared, you should include a project overview, table of contents (with contributors' names, if appropriate), your c.v. or resume, and any available sample materials (e.g., abstracts, draft chapters, previously published work on a related topic, copies of illustrations).

If you would like to submit a completed or nearly completed manuscript, you should send a brief inquiry (by mail or email) or speak with an editor first to discuss the book's appropriateness for our list. When you send the manuscript, you should include your c.v. or resume as well as a cover letter that tells us whether you are also submitting it to other publishers. Manuscripts should come in the form of unbound pages so that we can easily photocopy them if we decide to send them out for review.

You are welcome to suggest possible readers for your proposal or manuscript; if you do, please supply their current affiliations. Please do not, however, contact the potential reviewers yourself. The editor will discuss your work and review process with you before deciding whether to send the project out for further evaluation.

An envelope with return postage is customary if you would like your materials returned to you in the event that we do not pursue the project.

To Which Editor?

If you have a project that you would like to submit to the Press, you can send an inquiry to Janet Francendese, Editor-in-Chief, or directly to the editor who seems to be responsible for acquisitions in your field. Our list is highly interdisciplinary, so the right choice is not always obvious. Be assured, though, that your project will soon find its way to the appropriate person.

Categories: Nonfiction—African-American—Animals—Asian-American—Biography—Culture—Dance—Drama—Disabilities—Ecology—Education—Family—Feminism—Film/Video—Gay/Lesbian—General Interest—Health—Hispanic—History—Jewish Interest—Law—Literature—Multicultural—Music—Politics—Psychology—Regional—Religion—Sexuality—Sports/Recreation—Television/Radio—Theatre—Women's Issues—Ethnic—Public Policy

CONTACT: Janet M. Francendese, Editor-in-Chief
Material: History, American Studies, Asian American Studies, African American Studies, Film, Music, Disability Studies, Animals and Culture
E-mail: francendesej@mail.temple.edu
CONTACT: Micah Kleit, Senior Acquisitions Editor
Material: American Studies, Media & Television Studies, Political & Social Theory, Sociology, Education, Religion.
E-mail: kleit@mail.temple.edu
CONTACT: Peter Wissoker, Senior Acquisitions Editor
Material: Labor Studies/International Political Economy, Urban Studies, Geography, Sociology, Political Science, and Information.
University Services 083-42
1601 North Broad St., USB 306
Philadelphia PA 191212-6099
Phone: 215-204-8787
Fax: 215-204-4719
Website: www.temple.edu/tempress

Ten Speed Press
Celestial Arts & Tricycle Press

If you wish to submit a book proposal to Ten Speed Press or Celestial Arts, please include:

• A cover letter detailing the work as a whole—including any and all information that you think we should have in order to make a decision about your project. In particular, be sure to tell us who your target audience is, and why.

• A chapter-by-chapter outline of the entire work.

• One or two sample chapters—whatever you consider to be enough material to give us a sense of the work as a whole. It is not necessary to send the entire manuscript.

• A brief bio or a note describing who you are and why you are the right person to write this book. Needn't be a formal resume.

• A self-addressed, stamped envelope with sufficient postage for the return of all of your material. Without this, we cannot return your materials to you.

• Do NOT send originals of anything. We are not liable for artwork or manuscript submissions.

A few helpful hints:

• Do familiarize yourself with our house and our list before submitting your manuscript.

• Provide a rationale for why we are the best publishing house for your work.

• If you're not sure which publisher would be best for your proposal, there are resources available. A particularly good one is *Writer's Market*, available at most libraries and bookstores.

• Thank you for your interest in Ten Speed Press or Celestial Arts. We look forward to reading your proposal soon. Be prepared to wait about six to eight weeks for a reply.

Children's book submissions, Tricycle Press

All Tricycle Press submissions are considered on an individual basis, although a personalized response is not always possible due to the volume of submissions we receive. Please note that we do accept simultaneous submissions.

DO NOT SEND ORIGINALS OR YOUR ONLY COPY OF ANYTHING. We are not liable for artwork or manuscript submissions.

Send an appropriate SASE.

Allow 8 to 20 weeks for a reply.

Be sure your work is appropriate for us. Familiarize yourself with our list by going to bookstores or libraries. We encourage you to request our catalogue by mailing a 9 x 12 envelope with three first class stamps postage (no checks or cash, please).

Correspondence regarding status of manuscripts should be done by mail—no phone calls, please.

Please do not send queries.

Activity Books: Ages 3 to 12. One-third to one-half of the manuscript is usually sufficient. Submit a table of contents or outline. Illustration ideas are often helpful but not necessary.

Novels for Young Readers: Ages 8 and up. If it is in chapters, please submit two to three sample chapters; otherwise one-third to one-half of the manuscript is usually sufficient. Also submit a table of contents or outline.

Picture Books: Ages 3 and up. Complete story is necessary; illustration ideas are often helpful but not necessary.

Real Life Books: (books about and for kids to help them understand themselves and their world; includes parenting books): Ages 3 to 13. If it is in chapters, please submit two to three sample chapters; otherwise one-third to one-half of the manuscript is usually sufficient. Also submit a table of contents or outline.

We encourage you to look at the following book: *Children's Writer's Market.*

Categories: Nonfiction—Agriculture—Animals—Business—Careers—Children—College—Cooking—Crafts/Hobbies—Diet/Nutrition—Food/Drink—Gardening—General Interest—Humor—Interview—Juvenile—Money & Finances—Outdoors—Recreation—Reference—Regional—Travel

CONTACT: The Editors
Material: All
PO Box 7123-S
Berkeley CA 94707
Phone: 510-559-1600
Fax: 510-559-1629
Website: www.tenspeed.com

Texas A&M University Press

ACQUISITION/SUBMISSION

The Press has established a respected list in several disciplines and will continue to build on those strengths by publishing books in the following fields: regional, military, and business history; natural history and related nature subjects; economics; agriculture; nautical archaeology; literature of Texas and the American West, including some works of short fiction and creative nonfiction; Texas art and photography; and women's, Borderlands, regional, and environmental studies.

If your manuscript or book idea seems to fit in one of these categories, or if you think it is on a subject the Press might wish to explore, your first step is to send a letter to the Press to describe the book you are writing or have written and the audience for which it is intended. With the letter, provide a table of contents, with a short synopsis of each chapter, as well as the introduction and another sample chapter if they are available.

We will respond to your query promptly to let you know if your book is a candidate for full consideration by the Press. If it is, we will invite submission of the full work, which should include an indication of illustrative materials that will be available. Do not send original photographs or art work at that time.

The manuscript will be evaluated first by the Press staff. If it seems appropriate to our list, we will then send it to outside reviewers-specialists in the field-who usually remain anonymous to the author. The outside readers will be asked to provide specific recommendations for revision of the manuscript, if such are necessary, as well as general comments on its overall potential. The review process may take several weeks. To speed the process you may offer a second copy of the manuscript.

We will provide copies of the readers' reports, and you will be given the opportunity to respond to them. If extensive revisions are recommended by the readers, we may ask that you make those revisions before we continue with the review process. If the manuscript receives favorable reviews and does not need revision, or if recommended revisions are satisfactorily handled, the manuscript will be brought before the Faculty Advisory Committee, which meets monthly, for their approval to publish. Once the manuscript is approved, the Press staff prepare a preliminary estimate of its publishing costs and then offer a contract.

When the manuscript has been approved by the Faculty Advisory Committee and revised to the Press's satisfaction, and the contract has been signed, submit two copies of the final revised manuscript and a disk containing the files of the manuscript, as well as all illustrative material and copies of all permissions. The manuscript should be submitted as flat, loose sheets-unfolded, unbound, and unstapled-in a box. A more detailed description of how to prepare the final manuscript, on paper and on disk, and illustrations is included later in this guide.

Publishers normally divide the year into two publishing seasons: spring/summer (February through July) and fall/winter (August through January). We must work well ahead-sometimes as much as two to four seasons-and take many factors into account before deciding which season would be the appropriate time to publish a particular book. Because of these complexities and the unique requirements of every book, there is no rule of thumb to determine how long after acceptance a manuscript can be put into production and, ultimately, be offered for sale. Be assured, though, that we make every effort to produce every book that bears our imprint in a timely manner.

COPYEDITING

The manuscript will be edited by a copy editor, and the author will review the edited manuscript. When the house editor has resolved all editorial issues with the author and prepared a manuscript "package" of the book's parts, the manuscript is ready to be designed. This process of copyediting, review, and resolution normally takes three to four months. More time is required for large or difficult books.

DESIGN AND PRODUCTION

A book designer will specify type and layout for the book and design a dust jacket. Although the specifications and jacket design are ultimately the designer's and the Press's prerogative, authors are welcome to make suggestions to their editors.

The manuscript will be typeset, and the author will then proofread the typeset pages and prepare an index within the time agreed to in the contract.

The Press staff will check all subsequent proofs. After the book is printed and the bindery ships the finished books, the author will be sent the number of complimentary copies stipulated in the contract. The entire production process, from design through shipment of the books, normally takes six to eight months. More time is needed for books that are large, very complex, or heavily illustrated.

MARKETING

Near the time a fully executed contract is returned to the Press offices, the author will receive an author information form from the marketing department.

Authors should give the items on that questionnaire prompt and careful attention. Detailed responses on this form not only help the marketing staff as they prepare promotion plans but also serve as a reference for the house editor and the Library of Congress.

Books are promoted through advertising, publicity, direct mail, exhibits, on-line, classroom adoption, and trade sales programs, supported by national and international sales representation. Books are also entered in appropriate award competitions.

POST-PUBLICATION

Authors should contact the Press's order department if they wish to buy copies of their book (Phone Orders: 800-826-8911, FAX: 409-847-8752). Press authors receive a 40 percent discount on any book that TAMU Press publishes (excluding limited editions).

Physical Preparation of the Manuscript

Manuscripts submitted to Texas A&M University Press should be prepared according to the guidelines given here. Even if the book is to be typeset from the author's diskettes, three hard (paper) copies of the manuscript are needed.

THE HARD COPY

• All elements of the manuscript (including indented quotations often or more lines, epigraphs, captions, notes, and bibliography) should be typed or printed double-spaced.

• All pages should be printed or typed with ten-pitch (i.e., pica) type if possible, and word-processed manuscripts should be printed with a letter-quality or near-letter-quality printer.

• Turn off the right-justification and proportional letter spacing features on word processors and printers before printing a manuscript; it is difficult to make an accurate character count of the manuscript when lines have been justified.

• Late corrections may be made on the final copy by neatly writing them above the line in which they should be inserted. Longer revisions may be inserted as separate pages. Pages that have been corrected and reprinted using a word processor should be matched carefully to the preceding and following pages to be sure the newly printed page does not drop or duplicate any lines. To match such pages, it may be necessary to insert a temporary hard page code.

COMPUTER DISKS

The Press requires that all manuscripts be submitted on 3½" disks and can work with the following IBM-compatible word processor formats: Microsoft Word, MultiMate, NotaBene, PFS:Write, Sprint, Wang PC (IWP), WordPerfect, WordStar, XyWrite. Acceptable Apple Macintosh formats include Microsoft Word, WordPerfect, and MacWrite II. "Text only" or "generic" files are also acceptable. If you use some other word processor, you should check with your editor to determine compatibility.

The following general guidelines are excerpted from a brochure produced by the Association of American University Presses.

• Prepare your manuscript on the same system-both hardware and software-from start to finish.

• Name files sequentially: chap01, chap02, etc. A list of file names submitted with your disks is helpful.

• Front matter, bibliography, and other apparatus should be in separate files. (In other words, do not put an entire manuscript in one file.)

• Notes should be grouped together in one or more separate files-not at the bottoms of pages or at the ends of chapters. If your word-processing software has the capability to do on-page (embedded) footnotes, please do not use it. Instead, use superscript callouts for note numbering. The notes should all be together, in a separate file or files, grouped and numbered by chapter, double-spaced and paragraph-indented, with no extra spaces between notes.

• Keep formatting to a minimum. Most if not all formatting must be removed before typesetting can begin, and this can be time-consuming or even unfeasible if it cannot be accomplished on a global basis. If you do use any formatting, make certain you are consistent.

• The hard copy of the manuscript and computer files must match exactly.

PARTS OF A MANUSCRIPT

Front Matter

The completed manuscript should contain a title page, dedication (if desired), book epigraph (if desired), table of contents, lists of any illustrations or tables, and a preface, acknowledgments, introduction, or foreword, if desired. Authors should note the differences between a preface, introduction, and foreword. In the preface the author gives details about the writing of the book; it may include brief acknowledgments. An introduction, as the name implies, introduces the subject of the book and background for that subject. A foreword is written by someone other than the author of the book. It provides another viewpoint and should attest to the book's value in the field.

Text

The text consists of all material through the end of the last chapter, epilogue, or postscript. If you use chapter epigraphs, keep them brief, citing only the author of the words quoted and perhaps the title of the work in which they appeared. Epigraphs should not be documented with endnotes or footnotes.

Back Matter

Back matter comprises the notes, bibliography, and any appendixes or glossary that will appear at the end of the book. In a manuscript, as opposed to a finished book, the last pages are usually tables and captions.

Page Numbers and Running Heads

Pages should be numbered consecutively through the manuscript, not by chapters. It is not necessary to add a running head (a top-of-the-page label such as chapter title or author's name) to the page number.

Elements to Be Aware of when Preparing a Manuscript
RIGHTS AND PERMISSIONS

Authors who are in the process of writing book manuscripts should take care to see that their work does not violate copyright laws.

If any substantial part of your work has been previously published, you will need to show evidence that you have the right to allow us to republish it. Such evidence should be presented to the Press when the manuscript is submitted for consideration.

The term fair use in the copyright law designates the way in which copyrighted material may be quoted without permission. In general, authors may quote without permission up to five hundred words in order to illustrate a point, substantiate a position, clarify an argument, or fulfill some such scholarly need. Letters of permission should be submitted with the manuscript.

Always obtain written permission to use:
• Any copyrighted material that is an entity itself, such as a map, a table, photograph, chapter of a book, article in a journal or newspaper, short story, poem, essay, or chart. Permission should be obtained from the author or copyright holder as well as the publisher.
• A private letter (the letter writer, not the recipient, holds the rights.)
• More than one line of a short poem or one stanza of a long poem.
• Music or words to a song.
• A reproduction of a work of art such as a painting or statue. The authority to grant permission to reproduce works of art may be held by the museum in which the art is located, by the artist, or by a private owner. Permission should be obtained at the time reproduction is made.

Signed releases should also be obtained from the subjects of interviews. U.S. government publications, uncopyrighted publications, and publications for which the copyright has expired may be used without requesting permission. Copyright duration under U.S. law is summarized here:

WORKS COPYRIGHT TERM

Created or Published after 1978 Lifetime of author + 50 years

Anonymous, or made for hire 75 years from publication or 100 years from creation, whichever is sooner

Copyrighted between 1950 and 1978 28 years from original copyright date; may be renewed for 47 years more (for a total of 75 years); renewal is automatic for books published between 1964 and 1978

Copyrighted before 1950 and renewed 75 years from original copyright date

Copyrighted before 1950 and not renewed Expired

Works created before 1978 but not copyrighted or published Considered to be copyrighted as of January, 1978, except that copyright will not expire before December 31, 2002

To find out whether a copyright has been renewed, authors should consult the Catalog of Copyright Entries of the U.S. Copyright Office for the year in which the renewal should have been made (i.e., twenty-eight years after the original copyright date). It is best to send permis-

sions requests to the rights holder in duplicate so that one copy can be retained by the rights holder and the signed copy returned to the author, who should make an additional copy for the Press.

The author is responsible for any fees assessed by rights holders and for supplying any complimentary copies of the book requested by the rights holders as a condition of granting permission.

A form that may be used to request permission or to gain use of material under different conditions is reproduced below.

When in doubt about using copyrighted material, authors should consult a Press editor.

INCLUSIVE LANGUAGE

The language and tone of books published by Texas A&M University Press should not be offensive to persons of any race, ethnic origin, religion, physical or mental condition, or gender and should be as inclusive as possible.

Editors employed by the Press will ensure that the accepted terms for designating racial or ethnic origin are used, except in direct quotations where historical accuracy requires special usage. Racial, ethnic, and gender stereotypes should not be used, except when clearly attributed to a source in a scholarly work and then only when such usage furthers the scholarly purpose of the work. Words derived from proper names should be capitalized; others should be lowercased. Two-word designations that indicate national origin are not hyphenated.

Inclusive language omits words that imply exclusion of either gender. Although it may be a historical fact that all the members of a city council were men, the word councilmen suggests the assumption that there could be no women on the council. On the other hand, it would never be inaccurate to say that there were x council members making decisions, etc., and that phrase avoids gender-biased implications.

Because there are suitable, neutral synonyms for most gender-based words in common usage, we discourage the use of such awkward constructions as "he or she" or compounds ending with the suffix "-person." Texas A&M University Press advocates the use of neutral synonyms and the third-person plural to eliminate language that is gender-based.

For example, the sentence

A group of influential businessmen was behind the decision.

is gender-specific. A good way to recast it would be:Influential members of the business community were behind the decision.

Language that creates imagery based on gender should be avoided. The example below illustrates how gender-based language can be replaced.

The sea beckoned men to explore her.

The sea beckoned, inviting explorers.

To avoid the possibility of heavy editing later on, authors who have questions about inclusive language may want to contact the copyediting department at the Press while they are still drafting the manuscript.

HOUSE STYLE

In general, Texas A&M University Press follows the style guidelines of *The Chicago Manual of Style* and the spelling conventions of *Webster's Third New International Dictionary* or *Webster's New Collegiate Dictionary*. Dictionaries differ on preferred spellings, so the Press follows Webster's in order to have a standard source when questions arise.

On some points Texas A&M University Press house style will differ from that described in *The Chicago Manual*. For example, we use American-style dates, with commas before and after the year, rather than the inverted European style:

October 6, 1966, NOT 6 October 1966

April, 1977, NOT April 1977

TAMUP house style also differs from that of *The Chicago Manual* in the writing of inclusive numbers. Because inclusive numbers are most often found in the index, detailed rules are listed in the indexing subsection of this guide, under Design and Production.

A variant on usual house style exists for military history titles, and authors writing in this field may request a copy of the special style sheet from a Press editor.

An author using a specialized style guide for a particular field should notify the Press editor of this and discuss the decision before submitting the manuscript for copyediting.

MULTI-AUTHOR VOLUMES

The compiler or editor of a volume consisting of symposium papers or other unpublished papers by various authors must submit written permission to publish from each of those authors at the time the manuscript is submitted for consideration. The compiler of a manuscript containing any previously published articles must have written permission from both the author of the article and from the original publisher. This written permission must be provided when the manuscript is submitted for consideration. If the original publisher or author of an article refuses permission or charges a fee beyond the amount the compiler wishes to pay, the content of the book will change. The problems that would arise if permission were not requested early on need not be spelled out.

The volume editor should see that the manuscript is submitted in a form that is internally consistent and follows the guidelines in this manual.

Photocopies of journal or newspaper articles should not be submitted as part of the manuscript. All components of the manuscript should be typewritten or printed with the same equipment.

Documentation should be consistent; if one article has footnotes, another has endnotes, and another has author-date citations and a reference list, one system should be selected and the rest of the articles in the volume be revised to conform to that style.

See the section of this guide on manuscript apparatus for more specific details on style for notes, bibliographies, display,. and so forth.

Manuscript Apparatus

NOTES

For most scholarly works in the humanities and social sciences, endnotes have become the standard form of documentation. In some circumstances, however, footnotes may be used instead. Authors should talk with Press editors before putting documentation in footnote style.

In books that have a bibliography, the notes need contain only author's name, title of article and journal (plus volume and issue number) or book, and relevant page numbers. Books that have notes but no bibliography (typically, an anthology or volume of essays) will generally have chapter endnotes, which will contain full publication information at first citation.

BIBLIOGRAPHIES

The bibliography should be as concise and easy to use as the content of the manuscript allows. Division of the bibliography into numerous sections for magazine articles, books, newspapers, and archival materials may be unnecessary and make the bibliography difficult to use. Make sure each subdivision is absolutely necessary and logical.

Bibliographies that list not only those works cited in the notes but also those which are of major significance in the field should be discussed with and approved by the Press editor responsible for development of that manuscript.

Double-space bibliographies, listing entries in alphabetical order (by section, if sections are used), starting each entry flush left, and indenting runover lines. When two or more works by one author are listed, replace the author's name with five hyphens on the second and subsequent entries.

For multi-author works, invert only the first name, and separate the author's names with semicolons.

ILLUSTRATIONS

In most cases authors are responsible for obtaining any photographs or drawings to be used in their books, securing written permission to use these materials, and paying any usage fees. Illustrations may add considerably to the cost of manufacturing a book, so their use should be discussed with the editors before the author has incurred the costs of obtaining them. Illustrations of any kind (including maps) should contribute significantly to the text; they should not be mere decoration. The Press will determine, in consultation with the author, the final number and selection of illustrations used.

Author-furnished illustrations received by the Press will be logged in and placed in our vault. They will be returned to the author about one year after the book is published, unless the Press is requested to return them sooner. The Press will exercise due caution when working with illustrations but is not responsible for loss or damage.

Permissions and Credit

After obtaining written agreements to use material owned by institutions or individuals other than yourself, submit the illustrations, double-spaced captions with the appropriate credit lines, and copies of letters granting permission to reproduce illustrations in your book and in its promotion.

Photographs

Photographs should be submitted as glossy black-and-white prints of at least 5"X7" for best reproduction. Consult the editor regarding the suitability of other sizes. Photocopied items do not reproduce well and should not be submitted as book illustrations.

Photographs should be submitted for color reproduction only with the approval of the editor. If color transparencies or slides are submitted for color reproduction, a color print should be submitted with them to show color quality. Color prints should not be submitted for illustrations to be produced in black and white. A glossy, black-and-white reproduction of a color print or transparency made in a professional photo-processing lab (which has been instructed to provide camera-quality copy) is usually acceptable, however.

Drawings and Diagrams

All line art should be professionally drawn. Clean, clear drawings or photographic prints of the original drawings should be proportional to the book page and no more than 50 percent larger than the approximate page size. Consult with the Press before committing to graphs or diagrams of a certain size.

Black sans-serif lettering is preferable. It should be large enough to be legible after reduction to book page size. Lines should be black and heavy enough to hold up in reduction.

A tissue overlay may be used to protect the surface of the finished drawing.

Maps

Authors are responsible for supplying professional-quality maps to be used in their books, unless special arrangements are made and agreed to in writing by the director or acquiring editor. Maps are protected under copyright laws and cannot simply be copied and reprinted from other books.

Before proposing to use a map, authors must ask themselves if the map is necessary, what it adds to the words in the text, what the clearest way of presenting the information is, if the map will look good on the printed page, and if the quality of a particular map is good enough for use in a book.

A map may be for purposes of reference, showing point locations, or it may be thematic, with information conveyed by means of shading, to show, for example, areas of low annual rainfall.

To compile a base map for use by a professional cartographer, find a map of the area needed. Trace a sketch map from the base map, eliminating any irrelevant detail while adding any details from individual research or from other maps. Like drawings, maps should be no more than 50 percent larger than they will appear on the book page.

Press editors will assist authors in determining the number of maps needed and can provide the names of qualified cartographers.

In making arrangements with cartographers, authors should keep in mind that all maps should be prepared as one-piece, black-and-white camera-ready art (Velox or photographic prints) suitable for reduction. Photocopies of the finished maps to be supplied should be submitted to the Press before an author fully commits to a final rendering. Final approval must await the copy editor's checking of the map against the text.

Map Materials

BASE: Use heavy, smooth white graphic board. Avoid Mylar, which may cast shadows when photographed by the printer.

GRAPHICS: U.S. Geographical Survey standards should normally be used in designating features. Lines should be even and black and thick enough to hold in reduction. Roman type is used for labeling cities, town, and mountain, and italic type is used for bodies of water. Compass north designation and graphic scale in miles (with metric equivalent) should be given.

TYPE: Use calligraphy or typeset lettering in Times Roman or Century serif face, or Optima, Helvetica, or Univers sanserif face. Maps or map labels generated by computer must be reviewed by the Press for legibility and output capabilities.

SHADING: Use Zip-a-Tone patterns, tightly burnished to minimize shadows. Overlays for multiple exposures are strongly discouraged and can be used only with the prior approval of the Press staff.

COMPUTER GENERATED MAPS: Many people are using computers to generate maps and using patterns from the computer. Please show samples to your editor (for referral to the design and production departments) before producing final copy. When the final manuscript is submitted, font files used on the maps should be included on the disk.

NUMBERING ILLUSTRATIONS

Never write on the front of photographs. Number them (and drawings) on the back, preferably with a soft grease pencil or a stick-on label. Ballpoint pen or pencil can leave a visible line on the photograph's emulsion, and ink can permanently damage the front of a photograph stacked underneath. Paper clips can also damage photographs. Maps should be numbered on the front, outside the text area.

CAPTIONS

Write a caption for each illustration, putting any required credit line at the end. Captions should be numbered and typed double-spaced on a separate sheet of paper; captions should not be written on the illustrations themselves or attached to them. If an illustration is keyed to a particular page in the manuscript, indicate that page number on the caption sheet or an accompanying illustration identification list.

TABLES

• Separate the tables from the text, placing them with other text apparatus at the back of the manuscript.

• Tables should be numbered sequentially throughout the text unless (1) the manuscript is a compilation of essays, or (2) the manuscript is a reference work with figures and tables numbered to indicate chapter (e.g., Table 2.3, Fig. 3.1). In the text discussion, refer to each table by number, not by position.

• Each table should have a title of reasonable length.

• When preparing tables, keep in mind the size of a normal vertical book page. Tables that would require quarter-turns (sideways placement) should be avoided.

• Horizontal lines may be used to separate the table title from column heads and table text from table notes. Do not use vertical lines.

• Footnotes to a table should be called out by italic letters rather than by Arabic numerals.

• If the table is taken from a published source, the author must have the original author's and publisher's written permission to use it. Under the table text, above any footnotes, indicate the source of the table using standard bibliographical information.

• If tables are to be provided on disks with the manuscript, please consult with the editor, who will check with Design and Production on specific guidelines.

Copyediting

University presses can bring forth a high-quality book in ten to twelve months. More complicated books may take longer. The time required to actually produce the book begins when the manuscript is assigned to a copy editor.

A manuscript is a candidate for assignment to a copy editor when all materials are in house-two final, complete manuscript copies; all illustrations; and all permissions documents. At this time the tentative season of publication may be designated.

The copy editor will edit the manuscript for style, grammar, spelling, punctuation, and general integrity of text. Manuscripts edited on disk will show queries as footnotes on the edited printout and will usu-

ally also include a comparison printout showing changes made. Queries will be written on tabs attached to the margin of manuscripts not submitted on disk. At this stage, the editor may also select the illustrations to be used from those submitted. The editor also compares map text to manuscript text. If there are discrepancies, corrections may be needed on the map, and the authors should keep their cartographers aware of this possibility.

Discussion about the title of the book may not occur until the manuscript-editing stage. The editor may relay to the author suggestions for a new title or subtitle. Although the title of a book is ultimately the publisher's decision, we do everything possible to make sure that authors approve of the final titles of their books.

When copyediting is complete, the editor will draft some text to be used on the dust jacket flaps or on the back cover of a paperbound book. The editor then sends the edited manuscript and this draft of dust jacket or cover copy to the author for approval.

At this point, authors should read through the manuscript carefully, page by page, and answer all queries. Responses may be written at the point of the query, or check marks placed there to indicate concurrence with the editor's comment. If a response requires more space, the author may attach an additional query tab or page and write responses there.

The review of edited copy by authors represents the last opportunity to make changes in the text. Corrections to proofs are expensive and time consuming and may not be made unless the unaltered material would compromise the integrity of the book. Alterations required for this reason may be charged to the author.

Editors responsible for volumes of essays will likely be asked to send photocopies of the copyedited essays to the authors. The volume editor must be sure to convey the importance of retaining consistency, making sure that all changes are final, and meeting the deadline. Essays not returned by the deadline should be considered approved by the author.

The edited copy should be returned to the Press by the date requested. A missed deadline anytime during the copyediting and production phase can delay a book's publication and cause a host of related problems. Deadlines missed by a significant amount, such as a week or two, may translate into a publication delay of many weeks or even months.

The Press prefers that manuscripts be shipped by a private carrier whose shipping fee includes insurance and tracing services if the package is lost. Manuscripts sent by U.S. mail should go first class and be insured for fifty dollars.

The editor reviews the author's responses to queries, consulting with the author on any final points, and then submits the manuscript to the design and production departments.

Design and Production

DESIGN

Authors are invited to convey to the editor any ideas about their book's design or dust jacket. The editor will pass this information along to the designer, but the decision on all elements of design, including the dust jacket, belongs to the Press and the designers it employs.

PROOFREADING

After the manuscript has been designed and typeset, the author will receive proofs. The Press usually sends galley proofs (long sheets of unpaged type) to authors only when the book is very heavily illustrated. Most authors will receive only page proofs. These are facsimiles of the made-up pages.

Proofreading is the author's responsibility; page proofs will not necessarily be read by the editor or production staff. Most authors will receive two sets of page proof plus the edited manuscript. The first set of pages is to be proofread and marked for correction. The second set is to be marked up in preparation for indexing.

To proofread typeset text, compare it word for word to the edited manuscript. Pay close attention to the lines that contain an error; errors found in the same general vicinity are often missed. Also pay careful attention to display type; it is easy to pore carefully through ten-point text type and overlook typos in the large display type. Repeated or missing lines of manuscript text and substitution of one word for another can escape a careless proofreader.

Proofs must be marked clearly so that the editor and compositor know exactly what corrections are needed.

Make a small slash mark in the line of type that needs a correction, and in the margin place the appropriate proofreading symbol. If more than one alteration is needed in a line, the correction symbols in the margin should appear in the proper order, from left to right, separated by a vertical or diagonal line.

Use regular lead pencil to indicate typographic errors—those errors which differ from the edited manuscript. The compositor is obliged to follow the manuscript letter for letter, so any mistakes in proof that are copied from the manuscript should not be considered compositor's errors.

Use a colored pencil to indicate editorial errors or author's alterations. Such changes are expensive, both in time and money, and new errors could be introduced when the change is made. Pagination must not be affected in making a change, as the index must be prepared from this set of paginated proof.

If an author alteration is deemed necessary, however, make the altered line approximately the same length as the original line.

As specified in the contract, compositor's errors will be corrected without expense to you, but you will be charged for author alterations that exceed the percentage of the total typesetting cost specified in your contract. Correction of editorial errors will not be charged to you.

INDEXING

Indexing may not be the most enjoyable aspect of producing a book, but it is one of the most important for scholarly works. An inadequate or error-ridden index may lock the door to an otherwise valuable resource.

If the Press determines that an index will be needed for a particular book, it is the author's responsibility to provide one within the time allotted, typically a couple of weeks. Authors are strongly encouraged to prepare their own indexes and review indexing procedures well in advance. If the author chooses not to do so, the Press can hire a freelance indexer at the author's expense. If a freelancer prepares the index, there is rarely enough time for the author to review the product.

Although many authors now produce manuscripts on word processors, the software programs that include an "indexing" feature will still require the author's expertise in analyzing the text for main entries, subentries, and cross-references. Without a special program designed specifically for indexing complex material, a considerable amount of manual alphabetizing and editing will also be needed for the index sorted by computer.

The finished index should be typed or printed on 8½"x11" paper. Double-space the entire index, including subentries. If possible, a disk should be sent in addition to the printout.

Form

Texas A&M University Press follows closely the style recommendations of *The Chicago Manual of Style*. The Press will lend authors an offprint of the Chicago Manual's chapter on indexing. By following its guidelines, authors can be confident that their indexes will be acceptable in form.

Follow the example in the Chicago Manual that uses run-in subentries. Authors should consult their editors before deciding to prepare an index that may require a more elaborate breakdown of entries.

Content

In general, an index should be more than a proper-name list. It should include substantive entries (e.g., alcoholism; customs; dress; political parties) and conceptual entries (e.g., authority; imperialism; manifest destiny; natural law). Only in rare circumstances are separate indexes (e.g., for subjects as opposed to persons) advisable.

Alphabetizing
• Use the letter-by-letter system of alphabetizing described in the Chicago Manual.

Main
• Start main entries with a lowercase letter unless the entry is a proper name.
• Reverse the order of words in a main entry to place a descriptive adjective or phrase after it. If there are no subentries and the reversal places the beginning of the description in the reversed position, separate the entry from the page numbers with commas:
Subentries
• If subentries are used or if the descriptive phrase comes after the main entry, separate the main entry from the subentries or descriptive phrase with a colon:
• Use the run-in style for subentries unless instructed to do otherwise.
Page Numbers
• Use italics for page numbers that refer to illustration legends or caption. Place a note to that effect at the beginning of the index.
• Use no more than ten page numbers after a main entry. If more page numbers are required, break the entry down into subentries.
• Never use ff. after page numbers.
• Texas A&M University Press follows a style for inclusive numbers that is somewhat different from that suggested by the Chicago Manual. In preparing an index, please follow the style summarized here:
Use all digits if:
a) the first number is under 100:
3-10 32-37 97-129
b) the second number ends in 00-09:
704-705 997-1102 1002-1003 1895-1902
c) the second number goes into the next hundred or more:
996-1138 1697-1721 2,000-2,500
For all other inclusive numbers, use only the last two digits of the second number of the pair:
107-23 321-25 1304-29 1536-38

Authors who have read their proofs and prepared a satisfactory index have completed their work on the book. The editor will transfer all appropriate corrections to the master proofs and copyedit the index. After the compositors have set corrections and the index, the editor will proofread them.

The Press will send the author a finished dust jacket as soon as it is printed. The author will also receive one complimentary advance copy of the book; the remainder of the author's allotment of complimentary copies will be mailed after the main shipment of books has arrived at the Press.

If you have further questions about publishing with Texas A&M University Press, feel free to call or write and we will be glad to help in any way we can.

Categories: Nonfiction—Agriculture—Architecture—Business—Culture—Economics—Hispanic—History—Military—Multicultural—Native American—Regional—Women's Issues—Anthropology

CONTACT: Diane L. Vance
Material: All
Lindsey Building
Lewis St. 4354 TAMU
College Station TX 77843-4354
Phone: 409-845-1436
Fax: 409-847-8752
E-mail: dlv@tampress.edu

Texas Western Press

Before submitting a manuscript, check our mission statement to see whether your manuscript fits the literary focus of our press:

The mission of Texas Western Press of the University of Texas at El Paso is the publication of books on the history and cultures of the American Southwest, including particularly historical and biographical works about West Texas, New Mexico, northern Mexico and the U.S.-Mexico borderlands. The Press has also published books in the areas of regional art, photography, Native American studies, demographics, border issues, and natural history. Texas Western Press also publishes two series: Southwestern Studies, short books on personalities and events of the American southwest; and The Border/La Frontera, a series based on current research directed at enhancing understanding of the diversity of conditions and experiences represented in the United States-Mexico borderlands. Texas Western Press is a member of the Association of American University Presses.

Texas Western Press follows the guidelines of *The Chicago Manual of Style.*

A manuscript proposal should include the following:
• cover letter
• prospectus to include analysis of current market competition and what place your book will have within it
• curriculum vitae
• potential audience for work
• table of contents
• sample chapter
• estimated length of manuscript
• examples or descriptions of artwork, including number of illustrations. Do not send originals
• self-addressed, stamped envelope for reply. If you want your materials returned, make sure to include an envelope that is large enough to hold the materials and include sufficient postage. Otherwise, your material will be recycled.
• If the manuscript is not a completed work, give estimated date of completion.
• Do not send irreplaceable materials.
For more information, contact Bobbi Gonzales at bobbi@utep.edu.
Categories: Nonfiction—Biography—Civil War—Culture—Hispanic—Military

CONTACT: Bobbi Gonzales, Assistant to Director
Material: All
500 W. University Ave.
El Paso TX 79968-0633
Phone: 915-747-5688
E-mail: bobbi@utep.edu
Website: www.utep.edu/twp

Third World Press

Thank you for your interest in publishing with THIRD WORLD PRESS. Third World Press is an African-centered publishing house dedicated to the creation and dissemination of written work of the highest quality.

A progressive publisher of Black and African-centered material for more than thirty years, our goal is to be the best provider of material to expand the mind and reach to all backgrounds especially the African-American community, and other African communities in the Diaspora. Third World Press promotes maximum effect of creative expression and cultural enlightenment in all the written genres, including fiction, nonfiction, poetry, drama, young adult and children's books which other wise may not have an outlet.

Third World Press has published poetry works from noted writers including Gwendolyn Brooks, Sterling Plump, Haki R. Madhubuti, and Amiri Baraka. We value and support the talents of poets who wish to contribute to the literary world and showcase their poetics.

Third World Press welcomes the opportunity to review both solicited and unsolicited POETRY manuscripts that explore African-centered life and thought. When submitting poetry manuscripts for consideration, please adhere to the following guidelines.
POETRY MANUSCRIPTS MUST BE:
• At least fifty pages to be considered
• Typed and double-spaced
• Do not include more than one poem on a page

• Proofread for typographical and grammatical errors unless otherwise noted
SEND ONLY COPIES of any related artwork, photographs or layout boards. KEEP ALL ORIGINALS.
SEND ONLY COPIES of any other manuscripts-related materials. KEEP ALL ORIGINALS.
PLEASE INCLUDE THE FOLLOWING MATERIAL WITH THE SUBMITTED MANUSCRIPT:
• The subject of the manuscript, in a one-page synopsis form.
• Reasons why you, the author, are best qualified to write a book and why it needs to be published (what unmet needs in the literary market the book meets.)
Identify competition for your prospective book, and how your manuscript differs from those already existing.
• An identified market, and at least a preliminary outline of how your manuscript can be marketed to this segment.
Along with your manuscript, please attach one copy of these guidelines, as well as a self-address stamped envelope with correct postage and package size relative to your submissions. MANUSCRIPTS WILL ONLY BE ACCEPTED IN JULY OF EACH YEAR.
PLEASE REMEMBER THE FOLLOWING:
UNACCEPECTED MANUSCRIPTS MAILED WITHOUT PROPER POSTAGE AND PACKAGING WILL BE DISCARDED.
FAILURE TO ADHERE TO SUBMISSION GUIDELINES WILL RESULT IN THE IMMEDIATE RETURN OR ELMINATION OF YOUR MANUSCRIPT.
Once your manuscript has been mailed, allow anywhere from four to six months for a written response. THE staff will not accept telephone calls regarding the status or review of a manuscript.
Categories: Fiction—Nonfiction—African-American—Children—Drama—Poetry—Young Adult

CONTACT: Assistant to the Publisher
Material: All
PO Box 19730
Chicago, IL. 60619
Phone: 773-651-0700
E-mail: gwenmtwp@aol.com
Website: www.thirdworldpressinc.com

Three Forks

Please refer to Falcon Publishing.

Thriller Press

WHAT WE WILL CONSIDER
Thriller Press is a small publisher specializing in a narrow niche of fiction. We are not looking for new authors at this time. Please keep this in mind if you send us a submission and don't get a response from us.

Having said that, in the interest of our long term goals we will consider submissions in the following format.

You may send us ten pages in the body of an email. We will not open attachments. The email address to submit to is submissions@thrillerpress.com.

Your ten pages should consist of a one page letter with the remaining nine pages the opening of your novel. In your letter, please summarize your novel in 2 or 3 sentences. Also include any information about how you could help sell your book. (A critical part of selling books in today's market is author's own marketing efforts. i.e., if your job is being a Talk Show Host, let us know!) Please do not submit more than ten pages. If we're not hooked on your story by then, we won't respond anyway, no matter how great the rest of your novel may be.

We pay small advances, preferring to concentrate our resources on fantastic cover design, website marketing and direct contact with bookstores. If a book is successful it will earn royalties.

If, after reading our novels, you believe you have an intelligent, action-based thriller or mystery that would suit us, then please submit as described above.

Thank you,
—Tyler Larsson

CAVEATS

Please take a moment to consider that the typical successful fiction writer has done all of the following BEFORE submitting their work to agents and publishing companies:

• Taken multiple creative writing courses with a focus on fiction. You will find a range of courses at your local community college or through a university's extension program.

• Enthusiastically read and studied an enormous volume of work in the genre, i.e. mysteries and thrillers. If you don't read them voraciously, don't try to write them.

• Had their work scrutinized by a professional in the writing/editing field whether a writing teacher, a friend in the business or an editor hired from an ad in *Publishers Weekly*. Ask for referrals and check them out.• When you find one who comes well recommended, pay the few hundred dollars and see what you learn. Remember, you don't want someone who flatters you, you want someone who will pick apart every aspect of your writing, plot line, character development, dialogue, syntax, grammar, the works.

• Attended several writing conferences and submitted his or her work to multiple critiques. There are hundreds of writing conferences available throughout the year. You can find them on the internet, or advertised in *Writer's Digest* and other writing magazines. Pick three or four one week conferences and sign up for all of them. Bring your completed novel to the first one. After the conference is over you will have a thousand ideas of how to improve your work. Rewrite accordingly, then take the result to the second conference. At each stage you will see improvement that you didn't think was possible. After taking your novel through four conferences, four complete rewrites, a dozen minor rewrites and a year or two of extra polishing, you'll be amazed at what you learned. Furthermore, you'll be glad you were spared the embarrassment of sending your work out earlier.

WHY WORK IS REJECTED

Every editor can tell you a thousand stories about writers who weren't prepared. Here are some telltale signs that immediately show an editor that the writer is not a professional.

1. The writer's cover letter calls their work a fiction novel, an embarrassing redundancy.

2. The writer makes mistakes in grammar and spelling.

3. The writer's novel lacks a compelling hook or setup.

4. The writer's work has "purple prose" (excessively fancy writing) and does not demonstrate economy of words. Mark Twain said, "Never use a quarter word when a nickel word will do the job." E.B. White said, "Cross out any word or sentence that doesn't develop character or advance the plot. And eliminate all adverbs." Study Hemingway for writing economy.

5. The novel doesn't start off with an immediate problem. Fiction is all about conflict and resolution. Read any good novel, whether a commercial "beach read" or a serious literary work or a fairy tale and you'll find that the story starts with a problem.

Here is a short, very simplified example of typical rising plot curve. Note that these characteristics apply to most fiction, be it *Moby Dick* or *Jurassic Park* or *The Old Man In The Sea* or Harry Potter or *Star Wars*.

The novel starts with a problem. Our hero (the protagonist) tries to solve the initial problem, but the problem gets worse. The protagonist takes a different approach, but the difficulties multiply until the problem is overwhelming. Eventually, our hero has an epiphany about how to solve the dilemma. He or she gears up to take on the problem in a final do-or-die climactic battle, engaging the antagonist/bad guy on his own turf. The climax is followed by a short wrap-up/resolution.

Note that the "problem" can be Captain Ahab's whale or genetic manipulation of extinct dinosaurs which are now running amok or the old man's fish or the evil professor or Darth Vader. Also, every aspect of the novel can be literal or metaphorical.

Categories: Fiction

CONTACT: Submissions Editor
Material: All
E-mail: submissions@thrillerpress.com
Website: thrillerpress.com

Tilbury House Publishers

Tilbury House narrowed its editorial focus several years ago, and we would appreciate receiving only queries and manuscripts that fit within our current areas of interest. We receive hundreds of unsolicited manuscripts each year; it's a time-consuming task to read and answer them all-although we sometimes find a gem! If you are connected to the Internet, please take a moment to visit our web site at www.tilburyhouse.com to familiarize yourself with our catalog and the kinds of books we publish. We look forward to seeing your manuscript and appreciate your interest in Tilbury House.

Children's Books

We are primarily interested in children's picture books (for ages 7-12) that:

1. Deal with issues of cultural diversity (global), nature, or the environment (we don't publish "general" children's books about animals, fables, or fantasy);

2. Appeal to children and parents and offer enough learning content so that they will also appeal to the educational market;

3. Will sell to the national (not just regional) market; and

4. Offer possibilities for developing a separate teacher's guide (written by an educator) that will expand the focus of the book, offer additional information, and suggest learning activities and approaches.

Adult Books

1. Much of our effort goes into our children's books, and it was difficult in the past to effectively market a diverse adult list. As a result, we decided to limit our new adult books to non-fiction about Maine or the Northeast, particularly books that are documentary or about Maine's history. Because the market for these books is small, we often seek out co-publishing arrangements with museums, historical societies, or other organizations; this helps us produce high-quality books that might not otherwise be published, and benefits both parties.

2. Please do not send us fiction, short stories, memoirs, or poetry. Our current catalog will give you a good idea of the kinds of books that interest us. You'll find our complete catalog, excerpts from our books, and more on this web site. If your manuscript doesn't seem like a good fit for Tilbury, you'll find guidance in books like Writer's Market or Children's Writers and Illustrator's Market to help you locate a more likely publisher.

What to Send

1. A query letter (a short, concise letter about your project), is a good start, or send a partial manuscript and outline, unless you feel we must see the entire manuscript to adequately assess it. For children's books, we prefer to see a complete manuscript. If you query us by email, please put "Book Query" in the subject line, and do not send an attachment. We will not open attachments. Please do not send us large files over the Internet.

2. Work not accompanied by a self-addressed, stamped envelope will not be answered. If you want your materials returned, please be sure to enclose adequate postage, otherwise they will be recycled.

3. If you are making simultaneous submissions to other publishers, please note this in your query letter.

4. Please be patient with us; it usually takes us a month or so to respond.

We appreciate the opportunity to read your work. Thank you for your interest in Tilbury House, and for considering us as a possible publisher.

Categories: Fiction—Nonfiction—Children—Mulitcultural—Outdoors—Science

CONTACT: Audrey Maynard
Material: Children's Books Editor
2 Mechanic St., Ste. 3
Gardiner, ME 04345
Phone: 207-582-1899
E-mail: tilbury@tilburyhouse.com
Website: www.tilburyhouse.com

Time Warner Book Group

Time Warner Book Group, formerly known as Time Warner Trade Publishing, came into existence when Time Inc. and Warner Communications merged in 1990. Domestically, it consists of Warner Books and its various imprints: The Mysterious Press, Warner Vision, Warner Business Books, Aspect, Warner Faith, Warner Forever, and Little, Brown and Company and its various imprints: Little, Brown Adult Trade, Little, Brown Children's Books, Back Bay and Bulfinch Press. In addition, TWBG distributes publishing lines for Hyperion, Arcade, Disney, Harry Abrams, Time Life Books, and Microsoft. In 1996, Little, Brown opened a 750,000-square foot, state-of-the-art warehouse in Lebanon, Indiana. In addition to its New York and Indiana based companies, most of TWBG's back office operations are based in Boston.

Manuscript Submissions and Unsolicited Queries

Publishers in the Time Warner Book Group (including Warner Books, Warner Business Books, Warner Faith, Mysterious Press, Aspect, Little, Brown and Company, Back Bay Books, Bulfinch Press, Little, Brown Children's Books) are not able to consider unsolicited manuscript submissions and unsolicited queries. Many major publishers have a similar policy. Unfamiliar packages and letters mailed to our offices will be returned to sender unopened.

If you are interested in having a manuscript considered for publication, we recommend that you first enlist the services of an established literary agent. Many literary agencies can be located in Bowker's *Literary MarketPlace* (commonly known as the "LMP"), an annual reference publication which can be found in most major libraries. These literary agencies, in turn, have guidelines for submitting manuscripts. You can find out more about the LMP at *Literary MarketPlace*.

Categories: Fiction—Nonfiction

CONTACT: Submissions Editor
Material: All
1271 Ave of the Americas
New York NY 10020

Tom Doherty Associate, LLC
Tor Books, Forge Books, Orb, Starscape

About Tor Books

Tor Books, an imprint of Tom Doherty Associates, LLC, is a New York-based publisher of hardcover and softcover books, founded in 1980 and committed (although not limited) to SF and fantasy literature. Between our extensive hardcover and trade-softcover line, our Orb backlist program, and our stronghold in mass-market paperback, we annually publish what is arguably the largest and most diverse line of SF and fantasy ever produced by a single English-language publisher. Books from Tor have won every major award in the SF and fantasy fields, and for the last fourteen years in a row we have been named Best Publisher in the Locus Poll, the largest consumer poll in SF.

About Forge Books

Forge Books is an imprint of Tom Doherty Associates, and publishes fiction and nonfiction in a wide variety of genres and categories.

Its sister imprint Tor Books, while famous for its science fiction and fantasy, also publishes books in other genres.

Here are some good rules to follow when submitting your work to us:

• Do not submit work on disk, tape, or other electronic media; do not submit work by email.

Submit only the first three chapters of your book, and a synopsis of the entire book. (We're not big on query letters, since we can't tell whether we'll like the book until we see a chunk of the manuscript.) And please make sure you send the first three chapters. No matter how good your synopsis is, it's difficult for us to get a good sense of the book from chapters 4, 17, and 32.

• Your cover letter should state the genre of the submission, and previous sales or publications if relevant.

• Never send us the only copy of your book. The U.S. Post Office is no more perfect than the rest of us, and things do get lost in the mail. Always put your name and address on the manuscript. In addition, your name, the manuscript title, and the page number should appear on every page of the manuscript. If you wish your manuscript to be returned, enclose a stamped, self-addressed envelope large enough to hold your submission; publishers are not responsible for returning submissions unaccompanied by return postage. If you do not wish your manuscript to be returned, please say so on the cover letter, and enclose a stamped, self-addressed, business-sized envelope for our reply. If you enclose a stamped, self-addressed postcard, we will return it to verify receipt of the manuscript.

• Type your manuscript on plain white paper, double-spaced, using only one side of the page. Do not staple or otherwise bind your manuscript; a paper clip will suffice. If you use a computer and printer, do not submit low-resolution dot matrix printouts; they will not be read. Please do not use a fancy font (this is almost as difficult to read as the palest dot-matrix), and please make sure you use a font large enough to read easily. Please turn off margin justification and proportional spacing; pages with ragged right margins are easier for us to read, and easier for our production department to set.

• Please indicate italics by underlining and indicate boldface by drawing a wavy line beneath the affected characters. Copy to be typeset needs to be marked in very specific ways, and if you use italics or boldface in the manuscript, they will still need to be marked up by production.

• Please allow at least four to six months for your manuscript to be considered. If you haven't heard from us after four months, and wish to make sure your manuscript got here, please write a letter stating the genre, the date of submission, and the title of the manuscript, rather than calling. We will respond promptly.

• We do not accept simultaneous submissions.
Good luck!

Categories: Fiction—Civil War—Crime—Fantasy—Horror—Mystery—Occult—Paranormal—Science Fiction—Western

CONTACT: William Smith, Editorial Asst.
Material: General fiction
CONTACT: Fred Herman, Editorial Asst.
Material: Science fiction and fantasy
175 Fifth Ave.
New York NY 10010
Website: www.tor.com

Tor Books

Please refer to Tom Doherty Associate, LLC, in the Book Publishers section.

Books M-Z

Tower Publishing

Tower specializes in legal and professional business publications. Submittals should take the form of a listing of chapters offered and at least three sample chapters. The market should be business or legal.

Categories: Nonfiction—Business—Law—Reference

CONTACT: Michael Lyons, Publishers
Material: All
588 Saco Rd.
Standish ME 04084
Phone: 800-969-8693
Fax: 207-642-5463
Website: www.towerpub.com

Towlehouse Publishing Co.

I don't have proposal guidelines per se. Just send me a proposal, period. A cover letter, outline, two sample chapters, and SASE.

Categories: Nonfiction—Sports/Recreation—Golf

CONTACT: Mike Towle, President
Material: All
1312 Bell Grimes Ln.
Nashville TN 37207
Phone: 615-366-9120

Transaction Publishers Rutgers
The State University of New Jersey

Transaction Publishers is widely acknowledged as a major independent publisher of social scientific books, periodicals and serials. Transaction's mission is scholarly and professional inquiry into the nature of society. Transaction offers publications in older, established disciplines such as economics, political science, history, sociology, anthropology, psychology, as well as recently established disciplines ranging from area research to urban studies, policy analysis, philosophy of social science, organizational behavior, and criminology. Located on the campus of Rutgers University in Piscataway, New Jersey, Transaction has strong ties to the traditional mission of American university life as a center of learning, and to applied needs of public and private institutions in social research. Through its many publications, Transaction promotes mutually beneficial exchanges between academic and professional life.

Guidelines

Formal guidelines not available.
Send queries or book proposals to below address.

Categories: Nonfiction—Society

CONTACT: Irving Louis Horowitz, Publisher
Material: All
35 Berrue Circle
Piscataway NJ 08854
Phone: 732-445-2280
E-mail: ihorowitz@transactionpub.com
Website: www.transactionpub.com

Transnational Publishers, Inc.

Transnational is an independent publishing firm that has been producing material for the international community for over twenty years. We are distinguished for our well-crafted publications written by leading authorities on human rights law, public and private international law, international organizations, criminal law, dispute resolution, trade law, legal research, comparative law, taxation, foreign affairs, and political theory.

Transnational publications are innovative and thought provoking, provide need-to know information for legal practice, and explore the cutting edge of contemporary affairs. Scholars, students, and practitioners examining and working in the international arena will find Transnational publications significant resources.

For authors who wish to investigate publishing their work with Transnational, we offer a thorough review of proposed projects with a decision to publish within a month of submission. If we do agree to collaborate, authors will experience an open and cooperative atmosphere where they will be asked to be involved in all stages of production and marketing.

Our production process is set up to assure quality publications. Manuscripts are evaluated upon receipt and assigned to appropriate editors for copy editing. Once the edits have been approved by an author projects are sent to composition. The resulting page proof is sent to the author for review. When all corrections have been made and index completed, the book goes to press. In most cases a book will be published six weeks after going to the printer. We expedite the production of all projects but will work closely with authors who need to have a work available by a certain date.

The marketing of publications is of great concern to authors. As a publisher focused on the issues of international law and global affairs, Transnational is experienced in reaching those worldwide audiences seeking resources in these areas. We employ direct mail campaigns, an e-commerce enabled web site, internet booksellers, and an international network of agents and distributors to assure Transnational publications receive maximum exposure.

All Transnational books are sent out for review by major journals.

Categories: Environment—Human Rights—Law—Reference—Women's Issues

CONTACT: Submissions Editor
Material: All
410 Saw Mill River Rd.
Ardsley NY 10503
Phone: 914-693-5100
Website: www.transnationalpubs.com

Tricycle Press

Please refer to Ten Speed Press.

The Trinity Foundation

No formal guidelines, but only publishes books consistent with Westminster Confession of Faith.

Categories: Nonfiction—Book Reviews—Christian Interests—Culture—Economics—Education—Government—Politics—Religion—Science—Spiritual

CONTACT: Dr. John Robbins
Material: All
PO Box 68
Unicoi TN 37692
Phone: 423-743-0199
Fax: 423-743-2005
Website: www.trinityfoundation.org

Trinity Press International

Profile

Academic and trade religion titles. Titles: 30 per year, many from first time authors. Hardcover and paperback publisher. Accepts unsolicited mss. Response time: 2-6 weeks.

Editorial Focus

Trinity Press International publishes serious books on Bible and theology for a broad range of readers. Its books offer enlightening perspectives of biblical, cultural, ethical, theological, and religious issues. Trinity Press International publishes books that address many of humanity's deepest questions. Specific categories include biblical studies, theology, religion and science, religion and culture, and ethics. Trinity Press International seeks to publish books that express diverse biblical and theological views.

Submission and Payment Policy

Submit query with one page synopsis of the book, an annotated table of contents, one page comparing the book to others like it on the market, a resume, an introduction to the book, and one sample chapter to Henry L. Carrigan, Jr. More detailed submission guidelines are available from Henry L. Carrigan, Jr. Include a self-addressed mailer with adequate postage so the proposal can be returned at a later date. Manuscripts originating outside the USA will not be returned. Simultaneous submissions should be identified. Advances on royalties are negotiable and paid on signing of contract and final ms. submission.

Book Catalog

Call 1-800-877-0012 for a free copy.

Guidelines for Submitting a Book Proposal

Author Information. Name, mailing address, and daytime phone number. Enclose a current vita which indicates your present position, educational background, previous publications, and why you are qualified to write the book you are proposing.

Title of the Book. Indicate the tentative title of the book with possible alternative titles.

Description of the Book. In 250-500 words, summarize the book you are proposing. What is the nature, focus, purpose, or argument of the book? What is its thesis? Write the summary as if it were on the back cover of the book convincing a potential reader to buy this book. What unique contributions to the subject does this manuscript provide?

Audience. For what audience, specifically, is the book written: lay person? pastors, or other religious professionals? college students? seminary/graduate school students? professors? Why does someone need to read this book? Does the book have potential for textbook adoption? If so, in what courses?

Competition. Are there competing titles? If so, what are they? What does your book offer that these competing titles do not? How will your book be superior to or different from them?

Table of Contents. Give a tentative table of contents of the book by chapters. Beneath each chapter title, give a brief outline of the chapter and a brief summary of its contents. This summary should explain the focus and development of the chapter and indicate how the chapter advances the argument of the whole book.

Manuscript Length. What is the estimated length of the proposed manuscript, printed double-spaced on 8½" x 11" paper with 1" margins and 12-point type size?

Sample Pages. Enclose a sample of 15-25 pages, perhaps of the introduction or first chapter, which illustrates your writing style. These should be pages that are typical of the book as a whole, especially critical to your argument, potentially controversial, or that give an overview of the book.

Manuscript Submission. If your proposal is accepted and a complete manuscript requested, you should plan to submit a hard copy of the manuscript together with a 3½" disk in IBM or MAC compatible text files. Indicate what program and version you have used.

Completion Date. Indicate the date your would expect to submit a completed manuscript.

Categories: Nonfiction—Biography—Christian Interests—Culture—Religion—Spiritual

CONTACT: Henry Carrigan, Editorial Director
Material: All
4775 Linglestown Rd
Harrisburg PA 17112
Phone: 717-541-8130

Truman State University Press

TSUP publishes scholarly works in the humanities, nonfiction regional books, and poetry. Our series include the Sixteenth Century Essays & Studies, Bethsaida Excavation Project, Peter Martyr Library, and New Odyssey (poetry).

TSUP holds an annual poetry competition, the T. S. Eliot Prize, for the best unpublished book-length collection of poetry in English, in honor of T. S. Eliot's considerable intellectual and artistic legacy.

For nonfiction manuscripts, please submit a short, informative letter of inquiry with:

• a clear and concise description of your book and its notable features

• your intended audience for the book

• the current status of the manuscript and expected completion date

• the length, number of illustrations, tables, appendices

• a table of contents

• a preface, introduction, or other brief sample of your manuscript

• your curriculum vitae or biographical notes

If the press is interested, you will be invited to submit the complete manuscript. All manuscripts considered for publication are peer reviewed.

T. S. Eliot Prize manuscripts should be between 60 and 100 typed pages of original poetry in English. Each poem should begin on a separate page. Include two title pages: one with name, address, phone number, and manuscript title; one with only the manuscript title.

(Your name must not appear in the manuscript, since the poet's identity should not be known to the judge.) Include a table of contents and a list of acknowledgments for previously published individual poems, if applicable. Enclose a self-addressed, stamped envelope to be notified when we receive your manuscript. (No other postage-paid envelopes are necessary.) All entrants will receive notice of the results. Manuscripts will not be returned. Please do not send your only copy. Include $25 for the reading fee. Make checks payable to Truman State University Press. If you prefer to pay by Visa or MasterCard include your credit card number, expiration date, cardholder name, and signature. Manuscripts should be unbound, placed in manila file folder and mailer.

Categories: Nonfiction—History—Poetry—Regional—Religion

CONTACT: Nancy Rediger, Director
Material: All
100 E. Normal St.
Kirksville MO 63501-4221
Phone: 660-785-7336, 800-916-6802
Fax: 660-785-4480
E-mail: tsup@truman.edu
Website: tsup.truman.edu

Turtle Press

Turtle Press publishes a wide variety of books in the areas of sports, martial arts, Eastern philosophy, and self-improvement. We have also started a new line of children's martial arts books, both fiction and nonfiction. While we are open to a broad range of topics, we prefer that a manuscript be tightly focused and give thorough coverage to its subject.

Please query with a self-addressed stamped envelope before submitting a proposal. Your query letter will be answered within two to three weeks.

If requested to submit a proposal, please send the following:

a. outline or summary

b. table of contents

c. two to four sample chapters, including chapter one

d. market potential for the proposed manuscript

e. author credentials

f. sample photos or artwork

g. availability of manuscript on disk, including format

h. postage paid return envelope

Materials should be submitted on 8½" x 11" white paper, double spaced. Please allow two to four weeks for a response. Materials sent without a postage paid return envelope will not be returned.

Thank you for your interest in Turtle Press.

Categories: Nonfiction—Asian-American—Health—Multicultural—New Age—Physical Fitness—Sports/Recreation

CONTACT: Cynthia Kim, Acquisitions Editor
Material: All
S.K. Productions, PO Box 290206
Wethersfield CT 06129-0206

Two Dot

Please refer to Falcon Publishing.

Unity House

Unity House is a publishing imprint of Unity School of Christianity, a nondenominational religious organization founded more than one hundred years ago. It publishes books, cassettes and CDs both for and beyond the churches and congregants of the worldwide Unity movement.

Unity teachings are based on metaphysical interpretation of scriptures with an emphasis on practical application, and the demonstration of the spiritual Truth of life as taught by Jesus Christ as well as other spiritual masters. If you would like further information about Unity's teachings and beliefs, please contact Customer Service at the address on the last page of this brochure, or call 1-800-669-0282, 7:30-4:30 CST, Monday thru Thursday.

WHAT WE'RE LOOKING FOR

We publish spiritual books based on Unity principles, as well as inspirational books on self-help psychology and practical spirituality. All manuscripts must reflect a spiritual foundation and express the Unity philosophy of practical Christianity using universal principles, and/or metaphysics. We're looking for proposals (not complete manuscripts).

In reviewing proposals, one of the first things we consider is whether or not the subject would be appropriate for a person on a path of enlightenment and wholeness. The subject should be dealt with in such a way as to inform and uplift the reader, give hope, and assist with practical advice on meeting life's challenges creatively and positively. Emphasis should be on practical application of spiritual principles in everyday living. The following will give you an idea of a few of our editorial interests:

Nonfiction: Bible interpretation, biblical studies, children's issues (5-12 years), comparative religion, Eastern thought, family, finances, holistic health, humor, inspiration, leadership, meditation, marriage, mythology, New Thought, philosophy, parenting, personal experience, prayer, recovery, renewal, spirituality, teens, transpersonal psychology, and young adult issues

Fiction: Visionary fiction for adults and adolescents, children's stories (5-12 years) based on Unity principles

Some of our current titles and authors include: *Looking in for Number One* by Alan Cohen; *The Quest for Wholeness* by Robert Brumet; *The Vortex Shift* by Mario De Ferrari; *That's Just How My Spirit Travels* by Rosemary Fillmore Rhea; *Henrietta the Homely Duckling* by Phil Hahn and illustrated by Joe Coker, Jr.; *Angels Sing in Me* by James Dillet Freeman.

WHAT YOU SHOULD INCLUDE IN A PROPOSAL

When sending a proposal, you should send the following:

• A brief cover letter introducing yourself and a brief biographical resume describing your writing, education, and religious background

• A summary highlighting your proposal and its compelling, unique features–include suggested sales and publicity strategies

• A project outline and/or table of contents

• One to three sample chapters (if a children's picture book, send the entire text)

• Date your manuscript will be finished

• Self-addressed, stamped envelope (necessary for returns)

Please do not submit an entire manuscript at this stage. When we receive your proposal, we will review it and make our decision within eight weeks.

WHEN WE ASK FOR YOUR MANUSCRIPT

If we decide that your proposal will fit within the Unity House guidelines, we will request additional materials. Your manuscript must be printed with laser quality, double-spaced, and must be proofread for spelling and grammar. Should we decide to publish your manuscript, we will also require a computer disk of your manuscript.

We prefer that manuscripts be between 40,000 and 75,000 words in length, except for children's picture books. The pages should be numbered consecutively throughout the manuscript, with your book title at the top of each page.

If you quote an individual source more than casually (roughly more that 200 words in 200 pages of manuscript–less than this will usually constitute "fair use"), then you must seek formal permission from the publisher of your source. Furthermore, this guideline is not a legal guarantee of fair use nor a protection that we are offer as the publisher. Receiving permission to quote copyrighted material is your responsibility, and you are responsible for paying any fees (usually minimal) for this. Your manuscript draft will not be considered final until we have received a copy of each permission for our files.

All quotes must be verified by sending us a photocopy of the page on which the quote appears as well as a photocopy of the work's title and copyright page. If we cannot verify your quote, then we cannot use it. Please be sure all quoted material is quoted exactly.

If in your text you are referring to facts or statistics that are not easily verifiable with a good encyclopedia, world almanac, or unabridged dictionary, we require that you send us a copy of your source reference. This will help us assure that your book will be accurate.

We prefer to have Bible quotations conform to the *New Revised Standard Version*, but we will accept other translations if their version better makes your textual point. Please identify which version you are using.

We do not solicit artwork or graphic design. However, if your manuscript requires specific photographs that you can furnish, we will be happy to consider them. You are also responsible for providing an index or illustrations if you wish the book to have them.

IF WE PUBLISH YOUR MANUSCRIPT

After substantive editing is complete, expect publication in nine months. Payment contracts vary for the individual author. Copyrights are registered in the author's name.

Thank you for your interest in publishing through Unity House. If you have further questions regarding book publishing, please feel free to contact us.

Categories: Fiction—Nonfiction—New Age—Religion—Spiritual—New Thought/Metaphysical

CONTACT: BOOKS ACQUISITIONS
Material: All
Unity House
1901 NW Blue Parkway
Unity Village MO 64065-0001
Phone: 816-524-3550, ext. 3190

Fax: 816-251-3552
Website: www.unityonline.org

University of Idaho Press

The University of Idaho Press publishes titles in history and regional studies, Native American studies, folklore, western literature and literary criticism, natural sciences, and resource and policy studies. Individuals wishing to submit manuscripts should first request a current catalog to determine if the work fits the publishing program. If an author feels his or her work is appropriate for the UI Press, a cover letter explaining the purpose of the manuscript and the audience for which the book is intended should be sent along with a contents page, an introduction or preliminary chapter, and a bibliography indicating sources used.

When the director requests the entire manuscript for review, it should be prepared according to recommendations in *The Chicago Manual of Style*, Fourteenth Edition, *The Essential Guide for Writers, Editors, and Publishers* (Chicago and London: The University of Chicago Press, 1993) in all respects, including notes and bibliography. If you have followed another style guide in preparing the manuscript, please include that information when you submit the manuscript.

Please adhere to the following general guidelines:

1. Submit your manuscript on white 8 1/2 by 11 inch paper with all copy double spaced, including bibliographies, notes, and extracts (to distinguish extracts from text, draw a line next to the quoted material or use a second level of indent).

2. Include photocopies of all photographs or illustrations and indicate their approximate location in the text by numbering them consecutively and writing or circling the numbers in the left margin of the text.

3. Include all tables and indicate their location by using call-outs in the text (see *The Chicago Manual of Style*).

4. Hand number all pages consecutively in the upper right corner beginning with the first page and ending with the last page of the manuscript.

5. Use default settings and keep all special formatting to a minimum (i.e., chapter titles should be flush left in the upper and lowercase with bold or italic; subheads within chapters should be presented the same way and level of importance indicated by writing A, B, C circled in the left margin next to the headings).

6. Have the text unjustified.

7. Have no running heads or embedded page numbers.

8. Have consistent use of the tab key for paragraph indents.

9. Use one underlining command (not the italic code) for all words in a phrase (i.e., underline at the beginning of the first word and turn off the underline at the end of the last word).

10. Use the numeral 1, not the letter l, in all numbering.

11. Have notes grouped together in one or more files, numbered by chapter, double-spaced and paragraph indented, with no extra space between notes. Do not use on-page footnotes even if your software has this feature.

12. Please include a list of accented letters or special characters and hand-marked diacriticals instead of embedded diacritical marks.

The manuscript will be reviewed in-house. If the work seems a likely candidate for publication, it will be submitted to two or more readers. The readers may suggest the need for revisions and subsequent readings prior to the manuscript being presented to the editorial board, or the manuscript may be rejected at this stage. The editorial board provides final approval for all titles published by the UI Press.

Thank you for your interest in the University of Idaho Press. Please contact us if you have any questions.

Categories: Nonfiction—Folklore—History—Human Rights—Literature—Native American—Regional—Science

CONTACT: Candace J. Akins, Managing Editor
Material: All

PO Box 444416
Moscow ID 83844-4416
Phone: 208-885-3300
E-mail: candacea@uidaho.edu
Website: www.uidaho.edu/uipress

University of Maine Press

The University of Maine Press publishes scholarly books and original writing which focus on the intellectual concerns of the Maine region. Although the press occasionally publishes works of regional fiction (and works of nonfiction which are outside of its regional focus) the press is primarily interested in publishing scholarly studies in the sciences, the social sciences, and the humanities.

An author who is considering the University of Maine Press should send a letter of inquiry, a synopsis, and—if appropriate—a few representative chapters or sections from the manuscript of the proposed book. The entire manuscript should not be sent to the press with the initial inquiry. An author should not send the only copy of anything to the press. Although the press will make every effort to safeguard what it receives, it cannot be held responsible for lost manuscripts. A stamped envelope should be included with the letter and supportive material.

Since proposals for books need to be considered by the Director of the Press, the Board of Directors and outside expert readers, a thorough consideration of the initial manuscript material may take several months. The Director of the Press will make every attempt to expedite this process.

Inquires should be sent to Michael Alpert, Director of the Press. Correspondence about the status of a proposal should also be sent to the Director of the Press at the address below.

All manuscript material should be presented in a legible typeface, with ample margins and double line-spacing, to facilitate reading and annotation. Manuscript material in obvious need of basic copy-editing will not be considered by the press. In general, authors should prepare manuscript material by following the guidelines in *The Chicago Manual of Style* or a comparable standard style-manual in the author's discipline. Approved manuscripts must be submitted in hardcopy form and in Microsoft Word or a comparable electronic file that can be imported into commonly-used publishing software. AUG. 2002

Categories: Nonfiction—Agriculture—Arts—Biography—Civil War—History—Regional

CONTACT: Michael Alpert, Director of the Press
Material: All
126A College Ave.
Orono ME 04473
Phone: 207-866-0573
Fax: 207-866-2084

University of Nebraska Press

The Mission of the University of Nebraska Press

The University of Nebraska Press, founded in 1941, seeks to encourage, develop, publish, and disseminate research, literature, and the publishing arts. The Press is the largest academic publisher in the Great Plains and a major publisher of books about that region. It is the state"s largest repository of the knowledge, arts, and skills of publishing and advises the University and the people of Nebraska about book publishing. Reporting to the Vice-Chancellor for Research and having a faculty advisory board, the Press maintains scholarly standards and fosters innovations guided by refereed evaluations.

What is the University of Nebraska Press?

The University of Nebraska Press is the second largest state university press in the nation (following only the University of California Press) in terms of titles published, and is among the top ten university presses in the nation in terms of annual sales volume.

The Press is the largest and most diversified university press between Chicago and California, and seeks to serve as the publisher for that enormous region. We proudly publish excellent writers and scholars, including those of our own university system, and foster projects on the culture and history of the state and of the entire West. As the population and influence of the West increase, we intend to keep pace, providing our university, state, and region with a publishing program equal to the energies, needs and intelligence of the area.

We currently have influential programs in Native studies, the history of the American West, literary and cultural studies, music, and Jewish studies. We are among the leading scholarly publishers of books in translation. We have recently inaugurated successful lists in military history, sports history, and environmental history. Catalogs describing our new books are available, as are specialty catalogs for several of our publishing programs (please send e-mail to pressmail@unl.edu).

We have initiated programs in nonprint publishing, including cassettes, CD-ROM, and on-demand databases, and have an electronic media department that not only produces materials in the current technologies but is actively researching state-of-the-art technological developments to assess their likely opportunities and impact on scholarly publishing.

How Do I Choose a Publisher?

The most important work an aspiring author must do is read. The writer who does not read will seldom become an author. An author must read for two reasons: first, to be sure that what he or she writes is genuinely new; and second, to know which publishers are interested in different kinds of books.

Publishers tend to specialize. Some concentrate on gardening, some on children"s books, some on religion, computers, or stamp collecting. Look in a large library and look for recent books like the one you are writing. Write to those publishers that best match your needs. Don"t waste time, energy, and postage on publishers that have never shown any interest in the kind of book that interests you. Some guidebooks, available in the reference books section of public and university libraries, that may help in this search are *Literary MarketPlace*, an annual published by R. R. Bowker, and *Writer's Market*, an annual published by *Writer's Digest Books*.

Remember that publishers look upon publishing as a profession. They will want you to behave professionally. Very few amateurs can tolerate the stress and effort required to be a published author.

What does the University of Nebraska Press Publish?

We publish books and scholarly journals only, and have no programs in contemporary fiction or poetry. On occasion, we reprint previously published fiction of established reputation and we have several programs to publish literary works in translation. But we cannot undertake original fiction, regardless of topic, children's books, or the work of living poets. Our mission, defined by the University through the Press Advisory Board of faculty members working in concert with the Press, is to find, evaluate, and publish in the best fashion possible, serious works of non-fiction.

How Do I Approach a Publisher?

We prefer to see prospectuses prior to inviting completed manuscripts. Such prospectuses should include the following: an outline, with a paragraph describing each chapter; a cover letter describing the length and focus of the manuscript; and a copy of the author"s curriculum vitae or resume.

We receive more than 1000 inquiries each year. Although we are delighted to find so much interest in our press, we can only invite submission of a small fraction of these projects, and then publish an even smaller fraction of the manuscripts actually invited. Literary translations are especially competitive.

When we receive an invited manuscript an acknowledgment of receipt is immediately sent, and we evaluate the work promptly to determine whether it would fit our list. If we think it may be appropriate, we send it to two experts in the field for their comments. If both readers endorse publication, we take the manuscript and readers" reports to our faculty committee and request approval to publish. The entire review process usually takes four to six months, and can be longer if the expert readers counsel significant changes.

We are becoming increasingly adept at using computer disks. Nevertheless, we prefer to see printed pages for any prospectus or invited manuscript. All pages should be prepared in conformity with *The Chicago Manual of Style*, 14th edition.

A guide to manuscript preparation is available from our receptionist, or by mail upon request, or e-mail pressmail@unl.edu.

What if I Write Fiction, Poetry, or Children"s Books?

Again, be sure to read dozens if not hundreds of books to understand what other people are reading and writing. If you want to publish a book of fiction or poetry or a book for children, you must be prepared for a difficult challenge. These are the most competitive areas of publishing, with thousands of authors vying for attention. Publishers of fiction and poetry prefer authors who have published their work in journals. Most poets and fiction writers have begun publishing in literary magazines. When they have established a reputation they can collect their poems and stories into books.

Spend time in a large library looking at literary journals like *Prairie Schooner*, *Iowa Review*, *Chicago Review*, and *Tri-Quarterly*. Find a journal that you like which you believe will like you. Look for its editorial policy and rules for submission.

The University of Nebraska Press does not publish in the areas of fiction, poetry, or children's books.

Where Can I Go for Help?

For addresses of literary journals see *International Directory of Little Magazines and Small Presses*. For addresses of book publishers see *Literary MarketPlace*.

Should you try to find an agent?

Probably not until you have already published several works in different places.

What if the publisher asks for money? Be cautious and learn as much as you can about the publisher and its reputation, as you would in buying any product or service. Be sure you understand what is being offered for the money.

Should I Publish Myself?

Many of the most famous and beloved writers in American literature published their works themselves. These writers include Walt Whitman, Marianne Moore, Ezra Pound, John Neihardt, Edgar Allan Poe, and Upton Sinclair.

Family stories and family histories are best published by the authors themselves. It is very difficult to sell books you publish yourself, but you can give books to people whose affection and attention matters to you.

To publish yourself you need to find a printer you trust. Look in the phone book to find a list of printers, then call them to see whether they can print and bind books. If they do, visit their offices and see samples of their work. Check different printers to find the best quality at the best price.

There are several guides to publishing books yourself; also, there are professional consultants who offer assistance with the process (see section 64 in *Literary MarketPlace*). Additionally there are a number of guidebooks to the individual parts of book publishing (production, marketing, publicity, etc.). Large public libraries and writers" workshops may be able to suggest appropriate and useful titles.

Can the University of Nebraska Press Help Me?

Even if we can't publish your book (we, too, must specialize) we can offer some help to citizens of Nebraska. If you receive an offer from a publisher, we will be happy to discuss the offer with you.

If you have questions about publishing jargon, we can try to explain it.

Editorial Program

The University of Nebraska Press publishes on the following topical areas:

Agriculture
The American Indian
American literature
The American West
Anthropology, Ethnology, and Archaeology
Civil War studies
English literature
Environmental studies
The Great Plains
Jewish Studies
Latin American studies
Literature in translation
Military history
Modern history of Western Europe
Music
Natural history
Philosophy and religion
Political science
Psychology
Sociology
Sports history
Women's studies
Submissions are not invited in original poetry or fiction.
Special imprints: Bison Books; Bison Originals; Landmark Editions.

Categories: Nonfiction—African-American—Agriculture—Arts—Biography—Civil War—Conservation—Culture—Ecology—Environment—Feminism—Film/Video—Government—Hispanic—History—Jewish Interest—Language—Literature—Military—Music—Native American—Politics—Psychology—Regional—Rural America—Sports/Recreation—Western—Women's Issues—Ethnic—Philosophy—Public Policy

CONTACT: Submissions Editor
Material: All
233 N. 8th St.
Lincoln NE 68588-0255
Phone: 402-472-3584
Fax: 402-472-0308
E-mail: pressmail@unl.edu
Website: www.unp.unl.edu

University of Nevada Press

The University of Nevada Press is a public service division of the University and Community College System of Nevada. Its mission is to make a contribution to the State of Nevada, as well as to the national and international scholarly communities, by publishing books in the humanities, sciences, and social sciences that deal with the history, literature, natural history and resources, environment, economy, politics, anthropology, ethnic groups and cultures of Nevada and the West; the Basque people of Europe and the Americas; Native Americans; gambling and commercial gaming; and contemporary affairs.

In addition to books of general and scholarly interest, the Press publishes seven distinguished series of books: the Basque Series; the Wilbur S. Shepperson Series in Nevada History; the Western Literature Series; the Max C. Fleischmann Series in Great Basin Natural History; and the Gambling Studies Series. The Press also publishes original fiction, and creative nonfiction; and books on regional themes for a general audience.

INITIAL REVIEW

We ask authors interested in submitting their work to the University of Nevada Press to send us first a manuscript proposal, which should consist of a table of contents; a summary or chapter outline of the manuscript; information about its length, number and type of illustrations (if any are planned), and any special components, such as footnotes, bibliography, appendices, tables, glossaries, etc.; information about the book's intended audience and any competing works already in publication; and a representative sample section of the text, consisting of a chapter or two, or in the case of short fiction, a couple of sample stories. A brief vita of the author should accompany this material.

Once we have reviewed the proposal, we shall, if the project seems suited for our publishing program, invite the author to submit the entire manuscript for formal consideration.

FORMAL REVIEW

When we invite an author to submit a full manuscript for our consideration, we ask for two clean paper copies of the entire manuscript, including all notes, bibliography, appendices, and any other components.

If the book is to include illustrations, please send only photocopies at this time.

If the manuscript exists on an electronic disk, we do not need to have access to the disk during the review process. If the manuscript exists only on paper, please provide us with two clear photocopies.

Do not bind the manuscript or enclose it in a binder. Double-space everything (all text, quotations, footnotes, bibliography, figure captions, tables, lists, appendices, etc.). Number the pages consecutively from the beginning to the end of the manuscript. Long quotations (10 lines or more) should be indented an extra five spaces. Use paragraph indents if the quotations were indented in the original. Notes should be placed at the end of the manuscript (not at the bottoms of the pages or ends of the chapters).

Photographs, figures, charts, graphs, tables, etc., should be on separate pages, not on pages with text.

Authors of manuscripts that contain illustrations or large amounts of quoted material and editors of anthologies will be responsible, if the Press makes a publishing commitment, for obtaining all necessary permissions to reprint and for paying any related fees. Fiction authors should include information about any previous publication of this material, including date of first publication and titles of venue.

If the Press makes a publishing offer, the author is required to provide two paper copies of the final draft of the manuscript (which incorporates all revisions recommended by the Press's editors and outside readers) and a disk containing the manuscript formatted to the Press's specifications.

Helpful reference book: *The Chicago Manual of Style*, available at most libraries and books stores.

MANUSCRIPT EVALUATION PROCESS

The review process consists of several stages. Manuscripts are read first by an in-house editor. If they appear suited for our publishing program, they are evaluated by readers from outside the house who are recognized authorities in the subject matter of the manuscript or, in the case of literary work, by distinguished critics or writers in the genre of the manuscript (usually both). After two favorable outside evaluations, the manuscript is presented to the Press's Editorial Board, which consists of eight representatives from the campuses of the University and Community College System of Nevada and the Desert Research Institute, which controls the Press's imprint. Only after Board approval is the Press able to make a publishing commitment.

Publication takes place after negotiation and acceptance of a formal contract between the Press and the author or his/her agent. In most cases, the author receives a royalty on book sales, the amount of which is negotiated at the time the contract is offered.

Categories: Fiction—Nonfiction—Biography—Ecology—Environment—General Interest—History—Literature—Native American—Politics—Regional—Science—Ethnic

CONTACT: Joanne O'Hare, Director
Material: All
MS 166
Reno NV 89557-0076

Books M-Z

Phone: 775-784-6573
Fax: 775-784-6200
Website: www.nvbooks.nevada.edu

University of North Texas Press

The University of North Texas Press was established in August 1987, and its first books were published in 1989. We publish approximately 15 books a year, with more than 200 books currently in print. Our books are distributed and marketed nationally and internationally through a university press consortium.

The University of North Texas Press is dedicated to producing the highest quality scholarly, academic and general interest books for the Dallas-Fort Worth-Denton metroplex, state, national and international communities as part of an outreach activity. As a part of the largest and most comprehensive research university in North Texas, UNT Press holds to the philosophy that university presses should be on the cutting edge of publishing and thus is not averse to the different and unusual in its publishing agenda.

We are committed to serving all peoples by publishing stories of their cultures and their experiences that have been overlooked. We seek to nurture the development of writers by publishing first books and by publishing poetry. We strive to advance understanding and appreciation of the historical, intellectual, scientific and cultural milieu through our publications. Through sales, advertisements, and reviews of UNT Press books nationally and internationally, we strive to enhance and support the University of North Texas as an academic presence in education and community life.

Publishing Emphasis

The University of North Texas Press is the publisher of the Texas Folklore Society Publications. We also publish the following series: War and the Southwest, Texas Writers (critical biography), Western Life, Practical Guide, the Katherine Anne Porter Prize in Short Fiction, the Vassar Miller Prize in Poetry, and the North Texas Crime and Criminal Justice Series.

Please note that manuscripts for the Vassar Miller Prize in Poetry should be sent, along with the entry fee, directly to the editor of the series: Scott Cairns, English Department, Tate Hall 107, University of Missouri, Columbia, MO 65211.

Note also that manuscripts for the Katherine Anne Porter Prize in Short Fiction should be sent, along with the entry fee to: KAP contest, Department of English, University of North Texas, P.O. Box 311307, Denton, TX 76203.

Procedures

The decision-making process at UNT Press is like other university presses. If we feel your proposal fits with our publishing list and publishing schedule, we will ask for a complete manuscript, which will then be evaluated by at least two expert readers. These confidential reports are taken to the UNT Press Editorial Board, which has the final say on whether or not we will publish the book. Both the readers and the Editorial Board may have suggestions on revising and improving the manuscript. Sometimes their approval may be contingent on whether or not these changes are made.

The review process can take several months, depending upon the time necessary to receive and compile reports from the readers and the Editorial Board. Once the Editorial Board recommends publication, we will send you a contract for your consideration. Once the contract is signed by both parties, the publication process will usually be from nine months to a year.

Publication Process

UNT Press books are all printed on acid-free paper, according to the American National Standard for Permanence of paper for printed library materials. Many of our books are sent to the printer in electronic form, with design and typesetting done on computer, both by in-house and by outside designers and typesetters.

Editing is done by both in-house and freelance editors, with the author being given an opportunity to check the edited manuscript, answer questions asked by the editor and offer input on changes made. The author also sees the book in page proofs, for the final chance to correct typographical errors and other problems that may arise. If the book is to be indexed, it will be done at this time.

Once the book goes to the printer, it usually takes around 40 working days for a hardback book and around 35 working days for a paperback book to be printed, bound, wrapped and shipped to the warehouse for distribution to bookstores.

Marketing

You will be sent an author biography form to fill out which will help in marketing your book. You are encouraged to become actively involved in the marketing. It is our experience that the most successful books are the ones in which the author has been particularly aggressive in seeking out markets for the books, arranging speaking engagements with appropriate groups, arranging book signings and other venues offering opportunities for book sales. Contacting your sources for book reviews is another effective marketing tool.

We will have your book at most of the major conferences and will consider taking them to other meetings you notify us about.

Since we consider our backlist books the backbone of our publishing house, we actively promote the backlist titles and seek course adoptions for the books. Your book will be kept in print as long as demand justifies.

We have sales representatives throughout the United States, including Hawaii and Alaska. We have representation in Canada, Europe, Latin America, Asia, Australia, New Zealand, and the Pacific Islands.

We are part of a university press consortium that actively markets our books to major bookstore and library accounts and to national and regional distributors, as well as to individuals, through both extensive mailing lists and professional sales representation.

The Final Manuscript

Manuscripts submitted should be prepared according to the guidelines given here. Even if the book is to be typeset from diskettes provided by the author, one hard (paper) copy of the manuscript is needed.

Hard Copy:

• Once a contract is signed, we need two hard copies of the ms.

• Word-processed manuscripts printed with letter-quality or near letter-quality printer. No dot matrix.

• No right-justification or proportional interspacing on word-processed manuscripts.

• Number pages consecutively through the manuscript; DO NOT begin renumbering with each chapter.

• Include photocopies, with captions, of any photographs or illustrations. (If you have already signed a contract with us, at this point we need original photos or duplicate prints.)

Computer Disks:

• These are not necessary until after a decision to publish the book has been made. (At that time, we will also need actual photographs and art work submitted with disks and hard copy.)

• Use the same hardware and software systems from start to finish.

• Keep formatting and fonts to a minimum. Most of it must be removed before typesetting.

• Once you have printed out the hard copy, do not make further changes on the computer disks.

• Name files sequentially ("A. Front matter," "B. Ch 1," "C. Ch 2," etc.) Submit a list of file names with disks. Do not put an entire manuscript in a single document.

• Front matter (title page, dedication, book epigraph, table of contents, lists of illustrations or tables, preface, acknowledgments, introduction, and foreword) and back matter (notes, bibliography, appendixes, index, and/or glossary) should be in separate files.

- Use endnotes at the end of chapters rather than footnotes at the bottom of the page.
- Double-space endnotes and bibliography.
- Do not put two spaces after periods like you do in a type-written document. This causes formatting problems. Do not put two spaces after colons, or anywhere else in the manuscript.
- Do not double-space between paragraphs.
- Use tabs, not spaces, to indent paragraphs.

Style Manual:

In general, the University of North Texas Press follows *The Chicago Manual of Style*. However, we like to remain flexible to the needs of each manuscript, so alternate styles are open for discussion.

Categories: Fiction—Nonfiction—African-American—Animals—Biography—Civil War—Conservation—Cooking—Crime—Ecology—Environment—Feminism—Folklore—General Interest—History—Literature—Military—Multicultural—Music—Poetry—Short Stories—True Crime—Western—Women's Fiction—Texana/Texas Regional

CONTACT: Acquisitions Editor
Material: All
PO Box 311336
Denton TX 76203-1336
Phone: 940-565-2142
Fax: 940-565-4590

University of Oklahoma Press

University of Oklahoma Press

During its more than seventy years of continuous operation, the University of Oklahoma Press has gained international recognition as an outstanding source of scholarly literature. It was the first university press established in the Southwest, and the fourth in the western half of the country.

The Press began as an idea of a man of vision, William Bennett Bizzell, the fifth president of the University of Oklahoma and a wide-ranging humanist and book collector. Over the years, the Press has grown from a staff of one—the first director, Joseph A. Brandt—to an active and capable team of more than forty members.

The OU Press continues its dedication to the publication of outstanding scholarly works.

Under the guidance of the present director, John Drayton, the major editorial goal of the Press is to maintain its position as a preeminent publisher of books about the American West and American Indians, while expanding its program in other scholarly disciplines, including archaeology, classical studies, military history, language and literature, natural science, and women's studies.

GUIDELINES FOR AUTHORS
Introduction

The mission of the University of Oklahoma Press is to publish scholarly books of significance to the state, region, nation, and world both to convey the results of current research to other scholars and to offer broader presentations for the general public.

Founded in 1928, the University of Oklahoma Press was the first university press established in the Southwest and the fourth founded in the western half of the nation. Over time the Press has grown from a staff of one to a team of more than forty people who work in acquisitions, editing, design and production, marketing and sales, rights, distribution, accounting, and administration.

The University of Oklahoma Press is dedicated to publishing outstanding scholarly works by national and international scholars. The Press's ongoing editorial goal is to maintain its preeminent position as a publisher of books about the West and the American Indian and to expand its program in other scholarly disciplines, including archaeology, classical studies, energy studies, language and literature (excluding unsolicited fiction and poetry), natural sciences, political science, and women's studies. Books published by the Press, including those in the series listed below, have accumulated an impressive array of honors and awards.

Series currently published by the Press include:
- American Exploration and Travel
- American Indian Literature and Critical Studies
- Animal Natural History
- Campaigns and Commanders
- Centers of Civilization
- Chicana and Chicano Visions of the Americas
- Civilization of the American Indian
- Congressional Studies
- Gilcrease-Oklahoma Series on Western Art and Artists
- Julian J. Rothbaum Distinguished Lecture Series
- Literature of the American West
- Oklahoma Museum of Natural History Publications
- Oklahoma Series in Classical Culture
- Oklahoma Western Biographies
- Series for Science and Culture
- Variorum Chaucer
- Western Frontier Library

Manuscript Submission and the Review Process

Our decision to publish a book is based chiefly on its contribution to knowledge in fields compatible with our list, sound scholarship, clear writing style, and financial feasibility.

The Press often solicits manuscripts and manuscript proposals. For unsolicited inquiries we prefer to receive:

1. A letter of inquiry that briefly describes the manuscript, its approximate length (including number and kinds of illustrations), its purpose, and its relationship to other books in its field;

2. The author's qualifications to write such a book;

3. A table of contents or, in the case of a proposal, a description of projected contents;

4. A sample chapter.

Upon receipt of your proposal, we will evaluate it and respond to you. If we wish to pursue the project, we will ask to see the complete manuscript. Unless we are told otherwise, we will assume that no other publisher has it under consideration while we consider it for publication.

Manuscripts that pass initial in-house scrutiny are sent to experts in the subject area for evaluation and then considered by an in-house Editorial Committee. Authors of manuscripts not recommended for publication are informed immediately. Manuscripts still under consideration are either presented to the

Press's Faculty Advisory Board or returned to the author for revision and re-submission. If the Board approves publication, the Press offers the author a contract for publication. An in-house decision to publish a book is usually made in approximately three to six months.

Manuscript proposals should be directed to the appropriate editor at the University of Oklahoma.

Categories: Nonfiction—Biography—Civil War—History—Literature—Native American—Regional—Western—Archaeology

CONTACT: John Drayton, Director
Material: Classics
CONTACT: Charles Rankin, Editor-in-Chief
Material: History of the American West, military history, Oklahoma history
CONTACT: Jean Hurtado, Acquisitions Editor
Material: History of the American West, natural history, political science, women's studies

Books
M-Z

CONTACT: Jo Ann Reece, Acquisitions Editor
Material: American Indian anthropology and history,
Mesoamerican studies, Latin American studies
CONTACT: Daniel Simon, Acquisitions Editor
Material: Literature and paperback reprints of previously
published works in the above fields
1005 Asp Ave.
Norman OK 73019-6051
Phone: 405-325-5114
Fax: 405-325-4000
Website: www.oupress.com

UpstartBooks
Creative Ideas for Library
and Classroom Learning

General

UpstartBooks is an imprint of Highsmith Press. UpstartBooks accepts unsolicited proposals and manuscripts from prospective authors, and we welcome your inquiries. We recommend that you review our online catalog to see the types of materials we publish. Essentially, our primary interests are resources that aid media specialists, librarians and teachers to develop and stimulate reading interests, and facilitate library and information-seeking skills among youth (preschool through high school).

UpstartBooks has over 80 titles currently in print, and we publish approximately twelve new titles a year. We seek to reach a decision on each submission or proposal within 60 days, but in order to achieve this goal we need your cooperation by following these submission guidelines.

Specifics

For manuscripts which are less than 100 pages, we would like to receive the entire work for review, including illustrations.

For longer manuscripts, please send selected sections and illustrations that best describe the project, including the introduction.

We also welcome outlines of prospective projects, particularly if the manuscript is very lengthy.

Please include a cover letter summarizing the purpose of the work and its potential market. Identify any other recent books which have been published on a similar topic, and describe how your book differs.

In your letter state which computer software and platform you used (or plan to use) to develop your manuscript. We can accept a wide variety of Windows and Macintosh software programs. We do not need to receive an electronic version of your manuscript for initial evaluation, but we do require that final manuscripts be in an electronic format.

Attach a current resume listing your qualifications.

Include a self-addressed stamped envelope so we may return your material if we do not accept your manuscript for publication.

Do not send your only manuscript copy; send us a photocopy.

We are not troubled by manuscripts which are being simultaneously submitted to other publishers. We do not have any guidelines for artwork, although we will consider artwork submitted with manuscripts.

At present, we are interested in proposals or manuscripts on the following subjects:

• Creative reading activity books that can be used by children's and school librarians, and teachers to stimulate reading among youth.

• Basic guides for teachers and librarians that offer instructional activities, lesson plans and resources that develop library, information-seeking and computer skills among youth.

• Guides to library-realted resources on the Internet for youth.

• Storytelling resources for children's librarians, teachers and professional storytellers that feature interesting and easy-to-learn stories and storytelling techniques.

• The specific terms we can offer authors and illustrators will vary with the nature of each project. However, we do provide very competitive royalties and advances, and we emphasize quality design and high production standards. Please call Matt Mulder at (920) 563-9571 if you have any questions or concerns.

Categories: Fiction—Nonfiction—Children—Education—Juvenile—Teen

CONTACT: Matt Mulder, Director of Publications
Material: All
Highsmith Press
PO Box 800
Ft. Atkinson WI 53538-0800
Phone: 920-563-9571
Fax: 920-563-4801(8 pages or less only)
E-mail: mmulder@highsmith.com (4 pages or less)
Website: www.hpress.highsmith.com

USA Books, Inc

We publish: children's, non-fiction, and historical fiction (no crime) with a strong accent on current affairs.

Send two-page synopsis of the work + 3 sample chapters + 1-paragraph author's bio in word format by email to:
Reading committee; Att: Sean Besanger (sbesanger@aol.com).
Do not send whole work.
We respond within a week.
Categories: Fiction—Nonfiction—Biography—Children—History—Mystery—Self Help—Western

CONTACT: Submissions Editor
Material: All
244, Fifth Ave.
New York NY 10001-7604
Phone: 212-561 0849
E-mail: sbesanger@aol.com

Vanwell Publishing

Please refer to Howell Press, Inc.

Via Dolorosa Press

Background

Via Dolorosa Press began in February of 1994. It was originally created to showcase dark works for the goth music scene, but eventually took a more philanthropic role by providing quality reading material to suicidal and depressed individuals. VDP continues to fill this niche in the small press with our selection of cathartic works.

Our specialty is work that is dark, painful, and anguished. We take the opposite stance of conventional therapy as we feel that the sharing of catharsis is more helpful than mainstream inspirational work. (Please be aware that, despite the religious connotations of our name, VDP is *not* a Christian publisher.) It has been our mission to present quality literature helping suffering people see that they are not alone in their struggle and that they can conquer their pain through solidarity.

The majority of our readers are between the ages of 18 and 40. They are extremely well-read and veer from traditional styles and subject matter. Most are in college or have completed degrees. Also, many of our readers are writers themselves, so they pay closer attention to the quality and style of writing than does the average person. Our readers demand higher-level writing, and this makes us very particular about the work we accept.

What We Are Looking For

While we strongly encourage *all* people to write as catharsis, we primarily print writing that *results from* catharsis, not necessarily that *is* catharsis. There is a huge difference between the two and we expect writers to be able to distinguish this difference.

It is necessary to note that we are not interested in work which deals with recovery from abuse (be it physical, mental, sexual, etc.) nor mental health issues. VDP is not qualified to handle such subjects.

We will not accept works which involve incest, rape, abuse, mental health, or geriatric issues as primary subjects.

Works which are directed to children or which feature children as main characters are inappropriate. As stated before, we cater to an adult audience. However, works which feature *excessive* sexual scenes are also inappropriate. Erotica is a great genre (and you can send us some if you really want to put us in good moods!), but we don't print it. We have no aversions to obscene language, just make sure it fits the work.

It is also extremely necessary to reiterate that we are not a Christian publisher. This means that we do not and will not print works about Christianity or works with a Christian slant. We repeatedly receive manuscripts that are supposedly directed to an open audience—Christians and non-Christians alike—but have really only been glorified religious propaganda. There are many new and successful magazines and publishers these days which specialize in Christian-themed work (and the demand is high), so if your manuscript has that slant, we encourage you to submit to those places, not VDP. Our stance does not only apply to Christianity; however, we do not support *any* organized religion or political ideology. Any work which slants toward religion or politics is inappropriate for VDP and will be rejected.

Art will be reviewed with the manuscript as a whole. Please note that we do not print in color. Also, pen and ink drawings are preferred to photographs and paintings as they reproduce best with our mode of printing. Permission to use someone else's artwork must be obtained prior to submitting the manuscript; we do not contact the artist(s) on the author's behalf and will request written proof of permission before accepting the artwork for printing.

There are also specific details for each genre we print:

Poetry

As poetry is our specialty, we are very particular about the manuscripts we accept. We publish dark, introspective writing only. It is *highly* recommended that you read a selection of our books to see what we prefer. We do not accept traditional (rhyming) verse or concrete poetry. We will review and consider experimental poetry, but if it's too elusive we may decline it. Our preference is towards confessional, free verse poetry (like the style of Anne Sexton). We receive a high volume of poetry submissions that are quickly rejected because the style is not like something we'd publish. Please be familiar with our work.

Fiction

We only print fiction that is thematically and stylistically like what Nathanael West would write if he were still alive. Any work unlike that will not be reviewed. As with our usual style, we look for darker material. We are interested in existential, humanist, nihilist, phenomenologist, and solipsist slants.

Non-Fiction

We are looking primarily for literary and philosophical essays. Literary criticisms should cover writers, works, or movements from the 20th century that were typically ignored by mainstream America. We are interested in more works covering Scandinavian poets and novelists of 1930-50, especially Swedish writers. Philosophical criticisms should cover existentialism, humanism, nihilism, phenomenology, and/or solipsism. We are not interested in works on any other philosophical ideologies. We prefer thesis-length works that include a healthy bibliography/works cited section.

How to Submit

For poetry, we suggest that you submit the entire manuscript, along with a cover letter and a list of publishing credits.

For fiction, we suggest that you send a query letter with the approximate word count, a short synopsis, the first 3 pages of your story, and a list of publishing credits.

For non-fiction, we suggest that you send a query letter with the approximate word count, a short synopsis, your table of contents, a few sample pages from one of the chapters, and a list of publishing

credits.

Please note: At this time we are only accepting works under 12,500 words. (VDP primarily prints chapbooks which we hand-bind or staple saddleback. This word count limit is in place as have volume limitations. Within the next few years we will begin outsourcing our printing and all books will be trade paperbacks, at which time our word/page limit will be lifted.)

We do not accept submissions by email or fax; all manuscripts should be sent via post or courier with sufficient postage. Please do not send submissions by certified mail, registered mail, or any other form that requires signed receipt, as we are often unavailable when the mail is delivered. If you want confirmation of receipt prior to our acceptance/rejection letter, please include an additional SASE with your manuscript (foreign addresses send an IRC and SAE).

Agented submissions are *not* accepted. We work directly with writers and will reject any and all manuscripts submitted by agents.

All manuscripts should be formatted in the proper MLA style and typed; we do not accept handwritten manuscripts. Double-space lines for fiction and non-fiction. Poetry should be single-spaced. Please indicate on poems longer than one page where the stanza breaks should be.

Excessive spelling, punctuation, &/or grammatical errors will warrant rejection.

On a minor note, please refrain from using "he/she" and variations of it. Despite how politically-correct that form may be, we find it awkward and annoying. We prefer to see either "he" or "she" used consistently throughout the work. Pick a sex! If in doubt, use the masculine form. We also frown upon politically-correct forms of words when the original word is more recognized and sounds better. We will edit out all laborious politically-correct terms.

Rejected manuscripts are only returned to authors when a SASE with sufficient postage (or IRCs for foreign submissions) has been sent with the work.

One last word before submitting…

All magazines and publishing companies say this, and it's true: know your market. We can't stress enough how important it is to know the style and theme of the places you submit your work to. No editor wants to review something that has nothing to do with the type of work he prints. You should always read through the last year's worth of issues from a magazine you're planning to query or read recent books a publishing company you are interested in has released. We are reminding writers of this as 95% of the manuscripts we receive are not stylistically or thematically fitting for VDP.

Submission Address:

Submit all manuscripts to the address below. Include a SASE (or IRC) for a response; we do not respond via email and do not acknowledge submissions sent without a SASE.

Terms of Acceptance

Via Dolorosa Press has very straightforward terms which are standard for all works. We do not work on a negotiation basis as do many other publishing companies (which is why we discourage agented submissions). Our terms are listed below so that you may decide prior to submission if VDP is a worthwhile market for your work.

Like any other small press, our budget is very limited. We used to pay in copies only, but we are established enough now to also pay royalties. We cannot pay advances on works and do not purchase manuscripts outright. Please keep in mind, however, that we are not funded by any state or national grants, and we do not require authors to subsidize the printing of their works. We expect, though, that you know the plight of small presses and the difference between them and large publishing companies if you are considering VDP as your publisher.

Our terms are as follows:

We ask for first print rights and limited reprint rights. Authors retain all other rights to their work.

Authors receive initial payment as copies equaling 10% of the first print run. Our first print runs are small, usually between 50 and 250 copies. Many of the remaining 90% of copies are sent out to other journals and magazines for public review. Any remainders are for sale to the public and help fund the second printing.

Beginning with the first book of the second printing (and continuing until the book is no longer published), the author will receive a 25% royalty payment on the sale price of each copy sold.

Additional compensation may be provided based on each contract, and at the editor's discretion.

Royalty payments are made quarterly.

Specific information such as sale price, royalty amount, and royalty payment dates are different for each work accepted. These details are provided on our acceptance letter.

Categories: Fiction—Nonfiction—Drama—Experimental Fiction—Literature—Philosophy—Poetry—Short Stories

CONTACT: Ms. Hyacinthe L. Raven, Editor
Material: All
701 E. Schaaf Rd.
Cleveland, OH 44131-1227

Virginia Foundation for the Humanities Press

Please refer to Howell Press, Inc.

Volcano Press

No formal guidelines available.

A BRIEF HISTORY OF VOLCANO PRESS

We are often asked how Volcano Press began, inasmuch as the subject of domestic violence thirty years ago was hardly a household word.

Actually, I was on the publications staff of the Glide Foundation in San Francisco, back in the 70s. Glide was a very forward-looking proactive organization, engaged in many avant-garde programs. It reflected the mood and spirit of San Francisco and the Bay Area of that time, where almost anything new and innovative seemed possible. And, since we had adequate funding, it was like Camelot—"...where it only rained at night".

So we published many books which were the first of their kind. "Battered Wives", "Lesbian Woman, Menopause~Naturally, Senior Power: Growing Old Rebelliously, Jury Woman, Learning to Live Without Violence: A Workbook for Men, to name a few.

But eventually the Glide Foundation encountered other financial pressing needs in the community, including feeding the poor and homeless, and the publications program was acquired by me. What had been Glide Publications became Volcano Press, a woman-owned California corporation. Today, of course, I now have a wonderful partner, my son Adam, whose energy and skills are once again re-vitalizing our publishing activities.

A review of our ever-changing, expanding website is the best way to learn about us. And as ever, we welcome comments, queries-even pats on the back.

Categories: Human Rights—Marriage—Parenting—Relationships—Senior Citizen—Women's Issues

CONTACT: Ruth Gottstein, Publisher
Material: All
PO Box 270
Volcano, CA 95689
Website: www.volcanopress.com

Voyageur Press

Welcome to Voyageur Press, publisher of quality nonfiction books on nature, travel, and American heritage. Founded in 1972, Voyageur takes pride in publishing titles featuring exceptional four-color photography and informative, entertaining text. With more than two hundred titles in print and foreign editions throughout the world, Voyageur publishes an average of forty new books a year.

Nature

Voyageur's large-format natural history books detail the behavior, habitat, and conservation of the world's wildlife, including wolves, bears, deer, dolphins, sea turtles, reptiles, raptors, hummingbirds, and bluebirds. Our nature authors include wilderness experts Dr. L. David Mech, Doug Perrine, Dr. Leonard Lee Rue III, and the late Erwin Bauer.

Voyageur also publishes a range of titles on the natural world, including Ken Libbrecht's bestselling pop science book, The Snowflake, and Ted Kerasote's modern wilderness adventure, Out There: In the Wild in a Wired Age. In addition, we have a successful series celebrating our nation's wild places and promoting conservation, led by Judith Sellers's Colorado Wild.

Travel

Our travel titles take readers throughout the United States, exploring historic landmarks and natural wonders through stunning photography and narrative text. Destinations range from canoe country to wine country, from the graceful plantation homes of the South to the fascinating ghost towns of the West. Our popular state backroads series explores secluded roads and unique sites, while our regional lighthouses series tours the historic sentries of America's coasts. We also have an established series of city and state photography books. Titles include Joseph Arrigo's Louisiana Plantation Homes, Philip Varney's Ghost Towns of Northern California, Shawn Perich's Backroads of Minnesota, Jon Marcus's Lighthouses of New England, and J. C. Leacock's Our Colorado.

American Heritage

Voyageur celebrates our national heritage with an extensive list of books on country life and popular culture. Paying tribute to the tractors that cultivated America, our booklist features informative field guides, how-to texts on tractor restoration, and in-depth histories such as Ralph Sanders's Ultimate John Deere. We also look at the lighter side of rural living with titles such as Dolly Mu's The Tao of Cow, Pam Percy's The Complete Chicken, and Roger Welsch's Old Tractors Never Die.

Our popular culture line includes a diverse range of books on transportation, crafts, sports, and other Americana titles. Within transportation, we publish titles on railroading and Harley-Davidson, as well as Mustangs, Corvettes, and hot rods. Our craft books, including Helen Kelley's Every Quilt Tells a Story, celebrate the arts of quilting and knitting through narrative, pictures, and history; we hope to develop a how-to line of craft titles in the future. In sports, we publish entertaining titles on the nostalgic appeal of baseball, hunting, and fishing.

Proposing a Book

If you have a manuscript or book idea that fits our publishing categories, we invite you to submit a proposal. Please note that we specialize in nonfiction. We do not publish poetry and rarely publish fiction; we also do not publish children's books or self-help books. We are especially eager at this time to review proposals on wildlife, the natural world, the Southwest, Michigan, Chicago, railroading, quilting, knitting, and baseball. With your proposal, please submit the following:

• Cover letter introducing your book idea in 250 words or less, your writing qualifications, and an analysis of the potential audience. Who would buy your book and why? What's the appeal or hook?

• Outline or table of contents

• Sample chapter, if written (do not submit an entire manuscript at this stage)

• Published clips

• Sample photography, if applicable

• Self-addressed, stamped return envelope

Mail your proposal to Voyageur Press, Attn: Mary LaBarre/Book Proposals, 123 N. Second St., Stillwater, MN 55082. Please keep in mind that every book idea is unique. We attempt to respond to each proposal within thirty days but ask for your patience if the process takes longer. We'll let you know as soon as we've made a decision. Thank you for your interest in Voyageur Press, and we look forward to reviewing your proposal

Categories: Adventure—Agriculture—Animals—Automobiles—Crafts/Hobbies—Fishing—Photography—Science—Sports/Recreation

CONTACT: Mary LaBarre/Book Proposals
Material: All
123 N. 2nd St.
Stillwater, MN 55082
Phone: 651-430-2210
Website: www.voyageurpress.com

Walter Foster Publishing, Inc.

ARTIST SUBMISSIONS

Walter Foster Publishing welcomes art submissions from individual artists. Please send color copies of illustrations, paintings, and other works for us to review and keep on file. Do not send original images and other original materials as they cannot be returned unless you provide a self-addressed, stamped envelope.

Some categories that we're interested in (but we're open to others):
• painting (oil, acrylic, watercolor)
• drawing (ink, pencil, charcoal)
• illustrations (serious or whimsical)
• crafts for children
• crafts for adults

Fees will be discussed only after your art has been accepted for publication.

Categories: Nonfiction—Arts—Crafts/Hobbies

CONTACT: Artist Submissions
Material: All
A Quarto Group Company
23062 La Cadena Dr.
Laguna Hills CA 92653
Phone: 949-380-7510

Waltsan Publishing, LLC

Publishes 10-20 titles/year. Receives 1,500 queries and 1,000 mss/year. 95% of books from first-time authors; 95% from unagented writers. Pays 20% royalty on invoiced price. Publishes book 9 months to 2 years after acceptance of ms. Accepts simultaneous submissions. Responds in 1 month to queries; 1 month to proposals; 2 months to mss. Not accepting new queries until January 1, 2005.

Book catalog online at: www.waltsan.com

Ms guidelines: Waltsan Publishing does not charge a reading fee or any other type of fee to the author. We offer industry standard royalty contracts. We do not give advances against royalties. At this time, we are only looking for material suitable for publishing on CDs. Genres include non-fiction, fiction, science fiction, how-to's, romance, children's stories, cook books and collections of short stories and poetry. We do not publish porn of any kind.

When querying, please advise availability of illustrations and/or photos. Author must own the copyrights or have obtained permission

to use any and all material utilized in the manuscripts. Queries may be accompanied with the first two and last chapters of books or by three of the best works from a collection. 50,000 word minimum. Multiple submissions OK.

Nonfiction: Subjects include general nonfiction. "We look at any nonfiction subject." Query with SASE or via website or submit proposal package, including outline and 3 sample chapters or submit complete ms. Reviews artwork/photos as part of ms package. Send photocopies. Fiction: "We look at all fiction." Full-length or collections equal to full-length only. Query with SASE or submit proposal package including 3 sample chapter(s), synopsis or submit complete ms. Recent Title(s): *Shadows and Stones*, by Bernita Stark (dark fiction of shape changers and vampires); *Kite Paper, Papel de Barrilete*, by Sue Littleton (love poem with Spanish and English texts); *Jules Verne Classics*, edited by Walter Wellborn. Tips: Audience is computer literate, generally higher income and intelligent. "When possible, authors record their manuscript to include audio on the CD. Check our website for guidelines and sample contract." Only publishes on CDs and other removable media.

Categories: Fiction—Nonfiction

5000 Barnett St.
Fort Worth, TX 76103-2006
Phone: 817-492-0188
E-mail: sandra@waltsan.com
Website: www.waltsan.com

Warner Books

Due to the volume of submissions we receive, our policy is not to accept anything unsolicited, so we generally request that authors seek an agent. For our subject requirements, we are specifically interested in EPIC fantasy and science fiction for adults. Otherwise, the standard book proposal format applies: We prefer to receive a cover letter with the whole manuscript and a synopsis but are happy to review at least 3 chapters and a synopsis. We strongly encourage including a self addressed, stamped return package. When we are reviewing submissions, we are looking at both the plot and subject of the project as well as the author's writing ability and style.

—Jaime Levine, Editorial Director

Categories: Fiction—Fantasy—Science Fiction

CONTACT: Devi Pillalai, Assist. Director
Material: All
1271 Avenue of the Americas
New York NY 10020
Phone: 212-522-5113
Fax: 212-522-7990
Website: www.twbookmark.com

Warner Business Books

Please refer to Time Warner Book Group.

Warner Faith

Please refer to Time Warner Book Group.

Washington State University Press

Washington State University Press, a member of the Association of American University Presses, invites manuscripts focusing on the American West, particularly the prehistory, history, environment, politics, and culture of the greater Northwest region. The Press publishes in a wide variety of genres, including scholarly and trade monographs, reminiscences, essays, and biographies. We seek imaginative works that tell the story of the West in innovative ways. We are not at this time accepting novels, poetry, or literary criticism.

The secret to publishing with WSU Press is to write in a lively fashion. The WSU Press adheres to the belief that good scholarship and good writing are compatible. We are unlikely to spend much time with a manuscript exhibiting extensive academic jargon. On the other hand, when you write a work that requires documentation, we expect to see evidence that your research has been thorough and sound.

The Press publishes an average of 8-10 titles a year. First-time authors are encouraged to submit proposals. The majority of our submissions come from unagented authors, but we also accept agent queries. We respond to queries within two months; simultaneous submissions are acceptable, but please tell us if you are making a multiple submission. On average we publish 12 to 18 months after a contract has been finalized for a manuscript. In general, royalties start on the sale of the first book, and graduate up according to sales.

When querying the Press about a possible manuscript, please submit a cover letter, chapter outline, and sample chapter or chapters. Please do not send the entire manuscript or original artwork/photographs at the query stage. Although we will respond to general questions via e-mail, we prefer that manuscript submissions be submitted via regular mail.

Categories: Nonfiction—Biography—Culture—Environment—History—Native American—Politics—Regional

CONTACT: Glen Lindeman , Acquisitions Editor
Material: All
PO Box 645910
Pullman WA 99164-5910
Phone: 509- 335-3518
Fax: 509-335-8568
E-mail: lindeman@wsu.edu
Website: www.wsu.edu

WATERBROOK
PRESS

Waterbrook Press
A Division of Random House, Inc.

Guidelines for Submitting Fiction Proposals

The creativity, craftsmanship and care reflected in your proposal will help us see how those same qualities would be evidenced in your book. Your book must have a Christian message/theme (Psalm 15:2). This does not mean we want to be hit over the head with the Gospel—weave it in where you can naturally do so. We find the best way is to subtly show your readers what your characters are learning, and how that impacts their lives.

We are seeking quality fiction.

If it competes with the best you've read in our market, we want to see it:

• *Big Concept Fiction:* 90-120,000 words; strong theme or issue addressed; plays to either male or female audience.

• *Women's Fiction:* 100-120,000 words; strong romantic element, but love story does not necessarily have to be the central focus.

• *Suspense:* 90-120,000 words, a la Clancy, Grisham, etc.

• *Literary or Allegorical Fiction:* Must be truly incredible for us to consider. Undaunted by that warning? Send it in.

• *No Short Stories, Anthologies, Science Fiction, or Youth Fiction*

Your Proposal Must Include:

1) A cover letter detailing: writing experience and sales; educational or professional qualifications to write the book; why your book is unique or compelling; targeted reader profile; your name, address, and phone number; competition or similar novels already on the market.

2) A two page synopsis of the story. Emphasize message/theme within

3) Your first three chapters (not more, not less)

4) A SASE with enough postage to cover the package, should you wish to see your full proposal returned, a SASE (legal-size envelope) should you simply be seeking a reply. It is our experience that paper is less expensive than postage and would recommend you include a legal envelope only. Include SASE postcard if you want to verify that we received the package. *Response in four months. No query necessary.*

Guidelines for Submitting Children's Book Proposals

The creativity, craftsmanship and care reflected in your proposal will help us see how those same qualities would be evidenced in your book. There are a variety of proposal approaches that can work, so let your proposal demonstrate the uniqueness of both you and your children's book idea. Demonstrate your style, your enthusiasm, your expertise, and your professionalism.

Within this wide range of creative possibilities, here are some of your most important goals to accomplish in your project proposal:

1. Summarize in thirty words or less the unique, compelling appeal of your book. (Why would children enjoy it? What will make your book intriguing? What's fresh and unusual about yoru approach?)

2. Describe the realistic audience for this book. What age if the typical child who most enjoys the book?

3. Survey the competition. Give a content and market analysis of the major children's books now in print which would compete significantly with yours.

4. Outline your writing experience and provide an updated report on the market performance of your previously published works.

5. Outline your educational and career background.

6. Explain your qualifications to write this children's book and tell us about your natural "platform" (such as a speaking ministry) that allows you to promote the book.

7. Tell why you've written this book. What does it truly mean to you personally?

Please remember to include an SASE.

Categories: Fiction—Nonfiction—Adventure—African-American—Christian Interests—Drama—Family—Inspirational—Marriage—Men's Fiction—Mystery—Parenting—Relationships—Religion—Romance—Self Help—Society—Spiritual—Women's Fiction—Writing

CONTACT: Submissions Editor
Material: All
2375 Telstar Dr., Ste 160
Colorado Springs CO 80920
Phone: 719-590-4999
Fax: 719-590-8977
Website: www.randomhouse.com/waterbrook

Wescott Cove Publishing Co.

We only publish books on:
- Nautical
- Cruising guides

Please query first. No email submissions.

Categories: Nonfiction—Adventure—Boating—Outdoors—Recreation—Sports/Recreation—Travel

CONTACT: Editor
Material: All
PO Box 130
Stamford CT 06904
Phone: 203-353-8142
Fax: 203-353-8143

Westcliffe Publishers

BOOK PROPOSAL GUIDELINES

When you submit a book proposal to Westcliffe Publishers, your proposal should contain the following items in order to convey a solid "snapshot" of your book idea and its anticipated audience.

- A working title
- A brief description of the concept of the book
- A sample table of contents page, with a general idea of the ratio of text to photography, art, or illustrations
- A sample chapter or two, with at least two samples of proposed photographs or artwork • A resume, tear sheets from previously published work (if available), and brief description of your background and credibility as author/photographer/artist
- A list of similar books in print on a related subject or approach (include the year published, size, and price) • How your book idea differs from other similar books on the market
- Target market: Who would buy this book? Do you see this as potentially a mass-market book, or one targeted to a regional audience?
- A proposed date for completion of the manuscript.

ABOUT WESTCLIFFE

As an eco-publisher, Westcliffe's mission is to foster environmental awareness by showing the beauty and diversity of the natural world. Westcliffe specializes in high-quality nature photography books, calendars, recreational guidebooks, and books with a regional focus. To learn more about Westcliffe's current titles, please browse our catalog. Because production of large-format photography books is costly, Westcliffe is interested in co-publishing ventures whenever possible. If you have support for your book proposal from an environmental or nonprofit organization or a corporate entity, please be sure to include that information. You are invited to call or email also: Linda@westcliffepublishers.com /800-523-3692.

PHOTOGRAPHY PROPOSAL GUIDELINES

For the most part, Westcliffe books and calendars are single-photographer works focusing on states or regions within the United States. The majority of our photographers have established national reputations and are published regularly in magazines such as Sierra, Wilderness, and National Geographic. We generally publish large-format photography (4x5 or 2 1/4), though on occasion we publish 35 mm work. Westcliffe does not use stock photography.

If you would like to submit work for review by Westcliffe, it is suggested that you submit a specific book or calendar proposal, a concise overview of the project following the book proposal guidelines described above. Please look through our catalog and familiarize yourself with the types of titles we publish.

Westcliffe's current list of calendar titles focuses on individual states. We are, however, open to new ideas. Calendar proposals should be in line with or similar to the type of work Westcliffe publishes - regional nature photography. Submit calendar proposals with a resume and tear sheets.

Westcliffe will contact you if we would like you to submit transparencies. If you have questions or require further information, please contact the production manager at: craig@westcliffepublishers.com or 1-800-523-3692.

Thank you for your interest in Westcliffe Publishers.

Categories: Nonfiction—Ecology—Environment—Photography—Recreation—REgional

CONTACT: Linda Doyle, Associate Publisher
Material: All
PO Box 1261
Englewood, CO 80150-1261
Phone: 800-523-3692
Fax: 303-935-0903
Website: www.westcliffepublishers.com

Westwinds Press

Please refer to Graphic Arts Center Publishing Company

Whispering Coyote

Please refer to Charlesbridge Publishing.

White Cliffs Media, Inc.

White Cliffs Media publishes quality material about African, World and Popular Music that withstands the test of time.

White Cliffs Media works with the best authorities and performers in the world.

The content of our books and CDs is excellent, and now we're improving the graphics.

White Cliffs Media has been around for over fifteen years.

Categories: Nonfiction—Arts—Biography—Culture—Entertainment—Music

CONTACT: Editorial Dept.
Material: All
PO Box 6083
Incline Village NV 89450
E-mail: wcm@wc-media.com
Website: www.wc-media.com

White Mane Publishing Co., Inc.

What We Are Looking for:

White Mane Publishing Co., Inc. consists of four imprints. White Mane Books publishes quality military history non-fiction titles for the avid collector. Burd Street Press publishes general non-fiction military history books for the enjoyment of reading history. White Mane Kids publishes historical children's fiction for middle grade and young adult readers. Each book contains accurate historical information while captivating the readers with fascinating stories. White Mane Kids does not, however, publish picture books at this time. Finally, Ragged Edge Press aims to make a difference in people's lives with topics that focus on relationships and religion.

How to Submit Your Proposal:

Do not send a computer disk. Please submit printed proposals/

manuscripts. Please note only materials accompanied by a self-addressed, postage paid shipping envelope will be returned to you. While every care will be taken of the manuscript, we cannot be responsible for loss or damages, whether it be in our possession or in transit. If concerned about receipt of manuscript please send it by a carrier that provides tracking services.

Submissions should include the following:
- Title/subtitle of Manuscript
- Number of pages and/or words, photos, maps
- Does the manuscript include a bibliography or index?
- Statement of Purpose: A brief paragraph describing why you feel this topic is important. What new information, insights, or approach does your work add to existing works on this topic?
- Marketing Ideas: A brief paragraph outlining the marketing potential of your work. What types of contacts have you made in this field? Indicate any organizations or associations that may help in promoting the book.

Sample Dust Jacket Paragraph: A brief paragraph that describes your book to a potential buyer.
- Contact information including address, day/evening telephone numbers, fax, and email.

When to Expect an Answer:
Review of proposals generally takes one month. Review of full manuscripts generally takes 3 months.

Categories: Fiction—Civil War—Historical—Military—Religion—Self-Help—Young Adult

CONTACT: Acquisitions Department
Material: All
73 West Burd St.
PO Box 708
Shippensburg, PA 17257
Phone: 717-532-2237
Fax: 717-532-6110
E-mail: marketing@whitemane.com
E-mail: editorial@whitemane.com
Website: www.whitemane.com

Wild Flower Press

Please refer to Granite Publishing Group, LLC

Wilder Publishing Center

What We're Looking for
Wilder Publishing Center is looking for book proposals from experts in community development, nonprofit management and organizational development, and human services.

We want manuscripts that identify "best practice" and make it easy to understand. We feel our publications are successful if the reader can pick one up and put it to work immediately. Thus our publications emphasize practical experience and step-by-step directions. *To date, we've used three formats, although we are open to others:*
- Workbooks that explain a process and provide worksheets to guide the reader through that process.
- Research reports and literature reviews that sift through many studies to distill basic trends useful for community organizers and policy makers.
- Curricula that human services professionals can easily follow and adapt for their programs.

Our publications are used by nonprofit managers, community organizers, grassroots groups, policy makers, consultants, trainers, funders, and human service professionals. We seek proposals that appeal to one or more of these audiences.

How to Submit Your Proposal
Do not send a computer disk. You need not send an entire manuscript.

Your proposal should specify the following:
- Audience—who you see as the users of your information.
- Objective—one paragraph that describes the impact your book will make on its readers.
- Market-types of organizations most likely to purchase the book, and your estimate of the number of such organizations.
- Competing publications—competing or similar titles, if any; be sure to describe how your book will differ from them.
- Contents, including:
- A chapter outline with paragraphs or lists of all topics to be covered in each chapter.
- A sample worksheet, if worksheets are to be part of the book. Appendix headings, partial bibliography, and headings for other back matter.
- A description of any illustrations you feel are necessary.
- Sample chapter(s). This is optional. You may enclose a sample chapter if you've already written one, or save yourself the postage by waiting for us to respond to your detailed outline.
- Process—a brief description of the sources you will use as you write.
- Author qualifications—a brief description of yourself, relevant experience, any previous publications, and why you are qualified to write this book.

We encourage you to look through our publications brochure before sending us a proposal. Better still, get a hold of our books and review them first.

When to Expect an Answer
Within three months of receiving your proposal, we will respond telling you either:

We are not interested in the proposal, or we have an interest in the proposal, but need more time to study it.

If we have an interest in the proposal, the actual decision to publish may take another two to three months. During this time we will evaluate the manuscript for its fit with our mission, niche, existing publications, and marketing capacities; its uniqueness, contribution to the field, and impact on readers; and your qualifications as an author and expert. We may also send the proposal for peer review, ask for writing samples, request sample chapters (or a complete manuscript if available), and speak with you about timelines, funding, and other information as appropriate.

What Happens When We Accept Your Book
If we're interested in publishing the book, we work with you to develop a contract we're both happy with. In some cases, we are able to raise funds to pay for the writing of the book, in which case we prefer to purchase the manuscript outright. In others, we are able to work out a royalty agreement. Once you deliver the manuscript, expect rigorous editing and revision; your manuscript will be reviewed by a minimum of three outside experts and often many more. The amount of time it takes to produce the book varies with the scope and size of the work. Once the book is printed, it will be promoted a minimum of four times each year through direct mail.

About the Wilder Publishing Center
Based in St. Paul, Minnesota, the Wilder Publishing Center is a part of the Amherst H. Wilder Foundation, one of the oldest and largest nonprofit human service agencies in North America. Our first book, *Strategic Planning Workbook for Nonprofit Organizations*, has become a classic. Among our other titles are *Collaboration Handbook: Creating, Sustaining, and Enjoying the Journey* and *Community Economic Development Handbook*.

Categories: Nonfiction—Trade—Nonprofit—Nonprofit Management

CONTACT: Acquisitions Editor
Material: Nonprofit Management, Community Development
Wilder Publishing Center
919 Lafond Ave.
St. Paul MN 55104
Phone: 612-659-6013
Website: www.wilder.org

Will Hall Books

The mission of Will Hall, Inc. is threefold: books for children;, chapbooks for emerging writers (handmade, hand-sewn, 25 pp.) who manifestly deserve a broader readership; and, third, educational assistance to any artists, regardless of discipline, for the opportunity to travel, attend conferences, or complete course work.

Will Hall, Inc., which includes the title, Will Hall Books, is a 501(c)3 tax deductible public foundation whose mission is literary and cultural. Our philosophy holds that encouragement to authors, photographers, artists, and musicians is essential to the well-being of a civilized world. We publish books, donate to libraries, and, in doing so, give a "boost" to children and individual artists.

Our most recent endeavors have been supplying an honorarium for Irish Poet, Matthew Sweeney, to read in Fayetteville, donating money to enable a scholar to complete the editing of a book, and providing a scholarship fund for a music student to study in Italy. We are proud to be able to support the efforts of these and other talented individuals.

Will Hall Books publishes chapbooks in any genre. 20 poems submission all year round. once in a while we publish full length books in runs of 1,000 in any genre.

Categories: Nonfiction—Arts—Children—Education—Poetry

CONTACT: Rebecca Newth
Material: Queries
611 Oliver Ave.
Fayetteville AR 72701
E-mail: rharriso@uark.edu
Website: www.willhallbooks.com

Willow Creek Press

Willow Creek Press is a publisher whose primary commitment is to publish nonfiction books specializing in wildlife, nature, the outdoors, gardening, pets, fishing, and some cookbooks. We also publish nature, wildlife, fishing, and sporting calendars.

Personal memoirs and manuscripts dealing with limited regional subject matter may be considered, but generally stand little chance of acceptance. Children's books and fiction manuscripts are not being considered at the present time.

Please include the following details when submitting book proposals:

• Brief synopsis of the book being proposed
• Detailed outline or table of contents
• One or two sample chapters if available
• Samples of art, photos, or transparencies intended for use in the book (no originals, please)
• Author's background, credentials, other publications relevant to the project
Notation as to whether or not proposal is a simultaneous submission
SASE with sufficient postage for response and/or return of materials

Proposals submitted to Willow Creek Press are reviewed for style, content, appropriateness, conceptual integrity, author expertise, and marketability. Therefore, a rejection does not necessarily reflect any judgment regarding the literary merit of an author's work. Please note that Willow Creek Press is not responsible for the loss or damage of any materials submitted for consideration.

We use a standardized author contract, which may be modified upon mutual agreement by the author and publisher. Advances against royalties are negotiable, and royalties are paid semi-annually.

Please provide SASE with all correspondence if you want your materials returned.

Thank you for your interest in Willow Creek Press!

Categories: Nonfiction—Animals—Cooking—Fishing—Gardening—Outdoors—Recreation—Hunting/Birding

CONTACT: Andrea Donner, Managing Editor
Material: All
PO Box 147, 9931 Highway 70 W.
Minocqua WI 54548
Phone: 715-358-7010

Willowgate Press

Willowgate Press currently has six additional novels in press, which will occupy our time through calendar year 2003. We are therefore closed to new submissions until further notice. All submissions received prior to October 1, 2002 will be considered. All submissions received after that date will be returned without examination or comment.

As indicated, we are seeking book length fiction in all categories. We welcome both agented and unagented submissions. *We will be making judgments as to literary merit and commercial viability on the basis of submissions that should include the following:*

• A cover letter identifying the work, and giving a brief biographical sketch of the author and his or her history of publications;
• A brief (one to two page) double-spaced synopsis covering the entire plot, theme and structure of the book, including the conclusion (the synopsis should also identify the genre of the work, if appropriate, the length of the work in words and pages, and whether it is written in the first or third person);
• A chapter outline of no more than 4-5 pages, single-spaced, that gives us the pace and plot of the novel in detail;
• The first ten pages of the manuscript;
• Ten additional consecutive pages of the manuscript of the author's choosing;
• A self-addressed, stamped envelope sufficient to contain all submitted materials.

We will not editorialize, critique or communicate gratuitous judgments about the quality of the work on the basis of this submission. We will either return the material to you with our thanks or ask to see the entire manuscript.

If we do request the manuscript, we ask that it be forwarded in an envelope marked "requested material," and that it be one-sided, double-spaced and contain a "slug line" at the top stating title and author. It must contain an SASE or email address, to which we shall be happy to respond.

Due to the difficulties of supplying a SASE from countries other than the United States, we suggest that submissions from such nations be sent with an email address, rather than return postage.

We hope to respond to queries within two months, and to requested manuscripts within a six months of receipt.

Categories: Fiction—Adventure—Crime—Fantasy—General Interest—Horror—Literature—Mystery—Science Fiction

CONTACT: Submissions Editor
Material: All
PO Box 6529
Holliston MA 01746
Phone: 508-429-8774
Website: www.willowgatepress.com

Books
M-Z

Wilshire Book Co.

Publisher: Melvin Powers. **Acquisitions**: Rights Department. Estab. 1947. Publishes trade paperback originals and reprints. Publishes 25 titles/year. Receives 1,200 submissions/year. 80% of books from first-time authors; 75% from unagented writers. Pays standard royalty. Offers advance. Publishes 6 months after acceptance of ms. Accepts simultaneous submissions. Responds in 2 months.

Nonfiction: How-to, self-help, motivational, recovery. Subjects include psychology, personal success, entrepreneurship, humor, Internet marketing, mail order, horsemanship, trick training for horses. Minimum 50,000 words. Query or submit outline (synopsis for fiction) and 3 sample chapters or complete ms. Include SASE and e-mail address. No e-mail submissions. Reviews artwork/photos as part of ms package. Photocopies only. Guidelines online.

Fiction: Adult allegories that teach principles of psychological growth or offer guidance in living. Minimum 30,000 words. No standard fiction or short stories.

Recent Title(s): *The Dragon Slayer with a Heavy Heart* by Marcia Powers, *The Secret of Overcoming Verbal Abuse* by Albert Ellis, Ph.D. and Marcia Grad Powers, *The Princess Who Believed in Fairy Tales* by Marcia Grad, *The Knight in Rusty Armor* by Robert Fisher, *Think and Grow Rich* by Napoleon Hill.

Tips: "We are vitally interested in all new material we receive. Just as you are hopeful when submitting your manuscript for publication, we are hopeful as we read each one submitted, searching for those we believe could be successful in the marketplace. Writing and publishing must be a team effort. We need you to write what we can sell. We suggest you read successful books similar to the one you want to write. Analyze them to discover what elements make them winners. Duplicate those elements in your own style, using a creative new approach and fresh material, and you will have written a book we can catapult onto the bestseller list. You are welcome to telephone or e-mail us for immediate feedback on any book concept you may have. To learn more about us and what we publish, visit our website."

Categories: Fiction—Nonfiction—Animals—Business—Health—Hobbies—Humor—Inspirational—Internet—Psychology—Relationships—Romance—Self Help—Sexuality

CONTACT: Submissions Editor
Material: All
12015 Sherman Rd.
North Hollywood CA 91605-3781
Phone: 818-765-8579
Fax: 818-765-2922
E-mail: mnpowers@mpowers.com
Website: www.mpowers.com

Woodbine House

Woodbine House welcomes submissions from all writers-agented and unagented, previously published and unpublished. We will gladly consider book-length, nonfiction manuscripts on almost any subject related to disabilities, but we do not publish and will not consider fiction, poetry, and personal accounts.

We favor books that are one of a kind, but will also consider books that take fresh slants on old subjects. Regardless of a book's subject, we are always impressed by authors who 1) can write with clarity, au-

thority, and style; and 2) can demonstrate that their book has a clearly defined market that they know how to reach.

To submit a proposal, please send a query letter. *If you would like to submit more than a query letter, you can send the following information:*

1. The table of contents;
2. 2-3 sample chapters;
3. An annotated list of books in print on the subject, explaining how your book differs from the competition;
4. A list of potential markets, including specific organizations, book clubs, and groups of individuals that would buy your book;
5. A short biographical note describing your qualifications to write this book;
6. Estimated length and completion date.

Manuscripts should be typed. Send illustrations or copies if applicable. Photocopies and computer printouts are acceptable, as are simultaneous submissions, if so marked. Allow 8-12 weeks for a response.

Categories: Children—Disabilities—Education—Parenting—Self Help—Special Needs

CONTACT: Nancy Gray Paul, Acquisitions Editor
Material: All
6510 Bells Mill Rd.
Bethesda MD 20817
Phone: 301-897-3570
Fax: 301-897-5838

WoodenBoat Books

If you have a manuscript to submit, please take a look at these basic guidelines.

We publish books on boat building, design, nautical history, woodworking, as well as books with great photography.

If your book fits in that area, then you should send:

• A detailed outline / extended table of contents
• Sample chapters / photos / drawings
• Who you feel the target audience is
• What competition is already out there for this topic
• Format: length of the project, types and amount of illustrations
• What specialty marketing would you suggest
• Your information, contact, including email, as well as background
• Postage paid envelope, if you would like the materials returned
Categories: Nonfiction—Boating—History—Photography

CONTACT: Scot Bell
Material: All
Naskeag Rd.
PO Box 78
Brooklin ME 04616
Phone: 207-359-4651
Fax: 207-359-2048
E-mail: books@woodenboat.com
Website: www.woodenboat.com

Woodland Publishing

Does Woodland accept unsolicited manuscripts?

Yes, but we prefer that potential authors query first. Queries should be between 250 and 300 words and should convince us that your topic is timely and of interest to our readers, offer a description on how you would treat the subject and what research or other data you would use. Your query should also tell us if any other books have been written recently on your topic. Background information and credentials are also helpful. Also, because of the high volume of queries we receive, it may take us a while to get back to you.

We endeavor to respond to every query, but the high volume of queries and submissions can delay response time. Furthermore, queries for newsletter articles are not guaranteed a response. Do know that if you send a SASE with your manuscript submission, we will return your manuscript if it is not accepted. Please do not send us the only copy of your manuscript!

Categories: Diet/Nutrition—Health

CONTACT: Cord Udall, Managing Editor
Material: All
PO Box 160
Pleasant Grove, UT 84062
Phone: 801-785-8100
Fax: 801-785-8511
Website: www.woodlandpublishing.com

Word Dancer Press

Please refer to Quill Driver Books/Word Dancer Press, Inc.

World Leisure Corporation

Here are the submission guidelines you requested. We are publishing sports travel, family travel, gift/self-help books and some children's books.

Before any submissions will be considered please prepare:

• an introduction explaining why someone should read the materials you are presenting

• an annotated table of contents outlining each chapter of your proposed book

• at least one sample chapter so I can see your writing style

If I feel your book will fit into our coming book lists I will contact you. Do not send queries.

Send a SASE if you wish to have your manuscript returned or just your cover letter with my notes to you.

Sincerely, Charles Leocha, Publisher

Categories: Nonfiction—Children—Relationships—Sports/Recreation—Travel

CONTACT: Charles Leocha, Publisher
Material: All
177 Paris St.
Boston MA 02128
Phone: 617-569-1966
Fax: 617-561-7654
E-mail: WLEISURE@aol.com

The Writer Gazette

Please refer to The Writer Gazette, in the Periodical Section of this directory.

YMAA Publication Center

The proposed work should address some aspect of Chinese culture—martial arts, Qigong (Chi Kung), medicine, etc. No children's stories, please.

For fastest response, please use the following guidelines:

• Send a brief summary of each chapter and one complete sample chapter. Include sample photos or drawings, if available (photocopies or facsimiles acceptable).

• Include a one page (maximum) author biography. Relate salient experience and qualifications.

• Include a one page (maximum) cover letter. State your intention for writing the book, the proposed audience, and describe the unique, compelling features of the book.

• Letter quality computer printouts acceptable.

Categories: Nonfiction—Health—History—Military—New Age—Sports/Recreation—Martial Arts

CONTACT: David Ripianzi, Acquisitions Editor
Material: Chinese Martial Arts, Chinese Healing Arts
4354 Washington St.
Roslindale MA 02131
Phone: 617-323-7215
Fax: 617-323-7417
E-mail: ymaa@aol.com
Website: www.YMAA.com

ZondervanPublishingHouse
A Division of HarperCollinsPublishers

Zondervan and Zonderkidz

Zondervan and Zonderkidz No Longer Accepting Unsolicited Manuscripts and Book Proposals Sent by Air or Surface Mail

Since the events of 9-11-2001, Zondervan and Zonderkidz have established a new policy concerning unsolicited manuscripts and book proposals. We will no longer open and review any envelope or package that is not addressed to a particular individual or that does not come from an identified source that we recognize. Any such packages that we receive will be returned to the sender unopened; if there is no return address, such packages will be discarded.

We encourage you to submit your book proposal electronically to First Edition, The ECPA Manuscript Service on the ECPA website (www.ECPA.org). Book proposals posted on this website are available for review by all the member publishers of the Evangelical Christian Publishers Association, and Zondervan and Zonderkidz have assigned an editor to regularly review all new proposals posted on First Edition.

If you feel you must submit your book proposal directly to Zondervan or Zonderkidz, you may do so by faxing it to us. Your proposal should include the book title; a table of contents, including a 2 or 3 sentence description of each chapter; a brief description of the proposed book, including the unique contribution of the book and why you feel it must be published; your intended reader; and your Vita, including your qualifications to write the book. The proposal should be no more than 5 pages. If we are interested in reviewing more material from you, we will respond within 6 weeks. You may fax your proposal to the Book Proposal Review Editor, 616-698-3454.

Please note that we've never accepted email proposals.

Categories: Fiction—Nonfiction—Adventure—African-American—Biography—Children—Christian Interests—Family—Marriage—Parenting—Relationships—Spiritual—Women's Fiction

CONTACT: Acquisitions Editor
Material: All
Fax: 616-698-3454
Website: www.zondervan.com

Books
M-Z

Topic Index

This index provides the names of publishers interested in seeing
material on or relating to the topics listed.

-A-

Adventure

Periodicals:

America West, American Fitness, Arizona Highways, Artemis Magazine, Aspen Magazine, Backroads, Bibliophilos, Bike Magazine, Boating Life, Boys' Life, Boys' Quest, The Bugle, Cadet Quest, Canoe & Kayak Magazine, Cascades East Magazine: Central Oregon's Quarterly, Cobblestone Magazine, Country Magazine, Country Extra Magazine, Creative With Words!, Happy Times Monthly, Heartland USA, Home Times Family Newspaper, House, Home and Garden, The Iconoclast, Insider Magazine, Lake Michigan Travel Guide, Lake Superior Magazine, Lifeglow, Marlin, Men's Journal, My Legacy, The National Enquirer, Outdoor Life, Paddler, Passport, Persimmon Hill, Rack, Adventures in Trophy Hunting, Rocky Mountain Sports Magazine, Sandlapper, Ski, Skiing Magazine, Specialty Travel Index, Sports Afield, Springfield! Magazine, Swank, Texas Parks & Wildlife, Times News Service, Transitions Abroad, Western RV News & Recreation, Willow Springs, Wisconsin Trails, Young & Alive

Book Publishers:

American Literary Press, Inc.: Noble House, Black Forest Press: Arbenteuer Books, Dichter Books, Kinder Books, Bridge Works, Clover Park Press, The Conservatory of American Letters, Crossway Books, Denlinger's Publishers, Ltd., Dial Books for Young Readers, Dutton 's Books, The Globe Pequot Press, Graphic Arts Center Publishing Company, ImaJinn Books, The Lyons Press, Mayhaven Publishing, Mountain N' Air Books, Mountaineers Books, Narwhal Press, Inc., Paladin Press: Sycamore Island Books, Flying Machines Press, Prep Publishing, Puget Sound Books, Richard C. Owen Publishers, Inc., Voyageur Press, Waterbrook Press, Wescott Cove Publishing Co., Willowgate Press, Zondervan and Zonderkidz

African-American

Periodicals:

Affaire De Coeur, The African American Pulpit!, African American Review, American Profile, Arkansas Review, Blackfire, Calyx Journal, The Carolina Quarterly, Clubhouse, Diversity, Equal Opportunity Publications, Inc., Essence, Feminist Studies: University of Maryland, Footsteps, Futures Mysterious Anthology Magazine, Home Times Family Newspaper, Kuumba, Message Magazine, Metro Parent, Metro Baby, African American Family, Mother Jones, The New Centennial Review, Obsidian III, The Other Side, Passport, Reunions Magazine, South Florida History, Springfield! Magazine, Teaching Tolerance, Tequesta, Vibe, Willow Springs

BookPublishers:

Barricade Books, Branden Publishing Company, Calyx Books, Clarity Press, Inc., Face to Face Press, Fairleigh Dickinson University Press, Great Quotations Publishing, Holloway House Publishing Group, Intercultural Press, Judson Press, Just Us Books, Lerner Publishing, McFarland & Company, Inc., Mississippi, Pelican Publishing Company, Richard C. Owen Publishers, Inc., Rutledge Hill Press, Safari Press, Inc., Scarecrow Press, Inc., Southern Illinois University Press, Third World Press, Temple University Press, University of Nebraska Press, University of North Texas Press, Waterbrook Press, Zondervan and Zonderkidz

Agriculture

Periodicals:

Artemis Magazine, Capper's, Country Magazine, Country Extra Magazine, Digger Magazine, Farwest Magazine, Environment, Farm & Ranch Living, Farm Times, Beef Times, Feed-Lot, Futurific Magazine, Grit Magazine, The Growing Edge, The Maine Organic Farmer & Gardener, Mother Earth News, The New Centennial Review, The Old Farmer's Almanac, Onion World, Small Farm Today, Wines & Vines

Book Publishers:

Green Nature Books, Island Press, Stipes Publishing, LLC, Storey Publishing, LCC, Ten Speed Press, Celestial Arts, Tricycle Press, Texas A&M University Press, University of Maine Press, University of Nebraska Press, Voyageur Press

Alternate Lifestyle

Periodicals:

American Fitness, Body & Soul, Frontiers, Futures Mysterious Anthology Magazine, Genre, Gray Areas, In the Family, Magical Blend, The Maine Organic Farmer & Gardener, The National Enquirer, Natural Beauty & Health, Penthouse Variations, Rainbow Review, Syracuse New Times, Travel Naturally, Willow Springs

Book Publishers:

Alyson Publications, Inc., Face to Face Press, HiddenSpring, New Horizons Press, Small Horizons Imprint, Shambhala Publications

Animals

Periodicals:

America West, American Hunter, Animal People, The Animals' Agenda, Animals Magazine, Back Home in Kentucky, Bibliophilos, Birds & Blooms, Blue Ridge Country Magazine, Boys' Life, Boys' Quest, The Bugle, California Wild: California Academy of Sciences, Cat Fancy, Country Magazine, Country Extra Magazine, Creative With Words!, Defenders, Dog Gone, Environment, Equine Journal, Florida Wildlife, Fun for Kidz, Fur-Fish-Game, The Gaited Horse, Grit Magazine, Guideposts for Kids, Happy Times Monthly, Heartland USA, Hopscotch for Girls, Horse Illustrated, House, Home and Garden, I Love Cats, The Lutheran Digest, Magical Blend, The Maine Organic Farmer & Gardener, Mushing, My Legacy, The National Enquirer, Outdoor Life, Persimmon Hill, Polo Players' Edition, Saturday Evening Post, Spider, Springfield! Magazine, Transitions, Wildlife Art, Young & Alive

Book Publishers:

Alpine Publications, Angel Bea Publishing, Barrons Educational Series, Inc., Brookline Books, Chronicle Books LLC, Creative Publishing International, Inc., Cruden Bay Books, Dimi Press, Dutton Children's Books, Eclipse Press, Green Nature Books, Hancock House, J.N. Townsend Publishing, Lerner Publishing, The Lyons Press, The Magni Group, Inc., Mayhaven Publishing, Richard C. Owen Publishers, Inc., Safari Press, Inc., Soundprints, Storey Publishing, LCC, Temple University Press, Ten Speed Press, Celestial Arts, Tricycle Press, University of North Texas Press, Voyageur Press, Willow Creek Press, Wilshire Book Co.

Antiques

Periodicals:

Antique Trader Weekly, Antiques & Collecting Magazine, The Appraisers Standard, Art & Antiques, Atlanta Homes and Lifestyles, Back Home in Kentucky, Bibliophilos, Budget Living, Classic Toy Trains, Collectors News, Country Living, Early American Life, House, Home and

Garden, Long Island Woman, Mountain Living, The New Yorker, Persimmon Hill, River Town Gazette, Rug Hooking, Southern Accents, Town & Country

Architecture

Periodicals:

Adirondack Life, Architectural Digest, American Bungalow, Artemis Magazine, Atlanta Homes and Lifestyles, Back Home in Kentucky, Bibliophilos, Charleston Magazine, Colorado Homes & Lifestyles, Early American Life, Futurific Magazine, Home Improver Magazine, House Beautiful, House, Home and Garden, Joiners' Quarterly, LA Architect, Log Home Living, Timber Frame Homes, Metropolis, Metropolitan Home, Mountain Living, The New Centennial Review, Persimmon Hill, River Town Gazette, Seattle Homes and Lifestyles, Southern Accents, Springfield! Magazine, Sunset Magazine, Town & Country

Book Publishers:

Allworth Press, Balcony Press, Chronicle Books LLC, David R. Godine, Inc., Fairleigh Dickinson University Press, Mage Publishers, Mississippi: University Press of Mississippi, Pelican Publishing Company, Stipes Publishing, LLC, Storey Publishing, LCC, Texas A&M University Press

Arts

Periodicals:

5678 Swing, 96 Inc., Alberta Views, Alive Now, American Artist, American Indian Art Magazine, The American Legion Magazine, The American Scholar: Phi Beta Kappa, American Theatre, AmericanStyle, Antiques & Collecting Magazine, The Appraisers Standard, Arkansas Review, Art & Antiques, Art Papers, Art Times, Artemis Magazine, The Artist's Magazine, Asian Pacific American Journal, Aspen Magazine, Atlanta Homes and Lifestyles, Austin Monthly Magazine, BabyTalk, Back Home in Kentucky, Beadwork, The Bear Deluxe Magazine, The Beauty Spot, Bibliophilos, Body & Soul, Bridge, Buffalo Spree Magazine, Central PA Magazine, Ceramics Monthly, Charleston Magazine, Chiron Review, Chronogram, Chrysalis Reader, Cincinnati Woman Magazine, The Circle, Click Magazine, Crab Creek Review, The Cream City Review, Milwaukee, Cross & Quill, Dance Spirit, Dance Teacher, Decorative Artist's Workbook, Devo 'Zine, Doll World, Dream Network: A Quarterly Journal Exploring Dreams & Myth, Drum Early American Life, East End Lights, Fiberarts Magazine, Futures Mysterious Anthology Magazine, Game Developer, The Georgia Review, The Gettysburg Review, Gist Review, The Good Red Road, Grit Magazine, Handwoven, Harper's Magazine, Home Times Family Newspaper, Hope Magazine, House, Home and Garden, The Hudson Review, The Iconoclast, Insider Magazine, Interior Design Magazine, Jam Rag, The Journal of Asian Martial Arts, Kaleidoscope: Exploring the Experience of Disability through Literature & Fine Arts, Kalliope, Kentucky Monthly, The Kenyon Review, Ladies' Home Journal, Ladybug Parent's Companion, Left Curve, Letter Arts Review, Light of Consciousnes, Liquid Ohio, Literal Latte, Long Island Woman, Lynx Eye, Mama's Little Helper Newsletter, Metropolis, Mountain Living, The National Enquirer, Native Peoples, The New Centennial Review, New Letters, New Mexico Magazine, New Millennium Writings, The New Yorker, Nimrod: International Journal of Prose and Poetry (University of Tulsa), Northwest Review: University of Oregon, The Other Side, Over the Back Fence, Passages North: Northern Michigan University, Persimmon Hill, Phi Delta Kappan, Popular Photography, Potomac Review, Quilting Arts Magazine, Rearview, Redbook, Rhino, River Town Gazette, RiverSedge: The University of Texas-Pan American, The Roanoker, Rosebud, Rug Hooking, Salon, Sandlapper, SchoolArts, Shuttle Spindle & Dyepot, Smithsonian Magazine, Snake Nation Review, South Florida History, Southern Accents, Southern Humanities Review: Auburn University, Southwest Review: Southern Methodist University, Springfield! Magazine, Stone Soup, Sycamore Review: Purdue University, Syracuse New Times, Teaching Tolerance, Tequesta, Thema, The Threepenny Review, Town & Country, Tradition, Vanity Fair, Vibe, Watercolor, Watercolor Magic, Weavings, Wildlife Art, The William and Mary Review: College

of William and Mary, Willow Springs, Women Artists News Book Review, The World & I, Zoetrope: All-Story

Book Publishers:

Allworth Press, Anchorage Press Plays, Inc., Art Direction Book Company, Inc., Balcony Press, Branden Publishing Company, Chitra Publications, Chronicle Books LLC, Collectors Press, Cricket Books, David R. Godine, Inc., Down East Books, Fairleigh Dickinson University Press, Lerner Publishing, Limelight Editions, Maisonneuve Press, Meriwether Publishing Ltd: Contemporary Drama Service, Michael Wiese Productions, Midmarch Arts Press, Mississippi: University Press of Mississippi, Pelican Publishing Company, Players Press, Inc., QED Press, Santa Monica Press LLC, Scarecrow Press, Inc., Shambala Publications, Stone Bridge Press, Storey Publishing, LCC, University of Maine Press, University of Nebraska Press, Walter Foster Publishing, Inc., White Cliffs Media, Inc., Will Hall Books, Will Hall, Inc.

Asian-American

Periodicals:

American Profile, The Asian Pacific American Journal, Calyx Journal, Clubhouse, Equal Opportunity Publications, Inc., Filipinas, Futures Mysterious Anthology Magazine, Japanophile, The Journal of Asian Martial Arts, Kung Fu Tai Chi, Manoa, Mother Jones, Passport, South Florida History, Springfield! Magazine, T'ai Chi, Teaching Tolerance, Tequesta, Willow Springs

Book Publishers:

Bridge Works, Calyx Books, Clarity Press, Inc., Cross Cultural Publications, Inc., Fairleigh Dickinson University Press, Intercultural Press, Lehigh University Press, Mayhaven Publishing, McFarland & Company, Inc., Pacific View Press, Pelican Publishing Company, Richard C. Owen Publishers, Inc., Temple University Press, Turtle Press

Associations

Periodicals:

Authorship, Christian Camp & Conference Journal, Commercial Investment Real Estate Magazine, Cross & Quill, DECA Dimensions, The Elks Magazine, Equal Opportunity Publications, Inc., Hawaii Westways, Highways, Hope Magazine, The Kiwanis Magazine, The Lion Magazine, The Maine Organic Farmer & Gardener, Midwest Traveler, Muzzle Blasts, New Mexico Journey, The Old Farmer's Almanac, Paddler, Shuttle Spindle & Dyepot, South American Explorer, Southern Traveler, Springfield! Magazine, Teaching Tolerance, The Toastmaster, VFW Magazine, Westways, Women In Business, Southern California Lifestyle Magazine, WIN-Informer

Book Publishers:

Abbott, Langer & Associates, Graphic Arts Technical Foundation/GATFPress, Lerner Publishing, Pineapple Press, Inc., Shambhala Publications, Stone Bridge Press,

Automobiles

Periodicals:

4-Wheel Drive & Sport Utility, 5.0 Mustang & Super Fords, Aspen Magazine, Auto Sound & Security, Automobile Quarterly, The Beauty Spot, Better Homes and Gardens, Boys' Life, British Car Magazine, Business Fleet, Managing 10-5- Company Vehicles, Car and Driver, CC Motorcycle News Magazine, Circle Track, Corvette Fever, Custom Rodder, Futurific Magazine, Go Magazine,, Good Old Days/Good Old Days Specials, Hawaii Westways, Heartland USA, Insider Magazine, Midwest Traveler, Mopar Muscle, Motor Trend, Motorcycling, Muscle Mustang & Fast Fords, Mustang & Fords, Mustang Monthly, New Mexico Journey, Poptronics, Popular Mechanics, Popular Science, River Town Gazette, Smoke Magazine: Life's Burning Desires, Southern Traveler, Speedway Illustrated, Stock Car Racing, Toy Cars & Models, Trailer Boats, Via, Western RV News & Recreation, Westways, Southern California Lifestyle Magazine

Book Publishers:

Aeronautical Publishers, Howell Press, Inc., Iconografix, Inc., Voyageur Press

Aviation

Periodicals:

Artemis Magazine, Aviation Maintenance, Balloon Life, Boys' Life, The Elks Magazine, Futurific Magazine, General Aviation News, Heartland USA, Kitplanes, Popular Mechanics, Popular Science, Primedia History Group, The Southern Aviator

Book Publishers:

Aeronautical Publishers, Branden Publishing Company, Brassey's, Inc., Hancock House, Howell Press, Inc., Naval Institute Press, Southern Illinois University Press

-B-

Beauty

Periodicals:

The Beauty Spot, Christian Women Today, Elle, First for Women, Harper's Bazaar, Lucky Magazine, Redbook, Self, Seventeen, Town & Country, Woman's World, Women Today Magazine

Book Publishers:

Harvard Common Press,

Biography

Periodicals:

Acoustic Guitar Magazine, American Artist, Back Home in Kentucky, Bibliophilos, Cobblestone Magazine, Crone Chronicles, Doll World, Early American Life, East End Lights, The Elks Magazine, The Freeman: Ideas on Liberty, Grit Magazine, Heartland USA, The Iconoclast, Kalliope, Kentucky Monthly, Ladies' Home Journal, Lifeglow, Light of Consciousnes, Lilith: The Independent Jewish Women's Magazine, Minnesota Memories, The National Enquirer, The New Centennial Review, Nine, The Old Farmer's Almanac, Persimmon Hill, Plus Magazine, Redbook, Rosebud, Sandlapper, South Florida History, Springfield! Magazine, Tequesta, Transitions, Vanity Fair, Watercolor, Women Today Magazine, Young & Alive

Book Publishers:

Arden Press, Inc., Barricade Books, Black Forest Press: Arbenteuer Books, Dichter Books, Kinder Books, Branden Publishing Company, Brassey's, Inc., Charlesbridge Publishing, Clover Park Press, The Conservatory of American Letters, Cross Cultural Publications, Inc., David R. Godine, Inc., Dial Books for Young Readers, Down East Books, Excelsior Cee Publishing, Fairleigh Dickinson University Press, Granite Publishing Group, LLC, Hancock House, Heritage Books, Inc., HiddenSpring, Howells House, Inc., In Print Publishing, International Marine, Iron Horse Free Press, Ivan R. Dee, Inc., Publisher, Jewish Lights Publishing, Jona Books, Just Us Books, Kregel Publications/Kregel Kidzone, Lehigh University Press, Lerner Publishing, Mayhaven Publishing, The McDonald & Woodward Publishing Company, Mississippi: University Press of Mississippi, Mountain Press Publishing Company, Narwhal Press, Inc., North Ridge Books, North Street Publishers, The Overmountain Press, Paulist Press: HiddenSpring, Pelican Publishing Company, Prep Publishing, Quality Words In Print, Ragged Mountain Press, Rutledge Hill Press, Santa Monica Press LLC, Scarecrow Press, Inc., Schirmer Trade Book, Shambhala Publications, Sourcebooks, Inc., Sourcebooks Casablanca, Sourcebooks Hysteria, Sourcebooks Landmark, Sourcebooks MediaFusion, Sphinx Publishing, Temple University Press, Texas Western Press, Trinity Press International, University of Maine Press, University of Nebraska Press, University of Nevada Press, University of North Texas Press, University of Oklahoma Press, USA Books, Washington State University Press, White Cliffs Media, Inc., Zondervan and Zonderkidz

Boating

Periodicals:

Canoe & Kayak Magazine, Cruising World, Florida Wildlife, Heartland USA, Houseboat, Marlin, Offshore: Northeast Boating at Its Best,

Paddler, Popular Mechanics, Power & Motoryacht, River Town Gazette, Sailing Magazine, Sailing World, Sea Kayaker, Sea: The Magazine of Western Boating, Sport Fishing Magazine, Texas Parks & Wildlife, Trailer Boats, Yachting

Book Publishers:

Bristol Fashion Publications, Inc.: The World's Largest Nautical Publishing House, Cornell Maritime Press, Inc., David R. Godine, Inc., The Globe Pequot Press, Howell Press, Inc., International Marine, The Lyons Press, Narwhal Press, Inc., Naval Institute Press, Paradise Cay, Pelican Publishing Company, Wescott Cove Publishing Co., WoodenBoat Books

Book Reviews

Periodicals:

Absolute Write, The African American Pulpit!, American Turf Monthly, Anvil Magazine, Atlanta Homes and Lifestyles, Audubon, Authorship, BabyTalk, Balanced Living Magazine, The Bear Deluxe Magazine, The Beauty Spot, The Beloit Poetry Journal, Bibliophilos, Bloomsbury Review, Blue Ridge Country Magazine, Body & Soul, Book/Mark Small Press Quarterly Review, Boston Magazine, California Wild: California Academy of Sciences, The Carolina Quarterly, The Chattahoochee Review, Cicada, Cincinnati Woman Magazine, Clamor, Culture, Media and Life., CompulsiveReader.com, Confrontation, A Literary Journal, Cosmopolitan, Fellowship, First Things, French Forum, Genre, The Georgia Review, The Gettysburg Review, Gist Review, Glamour, The Good Red Road, Gray Areas, The Green Hills Literary Lantern: Truman State University, Home Times Family Newspaper, The Hudson Review, Indiana Review, Iris: A Journal about Women (University of Virginia), Japanophile, Kentucky Monthly, Legacy: A Journal of American Women Writers, The Literary Review: Fairleigh Dickinson University, Long Island Woman, Maelstrom, Magical Blend, The Maine Organic Farmer & Gardener, Mama's Little Helper Newsletter, Mental Floss, Mid-American Review: Green State University, The Missouri Review, Native Peoples, New Mexico Magazine, The New Yorker, Nine, Nineteenth-Century French Studies, Northwest Family News, Obsidian III, Outdoor Life, Parenting, Persimmon Hill, Pleiades: A Journal of New Writing, Poetry, Quarterly West: University of Utah, Redbook, River Town Gazette, Ruminator Review, Salon, Sewanee Review, Shenandoah: The Washington and Lee University Review, Shofar, Southern Accents, Southern Living, Springfield! Magazine, Stone Soup, Studies in American Jewish Literature, Syracuse New Times, Teaching Tolerance, The Threepenny Review, Transitions, West Coast Magazine, Willow Springs, WIN-Informer, The World & I

Book Publishers:

Gryphon Books—Paradise Cay, Safari Press, Inc., The Trinity Foundation

Business

Periodicals:

Alaska Business Monthly, American Business Review, The American Legion Magazine, American Salesman, Area Development, Artemis Magazine, The Artist's Magazine, Aspen Magazine, Austin Monthly Magazine, Automated Builder, The Beauty Spot, Boston Magazine, Business 2.0, ColoradoBiz Magazine, Commercial Investment Real Estate Magazine, Contract Management, The Cooperator: The Co-op and Condo Monthly, DECA Dimensions, Drum Business, Entrepreneur Magazine, Entrepreneur.com, Equities Magazine, Farm Times, Beef Times, Fast Company, Financial Planning, Florida Hotel & Motel Journal, Forester Communications, Fresh Cut, Futurific Magazine, Government Executive, Happy Times Monthly, Harper's Magazine, Home Business Magazine, Home Business Journal, Home Times Family Newspaper, Inc., The Labor Paper: Serving Southern Wisconsin, Long Island Woman, Model Retailer, Mortgage Banking, New Mexico Woman, Onion World, Oregon Business, Perdido: Leadership with a Conscience, Personal Branding Magazine, Playboy, Podiatry Management, Popular Mechanics, Presentations Magazine, Radio World, Redbook, River Town Gazette, The Roanoker, Salon, Sandlapper, Script,

Specialty Retail Report, Stamats Meetings Media, Succeed, Supervision, Supply Chain Systems Magazine, Supply Chain Systems Magazine, Toy Farmer, Toy Trucker & Contractor, Wines & Vines, Woman's World

Book Publishers:

Abbott, Langer & Associates, Addicus Books, Inc., Aegis Publishing Group, Ltd., Algora Publishing, Allworth Press, ATL Press: Science Technology, B. Klein Publications, Barrons Educational Series, Inc., Bay Tree Publishing, Berrett-Koehler Publishers, Black Forest Press: Arbenteuer Books, Dichter Books, Kinder Books, Bonus Books, Inc., Bookhaven Press LLC, Branden Publishing Company, The Business Group, Capital Books, Contemporary Books: A Division of McGraw-Hill Companies, Craftsman Book Company, Emerald Ink Publishing, Forum Publishing Company, Frederick Fell Publishers, Inc., The Globe Pequot Press, The Graduate Group, Harvard Common Press, Intercultural Press, International Foundation of Employee Benefit Plans, JIST Works/Park Avenue, Jodere Group Inc., Lehigh University Press, Markowski International Publishers, Possibility Press, Metamorphous Press, Millennium Publishing Company, New Society Publishers, New World Library, Origin Media, Inc.: "Books for the Integral Age", Pelican Publishing Company, Personal Branding Press, Possibility Press, Prep Publishing, Prima Publishing, PSI Research: The Oasis Press, Hellgate Press, Stipes Publishing, LLC, Stone Bridg Press, Ten Speed Press, Celestial Arts, Tricycle Press, Texas A&M University Press, Tower Publishing, Wilshire Book Co.

-C-

Campus Life

Periodicals:

Campus Life, Circle K, CollegeBound Teen Magazine, Kentucky Monthly, River Town Gazette, Syracuse New Times, Young & Alive

Book Publishers:

Stylus Publishing, LLC

Careers

Periodicals:

America West, American Careers, American Salesman, Artemis Magazine, The Beauty Spot, Boys' Life, Christian Women Today, Cosmopolitan, Cross & Quill, DECA Dimensions, Dialogue, Diversity, Dramatics, Equal Opportunity Publications, Inc., Glamour, Happy Times Monthly, Insider Magazine, The Labor Paper: Serving Southern Wisconsin, Lifeglow, Long Island Woman, Men's Health, Modern Maturity, Natural Beauty & Health, The New Centennial Review, Persimmon Hill, Personal Branding Magazine, Springfield! Magazine, Student Lawyer, Succeed, Supervision, Times News Service, Transitions, Unique Opportunities: The Physician's Resource, Wines & Vines, Women in Business, Women Today Magazine, Working Mother Magazine, Young & Alive

Book Publishers:

American Correctional Association (ACA) Book Publishing, Barrons Educational Series, Inc., Berrett-Koehler Publishers, Black Forest Press: Arbenteuer Books, Dichter Books, Kinder Books, Bookhaven Press LLC, Capital Books, Contemporary Books: A Division of McGraw-Hill Companies, Garth Gardner Company, The Globe Pequot Press, The Graduate Group, Harvard Common Press, Impact Publishers, JIST Works/Park Avenue, Millennium Publishing Company, Mustang Publishing Company, Pathfinder Publishing of California, Prep Publishing, Prima Publishing, Ronin Publishing, Inc., Sourcebooks, Inc., Sourcebooks Casablanca, Sourcebooks Hysteria, Sourcebooks Landmark, Sourcebooks MediaFusion, Sphinx Publishing, Stone Bridge Press, Ten Speed Press, Celestial Arts, Tricycle Press

Cartoons

Periodicals:

Artemis Magazine, BabyTalk, The Beauty Spot, Bibliophilos, Boys' Life, Boys' Quest, Chronogram, Funny Times, Futures Mysterious Anthol-

ogy Magazine, Happy Times Monthly, Heartland USA, Home Times Family Newspaper, Hopscotch for Girls, The Iconoclast, Inside Texas Running, Light, Liquid Ohio, The Lutheran Digest, Maelstrom, Model Retailer, The New Yorker, Passport, Phi Delta Kappan, Protooner, River Town Gazette, Saturday Evening Post, Short Stuff Magazine, Supervision, Teaching Tolerance, Thema, With: The Magazine for Radical Christian Youth, Young & Alive

Book Publishers:

Elderberry Press, LLC, Garth Gardner Company, Great Quotations Publishing, Pelican Publishing Company

Children

Periodicals:

African American Family, All About Kids, American Fitness, American Girl, The American Legion Magazine, American Profile, Appleseeds, Artemis Magazine, Atlanta Parent, Atlanta Baby, Austin Monthly Magazine, Babybug, Boys' Life, Boys' Quest, Calliope Magazine, Cat Fancy, Chess Life, School Mates, Child Magazine, Christian Parenting Today, Click Magazine, Club Connection, Clubhouse, Creative With Words!, Cricket, The Dollar Stretcher, Dream Network: A Quarterly Journal Exploring Dreams & Myth, Educator's Edition, Faces: The Magazine About People, Family Circle, Family Digest, Fun for Kidz, Girls' Life, Grit Magazine, Guideposts for Kids, Happy Times Monthly, Highlights for Children, Home Education Magazine, Home Times Family Newspaper, Hopscotch for Girls, House, Home and Garden, Instructor, Journal of Christian Nursing, Ladies' Home Journal, Ladybug Parent's Companion, Ladybug: The Magazine for Young Children, The Lutheran Digest, Mama's Little Helper Newsletter, Metro Parent, Metro Baby, MetroKids, Muse Magazine, My Legacy, Natural Beauty & Health, New Moon, Northwest Family Magazine, Odyssey Magazine, The Old Farmer's Almanac, Pack-o-Fun, Parenting, Parents Magazine, Parents' Press, Passport, Pediatrics For Parents, Pockets, Potluck Children's Literary Magazine, Potomac Review, Redbook, River Town Gazette, Sandlapper, SchoolArts, Scouting, Spider: The Magazine for Children, Sports Illustrated for Kids, Springfield! Magazine, Stone Soup, Swimming World, Junior Swimmer, Teaching Tolerance, Today's Christian Woman, United Parenting Publications, West Coast Magazine, Woman's World, Wonderful Ideas for Teaching, Learning, and Enjoying Mathematics!, Working Mother Magazine

Book Publishers:

American Literary Press, Inc.: Noble House, Anchorage Press Plays, Inc., Angel Bea Publishing, Atheneum Books, Barbed Wire Publishing, Barrons Educational Series, Inc., Bee-Con Books, Bethany House Publishers, Beyond Words Publishing, Black Forest Press: Arbenteuer Books, Dichter Books, Kinder Books, Branden Publishing Company, Charlesbridge Publishing, Cricket Books, David R. Godine, Inc., Dawn Publications, Down East Books, Dutton Children's Books, Edupress, Inc., Farrar, Straus and Giroux, Publishers, Inc: Books for Young Readers, Free Spirit Publishing, Front Street, Inc., G.P. Putnam's Sons, Graphic Arts Center Publishing Company, Guide, Hachai Publishing, Hearts 'N Tummies Cookbook Company, Hilliard & Harris, Holiday House, Inc., Incentive Publications, Inc., Jodere Group Inc., Judson Press, Just Us Books, Kar-Ben Publishing, Kids Books By Kids, Kregel Publications/Kregel Kidzone, Legacy Press, Lerner Publishing, Little Simon, Mayhaven Publishing, Meriwether Publishing Ltd: Contemporary Drama Service, Milkweed Editions, Millbrook Press, Munchweiler Press: Quality Books for Young Readers, New Horizons Press, Small Horizons Imprint, Pacific View Press, Pauline Books & Media, Peachtree Publishers, Peachtree Jr., Freestone, Pelican Publishing Company, Perspectives Press, Inc.: The Infertility and Adoption Publisher, Piano Press, Rainbow Publishers, Richard C. Owen Publishers, Inc., Roberts Rinehart, Running Review, Sasquatch Books, Soundprints, Ten Speed Press, Celestial Arts, Third World Press, Tilbury House Publishers, Tricycle Press, UpstartBooks, USA Books, Inc. Will Hall Books, Will Hall, Inc., Woodbine House, World Leisure Corporation, Zondervan and Zonderkidz

Christian Interests

Periodicals:

The African American Pulpit!, Alive! A Magazine for Christian Adults, Bible Advocate, Now What? E-zine, Books & Culture, Cadet Quest, Christian Camp & Conference Journal, Christian Century, Christian New Age Quarterly, Christian Parenting Today, Christian Single, Christian Social Action, Christian Women Today, Christianity Today, Chronicles, Club Connection, Clubhouse, CNEWA World, Cornerstone, Cross & Quill, Devo'Zine, Discipleship Journal, The Door Magazine, Evangel, First Things, Guideposts for Kids, Guideposts, Home Education Magazine, Home Times Family Newspaper, Insight, The Journal of Adventist Education, Journal of Christian Nursing, Leadership Journal, LifeWayonline.com, Ligourian, The Living Church, Living With Teenagers, The Lookout, The Lutheran Digest, Marriage Partnership, Mature Living, Mature Years, Men of Integrity, Message Magazine, Moody Magazine, My Legacy, The North American Voice of Fatima, Oblates, On Mission, The Other Side, Passport, Pentecostal Evangel, The Plain Truth, Pockets, Presbyterians Today, Seek The Abundant Life, Sports Spectrum, St. Anthony Messenger, Standard, Teaching Tolerance, Today's Christian, Today's Christian Woman, The Upper Room, Weavings, WIN-Informer, With: The Magazine for Radical Christian Youth, Woman's Touch, Women Today Magazine, Young & Alive,

Book Publishers:

Angel Bea Publishing, Baker Book House Company, Beyond Words Publishing, Black Forest Press: Arbenteuer Books, Dichter Books, Kinder Books, Broadman & Holman Publishers, Christian Ed. Publishers, Christian Publications, Inc. Cross Cultural Publications, Inc., Crossway Books, Daily Guideposts, ETC Publications, Genesis Communications, Inc.: Evergreen Press & Gazelle Press, God Allows U-Turns, Great Quotations Publishing, Guide, Judson Press, Just Us Books, Kregel Publications: Kregel Kidzone, Legacy Press, Loyola Press, Nelson Reference & Electronic Publishing, Possibility Press, PREP Publishing, Rainbow Publishers, Shambhala Publications, Sports Spectrum, St. Bede's Publications, Trinity Foundation, The Trinity Press International, Waterbrook Press, Zondervan and Zonderkidz

Civil War

Periodicals:

Back Home in Kentucky, Bibliophilos, Blue Ridge Country Magazine, Grit Magazine, Heartland USA, Kentucky Monthly, My Legacy, Primedia History Group, Sandlapper, Springfield! Magazine, Tequesta, Times News Service, Willow Springs, Young & Alive

Book Publishers:

Black Forest Press: Arbenteuer Books, Dichter Books, Kinder Books, Branden Publishing Company, Brassey's, Inc., Bridge Works, The Conservatory of American Letters, Fairleigh Dickinson University Press, Fordham University Press, Heritage Books, Inc., Mayhaven Publishing, McFarland & Company, Inc., Mississippi: University Press of Mississippi, Narwhal Press, Inc., Pelican Publishing Company, Rutledge Hill Press, Southern Illinois University Press, Texas Western Press, Tom Doherty Associate, LLC, Tor Books, Forge Books, Orb, Starscape, University of Maine Press, University of Nebraska Press, University of North Texas Press, University of Oklahoma Press, White Mane Publishing Company, Inc.

Collectibles

Periodicals:

American Bungalow, AmericanStyle, Antique Trader Weekly, The Appraisers Standard, Back Home in Kentucky, Bibliophilos, Classic Toy Trains, Collector Editions, Collectors News, Country Living, Doll World, Early American Life, Grit Magazine, House, Home and Garden, Kentucky Monthly, Knives Illustrated, Model Retailer, Persimmon Hill, Plus Magazine, River Town Gazette, Rug Hooking, Toy Farmer, Toy Trucker & Contractor, Toy Shop, Wildlife ArtBook

Book Publishers:

Collectors Press, Hobby House Press, Inc., Narwhal Press, Inc., Square One Publishers

College

Periodicals:

Bibliophilos, Change: The Magazine of Higher Learning, Circle K, CollegeBound Teen Magazine, Equal Opportunity Publications, Inc., Insider Magazine, Iris: A Journal about Women (University of Virginia), Kentucky Monthly, Liquid Ohio, The New Centennial Review, New Millennium Writings, Oregon Quarterly: The Magazine of the University of Oregon, RiverSedge: The University of Texas-Pan American, Sandlapper, Springfield! Magazine, Teaching Tolerance, Young & Alive

Book Publishers:

Barrons Educational Series, Inc., Black Forest Press: Arbenteuer Books, Dichter Books, Kinder Books, Cross Cultural Publications, Inc., The Denali Press, Frederick Fell Publishers, Inc., Garth Gardner Company, The Graduate Group, Great Quotations Publishing, Intercultural Press, Mustang Publishing Company, Nova Press, Oxendine Publishing, Sourcebooks, Inc., Sourcebooks Casablanca, Sourcebooks Hysteria, Sourcebooks Landmark, Sourcebooks MediaFusion, Sphinx Publishing, Ten Speed Press, Celestial Arts, Tricycle Press

Comedy

Periodicals:

America West, Artemis Magazine, Cadet Quest, The Circle, Creative With Words!, Happy Times Monthly, Home Times Family Newspaper, Light, The Lutheran Digest, New Millennium Writings, Plus Magazine, Protooner, River Town Gazette, Short Stuff Magazine, Springfield! Magazine, Transitions, Young & Alive

Book Publishers:

Bridge Works, CCC Publications, Diogenes Publishing, Great Quotations Publishing, Piccadilly Books, Ltd.

Computers

Periodicals:

American Hunter, Artemis Magazine, Aspen Magazine, Beauty Spot, Better Homes and Gardens, Boys' Life, Computer Bits, ComputorEdge, Desktop Engineering, Dialogue, Fast Company, Futurific Magazine, Game Developer, Genealogical Computing, House, Home and Garden, Insider Magazine, Memory Makers, Model Retailer, Mom Guess What Newspaper, PC Magazine, PCWorld, Popular Mechanics, Popular Science, Presentations Magazine, River Town Gazette, Supply Chain Systems Magazine, Wired, Women in Business, The Writer Gazette, Young & Alive

Book Publishers:

29th Press, Abbott, Langer & Associates, ATL Press: Science Technology, Franklin, Beedle & Associates, Garth Gardner Company, The Graduate Group, Millennium Publishing Company, Osborne/McGraw-Hill, Pathfinder Publishing of California, Prima Publishing, Scarecrow Press, Inc.

Confession

Periodicals:

Complete Woman, The Lutheran Digest, Springfield! Magazine

Conservation

Periodicals:

Adirondack Life, America West, American Forests, Artemis Magazine, Aspen Magazine, Audubon, BabyTalk, Bibliophilos, Boys' Life, The Bugle, California Wild: California Academy of Sciences, Country Living, Defenders, E Magazine: The Environmental Magazine, Field & Stream, Florida Wildlife, Flyfisher, Grit Magazine, Heartland USA, HerbalGram, Insider Magazine, Kentucky Monthly, The The Lutheran Digest, Magical Blend, The Maine Organic Farmer & Gardener, Marlin, Mother Earth News, Mountain Living, Natural Beauty & Health, Northwest Fly Fishing, Outdoor America, Outdoor Life, Paddler, Persimmon Hill, Safari, Sandlapper, Scouting, Sierra: The Magazine of the Sierra Club, Smithsonian Magazine, South American Explorer, South Florida History, Southwest Fly Fishing, Sport Fishing Magazine, Texas Parks & Wildlife, Transitions Abroad, Whole Life Times, Wildlife Art, Wisconsin Trails

Topics

Book Publishers:
Beyond Words Publishing, The Conservatory of American Letters, Cross Cultural Publications, Inc., Green Nature Books, Hancock House, Island Press, The McDonald & Woodward Publishing Company, Milkweed Editions, Mountaineers Books, New Society Publishers, Ragged Mountain Press, University of Nebraska Press, University of North Texas Press

Consumer

Periodicals:
American Fitness, American Profile, Artemis Magazine, Arthritis Today, Automobile Quarterly, The Beauty Spot, Budget Living, Canoe & Kayak Magazine, Child Magazine, Cincinnati Woman Magazine, Country Home, Country Woman Magazine, Dialogue, The Dollar Stretcher, Go Magazine, Guns & Ammo, Hawaii Westways, Home Improver Magazine, Insider Magazine, Kentucky Monthly, Knives Illustrated, The Labor Paper: Serving Southern Wisconsin, Ladies' Home Journal, Lake Superior Magazine, Leather The The Crafters & Saddlers Journal The Lutheran Digest, The Maine Organic Farmer & Gardener, Marlin, Marriage Partnership, Men's Fitness, Message Magazine, Metropolis, Midwest Traveler, Modern Bride, National Geographic Traveler, Native Peoples, Natural Beauty & Health, New Mexico Journey, North Dakota Horizons, Oklahoma Today Magazine, The Old Farmer's Almanac, Outdoor Life, Parenting, Popular Mechanics, Reunions Magazine, River Town Gazette, Rosebud, Sew News, Skiing Magazine, Southern Traveler, Toy Shop, Travel & Leisure, Veggie Life, Via, Westways, Southern California Lifestyle Magazine, Whole Life Times, Woman's World, Women In Business

Book Publishers:
Berrett-Koehler Publishers, Branden Publishing Company, Mustang Publishing Company, Santa Monica Press LLC

Cooking

Periodicals:
Alaska Business Monthly, America West, American Girl, Artemis Magazine, Atlanta Homes and Lifestyles, Austin Monthly Magazine, Back Home in Kentucky, The Beauty Spot, Better Homes and Gardens, Blue Ridge Country Magazine, Central PA Magazine, Cincinnati Woman Magazine, Clubhouse, Colorado Homes & Lifestyles, Cooking Light, Country Home, Country Living, Country Magazine, Country Extra Magazine, Country Woman Magazine, First for Women, Food & Wine, Glamour, Good Old Days/Good Old Days Specials, Gourmet, Grit Magazine, Happy Times Monthly, Health, Home Cooking, House, Home and Garden, Italian Cooking and Living, Kentucky Monthly, Ladies' Home Journal, Long Island Woman, The The Magazine of La Cucina Italiana, The Maine Organic Farmer & Gardener, Metropolitan Home, Modern Maturity, Mother Earth News, Mountain Living, Natural Beauty & Health, Northwest Palate, The Old Farmer's Almanac, Outdoor Life, Persimmon Hill, Prevention Magazine, Redbook, Sandlapper, Saveur, Shape Magazine, Southern Living, Sunset Magazine, Veggie Life, Whole Life Times, The Wild Foods Forum, Woman's World, Working Mother Magazine, Yankee, Young & Alive

Book Publishers:
American Literary Press, Inc.: Noble House, Barrons Educational Series, Inc., Berkshire House Publishers, Black Forest Press: Arbenteuer Books, Dichter Books, Kinder Books, Bonus Books, Inc., Bristol Publishing Enterprises: nitty gritty Cookbooks, Champion Press, Ltd., Chronicle Books LLC, Collectors Press, The Crossing Press, David R. Godine, Inc., Down East Books, Falcon Publishing/Falcon Guides, Two Dot, Three Forks, Frederick Fell Publishers, Inc., The Globe Pequot Press, Golden West Publishers, Graphic Arts Center Publishing Company, Harvard Common Press, Hay House, Inc., Hearts 'N Tummies Cookbook Company, Howell Press, Inc., Jewish Lights Publishing, Llewellyn Publications, The Lyons Press, Mage Publishers, The Magni Group, Inc., Mayhaven Publishing, Mountain N' Air Books, Paradise Cay, Pelican Publishing Company, Pineapple Press, Inc., Prima Publishing, Ragged Mountain Press, Rutledge Hill Press, Square One

Publishers, Storey Publishing, LCC, Taylor Trade, Ten Speed Press, Celestial Arts, Tricycle Press, University of North Texas Press, Willow Creek Press

Counseling

Periodicals:
Family Therapy

Book Publishers:
Baywood Publishing Company, Inc., Hazelden Publishing

Crafts/Hobbies

Periodicals:
American Girl, AmericanStyle, Antiques & Collecting Magazine, Art Times, Artemis Magazine, Back Home in Kentucky, Backwoodsman Magazine, Bead&Button, Beadwork, Boys' Life, Budget Living, Cat Fancy, Ceramics Monthly, Cincinnati Woman Magazine, Classic Toy Trains, Cloth Paper Scissors, Clubhouse, Country Living, Country Woman Magazine, Creative Crafter, Crochet World, Decorative Artist's Workbook, Doll World, Fast & Fun Crochet, Fiberarts Magazine, Fine Woodworking, Girls' Life, Grit Magazine, Guideposts for Kids, Handwoven, House, Home and Garden, Interweave Knits, Kentucky Monthly, Creative Knitting, Ladies' Home Journal, Ladybug: The Magazine for Young Children, Leather The Crafters & Saddlers Journal, Long Island Woman, Memory Makers, Model Railroader, Modeler's Resource, Modern Bride, Mother Earth News, The Old Farmer's Almanac, Outdoor Life, Pack-o-Fun, Passport, PieceWork: Needlework and History, Hand in Hand, Plastic Canvas Today, Popular Mechanics, Popular Woodworking, River Town Gazette, Rug Hooking, Scouting, Sew News, Shuttle Spindle & Dyepot, Spider, Spin-Off, Sunset Magazine, Traditional Quiltworks, Quick & Easy Quilting, Quilt World, Quilting Arts Magazine, Quilting Today, Miniature Quilts, Threads Magazine, Transitions, Woman's World, Woodall Publications, Corp., Young & Alive

Book Publishers:
Allworth Press, Barrons Educational Series, Inc., Chitra Publications, Chronicle Books LLC, Cricket Books, Down East Books, Gem Guides Book Company, Green Nature Books, Hobby House Press, Inc., Howell Press, Inc., Interweave Press, Jewish Lights Publishing, Legacy Press, The Magni Group, Inc., Railroading, Rainbow Publishers, Square One Publishers, Storey Publishing, LCC, Ten Speed Press, Celestial Arts, Tricycle Press, Voyageur Press, Walter Foster Publishing, Inc.

Crime

Periodicals:
Alfred Hitchcock Mystery Magazine, Corrections Compendium, Corrections Today, FBI Law Enforcement Bulletin, Futures Mysterious Anthology Magazine, Good Housekeeping, Gray Areas, Gryphon Books, Harper's Magazine, Heartland USA, Kentucky Monthly, My Legacy, Redbook, Smoke Magazine, Life's Burning Desires, Springfield! Magazine, Teaching Tolerance

Book Publishers:
American Correctional Association (ACA) Book Publishing, Bridge Works, David R. Godine, Inc., The Graduate Group, Gryphon Books, Holloway House Publishing Group, Howells House, Inc., Mayhaven Publishing, Narwhal Press, Inc., New Horizons Press, Small Horizons Imprint, Paladin Press: Sycamore Island Books, Flying Machines Press, Prep Publishing, Soho Press Inc, Soho, Soho Crime, Tom Doherty Associate, LLC, Tor Books, Forge Books, Orb, Starscape, University of North Texas Press, Willowgate Press

Culture

Periodicals:
Adirondack Life, Alaska Business Monthly, Alberta Views, America West, American Indian Quarterly, American Visions, Arizona Highways, Arkansas Review, Art Times, Aspen Magazine, Austin Monthly Magazine, The Beauty Spot, Bible Advocate, Now What? E-zine, Bibliophilos, The Black Table, Books & Culture, Boston Magazine, Boston Review, Bridge,

Capper's, Caribbean Travel & Life, Central PA Magazine, Chronicles, Chronogram, Cimarron Review, Cincinnati Woman Magazine, The Circle, Colorado Homes & Lifestyles Magazine, Commonweal, Computer Bits, CNEWA World, Creative With Words!, Crone Chronicles, Dream Network: A Quarterly Journal Exploring Dreams & Myth, East Bay Monthly, Faces: The Magazine About People, Family Digest, Feminist Studies: University of Maryland, First Things, Footsteps, German Life, Girlfriends Magazine, Gray Areas, Grit Magazine, Harper's Magazine, The Hellenic Calendar, Home Times Family Newspaper, Hurricane Alice, The Iconoclast, Insider Magazine, Italian Cooking and Living, The Journal of Asian Martial Arts, Kentucky Monthly, Kung Fu Tai Chi, Lake Michigan Travel Guide, Left Curve, Magical Blend, The Maine Organic Farmer & Gardener, Metro Parent, MetroKids, Metro Baby, African American Family, Metropolis, The Minnesota Review: University of Missouri, Columbia, Mississippi Magazine, More, Mother Jones, Mountain Living, My Legacy, Native Peoples, Natural Beauty & Health, The New Centennial Review, New Letters, New Mexico Magazine, The New Renaissance, New Yorker, Nimrod: International Journal of Prose and Poetry (University of Tulsa), Nine, Nineteenth-Century French Studies, North Dakota Horizons, Obsidian III, The Old Farmer's Almanac, Oregon Quarterly: The Magazine of the University of Oregon, Playboy, Points North, Potomac Review, River Town Gazette, The Roanoker, Russian Life, San Francisco, Sandlapper, Shofar, Shuttle Spindle & Dyepot, Smithsonian Magazine, Snake Nation Review, South Florida History, Southern Traveler, Southwest Review: Southern Methodist University, Specialty Travel Index, Spider, Springfield! Magazine, Studies in American Jewish Literature, symploke, Syracuse New Times, Teaching Tolerance, Tequesta, Texas Highways, The Travel Magazine of Texas, Tikkun, Transitions, Vanity Fair, Vibe, Vogue, Washington Monthly, Willow Springs, Wisconsin Trails, Women and Music, The World & I

Book Publishers:

Algora Publishing, BenBella Books, Beyond Words Publishing, Black Forest Press: Arbenteuer Books, Dichter Books, Kinder Books, Branden Publishing Company, Chronicle Books LLC, Cricket Books, Cross Cultural Publications, Inc., The Denali Press, Diogenes Publishing, Graphic Arts Center Publishing Company, HiddenSpring, Intercultural Press, Jewish Lights Publishing, Just Us Books, Lerner Publishing, Mage Publishers, Maisonneuve Press, Mississippi: University Press of Mississippi, Mustang Publishing Company, Paulist Press: HiddenSpring, Ronin Publishing, Inc., Santa Monica Press LLC, Scarecrow Press, Inc., Stone Bridge Press, Temple University Press, Texas A&M University Press, Texas Western Press, The Trinity Foundation, Trinity Press International, University of Nebraska Press, Washington State University Press, White Cliffs Media, Inc.

Current Affairs

Periodicals:

The Black Table, Newsweek, Ruminator Review, Salon, The World & I

Book Publishers:

Bay Tree Publishing, North Ridge Books

-D-

Dance

Periodicals:

5678 Country, 5678 Swing, Art Times, The Beauty Spot, Cincinnati Woman Magazine, Dance Spirit, Dance Teacher, The Hudson Review, Kentucky Monthly, Teaching Tolerance, Threads Magazine, The Threepenny Review, Tradition, Willow Springs

Book Publishers:

Allworth Press, Players Press, Inc., Temple University Press

Diet/Nutrition

Periodicals:

The Beauty Spot, Body & Soul, Cincinnati Woman Magazine, Complete Woman, Cooking Light, Cosmopolitan, Diabetes Self-Manage-

ment, Elle, Good Housekeeping, Health, House, Home and Garden, Ladies' Home Journal, Long Island Woman, The The Lutheran Digest, Magical Blend, The Maine Organic Farmer & Gardener, Men's Fitness, Men's Health, Muscle & Fitness, The National Enquirer, Natural Beauty & Health, The New Times, New York Runner, Plus Magazine, Prevention Magazine, River Town Gazette, Rocky Mountain Sports Magazine, Shape Magazine, Skating Magazine, Southern Living, Swim Magazine, Veggie Life, Weight Watchers Magazine, West Coast Magazine, Whole Life Times, The Wild Foods Forum, Wines & Vines, Woman's World, Women In Business Working Mother Magazine, Young & Alive

Book Publishers:

Barrons Educational Series, Inc., Contemporary Books: A Division of McGraw-Hill Companies, The Crossing Press, Empire Publishing Service, Fairview Press, Frederick Fell Publishers, Inc., Hay House, Inc., Hohm Press, Hunter House Publishers, Kali Press, Llewellyn Publications, Piccadilly Books, Ltd., Renders Wellness/Publishing, Shambhala Publicaitions, Sourcebooks, Inc., Sourcebooks Casablanca, Sourcebooks Hysteria, Sourcebooks Landmark, Sourcebooks MediaFusion, Sphinx Publishing, Ten Speed Press, Celestial Arts, Tricycle Press, Woodland Publishing

Directories

Periodicals:

The Beauty Spot, RiverSedge: The University of Texas-Pan American, Springfield! Magazine, Teaching Tolerance

Book Publishers:

B. Klein Publications, The Denali Press

Disabilities

Periodicals:

Abilities, American Profile, Dialogue, Equal Opportunity Publications, Inc., Heartland USA, Journal of Christian Nursing, Kaleidoscope: Exploring the Experience of Disability through Literature & Fine Arts, Lifeglow, The Ragged Edge, River Town Gazette, Teaching Tolerance, Transitions

Book Publishers:

American Correctional Association (ACA) Book Publishing, Black Forest Press: Arbenteuer Books, Dichter Books, Kinder Books, Branden Publishing Company, Brookline Books, Fairview Press, Future Horizons, Hunter House Publishers, Mayhaven Publishing, Pathfinder Publishing of California, Temple University Press, Woodbine House

Drama

Periodicals:

American Theatre, Art Times, The Asian Pacific American Journal, Bibliophilos, Cincinnati Woman Magazine, Confrontation, A Literary Journal, Dance Teacher, Dramatics, Fourteen Hills: The SFSU Review, Futures Mysterious Anthology Magazine, The Iconoclast, Kentucky Monthly, The Kenyon Review, Lilith: The Independent Jewish Women's Magazine, The New Centennial Review, Obsidian III, Pleiades: A Journal of New Writing, Rockford Review, Rosebud, Spinning Jenny, Springfield! Magazine, Sycamore Review: Purdue University, Teaching Theatre, Teaching Tolerance, The Threepenny Review, Today's Christian, Willow Springs

Book Publishers:

Allworth Press, Anchorage Press Plays, Inc., Black Forest Press: Arbenteuer Books, Dichter Books, Kinder Books, Branden Publishing Company, Bridge Works, The Conservatory of American Letters, Fairleigh Dickinson University Press, Limelight Editions, Mayhaven Publishing, Meriwether Publishing Ltd: Contemporary Drama Service, Players Press, Inc., Santa Monica Press LLC, Southern Illinois University Press, Temple University Press, Via Dolorosa Press, Waterbrook Press

Topics

-E-

Ecology

Periodicals:

Adirondack Life, American Forests, The American Gardener, Artemis Magazine, Audubon, BabyTalk, BackHome, Boys' Life, The Bugle, California Wild: California Academy of Sciences, Chronogram, Defenders, The Dollar Stretcher, E Magazine: The Environmental Magazine, Environment, Florida Wildlife, Flyfisher, Fur-Fish-Game, Girls' Life, Grit Magazine, Heartland USA, Kentucky Monthly, Magical Blend, The Maine Organic Farmer & Gardener, Mountain Living, National Geographic Traveler, The New Centennial Review, The The New Times Old Farmer's Almanac, Outdoor Life, Potomac Review, River Town Gazette, Scouting, Sierra: The Magazine of the Sierra Club, Smithsonian Magazine, South American Explorer, Springfield! Magazine, Whole Life Times, Wisconsin Trails

Book Publishers:

Beyond Words Publishing, Charlesbridge Publishing, Chelsea Green Publishing Company, Cross Cultural Publications, Inc., Dimi Press, Down East Books, Granite Publishing Group, LLC, Green Nature Books, HiddenSpring, In Print Publishing, Island Press, Jewish Lights Publishing, The McDonald & Woodward Publishing Company, Mountain Press Publishing Company, New Society Publishers, Ragged Mountain Press, Stipes Publishing, LLC, Temple University Press, University of Nebraska Press, University of Nevada Press, University of North Texas Press, Westcliffe Publishers

Economics

Periodicals:

Alberta Views, American Salesman, Artemis Magazine, Austin Monthly Magazine, Bibliophilos, Boston Magazine, Boston Review, Equities Magazine, Futurific Magazine, Home Times Family Newspaper, The Freeman:Ideas on Liberty, Insider Magazine, The Labor Paper: Serving Southern Wisconsin, Long Island Woman, Mortgage Banking, Mother Jones, National Geographic Traveler, The New Centennial Review, Tikkun, Woman's World, The World & I

Book Publishers:

Algora Publishing, Agathon Press, Berrett-Koehler Publishers, Cross Cultural Publications, Inc., Fordham University Press, The Globe Pequot Press, Paragon House, Texas A&M University Press, The Trinity Foundation

Education

Periodicals:

American Careers, The American Legion Magazine, American Libraries, American Profile, Artemis Magazine, Bibliophilos, Boston Magazine, Boston Review, Boys' Life, Campus Life, Central PA Magazine, Change: The Magazine of Higher Learning, Christian Home & School, Chronicles, Circle K, Click Magazine, CollegeBound Teen Magazine, Corrections Compendium, Corrections Today, Creative With Words!, Cross & Quill, DECA Dimensions, The Dollar Stretcher, Dramatics, Education in Focus, Educational Leadership, Education Week, Educator's Edition, The Electron: Cleveland Institute of Electronics and World College, Equal Opportunity Publications, Inc., Et cetera: A Review of General Semantics, Fast Company, First Things, Florida Leader: For College Students, Flyfisher, Futurific Magazine, The Growing Edge, Guideposts for Kids, Home Education Magazine, Home Times Family Newspaper, Hope Magazine, Ideas on Liberty, Instructor, The Journal of Adventist Education, Journal of Christian Nursing, Kentucky Monthly, Ladies' Home Journal, Ladybug Parent's Companion, Mama's Little Helper Newsletter, Mental Floss, Mercury: The Journal of the Astronomical Society of the Pacific, MetroKids, Midwifery Today, Muse Magazine, Muzzle Blasts, The National Enquirer, National Geographic Traveler, The New Centennial Review, New Millennium Writings, Onion World, Oregon Quarterly: The Magazine of the University of Oregon, Parenting, Pastoral Life, Phi Delta Kappan, Presentations Magazine, Radio World, Reader's Digest, The Roanoker, Sandlapper, SchoolArts, Scouting, Shuttle Spindle & Dyepot, Springfield! Magazine, Stone Soup, Student Lawyer, Succeed, Teacher Magazine, Teachers of Vision, Teaching Theatre, Teaching Tolerance, Tikkun, Today's Catholic Teacher, Today's School, Transitions, Transitions Abroad, West Coast Magazine, Wonderful Ideas for Teaching, Learning, and Enjoying Mathematics!

Book Publishers:

Agathon Press, Barrons Educational Series, Inc., Black Forest Press: Arbenteuer Books, Dichter Books, Kinder Books, Branden Publishing Company, Brookline Books, Bye Publishing, Carson-Dellosa Publishing Co., Inc., Champion Press, Ltd., Contemporary Books: A Division of McGraw-Hill Companies, Cottonwood Press, Inc., Cricket Books, Cross Cultural Publications, Inc., Crossway Books, Edupress, Inc., ETC Publications, Fordham University Press, Free Spirit Publishing, The Graduate Group, Great Quotations Publishing, Gryphon House, Inc., Incentive Publications, Inc., Intercultural Press, Kregel Publications/ Kregel Kidzone, Lerner Publishing, Maupin House, Metamorphous Press, Michael Wiese Productions, The Millbrook Press, Nova Press, Orange Frazer Press, Inc., Perron Press, The Phi Delta Kappa Educational Foundation, Pineapple Press, Inc., Players Press, Inc., Rainbow Publishers, Redleaf Press, Rodnik Publishing Co., Running Press Kids, Scarecrow Press, Inc., Soundprints, Stenhouse Publishers, Stylus Publishing, LLC, Temple University Press, The Trinity Foundation, UpstartBooks, Will Hall Books, Will Hall, Inc., Woodbine House

Electronics

Periodicals:

Artemis Magazine, Boys' Life, The Electron: Cleveland Institute of Electronics and World College, Electronic Servicing & Technology, Futurific Magazine, House, Home and Garden, The New Centennial Review, Poptronics, Popular Mechanics, Popular Science, Wired

Engineering

Periodicals:

Artemis Magazine, Cutting Tool Engineering, Desktop Engineering, The Engineering Economist, Equal Opportunity Publications, Inc., Futurific Magazine, Game Developer, Industrial Management, The Joiners' Quarterly, The New Centennial Review, Poptronics, Popular Mechanics, Progressive Engineer, Radio World

Book Publishers:

Craftsman Book Company, Stipes Publishing, LLC

Entertainment

Periodicals:

5678 Country, 5678 Swing, America West, American Girl, Art Times, Artemis Magazine, Aspen Magazine, The Beauty Spot, Boston Magazine, Boys' Life, Buffalo Spree Magazine, Caribbean Travel & Life, Central PA Magazine, Cincinnati Woman Magazine, Coastal Living, Complete Woman, Cosmopolitan, Country Living, Dance Spirit, Doll World, Dramatics, East End Lights, Elle, Fast Company, Food & Wine, Futures Mysterious Anthology Magazine, Girlfriends Magazine, Girls' Life, Glamour, Gourmet, Happy Times Monthly, Home Cooking, Home Times Family Newspaper, Horror Tales, House, Home and Garden, Insider Magazine, Jam Rag, Kentucky Monthly, Lacunae, Ladies' Home Journal, Martha Stewart Living, More, The The National Enquirer New Yorker, Northwest Palate, Penthouse, Persimmon Hill, Playboy, Plus Magazine, Redbook, River Town Gazette, The Roanoker, Salon, Sandlapper, Swank, Syracuse New Times, Teaching Tolerance, Times News Service, Tradition, Transitions, Vampire Tales, Vibe, West Coast Magazine, Willow Springs, Wisconsin Trails, Woman's World

Book Publishers:

Barricade Books, Branden Publishing Company, Chronicle Books LLC, Cross Cultural Publications, Inc., Empire Publishing Service, Frederick Fell Publishers, Inc., Great Quotations Publishing, Hannover House, Mustang Publishing Company, Orange Frazer Press, Inc., Piccadilly

Books, Ltd., Players Press, Inc., Rutledge Hill Press, Santa Monica Press LLC, Taylor Trade, White Cliffs Media, Inc.

Environment

Periodicals:

Adirondack Life, American Forests, The American Gardener, Archaeology, Arizona Highways, Artemis Magazine, Audubon, BabyTalk, BackHome, Balanced Living Magazine, Better Homes and Gardens, Bibliophilos, Blue Ridge Country Magazine, Body & Soul, Boys' Life, The Bugle, California Wild: California Academy of Sciences, Central PA Magazine, Chronicles, Defenders, The Dollar Stretcher, E Magazine: The Environmental Magazine, Environment, Field & Stream, Florida Wildlife, Flyfisher, Forester Communications, Fur-Fish-Game, Happy Times Monthly, Heartland USA, Insider Magazine, Joiners' Quarterly, Kentucky Monthly, Magical Blend, Metropolis, Mother Jones, Mountain Living, Natural History, Natural Home, New Millennium Writings, The New Times, Offshore: Northeast Boating at Its Best, The Other Side, Outdoor America, Paddler, Persimmon Hill, Popular Mechanics, Popular Science, Potomac Review, Power & Motoryacht, Sandlapper, Scouting, Sierra: The Magazine of the Sierra Club, Spider, Sports Afield, Springfield! Magazine, Sun Valley Magazine, Texas Parks & Wildlife, Tikkun, Transitions, Weatherwise Magazine, Whole Life Times, Wildlife Art, Willow Springs, Wisconsin Trails

Book Publishers:

Charlesbridge Publishing, Chelsea Green Publishing Company, Cross Cultural Publications, Inc., The Denali Press, Dimi Press, Falcon Publishing/Falcon Guides, Two Dot, Three Forks, The Graduate Group, Granite Publishing Group, Granite Publishing Group, LLC, Green Nature Books, Hay House, Inc., In Print Publishing, Island Press, Kali Press, The McDonald & Woodward Publishing Company, McFarland & Company, Inc., Milkweed Editions, Naturegraph Publishers, Pruett Publishing Company, Ragged Mountain Press, Richard C. Owen Publishers, Inc., Sierra Club Books, Transnational Publishers, Inc., University of Nebraska Press, University of Nevada Press, University of North Texas Press, Washington State University Press, Westcliffe Publishers

Erotica

Periodicals:

Blackfire, Eros, Horrorfind, In Touch/Indulge, Penthouse, Penthouse Variations, Playgirl, Rosebud, Springfield! Magazine, Swank

Book Publishers:

Bella Books, Companion Press, The Conservatory of American Letters

Experimental Fiction

Periodicals:

Bellingham Review, Confrontation, A Literary Journal, New Millennium Writings, Willow Spring

Book Publishers:

Dalkey Archive Press, Via Dolorosa Press

-F-

Family

Periodicals:

African American Family, America West, The American Legion Magazine, American Profile, Ancestry Magazine, Atlanta Parent, Atlanta Baby, Austin Monthly Magazine, Best of Times, Better Homes and Gardens, Bible Advocate, Now What? E-zine, Birds & Blooms, Blue Ridge Country Magazine, Bride's Magazine, Cadet Quest, Canoe & Kayak Magazine, Capper's, Catholic Digest, Central PA Magazine, Christian Home & School, Christian Parenting Today, Christian Women Today, Cincinnati Woman Magazine, Clubhouse, Country Living, Country Woman Magazine, Creative With Words!, Dialogue, Doll World, The Dollar Stretcher, Dovetail, Family Circle, Family Digest, Family Fun, Family Safety and Health, Family Therapy, Genealogical Computing, Good

Housekeeping, Grit Magazine, Guideposts for Kids, Happy Times Monthly, Health, Home Education Magazine, Home Times Family Newspaper, Hope Magazine, House, Home and Garden, In the Family and Their Loved Ones, Journal of Christian Nursing, Ladies' Home Journal, Ligourian, Long Island Woman, The Lookout, The Lutheran Digest, Marriage Partnership, Mature Years, Men of Integrity, Metro Parent, Metro Baby, MetroKids, Military Officer, Modern Bride, My Legacy, Northwest Family Magazine, Over the Back Fence, Parenting, Parents Magazine, Passport, Pentecostal Evangel, Pockets, Remembrance: A Celebration of Life, Reunions Magazine, River Town Gazette, RiverSedge: The University of Texas-Pan American, Rosebud, Sandlapper, Saturday Evening Post, Scouting, Short Stuff Magazine, Springfield! Magazine, St. Anthony Messenger, Sunset Magazine, Teaching Tolerance, Today's Christian Woman, Transitions, TWINS, United Parenting Publications, West Coast Magazine, Woman's World, Women Today Magazine, Working Mother Magazine, Young & Alive

Book Publishers:

Alba House, Bethany House Publishers, Beyond Words Publishing, Black Forest Press: Arbenteuer Books, Dichter Books, Kinder Books, Bookhaven Press LLC, Branden Publishing Company, Broadman & Holman Publishers, Capital Books, Charlesbridge Publishing, Cross Cultural Publications, Inc., Dial Books for Young Readers, Diogenes Publishing, Excelsior Cee Publishing, Fairview Press, Free Spirit Publishing, The Globe Pequot Press, God Allows U-Turns: Book Series, Great Quotations Publishing, Hazelden Publishing, Health Communications, Inc., Hunter House Publishers, Impact Publishers, Jewish Lights Publishing, Judson Press, Just Us Books, Kar-Ben Publishing, Kregel Publications/Kregel Kidzone, Mayhaven Publishing, McBooks Press, Mustang Publishing Company, New Horizons Press, Small Horizons Imprint, Pathfinder Publishing of California, Pelican Publishing Company, Perspectives Press, Inc.: The Infertility and Adoption Publisher, Prep Publishing, Ragged Mountain Press, Temple University Press, Waterbrook Press, Zondervan and Zonderkidz

Fantasy

Periodicals:

Asimov's Science Fiction, Blackfire, Complete Woman, Hadrosaur Tales, Horrorfind, Ladybug: The Magazine for Young Children, Fantasy & Science Fiction, The Magazine of Speculative Poetry, My Legacy, Playgirl, Rosebud, Space and Time, Spider, Weird Tales, With: The Magazine for Radical Christian Youth

Book Publishers:

Baen Books, Black Forest Press: Arbenteuer Books, DAW Books, Dichter Books, Kinder Books, Charlesbridge Publishing, The Conservatory of American Letters, Cricket Books, Gryphon Books, Highlands Keep Publishing, ImaJinn Books, Tom Doherty Associate, LLC, Tor Books, Forge Books, Orb, Starscape, Warner Books, Willowgate Press

Fashion

Periodicals:

Artemis Magazine, The Beauty Spot, Boston Magazine, Budget Living, Cincinnati Woman Magazine, Complete Woman, Cosmopolitan, Diamond Registry The Bulletin, Doll World, Elle, First for Women, Genre, Glamour, Harper's Bazaar, House, Home and Garden, Kentucky Monthly, Ladies' Home Journal, Long Island Woman, Lucky Magazine, Men's Health, Modern Bride, More, The National Enquirer, Parents Magazine, Penthouse, Persimmon Hill, Playboy, Playgirl, Redbook, River Town Gazette, Seventeen, Sew News, Shape Magazine, Shuttle Spindle & Dyepot, Springfield! Magazine, Town & Country, Travel & Leisure, Vibe, Vogue, Wall Fashions, Weight Watchers Magazine, West Coast Magazine, Woman's World, Working Mother Magazine

Book Publishers:

Players Press, Inc.

Feminism

Periodicals:

Affilia, The Beauty Spot, Calyx Journal, Crone Chronicles, Feminist Studies: University of Maryland, Frontiers: A Journal of Women Stud-

Topics

ies, *Girlfriends Magazine, House, Home and Garden, Hurricane Alice, Insider Magazine, Iris: A Journal about Women (University of Virginia), Journal of Christian Nursing, Liquid Ohio, Magical Blend, The Minnesota Review: University of Missouri, Columbia, Mom Guess What Newspaper, The New Centennial Review, New Moon, The The New Times Other Side, Playgirl, Rosebud, SageWoman, PanGaia,, The Blessed Bee, New Witch, Shofar, Springfield! Magazine, Studies in American Jewish Literature, Teaching Tolerance, Tikkun, Whole Life Times*

Book Publishers:

American Literary Press, Inc.: Noble House, Beyond Words Publishing, Bridge Works, Calyx Books, Cross Cultural Publications, Inc., David R. Godine, Inc., Hay House, Inc., Maisonneuve Press, Mississippi: University Press of Mississippi, New Society Publishers, New Victoria Publishers, Scarecrow Press, Inc., Spinsters Ink, Temple University Press, University of Nebraska Press, University of North Texas Press

Fiction

Periodicals:

5678 Country, 5678 Swing, 96 Inc., America West, ACM: Another Chicago Magazine, Affaire De Coeur, Agni, Alfred Hitchcock Mystery Magazine, Alive! A Magazine for Christian Senior Adults, American Girl, American Letters & Commentary, Analog Science Fiction and Fact, Antioch Review, AQR: Alaska Quarterly Review, Arkansas Review, Artemis Magazine, Artful Dodge: The College of Wooster, Asimov's Science Fiction, The Atlantic Monthly, Babybug, BabyTalk, The Bear Deluxe Magazine, Bellevue Literary Review, Bellingham Review, Bellowing Ark, Bibliophilos, Birds & Blooms, Black Warrior Review, Blackfire, Bloomsbury Review, Boston Review, Boys' Life, Boys' Quest, Bridal Guide, Bridge, Buffalo Spree Magazine, The Bugle, ByLine, Cadet Quest, Calyx Journal, The Carolina Quarterly, Cat Fancy, CC Motorcycle News Magazine, The Chattahoochee Review, Chicago Magazine, Chicago Review, Chrysalis Reader, Cicada, Cimarron Review, The Circle, Clubhouse, Coal People Magazine, Cobblestone Magazine, Confrontation, A Literary Journal, Conversely, The Cooperator: The Co-op and Condo Monthly, Cosmopolitan, The Cream City Review, Milwaukee, Creative With Words!, Cricket, CutBank: University of Montana, Downstate Story, Dream Network: A Quarterly Journal Exploring Dreams & Myth, East End Lights, Elle, Ellery Queen's Mystery Magazine, Erased, Sigh, Sigh., Eros, Essence, Evangel, Field & Stream, Flesh & Blood, Fourteen Hills: The SFSU Review, French Forum, Fun for Kidz, Futures Mysterious Anthology Magazine, The Georgia Review, The Gettysburg Review, Gist Review, Glimmer Train Stories, Golf Journal Magazine, Good Housekeeping, The Good Red Road, The Green Hills Literary Lantern: Truman State University, Green Mountains Review: Johnson State College, The Greensboro Review, Grit Magazine, Gryphon Books, Hadrosaur Tales, Harper's Bazaar, Harper's Magazine, Hawaii Review, Hayden's Ferry Review: Arizona State University, Home Business Magazine, Home Times Family Newspaper, Hopscotch for Girls, Horror Tales, Horrorfind, The Hudson Review, Hurricane Alice, I Love Cats, The Iconoclast, In the Family and Their Loved Ones, In Touch/Indulge, Indiana Review, Iris: A Journal about Women (University of Virginia), Japanophile, Kalliope, The Kenyon Review, Lacunae, Ladies' Home Journal, Ladybug: The Magazine for Young Children, Legacy: A Journal of American Women Writers, Light, Light of Consciousnes, Lilith: The Independent Jewish Women's Magazine, Liquid Ohio, The Literary Review: Fairleigh Dickinson University, The MacGuffin, Maelstrom, Fantasy & Science Fiction, The Massachusetts Review: University of Massachusetts, Mature Years, The Melic Review, Message Magazine, Mid-American Review: Bowling Green State University, The Minnesota Review: University of Missouri, Columbia, The Mississippi Review, The Mississippi Review online, The Missouri Review, My Legacy, Nebo: A Literary Journal (Arkansas Polytechnic University), The Nebraska Review: University of Nebraska-Omaha, New England Review: Middlebury College, New Letters, New Millennium Writings, New Moon, The New Renaissance, New Yorker, Nimrod: International Journal of Prose and Poetry (University of Tulsa), Nine, Northwest Review: University of Oregon, Obsidian III, Office Number

One, Ohio Writer, The Other Side, Other Voices: University of Illinois-Chicago, Over the Back Fence, Pangolin Papers, Passages North: Northern Michigan University, Passport, Pearl, The Pedestal Magazine, Penthouse, Penthouse Variations, Peregrine: History and Background of Amherst Writers and Artists, Phantasmagoria, Phoebe, Playgirl, Pleiades: A Journal of New Writing, Ploughshares: Emerson College, Potomac Review, Prairie Schooner: University of Nebraska Press, Primavera, Quarterly West: University of Utah, Red Rock Review, Redbook, Rhino, Rockford Review, Rosebud, Running Times, Saturday Evening Post, Seek The Abundant Life, Sewanee Review, Short Stuff Magazine, Slipstream, Snake Nation Review, The Southern California Anthology: University of Southern California, Southern Humanities Review: Auburn University, The Southern Review: Louisiana State University, Southwest Review: Southern Methodist University, Space and Time, Spider, Spinning Jenny, St. Anthony Messenger, The Sun, Swank, Sycamore Review: Purdue University, Tampa Review: Literary Journal of the University of Tampa, Thema, The Threepenny Review, Tikkun, Two Rivers Review, True Romance, Turkey Call, Women In The Outdoors, Wheelin' Sportsmen, The Caller, Jakes Magazine, The Urbanite, Vampire Tales, Verses Magazine, Virginia Quarterly Review, Weavings, Weird Tales, Western Humanities Review, The William and Mary Review: College of William and Mary, Willow Springs, Wired, With: The Magazine for Radical Christian Youth, The Worcester Review, Writer's Guidelines & News, The Yalobusha Review, Zoetrope: All-Story, ZYZZYVA

Book Publishers:

Alyson Publications, Inc., American Book Publishing, American Literary Press, Inc.: Noble House, Anchorage Press Plays, Inc., Time Warner Book Group, Apage4You Book Publishing, Arte Público Press: The University of Houston, Atheneum Books, Avalon Books, Baen Books, Bee-Con Books, Bella Books, Bethany House Publishers, BkMk Press: University of Missouri-Kansas City, Black Forest Press: Arbenteuer Books, Dichter Books, Kinder Books, Book Peddlers, Branden Publishing Company, Bridge Works, Brookline Books, Calyx Books, CCC Publications, Charlesbridge Publishing, Christian Ed. Publishers, Chronicle Books LLC, The Conservatory of American Letters, Cricket Books, Crossway Books, Dalkey Archive Press, David R. Godine, Inc., DAW Books, Dial Books for Young Readers, Denlinger's Publishers, Ltd., Dorchester Publishing Co., Inc., Down East Books, Dutton Children's Books, Edupress, Inc., Elderberry Press, LLC, Emquad International, Ltd., Farrar, Straus and Giroux, Publishers, Inc: Books for Young Readers, Fiesta City Publishers, Front Street, Inc., G.P. Putnam's Sons, Gryphon Books, Hampton Roads Publishing, Co., Hannover House, Harlequin, Hillbrook Publishing, Hilliard & Harris, Holloway House Publishing Group, ImaJinn Books, Intercontinental Publishing: New Amsterdam Publishing, J.N. Townsend Publishing, John Daniel & Company, Jona Books, Just Us Books, Kar-Ben Publishing, Latin American Literary Review Press, Llewellyn Publications, Lumen Editions, The Lyons Press, MacAdam/Cage, Mage Publishers, Maisonneuve Press, March Street Press, Parting Gifts, Mayhaven Publishing, McBooks Press, Metropolis Ink, Milkweed Editions, Mississippi: University Press of Mississippi, Moondance Publishing, Narwhal Press, Inc., Naval Institute Press, New Victoria Publishers, North Street Publishers, Origin Media, Inc.: "Books for the Integral Age", Padlock Mystery Press, Peachtree Publishers, Peachtree Jr, .Freestone, Pelican Publishing Company, The Permanent Press: Second Chance Press, Pineapple Press, Inc., The Post-Apollo Press, Prep Publishing, Puget Sound Books, QED Press, Quality Words In Print, Red Dress InkTM, Richard C. Owen Publishers, Inc., Roberts Rinehart, Sarabande Books, Serendipity Systems: Books-on-disks, Silver Dagger Mysteries, Soho Press Inc., Soho, Soho Crime, Sourcebooks, Inc., Sourcebooks Casablanca, Sourcebooks Hysteria, Sourcebooks Landmark, Sourcebooks MediaFusion, Sphinx Publishing, Spinsters Ink, Third World Press, Thriller Press, Tilbury House Publishers, Tom Doherty Associate, LLC, Tor Books, Forge Books, Orb, Starscape, Unity House, University of Nevada Press, University of North Texas Press, UpstartBooks, USA Books, Via Dolorosa Press, Waltsan Publishing,

LLC, Warner Books, Waterbrook Press, White Mane Publishing Company, Willowgate Press, Wilshire Book Co., Zondervan and Zonderkidz

Film/Video

Periodicals:

Art Times, Bibliophilos, Cincinnati Woman Magazine, Cineaste, Clamor, Culture, Media and Life., Dramatics, Film Quarterly, Girls' Life, Good Old Days/Good Old Days Specials, Gray Areas, Home Times Family Newspaper, The Hudson Review, Insider Magazine, Lilith: The Independent Jewish Women's Magazine, The Minnesota Review: University of Missouri, Columbia, Mom Guess What Newspaper, Mother Jones, The New Renaissance, New Yorker, River Town Gazette, Springfield! Magazine, Teaching Tolerance, The Threepenny Review, Times News Service, Vanity Fair, Zoetrope: All-Story

Book Publishers:

Allworth Press, Arden Press, Inc., Chronicle Books LLC, Companion Press, Fordham University Press, Garth Gardner Company, Hannover House, In Print Publishing, Intercultural Press, Lehigh University Press, Maisonneuve Press, McFarland & Company, Inc., Michael Wiese Productions, Mississippi: University Press of Mississippi, Players Press, Inc., Rutledge Hill Press, Santa Monica Press LLC, Scarecrow Press, Inc., Southern Illinois University Press, Stone Bridge Press, Temple University Press, University of Nebraska Press

Fishing

Periodicals:

Adirondack Life, American Hunter, Bass West, Blue Ridge Country Magazine, Boating Life, Boys' Life, Cascades East Magazine: Central Oregon's Quarterly, Dakota Outdoors: Premier Outdoor Magazine of the Dakotas, Field & Stream, Fishing Facts, Fly Fisherman, Fly Fishing in Salt Waters, Flyfisher, Flyfishing & Tying Journal, A Compendium for the Complete Fly Fisherman, Fur-Fish-Game, Grit Magazine, Happy Times Monthly, Heartland USA, Houseboat, Knives Illustrated, Marlin, Midwest Outdoors, Mountain Living, Northwest Fly Fishing, Offshore: Northeast Boating at Its Best, Outdoor America, Outdoor Life, Outdoor World, Pacific Fishing, Paddler, Power & Motoryacht, River Town Gazette, Salmon-Trout-Steelheader, Sandlapper, Scouting, Smoke Magazine, Life's Burning Desires, Southwest Fly Fishing, Sport Fishing Magazine, Springfield! Magazine, Texas Parks & Wildlife

Book Publishers:

The Conservatory of American Letters, Down East Books, Falcon Publishing/Falcon Guides, Two Dot, Three Forks, Frank Amato Publications, Inc., The Globe Pequot Press, Hearts 'N Tummies Cookbook Company, The Lyons Press, Mayhaven Publishing, Paradise Cay, Ragged Mountain Press, Stackpole Books, Voyageur Press, Willow Creek Press

Folklore

Periodicals:

Bibliophilos, Blue Ridge Country Magazine, Fate, Grit Magazine, The Old Farmer's Almanac, Parabola, Parenting, Persimmon Hill, River Town Gazette, Sandlapper, Short Stuff Magazine, Springfield! Magazine, Teaching Tolerance, Tradition, Willow Springs

Book Publishers:

Dial Books for Young Readers, Granite Publishing Group, LLC, Mayhaven Publishing, Santa Monica Press LLC, University of Idaho Press, University of North Texas Press

Food/Drink

Periodicals:

All for You, America West, American Fitness, Artemis Magazine, Atlanta Homes and Lifestyles, Austin Monthly Magazine, The Beauty Spot, Bibliophilos, Boston Magazine, Budget Living, Central PA Magazine, Chef Magazine, Cooking Light, Country Home, Country Living, Country Magazine, Country Extra Magazine, First for Women, Food & Wine, Fresh Cut, Glamour, Good Old Days/Good Old Days Specials, Health, Home Cooking, House, Home and Garden, Insider Magazine, Italian

Cooking and Living, Ladies' Home Journal, Lake Michigan Travel Guide, Long Island Woman, The Magazine of La Cucina Italiana, The Maine Organic Farmer & Gardener, MetroKids, Mississippi Magazine, Modern Maturity, Mom Guess What Newspaper, Mother Earth News, National Geographic Traveler, Native Peoples, The New Yorker, Northwest Palate, Penthouse, Points North, Prevention Magazine, Redbook, River Town Gazette, The Roanoker, Sandlapper, Saveur, Self, Shape Magazine, Smoke Magazine, Life's Burning Desires, Southern Living, Springfield! Magazine, Sunset Magazine, Syracuse New Times, Transitions, Travel & Leisure, Whole Life Times, The Wild Foods Forum, Wines & Vines, Wisconsin Trails, Woman's World, Women Today, Working Mother Magazine, Yankee

Book Publishers:

Bristol Publishing Enterprises: nitty gritty Cookbooks, Charlesbridge Publishing, Chronicle Books LLC, Collectors Press, David R. Godine, Inc., Frederick Fell Publishers, Inc., Gürze Books, Hearts 'N Tummies Cookbook Company, Lerner Publishing, The Lyons Press, Mayhaven Publishing, Mustang Publishing Company, Rutledge Hill Press, Sasquatch Books, Ten Speed Press, Celestial Arts, Tricycle Press

-G-

Games

Periodicals:

American Girl, American Turf Monthly, Artemis Magazine, Boys' Life, Boys' Quest, Card Player, Cat Fancy, Chess Life, School Mates, Clubhouse, Cobblestone Magazine, Game Developer, Guideposts for Kids, Happy Times Monthly, Ladybug: The Magazine for Young Children, Passport, River Town Gazette, Spider, Sports Illustrated for Kids, Young & Alive

Book Publishers:

Bonus Books, Inc., Chess Enterprises, Legacy Press, Mustang Publishing Company, Naturegraph Publishers, Rainbow Publishers, Square One Publishers

Gardening

Periodicals:

Adirondack Life, Alaska Business Monthly, The American Gardener, American Profile, Atlanta Homes and Lifestyles, BackHome, Better Homes and Gardens, Birds & Blooms, Blue Ridge Country Magazine, Bride's Magazine, Capper's, Central PA Magazine, Coastal Living, Colorado Homes & Lifestyles, Country Living, Creative With Words!, Fine Gardening, Gardening How-To, Grit Magazine, The Growing Edge, Happy Times Monthly, Heartland USA, Home Improver Magazine, Horticulture, House, Home and Garden, Ladies' Home Journal, Long Island Woman, The Lutheran Digest, The Maine Organic Farmer & Gardener, Metropolitan Home, Mississippi Magazine, Mother Earth News, Mountain Living, The Old Farmer's Almanac, Plus Magazine, Points North, River Town Gazette, Sandlapper, Saturday Evening Post, Seattle Homes and Lifestyles, Southern Living, Springfield! Magazine, Sunset Magazine, Texas Gardener, Transitions, Veggie Life, The Wild Foods Forum, Woman's World, Yankee

Book Publishers:

Barrons Educational Series, Inc., Bristol Publishing Enterprises: nitty gritty Cookbooks, Chelsea Green Publishing Company, David R. Godine, Inc., Down East Books, The Globe Pequot Press, Graphic Arts Center Publishing Company, Hearts 'N Tummies Cookbook Company, HiddenSpring, Llewellyn Publications, Mage Publishers, Mississippi: University Press of Mississippi, Sasquatch Books, Stipes Publishing, LLC, Storey Publishing, LCC, Taylor Trade, Ten Speed Press, Celestial Arts, Tricycle Press, Willow Creek Press

Gay/Lesbian

Periodicals:

And Baby, Blackfire, Calyx Journal, The Carolina Quarterly, Chiron Review, East End Lights, Feminist Studies: University of Maryland, Fourteen Hills: The SFSU Review, Frontiers: A Journal of Women Stud-

ies, Genre, Girlfriends Magazine, Hurricane Alice, In the Family and Their Loved Ones, In Touch/Indulge, Iris: A Journal about Women (University of Virginia), Kuumba, The Minnesota Review: University of Missouri, Columbia, Mom Guess What Newspaper, The The New Times Other Side, Penthouse Variations, Rainbow Review, fiction, and nonfiction, Teaching Tolerance

Book Publishers:

Alyson Publications, Inc., Barricade Books, Bella Books, Chronicle Books LLC, Companion Press, David R. Godine, Inc., New Victoria Publishers, Scarecrow Press, Inc., Spinsters Ink, Temple University Press

General Interest

Periodicals:

America West, American Forests, American Hunter, The American Scholar: Phi Beta Kappa, Arizona Foothills Magazine, Artemis Magazine, The Atlantic Monthly, Attaché, Austin Monthly Magazine, Baltimore Magazine, The Beauty Spot, The Beloit Poetry Journal, Bibliophilos, Blue Ridge Country Magazine, Boston Magazine, Boys' Life, Braveheart, California Lawyer, Calyx Journal, Capper's, Charleston Magazine, Cincinnati Woman Magazine, Colorado Homes & Lifestyles, Complete Woman, Creative Nonfiction, Dovetail, Dream Network: A Quarterly Journal Exploring Dreams & Myth, The Elks Magazine, Essence, Et cetera: A Review of General Semantics, Family Circle, Fate, First Things, Futures Mysterious Anthology Magazine, Futurific Magazine, Good Housekeeping, Grit Magazine, Guideposts for Kids, Happy Times Monthly, Heartland USA, HerbalGram, Home Education Magazine, Home Times Family Newspaper, Hope Magazine, The Hudson Review, The Iconoclast, Insider Magazine, Journal of Christian Nursing, Kentucky Monthly, The Kenyon Review, Knives Illustrated, Ligourian, Liquid Ohio, The Lutheran Digest, Men's Journal, Metropolis, Military Officer, Modern Bride, More, Mother Jones, The New Renaissance, Ohio Magazine, The Old Farmer's Almanac, Over the Back Fence, Parade, Passages North: Northern Michigan University, Playboy, Popular Science, Reader's Digest, Reunions Magazine, River Town Gazette, The Roanoker, Rosebud, San Francisco, Sandlapper, Senior Living, Short Stuff Magazine, Shuttle Spindle & Dyepot, Sports Illustrated for Kids, Teaching Tolerance, The Threepenny Review Toastmaster, Today's Christian, Today's Christian Woman, Town & Country, Transitions, Troika Magazine, West Coast Magazine, Whole Life Times, Willow Springs, Wisconsin Trails, Writer's Guidelines & News, Yankee, Young & Alive

Book Publishers:

Addicus Books, Inc., Arden Press, Inc., Aslan Publishing, Beyond Words Publishing, Black Forest Press: Arbenteuer Books, Dichter Books, Kinder Books, Branden Publishing Company, Bridge Works, Bright Mountain Books, Inc., Chronicle Books LLC, Cross Cultural Publications, Inc., Down East Books, Excelsior Cee Publishing, God Allows U-Turns: Book Series, The Graduate Group, Great Quotations Publishing, Hay House, Inc., HiddenSpring, Howells House, Inc., In Print Publishing, Johnston Associates International, Mayhaven Publishing, Millennium Publishing Company, Mississippi: University Press of Mississippi, Mustang Publishing Company, Paulist Press: HiddenSpring, Roberts Rinehart, Santa Monica Press LLC, Skinner House Books, Sourcebooks, Inc., Sourcebooks Casablanca, Sourcebooks Hysteria, Sourcebooks Landmark, Sourcebooks MediaFusion, Sphinx Publishing, Temple University Press, Ten Speed Press, Celestial Arts, Tricycle Press, University of Nevada Press, University of North Texas Press, Willowgate Press

Government

Periodicals:

American City & County, Artemis Magazine, Austin Monthly Magazine, Bibliophilos, California Journal, California Lawyer, Chronicles, Contract Management, FBI Law Enforcement Bulletin, First Things, Futures Mysterious Anthology Magazine, Government Executive, Home Times Family Newspaper, Ideas on Liberty, Insider Magazine, Ken-

tucky Monthly, The The Long Term View: Massachusetts School of Law Messenger, Mother Jones, The National Enquirer, The New Centennial Review, Penthouse, Presentations Magazine, Springfield! Magazine, Teaching Tolerance, Tikkun, Washington Monthly, Whole Life Times, Wines & Vines, Women In Business

Book Publishers:

Algora Publishing, Berrett-Koehler Publishers, Black Forest Press: Arbenteuer Books, Dichter Books, Kinder Books, Bookhaven Press LLC, Branden Publishing Company, Brassey's, Inc., Clarity Press, Inc., Cross Cultural Publications, Inc., Fairleigh Dickinson University Press, Fordham University Press, The Graduate Group, Lehigh University Press, Lerner Publishing, The Trinity Foundation, University of Nebraska Press

Graphics

Periodicals:

Futures Mysterious Anthology Magazine, Game Developer, Letter Arts Review

Book Publishers:

Garth Gardner Company, Graphic Arts Technical Foundation/ GATFPress

-H-

Health

Periodicals:

Alive! A Magazine for Christian Senior Adults, All for You, American Fitness, American Indian Quarterly, The American Legion Magazine, American Medical News, American Profile, Artemis Magazine, Arthritis Today, Aspen Magazine, Balanced Living Magazine, The Beauty Spot, Better Homes and Gardens, Body & Soul, Boston Magazine, Boys' Life, Bridal Guide, Buffalo Spree Magazine, Cat Fancy, Catholic Digest, Central PA Magazine, Children's Better Health Institute, Christian Women Today, Cooking Light, Cosmopolitan, Crone Chronicles, Dermascope, Diabetes Self-Management, Discover, Dream Network: A Quarterly Journal Exploring Dreams & Myth, Elle, Equal Opportunity Publications, Inc., Essence, Family Circle, Family Safety and Health, FirehouseMagazine, Firehouse.com, Fitness Management, Glamour, The Golfer, Good Housekeeping, Good Old Days/Good Old Days Specials, Grit Magazine, Health, HerbalGram, Home Times Family Newspaper, HomeLife, House, Home and Garden, International Sports Journal: University of West Haven, The Journal of Asian Martial Arts, Journal of Christian Nursing, Kentucky Monthly, Kung Fu Tai Chi, Ladies' Home Journal, Llewellyn Journal, Long Island Woman, The Lutheran Digest, Magical Blend, The Maine Organic Farmer & Gardener, Massage & Bodywork, Massage Magazine, Mature Years, Men's Fitness, Men's Health, Military Officer, Modern Bride, MetroKids, Modern Maturity, More, Mother Earth News, Muscle & Fitness, The National Enquirer, National Geographic Traveler, Natural Beauty & Health, Natural Home, The New Times, Onion World, Outdoor Life, Parenting, Parents Magazine, Pediatrics For Parents, Plus Magazine, Podiatry Management, Prevention Magazine, Psychology Today, Reader's Digest, Redbook, River Town Gazette, Rock and Ice, Rocky Mountain Sports Magazine, Runner's World, Running Times, Saturday Evening Post, Scouting, Self, Senior Living, Seventeen, Shape Magazine, Skin Inc. Magazine: The Complete Business Guide for Face & Body Care, Springfield! Magazine, Swim Magazine, Swimming Technique, Swimming World, Junior Swimmer, T'ai Chi, Town & Country, Trail Runner, Transitions, Veggie Life, Volleyball Magazine, Weight Watchers Magazine, West Coast Magazine, The Wild Foods Forum, Wines & Vines, Woman's World, Women In Business, Women Today Magazine, Yoga Journal, Young & Alive

Book Publishers:

Addicus Books, Inc., American Literary Press, Inc.: Noble House, Barrons Educational Series, Inc., Baywood Publishing Company, Inc.,

Press, Mustang Publishing Company, Storey Publishing, LCC, Wilshire Book Co.

Home

Periodicals:

Better Homes and Gardens, Clubhouse, Coastal Living, Colorado Homes & Lifestyles, Country Home, Fine Homebuilding, Home Furnishings Retailer, House Beautiful, Intertior Design Magazine, MetroKids, Mother Earth News, Natural Home, Pentecostal Evangel, Points North, Sew News, Town & Country, Woman's World

Book Publishers:

Bristol Publishing Enterprises: nitty gritty Cookbooks

Horror

Periodicals:

Flesh & Blood, Futures Mysterious Anthology Magazine, Horror Tales, Horrorfind, Lacunae, Fantasy & Science Fiction, The Magazine of Speculative Poetry, Office Number One, Space and Time, Swank, Vampire Tales, Weird Tales

Book Publishers:

American Literary Press, Inc.: Noble House, Denlinger's Publishers, Ltd., Dorchester Publishing Co., Inc., Tom Doherty Associate, LLC, Tor Books, Forge Books, Gryphon Books, Orb, Starscape, Willowgate Press

Human Rights

Periodicals:

Futures Mysterious Anthology Magazine, Home Times Family Newspaper, In the Family and Their Loved Ones, The Other Side, Springfield! Magazine, Syracuse New Times, Teaching Tolerance, Willow Springs

Book Publishers:

Berrett-Koehler Publishers, Brassey's, Inc., Clarity Press, Inc., The Denali Press, Maisonneuve Press, New Horizons Press, Small Horizons Imprint, Paragon House, QED Press, Transnational Publishers, Inc., University of Idaho Press, Volcano Press

Humor

Periodicals:

Annals of Improbable Research (AIR): The Journal of Record for Inflated Research and Personalities, The Black Table, The Bugle, Catholic Digest, CC Motorcycle News Magazine, Coastal Living, Funny Times, The Iconoclast, Minnesota Memories, Penthouse, Rosebud, Sandlapper, Saturday Evening Post, Short Stuff Magazine, Smithsonian Magazine, Society of American Baseball Research, Spider, Woodall Publications, Corp.

Book Publishers:

Calyx Books, CCC Publications, Great Quotations Publishing, Jona Books, Moondance Publishing, North Ridge Books, Ten Speed Press, Celestial Arts, Tricycle Press, Wilshire Book Co.

-I-

Inspirational

Periodicals:

The African American Pulpit!, Alive Now, America West, American Fitness, American Profile, AmericanStyle, Angels on Earth, Bible Advocate, Now What? E-zine, Body & Soul, Braveheart, Capper's, Christian Parenting Today, Club Connection, Crone Chronicles, Devo'Zine, Discipleship Journal, Dream Network: A Quarterly Journal Exploring Dreams & Myth, Evangel, Grit Magazine, Guideposts for Kids, Guideposts, Happy Times Monthly, Heartland USA, Home Times Family Newspaper, Journal of Christian Nursing, Kentucky Monthly, Lifeglow, Light of Consciousnes, The Lutheran Digest, Magical Blend, Mature Years, Memory Makers, Men's Fitness, Message Magazine, Minnesota Memories, My Legacy, The New Times, The North American Voice of Fatima, Oblates, The Other Side, Pastoral Life, The Plain Truth, Reader's Digest, Science of Mind, Seek The Abundant Life, Senior Living, Sports Illustrated for Kids, Springfield! Magazine, St. Anthony Messenger, Today's Christian, Today's Christian Woman, Transitions, True Romance, The Upper Room, Weight Watchers Magazine, West Coast Magazine, Whole Life Times, WIN-Informer, With: The Magazine for Radical Christian Youth, Woman's Touch, Young & Alive

Book Publishers:

Aslan Publishing, Berrett-Koehler Publishers, Beyond Words Publishing, Black Forest Press: Arbenteuer Books, Dichter Books, Kinder Books, Broadman & Holman Publishers, Bye Publishing, Christian Publications, Inc., Cross Cultural Publications, Inc., Daily Guideposts, Emerald Ink Publishing, Excelsior Cee Publishing, Fairview Press, Frederick Fell Publishers, Inc., Genesis Communications, Inc.: Evergreen Press & Gazelle Press, God Allows U-Turns: Book Series, Granite Publishing Group, Great Quotations Publishing, Green Nature Books, Guide, Hampton Roads Publishing, Harbor Press, Hay House, Inc., Health Communications, Inc., HiddenSpring, In Print Publishing, Jewish Lights Publishing, Jodere Group Inc., Judson Press, Kali Press, Kregel Publications/Kregel Kidzone, Legacy Press, Llewellyn Publications, Markowski International Publishers, Possibility Press, Mayhaven Publishing, New Horizons Press, Small Horizons Imprint, Paulist Press: HiddenSpring, Pelican Publishing Company, Prep Publishing, Rainbow Publishers, Red Wheel/Weiser, Rutledge Hill Press, Skinner House Books, Waterbrook Press, Wilshire Book Co.

Internet

Periodicals:

American Hunter, Annals of Improbable Research (AIR): The Journal of Record for Inflated Research and Personalities, The Beauty Spot, Cross & Quill, Diversity, Futurific Magazine, Gray Areas, Insider Magazine, Journal of Information Ethics: St. Cloud State University, Magical Blend, Memory Makers, Poptronics, Presentations Magazine, Radio World, River Town Gazette, Teaching Tolerance, Women In Business

Book Publishers:

Branden Publishing Company, Franklin, Beedle & Associates, The Graduate Group, Osborne/McGraw-Hill, Scarecrow Press, Inc., Serendipity Systems: Books-on-disks, Wilshire Book Co.

Interview

Periodicals:

Absolute Write, American Fitness, AmericanStyle, Annals of Improbable Research (AIR): The Journal of Record for Inflated Research and Personalities, Artemis Magazine, Audubon, The Bear Deluxe Magazine, The Beauty Spot, Bibliophilos, The Black Table, Bloomsbury Review, The Carolina Quarterly, Central PA Magazine, Chronogram, The Circle, Complete Woman, Crone Chronicles, Doll World, Dream Network: A Quarterly Journal Exploring Dreams & Myth, The Good Red Road, The Green Hills Literary Lantern: Truman State University, Home Times Family Newspaper, The Iconoclast, Insider Magazine, Journal of Christian Nursing, The Labor Paper: Serving Southern Wisconsin, Lacunae, Ladybug Parent's Companion, The Literary Review: Fairleigh Dickinson University, Magical Blend, Mama's Little Helper Newsletter, Memory Makers, The Missouri Review, Mother Jones, Natural Beauty & Health, The New Renaissance, New Times, New York Stories, Obsidian III, Outdoor Life, Passages North: Northern Michigan University, Penthouse, Playboy, Quarterly West: University of Utah, Reader's Digest, Redbook, The Roanoker, Ruminator Review, Sandlapper, Shape Magazine, The Southern Review: Louisiana State University, Southwest Review: Southern Methodist University, Sports Illustrated for Kids, Springfield! Magazine, St. Anthony Messenger, The Sun, Surfer, Swimming Technique, Sycamore Review: Purdue University, Today's Christian Woman, Transitions, Whole Life Times, Willow Springs, Wines & Vines, Wired, The Writer Gazette, Yankee, Young & Alive

Book Publishers:

The Graduate Group, JIST Works/Park Avenue, Ten Speed Press, Celestial Arts, Tricycle Press

-J-

Jewish Interest

Periodicals:

Cincinnati Woman Magazine, First Things, Home Times Family Newspaper, Jewish Action, Jewish Currents, Lilith: The Independent Jewish Women's Magazine, Moment, Passport, River Town Gazette, Shofar, South Florida History, Springfield! Magazine, Studies in American Jewish Literature, Teaching Tolerance, Tequesta, Tikkun,

Book Publishers:

Branden Publishing Company, Brookline Books, Calyx Books, Cross Cultural Publications, Inc., David R. Godine, Inc., The Denali Press, Fairleigh Dickinson University Press, Frederick Fell Publishers, Inc., Hachai Publishing, Jewish Lights Publishing, Kar-Ben Publishing, Latin American Literary Review Press, Lehigh University Press, Lumen Editions, Pelican Publishing Company, Temple University Press, University of Nebraska Press

Juvenile

Periodicals:

American Girl, Appleseeds, Boys' Life, Cadet Quest, Calliope Magazine, Campus Life, Cicada, Classic Toy Trains, Click Magazine, Clubhouse, Creative With Words!, Faces: The Magazine About People, Footsteps, Guideposts for Kids, Instructor, Muse Magazine, Northwest Family News, Odyssey Magazine, Parents' Press, Passport, Potluck Children's Literary Magazine, River Town Gazette, SchoolArts, Sports Illustrated for Kids, Springfield! Magazine, Stone Soup, Teaching Tolerance, United Parenting Publications, Wonderful Ideas for Teaching, Learning, and Enjoying Mathematics!

Book Publishers:

American Literary Press, Inc.: Noble House, Anchorage Press Plays, Inc., Arte Público Press: The University of Houston, Atheneum Books, ATL Press: Science Technology, Barrons Educational Series, Inc., Bethany House Publishers, Carolrhoda Books, Charlesbridge Publishing, Cricket Books, Crossway Books, David R. Godine, Inc., Farrar, Straus and Giroux, Publishers, Inc: Books for Young Readers, Free Spirit Publishing, Front Street, Inc., Guide, ImaJinn Books, Just Us Books, Kar-Ben Publishing, Kids Books By Kids, Kregel Publications/Kregel Kidzone, Legacy Press, Mayhaven Publishing, Peachtree Publishers, Peachtree Jr, .Freestone, Richard C. Owen Publishers, Inc., Ten Speed Press, Celestial Arts, Tricycle Press, UpstartBooks

-L-

Language

Periodicals:

America West, Bibliophilos, Cross & Quill, Et cetera: A Review of General Semantics, French Forum, Futures Mysterious Anthology Magazine, The Kenyon Review, The New Centennial Review, Nineteenth-Century French Studies, Obsidian III, Rhino, Rosebud, Springfield! Magazine, Teaching Tolerance, Thoughts for All Seasons, Transitions Abroad

Book Publishers:

Barbed Wire Publishing, Barrons Educational Series, Inc., Branden Publishing Company, Contemporary Books: A Division of McGraw-Hill Companies, The Globe Pequot Press, Lerner Publishing, Maupin House, Rodnik Publishing Co., Southern Illinois University Press, Stone Bridge Press, University of Nebraska Press

Law

Periodicals:

ABA Journal, American Hunter, Artemis Magazine, Bibliophilos, Cincinnati Woman Magazine, Corrections Compendium, Corrections Today, FBI Law Enforcement Bulletin, FirehouseMagazine, Firehouse.com, First Things, Gray Areas, Insider Magazine, Long Is-

land Woman, The The Long Term View: Massachusetts School of Law Messenger, Police and Security News, Police Times, Referee, Springfield! Magazine, Student Lawyer, Teaching Tolerance

Book Publishers:

BNA Books, Branden Publishing Company, Clarity Press, Inc., Do-It-Yourself Legal Publishers, Fordham University Press, The Graduate Group, Maisonneuve Press, Narwhal Press, Inc., Sourcebooks, Inc., Sourcebooks Casablanca, Sourcebooks Hysteria, Sourcebooks Landmark, Sourcebooks MediaFusion, Sphinx Publishing, Temple University Press, Tower Publishing, Transnational Publishers, Inc.

Lifestyle

Periodicals:

Abilities, Adirondack Life, Arizona Foothills Magazine, Artemis Magazine, Aspen Magazine, Atlanta Homes and Lifestyles, Atlanta Parent, Atlanta Baby, Austin Monthly Magazine, Balanced Living Magazine, The Beauty Spot, Bible Advocate, Now What? E-zine, Bibliophilos, Birds & Blooms, Blue Ridge Country Magazine, Boating Life, Body & Soul, Boston Magazine, Braveheart, Campus Life, Capper's, CC Motorcycle News Magazine, Central PA Magazine, Charleston Magazine, Christian Women Today, Cincinnati Woman Magazine, Coastal Living, CollegeBound Teen Magazine, Colorado Homes & Lifestyles, Complete Woman, Cosmopolitan, Country Home, Country Magazine, Country Extra Magazine, Country Woman Magazine, Crone Chronicles, Cruising World, East Bay Monthly, Elle, Farm & Ranch Living, Farm Times, Beef Times, Fast Company, FirehouseMagazine, Firehouse.com, Freeskier, Futures Mysterious Anthology Magazine, Genre, Glamour, Good Housekeeping, Grit Magazine, Happy Times Monthly, Highways, Home Improver Magazine, Home Times Family Newspaper, HomeLife, House Beautiful, Houseboat, Inc., Italian Cooking and Living, Kentucky Monthly, Lilith: The Independent Jewish Women's Magazine, Log Home Living, Timber Frame Homes, The Magazine of La Cucina Italiana, Magical Blend, The Maine Organic Farmer & Gardener, Marriage Partnership, Mature Living, Men of Integrity, Military Officer, Mom Guess What Newspaper, Motorcycling, Mountain Living, Natural Beauty & Health, The New Times, New York Runner, Northwest Palate, Paddler, Penthouse, Persimmon Hill, Points North, Rainbow Review, Remembrance: A Celebration of Life, Reunions Magazine, River Town Gazette, The Roanoker, Salon, San Francisco, Sandlapper, Seattle Homes and Lifestyles, Short Stuff Magazine, Ski, South Florida History, Springfield! Magazine, Surfer, Swim Magazine, Teaching Tolerance, Transitions, Travel & Leisure, Travel Naturally, Troika Magazine, True West, Vibe, Westchester Magazine, Western RV News & Recreation, Whole Life Times, Wired, Wisconsin Trails, The World & I

Book Publishers:

Apage4You Book Publishing, Aslan Publishing, Book Peddlers, Bookhaven Press LLC, Capital Books, Champion Press, Ltd., Chronicle Books LLC, Eclipse Press, Face to Face Press, Genesis Communications, Inc.: Evergreen Press & Gazelle Press, God Allows U-Turns: Book Series, Great Quotations Publishing, HiddenSpring, Hunter House Publishers, Mustang Publishing Company, New Horizons Press, Small Horizons Imprint, New Society Publishers, Paulist Press: HiddenSpring, Prima Publishing, Ronin Publishing, Inc., Swedenborg Foundation, Inc.: Chrysalis Books

Literature

Periodicals:

African American Review, America West, The American Dissident, The American Poetry Review, The American Scholar: Phi Beta Kappa, Anhinga Press, Antioch Review, Arkansas Review, Art Times, Artemis Magazine, Authorship, Babybug, The Bear Deluxe Magazine, The Beauty Spot, Bellowing Ark, The Beloit Poetry Journal, Bloomsbury Review, Book/Mark Small Press Quarterly Review, Books & Culture, Boston Review, Bridge, ByLine, Calyx Journal, The Carolina Quarterly, The Chattahoochee Review, Chicago Magazine, Chiron Review, Chronicles, Chrysalis Reader, Cimarron Review, Cincinnati Woman

Magazine, The Circle, Commonweal, Confrontation, A Literary Journal, The Cream City Review, Milwaukee, Creative Nonfiction, Cricket, Cross & Quill, Ellery Queen's Mystery Magazine, Erased, Sigh, Sigh., Et cetera: A Review of General Semantics, Feminist Studies: University of Maryland, Fourteen Hills: The SFSU Review, French Forum, Futures Mysterious Anthology Magazine, The Gettysburg Review, Gist Review, Glimmer Train Stories, Grain, Green Mountains Review: Johnson State College, Hadrosaur Tales, Harper's Magazine, The Hollins Critic, Home Times Family Newspaper, The Hudson Review, Hurricane Alice, The Iconoclast, Indiana Review, The Journal of Asian Martial Arts, Journal of Modern Literature: Temple University, Kaleidoscope: Exploring the Experience of Disability through Literature & Fine Arts, Kalliope, Kentucky Monthly, The Kenyon Review, Ladybug Parent's Companion, Left Curve, Legacy: A Journal of American Women Writers, Light, Literary Magazine Review, The Literary Review: Fairleigh Dickinson University, Lucky Magazine, The MacGuffin, The Magazine of Speculative Poetry, Manoa, The Minnesota Review: University of Missouri, Columbia, Native Peoples, The The Nebraska Review: University of Nebraska-Omaha, The New Centennial Review, New England Review: Middlebury College, New Letters, New Millennium Writings, The New Renaissance, New York Stories, Nineteenth-Century French Studies, Northwest Review: University of Oregon, Obsidian III, Ohio Writer, Other Voices: University of Illinois-Chicago, Pangolin Papers, Parnassus, Passages North: Northern Michigan University, Persimmon Hill, Phantasmagoria, Phoebe, Pleiades: A Journal of New Writing, Potluck Children's Literary Magazine, Potomac Review, Quarterly West: University of Utah, Rhino, RiverSedge: The University of Texas-Pan American, Rosebud, Sewanee Review, Shofar, Short Stuff Magazine, Slipstream, Southern Humanities Review: Auburn University, The Southern Review: Louisiana State University, Southwest Review: Southern Methodist University, Springfield! Magazine, Stone Soup, Studies in American Jewish Literature, The Sun, Sycamore Review: Purdue University, symploke, Tampa Review: Literary Journal of the University of Tampa, Thema, The Threepenny Review, Tikkun, Town & Country, Troika Magazine, Vanity Fair, Verses Magazine, Virginia Quarterly Review, Western Humanities Review, The William and Mary Review: College of William and Mary, Willow Springs, Women Artists News Book Review, The Worcester Review, The World & I, The Yalobusha Review

Book Publishers:

Arte Público Press: The University of Houston, Atheneum Books, BkMk Press: University of Missouri-Kansas City, Black Forest Press: Arbenteuer Books, Dichter Books, Kinder Books, Branden Publishing Company, Brookline Books, Calyx Books, Chatoyant, Chronicle Books LLC, The Conservatory of American Letters, Cross Cultural Publications, Inc., David R. Godine, Inc., Dutton Children's Books, Fairleigh Dickinson University Press, Front Street, Inc., Ivan R. Dee, Inc., Publisher, John Daniel & Company, Latin American Literary Review Press, Lumen Editions, The Lyons Press, Mage Publishers, Maisonneuve Press, Mayhaven Publishing, Midmarch Arts Press, Milkweed Editions, Mississippi: University Press of Mississippi, Prep Publishing, QED Press, Serendipity Systems: Books-on-disks, Soho Press Inc, Soho, Soho Crime, Southern Illinois University Press, Temple University Press, University of Idaho Press, University of Nebraska Press, University of Nevada Press, University of North Texas Press, University of Oklahoma Press, Via Dolorosa Press, Willowgate Press

-M-

Marriage

Periodicals:

Bible Advocate, Now What? E-zine, Bridal Guide, Bride's Magazine, Christian Home & School, Christian Women Today, Cincinnati Woman Magazine, Complete Woman, Country Living, Diamond Registry The Bulletin, The Dollar Stretcher, Family Therapy, Good Housekeeping,

Happy Times Monthly, Health, Home Times Family Newspaper, Ladies' Home Journal, Lifeglow, Long Island Woman, The Lutheran Digest, Marriage Partnership, Modern Bride, Natural Beauty & Health, Parenting, Parents Magazine, Redbook, River Town Gazette, Springfield! Magazine, St. Anthony Messenger, Today's Christian Woman, Transitions, Whole Life Times, Woman's World, Women Today Magazine, Working Mother Magazine

Book Publishers:

Alba House, God Allows U-Turns: Book Series, Great Quotations Publishing, Hay House, Inc., Impact Publishers, Kregel Publications/Kregel Kidzone, Sourcebooks, Inc., Sourcebooks Casablanca, Sourcebooks Hysteria, Sourcebooks Landmark, Sourcebooks MediaFusion, Sphinx Publishing, Volcano Press, Waterbrook Press, Zondervan and Zonderkidz

Mass Communications

Periodicals:

Clamor, Culture, Media and Life., The Journal of Asian Martial Arts, Radio World, Redbook, Springfield! Magazine

Book Publishers:

Barricade Books, Players Press, Inc., Santa Monica Press LLC

Men's Fiction

Periodicals:

Blackfire, The Carolina Quarterly, Futures Mysterious Anthology Magazine, Genre, In Touch/Indulge, Obsidian III, Rosebud, Sycamore Review: Purdue University, Willow Springs

Book Publishers:

The Conservatory of American Letters, David R. Godine, Inc., Narwhal Press, Inc., Waterbrook Press

Men's Issues

Periodicals:

The African American Pulpit!, The Beauty Spot, Blackfire, The Carolina Quarterly, Esquire, Genre, Happy Times Monthly, Heartland USA, Insider Magazine, Knives Illustrated, Magical Blend, Men of Integrity, Men's Journal, Mom Guess What Newspaper, Muscle & Fitness, Natural Beauty & Health, The New Times, Transitions, River Town Gazette, Rosebud, Smoke Magazine, Life's Burning Desires, Springfield! Magazine, Swank, Teaching Tolerance, Whole Life Times

Book Publishers:

God Allows U-Turns: Book Series, Hay House, Inc., Health Communications, Inc., Hunter House Publishers, Pathfinder Publishing of California

Military

Periodicals:

The American Legion Magazine, Army Magazine, Artemis Magazine, Bibliophilos, Futurific Magazine, Heartland USA, The Journal of Asian Martial Arts, Marine Corps Gazette, MHQ, The Quarterly Journal of Military History, Military Officer, Parameters: US Army War College Quarterly, Popular Mechanics, Primedia History Group, Reunions Magazine, Springfield! Magazine, Times News Service, VFW Magazine

Book Publishers:

B. Klein Publications, Black Forest Press: Arbenteuer Books, Dichter Books, Kinder Books, Branden Publishing Company, Brassey's, Inc., Elderberry Press, LLC, The Graduate Group, Highlands Keep Publishing, Howells House, Inc., Jona Books, The Lyons Press, Mayhaven Publishing, McBooks Press, Narwhal Press, Inc., Naval Institute Press, Paladin Press: Sycamore Island Books, Flying Machines Press, Prep Publishing, PSI Research: The Oasis Press, Hellgate Press, Scarecrow Press, Inc., Stackpole Books, Texas A&M University Press, Texas Western Press, University of Nebraska Press, University of North Texas Press, White Mane Publishing Company, Inc., YMAA Publication Center

Money & Finances

Periodicals:

Accounting Today, America West, American Business Review, American Profile, American Salesman, Artemis Magazine, The Beauty Spot, Better Homes and Gardens, Bridal Guide, Budget Living, Business 2.0, Christian Women Today, Cincinnati Woman Magazine, Commercial Investment Real Estate Magazine, Cosmopolitan, Diversity, The Dollar Stretcher, Drum Business, Family Circle, Financial Planning, Futurific Magazine, Home Business Journal, Home Times Family Newspaper, House, Home and Garden, Inc., Long Island Woman, The Lutheran Digest, Mature Years, Military Officer, Model Retailer, Modern Bride, Modern Maturity, More, Mortgage Banking, Mother Jones, National Geographic Traveler, Natural Beauty & Health, Personal Branding Magazine, Playboy, Redbook, River Town Gazette, Saturday Evening Post, Springfield! Magazine, Supervision, Technical Analysis of Stocks & Commodities, Times News Service, Transitions, West Coast Magazine, Whole Life Times, Women Today Magazine, Working Mother Magazine, Young & Alive

Book Publishers:

Allworth Press, B. Klein Publications, Bookhaven Press LLC, The Business Group, Contemporary Books: A Division of McGraw-Hill Companies, Do-It-Yourself Legal Publishers, Genesis Communications, Inc.: Evergreen Press & Gazelle Press, The Graduate Group, Markowski International Publishers, Possibility Press, Paladin Press: Sycamore Island Books, Flying Machines Press, Sourcebooks, Inc., Sourcebooks Casablanca, Sourcebooks Hysteria, Sourcebooks Landmark, Sourcebooks MediaFusion, Sphinx Publishing, Square One Publishers, Ten Speed Press, Celestial Arts, Tricycle Press

Multicultural

Periodicals:

The African American Pulpit!, America West, American Profile, Arkansas Review, Art Times, Blue Ridge Country Magazine, Boston Review, Calyx Journal, Central PA Magazine, Clubhouse, Country Magazine, Country Extra Magazine, Equal Opportunity Publications, Inc., Faces: The Magazine About People, Filipinas, Frontiers: A Journal of Women Studies, The Hellenic Calendar, Hurricane Alice, In the Family and Their Loved Ones, Iris: A Journal about Women (University of Virginia), The Journal of Asian Martial Arts, Journal of Christian Nursing, The Kenyon Review, Left Curve, Legacy: A Journal of American Women Writers, Magical Blend, Manoa, The Minnesota Review: University of Missouri, Columbia, Mother Jones, Native Peoples, The New Centennial Review, The New Renaissance, Obsidian III, Passport, RiverSedge: The University of Texas-Pan American, South Florida History, Southwest Review: Southern Methodist University, Springfield! Magazine, Teaching Tolerance, Tequesta, Transitions Abroad, Vibe, Whole Life Times, Willow Springs

Book Publishers:

Arte Público Press: The University of Houston, Black Forest Press: Arbenteuer Books, Dichter Books, Kinder Books, Branden Publishing Company, Clarity Press, Inc., Clover Park Press, Cross Cultural Publications, Inc., The Denali Press, Face to Face Press, HiddenSpring, Hunter House Publishers, Intercultural Press, Judson Press, Just Us Books, Lerner Publishing, Mage Publishers, McFarland & Company, Inc., New Horizons Press, New World Library, Small Horizons Imprint, Pacific View Press, Paulist Press: HiddenSpring, Pelican Publishing Company, Scarecrow Press, Inc., Temple University Press, Texas A&M University Press, Tilbury House Publishers, Turtle Press, University of North Texas Press

Music

Periodicals:

5678 Country, 5678 Swing, Acoustic Guitar Magazine, The African American Pulpit!, Arkansas Review, Art Times, Austin Monthly Magazine, Bibliophilos, Body & Soul, Bridge, Campus Life, Chronogram, The Circle, Clamor, Culture, Media and Life., Drum Business, East End Lights, Girls' Life, Gray Areas, Grit Magazine, Heartland USA,

Home Times Family Newspaper, Insider Magazine, Jam Rag, Journal of Christian Nursing, Kentucky Monthly, Lacunae, Ladybug: The Magazine for Young Children, Lilith: The Independent Jewish Women's Magazine, The Lutheran Digest, Modern Drummer, The New Renaissance New Yorker, Playboy, Playgirl, River Town Gazette, Rosebud, Shofar, Southern Humanities Review: Auburn University, Springfield! Magazine, Studies in American Jewish Literature, Teaching Tolerance, The Threepenny Review, Tradition, Vibe, Whole Life Times, Willow Springs, Women and Music

Book Publishers:

Allworth Press, Centerstream Publishing, Charlesbridge Publishing, Chronicle Books LLC, Fiesta City Publishers, Lehigh University Press, Limelight Editions, Mage Publishers, Mel Bay Publications, Meriwether Publishing Ltd: Contemporary Drama Service, Mississippi: University Press of Mississippi, Pelican Publishing Company, Piano Press, Players Press, Inc., Santa Monica Press LLC, Scarecrow Press, Inc., Schirmer Trade Book, Sourcebooks, Inc., Sourcebooks Casablanca, Sourcebooks Hysteria, Sourcebooks Landmark, Sourcebooks MediaFusion, Sphinx Publishing, Stipes Publishing, LLC, Temple University Press, University of Nebraska Press, University of North Texas Press, White Cliffs Media, Inc.

Mystery

Periodicals:

Alfred Hitchcock Mystery Magazine, Capper's, Ellery Queen's Mystery Magazine, Futures Mysterious Anthology Magazine, Grit Magazine, Lacunae, My Legacy, Passport, River Town Gazette, Rosebud, Short Stuff Magazine, Woman's World

Book Publishers:

Avalon Books, Bee-Con Books, Bella Books, Black Forest Press: Arbenteuer Books, Dichter Books, Kinder Books, The Conservatory of American Letters, Crossway Books, David R. Godine, Inc., Denlinger's Publishers, Ltd., Empire Publishing Service, Hilliard & Harris, Holloway House Publishing Group, Intercontinental Publishing: New Amsterdam Publishing, Mayhaven Publishing, Narwhal Press, Inc., New Victoria Publishers, North Street Publishers, Padlock Mystery Press, Prep Publishing, Puget Sound Books, Quality Words In Print, Silver Dagger Mysteries, Soho Press Inc, Soho, Soho Crime, Spinsters Ink, Tom Doherty Associate, LLC, Tor Books, Forge Books, Orb, Starscape, USA Books, Waterbrook Press, Willowgate Press

-N-

Native American

Periodicals:

Alaska Business Monthly, America West, American Indian Art Magazine, American Indian Quarterly, American Profile, Backwoodsman Magazine, Calyx Journal, Cimarron Review, Equal Opportunity Publications, Inc., Florida Wildlife, Futures Mysterious Anthology Magazine, The Good Red Road, Light, Light of Consciousnes, Magical Blend, My Legacy, Native Peoples, The New Times, Oklahoma Today Magazine, Persimmon Hill, River Town Gazette, Rosebud, South Florida History, Springfield! Magazine, Teaching Tolerance, Tequesta, Willow Springs

Book Publishers:

B. Klein Publications, Beyond Words Publishing, Black Forest Press: Arbenteuer Books, Dichter Books, Kinder Books, Bright Mountain Books, Inc., Calyx Books, Caxton Press, Clarity Press, Inc., Cross Cultural Publications, Inc., The Denali Press, Fairleigh Dickinson University Press, Gem Guides Book Company, Granite Publishing Group, Granite Publishing Group, LLC, Graphic Arts Center Publishing Company, Hearts 'N Tummies Cookbook Company, Heritage Books, Inc., Kali Press, Mayhaven Publishing, Mississippi: University Press of Mississippi, Mountain Press Publishing Company, Naturegraph Publishers, The Overmountain Press, Pelican Publishing Company, Roberts

Rinehart, Shambhala Publications, Texas A&M University Press, University of Idaho Press, University of Nebraska Press, University of Nevada Press, University of Oklahoma Press, Washington State University Press

Nature

Periodicals:

Birds & Blooms, Boys' Quest, Click Magazine, Country Magazine, Country Extra Magazine, Defenders, Florida Wildlife, Flyfisher, HerbalGram, Lake Michigan Travel Guide, Lifeglow, Manoa, Northwest Fly Fishing, Smithsonian Magazine, South American Explorer, Southwest Fly Fishing, Spider, Sun Valley Magazine, The Wild Foods Forum, Woman's World

Book Publishers:

Dawn Publications, Dimi Press, Harvard Common Press, Primer Publishers, Pruett Publishing Company, Roberts Rinehart, Sasquatch Books, Soundprints, Taylor Trade

New Age

Periodicals:

Balanced Living Magazine, Body & Soul, Christian New Age Quarterly, Dream Network: A Quarterly Journal Exploring Dreams & Myth, Fate, Futurific Magazine, Light, Light of Consciousnes, Llewellyn Journal, Magical Blend, My Legacy, The National Enquirer, New Millennium Writings, The New Times, River Town Gazette, Rosebud, Whole Life Times, Yoga Journal

Book Publishers:

American Literary Press, Inc.: Noble House, Beyond Words Publishing, Chronicle Books LLC, Cross Cultural Publications, Inc., The Crossing Press, Frederick Fell Publishers, Inc., Granite Publishing Group, Granite Publishing Group, LLC, Gryphon House, Inc., Hampton Roads Publishing, Harbor Press, Hay House, Inc., In Print Publishing, Llewellyn Publications, New Horizons Press, Small Horizons Imprint, New World Library, Paragon House, Sourcebooks, Inc., Sourcebooks Casablanca, Sourcebooks Hysteria, Sourcebooks Landmark, Sourcebooks MediaFusion, Sphinx Publishing, Square One Publishers, Turtle Press, Unity House, YMAA Publication Center

Nonfiction

Periodicals:

4-Wheel Drive & Sport Utility, 5.0 Mustang & Super Fords, 5678 Country, 5678 Swing, ABA Journal, Abilities, Absolute Write, Acoustic Guitar Magazine, Adirondack Life, Affilia, The African American Pulpit!, Alaska Business Monthly, Alberta Views, Alive! A Magazine for Christian Senior Adults, All About Kids, America West, American Bungalow, American Business Review, American Careers, American City & County, The American Dissident, American Fitness, American Forests, American Girl, American Hunter, American Indian Art Magazine, American Indian Quarterly, The American Legion Magazine, American Letters & Commentary, American Rifleman, The American Scholar: Phi Beta Kappa, American Snowmobiler, American Turf Monthly, Ancestry Magazine, Angels on Earth, Anhinga Press, Antioch Review, Antique Trader Weekly, Antiques & Collecting Magazine, Appleseeds, The Appraisers Standard, AQR: Alaska Quarterly Review, Archaeology, Architectural Digest, Arkansas Review, Art & Antiques, Artemis Magazine, Arthritis Today, The Artist's Magazine, Asian Pacific American Journal, Aspen Magazine, Atlanta Homes and Lifestyles, Atlanta Parent, Atlanta Baby, Audio Video Interiors, Audubon, Austin Monthly Magzazine, Authorship, Auto Sound & Security, Automated Builder, Automobile Quarterly, Aviation Maintenance, Babybug, BabyTalk, Back Home in Kentucky, Balanced Living Magazine, Balloon Life, Baltimore Magazine, Beadwork, The Beauty Spot, Bellevue Literary Review, Bellingham Review, Bend of the River Magazine, Better Homes and Gardens, Bible Advocate, Now What? E-zine, Bibliophilos, Bike Magazine, The Black Table, Black Warrior Review, Bloomsbury Review, Blue Ridge Country Magazine, Boating Life, Body & Soul, Book/Mark Small Press Quarterly Review, Boston Review, Boys' Life, Boys' Quest, Braveheart, Bridal

Guide, Bride's Magazine, Budget Living, Buffalo Spree Magazine, The Bugle, Business Fleet, Managing 10-5- Company Vehicles, Cadet Quest, California Lawyer, Calyx Journal, Canoe & Kayak Magazine, Car and Driver, Card Player, Caribbean Travel & Life, The Carolina Quarterly, Cat Fancy, Catholic Digest, CC Motorcycle News Magazine, Central PA Magazine, Change: The Magazine of Higher Learning, Charleston Magazine, The Chattahoochee Review, Chicago Magazine, Child Magazine, Children's Better Health Institute, Christian Home & School, Christian New Age Quarterly, Christian Parenting Today, Christian Single, Christian Social Action, Christian Women Today, Christianity Today, Chronicle of the Old West, Chronicles, Chronogram, Chrysalis Reader, Cicada, Cimarron Review, Cincinnati Woman Magazine, Circle Track, The Circle, Click Magazine, Club Connection, Clubhouse, Clubmex, CNEWA World, Coastal Living, Collectors News, CollegeBound Teen Magazine, ColoradoBiz Magazine, Colorado Homes & Lifestyles, Colored Stone, CompulsiverReader.com, Commercial Investment Real Estate Magazine, Commonweal, Computer Bits, ComputorEdge, Confrontation, A Literary Journal, Conscience, Contract Management, Conversely, Cooking Light, Corrections Compendium, Corrections Today, Corvette Fever, Cosmopolitan, Country Home, Country Living, Country Magazine, Country Extra Magazine, Crab Creek Review, The Cream City Review, Milwaukee, Creative Crafter, Creative Nonfiction, Cricket, Crochet World, Crone Chronicles, Cross & Quill, Cruising World, Custom Rodder, CutBank: University of Montana, Cutting Tool Engineering, Dance Spirit, Defenders, Dermascope, Desktop Engineering, Dialogue, Diamond Registry The Bulletin, Digger Magazine, Farwest Magazine, Discipleship Journal, Discover, Diver, Diversity, Dog Gone, Doll World, The Dollar Stretcher, The Door Magazine, Dramatics, Dream Network: A Quarterly Journal Exploring Dreams & Myth, Drum Business, East End Lights, East Texas Historical Journal, Education Week, Educational Leadership, The Elks Magazine, Benefits & Compensation Digest, Journal, Endless Vacation RCI, The Engineering Economist, Enrichment: A Journal for Pentecostal Ministry, Entrepreneur.com, Environment, Equal Opportunity Publications, Inc., Equine Journal, Equities Magazine, Erased, Sigh, Sigh., Essence, Evangel, Family Circle, Family Digest, Family Fun, Family Safety and Health, Family Therapy, Farm & Ranch Living, Farm Times, Beef Times, Fast & Fun Crochet, Fast Company, Fate, Fellowship, Fiberarts Magazine, Field & Stream, Filipinas, Financial Planning, Fine Gardening, Fine Homebuilding, Fine Woodworking, FineScale Modeler, FirehouseMagazine, Firehouse.com, First for Women, First Things, Fishing Facts, Florida Hotel & Motel Journal, Fly Fisherman, Flyfisher, Food & Wine, Footsteps, Forester Communications, Fourteen Hills: The SFSU Review, Freelance Philosophy, The Freeman: Ideas on Liberty, Freeskier, French Forum, Fresh Cut, Frontiers: A Journal of Women Studies, Fun for Kidz, Fur-Fish-Game, Futurific Magazine, The Gaited Horse, Game Developer, Gardening How-To, Genre, The Georgia Review, German Life, The Gettysburg Review, Girlfriends Magazine, Glamour, Go Magazine,, Golf Digest, Golf Journal Magazine, The Good Red Road, Gourmet, Government Executive, Green Mountains Review: Johnson State College, Grit Magazine, The Growing Edge, Guideposts, Guns & Ammo, Handwoven, Hang Loose, Happy Times Monthly, Hard Hat News, Harper's Bazaar, Harper's Magazine, Hawaii Review, Hawaii Westways, Health, Heartland USA, The Hellenic Calendar, HerbalGram, The Hollins Critic, Home Business Journal, Home Cooking, Home Furnishings Retailer, Home Improver Magazine, Home Times Family Newspaper, HomeLife, Hopscotch for Girls, Horticulture, Houseboat, The Hudson Review, Hurricane Alice, I Love Cats, The Iconoclast, In the Family and Their Loved Ones, Inc., Indiana Review, Inside Texas Running, Insider Magazine, Insight, Instructor, Interior Design Magazine, The International Railway Traveler, International Sports Journal: University of West Haven, Interweave Knits, Iris: A Journal about Women (University of Virginia), Islands, Japanophile, The Joiners' Quarterly, The Journal of Adventist Education, Journal of Asian Martial Arts, Journal of Christian Nursing, Journal of Information Ethics: St. Cloud State University, Kentucky Monthly, The Kenyon Review, Kitplanes, Knitting Digest, Knives Illustrated, Kung

Fu Tai Chi, LA Architect, The Labor Paper: Serving Southern Wisconsin, Ladies' Home Journal, Lake Michigan Travel Guide, Lake Superior Magazine, Leadership Journal, Leather The Crafters & Saddlers Journal, Legacy: A Journal of American Women Writers, Letter Arts Review, Lifeglow, LifeWayonline.com, Light, Light of Consciousnes, Lilith: The Independent Jewish Women's Magazine, Linn's Stamp News, The Lion Magazine, Literal Latte, The Literary Review: Fairleigh Dickinson University, The Living Church, Llewellyn Journal, Log Home Living, Timber Frame Homes, Long Island Woman, The Long Term View: Massachusetts School of Law, Lucky Magazine, The Lutheran Digest, The MacGuffin, The Magazine of La Cucina Italiana, Magical Blend, The Maine Organic Farmer & Gardener, Mama's Little Helper Newsletter, Manoa, Marlin, Marriage Partnership, Massage & Bodywork, Massage Magazine, Mature Years, Memory Makers, Men of Integrity, Men's Fitness, Men's Health, Mental Floss, Metropolis, Mid-American Review: Bowling Green State University, Midwest Outdoors, Midwifery Today, Minnesota Memories, The Minnesota Review: University of Missouri, Columbia, Mississippi Magazine, The Missouri Review, Model Railroader, Modeler's Resource, Modern Bride, Modern Drummer, Modern Maturity, Moment, Montana Magazine, Montana, Moody Magazine, Mopar Muscle, More, Mortgage Banking, Mother Earth News, Mother Jones, Motor Trend, Motorcycling, MotorHome, Muscle Mustang & Fast Fords, Muse Magazine, Mushing, Mustang & Fords, Mustang Monthly, The National Enquirer, National Geographic Traveler, National Review, Native Peoples, Natural Beauty & Health, Natural History, Natural Home, The Nebraska Review: University of Nebraska-Omaha, Nevada Magazine, The New Centennial Review, New England Review: Middlebury College, New Letters, New Mexico Journey, New Mexico Woman, New Millennium Writings, New Moon, The New Renaissance, New Times, New York Runner, Newsweek, Nimrod: International Journal of Prose and Poetry (University of Tulsa), Nine, Nineteenth-Century French Studies, Fabricator, The North American Voice of Fatima, North Dakota Horizons, Northwest Fly Fishing, Northwest Palate, Northwest Regional Magazines, Obsidian III, Odyssey Magazine, Offshore: Northeast Boating at Its Best, Ohio Writer, Oklahoma Today Magazine, The Old Farmer's Almanac, On Mission, Onion World, Orange Coast Magazine, Oregon Quarterly: The Magazine of the University of Oregon, The Other Side, Outdoor America, Outdoor Life, Outdoor World, Over the Back Fence, Overland Journal, Pacific Fishing, Paddler, Parabola, Parade, Parameters: US Army War College Quarterly, Parenting, Parents Magazine, Parents' Press, Passages North: Northern Michigan University, Passport, PC World, The Pedestal Magazine, Pediatrics For Parents, PEN America, Pennsylvania Magazine, Pentecostal Evangel, Penthouse, Perdido: Leadership with a Conscience, Persimmon Hill, Phi Delta Kappan, PieceWork: Needlework and History, Hand in Hand, The Plain Truth, Plastic Canvas Today, Playboy, Playgirl, Pleiades: A Journal of New Writing, Plus Magazine, Podiatry Management, Poetry, Points North, Police and Security News, Police Times, Poptronics, Popular Mechanics, Popular Photography, Popular Science, Popular Woodworking, Potomac Review, Presbyterians Today, Presentations Magazine, Prevention Magazine, Primedia History Group, Progressive Engineer, Psychology Today, Quarterly West: University of Utah, Quick & Easy Quilting, Quilt World, Rack, Adventures in Trophy Hunting, Radio World, Reader's Digest, Redbook, Referee, Reminisce Magazine, Reminisce Extra, Reunions Magazine, River Town Gazette, The Roanoker, Rock and Ice, Rocky Mountain Sports Magazine, Rosebud, Rug Hooking, Ruminator Review, Runner's World, Running Times, Rural Heritage, Russian Life, Sailing Magazine, Salon, Sandlapper, Saturday Evening Post, Saveur, SchoolArts, Science of Mind, Scouting, Sea Kayaker, Sea: The Magazine of Western Boating, Seattle Homes and Lifestyles, The Secret Place, Seek The Abundant Life, Senior Living, Seventeen, Sew News, Sewanee Review, Shape Magazine, Shenandoah: The Washington and Lee University Review, Shofar, Short Stuff Magazine, Signs of the Times, Ski, Skiing Magazine, Skin Inc. Magazine: The Complete Business Guide for Face & Body Care, Small Farm Today, Smithsonian Magazine, Smoke Magazine, Life's Burning Desires, Society of American Base-

ball Research, South American Explorer, South Florida History, Southern Humanities Review: Auburn University, Southern Living, The Southern Review: Louisiana State University, Southern Traveler, Southwest Fly Fishing, Southwest Review: Southern Methodist University, Specialty Travel Index, Speedway Illustrated, Spider, Spin-Off, Sport Fishing Magazine, Sports Afield, Sports Illustrated for Kids, Springfield! Magazine, St. Anthony Messenger, Stamats Meetings Media, Standard, Student Lawyer, Studies in American Jewish Literature, Succeed, Sun Valley Magazine, The Sun, Sunset Magazine, Supply Chain Systems Magazine, Supply Chain Systems Magazine, Surfer, Swank, Swim Magazine, Swimming Technique, Swimming World, Junior Swimmer, Sycamore Review: Purdue University, Syracuse New Times, T'ai Chi, Tampa Review: Literary Journal of the University of Tampa, Teacher Magazine, Teachers of Vision, Technical Analysis of Stocks & Commodities, Tennis Magazine, Tequesta, Texas Gardener, Texas Highways, The Travel Magazine of Texas, Texas Parks & Wildlife, Threads Magazine, The Threepenny Review, Tikkun, Times News Service, Tiny Lights: A Journal of Personal Essay, The Toastmaster, Today's Catholic Teacher, Today's Christian, Today's Christian Woman, Today's School, Town & Country, Toy Farmer, Toy Trucker & Contractor, Tradition, Traditional Quiltworks, Quilting Today, Miniature Quilts, Trail Runner, Transaction Publishers Rutgers, Transitions, Transitions Abroad, Travel & Leisure, Travel Naturally, Troika Magazine, True West, Turkey Call, Women In The Outdoors, Wheelin' Sportsmen, The Caller, Jakes Magazine, Unique Opportunities: The Physician's Resource, The Upper Room, USA Cycling, Veggie Life, VFW Magazine, Via, Virginia Quarterly Review, Volleyball Magazine, Voyageur: Northeast Wisconsin's Historical Review, Washington Monthly, Weavings, Weight Watchers Magazine, West Coast Magazine, Western Humanities Review, Western RV News & Recreation, Westways, Southern California Lifestyle Magazine, Whole Life Times, The Wild Foods Forum, The William and Mary Review: College of William and Mary, Willow Springs, Wines & Vines, Wired, Wisconsin Trails, With: The Magazine for Radical Christian Youth, Woman's Touch, Woman's World, Women Alive!, Women and Music, Women in Business, Women Today Magazine, Wonderful Ideas for Teaching, Learning, and Enjoying Mathematics!, Woodall Publications, Corp., Working Mother Magazine, The World & I, The Writer Gazette, Writer's Guidelines & News, Writers' Journal, The Yalobusha Review, Yankee, Young & Alive, ZYZZYVA

Book Publishers:

29th Press, Abbott, Langer & Associates, Addicus Books, Inc., Aegis Publishing Group, Ltd., Alba House, Algora Publishing, Agathon Press, Allworth Press, Alpine Publications, Alyson Publications, Inc., American Book Publishing, American Correctional Association (ACA) Book Publishing, The Americas Group, AMG Publishers, Anchorage Press Plays, Inc., Angel Bea Publishing, Time Warner Book Group, Apage4You Book Publishing, Arden Press, Inc., Arte Público Press: The University of Houston, Aslan Publishing, Atheneum Books, Aeronautical Publishers, B. Klein Publications, Balcony Press, Barbed Wire Publishing, Barricade Books, Barricade Books, Barrons Educational Series, Inc., Bay Tree Publishing, Baywood Publishing Company, Inc., Berkshire House Publishers, Berrett-Koehler Publishers, Bethany House Publishers, Beyond Words Publishing, BkMk Press: University of Missouri-Kansas City, Black Forest Press: Arbenteuer Books, Dichter Books, Kinder Books, Blue Poppy Press, Inc., BNA Books, Bonus Books, Inc., Book Peddlers, Bookhaven Press LLC, Branden Publishing Company, Brassey's Sports, Brassey's, Inc., Bridge Works, Bright Mountain Books, Inc., Bristol Fashion Publications, Inc.: The World's Largest Nautical Publishing House, Broadman & Holman Publishers, Brookline Books, The Business Group, Bye Publishing, Calyx Books, Carson-Dellosa Publishing Co., Inc., Caxton Press, CCC Publications, Charles River Media, Charlesbridge Publishing, Chelsea Green Publishing Company, Chess Enterprises, Chitra Publications, Christian Ed. Publishers, Chronicle Books LLC, Clarity Press, Inc., Clover Park Press, Collectors Press, Commonwealth Editions, The Conservatory of American Letters, Contemporary Books: A Division of McGraw-Hill Companies, Cornell Maritime Press, Inc., Creative Publishing International,

Inc., Cricket Books, The Crossing Press, Crossway Books, Cruden Bay Books, Daily Guideposts, David R. Godine, Inc., Dawn Publications, The Denali Press, Denlinger's Publishers, Ltd., Dial Books for Young Readers, Dimi Press, Diogenes Publishing, Do-It-Yourself Legal Publishers, Down East Books, Dutton Children's Books, Eclipse Press, Edupress, Inc., Elderberry Press, LLC, Emerald Ink Publishing, Emquad International, Ltd., ETC Publications, Excelsior Cee Publishing, Fairleigh Dickinson University Press, Fairview Press, Falcon Publishing/Falcon Guides, Two Dot, Three Forks, Fiesta City Publishers, Fordham University Press, Forum Publishing Company, Franklin, Beedle & Associates, Free Spirit Publishing, Frederick Fell Publishers, Inc., Front Street, Inc., Future Horizons, G.P. Putnam's Sons, Garth Gardner Company, Gem Guides Book Company, The Globe Pequot Press, God Allows U-Turns: Book Series, The Graduate Group, Granite Publishing Group, Granite Publishing Group, LLC, Graphic Arts Center Publishing Company, Graphic Arts Technical Foundation/GATFPress, Green Nature Books, Gryphon Books, Guide, Gürze Books, Hachai Publishing, Hampton Roads Publishing Co., Hancock House, Hannover House, Harbor Press, Harvard Common Press, Hatherleigh Press, Hay House, Inc., Hazelden Publishing, Health Communications, Inc., Heritage Books, Inc., HiddenSpring, Hillbrook Publishing, Historical Resources Press, Hobby House Press, Inc., Hohm Press, Holloway House Publishing Group, Howell Press, Inc., Human Kinetics, Hunter House Publishers, Iconografix, Inc., Impact Publishers, In Print Publishing, Incentive Publications, Inc., Intercultural Press, International Foundation of Employee Benefit Plans, International Marine, Interweave Press, Iron Horse Free Press, Island Press, Ivan R. Dee, Inc., Publisher, J.N. Townsend Publishing, Jewish Lights Publishing, JIST Works/Park Avenue, Jodere Group Inc., John Daniel & Company, Johnston Associates International, Jona Books, Judson Press, Just Us Books, Kali Press, Kar-Ben Publishing, Kids Books By Kids, Kregel Publications/Kregel Kidzone, Lake Claremont Press, Legacy Press, Lehigh University Press, Llewellyn Publications, Lerner Publishing, Loyola Press, Lumen Editions, The Lyons Press, MacAdam/Cage, Mage Publishers, The Magni Group, Inc., Maisonneuve Press, Marion Street Press, Inc., Mayhaven Publishing, The McDonald & Woodward Publishing Company, McKenna Publishing Group, Meadowbrook Press, Mel Bay Publications, Metamorphous Press, Metropolis Ink, Michael Wiese Productions, Milkweed Editions, The Millbrook Press, Millennium Publishing Company, Mississippi: University Press of Mississippi, Mountain N' Air Books, Mountain Press Publishing Company, Mountaineers Books, Mustang Publishing Company, Narwhal Press, Inc., Naval Institute Press, New Harbinger Publications, New Horizons Press, Small Horizons Imprint, New Society Publishers, New Victoria Publishers, New World Library, North Ridge Books, North Street Publishers, Northern Publishing, Nova Press, Omnibus Press, Orange Frazer Press, Inc., Orchises Press, The Overmountain Press, Pacific View Press, Paladin Press: Sycamore Island Books, Flying Machines Press, Paradise Cay, Parenting Press, Parkway Publishers, Inc., Pathfinder Publishing of California, Paulist Press: HiddenSpring, Peachtree Publishers, Peachtree Jr, .Freestone, Pelican Publishing Company, Perron Press, Perspectives Press, Inc.: The Infertility and Adoption Publisher, The Phi Delta Kappa Educational Foundation, Piccadilly Books, Ltd., Pineapple Press, Inc., Players Press, Inc., Possibility Press, Prep Publishing, Prima Publishing, Pruett Publishing Company, PSI Research: The Oasis Press, Hellgate Press, QED Press, Quality Words In Print, Ragged Mountain Press, Rainbow Publishers, Really Great Books, Red Wheel/Weiser, Redleaf Press, Renders Wellness/Publishing, Republic of Texas Press, Resurrection Press, Ltd., Richard C. Owen Publishers, Inc., RLN & Company, Roadman Press, Roberts Rinehart, Rodnik Publishing Co., Running Press Kids, Rutledge Hill Press, Safari Press, Inc., Safer Society Press, Santa Monica Press LLC, Sasquatch Books, Scarecrow Press, Inc., Schirmer Trade Book, Serendipity Systems: Books-on-disks, Shambhala Publications, Sierra Club Books, Skinner House Books, Soho Press Inc, Soho, Soho Crime, Sourcebooks, Inc., Sourcebooks Casablanca, Sourcebooks Hysteria, Sourcebooks Landmark, Sourcebooks MediaFusion, Solas Press, Sphinx Publish-

ing, Southern Illinois University Press, Spinsters Ink, Square One Publishers, St. Bede's Publications, Stackpole Books, Stipes Publishing, LLC, Stone Bridge Press, Storey Publishing, LCC, Stylus Publishing, LLC, Sunbelt Publications, Swedenborg Foundation, Inc.: Chrysalis Books, Taylor Trade, Temple University Press, Ten Speed Press, Celestial Arts, Third World Press, Tilbury House Publishers, Tricycle Press, Texas A&M University Press, Texas Western Press, Tower Publishing, Towlehouse Publishing Co., The Trinity Foundation, Trinity Press International, Truman State University Press, Turtle Press, Unity House/Books, University of Idaho Press, University of Maine Press, University of Nebraska Press, University of Nevada Press, University of North Texas Press, University of Oklahoma Press, UpstartBooks, USA Books, Via Dolorosa Press, Volcano Press, Voyageur Press, Walter Foster Publishing, Inc., Waltsan Publishing, LLC, Washington State University Press, Waterbrook Press, Weiser Books, Wescott Cove Publishing Co., Westcliff Publishers, White Cliffs Media, Inc., Wilder Publishing Center, Will Hall Books, Will Hall, Inc., Willow Creek Press, Wilshire Book Co., WoodenBoat Books, World Leisure Corporation, YMAA Publication Center, Zondervan and Zonderkidz

-O-

Occult

Periodicals:

Fate

Book Publishers:

Hampton Roads Publishing, In Print Publishing, Tom Doherty Associate, LLC, Tor Books, Forge Books, Orb, Starscape

Outdoors

Periodicals:

Adirondack Life, Alaska Business Monthly, American Forests, American Hunter, American Profile, American Snowmobiler, Artemis Magazine, Aspen Magazine, Audubon, Backpacker, Balloon Life, Birds & Blooms, Blue Ridge Country Magazine, Boating Life, Boys' Life, Boys' Quest, The Bugle, Canoe & Kayak Magazine, Capper's, Cascades East Magazine: Central Oregon's Quarterly, Central PA Magazine, Country Magazine, Country Extra Magazine, Creative With Words!, Cruising World, Dog Gone, Field & Stream, Florida Wildlife, Flyfishing & Tying Journal, A Compendium for the Complete Fly Fisherman, Fur-Fish-Game, The Gaited Horse, Girls' Life, Grit Magazine, Guns & Ammo, Happy Times Monthly, Heartland USA, Highways, House, Home and Garden, Inside Texas Running, Insider Magazine, Kentucky Monthly, Knives Illustrated, Lifeglow, The Lutheran Digest, Magical Blend, Marlin, Midwest Outdoors, Montana Magazine, Mushing, Muzzle Blasts, Nevada Magazine, Northwest Regional Magazines, The Old Farmer's Almanac, Outdoor America, Outdoor Life, Outdoor World, Over the Back Fence, Paddler, Persimmon Hill, Popular Mechanics, Power & Motoryacht, Rack, Adventures in Trophy Hunting, Ranger Rick, River Town Gazette, Rocky Mountain Sports Magazine, Safari, Sailing Magazine, Sailing World, Salmon-Trout-Steelheader, Sandlapper, Scouting, Skiing Magazine, Sports Afield, Springfield! Magazine, Sun Valley Magazine, Sunset Magazine, Texas Parks & Wildlife, Trailer Boats, Transitions, USA Cycling, Western RV News & Recreation, Whole Life Times, The Wild Foods Forum, Wildlife Art, Willow Springs, Wisconsin Trails, Woodall Publications, Corp., Young & Alive

Book Publishers:

Bright Mountain Books, Inc., Charlesbridge Publishing, The Conservatory of American Letters, Creative Publishing International, Inc., David R. Godine, Inc., Down East Books, Falcon Publishing/Falcon Guides, Two Dot, Three Forks, Frank Amato Publications, Inc., Gem Guides Book Company, The Globe Pequot Press, Graphic Arts Center Publishing Company, Hancock House, Hatherleigh Press, Hearts 'N Tummies Cookbook Company, International Marine, Johnston Associates International, The Lyons Press, Menasha Ridge Press, Mountain

N' Air Books, Mountain Press Publishing Company, Mountaineers Books, Naturegraph Publishers, Northern Publishing, Paladin Press: Sycamore Island Books, Flying Machines Press, Paradise Cay, Pelican Publishing Company, Primer Publishers, Pruett Publishing Company, Rutledge Hill Press, Soundprints, Stackpole Books, Sunbelt Publications, Ten Speed Press, Celestial Arts, Tilbury House Publishers, Tricycle Press, Wescott Cove Publishing Co., Willow Creek Press

-P-

Paranormal

Periodicals:

The Circle, Crone Chronicles, Dream Network: A Quarterly Journal Exploring Dreams & Myth, Fate, Flesh & Blood, Futures Mysterious Anthology Magazine, Horrorfind, Magical Blend, The New Times, Office Number One, Swank, Whole Life Times

Book Publishers:

Beyond Words Publishing, The Conservatory of American Letters, Crossway Books, Granite Publishing Group, Granite Publishing Group, LLC, Gryphon House, Inc., Hampton Roads Publishing, Hillbrook Publishing, ImaJinn Books, Llewellyn Publications, Mayhaven Publishing, Square One Publishers, Tom Doherty Associate, LLC, Tor Books, Forge Books, Orb, Starscape

Parenting

Periodicals:

African American Family, All About Kids, American Profile, And Baby, Atlanta Parent, Atlanta Baby, Better Homes and Gardens, Bible Advocate, Now What? E-zine, Bride's Magazine, Child Magazine, Christian Parenting Today, Christian Women Today, Cincinnati Woman Magazine, Dovetail, Dream Network: A Quarterly Journal Exploring Dreams & Myth, Family Digest, Grit Magazine, Happy Times Monthly, Home Education Magazine, Home Times Family Newspaper, HomeLife, Ladies' Home Journal, Ladybug Parent's Companion, Ligourian, The Lutheran Digest, Mama's Little Helper Newsletter, Men of Integrity, Metro Parent, Metro Baby, MetroKids, Natural Beauty & Health, Northwest Family News, Parenting, ParentLife, Parents' Press, Redbook, River Town Gazette, Scouting, Springfield! Magazine, St. Anthony Messenger, Teaching Tolerance, Today's Christian Woman, TWINS, Transitions, United Parenting Publications, West Coast Magazine, Whole Life Times, Women Today Magazine, Working Mother Magazine

Book Publishers:

Barrons Educational Series, Inc., Bethany House Publishers, Beyond Words Publishing, Brookline Books, Capital Books, Charlesbridge Publishing, Chronicle Books LLC, Contemporary Books: A Division of McGraw-Hill Companies, Fairview Press, Free Spirit Publishing, God Allows U-Turns: Book Series, Great Quotations Publishing, Gryphon House, Inc., Harbor Press, Harvard Common Press, Impact Publishers, Jewish Lights Publishing, Kali Press, Kregel Publications/Kregel Kidzone, McBooks Press, Meadowbrook Press, Mustang Publishing Company, New Society Publishers, New World Library, Parenting Pressm Perspectives Press, Inc.: The Infertility and Adoption Publisher, Sourcebooks, Inc., Sourcebooks Casablanca, Sourcebooks Hysteria, Sourcebooks Landmark, Sourcebooks MediaFusion, Sphinx Publishing, Square One Publishers, Volcano Press, Waterbrook Press, Woodbine House, Zondervan and Zonderkidz

Philosophy

Periodicals:

The Journal of Asian Martial Arts, Mental Floss, The Minnesota Review: University of Missouri, Columbia, symploke, The World & I, Yoga Journal

Book Publishers:

Alba House, Algora Publishing, Hazelden Publishing, Paragon House, Swedenborg Foundation, Inc.: Chrysalis Books

Photography

Periodicals:

Adirondack Life, Alive Now, America West, Artemis Magazine, Blue Ridge Country Magazine, The Bugle, The Circle, Devo'Zine, Doll World, Gist Review, Happy Times Monthly, Letter Arts Review, Liquid Ohio, Memory Makers, National Geographic Traveler, Northwest Fly Fishing, Outdoor Life, Popular Mechanics, Popular Photography, Popular Science, Rearview, Reminisce Magazine, Reminisce Extra, River Town Gazette, Rock and Ice, Sandlapper, Southwest Fly Fishing, Springfield! Magazine, The Sun, Surfer, Sycamore Review: Purdue University, Texas Highways, The Travel Magazine of Texas

Book Publishers:

Allworth Press, Amherst Media, Beyond Words Publishing, Chronicle Books LLC, David R. Godine, Inc., Down East Books, Graphic Arts Center Publishing Company, Green Nature Books, Mississippi: University Press of Mississippi, Voyageur Press, Westcliffe Publishers, WoodenBoat Books

Physical Fitness

Periodicals:

American Fitness, Artemis Magazine, Balanced Living Magazine, Better Homes and Gardens, Body & Soul, Cascades East Magazine: Central Oregon's Quarterly, Children's Better Health Institute, Cincinnati Woman Magazine, Complete Woman, Cooking Light, Cosmopolitan, Glamour, Golf Digest, The Golfer, Happy Times Monthly, Health, Home Times Family Newspaper, Inside Texas Running, International Sports Journal: University of West Haven, The Journal of Asian Martial Arts, Journal of Christian Nursing, Kung Fu Tai Chi, Long Island Woman, Men's Fitness, Men's Health, Men's Journal, Military Officer, Modern Bride, Muscle & Fitness, Muscle & Fitness Hers, The National Enquirer, Natural Beauty & Health, Outdoor Life, Paddler, Parenting, Parents Magazine, Prevention Magazine, Reader's Digest, Rock and Ice, Rocky Mountain Sports Magazine, Runner's World, Saturday Evening Post, Scouting, Self, Senior Living, Shape Magazine, Skating Magazine, Swim Magazine, Swimming World, Junior Swimmer, T'ai Chi, Tennis Magazine, Trail Runner, Transitions, Veggie Life, Volleyball Magazine, Weight Watchers Magazine, West Coast Magazine, Whole Life Times, Woman's World, Women Today Magazine, Yoga Journal, Young & Alive

Book Publishers:

Contemporary Books: A Division of McGraw-Hill Companies, Fairview Press, Front Row Experience, Human Kinetics, International Marine, The Lyons Press, Ragged Mountain Press, Turtle Press

Poetry

Periodicals:

12th Planet Literary Journal, 96 Inc., ACM: Another Chicago Magazine, The African American Pulpit!, Agni, Alive Now, The American Dissident, American Letters & Commentary, The American Poetry Review, Anhinga Press, Antioch Review, AQR: Alaska Quarterly Review, Arkansas Review, Art Times, Artful Dodge: The College of Wooster, The Asian Pacific American Journal, The Atlantic Monthly, Babybug, The Baltimore Review, Bear Deluxe Magazine, The Beauty Spot, Bellevue Literary Review, Bellingham Review, Bellowing Ark, The Beloit Poetry Journal, Bibliophilos, Birmingham Poetry Review, Black Warrior Review, Blackfire, Boston Review, Bridal Guide, Bridge, Buffalo Spree Magazine, ByLine, Calyx Journal, Capper's, The Carolina Quarterly, Cat Fancy, The Chattahoochee Review, Chicago Magazine, Chicago Review, Chiron Review, Chronicles, Chronogram, Chrysalis Reader, Cicada, Cimarron Review, The Circle, Cobblestone Magazine, Cornerstone, Crab Creek Review, The Cream City Review, Milwaukee, Creative With Words!, Cricket, Crone Chronicles, Cross & Quill, CutBank: University of Montana, Devo'Zine, Erased, Sigh, Sigh., Eros, Field: A Journal of Contemporary Poetry and Poetic, Flesh & Blood, Fourteen Hills: The SFSU Review, Futures Mysterious Anthology Magazine, The Georgia Review, The Gettysburg Review, Gist Review, The Good Red Road, Grain, The Green Hills Literary Lantern: Truman State University, Green Mountains Review: Johnson State College, The Greensboro Review, Grit Magazine, Guideposts for Kids,

Topics

Hadrosaur Tales, Harper's Magazine, Hawaii Review, Hayden's Ferry Review: Arizona State University, The Hollins Critic, Home Times Family Newspaper, House, Home and Garden, The Hudson Review, The Iconoclast, Indiana Review, Iris: A Journal about Women (University of Virginia), Japanophile, Kalliope, Kentucky Monthly, The Kenyon Review, Kuumba, Ladybug: The Magazine for Young Children, The Ledge Magazine, Left Curve, Light, Light of Consciousnes, Lilith: The Independent Jewish Women's Magazine, Liquid Ohio, Literal Latte, Literary Magazine Review, The Literary Review: Fairleigh Dickinson University, The Lutheran Digest, Lynx Eye, The MacGuffin, Maelstrom, The Magazine of Speculative Poetry, Mama's Little Helper Newsletter, Manoa, The Massachusetts Review: University of Massachusetts, Mature Years, The Melic Review, Mid-American Review: Bowling Green State University, The Minnesota Review: University of Missouri, Columbia, The Mississippi Review, The Mississippi Review online, The Missouri Review, Modern Haiku, Nebo: A Literary Journal (Arkansas Polytechnic University), The Nebraska Review: University of Nebraska-Omaha, New England Review: Middlebury College, New Letters, New Millennium Writings, The New Renaissance, New Yorker, Nimrod: International Journal of Prose and Poetry (University of Tulsa), Northwest Review: University of Oregon, Oblates, Obsidian III, Office Number One, Ohio Writer, Omnific, The Other Side, Parnassus, Passages North: Northern Michigan University, Pearl, The Pedestal Magazine, Peregrine: History and Background of Amherst Writers and Artists, Phantasmagoria, Phoebe, Pleiades: A Journal of New Writing, Ploughshares: Emerson College, Poem: University of Alabama-Huntsville, Poetic Realm, Poetry, Potluck Children's Literary Magazine, Potomac Review, Prairie Schooner: University of Nebraska Press, Primavera, Quarterly West: University of Utah, Rearview, Red Rock Review, Rhino, RiverSedge: The University of Texas-Pan American, Rockford Review, Rosebud, Science of Mind, SecondWind, The Secret Place, Seneca Review, Senior Living, Shenandoah: The Washington and Lee University Review, Slipstream, Snake Nation Review, Society of American Baseball Research, The Southern California Anthology: University of Southern California, Southern Humanities Review: Auburn University, The Southern Review: Louisiana State University, Southwest Review: Southern Methodist University, Spider, Spinning Jenny, The Spoon River Poetry Review, St. Anthony Messenger, Standard, Stone Soup, Studies in American Jewish Literature, The Sun, Sycamore Review: Purdue University, Tampa Review: Literary Journal of the University of Tampa, Teaching Tolerance, Thema, Thoughts for All Seasons, The Threepenny Review, Tikkun, Two Rivers Review, The Urbanite, Verses Magazine, Virginia Quarterly Review, Visions-International Arts, Weavings, Weird Tales, Western Humanities Review, The William and Mary Review: College of William and Mary, Willow Springs, Women Artists News Book Review, The Worcester Review, Writer's Guidelines & News, The Yalobusha Review, ZYZZYVA

Book Publishers:

American Literary Press, Inc.: Noble House, The Backwaters Press, BkMk Press: University of Missouri-Kansas City, Black Forest Press: Arbenteuer Books, Dichter Books, Kinder Books, Branden Publishing Company, Brookline Books, Bye Publishing, Calyx Books, Chatoyant, David R. Godine, Inc., Fairleigh Dickinson University Press, Front Street, Inc., Hilliard & Harris, John Daniel & Company, Latin American Literary Review Press, March Street Press, Parting Gifts, Mayhaven Publishing, Midmarch Arts Press, Milkweed Editions, Moondance Publishing, Orchises Press, Perugia Press, Piano Press, The Post-Apollo Press, QED Press, Sarabande Books, Southern Illinois University Press, SPS Studios, Inc., Publishers of Blue Mountain Arts, quality books, cards, calendars, and prints, Staplegun Press, Third World Press, Truman State University Press, University of North Texas Press, Via Dolorosa Press, Will Hall Books, Will Hall, Inc.

Politics

Periodicals:

Alberta Views, American Forests, American Hunter, The American Legion Magazine, Archaeology, Artemis Magazine, Austin Monthly Magazine, Bibliophilos, Boston Magazine, Boston Review, California Jour-

nal, California Lawyer, Chronicles, Commonweal, Conscience, Corrections Compendium, Corrections Today, Defenders, E Magazine: The Environmental Magazine, Fellowship, First Things, The Freeman: Ideas on Liberty, Futures Mysterious Anthology Magazine, Futurific Magazine, Girlfriends Magazine, The Good Red Road, Government Executive, Harper's Magazine, Home Times Family Newspaper, Insider Magazine, Jam Rag, Kentucky Monthly, Left Curve, The Long Term View: Massachusetts School of Law, The Minnesota Review: University of Missouri, Columbia, Mom Guess What Newspaper, Mother Jones, National Review, Natural Beauty & Health, The New Centennial Review, The New Renaissance, New Yorker, Newsweek, The Other Side, Parameters: US Army War College Quarterly, PEN America, Playboy, River Town Gazette, Salon, The Threepenny Review, Tikkun, Transitions, Vanity Fair, Vibe, Virginia Quarterly Review, Washington Monthly, Whole Life Times, The World & I

Book Publishers:

Algora Publishing, Agathon Press, Barbed Wire Publishing, Black Forest Press: Arbenteuer Books, Dichter Books, Kinder Books, Branden Publishing Company, Brassey's, Inc., Chelsea Gree Publishing Company, Clarity Press, Inc., Cross Cultural Publications, Inc., The Denali Press, Elderberry Press, LLC, Fairleigh Dickinson University Press, Howells House, Inc., In Print Publishing, Ivan R. Dee, Inc., Publisher, Maisonneuve Press, Mayhaven Publishing, Origin Media, Inc.: "Books for the Integral Age", Temple University Press, The Trinity Foundation, University of Nebraska Press, University of Nevada Press, Washington State University Press

Psychology

Periodicals:

Angels on Earth, Artemis Magazine, Balanced Living Magazine, Bibliophilos, Bridal Guide, Crone Chronicles, Dream Network: A Quarterly Journal Exploring Dreams & Myth, Et cetera: A Review of General Semantics, Family Therapy, Glamour, Health, Home Times Family Newspaper, In the Family and Their Loved Ones, Journal of Christian Nursing, Ladies' Home Journal, Long Island Woman, Magical Blend, Men's Fitness, Modern Bride, Natural Beauty & Health, The New Centennial Review, Parenting, Psychology Today, Redbook, River Town Gazette, Springfield! Magazine, St. Anthony Messenger, Teaching Tolerance, Tikkun, Transitions, West Coast Magazine, Whole Life Times,

Book Publishers:

Alba House, American Correctional Association (ACA) Book Publishing, B. Klein Publications, Bay Tree Publishing, Baywood Publishing Company, Inc., Black Forest Press: Arbenteuer Books, Dichter Books, Kinder Books, Brookline Books, Diogenes Publishing, Fairleigh Dickinson University Press, Fairview Press, Free Spirit Publishing, Hampton Roads Publishing, Harbor Press, Hatherleigh Press, Hay House, Inc., Health Communications, Inc., Hunter House Publishers, Impact Publishers, Jodere Group Inc., Llewellyn Publications, Metamorphous Press, New Harbinger Publications, Origin Media, Inc.: "Books for the Integral Age", Paragon House, Perron Press, Perspectives Press, Inc.: The Infertility and Adoption Publisher, Possibility Press, Safer Society Press, Swedenborg Foundation, Inc.: Chrysalis Books, Temple University Press, University of Nebraska Press, Wilshire Book Co.

Public Speaking

Periodicals:

The African American Pulpit!, The Beauty Spot, New Millennium Writings

Book Publishers:
Personal Branding Press

-R-

Real Estate

Periodicals:

Atlanta Homes and Lifestyles, The Beauty Spot, Boston Magazine, Cincinnati Woman Magazine, Commercial Investment Real Estate Magazine, The Cooperator: The Co-op and Condo Monthly, Country Living, House, Home and Garden, Log Home Living, Timber Frame Homes, Mortgage Banking, River Town Gazette, Springfield! Magazine, Transitions, West Coast Magazine

Recreation

Periodicals:

Adirondack Life, America West, American Forests, American Hunter, Artemis Magazine, Aspen Magazine, BabyTalk, Bike Magazine, Blue Ridge Country Magazine, Budget Living, The Bugle, Canoe & Kayak Magazine, Capper's, Car and Driver, Cascades East Magazine: Central Oregon's Quarterly, Country Magazine, Country Extra Magazine, Cruising World, Dialogue, Diver, Dog Gone, Fishing Facts, Florida Wildlife, Fly Fisherman, Flyfishing & Tying Journal, A Compendium for the Complete Fly Fisherman, Freeskier, Fur-Fish-Game, Golf Digest, Grit Magazine, Guns & Ammo, Happy Times Monthly, Heartland USA, Highways, Home Times Family Newspaper, Houseboat, Inside Texas Running, International Sports Journal: University of West Haven, The Lutheran Digest, Marlin, Men's Health, Midwest Outdoors, Montana Magazine, Mushing, Muzzle Blasts, National Geographic Traveler, Natural Beauty & Health, Nevada Magazine, New York Runner, Northwest Family News, Northwest Fly Fishing, Outdoor Life, Over the Back Fence, Pacific Fishing, Pack-o-Fun, Paddler, Penthouse, Playboy, Polo Players' Edition, Popular Mechanics, River Town Gazette, Rock and Ice, Rocky Mountain Sports Magazine, Rug Hooking, Runner's World, Running Times, Sailing Magazine, Salmon-Trout-Steelheader, Sandlapper, Scouting, Sea: The Magazine of Western Boating, Senior Living, Shape Magazine, Ski, Skiing Magazine, Smoke Magazine, Life's Burning Desires, Southwest Fly Fishing, Speedway Illustrated, Sport Fishing Magazine, Sports Afield, Sports Illustrated for Kids, Sun Valley Magazine, Sunset Magazine, Surfer, Swim Magazine, Swimming World, Junior Swimmer, Tennis Magazine, Tradition, Transitions, Travel & Leisure, Turkey Call, Women In The Outdoors, Wheelin' Sportsmen, The Caller, Jakes Magazine, Volleyball Magazine, Western RV News & Recreation, The Wild Foods Forum, Wisconsin Trails, Woodall Publications, Corp., Young & Alive

Book Publishers:

Bristol Fashion Publications, Inc.: The World's Largest Nautical Publishing House, Chitra Publications, Contemporary Books: A Division of McGraw-Hill Companies, Cruden Bay Books, Down East Books, Falcon Publishing/Falcon Guides, Two Dot, Three Forks, Frank Amato Publications, Inc., The Globe Pequot Press, Hatherleigh Press, International Marine, Johnston Associates International, The Lyons Press, Menasha Ridge Press, Mountain N' Air Books, Mountaineers Books, Mustang Publishing Company, Northern Publishing, Paradise Cay, Pruett Publishing Company, Ragged Mountain Press, Sunbelt Publications, Ten Speed Press, Celestial Arts, Tricycle Press, Wescott Cove Publishing Co., Westcliffe Publishers, Willow Creek Press

Recreation Vehicles

Periodicals:

Artemis Magazine, Camping Today, Coast to Coast, Grit Magazine, Highways, Plus Magazine, Smoke Magazine, Life's Burning Desires, Trailer Boats, Western RV News & Recreation, Woodall Publications, Corp.

Book Publishers
Iconografix, Inc.

Reference

Periodicals:

Affaire De Coeur, Alaska Business Monthly, American Forests, Artemis Magazine, California Journal, Obsidian III, The Old Farmer's Alma-nac, Shuttle Spindle & Dyepot, Springfield! Magazine, Sunset Magazine, Teaching Tolerance, Wall Fashions

Book Publishers:

Abbott, Langer & Associates, American Correctional Association (ACA) Book Publishing, Arden Press, Inc., B. Klein Publications, Barrons Educational Series, Inc., Black Forest Press: Arbenteuer Books, Dichter Books, Kinder Books, Contemporary Books: A Division of McGraw-Hill Companies, Craftsman Book Company, The Denali Press, Fairview Press, Garth Gardner Company, The Graduate Group, Graphic Arts Center Publishing Company, Heritage Books, Inc., International Marine, JIST Works/Park Avenue, Lehigh University Press, Marion Street Press, Inc., McFarland & Company, Inc., Mississippi: University Press of Mississippi, Mustang Publishing Company, Naval Institute Press, Nelson Reference & Electronic Publishing, North Ridge Books, Santa Monica Press LLC, Scarecrow Press, Inc., Schirmer Trade Book, Square One Publishers, Stone Bridge Press, Ten Speed Press, Celestial Arts, Tricycle Press, Tower Publishing, Transnational Publishers, Inc.

Regional

Periodicals:

Adirondack Life, African American Family, Alaska Business Monthly, Alberta Views, Arizona Foothills Magazine, Arizona Highways, Arkansas Review, Artemis Magazine, Aspen Magazine, Atlanta Homes and Lifestyles, Austin Monthly Magazine, Baltimore Magazine, Bend of the River Magazine, Bibliophilos, Blue Ridge Country Magazine, Buffalo Spree Magazine, Capper's, Caribbean Travel & Life, Central PA Magazine, Charleston Magazine, Chicago Magazine, Chronicles, Chronogram, Coastal Living, Commonweal, Diver, Gateway Heritage, Grit Magazine, Hawaii Westways, The Hellenic Calendar, Inside Texas Running, Insider Magazine, Kentucky Monthly, Lake Michigan Travel Guide, Lake Superior Magazine, The Maine Organic Farmer & Gardener, Metro Parent, Metro Baby, Michigan Historical Review: Central Michigan University, Midwest Outdoors, Minnesota Memories, Mississippi Magazine, The Mississippi Review, The Mississippi Review online, The Montana Catholic, Montana Magazine, Montana, National Geographic Traveler, Nevada Magazine, New Mexico Journey, New Mexico Magazine, New York Stories, North Dakota Horizons, Northwest Palate, Northwest Regional Magazines, Ohio Magazine, Oklahoma Today Magazine, Orange Coast Magazine, Oregon Business, Oregon Quarterly: The Magazine of the University of Oregon, Outdoor Life, Over the Back Fence, Paddler, Pennsylvania Magazine, Persimmon Hill, Pittsburgh, Points North, Potomac Review, Premier Tourism Marketing, Inc., Progressive Engineer, River Town Gazette, The Roanoker, San Francisco, Sandlapper, Seattle Homes and Lifestyles, South Florida History, Southern Living, Southern Traveler, Sun Valley Magazine, Sunset Magazine, Tequesta, Texas Highways, The Travel Magazine of Texas, Texas Parks & Wildlife, Timeline, Voyageur: Northeast Wisconsin's Historical Review, Westchester Magazine, Westways, Southern California Lifestyle Magazine, Whole Life Times, Willow Springs, Wisconsin Trails, Woodall Publications, Corp.

Book Publishers:

Barbed Wire Publishing, Barricade Books, BkMk Press: University of Missouri-Kansas City, Branden Publishing Company, Brassey's, Inc., Bright Mountain Books, Inc., Clover Park Press, Commonwealth Editions, Cornell Maritime Press, Inc., Cruden Bay Books, Down East Books, Falcon Publishing/Falcon Guides, Two Dot, Three Forks, Fordham University Press, Gem Guides Book Company, Golden West Publishers, Graphic Arts Center Publishing Company, Great Quotations Publishing, Hearts 'N Tummies Cookbook Company, Heritage Books, Inc., Howell Press, Inc., Johnston Associates International, Lake Claremont Press, Lehigh University Press, Mayhaven Publishing, McBooks Press, Mississippi: University Press of Mississippi, Mountain Press Publishing Company, Narwhal Press, Inc., Orange Frazer Press, Inc., The Overmountain Press, Paradise Cay, Parkway Publishers, Inc., Peachtree Publishers, Peachtree Jr, .Freestone, Pelican Publishing Company, Pineapple Press, Inc., Primer Publishers, Pruett

Topics

Publishing Company, Republic of Texas Press, Southern Illinois University Press, Stackpole Books, Sunbelt Publications, Taylor Trade, Temple University Press, Ten Speed Press, Celestial Arts, Tricycle Press, Texas A&M University Press, Truman State University Press, University of Idaho Press, University of Maine Press, University of Nebraska Press, University of Nevada Press, University of Oklahoma Press, Washington State University Press, Westcliffe Publishers

Relationships

Periodicals:

Alive! A Magazine for Christian Senior Adults, All About Kids, The Beauty Spot, Bible Advocate, Now What? E-zine, Bridal Guide, Bride's Magazine, Campus Life, Catholic Digest, Christian Women Today, Cincinnati Woman Magazine, Complete Woman, Conversely, Cosmopolitan, Creative With Words!, Crone Chronicles, Dovetail, Essence, Family Circle, Family Digest, Family Therapy, Girls' Life, Glamour, Happy Times Monthly, Health, Home Times Family Newspaper, HomeLife, In the Family and Their Loved Ones, Insider Magazine, Journal of Christian Nursing, Ladies' Home Journal, Lifeglow, Ligourian, Long Island Woman, The Lutheran Digest, Magical Blend, Marriage Partnership, Mature Years, Men's Health, Modern Bride, Modern Maturity, Mom Guess What Newspaper, The National Enquirer, Natural Beauty & Health, Parenting, Parents Magazine, Playgirl, River Town Gazette, Seventeen, Springfield! Magazine, Supervision, Teaching Tolerance, Today's Christian Woman, Transitions, West Coast Magazine, Whole Life Times, Women Today Magazine, Working Mother Magazine, Young & Alive

Book Publishers:

Algora Publishing, Aslan Publishing, Barricade Books, Bethany House Publishers, Beyond Words Publishing, Bye Publishing, Contemporary Books: A Division of McGraw-Hill Companies, Face to Face Press, Fairview Press, Great Quotations Publishing, Harbor Press, Hatherleigh Press, Hay House, Inc., Hazelden Publishing, Health Communications, Inc., Hunter House Publishers, Impact Publishers, Jodere Group Inc., Kregel Publications/Kregel Kidzone, Loyola Press, Mayhaven Publishing, New Horizons Press, Small Horizons Imprint, Perron Press, Possibility Press, Prep Publishing, Sourcebooks, Inc., Sourcebooks Casablanca, Sourcebooks Hysteria, Sourcebooks Landmark, Sourcebooks MediaFusion, Sphinx Publishing, Volcano Press, Waterbrook Press, Wilshire Book Co., World Leisure Corporation, Zondervan and Zonderkidz

Religion

Periodicals:

The African American Pulpit!, Alive Now, The American Legion Magazine, American Profile, Angels on Earth, Bible Advocate, Now What? E-zine, Books & Culture, Braveheart, Catholic Digest, Christian New Age Quarterly, Christian Parenting Today, The Christian Century, Christian Single, Christian Social Action, Christian Women Today, Christianity Today, Clubhouse, CNEWA World, Cadet Quest, Conscience, Crone Chronicles, Cross & Quill, Devo'Zine, The Door Magazine, Dovetail, Enrichment: A Journal for Pentecostal Ministry, Fellowship, First Things, The Good Red Road, Grit Magazine, Guideposts, Home Times Family Newspaper, Insight, Jewish Action, Journal of Christian Nursing, Leadership Journal, LifeWayonline.com, Light of Consciousnes, Ligourian, The The Living Church Lutheran Digest, Magical Blend, Mature Living, Mature Years, Men of Integrity, Message Magazine, Moment, The The Montana Catholic New Times, The North American Voice of Fatima, Oblates, On Mission, The Other Side, Parabola, Passport, Pastoral Life, Pentecostal Evangel, The Plain Truth, Pockets, Presbyterians Today, SageWoman, PanGaia,, The Blessed Bee, New Witch, Science of Mind, The Secret Place, Seek The Abundant Life, Shofar, Signs of the Times, Sports Spectrum, Springfield! Magazine, St. Anthony Messenger, Standard, Studies in American Jewish Literature, Teachers of Vision, Teaching Tolerance, Tikkun, Today's Catholic Teacher, Today's Christian, Today's Christian Woman, Transitions, The Upper Room, Weavings, WIN-Informer, With: The Magazine for Radical Christian Youth,

Book Publishers:

ACTA Publications: Assisting Christians to Act, Alba House, American Literary Press, Inc.: Noble House, AMG Publishers, Apage4You Book Publishing, Baker Book Publishing Group, Barbed Wire Publishing, Bethany House Publishers, Beyond Words Publishing, Black Forest Press: Arbenteuer Books, Dichter Books, Kinder Books, Branden Publishing Company, Bye Publishing, Christian Ed. Publishers, Christian Publications, Inc., Cross Cultural Publications, Inc., Crossway Books, Daily Guideposts, David R. Godine, Inc., Fordham University Press, God Allows U-Turns: Book Series, Guide, Hachai Publishing, HiddenSpring, Hohm Press, Intercultural Press, Jewish Lights Publishing, Judson Press, Kregel Publications/Kregel Kidzone, Legacy Press, Llewellyn Publications, Loyola Press, Meriwether Publishing Ltd: Contemporary Drama Service, Nelson Reference & Electronic Publishing, New World Library, Paragon House, Pauline Books & Media, Paulist Press: HiddenSpring, Pelican Publishing Company, Prep Publishing, Resurrection Press, Ltd., Shambhala Publications, Skinner House Books, Solas Press, St. Bede's Publications, Swedenborg Foundation, Inc.: Chrysalis Books, Temple University Press, The Trinity Foundation, Trinity Press International, Truman State University Press, Unity House/Books, Waterbrook Press, White Mane Publishing Company

Romance

Periodicals:

Affaire De Coeur, Braveheart, Capper's, Cosmopolitan, Grit Magazine, Happy Times Monthly, Playgirl, Short Stuff Magazine, Springfield! Magazine, True Romance, Woman's World

Book Publishers:

American Literary Press, Inc.: Noble House, Avalon Books, Black Forest Press: Arbenteuer Books, Bee-Con Books, Bella Books, Dichter Books, Kinder Books, The Conservatory of American Letters, Dorchester Publishing Co., Inc., Great Quotations Publishing, Harlequin, Hilliard & Harris, ImaJinn Books, LionHearted Publishing, Inc., New Victoria Publishers, Prep Publishing, Red Dress InkTM, Waterbrook Press, Wilshire Book Co.

Rural America

Periodicals:

America West, American Profile, Aspen Magazine, Back Home in Kentucky, BackHome, Blue Ridge Country Magazine, Capper's, Country Home, Country Magazine, Country Extra Magazine, Country Woman Magazine, The Elks Magazine, Farm & Ranch Living, Farm Times, Beef Times, Grit Magazine, Heartland USA, Home Times Family Newspaper, The The Lutheran Digest, The Maine Organic Farmer & Gardener, The Montana Catholic, My Legacy, North Dakota Horizons, The Old Farmer's Almanac, Over the Back Fence, Persimmon Hill, Rosebud, Rural Heritage, Sandlapper, Short Stuff Magazine, Teaching Tolerance, Tradition, True Romance, Young & Alive

Book Publishers:

The Conservatory of American Letters, David R. Godine, Inc., Falcon Publishing/Falcon Guides, Two Dot, Three Forks, The Globe Pequot Press, Mayhaven Publishing, University of Nebraska Press

Satire

Periodicals:

Artemis Magazine, Bibliophilos, The Black Table, Funny Times, Futures Mysterious Anthology Magazine, Home Times Family Newspaper, The Iconoclast, Office Number One, Rockford Review, Short Stuff Magazine, Springfield! Magazine, Thoughts for All Seasons, Willow Springs

Book Publishers:

Diogenes Publishing, Elderberry Press, LLC, Mayhaven Publishing

Science

Periodicals:

America West, Analog Science Fiction and Fact, Annals of Improbable Research (AIR): The Journal of Record for Inflated Research and Personalities, Appleseeds, Archaeology, Artemis Magazine, Boys' Life, The Bugle, California Wild: California Academy of Sciences, Catholic Digest, The Circle, Click Magazine, Discover, The Elks Magazine, Environment, Futurific Magazine, The Growing Edge, Harper's Magazine, HerbalGram, Home Times Family Newspaper, The Journal of Asian Martial Arts, The Magazine of Speculative Poetry, Magical Blend, Men's Fitness, Mental Floss, Mercury: The Journal of the Astronomical Society of the Pacific, The National Enquirer, Natural History, Odyssey Magazine, Playboy, Poptronics, Popular Mechanics, Popular Science, Psychology Today, Smithsonian Magazine, Spider, Springfield! Magazine, Transitions, Weatherwise Magazine, The World & I, Young & Alive

Book Publishers:

ATL Press: Science Technology, Bay Tree Publishing, Charlesbridge Publishing, Cricket Books, Dawn Publications, Green Nature Books, HiddenSpring, Island Press, Lerner Publishing, The Lyons Press, The Millbrook Press, Mountain Press Publishing Company, Tilbury House Publishers, The Trinity Foundation, University of Idaho Press, University of Nevada Press, Voyageur Press

Science Fiction

Periodicals:

Analog Science Fiction and Fact , Artemis Magazine, Asimov's Science Fiction, Boys' Life, The Circle, Futures Mysterious Anthology Magazine, Hadrosaur Tales, Horrorfind, Fantasy & Science Fiction, The Magazine of Speculative Poetry, My Legacy, Rosebud, Snake Nation Review, Space and Time, Weird Tales

Book Publishers:

American Literary Press, Inc.: Noble House, Baen Books, Bella Books, BenBella Books, Black Forest Press: Arbenteuer Books, Dichter Books, Kinder Books, Collectors Press, The Conservatory of American Letters, Cricket Books: Marcato Books, DAW Books, Gryphon House, ImaJinn Books, Jona Books, Mayhaven Publishing, Tom Doherty Associate, LLC, Tor Books, Forge Books, Orb, Starscape, Warner Books, Willowgate Press

Self Help

Periodicals:

Angels on Earth, Body & Soul, CollegeBound Teen Magazine, Complete Woman, Dream Network: A Quarterly Journal Exploring Dreams & Myth, Health, Home Times Family Newspaper, House, Home and Garden, Ladies' Home Journal, Lifeglow, Magical Blend, Massage Magazine, Men's Fitness, Modern Bride, The National Enquirer, Natural Beauty & Health, River Town Gazette, Springfield! Magazine, Today's Christian Woman, Transitions, Weight Watchers Magazine, West Coast Magazine, Women In Business, Young & Alive

Book Publishers:

Allworth Press, Aslan Publishing, Berrett-Koehler Publishers, Beyond Words Publishing, Bye Publishing, Calyx Books, Capital Books, CCC Publications, Champion Press, Ltd., Contemporary Books: A Division of McGraw-Hill Companies, Denlinger's Publishers, Ltd., Do-It-Yourself Legal Publishers, Fairview Press, Free Spirit Publishing, God Allows U-Turns: Book Series, Gürze Books, Hampton Roads Publishing, Harbor Press, Hatherleigh Press, Hay House, Inc., Hazelden Publishing, HiddenSpring, Hunter House Publishers, Impact Publishers, Jodere Group Inc., Markowski International Publishers, Possibility Press, Metamorphous Press, New Horizons Press, Small Horizons Imprint, Origin Media, Inc.: "Books for the Integral Age", Pathfinder Publishing of California, Possibility Press, Prima Publishing, Red Wheel/Weiser, Ronin Publishing, Inc., Safer Society Press, Shambhala Publications, Sourcebooks, Inc., Sourcebooks Casablanca, Sourcebooks Hysteria, Sourcebooks Landmark, Sourcebooks MediaFusion, Sphinx Publishing, Square One Publishers, Taylor Trade, USA Books, Waterbrook Press, White Mane Publishing Company, Wilshire Book Co., Woodbine House

Senior Citizen

Periodicals:

Alive! A Magazine for Christian Senior Adults, American Fitness, Best of Times, Blue Ridge Country Magazine, Capper's, Creative With Words!, Crone Chronicles, Dialogue, Dog Gone, Dream Network: A Quarterly Journal Exploring Dreams & Myth, Futures Mysterious Anthology Magazine, Grit Magazine, Happy Times Monthly, Highways, Home Times Family Newspaper, Ligourian, Long Island Woman, The Lutheran Digest, Mature Living, Mature Years, Modern Maturity, My Legacy, River Town Gazette, Sandlapper, Senior Living, Transitions, Western RV News & Recreation

Book Publishers:

American Correctional Association (ACA) Book Publishing, Calyx Books, Great Quotations Publishing, Impact Publishers, Johnston Associates International, Judson Press, Volcano Press

Sexuality

Periodicals:

Blackfire, Bridal Guide, Campus Life, Complete Woman, Cosmopolitan, Crone Chronicles, Genre, Girlfriends Magazine, Harper's Bazaar, In the Family and Their Loved Ones, Insider Magazine, Ladies' Home Journal, Libido, Long Island Woman, Magical Blend, Men's Fitness, Mom Guess What Newspaper, The National Enquirer, Natural Beauty & Health, New Millennium Writings, Penthouse, Penthouse Variations, Playboy, Playgirl, Redbook, Salon, Seventeen, Snake Nation Review, Springfield! Magazine, Tikkun, Transitions, Whole Life Times

Book Publishers:

Barricade Books, Bethany House Publishers, Companion Press, Frederick Fell Publishers, Inc., Hunter House Publishers, Metamorphous Press, Safer Society Press, Temple University Press, Wilshire Book Co.

Short Stories

Periodicals:

12th Planet Literary Journal, 96 Inc., ACM: Another Chicago Magazine, Agni, Alfred Hitchcock Mystery Magazine, Alive! A Magazine for Christian Senior Adults, America West, American Letters & Commentary, Arkansas Review, Art Times, Artemis Magazine, The Asian Pacific American Journal, Babybug, BabyTalk, The Baltimore Review, Bibliophilos, Boston Review, Boys' Life, Buffalo Spree Magazine, The Bugle, ByLine, Calyx Journal, The Carolina Quarterly, Cat Fancy, CC Motorcycle News Magazine, Chicago Magazine, Chicago Review, Cimarron Review, The Circle, Confrontation, A Literary Journal, Conversely, Crab Creek Review, The Cream City Review, Milwaukee, Creative With Words!, Cricket, CutBank: University of Montana, Downstate Story, Ellery Queen's Mystery Magazine, Flesh & Blood, Fourteen Hills: The SFSU Review, Futures Mysterious Anthology Magazine, Genre, The Gettysburg Review, Glimmer Train Stories, Golf Journal Magazine, Good Housekeeping, Grit Magazine, Guideposts for Kids, Happy Times Monthly, Home Times Family Newspaper, Horror Tales, Horrorfind, House, Home and Garden, The Hudson Review, Hurricane Alice, The Iconoclast, Iris: A Journal about Women (University of Virginia), Japanophile, Kentucky Monthly, The Kenyon Review, Ladybug: The Magazine for Young Children, Libido, Light, The Literary Review: Fairleigh Dickinson University, Lynx Eye, The MacGuffin, Manoa, Mature Years, The Melic Review, Minnesota Memories, The Minnesota Review: University of Missouri, Columbia, My Legacy, The Nebraska Review: University of Nebraska-Omaha, New Letters, New Millennium Writings, The New Renaissance, New York Stories, Nine, Obsidian III, Office Number One, Ohio Writer, Other Voices: University of Illinois-Chicago, Over the Back Fence, Paddler, Pangolin Papers, Passages North: Northern Michigan University, Passport, Pearl, Peregrine: History and Background of Amherst Writers and Artists, Phantasmagoria, Playgirl, Pleiades: A Journal of New Writing, Potluck Children's Literary Magazine, Potomac Review, Quarterly West: University of Utah, Red Rock Review, Reminisce Magazine, Reminisce Extra, Rhino, RiverSedge: The University of Texas-Pan

Topics

American, Rosebud, Seek The Abundant Life, Sewanee Review, Shenandoah: The Washington and Lee University Review, Slipstream, Southern Humanities Review: Auburn University, The Southern Review: Louisiana State University, St. Anthony Messenger, Standard, Stone Soup, Studies in American Jewish Literature, The Sun, Sycamore Review: Purdue University, Teaching Tolerance, Thema, The Threepenny Review, True Romance, Vampire Tales, Woman's World, Weird Tales, West Coast Magazine, The William and Mary Review: College of William and Mary, Willow Springs, Zoetrope: All-Story, ZYZZYVA

Book Publishers:

American Literary Press, Inc.: Noble House, Angel Bea Publishing, BkMk Press: University of Missouri-Kansas City, Black Forest Press: Arbenteuer Books, Dichter Books, Kinder Books, Brookline Books, The Conservatory of American Letters, David R. Godine, Inc., Genesis Communications, Inc.: Evergreen Press & Gazelle Press, God Allows U-Turns: Book Series, Gryphon Books, John Daniel & Company, Latin American Literary Review Press, Mage Publishers, Mayhaven Publishing, Milkweed Editions, Piano Press, Safari Press, Inc., Sarabande Books, University of North Texas Press, Via Dolorosa Press

Singles

Periodicals:

Christian Single, Complete Woman, Home Times Family Newspaper, Long Island Woman, River Town Gazette, Springfield! Magazine, Today's Christian Woman

Book Publishers:

God Allows U-Turns: Book Series, Kregel Publications/Kregel Kidzone, Sourcebooks, Inc., Sourcebooks Casablanca, Sourcebooks Hysteria, Sourcebooks Landmark, Sourcebooks MediaFusion, Sphinx Publishing, Square One Publishers

Society

Periodicals:

America West, The American Legion Magazine, Angels on Earth, Appleseeds, Artemis Magazine, Atlanta Homes and Lifestyles, Bible Advocate, Now What? E-zine, The Beauty Spot, Boston Review, California Lawyer, Christian Social Action, The Freeman: Ideas on Liberty, Futurific Magazine, Glamour, Gray Areas, Grit Magazine, Harper's Magazine, Home Times Family Newspaper, In the Family and Their Loved Ones, Insider Magazine, Jam Rag, Ladies' Home Journal, Left Curve, Legacy: A Journal of American Women Writers, Magical Blend, Modern Maturity, Natural Beauty & Health, The New Centennial Review, New Mexico Magazine, Nine, North Dakota Horizons, Penthouse, Reader's Digest, Redbook, River Town Gazette, The Roanoker, Smithsonian Magazine, St. Anthony Messenger, Studies in American Jewish Literature, Teaching Tolerance, Thoughts for All Seasons, Tikkun, Town & Country, Transaction Publishers Rutgers, Transitions, Vanity Fair, Vibe, Willow Springs

Book Publishers:

Algora Publishing, Agathon Press, Black Forest Press: Arbenteuer Books, Dichter Books, Kinder Books, Branden Publishing Company, Cross Cultural Publications, Inc., Diogenes Publishing, Face to Face Press, Pathfinder Publishing of California, Waterbrook Press

Software

Periodicals:

Artemis Magazine, Better Homes and Gardens, Memory Makers, Poptronics, Wired

Book Publishers:

Franklin, Beedle & Associates

Spiritual

Periodicals:

The African American Pulpit!, Alive Now, Alive! A Magazine for Christian Senior Adults, All for You, American Profile, Balanced Living Magazine, Bible Advocate, Now What? E-zine, Body & Soul, Books & Culture, Braveheart, Campus Life, Catholic Digest, Christian New Age

Quarterly, Christian Parenting Today, Christian Single, Christian Women Today, Christian Social Action, Christianity Today, Chrysalis Reader, Cincinnati Woman Magazine, Clubhouse, CNEWA World, Conscience, Crone Chronicles, Devo'Zine, Discipleship Journal, The Door Magazine, Dream Network: A Quarterly Journal Exploring Dreams & Myth, Enrichment: A Journal for Pentecostal Ministry, Fate, Fellowship, First Things, The Good Red Road, Guideposts, Home Times Family Newspaper, Journal of Christian Nursing, Leadership Journal, LifeWayonline.com, Light of Consciousnes, Ligourian, Llewellyn Journal, The Lutheran Digest, Magical Blend, Mature Living, Mature Years, Men of Integrity, Message Magazine, Moment, My Legacy, Natural Beauty & Health, New Millennium Writings, The New Times, The North American Voice of Fatima, The Other Side, Parabola, Pastoral Life, Pentecostal Evangel, The Plain Truth, Pockets, SageWoman, PanGaia,, The Blessed Bee, New Witch, Science of Mind, The Secret Place, Shofar, Sports Spectrum, St. Anthony Messenger, Standard, Studies in American Jewish Literature, Teaching Tolerance, Tikkun, Today's Christian, Today's Christian Woman, Transitions, The Upper Room, Weavings, Whole Life Times, Women Today Magazine, Yoga Journal, Young & Alive

Book Publishers:

ACTA Publications: Assisting Christians to Act, Alba House, AMG Publishers, Aslan Publishing, Baker Book Publishing Group, Berrett-Koehler Publishers, Black Forest Press: Arbenteuer Books, Dichter Books, Kinder Books, Bye Publishing, Christian Ed. Publishers, Christian Publications, Inc., Cross Cultural Publications, Inc., The Crossing Press, Daily Guideposts, God Allows U-Turns: Book Series, Granite Publishing Group, Great Quotations Publishing, Guide, Hachai Publishing, Hampton Roads Publishing, Harbor Press, Hay House, Inc., Hazelden Publishing, Health Communications, Inc., HiddenSpring, Hillbrook Publishing, Hohm Press, In Print Publishing, Jewish Lights Publishing, Jodere Group Inc., Judson Press, Kali Press, Kregel Publications/Kregel Kidzone, Legacy Press, Llewellyn Publications, Loyola Press, Mayhaven Publishing, Meriwether Publishing Ltd: Contemporary Drama Service, Nelson Reference & Electronic Publishing, New World Library, Origin Media, Inc.: "Books for the Integral Age", Paragon House, Pauline Books & Media, Paulist Press: HiddenSpring, Prep Publishing, Red Wheel/Weiser, Resurrection Press, Ltd., Solas Press, Shambhala Publications, St. Bede's Publications, Swedenborg Foundation, Inc.: Chrysalis Books, The Trinity Foundation, Trinity Press International, Unity House, Waterbrook Press, Zondervan and Zonderkidz

Sports/Recreation

Periodicals:

4-Wheel Drive & Sport Utility, Adirondack Life, American Fitness, American Hunter, American Profile, American Snowmobiler, American Turf Monthly, Artemis Magazine, Aspen Magazine, Backpacker, Balloon Life, Bike Magazine, Boating Life, Boys' Life, Boys' Quest, The Bugle, Cadet Quest, Canoe & Kayak Magazine, Car and Driver, Cascades East Magazine: Central Oregon's Quarterly, Chess Life, School Mates, Circle Track, Cruising World, Dialogue, Diver, Dog Gone, The Elks Magazine, Field & Stream, Fishing Facts, Fly Fisherman, Fly Fishing in Salt Waters, Flyfisher, Freeskier, Fur-Fish-Game, Girls' Life, Golf Digest, Golf Journal Magazine, The Golfer, Guideposts for Kids, Guns & Ammo, Heartland USA, Home Times Family Newspaper, Inside Texas Running, Insider Magazine, International Sports Journal: University of West Haven, The Journal of Asian Martial Arts, Kentucky Monthly, Kung Fu Tai chi, Long Island Woman, Marlin, Men's Health, Men's Journal, Mom Guess What Newspaper, Mushing, Muzzle Blasts, National Geographic Traveler, Natural Beauty & Health, New York Runner, Nine, Northwest Fly Fishing, Outdoor America, Outdoor Life, Pacific Fishing, Paddler, Penthouse, Playboy, Points North, Polo Players' Edition, Power & Motoryacht, Referee, River Town Gazette, Rock and Ice, Rocky Mountain Sports Magazine, Runner's World, Running Times, Sailing Magazine, Sailing World, Salmon-Trout-Steelheader, Sandlapper, Scouting, Sea Kayaker, Sea: The Magazine of Western Boating, Senior Living, Shape Magazine, Skating Magazine, Ski, Skiing Magazine, Smoke Magazine,

Life's Burning Desires, Society of American Baseball Research, Southwest Fly Fishing, Speedway Illustrated, Sport Fishing Magazine, Sports Afield, Sports Illustrated for Kids, Sports Spectrum, Springfield! Magazine, Sun Valley Magazine, Surfer, Swim Magazine, Swimming Technique, Swimming World, Junior Swimmer, T'ai Chi, Tennis Magazine, Trail Runner, Transitions, Turkey Call, Women In The Outdoors, Wheelin' Sportsmen, The Caller, Jakes Magazine, USA Cycling, Volleyball Magazine, Whole Life Times, Young & Alive

Book Publishers:

American Literary Press, Inc.: Noble House, Black Forest Press: Arbenteuer Books, Dichter Books, Kinder Books, Bonus Books, Inc., Branden Publishing Company, Brassey's Sports, Brassey's, Inc., Bristol Fashion Publications, Inc.: The World's Largest Nautical Publishing House, The Conservatory of American Letters, Contemporary Books: A Division of McGraw-Hill Companies, Down East Books, Eclipse Press, Fairleigh Dickinson University Press, Falcon Publishing/Falcon Guides, Two Dot, Three Forks, The Globe Pequot Press, Hatherleigh Press, International Marine, The Lyons Press, McBooks Press, McFarland & Company, Inc., Menasha Ridge Press, Mountain N' Air Books, Mustang Publishing Company, Northern Publishing, Orange Frazer Press, Inc., Paradise Cay, Pelican Publishing Company, Prima Publishing, Pruett Publishing Company, Ragged Mountain Press, Rutledge Hill Press, Sourcebooks, Inc., Sourcebooks Casablanca, Sourcebooks Hysteria, Sourcebooks Landmark, Sourcebooks MediaFusion, Southern Illinois University Press, Sphinx Publishing, Stackpole Books, Stipes Publishing, LLC, Taylor Trade, Temple University Press, Towlehouse Publishing Co., Turtle Press, University of Nebraska Press, Voyageur Press, Wescott Cove Publishing Co., World Leisure Corporation, YMAA Publication Center

-T-

Technical

Periodicals:

4-Wheel Drive & Sport Utility, 5.0 Mustang & Super Fords, Artemis Magazine, Audio Video Interiors, ComputorEdge, Corvette Fever, Cutting Tool Engineering, FirehouseMagazine, Firehouse.com, Game Developer, The Labor Paper: Serving Southern Wisconsin, Memory Makers, Muscle Mustang & Fast Fords, Mustang & Fords, Mustang Monthly, Poptronics, Popular Woodworking

Book Publishers:

Baywood Publishing Company, Inc., Bookhaven Press LLC, Charles River Media, Graphic Arts Technical Foundation/GATFPress, Medical Physics Publishing, Millennium Publishing Company, Railroading, Stipes Publishing, LLC

Technology

Periodicals:

Audio Video Interiors, Business 2.0, Circle Track, Click Magazine, Computer Bits, ComputorEdge, Doll World, Fast Company, Fresh Cut, Industrial Management, Radio World, PC Magazine, Smithsonian Magazine, Salon, Spider, Supply Chain Systems Magazine, Supply Chain Systems Magazine

Book Publishers:

Aegis Publishing Group, Ltd., Franklin, Beedle & Associates

Teen

Periodicals:

African American Family, All About Kids, American Girl, Cicada, CollegeBound Teen Magazine, Complete Woman, Creative With Words!, DECA Dimensions, Dramatics, Florida Leader: For High School Student, Girls' Life, Hang Loose, Ha)0ppy Times Monthly, Home Times Family Newspaper, Insight, Instructor, Living With Teenagers, The Lutheran Digest, Metro Parent, Metro Baby, MetroKids, Muse Magazine, New Moon, Northwest Family News, Odyssey Magazine, Oxendine Publishing, Inc., Parents' Press, Passport, Potluck Children's Literary

Magazine, River Town Gazette, SchoolArts, Scouting, Springfield! Magazine, Swimming World, Junior Swimmer, Teaching Tolerance, United Parenting Publications, With: The Magazine for Radical Christian Youth,

Book Publishers:

Atheneum Books, Beyond Words Publishing, Branden Publishing Company, Cricket Books, Dial Books for Young Readers, Free Spirit Publishing, Front Street, Inc., God Allows U-Turns: Book Series, Harbor Press, ImaJinn Books, Just Us Books, Kids Books By Kids, Kregel Publications/Kregel Kidzone, Mayhaven Publishing, Millennium Publishing Company, Scarecrow Press, Inc., UpstartBooks

Television/Radio

Periodicals:

Film Quarterly, Futurific Magazine, Home Times Family Newspaper, Kentucky Monthly, Playgirl, Plus Magazine, Poptronics, Radio World, River Town Gazette, Springfield! Magazine, Teaching Tolerance, Times News Service

Book Publishers:

Fordham University Press, McFarland & Company, Inc., Players Press, Inc., Santa Monica Press LLC, Temple University Press

Textbooks

Periodicals:

Calyx Journal, Northwoods Journal, RiverSedge: The University of Texas-Pan American, Springfield! Magazine, Teaching Tolerance

Book Publishers:

Barrons Educational Series, Inc., Baywood Publishing Company, Inc., Black Forest Press: Arbenteuer Books, Dichter Books, Kinder Books, Bonus Books, Inc., Branden Publishing Company, Brassey's, Inc., The Conservatory of American Letters, Cottonwood Press, Inc., ETC Publications, Garth Gardner Company, Graphic Arts Technical Foundation/GATFPress, Intercultural Press, Mississippi: University Press of Mississippi, Orchises Press, Paragon House, Pelican Publishing Company, Scarecrow Press, Inc., Stipes Publishing, LLC

Theatre

Periodicals:

American Theatre, Art Times, The Beauty Spot, Bibliophilos, Cincinnati Woman Magazine, Confrontation, A Literary Journal, Dramatics, Futures Mysterious Anthology Magazine, Home Times Family Newspaper, Insider Magazine, Kentucky Monthly, The New Centennial Review, New Yorker, Obsidian III, Rosebud, Springfield! Magazine, Teaching Tolerance, Vanity Fair, Willow Springs

Book Publishers:

Allworth Press, Anchorage Press Plays, Inc., Branden Publishing Company, Fairleigh Dickinson University Press, Ivan R. Dee, Inc., Publisher, Limelight Editions, McFarland & Company, Inc., Mississippi: University Press of Mississippi, Piccadilly Books, Ltd., Players Press, Inc., Santa Monica Press LLC, Southern Illinois University Press, Temple University Press

Trade

Periodicals:

The African American Pulpit!, American Artist, Ceramics Monthly, Chef Magazine, Desktop Engineering, Development Director's Letter, Digger Magazine, Farwest Magazine, Doll World, Fiberarts Magazine, Forester Communications, Oildom Publishing, Shuttle Spindle & Dyepot, Toy Farmer, Toy Trucker & Contractor, Vacation Industry Review, Watercolor

Book Publishers:

Forum Publishing Company, Paradise Cay, Wilder Publishing Center

Travel

Periodicals:

Adirondack Life, Alaska Business Monthly, Alive! A Magazine for Christian Senior Adults, America West, American Fitness, Arizona

Highways, Artemis Magazine, Aspen Magazine, ASU Travel Guide: The Guide for Airline Employee Discounts, Atlanta Homes and Lifestyles, Back Home in Kentucky, Backpacker, Backroads, The Beauty Spot, Better Homes and Gardens, Bibliophilos, Blue Ridge Country Magazine, Boating Life, Bridal Guide, Budget Living, Canoe & Kayak Magazine, Capper's, Caribbean Travel & Life, CC Motorcycle News Magazine, Clubmex, Coast to Coast, Cooking Light, Cosmopolitan, Country Living, Country Magazine, Country Extra Magazine, Creative With Words!, Dog Gone, Early American Life, Endless Vacation RCI, Fast Company, Florida Wildlife, Fly Fishing in Salt Waters, Freeskier, German Life, Glamour, Go Magazine,, Going Places, The Golfer, Grit Magazine, Hawaii Westways, Highways, House, Home and Garden, Inside Texas Running, Insider Magazine, The International Railway Traveler, Islands, Italian Cooking and Living, Kentucky Monthly, Ladies' Home Journal, Lake Michigan Travel Guide, Lifeglow, Log Home Living, Timber Frame Homes, The Magazine of La Cucina Italiana, Magical Blend, Mature Years, Men's Health, Men's Journal, Midwest Outdoors, Midwest Traveler, Modern Bride, Modern Maturity, Montana Magazine, More, Motorcycling, Mountain Living, National Geographic Traveler, Natural Beauty & Health, Nevada Magazine, New Mexico Journey, New Mexico Magazine, The New Yorker, North Dakota Horizons, Northwest Family News, Northwest Fly Fishing, Northwest Palate, Northwest Regional Magazines, Offshore: Northeast Boating at Its Best, Oklahoma Today Magazine, Outdoor Life, Over the Back Fence, Paddler, Persimmon Hill, Plus Magazine, Points North, Power & Motoryacht, Premier Tourism Marketing, Inc., Reunions Magazine, River Town Gazette, Russian Life, Sandlapper, Saturday Evening Post, Scouting, Sea: The Magazine of Western Boating, Shape Magazine, Sierra: The Magazine of the Sierra Club, Skiing Magazine, Smithsonian Magazine, South American Explorer, Southern Living, Southern Traveler, Southwest Fly Fishing, Specialty Travel Index, Sports Afield, Springfield! Magazine, Sunset Magazine, Surfer, Tennis Magazine, Texas Highways, The Travel Magazine of Texas, Texas Parks & Wildlife, Times News Service, Town & Country, Trailer Boats, Transitions, Transitions Abroad, Travel Naturally, Via, Western RV News & Recreation, Westways, Southern California Lifestyle Magazine, Whole Life Times, Wisconsin Trails, Woodall Publications, Corp., Working Mother Magazine, Yankee, Young & Alive

Book Publishers:

Berkshire House Publishers, Brookline Books, Capital Books, Chronicle Books LLC, Clover Park Press, Dimi Press, Down East Books, Falcon Publishing/Falcon Guides, Two Dot, Three Forks, Gem Guides Book Company, The Globe Pequot Press, Graphic Arts Center Publishing Company, Green Nature Books, HiddenSpring, Jewish Lights Publishing, Johnston Associates International, Lake Claremont Press, Lumen Editions, The Lyons Press, The McDonald & Woodward Publishing Company, Menasha Ridge Press, Millennium Publishing Company, Mountain N' Air Books, Mustang Publishing Company, North Ridge Books, Paradise Cay, Pelican Publishing Company, Pruett Publishing Company, Ragged Mountain Press, Roadman Press, Rutledge Hill Press, Sasquatch Books, Stone Bridge Press, Sunbelt Publications, Ten Speed Press, Celestial Arts, Tricycle Press, Wescott Cove Publishing Co., World Leisure Corporation

True Crime

Periodicals:
Futures Mysterious Anthology Magazine

Book Publishers:
Addicus Books, Inc., Branden Publishing Company, Holloway House Publishing, Jona Books, Mayhaven Publishing, New Horizons Press, Small Horizons Imprint, University of North Texas Press

-W-

Western

Periodicals:
America West, Arizona Highways, Backwoodsman Magazine, Bibliophilos, Capper's, Chronicle of the Old West, Grit Magazine, Horrorfind, Montana, My Legacy, New Mexico Magazine, Overland Journal, Persimmon Hill, Primedia History Group, Sunset Magazine, True West

Book Publishers:
American Literary Press, Inc.: Noble House, Avalon Books, Black Forest Press: Arbenteuer Books, Dichter Books, Kinder Books, Branden Publishing Company, Caxton Press, The Conservatory of American Letters, Crossway Books, Denlinger's Publishers, Ltd., Dorchester Publishing Co., Inc., Eclipse Press, Fairleigh Dickinson University Press, Hilliard & Harris, Jona Books, Mayhaven Publishing, Mountain N' Air Books, Pelican Publishing Company, Tom Doherty Associate, LLC, Tor Books, Forge Books, Orb, Starscape, University of Nebraska Press, University of North Texas Press, University of Oklahoma Press, USA Books

Women's Fiction

Periodicals:
Affaire De Coeur, Calyx Journal, The Carolina Quarterly, Cincinnati Woman Magazine, Feminist Studies: University of Maryland, Fourteen Hills: The SFSU Review, Frontiers: A Journal of Women Studies, Futures Mysterious Anthology Magazine, Good Housekeeping, Home Times Family Newspaper, Hurricane Alice, Iris: A Journal about Women (University of Virginia), Kalliope, Kentucky Monthly, Legacy: A Journal of American Women Writers, New Millennium Writings, New Moon, Obsidian III, Playgirl, Primavera, Redbook, Rosebud, Sycamore Review: Purdue University, True Romance, Willow Springs, Women's World

Book Publishers:
American Literary Press, Inc.: Noble House, Calyx Books, David R. Godine, Inc., Latin American Literary Review Press, Narwhal Press, Inc., Red Dress Ink, Soho Press Inc., Sourcebooks, Inc., Sourcebooks Casablanca, Sourcebooks Hysteria, Sourcebooks Landmark, Sourcebooks MediaFusion, University of Nebraska Press, Waterbrook Press, Zondervan and Zonderkidz

Women's Issues

Periodicals:
The African American Pulpit!, All About Kids, The Beauty Spot, Calyx Journal, The Carolina Quarterly, Cincinnati Woman Magazine, Complete Woman, Conscience, Cosmopolitan, Crone Chronicles, Elle, Equal Opportunity Publications, Inc., Feminist Studies: University of Maryland, Frontiers: A Journal of Women Studies, Glamour, Good Housekeeping, Home Times Family Newspaper, Hurricane Alice, Insider Magazine, Iris: A Journal about Women (University of Virginia), Journal of Christian Nursing, Kalliope, Kentucky Monthly, Ladies' Home Journal, Legacy: A Journal of American Women Writers, Lilith: The Independent Jewish Women's Magazine, Long Island Woman, Magical Blend, MetroKids, Midwifery Today, More, The National Enquirer, Natural Beauty & Health, New Mexico Woman Magazine, New Moon, The New Times, Parents Magazine, Playgirl, Redbook, Rosebud, SageWoman, PanGaia, The Blessed Bee, New Witch, Seventeen, Shape Magazine, Springfield! Magazine, Teaching Tolerance, Town & Country, Transitions, Whole Life Times, Woman's Touch, Woman's World, Women and Music, Women Artists News Book Review, Women In Business, Working Mother Magazine

Book Publishers:
Arden Press, Inc., Arte Público Press: The University of Houston, Beyond Words Publishing, Branden Publishing Company, Calyx Books, Champion Press, Ltd., Clover Park Press, Cross Cultural Publications, Inc., Fairleigh Dickinson University Press, God Allows U-Turns: Book

Series, Great Quotations Publishing, Hay House, Inc., Health Communications, Inc., Impact Publishers, Jewish Lights Publishing, Jodere Group Inc., Judson Press, Midmarch Arts Press, New Horizons Press, New World Library, Small Horizons Imprint, Prep Publishing, Ragged Mountain Press, Rutledge Hill Press, Sourcebooks, Inc., Sourcebooks Casablanca, Sourcebooks Hysteria, Sourcebooks Landmark, Sourcebooks MediaFusion, Sphinx Publishing, Spinsters Ink, Temple University Press, Texas A&M University Press, Transnational Publishers, Inc., University of Nebraska Press, University of North Texas Press, Volcano Press

Writing

Periodicals:

Absolute Write, America West, The American Poetry Review, Authorship, BabyTalk, Bibliophilos, Bloomsbury Review, Boston Review, By-Line, The Carolina Quarterly, The Chattahoochee Review, Chicago Magazine, Cimarron Review, The Circle, CompulsiveReader.com, Confrontation, A Literary Journal, The Cream City Review, Milwaukee, Creative Nonfiction, Creative With Words!, Cross & Quill, Et cetera: A Review of General Semantics, Freelance Writer's Report, The Gettysburg Review, Happy Times Monthly, Home Times Family Newspaper, Indiana Review, Iris: A Journal about Women (University of Virginia), Kalliope, The Kenyon Review, Lacunae, Light, The MacGuffin, My Legacy, The Nebraska Review: University of Nebraska-Omaha, New Millennium Writings, Nimrod: International Journal of Prose and Poetry (University of Tulsa), Obsidian III, Ohio Writer, Passages North: Northern Michigan University, PEN America, Peregrine: History and Background of Amherst Writers and Artists, Phoebe, Potluck Children's Literary Magazine, Potomac Review, Quarterly West: University of Utah, Rearview, Rhino, Rosebud, Script Magazine, Snake Nation Review, Springfield! Magazine, Stone Soup, Sycamore Review: Purdue University, Teaching Tolerance, Thoughts for All Seasons, Tikkun, Culture, & Society, Verses Magazine, Willow Springs, WIN-Informer, The Writer Gazette, Writer's Digest, Writer's Guidelines & News, Writers' Journal, The Yalobusha Review

Book Publishers:

Black Forest Press: Arbenteuer Books, Dichter Books, Kinder Books, Brookline Books, The Conservatory of American Letters, David R. Godine, Inc., Excelsior Cee Publishing, Front Street, Inc., Lumen Editions, Marion Street Press, Inc., Mountain N' Air Books, Players Press, Inc., Prep Publishing, Serendipity Systems: Books-on-disks, Square One Publishers, Waterbrook Press

-Y-

Young Adult

Periodicals:

Cadet Quest. Calliope Magazine, Campus Life, Chess Life, School Mates, Cicada, Circle K, CollegeBound Teen Magazine, Creative With Words!, DECA Dimensions, Faces: The Magazine About People, Futures Mysterious Anthology Magazine, Girls' Life, Home Times Family Newspaper, Ligourian, Living With Teenagers, New Moon, Potluck Children's Literary Magazine, School Mates, Scouting, Seventeen, Springfield! Magazine, Stone Soup, Swimming World, Junior Swimmer, Teaching Tolerance

Book Publishers:

American Literary Press, Inc.: Noble House, Arte Público Press: The University of Houston, Atheneum Books, Barrons Educational Series, Inc., Beyond Words Publishing, Branden Publishing Company, Chronicle Books LLC, Crossway Books, David R. Godine, Inc., Farrar, Straus and Giroux, Publishers, Inc: Books for Young Readers, Free Spirit Publishing, Front Street, Inc., G.P. Putnam's Sons, God Allows U-Turns: Book Series, Harbor Press, Just Us Books, Kar-Ben Publishing, Lerner Publishing, Little, Brown Children's Books, Mayhaven Publishing, Narwhal Press, Inc., Peachtree Publishers, Peachtree Jr., Freestone, Prep Publishing, Scarecrow Press, Inc., Third World Press, White Mane Publishing Company

Writers' and Artists' Hideouts

Great Getaways for Seducing the Muse
—by Andrea Brown

"...a must-have for the writer's and artist's soul"
Jack Canfield, author of
Chicken Soup for the Soul

GREAT GETAWAYS FOR SEDUCING THE MUSE

Andrea Brown

$14.95 ($23.50 Canada) · ISBN 1-884956-34-3

The desire to be creative is often at odds with the routines of daily life. Literary agent Andrea Brown combines her love of travel and adventure with her search for perfect places to seduce the muse and delivers a charming, practical guide that enlightens the curious traveler and provides astute advice from editors, literary agents, authors, illustrators, art directors and other creative people on harnessing one's creativity.

Listed are locations all over the country, from $19 per night hostels to $1,000 per night luxury hotels. There are ranches, lighthouses, boats, bed and breakfasts, and even a museum to sleep in, all listed by region.

"This book is a double treat—both a valuable and unique travel guide but also a useful writer's and artist's manual for accomplishing one's goals to publish or produce lasting creative works. A must have for the writer's and artist's soul—and bookshelf."
—Jack Canfield, author of *Chicken Soup for the Soul* series

Quit Your Day Job!

How to Sleep Late, Do What You Enjoy, and Make a Ton of Money *as a Writer!*
—by Jim Denney

A Writer's Digest Book Club Selection

Resolution and perseverance are required to build a writing career and if you're going to succeed, you don't need the hype or hyperbole so often dished out in other writer's guides. You need a candid, no-nonsense appraisal of the daily grind of the writer's life, with the potholes and pitfalls clearly marked.

This book is your road map, written by someone who's lived the writing life for years, with more than sixty published novels and nonfiction books to his credit.

"While there are always a few charmed souls, most career-bent writers are destined to struggle. Jim Denney has been there, done that. Read his book and save yourself much of the anguish."
—James N. Frey, author of *How to Write a Damn Good Novel*

Quit Your Day Job!

How to Sleep Late, Do What You Enjoy, and Make a Ton of Money *as a Writer!*

By Jim Denney

$14.95 (29.95 Canada) · ISBN 1-884956-04-1

Available at better brick and mortar bookstores, online bookstores, at QuillDriverBooks.com or by calling 1-800-497-4909

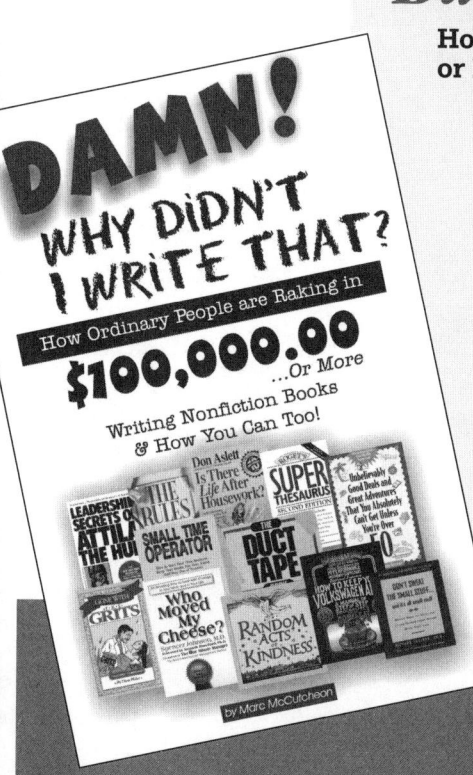
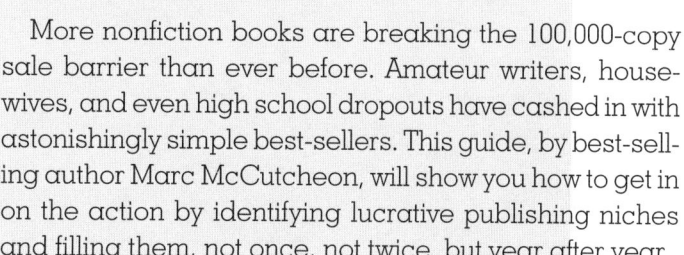

Notes

Notes

Notes